THE
Norton
Anthology
OF
American
Literature

Volume 2

THE

Norton

Anthology

OF

American

Literature

RONALD GOTTESMAN
University of Southern California

FRANCIS MURPHY
Smith College

LAURENCE B. HOLLAND
Johns Hopkins University

HERSHEL PARKER
University of Southern California

DAVID KALSTONE
Rutgers, The State University of New Jersey

WILLIAM H. PRITCHARD
Amherst College

Volume 2

W · W · NORTON & COMPANY
NEW YORK · LONDON

FIRST EDITION

Henry Adams: From *The Education of Henry Adams,* copyright 1918 by the Massachusetts Historical Society, copyright 1946 by Charles F. Adams. Reprinted by permission of Houghton Mifflin Company.
A. R. Ammons: Selections reprinted from *Collected Poems* by A. R. Ammons, with the permission of W. W. Norton & Company, Inc. Copyright © 1972 by A. R. Ammons.
Sherwood Anderson: From *Winesburg, Ohio,* copyright 1919 by B. W. Huebsch; renewed 1947 by Eleanor Copenhaver Anderson. Reprinted by permission of the Estate of Sherwood Anderson, Viking Penguin, Inc., and Jonathan Cape Ltd. From *A Story-Teller's Story,* copyright 1924 by B. W. Huebsch, Inc.; renewed 1952 by Eleanor Copenhaver Anderson. Reprinted by permission of Harold Ober Associates, Incorporated.
John Ashbery: "Illustration" and "Some Trees" from *Some Trees* by John Ashbery, copyright 1956 by John Ashbery. "Soonest Mended," "Definition of Blue," and "Summer" from *The Double Dream of Spring* by John Ashbery, copyright 1966, 1967, 1968, 1969, 1970 by John Ashbery. Reprinted by permission of John Ashbery. "Self-Portrait in a Convex Mirror" from *Self-Portrait in a Convex Mirror* by John Ashbery, copyright © 1974, 1977 by John Ashbery. Reprinted by permission of Viking Penguin, Inc. and Carcanet Press. "Wet Casements" from *Houseboat Days* by John Ashbery, copyright © 1976 by John Ashbery. Reprinted by permission of Viking Penguin, Inc. and John Ashbery.
James Baldwin: Excerpted from "Down at the Cross: Letter from a Region in My Mind" from the book *The Fire Next Time* by James Baldwin. Copyright © 1963, 1962 by James Baldwin. Reprinted by permission of The Dial Press and Edward J. Acton, Inc.
Imamu Amiri Baraka (Leroi Jones): Text of *The Dead Lecturer,* copyright © 1963, 1964, 1965, 1967 by Leroi Jones (Imamu Amiri Baraka). Reprinted by permission of Grove Press, Inc. and The Sterling Lord Agency, Inc. From *Black Magic Poetry, 1961–1967,* copyright © 1969 by Leroi Jones (Imamu Amiri Baraka). Reprinted by permission of the publisher, The Bobbs-Merrill Co., Inc., and the Sterling Lord Agency, Inc.
John Barth: "Life Story" from *Lost in the Funhouse* by John Barth. Copyright © 1968, 1969 by John Barth. Reprinted by permission of Doubleday & Company, Inc. and the author's agents, Blassingame, McCauley & Wood.
Saul Bellow: *Seize the Day,* copyright © 1956 by Saul Bellow. First published by Weidenfeld & Nicolson, London. Reprinted by permission of Viking Penguin, Inc. and George Weidenfeld and Nicolson Ltd.
John Berryman: From *His Toy, His Dream, His Rest* by John Berryman, Copyright © 1964, 1965, 1966, 1967, 1968 by John Berryman. From *77 Dream Songs* by John Berryman, Copyright © 1959, 1962, 1963, 1964 by John Berryman. A selection from *Homage to Mistress Bradstreet* by John Berryman, Copyright © 1956 by John Berryman. Reprinted with the permission of Farrar, Straus & Giroux, Inc. and Faber and Faber Ltd.
Elizabeth Bishop: From *The Complete Poems,* copyright © 1940, 1941, 1947, 1948, 1956, 1957, 1959, 1969 by Elizabeth Bishop; copyright renewed © 1974, 1975 by Elizabeth Bishop. Reprinted with the permission of Farrar, Straus & Giroux, Inc. "The Armadillo" appeared originally in *The New Yorker.* From *Geography III,* copyright © 1971, 1972, 1973, 1974, 1975, 1976 by Elizabeth Bishop. Reprinted with the permission of Farrar, Straus & Giroux, Inc., Elizabeth Bishop, and Chatto & Windus Ltd. "In the Waiting Room" and "One Art" appeared originally in *The New Yorker.*
Gwendolyn Brooks: From *The World of Gwendolyn Brooks,* copyright 1945, 1949, 1960, 1967 by Gwendolyn Brooks Blakely. Reprinted by permission of Harper & Row, Publishers, Inc.
Willa Cather: "Neighbour Rosicky," copyright 1932 by Willa Cather and renewed 1960 by the Executors of the Estate of Willa Cather. Reprinted from *Obscure Destinies,* by Willa Cather, by permission of Alfred A. Knopf, Inc.

Since this page cannot legibly accommodate all the copyright notices,
the following four pages constitute an extension of the copyright page.

Library of Congress Cataloging in Publication Data
Main entry under title:
The Norton Anthology of American Literature.
    1. American literature.   I. Gottesman, Ronald, *et al.*
PS507.N65   810'.8   78–27308

ISBN 0–393–95033–6 (v. 2)
ISBN 0–393–95035–2 (v. 2, pbk.)

1 2 3 4 5 6 7 8 9 0

Contents

American Literature
between the Wars 1914–1945 1015

Contemporary American Prose 1945–   1857

Contemporary American Poetry 1945– 2251

Preface

THIS ENTIRELY NEW anthology of American literature has been devised to close the ever-widening gap between the current conception and appraisal of the American literary heritage and the way in which American literature is represented in existing anthologies. To this end, the editors and their editorial advisers polled a large number of teachers and used the resulting consensus to supplement their own judgments. The present anthology, as a consequence, not only reprints traditional masterpieces of American literature, but includes a number of innovations both in organization and content, which bring the volume into accord with contemporary evaluations and points of view.

The most prominent change is that the break between the two volumes occurs not before (or in the middle of) Whitman, but after Emily Dickinson (Samuel Clemens beginning our Volume 2). When the first recognizable American anthologies were published sixty years or more ago, it made sense to start the second half of the course with Whitman. After all, at the end of World War I, the first edition of *Leaves of Grass* was a more recent publication than *The Waste Land* is today. Even Whitman's "deathbed edition" was more recent than such a "contemporary" book as *The Naked and the Dead* is now. But despite the immense proliferation of important American writing in those same sixty years, anthologists have continued to divide the volumes in the same old way, with the result of increasingly compressing and underrepresenting the American literature of recent years. More than 75 percent of the 1,700 teachers we polled agreed with our decision to include both Whitman and Dickinson in their appropriate period in the first volume.

This reorganization enables us to represent twentieth-century literature adequately for the first time in an anthology of American literature. The many new authors and selections are there not because of the glamor of contemporaneity, but because they are of high literary merit and because their presence is needed in order to make sense of the literary history of our age.

To help make such sense, the editors have subdivided the standard but amorphous category, twentieth-century literature. The section "American Literature between the Wars 1914–1945" recognizes that these three decades are a definable literary span with its own literary history. The body of literature after World War II has, in its turn, been divided into separate sections of prose and poetry. This division has enabled the editors to write introductions and other editorial aids, as well as to make their selections, in such a way as to assist students in understanding the movements, trends, and careers in contemporary prose and contemporary poetry and to stimulate them to carry on their reading after they have finished the course.

The other sections of the anthology are also freshly conceived. In all of them, we have dropped the traditional period names and have discontinued the practice of organizing writers according to "influences" and "schools." In our simplified arrangement, we merely assign time-span titles to the six sections into which the volumes are divided (e.g., "Early American Literature 1620–1820"), and, with very few exceptions, we arrange all the authors chronologically by date of birth. This change eliminates period labels, group labels, and topic labels that encourage students to prejudge the literature, while permitting teachers the utmost flexibility in organizing their own courses.

In all periods, teachers are offered more authors and (by at least major authors) more selections than, in all probability, they will have time to assign or teach. This principle of copiousness in selection is designed to allow teachers to set up their own reading lists, without the need to ask students to buy extra books. Out of the materials provided, instructors can teach, for example, their own selections of Thoreau, Whitman, Melville, Dickinson, Pound, Frost, or Williams; they can also vary the assignments from year to year as their interests or their students' interests change. Whenever possible, we have made selections that would show a writer's development; for example, instead of representing Adrienne Rich with a random handful of poems, we have chosen thirteen poems that demonstrate the arc of this notable poet's career, from her first to her most recent book.

On the principle of making the anthology self-sufficient—thereby eliminating heavy extra costs to the student and ensuring that the wrong book won't be brought to class—we print in their entirety a great many long works, all notable achievements in American literature: Franklin's *Autobiography* (newly edited from manuscript); Hawthorne's *The Scarlet Letter* (with the "Custom-House" preface); Thoreau's *Walden*; Melville's *Benito Cereno* and *Billy Budd, Sailor*; Twain's *Adventures of Huckleberry Finn*; James's *Daisy Miller*; Stephen Crane's *The Red Badge of Courage. An Episode of the American Civil War* (again, newly edited from manuscript); and Bellow's *Seize the Day*. In addition we also offer Rowlandson's complete *Captivity and Restoration*; Fuller's *The Great Lawsuit* (the first major document of American feminism); Chopin's novel *The Awakening*; Wharton's novella *Bunner Sisters*; and Faulkner's

Old Man. Longer poems printed in their entirety range from Cooke's *The Sot-Weed Factor* and Barlow's *The Hasty Pudding* through Pound's *Hugh Selwyn Mauberley* (complete with the 1920 "post-script"), Eliot's *The Waste Land*, Hart Crane's *Voyages* and *The Bridge*, and Ginsberg's elegy *Kaddish*.

A major responsibility of any new anthology is to redress the long neglect of woman writers in America. To this end, we profited from the advice of a large number of teachers who are women. In these two volumes, about 700 pages represent the work of some twenty-nine women. Some of these, of course, are familiar, but we also include the feminist Margaret Fuller; all three of the major woman local-colorists; the feminist-anarchist Emma Goldman; the influential innovator Gertrude Stein; and many other poets and writers of the twentieth century. Another responsibility of a new anthology is to do justice to the contributions of black writers to American literature and culture. We represent fourteen black authors.

This latest of "the Norton anthologies" incorporates the features that have established a new standard in literary texts for the class-room. The format is not that of the traditional anthology, but of a book to be read for pleasure. There are no forbidding double columns of prose and verse; the text is inviting to the eye; and the special paper makes it possible to keep each volume to a size and weight that make it easily carried—including to a classroom. Furthermore, the editorial materials—introductions, headnotes, footnotes—are terse but full, and designed to give the student the information needed, without pre-empting the interpretive function either of the student or the instructor. The "Selected Bibliographies" at the end of each volume provide guides to further readings and research, and complete the self-sufficiency of the anthology, which permits each of its selections to be read, understood, and placed in historical context without the need for access to a collection of reference books.

The editors have taken scrupulous care to provide the most accurate available version of each work that is represented. Indeed, several of the major texts—Franklin's *Autobiography*, some of the materials by Clemens, Howells's *Novel-Writing and Novel-Reading*, and *The Red Badge of Courage*—have been newly edited from the original manuscripts. And each text is printed in the form which accords, as closely as it is possible to determine, to the intentions of its author. There is one exception: we have modernized the spellings and (very sparingly) the punctuation in the section on early American literature, on the principle that nonfunctional features such as archaic spellings and typography pose unnecessary problems for beginning students. We have, however, since it is a new edition from the manuscript, left Franklin's *Autobiography* unchanged. For the convenience of the student, we have used square brackets to indicate titles supplied by the editors, and have, whenever a portion of a text has been omitted, indicated that omission by three asterisks.

The editors of this anthology were selected on the basis of their expertness in their individual areas, and also because they combine respect for the best that has been thought and said about literature in the past with an alertness (as participants, as well as observers) to the altering interests, procedures, and evaluations in contemporary scholarship and criticism. Each editor was given ultimate responsibility for his own period, but all collaborated in the total enterprise.

In preparing these volumes, we have incurred obligations to hundreds of teachers throughout the country who have answered our questions; we take this opportunity to thank them warmly for their invaluable assistance. Those teachers who prepared detailed critiques, or who offered special help in selecting or preparing texts, are listed under "Acknowledgments," on a separate page. The editors would like to express their appreciation to their own invaluable assistants: Jill Beerman, Mark Canner, Mary Eberle, Deborah Grossman, Mary Hathorn, William Kozlowski, Bea McLean, Patrick Merla, the staff of the Enoch Pratt Library, Heddy Richter (American Literature Librarian, Doheny Library, University of Southern California), Diane Rosenfeldt, and Tina Stough. The publishers would like, in turn, to express their thanks to Jennifer Sutherland, John W. N. Francis, Victor Schmalzer, and Neil Patterson, as well as to Diane O'Connor, Marjorie Flock, Nelda Freeman, Carol Flechner, Calvin Towle, Sue Lowe, Roy Tedoff, Hugh O'Neill, and James Mairs of Norton's production department; we also owe thanks to Valerie Eads, Karen Fischer, George J. Firmage, Mike McIver, and Barbara Zimmerman. Our greatest debt is to M. H. Abrams (Class of 1916 Professor of English at Cornell, and Norton's adviser on English texts), upon whose rich experience in making anthologies we drew often and profitably. All have helped us to achieve the task of representing adequately, in two convenient volumes, the extraordinary variety and quality of our American literary heritage.

Acknowledgments

A MONG OUR many critics, advisers, and friends, the following were of especial help in providing critiques of particular periods or of the anthology as a whole, or assisted in preparing texts and editorial matter: M. H. Abrams, (Cornell University); Frederick Anderson (late General Editor of *The Mark Twain Papers*, University of California at Berkeley); Nina Baym (University of Illinois); Henry Binder (University of California at Riverside); Sargent Bush (University of Wisconsin); Edwin H. Cady (Duke University); Evan B. Carton (University of Texas); Sarah Blacher Cohen (State University of New York at Albany); Thomas W. Cooley (Ohio State University); James M. Cox (Dartmouth College); Doris L. Eder (University of Rochester); Thomas R. Edwards (Rutgers University); Alison Ensor (University of Tennessee); Rosemary Franklin (University of Georgia); Vincent Freimarck (State University of New York at Binghamton); Albert Gelpi (Stanford University); Barbara Charlesworth Gelpi (Stanford University); William M. Gibson (University of Wisconsin); Seymour Gross (University of Detroit); Harrison Hayford (Northwestern University); Carolyn Heilbrun (Columbia University); Faith Mackey Holland; C. Hugh Holman (University of North Carolina); Myrl G. Jones (Radford College); Jerome F. Klinkowitz (University of Northern Iowa); J. A. Leo Lemay (University of Delaware); Perry Lentz (Kenyon College); Ilse Lind (New York University); Jay Martin (University of California at Irvine); Diane Middlebrook (Stanford University); Thomas Moser (Stanford University); Robert O'Clair (Manhattanville College); Nancy Packer (Stanford University); Marjorie Perloff (University of Maryland); Donald Pizer (Tulane University); Carol H. Poston (University of Illinois at Chicago Circle); Dorothy Redden (Douglass College); Adrienne Rich; M. L. Rosenthal (New York University); Daniel Shea (Washington University); Alan Shucard (University of Wisconsin at Parkside); Eleanor M. Tilton (Barnard College); Darwin T. Turner (University of Iowa); Linda W. Wagner (Radcliffe Institute); Kathleen Woodward (University of Wisconsin at Milwaukee).

American Literature
1865–1914

THE TRANSFORMATION OF A NATION

IN THE SECOND half of the nineteenth century, the fertile, mineral-rich American continent west of the Appalachians and Alleghenies was peopled and exploited. Americans, their numbers doubled by a continuous flow of immigrants, pushed westward to the Pacific coast, displacing Indians and the Spanish settlements where they stood in the way. Vast stands of timber were consumed; numberless herds of buffalo and other game gave way to cattle, sheep, farms, villages, and cities; various technologies converted the country's immense natural resources into industrial products both for its own burgeoning population and for foreign markets.

The result was that, between the end of the Civil War and the beginning of the First World War, the country was wholly transformed. Before the Civil War, America had been essentially a rural, agrarian, isolated republic whose idealistic, confident, and self-reliant inhabitants for the most part believed in God; by the time the United States entered World War I as a world power, it was an industrialized, urbanized, continental nation whose people had been forced to come to terms with the implications of Darwin's theory of evolution as well as with profound changes in its own social institutions and cultural values.

The Civil War cost some $8 billion and claimed 600,000 lives. It seems also to have left the country morally exhausted. Nonetheless, the country prospered materially over the five following decades in part because the war had stimulated technological development and had served as an occasion to test new methods of organization and management that were required to move efficiently large numbers of men and material, and which were then adapted to industrial modernization on a massive scale. The first transcontinental railroad was completed in 1869; industrial output grew at a geometric rate, and agricultural productivity increased dramatically; electricity was introduced on a large scale; new means of communication such as the telephone revolutionized many aspects of daily life; coal, oil, iron, gold, silver, and other kinds of mineral wealth were discovered and extracted to make large numbers of vast individual fortunes and to make the nation as a whole rich enough to capitalize for the first time on its own further development. By the end of the century, no longer a colony politically or economically, the United States could begin its own imperialist expansion (of which the Spanish-American War in 1898 was only one sign).

The central material fact of the period was industrialization, on a scale unprecedented in the earlier experiences of England and Europe. Between 1850 and 1880 capital invested in manufacturing industries more than quadrupled, while factory employment nearly doubled. By 1885 four transcontinental railroad lines were completed, using in their own construction and carrying to manufacturing centers in Pittsburgh, Cleveland, Detroit, and Chicago the nation's quintupled output of steel. This extensive railway system—and the invention of the refrigerated railway car—in turn made possible such economic developments as the centralization of the meat-packing industry in Chicago. Control over this enterprise as well as other industries passed to fewer and larger companies as time went on. In the two decades following the 1870s, a very small number of men controlled without significant competition the enormously profitable steel, railroad, oil, and meat-packing industries.

This group of men, known variously as buccaneers, captains of industry, self-made men, or robber barons, included Jay Gould, Jim Hill, Leland Stanford, Jim Fisk, Andrew Carnegie, J. P. Morgan, and John D. Rockefeller. However different in temperament and public behavior, all of these men successfully squeezed out their competitors and accumulated vast wealth and power. All were good examples of what the English novelist D. H. Lawrence described as "the lone hand and the huge success." These were the men who served as examplars of Mark Twain's Colonel Beriah Sellers, a character who in turn epitomizes much of the spirit of acquisitiveness excoriated by Twain in *The Gilded Age*, 1873 (a novel written in collaboration with Charles Dudley Warner).

In this half century, as industry flourished, America's cities grew. When the Civil War broke out, America, except for the northeastern seaboard, was a country of farms, villages, and small towns. Most of its citizens were involved in agricultural pursuits and small family businesses. By the turn of the century only about one third of the population lived on farms. New York had grown from a city of 500,000 in 1850 to a metropolis of nearly 3,500,000 persons by 1900, many of them recent immigrants from central, eastern, and southern Europe. Chicago, at mid-century a raw town of 20,000, had over 2,000,000 inhabitants by 1910. By the end of the First World War one half of the American population was concentrated in a dozen or so cities; the vast majority of all wage earners were employed by corporations and large enterprises, 8.5 million as factory workers. Millions of people participated in the prosperity that accompanied this explosive industrial expansion, but the social costs were immense.

The transformation of an entire continent, outlined above, was not accomplished, that is, without incalculable suffering. In the countryside increasing numbers of farmers, dependent for transportation of their crops on the monopolistic railroads, were squeezed off the land by what novelist Frank Norris characterized as the giant "octopus" that crisscrossed the continent. Everywhere independent farmers were placed "under the lion's paw" of land speculators and absentee landlords that Hamlin Garland's story made famous. For many, the great cities were also, as the radical novelist Upton Sinclair sensed, jungles where only the strongest, the most ruthless, and the luckiest survived. An oversupply of labor kept wages down and allowed the industrialists to maintain working conditions of notorious danger and discomfort for men, women, and children who competed for the scarce jobs.

Neither farmers nor urban laborers were effectively organized to pursue their own interests, and neither group had any significant political leverage until the 1880s. Legislators essentially served the interests of business and industry, and the scandals of President Grant's administration, the looting of the New York City Treasury by William Marcy ("Boss") Tweed in the 1870s, as well as the later horrors of municipal corruption exposed by journalist Lincoln Steffens and other "muckrakers" were symptomatic of what many writers of the time took to be the age of the "Great Barbecue." Early attempts by labor to organize were crude and often violent, and such groups as the notorious "Molly Maguires," which performed acts of terrorism in Pennsylvania, seemed to confirm the sense of the public and of the courts that labor organizations were "illegal conspiracies" and thus public enemies. Direct violence was probably, as young Emma Goldman believed, a necessary step toward establishing collective bargaining as a means of negotiating disputes between industrial workers and their employers; it was, in any event, not until such an alternative developed—really not until the 1930s—that labor acquired the unquestioned right to strike.

MARK TWAIN, W. D. HOWELLS, AND HENRY JAMES

This rapid transcontinental settlement and these new urban industrial circumstances were accompanied by the development of a national literature of great abundance and variety. New themes, new forms, new subjects, new regions, new authors, new audiences all emerged in the literature of this half century. As a result, at the onset of World War I, the spirit and substance of American literature had evolved remarkably, just as its center of production had shifted from Boston to New York in the late 1880s and the sources of its energy to Chicago and the Midwest. No longer was it produced, at least in its popular forms, in the main by solemn, typically moralistic men from New England and the Old South; no longer were polite, well-dressed, grammatically correct, middle-class young people the only central characters in its narratives; no longer were these narratives to be set in exotic places and remote times; no longer, indeed, were fiction, poetry, drama, and formal history the chief acceptable forms of literary expression; no longer, finally, was literature read primarily by young, middle-class women. In sum, American literature in these years fulfilled in considerable measure the condition Whitman called for in 1867 in describing *Leaves of Grass*: it treats, he said of his own major work, each state and region as peers "and expands from them, and includes the world . . . connecting an American citizen with the citizens of all nations." Self-educated men from the frontier, adventurers, and journalists introduced industrial workers and the rural poor, ambitious businessmen and vagrants, prostitutes and unheroic soldiers as major characters in fiction. At the same time, these years saw the emergence of what the critic Warner Berthoff aptly designates "the literature of argument," powerful works in sociology, philosophy, psychology, many of them impelled by the spirit of exposure and reform. Just as America learned to play a role in this half century as an autonomous international political, economic, and military power, so did its literature establish itself as a producer of major works. In its new security, moreover, it welcomed (in translation) the leading European figures of the time—Tolstoy, Ibsen, Chekhov, Hardy, Zola, Galdós, Verga—often in the columns of Henry James and William Dean Howells, who reviewed their works enthusiastically in *Harper's Weekly* and *Harper's Monthly*, the *North*

American Review, and other leading journals of the era. American writers in this period, like most writers of other times and places, wrote to earn money, earn fame, change the world, and—out of that mysterious compulsion to find the best order for the best words—express themselves in a permanent form and thus exorcise the demon that drove them.

The three figures who dominated prose fiction in the last quarter of the nineteenth century were Mark Twain, William Dean Howells, and Henry James. For half a century Howells was friend, editor, correspondent, and champion of both Twain and James. These latter two, however, knew each other little, and liked each other's work even less.

Twain was without doubt the most popular of the three, in part because of his unusual gift as a humorous public speaker. There is, indeed, much truth in the shrewd observation that Twain's art was in essence the art of the performer. Unlike many of his contemporaries who were successful on the platform, however, Twain had the even rarer ability to convert the humor of stage performance into written language. Twain is one of the few writers of any nationality who makes nearly all of his readers laugh out loud. He had flair; he shared the belief of one of his characters, that "you can't throw too much style into a miracle." To say this is not to deny Twain's skills as a craftsman, his consummate care with words. He was constitutionally incapable of writing—or speaking—a dull sentence. He was a master of style, and there is wide agreement among his fellow writers and literary historians alike that his masterpiece, *Adventures of Huckleberry Finn* (1885), is the fountainhead of American colloquial prose. Nor is there much dispute about Twain's ability to capture the enduring, archetypal, mythic images of America before the writer and the country came of age, or to create some of the most memorable characters in all of American fiction—Colonel Sellers, Tom Sawyer, Huck Finn and his Pap, the king and the duke, and Nigger Jim. Because of his "river" books—*The Adventures of Tom Sawyer* (1876), *Life on the Mississippi* (1883), and *Adventures of Huckleberry Finn* (1885)—we as Americans have a clearer (because it is mythic rather than historical) collective sense of life in the prewar Mississippi valley than we do of any other region of America at any other time.

Huck Finn might, at the end of his adventures, imagine lighting out "for the territory," the still uncivilized frontier, but for Twain there was to be no escape; *Huck Finn* was his last "evasion." Obliged to confront the moral, mental, and material squalor of postwar industrialized America (and to deal with a succession of personal catastrophes), Twain's work became more cerebral, contrived, and embittered. Only when he began in the late 1890s to dictate his autobiography, as the critic Jay Martin observes, did he once again become invisible in his words. Freed of the need to be respectable or to make large coherent narrative structures, Twain once more could function as an artist.

If Twain was the most popular of these three major figures, his friend and adviser Howells was unquestionably the most influential American writer in the last quarter of the century. Relentlessly productive, Howells wrote and published the equivalent of one hundred books during his sixty-year professional career. He wrote novels, travel books, biographies, plays, criticism, essays, autobiography—and made them pay. He was the first American writer self-consciously to conceive, to cite the title of one of his essays, of *The Man of Letters As a Man of Business*. Howells was, however, no mere acquisitive hack. He wrote always with a sense of his genteel, largely female audience; but if he generally observed the proprieties, he often took real risks and opened new territories for fiction. In Marcia Gaylord of *A Modern Instance* (1881) he traces with great subtlety the moral decline of an overindulged country girl as she turns into a vindictively jealous bitch. Nor can those who complain that Howells only wrote of the "smiling aspects" of life have read *The Landlord at Lion's Head* (1897), with its brutal Jeff Durgin, or *An Imperative Duty* (1892), a curious novel of miscegenation.

Starting with *The Rise of Silas Lapham* (1885), Howells addressed with deepening seriousness (and risk to his reputation) the relationship between the economic transformation of America and its moral condition. In *A Hazard of New Fortunes* (1890), written after his "conversion" to socialism by his reading of Tolstoy and what he described as the "civic murder" of the Haymarket anarchists in 1887, Howells offers his most extended interpretation of the decay of American life under the rule of competitive capitalism. Of the physical squalor and human misery he observes in the Bowery, his character Basil March (the central consciousness of the narrative) concludes:

> Accident and then exigency seemed the forces at work to this extraordinary effect; the play of energies as free and planless as those that force the forest from the soil to the sky; and then the fierce struggle for survival, with the stronger life persisting over the deformity, the mutilation, the destruction, the decay of the weaker. The whole at moments seemed to him lawless, Godless; the absence of intelligent, comprehensive purpose in the huge disorder, and the violent struggle to subordinate the result to the greater good, penetrated with its dumb appeal the consciousness of a man who had always been too self-inwrapt to perceive the chaos to which the individual selfishness must always lead.

Howells could see even more clearly in New York than he had in Boston that for the mass of their populations the cities had become infernos, the social environment degraded by the chasm that had opened between rich and poor, leaving the middle class trapped in their attitudes toward the poor between appalled sympathy and fear.

In his criticism, Howells had called for a literary realism that would treat commonplace Americans truthfully; "this truth given, the book *cannot* be wicked and cannot be weak; and without it all graces of style and feats of invention and cunning of construction are so many superfluities of naughtiness," he observed in "The Editor's Study" of *Harper's Monthly* for April, 1887. Critics are now pretty much in agreement that Howells's novels, especially those of the 1880s and 1890s, succeed in providing such a "truthful treatment." His lifelong friend Henry James observed in a letter on the occasion of Howells's seventy-fifth birthday: "Stroke by stroke and book by book your work was to become, for this exquisite notation of our whole democratic light and shade and give and take, in the highest degree *documentary*, so that none other . . . could approach it in value and amplitude." Whether Howells also had a truly "grasping imagination," the imagination to penetrate photographic surfaces, is the kind of question that finally each reader must decide; that it has become an active question at all is a sign of how far Howells's reputation has come since H. L. Mencken characterized him in 1919 as "an urbane and highly respectable old gentleman, a sitter on committees, an intimate of professors . . . , a placid conformist."

On his deathbed Howells was writing an essay on *The American James,* an essay which apparently would have defended James against charges that in moving to England permanently in the mid-1870s he had cut himself off from the sources of his imaginative power as well as sacrificed any hope of having a large audience for his work. In view of the critical praise lavished on James since World War II, and in the light of the highly successful film and television adaptations of his fiction, the need for any such defense may seem puzzling. Yet it is true that during his lifetime few of James's books had much popular success and that he was not a favorite of the American people.

There is more of American life and spirit represented in his literary production than is often thought, but James early came to believe the literary artist should not simply hold a mirror to the surface of social life in particular times and places. Instead, the writer should use language to probe the deepest reaches of the psychological and moral nature of human beings. At a time when novels were widely conceived as mere popular entertainment, James believed that the best fiction illuminates life by revealing it as an immensely complex process; and he demonstrated in work after work what a superb literary sensibility can do to dignify both life and art. He is a realist of the inner life; a dramatizer, typically, to put it crudely, of the tensions that develop between the young, innocent, selfless, and free woman and the older, sophisticated, and convention-bound man. That he is always on the side of freedom, Ezra Pound was to be one of the first to note.

Twain, James, and Howells together brought to fulfillment native trends in the realistic portrayal of the landscape and social surfaces, brought to perfection the vernacular style, and explored and exploited the literary possibilities of the interior life. Among them they recorded and made permanent the essential life of the eastern third of the continent as it was lived in the last half of the nineteenth century on the vanishing frontier, in the village, small town, or turbulent metropolis, and in European watering places and capitals. Among them they established the literary identity of distinctively American protagonists, specifically the vernacular hero and the "American Girl," the baffled and strained middle-class family, the businessman, the psychologically complicated citizens of a new international culture. Together, in short, they set the example and charted the future course for the subjects, themes, techniques, and styles of fiction we still call modern.

OTHER REALISTS AND NATURALISTS

Terms like *realism, naturalism, local color,* while useful shorthand for professors of literature trying to "cover" great numbers of books and long periods of time, probably do as much harm as they do good, especially for readers who are beginning their study of literature. The chief disservice these generalizing terms do to readers and authors is to divert attention away from the distinctive quality of an author's sense of life to a general body of ideas. In a letter turning down one of the many professorships he was offered, Howells observed that the study of literature should begin and end in pleasure, and it is far more rewarding to establish, in Emerson's phrase, "an original relationship" to particular texts and authors than it is an attempt to fit them into movements. However, since these generalizations are still in currency, we need to examine some of them.

One of the most far-reaching intellectual events of the last half of the nineteenth century was the publication in 1859 of Charles Darwin's *The Origin of Species*. This book, together with Darwin's *Descent of Man* (1870), hypothesized that over the millennia, man had evolved from lower forms of life. Humans were special, not—as the Bible taught—because God had created them in His image, but because they had successfully adapted to changing environmental conditions and had passed on their survival-making characteristics genetically. Though few American authors wrote treatises in reaction to Darwinism, nearly every writer had to come to terms somehow with this challenge to traditional conceptions of man, nature, and the social order.

One response was to accept the more negative implications of evolutionary theory and to use it to account for the behavior of characters in literary works. That is, characters were conceived as more or less complex combinations of inherited attributes and habits conditioned by social and economic forces. As Émile Zola, the influential French theorist and novelist, put the matter in his essay *The Experimental Novel*:

> In short, we must operate with characters, passions, human and social data as the chemist and the physicist work on inert bodies, as the physiologist works on living bodies. Determinism governs everything. It is scientific investigation; it is experimental reasoning that combats one by one the hypotheses of the idealists and will replace novels of pure imagination by novels of observation and experiment.

Many American writers adopted this pessimistic form of realism, this so-called "naturalistic" view of man, though each writer, of course, incorporated this assumption, and many others, into his or her work in highly individual ways.

Stephen Crane is a case in point. Crane believed, as he said of *Maggie*, that environment counts for a great deal in determining human fate. Nature is not hostile, he observes in *The Open Boat*, only "indifferent, flatly indifferent." Indeed, the earth, in *The Blue Hotel*, is described in one of the most famous passages in naturalistic fiction, as a "whirling, fire-smitten, ice-locked, disease-stricken, space-lost bulb." In Crane's *The Red Badge of Courage*—and this is especially clear in the text reconstituted for this anthology—Henry Fleming responds to the very end to the world of chaos and violence that surrounds him with alternating surges of panic and self-congratulation, not as a man who has understood himself and his place in a world which reveals order below its confused surface.

But after we have granted this ostensibly "naturalistic" perspective to Crane, we are still left with his distinctiveness as a writer, with his "personal honesty" in reporting what he saw (and concomitant rejection of accepted literary conventions), and with his use of impressionistic literary techniques to present incomplete characters and a broken world—a world more random than scientifically predictable. We are also left with the hardly pessimistic lesson of *The Open Boat*—that precisely because human beings are exposed to a savage world of chance where death is always imminent, they must learn the art of sympathetic identification with others and how to practice solidarity, often learned at the price of death. Without this deeply felt human connection, human experience is as meaningless as wind, sharks, and waves. It is Crane's power with words and his ability to live with paradox, then, that make him interesting, not his allegiance to philosophic or scientific theories.

Theodore Dreiser certainly did not share Crane's tendency to use words and images as if he were a composer or a painter. But he did share, at least early in his career, Crane's view that by and large human beings were more like moths drawn to flame than lords of creation. But, again, it is not Dreiser's beliefs that make him an enduring major figure in American letters: it is what his imagination and literary technique do with an extremely rich set of ideas, experiences, and emotions to create the "color of life" in his fictions that earns him an honored place. If Crane gave us through the personal honesty of his vision a new sense of the human consciousness under conditions of extreme pressure, Dreiser gave us for the first time in his unwieldy novels a sense of the fumbling, yearning, confused response to the simultaneously enchanting, exciting, ugly, and dangerous metropolis that had become the familiar residence for such large numbers of Americans by the turn of the century.

Best known as a novelist of manners in the tradition of Henry James and for her stories of the beleaguered upper class, Edith Wharton also wrote sympathetically of the "commonplace" people Howells believed should be the subjects of a democratic fiction. Unlike Howells, however, she depicted deeply frustrated people caught in the trap of life, people too poor, too weak, too unlucky, too dull to escape their miserable fates, their tragic isolation. Every bit as grim and relentless (if not as melodramatic) as the environment of Crane's *Maggie*, is the shabby cityscape in which the Bunner sisters play out their drama.

In sum, despite residual prohibitions that insisted on humanity's special place in the universe, and a status-conscious gentility that militated against the ugly as well as the "morally" unclean, America proved to be a fertile ground for naturalistic ideas and realistic literary technique, though the ideas were often undercut, and the technique, while commonly documentary, was adapted to highly individual uses. The country's democratic spirit (in any case, the principle of equality) and the harsh realities of country and urban life that accompanied industrialization and unbridled economic competitiveness made it receptive to a literature of familiar people and ordinary places keenly observed by eye and ear.

REGIONAL WRITING

Regional writing, another expression of the realistic impulse, resulted from the desire both to preserve distinctive ways of life before industrialization dispersed or homogenized them and to avoid the harsh realities that seemed to replace these early times. At a more practical level, much of the writing was a response to the opportunities presented by the rapid growth of magazines, which created a new market for short fiction. By the end of the century, in any case, virtually every region of the country, from Maine to California, from the northern plains to the Louisiana bayous, had its "local colorist" (the implied comparison is to painters of so-called "genre" scenes) to immortalize its distinctive natural, social, and linguistic features. Though often suffused with sentimentalism and nostalgia, the best work of these regionalists renders both a convincing surface of a particular time and location and penetrates below that surface to the depths that transform the local into the universal. This ambiguity of attitude may be seen even in an early example of local-color writing such as Bret Harte's *The Luck of Roaring Camp,* which made Harte a national celebrity in 1868. But Harte knew how to be entertaining, and the curiosity of the rest of the country about the gold-rush country was satisfied in this and other myth-making stories Harte produced early in his career.

Hamlin Garland, rather than creating a myth, set out to destroy one. Like so many other writers of the time, Garland was encouraged by W. D. Howells to write about what he knew best—the bleak and exhausting life of farmers of the upper Midwest. As he later said, his purpose in writing his early stories was to show that the "mystic quality connected with free land . . . was a myth." Garland's farmers are not the vigorous, sensuous peasants of Brueghel's paintings, but bent, drab figures reminiscent of Millet's *Sowers* or Edwin Markham's *Man with a Hoe.* In *Under the Lion's Paw,* from the collection *Main-Travelled Roads* (1891), we see local color not as nostalgia but as realism in the service of social protest.

Before the Civil War, New England—and Boston and Concord in particular—had long dominated the American literary scene, and its authors had created, in works such as Thoreau's *Walden* (1854), a strong image of itself as a bucolic landscape with still a suggestion of the wild at the edge of its clearings. Harriet Beecher Stowe had also provided in her *Old Town Folks* (1869) one of the most successful postwar evocations of a mode of life that had never quite existed. And her earlier novel, *Pearl of Orr's Island* (1862), inspired Sarah Orne Jewett of South Berwick, Maine, to become a writer.

In Jewett, particularly in her Dunnet Landing stories written at the turn of the century, the dramatic and narrative possibilities of local-color short fiction may be said to have reached their apotheosis. In *The Foreigner* (1900), Jewett found the perfect emblematic figure, setting, and form to represent her rich sense of the consequences for women of their emotional and social deprivation. Her Massachusetts contemporary, Mary E. Wilkins Freeman, produced no single work equal to Jewett's best, but this New England writer of some two hundred stories deserves the attention she continues to receive on the strength of a score of first-rate shorter fictions, which allowed her to perfect, with her special intensity, the sentimental regional tale. Alice Brown of New Hampshire and Rose Terry Cooke of Connecticut offer further excellent examples of New England regionalism at its best.

Chief among the southern local colorists are George Washington Cable, Joel Chandler Harris, Charles Waddell Chesnutt, and Kate Chopin. Like their Yankee counterparts, they become most universal when they are most faithfully particular. Harris's Georgia Negroes live permanently in our imagination because he knew them well and from within. He did not exploit or demean them; and Kate Chopin did not exploit or demean the characters who people her stories of the Louisiana bayous.

REALISM AS ARGUMENT

During these fifty years a vast body of nonfictional prose was devoted to the description, analysis, and critique of social, economic, and political institutions and to the unsolved social problems that were one consequence of the rapid growth and change of the time. Women's rights, political corruption, economic inequity, business deceptions, the exploitation of labor—these became the subjects of articles and books by a long list of journalists, historians, social critics, and economists. A surprising amount of this writing survives as literature, and much of it has genuine power that is often attributed only to the older, "purer" forms. Certainly in that most ambitious of all American works of moral instruction, *The Education of Henry Adams* (1918), Adams registers through a literary sensibility a sophisticated historian's sense of what we now recognize as the disorientation that accompanies rapid and continuous change. The result is one of the most essential books of and about the whole period, and it seems fitting that Adams should have the last—though surely not the conclusive—word about his own problematic times.

Of all the problems of the day, perhaps the most persistent and resistant to solution was the problem of racial inequality, more specifically what came to be known as the "Negro problem." Several of the selections in this anthology touch one aspect or another of the long, shameful history of white injustices to black Americans, but two items by major black writers and leaders have a special claim on our attention: the autobiography of Booker T. Washington, *Up from Slavery* (1900), and the brilliantly analytical essay on Washington in *The Souls of Black Folk* (1903) by W. E. B. DuBois. The Washington-DuBois controversy set the major terms of the continuing debate between black leaders and in the black community with respect to the future: Will blacks accept anything less than complete equality educationally, socially, politically, and economically?

In this half century, material, intellectual, social, and psychological changes in America went forward at such extreme speed and on such a massive scale that the enormously diverse writing of the time registers, at its core, degrees of shocked recognition of the human consequences of these radical transformations. Sometimes the shock is expressed in recoil and denial—thus the persistence, in the face of the ostensible triumph of realism, of the literature of diversion: nostalgic poetry, sentimental and melodramatic drama, and swashbuckling historical novels. The more enduring fictional and nonfictional prose forms of the era, however, come to terms imaginatively with the individual and collective dislocations and discontinuities associated with the closing out of the frontier, urbanization, intensified secularism, unprecedented immigration, the surge of national wealth unequally distributed, revised conceptions of human nature and destiny, the reordering of family and civil life, and the pervasive spread of mechanical and organizational technologies. The examples of courage, sympathy, and critical understanding on the part of our writers were a legacy to be drawn on, often unconsciously, often rebelliously, as America entered her next round of triumphs and tragedies, as the country self-consciously began its quest for a usable past.

SAMUEL CLEMENS
1835–1910

Samuel Langhorne Clemens, the third of five children, was born on November 30, 1835, in the village of Florida, Missouri, and grew up in the larger river town of Hannibal, that mixture of idyll and nightmare in and around which his two most famous characters, Tom Sawyer and Huck Finn, live out their adventure-filled summers. Sam's father, an ambitious and respected but unsuccessful country lawyer and storekeeper, died when Sam was twelve, and from that time on Sam worked to support himself and the rest of the family. Perhaps, as more than one critic has remarked, the shortness of his boyhood made him value it the more.

Sam was apprenticed to a printer after his father's death, and in 1851, when his brother Orion became a publisher in Hannibal, Sam went to work for him. In 1853 he began a three-year period of restless travel which took him to St. Louis, New York, Philadelphia, Keokuk (Iowa), and Cincinnati, in each of which he earned his living as a printer hired by the day. In 1856 he set out by steamboat for New Orleans, intending to go to the Amazon, where he expected to find adventure and perhaps wealth and fame besides. This scheme fell through, and instead, he apprenticed himself to Horace Bixby, the pilot of the Mississippi riverboat. After a training period of eighteen months, Clemens satisfied a boyhood ambition when he became a pilot himself. Clemens practiced this lucrative and prestigious trade until the Civil War virtually ended commercial river traffic in 1861. During this period he began to write humorous accounts of his activities for the *Keokuk Saturday Post*; though only three of these articles were published (under the pseudonym Thomas Jefferson Snodgrass), they established the pattern of peripatetic journalism—the pattern for much of the next ten years of his life.

After brief and rather inglorious service in the Confederate militia, Clemens made the first of the trips that would take him farther West and toward his ultimate careers as humorist, lecturer, and writer. In 1861, he accompanied Orion to the Nevada Territory, to which the latter had been appointed Secretary (chief record keeper for the territorial government) by President Lincoln. In *Roughing It*, written a decade later, Clemens told of the brothers' adventures on the way to Carson City and of the various schemes that, once there, Sam devised for getting rich quick on timber and silver. All of these schemes failed, however, and as usual Clemens was to get much more out of refining the ore of his experience into books than he was to earn from the actual experience of prospecting and claim staking. Soon enough Clemens was once again writing for newspapers, first for the *Territorial Enterprise* in Virginia City and then, after 1864, for the *Californian*. The fashion of the time called for a *nom de plume*, and Clemens used "Mark Twain," a term from his piloting days signifying "two fathoms deep" or "safe water." Twain's writing during these early years, while often distinctive and amusing, was largely imitative of the humorous journalism of the time and is important chiefly because it provided him with an opportunity to master the techniques of the short narrative and to try out a variety of subjects in a wide range of tones and modes. No less important than his writing during these formative Western years were his friendships with three master storytellers: the writer Bret Harte, the famous professional lecturer Artemus Ward, and the obscure amateur raconteur Jim Gillis. Twain owed his earliest national audience and critical recognition to his performances as lecturer and to his skillful retelling of a well-known tall tale, *The Jumping Frog of Calaveras County*, first published in 1865.

In this same year Twain signed up with the *Sacramento Union* to cover in a series of amusing letters the newly opened passenger service between San Francisco and Honolulu. In these letters Twain used a fictitious character, Mr. Brown, to present inelegant ideas, attitudes, and information, sometimes in impolite language. In this series Twain discovered that he could say almost anything he wanted—provided he could convincingly claim that he was simply reporting what others said and did. The refinement of this technique—a written equivalent of "dead-pan" lecturing—which allowed his fantasy a long leash and yet required him to anchor it in the circumstantial details of time and place, was to be his major technical accomplishment of the next two decades, the period of his best work.

The first book of this period—and still one of Twain's most popular—was *Innocents Abroad* (1869). It consists of a revised form of letters that Twain wrote for the *Alta California* and the *New York Tribune* during his 1867 excursion on the *Quaker City* to the Mediterranean and the Holy Land. The letters as they appeared in the newspaper—and later the book —were enormously popular, not only because they were exuberantly funny, but also because the satire they leveled against a pretentious, decadent, and undemocratic Old World was especially relished by a young country about to enter a period of explosive economic growth and political consolidation.

Twain still had no literary aspirations, nor any clear plans for a career. Nor did he have a permanent base of operations. To record the second half of his life is to record his acquisition of status, the mature development of his literary powers, and his transformation into a living public legend. A wife came first. Twain courted and finally won the hand of Olivia Langdon, the physically delicate daughter of a wealthy industrialist in Elmira, New York. This unlikely marriage brought both husband and wife the special pleasure that the union of apparent opposites sometimes yields. She was his "Angel"; he was her "Youth." The charge leveled in the 1920s by the critic Van Wyck Brooks that Livy's gentility emasculated Twain as a writer is no longer given serious credence. The complex comfort that this ebullient, whiskey-drinking, cigar-smoking, wild humorist took in his wife is suggested in the letter reproduced below that he wrote to his childhood friend Will Bowen.

The letter also makes clear just how deep the rich material of his Mississippi boyhood ran in his memory and imagination. To get to it, Twain had, in effect, to work chronologically backward and psychically inward. He made a tentative probe of this material as early as 1870 in an early version of *The Adventures of Tom Sawyer* called *A Boy's Manuscript*. But it was not until 1875, when he wrote *Old Times on the Mississippi* in seven installments of the *Atlantic Monthly* (edited by his lifelong friend W. D. Howells), that Twain arrived at the place his deepest imagination called home. For in this work, an account of Twain's apprenticeship to the pilot Horace Bixby, he evokes not only "the great Mississippi, the majestic, the magnificent Mississippi, rolling its mile-wide tide along, shining in the sun," but also his most intimate ties to the life on its surface and shores. With *Old Times* Twain is no longer a writer exploiting material; rather, he is a man expressing imaginatively a period of his life that he had deeply absorbed. The material he added to these installments to make the book *Life on the Mississippi* (1883) is often excellent, but it is clearly grafted on, not an organic development of the original story.

For all its charm and lasting appeal, *The Adventures of Tom Sawyer* (1876) is in certain respects a backward step. There is no mistaking its failure to integrate its self-consciously fine writing, addressed to adults, with its account in plain diction of thrilling adventures designed to appeal to young people. Twain had returned imaginatively to the Hannibal of his youth; before he could realize the deepest potential of this material he would have to put aside the psychological impediments of his civilized adulthood. *Tom Sawyer* creates a compelling myth of the endless summer of childhood pleasures mixed with terror, but as Twain hints in the opening sentence of *Huck Finn*, the earlier novel is important primarily as the place of origin of Huckleberry Finn—often described by critics and such fellow writers as Hemingway as the greatest American character in the greatest American book.

Adventures of Huckleberry Finn took Twain eight years to write. He began it in 1876, and completed it, after several stops and starts, in 1883. The fact that he devoted seven months to subsequent revision suggests that Twain was aware of the novel's sometimes discordant tones and illogical shifts in narrative intention. Any real or imagined flaws in the novel, however, have not bothered most readers; *Huck Finn* has enjoyed extraordinary popularity since its publication nearly one hundred years ago. Its unpretentious, colloquial, yet poetic style, its wide-ranging humor, its embodiment of the enduring and universally shared dream of perfect innocence and freedom, its recording of a vanished way of life in the pre–Civil War Mississippi valley has moved millions of people of all ages and conditions, and all over the world. It is one of those rare works that reveals to us the discrepancy between appearance and reality without leading us to despair of ourselves or others.

Though Twain made a number of attempts to return to the characters, themes, settings, and points of view of Tom and Huck, *Old Times*, *Tom Sawyer*, and *Huck Finn* had exhausted the rich themes of river and boyhood. Twain would live to write successful—even memorable—books, but the critical consensus is that his creative time had passed when he turned fifty. *A Connecticut Yankee at King Arthur's Court* (1889), for instance, is vividly imagined and very entertaining, but the satire, burlesque, moral outrage, and comic invention remain unintegrated.

A similar mood of despair informs and flaws *The Tragedy of Pudd'nhead Wilson* (1894). The book shows the disastrous effects of slavery on victimizer and victim alike—the unearned pride of whites and the undeserved self-hate of blacks. Satire turns to scorn, and beneath the drollery and fun one senses angry contempt for what Twain would soon refer to regularly as the "damned human race."

The decline of Twain's achievement as a writer between *Huck Finn* in 1884 and *Pudd'nhead Wilson* ten years later, however, is not nearly so precipitous as it turned out to be in the next decade, a decade which saw Twain's physical, economic, familial, and psychological supports collapse in a series of calamitous events. For forty years Twain had been fortune's favorite. Now, suddenly, his health was broken, his speculative investments in such enterprises as the Paige typesetting machine bankrupted him in the panic of 1893, his youngest daughter Jean was diagnosed as an epileptic, his oldest daughter Susy died of meningitis while he and Livy were in Europe, his wife began her decline into permanent invalidism, and Twain's grief for a time threatened his own sanity. For several years, as the critic Bernard DeVoto has shown, writing became both agonized labor and necessary therapy. The result of these circumstances was a dull book, *Following the Equator* (1897), which records Twain's round-the-world lecture tour undertaken to pay off debts; a sardonically preachy story, *The Man That Corrupted Hadleyburg* (1900); an embittered treatise on man's foibles, follies, and venality, *What Is Man?* (1906); and the bleakly despairing *The Mysterious Stranger*, first published in an "edited" version by Albert Bigelow Paine in 1916. Though the continuing study of the large bulk of Twain's unfinished (and, until recently, unpublished) work reveals much that is of interest to students of Twain, no one has come forward to claim that his final fifteen years represent a Henry Jamesian "major phase."

Unlike James, however, Twain in his last years became a revered public institution; his opinions were sought by the press on every subject of general interest. Though his opinions on many of these subjects—political, military, and social—were often tinged with vitriol, it was only to his best friends—who understood the complex roots of his despair and anger at the human race in general—that he vented his blackest rages. Much of this bitterness nonetheless informs such works, unpublished in his lifetime, as *The United States of Lyncherdom* (composed in 1901).

But early and late Twain maintained his magical power with language. What he said of one of his characters is a large part of his permanent appeal: "he could curl his tongue around the bulliest words in the language when he was a mind to, and lay them before you without a jint started, anywheres." This love of words and command over their arrangement, his mastery at distilling the rhythms and metaphors of oral speech into written prose, his vivid personality, his identification with the deepest centers of his fellow man's emotional and moral condition—all of these made Twain unique. As his friend Howells observed, he was unlike any of his contemporaries in American letters: "Emerson, Longfellow, Lowell, Holmes—I knew them all and all the rest of our sages, poets, seers, critics, humorists; they were like one another and like other literary men; but Clemens was sole, incomparable, the Lincoln of our literature." Like Lincoln, Clemens spoke to and for the common man of the American heartland that had nourished them both. And like Lincoln, who transcended the local political traditions in which he was trained to become the first great President of a continental nation, Clemens made out of the frontier humor and storytelling conventions of his journalistic influences a body of work of enduring value to the world of letters.

The editor is indebted to Frederick Anderson, editor of the Mark Twain Papers at the Bancroft Library, University of California, Berkeley, for textual advice and general counsel in preparing the Clemens materials.

Jim Smiley and His Jumping Frog[1]

Mr. A. Ward,

Dear Sir:—Well, I called on good-natured, garrulous old Simon Wheeler, and I inquired after your friend Leonidas W. Smiley, as you requested me to do, and I hereunto append the result. If you can get any information out of it you are cordially welcome to it. I have a lurking suspicion that your Leonidas W. Smiley is a myth—that you never knew such a personage, and that you only conjectured that if I asked old Wheeler about him it would remind him of his infamous *Jim* Smiley, and he would go to work and bore me nearly to death with some infernal reminiscence of him as long and tedious as it should be useless to me. If that was your design, Mr. Ward, it will gratify you to know that it succeeded.

I found Simon Wheeler dozing comfortably by the bar-room stove of the little old dilapidated tavern in the ancient mining camp of Boomerang,[2] and I noticed that he was fat and bald-headed, and had an expression of winning gentleness and simplicity upon his tranquil countenance. He roused up and gave me good-day. I told him a friend of mine had commissioned me to make some inquiries about a cherished companion of his boyhood named Leonidas W. Smiley—Rev. Leonidas W. Smiley—a young minister of the gospel, who he had heard was at one time a resident of this village of Boomerang. I added that if Mr. Wheeler could tell me anything about this Rev. Leonidas W. Smiley, I would feel under many obligations to him.

Simon Wheeler backed me into a corner and blockaded me there with his chair—and then sat down and reeled off the monotonous narrative which follows this paragraph. He never smiled, he never frowned, he never changed his voice from the quiet, gently-flowing key to which he turned the initial sentence, he never betrayed the slightest suspicion of enthusiasm—but all through the interminable narrative there ran a vein of impressive earnestness and sincerity, which showed me plainly that so far from his imagining that there was anything ridiculous or funny about his story, he regarded it as a really important matter, and admired its two heroes as men of transcendent genius in finesse. To me, the spectacle of a man drifting serenely along through such a queer yarn without ever smiling was exquisitely absurd. As I said before, I asked him to tell me what he knew of Rev. Leonidas W. Smiley, and he replied as follows. I let him go on in his own way, and never interrupted him once:

---

1. We reprint the original text as it appeared in *The New York Saturday Press* for November 18, 1865. It was later published as a short book entitled *The Celebrated Jumping Frog of Calaveras County* in 1867.
2. A booming camp in Calaveras County, northern California, during the gold rush. Calaveras County is now famous for its annual frog-jumping contest.

There was a feller here once by the name of *Jim* Smiley, in the winter of '49—or maybe it was the spring of '50—I don't recollect exactly, some how, though what makes me think it was one or the other is because I remember the big flume[3] wasn't finished when he first come to the camp; but anyway, he was the curiosest man about always betting on anything that turned up you ever see, if he could get anybody to bet on the other side, and if he couldn't he'd change sides—any way that suited the other man would suit *him*— any way just so's he got a bet, *he* was satisfied. But still, he was lucky—uncommon lucky; he most always come out winner. He was always ready and laying for a chance; there couldn't be no solitry thing mentioned but what that feller'd offer to bet on it—and take any side you please, as I was just telling you: if there was a horse race, you'd find him flush or you find him busted at the end of it; if there was a dog-fight, he'd bet on it; if there was a cat-fight, he'd bet on it; if there was a chicken-fight, he'd bet on it; why if there was two birds setting on a fence, he would bet you which one would fly first—or if there was a camp-meeting he would be there regular to bet on parson Walker, which he judged to be the best exhorter about here, and so he was, too, and a good man; if he even see a straddle-bug[4] start to go any wheres, he would bet you how long it would take him to get wherever he was going to, and if you took him up he would foller that straddle-bug to Mexico but what he would find out where he was bound for and how long he was on the road. Lots of the boys here has seen that Smiley and can tell you about him. Why, it never made no difference to *him*—he would bet on *anything*—the dangdest feller. Parson Walker's wife laid very sick, once, for a good while, and it seemed as if they warn't going to save her; but one morning he come in and Smiley asked him how she was, and he said she was considerable better— thank the Lord for his inf'nit mercy—and coming on so smart that with the blessing of Providence she'd get well yet—and Smiley, before he thought, says, "Well, I'll resk two-and-a-half that she don't, anyway."

Thish-yer Smiley had a mare—the boys called her the fifteen-min-ute nag, but that was only in fun, you know, because, of course, she was faster than that—and he used to win money on that horse, for all she was so slow and always had the asthma, or the distemper, or the consumption, or something of that kind. They used to give her two or three hundred yards' start, and then pass her under way; but always at the fag-end of the race she'd get excited and desperate-like, and come cavorting and spraddling up, and scattering her legs around limber, sometimes in the air, and sometimes out to one side amongst the fences, and kicking up m-o-r-e dust, and raising m-o-r-e racket with her coughing and sneezing and blowing her nose—and

3. An inclined channel which conveys water from a distance.
4. Long-legged beetle.

always fetch up at the stand just about a neck ahead, as near as you could cipher it down.

And he had a little small bull-pup, that to look at him you'd think he warn't worth a cent, but to set around and look ornery, and lay for a chance to steal something. But as soon as money was up on him he was a different dog—his under-jaw'd begin to stick out like the for'castle of a steamboat, and his teeth would uncover, and shine savage like the furnaces. And a dog might tackle him, and bully-rag him, and bite him, and throw him over his shoulder two or three times, and Andrew Jackson—which was the name of the pup—Andrew Jackson would never let on but what he was satisfied, and hadn't expected nothing else—and the bets being doubled and doubled on the other side all the time, till the money was all up— and then all of a sudden he would grab that other dog just by the joint of his hind legs and freeze to it—not chaw, you understand, but only just grip and hang on till they throwed up the sponge, if it was a year. Smiley always came out winner on that pup till he harnessed a dog once that didn't have no hind legs, because they'd been sawed off in a circular saw, and when the thing had gone along far enough, and the money was all up, and he came to make a snatch for his pet holt, he saw in a minute how he'd been imposed on, and how the other dog had him in the door, so to speak, and he 'peared surprised, and then he looked sorter discouraged like, and didn't try no more to win the fight, and so he got shucked out bad. He gave Smiley a look as much as to say his heart was broke, and it was *his* fault, for putting up a dog that hadn't no hind legs for him to take holt of, which was his main dependence in a fight, and then he limped off a piece, and laid down and died. It was a good pup, was that Andrew Jackson, and would have made a name for hisself if he'd lived, for the stuff was in him, and he had genius—I know it, because he hadn't had no opportunities to speak of, and it don't stand to reason that a dog could make such a fight as he could under them circumstances, if he hadn't no talent. It always makes me feel sorry when I think of that last fight of his'on, and the way it turned out.

Well, thish-yer Smiley had rat-terriers and chicken cocks, and tom-cats, and all them kind of things, till you couldn't rest, and you couldn't fetch nothing for him to bet on but he'd match you. He ketched a frog one day and took him home and said he cal'lated to educate him; and so he never done nothing for three months but set in his back yard and learn that frog to jump. And you bet you he *did* learn him, too. He'd give him a little hunch behind, and the next minute you'd see that frog whirling in the air like a doughnut —see him turn one summerset,[5] or maybe a couple, if he got a good start, and come down flat-footed and all right, like a cat. He got him up so in the matter of ketching flies, and kept him in prac-

5. Somersault.

tice so constant, that he'd nail a fly every time as far as he could see him. Smiley said all a frog wanted was education, and he could do most anything—and I believe him. Why, I've seen him set Dan'l Webster down here on this floor—Dan'l Webster was the name of the frog—and sing out, "Flies! Dan'l, flies," and quicker'n you could wink, he'd spring straight up, and snake a fly off'n the counter there, and flop down on the floor again as solid as a gob of mud, and fall to scratching the side of his head with his hind foot as indifferent as if he hadn't no idea he'd done any more'n any frog might do. You never see a frog so modest and straightfor'ard as he was, for all he was so gifted. And when it come to fair-and-square jumping on a dead level, he could get over more ground at one straddle than any animal of his breed you ever see. Jumping on a dead level was his strong suit, you understand, and when it come to that, Smiley would ante up money on him as long as he had a red.[6] Smiley was monstrous proud of his frog, and well he might be, for fellers that had travelled and ben everywheres all said he laid over any frog that ever *they* see.

Well, Smiley kept the beast in a little lattice box, and he used to fetch him down town sometimes and lay for a bet. One day a feller —a stranger in the camp, he was—come across him with his box, and says:

"What might it be that you've got in the box?"

And Smiley says, sorter indifferent like, "It might be a parrot, or it might be a canary, maybe, but it ain't—it's only just a frog."

And the feller took it, and looked at it careful, and turned it round this way and that, and says, "H'm—so 'tis. Well, what's *he* good for?"

"Well," Smiley says, easy and careless, "He's good enough for *one* thing I should judge—he can out-jump any frog in Calaveras county."

The feller took the box again, and took another long, particular look, and give it back to Smiley and says, very deliberate, "Well—I don't see no points about that frog that's any better'n any other frog."

"Maybe you don't," Smiley says. "Maybe you understand frogs, and maybe you don't understand 'em; maybe you've had experience, and maybe you ain't only a amature, as it were. Anyways, I've got *my* opinion, and I'll resk forty dollars that he can outjump ary frog in Calaveras county."

And the feller studied a minute, and then says, kinder sad, like, "Well—I'm only a stranger here, and I ain't got no frog—but if I had a frog I'd bet you."

And then Smiley says, "That's all right—that's all right—if you'll

6. I.e., a red cent.

hold my box a minute I'll go and get you a frog;" and so the feller took the box, and put up his forty dollars along with Smiley's, and set down to wait.

So he set there a good while thinking and thinking to hisself, and then he got the frog out and prized his mouth open and took a tea-spoon and filled him full of quail-shot—filled him pretty near up to his chin—and set him on the floor. Smiley he went out to the swamp and slopped around in thc mud for a long time, and finally he ketched a frog and fetched him in and give him to this feller and says:

"Now if you're ready, set him alongside of Dan'l, with his fore-paws just even with Dan'l's, and I'll give the word. Then he says, "one—two—three—jump!" and him and the feller touched up the frogs from behind, and the new frog hopped off lively, but Dan'l give a heave, and hysted up his shoulders—so—like a Frenchman, but it wasn't no use—he couldn't budge; he was planted as solid as a anvil, and he couldn't no more stir than if he was anchored out. Smiley was a good deal surprised, and he was disgusted too, but he didn't have no idea what the matter was, of course.

The feller took the money and started away, and when he was going out at the door he sorter jerked his thumb over his shoulder—this way—at Dan'l, and says again, very deliberate, "Well—I don't see no points about that frog that's any better'n any other frog."

Smiley he stood scratching his head and looking down at Dan'l a long time, and at last he says, "I do wonder what in the nation that frog throwed off for—I wonder if there ain't something the matter with him—he 'pears to look mighty baggy, somehow—and he ketched Dan'l by the nap of the neck, and lifted him up and says, "Why blame my cats if he don't weigh five pound"—and turned him upside down, and he belched out about a double-handful of shot. And then he see how it was, and he was the maddest man—he set the frog down and took out after that feller, but he never ketched him. And——

(Here Simon Wheeler heard his name called from the front-yard, and got up to go and see what was wanted.) And turning to me as he moved away, he said: "Just sit where you are, stranger, and rest easy—I ain't going to be gone a second."

But by your leave, I did not think that a continuation of the his-tory of the enterprising vagabond Jim Smiley would be likely to afford me much information concerning the Rev. Leonidas W. Smiley, and so I started away.

At the door I met the sociable Wheeler returning, and he but-tonholed me and recommenced:

"Well, thish-yer Smiley had a yaller one-eyed cow that didn't have no tail only just a short stump like a bannanner, and——"

"O, curse Smiley and his afflicted cow!" I muttered, good-naturedly, and bidding the old gentleman good-day, I departed.

Yours, truly,
Mark Twain

Letter to Will Bowen (February 6, 1870)[1]
[*The Matter of Hannibal*]

Sunday Afternoon,
At Home, 472 Delaware Avenue,
Buffalo Feb. 6. 1870

My First, & Oldest & Dearest Friend,

My heart goes out to you just the same as ever. Your letter has stirred me to the bottom. The fountains of my great deep are broken up & I have rained reminiscences for four & twenty hours. The old life has swept before me like a panorama; the old days have trooped by in their old glory, again; the old faces have looked out of the mists of the past; old footsteps have sounded in my listening ears; old hands have clasped mine, old voices have greeted me, & the songs I loved ages & ages ago have come wailing down the centuries! Heavens what eternities have swung their hoary cycles about us since those days were new!—Since we tore down Dick Hardy's stable; since you had the measles & I went to your house purposely to catch them; since Henry Beebe kept that envied slaughter-house, & Joe Craig sold him cats to kill in it; since old General Gaines used to say, "Whoop! Bow your neck & spread!"; since Jimmy Finn was town drunkard & we stole his dinner while he slept in the vat & fed it to the hogs in order to keep them still till we could mount them & have a ride; since Clint Levering was drowned; since we taught that one-legged nigger, Higgins, to offend Bill League's dignity by hailing him in public with his exasperating "Hello, League!"—since we used to undress & play Robin Hood in our shirt-tails, with lath swords, in the woods on Halliday's Hill on those long summer days; since we used to go in swimming above the still-house branch—& at mighty intervals wandered on vagrant fishing excursions clear up to "the Bay," & wondered what was curtained away in the great world beyond that remote point; since I jumped overboard from the ferry boat in the middle of the river that stormy day to get my hat, & swam two or three miles after it (& *got* it,) while all the town collected on the wharf & for an hour or so looked out across the angry waste of "white-caps" toward where people said Sam. Clemens was last seen before he went down; since we got up a rebellion against Miss Newcomb, under Ed. Stevens' leadership, (to force her to let us all go over to Miss Torry's side of the schoolroom,) & gallantly "sassed" Laura Hawk-

---

1. This letter to one of Clemens's best boyhood friends was originally published in 1938; in 1941 it appeared in *Mark Twain's Letters to Will Bowen*, the source of the present text.

ins when she came out the third time to call us in, & then afterward
marched in in threatening & bloodthirsty array,—& meekly yielded,
& took each his little thrashing, & resumed his old seat entirely
"reconstructed;" since we used to indulge in that very peculiar performance on that old bench outside the school-house to drive good
old Bill Brown crazy while he was eating his dinner; since we used
to remain at school at noon & go hungry, in order to persecute Bill
Brown in all possible ways—poor old Bill, who *could* be driven to
such extremity of vindictiveness as to call us "You *infernal* fools!" &
chase us round & round the school-house—& yet who never had the
heart to hurt us when he caught us, & who always loved us & always
took our part when the big boys wanted to thrash us; since we used
to lay in wait for Bill Pitts at the pump & whale him; (I saw him
two or three years ago, & was awful polite to his six feet two, &
mentioned no reminiscences); since we used to be in Dave Garth's
class in Sunday school & on week-days stole his leaf tobacco to run
our miniature tobacco presses with; since Owsley shot Smar; since
Ben Hawkins shot off his finger; since we accidentally burned up
that poor fellow in the calaboose;[2] since we used to shoot spool
cannons; & cannons made of keys, while that envied & hated Henry
Beebe drowned out our poor little pop-guns with his booming
brazen little artillery on wheels; since Laura Hawkins was my sweetheart——

Hold! *That* rouses me out of my dream, & brings me violently
back unto this day and this generation. For behold I have at this
moment the only sweetheart I ever *loved*, and bless her old heart
she is lying asleep upstairs in a bed that I sleep in every night, and
for four whole days she has been *Mrs. Samuel L. Clemens!*

I am 34 and she is 24; I am young and very handsome (I make
the statement with the fullest confidence, for I got it from her) and
she is much the most beautiful girl I ever saw (I said that before
she was anything to me,[3] and so it is worthy of all belief) and she
is the *best* girl, and the sweetest, and the gentlest, and the daintiest
and the most modest and unpretentious, and the wisest in all things
she should be wise in, and the most ignorant in all matters it would
not grace her to know, and she is sensible and quick, and loving and
faithful, forgiving, full of charity—and her beautiful life is ordered
by a religion that is all kindliness and unselfishness. Before the
gentle majesty of her purity all evil things and evil ways and evil
deeds stand abashed—then surrender. Wherefore, without effort, or
struggle, or spoken exorcism, all the old vices and shameful habits
that have possessed me these many many years, are falling away,
one by one, and departing into the darkness.

2. Small building that served as a jail;
Clemens continued to blame this death
on himself, though he had only supplied
matches to the prisoner so that the latter
could smoke.

3. Clemens fell in love with Olivia
Langdon when her brother showed him
her picture during a trip to the Holy
Land.

Bill, I know whereof I speak. I am too old and have moved about too much, and rubbed against too many people not to know human beings as well as we used to know "boils" from "breaks."[4]

She is the very most perfect gem of womankind that ever I saw in my life—and I will stand by that remark till I die.

William, old boy, her father surprised us a little, the other night. We all arrived here in a night train (my little wife and I were going to board) and under pretense of taking us to the private boarding house that had been selected for me while I was absent lecturing in New England, my new father-in-law and some old friends drove us in sleighs to the daintiest, darlingest, lovliest little palace in America—and when I said "Oh, this wont do—people who can afford to live in this sort of style wont take boarders," that same blessed father-in-law let out the secret that this was all *our* property—a present from himself. House & furniture cost $40,000 in cash, (including stable, horse & carriage), & is a most exquisite little palace (I saw no apartment in Europe so lovely as our drawing-room.)

Come along, you & Mollie, just whenever you can, & pay us a visit, (giving us a little notice beforehand,) & if we don't make you comfortable nobody in the world can.

And now my princess has come down for dinner (bless me, isn't it cosy, nobody but just us two, & three servants to wait on us & respectfully call us "Mr." and "Mrs. Clemens" instead of "Sam." & "Livy!") It took me many a year to work up to where I can put on style, but now I'll do it.—My book gives me an income like a small lord, & my paper is a good profitable concern.[5]

Dinner's ready. Good bye & God bless you, old friend, & keep your heart fresh & your memory green for the old days that will never come again.

Yrs always
Sam. Clemens

From Roughing It[1]
[*The Story of the Old Ram*]

Every now and then, in these days, the boys used to tell me I ought to get one Jim Blaine to tell me the stirring story of his grandfather's old ram—but they always added that I must not mention the matter unless Jim was drunk at the time—just comfortably and sociably drunk. They kept this up until my curiosity was on the rack to hear the story. I got to haunting Blaine; but it was of no

4. Eddylike disturbances on the surface of the water; a "break" is caused by a hidden solid object and is thus dangerous.
5. Clemens was part owner of the Buffalo *Express*; "My book": *Innocents Abroad* (1869).
1. The source of the present text is that of the 1872 edition (Hartford, Conn.:

American Publishing Co.). The story of the composition and publication of this episodic work is told fully by Franklin R. Rogers in the introduction to Volume 2 of *The Works of Mark Twain* (1972); the basis for the present text is Chapter 53. The time is 1863 in Virginia City; the "boys" are the local roughs. Twain was 28 at the time of this "incident."

use, the boys always found fault with his condition; he was often moderately but never satisfactorily drunk. I never watched a man's condition with such absorbing interest, such anxious solicitude; I never so pined to see a man uncompromisingly drunk before. At last, one evening I hurried to his cabin, for I learned that this time his situation was such that even the most fastidious could find no fault with it—he was tranquilly, serenely, symmetrically drunk—not a hiccup to mar his voice, not a cloud upon his brain thick enough to obscure his memory. As I entered, he was sitting upon an empty powder-keg, with a clay pipe in one hand and the other raised to command silence. His face was round, red, and very serious; his throat was bare and his hair tumbled; in general appearance and costume he was a stalwart miner of the period. On the pine table stood a candle, and its dim light revealed "the boys" sitting here and there on bunks, candle-boxes, powder-kegs, etc. They said:

"Sh—! Don't speak—he's going to commence."

THE STORY OF THE OLD RAM

I found a seat at once, and Blaine said:

"I don't reckon them times will ever come again. There never was a more bullier old ram than what he was. Grandfather fetched him from Illinois—got him of a man by the name of Yates—Bill Yates—maybe you might have heard of him; his father was a deacon—Baptist—and he was a rustler, too; a man had to get up ruther early to get the start of old Thankful Yates; it was him that put the Greens up to jining teams with my grandfather when he moved West. Seth Green was prob'ly the pick of the flock; he married a Wilkerson—Sarah Wilkerson—good cretur, she was—one of the likeliest heifers that was ever raised in old Stoddard, everybody said that knowed her. She could heft a bar'l of flour as easy as I can flirt a flapjack. And spin? Don't mention it! Independent? Humph! When Sile Hawkins come a-browsing around her, she let him know that for all his tin he couldn't trot in harness alongside of *her*. You see, Sile Hawkins was—no, it warn't Sile Hawkins, after all—it was a galoot by the name of Filkins—I disremember his first name; but he *was* a stump—come into pra'r meeting drunk, one night, hoor*a*ying for Nixon, becuz he thought it was a primary; and old deacon Ferguson up and scooted him through the window and he lit on old Miss Jefferson's head, poor old filly. She was a good soul—had a glass eye and used to lend it to old Miss Wagner, that hadn't any, to receive company in; it warn't big enough, and when Miss Wagner warn't noticing, it would get twisted around in the socket, and look up, maybe, or out to one side, and every which way, while t'other one was looking as straight ahead as a spy-glass. Grown people didn't mind it, but it most always made the children cry, it was so sort of scary. She tried packing it in raw cotton, but it wouldn't work, somehow—the cotton would get loose and stick out and look so kind of awful that the children couldn't stand it no way. She was always dropping it out, and turned up her old dead-light on the company empty, and making them oncomfortable, becuz *she* never could tell when it hopped out, being blind on that side, you see. So somebody would have to hunch her and say, 'Your game eye has fetched loose, Miss Wagner dear'—and then all of them would have to sit and wait till she jammed it in again—wrong side before, as a general thing, and green as a bird's egg, being a bashful cretur and easy sot back before company. But being wrong side before warn't much difference, anyway, becuz her own eye was sky-blue and the glass one was yaller on the front side, so whichever way she turned it it didn't match nohow. Old Miss Wagner was considerable on the borrow, she was. When she had a quilting, or Dorcas S'iety[2] at her house she gen'ally borrowed Miss Higgins's wooden leg to stump around on; it was considerable shorter than her other pin, but much *she* minded that. She said she couldn't abide crutches when she had company, becuz they were so slow; said when she had company and things had to be done, she wanted to get up and hump herself. She was as bald as a jug, and so she used to borrow Miss Jacops's wig—Miss Jacops was the coffin-peddler's wife—a ratty old buzzard, he was, that used to go roosting around where people was sick, waiting for 'em; and there that old rip would sit all day, in the shade, on a coffin that he judged would fit the can'idate; and if it was a slow customer and kind of uncertain, he'd fetch his rations and a blanket along and sleep in the coffin nights. He was anchored out that way, in frosty weather, for about three weeks, once, before old Robbins's place, waiting for him; and after that, for as much as two years, Jacops was not on speaking terms with the old man, on account of his disapp'inting him. He got one of his feet froze, and lost money, too, becuz old Robbins took a favorable turn and got well. The next time Robbins got sick, Jacops tried to make up with him, and varnished up the same old coffin and fetched it along; but old Robbins was too many for him; he had him in, and 'peared to be powerful weak; he bought the coffin for ten dollars and Jacops was to pay it back and twenty-five more besides if Robbins didn't like the coffin after he'd tried it. And then Robbins died, and at the funeral he bursted off the lid and riz up in his shroud and told the parson to let up on the performances, becuz he could *not* stand such a coffin as that. You see he had been in a trance once before, when he was young, and he took the chances on another, cal'lating that if he made the trip it was money in his pocket, and if he missed fire he couldn't lose a cent. And by George he sued Jacops for the rhino[3] and got jedgment; and he set up the coffin in his back parlor and said he

2. Dorcas Society, common name for charitable church societies. From the Biblical Dorcas (Acts 9.36–42), who per-formed charitable deeds, particularly sewing clothes for the poor.
3. Slang for cash, money.

'lowed to take his time, now. It was always an aggravation to Jacops, the way that miserable old thing acted. He moved back to Indiany pretty soon—went to Wellsville—Wellsville was the place the Hogadorns was from. Mighty fine family. Old Maryland stock. Old Squire Hogadorn could carry around more mixed licker, and cuss better than most any man I ever see. His second wife was the widder Billings—she that was Becky Martin; her dam was deacon Dunlap's first wife. Her oldest child, Maria, married a missionary and died in grace—et up by the savages. They et *him*, too, poor feller—biled him. It warn't the custom, so they say, but they explained to friends of his'n that went down there to bring away his things, that they'd tried missionaries every other way and never could get any good out of 'em—and so it annoyed all his relations to find out that that man's life was fooled away just out of a dern'd experiment, so to speak. But mind you, there ain't anything ever reely lost; everything that people can't understand and don't see the reason of does good if you only hold on and give it a fair shake; Prov'dence don't fire no blank ca'tridges, boys. That there missionary's substance, unbeknowns to himself, actu'ly converted every last one of them heathens that took a chance at the barbecue. Nothing ever fetched them but that. Don't tell *me* it was an accident that he was biled. There ain't no such a thing as an accident. When my uncle Lem was leaning up agin a scaffolding once, sick, or drunk, or suthin, an Irishman with a hod full of bricks fell on him out of the third story and broke the old man's back in two places. People said it was an accident. Much accident there was about that. He didn't know what he was there for, but he was there for a good object. If he hadn't been there the Irishman would have been killed. Nobody can ever make me believe anything different from that. Uncle Lem's dog was there. Why didn't the Irishman fall on the dog? Becuz the dog would a seen him a-coming and stood from under. That's the reason the dog warn't appinted. A dog can't be depended on to carry out a special providence. Mark my words it was a put-up thing. Accidents don't happen, boys. Uncle Lem's dog —I wish you could a seen that dog. He was a reglar shepherd—or ruther he was part bull and part shepherd—splendid animal; belonged to parson Hagar before Uncle Lem got him. Parson Hagar belonged to the Western Reserve Hagars; prime family; his mother was a Watson; one of his sisters married a Wheeler; they settled in Morgan County, and he got nipped by the machinery in a carpet factory and went through in less than a quarter of a minute; his widder bought the piece of carpet that had his remains wove in, and people come a hundred mile to 'tend the funeral. There was fourteen yards in the piece. She wouldn't let them roll him up, but planted him just so—full length. The church was middling small where they preached the funeral, and they had to let one end of the coffin stick out of the window. They didn't bury him—they planted one end, and let him stand up, same as a monument. And they nailed a sign on it and put—put on—put on it—sacred to—the m-e-m-o-r-y—of fourteen y-a-r-d-s—of three-ply—car - - - pet—containing all that was—m-o-r-t-a-l—of—of—W-i-l-l-i-a-m—W-h-e—"

Jim Blaine had been growing gradually drowsy and drowsier—his head nodded, once, twice, three times—dropped peacefully upon his breast, and he fell tranquilly asleep. The tears were running down the boys' cheeks—they were suffocating with suppressed laughter—and had been from the start, though I had never noticed it. I perceived that I was "sold." I learned then that Jim Blaine's peculiarity was that whenever he reached a certain stage of intoxication, no human power could keep him from setting out, with impressive unction, to tell about a wonderful adventure which he had once had with his grandfather's old ram—and the mention of the ram in the first sentence was as far as any man had ever heard him get, concerning it. He always maundered off, interminably, from one thing to another, till his whisky got the best of him and he fell asleep. What the thing was that happened to him and his grandfather's old ram is a dark mystery to this day, for nobody has ever yet found out.

1872

From Old Times on the Mississippi[1]

I

When I was a boy, there was but one permanent ambition among my comrades in our village on the west bank of the Mississippi River. That was, to be a steamboatman. We had transient ambitions of other sorts, but they were only transient. When a circus came and went, it left us all burning to become clowns; the first negro minstrel show that came to our section left us all suffering to try that kind of life; now and then we had a hope that if we lived and were good, God would permit us to be pirates. These ambitions faded out, each in its turn; but the ambition to be a steamboatman always remained.

Once a day a cheap, gaudy packet arrived upward from St. Louis, and another downward from Keokuk. Before these events had transpired, the day was glorious with expectancy; after they had transpired, the day was a dead and empty thing. Not only the boys, but the whole village, felt this. After all these years I can picture that old time to myself now, just as it was then: the white town drows-

1. Twain had considered writing an account of his apprenticeship and piloting days a few years after they came to an end, but he did not get around to writing about them until 1875, when he contributed a series of seven papers to the *Atlantic Monthly*, the source of the present text. The first essay appeared in the *Atlantic* for January, 1875, the second in the February issue. Together they constitute the story of his initiation into riverboat piloting. After a trip down the Mississippi in 1882 Twain more than doubled the bulk of the *Old Times* series to make *Life on the Mississippi* (1883).

ing in the sunshine of a summer's morning; the streets empty, or pretty nearly so; one or two clerks sitting in front of the Water Street stores, with their splint-bottomed chairs tilted back against the wall, chins on breasts, hats slouched over their faces, asleep— with shingle-shavings enough around to show what broke them down; a sow and a litter of pigs loafing along the sidewalk, doing a good business in water-melon rinds and seeds; two or three lonely little freight piles scattered about the "levee;"[2] a pile of "skids" on the slope of the stone-paved wharf, and the fragrant town drunkard asleep in the shadow of them; two or three wood flats at the head of the wharf, but nobody to listen to the peaceful lapping of the wavelets against them; the great Mississippi, the majestic, the magnificent Mississippi, rolling its mile-wide tide along, shining in the sun; the dense forest away on the other side; the "point" above the town, and the "point" below, bounding the river-glimpse and turning it into a sort of sea, and withal a very still and brilliant and lonely one. Presently a film of dark smoke appears above one of those remote "points;" instantly a negro drayman,[3] famous for his quick eye and prodigious voice, lifts up the cry, "S-t-e-a-m-boat a-comin'!" and the scene changes! The town drunkard stirs, the clerks wake up, a furious clatter of drays follows, every house and store pours out a human contribution, and all in a twinkling the dead town is alive and moving. Drays, carts, men, boys, all go hurrying from many quarters to a common centre, the wharf. Assembled there, the people fasten their eyes upon the coming boat as upon a wonder they are seeing for the first time. And the boat *is* rather a handsome sight, too. She is long and sharp and trim and pretty; she has two tall, fancy-topped chimneys, with a gilded device of some kind swung between them; a fanciful pilot-house, all glass and "gingerbread," perched on top of the "texas"[4] deck behind them; the paddle-boxes are gorgeous with a picture or with gilded rays above the boat's name; the boiler deck, the hurricane deck, and the texas deck are fenced and ornamented with clean white railings; there is a flag gallantly flying from the jack-staff; the furnace doors are open and the fires glaring bravely; the upper decks are black with passengers; the captain stands by the big bell, calm, imposing, the envy of all; great volumes of the blackest smoke are rolling and tumbling out of the chimneys—a husbanded grandeur created with a bit of pitch pine just before arriving at a town; the crew are grouped on the forecastle; the broad stage[5] is run far out over the port bow, and an envied deck-hand stands picturesquely on the end of it with a coil of rope in his hand; the pent steam is screaming through the gauge-cocks; the captain lifts his hand, a bell rings, the

2. A river landing place; "skids": low wooden platforms.
3. A "dray" is a strong, low cart or wagon without sides.
4. The deck of a Mississippi steamer just over the largest cabins, those of the officers; "paddle-boxes": covering of the paddlewheels on a sidewheel steamboat.
5. Plank for the landing and embarking of passengers and freight.

wheels stop; then they turn back, churning the water to foam, and
the steamer is at rest. Then such a scramble as there is to get
aboard, and to get ashore, and to take in freight and to discharge
freight, all at one and the same time; and such a yelling and cursing
as the mates facilitate it all with! Ten minutes later the steamer is
under way again, with no flag on the jack-staff and no black smoke
issuing from the chimneys. After ten more minutes the town is
dead again, and the town drunkard asleep by the skids once more.

My father was a justice of the peace, and I supposed he possessed
the power of life and death over all men and could hang anybody
that offended him. This was distinction enough for me as a general
thing; but the desire to be a steamboatman kept intruding, nevertheless. I first wanted to be a cabin-boy, so that I could come out
with a white apron on and shake a table-cloth over the side, where
all my old comrades could see me; later I thought I would rather be
the deck-hand who stood on the end of the stage-plank with the
coil of rope in his hand, because he was particularly conspicuous.
But these were only daydreams—they were too heavenly to be contemplated as real possibilities. By and by one of our boys went
away. He was not heard of for a long time. At last he turned up as
apprentice engineer or "striker" on a steamboat. This thing shook
the bottom out of all my Sunday-school teachings. That boy had
been notoriously worldly, and I just the reverse; yet he was exalted
to this eminence, and I left in obscurity and misery. There was
nothing generous about this fellow in his greatness. He would
always manage to have a rusty bolt to scrub while his boat tarried at
our town, and he would sit on the inside guard and scrub it, where
we could all see him and envy him and loathe him. And whenever
his boat was laid up he would come home and swell around the
town in his blackest and greasiest clothes, so that nobody could
help remembering that he was a steamboatman; and he used all
sorts of steamboat technicalities in his talk, as if he were so used to
them that he forgot common people could not understand them.
He would speak of the "labboard"[6] side of a horse in an easy, natural way that would make one wish he was dead. And he was always
talking about "St. Looy" like an old citizen; he would refer casually
to occasions when he "was coming down Fourth Street," or when
he was "passing by the Planter's House," or when there was a fire
and he took a turn on the brakes of "the old Big Missouri;" and
then he would go on and lie about how many towns the size of ours
were burned down there that day. Two or three of the boys had
long been persons of consideration among us because they had been
to St. Louis once and had a vague general knowledge of its wonders,
but the day of their glory was over now. They lapsed into a humble
silence, and learned to disappear when the ruthless "cub"-engineer
approached. This fellow had money, too, and hair oil. Also an igno-

6. I.e., larboard or port—the left-hand side of a ship.

rant silver watch and a showy brass watch chain. He wore a leather belt and used no suspenders. If ever a youth was cordially admired and hated by his comrades, this one was. No girl could withstand his charms. He "cut out" every boy in the village. When his boat blew up at last, it diffused a tranquil contentment among us such as we had not known for months. But when he came home the next week, alive, renowned, and appeared in church all battered up and bandaged, a shining hero, stared at and wondered over by everybody, it seemed to us that the partiality of Providence for an undeserving reptile had reached a point where it was open to criticism.

This creature's career could produce but one result, and it speedily followed. Boy after boy managed to get on the river. The minister's son became an engineer. The doctor's and the postmaster's sons became "mud clerks;"[7] the wholesale liquor dealer's son became a bar-keeper on a boat; four sons of the chief merchant, and two sons of the county judge, became pilots. Pilot was the grandest position of all. The pilot, even in those days of trivial wages, had a princely salary—from a hundred and fifty to two hundred and fifty dollars a month, and no board to pay. Two months of his wages would pay a preacher's salary for a year. Now some of us were left disconsolate. We could not get on the river—at least our parents would not let us.

So by and by I ran away. I said I never would come home again till I was a pilot and could come in glory. But somehow I could not manage it. I went meekly aboard a few of the boats that lay packed together like sardines at the long St. Louis wharf, and very humbly inquired for the pilots, but got only a cold shoulder and short words from mates and clerks. I had to make the best of this sort of treatment for the time being, but I had comforting day-dreams of a future when I should be a great and honored pilot, with plenty of money, and could kill some of these mates and clerks and pay for them.

Months afterward the hope within me struggled to a reluctant death, and I found myself without an ambition. But I was ashamed to go home. I was in Cincinnati, and I set to work to map out a new career. I had been reading about the recent exploration of the river Amazon by an expedition sent out by our government. It was said that the expedition, owing to difficulties, had not thoroughly explored a part of the country lying about the head-waters, some four thousand miles from the mouth of the river. It was only about fifteen hundred miles from Cincinnati to New Orleans, where I could doubtless get a ship. I had thirty dollars left; I would go and complete the exploration of the Amazon. This was all the thought I gave to the subject. I never was great in matters of detail. I packed

7. Assistants to steamboat clerks, so called because they had the task of receiving and delivering the freight on open wharves in all kinds of weather.

my valise, and took passage on an ancient tub called the Paul Jones, for New Orleans. For the sum of sixteen dollars I had the scarred and tarnished splendors of "her" main saloon principally to myself, for she was not a creature to attract the eye of wiser travelers.

When we presently got under way and went poking down the broad Ohio, I became a new being, and the subject of my own admiration. I was a traveler! A word never had tasted so good in my mouth before. I had an exultant sense of being bound for mysterious lands and distant climes which I never have felt in so uplifting a degree since. I was in such a glorified condition that all ignoble feelings departed out of me, and I was able to look down and pity the untraveled with a compassion that had hardly a trace of contempt in it. Still, when we stopped at villages and wood-yards, I could not help lolling carelessly upon the railings of the boiler deck to enjoy the envy of the country boys on the bank. If they did not seem to discover me, I presently sneezed to attract their attention, or moved to a position where they could not help seeing me. And as soon as I knew they saw me I gaped and stretched, and gave other signs of being mightily bored with traveling.

I kept my hat off all the time, and stayed where the wind and the sun could strike me, because I wanted to get the bronzed and weather-beaten look of an old traveler. Before the second day was half gone, I experienced a joy which filled me with the purest gratitude; for I saw that the skin had begun to blister and peel off my face and neck. I wished that the boys and girls at home could see me now.

We reached Louisville in time—at least the neighborhood of it. We stuck hard and fast on the rocks in the middle of the river and lay there four days. I was now beginning to feel a strong sense of being a part of the boat's family, a sort of infant son to the captain and younger brother to the officers. There is no estimating the pride I took in this grandeur, or the affection that began to swell and grow in me for those people. I could not know how the lordly steamboatman scorns that sort of presumption in a mere landsman. I particularly longed to acquire the least trifle of notice from the big stormy mate, and I was on the alert for an opportunity to do him a service to that end. It came at last. The riotous powwow of setting a spar was going on down on the forecastle, and I went down there and stood around in the way—or mostly skipping out of it—till the mate suddenly roared a general order for somebody to bring him a capstan bar.[8] I sprang to his side and said: "Tell me where it is— I'll fetch it!"

If a rag-picker had offered to do a diplomatic service for the Emperor of Russia, the monarch could not have been more astounded than the mate was. He even stopped swearing. He stood

8. Bar used to turn a capstan, a vertical spindle-mounted drum that is rotated to raise heavy weights by winding a heavy cable about it.

and stared down at me. It took him ten seconds to scrape his disjointed remains together again. Then he said impressively: "Well, if
this don't beat hell!" and turned to his work with the air of a man
who had been confronted with a problem too abstruse for solution.

I crept away, and courted solitude for the rest of the day. I did
not go to dinner; I stayed away from supper until everybody else
had finished. I did not feel so much like a member of the boat's
family now as before. However, my spirits returned, in installments,
as we pursued our way down the river. I was sorry I hated the mate
so, because it was not in (young) human nature not to admire him.
He was huge and muscular, his face was bearded and whiskered all
over; he had a red woman and a blue woman tattooed on his right
arm,—one on each side of a blue anchor with a red rope to it; and
in the matter of profanity he was perfect. When he was getting out
cargo at a landing, I was always where I could see and hear. He felt
all the sublimity of his great position, and made the world feel it,
too. When he gave even the simplest order, he discharged it like a
blast of lightning, and sent a long, reverberating peal of profanity
thundering after it. I could not help contrasting the way in which
the average landsman would give an order, with the mate's way of
doing it. If the landsman should wish the gangplank moved a foot
farther forward, he would probably say: "James, or Williams, one of
you, push that plank forward, please;" but put the mate in his
place, and he would roar out: "Here, now, start that gang-plank
for'ard! Lively, now! *What*'re you about! Snatch it! *snatch* it!
There! there! Aft again! aft again! Don't you hear me? Dash it to
dash! are you going to *sleep* over it! 'Vast heaving. 'Vast heaving, I
tell you! Going to heave it clear astern? WHERE're you going with
that barrel! *for'ard* with it 'fore I make you swallow it, you dash-
dash-dash-*dashed* split between a tired mud-turtle and a crippled
hearse-horse!"

I wished I could talk like that.

When the soreness of my adventure with the mate had somewhat worn off, I began timidly to make up to the humblest official
connected with the boat—the night watchman. He snubbed my
advances at first, but I presently ventured to offer him a new chalk
pipe, and that softened him. So he allowed me to sit with him by
the big bell on the hurricane deck, and in time he melted into conversation. He could not well have helped it, I hung with such
homage on his words and so plainly showed that I felt honored by
his notice. He told me the names of dim capes and shadowy islands
as we glided by them in the solemnity of the night, under the winking stars, and by and by got to talking about himself. He seemed
over-sentimental for a man whose salary was six dollars a week—or
rather he might have seemed so to an older person than I. But I
drank in his words hungrily, and with a faith that might have
moved mountains if it had been applied judiciously. What was it to

me that he was soiled and seedy and fragrant with gin? What was it
to me that his grammar was bad, his construction worse, and his
profanity so void of art that it was an element of weakness rather
than strength in his conversation? He was a wronged man, a man
who had seen trouble, and that was enough for me. As he mellowed
into his plaintive history his tears dripped upon the lantern in his
lap, and I cried, too, from sympathy. He said he was the son of an
English nobleman—either an earl or an alderman, he could not
remember which, but believed he was both; his father, the nobleman, loved him, but his mother hated him from the cradle; and so
while he was still a little boy he was sent to "one of them old,
ancient colleges"—he couldn't remember which; and by and by his
father died and his mother seized the property and "shook" him, as
he phrased it. After his mother shook him, members of the nobility
with whom he was acquainted used their influence to get him the
position of "lob-lolly-boy in a ship;" and from that point my watchman threw off all trammels of date and locality and branched out
into a narrative that bristled all along with incredible adventures; a
narrative that was so reeking with blood-shed and so crammed with
hair-breadth escapes and the most engaging and unconscious personal villainies, that I sat speechless, enjoying, shuddering, wondering, worshiping.

It was a sore blight to find out afterwards that he was a low,
vulgar, ignorant, sentimental, half-witted humbug, an untraveled
native of the wilds of Illinois, who had absorbed wildcat literature
and appropriated its marvels, until in time he had woven odds and
ends of the mess into this yarn, and then gone on telling it to fledg-
lings like me, until he had come to believe it himself.

II

A "CUB" PILOT'S EXPERIENCE; OR, LEARNING THE RIVER

What with lying on the rocks four days at Louisville, and some
other delays, the poor old Paul Jones fooled away about two weeks
in making the voyage from Cincinnati to New Orleans. This gave
me a chance to get acquainted with one of the pilots, and he taught
me how to steer the boat, and thus made the fascination of river
life more potent than ever for me.

It also gave me a chance to get acquainted with a youth who had
taken deck passage—more's the pity; for he easily borrowed six dollars of me on a promise to return to the boat and pay it back to me
the day after we should arrive. But he probably died or forgot, for
he never came. It was doubtless the former, since he had said his
parents were wealthy, and he only traveled deck passage[8] because it
was cooler.

I soon discovered two things. One was that a vessel would not be
likely to sail for the mouth of the Amazon under ten or twelve

9. " 'Deck' passage"—i.e., steerage passage [Clemens's note].

years; and the other was that the nine or ten dollars still left in my pocket would not suffice for so imposing an exploration as I had planned, even if I could afford to wait for a ship. Therefore it followed that I must contrive a new career. The Paul Jones was now bound for St. Louis. I planned a siege against my pilot, and at the end of three hard days he surrendered. He agreed to teach me the Mississippi River from New Orleans to St. Louis for five hundred dollars, payable out of the first wages I should receive after graduating. I entered upon the small enterprise of "learning" twelve or thirteen hundred miles of the great Mississippi River with the easy confidence of my time of life. If I had really known what I was about to require of my faculties, I should not have had the courage to begin. I supposed that all a pilot had to do was to keep his boat in the river, and I did not consider that that could be much of a trick, since it was so wide.

The boat backed out from New Orleans at four in the afternoon, and it was "our watch" until eight. Mr. B——, my chief, "straightened her up," plowed her along past the sterns of the other boats that lay at the Levee, and then said, "Here, take her; shave those steamships as close as you'd peel an apple." I took the wheel, and my heart went down into my boots; for it seemed to me that we were about to scrape the side off every ship in the line, we were so close. I held my breath and began to claw the boat away from the danger; and I had my own opinion of the pilot who had known no better than to get us into such peril, but I was too wise to express it. In half a minute I had a wide margin of safety intervening between the Paul Jones and the ships; and within ten seconds more I was set aside in disgrace, and Mr. B—— was going into danger again and flaying me alive with abuse of my cowardice. I was strung, but I was obliged to admire the easy confidence with which my chief loafed from side to side of his wheel, and trimmed the ships so closely that disaster seemed ceaselessly imminent. When he had cooled a little he told me that the easy water was close ashore and the current outside, and therefore we must hug the bank, upstream, to get the benefit of the former, and stay well out, downstream, to take advantage of the latter. In my own mind I resolved to be a down-stream pilot and leave the up-streaming to people dead to prudence.

Now and then Mr. B—— called my attention to certain things. Said he, "This is Six-Mile Point." I assented. It was pleasant enough information, but I could not see the bearing of it. I was not conscious that it was a matter of any interest to me. Another time he said, "This is Nine-Mile Point." Later he said, "This is Twelve-Mile Point." They were all about level with the water's edge; they all looked about alike to me; they were monotonously unpicturesque. I hoped Mr. B—— would change the subject. But no; he would crowd up around a point, hugging the shore with affection, and then say: "The slack water ends here, abreast this bunch of China-trees; now we cross over." So he crossed over. He gave me the wheel once or twice, but I had no luck. I either came near chipping off the edge of a sugar plantation, or else I yawed[1] too far from shore, and so I dropped back into disgrace again and got abused.

The watch was ended at last, and we took supper and went to bed. At midnight the glare of a lantern shone in my eyes, and the night watchman said:—

"Come! turn out!"

And then he left. I could not understand this extraordinary procedure; so I presently gave up trying to, and dozed off to sleep. Pretty soon the watchman was back again, and this time he was gruff. I was annoyed. I said:—

"What do you want to come bothering around here in the middle of the night for? Now as like as not I'll not get to sleep again to-night."

The watchman said;—

"Well, if this ain't good, I'm blest."

The "off-watch" was just turning in, and I heard some brutal laughter from them, and such remarks as "Hello, watchman! an't the new cub turned out yet? He's delicate, likely. Give him some sugar in a rag and send for the chambermaid to sing rock-a-by-baby to him."

About this time Mr. B—— appeared on the scene. Something like a minute later I was climbing the pilot-house steps with some of my clothes on and the rest in my arms. Mr. B—— was close behind, commenting. Here was something fresh—this thing of getting up in the middle of the night to go to work. It was a detail in piloting that had never occurred to me at all. I knew that boats ran all night, but somehow I had never happened to reflect that somebody had to get up out of a warm bed to run them. I began to fear that piloting was not quite so romantic as I had imagined it was; there was something very real and work-like about this new phase of it.

It was a rather dingy night, although a fair number of stars were out. The big mate was at the wheel, and he had the old tub pointed at a star and was holding her straight up the middle of the river. The shores on either hand were not much more than a mile apart, but they seemed wonderfully far away and ever so vague and indistinct. The mate said:—

"We've got to land at Jones's plantation, sir."

The vengeful spirit in me exulted. I said to myself, I wish you joy of your job, Mr. B——; you'll have a good time finding Mr. Jones's plantation such a night as this; and I hope you never *will* find it as long as you live.

1. Swerved.

Mr. B—— said to the mate:—

"Upper end of the plantation, or the lower?"

"Upper."

"I can't do it. The stumps there are out of water at this stage. It's no great distance to the lower, and you'll have to get along with that."

"All right, sir. If Jones don't like it he'll have to lump it, I reckon."

And then the mate left. My exultation began to cool and my wonder to come up. Here was a man who not only proposed to find this plantation on such a night, but to find either end of it you preferred. I dreadfully wanted to ask a question, but I was carrying about as many short answers as my cargo-room would admit of, so I held my peace. All I desired to ask Mr. B—— was the simple question whether he was ass enough to really imagine he was going to find that plantation on a night when all plantations were exactly alike and all the same color. But I held in. I used to have fine inspirations of prudence in those days.

Mr. B—— made for the shore and soon was scraping it, just the same as if it had been daylight. And not only that, but singing—

"Father in heaven the day is declining," etc.

It seemed to me that I had put my life in the keeping of a peculiarly reckless outcast. Presently he turned on me and said:—

"What's the name of the first point above New Orleans?"

I was gratified to be able to answer promptly, and I did. I said I didn't know.

"Don't *know*?"

This manner jolted me. I was down at the foot again, in a moment. But I had to say just what I had said before.

"Well, you're a smart one," said Mr. B——. "What's the name of the *next* point?"

Once more I didn't know.

"Well this beats anything. Tell me the name of *any* point or place I told you."

I studied a while and decided that I couldn't.

"Look-a-here! What do you start out from, above Twelve-Mile Point, to cross over?"

"I—I—don't know."

"You—you—don't know?" mimicking my drawling manner of speech. "What *do* you know?"

"I—I—nothing, for certain."

"By the great Caesar's ghost I believe you! You're the stupidest dunderhead I ever saw or ever heard of, so help me Moses! The idea of *you* being a pilot—*you!* Why, you don't know enough to pilot a cow down a lane."

Oh, but his wrath was up! He was a nervous man, and he shuffled from one side of his wheel to the other as if the floor was hot. He would boil a while to himself, and then overflow and scald me again.

"Look-a-here! What do you suppose I told you the names of those points for?"

I tremblingly considered a moment, and then the devil of temptation provoked me to say:—

"Well—to—to—be entertaining, I thought."

This was a red rag to the bull. He raged and stormed so (he was crossing the river at the time) that I judge it made him blind, because he ran over the steering-oar of a trading-scow. Of course the traders sent up a volley of red-hot profanity. Never was a man so grateful as Mr. B—— was: because he was brim full, and here were subjects who would *talk back*. He threw open a window, thrust his head out, and such an irruption followed as I never had heard before. The fainter and farther away the scowmen's curses drifted, the higher Mr. B—— lifted his voice and the weightier his adjectives grew. When he closed the window he was empty. You could have drawn a seine through his system and not caught curses enough to disturb your mother with. Presently he said to me in the gentlest way:—

"My boy, you must get a little memorandum-book, and every time I tell you a thing, put it down right away. There's only one way to be a pilot, and that is to get this entire river by heart. You have to know it just like A B C."

That was a dismal revelation to me; for my memory was never loaded with anything but blank cartridges. However, I did not feel discouraged long. I judged that it was best to make some allowances, for doubtless Mr. B—— was "stretching." Presently he pulled a rope and struck a few strokes on the big bell. The stars were all gone, now, and the night was as black as ink. I could hear the wheels churn along the bank, but I was not entirely certain that I could see the shore. The voice of the invisible watchman called up from the hurricane deck:—

"What's this, sir?"

"Jones's plantation."

I said to myself, I wish I might venture to offer a small bet that it isn't. But I did not chirp. I only waited to see. Mr. B—— handled the engine bells, and in due time the boat's nose came to the land, a torch glowed from the forecastle, a man skipped ashore, a darky's voice on the bank said, "Gimme de carpet-bag, Mars' Jones," and the next moment we were standing up the river again, all serene. I reflected deeply a while, and then said,—but not aloud, —Well, the finding of that plantation was the luckiest accident that ever happened; but it couldn't happen again in a hundred years. And I fully believed it *was* an accident, too.

By the time we had gone seven or eight hundred miles up the

river, I had learned to be a tolerably plucky up-stream steersman, in daylight, and before we reached St. Louis I had made a trifle of progress in night-work, but only a trifle. I had a note-book that fairly bristled with the names of towns, "points," bars, islands, bends, reaches, etc.; but the information was to be found only in the note-book—none of it was in my head. It made my heart ache to think I had only got half of the river set down; for as our watch was four hours off and four hours on, day and night, there was a long four-hour gap in my book for every time I had slept since the voyage began.

My chief was presently hired to go on a big New Orleans boat, and I packed my satchel and went with him. She was a grand affair. When I stood in her pilot-house I was so far above the water that I seemed perched on a mountain; and her decks stretched so far away, fore and aft, below me, that I wondered how I could ever have considered the little Paul Jones a large craft. There were other differences, too. The Paul Jones's pilot-house was a cheap, dingy, battered rattle-trap, cramped for room: but here was a sumptuous glass temple; room enough to have a dance in; showy red and gold window-curtains; an imposing sofa; leather cushions and a back to the high bench where visiting pilots sit, to spin yarns and "look at the river;" bright, fanciful "cuspadores" instead of a broad wooden box filled with sawdust; nice new oil-cloth on the floor; a hospitable big stove for winter; a wheel as high as my head, costly with inlaid work; a wire tiller-rope; bright brass knobs for the bells; and a tidy, white-aproned, black "texas-tender," to bring up tarts and ices and coffee during mid-watch, day and night. Now this was "something like;" and so I began to take heart once more to believe that piloting was a romantic sort of occupation after all. The moment we were under way I began to prowl about the great steamer and fill myself with joy. She was as clean and as dainty as a drawing-room; when I looked down her long, gilded saloon, it was like gazing through a splendid tunnel; she had an oil-picture, by some gifted sign-painter, on every state-room door; she glittered with no end of prism-fringed chandeliers; the clerk's office was elegant, the bar was marvelous, and the bar-keeper had been barbered and upholstered at incredible cost. The boiler deck (*i.e.*, the second story of the boat, so to speak) was as spacious as a church, it seemed to me; so with the forecastle; and there was no pitiful handful of deckhands, firemen, and roust-abouts down there, but a whole battalion of men. The fires were fiercely glaring from a long row of furnaces, and over them were eight huge boilers! This was unutterable pomp. The mighty engines—but enough of this. I had never felt so fine before. And when I found that the regiment of natty servants respectfully "sir'd" me, my satisfaction was complete.

When I returned to the pilot-house St. Louis was gone and I was lost. Here was a piece of river which was all down in my book, but I could make neither head nor tail of it: you understand, it was turned around. I had seen it, when coming up-stream, but I had never faced about to see how it looked when it was behind me. My heart broke again, for it was plain that I had got to learn this troublesome river *both ways.*

The pilot-house was full of pilots, going down to "look at the river." What is called the "upper river" (the two hundred miles between St. Louis and Cairo, where the Ohio comes in) was low; and the Mississippi changes its channel so constantly that the pilots used to always find it necessary to run down to Cairo to take a fresh look, when their boats were to lie in port a week, that is, when the water was at a low stage. A deal of this "looking at the river" was done by poor fellows who seldom had a berth, and whose only hope of getting one lay in their being always freshly posted and therefore ready to drop into the shoes of some reputable pilot, for a single trip, on account of such pilot's sudden illness, or some other necessity. And a good many of them constantly ran up and down inspecting the river, not because they ever really hoped to get a berth, but because (they being guests of the boat) it was cheaper to "look at the river" than stay ashore and pay board. In time these fellows grew dainty in their tastes, and only infested boats that had an established reputation for setting good tables. All visiting pilots were useful, for they were always ready and willing, winter or summer, night or day, to go out in the yawl and help buoy the channel or assist the boat's pilots in any way they could. They were likewise welcome because all pilots are tireless talkers, when gathered together, and as they talk only about the river they are always understood and are always interesting. Your true pilot cares nothing about anything on earth but the river, and his pride in his occupation surpasses the pride of kings.

We had a fine company of these river-inspectors along, this trip. There were eight or ten; and there was abundance of room for them in our great pilot-house. Two or three of them wore polished silk hats, elaborate shirt-fronts, diamond breastpins, kid gloves, and patent-leather boots. They were choice in their English, and bore themselves with a dignity proper to men of solid means and prodigious reputation as pilots. The others were more or less loosely clad, and wore upon their heads tall felt cones that were suggestive of the days of the Commonwealth.[2]

I was a cipher in this august company, and felt subdued, not to say torpid. I was not even of sufficient consequence to assist at the wheel when it was necessary to put the tiller hard down in a hurry; the guest that stood nearest did that when occasion required—and this was pretty much all the time, because of the crookedness of the channel and the scant water. I stood in a corner; and the talk I lis-

2. I.e., the government established in England by Oliver Cromwell from the execution of Charles I in 1649 to the Restoration of Charles II in 1660.

tened to took the hope all out of me. One visitor said to another:—

"Jim, how did you run Plum Point, coming up?"

"It was in the night, there, and I ran it the way one of the boys on the Diana told me; started out about fifty yards above the wood pile on the false point, and held on the cabin under Plum Point till I raised the reef—quarter less twain[3]—then straightened up for the middle bar[4] till I got well abreast the old one-limbed cotton-wood in the bend, then got my stern on the cotton-wood and head on the low place above the point, and came through a-booming—nine and a half."[5]

"Pretty square crossing, an't it?"

"Yes, but the upper bar's working down fast."

Another pilot spoke up and said:—

"I had better water than that, and ran it lower down; started out from the false point—mark twain[6]—raised the second reef abreast the big snag in the bend, and had quarter less twain."

One of the gorgeous ones remarked: "I don't want to find fault with your leadsmen,[7] but that's a good deal of water for Plum Point, it seems to me."

There was an approving nod all around as this quiet snub dropped on the boaster and "settled" him. And so they went on talk - talk - talking. Meantime, the thing that was running in my mind was, "Now if my ears hear aright, I have not only to get the names of all the towns and islands and bends, and so on, by heart, but I must even get up a warm personal acquaintanceship with every old snag and one-limbed cotton-wood and obscure wood pile that ornaments the banks of this river for twelve hundred miles; and more than that, I must actually know where these things are in the dark, unless these guests are gifted with eyes that can pierce through two miles of solid blackness; I wish the piloting business was in Jericho and I had never thought of it."

At dusk Mr. B—— tapped the big bell three times (the signal to land), and the captain emerged from his drawing-room in the forward end of the texts, and looked up inquiringly. Mr. B—— said:—

"We will lay up here all night, captain."

"Very well, sir."

That was all. The boat came to shore and was tied up for the night. It seemed to me a fine thing that the pilot could do as he pleased without asking so grand a captain's permission. I took my supper and went immediately to bed, discouraged by my day's observations and experiences. My late voyage's note-booking was but a confusion of meaningless names. It had tangled me all up in a

---

3. A quarter of a fathom less than two fathoms; i.e., 10½ feet of water.
4. I.e., submerged dirt bar in the middle of the river.
5. Nine and a half feet of water.

6. A two-fathom (12-foot) sounding; i.e., safe water.
7. Men who use sounding leads to determine the depth of water.

knot every time I had looked at it in the daytime. I now hoped for respite in sleep; but no, it reveled all through my head till sunrise again, a frantic and tireless nightmare.

Next morning I felt pretty rusty and low-spirited. We went booming along, taking a good many chances, for we were anxious to "get out of the river" (as getting out to Cairo was called) before night should overtake us. But Mr. B——'s partner, the other pilot, presently grounded the boat, and we lost so much time getting her off that it was plain the darkness would overtake us a good long way above the mouth. This was a great misfortune, especially to certain of our visiting pilots, whose boats would have to wait for their return, no matter how long that might be. It sobered the pilot-house talk a good deal. Coming up-stream, pilots did not mind low water or any kind of darkness; nothing stopped them but fog. But down-stream work was different; a boat was too nearly helpless, with a stiff current pushing behind her; so it was not customary to run down-stream at night in low water.

There seemed to be one small hope, however: if we could get through the intricate and dangerous Hat Island crossing before night, we could venture the rest, for we would have plainer sailing and better water. But it would be insanity to attempt Hat Island at night. So there was a deal of looking at watches all the rest of the day, and a constant ciphering upon the speed we were making; Hat Island was the eternal subject; sometimes hope was high and sometimes we were delayed in a bad crossing, and down it went again. For hours all hands lay under the burden of this suppressed excitement; it was even communicated to me, and I got to feeling so solicitous about Hat Island, and under such an awful pressure of responsibility, that I wished I might have five minutes on shore to draw a good, full, relieving breath, and start over again. We were standing no regular watches. Each of our pilots ran such portions of the river as he had run when coming up-stream, because of his greater familiarity with it; but both remained in the pilot-house constantly.

An hour before sunset, Mr. B—— took the wheel and Mr. W—— stepped aside. For the next thirty minutes every man held his watch in his hand and was restless, silent, and uneasy. At last somebody said, with a doomful sign.

"Well, yonder's Hat Island—and we can't make it."

All the watches closed with a snap, everybody sighed and muttered something about its being "too bad, too bad—ah, if we could *only* have got here half an hour sooner!" and the place was thick with the atmosphere of disappointment. Some started to go out, but loitered, hearing no bell-tap to land. The sun dipped behind the horizon, the boat went on. Inquiring looks passed from one guest to another; and one who had his hand on the doorknob, and had turned it, waited, then presently took away his hand and let the knob turn back again. We bore steadily down the bend. More looks were exchanged, and nods of surprised admiration—but no words. Insensibly the men drew together behind Mr. B—— as the sky darkened and one or two dim stars came out. The dead silence and sense of waiting became oppressive. Mr. B—— pulled the cord, and two deep, mellow notes from the big bell floated off on the night. Then a pause, and one more note was struck. The watchman's voice followed, from the hurricane deck:—

"Labboard lead, there! Stabboard lead!"

The cries of the leadsmen began to rise out of the distance, and were gruffly repeated by the word-passers on the hurricane deck.

"M-a-r-k three! M-a-r-k three! Quarter-less-three! Half twain! Quarter twain! M-a-r-k twain! Quarter-less"—

Mr. B—— pulled two bell-ropes, and was answered by faint jinglings far below in the engine-room, and our speed slackened. The steam began to whistle through the gauge-cocks. The cries of the leadsmen went on—and it is a weird sound, always, in the night. Every pilot in the lot was watching, now, with fixed eyes, and talking under his breath. Nobody was calm and easy but Mr. B——. He would put his wheel down and stand on a spoke, and as the steamer swung into her (to me) utterly invisible marks—for we seemed to be in the midst of a wide and gloomy sea—he would meet and fasten her there. Talk was going on, now, in low voices:-

"There; she's over the first reef all right!"

After a pause, another subdued voice:—

"Her stern's coming down just *exactly* right, by *George!* Now she's in the marks;[8] over she goes!"

Somebody else muttered:—

"Oh, it was done beautiful—*beautiful!*"

Now the engines were stopped altogether, and we drifted with the current. Not that I could see the boat drift, for I could not, the stars being all gone by this time. This drifting was the dismalest work; it held one's heart still. Presently I discovered a blacker gloom than that which surrounded us. It was the head of the island. We were closing right down upon it. We entered its deeper shadow, and so imminent seemed the peril that I was likely to suffocate; and I had the strongest impulse to do *something*, anything, to save the vessel. But still Mr. B—— stood by his wheel, silent, intent as a cat, and all the pilots stood shoulder to shoulder at his back.

"She'll not make it!" somebody whispered.

The water grew shoaler and shoaler by the leadsmen's cries, till it was down to—

"Eight-and-a-half! E-i-g-h-t feet! E-i-g-h-t feet! Seven-and"—

Mr. B—— said warningly through his speaking tube to the engineer:—

"Stand by, now!"

8. Safe water, measurable water on a sounding lead.

"Aye-aye, sir."

"Seven-and-a-half! Seven feet! *Six*-and"—

We touched bottom! Instantly Mr. B—— set a lot of bells ringing, shouted through the tube, "*Now* let her have it—every ounce you've got!" then to his partner, "Put her hard down! snatch her! snatch her!" The boat rasped and ground her way through the sand, hung upon the apex of disaster a single tremendous instant, and then over she went! And such a shout as went up at Mr. B——'s back never loosened the roof of a pilot-house before!

There was no more trouble after that. Mr. B—— was a hero that night; and it was some little time, too, before his exploit ceased to be talked about by river men.

Fully to realize the marvelous precision required in laying the great steamer in her marks in that murky waste of water, one should know that not only must she pick her intricate way through snags and blind reefs, and then shave the head of the island so closely as to brush the overhanging foliage with her stern, but at one place she must pass almost within arm's reach of a sunken and invisible wreck that would snatch the hull timbers from under her if she should strike it, and destroy a quarter of a million dollars' worth of steamboat and cargo in five minutes, and maybe a hundred and fifty human lives into the bargain.

The last remark I heard that night was a compliment to Mr. B——, uttered in soliloquy and with unction by one of our guests. He said:—

"By the Shadow of Death, but he's a lightning pilot!"

1875, 1883

Adventures of Huckleberry Finn[1]

(TOM SAWYER'S COMRADE)

SCENE: THE MISSISSIPPI

TIME: FORTY TO FIFTY YEARS AGO[2]

NOTICE

Persons attempting to find a motive in this narrative will be prosecuted; persons attempting to find a moral in it will be banished; persons attempting to find a plot in it will be shot.

BY ORDER OF THE AUTHOR

PER G. G., CHIEF OF ORDNANCE.

---

1. *Adventures of Huckleberry Finn* was first published in England in December, 1884. The present text is a corrected version of the first American edition of 1885.
2. That is, in 1835 or 1845—well before the Civil War.

Explanatory

In this book a number of dialects are used, to wit: the Missouri negro dialect; the extremest form of the backwoods South-Western dialect; the ordinary "Pike-County"[3] dialect; and four modified varieties of this last. The shadings have not been done in a hap-hazard fashion, or by guess-work; but pains-takingly, and with the trustworthy guidance and support of personal familiarity with these several forms of speech.

I make this explanation for the reason that without it many readers would suppose that all these characters were trying to talk alike and not succeeding.

THE AUTHOR

Chapter I

You don't know about me, without you have read a book by the name of "The Adventures of Tom Sawyer,"[4] but that ain't no matter. That book was made by Mr. Mark Twain, and he told the truth, mainly. There was things which he stretched, but mainly he told the truth. That is nothing. I never seen anybody but lied, one time or another, without it was Aunt Polly, or the widow, or maybe Mary. Aunt Polly—Tom's Aunt Polly, she is—and Mary, and the Widow Douglas, is all told about in that book—which is mostly a true book; with some stretchers, as I said before.

Now the way that the book winds up, is this: Tom and me found the money that the robbers hid in the cave, and it made us rich. We got six thousand dollars apiece—all gold. It was an awful sight of money when it was piled up. Well, Judge Thatcher, he took it and put it out at interest, and it fetched us a dollar a day apiece, all the year round—more than a body could tell what to do with. The Widow Douglas, she took me for her son, and allowed she would sivilize me; but it was rough living in the house all the time, considering how dismal regular and decent the widow was in all her ways; and so when I couldn't stand it no longer, I lit out. I got into my old rags, and my sugar-hogshead[5] again, and was free and satisfied. But Tom Sawyer, he hunted me up and said he was going to start a band of robbers, and I might join if I would go back to the widow and be respectable. So I went back.

The widow she cried over me, and called me a poor lost lamb, and she called me a lot of other names, too, but she never meant no harm by it. She put me in them new clothes again, and I couldn't do nothing but sweat and sweat, and feel all cramped up. Well, then, the old thing commenced again. The widow rung a bell for supper, and you had to come to time. When you got to the table you couldn't go right to eating, but you had to wait for the widow

3. Pike County, Missouri.
4. Published in 1876.
5. A large barrel.

to tuck down her head and grumble a little over the victuals,
though there warn't really anything the matter with them. That is,
nothing only everything was cooked by itself. In a barrel of odds
and ends it is different; things get mixed up, and the juice kind of
swaps around, and the things go better.

After supper she got out her book and learned me about Moses
and the Bulrushers;⁶ and I was in a sweat to find out all about him;
but by-and-by she let it out that Moses had been dead a considerable long time; so then I didn't care no more about him; because I
don't take no stock in dead people.

Pretty soon I wanted to smoke, and asked the widow to let me.
But she wouldn't. She said it was a mean practice and wasn't clean,
and I must try to not do it any more. That is just the way with
some people. They get down on a thing when they don't know
nothing about it. Here she was a bothering about Moses, which was
no kin to her, and no use to anybody, being gone, you see, yet
finding a power of fault with me for doing a thing that had some
good in it. And she took snuff too; of course that was all right,
because she done it herself.

Her sister, Miss Watson, a tolerable slim old maid, with goggles
on, had just come to live with her, and took a set at me now, with a
spelling-book. She worked me middling hard for about an hour, and
then the widow made her ease up. I couldn't stood it much longer.
Then for an hour it was deadly dull, and I was fidgety. Miss
Watson would say, "Dont put your feet up there, Huckleberry;"
and "dont scrunch up like that, Huckleberry—set up straight;" and
pretty soon she would say, "Don't gap and stretch like that, Huckleberry—why don't you try to behave?" Then she told me all about
the bad place, and I said I wished I was there. She got mad, then,
but I didn't mean no harm. All I wanted was to go somewheres; all
I wanted was a change, I warn't particular. She said it was wicked
to say what I said; said she wouldn't say it for the whole world; *she*
was going to live so as to go to the good place. Well, I couldn't see
no advantage in going where she was going, so I made up my mind
I wouldn't try for it. But I never said so, because it would only
make trouble, and wouldn't do no good.

Now she had got a start, and she went on and told me all about
the good place. She said all a body would have to do there was to
go around all day long with a harp and sing, forever and ever.⁷ So I
didn't think much of it. But I never said so. I asked her if she
reckoned Tom Sawyer would go there, and, she said, not by a considerable sight. I was glad about that, because I wanted him and me
to be together.

Miss Watson she kept pecking at me, and it got tiresome and

6. Pharoah's daughter discovered the infant Moses floating in the Nile in a basket woven from bulrushes (Exodus 2).
She adopted him into the royal family
just as the widow has adopted Huck.
7. Conventional conceptions of the
Christian heaven were satirized early
and late in Twain's writings.

lonesome. By-and-by they fetched the niggers[8] in and had prayers, and then everybody was off to bed. I went up to my room with a piece of candle and put it on the table. Then I set down in a chair by the window and tried to think of something cheerful, but it warn't no use. I felt so lonesome I most wished I was dead. The stars was shining, and the leaves rustled in the woods ever so mournful; and I heard an owl, away off, who-whooing about somebody that was dead, and a whippowill and a dog crying about somebody that was going to die; and the wind was trying to whisper something to me and I couldn't make out what it was, and so it made the cold shivers run over me. Then away out in the woods I heard that kind of a sound that a ghost makes when it wants to tell about something that's on its mind and can't make itself understood, and so can't rest easy in its grave and has to go about that way every night grieving. I got so down-hearted and scared, I did wish I had some company. Pretty soon a spider went crawling up my shoulder, and I slipped it off and it lit in the candle; and before I could budge it was all shriveled up. I didn't need anybody to tell me that that was an awful bad sign and would fetch me some bad luck, so I was scared and most shook the clothes off of me. I got up and turned around in my tracks three times and crossed my breast every time; and then I tied up a little lock of my hair with a thread to keep witches away. But I hadn't no confidence. You do that when you've lost a horse-shoe that you've found, instead of nailing it up over the door, but I hadn't ever heard anybody say it was any way to keep off bad luck when you'd killed a spider.

I set down again, a shaking all over, and got out my pipe for a smoke; for the house was all as still as death, now, and so the widow wouldn't know. Well, after a long time I heard the clock away off in the town go boom—boom—boom—twelve licks—and all still again—stiller than ever. Pretty soon I heard a twig snap, down in the dark amongst the trees—something was a stirring. I set still and listened. Directly I could just barely hear a *"me-yow! me-yow!"* down there. That was good! Says I, *"me-yow! me-yow!"* as soft as I could, and then I put out the light and scrambled out of the window onto the shed. Then I slipped down to the ground and crawled in amongst the trees, and sure enough there was Tom Sawyer waiting for me.

Chapter II

We went tip-toeing along a path amongst the trees back towards the end of the widow's garden, stooping down so as the branches wouldn't scrape our heads. When we was passing by the kitchen I fell over a root and made a noise. We scrouched down and laid

8. Huck appropriately speaks the colloquial word used in the South to describe black slaves; it is not used derisively or contemptuously.

still. Miss Watson's big nigger, named Jim, was setting in the kitchen door; we could see him pretty clear, because there was a light behind him. He got up and stretched his neck out about a minute, listening. Then he says,

"Who dah?"

He listened some more; then he come tip-toeing down and stood right between us; we could a touched him, nearly. Well, likely it was minutes and minutes that there warn't a sound, and we all there so close together. There was a place on my ankle that got to itching; but I dasn't scratch it; and then my ear begun to itch; and next my back, right between my shoulders. Seemed like I'd die if I couldn't scratch. Well, I've noticed that thing plenty of times since. If you are with the quality, or at a funeral, or trying to go to sleep when you ain't sleepy—if you are anywheres where it won't do for you to scratch, why you will itch all over in upwards of a thousand places. Pretty soon Jim says:

"Say—who is you? Whar is you? Dog my cats ef I didn' hear sumf'n. Well, I knows what I's gwyne to do. I's gwyne to set down here and listen tell I hears it agin."

So he set down on the ground betwixt me and Tom. He leaned his back up against a tree, and stretched his legs out till one of them most touched one of mine. My nose begun to itch. It itched till the tears come into my eyes. But I dasn't scratch. Then it begun to itch on the inside. Next I got to itching underneath. I didn't know how I was going to set still. This miserableness went on as much as six or seven minutes; but it seemed a sight longer than that. I was itching in eleven different places now. I reckoned I couldn't stand it more'n a minute longer, but I set my teeth hard and got ready to try. Just then Jim begun to breathe heavy; next he begun to snore—and then I was pretty soon comfortable again.

Tom he made a sign to me—kind of a little noise with his mouth —and we went creeping away on our hands and knees. When we was ten foot off, Tom whispered to me and wanted to tie Jim to the tree for fun; but I said no; he might wake and make a disturbance, and then they'd find out I warn't in. Then Tom said he hadn't got candles enough, and he would slip in the kitchen and get some more. I didn't want him to try. I said Jim might wake up and come. But Tom wanted to resk it; so we slid in there and got three candles, and Tom laid five cents on the table for pay. Then we got out, and I was in a sweat to get away; but nothing would do Tom but he must crawl to where Jim was, on his hands and knees, and play something on him. I waited, and it seemed a good while, everything was so still and lonesome.

As soon as Tom was back, we cut along the path, around the garden fence, and by-and-by fetched up on the steep top of the hill the other side of the house. Tom said he slipped Jim's hat off of his head and hung it on a limb right over him, and Jim stirred a little, but he didn't wake. Afterwards Jim said the witches bewitched him and put him in a trance, and rode him all over the State, and then set him under the trees again and hung his hat on a limb to show who done it. And next time Jim told it he said they rode him down to New Orleans; and after that, every time he told it he spread it more and more, till by-and-by he said they rode him all over the world, and tired him most to death, and his back was all over saddle-boils. Jim was monstrous proud about it, and he got so he wouldn't hardly notice the other niggers. Niggers would come miles to hear Jim tell about it, and he was more looked up to than any nigger in that country. Strange niggers[9] would stand with their mouths open and look him all over, same as if he was a wonder. Niggers is always talking about witches in the dark by the kitchen fire; but whenever one was talking and letting on to know all about such things, Jim would happen in and say, "Hm! What you know 'bout witches?" and that nigger was corked up and had to take a back seat. Jim always kept that five-center piece around his neck with a string and said it was a charm the devil give to him with his own hands and told him he could cure anybody with it and fetch witches whenever he wanted to, just by saying something to it; but he never told what it was he said to it. Niggers would come from all around there and give Jim anything they had, just for a sight of that five-center piece; but they wouldn't touch it, because the devil had had his hands on it. Jim was most ruined, for a servant, because he got so stuck up on account of having seen the devil and been rode by witches.

Well, when Tom and me got to the edge of the hill-top, we looked away down into the village[1] and could see three or four lights twinkling, where there was sick folks, may be; and the stars over us was sparkling ever so fine; and down by the village was the river, a whole mile broad, and awful still and grand. We went down the hill and found Jo Harper, and Ben Rogers, and two or three more of the boys, hid in the old tanyard. So we unhitched a skiff and pulled down the river two mile and a half, to the big scar on the hillside, and went ashore.

We went to a clump of bushes, and Tom made everybody swear to keep the secret, and then showed them a hole in the hill, right in the thickest part of the bushes. Then we lit the candles and crawled in on our hands and knees. We went about two hundred yards, and then the cave opened up. Tom poked about amongst the passages and pretty soon ducked under a wall where you wouldn't a noticed that there was a hole. We went along a narrow place and got into a kind of room, all damp and sweaty and cold, and there we stopped. Tom says:

9. Those who did not live in the immediate area.
1. The village, called St. Petersburg here and in *Tom Sawyer*, is modeled on Hannibal, Missouri.

"Now we'll start this band of robbers and call it Tom Sawyer's Gang. Everybody that wants to join has got to take an oath, and write his name in blood."

Everybody was willing. So Tom got out a sheet of paper that he had wrote the oath on, and read it. It swore every boy to stick to the band, and never tell any of the secrets; and if anybody done anything to any boy in the band, whichever boy was ordered to kill that person and his family must do it, and he mustn't eat and he mustn't sleep till he had killed them and hacked a cross in their breasts, which was the sign of the band. And nobody that didn't belong to the band could use that mark, and if he did he must be sued; and if he done it again he must be killed. And if anybody that belonged to the band told the secrets, he must have his throat cut, and then have his carcass burnt up and the ashes scattered all around, and his name blotted off of the list with blood and never mentioned again by the gang, but have a curse put on it and be forgot, forever.

Everybody said it was a real beautiful oath, and asked Tom if he got it out of his own head. He said, some of it, but the rest was out of pirate books, and robber books, and every gang that was high-toned had it.

Some thought it would be good to kill the *families* of boys that told the secrets. Tom said it was a good idea, so he took a pencil and wrote it in. Then Ben Rogers says:

"Here's Huck Finn, he hain't got no family—what you going to do 'bout him?"

"Well, hain't he got a father?" says Tom Sawyer.

"Yes, he's got a father, but you can't never find him, these days. He used to lay drunk with the hogs in the tanyard, but he hain't been seen in these parts for a year or more."

They talked it over, and they was going to rule me out, because they said every boy must have a family or somebody to kill, or else it wouldn't be fair and square for the others. Well, nobody could think of anything to do—everybody was stumped, and set still. I was most ready to cry; but all at once I thought of a way, and so I offered them Miss Watson—they could kill her. Everybody said:

"Oh, she'll do, she'll do. That's all right. Huck can come in."

Then they all stuck a pin in their fingers to get blood to sign with, and I made my mark on the paper.

"Now," says Ben Rogers, "what's the line of business of this Gang?"

"Nothing only robbery and murder," Tom said.

"But who are we going to rob? houses—or cattle—or—"

"Stuff! stealing cattle and such things ain't robbery, it's burglary," says Tom Sawyer. "We ain't burglars. That ain't no sort of style. We are highwaymen. We stop stages and carriages on the road, with masks on, and kill the people and take their watches and money."

"Must we always kill the people?"

"Oh, certainly. It's best. Some authorities think different, but mostly it's considered best to kill them. Except some that you bring to the cave here and keep them till they're ransomed."

"Ransomed? What's that?"

"I don't know. But that's what they do. I've seen it in books; and so of course that's what we've got to do."

"But how can we do it if we don't know what it is?"

"Why blame it all, we've *got* to do it. Don't I tell you it's in the books? Do you want to go to doing different from what's in the books, and get things all muddled up?"

"Oh, that's all very fine to *say*, Tom Sawyer, but how in the nation[2] are these fellows going to be ransomed if we don't know how to do it to them? that's the thing I want to get at. Now what do you *reckon* it is?"

"Well I don't know. But per'aps if we keep them till they're ransomed, it means that we keep them till they're dead."

"Now, that's something *like*. That'll answer. Why couldn't you said that before? We'll keep them till they're ransomed to death— and a bothersome lot they'll be, too, eating up everything and always trying to get loose."

"How you talk, Ben Rogers. How can they get loose when there's a guard over them, ready to shoot them down if they move a peg?"

"A guard. Well, that *is* good. So somebody's got to set up all night and never get any sleep, just so as to watch them. I think that's foolishness. Why can't a body take a club and ransom them as soon as they get here?"

"Because it ain't in the books so—that's why. Now Ben Rogers, do you want to do things regular, or don't you?—that's the idea. Don't you reckon that the people that made the books knows what's the correct thing to do? Do you reckon *you* can learn 'em anything? Not by a good deal. No, sir, we'll just go on and ransom them in the regular way."

"All right. I don't mind; but I say it's a fool way, anyhow. Say— do we kill the women, too?"

"Well, Ben Rogers, if I was as ignorant as you I wouldn't let on. Kill the women? No—nobody ever saw anything in the books like that. You fetch them to the cave, and you're always as polite as pie to them; and by-and-by they fall in love with you and never want to go home any more."

"Well, if that's the way, I'm agreed, but I don't take no stock in it. Mighty soon we'll have the cave so cluttered up with women,

2. **Damnation.**

and fellows waiting to be ransomed, that there won't be no place
for the robbers. But go ahead, I ain't got nothing to say."

Little Tommy Barnes was asleep, now, and when they waked him
up he was scared, and cried, and said he wanted to go home to his
ma, and didn't want to be a robber any more.

So they all made fun of him, and called him cry-baby, and that
made him mad, and he said he would go straight and tell all the
secrets. But Tom give him five cents to keep quiet, and said we
would all go home and meet next week and rob somebody and kill
some people.

Ben Rogers said he couldn't get out much, only Sundays, and so
he wanted to begin next Sunday; but all the boys said it would be
wicked to do it on Sunday, and that settled the thing. They agreed
to get together and fix a day as soon as they could, and then we
elected Tom Sawyer first captain and Jo Harper second captain of
the Gang, and so started home.

I clumb up the shed and crept into my window just before day
was breaking. My new clothes was all greased up and clayey, and I
was dog-tired.

Chapter III

Well, I got a good going-over in the morning, from old Miss
Watson, on account of my clothes; but the widow she didn't scold,
but only cleaned off the grease and clay and looked so sorry that I
thought I would behave a while if I could. Then Miss Watson she
took me in the closet[3] and prayed, but nothing come of it. She told
me to pray every day, and whatever I asked for I would get it. But
it warn't so. I tried it. Once I got a fish-line, but no hooks. It warn't
any good to me without hooks. I tried for the hooks three or four
times, but somehow I couldn't make it work. By-and-by, one day, I
asked Miss Watson to try for me, but she said I was a fool. She
never told me why, and I couldn't make it out no way.

I set down, one time, back in the woods, and had a long think
about it. I says to myself, if a body can get anything they pray for,
why don't Deacon Winn get back the money he lost on pork? Why
can't the widow get back her silver snuff-box that was stole? Why
can't Miss Watson fat up? No, says I to myself, there ain't nothing
in it. I went and told the widow about it, and she said the thing a
body could get by praying for it was "spiritual gifts." This was too
many for me, but she told me what she meant—I must help other
people, and do everything I could for other people, and look out for
them all the time, and never think about myself. This was including
Miss Watson, as I took it. I went out in the woods and turned it
over in my mind a long time, but I couldn't see no advantage about
it—except for the other people—so at last I reckoned I wouldn't

3. Matthew 6.6: "But thou, when thou
prayest, enter into thy closet" is apparently the admonition Miss Watson has in
mind.

worry about it any more, but just let it go. Sometimes the widow would take me one side and talk about Providence in a way to make a boy's mouth water; but maybe next day Miss Watson would take hold and knock it all down again. I judged I could see that there was two Providences, and a poor chap would stand considerable show with the widow's Providence, but if Miss Watson's got him there warn't no help for him any more. I thought it all out, and reckoned I would belong to the widow's, if he wanted me, though I couldn't make out how he was agoing to be any better off then than what he was before, seeing I was so ignorant and so kind of low-down and ornery.

Pap he hadn't been seen for more than a year, and that was comfortable for me; I didn't want to see him no more. He used to always whale me when he was sober and could get his hands on me; though I used to take to the woods most of the time when he was around. Well, about this time he was found in the river drowned, about twelve mile above town, so people said. They judged it was him, anyway; said this drowned man was just his size, and was ragged, and had uncommon long hair—which was all like pap—but they couldn't make nothing out of the face, because it had been in the water so long it warn't much like a face at all. They said he was floating on his back in the water. They took him and buried him on the bank. But I warn't comfortable long, because I happened to think of something. I knowed mighty well that a drownded man don't float on his back, but on his face. So I knowed, then, that this warn't pap, but a woman dressed up in a man's clothes. So I was uncomfortable again. I judged the old man would turn up again by-and-by, though I wished he wouldn't.

We played robber now and then about a month, and then I resigned. All the boys did. We hadn't robbed nobody, we hadn't killed any people, but only just pretended. We used to hop out of the woods and go charging down on hog-drovers and women in carts taking garden stuff to market, but we never hived[4] any of them. Tom Sawyer called the hogs "ingots," and he called the turnips and stuff "julery" and we would go to the cave and pow-wow over what we had done and how many people we had killed and marked. But I couldn't see no profit in it. One time Tom sent a boy to run about town with a blazing stick, which he called a slogan (which was the sign for the Gang to get together), and then he said he had got secret news by his spies that next day a whole parcel of Spanish merchants and rich A-rabs was going to camp in Cave Hollow with two hundred elephants, and six hundred camels, and over a thousand "sumter" mules,[5] all loaded with di'monds, and they didn't have only a guard of four hundred soldiers, and so we would lay in ambuscade, as he called it, and kill the lot and scoop the things. He said we must slick up our swords and guns,

4. **Captured, secured.**   5. **Pack mules.**

and get ready. He never could go after even a turnip-cart but he must have the swords and guns all scoured up for it; though they was only lath and broom-sticks, and you might scour at them till you rotted and then they warn't worth a mouthful of ashes more than what they was before. I didn't believe we could lick such a crowd of Spaniards and A-rabs, but I wanted to see the camels and elephants, so I was on hand next day, Saturday, in the ambuscade; and when we got the word, we rushed out of the woods and down the hill. But there warn't no Spaniards and A-rabs, and there warn't no camels nor no elephants. It warn't anything but a Sunday-school picnic, and only a primer-class at that. We busted it up, and chased the children up the hollow; but we never got anything but some doughnuts and jam, though Ben Rogers got a rag doll, and Jo Harper got a hymn-book and a tract; and then the teacher charged in and made us drop everything and cut. I didn't see no di'monds, and I told Tom Sawyer so. He said there was loads of them there, anyway; and he said there was A-rabs there, too, and elephants and things. I said, why couldn't we see them, then? He said if I warn't so ignorant, but had read a book called "Don Quixote,"[6] I would know without asking. He said it was all done by enchantment. He said there was hundreds of soldiers there, and elephants and treasure, and so on, but we had enemies which he called magicians, and they had turned the whole thing into an infant Sunday school, just out of spite. I said, all right, then the thing for us to do was to go for the magicians. Tom Sawyer said I was a numskull.

"Why," says he, "a magician could call up a lot of genies, and they would hash you up like nothing before you could say Jack Robinson. They are as tall as a tree and as big around as a church."

"Well," I says, "s'pose we got some genies to help *us*—can't we lick the other crowd then?"

"How you going to get them?"

"I don't know. How do *they* get them?"

"Why they rub an old tin lamp or an iron ring, and then the genies come tearing in, with the thunder and lightning a-ripping around and the smoke a-rolling, and everything they're told to do they up and do it. They don't think nothing of pulling a shot tower[7] up by the roots, and belting a Sunday-school superintendent over the head with it—or any other man."

"Who makes them tear around so?"

"Why, whoever rubs the lamp or the ring. They belong to whoever rubs the lamp or the ring, and they've got to do whatever he says. If he tells them to build a palace forty miles long, out of di'monds, and fill it full of chewing gum, or whatever you want, and fetch an emperor's daughter from China for you to marry,

6. Tom is here alluding to stories in *The Arabian Nights Entertainments* (1838–41) and to the hero in Cervantes's *Don Quixote* (1605).

7. A device in which gunshot was formed by dripping molten lead into water.

they've got to do it—and they've got to do it before sun-up next morning, too. And more—they've got to waltz that palace around over the country whenever you want it, you understand."

"Well," says I, "I think they are a pack of flatheads for not keeping the palace themselves 'stead of fooling them away like that. And what's more—if I was one of them I would see a man in Jericho before I would drop my business and come to him for the rubbing of an old tin lamp."

"How you talk, Huck Finn. Why, you'd *have* to come when he rubbed it, whether you wanted to or not."

"What, and I as high as a tree and as big as a church? All right, then; I *would* come; but I lay I'd make that man climb the highest tree there was in the country."

"Shucks, it ain't no use to talk to you, Huck Finn. You don't seem to know anything, somehow—perfect sap-head."

I thought all this over for two or three days, and then I reckoned I would see if there was anything in it. I got an old tin lamp and an iron ring and went out in the woods and rubbed and rubbed till I sweat like an Injun, calculating to build a palace and sell it; but it warn't no use, none of the genies come. So then I judged that all that stuff was only just one of Tom Sawyer's lies. I reckoned he believed in the A-rabs and the elephants, but as for me I think different. It had all the marks of a Sunday school.

Chapter IV

Well, three or four months run along, and it was well into the winter, now. I had been to school most all the time, and could spell, and read, and write just a little, and could say the multiplication table up to six times seven is thirty-five, and I don't reckon I could ever get any further than that if I was to live forever. I don't take no stock in mathematics, anyway.

At first I hated the school, but by-and-by I got so I could stand it. Whenever I got uncommon tired I played hookey, and the hiding I got next day done me good and cheered me up. So the longer I went to school the easier it got to be. I was getting sort of used to the widow's ways, too, and they warn't so raspy on me. Living in a house, and sleeping in a bed, pulled on me pretty tight, mostly, but before the cold weather I used to slide out and sleep in the woods, sometimes, and so that was a rest to me. I liked the old ways best, but I was getting so I liked the new ones, too, a little bit. The widow said I was coming along slow but sure, and doing very satisfactory. She said she warn't ashamed of me.

One morning I happened to turn over the salt-cellar at breakfast. I reached for some of it as quick as I could, to throw over my left shoulder and keep off the bad luck, but Miss Watson was in ahead of me, and crossed me off. She says, "Take your hands away, Huckleberry—what a mess you are always making." The widow put in a

good word for me, but that warn't going to keep off the bad luck, I
knowed that well enough. I started out, after breakfast, feeling worried and shaky, and wondering where it was going to fall on me,
and what it was going to be. There is ways to keep off some kinds
of bad luck, but this wasn't one of them kind; so I never tried to do
anything, but just poked along low-spirited and on the watch-out.

I went down the front garden and clumb over the stile,[8] where
you go through the high board fence. There was an inch of new
snow on the ground, and I seen somebody's tracks. They had come
up from the quarry and stood around the stile a while, and then
went on around the garden fence. It was funny they hadn't come
in, after standing around so. I couldn't make it out. It was very
curious, somehow. I was going to follow around, but I stooped
down to look at the tracks first. I didn't notice anything at first, but
next I did. There was a cross in the left boot-heel made with big
nails, to keep off the devil.

I was up in a second and shinning down the hill. I looked over
my shoulder every now and then, but I didn't see nobody. I was at
Judge Thatcher's as quick as I could get there. He said:

"Why, my boy, you are all out of breath. Did you come for your
interest?"

"No sir," I says; "is there some for me?"

"Oh, yes, a half-yearly is in, last night. Over a hundred and fifty
dollars. Quite a fortune for you. You better let me invest it along
with your six thousand, because if you take it you'll spend it."

"No sir," I says, "I don't want to spend it. I don't want it at all
—nor the six thousand, nuther. I want you to take it; I want to give
it to you—the six thousand and all."

He looked surprised. He couldn't seem to make it out. He says:

"Why, what can you mean, my boy?"

I says, "Don't you ask me no questions about it, please. You'll
take it—won't you?"

He says:

"Well I'm puzzled. Is something the matter?"

"Please take it," says I, "and don't ask me nothing—then I won't
have to tell no lies."

He studied a while, and then he says:

"Oho-o. I think I see. You want to *sell* all your property to me—
not give it. That's the correct idea."

Then he wrote something on a paper and read it over, and says:

"There—you see it says 'for a consideration.' That means I have
bought it of you and paid you for it. Here's a dollar for you. Now,
you sign it."

So I signed it, and left.

8. Steps which flank and straddle a fence.

Miss Watson's nigger, Jim, had a hair-ball as big as your fist, which had been took out of the fourth stomach of an ox, and he used to do magic with it.[9] He said there was a spirit inside of it, and it knowed everything. So I went to him that night and told him pap was here again, for I found his tracks in the snow. What I wanted to know, was, what he was going to do, and was he going to stay? Jim got out his hair-ball, and said something over it, and then he held it up and dropped it on the floor. It fell pretty solid, and only rolled about an inch. Jim tried it again, and then another time, and it acted just the same. Jim got down on his knees and put his ear against it and listened. But it warn't no use; he said it wouldn't talk. He said sometimes it wouldn't talk without money. I told him I had an old slick counterfeit quarter that warn't no good because the brass showed through the silver a little, and it wouldn't pass nohow, even if the brass didn't show, because it was so slick it felt greasy, and so that would tell on it every time. (I reckoned I wouldn't say nothing about the dollar I got from the judge.) I said it was pretty bad money, but maybe the hair-ball would take it, because maybe it wouldn't know the difference. Jim smelt it, and bit it, and rubbed it, and said he would manage so the hair-ball would think it was good. He said he would split open a raw Irish potato and stick the quarter in between and keep it there all night, and next morning you couldn't see no brass, and it wouldn't feel greasy no more, and so anybody in town would take it in a minute, let alone a hair-ball. Well, I knowed a potato would do that, before, but I had forgot it.

Jim put the quarter under the hair-ball and got down and listened again. This time he said the hair-ball was all right. He said it would tell my whole fortune if I wanted it to. I says, go on. So the hair-ball talked to Jim, and Jim told it to me. He says:

"Yo' ole father doan' know, yit, what he's a-gwyne to do. Sometimes he spec he'll go 'way, en den agin he spec he'll stay. De bes' way is to res' easy en let de ole man take his own way. Dey's two angels hoverin' roun' 'bout him. One uv 'em is white en shiny, en 'tother one is black. De white one gits him to go right, a little while, den de black one sail in en bust it all up. A body can't tell, yit, which one gwyne to fetch him at de las'. But you is all right. You gwyne to have considable trouble in yo' life, en considable joy. Sometimes you gwyne to git hurt, en sometimes you gwyne to git sick; but every time you's gwyne to git well agin. Dey's two gals flyin' 'bout you in yo' life. One uv 'em's light en 'tother one is dark. One is rich en 'tother is po'. You's gwyne to marry de po' one fust en de rich one by-en-by. You wants to keep 'way fum de water as

9. Though most of the superstitions in *Tom Sawyer* and *Huck Finn* have been traced to European sources, the belief in the magical powers of the hair ball found in the stomachs of oxen seems to be a Negro one.

much as you kin, en don't run no resk, 'kase it's down in de bills
dat you's gwyne to git hung."

When I lit my candle and went up to my room that night, there
set pap, his own self!

Chapter V

I had shut the door to. Then I turned around, and there he was.
I used to be scared of him all the time, he tanned me so much. I
reckoned I was scared now, too; but in a minute I see I was mistaken. That is, after the first jolt, as you may say, when my breath
sort of hitched—he being so unexpected; but right away after, I see
I warn't scared of him worth bothering about.

He was most fifty, and he looked it. His hair was long and tangled and greasy, and hung down, and you could see his eyes shining
through like he was behind vines. It was all black, no gray; so was
his long, mixed-up whiskers. There warn't no color in his face,
where his face showed; it was white; not like another man's white,
but a white to make a body sick, a white to make a body's flesh
crawl—a tree-toad white, a fish-belly white. As for his clothes—just
rags, that was all. He had one ankle resting on 'tother knee; the
boot on that foot was busted, and two of his toes stuck through,
and he worked them now and then. His hat was laying on the floor;
an old black slouch with the top caved in, like a lid.

I stood a-looking at him; he set there a-looking at me, with his
chair tilted back a little. I set the candle down. I noticed the
window was up; so he had clumb in by the shed. He kept a-looking
me all over. By-and-by he says:

"Starchy clothes—very. You think you're a good deal of a big-
bug, *don't* you?"

"Maybe I am, maybe I ain't," I says.

"Don't you give me none o' your lip," says he. "You've put on
considerble many frills since I been away. I'll take you down a peg
before I get done with you. You're educated, too, they say; can read
and write. You think you're better'n your father, now, don't you,
because he can't? *I'll* take it out of you. Who told you you might
meddle with such hifalut'n foolishness, hey?—who told you you
could?"

"The widow. She told me."

"The widow, hey?—and who told the widow she could put in her
shovel about a thing that ain't none of her business?"

"Nobody never told her."

"Well, I'll learn her how to meddle. And looky here—you drop
that school, you hear? I'll learn people to bring up a boy to put on
airs over his own father and let on to be better'n what *he* is. You
lemme catch you fooling around that school again, you hear? Your
mother couldn't read, and she couldn't write, nuther, before she
died. None of the family couldn't, before *they* died. I can't; and

here you're a-swelling yourself up like this. I ain't the man to stand it—you hear? Say—lemme hear you read."

I took up a book and begun something about General Washington and the wars. When I'd read about a half a minute, he fetched the book a whack with his hand and knocked it across the house. He says:

"It's so. You can do it. I had my doubts when you told me. Now looky here; you stop that putting on frills. I won't have it. I'll lay for you, my smarty; and if I catch you about that school I'll tan you good. First you know you'll get religion, too. I never see such a son."

He took up a little blue and yaller picture of some cows and a boy, and says:

"What's this?"

"It's something they give me for learning my lessons good."

He tore it up, and says—

"I'll give you something better—I'll give you a cowhide."[1]

He set there a-mumbling and a-growling a minute, and then he says—

"*Ain't* you a sweet-scented dandy, though? A bed; and bedclothes; and a look'n-glass; and a piece of carpet on the floor—and your own father got to sleep with the hogs in the tanyard. I never see such a son. I bet I'll take some o' these frills out o' you before I'm done with you. Why there ain't no end to your airs—they say you're rich. Hey?—how's that?"

"They lie—that's how."

"Looky here—mind how you talk to me; I'm a-standing about all I can stand, now—so don't gimme no sass. I've been in town two days, and I hain't heard nothing but about you bein' rich. I heard about it away down the river, too. That's why I come. You git me that money to-morrow—I want it."

"I hain't got no money."

"It's a lie. Judge Thatcher's got it. You git it. I want it."

"I hain't got no money, I tell you. You ask Judge Thatcher; he'll tell you the same."

"All right. I'll ask him; and I'll make him pungle,[2] too, or I'll know the reason why. Say—how much you got in your pocket? I want it."

"I hain't got only a dollar, and I want that to—"

"It don't make no difference what you want it for—you just shell it out."

He took it and bit it to see if it was good, and then he said he was going down town to get some whisky; said he hadn't had a drink all day. When he had got out on the shed, he put his head in again, and cussed me for putting on frills and trying to be better than him; and when I reckoned he was gone, he come back and put

1. A strapping with a cowhide whip.　　2. Turn over the money.

his head in again, and told me to mind about that school, because
he was going to lay for me and lick me if I didn't drop that.

Next day he was drunk, and he went to Judge Thatcher's and
bullyragged him and tried to make him give up the money, but he
couldn't, and then he swore he'd make the law force him.

The judge and the widow went to law to get the court to take me
away from him and let one of them be my guardian; but it was a
new judge that had just come, and he didn't know the old man; so
he said courts mustn't interfere and separate families if they could
help it; said he'd druther not take a child away from its father. So
Judge Thatcher and the widow had to quit on the business.

That pleased the old man till he couldn't rest. He said he'd
cowhide me till I was black and blue if I didn't raise some money
for him. I borrowed three dollars from Judge Thatcher, and pap
took it and got drunk and went a-blowing around and cussing and
whooping and carrying on; and he kept it up all over town, with a
tin pan, till most midnight; then they jailed him, and next day they
had him before court, and jailed him again for a week. But he said
he was satisfied; said he was boss of his son, and he'd make it warm
for *him*.

When he got out the new judge said he was agoing to make a
man of him. So he took him to his own house, and dressed him up
clean and nice, and had him to breakfast and dinner and supper
with the family, and was just old pie to him, so to speak. And after
supper he talked to him about temperance and such things till the
old man cried, and said he'd been a fool, and fooled away his life;
but now he was agoing to turn over a new leaf and be a man
nobody wouldn't be ashamed of, and he hoped the judge would
help him and not look down on him. The judge said he could hug
him for them words; so *he* cried, and his wife she cried again; pap
said he'd been a man that had always been misunderstood before,
and the judge said he believed it. The old man said that what a
man wanted that was down, was sympathy; and the judge said it
was so; so they cried again. And when it was bedtime, the old man
rose up and held out his hand, and says:

"Look at it gentlemen, and ladies all; take ahold of it; shake it.
There's a hand that was the hand of a hog; but it ain't so no more;
it's the hand of a man that's started in on a new life, and 'll die
before he'll go back. You mark them words—don't forget I said
them. It's a clean hand now; shake it—don't be afeard."

So they shook it, one after the other, all around, and cried. The
judge's wife she kissed it. Then the old man he signed a pledge—
made his mark. The judge said it was the holiest time on record, or
something like that. Then they tucked the old man into a beautiful
room, which was the spare room, and in the night sometime he got
powerful thirsty and clumb out onto the porch-roof and slid down a

stanchion and traded his new coat for a jug of forty-rod,[3] and clumb back again and had a good old time; and towards daylight he crawled out again, drunk as a fiddler, and rolled off the porch and broke his left arm in two places and was most froze to death when somebody found him after sun-up. And when they come to look at that spare room, they had to take soundings before they could navigate it.

The judge he felt kind of sore. He said he reckoned a body could reform the ole man with a shot-gun, maybe, but he didn't know no other way.

Chapter VI

Well, pretty soon the old man was up and around again, and then he went for Judge Thatcher in the courts to make him give up that money, and he went for me, too, for not stopping school. He catched me a couple of times and thrashed me, but I went to school just the same, and dodged him or out-run him most of the time. I didn't want to go to school much, before, but I reckoned I'd go now to spite pap. That law trial was a slow business; appeared like they warn't ever going to get started on it; so every now and then I'd borrow two or three dollars off of the judge for him, to keep from getting a cowhiding. Every time he got money he got drunk; and every time he got drunk he raised Cain around town; and every time he raised Cain he got jailed. He was just suited— this kind of thing was right in his line.

He got to hanging around the widow's too much, and so she told him at last, that if he didn't quit using around there she would make trouble for him. Well, *wasn't* he mad? He said he would show who was Huck Finn's boss. So he watched out for me one day in the spring, and catched me, and took me up the river about three mile, in a skiff, and crossed over to the Illinois shore where it was woody and there warn't no houses but an old log hut in a place where the timber was so thick you couldn't find it if you didn't know where it was.

He kept me with him all the time, and I never got a chance to run off. We lived in that old cabin, and he always locked the door and put the key under his head, nights. He had a gun which he had stole, I reckon, and we fished and hunted, and that was what we lived on. Every little while he locked me in and went down to the store, three miles, to the ferry, and traded fish and game for whisky and fetched it home and got drunk and had a good time, and licked me. The widow she found out where I was, by-and-by, and she sent a man over to try to get hold of me, but pap drove him off with the gun, and it warn't long after that till I was used to being where I was, and liked it, all but the cowhide part.

3. Home-distilled whiskey strong enough to knock a man 40 rods, or 60 yards.

It was kind of lazy and jolly, laying off comfortable all day, smoking and fishing, and no books nor study. Two months or more run along, and my clothes got to be all rags and dirt, and I didn't see how I'd ever got to like it so well at the widow's, where you had to wash, and eat on a plate, and comb up, and go to bed and get up regular, and be forever bothering over a book and have old Miss Watson pecking at you all the time. I didn't want to go back no more. I had stopped cussing, because the widow didn't like it; but now I took to it again because pap hadn't no objections. It was pretty good times up in the woods there, take it all around.

But by-and-by pap got too handy with his hick'ry, and I couldn't stand it. I was all over welts. He got to going away so much, too, and locking me in. Once he locked me in and was gone three days. It was dreadful lonesome. I judged he had got drowned and I wasn't ever going to get out any more. I was scared. I made up my mind I would fix up some way to leave there. I had tried to get out of that cabin many a time, but I couldn't find no way. There warn't window to it big enough for a dog to get through. I couldn't get up the chimbly, it was too narrow. The door was thick solid oak slabs. Pap was pretty careful not to leave a knife or anything in the cabin when he was away; I reckon I had hunted the place over as much as a hundred times; well, I was 'most all the time at it, because it was about the only way to put in the time. But this time I found something at last; I found an old rusty wood-saw without any handle; it was laid in between a rafter and the clapboards of the roof. I greased it up and went to work. There was an old horse-blanket nailed against the logs at the far end of the cabin behind the table, to keep the wind from blowing through the chinks and putting the candle out. I got under the table and raised the blanket and went to work to saw a section of the big bottom log out, big enough to let me through. Well, it was a good long job, but I was getting towards the end of it when I heard pap's gun in the woods. I got rid of the signs of my work, and dropped the blanket and hid my saw, and pretty soon pap come in.

Pap warn't in a good humor—so he was his natural self. He said he was down to town, and everything was going wrong. His lawyer said he reckoned he would win his lawsuit and get the money, if they ever got started on the trial; but then there was ways to put it off a long time, and Judge Thatcher knowed how to do it. And he said people allowed there'd be another trial to get me away from him and give me to the widow for my guardian, and they guessed it would win, this time. This shook me up considerable, because I didn't want to go back to the widow's any more and be so cramped up and sivilized, as they called it. Then the old man got to cussing, and cussed everything and everybody he could think of, and then cussed them all over again to make sure he hadn't skipped any, and after that he polished off with a kind of a general cuss all round, including a considerable parcel of people which he didn't know the names of, and so called them what's-his-name, when he got to them, and went right along with his cussing.

He said he would like to see the widow get me. He said he would watch out, and if they tried to come any such game on him he knowed of a place six or seven mile off, to stow me in, where they might hunt till they dropped and they couldn't find me. That made me pretty uneasy again, but only for a minute; I reckoned I wouldn't stay on hand till he got that chance.

The old man made me go to the skiff and fetch the things he had got. There was a fifty-pound sack of corn meal, and a side of bacon, ammunition, and a four-gallon jug of whisky, and an old book and two newspapers for wadding,[4] besides some tow. I toted up a load, and went back and set down on the bow of the skiff to rest. I thought it all over, and I reckoned I would walk off with the gun and some lines, and take to the woods when I run away. I guessed I wouldn't stay in one place, but just tramp right across the country, mostly night times, and hunt and fish to keep alive, and so get so far away that the old man nor the widow couldn't ever find me any more. I judged I would saw out and leave that night if pap got drunk enough, and I reckoned he would. I got so full of it I didn't notice how long I was staying, till the old man hollered and asked me whether I was asleep or drownded.

I got the things all up to the cabin, and then it was about dark. While I was cooking supper the old man took a swig or two and got sort of warmed up, and went to ripping again. He had been drunk over in town, and laid in the gutter all night, and he was a sight to look at. A body would a thought he was Adam, he was just all mud.[5] Whenever his liquor begun to work, he most always went for the govment. This time he says:

"Call this a govment! why, just look at it and see what it's like. Here's the law a-standing ready to take a man's son away from him —a man's own son, which he has had all the trouble and all the anxiety and all the expense of raising. Yes, just as that man has got that son raised at last, and ready to go to work and begin to do suthin' for *him* and give him a rest, the law up and goes for him. And they call *that* govment! That ain't all, nuther. The law backs that old Judge Thatcher up and helps him to keep me out o' my property. Here's what the law does. The law takes a man worth six thousand dollars and upards, and jams him into an old trap of a cabin like this, and lets him go round in clothes that ain't fitten for a hog. They call that govment! A man can't get his rights in a govment like this. Sometimes I've a mighty notion to just leave the country for good and all. Yes, and I *told* 'em so; I told old Thatcher so to his face. Lots of 'em heard me, and can tell what I said. Says

4. To pack the gunpowder in a rifle; "tow": cheap rope.
5. God created Adam from earth in Genesis 2.7.

I, for two cents I'd leave the blamed country and never come anear it agin. Them's the very words. I says, look at my hat—if you call it a hat—but the lid raises up and the rest of it goes down till it's below my chin, and then it ain't rightly a hat at all, but more like my head was shoved up through a jint o' stove-pipe. Look at it, says I—such a hat for me to wear—one of the wealthiest men in this town, if I could git my rights.

"Oh, yes, this is a wonderful govment, wonderful. Why, looky here. There was a free nigger there, from Ohio; a mulatter,[6] most as white as a white man. He had the whitest shirt on you ever see, too, and the shiniest hat; and there ain't a man in that town that's got as fine clothes as what he had; and he had a gold watch and chain and a silver-headed cane—the awfulest old gray-headed nabob in the State. And what do you think? they said he was a p'fessor in a college, and could talk all kinds of languages, and knowed everything. And that ain't the wust. They said he could *vote*, when he was at home. Well, that let me out. Thinks I, what is the country a-coming to? It was 'lection day, and I was just about to go and vote, myself, if I warn't too drunk to get there; but when they told me there was a State in this country where they'd let that nigger vote, I drawed out. I says I'll never vote agin. Them's the very words I said; they all heard me; and the country may rot for all me —I'll never vote agin as long as I live. And to see the cool way of that nigger—why, he wouldn't a give me the road if I hadn't shoved him out o' the way. I says to the people, why ain't this nigger put up at auction and sold?—that's what I want to know. And what do you reckon they said? Why, they said he couldn't be sold till he'd been in the State six months, and he hadn't been there that long yet. There, now—that's a specimen. They call that a govment that can't sell a free nigger till he's been in the State six months. Here's a govment that calls itself a govment, and lets on to be a govment, and thinks it is a govment, and yet's got to set stock-still for six whole months before it can take ahold of a prowling, thieving, infernal, white-shirted free nigger, and—"[7]

Pap was agoing on so, he never noticed where his old limber legs was taking him to, so he went head over heels over the tub of salt pork, and barked both shins, and the rest of his speech was all the hottest kind of language—mostly hove at the nigger and the govment, though he give the tub some, too, all along, here and there. He hopped around the cabin considerable, first on one leg and then on the other, holding first one shin and then the other one, and at last he let out with his left foot all of a sudden and fetched the tub a rattling kick. But it warn't good judgment, because that was the

6. **Person of mixed Caucasian and Negro ancestry.**
7. **Missouri's original constitution prohibited the entrance of freed slaves and mulattoes into the state, but the "second Missouri Compromise" of 1820 deleted the provision. In the 1830s and 1840s, however, increasingly strict anti-Negro laws were passed, and by 1850 a Negro without freedom papers could be sold down river with a mere sworn statement of ownership from a white man.**

boot that had a couple of his toes leaking out of the front end of it; so now he raised a howl that fairly made a body's hair raise, and down he went in the dirt, and rolled there, and held his toes; and the cussing he done then laid over anything he had ever done previous. He said so his own self, afterwards. He had heard old Sowberry Hagan in his best days, and he said it laid over him, too; but I reckon that was sort of piling it on, maybe.

After supper pap took the jug, and said he had enough whisky there for two drunks and one delirium tremens. That was always his word. I judged he would be blind drunk in about an hour, and then I would steal the key, or saw myself out, one or 'tother. He drank, and drank, and tumbled down on his blankets, by-and-by; but luck didn't run my way. He didn't go sound asleep, but was uneasy. He groaned, and moaned, and thrashed around this way and that, for a long time. At last I got so sleepy I couldn't keep my eyes open, all I could do, and so before I knowed what I was about I was sound asleep, and the candle burning.

I don't know how long I was asleep, but all of a sudden there was an awful scream and I was up. There was pap, looking wild and skipping around every which way and yelling about snakes. He said they was crawling up his legs; and then he would give a jump and scream, and say one had bit him on the cheek—but I couldn't see no snakes. He started and run round and round the cabin, hollering "take him off! take him off! he's biting me on the neck!" I never see a man look so wild in the eyes. Pretty soon he was all fagged out, and fell down panting; then he rolled over and over, wonderful fast, kicking things every which way, and striking and grabbing at the air with his hands, and screaming, and saying there was devils ahold of him. He wore out, by-and-by, and laid still a while, moaning. Then he laid stiller, and didn't make a sound. I could hear the owls and the wolves, away off in the woods, and it seemed terrible still. He was laying over by the corner. By-and-by he raised up, part way, and listened, with his head to one side. He says very low:

"Tramp—tramp—tramp; that's the dead; tramp—tramp—tramp; they're coming after me; but I won't go— Oh, they're here! don't touch me—don't! hands off—they're cold; let go— Oh, let a poor devil alone!"

Then he went down on all fours and crawled off begging them to let him alone, and he rolled himself up in his blanket and wallowed in under the old pine table, still a-begging; and then he went to crying. I could hear him through the blanket.

By-and-by he rolled out and jumped up on his feet looking wild, and he see me and went for me. He chased me round and round the place, with a clasp-knife, calling me the Angel of Death and saying he would kill me and then I couldn't come for him no more. I begged, and told him I was only Huck, but he laughed *such* a screechy laugh, and roared and cussed, and kept on chasing me up.

Once when I turned short and dodged under his arm he made a grab and got me by the jacket between my shoulders, and I thought I was gone; but I slid out of the jacket quick as lightning, and saved myself. Pretty soon he was all tired out, and dropped down with his back against the door, and said he would rest a minute and then kill me. He put his knife under him, and said he would sleep and get strong, and then he would see who was who.

So he dozed off, pretty soon. By-and-by I got the old split-bottom[8] chair and clumb up, as easy as I could, not to make any noise, and got down the gun. I slipped the ramrod down it to make sure it was loaded, and then I laid it across the turnip barrel, pointing towards pap, and set down behind it to wait for him to stir. And how slow and still the time did drag along.

Chapter VII

"Git up! what you 'bout!"

I opened my eyes and looked around, trying to make out where I was. It was after sun-up, and I had been sound asleep. Pap was standing over me, looking sour—and sick, too. He says—

"What you doin' with this gun?"

I judged he didn't know nothing about what he had been doing, so I says:

"Somebody tried to get in, so I was laying for him."

"Why didn't you roust me out?"

"Well I tried to, but I couldn't; I couldn't budge you."

"Well, all right. Don't stand there palavering all day, but out with you and see if there's a fish on the lines for breakfast. I'll be along in a minute."

He unlocked the door and I cleared out, up the river bank. I noticed some pieces of limbs and such things floating down, and a sprinkling of bark; so I knowed the river had begun to rise. I reckoned I would have great times, now, if I was over at the town. The June rise used to be always luck for me; because as soon as that rise begins, here comes cord-wood floating down, and pieces of log rafts—sometimes a dozen logs together; so all you have to do is to catch them and sell them to the wood yards and the sawmill.

I went along up the bank with one eye out for pap and 'tother one out for what the rise might fetch along. Well, all at once, here comes a canoe; just a beauty, too, about thirteen or fourteen foot long, riding high like a duck. I shot head first off of the bank, like a frog, clothes and all on, and struck out for the canoe. I just expected there'd be somebody laying down in it, because people often done that to fool folks, and when a chap had pulled a skiff out most to it they'd raise up and laugh at him. But it warn't so this time. It was a drift-canoe, sure enough, and I clumb in and paddled her ashore. Thinks I, the old man will be glad when he

8. I.e., splint-bottom, made by weaving thin strips of wood.

sees this—she's worth ten dollars. But when I got to shore pap wasn't in sight yet, and as I was running her into a little creek like a gully, all hung over with vines and willows, I struck another idea; I judged I'd hide her good, and then, stead of taking to the woods when I run off, I'd go down the river about fifty mile and camp in one place for good, and not have such a rough time tramping on foot.

It was pretty close to the shanty, and I thought I heard the old man coming, all the time; but I got her hid; and then I out and looked around a bunch of willows, and there was the old man down the path apiece just drawing a bead on a bird with his gun. So he hadn't seen anything.

When he got along, I was hard at it taking up a "trot" line.[9] He abused me a little for being so slow, but I told him I fell in the river and that was what made me so long. I knowed he would see I was wet, and then he would be asking questions. We got five catfish off of the lines and went home.

While we laid off, after breakfast, to sleep up, both of us being about wore out, I got to thinking that if I could fix up some way to keep pap and the widow from trying to follow me, it would be a certainer thing than trusting to luck to get far enough off before they missed me; you see, all kinds of things might happen. Well, I didn't see no way for a while, but by-and-by pap raised up a minute, to drink another barrel of water, and he says:

"Another time a man comes a-prowling round here, you roust me out, you hear? That man warn't here for no good. I'd a shot him. Next time, you roust me out, you hear?"

Then he dropped down and went to sleep again—but what he had been saying give me the very idea I wanted. I says to myself, I can fix it now so nobody won't think of following me.

About twelve o'clock we turned out and went along up the bank. The river was coming up pretty fast, and lots of drift-wood going by on the rise. By-and-by, along comes part of a log raft—nine logs fast together. We went out with the skiff and towed it ashore. Then we had dinner. Anybody but pap would a waited and seen the day through, so as to catch more stuff; but that warn't pap's style. Nine logs was enough for one time; he must shove right over to town and sell. So he locked me in and took the skiff and started off towing the raft about half-past three. I judged he wouldn't come back that night. I waited till I reckoned he had got a good start, then I out with my saw and went to work on that log again. Before he was 'tother side of the river I was out of the hole; him and his raft was just a speck on the water away off yonder.

I took the sack of corn meal and took it to where the canoe was hid, and shoved the vines and branches apart and put it in; then I

9. A long fishing line fastened across a stream and to which several shorter baited lines are attached.

done the same with the side of bacon; then the whisky jug; I took all the coffee and sugar there was, and all the ammunition; I took the wadding; I took the bucket and gourd, I took a dipper and a tin cup, and my old saw and two blankets, and the skillet and the coffee-pot. I took fish-lines and matches and other things—everything that was worth a cent. I cleaned out the place. I wanted an axe, but there wasn't any, only the one out at the wood pile, and I knowed why I was going to leave that. I fetched out the gun, and now I was done.

I had wore the ground a good deal, crawling out of the hole and dragging out so many things. So I fixed that as good as I could from the outside by scattering dust on the place, which covered up the smoothness and the sawdust. Then I fixed the piece of log back into its place, and put two rocks under it and one against it to hold it there,—for it was bent up at that place, and didn't quite touch ground. If you stood four or five foot away and didn't know it was sawed, you wouldn't ever notice it; and besides, this was the back of the cabin and it warn't likely anybody would go fooling around there.

It was all grass clear to the canoe; so I hadn't left a track. I followed around to see. I stood on the bank and looked out over the river. All safe. So I took the gun and went up a piece into the woods and was hunting around for some birds, when I see a wild pig; hogs soon went wild in them bottoms after they had got away from the prairie farms. I shot this fellow and took him into camp.

I took the axe and smashed in the door—I beat it and hacked it considerable, a-doing it. I fetched the pig in and took him back nearly to the table and hacked into his throat with the ax, and laid him down on the ground to bleed—I say ground, because it *was* ground—hard packed, and no boards. Well, next I took an old sack and put a lot of big rocks in it,—all I could drag—and I started it from the pig and dragged it to the door and through the woods down to the river and dumped it in, and down it sunk, out of sight. You could easy see that something had been dragged over the ground. I did wish Tom Sawyer was there, I knowed he would take an interest in this kind of business, and throw in the fancy touches. Nobody could spread himself like Tom Sawyer in such a thing as that.

Well, last I pulled out some of my hair, and bloodied the ax good, and stuck it on the back side, and slung the ax in the corner. Then I took up the pig and held him to my breast with my jacket (so he couldn't drip) till I got a good piece below the house and then dumped him into the river. Now I thought of something else. So I went and got the bag of meal and my old saw out of the canoe and fetched them to the house. I took the bag to where it used to stand, and ripped a hole in the bottom of it with the saw, for there warn't no knives and forks on the place—pap done everything with his clasp-knife, about the cooking. Then I carried the sack about a hundred yards across the grass and through the willows east of the house, to a shallow lake that was five mile wide and full of rushes —and ducks too, you might say, in the season. There was a slough or a creek leading out of it on the other side, that went miles away, I don't know where, but it didn't go to the river. The meal sifted out and made a little track all the way to the lake. I dropped pap's whetstone there too, so as to look like it had been done by accident. Then I tied up the rip in the meal sack with a string, so it wouldn't leak no more, and took it and my saw to the canoe again.

It was about dark, now; so I dropped the canoe down the river under some willows that hung over the bank, and waited for the moon to rise. I made fast to a willow; then I took a bite to eat, and by-and-by laid down in the canoe to smoke a pipe and lay out a plan. I says to myself, they'll follow the track of that sackful of rocks to the shore and then drag the river for me. And they'll follow that meal track to the lake and go browsing down the creek that leads out of it to find the robbers that killed me and took the things. They won't ever hunt the river for anything but my dead carcass. They'll soon get tired of that, and won't bother no more about me. All right; I can stop anywhere I want to. Jackson's Island[1] is good enough for me; I know that island pretty well, and nobody ever comes there. And then I can paddle over to town, nights, and slink around and pick up things I want. Jackson's Island's the place.

I was pretty tired, and the first thing I knowed, I was asleep. When I woke up I didn't know where I was, for a minute. I set up and looked around, a little scared. Then I remembered. The river looked miles and miles across. The moon was so bright I could a counted the drift logs that went a slipping along, black and still, hundred of yards from shore. Everything was dead quiet, and it looked late, and *smelt* late. You know what I mean—I don't know the words to put it in.

I took a good gap and a stretch, and was just going to unhitch and start, when I heard a sound away over the water. I listened. Pretty soon I made it out. It was that dull kind of a regular sound that comes from oars working in rowlocks when it's a still night. I peeped out through the willow branches, and there it was—a skiff, away across the water. I couldn't tell how many was in it. It kept a-coming, and when it was abreast of me I see there warn't but one man in it. Thinks I, maybe it's pap, though I warn't expecting him. He dropped below me, with the current, and by-and-by he come a-swinging up shore in the easy water, and he went by so close I could a reached out the gun and touched him. Well it *was* pap, sure enough—and sober, too, by the way he laid to his oars.

1. The same island which serves for an adventure in *Tom Sawyer* (Chapter XIII); actually known as Glasscock's Island, it has now been washed away.

I didn't lose no time. The next minute I was a-spinning down stream soft but quick in the shade of the bank. I made two mile and a half, and then struck out a quarter of a mile or more towards the middle of the river, because pretty soon I would be passing the ferry landing and people might see me and hail me. I got out amongst the drift-wood and then laid down in the bottom of the canoe and let her float. I laid there and had a good rest and a smoke out of my pipe, looking away into the sky, not a cloud in it. The sky looks ever so deep when you lay down on your back in the moonshine; I never knowed it before. And how far a body can hear on the water such nights! I heard people talking at the ferry landing. I heard what they said, too, every word of it. One man said it was getting towards the long days and the short nights, now. 'Tother one said *this* warn't one of the short ones, he reckoned— and then they laughed, and he said it over again and they laughed again; then they waked up another fellow and told him, and laughed, but he didn't laugh; he ripped out something brisk and said let him alone. The first fellow said he 'lowed to tell it to his old woman—she would think it was pretty good; but he said that warn't nothing to some things he had said in his time. I heard one man say it was nearly three o'clock, and he hoped daylight wouldn't wait more than about a week longer. After that, the talk got further and further away, and I couldn't make out the words any more, but I could near the mumble; and now and then a laugh, too, but it seemed a long ways off.

I was away below the ferry now. I rose up and there was Jackson's Island, about two mile and a half down stream, heavy-timbered and standing up out of the middle of the river, big and dark and solid, like a steamboat without any lights. There warn't any signs of the bar at the head—it was all under water, now.

It didn't take me long to get there. I shot past the head at a ripping rate, the current was so swift, and then I got into the dead water and landed on the side towards the Illinois shore. I run the canoe into a deep dent in the bank that I knowed about; I had to part the willow branches to get in; and when I made fast nobody could a seen the canoe from the outside.

I went up and set down on a log at the head of the island and looked out on the big river and the black driftwood, and away over to the town, three mile away, where there was three or four lights twinkling. A monstrous big lumber raft was about a mile up stream, coming along down, with a lantern in the middle of it. I watched it come creeping down, and when it was most abreast of where I stood I heard a man say, "Stern oars, there! heave her head to stabboard!"[2] I heard that just as plain as if the man was by my side.

2. Starboard, right-hand side facing forward.

There was a little gray in the sky, now; so I stepped into the woods and laid down for a nap before breakfast.

Chapter VIII

The sun was up so high when I waked, that I judged it was after eight o'clock. I laid there in the grass and the cool shade, thinking about things and feeling rested and ruther comfortable and satisfied. I could see the sun out at one or two holes, but mostly it was big trees all about, and gloomy in there amongst them. There was freckled places on the ground where the light sifted down through the leaves, and the freckled places swapped about a little, showing there was a little breeze up there. A couple of squirrels set on a limb and jabbered at me very friendly.

I was powerful lazy and comfortable—didn't want to get up and cook breakfast. Well, I was dozing off again, when I thinks I hears a deep sound of "boom!" away up the river. I rouses up and rests on my elbow and listens; pretty soon I hears it again. I hopped up and went and looked out at a hole in the leaves, and I see a bunch of smoke laying on the water a long ways up—about abreast the ferry. And there was the ferry-boat full of people, floating along down. I knowed what was the matter, now. "Boom!" I see the white smoke squirt out of the ferry-boat's side. You see, they was firing cannon over the water, trying to make my carcass come to the top.

I was pretty hungry, but it warn't going to do for me to start a fire, because they might see the smoke. So I set there and watched the cannon-smoke and listened to the boom. The river was a mile wide, there, and it always looks pretty on a summer morning—so I was having a good enough time seeing them hunt for my remainders, if I only had a bite to eat. Well, then I happened to think how they always put quicksilver in loaves of bread and float them off because they always go right to the drownded carcass and stop there. So says I, I'll keep a lookout, and if any of them's floating around after me, I'll give them a show. I changed to the Illinois edge of the island to see what luck I could have, and I warn't disappointed. A big double loaf come along, and I most got it, with a long stick, but my foot slipped and she floated out further. Of course I was where the current set in the closest to the shore—I knowed enough for that. But by-and-by along comes another one, and this time I won. I took out the plug and shook out the little dab of quicksilver, and set my teeth in. It was "baker's bread"— what the quality eat—none of your low-down corn-pone.[3]

I got a good place amongst the leaves, and set there on a log, munching the bread and watching the ferry-boat, and very well satisfied. And then something struck me. I says, now I reckon the

3. A simple Indian corn bread.

widow or the parson or somebody prayed that this bread would find me, and here it has gone and done it. So there ain't no doubt but there is something in that thing. That is, there's something in it when a body like the widow or the parson prays, but it don't work for me, and I reckon it don't work for only just the right kind.

I lit a pipe and had a good long smoke and went on watching. The ferry-boat was floating with the current, and I allowed I'd have a chance to see who was aboard when she come along, because she would come in close, where the bread did. When she'd got pretty well along down towards me, I put out my pipe and went to where I fished out the bread, and laid down behind a log on the bank in a little open place. Where the log forked I could peep through.

By-and-by she come along, and she drifted in so close that they could a run out a plank and walked ashore. Most everybody was on the boat. Pap, and Judge Thatcher, and Bessie Thatcher, and Jo Harper, and Tom Sawyer, and his old Aunt Polly, and Sid and Mary, and plenty more. Everybody was talking about the murder, but the captain broke in and says:

"Look sharp, now; the current sets in the closest here, and maybe he's washed ashore and got tangled amongst the brush at the water's edge. I hope so, anyway."

I didn't hope so. They all crowded up and leaned over the rails, nearly in my face, and kept still, watching with all their might. I could see them first-rate, but they couldn't see me. Then the captain sung out:

"Stand away!" and the cannon let off such a blast right before me that it made me deef with the noise and pretty near blind with the smoke, and I judged I was gone. If they'd a had some bullets in, I reckon they'd a got the corpse they was after. Well, I see I warn't hurt, thanks to goodness. The boat floated on and went out of sight around the shoulder of the island. I could hear the booming, now and then, further and further off, and by-and-by after an hour, I didn't hear it no more. The island was three mile long. I judged they had got to the foot, and was giving it up. But they didn't yet a while. They turned around the foot of the island and started up the channel on the Missouri side, under steam, and booming once in a while as they went. I crossed over to that side and watched them. When they got abreast the head of the island they quit shooting and dropped over to the Missouri shore and went home to the town.

I knowed I was all right now. Nobody else would come a-hunting after me. I got my traps out of the canoe and made me a nice camp in the thick woods. I made a kind of a tent out of my blankets to put my things under so the rain couldn't get at them. I catched a cat fish and haggled him open with my saw, and towards sundown I started my camp fire and had supper. Then I set out a line to catch some fish for breakfast.

When it was dark I set by my camp fire smoking, and feeling pretty satisfied; but by-and-by it got sort of lonesome, and so I went and set on the bank and listened to the currents washing along, and counted the stars and drift-logs and rafts that come down, and then went to bed; there ain't no better way to put in time when you are lonesome; you can't stay so, you soon get over it.

And so for three days and nights. No difference—just the same thing. But the next day I went exploring around down through the island. I was boss of it; it all belonged to me, so to say, and I wanted to know all about it; but mainly I wanted to put in the time. I found plenty strawberries, ripe and prime; and green summer-grapes, and green razberries; and the green blackberries was just beginning to show. They would all come handy by-and-by, I judged.

Well, I went fooling along in the deep woods till I judged I warn't far from the foot of the island. I had my gun along, but I hadn't shot nothing; it was for protection; thought I would kill some game nigh home. About this time I mighty near stepped on a good sized snake, and it went sliding off through the grass and flowers, and I after it, trying to get a shot at it. I clipped along, and all of a sudden I bounded right on to the ashes of a camp fire that was still smoking.

My heart jumped up amongst my lungs. I never waited for to look further, but uncocked my gun and went sneaking back on my tip-toes as fast as ever I could. Every now and then I stopped a second, amongst the thick leaves, and listened; but my breath come so hard I couldn't hear nothing else. I slunk along another piece further, then listened again; and so on, and so on; if I see a stump, I took it for a man; if I trod on a stick and broke it, it made me feel like a person had cut one of my breaths in two and I only got half, and the short half, too.

When I got to camp I warn't feeling very brash, there warn't much sand in my craw;[4] but I says, this ain't no time to be fooling around. So I got all my traps into my canoe again so as to have them out of sight, and I put out the fire and scattered the ashes around to look like an old last year's camp, and then clumb a tree.

I reckon I was up in the tree two hours; but I didn't see nothing, I didn't hear nothing—I only *thought* I heard and seen as much as a thousand things. Well, I couldn't stay up there forever; so at last I got down, but I kept in the thick woods and on the lookout all the time. All I could get to eat was berries and what was left over from breakfast.

By the time it was night I was pretty hungry. So when it was good and dark, I slid out from shore before moonrise and paddled over to the Illinois bank—about a quarter of a mile. I went out in the woods and cooked a supper, and I had about made up my mind I would stay there all night, when I hear a *plunkety-plunk, plunk-*

4. Slang for not feeling very brave.

ety-plunk, and says to myself, horses coming; and next I hear people's voices. I got everything into the canoe as quick as I could, and
then went creeping through the woods to see what I could find out.
I hadn't got far when I hear a man say:

"We better camp here, if we can find a good place; the horses is
about beat out. Let's look around."[5]

I didn't wait, but shoved out and paddled away easy. I tied up in
the old place, and reckoned I would sleep in the canoe.

I didn't sleep much. I couldn't, somehow, for thinking. And
every time I waked up I thought somebody had me by the neck. So
the sleep didn't do me no good. By-and-by I says to myself, I can't
live this way; I'm agoing to find out who it is that's here on the
island with me; I'll find it out or bust. Well, I felt better, right off.

So I took my paddle and slid out from shore just a step or two,
and then let the canoe drop along down amongst the shadows. The
moon was shining, and outside of the shadows it made it most as
light as day. I poked along well onto an hour, everything still as
rocks and sound asleep. Well by this time I was most down to the
foot of the island. A little ripply, cool breeze begun to blow, and
that was as good as saying the night was about done. I give her a
turn with the paddle and brung her nose to shore; then I got my
gun and slipped out and into the edge of the woods. I set down
there on a log and looked out through the leaves. I see the moon go
off watch and the darkness begin to blanket the river. But in a little
while I see a pale streak over the tree-tops, and knowed the day was
coming. So I took my gun and slipped off towards where I had run
across that camp fire, stopping every minute or two to listen. But I
hadn't no luck, somehow; I couldn't seem to find the place. But
by-and-by, sure enough, I catched a glimpse of fire, away through
the trees. I· went for it, cautious and slow. By-and-by I was close
enough to have a look, and there laid a man on the ground. It most
give me the fan-tods.[6] He had a blanket around his head, and his
head was nearly in the fire. I set there behind a clump of bushes, in
about six foot of him, and kept my eyes on him steady. It was getting gray daylight, now. Pretty soon he gapped, and stretched himself, and hove off the blanket, and it was Miss Watson's Jim! I bet
I was glad to see him. I says:

"Hello, Jim!" and skipped out.

He bounced up and stared at me wild. Then he drops down on
his knees, and puts his hands together and says:

"Doan' hurt me—don't! I hain't ever done no harm to a ghos'. I
awluz liked dead people, en done all I could for 'em. You go en git
in de river agin, whah you b'longs, en doan' do nuffin to Ole Jim,
'at 'uz awluz yo' fren'."

---

5. Apparently this episode is a vestige of
an early conception of the novel involving Pap in a murder plot and court trial.

6. Slang for the hallucinatory state associated with delirium tremens.

Well, I warn't long making him understand I warn't dead. I was ever so glad to see Jim. I warn't lonesome, now. I told him I warn't afraid of *him* telling the people where I was. I talked along, but he only set there and looked at me; never said nothing. Then I says:

"It's good daylight. Le's get breakfast. Make up your camp fire good."

"What's de use er makin' up de camp fire to cook strawbries en sich truck? But you got a gun, hain't you? Den we kin git sumfin better den strawbries."

"Strawberries and such truck," I says. "Is that what you live on?"

"I couldn't git nuffin else," he says.

"Why, how long you been on the island, Jim?"

"I come heah de night arter you's killed."

"What, all that time?"

"Yes-indeedy."

"And ain't you had nothing but that kind of rubbage to eat?"

"No, sah—nuffin else."

"Well, you must be most starved, ain't you?"

"I reck'n I could eat a hoss. I think I could. How long you ben on de islan'?"

"Since the night I got killed."

"No! W'y, what has you lived on? But you got a gun. Oh, yes, you got a gun. Dat's good. Now you kill sumfin en I'll make up de fire."

So we went over to where the canoe was, and while he built a fire in a grassy open place amongst the trees, I fetched meal and bacon and coffee, and coffee-pot and frying-pan, and sugar and tin cups, and the nigger was set back considerable, because he reckoned it was all done with witchcraft. I catched a good big cat-fish, too, and Jim cleaned him with his knife, and fried him.

When breakfast was ready, we lolled on the grass and eat it smoking hot. Jim laid it in with all his might, for he was most about starved. Then when we had got pretty well stuffed, we laid off and lazied.

By-and-by Jim says:

"But looky here, Huck, who wuz it dat 'uz killed in dat shanty, ef it warn't you?"

Then I told him the whole thing, and he said it was smart. He said Tom Sawyer couldn't get up no better plan than what I had. Then I says:

"How do you come to be here, Jim, and how'd you get here?"

He looked pretty uneasy, and didn't say nothing for a minute. Then he says:

"Maybe I better not tell."

"Why, Jim?"

"Well, dey's reasons. But you wouldn' tell on me ef I 'uz to tell you, would you, Huck?"

"Blamed if I would, Jim."

"Well, I b'lieve you, Huck. I—I *run off*."

"Jim!"

"But mind, you said you wouldn't tell—you know you said you wouldn't tell, Huck."

"Well, I did. I said I wouldn't, and I'll stick to it. Honest *injun* I will. People would call me a low down Ablitionist and despise me for keeping mum—but that don't make no difference. I ain't agoing to tell, and I ain't agoing back there anyways. So now, le's know all about it."

"Well, you see, it 'uz dis way. Ole Missus—dat's Miss Watson —she pecks on me all de time, en treats me pooty rough, but she awluz said she wouldn' sell me down to Orleans. But I noticed dey wuz a nigger trader roun' de place considable, lately, en I begin to git oneasy. Well, one night I creeps to de do', pooty late, en de do' warn't quite shet, en I hear ole missus tell de widder she gwyne to sell me down to Orleans, but she didn' want to, but she could git eight hund'd dollars for me,[7] en it 'uz sich a big stack o' money she couldn' resis'. De widder she try to git her to say she wouldn' do it, but I never waited to hear de res'. I lit out mighty quick, I tell you.

"I tuck out en shin down de hill en 'spec to steal a skift 'long de sho' som'ers 'bove de town, but dey wuz people a-stirrin' yit, so I hid in de ole tumble-down cooper shop on de bank to wait for everybody to go 'way. Well, I wuz dah all night. Dey wuz somebody roun' all de time. 'Long 'bout six in de mawnin', skifts begin to go by, en 'bout eight er nine every skift dat went 'long wuz talkin' 'bout how yo' pap come over to de town en say you's killed. Dese las' skifts wuz full o' ladies en genlmen agoin' over for to see de place. Sometimes dey'd pull up at de sho' en take a res' b'fo' dey started acrost, so by de talk I got to know all 'bout de killin'. I 'uz powerful sorry you's killed, Huck, but I ain't no mo', now.

"I laid dah under de shavins all day. I 'uz hungry, but I warn't afeared; bekase I knowed ole missus en de widder wuz goin' to start to de camp-meetn' right arter breakfas' en be gone all day, en dey knows I goes off wid de cattle 'bout daylight, so dey wouldn' 'spec to see me roun' de place, en so dey wouldn' miss me tell arter dark in de evenin'. De yuther servants wouldn' miss me, kase dey'd shin out en take holiday, soon as de ole folks 'uz out'n de way.

"Well, when it come dark I tuck out up de river road, en went 'bout two mile er more to whah dey warn't no houses. I'd made up my mind 'bout what I's agwyne to do. You see ef I kep' on tryin' to git away afoot, de dogs 'ud track me; ef I stole a skift to cross over, dey'd miss dat skift, you see, en dey'd know 'bout whah I'd lan' on de yuther side en whah to pick up my track. So I says, a raff is what I's arter; it doan' *make* no track.

7. A realistic price for a healthy male slave in the 1840s.

"I see a light a-comin' round' de p'int, bymeby, so I wade' in en shove' a log ahead o' me, en swum more'n half-way acrost de river, en got in 'mongst de drift-wood, en kep' my head down low, en kinder swum agin de current tell de raff come along. Den I swum to de stern uv it, en tuck aholt. It clouded up en 'uz pooty dark for a little while. So I clumb up en laid down on de planks. De men 'uz all 'way yonder in de middle,[8] whah de lantern wuz. De river wuz arisin' en dey wuz a good current; so I reck'n'd 'at by fo' in de mawnin' I'd be twenty-five mile down de river, en den I'd slip in, jis' b'fo' daylight, en swim asho' en take to de woods on de Illinoi side.[9]

"But I didn' have no luck. When we 'uz mos' down to de head er de islan', a man begin to come aft wid de lantern. I see it warn't no use fer to wait, so I slid overboard, en struck out fer de islan'. Well, I had a notion I could lan' mos' anywhers, but I couldn'—bank too bluff. I 'uz mos' to de foot er de islan' b'fo' I foun' a good place. I went into de woods en jedged I wouldn' fool wid raffs no mo', long as dey move de lantern roun' so. I had my pipe en a plug er dog-leg,[1] en some matches in my cap, en dey warn't wet, so I 'uz all right."

"And so you ain't had no meat nor bread to eat all this time? Why didn't you get mud-turkles?"

"How you gwyne to git'm? You can't slip up on um en grab um; en how's a body gwyne to hit um wid a rock? How could a body do it in de night? en I warn't gwyne to show myself on de bank in de daytime."

"Well, that's so. You've had to keep in the woods all the time, of course. Did you hear 'em shooting the cannon?"

"Oh, yes. I knowed dey was arter you. I see um go by heah; watched um thoo de bushes."

Some young birds come along, flying a yard or two at a time and lighting. Jim said it was a sign it was going to rain. He said it was a sign when young chickens flew that way, and so he reckoned it was the same way when young birds done it. I was going to catch some of them, but Jim wouldn't let me. He said it was death. He said his father laid mighty sick once, and some of them catched a bird, and his old granny said his father would die, and he did.

And Jim said you mustn't count the things you are going to cook for dinner, because that would bring bad luck. The same if you shook the table-cloth after sundown. And he said if a man owned a bee-hive, and that man died, the bees must be told about it before sun-up next morning, or else the bees would all weaken down and

8. A river raft would be large enough to make this easily possible.
9. Though Illinois was not a slave state, by state law any Negro without freedom papers could be arrested and subjected to forced labor. Jim's chances for escape would be improved if he went down the Mississippi and then up the Ohio.
1. Cheap tobacco.

quit work and die. Jim said bees wouldn't sting idiots; but I didn't believe that, because I had tried them lots of times myself, and they wouldn't sting me.

I had heard about some of these things before, but not all of them. Jim knowed all kinds of signs. He said he knowed most everything. I said it looked to me like all the signs was about bad luck, and so I asked him if there warn't any good-luck signs. He says:

"Mighty few—an' *dey* ain' no use to a body. What you want to know when good luck's a-comin' for? want to keep it off?" And he said: "Ef you's got hairy arms en a hairy breas', it's a sign dat you's agwyne to be rich. Well, dey's some use in a sign like dat, 'kase it's so fur ahead. You see, maybe you's got to be po' a long time fust, en so you might git discourage' en kill yo'self 'f you didn' know by de sign dat you gwyne to be rich bymeby."

"Have you got hairy arms and a hairy breast, Jim?"

"What's de use to ax dat question? don' you see I has?"

"Well, are you rich?"

"No, but I ben rich wunst, and gwyne to be rich agin. Wunst I had foteen dollars, but I tuck to specalat'n', en got busted out."

"What did you speculate in, Jim?"

"Well, fust I tackled stock."

"What kind of stock?"

"Why, live stock. Cattle, you know. I put ten dollars in a cow. But I ain't gwyne to resk no mo' money in stock. De cow up 'n' died on my han's."

"So you lost the ten dollars."

"No, I didn' lose it all. I on'y los' 'bout nine of it. I sole de hide en taller for a dollar en ten cents."

"You had five dollars and ten cents left. Did you speculate any more?"

"Yes. You know dat one-laigged nigger dat b'longs to old Misto Bradish? well, he sot up a bank, en say anybody dat put in a dollar would git fo' dollars mo' at de en' er de year. Well, all de niggers went in, but dey didn' have much. I wuz de on'y one dat had much. So I stuck out for mo' dan fo' dollars, en I said 'f I didn't git it I'd start a bank myself. Well o' course dat nigger want' to keep me out er de business, bekase he say dey warn't business 'nough for two banks, so he say I could put in my five dollars en he pay me thirty-five at de en' er de year.

"So I done it. Den I reck'n'd I'd inves' de thirty-five dollars right off en keep things a-movin'. Dey wuz a nigger name' Bob, dat had ketched a wood-flat,[2] en his marster didn' know it; en I bought it off'n him en told him to take de thirty-five dollars when de en' er de year come; but somebody stole de wood-flat dat night, en nex' day de one-laigged nigger say de bank 's busted. So dey didn' none uv us git no money."

2. A flat-bottomed boat used to transport timber.

"What did you do with the ten cents, Jim?"

"Well, I 'uz gwyne to spen' it, but I had a dream, en de dream tole me to give it to a nigger name' Balum—Balum's Ass[3] dey call him for short, he's one er dem chuckle-heads, you know. But he's lucky, dey say, en I see I warn't lucky. De dream say let Balum inves' de ten cents en he'd make a raise for me. Well, Balum he tuck de money, en when he wuz in church he hear de preacher say dat whoever give to de po' len' to de Lord, en boun' to git his money back a hund'd times. So Balum he tuck en give de ten cents to de po', en laid low to see what wuz gwyne to come of it."

"Well, what did come of it, Jim?"

"Nuffin' never come of it. I couldn' manage to k'leck dat money no way; en Balum he couldn'. I ain' gwyne to len' no mo' money 'dout I see de security. Boun' to git yo' money back a hund'd times, de preacher says! Ef I could git de ten *cents* back, I'd call it squah, en be glad er de chanst."

"Well, it's all right, anyway, Jim, long as you're going to be rich again some time or other."

"Yes—en I's rich now, come to look at it. I owns mysef, en I's wuth eight hund'd dollars. I wisht I had de money, I wouldn' want no mo'."

Chapter IX

I wanted to go and look at a place right about the middle of the island, that I'd found when I was exploring; so we started, and soon got to it, because the island was only three miles long and a quarter of a mile wide.

This place was a tolerable long steep hill or ridge, about forty foot high. We had a rough time getting to the top, the sides was so steep and the bushes so thick. We tramped and clumb around all over it, and by-and-by found a good big cavern in the rock, most up to the top on the side towards Illinois. The cavern was as big as two or three rooms bunched together, and Jim could stand up straight in it. It was cool in there. Jim was for putting our traps in there, right away, but I said we didn't want to be climbing up and down there all the time.

Jim said if we had the canoe hid in a good place, and had all the traps in the cavern, we could rush there if anybody was to come to the island, and they would never find us without dogs. And besides, he said them little birds had said it was going to rain, and did I want the things to get wet?

So we went back and got the canoe and paddled up abreast the cavern, and lugged all the traps up there. Then we hunted up a place close by to hide the canoe in, amongst the thick willows. We

---

3. Balaam, Old Testament prophet. God's avenging angel interrupted this prophet's journey to curse the Israelites by standing in the path of his progress. Balaam was blind to the angel's presence, but his ass saw the angel clearly and swerved off the road, much to Balaam's chagrin (Numbers 22).

took some fish off of the lines and set them again, and begun to get ready for dinner.

The door of the cavern was big enough to roll a hogshead in, and on one side of the door the floor stuck out a little bit and was flat and a good place to build a fire on. So we built it there and cooked dinner.

We spread the blankets inside for a carpet, and eat our dinner in there. We put all the other things handy at the back of the cavern. Pretty soon it darkened up and begun to thunder and lighten; so the birds was right about it. Directly it begun to rain, and it rained like all fury, too, and I never see the wind blow so. It was one of these regular summer storms. It would get so dark that it looked all blue-black outside, and lovely; and the rain would thrash along by so thick that the trees off a little ways looked dim and spider-webby; and here would come a blast of wind that would bend the trees down and turn up the pale underside of the leaves; and then a perfect ripper of a gust would follow along and set the branches to tossing their arms as if they was just wild; and next, when it was just about the bluest and blackest—*fst!* it was as bright as glory and you'd have a little glimpse of tree-tops a-plunging about, away off yonder in the storm, hundreds of yards further than you could see before; dark as sin again in a second, and now you'd hear the thunder let go with an awful crash and then go rumbling, grumbling, tumbling down the sky towards the under side of the world, like rolling empty barrels down stairs, where it's long stairs and they bounce a good deal, you know.

"Jim, this is nice," I says. "I wouldn't want to be nowhere else but here. Pass me along another hunk of fish and some hot corn-bread."

"Well, you wouldn't a ben here, 'f it hadn't a ben for Jim. You'd a ben down dah in de woods widout any dinner, en gittn' mos' drownded, too, dat you would, honey. Chickens knows when its gwyne to rain, en so do de birds, chile."

The river went on raising and raising for ten or twelve days, till at last it was over the banks. The water was three or four foot deep on the island in the low places and on the Illinois bottom. On that side it was a good many miles wide; but on the Missouri side it was the same old distance across—a half a mile—because the Missouri shore was just a wall of high bluffs.

Daytimes we paddled all over the island in the canoe. It was mighty cool and shady in the deep woods even if the sun was blazing outside. We went winding in and out amongst the trees; and sometimes the vines hung so thick we had to back away and go some other way. Well, on every old broken-down tree, you could see rabbits, and snakes, and such things; and when the island had been overflowed a day or two, they got so tame, on account of being hungry, that you could paddle right up and put your hand on them

if you wanted to; but not the snakes and turtles—they would slide
off in the water. The ridge our cavern was in, was full of them. We
could a had pets enough if we'd wanted them.

One night we catched a little section of a lumber raft—nice pine
planks. It was twelve foot wide and about fifteen or sixteen foot
long, and the top stood above water six or seven inches, a solid level
floor. We could see saw-logs go by in the daylight, sometimes, but
we let them go; we didn't show ourselves in daylight.

Another night, when we was up at the head of the island, just
before daylight, here comes a frame house down, on the west side.
She was a two-story, and tilted over, considerable. We paddled out
and got aboard—clumb in at an up-stairs window. But it was too
dark to see yet, so we made the canoe fast and set in her to wait for
daylight.

The light begun to come before we got to the foot of the island.
Then we looked in at the window. We could make out a bed, and a
table, and two old chairs, and lots of things around about on the
floor; and there was clothes hanging against the wall. There was
something laying on the floor in the far corner that looked like a
man. So Jim says:

"Hello, you!"

But it didn't budge. So I hollered again, and then Jim says:

"De man ain't asleep—he's dead. You hold still—I'll go en see."

He went and bent down and looked, and says:

"It's a dead man. Yes, indeedy; naked, too. He's ben shot in de
back. I reck'n he's ben dead two er three days. Come in, Huck, but
doan' look at his face—it's too gashly."

I didn't look at him at all. Jim throwed some old rags over him,
but he needn't done it; I didn't want to see him. There was heaps
of old greasy cards scattered around over the floor, and old whisky
bottles, and a couple of masks made out of black cloth; and all over
the walls was the ignorantest kind of words and pictures, made
with charcoal. There was two old dirty calico dresses, and a sun-
bonnet, and some women's under-clothes, hanging against the wall,
and some men's clothing, too. We put the lot into the canoe; it
might come good. There was a boy's old speckled straw hat on the
floor; I took that too. And there was a bottle that had had milk in
it; and it had a rag stopper for a baby to suck. We would a took the
bottle, but it was broke. There was a seedy old chest, and an old
hair trunk with the hinges broke. They stood open, but there warn't
nothing left in them that was any account. The way things was
scattered about, we reckoned the people left in a hurry and warn't
fixed so as to carry off most of their stuff.

We got an old tin lantern, and a butcher-knife without any
handle, and a bran-new Barlow knife[4] worth two bits in any store,
and a lot of tallow candles, and a tin candlestick, and a gourd, and

4. Pocketknife with one blade, named for the inventor.

a tin cup, and a ratty old bed-quilt off the bed, and a reticule with needles and pins and beeswax and buttons and thread and all such truck in it, and a hatchet and some nails, and a fish-line as thick as my little finger, with some monstrous hooks on it, and a roll of buckskin, and a leather dog-collar, and a horse-shoe, and some vials of medicine that didn't have no label on them; and just as we was leaving I found a tolerable good curry-comb, and Jim he found a ratty old fiddle-bow, and a wooden leg. The straps was broke off of it, but barring that, it was a good enough leg, though it was too long for me and not long enough for Jim, and we couldn't find the other one, though we hunted all around.

And so, take it all around, we made a good haul. When we was ready to shove off, we was a quarter of a mile below the island, and it was pretty broad day; so I made Jim lay down in the canoe and cover up with the quilt, because if he set up, people could tell he was a nigger a good ways off. I paddled over to the Illinois shore, and drifted down most a half a mile doing it. I crept up the dead water under the bank, and hadn't no accidents and didn't see nobody. We got home all safe.

Chapter X

After breakfast I wanted to talk about the dead man and guess out how he come to be killed, but Jim didn't want to. He said it would fetch bad luck; and besides, he said, he might come and ha'nt us; he said a man that warn't buried was more likely to go a-ha'nting around than one that was planted and comfortable. That sounded pretty reasonable, so I didn't say no more; but I couldn't keep from studying over it and wishing I knowed who shot the man, and what they done it for.

We rummaged the clothes we'd got, and found eight dollars in silver sewed up in the lining of an old blanket overcoat. Jim said he reckoned the people in that house stole the coat, because if they'd a knowed the money was there they wouldn't a left it. I said I reckoned they killed him, too; but Jim didn't want to talk about that. I says:

"Now you think it's bad luck; but what did you say when I fetched in the snake-skin that I found on the top of the ridge day before yesterday? You said it was the worst bad luck in the world to touch a snake-skin with my hands. Well, here's your bad luck! We've raked in all this truck and eight dollars besides. I wish we could have some bad luck like this every day, Jim."

"Never you mind, honey, never you mind. Don't you git too peart. It's a-comin'. Mind I tell you, it's a-comin'."

It did come, too. It was a Tuesday that we had that talk. Well, after dinner Friday, we was laying around in the grass at the upper end of the ridge, and got out of tobacco. I went to the cavern to get some, and found a rattlesnake in there. I killed him, and curled him up on the foot of Jim's blanket, ever so natural, thinking there'd be some fun when Jim found him there. Well, by night I forgot all about the snake, and when Jim flung himself down on the blanket while I struck a light, the snake's mate was there, and bit him.

He jumped up yelling, and the first thing the light showed was the varmint curled up and ready for another spring. I laid him out in a second with a stick, and Jim grabbed pap's whisky jug and began to pour it down.

He was barefooted, and the snake bit him right on the heel. That all comes of my being such a fool as to not remember that whenever you leave a dead snake its mate always comes there and curls around it. Jim told me to chop off the snake's head and throw it away, and then skin the body and roast a piece of it. I done it, and he eat it and said it would help cure him.[5] He made me take off the rattles and tie them around his wrist, too. He said that that would help. Then I slid out quiet and throwed the snakes clear away amongst the bushes; for I warn't going to let Jim find out it was all my fault, not if I could help it.

Jim sucked and sucked at the jug, and now and then he got out of his head and pitched around and yelled; but every time he come to himself he went to sucking at the jug again. His foot swelled up pretty big, and so did his leg; but by-and-by the drunk begun to come, and so I judged he was all right; but I'd druther been bit with a snake than pap's whisky.

Jim was laid up for four days and nights. Then the swelling was all gone and he was around again. I made up my mind I wouldn't ever take aholt of a snake-skin again with my hands, now that I see what had come of it. Jim said he reckoned I would believe him next time. And he said that handling a snake-skin was such awful bad luck that maybe we hadn't got to the end of it yet. He said he druther see the new moon over his left shoulder as much as a thousand times than take up a snake-skin in his hand. Well, I was getting to feel that way myself, though I've always reckoned that looking at the new moon over your left shoulder is one of the carelessest and foolishest things a body can do. Old Hank Bunker done it once, and bragged about it; and in less than two years he got drunk and fell off of the shot tower and spread himself out so that he was just a kind of layer, as you may say; and they slid him edgeways between two barn doors for a coffin, and buried him so, so they say, but I didn't see it. Pap told me. But anyway, it all come of looking at the moon that way, like a fool.

Well, the days went along, and the river went down between its banks again; and about the first thing we done was to bait one of the big hooks with a skinned rabbit and set it and catch a cat-fish that was as big as a man, being six foot two inches long, and weighed over two hundred pounds. We couldn't handle him, of

5. Jim's homeopathic remedy is a common folk-medical practice.

course; he would a flung us into Illinois. We just set there and watched him rip and tear around till he drowned. We found a brass button in his stomach, and a round ball, and lots of rubbage. We split the ball open with the hatchet, and there was a spool in it. Jim said he'd had it there a long time, to coat it over so and make a ball of it. It was as big a fish as was ever catched in the Mississippi, I reckon. Jim said he hadn't ever seen a bigger one. He would a been worth a good deal over at the village. They peddle out such a fish as that by the pound in the market house there; everybody buys some of him; his meat's as white as snow and makes a good fry.

Next morning I said it was getting slow and dull, and I wanted to get a stirring up, some way. I said I reckoned I would slip over the river and find out what was going on. Jim liked that notion; but he said I must go in the dark and look sharp. Then he studied it over and said, couldn't I put on some of them old things and dress up like a girl? That was a good notion, too. So we shortened up one of the calico gowns and I turned up my trowser-legs to my knees and got into it. Jim hitched it behind with the hooks, and it was a fair fit. I put on the sun-bonnet and tied it under my chin, and then for a body to look in and see my face was like looking down a joint of stove-pipe. Jim said nobody would know me, even in the daytime, hardly. I practiced around all day to get the hang of the things, and by-and-by I could do pretty well in them, only Jim said I didn't walk like a girl; and he said I must quit pulling up my gown to get at my britches pocket. I took notice, and done better.

I started up the Illinois shore in the canoe just after dark.

I started across to the town from a little below the ferry landing, and the drift of the current fetched me in at the bottom of the town. I tied up and started along the bank. There was a light burning in a little shanty that hadn't been lived in for a long time, and I wondered who had took up quarters there. I slipped up and peeped in at the window. There was a woman about forty year old in there, knitting by a candle that was on a pine table. I didn't know her face; she was a stranger, for you couldn't start a face in that town that I didn't know. Now this was lucky, because I was weakening; I was getting afraid I had come; people might know my voice and find me out. But if this woman had been in such a little town two days she could tell me all I wanted to know; so I knocked at the door, and made up my mind I wouldn't forget I was a girl.

Chapter XI

"Come in," says the woman, and I did. She says:
"Take a cheer."

I done it. She looked me all over with her little shiny eyes, and
says:

"What might your name be?"

"Sarah Williams."

"Where 'bouts do you live? In this neighborhood?"

"No'm. In Hookerville, seven mile below. I've walked all the way
and I'm all tired out."

"Hungry, too, I reckon. I'll find you something."

"No'm, I ain't hungry. I was so hungry I had to stop two mile
below here at a farm; so I ain't hungry no more. It's what makes
me so late. My mother's down sick, and out of money and everything, and I come to tell my uncle Abner Moore. He lives at the
upper end of the town, she says. I hain't ever been here before. Do
you know him?"

"No; but I don't know everybody yet. I haven't lived here quite
two weeks. It's a considerable ways to the upper end of the town.
You better stay here all night. Take off your bonnet."

"No," I says, "I'll rest a while, I reckon, and go on. I ain't afeard
of the dark."

She said she wouldn't let me go by myself, but her husband
would be in by-and-by, maybe in a hour and a half, and she'd send
him along with me. Then she got to talking about her husband,
and about her relations up the river, and her relations down the
river, and about how much better off they used to was, and how
they didn't know but they'd made a mistake coming to our town,
instead of letting well alone—and so on and so on, till I was afeard
I had made a mistake coming to her to find out what was going on
in the town; but by-and-by she dropped onto pap and the murder,
and then I was pretty willing to let her clatter right along. She told
about me and Tom Sawyer finding the six thousand dollars (only
she got it ten) and all about pap and what a hard lot he was, and
what a hard lot I was, and at last she got down to where I was murdered. I says:

"Who done it? We've heard considerable about these goings on,
down in Hookerville, but we don't know who 'twas that killed Huck
Finn."

"Well, I reckon there's a right smart chance of people *here*
that'd like to know who killed him. Some thinks old Finn done it
himself."

"No—is that so?"

"Most everybody thought it at first. He'll never know how nigh
he come to getting lynched. But before night they changed around
and judged it was done by a runaway nigger named Jim."

"Why *he*—"

I stopped. I reckoned I better keep still. She run on, and never
noticed I had put in at all.

"The nigger run off the very night Huck Finn was killed. So there's a reward out for him—three hundred dollars. And there's a reward out for old Finn too—two hundred dollars. You see, he come to town the morning after the murder, and told about it, and was out with 'em on the ferry-boat hunt, and right away after he up and left. Before night they wanted to lynch him, but he was gone, you see. Well, next day they found out the nigger was gone; they found out he hadn't ben seen sence ten o'clock the night the murder was done. So then they put it on him, you see, and while they was full of it, next day back comes old Finn and went boohooing to Judge Thatcher to get money to hunt for the nigger all over Illinois with. The judge give him some, and that evening he got drunk and was around till after midnight with a couple of mighty hard looking strangers, and then went off with them. Well, he hain't come back sence, and they ain't looking for him back till this thing blows over a little, for people thinks now that he killed his boy and fixed things so folks would think robbers done it, and then he'd get Huck's money without having to bother a long time with a lawsuit. People do say he warn't any too good to do it. Oh, he's sly, I reckon. If he don't come back for a year, he'll be all right. You can't prove anything on him, you know; everything will be quieted down then, and he'll walk into Huck's money as easy as nothing."

"Yes, I reckon so, 'm. I don't see nothing in the way of it. Has everybody quit thinking the nigger done it?"

"Oh, no, not everybody. A good many thinks he done it. But they'll get the nigger pretty soon, now, and maybe they can scare it out of him."

"Why, are they after him yet?"

"Well, you're innocent, ain't you! Does three hundred dollars lay round every day for people to pick up? Some folks thinks the nigger ain't far from here. I'm one of them—but I hain't talked it around. A few days ago I was talking with an old couple that lives next door in the log shanty, and they happened to say hardly anybody ever goes to that island over yonder that they call Jackson's Island. Don't anybody live there? says I. No, nobody, says they. I didn't say any more, but I done some thinking. I was pretty near certain I'd seen smoke over there, about the head of the island, a day or two before that, so I says to myself, like as not that nigger's hiding over there; anyway, says I, it's worth the trouble to give the place a hunt. I hain't seen any smoke sence, so I reckon maybe he's gone, if it was him; but husband's going over to see—him and another man. He was gone up the river; but he got back to-day and I told him as soon as he got here two hours ago."

I had got so uneasy I couldn't set still. I had to do something with my hands; so I took up a needle off of the table and went to threading it. My hands shook, and I was making a bad job of it.

When the woman stopped talking, I looked up, and she was looking at me pretty curious, and smiling a little. I put down the needle and thread and let on to be interested—and I was, too—and says:

"Three hundred dollars is a power of money. I wish my mother could get it. Is your husband going over there to-night?"

"Oh, yes. He went up town with the man I was telling you of, to get a boat and see if they could borrow another gun. They'll go over after midnight."

"Couldn't they see better if they was to wait till daytime?"

"Yes. And couldn't the nigger see better, too? After midnight he'll likely be asleep, and they can slip around through the woods and hunt up his camp fire all the better for the dark, if he's got one."

"I didn't think of that."

The woman kept looking at me pretty curious, and I didn't feel a bit comfortable. Pretty soon she says:

"What did you say your name was, honey?"

"M—Mary Williams."

Somehow it didn't seem to me that I said it was Mary before, so I didn't look up; seemed to me I said it was Sarah; so I felt sort of cornered, and was afeared maybe I was looking it, too. I wished the woman would say something more; the longer she set still, the uneasier I was. But now she says:

"Honey, I thought you said it was Sarah when you first come in?"

"Oh, yes'm, I did. Sarah Mary Williams. Sarah's my first name. Some calls me Sarah, some calls me Mary."

"Oh, that's the way of it?"

"Yes'm."

I was feeling better, then, but I wished I was out of there, anyway. I couldn't look up yet.

Well, the woman fell to talking about how hard times was, and how poor they had to live, and how the rats was as free as if they owned the place, and so forth, and so on, and then I got easy again. She was right about the rats. You'd see one stick his nose out of a hole in the corner every little while. She said she had to have things handy to throw at them when she was alone, or they wouldn't give her no peace. She showed me a bar of lead, twisted up into a knot, and she said she was a good shot with it generly, but she'd wrenched her arm a day or two ago, and didn't know whether she could throw true, now. But she watched for a chance, and directly she banged away at a rat, but she missed him wide, and said "Ouch!" it hurt her arm so. Then she told me to try for the next one. I wanted to be getting away before the old man got back, but of course I didn't let on. I got the thing, and the first rat that showed his nose I let drive, and if he'd a stayed where he was he'd a been a tolerable sick rat. She said that that was first-rate, and she reckoned I would hive[6] the next one. She went and got the lump of lead and fetched it back and brought along a hank of yarn, which she wanted me to help her with. I held up my two hands and she put the hank over them and went on talking about her and her husband's matters. But she broke off to say:

"Keep your eye on the rats. You better have the lead in your lap, handy."

So she dropped the lump into my lap, just at that moment, and I clapped my legs together on it and she went on talking. But only about a minute. Then she took off the hank and looked me straight in the face, but very pleasant, and says:

"Come, now—what's your real name?"

"Wh-what, mum?"

"What's your real name? Is it Bill, or Tom, or Bob?—or what is it?"

I reckon I shook like a leaf, and I didn't know hardly what to do. But I says:

"Please to don't poke fun at a poor girl like me, mum. If I'm in the way, here, I'll—"

"No, you won't. Set down and stay where you are. I ain't going to hurt you, and I ain't going to tell on you, nuther. You just tell me your secret, and trust me. I'll keep it; and what's more, I'll help you. So'll my old man, if you want him to. You see, you're a runaway 'prentice—that's all. It ain't anything. There ain't any harm in it. You've been treated bad, and you made up your mind to cut. Bless you, child, I wouldn't tell on you. Tell me all about it, now—that's a good boy."

So I said it wouldn't be no use to try to play it any longer, and I would just make a clean breast and tell her everything, but she mustn't go back on her promise. Then I told her my father and mother was dead, and the law had bound me out to a mean old farmer in the country thirty mile back from the river, and he treated me so bad I couldn't stand it no longer; he went away to be gone a couple of days, and so I took my chance and stole some of his daughter's old clothes, and cleared out, and I had been three nights coming the thirty miles; I traveled nights, and hid daytimes and slept, and the bag of bread and meat I carried from home lasted me all the way and I had a plenty. I said I believed my uncle Abner Moore would take care of me, and so that was why I struck out for this town of Goshen.

"Goshen, child? This ain't Goshen. This is St. Petersburg. Goshen's ten mile further up the river. Who told you this was Goshen?"

"Why, a man I met at day-break this morning, just as I was going to turn into the woods for my regular sleep. He told me when

6. Get, in the sense of hit and kill.

the roads forked I must take the right hand, and five mile would fetch me to Goshen."

"He was drunk I reckon. He told you just exactly wrong."

"Well, he did act like he was drunk, but it ain't no matter now. I got to be moving along. I'll fetch Goshen before day-light."

"Hold on a minute. I'll put you up a snack to eat. You might want it."

So she put me up a snack, and says:

"Say—when a cow's laying down, which end of her gets up first? Answer up prompt, now—don't stop to study over it. Which end gets up first?"

"The hind end, mum."

"Well, then, a horse?"

"The for'rard end, mum."

"Which side of a tree does the most moss grow on?"

"North side."

"If fifteen cows is browsing on a hillside, how many of them eats with their heads pointed the same direction?"

"The whole fifteen, mum."

"Well, I reckon you *have* lived in the country. I thought maybe you was trying to hocus me again. What's your real name, now?"

"George Peters, mum."

"Well, try to remember it, George. Don't forget and tell me it's Elexander before you go, and then get out by saying it's George Elexander when I catch you. And don't go about women in that old calico. You do a girl tolerable poor, but you might fool men, maybe. Bless you, child, when you set out to thread a needle, don't hold the thread still and fetch the needle up to it; hold the needle still and poke the thread at it—that's the way a woman most always does; but a man always does 'tother way. And when you throw at a rat or anything, hitch yourself up a tip-toe, and fetch your hand up over your head as awkard as you can, and miss your rat about six or seven foot. Throw stiff-armed from the shoulder, like there was a pivot there for it to turn on—like a girl; not from the wrist and elbow, with your arm out to one side, like a boy. And mind you, when a girl tries to catch anything in her lap, she throws her knees apart; she don't clap them together, the way you did when you catched the lump of lead. Why, I spotted you for a boy when you was threading the needle; and I contrived the other things just to make certain. Now trot along to your uncle, Sarah Mary Williams George Elexander Peters, and if you get into trouble you send word to Mrs. Judith Loftus, which is me, and I'll do what I can to get you out of it. Keep the river road, all the way, and next time you tramp, take shoes and socks with you. The river road's a rocky one, and your feet 'll be in a condition when you get to Goshen, I reckon."

I went up the bank about fifty yards, and then I doubled on my tracks and slipped back to where my canoe was, a good piece below the house. I jumped in and was off in a hurry. I went up stream far enough to make the head of the island, and then started across. I took off the sun-bonnet, for I didn't want no blinders on, then. When I was about the middle, I hear the clock begin to strike; so I stops and listens; the sound come faint over the water, but clear— eleven. When I struck the head of the island I never waited to blow, though I was most winded, but I shoved right into the timber where my old camp used to be, and started a good fire there on a high-and-dry spot.

Then I jumped in the canoe and dug out for our place a mile and a half below, as hard as I could go. I landed, and slopped through the timber and up the ridge and into the cavern. There Jim laid, sound asleep on the ground. I roused him out and says.

"Git up and hump yourself, Jim! There ain't a minute to lose. They're after us!"

Jim never asked no questions, he never said a word; but the way he worked for the next half an hour showed about how he was scared. By that time everything we had in the world was on our raft and she was ready to be shoved out from the willow cove where she was hid. We put out the camp fire at the cavern the first thing, and didn't show a candle outside after that.

I took the canoe out from shore a little piece and took a look, but if there was a boat around I couldn't see it, for stars and shadows ain't good to see by. Then we got out the raft and slipped along down in the shade, past the foot of the island dead still, never saying a word.

Chapter XII

It must a been close onto one o'clock when we got below the island at last, and the raft did seem to go mighty slow. If a boat was to come along, we was going to take to the canoe and break for the Illinois shore; and it was well a boat didn't come, for we hadn't ever thought to put the gun into the canoe, or a fishing-line or anything to eat. We was in ruther too much of a sweat to think of so many things. It warn't good judgment to put *everything* on the raft.

If the men went to the island, I just expect they found the camp fire I built, and watched it all night for Jim to come. Anyways, they stayed away from us, and if my building the fire never fooled them it warn't no fault of mine. I played it as low-down on them as I could.

When the first streak of day begun to show, we tied up to a tow-head in a big bend on the Illinois side, and hacked off cotton-wood branches with the hatchet and covered up the raft with them so she looked like there had been a cave-in in the bank there. A tow-head is a sand-bar that has cotton-woods on it as thick as harrow-teeth.

We had mountains on the Missouri shore and heavy timber on

the Illinois side, and the channel was down the Missouri shore at
that place, so we warn't afraid of anybody running across us. We
laid there all day and watched the rafts and steamboats spin down
the Missouri shore, and up-bound steamboats fight the big river in
the middle. I told Jim all about the time I had jabbering with that
woman; and Jim said she was a smart one, and if she was to start
after us herself *she* wouldn't set down and watch a camp fire—no,
sir, she'd fetch a dog. Well, then, I said, why couldn't she tell her
husband to fetch a dog? Jim said he bet she did think of it by the
time the men was ready to start, and he believed they must a gone
up town to get a dog and so they lost all that time, or else we
wouldn't be here on a tow-head sixteen or seventeen mile below the
village—no, indeedy, we would be in that same old town again. So
I said I didn't care what was the reason they didn't get us, as long
as they didn't.

When it was beginning to come on dark, we poked our heads out
of the cottonwood thicket and looked up, and down, and across;
nothing in sight; so Jim took up some of the top planks of the raft
and built a snug wigwam to get under in blazing weather and rainy,
and to keep the things dry. Jim made a floor for the wigwam, and
raised it a foot or more above the level of the raft, so now the blankets and all the traps was out of the reach of steamboat waves.
Right in the middle of the wigwam we made a layer of dirt about
five or six inches deep with a frame around it for to hold it to its
place; this was to build a fire on in sloppy weather or chilly; the
wigwam would keep it from being seen. We made an extra steering
oar, too, because one of the others might get broke, on a snag or
something. We fixed up a short forked stick to hang the old lantern
on; because we must always light the lantern whenever we see a
steamboat coming down stream, to keep from getting run over; but
we wouldn't have to light it up for upstream boats unless we see we
was in what they call "crossing;" for the river was pretty high yet,
very low banks being still a little under water; so up-bound boats
didn't always run the channel, but hunted easy water.

This second night we run between seven and eight hours, with a
current that was making over four mile an hour. We catched fish,
and talked, and we took a swim now and then to keep off sleepi-
ness. It was kind of solemn, drifting down the big still river, laying
on our backs looking up at the stars, and we didn't ever feel like
talking loud, and it warn't often that we laughed, only a little kind
of a low chuckle. We had mighty good weather, as a general thing,
and nothing ever happened to us at all, that night, nor the next,
nor the next.

Every night we passed towns, some of them away up on black
hillsides, nothing but just a shiny bed of lights, not a house could
you see. The fifth night we passed St. Louis, and it was like the
whole world lit up. In St. Petersburg they used to say there was

twenty or thirty thousand people in St. Louis,[7] but I never believed it till I see that wonderful spread of lights at two o'clock that still night. There warn't a sound there; everybody was asleep.

Every night, now, I used to slip ashore, towards ten o'clock, at some little village, and buy ten or fifteen cents' worth of meal or bacon or other stuff to eat; and sometimes I lifted a chicken that warn't roosting comfortable, and took him along. Pap always said, take a chicken when you get a chance, because if you don't want him yourself you can easy find somebody that does, and a good deed ain't ever forgot. I never see Pap when he didn't want the chicken himself, but that is what he used to say, anyway.

Mornings, before daylight, I slipped into corn fields and borrowed a watermelon, or a mushmelon, or a punkin, or some new corn, or things of that kind. Pap always said it warn't no harm to borrow things, if you was meaning to pay them back, sometime; but the widow said it warn't anything but a soft name for stealing, and no decent body would do it. Jim said he reckoned the widow was partly right and pap was partly right; so the best way would be for us to pick out two or three things from the list and say we wouldn't borrow them any more—then he reckoned it wouldn't be no harm to borrow the others. So we talked it over all one night, drifting along down the river, trying to make up our minds whether to drop the watermelons, or the cantelopes, or the mushmelons, or what. But towards daylight we got it all settled satisfactory, and concluded to drop crabapples and p'simmons. We warn't feeling just right, before that, but it was all comfortable now. I was glad the way it come out, too, because the crabapples ain't ever good, and the p'simmons wouldn't be ripe for two or three months yet.

We shot a water-fowl, now and then, that got up too early in the morning or didn't go to bed early enough in the evening. Take it all around, we lived pretty high.

The fifth night below St. Louis we had a big storm after midnight, with a power of thunder and lightning, and the rain poured down in a solid sheet. We stayed in the wigwam and let the raft take care of itself. When the lightning glared out we could see a big straight river ahead, and high rocky bluffs on both sides. By-and-by says I, "Hel-*lo* Jim, looky yonder!" It was a steamboat that had killed herself on a rock. We was drifting straight down for her. The lightning showed her very distinct. She was leaning over, with part of her upper deck above water, and you could see every little chimbly-guy[8] clean and clear, and a chair by the big bell, with an old slouch hat hanging on the back of it when the flashes come.

Well, it being away in the night, and stormy, and all so mysterious-like, I felt just the way any other boy would a felt when I see

7. St. Louis is 170 miles down the Mississippi from Hannibal.
8. Wires used to steady the chimney stacks.

that wreck laying there so mournful and lonesome in the middle of
the river. I wanted to get aboard of her and slink around a little,
and see what there was there. So I says:

"Le's land on her, Jim."

But Jim was dead against it, at first. He says:

"I doan' want to go fool'n 'long er no wrack. We's doin' blame'
well, en we better let blame' well alone, as de good book says. Like
as not dey's a watchman on dat wrack."

"Watchman your grandmother," I says; "there ain't nothing to
watch but the texas and the pilot-house;[9] and do you reckon anybody's going to resk his life for a texas and a pilot-house such a
night as this, when it's likely to break up and wash off down the
river any minute?" Jim couldn't say nothing to that, so he didn't
try. "And besides," I says, "we might borrow something worth
having, out of the captain's stateroom. Seegars, *I* bet you—and cost
five cents apiece, solid cash. Steamboat captains is always rich, and
get sixty dollars a month, and *they* don't care a cent what a thing
costs, you know, long as they want it. Stick a candle in your pocket;
I can't rest, Jim, till we give her a rummaging. Do you reckon Tom
Sawyer would ever go by this thing? Not for pie, he wouldn't. He'd
call it an adventure—that's what he'd call it; and he'd land on that
wreck if it was his last act. And wouldn't he throw style into it?—
wouldn't he spread himself, nor nothing? Why, you'd think it was
Christopher C'lumbus discovering Kingdom-Come. I wish Tom
Sawyer *was* here."

Jim he grumbled a little, but give in. He said we mustn't talk any
more than we could help, and then talk mighty low. The lightning
showed us the wreck again, just in time, and we fetched the starboard derrick,[1] and made fast there.

The deck was high out, here. We went sneaking down the slope
of it to labboard, in the dark, towards the texas, feeling our way
slow with our feet, and spreading our hands out to fend off the
guys, for it was so dark we couldn't see no sign of them. Pretty soon
we struck the forward end of the skylight, and clumb onto it; and
the next step fetched us in front of the captain's door, which was
open, and by Jimminy, away down through the texas-hall we see a
light! and all in the same second we seem to hear low voices in
yonder!

Jim whispered and said he was feeling powerful sick, and told me
to come along. I says, all right; and was going to start for the raft;
but just then I heard a voice wail out and say:

"Oh, please don't, boys; I swear I won't ever tell!"

Another voice said, pretty loud:

---

9. The texas is the large cabin on the
top deck located just behind or beneath
the pilot house; it serves as officers'
quarters.
1. Boom for lifting cargo.

"It's a lie, Jim Turner. You've acted this way before. You always want more'n your share of the truck, and you've always got it, too, because you've swore 't if you didn't you'd tell. But this time you've said it jest one time too many. You're the meanest, treacherousest hound in this country."

By this time Jim was gone for the raft. I was just a-biling with curiosity; and I says to myself, Tom Sawyer wouldn't back out now, and so I won't either; I'm agoing to see what's going on here. So I dropped on my hands and knees, in the little passage, and crept aft in the dark, till there warn't but about one stateroom betwixt me and the cross-hall of the texas. Then, in there I see a man stretched on the floor and tied hand and foot, and two men standing over him, and one of them had a dim lantern in his hand, and the other one had a pistol. This one kept pointing the pistol at the man's head on the floor and saying—

"I'd *like* to! And I orter, too, a mean skunk!"

The man on the floor would shrivel up, and say: "Oh, please don't, Bill—I hain't ever goin' to tell."

And every time he said that, the man with the lantern would laugh, and say:

" 'Deed you *ain't*! You never said no truer thing 'n that, you bet you." And once he said, "Hear him beg! and yit if we hadn't got the best of him and tied him, he'd a killed us both. And what *for*? Jist for noth'n. Jist because we stood on our *rights*—that's what for. But I lay you ain't agoin' to threaten nobody any more, Jim Turner. Put *up* that pistol, Bill."

Bill says:

"I don't want to, Jake Packard. I'm for killin' him—and didn't he kill old Hatfield jist the same way—and don't he deserve it?"

"But I don't *want* him killed, and I've got my reasons for it."

"Bless yo' heart for them words, Jake Packard! I'll never forgit you, long's I live!" says the man on the floor, sort of blubbering.

Packard didn't take no notice of that, but hung up his lantern on a nail, and started towards where I was, there in the dark, and motioned Bill to come. I crawfished[2] as fast as I could, about two yards, but the boat slanted so that I couldn't make very good time; so to keep from getting run over and catched I crawled into a stateroom on the upper side. The man come a-pawing along in the dark, and when Packard got to my stateroom, he says:

"Here—come in here."

And in he come, and Bill after him. But before they got in, I was up in the upper berth, cornered, and sorry I come. Then they stood there, with their hands on the ledge of the berth, and talked. I couldn't see them, but I could tell where they was, by the whisky they'd been having. I was glad I didn't drink whisky; but it

2. Crept backward on all fours.

wouldn't made much difference, anyway, because most of the time they couldn't a treed me because I didn't breathe. I was too scared. And besides, a body *couldn't* breathe, and hear such talk. They talked low and earnest. Bill wanted to kill Turner. He says:

"He's said he'll tell, and he will. If we was to give both our shares to him *now*, it wouldn't make no difference after the row, and the way we've served him. Shore's you're born, he'll turn State's evidence; now you hear *me*. I'm for putting him out of his troubles."

"So'm I," says Packard, very quiet.

"Blame it, I'd sorter begun to think you wasn't. Well, then, that's all right. Les' go and do it."

"Hold on a minute; I hain't had my say yit. You listen to me. Shooting's good, but there's quieter ways if the thing's *got* to be done. But what I say, is this; it ain't good sense to go court'n around after a halter[3] if you can git at what you're up to in some way that's jist as good and at the same time don't bring you into no resks. Ain't that so?"

"You bet it is. But how you goin' to manage it this time?"

"Well, my idea is this: we'll rustle around and gether up whatever pickins we've overlooked in the staterooms, and shove for shore and hide the truck. Then we'll wait. Now I say it ain't agoin' to be more 'n two hours befo' this wrack breaks up and washes off down the river. See? He'll be drownded, and won't have nobody to blame for it but his own self. I reckon that's a considerble sight better'n killin' of him. I'm unfavorable to killin' a man as long as you can git around it; it ain't good sense, it ain't good morals. Ain't I right?"

"Yes—I reck'n you are. But s'pose she *don't* break up and wash off?"

"Well, we can wait the two hours, anyway, and see, can't we?"

"All right, then; come along."

So they started, and I lit out, all in a cold sweat, and scrambled forward. It was dark as pitch there; but I said in a kind of a coarse whisper, "Jim!" and he answered up, right at my elbow, with a sort of a moan, and I says:

"Quick, Jim, it ain't no time for fooling around and moaning; there's a gang of murderers in yonder, and if we don't hunt up their boat and set her drifting down the river so these fellows can't get away from the wreck, there's one of 'em going to be in a bad fix. But if we find their boat we can put *all* of 'em in a bad fix—for the Sheriff 'll get 'em. Quick—hurry! I'll hunt the labboard side, you hunt the stabboard. You start at the raft, and—"

"Oh, my lordy, lordy! *Raf'*? Dey ain' no raf' no mo', she done broke loose en gone!—'en here we is!"

---

3. **Hangman's noose.**

Chapter XIII

Well, I catched my breath and most fainted. Shut up on a wreck with such a gang as that! But it warn't no time to be sentimentering. We'd *got* to find that boat, now—had to have it for ourselves. So we went a-quaking and shaking down the stabboard side, and slow work it was, too—seemed a week before we got to the stern. No sign of a boat. Jim said he didn't believe he could go any further—so scared he hadn't hardly any strength left, he said. But I said come on, if we get left on this wreck, we are in a fix, sure. So on we prowled, again. We struck for the stern of the texas, and found it, and then scrabbled along forwards on the skylight, hanging on from shutter to shutter, for the edge of the skylight was in the water. When we got pretty close to the cross-hall door there was the skiff, sure enough! I could just barely see her. I felt ever so thankful. In another second I would a been aboard of her; but just then the door opened. One of the men stuck his head out, only about a couple of foot from me, and I thought I was gone; but he jerked it in again, and says:

"Heave that blame lantern out o' sight, Bill!"

He flung a bag of something into the boat, and then got in himself, and set down. It was Packard. Then Bill *he* come out and got in. Packard says, in a low voice:

"All ready—shove off!"

I couldn't hardly hang onto the shutters, I was so weak. But Bill says:

"Hold on—'d you go through him?"

"No. Didn't you?"

"No. So he's got his share o' the cash, yet."

"Well, then, come along—no use to take truck and leave money."

"Say—won't he suspicion what we're up to?"

"Maybe he won't. But we got to have it anyway. Come along." So they got out and went in.

The door slammed to, because it was on the careened side; and in a half second I was in the boat, and Jim come a tumbling after me. I out with my knife and cut the rope, and away we went!

We didn't touch an oar, and we didn' speak nor whisper, nor hardly even breathe. We went gliding swift along, dead silent, past the tip of the paddle-box, and past the stern; then in a second or two more we was a hundred yards below the wreck, and the darkness soaked her up, every last sign of her, and we was safe, and knowed it.

When we was three or four hundred yards down stream, we see the lantern show like a little spark at the texas door, for a second, and we knowed by that that the rascals had missed their boat, and was beginning to understand that they was in just as much trouble, now, as Jim Turner was.

Then Jim manned the oars, and we took out after our raft. Now was the first time that I begun to worry about the men—I reckon I hadn't had time to before. I begun to think how dreadful it was, even for murderers, to be in such a fix. I says to myself, there ain't no telling but I might come to be a murderer myself, yet, and then how would *I* like it? So says I to Jim:

"The first light we see, we'll land a hundred yards below it or above it, in a place where it's a good hiding-place for you and the skiff, and then I'll go and fix up some kind of a yarn, and get somebody to go for that gang and get them out of their scrape, so they can be hung when their time comes."

But that idea was a failure; for pretty soon it begun to storm again, and this time worse than ever. The rain poured down, and never a light showed; everybody in bed, I reckon. We boomed along down the river, watching for lights and watching for our raft. After a long time the rain let up, but the clouds staid, and the lightning kept whimpering, and by-and-by a flash showed us a black thing ahead, floating, and we made for it.

It was the raft, and mighty glad was we to get aboard of it again. We seen a light, now, away down to the right, on shore. So I said I would go for it. The skiff was half full of plunder which that gang had stole, there on the wreck. We hustled it onto the raft in a pile, and I told Jim to float along down, and show a light when he judged he had gone about two mile, and keep it burning till I come; then I manned my oars and shoved for the light. As I got down towards it, three or four more showed—up on a hillside. It was a village. I closed in above the shore-light, and laid on my oars and floated. As I went by, I see it was a lantern hanging on the jackstaff of a double-hull ferry-boat. I skimmed around for the watchman, a-wondering whereabouts he slept; and by-and-by I found him roosting on the bitts,[4] forward, with his head down between his knees. I give his shoulder two or three little shoves, and begun to cry.

He stirred up, in a kind of startlish way; but when he see it was only me, he took a good gap and stretch, and then he says:

"Hello, what's up? Don't cry, bub. What's the trouble?"

I says:

"Pap, and mam, and sis, and—"

Then I broke down. He says:

"Oh, dang it, now, *don't* take on so, we all has to have our troubles and this'n 'll come out all right. What's the matter with 'em?"

"They're—they're—are you the watchman of the boat?"

"Yes," he says, kind of pretty-well-satisfied like. "I'm the captain and the owner, and the mate, and the pilot, and watchman, and

4. Vertical wooden posts to which cables can be secured.

head deck-hand; and sometimes I'm the freight and passengers. I
ain't as rich as old Jim Hornback, and I can't be so blame' generous
and good to Tom, Dick and Harry as what he is, and slam around
money the way he does; but I've told him a many a time 't I
wouldn't trade places with him; for, says I, a sailor's life's the life
for me, and I'm derned if *I'd* live two mile out o' town, where there
ain't nothing ever goin' on, not for all his spondulicks and as much
more on top of it. Says I—"

I broke in and says:

"They're in an awful peck of trouble, and—"

"*Who* is?"

"Why, pap, and mam, and sis, and Miss Hooker; and if you'd
take your ferry-boat and go up there—"

"Up where? Where are they?"

"On the wreck."

"What wreck?"

"Why, there ain't but one."

"What, you don't mean the *Walter Scott?*"[5]

"Yes."

"Good land! what are they doin' *there*, for gracious sakes?"

"Well, they didn't go there a-purpose."

"I bet they didn't! Why, great goodness, there ain't no chance
for 'em if they don't git off mighty quick! Why, how in the nation
did they ever git into such a scrape?"

"Easy enough. Miss Hooker was a-visiting, up there to the
town—"

"Yes, Booth's Landing—go on."

"She was a-visiting, there at Booth's Landing, and just in the
edge of the evening she started over with her nigger woman in the
horse-ferry,[6] to stay all night at her friend's house, Miss What-you-
may-call-her, I disremember her name, and they lost their steering-
oar, and swung around and went a-floating down, stern-first, about
two mile, and saddle-baggsed[7] on the wreck, and the ferry man and
the nigger woman and the horses was all lost, but Miss Hooker she
made a grab and got aboard the wreck. Well, about an hour after
dark, we come along down in our trading-scow, and it was so dark
we didn't notice the wreck till we was right on it; and so *we* saddle-
baggsed; but all of us was saved but Bill Whipple—and oh, he *was*
the best cretur!—I most wish't it had been me, I do."

"My George! It's the beatenest thing I ever struck. And *then*
what did you all do?"

---

5. Twain held Sir Walter Scott's romantic adventure novels set in feudal England responsible for the distorted anti-
democratic notions held by so many southerners and thus for the false ideology
they were willing to fight and die for in
the Civil War. Twain expressed himself
most vividly on this subject in *Life on*
the Mississippi (Chapter XLVI), where
he observes: "Sir Walter had so large a
hand in making Southern character, as it
existed before the war, that he is in
great measure responsible for the war."
6. A ferry large enough to take horses
and wagons.
7. Broken and doubled around the wreck.

"Well, we hollered and took on, but it's so wide there, we couldn't make nobody hear. So pap said somebody got to get ashore and get help somehow. I was the only one that could swim, so I made a dash for it, and Miss Hooker she said if I didn't strike help sooner, come here and hunt up her uncle, and he'd fix the thing. I made the land about a mile below, and been fooling along ever since, trying to get people to do something, but they said, 'What, in such a night and such a current? there ain't no sense in it; go for the steam-ferry.' Now if you'll go, and—"

"By Jackson, I'd *like* to, and blame it I don't know but I will; but who in the dingnation's agoin' to *pay* for it? Do you reckon your pap—"

"Why *that's* all right. Miss Hooker she told me, *particular*, that her uncle Hornback—"

"Great guns! is *he* her uncle? Looky here, you break for that light over yonder-way, and turn out west when you git there, and about a quarter of a mile out you'll come to the tavern; tell 'em to dart you out to Jim Hornback's and he'll foot the bill. And don't you fool around any, because he'll want to know the news. Tell him I'll have his niece all safe before he can get to town. Hump yourself, now; I'm agoing up around the corner here, to roust out my engineer."

I struck for the light, but as soon as he turned the corner I went back and got into my skiff and bailed her out and then pulled up shore in the easy water about six hundred yards, and tucked myself in among some woodboats; for I couldn't rest easy till I could see the ferry-boat start. But take it all around, I was feeling ruther comfortable on accounts of taking all this trouble for that gang, for not many would a done it. I wished the widow knowed about it. I judged she would be proud of me for helping these rapscallions, because rapscallions and dead beats is the kind the widow and good people takes the most interest in.

Well, before long, here comes the wreck, dim and dusky, sliding along down! A kind of cold shiver went through me, and then I struck out for her. She was very deep, and I see in a minute there warn't much chance for anybody being alive in her. I pulled all around her and hollered a little, but there wasn't any answer; all dead still. I felt a little bit heavy-hearted about the gang, but not much, for I reckoned if they could stand it, I could.

Then here comes the ferry-boat; so I shoved for the middle of the river on a long down-stream slant; and when I judged I was out of eye-reach, I laid on my oars, and looked back and see her go and smell around the wreck for Miss Hooker's remainders, because the captain would know her uncle Hornback would want them; and then pretty soon the ferry-boat give it up and went for shore, and I laid into my work and went a-booming down the river.

It did seem a powerful long time before Jim's light showed up; and when it did show, it looked like it was a thousand mile off. By the time I got there the sky was beginning to get a little gray in the east; so we struck for an island, and hid the raft, and sunk the skiff, and turned in and slept like dead people.

Chapter XIV

By-and-by, when we got up, we turned over the truck the gang had stole off of the wreck, and found boots, and blankets, and clothes, and all sorts of other things, and a lot of books, and a spy-glass, and three boxes of seegars. We hadn't ever been this rich before, in neither of our lives. The seegars was prime. We laid off all the afternoon in the woods talking, and me reading the books, and having a general good time. I told Jim all about what happened inside the wreck, and at the ferry-boat; and I said these kinds of things was adventures; but he said he didn't want no more adventures. He said that when I went in the texas and he crawled back to get on the raft and found her gone, he nearly died; because he judged it was all up with *him*, anyway it could be fixed; for if he didn't get saved he would get drownded; and if he did get saved, whoever saved him would send him back home so as to get the reward, and then Miss Watson would sell him South, sure. Well, he was right; he was most always right; he had an uncommon level head, for a nigger.

I read considerable to Jim about kings, and dukes, and earls, and such, and how gaudy they dressed, and how much style they put on, and called each other your majesty, and your grace, and your lord-ship, and so on, 'stead of mister; and Jim's eyes bugged out, and he was interested. He says:

"I didn' know dey was so many un um. I hain't hearn 'bout none un um, skasely, but ole King Sollermun, onless you counts dem kings dat's in a pack er k'yards. How much do a king git?"

"Get?" I says; "why, they get a thousand dollars a month if they want it; they can have just as much as they want; everything belongs to them."

"Ain' dat gay? En what dey got to do, Huck?"

"*They* don't do nothing! Why how you talk. They just set arou[.]d."

"No—is dat so?"

"Of course it is. They just set around. Except maybe when there 's a war; then they go to the war. But other times they just lazy around; or go hawking—just hawking and sp— Sh!—d' you hear a noise?"

We skipped out and looked; but it warn't nothing but the flutter of a steamboat's wheel, away down coming around the point; so we come back.

"Yes," says I, "and other times, when things is dull, they fuss with the parlyment; and if everybody don't go just so he whacks their heads off. But mostly they hang round the harem."

"Roun' de which?"

"Harem."

"What's de harem?"

"The place where he keep his wives. Don't you know about the harem? Solomon had one; he had about a million wives."

"Why, yes, dat's so; I—I'd done forgot it. A harem's a bo'd'n-house, I reck'n. Mos' likely dey has rackety times in de nussery. En I reck'n de wives quarrels considable; en dat 'crease de racket. Yit dey say Sollermun de wises' man dat ever live.' I doan' take no stock in dat. Bekase why: would a wise man want to live in de mids' er sich a blimblammin' all de time? No—'deed he wouldn't. A wise man 'ud take en buil' a biler-factry; en den he could shet *down* de biler-factry when he want to res'."

"Well, but he *was* the wisest man, anyway; because the widow she told me so, her own self."

"I doan k'yer what de widder say, he *warn't* no wise man, nuther. He had some er de dad-fetchedes' ways I ever see. Does you know 'bout dat chile dat he 'uz gwyne to chop in two?"[8]

"Yes, the widow told me all about it."

"*Well*, den! Warn' dat de beatenes' notion in de worl'? You jes' take en look at it a minute. Dah's de stump, dah—dat's one er de women; heah's you—dat's de yuther one; I's Sollermun; en dish-yer dollar bill's de chile. Bofe un you claims it. What does I do? Does I shin aroun' mongs' de neighbors en fine out which un you de bill do b'long to, en han' it over to de right one, all safe en soun', de way dat anybody dat had any gumption would? No—I take en whack de bill in *two*, en give half un it to you, en de yuther half to de yuther woman. Dat's de way Sollermun was gwyne to do wid de chile. Now I want to ast you: what's de use er dat half a bill?—can't buy noth'n wid it. En what use is a half a chile? I would'n give a dern for a million un um."

"But hang it, Jim, you've clean missed the point—blame it, you've missed it a thousand mile."

"Who? Me? Go 'long. Doan' talk to *me* 'bout yo' pints. I reck'n I knows sense when I sees it; en dey ain' no sense in sich doin's as dat. De 'spute warn't 'bout a half a chile, de 'spute was 'bout a whole chile; en de man dat think he kin settle a 'spute 'bout a whole chile wid a half a chile, doan' know enough to come in out'n de rain. Doan' talk to me 'bout Sollermun, Huck, I knows him by de back."

"But I tell you you don't get the point."

"Blame de pint! I reck'n I knows what I knows. En mine you, de *real* pint is down furder—it's down deeper. It lays in de way Sollermun was raised. You take a man dat's got on'y one er two chillen; is

8. In 1 Kings 3.16–28. When two women appeared before him claiming to be the mother of the same infant, Solomon ordered the child cut in two. The child's real mother pleaded with him to save the baby and to give it to the other woman, who maliciously agreed to Solomon's original plan.

dat man gwyne to be waseful o' chillen? No, he ain't; he can't 'ford it. *He* know how to value 'em. But you take a man dat's got 'bout five million chillen runnin' roun' de house, en it's diffunt. *He* as soon chop a chile in two as a cat. Dey's plenty mo'. A chile er two, mo' er less, warn't no consekens to Sollermun, dad fetch him!"

I never see such a nigger. If he got a notion in his head once, there warn't no getting it out again. He was the most down on Solomon of any nigger I ever see. So I went to talking about other kings, and let Solomon slide. I told about Louis Sixteenth that got his head cut off in France long time ago; and about his little boy the dolphin,[9] that would a been a king, but they took and shut him up in jail, and some say he died there.

"Po' little chap."

"But some says he got out and got away, and come to America."

"Dat's good! But he'll be pooty lonesome—dey ain' no kings here, is dey, Huck?"

"No."

"Den he cain't git no situation. What he gwyne to do?"

"Well, I don't know. Some of them gets on the police, and some of them learns people how to talk French."

"Why, Huck, doan' de French people talk de same way we does?"

"No, Jim; you couldn't understand a word they said—not a single word."

"Well, now, I be ding-busted! How do dat come?"

"*I* don't know; but it's so. I got some of their jabber out of a book. Spose a man was to come to you and say *Polly-voo-franzy*—what would you think?"

"I wouldn' think nuff'n; I'd take en bust him over de head. Dat is, if he warn't white. I wouldn't 'low no nigger to call me dat."

"Shucks, it ain't calling you anything. It's only saying do you know how to talk French."

"Well, den, why couldn't he *say* it?"

"Why, he *is* a-saying it. That's a Frenchman's *way* of saying it."

"Well, it's a blame' ridicklous way, en I doan' want to hear no mo' 'bout it. Dey ain' no sense in it."

"Looky here, Jim; does a cat talk like we do?"

"No, a cat don't."

"Well, does a cow?"

"No, a cow don't, nuther."

"Does a cat talk like a cow, or a cow talk like a cat?"

"No, dey don't."

---

9. The Dauphin, Louis Charles, next in line of the succession to the throne, was eight years old when his father, Louis XVI, was beheaded (1793). Though the boy died in prison, probably in 1795, legends of his escape to America (and elsewhere) persisted, and Clemens owned a book on the subject by Horace W. Fuller: *Imposters and Adventurers, Noted French Trials* (1882).

"It's natural and right for 'em to talk different from each other, ain't it?"

" 'Course."

"And ain't it natural and right for a cat and a cow to talk different from *us*?"

"Why, mos' sholy it is."

"Well, then, why ain't it natural and right for a *Frenchman* to talk different from us? You answer me that."

"Is a cat a man, Huck?"

"No."

"Well, den, dey ain't no sense in a cat talkin' like a man. Is a cow a man?—er is a cow a cat?"

"No, she ain't either of them."

"Well, den, she ain' got no business to talk like either one er the yuther of 'em. Is a Frenchman a man?"

"Yes."

"*Well*, den! Dad blame it, why doan' he *talk* like a man? You answer me *dat*!"

I see it warn't no use wasting words—you can't learn a nigger to argue. So I quit.

Chapter XV

We judged that three nights more would fetch us to Cairo,[1] at the bottom of Illinois, where the Ohio River comes in, and that was what we was after. We would sell the raft and get on a steamboat and go way up the Ohio amongst the free States, and then be out of trouble.[2]

Well, the second night a fog begun to come on, and we made for a tow-head to tie to, for it wouldn't do to try to run in fog; but when I paddled ahead in the canoe, with the line, to make fast, there warn't anything but little saplings to tie to. I passed the line around one of them right on the edge of the cut bank, but there was a stiff current, and the raft come booming down so lively she tore it out by the roots and away she went. I see the fog closing down, and it made me so sick and scared I couldn't budge for most a half a minute it seemed to me—and then there warn't no raft in sight; you couldn't see twenty yards. I jumped into the canoe and run back to the stern and grabbed the paddle and set her back a stroke. But she didn't come. I was in such a hurry I hadn't untied her. I got up and tried to untie her, but I was so excited my hands shook so I couldn't hardly do anything with them.

1. Pronounced "Kay-ro"; the town is 364 miles from Hannibal, 194 miles from St. Louis.
2. Southern Illinois was proslavery in sentiment. The state, moreover, had a system of indentured labor not unlike slavery to which a Negro without proof of his free status might be subjected. Though even among the "free States" there were similar dangers for Jim, the chances of making his way to freedom and safety in Canada from Ohio or Pennsylvania would be much greater.

As soon as I got started I took out after the raft, hot and heavy, right down the tow-head. That was all right as far as it went, but the tow-head warn't sixty yards long, and the minute I flew by the foot of it I shot out into the solid white fog, and hadn't no more idea which way I was going than a dead man.

Thinks I, it won't do to paddle; first I know I'll run into the bank or a tow-head or something; I got to set still and float, and yet it's mighty fidgety business to have to hold your hands still at such a time. I whooped and listened. Away down there, somewheres, I hears a small whoop, and up comes my spirits. I went tearing after it, listening sharp to hear it again. The next time it come, I see I warn't heading for it but heading away to the right of it. And the next time, I was heading away to the left of it—and not gaining on it much, either, for I was flying around, this way and that and 'tother, but it was going straight ahead all the time.

I did wish the fool would think to beat a tin pan, and beat it all the time, but he never did, and it was the still places between the whoops that was making the trouble for me. Well, I fought along, and directly I hears the whoops *behind* me. I was tangled good, now. That was somebody else's whoop, or else I was turned around.

I throwed the paddle down. I heard the whoop again; it was behind me yet, but in a different place; it kept coming, and kept changing its place, and I kept answering, till by-and-by it was in front of me again and I knowed the current had swung the canoe's head down stream and I was all right, if that was Jim and not some other raftsman hollering. I couldn't tell nothing about voices in a fog, for nothing don't look natural nor sound natural in a fog.

The whooping went on, and in about a minute I come a booming down on a cut bank[3] with smoky ghosts of big trees on it, and the current throwed me off to the left and shot by, amongst a lot of snags that fairly roared, the current was tearing by them so swift.

In another second or two it was solid white and still again. I set perfectly still, then, listening to my heart thump, and I reckon I didn't draw a breath while it thumped a hundred.

I just give up, then. I knowed what the matter was. That cut bank was an island, and Jim had gone down 'tother side of it. It warn't no tow-head, that you could float by in ten minutes. It had the big timber of a regular island; it might be five or six mile long and more than a half a mile wide.

I kept quiet, with my ears cocked, about fifteen minutes, I reckon. I was floating along, of course, four or five mile an hour; but you don't ever think of that. No, you *feel* like you are laying dead still on the water; and if a little glimpse of a snap slips by, you don't think to yourself how fast *you're* going, but you catch your breath and think, my! how that snag's tearing along. If you think it

3. Steep bank carved out by the force of the current.

ain't dismal and lonesome out in a fog that way, by yourself, in the night, you try it once—you'll see.

Next, for about a half an hour, I whoops now and then; at last I hears the answer a long ways off, and tries to follow it, but I couldn't do it, and directly I judged I'd got into a nest of tow-heads, for I had little dim glimpses of them on both sides of me, sometimes just a narrow channel between; and some that I couldn't see, I knowed was there, because I'd hear the wash of the current against the old dead brush and trash that hung over the banks. Well, I warn't long losing the whoops, down amongst the tow-heads; and I only tried to chase them a little while, anyway, because it was worse than chasing a Jack-o-lantern. You never knowed a sound dodge around so, and swap places so quick and so much.

I had to claw away from the bank pretty lively, four or five times, to keep from knocking the islands out of the river; and so I judged the raft must be butting into the bank every now and then, or else it would get further ahead and clear out of hearing—it was floating a little faster than what I was.

Well, I seemed to be in the open river again, by-and-by, but I couldn't hear no sign of a whoop nowheres. I reckoned Jim had fetched up on a snag, maybe, and it was all up with him. I was good and tired, so I laid down in the canoe and said I wouldn't bother no more. I didn't want to go to sleep, of course; but I was so sleepy I couldn't help it; so I thought I would take just one little cat-nap.

But I reckon it was more than a cat-nap, for when I waked up the stars was shining bright, the fog was all gone, and I was spinning down a big bend stern first. First I didn't know where I was; I thought I was dreaming; and when things begun to come back to me, they seemed to come up dim out of last week.

It was a monstrous big river here, with the tallest and the thickest kind of timber on both banks; just a solid wall, as well as I could see, by the stars. I looked away down stream, and seen a black speck on the water. I took out after it; but when I got to it it warn't nothing but a couple of saw-logs made fast together. Then I see another speck, and chased that; then another, and this time I was right. It was the raft.

When I got to it Jim was setting there with his head down between his knees, asleep, with his right arm hanging over the steering oar. The other oar was smashed off, and the raft was littered up with leaves and branches and dirt. So she'd had a rough time.

I made fast and laid down under Jim's nose on the raft, and begun to gap, and stretch my fists out against Jim, and says:

"Hello, Jim, have I been asleep? Why didn't you stir me up?"

"Goodness gracious, is dat you, Huck? En you ain' dead—you ain' drowned—you's back agin? It's too good for true, honey, it's too good for true. Lemme look at you, chile, lemme feel o' you. No, you ain' dead? you's back agin, 'live en soun', jis de same ole Huck —de same ole Huck, thanks to goodness!"

"What's the matter with you, Jim? You been a drinking?"

"Drinkin'? Has I ben a drinkin'? Has I had a chance to be a drinkin'?"

"Well, then, what makes you talk so wild?"

"How does I talk wild?"

"*How?* why, haint you been talking about my coming back, and all that stuff, as if I'd been gone away?"

"Huck—Huck Finn, you look me in de eye; look me in de eye. *Hain't* you ben gone away?"

"Gone away? Why, what in the nation do you mean? I hain't been gone anywheres. Where would I go to?"

"Well, looky here, boss, dey's sumf'n wrong, dey is. Is I *me*, or who *is* I? Is I heah, or whah *is* I? Now dat's what I wants to know?"

"Well, I think you're here, plain enough, but I think you're a tangle-headed old fool, Jim."

"I is, is I? Well you answer me dis. Didn't you tote out de line in de canoe, fer to make fas' to de tow-head?"

"No, I didn't. What tow-head? I hain't seen no tow-head."

"You hain't seen no tow-head? Looky here—didn't de line pull loose en de raf' go a hummin' down de river, en leave you en de canoe behine in de fog?"

"What fog?"

"Why *de* fog. De fog dat's ben aroun' all night. En didn't you whoop, en didn't I whoop, tell we got mix' up in de islands en one un us got los' en 'tother one was jis' as good as los', 'kase he didn' know whah he wuz? En didn't I bust up agin a lot er dem islands en have a turrible time en mos' git drownded? Now ain' dat so, boss —ain't it so? You answer me dat."

"Well, this is too many for me, Jim. I hain't seen no fog, nor no islands, nor no troubles, nor nothing. I been setting here talking with you all night till you went to sleep about ten minutes ago, and I reckon I done the same. You couldn't a got drunk in that time, so of course you've been dreaming."

"Dad fetch it, how is I gwyne to dream all dat in ten minutes?"

"Well, hang it all, you did dream it, because there didn't any of it happen."

"But Huck, it's all jis' as plain to me as—"

"It don't make no difference how plain it is, there ain't nothing in it. I know, because I've been here all the time."

Jim didn't say nothing for about five minutes, but set there studying over it. Then he says:

"Well, den, I reck'n I did dream it, Huck; but dog my cats ef it ain't de powerfullest dream I ever see. En I hain't ever had no dream b'fo' dat's tired me like dis one."

"Oh, well, that's all right, because a dream does tire a body like everything, sometimes. But this one was a staving[4] dream—tell me all about it, Jim."

So Jim went to work and told me the whole thing right through, just as it happened, only he painted it up considerable. Then he said he must start in and "'terpret" it, because it was sent for a warning. He said the first tow-head stood for a man that would try to do us some good, but the current was another man that would get us away from him. The whoops was warnings that would come to us every now and then, and if we didn't try hard to make out to understand them they'd just take us into bad luck, 'stead of keeping us out of it. The lot of tow-heads was troubles we was going to get into with quarrelsome people and all kinds of mean folks, but if we minded our business and didn't talk back and aggravate them, we would pull through and get out of the fog and into the big clear river, which was the free States, and wouldn't have no more trouble.

It had clouded up pretty dark just after I got onto the raft, but it was clearing up again, now.

"Oh, well, that's all interpreted well enough, as far as it goes, Jim," I says; "but what does *these* things stand for?"

It was the leaves and rubbish on the raft, and the smashed oar. You could see them first rate, now.

Jim looked at the trash, and then looked at me, and back at the trash again. He had got the dream fixed so strong in his head that he couldn't seem to shake it loose and get the facts back into its place again, right away. But when he did get the thing straightened around, he looked at me steady, without ever smiling, and says:

"What do dey stan' for? I's gwyne to tell you. When I got all wore out wid work, en wid de callin' for you, en went to sleep, my heart wuz mos' broke bekase you wuz los', en I didn' k'yer no mo' what become er me en de raf'. En when I wake up en fine you back agin', all safe en soun', de tears come en I could a got down on my knees en kiss yo' foot I's so thankful. En all you wuz thinkin' 'bout wuz how you could make a fool uv ole Jim wid a lie. Dat truck dah is *trash*; en trash is what people is dat puts dirt on de head er dey fren's en makes 'em ashamed."

Then he got up slow, and walked to the wigwam, and went in there, without saying anything but that. But that was enough. It made me feel so mean I could almost kissed *his* foot to get him to take it back.

It was fifteen minutes before I could work myself up to go and humble myself to a nigger—but I done it, and I warn't ever sorry for it afterwards, neither. I didn't do him no more mean tricks, and I wouldn't done that one if I'd a knowed it would make him feel that way.

4. **Vivid, compelling.**

Chapter XVI

We slept most all day, and started out at night, a little ways behind a monstrous long raft that was as long going by as a procession. She had four long sweeps[5] at each end, so we judged she carried as many as thirty men, likely. She had five big wigwams aboard, wide apart, and an open camp fire in the middle, and a tall flagpole at each end. There was a power of style about her. It *amounted* to something being a raftsman on such a craft as that.

We went drifting down into a big bend, and the night clouded up and got hot. The river was very wide, and was walled with solid timber on both sides; you couldn't see a break in it hardly ever, or a light. We talked about Cairo, and wondered whether we would know it when we got to it. I said likely we wouldn't, because I had heard say there warn't but about a dozen houses there, and if they didn't happen to have them lit up, how was we going to know we was passing a town? Jim said if the two big rivers joined together there, that would show. But I said maybe we might think we was passing the foot of an island and coming into the same old river again. That disturbed Jim—and me too. So the question was, what to do? I said, paddle ashore the first time a light showed, and tell them pap was behind, coming along with a trading-scow, and was a green hand at the business, and wanted to know how far it was to Cairo. Jim thought it was a good idea, so we took a smoke on it and waited.[6]

But you know a young person can't wait very well when he is impatient to find a thing out. We talked it over, and by and by Jim said it was such a black night, now, that it wouldn't be no risk to swim down to the big raft and crawl aboard and listen—they would talk about Cairo, because they would be calculating to go ashore there for a spree, maybe; or anyway they would send boats ashore to buy whisky or fresh meat or something. Jim had a wonderful level head, for a nigger: he could most always start a good plan when you wanted one.

I stood up and shook my rags off and jumped into the river, and struck out for the raft's light. By and by, when I got down nearly to her, I eased up and went slow and cautious. But everything was all right—nobody at the sweeps. So I swum down along the raft till I was most abreast the camp-fire in the middle, then I crawled aboard and inched along and got in among some bundles of shingles on the

5. Long oars used chiefly for steering.
6. The passage which follows was part of the final autograph manuscript for *Huck Finn* which Clemens sent to his nephew-publisher Charles L. Webster in April, 1884. Though Twain acquiesced to the cutting of this "Raft Passage" (on a suggestion made initially by W. D. Howells), the cut was made to save space and not on literary or aesthetic grounds, and the passage is there- fore reinstated in this text. The raft material had already appeared—with an introductory note explaining that it was part of a book in progress—as part of Chapter III of *Life on the Mississippi* (1883). For a further discussion of this textual crux see Walter Blair, *Mark Twain and "Huck Finn"* (1960), and Peter G. Beidier, "The Raft Episode in Huckleberry Finn," *Modern Fiction Studies*, XIV, 1 (Spring, 1965), 11–20.

weather side of the fire. There was thirteen men there—they was the watch on deck of course. And a mighty rough-looking lot, too. They had a jug, and tin cups, and they kept the jug moving. One man was singing—roaring, you may say; and it wasn't a nice song —for a parlor, anyway. He roared through his nose, and strung out the last word of every line very long. When he was done they all fetched a kind of Injun war-whoop, and then another was sung. It begun:

> "There was a woman in our towdn,
>   In our towdn did dwed'l [dwell],
> She loved her husband dear-i-lee,
>   But another man twyste as wed'l.

> "Singing too, riloo, riloo, riloo,
>   Ri-too, riloo, rilay - - - e,
> She loved her husband dear-i-lee,
>   But another man twyste as wed'l."

And so on—fourteen verses. It was kind of poor, and when he was going to start on the next verse one of them said it was the tune the old cow died on; and another one said: "Oh, give us a rest!" And another one told him to take a walk. They made fun of him till he got mad and jumped up and begun to cuss the crowd, and said he could lam any thief in the lot.

They was all about to make a break for him, but the biggest man there jumped up and says:

"Set whar you are, gentlemen. Leave him to me; he's my meat."

Then he jumped up in the air three times, and cracked his heels together every time. He flung off a buckskin coat that was all hung with fringes, and says, "You lay thar tell the chawin-up's done"; and flung his hat down, which was all over ribbons, and says, "You lay thar tell his sufferin's is over."

Then he jumped up in the air and cracked his heels together again, and shouted out:

"Whoo-oop! I'm the old original iron-jawed, brass-mounted, cop-per-bellied corpse-maker from the wilds of Arkansaw. Look at me! I'm the man they call Sudden Death and General Desolation! Sired by a hurricane, dam'd by an earthquake, half-brother to the cholera, nearly related to the smallpox on the mother's side! Look at me! I take nineteen alligators and a bar'l of whisky for breakfast when I'm in robust health, and a bushel of rattlesnakes and a dead body when I'm ailing. I split the everlasting rocks with my glance, and I squench[7] the thunder when I speak! Whoo-oop! Stand back and give me room according to my strength! Blood's my natural drink, and the wails of the dying is music to my ear. Cast your eye on me,

---

7. Outdo, overpower.

gentlemen! and lay low and hold your breath, for I'm 'bout to turn myself loose![8]

All the time he was getting this off, he was shaking his head and looking fierce, and kind of swelling around in a little circle, tucking up his wristbands, and now and then straightening up and beating his breast with his fist, saying, "Look at me, gentlemen!" When he got through, he jumped up and cracked his heels together three times, and let off a roaring "Whoo-oop! I'm the bloodiest son of a wildcat that lives!"

Then the man that had started the row tilted his old slouch hat down over his right eye; then he bent stooping forward, with his back sagged and his south end sticking out far, and his fists a-shoving out and drawing in in front of him, and so went around in a little circle about three times, swelling himself up and breathing hard. Then he straightened, and jumped up and cracked his heels together three times before he lit again (that made them cheer), and he began to shout like this:

"Whoo-oop! bow your neck and spread, for the kingdom of sorrow's a-coming! Hold me down to the earth, for I feel my powers a-working! whoo-oop! I'm a child of sin, *don't* let me get a start! Smoked glass, here, for all! Don't attempt to look at me with the naked eye, gentlemen! When I'm playful I use the meridians of longitude and parallels of latitude for a seine, and drag the Atlantic Ocean for whales! I scratch my head with the lightning and purr myself to sleep with the thunder! When I'm cold, I bile the Gulf of Mexico and bathe in it; when I'm hot I fan myself with an equinoctial storm; when I'm thirsty I reach up and suck a cloud dry like a sponge; when I range the earth hungry, famine follows in my tracks! Whoo-oop! Bow your neck and spread! I put my hand on the sun's face and make it night in the earth; I bite a piece out of the moon and hurry the seasons; I shake myself and crumble the mountains! Contemplate me through leather—*don't* use the naked eye! I'm the man with a petrified heart and biler-iron bowels! The massacre of isolated communities is the pastime of my idle moments, the destruction of nationalities the serious business of my life! The boundless vastness of the great American desert is my inclosed property, and I bury my dead on my own premises!" He jumped up and cracked his heels together three times before he lit (they cheered him again), and as he come down he shouted out: "Whoo-oop! bow your neck and spread, for the Pet Child of Calamity's a-coming!"

Then the other one went to swelling around and blowing again —the first one—the one they called Bob; next, the Child of Calam-

---

8. Twain here immortalizes the ritual boasting of the "ring-tailed roarers," chiefly associated with Kentucky but familiar both in the oral traditions of the frontier and in the writings of the southwestern humorists, in whose tradition Twain follows.

ity chipped in again, bigger than ever; then they both got at it at
the same time, swelling round and round each other and punching
their fists most into each other's faces, and whooping and jawing
like Injuns; then Bob called the Child names, and the Child called
him names back again; next, Bob called him a heap rougher names,
and the Child come back at him with the very worst kind of language; next, Bob knocked the Child's hat off, and the Child picked
it up and kicked Bob's ribbony hat about six foot; Bob went and
got it and said never mind, this warn't going to be the last of this
thing, because he was a man that never forgot and never forgive,
and so the Child better look out, for there was a time a-coming,
just as sure as he was a living man, that he would have to answer to
him with the best blood in his body. The Child said no man was
willinger than he for that time to come, and he would give Bob fair
warning, *now*, never to cross his path again, for he could never rest
till he had waded in his blood, for such was his nature, though he
was sparing him now on account of his family, if he had one.

Both of them was edging away in different directions, growling
and shaking their heads and going on about what they was going to
do; but a little black-whiskered chap skipped up and says:

"Come back here, you couple of chicken-livered cowards, and I'll
thrash the two of ye!"

And he done it, too. He snatched them, he jerked them this way
and that, he booted them around, he knocked them sprawling faster
than they could get up. Why, it warn't two minutes till they
begged like dogs—and how the other lot did yell and laugh and
clap their hands all the way through, and shout "Sail in, Corpse-
Maker!" "Hit at him again, Child of Calamity!" "Bully for you,
little Davy!" Well, it was a perfect pow-wow for a while. Bob and
the Child had red noses and black eyes when they got through.
Little Davy made them own up that they were sneaks and cowards
and not fit to eat with a dog or drink with a nigger; then Bob and
the Child shook hands with each other, very solemn, and said they
had always respected each other and was willing to let bygones be
bygones. So then they washed their faces in the river; and just then
there was a loud order to stand by for a crossing, and some of them
went forward to man the sweeps there, and the rest went aft to
handle the after sweeps.

I laid still and waited for fifteen minutes, and had a smoke out of
a pipe that one of them left in reach; then the crossing was
finished, and they stumped back and had a drink around and went
to talking and singing again. Next they got out an old fiddle, and
one played, and another patted juba, and the rest turned themselves
loose on a regular old-fashioned keelboat breakdown.[9] They

9. As the name suggests, a wild dance
with a rapid rhythm. The "juba" is a
strongly rhythmical dance that originated
among southern Negroes about 1880; to
pat a juba would be to clap the hands
or tap the feet to make the rhythm.

couldn't keep that up very long without getting winded, so by and by they settled around the jug again.

They sung "Jolly, Jolly Raftsman's the Life for Me," with a rousing chorus, and then they got to talking about differences betwixt hogs, and their different kind of habits, and next about women and their different ways; and next about the best ways to put out houses that was afire; and next about what ought to be done with the Injuns; and next about what a king had to do, and how much he got; and next about how to make cats fight; and next about what to do when a man has fits; and next about differences betwixt clear-water rivers and muddy-water ones. The man they called Ed said the muddy Mississippi water was wholesomer to drink than the clear water of the Ohio; he said if you let a pint of this yaller Mississippi water settle, you would have about a half to three-quarters of an inch of mud in the bottom, according to the stage of the river, and then it warn't no better than Ohio water—what you wanted to do was to keep it stirred up—and when the river was low, keep mud on hand to put in and thicken the water up the way it ought to be.

The Child of Calamity said that was so; he said there was nutritiousness in the mud, and a man that drunk Mississippi water could grow corn in his stomach if he wanted to. He says:

"You look at the graveyards; that tells the tale. Trees won't grow worth shucks in a Cincinnati graveyard, but in a Sent Louis graveyard they grow upwards of eight hundred foot high. It's all on account of the water the people drunk before they laid up. A Cincinnati corpse don't richen a soil any."

And they talked about how Ohio water didn't like to mix with Mississippi water. Ed said if you take the Mississippi on a rise when the Ohio is low, you'll find a wide band of clear water all the way down the east side of the Mississippi for a hundred mile or more, and the minute you get out a quarter of a mile from shore and pass the line, it is all thick and yaller the rest of the way across. Then they talked about how to keep tobacco from getting moldy, and from that they went into ghosts and told about a lot that other folks had seen; but Ed says:

"Why don't you tell something that you've seen yourselves? Now let me have a say. Five years ago I was on a raft as big as this, and right along here it was a bright moonshiny night, and I was on watch and boss of the stabboard oar forrard, and one of my pards was a man named Dick Allbright, and he come along to where I was sitting, forrard—gaping and stretching, he was—and stooped down on the edge of the raft and washed his face in the river, and come and set down by me and got out his pipe, and had just got it filled, when he looks up and says:

" 'Why looky-here,' he says, 'ain't that Buck Miller's place, over yander in the bend?'

" 'Yes,' says I, 'it is—why?' He laid his pipe down and leaned his head on his hand, and says:

" 'I thought we'd be furder down.' I says:

" 'I thought it, too, when I went off watch'—we was standing six hours on and six off—'but the boys told me,' I says, 'that the raft didn't seem to hardly move, for the last hour,' says I, 'though she's a-slipping along all right now,' says I. He give a kind of a groan, and says:

" 'I've seed a raft act so before, along here,' he says. ' 'pears to me the current has most quit above the head of this bend durin' the last two years,' he says.

"Well, he raised up two or three times, and looked away off and around on the water. That started me at it, too. A body is always doing what he sees somebody else doing, though there mayn't be no sense in it. Pretty soon I see a black something floating on the water away off to stabboard and quartering behind us. I see he was looking at it, too. I says:

" 'What's that?' He says, sort of pettish:

" ' 'Tain't nothing but an old empty bar'l.'

" 'An empty bar'l!' says I, 'why,' says I, 'a spy-glass is a fool to *your* eyes. How can you tell it's an empty bar'l?' He says:

" 'I don't know; I reckon it ain't a bar'l, but I thought it might be,' says he.

" 'Yes,' I says, 'so it might be, and it might be anything else too; a body can't tell nothing about it, such a distance as that,' I says.

"We hadn't nothing else to do, so we kept on watching it. By and by I says:

" 'Why, looky-here, Dick Allbright, that thing's a-gaining on us, I believe.'

"He never said nothing. The thing gained and gained, and I judged it must be a dog that was about tired out. Well, we swung down into the crossing, and the thing floated across the bright streak of the moonshine, and by George, it *was* a bar'l. Says I:

" 'Dick Allbright, what made you think that thing was a bar'l, when it was half a mile off?' says I. Says he:

" 'I don't know.' Says I:

" 'You tell me, Dick Allbright.' Says he:

" 'Well, I knowed it was a bar'l; I've seen it before; lots has seen it; they says it's a ha'nted bar'l.'

"I called the rest of the watch, and they come and stood there, and I told them what Dick said. It floated right along abreast, now, and didn't gain any more. It was about twenty foot off. Some was for having it aboard, but the rest didn't want to. Dick Allbright said rafts that had fooled with it had got bad luck by it. The captain of the watch said he didn't believe in it. He said he reckoned the bar'l gained on us because it was in a little better current than what we was. He said it would leave by and by.

"So then we went to talking about other things, and we had a song, and then a breakdown; and after that the captain of the watch called for another song; but it was clouding up now, and the bar'l stuck right thar in the same place, and the song didn't seem to have much warm-up to it, somehow, and so they didn't finish it, and there warn't any cheers, but it sort of dropped flat, and nobody said anything for a minute. Then everybody tried to talk at once, and one chap got off a joke, but it warn't no use, they didn't laugh, and even the chap that made the joke didn't laugh at it, which ain't usual. We all just settled down glum, and watched the bar'l, and was oneasy and oncomfortable. Well, sir, it shut down black and still, and then the wind began to moan around, and next the lightning began to play and the thunder to grumble. And pretty soon there was a regular storm, and in the middle of it a man that was running aft stumbled and fell and sprained his ankle so that he had to lay up. This made the boys shake their heads. And every time the lightning come, there was that bar'l, with the blue lights winking around it. We was always on the lookout for it. But by and by, toward dawn, she was gone. When the day come we couldn't see her anywhere, and we warn't sorry, either.

"But next night about half-past nine, when there was songs and high jinks going on, here she comes again, and took her old roost on the stabboard side. There warn't no more high jinks. Everybody got solemn; nobody talked; you couldn't get anybody to do anything but set around moody and look at the bar'l. It begun to cloud up again. When the watch changed, the off watch stayed up, 'stead of turning in. The storm ripped and roared around all night, and in the middle of it another man tripped and sprained his ankle, and had to knock off. The bar'l left toward day, and nobody see it go.

"Everybody was sober and down in the mouth all day. I don't mean the kind of sober that comes of leaving liquor alone—not that. They was quiet, but they all drunk more than usual—not together, but each man sidled off and took it private, by himself.

"After dark the off watch didn't turn in; nobody sung, nobody talked; the boys didn't scatter around, neither; they sort of huddled together, forrard; and for two hours they set there, perfectly still, looking steady in the one direction, and heaving a sigh once in a while. And then, here comes the bar'l again. She took up her old place. She stayed there all night; nobody turned in. The storm come on again, after midnight. It got awful dark; the rain poured down; hail, too; the thunder boomed and roared and bellowed; the wind blowed a hurricane; and the lightning spread over everything in big sheets of glare, and showed the whole raft as plain as day; and the river lashed up white as milk as far as you could see for miles, and there was that bar'l jiggering along, same as ever. The captain ordered the watch to man the after sweeps for a crossing, and nobody would go—no more sprained ankles for them, they said. They wouldn't even *walk* aft. Well, then, just then the sky split wide open, with a crash, and the lightning killed two men of the after watch, and crippled two more. Crippled them how, say you? Why, *sprained their ankles!*

"The bar'l left in the dark betwixt lightnings, toward dawn. Well, not a body eat a bite at breakfast that morning. After that the men loafed around, in twos and threes, and talked low together. But none of them herded with Dick Allbright. They all give him the cold shake. If he come around where any of the men was, they split up and sidled away. They wouldn't man the sweeps with him. The captain had all the skiffs hauled up on the raft, alongside of his wigwam, and wouldn't let the dead men be took ashore to be planted; he didn't believe a man that got ashore would come back; and he was right.

"After night come, you could see pretty plain that there was going to be trouble if that bar'l come again; there was such a muttering going on. A good many wanted to kill Dick Allbright, because he'd seen the bar'l on other trips, and that had an ugly look. Some wanted to put him ashore. Some said: 'Let's all go ashore in a pile, if the bar'l comes again.'

"This kind of whispers was still going on, the men being bunched together forrard watching for the bar'l, when lo and behold you! here she comes again. Down she comes, slow and steady, and settles into her old tracks. You could 'a' heard a pin drop. Then up comes the captain, and says:

" 'Boys, don't be a pack of children and fools; I don't want this bar'l to be dogging us all the way to Orleans, and *you* don't: Well, then, how's the best way to stop it? Burn it up—that's the way. I'm going to fetch it aboard,' he says. And before anybody could say a word, in he went.

"He swum to it, and as he come pushing it to the raft, the men spread to one side. But the old man got it aboard and busted in the head, and there was a baby in it! Yes, sir; a stark-naked baby. It was Dick Allbright's baby; he owned up and said so.

" 'Yes,' he says, a-leaning over it, 'yes, it is my own lamented darling, my poor lost Charles William Allbright deceased,' says he—for he could curl his tongue around the bulliest words in the language when he was a mind to, and lay them before you without a jint started anywheres.[1] Yes, he said, he used to live up at the head of this bend, and one night he choked his child, which was crying, not intending to kill it—which was prob'ly a lie—and then he was scared, and buried it in a bar'l, before his wife got hime, and off he went, and struck the northern trail and went to rafting; and this was the third year that the bar'l had chased him. He said the bad luck always begun light, and lasted till four men was killed, and then the bar'l didn't come any more after that. He said if the men would stand it one more night—and was a-going on like that—but

---

1. Without bending their joints; i.e., perfectly smoothly and eloquently.

the men had got enough. They started to get out a boat to take him ashore and lynch him, but he grabbed the little child all of a sudden and jumped overboard with it, hugged up to his breast and shedding tears, and we never see him again in this life, poor old suffering soul, nor Charles William neither."

"*Who* was shedding tears?" says Bob; "was it Allbright or the baby?"

"Why, Allbright, of course; didn't I tell you the baby was dead? Been dead three years—how could it cry?"

"Well, never mind how it could cry—how could it *keep* all that time?" says Davy. "You answer me that."

"I don't know how it done it," says Ed. "It done it, though—that's all I know about it."

"Say—what did they do with the bar'l?" says the Child of Calamity.

"Why, they hove it overboard, and it sunk like a chunk of lead."

"Edward, did the child look like it was choked?" says one.

"Did it have its hair parted?" says another.

"What was the brand on that bar'l, Eddy?" says a fellow they called Bill.

"Have you got the papers for them statistics, Edmund?" says Jimmy.

"Say, Edwin, was you one of the men that was killed by the lightning?" says Davy.

"Him? Oh, no! he was both of 'em," says Bob. Then they all haw-hawed.

"Say, Edward, don't you reckon you'd better take a pill? You look bad—don't you feel pale?" says the Child of Calamity.

"Oh, come, now, Eddy," says Jimmy, "show up; you must 'a' kept part of that bar'l to prove the thing by. Show us the bung-hole —do—and we'll all believe you."

"Say, boys," says Bill, "less divide it up. Thar's thirteen of us. I can swaller a thirteenth of the yarn, if you can worry down the rest."

Ed got up mad and said they could all go to some place which he ripped out pretty savage, and then walked off aft, cussing to himself, and they yelling and jeering at him, and roaring and laughing so you could hear them a mile.

"Boys, we'll split a watermelon on that," says the Child of Calamity; and he came rummaging around in the dark amongst the shingle bundles where I was, and put his hand on me. I was warm and soft and naked; so he says "Ouch!" and jumped back.

"Fetch a lantern or a chunk of fire here, boys—there's a snake here as big as a cow!"

So they run there with a lantern, and crowded up and looked in on me.

"Come out of that, you beggar!" says one.

"Who are you?" says another.

"What are you after here? Speak up prompt, or overboard you go."

"Snake him out, boys. Snatch him out by the heels."

I began to beg, and crept out amongst them trembling. They looked me over, wondering, and the Child of Calamity says:

"A cussed thief! Lend a hand and less heave him overboard!"

"No," says Big Bob, "less get out the paint-pot and paint him a sky-blue all over from head to heel, and *then* heave him over."

"Good! that's it. Go for the paint, Jimmy."

When the paint come, and Bob took the brush and was just going to begin, the others laughing and rubbing their hands, I begun to cry, and that sort of worked on Davy, and he says:

" 'Vast there. He's nothing but a cub. I'll paint the man that teches him!"

So I looked around on them, and some of them grumbled and growled, and Bob put down the paint, and the others didn't take it up.

"Come here to the fire, and less see what you're up to here," says Davy. "Now set down there and give an account of yourself. How long have you been aboard here?"

"Not over a quarter of a minute, sir," says I.

"How did you get dry so quick?"

"I don't know, sir. I'm always that way, mostly."

"Oh, you are, are you? What's your name?"

I warn't going to tell my name. I didn't know what to say, so I just says:

"Charles William Allbright, sir."

Then they roared—the whole crowd; and I was mighty glad I said that, because, maybe, laughing would get them in a better humor.

When they got done laughing, Davy says:

"It won't hardly do, Charles William. You couldn't have growed this much in five year, and you was a baby when you come out of the bar'l, you know, and dead at that. Come, now, tell a straight story, and nobody'll hurt you, if you ain't up to anything wrong. What *is* your name?"

"Aleck Hopkins, sir. Aleck James Hopkins."

"Well, Aleck, where did you come from, here?"

"From a trading-scow. She lays up the bend yonder. I was born on her. Pap has traded up and down here all his life; and he told me to swim off here, because when you went by he said he would like to get some of you to speak to a Mr. Jonas Turner, in Cairo, and tell him—"

"Oh, come!"

"Yes, sir, it's as true as the world. Pap he says—"

"Oh, your grandmother!"

They all laughed, and I tried again to talk, but they broke in on me and stopped me.

"Now, looky-here," says Davy; "you're scared, and so you talk wild. Honest, now, do you live in a scow, or is it a lie?"

"Yes, sir, in a trading-scow. She lays up at the head of the bend. But I warn't born in her. It's our first trip."

"Now you're talking! What did you come aboard here for? To steal?"

"No sir, I didn't. It was only to get a ride on the raft. All boys does that."

"Well, I know that. But what did you hide for?"

"Sometimes they drive the boys off."

"So they do. They might steal. Looky-here; if we let you off this time, will you keep out of these kind of scrapes hereafter?"

" 'Deed I will, boss. You try me."

"All right, then. You ain't but little ways from shore. Overboard with you, and don't you make a fool of yourself another time this way. Blast it, boy, some raftsmen would rawhide you till you were black and blue!"

I didn't wait to kiss good-by, but went overboard and broke for shore. When Jim come along by and by, the big raft was away out of sight around the point. I swum out and got aboard, and was mighty glad to see home again.[2]

There warn't nothing to do, now, but to look out sharp for the town, and not pass it without seeing it. He said he'd be mighty sure to see it, because he'd be a free man the minute he seen it, but if he missed it he'd be in the slave country again and no more show for freedom. Every little while he jumps up and says:

"Dah she is!"

But it warn't. It was Jack-o-lanterns, or lightning-bugs; so he set down again, and went to watching, same as before. Jim said it made him all over trembly and feverish to be so close to freedom. Well, I can tell you it made me all over trembly and feverish, too, to hear him, because I begun to get it through my head that he *was* most free—and who was to blame for it? Why, *me*. I couldn't get that out of my conscience, no how nor no way. It got to troubling me so I couldn't rest; I couldn't stay still in one place. It hadn't ever come home to me before, what this thing was that I was doing. But now it did; and it staid with me, and scorched me more and more. I tried to make out to myself that *I* warn't to blame, because I didn't run Jim off from his rightful owner; but it warn't no use, conscience up and says, every time, "But you knowed he was running for his freedom, and you could a paddled ashore and told somebody." That was so—I couldn't get around that, noway. That was where it

2. End of the interpolated passage.

pinched. Conscience says to me, "What had poor Miss Watson done to you, that you could see her nigger go off right under your eyes and never say one single word? What did that poor old woman do to you, that you could treat her so mean? Why, she tried to learn you your book, she tried to learn you your manners, she tried to be good to you every way she knowed how. *That's* what she done."

I got to feeling so mean and so miserable I most wished I was dead. I fidgeted up and down the raft, abusing myself to myself, and Jim was fidgeting up and down past me. We neither of us could keep still. Every time he danced around and says, "Dah's Cairo!" it went through me like a shot, and I thought if it *was* Cairo I reckoned I would die of miserableness.

Jim talked out loud all the time while I was talking to myself. He was saying how the first thing he would do when he got to a free State he would go to saving up money and never spend a single cent, and when he got enough he would buy his wife, which was owned on a farm close to where Miss Watson lived; and then they would both work to buy the two children, and if their master wouldn't sell them, they'd get an Ab'litionist to go and steal them.

It most froze me to hear such talk. He wouldn't ever dared to talk such talk in his life before. Just see what a difference it made in him the minute he judged he was about free. It was according to the old saying, "give a nigger an inch and he'll take an ell." Thinks I, this is what comes of my not thinking. Here was this nigger which I had as good as helped to run away, coming right out flat-footed and saying he would steal his children—children that belonged to a man I didn't even know; a man that hadn't ever done me no harm.

I was sorry to hear Jim say that, it was such a lowering of him. My conscience got to stirring me up hotter than ever, until at last I says to it, "Let up on me—it ain't too late, yet—I'll paddle ashore at the first light, and tell." I felt easy, and happy, and light as a feather, right off. All my troubles was gone. I went to looking out sharp for a light, and sort of singing to myself. By-and-by one showed. Jim sings out:

"We's safe, Huck, we's safe! Jump up and crack yo' heels, dat's de good ole Cairo at las', I jis knows it!"

I says:

"I'll take the canoe and go see, Jim. It mightn't be, you know."

He jumped and got the canoe ready, and put his old coat in the bottom for me to set on, and give me the paddle; and as I shoved off, he says:

"Pooty soon I'll be a-shout'n for joy, en I'll say, it's all on accounts o' Huck; I's a free man, en I couldn't ever ben free ef it hadn' ben for Huck; Huck done it. Jim won't ever forgit you, Huck;

you's de bes' fren' Jim's ever had; en you's de *only* fren' ole Jim's got now."

I was paddling off, all in a sweat to tell on him; but when he says this, it seemed to kind of take the tuck all out of me. I went along slow then, and I warn't right down certain whether I was glad I started or whether I warn't. When I was fifty yards off, Jim says:

"Dah you goes, de ole true Huck; de on'y white genlman dat ever kep' his promise to ole Jim."

Well, I just felt sick. But I says, I *got* to do it—I can't get *out* of it. Right then, along comes a skiff with two men in it, with guns, and they stopped and I stopped. One of them says:

"What's that, yonder?"

"A piece of raft," I says.

"Do you belong on it?"

"Yes, sir."

"Any men on it?"

"Only one, sir."

"Well, there's five niggers run off to-night, up yonder above the head of the bend. Is your man white or black?"

I didn't answer up prompt. I tried to, but the words wouldn't come. I tried, for a second or two, to brace up and out with it, but I warn't man enough—hadn't the spunk of a rabbit. I see I was weakening; so I just give up trying, and up and says—

"He's white."

"I reckon we'll go and see for ourselves."

"I wish you would," says I, "because it's pap that's there, and maybe you'd help me tow the raft ashore where the light is. He's sick—and so is mam and Mary Ann."

"Oh, the devil! we're in a hurry, boy. But I s'pose we've got to. Come—buckle to your paddle, and let's get along."

I buckled to my paddle and they laid to their oars. When we had made a stroke or two, I says:

"Pap'll be mighty much obleeged to you, I can tell you. Everybody goes away when I want them to help me tow the raft ashore, and I can't do it myself."

"Well, that's infernal mean. Odd, too. Say, boy, what's the matter with your father?"

"It's the—a—the—well, it ain't anything, much."

They stopped pulling. It warn't but a mighty little ways to the raft, now. One says:

"Boy, that's a lie. What *is* the matter with your pap? Answer up square, now, and it'll be the better for you."

"I will, sir, I will, honest—but don't leave us, please. It's the—the—gentlemen, if you'll only pull ahead, and let me heave you the head-line, you won't have to come a-near the raft—please do."

"Set her back, John, set her back!" says one. They backed water.

"Keep away, boy—keep to looard.[3] Confound it, I just expect the wind has blowed it to us. Your pap's got the small-pox,[4] and you know it precious well. Why didn't you come out and say so? Do you want to spread it all over?"

"Well," says I, a-blubbering, "I've told everybody before, and then they just went away and left us."

"Poor devil, there's something in that. We are right down sorry for you, but we—well, hang it, we don't want the small-pox, you see. Look here, I'll tell you what to do. Don't you try to land by yourself, or you'll smash everything to pieces. You float along down about twenty miles and you'll come to a town on the left-hand side of the river. It will be long after sun-up, then, and when you ask for help, you tell them your folks are all down with chills and fever. Don't be a fool again, and let people guess what is the matter. Now we're trying to do you a kindness; so you just put twenty miles between us, that's a good boy. It wouldn't do any good to land yonder where the light is—it's only a wood-yard. Say—I reckon your father's poor, and I'm bound to say he's in pretty hard luck. Here—I'll put a twenty dollar gold piece on this board, and you get it when it floats by. I feel mighty mean to leave you, but my kingdom! it won't do to fool with small-pox, don't you see?"

"Hold on, Parker," says the other man, "here's a twenty to put on the board for me. Good-bye boy, you do as Mr. Parker told you, and you'll be all right."

"That's so, my boy—good-bye, good-bye. If you see any runaway niggers, you get help and nab them, and you can make some money by it."

"Good-bye, sir," says I, "I won't let no runaway niggers get by me if I can help it."

They went off, and I got aboard the raft, feeling bad and low, because I knowed very well I had done wrong, and I see it warn't no use for me to try to learn to do right; a body that don't get *started* right when he's little, ain't got no show—when the pinch comes there ain't nothing to back him up and keep him to his work, and so he gets beat. Then I thought a minute, and says to myself, hold on,—s'pose you'd a done right and give Jim up; would you felt better than what you do now? No, says I, I'd feel bad—I'd feel just the same way I do now. Well, then, says I, what's the use you learning to do right, when it's troublesome to do right and ain't no trouble to do wrong, and the wages is just the same? I was stuck. I couldn't answer that. So I reckoned I wouldn't bother no more about it, but after this always do whichever come handiest at the time.

---

3. Nautical spelling of *leeward*.
4. At the time a highly infectious, often fatal disease.

I went into the wigwam; Jim warn't there. I looked all around; he warn't anywhere. I says:

"Jim!"

"Here I is, Huck. Is dey out o' sight yit? Don't talk loud."

He was in the river, under the stern oar, with just his nose out. I told him they was out of sight, so he come aboard. He says:

"I was a-listenin' to all de talk, en I slips into de river en was gwyne to shove for sho' if dey come aboard. Den I was gwyne to swim to de raf' agin when dey was gone. But lawsy, how you did fool 'em, Huck! Dat *wuz* de smartes' dodge! I tell you, chile, I 'speck it save' ole Jim—ole Jim ain't gwyne to forgit you for dat, honey."

Then we talked about the money. It was a pretty good raise, twenty dollars apiece. Jim said we could take deck passage on a steamboat now, and the money would last us as far as we wanted to go in the free States. He said twenty mile more warn't far for the raft to go, but he wished we was already there.

Towards daybreak we tied up, and Jim was mighty particular about hiding the raft good. Then he worked all day fixing things in bundles, and getting all ready to quit rafting.

That night about ten we hove in sight of the lights of a town away down in a left-hand bend.

I went off in the canoe, to ask about it. Pretty soon I found a man out in the river with a skiff, setting a trot-line. I ranged up and says:

"Mister, is that town Cairo?"

"Cairo? no. You must be a blame' fool."

"What town is it, mister?"

"If you want to know, go and find out. If you stay here botherin' around me for about a half a minute longer, you'll get something you won't want."

I paddled to the raft. Jim was awful disappointed, but I said never mind, Cairo would be the next place, I reckoned.

We passed another town before daylight, and I was going out again; but it was high ground, so I didn't go. No high ground about Cairo, Jim said. I had forgot it. We laid up for the day, on a tow-head tolerable close to the left-hand bank. I begun to suspicion something. So did Jim. I says:

"Maybe we went by Cairo in the fog that night."

He says:

"Doan' less' talk about it, Huck. Po' niggers can't have no luck. I awluz 'spected dat rattle-snake skin warn't done wid it's work."

"I wish I'd never seen that snake-skin, Jim—I do wish I'd never laid eyes on it."

"It ain't yo' fault, Huck; you didn' know. Don't you blame y'self 'bout it."

When it was daylight, here was the clear Ohio water in shore, sure enough, and outside was the old regular Muddy! So it was all up with Cairo.[5]

We talked it all over. It wouldn't do to take to the shore; we couldn't take the raft up the stream, of course. There warn't no way but to wait for dark, and start back in the canoe and take the chances. So we slept all day amongst the cotton-wood thicket, so as to be fresh for the work, and when we went back to the raft about dark the canoe was gone!

We didn't say a word for a good while. There warn't anything to say. We both knowed well enough it was some more work of the rattle-snake skin; so what was the use to talk about it? It would only look like we was finding fault, and that would be bound to fetch more bad luck—and keep on fetching it, too, till we knowed enough to keep still.

By-and-by we talked about what we better do, and found there warn't no way but just to go along down with the raft till we got a chance to buy a canoe to go back in. We warn't going to borrow it when there warn't anybody around, the way pap would do, for that might set people after us.

So we shoved out, after dark, on the raft.[6]

Anybody that don't believe yet, that it's foolishness to handle a snake-skin, after all that that snake-skin done for us, will believe it now, if they read on and see what more it done for us.

The place to buy canoes is off of rafts laying up at shore. But we didn't see no rafts laying up; so we went along during three hours and more. Well, the night got gray, and ruther thick, which is the next meanest thing to fog. You can't tell the shape of the river, and you can't see no distance. It got to be very late and still, and then along comes a steamboat up the river. We lit the lantern, and judged she would see it. Up-stream boats didn't generly come close to us; they go out and follow the bars and hunt for easy water under the reefs; but nights like this they bull right up the channel against the whole river.

We could hear her pounding along, but we didn't see her good till she was close. She aimed right for us. Often they do that and try to see how close they can come without touching; sometimes the wheel bites off a sweep, and then the pilot sticks his head out and laughs, and thinks he's mighty smart. Well, here she comes, and we said she was going to try to shave us; but she didn't seem to

5. Since Cairo is located at the confluence of the Ohio and Mississippi rivers, which in turn lies below the confluence of the Missouri (Big Muddy) and Mississippi, they know that they have passed Cairo and lost the opportunity to sell the raft and travel up the Ohio by steamboat to freedom.
6. Clemens was "stuck" at this point in the writing of the novel and put the 400-page manuscript aside for approximately three years. In the winter of 1879–80 he added the two chapters dealing with the feud (XVII and XVIII) and then the three chapters (XIX–XXI) in which the king and duke enter the story and for a time dominate the action. The novel was not completed until 1883, when Clemens wrote the last half of the novel in a few months of concentrated writing. As late as 1882, he was not confident he would ever complete the book. See Walter Blair, *Mark Twain and "Huck Finn"* (Berkeley, 1960).

be sheering off a bit. She was a big one, and she was coming in a hurry, too, looking like a black cloud with rows of glow-worms around it; but all of a sudden she bulged out, big and scary, with a long row of wide-open furnace doors shining like red-hot teeth, and her monstrous bows and guards hanging right over us. There was a yell at us, and a jingling of bells to stop the engines, a pow-wow of cussing, and whistling of steam—and as Jim went overboard on one side and I on the other, she come smashing straight through the raft.

I dived—and I aimed to find the bottom, too, for a thirty-foot wheel had got to go over me, and I wanted it to have plenty of room. I could always stay under water a minute; this time I reckon I staid under water a minute and a half. Then I bounced for the top in a hurry, for I was nearly busting. I popped out to my arm-pits and blowed the water out of my nose, and puffed a bit. Of course there was a booming current; and of course that boat started her engines again ten seconds after she stopped them, for they never cared much for raftsmen; so now she was churning along up the river, out of sight in the thick weather, though I could hear her.

I sung out for Jim about a dozen times, but I didn't get any answer; so I grabbed a plank that touched me while I was "treading water," and struck out for shore, shoving it ahead of me. But I made out to see that the drift of the current was towards the left-hand shore,[7] which meant that I was in a crossing; so I changed off and went that way.

It was one of these long, slanting, two-mile crossings; so I was a good long time in getting over. I made a safe landing, and clum up the bank. I couldn't see but a little ways, but I went poking along over rough ground for a quarter of a mile or more, and then I run across a big old-fashioned double log house before I noticed it. I was going to rush by and get away, but a lot of dogs jumped out and went to howling and barking at me, and I knowed better than to move another peg.

Chapter XVII

In about half a minute somebody spoke out of a window, without putting his head out, and says:

"Be done, boys! Who's there?"

I says:

"It's me."

"Who's me?"

"George Jackson, sir."

"What do you want?"

"I don't want nothing, sir. I only want to go along by, but the dogs won't let me."

---

7. Kentucky, where the feud in Chapters XVII and VXIII is set.

"What are you prowling around here this time of night, for—hey?"

"I warn't prowling around, sir; I fell overboard off of the steamboat."

"Oh, you did, did you? Strike a light there, somebody. What did you say your name was?"

"George Jackson, sir. I'm only a boy."

"Look here; if you're telling the truth, you needn't be afraid—nobody'll hurt you. But don't try to budge; stand right where you are. Rouse our Bob and Tom, some of you, and fetch the guns. George Jackson, is there anybody with you?"

"No, sir, nobody."

I heard the people stirring around in the house, now, and see a light. The man sung out:

"Snatch that light away, Betsy, you old fool—ain't you got any sense? Put it on the floor behind the front door. Bob, if you and Tom are ready, take your places."

"All ready."

"Now, George Jackson, do you know the Shepherdsons?"

"No, sir—I never heard of them."

"Well, that may be so, and it mayn't. Now, all ready. Step forward, George Jackson. And mind, don't you hurry—come mighty slow. If there's anybody with you, let him keep back—if he shows himself he'll be shot. Come along, now. Come slow; push the door open, yourself—just enough to squeeze in, d' you hear?"

I didn't hurry, I couldn't if I'd a wanted to. I took one slow step at a time, and there warn't a sound, only I thought I could hear my heart. The dogs were as still as the humans, but they followed a little behind me. When I got to the three log door-steps, I heard them unlocking and unbarring and unbolting. I put my hand on the door and pushed it a little and a little more, till somebody said, "There, that's enough—put your head in." I done it, but I judged they would take it off.

The candle was on the floor, and there they all was, looking at me, and me at them, for about a quarter of a minute. Three big men with guns pointed at me, which made me wince, I tell you; the oldest, gray and about sixty, the other two thirty or more—all of them fine and handsome—and the sweetest old gray-headed lady, and back of her two young women which I couldn't see right well. The old gentleman says:

"There—I reckon it's all right. Come in."

As soon as I was in, the old gentleman he locked the door and barred it and bolted it, and told the young men to come in with their guns, and they all went in a big parlor that had a new rag carpet on the floor, and got together in a corner that was out of range of the front windows—there warn't none on the side. They held the candle, and took a good look at me, and all said, "Why *he*

ain't a Shepherdson—no, there ain't any Shepherdson about him."
Then the old man said he hoped I wouldn't mind being searched
for arms, because he didn't mean no harm by it—it was only to
make sure. So he didn't pry into my pockets, but only felt outside
with his hands, and said it was all right. He told me to make myself
easy and at home, and tell all about myself; but the old lady says:

"Why bless you, Saul, the poor thing's as wet as he can be; and
don't you reckon it may be he's hungry?"

"True for you, Rachel—I forgot."

So the old lady says:

"Betsy" (this was a nigger woman), "you fly around and get him
something to eat, as quick as you can, poor thing; and one of you
girls go and wake up Buck and tell him— Oh, here he is himself.
Buck, take this little stranger and get the wet clothes off from him
and dress him up in some of yours that's dry."

Buck looked about as old as me—thirteen or fourteen[8] or along
there, though he was a little bigger than me. He hadn't on anything
but a shirt, and he was very frowsy-headed. He come in gaping and
digging one fist into his eyes, and he was dragging a gun along with
the other one. He says:

"Ain't they no Shepherdsons around?"

They said, no, 'twas a false alarm.

"Well," he says, "if they'd a ben some, I reckon I'd a got one."

They all laughed, and Bob says:

"Why, Buck, they might have scalped us all, you've been so slow
in coming."

"Well, nobody come after me, and it ain't right. I'm always kep'
down; I don't get no show."

"Never mind, Buck, my boy," says the old man, "you'll have
show enough, all in good time, don't you fret about that. Go 'long
with you now, and do as your mother told you."

When we got up stairs to his room, he got me a coarse shirt and
a roundabout[9] and pants of his, and I put them on. While I was at
it he asked me what my name was, but before I could tell him, he
started to telling me about a blue jay and a young rabbit he had
catched in the woods day before yesterday, and he asked me where
Moses was when the candle went out. I said I didn't know; I hadn't
heard about it before, no way.

"Well, guess," he says.

"How'm I going to guess," says I, "when I never heard tell about
it before?"

"But you can guess, can't you? It's just as easy."

"*Which* candle?" I says.

"Why, any candle," he says.

8. Clemens identifies Huck as "a boy of 14" in a notebook.
9. Short, close-fitting jacket.

"I don't know where he was," says I; "where was he?"

"Why he was in the *dark!* That's where he was!"

"Well, if you knowed where he was, what did you ask me for?"

"Why, blame it, it's a riddle, don't you see? Say, how long are you going to stay here? You got to stay always. We can just have booming times—they don't have no school now. Do you own a dog? I've got a dog—and he'll go in the river and bring out chips that you throw in. Do you like to comb up, Sundays, and all that kind of foolishness? You bet I don't, but ma she makes me. Confound these ole britches, I reckon I'd better put 'em on, but I'd ruther not, it's so warm. Are you all ready? All right—come along, old hoss."

Cold corn-pone, cold corn-beef, butter and butter-milk—that is what they had for me down there, and there ain't nothing better that ever I've come across yet. Buck and his ma and all of them smoked cob pipes, except the nigger woman, which was gone, and the two young women. They all smoked and talked, and I eat and talked. The young women had quilts around them, and their hair down their backs. They all asked me questions, and I told them how pap and me and all the family was living on a little farm down at the bottom of Arkansaw, and my sister Mary Ann run off and got married and never was heard of no more, and Bill went to hunt them and he warn't heard of no more, and Tom and Mort died, and then there warn't nobody but just me and pap left, and he was just trimmed down to nothing, on account of his troubles; so when he died I took what there was left, because the farm didn't belong to us, and started up the river, deck passage, and fell overboard; and that was how I come to be here. So they said I could have a home there as long as I wanted it. Then it was most daylight, and everybody went to bed, and I went to bed with Buck, and when I waked up in the morning, drat it all, I had forgot what my name was. So I laid there about an hour trying to think, and when Buck waked up, I says:

"Can you spell, Buck?"

"Yes," he says.

"I bet you can't spell my name," says I.

"I bet you what you dare I can," says he.

"All right," says I, "go ahead."

"G-o-r-g-e J-a-x-o-n—there now," he says.

"Well," says I, "you done it, but I didn't think you could. It ain't no slouch of a name to spell—right off without studying."

I set it down, private, because somebody might want *me* to spell it, next, and so I wanted to be handy with it and rattle it off like I was used to it.

It was a mighty nice family, and a mighty nice house, too. I hadn't seen no house out in the country before that was so nice and had so much style.[1] It didn't have an iron latch on the front door, nor a wooden one with a buckskin string, but a brass knob to turn, the same as houses in a town. There warn't no bed in the parlor, not a sign of a bed; but heaps of parlors in towns has beds in them. There was a big fireplace that was bricked on the bottom, and the bricks was kept clean and red by pouring water on them and scrubbing them with another brick; sometimes they washed them over with red water-paint that they call Spanish-brown, same as they do in town. They had big brass dog-irons that could hold up a saw-log.[2] There was a clock on the middle of the mantel-piece, with a picture of a town painted on the bottom half of the glass front, and a round place in the middle of it for the sun, and you could see the pendulum swing behind it. It was beautiful to hear that clock tick; and sometimes when one of these peddlers had been along and scoured her up and got her in good shape, she would start in and strike a hundred and fifty before she got tuckered out. They wouldn't took any money for her.

Well, there was a big outlandish parrot on each side of the clock, made out of something like chalk, and painted up gaudy. By one of the parrots was a cat made of crockery, and a crockery dog by the other; and when you pressed down on them they squeaked, but didn't open their mouths nor look different nor interested. They squeaked through underneath. There was a couple of big wild-turkey-wing fans spread out behind those things. On a table in the middle of the room was a kind of a lovely crockery basket that had apples and oranges and peaches and grapes piled up in it which was much redder and yellower and prettier than real ones is, but they warn't real because you could see where pieces had got chipped off and showed the white chalk or whatever it was, underneath.

This table had a cover made out of beautiful oil-cloth, with a red and blue spread-eagle painted on it, and a painted border all around. It come all the way from Philadelphia, they said. There was some books too, piled up perfectly exact, on each corner of the table. One was a big family Bible, full of pictures. One was "Pilgrim's Progress," about a man that left his family it didn't say why. I read considerable in it now and then. The statements was interesting, but tough. Another was "Friendship's Offering," full of beautiful stuff and poetry; but I didn't read the poetry. Another was Henry Clay's Speeches, and another was Dr. Gunn's Family Medicine, which told you all about what to do if a body was sick or dead. There was a Hymn Book, and a lot of other books.[3] And

1. Every detail of the furniture, furnishing, and decoration as well as the dress, speech, manners, and mores of the Grangerford household is carefully selected to epitomize satirically pre–Civil War culture of the lower Mississippi valley.
2. A log large enough to be sawed into planks.
3. The neatly stacked, unread books are meant to define the values and tastes of the time and place: the Bible, Bunyan's *Pilgrim's Progress,* and the Hymn Book establish Calvinistic piety; Clay's speeches suggest political orthodoxy; Gunn's *Domestic Medicine* suggests popular notions of science and medical practice; *Friendship's Offering* was a popular gift book.

there was nice split-bottom chairs, and perfectly sound, too—not bagged down in the middle and busted, like an old basket.

They had pictures hung on the walls—mainly Washingtons and Lafayettes, and battles, and Highland Marys,[4] and one called "Signing the Declaration." There was some that they called crayons, which one of the daughters which was dead made her own self when she was only fifteen years old. They was different from any pictures I ever see before; blacker, mostly, than is common. One was a woman in a slim black dress, belted small under the armpits, with bulges like a cabbage in the middle of the sleeves, and a large black scoop-shovel bonnet with a black veil, and white slim ankles crossed about with black tape, and very wee black slippers, like a chisel, and she was leaning pensive on a tombstone on her right elbow, under a weeping willow, and her other hand hanging down her side holding a white handkerchief and a reticule, and underneath the picture it said "Shall I Never See Thee More Alas." Another one was a young lady with her hair all combed up straight to the top of her head, and knotted there in front of a comb like a chair-back, and she was crying into a handkerchief and had a dead bird laying on its back in her other hand with its heels up, and underneath the picture it said "I Shall Never Hear Thy Sweet Chirrup More Alas." There was one where a young lady was at a window looking up at the moon, and tears running down her cheeks; and she had an open letter in one hand with black sealing-wax showing on one edge of it, and she was mashing a locket with a chain to it against her mouth, and underneath the picture it said "And Art Thou Gone Yes Thou Art Gone Alas." These was all nice pictures, I reckon, but I didn't somehow seem to take to them, because if ever I was down a little, they always give me the fan-tods. Everybody was sorry she died, because she had laid out a lot more of these pictures to do, and a body could see by what she had done what they had lost. But I reckoned, that with her disposition, she was having a better time in the graveyard. She was at work on what they said was her greatest picture when she took sick, and every day and every night it was her prayer to be allowed to live till she got it done, but she never got the chance. It was a picture of a young woman in a long white gown, standing on the rail of a bridge all ready to jump off, with her hair all down her back, and looking up to the moon, with the tears running down her face, and she had two arms folded across her breast, and two arms stretched out in front, and two more reaching up towards the moon—and the idea was, to see which pair would look best and then scratch out all the other arms; but, as I was saying, she died before she got her mind made up, and now they kept this picture over the head of the bed

4. The pictures similarly typify the culture of the region in the 1840s and 1850s. "Highland Mary" depicts poet Robert Burns's first love, who died a few months after they met. He memorialized her in several poems, especially *To Mary in Heaven.*

in her room, and every time her birthday come they hung flowers on it. Other times it was hid with a little curtain. The young woman in the picture had a kind of a nice sweet face, but there was so many arms it made her look too spidery, seemed to me.

This young girl kept a scrap-book when she was alive, and used to paste obituaries and accidents and cases of patient suffering in it out of the *Presbyterian Observer*, and write poetry after them out of her own head. It was very good poetry.[5] This is what she wrote about a boy by the name of Stephen Dowling Bots that fell down a well and was drownded:

ODE TO STEPHEN DOWLING BOTS, DEC'D

And did the mourners cry?
   And did young Stephen die?
And did the sad hearts thicken,
   And did young Stephen sicken,

No; such was not the fate of
   Young Stephen Dowling Bots;
Though sad hearts round him thickened,
   'Twas not from sickness' shots.

No whooping-cough did rack his frame,
   Nor measles drear, with spots;
Not these impaired the sacred name
   Of Stephen Dowling Bots.

Despised love struck not with woe
   That head of curly knots,
Nor stomach troubles laid him low,
   Young Stephen Dowling Bots.

O no. Then list with tearful eye,
   Whilst I his fate do tell.
His soul did from this cold world fly,
   By falling down a well.

They got him out and emptied him;
   Alas it was too late;
His spirit was gone for to sport aloft
   In the realms of the good and great.

If Emmeline Grangerford could make poetry like that before she was fourteen, there ain't no telling what she could a done by-and-

5. This parody derives in particular from two poems by "The Sweet Singer of Michigan," Julia A. Moore (1847–1920), whose sentimental poetry was popular at the time Clemens was writing *Huck Finn*. In one of the two poems, *Little Libbie*, the heroine "was choken on a piece of beef." The graveyard and obituary (or "sadful") schools of popular poetry are much older and widespread. See Walter Blair, *Mark Twain and "Huck Finn"* (Berkeley, 1960).

by. Buck said she could rattle off poetry like nothing. She didn't ever have to stop to think. He said she would slap down a line, and if she couldn't find anything to rhyme with it she would just scratch it out and slap down another one, and go ahead. She warn't particular, she could write about anything you choose to give her to write about, just so it was sadful. Every time a man died, or a woman died, or a child died, she would be on hand with her "tribute" before he was cold. She called them tributes. The neighbors said it was the doctor first, then Emmeline, then the undertaker—the undertaker never got in ahead of Emmeline but once, and then she hung fire on a rhyme for the dead person's name, which was Whistler. She warn't ever the same, after that; she never complained, but she kind of pined away and did not live long. Poor thing, many's the time I made myself go up to the little room that used to be hers and get out her poor old scrapbook and read in it when her pictures had been aggravating me and I had soured on her a little. I liked all that family, dead ones and all, and warn't going to let anything come between us. Poor Emmeline made poetry about all the dead people when she was alive, and it didn't seem right that there warn't nobody to make some about her, now she was gone; so I tried to sweat out a verse or two myself, but I couldn't seem to make it go, somehow. They kept Emmeline's room trim and nice and all the things fixed in it just the way she liked to have them when she was alive, and nobody ever slept there. The old lady took care of the room herself, though there was plenty of niggers, and she sewed there a good deal and read her Bible there, mostly.

Well, as I was saying about the parlor, there was beautiful curtains on the windows: white, with pictures painted on them, of castles with vines all down the walls, and cattle coming down to drink. There was a little old piano, too, that had tin pans in it, I reckon, and nothing was ever so lovely as to hear the young ladies sing, "The Last Link is Broken" and play "The Battle of Prague"[6] on it. The walls of all the rooms was plastered, and most had carpets on the floors, and the whole house was whitewashed on the outside.

It was a double house, and the big open place betwixt them was roofed and floored, and sometimes the table was set there in the middle of the day, and it was a cool, comfortable place. Nothing couldn't be better. And warn't the cooking good, and just bushels of it too!

Chapter XVIII

Col. Grangerford was a gentleman, you see. He was a gentleman all over; and so was his family. He was well born, as the saying is, and that's worth as much in a man as it is in a horse, so the Widow

---

6. William Clifton's *The Last Link Is Broken* was published about 1840; it is the musical equivalent of Mrs. Moore's poetry. *The Battle of Prague*, written by Czech composer Franz Kotswara in about 1788, is a bloody story told in clichéd style. Clemens first heard it in 1878.

Douglas said, and nobody ever denied that she was of the first aristocracy in our town; and pap he always said it, too, though he warn't no more quality than a mudcat,[7] himself. Col. Grangerford was very tall and very slim, and had a darkish-paly complexion, not a sign of red in it anywheres; he was clean-shaved every morning, all over his thin face, and he had the thinnest kind of lips, and the thinnest kind of nostrils, and a high nose, and heavy eyebrows, and the blackest kind of eyes, sunk so deep back that they seemed like they was looking out of caverns at you, as you may say. His forehead was high, and his hair was black and straight, and hung to his shoulders. His hands was long and thin, and every day of his life he put on a clean shirt and a full suit from head to foot made out of linen so white it hurt your eyes to look at it; and on Sundays he wore a blue tail-coat with brass buttons on it. He carried a mahogany cane with a silver head to it. There warn't no frivolishness about him, not a bit, and he warn't ever loud. He was as kind as he could be—you could feel that, you know, and so you had confidence. Sometimes he smiled, and it was good to see; but when he straightened himself up like a liberty-pole,[8] and the lightning begun to flicker out from under his eyebrows you wanted to climb a tree first, and find out what the matter was afterwards. He didn't ever have to tell anybody to mind their manners—everybody was always good mannered where he was. Everybody loved to have him around, too; he was sunshine most always—I mean he made it seem like good weather. When he turned into a cloud-bank it was awful dark for a half a minute and that was enough; there wouldn't nothing go wrong again for a week.

When him and the old lady come down in the morning, all the family got up out of their chairs and give them good-day, and didn't set down again till they had set down. Then Tom and Bob went to the sideboard where the decanters was, and mixed a glass of bitters and handed it to him, and he held it in his hand and waited till Tom's and Bob's was mixed, and then they bowed and said "Our duty to you, sir, and madam;" and *they* bowed the least bit in the world and said thank you, and so they drank, all three, and Bob and Tom poured a spoonful of water on the sugar and the mite of whisky or apple brandy in the bottom of their tumblers, and give it to me and Buck, and we drank to the old people too.

Bob was the oldest, and Tom next. Tall, beautiful men with very broad shoulders and brown faces, and long black hair and black eyes. They dressed in white linen from head to foot, like the old gentleman, and wore broad Panama hats.

Then there was Miss Charlotte, she was twenty-five, and tall and proud and grand, but as good as she could be, when she warn't

7. General term for a number of species of catfish; in this context the lowliest and least esteemed.
8. Flagpole.

stirred up; but when she was, she had a look that would make you wilt in your tracks, like her father. She was beautiful.

So was her sister, Miss Sophia, but it was a different kind. She was gentle and sweet, like a dove, and she was only twenty.

Each person had their own nigger to wait on them—Buck, too. My nigger had a monstrous easy time, because I warn't used to having anybody do anything for me, but Buck's was on the jump most of the time.

This was all there was of the family, now; but there used to be more—three sons; they got killed; and Emmeline that died.

The old gentleman owned a lot of farms, and over a hundred niggers. Sometimes a stack of people would come there, horseback, from ten or fifteen mile around, and stay five or six days, and have such junketings round about and on the river, and dances and picnics in the woods, day-times, and balls at the house, nights. These people was mostly kin-folks of the family. The men brought their guns with them. It was a handsome lot of quality, I tell you.

There was another clan of aristocracy around there—five or six families—mostly of the name of Shepherdson. They was as high-toned, and well born, and rich and grand, as the tribe of Granger-fords. The Shepherdsons and the Grangerfords used the same steamboat landing, which was about two mile above our house; so sometimes when I went up there with a lot of our folks I used to see a lot of Shepherdsons there, on their fine horses.

One day Buck and me was away out in the woods, hunting, and heard a horse coming. We was crossing the road. Buck says:

"Quick! Jump for the woods!"

We done it, and then peeped down the woods through the leaves. Pretty soon a splendid young man come galloping down the road, setting his horse easy and looking like a soldier. He had his gun across his pommel. I had seen him before. It was young Harney Shepherdson. I heard Buck's gun go off at my ear, and Harney's hat tumbled off from his head. He grabbed his gun and rode straight to the place where we was hid. But we didn't wait. We started through the woods on a run. The woods warn't thick, so I looked over my shoulder, to dodge the bullet, and twice I seen Harney cover Buck with his gun; and then he rode away the way he come —to get his hat, I reckon, but I couldn't see. We never stopped running till we got home. The old gentleman's eyes blazed a minute —'twas pleasure, mainly, I judged—then his face sort of smoothed down, and he says, kind of gentle:

"I don't like that shooting from behind a bush. Why didn't you step into the road, my boy?"

"The Shepherdsons don't, father. They always take advantage."

Miss Charlotte she held her head up like a queen while Buck was telling his tale, and her nostrils spread and her eyes snapped. The two young men looked dark, but never said nothing. Miss Sophia she turned pale, but the color come back when she found the man warn't hurt.

Soon as I could get Buck down by the corn-cribs under the trees by ourselves, I says:

"Did you want to kill him, Buck?"

"Well, I bet I did."

"What did he do to you?"

"Him? He never done nothing to me."

"Well, then, what did you want to kill him for?"

"Why nothing—only it's on account of the feud."

"What's a feud?"

"Why, where was you raised? Don't you know what a feud is?"

"Never heard of it before—tell me about it."

"Well," says Buck, "a feud is this way. A man has a quarrel with another man, and kills him; then that other man's brother kills *him*; then the other brothers, on both sides, goes for one another; then the *cousins* chip in—and by-and-by everybody's killed off, and there ain't no more feud. But it's kind of slow, and takes a long time."

"Has this one been going on long, Buck?"

"Well I should *reckon!* it started thirty year ago, or som'ers along there. There was trouble 'bout something and then a lawsuit to settle it; and the suit went agin one of the men, and so he up and shot the man that won the suit—which he would naturally do, of course. Anybody would."

"What was the trouble about, Buck?—land?"

"I reckon maybe—I don't know."

"Well, who done the shooting?—was it a Grangerford or a Shepherdson?"

"Laws, how do *I* know? it was so long ago."

"Don't anybody know?"

"Oh, yes, pa knows, I reckon, and some of the other old folks; but they don't know, now, what the row was about in the first place."

"Has there been many killed, Buck?"

"Yes—right smart chance of funerals. But they don't always kill. Pa's got a few buck-shot in him; but he don't mind it 'cuz he don't weigh much anyway. Bob's been carved up some with a bowie, and Tom's been hurt once or twice."

"Has anybody been killed this year, Buck?"

"Yes, we got one and they got one. 'Bout three months ago, my cousin Bud, fourteen year old, was riding through the woods, on t'other side of the river, and didn't have no weapon with him, which was blame' foolishness, and in a lonesome place he hears a horse a-coming behind him, and sees old Baldy Shepherdson a-linkin' after him with his gun in his hand and his white hair a-flying in the wind; and 'stead of jumping off and taking to the brush, Bud 'lowed he could outrun him; so they had it, nip and tuck, for five mile or more, the old man a-gaining all the time; so at last Bud seen it warn't any use, so he stopped and faced around so as to have the bullet holes in front, you know, and the old man he rode up and shot him down. But he didn't git much chance to enjoy his luck, for inside of a week our folks laid *him* out."

"I reckon that old man was a coward, Buck."

"I reckon he *warn't* a coward. Not by a blame' sight. There ain't a coward amongst them Shepherdsons—not a one. And there ain't no cowards amongst the Grangerfords, either. Why, that old man kep' up his end in a fight one day, for a half an hour, against three Grangerfords, and come out winner. They was all a-horseback; he lit off of his horse and got behind a little wood-pile, and kep' his horse before him to stop the bullets; but the Grangerfords staid on their horses and capered around the old man, and peppered away at him, and he peppered away at them. Him and his horse both went home pretty leaky and crippled, but the Grangerfords had to be *fetched* home—and one of 'em was dead, and another died the next day. No, sir, if a body's out hunting for cowards, he don't want to fool away any time amongst them Shepherdsons, becuz they don't breed any of that *kind*."

Next Sunday we all went to church, about three mile, everybody a-horseback. The men took their guns along, so did Buck, and kept them between their knees or stood them handy against the wall. The Shepherdsons done the same. It was pretty ornery preaching— all about brotherly love, and such-like tiresomeness; but everybody said it was a good sermon, and they all talked it over going home, and had such a powerful lot to say about faith, and good works, and free grace, and preforeordestination,[9] and I don't know what all, that it did seem to me to be one of the roughest Sundays I had run across yet.

About an hour after dinner everybody was dozing around, some in their chairs and some in their rooms, and it got to be pretty dull. Buck and a dog was stretched out on the grass in the sun, sound asleep. I went up to our room, and judged I would take a nap myself. I found that sweet Miss Sophia standing in her door, which was next to ours, and she took me in her room and shut the door very soft, and asked me if I liked her, and I said I did; and she asked me if I would do something for her and not tell anybody, and I said I would. Then she said she'd forgot her Testament, and left it in the seat at church, between two other books and would I slip out quiet and go there and fetch it to her, and not say nothing to nobody. I said I would. So I slid out and slipped off up the road, and there warn't anybody at the church, except maybe a hog or

9. Huck combines the closely related Presbyterian terms *predestination* and *fore-ordination*.

two, for there warn't any lock on the door, and hogs likes a pun-
cheon floor[1] in summer-time because it's cool. If you notice, most
folks don't go to church only when they've got to; but a hog is different.

Says I to myself something's up—it ain't natural for a girl to be
in such a sweat about a Testament; so I give it a shake, and out
drops a little piece of paper with "*Half-past two*" wrote on it with a
pencil. I ransacked it, but couldn't find anything else. I couldn't
make anything out of that, so I put the paper in the book again,
and when I got home and up stairs, there was Miss Sophia in her
door waiting for me. She pulled me in and shut the door; then she
looked in the Testament till she found the paper, and as soon as
she read it she looked glad; and before a body could think, she
grabbed me and give me a squeeze, and said I was the best boy in
the world, and not to tell anybody. She was mighty red in the face,
for a minute, and her eyes lighted up and it made her powerful
pretty. I was a good deal astonished, but when I got my breath I
asked her what the paper was about, and she asked me if I had read
it, and I said no, and she asked me if I could read writing, and I
told her "no, only coarse-hand,"[2] and then she said the paper
warn't anything but a book-mark to keep her place, and I might go
and play now.

I went off down to the river, studying over this thing, and pretty
soon I noticed that my nigger was following along behind. When
we was out of sight of the house, he looked back and around a
second, and then comes a-running, and says:

"Mars Jawge, if you'll come down into de swamp, I'll show you a
whole stack o' water-moccasins."

Thinks I, that's mighty curious; he said that yesterday. He oughter know a body don't love water-moccasins enough to go around
hunting for them. What is he up to anyway? So I says—

"All right, trot ahead."

I followed a half a mile, then he struck out over the swamp and
waded ankle deep as much as another half mile. We come to a
little flat piece of land which was dry and very thick with trees and
bushes and vines, and he says—

"You shove right in dah, jist a few steps, Mars Jawge, dah's whah
dey is. I's seed 'm befo', I don't k'yer to see 'em no mo'."

Then he slopped right along and went away, and pretty soon the
trees hid him. I poked into the place a-ways, and come to a little
open patch as big as a bedroom, all hung around with vines, and
found a man laying there asleep—and by jings it was my old Jim!

I waked him up, and I reckoned it was going to be a grand surprise to him to see me again, but it warn't. He nearly cried, he was
so glad, but he warn't surprised. Said he swum along behind me,

---

1. A crude floor made from log slabs in   rounded side is set in the dirt.
which the flat side is turned up and the   2. Block printing.

that night, and heard me yell every time, but dasn't answer, because he didn't want nobody to pick *him* up, and take him into slavery again. Says he—

"I got hurt a little, en couldn't swim fas', so I wuz a considable ways behind you, towards de las'; when you landed I reck'ned I could ketch up wid you on de lan' 'dout havin' to shout at you, but when I see dat house I begin to go slow. I 'uz off too fur to hear what dey say to you—I wuz 'fraid o' de dogs—but when it 'uz all quiet again, I knowed you's in de house, so I struck out for de woods to wait for day. Early in de mawnin' some er de niggers come along, gwyne to de fields, en dey tuck me en showed me dis place, whah de dogs can't track me on accounts o' de water, en dey brings me truck to eat every night, en tells me how you's a gitt'n along."

"Why didn't you tell my Jack to fetch me here sooner, Jim?"

"Well, 'twarn't no use to 'sturb you, Huck, tell we could do sumfn—but we's all right, now. I ben a-buyin' pots en pans en vittles, as I got a chanst, en a patchin' up de raf', nights, when—"

"*What* raft, Jim?"

"Our ole raf'."

"You mean to say our old raft warn't smashed all to flinders?"

"No, she warn't. She was tore up a good deal—one en' of her was—but dey warn't no great harm done, on'y our traps was mos' all los'. Ef we hadn' dive' so deep en swum so fur under water, en de night hadn' ben so dark, en we warn't so sk'yerd, en ben sich punkin-heads, as de sayin' is, we'd a seed de raf'. But it's jis' as well we didn't, 'kase now she's all fixed up agin mos' as good as new, en we's got a new lot o' stuff, too, in de place o' what 'uz los'."

"Why, how did you get hold of the raft again, Jim—did you catch her?"

"How I gwyne to ketch her, en I out in de woods? No, some er de niggers foun' her ketched on a snag, along heah in de ben', en dey hid her in a crick, 'mongst de willows, en dey wuz so much jawin' 'bout which un 'um she b'long to de mos', dat I come to heah 'bout it pooty soon, so I ups en settles de trouble by tellin' um she don't b'long to none uv um, but to you en me; en I ast 'm if dey gwyne to grab a young white genlman's propaty, en git a hid'n for it? Den I gin 'm ten cents apiece, en dey 'uz mighty well satisfied, en wisht some mo' raf's 'ud come along en make 'm rich agin. Dey's mighty good to me, dese niggers is, en whatever I wants 'm to do fur me, I doan' have to ast 'm twice, honey. Dat Jack's a good nigger, en pooty smart."

"Yes, he is. He ain't ever told me you was here; told me to come, and he'd show me a lot of water-moccasins. If anything happens, *he* ain't mixed up in it. He can say he never seen us together, and it'll be the truth."

I don't want to talk much about the next day. I reckon I'll cut it pretty short. I waked up about dawn, and was agoing to turn over and go to sleep again, when I noticed how still it was—didn't seem to be anybody stirring. That warn't usual. Next I noticed that Buck was up and gone. Well, I gets up, a-wondering, and goes down stairs—nobody around; everything as still as a mouse. Just the same outside; thinks I, what does it mean? Down by the wood-pile I comes across my Jack, and says:

"What's it all about?"

Says he:

"Don't you know, Mars Jawge?"

"No," says I, "I don't."

"Well, den, Miss Sophia's run off! 'deed she has. She run off in de night, sometime—nobody don't know jis' when—run off to git married to dat young Harney Shepherdson, you know—leastways, so dey 'spec. De fambly foun' it out, 'bout half an hour ago—maybe a little mo'—en' I *tell* you dey warn't no time los'. Sich another hurryin' up guns en hosses *you* never see! De women folks has gone for to stir up de relations, en ole Mars Saul en de boys tuck dey guns en rode up de river road for to try to ketch dat young man en kill him 'fo' he kin git acrost de river wid Miss Sophia. I reck'n dey's gwyne to be mighty rough times."

"Buck went off 'thout waking me up."

"Well I reck'n he *did!* Dey warn't gwyne to mix you up in it. Mars Buck he loaded up his gun en 'lowed he's gwyne to fetch home a Shepherdson or bust. Well, dey'll be plenty un 'm dah, I reck'n, en you bet you he'll fetch one ef he gits a chanst."

I took up the river road as hard as I could put. By-and-by I begin to hear guns a good ways off. When I come in sight of the log store and the wood-pile where the steamboats lands, I worked along under the trees and brush till I got to a good place, and then I clumb up into the forks of a cotton-wood that was out of reach, and watched. There was a wood-rank four foot high,[3] a little ways in front of the tree, and first I was going to hide behind that; but maybe it was luckier I didn't.

There was four or five men cavorting around on their horses in the open place before the log store, cussing and yelling, and trying to get at a couple of young chaps that was behind the wood-rank alongside of the steamboat landing—but they couldn't come it. Every time one of them showed himself on the river side of the wood-pile he got shot at. The two boys was squatting back to back behind the pile, so they could watch both ways.

By-and-by the men stopped cavorting around and yelling. They started riding towards the store; then up gets one of the boys, draws a steady bead over the wood-rank, and drops one of them out of his saddle. All the men jumped off of their horses and grabbed the hurt one and started to carry him to the store; and that minute the two boys started on the run. They got half-way to the tree I was in

3. Half a cord of stacked firewood.

before the men noticed. Then the men see them, and jumped on their horses and took out after them. They gained on the boys, but it didn't do no good, the boys had too good a start; they got to the wood-pile that was in front of my tree, and slipped in behind it, and so they had the bulge[4] on the men again. One of the boys was Buck, and the other was a slim young chap about nineteen years old.

The men ripped around awhile, and then rode away. As soon as they was out of sight, I sung out to Buck and told him. He didn't know what to make of my voice coming out of the tree, at first. He was awful surprised. He told me to watch out sharp and let him know when the men come in sight again; said they was up to some devilment or other—wouldn't be gone long. I wished I was out of that tree, but I dasn't come down. Buck begun to cry and rip, and 'lowed that him and his cousin Joe (that was the other young chap) would make up for this day, yet. He said his father and his two brothers was killed, and two or three of the enemy. Said the Shepherdsons laid for them, in ambush. Buck said his father and brothers ought to waited for their relations—the Shepherdsons was too strong for them. I asked him what was become of young Harney and Miss Sophia. He said they'd got across the river and was safe. I was glad of that; but the way Buck did take on because he didn't manage to kill Harney that day he shot at him—I hain't ever heard anything like it.

All of a sudden, bang! bang! bang! goes three or four guns—the men had slipped around through the woods and come in from behind without their horses! The boys jumped for the river—both of them hurt—and as they swum down the current the men run along the bank shooting at them and singing out, "Kill them, kill them!" It made me so sick I most fell out of the tree. I ain't agoing to tell *all* that happened—it would make me sick again if I was to do that. I wished I hadn't ever come ashore that night, to see such things. I ain't ever going to get shut of them—lots of times I dream about them.

I staid in the tree till it begun to get dark, afraid to come down. Sometimes I heard guns away off in the woods; and twice I seen little gangs of men gallop past the log store with guns; so I reckoned the trouble was still agoing on. I was mighty down-hearted; so I made up my mind I wouldn't ever go anear that house again, because I reckoned I was to blame, somehow. I judged that that piece of paper meant that Miss Sophia was to meet Harney somewheres at half-past two and run off; and I judged I ought to told her father about that paper and the curious way she acted, and then maybe he would a locked her up and this awful mess wouldn't ever happened.

When I got down out of the tree, I crept along down the river

4. Upper hand.

bank a piece, and found the two bodies laying in the edge of the water, and tugged at them till I got them ashore; then I covered up their faces, and got away as quick as I could. I cried a little when I was covering up Buck's face, for he was mighty good to me.

It was just dark, now. I never went near the house, but struck through the woods and made for the swamp. Jim warn't on his island, so I tramped off in a hurry for the crick, and crowded through the willows, red-hot to jump aboard and get out of that awful country—the raft was gone! My souls, but I was scared! I couldn't get my breath for most a minute. Then I raised a yell. A voice not twenty-five foot from me, says—

"Good lan'! is dat you, honey? Doan' make no noise."

It was Jim's voice—nothing ever sounded so good before. I run along the bank a piece and got aboard, and Jim he grabbed me and hugged me, he was so glad to see me. He says—

"Laws bless you, chile, I 'uz right down sho' you's dead agin. Jack's been heah, he say he reck'n you's ben shot, kase you didn' come home no mo'; so I's jes' dis minute a startin' de raf' down towards de mouf er de crick, so's to be all ready for to shove out en leave soon as Jack comes agin en tells me for certain you *is* dead. Lawsy, I's mighty glad to git you back agin, honey."

I says—

"All right—that's mighty good; they won't find me, and they'll think I've been killed, and floated down the river—there's something up there that'll help them to think so—so don't you lose no time, Jim, but just shove off for the big water as fast as ever you can."

I never felt easy till the raft was two mile below there and out in the middle of the Mississippi. Then we hung up our signal lantern, and judged that we was free and safe once more. I hadn't had a bite to eat since yesterday; so Jim he got out some corn-dodgers[5] and buttermilk, and pork and cabbage, and greens—there ain't nothing in the world so good, when it's cooked right—and whilst I eat my supper we talked, and had a good time. I was powerful glad to get away from the feuds, and so was Jim to get away from the swamp. We said there warn't no home like a raft, after all. Other places do seem so cramped up and smothery, but a raft don't. You feel mighty free and easy and comfortable on a raft.

Chapter XIX

Two or three days and nights went by; I reckon I might say they swum by, they slid along so quiet and smooth and lovely. Here is the way we put in the time. It was a monstrous big river down there —sometimes a mile and a half wide; we run nights, and laid up and hid day-times; soon as night was most gone, we stopped navigating and tied up—nearly always in the dead water under a tow-head; and

5. Hard corn-meal rolls or cakes.

then cut young cottonwoods and willows and hid the raft with them. Then we set out the lines. Next we slid into the river and had a swim, so as to freshen up and cool off; then we set down on the sandy bottom where the water was about knee deep, and watched the daylight come. Not a sound, anywheres—perfectly still —just like the whole world was asleep, only sometimes the bull-frogs a-cluttering, maybe. The first thing to see, looking away over the water, was a kind of dull line—that was the woods on t'other side—you couldn't make nothing else out; then a pale place in the sky; then more paleness, spreading around; then the river softened up, away off, and warn't black any more, but gray; you could see little dark spots drifting along, ever so far away—trading scows, and such things; and long black streaks—rafts; sometimes you could hear a sweep screaking; or jumbled up voices, it was so still, and sounds come so far; and by-and-by you could see a streak on the water which you know by the look of the streak that there's a snag there in a swift current which breaks on it and makes that streak look that way; and you see the mist curl up off of the water, and the east reddens up, and the river, and you make out a log cabin in the edge of the woods, away on the bank on t'other side of the river, being a wood-yard, likely, and piled by them cheats so you can throw a dog through it anywheres;[6] then the nice breeze springs up, and comes fanning you from over there, so cool and fresh, and sweet to smell, on account of the woods and the flowers; but some-times not that way, because they've left dead fish laying around, gars, and such, and they do get pretty rank; and next you've got the full day, and everything smiling in the sun, and the song-birds just going it!

A little smoke couldn't be noticed, now, so we would take some fish off of the lines, and cook up a hot breakfast. And afterwards we would watch the lonesomeness of the river, and kind of lazy along, and by-and-by lazy off to sleep. Wake up, by-and-by, and look to see what done it, and maybe see a steamboat coughing along up stream, so far off towards the other side you couldn't tell nothing about her only whether she was stern-wheel or side-wheel; then for about an hour there wouldn't be nothing to hear nor nothing to see—just solid lonesomeness. Next you'd see a raft sliding by, away off yonder, and maybe a galoot on it chopping, because they're almost always doing it on a raft; you'd see the ax flash, and come down— you don't hear nothing; you see that ax go up again, and by the time it's above the man's head, then you hear the *k'chunk!*—it had took all that time to come over the water. So we would put in the day, lazying around, listening to the stillness. Once there was a thick fog, and the rafts and things that went by was beating tin pans so the steamboats wouldn't run over them. A scow or a raft went by so close we could hear them talking and cussing and laugh-

6. Stacks of wood in this yard were sold by their volume, gappage included.

ing—heard them plain; but we wouldn't see no sign of them; it made you feel crawly, it was like spirits carrying on that way in the air. Jim said he believed it was spirits; but I says:

"No, spirits wouldn't say, 'dern the dern fog.'"

Soon as it was night, out we shoved; when we got her out to about the middle, we let her alone, and let her float wherever the current wanted her to; then we lit the pipes, and dangled our legs in the water and talked about all kinds of things—we was always naked, day and night, whenever the mosquitoes would let us—the new clothes Buck's folks made for me was too good to be comfortable, and besides I didn't go much on clothes, nohow.

Sometimes we'd have that whole river all to ourselves for the longest time. Yonder was the banks and the islands, across the water; and maybe a spark—which was a candle in a cabin window —and sometimes on the water you could see a spark or two—on a raft or a scow, you know; and maybe you could hear a fiddle or a song coming over from one of them crafts. It's lovely to live on a raft. We had the sky, up there, all speckled with stars, and we used to lay on our backs and look up at them, and discuss about whether they was made, or only just happened—Jim he allowed they was made, but I allowed they happened; I judged it would have took too long to *make* so many. Jim said the moon could a *laid* them; well, that looked kind of reasonable, so I didn't say nothing against it, because I've seen a frog lay most as many, so of course it could be done. We used to watch the stars that fell, too, and see them streak down. Jim allowed they'd got spoiled and was hove out of the nest.

Once or twice of a night we would see a steamboat slipping along in the dark, and now and then she would belch a whole world of sparks up out of her chimbleys, and they would rain down in the river and look awful pretty; then she would turn a corner and her lights would wink out and her pow-wow shut off and leave the river still again; and by-and-by her waves would get to us, a long time after she was gone, and joggle the raft a bit, and after that you wouldn't hear nothing for you couldn't tell how long, except maybe frogs or something.

After midnight the people on shore went to bed, and then for two or three hours the shores was black—no more sparks in the cabin windows. These sparks was our clock—the first one that showed again meant morning was coming, so we hunted a place to hide and tie up, right away.

One morning about day-break, I found a canoe and crossed over a chute[7] to the main shore—it was only two hundred yards—and paddled about a mile up a crick amongst the cypress woods, to see if I couldn't get some berries. Just as I was passing a place where a kind of a cow-path crossed the crick, here comes a couple of men

7. A narrow channel with swift-flowing water.

tearing up the path as tight as they could foot it. I thought I was a goner, for whenever anybody was after anybody I judged it was *me* —or maybe Jim. I was about to dig out from there in a hurry, but they was pretty close to me then, and sung out and begged me to save their lives—said they hadn't been doing nothing, and was being chased for it—said there was men and dogs a-coming. They wanted to jump right in, but I says—

"Don't you do it. I don't hear the dogs and horses yet; you've got time to crowd through the brush and get up the crick a little ways; then you take to the water and wade down to me and get in— that'll throw the dogs off the scent."

They done it, and soon as they was aboard I lit out for our tow-head, and in about five or ten minutes we heard the dogs and the men away off, shouting. We heard them come along towards the crick, but couldn't see them; they seemed to stop and fool around a while; then, as we got further and further away all the time, we couldn't hardly hear them at all; by the time we had left a mile of woods behind us and struck the river, everything was quiet, and we paddled over to the tow-head and hid in the cotton-woods and was safe.

One of these fellows was about seventy, or upwards, and had a bald head and very gray whiskers. He had an old battered-up slouch hat on, and a greasy blue woolen shirt, and ragged old blue jeans britches stuffed into his boot tops, and home-knit galluses[8]—no, he only had one. He had an old long-tailed blue jeans coat with slick brass buttons, flung over his arm, and both of them had big fat rat-ty-looking carpet-bags.

The other fellow was about thirty and dressed about as ornery. After breakfast we all laid off and talked, and the first thing that come out was that these chaps didn't know one another.

"What got you into trouble?" says the baldhead to t'other chap.

"Well, I'd been selling an article to take the tartar off the teeth —and it does take it off, too, and generly the enamel along with it —but I staid about one night longer than I ought to, and was just in the act of sliding out when I ran across you on the trail this side of town, and you told me they were coming, and begged me to help you to get off. So I told you I was expecting trouble myself and would scatter out *with* you. That's the whole yarn—what's yourn?"

"Well, I'd ben a-runnin' a little temperance revival thar, 'bout a week, and was the pet of the women-folks, big and little, for I was makin' it mighty warm for the rummies, I *tell* you, and takin' as much as five or six dollars a night—ten cents a head, children and niggers free—and business a growin' all the time; when somehow or another a little report got around, last night, that I had a way of puttin' in my time with a private jug, on the sly. A nigger rousted me out this mornin', and told me the people was getherin' on the

8. Suspenders.

quiet, with their dogs and horses, and they'd be along pretty soon and give me 'bout half an hour's start, and then run me down, if they could; and if they got me they'd tar and feather me and ride me on a rail, sure. I didn't wait for no breakfast—I warn't hungry."

"Old man," says the young one, "I reckon we might double-team it together; what do you think?"

"I ain't undisposed. What's your line—mainly?"

"Jour printer,[9] by trade; do a little in patent medicines; theatre-actor—tragedy, you know; take a turn at mesmerism[1] and phrenology, when there's a chance; teach singing-geography school for a change; sling a lecture, sometimes—oh, I do lots of things—most anything that comes handy, so it ain't work. What's your lay?"[2]

"I've done considerable in the doctoring way in my time. Layin' on o' hands is my best holt—for cancer, and paralysis, and sich things; and I k'n tell a fortune pretty good, when I've got somebody along to find out the facts for me. Preachin's my line, too; and workin' camp-meetin's; and missionaryin' around."

Nobody never said anything for a while; then the young man hove a sigh and says—

"Alas!"

"What're you alassin' about?" says the baldhead.

"To think I should have lived to be leading such a life, and be degraded down into such company." And he begun to wipe the corner of his eye with a rag.

"Dern your skin, ain't the company good enough for you?" says the baldhead, pretty pert and uppish.

"Yes, it *is* good enough for me; it's as good as I deserve; for who fetched me so low, when I was so high? *I* did myself. I don't blame *you*, gentlemen—far from it; I don't blame anybody. I deserve it all. Let the cold world do its worst; one thing I know—there's a grave somewhere for me. The world may go on just as its always done, and take everything from me—loved ones, property, everything—but it can't take that. Some day I'll lie down in it and forget it all, and my poor broken heart will be at rest." He went on a-wiping.

"Drot your pore broken heart," says the baldhead; "what are you heaving your pore broken heart at *us* f'r? *We* hain't done nothing."

"No, I know you haven't. I ain't blaming you, gentlemen. I brought myself down—yes, I did it myself. It's right I should suffer—perfectly right—I don't make any moan."

"Brought you down from whar? Whar was you brought down from?"

---

9. A journeyman-printer, not yet a salaried master-printer, who worked by the day.
1. Hypnotic induction involving animal magnetism; "phrenology": study of the shape of the skull as an indicator of mental acumen and character.
2. Work, in the sense here of hustle or scheme.

"Ah, you would not believe me; the world never believes—let it pass—'tis no matter. The secret of my birth—"

"The secret of your birth? Do you mean to say—"

"Gentlemen," says the young man, very solemn, "I will reveal it to you, for I feel I may have confidence in you. By rights I am a duke!"

Jim's eyes bugged out when he heard that; and I reckon mine did, too. Then the baldhead says: "No! you can't mean it?"

"Yes. My great-grandfather, eldest son of the Duke of Bridgewater, fled to this country about the end of the last century, to breathe the pure air of freedom; married here, and died, leaving a son, his own father dying about the same time. The second son of the late duke seized the title and estates—the infant real duke was ignored. I am the lineal descendant of that infant—I am the rightful Duke of Bridgewater; and here am I, forlorn, torn from my high estate, hunted of men, despised by the cold world, ragged, worn, heartbroken, and degraded to the companionship of felons on a raft!"

Jim pitied him ever so much, and so did I. We tried to comfort him, but he said it warn't much use, he couldn't be much comforted; said if we was a mind to acknowledge him, that would do him more good than most anything else; so we said we would, if he would tell us how. He said we ought to bow, when we spoke to him, and say "Your Grace," or "My Lord," or "Your Lordship"— and he wouldn't mind it if we called him plain "Bridgewater," which he said was a title, anyway, and not a name; and one of us ought to wait on him at dinner, and do any little thing for him he wanted done.

Well, that was all easy, so we done it. All through dinner Jim stood around and waited on him, and says, "Will yo' Grace have some o' dis, or some o' dat?" and so on, and a body could see it was mighty pleasing to him.

But the old man got pretty silent, by-and-by—didn't have much to say, and didn't look pretty comfortable over all that petting that was going on around that duke. He seemed to have something on his mind. So, along in the afternoon, he says:

"Looky here, Bilgewater," he says, "I'm nation sorry for you, but you ain't the only person that's had troubles like that."

"No?"

"No, you ain't. You ain't the only person that's ben snaked down wrongfully out'n a high place."

"Alas!"

"No, you ain't the only person that's had a secret of his birth." And by jings, *he* begins to cry.

"Hold! What do you mean?"

"Bilgewater, kin I trust you?" says the old man, still sort of sobbing.

"To the bitter death!" He took the old man by the hand and squeezed it, and says, "The secret of your being: speak!"

"Bilgewater, I am the late Dauphin!"[3]

You bet you Jim and me stared, this time. Then the duke says: "You are what?"

"Yes, my friend, it is too true—your eyes is lookin' at this very moment on the pore disappeared Dauphin, Looy the Seventeen, son of Looy the Sixteen and Marry Antonette."

"You! At your age! No! You mean you're the late Charlemagne;[4] you must be six or seven hundred years old, at the very least."

"Trouble has done it, Bilgewater, trouble has done it; trouble has brung these gray hairs and this premature balditude. Yes, gentlemen, you see before you, in blue jeans and misery, the wanderin', exiled, trampled-on and sufferin' rightful King of France."

Well, he cried and took on so, that me and Jim didn't know hardly what to do, we was so sorry—and so glad and proud we'd got him with us, too. So we set in, like we done before with the duke, and tried to comfort *him.* But he said it warn't no use, nothing but to be dead and done with it all could do him any good; though he said it often made him feel easier and better for a while if people treated him according to his rights, and got down on one knee to speak to him, and always called him "Your Majesty," and waited on him first at meals, and didn't set down in his presence till he asked them. So Jim and me set to majestying him, and doing this and that and t'other for him, and standing up till he told us we might set down. This done him heaps of good, and so he got cheerful and comfortable. But the duke kind of soured on him, and didn't look a bit satisfied with the way things was going; still, the king acted real friendly towards him, and said the duke's great-grandfather and all the other Dukes of Bilgewater was a good deal thought of by *his* father and was allowed to come to the palace considerable; but the duke staid huffy a good while, till by-and-by the king says:

"Like as not we got to be together a blamed long time, on this h-yer raft, Bilgewater, and so what's the use o' your bein' sour? It'll only make things oncomfortable. It ain't my fault I warn't born a duke, it ain't your fault you warn't born a king—so what's the use to worry? Make the best o' things the way you find 'em, says I— that's my motto. This ain't no bad thing that we've struck here— plenty grub and an easy life—come, give us your hand, Duke, and less all be friends."

The duke done it, and Jim and me was pretty glad to see it. It took away all the uncomfortableness, and we felt mighty good over it, because it would a been a miserable business to have any unfriendliness on the raft; for what you want, above all things, on a

3. The Dauphin, born in 1785, would have been in his mid-50s or 60s had he survived.

4. Charlemagne (742–814) established the Holy Roman Empire.

raft, is for everybody to be satisfied, and feel right and kind towards the others.

It didn't take me long to make up my mind that these liars warn't no kings nor dukes, at all, but just low-down humbugs and frauds. But I never said nothing, never let on; kept it to myself; it's the best way; then you don't have no quarrels, and don't get into no trouble. If they wanted us to call them kings and dukes, I hadn't no objections, 'long as it would keep peace in the family; and it warn't no use to tell Jim, so I didn't tell him. If I never learnt nothing else out of pap, I learnt that the best way to get along with his kind of people is to let them have their own way.

Chapter XX

They asked us considerable many questions; wanted to know what we covered up the raft that way for, and laid by in the day-time instead of running—was Jim a runaway nigger? Says I—

"Goodness sakes, would a runaway nigger run *south?*"

No, they allowed he wouldn't. I had to account for things some way, so I says:

"My folks was living in Pike County, in Missouri, where I was born, and they all died off but me and pa and my brother Ike. Pa, he 'lowed he'd break up and go down and live with Uncle Ben, who's got a little one-horse place on the river, forty-four mile below Orleans. Pa was pretty poor, and had some debts; so when he'd squared up there warn't nothing left but sixteen dollars and our nigger, Jim. That warn't enough to take us fourteen hundred mile, deck passage nor no other way. Well, when the river rose, pa had a streak of luck one day; he ketched this piece of a raft; so we reckoned we'd go down to Orleans on it. Pa's luck didn't hold out; a steamboat run over the forrard corner of the raft, one night, and we all went overboard and dove under the wheel; Jim and me come up, all right, but pa was drunk, and Ike was only four years old, so they never come up no more. Well, for the next day or two we had considerable trouble, because people was always coming out in skiffs and trying to take Jim away from me, saying they believed he was a runaway nigger. We don't run day-times no more, now; nights they don't bother us."

The duke says—

"Leave me alone to cipher out a way so we can run in the day-time if we want to. I'll think the thing over—I'll invent a plan that'll fix it. We'll let it alone for to-day, because of course we don't want to go by that town yonder in daylight—it mightn't be healthy."

Towards night it begun to darken up and look like rain; the heat lightning was squirting around, low down in the sky, and the leaves was beginning to shiver—it was going to be pretty ugly, it was easy to see that. So the duke and the king went to overhauling our wigwam, to see what the beds was like. My bed was a straw tick[5]—better than Jim's, which was a corn-shuck tick; there's always cobs around about in a shuck tick, and they poke into you and hurt; and when you roll over, the dry shucks sound like you was rolling over in a pile of dead leaves; it makes such a rustling that you wake up. Well, the duke allowed he would take my bed; but the king allowed he wouldn't. He says—

"I should a reckoned the difference in rank would a sejested to you that a corn-shuck bed warn't just fitten for me to sleep on. Your Grace'll take the shuck bed yourself."

Jim and me was in a sweat again, for a minute, being afraid there was going to be some more trouble amongst them; so we was pretty glad when the duke says—

" 'Tis my fate to be always ground into the mire under the iron heel of oppression. Misfortune has broken my once haughty spirit; I yield, I submit; 'tis my fate. I am alone in the world—let me suffer; I can bear it."

We got away as soon as it was good and dark. The king told us to stand well out towards the middle of the river, and not show a light till we got a long ways below the town. We come in sight of the little bunch of lights by-and-by—that was the town, you know —and slid by, about a half a mile out, all right. When we was three-quarters of a mile below, we hoisted up our signal lantern; and about ten o'clock it come on to rain and blow and thunder and lighten like everything; so the king told us to both stay on watch till the weather got better; then him and the duke crawled into the wigwam and turned in for the night. It was my watch below, till twelve, but I wouldn't a turned in, anyway, if I'd had a bed; because a body don't see such a storm as that every day in the week, not by a long sight. My souls, how the wind did scream along! And every second or two there'd come a glare that lit up the white-caps for a half a mile around, and you'd see the islands looking dusty through the rain, and the trees thrashing around in the wind; then comes a *h-wack!*—bum! bum! bumble-umble-um-bum-bum-bum-bum—and the thunder would go rumbling and grumbling away, and quit—and then *rip* comes another flash and another sock-dolager.[6] The waves most washed me off the raft, sometimes, but I hadn't any clothes on, and didn't mind. We didn't have no trouble about snags; the lightning was glaring and flittering around so constant that we could see them plenty soon enough to throw her head this way or that and miss them.

I had the middle watch, you know, but I was pretty sleepy by that time, so Jim he said he would stand the first half of it for me; he was always mighty good, that way, Jim was. I crawled into the wigwam, but the king and the duke had their legs sprawled around

5. Mattress.
6. Something exceptionally strong or climactic.

so there warn't no show for me; so I laid outside—I didn't mind the rain, because it was warm, and the waves warn't running so high, now. About two they come up again, though, and Jim was going to call me, but he changed his mind because he reckoned they warn't high enough yet to do any harm; but he was mistaken about that, for pretty soon all of a sudden along comes a regular ripper, and washed me overboard. It most killed Jim a-laughing. He was the easiest nigger to laugh that ever was, anyway.

I took the watch, and Jim he laid down and snored away; and by-and-by the storm let up for good and all; and the first cabin-light that showed, I rousted him out and we slid the raft into hiding-quarters for the day.

The king got out an old ratty deck of cards, after breakfast, and him and the duke played seven-up a while, five cents a game. Then they got tired of it, and allowed they would "lay out a campaign," as they called it. The duke went down into his carpet-bag and fetched up a lot of little printed bills, and read them out loud. One bill said "The celebrated Dr. Armand de Montalban of Paris," would "lecture on the Science of Phrenology" at such and such a place, on the blank day of blank, at ten cents admission, and "furnish charts of character at twenty-five cents apiece." The duke said that was *him*. In another bill he was the "world renowned Shaksperean tragedian, Garrick the Younger,[7] of Drury Lane, London." In other bills he had a lot of other names and done other wonderful things, like finding water and gold with a "divining rod," "dissipating witch-spells," and so on. By-and-by he says—

"But the histrionic muse is the darling. Have you ever trod the boards, Royalty?"

"No," says the king.

"You shall, then, before you're three days older, Fallen Grandeur," says the duke. "The first good town we come to, we'll hire a hall and do the sword-fight in Richard III. and the balcony scene in Romeo and Juliet. How does that strike you?"

"I'm in, up to the hub, for anything that will pay, Bilgewater, but you see I don't know nothing about play-actn', and hain't ever seen much of it. I was too small when pap used to have 'em at the palace. Do you reckon you can learn me?"

"Easy!"

"All right. I'm jist a-freezn' for something fresh, anyway. Less commence, right away."

So the duke he told him all about who Romeo was, and who Juliet was, and said he was used to being Romeo, so the king could be Juliet.

"But if Juliet's such a young gal, Duke, my peeled head and my white whiskers is goin' to look oncommon odd on her, maybe."

---

7. **David Garrick (1717–79) was a famous tragedian at the Theatre Royal in Drury Lane, London.**

"No, don't you worry—these country jakes won't ever think of that. Besides, you know, you'll be in costume, and that makes all the difference in the world; Juliet's in a balcony, enjoying the moonlight before she goes to bed, and she's got on her night-gown and her ruffled night-cap. Here are the costumes for the parts."

He got out two or three curtain-calico suits, which he said was meedyevil armor for Richard III. and t'other chap, and a long white cotton night-shirt and a ruffled night-cap to match. The king was satisfied; so the duke got out his book and read the parts over in the most splendid spread-eagle way, prancing around and acting at the same time, to show how it had got to be done; then he give the book to the king and told him to get his part by heart.

There was a little one-horse town about three mile down the bend, and after dinner the duke said he had ciphered out his idea about how to run in daylight without it being dangersome for Jim; so he allowed he would go down to the town and fix that thing. The king allowed he would go too, and see if he couldn't strike something. We was out of coffee, so Jim said I better go along with them in the canoe and get some.

When we got there, there warn't nobody stirring; streets empty, and perfectly dead and still, like Sunday. We found a sick nigger sunning himself in a back yard, and he said everybody that warn't too young or too sick or too old, was gone to camp-meeting, about two mile back in the woods. The king got the directions, and allowed he'd go and work that camp-meeting for all it was worth, and I might go, too.[8]

The duke said what he was after was a printing office. We found it; a little bit of a concern, up over a carpenter shop—carpenters and printers all gone to the meeting, and no doors locked. It was a dirty, littered-up place, and had ink marks, and handbills with pictures of horses and runaway niggers on them, all over the walls. The duke shed his coat and said he was all right, now. So me and the king lit out for the camp-meeting.

We got there in about a half an hour, fairly dripping, for it was a most awful hot day. There was as much as a thousand people there, from twenty mile around. The woods was full of teams and wagons, hitched everywheres, feeding out of the wagon troughs and stomping to keep off the flies. There was sheds made out of poles and roofed over with branches, where they had lemonade and gingerbread to sell, and piles of watermelons and green corn and such-like truck.

The preaching was going on under the same kinds of sheds, only they was bigger and held crowds of people. The benches was made

8. Camp meetings were notoriously easy pickings for confidence men. One of the best-known literary renderings of this stock situation was Johnson J. Johnson's *The Captain Attends a Camp-Meeting*.

Camp meetings are extended evangelical meetings held in the open air. Families camp nearby for the duration of the event.

out of outside slabs of logs, with holes bored in the round side to drive sticks into for legs. They didn't have no backs. The preachers had high platforms to stand on, at one end of the sheds. The women had on sunbonnets; and some had linsey-woolsey[9] frocks, some gingham ones, and a few of the young ones had on calico. Some of the young men was barefooted, and some of the children didn't have on any clothes but just a tow-linen shirt. Some of the old women was knitting, and some of the young folks was courting on the sly.

The first shed we come to, the preacher was lining out a hymn. He lined out two lines, everybody sung it, and it was kind of grand to hear it, there was so many of them and they done it in such a rousing way; then he lined out two more for them to sing—and so on. The people woke up more and more, and sung louder and louder; and towards the end, some begun to groan, and some begun to shout. Then the preacher begun to preach; and begun in earnest, too; and went weaving first to one side of the platform and then the other, and then a leaning down over the front of it, with his arms and his body going all the time, and shouting his words out with all his might; and every now and then he would hold up his Bible and spread it open, and kind of pass it around this way and that, shouting, "It's the brazen serpent in the wilderness! Look upon it and live!" And people would shout out, "Glory!—A-*a-men!*" And so he went on, and the people groaning and crying and saying amen:

"Oh, come to the mourners' bench![1] come, black with sin! (*amen!*) come, sick and sore! (*amen!*) come, lame and halt, and blind! (*amen!*) come, pore and needy, sunk in shame! (*a-a-men!*) come all that's worn, and soiled, and suffering!—come with a broken spirit! come with a contrite heart! come in your rags and sin and dirt! the waters that cleanse is free, the door of heaven stands open—oh, enter in and be at rest!" (*a-a-men! glory, glory hallelujah!*)

And so on. You couldn't make out what the preacher said, any more, on account of the shouting and crying. Folks got up, everywheres in the crowd, and worked their way, just by main strength, to the mourners' bench, with the tears running down their faces; and when all the mourners had got up there to the front benches in a crowd, they sung, and shouted, and flung themselves down on the straw, just crazy and wild.

Well, the first I knowed, the king got agoing; and you could hear him over everybody; and next he went a-charging up on to the platform and the preacher he begged him to speak to the people, and he done it. He told them he was a pirate—been a pirate for thirty years, out in the Indian Ocean, and his crew was thinned out considerable, last spring, in a fight, and he was home now, to take out some fresh men, and thanks to goodness he'd been robbed last

9. Cheap, often homespun, unpatterned cloth composed of wool and flax; gingham and calico are inexpensive, store-bought printed cotton; tow linen is coarse linen cloth.
1. Front-row pews filled by penitents.

night, and put ashore off of a steamboat without a cent, and he was glad of it, it was the blessedest thing that ever happened to him, because he was a changed man now, and happy for the first time in his life; and poor as he was, he was going to start right off and work his way back to the Indian Ocean and put in the rest of his life trying to turn the pirates into the true path; for he could do it better than anybody else, being acquainted with all the pirate crews in that ocean; and though it would take him a long time to get there, without money, he would get there anyway, and every time he convinced a pirate he would say to him, "Don't you thank me, don't you give me no credit, it all belongs to them dear people in Pokeville camp-meeting, natural brothers and benefactors of the race—and that dear preacher there, the truest friend a pirate ever had!"

And then he busted into tears, and so did everybody. Then somebody sings out, "Take up a collection for him, take up a collection!" Well, a half a dozen made a jump to do it, but somebody sings out, "Let *him* pass the hat around!" Then everybody said it, the preacher too.

So the king went all through the crowd with his hat, swabbing his eyes, and blessing the people and praising them and thanking them for being so good to the poor pirates away off there; and every little while the prettiest kind of girls, with the tears running down their cheeks, would up and ask him would he let them kiss him, for to remember him by; and he always done it; and some of them he hugged and kissed as many as five or six times—and he was invited to stay a week; and everybody wanted him to live in their houses, and said they'd think it was an honor; but he said as this was the last day of the camp-meeting he couldn't do no good, and besides he was in a sweat to get to the Indian Ocean right off and go to work on the pirates.

When we got back to the raft and he come to count up, he found he had collected eighty-seven dollars and seventy-five cents. And then he had fetched away a three-gallon jug of whisky, too, that he found under a wagon when we was starting home through the woods. The king said, take it all around, it laid over any day he'd ever put in in the missionarying line. He said it warn't no use talking, heathens don't amount to shucks, alongside of pirates, to work a campmeeting with.

The duke was thinking *he'd* been doing pretty well, till the king come to show up, but after that he didn't think so so much. He had set up and printed off two little jobs for farmers, in that printing office—horse bills—and took the money, four dollars. And he had got in ten dollars worth of advertisements for the paper, which he said he would put in for four dollars if they would pay in advance—so they done it. The price of the paper was two dollars a year, but he took in three subscriptions for half a dollar apiece on condition of them paying him in advance; they were going to pay in cord-wood and onions, as usual, but he said he had just bought the concern and knocked down the price as low as he could afford it, and was going to run it for cash. He set up a little piece of poetry, which he made, himself, out of his own head—three verses—kind of sweet and saddish—the name of it was, "Yes, crush, cold world, this breaking heart"—and he left that all set up and ready to print in the paper and didn't charge nothing for it. Well, he took in nine dollars and a half, and said he'd done a pretty square day's work for it.

Then he showed us another little job he'd printed and hadn't charged for, because it was for us. It had a picture of a runaway nigger, with a bundle on a stick, over his shoulder, and "$200 reward" under it. The reading was all about Jim, and just described him to a dot. It said he run away from St. Jacques' plantation, forty mile below New Orleans, last winter, and likely went north, and whoever would catch him and send him back, he could have the reward and expenses.

"Now," says the duke, "after to-night we can run in the daytime if we want to. Whenever we see anybody coming, we can tie Jim hand and foot with a rope, and lay him in the wigwam and show this handbill and say we captured him up the river, and were too poor to travel on a steamboat, so we got this little raft on credit from our friends and are going down to get the reward. Handcuffs and chains would look still better on Jim, but it wouldn't go well with the story of us being so poor. Too much like jewelry. Ropes are the correct thing—we must preserve the unities,[2] as we say on the boards."

We all said the duke was pretty smart, and there couldn't be no trouble about running daytimes. We judged we could make miles enough that night to get out of the reach of the pow-wow we reckoned the duke's work in the printing office was going to make in that little town—then we could boom right along, if we wanted to.

We laid low and kept still, and never shoved out till nearly ten o'clock; then we slid by, pretty wide away from the town, and didn't hoist our lantern till we was clear out of sight of it.

When Jim called me to take the watch at four in the morning, he says—

"Huck, does you reck'n we gwyne to run acrost any mo' kings on dis trip?"

"No," I says, "I reckon not."

"Well," says he, "dat's all right, den. I doan' mine one er two kings, but dat's enough. Dis one's powerful drunk, en de duke ain' much better."

---

2. Of time, place, and action in classical drama; here the duke is using the term to mean "consistent with the rest of our story."

I found Jim had been trying to get him to talk French, so he could hear what it was like; but he had been in this country so long, and had so much trouble, he'd forgot it.

Chapter XXI

It was after sun-up, now, but we went right on, and didn't tie up. The king and the duke turned out, by-and-by, looking pretty rusty; but after they'd jumped overboard and took a swim, it chippered them up a good deal. After breakfast the king he took a seat on a corner of the raft, and pulled off his boots and rolled up his britches, and let his legs dangle in the water, so as to be comfortable, and lit his pipe, and went to getting his Romeo and Juliet by heart. When he had got it pretty good, him and the duke begun to practice it together. The duke had to learn him over and over again, how to say every speech; and he made him sigh, and put his hand on his heart, and after while he said he done it pretty well; "only," he says, "you mustn't bellow out *Romeo!* that way, like a bull—you must say it soft, and sick, and languishy, so—R-o-o-meo! that is the idea; for Juliet's a dear sweet mere child of a girl, you know, and she don't bray like a jackass."

Well, next they got out a couple of long swords that the duke made out of oak laths, and begun to practice the sword-fight—the duke called himself Richard III.; and the way they laid on, and pranced around the raft was grand to see. But by-and-by the king tripped and fell overboard, and after that they took a rest, and had a talk about all kinds of adventures they'd had in other times along the river.

After dinner, the duke says:

"Well, Capet,[3] we'll want to make this a first-class show, you know, so I guess we'll add a little more to it. We want a little something to answer encores with, anyway."

"What's onkores, Bilgewater?"

The duke told him, and then says:

"I'll answer by doing the Highland fling or the sailor's hornpipe; and you—well, let me see—oh, I've got it—you can do Hamlet's soliloquy."

"Hamlet's which?"

"Hamlet's soliloquy, you know; the most celebrated thing in Shakespeare. Ah, it's sublime, sublime! Always fetches the house. I haven't got it in the book—I've only got one volume—but I reckon I can piece it out from memory. I'll just walk up and down a minute, and see if I can call it back from recollection's vaults."

So he went to marching up and down, thinking, and frowning horrible every now and then; then he would hoist up his eyebrows; next he would squeeze his hand on his forehead and stagger back and kind of moan; next he would sigh, and next he'd let on to drop

3. The family name of Louis XVI.

a tear. It was beautiful to see him. By-and-by he got it. He told us to give attention. Then he strikes a most noble attitude, with one leg shoved forwards, and his arms stretched away up, and his head tilted back, looking up at the sky; and then he begins to rip and rave and grit his teeth; and after that, all through his speech he howled, and spread around, and swelled up his chest, and just knocked the spots out of any acting ever I see before. This is the speech—I learned it, easy enough, while he was learning it to the king:[4]

To be, or not to be; that is the bare bodkin
That makes calamity of so long life;
For who would fardels bear, till Birnam Wood do come to Dunsi-
    nane,
But that the fear of something after death
Murders the innocent sleep,
Great nature's second course,
And makes us rather sling the arrows of outrageous fortune
Than fly to others that we know not of.
There's the respect must give us pause:
Wake Duncan with thy knocking! I would thou couldst;
For who would bear the whips and scorns of time,
The oppressor's wrong, the proud man's contumely,
The law's delay, and the quietus which his pangs might take,
In the dead waste and middle of the night, when churchyards yawn
In customary suits of solemn black,
But that the undiscovered country from whose bourne no traveler
    returns,
Breathes forth contagion on the world,
And thus the native hue of resolution, like the poor cat i' the adage,
Is sicklied o'er with care,
And all the clouds that lowered o'er our housetops,
With this regard their currents turn awry,
And lose the name of action.
'Tis a consummation devoutly to be wished. But soft you, the fair
    Ophelia:
Ope not thy ponderous and marble jaws,
But get thee to a nunnery—go!

Well, the old man he liked that speech, and he mighty soon got it so he could do it first rate. It seemed like he was just born for it; and when he had his hand in and was excited, it was perfectly lovely the way he would rip and tear and rair up behind when he was getting it off.

The first chance we got, the duke he had some show bills

4. The comical garbling of Shakespeare was another stock in trade of the south-western humorists in whose tradition Clemens follows. The soliloquy is com-posed chiefly of phrases from *Hamlet* and *Macbeth*; but several other plays are also drawn upon.

printed; and after that, for two or three days as we floated along, the raft was a most uncommon lively place, for there warn't nothing but sword-fighting and rehearsing—as the duke called it—going on all the time. One morning, when we was pretty well down the State of Arkansaw, we come in sight of a little one-horse town[5] in a big bend; so we tied up about three-quarters of a mile above it, in the mouth of a crick which was shut in like a tunnel by the cypress trees, and all of us but Jim took the canoe and went down there to see if there was any chance in that place for our show.

We struck it mighty lucky; there was going to be a circus there that afternoon, and the country people was already beginning to come in, in all kinds of old shackly wagons, and on horses. The circus would leave before night, so our show would have a pretty good chance. The duke he hired the court house, and we went around and stuck up our bills. They read like this:

Shaksperean Revival! ! !
Wonderful Attraction!
For One Night Only!
The world renowned tragedians,
David Garrick the younger, of Drury Lane Theatre, London,
and
Edmund Kean the elder,[6] of the Royal Haymarket Theatre, White-
chapel, Pudding Lane, Piccadilly, London, and the
Royal Continental Theatres, in their sublime
Shaksperean Spectacle entitled
The Balcony Scene
in
Romeo and Juliet! ! !

Romeo . . . . .Mr. Garrick.
Juliet . . . . .Mr. Kean.

Assisted by the whole strength of the company!
New customes, new scenery, new appointments!
Also:
The thrilling, masterly, and blood-curdling
Broad-sword conflict
In Richard III.! ! !

Richard III . . . . .Mr. Garrick.
Richmond . . . . .Mr. Kean.

also:
(by special request,)
Hamlet's Immortal Soliloquy! !
By the Illustrious Kean!
Done by him 30 consecutive nights in Paris!
For One Night Only,
On account of imperative European engagements!
Admission 25 cents; children and servants, 10 cents.

---

5. Clemens's Bricksville is apparently modeled after Napoleon, Arkansas, although certain unattractive elements of this river town and its inhabitants were common to most—including Hannibal.
6. Here, as elsewhere, the duke garbles the facts. David Garrick (1717–79), Edmund Kean (1787–1833), and Charles John Kean (1811–68) were all famous tragedians at the Theatre Royal in Drury Lane, London.

Then we went loafing around the town. The stores and houses
was most all old shackly dried-up frame concerns that hadn't ever
been painted; they was set up three or four foot above ground on
stilts, so as to be out of reach of the water when the river was overflowed. The houses had little gardens around them, but they didn't
seem to raise hardly anything in them but jimpson weeds, and sunflowers, and ash-piles, and old curled-up boots and shoes, and pieces
of bottles, and rags, and played-out tin-ware. The fences was made
of different kinds of boards, nailed on at different times; and they
leaned every which-way, and had gates that didn't generly have but
one hinge—a leather one. Some of the fences had been whitewashed, some time or another, but the duke said it was in Clum-
bus's time, like enough. There was generly hogs in the garden, and
people driving them out.

All the stores was along one street. They had white-domestic
awnings[7] in front, and the country people hitched their horses to
the awning-posts. There was empty dry-goods boxes under the awnings, and loafers roosting on them all day long, whittling them with
their Barlow knives; and chawing tobacco, and gaping and yawning
and stretching—a mighty ornery lot. They generly had on yellow
straw hats most as wide as an umbrella, but didn't wear no coats
nor waistcoats; they called one another Bill, and Buck, and Hank,
and Joe, and Andy, and talked lazy and drawly, and used considerable many cuss-words. There was as many as one loafer leaning up
against every awning-post, and he most always had his hands in his
britches pockets, except when he fetched them out to lend a chaw
of tobacco or scratch. What a body was hearing amongst them, all
the time was—

"Gimme a chaw 'v tobacker, Hank."

"Cain't—I hain't got but one chaw left. Ask Bill."

Maybe Bill he gives him a chaw; maybe he lies and says he ain't
got none. Some of them kinds of loafers never has a cent in the
world, nor a chaw of tobacco of their own. They get all their chawing by borrowing—they say to a fellow, "I wisht you'd len' me a
chaw, Jack, I jist this minute give Ben Thompson the last chaw I
had"—which is a lie, pretty much every time; it don't fool nobody
but a stranger; but Jack ain't no stranger, so he says—

"*You* give him a chaw, did you? so did your sister's cat's grandmother. You pay me back the chaws you've awready borry'd off'n
me, Lafe Buckner, then I'll loan you one or two ton of it, and
won't charge you no back intrust, nuther."

"Well, I *did* pay you back some of it wunst."

"Yes, you did—'bout six chaws. You borry'd store tobacker and
paid back nigger-head."

Store tobacco is flat black plug, but these fellows mostly chaws
the natural leaf twisted. When they borrow a chaw, they don't

7. **Awnings made from crude canvas.**

generly cut it off with a knife, but they set the plug in between their teeth, and gnaw with their teeth and tug at the plug with their hands till they get it in two—then sometimes the one that owns the tobacco looks mournful at it when it's handed back, and says, sarcastic—

"Here, gimme the *chaw*, and you take the *plug*."

All the streets and lanes was just mud, they warn't nothing else *but* mud—mud as black as tar, and nigh about a foot deep in some places; and two or three inches deep in *all* the places. The hogs loafed and grunted around, everywheres. You'd see a muddy sow and a litter of pigs come lazying along the street and whollop herself right down in the way, where folks had to walk around her, and she'd stretch out, and shut her eyes, and wave her ears, whilst the pigs was milking her, and look as happy as if she was on salary. And pretty soon you'd hear a loafer sing out, "Hi! *so* boy! sick him, Tige!" and away the sow would go, squealing most horrible, with a dog or two swinging to each ear, and three or four dozen more a-coming; and then you would see all the loafers get up and watch the thing out of sight, and laugh at the fun and look grateful for the noise. Then they'd settle back again till there was a dog-fight. There couldn't anything wake them up all over, and make them happy all over, like a dog-fight—unless it might be putting turpentine on a stray dog and setting fire to him, or tying a tin pan to his tail and see him run himself to death.

On the river front some of the houses was sticking out over the bank, and they was bowed and bent, and about ready to tumble in. The people had moved out of them. The bank was caved away under one corner of some others, and that corner was hanging over. People lived in them yet, but it was dangersome, because sometimes a strip of land as wide as a house caves in at a time. Sometimes a belt of land a quarter of a mile deep will start in and cave along and cave along till it all caves into the river in one summer. Such a town as that has to be always moving back, and back, and back, because the river's always gnawing at it.

The nearer it got to noon that day, the thicker and thicker was the wagons and horses in the streets, and more coming all the time. Families fetched their dinners with them, from the country, and eat them in the wagons. There was considerable whiskey drinking going on, and I seen three fights. By-and-by somebody sings out—

"Here comes old Boggs!—in from the country for his little old monthly drunk—here he comes, boys!"

All the loafers looked glad—I reckoned they was used to having fun out of Boggs. One of them says—

"Wonder who he's a gwyne to chaw up this time. If he'd a chawed up all the men he's ben a gwyne to chaw up in the last twenty year, he'd have considerble ruputation, now."

Another one says, "I wisht old Boggs'd threaten me, 'cuz then I'd know I warn't gwyne to die for a thousan' year."

Boggs comes a-tearing along on his horse, whooping and yelling like an Injun, and singing out—

"Cler the track, thar. I'm on the war-path, and the price uv coffins is a gwyne to raise."

He was drunk, and weaving about in his saddle; he was over fifty year old, and had a very red face. Everybody yelled at him, and laughed at him, and sassed him, and he sassed back, and said he'd attend to them and lay them out in their regular turns, but he couldn't wait now, because he'd come to town to kill old Colonel Sherburn, and his motto was, "meat first, and spoon vittles to top off on."

He see me, and rode up and says—

"Whar'd you come f'm, boy? You prepared to die?"

Then he rode on. I was scared; but a man says—

"He don't mean nothing; he's always a carryin' on like that, when he's drunk. He's the best-naturedest old fool in Arkansaw—never hurt nobody, drunk nor sober."

Boggs rode up before the biggest store in town and bent his head down so he could see under the curtain of the awning, and yells—

"Come out here, Sherburn! Come out and meet the man you've swindled. You're the houn' I'm after, and I'm a gwyne to have you, too!"

And so he went on, calling Sherburn everything he could lay his tongue to, and the whole street packed with people listening and laughing and going on. By-and-by a proud-looking man about fifty-five—and he was a heap the best dressed man in that town, too—steps out of the store, and the crowd drops back on each side to let him come. He says to Boggs, mighty ca'm and slow—he says:

"I'm tired of this; but I'll endure it till one o'clock. Till one o'clock, mind—no longer. If you open your mouth against me only once, after that time, you can't travel so far but I will find you."

Then he turns and goes in. The crowd looked mighty sober; nobody stirred, and there warn't no more laughing. Boggs rode off blackguarding Sherburn as loud as he could yell, all down the street; and pretty soon back he comes and stops before the store still keeping it up. Some men crowded around him and tried to get him to shut up, but he wouldn't; they told him it would be one o'clock in about fifteen minutes, and so he *must* go home—he must go right away. But it didn't do no good. He cussed away, with all his might, and throwed his hat down in the mud and rode over it, and pretty soon away he went a-raging down the street again, with his gray hair a-flying. Everybody that could get a chance at him tried their best to coax him off of his horse so they could lock him up and get him sober; but it warn't no use—up the street he would tear again, and give Sherburn another cussing. By-and-by somebody says—

"Go for his daughter!—quick, go for his daughter; sometimes

he'll listen to her. If anybody can persuade him, she can."

So somebody started on a run. I walked down street a ways, and stopped. In about five or ten minutes, here comes Boggs again—but not on his horse. He was a-reeling across the street towards me, bareheaded, with a friend on both sides of him aholt of his arms and hurrying him along. He was quiet, and looked uneasy; and he warn't hanging back any, but was doing some of the hurrying himself. Somebody sings out—

"Boggs!"

I looked over there to see who said it, and it was that Colonel Sherburn. He was standing perfectly still, in the street, and had a pistol raised in his right hand—not aiming it, but holding it out with the barrel tilted up towards the sky. The same second I see a young girl coming on the run, and two men with her. Boggs and the men turned round, to see who called him, and when they see the pistol the men jumped to one side, and the pistol barrel come down slow and steady to a level—both barrels cocked. Boggs throws up both of his hands, and says, "O Lord, don't shoot!" Bang! goes the first shot, and he staggers back clawing at the air—bang! goes the second one, and he tumbles backwards onto the ground, heavy and solid, with his arms spread out. That young girl screamed out, and comes rushing, and down she throws herself on her father, crying, and saying, "Oh, he's killed him, he's killed him!" The crowd closed up around them, and shouldered and jammed one another, with their necks stretched, trying to see, and people on the inside trying to shove them back, and shouting, "Back, back! give him air, give him air!"

Colonel Sherburn he tossed his pistol onto the ground, and turned around on his heels and walked off.

They took Boggs to a little drug store, the crowd pressing around, just the same, and the whole town following, and I rushed and got a good place at the window, where I was close to him and could see in. They laid him on the floor, and put one large Bible under his head, and opened another one and spread it on his breast—but they tore open his shirt first, and I seen where one of the bullets went in. He made about a dozen long gasps, his breast lifting the Bible up when he drawed in his breath, and letting it down again when he breathed it out—and after that he laid still; he was dead.[8] Then they pulled his daughter away from him, screaming and crying, and took her off. She was about sixteen, and very sweet and gentle-looking, but awful pale and scared.

Well, pretty soon the whole town was there, squirming and scrouging and pushing and shoving to get at the window and have a

8. Clemens had witnessed a shooting very much like this one when he was 10 years old. His father was judge at the trial, which ended in acquittal. Only the Bibles under the victim's head and on his chest seem to have been added by Clemens, who seldom could resist ironies at the expense of institutionalized religion.

look, but people that had the places wouldn't give them up, and
folks behind them was saying all the time, "Say, now, you've looked
enough, you fellows; 'taint right and 'taint fair, for you to stay thar
all the time, and never give nobody a chance; other folks has their
rights as well as you."

There was considerable jawing back, so I slid out, thinking maybe
there was going to be trouble. The streets was full, and everybody
was excited. Everybody that seen the shooting was telling how it
happened, and there was a big crowd packed around each one of
these fellows, stretching their necks and listening. One long lanky
man, with long hair and a big white fur stove-pipe hat on the back
of his head, and a crooked-handled cane, marked out the places on
the ground where Boggs stood, and where Sherburn stood, and the
people following him around from one place to t'other and watching everything he done, and bobbing their heads to show they
understood, and stooping a little and resting their hands on their
thighs to watch him mark the places on the ground with his cane;
and then he stood up straight and stiff where Sherburn had stood,
frowning and having his hat-brim down over his eyes, and sung out,
"Boggs!" and then fetched his cane down slow to a level, and says
"Bang!" staggered backwards, says "Bang!" again, and fell down flat
on his back. The people that had seen the thing said he done it perfect; said it was just exactly the way it all happened. Then as much
as a dozen people got out their bottles and treated him.

Well, by-and-by somebody said Sherburn ought to be lynched. In
about a minute everybody was saying it; so away they went, mad
and yelling, and snatching down every clothes-line they come to, to
do the hanging with.

Chapter XXII

They swarmed up the street towards Sherburn's house, a-whoop-
ing and yelling and raging like Injuns, and everything had to clear
the way or get run over and tromped to mush, and it was awful to
see. Children was heeling it ahead of the mob, screaming and trying
to get out of the way; and every window along the road was full of
women's heads, and there was nigger boys in every tree, and bucks
and wenches looking over every fence; and as soon as the mob
would get nearly to them they would break and skaddle back out of
reach. Lots of the women and girls was crying and taking on, scared
most to death.

They swarmed up in front of Sherburn's palings as thick as they
could jam together, and you couldn't hear yourself think for the
noise. It was a little twenty-foot yard. Some sung out "Tear down
the fence! tear down the fence!" Then there was a racket of ripping
and tearing and smashing, and down she goes, and the front wall of
the crowd begins to roll in like a wave.

Just then Sherburn steps out on to the roof of his little front porch, with a double-barrel gun in his hand, and takes his stand, perfectly ca'm and deliberate, not saying a word. The racket stopped, and the wave sucked back.

Sherburn never said a word—just stood there, looking down. The stillness was awful creepy and uncomfortable. Sherburn run his eye slow along the crowd; and wherever it struck, the people tried a little to outgaze him, but they couldn't; they dropped their eyes and looked sneaky. Then pretty soon Sherburn sort of laughed; not the pleasant kind, but the kind that makes you feel like when you are eating bread that's got sand in it.

Then he says, slow and scornful:

"The idea of *you* lynching anybody! It's amusing. The idea of you thinking you had pluck enough to lynch a *man!* Because you're brave enough to tar and feather poor friendless cast-out women that come along here, did that make you think you had grit enough to lay your hands on a *man?* Why, a *man's* safe in the hands of ten thousand of your kind—as long as it's day-time and you're not behind him.

"Do I know you? I know you clear through. I was born and raised in the South, and I've lived in the North; so I know the aver-age all around. The average man's a coward. In the North he lets anybody walk over him that wants to, and goes home and prays for a humble spirit to bear it. In the South one man, all by himself, has stopped a stage full of men, in the day-time, and robbed the lot. Your newspapers call you a brave people so much that you think you *are* braver than any other people—whereas you're just *as* brave, and no braver. Why don't your juries hang murderers? Because they're afraid the man's friends will shoot them in the back, in the dark—and it's just what they *would* do.

"So they always acquit; and then a *man* goes in the night, with a hundred masked cowards at his back, and lynches the rascal. Your mistake is, that you didn't bring a man with you; that's one mis-take, and the other is that you didn't come in the dark, and fetch your masks. You brought *part* of a man—Buck Harkness, there—and if you hadn't had him to start you, you'd a taken it out in blowing.

"You didn't want to come. The average man don't like trouble and danger. *You* don't like trouble and danger. But if only *half* a man—like Buck Harkness, there—shouts 'Lynch him, lynch him!' you're afraid to back down—afraid you'll be found out to be what you are—*cowards*—and so you raise a yell, and hang yourselves onto that half-a-man's coat tail, and come raging up here, swearing what big things you're going to do. The pitifulest thing out is a mob; that's what an army is—a mob; they don't fight with courage that's born in them, but with courage that's borrowed from their mass, and from their officers. But a mob without any *man* at the head of it, is *beneath* pitifulness. Now the thing for *you* to do, is to droop your tails and go home and crawl in a hole. If any real lynching's going to be done, it will be done in the dark, Southern fashion; and when they come they'll bring their masks, and fetch a *man* along. Now *leave*—and take your half-a-man with you"—tossing his gun up across his left arm and cocking it, when he says this.

The crowd washed back sudden, and then broke all apart and went tearing off every which way, and Buck Harkness he heeled it after them, looking tolerable cheap. I could a staid, if I'd a wanted to, but I didn't want to.

I went to the circus, and loafed around the back side till the watchman went by, and then dived in under the tent. I had my twenty-dollar gold piece and some other money, but I reckoned I better save it, because there ain't no telling how soon you are going to need it, away from home and amongst strangers, that way. You can't be too careful. I ain't opposed to spending money on circuses, when there ain't no other way, but there ain't no use in *wasting* it on them.

It was a real bully circus. It was the splendidest sight that ever was, when they all come riding in, two and two, a gentleman and lady, side by side, the men just in their drawers and under-shirts, and no shoes nor stirrups, and resting their hands on their thighs, easy and comfortable—there must a' been twenty of them—and every lady with a lovely complexion, and perfectly beautiful, and looking just like a gang of real sure-enough queens, and dressed in clothes that cost millions of dollars, and just littered with diamonds. It was a powerful fine sight; I never see anything so lovely. And then one by one they got up and stood, and went a-weaving around the ring so gentle and wavy and graceful, the men looking ever so tall and airy and straight, with their heads bobbing and skimming along, away up there under the tent-roof, and every lady's rose-leafy dress flapping soft and silky around her hips, and she looking like the most loveliest parasol.

And then faster and faster they went, all of them dancing, first one foot stuck out in the air and then the other, the horses leaning more and more, and the ring-master going round and round the centre-pole, cracking his whip and shouting "hi!—hi!" and the clown cracking jokes behind him; and by-and-by all hands dropped the reins, and every lady put her knuckles on her hips and every gentleman folded his arms, and then how the horses did lean over and jump themselves! And so, one after the other they all skipped off into the ring, and made the sweetest bow I ever see, and then scampered out, and everybody clapped their hands and went just about wild.

Well, all through the circus they done the most astonishing things; and all the time that clown carried on so it most killed the people. The ring-master couldn't ever say a word to him but he was back at him quick as a wink with the funniest things a body ever

said; and how he ever *could* think of so many of them, and so
sudden and so pat, was what I couldn't noway understand. Why, I
couldn't a thought of them in a year. And by-and-by a drunk man
tried to get into the ring—said he wanted to ride; said he could ride
as well as anybody that ever was. They argued and tried to keep
him out, but he wouldn't listen, and the whole show come to a
standstill. Then the people begun to holler at him and make fun of
him, and that made him mad, and be begun to rip and tear; so that
stirred up the people, and a lot of men began to pile down off of
the benches and swarm towards the ring, saying, "Knock him down!
throw him out!" and one or two women begun to scream. So, then,
the ring-master he made a little speech, and said he hoped there
wouldn't be no disturbance, and if the man would promise he
wouldn't make no more trouble, he would let him ride, if he
thought he could stay on the horse. So everybody laughed and said
all right, and the man got on. The minute he was on, the horse
begun to rip and tear and jump and cavort around, with two circus
men hanging onto his bridle trying to hold him, and the drunk man
hanging onto his neck, and his heels flying in the air every jump,
and the whole crowd of people standing up shouting and laughing
till the tears rolled down. And at last, sure enough, all the circus
men could do, the horse broke loose, and away he went like the
very nation, round and round the ring, with that sot laying down on
him and hanging to his neck, with first one leg hanging most to the
ground on one side, and then t'other one on t'other side, and the
people just crazy. It warn't funny to me, though; I was all of a
tremble to see his danger. But pretty soon he struggled up astraddle
and grabbed the bridle, a-reeling this way and that; and the next
minute he sprung up and dropped the bridle and stood! and the
horse agoing like a house afire too. He just stood up there, a-sailing
around as easy and comfortable as if he warn't ever drunk in his life
—and then he begun to pull off his clothes and sling them. He
shed them so thick they kind of clogged up the air, and altogether
he shed seventeen suits. And then, there he was, slim and handsome, and dressed the gaudiest and prettiest you ever saw, and he
lit int hat horse with his whip and made him fairly hum—and
finally skipped off, and made his bow and danced off to the dressing-room, and everybody just a-howling with pleasure and astonishment.

Then the ring-master he see how he had been fooled, and he *was*
the sickest ring-master you ever see, I reckon. Why, it was one of
his own men! He had got up that joke all out of his own head, and
never let on to nobody. Well, I felt sheepish enough, to be took in
so, but I wouldn't a been in that ring-master's place, not for a thousand dollars. I don't know; there may be bullier circuses than what
that one was, but I never struck them yet. Anyways it was plenty

good enough for *me*; and wherever I run across it, it can have all of *my* custom, everytime.

Well, that night we had *our* show; but there warn't only about twelve people there; just enough to pay expenses. And they laughed all the time, and that made the duke mad; and everybody left, anyway, before the show was over, but one boy which was asleep. So the duke said these Arkansaw lunkheads couldn't come up to Shakspeare; what they wanted was low comedy—and may be something ruther worse than low comedy, he reckoned. He said he could size their style. So next morning he got some big sheets of wrapping-paper and some black paint, and drawed off some handbills and stuck them up all over the village. The bills said:

AT THE COURT HOUSE!
FOR 3 NIGHTS ONLY!
The World-Renowned Tragedians
DAVID GARRICK THE YOUNGER
AND
EDMUND KEAN THE ELDER!
Of the London and Continental
Theatres,
In their Thrilling Tragedy of
THE KING'S CAMELOPARD
OR
THE ROYAL NONESUCH! ! !⁹
Admission 50 cents.

Then at the bottom was the biggest line of all—which said:

LADIES AND CHILDREN NOT ADMITTED.

"There," says he, "if that line don't fetch them, I dont know Arkansaw!"

Chapter XXIII

Well, all day him and the king was hard at it, rigging up a stage, and a curtain, and a row of candles for footlights; and that night the house was jam full of men in no time. When the place couldn't hold no more, the duke he quit tending door and went around the back way and come onto the stage and stood up before the curtain, and made a little speech, and praised up this tragedy, and said it was the most thrillingest one that ever was; and so he went on a-bragging about the tragedy and about Edmund Kean the Elder, which was to play the main principal part in it; and at last when he'd got everybody's expectations up high enough, he rolled up the curtain, and the next minute the king come a-prancing out on all fours, naked; and he was painted all over, ring-streaked-and-striped,

9. A camelopard is an archaic name for a giraffe, but also describes a legendary spotted beast the size of a camel. This hoax performance was a popular subject of comic stories, and Clemens had heard a version he referred to as *The Burning Shame* from his friend Jim Gillis in his California newspaper days.

all sorts of colors, as splendid as a rainbow. And—but never mind the rest of his outfit, it was just wild, but it was awful funny. The people most killed themselves laughing; and when the king got done capering, and capered off behind the scenes, they roared and clapped and stormed and haw-hawed till he come back and done it over again; and after that, they made him do it another time. Well, it would a made a cow laugh to see the shines that old idiot cut.

Then the duke he lets the curtain down, and bows to the people, and says the great tragedy will be performed only two nights more, on accounts of pressing London engagements, where the seats is all sold aready for it in Drury Lane; and then he makes them another bow, and says if he has succeeded in pleasing them and instructing them, he will be deeply obleeged if they will mention it to their friends and get them to come and see it.

Twenty people sings out:

"What, is it over? Is that *all?*"

The duke says yes. Then there was a fine time. Everybody sings out "sold," and rose up mad, and was agoing for that stage and them tragedians. But a big fine-looking man jumps up on a bench, and shouts:

"Hold on! Just a word, gentlemen." They stopped to listen. "We are sold—mighty badly sold. But we don't want to be the laughing-stock of this whole town, I reckon, and never hear the last of this thing as long as we live. *No.* What we want, is to go out of here quiet, and talk this show up, and sell the *rest* of the town! Then we'll all be in the same boat. Ain't that sensible?" ("You bet it is! —the jedge is right!" everybody sings out.) "All right, then—not a word about any sell. Go along home, and advise everybody to come and see the tragedy."

Next day you couldn't hear nothing around that town but how splendid that show was. House was jammed again, that night, and we sold this crowd the same way. When me and the king and the duke got home to the raft, we all had a supper; and by-and-by, about midnight, they made Jim and me back her out and float her down the middle of the river and fetch her in and hide her about two mile below town.

The third night the house was crammed again—and they warn't new-comers, this time, but people that was at the show the other two nights. I stood by the duke at the door, and I see that every man that went in had his pockets bulging, or something muffled up under his coat—and I see it warn't no perfumery neither, not by a long sight. I smelt sickly eggs by the barrel, and rotten cabbages, and such things; and if I know the signs of a dead cat being around, and I bet I do, there was sixty-four of them went in. I shoved in there for a minute, but it was too various for me, I couldn't stand it. Well, when the place couldn't hold no more people, the duke he give a fellow a quarter and told him to tend door for him a minute, and then he started around for the stage door, I after him; but the minute we turned the corner and was in the dark, he says:

"Walk fast, now, till you get away from the houses, and then shin for the raft like the dickens was after you!"

I done it, and he done the same. We struck the raft at the same time, and in less than two seconds we was gliding down stream, all dark and still, and edging towards the middle of the river, nobody saying a word. I reckoned the poor king was in for a gaudy time of it with the audience; but nothing of the sort; pretty soon he crawls out from under the wigwam, and says:

"Well, how'd the old thing pan out this time, Duke?"

He hadn't been up town at all.

We never showed a light till we was about ten mile below that village. Then we lit up and had a supper, and the king and the duke fairly laughed their bones loose over the way they'd served them people. The duke says:

"Greenhorns, flatheads! *I* knew the first house would keep mum and let the rest of the town get roped in; and I knew they'd lay for us the third night, and consider it was *their* turn now. Well, it *is* their turn, and I'd give something to know how much they'd take for it. I *would* just like to know how they're putting in their opportunity. They can turn it into a picnic, if they want to—they brought plenty provisions."

Them rapscallions took in four hundred and sixty-five dollars in that three nights. I never see money hauled in by the wagon-load like that, before.

By-and-by, when they was asleep and snoring, Jim says:

"Don't it 'sprise you, de way dem kings carries on, Huck?"

"No," I says, "it don't."

"Why don't it, Huck?"

"Well, it don't, because it's in the breed. I reckon they're all alike."

"But, Huck, dese kings o' ourn is regular rapscallions; dat's jist what dey is; dey's reglar rapscallions."

"Well, that's what I'm a-saying; all kings is mostly rapscallions, as fur as I can make out."

"Is dat so?"

"You read about them once—you'll see. Look at Henry the Eight; this'n a Sunday-School Superintendent to *him*. And look at Charles Second, and Louis Fourteen, and Louis Fifteen, and James Second, and Edward Second, and Richard Third, and forty more; besides all them Saxon heptarchies that used to rip around so in old times and raise Cain. My, you ought to seen old Henry the Eight when he was in bloom. He *was* a blossom. He used to marry a new wife every day, and chop off her head next morning. And he would do it just as indifferent as if he was ordering up eggs. 'Fetch up Nell Gwynn,' he says. They fetch her up. Next morning, 'Chop off her head!' And they chop it off. 'Fetch up Jane Shore,' he says; and up she comes. Next morning 'Chop off her head'—and they chop it off. 'Ring up Fair Rosamun.' Fair Rosamun answers the bell. Next morning, 'Chop off her head.' And he made every one of them tell him a tale every night; and he kept that up till he had hogged a thousand and one tales that way, and then he put them all in a book, and called it Domesday Book—which was a good name and stated the case. You don't know kings, Jim, but I know them; and this old rip of ourn is one of the cleanest I've struck in history. Well, Henry he takes a notion he wants to get up some trouble with this country. How does he go at it—give notice?—give the country a show? No. All of a sudden he heaves all the tea in Boston Harbor overboard, and whacks out a declaration of independence, and dares them to come on. That was *his* style—he never give anybody a chance. He had suspicions of his father, the Duke of Wellington. Well, what did he do?—ask him to show up? No—drownded him in a butt of mamsey, like a cat. Spose people left money laying around where he was—what did he do? He collared it. Spose he contracted to do a thing; and you paid him, and didn't set down there and see that he done it—what did he do? He always done the other thing. Spose he opened his mouth—what then? If he didn't shut it up powerful quick, he'd lose a lie, every time. That's the kind of a bug Henry was; and if we'd a had him along 'stead of our kings, he'd a fooled that town a heap worse than ourn done.[1] I don't say that ourn is lambs, because they ain't, when you come right down to the cold facts; but they ain't nothing to *that* old ram, anyway. All I say is, kings is kings, and you got to make allowances. Take them all around, they're a mighty ornery lot. It's the way they're raised."

"But dis one do *smell* so like de nation, Huck."

"Well, they all do, Jim. *We* can't help the way a king smells; history don't tell no way."

"Now de duke, he's a tolerble likely man, in some ways."

"Yes, a duke's different. But not very different. This one's a middling hard lot, for a duke. When he's drunk, there ain't no near-sighted man could tell him from a king."

"Well, anyways, I doan' hanker for no mo' un um, Huck. Dese is all I kin stan'."

1. Huck's "history" of kingly behavior is a farrago of fact and fiction. Henry VIII, King of England from 1509 to 1547, did execute two of his wives and divorced two others; Nell Gwynn, however, was the mistress of Charles II (reigned 1669–85); Jane Shore was mistress to Edward IV (who reigned in the 15th century); and Rosamund Clifford was mistress to Henry II in the 12th century. The Anglo-Saxon heptarchy (seven friendly kingdoms) ruled England 449–829. The Domesday Book, in which William the Conqueror of England had recorded all landowners and the value of their holdings, was completed in 1086; Huck confuses it with the stories in the *Arabian Nights*. The Duke of Wellington is a 19th-century personage; the Duke of Clarence was reportedly drowned in a wine butt in the early 16th century. The Boston Tea Party took place in 1773, and the Declaration of Independence was adopted in 1776; neither event, of course, has any connection with Henry VIII.

"It's the way I feel, too, Jim. But we've got them on our hands, and we got to remember what they are, and make allowances. Sometimes I wish we could hear of a country that's out of kings."

What was the use to tell Jim these warn't real kings and dukes? It wouldn't a done no good; and besides, it was just as I said; you couldn't tell them from the real kind.

I went to sleep, and Jim didn't call me when it was my turn. He often done that. When I waked up, just at day-break, he was setting there with his head down betwixt his knees, moaning and mourning to himself. I didn't take notice, nor let on. I knowed what it was about. He was thinking about his wife and his children, away up yonder, and he was low and homesick; because he hadn't ever been away from home before in his life; and I do believe he cared just as much for his people as white folks does for their'n. It don't seem natural, but I reckon it's so. He was often moaning and mourning that way, nights, when he judged I was asleep, and saying, "Po' little 'Lizabeth! po' little Johnny! its mighty hard; I spec' I ain't ever gwyne to see you no mo', no mo'!" He was a mighty good nigger, Jim was.

But this time I somehow got to talking to him about his wife and young ones; and by-and-by he says:

"What makes me feel so bad dis time, 'uz bekase I hear sumpn over yonder on de bank like a whack, er a slam, while ago, en it mine me er de time I treat my little 'Lizabeth so ornery. She warn't on'y 'bout fo' year ole, en she tuck de sk'yarlet-fever, en had a powful rough spell; but she got well, en one day she was a-stannin' aroun', en I says to her, I says:

" 'Shet de do'.'

"She never done it; jis' stood dar, kiner smilin' up at me. It make me mad; en I says agin, mighty loud, I says:

" 'Doan' you hear me?—shet de do'!'

"She jis' stood de same way, kiner smilin' up. I was a-bilin'! I says:

" 'I lay I *make* you mine!'

"En wid dat I fetch' her a slap side de head dat sont her a-sprawlin'. Den I went into de yuther room, en 'uz gone 'bout ten minutes; en when I come back, dah was dat do' a-stannin' open *yit*, en dat chile stannin' mos' right in it, a-lookin' down and mournin', en de tears runnin' down. My, but I *wuz* mad, I was agwyne for de chile, but jis' den—it was a do' dat open innerds—jis' den, 'long come de wind en slam it to, behine de chile, *ker-blam!*—en my lan', de chile never move'! My breff mos' hop outer me; en I feel so—so —I doan' know *how* I feel. I crope out, all a-tremblin', en crope aroun' en open de do' easy en slow, en poke my head in behine de chile, sof' en still, en all uv a sudden, I says *pow!* jis' as loud as I could yell. *She never budge!* Oh, Huck, I bust out a-cryin' en grab her up in my arms, en say, 'Oh, de po' little thing! de Lord God

Amighty fogive po' ole Jim, kaze he never gwyne to fogive hisself as long's he live!' Oh, she was plumb deef en dumb, Huck, plumb deef en dumb—en I'd ben a'treat'n her so!"

Chapter XXIV

Next day, towards night, we laid up under a little willow towhead out in the middle, where there was a village on each side of the river, and the duke and the king begun to lay out a plan for working them towns. Jim he spoke to the duke, and said he hoped it wouldn't take but a few hours, because it got mighty heavy and tiresome to him when he had to lay all day in the wigwam tied with the rope. You see, when we left him all alone we had to tie him, because if anybody happened on him all by himself and not tied, it wouldn't look much like he was a runaway nigger, you know. So the duke said it *was* kind of hard to have to lay roped all day, and he'd cipher out some way to get around it.

He was uncommon bright, the duke was, and he soon struck it. He dressed Jim up in King Lear's outfit—it was a long curtain-calico gown, and a white horse-hair wig and whiskers; and then he took his theatre-paint and painted Jim's face and hands and ears and neck all over a dead bull solid blue, like a man that's been drownded nine days. Blamed if he warn't the horriblest looking outrage I ever see. Then the duke took and wrote out a sign on a shingle so—

Sick Arab—but harmless when not out of his head.

And he nailed that shingle to a lath, and stood the lath up four or five foot in front of the wigwam. Jim was satisfied. He said it was a sight better than laying tied a couple of years every day and trembling all over every time there was a sound. The duke told him to make himself free and easy, and if anybody ever come meddling around, he must hop out of the wigwam, and carry on a little, and fetch a howl or two like a wild beast, and he reckoned they would light out and leave him alone. Which was sound enough judgment; but you take the average man, and he wouldn't wait for him to howl. Why, he didn't only look like he was dead, he looked considerable more than that.

These rapscallions wanted to try the Nonesuch again, because there was so much money in it, but they judged it wouldn't be safe, because maybe the news might a worked along down by this time. They couldn't hit no project that suited, exactly; so at last the duke said he reckoned he'd lay off and work his brains an hour or two and see if he couldn't put up something on the Arkansaw village; and the king he allowed he would drop over to t'other village, without any plan, but just trust in Providence to lead him the profitable way—meaning the devil, I reckon. We had all bought store clothes where we stopped last; and now the king put his'n on, and he told me to put mine on. I done it, of course. The king's duds was all black, and he did look real swell and starchy. I never knowed how clothes could change a body before. Why, before, he looked like the orneriest old rip that ever was; but now, when he'd take off his new white beaver and make a bow and do a smile, he looked that grand and good and pious that you'd say he had walked right out of the ark, and maybe was old Leviticus[2] himself. Jim cleaned up the canoe, and I got my paddle ready. There was a big steamboat laying at the shore away up under the point, about three mile above town —been there a couple of hours, taking on freight. Says the king:

"Seein' how I'm dressed, I reckon maybe I better arrive down from St. Louis or Cincinnati, or some other big place. Go for the steamboat, Huckleberry; we'll come down to the village on her."

I didn't have to be ordered twice, to go and take a steamboat ride. I fetched the shore a half a mile above the village, and then went scooting along the bluff bank in the easy water. Pretty soon we come to a nice innocent-looking young country jake setting on a log swabbing the sweat off of his face, for it was powerful warm weather; and he had a couple of big carpet-bags by him.

"Run her nose in shore," says the king. I done it. "Wher' you bound for, young man?"

"For the steamboat; going to Orleans."

"Git aboard," says the king. "Hold on a minute, my servant 'll he'p you with them bags. Jump out and he'p the gentleman, Adolphus"—meaning me, I see.

I done so, and then we all three started on again. The young chap was mighty thankful; said it was tough work toting his baggage such weather. He asked the king where he was going, and the king told him he'd come down the river and landed at the other village this morning, and now he was going up a few mile to see an old friend on a farm up there. The young fellow says:

"When I first see you, I says to myself, 'It's Mr. Wilks, sure, and he come mighty near getting here in time.' But then I says again, 'No, I reckon it ain't him, or else he wouldn't be paddling up the river.' You *ain't* him, are you?"

"No, my name's Blodgett—Elexander Blodgett—*Reverend* Elexander Blodgett, I spose I must say, as I'm one o' the Lord's poor servants. But still I'm jist as able to be sorry for Mr. Wilks for not arriving in time, all the same, if he's missed anything by it—which I hope he hasn't."

"Well, he don't miss any property by it, because he'll get that all right; but he's missed seeing his brother Peter die—which he mayn't mind, nobody can tell as to that—but his brother would a give anything in this world to see *him* before he died; never talked about nothing else all these three weeks; hadn't seen him since they was boys together—and hadn't ever seen his brother William at all

2. The third book of the Old Testament is here confused with Noah.

—that's the deef and dumb one—William ain't more than thirty or thirty-five. Peter and George was the only ones that come out here; George was the married brother; him and his wife both died last year. Harvey and William's the only ones that's left now; and, as I was saying, they haven't got here in time."

"Did anybody send 'em word?"

"Oh, yes; a month or two ago, when Peter was first took; because Peter said then that he sorter felt like he warn't going to get well this time. You see, he was pretty old, and George's g'yirls was too young to be much company for him, except Mary Jane the red-headed one; and so he was kinder lonesome after George and his wife died, and didn't seem to care much to live. He most desperately wanted to see Harvey—and William too, for that matter—because he was one of them kind that can't bear to make a will. He left a letter behind for Harvey, and said he'd told in it where his money was hid, and how he wanted the rest of the property divided up so George's g'yirls would be all right—for George didn't leave nothing. And that letter was all they could get him to put a pen to."

"Why do you reckon Harvey don't come? Wher' does he live?"

"Oh, he lives in England—Sheffield—preaches there—hasn't ever been in this country. He hasn't had any too much time—and besides he mightn't a got the letter at all, you know."

"Too bad, too bad he couldn't a lived to see his brothers, poor soul. You going to Orleans, you say?"

"Yes, but that ain't only a part of it. I'm going in a ship, next Wednesday, for Ryo Janeero, where my uncle lives."

"It's a pretty long journey. But it'll be lovely; I wisht I was agoing. Is Mary Jane the oldest? How old is the others?"

"Mary Jane's nineteen, Susan's fifteen, and Joanna's about fourteen—that's the one that gives herself to good works and has a hare-lip."

"Poor things! to be left alone in the cold world so."

"Well, they could be worse off. Old Peter had friends, and they ain't going to let them come to no harm. There's Hobson, the Babtis' preacher; and Deacon Lot Hovey, and Ben Rucker, and Abner Shackleford, and Levi Bell, the lawyer; and Dr. Robinson, and their wives, and the widow Bartley, and—well, there's a lot of them; but these are the ones that Peter was thickest with, and used to write about sometimes, when he wrote home; so Harvey'll know where to look for friends when he gets here."

Well, the old man he went on asking questions till he just fairly emptied that young fellow. Blamed if he didn't inquire about everybody and everything in that blessed town, and all about all the Wilkses; and about Peter's business—which was a tanner; and about George's—which was a carpenter; and about Harvey's—

which was a dissentering[3] minister, and so on, and so on. Then he says:

"What did you want to walk all the way up to the steamboat for?"

"Because she's a big Orleans boat, and I was afeard she mightn't stop there. When they're deep they won't stop for a hail. A Cincinnati boat will, but this is a St. Louis one."

"Was Peter Wilks well off?"

"Oh, yes, pretty well off. He had houses and land, and it's reckoned he left three or four thousand in cash hid up som'ers."

"When did you say he died?"

"I didn't say, but it was last night."

"Funeral to-morrow, likely?"

"Yes, 'bout the middle of the day."

"Well, it's all terrible sad; but we've all got to go, one time or another. So what we want to do is to be prepared; then we're all right."

"Yes, sir, it's the best way. Ma used to always say that."

When we struck the boat, she was about done loading, and pretty soon she got off. The king never said nothing about going aboard, so I lost my ride, after all. When the boat was gone, the king made me paddle up another mile to a lonesome place, and then he got ashore, and says:

"Now hustle back, right off, and fetch the duke up here, and the new carpet-bags. And if he's gone over to t'other side, go over there and git him. And tell him to git himself up regardless. Shove along, now."

I see what *he* was up to; but I never said nothing, of course. When I got back with the duke, we hid the canoe and then they set down on a log, and the king told him everything, just like the young fellow had said it—every last word of it. And all the time he was a doing it, he tried to talk like an Englishman; and he done it pretty well too, for a slouch. I can't imitate him, and so I ain't agoing to try to; but he really done it pretty good. Then he says:

"How are you on the deef and dumb, Bilgewater?"

The duke said, leave him alone for that; said he had played a deef and dumb person on the histrionic boards. So then they waited for a steamboat.

About the middle of the afternoon a couple of little boats come along, but they didn't come from high enough up the river; but at last there was a big one, and they hailed her. She sent out her yawl, and we went aboard, and she was from Cincinnati; and when they found we only wanted to go four or five mile, they was booming mad, and give us a cussing, and said they wouldn't land us. But the king was ca'm. He says:

3. Dissenting.

"If gentlemen kin afford to pay a dollar a mile apiece, to be took on and put off in a yawl, a steamboat kin afford to carry 'em, can't it?"

So they softened down and said it was all right; and when we got to the village, they yawled us ashore. About two dozen men flocked down, when they see the yawl a coming; and when the king says—

"Kin any of you gentlemen tell me wher' Mr. Peter Wilks lives?" they give a glance at one another, and nodded their heads, as much as to say, "What d' I tell you?" Then one of them says, kind of soft and gentle:

"I'm sorry, sir, but the best we can do is to tell you where he *did* live yesterday evening."

Sudden as winking, the ornery old cretur went all to smash, and fell up against the man, and put his chin on his shoulder, and cried down his back, and says:

"Alas, alas, our poor brother—gone, and we never got to see him; oh, it's too, *too* hard!"

Then he turns around, blubbering, and makes a lot of idiotic signs to the duke on his hands, and blamed if *he* didn't drop a carpet-bag and bust out a-crying. If they warn't the beatenest lot, them two frauds, that ever I struck.

Well, the men gethered around, and sympathized with them, and said all sorts of kind things to them, and carried their carpet-bags up the hill for them, and let them lean on them and cry, and told the king all about his brother's last moments, and the king he told it all over again on his hands to the duke, and both of them took on about that dead tanner like they'd lost the twelve disciples. Well, if ever I struck anything like it, I'm a nigger. It was enough to make a body ashamed of the human race.

Chapter XXV

The news was all over town in two minutes, and you could see the people tearing down on the run, from every which way, some of them putting on their coats as they come. Pretty soon we was in the middle of a crowd, and the noise of the tramping was like a soldier-march. The windows and dooryards was full; and every minute somebody would say, over a fence:

"Is it *them!*"

And somebody trotting along with the gang would answer back and say,

"You bet it is."

When we got to the house, the street in front of it was packed, and the three girls was standing in the door. Mary Jane *was* red-headed, but that don't make no difference, she was most awful beautiful, and her face and her eyes was all lit up like glory, she was so glad her uncles was come. The king he spread his arms, and Mary Jane she jumped for them, and the hare-lip jumped for the duke, and there they *had* it! Everybody most, leastways women, cried for joy to see them meet again at last and have such good times.

Then the king he hunched the duke, private—I see him do it—and then he looked around and see the coffin, over in the corner on two chairs; so then, him and the duke, with a hand across each other's shoulder, and t'other hand to their eyes, walked slow and solemn over there, everybody dropping back to give them room, and all the talk and noise stopping, people saying "Sh!" and all the men taking their hats off and drooping their heads, so you could a heard a pin fall. And when they got there, they bent over and looked in the coffin, and took one sight, and then they bust out a crying so you could a heard them to Orleans, most; and then they put their arms around each other's necks, and hung their chins over each other's shoulders; and then for three minutes, or maybe four, I never see two men leak the way they done. And mind you, everybody was doing the same; and the place was that damp I never see anything like it. Then one of them got on one side of the coffin, and t'other on t'other side, and they kneeled down and rested their foreheads on the coffin, and let on to pray all to theirselves. Well, when it come to that, it worked the crowd like you never see anything like it, and so everybody broke down and went to sobbing right out loud—the poor girls, too; and every woman, nearly, went up to the girls, without saying a word, and kissed them, solemn, on the forehead, and then put their hand on their head, and looked up towards the sky, with the tears running down, and then busted out and went off sobbing and swabbing, and give the next woman a show. I never see anything so disgusting.

Well, by-and-by the king he gets up and comes forward a little, and works himself up and slobbers out a speech, all full of tears and flapdoodle about its being a sore trial for him and his poor brother to lose the diseased, and to miss seeing diseased alive, after the long journey of four thousand mile, but its a trial that's sweetened and sanctified to us by this dear sympathy and these holy tears, and so he thanks them out of his heart and out of his brother's heart, because out of their mouths they can't, words being too weak and cold, and all that kind of rot and slush, till it was just sickening; and then he blubbers out a pious goody-goody Amen, and turns himself loose and goes to crying fit to bust.

And the minute the words was out of his mouth somebody over in the crowd struck up the doxolojer,[4] and everybody joined in with all their might, and it just warmed you up and made you feel as good as church letting out. Music *is* a good thing; and after all that soul-butter and hogwash, I never see it freshen up things so, and sound so honest and bully.

Then the king begins to work his jaw again, and says how him

4. Doxology or hymn of praise to God.

and his nieces would be glad if a few of the main principal friends of the family would take supper here with them this evening, and help set up with the ashes of the diseased; and says if his poor brother laying yonder could speak, he knows who he would name, for they was names that was very dear to him, and mentioned often in his letters; and so he will name the same, to-wit, as follows, vizz:—Rev. Mr. Hobson, and Deacon Lot Hovey, and Mr. Ben Rucker, and Abner Shackleford, and Levi Bell, and Dr. Robinson, and their wives, and the widow Bartley.

Rev. Hobson and Dr. Robinson was down to the end of the town, a-hunting together; that is, I mean the doctor was shipping a sick man to t'other world, and the preacher was pinting him right. Lawyer Bell was away up to Louisville on some business. But the rest was on hand, and so they all come and shook hands with the king and thanked him and talked to him; and then they shook hands with the duke, and didn't say nothing but just kept a-smiling and bobbing their heads like a passel of sapheads whilst he made all sorts of signs with his hands and said "Goo-goo—goo-goo-goo," all the time, like a baby that can't talk.

So the king he blatted along, and managed to inquire about pretty much everybody and dog in town, by his name, and mentioned all sorts of little things that happened one time or another in the town, or to George's family, or to Peter; and he always let on that Peter wrote him the things, but that was a lie, he got every blessed one of them out of that young flathead that we canoed up to the steamboat.

Then Mary Jane she fetched the letter her father left behind, and the king he read it out loud and cried over it. It give the dwelling-house and three thousand dollars, gold, to the girls; and it give the tanyard (which was doing a good business), along with some other houses and land (worth about seven thousand), and three thousand dollars in gold to Harvey and William, and told where the six thousand cash was hid, down cellar. So these two frauds said they'd go and fetch it up, and have everything square and above-board; and told me to come with a candle. We shut the cellar door behind us, and when they found the bag they spilt it out on the floor, and it was a lovely sight, all them yallerboys.[5] My, the way the king's eyes did shine! He slaps the duke on the shoulder, and says:

"Oh, *this* ain't bully, nor noth'n! Oh, no, I reckon not! Why, Biljy, it beats the Nonesuch, *don't* it!"

The duke allowed it did. They pawed the yaller-boys, and sifted them through their fingers and let them jingle down on the floor; and the king says:

"It ain't no use talkin'; bein' brothers to a rich dead man, and representatives of furrin heirs that's got left, is the line for you and

5. Gold coins.

me, Bilge. Thish-yer comes of trust'n to Providence. It's the best way, in the long run. I've tried 'em all, and ther' ain't no better way."

Most everybody would a been satisfied with the pile, and took it on trust; but no, they must count it. So they counts it, and it comes out four hundred and fifteen dollars short. Says the king:

"Dern him, I wonder what he done with that four hundred and fifteen dollars?"

They worried over that a while, and ransacked all around for it. Then the duke says:

"Well, he was a pretty sick man, and likely he made a mistake—I reckon that's the way of it. The best way's to let it go, and keep still about it. We can spare it."

"Oh, shucks, yes, we can *spare* it. I don't k'yer noth'n 'bout that—it's the *count* I'm thinkin' about. We want to be awful square and open and aboveboard, here, you know. We want to lug this h'yer money up stairs and count it before everybody—then ther' ain't noth'n suspicious. But when the dead man says ther's six thous'n dollars, you know, we don't want to—"

"Hold on," says the duke. "Less make up the deffisit"—and he begun to haul out yallerboys out of his pocket.

"It's a most amaz'n' good idea, duke—you *have* got a rattlin' clever head on you," says the king. "Blest if the old Nonesuch ain't a heppin' us out agin"—and *he* begun to haul out yallerjackets and stack them up.

It most busted them, but they made up the six thousand clean and clear.

"Say," says the duke, "I got another idea. Le's go up stairs and count this money, and then take and *give it to the girls*."

"Good land, duke, lemme hug you! It's the most dazzling idea 'at ever a man struck. You have cert'nly got the most astonishin' head I ever see. Oh, this is the boss dodge,[6] ther' ain't no mistake 'bout it. Let 'em fetch along their suspicions now, if they want to—this'll lay 'em out."

When we got up stairs, everybody gethered around the table, and the king he counted it and stacked it up, three hundred dollars in a pile—twenty elegant little piles. Everybody looked hungry at it, and licked their chops. Then they raked it into the bag again, and I see the king begin to swell himself up for another speech. He says:

"Friends all, my poor brother that lays yonder, has done generous by them that's left behind in the vale of sorrers. He has done generous by these-yer poor little lambs that he loved and sheltered, and that's left fatherless and motherless. Yes, and we that knowed him, knows that he would a done *more* generous by 'em if he hadn't been afeard o' woundin' his dear William and me. Now, *wouldn't*

6. **Best confidence trick.**

he? Ther' ain't no question 'bout it, in *my* mind. Well, then—what
kind o' brothers would it be, that 'd stand in his way at sech a
time? And what kind o' uncles would it be that 'd rob—yes, *rob*—
sech poor sweet lambs as these 'at he loved so, at sech a time? If I
know William—and I *think* I do—he—well, I'll jest ask him." He
turns around and begins to make a lot of signs to the duke with his
hands; and the duke he looks at him stupid and leather-headed a
while, then all of a sudden he seems to catch his meaning, and
jumps for the king, goo-gooing with all his might for joy, and hugs
him about fifteen times before he lets up. Then the king says, "I
knowed it; I reckon *that* 'll convince anybody the way *he* feels about
it. Here, Mary Jane, Susan, Joanner, take the money—take it *all*.
It's the gift of him that lays yonder, cold but joyful."

Mary Jane she went for him, Susan and the hare-lip went for the
duke, and then such another hugging and kissing I never see yet.
And everybody crowded up with the tears in their eyes, and most
shook the hands off of them frauds, saying all the time:

"You *dear* good souls!—how *lovely!*—how *could* you!"

Well, then, pretty soon all hands got to talking about the diseased again, and how good he was, and what a loss he was, and all
that; and before long a big iron-jawed man worked himself in there
from outside, and stood a listening and looking, and not saying anything; and nobody saying anything to him either, because the king
was talking and they was all busy listening. The king was saying—in
the middle of something he'd started in on—

"—they bein' partickler friends o' the diseased. That's why
they're invited here this evenin'; but to-morrow we want *all* to come
—everybody; for he respected everybody, he liked everybody, and so
it's fitten that his funeral orgies sh'd be public."

And so he went a-mooning on and on, liking to hear himself talk,
and every little while he fetched in his funeral orgies again, till the
duke he couldn't stand it no more; so he writes on a little scrap of
paper, "*obsequies*, you old fool," and folds it up and goes to goo-
gooing and reaching it over people's heads to him. The king he
reads it, and puts it in his pocket, and says:

"Poor William, afflicted as he is, his *heart's* aluz right. Asks me
to invite everybody to come to the funeral—wants me to make 'em
all welcome. But he needn't a worried—it was jest what I was at."

Then he weaves along again, perfectly ca'm, and goes to dropping in his funeral orgies again every now and then, just like he done
before. And when he done it the third time, he says:

"I say orgies, not because it's the common term, because it ain't
—obsequies bein' the common term—but because orgies is the
right term. Obsequies ain't used in England no more, now—it's
gone out. We say orgies now, in England. Orgies is better,
because it means the thing you're after, more exact. It's a word

that's made up out'n the Greek *orgo*, outside, open, abroad; and the Hebrew *jeesum*, to plant, cover up; hence in*ter*. So, you see, funeral orgies is an open er public funeral."[7]

He was the *worst* I ever struck. Well, the iron-jawed man he laughed right in his face. Everybody was shocked. Everybody says, "Why *doctor!*" and Abner Shackleford says:

"Why, Robinson, hain't you heard the news? This is Harvey Wilks."

The king he smiled eager, and shoved out his flapper, and says:

"*Is* it my poor brother's dear good friend and physician? I—"

"Keep your hands off of me!" says the doctor. "*You* talk like an Englishman—*don't* you? It's the worse imitation I ever heard. *You* Peter Wilks's brother. You're a fraud, that's what you are!"

Well, how they all took on! They crowded around the doctor, and tried to quiet him down, and tried to explain to him, and tell him how Harvey'd showed in forty ways that he *was* Harvey, and knowed everybody by name, and the names of the very dogs, and begged and *begged* him not to hurt Harvey's feelings and the poor girls' feelings, and all that; but it warn't no use, he stormed right along, and said any man that pretended to be an Englishman and couldn't imitate the lingo no better than what he did, was a fraud and a liar. The poor girls was hanging to the king and crying; and all of a sudden the doctor ups and turns on *them*. He says:

"I was your father's friend, and I'm your friend; and I warn you *as* a friend, and an honest one, that wants to protect you and keep you out of harm and trouble, to turn your backs on that scoundrel, and have nothing to do with him, the ignorant tramp, with his idiotic Greek and Hebrew as he calls it. He is the thinnest kind of an impostor—has come here with a lot of empty names and facts which he has picked up somewheres, and you take them for *proofs*, and are helped to fool yourselves by these foolish friends here, who ought to know better. Mary Jane Wilks, you know me for your friend, and for your unselfish friend, too. Now listen to me; turn this pitiful rascal out—I *beg* you to do it. Will you?"

Mary Jane straightened herself up, and my, but she was handsome! She says:

"*Here* is my answer." She hove up the bag of money and put it in the king's hands, and says, "Take this six thousand dollars, and invest it for me and my sisters any way you want to, and don't give us no receipt for it."

Then she put her arm around the king on one side, and Susan and the hare-lip done the same on the other. Everybody clapped their hands and stomped on the floor like a perfect storm, whilst the king held up his head and smiled proud. The doctor says:

---

7. The comic etymology was a stock in trade of the southwestern humorists and is still popular in comedy routines.

"All right, I wash *my* hands of the matter. But I warn you all that a time's coming when you're going to feel sick whenever you think of this day"—and away he went.

"All right, doctor," says the king, kinder mocking him, "we'll try and get 'em to send for you"—which made them all laugh, and they said it was a prime good hit.

Chapter XXVI

Well, when they was all gone, the king he asks Mary Jane how they was off for spare rooms, and she said she had one spare room, which would do for Uncle William, and she'd give her own room to Uncle Harvey, which was a little bigger, and she would turn into the room with her sisters and sleep on a cot; and up garret was a little cubby, with a pallet in it. The king said the cubby would do for his valley—meaning me.

So Mary Jane took us up, and she showed them their rooms, which was plain but nice. She said she'd have her frocks and a lot of other traps took out of her room if they was in Uncle Harvey's way, but he said they warn't. The frocks was hung along the wall, and before them was a curtain made out of calico that hung down to the floor. There was an old hair trunk in one corner, and a guitar box in another, and all sorts of little knickknacks and jim-cracks around, like girls brisken up a room with. The king said it was all the more homely and more pleasanter for these fixings, and so don't disturb them. The duke's room was pretty small, but plenty good enough, and so was my cubby.

That night they had a big supper, and all them men and women was there, and I stood behind the king and the duke's chairs and waited on them, and the niggers waited on the rest. Mary Jane she set at the head of the table, with Susan along side of her, and said how bad the biscuits was, and how mean the preserves was, and how ornery and tough the fried chickens was—and all that kind of rot, the way women always do for to force out compliments; and the people all knowed everything was tip top, and said so—said "How *do* you get biscuits to brown so nice?" and "Where, for the land's sake *did* you get these amaz'n pickles?" and all that kind of humbug talky-talk, just the way people always does at a supper, you know.

And when it was all done, me and the hare-lip had supper in the kitchen off of the leavings, whilst the others was helping the niggers clean up the things. The hare-lip she got to pumping me about England, and blest if I didn't think the ice was getting mighty thin, sometimes. She says:

"Did you ever see the king?"

"Who? William Fourth? Well, I bet I have—he goes to our church." I knowed he was dead years ago, but I never let on. So when I says he goes to our church, she says:

"What—regular?"

"Yes—regular. His pew's right over opposite ourn—on 'tother side the pulpit."

"I thought he lived in London?"

"Well, he does. Where *would* he live?"

"But I thought *you* lived in Sheffield?"

I see I was up a stump. I had to let on to get choked with a chicken bone, so as to get time to think how to get down again. Then I says:

"I mean he goes to our church regular when he's in Sheffield. That's only in the summer-time, when he comes there to take the sea baths."

"Why, how you talk—Sheffield ain't on the sea."

"Well, who said it was?"

"Why, you did."

"I *didn't*, nuther."

"You did!"

"I didn't."

"You did."

"I never said nothing of the kind."

"Well, what *did* you say, then?"

"Said he come to take the sea *baths*—that's what I said."

"Well, then! how's he going to take the sea baths if it ain't on the sea?"

"Looky here," I says; "did you ever see any Congress water?"[8]

"Yes."

"Well, did you have to go to Congress to get it?"

"Why, no."

"Well, neither does William Fourth have to go to the sea to get a sea bath."

"How does he get it, then?"

"Gets it the way people down here gets Congress water—in barrels. There in the palace at Sheffield they've got furnaces, and he wants his water hot. They can't bile that amount of water away off there at the sea. They haven't got no conveniences for it."

"Oh, I see, now. You might a said that in the first place and saved time."

When she said that, I see I was out of the woods again, and so I was comfortable and glad. Next, she says:

"Do you go to church, too?"

"Yes—regular."

"Where do you set?"

"Why, in our pew."

"*Who*se pew?"

"Why, *ourn*—your Uncle Harvey's."

---

8. Famous mineral water from the Congress Spring in Saratoga, New York.

"His'n? What does *he* want with a pew?"

"Wants it to set in. What did you *reckon* he wanted with it?"

"Why, I thought he'd be in the pulpit."

Rot him, I forgot he was a preacher. I see I was up a stump again, so I played another chicken bone and got another think. Then I says:

"Blame it, do you suppose there ain't but one preacher to a church?"

"Why, what do they want with more?"

"What!—to preach before a king? I never see such a girl as you. They don't have no less than seventeen."

"Seventeen! My land! Why, I wouldn't set out such a string as that, not if I *never* got to glory. It must take 'em a week."

"Shucks, they don't *all* of 'em preach the same day—only *one* of 'em."

"Well, then, what does the rest of 'em do?"

"Oh, nothing much. Loll around, pass the plate—and one thing or another. But mainly they don't do nothing."

"Well, then, what are they *for?*"

"Why, they're for *style*. Don't you know nothing?"

"Well, I don't *want* to know no such foolishness as that. How is servants treated in England? Do they treat 'em better 'n we treat our niggers?"

"*No!* A servant ain't nobody there. They treat them worse than dogs."

"Don't they give 'em holidays, the way we do, Christmas and New Year's week, and Fourth of July?"

"Oh, just listen! A body could tell *you* hain't ever been to England, by that. Why, Hare-l—why, Joanna, they never see a holiday from year's end to year's end; never go to the circus, nor theatre, nor nigger shows, nor nowheres."

"Nor church?"

"Nor church."

"But *you* always went to church."

Well, I was gone up again. I forgot I was the old man's servant. But next minute I whirled in on a kind of an explanation how a valley was different from a common servant, and *had* to go to church whether he wanted to or not, and set with the family, on account of it's being the law. But I didn't do it pretty good, and when I got done I see she warn't satisfied. She says:

"Honest injun, now, hain't you been telling me a lot of lies?"

"Honest injun," says I.

"None of it at all?"

"None of it at all. Not a lie in it," says I.

"Lay your hand on this book and say it."

I see it warn't nothing but a dictionary, so I laid my hand on it and said it. So then she looked a little better satisfied, and says:

"Well, then, I'll believe some of it; but I hope to gracious if I'll believe the rest."

"What is it you won't believe, Joe?" says Mary Jane, stepping in with Susan behind her. "It ain't right nor kind for you to talk so to him, and him a stranger and so far from his people. How would you like to be treated so?"

"That's always your way, Maim—always sailing in to help somebody before they're hurt. I hain't done nothing to him. He's told some stretchers, I reckon; and I said I wouldn't swallow it all; and that's every bit and grain I *did* say. I reckon he can stand a little thing like that, can't he?"

"I don't care whether 'twas little or whether 'twas big, he's here in our house and a stranger, and it wasn't good of you to say it. If you was in his place, it would make you feel ashamed; and so you ought'nt to say a thing to another person that will make *them* feel ashamed."

"Why, Maim, he said—"

"It don't make no difference what he *said*—that ain't the thing. The thing is for you to treat him *kind*, and not be saying things to make him remember he ain't in his own country and amongst his own folks."

I says to myself, *this* is a girl that I'm letting that old reptle rob her of her money!

Then Susan *she* waltzed in; and if you'll believe me, she did give Hare-lip hark from the tomb![9]

Says I to myself, And this is *another* one that I'm letting him rob her of her money!

Then Mary Jane she took another inning, and went in sweet and lovely again—which was her way—but when she got done there warn't hardly anything left o' poor Hare-lip. So she hollered.

"All right, then," says the other girls, "you just ask his pardon."

She done it, too. And she done it beautiful. She done it so beautiful it was good to hear; and I wished I could tell her a thousand lies, so she could do it again.

I says to myself, this is *another* one that I'm letting him rob her of her money. And when she got through, they all jest laid their-selves out to make me feel at home and know I was amongst friends. I felt so ornery and low down and mean, that I says to myself, My mind's made up; I'll hive that money for them or bust.

So then I lit out—for bed, I said, meaning some time or another. When I got by myself, I went to thinking the thing over. I says to myself, shall I go to that doctor, private, and blow on these frauds? No—that won't do. He might tell who told him; then the king and the duke would make it warm for me. Shall I go, private, and tell Mary Jane? No—I dasn't do it. Her face would give them a hint, sure; they've got the money, and they'd slide right out and get away

9. A chewing out.

with it. If she was to fetch in help, I'd get mixed up in the business, before it was done with, I judge. No, there ain't no good way but one. I got to steal that money, somehow; and I got to steal it some way that they won't suspicion that I done it. They've got a good thing, here; and they ain't agoing to leave till they've played this family and this town for all they're worth, so I'll find a chance time enough. I'll steal it, and hide it; and by-and-by, when I'm away down the river, I'll write a letter and tell Mary Jane where it's hid. But I better hive it to-night, if I can, because the doctor maybe hasn't let up as much as he lets on he has; he might scare them out of here, yet.

So, thinks I, I'll go and search them rooms. Up stairs the hall was dark, but I found the duke's room, and started to paw around it with my hands; but I recollected it wouldn't be much like the king to let anybody else take care of that money but his own self; so then I went to his room and begun to paw around there. But I see I couldn't do nothing without a candle, and I dasn't light one, of course. So I judged I'd got to do the other thing—lay for them, and eavesdrop. About that time, I hears their footsteps coming, and was going to skip under the bed; I reached for it, but it wasn't where I thought it would be; but I touched the curtain that hid Mary Jane's frocks, so I jumped in behind that and snuggled in amongst the gowns, and stood there perfectly still.

They come in and shut the door; and the first thing the duke done was to get down and look under the bed. Then I was glad I hadn't found the bed when I wanted it. And yet, you know, it's kind of natural to hide under the bed when you are up to anything private. They sets down, then, and the king says:

"Well, what is it? and cut it middlin' short, because it's better for us to be down there a whoopin'-up the mournin', than up here givin' 'em a chance to talk us over."

"Well, this is it, Capet. I ain't easy; I ain't comfortable. That doctor lays on my mind. I wanted to know your plans. I've got a notion, and I think it's a sound one."

"What is it, duke?"

"That we better glide out of this, before three in the morning, and clip it down the river with what we've got. Specially, seeing we got it so easy—*given* back to us, flung at our heads, as you may say, when of course we allowed to have to steal it back. I'm for knocking off and lighting out."

That made me feel pretty bad. About an hour or two ago, it would a been a little different, but now it made me feel bad and disappointed. The king rips out and says:

"What! And not sell out the rest o' the property? March off like a passel o' fools and leave eight or nine thous'n' dollars' worth o' property layin' around jest sufferin' to be scooped in?—and all good salable stuff, too."

The duke he grumbled; said the bag of gold was enough, and he didn't want to go no deeper—didn't want to rob a lot of orphans of *everything* they had.

"Why, how you talk!" says the king. "We shan't rob 'em of nothing at all but jest this money. The people that *buys* the property is the suff'rers; because as soon's it's found out 'at we didn't own it—which won't be long after we've slid—the sale won't be valid, and it'll all go back to the estate. These-yer orphans 'll git their house back agin, and that's enough for *them;* they're young and spry, and k'n easy earn a livin'. *They* ain't agoing to suffer. Why, jest think—there's thous'n's and thous'n's that ain't nigh so well off. Bless you, *they* ain't got noth'n to complain of."

Well, the king he talked him blind; so at last he give in, and said all right, but said he believed it was blame foolishness to stay, and that doctor hanging over them. But the king says:

"Cuss the doctor! What do we k'yer for *him?* Hain't we got all the fools in town on our side? and ain't that a big enough majority in any town?"

So they got ready to go down stairs again. The duke says:

"I don't think we put that money in a good place."

That cheered me up. I'd begun to think I warn't going to get a hint of no kind to help me. The king says:

"Why?"

"Because Mary Jane'll be in mourning from this out; and first you know the nigger that does up the rooms will get an order to box these duds up and put 'em away; and do you reckon a nigger can run across money and not borrow some of it?"

"Your head's level, agin, Duke," says the king; and he come a fumbling under the curtain two or three foot from where I was. I stuck tight to the wall, and kept mighty still, though quivery; and I wondered what them fellows would say to me if they catched me; and I tried to think what I'd better do if they did catch me. But the king he got the bag before I could think more than about a half a thought, and he never suspicioned I was around. They took and shoved the bag through a rip in the straw tick that was under the feather bed, and crammed it in a foot or two amongst the straw and said it was all right, now, because a nigger only makes up the feather bed, and don't turn over the straw tick only about twice a year, and so it warn't in no danger of getting stole, now.

But I knowed better. I had it out of there before they was half-way down stairs. I groped along up to my cubby, and hid it there till I could get a chance to do better. I judged I better hide it outside of the house somewheres, because if they missed it they would give the house a good ransacking. I knowed that very well. Then I turned in, with my clothes all on; but I couldn't a gone to sleep, if I'd a wanted to, I was in such a sweat to get through with the business. By-and-by I heard the king and the duke come up; so I rolled off of my pallet and laid with my chin at the top of my ladder and waited to see if anything was going to happen. But nothing did.

So I held on till all the late sounds had quit and the early ones hadn't begun, yet; and then I slipped down the ladder.

Chapter XXVII

I crept to their doors and listened; they was snoring, so I tip-toed along, and got down stairs all right. There warn't a sound any-wheres. I peeped through a crack of the dining-room door, and see the men that was watching the corpse all sound asleep on their chairs. The door was open into the parlor, where the corpse was laying, and there was a candle in both rooms, I passed along, and the parlor door was open; but I see there warn't nobody in there but the remainders of Peter; so I shoved on by; but the front door was locked, and the key wasn't there. Just then I heard somebody coming down the stairs, back behind me. I run in the parlor, and took a swift look around, and the only place I see to hide the bag was in the coffin. The lid was shoved along about a foot, showing the dead man's face down in there, with a wet cloth over it, and his shroud on. I tucked the money-bag in under the lid, just down beyond where his hands was crossed, which made me creep, they was so cold, and then I run back across the room and in behind the door.

The person coming was Mary Jane. She went to the coffin, very soft, and kneeled down and looked in; then she put up her handker-chief and I see she begun to cry, though I couldn't hear her, and her back was to me. I slid out, and as I passed the dining-room I thought I'd make sure them watchers hadn't seen me; so I looked through the crack and everything was all right. They hadn't stirred.

I slipped up to bed, feeling ruther blue, on accounts of the thing playing out that way after I had took so much trouble and run so much resk about it. Says I, if it could stay where it is, all right; because when we get down the river a hundred mile or two, I could write back to Mary Jane, and she could dig him up again and get it; but that ain't the thing that's going to happen; the thing that's going to happen is, the money 'll be found when they come to screw on the lid. Then the king 'll get it again, and it 'll be a long day before he gives anybody another chance to smouch it from him. Of course I *wanted* to slide down and get it out of there, but I dasn't try it. Every minute it was getting earlier, now, and pretty soon some of them watchers would begin to stir, and I might get catched—catched with six thousand dollars in my hands that nobody hadn't hired me to take care of. I don't wish to be mixed up in no such business as that, I says to myself.

When I got down stairs in the morning, the parlor was shut up, and the watchers was gone. There warn't nobody around but the family and the widow Bartley and our tribe. I watched their faces to see if anything had been happening, but I couldn't tell.

Towards the middle of the day the undertaker come, with his man, and they set the coffin in the middle of the room on a couple of chairs, and then set all our chairs in rows, and borrowed more from the neighbors till the hall and the parlor and the dining-room was full. I see the coffin lid was the way it was before, but I dasn't go to look in under it, with folks around.

Then the people begun to flock in, and the beats and the girls took seats in the front row at the head of the coffin, and for a half an hour the people filed around slow, in single rank, and looked down at the dead man's face a minute, and some dropped in a tear, and it was all very still and solemn, only the girls and the beats holding handkerchiefs to their eyes and keeping their heads bent, and sobbing a little. There warn't no other sound but the scraping of the feet on the floor, and blowing noses—because people always blows them more at a funeral than they do at other places except church.

When the place was packed full, the undertaker he slid around in his black gloves with his softy soothering ways, putting on the last touches, and getting people and things all shipshape and comfortable, and making no more sound than a cat. He never spoke; he moved people around, he squeezed in late ones, he opened up passage-ways, and done it all with nods, and signs with his hands. Then he took his place over against the wall. He was the softest, glidingest, stealthiest man I ever see; and there warn't no more smile to him than there is to a ham.

They had borrowed a melodeum[1]—a sick one; and when everything was ready, a young woman set down and worked it, and it was pretty skreeky and colicky, and everybody joined in and sung, and Peter was the only one that had a good thing, according to my notion. Then the Reverend Hobson opened up, slow and solemn, and begun to talk; and straight off the most outrageous row busted out in the cellar a body ever heard; it was only one dog, but he made a most powerful racket, and he kept it up, right along; the parson he had to stand there, over the coffin, and wait—you couldn't hear yourself think. It was right down awkward, and nobody didn't seem to know what to do. But pretty soon they see that long-legged undertaker make a sign to the preacher as much as to say, "Don't you worry—just depend on me." Then he stooped down and begun to glide along the wall, just his shoulders showing over the people's heads. So he glided along, and the pow-wow and racket getting more and more outrageous all the time; and at last, when he had gone around two sides of the room, he disappears down cellar. Then, in about two seconds we heard a whack, and the dog he finished up with a most amazing howl or two, and then

1. A melodeon, small keyboard organ.

everything was dead still, and the parson begun his solemn talk where he left off. In a minute or two here comes this undertaker's back and shoulders gliding along the wall again; and so he glided, and glided, around three sides of the room, and then rose up, and shaded his mouth with his hands, and stretched his neck out towards the preacher, over the people's heads, and says, in a kind of a coarse whisper, *"He had a rat!"* Then he drooped down and glided along the wall again to his place. You could see it was a great satisfaction to the people, because naturally they wanted to know. A little thing like that don't cost nothing, and it's just the little things that makes a man to be looked up to and liked. There warn't no more popular man in town than what that undertaker was.

Well, the funeral sermon was very good, but pison long and tiresome; and then the king he shoved in and got off some of his usual rubbage, and at last the job was through, and the undertaker begun to sneak up on the coffin with his screw-driver. I was in a sweat then, and watched him pretty keen. But he never meddled at all; just slid the lid along, as soft as mush, and screwed it down tight and fast. So there I was! I didn't know whether the money was in there, or not. So, says I, spose somebody has hogged that bag on the sly?—now how do *I* know whether to write to Mary Jane or not? 'Spose she dug him up and didn't find nothing—what would she think of me? Blame it, I says, I might get hunted up and jailed; I'd better lay low and keep dark, and not write at all; the thing's awful mixed, now; trying to better it, I've worsened it a hundred times, and I wish to goodness I'd just let it alone, dad fetch the whole business!

They buried him, and we come back home, and I went to watching faces again—I couldn't help it, and I couldn't rest easy. But nothing come of it; the faces didn't tell me nothing.

The king he visited around, in the evening, and sweetened everybody up, and made himself ever so friendly; and he give out the idea that his congregation over in England would be in a sweat about him, so he must hurry and settle up the estate right away, and leave for home. He was very sorry he was so pushed, and so was everybody; they wished he could stay longer, but they said they could see it couldn't be done. And he said of course him and William would take the girls home with them; and that pleased everybody too, because then the girls would be well fixed, and amongst their own relations; and it pleased the girls, too—tickled them so they clean forgot they ever had a trouble in the world; and told him to sell out as quick as he wanted to, they would be ready. Them poor things was that glad and happy it made my heart ache to see them getting fooled and lied to so, but I didn't see no safe way for me to chip in and change the general tune.

Well, blamed if the king didn't bill the house and the niggers and all the property for auction straight off—sale two days after the funeral; but anybody could buy private beforehand if they wanted to.

So the next day after the funeral, along about noontime, the girls' joy got the first jolt; a couple of nigger traders come along, and the king sold them the niggers reasonable, for three-day drafts as they called it,[2] and away they went, the two sons up the river to Memphis, and their mother down the river to Orleans. I thought them poor girls and them niggers would break their hearts for grief; they cried around each other, and took on so it most made me down sick to see it. The girls said they hadn't ever dreamed of seeing the family separated or sold away from the town. I can't ever get it out of my memory, the sight of them poor miserable girls and niggers hanging around each other's necks and crying; and I reckon I couldn't a stood it all but would a had to bust out and tell on our gang if I hadn't knowed the sale warn't no account and the niggers would be back home in a week or two.

The thing made a big stir in the town, too, and a good many come out flatfooted and said it was scandalous to separate the mother and the children that way. It injured the frauds some; but the old fool he bulled right along, spite of all the duke could say or do, and I tell you the duke was powerful uneasy.

Next day was auction day. About broad-day in the morning, the king and the duke come up in the garret and woke me up, and I see by their look that there was trouble. The king says:

"Was you in my room night before last?"

"No, your majesty"—which was the way I always called him when nobody but our gang warn't around.

"Was you in there yisterday er last night?"

"No, your majesty."

"Honor bright, now—no lies."

"Honor bright, your majesty, I'm telling you the truth. I hain't been anear your room since Miss Mary Jane took you and the duke and showed it to you."

The duke says:

"Have you seen anybody else go in there?"

"No, your grace, not as I remember, I believe."

"Stop and think."

I studied a while, and see my chance, then I says:

"Well, I see the niggers go in there several times."

Both of them give a little jump; and looked like they hadn't ever expected it, and then like they *had*. Then the duke says:

"What, *all* of them?"

"No—leastways not all at once. That is, I don't think I ever see them all come *out* at once but just one time."

"Hello—when was that?"

2. Bank drafts or checks payable three days later.

"It was the day we had the funeral. In the morning. It warn't early, because I overslept. I was just starting down the ladder, and I see them."

"Well, go on, *go on*—what did they do? How'd they act?"

"They didn't do nothing. And they didn't act anyway, much, as fur as I see. They tip-toed away; so I seen, easy enough, that they'd shoved in there to do up your majesty's room, or something, sposing you was up; and found you *warn't* up, and so they was hoping to slide out of the way of trouble without waking you up, if they hadn't already waked you up."

"Great guns, *this* is a go!" says the king; and both of them looked pretty sick, and tolerable silly. They stood there a thinking and scratching their heads, a minute, and then the duke he bust into a kind of a little raspy chuckle, and says:

"It does beat all, how neat the niggers played their hand. They let on to be *sorry* they was going out of this region! and I believed they *was* sorry. And so did you, and so did everybody. Don't ever tell *me* any more that a nigger ain't got any histrionic talent. Why, the way they played that thing, it would fool *anybody*. In my opinion there's a fortune in 'em. If I had capital and a theatre, I wouldn't want a better lay out than that—and here we've gone and sold 'em for a song. Yes, and ain't privileged to sing the song, yet. Say, where *is* that song?—that draft."

"In the bank for to be collected. Where *would* it be?"

"Well, *that's* all right then, thank goodness."

Says I, kind of timid-like:

"Is something gone wrong?"

The king whirls on me and rips out:

"None o' your business! You keep your head shet, and mind y'r own affairs—if you got any. Long as you're in this town, don't you forgit *that*, you hear?" Then he says to the duke, "We got to jest swaller it, and say noth'n: mum's the word for *us*."

As they was starting down the ladder, the duke he chuckles again, and says:

"Quick sales *and* small profits! It's a good business—yes."

The king snarls around on him and says,

"I was trying to do for the best, in sellin' 'm out so quick. If the profits has turned out to be none, lackin' considable, and none to carry, is it my fault any more'n it's yourn?"

"Well, *they'd* be in this house yet, and we *wouldn't* if I could a got my advice listened to."

The king sassed back, as much as was safe for him, and then swapped around and lit into *me* again. He give me down the banks[3] for not coming and *telling* him I see the niggers come out

---

3. A cussing out.

of his room acting that way—said any fool would a *knowed* something was up. And then waltzed in and cussed *himself* a while; and
said it all come of him not laying late and taking his natural rest
that morning, and he'd be blamed if he'd ever do it again. So they
went off a jawing; and I felt dreadful glad I'd worked it all off onto
the niggers and yet hadn't done the niggers no harm by it.

Chapter XXVIII

By-and-by it was getting-up time; so I come down the ladder and
started for down stairs, but as I come to the girls' room, the door
was open, and I see Mary Jane setting by her old hair trunk, which
was open and she'd been packing things in it—getting ready to go
to England. But she had stopped now, with a folded gown in her
lap, and had her face in her hands, crying. I felt awful bad to see it;
of course anybody would. I went in there, and says:

"Miss Mary Jane, you can't abear to see people in trouble, and I
can't—most always. Tell me about it."

So she done it. And it was the niggers—I just expected it. She
said the beautiful trip to England was most about spoiled for her;
she didn't know *how* she was ever going to be happy there, knowing
the mother and the children warn't ever going to see each other no
more—and then busted out bitterer than ever, and flung up her
hands, and says

"Oh, dear, dear, to think they ain't *ever* going to see each other
any more!"

"But they *will*—and inside of two weeks—and I *know* it!" says I.

Laws it was out before I could think!—and before I could budge,
she throws her arms around my neck, and told me to say it *again*,
say it *again*, say it *again!*

I see I had spoke too sudden, and said too much, and was in a
close place. I asked her to let me think a minute; and she set there,
very impatient and excited, and handsome, but looking kind of
happy and eased-up, like a person that's had a tooth pulled out. So
I went to studying it out. I says to myself, I reckon a body that ups
and tells the truth when he is in a tight place, is taking considerable
many resks, though I ain't had no experience, and can't say for certain; but it looks so to me, anyway; and yet here's a case where I'm
blest if it don't look to me like the truth is better, and actuly *safer*,
than a lie. I must lay it by in my mind, and think it over some time
or other, it's so kind of strange and unregular. I never see nothing
like it. Well, I says to myself at last, I'm agoing to chance it; I'll up
and tell the truth this time, though it does seem most like setting
down on a kag of powder and touching it off just to see where
you'll go to. Then I says:

"Miss Mary Jane, is there any place out of town a little ways,
where you could go and stay three or four days?"

"Yes—Mr. Lothrop's. Why?"

"Never mind why, yet. If I'll tell you how I know the niggers will see each other again—inside of two weeks—here in this house—and *prove* how I know it—will you go to Mr. Lothrop's and stay four days?"

"Four days!" she says; "I'll stay a year!"

"All right," I says, "I don't want nothing more out of *you* than just your word—I druther have it than another man's kiss-the-Bible." She smiled, and reddened up very sweet, and I says, "If you don't mind it, I'll shut the door—and bolt it."

Then I come back and set down again, and says:

"Don't you holler. Just set still, and take it like a man. I got to tell the truth, and you want to brace up, Miss Mary, because it's a bad kind, and going to be hard to take, but there ain't no help for it. These uncles of yourn ain't no uncles at all—they're a couple of frauds—regular dead-beats. There, now we're over the worst of it—you can stand the rest middling easy."

It jolted her up like everything, of course; but I was over the shoal water now, so I went right along, her eyes a blazing higher and higher all the time, and told her every blame thing, from where we first struck that young fool going up to the steamboat, clear through to where she flung herself onto the king's breast at the front door and he kissed her sixteen or seventeen times—and then up she jumps, with her face afire like sunset, and says:

"The brute! Come—don't waste a minute—not a *second*—we'll have them tarred and feathered, and flung in the river!"[4]

Says I:

"Cert'nly. But do you mean, *before* you go to Mr. Lothrop's, or—"

"Oh," she says, "what am I *thinking* about!" she says, and set right down again. "Don't mind what I said—please don't—you *won't*, now, *will* you?" Laying her silky hand on mine in that kind of a way that I said I would die first. "I never thought, I was so stirred up," she says; "now go on, and I won't do so any more. You tell me what to do, and whatever you say, I'll do it."

"Well," I says, "it's a rough gang, them two frauds, and I'm fixed so I got to travel with them a while longer, whether I want to or not—I druther not tell you why—and if you was to blow on them this town would get me out of their claws, and *I'd* be all right, but there'd be another person that you don't know about who'd be in big trouble. Well, we got to save *him*, hain't we? Of course. Well, then, we won't blow on them."

Saying them words put a good idea in my head. I see how maybe I could get me and Jim rid of the frauds; get them jailed here, and

4. The victim of this fairly commonplace mob punishment was tied to a rail, smeared with hot tar, and covered with feathers. Then he would be ridden out of town on the rail to the jeers of the mob.

then leave. But I didn't want to run the raft in day-time, without anybody aboard to answer questions but me; so I didn't want the plan to begin working till pretty late to-night. I says:

"Miss Mary Jane, I'll tell you what we'll do—and you won't have to stay at Mr. Lothrop's so long, nuther. How fur is it?"

"A little short of four miles—right out in the country, back here."

"Well, that'll answer. Now you go along out there, and lay low till nine or half-past, to-night, and then get them to fetch you home again—tell them you've thought of something. If you get here before eleven, put a candle in this window, and if I don't turn up, wait *till* eleven, and *then* if I don't turn up it means I'm gone, and out of the way, and safe. Then you come out and spread the news around, and get these beats jailed."

"Good," she says, "I'll do it."

"And if it just happens so that I don't get away, but get took up along with them, you must up and say I told you the whole thing beforehand, and you must stand by me all you can."

"Stand by you, indeed I will. They sha'n't touch a hair of your head!" she says, and I see her nostrils spread and her eyes snap when she said it, too.

"If I get away, I sha'n't be here," I says, "to prove these rapscallions ain't your uncles, and I couldn't do it if I *was* here. I could swear they was beats and bummers, that's all; though that's worth something. Well, there's others can do that better than what I can—and they're people that ain't going to be doubted as quick as I'd be. I'll tell you how to find them. Gimme a pencil and a piece of paper. There—'*Royal Nonesuch, Bricksville.*' Put it away, and don't lose it. When the court wants to find out something about these two, let them send up to Bricksville and say they've got the men that played the Royal Nonesuch, and ask for some witnesses—why, you'll have that entire town down here before you can hardly wink, Miss Mary. And they'll come a-biling, too."

I judged we had got everything fixed about right, now. So I says:

"Just let the auction go right along, and don't worry. Nobody don't have to pay for the things they buy till a whole day after the auction, on accounts of the short notice, and they ain't going out of this till they get that money—and the way we've fixed it the sale ain't going to count, and they ain't going to *get* no money. It's just like the way it was with the niggers—it warn't no sale, and the niggers will be back before long. Why, they can't collect the money for the *niggers*, yet—they're in the worst kind of a fix, Miss Mary."

"Well," she says, "I'll run down to breakfast now, and then I'll start straight for Mr. Lothrop's."

" 'Deed, *that* ain't the ticket, Miss Mary Jane," I says, "by no manner of means; go *before* breakfast."

"Why?"

"What did you reckon I wanted you to go at all for, Miss Mary?"

"Well, I never thought—and come to think, I don't know. What was it?"

"Why, it's because you ain't one of these leather-face people. I don't want no better book than what your face is. A body can set down and read it off like coarse print. Do you reckon you can go and face your uncles, when they come to kiss you good-morning, and never—"

"There, there, don't! Yes, I'll go before breakfast—I'll be glad to. And leave my sisters with them?"

"Yes—never mind about them. They've got to stand it yet a while. They might suspicion something if all of you was to go. I don't want you to see them, nor your sisters, nor nobody in this town—if a neighbor was to ask how is your uncles this morning, your face would tell something. No, you go right along, Miss Mary Jane, and I'll fix it with all of them. I'll tell Miss Susan to give your love to your uncles and say you've went away for a few hours for to get a little rest and change, or to see a friend, and you'll be back to-night or early in the morning."

"Gone to see a friend is all right, but I won't have my love given to them."

"Well, then, it sha'n't be." It was well enough to tell *her* so—no harm in it. It was only a little thing to do, and no trouble; and it's the little things that smoothes people's roads the most, down here below; it would make Mary Jane comfortable, and it wouldn't cost nothing. Then I says: "There's one more thing—that bag of money."

"Well, they've got that; and it makes me feel pretty silly to think *how* they got it."

"No, you're out, there. They hain't got it."

"Why, who's got it?"

"I wish I knowed, but I don't. I *had* it, because I stole it from them: and I stole it to give to you; and I know where I hid it, but I'm afraid it ain't there no more. I'm awful sorry, Miss Mary Jane, I'm just as sorry as I can be; but I done the best I could; I did, honest. I come nigh getting caught, and I had to shove it into the first place I come to, and run—and it warn't a good place."

"Oh, stop blaming yourself—it's too bad to do it, and I won't allow it—you couldn't help it; it wasn't you fault. Where did you hide it?"

I didn't want to set her to thinking about her troubles again; and I couldn't seem to get my mouth to tell her what would make her see that corpse laying in the coffin with that bag of money on his stomach. So for a minute I didn't say nothing—then I says:

"I'd ruther not *tell* you where I put it, Miss Mary Jane, if you don't mind letting me off; but I'll write it for you on a piece of paper, and you can read it along the road to Mr. Lothrop's, if you want to. Do you reckon that'll do?"

"Oh, yes."

So I wrote: "I put it in the coffin. It was in there when you was crying there, away in the night. I was behind the door, and I was mighty sorry for you, Miss Mary Jane."

It made my eyes water a little, to remember her crying there all by herself in the night, and them devils laying there right under her own roof, shaming her and robbing her; and when I folded it up and give it to her, I see the water come into her eyes, too; and she shook me by the hand, hard, and says:

"Good-bye—I'm going to do everything just as you've told me; and if I don't ever see you again, I sha'n't ever forget you, and I'll think of you a many and a many a time, and I'll *pray* for you, too!" —and she was gone.

Pray for me! I reckoned if she knowed me she'd take a job that was more nearer her size. But I bet she done it, just the same—she was just that kind. She had the grit to pray for Judus if she took the notion—there warn't no backdown to her, I judge. You may say what you want to, but in my opinion she had more sand in her than any girl I ever see; in my opinion she was just full of sand.[5] It sounds like flattery, but it ain't no flattery. And when it comes to beauty—and goodness too—she lays over them all. I hain't ever seen her since that time that I see her go out of that door; no, I hain't ever seen her since, but I reckon I've thought of her a many and a many a million times, and of her saying she would pray for me; and if ever I'd a thought it would do any good for me to pray for *her*, blamed if I wouldn't a done it or bust.

Well, Mary Jane she lit out the back way, I reckon; because nobody see her go. When I struck Susan and the hare-lip, I says:

"What's the name of them people over on t'other side of the river that you all goes to see sometimes?"

They says:

"There's several; but it's the Proctors, mainly."

"That's the name," I says; "I most forgot it. Well, Miss Mary Jane she told me to tell you she's gone over there in a dreadful hurry —one of them's sick."

"Which one?"

"I don't know; leastways I kinder forget; but I think it's—"

"Sakes alive, I hope it ain't *Hanner*?"

"I'm sorry to say it," I says, "but Hanner's the very one."

"My goodness—and she so well only last week! Is she took bad?"

"It ain't no name for it. They set up with her all night, Miss Mary Jane said, and they don't think she'll last many hours."

"Only think of that, now! What's the matter with her!"

5. **Courage, guts.**

I couldn't think of anything reasonable, right off that way, so I says:

"Mumps."

"Mumps your granny! They don't set up with people that's got the mumps."

"They don't, don't they? You better bet they do with *these* mumps. These mumps is different. It's a new kind, Miss Mary Jane said."

"How's it a new kind?"

"Because it's mixed up with other things."

"What other things?"

"Well, measles, and whooping-cough, and erysiplas, and consumption, and yaller janders, and brain fever, and I don't know what all."

"My land! And they call it the *mumps?*"

"That's what Miss Mary Jane said."

"Well, what in the nation do they call it the *mumps* for?"

"Why, because it *is* the mumps. That's what it starts with."

"Well, ther' ain't no sense in it. A body might stump his toe, and take pison, and fall down the well, and break his neck, and bust his brains out, and somebody come along and ask what killed him, and some numskull up and say, 'Why, he stumped his *toe.*' Would ther' be any sense in that? No. And ther' ain't no sense in *this*, nuther. Is it ketching?"

"Is it *ketching?* Why, how you talk. Is a *harrow* catching?—in the dark? If you don't hitch onto one tooth, you're bound to on another, ain't you? And you can't get away with that tooth without fetching the whole harrow along, can you? Well, these kind of mumps is a kind of a harrow, as you may say—and it ain't no slouch of a harrow, nuther, you come to get it hitched on good."

"Well, it's awful, I think," says the hare-lip. "I'll go to Uncle Harvey and—"

"Oh, yes," I says, "I *would*. Of *course* I would. I wouldn't lose no time."

"Well, why wouldn't you?"

"Just look at it a minute, and maybe you can see. Hain't your uncles obleeged to get along home to England as fast as they can? And do you reckon they'd be mean enough to go off and leave you to go all that journey by yourselves? *You* know they'll wait for you. So fur, so good. Your uncle Harvey's a preacher, ain't he? Very well, then; is a *preacher* going to deceive a steamboat clerk? is he going to deceive a *ship clerk?*—so as to get them to let Miss Mary Jane go aboard? Now *you* know he ain't. What *will* he do, then? Why, he'll say, 'It's a great pity, but my church matters has got to get along the best way they can; for my niece has been exposed to the dreadful pluribus-unum[6] mumps, and so it's my bounden duty

6. Huck reaches for the handiest Latin phrase he could be expected to know.

to set down here and wait the three months it takes to show on her if she's got it.' But never mind, if you think it's best to tell your uncle Harvey—"

"Shucks, and stay fooling around here when we could all be having good times in England whilst we was waiting to find out whether Mary Jane's got it or not? Why, you talk like a muggins."[7]

"Well, anyway, maybe you better tell some of the neighbors."

"Listen at that, now. You do beat all, for natural stupidness. Can't you *see* that *they'd* go and tell? Ther' ain't no way but just to not tell anybody at *all*."

"Well, maybe you're right—yes, I judge you *are* right."

"But I reckon we ought to tell Uncle Harvey she's gone out a while, anyway, so he wont be uneasy about her?"

"Yes, Miss Mary Jane she wanted you to do that. She says, 'Tell them to give Uncle Harvey and William my love and a kiss, and say I've run over the river to see Mr.—Mr.—what *is* the name of that rich family your uncle Peter used to think so much of?—I mean the one that—"

"Why, you must mean the Apthorps, ain't it?"

"Of course; bother them kind of names, a body can't ever seem to remember them, half the time, somehow. Yes, she said, say she has run over for to ask the Apthorps to be sure and come to the auction and buy this house, because she allowed her uncle Peter would ruther they had it than anybody else; and she's going to stick to them till they say they'll come, and then, if she ain't too tired, she's coming home; and if she is, she'll be home in the morning anyway. She said, don't say nothing about the Proctors, but only about the Apthorps—which'll be perfectly true, because she *is* going there to speak about their buying the house; I know it, because she told me so, herself."

"All right," they said, and cleared out to lay for their uncles, and give them the love and the kisses, and tell them the message.

Everything was all right now. The girls wouldn't say nothing because they wanted to go to England; and the king and the duke would ruther Mary Jane was off working for the auction than around in reach of Doctor Robinson. I felt very good; I judged I had done it pretty neat—I reckoned Tom Sawyer couldn't a done it no neater himself. Of course he would a throwed more style into it, but I can't do that very handy, not being brung up to it.

Well, they held the auction in the public square, along towards the end of the afternoon, and it strung along, and strung along, and the old man he was on hand and looking his level piousest, up there longside of the auctioneer, and chipping in a little Scripture, now and then, or a little goody-goody saying, of some kind, and the duke he was around goo-gooing for sympathy all he knowed how, and just spreading himself genly.

7. A fool.

But by-and-by the thing dragged through, and everything was sold. Everything but a little old trifling lot in the graveyard. So they'd got to work *that* off—I never see such a girafft as the king was for wanting to swallow *everything*. Well, whilst they was at it, a steamboat landed, and in about two minutes up comes a crowd a whooping and yelling and laughing and carrying on, and singing out:

"*Here's* your opposition line! here's your two sets o' heirs to old Peter Wilks—and you pays your money and you takes your choice!"

Chapter XXIX

They was fetching a very nice looking old gentleman along, and a nice looking younger one, with his right arm in a sling. And my souls, how the people yelled, and laughed, and kept it up. But I didn't see no joke about it, and I judged it would strain the duke and the king some to see any. I reckoned they'd turn pale. But no, nary a pale did *they* turn. The duke he never let on he suspicioned what was up, but just went a goo-gooing around, happy and satisfied, like a jug that's googling out buttermilk; and as for the king, he just gazed and gazed down sorrowful on them newcomers like it give him the stomach-ache in his very heart to think there could be such frauds and rascals in the world. Oh, he done it admirable. Lots of the principal people gethered around the king, to let him see they was on his side. That old gentleman that had just come looked all puzzled to death. Pretty soon he begun to speak, and I see, straight off, he pronounced *like* an Englishman, not the king's way, though the king's *was* pretty good, for an imitation. I can't give the old gent's words, nor I can't imitate him; but he turned around to the crowd, and says, about like this:

"This is a surprise to me which I wasn't looking for; and I'll acknowledge, candid and frank, I ain't very well fixed to meet it and answer it; for my brother and me has had misfortunes, he's broke his arm, and our baggage got put off at a town above here, last night in the night by a mistake. I am Peter Wilks's brother Harvey, and this is his brother William, which can't hear nor speak —and can't even make signs to amount to much, now 't he's only got one hand to work them with. We are who we say we are; and in a day or two, when I get the baggage, I can prove it. But, up till then, I won't say nothing more, but go to the hotel and wait."

So him and the new dummy started off; and the king he laughs, and blethers out:

"Broke his arm—*very* likely *ain't* it?—and very convenient, too, for a fraud that's got to make signs, and hain't learnt how. Lost their baggage! That's *mighty* good!—and mighty ingenious—under the *circumstances!*"

So he laughed again; and so did everybody else, except three or four, or maybe half a dozen. One of these was that doctor; another one was a sharp looking gentleman, with a carpet-bag of the old-fashioned kind made out of carpet-stuff, that had just come off of the steamboat and was talking to him in a low voice, and glancing towards the king now and then and nodding their heads—it was Levi Bell, the lawyer that was gone up to Louisville; and another one was a big rough husky that come along and listened to all the old gentleman said, and was listening to the king now. And when the king got done, this husky up and says:

"Say, looky here; if you are Harvey Wilks, when'd you come to this town?"

"The day before the funeral, friend," says the king.

"But what time o' day?"

"In the evenin'—'bout an hour er two before sundown."

"*How'd* you come?"

"I come down on the *Susan Powell*, from Cincinnati."

"Well, then, how'd you come to be up at the Pint in the *mornin'*—in a canoe?"

"I warn't up at the Pint in the mornin'."

"It's a lie."

Several of them jumped for him and begged him not to talk that way to an old man and a preacher.

"Preacher be hanged, he's a fraud and a liar. He was up at the Pint that mornin'. I live up there, don't I? Well, I was up there, and he was up there. I *see* him there. He come in a canoe, along with Tim Collins and a boy."

The doctor he up and says:

"Would you know the boy again if you was to see him, Hines?"

"I reckon I would, but I don't know. Why, yonder he is, now. I know him perfectly easy."

It was me he pointed at. The doctor says:

"Neighbors, I don't know whether the new couple is frauds or not; but if *these* two ain't frauds, I am an idiot, that's all. I think it's our duty to see that they don't get away from here till we've looked into this thing. Come along, Hines; come along, the rest of you. We'll take these fellows to the tavern and affront them with t'other couple, and I reckon we'll find out *something* before we get through."

It was nuts for the crowd, though maybe not for the king's friends; so we all started. It was about sundown. The doctor he led me along by the hand, and was plenty kind enough, but he never let *go* my hand.

We all got in a big room in the hotel, and lit up some candles, and fetched in the new couple. First, the doctor says:

"I don't wish to be too hard on these two men, but I think they're frauds, and they may have complices that we don't know nothing about. If they have, won't the complices get away with that bag of gold Peter Wilks left? It ain't unlikely. If these men ain't frauds, they won't object to sending for that money and letting us keep it till they prove they're all right—ain't that so?"

Everybody agreed to that. So I judged they had our gang in a pretty tight place, right at the outstart. But the king he only looked sorrowful, and says:

"Gentlemen, I wish the money was there, for I ain't got no disposition to throw anything in the way of a fair, open, out-and-out investigation o' this misable business; but alas, the money ain't there; you k'n send and see, if you want to."

"Where is it, then?"

"Well, when my niece give it to me to keep for her, I took and hid it inside o' the straw tick o' my bed, not wishin' to bank it for the few days we'd be here, and considerin' the bed a safe place, we not bein' used to niggers, and suppos'n' 'em honest, like servants in England. The niggers stole it the very next mornin' after I had went down stairs; and when I sold 'em, I hadn't missed the money yit, so they got clean away with it. My servant here k'n tell you 'bout it gentlemen."

The doctor and several said "Shucks!" and I see nobody didn't altogether believe him. One man asked me if I see the niggers steal it. I said no, but I see them sneaking out of the room and hustling away, and I never thought nothing, only I reckoned they was afraid they had waked up my master and was trying to get away before he made trouble with them. That was all they asked me. Then the doctor whirls on me and says:

"Are *you* English too?"

I says yes; and him and some others laughed, and said, "Stuff!"

Well, then they sailed in on the general investigation, and there we had it, up and down, hour in, hour out, and nobody never said a word about supper, nor ever seemed to think about it—and so they kept it up, and kept it up; and it *was* the worst mixed-up thing you ever see. They made the king tell his yarn, and they made the old gentleman tell his'n; and anybody but a lot of prejudiced chuckleheads would a *seen* that the old gentleman was spinning truth and t'other one lies. And by-and-by they had me up to tell what I knowed. The king he give me a left-handed look out of the corner of his eye, and so I knowed enough to talk on the right side. I begun to tell about Sheffield, and how we lived there, and all about the English Wilkses, and so on; but I didn't get pretty fur till the doctor begun to laugh; and Levi Bell, the lawyer, says:

"Set down, my boy, I wouldn't strain myself, if I was you. I reckon you ain't used to lying, it don't seem to come handy; what you want is practice. You do it pretty awkward."

I didn't care nothing for the compliment, but I was glad to be let off, anyway.

The doctor he started to say something, and turns and says:

"If you'd been in town at first, Levi Bell—"

The king broke in and reached out his hand, and says:

"Why, is this my poor dead brother's old friend that he's wrote so often about?"

The lawyer and him shook hands, and the lawyer smiled and looked pleased, and they talked right along a while, and then got to one side and talked low; and at last the lawyer speaks up and says:

"That'll fix it. I'll take the order and send it, along with your brother's, and then they'll know it's all right."

So they got some paper and a pen, and the king he set down and twisted his head to one side, and chawed his tongue, and scrawled off something; and then they give the pen to the duke—and then for the first time, the duke looked sick. But he took the pen and wrote. So then the lawyer turns to the new old gentleman and says:

"You and your brother please write a line or two and sign your names."

The old gentleman wrote, but nobody couldn't read it. The lawyer looked powerful astonished, and says:

"Well, it beats *me*"—and snaked a lot of old letters out of his pocket, and examined them, and then examined the old man's writing, and then *them* again; and then says: "These old letters is from Harvey Wilks; and here's~*these* two's handwritings, and anybody can see *they* didn't write them" (the king and the duke looked sold and foolish, I tell you, to see how the lawyer had took them in), "and here's *this* old gentleman's handwriting, and anybody can tell, easy enough, *he* didn't write them—fact is, the scratches he makes ain't properly *writing*, at all. Now here's some letters from—"

The new old gentleman says:

"If you please, let me explain. Nobody can read my hand but my brother there—so he copies for me. It's *his* hand you've got there, not mine."

"*Well!*" says the lawyer, "this *is* a state of things. I've got some of William's letters too; so if you'll get him to write a line or so we can com—"

"He *can't* write with his left hand," says the old gentleman. "If he could use his right hand, you would see that he wrote his own letters and mine too. Look at both, please—they're by the same hand."

The lawyer done it, and says:

"I believe it's so—and if it ain't so, there's a heap stronger resemblance than I'd noticed before, anyway. Well, well, well! I thought we was right on the track of a slution, but it's gone to grass, partly. But anyway, *one* thing is proved—*these* two ain't either of 'em Wilkses"—and he wagged his head towards the king and the duke.

Well, what do you think?—that muleheaded old fool wouldn't give in *then!* Indeed he wouldn't. Said it warn't no fair test. Said his brother William was the cussedest joker in the world, and hadn't *tried* to write—*he* see William was going to play one of his jokes the minute he put the pen to paper. And so he warmed up and went warbling and warbling right along, till he was actuly beginning to believe what he was saying, *himself*—but pretty soon the new old gentleman broke in, and says:

"I've thought of something. Is there anybody here that helped to lay out my br—helped to lay out the late Peter Wilks for burying?"

"Yes," says somebody, "me and Ab Turner done it. We're both here."

Then the old man turns towards the king, and says:

"Peraps this gentleman can tell me what was tatooed on his breast?"

Blamed if the king didn't have to brace up mighty quick, or he'd a squshed down like a bluff bank that the river has cut under, it took him so sudden—and mind you, it was a thing that was calculated to make most *anybody* sqush to get fetched such a solid one as that without any notice—because how was *he* going to know what was tatooed on the man? He whitened a little; he couldn't help it; and it was mighty still in there, and everybody bending a little forwards and gazing at him. Says I to myself, *Now* he'll throw up the sponge—there ain't no more use. Well, did he? A body can't hardly believe it, but he didn't. I reckon he thought he'd keep the thing up till he tired them people out, so they'd thin out, and him and the duke could break loose and get away. Anyway, he set there, and pretty soon he begun to smile, and says:

"Mf! It's a *very* tough question, *ain't* it! *Yes*, sir, I k'n tell you what's tatooed on his breast. It's jest a small, thin, blue arrow—that's what it is; and if you don't look clost, you can't see it. *Now* what do you say—hey?"

Well, *I* never see anything like that old blister for clean out-and-out cheek.

The new old gentleman turns brisk towards Ab Turner and his pard, and his eye lights up like he judged he'd got the king *this* time, and says:

"There—you've heard what he said! Was there any such mark on Peter Wilks's breast?"

Both of them spoke up and says:

"We didn't see no such mark."

"Good!" says the old gentleman. "Now, what you *did* see on his breast was a small dim P, and a B (which is an initial he dropped when he was young), and a W, with dashes between them, so: P—B—W"—and he marked them that way on a piece of paper. "Come—ain't that what you saw?"

Both of them spoke up again, and says:

"No, we *didn't*. We never seen any marks at all."

Well, everybody *was* in a state of mind, now; and they sings out:

"The whole *bilin*' of 'm 's frauds! Le's duck 'em! le's drown 'em! le's ride 'em on a rail!" and everybody was whooping at once, and there was a rattling pow-wow. But the lawyer he jumps on the table and yells, and says:

"Gentlemen—*gentlemen!* Hear me just a word—just a *single* word—if you PLEASE! There's one way yet—let's go and dig up the corpse and look."

That took them.

"Hooray!" they all shouted, and was starting right off; but the lawyer and the doctor sung out:

"Hold on, hold on! Collar all these four men and the boy, and fetch *them* along, too!"

"We'll do it!" they all shouted: "and if we don't find them marks we'll lynch the whole gang!"

I *was* scared, now, I tell you. But there warn't no getting away, you know. They gripped us all, and marched us right along, straight for the graveyard, which was a mile and a half down the river, and the whole town at our heels, for we made noise enough, and it was only nine in the evening.

As we went by our house I wished I hadn't sent Mary Jane out of town; because now if I could tip her the wink, she'd light out and save me, and blow on our dead-beats.

Well, we swarmed along down the river road, just carrying on like wild-cats; and to make it more scary, the sky was darking up, and the lightning beginning to wink and flitter, and the wind to shiver amongst the leaves. This was the most awful trouble and most dangersome I ever was in; and I was kinder stunned; everything was going so different from what I had allowed for; stead of being fixed so I could take my own time, if I wanted to, and see all the fun, and have Mary Jane at my back to save me and set me free when the close-fit come, here was nothing in the world betwixt me and sudden death but just them tatoo-marks. If they didn't find them—

I couldn't bear to think about it; and yet, somehow, I couldn't think about nothing else. It got darker and darker, and it was a beautiful time to give the crowd the slip; but that big husky had me by the wrist—Hines—and a body might as well try to give Goliar[8] the slip. He dragged me right along, he was so excited; and I had to run to keep up.

When they got there they swarmed into the graveyard and washed over it like an overflow. And when they got to the grave, they found they had about a hundred times as many shovels as they wanted, but nobody hadn't thought to fetch a lantern. But they sailed into digging, anyway, by the flicker of the lightning, and sent a man to the nearest house a half a mile off, to borrow one.

So they dug and dug, like everything; and it got awful dark, and

---

8. Goliath, a Philistine giant who challenged the Israelites. David, a young shepherd boy, accepted his challenge and killed him with a stone thrown from a sling.

the rain started, and the wind swished and swushed along, and the lightning come brisker and brisker, and the thunder boomed; but them people never took no notice of it, they was so full of this business; and one minute you could see everything and every face in that big crowd, and the shovelfuls of dirt sailing up out of the grave, and the next second the dark wiped it all out, and you couldn't see nothing at all.

At last they got out the coffin, and begun to unscrew the lid, and then such another crowding, and shouldering, and shoving as there was, to scrouge in and get a sight, you never see; and in the dark, that way, it was awful. Hines he hurt my wrist dreadful, pulling and tugging so, and I reckon he clean forgot I was in the world, he was so excited and panting.

All of a sudden the lightning let go a perfect sluice of white glare, and somebody sings out:

"By the living jingo, here's the bag of gold on his breast!"

Hines let out a whoop, like everybody else, and dropped my wrist and give a big surge to bust his way in and get a look, and the way I lit out and shinned for the road in the dark, there ain't nobody can tell.

I had the road all to myself, and I fairly flew—leastways I had it all to myself except the solid dark, and the now-and-then glares, and the buzzing of the rain, and the thrashing of the wind, and the splitting of the thunder; and sure as you are born I did clip it along!

When I struck the town, I see there warn't nobody out in the storm, so I never hunted for no back streets, but humped it straight through the main one; and when I begun to get towards our house I aimed my eye and set it. No light there; the house all dark— which made me feel sorry and disappointed, I didn't know why. But at last, just as I was sailing by, *flash* comes the light in Mary Jane's window! and my heart swelled up sudden, like to bust; and the same second the house and all was behind me in the dark, and wasn't ever going to be before me no more in this world. She *was* the best girl I ever see, and had the most sand.

The minute I was far enough above the town to see I could make the tow-head, I begun to look sharp for a boat to borrow; and the first time the lightning showed me one that wasn't chained, I snatched it and shoved. It was a canoe, and warn't fastened with nothing but a rope. The tow-head was a rattling big distance off, away out there in the middle of the river, but I didn't lose no time; and when I struck the raft at last, I was so fagged I would a just laid down to blow and gasp if I could afforded it. But I didn't. As I sprung aboard I sung out:

"Out with you Jim, and set her loose! Glory be to goodness, we're shut of them!"

Jim lit out, and was a coming for me with both arms spread, he was so full of joy; but when I glimpsed him in the lightning, my heart shot up in my mouth, and I went overboard backwards; for I forgot he was old King Lear and a drownded A-rab all in one, and it most scared the livers and lights out of me. But Jim fished me out, and was going to hug me and bless me, and so on, he was so glad I was back and we was shut of the king and the duke, but I says:

"Not now—have it for breakfast, have it for breakfast! Cut loose and let her slide!"

So, in two seconds, away we went, a sliding down the river, and it *did* seem so good to be free again and all by ourselves on the big river and nobody to bother us. I had to skip around a bit, and jump up and crack my heels a few times, I couldn't help it; but about the third crack, I noticed a sound that I knowed mighty well—and held my breath and listened and waited—and sure enough, when the next flash busted out over the water, here they come!—and just a laying to their oars and making their skiff hum! It was the king and the duke.

So I wilted right down onto the planks, then, and give up; and it was all I could do to keep from crying.

Chapter XXX

When they got aboard, the king went for me, and shook me by the collar, and says:

"Tryin' to give us the slip, was ye, you pup! Tired of our company—hey!"

I says:

"No, your majesty, we warn't—*please* don't, your majesty!"

"Quick, then, and tell us what *was* your idea, or I'll shake the insides out o' you!"

"Honest, I'll tell you everything, just as it happened, your majesty. The man that had aholt of me was very good to me, and kept saying he had a boy about as big as me that died last year, and he was sorry to see a boy in such a dangerous fix; and when they was all took by surprise by finding the gold, and made a rush for the coffin, he lets go of me and whispers, 'Heel it, now, or they'll hang ye, sure!' and I lit out. It didn't seem no good for *me* to stay—I couldn't do nothing, and I didn't want to be hung if I could get away. So I never stopped running till I found the canoe; and when I got here I told Jim to hurry, or they'd catch me and hang me yet, and said I was afeard you and the duke wasn't alive, now, and I was awful sorry, and so was Jim, and was awful glad when we see you coming, you may ask Jim if I didn't."

Jim said it was so; and the king told him to shut up, and said, "Oh, yes, it's *mighty* likely!" and shook me up again, and said he reckoned he'd drownd me. But the duke says:

"Leggo the boy, you old idiot! Would *you* done any different? Did you inquire around for *him*, when you got loose? *I* don't remember it."

So the king let go of me, and begun to cuss that town and every-body in it. But the duke says:

"You better a blame sight give *yourself* a good cussing, for you're the one that's entitled to it most. You hain't done a thing, from the start, that had any sense in it, except coming out so cool and cheeky with that imaginary blue-arrow mark. That *was* bright—it was right down bully; and it was the thing that saved us. For if it hadn't been for that, they'd a jailed us till them Englishmen's baggage come—and then—the penitentiary, you bet! But that trick took 'em to the graveyard, and the gold done us a still bigger kindness; for if the excited fools hadn't let go all holts and made that rush to get a look, we'd a slept in our cravats to-night—cravats warranted to *wear*, too—longer than *we'd* need 'em."

They was still a minute—thinking—then the king says, kind of absent-minded like:

"Mf! And we reckoned the *niggers* stole it!"

That made me squirm!

"Yes," says the duke, kinder slow, and deliberate, and sarcastic, "*We* did."

After about a half a minute, the king drawls out:

"Leastways—*I* did."

The duke says, the same way:

"On the contrary—*I* did."

The king kind of ruffles up, and says:

"Looky here, Bilgewater, what'r you referrin' to?"

The duke says, pretty brisk:

"When it comes to that, maybe you'll let me ask, what was *you* referring to?"

"Shucks!" says the king, very sarcastic; "but *I* don't know—maybe you was asleep, and didn't know what you was about."

The duke bristles right up, now, and says:

"Oh, let *up* on this cussed nonsense—do you take me for a blame' fool? Don't you reckon *I* know who hid that money in that coffin?"

"*Yes*, sir! I know you *do* know—because you done it yourself!"

"It's a lie!"—and the duke went for him. The king sings out:

"Take y'r hands off!—leggo my throat!—I take it all back!"

The duke says:

"Well, you just own up, first, that you *did* hide that money there, intending to give me the slip one of these days, and come back and dig it up, and have it all to yourself."

"Wait jest a minute, duke—answer me this one question, honest and fair; if you didn't put the money there, say it, and I'll b'lieve you, and take back everything I said."

"You old scoundrel, I didn't, and you know I didn't. There, now!"

"Well, then, I b'lieve you. But answer me only jest this one more

—now *don't* git mad; didn't you have it in your *mind* to hook the money and hide it?"

The duke never said nothing for a little bit; then he says:

"Well—I don't care if I *did*, I didn't *do* it, anyway. But you not only had it in mind to do it, but you *done* it."

"I wisht I may never die if I done it, duke, and that's honest. I won't say I warn't *goin'* to do it, because I *was*; but you—I mean somebody—got in ahead o' me."

"It's a lie! You done it, and you got to *say* you done it, or—"

The king begun to gurgle, and then he gasps out:

" 'Nough!—I *own up!*"

I was very glad to hear him say that, it made me feel much more easlier than what I was feeling before. So the duke took his hands off, and says:

"If you ever deny it again, I'll drown you. It's *well* for you to set there and blubber like a baby—it's fitten for you, after the way you've acted. I never see such an old ostrich for wanting to gobble everything—and I a trusting you all the time, like you was my own father. You ought to be ashamed of yourself to stand by and hear it saddled onto a lot of poor niggers and you never say a word for 'em. It makes me feel ridiculous to think I was soft enough to *believe* that rubbage. Cuss you, I can see, now, why you was so anxious to make up the deffesit—you wanted to get what money I'd got out of the Nonesuch and one thing or another, and scoop it *all!*"

The king says, timid, and still a snuffling:

"Why, duke, it was you that said make up the deffersit, it warn't me."

"Dry up! I don't want to hear no more *out* of you!" says the duke. "And *now* you see what you *got* by it. They've got all their own money back, and all of *ourn* but a sheckel or two, *besides*. G'long to bed—and don't you deffersit *me* no more deffersits, long 's *you* live!"

So the king sneaked into the wigwam, and took to his bottle for comfort; and before long the duke tackled *his* bottle; and so in about a half an hour they was as thick as thieves again, and the tighter they got, the lovinger they got; and went off a snoring in each other's arms. They both got powerful mellow, but I noticed the king didn't get mellow enough to forget to remember to not deny about hiding the money-bag again. That made me feel easy and satisfied. Of course when they got to snoring, we had a long gabble, and I told Jim everything.

Chapter *XXXI*

We dasn't stop again at any town, for days and days; kept right along down the river. We was down south in the warm weather, now, and a mighty long ways from home. We begun to come to trees with Spanish moss on them, hanging down from the limbs like long gray beards. It was the first I ever see it growing, and it made the woods look solemn and dismal. So now the frauds reckoned they was out of danger, and they begun to work the villages again.

First they done a lecture on temperance; but they didn't make enough for them both to get drunk on. Then in another village they started a dancing school; but they didn't know no more how to dance than a kangaroo does; so the first prance they made, the general public jumped in and pranced them out of town. Another time they tried a go at yellocution; but they didn't yellocute long till the audience got up and give them a solid good cussing and made them skip out. They tackled missionarying, and mesmerizering, and doctoring, and telling fortunes, and a little of everything; but they couldn't seem to have no luck. So at last they got just about dead broke, and laid around the raft, as she floated along, thinking, and thinking, and never saying nothing, by the half a day at a time, and dreadful blue and desperate.

And at last they took a change, and begun to lay their heads together in the wigwam and talk low and confidential two or three hours at a time. Jim and me got uneasy. We didn't like the look of it. We judged they was studying up some kind of worse deviltry than ever. We turned it over and over, and at last we made up our minds they was going to break into somebody's house or store, or was going into the counterfeit-money business, or something. So then we was pretty scared, and made up an agreement that we wouldn't have nothing in the world to do with such actions, and if we ever got the least show we would give them the cold shake, and clear out and leave them behind. Well, early one morning we hid the raft in a good safe place about two mile below a little bit of a shabby village, named Pikesville, and the king he went ashore, and told us all to stay hid whilst he went up to town and smelt around to see if anybody had got any wind of the Royal Nonesuch there yet. ("House to rob, you *mean*," says I to myself; "and when you get through robbing it you'll come back here and wonder what's become of me and Jim and the raft—and you'll have to take it out in wondering.") And he said if he warn't back by midday, the duke and me would know it was all right, and we was to come along.

So we staid where we was. The duke he fretted and sweated around, and was in a mighty sour way. He scolded us for everything, and we couldn't seem to do nothing right; he found fault with every little thing. Something was a-brewing, sure. I was good and glad when midday come and no king; we could have a change, anyway—and maybe a chance for *the* change, on top of it. So me and the duke went up to the village, and hunted around there for the king, and by-and-by we found him in the back room of a little low doggery,[9] very tight, and a lot of loafers bullyragging him for sport, and he a cussing and threatening with all his might, and so

9. Cheap barroom.

tight he couldn't walk, and couldn't do nothing to them. The duke he begun to abuse him for an old fool, and the king begun to sass back; and the minute they was fairly at it, I lit out, and shook the reefs out of my hind legs, and spun down the river road like a deer —for I see our chance; and I made up my mind that it would be a long day before they ever see me and Jim again. I got down there all out of breath but loaded up with joy, and sung out—

"Set her loose, Jim, we're all right, now!"

But there warn't no answer, and nobody come out of the wigwam. Jim was gone! I set up a shout—and then another—and then another one; and run this way and that in the woods, whooping and screeching; but it warn't no use—old Jim was gone. Then I set down and cried; I couldn't help it. But I couldn't set still long. Pretty soon I went out on the road, trying to think what I better do, and I run across a boy walking, and asked him if he'd seen a strange nigger, dressed so and so, and he says:

"Yes."

"Whereabouts?" says I.

"Down to Silas Phelps's place, two mile below here. He's a runaway nigger, and they've got him. Was you looking for him?"

"You bet I ain't! I run across him in the woods about an hour or two ago, and he said if I hollered he'd cut my livers out—and told me to lay down and stay where I was; and I done it. Been there ever since; afeard to come out."

"Well," he says, "you needn't be afraid no more, becuz they've got him. He run off f'm down South, som'ers."

"It's a good job they got him."

"Well, I *reckon!* There's two hunderd dollars reward on him. It's like picking up money out'n the road."

"Yes, it is—and *I* could a had it if I'd been big enough; I see him *first.* Who nailed him?"

"It was an old fellow—a stranger—and he sold out his chance in him for forty dollars, becuz he's got to go up the river and can't wait. Think o' that, now! You bet *I'd* wait, if it was seven year."

"That's me, every time," says I. "But maybe his chance ain't worth no more than that, if he'll sell it so cheap. Maybe there's something ain't straight about it."

"But it *is*, though—straight as a string. I see the handbill myself. It tells all about him, to a dot—paints him like a picture, and tells the plantation he's frum, below New*r*leans. No-siree-*bob*, they ain't no trouble 'bout *that* speculation, you bet you. Say, gimme a chaw tobacker, won't ye?"

I didn't have none, so he left. I went to the raft, and set down in the wigwam to think. But I couldn't come to nothing. I thought till I wore my head sore, but I couldn't see no way out of the trouble. After all this long journey, and after all we'd done for them scoundrels, here was it all come to nothing, everything all busted up and ruined, because they could have the heart to serve Jim such a trick as that, and make him a slave again all his life, and amongst strangers, too, for forty dirty dollars.

Once I said to myself it would be a thousand times better for Jim to be a slave at home where his family was, as long as he'd *got* to be a slave, and so I'd better write a letter to Tom Sawyer and tell him to tell Miss Watson where he was. But I soon give up that notion, for two things: she'd be mad and disgusted at his rascality and ungratefulness for leaving her, and so she'd sell him straight down the river again; and if she didn't, everybody naturally despises an ungrateful nigger, and they'd make Jim feel it all the time, and so he'd feel ornery and disgraced. And then think of *me!* It would get all round, that Huck Finn helped a nigger to get his freedom; and if I was to ever see anybody from that town again, I'd be ready to get down and lick his boots for shame. That's just the way: a person does a low-down thing, and then he don't want to take no consequences of it. Thinks as long as he can hide it, it ain't no disgrace. That was my fix exactly. The more I studied about this, the more my conscience went to grinding me, and the more wicked and low-down and ornery I got to feeling. And at last, when it hit me all of a sudden that here was the plain hand of Providence slapping me in the face and letting me know my wickedness was being watched all the time from up there in heaven, whilst I was stealing a poor old woman's nigger that hadn't ever done me no harm, and now was showing me there's One that's always on the lookout, and ain't agoing to allow no such miserable doings to go only just so fur and no further, I most dropped in my tracks I was so scared. Well, I tried the best I could to kinder soften it up somehow for myself, by saying I was brung up wicked, and so I warn't so much to blame; but something inside of me kept saying, "There was the Sunday school, you could a gone to it; and if you'd a done it they'd a learnt you, there, that people that acts as I'd been acting about that nigger goes to everlasting fire."

It made me shiver. And I about made up my mind to pray; and see if I couldn't try to quit being the kind of a boy I was, and be better. So I kneeled down. But the words wouldn't come. Why wouldn't they? It warn't no use to try and hide it from Him. Nor from *me*, neither. I knowed very well why they wouldn't come. It was because my heart warn't right; it was because I warn't square; it was because I was playing double. I was letting *on* to give up sin, but away inside of me I was holding on to the biggest one of all. I was trying to make my mouth *say* I would do the right thing and the clean thing, and go and write to that nigger's owner and tell where he was; but deep down in me I knowed it was a lie—and He knowed it. You can't pray a lie—I found that out.

So I was full of trouble, full as I could be; and didn't know what to do. At last I had an idea; and I says, I'll go and write the letter

—and *then* see if I can pray. Why, it was astonishing, the way I felt as light as a feather, right straight off, and my troubles all gone. So I got a piece of paper and a pencil, all glad and excited, and set down and wrote:

> Miss Watson your runaway nigger Jim is down here two mile below Pikesville and Mr. Phelps has got him and he will give him up for the reward if you send.
>
> Huck Finn

I felt good and all washed clean of sin for the first time I had ever felt so in my life, and I knowed I could pray now. But I didn't do it straight off, but laid the paper down and set there thinking—thinking how good it was all this happened so, and how near I come to being lost and going to hell. And went on thinking. And got to thinking over our trip down the river; and I see Jim before me, all the time, in the day, and in the night-time, sometimes moonlight, sometimes storms, and we a floating along, talking, and singing, and laughing. But somehow I couldn't seem to strike no places to harden me against him, but only the other kind. I'd see him standing my watch on top of his'n, stead of calling me, so I could go on sleeping; and see him how glad he was when I come back out of the fog; and when I come to him again in the swamp, up there where the feud was; and such-likes times; and would always call me honey, and pet me, and do everything he could think of for me, and how good he always was; and at last I struck the time I saved him by telling the men we had small-pox aboard, and he was so grateful, and said I was the best friend old Jim ever had in the world, and the *only* one he's got now; and then I happened to look around, and see that paper.

It was a close place. I took it up, and held it in my hand. I was a trembling, because I'd got to decide, forever, betwixt two things, and I knowed it. I studied a minute, sort of holding my breath, and then says to myself:

"All right, then, I'll *go* to hell"—and tore it up.

It was awful thoughts, and awful words, but they was said. And I let them stay said; and never thought no more about reforming. I shoved the whole thing out of my head; and said I would take up wickedness again, which was in my line, being brung up to it, and the other warn't. And for a starter, I would go to work and steal Jim out of slavery again; and if I could think up anything worse, I would do that, too; because as long as I was in, and in for good, I might as well go the whole hog.

Then I set to thinking over how to get at it, and turned over considerable many ways in my mind; and at last fixed up a plan that suited me. So then I took the bearings of a woody island that was down the river a piece, and as soon as it was fairly dark I crept out with my raft and went for it, and hid it there, and then turned in. I slept the night through, and got up before it was light, and had my breakfast, and put on my store clothes, and tied up some others and one thing or another in a bundle, and took the canoe and cleared for shore. I landed below where I judged was Phelps's place, and hid my bundle in the woods, and then filled up the canoe with water, and loaded rocks into her and sunk her where I could find her again when I wanted her, about a quarter of a mile below a little stream sawmill that was on the bank.

Then I struck up the road, and when I passed the mill I see a sign on it, "Phelps's Sawmill," and when I come to the farmhouses, two or three hundred yards further along, I kept my eyes peeled, but didn't see nobody around, though it was good daylight, now. But I didn't mind, because I didn't want to see nobody just yet—I only wanted to get the lay of the land. According to my plan, I was going to turn up there from the village, not from below. So I just took a look, and shoved along, straight for town. Well, the very first man I see, when I got there, was the duke. He was sticking up a bill for the Royal Nonesuch—three-night performance—like that other time. *They* had the cheek, them frauds! I was right on him, before I could shirk. He looked astonished, and says:

"Hel-*lo!* Where'd *you* come from?" Then he says, kind of glad and eager, "Where's the raft?—got her in a good place?"

I says:

"Why, that's just what I was agoing to ask your grace."

Then he didn't look so joyful—and says:

"What was your idea for asking *me?*" he says.

"Well," I says, "when I see the king in that doggery yesterday, I says to myself, we can't get him home for hours, till he's soberer; so I went a loafing around town to put in the time, and wait. A man up and offered me ten cents to help him pull a skiff over the river and back to fetch a sheep, and so I went along; but when we was dragging him to the boat, and the man left me aholt of the rope and went behind him to shove him along, he was too strong·for me, and jerked loose and run, and we after him. We didn't have no dog, and so we had to chase him all over the country till we tired him out. We never got him till dark, then we fetched him over, and I started down for the raft. When I got there and see it was gone, I says to myself, 'they've got into trouble and had to leave; and they've took my nigger, which is the only nigger I've got in the world, and now I'm in a strange country, and ain't got no property no more, nor nothing, and no way to make my living;' so I set down and cried. I slept in the woods all night. But what *did* become of the raft then?—and Jim, poor Jim!"

"Blamed if *I* know—that is, what's become of the raft. That old fool had made a trade and got forty dollars, and when we found him in the doggery the loafers had matched half dollars with him and got every cent but what he'd spent for whisky; and when I got him home late last night and found the raft gone, we said, 'That little rascal has stole our raft and shook us, and run off down the river.' "

"I wouldn't shake my *nigger*, would I?—the only nigger I had in the world, and the only property."

"We never thought of that. Fact is, I reckon we'd come to consider him *our* nigger; yes, we did consider him so—goodness knows we had trouble enough for him. So when we see the raft was gone, and we flat broke, there warn't anything for it but to try the Royal Nonesuch another shake. And I've pegged along ever since, dry as a powderhorn. Where's that ten cents? Give it here."

I had considerable money, so I give him ten cents, but begged him to spend it for something to eat, and give me some, because it was all the money I had, and I hadn't had nothing to eat since yesterday. He never said nothing. The next minute he whirls on me and says:

"Do you reckon that nigger would blow on us? We'd skin him if he done that!"

"How can he blow? Hain't he run off?"

"No! That old fool sold him, and never divided with me, and the money's gone."

"*Sold* him?" I says, and begun to cry; "why, he was *my* nigger, and that was my money. Where is he?—I want my nigger."

"Well, you can't *get* your nigger, that's all—so dry up your blubbering. Looky here—do you think *you'd* venture to blow on us? Blamed if I think I'd trust you. Why, if you *was* to blow on us—"

He stopped, but I never see the duke look so ugly out of his eyes before. I went on a-whimpering, and says:

"I don't want to blow on nobody; and I ain't got no time to blow, nohow. I got to turn out and find my nigger."

He looked kinder bothered, and stood there with his bills fluttering on his arm, thinking, and wrinkling up his forehead. At last he says:

"I'll tell you something. We got to be here three days. If you'll promise you won't blow, and won't let the nigger blow, I'll tell you where to find him."

So I promised, and he says:

"A farmer by the name of Silas Ph——" and then he stopped. You see he started to tell me the truth; but when he stopped, that way, and begun to study and think again, I reckoned he was changing his mind. And so he was. He wouldn't trust me; he wanted to make sure of having me out of the way the whole three days. So pretty soon he says: "The man that bought him is named Abram Foster—Abram G. Foster—and he lives forty mile back here in the country, on the road to Lafayette."

"All right," I says, "I can walk it in three days. And I'll start this very afternoon."

"No you won't, you'll start *now*; and don't you lose any time about it, neither, nor do any gabbling by the way. Just keep a tight tongue in your head and move right along, and then you won't get into trouble with *us*, d'ye hear?"

That was the order I wanted, and that was the one I played for. I wanted to be left free to work my plans.

"So clear out," he says; "and you can tell Mr. Foster whatever you want to. Maybe you can get him to believe that Jim *is* your nigger—some idiots don't require documents—leastways I've heard there's such down South here. And when you tell him the handbill and the reward's bogus, maybe he'll believe you when you explain to him what the idea was for getting 'em out. Go 'long, now, and tell him anything you want to; but mind you don't work your jaw any *between* here and there."

So I left, and struck for the back country. I didn't look around, but I kinder felt like he was watching me. But I knowed I could tire him out at that. I went straight out in the country as much as a mile, before I stopped; then I doubled back through the woods towards Phelps's. I reckoned I better start in on my plan straight off, without fooling around, because I wanted to stop Jim's mouth till these fellows could get away. I didn't want no trouble with their kind. I'd seen all I wanted to of them, and wanted to get entirely shut of them.

Chapter XXXII

When I got there it was all still and Sunday-like, and hot and sunshiny—the hands was gone to the fields; and there was them kind of faint dronings of bugs and flies in the air that makes it seem so lonesome and like everybody's dead and gone; and if a breeze fans along and quivers the leaves, it makes you feel mournful, because you feel like it's spirits whispering—spirits that's been dead ever so many years—and you always think they're talking about *you*. As a general thing it makes a body wish *he* was dead, too, and done with it all.

Phelps's was one of these little one-horse cotton plantations; and they all look alike. A rail fence round a two-acre yard; a stile, made out of logs sawed off and up-ended, in steps, like barrels of a different length, to climb over the fence with, and for the women to stand on when they are going to jump onto a horse; some sickly grass-patches in the big yard, but mostly it was bare and smooth, like an old hat with the nap rubbed off; big double log house for the white folks—hewed logs, with the chinks stopped up with mud or mortar, and these mud-stripes been whitewashed some time or another; round-log kitchen, with a big broad, open but roofed passage joining in to the house; log smoke-house back of the kitchen; three little log nigger-cabins in a row t'other side the smokehouse; one little hut all by itself away down against the back fence, and some outbuildings down a piece the other side; ash-hopper,[1] and big kettle to bile soap in, by the little hut; bench by the kitchen door, with bucket of water and a gourd; hound asleep there, in the sun; more hounds asleep, round about; about three shade-trees away off in a corner; some currant bushes and gooseberry bushes in one place by the fence; outside of the fence a garden and a water-melon patch; then the cotton fields begins; and after the fields, the woods.

I went around and clumb over the back stile by the ash-hopper, and started for the kitchen. When I got a little ways, I heard the dim hum of a spinning-wheel wailing along up and sinking along down again; and then I knowed for certain I wished I was dead—for that *is* the lonesomest sound in the whole world.[2]

I went right along, not fixing up any particular plan, but just trusting to Providence to put the right words in my mouth when the time come; for I'd noticed that Providence always did put the right words in my mouth, if I left it alone.

When I got half-way, first one hound and then another got up and went for me, and of course I stopped and faced them, and kept still. And such another pow-wow as they made! In a quarter of a minute I was a kind of a hub of a wheel, as you may say—spokes made out of dogs—circle of fifteen of them packed together around me, with their necks and noses stretched up towards me, a barking and howling; and more a coming; you could see them sailing over fences and around corners from everywheres.

A nigger woman come tearing out of the kitchen with a rolling-pin in her hand, singing out, "Begone! *you* Tige! you Spot! begone, sah!" and she fetched first one and then another of them a clip and sent him howling, and then the rest followed; and the next second, half of them come back, wagging their tails around me and making friends with me. There ain't no harm in a hound, nohow.

And behind the woman comes a little nigger girl and two little nigger boys, without anything on but tow-linen shirts, and they hung onto their mother's gown, and peeped out from behind her at me, bashful, the way they always do. And here comes the white woman running from the house, about forty-five or fifty year old, bare-headed, and her spinning-stick in her hand; and behind her comes her little white children, acting the same way the little niggers was doing. She was smiling all over so she could hardly stand —and says:

"It's *you*, at last!—*ain't* it?"

I out with a "Yes'm," before I thought.

She grabbed me and hugged me tight; and then gripped me by both hands and shook and shook; and the tears come in her eyes, and run down over; and she couldn't seem to hug and shake

1. A container for lye used in making soap.
2. For the details of the Phelps plantation Clemens drew on his memories of vacations at his Uncle John Quarles's farm near Hannibal. See Twain's *Autobiography* for his vivid evocation of the farm.

enough, and kept saying, "You don't look as much like your mother as I reckoned you would, but law sakes, I don't care for that, I'm *so* glad to see you! Dear, dear, it does seem like I could eat you up! Childern, it's your cousin Tom!—tell him howdy."

But they ducked their heads, and put their fingers in their mouths, and hid behind her. So she run on:

"Lize, hurry up and get him a hot breakfast, right away—or did you get your breakfast on the boat?"

I said I had got it on the boat. So then she started for the house, leading me by the hand, and the children tagging after. When we got there, she set me down in a split-bottomed chair, and set herself down on a little low stool in front of me, holding both of my hands, and says:

"Now I can have a *good* look at you; and laws-a-me, I've been hungry for it a many and a many a time, all these long years, and it's come at last! We been expecting you a couple of days and more. What's kep' you?—boat get aground?"

"Yes'm—she—"

"Don't say yes'm—say Aunt Sally. Where'd she get aground?"

I didn't rightly know what to say, because I didn't know whether the boat would be coming up the river or down. But I go a good deal on instinct; and my instinct said she would be coming up—from down towards Orleans. That didn't help me much, though; for I didn't know the names of bars down that way. I see I'd got to invent a bar, or forget the name of the one we got aground on—or —Now I struck an idea, and fetched it out:

"It warn't the grounding—that didn't keep us back but a little. We blowed out a cylinder-head."

"Good gracious! anybody hurt?"

"No'm. Killed a nigger."

"Well, it's lucky; because sometimes people do get hurt. Two years ago last Christmas, your uncle Silas was coming up from Newrleans on the old *Lally Rook*,[3] and she blowed out a cylinder-head and crippled a man. And I think he died afterwards. He was a Babtist. Your uncle Silas knowed a family in Baton Rouge that knowed his people very well. Yes, I remember, now he *did* die. Mortification[4] set in, and they had to amputate him. But it didn't save him. Yes, it was mortification—that was it. He turned blue all over, and died in the hope of a glorious resurrection. They say he was a sight to look at. Your uncle's been up to the town every day to fetch you. And he's gone again, not more'n an hour ago; he'll be back any minute, now. You must a met him on the road, didn't you?—oldish man, with a—"

"No, I didn't see nobody, Aunt Sally. The boat landed just at daylight, and I left my baggage on the wharf-boat and went looking

---

3. *Lalla Rookh* (1817) is a popular Romantic poem by Thomas Moore.
4. Gangrene.

around the town and out a piece in the country, to put in the time and not get here too soon; and so I come down the back way."

"Who'd you give the baggage to?"

"Nobody."

"Why, child, it'll be stole!"

"Not where *I* hid it I reckon it won't," I says.

"How'd you get your breakfast so early on the boat?"

It was kinder thin ice, but I says:

"The captain see me standing around, and told me I better have something to eat before I went ashore; so he took me in the texas to the officers' lunch, and give me all I wanted."

I was getting so uneasy I couldn't listen good. I had my mind on the children all the time; I wanted to get them out to one side, and pump them a little, and find out who I was. But I couldn't get no show, Mrs. Phelps kept it up and run on so. Pretty soon she made the cold chills streak all down my back, because she says:

"But here we're a running on this way, and you hain't told me a word about Sis, nor any of them. Now I'll rest my works a little, and you start up yourn; just tell me *everything*—tell me all about 'm all—every one of 'm; and how they are, and what they're doing, and what they told you to tell me; and every last thing you can think of."

Well, I see I was up a stump—and up it good. Providence had stood by me this fur, all right, but I was hard and tight aground, now. I see it warn't a bit of use to try to go ahead—I'd *got* to throw up my hand. So I says to myself, here's another place where I got to resk the truth. I opened my mouth to begin; but she grabbed me and huntled me in behind the bed, and says:

"Here he comes! stick your head down lower—there, that'll do; you can't be seen, now. Don't you let on you're here. I'll play a joke on him. Children, don't you say a word."

I see I was in a fix, now. But it warn't no use to worry; there warn't nothing to do but just hold still, and try to be ready to stand from under when the lightning struck.

I had just one little glimpse of the old gentleman when he come in, then the bed hid him. Mrs. Phelps she jumps for him and says:

"Has he come?"

"No," says her husband.

"Good-*ness* gracious!" she says, "what in the world *can* have become of him?"

"I can't imagine," says the old gentleman; "and I must say, it makes me dreadful uneasy."

"Uneasy!" she says, "I'm ready to go distracted! He *must* a come; and you've missed him along the road. I *know* it's so—something *tells* me so."

"Why Sally, I *couldn't* miss him along the road—*you* know that."

"But oh, dear, dear, what *will* Sis say! He must a come! You must a missed him. He—"

"Oh, don't distress me any more'n I'm already distressed. I don't know what in the world to make of it. I'm at my wit's end, and I don't mind acknowledging 't I'm right down scared. But there's no hope that he's come; for he *couldn't* come and me miss him. Sally, it's terrible—just terrible—something's happened to the boat, sure!"

"Why, Silas! Look yonder!—up the road!—ain't that somebody coming?"

He sprung to the window at the head of the bed, and that give Mrs. Phelps the chance she wanted. She stooped down quick, at the foot of the bed, and give me a pull, and out I come; and when he turned back from the window, there she stood, a-beaming and a-smiling like a house afire, and I standing pretty meek and sweaty alongside. The old gentleman stared, and says:

"Why, who's that?"

"Who do you reckon 't is?"

"I haint no idea. Who *is* it?"

"It's *Tom Sawyer!*"

By jings, I most slumped through the floor. But there warn't no time to swap knives;[5] the old man grabbed me by the hand and shook, and kept on shaking; and all the time, how the woman did dance around and laugh and cry; and then how they both did fire off questions about Sid, and Mary, and the rest of the tribe.

But if they was joyful, it warn't nothing to what I was; for it was like being born again, I was so glad to find out who I was. Well, they froze to me for two hours; and at last when my chin was so tired it couldn't hardly go, any more, I had told them more about my family—I mean the Sawyer family—than ever happened to any six Sawyer families. And I explained all about how we blowed out a cylinder-head at the mouth of White River and it took us three days to fix it. Which was all right, and worked first rate; because *they* didn't know but what it would take three days to fix it. If I'd a called it a bolt-head it would a done just as well.

Now I was feeling pretty comfortable all down one side, and pretty uncomfortable all up the other. Being Tom Sawyer was easy and comfortable; and it stayed easy and comfortable till by-and-by I hear a steamboat coughing along down the river—then I says to myself, spose Tom Sawyer come down on that boat?—and spose he steps in here, any minute, and sings out my name before I can throw him a wink to keep quiet? Well, I couldn't *have* it that way —it wouldn't do at all. I must go up the road and waylay him. So I told the folks I reckoned I would go up to the town and fetch down my baggage. The old gentleman was for going along with me, but I

5. Change plans.

said no, I could drive the horse myself, and I druther he wouldn't take no trouble about me.

Chapter XXXIII

So I started for town, in the wagon, and when I was half-way I see a wagon coming, and sure enough it was Tom Sawyer, and I stopped and waited till he come along. I says "Hold on!" and it stopped alongside, and his mouth opened up like a trunk, and staid so; and he swallowed two or three times like a person that's got a dry throat, and then says:

"I hain't ever done you no harm. You know that. So then, what you want to come back and ha'nt *me* for?"

I says:

"I hain't come back—I hain't been *gone*."

When he heard my voice, it righted him up some, but he warn't quite satisfied yet. He says:

"Don't you play nothing on me, because I wouldn't on you. Honest injun, now, you ain't a ghost?"

"Honest injun, I ain't," I says.

"Well—I—well, that ought to settle it, of course; but I can't somehow seem to understand it, no way. Looky here, warn't you ever murdered *at all?*"

"No. I warn't ever murdered at all—I played it on them. You come in here and feel of me if you don't believe me."

So he done it; and it satisfied him; and he was that glad to see me again, he didn't know what to do. And he wanted to know all about it right off; because it was a grand adventure, and mysterious, and so it hit him where he lived. But I said, leave it alone till by-and-by; and told his driver to wait, and we drove off a little piece, and I told him the kind of a fix I was in, and what did he reckon we better do? He said, let him alone a minute, and don't disturb him. So he thought and thought, and pretty soon he says:

"It's all right, I've got it. Take my trunk in your wagon, and let on it's your'n; and you turn back and fool along slow, so as to get to the house about the time you ought to; and I'll go towards town a piece, and take a fresh start, and get there a quarter or a half an hour after you; and you needn't let on to know me, at first."

I says:

"All right; but wait a minute. There's one more thing—a thing that *nobody* don't know but me. And that is, there's a nigger here that I'm a trying to steal out of slavery—and his name is *Jim*—old Miss Watson's Jim."

He says:

"What! Why Jim is—"

He stopped and went to studying. I says:

"*I* know what you'll say. You'll say it's dirty low-down business;

but what if it is?—*I'm* low down; and I'm agoing to steal him, and I want you to keep mum and not let on. Will you?"

His eye lit up, and he says:

"I'll *help* you steal him!"

Well, I let go all holts then, like I was shot. It was the most astonishing speech I ever heard—and I'm bound to say Tom Sawyer fell, considerable, in my estimation. Only I couldn't believe it. Tom Sawyer a *nigger stealer!*

"Oh, shucks," I says, "you're joking."

"I ain't joking, either."

"Well, then," I says, "joking or no joking, if you hear anything said about a runaway nigger, don't forget to remember that *you* don't know nothing about him, and *I* don't know nothing about him."

Then we took the trunk and put it in my wagon, and he drove off his way, and I drove mine. But of course I forgot all about driving slow, on accounts of being glad and full of thinking; so I got home a heap too quick for that length of a trip. The old gentleman was at the door, and he says.

"Why, this is wonderful. Who ever would a thought it was in that mare to do it. I wish we'd a timed her. And she hain't sweated a hair—not a hair. It's wonderful. Why, I wouldn't take a hunderd dollars for that horse now; I wouldn't, honest; and yet I'd a sold her for fifteen before, and thought 'twas all she was worth."

That's all he said. He was the innocentest, best old soul I ever see. But it warn't surprising; because he warn't only just a farmer, he was a preacher, too, and had a little one-horse log church down back of the plantation, which he built it himself at his own expense, for a church and school-house, and never charged nothing for his preaching, and it was worth it, too. There was plenty other farmer-preachers like that, and done the same way, down South.

In about half an hour Tom's wagon drove up to the front stile, and Aunt Sally she see it through the window because it was only about fifty yards, and says:

"Why, there's somebody come! I wonder who 'tis? Why, I do believe it's a stranger. Jimmy" (that's one of the children), "run and tell Lize to put on another plate for dinner."

Everybody made a rush for the front door, because, of course, a stranger don't come *every* year, and so he lays over the yaller fever, for interest, when he does come. Tom was over the stile and starting for the house; the wagon was spinning up the road for the village, and we was all bunched in the front door. Tom had his store clothes on, and an audience—and that was always nuts for Tom Sawyer. In them circumstances it warn't no trouble to him to throw in an amount of style that was suitable. He warn't a boy to meeky along up that yard like a sheep; no, he come ca'm and important, like the ram. When he got afront of us, he lifts his hat ever so gracious and dainty, like it was the lid of a box that had butterflies asleep in it and he didn't want to disturb them, and says:

"Mr. Archibald Nichols, I presume?"

"No, my boy," says the old gentleman, "I'm sorry to say 't your driver has deceived you; Nichols's place is down a matter of three mile more. Come in, come in."

Tom he took a look back over his shoulder, and says, "Too late —he's out of sight."

"Yes, he's gone, my son, and you must come in and eat your dinner with us; and then we'll hitch up and take you down to Nichols's."

"Oh, I *can't* make you so much trouble; I couldn't think of it. I'll walk—I don't mind the distance."

"But we won't *let* you walk—it wouldn't be Southern hospitality to do it. Come right in."

"Oh, *do*," says Aunt Sally; "it ain't a bit of trouble to us, not a bit in the world. You *must* stay. It's a long, dusty three mile, and we *can't* let you walk. And besides, I've already told 'em to put on another plate, when I see you coming; so you mustn't disappoint us. Come right in, and make yourself at home."

So Tom he thanked them very hearty and handsome, and let himself be persuaded, and come in; and when he was in, he said he was a stranger from Hicksville, Ohio, and his name was William Thompson—and he made another bow.

Well, he run on, and on, and on, making up stuff about Hicksville and everybody in it he could invent, and I getting a little nervous, and wondering how this was going to help me out of my scrape; and at last, still talking along, he reached over and kissed Aunt Sally right on the mouth, and then settled back again in his chair, comfortable, and was going on talking; but she jumped up and wiped it off with the back of her hand, and says:

"You owdacious puppy!"

He looked kind of hurt, and says:

"I'm surprised at you, m'am."

"You're s'rp— Why, what do you reckon *I* am? I've a good notion to take and—say, what do you mean by kissing me?"

He looked kind of humble, and says:

"I didn't mean nothing, m'am. I didn't mean no harm. I—I— thought you'd like it."

"Why, you born fool!" She took up the spinning-stick, and it looked like it was all she could do to keep from giving him a crack with it. "What made you think I'd like it?"

"Well, I don't know. Only, they—they—told me you would."

"*They* told you I would. Whoever told you's *another* lunatic. I never heard the beat of it. Who's *they*?"

"Why—everybody. They all said so, m'am."

It was all she could do to hold in; and her eyes snapped, and her fingers worked like she wanted to scratch him; and she says:

"Who's 'everybody?' Out with their names—or ther'll be an idiot short."

He got up and looked distressed, and fumbled his hat, and says:

"I'm sorry, and I warn't expecting it. They told me to. They all told me to. They all said kiss her; and said she'll like it. They all said it—every one of them. But I'm sorry, m'am, and I won't do it no more—I won't, honest."

"You won't, wont you? Well, I sh'd *reckon* you won't!"

"No'm, I'm honest about it; I won't ever do it again. Till you ask me."

"Till I *ask* you! Well, I never see the beat of it in my born days! I lay you'll be the Methusalem-numskull[6] of creation before ever *I* ask you—or the likes of you."

"Well," he says, "it does surprise me so. I can't make it out, somehow. They said you would, and I thought you would. But—" He stopped and looked around slow, like he wished he could run across a friendly eye, somewhere's; and fetched up on the old gentleman's, and says, "Didn't *you* think she'd like me to kiss her, sir?"

"Why, no, I—I—well, no, I b'lieve I didn't."

Then he looks on around, the same way, to me—and says:

"Tom, didn't *you* think Aunt Sally 'd open out her arms and say, 'Sid Sawyer—' "

"My land!" she says, breaking in and jumping for him, "you impudent young rascal, to fool a body so—" and was going to hug him, but he fended her off, and says:

"No, not till you've asked me, first."

So she didn't lose no time, but asked him; and hugged him and kissed him, over and over again, and then turned him over to the old man, and he took what was left. And after they got a little quiet again, she says:

"Why, dear me, I never see such a surprise. We warn't looking for *you*, at all, but only Tom. Sis never wrote to me about anybody coming but him."

"It's because it warn't *intended* for any of us to come but Tom," he says; "but I begged and begged, and at the last minute she let me come, too; so, coming down the river, me and Tom thought it would be a first-rate surprise for him to come here to the house first, and for me to by-and-by tag along and drop in and let on to be a stranger. But it was a mistake, Aunt Sally. This ain't no healthy place for a stranger to come."

"No—not impudent whelps, Sid. You ought to had your jaws boxed; I hain't been so put out since I don't know when. But I don't care, I don't mind the terms—I'd be willing to stand a thou-

6. Methuselah was a Biblical patriarch said to have lived 969 years.

sand such jokes to have you here. Well, to think of that performance! I don't deny it, I was most putrified[7] with astonishment
when you give me that smack."

We had dinner out in that broad open passage betwixt the house
and the kitchen; and there was things enough on that table for
seven families—and all hot, too; none of your flabby tough meat
that's laid in a cupboard in a damp cellar all night and tastes like a
hunk of old cold cannibal in the morning. Uncle Silas he asked a
pretty long blessing over it, but it was worth it; and it didn't cool it
a bit, neither, the way I've seen them kind of interruptions do, lots
of times.

There was a considerable good deal of talk, all the afternoon, and
me and Tom was on the lookout all the time, but it warn't no use,
they didn't happen to say nothing about any runaway nigger, and
we was afraid to try to work up to it. But at supper, at night, one of
the little boys says:

"Pa, mayn't Tom and Sid and me go to the show?"

"No," says the old man, "I reckon there ain't going to be any;
and you couldn't go if there was; because the runaway nigger told
Burton and me all about that scandalous show, and Burton said he
would tell the people; so I reckon they've drove the owdacious loafers out of town before this time."

So there it was!—but *I* couldn't help it. Tom and me was to
sleep in the same room and bed; so, being tired, we bid good-night
and went up to bed, right after supper, and clumb out of the
window and down the lightning-rod, and shoved for the town; for I
didn't believe anybody was going to give the king and the duke a
hint, and so, if I didn't hurry up and give them one they'd get into
trouble sure.

On the road Tom he told me all about how it was reckoned I
was murdered, and how pap disappeared, pretty soon, and didn't
come back no more, and what a stir there was when Jim run away;
and I told Tom all about our Royal Nonesuch rapscallions, and as
much of the raft-voyage as I had time to; and as we struck into the
town and up through the middle of it—it was as much as half-after
eight, then—here comes a raging rush of people, with torches, and
an awful whooping and yelling, and banging tin pans and blowing
horns; and we jumped to one side to let them go by; and as they
went by, I see they had the king and the duke astraddle of a rail—
that is, I knowed it *was* the king and the duke, though they was all
over tar and feathers, and didn't look like nothing in the world that
was human—just looked like a couple of monstrous big soldier-
plumes. Well, it made me sick to see it; and I was sorry for them
poor pitiful rascals, it seemed like I couldn't ever feel any hardness
against them any more in the world. It was a dreadful thing to see.
Human beings *can* be awful cruel to one another.

7. Petrified or stunned.

We see we was too late—couldn't do no good. We asked some stragglers about it, and they said everybody went to the show looking very innocent; and laid low and kept dark till the poor old king was in the middle of his cavortings on the stage; then somebody give a signal, and the house rose up and went for them.

So we poked along back home, and I warn't feeling so brash as I was before, but kind of ornery, and humble, and to blame, somehow—though *I* hadn't done nothing. But that's always the way; it don't make no difference whether you do right or wrong, a person's conscience ain't got no sense, and just goes for him *anyway*. If I had a yaller dog that didn't know no more than a person's conscience does, I would pison him. It takes up more room than all the rest of a person's insides, and yet ain't no good, nohow. Tom Sawyer he says the same.

Chapter XXXIV

We stopped talking, and got to thinking. By-and-by Tom says:

"Looky here, Huck, what fools we are, to not think of it before! I bet I know where Jim is."

"No! Where?"

"In that hut down by the ash-hopper. Why, looky here. When we was at dinner, didn't you see a nigger man go in there with some vittles?"

"Yes."

"What did you think the vittles was for?"

"For a dog."

"So'd I. Well, it wasn't for a dog."

"Why?"

"Because part of it was watermelon."

"So it was—I noticed it. Well, it does beat all, that I never thought about a dog not eating watermelon. It shows how a body can see and don't see at the same time."

"Well, the nigger unlocked the padlock when he went in, and he locked it again when he come out. He fetched uncle a key, about the time we got up from table—same key, I bet. Watermelon shows man, lock shows prisoner; and it ain't likely there's two prisoners on such a little plantation, and where the people's all so kind and good. Jim's the prisoner. All right—I'm glad we found it out detective fashion; I wouldn't give shucks for any other way. Now you work your mind and study out a plan to steal Jim, and I will study out one, too; and we'll take the one we like the best."

What a head for just a boy to have! If I had Tom Sawyer's head, I wouldn't trade it off to be a duke, nor mate of a steamboat, nor clown in a circus, nor nothing I can think of. I went to thinking out a plan, but only just to be doing something; I knowed very well where the right plan was going to come from. Pretty soon, Tom says:

"Ready?"

"Yes," I says.

"All right—bring it out."

"My plan is this," I says. "We can easy find out if it's Jim in there. Then get up my canoe to-morrow night, and fetch my raft over from the island. Then the first dark night that comes, steal the key out of the old man's britches, after he goes to bed, and shove off down the river on the raft, with Jim, hiding daytimes and running nights, the way me and Jim used to do before. Wouldn't that plan work?"

"*Work?* Why cert'nly, it would work, like rats a fighting. But it's too blame' simple; there ain't nothing *to* it. What's the good of a plan that ain't no more trouble than that? It's as mild as goose-milk. Why, Huck, it wouldn't make no more talk than breaking into a soap factory."

I never said nothing, because I warn't expecting nothing different; but I knowed mighty well that whenever he got *his* plan ready it wouldn't have none of them objections to it.

And it didn't. He told me what it was, and I see in a minute it was worth fifteen of mine, for style, and would make Jim just as free a man as mine would, and maybe get us all killed besides. So I was satisfied, and said we would waltz in on it. I needn't tell what it was, here, because I knowed it wouldn't stay the way it was. I knowed he would be changing it around, every which way, as we went along, and heaving in new bullinesses wherever he got a chance. And that is what he done.

Well, one thing was dead sure; and that was, that Tom Sawyer was in earnest and was actuly going to help steal that nigger out of slavery. That was the thing that was too many for me. Here was a boy that was respectable, and well brung up; and had a character to lose; and folks at home that had characters; and he was bright and not leather-headed; and knowing and not ignorant; and not mean, but kind; and yet here he was, without any more pride, or rightness, or feeling, than to stoop to this business, and make himself a shame, and his family a shame, before everybody. I *couldn't* understand it, no way at all. It was outrageous, and I knowed I ought to just up and tell him so; and so be his true friend, and let him quit the thing right where he was, and save himself. And I *did* start to tell him; but he shut me up, and says:

"Don't you reckon I know what I'm about? Don't I generly know what I'm about?"

"Yes."

"Didn't I *say* I was going to help steal the nigger?"

"Yes."

"*Well* then."

That's all he said, and that's all I said. It warn't no use to say any more; because when he said he'd do a thing, he always done it. But

I couldn't make out how he was willing to go into this thing; so I just let it go, and never bothered no more about it. If he was bound to have it so, I couldn't help it.

When we got home, the house was all dark and still; so we went on down to the hut by the ash-hopper, for to examine it. We went through the yard, so as to see what the hounds would do. They knowed us, and didn't make no more noise than country dogs is always doing when anything comes by in the night. When we got to the cabin, we took a look at the front and two sides; and on the side I warn't acquainted with—which was the north side—we found a square window-hole, up tolerable high, with just one stout board nailed across it. I says:

"Here's the ticket. This hole's big enough for Jim to get through, if we wrench off the board."

Tom says:

"It's as simple as tit-tat-toe, three-in-a-row, and as easy as playing hooky. I should *hope* we can find a way that's a little more complicated than *that*, Huck Finn."

"Well, then," I says, "how'll it do to saw him out, the way I done before I was murdered, that time?"

"That's more *like*," he says. "It's real mysterious, and troublesome, and good," he says; "but I bet we can find a way that's twice as long. There ain't no hurry; le's keep on looking around."

Betwixt the hut and the fence, on the back side, was a lean-to, that joined the hut at the eaves, and was made out of plank. It was as long as the hut, but narrow—only about six foot wide. The door to it was at the south end, and was padlocked. Tom he went to the soap kettle, and searched around and fetched back the iron thing they lift the lid with; so he took it and prized out one of the staples. The chain fell down, and we opened the door and went in, and shut it, and struck a match, and see the shed was only built against the cabin and hadn't no connection with it; and there warn't no floor to the shed, nor nothing in it but some old rusty played-out hoes, and spades, and picks, and a crippled plow. The match went out, and so did we, and shoved in the staple again, and the door was locked as good as ever. Tom was joyful. He says:

"Now we're all right. We'll *dig* him out. It'll take about a week!"

Then we started for the house, and I went in the back door—you only have to pull a buckskin latch-string, they don't fasten the doors —but that warn't romantical enough for Tom Sawyer: no way would do him but he must climb up the lightning-rod. But after he got up half-way about three times, and missed fire and fell every time, and the last time most busted his brains out, he thought he'd got to give it up; but after he rested, he allowed he would give her one more turn for luck, and this time he made the trip.

In the morning we was up at break of day, and down to the nigger cabins to pet the dogs and make friends with the nigger that fed Jim—if it *was* Jim that was being fed. The niggers was just getting through breakfast and starting for the fields; and Jim's nigger was piling up a tin pan with bread and meat and things; and whilst the other was leaving, the key come from the house.

This nigger had a good-natured, chuckle-headed face, and his wool was all tied up in little bunches with thread. That was to keep witches off. He said the witches was pestering him awful, these nights, and making him see all kinds of strange things, and hear all kinds of strange words and noises, and he didn't believe he was ever witched so long, before, in his life. He got so worked up, and got to running on so about his troubles, he forgot all about what he'd been agoing to do. So Tom says:

"What's the vittles for? Going to feed the dogs?"

The nigger kind of smiled around gradully over his face, like when you heave a brickbat in a mid puddle, and he says:

"Yes, Mars Sid, *a* dog. Cur'us dog, too. Does you want to go en look at 'im?"

"Yes."

I hunched Tom, and whispers:

"You going, right here in the day-break? *That* warn't the plan."

"No, it warn't—but it's the plan *now*."

So, drat him, we went along, but I didn't like it much. When we got in, we couldn't hardly see anything, it was so dark; but Jim was there, sure enough, and could see us; and he sings out:

"Why, *Huck!* En good *lan'!* ain' dat Misto Tom?"

I just knowed how it would be; I just expected it. *I* didn't know nothing to do; and if I had, I couldn't a done it; because that nigger busted in and says:

"Why, de gracious sakes! do he know you genlmen?"

We could see pretty well, now. Tom he looked at the nigger, steady and kind of wondering, and says:

"Does *who* know us?"

"Why, dish-yer runaway nigger."

"I don't reckon he does; but what put that into your head?"

"What *put* it dar? Didn' he jis' dis minute sing out like he knowed you?"

Tom says, in a puzzled-up kind of way:

"Well, that's mighty curious. *Who* sung out? *When* did he sing out. *What* did he sing out?" And turns to me, perfectly ca'm, and says, "Did *you* hear anybody sing out?"

Of course there warn't nothing to be said but the one thing; so I says:

"No; I ain't heard nobody say nothing."

Then he turns to Jim, and looks him over like he never see him before; and says:

"Did you sing out?"

"No, sah," says Jim; "*I* hain't said nothing, sah."

"Not a word?"

"No, sah, I hain't said a word."

"Did you ever see us before?"

"No, sah; not as *I* knows on."

So Tom turns to the nigger, which was looking wild and distressed, and says, kind of severe:

"What do you reckon's the matter with you, anyway? What
made you think somebody sung out?"

"Oh, it's de dad-blame' witches, sah, en I wisht I was dead, I do.
Dey's awluz at it, sah, en dey do mos' kill me, dey sk'yers me so.
Please to don't tell nobody 'bout it sah, er ole Mars Silas he'll scole
me; 'kase he say dey *ain't* no witches. I jis' wish to goodness he was
heah now—*den* what would he say! I jis' bet he couldn' fine no way
to git aroun' it *dis* time. But it's awluz jis' so; people dat's *sot*, stays
sot; dey won't look into nothn' en fine it out f'r deyselves, en when
you fine it out en tell um 'bout it, dey doan' b'lieve you."

Tom give him a dime, and said we wouldn't tell nobody; and
told him to buy some more thread to tie up his wool with; and then
looks at Jim, and says:

"I wonder if Uncle Silas is going to hang this nigger. If I was to
catch a nigger that was ungrateful enough to run away, *I* wouldn't
give him up, I'd hang him." And whilst the nigger stepped to the
door to look at the dime and bite it to see if it was good, he whispers to Jim, and says:

"Don't ever let on to know us. And if you hear any digging going
on nights, it's us: we're going to set you free."

Jim only had time to grab us by the hand and squeeze it, then
the nigger come back, and we said we'd come again some time if
the nigger wanted us to; and he said he would, more particular if it
was dark, because the witches went for him mostly in the dark, and
it was good to have folks around then.

Chapter XXXV

It would be most an hour, yet, till breakfast, so we left, and
struck down into the woods; because Tom said we got to have *some*
light to see how to dig by, and a lantern makes too much, and
might get us into trouble; what we must have was a lot of them
rotten chunks that's called fox-fire[8] and just makes a soft kind of a
glow when you lay them in a dark place. We fetched an armful and
hid it in the weeds, and set down to rest, and Tom says, kind of dissatisfied:

"Blame it, this whole thing is just as easy and awkard as it can
be. And so it makes it so rotten difficult to get up a difficult plan.
There ain't no watchman to be drugged—now there *ought* to be a
watchman. There ain't even a dog to give a sleeping-mixture to.
And there's Jim chained by one leg, with a ten-foot chain, to the

---

8. Phosphorescent glow of fungus on rotting wood.

leg of his bed: why, all you got to do is to lift up the bedstead and slip off the chain. And Uncle Silas he trusts everybody; sends the key to the punkin-headed nigger, and don't send nobody to watch the nigger. Jim could a got out of that window hole before this, only there wouldn't be no use trying to travel with a ten-foot chain on his leg. Why, drat it, Huck, it's the stupidest arrangement I ever see. You got to invent *all* the difficulties. Well, we can't help it, we got to do the best we can with the materials we've got. Anyhow, there's one thing—there's more honor in getting him out through a lot of difficulties and dangers, where there warn't one of them furnished to you by the people who it was their duty to furnish them, and you had to contrive them all out of your own head. Now look at just that one thing of the lantern. When you come down to the cold facts, we simply got to *let on* that a lantern's resky. Why, we could work with a torchlight procession if we wanted to, *I* believe. Now, whilst I think of it, we got to hunt up something to make a saw out of, the first chance we get."

"What do we want of a saw?"

"What do we *want* of it? Hain't we got to saw the leg of Jim's bed off, so as to get the chain loose?"

"Why, you just said a body could lift up the bedstead and slip the chain off."

"Well, if that ain't just like you, Huck Finn. You *can* get up the infant-schooliest ways of going at a thing. Why, hain't you ever read any books at all?—Baron Trenck, nor Casanova, nor Benvenuto Chelleeny, nor Henri IV.,[9] nor none of them heroes? Whoever heard of getting a prisoner loose in such an old-maidy way as that? No; the way all the best authorities does, is to saw the bedleg in two, and leave it just so, and swallow the sawdust, so it can't be found, and put some dirt and grease around the sawed place so the very keenest seneskal[1] can't see no sign of it's being sawed, and thinks the bed-leg is perfectly sound. Then, the night you're ready, fetch the leg a kick, down she goes; slip off your chain, and there you are. Nothing to do but hitch your rope-ladder to the battlements, shin down it, break your leg in the moat—because a rope-ladder is nineteen foot too short, you know—and there's your horses and your trusty vassles, and they scoop you up and fling you across a saddle and away you go, to your native Langudoc, or Navarre,[2] or wherever it is. It's gaudy, Huck. I wish there was a moat to this cabin. If we get time, the night of the escape, we'll dig one."

I says:

9. Baron Friedrich von der Trenck (1726–94), an Austrian soldier, and Henry IV of France (1553–1610) were military heroes; Benvenuto Cellini (1500–71), an artist, and Giovanni Jacopo Casanova (1725–98), were both famous lovers. All four were involved in daring escape attempts.
1. Seneschal, powerful official in the service of medieval nobles.
2. Provinces in France and Spain, respectively.

"What do we want of a moat, when we're going to snake him out from under the cabin?"

But he never heard me. He had forgot me and everything else. He had his chin in his hand, thinking. Pretty soon, he sighs, and shakes his head; then sighs again, and says:

"No, it wouldn't do—there ain't necessity enough for it."

"For what?" I says.

"Why, to saw Jim's leg off," he says.

"Good land!" I says, "why, there ain't *no* necessity for it. And what would you want to saw his leg off for, anyway?"

"Well, some of the best authorities has done it. They couldn't get the chain off, so they just cut their hand off, and shoved. And a leg would be better still. But we got to let that go. There ain't necessity enough in this case; and besides, Jim's a nigger and wouldn't understand the reasons for it, and how it's the custom in Europe; so we'll let it go. But there's one thing—he can have a rope-ladder; we can tear up our sheets and make him a rope-ladder easy enough. And we can send it to him in a pie; it's mostly done that way. And I've et worse pies."

"Why, Tom Sawyer, how you talk," I says; "Jim ain't got no use for a rope-ladder."

"He *has* got use for it. How *you* talk, you better say; you don't know nothing about it. He's *got* to have a rope ladder; they all do."

"What in the nation can he *do* with it?"

"*Do* with it? He can hide it in his bed, can't he? That's what they all do; and he's got to, too. Huck, you don't ever seem to want to do anything that's regular; you want to be starting something fresh all the time. Spose he *don't* do nothing with it? ain't it there in his bed, for a clew, after he's gone? and don't you reckon they'll want clews? Of course they will. And you wouldn't leave them any? That would be a *pretty* howdy-do, *wouldn't* it! I never heard of such a thing."

"Well," I says, "if it's in the regulations, and he's got to have it, all right, let him have it; because I don't wish to go back on no regulations; but there's one thing, Tom Sawyer—if we go to tearing up our sheets to make Jim a rope-ladder, we're going to get into trouble with Aunt Sally, just as sure as you're born. Now, the way I look at it, a hickry-bark ladder don't cost nothing, and don't waste nothing, and is just as good to load up a pie with, and hide in a straw tick, as any rag ladder you can start; and as for Jim, he ain't had no experience, and so *he* don't care what kind of a—"

"Oh, shucks, Huck Finn, if I was as ignorant as you, I'd keep still —that's what *I'd* do. Who ever heard of a state prisoner escaping by a hickry-bark ladder? Why, it's perfectly ridiculous."

"Well, all right, Tom, fix it your own way; but if you'll take my advice, you'll let me borrow a sheet off of the clothes-line."

He said that would do. And that give him another idea, and he says:

"Borrow a shirt, too."

"What do we want of a shirt, Tom?"

"Want it for Jim to keep a journal on."

"Journal your granny—*Jim* can't write."

"Spose he *can't* write—he can make marks on the shirt, can't he, if we make him a pen out of an old pewter spoon or a piece of an old iron barrel-hoop?"

"Why, Tom, we can pull a feather out of a goose and make him a better one; and quicker, too."

"*Prisoners* don't have geese running around the donjon-keep to pull pens out of, you muggins. They *always* make their pens out of the hardest, toughest, troublesomest piece of old brass candlestick or something like that they can get their hands on; and it takes them weeks and weeks, and months and months to file it out, too, because they've got to do it by rubbing it on the wall. *They* wouldn't use a goose-quill if they had it. It ain't regular."

"Well, then, what'll we make him the ink out of?"

"Many makes it out of iron-rust and tears; but that's the common sort and women; the best authorities uses their own blood. Jim can do that; and when he wants to send any little common ordinary mysterious message to let the world know where he's captivated, he can write it on the bottom of a tin plate with a fork and throw it out of the window. The Iron Mask[3] always done that, and it's a blame' good way, too."

"Jim ain't got no tin plates. They feed him in a pan."

"That ain't anything; we can get him some."

"Can't nobody *read* his plates."

"That ain't got nothing to *do* with it, Huck Finn. All *he's* got to do is to write on the plate and throw it out. You don't *have* to be able to read it. Why, half the time you can't read anything a prisoner writes on a tin plate, or anywhere else."

"Well, then, what's the sense in wasting the plates?"

"Why, blame it all, it ain't the *prisoner's* plates."

"But it's *somebody's* plates, ain't it?"

"Well, spos'n it is? What does the *prisoner* care whose—"

He broke off there, because we heard the breakfast-horn blowing. So we cleared out for the house.

Along during that morning I borrowed a sheet and a white shirt off of the clothes-line; and I found an old sack and put them in it, and we went down and got the fox-fire, and put that in too. I called it borrowing, because that was what pap always called it; but Tom

3. The chief character in Alexandre Dumas's novel *Le Vicomte de Bragelonne* (1848–50), part of which was soon after translated into English as *The Man in the Iron Mask.*

said it warn't borrowing, it was stealing. He said we was representing prisoners; and prisoners don't care how they get a thing so they
get it, and nobody don't blame them for it, either. It ain't no crime
in a prisoner to steal the thing he needs to get away with, Tom
said; it's his right; and so, as long as we was representing a prisoner,
we had a perfect right to steal anything on this place we had the
least use for, to get ourselves out of prison with. He said if we
warn't prisoners it would be a very different thing, and nobody but
a mean ornery person would steal when he warn't a prisoner. So we
allowed we would steal everything there was that come handy. And
yet he made a mighty fuss, one day, after that, when I stole a watermelon out of the nigger patch and eat it; and he made me go and
give the niggers a dime, without telling them what it was for. Tom
said that what he meant was, we could steal anything we *needed*.
Well, I says, I needed the watermelon. But he said I didn't need it
to get out of prison with, there's where the difference was. He said
if I'd a wanted it to hide a knife in, and smuggle it to Jim to kill
the seneskal with, it would a been all right. So I let it go at that,
though I couldn't see no advantage in my representing a prisoner, if
I got to set down and chaw over a lot of golf-leaf distinctions like
that, every time I see a chance to hog a watermelon.

Well, as I was saying, we waited that morning till everybody was
settled down to business, and nobody in sight around the yard; then
Tom he carried the sack into the lean-to whilst I stood off a piece
to keep watch. By-and-by he come out, and we went and set down
on the wood-pile, to talk. He says:

"Everything's all right, now, except tools; and that's easy fixed."

"Tools?" I says.

"Yes."

"Tools for what?"

"Why, to dig with. We ain't agoing to *gnaw* him out, are we?"

"Ain't them old crippled picks and things in there good enough
to dig a nigger out with?" I says.

He turns on me looking pitying enough to make a body cry, and
says:

"Huck Finn, did you *ever* hear of a prisoner having picks and
shovels, and all the modern conveniences in his wardrobe to dig
himself out with? Now I want to ask you—if you got any reason-
ableness in you at all—what kind of a show would *that* give him to
be a hero? Why, they might as well lend him the key, and done
with it. Picks and shovels—why they wouldn't furnish 'em to a
king."

"Well, then," I says, "if we don't want the picks and shovels,
what do we want?"

"A couple of case-knives."[4]

"To dig the foundations out from under that cabin with?"

4. Ordinary kitchen knives.

"Yes."

"Confound it, it's foolish, Tom."

"It don't make no difference how foolish it is, it's the *right* way —and it's the regular way. And there ain't no *other* way, that ever I heard of, and I've read all the books that gives any information about these things. They always dig out with a case-knife—and not through dirt, mind you; generly it's through solid rock. And it takes them weeks and weeks and weeks, and for ever and ever. Why, look at one of them prisoners in the bottom dungeon of the Castle Deef,[5] in the harbor of Marseilles, that dug himself out that way; how long was *he* at it, you reckon?"

"I don't know."

"Well, guess."

"I don't know. A month and a half?"

"*Thirty-seven year*—and he come out in China. *That's* the kind. I wish the bottom of *this* fortress was solid rock."

"*Jim* don't know nobody in China."

"What's *that* got to do with it? Neither did that other fellow. But you're always a-wandering off on a side issue. Why can't you stick to the main point?"

"All right—I don't care where he comes out, so he *comes* out; and Jim don't, either, I reckon. But there's one thing, anyway— Jim's too old to be dug out with a case-knife. He won't last."

"Yes he will *last*, too. You don't reckon it's going to take thirty-seven years to dig out through a *dirt* foundation, do you?"

"How long will it take, Tom?"

"Well, we can't resk being as long as we ought to, because it mayn't take very long for Uncle Silas to hear from down there by New Orleans. He'll hear Jim ain't from there. Then his next move will be to advertise Jim, or something like that. So we can't resk being as long digging him out as we ought to. By rights I reckon we ought to be a couple of years; but we can't. Things being so uncertain, what I recommend is this: that we really dig right in, as quick as we can; and after that, we can *let on*, to ourselves, that we was at it thirty-seven years. Then we can snatch him out and rush him away the first time there's an alarm. Yes, I reckon that'll be the best way."

"Now, there's *sense* in that," I says. "Letting on don't cost nothing; letting on ain't no trouble; and if it's any object, I don't mind letting on we was at it a hundred and fifty year. It wouldn't strain me none, after I got my hand in. So I'll mosey along now, and smouch a couple of case-knives."

"Smouch three," he says; "we want one to make a saw out of."

"Tom, if it ain't unregular and irreligious to sejest it," I says,

5. The hero of Alexandre Dumas's popular Romantic novel *The Count of Monte Cristo* (1844) was held prisoner at the Chateau d'If, a castle built by Francis I in 1524 on a small island in Marseilles harbor and used for many years as a state prison.

"there's an old rusty saw-blade around yonder sticking under the weatherboarding behind the smoke-house."

He looked kind of weary and discouraged-like, and says:

"It ain't no use to try to learn you nothing, Huck. Run along and smouch the knives—three of them." So I done it.

Chapter XXXVI

As soon as we reckoned everybody was asleep, that night, we went down the lightning-rod, and shut ourselves up in the lean-to, and got out our pile of fox-fire, and went to work. We cleared everything out of the way, about four or five foot along the middle of the bottom log. Tom said he was right behind Jim's bed now, and we'd dig in under it, and when we got through there couldn't nobody in the cabin ever know there was any hole there, because Jim's counterpin[6] hung down most to the ground, and you'd have to raise it up and look under to see the hole. So we dug and dug, with the case-knives, till most midnight; and then we was dog-tired, and our hands was blistered, and yet you couldn't see we'd done anything, hardly. At last I says:

"This ain't no thirty-seven year job, this is a thirty-eight year job, Tom Sawyer."

He never said nothing. But he sighed, and pretty soon he stopped digging, and then for a good little while I knowed he was thinking. Then he says:

"It ain't no use, Huck, it ain't agoing to work. If we was prisoners it would, because then we'd have as many years as we wanted, and no hurry; and we wouldn't get but a few minutes to dig, every day, while they was changing watches, and so our hands wouldn't get blistered, and we could keep it up right along, year in and year out, and do it right, and the way it ought to be done. But *we* can't fool along, we got to rush; we ain't got no time to spare. If we was to put in another night this way, we'd have to knock off for a week to let our hands get well—couldn't touch a case-knife with them sooner."

"Well, then, what we going to do, Tom?"

"I'll tell you. It ain't right, and it ain't moral, and I wouldn't like it to get out—but there ain't only just the one way; we got to dig him out with the picks, and *let on* it's case-knives."

"*Now* you're *talking!*" I says; "your head gets leveler and leveler all the time, Tom Sawyer," I says. "Picks is the thing, moral or no moral; and as for me, I don't care shucks for the morality of it, nohow. When I start in to steal a nigger, or a watermelon, or a Sunday-school book, I ain't no ways particular how it's done so it's done. What I want is my nigger; or what I want is my watermelon; or what I want is my Sunday-school book; and if a pick's the handiest thing, that's the thing I'm agoing to dig that nigger or that wat-

6. Counterpane or bedspread.

ermelon or that Sunday-school book out with; and I don't give a dead rat what the authorities thinks about it nuther."

"Well," he says, "there's excuse for picks and letting-on in a case like this; if it warn't so, I wouldn't approve of it, nor I wouldn't stand by and see the rules broke—because right is right, and wrong is wrong, and a body ain't got no business doing wrong when he ain't ignorant and knows better. It might answer for *you* to dig Jim out with a pick, *without* any letting-on, because you don't know no better; but it wouldn't for me, because I do know better. Gimme a case-knife."

He had his own by him, but I handed him mine. He flung it down, and says:

"Gimme a *case-knife*."

I didn't know just what to do—but then I thought. I scratched around amongst the old tools, and got a pick-ax and give it to him, and he took it and went to work, and never said a word.

He was always just that particular. Full of principle.

So then I got a shovel, and then we picked and shoveled, turn about, and made the fur fly. We stuck to it about a half an hour, which was as long as we could stand up; but we had a good deal of a hole to show for it. When I got up stairs, I looked out at the window and see Tom doing his level best with the lightning-rod, but he couldn't come it, his hands was so sore. At last he says:

"It ain't no use, it can't be done. What you reckon I better do? Can't you think up no way?"

"Yes," I says, "but I reckon it ain't regular. Come up the stairs, and let on it's a lightning-rod."

So he done it.

Next day Tom stole a pewter spoon and a brass candlestick in the house, for to make some pens for Jim out of, and six tallow candles; and I hung around the nigger cabins, and laid for a chance, and stole three tin plates. Tom said it wasn't enough; but I said nobody wouldn't ever see the plates that Jim throwed out, because they'd fall in the dog-fennel and jimpson weeds under the window-hole— then we could tote them back and he could use them over again. So Tom was satisfied. Then he says:

"Now, the thing to study out is, how to get the things to Jim."

"Take them in through the hole," I says, "when we get it done."

He only just looked scornful, and said something about nobody ever heard of such an idiotic idea, and then he went to studying. By-and-by he said he had ciphered out two or three ways, but there warn't no need to decide on any of them yet. Said we'd got to post Jim first.

That night we went down the lightning-rod a little after ten, and took one of the candles along, and listened under the window-hole, and heard Jim snoring; so we pitched it in, and it didn't wake him. Then we whirled in with the pick and shovel, and in about two hours and a half the job was done. We crept in under Jim's bed and into the cabin, and pawed around and found the candle and lit it, and stood over Jim a while, and found him looking hearty and healthy, and then we woke him up gentle and gradual. He was so glad to see us he most cried; and called us honey, and all the pet names he could think of; and was for having us hunt up a cold chisel to cut the chain off of his leg with, right away, and clearing out without losing any time. But Tom he showed him how unregular it would be, and set down and told him all about our plans, and how we could alter them in a minute any time there was an alarm; and not to be the least afraid, because we would see he got away, *sure*. So Jim he said it was all right, and we set there and talked over old times a while, and then Tom asked a lot of questions, and when Jim told him Uncle Silas come in every day or two to pray with him, and Aunt Sally come in to see if he was comfortable and had plenty to eat, and both of them was kind as they could be, Tom says:

"Now I know how to fix it. We'll send you some things by them."

I said, "Don't do nothing of the kind; it's one of the most jackass ideas I ever struck;" but he never paid no attention to me; went right on. It was his way when he'd got his plans set.

So he told Jim how we'd have to smuggle in the rope-ladder pie, and other large things, by Nat, the nigger that fed him, and he must be on the lookout, and not be surprised, and not let Nat see him open them; and we would put small things in uncle's coat pockets and he must steal them out; and we would tie things to aunt's apron strings or put them in her apron pocket, if we got a chance; and told him what they would be and what they was for. And told him how to keep a journal on the shirt with his blood, and all that. He told him everything. Jim he couldn't see no sense in the most of it, but he allowed we was white folks and knowed better than him; so he was satisfied, and said he would do it all just as Tom said.

Jim had plenty corn-cob pipes and tobacco; so we had a right down good sociable time; then we crawled out through the hole, and so home to bed, with hands that looked like they'd been chawed. Tom was in high spirits. He said it was the best fun he ever had in his life, and the most intellectural; and said if he only could see his way to it we would keep it up all the rest of our lives and leave Jim to our children to get out; for he believed Jim would come to like it better and better the more he got used to it. He said that in that way it could be strung out to as much as eighty year, and would be the best time on record. And he said it would make us all celebrated that had a hand in it.

In the morning we went out to the wood-pile and chopped up

the brass candlestick into handy sizes, and Tom put them and the pewter spoon in his pocket. Then we went to the nigger cabins, and while I got Nat's notice off, Tom shoved a piece of candlestick into the middle of a corn-pone that was in Jim's pan, and we went along with Nat to see how it would work, and it just worked noble; when Jim bit into it it most mashed all his teeth out; and there warn't ever anything could a worked better. Tom said so himself. Jim he never let on but what it was only just a piece of rock or something like that that's always getting into bread, you know; but after that he never bit into nothing but what he jabbed his fork into it in three or four places, first.

And whilst we was a standing there in the dimmish light, here comes a couple of the hounds bulging in, from under Jim's bed; and they kept on piling in till there was eleven of them, and there warn't hardly room in there to get your breath. By jings, we forgot to fasten that lean-to door. The nigger Nat he only just hollered "witches!" once, and kneeled over onto the floor amongst the dogs, and begun to groan like he was dying. Tom jerked the door open and flung out a slab of Jim's meat, and the dogs went for it, and in two seconds he was out himself and back again and shut the door, and I knowed he'd fixed the other door too. Then he went to work on the nigger, coaxing him and petting him, and asking him if he'd been imagining he saw something again. He raised up, and blinked his eyes around, and says:

"Mars Sid, you'll say I's a fool, but if I didn't b'lieve I see most a million dogs, er devils, er some'n, I wisht I may die right heah in dese tracks. I did, mos' sholy. Mars Sid, I *felt* um—I *felt* um, sah; dey was all over me. Dad fetch it, I jis' wisht I could git my han's on one er dem witches jis' wunst—on'y jis' wunst—it's all *I'd* ast. But mos'ly I wisht dey'd lemme 'lone, I does."

Tom says:

"Well, I tell you what *I* think. What makes them come here just at this runaway nigger's breakfast-time? It's because they're hungry; that's the reason. You make them a witch pie; that's the thing for *you* to do."

"But my lan', Mars Sid, how's I gwyne to make 'm a witch pie? I doan' know how to make it. I hain't ever hearn er sich a thing b'fo.' "

"Well, then, I'll have to make it myself."

"Will you do it, honey?—will you? I'll wusshup de groun' und' yo' foot, I will!"

"All right, I'll do it, seeing it's you, and you've been good to us and showed us the runaway nigger. But you got to be mighty care-ful. When we come around, you turn your back; and then whatever we've put in the pan, don't you let on you see it at all. And don't you look, when Jim unloads the pan—something might happen, I don't know what. And above all, don't you *handle* the witch-things."

"*Hannel* 'm Mars Sid? What *is* you a talkin' 'bout? I wouldn' lay de weight er my finger on um, not f'r ten hund'd thous'n' billion dollars, I wouldn't."

Chapter XXXVII

That was all fixed. So then we went away and went to the rub-bage-pile in the back yard where they keep the old boots, and rags, and pieces of bottles, and wore-out tin things, and all such truck, and scratched around and found an old tin washpan and stopped up the holes as well as we could, to bake the pie in, and took it down cellar and stole it full of flour, and started for breakfast and found a couple of shingle-nails that Tom said would be handy for a prisoner to scrabble his name and sorrows on the dungeon walls with, and dropped one of them in Aunt Sally's apron pocket which was hanging on a chair, and t'other we stuck in the band of Uncle Silas's hat, which was on the bureau, because we heard the children say their pa and ma was going to the runaway nigger's house this morning, and then went to breakfast, and Tom dropped the pewter spoon in Uncle Silas's coat pocket, and Aunt Sally wasn't come yet, so we had to wait a little while.

And when she come she was hot, and red, and cross, and couldn't hardly wait for the blessing; and then she went to sluicing out coffee with one hand and cracking the handiest child's head with her thimble with the other, and says:

"I've hunted high, and I've hunted low, and it does beat all, what *has* become of your other shirt."

My heart fell down amongst my lungs and livers and things, and a hard piece of corn-crust started down my throat after it and got met on the road with a cough and was shot across the table and took one of the children in the eye and curled him up like a fishing-worm, and let a cry out of him the size of a war-whoop, and Tom he turned kinder blue around the gills, and it all amounted to a considerable state of things for about a quarter of a minute or as much as that, and I would a sold out for half price if there was a bidder. But after that we was all right again—it was the sudden surprise of it that knocked us so kind of cold. Uncle Silas he says:

"It's most uncommon curious, I can't understand it. I know perfectly well I took it *off*, because——"

"Because you hain't got but one on. Just *listen* at the man! I know you took it off, and know it by a better way than your wool-gethering memory, too, because it was on the clo'es-line yesterday —I see it there myself. But it's gone—that's the long and the short of it, and you'll just have to change to a red flann'l one till I can get time to make a new one. And it'll be the third I've made in two years; it just keeps a body on the jump to keep you in shirts; and whatever you do manage to *do* with 'm all, is more'n I can make out. A body'd think you *would* learn to take some sort of care of 'em, at your time of life."

"I know it, Sally, and I do try all I can. But it oughtn't to be altogether my fault, because you know I don't see them nor have nothing to do with them except when they're on me; and I don't believe I've ever lost one of them *off* of me."

"Well, it ain't *your* fault if you havent', Silas—you'd a done it if you could, I reckon. And the shirt ain't all that's gone, nuther. Ther's a spoon gone; and *that* ain't all. There was ten, and now ther's only nine. The calf got the shirt I reckon, but the calf never took the spoon, *that's* certain."

"Why, what else is gone, Sally?"

"Ther's six *candles* gone—that's what. The rats could a got the candles, and I reckon they did; I wonder they don't walk off with the whole place, the way you're always going to stop their holes and don't do it; and if they warn't fools they'd sleep in your hair, Silas —*you'd* never find it out; but you can't lay the *spoon* on the rats, and that I *know*."

"Well, Sally, I'm in fault, and I acknowledge it; I've been remiss; but I won't let to-morrow go by without stopping up them holes."

"Oh, I wouldn't hurry, next year'll do. Matilda Angelina Araminta *Phelps!*"

Whack comes the thinble, and the child snatches her claws out of the sugar-bowl without fooling around any. Just then, the nigger woman steps onto the passage, and says:

"Missus, dey's a sheet gone."

"A *sheet* gone! Well, for the land's sake!"

"I'll stop up them holes *to-day*," says Uncle Silas, looking sorrowful.

"Oh, *do* shet up!—spose the rats took the *sheet?* *Where's* it gone, Lize?"

"Clah to goodness I hain't no notion, Miss Sally. She wuz on de clo's-line yistiddy, but she done gone; she ain' dah no mo', now."

"I reckon the world *is* coming to an end. I *never* see the beat of it, in all my born days. A shirt, and a sheet, and a spoon, and six can—"

"Missus," comes a young yaller wench, "dey's a brass cannelstick miss'n."

"Cler out from here, you hussy, er I'll take a skillet to ye!"

Well, she was just a biling. I begun to lay for a chance; I reckoned I would sneak out and go for the woods till the weather moderated. She kept a raging right along, running her insurrection all by herself, and everybody else mighty meek and quiet; and at last Uncle Silas, looking kind of foolish, fishes up that spoon out of his pocket. She stopped, with her mouth open and her hands up; and as for me, I wished I was in Jeruslem or somewheres. But not long; because she says:

"It's *just* as I expected. So you had it in your pocket all the time; and like as not you've got the other things there, too. How'd it get there?"

"I reely don't know, Sally," he says, kind of apologizing, "or you know I would tell. I was a-studying over my text in Acts Seventeen, before breakfast, and I reckon I put it in there, not noticing, meaning to put my Testament in, and it must be so, because my Testament ain't in, but I'll go and see, and if the Testament is where I had it, I'll know I didn't put it in, and that will show that I laid the Testament down and took up the spoon, and——'

"Oh, for the land's sake! Give a body a rest! Go 'long now, the whole kit and biling of ye; and don't come nigh me again till I've got back my peace of mind."

I'd a heard her, if she'd a said it to herself, let alone speaking it out; and I'd a got up and obeyed her, if I'd a been dead. As we was passing through the setting-room, the old man he took up his hat, and the shingle-nail fell out on the floor, and he just merely picked it up and laid it on the mantel-shelf, and never said nothing, and went out. Tom see him do it, and remembered about the spoon, and says:

"Well, it ain't no use to send things by *him* no more, he ain't reliable." Then he says: "But he done us a good turn with the spoon, anyway, without knowing it, and so we'll go and do him one without *him* knowing it—stop up his rat-holes."

There was a noble good lot of them, down cellar, and it took us a whole hour, but we done the job tight and good, and ship-shape. Then we heard steps on the stairs, and blowed out our light, and hid; and here comes the old man, with a candle in one hand and a bundle of stuff in t'other, looking as absent-minded as year before last. He went a mooning around, first to one rat-hole and then another, till he'd been to them all. Then he stood about five minutes, picking tallow-drip off of his candle and thinking. Then he turns off slow and dreamy towards the stairs, saying:

"Well, for the life of me I can't remember when I done it. I could show her now that I warn't to blame on account of the rats. But never mind—let it go. I reckon it wouldn't do no good."

And so he went on a mumbling up stairs, and then we left. He was a mighty nice old man. And always is.

Tom was a good deal bothered about what to do for a spoon, but he said we'd got to have it; so he took a think. When he had ciphered it out, he told me how we was to do; then we went and waited around the spoon-basket till we see Aunt Sally coming, and then Tom went to counting the spoons and laying them out to one side, and I slid one of them up my sleeve, and Tom says:

"Why, Aunt Sally, there ain't but nine spoons, *yet*."

She says:

"Go 'long to your play, and don't bother me. I know better, I counted 'm myself."

"Well, I've counted them twice, Aunty, and I can't make but nine."

She looked out of all patience, but of course she come to count —anybody would.

"I declare to gracious ther' *ain't* but nine!" she says. "Why, what in the world—plague *take* the things, I'll count 'm again."

So I slipped back the one I had, and when she got done counting, she says:

"Hang the troublesome rubbage, ther's *ten*, now!" and she looked huffy and bothered both. But Tom says:

"Why, Aunty, I don't think there's ten."

"You numskull, didn't you see me *count* 'm?"

"I know, but—"

"Well, I'll count 'm *again*."

So I smouched one, and they come out nine same as the other time. Well, she *was* in a tearing way—just a trembling all over, she was so mad. But she counted and counted, till she got that addled she'd start to count-in the *basket* for a spoon, sometimes; and so, three times they come out right, and three times they come out wrong. Then she grabbed up the basket and slammed it across the house and knocked the cat galley-west;[7] and she said cle'r out and let her have some peace, and if we come bothering around her again betwixt that and dinner, she'd skin us. So we had the odd spoon; and dropped it in her apron pocket whilst she was a giving us our sailing-orders, and Jim got it all right, along with her shingle-nail, before noon. We was very well satisfied with this business, and Tom allowed it was worth twice the trouble it took, because he said *now* she couldn't ever count them spoons twice alike again to save her life; and wouldn't believe she'd counted them right, if she *did*; and said that after she'd about counted her head off, for the next three days, he judged she'd give it up and offer to kill anybody that wanted her to ever count them any more.

So we put the sheet back on the line, that night, and stole one out of her closet; and kept on putting it back and stealing it again, for a couple of days, till she didn't know how many sheets she had, any more, and said she didn't *care*, and warn't agoing to bullyrag[8] the rest of her soul out about it, and wouldn't count them again not to save her life, she druther die first.

So we was all right now, as to the shirt and the sheet and the spoon and the candles, by the help of the calf and the rats and the mixed-up counting; and as to the candlestick, it warn't no consequence, it would blow over by-and-by.

---

7. Knocked out completely.   8. To nag mercilessly.

But that pie was a job; we had no end of trouble with that pie. We fixed it up away down in the woods, and cooked it there; and we got it done at last, and very satisfactory, too; but not all in one day; and we had to use up three washpans full of flour, before we got through, and we got burnt pretty much all over, in places, and eyes put out with the smoke; because, you see, we didn't want nothing but a crust, and we couldn't prop it up right, and she would always cave in. But of course we thought of the right way at last; which was to cook the ladder, too, in the pie. So then we laid in with Jim, the second night, and tore up the sheet all in little strings, and twisted them together, and long before daylight we had a lovely rope, that you could a hung a person with. We let on it took nine months to make it.

And in the forenoon we took it down to the woods, but it wouldn't go in the pie. Being made of a whole sheet, that way, there was rope enough for forty pies, if we'd a wanted them, and plenty left over for soup, or sausage, or anything you choose. We could a had a whole dinner.

But we didn't need it. All we needed was just enough for the pie, and so we throwed the rest away. We didn't cook none of the pies in the washpan, afraid the solder would melt; but Uncle Silas he had a noble brass warming-pan which he thought considerable of, because it belonged to one of his ancestors with a long wooden handle that come over from England with William the Conqueror in the *Mayflower*[9] or one of them early ships and was hid away up garret with a lot of other old pots and things that was valuable, not on account of being any account because they warn't, but on account of them being relicts, you know, and we snaked her out, private, and took her down there, but she failed on the first pies, because we didn't know how, but she come up smiling on the last one. We took and lined her with dough, and set her in the coals, and loaded her up with rag-rope, and put on a dough roof, and shut down the lid, and put hot embers on top, and stood off five foot, with the long handle, cool and comfortable, and in fifteen minutes she turned out a pie that was a satisfaction to look at. But the person that et it would want to fetch a couple of kags of toothpicks along, for if that rope-ladder wouldn't cramp him down to business, I don't know nothing what I'm talking about, and lay him in enough stomach-ache to last him till next time, too.

Nat didn't look, when we put the witch-pie in Jim's pan; and we put the three tin plates in the bottom of the pan under the vittles; and so Jim got everything all right, and as soon as he was by himself he busted into the pie and hid the rope-ladder inside of his straw tick, and scratched some marks on a tin plate and throwed it out of the window-hole.

9. William the Conqueror lived in the 11th century; the *Mayflower* made its historic crossing in 1620.

Chapter XXXVIII

Making them pens was a distressid-tough job, and so was the saw; and Jim allowed the inscription was going to be the toughest of all. That's the one which the prisoner has to scrabble on the wall. But we had to have it; Tom said we'd *got* to; there warn't no case of a state prisoner not scrabbling his inscription to leave behind, and his coat of arms.

"Look at Lady Jane Grey," he says; "look at Gilford Dudley; look at old Northumberland![1] Why, Huck, spose it *is* considerble trouble?—what you going to do?—how you going to get around it? Jim's *got* to do his inscription and coat of arms. They all do."

Jim says:

"Why, Mars Tom, I hain't got no coat o' arms; I hain't got nuffn but dish-yer ole shirt, en you knows I got to keep de journal on dat."

"Oh, you don't understand, Jim; a coat of arms is very different."

"Well," I says, "Jim's right, anyway, when he says he hain't got no coat of arms, because he hain't."

"I reckon *I* knowed that," Tom says, "but you bet he'll have one before he goes out of this—because he's going out *right*, and there ain't going to be no flaws in his record."

So whilst me and Jim filed away at the pens on a brickbat[2] apiece, Jim a making his'n out of the brass and I making mine out of the spoon, Tom set to work to think out the coat of arms. By-and-by he said he'd struck so many good ones he didn't hardly know which to take, but there was one which he reckoned he'd decide on. He says:

"On the scutcheon we'll have a bend *or* in the dexter base, a saltire *murrey* in the fess, with a dog, couchant, for common charge, and under his foot a chain embattled, for slavery, with a chevron *vert* in a chief engrailed, and three invected lines on a field *azure*, with the nombril points rampant on a dancette indented; crest, a runaway nigger, *sable*, with his bundle over his shoulder on a bar sinister: and a couple of gules for supporters, which is you and me; motto, *Maggiore fretta, minore atto*. Got it out of a book—means, the more haste, the less speed."[3]

"Geewhillikins," I says, "but what does the rest of it mean?"

"We ain't got no time to bother over that," he says, "we got to dig in like all git-out."

"Well, anyway," I says, "what's *some* of it? What's a fess?"

1. The story of Lady Jane Grey (1537–54), her husband Guildford Dudley, and his father the Duke of Northumberland was told in W. H. Ainsworth's romance *The Tower of London* (1840). The duke was at work carving a poem on the wall of his cell when the executioners came for him.
2. A brick.
3. An escutcheon is the shield-shaped surface on which the coat of arms is inscribed. The details are expressed in the technical argot of heraldry.

"A fess—a fess is—*you* don't need to know what a fess is. I'll show him how to make it when he gets to it."

"Shucks, Tom," I says, "I think you might tell a person. What's a bar sinister?"

"Oh, *I* don't know. But he's got to have it. All the nobility does."

That was just his way. If it didn't suit him to explain a thing to you, he wouldn't do it. You might pump at him a week, it wouldn't make no difference.

He'd got all that coat of arms business fixed, so now he started in to finish up the rest of that part of the work, which was to plan out a mournful inscription—said Jim got to have one, like they all done. He made up a lot, and wrote them out on a paper, and read them off, so:

1. *Here a captive heart busted.*

2. *Here a poor prisoner, forsook by the world and friends, fretted out his sorrowful life.*

3. *Here a lonely heart broke, and a worn spirit went to its rest, after thirty-seven years of solitary captivity.*

4. *Here, homeless and friendless, after thirty-seven years of bitter captivity, perished a noble stranger, natural son of Louis XIV.*

Tom's voice trembled, whilst he was reading them, and he most broke down. When he got done, he couldn't no way make up his mind which one for Jim to scrabble onto the wall, they was all so good; but at last he allowed he would let him scrabble them all on. Jim said it would take him a year to scrabble such a lot of truck onto the logs with a nail, and he didn't know how to make letters, besides; but Tom said he would block them out for him, and then he wouldn't have nothing to do but just follow the lines. Then pretty soon he says:

"Come to think, the logs ain't agoing to do; they don't have log walls in a dungeon: we got to dig the inscriptions into a rock. We'll fetch a rock."

Jim said the rock was worse than the logs; he said it would take him such a pison long time to dig them into a rock, he wouldn't ever get out. But Tom said he would let me help him do it. Then he took a look to see how me and Jim was getting along with the pens. It was most pesky tedious hard work and slow, and didn't give my hands no show to get well of the sores, and we didn't seem to make no headway, hardly. So Tom says:

"I know how to fix it. We got to have a rock for the coat of arms and mournful inscriptions, and we can kill two birds with that same rock. There's a gaudy big grindstone down at the mill, and we'll smouch it, and carve the things on it, and file out the pens and the saw on it, too."

It warn't no slouch of an idea; and it warn't no slouch of a grindstone nuther; but we allowed we'd tackle it. It warn't quite midnight, yet, so we cleared out for the mill, leaving Jim at work. We smouched the grindstone, and set out to roll her home, but it was a most nation tough job. Sometimes, do what we could, we couldn't keep her from falling over, and she come mighty near mashing us, every time. Tom said she was going to get one of us, sure, before we got through. We got her half way; and then we was plumb played out, and most drownded with sweat. We see it warn't no use, we got to go and fetch Jim. So he raised up his bed and slid the chain off of the bed-leg, and wrapt it round and round his neck, and we crawled out through our hole and down there, and Jim and me laid into that grindstone and walked her along like nothing; and Tom superintended. He could out-superintend any boy I ever see. He knowed how to do everything.

Our hole was pretty big, but it warn't big enough to get the grindstone through; but Jim he took the pick and soon made it big enough. Then Tom marked out them things on it with the nail, and set Jim to work on them, with the nail for a chisel and an iron bolt from the rubbage in the lean-to for a hammer, and told him to work till the rest of his candle quit on him, and then he could go to bed, and hide the grindstone under his straw tick and sleep on it. Then we helped him fix his chain back on the bed-leg, and was ready for bed ourselves. But Tom thought of something, and says:

"You got any spiders in here, Jim?"

"No, sah, thanks to goodness I hain't, Mars Tom."

"All right, we'll get you some."

"But bless you, honey, I doan' *want* none. I's afeard un um. I jis' 's soon have rattlesnakes aroun'."

Tom thought a minute or two, and says:

"It's a good idea. And I reckon it's been done. It *must* a been done; it stands to reason. Yes, it's a prime good idea. Where could you keep it?"

"Keep what, Mars Tom?"

"Why, a rattlesnake."

"De goodness gracious alive, Mars Tom! Why, if dey was a rattlesnake to come in heah, I'd take en bust right out thoo dat log wall, I would, wid my head."

"Why, Jim, you wouldn't be afraid of it, after a little. You could tame it."

"*Tame* it!"

"Yes—easy enough. Every animal is grateful for kindness and petting, and they wouldn't *think* of hurting a person that pets them. Any book will tell you that. You try—that's all I ask; just try for two or three days. Why, you can get him so, in a little while, that he'll love you; and sleep with you; and won't stay away from you a minute; and will let you wrap him round your neck and put his head in your mouth."

"*Please*, Mars Tom—*doan'* talk so! I can't *stan'* it! He'd *let* me shove his head in my mouf—fer a favor, hain't it? I lay he'd wait a pow'ful long time 'fo' I *ast* him. En mo' en dat, I doan' *want* him to sleep wid me."

"Jim, don't act so foolish. A prisoner's *got* to have some kind of a dumb pet, and if a rattlesnake hain't ever been tried, why, there's more glory to be gained in your being the first to ever try it than any other way you could ever think of to save your life."

"Why, Mars Tom, I doan' *want* no sich glory. Snake take 'n bite Jim's chin off, den *whah* is de glory? No, sah, I doan' want no sich doin's."

"Blame it, can't you *try*? I only *want* you to try—you needn't keep it up if it don't work."

"But de trouble all *done*, ef de snake bite me while I's a tryin' him. Mars Tom, I's willin' to tackle mos' anything 'at ain't onreasonable, but ef you en Huck fetches a rattlesnake in heah for me to tame, I's gwyne to *leave*, dat's *shore*."

"Well, then, let it go, let it go, if you're so bullheaded about it. We can get you some garter-snakes and you can tie some buttons on their tails, and let on they're rattlesnakes, and I reckon that'll have to do."

"I k'n stan' *dem*, Mars Tom, but blame' 'f I couldn' get along widout um, I tell you dat. I never knowed b'fo', 't was so much bother and trouble to be a prisoner."

"Well, it *always* is, when it's done right. You got any rats around here?"

"No, sah, I hain't seed none."

"Well, we'll get you some rats."

"Why, Mars Tom, I doan' *want* no rats. Dey's de dad-blamedest creturs to sturb a body, en rustle roun' over 'im, en bite his feet, when he's tryin' to sleep, I ever see. No, sah, gimme g'yarter-snakes, 'f I's got to have 'm, but doan' gimme no rats, I ain' got no use f'r um, skasely."

"But Jim, you *got* to have 'em—they all do. So don't make no more fuss about it. Prisoners ain't ever without rats. There ain't no instance of it. And they train them, and pet them, and learn them tricks, and they get to be as sociable as flies. But you got to play music to them. You got anything to play music on?"

"I ain't got nuffn but a coase comb en a piece o' paper, en a juice-harp; but I reck'n dey wouldn' take no stock in a juice-harp."

"Yes they would. *They* don't care what kind of music 'tis. A jews-harp's plenty good enough for a rat. All animals likes music—in a prison they dote on it. Specially, painful music; and you can't get no other kind out of a jews-harp. It always interests them; they come out to see what's the matter with you. Yes, you're all right; you're fixed very well. You want to set on your bed, nights, before you go to sleep, and early in the mornings, and play your jews-harp; play The Last Link is Broken—that's the thing that'll scoop a rat,

quicker'n anything else: and when you've played about two minutes, you'll see all the rats, and the snakes, and spiders, and things
begin to feel worried about you, and come. And they'll just fairly
swarm over you, and have a noble good time."

"Yes, *dey* will, I reck'n, Mars Tom, but what kine er time is *Jim*
havin'? Blest if I kin see de pint. But I'll do it ef I got to. I reck'n I
better keep de animals satisfied, en not have no trouble in de
house."

Tom waited to think over, and see if there wasn't nothing else;
and pretty soon he says:

"Oh—there's one thing I forgot. Could you raise a flower here,
do you reckon?"

"I doan' know but maybe I could, Mars Tom; but it's tolable
dark in heah, en I ain' got no use f'r no flower, nohow, en she'd be
a pow'ful sight o' trouble."

"Well, you try it, anyway. Some other prisoners has done it."

"One er dem big cat-tail-lookin' mullen-stalks would grow in
heah, Mars Tom, I reck'n, but she wouldn' be wuth half de trouble
she'd coss."

"Don't you believe it. We'll fetch you a little one, and you plant
it in the corner, over there, and raise it. And don't call it mullen,
call it Pitchiola—that's its right name, when it's in a prison.[4] And
you want to water it with your tears."

"Why, I got plenty spring water, Mars Tom."

"You don't *want* spring water; you want to water it with your
tears. It's the way they always do."

"Why, Mars Tom, I lay I kin raise one er dem mullen-stalks
twyste wid spring water whiles another man's a *start'n* one wid
tears."

"That ain't the idea. You *got* to do it with tears."

"She'll die on my han's, Mars Tom, she sholy will; kase I doan'
skasely ever cry."

So Tom was stumped. But he studied it over, and then said Jim
would have to worry along the best he could with an onion. He
promised he would go to the nigger cabins and drop one, private, in
Jim's coffee-pot, in the morning. Jim said he would "jis' 's soon
have tobacker in his coffee;" and found so much fault with it, and
with the work and bother of raising the mullen, and jews-harping
the rats, and petting and flattering up the snakes and spiders and
things, on top of all the other work he had to do on pens, and
inscriptions, and journals, and things, which made it more trouble
and worry and responsibility to be a prisoner than anything he ever
undertook, that Tom most lost all patience with him; and said he
was just loadened down with more gaudier chances than a prisoner

---

4. *Picciola* (1836) was a popular romantic story by Xavier Saintine (pseudonym
for Joseph Xavier Boniface, 1798–1865),
in which a plant helps sustain a prisoner.

ever had in the world to make a name for himself, and yet he didn't know enough to appreciate them, and they was just about wasted on him. So Jim he was sorry, and said he wouldn't behave so no more, and then me and Tom shoved for bed.

Chapter XXXIX

In the morning we went up to the village and bought a wire rat trap and fetched it down, and unstopped the best rat hole, and in about an hour we had fifteen of the bulliest kind of ones; and then we took it and put it in a safe place under Aunt Sally's bed. But while we was gone for spiders, little Thomas Franklin Benjamin Jefferson Elexander Phelps found it there, and opened the door of it to see if the rats would come out, and they did; and Aunt Sally she come in, and when we got back she was standing on top of the bed raising Cain, and the rats was doing what they could to keep off the dull times for her. So she took and dusted us both with the hickry, and we was as much as two hours catching another fifteen or sixteen, drat that meddlesome cub, and they warn't the likeliest, nuther, because the first haul was the pick of the flock. I never see a likelier lot of rats than what that first haul was.

We got a splendid stock of sorted spiders, and bugs, and frogs, and caterpillars, and one thing or another; and we like to got a hornet's nest, but we didn't. The family was at home. We didn't give it right up, but staid with them as long as we could; because we allowed we'd tire them out or they'd got to tire us out, and they done it. Then we got allycumpain[5] and rubbed on the places, and was pretty near all right again, but couldn't set down convenient. And so we went for the snakes, and grabbed a couple of dozen garters and house-snakes, and put them in a bag, and put it in our room, and by that time it was supper time, and a rattling good honest day's work; and hungry?—oh, no, I reckon not! And there warn't a blessed snake up there, when we went back—we didn't half tie the sack, and they worked out, somehow, and left. But it didn't matter much, because they was still on the premises somewheres. So we judged we could get some of them again. No, there warn't no real scarcity of snakes about the house for a considerable spell. You'd see them dripping from the rafters and places, every now and then; and they generly landed in your plate, or down the back of your neck, and most of the time where you didn't want them. Well, they was handsome, and striped, and there warn't no harm in a million of them; but that never made no difference to Aunt Sally, she despised snakes, be the breed what they might, and she couldn't stand them no way you could fix it; and every time one of them flopped down on her, it didn't make no difference what she was doing, she would just lay that work down and light out. I never see such a woman. And you could hear her whoop to Jericho. You

5. Elecampane is an herb used to relieve the pain of the hornet sting.

couldn't get her to take aholt of one of them with the tongs. And if she turned over and found one in bed, she would scramble out and lift a howl that you would think the house was afire. She disturbed the old man so, that he said he could most wish there hadn't ever been no snakes created. Why, after every last snake had been gone clear out of the house for as much as a week, Aunt Sally warn't over it yet; she warn't near over it; when she was setting thinking about something, you could touch her on the back of her neck with a feather and she would jump right out of her stockings. It was very curious. But Tom said all women was just so. He said they was made that way; for some reason or other.

We got a licking every time one of our snakes come in her way; and she allowed these lickings warn't nothing to what she would do if we ever loaded up the place again with them. I didn't mind the lickings, because they didn't amount to nothing; but I minded the trouble we had, to lay in another lot. But we got them laid in, and all the other things; and you never see a cabin as blithesome as Jim's was when they'd all swarm out for music and go for him. Jim didn't like the spiders, and the spiders didn't like Jim; and so they'd lay for him and make it mighty warm for him. And he said that between the rats, and the snakes, and the grindstone, there warn't no room in bed for him, skasely; and when there was, a body couldn't sleep, it was so lively, and it was always lively, he said, because *they* never all slept at one time, but took turn about, so when the snakes was asleep the rats was on deck, and when the rats turned in the snakes come on watch, so he always had one gang under him, in his way, and t'other gang having a circus over him, and if he got up to hunt a new place, the spiders would take a chance at him as he crossed over. He said if he ever got out, this time, he wouldn't ever be a prisoner again, not for a salary.

Well, by the end of three weeks, everything was in pretty good shape. The shirt was sent in early, in a pie, and every time a rat bit Jim he would get up and write a little in his journal whilst the ink was fresh; the pens was made, the inscriptions and so on was all carved on the grindstone; the bed-leg was sawed in two, and we had et up the sawdust, and it give us a most amazing stomach-ache. We reckoned we was all going to die, but didn't. It was the most undigestible sawdust I ever see; and Tom said the same. But as I was saying, we'd got all the work done, now, at last; and we was all pretty much fagged out, too, but mainly Jim. The old man had wrote a couple of times to the plantation below Orleans to come and get their runaway nigger, but hadn't got no answer, because there warn't no such plantation; so he allowed he would advertise Jim in the St. Louis and New Orleans papers; and when he mentioned the St. Louis ones, it give me the cold shivers, and I see we hadn't no time to lose. So Tom said, now for the nonnamous letters.

"What's them?" I says.

"Warnings to the people that something is up. Sometimes it's done one way, sometimes another. But there's always somebody spying around, that gives notice to the governor of the castle. When Louis XVI was going to light out of the Tooleries,[6] a servant girl done it. It's a very good way, and so is the nonnamous letters. We'll use them both. And it's usual for the prisoner's mother to change clothes with him, and she stays in, and he slides out in her clothes. We'll do that too."

"But looky here, Tom, what do we want to *warn* anybody for, that something's up? Let them find it out for themselves—it's their lookout."

"Yes, I know; but you can't depend on them. It's the way they've acted from the very start—left us to do *everything*. They're so confiding and mullet-headed they don't take notice of nothing at all. So if we don't *give* them notice, there won't be nobody nor nothing to interfere with us, and so after all our hard work and trouble this escape 'll go off perfectly flat: won't amount to nothing—won't be nothing *to* it."

"Well, as for me, Tom, that's the way I'd like."

"Shucks," he says, and looked disgusted. So I says:

"But I ain't going to make no complaint. Anyway that suits you suits me. What you going to do about the servant-girl?"

"You'll be her. You slide in, in the middle of the night, and hook that yaller girl's frock."

"Why, Tom, that'll make trouble next morning; because of course she prob'bly hain't got any but that one."

"I know; but you don't want it but fifteen minutes, to carry the nonnamous letter and shove it under the front door."

"All right, then, I'll do it; but I could carry it just as handy in my own togs."

"You wouldn't look like a servant-girl *then*, would you?"

"No, but there won't be nobody to see what I look like, *anyway*."

"That ain't got nothing to do with it. The thing for us to do, is just to do our *duty*, and not worry about whether anybody *sees* us do it or not. Hain't you got no principle at all?"

"All right, I ain't saying nothing; I'm the servant-girl. Who's Jim's mother?"

"I'm his mother. I'll hook a gown from Aunt Sally."

"Well, then, you'll have to stay in the cabin when me and Jim leaves."

"Not much. I'll stuff Jim's clothes full of straw and lay it on his bed to represent his mother in dusguise, and Jim 'll take Aunt Sally's gown off of me and wear it, and we'll all evade together. When a prisoner of style escapes, it's called an evasion. It's always

---

6. Clemens probably read this episode of the Tuileries, a palace in Paris, in Thomas Carlyle's *French Revolution* (1837).

called so when a king escapes, f'rinstance. And the same with a king's son; it don't make no difference whether he's a natural one or an unnatural one."

So Tom he wrote the nonamous letter, and I smouched the yaller wench's frock, that night, and put it on, and shoved it under the front door, the way Tom told me to. It said:

> *Beware. Trouble is brewing. Keep a sharp lookout.*
>
> Unknown Friend

Next night we stuck a picture which Tom drawed in blood, of a skull and crossbones, on the front door; and next night another one of a coffin, on the back door. I never see a family in such a sweat. They couldn't a been worse scared if the place had a been full of ghosts laying for them behind everything and under the beds and shivering through the air. If a door banged, Aunt Sally she jumped, and said "ouch!" if anything fell, she jumped and said "ouch!" if you happened to touch her, when she warn't noticing, she done the same; she couldn't face noway and be satisfied, because she allowed there was something behind her every time—so she was always a whirling around, sudden, and saying "ouch," and before she'd get two-thirds around, she'd whirl back again, and say it again; and she was afraid to go to bed, but she dasn't set up. So the thing was working very well, Tom said; he said he never see a thing work more satisfactory. He said it showed it was done right.

So he said, now for the grand bulge! So the very next morning at the streak of dawn we got another letter ready, and was wondering what we better do with it, because we heard them say at supper they was going to have a nigger on watch at both doors all night. Tom he went down the lightning-rod to spy around; and the nigger at the back door was asleep, and he stuck it in the back of his neck and come back. This letter said:

> *Don't betray me, I wish to be your friend. There is a desprate gang of cutthroats from over in the Ingean Territory[7] going to steal your runaway nigger to-night, and they have been trying to scare you so as you will stay in the house and not bother them. I am one of the gang, but have got religion and wish to quit it and lead a honest life again, and will betray the helish design. They will sneak down from northards, along the fence, at midnight exact, with a false key, and go in the nigger's cabin to get him. I am to be off a piece and blow a tin horn if I see any danger; but stead of that, I will* BA *like a sheep soon as they get in and not blow at all; then whilst they are getting his chains loose, you slip there and lock them in, and can kill them at your leasure. Don't do anything but just the way I am telling you, if you do they will suspicion some-*

---

7. The area now the state of Oklahoma was granted to the Indians and became a base of operations for outlaws for most of the 19th century.

*thing and raise whoopjamboreehoo. I do not wish any reward but to
know I have done the right thing.*

Unknown Friend

Chapter XL

We was feeling pretty good, after breakfast, and took my canoe
and went over the river a fishing, with a lunch, and had a good
time, and took a look at the raft and found her all right, and got
home late to supper, and found them in such a sweat and worry
they didn't know which end they was standing on, and made us go
right off to bed the minute we was done supper, and wouldn't tell
us what the trouble was, and never let on a word about the new
letter, but didn't need to, because we knowed as much about it as
anybody did, and as soon as we was half up stairs and her back was
turned, we slid for the cellar cubboard and loaded up a good lunch
and took it up to our room and went to bed, and got up about
half-past eleven, and Tom put on Aunt Sally's dress that he stole
and was going to start with the lunch, but says:

"Where's the butter?"

"I laid out a hunk of it," I says, "on a piece of a corn-pone."

"Well, you *left* it laid out, then—it ain't here."

"We can get along without it," I says.

"We can get along *with* it, too," he says; "just you slide down
cellar and fetch it. And then mosey right down the lightning-rod
and come along. I'll go and stuff the straw into Jim's clothes to represent his mother in disguise, and be ready to *ba* like a sheep and
shove soon as you get there."

So out he went, and down cellar went I. The hunk of butter, big
as a person's fist, was where I had left it, so I took up the slab of
corn-pone with it on, and blowed out my light, and started up
stairs, very stealthy, and got up to the main floor all right, but here
comes Aunt Sally with a candle, and I clapped the truck in my hat,
and clapped my hat on my head, and the next second she see me;
and she says:

"You been down cellar?"

"Yes'm."

"What you been doing down there?"

"Noth'n."

"*Noth'n!*"

"No'm."

"Well, then, what possessed you to go down there, this time of
night?"

"I don't know'm."

"You don't *know?* Don't answer me that way, Tom, I want to
know what you been *doing* down there?"

"I hain't been doing a single thing, Aunt Sally, I hope to gracious if I have."

I reckoned she'd let me go, now, and as a generl thing she would; but I spose there was so many strange things going on she was just in a sweat about every little thing that warn't yard-stick straight; so she says, very decided:

"You just march into that setting-room and stay there till I come. You been up to something you no business to, and I lay I'll find out what it is before I'*m* done with you."

So she went away as I opened the door and walked into the setting-room. My, but there was a crowd there! Fifteen farmers, and every one of them had a gun. I was most powerful sick, and slunk to a chair and set down. They was setting around, some of them talking a little, in a low voice, and all of them fidgety and uneasy, but trying to look like they warn't; but I knowed they was, because they was always taking off their hats, and putting them on, and scratching their heads, and changing their seats, and fumbling with their buttons. I warn't easy myself, but I didn't take my hat off, all the same.

I did wish Aunt Sally would come, and get done with me, and lick me, if she wanted to, and let me get away and tell Tom how we'd overdone this thing, and what a thundering hornet's nest we'd got ourselves into, so we could stop fooling around, straight off, and clear out with Jim before these rips got out of patience and come for us.

At last she come, and begun to ask me questions, but I *couldn't* answer them straight, I didn't know which end of me was up; because these men was in such a fidget now, that some was wanting to start right *now* and lay for them desperadoes, and saying it warn't but a few minutes to midnight; and others was trying to get them to hold on and wait for the sheep-signal; and here was aunty pegging away at the questions, and me a shaking all over and ready to sink down in my tracks I was that scared; and the place getting hotter and hotter, and the butter beginning to melt and run down my neck and behind my ears: and pretty soon, when one of them says, "I'*m* for going and getting in the cabin *first*, and right *now*, and catching them when they come," I most dropped; and a streak of butter come a trickling down my forehead, and Aunt Sally she see it, and turns white as a sheet, and says:

"For the land's sake what *is* the matter with the child!—he's got the brain fever as shore as you're born, and they're oozing out!"

And everybody runs to see, and she snatches off my hat, and out comes the bread, and what was left of the butter, and she grabbed me, and hugged me, and says:

"Oh, what a turn you did give me! and how glad and grateful I am it ain't no worse; for luck's against us, and it never rains but it pours, and when I see that truck I thought we'd lost you, for I knowed by the color and all, it was just like your brains would be if —Dear, dear, whyd'nt you *tell* me that was what you'd been down there for, *I* wouldn't a cared. Now cler out to bed, and don't lemme see no more of you till morning!"

I was up stairs in a second, and down the lightning-rod in another one, and shinning through the dark for the lean-to. I couldn't hardly get my words out, I was so anxious; but I told Tom as quick as I could, we must jump for it, now, and not a minute to lose—the house full of men, yonder, with guns!

His eyes just blazed; and he says:

"No!—is that so? *Ain't* it bully! Why, Huck, if it was to do over again, I bet I could fetch two hundred! If we could put it off till—"

"Hurry! *hurry!*" I says. "Where's Jim?"

"Right at your elbow; if you reach out your arm you can touch him. He's dressed, and everything's ready. Now we'll slide out and give the sheep-signal."

But then we heard the tramp of men, coming to the door, and heard them begin to fumble with the padlock; and heard a man say:

"I *told* you we'd be too soon; they haven't come—the door is locked. Here, I'll lock some of you into the cabin and you lay for 'em in the dark and kill 'em when they come; and the rest scatter around a piece, and listen if you can hear 'em coming."

So in they come, but couldn't see us in the dark, and most trod on us whilst we was hustling to get under the bed. But we got under all right, and out through the hole, swift but soft—Jim first, me next, and Tom last, which was according to Tom's orders. Now we was in the lean-to, and heard trampings close by outside. So we crept to the door, and Tom stopped us there and put his eye to the crack, but couldn't make out nothing, it was so dark; and whispered and said he would listen for the steps to get further, and when he nudged us Jim must glide out first, and him last. So he set his ear to the crack and listened, and listened, and listened, and the steps a scraping around, out there, all the time; and at last he nudged us, and we slid out, and stooped down, not breathing, and not making the least noise, and slipped stealthy towards the fence, in Injun file, and got to it, all right, and me and Jim over it; but Tom's britches catched fast on a splinter on the top rail, and then he hear the steps coming, so he had to pull loose, which snapped the splinter and made a noise; and as he dropped in our tracks and started, somebody sings out:

"Who's that? Answer, or I'll shoot!"

But we didn't answer; we just unfurled our heels and shoved. Then there was a rush, and a *bang, bang, bang!* and the bullets fairly whizzed around us! We heard them sing out:

"Here they are! They've broke for the river! after 'em, boys! And turn loose the dogs!"

So here they come, full tilt. We could hear them, because they wore boots, and yelled, but we didn't wear no boots, and didn't yell.

We was in the path to the mill; and when they got pretty close onto us, we dodged into the bush and let them go by, and then dropped in behind them. They'd had all the dogs shut up, so they wouldn't scare off the robbers; but by this time somebody had let them loose, and here they come, making pow-wow enough for a million; but they was our dogs; so we stopped in our tracks till they catched up; and when they see it warn't nobody but us, and no excitement to offer them, they only just said howdy, and tore right ahead towards the shouting and clattering; and then we up steam again and whizzed along after them till we was nearly to the mill, and then struck up through the bush to where my canoe was tied, and hopped in and pulled for dear life towards the middle of the river, but didn't make no more noise than we was obleeged to. Then we struck out, easy and comfortable, for the island where my raft was; and we could hear them yelling and barking at each other all up and down the bank, till we was so far away the sounds got dim and died out. And when we stepped onto the raft, I says:

"*Now*, old Jim, you're a free man *again*, and I bet you won't ever be a slave no more."

"En a mighty good job it wuz, too, Huck. It 'uz planned beautiful, en it 'uz *done* beautiful; en dey ain't *nobody* kin git up a plan dat's mo' mixed-up en splendid den what dat one wuz."

We was all glad as we could be, but Tom was the gladdest of all, because he had a bullet in the calf of his leg.

When me and Jim heard that, we didn't feel so brash as what we did before. It was hurting him considerble, and bleeding; so we laid him in the wigwam and tore up one of the duke's shirts for to bandage him, but he says:

"Gimme the rags, I can do it myself. Don't stop, now; don't fool around here, and the evasion booming along so handsome; man the sweeps, and set her loose! Boys, we done it elegant!—'deed we did. I wish *we'd* a had the handling of Louis XVI, there wouldn't a been no "Son of Saint Louis, ascend to heaven!'[8] wrote down in *his* biography: no, sir, we'd a whooped him over the *border*—that's what we'd a done with *him*—and done it just as slick as nothing at all, too. Man the sweeps—man the sweeps!"

But me and Jim was consulting—and thinking. And after we'd thought a minute, I says:

"Say it, Jim."

So he says:

"Well, den, dis is de way it look to me, Huck. Ef it wuz *him* dat 'uz bein' sot free, en one er de boys wuz to git shot, would he say, 'Go on en save me, nemmine 'bout a doctor f'r to save dis one? Is dat like Mars Tom Sawyer? Would he say dat? You *bet* he wouldn't! *Well*, den, is *Jim* gwyne to say it? No, sah—I doan'

---

8. Taken from Carlyle's rendering of the King's execution in his *French Revolution* (1837).

budge a step out'n dis place, 'dout a *doctor*; not if it's forty year!"

I knowed he was white inside, and I reckoned he'd say what he did say—so it was all right, now, and I told Tom I was agoing for a doctor. He raised considerble row about it, but me and Jim stuck to it and wouldn't budge; so he was for crawling out and setting the raft loose himself; but we wouldn't let him. Then he give us a piece of his mind—but it didn't do no good.

So when he see me getting the canoe ready, he says:

"Well, then, if you're bound to go, I'll tell you the way to do, when you get to the village. Shut the door, and blindfold the doctor tight and fast, and make him swear to be silent as the grave, and put a purse full of gold in his hand, and then take and lead him all around the back alleys and everywheres, in the dark, and then fetch him here in the canoe, in a roundabout way amongst the islands, and search him and take his chalk away from him, and don't give it back to him till you get him back to the village, or else he will chalk this raft so he can find it again. It's the way they all do."

So I said I would, and left, and Jim was to hide in the woods when he see the doctor coming, till he was gone again.

Chapter XLI

The doctor was an old man; a very nice, kind-looking old man, when I got him up. I told him me and my brother was over on Spanish Island hunting, yesterday afternoon, and camped on a piece of a raft we found, and about midnight he must a kicked his gun in his dreams, for it went off and shot him in the leg, and we wanted him to go over there and fix it and not say nothing about it, nor let anybody know, because we wanted to come home this evening, and surprise the folks.

"Who is your folks?" he says.

"The Phelpses, down yonder."

"Oh," he says. And after a minute, he says: "How'd you say he got shot?"

"He had a dream," I says, "and it shot him."

"Singular dream," he says.

So he lit up his lantern, and got his saddle-bags, and we started. But when he see the canoe, he didn't like the look of her—said she was big enough for one, but didn't look pretty safe for two. I says:

"Oh, you needn't be afeard, sir, she carried the three of us, easy enough."

"What three?"

"Why, me and Sid, and—and—and *the guns*; that's what I mean."

"Oh," he says.

But he put his foot on the gunnel, and rocked her; and shook his head, and said he reckoned he'd look around for a bigger one. But they was all locked and chained; so he took my canoe, and said for me to wait till he come back, or I could hunt around further, or maybe I better go down home and get them ready for the surprise, if I wanted to. But I said I didn't; so I told him just how to find the raft, and then he started.

I struck an idea, pretty soon. I says to myself, spos'n he can't fix that leg just in three shakes of a sheep's tail, as the saying is? spos'n it takes him three or four days? What are we going to do?—lay around there till he lets the cat out of the bag? No, sir, I know what *I'll* do. I'll wait, and when he comes back, if he says he's got to go any more, I'll get down there, too, if I swim; and we'll take and tie him, and keep him, and shove out down the river; and when Tom's done with him, we'll give him what it's worth, or all we got, and then let him get shore.

So then I crept into a lumber pile to get some sleep; and next time I waked up the sun was away up over my head! I shot out and went for the doctor's house, but they told me he'd gone away in the night, some time or other, and warn't back yet. Well, thinks I, that looks powerful bad for *Tom*, and I'll dig out for the island, right off. So away I shoved, and turned the corner, and nearly rammed my head into Uncle Silas's stomach! He says:

"Why, Tom! Where you been, all this time, you rascal?"

"I hain't been nowheres," I says, "only just hunting for the runaway nigger—me and Sid."

"Why, where ever did you go?" he says. "Your aunt's been mighty uneasy."

"She needn't," I says, "because we was all right. We followed the men and the dogs, but they out-run us, and we lost them; but we thought we heard them on the water, so we got a canoe and took out after them, and crossed over but couldn't find nothing of them; so we cruised along up-shore till we got kind of tired and beat out; and tied up the canoe and went to sleep, and never waked up till about an hour ago, then we paddled over here to hear the news, and Sid's at the post-office to see what he can hear, and I'm a branching out to get something to eat for us, and then we're going home."

So then we went to the post-office to get "Sid"; but just as I suspicioned, he warn't there; so the old man he got a letter out of the office, and we waited a while longer but Sid didn't come; so the old man said come along, let Sid foot it home, or canoe-it, when he got done fooling around—but we would ride. I couldn't get him to let me stay and wait for Sid; and he said there warn't no use in it, and I must come along, and let Aunt Sally see we was all right.

When we got home, Aunt Sally was that glad to see me she laughed and cried both, and hugged me, and give me one of them lickings of hern that don't amount to shucks, and said she'd serve Sid the same when he come.

And the place was plumb full of farmers and farmers' wives, to dinner; and such another clack a body never heard. Old Mrs.

Hotchkiss was the worst; her tongue was agoing all the time. She says:

"Well, Sister Phelps, I've ransacked that-air cabin over an' I b'lieve the nigger was crazy. I says so to Sister Damrell—didn't I, Sister Damrell?—s'I, he's crazy, s'I—them's the very words I said. You all hearn me: he's crazy, s'I; everything shows it, s'I. Look at that-air grindstone, s'I; want to tell *me*'t any cretur 'ts in his right mind 's agoin' to scrabble all them crazy things onto a grindstone, s'I? Here sich 'n' sich a person busted his heart; 'n' here so 'n' so pegged along for thirty-seven year, 'n' all that—natcherl son o' Louis somebody, 'n' sich everlast'n rubbage. He's plumb crazy, s'I; it's what I says in the fust place, it's what I says in the middle, 'n' it's what I says last 'n' all the time—the nigger's crazy—crazy's Nebokoodneezer,[9] s'I."

"An' look at that-air ladder made out'n rags, Sister Hotchkiss," says old Mrs. Damrell, "what in the name o' goodness *could* he ever want of—"

"The very words I was a-sayin' no longer ago th'n this minute to Sister Utterback, 'n' she'll tell you so herself. Sh-she, look at that-air rag ladder, sh-she; 'n' s'I, yes, *look* at it, s'I—what *could* he a wanted of it, s'I. Sh-she, Sister Hotchkiss, sh-she—"

"But how in the nation'd they ever *git* that grindstone *in* there, *any*way? 'n' who dug that-air *hole?* 'n' who—"

"My very *words*, Brer Penrod! I was a-sayin'—pass that-air sasser o' m'lasses, won't ye?—I was a-sayin' to Sister Dunlap, jist this minute, how *did* they git that grindstone in there, s'I. Without *help*, mind you—'thout *help! Thar's* wher' 'tis. Don't tell *me*, s'I; there *wuz* help, s'I; 'n' ther' wuz a *plenty* help, too, s'I; ther's ben a *doz*en a-helpin' that nigger, 'n' I lay I'd skin every last nigger on this place, but *I'd* find out who done it, s'I; 'n' moreover, s'I—"

"A *dozen* says you!—*forty* couldn't a done everything that's been done. Look at them case-knife saws and things, how tedious they've been made; look at that bed-leg sawed off with 'em, a week's work for six men; look at that nigger made out'n straw on the bed; and look at—"

"You may *well* say it, Brer Hightower! It's jist as I was a-sayin' to Brer Phelps, his own sel   S'e, what do *you* think of it, Sister Hotchkiss, s'e? think o' what, Brer Phelps, s'I? think o' that bed-leg sawed off that a way, s'e? *think* of it, s'I? I lay it never sawed *itself* off, s'I —somebody sawed it, s'I; that's my opinion, take it or leave it, it mayn't be no 'count, s'I, but sich as 't is, it's my opinion, s'I, 'n' if anybody k'n start a better one, s'I, let him *do* it, s'I, that's all. I says to Sister Dunlap, s'I—"

"Why, dog my cats, they must a ben a house-full o' niggers in

<hr>

9. Nebuchadnezzar (605–562 B.C.), King of Babylon, is described in Daniel 4.33 as going mad and eating grass.

there every night for four weeks, to a done all that work, Sister Phelps. Look at that shirt—every last inch of it kivered over with secret African writ'n done with blood! Must a ben a raft uv 'm at it right along, all the time, amost. Why, I'd give two dollars to have it read to me; 'n' as for the niggers that wrote it, I 'low I'd take 'n' lash 'm t'll—"

"People to *help* him, Brother Marples! Well, I reckon you'd *think* so, if you'd a been in this house for a while back. Why, they've stole everything they could lay their hands on—and we a watching, all the time, mind you. They stole that shirt right off o' the line! and as for that sheet they made the rag ladder out of ther' ain't no telling how many times they *didn't* steal that; and flour, and candles, and candlesticks, and spoons, and the old warming-pan, and most a thousand things that I disremember, now, and my new calico dress; and me, and Silas, and my Sid and Tom on the constant watch day *and* night, as I was a telling you, and not a one of us could catch hide nor hair, nor sight nor sound of them; and here at the last minute, lo and behold you, they slides right in under our noses, and fools us, and not only fools *us* but the Injun Territory robbers too, and actuly gets *away* with that nigger, safe and sound, and that with sixteen men and twenty-two dogs right on their very heels at that very time! I tell you, it just bangs anything I ever *heard* of. Why, *sperits* couldn't a done better, and been no smarter. And I reckon they must a *been* sperits—because, *you* know our dogs, and ther' ain't no better; well, them dogs never even got on the track of 'm, once! You explain *that* to me, if you can!—*any* of you!"

"Well, it does beat—"

"Laws alive, I never—"

"So help me, I wouldn't a be—"

"*House* thieves as well as—"

"Goodnessgracioussakes, I'd a ben afeard to *live* in sich a—"

" 'Fraid to *live!*—why, I was that scared I dasn't hardly go to bed, or get up, or lay down, or *set* down, Sister Ridgeway. Why, they'd steal the very—why, goodness sakes, you can guess what kind of a fluster I was in by the time midnight come, last night. I hope to gracious if I warn't afraid they'd steal some o' the family! I was just to that pass, I didn't have no reasoning faculties no more. It looks foolish enough, *now*, in the day-time; but I says to myself, there's my two poor boys asleep, 'way up stairs in that lonesome room, and I declare to goodness I was that uneasy 't I crep' up there and locked 'em in! I *did*. And anybody would. Because, you know, when you get scared that way, and it keeps running on, and getting worse and worse, all the time, and your wits gets to addling, and you get to doing all sorts o' wild things, and by-and-by you think to yourself, spos'n I was a boy, and was away up there, and the door ain't locked, and you—" She stopped, looking kind of wondering, and then she turned her head around slow, and when her eye lit on me—I got up and took a walk.

Says I to myself, I can explain better how we come to not be in that room this morning, if I go out to one side and study over it a little. So I done it. But I dasn't go fur, or she'd a sent for me. And when it was late in the day, the people all went, and then I come in and told her the noise and shooting waked up me and "Sid," and the door was locked, and we wanted to see the fun, so we went down the lightning-rod, and both of us got hurt a little, and we didn't never want to try *that* no more. And then I went on and told her all what I told Uncle Silas before; and then she said she'd forgive us, and maybe it was all right enough anyway, and about what a body might expect of boys, for all boys was a pretty harum-scarum lot, as fur as she could see; and so, as long as no harm hadn't come of it, she judged she better put in her time being grateful we was alive and well and she had us still, stead of fretting over what was past and done. So then she kissed me, and patted me on the head, and dropped into a kind of a brown study; and pretty soon jumps up, and says:

"Why, lawsamercy, it's most night, and Sid not come yet! What *has* become of that boy?"

I see my chance; so I skips up and says:

"I'll run right up to town and get him," I says.

"No you won't," she says. "You'll stay right wher' you are; *one's* enough to be lost at a time. If he ain't here to supper, your uncle 'll go."

Well, he warn't there to supper; so right after supper uncle went.

He come back about ten, a little bit uneasy; hadn't run across Tom's track. Aunt Sally was a good *deal* uneasy; but Uncle Silas he said there warn't no occasion to be—boys will be boys, he said, and you'll see this one turn up in the morning, all sound and right. So she had to be satisfied. But she said she'd set up for him a while, anyway, and keep a light burning, so he could see it.

And then when I went up to bed she come up with me and fetched her candle, and tucked me in, and mothered me so good I felt mean, and like I couldn't look her in the face; and she set down on the bed and talked with me a long time, and said what a splendid boy Sid was, and didn't seem to want to ever stop talking about him; and kept asking me every now and then, if I reckoned he could a got lost, or hurt, or maybe drownded, and might be laying at this minute, somewheres, suffering or dead, and she not by him to help him, and so the tears would drip down, silent, and I would tell her that Sid was all right, and would be home in the morning, sure; and she would squeeze my hand, or maybe kiss me, and tell me to say it again, and keep on saying it, because it done her good, and she was in so much trouble. And when she was going away, she looked down in my eyes, so steady and gentle, and says:

"The door ain't going to be locked, Tom; and there's the window and the rod; but you'll be good, *won't* you? And you won't go? For *my* sake."

Laws knows I *wanted* to go, bad enough, to see about Tom, and was all intending to go; but after that, I wouldn't a went, not for kingdoms.

But she was on my mind, and Tom was on my mind; so I slept very restless. And twice I went down the rod, away in the night, and slipped around front, and see her setting there by her candle in the window with her eyes towards the road and the tears in them; and I wished I could do something for her, but I couldn't, only to swear that I wouldn't never do nothing to grieve her any more. And the third time, I waked up at dawn, and slid down, and she was there yet, and her candle was most out, and her old gray head was resting on her hand, and she was asleep.

Chapter XLII

The old man was up town again, before breakfast, but couldn't get no track of Tom; and both of them set at the table, thinking, and not saying nothing, and looking mournful, and their coffee getting cold, and not eating anything. And by-and-by the old man says:

"Did I give you the letter?"

"What letter?"

"The one I got yesterday out of the post-office."

"No, you didn't give me no letter."

"Well, I must a forgot it."

So he rummaged his pockets, and then went off somewheres where he had laid it down, and fetched it, and give it to her. She says:

"Why, it's from St. Petersburg—it's from Sis."

I allowed another walk would do me good; but I couldn't stir. But before she could break it open, she dropped it and run—for she see something. And so did I. It was Tom Sawyer on a mattress; and that old doctor; and Jim, in *her* calico dress, with his hands tied behind him; and a lot of people. I hid the letter behind the first thing that come handy, and rushed. She flung herself at Tom, crying, and says:

"Oh, he's dead, he's dead, I know he's dead!"

And Tom he turned his head a little, and muttered something or other, which showed he warn't in his right mind; then she flung up her hands, and says:

"He's alive, thank God! And that's enough!" and she snatched a kiss of him, and flew for the house to get the bed ready, and scattering orders right and left at the niggers and everybody else, as fast as her tongue could go, every jump of the way.

I followed the men to see what they was going to do with Jim; and the old doctor and Uncle Silas followed after Tom into the house. The men was very huffy, and some of them wanted to hang Jim, for an example to all the other niggers around there, so they wouldn't be trying to run away, like Jim done, and making such a raft of trouble, and keeping a whole family scared most to death for days and nights. But the others said, don't do it, it wouldn't answer at all, he ain't our nigger, and his owner would turn up and make us pay for him, sure. So that cooled them down a little, because the people that's always the most anxious for to hang a nigger that hain't done just right, is always the very ones that ain't the most anxious to pay for him when they've got their satisfaction out of him.

They cussed Jim considerble, though, and give him a cuff or two, side the head, once in a while, but Jim never said nothing, and he never let on to know me, and they took him to the same cabin, and put his own clothes on him, and chained him again, and not to no bed-leg, this time, but to a big staple drove into the bottom log, and chained his hands, too, and both legs, and said he warn't to have nothing but bread and water to eat, after this, till his owner come or he was sold at auction, because he didn't come in a certain length of time, and filled up our hole, and said a couple of farmers with guns must stand watch around about the cabin every night, and a bull-dog tied to the door in the day time; and about this time they was through with the job and was tapering off with a kind of generl good-bye cussing, and then the old doctor comes and takes a look and says:

"Don't be no rougher on him than you're obleeged to, because he ain't a bad nigger. When I got to where I found the boy, I see I couldn't cut the bullet out without some help, and he warn't in no condition for me to leave, to go and get help; and he got a little worse and a little worse, and after a long time he went out of his head, and wouldn't let me come anigh him, any more, and said if I chalked his raft he'd kill me, and no end of wild foolishness like that, and I see I couldn't do anything at all with him; so I says, I got to have *help*, somehow; and the minute I says it, out crawls this nigger from somewheres, and says he'll help, and he done it, too, and done it very well. Of course I judged he must be a runaway nigger, and there I *was!* and there I had to stick, right straight along all the rest of the day, and all night. It was a fix, I tell you! I had a couple of patients with the chills, and of course I'd of liked to run up to town and see them, but I dasn't, because the nigger might get away, and then I'd be to blame; and yet never a skiff come close enough for me to hail. So there I had to stick, plumb till daylight this morning; and I never see a nigger that was a better nuss or faithfuller, and yet he was resking his freedom to do it, and was all tired out, too, and I see plain enough he'd been worked main hard, lately. I liked the nigger for that; I tell you, gentlemen, a nigger like that is worth a thousand dollars—and kind treatment, too. I had everything I needed, and the boy was doing as well there as he would a done at home—better, maybe, because it was so quiet; but there I *was*, with both of 'm on my hands; and there I had to stick, till about dawn this morning; then some men in a skiff come by, and as good luck would have it, the nigger was setting by the pallet with his head propped on his knees, sound asleep; so I motioned them in, quiet, and they slipped up on him and grabbed him and tied him before he knowed what he was about, and we never had no trouble. And the boy being in a kind of a flighty sleep, too, we muffled the oars and hitched the raft on, and towed her over very nice and quiet, and the nigger never made the least row nor said a word, from the start. He ain't no bad nigger, gentlemen; that's what I think about him."

Somebody says:

"Well, it sounds very good, doctor, I'm obleeged to say."

Then the others softened up a little, too, and I was mighty thankful to that old doctor for doing Jim that good turn; and I was glad it was according to my judgment of him, too; because I thought he had a good heart in him and was a good man, the first time I see him. Then they all agreed that Jim had acted very well, and was deserving to have some notice took of it, and reward. So every one of them promised, right out and hearty, that they wouldn't cuss him no more.

Then they come out and locked him up. I hoped they was going to say he could have one or two of the chains took off, because they was rotten heavy, or could have meat and greens with his bread and water, but they didn't think of it, and I reckoned it warn't best for me to mix in, but I judged I'd get the doctor's yarn to Aunt Sally, somehow or other, as soon as I'd got through the breakers that was laying just ahead of me. Explanations, I mean, of how I forgot to mention about Sid being shot, when I was telling how him and me put in that dratted night paddling around hunting the runaway nigger.

But I had plenty time. Aunt Sally she stuck to the sick-room all day and all night; and every time I see Uncle Silas mooning around, I dodged him.

Next morning I heard Tom was a good deal better, and they said Aunt Sally was gone to get a nap. So I slips to the sick-room, and if I found him awake I reckoned we could put up a yarn for the family that would wash. But he was sleeping, and sleeping very peaceful, too; and pale, not fire-faced the way he was when he come. So I set down and laid for him to wake. In about a half an hour, Aunt Sally comes gliding in, and there I was, up a stump again! She motioned me to be still, and set down by me, and begun to whisper, and said we could all be joyful now, because all the symptoms was first rate, and he'd been sleeping like that for ever so long, and looking better and peacefuller all the time, and ten to one he'd wake up in his right mind.

So we set there watching, and by-and-by he stirs a bit, and opened his eyes very natural, and takes a look, and says:

"Hello, why I'm at *home!* How's that? Where's the raft?"

"It's all right," I says.

"And *Jim?*"

"The same," I says, but couldn't say it pretty brash. But he never noticed, but says:

"Good! Splendid! *Now* we're all right and safe! Did you tell Aunty?"

I was going to say yes; but she chipped in and says:

"About what, Sid?"

"Why, about the way the whole thing was done."

"What whole thing?"

"Why, *the* whole thing. There ain't but one; how we set the runaway nigger free—me and Tom."

"Good land! Set the run— What *is* the child talking about! Dear, dear, out of his head again!"

"No, I ain't out of my HEAD; I know all what I'm talking about. We *did* set him free—me and Tom. We laid out to do it, and we *done* it. And we done it elegant, too." He'd got a start, and she never checked him up, just set and stared and stared, and let him clip along, and I see it warn't no use for *me* to put in. "Why, Aunty, it cost us a power of work—weeks of it—hours and hours, every night, whilst you was all asleep. And we had to steal candles, and the sheet, and the shirt, and your dress, and spoons, and tin plates, and case-knives, and the warming-pan, and the grindstone, and flour, and just no end of things, and you can't think what work it was to make the saws, and pens, and inscriptions, and one thing or another, and you can't think *half* the fun it was. And we had to make up the pictures of coffins and things, and nonnamous letters from the robbers, and get up and down the lightning-rod, and dig the hole into the cabin, and make the rope-ladder and send it in cooked up in a pie, and send in spoons and things to work with, in your apron pocket"—

"Mercy sakes!"

—"and load up the cabin with rats and snakes and so on, for company for Jim; and then you kept Tom here so long with the butter in his hat that you come near spiling the whole business, because the men come before we was out of the cabin, and we had to rush, and they heard us and let drive at us, and I got my share, and we dodged out of the path and let them go by, and when the dogs come they warn't interested in us, but went for the most noise, and we got our canoe, and made for the raft, and was all safe, and Jim was a free man, and we done it all by ourselves, and *wasn't* it bully, Aunty!"

"Well, I never heard the likes of it in all my born days! So it was *you*, you little rapscallions, that's been making all this trouble, and turn everybody's wits clean inside out and scared us all most to death. I've as good a notion as ever I had in my life, to take it out o' you this very minute. To think, here I've been, night after night, a—*you* just get well once, you young scamp, and I lay I'll tan the Old Harry out o' both o' ye!"

But Tom, he *was* so proud and joyful, he just *couldn't* hold in, and his tongue just *went* it—she a-chipping in, and spitting fire all along, and both of them going it at once, like a cat-convention; and she says:

"*Well*, you get all the enjoyment you can out of it *now*, for mind I tell you if I catch you meddling with him again—"

"Meddling with *who*?" Tom says, dropping his smile and looking surprised.

"With *who*? Why, the runaway nigger, of course. Who'd you reckon?"

Tom looks at me very grave, and says:

"Tom, didn't you just tell me he was all right? Hasn't he got away?"

"*Him*?" says Aunt Sally; "the runaway nigger? 'Deed he hasn't. They've got him back, safe and sound, and he's in that cabin again, on bread and water, and loaded down with chains, till he's claimed or sold!"

Tom rose square up in bed, with his eye hot, and his nostrils opening and shutting like gills, and sings out to me:

"They hain't no *right* to shut him up! *Shove!*—and don't you lose a minute. Turn him loose! he ain't no slave; he's as free as any cretur that walks this earth!"

"What *does* the child mean?"

"I mean every word I *say*, Aunt Sally, and if somebody don't go, *I'll* go. I've knowed him all his life, and so has Tom, there. Old Miss Watson died two months ago, and she was ashamed she ever was going to sell him down the river, and *said* so; and she set him free in her will."

"Then what on earth did *you* want to set him free for, seeing he was already free?"

"Well, that *is* a question, I must say; and *just* like women! Why, I wanted the *adventure* of it; and I'd a waded neck-deep in blood to —goodness alive, AUNT POLLY!"[1]

If she warn't standing right there, just inside the door, looking as sweet and contented as an angel half-full of pie, I wish I may never!

---

1. Tom Sawyer's aunt and guardian.

Aunt Sally jumped for her, and most hugged the head off of her, and cried over her, and I found a good enough place for me under the bed, for it was getting pretty sultry for *us*, seemed to me. And I peeped out, and in a little while Tom's Aunt Polly shook herself loose and stood there looking across at Tom over her spectacles—kind of grinding him into the earth, you know. And then she says:

"Yes, you *better* turn y'r head away—I would if I was you, Tom."

"Oh, deary me!" says Aunt Sally; "*is* he changed so? Why, that ain't *Tom* it's Sid; Tom's—Tom's—why, where is Tom? He was here a minute ago."

"You mean where's Huck *Finn*—that's what you mean! I reckon I hain't raised such a scamp as my Tom all these years, not to know him when I *see* him. That *would* be a pretty howdy-do. Come out from under the bed, Huck Finn."

So I done it. But not feeling brash.

Aunt Sally she was one of the mixed-upest looking persons I ever see; except one, and that was Uncle Silas, when he come in, and they told it all to him. It kind of made him drunk, as you may say, and he didn't know nothing at all the rest of the day, and preached a prayer-meeting sermon that night that give him a rattling ruputation, because the oldest man in the world couldn't a understood it. So Tom's Aunt Polly, she told all about who I was, and what; and I had to up and tell how I was in such a tight place that when Mrs. Phelps took me for Tom Sawyer—she chipped in and says, "Oh, go on and call me Aunt Sally, I'm used to it, now, and 'tain't no need to change"—that when Aunt Sally took me for Tom Sawyer, I had to stand it—there warn't no other way, and I knowed he wouldn't mind, because it would be nuts for him, being a mystery, and he'd make an adventure out of it and be perfectly satisfied. And so it turned out, and he let on to be Sid, and made things as soft as he could for me.

And his Aunt Polly she said Tom was right about old Miss Watson setting Jim free in her will; and so, sure enough, Tom Sawyer had gone and took all that trouble and bother to set a free nigger free! and I couldn't ever understand, before, until that minute and that talk, how he *could* help a body set a nigger free, with his bringing-up.

Well, Aunt Polly she said that when Aunt Sally wrote to her that Tom and *Sid* had come, all right and safe, she says to herself:

"Look at that, now! I might have expected it, letting him go off that way without anybody to watch him. So now I got to go and trapse all the way down the river, eleven hundred mile,[2] and find out what that creetur's up to, *this* time; as long as I couldn't seem to get any answer out of you about it."

2. This distance from Hannibal would place the Phelps plantation in northern Louisiana.

"Why, I never heard nothing from you," says Aunt Sally.

"Well, I wonder! Why, I wrote to you twice, to ask you what you could mean by Sid being here."

"Well, I never got 'em, Sis."

Aunt Polly, she turns around slow and severe, and says:

"You, Tom!"

"Well—*what?*" he says, kind of pettish.

"Don't you what me, you impudent thing—hand out them letters."

"What letters?"

"*Them* letters. I be bound, if I have to take aholt of you I'll—"

"They're in the trunk. There, now. And they're just the same as they was when I got them out of the office. I hain't looked into them, I hain't touched them. But I knowed they'd make trouble, and I thought if you warn't in no hurry, I'd—"

"Well, you *do* need skinning, there ain't no mistake about it. And I wrote another one to tell you I was coming; and I spose he—"

"No, it come yesterday; I hain't read it yet, but *it's* all right, I've got that one."

I wanted to offer to bet two dollars she hadn't, but I reckoned maybe it was just as safe to not to. So I never said nothing.

Chapter the Last

The first time I catched Tom, private, I asked him what was his idea, time of the evasion?—what it was he'd planned to do if the evasion worked all right and he managed to set a nigger free that was already free before? And he said, what he had planned in his head, from the start, if we got Jim out all safe, was for us to run him down the river, on the raft, and have adventures plumb to the mouth of the river, and then tell him about his being free, and take him back up home on a steamboat, in style, and pay him for his lost time, and write word ahead and get out all the niggers around, and have them waltz him into town with a torchlight procession and a brass band, and then he would be a hero, and so would we. But I reckened it was about as well the way it was.

We had Jim out of the chains in no time, and when Aunt Polly and Uncle Silas and Aunt Sally found out how good he helped the doctor nurse Tom, they made a heap of fuss over him, and fixed him up prime, and give him all he wanted to eat, and a good time, and nothing to do. And we had him up to the sickroom; and had a high talk; and Tom give Jim forty dollars for being prisoner for us so patient, and doing it up so good, and Jim was pleased most to death, and busted out, and says:

"*Dah*, now, Huck, what I tell you?—what I tell you up dah on Jackson islan'? I *tole* you I got a hairy breas', en what's de sign un it; en I *tole* you I ben rich wunst, en gwineter to be rich *agin*; en it's come true; en heah she *is! Dah*, now! doan' talk to *me*—signs is *signs*, mine I tell you; en I knowed jis' 's well 'at I 'uz gwineter be rich agin as I's a stannin' heah dis minute!"

And then Tom he talked along, and talked along, and says, le's all three slide out of here, one of these nights, and get an outfit, and go for howling adventures amongst the Injuns, over in the Territory, for a couple of weeks or two; and I says, all right, that suits me, but I ain't got no money for to buy the outfit, and I reckon I couldn't get none from home, because it's likely pap's been back before now, and got it all away from Judge Thatcher and drunk it up.

"No he hain't," Tom says; "it's all there, yet—six thousand dollars and more; and your pap hain't ever been back since. Hadn't when I come away, anyhow."

Jim says, kind of solemn:

"He ain't a comin' back no mo', Huck."

I says:

"Why, Jim?"

"Nemmine why, Huck—but he ain't comin' back no mo'."

But I kept at him; so at last he says:

"Doan' you 'member de house dat was float'n down de river, en dey wuz a man in dah, kivered up, en I went in en unkivered him and didn' let you come in? Well, den, you k'n git yo' money when you wants it; kase dat wuz him."

Tom's most well, now, and got his bullet around his neck on a watch-guard for a watch, and is always seeing what time it is, and so there ain't nothing more to write about, and I am rotten glad of it, because if I'd a knowed what a trouble it was to make a book I wouldn't a tackled it and ain't agoing to no more. But I reckon I got to light out for the Territory ahead of the rest, because Aunt Sally she's going to adopt me and sivilize me and I can't stand it. I been there before.

The End. Yours Truly, Huck Finn

1876–83   1884

Fenimore Cooper's Literary Offences[1]

The Pathfinder and *The Deerslayer* stand at the head óf Cooper's novels as artistic creations. There are others of his works which contain parts as perfect as are to be found in these, and scenes even more thrilling. Not one can be compared with either of them as a finished whole.

The defects in both of these tales are comparatively slight. They were pure works of art.—*Prof. Lounsbury.*

The five tales reveal an extraordinary fulness of invention.

1. James Fenimore Cooper (1789–1851) is best known for his series of historical novels in which the hero is variously called Leatherstocking, Natty Bumppo, Hawkeye, and Deerslayer. The novels are *The Pioneers* (1823), *The Last of the Mohicans* (1826), *The Prairie* (1827), *The Pathfinder* (1840), and *The Deerslayer* (1841). This essay was first published in July, 1895, in *North American Review*, the source for the present text, and later in the collection *How to Tell a Story and Other Essays* in 1897.

. . . One of the very greatest characters in fiction, "Natty Bumppo." . . .

The craft of the woodsman, the tricks of the trapper, all the delicate art of the forest, were familiar to Cooper from his youth up.—*Prof. Brander Matthews.*

Cooper is the greatest artist in the domain of romantic fiction yet produced by America.—*Wilkie Collins.*[2]

It seems to me that it was far from right for the Professor of English Literature in Yale, the Professor of English Literature in Columbia, and Wilkie Collins, to deliver opinions on Cooper's literature without having read some of it. It would have been much more decorous to keep silent and let persons talk who have read Cooper.

Cooper's art has some defects. In one place in *Deerslayer*, and in the restricted space of two-thirds of a page, Cooper has scored 114 offences against literary art out of a possible 115. It breaks the record.

There are nineteen rules governing literary art in the domain of romantic fiction—some say twenty-two. In *Deerslayer* Cooper violated eighteen of them. These eighteen require:

1. That a tale shall accomplish something and arrive somewhere. But the *Deerslayer* tale accomplishes nothing and arrives in the air.

2. They require that the episodes of a tale shall be necessary parts of the tale, and shall help to develop it. But as the *Deerslayer* tale is not a tale, and accomplishes nothing and arrives nowhere, the episodes have no rightful place in the work, since there was nothing for them to develop.

3. They require that the personages in a tale shall be alive, except in the case of corpses, and that always the reader shall be able to tell the corpses from the others. But this detail has often been overlooked in the *Deerslayer* tale.

4. They require that the personages in a tale, both dead and alive, shall exhibit a sufficient excuse for being there. But this detail also has been overlooked in the *Deerslayer* tale.

5. They require that when the personages of a tale deal in conversation, the talk shall sound like human talk, and be talk such as human beings would be likely to talk in the given circumstances, and have a discoverable meaning, also a discoverable purpose, and a show of relevancy, and remain in the neighborhood of the subject in hand, and be interesting to the reader, and help out the tale, and stop when the people cannot think of anything more to say. But this requirement has been ignored from the beginning of the *Deerslayer* tale to the end of it.

6. They require that when the author describes the character of a

2. Thomas Raynesford Lounsbury (1838–1915), American scholar and editor; professor at Yale University; James Brander Matthews (1852–1929), American educator and author, professor at Columbia University; William Wilkie Collins (1824–89), English novelist.

personage in his tale, the conduct and conversation of that personage shall justify said description. But this law gets little or no attention in the *Deerslayer* tale, as "Natty Bumppo's" case will amply prove.

7. They require that when a personage talks like an illustrated, gilt-edged, tree-calf, hand-tooled, seven-dollar Friendship's Offering[3] in the beginning of a paragraph, he shall not talk like a negro minstrel in the end of it. But this rule is flung down and danced upon in the *Deerslayer* tale.

8. They require that crass stupidities shall not be played upon the reader as "the craft of the woodsman, the delicate art of the forest," by either the author or the people in the tale. But this rule is persistently violated in the *Deerslayer* tale.

9. They require that the personages of a tale shall confine themselves to possibilities and let miracles alone; or, if they venture a miracle, the author must so plausibly set it forth as to make it look possible and reasonable. But these rules are not respected in the *Deerslayer* tale.

10. They require that the author shall make the reader feel a deep interest in the personages of his tale and in their fate; and that he shall make the reader love the good people in the tale and hate the bad ones. But the reader of the *Deerslayer* tale dislikes the good people in it, is indifferent to the others, and wishes they would all get drowned together.

11. They require that the characters in a tale shall be so clearly defined that the reader can tell beforehand what each will do in a given emergency. But in the *Deerslayer* tale this rule is vacated.

In addition to these large rules there are some little ones. These require that the author shall

12. *Say* what he is proposing to say, not merely come near it.

13. Use the right word, not its second cousin.

14. Eschew surplusage.

15. Not omit necessary details.

16. Avoid slovenliness of form.

17. Use good grammar.

18. Employ a simple and straightforward style.

Even these seven are coldly and persistently violated in the *Deerslayer* tale.

Cooper's gift in the way of invention was not a rich endowment; but such as it was he liked to work it, he was pleased with the effects, and indeed he did some quite sweet things with it. In his little box of stage properties he kept six or eight cunning devices, tricks, artifices for his savages and woodsmen to deceive and circumvent each other with, and he was never so happy as when he was working these innocent things and seeing them go. A favorite one

3. I.e., like one of the then-popular expensive, illustrated literary miscellanies ("tree-calf" was leather chemically treated to produce a treelike design).

was to make a moccasined person tread in the tracks of the moccasined enemy, and thus hide his own trail. Cooper wore out barrels
and barrels of moccasins in working that trick. Another stage-prop-
erty that he pulled out of his box pretty frequently was his broken
twig. He prized his broken twig above all the rest of his effects, and
worked it the hardest. It is a restful chapter in any book of his
when somebody doesn't step on a dry twig and alarm all the reds
and whites for two hundred yards around. Every time a Cooper
person is in peril, and absolute silence is worth four dollars a
minute, he is sure to step on a dry twig. There may be a hundred
handier things to step on, but that wouldn't satisfy Cooper. Cooper
requires him to turn out and find a dry twig; and if he can't do it,
go and borrow one. In fact the Leather Stocking Series ought to
have been called the Broken Twig Series.

I am sorry there is not room to put in a few dozen instances of
the delicate art of the forest, as practiced by Natty Bumppo and
some of the other Cooperian experts. Perhaps we may venture two
or three samples. Cooper was a sailor—a naval officer; yet he gravely
tells us how a vessel, driving toward a lee shore[4] in a gale, is steered
for a particular spot by her skipper because he knows of an *under-
tow* there which will hold her back against the gale and save her.
For just pure woodcraft, or sailor-craft, or whatever it is, isn't that
neat? For several years Cooper was daily in the society of artillery,
and he ought to have noticed that when a cannon ball strikes the
ground it either buries itself or skips a hundred feet or so; skips
again a hundred feet or so—and so on, till it finally gets tired and
rolls. Now in one place he loses some "females"—as he always calls
women—in the edge of a wood near a plain at night in a fog, on
purpose to give Bumppo a chance to show off the delicate art of the
forest before the reader. These mislaid people are hunting for a fort.
They hear a cannon-blast, and a cannon-ball presently comes rolling
into the wood and stops at their feet. To the females this suggests
nothing. The case is very different with the admirable Bumppo. I
wish I may never know peace again if he doesn't strike out
promptly and *follow the track* of that cannon-ball across the plain
through the dense fog and find the fort. Isn't it a daisy? If Cooper
had any real knowledge of Nature's ways of doing things, he had a
most delicate art in concealing the fact. For instance: one of his
acute Indian experts, Chingachgook[5] (pronounced Chicago, I
think), has lost the trail of a person he is tracking through the
forest. Apparently that trail is hopelessly lost. Neither you nor I
could ever have guessed out the way to find it. It was very different
with Chicago. Chicago was not stumped for long. He turned a running stream out of its course, and there, in the slush in its old bed,
were that person's moccasin-tracks. The current did not wash them
away, as it would have done in all other like cases—no, even the

4. Shore that is protected from the wind.   5. Natty Bumppo's Indian friend.

of it. Then No. 3 jumped for the boat, and fell a good way astern
of it. Then No. 4 jumped for the boat, and fell in the water *away*
astern. Then even No. 5 made a jump for the boat—for he was a
Cooper Indian. In the matter of intellect, the difference between a
Cooper Indian and the Indian that stands in front of the cigar shop
is not spacious. The scow episode is really a sublime burst of invention; but it does not thrill, because the inaccuracy of the details
throws a sort of air of fictitiousness and general improbability over
it. This comes of Cooper's inadequacy as an observer.

The reader will find some examples of Cooper's high talent for
inaccurate observation in the account of the shooting match in *The
Pathfinder.* "A common wrought nail was driven lightly into the
target, its head having been first touched with paint." The color of
the paint is not stated—an important omission, but Cooper deals
freely in important omissions. No, after all, it was not an important
omission; for this nail head is *a hundred yards* from the marksman
and could not be seen by them at that distance no matter what its
color might be. How far can the best eyes see a common house fly?
A hundred yards? It is quite impossible. Very well, eyes that cannot
see a house fly that is a hundred yards away cannot see an ordinary
nail head at that distance, for the size of the two objects is the
same. It takes a keen eye to see a fly or a nail head at fifty yards—
one hundred and fifty feet. Can the reader do it?

The nail was lightly driven, its head painted, and game called.
Then the Cooper miracles began. The bullet of the first marksman
chipped an edge of the nail head; the next man's bullet drove the
nail a little way into the target—and removed all the paint. Haven't
the miracles gone far enough now? Not to suit Cooper; for the purpose of this whole scheme is to show off his prodigy, Deerslayer-
Hawkeye-Long-Rifle-Leather-Stocking-Pathfinder-Bumppo before the
ladies.

"Be all ready to clench it, boys!" cried out Pathfinder, stepping into his friend's tracks the instant they were vacant.
"Never mind a new nail; I can see that, though the paint is
gone, and what I can see, I can hit at a hundred yards, though
it were only a mosquitos's eye. Be ready to clench!"

The rifle cracked, the bullet sped its way and the head of
the nail was buried in the wood, covered by the piece of flattened lead.

There, you see, is a man who could hunt flies with a rifle, and
command a ducal salary in a Wild West show to-day, if we had
him back with us.

The recorded feat is certainly surprising, just as it stands; but it is
not surprising enough for Cooper. Cooper adds a touch. He has
made Pathfinder do this miracle with another man's rifle, and not
only that, but Pathfinder did not have even the advantage of loading it himself. He had everything against him, and yet he made that

impossible shot, and not only made it, but did it with absolute confidence, saying, "Be ready to clench." Now a person like that would have undertaken that same feat with a brickbat, and with Cooper to help he would have achieved it, too.

Pathfinder showed off handsomely that day before the ladies. His very first feat was a thing which no Wild West show can touch. He was standing with the group of marksmen, observing—a hundred yards from the target, mind: one Jasper raised his rifle and drove the centre of the bull's-eye. Then the quartermaster fired. The target exhibited no result this time. There was a laugh. "It's a dead miss," said Major Lundie. Pathfinder waited an impressive moment or two, then said in that calm, indifferent, know-it-all way of his, "No, Major—he has covered Jasper's bullet, as will be seen if any one will take the trouble to examine the target."

Wasn't it remarkable! How *could* he see that little pellet fly through the air and enter that distant bullet-hole? Yet that is what he did; for nothing is impossible to a Cooper person. Did any of those people have any deep-seated doubts about this thing? No; for that would imply sanity, and these were all Cooper people.

> The respect for Pathfinder's skill and for his *quickness and accuracy of sight* (the italics are mine) was so profound and general, that the instant he made this declaration the spectators began to distrust their own opinions, and a dozen rushed to the target in order to ascertain the fact. There, sure enough, it was found that the quartermaster's bullet had gone through the hole made by Jasper's, and that, too, so accurately as to require a minute examination to be certain of the circumstance, which, however, was soon clearly established by discovering one bullet over the other in the stump against which the target was placed.

They made a "minute" examination; but never mind, how could they know that there were two bullets in that hole without digging the latest one out? for neither probe nor eyesight could prove the presence of any more than one bullet. Did they dig? No; as we shall see. It is the Pathfinder's turn now; he steps out before the ladies, takes aim, and fires.

But alas! here is a disappointment; an incredible, an unimaginable disappointment—for the target's aspect is unchanged; there is nothing there but that same old bullet hole!

> "If one dared to hint at such a thing," cried Major Duncan, "I should say that the Pathfinder has also missed the target."

As nobody had missed it yet, the "also" was not necessary; but never mind about that, for the Pathfinder is going to speak.

> "No, no, Major," said he, confidently, "that *would* be a risky declaration. I didn't load the piece, and can't say what was in it, but if it was lead, you will find the bullet driving

eternal laws of Nature have to vacate when Cooper wants to put up a delicate job of woodcraft on the reader.

We must be a little wary when Brander Matthews tells us that Cooper's books "reveal an extraordinary fulness of invention." As a rule, I am quite willing to accept Brander Matthews's literary judgments and applaud his lucid and graceful phrasing of them; but that particular statement needs to be taken with a few tons of salt. Bless your heart, Cooper hadn't any more invention than a horse; and I don't mean a high-class horse, either; I mean a clothes-horse. It would be very difficult to find a really clever "situation" in Cooper's books; and still more difficult to find one of any kind which he has failed to render absurd by his handling of it. Look at the episodes of "the caves;" and at the celebrated scuffle between Maqua and those others on the table-land a few days later; and at Hurry Harry's queer water-transit from the castle to the ark; and at Deerslayer's half hour with his first corpse; and at the quarrel between Hurry Harry and Deerslayer later; and at—but choose for yourself; you can't go amiss.

If Cooper had been an observer, his inventive faculty would have worked better, not more interestingly, but more rationally, more plausibly. Cooper's proudest creations in the way of "situations" suffer noticeably from the absence of the observer's protecting gift. Cooper's eye was splendidly inaccurate. Cooper seldom saw anything correctly. He saw nearly all things as through a glass eye, darkly.[6] Of course a man who cannot see the commonest little everyday matters accurately is working at a disadvantage when he is constructing a "situation." In the *Deerslayer* tale Cooper has a stream which is fifty feet wide, where it flows out of a lake; it presently narrows to twenty as it meanders along for no given reason, and yet, when a stream acts like that it ought to be required to explain itself. Fourteen pages later the width of the brook's outlet from the lake has suddenly shrunk thirty feet, and become "the narrowest part of the stream." This shrinkage is not accounted for. The stream has bends in it, a sure indication that it has alluvial banks, and cuts them; yet these bends are only thirty and fifty feet long. If Cooper had been a nice[7] and punctilious observer he would have noticed that the bends were oftener nine hundred feet long than short of it.

Cooper made the exit of that stream fifty feet wide in the first place, for no particular reason; in the second place, he narrowed it to less than twenty to accommodate some Indians. He bends a "sapling" to the form of an arch over this narrow passage, and conceals six Indians in its foliage. They are "laying" for a settler's scow or ark which is coming up the stream on its way to the lake; it is being hauled against the stiff current by a rope whose stationary end

6. Humorous turn of the Biblical
"through a glass, darkly" (1 Corinthians

13.12).
7. I.e., meticulous.

is anchored in the lake; its rate of progress cannot be more than a mile an hour. Cooper describes the ark, but pretty obscurely. In the matter of dimensions "it was little more than a modern canal boat." Let us guess, then, that it was about 140 feet long. It was of "greater breadth than common." Let us guess, then, that it was about sixteen feet wide. This leviathan had been prowling down bends which were but a third as long as itself, and scraping between banks where it had only two feet of space to spare on each side. We cannot too much admire this miracle. A low-roofed log dwelling occupies "two-third's of the ark's length"—a dwelling ninety feet long and sixteen feet wide, let us say—a kind of vestibule train. The dwelling has two rooms—each forty-five feet long and sixteen feet wide, let us guess. One of them is the bed-room of the Hutter girls, Judith and Hetty; the other is the parlor, in the day time, at night it is papa's bed chamber. The ark is arriving at the stream's exit, now, whose width has been reduced to less than twenty feet to accommodate the Indians—say to eighteen. There is a foot to spare on each side of the boat. Did the Indians notice that there was going to be a tight squeeze there? Did they notice that they could make money by climbing down out of that arched sapling and just stepping aboard when the ark scraped by? No; other Indians would have noticed these things, but Cooper's Indians never notice anything. Cooper thinks they are marvellous creatures for noticing, but he was almost always in error about his Indians. There was seldom a sane one among them.

The ark is 140 feet long; the dwelling is 90 feet long. The idea of the Indians is to drop softly and secretly from the arched sapling to the dwelling as the ark creeps along under it at the rate of a mile an hour, and butcher the family. It will take the ark a minute and a half to pass under. It will take the 90-foot dwelling a minute to pass under. Now, then, what did the six Indians do? It would take you thirty years to guess, and even then you would have to give it up, I believe. Therefore, I will tell you what the Indians did. Their chief, a person of quite extraordinary intellect for a Cooper Indian, warily watched the canal boat as it squeezed along under him, and when he had got his calculations fined down to exactly the right shade, as he judged, he let go and dropped. And *missed the house!* That is actually what he did. He missed the house, and landed in the stern of the scow. It was not much of a fall, yet it knocked him silly. He lay there unconscious. If the house had been 97 feet long, he would have made the trip. The fault was Cooper's, not his. The error lay in the construction of the house. Cooper was no architect.

There still remained in the roost five Indians. The boat has passed under and is now out of their reach. Let me explain what the five did—you would not be able to reason it out for yourself. No. 1 jumped for the boat, but fell in the water astern of it. Then No. 2 jumped for the boat, but fell in the water still further astern

down those of the Quartermaster and Jasper, else is not my name Pathfinder."

A shout from the target announced the truth of this assertion.

Is the miracle sufficient as it stands? Not for Cooper. The Pathfinder speaks again, as he "now slowly advances towards the stage occupied by the females:"

"That's not all, boys, that's not all; if you find the target touched at all, I'll own to a miss. The Quartermaster cut the wood, but you'll find no wood cut by that last messenger."

The miracle is at last complete. He knew—doubtless *saw*—at the distance of a hundred yards—that his bullet had passed into the hole *without fraying the edges*. There were now three bullets in that one hole—three bullets imbedded processionally in the body of the stump back of the target. Everybody knew this—somehow or other—and yet nobody had dug any of them out to make sure. Cooper is not a close observer, but he is interesting. He is certainly always that, no matter what happens. And he is more interesting when he is not noticing what he is about than when he is. This is a considerable merit.

The conversations in the Cooper books have a curious sound in our modern ears. To believe that such talk really ever came out of people's mouths would be to believe that there was a time when time was of no value to a person who thought he had something to say; when it was the custom to spread a two-minute remark out to ten; when a man's mouth was a rolling-mill, and busied itself all day long in turning four-foot pigs[8] of thought into thirty-foot bars of conversational railroad iron by attenuation; when subjects were seldom faithfully stuck to, but the talk wandered all around and arrived nowhere; when conversations consisted mainly of irrelevances, with here and there a relevancy, a relevancy with an embarrassed look, as not being able to explain how it got there.

Cooper was certainly not a master in the construction of dialogue. Inaccurate observation defeated him here as it defeated him in so many other enterprises of his. He even failed to notice that the man who talks corrupt English six days in the week must and will talk it on the seventh, and can't help himself. In the *Deerslayer* story he lets Deerslayer talk the showiest kind of book talk sometimes, and at other times the basest of base dialects. For instance, when some one asks him if he has a sweetheart, and if so, where she abides, this is his majestic answer:

"She's in the forest—hanging from the boughs of the trees, in a soft rain—in the dew on the open grass—the clouds that float about in the blue heavens—the birds that sing in the

---

8. Crude castings of iron.

woods—the sweet springs where I slake my thirst—and in all the other glorious gifts that come from God's Providence!"

And he preceded that, a little before, with this:

"It consarns me as all things that touches a fri'nd consarns a fri'nd."

And this is another of his remarks:

"If I was Injun born, now, I might tell of this, or carry in the scalp and boast of the expl'ite afore the whole tribe; or if my inimy had only been a bear"—and so on.

We cannot imagine such a thing as a veteran Scotch Commander-in-Chief comporting himself in the field like a windy melodramatic actor, but Cooper could. On one occasion Alice and Cora were being chased by the French through a fog in the neighborhood of their father's fort:

"*Point de quartier aux coquins!*"[9] cried an eager pursuer, who seemed to direct the operations of the enemy.
"Stand firm and be ready, my gallant 6oths!" suddenly exclaimed a voice above them; "wait to see the enemy; fire low, and sweep the glacis."[1]
"Father! father!" exclaimed a piercing cry from out the mist; "it is I! Alice! thy own Elsie! spare, O! save your daughters!"
"Hold!" shouted the former speaker, in the awful tones of parental agony, the sound reaching even to the woods, and rolling back in solemn echo. "'Tis she! God has restored me my children! Throw open the sally-port;[2] to the field, 6oths, to the field; pull not a trigger, lest ye kill my lambs! Drive off these dogs of France with your steel."

Cooper's word-sense was singularly dull. When a person has a poor ear for music he will flat and sharp right along without knowing it. He keeps near the tune, but it is *not* the tune. When a person has a poor ear for words, the result is a literary flatting and sharping; you perceive what he is intending to say, but you also perceive that he doesn't *say* it. This is Cooper. He was not a word-musician. His ear was satisfied with the *approximate* word. I will furnish some circumstantial evidence in support of this charge. My instances are gathered from half a dozen pages of the tale called *Deerslayer.* He uses "verbal," for "oral"; "precision," for "facility"; "phenomena," for "marvels"; "necessary," for "predetermined"; "unsophisticated," for "primitive"; "preparation," for "expectancy"; "rebuked," for "subdued"; "dependent on," for "resulting from"; "fact," for "condition"; "fact," for "conjecture"; "precaution," for "caution"; "explain," for "determine"; "mortified," for "disappointed"; "meretricious," for "factitious"; "materially," for "consid-

---

9. "No quarter for the rascals!"
1. Slope that runs downward from a fortification.

2. Gate or passage in a fortified place for use of troops making a sortie.

erably"; "decreasing," for "deepening"; "increasing," for "disappearing"; "embedded," for "enclosed"; "treacherous," for "hostile"; "stood," for "stooped"; "softened," for "replaced"; "rejoined," for "remarked"; "situation," for "condition"; "different," for "differing"; "insensible," for "unsentient"; "brevity," for "celerity"; "distrusted," for "suspicious"; "mental imbecility," for "imbecility"; "eyes," for "sight"; "counteracting," for "opposing"; "funeral obsequies," for "obsequies."

There have been daring people in the world who claimed that Cooper could write English, but they are all dead now—all dead but Lounsbury. I don't remember that Lounsbury makes the claim in so many words, still he makes it, for he says that *Deerslayer* is a "pure work of art." Pure, in that connection, means faultless—faultless in all details—and language is a detail. If Mr. Lounsbury had only compared Cooper's English with the English which he writes himself—but it is plain that he didn't; and so it is likely that he imagines until this day that Cooper's is as clean and compact as his own. Now I feel sure, deep down in my heart, that Cooper wrote about the poorest English that exists in our language, and that the English of *Deerslayer* is the very worst than even Cooper ever wrote.

I may be mistaken, but it does seem to me that *Deerslayer* is not a work of art in any sense; it does seem to me that it is destitute of every detail that goes to the making of a work of art; in truth, it seems to me that *Deerslayer* is just simply a literary *delirium tremens*.

A work of art? It has no invention; it has no order, system, sequence, or result; it has no lifelikeness, no thrill, no stir, no seeming of reality; its characters are confusedly drawn, and by their acts and words they prove that they are not the sort of people the author claims that they are; its humor is pathetic; its pathos is funny; its conversations are—oh! indescribable; its love-scenes odious; its English a crime against the language.

Counting these out, what is left is Art. I think we must all admit that.

1895, 1897

The United States of Lyncherdom[1]

I

And so Missouri has fallen, that great state! Certain of her children have joined the lynchers, and the smirch is upon the rest of us.

1. This essay was not published during Mark Twain's lifetime. When Albert Bigelow Paine edited the essay for inclusion in *Europe and Elsewhere* (1923), he took considerable liberties with the manuscript that Twain had left behind. The present text is freshly edited from the manuscript with the cooperation of Frederick Anderson, editor of the Mark Twain Papers, University of California, Berkeley. It will appear in a forthcoming volume of the California edition of Twain's works.

That handful of her children have given us a character and labeled us with a name; and to the dwellers in the four quarters of the earth we are "lynchers," now, and ever shall be. For the world will not stop and think—it never does, it is not its way; its way is to generalize from a single sample. It will not say "Those Missourians have been busy eighty years in building an honorable good name for themselves; these hundred lynchers down in the corner of the State are not real Missourians, they are bastards." No, that truth will not enter its mind; it will generalize from the one or two misleading samples and say "The Missourians are lynchers." It has no reflection, no logic, no sense of proportion. With it, figures go for nothing; to it, figures reveal nothing, it cannot reason upon them rationally; it is Brother J.-J. infinitely multiplied; it would say, with him, that China is being swiftly and surely Christianized, since 9 Chinese Christians are being made every day; and it would fail, with him, to notice that the fact that 33,000 pagans are *born* there every day, damages the argument. It would J-J Missouri, and say "There are a hundred lynchers there, therefore the Missourians are lynchers;" the considerable fact that there are two and a half million Missourians who are *not* lynchers would not affect their verdict any more than it would affect Bro. J.-J.'s.

What, then, results from this curious fashion of the world? A chief and dismal result is, that the reputations of States and nations are made by the conduct of a few of their noisiest and worst representatives, and not by the conduct of the clean and sober multitude of their populations. In the eyes of the world are all Englishmen Alfreds the Great? no, they are all Chamberlains; are all Frenchmen Saints Louis? no, they are all Melines; are all New Yorkers Odells? no, they are all Crokers;[2] are all but three of our States honest and honorable? no, in foreign eyes we are all repudiators of our bonds; are we Southerners all Dr. Lazears,[3] General Lees, Stonewall Jacksons? no, we are all lynchers.

Since, then, a nation's foreign reputation must depend upon the conduct of its handful of Chamberlains, bond-repudiators, Quays,[4] Crokers, and such, it ought to be a good idea to suppress these people—is it not so? How is it to be done? It is an easy question—to ask.

2. Alfred (849–899), King of the West Saxons (871–899), known as Alfred the Great; Joseph Chamberlain (1836–1914), British statesman who finally resigned from office in 1903 after controversy surrounded his political affairs; Louis IX (1214–70), King of France (1226–70), went on the Sixth Crusade and planned another; Félix Jules Méline (1838–1925), French statesman forced to resign because he refused to rely solely on the left-wing republicans; Benjamin Barker Odell (1854–1926), Governor of New York, much lauded for reduced direct taxation; Richard Croker (1841–1922), New York City machine politician.
3. Jesse William Lazear (1866–1900), American physician and member of the commission which proved that yellow fever was transmitted through mosquitoes. As proof of the commission's thesis, he allowed a mosquito to bite him and died a week later.
4. Matthew Stanley Quay (1833–1904), Pennsylvania politician who controlled the state's Republican machine.

II

Oh, Missouri!

The tragedy occurred near Pierce City, down in the southwestern corner of the State. On a Sunday afternoon a young white woman who had started homeward alone from church, was found murdered. From church. For there are churches there; in my time religion was more general, more pervasive, in the South than it was in the North, and more virile and earnest, too, I think; I have some reason to believe that this is still the case. The young woman was found murdered. Although it was a region of churches and schools, the people rose, lynched three negroes—two of them very aged ones —burned out five negro households, and drove thirty negro families to the woods.

I do not dwell upon the provocation which moved the people to these crimes, for that has nothing to do with the matter. We know by the recent Keller case in a Jersey court, that evidence to show that an assassin was moved by great provocation is not admissible and cannot be listened to; the only question is, did the assassin *take the law into his own hands?* It is very simple, and very just. If the assassin be proved to have usurped the law's prerogative in righting his wrongs, that ends the matter; a thousand provocations are no defence. The Pierce City people had bitter provocation—indeed, as revealed by certain of the particulars, the bitterest of all provocations—but no matter, they took the law into their own hands, and by the terms of their own statutes they are assassins and should hang—in Jersey, let us believe, that is what would happen to them. Also, in Jersey the assassin of that helpless poor white woman would hang—and we know that Pierce City's courts would have hanged him if the law had been allowed to take its course, for there are but few negroes in that region and they are without authority and without influence in overawing juries.

III

Why has lynching, with various barbaric accompaniments, become a favorite regulator in cases of "the usual crime" in several parts of the country? Is it because men think a lurid and terrible punishment a more forcible object-lesson and a more effective deterrent than a sober and colorless hanging, done privately in a jail, would be? Surely sane men do not think that. Even the average child should know better. It should know that any strange and much-talked-of event is always followed by imitations, the world being so well supplied with excitable people who only need a little stirring up to make them lose what is left of their heads and do mad things which they would not have thought of ordinarily. It should know that if a man jump off Brooklyn Bridge another will imitate him; that if a person venture down Niagara Whirlpool in a barrel another will imitate him; that if a Jack the Ripper make notoriety by slaughtering women in dark alleys he will be imitated; that if a man attempt a king's life and the newspapers carry the noise of it around the globe, regicides will crop up all around. The child should know that one much-talked-of outrage and murder committed by a negro will upset the disturbed intellects of several other negroes and produce a series of the very tragedies the community would so strenuously wish to prevent; that each of these crimes will produce another series, and year by year steadily increase the tale of these disasters instead of diminishing it; that, in a word, the lynchers are themselves the worst enemies of their women. The child should also know that by a law of our make, communities, as well as individuals, are imitators; and that a much-talked-of lynching will infallibly produce other lynchings here and there and yonder, and that in time these will breed a mania, a fashion; a fashion which will spread wide and wider, year by year, covering State after State, as with an advancing disease. Lynching has reached Colorado, it has reached California, it has reached Indiana—and now Missouri! I shall live to see a negro burned in Union Square, New York, with fifty thousand people present, and not a sheriff visible, not a governor, not a constable, not a colonel, not a clergyman, not a law-and-order representative of any sort.

> *Increase in Lynching.*—In 1900 there were eight more cases than in 1899, and probably this year there will be more than there were last year. The year is little more than half gone, and yet there are eighty-eight cases as compared with one hundred and fifteen for all of last year. Four Southern states, Alabama, Georgia, Louisiana, and Mississippi are the worst offenders. Last year there were eight cases in Alabama, sixteen in Georgia, twenty in Louisiana, and twenty in Mississippi—over one-half the total. This year to date there have been nine in Alabama, twelve in Georgia, eleven in Louisiana, and thirteen in Mississippi—again more than one-half the total number in the whole United States.—*Chicago Tribune.*

It must be that the increase comes of the inborn human instinct to imitate—that and man's commonest weakness, his aversion to being unpleasantly conspicuous, pointed at, shunned, as being on the unpopular side. Its other name is Moral Cowardice, and is the supreme feature of the make-up of 9,999 men in the 10,000. I am not offering this as a discovery; privately the dullest of us knows it to be true. History will not allow us to forget or ignore this commanding trait of our character. It persistently and sardonically reminds us that from the beginning of the world no revolt against a public infamy or oppression has ever been begun but by the one daring man in the 10,000, the rest timidly waiting, and slowly and reluctantly joining, under the influence of that man and his fellows from the other ten thousands. The abolitionists remember. Privately the public feeling was with them early, but each man was afraid to speak out until he got some hint that his neighbor was privately feeling as he privately felt himself. Then the boom followed. It always does. It will occur in New York, some day; and even in Pennsylvania.

IV

It has been supposed—and said—that the people at a lynching enjoy the spectacle, and are glad of a chance to see it. It cannot be true; all experience is against it. The people in the South are made like the people in the North—the vast majority of whom are right-hearted and compassionate, and would be cruelly pained by such a spectacle—and *would attend it*, and let on to be pleased with it if the public approval seemed to require it. We are made like that, and we cannot help it. The other animals are not so, but we cannot help that, either. They lack the Moral Sense; we have no way of trading ours off, for a nickel or some other thing above its value. The Moral Sense teaches us what is right and how to avoid it. When unpopular.

It is thought, as I have said, that a lynching-crowd enjoys a lynching. It certainly is not true; it is impossible of belief. It is freely asserted—you have seen it in print many times of late—that the lynching impulse has been misinterpreted: that it is *not* the outcome of a spirit of revenge, but of a "mere atrocious hunger *to look upon human suffering.*" If that were so, the crowds that saw the Windsor Hotel[5] burn down would have enjoyed the horrors that fell under their eyes. Did they? No one will think that of them, no one will make that charge. Many risked their lives to save the men and women who were in peril. Why did they do that? Because *none would disapprove.* There was no restraint; they could follow their natural impulse. Why does a crowd of the same kind of people in Texas, Colorado, Indiana, stand by, smitten to the heart and miserable, and by ostentatious outward signs pretend to enjoy a lynching? Why does it lift no hand nor voice in protest? Only because it would be unpopular to do it, I think; each man is afraid of his neighbor's disapproval—a thing which to the general run of the race is more dreaded than wounds and death. When there is to be a lynching the people hitch up and come miles to see it, bringing their wives and children. Really to see it? No—they come only because they are afraid to stay at home, lest it be noticed and offensively commented upon. We may believe this, for we all know how *we* feel about such spectacles—also, how we would act under the like pressure. We are not any better nor any braver than anybody else, and we must not try to creep out of it.

5. The grand Windsor Hotel in New York City was reduced to ashes on March 17, 1899.

V

A Savonarola[6] can quell and scatter a mob of lynchers with a mere glance of his eye; so can a Merrill[7] or a Beloat. For no mob has any sand in the presence of a man known to be splendidly brave. Besides, a lynching-mob would *like* to be scattered, for of a certainty there are never ten men in it who would not prefer to be somewhere else—and would be, if they but had the courage to go. When I was a boy I saw a brave gentleman deride and insult a mob and drive it away; and afterward, in Nevada, I saw a noted desperado make two hundred men sit still, with the house burning under them, until he gave them permission to retire. A plucky man can rob a whole passenger train by himself; and the half of a brave man can hold up a stagecoach and strip its occupants.

Then perhaps the remedy for lynchings comes to this: station a brave man in each affected community to encourage, support, and bring to light the deep disapproval of lynching hidden in the secret places of its heart—for it is there, beyond question. Then those communities will find something better to imitate—of course, being human they must imitate something. Where shall these brave men be found? That is indeed a difficulty; there are not three hundred of them in the earth. If merely *physically* brave men would do, then it were easy; they could be furnished by the cargo. When Hobson[8] called for seven volunteers to go with him to what promised to be certain death, four thousand men responded—the whole fleet, in fact. Because *all the world would approve.* They knew that; but if Hobson's project had been charged with the scoffs and jeers of the friends and associates, whose good opinion and approval the sailors valued, he could not have got his seven.

No, upon reflection, the scheme will not work. There are not enough morally brave men in stock. We are out of moral-courage material; we are in a condition of profound poverty. We have those two sheriffs down South who—but never mind, it is not enough to go around; they have to stay and take care of their own communities.

But if we only *could* have three or four more sheriffs of that great breed! Would it help? I think so. For we are all imitators: other brave sheriffs would follow; to be a dauntless sheriff would come to be recognized as the correct and only thing, and the dreaded disapproval would fall to the share of the other kind; courage in this office would become custom, the absence of it a dishonor, just as

6. Girolamo Savonarola (1452–98), Florentine religious reformer known for his eloquence and rousing speeches.
7. "Merrill": "sheriff of Carroll County, Georgia" [Clemens's note]. "Beloat": "sheriff, Princeton, Indiana. By that formidable power which lies in an established reputation for cold pluck they faced lynching mobs and securely held the field against them" [Clemens's note].
8. Edward Henry Hobson (1825–1901), Union soldier who recruited the 13th Union Infantry from Kentucky and was promoted to Brigadier-General of the Volunteers.

courage presently replaces the timidity of the new soldier; then the mobs and the lynchings would disappear, and——

However. It can never be done without some starters, and where are we to get the starters? Advertise? Very well, then, let us advertise.

VI

In the meantime, there is another plan. Let us import American missionaries from China, and send them into the lynching field. With 1511 of them out there converting 2 Chinamen apiece per annum against an uphill birthrate of 33,000 pagans per day,[9] it will take upwards of a million years to make the conversions balance the output and bring the Christianizing of the country in sight with the naked eye; therefore, if we can offer our missionaries as rich a field at home, at lighter expense and quite satisfactory in the matter of danger, why shouldn't they find it fair and right to come back and give us a trial? The Chinese are universally conceded to be excellent people, honest, honorable, industrious, trustworthy, kind-hearted, and all that—leave them alone, they are plenty good enough just as they are; and besides, almost every convert runs a risk of catching our Civilization. We ought to be careful. We ought to think twice before we encourage a risk like that; for, *once civilized, China can never be uncivilized again.* We have not been thinking of that. Very well, we ought to think of it now. Our missionaries will find that we have a field for them—and not only for the 1511, but for 15,011. Let them look at the following telegram, and see if they have anything in China that is more appetizing. It is from Texas:

> The negro was taken to a tree, and swung in the air. Wood and fodder were piled beneath his body and a hot fire was made. *Then it was suggested that the man ought not to die too quickly, and he was let down to the ground, while a party went to Dexter about two miles distant, to procure coal oil. This was thrown on the flames and the work completed.*

We implore them to come back and help us in our need. Patriotism imposes this duty upon them. Our country is worse off than China; they are our countrymen, their motherland supplicates their aid in this her hour of deep distress. They are competent, our people are not; they are used to scoffs, sneers, revilings, danger; our people are not; they have the martyr spirit, nothing but the martyr spirit can brave a lynching-mob and cow it and scatter it; they can save their country, we beseech them to come home and do it. We ask them to read that telegram again, and yet again, and picture the scene in their minds, and soberly ponder it; then multiply it by 115; add 88; place the 203 in a row, allowing 600 feet of space for each

9. "These figures are not fanciful; all of them are genuine and authentic. They are from official missionary records in China. See Dr. Morrison's book on his pedestrian journey across China; he quotes them and gives his authorities. For several years he has been the London *Times*'s representative in Peking, and was there through the siege" [Clemens's note].

human torch, so that there may be viewing-room around it for 5,000 Christian American men, women and children, youths and maidens; make it night, for grim effect; have the show in a gradually rising plain, and let the course of the stakes be up-hill; the eye can then take in the whole line of twenty-four miles of blood-and-flesh bonfires unbroken, whereas if it occupied level ground the ends of the line would bend down and be hidden from view by the curvature of the earth; all being ready, now, and the darkness opaque, the stillness impressive—for there should be no sound but the soft moaning of the night-wind and the muffled sobbing of the sacrifices—let all the far stretch of kerosened pyres be touched off simultaneously and the glare and the shrieks and the agonies burst heavenward to the Throne.

There are more than a million persons present; the light from the fires flushes into vague outline against the night the spires of five thousand churches. Oh kind missionary, oh compassionate missionary, leave China! come home and convert these Christians!

VII

I believe that if anything can stop this epidemic of bloody insanities it is martial personalities that can face mobs without flinching; and as such personalities are developed only by familiarity with danger and by the training and seasoning which come of resisting it, the likeliest place to find them must be among the missionaries who have been under tuition in China during the past year or two. We have abundance of work for them, and for hundreds and thousands more, and the field is daily growing and spreading. We shall add 60 lynchings to our 88 before the year is out; we shall reach the 300-mark next year, the 500-mark in 1903, we shall lynch a thousand negroes in 1904; in 1905 there will be lynchings in every State and Territory and Possession, for our morals follow the flag, let the Constitution do as it may; and by 1910 my prediction will mature and I shall see a negro burned in Union Square. For murder? No, for being in the country against the country's will—like the Chinaman in America and the missionary in China. By that time we shall be known abroad as the United States of Lyncherdom, and be no more respected than a Chamberlain-war[1] for South African swag.

This must all happen. That is, unless we find those seasoned great braves—in the China missions or elsewhere—with the Savonarola glance which withers mobs with its stern rebuke and disperses them in shame and fear. Shall we find them? We can try. In 75,000,000 there must be other Merrills and Beloats; and it is the law of our make that each example shall wake up drowsing chevaliers of the same great knighthood and bring them to the front.

1901   1923

1. I.e., the Boer War (1899–1902) between the Boers, descendants of the Dutch settlers, and England over possession of South Africa. England eventually won.

BRET HARTE
1836–1902

Francis Brett Harte was born August 25, 1836, in Albany, New York, of
Jewish, English, and Dutch descent. His schoolteacher father died in 1845,
and four years later Harte left school to work in a lawyer's office and then
in the counting room of a merchant. In 1854 he followed his mother and
elder sister and brother to Oakland, California, and for a year he lived with
his mother and stepfather, Colonel Andrew Williams, the first Mayor of
Oakland. During this time he contributed some stories and poems to eastern magazines, but he had by no means settled on a career as a writer.
When he turned twenty-one he left Williams's house to wander in northern California, where he rode shotgun for Wells Fargo and held less romantic jobs as miner, teacher, apothecary's clerk, and in the printing room of
the *Humbolt Times.*

In San Francisco in 1860, Harte set type for the newspaper the *Golden
Era* and began contributing to it. Shortly after the Civil War started, he
quit the *Golden Era* and became a clerk in the Surveyor-General's office.
Soon after he married Anna Griswold in 1862, Harte secured the unde-
manding position of Secretary to the Superintendent in the U.S. Branch
Mint in San Francisco and began to establish himself as a journalist, contributing together with Mark Twain and others to the first issue of the
weekly *Californian.* Harte's career as a writer was confirmed in 1868 when
he became the first editor of the newly established magazine *Overland
Monthly,* for which he wrote the works that made him—and the magazine
—famous. Two of his poems were printed in the first issue, followed in the
second by *The Luck of Roaring Camp,* the story that made him a celebrity
from coast to coast, and then by *The Outcasts of Poker Flat* and his best-
known poem, *Plain Language from Truthful James,* commonly referred to
as *The Heathen Chinee.*

Harte left San Francisco with his family early in 1871 at the height of
his fame. After a journey cross-country that was covered by the daily press,
the Hartes were entertained in Boston for a week as guests of the new
editor of the *Atlantic Monthly,* William Dean Howells. James T. Fields,
who owned the prestigious *Atlantic,* had offered Harte the unheard of sum
of ten thousand dollars to write twelve or more poems and sketches within
a year to be published in the *Atlantic* and *Every Saturday.* Unfortunately,
Harte could not meet his deadline, and it was not until several months later
that he satisfied Fields. The contract was not renewed.

The last three decades of Harte's life constitute a decline in his personal
and literary fortunes. Though he lectured and wrote feverishly for the next
few years, his extravagant life style kept him continually in debt. His novel
Gabriel Conroy (1876) earned a "small fortune," but he soon spent it. For
a time he turned to the theater; though his plays *Two Men of Sandy Bar*
(1876) and *Ah Sin* (1877) were produced (the latter after an unhappy
attempt to collaborate with Mark Twain), neither was successful.
Appointed Consul to Crefield, Prussia, by President Rutherford B. Hayes,
Harte, by this time on bad terms with his wife, went alone to this post in

1878. He never saw his wife again. He was transferred to Glasgow, Scotland, in 1880 at his request. On visits to London and Bournemouthe, he often stayed with a Belgian couple, the Van de Veldes. From the beginning, Harte's relationship with Mrs. Van de Velde caused much gossip, and rumors of a *ménage à trois* floated through society. When Grover Cleveland became President in 1885, Harte lost his consulship and became a permanent guest of the Van de Veldes.

Harte's English readers continued to receive his work favorably until his death, although the American audience had long since tired of the sentimental depictions of stock frontier types that brought him initial fame. By the turn of the century, what in 1870 had seemed like a bold, realistic treatment of sex and love seemed rather tame, and the appeal of the Wild West that Harte had pioneered in implanting in the American imagination had become the stuff of myth. When Harte died on May 5, 1902, he had outlived his distinctive contribution to American letters by a generation.

The Outcasts of Poker Flat[1]

As Mr. John Oakhurst, gambler, stepped into the main street of Poker Flat on the morning of the twenty-third of November, 1850, he was conscious of a change in its moral atmosphere from the preceding night. Two or three men, conversing earnestly together, ceased as he approached, and exchanged significant glances. There was a Sabbath lull in the air, which, in a settlement unused to Sabbath influences, looked ominous.

Mr. Oakhurst's calm, handsome face betrayed small concern of these indications. Whether he was conscious of any predisposing cause, was another question. "I reckon they're after somebody," he reflected; "likely it's me." He returned to his pocket the handkerchief with which he had been whipping away the red dust of Poker Flat from his neat boots, and quietly discharged his mind of any further conjecture.

In point of fact, Poker Flat was "after somebody." It had lately suffered the loss of several thousand dollars, two valuable horses, and a prominent citizen. It was experiencing a spasm of virtuous reaction, quite as lawless and ungovernable as any of the acts that had provoked it. A secret committee[2] had determined to rid the town of all improper persons. This was done permanently in regard of two men who were then hanging from the boughs of a sycamore in the gulch, and temporarily in the banishment of certain other objectionable characters. I regret to say that some of these were ladies. It is but due to the sex, however, to state that their impropriety was professional, and it was only in such easily established standards of evil that Poker Flat ventured to sit in judgment.

1. First published in *Overland Monthly*, January, 1869, the source of the present text, and collected in the *Luck of Roaring Camp and Other Sketches* (Boston: Fields, Osgood, 1870).

2. I.e., vigilance committee—a volunteer committee of citizens organized to suppress and punish crime summarily when the processes of law appear inadequate.

Mr. Oakhurst was right in supposing that he was included in this category. A few of the committee had urged hanging him as a possible example, and a sure method of reimbursing themselves from his pockets of the sums he had won from them. "It's agin justice," said Jim Wheeler, "to let this yer young man from Roaring Camp—an entire stranger—carry away our money." But a crude sentiment of equity residing in the breasts of those who had been fortunate enough to win from Mr. Oakhurst, overruled this narrower local prejudice.

Mr. Oakhurst received his sentence with philosophic calmness, none the less coolly, that he was aware of the hesitation of his judges. He was too much of a gambler not to accept Fate. With him life was at best an uncertain game, and he recognized the usual percentage in favor of the dealer.

A body of armed men accompanied the deported wickedness of Poker Flat to the outskirts of the settlement. Besides Mr. Oakhurst, who was known to be a coolly desperate man, and for whose intimidation the armed escort was intended, the expatriated party consisted of a young woman familiarly known as "The Duchess;" another, who had gained the infelicitous title of "Mother Shipton,"[3] and "Uncle Billy," a suspected sluice-robber[4] and confirmed drunkard. The cavalcade provoked no comments from the spectators, nor was any word uttered by the escort. Only when the gulch which marked the uttermost limit of Poker Flat was reached, the leader spoke briefly and to the point. The exiles were forbidden to return at the peril of their lives.

As the escort disappeared, their pent-up feelings found vent in a few hysterical tears from "The Duchess," some bad language from Mother Shipton, and a Partheian[5] volley of expletives from Uncle Billy. The philosophic Oakhurst alone remained silent. He listened calmly to Mother Shipton's desire to cut somebody's heart out, to the repeated statements of "The Duchess" that she would die in the road, and to the alarming oaths that seemed to be bumped out of Uncle Billy as he rode forward. With the easy good-humor characteristic of his class, he insisted upon exchanging his own riding-horse, "Five Spot," for the sorry mule which the Duchess rode. But even this act did not draw the party into any closer sympathy. The young woman readjusted her somewhat draggled plumes with a feeble, faded coquetry; Mother Shipton eyed the possessor of "Five Spot" with malevolence, and Uncle Billy included the whole party in one sweeping anathema.

The road to Sandy Bar—a camp that not having as yet experienced the regenerating influences of Poker Flat, consequently

---

3. Mother Shipton (1488–1560), an English witch who was carried off by the devil and bore him an imp. Her prophecies were edited by S. Baker in 1797.
4. A sluice is an inclined trough or flume for washing or separating gold from earth.
5. An ancient people of southwest Asia noted for firing shots while in real or feigned retreat.

seemed to offer some invitation to the emigrants—lay over a steep mountain range. It was distant a day's severe journey. In that advanced season, the party soon passed out of the moist, temperate regions of the foot-hills, into the dry, cold, bracing air of the Sierras. The trail was narrow and difficult. At noon the Duchess, rolling out of her saddle upon the ground, declared her intention of going no further, and the party halted.

The spot was singularly wild and impressive. A wooded amphitheatre, surrounded on three sides by precipitous cliffs of naked granite, sloped gently toward the crest of another precipice that overlooked the valley. It was undoubtedly the most suitable spot for a camp, had camping been advisable. But Mr. Oakhurst knew that scarcely half the journey to Sandy Bar was accomplished, and the party were not equipped or provisioned for delay. This fact he pointed out to his companions curtly, with a philosophic commentary on the folly of "throwing up their hand before the game was played out." But they were furnished with liquor, which in this emergency stood them in place of food, fuel, rest and prescience. In spite of his remonstrances, it was not long before they were more or less under its influence. Uncle Billy passed rapidly from a bellicose state into one of stupor, the Duchess became maudlin, and Mother Shipton snored. Mr. Oakhurst alone remained erect, leaning against a rock, calmly surveying them.

Mr. Oakhurst did not drink. It interfered with a profession which required coolness, impassiveness and presence of mind, and, in his own language, he "couldn't afford it." As he gazed at his recumbent fellow-exiles, the loneliness begotten of his pariah-trade, his habits of life, his very vices, for the first time seriously oppressed him. He bestirred himself in dusting his black clothes, washing his hands and face, and other acts characteristic of his studiously neat habits, and for a moment forgot his annoyance. The thought of deserting his weaker and more pitiable companions never perhaps occurred to him. Yet he could not help feeling the want of that excitement, which singularly enough was most conducive to that calm equanimity for which he was notorious. He looked at the gloomy walls that rose a thousand feet sheer above the circling pines around him; at the sky, ominously clouded; at the valley below, already deepening into shadow. And doing so, suddenly he heard his own name called.

A horseman slowly ascended the trail. In the fresh, open face of the new-comer, Mr. Oakhurst recognized Tom Simson, otherwise known as "The Innocent" of Sandy Bar. He had met him some months before over a "little game," and had, with perfect equanimity, won the entire fortune—amounting to some forty dollars—of that guileless youth. After the game was finished. Mr. Oakhurst drew the youthful speculator behind the door and thus addressed him: "Tommy, you're a good little man, but you can't gamble worth a cent. Don't try it over again." He then handed him his money back, pushed him gently from the room, and so made a devoted slave of Tom Simson.

There was a remembrance of this in his boyish and enthusiastic greeting of Mr. Oakhurst. He had started, he said, to go to Poker Flat to seek his fortune. "Alone?" No, not exactly alone; in fact—a giggle—he had run away with Piney Woods. Didn't Mr. Oakhurst remember Piney? She that used to wait on the table at the Temperance House? They had been engaged a long time, but old Jake Woods had objected, and so they had run away, and were going to Poker Flat to be married, and here they were. And they were tired out, and how lucky it was they had found a place to camp and company. All this The Innocent delivered rapidly, while Piney—a stout, comely damsel of fifteen—emerged from behind the pine tree, where she had been blushing unseen, and rode to the side of her lover.

Mr. Oakhurst seldom troubled himself with sentiment. Still less with propriety. But he had a vague idea that the situation was not felicitous. He retained, however, his presence of mind sufficiently to kick Uncle Billy, who was about to say something, and Uncle Billy was sober enough to recognize in Mr. Oakhurst's kick a superior power that would not bear trifling. He then endeavored to dissuade Tom Simson from delaying further, but in vain. He even pointed out the fact that there was no provision, nor means of making a camp. But, unluckily, "The Innocent" met this objection by assuring the party that he was provided with an extra mule loaded with provisions, and by the discovery of a rude attempt at a log-house near the trail. "Piney can stay with Mrs. Oakhurst," said The Innocent, pointing to the Duchess, "and I can shift for myself."

Nothing but Mr. Oakhurst's admonishing foot saved Uncle Billy from bursting into a roar of laughter. As it was, he felt compelled to retire up the cañon until he could recover his gravity. There he confided the joke to the tall pine trees, with many slaps of his leg, contortions of his face, and the usual profanity. But when he returned to the party, he found them seated by a fire—for the air had grown strangely chill and the sky overcast—in apparently amicable conversation. Piney was actually talking in an impulsive, girlish fashion to the Duchess, who was listening with an interest and animation she had not shown for many days. The Innocent was holding forth, apparently with equal effect, to Mr. Oakhurst and Mother Shipton, who was actually relaxing into amiability. "Is this yer a d——d picnic?" said Uncle Billy, with inward scorn, as he surveyed the sylvan group, the glancing fire-light and the tethered animals in the foreground. Suddenly an idea mingled with the alcoholic fumes that disturbed his brain. It was apparently of a jocular nature, for he felt impelled to slap his leg again and cram his fist into his mouth.

As the shadows crept slowly up the mountain, a slight breeze rocked the tops of the pine trees, and moaned through their long and gloomy aisles. The ruined cabin, patched and covered with pine boughs, was set apart for the ladies. As the lovers parted, they unaffectedly exchanged a parting kiss, so honest and sincere that it might have been heard above the swaying pines. The frail Duchess and the malevolent Mother Shipton were probably too stunned to remark upon this last evidence of simplicity, and so turned without a word to the hut. The fire was replenished, the men lay down before the door, and in a few minutes were asleep.

Mr. Oakhurst was a light sleeper. Toward morning he awoke benumbed and cold. As he stirred the dying fire, the wind, which was now blowing strongly, brought to his cheek that which caused the blood to leave it—snow!

He started to his feet with the intention of awakening the sleepers, for there was no time to lose. But turning to where Uncle Billy had been lying he found him gone. A suspicion leaped to his brain and a curse to his lips. He ran to the spot where the mules had been tethered; they were no longer there. The tracks were already rapidly disappearing in the snow.

The momentary excitement brought Mr. Oakhurst back to the fire with his usual calm. He did not waken the sleepers. The Innocent slumbered peacefully, with a smile on his good-humored, freckled face; the virgin Piney slept beside her frailer sisters as sweetly as though attended by celestial guardians, and Mr. Oakhurst, drawing his blanket over his shoulders, stroked his mustachios and waited for the dawn. It came slowly in a whirling mist of snowflakes, that dazzled and confused the eye. What could be seen of the landscape appeared magically changed. He looked over the valley, and summed up the present and future in two words—"Snowed in!"

A careful inventory of the provisions, which, fortunately for the party, had been stored within the hut, and so escaped the felonious fingers of Uncle Billy, disclosed the fact that with care and prudence they might last ten days longer. "That is," said Mr. Oakhurst, *sotto voce*[6] to The Innocent, "if you're willing to board us. If you aint—and perhaps you'd better not—you can wait till Uncle Billy gets back with provisions." For some occult reason, Mr. Oakhurst could not bring himself to disclose Uncle Billy's rascality, and so offered the hypothesis that he had wandered from the camp and had accidentally stampeded the animals. He dropped a warning to the Duchess and Mother Shipton, who of course knew the facts of their associate's defection. "They'll find out the truth about us *all*, when they find out anything," he added, significantly, "and there's no good frightening them now."

Tom Simson not only put all his worldly store at the disposal of Mr. Oakhurst, but seemed to enjoy the prospect of their enforced seclusion. "We'll have a good camp for a week, and then the

6. In an undertone.

snow'll melt, and we'll all go back together." The cheerful gayety of the young man and Mr. Oakhurst's calm infected the others. The Innocent, with the aid of pine boughs, extemporized a thatch for the roofless cabin, and the Duchess directed Piney in the reärrangement of the interior with a taste and tact that opened the blue eyes of that provincial maiden to their fullest extent. "I reckon now you're used to fine things at Poker Flat," said Piney. The Duchess turned away sharply to conceal something that reddened her cheeks through its professional tint, and Mother Shipton requested Piney not to "chatter." But when Mr. Oakhurst returned from a weary search for the trail, he heard the sound of happy laughter echoed from the rocks. He stopped in some alarm, and his thoughts first naturally reverted to the whiskey—which he had prudently *cachéd*. "And yet it don't somehow sound like whiskey," said the gambler. It was not until he caught sight of the blazing fire through the still blinding storm, and the group around it, that he settled to the conviction that it was "square fun."

Whether Mr. Oakhurst had *cachéd* his cards with the whiskey as something debarred the free access of the community, I cannot say. It was certain that, in Mother Shipton's words, he "didn't say cards once" during that evening. Haply the time was beguiled by an accordeon, produced somewhat ostentatiously by Tom Simson, from his pack. Notwithstanding some difficulties attending the manipulation of this instrument, Piney Woods managed to pluck several reluctant melodies from its keys, to an accompaniment by The Innocent on a pair of bone castinets. But the crowning festivity of the evening was reached in a rude camp-meeting hymn, which the lovers, joining hands, sang with great earnestness and vociferation. I fear that a certain defiant tone and Covenanter's swing[7] to its chorus, rather than any devotional quality, caused it to speedily infect the others, who at last joined in the refrain:

> "I'm proud to live in the service of the Lord,
> And I'm bound to die in His army."[8]

The pines rocked, the storm eddied and whirled above the miserable group, and the flames of their altar leaped heavenward, as if in token of the vow.

At midnight the storm abated, the rolling clouds parted, and the stars glittered keenly above the sleeping camp. Mr. Oakhurst, whose professional habits had enabled him to live on the smallest possible amount of sleep, in dividing the watch with Tom Simson, somehow managed to take upon himself the greater part of that duty. He excused himself to The Innocent, by saying that he had "often

---

7. Covenanters were Scottish Presbyterians of the 16th and 17th centuries who bound themselves by a series of oaths or covenants to the Presbyterian doctrine and demanded separation from the Church of England. "Covenanter's swing" would indicate that the hymn would be sung with a vigorous rhythm with a martial beat.
8. Refrain of the early American spiritual *Service of the Lord*.

been a week without sleep." "Doing what?" asked Tom. "Poker!"
replied Oakhurst, sententiously; "when a man gets a streak of luck
—nigger-luck[9]—he don't get tired. The luck gives in first. Luck,"
continued the gambler, reflectively, "is a mighty queer thing. All
you know about it for certain is that it's bound to change. And it's
finding out when it's going to change that makes you. We've had a
streak of bad luck since we left Poker Flat—you come along and
slap you get into it, too. If you can hold your cards right along
you're all right. For," added the gambler, with cheerful irrelevance,

> "I'm proud to live in the service of the Lord,
> And I'm bound to die in His army."

The third day came, and the sun, looking through the white-cur-
tained valley, saw the outcasts divide their slowly decreasing store of
provisions for the morning meal. It was one of the peculiarities of that
mountain climate that its rays diffused a kindly warmth over the
wintry landscape, as if in regretful commiseration of the past. But it
revealed drift on drift of snow piled high around the hut; a hopeless,
uncharted, trackless sea of white lying below the rocky shores to
which the castaways still clung. Through the marvellously clear air,
the smoke of the pastoral village of Poker Flat rose miles away.
Mother Shipton saw it, and from a remote pinnacle of her rocky
fastness, hurled in that direction a final malediction. It was her last
vituperative attempt, and perhaps for that reason was invested with
a certain degree of sublimity. It did her good, she privately
informed the Duchess. "Just you go out there and cuss, and see."
She then set herself to the task of amusing 'the child," as she and
the Duchess were pleased to call Piney. Piney was no chicken, but
it was a soothing and ingenious theory of the pair to thus account
for the fact that she didn't swear and wasn't improper.

When night crept up again through the gorges, the reedy notes
of the accordeon rose and fell in fitful spasms and long-drawn gasps
by the flickering camp-fire. But music failed to fill entirely the
aching void left by insufficient food, and a new diversion was proposed by Piney—story-telling. Neither Mr. Oakhurst nor his
female companions caring to relate their personal experiences, this
plan would have failed, too, but for The Innocent. Some months
before he had chanced upon a stray copy of Mr. Pope's[1] ingenious
translation of the Iliad. He now proposed to narrate the principal
incidents of that poem—having thoroughly mastered the argument
and fairly forgotten the words—in the current vernacular of Sandy
Bar. And so for the rest of that night the Homeric demi-gods again
walked the earth. Trojan bully and wily Greek wrestled in the
winds, and the great pines in the cañon seemed to bow to the wrath
of the son of Peleus.[2] Mr. Oakhurst listened with quiet satisfaction.

9. I.e., very good fortune.
1. Alexander Pope (1688–1744), English
poet who translated Homer's *Iliad* (and
Odyssey) into the Heroic couplets for
which Pope is famous.
2. Achilles, chief hero on the Greek side
of the Trojan War.

Most especially was he interested in the fate of "Ash-heels,"[3] as The Innocent persisted in denominating the "swift-footed Achilles."

So with small food and much of Homer and the accordeon, a week passed over the heads of the outcasts. The sun again forsook them, and again from leaden skies the snow-flakes were sifted over the land. Day by day closer around them drew the snowy circle, until at last they looked from their prison over drifted walls of dazzling white, that towered twenty feet above their heads. It became more and more difficult to replenish their fires, even from the fallen trees beside them, now half-hidden in the drifts. And yet no one complained. The lovers turned from the dreary prospect and looked into each other's eyes, and were happy. Mr. Oakhurst settled himself coolly to the losing game before him. The Duchess, more cheerful than she had been, assumed the care of Piney. Only Mother Shipton—once the strongest of the party—seemed to sicken and fade. At midnight on the tenth day she called Oakhurst to her side. "I'm going," she said, in a voice of querulous weakness, "but don't say anything about it. Don't waken the kids. Take the bundle from under my head and open it." Mr. Oakhurst did so. It contained Mother Shipton's rations for the last week, untouched. "Give 'em to the child," she said, pointing to the sleeping Piney. "You've starved yourself," said the gambler. "That's what they call it," said the woman querulously, as she lay down again, and turning her face to the wall, passed quietly away.

The accordeon and the bones were put aside that day, and Homer was forgotten. When the body of Mother Shipton had been committed to the snow, Mr. Oakhurst took The Innocent aside, and showed him a pair of snow-shoes, which he had fashioned from the old pack-saddle. "There's one chance in a hundred to save her yet," he said, pointing to Piney; "but it's there," he added, pointing toward Poker Flat. "If you can reach there in two days she's safe." "And you?" asked Tom Simson. "I'll stay here," was the curt reply.

The lovers parted with a long embrace. "You are not going, too," said the Duchess, as she saw Mr. Oakhurst apparently waiting to accompany him. "As far as the cañon," he replied. He turned suddenly, and kissed the Duchess, leaving her pallid face aflame, and her trembling limbs rigid with amazement.

Night came, but not Mr. Oakhurst. It brought the storm again and the whirling snow. Then the Duchess, feeding the fire, found that some one had quietly piled beside the hut enough fuel to last a few days longer. The tears rose to her eyes, but she hid them from Piney.

The women slept but little. In the morning, looking into each

---

3. The mispronunciation emphasizes Achilles' one vulnerable spot, his heel, by which his mother Thetis held him when she dipped him in the River Styx to make him invulnerable.

other's faces, they read their fate. Neither spoke; but Piney, accepting the position of the stronger, drew near and placed her arm around the Duchess's waist. They kept this attitude for the rest of the day. That night the storm reached its greatest fury, and rending asunder the protecting pines, invaded the very hut.

Toward morning they found themselves unable to feed the fire, which gradually died away. As the embers slowly blackened, the Duchess crept closer to Piney, and broke the silence of many hours: "Piney, can you pray?" "No, dear," said Piney, simply. The Duchess, without knowing exactly why, felt relieved, and putting her head upon Piney's shoulder, spoke no more. And so reclining, the younger and purer pillowing the head of her soiled sister upon her virgin breast, they fell asleep.

The wind lulled as if it feared to waken them. Feathery drifts of snow, shaken from the long pine boughs, flew like white-winged birds, and settled about them as they slept. The moon through the rifted clouds looked down upon what had been the camp. But all human stain, all trace of earthly travail, was hidden beneath the spotless mantle mercifully flung from above.

They slept all that day and the next, nor did they waken when voices and footsteps broke the silence of the camp. And when pitying fingers brushed the snow from their wan faces, you could scarcely have told from the equal peace that dwelt upon them, which was she that had sinned. Even the Law of Poker Flat recognized this, and turned away, leaving them still locked in each other's arms.

But at the head of the gulch, on one of the largest pine trees, they found the deuce of clubs pinned to the bark with a bowie knife. It bore the following, written in pencil, in a firm hand:

✝

BENEATH THIS TREE

LIES THE BODY

OF

JOHN OAKHURST,

WHO STRUCK A STREAK OF BAD LUCK

ON THE 23D OF NOVEMBER, 1850,

AND

HANDED IN HIS CHECKS

ON THE 7TH DECEMBER, 1850

✝

And pulseless and cold, with a Derringer[4] by his side and a bullet in his heart, though still calm as in life, beneath the snow, lay he who was at once the strongest and yet the weakest of the outcasts of Poker Flat.   1869, 1870

---

4. Short-barreled pocket pistol, named after its 19th-century American inventor, Henry Deringer.

W. D. HOWELLS
1837–1920

No other American writer has dominated the literary scene the way William Dean Howells did in his prime. As a steadily productive novelist, playwright, critic, essayist, and editor, Howells was always in the public eye, and his influence during the 1880s and 1890s on a growing, serious middle-class readership was incalculable. He made that emerging middle class aware of itself: in his writings an entire generation discovered through his faithful description of familiar places, his dramatizations of ordinary lives, and his shrewd analyses of shared moral issues, its tastes, its social behavior, its values, and its problems. Howells was by temperament genial and modest, but he was also forthright and tough-minded. He was, as the critic Lionel Trilling has observed, a deeply civil man with a balanced sense of life. Perhaps that is why, when he died in 1920, the spontaneous outpouring of sorrow and admiration was the kind reserved for national heroes.

Howells's eminence had its roots in humble beginnings. He was born, one of eight children, in the postfrontier village of Martin's Ferry, Ohio, on March 1, 1837, to a poor, respectable, proud, and culturally informed family. Like his contemporary Mark Twain and their predecessor Ben Franklin, Howells went to school at the printer's office, setting type for the series of unsuccessful newspapers that his good-natured, somewhat impractical father owned. Though the family moved around a good deal in Ohio, Howells's youth was secure and, on the whole, happy. His mother, he observed, had the gift of making each child feel that he or she was the center of the world.

From his earliest years Howells had both literary passions and literary ambitions. When he was not setting type or reading Goldsmith, Irving, Shakespeare, Dickens, Thackeray, or other favorites, he was teaching himself several foreign languages. Howells tried his hand at a number of literary forms in his teens, but his first regular jobs involved writing for newspapers in Columbus and Cincinnati. It was as a journalist that he made his first pilgrimage to New England in 1860, where he was treated with remarkable generosity by such literary readers as Lowell, Holmes, Emerson, and Hawthorne, who must have recognized that he possessed talent and the will to succeed, as well as courtesy and deference.

A campaign biography of Lincoln, his first significant book, won for Howells the consulship at Venice in 1861. There he wrote the series of travel letters that eventually became *Venetian Life* (1866); more importantly, they made his name known in eastern literary circles. When he returned to America in 1866, he went to work in New York briefly for the *Nation* until James T. Fields offered him the assistant editorship of the enormously prestigious and influential *Atlantic Monthly*, to which he had contributed some of his earliest verse before the war. In effect Howells assumed active control of the magazine from the very beginning, and he succeeded officially to the editorship in 1871, a position he held until he resigned in 1881 in order to have more time to write fiction. Because the *Atlantic* was the pre-eminent literary magazine of the day, Howells had, as a young man, the power to make or break careers, a power he exercised tactfully and responsibly.

Howells had been finding his way as a novelist during his ten years as editor, publishing seven novels in this period, beginning with *Their Wedding Journey* (1872) and concluding with *The Undiscovered Country* (1880). These first novels are short, uncomplicated linear narratives which deliberately eschew the passionate, heroic, action-packed, and exciting adventures that were the staple of American fiction of the time, a fiction read chiefly by middle-class women.

In the 1880s Howells came into his own as novelist and critic. A *Modern Instance* (1882) examines psychic, familial, and social disintegration under the pressure of the secularization and urbanization of post–Civil War America, the disintegration that is Howells's central and deepest subject. Three years later Howells published his most famous novel, *The Rise of Silas Lapham* (1885). Within a year of its publication Howells, who was ostensibly successful and financially secure, suddenly felt that "the bottom had dropped out" of his life, had been profoundly affected by Tolstoy's Christian socialism, and publicly defended the "Haymarket Anarchists," a group of Chicago workers, several of whom were executed without clear proof of their complicity in a dynamiting at a public demonstration. After *Lapham*, Howells offered more direct, ethical criticism of social and economic anomalies and inequities in such succeeding novels as the popular, large-canvassed *A Hazard of New Fortunes* (1890) and the utopian romance *A Traveler from Altruria* (1894). In these same years Howells also penetrated more deeply into individual consciousness, particularly in two short novels, *The Shadow of a Dream* (1890) and *An Imperative Duty* (1892).

In his later years Howells sustained and deepened his varied literary output. Among his novels of consequence in this period are the naturalistic *The Landlord at Lion's Head* (1897) and the elegiac *The Vacation of the Kelwyns* (published posthumously, 1920). He also wrote charming and vivid autobiography and reminiscence in *A Boy's Town* (1890) and *Years of My Youth* (1916), and as he had since the 1870s, Howells continued to produce plays and farces which served, as one critic has remarked, as "finger exercises for his novels."

In the mid 1880s Howells had aggressively argued the case for realism and against the "romanticistic," promoting Henry James in particular at the expense of such English novelists as Scott, Dickens, and Thackeray. In *The Editor's Study* essays he wrote for *Harper's Monthly* starting in 1886 (and some of which in 1891 he made into *Criticism and Fiction*), Howells attacked sentimentality of thought and feeling and the falsification of moral nature and ethical options wherever he found them in fiction. He believed that realism "was nothing more or less than the truthful treatment of material," especially the motives and actions of *ordinary* men and women. He insisted, sooner and more vigorously than any other American critic, that the novel be objective or dramatic in point of view; solidly based in convincingly motivated characters speaking the language of actual men and women; free of contrived events or melodramatic effects; true to the particulars of a recent time and specific place; ethically and aesthetically a seamless piece. Indeed, perhaps the polemical nature of his critical stance in the 1880s did as much as anything to obscure until recently the flexibility and range of his sensibility. Certainly *Novel-Writing and Novel-Reading*, first delivered as a lecture in 1899, suggests more accurately than *Criticism and*

Fiction (1891) the shrewdness, common sense, and penetrating thoughtfulness that characterize his criticism at its best.

In the course of his life-long career as literary arbiter, Howells was remarkably international in outlook, and promoted in his diverse critical writings such non-American contemporaries as Ivan Turgenev, Benito Pérez Galdós, Björnstjerne Björnson, Leo Tolstoy, Henrik Ibsen, Émile Zola, George Eliot, and Thomas Hardy. Howells also championed many younger American writers and early recognized many talented women writers in the relentless stream of reviews he wrote over six decades—among them Sarah Orne Jewett, Mary E. Wilkins Freeman, Edith Wharton, and Emily Dickinson. He is even better known for actively promoting the careers of such emerging realists and naturalists as Stephen Crane, Hamlin Garland, and Frank Norris. His chief fault as critic—if it is one—was excessive generosity, though he never falsely flattered or encouraged anyone.

The two contemporaries in whom Howells had the greatest critical confidence were Henry James and Mark Twain, both of whom he served since the 1860s as editor and with both of whom he also sustained a personal friendship of forty years and more. In the late 1860s, Howells had walked the Cambridge streets with James, discussing the present state and future prospects for the substance and techniques of fiction. As editor of *Atlantic Monthly*, Howells had accepted a number of James's early tales. Throughout his career he wrote essays and reviews in praise of James's work; on his deathbed Howells was working on an essay, *The American James*. He genuinely admired and was friendly with the patrician James, but he clearly loved and was more intimate with the rough-textured Twain. *My Mark Twain*, written immediately after his friend's death in 1910, records that affection in one of the enduring memoirs of our literary history.

By the time Howells died, he had served for thirteen years as first president of the American Academy of Arts and Letters, the organization which seeks to identify and honor the most distinguished work in these fields, and was himself a national institution. For rebels and iconoclasts like H. L. Mencken, Sinclair Lewis, and a young Van Wyck Brooks, he epitomized the dead hand of the past, the genteel, Victorian enemy. Since the 1930s, however, Howells's reputation has slowly recovered from these charges. The courage of his liberal—at times radical—perspective in his own time has been acknowledged; his steady, masterful style has been given its due; and his intelligent civility has been commended.

Novel-Writing and Novel-Reading: An Impersonal Explanation[1]

It was Thackeray[2] who noted how actors, when they had a holiday, always went and saw a play. I fancy that they form the kindest

1. This essay is a corrected transcription of a draft manuscript of one of two lectures Howells gave during a tour of the East and Midwest he made in 1899 under the auspices of the lecture agent James B. Pond. The manuscript survives in the Rutherford B. Hayes Library, Fremont, Ohio; while Howells himself never prepared it for publication, a slightly different version was edited by William M. Gibson and published, first, in the *Bulletin* of the New York Public Library in January, 1958, and later as a monograph, also by the New York Public Library. The present text, copyright 1978 by the Indiana University Press and the Howells Edition Editorial Board, was prepared for *A Selected Edition of W. D. Howells* and is used with permission. The notes were prepared by the present editor.

2. William Makepeace Thackeray (1811–63), English novelist.

and best part of the house at such times. They know how hard it is to do what the people on the stage are doing; if they are quick to what is ill-done, they are quick to what is well done, too; and from what I have seen of their behavior at actors' matinées,[3] as they are called, when the profession pretty much fills the house, I am ready to say, that they are the most lenient, the most generous of all the spectators.

It is much the same, I believe, with novelists, whom I will assume for the purposes of illustration, to be so largely of my own mind and make, that I need not consider those who are otherwise. In fact, I will assume, as a working hypothesis that I am exactly like every other novelist, and I will speak for the whole body of fiction-mongers in saying that when I get a day off from a novel of my own, there is nothing I like so much as to lose myself in the novel of some one else. When I have not a whole day, I am very glad of a half day, or even such hours and halfhours as I can steal from sleep after going to bed at night, and before getting up in the morning. I do not despise other kinds of reading. I like history, I like biography, I like travels, I like poetry, I like drama, I like metaphysics; but I suspect that if I could once be got to tell the whole truth, it would appear that I liked all these in the measure they reminded me of the supreme literary form, the fine flower of the human story, the novel; and if I have anywhere said anything else to the contrary, I take it back, at least for the time being.

You would have thought perhaps that having written so many novels myself,—the procession has now been some twenty-five years in passing a given point,—I would not care to read any; but we novelists, like the actors, are so in love with our art that we cannot get enough of it; and rather than read no novels at all, I would read my own, over and over again. In fact I often do this, and I have probably read them more times than any person present, not because I admire them so very much, but because when I find myself in a difficult place in some new one, I can learn from the old ones how I once behaved in another difficult place. If I go to some other novelist's book to take a leaf from it, I am apt to become so interested in the story, that I forget what I went to it for, and rise from it as honest as I sat down. But I know the story in my own books so thoroughly that I can give myself without hindrance to the study of the method, which is what I want.

That is what we go to one another's novels for. We read them for pleasure, of course, but for a pleasure quite different from that which other readers find in them. The pleasure they yield is probably greater for us than for any other kind of reader; but again we are like the actors at the play: we are all the time, consciously or unconsciously, taking note how the thing is done. We may forget the shop, as I have just now pretended, but the shop does not forget

3. I.e., afternoon benefit performances.

us; sooner or later we find that we have had it with us; and here appears that chasmal difference between the author and the reader, which Goethe[4] says can never be bridged. The reader who is not an author considers what the book is; the author who is a reader, considers, will he, nill he, how the book has been done. It is so in every art. The painter, sculptor, architect, musician feels to his inmost soul the beauty of the picture, statue, edifice, symphony, but he feels still more thoroughly the skill which manifests that beauty. This difference is from everlasting to everlasting, and it disposes instantly of the grotesque pretension that the artist is not the best critic of his art. He is the best of all possible critics. Others may learn to enjoy, to reason and to infer in the presence of a work of art; but he alone who has wrought in the same kind can feel and know concerning it from instinct and from experience. Construction and criticism go hand in hand. No man ever yet imagined beauty without imagining more beauty and less; he *senses*, as the good common phrase has it, the limitations to the expression of beauty; and if he is an artist he puts himself in the place of the man who made the thing of beauty before him, clothes himself in his possibilities, and lives the failure and the success which it records. His word, if honest, is the supreme criticism.

By beauty of course I mean truth, for the one involves the other; it is only the false in art which is ugly, and it is only the false which is immoral. The truth may be indecent, but it cannot be vicious, it can never corrupt or deprave; and I should say this in defence of the grossest material honestly treated in modern novels as against the painted and perfumed meretriciousness of the novels that went before them. I conceive that apart from all the clamor about schools of fiction is the question of truth, how to get it in, so that it may get itself out again as beauty, the divinely living thing, which all men love and worship. So I make truth the prime test of a novel. If I do not find that it is like life, then it does not exist for me as art; it is ugly, it is ludicrous, it is impossible. I do not expect a novel to be wholly true; I have never read one that seemed to me so except Tolstoy's[5] novels; but I expect it to be a constant endeavor for the truth, and I perceive beauty in it so far as it fulfills this endeavor. I am quite willing to recognize and enjoy whatever measure of truth I find in a novel that is partly or mainly false; only, if I come upon the falsehood at the outset I am apt not to read that novel. But I do not bear such a grudge against it as I do against the novel which lures me on with a fair face of truth, and drops the mask midway. If you ask me for illustrations, I am somewhat at a loss, but if you ask me for examples, they are manifold. In English I should say the truthful novelists or those working with an ideal of truth were Jane

4. Johann Wolfgang von Goethe (1749–1832), German poet, dramatist, novelist, and scientist.

5. Leo Tolstoy (1828–1910), Russian novelist and religious philosopher.

Austen, George Eliot, Anthony Trollope, Thomas Hardy, Mrs. Humphrey Ward, George Moore; in French, Flaubert, Maupassant, the Goncourts, Daudet and Zola; in Russian, Tourguenief and Tolstoy; in Spanish, Valdés, Galdós and Pardo-Bazan; in Norwegian, Björnson, Lie, and Kielland. In English, some untruthful novelists, or those working from an ideal of effect, are Thackeray, Dickens, Bulwer, Reade, and all their living followers; in French, Dumas, Feuillet, Ohnet; in Spanish Valera; in Russian, measurably Doystoyevsky;[6] in Norwegian, none that I know of. It is right to say, however that of some of the untruthful novelists, and notably of Thackeray, that they were the victims of their period. If Thackeray had been writing in our time, I have no question but he would have been one of its most truthful artists.

The truth which I mean, the truth which is the only beauty, is truth to human experience, and human experience is so manifold and so recondite, that no scheme can be too remote, too airy for the test. It is a well ascertained fact concerning the imagination that it can work only with the stuff of experience. It can absolutely create nothing; it can only compose. The most fantastic extravagance comes under the same law that exacts likeness to the known as well as the closest and severest study of life. Once for all, then, obedience to this law is the creed of the realist, and rebellion is the creed of the romanticist. Both necessarily work under it, but one willingly, to beautiful effect, and the other unwillingly to ugly effect.

For the reader, whether he is an author too, or not, the only test of a novel's truth is his own knowledge of life. Is it like what he has seen or felt? Then it is true, and for him it cannot otherwise be true, that is to say beautiful. It will not avail that it has style, learning, thinking, feeling; it is no more beautiful without truth than the pretty statue which cannot stand on its feet. It is very astonishing to me that any sort of people can find pleasure in such a thing; but I know that there are many who do; and I should not think of consigning them to the police for their bad taste so long as their taste alone is bad. At the same time I confess that I should suspect an unreality, an insincerity in a mature and educated person whom I found liking an unreal, an insincere novel. You see, I take novels rather seriously, and I would hold them to a much stricter account

6. Jane Austen (1775–1817), George Eliot (1819–80), Anthony Trollope (1815–82), Thomas Hardy (1840–1928), Mrs. Humphrey Ward (1851–1920), and George Moore (1852–1933), English novelists; Gustave Flaubert (1821–80), Guy de Maupassant (1850–93), Edmond de Goncourt (1822–96) and Jules de Goncourt (1830–70), Alphonse Daudet (1840–97), Émile Zola (1840–1902), French novelists; Ivan Turgenev (1818–83) and Leo Tolstoy (1828–1910), Russian novelists; Armando Palacio Valdés (1853–1938), Benito Pérez Galdós (1843–1920), Emilia Pardo Bazán (1852–1921), Spanish novelists; Björnstjerne Martinius Björnson (1832–1910), Jonas Lauritz Idemil Lie (1833–1909), Alexander Lange Kielland (1849–1906), Norwegian novelists; William Makepeace Thackeray (1811–63), Charles Dickens (1812–70), Edward George Earle Lytton Bulwer-Lytton (1803–73), Charles Reade (1814–84), English novelists; Alexandre Dumas (1802–70), Octave Feuillet (1821–90), Georges Ohnet (1848–1918), French novelists; Juan Valera y Alcalá Galiano (1824–1905), Spanish novelist; Feodor Dostoevsky (1821–81), Russian novelist.

than they are commonly held to. If I could, I would have them all subject to the principles that govern an honest man, and do not suffer him to tell lies of any sort. I think the novelist is rarely the victim of such a possession, or obsession, that he does not know when he is representing and when he is misrepresenting life. If he does not know it fully at the time, he cannot fail to be aware of it upon review of his work. In the frenzy of inspiration, he may not know that he has been lying; but a time will quickly come to him, if he is at all an artist, when he will know it, and will see that the work he has done is ugly because of it. That is the time for him to tear up his work, and to begin anew.

Of course, there are several ways of regarding life in fiction, and in order to do justice to the different kinds we ought to distinguish very clearly between them. There are three forms, which I think of, and which I will name in the order of their greatness: the novel, the romance, and the romanticistic novel.

The novel I take to be the sincere and conscientious endeavor to picture life just as it is, to deal with character as we witness it in living people, and to record the incidents that grow out of character. This is the supreme form of fiction, and I offer as supreme examples of it, Pride and Prejudice, Middlemarch, Anna Karenina, Fathers and Sons, Doña Perfecta & Marta y María,[7] sufficiently varied in their origin and material and method, but all of the same absolute honesty in their intention. They all rely for their moral effect simply and solely upon their truth to nature.

The romance is of as great purity of intention as the novel, but it deals with life allegorically and not representatively; it employs types rather than characters, and studies them in the ideal rather than the real; it handles the passions broadly. Altogether the greatest in this kind are The Scarlet Letter and The Marble Faun of Hawthorne, which partake of the nature of poems, and which, as they frankly place themselves outside of familiar experience and circumstance, are not to be judged by the rules of criticism that apply to the novel. In this sort, Judd's Margaret is another eminent example that occurs to me; and some of you will think of Mrs. Shelley's Frankenstein, & of Stevenson's Jekyll and Hyde. I suggest also Chamisso's Peter Schlemihl.[8]

The romanticistic novel professes like the real novel to portray actual life, but it does this with an excess of drawing and coloring

7. Pride and Prejudice (1813) by Jane Austen; Middlemarch (1871–72) by George Eliot; Anna Karenina (1875–77) by Leo Tolstoy; Fathers and Sons (1861) by Ivan Turgenev; Doña Perfecta (1876) by Benito Pérez Galdós; and Marta y María (1883) by Armando Palacio Valdés.
8. The Scarlet Letter (1859), The Marble Faun (1860). Sylvester Judd III (1813–53), American novelist, published Margaret, a Tale of the Real and Ideal, Including Sketches of a Place Not Before Described, Called Mons Christi in 1845; Mary Wollstonecraft Godwin Shelley (1797–1851), English novelist, published Frankenstein in 1818; Robert Louis Stevenson (1850–94), English novelist, published The Strange Case of Dr. Jeckyll and Mr. Hyde in 1886; Adelbert von Chamisso (1781–1838), German writer, published Peter Schlemihls wunderbare Geschichte in 1814.

which are false to nature. It attributes motives to people which do not govern real people, and its characters are of the quality of types; they are heroic, for good or for bad. It seeks effect rather than truth; and endeavors to hide in a cloud of incident the deformity and artificiality of its creations. It revels in the extravagant, the unusual and the bizarre. The worst examples of it are to be found in the fictions of two very great men: Charles Dickens and Victor Hugo;[9] but it prevailed in all languages, except the Russian, from the rise of Bulwer and Balzac to the death of Dickens, in spite of the influence of George Eliot and Thackeray. Both these writers contemned it, but not effectively; the one was too much a moralist, the other too much a sentimentalist and caricaturist; I am speaking broadly. In all that time the most artistic, that is to say the most truthful, English novelist was Anthony Trollope, and he was so unconscious of his excellence, that at times he strove hard for the most inartistic, the most untruthful attitudes of Thackeray. Now, all is changed: not one *great* novelist, not a single one in any European language, in any country, has for the last twenty five years been a romanticistic novelist; while literature swarms with second-rate, third-rate romanticistic novelists. The great novelists of China, of Abyssinia, of Polynesia, may still be romanticists, but they are not so in any Western civilization. If you wish to darken council by asking how it is that these inferior romanticists are still incomparably the most popular novelists, I can only whisper, in strict confidence, that by far the greatest number of people in the world, even the civilized world, are people of weak and childish imagination, pleased with gross fables, fond of prodigies, heroes, heroines, portents and improbabilities, without self-knowledge, and without the wish for it. Only in some such exceptional assemblage as the present, do they even prefer truth to lies in art, and it is a great advance for them to prefer the half-lies which they get in romanticistic novels.

I believe, nevertheless, that the novelist has a grave duty to his reader; and I wish his reader realized that he has a grave duty to the novelist, and ought to exact the truth of him. But most readers think that they ought only to exact amusement of him. They are satisfied if they can get that, and often they have to be satisfied without it. In spite of the fact that the novelist is usually so great a novel-reader himself, I doubt if he is fully conscious of the mind the novel reader commonly brings to the work he has taken so much pains with. Once, a great while ago, when a story of mine was appearing from month to month, a young lady wrote me that she was reading it, with nine other serials, besides novels out of the circulating library,[1] and she liked mine the best of all. I thought it was very kind of her, and I could not help wondering what the

---

9. Victor Hugo (1802–85) and Honoré de Balzac (1779–1850), French novelists.

1. A circulating library rented popular fiction at a low daily rate.

inside of her mind could be like. But the mind of youth, before the world has yet filled it, is hospitable to many guests, and perhaps with all the people of all those stories in it, the mind of this young lady was still tolerably empty. I dare say there is not a person here present but has at some time or other read a novel; it is possible that several may have read two or three serials at the same time; and I would like these to understand that I do not at all object to that way of reading novels. It is much better than not to read novels at all, and I do not know that I felt any reproach for another young lady whose teacher evolved from her the fact that she knew all of what she called the love-parts of my novels, but supposed that I was an Englishman, and that I was dead. It would be no bad thing, I suppose, to be an Englishman if one were dead; and perhaps this may be my palingenesis;[2] but if I were to rise an English novelist I should like to be allowed a choice which.

It is not of novel writers however, that I now wish to speak, but a little more of novel readers, as I have known them. When another story of mine was appearing I had a bill for $30 sent me from a tailor in Chicago for a spring overcoat, against a certain Mr. Ferris. The hero of my novel—he was, as usual,—very unheroic—was Henry Ferris,[3] and the tailor naturally thought that from my intimacy with one member of the family, I would very likely know the address of another.

Only last summer a lady said to me that she wondered I could remember so exactly all that was said and done in a current story of mine; and it appeared that she thought it had all really happened as I had set it down. This was very gratifying in a way, but it was a little dismaying, too; and I fancy it would not be well to peer too earnestly into that chasm which parts authors and readers. Many people read your book without ever looking at the title page, or knowing who wrote it, or caring. This is the wholly unliterary sort, who do not know apparently how books come to be, or how they differ in origin from products of the loom or plough. There is another sort who amiably confuse you with some brother author, and praise you for novels that you have never written. I remember that one night at the White House one of the ladies who was receiving had the goodness to say that she was reading my story of The Bostonians with so much interest. I was forced to disclaim the honor done me; I could only thank her and add that I liked The Bostonians too, as I did everything that Henry James wrote.[4] Upon this we both fell into some embarrassment, I do know why; she excused herself for her blunder; of course, the story was Mr. James's; she knew that; and she asked me if I would be introduced to the Secretary of the Periphery (that was not really the office)

2. I.e., rebirth.
3. Henry Ferris was the sensitive young observer of Howells's *A Foregone Con-* clusion (1875).
4. *The Bostonians* was published in 1886.

who liked my books, and greatly wished to see me. The secretary was very cordial, and told me that he always kept my Stillwater Tragedy lying on his desk, he liked so much to take it up and read it at leisure moments. What could I do? I answered that I should be glad to tell Mr. Aldrich[5] when I went back to Boston, what a favorite his book was with the Secretary of the Periphery; and I really forget how we got rid of each other.

But anything so disastrous as this does not often happen to a novelist, I fancy. Those crushing blows, which fell within ten minutes of each other, were probably meant to cure me of vanity, and I can confidently say that they did so. I have not felt since the slightest motion of pride or conceit when the reader has failed to confound me with some one else, or even when he knows distinctly who I am and what I have written, and seizes with exquisite intelligence my lightest and slightest intention in a book. There *are* such readers; and I feel sure that nothing good that the author puts into a novel is ever lost. Some one sees it, feels it, loves it, and loves him for it. This is the sweet compensation for much negligence, much coldness, much dullness. Readers are not so bad, I should like to say to my brother novelists; they are really very good, and at any rate we could not get on without them. I myself think they are better in the small towns, where the excitements and the distractions are few, than in the cities where there are many. I have said before, somewhere, that in the cities people do not read books, they read about them; and I believe that it is far from these nervous centres, that the author finds his closest, truest, loveliest appreciation. For my part I like best to think of my stories, if they are so blest, as befriending the loneliness of outlying farms, dull villages, distant exile. I cannot express the joy it gave me to have General Greeley[6] say that he had read me amidst the frozen blackness of the arctic night; and the other day I had a letter from a man who had followed the fortunes of some imaginary people of mine through a long cruise in the South Seas. I answered him that it was the knowledge of such things which made it sweet to be a novelist; and I may add, to you, that to have a letter like that I would willingly disown all the books that Mr. James ever wrote, or Mr. Aldrich either.

While I am about these confidences, which I make very frank because they are typical rather than personal, and deal with things that happen to all authors more or less, I will confess that I have never yet seen one novel of mine sold. Once, in a book store, I saw a lady take up my latest, and look into it; I waited breathless; but she laid it down again, and went out directly, as if it had perhaps been too much for her. Yet, unless the publishers have abused my fondness,[7] some of my novels have had a pretty sale enough; and I

5. Thomas Bailey Aldrich (1836–1907), American writer and editor, published *The Stillwater Tragedy* in 1880.
6. General Adolphus W. Greely (1844–
1935), American army officer and explorer, led an expedition to the arctic in 1881.
7. I.e., my willingness to believe.

have at least overheard them talked about. In a railway train once, I listened to a gentleman in the seat before me commending them to a young lady for their blameless morality; another day, at the table next mine, in a restaurant, a young man went critically through most of them to his commensal.[8]

I believe he was rather lenient to them; but you cannot always depend upon the flattering quality of such eavesdroppings, and I think it is best to get away from them. At a table d'hôte[9] in Florence a charming young English lady, who knew me for an American by my speech began the talk by saying that she was just from Venice, where she had read a book which a countryman of mine had written about that city, and named a book of my own. I did not think it would be fair to let her go on if she had any censure to pronounce, and I knew it would not be pleasant; so I made haste to say that I was myself the countryman of mine whom she meant; after that she had nothing but praise for my book. The trouble is you cannot be sure what people will say, and it is best to forego anything surreptitious in the collection of opinion. I once wrote a novel in which I thought I had been very deeply, and was perhaps only too subtly, serious; but a young gentleman in a waltz, when his partner asked him if he were reading it, said, "No; too trivial." I did not overhear this, and so I do not feel justly punished by it. Neither do I consider that I quite merit the blame bestowed upon another novel of mine,[1] but I will report the fact because it shows that there may be two views of my morality. This story was of a young girl who, by a series of misunderstandings, finds herself the only woman on board a vessel going to Italy, with three young men for her fellow passengers. They do everything they can to keep her from embarrassment or even consciousness, and one of them marries her when they get to Venice. I thought this a very harmless scheme, and so did a friend of mine,[2] who was in France when the book came out, and who recommended it, perhaps too confidently, to a French mother of daughters anxious for some novel in English proper for a young girl to read. He lent it her, but when she had read it herself, she brought it back, and said the situation imagined in it was immoral and altogether unfit to be presented to the mind of a *jeune fille*.[3]

To tell the truth, I do not think it would be well for the author to aim at the good opinion of the reader in this or anything else. That cannot be trusted to keep the author's literary or moral conscience clean and that is the main thing with him. His affair is to do the best he can with the material he has chosen, to make the truest possible picture of life, and this is what I believe he always does, if he is worthy of the name of artist. He had better not aim to

---

8. I.e., those who shared the table with him.
9. Common dining table in a hotel.

1. *Lady of the Aroostook* (1879).
2. Henry James.
3. Young lady.

please, and he had still better not aim to instruct; the pleasure and
the instruction will follow from such measure of truth as the author
has in him to such measure of truth as the reader has in him. You
will sometimes find it said by the critics that such and such a novel
has evidently been written with such and such an object; but unless
it is the work of a mere artizan, and no artist at all, I believe this is
never the fact. If it is a work of art, it promptly takes itself out of
the order of polemics or of ethics, and primarily consents to be
nothing if not aesthetical. Its story is the thing that tells, first of all,
and if that does not tell, nothing in it tells. It is said that one
reason why Tolstoy, when he felt the sorrow of the world laid upon
him, decided to write no more novels, because no matter how full
he filled these with the desire of his soul to help them that have no
helper, he found that what went into the minds of most readers was
merely the story.

Then shall the novel have no purpose? Shall it not try to do good?
Shall this unrivalled, this inapproachable form, beside which epic
and drama dwindle to puny dwarfishness, and are so little that
they can both be lost in its vast room, shall this do nothing to
better men and uplift them? Shall it only amuse them? No, and a
thousand times, no! But it shall be a mission to their higher selves
only so far as it shall charm their minds and win their hearts. It
shall do no good directly. It shall not be the bread, but the grain of
wheat which must sprout and grow in the reader's soul, and be harvested in his experience, and in the mills of the gods ground slowly
perhaps many years before it shall duly nourish him. I do not mean
that there can never be any immediate good from novels. I do not see
how any one can read The Scarlet Letter, or Middlemarch, or Romola,[4] without being instantly seized with the dread of falsehood. This
is in the way to the love of truth. It is the first step, the indispensable
first step towards that love, but it is by no means arrival at it. The
novel can teach, and for shame's sake, it must teach, but only by
painting life truly. This is what it must above all things strive to do.
If it succeeds, every good effect shall come from it: delight, use, wisdom. If it does not succeed in this, no good can come of it. Let no
reader, and let no intending novelist suppose that this fidelity to life
can be carried too far. After all, and when the artist has given his
whole might to the realization of his ideal, he will have only an
effect of life. I think the effect is like that in those cycloramas
where up to a certain point there is real ground and real grass, and
then carried indivisibly on to the canvas the best that the painter
can do to imitate real ground and real grass. We start in our novels
with something we have known of life, that is, with life itself; and
then we go on and imitate what we have known of life. If we are
very skilful and very patient we can *hide the joint*. But the joint is
always there, and on one side of it are real ground and real grass,

4. *Romola* (1862–63), by George Eliot.

and on the other are the painted images of ground and grass. I do not believe that there was ever any one who longed more strenuously or endeavored more constantly to make the painted ground and grass exactly like the real, than I have done in my cycloramas. But I have to own that I have never yet succeeded to my own satisfaction. Some touch of color, some tone of texture is always wanting; the light is different; it is all in another region. At the same time I have the immense, the sufficient consolation, of knowing that I have not denied such truth as was in me by imitating unreal ground and unreal grass, or even copying the effect of some other's effort to represent real ground and real grass.

Early in the practice of my art I perceived that what I must do in fiction, if I were to do anything worth while, was to get into it from life the things that had not been got into fiction before. At the very first, of course I tried to do the things that I found done already, or the kind of things, especially as I found them in English novels. These had been approved as fit for literature, and they alone were imaginably fit for it. But I tried some other things, and found them fit too. Then I said to myself that I would throw away my English glasses, and look at American life with my own American eyes, and report the things I saw there, whether they were like the things in English fiction or not. In a modest measure this plan succeeded, and I could not commend any other to the American novelist.

I do not mean to say, however, that one's work is always of this intentional, this voluntary sort. On the contrary, there is so much which is unintentional and involuntary, that one might very well believe one's self inspired if one did not know better. For instance, each novel has a law of its own, which it seems to create for itself. Almost from the beginning it has its peculiar temperament and quality, and if you happen to be writing that novel you feel that you must respect its law. You, who are master of the whole affair, cannot violate its law without taking its life. It may grow again, but it will be of another generation and another allegiance. No more can you change the nature of any character in it without spoiling it. You cannot even change the name of a character without running great risk of affecting its vital principle; and by the way where do one's characters get their names? They mostly appear with their names on, an integral part of themselves. This is very curious; but it does not evince inspiration. It merely suggests that the materials which the imagination deals with are not fluid, not flexible, not ductile; but when they have once taken form have a plaster of paris fixity, which is scarcely more subject to the author's will than the reader's. Either one of these may shatter the form, but one is almost as able to reconstitute it as the other. I hope this is not very mystical for I hate anything of that sort, and would have all in plain day if I could. The most that I will allow is that the mind fathers creatures which are apparently as self-regulated as any other offspring. They are the children of a given mind; they bear a likeness to it; they are qualified by it; but they seem to have their own life and their own being apart from it. Perhaps this is allowing a good deal.

Another, and much simpler, fact of my experience has been that you never master your art as a whole. I used vainly to suppose, when I began to write fiction, that after I had struck my gait I had merely to keep on at that pace forever. But I discovered to my vast surprise that I had struck my gait for this or that book only, and that the pace would not serve for another novel. I must strike a new gait, I must get a new pace for every new story. I could issue master from the last, but I must begin prentice with the next; and I suppose this is the great difference between an art and a trade, or even a science. The art is always both a teaching and a learning. In virtue of never being twice the same, it is a perpetual delight, a perpetual ordeal to the artist. He enjoys and he suffers in it, as no other man enjoys or suffers in his work.

In fiction you cannot, if you would, strike twice in the same place, and you certainly had better not, if you could. It is interesting to note how, if you carry a character from one story to another, it can scarcely be important in both. If you have first given it a leading part, you have exhausted its possibilities, but if it has been at first subordinate, then you may develop it into something important in the second handling. Still less can you twice treat the same theme twice. For the novelist there is no replica; and I would ask those readers who sometimes complain of sameness in an author's books to consider whether it is anything more than that family likeness which they must inevitably have. All Mr. James's book are like Mr. James; all Tourguenieff's books are like Tourguenieff; all Hawthorne's books are like Hawthorne. You cannot read a page in any of them without knowing them for this author or that; but the books of no author resemble one another than through this sort of blood-relationship.

Indefinite patience is requisite to a fine or true effect in this art which I am speaking of. In my beginning, I sometimes imagined that a novel might be blocked out by writing all the vital scenes first from the earliest to the latest, and then going back, and supplying the spaces of dead color between them. But this is so obviously impossible that I never even tried it. The events of a real novel grow slowly and necessarily out of the development of its characters, and the author cannot fully forecast these. He creates them, but he has to get acquainted with them in great measure afterwards. He knows the nature of each, but he does not know how they will affect one another till he tries. Sometimes, I have hurried forward to an effect, impatient of intervening detail, but when I have got the effect by this haste I find that it is weak and false because the detail was wanting. That is the soil which it must grow out of; without that, and the slow, careful thinking which supplies it, the effect is a sickly and spindling growth.

The novel reader, who is on the outside of all these processes, cannot consider them in liking or disliking a novel. Yet it is the readers and not the writers of novels who decide their fate, and whom novels must first appeal to upon some broad principle common to all men, and especially to that kind of men who are called women. The favor of all the novel writers in the world could not solely make a novel successful; and yet if the novelists liked it I should say it was surely a good novel. I do not say, on the other hand that readers choose falsely, although they often choose foolishly. One could bring up a terrible array of foolish choices against them; novels that sold by the hundred thousand, and yet were disgracefully bad, and are now wholly forgotten. They met a momentary want, they caught a passing fancy; perhaps they touched with artless fortune a chord of real feeling. They pleased vastly, if not mightily, and till they blew over, as Douglass Jerrold[5] used to say of such books, the few who knew better had to hang their heads in shame for the rest.

But there are also novels that please mightily as well as vastly, and then cease to please at all and are as if they had never been. Who is it that now speaks of —— I was going to speak of it, but I will not; everyone knows what I mean and is sick of it. Yet it was a charming book, full of fun and airy fancy, and of a certain truth, generous, spirited, gay and heartbreaking. Why should not it please forever? It must simply be that the principles which in their peculiar combination it appealed to were worn out, as the capacity for being amused by a certain joke is exhausted by familiarity. The joke is as droll as ever: why do not you laugh still? That air, that song, which ravished your sense ninety times was torture the hundredth. Your beloved who died ten years ago, is more lost to you now than then: where are your tears?

> "All things are taken from us and become
> Portions and parcels of the dreadful past."[6]

Laughter passes; grief gluts itself and can no more; laughter dies, spent with its own joy.

That book *was* charming; I say it again; but nothing could make me read it again. Yet there are stories that I can read again and again, and not tire of. They are not such as appeal so much to the passions, or else they appeal to them in a different way. In them, the elements are more fortunately mixed and more skilfully; but it would be hard to say what makes a work of art lastingly please, and what makes a work of art please transiently. If you ask me, I will own frankly I do not know. I can only offer some such makeshift of

5. Douglas William Jerrold (1803–57), English dramatist and journalist.
6. Apparently Howells's parody of a clichéd verse.

an explanation as that it is repose which causes the enduring charm; but who can say just what repose is?

It is taken for granted that one thing which always pleases in a novel is the love-making; but I doubt it. A good deal of the lovemaking in novels is vulgar and offensive. Love is a passion which must be delicately handled by a novelist, or else his lovers will be as disgusting as those who betray their fondness in society, and make the spectator sick; they will be as bad as those poor things who sit with their arms round each other on the benches in the park. Really some of the lovescenes even in so great a novelist as George Eliot, stomach one. But there is nothing better than a love scene when it is well done, though there can be other things quite as good. I think that to make it very acceptable, there should be a little humorous consciousness, a little self-irony in the lovers; though when I think of such noble tragedy as the love-passages in Tourguenieff, I am not sure of my position. Still, still, I think I prefer the love-making of Jane Austen's people; but what do not I prefer of Jane Austen's?

As for my own modest attempts in that direction, I should be far too shame-faced to allege them, if I had not once received a singular proof of their success. I do not mean in the favor of that young lady who had read all the love parts in my books, and supposed I was a dead Englishman, or that other young lady who liked my story best of all out of the nine serials and novels from the library which she was reading. It was such testimony as the boys and the blackbirds bear to the flavor of fruit, and it came about through the printers' leaving the copy of one of my love scenes out overnight where the mice could get at it. The mice ate the delicious morsel all up but a few tattered fragments. It was excessively gratifying to my vanity as author; more, for me, mice could not do; but I did not find it so agreeable when the printers sent me these remnants, and asked me to supply the paragraphs which had been devoured with such eager interest. If you have never had a like experience you can not have any notion how difficult it is to reproduce a love-passage which the mice have eaten.

When I began to write fiction we were under the romantic superstition that the hero must do something to *win* the heroine; perform some valorous or generous act; save her from danger, as a burning building or a breaking bridge, or the like, or at least be nursed by her through a long and dangerous sickness. In compliance with this burdensome tradition, I had my hero rescue my heroine from a ferocious bulldog, which I remember was thought rather *infra dig.*[7] by some of the critics; but I had no other mortal peril handy, and a bulldog is really a very dangerous animal. This was in my first novel; but after that I began to look about me and consider. I observed that none of the loved husbands of the happy wives I knew

7. Abbreviation for *infra dignitatem*, beneath one's dignity.

had done anything to "win" them except pay a certain number of visits, send them flowers, dance or sit out dances with them at parties, and then muster courage to ask if they would have them. Amongst the young people of my acquaintance, I noticed that this simple and convenient sort of conquest was still going on; and I asked myself why it should be different in books. It was certainly very delightful as I saw it in nature, and why try to paint the lily or tint the rose? After that I let my heroes win my heroines by being as nice fellows as I could make them. But even then I felt that they both expected too much of me; and it was about this time that I had many long and serious talks with my friend, Mr. Henry James, as to how we might eliminate the everlasting young man and young woman, as we called them. We imagined a great many intrigues in which they should *not* be the principal personages; I remember he had one very notable scheme for a novel whose interest should centre about a mother and a son. Still, however, he is writing stories, as I still am, about the everlasting man and young woman; though I do think we have managed somewhat to moderate them a little as to their importance in fiction. I suppose we must always have them there, as we must always have them in life, if the race is to go on; but I think the modern novel is more clearly ascertaining their place. Their dominance of course was owing to the belief that young people were the chief readers of fiction. I dare say this is true yet; but I doubt if it is the young people who make the fortune of a novel. Rather, I fancy, its prosperity lies in the favor of women of all ages—and (I was going to say) sexes. These are the most devoted novel-readers, the most intelligent (after the novelists themselves) and the most influential, by far. It is the man of feminine refinement and of feminine culture, with us so much greater than masculine culture, who loves fiction, but amongst other sorts of men I have observed that lawyers are the greatest novel-readers. They read, however, for the story, the distraction, the relief; and after them come physicians, who read novels for much the same reasons, but more for the psychological interest than lawyers. The more liberal sorts of ministers read novels, with an eye to the ethical problems treated; but none of these read so nearly from the novelists' own standpoint as the women. Like the novelists, these read with sympathy for the way the thing is done, with an eye for the shades of character, the distribution of motive, the management of the intrigue, and not merely for the story, or so much for the psychological and ethical aspects of it. Business men, I fancy, seldom read novels at all; they read newspapers.

Fiction is the chief intellectual stimulus of our time, whether we like the fact or not, and taking it in the broad sense if not the deep sense, it is the chief intellectual influence. I should say moral influence, too; but it is often a moral stimulus without being a moral influence; it reaches the mind, and stops short of the conduct. As to the prime fact involved, I think we have but to recall the books of any last year of modern times, and we cannot question it. It is ninety-nine chances out of a hundred that the book which at any given moment is making the world talk, and making the world think is a novel. Within the last generation, I can remember only one book making the impression that a dozen of novels have each made, and against Renan's Life of Jesus,[8] I will set Les Miserable, Romola and Middlemarch and Daniel Deronda, Le'Assomoir and Nana, Tess of the D'Urbervilles, Anna Karénina and the Kreuzer Sonata, Robert Elsmere, Trilby, Ben Hur, not all, or at all, of the same artistic value, but all somehow, of a mighty human interest. We must leave Uncle Tom's Cabin out of the count because it was of an earlier period; if we counted it, the proof of my assertion would be overwhelming.

The novel is easily first among books that people read willingly, and it is rightfully first. It has known how to keep the charm of the story, and to add to it the attraction of almost every interest. It still beguiles, as in the hands of the Byzantine romancers,[9] not to go unnumbered centuries back to the Greek novel of Homer, the Odyssey; and it has learnt how to warn, to question, to teach in every concern of life. Scarcely any predicament, moral or psychological has escaped its study, and it has so refined and perfected its methods that antiseptic surgery itself has hardly made a more beneficent advance. It began with the merest fable, excluding from the reader's interest all but the fortunes of princes and the other dignified personages, for whose entertainment it existed until now it includes all sorts and conditions of men, who turn to it for instruction, inspiration, consolation. It has broadened and deepened down and out till it compasses the whole of human nature; and no cause important to the race has been unfriended of it. Sometimes I have been vexed at its vicious pandering to passion, but I cannot think, after all, of any great modern novel which has not been distinctly moral in effect. I am not sorry to have had it go into the dark places of the soul, the filthy and squalid places of society, high and low, and shed there its great light. Let us know with its help what we are, and where we are. Let all the hidden things be brought into the sun, and let every day be the day of judgment. If the sermon cannot any longer serve this end, let the novel do it.

8. Ernest Renan's *Life of Jesus* (1863) was one of the first such books to take a (what was for the time scandalous) scientific-historical approach to its subject. Victor Hugo published *Les Miserables* in 1862; George Eliot published *Daniel Deronda* in 1876; Émile Zola published *L'Assommoir* in 1877 and *Nana* in 1880; Thomas Hardy published *Tess of the D'Urbervilles* in 1891; Leo Tolstoy published *Kreuzer Sonata* in 1889; Mary Augusta Ward (1851–1920), American novelist, published *Robert Elsmere* in 1888; George du Maurier (1834–96), English artist and writer, published *Trilby* in 1894; General Lew Wallace (1827–1905), American soldier and novelist, published *Ben Hur; A Tale of the Christ* in 1880; Harriett Beecher Stowe (1811–96), American writer, published *Uncle Tom's Cabin* in 1851–52.

9. Perhaps Howells has in mind works such as *The Arabian Nights* or *Thousand and One Nights*, though these were not published until the 18th century.

But in doing this it will have to render a stricter account than it has yet been held to. The old superstition of a dramatic situation as the supreme representation of life must be discarded, and the novelist must endeavor to give exactly the effect of life. I believe he will yet come to do this. I can never do it, for I was bred in a false school whose trammels I have never been quite able to burst; but the novelist who begins where I leave off, will yet write the novel which has been my ideal. He will not reject anything because he cannot make it picturesque or dramatic; but he will feel the beauty of truth so intimately, and will value it so supremely that he will seek the effect of that solely. He cannot transport life really into his story, any more than the cycloramist could carry the real ground and the real grass into his picture. But he will not rest till he has made his story as like life as he can, with the same mixed motives, the same voluntary and involuntary actions, the same unaccountable advances and perplexing pauses, the same moments of rapture, the same days and weeks of horrible dullness, the same conflict of the higher and lower purposes, the same vices and virtues, inspirations and propensities. He will not shun any aspect of life because its image will be stupid and gross, still less because its image will be incredibly noble and glorious. He will try to give that general resemblance which can come only from the most devoted fidelity to particulars. As it is now the representation of life in novels, even the most conscientious in its details, is warped and distorted by the novelist's anxiety to produce an image that is startling and impressive, as well as true. But if he can once conceive the notion of letting the reader's imagination care for these things; if he can convince himself that his own affair is to arrange a correct perspective, in which all things shall appear in their very proportion and relation, he will have mastered the secret of repose, which is the soul of beauty in all its forms.

The hope of this may be the vainest of dreams, but I do not think so. Already I see the promise, the prophesy of such a novel in the work of some of the younger men. That work often seems to me crude and faulty, but I feel that it is in the right direction, and I value it for that reason with a faith which only work in the right direction can inspire. Good work in the wrong direction fills me with despair, and my heart sinks lower the better the work is. In a picture of life which is fundamentally or structurally false, I cannot value coloring or drawing, composition or sentiment; the lie at the from my own work when I have made a false start, and then I keep trying to hark back to the truth as I know it, and start afresh. A hundred times in the course of a story I have to retrace my steps, and efface them. Often the whole process is a series of arduous experiments, trying it this way, trying it that; testing it by my knowledge of myself and my acquaintance with others; asking if it would be true of me, or true of my friend or my enemy; and not possibly resting content with anything I thought gracious or pleasing in my performance till I have got the setting of truth for it. This sort of scrutiny goes on perpetually in the novelist's mind. His story is never out of it. He lies down with it in his last waking thought and rises up with it in his first. Throughout the day, in crowds or in solitude, it is dimly or distinctly in his thought, a joy, a torment. He shakes hands with a friend and asks after his sick wife, but he is really wondering whether his hero would probably marry his heroine. In his talk at dinner he brings covertly to the test of his neighbor's experience the question of the situation he is developing. He escapes with his life from a cable-car, and at the same instant the solution of a difficult problem flashes upon him. Till he has cannot dismiss it; consciously or unconsciously it pervades his being. written finis at the end of his book, it literally obsesses him. He thing's heart taints and blights every part of it. This happens to me

Is this a normal, a healthful state for a man to be in? I suppose it is measurably the state of every manner of artist, and I am not describing a condition that will seem strange to any artist. I am not at all sure that it is morbid or unwholesome. The best thing that can fill man's mind is his work, for if his work does not fill it, his self will fill it, and it can have no worse tenant. Of one thing I am certain, and that is that the preoccupation with work that constantly exacts reference to life, makes life incessantly interesting. In my quality of novelist I defy the deadliest bore to afflict me. I have but to test some bore in my story by him, and he becomes a boon, a favor of heaven, an invaluable and exquisitely interesting opportunity.

As to the outward shape of the inward life of the novel, which must invariably be truth, there is some choice, but mainly between three sorts: the autobiographical, the biographical and the historical. The first of these I have always considered the most perfect literary form after the drama. If you tell the story as apparently your own, you are completely master of the situation, and you can report everything as if it were a real incident. What goes on in your own mind concerning persons and events you can give with absolute authority, and you are not tempted to say what goes on in the minds of others, except in the way of conjecture, as one does in life. But the conditions are that you must not go outside of your own observation and experience; you cannot tell what you have not yourself seen and known to happen. If you do, you at once break the illusion; and you cannot even repeat things that you have at second hand, without some danger of this. Within its narrow range the autobiographical story[1] operates itself as much as the play does. Perhaps because of its limitations none of the greatest novels have been written in that form perfect as it is, and delightful as it is to

---

1. I.e., novels with a first-person narrator.

the reader, except Gil Blas[2] only. But Thackeray was always fond of it, and he wrote his best book, The Luck of Barry Lyndon, in it, and his next best, Henry Esmond. In many other novels of his, it is employed; in the very last, The Adventures of Philip, Pendennis tells the story of Firman as if he were knowing to it. Hawthorne chose the autobiographic form for what I think his greatest novel, The Blithedale Romance, and many others have used it. The old fashioned novels in letters, like Pamela and Evalina, were modifications of it; and some next-to-modern novelists, like Wilkie Collins have used the narratives, or statements, of several persons concerning the same fact to much the effect of the autobiographic novel. Gil Blas is possibly the most famous story in this form, and David Copperfield next.

The biographical novel is that in which the author chooses a central figure and refers to it and reports from it all the facts and feelings involved. The central figure must be of very paramount importance to justify this form, which is nearly as cramping as the autobiographical, and has not its intimate charm. Mr. James used it in his Roderick Hudson,[3] but to immeasurably less beautiful effect than he has used the autobiographical, in some of his incomparable short stories. He seems of late to prefer it to any other, and he has cast in it work of really unimpeachable perfection.

After all, however, the historical is the great form, impure and imperfect as it is. But here I wish you to note that I am talking of the historical form in novel writing, and not at all of the historical novel. The historical novel may be written in either the autobiographical, the biographical, or the historical form; but it is not now specifically under discussion. What is under discussion is any sort of novel whose material is treated as if it were real history. In this the novelist supposes himself to be narrating a series of events, indefinite in compass, and known to him from the original documents, as a certain passage in the real life of the race is known to the historian. If, then, he could work entirely in the historian's spirit, and content himself and his reader with conjecture as to his people's motives and with report of them from hearsay, I should not call this form impure or imperfect. But he cannot do this, apparently, or at least he never has done it. He enters into the minds and hearts of his characters; he gives long passages of dialogue among them, and invents speeches for them, as the real historians used to do for their real personages; and he not only does this, but he makes his reader privy to their most secret thoughts, feelings and desires. At times his work is dramatic, and at times narrative; he makes it either at

---

2. A picaresque novel by Alain René Lesage (1668–1747), French dramatist and novelist. The Luck of Barry Lyndon (1844), Henry Esmond (1852), The Adventures of Philip Pendennis (1848) by William Makepeace Thackeray; The Blithedale Romance (1852) by Nathaniel Hawthorne; Pamela, or Virtue Rewarded (1740–41) by Samuel Richardson; and Evelina (1778) by Frances Burney (1752–1840). Wilkie Collins (1824–89), English novelist. David Copperfield by Charles Dickens was published in 1850. 3. Published in 1876.

will. He dwells in a world of his own creating, where he is a universal intelligence, comprehending and interpreting everything, not indirectly or with any artistic conditions, but frankly and straightforwardly, without accounting in any way for his knowledge of the facts. The form involves a thousand contradictions, impossibilities. There is no point where it cannot be convicted of the most grotesque absurdity. The historian has got the facts from some one who witnessed them; but the novelist employing the historic form has no proof of them; he gives his word alone for them. He visits this situation and that and reports what no one but himself could have seen. He has the intimate confidence of his character in the hour of passion, the hour of remorse, the hour of death itself. Tourguenief and Tolstoy came back from following theirs to the verge of the other world. They tell what they thought and felt as this world faded from them, and nothing in fiction is more impressive, more convincing of its truth.

The historical form, though it involves every contradiction, every impossibility, is the only form which can fully represent any passage of life in its inner and outer entirety. It alone leaves nothing untouched, nothing unsearched. It is the primal form of fiction; it is epic. The first great novels, the Illiad and the Odyssey were cast in it; and the last, if there is ever any last novel while the human race endures, will probably wear it. The subtlest, the greatest achievements of fiction in other forms are nothing beside it. Think of Don Quixote, of Wilhelm Meister, of the Bride of Lammermoor, of I Promessi Sposi, of War and Peace, of Fathers and Sons, of Middlemarch, of Pendennis, of Bleak House, of Uncle Tom's Cabin, of The Scarlet Letter, of L'Assomoir, of The Grandissimes, of Princess Casamassima, of Far from the Madding Crowd:[4] the list of masterpieces in this form is interminable.

When Homer wrote his novels, he feigned that he had his facts from the Muse, and that saved appearances; but hardly any novelist since has seriously done so. The later novelist boldly asks you to believe, as a premise, that he knows all about things that no one man can imaginably know all about, and you are forced to grant it because he has the power of convincing you against your reason. The form which is the least artistic, is the least artificial; the novel of historic form is the novel par excellence; all other forms are clever feats in fiction, literary, conscious. This supreme form is almost shapeless, as it is with the greatest difficulty, with serious limitations of its effects, that you can give it symmetry. Left to

---

4. *Don Quixote* (1605, 1615), by Cervantes; *Wilhelm Meister* (1796), by Johann Wolfgang von Goethe; *Bride of Lammermoor* (1819), by Sir Walter Scott (1771–1832); *I Promessi Sposi* (1825–26), by Alessandro Manzoni (1785–1873); *War and Peace* (1862–69) by Leo Tolstoy; *The History of Pendennis* (1848–50), by William Makepeace Thackeray; *Bleak House* (1853), by Charles Dickens; *L'Assommoir* (1877), by Émile Zola; *The Grandissimes* (1880), by George Washington Cable (1844–1925); *Princess Casamassima* (1886), by Henry James; *Far from the Madding Crowd* (1874), by Thomas Hardy.

itself, it is sprawling, splay-footed, gangling, proportionless and inchoate; but if it is true to the life which it can give no authority for seeming to know, it is full of beauty and symmetry.

In fine, at the end of the ends, as the Italians say, truth to life is the supreme office of the novel, in whatever form. I am always saying this, and I can say no other. If you like to have it in different words, the business of the novelist is to make you understand the real world through his faithful effigy of it; or, as I have said before, to arrange a perspective for you with everything in its proper relation and proportion to everything else, and this so manifest that you cannot err in it however myopic or astigmatic you may be. It is his function to help you to be kinder to your fellows, juster to yourself, truer to all.

Mostly, I should say, he has failed. I can think of no one, except Tolstoy alone, who has met the high requirements of his gift, though I am tempted to add Björnson in some of his later books. But in spite of his long and almost invariable failure, I have great hopes of the novelist. His art, which is as old as the world, is yet the newest in it, and still very imperfect. But no novelist can think of it without feeling its immeasurable possibilities, without owning that in every instance the weakness, the wrong is in himself, and not in his art.

1899   1958, 1979

From A Boy's Town[1]
IX. Circuses and Shows

What every boy expected to do, some time or other, was to run off. He expected to do this because the scheme offered an unlimited field to the imagination, and because its fulfilment would give him the highest distinction among the other fellows. To run off was held to be the only way for a boy to right himself against the wrongs and hardships of a boy's life. As far as the Boy's Town[2] was concerned, no boy had anything to complain of; the boys had the best time in the world there, and in a manner they knew it. But there were certain things that they felt no boy ought to stand, and these things were sometimes put upon them at school, but usually at home. In fact, nearly all the things that a fellow intended to run off for were done to him by those who ought to have been the kindest to him. Some boys' mothers had the habit of making them stop and do something for them just when they were going away with the fellows. Others would not let them go in swimming as often as they wanted, and, if they saw them with their shirts on wrong side out, would not believe that they could get turned in climbing a fence. Others made them split kindling and carry in wood, and even

---

1. First published as Chapter IX of *A Boy's Town* in 1890, the source for the present text. 2. Hamilton, Ohio.

saw wood. None of these things, in a simple form, was enough to make a boy run off, but they prepared his mind for it, and when complicated with whipping they were just cause for it. Weeding the garden, though, was a thing that almost, in itself, was enough to make a fellow run off.

Not many of the boys really had to saw wood, though a good many of the fellows' fathers had saws and bucks[3] in their wood-sheds. There were public sawyers who did most of the wood-sawing; and they came up with their bucks on their shoulders, and asked for the job almost as soon as the wood was unloaded before your door. The most popular one with the boys was a poor half-wit known among them as Morn; and he was a favorite with them because he had fits, and because, when he had a fit, he would seem to fly all over the wood-pile. The boys would leave anything to see Morn in a fit, and he always had a large crowd round him as soon as the cry went out that he was beginning to have one. They watched the hapless creature with grave, unpitying, yet not unfriendly interest, too ignorant of the dark ills of life to know how deeply tragic was the spectacle that entertained them, and how awfully present in Morn's contortions was the mystery of God's ways with his children, some of whom he gives to happiness and some to misery. When Morn began to pick himself weakly up, with eyes of pathetic bewilderment, they helped him find his cap, and tried to engage him in conversation, for the pleasure of seeing him twist his mouth when he said, of a famous town drunkard whom he admired, "He's a strong man; he eats liquor." It was probably poor Morn's ambition to eat liquor himself, and the boys who followed that drunkard about to plague him had a vague respect for his lamentable appetite.

None of the boys ever did run off, except the son of one of the preachers. He was a big boy, whom my boy remotely heard of, but never saw, for he lived in another part of the town; but his adventure was known to all the boys, and his heroism rated high among them. It took nothing from this, in their eyes, that he was found, homesick and crying in Cincinnati, and was glad to come back—the great fact was that he had run off; nothing could change or annul that. If he had made any mistake, it was in not running off with a circus, for that was the true way of running off. Then, if you were ever seen away from home, you were seen tumbling through a hoop and alighting on the crupper of a bare-backed piebald, and if you ever came home you came home in a gilded chariot, and you flashed upon the domestic circle in flesh-colored tights and spangled breechcloth. As soon as the circus-bills began to be put up you began to hear that certain boys were going to run off with that circus, and the morning after it left town you heard they had gone, but they always turned up at school just the same. It was believed

3. Sawhorses.

that the circus-men would take any boy who wanted to go with them, and would fight off his friends if they tried to get him away.

The boys made a very careful study of the circus-bills, and afterwards, when the circus came, they held the performance to a strict account for any difference between the feats and their representation. For a fortnight beforehand they worked themselves up for the arrival of the circus into a fever of fear and hope, for it was always a question with a great many whether they could get their fathers to give them the money to go in. The full price was two bits, and the half-price was a bit, or a Spanish *real*, then a commoner coin than the American dime in the West; and every boy, for that time only, wished to be little enough to look young enough to go in for a bit. Editors of newspapers had a free ticket for every member of their families; and my boy was sure of going to the circus from the first rumor of its coming. But he was none the less deeply thrilled by the coming event, and he was up early on the morning of the great day, to go out and meet the circus procession beyond the corporation line.

I do not really know how boys live through the wonder and the glory of such a sight. Once there were two chariots—one held the band in red-and-blue uniforms, and was drawn by eighteen piebald horses; and the other was drawn by a troop of Shetland ponies, and carried in a vast mythical sea-shell little boys in spangled tights and little girls in the gauze skirts and wings of fairies. There was not a flaw in this splendor to the young eyes that gloated on it, and that followed it in rapture through every turn and winding of its course in the Boy's Town; nor in the magnificence of the actors and actresses, who came riding two by two in their circus-dresses after the chariots, and looking some haughty and contemptuous, and others quiet and even bored, as if it were nothing to be part of such a procession. The boys tried to make them out by the pictures and names on the bills: which was Rivers, the bare-back rider, and which was O'Dale, the champion tumbler; which was the India-rubber man, which the ring-master, which the clown. Covered with dust, gasping with the fatigue of a three hours' run beside the procession, but fresh at heart as in the beginning, they arrived with it on the Commons,[4] where the tent-wagons were already drawn up, and the ring was made, and mighty men were driving the iron-headed tent-stakes, and stretching the ropes of the great skeleton of the pavilion which they were just going to clothe with canvas. The boys were not allowed to come anywhere near, except three or four who got leave to fetch water from a neighboring well, and thought themselves richly paid with half-price tickets. The other boys were proud to pass a word with them as they went by with their brimming buckets; fellows who had money to go in would have been glad to carry water just for the glory of coming close to the

4. Land subject to common or public use.

circus-men. They stood about in two or threes, and lay upon the grass in groups debating whether a tan-bark[5] ring was better than a sawdust ring; there were different opinions. They came as near the wagons as they dared, and looked at the circus-horses munching hay from the tail-boards, just like common horses. The wagons were left standing outside of the tent; but when it was up, the horses were taken into the dressing-room, and then the boys, with many a backward look at the wide spread of canvas, and the flags and streamers floating over it from the centre-pole (the centre-pole was revered almost like a distinguished personage), ran home to dinner so as to get back good and early, and be among the first to go in. All round, before the circus doors were open, the doorkeepers of the side-shows were inviting people to come in and see the giants and fat woman and boa-constrictors, and there were stands for peanuts and candy and lemonade; the vendors cried, "Ice-cold lemonade, from fifteen hundred miles under ground! Walk up, roll up, tumble up, any way to get up!" The boys thought this brilliant drolling, but they had no time to listen after the doors were open, and they had no money to spend on side-shows or dainties, anyway. Inside the tent, they found it dark and cool, and their hearts thumped in their throats with the wild joy of being there; they recognized one another with amaze, as if they had not met for years, and the excitement kept growing, as other fellows came in. It was lots of fun, too, watching the country-jakes, as the boys called the farmer-folk, and seeing how green they looked, and how some of them tried to act smart with the circus-men that came round with oranges to sell. But the great thing was to see whether fellows that said they were going to hook in really got in. The boys held it to be a high and creditable thing to hook into a show of any kind, but hooking into a circus was something that a fellow ought to be held in special honor for doing. He ran great risks, and if he escaped the vigilance of the massive circus-man who patrolled the outside of the tent with a cowhide and a bulldog, perhaps he merited the fame he was sure to win.

I do not know where boys get some of the notions of morality that govern them. These notions are like the sports and plays that a boy leaves off as he gets older to the boys that are younger. He outgrows them, and other boys grow into them, and then outgrow them as he did. Perhaps they come down to the boyhood of our time from the boyhood of the race, and the unwritten laws of conduct may have prevailed among the earliest Aryans on the plains of Asia that I now find so strange in a retrospect of the Boy's Town. The standard of honor there was, in a certain way, very high among the boys; they would have despised a thief as he deserved, and I cannot remember one of them who might not have been safely

5. Pieces of bark from which tannin, used in the leather-tanning process, has been removed.

trusted. None of them would have taken an apple out of a market-wagon, or stolen a melon from a farmer who came to town with it; but they would all have thought it fun, if not right, to rob an orchard or hook a watermelon out of a patch. This would have been a foray into the enemy's country, and the fruit of the adventure would have been the same as the plunder of a city, or the capture of a vessel belonging to him on the high seas. In the same way, if one of the boys had seen a circus-man drop a quarter, he would have hurried to give it back to him, but he would only have been proud to hook into the circus-man's show, and the other fellows would have been proud of his exploit, too, as something that did honor to them all. As a person who enclosed bounds and forbade trespass, the circus-man constituted himself the enemy of every boy who respected himself, and challenged him to practise any sort of strategy. There was not a boy in the crowd that my boy went with who would have been allowed to hook into a circus by his parents; yet hooking in was an ideal that was cherished among them, that was talked of, and that was even sometimes attempted, though not often. Once, when a fellow really hooked in, and joined the crowd that had ignobly paid, one of the fellows could not stand it. He asked him just how and where he got in, and then he went to the door, and got back his money from the doorkeeper upon the plea that he did not feel well; and in five or ten minutes he was back among the boys, a hero of such moral grandeur as would be hard to describe. Not one of the fellows saw him as he really was—a little lying, thievish scoundrel. Not even my boy saw him so, though he had on some other point of personal honesty the most fantastic scruples.

The boys liked to be at the circus early so as to make sure of the grand entry of the performers into the ring, where they caracoled[6] round on horseback, and gave a delicious foretaste of the wonders to come. The fellows were united in this, but upon other matters feeling varied—some liked tumbling best; some the slack-rope;[7] some bare-back riding; some the feats of tossing knives and balls and catching them. There never was more than one ring in those days; and you were not tempted to break your neck and set your eyes forever askew, by trying to watch all the things that went on at once in two or three rings. The boys did not miss the smallest feats of any performance, and they enjoyed them every one, not equally, but fully. They had their preferences, of course, as I have hinted; and one of the most popular acts was that where a horse has been trained to misbehave, so that nobody can mount him; and after the actors have tried him, the ring-master turns to the audience, and asks if some gentleman among them wants to try it. Nobody stirs, till at last a tipsy country-jake is seen making his way down from

6. Made turning or capering movements.
7. Loosely stretched rope on which acrobats perform.

one of the top-seats towards the ring. He can hardly walk, he is so drunk, and the clown has to help him across the ring-board, and even then he trips and rolls over on the sawdust, and has to be pulled to his feet. When they bring him up to the horse, he falls against it; and the little fellows think he will certainly get killed. But the big boys tell the little fellows to shut up and watch out. The ring-master and the clown manage to get the country-jake on to the broad platform on the horse's back, and then the ring-master cracks his whip, and the two supes[8] who have been holding the horse's head let go, and the horse begins cantering round the ring. The little fellows are just sure the country-jake is going to fall off, he reels and totters so; but the big boys tell them to keep watching out; and pretty soon the country-jake begins to straighten up. He begins to unbutton his long gray overcoat, and then he takes it off and throws it into the ring, where one of the supes catches it. Then he sticks a short pipe into his mouth, and pulls on an old wool hat, and flourishes a stick that the supe throws to him, and you see that he is an Irishman just come across the sea; and then off goes another coat, and he comes out a British soldier in white duck trousers and red coat. That comes off, and he is an American sailor, with his hands on his hips dancing a hornpipe. Suddenly away flash wig and beard and false-face, the pantaloons are stripped off with the same movement, the actor stoops for the reins lying on the horse's neck, and James Rivers, the greatest three-horse rider in the world nimbly capers on the broad pad, and kisses his hand to the shouting and cheering spectators as he dashes from the ring past the braying and bellowing brass-band into the dressing-room!

The big boys have known all along that he was not a real country-jake; but when the trained mule begins, and shakes everybody off, just like the horse, and another country-jake gets up, and offers to bet that he can ride that mule, nobody can tell whether he is a real country-jake or not. This is always the last thing in the performance, and the boys have seen with heavy hearts many signs openly betokening the end which they knew was at hand. The actors have come out of the dressing-room door, some in their every-day clothes, and some with just overcoats on over their circus-dresses, and they lounge about near the band-stand watching the performance in the ring. Some of the people are already getting up to go out, and stand for this last act, and will not mind the shouts of "Down in front! Down there!" which the boys eagerly join in, to eke out their bliss a little longer by keeping away even the appearance of anything transitory in it. The country-jake comes stumbling awkwardly into the ring, but he is perfectly sober, and he boldly leaps astride the mule, which tries all its arts to shake him off, plunging, kicking, rearing. He sticks on, and everybody cheers him, and the owner of the mule begins to get mad and to make it do

8. Supernumerary performers.

more things to shake the country-jake off. At last, with one convulsive spring, it flings him from its back, and dashes into the dressing-room, while the country-jake picks himself up and vanishes among the crowd.

A man mounted on a platform in the ring is imploring the ladies and gentlemen to keep their seats, and to buy tickets for the negro-minstrel entertainment which is to follow, but which is not included in the price of admission. The boys would like to stay, but they have not the money, and they go out clamoring over the performance, and trying to decide which was the best feat. As to which was the best actor, there is never any question; it is the clown, who showed by the way he turned a double somersault that he can do anything, and who chooses to be clown simply because he is too great a creature to enter into rivalry with the other actors.

There will be another performance in the evening, with real fights outside between the circus-men and the country-jakes, and perhaps some of the Basin rounders,[9] but the boys do not expect to come; that would be too much. The boy's brother once stayed away in the afternoon, and went at night with one of the jour printers;[1] but he was not able to report that the show was better than it was in the afternoon. He did not get home till nearly ten o'clock, though, and he saw the sides of the tent dropped before the people got out; that was a great thing; and what was greater yet, and reflected a kind of splendor on the boy at second hand, was that the jour printer and the clown turned out to be old friends. After the circus, the boy actually saw them standing near the centre-pole talking together; and the next day the jour showed the grease that had dripped on his coat from the candles. Otherwise the boy might have thought it was a dream, that some one he knew had talked on equal terms with the clown. The boys were always intending to stay up and see the circus go out of town, and they would have done so, but their mothers would not let them. This may have been one reason why none of them ever ran off with a circus.

As soon as a circus had been in town, the boys began to have circuses of their own, and to practise for them. Everywhere you could see boys upside down, walking on their hands or standing on them with their legs dangling over, or stayed against house walls. It was easy to stand on your head; one boy stood on his head so much that he had to have it shaved, in the brain fever that he got from standing on it; but that did not stop the other fellows. Another boy fell head downwards from a rail where he was skinning-the-cat, and nearly broke his neck, and made it so sore that it was stiff ever so long. Another boy, who was playing Samson, almost had his leg torn off by the fellows that were pulling at it with a hook; and he did have the leg of his pantaloons torn off. Nothing could stop the

9. Rough laborers who worked on the Erie Canal.
1. Journeyman printers work by the day.

boys but time, or some other play coming in; and circuses lasted a good while. Some of the boys learned to turn hand-springs; anybody could turn cart-wheels; one fellow, across the river, could just run along and throw a somersault and light on his feet; lots of fellows could light on their backs; but if you had a spring-board, or shavings under a bank, like those by the turning-shop,[2] you could practise for somersaults pretty safely.

All the time you were practising you were forming your circus company. The great trouble was not that any boy minded paying five or ten pins to come in, but that so many fellows wanted to belong there were hardly any left to form an audience. You could get girls, but even as spectators girls were a little *too* despicable; they did not know anything; they had no sense; if a fellow got hurt they cried. Then another thing was, where to have the circus. Of course it was simply hopeless to think of a tent, and a boy's circus was very glad to get a barn. The boy whose father owned the barn had to get it for the circus without his father knowing it; and just as likely as not his mother would hear the noise and come out and break the whole thing up while you were in the very middle of it. Then there were all sorts of anxieties and perplexities about the dress. You could do something by turning your roundabout[3] inside out, and rolling your trousers up as far as they would go; but what a fellow wanted to make him a real circus actor was a long pair of white cotton stockings, and I never knew a fellow that got a pair; I heard of many a fellow who was said to have got a pair; but when you came down to the fact, they vanished like ghosts when you try to verify them. I believe the fellows always expected to get them out of a bureau-drawer or the clothes-line at home, but failed. In most other ways, a boy's circus was always a failure, like most other things boys undertake. They usually broke up under the strain of rivalry; everybody wanted to be the clown or ring-master; or else the boy they got the barn of behaved badly, and went into the house crying, and all the fellows had to run.

There were only two kinds of show known by that name in the Boy's Town: a Nigger Show, or a performance of burnt-cork minstrels; and an Animal Show, or a strolling menagerie; and the boys always meant a menagerie when they spoke of a show, unless they said just what sort of show. The only perfect joy on earth in the way of an entertainment, of course, was a circus, but after the circus the show came unquestionably next. It made a processional entry into the town almost as impressive as the circus's, and the boys went out to meet it beyond the corporation line in the same way. It always had two elephants, at least, and four or five camels, and sometimes there was a giraffe. These headed the procession, the elephants in the very front, with their keepers at their heads, and then the camels led by halters dangling from their sneering lips and con-

---

2. Shop that forms articles on a lathe.   3. Short, close-fitting jacket.

temptuous noses. After these began to come the show-wagons, with pictures on their sides, very flattered portraits of the wild beasts and birds inside; lions first, then tigers (never meaner than Royal Bengal ones, which the boys understood to be a superior breed), then leopards, then pumas and panthers; then bears, then jackals and hyenas; then bears and wolves; then kangaroos, musk-oxen, deer, and such harmless cattle; and then ostriches, emus, lyre-birds, birds-of-Paradise and all the rest. From time to time the boys ran back from the elephants and camels to get what good they could out of the scenes in which these hidden wonders were dramatized in acts of rapine or the chase, but they always came forward to the elephants and camels again. Even with them they had to endure a degree of denial, for although you could see most of the camels' figures, the elephants were so heavily draped that it was a kind of disappointment to look at them. The boys kept as close as they could, and came as near getting under the elephants' feet as the keepers would allow; but, after all, they were driven off a good deal and had to keep stealing back. They gave the elephants apples and bits of cracker and cake, and some tried to put tobacco into their trunks; though they knew very well that it was nearly certain death to do so; for any elephant that was deceived that way would recognize the boy that did it, and kill him the next time he came, if it was twenty years afterwards. The boys used to believe that the Miami[4] bridge would break down under the elephants if they tried to cross it, and they would have liked to see it do it, but no one ever saw it, perhaps because the elephants always waded the river. Some boys had seen them wading it, and stopping to drink and squirt the water out of their trunks. If an elephant got a boy that had given him tobacco into the river, he would squirt water on him till he drowned him. Still, some boys always tried to give the elephants tobacco, just to see how they would act for the time being.

A show was not so much in favor as a circus, because there was so little performance in the ring. You could go round and look at the animals, mostly very sleepy in their cages, but you were not allowed to poke them through the bars, or anything; and when you took your seat there was nothing much till Herr Driesbach entered the lions' cage, and began to make them jump over his whip. It was some pleasure to see him put his head between the jaws of the great African King of Beasts, but the lion never did anything to him, and so the act wanted a true dramatic climax. The boys would really rather have seen a bare-back rider, like James Rivers, turn a back-somersault and light on his horse's crupper, any time, though they respected Herr Driesbach, too; they did not care much for a woman who once went into the lions' cage and made them jump round.

If you had the courage you could go up the ladder into the cur-

4. The Miami River flows through Hamilton into the Ohio very near the border of Indiana.

tained tower on the elephant's back, and ride round the ring with
some of the other fellows; but my boy at least never had the courage; and he never was of those who mounted the trick pony and
were shaken off as soon as they got on. It seemed to be a good deal
of fun, but he did not dare to risk it; and he had an obscure trouble
of mind when, the last thing, four or five ponies were brought out
with as many monkeys tied on their backs, and set to run a race
round the ring. The monkeys always looked very miserable, and
even the one who won the race, and rode round afterwards with an
American flag in his hand and his cap very much cocked over his
left eye, did not seem to cheer up any.

The boys had their own beliefs about the different animals, and
one of these concerned the inappeasable ferocity of the zebra. I do
not know why the zebra should have had this repute, for he certainly never did anything to deserve it; but, for the matter of that,
he was like all the other animals. Bears were not much esteemed,
but they would have been if they could have been really seen hugging anybody to death. It was always hoped that some of the fiercest
animals would get away and have to be hunted down, and
retaken after they had killed a lot of dogs. If the elephants, some of
them, had gone crazy, it would have been something, for then they
would have roamed up and down the turnpike smashing buggies
and wagons, and had to be shot with the six-pound cannon that was
used to celebrate the Fourth of July with.

Another thing that was against the show was that the animals
were fed after it was out, and you could not see the tigers tearing
their prey when the great lumps of beef were thrown them. There
was somehow not so much chance of hooking into a show as a
circus, because the seats did not go all round, and you could be seen
under the cages as soon as you got in under the canvas. I never
heard of a boy that hooked into a show; perhaps nobody ever tried.

A show had the same kind of smell as a circus, up to a certain
point, and then its smell began to be different. Both smelt of tan-
bark or saw-dust and trodden grass, and both smelt of lemonade
and cigars; but after that a show had its own smell of animals. I
have found in later life that this is a very offensive smell on a hot
day; but I do not believe a boy ever thinks so; for him it is just a
different smell from a circus smell. There were two other reasons
why a show was not as much fun as a circus, and one was that it
was thought instructive, and fellows went who were not allowed to
go to circuses. But the great reason of all was that you could not
have an animal show of your own as you could a circus. You could
not get the animals; and no boy living could act a camel, or a Royal
Bengal tiger, or an elephant so as to look the least like one.

Of course you could have negro shows, and the boys often had
them; but they were not much fun, and you were always getting the
black on your shirt-sleeves.

1890

AMBROSE BIERCE
1842–1914?

Ambrose Gwinnett Bierce was born on June 24, 1842, in Meigs County, Ohio, the last of nine children of strongly religious parents. He led an unhappy childhood, and as an adult he cut himself off from his parents and all but one of his brothers and sisters. Perhaps his fascination with the supernatural in his fiction is similarly an attempt to escape the ordinary society of men he observed closely and claimed to detest. In any case, from his earliest days "Bitter Bierce," as he came to be called, seemed disappointed with what had been, displeased with his present condition, and pessimistic about what lay ahead.

Not long after he had spent one year at a military academy in Kentucky —his only formal schooling—the Civil War broke out and Bierce volunteered for the Union Army. He began as a drummer boy, was involved in several battles, and was mustered out a lieutenant. Bierce later defined war (in his *Devil's Dictionary*) as a "by-product of the arts of peace," and peace as "a period of cheating between two periods of fighting," and it is hard to believe that, even while a soldier, he had been a zealous military man. The Civil War experience, however, was an important source of some of his best fiction, including the spare and shocking *Chickamauga* and *An Occurrence at Owl Creek Bridge.*

After the war, Bierce moved to San Francisco. By 1866 he had secured a job as a journalist, the career he pursued for the rest of his life. He began as a columnist for the *News Letter* and in 1868 became its editor. Among his writer friends in San Francisco were Mark Twain, Bret Harte, Joaquin Miller, and George Sterling, all of whom were involved as journalists, lecturers, and writers in establishing San Francisco as a literary center. Bierce married in 1872 and took his bride to England, where they lived until 1876. There, under the influence of literary sophisticates such as George Augustus Sala and Thomas Hood, he developed from a crude western humorist into a satirist of elegance and bite. His best early work appeared in the "Prattler" column written first for *The Argonaut* (1877–79), and then for the *Wasp* until 1886. In that year the popular column was picked up by William Randolph Hearst's *San Francisco Sunday Examiner*, where it continued until 1896. A mixture of reviews, gossip, political and social commentary, the "Prattler" also served as outlet for a number of Bierce's best short stories.

Bierce's personal life was a series of disasters. His definition of marriage —"the state or condition of a community consisting of a master, a mistress, and two slaves, making in all, two"—reflected his views of his own marriage (which ended in divorce in 1891). In 1889 his elder son was shot to death during a fight over a girl; in 1901 his younger son died of alcoholism. In 1913, he went to Mexico and disappeared without a trace, though there is a story that he was killed in the revolutionary war which pitted Pancho Villa and Venustiano Carranza against General Victoriano Huerta.

Bierce's pessimism, cynicism, nihilism, and gallows humor are in the tradition of no-saying which runs from Herman Melville to Thomas Pynchon.

It is not the mordant wit of *The Devil's Dictionary* (first published in 1906 as *The Cynic's Word Book*) or Bierce's penchant for the grotesque, however, which finally makes him significant. In his best work, such as *Tales of Soldiers and Civilians* (1891; later retitled *In the Midst of Life*), Bierce, like Stephen Crane, Ernest Hemingway, and Norman Mailer after him, converted the disordered experience of man at war into resonant and dramatic fictional moments.

An Occurrence at Owl Creek Bridge[1]

I

A man stood upon a railroad bridge in northern Alabama, looking down into the swift water twenty feet below. The man's hands were behind his back, the wrists bound with a cord. A rope closely encircled his neck. It was attached to a stout cross-timber above his head and the slack fell to the level of his knees. Some loose boards laid upon the sleepers[2] supporting the metals of the railway supplied a footing for him and his executioners—two private soldiers of the Federal army, directed by a sergeant who in civil life may have been a deputy sheriff. At a short remove upon the same temporary platform was an officer in the uniform of his rank, armed. He was a captain. A sentinel at each end of the bridge stood with his rifle in the position known as "support," that is to say, vertical in front of the left shoulder, the hammer resting on the forearm thrown straight across the chest—a formal and unnatural position, enforcing an erect carriage of the body. It did not appear to be the duty of these two men to know what was occurring at the centre of the bridge; they merely blockaded the two ends of the foot planking that traversed it.

Beyond one of the sentinels nobody was in sight; the railroad ran straight away into a forest for a hundred yards, then, curving, was lost to view. Doubtless there was an outpost farther along. The other bank of the stream was open ground—a gentle acclivity topped with a stockade of vertical tree trunks, loopholed for rifles, with a single embrasure through which protruded the muzzle of a brass cannon commanding the bridge. Midway of the slope between bridge and fort were the spectators—a single company of infantry in line, at "parade rest," the butts of the rifles on the ground, the barrels inclining slightly backward against the right shoulder, the hands crossed upon the stock. A lieutenant stood at the right of the line, the point of his sword upon the ground, his left hand resting upon his right. Excepting the group of four at the centre of the

1. First published in the *San Francisco Examiner* on July 13, 1890, this story was subsequently reprinted as part of the collection *Tales of Soldiers and Civilians* (1891; retitled *In the Midst of Life* in 1898) and in Volume II of *The Col-*lected *Works of Ambrose Bierce* (1909–12), the basis of the present text.
2. Piece of timber, stone, or steel on or near the ground to keep railroad rails in place.

bridge, not a man moved. The company faced the bridge, staring stonily, motionless. The sentinels, facing the banks of the stream, might have been statues to adorn the bridge. The captain stood with folded arms, silent, observing the work of his subordinates, but making no sign. Death is a dignitary who when he comes announced is to be received with formal manifestations of respect, even by those most familiar with him. In the code of military etiquette silence and fixity are forms of deference.

The man who was engaged in being hanged was apparently about thirty-five years of age. He was a civilian, if one might judge from his habit, which was that of a planter. His features were good—a straight nose, firm mouth, broad forehead, from which his long, dark hair was combed straight back, falling behind his ears to the collar of his well-fitting frock-coat. He wore a mustache and pointed beard, but no whiskers; his eyes were large and dark gray, and had a kindly expression which one would hardly have expected in one whose neck was in the hemp. Evidently this was no vulgar assassin. The liberal military code makes provision for hanging many kinds of persons, and gentlemen are not excluded.

The preparations being complete, the two private soldiers stepped aside and each drew away the plank upon which he had been standing. The sergeant turned to the captain, saluted and placed himself immediately behind that officer, who in turn moved apart one pace. These movements left the condemned man and the sergeant standing on the two ends of the same plank, which spanned three of the cross-ties of the bridge. The end upon which the civilian stood almost, but not quite, reached a fourth. This plank had been held in place by the weight of the captain; it was now held by that of the sergeant. At a signal from the former the latter would step aside, the plank would tilt and the condemned man go down between two ties. The arrangement commended itself to his judgment as simple and effective. His face had not been covered nor his eyes bandaged. He looked a moment at his "unsteadfast footing," then let his gaze wander to the swirling water of the stream racing madly beneath his feet. A piece of dancing driftwood caught his attention and his eyes followed it down the current. How slowly it appeared to move! What a sluggish stream!

He closed his eyes in order to fix his last thoughts upon his wife and children. The water, touched to gold by the early sun, the brooding mists under the banks at some distance down the stream, the fort, the soldiers, the piece of drift—all had distracted him. And now he became conscious of a new disturbance. Striking through the thought of his dear ones was a sound which he could neither ignore nor understand, a sharp, distinct, metallic percussion like the stroke of a blacksmith's hammer upon the anvil; it had the same ringing quality. He wondered what it was, and whether immeasurably distant or near by—it seemed both. Its recurrence was regular, but as slow as the tolling of a death knell. He awaited each stroke with impatience and—he knew not why—apprehension. The intervals of silence grew progressively longer; the delays became maddening. With their greater infrequency the sounds increased in strength and sharpness. They hurt his ear like the thrust of a knife; he feared he would shriek. What he heard was the ticking of his watch.

He unclosed his eyes and saw again the water below him. "If I could free my hands," he thought, "I might throw off the noose and spring into the stream. By diving I could evade the bullets and, swimming vigorously, reach the bank, take to the woods and get away home. My home, thank God, is as yet outside their lines; my wife and little ones are still beyond the invader's farthest advance."

As these thoughts, which have here to be set down in words, were flashed into the doomed man's brain rather than evolved from it the captain nodded to the sergeant. The sergeant stepped aside.

II

Peyton Farquhar was a well-to-do planter, of an old and highly respected Alabama family. Being a slave owner and like other slave owners a politician he was naturally an original secessionist and ardently devoted to the Southern cause. Circumstances of an imperious nature, which it is unnecesary to relate here, had prevented him from taking service with the gallant army that had fought the disastrous campaigns ending with the fall of Corinth,[3] and he chafed under the inglorious restraint, longing for the release of his energies, the larger life of the soldier, the opportunity for distinction. That opportunity, he felt, would come, as it comes to all in war time. Meanwhile he did what he could. No service was too humble for him to perform in aid of the South, no adventure too perilous for him to undertake if consistent with the character of a civilian who was at heart a soldier, and who in good faith and without too much qualification assented to at least a part of the frankly villainous dictum that all is fair in love and war.

One evening while Farquhar and his wife were sitting on a rustic bench near the entrance to his grounds, a gray-clad soldier rode up to the gate and asked for a drink of water. Mrs. Farquhar was only too happy to serve him with her own white hands. While she was fetching the water her husband approached the dusty horseman and inquired eagerly for news from the front.

"The Yanks are repairing the railroads," said the man, "and are getting ready for another advance. They have reached the Owl Creek bridge, put it in order and built a stockade on the north bank. The commandant has issued an order, which is posted every-where, declaring that any civilian caught interfering with the rail-

---

3. Corinth, Mississippi, fell to the Union forces on April 6 and 7, 1862, under General Ulysses S. Grant in the Battle of Shiloh.

road, its bridges, tunnels or trains will be summarily hanged. I saw the order."

"How far is it to the Owl Creek bridge?" Farquhar asked.

"About thirty miles."

"Is there no force on this side the creek?"

"Only a picket post half a mile out, on the railroad, and a single sentinel at this end of the bridge."

"Suppose a man—a civilian and student of hanging—should elude the picket post and perhaps get the better of the sentinel," said Farquhar, smiling, "what could he accomplish?"

The soldier reflected. "I was there a month ago," he replied. "I observed that the flood of last winter had lodged a great quantity of driftwood against the wooden pier at this end of the bridge. It is now dry and would burn like tow."

The lady had now brought the water, which the soldier drank. He thanked her ceremoniously, bowed to her husband and rode away. An hour later, after nightfall, he repassed the plantation, going northward in the direction from which he had come. He was a Federal scout.

III

As Peyton Farquhar fell straight downward through the bridge he lost consciousness and was as one already dead. From this state he was awakened—ages later, it seemed to him—by the pain of a sharp pressure upon his throat, followed by a sense of suffocation. Keen, poignant agonies seemed to shoot from his neck downward through every fibre of his body and limbs. These pains appeared to flash along well-defined lines of ramification and to beat with an inconceivably rapid periodicity. They seemed like streams of pulsating fire heating him to an intolerable temperature. As to his head, he was conscious of nothing but a feeling of fulness—of congestion. These sensations were unaccompanied by thought. The intellectual part of his nature was already effaced; he had power only to feel, and feeling was torment. He was conscious of motion. Encompassed in a luminous cloud, of which he was now merely the fiery heart, without material substance, he swung through unthinkable arcs of oscillation, like a vast pendulum. Then all at once, with terrible suddenness, the light about him shot upward with the noise of a loud plash; a frightful roaring was in his ears, and all was cold and dark. The power of thought was restored; he knew that the rope had broken and he had fallen into the stream. There was no additional strangulation; the noose about his neck was already suffocating him and kept the water from his lungs. To die of hanging at the bottom of a river!—the idea seemed to him ludicrous. He opened his eyes in the darkness and saw above him a gleam of light, but how distant, how inaccessible! He was still sinking, for the light became fainter and fainter until it was a mere glimmer. Then it began to grow and brighten, and he knew that he was rising toward the surface—knew it with reluctance, for he was now very comfortable. "To be hanged and drowned," he thought, "that is not so bad; but I do not wish to be shot. No; I will not be shot; that is not fair."

He was not conscious of an effort, but a sharp pain in his wrist apprised him that he was trying to free his hands. He gave the struggle his attention, as an idler might observe the feat of a juggler, without interest in the outcome. What splendid effort!—what magnificent, what superhuman strength! Ah, that was a fine endeavor! Bravo! The cord fell away; his arms parted and floated upward, the hands dimly seen on each side in the growing light. He watched them with a new interest as first one and then the other pounced upon the noose at his neck. They tore it away and thrust it fiercely aside, its undulations resembling those of a water-snake. "Put it back, put it back!" He thought he shouted these words to his hands, for the undoing of the noose had been succeeded by the direst pang that he had yet experienced. His neck ached horribly; his brain was on fire; his heart, which had been fluttering faintly, gave a great leap, trying to force itself out at his mouth. His whole body was racked and wrenched with an insupportable anguish! But his disobedient hands gave no heed to the command. They beat the water vigorously with quick, downward strokes, forcing him to the surface. He felt his head emerge; his eyes were blinded by the sunlight; his chest expanded convulsively, and with a supreme and crowning agony his lungs engulfed a great draught of air, which instantly he expelled in a shriek!

He was now in full possession of his physical senses. They were, indeed, preternaturally keen and alert. Something in the awful disturbance of his organic system had so exalted and refined them that they made record of things never before perceived. He felt the ripples upon his face and heard their separate sounds as they struck. He looked at the forest on the bank of the stream, saw the individual trees, the leaves and the veining of each leaf—saw the very insects upon them: the locusts, the brilliant-bodied flies, the gray spiders stretching their webs from twig to twig. He noted the prismatic colors in all the dewdrops upon a million blades of grass. The humming of the gnats that danced above the eddies of the stream, the beating of the dragon-flies' wings, the strokes of the water-spiders' legs, like oars which had lifted their boat—all these made audible music. A fish slid along beneath his eyes and he heard the rush of its body parting the water.

He had come to the surface facing down the stream; in a moment the visible world seemed to wheel slowly round, himself the pivotal point, and he saw the bridge, the fort, the soldiers upon the bridge, the captain, the sergeant, the two privates, his executioners. They were in silhouette against the blue sky. They shouted and gesticulated, pointing at him. The captain had drawn his pistol, but did not fire; the others were unarmed. Their movements were grotesque and horrible, their forms gigantic.

Suddenly he heard a sharp report and something struck the water smartly within a few inches of his head, spattering his face with spray. He heard a second report, and saw one of the sentinels with his rifle at his shoulder, a light cloud of blue smoke rising from the muzzle. The man in the water saw the eye of the man on the bridge gazing into his own through the sights of the rifle. He observed that it was a gray eye and remembered having read that gray eyes were keenest, and that all famous markmen had them. Nevertheless, this one had missed.

A counter-swirl had caught Farquhar and turned him half round; he was again looking into the forest on the bank opposite the fort. The sound of a clear, high voice in a monotonous singsong now rang out behind him and came across the water with a distinctness that pierced and subdued all other sounds, even the beating of the ripples in his ears. Although no soldier, he had frequented camps enough to know the dread significance of that deliberate, drawling, aspirated chant; the lieutenant on shore was taking a part in the morning's work. How coldly and pitilessly—with what an even, calm intonation, presaging, and enforcing tranquillity in the men—with what accurately measured intervals fell those cruel words:

"Attention, company! . . . Shoulder arms! . . . Ready! . . . Aim! . . . Fire!"

Farquhar dived—dived as deeply as he could. The water roared in his ears like the voice of Niagara, yet he heard the dulled thunder of the volley and, rising again toward the surface, met shining bits of metal, singularly flattened, oscillating slowly downward. Some of them touched him on the face and hands, then fell away, continuing their descent. One lodged between his collar and neck; it was uncomfortably warm and he snatched it out.

As he rose to the surface, gasping for breath, he saw that he had been a long time under water; he was perceptibly farther down stream—nearer to safety. The soldiers had almost finished reloading; the metal ramrods flashed all at once in the sunshine as they were drawn from the barrels, turned in the air, and thrust into their sockets. The two sentinels fired again, independently and ineffectually.

The hunted man saw all this over his shoulder; he was now swimming vigorously with the current. His brain was as energetic as his arms and legs; he thought with the rapidity of lightning.

"The officer," he reasoned, "will not make that martinet's error a second time. It is as easy to dodge a volley as a single shot. He has probably already given the command to fire at will. God help me, I cannot dodge them all!"

An appalling plash within two yards of him was followed by a loud, rushing sound, *diminuendo*, which seemed to travel back through the air to the fort and died in an explosion which stirred the very river to its deeps! A rising sheet of water curved over him, fell down upon him, blinded him, strangled him! The cannon had taken a hand in the game. As he shook his head free from the commotion of the smitten water he heard the deflected shot humming through the air ahead, and in an instant it was cracking and smashing the branches in the forest beyond.

"They will not do that again," he thought; "the next time they will use a charge of grape.[4] I must keep my eye upon the gun; the smoke will apprise me—the report arrives too late; it lags behind the missile. That is a good gun."

Suddenly he felt himself whirled round and round—spinning like a top. The water, the banks, the forests, the now distant bridge, fort and men—all were commingled and blurred. Objects were represented by their colors only; circular horizontal streaks of color—that was all he saw. He had been caught in a vortex and was being whirled on with a velocity of advance and gyration that made him giddy and sick. In a few moments he was flung upon the gravel at the foot of the left bank of the stream—the southern bank—and behind a projecting point which concealed him from his enemies. The sudden arrest of his motion, the abrasion of one of his hands on the gravel, restored him, and he wept with delight. He dug his fingers into the sand, threw it over himself in handfuls and audibly blessed it. It looked like diamonds, rubies, emeralds; he could think of nothing beautiful which it did not resemble. The trees upon the bank were giant garden plants; he noted a definite order in their arrangement, inhaled the fragrance of their blooms. A strange, roseate light shone through the spaces among their trunks and the wind made in their branches the music of aeolian harps.[5] He had no wish to perfect his escape—was content to remain in that enchanting spot until retaken.

A whiz and rattle of grapeshot among the branches high above his head roused him from his dream. The baffled cannoneer had fired him a random farewell. He sprang to his feet, rushed up the sloping bank, and plunged into the forest.

All that day he traveled, laying his course by the rounding sun. The forest seemed interminable; nowhere did he discover a break in it, not even a woodman's road. He had not known that he lived in so wild a region. There was something uncanny in the revelation.

By nightfall he was fatigued, footsore, famishing. The thought of his wife and children urged him on. At last he found a road which led him in what he knew to be the right direction. It was as wide and straight as a city street, yet it seemed untraveled. No fields bordered it, no dwelling anywhere. Not so much as the barking of a dog sug-

---

4. Grapeshot, a cluster of small iron balls used as a cannon charge.
5. Stringed instruments activated by the wind (Aeolus was the keeper of the winds in classical mythology).

gested human habitation. The black bodies of the trees formed a straight wall on both sides, terminating on the horizon in a point, like a diagram in a lesson in perspective. Overhead, as he looked up through this rift in the wood, shone great golden stars looking unfamiliar and grouped in strange constellations. He was sure they were arranged in some order which had a secret and malign significance. The wood on either side was full of singular noises, among which—once, twice, and again—he distinctly heard whispers in an unknown tongue.

His neck was in pain and lifting his hand to it he found it horribly swollen. He knew that it had a circle of black where the rope had bruised it. His eyes felt congested; he could no longer close them. His tongue was swollen with thirst; he relieved its fever by thrusting it forward from between his teeth into the cold air. How softly the turf had carpeted the untraveled avenue—he could no longer feel the roadway beneath his feet!

Doubtless, despite his suffering, he had fallen asleep while walking, for now he sees another scene—perhaps he has merely recovered from a delirium. He stands at the gate of his own home. All is as he left it, and all bright and beautiful in the morning sunshine. He must have traveled the entire night. As he pushes open the gate and passes up the wide white walk, he sees a flutter of female garments; his wife, looking fresh and cool and sweet, steps down from the veranda to meet him. At the bottom of the steps she stands waiting, with a smile of ineffable joy, an attitude of matchless grace and dignity. Ah, how beautiful she is! He springs forward with extended arms. As he is about to clasp her he feels a stunning blow upon the back of the neck; a blinding white light blazes all about him with a sound like the shock of a cannon—then all is darkness and silence!

Peyton Farquhar was dead; his body, with a broken neck, swung gently from side to side beneath the timbers of the Owl Creek bridge.

1890, 1891

HENRY JAMES
1843–1916

Henry James was the first American writer to conceive his career in international terms; he set out, that is, to be a "literary master" in the European sense. Partly because of this grandiose self-conception, partly because he spent most of his adult life in England, partly because his intricate style and choices of cultivated characters ran counter to the dominant vernacular tradition initiated by Mark Twain, James attracted, in his own lifetime, only a select company of admirers. The recognition of his intrinsic importance, as well as his wide influence as novelist and critic, did not emerge until the years between the world wars, when American literary taste reached a new level of sophistication. Only quite recently has his playful prediction that "some day all my buried prose will kick off its various tombstones at once" largely come to pass. James is now firmly established as one of America's major novelists and critics and as a psychological realist of unsurpassed subtlety.

James was born in New York City on April 15, 1843. His father was an eccentric, independently wealthy philosopher and religious visionary; his slightly older brother William was the first notable American psychologist and perhaps our country's most influential philosopher; two younger brothers and a sister completed one of the most remarkable of American families. First taken to Europe as an infant, James spent his boyhood in a still almost bucolic New York City before the family once again left for the Continent when he was twelve. His father wanted the children to have a rich, "sensuous education," and during the next four years, with stays in England, Switzerland, and France, they were endlessly exposed to galleries, libraries, museums, and (of special interest to Henry) theaters. Henry's formal schooling was unsystematic, but he mastered French well enough to begin his lifelong study of its literature, and he thoroughly absorbed the ambiance of the Old World. From childhood on he was aware of the intricate network of institutions and traditions that he later lamented (in his study of Hawthorne and elsewhere) American novelists had to do without.

James early developed what he described in *A Small Boy and Others* (1913) as the "practice of wondering and dawdling and gaping." In that same memoir he also relates how he suffered the "obscure hurt" to his back which disqualified him from service in the Civil War and which must have helped to reinforce his inclination to be an observer rather than a participator. In his late teens his interest in literature and in writing intensified, and by the time he reached his majority he was publishing reviews and stories in some of the leading American journals—*Atlantic Monthly, North American Review, Galaxy,* and *Nation.* Though the crucial decision to establish his base of operations in England in 1876 remained to be made (after much shuttling back and forth between America and Europe, and after trial residence in France and Italy), the direction of James's single-minded career as man of letters was clearly marked in his early manhood. James never married. He maintained close ties with his family, kept up a large correspondence, was extremely sociable and a famous diner-out, knew most of his great contemporaries in the arts, many intimately—but he lived and worked alone. His emotional life and prodigious creative energy were invested for fifty years in what he called the "sacred rage" of his art.

Leon Edel, James's biographer, divides the writer's mature career into three parts. In the first, which culminated with *The Portrait of a Lady* (1881), he felt his way toward and appropriated the so-called international theme—the drama, comic and tragic, of Americans in Europe and Europeans in America. In the tripartite second period, he experimented with diverse themes and forms—first with novels dealing explicitly with strong social and political currents of the 1870s and 1880s, then with writing for the theater, and finally with shorter fictions that explore the relationship of artists to society and the troubled psychology of oppressed children and haunted or obsessed men and women. In James's last period—the so-called "major phase"—he returned to international or cosmopolitan subjects in an extraordinary series of elaborately developed novels, shorter fiction, and criticism.

Three of his earliest books—*A Passionate Pilgrim*, a collection of stories; *Transatlantic Sketches*, a collection of travel pieces; and *Roderick Hudson*, a novel—were all published in 1875. *The American* (1877) was his first successful and extended treatment of the naïve young American (Christopher Newman) from the New World in tension with the traditions, customs, and values of the Old. *Daisy Miller* (1878) was the work with which he first achieved widespread popularity. In this "sketch," as it was originally subtitled, the dangerously naïve young American girl (a subject to be treated often by James and his friend W. D. Howells) pays for her innocence of European social mores—and her willfulness—with her life. These stories make it clear that James was neither a chauvinist nor a resentful émigré, but a cosmopolitan whose concern was to explore the moral qualities of men and women forced to deal with the dilemmas of cultural displacement.

Despite their appeal, the characters of Daisy Miller and Christopher Newman are reductively simple and typecast, and this makes romance, melodrama, and pathos (whatever their charms) more likely than psychological complexity and genuine tragedy, which require, especially for James, a broad canvas. In the character and career of Isabel Archer—for which he drew on the tragically blighted life of his beloved cousin, Mary Temple, who died of tuberculosis in 1870 at the age of twenty-four—he found the focus for his first masterpiece on the international theme, *The Portrait of a Lady* (1881). Here, for the first time, the complex inner life of his characters—compounded of desire, will, thought, impulse—is fully and realistically projected. All the same, even in a relatively short work like *Daisy Miller*, James's essential themes and procedures are available.

From 1885 to 1890 James was largely occupied writing three novels in the naturalistic mode—*The Bostonians* (1886), *The Princess Casamassima* (1886), and *The Tragic Muse* (1889). James may have been right to put aside temporarily the "American-European legend" as subject, but he could not finally accept philosophic determinism of his characters' behavior or render his materials in documentary detail or depend for interest and effect on violent, physical action. These three novels have their virtues, but they are not the virtues of the mode as practiced by Zola, Norris, or Dreiser. For better *and* for worse, the English novelist Joseph Conrad observed, James was the "historian of fine consciences."

These stories of reformers, radicals, and revolutionaries, better appreciated in our own time than in his, alienated James's hard-won audience. Out of a sense of artistic challenge as well as financial need (he was never rich), James attempted to regain popularity and earn money by turning dramatist. Between 1890 and 1895 he wrote seven plays; two were produced, neither was a success. Humiliated by the boos and hooting of a hostile first-night crowd for *Guy Domville* (1895), James gave up the attempt to master this new form.

Between 1895 and 1900 James returned to fiction, especially to experiment in shorter works with three dominant subjects which he often combined: misunderstood or troubled writers and artists, ghosts and apparitions, and doomed or threatened children and adolescents. *The Real Thing* is an excellent example of a special kind of artistic dilemma that fascinated James, while *The Turn of the Screw* (1898), in which a whole household,

including two young children, is terrorized by "ghosts," is the most powerful and famous of those stories in which, as James put it, "the strange and
sinister is embroidered on the very type of the normal and the easy."
Almost as well known, *The Beast in the Jungle* (1903) projects the pathetic
career of a man who allows his obsessive imagination of personal disaster in
the future to destroy his chances for love and life in the present. This
theme of the wasted life is played out once again in the tantalizingly autobiographical *The Jolly Corner* (1907).

Following his own advice to other novelists to "dramatize, dramatize,
dramatize," James increasingly removed himself as controlling narrator—became "invisible," in T. S. Eliot's phrase—from the reader's awareness. The
benefits of this heightened emphasis on showing rather than telling were
compression or intensification and enhanced opportunity for ambiguity. The
more the author withdrew, the more the reader was forced to enter the
process of creating meaning. We are accustomed now to having our fiction
thus "objectified," but it is James who is largely responsible for this development in narrative technique.

The Wings of the Dove (1902), *The Ambassadors* (1903), which James
thought was "the best 'all round' " of his productions, and *The Golden
Bowl* (1904) are demanding novels. The first two deal with subjects he had
treated earlier in *The American* and *The Portrait of a Lady,* and all three
concern themselves with James's grand theme of freedom through perception: only awareness of one's own character and others' provides the
wisdom to live well. The treatment of this theme in these books, however,
is characterized by richness of syntax, characterization, point of view, symbolic resonance, metaphoric texture, and organizing rhythms. The world of
these novels is, as a critic has remarked, like the very atmosphere of the
mind. These dramas of perception are widely considered to be James's
most influential contribution to the craft of fiction.

When James was not writing fiction, he was most often writing about it
—either his own or others. He was, as he noted in one of his letters, "a critical, a *non-naif,* a questioning, worrying reader." If he was somewhat narrow
in his reading—restricting himself chiefly to nineteenth-century fiction—he
made his limited experience count for as much in criticism as it did in
fiction. His inquiries into the achievement of other writers—preserved in
such volumes as *French Poets and Novelists* (1878), *Partial Portraits*
(1888), and *Notes on Novelists* (1914)—are remarkable for their breadth,
balance, and acuteness. His taste and judgments have been largely confirmed
by time.

More broadly philosophic than the reviews or even the essays on individual writers, *The Art of the Novel* (1884) fairly represents James's central
aesthetic conceptions. Calling attention to the unparalleled opportunities
open to the artist of fiction and the beauty of the novel which creates a
new form, James also insists that "the deepest quality of a work of art will
always be the quality of the mind of the producer" and that "no good
novel will ever proceed from a superficial mind." James left no better
record than this essay of his always twinned concerns over the moral and
formal qualities of fiction, of the relationship between aesthetic and moral
perception.

James was an extremely self-conscious writer, and his *Notebooks* (published in 1947) reveal a subtle, intense mind in the act of discovering subjects, methods, and principles. The prefaces he wrote for the definitive New

York edition of his extensively revised novels and tales (gathered and published in 1934 as *The Art of the Novel*) contain James's final study of the works that he considered best represented his achievement. The culmination of an entire lifetime of reflection on the craft of fiction, they provide extraordinary accounts of the origins and growth of his major writings and exquisite analyses of the fictional problems that each work posed. Despite their occasional opacity, they also serve, as he wrote Howells he hoped they would, as a "sort of comprehensive manual or *vade-mecum* for aspirants in our arduous profession." These prefaces provided both vocabulary and example for the close textual analysis of prose fiction in the New Criticism that was dominant in America in the generation following World War II.

While James was in the United States arranging for Scribner's New York edition of his novels and tales, he also took the occasion to travel extensively and to lecture in his native land and Canada. The chief fruit of this experience was *The American Scene* (1907), which carried the art of travel writing to the same sophisticated level he had carried the art of fiction in *The Ambassadors*, *The Wings of the Dove*, and *The Golden Bowl*. This "absolutely personal" book is perhaps the most vividly particular account we have of the vast and profound changes that occurred in America between the Civil War and World War I, the period James later characterized as the "Age of the Mistake."

The same intricate, ruminative richness marks the three autobiographical reminiscences he wrote late in life: *A Small Boy and Others* (1913), *Notes of a Son and Brother* (1914), and the fragmentary and posthumously published *The Middle Years* (1917). Henry James died in 1916, a year after he became a naturalized British subject out of impatience with America's reluctance to enter World War I.

At one time or another James has been characterized as a snob, a deserter from his native land, an old maid, a mere aesthete; his fiction has been deprecated as narrowly concerned with the rich, the bloodless, and the sexless, as needlessly elaborate and long-winded, and as excessively introspective and autobiographical. But James, who always believed in his own genius, has been vindicated because he understood the mixed nature of men and women profoundly, because he judged them humanely, and because he gave enduring and compelling shape to his sense of life.

Daisy Miller[1]

I

At a little town of Vevey, in Switzerland, there is a particularly comfortable hotel; there are indeed many hotels, since the entertainment of tourists is the business of the place, which, as many travellers will remember, is seated upon the edge of a remarkably blue lake[2]—a lake that it behoves every tourist to visit. The shore of the lake presents an unbroken array of establishments of this

---

1. *Daisy Miller* first appeared in *Cornhill Magazine* in June–July, 1878, was reprinted (and pirated) many times in James's lifetime, and was carefully revised for inclusion in the New York edition, Vol. XVIII (1909), the source of the present text.
2. Lac Léman, or Lake of Geneva.

order, of every category, from the "grand hotel" of the newest fashion, with a chalk-white front, a hundred balconies, and a dozen flags flying from its roof, to the small Swiss pension of an elder day, with its name inscribed in German-looking lettering upon a pink or yellow wall and an awkward summer-house in the angle of the garden. One of the hotels at Vevey, however, is famous, even classical, being distinguished from many of its upstart neighbours by an air both of luxury and of maturity. In this region, through the month of June, American travellers are extremely numerous; it may be said indeed that Vevey assumes at that time some of the characteristics of an American watering-place. There are sights and sounds that evoke a vision, an echo, of Newport and Saratoga.[3] There is a flitting hither and thither of "stylish" young girls, a rustling of muslin flounces, a rattle of dance-music in the morning hours, a sound of high-pitched voices at all times. You receive an impression of these things at the excellent inn of the "Trois Couronnes,"[4] and are transported in fancy to the Ocean House or to Congress Hall. But at the "Trois Couronnes," it must be added, there are other features much at variance with these suggestions; neat German waiters who look like secretaries of legation; Russian princesses sitting in the garden; little Polish boys walking about, held by the hand, with their governors; a view of the snowy crest of the Dent du Midi[5] and the picturesque towers of the Castle of Chillon.

I hardly know whether it was the analogies or the differences that were uppermost in the mind of a young American, who, two or three years ago, sat in the garden of the "Trois Couronnes," looking about him rather idly at some of the graceful objects I have mentioned. It was a beautiful summer morning, and in whatever fashion the young American looked at things they must have seemed to him charming. He had come from Geneva the day before, by the little steamer, to see his aunt, who was staying at the hotel—Geneva having been for a long time his place of residence. But his aunt had a headache—his aunt had almost always a headache—and she was now shut up in her room smelling camphor so that he was at liberty to wander about. He was some seven-and-twenty years of age; when his friends spoke of him they usually said that he was at Geneva "studying." When his enemies spoke of him they said—but after all he had no enemies: he was extremely amiable and generally liked. What I should say is simply that when certain persons spoke of him they conveyed that the reason of his spending so much time at Geneva was that he was extremely devoted to a lady who lived there—a foreign lady, a person older than himself. Very few Americans—truly I think none—had ever seen this lady, about

---

3. Newport, Rhode Island, and Saratoga, New York, resort areas for the rich, where the Ocean House and Congress Hall are located.

4. "Three Crowns."

5. A peak of Mont Blanc; "Castle of Chillon": the setting for Byron's *The Prisoner of Chillon*.

whom there were some singular stories. But Winterbourne had an old attachment for the little capital of Calvinism;[6] he had been put to school there as a boy and had afterwards even gone, on trial —trial of the grey old "Academy"[7] on the steep and stony hillside —to college there; circumstances which had led to his forming a great many youthful friendships. Many of these he had kept, and they were a source of great satisfaction to him.

After knocking at his aunt's door and learning that she was indisposed he had taken a walk about the town and then he had come in to his breakfast. He had now finished that repast, but was enjoying a small cup of coffee which had been served him on a little table in the garden by one of the waiters who looked like *attachés*.[8] At last he finished his coffee and lit a cigarette. Presently a small boy came walking along the path—an urchin of nine or ten. The child, who was diminutive for his years, had an aged expression of countenance, a pale complexion and sharp little features. He was dressed in knickerbockers and had red stockings that displayed his poor little spindle-shanks; he also wore a brilliant red cravat. He carried in his hand a long alpenstock, the sharp point of which he thrust into everything he approached—the flower-beds, the garden-benches, the trains of the ladies' dresses. In front of Winterbourne he paused, looking at him with a pair of bright and penetrating little eyes.

"Will you give me a lump of sugar?" he asked in a small sharp hard voice—a voice immature and yet somehow not young.

Winterbourne glanced at the light table near him, on which his coffee-service rested, and saw that several morsels of sugar remained. "Yes, you may take one," he answered; "but I don't think too much sugar good for little boys."

This little boy stepped forward and carefully selected three of the coveted fragments, two of which he buried in the pocket of his knickerbockers, depositing the other as promptly in another place. He poked his alpenstock, lance-fashion, into Winterbourne's bench and tried to crack the lump of sugar with his teeth.

"Oh blazes; it's har-r-d!" he exclaimed, divesting vowel and consonants, pertinently enough, of any taint of softness.

Winterbourne had immediately gathered that he might have the honour of claiming him as a countryman. "Take care you don't hurt your teeth," he said paternally.

"I haven't got any teeth to hurt. They've all come out. I've only got seven teeth. Mother counted them last night, and one came out right afterwards. She said she'd slap me if any more came out. I can't help it. It's this old Europe. It's the climate that makes them come out. In America they didn't come out. It's these hotels."

---

6. Geneva, where John Calvin (1509–64) centered his Protestant regime.
7. I.e., University of Geneva.

8. I.e., like members of the diplomatic corps.

Winterbourne was much amused. "If you eat three lumps of sugar your mother will certainly slap you," he ventured.

"She's got to give me some candy then," rejoined his young interlocutor. "I can't get any candy here—any American candy. American candy's the best candy."

"And are American little boys the best little boys?" Winterbourne asked.

"I don't know. *I'm* an American boy," said the child.

"I see you're one of the best!" the young man laughed.

"Are you an American man?" pursued this vivacious infant. And then on his friend's affirmative reply, "American men are the best," he declared with assurance.

His companion thanked him for the compliment, and the child, who had now got astride of his alpenstock, stood looking about him while he attacked another lump of sugar. Winterbourne wondered if he himself had been like this in his infancy, for he had been brought to Europe at about the same age.

"Here comes my sister!" cried his young compatriot. "She's an American girl, you bet!"

Winterbourne looked along the path and saw a beautiful young lady advancing. "American girls are the best girls," he thereupon cheerfully remarked to his visitor.

"My sister ain't the best!" the child promptly returned. "She's always blowing at me."

"I imagine that's your fault, not hers," said Winterbourne. The young lady meanwhile had drawn near. She was dressed in white muslin, with a hundred frills and flounces and knots of pale-coloured ribbon. Bareheaded, she balanced in her hand a large parasol with a deep border of embroidery; and she was strikingly, admirably pretty. "How pretty they are!" thought our friend, who straightened himself in his seat as if he were ready to rise.

The young lady paused in front of his bench, near the parapet of the garden, which overlooked the lake. The small boy had now converted his alpenstock into a vaulting-pole, by the aid of which he was springing about in the gravel and kicking it up not a little. "Why Randolph," she freely began, "what *are* you doing?"

"I'm going up the Alps!" cried Randolph. "This is the way!" And he gave another extravagant jump, scattering the pebbles about Winterbourne's ears.

"That's the way they come down," said Winterbourne.

"He's an American man!" proclaimed Randolph in his harsh little voice.

The young lady gave no heed to this circumstance, but looked straight at her brother. "Well, I guess you'd better be quiet," she simply observed.

It seemed to Winterbourne that he had been in a manner presented. He got up and stepped slowly toward the charming creature, throwing away his cigarette. "This little boy and I have made acquaintance," he said with great civility. In Geneva, as he had been perfectly aware, a young man wasn't at liberty to speak to a young unmarried lady save under certain rarely-occurring conditions: but here at Vevey what conditions could be better than these?—a pretty American girl coming to stand in front of you in a garden with all the confidence in life. This pretty American girl, whatever that might prove, on hearing Winterbourne's observation simply glanced at him; she turned her head and looked over the parapet, at the lake and the opposite mountains. He wondered whether he had gone too far, but decided that he must gallantly advance rather than retreat. While he was thinking of something else to say the young lady turned again to the little boy, whom she addressed quite as if they were alone together. "I should like to know where you got that pole."

"I bought it!" Randolph shouted.

"You don't mean to say you're going to take it to Italy!"

"Yes, I'm going to take it t'Italy!" the child rang out.

She glanced over the front of her dress and smoothed out a knot or two of ribbon. Then she gave her sweet eyes to the prospect again. "Well, I guess you'd better leave it somewhere," she dropped after a moment.

"Are you going to Italy?" Winterbourne now decided very respectfully to enquire.

She glanced at him with lovely remoteness. "Yes sir," she then replied. And she said nothing more.

"And are you—a—thinking of the Simplon?"[9] he pursued with a slight drop of assurance.

"I don't know," she said. "I suppose it's some mountain. Randolph, what mountain are we thinking of?"

"Thinking of?"—the boy stared.

"Why going right over."

"Going to where?" he demanded.

"Why right down to Italy"—Winerbourne felt vague emulations.

"I don't know," said Randolph. "I don't want to go t' Italy. I want to go to America."

"Oh Italy's a beautiful place!" the young man laughed.

"Can you get candy there?" Randolph asked of all the echoes.

"I hope not," said his sister. "I guess you've had enough candy, and mother thinks so too."

"I haven't had any for ever so long—for a hundred weeks!" cried the boy, still jumping about.

The young lady inspected her flounces and smoothed her ribbons again; and Winterbourne presently risked an observation on the beauty of the view. He was ceasing to be in doubt, for he had begun to perceive that she was really not in the least embarrassed.

9. A pass in the Alps between Switzerland and Italy.

She might be cold, she might be austere, she might even be prim; for that was apparently—he had already so generalised—what the most "distant" American girls did: they came and planted themselves straight in front of you to show how rigidly unapproachable they were. There hadn't been the slightest flush in her fresh fairness however; so that she was clearly neither offended nor fluttered. Only she was composed—he had seen that before too—of charming little parts that didn't match and that made no *ensemble*;[1] and if she looked another way when he spoke to her, and seemed not particularly to hear him, this was simply her habit, her manner, the result of her having no idea whatever of "form" (with such a tell-tale appendage as Randolph where in the world would she have got it?) in any such connexion. As he talked a little more and pointed out some of the objects of interest in the view, with which she appeared wholly unacquainted, she gradually, none the less, gave him more of the benefit of her attention; and then he saw that act unqualified by the faintest shadow of reserve. It wasn't however what would have been called a "bold" front that she presented, for her expression was as decently limpid as the very cleanest water. Her eyes were the very prettiest conceivable, and indeed Winterbourne hadn't for a long time seen anything prettier than his fair country-woman's various features—her complexion, her nose, her ears, her teeth. He took a great interest generally in that range of effects and was addicted to noting and, as it were, recording them; so that in regard to this young lady's face he made several observations. It wasn't at all insipid, yet at the same time wasn't pointedly—what point, on earth, could she ever make?—expressive; and though it offered such a collection of small finenesses and neatnesses he mentally accused it—very forgivingly—of a want of finish. He thought nothing more likely than that its wearer would have had her own experience of the action of her charms, as she would certainly have acquired a resulting confidence; but even should she depend on this for her main amusement her bright sweet superficial little visage gave out neither mockery nor irony. Before long it became clear that, however these things might be, she was much disposed to conversation. She remarked to Winterbourne that they were going to Rome for the winter—she and her mother and Randolph. She asked him if he was a "real American"; she wouldn't have taken him for one: he seemed more like a German—this flower was gathered as from a large field of comparison—especially when he spoke. Winterbourne, laughing, answered that he had met Germans who spoke like Americans, but not, so far as he remembered, any American with the resemblance she noted. Then he asked her if she mightn't be more at ease should she occupy the bench he had just quitted. She answered that she liked hanging round, but she none the less resignedly, after a little, dropped to the bench. She told him she was from New York

1. Integrated whole.

State—"if you know where that is"; but our friend really quickened this current by catching hold of her small slippery brother and making him stand a few minutes by his side.

"Tell me your honest name, my boy." So he artfully proceeded.

In response to which the child was indeed unvarnished truth. "Randolph C. Miller. And I'll tell you hers." With which he levelled his alpenstock at his sister.

"You had better wait till you're asked!" said this young lady quite at her leisure.

"I should like very much to know *your* name," Winterbourne made free to reply.

"Her name's Daisy Miller!" cried the urchin. "But that ain't her real name; that ain't her name on her cards."

"It's a pity you haven't got one of my cards!" Miss Miller quite as naturally remarked.

"Her real name's Annie P. Miller," the boy went on.

It seemed, all amazingly, to do her good. "Ask him *his* now" —and she indicated their friend.

But to this point Randolph seemed perfectly indifferent; he continued to supply information with regard to his own family. "My father's name is Ezra B. Miller. My father ain't in Europe—he's in a better place than Europe." Winterbourne for a moment supposed this the manner in which the child had been taught to intimate that Mr. Miller had been removed to the sphere of celestial rewards. But Randolph immediately added: "My father's in Schenectady. He's got a big business. My father's rich, you bet."

"Well!" ejaculated Miss Miller, lowering her parasol and looking at the embroidered border. Winterbourne presently released the child, who departed, dragging his alpenstock along the path. "He don't like Europe," said the girl as with an artless instinct for historic truth. "He wants to go back."

"To Schenectady, you mean?"

"Yes, he wants to go right home. He hasn't got any boys here. There's one boy here, but he always goes round with a teacher. They won't let him play."

"And your brother hasn't any teacher?" Winterbourne enquired

It tapped, at a touch, the spring of confidence. "Mother thought of getting him one—to travel round with us. There was a lady told her of a very good teacher; an American lady—perhaps you know her—Mrs. Sanders. I think she came from Boston. She told her of this teacher, and we thought of getting him to travel round with us. But Randolph said he didn't want a teacher travelling round with us. He said he wouldn't have lessons when he was in the cars.[2] And we *are* in the cars about half the time. There was an English lady we met in the cars—I think her name was Miss Featherstone; perhaps you know her. She wanted to know why I didn't give Ran-

2. Railway cars.

dolph lessons—give him 'instruction,' she called it. I guess he could give me more instruction than I could give him. He's very smart.'

"Yes," said, Winterbourne; "he seems very smart."

"Mother's going to get a teacher for him as soon as we get t'Italy. Can you get good teachers in Italy?"

"Very good, I should think," Winterbourne hastened to reply.

"Or else she's going to find some school. He ought to learn some more. He's only nine. He's going to college." And in this way Miss Miller continued to converse upon the affairs of her family and upon other topics. She sat there with her extremely pretty hands, ornamented with very brilliant rings, folded in her lap, and with her pretty eyes now resting upon those of Winterbourne, now wandering over the garden, the people who passed before her and the beautiful view. She addressed her new acquaintance as if she had known him a long time. He found it very pleasant. It was many years since he had heard a young girl talk so much. It might have been said of this wandering maiden who had come and sat down beside him upon a bench that she chattered. She was very quiet, she sat in a charming tranquil attitude; but her lips and her eyes were constantly moving. She had a soft slender agreeable voice, and her tone was distinctly sociable. She gave Winterbourne a report of her movements and intentions, and those of her mother and brother, in Europe, and enumerated in particular the various hotels at which they had stopped. "That English lady in the cars," she said—"Miss Featherstone—asked me if we didn't all live in hotels in America. I told her I had never been in so many hotels in my life as since I came to Europe. I've never seen so many—it's nothing but hotels." But Miss Miller made this remark with no querulous accent: she appeared to be in the best humour with everything. She declared that the hotels were very good when once you got used to their ways and that Europe was perfectly entrancing. She wasn't disappointed—not a bit. Perhaps it was because she had heard so much about it before. She had ever so many intimate friends who had been there ever so many times, and that way she had got thoroughly posted. And then she had had ever so many dresses and things from Paris. Whenever she put on a Paris dress she felt as if she were in Europe.

"It was a kind of a wishing-cap," Winterbourne smiled.

"Yes," said Miss Miller at once and without examining this analogy; "it always made me wish I was here. But I needn't have done that for dresses. I'm sure they send all the pretty ones to America; you see the most frightful things here. The only thing I don't like," she proceeded, "is the society. There ain't any society—or if there is I don't know where it keeps itself. Do you? I suppose there's some society somewhere, but I haven't seen anything of it. I'm very fond of society and I've always had plenty of it. I don't mean only in Schenectady, but in New York. I used to go to New York every winter. In New York I had lots of society. Last winter I had seventeen dinners given me, and three of them were by gentlemen," added Daisy Miller. "I've more friends in New York than in Schenectady—more gentlemen friends; and more young lady friends too," she resumed in a moment. She paused again for an instant; she was looking at Winterbourne with all her prettiness in her frank gay eyes and in her clear rather uniform smile. "I've always had," she said, "a great deal of gentlemen's society."

Poor Winterbourne was amused and perplexed—above all he was charmed. He had never yet heard a young girl express herself in just this fashion; never at least save in cases where to say such things was to have at the same time some rather complicated consciousness about them. And yet was he to accuse Miss Daisy Miller of an actual or a potential *arrière-pensée*, as they said at Geneva? He felt he had lived at Geneva so long as to have got morally muddled; he had lost the right sense for the young American tone. Never indeed since he had grown old enough to appreciate things had he encountered a young compatriot of so "strong" a type as this. Certainly she was very charming, but how extraordinarily communicative and how tremendously easy! Was she simply a pretty girl from New York State—were they all like that, the pretty girls who had had a good deal of gentlemen's society? Or was she also a designing, an audacious, in short an expert young person? Yes, his instinct for such a question had ceased to serve him, and his reason could but mislead. Miss Daisy Miller looked extremely innocent. Some people had told him that after all American girls *were* exceedingly innocent, and others had told him that after all they weren't. He must on the whole take Miss Daisy Miller for a flirt—a pretty American flirt. He had never as yet had relations with representatives of that class. He had known here in Europe two or three women—persons older than Miss Daisy Miller and provided, for respectability's sake, with husbands—who were great coquettes; dangerous terrible women with whom one's light commerce might indeed take a serious turn. But this charming apparition wasn't a coquette in that sense; she was very unsophisticated; she was only a pretty American flirt. Winterbourne was almost grateful for having found the formula that applied to Miss Daisy Miller. He leaned back in his seat; he remarked to himself that she had the finest little nose he had ever seen; he wondered what were the regular conditions and limitations of one's intercourse with a pretty American flirt. It presently became apparent that he was on the way to learn.

"Have you been to that old castle?" the girl soon asked, pointing with her parasol to the far-shining walls of the Château de Chillon.

"Yes, formerly, more than once," said Winterbourne. "You too, I suppose, have seen it?"

3. Mental reservation.

"No, we haven't been there. I want to go there dreadfully. Of course I mean to go there. I wouldn't go away from here without having seen that old castle."

"It's a very pretty excursion," the young man returned, "and very easy to make. You can drive, you know, or you can go by the little steamer."

"You can go in the cars," said Miss Miller.

"Yes, you can go in the cars," Winterbourne assented.

"Our courier says they take you right up to the castle," she continued. "We were going last week, but mother gave out. She suffers dreadfully from dyspepsia. She said she couldn't any more go—!" But this sketch of Mrs. Miller's plea remained unfinished. "Randolph wouldn't go either; he says he don't think much of old castles. But I guess we'll go this week if we can get Randolph."

"Your brother isn't interested in ancient monuments?" Winterbourne indulgently asked.

He now drew her, as he guessed she would herself have said, every time. "Why no, he says he don't care much about old castles. He's only nine. He wants to stay at the hotel. Mother's afraid to leave him alone, and the courier won't stay with him; so we haven't been to many places. But it will be too bad if we don't go up there." And Miss Miller pointed again at the Château de Chillon.

"I should think it might be arranged," Winterbourne was thus emboldened to reply. "Couldn't you get some one to stay—for the afternoon—with Randolph?"

Miss Miller looked at him a moment, and then with all serenity, "I wish *you'd* stay with him!" she said.

He pretended to consider it. "I'd much rather go to Chillon with you."

"With me?" she asked without a shadow of emotion.

She didn't rise blushing, as a young person at Geneva would have done; and yet, conscious that he had gone very far, he thought it possible she had drawn back. "And with your mother," he answered very respectfully.

But it seemed that both his audacity and his respect were lost on Miss Daisy Miller. "I guess mother wouldn't go—for *you*," she smiled. "And she ain't much *bent* on going, anyway. She don't like to ride round in the afternoon." After which she familiarly proceeded: "But did you really mean what you said just now—that you'd like to go up there?"

"Most earnestly I meant it," Winterbourne declared.

"Then we may arrange it. If mother will stay with Randolph I guess Eugenio will."

"Eugenio?" the young man echoed.

"Eugenio's our courier.[4] He doesn't like to stay with Randolph —he's the most fastidious man I ever saw. But he's a splendid cou-

4. Social guide.

rier. I guess he'll stay at home with Randolph if mother does, and then we can go to the castle."

Winterbourne reflected for an instant as lucidly as possible: "we" could only mean Miss Miller and himself. This prospect seemed almost too good to believe; he felt as if he ought to kiss the young lady's hand. Possibly he would have done so,—and quite spoiled his chance; but at this moment another person—presumably Eugenio —appeared. A tall handsome man, with superb whiskers and wearing a velvet morning-coat and a voluminous watch-guard, approached the young lady, looking sharply at her companion. "Oh Eugenio!" she said with the friendliest accent.

Eugenio had eyed Winterbourne from head to foot; he now bowed gravely to Miss Miller. "I have the honour to inform Mademoiselle that luncheon's on table."

Mademoiselle slowly rose. "See here, Eugenio, I'm going to that old castle anyway."

"To the Château de Chillon, Mademoiselle?" the courier enquired. "Mademoiselle has made arrangements?" he added in a tone that struck Winterbourne as impertinent.

Eugenio's tone apparently threw, even to Miss Miller's own apprehension, a slightly ironical light on her position. She turned to Winterbourne with the slightest blush. "You won't back out?"

"I shall not be happy till we go!" he protested.

"And you're staying in this hotel?" she went on. "And you're really American?"

The courier still stood there with an effect of offence for the young man so far as the latter saw in it a tacit reflexion on Miss Miller's behaviour and an insinuation that she "picked up" acquaintances. "I shall have the honour of presenting to you a person who'll tell you all about me," he said, smiling, and referring to his aunt.

"Oh well, we'll go some day," she beautifully answered; with which she gave him a smile and turned away. She put up her parasol and walked back to the inn beside Eugenio. Winterbourne stood watching her, and as she moved away, drawing her muslin furbelows over the walk, he spoke to himself of her natural elegance.

II

He had, however, engaged to do more than proved feasible in promising to present his aunt, Mrs. Costello, to Miss Daisy Miller. As soon as that lady had got better of her headache he waited on her in her apartment and, after a show of the proper solicitude about her health, asked if she had noticed in the hotel an American family—a mamma, daughter and an obstreperous little boy.

"An obstreperous little boy and a preposterous big courier?" said Mrs. Costello. "Oh yes, I've noticed them. Seen them, heard them and kept out of their way." Mrs. Costello was a widow of fortune, a person of much distinction and who frequently intimated that if she hadn't been so dreadfully liable to sick-headaches she would probably have left a deeper impress on her time. She had a long pale face, a high nose and a great deal of very striking white hair, which she wore in large puffs and over the top of her head. She had two sons married in New York and another who was now in Europe. This young man was amusing himself at Homburg[5] and, though guided by his taste, was rarely observed to visit any particular city at the moment selected by his mother for her appearance there. Her nephew, who had come to Vevey expressly to see her, was therefore more attentive than, as she said, her very own. He had imbibed at Geneva the idea that one must be irreproachable in all such forms. Mrs. Costello hadn't seen him for many years and was now greatly pleased with him, manifesting her approbation by initiating him into many of the secrets of that social sway which, as he could see she would like him to think, she exerted from her stronghold in Forty-Second Street. She admitted that she was very exclusive, but if he had been better acquainted with New York he would see that one had to be. And her picture of the minutely hierarchical constitution of the society of that city, which she presented to him in many different lights, was, to Winterbourne's imagination, almost oppressively striking.

He at once recognised from her tone that Miss Daisy Miller's place in the social scale was low. "I'm afraid you don't approve of them," he pursued in reference to his new friends.

"They're horribly common"—it was perfectly simple. "They're the sort of Americans that one does one's duty by just ignoring."

"Ah you just ignore them?"—the young man took it in.

"I can't *not*, my dear Frederick. I wouldn't if I hadn't to, but I have to."

"The little girl's very pretty," he went on in a moment.

"Of course she's very pretty. But she's of the last crudity."

"I see what you mean of course," he allowed after another pause.

"She has that charming look they all have," his aunt resumed. "I can't think where they pick it up; and she dresses in perfection— no, you don't know how well she dresses. I can't think where they get their taste."

"But, my dear aunt, she's not, after all, a Comanche savage."

"She is a young lady," said Mrs. Costello, "who has an intimacy with her mamma's courier?"

"An 'intimacy' with him?" Ah there it was!

"There's no other name for such a relation. But the skinny little mother's just as bad! They treat the courier as a familiar friend—as a gentleman and scholar. I shouldn't wonder if he dines with them. Very likely they've never seen a man with such good manners, such fine clothes, so *like* a gentleman—or a scholar. He probably corre-

5. A resort in Germany.

sponds to the young lady's idea of a count. He sits with them in the garden of an evening. I think he smokes in their faces."

Winterbourne listened with interest to these disclosures; they helped him to make up his mind about Miss Daisy. Evidently she was rather wild. "Well," he said, "I'm not a courier and I didn't smoke in her face, and yet she was very charming to me."

"You had better have mentioned at first," Mrs. Costllo returned with dignity, "that you had made her valuable acquaintance."

"We simply met in the garden and talked a bit."

"By appointment—no? Ah that's still to come! Pray what did you say?"

"I said I should take the liberty of introducing her to my admirable aunt."

"Your admirable aunt's a thousand times obliged to you."

"It was to guarantee my respectability."

"And pray who's to guarantee hers?"

"Ah you're cruel!" said the young man. "She's a very innocent girl."

"You don't say that as if you believed it," Mrs. Costello returned.

"She's completely uneducated," Winterbourne acknowledged, "but she's wonderfully pretty, and in short she's very nice. To prove I believe it I'm going to take her to the Château de Chillon."

Mrs. Costello made a wondrous face. "You two are going off there together? I should say it proved just the contrary. How long had you known her, may I ask, when this interesting project was formed? You haven't been twenty-four hours in the house."

"I had known her half an hour!" Winterbourne smiled.

"Then she's just what I supposed."

"And what do you suppose?"

"Why that she's a horror."

Our youth was silent for some moments. "You really think then," he presently began, and with a desire for trustworthy information, "you really think that—" But he paused again while his aunt waited.

"Think what, sir?"

"That she's the sort of young lady who expects a man sooner or later to—well, we'll call it carry her off?"

"I haven't the least idea what such young ladies expect a man to do. But I really consider you had better not meddle with little American girls who are uneducated, as you mildly put it. You've lived too long out of the country. You'll be sure to make some great mistake. You're too innocent."

"My dear aunt, not so much as that comes to!" he protested with a laugh and a curl of his moustache.

"You're too guilty then!"

He continued all thoughtfully to finger the ornament in question.

"You won't let the poor girl know you then?" he asked at last.

"Is it literally true that she's going to the Château de Chillon with you?"

"I've no doubt she fully intends it."

"Then, my dear Frederick," said Mrs. Costello, "I must decline the honour of her acquaintance. I'm an old woman, but I'm not too old—thank heaven—to be honestly shocked!"

"But don't they all do these things—the little American girls at home?" Winterbourne enquired.

Mrs. Costello stared at moment. "I should like to see my granddaughters do them!" she then grimly returned.

This seemed to throw some light on the matter, for Winterbourne remembered to have heard his pretty cousins in New York, the daughters of this lady's two daughters, called "tremendous flirts." If therefore Miss Daisy Miller exceeded the liberal licence allowed to these young women it was probable she did go even by the American allowance rather far. Winterbourne was impatient to see her again, and it vexed, it even a little humiliated him, that he shouldn't by instinct appreciate her justly.

Though so impatient to see her again he hardly knew what ground he should give for his aunt's refusal to become acquainted with her; but he discovered promptly enough that with Miss Daisy Miller there was no great need of walking on tiptoe. He found her that evening in the garden, wandering about in the warm starlight after the manner of an indolent sylph and swinging to and fro the largest fan he had ever beheld. It was ten o'clock. He had dined with his aunt, had been sitting with her since dinner, and had just taken leave of her till the morrow. His young friend frankly rejoiced to renew their intercourse; she pronounced it the stupidest evening she had ever passed.

"Have you been all alone?" he asked with no intention of an epigram and no effect of her perceiving one.

"I've been walking round with mother. But mother gets tired walking round," Miss Miller explained.

"Has she gone to bed?"

"No, she doesn't like to go to bed. She doesn't sleep scarcely any —not three hours. She says she doesn't know how she lives. She's dreadfully nervous. I guess she sleeps more than she thinks. She's gone somewhere after Randolph; she wants to try to get him to go to bed. He doesn't like to go to bed."

The soft impartiality of her *constatations*,[6] as Winterbourne would have termed them, was a thing by itself—exquisite little fatalist as they seemed to make her. "Let us hope she'll persuade him," he encouragingly said.

"Well, she'll talk to him all she can—but he doesn't like her to talk to him": with which Miss Daisy opened and closed her fan.

6. Factual conclusions.

"She's going to try to get Eugenio to talk to him. But Randolph ain't afraid of Eugenio. Eugenio's a splendid courier, but he can't make much impression on Randolph! I don't believe he'll go to bed before eleven." Her detachment from any invidious judgment of this was, to her companion's sense, inimitable; and it appeared that Randolph's vigil was in fact triumphantly prolonged, for Winterbourne attended her in her stroll for some time without meeting her mother. "I've been looking round for that lady you want to introduce me to," she resumed—"I guess she's your aunt." Then on his admitting the fact and expressing some curiosity as to how she had learned it, she said she had heard all about Mrs. Costello from the chambermaid. She was very quiet and very *comme il faut*;[7] she wore white puffs; she spoke to no one and she never dined at the common table. Every two days she had a headache. "I think that's a lovely description, headache and all!" said Miss Daisy, chattering along in her thin gay voice. "I want to know her ever so much. I know just what *your* aunt would be; I know I'd like her. She'd be very exclusive. I like a lady to be exclusive; I'm dying to be exclusive myself. Well, I guess we *are* exclusive, mother and I. We don't speak to any one—or they don't speak to us. I suppose it's about the same thing. Anyway, I shall be ever so glad to meet your aunt."

Winterbourne was embarrassed—he could but trump up some evasion. "She'd be most happy, but I'm afraid those tiresome headaches are always to be reckoned with."

The girl looked at him through the fine dusk. "Well, I suppose she doesn't have a headache every day."

He had to make the best of it. "She tells me she wonderfully does." He didn't know what else to say.

Miss Miller stopped and stood looking at him. Her prettiness was still visible in the darkness; she kept flapping to and fro her enormous fan. "She doesn't want to know me!" she then lightly broke out. "Why don't you say so? You needn't be afraid. *I'm* not afraid!" And she quite crowed for the fun of it.

Winterbourne distinguished however a wee false note in this: he was touched, shocked, mortified by it. "My dear young lady, she knows no one. She goes through life immured. It's her wretched health."

The young girl walked on a few steps in the glee of the thing. "You needn't be afraid," she repeated. "Why should she want to know me?" Then she paused again; she was close to the parapet of the garden, and in front of her was the starlit lake. There was a vague sheen on its surface, and in the distance were dimly-seen mountain forms. Daisy Miller looked out at these great lights and shades and again proclaimed a gay indifference—"Gracious! she *is* exclusive!" Winterbourne wondered if she were seriously wounded and for a moment almost wished her sense of injury might be such

7. **Well mannered.**

as to make it becoming in him to reassure and comfort her. He had
a pleasant sense that she would be all accessible to a respectful tenderness at that moment. He felt quite ready to sacrifice his aunt—
conversationally; to acknowledge she was a proud rude woman and
to make the point that they needn't mind her. But before he had
time to commit herself to this questionable mixture of gallantry and
impiety, the young lady, resuming her walk, gave an exclamation in
quite another tone. "Well, here's mother! I guess she *hasn't* got
Randolph to go to bed.'" The figure of a lady appeared, at a distance, very indistinct in the darkness; it advanced with a slow and
wavering step and then suddenly seemed to pause.

"Are you sure it's your mother? Can you make her out in this
thick dusk?" Winterbourne asked.

"Well," the girl laughed, "I guess I know my own mother! And
when she has got on my shawl too. She's always wearing my
things."

The lady in question, ceasing now to approach, hovered vaguely
about the spot at which she had checked her steps.

"I'm afraid your mother doesn't see you," said Winterbourne.
"Or perhaps," he added—thinking, with Miss Miller, the joke permissible—"perhaps she feels guilty about your shawl."

"Oh it's a fearful old thing!" his companion placidly answered.
"I told her she could wear it if she didn't mind looking like a
fright. She won't come here because she sees you."

"Ah then," said Winterbourne, "I had better leave you."

"Oh no—come on!" the girl insisted.

"I'm afraid your mother doesn't approve of my walking with
you."

She gave him, he thought, the oddest glance. "It isn't for me; it's
for you—that is it's for *her*. Well, I don't know who it's for! But
mother doesn't like any of my gentlemen friends. She's right down
timid. She always makes a fuss if I introduce a gentleman. But I *do*
introduce them—almost always. If I didn't introduce my gentlemen
friends to mother," Miss Miller added, in her small flat monotone,
"I shouldn't think I was natural."

"Well, to introduce me," Winterbourne remarked, "you must
know my name. And he proceeded to pronounce it.

"Oh my—I can't say all that!" cried his companion, much
amused. But by this time they had come up to Mrs. Miller, who,
as they drew near, walked to the parapet of the garden and leaned
on it, looking intently at the lake and presenting her back to them.
"Mother!" said the girl in a tone of decision— upon which the
elder lady turned round. "Mr. Frederick Forsyth Winterbourne,"
said the latter's young friend, repeating his lesson of a moment
before and introducing him very frankly and prettily. "Common"
she might be, as Mrs. Costello had pronounced her; yet what provision was made by that epithet for her queer little native grace?

Her mother was a small spare light person, with a wandering eye, a scarce perceptible nose, and, as to make up for it, an unmistakeable forehead, decorated—but too far back, as Winterbourne mentally described it—with thin much-frizzled hair. Like her daughter Mrs. Miller was dressed with extreme elegance; she had enormous diamonds in her ears. So far as the young man could observe, she gave him no greeting—she certainly wasn't looking at him. Daisy was near her, pulling her shawl straight. "What are you doing, poking round here?" this young lady enquired—yet by no means with the harshness of accent her choice of words might have implied.

"Well, I don't know"—and the new-comer turned to the lake again.

"I shouldn't think you'd want that shawl!" Daisy familiarly proceeded.

"Well—I do!" her mother answered with a sound that partook for Winterbourne of an odd strain between mirth and woe.

"Did you get Randolph to go to bed?" Daisy asked.

"No, I couldn't induce him"—and Mrs. Miller seemed to confess to the same mild fatalism as her daughter. "He wants to talk to the waiter. He *likes* to talk to that waiter."

"I was just telling Mr. Winterbourne," the girl went on; and to the young man's ear her tone might have indicated that she had been uttering his name all her life.

"Oh yes!" he concurred— "I've the pleasure of knowing your son."

Randolph's mamma was silent; she kept her attention on the lake. But at last a sigh broke from her. "Well, I don't see how he lives!"

"Anyhow, it isn't so bad as it was at Dover," Daisy at least opined.

"And what occurred at Dover?" Winterbourne desired to know.

"He wouldn't go to bed at all. I guess he sat up all night—in the public parlour. He wasn't in bed at twelve o'clock: it seemed as if he couldn't budge."

"It ⸱ ⸱⸱ half-past twelve when I gave up," Mrs. Miller recorded with passionless accuracy.

It was of great interest to Winterbourne. "Does he sleep much during the day?"

"I guess he doesn't sleep *very* much," Daisy rejoined.

"I wish he just *would!*" said her mother. "It seems as if he *must* make it up somehow."

"Well, I guess it's we that make it up. I think he's real tiresome," Daisy pursued.

After which, for some moments, there was silence. "Well, Daisy Miller," the elder lady then unexpectedly broke out, "I shouldn't think you'd want to talk against your own brother!"

"Well, he *is* tiresome, mother," said the girl, but with no sharp-ness of insistence.

"Well, he's only nine," Mrs. Miller lucidly urged.

"Well, he wouldn't go up to that castle, anyway," her daughter replied as for accommodation. "I'm going up there with Mr. Win-terbourne."

To this announcement, very placidly made, Daisy's parent offered no response. Winterbourne took for granted on this that she opposed such a course; but he said to himself at the same time that she was a simple easily-managed person and that a few deferential protestations would modify her attitude. "Yes," he therefore inter-posed, "your daughter has kindly allowed me the honour of being her guide."

Mrs. Miller's wandering eyes attached themselves with an appeal-ing air to her other companion, who, however, strolled a few steps further, gently humming to herself. "I presume you'll go in the cars," she then quite colourlessly remarked.

"Yes, or in the boat," said Winterbourne.

"Well, of course I don't know," Mrs. Miller returned. "I've never been up to that castle."

"It is a pity you shouldn't go," he observed, beginning to feel reassured as to her opposition. And yet he was quite prepared to find that as a matter of course she meant to accompany her daugh-ter.

It was on this view accordingly that light was projected for him. "We've been thinking ever so much about going, but it seems as if we couldn't. Of course Daisy—she wants to go round everywhere. But there's a lady here—I don't know her name—she says she shouldn't think we'd want to go to see castles *here*; she should think we'd want to wait till we got t'Italy. It seems as if there would be so many there," continued Mrs. Miller with an air of increasing confidence. "Of course we only want to see the principal ones. We visited several in England," she presently added.

"Ah yes, in England there are beautiful castles," said Winter-bourne. "But Chillon here is very well worth seeing."

"Well, if Daisy feels up to it—" said Mrs. Miller in a tone that seemed to break under the burden of such conceptions. "It seems as if there's nothing she won't undertake."

"Oh I'm pretty sure she'll enjoy it!" Winterbourne declared. And he desired more and more to make it a certainty that he was to have the privilege of a *tête-à-tête* with the young lady who was still strolling along in front of them and softly vocalising. "You're not disposed, madam," he enquired, "to make the so interesting excur-sion yourself?"

So addressed Daisy's mother looked at him an instant with a cer-tain scared obliquity and then walked forward in silence. Then, "I guess she had better go alone," she said simply.

It gave him occasion to note that this was a very different type of maternity from that of the vigilant matrons who massed themselves in the forefront of social intercourse in the dark old city at the other end of the lake. But his meditations were interrupted by hearing his name very distinctly pronounced by Mrs. Miller's unprotected daughter. "Mr. Winterbourne!" she piped from a considerable distance.

"Mademoiselle!" said the young man.

"Don't you want to take me out in a boat?"

"At present?" he asked.

"Why of course!" she gaily returned.

"Well, Annie Miller!" exclaimed her mother.

"I beg you, madam, to let her go," he hereupon eagerly pleaded; so instantly had he been struck with the romantic side of this chance to guide through the summer starlight a skiff freighted with a fresh and beautiful young girl.

"I shouldn't think she'd want to," said her mother. "I should think she'd rather go indoors."

"I'm sure Mr. Winterbourne wants to *take* me," Daisy declared. "He's so awfully devoted!"

"I'll row you over to Chillon under the stars."

"I don't believe it!" Daisy laughed.

"Well!" the elder lady again gasped, as in rebuke of this freedom.

"You haven't spoken to me for half an hour," her daughter went on.

"I've been having some very pleasant conversation with your mother," Winterbourne replied.

"Oh pshaw! I want you to take me out in a boat!" Daisy went on as if nothing else had been said. They had all stopped and she had turned round and was looking at her friend. Her face wore a charming smile, her pretty eyes gleamed in the darkness, she swung her great fan about. No, he felt, it was impossible to be prettier than that.

"There are half a dozen boats moored at that landing-place," and he pointed to a range of steps that descended from the garden to the lake. "If you'll do me the honour to accept my arm we'll go and select one of them."

She stood there smiling; she threw back her head; she laughed as for the drollery of this. "I like a gentleman to be formal!"

"I assure you it's a formal offer."

"I was bound I'd make you say something," Daisy agreeably mocked.

"You see it's not very difficult," said Winterbourne. "But I'm afraid you're chaffing me."

"I think not, sir," Mrs. Miller shyly pleaded.

"Do then let me give you a row," he persisted to Daisy.

"It's quite lovely, the way you say that!" she cried in reward.

"It will be still more lovely to do it."

"Yes, it would be lovely!" But she made no movement to accompany him; she only remained an elegant image of free light irony.

"I guess you'd better find out what time it is," her mother impartially contributed.

"It's eleven o'clock, Madam," said a voice with a foreign accent out of the neighbouring darkness; and Winterbourne, turning, recognised the florid personage he had already seen in attendance. He had apparently just approached.

"Oh Eugenio," said Daisy, "I'm going out with Mr. Winterbourne in a boat!"

Eugenio bowed. "At this hour of the night, Mademoiselle?"

"I'm going with Mr. Winterbourne," she repeated with her shining smile. "I'm going this very minute."

"Do tell her she can't, Eugenio," Mrs. Miller said to the courier.

"I think you had better not go out in a boat, Mademoiselle," the man declared.

Winterbourne wished to goodness this pretty girl were not on such familiar terms with her courier; but he said nothing, and she meanwhile added to his ground. "I suppose you don't think it's proper! My!" she wailed; "Eugenio doesn't think anything's proper."

"I'm nevertheless quite at your service," Winterbourne hastened to remark.

"Does Mademoiselle propose to go alone?" Eugenio asked of Mrs. Miller.

"Oh, no, with this gentleman!" cried Daisy's mamma for reassurance.

"I *meant* alone with the gentleman." The courier looked for a moment at Winterbourne—the latter seemed to make out in his face a vague presumptuous intelligence as at the expense of their companions—and then solemnly and with a bow, "As Mademoiselle pleases!" he said.

But Daisy broke off at this. "Oh I hoped you'd make a fuss! I don't care to go now."

"Ah but I myself shall make a fuss if you don't go," Winterbourne declared with spirit.

"That's all I want—a little fuss!" With which she began to laugh again.

"Mr. Randolph has retired for the night!" the courier hereupon importantly announced.

"Oh Daisy, now we can go then!" cried Mrs. Miller.

Her daughter turned away from their friend, all lighted with her odd perversity. "Good-night—I hope you're disappointed or disgusted or something!"

He looked at her gravely, taking her by the hand she offered.

"I'm puzzled, if you want to know!" he answered.

"Well, I hope it won't keep you awake!" she said very smartly; and, under the escort of the privileged Eugenio, the two ladies passed toward the house.

Winterbourne's eyes followed them; he was indeed quite mystified. He lingered beside the lake a quarter of an hour, baffled by the question of the girl's sudden familiarities and caprices. But the only very definite conclusion he came to was that he should enjoy deucedly "going off" with her somewhere.

Two days later he went off with her to the Castle of Chillon. He waited for her in the large hall of the hotel, where the couriers, the servants, the foreign tourists were lounging about and staring. It wasn't the place he would have chosen for a tryst, but she had placidly appointed it. She came tripping downstairs, buttoning her long gloves, squeezing her folded parasol against her pretty figure, dressed exactly in the way that consorted best, to his fancy, with their adventure. He was a man of imagination and, as our ancestors used to say, of sensibility; as he took in her charming air and caught from the great staircase her impatient confiding step the note of some small sweet strain of romance, not intense but clear and sweet, seemed to sound for their start. He could have believed he was *really* going "off" with her. He led her out through all the idle people assembled—they all looked at her straight and hard: she had begun to chatter as soon as she joined him. His preference had been that they should be conveyed to Chillon in a carriage, but she expressed a lively wish to go in the little steamer— there would be such a lovely breeze upon the water and they should see such lots of people. The sail wasn't long, but Winterbourne's companion found time for many characteristic remarks and other demonstrations, not a few of which were, from the extremity of their candour, slightly disconcerting. To the young man himself their small excursion showed so for delightfully irregular and incongruously intimate that, even allowing for her habitual sense of freedom, he had some expectation of seeing her appear to find in it the same savour. But it must be confessed that he was in this particular rather disappointed. Miss Miller was highly animated, she was in the brightest spirits; but she was clearly not at all in a nervous flutter—as she should have been to match *his* tension; she avoided neither his eyes nor those of any one else; she neither coloured from an awkward consciousness when she looked at him nor when she saw that people were looking at herself. People continued to look at her a great deal, and Winterbourne could at least take pleasure in his pretty companion's distinguished air. He had been privately afraid she would talk loud, laugh overmuch, and even perhaps desire to move extravagantly about the boat. But he quite forgot his fears; he sat smiling with his eyes on her face while, without stirring from her place, she delivered herself of a great number of original reflexions. It was the most charming innocent prattle he had ever heard, for by his own experience hitherto, when young persons were so ingenuous they were less articulate and when they were so confident were more sophisticated. If he had assented to the idea that she was "common," at any rate, *was* she proving so, after all, or was he simply getting used to her commonness? Her discourse was for the most part of what immediately and superficially surrounded them, but there were moments when it threw out a longer look or took a sudden straight plunge.

"What on *earth* are you so solemn about?" she suddenly demanded, fixing her agreeable eyes on her friend's.

"Am I solemn?" he asked. "I had an idea I was grinning from ear to ear."

"You look as if you were taking me to a prayer-meeting or a funeral. If that's a grin your ears are very near together."

"Should you like me to dance a hornpipe on the deck?"

"Pray do, and I'll carry round your hat. It will pay the expenses of our journey."

"I never was better pleased in my life," Winterbourne returned.

She looked at him a moment, then let it renew her amusement. "I like to make you say those things. You're a queer mixture!"

In the castle, after they had landed, nothing could exceed the light independence of her humour. She tripped about the vaulted chambers, rustled her skirts in the corkscrew staircases, flirted back with a pretty little cry and a shudder from the edge of the oubliettes[8] and turned a singularly well-shaped ear to everything Winterbourne told her about the place. But he saw she cared little for mediæval history and that the grim ghosts of Chillon loomed but faintly before her. They had the good fortune to have been able to wander without other society than that of their guide; and Winterbourne arranged with this companion that they shouldn't be hurried—that they should linger and pause wherever they chose. He interpreted the bargain generously—Winterbourne on his side had been generous—and ended by leaving them quite to themselves. Miss Miller's observations were marked by no logical consistency; for anything she wanted to say she was sure to find a pretext. She found a great many, in the tortuous passages and rugged embrasures of the place, for asking her young man sudden questions about himself, his family, his previous history, his tastes, his habits, his designs, and for supplying information on corresponding points in her own situation. Of her own tastes, habits and designs the charming creature was prepared to give the most definite and indeed the most favourable account.

"Well, I hope you know enough!" she exclaimed after Winterbourne had sketched for her something of the story of the unhappy

8. Secret pitlike dungeons with an opening only at the top; places where one is forgotten.

Bonnivard.[9] "I never saw a man that knew so much!" The history of Bonnivard had evidently, as they say, gone into one ear and out of the other. But this easy erudition struck her none the less as wonderful, and she was soon quite sure she wished Winterbourne would travel with them and "go round" with them: they too in that case might learn something about something. "Don't you want to come and teach Randolph?" she asked; "I guess he'd improve with a gentleman teacher." Winterbourne was certain that nothing could possibly please him so much, but that he had unfortunately other occupations. "Other occupations? I don't believe a speck of it!" she protested. "What do you mean now? You're not in business." The young man allowed that he was not in business, but he had engagements which even within a day or two would necessitate his return to Geneva. "Oh bother!" she panted, "I don't believe it!" and she began to talk about something else. But a few moments later, when he was pointing out to her the interesting design of an antique fireplace, she broke out irrelevantly: "You don't mean to say you're going back to Geneva?"

"It is a melancholy fact that I shall have to report myself there to-morrow."

She met it with a vivacity that could only flatter him. "Well, Mr. Winterbourne, I think you're horrid!"

"Oh don't say such dreadful things!" he quite sincerely pleaded —"just at the last."

"The last?" the girl cried; "I call it the very first! I've half a mind to leave you here and go straight back to the hotel alone." And for the next ten minutes she did nothing but call him horrid. Poor Winterbourne was fairly bewildered; no young lady had as yet done him the honour to be so agitated by the mention of his personal plans. His companion, after this, ceased to pay any attention to the curiosities of Chillon or the beauties of the lake; she opened fire on the special charmer in Geneva whom she appeared to have instantly taken it for granted that he was hurrying back to see. How did Miss Daisy Miller know of that agent of his fate in Geneva? Winterbourne, who denied the existence of such a person, was quite unable to discover; and he was divided between amazement at the rapidity of her induction and amusement at the directness of her criticism. She struck him afresh, in all this, as an extraordinary mixture of innocence and crudity. "Does she never allow you more than three days at a time?" Miss Miller wished ironically to know. "Doesn't she give you a vacation in summer? There's no one so hard-worked but they can get leave to go off somewhere at this season. I suppose if you stay another day she'll come right after you in the boat. Do wait over till Friday and I'll go down to the landing

9. Hero of Byron's poem *The Prisoner of Chillon*; François de Bonnivard (1496–1570), Swiss patriot and martyr, was con-fined for seven years in the Castle of Chillon.

to see her arrive!" He began at last even to feel he had been wrong to be disappointed in the temper in which his young lady had embarked. If he had missed the personal accent, the personal accent was now making its appearance. It sounded very distinctly, toward the end, in her telling him she'd stop "teasing" him if he'd promise her solemnly to come down to Rome that winter.

"That's not a difficult promise to make," he hastened to acknowledge. "My aunt has taken an apartment in Rome from January and has already asked me to come and see her."

"I don't want you to come for your aunt," said Daisy; "I want you just to come for me." And this was the only allusion he was ever to hear her make again to his invidious kinswoman. He promised her that at any rate he would certainly come, and after this she forbore from teasing. Winterbourne took a carriage and they drove back to Vevey in the dusk; the girl at his side, her animation a little spent, was now quite distractingly passive.

In the evening he mentioned to Mrs. Costello that he had spent the afternoon at Chillon with Miss Daisy Miller.

"The Americans—of the courier?" asked this lady.

"Ah happily the courier stayed at home."

"She went with you all alone?"

"All alone."

Mrs. Costello sniffed a little at her smelling-bottle. "And that," she exclaimed, "is the little abomination you wanted me to know!"

III

Winterbourne, who had returned to Geneva the day after his excursion to Chillon, went to Rome toward the end of January. His aunt had been established there a considerable time and he had received from her a couple of characteristic letters. "Those people you were so devoted to last summer at Vevey have turned up here, courier and all," she wrote. "They seem to have made several acquaintances, but the courier continues to be the most *intime*. The young lady, however, is also very intimate with various third-rate Italians, with whom she rackets about in a way that makes much talk. Bring me that pretty novel of Cherbuliez's[1]—'Paule Méré'— and don't come later than the 23d."

Our friend would in the natural course of events, on arriving in Rome, have presently ascertained Mrs. Miller's address at the American banker's and gone to pay his compliments to Miss Daisy. "After what happened at Vevey I certainly think I may call upon them," he said to Mrs. Costello.

"If after what happens—at Vevey and everywhere—you desire to keep up the acquaintance, you're very welcome. Of course you're not squeamish—a man may know everyone. Men are welcome to the privilege!"

1. Victor Cherbuliez (1829–99), a minor French novelist of Swiss origin.

"Pray what is it then that 'happens'—here for instance?" Winterbourne asked.

"Well, the girl tears about alone with her unmistakeably low foreigners. As to what happens further you must apply elsewhere for information. She has picked up half a dozen of the regular Roman fortune hunters of the inferior sort and she takes them about to such houses as she may put *her* nose into. When she comes to a party—such a party as she can come to—she brings with her a gentleman with a good deal of manner and a wonderful moustache."

"And where's the mother?"

"I haven't the least idea. They're very dreadful people."

Winterbourne thought them over in these new lights. "They're very ignorant—very innocent only, and utterly uncivilised. Depend on it they're not 'bad.'"

"They're hopelessly vulgar," said Mrs. Costello. "Whether or no being hopelessly vulgar is being 'bad' is a question for the metaphysicians. They're bad enough to blush for, at any rate, and for this short life that's quite enough."

The news that his little friend the child of nature of the Swiss lakeside was now surrounded by half a dozen wonderful moustaches checked Winterbourne's impulse to go straightway to see her. He had perhaps not definitely flattered himself that he had made an ineffaceable impression upon her heart, but he was annoyed at hearing of a state of affairs so little in harmony with an image that had lately flitted in and out of his own meditations; the image of a very pretty girl looking out of an old Roman window and asking herself urgently when Mr. Winterbourne would arrive. If, however, he determined to wait a little before reminding this young lady of his claim to her faithful remembrance, he called with more promptitude on two or three other friends. One of these friends was an American lady who had spent several winters at Geneva, where she had placed her children at school. She was a very accomplished woman and she lived in Via Gregoriana. Winterbourne found her in a little crimson drawing-room on a third floor; the room was filled with southern sunshine. He hadn't been there ten minutes when the servant, appearing in the doorway, announced complacently "Madame Mila!" This announcement was presently followed by the entrance of little Randolph Miller, who stopped in the middle of the room and stood staring at Winterbourne. An instant later his pretty sister crossed the threshold; and then, after a considerable interval, the parent of the pair slowly advanced.

"I guess I know you!" Randolph broke ground without delay.

"I'm sure you know a great many things"—and his old friend clutched him all interestedly by the arm. "How's your education coming on?"

Daisy was engaged in some pretty babble with her hostess, but when she heard Winterbourne's voice she quickly turned her head with a "Well, I declare!" which he met smiling. "I told you I should come, you know."

"Well, I didn't believe it," she answered.

"I'm much obliged to you for that," laughed the young man.

"You might have come to see me then," Daisy went on as if they had parted the week before.

"I arrived only yesterday."

"I don't believe any such thing!" the girl declared afresh.

Winterbourne turned with a protesting smile to her mother, but this lady evaded his glance and, seating herself, fixed her eyes on her son. "We've got a bigger place than this," Randolph hereupon broke out. "It's all gold on the walls."

Mrs. Miller, more of a fatalist apparently than ever, turned uneasily in her chair. "I told you if I was to bring you you'd say something!" she stated as for the benefit of such of the company as might hear it.

"I told *you!*" Randolph retorted. "I tell *you,* sir!" he added jocosely, giving Winterbourne a thump on the knee. "It *is* bigger too!"

As Daisy's conversation with her hostess still occupied her Winterbourne judged it becoming to address a few words to her mother —such as "I hope you've been well since we parted at Vevey."

Mrs. Miller now certainly looked at him—at his chin. "Not very well, sir," she answered.

"She's got the dyspepsia," said Randolph. "I've got it too. Father's got it bad. But I've got it worst!"

This proclamation, instead of embarrassing Mrs. Miller, seemed to soothe her by reconstituting the environment to which she was most accustomed. "I suffer from the liver," she amiably whined to Winterbourne. "I think it's the climate; it's less bracing than Schenectady, especially in the winter season. I don't know whether you know we reside at Schenectady. I was saying to Daisy that I certainly hadn't found any one like Dr. Davis and I didn't believe I *would*. Oh up in Schenectady, he stands first; they think everything of Dr. Davis. He has so much to do, and yet there was nothing he wouldn't do for *me*. He said he never saw anything like my dyspepsia, but he was bound to get at it. I'm sure there was nothing he wouldn't try, and I didn't care what he did to me if he only brought me relief. He was just going to try something new, and I just longed for it, when we came right off. Mr. Miller felt as if he wanted Daisy to see Europe for herself. But I couldn't help writing the other day that I supposed it was all right for Daisy, but that I didn't know as I *could* get on much longer without Dr. Davis. At Schenectady he stands at the very top; and there's a great deal of sickness there too. It affects my sleep."

Winterbourne had a good deal of pathological gossip with Dr. Davis's patient, during which Daisy chattered unremittingly to her companion. The young man asked Mrs. Miller how she was pleased with Rome. "Well, I must say I'm disappointed," she confessed. "We had heard so much about it—I suppose we had heard too much. But we couldn't help that. We had been led to expect something different."

Winterbourne, however, abounded in reassurance. "Ah wait a little, and you'll grow very fond of it."

"I hate it worse and worse every day!" cried Randolph.

"You're like the infant Hannibal,"[2] his friend laughed.

"No I ain't—like any infant!" Randolph declared at a venture.

"Well, that's so—and you never *were!*" his mother concurred. "But we've seen places," she resumed, "that I'd put a long way ahead of Rome." And in reply to Winterbourne's interrogation, "There's Zürich—up there in the mountains," she instanced; "I think Zürich's real lovely, and we hadn't heard half so much about it."

"The best place we've seen's the *City of Richmond!*" said Randolph.

"He means the ship," Mrs. Miller explained. "We crossed in that ship. Randolph had a good time on the *City of Richmond.*

"It's the best place *I've* struck," the child repeated. "Only it was turned the wrong way."

"Well, we've got to turn the right way sometime," said Mrs. Miller with strained but weak optimism. Winterbourne expressed the hope that her daughter at least appreciated the so various interest of Rome, and she declared with some spirit that Daisy was quite carried away. "It's on account of the society—the society's splendid. She goes round everywhere; she has made a great number of acquaintances. Of course she goes round more than I do. I must say they've all been very sweet—they've taken her right in. And then she knows a great many gentlemen. Oh she thinks there's nothing like Rome. Of course it's a great deal pleasanter for a young lady if she knows plenty of gentlemen."

By this time Daisy had turned her attention again to Winterbourne, but in quite the same free form. "I've been telling Mrs. Walker how mean you were!"

"And what's the evidence you've offered?" he asked, a trifle disconcerted, for all his superior gallantry, by her inadequate measure of the zeal of an admirer who on his way down to Rome had stopped neither at Bologna nor at Florence, simply because of a certain sweet appeal to his fond fancy, not to say to his finest curiosity. He remembered how a cynical compatriot had once told him that American women—the pretty ones, and this gave a largeness to the

---

2. The Carthaginian General (247–183 B.C.) was sworn at his birth to an eternal hatred of Rome.

axiom—were at once the most exacting in the world and the least endowed with a sense of indebtedness.

"Why you were awfully mean up at Vevey," Daisy said. "You wouldn't do most anything. You wouldn't stay there when I asked you."

"Dearest young lady," cried Winterbourne, with generous passion, "have I come all the way to Rome only to be riddled by your silver shafts?"

"Just hear him say that!"—and she gave an affectionate twist to a bow on her hostess's dress. "Did you ever hear anything so quaint?"

"So 'quaint,' my dear?" echoed Mrs. Walker more critically—quite in the tone of a partisan of Winterbourne.

"Well, I don't know"—and the girl continued to finger her ribbons. "Mrs. Walker, I want to tell you something."

"Say, mother-r," broke in Randolph with his rough ends to his words, "I tell you you've got to go. Eugenio'll raise something!"

"I'm not afraid of Eugenio," said Daisy with a toss of her head. "Look here, Mrs. Walker," she went on, "You know I'm coming to your party."

"I'm delighted to hear it."

"I've got a lovely dress."

"I'm very sure of that."

"But I want to ask a favour—permission to bring a friend."

"I shall be happy to see any of your friends," said Mrs. Walker, who turned with a smile to Mrs. Miller.

"Oh they're not my friends," cried that lady, squirming in shy repudiation. "It seems as if they didn't take to *me*—I never spoke to one of them!"

"It's an intimate friend of mine, Mr. Giovanelli," Daisy pursued without a tremor in her young clearness or a shadow on her shining bloom.

Mrs. Walker had a pause and gave a rapid glance at Winterbourne. "I shall be glad to see Mr. Giovanelli," she then returned.

"He's just the finest kind of Italian," Daisy pursued with the-prettiest serenity. "He's a great friend of mine and the handsomest man in the world—except Mr. Winterbourne! He knows plenty of Italians, but he wants to know some Americans. It seems as if he was crazy about Americans. He's tremendously bright. He's perfectly lovely!"

It was settled that this paragon should be brought to Mrs. Walker's party, and then Mrs. Miller prepared to take her leave. "I guess we'll go right back to the hotel," she remarked with a confessed failure of the larger imagination.

"You may go back to the hotel, mother," Daisy replied, "but I'm just going to walk round."

"She's going to go it with Mr. Giovanelli," Randolph unscrupulously commented.

"I'm going to go it on the Pincio," Daisy peaceably smiled, while the way that she "condoned" these things almost melted Winterbourne's heart.

"Alone, my dear—at this hour?" Mrs. Walker asked. The afternoon was drawing to a close—it was the hour for the throng of carriages and of contemplative pedestrians. "I don't consider it's safe, Daisy," her hostess firmly asserted.

"Neither do I then," Mrs. Miller thus borrowed confidence to add. "You'll catch the fever as sure as you live. Remember what Dr. Davis told you!"

"Give her some of that medicine before she starts in," Randolph suggested.

The company had risen to its feet; Daisy, still showing her pretty teeth, bent over and kissed her hostess. "Mrs. Walker, you're too perfect," she simply said. "I'm not going alone; I'm going to meet a friend."

"Your friend won't keep you from catching the fever even if it *is* his own second nature," Mrs. Miller observed.

"Is it Mr. Giovanelli that's the dangerous attraction?" Mrs. Walker asked without mercy.

Winterbourne was watching the challenged girl; at this question his attention quickened. She stood there smiling and smoothing her bonnet-ribbons; she glanced at Winterbourne. Then, while she glanced and smiled, she brought out all affirmatively and without a shade of hesitation: "Mr. Giovanelli—the beautiful Giovanelli."

"My dear young friend"—and, taking her hand, Mrs. Walker turned to pleading—"don't prowl off to the Pincio at this hour to meet a beautiful Italian."

"Well, he speaks first-rate English," Mrs. Miller incoherently mentioned.

"Gracious me," Daisy piped up, "I don't want to do anything that's going to affect my health—or my character either! There's an easy way to settle it." Her eyes continued to play over Winterbourne. "The Pincio's only a hundred yards off, and if Mr. Winterbourne were as polite as he pretends he'd offer to walk right in with me!"

Winterbourne's politeness hastened to proclaim itself, and the girl gave him gracious leave to accompany her. They passed downstairs before her mother, and at the door he saw Mrs. Miller's carriage drawn up, with the ornamental courier whose acquaintance he had made at Vevey seated within. "Goodbye, Eugenio," cried Daisy; "I'm going to take a walk!" The distance from Via Gregoriana to the beautiful garden at the other end of the Pincian Hill is in fact rapidly traversed. As the day was splendid, however, and the concourse of vehicles, walkers and loungers numerous, the young Americans found their progress much delayed. This fact was highly agreeable to Winterbourne, in spite of his consciousness of his singular situation. The slow-moving, idly-gazing Roman crowd bestowed much attention on the extremely pretty young woman of English race who passed through it, with some difficulty, on his arm; and he wondered what on earth had been in Daisy's mind when she proposed to exhibit herself unattended to its appreciation. His own mission, to her sense, was apparently to consign her to the hands of Mr. Giovanelli; but, at once annoyed and gratified, he resolved that he would do no such thing.

"Why haven't you been to see me?" she meanwhile asked. "You can't get out of that."

"I've had the honour of telling you that I've only just stepped out of the train."

"You must have stayed in the train a good while after it stopped!" she derisively cried. "I suppose you were asleep. You've had time to go to see Mrs. Walker."

"I knew Mrs. Walker—" Winterbourne began to explain.

"I know where you knew her. You knew her at Geneva. She told me so. Well, you knew me at Vevey. That's just as good. So you ought to have come." She asked him no other question than this; she began to prattle about her own affairs. "We've got splendid rooms at the hotel; Eugenio says they're the best rooms in Rome. We're going to stay all winter—if we don't die of the fever; and I guess we'll stay then! It's a great deal nicer than I thought; I thought it would be fearfully quiet—in fact I was sure it would be deadly pokey. I foresaw we should be going round all the time with one of those dreadful old men who explain about the pictures and things. But we only had about a week of that, and now I'm enjoying myself. I know ever so many people, and they're all so charming. The society's extremely select. There are all kinds—English and Germans and Italians. I think I like the English best. I like their style of conversation. But there are some lovely Americans. I never saw anything so hospitable. There's something or other every day. There's not much dancing—but I must say I never thought dancing was everything. I was always fond of conversation. I guess I'll have plenty at Mrs. Walker's—her rooms are so small." When they had passed the gate of the Pincian Gardens Miss Miller began to wonder where Mr. Giovanelli might be. "We had better go straight to that place in front, where you look at the view."

Winterbourne at this took a stand. "I certainly shan't help you to find him."

"Then I shall find him without you," Daisy said with spirit.

"You certainly won't leave me!" he protested.

She burst into her familiar little laugh. "Are you afraid you'll get lost—or run over? But there's Giovanelli leaning against that tree. He's staring at the women in the carriages; did you ever see anything so cool?"

Winterbourne descried hereupon at some distance a little figure

that stood with folded arms and nursing its cane. It had a handsome face, a hat artfully poised, a glass in one eye and a nosegay in
its buttonhole. Daisy's friend looked at it a moment and then said:
"Do you mean to speak to that thing?"

"Do I mean to speak to him? Why you don't suppose I mean to
communicate by signs!"

"Pray understand then," the young man returned, "that I intend
to remain with you."

Daisy stopped and looked at him without a sign of troubled consciousness, with nothing in her face but her charming eyes, her
charming teeth and her happy dimples. "Well she's a cool one!" he
thought.

"I don't like the way you say that," she declared. "It's too imperious."

"I beg your pardon if I say it wrong. The main point's to give
you an idea of my meaning."

The girl looked at him more gravely, but with eyes that were
prettier than ever. "I've never allowed a gentleman to dictate to me
or to interfere with anything I do."

"I think that's just where your mistake has come in," he retorted.
"You should sometimes listen to a gentleman—the right one."

At this she began to laugh again. "I do nothing but listen to gentlemen! Tell me if Mr. Giovanelli is the right one."

The gentleman with the nosegay in his bosom had now made out
our two friends and was approaching Miss Miller with obsequious
rapidity. He bowed to Winterbourne as well as to the latter's compatriot; he seemed to shine, in his coxcombical way, with the desire
to please and the fact of his own intelligent joy, though Winterbourne thought him not a bad-looking fellow. But he nevertheless
said to Daisy: "No, he's not the right one."

She had clearly a natural turn for free introductions; she mentioned with the easiest grace the name of each of her companions
to the other. She strolled forward with one of them on either hand;
Mr. Giovanelli, who spoke English very clearly—Winterbourne
afterwards learned that he had practised the idiom upon a great
many American heiresses—addressed her a great deal of very polite
nonsense. He had the best possible manners, and the young American, who said nothing, reflected on that depth of Italian subtlety, so
strangely opposed to Anglo-Saxon simplicity, which enables people
to show a smoother surface in proportion as they're more acutely
displeased. Giovanelli of course had counted upon something more
intimate—he had not bargained for a party of three; but he kept his
temper in a manner that suggested far-stretching intentions. Winterbourne flattered himself he had taken his measure. "He's anything but a gentleman," said the young American; "he isn't even a
very plausible imitation of one. He's a music-master or a penny-a-
liner or a third-rate artist. He's awfully on his good behaviour, but

damn his fine eyes!" Mr. Giovanelli had indeed great advantages; but it was deeply disgusting to Daisy's other friend that something in her shouldn't have instinctively discriminated against such a type. Giovanelli chattered and jested and made himself agreeable according to his honest Roman lights. It was true that if he was an imitation the imitation was studied. "Nevertheless," Winterbourne said to himself, "a nice girl ought to know!" And then he came back to the dreadful question of whether this *was* in fact a nice girl. Would a nice girl—even allowing for her being a little American flirt—make a rendezvous with a presumably low-lived foreigner? The rendezvous in this case indeed had been in broad daylight and in the most crowded corner of Rome; but wasn't it possible to regard the choice of these very circumstances as a proof more of vulgarity than of anything else? Singular though it may seem, Winterbourne was vexed that the girl, in joining her *amoroso*,[3] shouldn't appear more impatient of his own company, and he was vexed precisely because of his inclination. It was impossible to regard her as a wholly unspotted flower—she lacked a certain indispensable fineness; and it would therefore much simplify the situation to be able to treat her as the subject of one of the visitations known to romancers as "lawless passions." That she should seem to wish to get rid of him would have helped him to think more lightly of her, just as to be able to think more lightly of her would have made her less perplexing. Daisy at any rate continued on this occasion to present herself as an inscrutable combination of audacity and innocence.

She had been walking some quarter of an hour, attended by her two cavaliers and responding in a tone of very childish gaiety, as it after all struck one of them, to the pretty speeches of the other, when a carriage that had detached itself from the revolving train drew up beside the path. At the same moment Winterbourne noticed that his friend Mrs. Walker—the lady whose house he had lately left—was seated in the vehicle and was beckoning to him. Leaving Miss Miller's side, he hastened to obey her summons—and all to find her flushed, excited, scandalised. "It's really too dreadful" —she earnestly appealed to him. "That crazy girl mustn't do this sort of thing. She mustn't walk here with you two men. Fifty people have remarked her."

Winterbourne—suddenly and rather oddly rubbed the wrong way by this—raised his grave eyebrows. "I think it's a pity to make too much fuss about it."

"It's a pity to let the girl ruin herself!"

"She's very innocent," he reasoned in his own troubled interest.

"She's very reckless," cried Mrs. Walker, "and goodness knows how far—left to itself—it may go. Did you ever," she proceeded to enquire, "see anything so blatantly imbecile as the mother? After you had all left me just now I couldn't sit still for thinking of it. It

3. **Lover.**

seemed too pitiful not even to attempt to save them. I ordered the carriage and put on my bonnet and came here as quickly as possible. Thank heaven I've found you!"

"What do you propose to do with us?" Winterbourne uncomfortably smiled.

"To ask her to get in, to drive her about here for half an hour—so that the world may see she's not running absolutely wild—and then take her safely home."

"I don't think it's a very happy thought," he said after reflexion, "but you're at liberty to try."

Mrs. Walker accordingly tried. The young man went in pursuit of their young lady who had simply nodded and smiled, from her distance, at her recent patroness in the carriage and then had gone her way with her own companion. On learning, in the event, that Mrs. Walker had followed her, she retraced her steps, however, with a perfect good grace and with Mr. Giovanelli at her side. She professed herself "enchanted" to have a chance to present this gentleman to her good friend, and immediately achieved the introduction; declaring with it, and as if it were of as little importance, that she had never in her life seen anything so lovely as that lady's carriage-rug.

"I'm glad you admire it," said her poor pursuer, smiling sweetly. "Will you get in and let me put it over you?"

"Oh no, thank you!"—Daisy knew her mind. "I'll admire it ever so much more as I see you driving round with it."

"Do get in and drive round *with* me," Mrs. Walker pleaded.

"That would be charming, but it's so fascinating just as I am!"—with which the girl radiantly took in the gentlemen on either side of her.

"It may be fascinating, dear child, but it's not the custom here," urged the lady of the victoria,[4] leaning forward in this vehicle with her hands devoutly clasped.

"Well, it ought to be then!" 'Daisy imperturbably laughed. "If I didn't walk I'd expire."

"You should walk with your mother, dear," cried Mrs. Walker with a loss of patience.

"With my mother dear?" the girl amusedly echoed. Winterbourne saw she scented interference. "My mother never walked ten steps in her life. And then, you know," she blandly added, "I'm more than five years old."

"You're old enough to be more reasonable. You're old enough, dear Miss Miller, to be talked about."

Daisy wondered to extravagance. "Talked about? What do you mean?"

"Come into my carriage and I'll tell you."

---

4. A horse-drawn carriage for two with a raised seat in front for the driver.

Daisy turned shining eyes again from one of the gentlemen beside her to the other. Mr. Giovanelli was bowing to and fro, rubbing down his gloves and laughing irresponsibly; Winterbourne thought the scene the most unpleasant possible. "I don't think I want to know what you mean," the girl presently said. "I don't think I should like it."

Winterbourne only wished Mrs. Walker would tuck up her carriage-rug and drive away; but this lady, as she afterwards told him, didn't feel she could "rest there." "Should you prefer being thought a very reckless girl?" she accordingly asked.

"Gracious me!" exclaimed Daisy. She looked again at Mr. Giovanelli, then she turned to her other companion. There was a small pink flush in her cheek; she was tremendously pretty. "Does Mr. Winterbourne think," she put to him with a wonderful bright intensity of appeal, "that—to save my reputation—I ought to get into the carriage?"

It really embarrassed him; for an instant he cast about—so strange was it to hear her speak that way of her "reputation." But he himself in fact had to speak in accordance with gallantry. The finest gallantry here was surely just to tell her the truth; and the truth, for our young man, as the few indications I have been able to give have made him known to the reader, was that his charming friend should listen to the voice of civilised society. He took in again her exquisite prettiness and then said the more distinctly: "I think you should get into the carriage."

Daisy gave the rein to her amusement. "I never heard anything so stiff! If this is improper, Mrs. Walker," she pursued, "then I'm *all* improper, and you had better give me right up. Good-bye; I hope you'll have a lovely ride!"—and with Mr. Giovanelli, who made a triumphantly obsequious salute, she turned away.

Mrs. Walker sat looking after her, and there were tears in Mrs. Walker's eyes. "Get in here, sir," she said to Winterbourne, indicating the place beside her. The young man answered that he felt bound to accompany Miss Miller; whereupon the lady of the victoria declared that if he refused her this favour she would never speak to him again. She was evidently wound up. He accordingly hastened to overtake Daisy and her more faithful ally, and, offering her his hand, told her that Mrs. Walker had made a stringent claim on his presence. He had expected her to answer with something rather free, something still more significant of the perversity from which the voice of society, through the lips of their distressed friend, had so earnestly endeavoured to dissuade her. But she only let her hand slip, as she scarce looked at him, through his slightly awkward grasp; while Mr. Giovanelli, to make it worse, bade him farewell with too emphatic a flourish of the hat.

Winterbourne was not in the best possible humour as he took his seat beside the author of his sacrifice. "That was not clever of you," he said candidly, as the vehicle mingled again with the throng of carriages.

"In such a case," his companion answered, "I don't want to be clever—I only want to be *true!*"

"Well, your truth has only offended the strange little creature—it has only put her off."

"It has happened very well"—Mrs. Walker accepted her work. "If she's so perfectly determined to compromise herself the sooner one knows it the better—one can act accordingly."

"I suspect she meant no great harm, you know," Winterbourne maturely opined.

"So I thought a month ago. But she has been going too far."

"What has she been doing?"

"Everything that's not done here. Flirting with any man she can pick up; sitting in corners with mysterious Italians; dancing all the evening with the same partners; receiving visits at eleven o'clock at night. Her mother melts away when the visitors come."

"But her brother," laughed Winterbourne, "sits up till two in the morning."

"He must be edified by what he sees. I'm told that at their hotel every one's talking about her and that a smile goes round among the servants when a gentleman comes and asks for Miss Miller."

"Ah we needn't mind the servants!" Winterbourne compassionately signified. "The poor girl's only fault," he presently added, "is her complete lack of education."

"She's naturally indelicate," Mrs. Walker, on her side, reasoned. "Take that example this morning. How long had you known her at Vevey?"

"A couple of days."

"Imagine then the taste of her making it a personal matter that you should have left the place!"

He agreed that taste wasn't the strong point of the Millers—after which he was silent for some moments; but only at last to add: "I suspect, Mrs. Walker, that you and I have lived too long at Geneva!" And he further noted that he should be glad to learn with what particular design she had made him enter her carriage.

"I wanted to enjoin on you the importance of your ceasing your relations with Miss Miller; that of your not appearing to flirt with her; that of your giving her no further opportunity to expose herself; that of your in short letting her alone."

"I'm afraid I can't do anything quite so enlightened as *that*," he returned. "I like her awfully, you know."

"All the more reason you shouldn't help her to make a scandal."

"Well, there shall be nothing scandalous in my attentions to her," he was willing to promise.

"There certainly will be in the way she takes them. But I've said what I had on my conscience," Mrs. Walker pursued. "If you wish to rejoin the young lady I'll put you down. Here, by the way, you have a chance."

The carriage was engaged in that part of the Pincian drive which overhangs the wall of Rome and overlooks the beautiful Villa Borghese. It is bordered by a large parapet, near which are several seats. One of these, at a distance, was occupied by a gentleman and a lady, toward whom Mrs. Walker gave a toss of her head. At the same moment these persons rose and walked to the parapet. Winterbourne had asked the coachman to stop; he now descended from the carriage. His companion looked at him a moment in silence and then, while he raised his hat, drove majestically away. He stood where he had alighted; he had turned his eyes toward Daisy and her cavalier. They evidently saw no one; they were too deeply occupied with each other. When they reached the low garden-wall they remained a little looking off at the great flat-topped pine-clusters of Villa Borghese; then the girl's attendant admirer seated himself familiarly on the broad ledge of the wall. The western sun in the opposite sky sent out a brilliant shaft through a couple of cloud-bars; whereupon the gallant Giovanelli took her parasol out of her hands and opened it. She came a little nearer and he held the parasol over her; then, still holding it, he let it so rest on her shoulder that both of their heads were hidden from Winterbourne. This young man stayed but a moment longer; then he began to walk. But he walked—not toward the couple united beneath the parasol, rather toward the residence of his aunt Mrs. Costello.

IV

He flattered himself on the following day that there was no smiling among the servants when he at least asked for Mrs. Miller at her hotel. This lady and her daughter, however, were not at home; and on the next day after, repeating his visit, Winterbourne again was met by a denial. Mrs. Walker's party took place on the evening of the third day, and in spite of the final reserves that had marked his last interview with that social critic our young man was among the guests. Mrs. Walker was one of those pilgrims from the younger world who, while in contact with the elder, make a point, in their own phrase, of studying European society; and she had on this occasion collected several specimens of diversely-born humanity to serve, as might be, for text-books. When Winterbourne arrived the little person he desired most to find wasn't there; but in a few moments he saw Mrs. Miller come in alone, very shyly and ruefully. This lady's hair, above the dead waste of her temples, was more frizzled than ever. As she approached their hostess Winterbourne also drew near.

"You see I've come all alone," said Daisy's unsupported parent. "I'm so frightened I don't know what to do; it's the first time I've

ever been to a party alone—especially in this country. I wanted to
bring Randolph or Eugenio or some one, but Daisy just pushed me
off by myself. I ain't used to going round alone."

"And doesn't your daughter intend to favour us with her
society?" Mrs. Walker impressively enquired.

"Well, Daisy's all dressed," Mrs. Miller testified with that accent
of the dispassionate, if not of the philosophic, historian with which
she always recorded the current incidents of her daughter's career.
"She got dressed on purpose before dinner. But she has a friend of
hers there; that gentleman—the handsomest of the Italians—that
she wanted to bring. They've got going at the piano—it seems as if
they couldn't leave off. Mr. Giovanelli does sing splendidly. But I
guess they'll come before very long," Mrs. Miller hopefully concluded.

"I'm sorry she should come—in that particular way," Mrs.
Walker permitted herself to observe.

"Well, I told her there was no use in her getting dressed before
dinner if she was going to wait three hours," returned Daisy's
mamma. "I didn't see the use of her putting on such a dress as that
to sit round with Mr. Giovanelli."

"This is most horrible!" said Mrs. Walker, turning away and
addressing herself to Winterbourne. "*Elle s'affiche, la malheureuse.*[5]
It's her revenge for my having ventured to remonstrate with her.
When she comes I shan't speak to her."

Daisy came after eleven o'clock, but she wasn't, on such an occasion, a young lady to wait to be spoken to. She rustled forward in
radiant loveliness, smiling and chattering, carrying a large bouquet
and attended by Mr. Giovanelli. Every one stopped talking and
turned and looked at her while she floated up to Mrs. Walker. "I'm
afraid you thought I never was coming, so I sent mother off to tell
you. I wanted to make Mr. Giovanelli practise some things before
he came; you know he sings beautifully, and I want you to ask him
to sing. This is Mr. Giovanelli; you know I introduced him to you;
he's got the most lovely voice and he knows the most charming set
of songs. I made him go over them this evening on purpose; we had
the greatest time at the hotel." Of all this Daisy delivered herself
with the sweetest brightest loudest confidence, looking now at her
hostess and now at all the room, while she gave a series of little
pats, round her very white shoulders, to the edges of her dress. "Is
there any one I know?" she as undiscourageably asked.

"I think every one knows you!" said Mrs. Walker as with a grand
intention; and she gave a very cursory greeting to Mr. Giovanelli.
This gentleman bore himself gallantly; he smiled and bowed and
showed his white teeth, he curled his moustaches and rolled his eyes
and performed all the proper functions of a handsome Italian at an
evening party. He sang, very prettily, half a dozen songs, though

5. "She's making a spectacle of herself, poor girl."

Mrs. Walker afterwards declared that she had been quite unable to find out who asked him. It was apparently not Daisy who had set him in motion—this young lady being seated a distance from the piano and though she had publicly, as it were, professed herself his musical patroness or guarantor, giving herself to gay and audible dis-course while he warbled.

"It's a pity these rooms are so small; we can't dance," she re-marked to Winterbourne as if she had seen him five minutes before.

"I'm not sorry we can't dance," he candidly returned. "I'm incap-able of a step."

"Of course you're incapable of a step," the girl assented. "I should think your legs *would* be stiff cooped in there so much of the time in that victoria."

"Well, they were very restless there three days ago," he amicably laughed; "all they really wanted was to dance attendance on you."

"Oh my other friend—my friend in need—stuck to me; he seems more at one with his limbs than you are—I'll say that for him. But did you ever hear anything so cool," Daisy demanded, "as Mrs. Walker's wanting me to get into her carriage and drop poor Mr. Giovanelli, and under the pretext that it was proper? People have different ideas! It would have been most unkind; he had been talking about that walk for ten days."

"He shouldn't have talked about it at all," Winterbourne decided to make answer on this: "he would never have proposed to a young lady of his country to walk about the streets of Rome with him."

"About the streets?" she cried with her pretty stare. "Where then would he have proposed to her to walk? The Pincio ain't the streets either, I guess; and I besides, thank goodness, am not a young lady of this country. The young ladies of this country have a dreadfully pokey time of it, by what I can discover; I don't see why I should change my habits for *such* stupids."

"I'm afraid your habits are those of a ruthless flirt," said Winter-bourne with studied severity.

"Of course they are!"—and she hoped, evidently, by the manner of it, to take his breath away. "I'm a fearful frightful flirt! Did you ever hear of a nice girl that wasn't? But I suppose you'll tell me now I'm not a nice girl."

He remained grave indeed under the shock of her cynical profes-sion. "You're a very nice girl, but I wish you'd flirt with me, and me only."

"Ah thank you, thank you very much: you're the last man I should think of flirting with. As I've had the pleasure of informing you, you're too stiff."

"You say that too often," he resentfully remarked.

Daisy gave a delighted laugh. "If I could have the sweet hope of making you angry I'd say it again."

"Don't do that—when I'm angry I'm stiffer than ever. But if you won't flirt with me do cease at least to flirt with your friend at the piano. They don't," he declared as in full sympathy with "them," "understand that sort of thing here."

"I thought they understood nothing else!" Daisy cried with startling world-knowledge.

"Not in young unmarried women."

"It seems to me much more proper in young unmarried than in old married ones," she retorted.

"Well," said Winterbourne, "when you deal with natives you must go by the custom of the country. American flirting is a purely American silliness; it has—in its ineptitude of innocence—no place in *this* system. So when you show yourself in public with Mr. Giovanelli and without your mother—"

"Gracious, poor mother!"—and she made it beautifully unspeakable.

Winterbourne had a touched sense for this, but it didn't alter his attitude. "Though *you* may be flirting Mr. Giovanelli isn't—he means something else."

"He isn't preaching at any rate," she returned. "And if you want very much to know, we're neither of us flirting—not a little speck. We're too good friends for that. We're real intimate friends."

He was to continue to find her thus at moments inimitable. "Ah," he then judged, "if you're in love with each other it's another affair altogether!"

She had allowed him up to this point to speak so frankly that he had no thought of shocking her by the force of his logic; yet she now none the less immediately rose, blushing visibly and leaving him mentally to exclaim that the name of little American flirts was incoherence. "Mr. Giovanelli at least," she answered, sparing but a single small queer glance for it, a queerer small glance, he felt, than he had ever yet had from her—"Mr. Giovanelli never says to me such very disagreeable things."

It had an effect on him—he stood staring. The subject of their contention had finished singing; he left the piano, and his recognition of what—a little awkwardly—didn't take place in celebration of this might nevertheless have been an acclaimed operatic tenor's series of repeated ducks before the curtain. So he bowed himself over to Daisy. "Won't you come to the other room and have some tea?" he asked—offering Mrs. Walker's slightly thin refreshment as he might have done all the kingdoms of the earth.

Daisy at last turned on Winterbourne a more natural and calculable light. He was but the more muddled by it, however, since so inconsequent a smile made nothing clear—it seemed at the most to prove in her a sweetness and softness that reverted instinctively to the pardon of offences. "It has never occurred to Mr. Winterbourne

to offer me any tea," she said with her finest little intention of torment and triumph.

"I've offered you excellent advice," the young man permitted
himself to growl.

"I prefer weak tea!" cried Daisy, and she went off with the brilliant Giovanelli. She sat with him in the adjoining room, in the
embrasure of the window, for the rest of the evening. There was an
interesting performance at the piano, but neither of these conversers
gave heed to it. When Daisy came to take leave of Mrs. Walker
this lady conscientiously repaired the weakness of which she had
been guilty at the moment of the girl's arrival—she turned her back
straight on Miss Miller and left her to depart with what grace she
might. Winterbourne happened to be near the door; he saw it all.
Daisy turned very pale and looked at her mother, but Mrs. Miller
was humbly unconscious of any rupture of any law or of any deviation from any custom. She appeared indeed to have felt an incongruous impulse to draw attention to her own striking conformity.
"Good-night, Mrs. Walker," she said; "we've had a beautiful evening. You see if I let Daisy come to parties without me I don't
want her to go away without me." Daisy turned away, looking with
a small white prettiness, a blighted grace, at the circle near the
door: Winterbourne saw that for the first moment she was too
much shocked and puzzled for indignation. He on his side was
greatly touched.

"That was very cruel," he promptly remarked to Mrs. Walker.

But this lady's face was also as a stone. "She never enters my
drawing-room again."

Since Winterbourne then, hereupon, was not to meet her in Mrs.
Walker's drawing-room he went as often as possible to Mrs. Miller's
hotel. The ladies were rarely at home, but when he found them the
devoted Giovanelli was always present. Very often the glossy little
Roman, serene in success, but not unduly presumptuous, occupied
with Daisy alone the florid salon enjoyed by Eugenio's care, Mrs.
Miller being apparently ever of the opinion that discretion is the
better part of solicitude. Winterbourne noted, at first with surprise,
that Daisy on these occasions was neither embarrassed nor annoyed
by his own entrance; but he presently began to feel that she had no
more surprises for him and that he really liked, after all, not making
out what she was "up to." She showed no displeasure for the interruption of her *tête-à-tête* with Giovanelli; she could chatter as
freshly and freely with two gentlemen as with one, and this easy
flow had ever the same anomaly for her earlier friend that it was so
free without availing itself of its freedom. Winterbourne reflected
that if she was seriously interested in the Italian it was odd she
shouldn't take more trouble to preserve the sanctity of their interviews, and he liked her the better for her innocent-looking indiffer-

ence and her inexhaustible gaiety. He could hardly have said why, but she struck him as a young person not formed for a troublesome jealousy. Smile at such a betrayal though the reader may, it was a fact with regard to the women who had hitherto interested him that, given certain contingencies, Winterbourne could see himself afraid—literally afraid—of these ladies. It pleased him to believe that even were twenty other things different and Daisy should love him and he should know it and like it, he would still never be afraid of Daisy. It must be added that this conviction was not altogether flattering to her: it represented that she was nothing every way if not light.

But she was evidently very much interested in Giovanelli. She looked at him whenever he spoke; she was perpetually telling him to do this and to do that; she was constantly chaffing and abusing him. She appeared completely to have forgotten that her other friend had said anything to displease her at Mrs. Walker's entertainment. One Sunday afternoon, having gone to Saint Peter's with his aunt, Winterbourne became aware that the young woman held in horror by that lady was strolling about the great church under escort of her coxcomb of the Corso. It amused him, after a debate, to point out the exemplary pair—even at the cost, as it proved, of Mrs. Costello's saying when she had taken them in through her eye-glass: "That's what makes you so pensive in these days, eh?"

"I hadn't the least idea I was pensive," he pleaded.

"You're very much preoccupied; you're always thinking of something."

"And what is it," he asked, "that you accuse me of thinking of?"

"Of that young lady's, Miss Baker's, Miss Chandler's—what's her name?—Miss Miller's intrigue with that little barber's block."

"Do you call it an intrigue," he asked—"an affair that goes on with such peculiar publicity?"

"That's their folly," said Mrs. Costello "it's not their merit."

"No," he insisted with a hint perhaps of the preoccupation to which his aunt had alluded—"I don't believe there's anything to be called an intrigue."

"Well"—and Mrs. Costello dropped her glass—"I've heard a dozen people speak of it: they say she's quite carried away by him."

"They're certainly as thick as thieves," our embarrassed young man allowed.

Mrs. Costello came back to them, however, after a little; and Winterbourne recognised in this a further illustration—than that supplied by his own condition—of the spell projected by the case. "He's certainly very handsome. One easily sees how it is. She thinks him the most elegant man in the world, the finest gentleman possible. She has never seen anything like him—he's better even than the courier. It was the courier probably who introduced him, and if he succeeds in marrying the young lady the courier will come in for a magnificent commission."

"I don't believe she thinks of marrying him," Winterbourne reasoned, "and I don't believe he hopes to marry her."

"You may be very sure she thinks of nothing at all. She romps on from day to day, from hour to hour, as they did in the Golden Age. I can imagine nothing more vulgar," said Mrs. Costello, whose figure of speech scarcely went on all fours. "And at the same time," she added, "depend upon it she may tell you any moment that she is 'engaged.'"

"I think that's more than Giovanelli really expects," said Winterbourne.

"And who is Giovanelli?"

"The shiny—but, to do him justice, not greasy—little Roman. I've asked questions about him and learned something. He's apparently a perfectly respectable little man. I believe he's in a small way a *cavaliere avvocato.*[6] But he doesn't move in what are called the first circles. I think it really not absolutely impossible the courier introduced him. He's evidently immensely charmed with Miss Miller. If she thinks him the finest gentleman in the world, he, on his side, has never found himself in personal contact with such splendour, such opulence, such personal daintiness, as this young lady's. And then she must seem to him wonderfully pretty and interesting. Yes, he can't really hope to pull it off. That must appear to him too impossible a piece of luck. He has nothing but his handsome face to offer, and there's a substantial, a possibly explosive Mr. Miller in that mysterious land of dollars asd six-shooters. Giovanelli's but too conscious that he hasn't a title to offer. If he were only a count or a *marchese!*[7] What on earth can he make of the way they've taken him up?"

"He accounts for it by his handsome face and thinks Miss Miller a young lady *qui se passe ses fantaisies!*"[8]

"It's very true," Winterbourne pursued, "that Daisy and her mamma haven't yet risen to that stage of—what shall I call it?—of culture, at which the idea of catching a count or *marchese* begins. I believe them intellectually incapable of that conception."

"Ah, but the *cavaliere avvocato* doesn't believe them!" cried Mrs. Costello.

Of the observation excited by Daisy's "intrigue" Winterbourne gathered that day at Saint Peter's sufficient evidence. A dozen of the American colonists in Rome came to talk with his relative, who sat on a small portable stool at the base of one of the great pilasters.

6. Lawyer; the *cavaliere* is merely honorific.
7. Marquis.
8. "Who is indulging her whims."

The vesper-service was going forward in splendid chants and organ-tones in the adjacent choir, and meanwhile, between Mrs. Costello and her friends, much was said about poor little Miss Miller's going really "too far." Winterbourne was not pleased with what he heard; but when, coming out upon the great steps of the church, he saw Daisy, who had emerged before him, get into an open cab with her accomplice and roll away through the cynical streets of Rome, the measure of her course struck him as simply there to take. He felt very sorry for her—not exactly that he believed she had completely lost her wits, but because it was painful to see so much that was pretty and undefended and natural sink so low in human estimation. He made an attempt after this to give a hint to Mrs. Miller. He met one day in the Corso a friend—a tourist like himself—who had just come out of the Doria Palace, where he had been walking through the beautiful gallery. His friend "went on" for some moments about the great portrait of Innocent X, by Velasquez,[9] suspended in one of the cabinets of the palace, and then said: "And in the same cabinet, by the way, I enjoyed sight of an image of a different kind; that little American who's so much more a work of nature than of art and whom you pointed out to me last week." In answer to Winterbourne's enquiries his friend narrated that the little American—prettier now than ever—was seated with a companion in the secluded nook in which the papal presence is enshrined.

"All alone?" the young man heard himself disingenuously ask.

"Alone with a little Italian who sports in his button-hole a stack of flowers. The girl's a charming beauty, but I thought I understood from you the other day that she's a young lady *du meilleur monde*."[1]

"So she is!" said Winterbourne; and having assured himself that his informant had seen the interesting pair but ten minutes before, he jumped into a cab and went to call on Mrs. Miller. She was at home, but she apologised for receiving him in Daisy's absence.

"She's gone out somewhere with Mr. Giovanelli. She's always going round with Mr. Giovanelli."

"I've noticed they're intimate indeed," Winterbourne concurred.

"Oh it seems as if they couldn't live without each other!" said Mrs. Miller. "Well, he's a real gentleman anyhow. I guess I have the joke on Daisy—that she *must* be engaged!"

"And how does your daughter *take* the joke?"

"Oh she just says she ain't. But she might as *well* be!" this philosophic parent resumed. "She goes on as if she was. But I've made Mr. Giovanelli promise to tell me if Daisy don't. I'd want to write to Mr. Miller about it—wouldn't you?" '

---

9. Diego Rodríguez de Silva y Velázquez (1599–1660), Spanish painter.
1. "Of the better society."

Winterbourne replied that he certainly should; and the state of mind of Daisy's mamma struck him as so unprecedented in the annals of parental vigilance that he recoiled before the attempt to educate at a single interview either her conscience or her wit.

After this Daisy was never at home and he ceased to meet her at the houses of their common acquaintance, because, as he perceived, these shrewd people had quite made up their minds as to the length she must have gone. They ceased to invite her, intimating that they wished to make, and make strongly, for the benefit of observant Europeans, the point that though Miss Daisy Miller was a pretty American girl all right, her behaviour wasn't pretty at all—was in fact regarded by her compatriots as quite monstrous. Winterbourne wondered how she felt about all the cold shoulders that were turned upon her, and sometimes found himself suspecting with impatience that she simply didn't feel and didn't know. He set her down as hopelessly childish and shallow, as such mere giddiness and ignorance incarnate as was powerless either to heed or to suffer. Then at other moments he couldn't doubt that she carried about in her elegant and irresponsible little organism a defiant, passionate, perfectly observant consciousness of the impression she produced. He asked himself whether the defiance would come from the consciousness of innocence or from her being essentially a young person of the reckless class. Then it had to be admitted, he felt, that holding fast to a belief in her "innocence" was more and more but a matter of gallantry too fine-spun for use. As I have already had occasion to relate, he was reduced without pleasure to this chopping of logic and vexed at his poor fallibility, his want of instinctive certitude as to how far extavagance was generic and national and how far it was crudely personal. Whatever it was he had helplessly missed her, and now it was too late. She was "carried away" by Mr. Giovanelli.

A few days after his brief interview with her mother he came across her at that supreme seat of flowering desolation known as the Palace of the Caesars. The early Roman spring had filled the air with bloom and perfume, and the rugged surface of the Palatine was muffled with tender verdure. Daisy moved at her ease over the great mounds of ruin that are embanked with mossy marble and paved with monumental inscriptions. It seemed to him he had never known Rome so lovely as just then. He looked off at the enchanting harmony of line and colour that remotely encircles the city—he inhaled the softly humid odours and felt the freshness of the year and the antiquity of the place reaffirm themselves in deep interfusion. It struck him also that Daisy had never showed to the eye for so utterly charming; but this had been his conviction on every occasion of their meeting. Giovanelli was of course at her side, and Giovanelli too glowed as never before with something of the glory of his race.

"Well," she broke out upon the friend it would have been such mockery to designate as the latter's rival, "I should think you'd be quite lonesome!"

"Lonesome?" Winterbourne resignedly echoed.

"You're always going round by yourself. Can't you get any one to walk with you?"

"I'm not so fortunate," he answered, "as your gallant companion."

Giovanelli had from the first treated him with distinguished politeness; he listened with a deferential air to his remarks; he laughed punctiliously at his pleasantries; he attached such importance as he could find terms for to Miss Miller's cold compatriot. He carried himself in no degree like a jealous wooer; he had obviously a great deal of tact; he had no objection to any one's expecting a little humility of him. It even struck Winterbourne that he almost yearned at times for some private communication in the interest of his character for common sense; a chance to remark to him as another intelligent man that, bless him, *he* knew how extraordinary was their young lady and didn't flatter himself with confident—at least *too* confident and too delusive—hopes of matrimony and dollars. On this occasion he strolled away from his charming charge to pluck a sprig of almond-blossom which he carefully arranged in his button-hole.

"I know why you say that," Daisy meanwhile observed. "Because you think I go round too much with *him*!" And she nodded at her discreet attendant.

"Every one thinks so—if you care to know," was all Winterbourne found to reply.

"Of course I care to know!"—she made this point with much expression. "But I don't believe a word of it. They're only pretending to be shocked. They don't really care a straw what I do. Besides, I don't go round so much."

"I think you'll find they do care. They'll show it—disagreeably," he took on himself to state.

Daisy weighed the importance of that idea. "How—disagreeably?"

"Haven't you noticed anything?" he compassionately asked.

"I've noticed *you*. But I noticed you've no more 'give' than a ramrod the first time ever I saw you."

"You'll find at least that I've more 'give' than several others," he patiently smiled.

"How shall I find it?"

"By going to see the others."

"What will they do to me?"

"They'll show you the cold shoulder. Do you know what that means?"

Daisy was looking at him intently; she began to colour. "Do you mean as Mrs. Walker did the other night?"

"Exactly as Mrs. Walker did the other night."

She looked away at Giovanelli, still titivating with his almond-blossom. Then with her attention again on the important subject: "I shouldn't think you'd let people be so unkind!"

"How can I help it?"

"I should think you'd want to say something."

"I do want to say something"—and Winterbourne paused a moment. "I want to say that your mother tells me she believes you engaged."

"Well, I guess she does," said Daisy very simply.

The young man began to laugh. "And does Randolph believe it?"

"I guess Randolph doesn't believe anything." This testimony to Randolph's scepticism excited Winterbourne to further mirth, and he noticed that Giovanelli was coming back to them. Daisy, observing it as well, addressed herself again to her countryman. "Since you've mentioned it," she said, "I *am* engaged." He looked at her hard—he had stopped laughing. "You don't believe it!" she added.

He asked himself, and it was for a moment like testing a heartbeat; after which, "Yes, I believe it!" he said.

"Oh no, you don't," she answered. "But *if* you possibly do," she still more perversely pursued—"well, I ain't!"

Miss Miller and her constant guide were on their way to the gate of the enclosure, so that Winterbourne, who had but lately entered, presently took leave of them. A week later on he went to dine at a beautiful villa on the Caelian Hill, and, on arriving, dismissed his hired vehicle. The evening was perfect and he promised himself the satisfaction of walking home beneath the Arch of Constantine and past the vaguely-lighted monuments of the Forum. Above was a moon half-developed, whose radiance was not brilliant but veiled in a thin cloud-curtain that seemed to diffuse and equalise it. When on his return from the villa at eleven o'clock he approached the dusky circle of the Colosseum the sense of the romantic in him easily suggested that the interior, in such an atmosphere, would well repay a glance. He turned aside and walked to one of the empty arches, near which, as he observed, an open carriage—one of the little Roman street-cabs—was stationed. Then he passed in among the cavernous shadows of the great structure and emerged upon the clear and silent arena. The place had never seemed to him more impressive. One half of the gigantic circus was in deep shade while the other slept in the luminous dusk. As he stood there he began to murmur Byron's famous lines out of "Manfred"; but before he had finished his quotation he remembered that if nocturnal meditation thereabouts was the fruit of a rich literary culture it was none the less deprecated by medical science. The air of other ages surrounded one; but the air of other ages, coldly analysed, was no better than a villainous miasma. Winterbourne sought, however, toward the middle of the arena, a further reach of vision, intending the next moment a hasty retreat. The great cross in the centre was almost obscured; only as he drew near did he make it out distinctly. He thus also distinguished two persons stationed on the low steps that formed its base. One of these was a woman seated; her companion hovered before her.

Presently the sound of the woman's voice came to him distinctly in the warm night-air. "Well, he looks at us as one of the old lions or tigers may have looked at the Christian martyrs!" These words were winged with their accent, so that they fluttered and settled about him in the darkness like vague white doves. It was Miss Daisy Miller who had released them for flight.

"Let us hope he's not very hungry"—the bland Giovanelli fell in with her humour. "He'll have to take *me* first; you'll serve for dessert."

Winterbourne felt himself pulled up with final horror now—and, it must be added, with final relief. It was as if a sudden clearance had taken place in the ambiguity of the poor girl's appearances and the whole riddle of her contradictions had grown easy to read. She was a young lady about the *shades* of whose perversity a foolish puzzled gentleman need no longer trouble his head or his heart. That once questionable quantity *had* no shades—it was a mere black little blot. He stood there looking at her, looking at her companion too, and not reflecting that though he saw them vaguely he himself must have been more brightly presented. He felt angry at all his shiftings of view—he felt ashamed of all his tender little scruples and all his witless little mercies. He was about to advance again, and then again checked himself; not from the fear of doing her injustice, but from a sense of the danger of showing undue exhilaration for this disburdenment of cautious criticism. He turned away toward the entrance of the place; but as he did so he heard Daisy speak again.

"Why it was Mr. Winterbourne! He saw me and he cuts me dead!"

What a clever little reprobate she was, he was amply able to reflect at this, and how smartly she feigned, how promptly she sought to play off on him, a surprised and injured innocence! But nothing would induce him to cut her either "dead" or to within any measurable distance even of the famous "inch" of her life. He came forward again and went toward the great cross. Daisy had got up and Giovanelli lifted his hat. Winterbourne had now begun to think simply of the madness, on the ground of exposure and infection, of a frail young creature's lounging away such hours in a nest of malaria. What if she *were* the most plausible of little reprobates? That was no reason for her denying of the *perniciosa*.[2] "How long have you been 'fooling round' here?" he asked with conscious roughness.

2. Malaria.

Daisy, lovely in the sinister silver radiance, appraised him a moment, roughness and all. "Well, I guess all the evening." She answered with spirit and, he could see even then, with exaggeration. "I never saw anything so quaint."

"I'm afraid," he returned, "you'll not think a bad attack of Roman fever very quaint. This is the way people catch it. I wonder," he added to Giovanelli, "that you, a native Roman, should countenance such extraordinary rashness."

"Ah" said this seasoned subject, "for myself I have no fear."

"Neither have I—for you!" Winterbourne retorted in French. "I'm speaking for this young lady."

Giovanelli raised his well-shaped eyebrows and showed his shining teeth, but took his critic's rebuke with docility. "I assured Mademoiselle it was a grave indiscretion, but when was Mademoiselle ever prudent?"

"I never was sick, and I don't mean to be!" Mademoiselle declared. "I don't look like much, but I'm healthy! I was bound to see the Colosseum by moonlight—I wouldn't have wanted to go home without *that*; and we've had the most beautiful time, haven't we, Mr. Giovanelli? If there has been any danger Eugenio can give me some pills. Eugenio has got some splendid pills."

"*I* should advise you then," said Winterbourne, "to drive home as fast as possible and take one!"

Giovanelli smiled as for the striking happy thought. "What you say is very wise. I'll go and make sure the carriage is at hand." And he went forward rapidly.

Daisy followed with Winterbourne. He tried to deny himself the small fine anguish of looking at her, but his eyes themselves refused to spare him, and she seemed moreover not in the least embarrassed. He spoke no word; Daisy chattered over the beauty of the place: "Well, I *have* seen the Colosseum by moonlight—that's one thing I can rave about!" Then noticing her companion's silence she asked him why he was so stiff—it had always been her great word. He made no answer, but he felt his laugh an immense negation of stiffness. They passed under one of the dark archways; Giovanelli was in front with the carriage. Here Daisy stopped a moment, looking at her compatriot. "*Did* you believe I was engaged the other day?"

"It doesn't matter now what I believed the other day!" he replied with infinite point.

It was a wonder how she didn't wince for it. "Well, what do you believe now?"

"I believe it makes very little difference whether you're engaged or not!"

He felt her lighted eyes fairly penetrate the thick gloom of the vaulted passage—as if to seek some access to him she hadn't yet compassed. But Giovanelli, with a graceful inconsequence, was at present all for retreat. "Quick, quick; if we get in by midnight we're quite safe!"

Daisy took her seat in the carriage and the fortunate Italian placed himself beside her. "Don't forget Eugenio's pills!" said Winterbourne as he lifted his hat.

"I don't care," she unexpectedly cried out for this, "whether I have Roman fever or not!" On which the cab-driver cracked his whip and they rolled across the desultory patches of antique pavement.

Winterbourne—to do him justice, as it were—mentioned to no one that he had encountered Miss Miller at midnight in the Colosseum with a gentleman; in spite of which deep discretion, however, the fact of the scandalous adventure was known a couple of days later, with a dozen vivid details, to every member of the little American circle, and was commented accordingly. Winterbourne judged thus that the people about the hotel had been thoroughly empowered to testify, and that after Daisy's return there would have been an exchange of jokes between the porter and the cab-driver. But the young man became aware at the same moment of how thoroughly it had ceased to ruffle him that the little American flirt should be "talked about" by low-minded menials. These sources of current criticism a day or two later abounded still further: the little American flirt was alarmingly ill and the doctors now in possession of the scene. Winterbourne, when the rumour came to him, immediately went to the hotel for more news. He found that two or three charitable friends had proceded him and that they were being entertained in Mrs. Miller's salon by the all-efficient Randolph.

"It's going round at night that way, you bet—that's what has made her so sick. She's always going round at night. I shouldn't think she'd want to—it's so plaguey dark over here. You can't see anything over here without the moon's right up. In America they don't go round by the moon!" Mrs. Miller meanwhile wholly surrendered to her genius for unapparent uses; her salon knew her less than ever, and she was presumably now at least giving her daughter the advantage of her society. It was clear that Daisy was dangerously ill.

Winterbourne constantly attended for news from the sick-room, which reached him, however, but with worrying indirectness, though he once had speech, for a moment, of the poor girl's physician and once saw Mrs. Miller, who, sharply alarmed, struck him as thereby more happily inspired than he could have conceived and indeed as the most noiseless and light-handed of nurses. She invoked a good deal the remote shade of Dr. Davis, but Winterbourne paid her the compliment of taking her after all for less monstrous a goose. To this indulgence indeed something she further said perhaps even more insidiously disposed him. "Daisy spoke of you the other day quite pleasantly. Half the time she doesn't know what

she's saying, but that time I think she did. She gave me a message
—she told me to tell you. She wanted you to know she never was
engaged to that handsome Italian who was always round. I'm sure
I'm very glad; Mr. Giovanelli hasn't been near us since she was
taken ill. I thought he was so much of a gentleman, but I don't
call that very polite! A lady told me he was afraid I hadn't approved
of his being round with her so much evenings. Of course it ain't as
if their evenings were as pleasant as ours—since *we* don't seem to
feel that way about the poison. I guess I *don't* see the point now;
but I suppose he knows I'm a lady and I'd scorn to raise a fuss.
Anyway, she wants you to realise she ain't engaged. I don't know
why she makes so much of it, but she said to me three times 'Mind
you tell Mr. Winterbourne.' And then she told me to ask if you
remembered the time you went up to that castle in Switzerland.
But I said I wouldn't give any such messages as *that*. Only if she
ain't engaged I guess I'm glad to realise it too."

But, as Winterbourne had originally judged, the truth on this
question had small actual relevance. A week after this the poor girl
died; it had been indeed a terrible case of the *perniciosa*. A grave
was found for her in the little Protestant cemetery, by an angle of
the wall of imperial Rome, beneath the cypresses and the thick
spring-flowers. Winterbourne stood there beside it with a number of
other mourners; a number larger than the scandal excited by the
young lady's career might have made probable. Near him stood
Giovanelli, who came nearer still before Winterbourne turned away.
Giovanelli, in decorous mourning, showed but a whiter face; his
button-hole lacked its nosegay and he had visibly something urgent
—and even to distress—to say, which he scarce knew how to
"place." He decided at last to confide it with a pale convulsion to
Winterbourne. "She was the most beautiful young lady I ever saw,
and the most amiable." To which he added in a moment: "Also—
naturally!—the most innocent."

Winterbourne sounded him with hard dry eyes, but presently
repeated his words, "The most innocent?"

"The most innocent!"

It came somehow so much too late that our friend could only
glare at its having come at all. "Why the devil," he asked, "did you
take her to that fatal place?"

Giovanelli raised his neat shoulders and eyebrows to within suspicion of a shrug. "For myself I had no fear; and *she*—she did what
she liked."

Winterbourne's eyes attached themselves to the ground. "She did
what she liked!"

It determined on the part of poor Giovanelli a further pious, a
further candid, confidence. "If she had lived I should have got
nothing. She never would have married me."

It had been spoken as if to attest, in all sincerity, his disinterestedness, but Winterbourne scarce knew what welcome to give it. He said, however, with a grace inferior to his friend's: "I dare say not."

The latter was even by this not discouraged. "For a moment I hoped so. But no. I'm convinced."

Winterbourne took it in; he stood staring at the raw protuberance among the April daisies. When he turned round again his fellow mourner had stepped back.

He almost immediately left Rome, but the following summer he again met his aunt Mrs. Costello at Vevey. Mrs. Costello extracted from the charming old hotel there a value that the Miller family hadn't mastered the secret of. In the interval Winterbourne had often thought of the most interesting member of that trio—of her mystifying manners and her queer adventure. One day he spoke of her to his aunt—said it was on his conscience he had done her injustice.

"I'm sure I don't know"—that lady showed caution. "How did your injustice affect her?"

"She sent me a message before her death which I didn't understand at the time. But I've understood it since. She would have appreciated one's esteem."

"She took an odd way to gain it! But do you mean by what you say," Mrs. Costello asked, "that she would have reciprocated one's affection?"

As he made no answer to this she after a little looked round at him—he hadn't been directly within sight; but the effect of that wasn't to make her repeat her question. He spoke, however, after a while. "You were right in that remark that you made last summer. I was booked to make a mistake. I've lived too long in foreign parts." And this time she herself said nothing.

Nevertheless he soon went back to live at Geneva, whence there continue to come the most contradictory accounts of his motives of sojourn: a report that he's "studying" hard—an intimation that he's much interested in a very clever foreign lady.

1878, 1879

The Real Thing[1]

I

When the porter's wife, who used to answer the house-bell, announced "A gentleman and a lady, sir" I had, as I often had in those days—the wish being father to the thought—an immediate vision of sitters. Sitters my visitors in this case proved to be; but not

---

1. This "little gem of bright, quick, vivid form," as James called it, first appeared in *Black and White* on April 16, 1892, in *The Real Thing and Other Tales* (1893), and finally in Vol. XVIII (1909) of the New York edition, the source of the present text.

in the sense I should have preferred. There was nothing at first however to indicate that they mightn't have come for a portrait. The gentleman, a man of fifty, very high and very straight, with a moustache slightly grizzled and a dark grey walking-coat admirably fitted, both of which I noted professionally—I don't mean as a barber or yet as a tailor—would have struck me as a celebrity if celebrities often were striking. It was a truth of which I had for some time been conscious that a figure with a good deal of frontage was, as one might say, almost never a public institution. A glance at the lady helped to remind me of this paradoxical law: she also looked too distinguished to be a "personality." Moreover one would scarcely come across two variations together.

Neither of the pair immediately spoke—they only prolonged the preliminary gaze suggesting that each wished to give the other a chance. They were visibly shy; they stood there letting me take them in—which, as I afterwards perceived, was the most practical thing they could have done. In this way their embarrassment served their cause. I had seen people painfully reluctant to mention that they desired anything so gross as to be represented on canvas; but the scruples of my new friends appeared almost insurmountable. Yet the gentleman might have said "I should like a portrait of my wife," and the lady might have said "I should like a portrait of my husband." Perhaps they weren't husband and wife—this naturally would make the matter more delicate. Perhaps they wished to be done together—in which case they ought to have brought a third person to break the news.

"We come from Mr. Rivet," the lady finally said with a dim smile that had the effect of a moist sponge passed over a "sunk"[2] piece of painting, as well as of a vague allusion to vanished beauty. She was as tall and straight, in her degree, as her companion, and with ten years less to carry. She looked as sad as a woman could look whose face was not charged with expression; that is her tinted oval mask showed waste as an exposed surface shows friction. The hand of time had played over her freely, but to an effect of elimination. She was slim and stiff, and so well-dressed, in dark blue cloth, with lappets and pockets and buttons, that it was clear she employed the same tailor as her husband. The couple had an indefinable air of prosperous thrift—they evidently got a good deal of luxury for their money. If I was to be one of their luxuries it would behove me to consider my terms.

"Ah Claude Rivet recommended me?" I echoed; and I added that it was very kind of him, though I could reflect that, as he only painted landscape, this wasn't a sacrifice.

The lady looked very hard at the gentleman, and the gentleman looked round the room. Then staring at the floor a moment and

2. When colors lose their brilliance after they have dried on the canvas, they are said to have "sunk in."

stroking his moustache, he rested his pleasant eyes on me with the remark: "He said you were the right one."

"I try to be, when people want to sit.

"Yes, we should like to," said the lady anxiously.

"Do you mean together?"

My visitors exchanged a glance. "If you could do anything with *me* I suppose it would be double," the gentleman stammered.

"Oh yes, there's naturally a higher charge for two figures than for one."

"We should like to make it pay," the husband confessed.

"That's very good of you," I returned, appreciating so unwonted a sympathy—for I supposed he meant pay the artist.

A sense of strangeness seemed to dawn on the lady.

"We mean for the illustrations—Mr. Rivet said you might put one in."

"Put in—an illustration?" I was equally confused.

"Sketch her off, you know," said the gentleman, colouring.

It was only then that I understood the service Claude Rivet had rendered me; he had told them how I worked in black-and-white, for magazines, for storybooks, for sketches of contemporary life, and consequently had copious employment for models. These things were true, but it was not less true—I may confess it now; whether because the aspiration was to lead to everything or to nothing I leave the reader to guess—that I couldn't get the honours, to say nothing of the emoluments, of a great painter of portraits out of my head. My "illustrations" were my pot-boilers; I looked to a different branch of art—far and away the most interesting it had always seemed to me—to perpetuate my fame. There was no shame in looking to it also to make my fortune; but that fortune was by so much further from being made from the moment my visitors wished to be "done" for nothing. I was disappointed; for in the pictorial sense I had immediately *seen* them. I had seized their type —I had already settled what I would do with it. Something that wouldn't absolutely have pleased them, I afterwards reflected.

"Ah you're—you're—a—?" I began as soon as I had mastered my surprise. I couldn't bring out the dingy word "models": it seemed so little to fit the case.

"We haven't had much practice," said the lady.

"We've got to *do* something, and we've thought that an artist in your line might perhaps make something of us," her husband threw off. He further mentioned that they didn't know many artists and that they had gone first, on the off-chance—he painted views of course, but sometimes put in figures; perhaps I remembered—to Mr. Rivet, whom they had met a few years before at a place in Norfolk where he was sketching.

"We used to sketch a little ourselves," the lady hinted.

"It's very awkward, but we absolutely *must* do something," her husband went on.

"Of course we're not so *very* young," she admitted with a wan smile.

With the remark that I might as well know something more about them the husband had handed me a card extracted from a neat new pocket-book—their appurtenances were all of the freshest —and inscribed with the words "Major Monarch." Impressive as these words were they didn't carry my knowledge much further; but my visitor presently added: "I've left the army and we've had the misfortune to lose our money. In fact our means are dreadfully small."

"It's awfully trying—a regular strain," said Mrs. Monarch.

They evidently wished to be discreet—to take care not to swagger because they were gentlefolk. I felt them willing to recognise this as something of a drawback, at the same time that I guessed at an underlying sense—their consolation in adversity—that they *had* their points. They certainly had; but these advantages struck me as pre-ponderantly social; such for instance as would help to make a draw-ing-room look well. However, a drawing-room was always, or ought to be, a picture.

In consequence of his wife's allusion to their age Major Monarch observed: "Naturally it's more for the figure that we thought of going in. We can still hold ourselves up." On the instant I saw that the figure was indeed their strong point. His "naturally" didn't sound vain, but it lighted up the question. "*She* has the best one," he continued, nodding at his wife with a pleasant after-dinner absence of circumlocution. I could only reply, as if we were in fact sitting over our wine, that this didn't prevent his own from being very good; which led him in turn to make answer: "We thought that if you ever have to do people like us we might be something like it. *She* particularly—for a lady in a book, you know."

I was so amused by them that, to get more of it, I did my best to take their point of view; and though it was an embarrassment to find myself appraising physically, as if they were animals on hire or useful blacks, a pair whom I should have expected to meet only in one of the relations in which criticism is tacit, I looked at Mrs. Monarch judicially enough to be able to exclaim after a moment with conviction: "Oh yes, a lady in a book!" She was singularly like a bad illustration.

"We'll stand up, if you like," said the Major; and he raised him-self before me with a really grand air.

I could take his measure at a glance—he was six feet two and a perfect gentleman. It would have paid any club in process of forma-tion and in want of a stamp to engage him at a salary to stand in the principal window. What struck me at once was that in coming to me they had rather missed their vocation; they could surely have been turned to better account for advertising purposes. I couldn't of course see the thing in detail, but I could see them make somebody's fortune—I don't mean their own. There was something in them for a waistcoat-maker, an hotel-keeper or a soap-vendor. I could imagine "We always use it" pinned on their bosoms with the greatest effect; I had a vision of the brilliancy with which they would launch a table d'hôte.[3]

Mrs. Monarch sat still, not from pride but from shyness, and presently her husband said to her: "Get up, my dear, and show how smart you are." She obeyed, but she had no need to get up to show it. She walked to the end of the studio and then came back blushing, her fluttered eyes on the partner of her appeal. I was reminded of an incident I had accidentally had a glimpse of in Paris being with a friend there, a dramatist about to produce a play, when an actress came to him to ask to be entrusted with a part. She went through her paces before him, walked up and down as Mrs. Monarch was doing. Mrs. Monarch did it quite as well, but I abstained from applauding. It was very odd to see such people apply for such poor pay. She looked as if she had ten thousand a year. Her husband had used the word that described her: she was in the London current jargon essentially and typically "smart." Her figure was, in the same order of ideas, conspicuously and irreproachably "good." For a woman of her age her waist was surprisingly small; her elbow moreover had the orthodox crook. She held her head at the conventional angle, but why did she come to *me*? She ought to have tried on jackets at a big shop. I feared my visitors were not only destitute but "artistic"—which would be a great complication. When she sat down again I thanked her, observing that what a draughtsman most valued in his model was the faculty of keeping quiet.

"Oh *she* can keep quiet," said Major Monarch. Then he added jocosely: "I've always kept her quiet."

"I'm not a nasty fidget, am I?" It was going to wring tears from me, I felt, the way she hid her head, ostrich-like, in the other broad bosom.

The owner of this expanse addressed his answer to me. "Perhaps it isn't out of place to mention—because we ought to be quite business-like, oughtn't we?—that when I married her she was known as the Beautiful Statue."

"Oh dear!" said Mrs. Monarch ruefully.

"Of course I should want a certain amount of expression," I rejoined.

"Of *course*!"—and I had never heard such unanimity.

"And then I suppose you know that you'll get awfully tired."

"Oh we *never* get tired!" they eagerly cried.

"Have you had any kind of practice?"

3. A common table for guests at a hotel.

They hesitated—they looked at each other. "We've been photographed—*immensely*," said Mrs. Monarch.

"She means the fellows have asked us themselves," added the Major.

"I see—because you're so good-looking."

"I don't know what they thought, but they were always after us."

"We always got our photographs for nothing," smiled Mrs. Monarch.

"We might have brought some, my dear," her husband remarked.

"I'm not sure we have any left. We've given quantities away," she explained to me.

"With our autographs and that sort of thing," said the Major.

"Are they to be got in the shops?" I enquired as a harmless pleasantry.

"Oh yes, *hers*—they used to be."

"Not now," said Mrs. Monarch with her eyes on the floor.

II

I could fancy the "sort of thing" they put on the presentation copies of their photographs, and I was sure they wrote a beautiful hand. It was odd how quickly I was sure of everything that concerned them. If they were now so poor as to have to earn shillings and pence they could never have had much of a margin. Their good looks had been their capital, and they had good-humouredly made the most of the career that this resource marked out for them. It was in their faces, the blankness, the deep intellectual repose of the twenty years of country-house visiting that had given them pleasant intonations. I could see the sunny drawing-rooms, sprinkled with periodicals she didn't read, in which Mrs. Monarch had continuously sat; I could see the wet shrubberies in which she had walked, equipped to admiration for either exercise. I could see the rich covers[4] the Major had helped to shoot and the wonderful garments in which, late at night, he repaired to the smoking-room to talk about them. I could imagine their leggings and waterproofs, their knowing tweeds and rugs, their rolls of sticks and cases of tackle and neat umbrellas; and I could evoke the exact appearance of their servants and the compact variety of their luggage on the platforms of country stations.

They gave small tips, but they were liked; they didn't do anything themselves, but they were welcome. They looked so well everywhere; they gratified the general relish for stature, complexion and "form." They knew it without fatuity or vulgarity, and they respected themselves in consequence. They weren't superficial; they were thorough and kept themselves up—it had been their line. People with such a taste for activity had to have some line. I could

4. Magazine covers.

feel how even in a dull house they could have been counted on for the joy of life. At present something had happened—it didn't matter what, their little income had grown less, it had grown least —and they had to do something for pocket-money. Their friends could like them, I made out, without liking to support them. There was something about them that represented credit—their clothes, their manners, their type; but if credit is a large empty pocket in which an occasional chink reverberates, the chink at least must be audible. What they wanted of me was to help to make it so. Fortunately they had no children—I soon divined that. They would also perhaps wish our relations to be kept secret: this was why it was "for the figure"—the reproduction of the face would betray them.

I liked them—I felt, quite as their friends must have done—they were so simple; and I had no objection to them if they would suit. But somehow with all their perfections I didn't easily believe in them. After all they were amateurs, and the ruling passion of my life was the detestation of the amateur. Combined with this was another perversity—an innate preference for the represented subject over the real one: the defect of the real one was so apt to be a lack of representation. I liked things that appeared; then one was sure. Whether they *were* or not was a subordinate and almost always a profitless question. There were other considerations, the first of which was that I already had two or three recruits in use, notably a young person with big feet, in alpaca, from Kilburn, who for a couple of years had come to me regularly for my illustrations and with whom I was still—perhaps ignobly—satisfied. I frankly explained to my visitors how the case stood, but they had taken more precautions than I supposed. They had reasoned out their opportunity, for Claude Rivet had told them of the projected *édition de luxe* of one of the writers of our day—the rarest of the novelists—who, long neglected by the multitudinous vulgar and dearly prized by the attentive (need I mention Philip Vincent?)[5] had had the happy fortune of seeing, late in life, the dawn and then the full light of a higher criticism; an estimate in which on the part of the public there was something really of expiation. The edition preparing, planned by a publisher of taste, was practically an act of high reparation; the wood-cuts with which it was to be enriched were the homage of English art to one of the most independent representatives of English letters. Major and Mrs. Monarch confessed to me they had hoped I might be able to work *them* into my branch of the enterprise. They knew I was to do the first of the books, "Rutland Ramsay," but I had to make clear to them that my participation in the rest of the affair—this first book was to be a test—must depend on the satisfaction I should give. If this should be limited my employers would drop me with scarce common

5. Obviously James, here indulging in some good-natured complaining and fantasizing.

forms. It was therefore a crisis for me, and naturally I was making special preparations, looking about for new people, should they be necessary, and securing the best types. I admitted however that I should like to settle down to two or three good models who would do for everything.

"Should we have often to—a—put on special clothes?" Mrs. Monarch timidly demanded.

"Dear yes—that's half the business."

"And should we be expected to supply our own costumes?"

"Oh no; I've got a lot of things. A painter's models put on—or put off—anything he likes."

"And you mean—a—the same?"

"The same?"

Mrs. Monarch looked at her husband again.

"Oh she was just wondering," he explained, "if the costumes are in *general* use." I had to confess that they were, and I mentioned further that some of them—I had a lot of genuine greasy last-century things—had served their time, a hundred years ago, on living world-stained men and women; on figures not perhaps so far removed, in that vanished world, from *their* type, the Monarchs', *quoi!*[6] of a breeched and bewigged age. "We'll put on anything that *fits*," said the Major.

"Oh I arrange that—they fit in the pictures."

"I'm afraid I should do better for the modern books. I'd come as you like," said Mrs. Monarch.

"She has got a lot of clothes at home: they might do for contemporary life," her husband continued.

"Oh I can fancy scenes in which you'd be quite natural." And indeed I could see the slipshod rearrangements of stale properties—the stories I tried to produce pictures for without the exasperation of reading them—whose sandy tracts the good lady might help to people. But I had to return to the fact that for this sort of work—the daily mechanical grind—I was already equipped: the people I was working with were fully adequate.

"We only thought we might be more like *some* characters," said Mrs. Monarch mildly, getting up.

Her husband also rose; he stood looking at me with a dim wistfulness that was touching in so fine a man.

"Wouldn't it be rather a pull sometimes to have—a—to have—?" He hung fire; he wanted me to help him by phrasing what he meant. But I couldn't—I didn't know. So he brought it out awkwardly: "The *real* thing; a gentleman, you know, or a lady." I was quite ready to give a general assent—I admitted that there was a great deal in that. This encouraged Major Monarch to say, following up his appeal with an unacted gulp: "It's awfully hard—we've tried everything." The gulp was communicative; it proved too much

6. What!

for his wife. Before I knew it Mrs. Monarch had dropped again upon a divan and burst into tears. Her husband sat down beside her, holding one of her hands; whereupon she quickly dried her eyes with the other, while I felt embarrassed as she looked up at me. "There isn't a confounded job I haven't applied for—waited for— prayed for. You can fancy we'd be pretty bad first. Secretaryships and that sort of thing? You might as well ask for a peerage. I'd be *anything*—I'm strong; a messenger or a coalheaver. I'd put on a gold-laced cap and open carriage-doors in front of the haberdasher's; I'd hang about a station to carry portmanteaux; I'd be a postman. But they won't *look* at you; there are thousands as good as yourself already on the ground. *Gentlemen,* poor beggars, who've drunk their wine, who've kept their hunters!"

I was as reassuring as I knew how to be, and my visitors were presently on their feet again while, for the experiment, we agreed on an hour. We were discussing it when the door opened and Miss Churm came in with a wet umbrella. Miss Churm had to take the omnibus to Maida Vale and then walk half a mile. She looked a trifle blowsy and slightly splashed. I scarcely ever saw her come in without thinking fresh how odd it was that, being so little in her-self, she should yet be so much in others. She was a meagre little Miss Churm, but was such an ample heroine of romance. She was only a freckled cockney,[7] but she could represent everything, from a fine lady to a shepherdess; she had the faculty as she might have had a fine voice or long hair. She couldn't spell and she loved beer, but she had two or three "points," and practice, and a knack, and mother-wit, and a whimsical sensibility, and a love of the theatre, and seven sisters, and not an ounce of respect, especially for the *h*. The first thing my visitors saw was that her umbrella was wet, and in their spotless perfection they visibly winced at it. The rain had come on since their arrival.

"I'm all in a soak; there *was* a mess of people in the 'bus. I wish you lived near a stytion," said Miss Churm. I requested her to get ready as quickly as possible, and she passed into the room in which she always changed her dress. But before going out she asked me what she was to get into this time.

"It's the Russian princess, don't you know?" I answered; "the one with the 'golden eyes,' in black velvet, for the long thing in the *Cheapside*."[8]

"Golden eyes? I *say!*" cried Miss Churm, while my companions watched her with intensity as she withdrew. She always arranged herself, when she was late, before I could turn around; and I kept my visitors a little on purpose, so that they might get an idea, from seeing her, what would be expected of themselves. I mentioned that

---

7. Native of London, especially the East End. The cockney dialect is known for dropping *h*'s; for example, *hair* would be pronounced *air*.

8. Imaginary magazine named after a main business street in London.

she was quite my notion of an excellent model—she was really very clever.

"Do you think she looks like a Russian princess?" Major Monarch asked with lurking alarm.

"When I make her, yes."

"Oh if you have to *make* her—!" he reasoned, not without point.

"That's the most you can ask. There are so many who are not makeable."

"Well now, *here's* a lady"—and with a persuasive smile he passed his arm into his wife's—"who's already made!"

"Oh I'm not a Russian princess," Mrs. Monarch protested a little coldly. I could see she had known some and didn't like them. There at once was a complication of a kind I never had to fear with Miss Churm.

This young lady came back in black velvet—the gown was rather rusty and very low on her lean shoulders—and with a Japanese fan in her red hands. I reminded her that in the scene I was doing she had to look over some one's head. "I forget whose it is; but it doesn't matter. Just look over a head."

"I'd rather look over a stove," said Miss Churm; and she took her station near the fire. She fell into position, settled herself into a tall attitude, gave a certain backward inclination to her head and a certain forward droop to her fan, and looked, at least to my prejudiced sense, distinguished and charming, foreign and dangerous. We left her looking so while I went downstairs with Major and Mrs. Monarch.

"I believe I could come about as near it as that," said Mrs. Monarch.

"Oh, you think she's shabby, but you must allow for the alchemy of art."

However, they went off with an evident increase of comfort founded on their demonstrable advantage in being the real thing. I could fancy them shuddering over Miss Churm. She was very droll about them when I went back, for I told her what they wanted.

"Well, if *she* can sit I'll tyke to bookkeeping," said my model.

"She's very ladylike," I replied as an innocent form of aggravation.

"So much the worse for *you*. That means she can't turn round."

"She'll do for the fashionable novels."

"Oh yes, she'll *do* for them!" my model humorously declared. "Ain't they bad enough without her?" I had often sociably denounced them to Miss Churm.

III

It was for the elucidation of a mystery in one of these works that I first tried Mrs. Monarch. Her husband came with her, to be useful if necessary—it was sufficiently clear that as a general thing he would prefer to come with her. At first I wondered if this were for "propriety's" sake—if he were going to be jealous and meddling. The idea was too tiresome, and if it had been confirmed it would speedily have brought our acquaintance to a close. But I soon saw there was nothing in it and that if he accompanied Mrs. Monarch it was—in addition to the chance of being wanted—simply because he had nothing else to do. When they were separate his occupation was gone and they never *had* been separate. I judged rightly that in their awkward situation their close union was their main comfort and that this union had no weak spot. It was a real marriage, an encouragement to the hesitating, a nut for pessimists to crack. Their address was humble—I remember afterwards thinking it had been the only thing about them that was really professional—and I could fancy the lamentable lodgings in which the Major would have been left alone. He could sit there more or less grimly with his wife—he couldn't sit there anyhow without her.

He had too much tact to try and make himself agreeable when he couldn't be useful; so when I was too absorbed in my work to talk he simply sat and waited. But I liked to hear him talk—it made my work, when not interrupting it, less mechanical, less special. To listen to him was to combine the excitement of going out with the economy of staying at home. There was only one hindrance—that I seemed not to know any of the people this brilliant couple had known. I think he wondered extremely, during the term of our intercourse, whom the deuce I *did* know. He hadn't a stray sixpence of an idea to fumble for, so we didn't spin it very fine; we confined ourselves to questions of leather and even of liquor—saddlers and breeches-makers and how to get excellent claret cheap—and matters like "good trains" and the habits of small game. His lore on these last subjects was astonishing—he managed to interweave the station-master with the ornithologist. When he couldn't talk about greater things he could talk cheerfully about smaller, and since I couldn't accompany him into reminiscences of the fashionable world he could lower the conversation without a visible effort to my level.

So earnest a desire to please was touching in a man who could so easily have knocked one down. He looked after the fire and had an opinion on the draught of the stove without my asking him, and I could see that he thought many of my arrangements not half knowing. I remember telling him that if I were only rich I'd offer him a salary to come and teach me how to live. Sometimes he gave a random sigh of which the essence might have been: "Give me even such a bare old barrack as *this*, and I'd do something with it!" When I wanted to use him he came alone; which was an illustration of the superior courage of women. His wife could bear her solitary second floor, and she was in general more discreet; showing by various small reserves that she was alive to the propriety of keeping our relations markedly professional—not letting them slide into sociability. She wished it to remain clear that she and the Major were employed, not cultivated, and if she approved of me as a superior, who could be kept in his place, she never thought me quite good enough for an equal.

She sat with great intensity, giving the whole of her mind to it, and was capable of remaining for an hour almost as motionless as before a photographer's lens. I could see she had been photographed often, but somehow the very habit that made her good for that purpose unfitted her for mine. At first I was extremely pleased with her ladylike air, and it was a satisfaction, on coming to follow her lines, to see how good they were and how far they could lead the pencil. But after a little skirmishing I began to find her too insurmountably stiff; do what I would with it my drawing looked like a photograph or a copy of a photograph. Her figure had no variety of expression—she herself had no sense of variety. You may say that this was my business and was only a question of placing her. Yet I placed her in every conceivable position and she managed to obliterate their differences. She was always a lady certainly, and into the bargain was always the same lady. She was the real thing, but always the same thing. There were moments when I rather writhed under the serenity of her confidence that she *was* the real thing. All her dealings with me and all her husband's were an implication that this was lucky for *me*. Meanwhile I found myself trying to invent types that approached her own, instead of making her own transform itself—in the clever way that was not impossible for instance to poor Miss Churm. Arrange as I would and take the precautions I would, she always came out, in my pictures, too tall—landing me in the dilemma of having represented a fascinating woman as seven feet high, which (out of respect perhaps to my own very much scantier inches) was far from my idea of such personage.

The case was worse with the Major—nothing I could do would keep *him* down, so that he became useful only for the representation of brawny giants. I adored variety and range, I cherished human accidents, the illustrative note; I wanted to characterise closely, and the thing in the world I most hated was the danger of being ridden by a type. I had quarrelled with some of my friends about it; I had parted company with them for maintaining that one *had* to be, and that if the type was beautiful—witness Raphael[9] and Leonardo—the servitude was only a gain. I was neither Leonardo nor Raphael—I might only be a presumptuous young modern searcher; but I held that everything was to be sacrificed sooner than character. When they claimed that the obsessional form could

9. Raffaello Santi or Sanzio (1483–1520), Italian painter; Leonardo da Vinci (1452–1519), Florentine painter, sculptor, architect, and engineer.

easily *be* character I retorted, perhaps superficially, "Whose?" It couldn't be everybody's—it might end in being nobody's.

After I had drawn Mrs. Monarch a dozen times I felt surer even than before that the value of such a model as Miss Churm resided precisely in the fact that she had no positive stamp, combined of course with the other fact that what she did have was a curious and inexplicable talent for imitation. Her usual appearance was like a curtain which she could draw up at request for a capital perform-ance. This performance was simply suggestive; but it was a word to the wise—it was vivid and pretty. Sometimes even I thought it, though she was plain herself, too insipidly pretty; I made it a reproach to her that the figures drawn from her were monotonously (*bêtement,*[1] as we used to say) graceful. Nothing made her more angry: it was so much her pride to feel she could sit for characters that had nothing in common with each other. She would accuse me at such moments of taking away her "reputytion."

It suffered a certain shrinkage, this queer quantity, from the repeated visits of my new friends. Miss Churm was greatly in demand, never in want of employment, so I had no scruple in put-ting her off occasionally, to try them more at my ease. It was cer-tainly amusing at first to do the real thing—it was amusing to do Major Monarch's trousers. They *were* the real thing, even if he did come out colossal. It was amusing to do his wife's back hair—it was so mathematically neat—and the particular "smart" tension of her tight stays. She lent herself especially to positions in which the face was somewhat averted or blurred; she abounded in ladylike back views and *profils perdus.*[2] When she stood erect she took naturally one of the attitudes in which court-painters represent queens and princesses; so that I found myself wondering whether, to draw out this accomplishment, I couldn't get the editor of the *Cheapside* to publish a really royal romance, "A Tale of Buckingham Palace." Sometimes however the real thing and the make-believe came into contact; by which I mean that Miss Churm, keeping an appoint-ment or coming to make one on days when I had much work in hand, encountered her invidious rivals. The encounter was not on their part, for they noticed her no more than if she had been the housemaid; not from intentional loftiness, but simply because as yet, professionally, they didn't know how to fraternise, as I could imagine they would have liked—or at least that the Major would. They couldn't talk about the omnibus—they always walked; and they didn't know what else to try—she wasn't interested in good trains or cheap claret. Besides, they must have felt—in the air—that she was amused at them, secretly derisive of their ever knowing how. She wasn't a person to conceal the limits of her faith if she had had a chance to show them. On the other hand Mrs. Monarch didn't think her tidy; for why else did she take pains to say to me

1. Foolishly.   2. Averted glances.

—it was going out of the way, for Mrs. Monarch—that she didn't like dirty women?

One day when my young lady happened to be present with my other sitters—she even dropped in, when it was convenient, for a chat—I asked her to be so good as to lend a hand in getting tea, a service with which she was familiar and which was one of a class that, living as I did in a small way, with slender domestic resources, I often appealed to my models to render. They liked to lay hands on my property, to break the sitting, and sometimes the china—it made them feel Bohemian. The next time I saw Miss Churm after this incident she surprised me greatly by making a scene about it— she accused me of having wished to humiliate her. She hadn't resented the outrage at the time, but had seemed obliging and amused, enjoying the comedy of asking Mrs. Monarch, who sat vague and silent, whether she would have cream and sugar, and putting an exaggerated simper into the question. She had tried intonations—as if she too wished to pass for the real thing—till I was afraid my other visitors would take offence.

Oh they were determined not to do this, and their touching patience was the measure of their great need. They would sit by the hour, uncomplaining, till I was ready to use them; they would come back on the chance of being wanted and would walk away cheerfully if it failed. I used to go to the door with them to see in what magnificent order they retreated. I tried to find other employment for them—I introduced them to several artists. But they didn't "take," for reasons I could appreciate, and I became rather anxiously aware that after such disappointments they fell back upon me with a heavier weight. They did me the honor to think me most *their* form. They weren't romantic enough for the painters, and in those days there were few serious workers in black-and-white. Besides, they had an eye to the great job I had mentioned to them—they had secretly set their hearts on supplying the right essence for my pictorial vindication of our fine novelist. They knew that for this undertaking I should want no costume-effects, none of the frippery of past ages—that it was a case in which everything would be contemporary and satirical and presumably genteel. If I could work them into it their future would be assured, for the labour would of course be long and the occupation steady.

One day Mrs. Monarch came without her husband—she explained his absence by his having had to go to the City.[3] While she sat there in her usual relaxed majesty there came at the door a knock which I immediately recognised as the subdued appeal of a model out of work. It was followed by the entrance of a young man whom I at once saw to be a foreigner and who proved in fact an Italian acquainted with no English word but my name, which he uttered in a way that made it seem to include all others. I hadn't

3. London.

then visited his country, nor was I proficient in his tongue; but as he was not so meanly constituted—what Italian is?—as to depend only on that member for expression he conveyed to me, in familiar but graceful mimicry, that he was in search of exactly the employment in which the lady before me was engaged. I was not struck with him at first, and while I continued to draw I dropped few signs of interest or encouragement. He stood his ground however— not importunately, but with a dumb dog-like fidelity in his eyes that amounted to innocent impudence, the manner of a devoted servant —he might have been in the house for years—unjustly suspected. Suddenly it struck me that this very attitude and expression made a picture; whereupon I told him to sit down and wait till I should be free. There was another picture in the way he obeyed me, and I observed as I worked that there were others still in the way he looked wonderingly, with his head thrown back, about the high studio. He might have been crossing himself in Saint Peter's. Before I finished I said to myself "The fellow's a bankrupt orange-monger, but a treasure."

When Mrs. Monarch withdrew he passed across the room like a flash to open the door for her, standing there with the rapt pure gaze of the young Dante spellbound by the young Beatrice.[4] As I never insisted, in such situations, on the blankness of the British domestic, I reflected that he had the making of a servant—and I needed one, but couldn't pay him to be only that—as well as of a model; in short I resolved to adopt my bright adventurer if he would agree to officiate in the double capacity. He jumped at my offer, and in the event my rashness—for I had really known nothing about him—wasn't brought home to me. He proved a sympathetic though a desultory ministrant, and had in a wonderful degree the *sentiment de la pose*.[5] It was uncultivated, instinctive, a part of the happy instinct that had guided him to my door and helped him to spell out my name on the card nailed to it. He had had no other introduction to me than a guess, from the shape of my high north window, seen outside, that my place was a studio and that as a studio it would contain an artist. He had wandered to England in search of fortune, like other itinerants, and had embarked, with a partner and a small green hand-cart, on the sale of penny ices. The ices had melted away and the partner had dissolved in their train. My young man wore tight yellow trousers with reddish stripes and his name was Oronte. He was sallow but fair, and when I put him into some old clothes of my own he looked like an Englishman. He was as good as Miss Churm, who could look, when requested, like an Italian.

4. Dante Alighieri (1265–1321), Italian poet, first saw Beatrice Portinari when they were both nine. Though he only saw her a few times, she made a lasting impression on him and became his ideal, his life's inspiration, and direct agent of his salvation (as his greatest work, *The Divine Comedy*, makes clear).
5. Instinct for striking poses.

IV

I thought Mrs. Monarch's face slightly convulsed when, on her coming back with her husband, she found Oronte installed. It was strange to have to recognise in a scrap of a lazzarone[6] a competitor to her magnificent Major. It was she who scented danger first, for the Major was anecdotically unconscious. But Oronte gave us tea, with a hundred eager confusions—he had never been concerned in so queer a process—and I think she thought better of me for having at last an "establishment." They saw a couple of drawings that I had made of the establishment, and Mrs. Monarch hinted that it never would have struck her he had sat for them. "Now the drawings you make from *us*, they look exactly like us," she reminded me, smiling in triumph; and I recognized that this was indeed just their defect. When I drew the Monarchs I couldn't anyhow get away from them—get into the character I wanted to represent; and I hadn't the least desire my model should be discoverable in my picture. Miss Churm never was, and Mrs. Monarch thought I hid her, very properly, because she was vulgar; whereas if she was lost it was only as the dead who go to heaven are lost—in the gain of an angel the more.

By this time I had got a certain start with "Rutland Ramsay," the first novel in the great projected series; that is I had produced a dozen drawings, several with the help of the Major and his wife, and I had sent them in for approval. My understanding with the publishers, as I have already hinted, had been that I was to be left to do my work, in this particular case, as I liked, with the whole book committed to me; but my connexion with the rest of the series was only contingent. There were moments when, frankly, it *was* a comfort to have the real thing under one's hand; for there were characters in "Rutland Ramsay" that were very much like it. There were people presumably as erect as the Major and women of as good a fashion as Mrs. Monarch. There was a great deal of country-house life—treated, it is true, in a fine fanciful ironical generalised way—and there was a considerable implication of knickerbockers and kilts.[7] There were certain things I had to settle at the outset; such things for instance as the exact appearance of the hero and the particular bloom and figure of the heroine. The author of course gave me a lead, but there was a margin for interpretation. I took the Monarchs into my confidence, I told them frankly what I was about, I mentioned my embarrassments and alternatives. "Oh take *him!*" Mrs. Monarch murmured sweetly, looking at her husband; and "What could you want better than my wife?" the Major enquired with the comfortable candour that now prevailed between us.

6. Beggar.
7. Knickerbockers (close-fitting short pants gathered at the knee) and kilts (a knee-length pleated skirt, usually of tartan, worn by Scottish men) are suggestive of rural, outdoors attire.

I wasn't obliged to answer these remarks—I was only obliged to place my sitters. I wasn't easy in mind, and I postponed a little timidly perhaps the solving of my question. The book was a large canvas, the other figures were numerous, and I worked off at first some of the episodes in which the hero and the heroine were not concerned. When once I had set *them* up I should have to stick to them—I couldn't make my young man seven feet high in one place and five feet nine in another. I inclined on the whole to the latter measurement, though the Major more than once reminded me that *he* looked about as young as any one. It was indeed quite possible to arrange him, for the figure, so that it would have been difficult to detect his age. After the spontaneous Oronte had been with me a month, and after I had given him to understand several times over that his native exuberance would presently constitute an insurmountable barrier to our further intercourse, I waked to a sense of his heroic capacity. He was only five feet seven, but the remaining inches were latent. I tried him almost secretly at first, for I was really rather afraid of the judgment my other models would pass on such a choice. If they regarded Miss Churm as little better than a snare what would they think of the representation by a person so little the real thing as an Italian street-vendor of a protagonist formed by a public school?

If I went a little in fear of them it wasn't because they bullied me, because they had got an oppressive foothold, but because in their really pathetic decorum and mysteriously permanent newness they counted on me so intensely. I was therefore very glad when Jack Hawley came home: he was always of such good counsel. He painted badly himself, but there was no one like him for putting his finger on the place. He had been absent from England for a year; he had been somewhere—I don't remember where—to get a fresh eye. I was in a good deal of dread of any such organ, but we were old friends; he had been away for months and a sense of emptiness was creeping into my life. I hadn't dodged a missile for a year.

He came back with a fresh eye, but with the same old black velvet blouse, and the first evening he spent in my studio we smoked cigarettes till the small hours. He had done no work himself, he had only got the eye; so the field was clear for the production of my little things. He wanted to see what I had produced for the *Cheapside*, but he was disappointed in the exhibition. That at least seemed the meaning of two or three comprehensive groans which, as he lounged on my big divan, his leg folded under him, looking at my latest drawings, issued from his lips with the smoke of the cigarette.

"What's the matter with you?" I asked.

"What's the matter with *you?*"

"Nothing save that I'm mystified."

"You are indeed. You're quite off the hinge. What's the meaning of this new fad?" And he tossed me, with visible irreverence, a drawing in which I happened to have depicted both my elegant models. I asked if he didn't think it good, and he replied that it struck him as execrable, given the sort of thing I had always represented myself to him as wishing to arrive at; but I let that pass—I was so anxious to see exactly what he meant. The two figures in the picture looked colossal, but I supposed this was *not* what he meant, inasmuch as, for aught he knew to the contrary, I might have been trying for some such effect. I maintained that I was working exactly in the same way as when he last had done me the honour to tell me I might do something some day. "Well, there's a screw loose somewhere," he answered; "wait a bit and I'll discover it." I depended upon him to do so: where else was the fresh eye? But he produced at last nothing more luminous than "I don't know—I don't like your types." This was lame for a critic who had never consented to discuss with me anything but the question of execution, the direction of strokes and the mystery of values.

"In the drawings you've been looking at I think my types are very handsome."

"Oh they won't do!"

"I've been working with new models."

"I see you have. *They* won't do."

"Are you very sure of that?"

"Absolutely—they're stupid."

"You mean *I* am—for I ought to get round that."

"You *can't*—with such people. Who are they?"

I told him, so far as was necessary, and he concluded heartlessly: "Ce sont des gens qu'il faut mettre à la porte."[8]

"You've never seen them; they're awfully good"—I flew to their defence.

"Not seen them? Why all this recent work of yours drops to pieces with them. It's all I want to see of them."

"No one else has said anything against it—the *Cheapside* people are pleased."

"Every one else is an ass, and the *Cheapside* people the biggest asses of all. Come, don't pretend at this time of day to have pretty illusions about the public, especially about publishers and editors. It's not for *such* animals you work—it's for those who know, *coloro che sanno;*[9] so keep straight for *me* if you can't keep straight for yourself. There was a certain sort of thing you used to try for—and a very good thing it was. But this twaddle isn't *in* it." When I talked with Hawley later about "Rutland Ramsay" and its possible successors he declared that I must get back into my boat again or I

8. "Such people should be shown the door."
9. A misquotation of a phrase Dante applied to Aristotle in *The Divine Comedy*, "Inferno," IV.131, which reads, "*el maestro di color che sanno,*" literally "the master of those who know."

should go to the bottom. His voice in short was the voice of warning.

I noted the warning, but I didn't turn my friends out of doors. They bored me a good deal; but the very fact that they bored me admonished me not to sacrifice them—if there was anything to be done with them—simply to irritation. As I look back at this phase they seem to me to have pervaded my life not a little. I have a vision of them as most of the time in my studio, seated against the wall on an old velvet bench to be out of the way, and resembling the while a pair of patient courtiers in a royal ante-chamber. I'm convinced that during the coldest weeks of the winter they held their ground because it saved them fire. Their newness was losing its gloss, and it was impossible not to feel them objects of charity. Whenever Miss Churm arrived they went away, and after I was fairly launched in "Rutland Ramsay" Miss Churm arrived pretty often. They managed to express to me tacitly that they supposed I wanted her for the low life of the book, and I let them suppose it, since they had attempted to study the work—it was lying about the studio—without discovering that it dealt only with the highest circles. They had dipped into the most brilliant of our novelists without deciphering many passages. I still took an hour from them, now and again, in spite of Jack Hawley's warning: it would be time enough to dismiss them, if dismissal should be necessary, when the rigour of the season was over. Hawley had made their acquaintance —he had met them at my fireside—and thought them a ridiculous pair. Learning that he was a painter they tried to approach him, to show him too that they were the real thing; but he looked at them, across the big room, as if they were miles away: they were a compendium of everything he most objected to in the social system of his country. Such people as that, all convention and patent-leather, with ejaculations that stopped conversation, had no business in a studio. A studio was a place to learn to see, and how could you see through a pair of feather-beds?

The main inconvenience I suffered at their hands was that at first I was shy of letting it break upon them that my artful little servant had begun to sit to me for "Rutland Ramsay." They knew I had been odd enough—they were prepared by this time to allow oddity to artists—to pick a foreign vagabond out of the streets when I might have had a person with whiskers and credentials; but it was some time before they learned how high I rated his accomplishments. They found him in an attitude more than once, but they never doubted I was doing him as an organ-grinder. There were several things they never guessed, and one of them was that for a striking scene in the novel, in which a footman briefly figured, it occurred to me to make use of Major Monarch as the menial. I kept putting this off, I didn't like to ask him to don the livery—besides the difficulty of finding a livery to fit him. At last, one day late in the winter, when I was at work on the despised Oronte, who caught one's idea on the wing, and was in the glow of feeling myself go very straight, they came in, the Major and his wife, with their society laugh about nothing (there was less and less to laugh at); came on like country-callers—they always reminded me of that—who have walked across the park after church and are presently persuaded to stay to luncheon. Luncheon was over, but they could stay to tea—I knew they wanted it. The fit was on me, however, and I couldn't let my ardour cool and my work wait, with the fading daylight, while my model prepared it. So I asked Mrs. Monarch if she would mind laying it out—a request which for an instant brought all the blood to her face. Her eyes were on her husband's for a second, and some mute telegraphy passed between them. Their folly was over the next instant; his cheerful shrewdness put an end to it. So far from pitying their wounded pride, I must add, I was moved to give it as complete a lesson as I could. They bustled about together and got out the cups and saucers and made the kettle boil. I know they felt as if they were waiting on my servant, and when the tea was prepared I said: "He'll have a cup, please—he's tired." Mrs. Monarch brought him one where he stood, and he took it from her, as if he had been a gentleman at a party squeezing a crush-hat with an elbow.

Then it came over me that she had made a great effort for me— made it with a kind of nobleness—and that I owed her a compensation. Each time I saw her after this I wondered what the compensation could be. I couldn't go on doing the wrong thing to oblige them. Oh it *was* the wrong thing, the stamp of the work for which they sat—Hawley was not the only person to say it now. I sent in a large number of the drawings I had made for "Rutland Ramsay," and I received a warning that was more to the point than Hawley's. The artistic adviser of the house for which I was working was of opinion that many of my illustrations were not what had been looked for. Most of these illustrations were the subjects in which the Monarchs had figured. Without going into the question of what *had* been looked for, I had to face the fact that at this rate I shouldn't get the other books to do. I hurled myself in despair on Miss Churm—I put her through all her paces. I not only adopted Oronte publicly as my hero, but one morning when the Major looked in to see if I didn't require him to finish a *Cheapside* figure for which he had begun to sit the week before, I told him I had changed my mind—I'd do the drawing from my man. At this my visitor turned pale and stood looking at me. "Is *he* your idea of an English gentleman?" he asked.

I was disappointed, I was nervous, I wanted to get on with my work; so I replied with irritation: "Oh my dear Major—I can't be ruined for *you*!". .

It was a horrid speech, but he stood another moment—after

which, without a word, he quitted the studio. I drew a long breath, for I said to myself that I shouldn't see him again. I hadn't told him definitely that I was in danger of having my work rejected, but I was vexed at his not having felt the catastrophe in the air, read with me the moral of our fruitless collaboration, the lesson that in the deceptive atmosphere of art even the highest respectability may fail of being plastic.

I didn't owe my friends money, but I did see them again. They reappeared together three days later, and, given all the other facts, there was something tragic in that one. It was a clear proof they could find nothing else in life to do. They had threshed the matter out in a dismal conference—they had digested the bad news that they were not in for the series. If they weren't useful to me even for the *Cheapside* their function seemed difficult to determine, and I could only judge at first that they had come, forgivingly, decorously, to take a last leave. This made me rejoice in secret that I had little leisure for a scene; for I had placed both my other models in position together and I was pegging away at a drawing from which I hoped to derive glory. It had been suggested by the passage in which Rutland Ramsay, drawing up a chair to Artemisia's piano-stool, says extraordinary things to her while she ostensibly fingers out a difficult piece of music. I had done Miss Churm at the piano before—it was an attitude in which she knew how to take on an absolutely poetic grace. I wished the two figures to "compose" together with intensity, and my little Italian had entered perfectly into my conception. The pair were vividly before me, the piano had been pulled out; it was a charming show of blended youth and murmured love, which I had only to catch and keep. My visitors stood and looked at it, and I was friendly to them over my shoulder.

They made no response, but I was used to silent company and went on with my work, only a little disconcerted—even though exhilarated by the sense that *this* was at least the ideal thing—at not having got rid of them after all. Presently I heard Mrs. Monarch's sweet voice beside or rather above me: "I wish her hair were a little better done." I looked up and she was staring with a strange fixedness at Miss Churm, whose back was turned to her. "Do you mind my just touching it?" she went on—a question which made me spring up for an instant as with the instinctive fear that she might do the young lady a harm. But she quieted me with a glance I shall never forget—I confess I should like to have been able to paint *that* —and went for a moment to my model. She spoke to her softly, laying a hand on her shoulder and bending over her; and as the girl, understanding, gratefully assented, she disposed her rough curls, with a few quick passes, in such a way as to make Miss Churm's head twice as charming. It was one of the most heroic personal services I've ever seen rendered. Then Mrs. Monarch turned away with a low sigh and, looking about her as if for something to do, stooped to the floor with a noble humility and picked up a dirty rag that had dropped out of my paint-box.

The Major meanwhile had also been looking for something to do, and, wandering to the other end of the studio, saw before him my breakfast-things neglected, unremoved. "I say, can't I be useful *here?*" he called out to me with an irrepressible quaver. I assented with a laugh that I fear was awkward, and for the next ten minutes, while I worked, I heard the light clatter of china and the tinkle of spoons and glass. Mrs. Monarch assisted her husband—they washed up my crockery, they put it away. They wandered off into my little scullery, and I afterwards found that they had cleaned my knives and that my slender stock of plate had an unprecedented surface. When it came over me, the latent eloquence of what they were doing, I confess that my drawing was blurred for a moment—the picture swam. They had accepted their failure, but they couldn't accept their fate. They had bowed their heads in bewilderment to the perverse and cruel law in virtue of which the real thing could be so much less precious than the unreal; but they didn't want to starve. If my servants were my models; then my models might be my servants. They would reverse the parts—the others would sit for the ladies and gentlemen and *they* would do the work. They would still be in the studio—it was an intense dumb appeal to me not to turn them out. "Take us on," they wanted to say—"we'll do *anything.*"

My pencil dropped from my hand; my sitting was spoiled and I got rid of my sitters, who were also evidently rather mystified and awestruck. Then, alone with the Major and his wife I had a most uncomfortable moment. He put their prayer into a single sentence: "I say, you know—just let *us* do for you, can't you?" I couldn't—it was dreadful to see them emptying my slops; but I pretended I could, to oblige them, for about a week. Then I gave them a sum of money to go away, and I never saw them again, I obtained the remaining books, but my friend Hawley repeats that Major and Mrs. Monarch did me a permanent harm, got me into false ways. If it be true I'm content to have paid the price—for the memory. 1892, 1909

From The Notebooks

[*The Real Thing*][1]

Paris, Hotel Westminster, February 22d, 1891.

In pursuance of my plan of writing some very short tales—things of from 7000 to 10,000 words, the easiest length to 'place,' I began yesterday the little story that was suggested to me some time ago by

1. The nine surviving notebooks of Henry James cover the period from November 7, 1878, through May 10, 1911, and record the germination and growth of individual works and his thoughts about technical problems and themes. They were edited in 1947 by F. O. Matthiessen and Kenneth B. Murdock as *The Notebooks of Henry James.*

an incident related to me by George du Maurier[2]—the lady and
gentleman who called upon him with a word from Frith, an oldish,
faded, ruined pair—he an officer in the army—who unable to turn a
penny in any other way, were trying to find employment as models.
I was struck with the pathos, the oddity and typicalness of the situation—the little tragedy of good-looking gentlefolk, who had been
all their life stupid and well-dressed, living, on a fixed income, at
country-houses, watering places and clubs, like so many others of
their class in England, and were now utterly unable to do anything,
had no cleverness, no art or craft to make use of as a *gagne-pain*[3]
—could only *show* themselves, clumsily, for the fine, clean, well-
groomed animals that they were, only hope to make a little money
by—in this manner—just simply *being*. I thought I saw a subject
for very brief treatment in this *donnée*[4] and I think I do still; but
to do anything worth while with it I must (as always, great Heavens!) be very clear as to what is in it and what I wish to get out of
it. I tried a beginning yesterday, but I instantly became conscious
that I must straighten out the little idea. It must be an idea—it
can't be a 'story' in the vulgar sense of the word. It must be a picture; it must illustrate something. God knows that's enough—if the
thing *does* illustrate. To make little anecdotes of this kind real
morceaux de vie[5] is a plan quite inspiring enough. *Voyons, un peu,*[6]
therefore, what one can put into this one—I mean how much of
life. One must put a little action—not a stupid, mechanical, arbitrary
action, but something that is of the real essence of the subject. I
thought of representing the husband as jealous of the wife—that is,
jealous of the artist employing her, from the moment that, in point
of fact, she begins to sit. But this is vulgar and obvious—worth
nothing. What I wish to represent is the baffled, ineffectual, incompetent character of their attempt, and how it illustrates once again
the everlasting English amateurishness—the way superficial,
untrained, unprofessional effort goes to the wall when confronted
with trained, competitive, intelligent, *qualified* art—in whatever
line it may be a question of. It is out of *that* element that my little
action and movement must come; and now I begin to see just how
—as one always *does*—Glory be to the Highest—when one begins
to look at a thing hard and straight and seriously—to fix it—as I
am so sadly lax and desultory about doing. What subjects I should
find—for *everything*—if I could only achieve this more as a habit!
Let my contrast and complication here come from the opposition
—to my melancholy Major and his wife—of a couple of little
vulgar professional people *who know*, with the consequent bewilderment, vagueness, depression of the former—their failure to understand how such people can be better than *they*—their failure, disap-

2. "George du Maurier": artist and il-
lustrator (1834–96), William Powell
Frith (1819–1909), English painter.
3. Breadwinner.

4. Idea, theme for a story, play, or
poem.
5. Pieces of life.
6. Let's take a little look.

pointment, disappearance—going forth into the vague again. *Il y a bien quelque chose à tirer de ça.*[7] They have no pictorial sense. They are only clean and stiff and stupid. The others are dirty, even —the melancholy Major and his wife remark on it, wondering. The artist is beginning a big illustrated book, a new edition of a famous novel—say *Tom Jones*: and he is willing to try to work them in —for he takes an interest in their predicament, and feels—sceptically, but, with his flexible artistic sympathy—the appeal of their type. He is willing to give them a trial. Make it out that *he* himself is on trial—he is young and 'rising,' but he has still his golden spurs to win. He can't afford, *en somme*,[8] to make many mistakes. He has regular work in drawing every week for a serial novel in an illustrated paper; but the great project—that of a big house—of issuing an illustrated Fielding[9] promises him a big lift. He has been intrusted with (say) *Joseph Andrews*, experimentally; he will have to do this brilliantly in order to have the engagement for the rest confirmed. He has already 2 models in his service—the 'complication' must come from *them*. One is a common, clever, London girl, of the smallest origin and without conventional beauty, but of aptitude, of perceptions—knowing thoroughly *how*. She says 'lydy' and 'plice,' but she has the pictorial sense, and can look like anything he wants her to look like. She poses, in short, in perfection. So does her colleague, a professional Italian, a little fellow—ill dressed, smelling of garlic, but admirably serviceable, quite universal. They must be contrasted, confronted, *juxtaposed* with the others; whom they take for people who *pay*, themselves, till they learn the truth when they are overwhelmed with derisive amazement. The denouement simply that the melancholy Major and his wife won't do—they're not 'in it.' Their surprise—their helpless, proud assent —without other prospects: yet at the same time *their* degree of more silent amazement at the success of the two inferior people— who are so much less nice-looking than themselves. Frankly, however, is this contrast enough of a *story*, by itself? It seems to me Yes —for it's an IDEA—and how the deuce should I get *more* into 7000 words? It must be simply 50 pp. of my manuscript. The little tale of *The Servant* (*Brooksmith*)[1] which I did the other day for *Black and White* and which I thought of at the same time as this, proved a very tight squeeze into the same tiny number of words, and I probably shall find that there is much more to be done with this than the compass will admit of. Make it tremendously succinct— with a very short pulse or rhythm—and the closest selection of detail—in other words *summarize* intensely and keep down the lateral development. It *should* be a little gem of bright, quick, vivid form. I shall get every grain of 'action' that the space admits of if I

7. Something good may be deduced from that.
8. In short.
9. Henry Fielding (1707–54), English

novelist, author of *Tom Jones* (1747) and *Joseph Andrews* (1742).
1. *The Servant* (*Brooksmith*) (1891).

make something, for the artist, hang in the balance—depend on the
way he does this particular work. It's when he finds that he shall
lose his great opportunity if he keeps on with them, that he has to
tell the gentlemanly couple, that, frankly, they won't serve his turn
—and make them wander forth into the cold world again. I must
keep them the age I've made them—50 and 40—because it's more
touching; but I must bring up the age of the 2 real models to
almost the same thing. That increases the incomprehensibility (to
the amateurs) of their usefulness. Picture the immanence, in the
latter, of the idle, provided-for, country-house habit—the blankness
of their *manière d'être*.[2] But in how tremendously few words I
must do it. This is a lesson—a *magnificent* lesson—if I'm to do a
good many. Something as admirably compact and *selected* as Maupassant.[3]

1947

The Beast in the Jungle[1]

I

What determined the speech that startled him in the course of
their encounter scarcely matters, being probably but some words
spoken by himself quite without intention—spoken as they lingered
and slowly moved together after their renewal of acquaintance. He
had been conveyed by friends an hour or two before to the house at
which she was staying; the party of visitors at the other house, of
whom he was one, and thanks to whom it was his theory, as always,
that he was lost in the crowd, had been invited over to luncheon.
There had been after luncheon much dispersal, all in the interest of
the original motive, a view of Weatherend itself and the fine
things, intrinsic features, pictures, heirlooms, treasures of all the
arts, that made the place almost famous; and the great rooms were
so numerous that guests could wander at their will, hang back from
the principal group and in cases where they took such matters with
the last seriousness give themselves up to mysterious appreciations
and measurements. There were persons to be observed, singly or in
couples, bending toward objects in out-of-the-way corners with their
hands on their knees and their heads nodding quite as with the
emphasis of an excited sense of smell. When they were two they
either mingled their sounds of ecstasy or melted into silences of
even deeper import, so that there were aspects of the occasion that
gave it for Marcher much the air of the "look round," previous to a
sale highly advertised, that excites or quenches, as may be, the
dream of acquisition. The dream of acquisition at Weatherend

2. Mode of being.
3. Guy de Maupassant (1850–93),
French author, best known for his carefully crafted short stories.
1. James initially recorded the "germ"
for this story in 1895, but it first ap-

peared in the collection *The Better Sort*
(1903). It was reprinted, with minor revisions, in the *Altar of the Dead* volume
of the New York edition, Vol. XVII
(1909), the source of the present text.

would have had to be wild indeed, and John Marcher found himself, among such suggestions, disconcerted almost equally by the presence of those who knew too much and by that of those who knew nothing. The great rooms caused so much poetry and history to press upon him that he needed some straying apart to feel in a proper relation with them, though this impulse was not, as happened, like the gloating of some of his companions, to be compared to the movements of a dog sniffing a cupboard. It had an issue promptly enough in a direction that was not to have been calculated.

It led, briefly, in the course of the October afternoon, to his closer meeting with May Bartram, whose face, a reminder, yet not quite a remembrance, as they sat much separated at a very long table, had begun merely by troubling him rather pleasantly. It affected him as the sequel of something of which he had lost the beginning. He knew it, and for the time quite welcomed it, as a continuation, but didn't know what it continued, which was an interest or an amusement the greater as he was also somehow aware —yet without a direct sign from her—that the young woman herself hadn't lost the thread. She hadn't lost it, but she wouldn't give it back to him, he saw, without some putting forth of his hand for it; and he not only saw that, but saw several things more, things odd enough in the light of the fact that at the moment some accident of grouping brought them face to face he was still merely fumbling with the idea that any contact between them in the past would have had no importance. If it had had no importance he scarcely knew why his actual impression of her should so seem to have so much; the answer to which, however, was that in such a life as they all appeared to be leading for the moment one could but take things as they came. He was satisfied, without in the least being able to say why, that this young lady might roughly have ranked in the house as a poor relation; satisfied also that she was not there on a brief visit, but was more or less a part of the establishment—almost a working, a remunerated part. Didn't she enjoy at periods a protection that she paid for by helping, among other services, to show the place and explain it, deal with the tiresome people, answer questions about the dates of the building, the styles of the furniture, the authorship of the pictures, the favourite haunts of the ghost? It wasn't that she looked as if you could have given her shillings—it was impossible to look less so. Yet when she finally drifted toward him, distinctly handsome, though ever so much older —older than when he had seen her before— it might have been as an effect of her guessing that he had, within the couple of hours, devoted more imagination to her than to all the others put together, and had thereby penetrated to a kind of truth that the others were too stupid for. She *was* there on harder terms than any one; she was there as a consequence of things suffered, one way and another, in the interval of years; and she remembered him very much as she was remembered—only a good deal better.

By the time they at last thus came to speech they were alone in one of the rooms—remarkable for a fine portrait over the chimney-place—out of which their friends had passed, and the charm of it was that even before they had spoken they had practically arranged with each other to stay behind for talk. The charm, happily, was in other things too—partly in there being scarce a spot at Weatherend without something to stay behind for. It was in the way the autumn day looked into the high windows as it waned; the way the red light, breaking at the close from under a low sombre sky, reached out in a long shaft and played over old wainscots, old tapestry, old gold, old colour. It was most of all perhaps in the way she came to him as if, since she had been turned on to deal with the simpler sort, he might, should he choose to keep the whole thing down, just take her mild attention for a part of her general business. As soon as he heard her voice, however, the gap was filled up and the missing link supplied; the slight irony he divined in her attitude lost its advantage. He almost jumped at it to get there before her. "I met you years and years ago in Rome. I remember all about it." She confessed to disappointment—she had been so sure he didn't; and to prove how well he did he began to pour forth the particular recollections that popped up as he called for them. Her face and her voice, all at his service now, worked the miracle—the impression operating like the torch of a lamplighter who touches into flame, one by one, a long row of gas-jets. Marcher flattered himself the illumination was brilliant, yet he was really still more pleased on her showing him, with amusement, that in his haste to make everything right he had got most things rather wrong. It hadn't been at Rome —it had been at Naples; and it hadn't been eight years before—it had been more nearly ten. She hadn't been, either, with her uncle and aunt, but with her mother and her brother; in addition to which it was not with the Pembles *he* had been, but with the Boyers, coming down in their company from Rome—a point on which she insisted, a little to his confusion, and as to which she had her evidence in hand. The Boyers she had known, but didn't know the Pembles, though she had heard of them, and it was the people he was with who had made them acquainted. The incident of the thunderstorm that had raged round them with such violence as to drive them for refuge into an excavation—this incident had not occurred at the Palace of the Cæsars, but at Pompeii,[2] on an occasion when they had been present there at an important find.

He accepted her amendments, he enjoyed her corrections, though the moral of them was, she pointed out, that he *really* didn't remember the least thing about her; and he only felt it as a draw-

2. Pompeii is near Naples, not Rome.

back that when all was made strictly historic there didn't appear much of anything left. They lingered together still, she neglecting her office—for from the moment he was so clever she had no proper right to him—and both neglecting the house, just waiting as to see if a memory or two more wouldn't again breathe on them. It hadn't taken them many minutes, after all, to put down on the table, like the cards of a pack, those that constituted their respective hands; only what came out was that the pack was unfortunately not perfect —that the past, invoked, invited, encouraged, could give them, naturally, no more than it had. It had made them anciently meet—her at twenty, him at twenty-five; but nothing was so strange, they seemed to say to each other, as that, while so occupied, it hadn't done a little more for them. They looked at each other as with the feeling of an occasion missed; the present would have been so much better if the other, in the far distance, in the foreign land, hadn't been so stupidly meagre. There weren't apparently, all counted, more than a dozen little old things that had succeeded in coming to pass between them; trivialities of youth, simplicities of freshness, stupidities of ignorance, small possible germs, but too deeply buried —too deeply (didn't it seem?) to sprout after so many years. Marcher could only feel he ought to have rendered her some service —saved her from a capsized boat in the Bay or at least recovered her dressing-bag, filched from her cab in the streets of Naples by a lazzarone[3] with a stiletto. Or it would have been nice if he could have been taken with fever all alone at his hotel, and she could have come to look after him, to write to his people, to drive him out in convalescence. *Then* they would be in possession of the something or other that their actual show seemed to lack. It yet somehow presented itself, this show, as too good to be spoiled; so that they were reduced for a few minutes more to wondering a little helplessly why —since they seemed to know a certain number of the same people —their reunion had been so long averted. They didn't use that name for it, but their delay from minute to minute to join the others was a kind of confession that they didn't quite want it to be a failure. Their attempted supposition of reasons for their not having met but showed how little they knew of each other. There came in fact a moment when Marcher felt a positive pang. It was vain to pretend she was an old friend, for all the communities were wanting, in spite of which it was as an old friend that he saw she would have suited him. He had new ones enough—was surrounded with them for instance on the stage of the other house; as a new one he probably wouldn't have so much as noticed her. He would have liked to invent something, get her to make-believe with him that some passage of a romantic or critical kind *had* originally occurred. He was really almost reaching out in imagination—as against time—for something that would do, and saying to himself

3. Beggar.

that if it didn't come this sketch of a fresh start would show for quite awkwardly bungled. They would separate, and now for no second or no third chance. They would have tried and not succeeded. Then it was, just at the turn, as he afterwards made it out to himself, that, everything else failing, she herself decided to take up the case and, as it were, save the situation. He felt as soon as she spoke that she had been consciously keeping back what she said and hoping to get on without it; a scruple in her that immensely touched him when, by the end of three or four minutes more, he was able to measure it. What she brought out, at any rate, quite cleared the air and supplied the link—the link it was so odd he should frivolously have managed to lose.

"You know you told me something I've never forgotten and that again and again has made me think of you since; it was that tremendously hot day when we went to Sorrento,[4] across the bay, for the breeze. What I allude to was what you said to me, on the way back, as we sat under the awning of the boat enjoying the cool. Have you forgotten?"

He had forgotten and was even more surprised than ashamed. But the great thing was that he saw in this no vulgar reminder of any "sweet" speech. The vanity of women had long memories, but she was making no claim on him of a compliment or a mistake. With another woman, a totally different one, he might have feared the recall possibly even some imbecile "offer." So, in having to say that he had indeed forgotten, he was conscious rather of a loss than of a gain; he already saw an interest in the matter of her mention. "I try to think—but I give it up. Yet I remember the Sorrento day."

"I'm not very sure you do," May Bartram after a moment said; "and I'm not very sure I ought to want you to. It's dreadful to bring a person back at any time to what he was ten years before. If you've lived away from it," she smiled, "so much the better."

"Ah if *you* haven't why should I?" he asked.

"Lived away, you mean, from what I myself was?"

"From what *I* was. I was of course an ass," Marcher went on; "but I would rather know from you just the sort of ass I was than—from the moment you have something in your mind—not know anything."

Still, however, she hesitated. "But if you've completely ceased to be that sort—?"

"Why I can then all the more bear to know. Besides, perhaps I haven't."

"Perhaps. Yet if you haven't," she added, "I should suppose you'd remember. Not indeed that *I* in the least connect with my impression the invidious name you use. If I had only thought you foolish," she explained, "the thing I speak of wouldn't so have

4. Across the bay from Naples.

remained with me. It was about yourself." She waited as if it might come to him; but as, only meeting her eyes in wonder, he gave no sign, she burnt her ships. "Has it ever happened?"

Then it was that, while he continued to stare, a light broke for him and the blood slowly came to his face, which began to burn with recognition. "Do you mean I told you—?" But he faltered, lest what came to him shouldn't be right, lest he should only give himself away.

"It was something about yourself that it was natural one shouldn't forget—that is if one remembered you at all. That's why I ask you," she smiled, "if the thing you then spoke of has ever come to pass?"

Oh then he saw, but he was lost in wonder and found himself embarrassed. This, he also saw, made her sorry for him, as if her allusion had been a mistake. It took him but a moment, however, to feel it hadn't been, much as it had been a surprise. After the first little shock of it her knowledge on the contrary began, even if rather strangely, to taste sweet to him. She was the only other person in the world then who would have it, and she had had it all these years, while the fact of his having so breathed his secret had unaccountably faded from him. No wonder they couldn't have met as if nothing had happened. "I judge," he finally said, "that I know what you mean. Only I had strangely enough lost any sense of having taken you so far into my confidence."

"Is it because you've taken so many others as well?"

"I've taken nobody. Not a creature since then."

"So that I'm the only person who knows?"

"The only person in the world."

"Well," she quickly replied, "I myself have never spoken. I've never, never repeated of you what you told me." She looked at him so that he perfectly believed her. Their eyes met over it in such a way that he was without a doubt. "And I never will."

She spoke with an earnestness that, as if almost excessive, put him at ease about her possible derision. Somehow the whole question was a new luxury to him—that is from the moment she was in possession. If she didn't take the sarcastic view she clearly took the sympathetic, and that was what he had had, in all the long time, from no one whomsoever. What he felt was that he couldn't at present have begun to tell her, and yet could profit perhaps exquisitely by the accident of having done so of old. "Please don't then. We're just right as it is."

"Oh I am," she laughed, "if you are!" To which she added: "Then you do still feel in the same way?"

It was impossible he shouldn't take to himself that she was really interested, though it all kept coming as perfect surprise. He had thought of himself so long as abominably alone, and lo he wasn't alone a bit. He hadn't been, it appeared, for an hour—since those

moments on the Sorrento boat. It was *she* who had been, he
seemed to see as he looked at her—she who had been made so by
the graceless fact of his lapse of fidelity. To tell her what he had
told her—what had it been but to ask something of her? something
that she had given, in her charity, without his having, by a remembrance, by a return of the spirit, failing another encounter, so much
as thanked her. What he had asked of her had been simply at first
not to laugh at him. She had beautifully not done so for ten years,
and she was not doing so now. So he had endless gratitude to make
up. Only for that he must see just how he had figured to her.
"What, exactly, was the account I gave—?"

"Of the way you did feel? Well, it was very simple. You said you
had had from your earliest time, as the deepest thing within you,
the sense of being kept for something rare and strange, possibly prodigious and terrible, that was sooner or later to happen to you, that
you had in your bones the foreboding and the conviction of, and
that would perhaps overwhelm you."

"Do you call that very simple?" John Marcher asked.

She thought a moment. "It was perhaps because I seemed, as you
spoke, to understand it."

"You do understand it?" he eagerly asked.

Again she kept her kind eyes on him. "You still have the belief?"

"Oh!" he exclaimed helplessly. There was too much to say.

"Whatever it's to be," she clearly made out, "it hasn't yet
come."

He shook his head in complete surrender now. "It hasn't yet
come. Only, you know, it isn't anything I'm to *do* to achieve in the
world, to be distinguished or admired for. I'm not such an ass as
that. It would be much better, no doubt, if I were."

"It's to be something you're merely to suffer?"

"Well, say to wait for—to have to meet, to face, to see suddenly
break out in my life; possibly destroying all further consciousness,
possibly annihilating me; possibly, on the other hand, only altering
everything, striking at the root of all my world and leaving me to
the consequences, however they shape themselves."

She took this in, but the light in her eyes continued for him not
to be that of mockery. "Isn't what you describe perhaps but the
expectation—of at any rate the sense of danger, familiar to so many
people—of falling in love?"

John Marcher wondered. "Did you ask me that before?"

"No—I wasn't so free-and-easy then. But it's what strikes me
now."

"Of course," he said after a moment, "it strikes you. Of course it
strikes *me*. Of course what's in store for me may be no more than
that. The only thing is," he went on, "that I think if it had been
that I should by this time know."

"Do you mean because you've *been* in love?" And then as he but looked at her in silence: "You've been in love, and it hasn't meant such a cataclysm, hasn't proved the great affair?"

"Here I am, you see. It hasn't been overwhelming."

"Then it hasn't been love," said May Bartram.

"Well, I at least thought it was. I took it for that—I've taken it till now. It was agreeable, it was delightful, it was miserable," he explained. "But it wasn't strange. It wasn't what *my* affair's to be."

"You want something all to yourself—something that nobody else knows or *has* known?"

It isn't a question of what I 'want'—God knows I don't want anything. It's only a question of the apprehension that haunts me —that I live with day by day."

He said this so lucidly and consistently that he could see it further impose itself. If she hadn't been interested before she'd have been interested now. "Is it a sense of coming violence?"

Evidently now too again he liked to talk of it. "I don't think of it as—when it does come—necessarily violent. I only think of it as natural and as of course above all unmistakeable. I think of it simply as *the* thing. *The* thing will of itself appear natural."

"Then how will it appear strange?"

Marcher bethought himself. "It won't—to *me*."

"To whom then?"

"Well," he replied, smiling at last, "say to you."

"Oh then I'm to be present?"

"Why you *are* present—since you know."

"I see." She turned it over. "But I mean at the catastrophe."

At this, for a minute, their lightness gave way to their gravity; it was as if the long look they exchanged held them together. "It will only depend on yourself—if you'll watch with me."

"Are you afraid?" she asked.

"Don't leave me *now*," he went on.

"Are you afraid?" she repeated.

"Do you think me simply out of my mind?" he pursued instead of answering. "Do I merely strike you as a harmless lunatic?"

"No," said May Bartram. "I understand you. I believe you."

"You mean you feel how my obsession—poor old thing!—may correspond to some possible reality?"

"To some possible reality."

"Then you *will* watch with me?"

She hesitated, then for the third time put her question. "Are you afraid?"

"Did I tell you I was—at Naples?"

"No, you said nothing about it."

"Then I don't know. And I should *like* to know," said John Marcher. "You'll tell me yourself whether you think so. If you'll watch with me you'll see."

"Very good then." They had been moving by this time across the room, and at the door, before passing out, they paused as for the full wind-up of their understanding. "I'll watch with you," said May Bartram.

II

The fact that she "knew"—knew and yet neither chaffed him nor betrayed him—had in a short time begun to constitute between them a goodly bond, which became more marked when, within the year that followed their afternoon at Weatherend, the opportunities for meeting multiplied. The event that thus promoted these occasions was the death of the ancient lady her great-aunt, under whose wing, since losing her mother, she had to such an extent found shelter, and who, though but the widowed mother of the new successor to the property, had succeeded—thanks to a high tone and a high temper—in not forfeiting the supreme position at the great house. The deposition of this personage arrived but with her death, which, followed by many changes, made in particular a difference for the young woman in whom Marcher's expert attention had recognized from the first a dependent with a pride that might ache though it didn't bristle. Nothing for a long time had made him easier than the thought that the aching must have been much soothed by Miss Bartram's now finding herself able to set up a small home in London. She had acquired property, to an amount that made that luxury just possible, under her aunt's extremely complicated will, and when the whole matter began to be straightened out, which indeed took time, she let him know that the happy issue was at last in view. He had seen her again before that day, because she had more than once accompanied the ancient lady to town and because he had paid another visit to the friends who so conveniently made of Weatherend one of the charms of their own hospitality. These friends had taken him back there; he had achieved there again with Miss Bartram some quiet detachment; and he had in London succeeded in persuading her to more than one brief absence from her aunt. They went together, on these latter occasions, to the National Gallery and the South Kensington Museum, where, among vivid reminders, they talked of Italy at large—not now attempting to recover, as at first, the taste of their youth and their ignorance. That recovery, the first day at Weatherend, had served its purpose well, had given them quite enough; so that they were, to Marcher's sense, no longer hovering about the headwaters of their stream, but had felt their boat pushed sharply off and down the current.

They were literally afloat together; for our gentleman this was marked, quite as marked as that the fortunate cause of it was just the buried treasure of her knowledge. He had with his own hands dug up this little hoard, brought to light—that is to within reach of the dim day constituted by their discretions and privacies—the object of value the hiding-place of which he had, after putting it into the ground himself, so strangely, so long forgotten. The rare luck of his having again just stumbled on the spot made him indifferent to any other question; he would doubtless have devoted more time to the odd accident of his lapse of memory if he hadn't been moved to devote so much to the sweetness, the comfort, as he felt, for the future, that this accident itself had helped to keep fresh. It had never entered into his plan that any one should "know," and mainly for the reason that it wasn't in him to tell any one. That would have been impossible, for nothing but the amusement of a cold world would have waited on it. Since, however, a mysterious fate had opened his mouth betimes, in spite of him, he would count that a compensation and profit by it to the utmost. That the right person *should* know tempered the asperity of his secret more even than his shyness had permitted him to imagine; and May Bartram was clearly right, because—well, because there she was. Her knowledge simply settled it; he would have been sure enough by this time had she been wrong. There was that in his situation, no doubt, that disposed him too much to see her as a mere confidant, taking all her light for him from the fact—the fact only—of her interest in his predicament; from her mercy, sympathy, seriousness, her consent not to regard him as the funniest of the funny. Aware, in fine, that her price for him was just in her giving him this constant sense of his being admirably spared, he was careful to remember that she had also a life of her own, with things that might happen to *her*, things that in friendship one should likewise take account of. Something fairly remarkable came to pass with him, for that matter, in this connexion—something represented by a certain passage of his consciousness, in the suddenest way, from one extreme to the other.

He had thought himself, so long as nobody knew, the most disinterested person in the world, carrying his concentrated burden, his perpetual suspense, ever so quietly, holding his tongue about it, giving others no glimpse of it nor of its effect upon his life, asking of them no allowance and only making on his side all those that were asked. He hadn't disturbed people with the queerness of their having to know a haunted man, though he had had moments of rather special temptation on hearing them say they were forsooth "unsettled." If they were as unsettled as he was—he who had never been settled for an hour in his life—they would know what it meant. Yet it wasn't, all the same, for him to make them, and he listened to them civilly enough. This was why he had such good— though possibly such rather colourless—manners; this was why, above all, he could regard himself, in a greedy world, as decently— as in fact perhaps even a little sublimely—unselfish. Our point is accordingly that he valued this character quite sufficiently to measure his present danger of letting it lapse, against which he promised himself to be much on his guard. He was quite ready, none the less,

to be selfish just a little, since surely no more charming occasion for
it had come to him. "Just a little," in a word, was just as much as
Miss Bartram, taking one day with another, would let him. He
never would be in the least coercive, and would keep well before
him the lines on which consideration for her—the very highest—
ought to proceed. He would thoroughly establish the heads under
which her affairs, her requirements, her peculiarities—he went so
far as to give them the latitude of that name—would come into
their intercourse. All this naturally was a sign of how much he took
the intercourse itself for granted. There was nothing more to be
done about *that*. It simply existed; had sprung into being with her
first penetrating question to him in the autumn light there at
Weatherend. The real form it should have taken on the basis that
stood out large was the form of their marrying. But the devil in this
was that the very basis itself put marrying out of the question. His
conviction, his apprehension, his obsession, in short, wasn't a privilege he could invite a woman to share; and that consequence of it
was precisely what was the matter with him. Something or other lay
in wait for him, amid the twists and the turns of the months and
the years, like a crouching beast in the jungle. It signified little
whether the crouching beast were destined to slay him or to be
slain. The definite point was the inevitable spring of the creature;
and the definite lesson from that was that a man of feeling didn't
cause himself to be accompanied by a lady on a tiger-hunt. Such
was the image under which he had ended by figuring his life.

They had at first, none the less, in the scattered hours spent
together, made no allusion to that view of it; which was a sign he
was handsomely alert to give that he didn't expect, that he in fact
didn't care, always to be talking about it. Such a feature in one's
outlook was really like a hump on one's back. The difference it
made every minute of the day existed quite independently of discussion. One discussed of course *like* a hunchback, for there was
always, if nothing else, the hunchback face. That remained, and she
was watching him; but people watched best, as a general thing, in
silence, so that such would be predominantly the manner of their
vigil. Yet he didn't want, at the same time, to be tense and solemn;
tense and solemn was what he imagined he too much showed for
with other people. The thing to be, with the one person who knew,
was easy and natural—to make the reference rather than be seeming
to avoid it, to avoid it rather than be seeming to make it, and to
keep it, in any case, familiar, facetious even, rather than pedantic
and portentous. Some such consideration as the latter was doubtless
in his mind for instance when he wrote pleasantly to Miss Bartram
that perhaps the great thing he had so long felt as in the lap of the
gods was no more than this circumstance, which touched him so
nearly, of her acquiring a house in London. It was the first allusion
they had yet again made, needing any other hitherto so little; but

when she replied, after having given him the news, that she was by no means satisfied with such a trifle as the climax to so special a suspense, she almost set him wondering if she hadn't even a larger conception of singularity for him than he had for himself. He was at all events destined to become aware little by little, as time went by, that she was all the while looking at his life, judging it, measuring it, in the light of the thing she knew, which grew to be at last, with the consecration of the years, never mentioned between them save as "the real truth" about him. That had always been his own form of reference to it, but she adopted the form so quietly that, looking back at the end of a period, he knew there was no moment at which it was traceable that she had, as he might say, got inside his idea, or exchanged the attitude of beautifully indulging for that of still more beautifully believing him.

It was always open to him to accuse her of seeing him but as the most harmless of maniacs, and this, in the long run—since it covered so much ground—was his easiest description of their friendship. He had a screw loose for her, but she liked him in spite of it and was practically, against the rest of the world, his kind wise keeper, unremunerated but fairly amused and, in the absence of other near ties, not disreputably occupied. The rest of the world of course thought him queer, but she, she only, knew how, and above all why, queer; which was precisely what enabled her to dispose the concealing veil in the right folds. She took his gaiety from him— since it had to pass with them for gaiety—as she took everything else; but she certainly so far justified by her unerring touch his finer sense of the degree to which he had ended by convincing her. *She* at least never spoke of the secret of his life except as "the real truth about you," and she had in fact a wonderful way of making it seem, as such, the secret of her own life too. That was in fine how he so constantly felt her as allowing for him; he couldn't on the whole call it anything else. He allowed for himself, but she, exactly, allowed still more; partly because, better placed for a sight of the matter, she traced his unhappy perversion through reaches of its course into which he could scarce follow it. He knew how he felt, but, besides knowing that, she knew how he *looked* as well; he knew each of the things of importance he was insidiously kept from doing, but she could add up the amount they made, understand how much, with a lighter weight on his spirit, he might have done, and thereby establish how, clever as he was, he fell short. Above all she was in the secret of the difference between the forms he went through—those of his little office under Government, those of caring for his modest patrimony, for his library, for his garden in the country, for the people in London whose invitations he accepted and repaid—and the detachment that reigned beneath them and that made of all behaviour, all that could in the least be called behaviour, a long act of dissimulation. What it had come to was that he wore a mask painted with the social simper, out of the eye-holes of which there looked eyes of an expression not in the least matching the other features. This the stupid world, even after years, had never more than half-discovered. It was only May Bartram who had, and she achieved, by an art indescribable, the feat of at once —or perhaps it was only alternately—meeting the eyes from in front and mingling her own vision, as from over his shoulder, with their peep through the apertures.

So while they grew older together she did watch with him, and so she let this association give shape and colour to her own existence. Beneath *her* forms as well detachment had learned to sit, and behaviour had become for her, in the social sense, a false account of herself. There was but one account of her that would have been true all the while and that she could give straight to nobody, least of all to John Marcher. Her whole attitude was a virtual statement, but the perception of that only seemed called to take its place for him as one of the many things necessarily crowded out of his con-sciousness. If she had moreover, like himself, to make sacrifices to their real truth, it was to be granted that her compensation might have affected her as more prompt and more natural. They had long periods, in this London time, during which, when they were together, a stranger might have listened to them without in the least pricking up his ears; on the other hand the real truth was equally liable at any moment to rise to the surface, and the auditor would then have wondered indeed what they were talking about. They had from an early hour made up their mind that society was, luckily, unintelligent, and the margin allowed them by this had fairly become one of their commonplaces. Yet there were still moments when the situation turned almost fresh—usually under the effect of some expression drawn from herself. Her expressions doubtless repeated themselves, but her intervals were generous. "What saves us, you know, is that we answer so completely to so usual an appearance: that of the man and woman whose friendship has become such a daily habit—or almost—as to be at last indispen-sable." That for instance was a remark she had frequently enough had occasion to make, though she had given it at different times different developments. What we are especially concerned with is the turn it happened to take from her one afternoon when he had come to see her in honour of her birthday. This anniversary had fallen on a Sunday, at a season of thick fog and general outward gloom; but he had brought her his customary offering, having known her now long enough to have established a hundred small traditions. It was one of his proofs to himself, the present he made her on her birthday, that he hadn't sunk into real selfishness. It was mostly nothing more than a small trinket, but it was always fine of its kind, and he was regularly careful to pay for it more than he thought he could afford. "Our habit saves you at least, don't you see? because it makes you, after all, for the vulgar, indistinguishable from other men. What's the most inveterate mark of men in general? Why the capacity to spend endless time with dull women—to spend it I won't say without being bored, but without minding that they are, without being driven off at a tangent by it; which comes to the same thing. I'm your dull woman, a part of the daily bread for which you pray at church. That covers your tracks more than anything."

"And what covers yours?" asked Marcher, whom his dull woman could mostly to this extent amuse. "I see of course what you mean by your saving me, in this way and that, so far as other people are concerned—I've seen it all along. Only what is it that saves *you*? I often think, you know, of that."

She looked as if she sometimes thought of that too, but rather in a different way. "Where other people, you mean, are concerned?"

"Well, you're really so in with me, you know—as a sort of result of my being so in with yourself. I mean of my having such an immense regard for you, being so tremendously mindful of all you've done for me. I sometimes ask myself if it's quite fair. Fair I mean to have so involved and—since one may say it—interested you. I almost feel as if you hadn't really had time to do anything else."

"Anything else but be interested?" she asked. "Ah what else does one ever want to be? If I've been 'watching' with you, as we long ago agreed I was to do, watching's always in itself an absorption."

"Oh certainly," John Marcher said, "if you hadn't had your curiosity—! Only doesn't it sometimes come to you as time goes on that your curiosity isn't being particularly repaid?"

May Bartram had a pause. "Do you ask that, by any chance, because you feel at all that yours isn't? I mean because you have to wait so long."

Oh he understood what she meant! "For the thing to happen that never does happen? For the beast to jump out? No, I'm just where I was about it. It isn't a matter as to which I can *choose*, I can decide for a change. It isn't one as to which there *can* be a change. It's in the lap of the gods. One's in the hands of one's law —there one is. As to the form the law will take, the way it will operate, that's its own affair."

"Yes," Miss Bartram replied; "of course one's fate's coming, of course it *has* come in its own form and its own way, all the while. Only, you know, the form and the way in your case were to have been—well, something so exceptional and, as one may say, so particularly *your* own."

Something in this made him look at her with suspicion. "You say 'were to *have* been,' as if in your heart you had begun to doubt."

"Oh!" she vaguely protested.

"As if you believed," he went on, "that nothing will now take place."

She shook her head slowly but rather inscrutably. "You're far from my thought."

He continued to look at her. "What then is the matter with you?"

"Well," she said after another wait, "the matter with me is simply that I'm more sure than ever my curiosity, as you call it, will be but too well repaid."

They were frankly grave now; he had got up from his seat, had turned once more about the little drawing-room to which, year after year, he brought his inevitable topic; in which he had, as he might have said, tasted their intimate community with every sauce, where every object was as familiar to him as the things of his own house and the very carpets were worn with his fitful walk very much as the desks in old counting-houses are worn by the elbows of generations of clerks. The generations of his nervous moods had been at work there, and the place was the written history of his whole middle life. Under the impression of what his friend had just said he knew himself, for some reason, more aware of these things; which made him, after a moment, stop again before her. "Is it possibly that you've grown afraid?"

"Afraid?" He thought, as she repeated the word, that his question had made her, a little, change colour; so that, lest he should have touched on a truth, he explained very kindly: "You remember that that was what you asked *me* long ago—that first day at Weatherend."

"Oh yes, and you told me you didn't know—that I was to see for myself. We've said little about it since, even in so long a time."

"Precisely," Marcher interposed—"quite as if it were too delicate a matter for us to make free with. Quite as if we might find, on pressure, that I *am* afraid. For then," he said, "we shouldn't, should we? quite know what to do."

She had for the time no answer to his question. "There have been days when I thought you were. Only, of course," she added, "there have been days when we have thought almost anything."

"Everything. Oh!" Marcher softly groaned as with a gasp, half-spent, at the face, more uncovered just then than it had been for a long while, of the imagination always with them. It had always had its incalculable moments of glaring out, quite as with the very eyes of the very Beast, and, used as he was to them, they could still draw from him the tribute of a sigh that rose from the depths of his being. All they had thought, first and last, rolled over him; the past seemed to have been reduced to mere barren speculation. This in fact was what the place had just struck him as so full of—the simplification of everything but the state of suspense. That remained only by seeming to hang in the void surrounding it. Even his original fear, if fear it had been, had lost itself in the desert. "I judge, however," he continued, "that you see I'm not afraid now."

"What I see, as I make it out, is that you've achieved something almost unprecedented in the way of getting used to danger. Living with it so long and so closely you've lost your sense of it; you know it's there, but you're indifferent, and you cease even, as of old, to have to whistle in the dark. Considering what the danger is," May Bartram wound up, "I'm bound to say I don't think your attitude could well be surpassed."

John Marcher faintly smiled. "It's heroic?"

"Certainly—call it that."

It was what he would have liked indeed to call it. "I *am* then a man of courage?"

"That's what you were to show me."

He still, however, wondered. "But doesn't the man of courage know what he's afraid of—or *not* afraid of? I don't know *that*, you see. I don't focus it. I can't name it. I only know I'm exposed."

"Yes, but exposed—how shall I say?—so directly. So intimately. That's surely enough."

"Enough to make you feel then—as what we may call the end and the upshot of our watch—that I'm not afraid?"

"You're not afraid. But it isn't," she said, "the end of our watch. That is it isn't the end of yours. You've everything still to see."

"Then why haven't *you?*" he asked. He had had, all along, to-day, the sense of her keeping something back, and he still had it. As this was his first impression of that it quite made a date. The case was the more marked as she didn't at first answer; which in turn made him go on. "You know something I don't." Then his voice, for that of a man of courage, trembled a little. "You know what's to happen." Her silence, with the face she showed, was almost a confession—it made him sure. "You know, and you're afraid to tell me. It's so bad that you're afraid I'll find out."

All this might be true, for she did look as if, unexpectedly to her, he had crossed some mystic line that she had secretly drawn around her. Yet she might, after all, not have worried; and the real climax was that he himself at all events, needn't. "You'll never find out."

III

It was all to have made, none the less, as I have said, a date; which came out in the fact that again and again, even after long intervals, other things that passed between them wore in relation to this hour but the character of recalls and results. Its immediate effect had been indeed rather to lighten insistence—almost to provoke a reaction; as if their topic had dropped by its own weight and as if moreover, for that matter, Marcher had been visited by one of his occasional warnings against egotism. He had kept up, he felt, and very decently on the whole, his consciousness of the importance of not being selfish, and it was true that he had never sinned in that direction without promptly enough trying to press the scales the other way. He often repaired his fault, the season permitting, by inviting his friend to accompany him to the opera; and it not infrequently thus happened that, to show he didn't wish her to have but one sort of food for her mind, he was the cause of her appearing there with him a dozen nights in the month. It even happened that, seeing her home at such times, he occasionally went in with her to finish, as he called it, the evening, and, the better to make his point, sat down to the frugal but always careful little supper that awaited his pleasure. His point was made, he thought, by his not eternally insisting with her on himself; made for instance, at such hours, when it befell that, her piano at hand and each of them familiar with it, they went over passages of the opera together. It chanced to be on one of these occasions, however, that he reminded her of not having answered a certain question he had put to her during the talk that had taken place between them on her last birthday. "What is it that saves *you?*"—saved her, he meant, from that appearance of variation from the usual human type. If he had practically escaped remark, as she pretended, by doing, in the most important particular, what most men do—find the answer to life in patching up an alliance of a sort with a woman no better than himself—how had she escaped it, and how could the alliance, such as it was, since they must suppose it had been more or less noticed, have failed to make her rather positively talked about?

"I never said," May Bartram replied, "that it hadn't made me a good deal talked about."

"Ah well then you're not 'saved.' "

"It hasn't been a question for me. If you've had your woman I've had," she said, "my man."

"And you mean that makes you all right?"

Oh it was always as if there were so much to say! "I don't know why it shouldn't make me—humanly, which is what we're speaking of—as right as it makes you."

"I see," Marcher returned. " 'Humanly,' no doubt, as showing that you're living for something. Not, that is, just for me and my secret."

May Bartram smiled. "I don't pretend it exactly shows that I'm not living for you. It's my intimacy with you that's in question."

He laughed as he saw what she meant. "Yes, but since, as you say, I'm only, so far as people make out, ordinary, you're—aren't you?—no more than ordinary either. You help me to pass for a man like another. So if I *am,* as I understand you, you're not compromised. Is that it?"

She had another of her waits, but she spoke clearly enough.

"That's it. It's all that concerns me—to help you to pass for a man like another."

He was careful to acknowledge the remark handsomely. "How kind, how beautiful, you are to me! How shall I ever repay you?"

She had her last grave pause, as if there might be a choice of ways. But she chose. "By going on as you are."

It was into this going on as he was that they relapsed, and really for so long a time that the day inevitably came for a further sounding of their depths. These depths, constantly bridged over by a structure firm enough in spite of its lightness and of its occasional oscillation in the somewhat vertiginous air, invited on occasion, in the interest of their nerves, a dropping of the plummet and a measurement of the abyss. A difference had been made moreover, once for all, by the fact that she had all the while not appeared to feel the need of rebutting his charge of an idea within her that she didn't dare to express—a charge uttered just before one of the fullest of their later discussions ended. It had come up for him then that she "knew" something and that what she knew was bad—too bad to tell him. When he had spoken of it as visibly so bad that she was afraid he might find it out, her reply had left the matter too equivocal to be let alone and yet, for Marcher's special sensibility, almost too formidable again to touch. He circled about it at a distance that alternately narrowed and widened and that still wasn't much affected by the consciousness in him that there was nothing she could "know," after all, any better than he did. She had no source of knowledge he hadn't equally—except of course that she might have finer nerves. That was what women had where they were interested; they made out things, where people were concerned, that the people often couldn't have made out for themselves. Their nerves, their sensibility, their imagination, were conductors and revealers, and the beauty of May Bartram was in particular that she had given herself so to his case. He felt in these days what, oddly enough, he had never felt before, the growth of a dread of losing her by some catastrophe—some catastrophe that yet wouldn't at all be *the* catastrophe: partly because she had almost of a sudden begun to strike him as more useful to him than ever yet, and partly by reason of an appearance of uncertainty in her health, coincident and equally new. It was characteristic of the inner detachment he had hitherto so successfully cultivated and to which our whole account of him is a reference, it was characteristic that his complications, such as they were, had never yet seemed so as at this crisis to thicken about him, even to the point of making him ask himself if he were, by any chance, of a truth, within sight or sound, within touch or reach, within the immediate jurisdiction, of the thing that waited.

When the day came, as come it had to, that his friend confessed to him her fear of a deep disorder in her blood, he felt somehow the shadow of a change and the chill of a shock. He immediately began to imagine aggravations and disasters, and above all to think of her peril as the direct menace for himself of personal privation. This indeed gave him one of those partial recoveries of equanimity that were agreeable to him—it showed him that what was still first in his mind was the loss she herself might suffer. "What if she should have to die before knowing, before seeing—?" It would have been brutal, in the early stages of her trouble, to put that question to her; but it had immediately sounded for him to his own concern, and the possibility was what most made him sorry for her. If she did "know," moreover, in the sense of her having had some—what should he think?—mystical irresistible light, this would make the matter not better, but worse, inasmuch as her original adoption of his own curiosity had quite become the basis of her life. She had been living to see what would *be* to be seen, and it would quite lacerate her to have to give up before the accomplishment of the vision. These reflexions, as I say, quickened his generosity; yet, make them as he might, he saw himself, with the lapse of the period, more and more disconcerted. It lapsed for him with a strange steady sweep, and the oddest oddity was that it gave him, independently of the threat of much inconvenience, almost the only positive surprise his career, if career it could be called, had yet offered him. She kept the house as she had never done; he had to go to her to see her—she could meet him nowhere now, though there was scarce a corner of their loved old London in which she hadn't in the past, at one time or another, done so; and he found her always seated by her fire in the deep old-fashioned chair she was less and less able to leave. He had been struck one day, after an absence exceeding his usual measure, with her suddenly looking much older to him than he had ever thought of her being; then he recognised that the suddenness was all on his side—he had just simply and suddenly noticed. She looked older because inevitably, after so many years, she *was* old, or almost; which was of course true in still greater measure of her companion. If she was old, or almost, John Marcher assuredly was, and yet it was her showing of the lesson, not his own, that brought the truth home to him. His surprises began here; when once they had begun they multiplied; they came rather with a rush: it was as if, in the oddest way in the world, they had all been kept back, sown in a thick cluster, for the late afternoon of life, the time at which for people in general the unexpected has died out.

One of them was that he should have caught himself—for he *had* so done—*really* wondering if the great accident would take form now as nothing more than his being condemned to see this charming woman, this admirable friend, pass away from him. He had never so unreservedly qualified her as while confronted in thought with such a possibility; in spite of which there was small

doubt for him that as an answer to his long riddle the mere effacement of even so fine a feature of his situation would be an abject
anti-climax. It would represent, as connected with his past attitude,
a drop of dignity under the shadow of which his existence could
only become the most grotesque of failures. He had been far from
holding it a failure—long as he had waited for the appearance that
was to make it a success. He had waited for quite another thing,
not for such a thing as that. The breath of his good faith came
short, however, as he recognised how long he had waited, or how
long at least his companion had. That she, at all events, might be
recorded as having waited in vain—this affected him sharply, and
all the more because of his at first having done little more than
amuse himself with the idea. It grew more grave as the gravity of
her condition grew, and the state of mind it produced in him,
which he himself ended by watching as if it had been some definite
disfigurement of his outer person, may pass for another of his surprises. This conjoined itself still with another, the really stupefying
consciousness of a question that he would have allowed to shape
itself had he dared. What did everything mean—what, that is, did
she mean, she and her vain waiting and her probable death and the
soundless admonition of it all—unless that, at this time of day, it
was simply, it was overwhelmingly too late? He had never at any
stage of his queer consciousness admitted the whisper of such a
correction; he had never till within these last few months been so
false to his conviction as not to hold that what was to come to him
had time, whether *he* struck himself as having it or not. That at
last, at last, he certainly hadn't it, to speak of, or had it but in the
scantiest measure—such, soon enough, as things went with him,
became the inference with which his old obsession had to reckon:
and this it was not helped to do by the more and more confirmed
appearance that the great vagueness casting the long shadow in
which he had lived had, to attest itself, almost no margin left. Since
it was in Time that he was to have met his fate, so it was in Time
that his fate was to have acted; and as he waked up to the sense of
no longer being young, which was exactly the sense of being stale,
just as that, in turn, was the sense of being weak, he waked up to
another matter beside. It all hung together; they were subject, he
and the great vagueness, to an equal and indivisible law. When the
possibilities themselves had accordingly turned stale, when the
secret of the gods had grown faint, had perhaps even quite evapo-
rated, that, and that only, was failure. It wouldn't have been failure
to be bankrupt, dishonoured, pilloried, hanged; it was failure not to
be anything. And so, in the dark valley into which his path had
taken its unlooked-for twist, he wondered not a little as he groped.
He didn't care what awful crash might overtake him, with what
ignominy or what monstrosity he might yet be associated—since he
wasn't after all too utterly old to suffer—if it would only be

decently proportionate to the posture he had kept, all his life, in the threatened presence of it. He had but one desire left—that he shouldn't have been "sold."

IV

Then it was that, one afternoon, while the spring of the year was young and new she met all in her own way his frankest betrayal of these alarms. He had gone in late to see her, but evening hadn't settled and she was presented to him in that long fresh light of waning April days which affects us often with a sadness sharper than the greyest hours of autumn. The week had been warm, the spring was supposed to have begun early, and May Bartram sat, for the first time in the year, without a fire; a fact that, to Marcher's sense, gave the scene of which she formed part a smooth and ultimate look, an air of knowing, in its immaculate order and cold meaningless cheer, that it would never see a fire again. Her own aspect—he could scarce have said why—intensified this note. Almost as white as wax, with the marks and signs in her face as numerous and as fine as if they had been etched by a needle, with soft white draperies relieved by a faded green scarf on the delicate tone of which the years had further refined, she was the picture of a serene and exquisite but impenetrable sphinx, whose head, or indeed all whose person, might have been powdered with silver. She was a sphinx, yet with her white petals and green fronds she might have been a lily too—only an artificial lily, wonderfully imitated and constantly kept, without dust or stain, though not exempt from a slight droop and a complexity of faint creases, under some clear glass bell. The perfection of household care, of high polish and finish, always reigned in her rooms, but they now looked most as if everything had been wound up, tucked in, put away, so that she might sit with folded hands and with nothing more to do. She was "out of it," to Marcher's vision; her work was over; she communicated with him as across some gulf or from some island of rest that she had already reached, and it made him feel strangely abandoned. Was it—or rather wasn't it—that if for so long she had been watching with him the answer to their question must have swum into her ken and taken on its name, so that her occupation was verily gone? He had as much as charged her with this in saying to her, many months before, that she even then knew something she was keeping from him. It was a point he had never since ventured to press, vaguely fearing as he did that it might become a difference, perhaps a disagreement, between them. He had in this later time turned nervous, which was what he in all the other years had never been; and the oddity was that his nervousness should have waited till he had begun to doubt, should have held off so long as he was sure. There was something, it seemed to him, that the wrong word would bring down on his head, something that would so at least ease off his tension. But he wanted not to speak the wrong word; that would make everything ugly. He wanted the knowledge he lacked to drop on him, if drop it could, by its own august weight. If she was to forsake him it was surely for her to take leave. This was why he didn't directly ask her again what she knew; but it was also why, approaching the matter from another side, he said to her in the course of his visit: "What do you regard as the very worst that at this time of day *can* happen to me?"

He had asked her that in the past often enough; they had, with the odd irregular rhythm of their intensities and avoidances, exchanged ideas about it and then had seen the ideas washed away by cool intervals, washed like figures traced in sea-sand. It had ever been the mark of their talk that the oldest allusions in it required but a little dismissal and reaction to come out again, sounding for the hour as new. She could thus at present meet his enquiry quite freshly and patiently. "Oh yes, I've repeatedly thought, only it always seemed to me of old that I couldn't quite make up my mind. I thought of dreadful things, between which it was difficult to choose; and so must you have done."

"Rather! I feel now as if I had scarce done anything else. I appear to myself to have spent my life in thinking of nothing *but* dreadful things. A great many of them I've at different times named to you, but there were others I couldn't name."

"They were too, too dreadful?"

"Too, too dreadful—some of them."

She looked at him a minute, and there came to him as he met it an inconsequent sense that her eyes, when one got their full clearness, were still as beautiful as they had been in youth, only beautiful with a strange cold light—a light that somehow was a part of the effect, if it wasn't rather a part of the cause, of the pale hard sweetness of the season and the hour. "And yet," she said at last, "there are horrors we've mentioned."

It deepened the strangeness to see her, as such a figure in such a picture, talk of "horrors," but she was to do in a few minutes something stranger yet—though even of this he was to take the full measure but afterwards—and the note of it already trembled. It was, for the matter of that, one of the signs that her eyes were having again the high flicker of their prime. He had to admit, however, what she said. "Oh yes, there were times when we did go far." He caught himself in the act of speaking as if it all were over. Well, he wished it were; and the consummation depended for him clearly more and more on his friend.

But she had now a soft smile. "Oh far—!"

It was oddly ironic. "Do you mean you're prepared to go further?"

She was frail and ancient and charming as she continued to look at him, yet it was rather as if she had lost the thread. "Do you consider that we went far?"

"Why I thought it the point you were just making—that we *had* looked most things in the face."

"Including each other?" She still smiled. "But you're quite right. We've had together great imaginations, often great fears; but some of them have been unspoken."

"Then the worst—we haven't faced that. I *could* face it, I believe, if I knew what you think it. I feel," he explained, "as if I had lost my power to conceive such things." And he wondered if he looked as blank as he sounded. "It's spent."

"Then why do you assume," she asked, "that mine isn't?"

"Because you've given me signs to the contrary. It isn't a question for you of conceiving, imagining, comparing. It isn't a question now of choosing." At last he came out with it. "You know something I don't. You've shown me that before."

These last words had affected her, he made out in a moment, exceedingly, and she spoke with firmness. "I've shown you, my dear, nothing."

He shook his head. "You can't hide it."

"Oh, oh!" May Bartram sounded over what she couldn't hide. It was almost a smothered groan.

"You admitted it months ago, when I spoke of it to you as of something you were afraid I should find out. Your answer was that I couldn't, that I wouldn't, and I don't pretend I have. But you had something therefore in mind, and I now see how it must have been, how it still is, the possibility that, of all possibilities, has settled itself for you as the worst. This," he went on, "is why I appeal to you. I'm only afraid of ignorance to-day—I'm not afraid of knowledge." And then as for a while she said nothing: "What makes me sure is that I see in your face and feel here, in this air and amid these appearances, that you're out of it. You've done. You've had your experience. You leave me to my fate."

Well, she listened, motionless and white in her chair, as on a decision to be made, so that her manner was fairly an avowal, though still, with a small fine inner stiffness, an imperfect surrender. "It *would* be the worst," she finally let herself say. "I mean the thing I've never said."

It hushed him a moment. "More monstrous than all the monstrosities we've named?"

"More monstrous. Isn't that what you sufficiently express," she asked, "in calling it the worst?"

Marcher thought. "Assuredly—if you mean, as I do, something that includes all the loss and all the shame that are thinkable."

"It would if it *should* happen," said May Bartram. "What we're speaking of, remember, is only my idea."

"It's your belief," Marcher returned. "That's enough for me. I feel your beliefs are right. Therefore if, having this one, you give me no more light on it, you abandon me."

"No, no!" she repeated. "I'm with you—don't you see?—still." And as to make it more vivid to him she rose from her chair—a movement she seldom risked in these days—and showed herself, all draped and all soft, in her fairness and slimness. "I haven't forsaken you."

It was really, in its effort against weakness, a generous assurance, and had the success of the impulse not, happily, been great, it would have touched him to pain more then to pleasure. But the cold charm in her eyes had spread, as she hovered before him, to all the rest of her person, so that it was for the minute almost a recovery of youth. He couldn't pity her for that; he could only take her as she showed—as capable even yet of helping him. It was as if, at the same time, her light might at any instant go out; wherefore he must make the most of it. There passed before him with intensity the three or four things he wanted most to know; but the question that came of itself to his lips really covered the others. "Then tell me if I shall consciously suffer."

She promptly shook her head. "Never!"

It confirmed the authority he imputed to her, and it produced on him an extraordinary effect. "Well, what's better than that? Do you call that the worst?"

"You think nothing is better?" she asked.

She seemed to mean something so special that he again sharply wondered, though still with the dawn of a prospect of relief. "Why not, if one doesn't *know*?" After which, as their eyes, over his question, met in a silence, the dawn deepened and something to his purpose came prodigiously out of her very face. His own, as he took it in, suddenly flushed to the forehead, and he gasped with the force of a perception to which, on the instant, everything fitted. The sound of his gasp filled the air; then he became articulate. "I see—if I don't suffer!"

In her own look, however, was doubt. "You see what?"

"Why what you mean—what you've always meant."

She again shook her head. "What I mean isn't what I've always meant. It's different."

"It's something new?"

She hung back from it a little. "Something new. It's not what you think. I see what you think."

His divination drew breath then; only her correction might be wrong. "It isn't that I *am* a blockhead?" he asked between faintness and grimness. "It isn't that it's all a mistake?"

"A mistake?" she pityingly echoed. *That* possibility, for her, he saw, would be monstrous; and if she guaranteed him the immunity from pain it would accordingly not be what she had in mind. "Oh no," she declared; "it's nothing of that sort. You've been right."

Yet he couldn't help asking himself if she weren't, thus pressed, speaking but to save him. It seemed to him he should be most in a hole if his history should prove all a platitude. "Are you telling me the truth, so that I shan't have been a bigger idiot than I can bear to know? I *haven't* lived with a vain imagination, in the most besotted illusion? I haven't waited but to see the door shut in my face?"

She shook her head again. "However the case stands *that* isn't the truth. Whatever the reality, it *is* a reality. The door isn't shut. The door's open," said May Bartram.

"Then something's to come?"

She waited once again, always with her cold sweet eyes on him. "It's never too late." She had, with her gliding step, diminished the distance between them, and she stood nearer to him, close to him, a minute, as if still charged with the unspoken. Her movement might have been for some finer emphasis of what she was at once hesitating and deciding to say. He had been standing by the chimney-piece, fireless and sparely adorned, a small perfect old French clock and two morsels of rosy Dresden constituting all its furniture; and her hand grasped the shelf while she kept him waiting, grasped it a little as for support and encouragement. She only kept him waiting, however; that is he only waited. It had become suddenly, from her movement and attitude, beautiful and vivid to him that she had something more to give him; her wasted face delicately shone with it—it glittered almost as with the white lustre of silver in her expression. She was right, incontestably, for what he saw in her face was the truth, and strangely, without consequence, while their talk of it as dreadful was still in the air, she appeared to present it as inordinately soft. This, prompting bewilderment, made him but gape the more gratefully for her revelation, so that they continued for some minutes silent, her face shining at him, her contact imponderably pressing, and his stare all kind but all expectant. The end, none the less, was that what he had expected failed to come to him. Something else took place instead, which seemed to consist at first in the mere closing of her eyes. She gave way at the same instant to a slow fine shudder, and though he remained staring—though he stared in fact but the harder—turned off and regained her chair. It was the end of what she had been intending, but it left him thinking only of that.

"Well, you don't say—?"

She had touched in her passage a bell near the chimney and had sunk back strangely pale. "I'm afraid I'm too ill."

"Too ill to tell me?" It sprang up sharp to him, and almost to his lips, the fear she might die without giving him light. He checked himself in time from so expressing his question, but she answered as if she had heard the words.

"Don't you know—now?"

" 'Now'—?" She had spoken as if some difference had been made within the moment. But her maid, quickly obedient to her bell, was already with them. "I know nothing." And he was afterwards to say to himself that he must have spoken with odious impatience, such an impatience as to show that, supremely disconcerted, he washed his hands of the whole question.

"Oh!" said May Bartram.

"Are you in pain?" he asked as the woman went to her.

"No," said May Bartram.

Her maid, who had put an arm round her as if to take her to her room, fixed on him eyes that appealingly contradicted her; in spite of which, however, he showed once more his mystification. "What then has happened?"

She was once more, with her companion's help, on her feet, and, feeling withdrawal imposed on him, he had blankly found his hat and gloves and had reached the door. Yet he waited for her answer. "What *was* to," she said.

V

He came back the next day, but she was then unable to see him, and as it was literally the first time this had occurred in the long stretch of their acquaintance he turned away, defeated and sore, almost angry—or feeling at least that such a break in their custom was really the beginning of the end—and wandered alone with his thoughts, especially with the one he was least able to keep down. She was dying and he would lose her; she was dying and his life would end. He stopped in the Park, into which he had passed, and stared before him at his recurrent doubt. Away from her the doubt pressed again; in her presence he had believed her, but as he felt his forlornness he threw himself into the explanation that, nearest at hand, had most of a miserable warmth for him and least of a cold torment. She had deceived him to save him—to put him off with something in which he should be able to rest. What could the thing that was to happen to him be, after all, but just this thing that had begun to happen? Her dying, her death, his consequent solitude—*that* was what he had figured as the Beast in the Jungle, that was what had been in the lap of the gods. He had had her word for it as he left her—what else on earth could she have meant? It wasn't a thing of a monstrous order; not a fate rare and distinguished; not a stroke of fortune that overwhelmed and immortalised; it had only the stamp of the common doom. But poor Marcher at this hour judged the common doom sufficient. It would serve his turn, and even as the consummation of infinite waiting he would bend his pride to accept it. He sat down on a bench in the twilight. He hadn't been a fool. Something had *been*, as she had said, to come. Before he rose indeed it had quite struck him that the final fact really matched with the long avenue through which he had had to reach it. As sharing his suspense and as giving herself all, giving her life, to bring it to an end, she had come with him every step of the way. He had lived by her aid, and to leave her behind would be cruelly, damnably to miss her. What could be more overwhelming than that?

Well, he was to know within the week, for though she kept him a while at bay, left him restless and wretched during a series of days on each of which he asked about her only again to have to turn away, she ended his trial by receiving him where she had always received him. Yet she had been brought out at some hazard into the presence of so many of the things that were, consciously, vainly, half their past, and there was scant service left in the gentleness of her mere desire, all too visible, to check his obsession and wind up his long trouble. That was clearly what she wanted, the one thing more for her own peace while she could still put out her hand. He was so affected by her state that, once seated by her chair, he was moved to let everything go; it was she herself therefore who brought him back, took up again, before she dismissed him, her last word of the other time. She showed how she wished to leave their business in order. "I'm not sure you understood. You've nothing to wait for more. It *has* come."

Oh how he looked at her! "Really?"

"Really."

"The thing that, as you said, *was* to?"

"The thing that we began in our youth to watch for."

Face to face with her once more he believed her; it was a claim to which he had so abjectly little to oppose. "You mean that it has come as a positive definite occurrence, with a name and a date?"

"Positive. Definite. I don't know about the 'name,' but oh with a date!"

He found himself again too helplessly at sea. "But come in the night—come and passed me by?"

May Bartram had her strange faint smile. "Oh no, it hasn't passed you by!"

"But if I haven't been aware of it and it hasn't touched me—?"

"Ah your not being aware of it"—and she seemed to hesitate an instant to deal with this—"your not being aware of it is the strangeness *in* the strangeness. It's the wonder *of* the wonder." She spoke as with the softness almost of a sick child, yet now at last, at the end of all, with the perfect straightness of a sibyl. She visibly knew that she knew, and the effect on him was of something co-ordinate, in its high character, with the law that had ruled him. It was the true voice of the law; so on her lips would the law itself have sounded. "It *has* touched you," she went on. "It has done its office. It has made you all its own."

"So utterly without my knowing it?"

"So utterly without your knowing it." His hand, as he leaned to her, was on the arm of her chair, and, dimly smiling always now, she placed her own on it. "It's enough if *I* know it."

"Oh!" he confusedly breathed, as she herself of late so often had done.

"What I long ago said is true. You'll never know now, and I think you ought to be content. You've *had* it," said May Bartram.

"But had what?"

"Why what was to have marked you out. The proof of your law. It has acted. I'm too glad," she then bravely added, "to have been able to see what it's *not*."

He continued to attach his eyes to her, and with the sense that it was all beyond him, and that *she* was too, he would still have sharply challenged her hadn't he so felt it an abuse of her weakness to do more than take devoutly what she gave him, take it hushed as to a revelation. If he did speak, it was out of the foreknowledge of his loneliness to come. "If you're glad of what it's 'not' it might then have been worse?"

She turned her eyes away, she looked straight before her; with which after a moment: "Well, you know our fears."

He wondered. "It's something then we never feared?"

On this slowly she turned to him. "Did we ever dream, with all our dreams, that we should sit and talk of it thus?"

He tried for a little to make out that they had; but it was as if their dreams, numberless enough, were in solution in some thick cold mist through which thought lost itself. "It might have been that we couldn't talk?"

"Well"—she did her best for him—"not from this side. This, you see," she said, "is the *other* side."

"I think," poor Marcher returned, "that all sides are the same to me." Then, however, as she gently shook her head in correction: "We mightn't, as it were, have got across—?"

"To where we are—no. We're *here*"—she made her weak emphasis.

"And much good does it do us!" was her friend's frank comment.

"It does us the good it can. It does us the good that *it* isn't here. It's past. It's behind," said May Bartram. "Before—" but her voice dropped.

He had got up, not to tire her, but it was hard to combat his yearning. She after all told him nothing but that his light had failed —which he knew well enough without her. "Before—?" he blankly echoed.

"Before, you see, it was always to *come*. That kept it present."

"Oh I don't care what comes now! Besides," Marcher added, "it seems to me I liked it better present, as you say, than I can like it absent with *your* absence."

"Oh mine!"—and her pale hands made light of it.

"With the absence of everything." He had a dreadful sense of standing there before her for—so far as anything but this proved, this bottomless drop was concerned—the last time of their life. It rested on him with a weight he felt he could scarce bear, and this weight it apparently was that still pressed out what remained in him of speakable protest. "I believe you; but I can't begin to pretend I understand. *Nothing*, for me, is past; nothing *will* pass till I pass myself, which I pray my stars may be as soon as possible. Say, however," he added, "that I've eaten my cake, as you contend, to the last crumb—how can the thing I've never felt at all be the thing I was marked out to feel?"

She met him perhaps less directly, but she met him unperturbed. "You take your 'feelings' for granted. You were to suffer your fate. That was not necessarily to know it."

"How in the world—when what is such knowledge but suffering?"

She looked up at him a while in silence. "No— you don't understand."

"I suffer," said John Marcher.

"Don't, don't!"

"How can I help at least *that?*"

"*Don't!*" May Bartram repeated.

She spoke it in a tone so special, in spite of her weakness, that he stared an instant—stared as if some light, hitherto hidden, had shimmered across his vision. Darkness again closed over it, but the gleam had already become for him an idea. "Because I haven't the right—?"

"Don't *know*—when you needn't," she mercifully urged. "You needn't—for we shouldn't."

"Shouldn't?" If he could but know what she meant!

"No—it's too much."

"Too much?" he still asked but, with a mystification that was the next moment of a sudden to give way. Her words, if they meant something, affected him in this light—the light also of her wasted face—as meaning *all*, and the sense of what knowledge had been for herself came over him with a rush which broke through into a question. "Is it of that then you're dying?"

She but watched him, gravely at first, as to see, with this, where he was, and she might have seen something or feared something that moved her sympathy. "I would live for you still—if I could." Her eyes closed for a little, as if, withdrawn into herself, she were for a last time trying. "But I can't!" she said as she raised them again to take leave of him.

She couldn't indeed, as but too promptly and sharply appeared, and he had no vision of her after this that was anything but darkness and doom. They had parted for ever in that strange talk; access to her chamber of pain, rigidly guarded, was almost wholly forbidden him; he was feeling now moreover, in the face of doctors, nurses, the two or three relatives attracted doubtless by the presumption of what she had to "leave," how few were the rights, as they were called in such cases, that he had to put forward, and how odd it might even seem that their intimacy shouldn't have given him more of them. The stupidest fourth cousin had more, even though she had been nothing in such a person's life. She had been a feature of features in *his*, for what else was it to have been so indispensable? Strange beyond saying were the ways of existence, baffling for him the anomaly of his lack, as he felt it to be, of producible claim. A woman might have been, as it were, everything to him, and it might yet present him in no connexion that any one seemed held to recognise. If this was the case in these closing weeks it was the case more sharply on the occasion of the last offices rendered, in the great grey London cemetery, to what had been mortal, to what had been precious, in his freind. The concourse at her grave was not numerous, but he saw himself treated as scarce more nearly concerned with it than if there had been a thousand others. He was in short from this moment face to face with the fact that he was to profit extraordinarily little by the interest May Bartram had taken in him. He couldn't quite have said what he expected, but he hadn't surely expected this approach to a double privation. Not only had her interest failed him, but he seemed to feel himself unattended—and for a reason he couldn't seize—by the distinction, the dignity, the propriety, if nothing else, of the man markedly bereaved. It was as if in the view of society he had not *been* markedly bereaved, as if there still failed some sign or proof of it, and as if none the less his character could never be affirmed nor the deficiency ever made up. There were moments as the weeks went by when he would have liked, by some almost aggressive act, to take his stand on the intimacy of his loss, in order that it *might* be questioned and his retort, to the relief of his spirit, so recorded; but the moments of an irritation more helpless followed fast on these, the moments during which, turning things over with a good conscience but with a bare horizon, he found himself wondering if he oughtn't to have begun, so to speak, further back.

He found himself wondering at many things, and this last speculation had others to keep it company. What could he have done, after all, in her lifetime, without giving them both, as it were, away? He couldn't have made known she was watching him, for that would have published the superstition of the Beast. This was what closed his mouth now—now that the Jungle had been threshed to vacancy and that the Beast had stolen away. It sounded too foolish and too flat; the difference for him in this particular, the extinction in his life of the element of suspense, was such as in fact to surprise him. He could scarce have said what the effect resembled; the abrupt cessation, the positive prohibition, of music perhaps, more than anything else, in some place all adjusted and all

accustomed to sonority and to attention. If he could at any rate have
conceived lifting the veil from his image at some moment of the
past (what had he done, after all, if not lift it to *her?*) so to do this
to-day, to talk to people at large of the Jungle cleared and confide
to them that he now felt it as safe, would have been not only to see
them listen as to a goodwife's tale, but really ro hear himself tell
one. What it presently came to in truth was that poor Marcher
waded through his beaten grass, where no life stirred, where no
breath sounded, where no evil eye seemed to gleam from a possible
lair, very much as if vaguely looking for the Beast, and still more as
if acutely missing it. He walked about in an existence that had
grown strangely more spacious, and, stopping fitfully in places
where the undergrowth of life struck him as closer, asked himself
yearningly, wondered secretly and sorely, if it would have lurked
here or there. It would have at all events *sprung*; what was at least
complete was his belief in the truth of the assurance given him.
The change from his old sense to his new was absolute and final:
what was to happen *had* so absolutely and finally happened that he
was as little able to know a fear for his future as to know a hope; so
absent in short was any question of anything still to come. He was
to live entirely with the other question, that of his unidentified
past, that of his having to see his fortune impenetrably muffled and
masked.

The torment of this vision became then his occupation; he
couldn't perhaps have consented to live but for the possibility of
guessing. She had told him, his friend, not to guess; she had forbidden him, so far as he might, to know, and she had even in a sort
denied the power in him to learn: which were so many things, precisely, to deprive him of rest. It wasn't that he wanted, he argued for
fairness, that anything past and done should repeat itself; it was
only that he shouldn't, as an anticlimax, have been taken sleeping
so sound as not to be able to win back by an effort of thought the
lost stuff of consciousness. He declared to himself at moments that
he would either win it back or have done with consciousness for
ever; he made this idea his one motive in fine, made it so much his
passion that none other, to compare with it, seemed ever to have
touched him. The lost stuff of consciousness became thus for him
as a strayed or stolen child to an unappeasable father; he hunted it
up and down very much as if he were knocking at doors and enquiring of the police. This was the spirit in which, inevitably, he set
himself to travel; he started on a journey that was to be as long as
he could make it; it danced before him that, as the other side of the
globe couldn't possibly have less to say to him, it might, by a possibility of suggestion, have more. Before he quitted London, however,
he made a pilgrimage to May Bartram's grave, took his way to it
through the endless avenues of the grim suburban metropolis,

sought it out in the wilderness of tombs, and, though he had come but for the renewal of the act of farewell, found himself, when he had at last stood by it, beguiled into long intensities. He stood for an hour, powerless to turn away and yet powerless to penetrate the darkness of death; fixing with his eyes her inscribed name and date, beating his forehead against the fact of the secret they kept, drawing his breath, while he waited, as if some sense would in pity of him rise from the stones. He kneeled on the stones, however, in vain; they kept what they concealed; and if the face of the tomb did become a face for him it was because her two names became a pair of eyes that didn't know him. He gave them a last long look, but no palest light broke.

VI

He stayed away, after this, for a year; he visited the depths of Asia, spending himself on scenes of romantic interest, of superlative sanctity; but what was present to him everywhere was that for a man who had known what *he* had known the world was vulgar and vain. The state of mind in which he had lived for so many years shone out to him, in reflexion, as a light that coloured and refined, a light beside which the glow of the East was garish cheap and thin. The terrible truth was that he had lost—with everything else—a distinction as well; the things he saw couldn't help being common when he had become common to look at them. He was simply now one of them himself—he was in the dust, without a peg for the sense of difference; and there were hours when, before the temples of gods and the sepulchres of kings, his spirit turned for nobleness of association to the barely discriminated slab in the London suburb. That had become for him, and more intensely with time and distance, his one witness of a past glory. It was all that was left to him for proof or pride, yet the past glories of Pharaohs were nothing to him as he thought of it. Small wonder then that he came back to it on the morrow of his return. He was drawn there this time as irresistibly as the other, yet with a confidence, almost, that was doubtless the effect of the many months that had elapsed. He had lived, in spite of himself, into his change of feeling, and in wandering over the earth had wandered, as might be said, from the circumference to the centre of his desert. He had settled to his safety and accepted perforce his extinction; figuring to himself, with some colour, in the likeness of certain little old men he remembered to have seen, of whom, all meagre and wizened as they might look, it was related that they had in their time fought twenty duels or been loved by ten princesses. They indeed had been wondrous for others while he was but wondrous for himself; which, however, was exactly the cause of his haste to renew the wonder by getting back, as he might put it, into his own presence. That had quickened his steps and checked his delay. If his visit was prompt it was because he had been separated so long from the part of himself that alone he now valued.

It's accordingly not false to say that he reached his goal with a certain elation and stood there again with a certain assurance. The creature beneath the sod *knew* of his rare experience, so that, strangely now, the place had lost for him its mere blankness of expression. It met him in mildness—not, as before, in mockery; it wore for him the air of conscious greeting that we find, after absence, in things that have closely belonged to us and which seem to confess of themselves to the connexion. The plot of ground, the graven tablet, the tended flowers affected him so as belonging to him that he resembled for the hour a contented landlord reviewing a piece of property. Whatever had happened—well, had happened. He had not come back this time with the vanity of that question, his former worrying "What, *what?*" now practically so spent. Yet he would none the less never again so cut himself off from the spot; he would come back to it every month, for if he did nothing else by its aid he at least held up his head. It thus grew for him, in the oddest way, a positive resource; he carried out his idea of periodical returns, which took their place at last among the most inveterate of his habits. What it all amounted to, oddly enough, was that in his finally so simplified world this garden of death gave him the few square feet of earth on which he could still most live. It was as if, being nothing anywhere else for any one, nothing even for himself, he were just everything here, and if not for a crowd of witnesses or indeed for any witness but John Marcher, then by clear right of the register that he could scan like an open page. The open page was the tomb of his friend, and *there* were the facts of the past, there the truth of his life, there the backward reaches in which he could lose himself. He did this from time to time with such effect that he seemed to wander through the old years with his hand in the arm of a companion who was, in the most extraordinary manner, his other, his younger self; and to wander, which was more extraordinary yet, round and round a third presence—not wandering she, but stationary, still, whose eyes, turning with his revolution, never ceased to follow him, and whose seat was his point, so to speak, of orientation. Thus in short he settled to live—feeding all on the sense that he once *had* lived, and dependent on it not alone for a support but for an identity.

It sufficed him in its way for months and the year elapsed; it would doubtless even have carried him further but for an accident, superficially slight, which moved him, quite in another direction, with a force beyond any of his impressions of Egypt or of India. It was a thing of the merest chance—the turn, as he afterwards felt, of a hair, though he was indeed to live to believe that if light hadn't come to him in this particular fashion it would still have come in

another. He was to live to believe this, I say, though he was not to
live, I may not less definitely mention, to do much else. We allow
him at any rate the benefit of the conviction, struggling up for him
at the end, that, whatever might have happened or not happened,
he would have come round of himself to the light. The incident of
an autumn day had put the match to the train laid from of old by
his misery. With the light before him he knew that even of late his
ache had only been smothered. It was strangely drugged, but it
throbbed; at the touch it began to bleed. And the touch, in the
event, was the face of a fellow mortal. This face, one grey afternoon
when the leaves were thick in the alleys, looked into Marcher's own,
at the cemetery, with an expression like the cut of a blade. He felt
it, that is, so deep down that he winced at the steady thrust. The
person who so mutely assaulted him was a figure he had noticed, on
reaching his own goal, absorbed by a grave a short distance away, a
grave apparently fresh, so that the emotion of the visitor would
probably match it for frankness. This fact alone forbade further
attention, though during the time he stayed he remained vaguely
conscious of his neighbour, a middle-aged man apparently, in
mourning, whose bowed back, among the clustered monuments and
mortuary yews, was constantly presented. Marcher's theory that
these were elements in contact with which he himself revived, had
suffered, on this occasion, it may be granted, a marked, an excessive
check. The autumn day was dire for him as none had recently been,
and he rested with a heaviness he had not yet known on the low
stone table that bore May Bartram's name. He rested without
power to move, as if some spring in him, some spell vouchsafed, had
suddenly been broken for ever. If he could have done that moment
as he wanted he would simply have stretched himself on the slab
that was ready to take him, treating it as a place prepared to receive
his last sleep. What in all the wide world had he now to keep
awake for? He stared before him with the question, and it was then
that, as one of the cemetery walks passed near him, he caught the
shock of the face.

His neighbour at the other grave had withdrawn, as he himself,
with force enough in him, would have done by now, and was advancing along the path on his way to one of the gates. This brought
him close, and his pace was slow, so that—and all the more as there
was a kind of hunger in his look—the two men were for a minute
directly confronted. Marcher knew him at once for one of the
deeply stricken—a perception so sharp that nothing else in the picture comparatively lived, neither his dress, his age, nor his presuma-
ble character and class; nothing lived but the deep ravage of the features he showed. He *showed* them—that was was the point; he was
moved, as he passed, by some impulse that was either a signal for
sympathy or, more possibly, a challenge to an opposed sorrow. He
might already have been aware of our friend, might at some pre-

vious hour have noticed in him the smooth habit of the scene, with which the state of his own senses so scantly consorted, and might thereby have been stirred as by an overt discord. What Marcher was at all events conscious of was in the first place that the image of scarred passion presented to him was conscious too—of something that profaned the air; and in the second that, roused, startled, shocked, he was yet the next moment looking after it, as it went, with envy. The most extraordinary thing that had happened to him —though he had given that name to other matters as well—took place, after his immediate vague stare, as a consequence of this impression. The stranger passed, but the raw glare of his grief remained, making our friend wonder in pity what wrong, what wound it expressed, what injury not to be healed. What had the man *had*, to make him by the loss of it so bleed and yet live?

Something—and this reached him with a pang—that *he*, John Marcher, hadn't; the proof of which was precisely John Marcher's arid end. No passion had ever touched him, for this was what passion meant; he had survived and maundered and pined, but where had been *his* deep ravage? The extraordinary thing we speak of was the sudden rush of the result of this question. The sight that had just met his eyes named to him, as in letters of quick flame, something he had utterly, insanely missed, and what he had missed made these things a train of fire, made them mark themselves in an anguish of inward throbs. He had seen *outside* of his life, not learned it within, the way a woman was mourned when she had been loved for herself: such was the force of his conviction of the meaning of the stranger's face, which still flared for him as a smoky torch. It hadn't come to him, the knowledge, on the wings of experience; it had brushed him, jostled him, upset him, with the disrespect of chance, the insolence of accident. Now that the illumination had begun, however, it blazed to the zenith, and what he presently stood there gazing at was the sounded void of his life. He gazed, he drew breath, in pain; he turned in his dismay, and, turning, he had before him in sharper incision than ever the open page of his story. The name on the table smote him as the passage of his neighbour had done, and what it said to him, full in the face, was that *she* was what he had missed. This was the awful thought, the answer to all the past, the vision at the dread clearness of which he grew as cold as the stone beneath him. Everything fell together, confessed, explained, overwhelmed; leaving him most of all stupefied at the blindness he had cherished. The fate he had been marked for he had met with a vengeance—he had emptied the cup to the lees; he had been the man of his time, *the* man, to whom nothing on earth was to have happened. That was the rare stroke—that was his visitation. So he saw it, as we say, in pale horror, while the pieces fitted and fitted. So *she* had seen it while he didn't, and so she served at this hour to drive the truth home. It was the truth, vivid and monstrous, that all the while he had waited the wait was itself his portion. This the companion of his vigil had at a given moment made out, and she had then offered him the chance to baffle his doom. One's doom, however, was never baffled, and on the day she told him his own had come down she had seen him but stupidly stare at the escape she offered him.

The escape would have been to love her; then, *then* he would have lived. *She* had lived—who could say now with what passion? —since she had loved him for himself; whereas he had never thought of her (ah how it hugely glared at him!) but in the chill of his egotism and the light of her use. Her spoken words came back to him—the chain stretched and stretched. The Beast had lurked indeed, and the Beast, at its hour, had sprung; it had sprung in that twilight of the cold April when, pale, ill, wasted, but all beautiful, and perhaps even then recoverable, she had risen from her chair to stand before him and let him imaginably guess. It had sprung as he didn't guess; it had sprung as she hopelessly turned from him, and the mark, by the time he left her, had fallen where it *was* to fall. He had justified his fear and achieved his fate; he had failed, with the last exactitude, of all he was to fail of; and a moan now rose to his lips as he remembered she had prayed he mightn't know. This horror of waking—*this* was knowledge, knowledge under the breath of which the very tears in his eyes seemed to freeze. Through them, none the less, he tried to fix it and hold it; he kept it there before him so that he might feel the pain. That at least, belated and bitter, had something of the taste of life. But the bitterness suddenly sickened him, and it was as if, horribly, he saw in the truth, in the cruelty of his image, what had been appointed and done. He saw the Jungle of his life and saw the lurking Beast; then, while he looked, perceived it, as by a stir of the air, rise, huge and hideous, for the leap that was to settle him. His eyes darkened—it was close; and, instinctively turning, in his hallucination, to avoid it, he flung himself, face down, on the tomb.

1901   1903, 1909

From The Art of the Novel[1]
[The Beast in the Jungle]

To desire, amid those collocations, to place, so far as possible, like with like, was to invite "The Beast in the Jungle" to stand here next in order. As to the accidental determinant of which composition, once more—of comparatively recent date and destined, like its predecessor, first to see the light in a volume of miscellanies ("The Better Sort," 1903)—I remount the stream of time, all enquiringly, but to come back empty-handed. The subject of this

---

1. The prefaces James wrote to the individual volumes of the New York edition of his works were collected, in 1934, by R. P. Blackmur under the title *The Art* *of the Novel.* The text here reprinted is drawn from the original preface to Volume XVII of the New York edition.

elaborated fantasy—which, I must add, I hold a successful thing only as its motive may seem to the reader to stand out sharp—can't quite have belonged to the immemorial company of such solicitations; though in spite of this I meet it, in ten lines of an old notebook, but as a recorded conceit and an accomplished fact. Another poor sensitive gentleman, fit indeed to mate with Stransom of "The Altar"[2]—my attested predilection for poor sensitive gentlemen almost embarrasses me as I march!—was to have been, after a strange fashion and from the threshold of his career, condemned to keep counting with the unreasoned prevision of some extraordinary fate; the conviction, lodged in his brain, part and parcel of his imagination from far back, that experience would be marked for him, and whether for good or for ill, by some rare distinction, some incalculable violence or unprecedented stroke. So I seemed to see him start in life—under the so mixed star of the extreme of apprehension and the extreme of confidence; all to the logical, the quite inevitable effect of the complication aforesaid: his having to wait and wait for the right recognition; none of the mere usual and normal human adventures, whether delights or disconcertments, appearing to conform to the great type of his fortune. So it is that he's depicted. No gathering appearance, no descried or interpreted promise or portent, affects his superstitious soul either as a damnation deep enough (if damnation be in question) for his appointed *quality* of consciousness, or as a translation into bliss sublime enough (on *that* hypothesis) to fill, in vulgar parlance, the bill. Therefore as each item of experience comes, with its possibilities, into view, he can but dismiss it under this sterilising habit of the failure to find it good enough and thence to appropriate it.

His one desire remains of course to meet his fate, or at least to divine it, to see it as intelligible, to learn it, in a word; but none of its harbingers, pretended or supposed, speak his ear in the true voice; they wait their moment at his door only to pass on unheeded, and the years ebb while he holds his breath and stays his hand and —from the dread not less of imputed pride than of imputed pusillanimity—stifles his distinguished secret. He perforce lets everything go—leaving all the while his general presumption disguised and his general abstention unexplained; since he's ridden by the idea of what things may lead to, since they mostly always lead to human communities, wider or intenser, of experience, and since, above all, in his uncertainty, he mustn't compromise others. Like the blinded seeker in the old-fashioned game he "burns," on occasion, as with the sense of the hidden thing near—only to deviate again however into the chill; the chill that indeed settles on him as the striking of his hour is deferred. His career thus resolves itself into a great negative adventure, my report of which presents, for its centre, the fine

---

2. Stransom is the hero of the *Altar of the Dead,* another story in Volume XVII.

case that has caused him most tormentedly to "burn," and then most unprofitably to stray. He is afraid to recognise what he incidentally misses, since what his high belief amounts to is not that he shall have felt and vibrated less than any one else, but that he shall have felt and vibrated more; which no acknowledgement of the minor loss must conflict with. Such a course of existence naturally involves a climax—the final flash of the light under which he reads his lifelong riddle and sees his conviction proved. He has indeed been marked and indeed suffered his fortune—which is precisely to have been the man in the world to whom nothing whatever was to happen. My picture leaves him overwhelmed—at last he has understood; though in thus disengaging my treated theme for the reader's benefit I seem to acknowledge that this more detached witness may not successfully have done so. I certainly grant that any felt merit in the thing must all depend on the clearness and charm with which the subject just noted expresses itself.

1909, 1934

From The Notebooks
[The Beast in the Jungle][1]

L.H.,[2] August 27th, 1901.

Meanwhile there is something else—a very tiny *fantaisie* probably —in small notion that comes to me of a man haunted by the fear, more and more, throughout life, that *something will happen to him:* he doesn't quite know what. His life *seems* safe and ordered, his liabilities and exposures (as a *result* of the fear) a good deal curtailed and cut down, so that the years go by and the stroke doesn't fall. Yet 'It *will* come, it will still come,' he finds himself believing —and indeed saying to some one, some second-consciousness in the anecdote. 'It will come before death; I shan't die without it.' Finally I think it must be *he* who sees—not the 2d consciousness. Mustn't indeed the '2d consciousness' be some woman, and it be she who *helps* him to see? She has always loved him—yes, *that,* for the story, 'pretty,' and he, saving, protecting, exempting his life (always, really, with and *for* the fear), has never known it. He likes her, talks to her, confides in her, sees her often—*la côtoie,* as to her hidden passion, but never guesses. She meanwhile, all the time, sees his life as it is. It is to her that he tells his fear—yes, she is the '2d consciousness.' At first she *feels,* herself, for him, his feeling of his fear, and is tender, reassuring, protective. Then she reads, as I say, his real case, and is, though unexpressedly, *lucid.* The years go by and *she sees the thing not happen.* At last one day they are somehow, some day, face to face over it, and then she speaks. 'It *has,* the great thing you've always lived in dread of, had the foreboding

1. This selection is taken from *The Notebooks of Henry James,* ed. F. O. Matthiessen and Kenneth B. Murdock (1947).

2. "L.H.": Lamb House.

of—it *has* happened to you.' He wonders—when, how, what? 'What is it?—why, it is that *nothing* has happened!' Then, later on, I think, to keep up the prettiness, it must be that HE sees, that he understands. She has loved him always—and *that* might have happened. But it's too late—she's dead. That, I think, at least, he comes to later on, after an interval, after her death. She is dying, or ill, when she says it. He *then* DOESN'T understand, doesn't see—or so far, only, as to agree with her, ruefully, that that very well *may* be it: that nothing has happened. He goes back; she is gone; she is dead. *What* she has said to him has in a way, by its truth, created the need for her, made him want her, *positively* want her, more. But she is gone, he has lost her, and *then* he sees all she has meant. She has loved him. (*It must come for the* READER *thus, at this moment.*) With his base safety and shrinkage he never knew. *That* was what might have happened, and what *has* happened is that it didn't.

1947

The Jolly Corner[1]

I

"Every one asks me what I 'think' of everything," said Spencer Brydon; "and I make answer as I can—begging or dodging the question, putting them off with any nonsense. It wouldn't matter to any of them really," he went on, "for even were it possible to meet in that stand-and-deliver way so silly a demand on so big a subject, my 'thoughts' would still be almost altogether about something that concerns only myself." He was talking to Miss Staverton, with whom for a couple of months now he had availed himself of every possible occasion to talk; this disposition and this resource, this comfort and support, as the situation in fact presented itself, having promptly enough taken the first place in the considerable array of rather unattenuated surprises attending his so strangely belated return to America. Everything was somehow a surprise; and that might be natural when one had so long and so consistently neglected everything, taken pains to give surprises so much margin for play. He had given them more than thirty years—thirty-three, to be exact; and they now seemed to him to have organised their performance quite on the scale of that licence. He had been twenty-three on leaving New York—he was fifty-six to-day: unless indeed he were to reckon as he had sometimes, since his repatriation, found himself feeling; in which case he would have lived longer than is often allotted to man. It would have taken a century, he repeatedly said to himself, and said also to Alice Staverton, it would have taken a longer absence and a more averted mind than those

1. Shortly after its appearance in the *English Review* for December, 1908, *The Jolly Corner* was thoroughly revised for inclusion as part of Volume XVII of the New York edition (1909), the source of the present text.

even of which he had been guilty, to pile up the differences, the newnesses, the queernesses, above all the bignesses, for the better or the worse, that at present assaulted his vision wherever he looked.

The great fact all the while however had been the incalculability; since he *had* supposed himself, from decade to decade, to be allowing, and in the most liberal and intelligent manner, for brilliancy of change. He actually saw that he had allowed for nothing; he missed what he would have been sure of finding, he found what he would never have imagined. Proportions and values were upside-down; the ugly things he had expected, the ugly things of his far-away youth, when he had too promptly waked up to a sense of the ugly—these uncanny phenomena placed him rather, as it happened, under the charm; whereas the "swagger" things, the modern, the monstrous, the famous things, those he had more particularly, like thousands of ingenuous enquirers every year, come over to see, were exactly his sources of dismay. They were as so many set traps for displeasure, above all for reaction, of which his restless tread was constantly pressing the spring. It was interesting, doubtless, the whole show, but it would have been too disconcerting hadn't a certain finer truth saved the situation. He had distinctly not, in this steadier light, come over *all* for the monstrosities; he had come, not only in the last analysis but quite on the face of the act, under an impulse with which they had nothing to do. He had come —putting the thing pompously—to look at his "property," which he had thus for a third of a century not been within four thousand miles of; or, expressing it less sordidly, he had yielded to the humour of seeing again his house on the jolly corner, as he usually, and quite fondly, described it—the one in which he had first seen the light, in which various members of his family had lived and had died, in which the holidays of his overschooled boyhood had been passed and the few social flowers of his chilled adolescence gathered, and which, alienated then for so long a period, had, through the successive deaths of his two brothers and the termination of old arrangements, come wholly into his hands. He was the owner of another, not quite so "good"—the jolly corner having been, from far back, superlatively extended and consecrated; and the value of the pair represented his main capital, with an income consisting, in these later years, of their respective rents which (thanks precisely to their original excellent type) had never been depressingly low. He could live in "Europe," as he had been in the habit of living, on the product of these flourishing New York leases, and all the better since, that of the second structure, the mere number in its long row, having within a twelvemonth fallen in, renovation at a high advance had proved beautifully possible.

These were items of property indeed, but he had found himself since his arrival distinguishing more than ever between them. The house within the street, two bristling blocks westward, was already in course of reconstruction as a tall mass of flats; he had acceded, some time before, to overtures for this conversion—in which, now that it was going forward, it had been not the least of his astonishments to find himself able, on the spot, and though without a previous ounce of such experience, to participate with a certain intelligence, almost with a certain authority. He had lived his life with his back so turned to such concerns and his face addressed to those of so different an order that he scarce knew what to make of this lively stir, in a compartment of his mind never yet penetrated, of a capacity for business and a sense for construction. These virtues, so common all round him now, had been dormant in his own organism—where it might be said of them perhaps that they had slept the sleep of the just. At present, in the splendid autumn weather—the autumn at least was a pure boon in the terrible place—he loafed about his "work" undeterred, secretly agitated; not in the least "minding" that the whole proposition, as they said, was vulgar and sordid, and ready to climb ladders, to walk the plank, to handle materials and look wise about them, to ask questions, in fine, and challenge explanations and really "go into" figures.

It amused, it verily quite charmed him; and, by the same stroke, it amused, and even more, Alice Staverton, though perhaps charming her perceptibly less. She wasn't however going to be better-off for it, as *he* was—and so astonishingly much: nothing was now likely, he knew, ever to make her better-off than she found herself, in the afternoon of life, as the delicately frugal possessor and tenant of the small house in Irving Place to which she had subtly managed to cling through her almost unbroken New York career. If he knew the way to it now better than to any other address among the dreadful multiplied numberings which seemed to him to reduce the whole place to some vast ledger-page, overgrown, fantastic, of ruled and criss-crossed lines and figures—if he had formed, for his consolation, that habit, it was really not a little because of the charm of his having encountered and recognised, in the vast wilderness of the wholesale, breaking through the mere gross generalisation of wealth and force and success, a small still scene where items and shades, all delicate things, kept the sharpness of the notes of a high voice perfectly trained, and where economy hung about like the scent of a garden. His old friend lived with one maid and herself dusted her relics and trimmed her lamps and polished her silver; she stood off, in the awful modern crush, when she could, but she sallied forth and did battle when the challenge was really to "spirit," the spirit she after all confessed to, proudly and a little shyly, as to that of the better time, that of *their* common, their quite far-away and antediluvian social period and order. She made use of the street-cars when need be, the terrible things that people scrambled for as the panic-stricken at sea scramble for the boats; she affronted, inscrutably, under stress, all the public concussions and ordeals; and yet, with that slim mystifying grace of her appearance, which defied you to say if she were a fair young woman who looked older through trouble, or a fine smooth older one who looked young through successful indifference; with her precious reference, above all, to memories and histories into which he could enter, she was as exquisite for him as some pale pressed flower (a rarity to begin with), and, failing other sweetnesses, she was a sufficient reward of his effort. They had communities of knowledge, "their" knowledge (this discriminating possessive was always on her lips) of presences of the other age, presences all overlaid, in his case, by the experience of a man and the freedom of a wanderer, overlaid by pleasure, by infidelity, by passages of life that were strange and dim to her, just by "Europe" in short, but still unobscured, still exposed and cherished, under that pious visitation of the spirit from which she had never been diverted.

She had come with him one day to see how his "apartment-house" was rising; he had helped her over gaps and explained to her plans, and while they were there had happened to have, before her, a brief but lively discussion with the man in charge, the representative of the building-firm that had undertaken his work. He had found himself quite "standing-up" to this personage over a failure on the latter's part to observe some detail of one of their noted conditions, and had so lucidly argued his case that, besides ever so prettily flushing, at the time, for sympathy in his triumph, she had afterwards said to him (though to a slightly greater effect of irony) that he had clearly for too many years neglected a real gift. If he had but stayed at home he would have anticipated the inventor of the skyscraper. If he had but stayed at home he would have discovered his genius in time really to start some new variety of awful architectural hare and run it till it burrowed in a gold mine. He was to remember these words, while the weeks elapsed, for the small silver ring they had sounded over the queerest and deepest of his own lately most disguised and most muffled vibrations.

It had begun to be present to him after the first fortnight, it had broken out with the oddest abruptness, this particular wanton wonderment: it met him there—and this was the image under which he himself judged the matter, or at least, not a little, thrilled and flushed with it—very much as he might have been met by some strange figure, some unexpected occupant, at a turn of one of the dim passages of an empty house. The quaint analogy quite hauntingly remained with him, when he didn't indeed rather improve it by a still intenser form: that of his opening a door behind which he would have made sure of finding nothing, a door into a room shuttered and void, and yet so coming, with a great suppressed start, on some quite erect confronting presence, something planted in the middle of the place and facing him through the dusk. After that visit to the house in construction he walked with his companion to see the other and always so much the better one, which in the eastward direction formed one of the corners, the "jolly" one precisely, of the street now so generally dishonoured and disfigured in its westward reaches, and of the comparatively conservative Avenue.[2] The Avenue still had pretensions, as Miss Staverton said, to decency; the old people had mostly gone, the old names were unknown, and here and there an old association seemed to stray, all vaguely, like some very aged person, out too late, whom you might meet and feel the impulse to watch or follow, in kindness, for safe restoration to shelter.

They went in together, our friends; he admitted himself with his key, as he kept no one there, he explained, preferring, for his reasons, to leave the place empty, under a simple arrangement with a good woman living in the neighbourhood and who came for a daily hour to open windows and dust and sweep. Spencer Brydon had his reasons and was growingly aware of them; they seemed to him better each time he was there, though he didn't name them all to his companion, any more than he told her as yet how often, how quite absurdly often, he himself came. He only let her see for the present, while they walked through the great blank rooms, that absolute vacancy reigned and that, from top to bottom, there was nothing but Mrs. Muldoon's broomstick, in a corner, to tempt the burglar. Mrs. Muldoon was then on the premises, and she loquaciously attended the visitors, preceding them from room to room and pushing back shutters and throwing up sashes—all to show them, as she remarked, how little there was to see. There was little indeed to see in the great gaunt shell where the main dispositions and the general apportionment of space, the style of an age of ampler allowances, had nevertheless for its master their honest pleading message, affecting him as some good old servant's, some lifelong retainer's appeal for a character, or even for a retiring-pension; yet it was also a remark of Mrs. Muldoon's that, glad as she was to oblige him by her noonday round, there was a request she greatly hoped he would never make of her. If he should wish her for any reason to come in after dark she would just tell him, if he "plased," that he must ask it of somebody else.

The fact that there was nothing to see didn't militate for the worthy woman against what one *might* see, and she put it frankly to Miss Staverton that no lady could be expected to like, could she? "craping up to thim top storeys in the ayvil hours." The gas and the electric light were off the house, and she fairly evoked a gruesome vision of her march through the great grey rooms—so many of them as there were too!—with her glimmering taper. Miss Staver-

2. The story is set in the area of Fifth Avenue and 14th Street in Manhattan, where James spent his childhood years.

This detail is one among many which make the story tantalizingly autobiographical.

ton met her honest glare with a smile and the profession that she herself certainly would recoil from such an adventure. Spencer Brydon meanwhile held his peace—for the moment; the question of the "evil" hours in his old home had already become too grave for him. He had begun some time since to "crape," and he knew just why a packet of candles addressed to that pursuit had been stowed by his own hand, three weeks before, at the back of a drawer of the fine old sideboard that occupied, as a "fixture," the deep recess in the dining-room. Just now he laughed at his companions—quickly however changing the subject; for the reason that, in the first place, his laugh struck him even at that moment as starting the odd echo, the conscious human resonance (he scarce knew how to qualify it) that sounds made while he was there alone sent back to his ear or his fancy; and that, in the second, he imagined Alice Staverton for the instant on the point of asking him, with a divination, if he ever so prowled. There were divinations he was unprepared for, and he had at all events averted enquiry by the time Mrs. Muldoon had left them, passing on to other parts.

There was happily enough to say, on so consecrated a spot, that could be said freely and fairly; so that a whole train of declarations was precipitated by his friend's having herself broken out, after a yearning look round: "But I hope you don't mean they want you to pull *this* to pieces!" His answer came, promptly, with his re-awakened wrath: it was of course exactly what they wanted, and what they were "at" him for, daily, with the iteration of people who couldn't for their life understand a man's liability to decent feelings. He had found the place, just as it stood and beyond what he could express, an interest and a joy. There were values other than the beastly rent-values, and in short, in short—! But it was thus Miss Staverton took him up. "In short you're to make so good a thing of your sky-scraper that, living in luxury on *those* ill-gotten gains, you can afford for a while to be sentimental here!" Her smile had for him, with the words, the particular mild irony with which he found half her talk suffused; an irony without bitterness and that came, exactly, from her having so much imagination—not, like the cheap sarcasms with which one heard most people, about the world of "society," bid for the reputation of cleverness, from nobody's really having any. It was agreeable to him at this very moment to be sure that when he had answered, after a brief demur, "Well, yes: so, precisely, you may put it!" her imagination would still do him justice. He explained that even if never a dollar were to come to him from the other house he would nevertheless cherish this one; and he dwelt, further, while they lingered and wandered, on the fact of the stupefaction he was already exciting, the positive mystification he felt himself create.

He spoke of the value of all he read into it, the mere sight of the walls, mere shapes of the rooms, mere sound of the floors, mere feel, in his hand, of the old silver-plate knobs of the several mahogany doors, which suggested the pressure of the palms of the dead; the seventy years of the past in fine that these things represented, the annals of nearly three generations, counting his grandfather's, the one that had ended there, and the impalpable ashes of his long-extinct youth, afloat in the very air like microscopic motes. She listened to everything; she was a woman who answered intimately but who utterly didn't chatter. She scattered abroad therefore no cloud of words; she could assent, she could agree, above all she could encourage, without doing that. Only at the last she went a little further than he had done himself. "And then how do you know? You may still, after all, want to live here." It rather indeed pulled him up, for it wasn't what he had been thinking, at least in her sense of the words. "You mean I may decide to stay on for the sake of it?"

"Well, *with* such a home—!" But, quite beautifully, she had too much tact to dot so monstrous an *i*, and it was precisely an illustration of the way she didn't rattle. How could any one—of any wit—insist on any one else's "wanting" to live in New York?

"Oh," he said, "I *might* have lived here (since I had my opportunity early in life); I might have put in here all these years. Then everything would have been different enough—and, I dare say, 'funny' enough. But that's another matter. And then the beauty of it—I mean of my perversity, of my refusal to agree to a 'deal'—is just in the total absence of a reason. Don't you see that if I had a reason about the matter at all it would *have* to be the other way, and would then be inevitably a reason of dollars? There are no reasons here *but* of dollars. Let us therefore have none whatever—not the ghost of one."

They were back in the hall then for departure, but from where they stood the vista was large, through an open door, into the great square main saloon, with its almost antique felicity of brave spaces between windows. Her eyes came back from that reach and met his own a moment. "Are you very sure the 'ghost' of one doesn't, much rather, serve—?"

He had a positive sense of turning pale. But it was as near as they were then to come. For he made answer, he believed, between a glare and a grin: "Oh ghosts—of course the place must swarm with them! I should be ashamed of it if it didn't. Poor Mrs. Muldoon's right, and it's why I haven't asked her to do more than look in."

Miss Staverton's gaze again lost itself, and things she didn't utter, it was clear, came and went in her mind. She might even for the minute, off there in the fine room, have imagined some element dimly gathering. Simplified like the death-mask of a handsome face, it perhaps produced for her just then an effect akin to the stir of an expression in the "set" commemorative plaster. Yet whatever her impression may have been she produced instead a vague platitude. "Well, if it were only furnished and lived in—!"

She appeared to imply that in case of its being still furnished he might have been a little less opposed to the idea of a return. But she passed straight into the vestibule, as if to leave her words behind her, and the next moment he had opened the house-door and was standing with her on the steps. He closed the door and, while he re-pocketed his key, looking up and down, they took in the compara-tively harsh actuality of the Avenue, which reminded him of the assault of the outer light of the Desert on the traveller emerging from an Egyptian tomb. But he risked before they stepped into the street his gathered answer to her speech. "For me it *is* lived in. For me it *is* furnished." At which it was easy for her to sigh "Ah yes—!" all vaguely and discreetly; since his parents and his favour-ite sister, to say nothing of other kin, in numbers, had run their course and met their end there. That represented, within the walls, ineffaceable life.

It was a few days after this that, during an hour passed with her again, he had expressed his impatience of the too flattering curiosity —among the people he met—about his appreciation of New York. He had arrived at none at all that was socially producible, and as for that matter of his "thinking" (thinking the better or the worse of anything there) he was wholly taken up with one subject of thought. It was mere vain egoism, and it was moreover, if she liked, a morbid obsession. He found all things come back to the question of what he personally might have been, how he might have led his life and "turned out," if he had not so, at the outset, given it up. And confessing for the first time to the intensity within him of this absurd speculation—which but proved also, no doubt, the habit of too selfishly thinking— he affirmed the impotence there of any other source of interest, any other native appeal. "What would it have made of me, what would it have made of me? I keep for ever wondering, all idiotically; as if I could possibly know! I see what it has made of dozens of others, those I meet, and it positively aches within me, to the point of exasperation, that it would have made something of me as well. Only I can't make out *what*, and the worry of it, the small rage of curiosity never to be satisfied, brings back what I remember to have felt, once or twice, after judging best, for reasons, to burn some important letter unopened. I've been sorry, I've hated it—I've never known what was in the letter. You may of course say it's a trifle—!"

"I don't say it's a trifle," Miss Staverton gravely interrupted.

She was seated by her fire, and before her, on his feet and rest-less, he turned to and fro between this intensity of his idea and a fitful and unseeing inspection, through his single eye-glass, of the dear little old objects on her chimney-piece. Her interruption made him for an instant look at her harder. "I shouldn't care if you did!" he laughed, however; "and it's only a figure, at any rate, for the way I now feel. *Not* to have followed my perverse young course—and almost in the teeth of my father's curse, as I may say; not to have kept it up, so, 'over there,' from that day to this, without a doubt or a pang; not, above all, to have liked it, to have loved it, so much, loved it, no doubt, with such an abysmal conceit of my own preference: some variation from *that*, I say, must have produced some different effect for my life and for my 'form.' I should have stuck here —if it had been possible; and I was too young, at twenty-three, to judge, *pour deux sous*,[3] whether it *were* possible. If I had waited I might have seen it was, and then I might have been, by staying here, something nearer to one of these types who have been hammered so hard and made so keen by their conditions. It isn't that I admire them so much—the question of any charm in them, or of any charm, beyond that of the rank money-passion, exerted by their conditions *for* them, has nothing to do with the matter: it's only a question of what fantastic, yet perfectly possible, development of my own nature I mayn't have missed. It comes over me that I had then a strange *alter ego* deep down somewhere within me, as the full-blown flower is in the small tight bud, and that I took the course, I just transferred him to the climate, that blighted him for once and for ever."

"And you wonder about the flower," Miss Staverton said. "So do I, if you want to know; and so I've been wondering these several weeks. I believe in the flower," she continued, "I feel it would have been quite splendid, quite huge and monstrous."

"Monstrous above all!" her visitor echoed; "and I imagine, by the same stroke, quite hideous and offensive."

"You don't believe that," she returned; "if you did you wouldn't wonder. You'd know, and that would be enough for you. What you feel—and what I feel *for* you—is that you'd have had power."

"You'd have liked me that way?" he asked.

She barely hung fire. "How should I not have liked you?"

"I see. You'd have liked me, have preferred me, a billionaire!"

"How should I not have liked you?" she simply again asked.

He stood before her still—her question kept him motionless. He took it in, so much there was of it; and indeed his not otherwise meeting it testified to that. "I know at least what I am," he simply went on; "the other side of the medal's clear enough. I've not been edifying—I believe I'm thought in a hundred quarters to have been barely decent. I've followed strange paths and worshipped strange gods; it must have come to you again and again—in fact you've admitted to me as much—that I was leading, at any time these thirty years, a selfish frivolous scandalous life. And you see what it has made of me."

She just waited, smiling at him. "You see what it has made of *me*."

3. "For two cents," i.e., with my limited experience.

"Oh you're a person whom nothing can have altered. You were born to be what you are, anywhere, anyway: you've the perfection nothing else could have blighted. And don't you see how, without my exile, I shouldn't have been waiting till now——?" But he pulled up for the strange pang.

"The great thing to see," she presently said, "seems to me to be that it has spoiled nothing. It hasn't spoiled your being here at last. It hasn't spoiled this. It hasn't spoiled your speaking——" She also however faltered.

He wondered at everything her controlled emotion might mean. "Do you believe then—too dreadfully!—that I *am* as good as I might ever have been?"

"Oh no! Far from it!" With which she got up from her chair and was nearer to him. "But I don't care," she smiled.

"You mean I'm good enough?"

She considered a little. "Will you believe it if I say so? I mean will you let that settle your question for you?" And then as if making out in his face that he drew back from this, that he had some idea which, however absurd, he couldn't yet bargain away: "Oh you don't care either—but very differently: you don't care for anything but yourself."

Spencer Brydon recognised it—it was in fact what he had absolutely professed. Yet he importantly qualified. "*He* isn't myself. He's the just so totally other person. But I do want to see him," he added. "And I can. And I shall."

Their eyes met for a minute while he guessed from something in hers that she divined his strange sense. But neither of them otherwise expressed it, and her apparent understanding, with no protesting shock, no easy derision, touched him more deeply than anything yet, constituting for his stifled perversity, on the spot, an element that was like breatheable air. What she said however was unexpected. "Well, *I've* seen him."

"You——?"

"I've seen him in a dream."

"Oh a 'dream'—!" It let him down.

"But twice over," she continued. "I saw him as I see you now."

"You've dreamed the same dream——?"

"Twice over," she repeated. "The very same."

This did somehow a little speak to him, as it also gratified him. "You dream about me at that rate?"

"Ah about *him!*" she smiled.

His eyes again sounded her. "Then you know all about him." And as she said nothing more: "What's the wretch like?"

She hesitated, and it was as if he were pressing her so hard that, resisting for reasons of her own, she had to turn away. "I'll tell you some other time!"

II

It was after this that there was most of a virtue for him, most of a cultivated charm, most of a preposterous secret thrill, in the particular form of surrender to his obsession and of address to what he more and more believed to be his privilege. It was what in these weeks he was living for—since he really felt life to begin but after Mrs. Muldoon had retired from the scene and, visiting the ample house from attic to cellar, making sure he was alone, he knew himself in safe possession and, as he tacitly expressed it, let himself go. He sometimes came twice in the twenty-four hours; the moments he liked best were those of gathering dusk, of the short autumn twilight; this was the time of which, again and again, he found himself hoping most. Then he could, as seemed to him, most intimately wander and wait, linger and listen, feel his fine attention, never in his life before so fine, on the pulse of the great vague place: he preferred the lampless hour and only wished he might have prolonged each day the deep crepuscular spell. Later—rarely much before midnight, but then for a considerable vigil—he watched with his glimmering light; moving slowly, holding it high, playing it far, rejoicing above all, as much as he might, in open vistas, reaches of communication between rooms and by passages; the long straight chance or show, as he would have called it, for the revelation he pretended to invite. It was a practice he found he could perfectly "work" without exciting remark; no one was in the least the wiser for it; even Alice Staverton, who was moreover a well of discretion, didn't quite fully imagine.

He let himself in and let himself out with the assurance of calm proprietorship; and accident so far favoured him that, if a fat Avenue "officer" had happened on occasion to see him entering at eleven-thirty, he had never yet, to the best of his belief, been noticed as emerging at two. He walked there on the crisp November nights, arrived regularly at the evening's end; it was as easy to do this after dining out as to take his way to a club or to his hotel. When he left his club, if he hadn't been dining out, it was ostensibly to go to his hotel; and when he left his hotel, if he had spent a part of the evening there, it was ostensibly to go to his club. Everything was easy in fine; everything conspired and promoted: there was truly even in the strain of his experience something that glossed over, something that salved and simplified, all the rest of consciousness. He circulated, talked, renewed, loosely and pleasantly, old relations—met indeed, so far as he could, new expectations and seemed to make out on the whole that in spite of the career, of such different contacts, which he had spoken of to Miss Staverton as ministering so little, for those who might have watched it, to edification, he was positively rather liked than not. He was a dim secondary social success—and all with people who had truly not an idea of him. It was all mere surface sound, this murmur of their welcome, this popping of their corks—just as his gestures of response were the extravagant shadows, emphatic in proportion as they meant little, of some game of *ombres chinoises*.[4] He projected himself all day, in thought, straight over the bristling line of hard unconscious heads and into the other, the real, the waiting life; the life that, as soon as he had heard behind him the click of his great house-door, began for him, on the jolly corner, as beguilingly as the slow opening bars of some rich music follows the tap of the conductor's wand.

He always caught the first effect of the steel point of his stick on the old marble of the hall pavement, large black-and-white squares that he remembered as the admiration of his childhood and that had then made in him, as he now saw, for the growth of an early conception of style. The effect was the dim reverberating tinkle as of some far-off bell hung who should say where?— in the depths of the house, of the past, of that mystical other world that might have flourished for him had he not, for weal or woe, abandoned it. On this impression he did ever the same thing; he put his stick noiselessly away in a corner—feeling the place once more in the likeness of some great glass bowl, all precious concave crystal, set delicately humming by the play of a moist finger round its edge. The concave crystal held, as it were, this mystical other world, and the indescribably fine murmur of its rim was the sigh there, the scarce audible pathetic wail to his strained ear, of all the old baffled forsworn possibilities. What he did therefore by this appeal of his hushed presence was to wake them into such measure of ghostly life as they might still enjoy. They were shy, all but unappeasably shy, but they weren't really sinister; at least they weren't as he had hitherto felt them—before they had taken the Form he so yearned to make them take, the Form he at moments saw himself in the light of fairly hunting on tiptoe, the points of his evening-shoes, from room to room and from storey to storey.

That was the essence of his vision—which was all rank folly, if one would, while he was out of the house and otherwise occupied, but which took on the last verisimilitude as soon as he was placed and posted. He knew what he meant and what he wanted; it was as clear as the figure on a cheque presented in demand for cash. His *alter ego* "walked"—that was the note of his image of him, while his image of his motive for his own odd pastime was the desire to waylay him and meet him. He roamed, slowly, warily, but all restlessly, he himself did—Mrs. Muldoon had been right, absolutely, with her figure of their "craping"; and the presence he watched for would roam restlessly too. But it would be as cautious and as shifty; the conviction of its probable, in fact its already quite sensible, quite audible evasion of pursuit grew for him from night to night,

4. I.e., Oriental shadow plays.

laying on him finally a rigour to which nothing in his life had been comparable. It had been the theory of many superficially-judging persons, he knew, that he was wasting that life in a surrender to sensations, but he had tasted of no pleasure so fine as his actual tension, had been introduced to no sport that demanded at once the patience and the nerve of this stalking of a creature more subtle, yet at bay perhaps more formidable, than any beast of the forest. The terms, the comparisons, the very practices of the chase positively came again into play; there were even moments when passages of his occasional experience as a sportsman, stirred memories, from his younger time, of moor and mountain and desert, revived for him— and to the increase of his keenness—by the tremendous force of analogy. He found himself at moments—once he had placed his single light on some mantel-shelf or in some recess—stepping back into shelter or shade, effacing himself behind a door or in an embrasure, as he had sought of old the vantage of rock and tree; he found himself holding his breath and living in the joy of the instant, the supreme suspense created by big game alone.

He wasn't afraid (though putting himself the question as he believed gentlemen on Bengal tiger-shoots or in close quarters with the great bear of the Rockies had been known to confess to having put it); and this indeed—since here at least he might be frank!— because of the impression, so intimate and so strange, that he himself produced as yet a dread, produced certainly a strain, beyond the liveliest he was likely to feel. They fell for him into categories, they fairly became familiar, the signs, for his own perception, of the alarm his presence and his vigilance created; though leaving him always to remark, portentously, on his probably having formed a relation, his probably enjoying a consciousness, unique in the experience of man. People enough, first and last, had been in terror of apparitions, but who had ever before so turned the tables and become himself, in the apparitional world, an incalculable terror? He might have found this sublime had he quite dared to think of it; but he didn't too much insist, truly, on that side of his privilege. With habit and repetition he gained to an extraordinary degree the power to penetrate the dusk of distances and the darkness of corners, to resolve back into their innocence the treacheries of uncertain light, the evil-looking forms taken in the gloom by mere shadows, by accidents of the air, by shifting effects of perspective; putting down his dim luminary he could still wander on without it, pass into other rooms and, only knowing it was there behind him in case of need, see his way about, visually project for his purpose a comparative clearness. It made him feel, this acquired faculty, like some monstrous stealthy cat; he wondered if he would have glared at these moments with large shining yellow eyes, and what it mightn't verily be, for the poor hard-pressed *alter ego,* to be confronted with such a type.

He liked however the open shutters; he opened everywhere those Mrs. Muldoon had closed, closing them as carefully afterwards, so that she shouldn't notice: he liked—oh this he did like, and above all in the upper rooms!—the sense of the hard silver of the autumn stars through the window-panes, and scarcely less the flare of the street-lamps below, the white electric lustre which it would have taken curtains to keep out. This was human actual social; this was of the world he had lived in, and he was more at his ease certainly for the countenance, coldly general and impersonal, that all the while and in spite of his detachment it seemed to give him. He had support of course mostly in the rooms at the wide front and the prolonged side; it failed him considerably in the central shades and the parts of the back. But if he sometimes, on his rounds, was glad of his optical reach, so none the less often the rear of the house affected him as the very jungle of his prey. The place was there more subdivided; a large "extension" in particular, where small rooms for servants had been multiplied, abounded in nooks and corners, in closets and passages, in the ramifications especially of an ample back staircase over which he leaned, many a time, to look far down—not deterred from his gravity even while aware that he might, for a spectator, have figured some solemn simpleton playing at hide-and-seek. Outside in fact he might himself make that ironic *rapprochement*;[5] but within the walls, and in spite of the clear windows, his consistency was proof against the cynical light of New York.

It had belonged to that idea of the exasperated consciousness of his victim to become a real test for him; since had quite put it to himself from the first that, oh distinctly! he could "cultivate" his whole perception. He had felt it as above all open to cultivation—which indeed was but another name for his manner of spending his time. He was bringing it on, bringing it to perfection, by practice; in consequence of which it had grown so fine that he was now aware of impressions, attestations of his general postulate, that couldn't have broken upon him at once. This was the case more specifically with a phenomenon at last quite frequent for him in the upper rooms, the recognition—absolutely unmistakeable, and by a turn dating from a particular hour, his resumption of his campaign after a diplomatic drop, a calculated absence of three nights—of his being definitely followed, tracked at a distance carefully taken and to the express end that he should the less confidently, less arrogantly, appear to himself merely to pursue. It worried, it finally quite broke him up, for it proved, of all the conceivable impressions, the one least suited to his book. He was kept in sight while remaining himself—as regards the essence of his position—sightless, and his only recourse then was in abrupt turns, rapid recoveries of ground. He wheeled about, retracing his steps, as if he might so catch in his face at least the stirred air of some other quick revolution. It was

5. Reconciliation.

indeed true that his fully dislocalised thought of these manœuvres recalled to him Pantaloon, at the Christmas farce, buffeted and tricked from behind by ubiquitous Harlequin;[6] but it left intact the influence of the conditions themselves each time he was re-exposed to them, so that in fact this association, had he suffered it to become constant, would on a certain side have but ministered to his intenser gravity. He had made, as I have said, to create on the premises the baseless sense of a reprieve, his three absences; and the result of the third was to confirm the after-effect of the second.

On his return, that night—the night succeeding his last intermission—he stood in the hall and looked up the staircase with a certainty more intimate than any he had yet known. "He's *there*, at the top, and waiting—not, as in general, falling back for disappearance. He's holding his ground, and it's the first time—which is a proof, isn't it? that something has happened for him." So Brydon argued with his hand on the banister and his foot on the lowest stair; in which position he felt as never before the air chilled by his logic. He himself turned cold in it, for he seemed of a sudden to know what now was involved. "Harder pressed?—yes, he takes it in, with its thus making clear to him that I've come, as they say, 'to stay.' He finally doesn't like and can't bear it, in the sense, I mean, that his wrath, his menaced interest, now balances with his dread. I've hunted him till he has 'turned': that, up there, is what has happened—he's the fanged or the antlered animals brought at last to bay." There came to him, as I say—but determined by an influence beyond my notation!—the acuteness of this certainty; under which however the next moment he had broken into a sweat that he would as little have consented to attribute to fear as he would have dared immediately to act upon it for enterprise. It marked none the less a prodigious thrill, a thrill that represented sudden dismay, no doubt, but also represented, and with the selfsame throb, the strangest, the most joyous, possibly the next minute almost the proudest, duplication of consciousness.

"He has been dodging, retreating, hiding, but now, worked up to anger, he'll fight!"—this intense impression made a single mouthful, as it were, of terror and applause. But what was wondrous was that the applause, for the felt fact, was so eager, since, if it was his other self he was running to earth, this ineffable identity was thus in the last resort not unworthy of him. It bristled there—somewhere near at hand, however unseen still—as the hunted thing, even as the trodden worm of the adage *must* at last bristle; and Brydon at this instant tasted probably of a sensation more complex than had ever before found itself consistent with sanity. It was as if it would have shamed him that a character so associated with his own should triumphantly succeed in just skulking, should to the

6. Harlequin is a character in comedy and pantomime who plays tricks on Pantaloon, a lean, old dotard.

end not risk the open; so that the drop of his danger was, on the spot, a great lift of the whole situation. Yet with another rare shift of the same subtlety he was already trying to measure by how much more he himself might now be in peril of fear; so rejoicing that he could, in another form, actively inspire that fear, and simultaneously quaking for the form in which he might passively know it.

The apprehension of knowing it must after a little have grown in him, and the strangest moment of his adventure perhaps, the most memorable or really most interesting, afterwards, of his crisis, was the lapse of certain instants of concentrated conscious *combat*, the sense of a need to hold on to something, even after the manner of a man slipping and slipping on some awful incline; the vivid impulse, above all, to move, to act, to charge, somehow and upon something —to show himself, in a word, that he wasn't afraid. The state of "holding-on" was thus the state to which he was momentarily reduced; if there had been anything, in the great vacancy, to seize, he would presently have been aware of having clutched it as he might under a shock at home have clutched the nearest chair-back. He had been surprised at any rate—of this he *was* aware—into something unprecedented since his original appropriation of the place; he had closed his eyes, held them tight, for a long minute, as with that instinct of dismay and that terror of vision. When he opened them the room, the other contiguous rooms, extraordinarily, seemed lighter—so light, almost, that at first he took the change for day. He stood firm, however that might be, just where he had paused; his resistance had helped him—it was as if there were something he had tided over. He knew after a little what this was—it had been in the imminent danger of flight. He had stiffened his will against going; without this he would have made for the stairs, and it seemed to him that, still with his eyes closed, he would have descended them, would have known how, straight and swiftly, to the bottom.

Well, as he had held out, here he was—still at the top, among the more intricate upper rooms and with the gauntlet of the others, of all the rest of the house, still to run when it should be his time to go. He would go at his time—only at his time: didn't he go every night very much at the same hour? He took out his watch— there was light for that: it was scarcely a quarter past one, and he had never withdrawn so soon. He reached his lodgings for the most part at two—with his walk of a quarter of an hour. He would wait for the last quarter—he wouldn't stir till then; and he kept his watch there with his eyes on it, reflecting while he held it that this deliberate wait, a wait with an effort, which he recognised, would serve perfectly for the attestation he desired to make. It would prove his courage—unless indeed the latter might most be proved by his budging at last from his place. What he mainly felt now was that, since he hadn't originally scuttled, he had his dignities—which had never in his life seemed so many—all to preserve and to carry aloft. This was before him in truth as a physical image, an image almost worthy of an age of greater romance. That remark indeed glimmered for him only to glow the next instant with a finer light; since what age of romance, after all, could have matched either the state of his mind or, "objectively," as they said, the wonder of his situation? The only difference would have been that, brandishing his dignities over his head as in a parchment scroll, he might then— that is in the heroic time—have proceeded downstairs with a drawn sword in his other grasp.

At present, really, the light he had set down on the mantel of the next room would have to figure his sword; which utensil, in the course of a minute, he had taken the requisite number of steps to possess himself of. The door between the rooms was open, and from the second another door opened to a third. These rooms, as he remembered, gave all three upon a common corridor as well, but there was a fourth, beyond them, without issue save through the preceding. To have moved, to have heard his step again, was appreciably a help; though even in recognising this he lingered once more a little by the chimney-piece on which his light had rested. When he next moved, just hesitating where to turn, he found himself considering a circumstance that, after his first and comparatively vague apprehension of it, produced in him the start that often attends some pang of recollection, the violent shock of having ceased happily to forget. He had come into sight of the door in which the brief chain of communication ended and which he now surveyed from the nearer threshold, the one not directly facing it. Placed at some distance to the left of this point, it would have admitted him to the last room of the four, the room without other approach or egress, had it not, to his intimate conviction, been closed *since* his former visitation, the matter probably of a quarter of an hour before. He stared with all his eyes at the wonder of the fact, arrested again where he stood and again holding his breath while he sounded its sense. Surely it had been *subsequently* closed—that is it had been on his previous passage indubitably open!

He took it full in the face that something had happened between —that he couldn't not have noticed before (by which he meant on his original tour of all the rooms that evening) that such a barrier had exceptionally presented itself. He had indeed since that moment undergone an agitation so extraordinary that it might have muddled for him any earlier view; and he tried to convince himself that he might perhaps then have gone into the room and, inadvertently, automatically, on coming out, have drawn the door after him. The difficulty was that this exactly was what he never did; it was against his whole policy, as he might have said, the essence of which was to keep vistas clear. He had them from the first, as he was well aware, quite on the brain: the strange apparition, at the far end of one of them, of his baffled "prey" (which had become by so sharp an irony so little the term now to apply!) was the form of success his imagination had most cherished, projecting into it always a refinement of beauty. He had known fifty times the start of perception that had afterwards dropped; had fifty times gasped to himself "There!" under some fond brief hallucination. The house, as the case stood, admirably lent itself; he might wonder at the taste, the native architecture of the particular time, which could rejoice so in the multiplication of doors—the opposite extreme to the modern, the actual almost complete proscription of them; but it had fairly contributed to provoke this obsession of the presence encountered telescopically, as he might say, focussed and studied in diminishing perspective and as by a rest for the elbow.

It was with these considerations that his present attention was charged—they perfectly availed to make what he saw portentous. He *couldn't*, by any lapse, have blocked that aperture; and if he hadn't, if it was unthinkable, why what else was clear but that there had been another agent? Another agent?—he had been catching, as he felt, a moment back, the very breath of him; but when had he been so close as in this simple, this logical, this completely personal act? It was so logical, that is, that one might have *taken* it for personal; yet for what did Brydon take it, he asked himself, while, softly panting, he felt his eyes almost leave their sockets. Ah this time at last they *were*, the two, the opposed projections of him, in presence; and this time, as much as one would, the question of danger loomed. With it rose, as not before, the question of courage—for what he knew the blank face of the door to say to him was "Show us how much you have!" It stared, it glared back at him with that challenge; it put to him the two alternatives: should he just push it open or not? Oh to have this consicousness was to *think*—and to think, Brydon knew, as he stood there, was, with the lapsing moments, not to have acted! Not to have acted—that was the misery and the pang—was even still not to act; was in fact *all* to feel the thing in another, in a new and terrible way. How long did he pause and how long did he debate? There was presently nothing to measure it; for his vibration had already changed—as just by the effect of its intensity. Shut up there, at bay, defiant, and with the prodigy of the thing palpably proveably *done*, thus giving notice like some stark signboard—under that accession of accent the situation itself had turned; and Brydon at last remarkably made up his mind on what it had turned to.

It had turned altogether to a different admonition; to a supreme hint, for him, of the value of Discretion! This slowly dawned, no doubt—for it could take its time; so perfectly, on his threshold, had he been stayed, so little as yet had he either advanced or retreated. It was the strangest of all things that now when, by his taking ten steps and applying his hand to a latch, or even his shoulder and his knee, if necessary, to a panel, all the hunger of his prime need might have been met, his high curiosity crowned, his unrest assuaged—it was amazing, but it was also exquisite and rare, that insistence should have, at a touch, quite dropped from him. Discretion—he jumped at that; and yet not, verily, at such a pitch, because it saved his nerves or his skin, but because, much more valuably, it saved the situation. When I say he "jumped" at it I feel the consonance of this term with the fact that—at the end indeed of I know not how long—he did move again, he crossed straight to the door. He wouldn't touch it—it seemed now that he might *if* he would: he would only just wait there a little, to show, to prove, that he wouldn't. He had thus another station, close to the thin partition by which revelation was denied him; but with his eyes bent and his hands held off in a mere intensity of stillness. He listened as if there had been something to hear, but this attitude, while it lasted, was his own communication. "If you won't then—good: I spare you and I give up. You affect me as by the appeal positively for pity: you convince me that for reasons rigid and sublime—what do I know?—we both of us should have suffered. I respect them then, and, though moved and privileged as, I believe, it has never been given to man, I retire, I renounce—never, on my honour, to try again. So rest for ever—and let *me!*"

That, for Brydon was the deep sense of this last demonstration—solemn, measured, directed, as he felt it to be. He brought it to a close, he turned away; and now verily he knew how deeply he had been stirred. He retraced his steps, taking up his candle, burnt, he observed, well-nigh to the socket, and marking again, lighten it as he would, the distinctness of his footfall; after which in a moment, he knew himself at the other side of the house. He did here what he had not yet done at these hours—he opened half a casement, one of those in the front, and let in the air of the night; a thing he would have taken at any time previous for a sharp rupture of his spell. His spell was broken now, and it didn't matter—broken by his concession and his surrender, which made it idle henceforth that he should ever come back. The empty street—its other life so marked even by the great lamplit vacancy—was within call, within touch; he stayed there as to be in it again, high above it though he was still perched; he watched as for some comforting common fact, some vulgar human note, the passage of a scavenger or a thief, some night-bird however base. He would have blessed that sign of life; he would have welcomed positively the slow approach of his friend the policeman, whom he had hitherto only sought to avoid, and was not sure that if the patrol had come into sight he mightn't have felt the impulse to get into relation with it, to hail it, on some pretext, from his fourth floor.

The pretext that wouldn't have been too silly or too compromising, the explanation that would have saved his dignity and kept his name, in such a case, out of the papers, was not definite to him: he was so occupied with the thought of recording his Discretion—as an effect of the vow he had just uttered to his intimate adversary— that the importance of this loomed large and something had over- taken all ironically his sense of proportion. If there had been a ladder applied to the front of the house, even one of the vertiginous perpendiculars employed by painters and roofers and sometimes left standing overnight, he would have managed somehow, astride of the windowsill, to compass by outstretched leg and arm that mode of descent. If there had been some such uncanny thing as he had found in his room at hotels, a workable fire-escape in the form of notched cable or a canvas shoot, he would have availed himself of it as a proof—well, of his present delicacy. He nursed that sentiment, as the question stood, a little in vain, and even—at the end of he scarce knew, once more, how long—found it, as by the action on his mind of the failure of response of the outer world, sinking back to vague anguish. It seemed to him he had waited an age for some stir of the great grim hush; the life of the town was itself under a spell —so unnaturally, up and down the whole prospect of known and rather ugly objects, the blankness and the silence lasted. Had they ever, he asked himself, the hard-faced houses, which had begun to look livid in the dim dawn, had they ever spoken so little to any need of his spirit? Great builded voids, great crowded stillnesses put on, often, in the heart of cities, for the small hours, a sort of sinister mask, and it was of this large collective negation that Brydon pres- ently became conscious—all the more that the break of day was, almost incredibly, now at hand, proving to him what a night he had made of it.

He looked again at his watch, saw what had become of his time- values (he had taken hours for minutes—not, as in other tense situ- ations, minutes for hours) and the strange air of the streets was but the weak, the sullen flush of a dawn in which everything was still locked up. His choked appeal from his own open window had been the sole note of life, and he could but break off at last as for a worse despair. Yet while so deeply demoralised he was capable again of an impulse denoting—at least by his present measure—extraordi- nary resolution; of retracing his steps to the spot where he had turned cold with the extinction of his last pulse of doubt as to there being in the place another presence than his own. This required an effort strong enough to sicken him; but he had his reason, which overmas- tered for the moment everything else. There was the whole of the rest of the house to traverse, and how should he screw himself to that if the door he had seen closed were at present open? He could hold to the idea that the closing had practically been for him an act of mercy, a chance offered him to descend, depart, get off the ground and never again profane it. This conception held together, it worked; but what it meant for him depended now clearly on the amount of forbearance his recent action, or rather his recent inaction, had engendered. The image of the "presence," whatever it was, waiting there for him to go—this image had not yet been so concrete for his nerves as when he stopped short of the point at which certainty would have come to him. For, with all his resolution, or more exactly with all his dread, he did stop short—he hung back from really seeing. The risk was too great and his fear too definite: it took at this moment an awful specific form.

He knew—yes, as he had never known anything—that, *should* he see the door open, it would all too abjectly be the end of him. It would mean that the agent of his shame—for his shame was the deep abjection—was once more at large and in general possession; and what glared him thus in the face was the act that this would determine for him. It would send him straight about to the window he had left open, and by that window, be long ladder and dangling rope as absent as they would, he saw himself uncontrollably insanely fatally take his way to the street. The hideous chance of this he at least could avert; but he could only avert it by recoiling in time from assurance. He had the whole house to deal with, this fact was still there; only he now knew that uncertainty alone could start him. He stole back from where he had checked himself—merely to do so was suddenly like safety—and, making blindly for the greater staircase, left gaping rooms and sounding passages behind. Here was the top of the stairs, with a fine large dim descent and three spacious landings to mark off. His instinct was all for mildness, but his feet were harsh on the floors, and, strangely, when he had in a couple of minutes become aware of this, it counted somehow for help. He couldn't have spoken, the tone of his voice would have scared him, and the common conceit or resource of "whistling in the dark" (whether literally or figuratively) have appeared basely vulgar; yet he liked none the less to hear himself go, and when he had reached his first landing—taking it all with no rush, but quite steadily—that stage of success drew from him a gasp of relief.

The house, withal, seemed immense, the scale of space again inordinate; the open rooms, to no one of which his eyes deflected, gloomed in their shuttered state like mouths of caverns; only the high skylight that formed the crown of the deep well created for him a medium in which he could advance, but which might have been, for queerness of colour, some watery under-world. He tried to think of something noble, as that his property was really grand, a splendid possession; but this nobleness took the form too of the clear delight with which he was finally to sacrifice it. They might come in now, the builders, the destroyers—they might come as soon as they would. At the end of two flights he had dropped to another zone, and from the middle of the third, with only one more left, he recognised the influence of the lower windows, of half-drawn blinds, of the occasional gleam of street-lamps, of the glazed spaces of the

vestibule. This was the bottom of the sea, which showed an illumination of its own and which he even saw paved—when at a given
moment he drew up to sink a long look over the banisters—with
the marble squares of his childhood. By that time indubitably he
felt, as he might have said in a commoner cause, better; it had
allowed him to stop and draw breath; and the ease increased with
the sight of the old black-and-white slabs. But what he most felt
was that now surely, with the element of impunity pulling him as
by hard firm hands, the case was settled for what he might have
seen above had he dared that last look. The closed door, blessedly
remote now, was still closed—and he had only in short to reach
that of the house.

He came down further, he crossed the passage forming the access
to the last flight; and if here again he stopped an instant it was
almost for the sharpness of the thrill of assured escape. It made him
shut his eyes—which opened again to the straight slope of the
remainder of the stairs. Here was impunity still, but impunity almost
excessive; inasmuch as the sidelights and the high fan-tracery of the
entrance were glimmering straight into the hall; an appearance produced, he the next instant saw, by the fact that the vestibule gaped
wide, that the hinged halves of the inner door had been thrown far
back. Out of that again the *question* sprang at him, making his
eyes, as he felt, half-start from his head, as they had done, at the
top of the house, before the sign of the other door. If he had left
that one open, hadn't he left this one closed, and wasn't he now in
most immediate presence of some inconceivable occult activity? It
was as sharp, the question, as a knife in his side, but the answer
hung fire still and seemed to lose itself in the vague darkness to
which the thin admitted dawn, glimmering archwise over the whole
outer door, made a semicircular margin, a cold silvery nimbus that
seemed to play a little as he looked—to shift and expand and contract.

It was as if there had been something within it, protected by
indistinctness and corresponding in extent with the opaque surface
behind, the painted panels of the last barrier to his escape, of which
the key was in his pocket. The indistinctness mocked him even
while he stared, affected him as somehow shrouding or challenging
certitude, so that after faltering an instant on his step he let himself
go with the sense that here *was* at last something to meet, to touch,
to take, to know—something all unnatural and dreadful, but to
advance upon which was the condition for him either of liberation
or of supreme defeat. The penumbra, dense and dark, was the virtual screen of a figure which stood in it as still as some image erect
in a niche or as some black-vizored sentinel guarding a treasure.
Brydon was to know afterwards, was to recall and make out, the
particular thing he had believed during the rest of his descent. He
saw, in its great grey glimmering margin, the central vagueness di-

minish, and he felt it to be taking the very form toward which, for so
many days, the passion of his curiosity had yearned. It gloomed, it
loomed, it was something, it was somebody, the prodigy of a personal presence.

Rigid and conscious, spectral yet human, a man of his own substance and stature waited there to measure himself with his power
to dismay. This only could it be—this only till he recognised, with
his advance, that what made the face dim was the pair of raised
hands that covered it and in which, so far from being offered in
defiance, it was buried as for dark deprecation. So Brydon, before
him, took him in; with every fact of him now, in the higher light,
hard and acute—his planted stillness, his vivid truth, his grizzled
bent head and white masking hands, his queer actuality of evening-
dress, of dangling double eye-glass, of gleaming silk lappet and
white linen, of pearl button and gold watch-guard and polished
shoe. No portrait by a great modern master could have presented
him with more intensity, thrust him out of his frame with more art,
as if there had been "treatment," of the consummate sort, in his
every shade and salience. The revulsion, for our friend, had become,
before he knew it, immense—this drop, in the act of apprehension,
to the sense of his adversary's inscrutable manœuvre. That meaning
at least, while he gaped, it offered him; for he could but gape at his
other self in this other anguish, gape as a proof that *he*, standing
there for the achieved, the enjoyed, the triumphant life, couldn't be
faced in his triumph. Wasn't the proof in the splendid covering
hands, strong and completely spread?—so spread and so intentional
that, in spite of a special verity that surpassed every other, the fact
that one of these hands had lost two fingers, which were reduced to
stumps, as if accidentally shot away, the face was effectually
guarded and saved.

"Saved," though, *would* it be?—Brydon breathed his wonder till
the very impunity of his attitude and the very insistence of his eyes
produced, as he felt, a sudden stir which showed the next instant as
a deeper portent, while the head raised itself, the betrayal of a
braver purpose. The hands, as he looked, began to move, to open;
then, as if deciding in a flash, dropped from the face and left it
uncovered and presented. Horror, with the sight, had leaped into
Brydon's throat, gasping there in a sound he couldn't utter; for the
bared identity was too hideous as *his*, and his glare was the passion
of his protest. The face, *that* face, Spencer Brydon's?—he searched
it still, but looking away from it in dismay and denial, falling
straight from his height of sublimity. It was unknown, inconceivable, awful, disconnected from any possibility—! He had been
"sold," he inwardly moaned, stalking such game as this: the presence before him was a presence, the horror within him a horror, but
the waste of his nights had been only grotesque and the success of
his adventure an irony. Such an identity fitted his at *no* point, made

its alternative monstrous. A thousand times yes, as it came upon him nearer now—the face was the face of a stranger. It came upon him nearer now, quite as one of those expanding fantastic images projected by the magic lantern of childhood; for the stranger, whoever he might be, evil, odious, blatant, vulgar, had advanced as for aggression, and he knew himself give ground. Then harder pressed still, sick with the force of his shock, and falling back as under the hot breath and the roused passion of a life larger than his own, a rage of personality before which his own collapsed, he felt the whole vision turn to darkness and his very feet give way. His head went round; he was going; he had gone.

III

What had next brought him back, clearly—though after how long?—was Mrs. Muldoon's voice, coming to him from quite near, from so near that he seemed presently to see her as kneeling on the ground before him while he lay looking up at her; himself not wholly on the ground, but half-raised and upheld—conscious, yes, of tenderness of support and, more particularly, of a head pillowed in extraordinary softness and faintly refreshing fragrance. He considered, he wondered, his wit but half at his service; then another face intervened, bending more directly over him, and he finally knew that Alice Staverton had made her lap an ample and perfect cushion to him, and that she had to this end seated herself on the lowest degree of the staircase, the rest of his long person remaining stretched on his old black-and-white slabs. They were cold, these marble squares of his youth; but *he* somehow was not, in this rich return of consciousness—the most wonderful hour, little by little, that he had ever known, leaving him, as it did, so gratefully, so abysmally passive, and yet as with a treasure of intelligence waiting all round him for quiet appropriation; dissolved, he might call it, in the air of the place and producing the golden glow of a late autumn afternoon. He had come back, yes—come back from further away than any man but himself had ever travelled; but it was strange how with this sense what he had come back *to* seemed really the great thing, and as if his prodigious journey had been all for the sake of it. Slowly but surely his consciousness grew, his vision of his state thus completing itself: he had been miraculously *carried* back—lifted and carefully borne as from where he had been picked up, the uttermost end of an interminable grey passage. Even with this he was suffered to rest, and what had now brought him to knowledge was the break in the long mild motion.

It had brought him to knowledge, to knowledge—yes, this was the beauty of his state; which came to resemble more and more that of a man who has gone to sleep on some news of a great inheritance, and then, after dreaming it away, after profaning it with matters strange to it, has waked up again to serenity of certitude and has only to lie and watch it grow. This was the drift of his patience —that he had only to let it shine on him. He must moreover, with intermissions, still have been lifted and borne; since why and how else should he have known himself, later on, with the afternoon glow intenser, no longer at the foot of his stairs—situated as these now seemed at that dark other end of his tunnel—but on a deep window-bench of his high saloon, over which had been spread, couch-fashion, a mantle of soft stuff lined with grey fur that was familiar to his eyes and that one of his hands kept fondly feeling as for its pledge of truth. Mrs. Muldoon's face had gone, but the other, the second he had recognised, hung over him in a way that showed how he was still propped and pillowed. He took it all in, and the more he took it the more it seemed to suffice: he was as much at peace as if he had had food and drink. It was the two women who had found him, on Mrs. Muldoon's having plied, at her usual hour, her latch-key—and on her having above all arrived while Miss Staverton still lingered near the house. She had been turning away, all anxiety, from worrying the vain bell-handle—her calculation having been of the hour of the good woman's visit; but the latter, blessedly, had come up while she was still there, and they had entered together. He had then lain, beyond the vestibule, very much as he was lying now—quite, that is, as he appeared to have fallen, but all so wondrously without bruise or gash; only in a depth of stupor. What he most took in, however, at present, with the steadier clearance, was that Alice Staverton had for a long unspeakable moment not doubted he was dead.

"It must have been that I *was*." He made it out as she held him. "Yes—I can only have died. You brought me literally to life. Only," he wondered, his eyes rising to her, "only, in the name of all the benedictions, how?"

It took her but an instant to bend her face and kiss him, and something in the manner of it, and in the way her hands clasped and locked his head while he felt the cool charity and virtue of her lips, something in all this beatitude somehow answered everything. "And now I keep you," she said.

"Oh keep me, keep me!" he pleaded while her face still hung over him: in response to which it dropped again and stayed close, clingingly close. It was the seal of their situation—of which he tasted the impress for a long blissful moment in silence. But he came back. "Yet how did you know—?"

"I was uneasy. You were to have come, you remember—and you had sent no word."

"Yes, I remember—I was to have gone to you at one to-day." It caught on to their "old" life and relation—which were so near and so far. "I was still out there in my strange darkness—where was it, what was it? I must have stayed there so long." He could but wonder at depth and the duration of his swoon.

"Since last night?" she asked with a shade of fear for her possible indiscretion.

"Since this morning—it must have been: the cold dim dawn of to-day. Where have I been," he vaguely wailed, "where have I been?" He felt her hold him close, and it was as if this helped him now to make in all security his mild moan. "What a long dark day!"

All in her tenderness she had waited a moment. "In the cold dim dawn?" she quavered.

But he had already gone on piecing together the parts of the whole prodigy. "As I didn't turn up you came straight—?"

She barely cast about. "I went first to your hotel—where they told me of your absence. You had dined out last evening and hadn't been back since. But they appeared to know you had been at your club."

"So you had the idea of *this*—?"

"Of what?" she asked in a moment.

"Well—of what has happened."

"I believed at least you'd have been here. I've known, all along," she said, "that you've been coming."

" 'Known' it—?"

"Well, I've believed it. I said nothing to you after that talk we had a month ago—but I felt sure. I knew you *would*," she declared.

"That I'd persist, you mean?"

"That you'd see him."

"Ah but I didn't!" cried Brydon with his long wail. "There's somebody—an awful beast; whom I brought, too horribly, to bay. But it's not me."

At this she bent over him again, and her eyes were in his eyes. "No—it's not you." And it was as if, while her face hovered, he might have made out in it, hadn't it been so near, some particular meaning blurred by a smile. "No, thank heaven," she repeated—"it's not you! Of course it wasn't to have been."

"Ah but it *was*," he gently insisted. And he stared before him now as he had been staring for so many weeks. "I was to have known myself."

"You couldn't!" she returned consolingly. And then reverting, and as if to account further for what she had herself done, "But it wasn't only *that*, that you hadn't been at home," she went on. "I waited till the hour at which we had found Mrs. Muldoon that day of my going with you; and she arrived, as I've told you, while, failing to bring any one to the door, I lingered in my despair on the steps. After a little, if she hadn't come, by such a mercy, I should have found means to hunt her up. But it wasn't," said Alice Staverton, as if once more with her fine intention—"it wasn't only that."

His eyes, as he lay, turned back to her. "What more then?"

She met it, the wonder she had stirred. "In the cold dim dawn, you say? Well, in the cold dim dawn of this morning I too saw you."

"Saw *me*—?"

"Saw *him*," said Alice Staverton. "It must have been at the same moment."

He lay an instant taking it in—as if he wished to be quite reasonable. "At the same moment?"

"Yes—in my dream again, the same one I've named to you. He came back to me. Then I knew it for a sign. He had come to you."

At this Brydon raised himself; he had to see her better. She helped him when she understood his movements, and he sat up, steadying himself beside her there on the window-bench and with his right hand grasping her left. "*He* didn't come to me."

"You came to yourself," she beautifully smiled.

"Ah I've come to myself now—thanks to you, dearest. But this brute, with his awful face—this brute's a black stranger. He's none of *me*, even as I *might* have been," Brydon sturdily declared.

But she kept the clearness that was like the breath of infallibility. "Isn't the whole point that you'd have been different?"

He almost scowled for it. "As different as *that*—?"

Her look again was more beautiful to him than the things of this world. "Haven't you exactly wanted to know *how* different? So this morning," she said, "you appeared to me."

"Like *him*?"

"A black stranger!"

"Then how did you know it was I?"

"Because, as I told you weeks ago, my mind, my imagination, had worked so over what you might, what you mightn't have been —to show you, you see, how I've thought of you. In the midst of that you came to me—that my wonder might be answered. So I knew," she went on; "and believed that, since the question held you too so fast, as you told me that day, you too would see for yourself. And when this morning I again saw I knew it would be because you had—and also then, from the first moment, because you somehow wanted me. *He* seemed to tell me of that. So why," she strangely smiled, "shouldn't I like him?"

It brought Spencer Brydon to his feet. "You 'like' that horror—?"

"I *could* have liked him. And to me," she said, "he was no horror. I had accepted him."

" 'Accepted'—?" Brydon oddly sounded.

"Before, for the interest of his difference—yes. And as *I* didn't disown him, as *I* knew him—which you at last, confronted with him in his difference, so cruelly didn't, my dear—well, he must have been, you see, less dreadful to me. And it may have pleased him that I pitied him."

She was beside him on her feet, but still holding his hand—still with her arm supporting him. But though it all brought for him thus a dim light, "You 'pitied' him?" he grudgingly, resentfully asked.

"He has been unhappy, he has been ravaged," she said.

"And haven't I been unhappy? Am not I—you've only to look at me!— ravaged?"

"Ah I don't say I like him *better*," she granted after a thought. "But he's grim, he's worn—and things have happened to him. He doesn't make shift, for sight, with your charming monocle."

"No"—it struck Brydon: "I couldn't have sported mine 'downtown.' They'd have guyed[7] me there."

"His great convex pince-nez—I saw it, I recognised the kind—is for his poor ruined sight. And his poor right hand—!"

"Ah!" Brydon winced—whether for his proved identity or for his lost fingers. Then, "He has a million a year," he lucidly added. "But he hasn't you."

"And he isn't—no, he isn't—*you!*" she murmured as he drew her to his breast.

1908, 1909

From A Small Boy and Others[1]
[*A Source for* The Jolly Corner]

* * * But who shall count the sources at which an intense young fancy (when a young fancy *is* intense) capriciously, absurdly drinks? —so that the effect is, in twenty connections, that of a love-philtre or fear-philtre which fixes for the senses their supreme symbol of the fair or the strange. The Galerie d'Apollon[2] became for years what I can only term a splendid scene of things, even of the quite irrelevant or, as might be, almost unworthy; and I recall to this hour, with the last vividness, what a precious part it played for me, and exactly by that continuity of honour, on my awaking, in a summer dawn many years later, to the fortunate, the instantaneous recovery and capture of the most appalling yet most admirable nightmare of my life. The climax of this extraordinary experience—which stands alone for me as a dream-adventure foun d in the deepest, quickest, clearest act of cogitation and comparison, act indeed of life-saving energy, as well as in unutterable fear—was the sudden pursuit, through an open door, along a huge high saloon, of a just dimly-descried figure that retreated in terror before my rush and dash (a glare of inspired reaction from irresistible but shameful dread,) out of the room I had a moment before been desperately, and all the more abjectly, defending by the push of my shoulder against hard pressure on lock and bar from the other side. The lucidity, not to say the sublimity, of the crisis had consisted of the great thought that I, in my appalled state, was probably still more appalling than the awful agent, creature or presence, whatever he was, whom I had

7. Ridiculed.
1. *A Small Boy and Others* (New York: Scribner's, 1913) was the first of three autobiographical reminiscences that

James wrote in his later years.
2. The great hall in the Palais du Louvre, the famous French art museum.

guessed, in the suddenest wild start from sleep, the sleep within my sleep, to be making for my place of rest. The triumph of my impulse, perceived in a flash as I acted on it by myself at a bound, forcing the door outward, was the grand thing, but the great point of the whole was the wonder of my final recognition. Routed, dismayed, the tables turned upon him by my so surpassing him for straight aggression and dire intention, my visitant was already but a diminished spot in the long perspective, the tremendous, glorious hall, as I say, over the far-gleaming floor of which, cleared for the occasion of its great line of priceless vitrines down the middle, he sped for *his* life, while a great storm of thunder and lightning played through the deep embrasures of high windows at the right. The lightning that revealed the retreat revealed also the wondrous place and, by the same amazing play, my young imaginative life in it of long before, the sense of which, deep within me, had kept it whole, preserved it to this thrilling use; for what in the world were the deep embrasures and the so polished floor but those of the Galerie d'Apollon of my childhood? The "scene of something" I had vaguely then felt it? Well I might, since it was to be the scene of that immense hallucination.

1913

From Hawthorne[1]

["The Lightness of the Diet to Which His Observation Was Condemned"]

I know not at what age he began to keep a diary;[2] the first entries in the American volumes are of the summer of 1835. There is a phrase in the preface to his novel of *Transformation*,[3] which must have lingered in the minds of many Americans who have tried to write novels and to lay the scene of them in the western world. 'No author, without a trial, can conceive of the difficulty of writing a romance about a country where there is no shadow, no antiquity, no mystery, no picturesque and gloomy wrong, nor anything but a commonplace prosperity, in broad and simple daylight, as is happily the case with my dear native land.' The perusal of Hawthorne's American Note-Books operates as a practical commentary upon this somewhat ominous text. It does so at least to my own mind; it would be too much perhaps to say that the effect would be the same for the usual English reader. An Amer-

1. James had only recently decided to settle permanently in London when he was invited by John Morley to contribute a book on Hawthorne to the English Men of Letters series. The volume, published in 1879, is as much an index to James's attitudes at the time as it is a study of a writer to whom he was—and remained—deeply attached and indebted.
2. Hawthorne's notebooks have been

published as *The American Notebooks*, ed. Randall Stewart (New Haven, Conn.: Yale University Press, 1952); *The English Notebooks*, ed. Randall Stewart (New York: Modern Language Association of America; London: Oxford University Press, 1941); and *Hawthorne's First Diary*, ed. S. T. Pickard (1897).
3. English title for his *The Marble Faun* (1860).

ican reads between the lines—he completes the suggestions—he constructs a picture. I think I am not guilty of any gross injustice in saying that the picture he constructs from Hawthorne's American diaries, though by no means without charms of its own, is not, on the whole, an interesting one. It is characterised by an extraordinary blankness—a curious paleness of colour and paucity of detail. Hawthorne, as I have said, has a large and healthy appetite for detail, and one is therefore the more struck with the lightness of the diet to which his observation was condemned. For myself, as I turn the pages of his journals, I seem to see the image of the crude and simple society in which he lived. I use these epithets, of course, not invidiously, but descriptively; if one desires to enter as closely as possible into Hawthorne's situation, one must endeavour to reproduce his circumstances. We are struck with the large number of elements that were absent from them, and the coldness, the thinness, the blankness, to repeat my epithet, present themselves so vividly that our foremost feeling is that of compassion for a romancer looking for subjects in such a field. It takes so many things, as Hawthorne must have felt later in life, when he made the acquaintance of the denser, richer, warmer European spectacle—it takes such an accumulation of history and custom, such a complexity of manners and types, to form a fund of suggestion for a novelist. If Hawthorne had been a young Englishman, or a young Frenchman of the same degree of genius, the same cast of mind, the same habits, his consciousness of the world around him would have been a very different affair; however obscure, however reserved, his own personal life, his sense of the life of his fellow-mortals would have been almost infinitely more various. The negative side of the spectacle on which Hawthorne looked out, in his contemplative saunterings and reveries, might, indeed, with a little ingenuity, be made almost ludicrous; one might enumerate the items of high civilization, as it exists in other countries, which are absent from the texture of American life, until it should become a wonder to know what was left. No State, in the European sense of the word, and indeed barely a specific national name. No sovereign, no court, no personal loyalty, no aristocracy, no church, no clergy, no army, no diplomatic service, no country gentlemen, no palaces, no castles, nor manors, nor old country-houses, no parsonages, nor thatched cottages nor ivied ruins; no cathedrals, nor abbeys, nor little Norman churches; no great Universities nor public schools—no Oxford, nor Eton, nor Harrow; no literature, no novels, no museums, no pictures, no political society, no sporting class—no Epsom nor Ascot![4] Some such list as that might be drawn up of the absent things in American life—especially in the American life of forty years ago, the effect of which, upon an English or a French imagination, would probably as a general thing be appalling. The natural remark, in the almost

4. English towns noted for their horse races.

lurid light of such an indictment, would be that if these things are
left out, everything is left out. The American knows that a good
deal remains; what it is that remains—that is his secret, his joke, as
one may say. It would be cruel, in this terrible denudation, to deny
him the consolation of his national gift, that 'American humour' of
which of late years we have heard so much.

But in helping us to measure what remains, our author's Diaries,
as I have already intimated, would give comfort rather to persons
who might have taken the alarm from the brief sketch I have just
attempted of what I have called the negative side of the American
social situation, than to those reminding themselves of its fine compensations. Hawthorne's entries are to a great degree accounts of
walks in the country, drives in stage-coaches, people he met in tav-
erns. The minuteness of the things that attract his attention and
that he deems worthy of being commemorated is frequently
extreme, and from this fact we get the impression of a general
vacancy in the field of vision. 'Sunday evening, going by the jail, the
setting sun kindled up the windows most cheerfully; as if there were
a bright, comfortable light within its darksome stone wall.' 'I went
yesterday with Monsieur S——to pick raspberries. He fell through
an old log-bridge, thrown over a hollow; looking back, only his head
and shoulders appeared through the rotten logs and among the
bushes. A shower coming on, the rapid running of a little barefooted boy, coming up unheard, and dashing swiftly past us, and
showing us the soles of his naked feet as he ran adown the path and
up the opposite side.' In another place he devotes a page to a
description of a dog whom he saw running round after its tail; in
still another he remarks, in a paragraph by itself—'The aromatic
odor of peat-smoke, in the sunny autumnal air is very pleasant.' The
reader says to himself that when a man turned thirty gives a place
in his mind—and his inkstand—to such trifles as these, it is
because nothing else of superior importance demands admission.
Everything in the Notes indicates a simple, democratic, thinly-com-
posed society; there is no evidence of the writer finding himself in
any variety or intimacy of relations with any one or with anything.
We find a good deal of warrant for believing that if we add that
statement of Mr. Lathrop's[5] about his meals being left at the door
of his room, to rural rambles of which an impression of the temporary phases of the local apple-crop were the usual, and an encounter
with an organ-grinder, or an eccentric dog, the rarer, outcome, we
construct a rough image of our author's daily life during the several
years that preceded his marriage. He appears to have read a good
deal, and that he must have been familiar with the sources of good
English we see from his charming, expressive, slightly self-conscious,
cultivated, but not too cultivated, style. Yet neither in these early

---

5. George Parsons Lathrop (1851–98), author of *A Study of Hawthorne* (1876) and
later editor of Hawthorne's *Works*.

volumes of his Note-Books, nor in the later, is there any mention of his reading. There are no literary judgments or impressions—there is almost no allusion to works or to authors. The allusions to individuals of any kind are indeed much less numerous than one might have expected; there is little psychology, little description of manners. We are told by Mr. Lathrop that there existed at Salem during the early part of Hawthorne's life 'a strong circle of wealthy families', which 'maintained rigorously the distinctions of class', and whose 'entertainments were splendid, their manners magnificent'. This is a rather pictorial way of saying that there were a number of people in the place—the commercial and professional aristocracy, as it were—who lived in high comfort and respectability, and who, in their small provincial way, doubtless had pretensions to be exclusive. Into this delectable company Mr. Lathrop intimates that his hero was free to penetrate. It is easy to believe it, and it would be difficult to perceive why the privilege should have been denied to a young man of genius and culture, who was very good-looking (Hawthorne must have been in these days, judging by his appearance later in life, a strikingly handsome fellow), and whose American pedigree was virtually as long as the longest they could show. But in fact Hawthorne appears to have ignored the good society of his native place almost completely; no echo of its conversation is to be found in his tales or his journals. Such an echo would possibly not have been especially melodious, and if we regret the shyness and stiffness, the reserve, the timidity, the suspicion, or whatever it was, that kept him from knowing what there was to be known, it is not because we have any very definite assurance that his gains would have been great. Still, since a beautiful writer was growing up in Salem, it is a pity that he should not have given himself a chance to commemorate some of the types that flourished in the richest soil of the place. Like almost all people who possess in a strong degree the story-telling faculty, Hawthorne had a democratic strain in his composition and a relish for the commoner stuff of human nature. Thoroughly American in all ways, he was in none more so than in the vagueness of his sense of social distinctions and his readiness to forget them if a moral or intellectual sensation were to be gained by it. He liked to fraternise with plain people, to take them on their own terms, and put himself if possible into their shoes. His Note-Books, and even his tales, are full of evidence of this easy and natural feeling about all his unconventional fellow-mortals—this imaginative interest and contemplative curiosity—and it sometimes takes the most charming and graceful forms. Commingled as it is with his own subtlety and delicacy, his complete exemption from vulgarity, it is one of the points in his character which his reader comes most to appreciate—that reader I mean for whom he is not as for some few, a dusky and malarious genius.

1879

The Art of Fiction[1]

I should not have affixed so comprehensive a title to these few remarks, necessarily wanting in any completeness upon a subject the full consideration of which would carry us far, did I not seem to discover a pretext for my temerity in the interesting pamphlet lately published under this name by Mr. Walter Besant. Mr. Besant's lecture at the Royal Institution—the original form of his pamphlet—appears to indicate that many persons are interested in the art of fiction, and are not indifferent to such remarks, as those who practise it may attempt to make about it. I am therefore anxious not to lose the benefit of this favourable association, and to edge in a few words under cover of the attention which Mr. Besant is sure to have excited. There is something very encouraging in his having put into form certain of his ideas on the mystery of story-telling.

It is a proof of life and curiosity—curiosity on the part of the brotherhood of novelists as well as on the part of their readers. Only a short time ago it might have been supposed that the English novel was not what the French call *discutable*.[2] It had no air of having a theory, a conviction, a consciousness of itself behind it— of being the expression of an artistic faith, the result of choice and comparison. I do not say it was necessarily the worse for that: it would take much more courage than I possess to intimate that the form of the novel as Dickens and Thackeray (for instance) saw it had any taint of incompleteness. It was, however, *naïf* (if I may help myself out with another French word); and evidently if it be destined to suffer in any way for having lost its *naïveté* it has now an idea of making sure of the corresponding advantages. During the period I have alluded to there was a comfortable, good-humoured feeling abroad that a novel is a novel, as a pudding is a pudding, and that our only business with it could be to swallow it. But within a year or two, for some reason or other, there have been signs of returning animation—the era of discussion would appear to have been to a certain extent opened. Art lives upon discussion, upon experiment, upon curiosity, upon variety of attempt, upon the exchange of views and the comparison of standpoints; and there is a presumption that those times when no one has anything particular to say about it, and has no reason to give for practice or preference, though they may be times of honour, are not times of development —are times, possibly even, a little of dulness. The successful application of any art is a delightful spectacle, but the theory too is interesting; and though there is a great deal of the latter without the former I suspect there has never been a genuine success that has not

1. James's most famous (and influential) critical essay was written in response to a lecture on fiction delivered by the English novelist and historian Walter Besant (1836–1901) at the Royal Institution (London) on April 25, 1884. First pub- lished in *Longman's Magazine* for September, 1884, the essay was reprinted in book form the next year and in *Partial Portraits* (1888), the source of the present text.
2. Debatable.

had a latent core of conviction. Discussion, suggestion, formulation, these things are fertilising when they are frank and sincere. Mr. Besant has set an excellent example in saying what he thinks, for his part, about the way in which fiction should be written, as well as about the way in which it should be published; for his view of the "art," carried on into an appendix, covers that too. Other labourers in the same field will doubtless take up the argument, they will give it the light of their experience, and the effect will surely be to make our interest in the novel a little more what it had for some time threatened to fail to be—a serious, active, inquiring interest, under protection of which this delightful study may, in moments of confidence, venture to say a little more what it thinks of itself.

It must take itself seriously for the public to take it so. The old superstition about fiction being "wicked" has doubtless died out in England; but the spirit of it lingers in a certain oblique regard directed toward any story which does not more or less admit that it is only a joke. Even the most jocular novel feels in some degree the weight of the proscription that was formerly directed against literary levity: the jocularity does not always succeed in passing for orthodoxy. It is still expected, though perhaps people are ashamed to say it, that a production which is after all only a "make-believe" (for what else is a "story"?) shall be in some degree apologetic—shall renounce the pretension of attempting really to represent life. This, of course, any sensible, wide-awake story declines to do, for it quickly perceives that the tolerance granted to it on such a condition is only an attempt to stifle it disguised in the form of generosity. The old evangelical hostility to the novel, which was as explicit as it was narrow, and which regarded it as little less favourable to our immortal part than a stage-play, was in reality far less insulting. The only reason for the existence of a novel is that it does attempt to represent life. When it relinquishes this attempt, the same attempt that we see on the canvas of the painter, it will have arrived at a very strange pass. It is not expected of the picture that it will make itself humble in order to be forgiven; and the analogy between the art of the painter and the art of the novelist is, so far as I am able to see, complete. Their inspiration is the same, their process (allowing for the different quality of the vehicle), is the same, their success is the same. They may learn from each other, they may explain and sustain each other. Their cause is the same, and the honour of one is the honour of another. The Mahometans think a picture an unholy thing, but it is a long time since any Christian did, and it is therefore the more odd that in the Christian mind the traces (dissimulated though they may be) of a suspicion of the sister art should linger to this day. The only effectual way to lay it to rest is to emphasise the analogy to which I just alluded—to insist on the fact that as the picture is reality, so the novel is history. That is the only general description (which does it justice) that we may give of the novel. But history also is allowed to represent life; it is not, any more than painting, expected to apologise. The subject-matter of fiction is stored up likewise in documents and records, and if it will not give itself away, as they say in California, it must speak with assurance, with the tone of the historian. Certain accomplished novelists have a habit of giving themselves away which must often bring tears to the eyes of people who take their fiction seriously. I was lately struck, in reading over many pages of Anthony Trollope,[3] with his want of discretion in this particular. In a digression, a parenthesis or an aside, he concedes to the reader that he and this trusting friend are only "making believe." He admits that the events he narrates have not really happened, and that he can give his narrative any turn the reader may like best. Such a betrayal of a sacred office seems to me, I confess, a terrible crime; it is what I mean by the attitude of apology, and it shocks me every whit as much in Trollope as it would have shocked me in Gibbon or Macaulay.[4] It implies that the novelist is less occupied in looking for the truth (the truth, of course I mean, that he assumes, the premises that we must grant him, whatever they may be), than the historian, and in doing so it deprives him at a stroke of all his standing-room. To represent and illustrate the past, the actions of men, is the task of either writer, and the only difference that I can see is, in proportion as he succeeds, to the honour of the novelist, consisting as it does in his having more difficulty in collecting his evidence, which is so far from being purely literary. It seems to me to give him a great character, the fact that he has at once so much in common with the philosopher and the painter; this double analogy is a magnificent heritage.

It is of all this evidently that Mr. Besant is full when he insists upon the fact that fiction is one of the *fine* arts, deserving in its turn of all the honours and emoluments that have hitherto been reserved for the successful profession of music, poetry, painting, architecture. It is impossible to insist too much on so important a truth, and the place that Mr. Besant demands for the work of the novelist may be represented, a trifle less abstractly, by saying that he demands not only that it shall be reputed artistic, but that it shall be reputed very artistic indeed. It is excellent that he should have struck this note, for his doing so indicates that there was need of it, that his proposition may be to many people a novelty. One rubs one's eyes at the thought; but the rest of Mr. Besant's essay confirms the revelation. I suspect in truth that it would be possible to confirm it still further, and that one would not be far wrong in saying that in addition to the people to whom it has never occurred that a novel ought to be artistic, there are a great many others who, if this principle were urged upon them, would be filled with an indefinable mistrust.

3. English novelist (1815–82).
4. Edward Gibbon (1737–94) and

Thomas Babington Macaulay (1800–59), English historians.

They would find it difficult to explain their repugnance, but it would operate strongly to put them on their guard. "Art," in our Protestant communities, where so many things have got so strangely twisted about, is supposed in certain circles to have some vaguely injurious effect upon those who make it an important consideration, who let it weigh in the balance. It is assumed to be opposed in some mysterous manner to morality, to amusement, to instruction. When it is embodied in the work of the painter (the sculptor is another affair!) you know what it is: it stands there before you, in the honesty of pink and green and a gilt frame; you can see the worst of it at a glance, and you can be on your guard. But when it is introduced into literature it becomes more insidious—there is danger of its hurting you before you know it. Literature should be either instructive or amusing, and there is in many minds an impression that these artistic preoccupations, the search for form, contribute to neither end, interfere indeed with both. They are too frivolous to be edifying, and too serious to be diverting; and they are moreover priggish and paradoxical and superfluous. That, I think, represents the manner in which the latent thought of many people who read novels as an exercise in skipping would explain itself if it were to become articulate. They would argue, of course, that a novel ought to be "good," but they would interpret this term in a fashion of their own, which indeed would vary considerably from one critic to another. One would say that being good means representing virtuous and aspiring characters, placed in prominent positions; another would say that it depends on a "happy ending," on a distribution at the last of prizes, pensions, husbands, wives, babies, millions, appended paragraphs, and cheerful remarks. Another still would say that it means being full of incident and movement, so that we shall wish to jump ahead, to see who was the mysterious stranger, and if the stolen will was ever found, and shall not be distracted from this pleasure by any tiresome analysis or "description." But they would all agree that the "artistic" idea would spoil some of their fun. One would hold it accountable for all the description, another would see it revealed in the absence of sympathy. Its hostility to a happy ending would be evident, and it might even in some cases render any ending at all impossible. The "ending" of a novel is, for many persons, like that of a good dinner, a course of dessert and ices, and the artist in fiction is regarded as a sort of meddlesome doctor who forbids agreeable aftertastes. It is therefore true that this conception of Mr. Besant's of the novel as a superior form encounters not only a negative but a positive indifference. It matters little that as a work of art it should really be as little or as much of its essence to supply happy endings, sympathetic characters, and an objective tone, as if it were a work of mechanics: the association of ideas, however incongruous, might easily be too much for it if an eloquent voice were not sometimes raised to call attention to the fact that it is at once as free and as serious a branch of literature as any other.

Certainly this might sometimes be doubted in presence of the enormous number of works of fiction that appeal to the credulity of our generation, for it might easily seem that there could be no great character in a commodity so quickly and easily produced. It must be admitted that good novels are much compromised by bad ones, and that the field at large suffers discredit from overcrowding. I think, however, that this injury is only superficial, and that the superabundance of written fiction proves nothing against the principle itself. It has been vulgarised, like all other kinds of literature, like everything else to-day, and it has proved more than some kinds accessible to vulgarisation. But there is as much difference as there ever was between a good novel and a bad one: the bad is swept with all the daubed canvases and spoiled marble into some unvisited limbo, or infinite rubbish-yard beneath the back-windows of the world, and the good subsists and emits its light and stimulates our desire for perfection. As I shall take the liberty of making but a single criticism of Mr. Besant, whose tone is so full of the love of his art, I may as well have done with it at once. He seems to me to mistake in attempting to say so definitely beforehand what sort of an affair the good novel will be. To indicate the danger of such an error as that has been the purpose of these few pages; to suggest that certain traditions on the subject, applied *a priori*, have already had much to answer for, and that the good health of an art which undertakes so immediately to reproduce life must demand that it be perfectly free. It lives upon exercise, and the very meaning of exercise is freedom. The only obligation to which in advance we may hold a novel, without incurring the accusation of being arbitrary, is that it be interesting. That general responsibility rests upon it, but it is the only one I can think of. The ways in which it is at liberty to accomplish this result (of interesting us) strike me as innumerable, and such as can only suffer from being marked out or fenced in by prescription. They are as various as the temperament of man, and they are successful in proportion as they reveal a particular mind, different from others. A novel is in its broadest definition a personal, a direct impression of life: that, to begin with, constitutes its value, which is greater or less according to the intensity of the impression. But there will be no intensity at all, and therefore no value, unless there is freedom to feel and say. The tracing of a line to be followed, of a tone to be taken, of a form to be filled out, is a limitation of that freedom and a suppression of the very thing that we are most curious about. The form, it seems to me, is to be appreciated after the fact: then the author's choice has been made, his standard has been indicated; then we can follow lines and directions and compare tones and resemblances. Then in a word we can enjoy one of the most charming of pleasures, we can estimate quality, we can apply the test of execution. The execution belongs to the author alone; it is what is most personal to him, and we measure him by that. The advantage, the luxury, as well as the torment and responsibility of the novelist, is that there is no limit to what he may attempt as an executant—no limit to his possible experiments, efforts, discoveries, successes. Here it is especially that he works, step by step, like his brother of the brush, of whom we may always say that he has painted his picture in a manner best known to himself. His manner is his secret, not necessarily a jealous one. He cannot disclose it as a general thing if he would; he would be at a loss to teach it to others. I say this with a due recollection of having insisted on the community of method of the artist who paints a picture and the artist who writes a novel. The painter *is* able to teach the rudiments of his practice, and it is possible, from the study of good work (granted the aptitude), both to learn how to paint and to learn how to write. Yet it remains true, without injury to the *rapprochement,* that the literary artist would be obliged to say to his pupil much more than the other, "Ah, well, you must do it as you can!" It is a question of degree, a matter of delicacy. If there are exact sciences, there are also exact arts, and the grammar of painting is so much more definite that it makes the difference.

I ought to add, however, that if Mr. Besant says at the beginning of his essay that the "laws of fiction may be laid down and taught with as much precision and exactness as the laws of harmony, perspective, and proportion," he mitigates what might appear to be an extravagance by applying his remark to "general" laws, and by expressing most of these rules in a manner with which it would certainly be unaccommodating to disagree. That the novelist must write from his experience, that his "characters must be real and such as might be met with in actual life;" that "a young lady brought up in a quiet country village should avoid descriptions of garrison life," and "a writer whose friends and personal experiences belong to the lower middle-class should carefully avoid introducing his characters into society;" that one should enter one's notes in a common-place book; that one's figures should be clear in outline; that making them clear by some trick of speech or of carriage is a bad method, and "describing them at length" is a worse one; that English Fiction should have a "conscious moral purpose;" that "it is almost impossible to estimate too highly the value of careful workmanship—that is, of style;" that "the most important point of all is the story," that "the story is everything": these are principles with most of which it is surely impossible not to sympathise. That remark about the lower middle-class writer and his knowing his place is perhaps rather chilling; but for the rest I should find it difficult to dissent from any one of these recommendations. At the same time, I should find it difficult positively to assent to them, with the exception, perhaps, of the injunction as to entering one's notes in a common-place book. They scarcely seem to me to have the quality that Mr. Besant attributes to the rules of the novelist— the "precision and exactness" of "the laws of harmony, perspective, and proportion." They are suggestive, they are even inspiring, but they are not exact, though they are doubtless as much so as the case admits of: which is a proof of that liberty of interpretation for which I just contended. For the value of these different injunctions —so beautiful and so vague—is wholly in the meaning one attaches to them. The characters, the situation, which strike one as real will be those that touch and interest one most, but the measure of reality is very difficult to fix. The reality of Don Quixote or of Mr. Micawber[5] is a very delicate shade; it is a reality so coloured by the author's vision that, vivid as it may be, one would hesitate to propose it as a model: one would expose one's self to some very embarrassing questions on the part of a pupil. It goes without saying that you will not write a good novel unless you possess the sense of reality; but it will be difficult to give you a recipe for calling that sense into being. Humanity is immense, and reality has a myriad forms; the most one can affirm is that some of the flowers of fiction have the odour of it, and others have not; as for telling you in advance how your nosegay should be composed, that is another affair. It is equally excellent and inconclusive to say that one must write from experience; to our supposititious aspirant such a declaration might savour of mockery. What kind of experience is intended, and where does it begin and end? Experience is never limited, and it is never complete; it is an immense sensibility, a kind of huge spiderweb of the finest silken threads suspended in the chamber of consciousness, and catching every airborne particle in its tissue. It is the very atmosphere of the mind; and when the mind is imaginative—much more when it happens to be that of a man of genius—it takes to itself the faintest hints of life, it converts the very pulses of the air into revelations. The young lady living in a village has only to be a damsel upon whom nothing is lost to make it quite unfair (as it seems to me) to declare to her that she shall have nothing to say about the military. Greater miracles have been seen than that, imagination assisting, she should speak the truth about some of these gentlemen. I remember an English novelist, a woman of genius,[6] telling me that she was much commended for the impression she had managed to give in one of her tales of the nature and way of life of the French Protestant youth. She had been asked where she learned so much about this recondite being, she had been congratulated on her peculiar opportunities. These opportunities consisted in her having once, in Paris, as she ascended a staircase, passed an

---

5. Main characters in the novel by Cervantes and in Dickens's *David Copperfield.*

6. **Leon Edel identifies her as novelist**

Thackeray's daughter Anne, whose first novel contains many of the elements of James's description.

open door where, in the household of a *pasteur*,⁷ some of the young
Protestants were seated at table round a finished meal. The glimpse
made a picture; it lasted only a moment, but that moment was
experience. She had got her direct personal impression, and she
turned out her type. She knew what youth was, and what Protest-
antism; she also had the advantage of having seen what it was to be
French, so that she converted these ideas into a concrete image and
produced a reality. Above all, however, she was blessed with the faculty which when you give it an inch takes an ell, and which for the
artist is a much greater source of strength than any accident of residence or of place in the social scale. The power to guess the unseen
from the seen, to trace the implication of things, to judge the whole
piece by the pattern, the condition of feeling life in general so completely that you are well on your way to knowing any particular
corner of it—this cluster of gifts may almost be said to constitute
experience, and they occur in country and in town, and in the most
differing stages of education. If experience consists of impressions, it
may be said that impressions *are* experience, just as (have we not
seen it?) they are the very air we breathe. Therefore, if I should certainly say to a novice, "Write from experience and experience only,"
I should feel that this was rather a tantalising monition if I were
not careful immediately to add, "Try to be one of the people on
whom nothing is lost!"

I am far from intending by this to minimise the importance of
exactness—of truth of detail. One can speak best from one's own
taste, and I may therefore venture to say that the air of reality (solidity of specification) seems to me to be the supreme virtue of a
novel—the merit on which all its other merits (including that conscious moral purpose of which Mr. Besant speaks) helplessly and
submissively depend. If it be not there they are all as nothing, and
if these be there, they owe their effect to the success with which the
author has produced the illusion of life. The cultivation of this success, the study of this exquisite process, form, to my taste, the
beginning and the end of the art of the novelist. They are his inspiration, his despair, his reward, his torment, his delight. It is here in
very truth that he competes with life; it is here that he competes with his brother the painter in *his* attempt to render
the look of things, the look that conveys their meaning, to
catch the colour, the relief, the expression, the surface, the substance of the human spectacle. It is in regard to this that Mr.
Besant is well inspired when he bids him take notes. He cannot
possibly take too many, he cannot possibly take enough. All life
solicits him, and to "render" the simplest surface, to produce the most
momentary illusion, is a very complicated business. His case would
be easier, and the rule would be more exact, if Mr. Besant had been
able to tell him what notes to take. But this, I fear, he can never

7. Pastor, minister.

learn in any manual; it is the business of his life. He has to take a
great many in order to select a few, he has to work them up as he
can, and even the guides and philosophers who might have most to
say to him must leave him alone when it comes to the application
of precepts, as we leave the painter in communion with his palette.
That his characters "must be clear in outline," as Mr. Besant says
—he feels that down to his boots; but how he shall make them so is
a secret between his good angel and himself. It would be absurdly
simple if he could be taught that a great deal of "description"
would make them so, or that on the contrary the absence of description and the cultivation of dialogue, or the absence of dialogue and
the multiplication of "incident," would rescue him from his
difficulties. Nothing, for instance, is more possible than that he be
of a turn of mind for which this odd, literal opposition of description and dialogue, incident and description, has little meaning and
light. People often talk of these things as if they had a kind of
internecine distinctness, instead of melting into each other at every
breath, and being intimately associated parts of one general effort of
expression. I cannot imagine composition existing in a series of
blocks, nor conceive, in any novel worth discussing at all, of a passage of description that is not in its intention narrative, a passage of
dialogue that is not in its intention descriptive, a touch of truth of
any sort that does not partake of the nature of incident, or an incident that derives its interest from any other source than the general
and only source of the success of a work of art—that of being illustrative. A novel is a living thing, all one and continuous, like any
other organism, and in proportion as it lives will it be found, I
think, that in each of the parts there is something of each of the
other parts. The critic who over the close texture of a finished work
shall pretend to trace a geography of items will mark some frontiers
as artificial, I fear, as any that have been known to history. There is
an old-fashioned distinction between the novel of character and the
novel of incident which must have cost many a smile to the intending fabulist who was keen about his work. It apppears to me as little
to the point as the equally celebrated distinction between the novel
and the romance—to answer as little to any reality. There are bad
novels and good novels, as there are bad pictures and good pictures;
but that is the only distinction in which I see any meaning, and I
can as little imagine speaking of a novel of character as I can imagine speaking of a picture of character. When one says picture one
says of character, when one says novel one says of incident, and the
terms may be transposed at will. What is character but the determination of incident? What is incident but the illustration of character? What is either a picture or a novel that is *not* of character?
What else do we seek in it and find in it? It is an incident for a
woman to stand up with her hand resting on a table and look out at
you in a certain way; or if it be not an incident I think it will be

hard to say what it is. At the same time it is an expression of character. If you say you don't see it (character in *that—allons donc!*[8]), this is exactly what the artist who has reasons of his own for thinking he *does* see it undertakes to show you. When a young man makes up his mind that he has not faith enough after all to enter the church as he intended, that is an incident, though you may not hurry to the end of the chapter to see whether perhaps he doesn't change once more. I do not say that these are extraordinary or startling incidents. I do not pretend to estimate the degree of interest proceeding from them, for this will depend upon the skill of the painter. It sounds almost puerile to say that some incidents are intrinsically much more important than others, and I need not take this precaution after having professed my sympathy for the major ones in remarking that the only classification of the novel that I can understand is into that which has life and that which has it not.

The novel and the romance, the novel of incident and that of character—these clumsy separations appear to me to have been made by critics and readers for their own convenience, and to help them out of some of their occasional queer predicaments, but to have little reality or interest for the producer, from whose point of view it is of course that we are attempting to consider the art of fiction. The case is the same with another shadowy category which Mr. Besant apparently is disposed to set up—that of the "modern English novel"; unless indeed it be that in this matter he has fallen into an accidental confusion of standpoints. It is not quite clear whether he intends the remarks in which he alludes to it to be didactic or historical. It is as difficult to suppose a person intending to write a modern English as to suppose him writing an ancient English novel: that is a label which begs the question. One writes the novel, one paints the picture, of one's language and of one's time, and calling it modern English will not, alas! make the difficult task any easier. No more, unfortunately, will calling this or that work of one's fellow-artist a romance—unless it be, of course, simply for the pleasantness of the thing, as for instance when Hawthorne gave this heading to his story of *Blithedale*.[9] The French, who have brought the theory of fiction to remarkable completeness, have but one name for the novel, and have not attempted smaller things in it, that I can see, for that. I can think of no obligation to which the "romancer" would not be held equally with the novelist; the standard of execution is equally high for each. Of course it is of execution that we are talking—that being the only point of a novel that is open to contention. This is perhaps too often lost sight of, only to produce interminable confusions and cross-purposes. We must grant the artist his subject, his idea, his *donnée*:[1] our criticism is applied only to what he makes of it. Naturally I do not mean that

8. Come now!—i.e., nonsense!
9. *The Blithedale Romance* was published in 1852.
1. That which is given.

we are bound to like it or find it interesting: in case we do not our course is perfectly simple—to let it alone. We may believe that of a certain idea even the most sincere novelist can make nothing at all, and the event may perfectly justify our belief; but the failure will have been a failure to execute, and it is in the execution that the fatal weakness is recorded. If we pretend to respect the artist at all, we must allow him his freedom of choice, in the face, in particular cases, of innumerable presumptions that the choice will not fructify. Art derives a considerable part of its beneficial exercise from flying in the face of presumptions, and some of the most interesting experiments of which it is capable are hidden in the bosom of common things. Gustave Flaubert has written a story about the devotion of a servant-girl to a parrot,[2] and the production, highly finished as it is, cannot on the whole be called a success. We are perfectly free to find it flat, but I think it might have been interesting; and I, for my part, am extremely glad he should have written it; it is a contribution to our knowledge of what can be done—or what cannot. Ivan Turgénieff has written a tale about a deaf and dumb serf and a lap-dog,[3] and the thing is touching, loving, a little masterpiece. He struck the note of life where Gustave Flaubert missed it—he flew in the face of a presumption and achieved a victory.

Nothing, of course, will ever take the place of the good old fashion of "liking" a work of art or not liking it: the most improved criticism will not abolish that primitive, that ultimate test. I mention this to guard myself from the accusation of intimating that the idea, the subject, of a novel or a picture, does not matter. It matters, to my sense, in the highest degree, and if I might put up a prayer it would be that artists should select none but the richest. Some, as I have already hastened to admit, are much more remunerative than others, and it would be a world happily arranged in which persons intending to treat them should be exempt from confusions and mistakes. This fortunate condition will arrive only, I fear, on the same day that critics become purged from error. Meanwhile, I repeat, we do not judge the artist with fairness unless we say to him, "Oh, I grant you your starting-point, because if I did not I should seem to prescribe to you, and heaven forbid I should take that responsibility. If I pretend to tell you what you must not take, you will call upon me to tell you then what you must take; in which case I shall be prettily caught. Moreover, it isn't till I have accepted your data that I can begin to measure you. I have the standard, the pitch; I have no right to tamper with your flute and then criticise your music. Of course I may not care for your idea at all; I may think it silly, or stale, or unclean; in which case I wash my hands of you altogether. I may content myself with believing that you will not have succeeded in being interesting, but I shall, of course, not

---

2. *A Simple Soul,* by Gustave Flaubert (1821–80). 3. *Mumu,* by Ivan Turgenev (1818–83).

attempt to demonstrate it, and you will be as indifferent to me as I am to you. I needn't remind you that there are all sorts of tastes: who can know it better? Some people, for excellent reasons, don't like to read about carpenters; others, for reasons even better, don't like to read about courtesans. Many object to Americans. Others (I believe they are mainly editors and publishers) won't look at Italians. Some readers don't like quiet subjects; others don't like bustling ones. Some enjoy a complete illusion, others the consciousness of large concessions. They choose their novels accordingly, and if they don't care about your idea they won't, *a fortiori*,[4] care about your treatment."

So that it comes back very quickly, as I have said, to the liking: in spite of M. Zola,[5] who reasons less powerfully than he represents, and who will not reconcile himself to this absoluteness of taste, thinking that there are certain things that people ought to like, and that they can be made to like. I am quite at a loss to imagine anything (at any rate in this matter of fiction) that people *ought* to like or to dislike. Selection will be sure to take care of itself, for it has a constant motive behind it. That motive is simply experience. As people feel life, so they will feel the art that is most closely related to it. This closeness of relation is what we should never forget in talking of the effort of the novel. Many people speak of it as a factitious, artificial form, a product of ingenuity, the business of which is to alter and arrange the things that surround us, to translate them into conventional, traditional moulds. This however, is a view of the matter which carries us but a very short way, condemns the art to an eternal repetition of a few familiar *clichés*, cuts short its development, and leads us straight up to a dead wall. Catching the very note and trick, the strange irregular rhythm of life, that is the attempt whose strenuous force keeps Fiction upon her feet. In proportion as in what she offers us we see life *without* rearrangement do we feel that we are touching the truth; in proportion as we see it *with* rearrangement do we feel that we are being put off with a substitute, a compromise and convention. It is not uncommon to hear an extraordinary assurance of remark in regard to this matter of rearranging, which is often spoken of as if it were the last word of art. Mr. Besant seems to me in danger of falling into the great error with his rather unguarded talk about "selection." Art is essentially selection, but it is a selection whose main care is to be typical, to be inclusive. For many people art means rose-coloured windowpanes, and selection means picking a bouquet for Mrs. Grundy.[6] They will tell you glibly that artistic considerations have nothing to do with the disagreeable, with the ugly; they will rattle off shallow

---

4. All the more reason.
5. Émile Zola (1840–1902), French naturalistic novelist and literary theorist who argued that people should like best what was represented with the greatest measure of scientific objectivity.
6. A stock character marked by prudishness who is alluded to in Thomas Morton's *Speed the Plough* (1798).

commonplaces about the province of art and the limits of art till you are moved to some wonder in return as to the province and the limits of ignorance. It appears to me that no one can ever have made a seriously artistic attempt without becoming conscious of an immense increase—a kind of revelation—of freedom. One perceives in that case—by the light of a heavenly ray—that the province of art is all life, all feeling, all observation, all vision. As Mr. Besant so justly intimates, it is all experience. That is a sufficient answer to those who maintain that it must not touch the sad things of life, who stick into its divine unconscious bosom little prohibitory inscriptions on the end of sticks, such as we see in public gardens—"It is forbidden to walk on the grass; it is forbidden to touch the flowers; it is not allowed to introduce dogs or to remain after dark; it is requested to keep to the right." The young aspirant in the line of fiction whom we continue to imagine will do nothing without taste, for in that case his freedom would be of little use to him; but the first advantage of his taste will be to reveal to him the absurdity of the little sticks and tickets. If he have taste, I must add, of course he will have ingenuity, and my disrespectful reference to that quality just now was not meant to imply that it is useless in fiction. But it is only a secondary aid; the first is a capacity for receiving straight impressions.

Mr. Besant has some remarks on the question of "the story" which I shall not attempt to criticise, though they seem to me to contain a singular ambiguity, because I do not think I understand them. I cannot see what is meant by talking as if there were a part of a novel which is the story and part of it which for mystical reasons is not—unless indeed the distinction be made in a sense in which it is difficult to suppose that any one should attempt to convey anything. "The story," if it represents anything, represents the subject, the idea, the *donnée* of the novel; and there is surely no "school"—Mr. Besant speaks of a school—which urges that a novel should be all treatment and no subject. There must assuredly be something to treat; every school is intimately conscious of that. This sense of the story being the idea, the starting-point, of the novel, is the only one that I see in which it can be spoken of as something different from its organic whole; and since in proportion as the work is successful the idea permeates and penetrates it, informs and animates it, so that every word and every punctuation-point contribute directly to the expression, in that proportion do we lose our sense of the story being a blade which may be drawn more or less out of its sheath. The story and the novel, the idea and the form, are the needle and thread, and I never heard of a guild of tailors who recommended the use of the thread without the needle, or the needle without the thread. Mr. Besant is not the only critic who may be observed to have spoken as if there were certain things in life which constitute stories, and certain others which do not. I find the same odd implication in an entertaining article in the *Pall Mall Gazette*, devoted, as it happens, to Mr. Besant's lecture. "The story is the thing!" says this graceful writer, as if with a tone of opposition to some other idea. I should think it was, as every painter who, as the time for "sending in"[7] his picture looms in the distance, finds himself still in quest of a subject—as every belated artist not fixed about his theme will heartily agree. There are some subjects which speak to us and others which do not, but he would be a clever man who should undertake to give a rule—an index expurgatorius[8]—by which the story and the no-story should be known apart. It is impossible (to me at least) to imagine any such rule which shall not be altogether arbitrary. The writer in the *Pall Mall* opposes the delightful (as I suppose) novel of *Margot la Balafrée*[9] to certain tales in which "Bostonian nymphs" appear to have "rejected English dukes for psychological reasons." I am not acquainted with the romance just designated, and can scarcely forgive the *Pall Mall* critic for not mentioning the name of the author, but the title appears to refer to a lady who may have received a scar in some heroic adventure. I am inconsolable at not being acquainted with this episode,[1] but am utterly at a loss to see why it is a story when the rejection (or acceptance) of a duke is not, and why a reason, psychological or other, is not a subject when a cicatrix[2] is. They are all particles of the multitudinous life with which the novel deals, and surely no dogma which pretends to make it lawful to touch the one and unlawful to touch the other will stand for a moment on its feet. It is the special picture that must stand or fall, according as it seem to possess truth or to lack it. Mr. Besant does not, to my sense, light up the subject by intimating that a story must, under penalty of not being a story, consist of "adventures." Why of adventures more than of green spectacles? He mentions a category of impossible things, and among them he places "fiction without adventure." Why without adventure, more than without matrimony, or celibacy, or parturition, or cholera, or hydropathy,[3] or Jansenism? This seems to me to bring the novel back to the hapless little *rôle* of being an artificial, ingenious thing—bring it down from its large, free character of an immense and exquisite correspondence with life. And what *is* adventure, when it comes to that, and by what sign is the listening pupil to recognise it? It is an adventure—an immense one—for me to write this little article; and for a Bostonian nymph to reject an English duke is an adventure only less stirring, I should say, than for an English duke to be rejected by a Bostonian nymph. I see dramas within dramas in

7. I.e., at the time of shipping his painting to a Royal Academy exhibit.
8. The list of books from which condemned passages must be removed before the book could be read by Catholics.
9. *Margot the Scarred Woman* (1884) by Fortuné du Boisgobey.
1. In truth James's *An International Ep-* isode (1879).
2. Scar.
3. Hydropathy involves the use of water in the treatment of disease; Jansenism is a theological doctrine named after Cornelis Jansen (1585–1638), Dutch theologian who emphasized predestination and the necessity of belonging to the Catholic Church for salvation.

that, and innumerable points of view. A psychological reason is, to my imagination, an object adorably pictorial; to catch the tint of its complexion—I feel as if that idea might inspire one to Titianesque[4] efforts. There are few things more exciting to me, in short, than a psychological reason, and yet, I protest, the novel seems to me the most magnificent form of art. I have just been reading, at the same time, the delightful story of *Treasure Island*,[5] by Mr. Robert Louis Stevenson and, in a manner less consecutive, the last tale from M. Edmond de Goncourt, which is entitled *Chérie*. One of these works treats of murders, mysteries, islands of dreadful renown, hairbreadth escapes, miraculous coincidences and buried doubloons. The other treats of a little French girl who lived in a finé house in Paris, and died of wounded sensibility because no one would marry her. I call *Treasure Island* delightful, because it appears to me to have succeeded wonderfully in what it attempts; and I venture to bestow no epithet upon *Chérie*, which strikes me as having failed deplorably in what it attempts—that is in tracing the development of the moral consciousness of a child. But one of these productions strikes me as exactly as much of a novel as the other, and as having a "story" quite as much. The moral consciousness of a child is as much a part of life as the islands of the Spanish Main, and the one sort of geography seems to me to have those "surprises"—of which Mr. Besant speaks quite as much as the other. For myself (since it comes back in the last resort, as I say, to the preference of the individual), the picture of the child's experience has the advantage that I can at successive steps (an immense luxury, near to the "sensual pleasure" of which Mr. Besant's critic in the *Pall Mall* speaks) say Yes or No, as it may be, to what the artist puts before me. I have been a child in fact, but I have been on a quest for a buried treasure only in supposition, and it is a simple accident that with M. de Goncourt I should have for the most part to say No. With George Eliot,[6] when she painted that country with a far other intelligence, I always said Yes.

The most interesting part of Mr. Besant's lecture is unfortunately the briefest passage—his very cursory allusion to the "conscious moral purpose" of the novel. Here again it is not very clear whether he be recording a fact or laying down a principle; it is a great pity that in the latter case he should not have developed his idea. This branch of the subject is of immense importance, and Mr. Besant's few words point to considerations of the widest reach, not to be lightly disposed of. He will have treated the art of fiction but superficially who is not prepared to go every inch of the way that these considerations will carry him. It is for this reason that at the begin-

4. Titian (1477–1576), Italian painter highly regarded for his use of color.
5. *Treasure Island* was published in 1883, *Chérie* in 1884.

6. George Eliot is the pseudonym for Marian Evans (1819–80), English novelist; "that country": imaginative country of buried treasure.

ning of these remarks I was careful to notify the reader that my reflections on so large a theme have no pretension to be exhaustive. Like Mr. Besant, I have left the question of the morality of the novel till the last, and at the last I find I have used up my space. It is a question surrounded with difficulties, as witness the very first that meets us, in the form of a definite question, on the threshold. Vagueness, in such a discussion, is fatal, and what is the meaning of your morality and your conscious moral purpose? Will you not define your terms and explain how (a novel being a picture) a picture can be either moral or immoral? You wish to paint a moral picture or carve a moral statue: will you not tell us how you would set about it? We are discussing the Art of Fiction; questions of art are questions (in the widest sense) of execution; questions of morality are quite another affair, and will you not let us see how it is that you find it so easy to mix them up? These things are so clear to Mr. Besant that he has deduced from them a law which he sees embodied in English Fiction, and which is "a truly admirable thing and a great cause for congratulation." It is a great cause for congratulation indeed when such thorny problems become as smooth as silk. I may add that in so far as Mr. Besant perceives that in point of fact English Fiction has addressed itself preponderantly to these delicate questions he will appear to many people to have made a vain discovery. They will have been positively struck, on the contrary, with the moral timidity of the usual English novelist; with his (or with her) aversion to face the difficulties with which on every side the treatment of reality bristles. He is apt to be extremely shy (whereas the picture that Mr. Besant draws is a picture of boldness), and the sign of his work, for the most part, is a cautious silence on certain subjects. In the English novel (by which of course I mean the American as well), more than in any other, there is a traditional difference between that which people know and that which they agree to admit that they know, that which they see and that which they speak of, that which they feel to be a part of life and that which they allow to enter into literature. There is the great difference, in short, between what they talk of in conversation and what they talk of in print. The essence of moral energy is to survey the whole field, and I should directly reverse Mr. Besant's remark and say not that the English novel has a purpose, but that it has a diffidence. To what degree a purpose in a work of art is a source of corruption I shall not attempt to inquire; the one that seems to me least dangerous is the purpose of making a perfect work. As for our novel, I may say lastly on this score that as we find it in England to-day it strikes me as addressed in a large degree to "young people," and that this in itself constitutes a presumption that it will be rather shy. There are certain things which it is generally agreed not to discuss, not even to mention, before young people. That is very well, but the absence of dis-

cussion is not a symptom of the moral passion. The purpose of the
English novel—"a truly admirable thing, and a great cause for congratulation"—strikes me therefore as rather negative.

There is one point at which the moral sense and the artistic sense
lie very near together; that is in the light of the very obvious truth
that the deepest quality of a work of art will always be the quality
of the mind of the producer. In proportion as that intelligence is
fine will the novel, the picture, the statue partake of the substance
of beauty and truth. To be constituted of such elements is, to my
vision, to have purpose enough. No good novel will ever proceed
from a superficial mind; that seems to me an axiom which, for the
artist in fiction, will cover all needful moral ground: if the youthful
aspirant take it to heart it will illuminate for him many of the mysteries of "purpose." There are many other useful things that might
be said to him, but I have come to the end of my article, and can
only touch them as I pass. The critic in the *Pall Mall Gazette*,
whom I have already quoted, draws attention to the danger, in
speaking of the art of fiction, of generalising. The danger that he has
in mind is rather, I imagine, that of particularising, for there are
some comprehensive remarks which, in addition to those embodied
in Mr. Besant's suggestive lecture, might without fear of misleading
him be addressed to the ingenuous student. I should remind him
first of the magnificence of the form that is open to him, which
offers to sight so few restrictions and such innumerable opportunities. The other arts, in comparison, appear confined and hampered;
the various conditions under which they are exercised are so rigid
and definite. But the only condition that I can think of attaching to
the composition of the novel is, as I have already said, that it be
sincere. This freedom is a splendid privilege, and the first lesson of
the young novelist is to learn to be worthy of it. "Enjoy it as it
deserves," I should say to him; "take possession of it, explore it to its
utmost extent, publish it, rejoice in it. All life belongs to you, and
do not listen either to those who would shut you up into corners of
it and tell you that it is only here and there that art inhabits, or to
those who would persuade you that this heavenly messenger wings
her way outside of life altogether, breathing a superfine air, and
turning away her head from the truth of things. There is no impression of life, no manner of seeing it and feeling it, to which the plan
of the novelist may not offer a place; you have only to remember
that talents so dissimilar as those of Alexandre Dumas and Jane
Austen, Charles Dickens and Gustave Flaubert have worked in this
field with equal glory. Do not think too much about optimism and
pessimism; try and catch the colour of life itself. In France to-day
we see a prodigious effort (that of Emile Zola, to whose solid and
serious work no explorer of the capacity of the novel can allude without respect), we see an extraordinary effort vitiated by a spirit of pessimism on a narrow basis. M. Zola is magnificent, but he strikes an

English reader as ignorant; he has an air of working in the dark; if he had as much light as energy, his results would be of the highest value. As for the aberrations of a shallow optimism, the ground (of English fiction especially) is strewn with their brittle particles as with broken glass. If you must indulge in conclusions, let them have the taste of a wide knowledge. Remember that your first duty is to be as complete as possible—to make as perfect a work. Be generous and delicate and pursue the prize."

1884, 1888

From The American Scene[1]
[*The New Jerusalem*][2]

New York really, I think, is all formidable foreground; or, if it be not, there is more than enough of this pressure of the present and the immediate to cut out the close sketcher's work for him. These things are a thick growth all round him, and when I recall the intensity of the material picture in the dense Yiddish quarter, for instance, I wonder at its not having forestalled, on my page, mere musings and, as they will doubtless be called, moonings. There abides with me, ineffaceably, the memory of a summer evening spent there by invitation of a high public functionary domiciled on the spot—to the extreme enhancement of the romantic interest his visitor found him foredoomed to inspire—who was to prove one of the most liberal of hosts and most luminous of guides. I can scarce help it if this brilliant personality, on that occasion the very medium itself through which the whole spectacle showed, so colours my impressions that if I speak, by intention, of the facts that played into them I may really but reflect the rich talk and the general privilege of the hour. That accident moreover must take its place simply as the highest value and the strongest note in the total show—so much did it testify to the quality of appealing, surrounding life. The sense of this quality was already strong in my drive, with a companion, through the long, warm June twilight, from a comparatively conventional neighbourhood; it was the sense, after all, of a great swarming, a swarming that had begun to thicken, infinitely, as soon as we had crossed to the East side and long before we had got to Rutgers Street. There is no swarming like that of Israel when once Israel has got a start, and the scene here bristled, at every step, with the signs and sounds, immitigable, unmistakable, of a Jewry that had burst all bounds. That it has burst all bounds in

1. Written after an absence on James's part of 20 years, *The American Scene* (1907) records the impressions James gathered in 10 months of 1904 and 1905 in New York, New England, and the eastern seaboard south to Florida. The two excerpts are from Chapters 3 and 14. Most of the book appeared serially in several journals before it was published in book form, first in England by Chapman and Hall and soon after by Harper & Brothers in New York. Section VII of the essay on Florida was omitted from the American edition; both excerpts printed here are based on the English edition.

2. In the Book of Revelation the New Jerusalem is the resting place of the redeemed.

New York, almost any combination of figures or of objects taken at hazard sufficiently proclaims; but I remember how the rising waters, on this summer night, rose, to the imagination, even above the housetops and seemed to sound their murmur to the pale distant stars. It was as if we had been thus, in the crowded, hustled roadway, where multiplication, multiplication of everything, was the dominant note, at the bottom of some vast sallow aquarium in which innumerable fish, of over-developed proboscis, were to bump together, for ever, amid heaped spoils of the sea.

The children swarmed above all—here was multiplication with a vengeance; and the number of very old persons, of either sex, was almost equally remarkable; the very old persons being in equal vague occupation of the doorstep, pavement, curbstone, gutter, roadway, and every one alike using the street for overflow. As overflow, in the whole quarter, is the main fact of life—I was to learn later on that, with the exception of some shy corner of Asia, no district in the world known to the statistician has so many inhabitants to the yard—the scene hummed with the human presence beyond any I had ever faced in quest even of refreshment; producing part of the impression, moreover, no doubt, as a direct consequence of the intensity of the Jewish aspect. This, I think, makes the individual Jew more of a concentrated person, savingly possessed of everything that is in him, than any other human, noted at random—or is it simply, rather, that the unsurpassed strength of the race permits of the chopping into myriads of fine fragments without loss of race-quality? There are small strange animals, known to natural history, snakes or worms, I believe, who, when cut into pieces, wriggle away contentedly and live in the snippet as completely as in the whole. So the denizens of the New York Ghetto, heaped as thick as the splinters on the table of a glass-blower, had each, like the fine glass particle, his or her individual share of the whole hard glitter of Israel. This diffused intensity, as I have called it, causes any array of Jews to resemble (if I may be allowed another image) some long nocturnal street where every window in every house shows a maintained light. The advanced age of so many of the figures, the ubiquity of the children, carried out in fact this analogy; they were all there for race, and not, as it were, for reason: that excess of lurid meaning, in some of the old men's and old women's faces in particular, would have been absurd, in the conditions, as a really directed attention—it could only be the gathered past of Israel mechanically pushing through. The way, at the same time, this chapter of history did, all that evening, seem to push, was a matter that made the "ethnic" apparition again sit like a skeleton at the feast. It was fairly as if I could see the spectre grin while the talk of the hour gave me, across the board, facts and figures, chapter and verse, for the extent of the Hebrew conquest of New York. With a reverence for intellect, one should doubtless have drunk in tribute to an intel-

lectual people; but I remember being at no time more conscious of
that merely portentous element, in the aspects of American growth,
which reduces to inanity any marked dismay quite as much as any
high elation. The portent is one of too many—you always come
back, as I have hinted, with your easier gasp, to *that*: it will be time
enough to sigh or to shout when the relation of the particular
appearance to all the other relations shall have cleared itself up.
Phantasmagoric for me, accordingly, in a high degree, are the interesting hours I here glance at content to remain—setting in this respect,
I recognize, an excellent example to all the rest of the New York
phantasmagoria. Let me speak of the remainder only as phantasmagoric too, so that I may both the more kindly recall it and the
sooner have done with it.

I have not done, however, with the impression of that large evening in the Ghetto; there was too much in the vision, and it has
left too much the sense of a rare experience. For what did it all
really come to but that one had seen with one's eyes the New Jerusalem on earth? What less than that could it all have been, in its
far-spreading light and its celestial serenity of multiplication? There
it was, there it is, and when I think of the dark, foul, stifling Ghettos of other remembered cities, I shall think by the same stroke of
the city of redemption, and evoke in particular the rich Rutgers
Street perspective—rich, so peculiarly, for the eye, in that complexity of fire-escapes with which each house-front bristles and which
gives the whole vista so modernized and appointed a look. Omnipresent in the "poor" regions, this neat applied machinery has, for
the stranger, a common side with the electric light and the telephone, suggests the distance achieved from the old Jerusalem.
(These frontal iron ladders and platforms, by the way, so numerous
throughout New York, strike more New York notes than can be
parenthetically named—and among them perhaps most sharply the
note of the ease with which, in the terrible town, on opportunity,
"architecture" goes by the board; but the appearance to which they
often most conduce is that of the spaciously organized cage for the
nimbler class of animals in some great zoological garden. This general analogy is irresistible—it seems to offer, in each district, a little
world of bars and perches and swings for human squirrels and monkeys. The very name of architecture perishes, for the fire-escapes
look like abashed afterthoughts, staircases and communications forgotten in the construction; but the inhabitants lead, like the squirrels and monkeys, all the merrier life.) It was while I hung over the
prospect from the windows of my friend, however, the presiding
genius of the district, and it was while, at a later hour, I proceeded
in his company, and in that of a trio of contributive fellow-pilgrims,
from one "characteristic" place of public entertainment to another:
it was during this rich climax, I say, that the city of redemption was
least to be taken for anything less than it was. The windows, while

we sat at meat, looked out on a swarming little square in which an ant-like population darted to and fro; the square consisted in part of a "district" public garden, or public lounge rather, one of those small backwaters or refuges, artfully economized for rest, here and there, in the very heart of the New York whirlpool, and which spoke louder than anything else of a Jerusalem disinfected. What spoke loudest, no doubt, was the great overtowering School which formed a main boundary and in the shadow of which we all comparatively crouched.

But the School must not lead me on just yet—so colossally has its presence still to loom for us; that presence which profits so, for predominance, in America, by the failure of concurrent and competitive presences, the failure of any others looming at all on the same scale save that of Business, those in particular of a visible Church, a visible State, a visible Society, a visible Past; those of the many visibilities, in short, that warmly cumber the ground in older countries. Yet it also spoke loud that my friend was quartered, for the interest of the thing (from his so interesting point of view), in a "tenement-house"; the New Jerusalem would so have triumphed, had it triumphed nowhere else, in the fact that this charming little structure *could* be ranged, on the wonderful little square, under that invidious head. On my asking to what latent vice it owed its stigma, I was asked in return if it didn't sufficiently pay for its name by harbouring some five-and-twenty families. But this, exactly, was the way it testified—this circumstance of the simultaneous enjoyment by five-and-twenty families, on "tenement" lines, of conditions so little sordid, so highly "evolved." I remembered the evolved fireproof staircase, a thing of scientific surfaces, impenetrable to the microbe, and above all plated, against side friction, with white marble of a goodly grain. The white marble was surely the New Jerusalem note, and we followed that note, up and down the district, the rest of the evening, through more happy changes than I may take time to count. What struck me in the flaring streets (over and beyond the everywhere insistent, defiant, unhumorous, exotic face) was the blaze of the shops addressed to the New Jerusalem wants and the splendour with which these were taken for granted; the only thing indeed a little ambiguous was just this look of the trap too brilliantly, too candidly baited for the wary side of Israel itself. It is not *for* Israel, in general, that Israel so artfully shines—yet its being moved to do so, at last, in that luxurious style, might be precisely the grand side of the city of redemption. Who can ever tell, moreover, in any conditions and in presence of any apparent anomaly, what the genius of Israel may, or may not, really be "up to"?

The grateful way to take it all, at any rate, was with the sense of its coming back again to the inveterate rise, in the American air, of every value, and especially of the lower ones, those most subject to multiplication; such a wealth of meaning did this keep appearing to pour into the value and function of the country at large. Importances are all strikingly shifted and reconstituted, in the United States, for the visitor attuned, from far back, to "European" importances; but I think of no other moment of my total impression as so sharply working over my own benighted vision of them. The scale, in this light of the New Jerusalem, seemed completely rearranged; or, to put it more simply, the wants, the gratifications, the aspirations of the "poor," as expressed in the shops (which were the shops of the "poor"), denoted a new style of poverty; and this new style of poverty, from street to street, stuck out of the possible purchasers, one's jostling fellow-pedestrians, and made them, to every man and woman, individual throbs in the larger harmony. One can speak only of what one has seen, and there were grosser elements of the sordid and the squalid that I doubtless never saw. That, with a good deal of observation and of curiosity, I should have failed of this, the country over, affected me as by itself something of an indication. To miss that part of the spectacle, or to know it only by its having so unfamiliar a pitch, was an indication that made up for a great many others. It is when this one in particular is forced home to you—this immense, vivid *general* lift of poverty and general appreciation of the living unit's paying property in himself—that the picture seems most to clear and the way to jubilation most to open. For it meets you there, at every turn, as the result most definitely attested. You are as constantly reminded, no doubt, that these rises in enjoyed value shrink and dwindle under the icy breath of Trusts and the weight of the new remorseless monopolies that operate as no madnesses of ancient personal power thrilling us on the historic page ever operated; the living unit's property in himself becoming more and more merely such a property as may consist with a relation to properties overwhelmingly greater and that allow the asking of no questions and the making, for co-existence with them, of no conditions. But that, in the fortunate phrase, is another story, and will be altogether, evidently, a new and different drama. There is such a thing, in the United States, it is hence to be inferred, as freedom to grow up to be blighted, and it may be the only freedom in store for the smaller fry of future generations. If it is accordingly of the smaller fry I speak, and of how large they massed on that evening of endless admonitions, this will be because I caught them thus in their comparative humility and at an early stage of their American growth. The life-thread has, I suppose, to be of a certain thickness for the great shears of Fate to feel for it. Put it, at the worst, that the Ogres were to devour them, they were but the more certainly to fatten into food for the Ogres.

Their dream, at all events, as I noted it, was meanwhile sweet and undisguised—nowhere sweeter than in the half-dozen picked beer-houses and cafés in which our ingenuous *enquête*,[3] that of my

3. Inquest.

fellow-pilgrims and I, wound up. These establishments had each been selected for its playing off some facet of the jewel, and they wondrously testified, by their range and their individual colour, to the spread of that lustre. It was a pious rosary of which I should like to tell each bead, but I must let the general sense of the adventure serve. Our successive stations were in no case of the "seamy" order, an inquiry into seaminess having been unanimously pronounced futile, but each had its separate social connotation, and it was for the number and variety of these connotations, and their individual plenitude and prosperity, to set one thinking. Truly the Yiddish world was a vast world, with its own deeps and complexities, and what struck one above all was that it sat there at its cups (and in no instance vulgarly the worse for them) with a sublimity of good conscience that took away the breath, a protrusion of elbow never aggressive, but absolutely proof against jostling. It was the incurable man of letters under the skin of one of the party who gasped, I confess; for it was in the light of letters, that is in the light of our language as literature has hitherto known it, that one stared at this all-unconscious impudence of the agency of future ravage. The man of letters, in the United States, has his own difficulties to face and his own current to stem—for dealing with which his liveliest inspiration may be, I think, that they are still very much his own, even in an Americanized world, and that more than elsewhere they press him to intimate communion with his honour. For that honour, the honour that sits astride of the consecrated English tradition, to his mind, quite as old knighthood astride of its caparisoned charger, the dragon most rousing, over the land, the proper spirit of St. George,[4] is just this immensity of the alien presence climbing higher and higher, climbing itself into the very light of publicity.

I scarce know why, but I saw it that evening as in some dim dawn of that promise to its own consciousness, and perhaps this was precisely what made it a little exasperating. Under the impression of the mere mob the question doesn't come up, but in these haunts of comparative civility we saw the mob sifted and strained, and the exasperation was the sharper, no doubt, because what the process had left most visible was just the various possibilities of the waiting spring of intelligence. Such elements constituted the germ of a "public," and it was impossible (possessed of a sensibility worth speaking of) to be exposed to them without feeling how new a thing under the sun the resulting public would be. That was where one's "lettered" anguish came in—in the turn of one's eye from face to face for some betrayal of a prehensile hook for the linguistic tradition as one had known it. Each warm lighted and supplied circle, each group of served tables and smoked pipes and fostered decencies and unprecedented accents, beneath the extravagant lamps, took on

---

4. Saint George (fourth century), patron saint of England, depicted in drama and art as the slayer of a dragon.

thus, for the brooding critic, a likeness to that terrible modernized and civilized room in the Tower of London, haunted by the shade of Guy Fawkes,[5] which had more than once formed part of the scene of the critic's taking tea there. In this chamber of the present urbanities the wretched man had been stretched on the rack, and the critic's ear (how else should it have been a critic's?) could still always catch, in pauses of talk, the faint groan of his ghost. Just so the East side cafés—and increasingly as their place in the scale was higher—showed to my inner sense, beneath their bedizenment, as torture-rooms of the living idiom; the piteous gasp of which at the portent of lacerations to come could reach me in any drop of the surrounding Accent of the Future. The accent of the very ultimate future, in the States, may be destined to become the most beautiful on the globe and the very music of humanity (here the "ethnic" synthesis shrouds itself thicker than ever); but whatever we shall know it for, certainly, we shall not know it for English—in any sense for which there is an existing literary measure.

[*"A Florida Adorable"*]

This last impression had indeed everything to gain from the sad rigour of steps retraced, an inevitable return to the North (in the interest of a directly subsequent, and thereby gracelessly roundabout, move Westward); and I confess to having felt on that occasion, before the dire backwardness of the Northern spring, as if I had, while travelling in the other sense, but blasphemed against the want of forwardness of the Southern. Every breath that one might still have drawn in the South—might if twenty other matters had been different—haunted me as the thought of a lost treasure, and I settled, at the eternal car window, to the mere sightless contemplation, the forlorn view, of an ugly—ah, such an ugly, wintering, waiting world. My eye had perhaps been jaundiced by the breach of a happy spell—inasmuch as on thus leaving the sad fragments there where they had fallen I tasted again the quite saccharine sweetness of my last experience of Palm Beach, and knew how I should wish to note for remembrance the passage, supremely charged with that quality, in which it had culminated. I asked myself what other expression I should find for the incident, the afternoon before I left the place, of one of those mild progresses to the head of Lake Worth which distil, for the good children of the Pair,[6] the purest poetry of their cup. The poetic effect had braved the compromising aid of the highly-developed electric launch in which the pilgrim embarks, and braved as well the immitigable fact that his shrine, at the end of a couple of hours, is, in the vast and exquisite void, but an institution of yesterday, a wondrous floating tea-house or restau-

5. Guy Fawkes (1570–1606), who conspired to blow up the Houses of Parliament in 1604–5.
6. The two outstanding hotels in Palm Beach, Florida, the Royal Poinciana and the Cocoa-Nut Grove. Thus, the good children of "the Pair" are tourists.

rant, inflated again with the hotel-spirit and exhaling modernity at every pore.

These associations are—so far as association goes—the only ones; but the whole impression, for simply sitting there in the softest lap the whole South had to offer, seemed to me to dispense with any aid but that of its own absolute felicity. It was, for the late return at least, the return in the divine dusk, with the flushed West at one's right, a concert of but two or three notes—the alignment, against the golden sky, of the individual black palms, a frieze of chiselled ebony, and the texture, for faintly-brushed cheek and brow, of an air of such silkiness of velvet, the very throne-robe of the star-crowned night, as one can scarce commemorate but in the language of the loom. The shore of the sunset and the palms, what was that, meanwhile, like, and yet with what did it, at the moment one asked the question, refuse to have anything to do? It was like a myriad pictures of the Nile; with much of the modern life of which it suggested more than one analogy. These indeed all dropped, I found, before I had done—it would have been a Nile so simplified out of the various fine senses attachable. One had to put the case, I mean, to *make* a fine sense, that here surely then was the greater antiquity of the two, the antiquity of the infinite *previous*, of the time, before Pharaohs and Pyramids, when everything was still to come. It was a Nile, in short, without the least little implication of a Sphinx or, still more if possible, of a Cleopatra. I had the foretaste of what I was presently to feel in California—when the general aspect of that wondrous realm kept suggesting to me a sort of prepared but unconscious and inexperienced Italy, the primitive *plate*, in perfect condition, but with the impression of History all yet to be made.

Of how grimly, meanwhile, under the annual rigour, the world, for the most part, waits to be less ugly again, less despoiled of interest, less abandoned to monotony, less forsaken of the presence that forms its only resource, of the one friend to whom it owes all it ever gets, of the pitying season that shall save it from its huge insignificance—of so much as this, no doubt, I sufficiently renewed my vision, and with plenty of the reviving ache of a question already familiar. To what extent was hugeness, to what extent *could* it be, a ground for complacency of view, in any country not visited for the very love of wildness, for positive joy in barbarism? Where was the charm of boundless immensity as overlooked from a car-window?— with the general pretension to charm, the general conquest of nature and space, affirmed, immediately round about you, by the general pretension of the Pullman,[7] the great monotonous rumble of which seems forever to say to you: "See what I'm making of all this —see what I'm making, what I'm making!" I was to become later on still more intimately aware of the spirit of one's possible reply to

7. Sleeping-car train coaches, named after George Pullman, whose company manufactured them.

that, but even then my consciousness served, and the eloquence of my exasperation seems, in its rude accents, to come back to me.

"I see what you are *not* making, oh, what you are ever so vividly not; and how can I help it if I am subject to that lucidity?—which appears never so welcome to you, for its measure of truth, as it ought to be! How can I not be so subject, from the moment I don't just irreflectively gape? If I were one of the painted savages you have dispossessed, or even some tough reactionary trying to emulate him, what you are making would doubtless impress me more than what you are leaving unmade; for in that case it wouldn't be to *you* I should be looking in any degree for beauty or for charm. Beauty and charm would be for me in the solitude you have ravaged, and I should owe you my grudge for every disfigurement and every violence, for every wound with which you have caused the face of the land to bleed. No, since I accept your ravage, what strikes me is the long list of the arrears of your undone; and so constantly, right and left, that your pretended message of civilization is but a colossal recipe for the *creation* of arrears, and of such as can but remain forever out of hand. You touch the great lonely land—as one feels it still to be—only to plant upon it some ugliness about which, never dreaming of the grace of apology or contrition, you then proceed to brag with a cynicism all your own. You convert the large and noble sanities that I see around me, you convert them one after the other to crudities, to invalidities, hideous and unashamed; and you so leave them to add to the number of the myriad aspects you simply spoil, of the myriad unanswerable questions that you scatter about as some monstrous unnatural mother might leave a family of unfathered infants on doorsteps or in waiting-rooms. This is the meaning surely of the inveterate rule that you shall multiply the perpetrations you call 'places'—by the sign of some name as senseless, mostly, as themselves—to the sole end of multiplying to the eye, as one approaches, every possible source of displeasure. When nobody cares or notices or suffers, by all one makes out, when no displeasure, by what one can see, is ever felt or ever registered, why shouldn't you, you may indeed ask, be as much in your right as you need? But in that fact itself, that fact of the vast general unconsciousness and indifference, looms, for any restless analyst who may come along, the accumulation, on your hands, of the unretrieved and the irretrievable!"

I remember how it was to come to me elsewhere, in such hours as those, that south of Pennsylvania, for instance, or beyond the radius of Washington, I had caught no glimpse of anything that was to be called, for more than a few miles and by a stretch of courtesy, the honour, the decency or dignity of a road—that most exemplary of all civil creations, and greater even as a note of morality, one often thinks, than as a note of facility; and yet had nowhere heard these particular arrears spoken of as matters ever conceivably to be made

up. I was doubtless aware that if I had been a beautiful red man
with a tomahawk I should of course have rejoiced in the occasional
sandy track, or in the occasional mud-channel, just in proportion as
they fell so short of the type. Only in that case I shouldn't have
been seated by the great square of plate-glass through which the
missionary Pullman appeared to invite me to admire the achievements it proclaimed. It was in this respect the great symbolic agent;
it seemed to stand for all the irresponsibility behind it; and I am
not sure that I didn't continue, so long as I was in it, to "slang" it
for relief of the o'erfraught heart. "You deal your wounds—that is
the 'trouble,' as you say—in numbers so out of proportion to any
hint of responsibility for them that you seem ever moved to take;
which is the devil's dance, precisely, that your vast expanse of level
floor leads you to caper through with more kinds of outward clumsi-
ness—even if also with more kinds of inward impatience and avidity, more leaps and bounds of the spirit at any cost to grace—than
have ever before been collectively displayed. The expanse of the
floor, the material opportunity itself, has elsewhere failed; so that
what is the positive effect of their inordinate presence but to make
the lone observer, here and there, but measure with dismay the trap
laid by the scale, if he be not tempted even to say by the superstition, of continuity? Is the germ of anything finely human, of anything agreeably or successfully social, supposably planted in conditions of such endless stretching and such boundless spreading as
shall appear finally to minister but to the triumph of the superficial
and the apotheosis of the raw? Oh for a split or a chasm, one
groans beside your plate-glass, oh for an unbridgeable abyss or an
insuperable mountain!"—and I could so indulge myself though still
ignorant of how one was to groan later on, in particular, after
taking yet further home the portentous truth that this same criminal continuity, scorning its grandest chance to break down, makes
but a mouthful of the mighty Mississippi. That was to be in fact
my very next "big" impression.

1907

JOEL CHANDLER HARRIS
1848–1908

Joel Chandler Harris was born in Putnam County, Georgia, on December
9, 1848, the son of an Irish day laborer who deserted his mother Mary
Harris, a seamstress, near the time of his birth. The townspeople helped the
small, red-haired boy and his mother, however, and paid his school fees. At
age fourteen he went to work on Joseph Addison Turner's newly established newspaper *The Countryman*, and lived on Turner's plantation Turnwold until 1866. He began as a printer's apprentice, but before long he

was contributing articles, humorous paragraphs, and reviews. Later that same year, Harris took a job briefly as a printer on the Macon *Telegraph* before becoming private secretary to William Evelyn, publisher of the New Orleans *Crescent Monthly*. In the fall of 1870 he accepted a position as associate editor on the Savannah *Morning News*; there his comic writings and his daily column on Georgia affairs soon earned him the reputation as Georgia's foremost newspaper humorist.

On April 20, 1873, Harris married Esther La Rose. To avoid a yellow fever epidemic, he took his family to Atlanta in 1876 in what turned out to be a permanent move. He went to work for the Atlanta *Constitution* as an associate editor, and initiated a column called "Round About in Georgia," similar to the one he had written for the *Morning News*. In time Harris became one of the leading editorial voices promoting the "New South" that was emerging from the ruin of the Civil War. More significantly, he wrote his first Uncle Remus story for the issue of October 26, 1876.

Harris's first Uncle Remus book, *Uncle Remus: His Songs and Sayings*, was published in 1881, and over the next twenty-five years five other collections of Remus stories and poems followed. For these immensely popular stories, Harris drew on his Turnwold experience as a fascinated listener to Negro folklore and storytelling, a tradition which in turn drew on a mixture of African and European models. It is Harris's painstaking reshaping and retelling of these stories through the shrewd and inventive persona of Uncle Remus that is his most important contribution to American letters. As the critic Jay Martin has suggested, the initiation of the young white child in the stories to the values of an earlier day constitutes an oblique satire on the commercial values of the New South espoused by Harris the journalist. But surely the enduring appeal of these stories rests in their offering wise commentary on universal features of human character in a satisfying narrative form.

Harris published in these same years another score of volumes of tales, sketches, novels, and children's stories featuring a wide range of characters both fanciful and real. Best known among these works is *Free Joe and Other Georgian Sketches* (1887), the title story of which explores the tragic displacement of a free black man in the pre–Civil War South. A shy man, Harris was rarely available to anyone but his closest friends and family. It was among them that he died on July 2, 1908, a week after being baptized as a Catholic.

The Wonderful Tar-Baby Story[1]

"Didn't the fox *never* catch the rabbit, Uncle Remus?" asked the little boy the next evening.

"He come mighty nigh it, honey, sho's you born—Brer Fox did. One day atter Brer Rabbit fool 'im wid dat calamus root, Brer Fox went ter wuk en got 'im some tar, en mix it wid some turkentime, en fix up a contrapshun wat he call a Tar-Baby, en he tuck dish yer Tar-Baby en he sot 'er in de big road, en den he lay off in de bushes fer to see wat de news wuz gwineter be. En he didn't hatter wait long, nudder, kaze bimeby here come Brer Rabbit pacin' down de

---

1. This story was first published in *Uncle Remus: His Songs and His Sayings* (1881), the source of the present text.

road—lippity-clippity, clippity-lippity—dez ez sassy ez a jay-bird. Brer Fox, he lay low. Brer Rabbit come prancin' 'long twel he spy de Tar-Baby, en den he fotch up on his behime legs like he wuz 'stonished. De Tar-Baby, she sot dar, she did, en Brer Fox, he lay low.

" 'Mawnin'!' sez Brer Rabbit, sezee—'nice wedder dis mawnin',' sezee.

"Tar-Baby ain't sayin' nothin', en Brer Fox, he lay low.

" 'How duz yo' sym'tums seem ter segashuate?' sez Brer Rabbit, sezee.

"Brer Fox, he wink his eye slow, en lay low, en de Tar-Baby, she ain't sayin' nothin'.

" 'How you come on, den? Is you deaf?' sez Brer Rabbit, sezee. 'Kaze if you is, I kin holler louder,' sezee.

"Tar-Baby stay still, en Brer Fox, he lay low.

" 'Youer stuck up, dat's w'at you is,' says Brer Rabbit, sezee, 'en I'm gwineter kyore you, dat's w'at I'm a gwineter do,' sezee.

"Brer Fox, he sorter chuckle in his stummuck, he did, but Tar-Baby ain't sayin' nothin'.

" 'I'm gwineter larn you howter talk ter 'specttubble fokes ef hit's de las' ack', sez Brer Rabbit, sezee. 'Ef you don't take off dat hat en tell me howdy, I'm gwineter bus' you wide open,' sezee.

"Tar-Baby stay still, en Brer Fox, he lay low.

"Brer Rabbit keep on axin' 'im, en de Tar-Baby, she keep on sayin' nothin', twel present'y Brer Rabbit draw back wid his fis', he did, en blip he tuck 'er side er de head. Right dar's whar he broke his merlasses jug. His fis' stuck, en he can't pull loose. De tar hilt 'im. But Tar-Baby, she stay still, en Brer Fox, he lay low.

" 'Ef you don't lemme loose, I'll knock you agin,' sez Brer Rabbit, sezee, en wid dat he fotch 'er a wipe wid de udder han', en dat stuck. Tar-Baby, she ain't sayin' nothin', en Brer Fox, he lay low.

" 'Tu'n me loose, fo' I kick de natal stuffin' outen you,' sez Brer Rabbit, sezee, but de Tar-Baby, she ain't sayin' nothin. She des hilt on, en den Brer Rabbit lose de use er his feet in de same way. Brer Fox, he lay low. Den Brer Rabbit squall out dat ef de Tar-Baby don't tu'n 'im loose he butt 'er cranksided. En den he butted, en his head got stuck. Den Brer Fox, he sa'ntered fort', lookin' des ez innercent ez one er yo' mammy's mockin'-birds.

" 'Howdy, Brer Rabbit,' sez Brer Fox, sezee. 'You look sorter stuck up dis mawnin',' sezee, en den he rolled on de groun', en laughed en laughed twel he couldn't laugh no mo'. 'I speck you'll take dinner wid me dis time, Brer Rabbit. I done laid in some calamus root, en I ain't gwineter take no skuse,' sez Brer Fox, sezee."

Here Uncle Remus paused, and drew a two-pound yam out of the ashes.

"Did the fox eat the rabbit?" asked the little boy to whom the story had been told.

"Dat's all de fur de tale goes," replied the old man. "He mout, en den agin he moutent. Some say Jedge B'ar come 'long en loosed 'im—some say he didn't. I hear Miss Sally callin'. You better run 'long."

1881

Mr. Rabbit Grossly Deceives Mr. Fox[1]

One evening when the little boy, whose nights with Uncle Remus are as entertaining as those Arabian ones of blessed memory, had finished supper and hurried out to sit with his venerable patron, he found the old man in great glee. Indeed, Uncle Remus was talking and laughing to himself at such a rate that the little boy was afraid he had company. The truth is, Uncle Remus had heard the child coming, and, when the rosy-cheeked chap put his head in at the door, was engaged in a monologue, the burden of which seemed to be—

> "Ole Molly Har',
> W'at you doin' dar,
> Settin' in de cornder
> Smokin' yo' seegyar?"

As a matter of course this vague allusion reminded the little boy of the fact that the wicked Fox was still in pursuit of the Rabbit, and he immediately put his curiosity in the shape of a question.

"Uncle Remus, did the Rabbit have to go clean away when he got loose from the Tar-Baby?"

"Bless grashus, honey, dat he didn't. Who? Him? You dunno nuthin' 'tall 'bout Brer Rabbit ef dat's de way you puttin' 'im down. W'at he gwine 'way fer? He mouter stayed sorter close twel de pitch rub off'n his ha'r, but twern't menny days 'fo' he wuz lopin' up en down de naberhood same ez ever, en I dunno ef he wern't mo' sassier dan befo'.

"Seem like dat de tale 'bout how he got mixt up wid de Tar-Baby got 'roun' 'mongst de nabers. Leas'ways, Miss Meadows en de gals got win' un' it, en de nex' time Brer Rabbit paid um a visit Miss Meadows tackled 'im 'bout it, en de gals sot up a monstus giggle-ment. Brer Rabbit, he sot up des ez cool ez a cowcumber, he did, en let 'em run on."

"Who was Miss Meadows, Uncle Remus?" inquired the little boy.

"Don't ax me, honey. She wuz in de tale, Miss Meadows en de gals wuz, en de tale I give you like hi't wer' gun ter me. Brer

---

1. This story was first published in *Uncle Remus: His Songs and His Sayings* (1881), the source of the present text.

Rabbit, he sot dar, he did, sorter lam' like, en den bimeby he cross his legs, he did, and wink his eye slow, en up en say, sezee:

" 'Ladies, Brer Fox wuz my daddy's ridin'-hoss for thirty year; maybe mo', but thirty year dat I knows un,' sezee; en den he paid um his 'specks, en tip his beaver, en march off, he did, des ez stiff en ez stuck up ez a fire-stick.

"Nex' day, Brer Fox cum a callin', and w'en he gun fer ter laff 'bout Brer Rabbit, Miss Meadows en de gals, dey ups en tells 'im 'bout w'at Brer Rabbit say. Den Brer Fox grit his toof sho' nuff, he did, en he look mighty dumpy, but w'en he riz fer ter go he up en say, sezee:

" 'Ladies, I ain't 'sputin' w'at you say, but I'll make Brer Rabbit chaw up his words en spit um out right yer whar you kin see 'im,' sezee, en wid dat off Brer Fox marcht.

"En w'en he got in de big road, he shuck de dew off'n his tail, en made a straight shoot for Brer Rabbit's house. W'en he got dar, Brer Rabbit wuz spectin' un 'im, en de do' wuz shet fas'. Brer Fox knock. Nobody ain't ans'er. Brer Fox knock. Nobody ans'er. Den he knock agin—blam! blam! Den Brer Rabbit holler out mighty weak:

" 'Is dat you, Brer Fox? I want you ter run en fetch de doctor. Dat bait er pusly w'at I e't dis mawnin' is gittin' 'way wid me. Do, please, Brer Fox, run quick,' sez Brer Rabbit, sezee.

" 'I come atter you, Brer Rabbit,' sez Brer Fox, sezee. 'Dere's gwineter be a party up at Miss Meadows's,' sezee. 'All de gals 'll be dere, en I promus' dat I'd fetch you. De gals, dey 'lowed dat hit wouldn't be no party 'ceppin' I fetch you,' sez Brer Fox, sezee.

" 'Den Brer Rabbit say he wuz too sick, en Brer Fox say he wuzzent, en dar dey had it up and down, 'sputin' en contendin'. Brer Rabbit say he can't walk. Brer Fox say he tote 'im. Brer Rabbit say how? Brer Fox say in his arms. Brer Rabbit say he drap 'im. Brer Fox 'low he won't. Bimeby Brer Rabbit say he go ef Brer Fox tote 'im on his back. Brer Fox say he would. Brer Rabbit say he can't ride widout a saddle. Brer Fox say he git de saddle. Brer Rabbit say he can't set in saddle less he have bridle fer ter hol' by. Brer Fox say he git de bridle. Brer Rabbit say he can't ride widout bline bridle, kaze Brer Fox be shyin' at stumps 'long de road, en fling 'im off. Brer Fox say he git bline bridle. Den Brer Rabbit say he go. Den Brer Fox say he ride Brer Rabbit mos' up ter Miss Meadows's, en den he could git down en walk de balance er de way. Brer Rabbit 'greed, en den Brer Fox lipt out atter de saddle en de bridle.

"Co'se Brer Rabbit know de game dat Brer Fox wuz fixin' fer ter play, en he 'termin' fer ter outdo 'im, en by de time he koam his ha'r en twis' his mustarsh, en sorter rig up, yer come Brer Fox, saddle en bridle on, en lookin' ez peart ez a circus pony. He trot up ter de do' en stan' dar pawin' de ground en chompin' de bit same like sho 'nuff hoss, en Brer Rabbit he mount, he did, en dey amble off. Brer Fox can't see behime wid de bline bridle on, but bimeby he feel Brer Rabbit raise one er his foots.

" 'W'at you doin' now, Brer Rabbit?' sezee.

" 'Short'nin' de lef stir'p, Brer Fox,' sezee.

"Bimeby Brer Rabbit raise up de udder foot.

" 'W'at you doin' now, Brer Rabbit?' sezee.

" 'Pullin' down my pants, Brer Fox,' sezee.

"All de time, bless grashus, honey, Brer Rabbit wer puttin' on his spurrers, en w'en dey got close to Miss Meadows's, whar Brer Rabbit wuz to git off, en Brer Fox made a motion fer ter stan' still, Brer Rabbit slap de spurrers inter Brer Fox flanks, en you better b'leeve he got over groun'. W'en dey got ter de house, Miss Meadows en all de gals wuz settin' on de peazzer, en stidder stoppin' at de gate, Brer Rabbit rid on by, he did, en den come gallopin' down de road en up ter de hoss-rack, w'ich he hitch Brer Fox at, en den he santer inter de house, he did, en shake han's wid de gals, en set dar, smokin' his seegyar same ez a town man. Bimeby he draw in long puff, en den let hit out in a cloud, en squar hisse'f back en holler out, he did:

" 'Ladies, ain't I done tell you Brer Fox wuz de ridin'-hoss fer our fambly? He sorter losin' his gait' now, but I speck I kin fetch 'im all right in a mont' er so,' sezee.

"En den Brer Rabbit sorter grin, he did, en de gals giggle, en Miss Meadows, she praise up de pony, en dar wuz Brer Fox hitch fas' ter de rack, en couldn't he'p hisse'f."

"Is that all, Uncle Remus?" asked the little boy as the old man paused.

"Dat ain't all, honey, but 'twon't do fer ter give out too much cloff fer ter cut one pa'r pants," replied the old man sententiously.

1881

Free Joe and the Rest of the World[1]

The name of Free Joe strikes humorously upon the ear of memory. It is impossible to say why, for he was the humblest, the simplest, and the most serious of all God's living creatures, sadly lacking in all those elements that suggest the humorous. It is certain, moreover, that in 1850 the sober-minded citizens of the little Georgian village of Hillsborough were not inclined to take a humorous view of Free Joe, and neither his name nor his presence provoked a smile. He was a black atom, drifting hither and thither without an owner, blown about by all the winds of circumstance, and given over to shiftlessness.

The problems of one generation are the paradoxes of a succeeding one, particularly if war, or some such incident, intervenes to

1. This story was first published in *Free Joe and Other Georgia Sketches* (1887), the source of the present text.

clarify the atmosphere and strengthen the understanding. Thus, in 1850, Free Joe represented not only a problem of large concern, but, in the watchful eyes of Hillsborough, he was the embodiment of that vague and mysterious danger that seemed to be forever lurking on the outskirts of slavery, ready to sound a shrill and ghostly signal in the impenetrable swamps, and steal forth under the midnight stars to murder, rapine, and pillage—a danger always threatening, and yet never assuming shape; intangible, and yet real; impossible, and yet not improbable. Across the serene and smiling front of safety, the pale outlines of the awful shadow of insurrection some-times fell. With this invisible panorama as a background, it was natural that the figure of Free Joe, simple and humble as it was, should assume undue proportions. Go where he would, do what he might, he could not escape the finger of observation and the kin-dling eye of suspicion. His lightest words were noted, his slightest actions marked.

Under all the circumstances it was natural that his peculiar con-dition should reflect itself in his habits and manners. The slaves laughed loudly day by day, but Free Joe rarely laughed. The slaves sang at their work and danced at their frolics, but no one ever heard Free Joe sing or saw him dance. There was something painfully plaintive and appealing in his attitude, something touching in his anxiety to please. He was of the friendliest nature, and seemed to be delighted when he could amuse the little children who had made a playground of the public square. At times he would please them by making his little dog Dan perform all sorts of curious tricks, or he would tell them quaint stories of the beasts of the field and birds of the air; and frequently he was coaxed into relating the story of his own freedom. That story was brief, but tragical.

In the year of our Lord 1840, when a negro speculator of a spor-tive turn of mind reached the little village of Hillsborough on his way to the Mississippi region, with a caravan of likely negroes of both sexes, he found much to interest him. In that day and at that time there were a number of young men in the village who had not bound themselves over to repentance for the various misdeeds of the flesh. To these young men the negro speculator (Major Framp-ton was his name) proceeded to address himself. He was a Virginian, he declared; and, to prove the statement, he referred all the festively inclined young men of Hillsborough to a barrel of peach-brandy in one of his covered wagons. In the minds of these young men there was less doubt in regard to the age and quality of the brandy than there was in regard to the negro trader's birthplace. Major Framp-ton might or might not have been born in the Old Dominion—that was a matter for consideration and inquiry—but there could be no question as to the mellow pungency of the peach-brandy.

In his own estimation, Major Frampton was one of the most accomplished of men. He had summered at the Virginia Springs;

he had been to Philadelphia, to Washington, to Richmond, to Lynchburg, and to Charleston, and had accumulated a great deal of experience which he found useful. Hillsborough was hid in the woods of Middle Georgia, and its general aspect of innocence impressed him. He looked on the young men who had shown their readiness to test his peach-brandy as overgrown country boys who needed to be introduced to some of the arts and sciences he had at his command. Thereupon the major pitched his tents, figuratively speaking, and became, for the time being, a part and parcel of the innocence that characterized Hillsborough. A wiser man would doubtless have made the same mistake.

The little village possessed advantages that seemed to be providentially arranged to fit the various enterprises that Major Frampton had in view. There was the auction block in front of the stuccoed court-house, if he desired to dispose of a few of his negroes; there was a quarter-track, laid out to his hand and in excellent order, if he chose to enjoy the pleasures of horse-racing; there were secluded pine thickets within easy reach, if he desired to indulge in the exciting pastime of cock-fighting; and variously lonely and unoccupied rooms in the second story of the tavern, if he cared to challenge the chances of dice or cards.

Major Frampton tried them all with varying luck, until he began his famous game of poker with Judge Alfred Wellington, a stately gentleman with a flowing white beard and mild blue eyes that gave him the appearance of a benevolent patriarch. The history of the game in which Major Frampton and Judge Alfred Wellington took part is something more than a tradition in Hillsborough, for there are still living three or four men who sat around the table and watched its progress. It is said that at various stages of the game Major Frampton would destroy the cards with which they were playing, and send for a new pack, but the result was always the same. The mild blue eyes of Judge Wellington, with few exceptions, continued to overlook "hands" that were invincible—a habit they had acquired during a long and arduous course of training from Saratoga to New Orleans. Major Frampton lost his money, his horses, his wagons, and all his negroes but one, his body-servant. When his misfortune had reached this limit, the major adjourned the game. The sun was shining brightly, and all nature was cheerful. It is said that the major also seemed to be cheerful. However this may be, he visited the court-house, and executed the papers that gave his body-servant his freedom. This being done, Major Frampton sauntered into a convenient pine thicket, and blew out his brains.

The negro thus freed came to be known as Free Joe. Compelled, under the law, to choose a guardian, he chose Judge Wellington, chiefly because his wife Lucinda was among the negroes won from Major Frampton. For several years Free Joe had what may be called a jovial time. His wife Lucinda was well provided for, and he found it a comparatively easy matter to provide for himself; so that, taking all the circumstances into consideration, it is not matter for astonishment that he became somewhat shiftless.

When Judge Wellington died, Free Joe's troubles began. The judge's negroes, including Lucinda, went to his half-brother, a man named Calderwood, who was a hard master and a rough customer generally—a man of many eccentricities of mind and character. His neighbors had a habit of alluding to him as "Old Spite"; and the name seemed to fit him so completely that he was known far and near as "Spite" Calderwood. He probably enjoyed the distinction the name gave him, at any rate he never resented it, and it was not often he missed an opportunity to show that he deserved it. Calderwood's place was two or three miles from the village of Hillsborough, and Free Joe visited his wife twice a week, Wednesday and Saturday nights.

One Sunday he was sitting in front of Lucinda's cabin, when Calderwood happened to pass that way.

"Howdy, marster?" said Free Joe, taking off his hat.

"Who are you?" exclaimed Calderwood abruptly, halting and staring at the negro.

"I'm name' Joe, marster. I'm Lucindy's ole man."

"Who do you belong to?"

"Marse John Evans is my gyardeen, marster."

"Big name—gyardeen. Show your pass."

Free Joe produced that document, and Calderwood read it aloud slowly, as if he found it difficult to get at the meaning:

"*To whom it may concern: This is to certify that the boy Joe Frampton has my permission to visit his wife Lucinda.*"

This was dated at Hillsborough, and signed "*John W. Evans.*"

Calderwood read it twice, and then looked at Free Joe, elevating his eyebrows, and showing his discolored teeth.

"Some mighty big words in that there. Evans owns this place, I reckon. When's he comin' down to take hold?"

Free Joe fumbled with his hat. He was badly frightened.

"Lucindy say she speck you wouldn't min' my comin', long ez I behave, marster."

Calderwood tore the pass in pieces and flung it away.

"Don't want no free niggers 'round here," he exclaimed. "There's the big road. It'll carry you to town. Don't let me catch you here no more. Now, mind what I tell you."

Free Joe presented a shabby spectacle as he moved off with his little dog Dan slinking at his heels. It should be said in behalf of Dan, however, that his bristles were up, and that he looked back and growled. It may be that the dog had the advantage of insignificance, but it is difficult to conceive how a dog bold enough to raise his bristles under Calderwood's very eyes could be as insignificant as Free Joe. But both the negro and his little dog seemed to give a new and more dismal aspect to forlornness as they turned into the road and went toward Hillsborough.

After this incident Free Joe appeared to have clearer ideas concerning his peculiar condition. He realized the fact that though he was free he was more helpless than any slave. Having no owner, every man was his master. He knew that he was the object of suspicion, and therefore all his slender resources (ah! how pitifully slender they were!) were devoted to winning, not kindness and appreciation, but toleration; all his efforts were in the direction of mitigating the circumstances that tended to make his condition so much worse than that of the negroes around him—negroes who had friends because they had masters.

So far as his own race was concerned, Free Joe was an exile. If the slaves secretly envied him his freedom (which is to be doubted, considering his miserable condition), they openly despised him, and lost no opportunity to treat him with contumely. Perhaps this was in some measure the result of the attitude which Free Joe chose to maintain toward them. No doubt his instinct taught him that to hold himself aloof from the slaves would be to invite from the whites the toleration which he coveted, and without which even his miserable condition would be rendered more miserable still.

His greatest trouble was the fact that he was not allowed to visit his wife; but he soon found a way out of his difficulty. After he had been ordered away from the Calderwood place, he was in the habit of wandering as far in that direction as prudence would permit. Near the Calderwood place, but not on Calderwood's land, lived an old man named Micajah Staley and his sister Becky Staley. These people were old and very poor. Old Micajah had a palsied arm and hand; but, in spite of this, he managed to earn a precarious living with his turning-lathe.

When he was a slave Free Joe would have scorned these representatives of a class known as poor white trash, but now he found them sympathetic and helpful in various ways. From the back door of their cabin he could hear the Calderwood negroes singing at night, and he sometimes fancied he could distinguish Lucinda's shrill treble rising above the other voices. A large poplar grew in the woods some distance from the Staley cabin, and at the foot of this tree Free Joe would sit for hours with his face turned toward Calderwood's. His little dog Dan would curl up in the leaves near by, and the two seemed to be as comfortable as possible.

One Saturday afternoon Free Joe, sitting at the foot of this friendly poplar, fell asleep. How long he slept, he could not tell; but when he awoke little Dan was licking his face, the moon was shining brightly, and Lucinda his wife stood before him laughing. The dog, seeing that Free Joe was asleep, had grown somewhat impatient, and he concluded to make an excursion to the Calderwood place on his own account. Lucinda was inclined to give the incident a twist in the direction of superstition.

"I 'uz settn' down front er de fireplace," she said, "cookin' me some meat, w'en all of a sudden I year sumpin at de do'—scratch, scratch. I tuck'n tu'n de meat over, en make out I ain't year it. Bimeby it come dar 'gin—scratch, scratch. I up en open de do', I did, en, bless de Lord! dar wuz little Dan, en it look like ter me dat his ribs done grow terge'er. I gin 'im some bread, en den, w'en he start out, I tuck'n foller 'im, kaze, I say ter myse'f, maybe my nigger man mought be some'rs 'roun'. Dat ar little dog got sense, mon."

Free Joe laughed and dropped his hand lightly on Dan's head. For a long time after that he had no difficulty in seeing his wife. He had only to sit by the poplar tree until little Dan could run and fetch her. But after a while the other negroes discovered that Lucinda was meeting Free Joe in the woods, and information of the fact soon reached Calderwood's ears. Calderwood was what is called a man of action. He said nothing; but one day he put Lucinda in his buggy, and carried her to Macon, sixty miles away. He carried her to Macon, and came back without her; and nobody in or around Hillsborough, or in that section, ever saw her again.

For many a night after that Free Joe sat in the woods and waited. Little Dan would run merrily off and be gone a long time, but he always came back without Lucinda. This happened over and over again. The "willis-whistlers"[2] would call and call, like fantom huntsmen wandering on a far-off shore; the screech-owl would shake and shiver in the depths of the woods; the night-hawks, sweeping by on noiseless wings, would snap their beaks as though they enjoyed the huge joke of which Free Joe and little Dan were the victims; and the whippoor-wills would cry to each other through the gloom. Each night seemed to be lonelier than the preceding, but Free Joe's patience was proof against loneliness. There came a time, however, when little Dan refused to go after Lucinda. When Free Joe motioned him in the direction of the Calderwood place, he would simply move about uneasily and whine; then he would curl up in the leaves and make himself comfortable.

One night, instead of going to the poplar tree to wait for Lucinda, Free Joe went to the Staley cabin, and, in order to make his welcome good, as he expressed it, he carried with him an armful of fat-pine splinters. Miss Becky Staley had a great reputation in those parts as a fortune-teller, and the schoolgirls, as well as older people, often tested her powers in this direction, some in jest and some in earnest. Free Joe placed his humble offering of light-wood in the chimney corner, and then seated himself on the steps, dropping his hat on the ground outside.

2. Probably the willet, a bird whose call was a piercing, shrill whistle.

"Miss Becky," he said presently, "whar in de name er gracious you reckon Lucindy is?"

"Well, the Lord he'p the nigger!" exclaimed Miss Becky, in a tone that seemed to reproduce, by some curious agreement of sight with sound, her general aspect of peakedness. "Well, the Lord he'p the nigger! hain't you been a-seein' her all this blessed time? She's over at old Spite Calderwood's, if she's anywheres, I reckon."

"No'm, dat I ain't, Miss Becky. I ain't seen Lucindy in now gwine on mighty nigh a mont'."

"Well, it hain't a-gwine to hurt you," said Miss Becky, somewhat sharply. "In my day an' time it wuz allers took to be a bad sign when niggers got to honeyin' 'roun' an' gwine on."

"Yessum," said Free Joe, cheerfully assenting to the proposition —"yessum, dat's so, but me an' my ole 'oman, we 'uz raise terge'er, en dey ain't bin many days w'en we 'uz 'way fum one 'n'er like we is now."

"Maybe she's up an' took up wi' some un else," said Micajah Staley from the corner. "You know what the sayin' is: 'New master, new nigger.'"

"Dat's so, dat's de sayin', but tain't wid my ole 'oman like 'tis wid yuther niggers. Me en her wuz des natally raise up terge'er. Dey's lots likelier niggers dan w'at I is," said Free Joe, viewing his shabbiness with a critical eye, "but I knows Lucindy mos' good ez I does little Dan dar—dat I does."

There was no reply to this, and Free Joe continued:

"Miss Becky, I wish you please, ma'am, take en run yo' kyards en see sump'n n'er 'bout Lucindy; kaze ef she sick, I'm gwine dar. Dey ken take en take me up en gimme a stroppin', but I'm gwine dar."

Miss Becky got her cards, but first she picked up a cup, in the bottom of which were some coffee-grounds. These she whirled slowly round and round, ending finally by turning the cup upside down on the hearth and allowing it to remain in that position.

"I'll turn the cup first," said Miss Becky, "and then I'll run the cards and see what they say."

As she shuffled the cards the fire on the hearth burned low, and in its fitful light the gray-haired, thin-featured woman seemed to deserve the weird reputation which rumor and gossip had given her. She shuffled the cards for some moments, gazing intently in the dying fire; then, throwing a piece of pine on the coals, she made three divisions of the pack, disposing them about in her lap. Then she took the first pile, ran the cards slowly through her fingers, and studied them carefully. To the first she added the second pile. The study of these was evidently not satisfactory. She said nothing, but frowned heavily; and the frown deepened as she added the rest of the cards until the entire fifty-two had passed in review before her. Though she frowned, she seemed to be deeply interested. Without changing the relative position of the cards, she ran them all over again. Then she threw a larger piece of pine on the fire, shuffled the cards afresh, divided them into three piles, and subjected them to the same careful and critical examination.

"I can't tell the day when I've seen the cards run this a-way," she said after a while. "What is an' what ain't, I'll never tell you; but I know what the cards sez."

"W'at does dey say, Miss Becky?" the negro inquired, in a tone the solemnity of which was heightened by its eagerness.

"They er runnin' quare. These here that I'm a-lookin' at," said Miss Becky, "they stan' for the past. Them there, they er the present; and the t'others, they er the future. Here's a bundle"—tapping the ace of clubs with her thumb—"an' here's a journey as plain as the nose on a man's face. Here's Lucinda—"

"Whar she, Miss Becky?"

"Here she is—the queen of spades."

Free Joe grinned. The idea seemed to please him immensely.

"Well, well, well!" he exclaimed. "Ef dat don't beat my time! De queen er spades! W'en Lucindy year dat hit'll tickle 'er, sho'!"

Miss Becky continued to run the cards back and forth through her fingers.

"Here's a bundle an' a journey, and here's Lucinda. An' here's ole Spite Calderwood."

She held the cards toward the negro and touched the king of clubs.

"De Lord he'p my soul!" exclaimed Free Joe with a chuckle. "De faver's[3] dar. Yesser, dat's him! W'at de matter 'long wid all un um, Miss Becky?"

The old woman added the second pile of cards to the first, and then the third, still running them through her fingers slowly and critically. By this time the piece of pine in the fireplace had wrapped itself in a mantle of flame, illuminating the cabin and throwing into strange relief the figure of Miss Becky as she sat studying the cards. She frowned ominously at the cards and mumbled a few words to herself. Then she dropped her hands in her lap and gazed once more into the fire. Her shadow danced and capered on the wall and floor behind her, as if, looking over her shoulder into the future, it could behold a rare spectacle. After a while she picked up the cup that had been turned on the hearth. The coffee-grounds, shaken around, presented what seemed to be a most intricate map.

"Here's the journey," said Miss Becky, presently; "here's the big road, here's rivers to cross, here's the bundle to tote." She paused and sighed. "They hain't no names writ here, an' what it all means I'll never tell you. Cajy, I wish you'd be so good as to han' me my pipe."

"I hain't no hand wi' the kyards," said Cajy, as he handed the pipe, "but I reckon I can patch out your misinformation, Becky,

3. Resemblance.

bekaze the other day, whiles I was a-finishin' up Mizzers Perdue's rollin'-pin, I hearn a rattlin' in the road. I looked out, an' Spite Calderwood was a-drivin' by in his buggy, an' thar sot Lucinda by him. It'd in-about drapt out er my min'."

Free Joe sat on the door-sill and fumbled at his hat, flinging it from one hand to the other.

"You ain't see um gwine back, is you, Mars Cajy?" he asked after a while.

"Ef they went back by this road," said Mr. Staley, with the air of one who is accustomed to weigh well his words, "it must 'a' bin endurin' of the time whiles I was asleep, bekaze I hain't bin no furder from my shop than to yon bed."

"Well, sir!" exclaimed Free Joe in an awed tone, which Mr. Staley seemed to regard as a tribute to his extraordinary powers of statement.

"Ef it's my beliefs you want," continued the old man, "I'll pitch 'em at you fair and free. My beliefs is that Spite Calderwood is gone an' took Lucindy outen the county. Bless your heart and soul! when Spite Calderwood meets the Old Boy[4] in the road they'll be a turrible scuffle. You mark what I tell you."

Free Joe, still fumbling with his hat, rose and leaned against the door-facing. He seemed to be embarrassed. Presently he said:

"I speck I better be gittin' 'long. Nex' time I see Lucindy, I'm gwine tell 'er w'at Miss Becky say 'bout de queen er spades—dat I is. Ef dat don't tickle 'er, dey ain't no nigger 'oman never bin tickle'."

He paused a moment, as though waiting for some remark or comment, some confirmation of misfortune, or, at the very least, some endorsement of his suggestion that Lucinda would be greatly pleased to know that she had figured as the queen of spades; but neither Miss Becky nor her brother said anything.

"One minnit ridin' in the buggy 'longside er Mars Spite, en de nex' highfalutin' 'roun' playin' de queen er spades. Mon, deze yer nigger gals gittin' up in de pictur's; dey sholy is."

With a brief "Good night, Miss Becky, Mars Cajy," Free Joe went out into the darkness, followed by little Dan. He made his way to the poplar, where Lucinda had been in the habit of meeting him, and sat down. He sat there a long time; he sat there until little Dan, growing restless, trotted off in the direction of the Calderwood place. Dozing against the poplar, in the gray dawn of the morning, Free Joe heard Spite Calderwood's fox-hounds in full cry a mile away.

"Shoo!" he exclaimed, scratching his head, and laughing to himself, "dem ar dogs is des a-warmin' dat old fox up."

But it was Dan the hounds were after, and the little dog came back no more. Free Joe waited and waited, until he grew tired of

4. The devil.

waiting. He went back the next night and waited, and for many nights thereafter. His waiting was in vain, and yet he never regarded it as in vain. Careless and shabby as he was, Free Joe was thoughtful enough to have his theory. He was convinced that little Dan had found Lucinda, and that some night when the moon was shining brightly through the trees, the dog would rouse him from his dreams as he sat sleeping at the foot of the poplar tree, and he would open his eyes and behold Lucinda standing over him, laughing merrily as of old; and then he thought what fun they would have about the queen of spades.

How many long nights Free Joe waited at the foot of the poplar tree for Lucinda and little Dan no one can ever know. He kept no account of them, and they were not recorded by Micajah Staley nor by Miss Becky. The season ran into summer and then into fall. One night he went to the Staley cabin, cut the two old people an armful of wood, and seated himself on the door-steps, where he rested. He was always thankful—and proud, as it seemed—when Miss Becky gave him a cup of coffee, which she was sometimes thoughtful enough to do. He was especially thankful on this particular night.

"You er still layin' off for to strike up wi' Lucindy out thar in the woods, I reckon," said Micajah Staley, smiling grimly. The situation was not without its humorous aspects.

"Oh, dey er comin', Mars Cajy, dey er comin', sho," Free Joe replied. "I boun' you dey'll come; en w'en dey does come, I'll des take en fetch um yer, whar you kin see um wid you own eyes, you en Miss Becky."

"No," said Mr. Staley, with a quick and emphatic gesture of disapproval. "Don't! don't fetch 'em anywheres. Stay right wi' 'em as long as may be."

Free Joe chuckled, and slipped away into the night, while the two old people sat gazing in the fire. Finally Micajah spoke.

"Look at that nigger; look at 'im. He's pine-blank as happy now as a killdee by a mill-race.[5] You can't faze 'em. I'd inabout give up my t'other hand ef I could stan' flat-footed, an' grin at trouble like that there nigger."

"Niggers is niggers," said Miss Becky, smiling grimly, "an' you can't rub it out; yit I lay I've seed a heap of white people lots meaner'n Free Joe. He grins—an' that's nigger—but I've ketched his under jaw a-tremblin' when Lucindy's name uz brung up. An' I tell you," she went on, bridling up a little, and speaking with almost fierce emphasis, "the Old Boy's done sharpened his claws for Spite Calderwood. You'll see it."

"Me, Rebecca?" said Mr. Staley, hugging his palsied arm; "me? I hope not."

"Well, you'll know it then," said Miss Becky, laughing heartily at her brother's look of alarm.

5. A small bird by a stream where seed was ground for flour.

The next morning Micajah Staley had occasion to go into the woods after a piece of timber. He saw Free Joe sitting at the foot of the poplar, and the sight vexed him somewhat.

"Git up from there," he cried, "an' go an' arn your livin'. A mighty purty pass it's come to, when great big buck niggers can lie a-snorin' in the woods all day, when t'other folks is got to be up an' a-gwine. Git up from there!"

Receiving no response, Mr. Staley went to Free Joe, and shook him by the shoulder; but the negro made no response. He was dead. His hat was off, his head was bent, and a smile was on his face. It was as if he had bowed and smiled when death stood before him, humble to the last. His clothes were ragged; his hands were rough and callous; his shoes were literally tied together with strings; he was shabby in the extreme. A passer-by, glancing at him, could have no idea that such a humble creature had been summoned as a witness before the Lord God of Hosts.

1887

SARAH ORNE JEWETT
1849–1909

When Sarah Orne Jewett was born in South Berwick, Maine, in 1849, the town and region she was to memorialize in her fiction were already changing rapidly. Her grandfather had been a sea captain, shipowner, and merchant, and as a child she was exposed to the bustle of this small inland port. By the end of the Civil War, however, textile mills and a cannery had largely replaced agriculture, shipbuilding, and logging as the economic base of the community, and the arrival of new French Canadian and Irish immigrants signaled a change in the ethnic character of the town from English to a more heterogeneous mixture. The stable, secure, and remote small town she knew and loved as a child was yielding to the economic, technological, and demographic pressures that transformed America in her lifetime.

Jewett's family life was stable and affectionate; she and her two sisters led happy and generally carefree childhoods. Their father was a kindly, hardworking obstetrician who indulged all three of his daughters, but Sarah most of all. He encouraged her reading, and even as a small child she accompanied him on his horse-and-buggy rounds, meeting the rural people who would later populate her fiction. Jewett loved her father deeply, and some of her strong feelings for him are invested in the novel *A Country Doctor* (1884).

In part under influence of Harriet Beecher Stowe's novel about Maine seacoast life, *The Pearl of Orr's Island* (1862), Jewett began to write and publish verse and stories while still in her teens. One of her first efforts was accepted in 1869 by the influential editor W. D. Howells for publication in the prestigious *Atlantic Monthly*. In her early twenties, encouraged by Howells, she wrote a group of stories and sketches about a fictional coastal town in Maine to which she gave the name Deephaven; under that title she published her first collection of short pieces in 1877. With the publication of this book, she entered the company of Mark Twain, Bret Harte, George Washington Cable, Harriet Beecher Stowe, and other "local colorists" who were depicting realistically the settings, people, speech patterns, and modes of life of many distinctive regions of the country. Many critics believe that these writers sensed early the profound changes that industrialization would bring as it spread across the continent in the decades following the Civil War, and that they wished to capture and reaffirm the conditions and values of an earlier time before they disappeared. Given this impulse, it is easy to understand why the characteristic realism of this group was tempered by a strong note of idealizing nostalgia. At their best, though, the "local colorists" created works whose themes are universally appealing and valid. Certainly Jewett's depiction of the courageous response of women to frustration and loneliness is a case in point.

Jewett reached maturity with the publication of the collection *The White Heron* in 1886; later collections of sketches and stories include *The King of Folly Island* (1888), *A Native of Winby* (1893), and *The Life of Nancy* (1895). In these works the careful documentary record of landscape, people, and dialect is suffused with a ripe understanding and sympathy that adds dimension to these fragments of remembered life. It is to this late period that the recently rediscovered *The Foreigner* (1900) belongs. Jewett's most enduring work is a group of loosely connected sketches called *The Country of the Pointed Firs* (1896). What most distinguishes it and *The Foreigner* from *Deephaven*, published two decades earlier, is the resonance —not quite tragic—that comes from a mature lifetime of conscious and subconscious mulling over of familiar material. In this work, bits and pieces of the lives of a small group of variously blighted characters are converted by Jewett's art into a quasi-mythic total community.

The Foreigner[1]

I

One evening, at the end of August, in Dunnet Landing, I heard Mrs. Todd's firm footstep crossing the small front entry outside my door, and her conventional cough which served as a herald's trumpet, or a plain New England knock, in the harmony of our fellowship.

"Oh, please come in!" I cried, for it had been so still in the house that I supposed my friend and hostess had gone to see one of her neighbors. The first cold northeasterly storm of the season was blowing hard outside. Now and then there was a dash of great raindrops and a flick of wet lilac leaves against the window, but I could hear that the sea was already stirred to its dark depths, and the great rollers were coming in heavily against the shore. One might well believe that Summer was coming to a sad end that night, in the darkness and rain and sudden access of autumnal cold. It

1. *The Foreigner* was first published in the *Atlantic Monthly*, Vol. LXXXVI (August, 1900), the source of the present text. Jewett never incorporated the story into a collection, but the story draws on the setting (Dunnet Landing), ambience, and some characters—especially Almira Todd—of *The Country of the Pointed Firs*.

seemed as if there must be danger offshore among the outer islands.

"Oh, there!" exclaimed Mrs. Todd, as she entered. "I know nothing ain't ever happened out to Green Island since the world began, but I always do worry about mother in these great gales. You know those tidal waves occur sometimes down to the West Indies, and I get dwellin' on 'em so I can't set still in my chair, nor knit a common row to a stocking. William might get mooning, out in his small bo't, and not observe how the sea was making, an' meet with some accident. Yes, I thought I'd come in and set with you if you wa'n't busy. No, I never feel any concern about 'em in winter 'cause then they're prepared, and all ashore and everything snug. William ought to keep help, as I tell him; yes, he ought to keep help."

I hastened to reassure my anxious guest by saying that Elijah Tilley had told me in the afternoon, when I came along the shore past the fish houses, that Johnny Bowden and the Captain were out at Green Island; he had seen them beating up the bay, and thought they must have put into Burnt Island cove, but one of the lobstermen brought word later that he saw them hauling out at Green Island as he came by, and Captain Bowden pointed ashore and shook his head to say that he did not mean to try to get in. "The old Miranda just managed it, but she will have to stay at home a day or two and put new patches in her sail," I ended, not without pride in so much circumstantial evidence.

Mrs. Todd was alert in a moment. "Then they'll all have a very pleasant evening," she assured me, apparently dismissing all fears of tidal waves and other sea-going disasters. "I was urging Alick Bowden to go ashore some day and see mother before cold weather. He's her own nephew; she sets a great deal by him. And Johnny's a great chum o' William's; don't you know the first day we had Johnny out 'long of us, he took an' give William his money to keep for him that he'd been a-savin', and William showed it to me an' was so affected I thought he was goin' to shed tears? 'Twas a dollar an' eighty cents; yes, they'll have a beautiful evenin' all together, and like's not the sea'll be flat as a doorstep come morning."

I had drawn a large wooden rocking-chair before the fire, and Mrs. Todd was sitting there jogging herself a little, knitting fast, and wonderfully placid of countenance. There came a fresh gust of wind and rain, and we could feel the small wooden house rock and hear it creak as if it were a ship at sea.

"Lord, hear the great breakers!" exclaimed Mrs. Todd. "How they pound!—there, there! I always run of an idea that the sea knows anger these nights and gets full o' fight. I can hear the rote[2] o' them old black ledges way down the thoroughfare. Calls up all those stormy verses in the Book o' Psalms; David he knew how old sea-goin' folks have to quake at the heart."

I thought as I had never thought before of such anxieties. The

---

2. Noise of the surf on the shore.

families of sailors and coastwise adventurers by sea must always be worrying about somebody, this side of the world or the other. There was hardly one of Mrs. Todd's elder acquaintances, men or women, who had not at some time or other made a sea voyage, and there was often no news until the voyagers themselves came back to bring it.

"There's a roaring high overhead, and a roaring in the deep sea," said Mrs. Todd solemnly, "and they battle together nights like this. No, I couldn't sleep; some women folks always goes right to bed an' to sleep, so's to forget, but 't aint my way. Well, it's a blessin' we don't all feel alike; there's hardly any of our folks at sea to worry about, nowadays, but I can't help my feelin's, an' I got thinking of mother all alone, if William had happened to be out lobsterin' and couldn't make the cove gettin' back."

"They will have a pleasant evening," I repeated. "Captain Bowden is the best of good company."

"Mother'll make him some pancakes for his supper, like's not," said Mrs. Todd, clicking her knitting needles and giving a pull at her yarn. Just then the old cat pushed open the unlatched door and came straight toward her mistress's lap. She was regarded severely as she stepped about and turned on the broad expanse, and then made herself into a round cushion of fur, but was not openly admonished. There was another great blast of wind overhead, and a puff of smoke came down the chimney.

"This makes me think o' the night Mis' Cap'n Tolland died," said Mrs. Todd, half to herself. "Folks used to say these gales only blew when somebody's a-dyin', or the devil was a-comin' for his own, but the worst man I ever knew died a real pretty mornin' in June."

"You have never told me any ghost stories," said I; and such was the gloomy weather and the influence of the night that I was instantly filled with reluctance to have this suggestion followed. I had not chosen the best of moments; just before I spoke we had begun to feel as cheerful as possible. Mrs. Todd glanced doubtfully at the cat and then at me, with a strange absent look, and I was really afraid that she was going to tell me something that would haunt my thoughts on every dark stormy night as long as I lived.

"Never mind now; tell me to-morrow by daylight, Mrs. Todd," I hastened to say, but she still looked at me full of doubt and deliberation.

"Ghost stories!" she answered. "Yes, I don't know but I've heard a plenty of 'em first an' last. I was just sayin' to myself that this is like the night Mis' Cap'n Tolland died. 'Twas the great line storm in September all of thirty, or maybe forty, year ago. I ain't one that keeps much account o' time."

"Tolland? That's a name I have never heard in Dunnet," I said.

"Then you haven't looked well about the old part o' the buryin' ground, no'theast corner," replied Mrs. Todd. "All their women folks lies there; the sea's got most o' the men. They were a known family o' shipmasters in early times. Mother had a mate, Ellen Tolland, that she mourns to this day; died right in her bloom with quick consumption, but the rest o' that family was all boys but one, and older than she, an' they lived hard seafarin' lives an' all died hard. They were called very smart seamen. I've heard that when the youngest went into one o' the old shippin' houses in Boston, the head o' the firm called out to him: 'Did you say Tolland from Dunnet? That's recommendation enough for any vessel!' There was some o' them old shipmasters as tough as iron, an' they had the name o' usin' their crews very severe, but there wa'n't a man that wouldn't rather sign with 'em an' take his chances, than with the slack ones that didn't know how to meet accidents."

II

There was so long a pause, and Mrs. Todd still looked so absent-minded, that I was afraid she and the cat were growing drowsy together before the fire, and I should have no reminiscences at all. The wind struck the house again, so that we both started in our chairs and Mrs. Todd gave a curious, startled look at me. The cat lifted her head and listened too, in the silence that followed, while after the wind sank we were more conscious than ever of the awful roar of the sea. The house jarred now and then, in a strange, disturbing way.

"Yes, they'll have a beautiful evening out to the island," said Mrs. Todd again; but she did not say it gayly. I had not seen her before in her weaker moments.

"Who was Mrs. Captain Tolland?" I asked eagerly, to change the current of our thoughts.

"I never knew her maiden name; if I ever heard it, I've gone an' forgot; 't would mean nothing to me," answered Mrs. Todd.

"She was a foreigner, an' he met with her out in the Island o' Jamaica. They said she'd been left a widow with property. Land knows what become of it; she was French born, an' her first husband was a Portugee, or somethin'."

I kept silence now, a poor and insufficient question being worse than none.

"Cap'n John Tolland was the least smartest of any of 'em, but he was full smart enough, an' commanded a good brig at the time, in the sugar trade; he'd taken out a cargo o' pine lumber to the islands from somewheres up the river, an' had been loadin' for home in the port o' Kingston, an' had gone ashore that afternoon for his papers, an' remained afterwards 'long of three friends o' his, shipmasters. They was havin' their suppers together in a tavern; 'twas late in the evenin' an' they was more lively than usual, an' felt boyish; and over opposite was another house full o' company, real bright and pleasant lookin', with a lot o' lights, an' they heard somebody

singin' very pretty to a guitar. They wa'n't in no go-to-meetin' condition, an' one of 'em, he slapped the table an' said, 'Le' 's go over
an' hear that lady sing!" an' over they all went, good honest sailors,
but three sheets in the wind, and stepped in as if they was invited,
an' made their bows inside the door, an' asked if they could hear
the music; they were all respectable well-dressed men. They saw the
woman that had the guitar, an' there was a company a-listenin', regular high binders all of 'em; an' there was a long table all spread out
with big candlesticks like little trees o' light, and a sight o' glass an'
silver ware; an' part o' the men was young officers in uniform, an'
the colored folks was steppin' round servin' 'em, an' they had the
lady singin'. 'Twas a wasteful scene, an' a loud talkin' company, an'
though they was three sheets in the wind themselves there wa'n't
one o' them cap'ns but had sense to perceive it. The others had
pushed back their chairs, an' their decanters an' glasses was standin'
thick about, an' they was teasin' the one that was singin' as if
they'd just got her in to amuse 'em. But they quieted down; one o'
the young officers had beautiful manners, an' invited the four cap'ns
to join 'em, very polite; 'twas a kind of public house, and after
they'd all heard another song, he come to consult with 'em whether
they wouldn't git up and dance a hornpipe or somethin' to the
lady's music.

"They was all elderly men an' shipmasters, and owned property;
two of 'em was church members in good standin'," continued Mrs.
Todd loftily, "an' they wouldn't lend theirselves to no such kick-
shows as that, an' spite o' bein' three sheets in the wind, as I have
once observed; they waved aside the tumblers of wine the young
officer was pourin' out for 'em so freehanded, and said they should
rather be excused. An' when they all rose, still very dignified, as I've
been well informed, and made their partin' bows and was goin' out,
them young sports got round 'em an' tried to prevent 'em, and they
had to push an' strive considerable, but out they come. There was
this Cap'n Tolland and two Cap'n Bowdens, and the fourth was my
own father." (Mrs. Todd spoke slowly, as if to impress the value of
her authority.) "Two of them was very religious, upright men, but
they would have their night off sometimes, all o' them old-fashioned cap'ns, when they was free of business and ready to leave
port.

"An' they went back to their tavern an' got their bills paid, an'
set down kind o' mad with everybody by the front windows, mis-
trusting some o' their tavern charges, like's not, by that time, an'
when they got tempered down, they watched the house over across,
where the party was.

"There was a kind of a grove o' trees between the house an' the
road, an' they heard the guitar a-goin' an' a-stoppin' short by turns,
and pretty soon somebody began to screech, an' they saw a white
dress come runnin' out through the bushes, an' tumbled over each

other in their haste to offer help; an' out she come, with the guitar, cryin' into the street, and they just walked off four square with her amongst 'em, down toward the wharves where they felt more to home. They couldn't make out at first what 'twas she spoke,— Cap'n Lorenzo Bowden was well acquainted in Havre an' Bordeaux,[3] an' spoke a poor quality o' French, an' she knew a little mite o' English, but not much; and they come somehow or other to discern that she was in real distress. Her husband and her children had died o' yellow fever; they'd all come up to Kingston from one o' the far Wind'ard Islands to get passage on a steamer to France, an' a negro had stole their money off her husband while he lay sick o' the fever, an' she had been befriended some, but the folks that knew about her had died too; it had been a dreadful run o' the fever that season, an' she fell at last to playin' an' singin' for hire, and for what money they'd throw to her round them harbor houses.

" 'Twas a real hard case, an' when them cap'ns made out about it, there wa'n't one that meant to take leave without helpin' of her. They was pretty mellow, an' whatever they might lack o' prudence they more'n made up with charity: they didn't want to see nobody abused, an' she was sort of a pretty woman, an' they stopped in the street then an' there an' drew lots who should take her aboard, bein' all bound home. An' the lot fell to Cap'n Jonathan Bowden who did act discouraged; his vessel had but small accommodations, though he could stow a big freight, an' she was a dreadful slow sailer through bein' square as a box, an' his first wife, that was livin' then, was a dreadful jealous woman. He threw himself right onto the mercy o' Cap'n Tolland."

Mrs. Todd indulged herself for a short time in a season of calm reflection.

"I always thought they'd have done better, and more reasonable, to give her some money to pay her passage home to France, or wherever she may have wanted to go," she continued.

I nodded and looked for the rest of the story.

"Father told mother," said Mrs. Todd confidentially, "that Cap'n Jonathan Bowden an' Cap'n John Tolland had both taken a little more than usual; I wouldn't have you think, either, that they both wasn't the best o' men, an' they was solemn as owls, and argued the matter between 'em, an' waved aside the other two when they tried to put their oars in. An' spite o' Cap'n Tolland's bein' a settled old bachelor they fixed it that he was to take the prize on his brig; she was a fast sailer, and there was a good spare cabin or two where he'd sometimes carried passengers, but he'd filled 'em with bags o' sugar on his own account an' was loaded very heavy beside. He said he'd shift the sugar an' get along somehow, an' the last the other three cap'ns saw of the party was Cap'n John handing the lady into his bo't, guitar and all, an' off they all set tow'ds their

3. French seaport cities.

ships with their men rowin' 'em in the bright moonlight down to
Port Royal where the anchorage was, an' where they all lay, goin'
out with the tide an' mornin' wind at break o' day. An' the others
thought they heard music of the guitar, two o' the bo'ts kept well
together, but it may have come from another source."

"Well; and then?" I asked eagerly after a pause. Mrs. Todd was
almost laughing aloud over her knitting and nodding emphatically.
We had forgotten all about the noise of the wind and sea.

"Lord bless you! he come sailing into Portland with his sugar, all
in good time, an' they stepped right afore a justice o' the peace, and
Cap'n John Tolland come paradin' home to Dunnet Landin' a married man. He owned one o' them thin, narrow-lookin' houses with
one room each side o' the front door, and two slim black spruces
spindlin' up against the front windows to make it gloomy inside.
There was no horse nor cattle of course, though he owned pasture
land, an' you could see rifts o' light right through the barn as you
drove by. And there was a good excellent kitchen, but his sister
reigned over that; she had a right to two rooms, and took the
kitchen an' a bedroom that led out of it; an' bein' given no rights in
the kitchen had angered the cap'n so they weren't on no kind o'
speakin' terms. He preferred his old brig for comfort, but now and
then, between voyages, he'd come home for a few days, just to show
he was master over his part o' the house, and show Eliza she
couldn't commit no trespass.

"They stayed a little while; 'twas pretty spring weather, an' I
used to see Cap'n John rollin' by with his arms full o' bundles from
the store, lookin' as pleased and important as a boy; an' then they
went right off to sea again, an' was gone a good many months. Next
time he left her to live there alone, after they'd stopped at home
together some weeks, an' they said she suffered from bein' at sea, but
some said that the owners wouldn't have a woman aboard. 'Twas
before father was lost on that last voyage of his, an' he and
mother went up once or twice to see them. Father said there wa'n't
a mite o' harm in her, but somehow or other a sight o' prejudice
arose; it may have been caused by the remarks of Eliza an' her feelin's tow'ds her brother. Even my mother had no regard for Eliza
Tolland. But mother asked the cap'n's wife to come with her one
evenin' to a social circle, that was down to the meetin'-house vestry,
so she'd get acquainted a little, an' she appeared very pretty until
they started to have some singin' to the melodeon. Mari' Harris an'
one o' the younger Caplin girls undertook to sing a duet, an' they
sort o' flatted, an' she put her hands right up to her ears, and gave a
little squeal, an' went quick as could be an' give 'em the right notes,
for she could read the music like plain print, an' made 'em try it
over again. She was real willin' an' pleasant, but that didn't suit,
an' she made faces when they got it wrong. An' then there fell a

dead calm, an' we was all settin' round prim as dishes, an' my mother, that never expects ill feelin', asked her if she wouldn't sing somethin', an' up she got,—poor creatur', it all seems so different to me now,—an' sung a lovely little song standin' in the floor; it seemed to have something gay about it that kept a-repeatin', an' nobody could help keepin' time, an' all of a sudden she looked round at the tables and caught up a tin plate that somebody'd fetched a Washin'ton pie in, an' she begun to drum on it with her fingers like one o' them tambourines, an' went right on singin' faster an' faster, and next minute she began to dance a little pretty dance between the verses, just as light and pleasant as a child. You couldn't help seein' how pretty 'twas; we all got to trottin' a foot, an' some o' the men clapped their hands quite loud, a-keepin' time, 'twas so catchin', an' seemed so natural to her. There wa'n't one of 'em but enjoyed it; she just tried to do her part, an' some urged her on, till she stopped with a little twirl of her skirts an' went to her place again by mother. And I can see mother now, reachin' over an' smilin' and pattin' her hand.

"But next day there was an awful scandal goin' in the parish, an' Mari' Harris reproached my mother to her face, an' I never wanted to see her since, but I've had to a good many times. I said Mis' Tolland didn't intend no impropriety,—I reminded her of David's dancin' before the Lord; but she said such a man as David never would have thought o' dancin' right there in the Orthodox vestry, and she felt I spoke with irreverence.

"And next Sunday Mis' Tolland come walkin' into our meeting, but I must say she acted like a cat in a strange garret, and went right out down the aisle with her head in the air, from the pew Deacon Caplin had showed her into. 'Twas just in the beginning of the long prayer. I wished she'd stayed through, whatever her reasons were. Whether she'd expected somethin' different, or misunderstood some o' the pastor's remarks, or what 'twas, I don't really feel able to explain, but she kind o' declared war, at least folks thought so, an' war 'twas from that time. I see she was cryin', or had been, as she passed by me; perhaps bein' in meetin' was what had power to make her feel homesick and strange.

"Cap'n John Tolland was away fittin' out; that next week he come home to see her and say farewell. He was lost with his ship in the Straits of Malacca, and she lived there alone in the old house a few months longer till she died. He left her well off; 'twas said he hid his money about the house and she knew where 'twas. Oh, I expect you've heard that story told over an' over twenty times, since you've been here at the Landin'?"

"Never one word," I insisted.

"It was a good while ago," explained Mrs. Todd, with reassurance. "Yes, it all happened a great while ago."

III

At this moment, with a sudden flaw of the wind, some wet twigs outside blew against the window panes and made a noise like a distressed creature trying to get in. I started with sudden fear, and so did the cat, but Mrs. Todd knitted away and did not even look over her shoulder.

"She was a good-looking woman; yes, I always thought Mis' Tolland was good-looking, though she had, as was reasonable, a sort of foreign cast, and she spoke very broken English, no better than a child. She was always at work about her house, or settin' at a front window with her sewing; she was a beautiful hand to embroider. Sometimes, summer evenings, when the windows was open, she'd set an' drum on her guitar, but I don't know as I ever heard her sing but once after the cap'n went away. She appeared very happy about havin' him, and took on dreadful at partin' when he was down here on the wharf, going back to Portland by boat to take ship for that last v'y'ge. He acted kind of ashamed, Cap'n John did; folks about here ain't so much accustomed to show their feelings. The whistle had blown an' they was waitin' for him to get aboard, an' he was put to it to know what to do and treated her very affectionate in spite of all impatience; but mother happened to be there and she went an' spoke, and I remember what a comfort she seemed to be. Mis' Tolland clung to her then, and she wouldn't give a glance after the boat when it had started, though the captain was very eager a-wavin' to her. She wanted mother to come home with her an' wouldn't let go her hand, and mother had just come in to stop all night with me an' had plenty o' time ashore, which didn't always happen, so they walked off together, an' 'twas some considerable time before she got back.

" 'I want you to neighbor with that poor lonesome creatur',' says mother to me, lookin' reproachful. 'She's a stranger in a strange land,' says mother. 'I want you to make her have a sense that somebody feels kind to her.'

" 'Why, since that time she flaunted out o' meetin', folks have felt she liked other ways better'n our'n,' says I. I was provoked, because I'd had a nice supper ready, an' mother'd let it wait so long 't was spoiled. 'I hope you'll like your supper!' I told her. I was dreadful ashamed afterward of speakin' so to mother.

" 'What consequence is my supper?' says she to me; mother can be very stern,—'or your comfort or mine, beside letting a foreign person an' a stranger feel so desolate; she's done the best a woman could do in her lonesome place, and she asks nothing of anybody except a little common kindness. Think if 't was you in a foreign land!'

"And mother set down to drink her tea, an' I set down humbled enough over by the wall to wait till she finished. An' I did think it all over, an' next day I never said nothin', but I put on my bonnet, and went to see Mis' Cap'n Tolland, if 'twas only for mother's sake. 'Twas about three quarters of a mile up the road here, beyond the school-house. I forgot to tell you that the cap'n had bought out his sister's right at three or four times what 'twas worth, to save trouble, so they'd got clear o' her, an' I went round into the side yard sort o' friendly an' sociable, rather than stop an' deal with the knocker an' the front door. It looked so pleasant an' pretty I was glad I come; she had set a little table for supper, though 'twas still early, with a white cloth on it, right out under an old apple tree close by the house. I noticed 'twas same as with me at home, there was only one plate. She was just coming out with a dish; you couldn't see the door nor the table from the road.

"In the few weeks she'd been there she'd got some bloomin' pinks an' other flowers next the doorstep. Somehow it looked as if she'd known how to make it homelike for the cap'n. She asked me to set down; she was very polite, but she looked very mournful, and I spoke of mother, an' she put down her dish and caught holt o' me with both hands an' said my mother was an angel. When I see the tears in her eyes 't was all right between us, and we were always friendly after that, and mother had us come out and make a little visit that summer; but she come a foreigner and she went a foreigner, and never was anything but a stranger among our folks. She taught me a sight o' things about herbs I never knew before nor since; she was well acquainted with the virtues o' plants. She'd act awful secret about some things too, an' used to work charms for herself sometimes, an' some o' the neighbors told to an' fro after she died that they knew enough not to provoke her, but 'twas all nonsense; 't is the believin' in such things that causes 'em to be any harm, an' so I told 'em," confided Mrs. Todd contemptuously. "That first night I stopped to tea witih her she'd cooked some eggs with some herb or other sprinkled all through, and 'twas she that first led me to discern mushrooms; an' she went right down on her knees in my garden here when she saw I had my different officious herbs. Yes, 't was she that learned me the proper use o' parsley too; she was a beautiful cook."

Mrs. Todd stopped talking, and rose, putting the cat gently in the chair, while she went away to get another stick of apple-tree wood. It was not an evening when one wished to let the fire go down, and we had a splendid bank of bright coals. I had always wondered where Mrs. Todd had got such an unusual knowledge of cookery, of the varieties of mushrooms, and the use of sorrel as a vegetable, and other blessings of that sort. I had long ago learned that she could vary her omelettes like a child of France, which was indeed a surprise in Dunnet Landing.

IV

All these revelations were of the deepest interest, and I was ready with a question as soon as Mrs. Todd came in and had well settled the fire and herself and the cat again.

"I wonder why she never went back to France, after she was left alone?"

"She come here from the French islands," explained Mrs. Todd. "I asked her once about her folks, an' she said they were all dead; 'twas the fever took 'em. She made this her home, lonesome as 'twas; she told me she hadn't been in France since she was 'so small,' and measured me off a child o' six. She'd lived right out in the country before, so that part wa'n't unusual to her. Oh yes, there was something very strange about her, and she hadn't been brought up in high circles nor nothing o' that kind. I think she'd been really pleased to have the cap'n marry her an' give her a good home, after all she'd passed through, and leave her free with his money an' all that. An' she got over bein' so strange-looking to me after a while, but 'twas a very singular expression: she wore a fixed smile that wa'n't a smile; there wa'n't no light behind it, same's a lamp can't shine if it ain't lit. I don't know just how to express it, 'twas a sort of made countenance."

One could not help thinking of Sir Philip Sidney's phrase, "A made countenance, between simpering and smiling."[4]

"She took it hard, havin' the captain go off on that last voyage," Mrs. Todd went on. "She said somethin' told her when they was partin' that he would never come back. He was lucky to speak a home-bound ship this side o' the Cape o' Good Hope, an' got a chance to send her a letter, an' that cheered her up. You often felt as if you was dealin' with a child's mind, for all she had so much information that other folks hadn't. I was a sight younger than I be now, and she made me imagine new things, and I got interested watchin' her an' findin' out what she had to say, but you couldn't get to no affectionateness with her. I used to blame me sometimes; we used to be real good comrades goin' off for an afternoon, but I never gave her a kiss till the day she laid in her coffin and it come to my heart there wa'n't no one else to do it."

"And Captain Tolland died," I suggested after a while.

"Yes, the cap'n was lost," said Mrs. Todd, "and of course word didn't come for a good while after it happened. The letter come from the owners to my uncle, Cap'n Lorenzo Bowden, who was in charge of Cap'n Tolland's affairs at home, and he come right up for me an' said I must go with him to the house. I had known what it was to be a widow, myself, for near a year, an' there was plenty o'

4. From *The Countess of Pembrokes Arcadia*, Book I, Chapter 16. The quotation actually reads "with a made countenance about her mouth, betweene simpering and smyling" in the 1590 quarto edition. The 1593 folio and following editions read "a made countenance."

widow women along this coast that the sea had made desolate, but I never saw a heart break as I did then.

" 'Twas this way: we walked together along the road, me an' uncle Lorenzo. You know how it leads straight from just above the schoolhouse to the brook bridge, and their house was just this side o' the brook bridge on the left hand; the cellar's there now, and a couple or three good-sized gray birches growin' in it. And when we come near enough I saw that the best room, this way, where she most never set, was all lighted up, and the curtains up so that the light shone bright down the road, and as we walked, those lights would dazzle and dazzle in my eyes, and I could hear the guitar a-goin', an' she was singin'. She heard our steps with her quick ears and come running to the door with her eyes a-shinin', and all that set look gone out of her face, an' begun to talk French, gay as a bird, an' shook hands and behaved very pretty an' girlish, sayin' 'twas her fête day. I didn't know what she meant then. And she had gone an' put a wreath o' flowers on her hair an' wore a handsome gold chain that the cap'n had given her; an' there she was, poor creatur', makin' believe have a party all alone in her best room; 'twas prim enough to discourage a person, with too many chairs set close to the walls, just as the cap'n's mother had left it, but she had put sort o' long garlands on the walls, droopin' very graceful, and a sight of green boughs in the corners, till it looked lovely, and all lit up with a lot o' candles."

"Oh dear!" I sighed. "Oh, Mrs. Todd, what did you do?"

"She beheld our countenances," answered Mrs. Todd solemnly. "I expect they was telling everything plain enough, but Cap'n Lorenzo spoke the sad words to her as if he had been her father; and she wavered a minute and then over she went on the floor before we could catch hold of her, and then we tried to bring her to herself and failed, and at last we carried her upstairs, an' I told uncle to run down and put out the lights, and then go fast as he could for Mrs. Begg, being very experienced in sickness, an' he so did. I got off her clothes and her poor wreath, and I cried as I done it. We both stayed there that night, and the doctor said 'twas a shock when he come in the morning; he'd been over to Black Island an' had to stay all night with a very sick child."

"You said that she lived alone some time after the news came," I reminded Mrs. Todd then.

"Oh yes, dear," answered my friend sadly, "but it wa'n't what you'd call livin'; no, it was only dyin', though at a snail's pace. She never went out again those few months, but for a while she could manage to get about the house a little, and do what was needed, an' I never let two days go by without seein' her or hearin' from her. She never took much notice as I came an' went except to answer if I asked her anything. Mother was the one who gave her the only comfort."

"What was that?" I asked softly.

"She said that anybody in such trouble ought to see their minister, mother did, and one day she spoke to Mis' Tolland, and found
that the poor soul had been believin' all the time that there weren't
any priests here. We'd come to know she was a Catholic by her
beads and all, and that had set some narrow minds against her. And
mother explained it just as she would to a child; and uncle Lorenzo
sent word right off somewhere up river by a packet that was bound
up the bay, and the first o' the week a priest come by the boat, an'
uncle Lorenzo was on the wharf 'tendin' to some business; so they
just come up for me, and I walked with him to show him the
house. He was a kind-hearted old man; he looked so benevolent an'
fatherly I could ha' stopped an' told him my own troubles; yes, I
was satisfied when I first saw his face, an' when poor Mis' Tolland
beheld him enter the room, she went right down on her knees and
clasped her hands together to him as if he'd come to save her life,
and he lifted her up and blessed her, an' I left 'em together, and
slipped out into the open field and walked there in sight so if they
needed to call me, and I had my own thoughts. At last I saw him
at the door; he had to catch the return boat. I meant to walk back
with him and offer him some supper, but he said no, and said he was
comin' again if needed, and signed me to go into the house to her,
and shook his head in a way that meant he understood everything. I
can see him now; he walked with a cane, rather tired and feeble; I
wished somebody would come along, so's to carry him down to the
shore.

"Mis' Tolland looked up at me with a new look when I went in,
an' she even took hold o' my hand and kept it. He had put some oil
on her forehead, but nothing anybody could do would keep her alive
very long; 'twas his medicine for the soul rather 'n the body. I
helped her to bed, and next morning she couldn't get up to dress
her, and that was Monday, and she began to fail, and 't was Friday
night she died." (Mrs. Todd spoke with unusual haste and lack of
detail.) "Mrs. Begg and I watched with her, and made everything
nice and proper, and after all the ill will there was a good number
gathered to the funeral. 'Twas in Reverend Mr. Bascom's day,
and he done very well in his prayer, considering he couldn't fill in with
mentioning all the near connections by name as was his habit. He
spoke very feeling about her being a stranger and twice widowed,
and all he said about her being reared among the heathen was to
observe that there might be roads leadin' up to the New Jerusalem
from various points. I says to myself that I guessed quite a number
must ha' reached there that wa'n't able to set out from Dunnet
Landin'!"

Mrs. Todd gave an odd little laugh as she bent toward the firelight to pick up a dropped stitch in her knitting, and then I heard
a heartfelt sigh.

" 'Twas most forty years ago," she said; "most everybody's gone a'ready that was there that day."

V

Suddenly Mrs. Todd gave an energetic shrug of her shoulders, and a quick look at me, and I saw that the sails of her narrative were filled with a fresh breeze.

"Uncle Lorenzo, Cap'n Bowden that I have referred to"—

"Certainly!" I agreed with eager expectation.

"He was the one that had been left in charge of Cap'n John Tolland's affairs, and had now come to be of unforeseen importance.

"Mrs. Begg an' I had stayed in the house both before an' after Mis' Tolland's decease, and she was now in haste to be gone, having affairs to call her home; but uncle come to me as the exercises was beginning, and said he thought I'd better remain at the house while they went to the buryin' ground. I couldn't understand his reasons, an' I felt disappointed, bein' as near to her as most anybody; 'twas rough weather, so mother couldn't get in, and didn't even hear Mis' Tolland was gone till next day. I just nodded to satisfy him, 'twas'n't no time to discuss anything. Uncle seemed flustered; he'd gone out deep-sea fishin' the day she died, and the storm I told you of rose very sudden, so they got blown off way down the coast beyond Monhegan, and he'd just got back in time to dress himself and come.

"I set there in the house after I'd watched her away down the straight road far's I could see from the door; 'twas a little short walkin' funeral an' a cloudy sky, so everything looked dull an' gray, an' it crawled along all in one piece, same's walking funerals do, an' I wondered how it ever come to the Lord's mind to let her begin down among them gay islands all heat and sun, and end up here among the rocks with a north wind blowin'. 'Twas a gale that begun the afternoon before she died, and had kept blowin' off an' on ever since. I'd thought more than once how glad I should be to get home an' out o' sound o' them black spruces a-beatin' an' scratchin' at the front windows.

"I set to work pretty soon to put the chairs back, an' set outdoors some that was borrowed, an' I went out in the kitchen, an' I made up a good fire in case somebody come an' wanted a cup o' tea; but I didn't expect any one to travel way back to the house unless 'twas uncle Lorenzo. 'Twas growin' so chilly that I fetched some kindlin' wood and made fires in both the fore rooms. Then I set down an' begun to feel as usual, and I got my knittin' out of a drawer. You can't be sorry for a poor creatur' that's come to the end o' all her troubles; my only discomfort was I thought I'd ought to feel worse at losin' her than I did; I was younger then than I be now. And as I set there, I begun to hear some long notes o' dronin' music from upstairs that chilled me to the bone."

Mrs. Todd gave a hasty glance at me.

"Quick's I could gather me, I went right upstairs to see what 'twas," she added eagerly, "an' 'twas just what I might ha' known. She'd always kept her guitar hangin' right against the wall in her room; 'twas tied by a blue ribbon, and there was a window left wide open; the wind was veerin' a good deal, an' it slanted in and searched the room. The strings was jarrin' yet.

" 'Twas growin' pretty late in the afternoon, an' I begun to feel lonesome as I shouldn't now, and I was disappointed at having to stay there, the more I thought it over, but after a while I saw Cap'n Lorenzo polin' back up the road all alone, and when he come nearer I could see he had a bundle under his arm and had shifted his best black clothes for his everyday ones. I run out and put some tea into the teapot and set it back on the stove to draw, an' when he come in I reached down a little jug o' spirits,—Cap'n Tolland had left his house well provisioned as if his wife was goin' to put to sea same's himself, an' there she'd gone an' left it. There was some cake that Mis' Begg an' I had made the day before. I thought that uncle an' me had a good right to the funeral supper, even if there wa'n't any one to join us. I was lookin' forward to my cup o' tea; 'twas beautiful tea out of a green lacquered chest that I've got now."

"You must have felt very tired," said I, eagerly listening.

"I was 'most beat out, with watchin' an' tendin' and all," answered Mrs. Todd, with as much sympathy in her voice as if she were speaking of another person. "But I called out to uncle as he came in, 'Well, I expect it's all over now, an' we've all done what we could. I thought we'd better have some tea or somethin' before we go home. Come right out in the kitchen, sir,' says I, never thinking but we only had to let the fires out and lock up everything safe an' eat our refreshment, an' go home.

" 'I want both of us to stop here tonight,' says uncle, looking at me very important.

" 'Oh, what for?' says I, kind o' fretful.

" 'I've got my proper reasons,' says uncle. 'I'll see you well satisfied, Almira. Your tongue ain't so easy-goin' as some o' the women folks, an' there's property here to take charge of that you don't know nothin' at all about.'

" 'What do you mean?' says I.

" 'Cap'n Tolland acquainted me with his affairs; he hadn't no sort o' confidence in nobody but me an' his wife, after he was tricked into signin' that Portland note, an' lost money. An' she didn't know nothin' about business; but what he didn't take to sea to be sunk with him he's hid somewhere in this house. I expect Mis' Tolland may have told you where she kept things?' said uncle.

"I see he was dependin' a good deal on my answer," said Mrs. Todd, "but I had to disappoint him; no, she had never said nothin' to me.

" 'Well, then, we've got to make a search,' says he, with considerable relish; but he was all tired and worked up, and we set down to the table, an' he had somethin', an' I took my desired cup o' tea, and then I begun to feel more interested.

" 'Where you goin' to look first?' says I, but he give me a short look an' made no answer, an begun to mix me a very small portion out of the jug, in another glass. I took it to please him; he said I looked tired, speakin' real fatherly, and I did feel better for it, and we set talkin' a few minutes, an' then he started for the cellar, carrying an old ship's lantern he fetched out o' the stairway an' lit.

" 'What are you lookin' for, some kind of a chist?' I inquired, and he said yes. All of a sudden it come to me to ask who was the heirs; Eliza Tolland, Cap'n John's own sister, had never demeaned herself to come near the funeral, and uncle Lorenzo faced right about and begun to laugh, sort o' pleased. I thought queer of it; 'twa'n't what he'd taken, which would be nothin' to an old weathered sailor like him.

" 'Who's the heir?' says I the second time.

" 'Why, it's *you*, Almiry,' says he; and I was so took aback I set right down on the turn o' the cellar stairs.

" 'Yes 'tis,' said uncle Lorenzo. 'I'm glad of it too. Some thought she didn't have no sense but foreign sense, an' a poor stock o' that, but she said you was friendly to her, an' one day after she got news of Tolland's death, an' I had fetched up his will that left everything to her, she said she was goin' to make a writin', so's you could have things after she was gone, an' she give five hundred to me for bein' executor. Square[5] Pease fixed up the paper, an' she signed it; it's all accordin' to law.' "There, I begun to cry," said Mrs. Todd; "I couldn't help it. I wished I had her back again to do somethin' for, an' to make her know I felt sisterly to her more'n I'd ever showed, an' it come over me 'twas all too late, an' I cried the more, till uncle showed impatience, an' I got up an' stumbled along down cellar with my apern to my eyes the greater part of the time.

" 'I'm goin' to have a clean search,' says he; 'you hold the light.' An' I held it and he rummaged in the arches an' under the stairs, an' over in some old closet where he reached out bottles an' stone jugs an' canted[6] some kags an' one or two casks, an' chuckled well when he heard there was somethin' inside,—but there wa'n't nothin' to find but things usual in a cellar, an' then the old lantern was givin' out an' we come away.

" 'He spoke to me of a chist, Cap'n Tolland did,' says uncle in a whisper. 'He said a good sound chist was as safe a bank as there was, an' I beat him out of such nonsense, 'count o' fire an' other risks.' 'There's no chist in the rooms above,' says I; 'no, uncle, there ain't no sea-chist, for I've been here long enough to see what there was to be seen.' Yet he wouldn't feel contented till he'd mounted

---

5. I.e., Squire.   6. Tipped or tilted.

up into the toploft; 'twas one o' them single, hip roofed houses
that don't give proper accommodation for a real garret, like Cap'n
Littlepage's down here at the Landin'. There was broken furniture
and rubbish, an' he let down a terrible sight o' dust into the front
entry, but sure enough there wasn't no chist. I had it all to sweep
up next day.

" 'He must have took it away to sea,' says I to the cap'n, an' even
then he didn't want to agree, but we was both beat out. I told him
where I'd always seen Mis' Tolland get her money from, and we
found much as a hundred dollars there in an old red morocco
wallet. Cap'n John had been gone a good while a'ready, and she
had spent what she needed. 'Twas in an old desk o' his in the
settin' room that we found the wallet."

"At the last minute he may have taken his money to sea," I suggested.

"Oh yes," agreed Mrs. Todd. "He did take considerable to make
his venture to bring home, as was customary, an' that was drowned
with him as uncle agreed; but he had other property in shipping,
and a thousand dollars invested in Portland in a cordage shop, but
'twas about the time shipping begun to decay, and the cordage
shop failed, and in the end I wa'n't so rich as I thought I was goin'
to be for those few minutes on the cellar stairs. There was an auction that accumulated something. Old Mis' Tolland, the cap'n's
mother, had heired some good furniture from a sister: there was
above thirty chairs in all, and they're apt to sell well. I got over a
thousand dollars when we come to settle up, and I made uncle take
his five hundred; he was getting along in years and had met with
losses in navigation, and he left it back to me when he died, so I
had a real good lift. It all lays in the bank over to Rockland, and I
draw my interest fall an' spring, with the little Mr. Todd was able
to leave me; but that's kind o' sacred money; 'twas earnt and saved
with the hope o' youth, an' I'm very particular what I spend it for.
Oh yes, what with ownin' my house, I've been enabled to get along
very well, with prudence!" said Mrs. Todd contentedly.

"But there was the house and land," I asked, — "what became
of that part of the property?"

Mrs. Todd looked into the fire, and a shadow of disapproval
flitted over her face.

"Poor old uncle!" she said, "he got childish about the matter. I
was hoping to sell at first, and I had an offer, but he always run of
an idea that there was more money hid away, and kept wanting me
to delay; an' he used to go up there all alone and search, and dig in
the cellar, empty an' bleak as 'twas in winter weather or any time.
An' he'd come and tell me he'd dreamed he found gold behind a
stone in the cellar wall, or somethin.' And one night we all see the
light o' fire up that way, an' the whole Landin' took the road, and
run to look, and the Tolland property was all in a light blaze. I

expect the old gentleman had dropped fire about; he said he'd been up there to see if everything was safe in the afternoon. As for the land, 'twas so poor that everybody used to have a joke that the Tolland boys preferred to farm the sea instead. It's 'most all grown up to bushes now where it ain't poor water grass in the low places. There's some upland that has a pretty view, after you cross the brook bridge. Years an' years after she died, there was some o' her flowers used to come up an' bloom in the door garden. I brought two or three that was unusual down here; they always come up and remind me of her, constant as the spring. But I never did want to fetch home that guitar, some way or 'nother; I wouldn't let it go at the auction, either. It was hangin' right there in the house when the fire took place. I've got some o' her other little things scattered about the house: that picture on the mantelpiece belonged to her."

I had often wondered where such a picture had come from, and why Mrs. Todd had chosen it; it was a French print of the statue of the Empress Josephine in the Savane at old Fort Royal, in Martinique.[7]

VI

Mrs. Todd drew her chair closer to mine; she held the cat and her knitting with one hand as she moved, but the cat was so warm and so sound asleep that she only stretched a lazy paw in spite of what must have felt like a slight earthquake. Mrs. Todd began to speak almost in a whisper.

"I ain't told you all," she continued; "no, I haven't spoken of all to but very few. The way it came was this," she said solemnly, and then stopped to listen to the wind, and sat for a moment in deferential silence, as if she waited for the wind to speak first. The cat suddenly lifted her head with quick excitement and gleaming eyes, and her mistress was leaning forward toward the fire with an arm laid on either knee, as if they were consulting the glowing coals for some augury. Mrs. Todd looked like an old prophetess as she sat there with the firelight shining on her strong face; she was posed for some great painter. The woman with the cat was as unconscious and as mysterious as any sibyl of the Sistine Chapel.

"There, that's the last struggle o' the gale," said Mrs. Todd, nodding her head with impressive certainty and still looking into the bright embers of the fire. "You'll see!" She gave me another quick glance, and spoke in a low tone as if we might be overheard.

"'Twas such a gale as this the night Mis' Tolland died. She appeared more comfortable the first o' the evenin'; and Mrs. Begg was more spent than I, bein' older, and a beautiful nurse that was the first to see and think of everything, but perfectly quiet an' never asked a useless question. You remember her funeral when you first

7. A statue of the Empress Josephine (1763–1814) stands in the public gardens of Fort-de-France on Martinique, an island in the West Indies.

come to the Landing? And she consented to goin' an' havin' a good sleep while she could, and left me one o' those good little pewter lamps that burnt whale oil an' made plenty o' light in the room, but not too bright to be disturbin'.'

"Poor Mis' Tolland had been distressed the night before, an' all that day, but as night came on she grew more and more easy, an' was layin' there asleep; 'twas like settin' by any sleepin' person, and I had none but usual thoughts. When the wind lulled and the rain, I could hear the seas, though more distant than this, and I don' know's I observed any other sound than what the weather made; 'twas a very solemn feelin' night. I set close by the bed; there was times she looked to find somebody when she was awake. The light was on her face, so I could see her plain; there was always times when she wore a look that made her seem a stranger you'd never set eyes on before. I did think what a world it was that her an' me should have come together so, and she have nobody but Dunnet Landin' folks about her in her extremity. 'You're one o' the stray ones, poor creatur',' I said. I remember those very words passin' through my mind, but I saw reason to be glad she had some comforts, and didn't lack friends at the last, though she'd seen misery an' pain. I was glad she was quiet; all day she'd been restless, and we couldn't understand what she wanted from her French speech. We had the window open to give her air, an' now an' then a gust would strike that guitar that was on the wall and set it swinging by the blue ribbon, and soundin' as if somebody begun to play it. I come near takin' it down, but you never know what'll fret a sick person an' put 'em on the rack, an' that guitar was one o' the few things she'd brought with her."

I nodded assent, and Mrs. Todd spoke still lower.

"I set there close by the bed; I'd been through a good deal for some days back, and I thought I might's well be droppin' asleep too, bein' a quick person to wake. She looked to me as if she might last a day longer, certain, now she'd got more comfortable, but I was real tired, an' sort o' cramped as watchers will get, an' a fretful feeling begun to creep over me such as they often do have. If you give way, there ain't no support for the sick person; they can't count on no composure o' their own. Mis' Tolland moved then, a little restless, an' I forgot me quick enough, an' begun to hum out a little part of a hymn tune just to make her feel everything was as usual an' not wake up into a poor uncertainty. All of a sudden she set right up in bed with her eyes wide open, an' I stood an' put my arm behind her; she hadn't moved like that for days. And she reached out both her arms toward the door, an' I looked the way she was lookin', an' I see some one was standin' there against the dark. No, 't wa'n't Mis' Begg; 'twas somebody a good deal shorter than Mis' Begg. The lamplight struck across the room between us. I couldn't tell the shape, but 'twas a woman's dark face lookin' right at us; 'twa'n't but an instant I could see. I felt dreadful cold, and my head begun to swim; I thought the light went out; 'twa'n't but an instant, as I say, an' when my sight come back I couldn't see nothing there. I was one that didn't know what it was to faint away, no matter what happened; time was I felt above it in others, but 'twas somethin' that made poor human natur' quail. I saw very plain while I could see; 'twas a pleasant enough face, shaped somethin' like Mis' Tolland's, and a kind of expectin' look.

"No, I don't expect I was asleep," Mrs. Todd assured me quietly, after a moment's pause, though I had not spoken. She gave a heavy sigh before she went on. I could see that the recollection moved her in the deepest way.

"I suppose if I hadn't been so spent an' quavery with long watchin', I might have kept my head an' observed much better," she added humbly; 'but I see all I could bear. I did try to act calm, an' I laid Mis' Tolland down on her pillow, an' I was a-shakin' as I done it. All she did was to look up to me so satisfied and sort o' questioning, an' I looked back to her.

"'You saw her, didn't you?' she says to me, speakin' perfectly reasonable. ''T is my mother,' she says again, very feeble, but lookin' straight up at me, kind of surprised with the pleasure, and smiling as if she saw I was overcome, an' would have said more if she could, but we had hold of hands. I see then her change was comin', but I didn't call Mis' Begg, nor make no uproar. I felt calm then, an' lifted to somethin' different as I never was since. She opened her eyes just as she was goin'—

"'You saw her, didn't you?' she said the second time, an' I says, 'Yes, dear, I did; you ain't never goin' to feel strange an' lonesome no more.' An' then in a few quiet minutes 'twas all over. I felt they'd gone away together. No, I wa'n't alarmed afterward; 'twas just that one moment I couldn't live under, but I never called it beyond reason I should see the other watcher. I saw plain enough there was somebody there with me in the room.

VII

"'Twas just such a night as this Mis' Tolland died," repeated Mrs. Todd, returning to her usual tone and leaning back comfortably in her chair as she took up her knitting. "'Twas just such a night as this. I've told the circumstances to but very few; but I don't call it beyond reason. When folks is goin' 'tis all natural, and only common things can jar upon the mind. You know plain enough there's somethin' beyond this world; the doors stand wide open. There's somethin' of us that must still live on; we've got to join both worlds together an' live in one but for the other.' The doctor said that to me one day, an' I never could forget it; he said 'twas in one o' his old doctor's books.'"

We sat together in silence in the warm little room; the rain dropped heavily from the eaves, and the sea still roared, but the high wind had done blowing. We heard the far complaining fog horn of a steamer up the Bay.

"There goes the Boston boat out, pretty near on time," said Mrs. Todd with satisfaction. "Sometimes these late August storms'll sound a good deal worse than they really be. I do hate to hear the poor steamers callin' when they're bewildered in thick nights in winter, comin' on the coast. Yes, there goes the boat; they'll find it rough at sea, but the storm's all over."

1900

KATE CHOPIN
1851–1904

Katherine O'Flaherty did not appear to be destined for a literary career, certainly not one which would end with the overtones of scandal. Her father was a successful businessman, the family enjoyed a high place in St. Louis society, and her mother, grandmother, and great-grandmother were active, pious Catholics. But in part under the influence of her strong-willed great-grandmother (who was also a compelling and tireless storyteller), and long before she began to compose and submit stories in the 1880s for publication, the young Katherine asserted her independence by smoking in company and going about the streets without a companion of either sex—both rather daring acts for the time.

At the age of twenty she married Oscar Chopin (who pronounced his name Show-pan) and spent the next decade in New Orleans, where her husband first prospered, then failed, in the cotton business. After spending a few years in Cloutierville in northwest Louisiana, where her husband opened a general store and taken over the management of a family cotton plantation, she returned to St. Louis in 1884, a year after her husband's sudden death from swamp fever. A year later her mother died, and at the age of thirty-five Kate Chopin was left essentially alone to raise her children and to fashion a literary career out of her experience of Louisiana life, and her reading of such French contemporary realists as Émile Zola and Guy de Maupassant.

Chopin wrote on a lapboard in the center of a swirl of children. She claimed, moreover, that she wrote on impulse, that she was "completely at the mercy of unconscious selection" of subject, and that "the polishing up process * * * always proved disastrous." This method, while it insured freshness and sincerity, made some of her stories seem anecdotal, and sometimes too loose or thin. In the relatively few years of her writing career— scarcely more than a decade—she completed two novels, over 150 stories and sketches, and a substantial body of poetry, reviews, and criticism. A first novel, *At Fault*, was published in 1890; but it was her early stories of Louisiana rural life, especially the collection *Bayou Folk* (1894), which won her national recognition as a leading practitioner of local-color fiction.

She made the Catholic Creoles with their old-fashioned European customs, their polyglot, witty speech, and the lush, semitropical landscape of picturesque Natchitoches Parish as familiar to Americans as Sarah Orne Jewett (whom she admired) was making the townspeople of the coastal region of Maine. A second collection of her stories, A *Night in Acadie*, was published three years later and enhanced that reputation.

Chopin's major work, *The Awakening*, was published in 1899. The novel, which traces the psychological and sexual coming to consciousness of a young woman, predictably aroused hostility among contemporary reviewers, just as Whitman's *Leaves of Grass*, which she admired, had done half a century earlier. The "new woman" of the time, demanding social. economic, and political equality, was already a common topic of public discussion and subject for fiction. But the depiction of such an unrepentant sensualist as Edna Pontellier was more than the critics of the time could allow to pass. The book was described as "trite and sordid," "essentially vulgar," and "unhealthily introspective and morbid in feeling." Chopin was hurt by this criticism and the social ostracism that accompanied it. Her only published response, however, was to claim, tongue in cheek: "I never dreamed of Mrs. Pontellier making such a mess of things and working out her own damnation as she did. If I had had the slightest intimation of such a thing I would have excluded her from the company." Though the book and its author fell into obscurity for half a century, they have now secured an honored place in American literary history.

In *The Awakening*, more impressively because on a grander scale than in a number of her shorter fictions, Chopin demonstrates her unusual capacity to make the alien, somewhat exotic world of New Orleans and the Gulf islands real, and to people it with complex and often baffled men and women whose humanity she confirms by refusing to use it to support a thesis or to judge it.

The notes to the present text of *The Awakening* (a corrected version of the first edition) owe much to the Norton Critical Edition prepared by Margaret Culley.

The Awakening

I

A green and yellow parrot, which hung in a cage outside the door, kept repeating over and over:

"*Allez vous-en! Allez vous-en! Sapristi!*[1] That's all right!"

He could speak a little Spanish, and also a language which nobody understood, unless it was the mocking-bird that hung on the other side of the door, whistling his fluty notes out upon the breeze with maddening persistence.

Mr. Pontellier, unable to read his newspaper with any degree of comfort, arose with an expression and an exclamation of disgust. He walked down the gallery and across the narrow "bridges" which connected the Lebrun cottages one with the other. He had been seated before the door of the main house. The parrot and the mocking-bird were the property of Madame Lebrun, and they had the right to make all the noise they wished. Mr. Pontellier had the priv-

1. "Go away! Go away! For God's sake!"

ilege of quitting their society when they ceased to be entertaining.

He stopped before the door of his own cottage, which was the fourth one from the main building and next to the last. Seating himself in a wicker rocker which was there, he once more applied himself to the task of reading the newspaper. The day was Sunday; the paper was a day old. The Sunday papers had not yet reached Grand Isle.[2] He was already acquainted with the market reports, and he glanced restlessly over the editorials and bits of news which he had not had time to read before quitting New Orleans the day before.

Mr. Pontellier wore eye-glasses. He was a man of forty, of medium height and rather slender build; he stooped a little. His hair was brown and straight, parted on one side. His beard was neatly and closely trimmed.

Once in a while he withdrew his glance from the newspaper and looked about him. There was more noise than ever over at the house. The main building was called "the house," to distinguish it from the cottages. The chattering and whistling birds were still at it. Two young girls, the Farival twins, were playing a duet from "Zampa"[3] upon the piano. Madame Lebrun was bustling in and out, giving orders in a high key to a yard-boy whenever she got inside the house, and directions in an equally high voice to a dining-room servant whenever she got outside. She was a fresh, pretty woman, clad always in white with elbow sleeves. Her starched skirts crinkled as she came and went. Farther down, before one of the cottages, a lady in black was walking demurely up and down, telling her beads. A good many persons of the *pension* had gone over to the *Chênière Caminada* in Beaudelet's lugger[4] to hear mass. Some young people were out under the water-oaks playing croquet. Mr. Pontellier's two children were there—sturdy little fellows of four and five. A qua-droon[5] nurse followed them about with a far-away, meditative air.

Mr. Pontellier finally lit a cigar and began to smoke, letting the paper drag idly from his hand. He fixed his gaze upon a white sunshade[6] that was advancing at snail's pace from the beach. He could see it plainly between the gaunt trunks of the water-oaks and acros the stretch of yellow camomile. The gulf looked far away, melting hazily into the blue of the horizon. The sunshade continued to approach slowly. Beneath its pink-lined shelter were his wife, Mrs. Pontellier, and young Robert Lebrun. When they reached the cottage, the two seated themselves with some appearance of fatigue upon the step of the porch, facing each other, each leaning against a supporting post.

2. A resort island, 50 miles south of New Orleans, between the Gulf of Mexico and Caminada Bay.
3. Romantic opera by Louis Hérold (1791–1833).
4. A *pension* is a bed-and-board hotel;

"*Chênière Caminada*": an island between Grande Isle and the Louisiana coast; "lugger": passenger boat.
5. A person with one-fourth ("quad") black ancestry.
6. I.e., parasol.

"What folly! to bathe at such an hour in such heat!" exclaimed Mr. Pontellier. He himself had taken a plunge at daylight. That was why the morning seemed long to him.

"You are burnt beyond recognition," he added, looking at his wife as one looks at a valuable piece of personal property which has suffered some damage. She held up her hands, strong, shapely hands, and surveyed them critically, drawing up her lawn[7] sleeves above the wrists. Looking at them reminded her of her rings, which she had given to her husband before leaving for the beach. She silently reached out to him, and he, understanding, took the rings from his vest pocket and dropped them into her open palm. She slipped them upon her fingers; then clasping her knees, she looked across at Robert and began to laugh. The rings sparkled upon her fingers. He sent back an answering smile.

"What is it?" asked Pontellier, looking lazily and amused from one to the other. It was some utter nonsense; some adventure out there in the water, and they both tried to relate it at once. It did not seem half so amusing when told. They realized this, and so did Mr. Pontellier. He yawned and stretched himself. Then he got up, saying he had half a mind to go over to Klein's hotel[8] and play a game of billiards.

"Come go along, Lebrun," he proposed to Robert. But Robert admitted quite frankly that he preferred to stay where he was and talk to Mrs. Pontellier.

"Well, send him about his business when he bores you, Edna," instructed her husband as he prepared to leave.

"Here, take the umbrella," she exclaimed, holding it out to him. He accepted the sunshade, and lifting it over his head descended the steps and walked away.

"Coming back to dinner?" his wife called after him. He halted a moment and shrugged his shoulders. He felt in his vest pocket; there was a ten-dollar bill there. He did not know; perhaps he would return for the early dinner and perhaps he would not. It all depended upon the company which he found over at Klein's and the size of "the game." He did not say this, but she understood it, and laughed, nodding good-by to him.

Both children wanted to follow their father when they saw him starting out. He kissed them and promised to bring them back bonbons and peanuts.

II

Mrs. Pontellier's eyes were quick and bright; they were a yellowish brown, about the color of her hair. She had a way of turning them swiftly upon an object and holding them there as if lost in some inward maze of contemplation or thought.

7. Fine linen or sheer muslin.
8. Probably based on Kranz's Hotel, a well-known establishment of the time.

Her eyebrows were a shade darker than her hair. They were thick and almost horizontal, emphasizing the depth of her eyes. She was rather handsome than beautiful. Her face was captivating by reason of a certain frankness of expression and a contradictory subtle play of features. Her manner was engaging.

Robert rolled a cigarette. He smoked cigarettes because he could not afford cigars, he said. He had a cigar in his pocket which Mr. Pontellier had presented him with, and he was saving it for his after-dinner smoke.

This seemed quite proper and natural on his part. In coloring he was not unlike his companion. A clean-shaven face made the resemblance more pronounced than it would otherwise have been. There rested no shadow of care upon his open countenance. His eyes gathered in and reflected the light and languor of the summer day.

Mrs. Pontellier reached over for a palmleaf fan that lay on the porch and began to fan herself, while Robert sent between his lips light puffs from his cigarette. They chatted incessantly: about the things around them; their amusing adventure out in the water—it had again assumed its entertaining aspect; about the wind, the trees, the people who had gone to the *Chênière*; about the children playing croquet under the oaks, and the Farival twins, who were now performing the overture to "The Poet and Peasant."[9]

Robert talked a good deal about himself. He was very young, and did not know any better. Mrs. Pontellier talked a little about herself for the same reason. Each was interested in what the other said. Robert spoke of his intention to go to Mexico in the autumn, where fortune awaited him. He was always intending to go to Mexico, but some way never got there. Meanwhile he held on to his modest position in a mercantile house in New Orleans, where an equal familiarity with English, French and Spanish gave him no small value as a clerk and correspondent.

He was spending his summer vacation, as he always did, with his mother at Grand Isle. In former times, before Robert could remember, "the house" had been a summer luxury of the Lebruns. Now, flanked by its dozen or more cottages, which were always filled with exclusive visitors from the *"Quartier Français,"*[1] it enabled Madame Lebrun to maintain the easy and comfortable existence which appeared to be her birthright.

Mrs. Pontellier talked about her father's Mississippi plantation and her girlhood home in the old Kentucky blue-grass country. She was an American woman, with a small infusion of French which seemed to have been lost in dilution. She read a letter from her sister, who was away in the East, and who had engaged herself to be married. Robert was interested, and wanted to know what manner

9. An operetta by Franz von Suppé (1819–95).
1. The French Quarter of New Orleans, settled by the French in the early 1700s and occupied by wealthy, older families.

of girls the sisters were, what the father was like, and how long the mother had been dead.

When Mrs. Pontellier folded the letter it was time for her to dress for the early dinner.

"I see Léonce isn't coming back," she said, with a glance in the direction whence her husband had disappeared. Robert supposed he was not, as there were a good many New Orleans club men over at Klein's.

When Mrs. Pontellier left him to enter her room, the young man descended the steps and strolled over toward the croquet players, where, during the half-hour before dinner, he amused himself with the little Pontellier children, who were very fond of him.

III

It was eleven o'clock that night when Mr. Pontellier returned from Klein's hotel. He was in an excellent humor, in high spirits, and very talkative. His entrance awoke his wife, who was in bed and fast asleep when he came in. He talked to her while he undressed, telling her anecdotes and bits of news and gossip that he had gathered during the day. From his trousers pockets he took a fistful of crumpled bank notes and a good deal of silver coin, which he piled on the bureau indiscriminately with keys, knife, handkerchief, and whatever else happened to be in his pockets. She was overcome with sleep, and answered him with little half utterances.

He thought it very discouraging that his wife, who was the sole object of his existence, evinced so little interest in things which concerned him and valued so little his conversation.

Mr. Pontellier had forgotten the bonbons and peanuts for the boys. Notwithstanding he loved them very much, and went into the adjoining room where they slept to take a look at them and make sure that they were resting comfortably. The result of his investigation was far from satisfactory. He turned and shifted the youngsters about in bed. One of them began to kick and talk about a basket full of crabs.

Mr. Pontellier returned to his wife with the information that Raoul had a high fever and needed looking after. Then he lit a cigar and went and sat near the open door to smoke it.

Mrs. Pontellier was quite sure Raoul had no fever. He had gone to bed perfectly well, she said, and nothing had ailed him all day. Mr. Pontellier was too well acquainted with fever symptoms to be mistaken. He assured her the child was consuming[2] at that moment in the next room.

He reproached his wife with her inattention, her habitual neglect of the children. If it was not a mother's place to look after children, whose on earth was it? He himself had his hands full with his brokerage business. He could not be in two places at once; making a

2. I.e., feverish.

living for his family on the street, and staying at home to see that no harm befell them. He talked in a monotonous, insistent way.

Mrs. Pontellier sprang out of bed and went into the next room. She soon came back and sat on the edge of the bed, leaning her head down on the pillow. She said nothing, and refused to answer her husband when he questioned her. When his cigar was smoked out he went to bed, and in half a minute he was fast asleep.

Mrs. Pontellier was by that time thoroughly awake. She began to cry a little, and wiped her eyes on the sleeve of her *peignoir.* Blowing out the candle, which her husband had left burning, she slipped her bare feet into a pair of satin *mules* at the foot of the bed and went out on the porch, where she sat down in the wicker chair and began to rock gently to and fro.

It was then past midnight. The cottages were all dark. A single faint light gleamed out from the hallway of the house. There was no sound abroad except the hooting of an old owl in the top of a water-oak, and the everlasting voice of the sea, that was not uplifted at that soft hour. It broke like a mournful lullaby upon the night.

The tears came so fast to Mrs. Pontellier's eyes that the damp sleeve of her *peignoir* no longer served to dry them. She was holding the back of her chair with one hand; her loose sleeve had slipped almost to the shoulder of her uplifted arm. Turning, she thrust her face, steaming and wet, into the bend of her arm, and she went on crying there, not caring any longer to dry her face, her eyes, her arms. She could not have told why she was crying. Such experiences as the foregoing were not uncommon in her married life. They seemed never before to have weighed much against the abundance of her husband's kindness and a uniform devotion which had come to be tacit and self-understood.

An indescribable oppression, which seemed to generate in some unfamiliar part of her consciousness, filled her whole being with a vague anguish. It was like a shadow, like a mist passing across her soul's summer day. It was strange and unfamiliar; it was a mood. She did not sit there inwardly upbraiding her husband, lamenting at Fate, which had directed her footsteps to the path which they had taken. She was just having a good cry all to herself. The mosquitoes made merry over her, biting her firm, round arms and nipping at her bare insteps.

The little stinging, buzzing imps succeeded in dispelling a mood which might have held her there in the darkness half a night longer.

The following morning Mr. Pontellier was up in good time to take the rockaway[3] which was to convey him to the steamer at the wharf. He was returning to the city to his business, and they would not see him again at the Island till the coming Saturday. He had

---

3. A four-wheeled carriage (manufactured in Rockaway, New Jersey).

regained his composure, which seemed to have been somewhat impaired the night before. He was eager to be gone, as he looked forward to a lively week in Carondelet Street.[4]

Mr. Pontellier gave his wife half the money which he had brought away from Klein's hotel the evening before. She liked money as well as most women, and accepted it with no little satisfaction.

"It will buy a handsome wedding present for Sister Janet!" she exclaimed, smoothing out the bills as she counted them one by one.

"Oh! we'll treat Sister Janet better than that, my dear," he laughed, as he prepared to kiss her good-by.

The boys were tumbling about, clinging to his legs, imploring that numerous things be brought back to them. Mr. Pontellier was a great favorite, and ladies, men, children, even nurses, were always on hand to say good-by to him. His wife stood smiling and waving, the boys shouting, as he disappeared in the old rockaway down the sandy road.

A few days later a box arrived for Mrs. Pontellier from New Orleans. It was from her husband. It was filled with *friandises*, with luscious and toothsome bits—the finest of fruits, *patés*, a rare bottle or two, delicious syrups, and bonbons in abundance.

Mrs. Pontellier was always very generous with the contents of such a box; she was quite used to receiving them when away from home. The *patés* and fruit were brought to the dining-room; the bonbons were passed around. And the ladies, selecting with dainty and discriminating fingers and a little greedily, all declared that Mr. Pontellier was the best husband in the world. Mrs. Pontellier was forced to admit that she knew of none better.

IV

It would have been a difficult matter for Mr. Pontellier to define to his own satisfaction or any one else's wherein his wife failed in her duty toward their children. It was something which he felt rather than perceived, and he never voiced the feeling without subsequent regret and ample atonement.

If one of the little Pontellier boys took a tumble whilst at play, he was not apt to rush crying to his mother's arms for comfort; he would more likely pick himself up, wipe the water out of his eyes and the sand out of his mouth, and go on playing. Tots as they were, they pulled together and stood their ground in childish battles with doubled fists and uplifted voices, which usually prevailed against the other mother-tots. The quadroon nurse was looked upon as a huge encumbrance, only good to button up waists and panties and to brush and part hair; since it seemed to be a law of society that hair must be parted and brushed.

---

4. New Orleans's equivalent of Wall Street, and the location of the Cotton Exchange.

In short, Mrs. Pontellier was not a mother-woman. The mother-women seemed to prevail that summer at Grand Isle. It was easy to know them, fluttering about with extended, protecting wings when any harm, real or imaginary, threatened their precious brood. They were women who idolized their children, worshiped their husbands, and esteemed it a holy privilege to efface themselves as individuals and grow wings as ministering angels.

Many of them were delicious in the rôle; one of them was the embodiment of every womanly grace and charm. If her husband did not adore her, he was a brute, deserving of death by slow torture. Her name was Adèle Ratignolle. There are no words to describe her save the old ones that have served so often to picture the bygone heroine of romance and the fair lady of our dreams. There was nothing subtle or hidden about her charms; her beauty was all there, flaming and apparent: the spun-gold hair that comb nor confining pin could restrain; the blue eyes that were like nothing but sapphires; two lips that pouted, that were so red one could only think of cherries or some other delicious crimson fruit in looking at them. She was growing a little stout, but it did not seem to detract an iota from the grace of every step, pose, gesture. One would not have wanted her white neck a mite less full or her beautiful arms more slender. Never were hands more exquisite than hers, and it was a joy to look at them when she threaded her needle or adjusted her gold thimble to her taper[5] middle finger as she sewed away on the little night-drawers or fashioned a bodice or a bib.

Madame Ratignolle was very fond of Mrs. Pontellier, and often she took her sewing and went over to sit with her in the afternoons. She was sitting there the afternoon of the day the box arrived from New Orleans. She had possession of the rocker, and she was busily engaged in sewing upon a diminutive pair of night-drawers.

She had brought the pattern of the drawers for Mrs. Pontellier to cut out—a marvel of construction, fashioned to enclose a baby's body so effectually that only two small eyes might look out from the garment, like an Eskimo's. They were designed for winter wear, when treacherous drafts came down chimneys and insidious currents of deadly cold found their way through key-holes.

Mrs. Pontellier's mind was quite at rest concerning the present material needs of her children, and she could not see the use of anticipating and making winter night garments the subject of her summer meditations. But she did not want to appear unamiable and uninterested, so she had brought forth newspapers which she spread upon the floor of the gallery, and under Madame Ratignolle's directions she had cut a pattern of the impervious garment.

Robert was there, seated as he had been the Sunday before, and

5. I.e., tapered.

Mrs. Pontellier also occupied her former position on the upper step, leaning listlessly against the post. Beside her was a box of bonbons, which she held out at intervals to Madame Ratignolle.

That lady seemed at a loss to make a selection, but finally settled upon a stick of nugat, wondering if it were not too rich; whether it could possibly hurt her. Madame Ratignolle had been married seven years. About every two years she had a baby. At that time she had three babies, and was beginning to think of a fourth one. She was always talking about her "condition." Her "condition" was in no way apparent, and no one would have known a thing about it but for her persistence in making it the subject of conversation.

Robert started to reassure her, asserting that he had known a lady who had subsisted upon nugat during the entire—but seeing the color mount into Mrs. Pontellier's face he checked himself and changed the subject.

Mrs. Pontellier, though she had married a Creole,[6] was not thoroughly at home in the society of Creoles; never before had she been thrown so intimately among them. There were only Creoles that summer at Lebrun's. They all knew each other, and felt like one large family, among whom existed the most amicable relations. A characteristic which distinguished them and which impressed Mrs. Pontellier most forcibly was their entire absence of prudery. Their freedom of expression was at first incomprehensible to her, though she had no difficulty in reconciling it with a lofty chastity which in the Creole woman seems to be inborn and unmistakable.

Never would Edna Pontellier forget the shock with which she heard Madame Ratignolle relating to old Monsieur Farival the harrowing story of one of her *accouchements*,[7] withholding no intimate detail. She was growing accustomed to like shocks, but she could not keep the mounting color back from her cheeks. Oftener than once her coming had interrupted the droll story with which Robert was entertaining some amused group of married women.

A book had gone the rounds of the *pension*. When it came her turn to read it, she did so with profound astonishment. She felt moved to read the book in secret and soilitude, though none of the others had done so—to hide it from view at the sound of approaching footsteps. It was openly criticised and freely discussed at table. Mrs. Pontellier gave over being astonished, and concluded that wonders would never cease.

V

They formed a congenial group sitting there that summer afternoon—Madame Ratignolle sewing away, often stopping to relate a story or incident with much expressive gesture of her perfect hands; Robert and Mrs. Pontellier sitting idle, exchanging occasional

6. A person descended from the original French and Spanish settlers of New Or- leans; thus, at this time, an aristocrat.
7. The birth of one of her children.

words, glances or smiles which indicated a certain advanced stage of intimacy and *camaraderie*.

He had lived in her shadow during the past month. No one thought anything of it. Many had predicted that Robert would devote himself to Mrs. Pontellier when he arrived. Since the age of fifteen, which was eleven years before, Robert each summer at Grand Isle had constituted himself the devoted attendant of some fair dame or damsel. Sometimes it was a young girl, again a widow; but as often as not it was some interesting married woman.

For two consecutive seasons he lived in the sunlight of Mademoiselle Duvigné's presence. But she died between summers; then Robert posed as an inconsolable, prostrating himself at the feet of Madame Ratignolle for whatever crumbs of sympathy and comfort she might be pleased to vouchsafe.

Mrs. Pontellier liked to sit and gaze at her fair companion as she might look upon a faultless Madonna.

"Could any one fathom the cruelty beneath that fair exterior?" murmured Robert. "She knew that I adored her once, and she let me adore her. It was 'Robert, come; go; stand up; sit down; do this; do that; see if the baby sleeps; my thimble, please, that I left God knows where. Come and read Daudet[8] to me while I sew.' "

"*Par exemple!*[9] I never had to ask. You were always there under my feet, like a troublesome cat."

"You mean like an adoring dog. And just as soon as Ratignolle appeared on the scene, then it *was* like a dog. '*Passez! Adieu! Allez vous-en!*' "[1]

"Perhaps I feared to make Alphonse jealous," she interjoined, with excessive naïveté. That made them all laugh. The right hand jealous of the left! The heart jealous of the soul! But for that matter, the Creole husband is never jealous; with him the gangrene passion is one which has become dwarfed by disuse.

Meanwhile Robert, addressing Mrs. Pontellier, continued to tell of his one time hopeless passion for Madame Ratignolle; of sleepless nights, of consuming flames till the very sea sizzled when he took his daily plunge. While the lady at the needle kept up a little running, contemptuous comment:

"*Blagueur—farceur—gros bête, va!*"[2]

He never assumed this serio-comic tone when alone with Mrs. Pontellier. She never knew precisely what to make of it; at that moment it was impossible for her to guess how much of it was jest and what proportion was earnest. It was understood that he had often spoken words of love to Madame Ratignolle, without any thought of being taken seriously. Mrs. Pontellier was glad he had

---

8. Alphonse Daudet (1840–87), French novelist.
9. "For goodness sake!"

1. "Go on! Good-by! Go away!"
2. "Liar—comedian—silly, come off it!"

not assumed a similar rôle toward herself. It would have been unac-
ceptable and annoying.

Mrs. Pontellier had brought her sketching materials, which she
sometimes dabbled with in an unprofessional way. She liked the
dabbling. She felt in it satisfaction of a kind which no other
employment afforded her.

She had long wished to try herself on Madame Ratignolle. Never
had that lady seemed a more tempting subject than at that
moment, seated there like some sensuous Madonna, with the gleam
of the fading day enriching her splendid color.

Robert crossed over and seated himself upon the step below
Mrs. Pontellier, that he might watch her work. She handled her
brushes with a certain ease and freedom which came, not from long
and close acquaintance with them, but from a natural aptitude.
Robert followed her work with close attention, giving forth little
ejaculatory expressions of appreciation in French, which he
addressed to Madame Ratignolle.

"*Mais ce n'est pas mal! Elle s'y connait, elle a de la force, oui.*"[3]

During his oblivious attention he once quietly rested his head
against Mrs. Pontellier's arm. As gently she repulsed him. Once
again he repeated the offense. She could not but believe it to be
thoughtlessness on his part; yet that was no reason she should
submit to it. She did not remonstrate, except again to repulse him
quietly but firmly. He offered no apology.

The picture completed bore no resemblance to Madame Ratignolle. She was greatly disappointed to find that it did not look like
her. But it was a fair enough piece of work, and in many respects
satisfying.

Mrs. Pontellier evidently did not think so. After surveying the
sketch critically she drew a broad smudge of paint across its surface,
and crumpled the paper between her hands.

The youngsters came tumbling up the steps, the quadroon following at the respectful distance which they required her to observe.
Mrs. Pontellier made them carry her paints and things into the
house. She sought to detain them for a little talk and some pleasantry. But they were greatly in earnest. They had only come to investigate the contents of the bonbon box. They accepted without
murmuring what she chose to give them, each holding out two
chubby hands scoop-like, in the vain hope that they might be filled;
and then away they went.

The sun was low in the west, and the breeze soft and languorous
that came up from the south, charged with the seductive odor of
the sea. Children, freshly befurbeloved,[4] were gathering for their
games under the oaks. Their voices were high and penetrating.

3. "Not bad at all! She knows what she's doing, she has talent."
4. Dressed up in petticoats.

Madame Ratignolle folded her sewing, placing thimble, scissors and thread all neatly together in the roll, which she pinned securely. She complained of faintness. Mrs. Pontellier flew for the cologne water and a fan. She bathed Madame Ratignolle's face with cologne, while Robert plied the fan with unnecessary vigor.

The spell was soon over, and Mrs. Pontellier could not help wondering if there were not a little imagination responsible for its origin, for the rose tint had never faded from her friend's face.

She stood watching the fair woman walk down the long line of galleries with the grace and majesty which queens are sometimes supposed to possess. Her little ones ran to meet her. Two of them clung about her white skirts, the third she took from its nurse and with a thousand endearments bore it along in her own fond, encircling arms. Though, as everybody well knew, the doctor had forbidden her to lift so much as a pin!

"Are you going bathing?" asked Robert of Mrs. Pontellier. It was not so much a question as a reminder.

"Oh, no," she answered, with a tone of indecision. "I'm tired; I think not." Her glance wandered from his face away toward the Gulf, whose sonorous murmur reached her like a loving but imperative entreaty.

"Oh, come!" he insisted. "You mustn't miss your bath. Come on. The water must be delicious; it will not hurt you. Come."

He reached up for her big, rough straw hat that hung on a peg outside the door, and put it on her head. They descended the steps, and walked away together toward the beach. The sun was low in the west and the breeze was soft and warm.

VI

Edna Pontellier could not have told why, wishing to go to the beach with Robert, she should in the first place have declined, and in the second place have followed in obedience to one of the two contradictory impulses which impelled her.

A certain light was beginning to dawn dimly within her,—the light which, showing the way, forbids it.

At that early period it served but to bewilder her. It moved her to dreams, to thoughtfulness, to the shadowy anguish which had overcome her the midnight when she had abandoned herself to tears.

In short, Mrs. Pontellier was beginning to realize her position in the universe as a human being, and to recognize her relations as an individual to the world within and about her. This may seem like a ponderous weight of wisdom to descend upon the soul of a young woman of twenty-eight—perhaps more wisdom than the Holy Ghost is usually pleased to vouchsafe to any woman.

But the beginning of things, of a world especially, is necessarily vague, tangled, chaotic, and exceedingly disturbing. How few of us ever emerge from such beginning! How many souls perish in its tumult!

The voice of the sea is seductive; never ceasing, whispering, clamoring, murmuring, inviting the soul to wander for a spell in abysses of solitude; to lose itself in mazes of inward contemplation.

The voice of the sea speaks to the soul. The touch of the sea is sensuous, enfolding the body in its soft, close embrace.

VII

Mrs. Pontellier was not a woman given to confidences, a characteristic hitherto contrary to her nature. Even as a child she had lived her own small life all within herself. At a very early period she had apprehended instinctively the dual life—that outward existence which conforms, the inward life which questions.

That summer at Grand Isle she began to loosen a little the mantle of reserve that had always enveloped her. There may have been—there must have been—influences, both subtle and apparent, working in their several ways to induce her to do this; but the most obvious was the influence of Adèle Ratignolle. The excessive physical charm of the Creole had first attracted her, for Edna had a sensuous susceptibility to beauty. Then the candor of the woman's whole existence, which everyone might read, and which formed so striking a contrast to her own habitual reserve—this might have furnished a link. Who can tell what metals the gods use in forging the subtle bond which we call sympathy, which we might as well call love.

The two women went away one morning to the beach together, arm in arm, under the huge white sunshade. Edna had prevailed upon Madame Ratignolle to leave the children behind, though she could not induce her to relinquish a diminutive roll of needlework, which Adèle begged to be allowed to slip into the depths of her pocket. In some unaccountable way they had escaped from Robert.

The walk to the beach was no inconsiderable one, consisting as it did of a long, sandy path, upon which a sporadic and tangled growth that bordered it on either side made frequent and unexpected inroads. There were acres of yellow camomile reaching out on either hand. Further away still, vegetable gardens abounded, with frequent small plantations of orange or lemon trees intervening. The dark green clusters glistened from afar in the sun.

The women were both of goodly height, Madame Ratignolle possessing the more feminine and matronly figure. The charm of Edna Pontellier's physique stole insensibly upon you. The lines of her body were long, clean and symmetrical; it was a body which occasionally fell into splendid poses; there was no suggestion of the trim, stereotyped fashion-plate about it. A casual and indiscriminating observer, in passing, might not cast a second glance upon the figure. But with more feeling and discernment he would have recognized the noble beauty of its modeling, and the graceful severity of poise and movement, which made Edna Pontellier different from the crowd.

She wore a cool muslin that morning—white, with a waving vertical line of brown running through it; also a white linen collar and the big straw hat which she had taken from the peg outside the door. The hat rested any way on her yellow-brown hair, that waved a little, was heavy, and clung close to her head.

Madame Ratignolle, more careful of her complexion, had twined a gauze veil about her head. She wore dogskin gloves, white gauntlets that protected her wrists. She was dressed in pure white, with a fluffiness of ruffles that became her. The draperies and fluttering things which she wore suited her rich, luxuriant beauty as a greater severity of line could not have done.

There were a number of bath-houses along the beach, of rough but solid construction, built with small, protecting galleries facing the water. Each house consisted of two compartments, and each family at Lebrun's possessed a compartment for itself, fitted out with all the essential paraphernalia of the bath and whatever other conveniences the owners might desire. The two women had no intention of bathing; they had just strolled down to the beach for a walk and to be alone and near the water. The Pontellier and Ratignolle compartments adjoined one another under the same roof.

Mrs. Pontellier had brought down her key through force of habit. Unlocking the door of her bath-room she went inside, and soon emerged, bringing a rug,[5] which she spread upon the floor of the gallery, and two huge hair pillows covered with crash,[6] which she placed against the front of the building.

The two seated themselves there in the shade of the porch, side by side, with their backs against the pillows and their feet extended. Madame Ratignolle removed her veil, wiped her face with a rather delicate handkerchief, and fanned herself with the fan which she always carried suspended somewhere about her person by a long, narrow ribbon. Edna removed her collar and opened her dress at the th oat. She took the fan from Madame Ratignolle and began to fan both herself and her companion. It was very warm, and for a while they did nothing but exchange remarks about the heat, the sun, the glare. But there was a breeze blowing, a choppy stiff wind that whipped the water into froth. It fluttered the skirts of the two women and kept them for a while engaged in adjusting, readjusting, tucking in, securing hair-pins and hat-pins. A few persons were sporting some distance away in the water. The beach was very still of human sound at that hour. The lady in black was reading her morning devotions on the porch of a neighboring bath-house. Two

5. Blanket.   6. Heavy linen fabric.

young lovers were exchanging their hearts' yearnings beneath the children's tent, which they had found unoccupied.

Edna Pontellier, casting her eyes about had finally kept them at rest upon the sea. The day was clear and carried the gaze out as far as the blue sky went; there were a few white clouds suspended idly over the horizon. A lateen[7] sail was visible in the direction of Cat Island, and others to the south seemed almost motionless in the far distance.

"Of whom—of what are you thinking?" asked Adèle of her companion, whose countenance she had been watching with a little amused attention, arrested by the absorbed expresson which seemed to have seized and fixed every feature into a statuesque repose.

"Nothing," returned Mrs. Pontellier, with a start, adding at once: "How stupid! But it seems to me it is the reply we make instinctively to such a question. Let me see," she went on, throwing back her head and narrowing her fine eyes till they shone like two vivid points of light. "Let me see. I was really not conscious of thinking of anything; but perhaps I can retrace my thoughts."

"Oh! never mind!" laughed Madame Ratignolle. "I am not quite so exacting. I will let you off this time. It is really too hot to think, especially to think about thinking."

"But for the fun of it," persisted Edna. "First of all, the sight of the water stretching so far away, those motionless sails against the blue sky, made a delicious picture that I just wanted to sit and look at. The hot wind beating in my face made me think—without any connection that I can trace—of a summer day in Kentucky, of a meadow that seemed as big as the ocean to the very little girl walking through the grass, which was higher than her waist. She threw out her arms as if swimming when she walked, beating the tall grass as one strikes out in the water. Oh, I see the connection now!"

"Where were you going that day in Kentucky, walking through the grass?"

"I don't remember now. I was just walking diagonally across a big field. My sun-bonnet obstructed the view. I could see only the stretch of green before me, and I felt as if I must walk on forever, without coming to the end of it. I don't remember whether I was frightened or pleased. I must have been entertained.

"Likely as not it was Sunday," she laughed; "and I was running away from prayers, from the Presbyterian service, read in a spirit of gloom by my father that chills me yet to think of."

"And have you been running away from prayers ever since, *ma chère?*" asked Madame Ratignolle, amused.

"No! oh, no!" Edna hastened to say. "I was a little unthinking child in those days, just following a misleading impulse without question. On the contrary, during one period of my life religion

7. Triangular sail extended by a long spar that is slung to a usually low mast.

took a firm hold upon me; after I was twelve and until—until—
why, I suppose until now, though I never thought much about it—
just driven along by habit. But do you know," she broke off, turning
her quick eyes upon Madame Ratignolle and leaning forward a little
so as to bring her face quite close to that of her companion, "sometimes I feel this summer as if I were walking through the green
meadow again; idly, aimlessly, unthinking and unguided."

Madame Ratignolle laid her hand over that of Mrs. Pontellier,
which was near her. Seeing that the hand was not withdrawn, she
clapsed it firmly and warmly. She even stroked it a little, fondly,
with the other hand, murmuring in an undertone, "*Pauvre chérie.*"[8]

The action was at first a little confusing to Edna, but she soon
lent herself readily to the Creole's gentle caress. She was not accustomed to an outward and spoken expression of affection, either in
herself or in others. She and her younger sister, Janet, had quarreled a good deal through force of unfortunate habit. Her older sister, Margaret, was matronly and dignified, probably from having
assumed matronly and house-wifely responsibilities too early in life,
their mother having died when they were quite young. Margaret
was not effusive; she was practical. Edna had had an occasional girl
friend, but whether accidentally or not, they seemed to have been
all of one type—the self-contained. She never realized that the
reserve of her own character had much, perhaps everything, to do
with this. Her most intimate friend at school had been one ʻof
rather exceptional intellectual gifts, who wrote fine-sounding essays,
which Edna admired and strove to imitate; and with her she talked
and glowed over the English classics, and sometimes held religious
and political controversies.

Edna often wondered at one propensity which sometimes had
inwardly disturbed her without causing any outward show or manifestation on her part. At a very early age—perhaps it was when she
traversed the ocean of waving grass—she remembered that she had
been passionately enamored of a dignified and sad-eyed cavalry
officer who visited her father in Kentucky. She could not leave his
presence when he was there, nor remove her eyes from his face,
which was something like Napoleon's, with a lock of black hair falling across the forehead. But the cavalry officer melted imperceptibly
out of her existence.

At another time her affections were deeply engaged by a young
gentleman who visited a lady on a neighboring plantation. It was
after they went to Mississippi to live. The young man was engaged
to be married to the young lady, and they sometimes called upon
Margaret, driving over of afternoons in a buggy. Edna was a little
miss, just merging into her teens; and the realization that she herself was nothing, nothing, nothing to the engaged young man was a
bitter affliction to her. But he, too, went the way of dreams.

8. "Poor dear."

She was a grown young woman when she was overtaken by what she supposed to be the climax of her fate. It was when the face and figure of a great tragedian[9] began to haunt her imagination and stir her senses. The persistence of the infatuation lent it an aspect of genuineness. The hopelessness of it colored it with the lofty tones of a great passion.

The picture of the tragedian stood enframed upon her desk. Any one may possess the portrait of a tragedian without exciting suspicion or comment. (This was a sinister reflection which she cherished.) In the presence of others she expressed admiration for his exalted gifts, as she handed the photograph around and dwelt upon the fidelity of the likeness. When alone she sometimes picked it up and kissed the cold glass passionately.

Her marriage to Léonce Pontellier was purely an accident, in this respect resembling many other marriages which masquerade as the decrees of Fate. It was in the midst of her secret great passion that she met him. He fell in love, as men are in the habit of doing, and pressed his suit with an earnestness and an ardor which left nothing to be desired. He pleased her; his absolute devotion flattered her. She fancied there was a sympathy of thought and taste between them, in which fancy she was mistaken. Add to this the violent opposition of her father and her sister Margaret to her marriage with a Catholic, and we need seek no further for the motives which led her to accept Monsieur Pontellier for her husband.

The acme of bliss, which would have been a marriage with the tragedian, was not for her in this world. As the devoted wife of a man who worshiped her, she felt she would take her place with a certain dignity in the world of reality, closing the portals forever behind her upon the realm of romance and dreams.

But it was not long before the tragedian had gone to join the cavalry officer and the engaged young man and a few others; and Edna found herself face to face with the realities. She grew fond of her husband, realizing with some unaccountable satisfaction that no trace of passion or excessive and fictitious warmth colored her affection, thereby threatening its dissolution.

She was fond of her children in an uneven, impulsive way. She would sometimes gather them passionately to her heart; she would sometimes forget them. The year before they had spent part of the summer with their grandmother Pontellier in Iberville. Feeling secure regarding their happiness and welfare, she did not miss them except with an occasional intense longing. Their absence was a sort of relief, though she did not admit this, even to herself. It seemed to free her of a responsibility which she had blindly assumed and for which Fate had not fitted her.

Edna did not reveal so much as all this to Madame Ratignolle

---

9. Probably Edwin Booth (1833–93), the Shakespearean actor particularly acclaimed for his Hamlet.

that summer day when they sat with faces turned to the sea. But a good part of it escaped her. She had put her head down on Madame Ratignolle's shoulder. She was flushed and felt intoxicated with the sound of her own voice and the unaccustomed taste of candor. It muddled her like wine, or like a first breath of freedom.

There was the sound of approaching voices. It was Robert, surrounded by a troop of children, searching for them. The two little Pontelliers were with him, and he carried Madame Ratignolle's little girl in his arms. There were other children beside, and two nursemaids followed, looking disagreeable and resigned.

The women at once rose and began to shake out their draperies and relax their muscles. Mrs. Pontellier threw the cushions and rug into the bath-house. The children all scampered off to the awning, and they stood there in a line, gazing upon the intruding lovers, still exchanging their vows and sighs. The lovers got up, with only a silent protest, and walked slowly away somewhere else.

The children possessed themselves of the tent, and Mrs. Pontellier went over to join them.

Madame Ratignolle begged Robert to accompany her to the house; she complained of cramp in her limbs and stiffness of the joints. She leaned draggingly upon his arm as they walked.

VIII

"Do me a favor, Robert," spoke the pretty woman at his side, almost as soon as she and Robert had started on their slow, homeward way. She looked up in his face, leaning on his arm beneath the encircling shadow of the umbrella which he had lifted.

"Granted; as many as you like," he returned, glancing down into her eyes that were full of thoughtfulness and some speculation.

"I only ask for one; let Mrs. Pontellier alone."

"*Tiens!*" he exclaimed, with a sudden, boyish laugh. "*Voilà que Madame Ratignolle est jalouse!*"[1]

"Nonsense! I'm in earnest; I mean what I say. Let Mrs. Pontellier alone."

"Why?" he asked; himself growing serious at his companion's solicitation.

"She is not one of us; she is not like us. She might make the unfortunate blunder of taking you seriously."

His face flushed with annoyance, and taking off his soft hat he began to beat it impatiently against his leg as he walked. "Why shouldn't she take me seriously?" he demanded sharply. "Am I a comedian, a clown, a jack-in-the-box? Why shouldn't she? You Creoles! I have no patience with you! Am I always to be regarded as a feature of an amusing programme? I hope Mrs. Pontellier does take me seriously. I hope she has discernment enough to find in me something besides the *blagueur.*[2] If I thought there was any doubt—"

1. "So, Madame Ratignolle is jealous!"   2. "Joker."

"Oh, enough, Robert!" she broke into his heated outburst. "You are not thinking of what you are saying. You speak with about as little reflection as we might expect from one of those children down there playing in the sand. If your attentions to any married women here were ever offered with any intention of being convincing, you would not be the gentleman we all know you to be, and you would be unfit to associate with the wives and daughters of the people who trust you."

Madame Ratignolle had spoken what she believed to be the law and the gospel. The young man shrugged his shoulders impatiently.

"Oh! well! That isn't it," slamming his hat down vehemently upon his head. "You ought to feel that such things are not flattering to say to a fellow."

"Should our whole intercourse consist of an exchange of compliments? *Ma foi!*"[3]

"It isn't pleasant to have a woman tell you—" he went on, unheedingly, but breaking off suddenly: "Now if I were like Arobin —you remember Alcée Arobin and that story of the consul's wife at Biloxi?"[4] And he related the story of Alcée Arobin and the consul's wife; and another about the tenor of the French Opera,[5] who received letters which should never have been written; and still other stories, grave and gay, till Mrs. Pontellier and her possible propensity for taking young men seriously was apparently forgotten.

Madame Ratignolle, when they had regained her cottage, went in to take the hour's rest which she considered helpful. Before leaving her, Robert begged her pardon for the impatience—he called it rudeness—with which he had received her well-meant caution.

"You made one mistake, Adèle," he said, with a light smile; "there is no earthly possibility of Mrs. Pontellier ever taking me seriously. You should have warned me against taking myself seriously. Your advice might then have carried some weight and given me subject for some reflection. *Au revoir*. But you look tired," he added, solicitously. "Would you like a cup of bouillon? Shall I stir you a toddy? Let me mix you a toddy with a drop of Angostura."[6]

She acceded to the suggestion of bouillon, which was grateful and acceptable. He went himself to the kitchen, which was a building apart from the cottages and lying to the rear of the house. And he himself brought her the golden-brown bouillon, in a dainty Sèvres[7] cup, with a flaky cracker or two on the saucer.

She thrust a bare, white arm from the curtain which shielded her open door, and received the cup from his hands. She told him he was a *bon garçon*,[8] and she meant it. Robert thanked her and turned away toward "the house."

3. "For heaven's sake!"
4. A coastal resort town in Mississippi near New Orleans.
5. The French Opera in New Orleans, perhaps the most distinguished opera company in 19th-century America.
6. Aromatic bitters.
7. Fine porcelain made in Sèvres, France.
8. The phrase means both "nice fellow" and "good waiter."

The lovers were just entering the grounds of the *pension*. They were leaning toward each other as the water-oaks bent from the sea. There was not a particle of earth beneath their feet. Their heads might have been turned upside-down, so absolutely did they tread upon blue ether. The lady in black, creeping behind them, looked a trifle paler and more jaded than usual. There was no sign of Mrs. Pontellier and the children. Robert scanned the distance for any such apparition. They would doubtless remain away till the dinner hour. The young man ascended to his mother's room. It was situated at the top of the house, made up of odd angles and a queer, sloping ceiling. Two broad dormer windows looked out toward the Gulf, and as far across it as a man's eye might reach. The furnishings of the room were light, cool, and practical.

Madame Lebrun was busily engaged at the sewing-machine. A little black girl sat on the floor, and with her hands worked the treadle of the machine. The Creole woman does not take any chances which may be avoided of imperiling her health.

Robert went over and seated himself on the broad sill of one of the dormer windows. He took a book from his pocket and began energetically to read it, judging by the precision and frequency with which he turned the leaves. The sewing-machine made a resounding clatter in the room; it was of a ponderous, by-gone make. In the lulls, Robert and his mother exchanged bits of desultory conversation.

"Where is Mrs. Pontellier?"

"Down at the beach with the children."

"I promised to lend her the Goncourt.[9] Don't forget to take it down when you go; it's there on the bookshelf over the small table." Clatter, clatter, clatter, bang! for the next five or eight minutes.

"Where is Victor going with the rockaway?"

"The rockaway? Victor?"

"Yes; down there in front. He seems to be getting ready to drive away somewhere."

"Call him." Clatter, clatter!

Robert uttered a shrill, piercing whistle which might have been heard back at the wharf.

"He won't look up."

Madame Lebrun flew to the window. She called "Victor!" She waved a handkerchief and called again. The young fellow below got into the vehicle and started the horse off at a gallop.

Madame Lebrun went back to the machine, crimson with annoyance. Victor was the younger son and brother—a *tête montée*,[1] with a temper which invited violence and a will which no ax could break.

9. A French novel by Edmond de Goncourt (1822–96).
1. Impulsive character.

"Whenever you say the word I'm ready to thrash any amount of reason into him that he's able to hold."

"If your father had only lived!" Clatter, clatter, clatter, clatter, bang! It was a fixed belief with Madame Lebrun that the conduct of the universe and all things pertaining thereto would have been manifestly of a more intelligent and higher order had not Monsieur Lebrun been removed to other spheres during the early years of their married life.

"What do you hear from Montel?" Montel was a middle-aged gentleman whose vain ambition and desire for the past twenty years had been to fill the void which Monsieur Lebrun's taking off had left in the Lebrun household. Clatter, clatter, bang, clatter!

"I have a letter somewhere," looking in the machine drawer and finding the letter in the bottom of the work-basket. "He says to tell you he will be in Vera Cruz[2] the beginning of next month"—clatter, clatter!—"and if you still have the intention of joining him"—bang! clatter, clatter, bang!

"Why didn't you tell me so before, mother? You know I wanted—" Clatter, clatter, clatter!

"Do you see Mrs. Pontellier starting back with the children? She will be in late to luncheon again. She never starts to get ready for luncheon till the last minute." Clatter, clatter! "Where are you going?"

"Where did you say the Goncourt was?"

IX

Every light in the hall was ablaze; every lamp turned as high as it could be without smoking the chimney or threatening explosion. The lamps were fixed at intervals against the wall, encircling the whole room. Some one had gathered orange and lemon branches and with these fashioned graceful festoons between. The dark green of the branches stood out and glistened against the white muslin curtains which draped the windows, and which puffed, floated, and flapped at the capricious will of a stiff breeze that swept up from the Gulf.

It was Saturday night a few weeks after the intimate conversation held between Robert and Madame Ratignolle on their way from the beach. An unusual number of husbands, fathers, and friends had come down to stay over Sunday; and they were being suitably entertained by their families, with the material help of Madame Lebrun. The dining tables had all been removed to one end of the hall, and the chairs ranged about in rows and in clusters. Each little family group had had its say and exchanged its domestic gossip earlier in the evening. There was now an apparent disposition to relax; to widen the circle of confidences and give a more general tone to the conversation.

2. City in the state of Vera Cruz, Mexico, on the Gulf of Mexico.

Many of the children had been permitted to sit up beyond their usual bedtime. A small band of them were lying on their stomachs on the floor looking at the colored sheets of the comic papers which Mr. Pontellier had brought down. The little Pontellier boys were permitting them to do so, and making their authority felt.

Music, dancing, and a recitation or two were the entertainments furnished, or rather, offered. But there was nothing systematic about the programme, no appearance of prearrangement nor even premeditation.

At an early hour in the evening the Farival twins were prevailed upon to play the piano. They were girls of fourteen, always clad in the Virgin's colors, blue and white, having been dedicated to the Blessed Virgin at their baptism. They played a duet from "Zampa," and at the earnest solicitation of every one present followed it with the overture to "The Poet and the Peasant."

"*Allez vous-en! Sapristi!*" shrieked the parrot outside the door. He was the only being present who possessed sufficient candor to admit that he was not listening to these gracious performances for the first time that summer. Old Monsieur Farival, grandfather of the twins, grew indignant over the interruption, and insisted upon having the bird removed and consigned to regions of darkness. Victor Lebrun objected; and his decrees were as immutable as those of Fate. The parrot fortunately offered no further interruption to the entertainment, the whole venom of his nature apparently having been cherished up and hurled against the twins in that one impetuous outburst.

Later a young brother and sister gave recitations, which every one present had heard many times at winter evening entertainments in the city.

A little girl performed a skirt dance in the center of the floor. The mother played her accompaniments and at the same time watched her daughter with greedy admiration and nervous apprehension. She need have had no apprehension. The child was mistress of the situation. She had been properly dressed for the occasion in black tulle and black silk tights. Her little neck and arms were bare, and her hair, artificially crimped, stood out like fluffy black plumes over her head. Her poses were full of grace, and her little black-shod toes twinkled as they shot out and upward with a rapidity and a suddenness which were bewildering.

But there was no reason why every one should not dance. Madame Ratignolle could not, so it was she who gaily consented to play for the others. She played very well, keeping excellent waltz time and infusing an expression into the strains which was indeed inspiring. She was keeping up her music on account of the children, she said; because she and her husband both considered it a means of brightening the home and making it attractive.

Almost every one danced but the twins, who could not be

induced to separate during the brief period when one or the other should be whirling around the room in the arms of a man. They might have danced together, but they did not think of it.

The children were sent to bed. Some went submissively; others with shrieks and protests as they were dragged away. They had been permitted to sit up till after the ice-cream, which naturally marked the limit of human indulgence.

The ice-cream was passed around with cake—gold and silver cake arranged on platters in alternate slices; it had been made and frozen during the afternoon back of the kitchen by two black women, under the supervision of Victor. It was pronounced a great success —excellent if it had only contained a little less vanilla or a little more sugar, if it had been frozen a degree harder, and if the salt might have been kept out of portions of it. Victor was proud of his achievement, and went about recommending it and urging every one to partake of it to excess.

After Mrs. Pontellier had danced twice with her husband, once with Robert, and once with Monsieur Ratignolle, who was thin and tall and swayed like a reed in the wind when he danced, she went out on the gallery and seated herself on the low window-sill, where she commanded a view of all that went on in the hall and could look out toward the Gulf. There was a soft effulgence in the east. The moon was coming up, and its mystic shimmer was casting a million lights across the distant, restless water.

"Would you like to hear Mademoiselle Reisz play?" asked Robert, coming out on the porch where she was. Of course Edna would like to hear Mademoiselle Reisz play; but she feared it would be useless to entreat her.

"I'll ask her," he said. "I'll tell her that you want to hear her. She likes you. She will come." He turned and hurried away to one of the far cottages, where Mademoiselle Reisz was shuffling away. She was dragging a chair in and out of her room, and at intervals objecting to the crying of a baby, which a nurse in the adjoining cottage was endeavoring to put to sleep. She was a disagreeable little woman, no longer young, who had quarreled with almost every one, owing to a temper which was self-assertive and a disposition to trample upon the rights of others. Robert prevailed upon her without any too great difficulty.

She entered the hall with him during a lull in the dance. She made an awkward, imperious little bow as she went in. She was a homely woman, with a small weazened face and body and eyes that glowed. She had absolutely no taste in dress, and wore a batch of rusty black lace with a bunch of artificial violets pinned to the side of her hair.

"Ask Mrs. Pontellier what she would like to hear me play," she requested of Robert. She sat perfectly still before the piano, not touching the keys, while Robert carried her message to Edna at the window. A general air of surprise and genuine satisfaction fell upon every one as they saw the pianist enter. There was a settling down, and a prevailing air of expectancy everywhere. Edna was a trifle embarrassed at being thus signaled out for the imperious little woman's favor. She would not dare to choose, and begged that Mademoiselle Reisz would please herself in her selections.

Edna was what she herself called very fond of music. Musical strains, well rendered, had a way of evoking pictures in her mind. She sometimes liked to sit in the room of mornings when Madame Ratignolle played or practiced. One piece which that lady played Edna had entitled "Solitude." It was a short, plaintive, minor strain. The name of the piece was something else, but she called it "Solitude." When she heard it there came before her imagination the figure of a man standing beside a desolate rock on the seashore. He was naked. His attitude was one of hopeless resignation as he looked toward a distant bird winging its flight away from him.

Another piece called to her mind a dainty young woman clad in an Empire gown, taking mincing dancing steps as she came down a long avenue between tall hedges. Again, another reminded her of children at play, and still another of nothing on earth but a demure lady stroking a cat.

The very first chords which Mademoiselle Reisz struck upon the piano sent a keen tremor down Mrs. Pontellier's spinal column. It was not the first time she had heard an artist at the piano. Perhaps it was the first time she was ready, perhaps the first time her being was tempered to take an impress of the abiding truth.

She waited for the material pictures which she thought would gather and blaze before her imagination. She waited in vain. She saw no pictures of solitude, of hope, of longing, or of despair. But the very passions themselves were aroused within her soul, swaying it, lashing it, as the waves daily beat upon her splendid body. She trembled, she was choking, and the tears blinded her.

Mademoiselle had finished. She arose, and bowing her stiff, lofty bow, she went away, stopping for neither thanks nor applause. As she passed along the gallery she patted Edna upon the shoulder.

"Well, how did you like my music?" she asked. The young woman was unable to answer; she pressed the hand of the pianist convulsively. Mademoiselle Reisz perceived her agitation and even her tears. She patted her again upon the shoulder as she said:

"You are the only one worth playing for. Those others? Bah!" and she went shuffling and sidling on down the gallery toward her room.

But she was mistaken about "those others." Her playing had aroused a fever of enthusiasm. "What passion!" "What an artist!" "I have always said no one could play Chopin[3] like Mademoiselle

---

3. Frédéric Chopin (1810–49), Polish composer.

Reisz!" "That last prelude! Bon Dieu! It shakes a man!"

It was growing late, and there was a general disposition to disband. But someone, perhaps it was Robert, thought of a bath at that mystic hour and under that mystic moon.

X

At all events Robert proposed it, and there was not a dissenting voice. There was not one but was ready to follow when he led the way. He did not lead the way, however, he directed the way; and he himself loitered behind with the lovers, who had betrayed a disposition to linger and hold themselves apart. He walked between them, whether with malicious or mischievous intent was not wholly clear, even to himself.

The Pontelliers and Ratignolles walked ahead; the women leaning upon the arms of their husbands. Edna could hear Robert's voice behind them, and could sometimes hear what he said. She wondered why he did not join them. It was unlike him not to. Of late he had sometimes held away from her for an entire day, redoubling his devotion upon the next and the next, as though to make up for hours that had been lost. She missed him the days when some pretext served to take him away from her, just as one misses the sun on a cloudy day without having thought much about the sun when it was shining.

The people walked in little groups toward the beach. They talked and laughed; some of them sang. There was a band playing down at Klein's hotel, and the strains reached them faintly, tempered by the distance. There were strange, rare odors abroad—a tangle of the sea smell and of weeds and damp, new-plowed earth, mingled with the heavy perfume of a field of white blossoms somewhere near. But the night sat light upon the sea and the land. There was no weight of darkness; there were no shadows. The white light of the moon had fallen upon the world like the mystery and the softness of sleep.

Most of them walked into the water as though into a native element. The sea was quiet now, and swelled lazily in broad billows that melted into one another and did not break except upon the beach in little foamy crests that coiled back like slow, white serpents.

Edna had attempted all summer to learn to swim. She had received instructions from both the men and women; in some instances from the children. Robert had pursued a system of lessons almost daily; and he was nearly at the point of discouragement in realizing the futility of his efforts. A certain ungovernable dread hung about her when in the water, unless there was a hand near by that might reach out and reassure her.

But that night she was like the little tottering, stumbling, clutching child, who of a sudden realizes its powers, and walks for the first time alone, boldly and with over-confidence. She could have shouted for joy. She did shout for joy, as with a sweeping stroke or two she lifted her body to the surface of the water.

A feeling of exultation overtook her, as if some power of significant import had been given her soul. She grew daring and reckless, overestimating her strength. She wanted to swim far out, where no woman had swum before.

Her unlooked-for achievement was the subject of wonder, applause, and admiration. Each one congratulated himself that his special teachings had accomplished this desired end.

"How easy it is!" she thought. "It is nothing," she said aloud; "why did I not discover before that it was nothing. Think of the time I have lost splashing about like a baby!" She would not join the groups in their sports and bouts, but intoxicated with her newly conquered power, she swam out alone.

She turned her face seaward to gather in an impression of space and solitude, which the vast expanse of water, meeting and melting with moonlit sky, conveyed to her excited fancy. As she swam she seemed to be reaching out for the unlimited in which to lose herself.

Once she turned and looked toward the shore, toward the people she had left there. She had not gone any great distance— that is, what would have been great distance for an experienced swimmer. But to her unaccustomed vision the stretch of water behind her assumed the aspect of a barrier which her unaided strength would never be able to overcome.

A quick vision of death smote her soul, and for a second of time appalled and enfeebled her senses. But by an effort she rallied her staggering faculties and managed to regain the land.

She made no mention of her encounter with death and her flash of terror, except to say to her husband, "I thought I should have perished out there alone."

"You were not so very far, my dear; I was watching you," he told her.

Edna went at once to the bath-house, and she had put on her dry clothes and was ready to return home before the others had left the water. She started to walk away alone. They all called to her and shouted to her. She waved a dissenting hand, and went on, paying no further heed to their renewed cries which sought to detain her.

"Sometimes I am tempted to think that Mrs. Pontellier is capricious," said Madame Lebrun, who was amusing herself immensely and feared that Edna's abrupt departure might put an end to the pleasure.

"I know she is," assented Mr. Pontellier; "sometimes, not often."

Edna had not traversed a quarter of the distance on her way home before she was overtaken by Robert.

"Did you think I was afraid?" she asked him, without a shade of annoyance.

"No; I knew you weren't afraid."

"Then why did you come? Why didn't you stay out there with the others?"

"I never thought of it."

"Thought of what?"

"Of anything. What difference does it make?"

"I'm very tired," she uttered, complainingly.

"I know you are."

"You don't know anything about it. Why should you know? I never was so exhausted in my life. But it isn't unpleasant. A thousand emotions have swept through me to-night. I don't comprehend half of them. Don't mind what I'm saying; I am just thinking aloud. I wonder if I shall ever be stirred again as Mademoiselle Reisz's playing moved me to-night. I wonder if any night on earth will ever again be like this one. It is like a night in a dream. The people about me are like some uncanny, half-human beings. There must be spirits abroad to-night."

"There are," whispered Robert. "Didn't you know this was the twenty-eighth of August?"

"The twenty-eighth of August?"

"Yes. On the twenty-eighth of August, at the hour of midnight, and if the moon is shining—the moon must be shining—a spirit that has haunted these shores for ages rises up from the Gulf. With its own penetrating vision the spirit seeks some one mortal worthy to hold him company, worthy of being exalted for a few hours into realms of the semi-celestials. His search has always hitherto been fruitless, and he has sunk back, disheartened, into the sea. But to-night he found Mrs. Pontellier. Perhaps he will never wholly release her from the spell. Perhaps she will never again suffer a poor, unworthy earthling to walk in the shadow of her divine presence."

"Don't banter me," she said, wounded at what appeared to be his flippancy. He did not mind the entreaty, but the tone with its delicate note of pathos was like a reproach. He could not explain; he could not tell her that he had penetrated her mood and understood. He said nothing except to offer her his arm, for, by her own admission, she was exhausted. She had been walking alone with her arms hanging limp, letting her white skirts trail along the dewy path. She took his arm, but she did not lean upon it. She let her hand lie listlessly, as though her thoughts were elsewhere—somewhere in advance of her body, and she was striving to overtake them.

Robert assisted her into the hammock which swung from the post before her door out to the trunk of a tree.

"Will you stay out here and wait for Mr. Pontellier?" he asked.

"I'll stay out here. Good-night."

"Shall I get you a pillow?"

"There's one here," she said, feeling about, for they were in the shadow.

"It must be soiled; the children have been tumbling it about."

"No matter." And having discovered the pillow, she adjusted it beneath her head. She extended herself in the hammock with a deep breath of relief. She was not a supercilious or an over-dainty woman. She was not much given to reclining in the hammock, and when she did so it was with no cat-like suggestion of voluptuous ease, but with a beneficent repose which seemed to invade her whole body.

"Shall I stay with you till Mr. Pontellier comes?" asked Robert, seating himself on the outer edge of one of the steps and taking hold of the hammock rope which was fastened to the post.

"If you wish. Don't swing the hammock. Will you get my white shawl which I left on the window-sill over at the house?"

"Are you chilly?"

"No; but I shall be presently."

"Presently?" he laughed. "Do you know what time it is? How long are you going to stay out here?"

"I don't know. Will you get the shawl?"

"Of course I will," he said, rising. He went over to the house, walking along the grass. She watched his figure pass in and out of the strips of moonlight. It was past midnight. It was very quiet.

When he returned with the shawl she took it and kept it in her hand. She did not put it around her.

"Did you say I should stay till Mr. Pontellier came back?"

"I said you might if you wished to."

He seated himself again and rolled a cigarette, which he smoked in silence. Neither did Mrs. Pontellier speak. No multitude of words could have been more significant than those moments of silence, or more pregnant with the first-felt throbbings of desire.

When the voices of the bathers were heard approaching, Robert said good-night. She did not answer him. He thought she was asleep. Again she watched his figure pass in and out of the strips of moonlight as he walked away.

XI

"What are you doing out here, Edna? I thought I should find you in bed," said her husband, when he discovered her lying there. He had walked up with Madame Lebrun and left her at the house. His wife did not reply.

"Are you asleep?" he asked, bending down close to look at her.

"No." Her eyes gleamed bright and intense, with no sleepy shadows, as they looked into his.

"Do you know it is past one o'clock? Come on," and he mounted the steps and went into their room.

"Edna!" called Mr. Pontellier from within, after a few moments had gone by.

"Don't wait for me," she answered. He thrust his head through the door.

"You will take cold out there," he said, irritably. "What folly is this? Why don't you come in?"

"It isn't cold; I have my shawl."

"The mosquitoes will devour you."

"There are no mosquitoes."

She heard him moving about the room; every sound indicating impatience and irritation. Another time she would have gone in at his request. She would, through habit, have yielded to his desire; not with any sense of submission or obedience to his compelling wishes, but unthinkingly, as we walk, move, sit, stand, go through the daily treadmill of the life which has been portioned out to us.

"Edna, dear, are you not coming in soon?" he asked again, this time fondly, with a note of entreaty.

"No; I am going to stay out here."

"This is more than folly," he blurted out. "I can't permit you to stay out there all night. You must come in the house instantly."

With a writhing motion she settled herself more securely in the hammock. She perceived that her will had blazed up, stubborn and resistant. She could not at that moment have done other than denied and resisted. She wondered if her husband had ever spoken to her like that before, and if she had submitted to his command. Of course she had; she remembered that she had. But she could not realize why or how she should have yielded, feeling as she then did.

"Léonce, go to bed," she said. "I mean to stay out here. I don't wish to go in, and I don't intend to. Don't speak to me like that again; I shall not answer you."

Mr. Pontellier had prepared for bed, but he slipped on an extra garment. He opened a bottle of wine, of which he kept a small and select supply in a buffet of his own. He drank a glass of the wine and went out on the gallery and offered a glass to his wife. She did not wish any. He drew up the rocker, hoisted his slippered feet on the rail, and proceeded to smoke a cigar. He smoked two cigars; then he went inside and drank another glass of wine. Mrs. Pontellier again declined to accept a glass when it was offered to her. Mr. Pontellier once more seated himself with elevated feet, and after a reasonable interval of time smoked some more cigars.

Edna began to feel like one who awakens gradually out of a dream, a delicious, grotesque, impossible dream, to feel again the realities pressing into her soul. The physical need for sleep began to overtake her; the exuberance which had sustained and exalted her spirit left her helpless and yielding to the conditions which crowded her in.

The stillest hour of the night had come, the hour before dawn, when the world seems to hold its breath. The moon hung low, and had turned from silver to copper in the sleeping sky. The old owl no longer hooted, and the water-oaks had ceased to moan as they bent their heads.

Edna arose, cramped from lying so long and still in the hammock. She tottered up the steps, clutching feebly at the post before passing into the house.

"Are you coming in, Léonce?" she asked, turning her face toward her husband.

"Yes, dear," he answered, with a glance following a misty puff of smoke. "Just as soon as I have finished my cigar."

XII

She slept but a few hours. They were troubled and feverish hours, disturbed with dreams that were intangible, that eluded her, leaving only an impression upon her half-awakened senses of something unattainable. She was up and dressed in the cool of the early morning. The air was invigorating and steadied somewhat her faculties. However, she was not seeking refreshment or help from any source, either external or from within. She was blindly following whatever impulse moved her, as if she had placed herself in alien hands for direction, and freed her soul of responsibility.

Most of the people at that early hour were still in bed and asleep. A few, who intended to go over to the *Chênière* for mass, were moving about. The lovers, who had laid their plans the night before, were already strolling toward the wharf. The lady in black, with her Sunday prayer book, velvet and gold-clasped, and her Sunday silver beads, was following them at no great distance. Old Monsieur Farival was up, and was more than half inclined to do anything that suggested itself. He put on his big straw hat, and taking his umbrella from the stand in the hall, followed the lady in black, never overtaking her.

The little negro girl who worked Madame Lebrun's sewing-machine was sweeping the galleries with long, absent-minded strokes of the broom. Edna sent her up into the house to awaken Robert.

"Tell him I am going to the *Chênière*. The boat is ready; tell him to hurry."

He had soon joined her. She had never sent for him before. She had never asked for him. She had never seemed to want him before. She did not appear conscious that she had done anything unusual in commanding his presence. He was apparently equally unconscious of anything extraordinary in the situation. But his face was suffused with a quiet glow when he met her.

They went together back to the kitchen to drink coffee. There was no time to wait for any nicety of service. They stood outside the window and the cook passed them their coffee and a roll, which they drank and ate from the window-sill. Edna said it tasted good.

She had not thought of coffee nor of anything. He told her he had often noticed that she lacked forethought.

"Wasn't it enough to think of going to the *Chênière* and waking you up?" she laughed. "Do I have to think of everything?—as Léonce says when he's in a bad humor. I don't blame him; he'd never be in a bad humor if it weren't for me."

They took a short cut across the sands. At a distance they could see the curious procession moving toward the wharf—the lovers, shoulder to shoulder, creeping; the lady in black, gaining steadily upon them; old Monsieur Farival, losing ground inch by inch, and a young barefooted Spanish girl, with a red kerchief on her head and a basket on her arm, bringing up the rear.

Robert knew the girl, and he talked to her a little in the boat. No one present understood what they said. Her name was Mariequita. She had a round, sly, piquant face and pretty black eyes. Her hands were small, and kept them folded over the handle of her basket. Her feet were broad and coarse. She did not strive to hide them. Edna looked at her feet, and noticed the sand and slime between her brown toes.

Beaudelet grumbled because Mariequita was there, taking up so much room. In reality he was annoyed at having old Monsieur Farival, who considered himself the better sailor of the two. But he would not quarrel with so old a man as Monsieur Farival, so he quarreled with Mariequita. The girl was deprecatory at one moment, appealing to Robert. She was saucy the next, moving her head up and down, making "eyes" at Robert and making "mouths" at Beaudelet.

The lovers were all alone. They saw nothing, they heard nothing. The lady in black was counting her beads for the third time. Old Monsieur Farival talked incessantly of what he knew about handling a boat, and of what Beaudelet did not know on the same subject.

Edna liked it all. She looked Mariequita up and down, from her ugly brown toes to her pretty black eyes, and back again.

"Why does she look at me like that?" inquired the girl of Robert.

"Maybe she thinks you are pretty. Shall I ask her?"

"No. Is she your sweetheart?"

"She's a married lady, and has two children."

"Oh! well! Francisco ran away with Sylvano's wife, who had four children. They took all his money and one of the children and stole his boat."

"Shut up!"

"Does she understand?"

"Oh, hush!"

"Are those two married over there—leaning on each other?"

"Of course not," laughed Robert.

"Of course not," echoed Mariequita, with a serious, confirmatory bob of the head.

The sun was high up and beginning to bite. The swift breeze seemed to Edna to bury the sting of it into the pores of her face and hands. Robert held his umbrella over her.

As they went cutting sidewise through the water, the sails bellied taut, with the wind filling and overflowing them. Old Monsieur Farival laughed sardonically at something as he looked at the sails, and Beaudelet swore at the old man under his breath.

Sailing across the bay to the *Chênière Caminada*, Edna felt as if she were being borne away from some anchorage which had held her fast, whose chains had been loosening—had snapped the night before when the mystic spirit was abroad, leaving her free to drift whithersoever she chose to set her sails. Robert spoke to her incessantly; he no longer noticed Mariequita. The girl had shrimps in her bamboo basket. They were covered with Spanish moss. She beat the moss impatiently, and muttered to herself sullenly.

"Let us go to Grande Terre[4] to-morrow?" said Robert in a low voice.

"What shall we do there?"

"Climb up the hill to the old fort and look at the little wriggling gold snakes, and watch the lizards sun themselves."

She gazed away toward Grande Terre and thought she would like to be alone there with Robert, in the sun, listening to the ocean's roar and watching the slimy lizards writhe in and out among the ruins of the old fort.

"And the next day or the next we can sail to the Bayou Brulow,"[5] he went on.

"What shall we do there?"

"Anything—cast bait for fish."

"No; we'll go back to Grande Terre. Let the fish alone."

"We'll go wherever you like," he said. "I'll have Tonie come over and help me patch and trim my boat. We shall not need Beaudelet nor any one. Are you afraid of the pirogue?"[6]

"Oh, no."

"Then I'll take you some night in the pirogue when the moon shines. Maybe your Gulf spirit will whisper to you in which of these islands the treasures are hidden—direct you to the very spot, perhaps."

"And in a day we should be rich!" she laughed. "I'd give it all to you, the pirate gold and every bit of treasure we could dig up. I think you would know how to spend it. Pirate gold isn't a thing to be hoarded or utilized. It is something to squander and throw to the four winds, for the fun of seeing the golden specks fly."

"We'd share it, and scatter it together," he said. His face flushed.

---

4. An island adjacent to Grande Isle.
5. Bayou Brulow (or Bruleau) was the nearest to Grande Isle of a series of villages built on stilts or platforms in large marshy areas called "bayous." Inhabited by Acadians, descendants of French-Canadians, expelled from Nova Scotia in 1755.
6. Canoe.

They all went together up to the quaint little Gothic church of Our Lady of Lourdes, gleaming all brown and yellow with paint in the sun's glare.

Only Beaudelet remained behind, tinkering at his boat, and Mariequita walked away with her basket of shrimps, casting a look of childish ill-humor and reproach at Robert from the corner of her eye.

XIII

A feeling of oppression and drowsiness overcame Edna during the service. Her head began to ache, and the lights on the altar swayed before her eyes. Another time she might have made an effort to regain her composure; but her one thought was to quit the stifling atmosphere of the church and reach the open air. She arose, climbing over Robert's feet with a muttered apology. Old Monsieur Farival, flurried, curious, stood up, but upon seeing that Robert had followed Mrs. Pontellier, he sank back into his seat. He whispered an anxious inquiry of the lady in black, who did not notice him or reply, but kept her eyes fastened upon the pages of her velvet prayer-book.

"I felt giddy and almost overcome," Edna said, lifting her hands instinctively to her head and pushing her straw hat up from her forehead. "I couldn't have stayed through the service." They were outside in the shadow of the church. Robert was full of solicitude.

"It was folly to have thought of going in the first place, let alone staying. Come over to Madame Antoine's; you can rest there." He took her arm and led her away, looking anxiously and continuously down into her face.

How still it was, with only the voice of the sea whispering through the reeds that grew in the salt-water pools! The long line of little gray, weather-beaten houses nestled peacefully among the orange trees. It must always have been God's day on that low, drowsy island, Edna thought. They stopped, leaning over a jagged fence made of sea-drift, to ask for water. A youth, a mild-faced Acadian, was drawing water from the cistern, which was nothing more than a rusty buoy, with an opening on one side, sunk in the ground. The water which the youth handed to them in a tin pail was not cold to taste, but it was cool to her heated face, and it greatly revived and refreshed her.

Madame Antoine's cot[7] was at the far end of the village. She welcomed them with all the native hospitality, as she would have opened her door to let the sunlight in. She was fat, and walked heavily and clumsily across the floor. She could speak no English, but when Robert made her understand that the lady who accompanied him was ill and desired to rest, she was all eagerness to make Edna feel at home and to dispose of her comfortably.

7. Cottage.

The whole place was immaculately clean, and the big, four-posted bed, snow-white, invited one to repose. It stood in a small side room which looked out across a narrow grass plot toward the shed, where there was a disabled boat lying keel upward.

Madame Antoine had not gone to mass. Her son Tonie had, but she supposed he would soon be back, and she invited Robert to be seated and wait for him. But he went and sat outside the door and smoked. Madame Antoine busied herself in the large front room preparing dinner. She was boiling mullets[8] over a few red coals in the huge fireplace.

Edna, left alone in the little side room, loosened her clothes, removing the greater part of them. She bathed her face, her neck and arms in the basin that stood between the windows. She took off her shoes and stockings and stretched herself in the very center of the high, white bed. How luxurious it felt to rest thus in a strange, quaint bed, with its sweet country odor of laurel lingering about the sheets and mattress! She stretched her strong limbs that ached a little. She ran her fingers through her loosened hair for a while. She looked at her round arms as she held them straight up and rubbed them one after the other, observing closely, as if it were something she saw for the first time, the fine, firm quality and texture of her flesh. She clasped her hands easily above her head, and it was thus she fell asleep.

She slept lightly at first, half awake and drowsily attentive to the things about her. She could hear Madame Antoine's heavy, scraping tread as she walked back and forth on the sanded floor. Some chickens were clucking outside the windows, scratching for bits of gravel in the grass. Later she half heard the voices of Robert and Tonie talking under the shed. She did not stir. Even her eyelids rested numb and heavily over her sleepy eyes. The voices went on— Tonie's slow, Acadian drawl, Robert's quick, soft, smooth French. She understood French imperfectly unless directly addressed, and the voices were only part of the other drowsy, muffled sounds lulling her.

When Edna awoke it was with the conviction that she had slept long and soundly. The voices were hushed under the shed. Madame Antoine's step was no longer to be heard in the adjoining room. Even the chickens had gone elsewhere to scratch and cluck. The mosquito bar was drawn over her; the old woman had come in while she slept and let down the bar. Edna arose quietly from the bed, and looking between the curtains of the window, she saw by the slanting rays of the sun that the afternoon was far advanced. Robert was out there under the shed, reclining in the shade against the sloping keel of the overturned boat. He was reading from a book. Tonie was no longer with him. She wondered what had

8. Small fish.

become of the rest of the party. She peeped out at him two or three times as she stood washing herself in the little basin between the windows.

Madame Antoine had laid some coarse, clean towels upon a chair, and had placed a box of *poudre de riz*[9] within easy reach. Edna dabbed the powder upon her nose and cheeks as she looked at herself closely in the little distorted mirror which hung on the wall above the basin. Her eyes were bright and wide awake and her face glowed.

When she had completed her toilet she walked into the adjoining room. She was very hungry. No one was there. But there was a cloth spread upon the table that stood against the wall, and a cover was laid for one, with a crusty brown loaf and a bottle of wine beside the plate. Edna bit a piece from the brown loaf, tearing it with her strong, white teeth. She poured some of the wine into the glass and drank it down. Then she went softly out of doors, and plucking an orange from the low-hanging bough of a tree, threw it at Robert, who did not know she was awake and up.

An illumination broke over his whole face when he saw her and joined her under the orange tree.

"How many years have I slept?" she inquired. "The whole island seems changed. A new race of beings must have sprung up, leaving only you and me as past relics. How many ages ago did Madame Antoine and Tonie die? and when did our people from Grand Isle disappear from the earth?"

He familiarly adjusted a ruffle upon her shoulder.

"You have slept precisely one hundred years. I was left here to guard your slumbers; and for one hundred years I have been out under the shed reading a book. The only evil I couldn't prevent was to keep a broiled fowl from drying up."

"If it had turned to stone, still will I eat it," said Edna, moving with him into the house. "But really, what has become of Monsieur Farival and the others?"

"Gone hours ago. When they found that you were sleeping they thought it best not to awake you. Any way, I wouldn't have let them. What was I here for?"

"I wonder if Léonce will be uneasy!" she speculated, as she seated herself at table.

"Of course not; he knows you are with me," Robert replied, as he busied himself among sundry pans and covered dishes which had been left standing on the hearth.

"Where are Madame Antoine and her son?" asked Edna.

"Gone to Vespers,[1] and to visit some friends, I believe. I am to take you back in Tonie's boat whenever you are ready to go."

He stirred the smoldering ashes till the broiled fowl began to

9. Talcum powder.   1. Evening church service.

sizzle afresh. He served her with no mean repast, dripping the coffee anew and sharing it with her. Madame Antoine had cooked little else than the mullets, but while Edna slept Robert had foraged the island. He was childishly gratified to discover her appetite, and to see the relish with which she ate the food which he had procured for her.

"Shall we go right away?" she asked, after draining her glass and brushing together the crumbs of the crusty loaf.

"The sun isn't as low as it will be in two hours," he answered.

"The sun will be gone in two hours."

"Well, let it go; who cares!"

They waited a good while under the orange trees, till Madame Antoine came back, panting, waddling, with a thousand apologies to explain her absence. Tonie did not dare to return. He was shy, and would not willingly face any woman except his mother.

It was very pleasant to stay there under the orange trees, while the sun dipped lower and lower, turning the western sky to flaming copper and gold. The shadows lengthened and crept out like stealthy, grotesque monsters across the grass.

Edna and Robert both sat upon the ground—that is, he lay upon the ground beside her, occasionally picking at the hem of her muslin gown.

Madame Antoine seated her fat body, broad and squat, upon a bench beside the door. She had been talking all the afternoon, and had wound herself up to the story-telling pitch.

And what stories she told them! But twice in her life she had left the *Chênière Caminada*, and then for the briefest span. All her years she had squatted and waddled there upon the island, gathering legends of the Baratarians[2] and the sea. The night came on, with the moon to lighten it. Edna could hear the whispering voices of dead men and the click of muffled gold.

When she and Robert stepped into Tonie's boat, with the red lateen sail, misty spirit forms were prowling in the shadows and among the reeds, and upon the water were phantom ships, speeding to cover.

XIV

The youngest boy, Etienne, had been very naughty, Madame Ratignolle said, as she delivered him into the hands of his mother. He had been unwilling to go to bed and had made a scene; whereupon she had taken charge of him and pacified him as well as she could. Raoul had been in bed and asleep for two hours.

The youngster was in his long white nightgown, that kept tripping him up as Madame Ratignolle led him along by the hand.

2. Pirates, most notably the legendary Jean Lafitte, who operated in the area of Barataria Bay.

With the other chubby fist he rubbed his eyes, which were heavy with sleep and ill humor. Edna took him in her arms, and seating herself in the rocker, began to coddle and caress him, calling him all manner of tender names, soothing him to sleep.

It was not more than nine o'clock. No one had yet gone to bed but the children.

Léonce had been very uneasy at first, Madame Ratignolle said, and had wanted to start at once for the *Chênière*. But Monsieur Farival had assured him that his wife was only overcome with sleep and fatigue, that Tonie would bring her safely back later in the day; and he had thus been dissuaded from crossing the bay. He had gone over to Klein's, looking up some cotton broker whom he wished to see in regard to securities, exchanges, stocks, bonds, or something of the sort, Madame Ratignolle did not remember what. He said he would not remain away late. She herself was suffering from heat and oppression, she said. She carried a bottle of salts and a large fan. She would not consent to remain with Edna, for Monsieur Ratignolle was alone, and he detested above all things to be left alone.

When Etienne had fallen asleep Edna bore him into the back room, and Robert went and lifted the mosquito bar that she might lay the child comfortably in his bed. The quadroon had vanished. When they emerged from the cottage Robert bade Edna good-night.

"Do you know we have been together the whole livelong day, Robert—since early this morning?" she said at parting.

"All but the hundred years when you were sleeping. Good-night."

He pressed her hand and went away in the direction of the beach. He did not join any of the others, but walked alone toward the Gulf.

Edna stayed outside, awaiting her husband's return. She had no desire to sleep or to retire; nor did she feel like going over to sit with the Ratignolles, or to join Madame Lebrun and a group whose animated voices reached her as they sat in conversation before the house. She let her mind wander back over her stay at Grand Isle; and she tried to discover wherein this summer had been different from any and every other summer of her life. She could only realize that she herself—her present self—was in some way different from the other self. That she was seeing with different eyes and making the acquaintance of new conditions in herself that colored and changed her environment, she did not yet suspect.

She wondered why Robert had gone away and left her. It did not occur to her to think he might have grown tired of being with her the livelong day. She was not tired, and she felt that he was not. She regretted that he had gone. It was so much more natural to have him stay, when he was not absolutely required to leave her.

As Edna waited for her husband she sang low a little song that

Robert had sung as they crossed the bay. It began with "Ah! *Si tu savais*," and every verse ended with "*si tu savais*."[3]

Robert's voice was not pretentious. It was musical and true. The voice, the notes, the whole refrain haunted her memory.

XV

When Edna entered the dining-room one evening a little late, as was her habit, an unusually animated conversation seemed to be going on. Several persons were talking at once, and Victor's voice was predominating, even over that of his mother. Edna had returned late from her bath, had dressed in some haste, and her face was flushed. Her head, set off by the dainty white gown, suggested a rich, rare blossom. She took her seat at table between old Monsieur Farival and Madame Ratignolle.

As she seated herself and was about to begin to eat her soup, which had been served when she entered the room, several persons informed her simultaneously that Robert was going to Mexico. She laid her spoon down and looked about her bewildered. He had been with her, reading to her all the morning, and had never even mentioned such a place as Mexico. She had not seen him during the afternoon; she had heard some one say he was at the house, upstairs with his mother. This she had thought nothing of, though she was surprised when he did not join her later in the afternoon, when she went down to the beach.

She looked across at him, where he sat beside Madame Lebrun, who presided. Edna's face was a blank picture of bewilderment, which she never thought of disguising. He lifted his eyebrows with the pretext of a smile as he returned her glance. He looked embarrassed and uneasy.

"When is he going?" she asked of everybody in general, as if Robert were not there to answer for himself.

"To-night!" "This very evening!" "Did you ever!" "What possesses him!" some of the replies she gathered, uttered simultaneously in French and English.

"Impossible!" she exclaimed. "How can a person start off from Grand Isle to Mexico at a moment's notice, as if he were going over to Klein's or to the wharf or down to the beach?"

"I said all along I was going to Mexico; I've been saying so for years!" cried Robert, in an excited and irritable tone, with the air of a man defending himself against a swarm of stinging insects.

Madame Lebrun knocked on the table with her knife handle.

"Please let Robert explain why he is going, and why he is going to-night," she called out. "Really, this table is getting to be more and more like Bedlam[4] every day, with everybody talking at once.

3. *Couldst Thou but Know* is the title of a song—and its refrain—written by Mi- chael William Balfe (1808–70). 4. Notorious lunatic asylum in London.

Sometimes—I hope God will forgive me—but positively, sometimes I wish Victor would lose the power of speech."

Victor laughed sardonically as he thanked his mother for her holy wish, of which he failed to see the benefit to anybody, except that it might afford her a more ample opportunity and license to talk herself.

Monsieur Farival thought that Victor should have been taken out in mid-ocean in his earliest youth and drowned. Victor thought there would be more logic in thus disposing of old people with an established claim for making themselves universally obnoxious. Madame Lebrun grew a trifle hysterical; Robert called his brother some sharp, hard names.

"There's nothing much to explain, mother," he said; though he explained, nevertheless—looking chiefly at Edna—that he could only meet the gentleman whom he intended to join at Vera Cruz by taking such and such a steamer, which left New Orleans on such a day; that Beaudelet was going out with his lugger-load of vegetables that night, which gave him an opportunity of reaching the city and making his vessel in time.

"But when did you make up your mind to all this?" demanded Monsieur Farival.

"This afternoon," returned Robert, with a shade of annoyance.

"At what time this afternoon?" persisted the old gentleman, with nagging determination, as if he were cross-questioning a criminal in a court of justice.

"At four o'clock this afternoon, Monsieur Farival," Robert replied, in a high voice and wiith a lofty air, which reminded Edna of some gentleman on the stage.

She had forced herself to eat most of her soup, and now she was picking the flaky bits of a *court bouillon*[5] with her fork.

The lovers were profiting by the general conversation on Mexico to speak in whispers of matters which they rightly considered were interesting to no one but themselves. The lady in black had once received a pair of prayer-beads of curious workmanship from Mexico, with very special indulgence[6] attached to them, but she had never been able to ascertain whether the indulgence extended outside the Mexican border. Father Fochel of the Cathedral had attempted to explain it; but he had not done so to her satisfaction. And she begged that Robert would interest himself, and discover, if possible, whether she was entitled to the indulgence accompanying the remarkably curious Mexican prayer-beads.

Madame Ratignolle hoped that Robert would exercise extreme caution in dealing with the Mexicans, who, she considered, were a

5. Broth in which fish is poached.
6. According to a Roman Catholic belief, some religious articles, through contact with a holy person or a special blessing, had the power to remit part of the punishment for sins which would otherwise be meted out to the sinner after death.

treacherous people, unscrupulous and revengeful. She trusted she did them no injustice in thus condemning them as a race. She had known personally but one Mexican, who made and sold excellent tamales, and whom she would have trusted implicitly, so soft-spoken was he. One day he was arrested for stabbing his wife. She never knew whether he had been hanged or not.

Victor had grown hilarious, and was attempting to tell an anecdote about a Mexican girl who served chocolate one winter in a restaurant in Dauphine Street.[7] No one would listen to him but old Monsieur Farival, who went into convulsions over the droll story.

Edna wondered if they had all gone mad, to be talking and clamoring at that rate. She herself could think of nothing to say about Mexico or the Mexicans.

"At what time do you leave?" she asked Robert.

"At ten," he told her. "Beaudelet wants to wait for the moon."

"Are you all ready to go?"

"Quite ready. I shall only take a handbag, and shall pack my trunk in the city."

He turned to answer some question put to him by his mother, and Edna, having finished her black coffee, left the table.

She went directly to her room. The little cottage was close and stuffy after leaving the outer air. But she did not mind; there appeared to be a hundred different things demanding her attention indoors. She began to set the toilet-stand to rights, grumbling at the negligence of the quadroon, who was in the adjoining room putting the children to bed. She gathered together stray garments that were hanging on the backs of chairs, and put each where it belonged in closet or bureau drawer. She changed her gown for a more comfortable and commodious wrapper. She rearranged her hair, combing and brushing it with unusual energy. Then she went in and assisted the quadroon in getting the boys to bed.

They were very playful and inclined to talk—to do anything but lie quiet and go to sleep. Edna sent the quadroon away to her supper and told her she need not return. Then she sat and told the child a story. Instead of soothing it excited them, and added to their wakefulness. She left them in heated argument, speculating about the conclusion of the tale which their mother promised to finish the following night.

The little black girl came in to say that Madame Lebrun would like to have Mrs. Pontellier go and sit with them over at the house till Mr. Robert went away. Edna returned answer that she had already undressed, that she did not feel quite well, but perhaps she would go over to the house later. She started to dress again, and got as far advanced as to remove her *peignoir*. But changing her mind once more she resumed the *peignoir*, and went outside and sat down before her door. She was overheated and irritable, and fanned

7. In the French Quarter.

herself energetically for a while. Madame Ratignolle came down to discover what was the matter.

"All that noise and confusion at the table must have upset me," replied Edna, "and moreover, I hate shocks and surprises. The idea of Robert starting off in such a ridiculously sudden and dramatic way! As if it were a matter of life and death! Never saying a word about it all morning when he was with me."

"Yes," agreed Madame Ratignolle. "I think it was showing us all —you especially—very little consideration. It wouldn't have surprised me in any of the others; those Lebruns are all given to heroics. But I must say I should never have expected such a thing from Robert. Are you not coming down? Come on, dear; it doesn't look friendly."

"No," said Edna, a little sullenly. "I can't go to the trouble of dressing again; I don't feel like it."

"You needn't dress; you look all right; fasten a belt around your waist. Just look at me!"

"No," persisted Edna; "but you go on. Madame Lebrun might be offended if we both stayed away."

Madame Ratignolle kissed Edna good-night, and went away, being in truth rather desirous of joining in the general and animated conversation which was still in progress concerning Mexico and the Mexicans.

Somewhat later Robert came up, carrying his hand-bag.

"Aren't you feeling well?" he asked.

"Oh, well enough. Are you going right away?"

He lit a match and looked at his watch. "In twenty minutes," he said. The sudden and brief flare of the match emphasized the darkness for a while. He sat down upon a stool which the children had left out on the porch.

"Get a chair," said Edna.

"This will do," he replied. He put on his soft hat and nervously took it off again, and wiping his face with his handkerchief, complained of the heat.

"Take the fan," said Edna, offering it to him.

"Oh, no! Thank you. It does no good; you have to stop fanning some time, and feel all the more uncomfortable afterward."

"That's one of the ridiculous things which men always say. I have never known one to speak otherwise of fanning. How long will you be gone?"

"Forever, perhaps. I don't know. It depends upon a good many things."

"Well, in case it shouldn't be forever, how long will it be?"

"I don't know."

"This seems to me perfectly preposterous and uncalled for. I don't like it. I don't understand your motive for silence and mystery, never saying a word to me about it this morning." He remained silent, not offering to defend himself. He only said, after a moment:

"Don't part from me in an ill-humor. I never knew you to be out of patience with me before."

"I don't want to part in any ill-humor," said she. "But can't you understand? I've grown used to seeing you, to having you with me all the time, and your action seems unfriendly, even unkind. You don't even offer an excuse for it. Why, I was planning to be together, thinking of how pleasant it would be to see you in the city next winter."

"So was I," he blurted. "Perhaps that's the—" He stood up suddenly and held out his hand. "Good-by, my dear Mrs. Pontellier; good-by. You won't—I hope you won't completely forget me." She clung to his hand, striving to detain him.

"Write to me when you get there, won't you, Robert?" she entreated.

"I will, thank you. Good-by."

How unlike Robert! The merest acquaintance would have said something more emphatic than "I will, thank you; good-by," to such a request.

He had evidently already taken leave of the people over at the house, for he descended the steps and went to join Beaudelet, who was out there with an oar across his shoulder waiting for Robert. They walked away in the darkness. She could only hear Beaudelet's voice; Robert had apparently not even spoken a word of greeting to his companion.

Edna bit her handkerchief convulsively, striving to hold back and to hide, even from herself as she would have hidden from another, the emotion which was troubling—tearing—her. Her eyes were brimming with tears.

For the first time she recognized anew the symptoms of infatuation which she felt incipiently as a child, as a girl in her earliest teens, and later as a young woman. The recognition did not lessen the reality, the poignancy of the revelation by any suggestion or promise of instability. The past was nothing to her; offered no lesson which she was willing to heed. The future was a mystery which she never attempted to penetrate. The present alone was significant; was hers, to torture her as it was doing then with the biting conviction that she had lost that which she had held, that she had been denied that which her impassioned, newly awakened being demanded.

XVI

"Do you miss your friend greatly?" asked Mademoiselle Reisz one morning as she came creeping up behind Edna, who had just left her cottage on her way to the beach. She spent much of her time in the water since she had acquired finally the art of swimming. As their stay at Grand Isle drew near its close, she felt that she could not give too much time to a diversion which afforded her the only real pleasurable moments that she knew. When Mademoiselle Reisz came and touched her upon the shoulder and spoke to her, the woman seemed to echo the thought which was ever in Edna's mind; or, better, the feeling which constantly possessed her.

Robert's going had some way taken the brightness, the color, the meaning out of everything. The conditions of her life were in no way changed, but her whole existence was dulled, like a faded garment which seems to be no longer worth wearing. She sought him everywhere—in others whom she induced to talk about him. She went up in the mornings to Madame Lebrun's room, braving the clatter of the old sewing-machine. She sat there and chatted at intervals as Robert had done. She gazed around the room at the pictures and photographs hanging upon the wall, and discovered in some corner an old family album, which she examined with the keenest interest, appealing to Madame Lebrun for enlightenment concerning the many figures and faces which she discovered between its pages.

There was a picture of Madame Lebrun with Robert as a baby, seated in her lap, a round-faced infant with a fist in his mouth. The eyes alone in the baby suggested the man. And that was he also in kilts, at the age of five, wearing long curls and holding a whip in his hand. It made Edna laugh, and she laughed, too, at the portrait in his first long trousers; while another interested her, taken when he left for college, looking thin, long-faced, with eyes full of fire, ambition and great intentions. But there was no recent picture, none which suggested the Robert who had gone away five days ago, leaving a void and wilderness behind him.

"Oh, Robert stopped having his pictures taken when he had to pay for them himself! He found wiser use for his money, he says," explained Madame Lebrun. She had a letter from him, written before he left New Orleans. Edna wished to see the letter, and Madame Lebrun told her to look for it either on the table or the dresser, or perhaps it was on the mantelpiece.

The letter was on the bookshelf. It possessed the greatest interest and attraction for Edna; the envelope, its size and shape, the postmark, the handwriting. She examined every detail of the outside before opening it. There were only a few lines, setting forth that he would leave the city that afternoon, that he had packed his trunk in good shape, that he was well, and sent her his love and begged to be affectionately remembered to all. There was no special message to Edna except a postscript saying that if Mrs. Pontellier desired to finish the book which he had been reading to her, his mother would find it in his room, among other books there on the table. Edna experienced a pang of jealousy because he had written to his mother rather than to her.

Every one seemed to take for granted that she missed him. Even her husband, when he came down the Saturday following Robert's departure, expressed regret that he had gone.

"How do you get on without him, Edna?" he asked.

"It's very dull without him," she admitted. Mr. Pontellier had seen Robert in the city, and Edna asked him a dozen questions or more. Where had they met? On Carondelet Street, in the morning. They had gone "in" and had a drink and a cigar together. What had they talked about? Chiefly about his prospects in Mexico, which Mr. Pontellier thought were promising. How did he look? How did he seem—grave, or gay, or how? Quite cheerful, and wholly taken up with the idea of his trip, which Mr. Pontellier found altogether natural in a young fellow about to seek fortune and adventure in a strange, queer country.

Edna tapped her foot impatiently, and wondered why the children persisted in playing in the sun when they might be under the trees. She went down and led them out of the sun, scolding the quadroon for not being more attentive.

It did not strike her as in the least grotesque that she should be making of Robert the object of conversation and leading her husband to speak of him. The sentiment which she entertained for Robert in no way resembled that which she felt for her husband, or had ever felt, or ever expected to feel. She had all her life long been accustomed to harbor thoughts and emotions which never voiced themselves. They had never taken the form of struggles. They belonged to her and were her own, and she entertained the conviction that she had a right to them and that they concerned no one but herself. Edna had once told Madame Ratignolle that she would never sacrifice herself for her children, or for any one. Then had followed a rather heated argument; the two women did not appear to understand each other or to be talking the same language. Edna tried to appease her friend, to explain.

"I would give up the unessential; I would give my money, I would give my life for my children; but I wouldn't give myself. I can't make it more clear; it's only something which I am beginning to comprehend, which is revealing itself to me."

"I don't know what you would call the essential, or what you mean by the unessential," said Madame Ratignolle, cheerfully; "but a woman who would give her life for her children could do no more than that—your Bible tells you so. I'm sure I couldn't do more than that."

"Oh, yes you could!" laughed Edna.

She was not surprised at Mademoiselle Reisz's question the morning that lady, following her to the beach, tapped her on the shoulder and asked if she did not greatly miss her young friend.

"Oh, good morning, Mademoiselle; it is you? Why, of course I miss Robert. Are you going down to bathe?"

"Why should I go down to bathe at the very end of the season when I haven't been in the surf all summer?" replied the woman, disagreeably.

"I beg your pardon," offered Edna, in some embarrassment, for she should have remembered that Mademoiselle Reisz's avoidance of the water had furnished a theme for much pleasantry. Some among them thought it was on account of her false hair, or the dread of getting the violets wet, while others attributed it to the natural aversion for water sometimes believed to accompany the artistic temperament. Mademoiselle offered Edna some chocolates in a paper bag, which she took from her pocket, by way of showing that she bore no ill feeling. She habitually ate chocolates for their sustaining quality; they contained much nutriment in small compass, she said. They saved her from starvation, as Madame Lebrun's table was utterly impossible; and no one save so impertinent a woman as Madame Lebrun could think of offering such food to people and requiring them to pay for it.

"She must feel very lonely without her son," said Edna, desiring to change the subject. "Her favorite son, too. It must have been quite hard to let him go."

Mademoiselle laughed maliciously.

"Her favorite son! Oh dear! Who could have been imposing such a tale upon you? Aline Lebrun lives for Victor, and for Victor alone. She has spoiled him into the worthless creature he is. She worships him and the ground he walks on. Robert is very well in a way, to give up all the money he can earn to the family, and keep the barest pittance for himself. Favorite son, indeed! I miss the poor fellow myself, my dear. I liked to see him and to hear him about the place—the only Lebrun who is worth a pinch of salt. He comes to see me often in the city. I like to play to him. That Victor! hanging would be too good for him. It's a wonder Robert hasn't beaten him to death long ago."

"I thought he had great patience with his brother," offered Edna, glad to be talking about Robert, no matter what was said.

"Oh! he thrashed him well enough a year or two ago," said Mademoiselle. "It was about a Spanish girl, whom Victor considered that he had some sort of claim upon. He met Robert one day talking to the girl, or walking with her, or bathing with her, or carrying her basket—I don't remember what;—and he became so insulting and abusive that Robert gave him a thrashing on the spot that has kept him comparatively in order for a good while. It's about time he was getting another."

"Was her name Mariequita?" asked Edna.

"Mariequita—yes, that was it. Mariequita. I had forgotten. Oh, she's a sly one, and a bad one, that Mariequita!"

Edna looked down at Mademoiselle Reisz and wondered how she could have listened to her venom so long. For some reason she felt depressed, almost unhappy. She had not intended to go into the water; but she donned her bathing suit, and left Mademoiselle alone, seated under the shade of the children's tent. The water was growing cooler as the season advanced. Edna plunged and swam about with an abandon that thrilled and invigorated her. She remained a long time in the water, half hoping that Mademoiselle Reisz would not wait for her.

But Mademoiselle waited. She was very amiable during the walk back, and raved much over Edna's appearance in her bathing suit. She talked about music. She hoped that Edna would go to see her in the city, and wrote her address with the stub of a pencil on a piece of card which she found in her pocket.

"When do you leave?" asked Edna.

"Next Monday; and you?"

"The following week," answered Edna, adding, "It has been a pleasant summer, hasn't it, Mademoiselle?"

"Well," agreed Mademoiselle Reiz, with a shrug, "rather pleasant, if it hadn't been for the mosquitoes and the Farival twins."

XVII

The Pontelliers possessed a very charming home on Esplanade Street[8] in New Orleans. It was a large, double cottage, with a broad front veranda, whose round, fluted columns supported the sloping roof. The house was painted a dazzling white; the outside shutters, or jalousies, were green. In the yard, which was kept scrupulously neat, were flowers and plants of every description which flourishes in South Louisiana. Within doors the appointments were perfect after the conventional type. The softest carpets and rugs covered the floors; rich and tasteful draperies hung at doors and windows. There were paintings, selected with judgment and discrimination, upon the walls. The cut glass, the silver, the heavy damask which daily appeared upon the table were the envy of many women whose husbands were less generous than Mr. Pontellier.

Mr. Pontellier was very fond of walking about his house examining its various appointments and details, to see that nothing was amiss. He greatly valued his possessions, chiefly because they were his, and derived genuine pleasure from contemplating a painting, a statuette, a rare lace curtain—no matter what—after he had bought it and placed it among his household goods.

On Tuesday afternoons—Tuesday being Mrs. Pontellier's reception day[9]—there was a constant stream of callers—women who came in carriages or in the street cars, or walked when the air was soft and distance permitted. A light-colored mulatto boy, in dress coat and bearing a diminutive silver tray for the reception of cards,

8. The most exclusive address of the Creole aristocracy; it was a street of palatial homes shaded by oaks, palms, and magnolias.

9. A day once a week when a woman was expected to be "at home" to receive visitors.

admitted them. A maid, in white fluted cap, offered the callers liqueur, coffee, or chocolate, as they might desire. Mrs. Pontellier, attired in a handsome reception gown, remained in the drawing-room the entire afternoon receiving her visitors. Men sometimes called in the evening with their wives.

This had been the programme which Mrs. Pontellier had religiously followed since her marriage, six years before. Certain evenings during the week she and her husband attended the opera or sometimes the play.

Mr. Pontellier left his home in the mornings between nine and ten o'clock, and rarely returned before half-past six or seven in the evening—dinner being served at half-past seven.

He and his wife seated themselves at table on Tuesday evening, a few weeks after their return from Grand Isle. They were alone together. The boys were being put to bed; the patter of their bare, escaping feet could be heard occasionally, as well as the pursuing voice of the quadroon, lifted in mild protest and entreaty. Mrs. Pontellier did not wear her usual Tuesday reception gown; she was in ordinary house dress. Mr. Pontellier, who was observant about such things, noticed it, as he served the soup and handed it to the boy in waiting.

"Tired out, Edna? Whom did you have? Many callers?" he asked. He tasted his soup and began to season it with pepper, salt, vinegar, mustard—everything within reach.

"There were a good many," replied Edna, who was eating her soup with evident satisfaction. "I found their cards when I got home; I was out."

"Out!" exclaimed her husband, with something like genuine consternation in his voice as he laid down the vinegar cruet and looked at her through his glasses. "Why, what could have taken you out on Tuesday? What did you have to do?"

"Nothing. I simply felt like going out, and I went out."

"Well, I hope you left some suitable excuse," said her husband, somewhat appeased, as he added a dash of cayenne pepper to the soup.

"No, I left no excuse. I told Joe to say I was out, that was all."

"Why, my dear, I should think you'd understand by this time that people don't do such things; we've got to observe *les convenances*[1] if we ever expect to get on and keep up with procession. If you felt that you had to leave home this afternoon, you should have left some suitable explanation for your absence.

"This soup is really impossible; it's strange that woman hasn't learned yet to make a decent soup. Any free-lunch stand in town serves a better one. Was Mrs. Belthrop here?"

"Bring the tray with the cards, Joe. I don't remember who was here."

1. Proprieties, social conventions.

The boy retired and returned after a moment, bringing the tiny silver tray, which was covered with ladies' visiting cards. He handed it to Mrs. Pontellier.

"Give it to Mr. Pontellier," she said.

Joe offered the tray to Mr. Pontellier, and removed the soup.

Mr. Pontellier scanned the names of his wife's callers, reading some of them aloud, with comments as he read.

" 'The Misses Delasidas.' I worked a big deal in futures[2] for their father this morning; nice girls; it's time they were getting married. 'Mrs. Belthrop.' I tell you what it is, Edna; you can't afford to snub Mrs. Belthrop. Why, Belthrop could buy and sell us ten times over. His business is worth a good, round sum to me. You'd better write her a note. 'Mrs. James Highcamp.' Hugh! the less you have to do with Mrs. Highcamp, the better. 'Madame Laforcé.' Came all the way from Carrolton,[3] too, poor old soul. 'Miss Wiggs,' 'Mrs. Eleanor Boltons.' " He pushed the cards aside.

"Mercy!" exclaimed Edna, who had been fuming. "Why are you taking the thing so seriously and making such a fuss over it?"

"I'm not making any fuss over it. But it's just such seeming trifles that we've got to take seriously; such things count."

The fish was scorched. Mr. Pontellier would not touch it. Edna said she did not mind a little scorched taste. The roast was in some way not to his fancy, and he did not like the manner in which the vegetables were served.

"It seems to me," he said, "we spend money enough in this house to procure at least one meal a day which a man could eat and retain his self-respect."

"You used to think the cook was a treasure," returned Edna, indifferently.

"Perhaps she was when she first came; but cooks are only human. They need looking after, like any other class of persons that you employ. Suppose I didn't look after the clerks in my office, just let them run things their own way; they'd soon make a nice mess of me and my business."

"Where are you going?'" asked Edna, seeing that her husband arose from table without having eaten a morsel except a taste of the highly-seasoned soup.

"'I'm going to get my dinner at the club. Good night." He went into the hall, took his hat and stick from the stand, and left the house.

She was somewhat familiar with such scenes. They had often made her very unhappy. On a few previous occasions she had been completely deprived of any desire to finish her dinner. Sometimes she had gone into the kitchen to administer a tardy rebuke to the

2. Commodities bought and sold for delivery at a future time and thus a form of speculation.

3. Village to the west of New Orleans later absorbed by the city.

cook. Once she went to her room and studied the cookbook during an entire evening, finally writing out a menu for the week, which left her harassed with a feeling that, after all, she had accomplished no good that was worth the name.

But that evening Edna finished her dinner alone, with forced deliberation. Her face was flushed and her eyes flamed with some inward fire that lighted them. After finishing her dinner she went to her room, having instructed the boy to tell any other callers that she was indisposed.

It was a large, beautiful room, rich and picturesque in the soft, dim light which the maid had turned low. She went and stood at an open window and looked out upon the deep tangle of the garden below. All the mystery and witchery of the night seemed to have gathered there amid the perfumes and the dusky and tortuous out-lines of flowers and foliage. She was seeking herself and finding herself in just such sweet, half-darkness which met her moods. But the voices were not soothing that came to her from the darkness and the sky above and the stars. They jeered and sounded mournful notes without promise, devoid even of hope. She turned back into the room and began to walk to and fro down its whole length, without stopping, without resting. She carried in her hands a thin handkerchief, which she tore into ribbons, rolled into a ball, and flung from her. Once she stopped, and taking off her wedding ring, flung it upon the carpet. When she saw it lying there, she stamped her heel upon it, striving to crush it. But her small boot heel did not make an indenture, not a mark upon the little glittering circlet.

In a sweeping passion she seized a glass vase from the table and flung it upon the tiles of the hearth. She wanted to destroy something. The crash and clatter were what she wanted to hear.

A maid, alarmed at the din of breaking glass, entered the room to discover what was the matter.

"A vase fell upon the hearth," said Edna. "Never mind; leave it till morning."

"Oh! you might get some of the glass in your feet, ma'am," insisted the young woman, picking up bits of the broken vase that were scattered upon the carpet. "And here's your ring, ma'am, under the chair."

Edna held out her hand, and taking the ring, slipped it upon her finger.

XVIII

The following morning Mr. Pontellier, upon leaving for his office, asked Edna if she would not meet him in town in order to look at some new fixtures for the library.

"I hardly think we need new fixtures, Léonce. Don't let us get anything new; you are too extravagant. I don't believe you ever think of saving or putting by."

"The way to become rich is to make money, my dear Edna, not to save it," he said. He regretted that she did not feel inclined to go with him and select new fixtures. He kissed her good-by, and told her she was not looking well and must take care of herself. She was unusually pale and very quiet.

She stood on the front veranda as he quitted the house, and absently picked a few sprays of jessamine[4] that grew upon a trellis near by. She inhaled the odor of the blossoms and thrust them into the bosom of her white morning gown. The boys were dragging along the banquette[5] a small "express wagon," which they had filled with blocks and sticks. The quadroon was following them with little quick steps, having assumed a fictitious animation and alacrity for the occasion. A fruit vender was crying his wares in the street.

Edna looked straight before her with a self-absorbed expression upon her face. She felt no interest in anything about her. The street, the children, the fruit vender, the flowers growing there under her eyes, were all part and parcel of an alien world which had suddenly become antagonistic.

She went back into the house. She had thought of speaking to the cook concerning her blunders of the previous night; but Mr. Pontellier had saved her that disagreeable mission, for which she was so poorly fitted. Mr. Pontellier's arguments were usually convincing with those whom he employed. He left home feeling quite sure that he and Edna would sit down that evening, and possibly a few subsequent evenings, to a dinner deserving of the name.

Edna spent an hour or two in looking over some of her old sketches. She could see their shortcomings and defects, which were glaring in her eyes. She tried to work a little, but found she was not in the humor. Finally she gathered together a few of the sketches —those which she considered the least discreditable; and she carried them with her when, a little later, she dressed and left the house. She looked handsome and distinguished in her street gown. The tan of the seashore had left her face, and her forehead was smooth, white, and polished beneath her heavy, yellow-brown hair. There were a few freckles on her face, and a small, dark mole near the under lip and one on the temple, half-hidden in her hair.

As Edna walked along the street she was thinking of Robert. She was still under the spell of her infatuation. She had tried to forget him, realizing the inutility of remembering. But the thought of him was like an obsession, ever pressing itself upon her. It was not that she dwelt upon details of their acquaintance, or recalled in any special or peculiar way his personality; it was his being, his existence, which dominated her thought, fading sometimes as if it would melt into the mist of the forgotten, reviving again with an intensity which filled her with an incomprehensible longing.

---

4. Jasmine.   5. Sidewalk.

Edna was on her way to Madame Ratignolle's. Their intimacy, begun at Grand Isle, had not declined, and they had seen each other with some frequency since their return to the city. The Ratignolles lived at no great distance from Edna's home, on the corner of a side street, where Monsieur Ratignolle owned and conducted a drug store which enjoyed a steady and prosperous trade. His father had been in the business before him, and Monsieur Ratignolle stood well in the community and bore an enviable reputation for integrity and clear-headedness. His family lived in commodious apartments over the store, having an entrance on the side within the *porte cochère*.[6] There was something which Edna thought very French, very foreign, about their whole manner of living. In the large and pleasant salon which extended across the width of the house, the Ratignolles entertained their friends once a fortnight with a *soirée musicale*,[7] sometimes diversified by card-playing. There was a friend who played upon the 'cello. One brought his flute and another his violin, while there were some who sang and a number who performed upon the piano with various degrees of taste and agility. The Ratignolles' *soirées musicales* were widely known, and it was considered a privilege to be invited to them.

Edna found her friend engaged in assorting the clothes which had returned that morning from the laundry. She at once abandoned her occupation upon seeing Edna, who had been ushered without ceremony into her presence.

"'Cité can do it as well as I; it is really her business," she explained to Edna, who apologized for interrupting her. And she summoned a young black woman, whom she instructed, in French, to be very careful in checking off the list which she handed her. She told her to notice particularly if a fine linen handkerchief of Monsieur Ratignolle's, which was missing last week, had been returned; and to be sure to set to one side such pieces as required mending and darning.

Then placing an arm around Edna's waist, she led her to the front of the house, to the salon, where it was cool and sweet with the odor of great roses that stood upon the hearth in jars.

Madame Ratignolle looked more beautiful than ever there at home, in a negligé which left her arms almost wholly bare and exposed the rich, melting curves of her white throat.

"Perhaps I shall be able to paint your picture some day," said Edna with a smile when they were seated. She produced the roll of sketches and started to unfold them. "I believe I ought to work again. I feel as if I wanted to be doing something. What do you think of them? Do you think it worth while to take it up again and study some more? I might study for a while with Laidpore."

She knew that Madame Ratignolle's opinion in such a matter

6. In America, a porch under which a   travelers alighting or boarding.
conveyance is driven in order to protect   7. An evening of music.

would be next to valueless, that she herself had not alone decided, but determined; but she sought the words and praise and encouragement that would help her to put heart into her venture.

"Your talent is immense, dear!"

"'Nonsense!" protested Edna, well pleased.

"Immense, I tell you," persisted Madame Ratignolle, surveying the sketches one by one, at close range, then holding them at arm's length, narrowing her eyes, and dropping her head on one side. "Surely, this Bavarian peasant is worthy of framing; and this basket of apples! never have I seen anything more lifelike. One might almost be tempted to reach out a hand and take one."

Edna could not control a feeling which bordered upon complacency at her friend's praise, even realizing, as she did, its true worth. She retained a few of the sketches, and gave all the rest to Madame Ratignolle, who appreciated the gift far beyond its value and proudly exhibited the pictures to her husband when he came up from the store a little later for his midday dinner.

Mr. Ratignolle was one of those men who are called the salt of the earth. His cheerfulness was unbounded, and it was matched by his goodness of heart, his broad charity, and common sense. He and his wife spoke English with an accent which was only discernible through its un-English emphasis and a certain carefulness and deliberation. Edna's husband spoke English with no accent whatever. The Ratignolles understood each other perfectly. If ever the fusion of two human beings into one has been accomplished on this sphere it was surely in their union.

As Edna seated herself at table with them she thought, "Better a dinner of herbs," though it did not take her long to discover that was no dinner of herbs, but a delicious repast, simple, choice, and in every way satisfying.

Monsieur Ratignolle was delighted to see her, though he found her looking not so well as at Grand Isle, and he advised a tonic. He talked a good deal on various topics, a little politics, some city news and neighborhood gossip. He spoke with an animation and earnestness that gave an exaggerated importance to every syllable he uttered. His wife was keenly interested in everything he said, laying down her fork the better to listen, chiming in, taking the words out of his mouth.

Edna felt depressed rather than soothed after leaving them. The little glimpse of domestic harmony which had been offered her, gave her no regret, no longing. It was not a condition of life which fitted her, and she could see in it but an appalling and hopeless ennui. She was moved by a kind of commiseration for Madame Ratignolle,—a pity for that colorless existence which never uplifted its possessor beyond the region of blind contentment, in which no moment of anguish ever visited her soul, in which she would never have the taste of life's delirium. Edna vaguely wondered what she meant by "life's delirium." It had crossed her thought like some unsought, extraneous impression.

XIX

Edna could not help but think that it was very foolish, very childish, to have stamped upon her wedding ring and smashed the crystal vase upon the tiles. She was visited by no more outbursts, moving her to such futile expedients. She began to do as she liked and to feel as she liked. She completely abandoned her Tuesdays at home, and did not return the visits of those who had called upon her. She made no ineffectual efforts to conduct her household *en bonne ménagère*,[8] going and coming as it suited her fancy, and, so far as she was able, lending herself to any passing caprice.

Mr. Pontellier had been a rather courteous husband so long as he met a certain tacit submissiveness in his wife. But her new and unexpected line of conduct completely bewildered him. It shocked him. Then her absolute disregard for her duties as a wife angered him. When Mr. Pontellier became rude, Edna grew insolent. She had resolved never to take another step backward.

"It seems to me the utmost folly for a woman at the head of a household, and the mother of children, to spend in an atelier[9] days which would be better employed contriving for the comfort of her family."

"I feel like painting," answered Edna. "Perhaps I shan't always feel like it."

"Then in God's name paint! but don't let the family go to the devil. There's Madame Ratignolle; because she keeps up her music, she doesn't let everything go to chaos. And she's more of a musician than you are a painter."

"She isn't a musician, and I'm not a painter. It isn't on account of painting that I let things go."

"On account of what, then?"

"Oh! I don't know. Let me alone; you bother me."

It sometimes entered Mr. Pontellier's mind to wonder if his wife were not growing a little unbalanced mentally. He could see plainly that she was not herself. That is, he could not see that she was becoming herself and daily casting aside that fictitious self which we assume like a garment with which to appear before the world.

Her husband let her alone as she requested, and went away to his office. Edna went up to her atelier—a bright room in the top of the house. She was working with great energy and interest, without accomplishing anything, however, which satisfied her even in the smallest degree. For a time she had the whole household enrolled in the service of art. The boys posed for her. They thought it amusing at first, but the occupation soon lost its attractiveness when they

8. As a good housewife.   9. Studio.

discovered that it was not a game arranged especially for their entertainment. The quadroon sat for hours before Edna's palette, patient
as a savage, while the housemaid took charge of the children, and
the drawing-room went undusted. But the house-maid, too, served
her term as model when Edna perceived that the young woman's
back and shoulders were molded on classic lines, and that her hair,
loosened from its confining cap, became an inspiration. While Edna
worked she sometimes sang low the little air, "*Ah! si tu savais!*"

It moved her with recollections. She could hear again the ripple
of the water, the flapping sail. She could see the glint of the moon
upon the bay, and could feel the soft, gusty beating of the hot
south wind. A subtle current of desire passed through her body,
weakening her hold upon the brushes and making her eyes burn.

There were days when she was very happy without knowing why.
She was happy to be alive and breathing, when her whole being
seemed to be one with the sunlight, the color, the odors, the luxuriant warmth of some perfect Southern day. She liked then to
wander alone into strange and unfamiliar places. She discovered
many a sunny, sleepy corner, fashioned to dream in. And she found
it good to dream and to be alone and unmolested.

There were days when she was unhappy, she did not know why,
—when it did not seem worth while to be glad or sorry, to be alive
or dead; when life appeared to her like a grotesque pandemonium
and humanity like worms struggling blindly toward inevitable annihilation. She could not work on such a day, nor weave fancies to
stir her pulses and warm her blood.

XX

It was during such a mood that Edna hunted up Mademoiselle
Reisz. She had not forgotten the rather disagreeable impression
left upon her by their last interview; but she nevertheless felt
a desire to see her—above all, to listen while she played upon
the piano. Quite early in the afternoon she started upon her quest
for the pianist. Unfortunately she had mislaid or lost Mademoiselle
Reisz's card, and looking up her address in the city directory, she
found that the woman lived on Bienville Street,[1] some distance
away. The directory which fell into her hands was a year or more
old, however, and upon reaching the number indicated, Edna discovered that the house was occupied by a respectable family of
mulattoes who had *chambres garnies*[2] to let. They had been living
there for six months, and knew absolutely nothing of a Mademoiselle Reisz. In fact, they knew nothing of any of their neighbors; their lodgers were all people of the highest distinction,
they assured Edna. She did not linger to discuss class distinctions
with Madame Pouponne, but hastened to a neighboring grocery

1. On the opposite side of the French Quarter from the Pontelliers' house.
2. Furnished rooms.

store, feeling sure that Mademoiselle would have left her address with the proprietor.

He knew Mademoiselle Reisz a good deal better than he wanted to know her, he informed his questioner. In truth, he did not want to know her at all, anything concerning her—the most disagreeable and unpopular woman who ever lived in Bienville Street. He thanked heaven she had left the neighborhood, and was equally thankful that he did not know where she had gone.

Edna's desire to see Mademoiselle Reisz had increased tenfold since these unlooked-for obstacles had arisen to thwart it. She was wondering who could give her the information she sought, when it suddenly occurred to her that Madame Lebrun would be the one most likely to do so. She knew it was useless to ask Madame Ratignolle, who was on the most distant terms with the musician, and preferred to know nothing concerning her. She had once been almost as emphatic in expressing herself upon the subject as the corner grocer.

Edna knew that Madame Lebrun had returned to the city, for it was the middle of November. And she also knew where the Lebruns lived, on Chartres Street.[3]

Their home from the outside looked like a prison, with iron bars before the door and lower windows. The iron bars were a relic of the old *régime*,[4] and no one had ever thought of dislodging them. At the side was a high fence enclosing the garden. A gate or door opening upon the street was locked. Edna rang the bell at this side garden gate, and stood upon the banquette, waiting to be admitted.

It was Victor who opened the gate for her. A black woman, wiping her hands upon her apron, was close at his heels. Before she saw them Edna could hear them in altercation, the woman—plainly an anomaly—claiming the right to be allowed to perform her duties, one of which was to answer the bell.

Victor was surprised and delighted to see Mrs. Pontellier, and he made no attempt to conceal either his astonishment or his delight. He was a dark-browed, good-looking youngster of nineteen, greatly resembling his mother, but with ten times her impetuosity. He instructed the black woman to go at once and inform Madame Lebrun that Mrs. Pontellier desired to see her. The woman grumbled a refusal to do part of her duty when she had not been permitted to do it all, and started back to her interrupted task of weeding the garden. Whereupon Victor administered a rebuke in the form of a volley of abuse, which owing to its rapidity and incoherence, was all but incomprehensible to Edna. Whatever it was, the rebuke was convincing, for the woman dropped her hoe and went mumbling into the house.

Edna did not wish to enter. It was very pleasant there on the side

3. In the heart of the French Quarter.   4. The Spanish regime (1766–1803).

porch, where there were chairs, a wicker lounge, and a small table. She seated herself, for she was tired from her long tramp; and she began to rock gently and smooth out the folds of her silk parasol. Victor drew up his chair beside her. He at once explained that the black woman's offensive conduct was all due to imperfect training, as he was not there to take her in hand. He had only come up from the island the morning before, expected to return next day. He stayed all winter at the island; he lived there, and kept the place in order and got things ready for the summer visitors.

But a man needed occasional relaxation, he informed Mrs. Pontellier, and every now and again he drummed up a pretext to bring him to the city. My! but he had had a time of it the evening before! He wouldn't want his mother to know, and he began to talk in a whisper. He was scintillant with recollections. Of course, he couldn't think of telling Mrs. Pontellier all about it, she being a woman and not comprehending such things. But it all began with a girl peeping and smiling at him through the shutters as he passed by. Oh! but she was a beauty! Certainly he smiled back, and went up and talked to her. Mrs. Pontellier did not know him if she supposed he was one to let an opportunity like that escape him. Despite herself, the youngster amused her. She must have betrayed in her look some degree of interest or entertainment. The boy grew more daring, and Mrs. Pontellier might have found herself, in a little while, listening to a highly colored story but for the timely appearance of Madame Lebrun.

That lady was still clad in white, according to her custom of the summer. Her eyes beamed an effusive welcome. Would not Mrs. Pontellier go inside? Would she partake of some refreshment? Why had she not been there before? How was that dear Mr. Pontellier and how were those sweet children? Has Mrs. Pontellier ever known such a warm November?

Victor went and reclined on the wicker lounge behind his mother's chair, where he commanded a view of Edna's face. He had taken her parasol from her hands while he spoke to her, and he now lifted it and twirled it above him as he lay on his back. When Madame Lebrun complained that it was so dull coming back to the city; that she saw so few people now; that even Victor, when he came up from the island for a day or two, had so much to occupy him and engage his time, then it was that the youth went into contortions on the lounge and winked mischievously at Edna. She somehow felt like a confederate in crime, and tried to look severe and disapproving.

There had been but two letters from Robert, with little in them, they told her. Victor said it was really not worth while to go inside for the letters, when his mother entreated him to go in search of them. He remembered the contents, which in truth he rattled off very glibly when put to the test.

One letter was written from Vera Cruz and the other from the City of Mexico. He had met Montel, who was doing everything toward his advancement. So far, the financial situation was no improvement over the one he had left in New Orleans, but of course the prospects were vastly better. He wrote of the City of Mexico, the buildings, the people and their habits, the conditions of life which he found there. He sent his love to the family. He inclosed a check to his mother, and hoped she would affectionately remember him to all his friends. That was about the substance of the two letters. Edna felt that if there had been a message for her, she would have received it. The despondent frame of mind in which she had left home began again to overtake her, and she remembered that she wished to find Mademoiselle Reisz.

Madame Lebrun knew where Mademoiselle Reisz lived. She gave Edna the address, regretting that she would not consent to stay and spend the remainder of the afternoon, and pay a visit to Mademoiselle Reisz some other day. The afternoon was already well advanced.

Victor escorted her out upon the banquette, lifted her parasol, and held it over her while he walked to the car with her. He entreated her to bear in mind that the disclosures of the afternoon were strictly confidential. She laughed and bantered him a little, remembering too late that she should have been dignified and reserved.

"How handsome Mrs. Pontellier looked!" said Madame Lebrun to her son.

"Ravishing!" he admitted. "The city atmosphere has improved her. Some way he doesn't seem like the same woman."

XXI

Some people contended that the reason Mademoiselle Reisz always chose apartments up under the roof was to discourage the approach of beggars, peddlars and callers. There were plenty of windows in her little front room. They were for the most part dingy, but as they were nearly always open it did not make so much difference. They often admitted into the room a good deal of smoke and soot; but at the same time all the light and air that there was came through them. From her windows could be seen the crescent of the river, the masts of ships and the big chimneys of the Mississippi steamers. A magnificent piano crowded the apartment. In the next room she slept, and in the third and last she harbored a gasoline stove on which she cooked her meals when disinclined to descend to the neighboring restaurant. It was there also that she ate, keeping her belongings in a rare old buffet, dingy and battered from a hundred years of use.

When Edna knocked at Mademoiselle Reisz's front room door and entered, she discovered that person standing beside the window, engaged in mending or patching an old prunella gaiter.[5]

5. A cloth button shoe with leather soles.

The little musician laughed all over when she saw Edna. Her laugh consisted of a contortion of the face and all the muscles of the body. She seemed strikingly homely, standing there in the afternoon light. She still wore the shabby lace and the artificial bunch of violets on the side of her head.

"So you remembered me at last," said Mademoiselle. "I had said to myself, 'Ah, bah! she will never come.' "

"Did you want me to come?" asked Edna with a smile.

"I had not thought much about it," answered Mademoiselle. The two had seated themselves on a little bumpy sofa which stood against the wall. "'I am glad, however, that you came. I have the water boiling back there, and was just about to make some coffee. You will drink a cup with me. And how is *la belle dame?*[6] Always handsome! always healthy! always contented!" She took Edna's hand between her strong wiry fingers, holding it loosely without warmth, and executing a sort of double theme upon the back and palm.

"Yes," she went on; "I sometimes thought: 'She will never come. She promised as those women in society always do, without meaning it. She will not come.' For I really don't believe you like me, Mrs. Pontellier."

"I don't know whether I like you or not," replied Edna, gazing down at the little woman with a quizzical look.

The candor of Mrs. Pontellier's admission greatly pleased Mademoiselle Reisz. She expressed her gratification by repairing forthwith to the region of the gasoline stove and rewarding her guest with the promised cup of coffee. The coffee and the biscuit accompanying it proved very acceptable to Edna, who had declined refreshment at Madame Lebrun's and was now beginning to feel hungry. Mademoiselle set the tray which she brought in upon a small table near at hand, and seated herself once again on the lumpy sofa.

"I have had a letter from your friend," she remarked, as she poured a little cream into Edna's cup and handed it to her.

"My friend?"

"Yes, your friend Robert. He wrote to me from the City of Mexico."

"Wrote to *you?*" repeated Edna in amazement, stirring her coffee absently.

"Yes, to me. Why not? Don't stir all the warmth out of your coffee; drink it. Though the letter might as well have been sent to you; it was nothing but Mrs. Pontellier from beginning to end."

"Let me see it," requested the young woman, entreatingly.

"No; a letter concerns no one but the person who writes it and the one to whom it is written."

"Haven't you just said it concerned me from beginning to end?"

"It was written about you, not to you. 'Have you seen Mrs. Pon-

6. The lovely lady.

tellier? How is she looking?' he asks. 'As Mrs. Pontellier says,' or 'as Mrs. Pontellier once said.' 'If Mrs. Pontellier should call upon you, play for her that Impromptu of Chopin's, my favorite. I heard it here a day or two ago, but not as you play it. I should like to know how it affects her,' and so on, as if he supposed we were constantly in each other's society."

"Let me see the letter."

"Oh, no."

"Have you answered it?"

"No."

"Let me see the letter."

"No, and again, no."

"Then play the Impromptu for me."

"It is growing late; what time do you have to be home?"

"Time doesn't concern me. Your question seems a little rude. Play the Impromptu."

"But you have told me nothing of yourself. What are you doing?"

"Painting!" laughed Edna. "I am becoming an artist. Think of it!"

"Ah! an artist! You have pretensions, Madame."

"Why pretensions? Do you think I could not become an artist?"

"I do not know you well enough to say. I do not know your talent or your temperament. To be an artist includes much; one must possess many gifts—absolute gifts—which have not been acquired by one's own effort. And, moreover, to succeed, the artist must possess the courageous soul."

"What do you mean by the courageous soul?"

"Courageous, *ma foi!* The brave soul. The soul that dares and defies."

"Show me the letter and play for me the Impromptu. You see that I have persistence. Does that quality count for anything in art?"

"It counts with a foolish old woman whom you have captivated," replied Mademoiselle, with her wriggling laugh.

The letter was right there at hand in the drawer of the little table upon which Edna had just placed her coffee cup. Mademoiselle opened the drawer and drew forth the letter, the topmost one. She placed it in Edna's hands, and without further comment arose and went to the piano.

Mademoiselle played a soft interlude. It was an improvisation. She sat low at the instrument, and the lines of her body settled into ungraceful curves and angles that gave it an appearance of deformity. Gradually and imperceptibly the interlude melted into the soft opening minor chords of the Chopin Impromptu.

Edna did not know when the impromptu began or ended. She sat in the sofa corner reading Robert's letter by the fading light.

Mademoiselle had glided from the Chopin into the quivering love-notes of Isolde's song,[7] and back again to the Impromptu with its soulful and poignant longing.

The shadows deepened in the little room. The music grew strange and fantastic—turbulent, insistent, plaintive and soft with entreaty. The shadows grew deeper. The music filled the room. It floated out upon the night, over the housetops, the crescent of the river, losing itself in the silence of the upper air.

Edna was sobbing, just as she had wept one midnight at Grand Isle when strange, new voices awoke in her. She arose in some agitation to take her departure. "May I come again, Mademoiselle?" she asked at the threshold.

"Come whenever you feel like it. Be careful; the stairs and landings are dark; don't stumble."

Mademoiselle reëntered and lit a candle. Robert's letter was on the floor. She stooped and picked it up. It was crumpled and damp with tears. Mademoiselle smoothed the letter out, restored it to the envelope, and replaced it in the table drawer.

XXII

One morning on his way into town Mr. Pontellier stopped at the house of his old friend and family physician, Doctor Mandelet. The Doctor was a semi-retired physician, resting, as the saying is, upon his laurels. He bore a reputation for wisdom rather than skill—leaving the active practice of medicine to his assistants and younger contemporaries—and was much sought for in matters of consultation. A few families, united to him by bonds of friendship, he still attended when they required the services of a physician. The Pontelliers were among these.

Mr. Pontellier found the Doctor reading at the open window of his study. His house stood rather far back from the street, in the center of a delightful garden, so that it was quiet and peaceful at the old gentleman's study window. He was a great reader. He stared up disapprovingly over his eyeglasses as Mr. Pontellier entered, wondering who had the temerity to disturb him at that hour of the morning.

"Ah, Pontellier! Not sick, I hope. Come and have a seat. What news do you bring this morning?" He was quite portly, with a profusion of gray hair, and small blue eyes which age had robbed of much of their brightness but none of their penetration.

"Oh! I'm never sick, Doctor. You know that I come of tough fiber—of that old Creole race of Pontelliers that dry up and finally blow away. I came to consult—no, not precisely to consult—to talk to you about Edna. I don't know what ails her."

---

7. From Richard Wagner's opera *Tristan und Isolde* (1857–59), based on a medieval legend of ill-fated love. Isolde's *Lie-* *bestod* ("love-death") is sung as she bids her dead lover farewell and falls dead herself in his arms.

"Madame Pontellier not well?" marveled the Doctor. "Why I saw her—I think it was a week ago—walking along Canal Street,[8] the picture of health, it seemed to me."

"Yes, yes; she seems quite well,'" said Mr. Pontellier, leaning forward and whirling his stick between his two hands; "but she doesn't act well. She's odd, she's not like herself. I can't make her out, and I thought perhaps you'd help me."

"How does she act?" inquired the doctor.

"Well, it isn't easy to explain," said Mr. Pontellier, throwing himself back in his chair. "She lets the housekeeping go to the dickens."

"Well, well; women are not all alike, my dear Pontellier. We've got to consider—"

"I know that; I told you I couldn't explain. Her whole attitude —toward me and everybody and everything—has changed. You know I have a quick temper, but I don't want to quarrel or be rude to a woman, especially my wife; yet I'm driven to it, and feel like ten thousand devils after I've made a fool of myself. She's making it devilishly uncomfortable for me," he went on nervously. "She's got some sort of notion in her head concerning the eternal rights of women; and—you understand—we meet in the morning at the breakfast table."

The old gentleman lifted his shaggy eyebrows, protruded his thick nether lip, and tapped the arms of his chair with his cushioned finger-tips.

"What have you been doing to her, Pontellier?"

"Doing! *Parbleu!*"[9]

"Has she," asked the Doctor, with a smile, "has she been associating of late with a circle of pseudo-intellectual women[1]— superspiritual superior beings? My wife has been telling me about them."

"That's the trouble," broke in Mr. Pontellier, "she hasn't been associating with any one. She has abandoned her Tuesdays at home, has thrown over all her acquaintances, and goes tramping about by herself, moping in the street-cars, getting in after dark. I tell you she's peculiar. I don't like it; I feel a little worried over it."

This was a new aspect for the Doctor. "Nothing hereditary?" he asked, seriously. "Nothing peculiar about her family antecedents, is there?"

"Oh, no, indeed! She comes of sound old Presbyterian Kentucky stock. The old gentleman, her father, I have heard, used to atone for his week-day sins with his Sunday devotions. I know for a fact,

8. The main street of downtown New Orleans, separating the old French city from the new American section.
9. "For heaven's sake!"
1. Women's clubs flourished during the late 19th century in America. They were a source of education for women as well as an arena for political organization. As the Doctor's remark indicates, the club movement was met with scorn in some quarters [Culley's note].

that his race horses literally ran away with the prettiest bit of Kentucky farming land I ever laid eyes upon. Margaret—you know Margaret—she has all the Presbyterianism undiluted. And the youngest is something of a vixen. By the way, she gets married in a couple of weeks from now."

"Send your wife up to the wedding," exclaimed the Doctor, foreseeing a happy solution. "Let her stay among her own people for a while; it will do her good."

"That's what I want her to do. She won't go to the marriage. She says a wedding is one of the most lamentable spectacles on earth. Nice thing for a woman to say to her husband!" exclaimed Mr. Pontellier, fuming anew at the recollection.

"Pontellier," said the Doctor, after a moment's reflection, "let your wife alone for a while. Don't bother her, and don't let her bother you. Woman, my dear friend, is a very peculiar and delicate organism—a sensitive and highly organized woman, such as I know Mrs. Pontellier to be, is especially peculiar. It would require an inspired psychologist to deal successfully with them. And when ordinary fellows like you and me attempt to cope with their idiosyncrasies the result is bungling. Most women are moody and whimsical. This is some passing whim of your wife, due to some cause or causes which you and I needn't try to fathom. But it will pass happily over, especially if you let her alone. Send her around to see me."

"Oh! I couldn't do that; there'd be no reason for it," objected Mr. Pontellier.

"Then I'll go around and see her," said the Doctor. "I'll drop in to dinner some evening *en bon ami*."[2]

"Do! by all means," urged Mr. Pontellier. "What evening will you come? Say Thursday. Will you come Thursday?" he asked, rising to take his leave.

"Very well; Thursday. My wife may possibly have some engagement for me Thursday. In case she has, I shall let you know. Otherwise, you may expect me."

Mr. Pontellier turned before leaving to say:

"I am going to New York on business very soon. I have a big scheme on hand, and want to be on the field proper to pull the ropes and handle the ribbons.[3] We'll let you in on the inside if you say so, Doctor," he laughed.

"No, I thank you, my dear sir," returned the Doctor. "I leave such ventures to you younger men with the fever of life still in your blood."

"What I wanted to say," continued Mr. Pontellier, with his hand on the knob; "I may have to be absent a good while. Would you advise me to take Edna along?"

2. "As a friend."   3. I.e., the reins.

"By all means, if she wishes to go. If not, leave her here. Don't contradict her. The mood will pass, I assure you. It may take a month, two, three months—possibly longer, but it will pass; have patience."

"Well, good-by, *à jeudi*,"[4] said Mr. Pontellier, as he let himself out.

The Doctor would have liked during the course of conversation to ask, "Is there any man in the case?" but he knew his Creole too well to make such a blunder as that.

He did not resume his book immediately, but sat for a while meditatively looking out into the garden.

XXIII

Edna's father was in the city, and had been with them several days. She was not very warmly or deeply attached to him, but they had certain tastes in common, and when together they were companionable. His coming was in the nature of a welcome disturbance; it seemed to furnish a new direction for her emotions.

He had come to purchase a wedding gift for his daughter, Janet, and an outfit for himself in which he might make a creditable appearance at her marriage. Mr. Pontellier had selected the bridal gift, as every one immediately connected with him always deferred to his taste in such matters. And his suggestions on the question of dress—which too often assumes the nature of a problem—were of inestimable value to his father-in-law. But for the past few days the old gentleman had been upon Edna's hands, and in his society she was becoming acquainted with a new set of sensations. He had been a colonel in the Confederate army, and still maintained, with the title, the military bearing which had always accompanied it. His hair and mustache were white and silky, emphasizing the rugged bronze of his face. He was tall and thin, and wore his coats padded, which gave a fictitious breadth and depth to his shoulders and chest. Edna and her father looked very distinguished together, and excited a good deal of notice during their perambulations. Upon his arrival she began by introducing him to her atelier and making a sketch of him. He took the whole matter very seriously. If her talent had been ten-fold greater than it was, it would not have surprised him, convinced as he was that he had bequeathed to all of his daughters the germs of a masterful capability, which only depended upon their own efforts to be directed toward successful achievement.

Before her pencil he sat rigid and unflinching, as he had faced the cannon's mouth in days gone by. He resented the intrusion of the children, who gaped with wondering eyes at him, sitting so stiff up there in their mother's bright atelier. When they drew near

4. "Until Thursday."

he motioned them away with an expressive action of the foot, loath to disturb the fixed lines of his countenance, his arms, or his rigid shoulders.

Edna, anxious to entertain him, invited Mademoiselle Reisz to meet him, having promised him a treat in her piano playing; but Mademoiselle declined the invitation. So together they attended a *soirée musicale* at the Ratignolle's. Monsieur and Madame Ratignolle made much of the Colonel, installing him as the guest of honor and engaging him at once to dine with them the following Sunday, or any day which he might select. Madame coquetted with him in the most captivating and naïve manner, with eyes, gestures, and a profusion of compliments, till the Colonel's old head felt thirty years younger on his padded shoulders. Edna marveled, not comprehending. She herself was almost devoid of coquetry.

There were one or two men whom she observed at the *soirée musicale*; but she would never have felt moved to any kittenish display to attract their notice—to any feline or feminine wiles to express herself toward them. Their personality attracted her in an agreeable way. Her fancy selected them, and she was glad when a lull in the music gave them an opportunity to meet her and talk with her. Often on the street the glance of strange eyes had lingered in her memory, and sometimes had disturbed her.

Mr. Pontellier did not attend these *soirées musicales*. He considered them *bourgeois*, and found more diversion at the club. To Madame Ratignolle he said the music dispensed at her *soirées* was too "heavy," too far beyond his untrained comprehension. His excuse flattered her. But she disapproved of Mr. Pontellier's club, and she was frank enough to tell Edna so.

"It's a pity Mr. Pontellier doesn't stay home more in the evenings. I think you would be more—well, if you don't mind my saying it—more united, if he did."

"Oh! dear no!" said Edna, with a blank look in her eyes. "What should I do if he stayed home? We wouldn't have anything to say to each other."

She had not much of anything to say to her father, for that matter; but he did not antagonize her. She discovered that he interested her, though she realized that he might not interest her long; and for the first time in her life she felt as if she were thoroughly acquainted with him. He kept her busy serving him and ministering to his wants. It amused her to do so. She would not permit a servant or one of the children to do anything for him which she might do herself. Her husband noticed, and thought it was the expression of a deep filial attachment which he had never suspected.

The Colonel drank numerous "toddies" during the course of the day, which left him, however, imperturbed. He was an expert at concocting strong drinks. He had even invented some, to which he had given fantastic names, and for whose manufacture he required diverse ingredients that it devolved upon Edna to procure for him.

When Doctor Mandelet dined with the Pontelliers on Thursday he could discern in Mrs. Pontellier no trace of that morbid condition which her husband had reported to him. She was excited and in a manner radiant. She and her father had been to the race course, and their thoughts when they seated themselves at table were still occupied with the events of the afternoon, and their talk was still of the track. The Doctor had not kept pace with turf affairs. He had certain recollections of racing in what he called "the good old times" when the Lecompte stables[5] flourished, and he drew upon this fund of memories so that he might not be left out and seem wholly devoid of the modern spirit. But he failed to impose upon the Colonel, and was even far from impressing him with this trumped-up knowledge of bygone days. Edna had staked her father on his last venture, with the most gratifying results to both of them. Besides, they had met some very charming people, according to the Colonel's impressions. Mrs. Mortimer Merriman and Mrs. James Highcamp, who were there with Alcée Arobin, had joined them and had enlivened the hours in a fashion that warmed him to think of.

Mr. Pontellier himself had no particular leaning toward horse-racing, and was even rather inclined to discourage it as a pastime, especially when he considered the fate of that blue-grass farm in Kentucky. He endeavored, in a general way, to express a particular disapproval, and only succeeded in arousing the ire and opposition of his father-in-law. A pretty dispute followed in which Edna warmly espoused her father's cause and the Doctor remained neutral.

He observed his hostess attentively from under his shaggy brows, and noted a subtle change which had transformed her from the listless woman he had known into a being who, for the moment, seemed palpitant with the forces of life. Her speech was warm and energetic. There was no repression in her glance or gesture. She reminded him of some beautiful, sleek animal waking up in the sun.

The dinner was excellent. The claret was warm and the champagne was cold, and under their beneficent influence the threatened unpleasantness melted and vanished with the fumes of the wine.

Mr. Pontellier warmed up and grew reminiscent. He told some amusing plantation experiences, recollections of old Iberville and his youth, when he hunted 'possum in company with some friendly darky; thrashed the pecan trees, shot the grosbec,[6] and roamed the woods and fields in mischievous idleness.

---

5. New Orleans was a celebrated racing center before the Civil War, boasting four race tracks. The Lecompte stables were owned by a famous Creole racing family.

6. Grosbeak, game birds distinguished by their large ("gros") bills.

The Colonel, with little sense of humor and of the fitness of things, related a somber episode of those dark and bitter days, in which he had acted a conspicuous part and always formed a central figure. Nor was the Doctor happier in his selection, when he told the old, ever new and curious story of the waning of a woman's love, seeking strange, new channels, only to return to its legitimate source after days of fierce unrest. It was one of the many little human documents which had been unfolded to him during his long career as a physician. The story did not seem especially to impress Edna. She had one of her own to tell, of a woman who paddled away with her lover one night in a pirogue and never came back. They were lost amid the Baratarian Islands, and no one ever heard of them or found trace of them from that day to this. It was a pure invention. She said that Madame Antoine had related it to her. That, also, was an invention. Perhaps it was a dream she had had. But every glowing word seemed real to those who listened. They could feel the hot breath of the Southern night; they could hear the long sweep of the pirogue through the glistening moonlit water, the beating of birds' wings, rising startled from among the reeds in the salt-water pools; they could see the faces of the lovers, pale, close together, rapt in oblivious forgetfulness, drifting into the unknown.

The champagne was cold, and its subtle fumes played fantastic tricks with Edna's memory that night.

Outside, away from the glow of the fire and the soft lamplight, the night was chill and murky. The Doctor doubled his old-fashioned cloak across his breast as he strode home through the darkness. He knew his fellow-creatures better than most men; knew that inner life which so seldom unfolds itself to unanointed eyes. He was sorry he had accepted Pontellier's invitation. He was growing old, and beginning to need rest and an imperturbed spirit. He did not want the secrets of other lives thrust upon him.

"I hope it isn't Arobin," he muttered to himself as he walked. "I hope to heaven it isn't Alcée Arobin."

XXIV

E .n1 and her father had a warm, and almost violent dispute upon the subject of her refusal to attend her sister's wedding. Mr. Pontellier declined to interfere, to interpose either his influence or his authority. He was following Doctor Mandelet's advice, and letting her do as she liked. The Colonel reproached his daughter for her lack of filial kindness and respect, her want of sisterly affection and womanly consideration. His arguments were labored and unconvincing. He doubted if Janet would accept any excuse—forgetting that Edna had offered none. He doubted if Janet would ever speak to her again, and he was sure Margaret would not.

Edna was glad to be rid of her father when he finally took himself off with his wedding garments and his bridal gifts, with his padded shoulders, his Bible reading, his "toddies" and ponderous oaths.

Mr. Pontellier followed him closely. He meant to stop at the wedding on his way to New York and endeavor by every means which money and love could devise to atone somewhat for Edna's incomprehensible action.

"You are too lenient, too lenient by far, Léonce,'" asserted the Colonel. "Authority, coercion are what is needed. Put your foot down good and hard; the only way to manage a wife. Take my word for it."

The Colonel was perhaps unaware that he had coerced his own wife into her grave. Mr. Pontellier had a vague suspicion of it which he thought it needless to mention at that late day.

Edna was not so consciously gratified at her husband's leaving home as she had been over the departure of her father. As the day approached when he was to leave her for a comparatively long stay, she grew melting and affectionate, remembering his many acts of consideration and his repeated expressions of an ardent attachment. She was solicitous about his health and his welfare. She bustled around, looking after his clothing, thinking about heavy underwear, quite as Madame Ratignolle would have done under similar circumstances. She cried when he went away, calling him her dear, good friend, and she was quite certain she would grow lonely before very long and go to join him in New York.

But after all, a radiant peace settled upon her when she at last found herself alone. Even the children were gone. Old Madame Pontellier had come herself and carried them off to Iberville with their quadroon. The old madame did not venture to say she was afraid they would be neglected during Léonce's absence; she hardly ventured to think so. She was hungry for them—even a little fierce in her attachment. She did not want them to be wholly "children of the pavement," she always said when begging to have them for a space. She wished them to know the country, with its streams, its fields, its woods, its freedom, so delicious to the young. She wished them to taste something of the life their father had lived and known and loved when he, too, was a little child.

When Edna was at last alone, she breathed a big, genuine sigh of relief. A feeling that was unfamiliar but very delicious came over her. She walked all through the house, from one room to another, as if inspecting it for the first time. She tried the various chairs and lounges, as if she had never sat and reclined upon them before. And she perambulated around the outside of the house, investigating, looking to see if windows and shutters were secure and in order. The flowers were like new acquaintances; she approached them in a familiar spirit, and made herself at home among them. The garden walks were damp, and Edna called to the maid to bring out her rubber sandals. And there she stayed, and stooped, digging around the plants, trimming, picking dead, dry leaves. The children's little dog came out, interfering, getting in her way. She scolded him, laughing at him, played with him. The garden smelled so good and looked so pretty in the afternoon sunlight. Edna plucked all the bright flowers she could find, and went into the house with them, she and the little dog.

Even the kitchen assumed a sudden interesting character which she had never before perceived. She went in to give directions to the cook, to say that the butcher would have to bring much less meat, that they would require only half their usual quantity of bread, of milk and groceries. She told the cook that she herself would be greatly occupied during Mr. Pontellier's alsence, and she begged her to take all thought and responsibility of the larder upon her own shoulders.

That night Edna dined alone. The candelabra, with a few candles in the center of the table, gave all the light she needed. Outside the circle of light in which she sat, the large dining-room looked solemn and shadowy. The cook, placed upon her nettle, served a delicious repast—a luscious tenderloin broiled à point.[7] The wine tasted good; the marron glacé[8] seemed to be just what she wanted. It was so pleasant, too, to dine in a comfortable peignoir.

She thought a little sentimentally about Léonce and the children, and wondered what they were doing. As she gave a dainty scrap or two to the doggie, she talked intimately to him about Etienne and Raoul. He was beside himself with astonishment and. delight over these companionable advances, and showed his appreciation by his little quick, snappy barks and a lively agitation.

Then Edna sat in the library after dinner and read Emerson[9] until she grew sleepy. She realized that she had neglected her reading, and determined to start anew upon a course of improving studies, now that her time was completely her own to do with as she liked.

After a refreshing bath, Edna went to bed. And as she snuggled comfortably beneath the eiderdown a sense of restfulness invaded her, such as she had not known before.

XXV

When the weather was dark and cloudy Edna could not work. She needed the sun to mellow and temper her mood to the sticking point. She had reached a stage when she seemed to be no longer feeling her way, working, when in the humor, with sureness and ease. And being devoid of ambition, and striving not toward accomplishment, she drew satisfaction from the work in itself.

On rainy or melancholy days Edna went out and sought the

---

7. To a turn.
8. Glazed chestnuts.

9. Ralph Waldo Emerson (1803–82), American philosopher, essayist, and poet.

society of the friends she had made at Grand Isle. Or else she
stayed indoors and nursed a mood with which she was becoming
too familiar for her own comfort and peace of mind. It was not
despair; but it seemed to her as if life were passing by, leaving its
promise broken and unfulfilled. Yet there were other days when
she listened, was led on and deceived by fresh promises which her
youth held out to her.

She went again to the races, and again. Alcée Arobin and Mrs.
Highcamp called for her one bright afternoon in Arobin's drag.[1]

Mrs. Highcamp was a worldly but unaffected, intelligent, slim,
tall blonde woman in the forties, with an indifferent manner and
blue eyes that stared. She had a daughter who served her as a pretext for cultivating the society of young men of fashion. Alcée
Arobin was one of them. He was a familiar figure at the race
course, the opera, the fashionable clubs. There was a perpetual
smile in his eyes, which seldom failed to awaken a corresponding
cheerfulness in any one who looked into them and listened to his
good-humored voice. His manner was quiet, and at times a little
insolent. He possessed a good figure, a pleasing face, not overburdened with depth of thought or feeling; and his dress was that
of the conventional man of fashion.

He admired Edna extravagantly, after meeting her at the races
with her father. He had met her before on other occasions, but
she had seemed to him unapproachable until that day. It was at
his instigation that Mrs. Highcamp called to ask her to go with
them to the Jockey Club[2] to witness the turf event of the season.

There were possibly a few track men out there who knew the race
horse as well as Edna, but there was certainly none who knew it
better. She sat between her two companions as one having authority
to speak. She laughed at Arobin's pretensions, and deplored Mrs.
Highcamp's ignorance. The race horse was a friend and intimate
associate of her childhood. The atmosphere of the stables and the
breath of the blue grass paddock revived in her memory and lingered in her nostrils. She did not perceive that she was talking like
her father as the sleek geldings ambled in review before them. She
played for very high stakes, and fortune favored her. The fever of
the game flamed in her cheeks and eyes, and it got into her blood
and into her brain like an intoxicant. People turned their heads to
look at her, and more than one lent an attentive ear to her utterances, hoping thereby to secure the elusive but ever-desired "tip."
Arobin caught the contagion of excitement which drew him to
Edna like a magnet. Mrs. Highcamp remained, as usual, unmoved,
with her indifferent stare and uplifted eyebrows.

Edna stayed and dined with Mrs. Highcamp upon being urged to
do so. Arobin also remained and sent away his drag.

1. Heavy coach drawn by four horses.
2. The New Louisiana Jockey Club, an exclusive social club.

The dinner was quiet and uninteresting, save for the cheerful efforts of Arobin to enliven things. Mrs. Highcamp deplored the absence of her daughter from the races, and tried to convey to her what she had missed by going to the "Dante[3] reading" instead of joining them. The girl held a geranium leaf up to her nose and said nothing, but looked knowing and noncommittal. Mr. Highcamp was a plain, bald-headed man, who only talked under compulsion. He was unresponsive. Mrs. Highcamp was full of delicate courtesy and consideration toward her husband. She addressed most of her conversation to him at table. They sat in the library after dinner and read the evening papers together under the drop-light;[4] while the younger people went into the drawing-room near by and talked. Miss Highcamp played some selections from Grieg[5] upon the piano. She seemed to have apprehended all of the composer's coldness and none of his poetry. While Edna listened she could not help wondering if she had lost her taste for music.

When the time came for her to go home, Mr. Highcamp grunted a lame offer to escort her, looking down at his slippered feet with tactless concern. It was Arobin who took her home. The car ride was long, and it was late when they reached Esplanade Street. Arobin asked permission to enter for a second to light his cigarette—his match safe[6] was empty. He filled his match safe, but did not light his cigarette until he left her, after she had expressed her willingness to go to the races with him again.

Edna was neither tired nor sleepy. She was hungry again, for the Highcamp dinner, though of excellent quality, had lacked abundance. She rummaged in the larder and brought forth a slice of "Gruyère"[7] and some crackers. She opened a bottle of beer which she found in the ice-box. Edna felt extremely restless and excited. She vacantly hummed a fantastic tune as she poked at the wood embers on the hearth and munched a cracker.

She wanted something to happen—something, anything; she did not know what. She regretted that she had not made Arobin stay a half hour to talk over the horses with her. She counted the money she had won. But there was nothing else to do, so she went to bed, and tossed there for hours in a sort of monotonous agitation.

In the middle of the night she remembered that she had forgotten to write her regular letter to her husband; and she decided to do so next day and tell him about her afternoon at the Jockey Club. She lay wide awake composing a letter which was nothing like the one which she wrote the next day. When the maid awoke her in the morning Edna was dreaming of Mr. Highcamp playing the

---

3. Dante Alighieri (1265–1321), Italian poet, author of *The Divine Comedy*; her daughter preferred intellectual activities to the social frivolity of racing.
4. Gas lamp which could be lowered for reading.
5. Edvard Grieg (1843–1907), Norwegian composer.
6. Box for friction matches.
7. Cheese originally made in Gruyère, Switzerland.

piano at the entrance of a music store on Canal Street, while his wife was saying to Alcée Arobin, as they boarded an Esplanade Street car:

"What a pity that so much talent has been neglected! but I must go."

When a few days later, Alcée Arobin again called for Edna in his drag, Mrs. Highcamp was not with him. He said they would pick her up. But as the lady had not been apprised of his intention of picking her up, she was not at home. The daughter was just leaving the house to attend the meeting of a branch Folk Lore Society,[8] and regretted that she could not accompany them. Arobin appeared nonplused, and asked Edna if there were any one else she cared to ask.

She did not deem it worthwhile to go in search of any of the fashionable acquaintances from whom she had withdrawn herself. She thought of Madame Ratignolle, but knew that her fair friend did not leave the house, except to take a languid walk around the block with her husband after nightfall. Mademoiselle Reisz would have laughed at such a request from Edna. Madame Lebrun might have enjoyed the outing, but for some reason Edna did not want her. So they went alone, she and Arobin.

The afternoon was intensely interesting to her. The excitement came back upon her like a remittent fever. Her talk grew familiar and confidential. It was no labor to become intimate with Arobin. His manner invited easy confidence. The preliminary stage of becoming acquainted was one which he always endeavored to ignore when a pretty and engaging woman was concerned.

He stayed and dined with Edna. He stayed and sat beside the wood fire. They laughed and talked; and before it was time to go he was telling her how different life might have been if he had known her years before. With ingenuous frankness he spoke of what a wicked, ill-disciplined boy he had been, and impulsively drew up his cuff to exhibit upon his wrist the scar from a saber cut which he had received in a duel outside of Paris when he was nineteen. She touched his hand as she scanned the red cicatrice[9] on the inside of his white wrist. A quick impulse that was somewhat spasmodic impelled her fingers to close in a sort of clutch upon his hand. He felt the pressure of her pointed nails in the flesh of his palm.

She arose hastily and walked toward the mantel.

"The sight of a wound or scar always agitates and sickens me," she said. "I shouldn't have looked at it."

"I beg your pardon," he entreated, following her; "it never occurred to me that it might be repulsive."

He stood close to her, and the effrontery in his eyes repelled the old, vanishing self in her, yet drew all her awakening sensousness.

---

8. The New Orleans Association of the American Folklore Society, founded in 1872 by Alcée Fortier of Tulane University, was very active from 1892 to 1895.
9. Scar.

He saw enough in her face to impel him to take her hand and hold it while he said his lingering good night.

"Will you go to the races again?" he asked.

"No," she said. "I've had enough of the races. I don't want to lose all the money I've won, and I've got to work when the weather is bright, instead of—"

"Yes; work; to be sure. You promised to show me your work. What morning may I come up to your atelier? To-morrow?"

"No!"

"Day after?"

"No, no."

"Oh, please don't refuse me! I know something of such things, I might help you with a stray suggestion or two."

"No. Good night. Why don't you go after you have said good night? I don't like you," she went on in a high, excited pitch, attempting to draw away her hand. She felt that her words lacked dignity and sincerity, and she knew that he felt it.

"I'm sorry you don't like me. I'm sorry I offended you. How have I offended you? What have I done? Can't you forgive me?" And he bent and pressed his lips upon her hand as if he wished never more to withdraw them.

"Mr. Arobin," she complained, "I'm greatly upset by the excitement of the afternoon; I'm not myself. My manner must have misled you in some way. I wish you to go, please." She spoke in a monotonous, dull tone. He took his hat from the table, and stood with eyes turned from her, looking into the dying fire. For a moment or two he kept an impressive silence.

"Your manner has not misled me, Mrs. Pontellier," he said finally. "My own emotions have done that. I couldn't help it. When I'm near you, how could I help it? Don't think anything of it, don't bother, please. You see, I go when you command me. If you wish me to stay away, I shall do so. If you let me come back, I—oh! you will let me come back?"

He cast one appealing glance at her, to which she made no response. Alcée Arobin's manner was so genuine that it often deceived even himself.

Edna did not care or think whether it were genuine or not. When she was alone she looked mechanically at the back of her hand which he had kissed so warmly. Then she leaned her head down on the mantelpiece. She felt somewhat like a woman who in a moment of passion is betrayed into an act of infidelity, and realizes the significance of the act without being wholly awakened from its glamour. The thought was passing vaguely through her mind, "what would he think?"

She did not mean her husband; she was thinking of Robert Lebrun. Her husband seemed to her now like a person whom she had married without love as an excuse.

She lit a candle and went up to her room. Alcée Arobin was absolutely nothing to her. Yet his presence, his manners, the warmth of his glances, and above all the touch of his lips upon her hand had acted like a narcotic upon her.

She slept a languorous sleep, interwoven with vanishing dreams.

XXVI

Alcée Arobin wrote Edna an elaborate note of apology, palpitant with sincerity. It embarrassed her; for in a cooler, quieter moment it appeared to her absurd that she should have taken his action so seriously, so dramatically. She felt sure that the significance of the whole occurrence had lain in her own self-consciousness. If she ignored his note it would give undue importance to a trivial affair. If she replied to it in a serious spirit it would still leave in his mind the impression that she had in a susceptible moment yielded to his influence. After all, it was no great matter to have one's hand kissed. She was provoked at his having written the apology. She answered in as light and bantering a spirit as she fancied it deserved, and said she would be glad to have him look in upon her at work whenever he felt the inclination and his business gave him the opportunity.

He responded at once by presenting himself at her home with all his disarming naïveté. And then there was scarcely a day which followed that she did not see him or was not reminded of him. He was prolific in pretexts. His attitude became one of good-humored subservience and tacit adoration. He was ready at all times to submit to her moods, which were as often kind as they were cold. She grew accustomed to him. They became intimate and friendly by imperceptible degrees, and then by leaps. He sometimes talked in a way that astonished her at first and brought the crimson into her face; in a way that pleased her at last, appealing to the animalism that stirrred impatiently within her.

There was nothing which so quieted the turmoil of Edna's senses as a visit to Mademoiselle Reisz. It was then, in the presence of that personality which was offensive to her, that the woman, by her divine art, seemed to reach Edna's spirit and set it free.

It was misty, with heavy, lowering atmosphere, one afternoon, when Edna climbed the stairs to the pianist's apartments under the roof. Her clothes were dripping with moisture. She felt chilled and pinched as she entered the room. Mademoiselle was poking at a rusty stove that smoked a little and warmed the room indifferently. She was endeavoring to heat a pot of chocolate on the stove. The room looked cheerless and dingy to Edna as she entered. A bust of Beethoven, covered with a hood of dust, scowled at her from the mantelpiece.

"Ah! here comes the sunlight!" exclaimed Mademoiselle, rising from her knees before the stove. "Now it will be warm and bright enough; I can let the fire alone."

She closed the stove door with a bang, and approaching assisted in removing Edna's dripping mackintosh.

"You are cold; you look miserable. The chocolate will soon be hot. But would you rather have a taste of brandy? I have scarcely touched the bottle which you brought me for my cold." A piece of red flannel was wrapped around Mademoiselle's throat; a stiff neck compelled her to hold her head on one side.

"I will take some brandy," said Edna, shivering as she removed her gloves and overshoes. She drank the liquor from the glass as a man would have done. Then flinging herself upon the uncomfortable sofa she said, "Mademoiselle, I am going to move away from my house on Esplanade Street."

"Ah!" ejaculated the musician, neither surprised nor especially interested. Nothing ever seemed to astonish her very much. She was endeavoring to adjust the bunch of violets which had become loose from its fastening in her hair. Edna drew her down upon the sofa and taking a pin from her own hair, secured the shabby artificial flowers in their accustomed place.

"Aren't you astonished?"

"Passably. Where are you going? To New York? to Iberville? to your father in Mississippi? where?"

"Just two steps away," laughed Edna, "in a little four-room house around the corner. It looks so cozy, so inviting and restful, whenever I pass by; and it's for rent. I'm tired looking after that big house. It never seemed like mine, anyway—like home. It's too much trouble. I have to keep too many servants. I am tired bothering with them."

"That is not your true reason, *ma belle*. There is no use in telling me lies. I don't know your reason, but you have not told me the truth." Edna did not protest or endeavor to justify herself.

"The house, the money that provides for it, are not mine. Isn't that enough reason?"

"They are your husband's," returned Mademoiselle, with a shrug and a malicious elevation of the eyebrows.

"Oh! I see there is no deceiving you. Then let me tell you: it is a caprice. I have a little money of my own from my mother's estate, which my father sends me by driblets. I won a large sum this winter on the races, and I am beginning to sell my sketches. Laidpore is more and more pleased with my work; he says it grows in force and individuality. I cannot judge of that myself, but I feel that I have gained in ease and confidence. However, as I said, I have sold a good many through Laidpore. I can live in the tiny house for little or nothing, with one servant. Old Celestine, who works occasionally for me, says she will come stay with me and do my work. I know I shall like it, like the feeling of freedom and independence.

"What does your husband say?"

"I have not told him yet. I only thought of it this morning. He will think I am demented, no doubt. Perhaps you think so."

Mademoiselle shook her head slowly. "Your reason is not yet clear to me," she said.

Neither was it quite clear to Edna herself; but it unfolded itself as she sat for a while in silence. Instinct had prompted her to put away her husband's bounty in casting off her allegiance. She did not know how it would be when he returned. There would have to be an understanding, an explanation. Conditions would some way adjust themselves, she felt, but whatever came, she had resolved never again to belong to another than herself.

"I shall give a grand dinner before I leave the old house!" Edna exclaimed. "You will have to come to it, Mademoiselle. I will give you everything that you like to eat and to drink. We shall sing and laugh and be merry for once." And she uttered a sigh that came from the very depth of her being.

If Mademoiselle happened to have received a letter from Robert during the interval of Edna's visits, she would give her the letter unsolicited. And she would seat herself at the piano and play as her humor prompted her while the young woman read the letter.

The little stove was roaring; it was red-hot, and the chocolate in the tin sizzled and sputtered. Edna went forward and opened the stove door, and Mademoiselle rising took a letter from under the bust of Beethoven and handed it to Edna.

"Another! so soon!" she exclaimed, her eyes filled with delight. "Tell me, Mademoiselle, does he know that I see his letters?"

"Never in the world! He would be angry and would never write to me again if he thought so. Does he write to you? Never a line. Does he send you a message? Never a word. It is because he loves you, poor fool, and is trying to forget you, since you are not free to listen to him or to belong to him."

"Why do you show me his letters, then?"

"Haven't you begged for them? Can I refuse you anything? Oh! you cannot deceive me," and Mademoiselle approached her beloved instrument and began to play. Edna did not at once read the letter. She sat holding it in her hand, while the music penetrated her whole being like an effulgence, warming and brightening the dark places of her soul. It prepared her for joy and exultation.

"Oh!" she exclaimed, letting the letter fall to the floor. "Why did you not tell me?" She went and grasped Mademoiselle's hands up from the keys. "Oh! unkind! malicious! Why did you not tell me?"

"That he was coming back? No great news, *ma foi.*[1] I wonder he did not come long ago."

---

1. "In fact."

"But when, when?" cried Edna, impatiently. "He does not say when."

"He says 'very soon.' You know as much about it as I do, it is all in the letter."

"But why? Why is he coming? Oh, if I thought—" and she snatched the letters from the floor and turned the pages this way and that way, looking for the reason, which was left untold.

"If I were young and in love with a man," said Mademoiselle, turning on the stool and pressing her wiry hands between her knees as she looked down at Edna, who sat on the floor holding the letter, "it seems to me he would have to be some *grand esprit*,[2] a man with lofty aims and ability to reach them; one who stood high enough to attract the notice of his fellow-men. It seems to me if I were young and in love I should never deem a man of ordinary caliber worthy of my devotion."

"Now it is you who are telling lies and seeking to deceive me, Mademoiselle; or else you have never been in love, and know nothing about it. Why," went on Edna, clasping her knees and looking up into Mademoiselle's twisted face, "do you suppose a woman knows why she loves? Does she select? Does she say to herself: 'Go to! Here is a distinguished statesman with presidential possibilities; I shall proceed to fall in love with him.' Or, 'I shall set my heart upon this musician, whose fame is on every tongue?' Or, 'This financier, who controls the world's money markets?'"

"You are purposely misunderstanding me, *ma reine*.[3] Are you in love with Robert?"

"Yes," said Edna. It was the first time she had admitted it, and a glow overspread her face, blotching it with red spots.

"Why?" asked her companion. "Why do you love him when you ought not to?"

Edna, with a motion or two, dragged herself on her knees before Mademoiselle Reisz, who took the glowing face between her two hands.

"Why? Because his hair is brown and grows away from his temples; because he opens and shuts his eyes, and his nose is a little out of drawing; because he has two lips and a square chin, and a little finger which he can't straighten from having played baseball too energetically in his youth. Because—"

"Because you do, in short," laughed Mademoiselle. "What will you do when he comes back?" she asked.

"Do? Nothing, except feel glad and happy to be alive."

She was already glad and happy to be alive at the mere thought of his return. The murky, lowering sky, which had depressed her a few hours before, seemed bracing and invigorating as she splashed through the streets on her way home.

She stopped at a confectioner's and ordered a huge box of bon-

2. Literally, "grand spirit"; noble soul. 3. "My queen."

bons for the children in Iberville. She slipped a card in the box, on which she scribbled a tender message and sent an abundance of kisses.

Before dinner in the evening Edna wrote a charming letter to her husband, telling him of her intention to move for a while into the little house around the block, and to give a farewell dinner before leaving, regretting that he was not there to share it, to help her out with the menu and assist her in entertaining the guests. Her letter was brilliant and brimming with cheerfulness.

XXVII

"What is the matter with you?" asked Arobin that evening. "I never found you in such a happy mood." Edna was tired by that time, and was reclining on the lounge before the fire.

"Don't you know the weather prophet has told us we shall see the sun pretty soon?"

"Well, that ought to be reason enough," he acquiesced. "You wouldn't give me another if I sat here all right imploring you." He sat close to her on a low tabouret,[4] and as he spoke his fingers lightly touched the hair that fell a little over her forehead. She liked the touch of his fingers through her hair, and closed her eyes sensitively.

"One of these days," she said, "I'm going to pull myself together for a while and think—try to determine what character of a woman I am; for, candidly, I don't know. By all the codes which I am acquainted with, I am a devilishly wicked specimen of the sex. But some way I can't convince myself that I am. I must think about it."

"Don't. What's the use? Why should you bother thinking about it when I can tell you what manner of woman you are." His fingers strayed occasionally down to her warm, smooth cheeks and firm chin, which was growing a little full and double.

"Oh, yes! You will tell me that I am adorable; everything that is captivating. Spare yourself the effort."

"No; I shan't tell you anything of the sort, though I shouldn't be lying if I did."

"Do you know Mademoiselle Reisz?" she asked irrelevantly.

"The pianist? I know her by sight. I've heard her play."

"She says queer things sometimes in a bantering way that you don't notice at the time and you feel yourself thinking about afterward."

"For instance?"

"Well, for instance, when I left her today, she put her arms around me and felt my shoulder blades, to see if my wings were strong, she said. 'The bird that would soar above the level plain of tradition and prejudice must have strong wings. It is a sad spectacle

4. Cylindrical seat or stool without arms or back.

to see the weaklings bruised, exhausted, fluttering back to earth.'"

"Whither would you soar?"

"I'm not thinking of any extraordinary flights. I only half comprehend her."

"I've heard she's partially demented," said Arobin.

"She seems to me wonderfully sane," Edna replied.

"I'm told she's extremely disagreeable and unpleasant. Why have you introduced her at a moment when I desired to talk of you?"

"Oh! talk of me if you like," cried Edna, clasping her hands beneath her head; "but let me think of something else while you do."

"I'm jealous of your thoughts to-night. They're making you a little kinder than usual; but some way I feel as if they were wandering, as if they were not here with me." She only looked at him and smiled. His eyes were very near. He leaned upon the lounge with an arm extended across her, while the other hand still rested upon her hair. They continued silently to look into each other's eyes. When he leaned forward and kissed her, she clasped his head, holding his lips to hers.

It was the first kiss of her life to which her nature had really responded. It was a flaming torch that kindled desire.

XXVIII

Edna cried a little that night after Arobin left her. It was only one phase of the multitudinous emotions which had assailed her. There was with her an overwhelming feeling of irresponsibility. There was the shock of the unexpected and the unaccustomed. There was her husband's reproach looking at her from external existence. There was Robert's reproach making itself felt by a quicker, fiercer, more overpowering love, which had awakened within her toward him. Above all, there was understanding. She felt as if a mist had been lifted from her eyes, enabling her to look upon and comprehend the significance of life, that monster made up of beauty and brutality. But among the conflicting sensations which assailed her, there was neither shame nor remorse. There was a dull pang of regret because it was not the kiss of love which had inflamed her, because it was not love which had held this cup of life to her lips.

XXIX

Without even waiting for an answer from her husband regarding his opinion or wishes in the matter, Edna hastened her preparations for quitting her home on Esplanade Street and moving into the little house around the block. A feverish anxiety attended her every action in that direction. There was no moment of deliberation, no interval of repose between the thought and its fulfillment. Early upon the morning following those hours passed in Arobin's society, Edna set about securing her new abode and hurrying her arrangements for occupying it. Within the precincts of her home she felt like one who has entered and lingered within the portals of some forbidden temple in which a thousand muffled voices bade her begone.

Whatever was her own in the house, everything which she had acquired aside from her husband's bounty, she caused to be transported to the other house, supplying simple and meager deficiencies from her own resources.

Arobin found her with rolled sleeves, working in company with the house-maid when he looked in during the afternoon. She was splendid and robust, and had never appeared handsomer than in the old blue gown, with a red silk handkerchief knotted at random around her head to protect her hair from the dust. She was mounted upon a high step-ladder, unhooking a picture from the wall when he entered. He had found the front door open, and had followed his ring by walking in unceremoniously.

"Come down!" he said. "Do you want kill yourself?" She greeted him with affected carelessness, and appeared absorbed in her occupation.

If he had expected to find her languishing, reproachful, or indulging in sentimental tears, he must have been greatly surprised.

He was no doubt prepared for any emergency, ready for any one of the foregoing attitudes, just as he bent himself easily and naturally to the situation which confronted him.

"Please come down," he insisted, holding the ladder and looking up at her.

"No," she answered; "Ellen is afraid to mount the ladder. Joe is working at the 'pigeon house'—that's the name Ellen gives it, because it's so small and looks like a pigeon house[5]—and some one has to do this."

Arobin pulled off his coat, and expressed himself ready and willing to tempt fate in her place. Ellen brought him one of her dustcaps, and went into contortions of mirth, which she found it impossible to control, when she saw him put it on before the mirror as grotesquely as he could. Edna herself could not refrain from smiling when she fastened it at his request. So it was he who in turn mounted the ladder, unhooking pictures and curtains, and dislodging ornaments as Edna directed. When he had finished he took off his dustcap and went out to wash his hands.

Edna was sitting on the tabouret, idly brushing the tips of a feather duster along the carpet when he came in again.

"Is there anything more you will let me do?" he asked.

"That is all," she answered. "Ellen can manage the rest." She kept the young woman occupied in the drawing-room, unwilling to be left alone with Arobin.

---

5. A house for domesticated birds kept for show or sport.

"What about the dinner?" he asked; "the grand event, the *coup
d'état?*"

"It will be day after to-morrow. Why do you call it the '*coup
d'état?*' Oh! it will be very fine; all my best of everything—crystal,
silver and gold. Sèvres, flowers, music, and champagne to swim in. I'll
let Léonce pay the bills. I wonder what he'll say when he sees the
bills."

"And you ask me why I call it a *coup d'état?*" Arobin had put
on his coat, and he stood before her and asked if his cravat was
plumb. She told him it was, looking no higher than the tip of his
collar.

"When do you go to the 'pigeon house?'—with all due acknowledgment to Ellen."

"Day after to-morrow, after the dinner. I shall sleep there."

"Ellen, will you very kindly get me a glass of water?" asked
Arobin. "The dust in the curtains, if you will pardon me for hinting
such a thing, has parched my throat to a crisp."

"While Ellen gets the water," said Edna, rising, "I will say
good-by and let you go. I must get rid of this grime, and I have a
million things to do and think of."

"When shall I see you? " asked Arobin, seeking to detain her,
the maid having left the room.

"At the dinner, of course. You are invited."

"Not before?—not to-night or to-morrow morning or to-morrow
noon or night? or the day after morning or noon? Can't you see
yourself, without my telling you, what an eternity it is?"

He had followed her into the hall and to the foot of the stairway,
looking up at her as she mounted with her face half turned to him.

"Not an instant sooner," she said. But she laughed and looked at
him with eyes that at once gave him courage to wait and made it
torture to wait.

XXX

Though Edna had spoken of the dinner as a very grand affair, it
was in truth a very small affair and very select, in so much as the
invited were few and were selected with discrimination. She had
counted upon an even dozen seating themselves at her round
mahogany board, forgetting for the moment that Madame Ratignolle was to the last degree *souffrante*[6] and unpresentable, and not
foreseeing that Madame Lebrun would send a thousand regrets at
the last moment. So there were only ten, after all, which made a
cozy, comfortable number.

There were Mr. and Mrs. Merriman, a pretty vivacious little
woman in the thirties; her husband, a jovial fellow, something
of a shallow-pate, who laughed a good deal at other people's

6. III.

witticisms, and had thereby made himself extremely popular. Mrs. Highcamp had accompanied them. Of course, there was Alcée Arobin; and Mademoiselle Reisz had consented to come. Edna had sent her a fresh bunch of violets with black lace trimmings for her hair. Monsieur Ratignolle brought himself and his wife's excuses. Victor Lebrun, who happened to be in the city, bent upon relaxation, had accepted with alacrity. There was a Miss Mayblunt, no longer in her teens, who looked at the world through lorgnettes and with the keenest interest. It was thought and said that she was intellectual; it was suspected of her that she wrote under a *nom de guerre*.[7] She had come with a gentleman by the name of Gouvernail, connected with one of the daily papers, of whom nothing special could be said, except that he was observant and seemed quiet and inoffensive. Edna herself made the tenth, and at half-past eight they seated themselves at table, Arobin and Monsieur Ratignolle on either side of their hostess.

Mrs. Highcamp sat between Arobin and Victor Lebrun. Then came Mrs. Merriman, Mr. Gouvernail, Miss Mayblunt, Mr. Merriman, and Mademoiselle Reisz next to Monsieur Ratignolle.

There was something extremely gorgeous about the appearance of the table, an effect of splendor conveyed by a cover of pale yellow satin under strips of lace-work. There were wax candles in massive brass candelabra, burning softly under yellow silk shades; full, fragrant roses, yellow and red, abounded. There were silver and gold, as she had said there would be, and crystal which glittered like the gems which the women wore.

The ordinary stiff dining chairs had been discarded for the occasion and replaced by the most commodious and luxurious which could be collected throughout the house. Mademoiselle Reisz, being exceedingly diminutive, was elevated upon cushions, as small children are sometimes hoisted at table upon bulky volumes.

"Something new, Edna?" exclaimed Miss Mayblunt, with lorgnette directed toward a magnificent cluster of diamonds that sparkled, that almost sputtered, in Edna's hair, just over the center of her forehead.

"Quite new; 'brand' new, in fact; a present from my husband. It arrived this morning from New York. I may as well admit that this is my birthday, and that I am twenty-nine. In good time I expect you to drink my health. Meanwhile, I shall ask you to begin with this cocktail, composed—would you say 'composed?' " with an appeal to Miss Mayblunt—"composed by my father in honor of Sister Janet's wedding."

Before each guest stood a tiny glass that looked and sparkled like a garnet gem.

"Then, all things considered," spoke Arobin, "it might not be

---

7. Pseudonym.

amiss to start out by drinking the Colonel's health in the cocktail which he composed, on the birthday of the most charming of women—the daughter whom he invented."

Mr. Merriman's laugh at this sally was such a genuine outburst and so contagious that it started the dinner with an agreeable swing that never slackened.

Miss Mayblunt begged to be allowed to keep her cocktail untouched before her, just to look at. The color was marvelous! She could compare it to nothing she had ever seen, and the garnet lights which it emitted were unspeakably rare. She pronounced the Colonel an artist, and stuck to it.

Monsieur Ratignolle was prepared to take things seriously; the *mets*, and *entre-mets*,[8] the service, the decorations, even the people. He looked up from his pompono[9] and inquired of Arobin if he were related to the gentleman of that name who formed one of the firm of Laitner and Arobin, lawyers. The young man admitted that Laitner was a warm personal friend, who permitted Arobin's name to decorate the firm's letterheads and to appear upon a shingle that graced Perdido Street.

"There are so many inquisitive people and institutions abounding," said Arobin, "that one is really forced as a matter of convenience these days to assume the virtue of an occupation if he has it not."

Monsieur Ratignolle stared a little, and turned to ask Mademoiselle Reisz if she considered the symphony concerts up to the standard which had been set the previous winter. Mademoiselle Reisz answered Monseiur Ratignolle in French, which Edna thought a little rude, under the circumstances, but characteristic. Mademoiselle had only disagreeable things to say of the symphony concerts, and insulting remarks to make of all the musicians of New Orleans, singly and collectively. All her interest seemed to be centered upon the delicacies placed before her.

Mr. Merriman said that Mr. Arobin's remark about inquisitive people reminded him of a man from Waco[1] the other day at the St. Charles Hotel—but as Mr. Merriman's stories were always lame and lacking point, his wife seldom permitted him to complete them. She interrupted him to ask if he remembered the name of the author whose book she had bought the week before to send to a friend in Geneva. She was talking "books" with Mr. Gouvernail and trying to draw from him his opinion upon current literary topics. Her husband told the story of the Waco man privately to Miss Mayblunt, who pretended to be greatly amused and to think it extremely clever.

Mrs. Highcamp hung with languid but unaffected interest upon the warm and impetuous volubility of her left-hand neighbor. Victor Lebrun. Her attention was never for a moment withdrawn

8. Main course and side dishes.
9. Pompano, fish of the southern Atlan-

tic and Gulf coasts of North America.
1. A town in Texas.

from him after seating herself at table; and when he turned to Mrs. Merriman, who was prettier and more vivacious than Mrs. High-camp, she waited with easy indifference for an opportunity to reclaim his attention. There was the occasional sound of music, of mandolins, sufficiently removed to be an agreeable accompaniment rather than an interruption to the conversation. Outside the soft, monotonous splash of a fountain could be heard; the sound pene-trated into the room wiith the heavy odor of jessamine that came through the open windows.

The golden shimmer of Edna's satin gown spread in rich folds on either side of her. There was a soft fall of lace encircling her shoulders. It was the color of her skin, without the glow, the myriad living tints that one may sometimes discover in vibrant flesh. There was something in her attitude, in her whole appear-ance when she leaned her head against the high-backed chair and spread her arms, which suggested the regal woman, the one who rules, who looks on, who stands alone.

But as she sat there amid her guests, she felt the old ennui over-taking her; the hopelessness which so often assailed her, which came upon her like an obsession, like something extraneous, independent of volition. It was something which announced itself; a chill breath that seemed to issue from some vast cavern wherein discords wailed. There came over her the acute longing which always summoned into her spiritual vision the presence of the beloved one, overpower-ing her at once with a sense of the unattainable.

The moments glided on, while a feeling of good fellowship passed around the circle like a mystic cord, holding and binding these people together with jest and laughter. Monsieur Ratignolle was the first to break the pleasant charm. At ten o'clock he excused himself. Madame Ratignolle was waiting for him at home. She was *bien souffrante*,[2] and she was filled with vague dread, which only her husband's presence could allay.

Mademoiselle Reisz arose with Monsieur Ratignolle, who offered to escort her to the car. She had eaten well; she had tasted the good rich wines, and they must have turned her head, for she bowed pleasantly to all as she withdrew from table. She kissed Edna upon the shoulder, and whispered: *"Bonne nuit, ma reine; soyez sage."*[3] She had been a little bewildered upon rising, or rather, descending from her cushions, and Monsieur Ratignolle gallantly took her arm and led her away.

Mrs. Highcamp was weaving a garland of roses, yellow and red. When she had finished the garland, she laid it lightly upon Victor's black curls. He was reclining far back in the luxurious chair, hold-ing a glass of champagne to the light.

As if a magician's wand had touched him, the garland of roses transformed him into a vision of Oriental beauty. His cheeks were

2. Very ill.　　　　3. "Good night, my love; be good."

the color of crushed grapes, and his dusky eyes glowed with a languishing fire.

"*Sapristi!*" exclaimed Arobin.

But Mrs. Highcamp had one more touch to add to the picture. She took from the back of her chair a white silken scarf, with which she had covered her shoulders in the early part of the evening. She draped it across the boy in graceful folds, and in a way to conceal his black, conventional evening dress. He did not seem to mind what she did to him, only smiled, showing a faint gleam of white teeth, while he continued to gaze with narrowing eyes at the light through his glass of champagne.

"Oh! to be able to paint in color rather than in words!" exclaimed Miss Mayblunt, losing herself in a rhapsodic dream as she looked at him.

" 'There was a graven image of Desire
Painted with red blood on a ground of gold.' "[4]
murmured Gouvernail, under his breath.

The effect of the wine upon Victor was, to change his accustomed volubility into silence. He seemed to have abandoned himself to a reverie, and to be seeing pleasing visions in the amber bead.

"Sing," entreated Mrs. Highcamp. "Won't you sing to us?"

"Let him alone," said Arobin.

"He's posing," offered Mr. Merriman; "let him have it out."

"I believe he's paralyzed," laughed Mrs. Merriman. And leaning over the youth's chair, she took the glass from his hand and held it to his lips. He sipped the wine slowly, and when he had drained the glass she laid it upon the table and wiped his lips with her little filmy handkerchief.

"Yes, I'll sing for you," he said, turning in his chair toward Mrs. Highcamp. He clasped his hands behind his head, and looking up at the ceiling began to hum a little, trying his voice like a musician tuning an instrument. Then, looking at Edna, he began to sing:
"Ah! si tu savais!"

"Stop!" she cried, "don't sing that. I don't want you to sing it," and she laid her glass so impetuously and blindly upon the table as to shatter it against a caraffe. The wine spilled over Arobin's legs and some of it trickled down upon Mrs. Highcamp's black gauze gown. Victor had lost all idea of courtesy, or else he thought his hostess was not in earnest, for he laughed and went on:
"Ah! si tu savais
Ce que tes yeux me disent"—

"Oh! you mustn't! you mustn't," exclaimed Edna, and pushing back her chair she got up, and going behind him placed her hand over his mouth. He kissed the soft palm that pressed upon his lips.

"No, no, I won't, Mrs. Pontellier. I didn't know you meant it,"

4. Lines from the sonnet *A Cameo*, by A. C. Swinburne (1837–1909).

looking up at her with caressing eyes. The touch of his lips was like a pleasing sting to her hand. She lifted the garland of roses from his head and flung it across the room.

"Come, Victor; you've posed long enough. Give Mrs. Highcamp her scarf."

Mrs. Highcamp undraped the scarf from about him with her own hands. Miss Mayblunt and Mr. Gouvernail suddenly conceived the notion that it was time to say good night. And Mr. and Mrs. Merriman wondered how it could be so late.

Before parting from Victor, Mrs. Highcamp invited him to call upon her daughter, who she knew would be charmed to meet him and talk French and sing French songs with him. Victor expressed his desire and intention to call upon Miss Highcamp at the first opportunity which presented itself. He asked if Arobin were going his way. Arobin was not.

The mandolin players had long since stolen away. A profound stillness had fallen upon the broad, beautiful street. The voices of Edna's disbanding guests jarred like a discordant note upon the quiet harmony of the night.

XXXI

"Well?" questioned Arobin, who had remained with Edna after the others had departed.

"Well," she reiterated, and stood up, stretching her arms, and feeling the need to relax her muscles after having been so long seated.

"What next?" he asked.

"The servants are all gone. They left when the musicians did. I have dismissed them. The house has to be closed and locked, and I shall trot around to the pigeon house, and shall send Celestine over in the morning to straighten things up."

He looked around, and began to turn out some of the lights.

"What about upstairs?" he inquired.

"I think it is all right; but there may be a window or two unlatched. We had better look; you might take a candle and see. And bring me my wrap and hat on the foot of the bed in the middle room."

He went up with the light, and Edna began closing doors and windows. She hated to shut in the smoke and the fumes of the wine. Arobin found her cape and hat, which he brought down and helped her to put on.

When everything was secured and the lights put out, they left through the front door, Arobin locking it and taking the key, which he carried for Edna. He helped her down the steps.

"Will you have a spray of jessamine?" he asked, breaking off a few blossoms as he passed.

"No; I don't want anything."

She seemed disheartened, and had nothing to say. She took his arm, which he offered her, holding up the weight of her satin train with the other hand. She looked down, noticing the black line of his leg moving in and out so close to her against the yellow shimmer of her gown. There was the whistle of a railway train somewhere in the distance, and the midnight bells were ringing. They met no one in their short walk.

The "pigeon-house" stood behind a locked gate, and a shallow *parterre*[5] that had been somewhat neglected. There was a small front porch, upon which a long window and the front door opened. The door opened directly into the parlor; there was no side entry. Back in the yard was a room for servants, in which old Celestine had been ensconced.

Edna had left a lamp burning low upon the table. She had succeeded in making the room look habitable and homelike. There were some books on the table and a lounge near at hand. On the floor was a fresh matting, covered with a rug or two; and on the walls hung a few tasteful pictures. But the room was filled with flowers. These were a surprise to her. Arobin had sent them, and had had Celestine distribute them during Edna's absence. Her bedroom was adjoining, and across a small passage were the dining-room and kitchen.

Edna seated herself with every appearance of discomfort.

"Are you tired?" he asked.

"Yes, and chilled and miserable. I feel as if I had been wound up to a certain pitch—too tight—and something inside of me had snapped." She rested her head against the table upon her bare arm.

"You want to rest," he said, "and to be quiet. I'll go; I'll leave you and let you rest."

"Yes," she replied.

He stood up beside her and smoothed her hair with his soft magnetic hand. His touch conveyed to her a certain physical comfort. She could have fallen quietly asleep there if he had continued to pass his hand over her hair. He brushed the hair upward from the nape of her neck.

"I hope you will feel better and happier in the morning," he said. "You have tried to do too much in the past few days. The dinner was the last straw; you might have dispensed with it."

"Yes," she admitted; "it was stupid."

"No, it was delightful; but it has worn you out." His hand had strayed to her beautiful shoulders, and he could feel the response of her flesh to his touch. He seated himself beside her and kissed her lightly upon the shoulder.

"I thought you were going away," she said, in an uneven voice.

"I am, after I have said good night."

"Good night," she murmured.

5. Garden.

He did not answer, except to continue to caress her. He did not say good night until she had become supple to his gentle, seductive entreaties.

XXXII

When Mr. Pontellier learned of his wife's intention to abandon her home and take up her residence elsewhere, he immediately wrote her a letter of unqualified disapproval and remonstrance. She had given reasons which he was unwilling to acknowledge as adequate. He hoped she had not acted upon her rash impulse; and he begged her to consider first, foremost, and above all else, what people would say. He was not dreaming of scandal when he uttered this warning; that was a thing which would never have entered into his mind to consider in connection with his wife's name or his own. He was simply thinking of his financial integrity. It might get noised about that the Pontelliers had met with reverses, and were forced to conduct their *ménage*[6] on a humbler scale than heretofore. It might do incalculable mischief to his business prospects.

But remembering Edna's whimsical turn of mind of late, and foreseeing that she had immediately acted upon her impetuous determination, he grasped the situation with his usual promptness and handled it with his well-known business tact and cleverness.

The same mail which brought to Edna his letter of disapproval carried instructions—the most minute instructions—to a well-known architect concerning the remodeling of his home, changes which he had long contemplated, and which he desired carried forward during his temporary absence.

Expert and reliable packers and movers were engaged to convey the furniture, carpets, pictures—everything movable, in short—to places of security. And in an incredibly short time the Pontellier house was turned over to the artisans. There was to be an addition —a small snuggery; there was to be frescoing, and hardwood flooring was to be put into such rooms as had not yet been subjected to this improvement.

Furthermore, in one of the daily papers appeared a brief notice to the effect that Mr. and Mrs. Pontellier were contemplating a summer sojourn abroad, and that their handsome residence on Esplanade Street was undergoing sumptuous alterations, and would not be ready for occupancy until their return. Mr. Pontellier had saved appearances!

Edna admired the skill of his maneuver, and avoided any occasion to balk his intentions. When the situation as set forth by Mr. Pontellier was accepted and taken for granted, she was apparently satisfied that it should be so.

The pigeon-house pleased her. It at once assumed the intimate character of a home, while she herself invested it with a charm

6. Household.

which it reflected like a warm glow. There was with her a feeling of
having descended in the social scale, with a corresponding sense of
having risen in the spiritual. Every step which she took toward
relieving herself from obligations added to her strength and expansion as an individual. She began to look with her own eyes; to see
and to apprehend the deeper undercurrents of life. No longer was
she content to "feed upon opinion" when her own soul had invited
her.

After a little while, a few days, in fact, Edna went up and spent a
week with her children in Iberville. They were delicious February
days, with all the summer's promises hovering in the air.

How glad she was to see the children! She wept for very pleasure
when she felt their little arms clasping her; their hard, ruddy cheeks
pressed against her own glowing cheeks. She looked into their faces
with hungry eyes that could not be satisfied with looking. And what
stories they had to tell their mother! About the pigs, the cows, the
mules! About riding to the mill behind Gluglu; fishing back in the
lake with their Uncle Jasper; picking pecans with Lidie's little black
brood, and hauling chips in their express wagon. It was a thousand
times more fun to haul real chips for old lame Susie's real fire than
to drag painted blocks along the banquette on Esplanade Street!

She went with them herself to see the pigs and the cows, to look
at the darkies laying the cane, to thrash the pecan trees, and catch
fish in the back lake. She lived with them a whole week long, giving
them all of herself, and gathering and filling herself with their young
existence. They listened, breathless, when she told them the house
in Esplanade Street was crowded with workmen, hammering, nailing,
sawing, and filling the place with clatter. They wanted to know
where their bed was; what had been done with their rocking-horse;
and where did Joe sleep, and where had Ellen gone, and the cook?
But, above all, they were fired with a desire to see the little house
around the block. Was there any place to play? Were there any boys
next door? Raoul, with pessimistic foreboding, was convinced that
there were only girls next door. Where would they sleep, and where
would papa sleep? She told them the fairies would fix it all right.

The old Madame was charmed with Edna's visit, and showered
all manner of delicate attentions upon her. She was delighted to
know that the Esplanade Street house was in a dismantled condition. It gave her the promise and pretext to keep the children indefinitely.

It was with a wrench and a pang that Edna left her children.
She carried away with her the sound of their voices and the touch
of their cheeks. All along the journey homeward their presence lingered with her like the memory of a delicious song. But by the
time she had regained the city the song no longer echoed in her
soul. She was again alone.

XXXIII

It happened sometimes when Edna went to see Mademoiselle Reisz that the little musician was absent, giving a lesson or making some small necessary household purchase. The key was always left in a secret hiding-place in the entry, which Edna knew. If Mademoiselle happened to be away, Edna would usually enter and wait for her return.

When she knocked at Mademoiselle Reisz's door one afternoon there was no response; so unlocking the door, as usual, she entered and found the apartment deserted, as she had expected. Her day had been quite filled up, and it was for a rest, for a refuge, and to talk about Robert, that she sought out her friend.

She had worked at her canvas—a young Italian character study —all the morning, completing the work without the model; but there had been many interruptions, some incident to her modest housekeeping, and others of a social nature.

Madame Ratignolle had dragged herself over, avoiding the too public thoroughfares, she said. She complained that Edna had neglected her much of late. Besides, she was consumed with curiosity to see the little house and the manner in which it was conducted. She wanted to hear all about the dinner party; Monsieur Ratignolle had left *so* early. What had happened after he left? The champagne and grapes which Edna sent over were *too* delicious. She had so little appetite; they had refreshed and toned her stomach. Where on earth was she going to put Mr. Pontellier in that little house, and the boys? And then she made Edna promise to go to her when her hour of trial overtook her.

"At any time—any time of the day or night, dear," Edna assured her.

Before leaving Madame Ratignolle said:

"In some way you seem to me like a child, Edna. You seem to act without a certain amount of reflection which is necessary in this life. That is the reason I want to say you mustn't mind if I advise you to be a little careful while you are living here alone. Why don't you have some one come and stay with you? Wouldn't Mademoiselle Reisz come?"

"No; she wouldn't wish to come, and I shouldn't want her always with me."

"Well, the reason—you know how evil-minded the world is— some one was talking of Alcée Arobin visiting you. Of course, it wouldn't matter if Mr. Arobin had not such a dreadful reputation. Monsieur Ratignolle was telling me that his attentions alone are considered enough to ruin a woman's name."

"Does he boast of his successes?" asked Edna, indifferently, squinting at her picture.

"No, I think not. I believe he is a decent fellow as far as that goes. But his character is so well known among the men. I shan't be able to come back and see you; it was very, very imprudent today."

"Mind the step!" cried Edna.

"Don't neglect me," entreated Madame Ratignolle; "and don't mind what I said about Arobin, or having some one to stay with you."

"Of course not," Edna laughed. "You may say anything you like to me." They kissed each other good-bye. Madame Ratignolle had not far to go, and Edna stood on the porch a while watching her walk down the street.

Then in the afternoon Mrs. Merriman and Mrs. Highcamp had made their "party call." Edna felt that they might have dispensed with the formality. They had also come to invite her to play *vingt-et-un*[7] one evening at Mrs. Merriman's. She was asked to go early, to dinner, and Mr. Merriman or Mr. Arobin would take her home. Edna accepted in a half-hearted way. She sometimes felt very tired of Mrs. Highcamp and Mrs. Merriman.

Late in the afternoon she sought refuge with Mademoiselle Reisz, and stayed there alone, waiting for her, feeling a kind of repose invade her with the very atmosphere of the shabby, unpretentious little room.

Edna sat at the window, which looked out over the house-tops and across the river. The window frame was filled with pots of flowers, and she sat and picked the dry leaves from a rose geranium. The day was warm, and the breeze which blew from the river was very pleasant. She removed her hat and laid it on the piano. She went on picking the leaves and digging around the plants with her hat pin. Once she thought she heard Mademoiselle Reisz approaching. But it was a young black girl, who came in, bringing a small bundle of laundry, which she deposited in the adjoining room, and went away.

Edna seated herself at the piano, and softly picked out with one hand the bars of a piece of music which lay open before her. A half-hour went by. There was the occasional sound of people going and coming in the lower hall. She was growing interested in her occupation of picking out the aria, when there was a second rap at the door. She vaguely wondered what these people did when they found Mademoiselle's door locked.

"Come in," she called, turning her face toward the door. And this time it was Robert Lebrun who presented himself. She attempted to rise; she could not have done so without betraying the agitation which mastered her at sight of him, so she fell back upon the stool, only exclaiming, "Why Robert!"

He came and clasped her hand, seemingly without knowing what he was saying or doing.

7. Twenty-one, a card game.

"Mrs. Pontellier! How do you happen—oh! how well you look! Is Mademoiselle Reisz not here? I never expected to see you."

"When did you come back?" asked Edna in an unsteady voice, wiping her face with her handkerchief. She seemed ill at ease on the piano stool, and he begged her to take the chair by the window. She did so, mechanically, while he seated himself on the stool.

"I returned day before yesterday," he answered, while he leaned his arm on the keys, bringing forth a crash of discordant sound.

"Day before yesterday!" she repeated, aloud, and went on thinking to herself, "day before yesterday," in a sort of an uncomprehending way. She had pictured him seeking her at the very first hour, and he had lived under the same sky since day before yesterday; while only by accident had he stumbled upon her. Mademoiselle must have lied when she said, "Poor fool, he loves you."

"Day before yesterday," she repeated, breaking off a spray of Mademoiselle's geranium; "then if you had not met me here to-day you wouldn't—when—that is, didn't you mean to come and see me?"

"Of course, I should have gone to see you. There have been so many things—" he turned the leaves of Mademoiselle's music nervously. "I started in at once yesterday with the old firm. After all there is as much chance for me here as there was there—that is, I might find it profitable some day. The Mexicans were not very congenial."

So he had come back because the Mexicans were not congenial; because business was as profitable here as there; because of any reason, and not because he cared to be near her. She remembered the day she sat on the floor, turning the pages of his letter, seeking the reason which was left untold.

She had not noticed how he looked—only feeling his presence; but she turned deliberately and observed him. After all, he had been absent but a few months, and was not changed. His hair—the color of hers—waved back from his temples in the same way as before. His skin was not more burned than it had been at Grand Isle. She found in his eyes, when he looked at her for one silent moment, the same tender caress, with an added warmth and entreaty which had not been there before—the same glance which had penetrated to the sleeping places of her soul and awakened them.

A hundred times Edna had pictured Robert's return, and imagined their first meeting. It was usually at her home, whither he had sought her out at once. She always fancied him expressing or betraying in some way his love for her. And here, the reality was that they sat ten feet apart, she at the window, crushing geranium leaves in her hand and smelling them, he twirling around on the piano stool, saying:

"I was very much surprised to hear of Mr. Pontellier's absence;

it's a wonder Mademoiselle Reisz did not tell me; and your moving —mother told me yesterday. I should think you would have gone to New York with him, or to Iberville with the children, rather than be bothered here with housekeeping. And you are going abroad, too, I hear. We shan't have you at Grand Isle next summer; it won't seem—do you see much of Mademoiselle Reisz? She often spoke of you in the few letters she wrote."

"Do you remember that you promised to write to me when you went away?" A flush overspread his whole face.

"I couldn't believe that my letters would be of any interest to you."

"That is an excuse; it isn't the truth." Edna reached for her hat on the piano. She adjusted it, sticking the hat pin through the heavy coil of hair with some deliberation.

"Are you not going to wait for Mademoiselle Reisz?" asked Robert.

"No; I have found when she is absent this long, she is liable not to come back till late." She drew on her gloves, and Robert picked up his hat.

"Won't you wait for her?" asked Edna.

"Not if you think she will not be back till late," adding, as if suddenly aware of some discourtesy in his speech, "and I should miss the pleasure of walking home with you." Edna locked the door and put the key back in its hiding place.

They went together, picking their way across muddy streets and sidewalks encumbered with the cheap display of small tradesmen. Part of the distance they rode in the car, and after disembarking, passed the Pontellier mansion, which looked broken and half torn asunder. Robert had never known the house, and looked at it with interest.

"I never knew you in your home," he remarked.

"I am glad you did not."

"Why?" She did not answer. They went on around the corner, and it seemed as if her dreams were coming true after all, when he followed her into the little house.

"You must stay and dine with me, Robert. You see I am all alone, and it is so long since I have seen you. There is so much I want to ask you."

She took off her hat and gloves. He stood irresolute, making some excuse about his mother who expected him; he even muttered something about an engagement. She struck a match and lit the lamp on the table; it was growing dusk. When he saw her face in the lamplight, looking pained, with all the soft lines gone out of it, he threw his hat aside and seated himself.

"Oh! you know I want to stay if you will let me!" he exclaimed. All the softness came back. She laughed, and went and put her hand on his shoulder.

"This is the first moment you have seemed like the old Robert.

I'll go tell Celestine." She hurried away to tell Celestine to set an extra place. She even sent her off in search of some added delicacy which she had not thought of for herself. And she recommended great care in dripping the coffee and having the omelet done to a proper turn.

When she reëntered, Robert was turning over magazines, sketches, and things that lay upon the table in great disorder. He picked up a photograph, and exclaimed:

"Alcée Arobin! What on earth is his picture doing here?"

"I tried to make a sketch of his head one day," answered Edna, "and he thought the photograph might help me. It was at the other house. I thought it had been left there. I must have picked it up with my drawing materials."

"I should think you would give it back to him if you have finished with it."

"Oh! I have a great many such photographs. I never think of returning them. They don't amount to anything." Robert kept on looking at the picture.

"It seems to me—do you think his head worth drawing? Is he a friend of Mr. Pontellier's? You never said you knew him."

"He isn't a friend of Mr. Pontellier's; he's a friend of mine. I always knew him—that is, it is only of late that I know him pretty well. But I'd rather talk about you, and know what you have been seeing and doing and feeling out there in Mexico." Robert threw aside the picture.

"I've been seeing the waves and the white beach of Grand Isle; the quiet, grassy street of the *Chênière*; the old fort at Grande Terre. I've been working like a machine, and feeling like a lost soul. There was nothing interesting."

She leaned her head upon her hand to shade her eyes from the light.

"And what have you been seeing and doing and feeling all these days?" he asked.

"I've been seeing the waves and the white beach of Grand Isle; the quiet, grassy street of the *Chênière Caminada*; the old sunny fort at Grande Terre. I've been working with little more comprehension than a machine, and still feeling like a lost soul. There was nothing interesting."

"Mrs. Pontellier, you are cruel," he said, with feeling, closing his eyes and resting his head back in his chair. They remained in silence till old Celestine announced dinner.

XXXIV

The dining-room was very small. Edna's round mahogany would have almost filled it. As it was there was but a step or two from the little table in the kitchen, to the mantel, the small buffet, and the side door that opened out on the narrow brick-paved yard.

A certain degree of ceremony settled upon them with the announcement of dinner. There was no return to personalities. Robert related incidents of his sojourn in Mexico, and Edna talked of events likely to interest him, which had occurred during his absence. The dinner was of ordinary quality, except for the few delicacies which she had sent out to purchase. Old Celestine, with a bandana *tignon*[8] twisted about her head, hobbled in and out, taking a personal interest in everything; and she lingered occasionally to talk *patois*[9] with Robert, whom she had known as a boy.

He went out to a neighboring cigar stand to purchase cigarette papers, and when he came back he found that Celestine had served the black coffee in the parlor.

"Perhaps I shouldn't have come back," he said. "When you are tired of me, tell me to go."

"You never tire me. You must have forgotten the hours and hours at Grand Isle in which we grew accustomed to each other and used to being together."

"I have forgotten nothing at Grand Isle," he said, not looking at her, but rolling a cigarette. His tobacco pouch, which he laid upon the table, was a fantastic embroidered silk affair, evidently the handiwork of a woman.

"You used to carry your tobacco in a rubber pouch," said Edna, picking up the pouch and examining the needlework.

"Yes; it was lost."

"Where did you buy this one? In Mexico?"

"It was given to me by a Vera Cruz girl; they are very generous," he replied, striking a match and lighting his cigarette.

"They are very handsome, I suppose, those Mexican women; very picturesque, with their black eyes and their lace scarfs."

"Some are; others are hideous. Just as you find women everywhere."

"What was she like—the one who gave you the pouch? You must have known her very well."

"She was very ordinary. She wasn't of the slightest importance. I knew her well enough."

"Did you visit at her house? Was it interesting? I should like to know and hear about the people you met, and the impressions they made on you."

"There are some people who leave impressions not so lasting as the imprint of an oar upon the water."

"Was she such a one?"

"It would be ungenerous for me to admit that she was of that order and kind." He thrust the pouch back in his pocket, as if to put away the subject with the trifle which had brought it up.

8. Archaic form of the word *chignon*, a "coil of hair," a "bun." She has her hair tied up with a scarf.
9. A dialect of archaic French mixed with English, Spanish, German, and American Indian words spoken by the descendants of the Acadians.

Arobin dropped in with a message from Mrs. Merriman, to say that the card party was postponed on account of the illness of one of her children.

"How do you do, Arobin?" said Robert, rising from the obscurity.

"Oh! Lebrun. To be sure! I heard yesterday you were back. How did they treat you down in Mexico?"

"Fairly well."

"But not well enough to keep you there. Stunning girls, though, in Mexico. I thought I should never get away from Vera Cruz when I was down there a couple of years ago."

"Did they embroider slippers and tobacco pouches and hat bands and things for you?" asked Edna.

"Oh! my! no! I didn't get so deep in their regard. I fear they made more impression on me than I made on them."

"You were less fortunate than Robert, then."

"I am always less fortunate than Robert. Has he been imparting tender confidences?"

"I've been imposing myself long enough," said Robert, rising, and shaking hands with Edna. "Please convey my regards to Mr. Pontellier when you write."

He shook hands with Arobin and went away.

"Fine fellow, that Lebrun," said Arobin when Robert had gone. "I never heard you speak of him."

"I knew him last summer at Grand Isle," she replied. "Here is that photograph of yours. Don't you want it?"

"What do I want with it? Throw it away." She threw it back on the table.

"I'm not going to Mrs. Merriman's," she said. "If you see her, tell her so. But perhaps I had better write. I think I shall write now, and say that I am sorry her child is sick, and tell her not to count on me."

"It would be a good scheme," acquiesced Arobin. "I don't blame you; stupid lot!"

Edna opened the blotter, and having procured paper and pen, began to write the note. Arobin lit a cigar and read the evening paper, which he had in his pocket.

"What is the date?" she asked. He told her.

"Will you mail this for me when you go out?"

"Certainly." He read to her little bits out of the newspaper, while she straightened things on the table.

"What do you want to do?" he asked, throwing aside the paper. "Do you want to go out for a walk or a drive or anything? It would be a fine night to drive."

"No; I don't want to do anything but just be quiet. You go away and amuse yourself. Don't stay."

"I'll go away if I must; but I shan't amuse myself. You know that I only live when I am near you."

He stood up to bid her good night.

"Is that one of the things you always say to women?"

"I have said it before, but I don't think I ever came so near meaning it," he answered with a smile. There were no warm lights in her eyes; only a dreamy, absent look.

"Good night. I adore you. Sleep well," he said, and he kissed her hand and went away.

She stayed alone in a kind of reverie—a sort of stupor. Step by step she lived over every instant of the time she had been with Robert after he had entered Mademoiselle Reisz's door. She recalled his words, his looks. How few and meager they had been for her hungry heart! A vision—a transcendently seductive vision of a Mexican girl arose before her. She writhed with a jealous pang. She wondered when he would come back. He had not said he would come back. She had been with him, had heard his voice and touched his hand. But some way he had seemed nearer to her off there in Mexico.

XXXV

The morning was full of sunlight and hope. Edna could see before her no denial—only the promise of excessive joy. She lay in bed awake, with bright eyes full of speculation. "He loves you, poor fool." If she could but get that conviction firmly fixed in her mind, what mattered about the rest? She felt she had been childish and unwise the night before in giving herself over to despondency. She recapitulated the motives which no doubt explained Robert's reserve. They were not insurmountable; they would not hold if he really loved her; they could not hold against her own passion, which he must come to realize in time. She pictured him going to his business that morning. She even saw how he was dressed; how he walked down one street, and turned the corner of another; saw him bending over his desk, talking to people who entered the office, going to his lunch, and perhaps watching for her on the street. He would come to her in the afternoon or evening, sit and roll his cigarette, talk a little, and go away as he had done the night before. But how delicious it would be to have him there with her! She would have no regrets, nor seek to penetrate his reserve if he still chose to wear it.

Edna ate her breakfast only half dressed. The maid brought her a delicious printed scrawl from Raoul, expressing his love, asking her to send him some bonbons, and telling her they had found that morning ten tiny white pigs all lying in a row beside Lidie's big white pig.

A letter also came from her husband, saying he hoped to be back early in March, and then they would get ready for that journey abroad which he had promised her so long, which he felt now fully able to afford; he felt able to travel as people should, without any thought of small economies—thanks to his recent speculations in Wall Street.

Much to her surprise she received a note from Arobin, written at midnight from the club. It was to say good morning to her, to hope that she had slept well, to assure her of his devotion, which he trusted she in some faintest manner returned.

All these letters were pleasing to her. She answered the children in a cheerful frame of mind, promising them bonbons, and congratulating them upon their happy find of the little pigs.

She answered her husband with friendly evasiveness,—not with any fixed design to mislead him, only because all sense of reality had gone out of her life, she had abandoned herslf to Fate, and awaited the consequences with indifference.

To Arobin's note she made no reply. She put it under Celestine's stove-lid.

Edna worked several hours with much spirit. She saw no one but a picture dealer, who asked her if it were true that she was going abroad to study in Paris.

She said possibly she might, and he negotiated with her for some Parisian studies to reach him in time for the holiday trade in December.

Robert did not come that day. She was keenly disappointed. He did not come the following day, nor the next. Each morning she awoke with hope, and each night she was a prey to despondency. She was tempted to seek him out. But far from yielding to the impulse, she avoided any occasion which might throw her in his way. She did not go to Mademoiselle Reisz's nor pass by Madame Lebrun's, as she might have done if he had still been in Mexico.

When Arobin, one night, urged her to drive with him, she went —out to the lake, on the Shell Road.[1] His horses were full of mettle, and even a little unmanageable. She liked the rapid gait at which they spun along, and the quick, sharp sound of the horses' hoofs on the hard road. They did not stop anywhere to eat or to drink. Arobin was not needlessly imprudent. But they ate and they drank when they regained Edna's little dining-room—which was comparatively early in the evening.

It was late when he left her. It was getting to be more than a passing whim with Arobin to see her and be with her. He had detected the latent sensuality, which unfolded under his delicate sense of her nature's requirements like a torpid, torrid, sensitive blossom.

There was no despondency when she fell asleep that night; nor was there hope when she awoke in the morning.

---

1. A road along Lake Pontchartrain, a favorite for testing the speed of horses.

XXXVI

There was a garden out in the suburbs; a small, leafy corner, with a few green tables under the orange trees. An old cat slept all day on the stone step in the sun, and an old *mulatresse*[2] slept her idle hours away in her chair at the open window, till some one happened to knock on one of the green tables. She had milk and cream cheese to sell, and bread and butter. There was no one who could make such excellent coffee or fry a chicken so golden brown as she.

The place was too modest to attract the attention of people of fashion, and so quiet as to have escaped the notice of those in search of pleasure and dissipation. Edna had discovered it accidentally one day when the high-board gate stood ajar. She caught sight of a little green table, blotched with the checkered sunlight that filtered through the quivering leaves overhead. Within she had found the slumbering *mulatresse*, the drowsy cat, and a glass of milk which reminded her of the milk she had tasted in Iberville.

She often stopped there during her perambulations; sometimes taking a book with her, and sitting an hour or two under the trees when she found the place deserted. Once or twice she took a quiet dinner there alone, having instructed Celestine beforehand to prepare no dinner at home. It was the last place in the city where she would have expected to meet any one she knew.

Still she was not astonished when, as she was partaking of a modest dinner late in the afternoon, looking into an open book, stroking the cat, which had made friends with her—she was not greatly astonished to see Robert come in at the tall garden gate.

"I am destined to see you only by accident," she said, shoving the cat off the chair beside her. He was surprised, ill at ease, almost embarrassed at meeting her thus so unexpectedly.

"Do you come here often?" he asked.

"I almost live here," she said.

"I used to drop in very often for a cup of Catiche's good coffee. This is the first time since I came back."

"She'll bring you a plate, and you will share my dinner. There's always enough for two—even three." Edna had intended to be indifferent and as reserved as he when she met him; she had reached the determination by a laborious train of reasoning, incident to one of her despondent moods. But her resolve melted when she saw him before her, seated there beside her in the little garden, as if a designing Providence had led him into her path.

"'Why have you kept away from me, Robert?" she asked, closing the book that lay open upon the table.

"Why are you so personal, Mrs. Pontellier? Why do you force me to idiotic subterfuges?" he exclaimed with sudden warmth. "I

2. A woman of mixed black and white blood.

suppose there's no use telling you I've been very busy, or that I've been sick, or that I've been to see you and not found you at home. Please let me off with any one of those excuses."

"You are the embodiment of selfishness," she said. "You save yourself something—I don't know what—but there is some selfish motive, and in sparing yourself you never consider for a moment what I think, or how I feel your neglect and indifference. I suppose this is what you would call unwomanly; but I have got into a habit of expressing myself. It doesn't matter to me, and you may think me unwomanly if you like."

"No; I only think you cruel, as I said the other day. Maybe not intentionally cruel; but you seem to be forcing me into disclosures which can result in nothing; as if you would have me bare a wound for the pleasure of looking at it, without the intention or power of healing it."

"I'm spoiling your dinner, Robert; never mind what I say. You haven't eaten a morsel."

"I only came in for a cup of coffee." His sensitive face was all disfigured with excitement.

"Isn't this a delightful place?" she remarked. "I am so glad it has never actually been discovered. It is so quiet, so sweet here. Do you notice there is scarcely a sound to be heard? It's so out of the way; and a good walk from the car. However, I don't mind walking. I always feel so sorry for women who don't like to walk; they miss so much—so many rare little glimpses of life; and we women learn so little of life on the whole.

"Catiche's coffee is always hot. I don't know how she manages it, here in the open air. Celestine's coffee gets cold bringing it from the kitchen to the dining-room. Three lumps! How can you drink it so sweet? Take some of the cress with your chop; it's so biting and crisp. Then there's the advantage of being able to smoke with your coffee out here. Now, in the city—aren't you going to smoke?"

"After a while," he said, laying a cigar on the table.

"Who gave it to you?" she laughed.

"I bought it. I suppose I'm getting reckless; I bought a whole box." She was determined not to be personal again and make him uncomfortable.

The cat made friends with him, and climbed into his lap when he smoked his cigar. He stroked her silky fur, and talked a little about her. He looked at Edna's book, which he had read; and he told her the end, to save her the trouble of wading through it, he said.

Again he accompanied her back to her home; and it was after dusk when they reached the little "pigeon-house." She did not ask him to remain, which he was grateful for, as it permitted him to stay without the discomfort of blundering through an excuse which he had no intention of considering. He helped her to light the lamp; then she went into her room to take off her hat and to bathe her face and hands.

When she came back Robert was not examining the pictures and magazines as before; he sat off in the shadow, leaning his head back on the chair as if in a reverie. Edna lingered a moment beside the table, arranging the books there. Then she went across the room to where he sat. She bent over the arm of his chair and called his name.

"Robert," she said, "are you asleep?"

"No," he answered, looking up at her.

She leaned over and kissed him—a soft, cool, delicate kiss, whose voluptuous sting penetrated his whole being—then she moved away from him. He followed, and took her in his arms, just holding her close to him. She put her hand up to his face and pressed his cheek against her own. The action was full of love and tenderness. He sought her lips again. Then he drew her down upon the sofa beside him and held her hand in both of his.

"Now you know," he said, "now you know what I have been fighting against since last summer at Grand Isle; what drove me away and drove me back again."

"Why have you been fighting against it?" she asked. Her face glowed with soft lights.

"Why? Because you were not free; you were Léonce Pontellier's wife. I couldn't help loving you if you were ten times his wife, but so long as I went away from you and kept away I could help telling you so." She put her free hand up to his shoulder, and then against his cheek, rubbing it softly. He kissed her again. His face was warm and flushed.

"There in Mexico I was thinking of you all the time, and longing for you."

"But not writing to me," she interrupted.

"Something put into my head that you cared for me; and I lost my senses. I forgot everything but a wild dream of your some way becoming my wife."

"Your wife!"

"Religion, loyalty, everything would give way if only you cared."

"Then you must have forgotten that I was Léonce Pontellier's wife."

"Oh! I was demented, dreaming of wild, impossible things, recalling men who had set their wives free, we have heard of such things."

"Yes, we have heard of such things."

"I came back full of vague, mad intentions. And when I got here—"

"When you got here you never came near me!" She was still caressing his cheek.

"I realized what a cur I was to dream of such a thing, even if you had been willing."

She took his face between her hands and looked into it as if she would never withdraw her eyes more. She kissed him on the forehead, the eyes, the cheeks, and the lips.

"You have been a very, very foolish boy, wasting your time dreaming of impossible things when you speak of Mr. Pontellier setting me free! I am no longer one of Mr. Pontellier's possessions to dispose of or not. I give myself where I choose. If he were to say, 'Here, Robert, take her and be happy; she is yours,' I should laugh at you both."

His face grew a little white. "What do you mean?" he asked.

There was a knock at the door. Old Celestine came in to say that Madame Ratignolle's servant had come around the back way with a message that Madame had been taken sick and begged Mrs. Pontellier to go to her immediately.

"Yes, yes," said Edna, rising; "I promised. Tell her yes—to wait for me. I'll go back with her."

"Let me walk over with you," offered Robert.

"No," she said; "I will go with the servant." She went into her room to put on her hat, and when she came in again she sat once more upon the sofa beside him. He had not stirred. She put her arms about his neck.

"Good-by, my sweet Robert. Tell me good-by." He kissed her with a degree of passion which had not before entered into his caress, and strained her to him.

"I love you," she whispered, "only you; no one but you. It was you who awoke me last summer out of a life-long, stupid dream. Oh! you have made me so unhappy with your indifference. Oh! I have suffered, suffered! Now you are here we shall love each other, my Robert. We shall be everything to each other. Nothing else in the world is of any consequence. I must go to my friend; but you will wait for me? No matter how late; you will wait for me, Robert?"

"Don't go; don't go! Oh! Edna, stay with me," he pleaded. "Why should you go? Stay with me, stay with me."

"I shall come back as soon as I can; I shall find you here." She buried her face in his neck, and said good-by again. Her seductive voice, together with his great love for her, had enthralled his senses, had deprived him of every impulse but the longing to hold her and keep her.

XXXVII

Edna looked in at the drug store. Monsieur Ratignolle was putting up a mixture himself, very carefully, dropping a red liquid into a tiny glass. He was grateful to Edna for having come; her presence would be a comfort to his wife. Madame Ratignolle's sister, who had always been with her at such trying times, had not been able to come up from the plantation, and Adèle had been inconsolable until Mrs. Pontellier so kindly promised to come to her. The nurse had been with them at night for the past week, as she lived a great distance away. And Dr. Mandelet had been coming and going all the afternoon. They were then looking for him any moment.

Edna hastened upstairs by a private stairway that led from the rear of the store to the apartments above. The children were all sleeping in a back room. Madame Ratignolle was in the salon, whither she had strayed in her suffering impatience. She sat on the sofa, clad in an ample white *peignoir*, holding a handkerchief tight in her hand with a nervous clutch. Her face was drawn and pinched, her sweet blue eyes haggard and unnatural. All her beautiful hair had been drawn back and plaited. It lay in a long braid on the sofa pillow, coiled like a golden serpent. The nurse, a comfortable looking *Griffe* woman[3] in white apron and cap, was urging her to return to her bedroom.

"There is no use, there is no use," she said at once to Edna. "We must get rid of Mandelet; he is getting too old and careless. He said he would be here at half-past seven; now it must be eight. See what time it is, Joséphine."

The woman was possessed of a cheerful nature, and refused to take any situation too seriously, especially a situation with which she was so familiar. She urged Madame to have courage and patience. But Madame only set her teeth hard into her under lip, and Edna saw the sweat gather in beads on her white forehead. After a moment or two she uttered a profound sigh and wiped her face with the handkerchief rolled in a ball. She appeared exhausted. The nurse gave her a fresh handkerchief, sprinkled with cologne water.

"This is too much!" she cried. "Mandelet ought to be killed! Where is Alphonse? Is it possible I am to be abandoned like this— neglected by every one?"

"Neglected, indeed!" exclaimed the nurse. Wasn't she there? And here was Mrs. Pontellier leaving, no doubt, a pleasant evening at home to devote to her? And wasn't Monsieur Ratignolle coming that very instant through the hall? And Joséphine was quite sure she had heard Doctor Mandelet's coupé. Yes, there it was, down at the door.

Adèle consented to go back to her room. She sat on the edge of a little low couch next to her bed.

Doctor Mandelet paid no attention to Madame Ratignolle's upbraidings. He was accustomed to them at such times, and was too well convinced of her loyalty to doubt it.

3. The daughter of a mulatto and a black, or of a mulatto and an American Indian.

He was glad to see Edna, and wanted her to go with him into the salon and entertain him. But Madame Ratignolle would not consent that Edna should leave her for an instant. Between agonizing moments, she chatted a little, and said it took her mind off her sufferings.

Edna began to feel uneasy. She was seized with a vague dread. Her own like experiences seemed far away, unreal, and only half remembered. She recalled faintly an ecstasy of pain, the heavy odor of chloroform, a stupor which had deadened sensation, and an awakening to find a little new life to which she had given being, added to the great unnumbered multitude of souls that come and go.

She began to wish she had not come; her presence was not necessary. She might have invented a pretext for staying away; she might even invent a pretext now for going. But Edna did not go. With an inward agony, with a flaming, outspoken revolt against the ways of Nature, she witnessed the scene [of] torture.

She was still stunned and speechless with emotion when later she leaned over her friend to kiss her and softly say good-by. Adèle, pressing her cheek, whispered in an exhausted voice: "Think of the children, Edna. Oh think of the children! Remember them!"

XXXVIII

Edna still felt dazed when she got outside in the open air. The Doctor's coupé had returned for him and stood before the *porte cochère.* She did not wish to enter the coupé, and told Doctor Mandelet she would walk; she was not afraid, and would go alone. He directed his carriage to meet him at Mrs. Pontellier's, and he started to walk home with her.

Up—away up, over the narrow street between the tall houses, the stars were blazing. The air was mild and caressing, but cool with the breath of spring and the night. They walked slowly, the Doctor with a heavy, measured tread and his hands behind him; Edna, in an absent-minded way, as she had walked one night at Grand Isle, as if her thoughts had gone ahead of her and she was striving to overtake them.

"You shouldn't have been there, Mrs. Pontellier," he said. "That was no place for you. Adèle is full of whims at such times. There were a dozen women she might have had with her, unimpressionable women. I felt that it was cruel, cruel. You shouldn't have gone."

"Oh, well!" she answered, indifferently. "I don't know that it matters after all. One has to think of the children some time or other; the sooner the better."

"When is Léonce coming back?"

"Quite soon. Some time in March."

"And you are going abroad?"

"Perhaps—no, I am not going. I'm not going to be forced into doing things. I don't want to go abroad. I want to be let alone. Nobody has any right—except children, perhaps—and even then, it seems to me—or it did seem—" She felt that her speech was voicing the incoherency of her thoughts, and stopped abruptly.

"The trouble is," sighed the Doctor, grasping her meaning intuitively, "that youth is given up to illusions. It seems to be a provision of Nature; a decoy to secure mothers for the race. And Nature takes no account of moral consequences, of arbitrary conditions which we create, and which we feel obliged to maintain at any cost."

"Yes," she said. "The years that are gone seem like dreams—if one might go on sleeping and dreaming—but to wake up and find —oh! well! perhaps it is better to wake up after all, even to suffer, rather than to remain a dupe to illusions all one's life."

"It seems to me, my dear child," said the Doctor at parting, holding her hand, "you seem to me to be in trouble. I am not going to ask for your confidence. I will only say that if ever you feel moved to give it to me, perhaps I might help you. I know I would understand, and I tell you there are not many who would—not many, my dear."

"Some way I don't feel moved to speak of things that trouble me. Don't think I am ungrateful or that I don't appreciate your sympathy. There are periods of despondency and suffering which take possession of me. But I don't want anything but my own way. That is wanting a good deal, of course, when you have to trample upon the lives, the hearts, the prejudices of others—but no matter —still, I shouldn't want to trample upon the little lives. Oh! I don't know what I'm saying, Doctor. Good night. Don't blame me for anything."

"Yes, I will blame you if you don't come and see me soon. We will talk of things you never have dreamt of talking about before. It will do us both good. I don't want you to blame yourself, whatever comes. Good night, my child."

She let herself in at the gate, but instead of entering she sat upon the step of the porch. The night was quiet and soothing. All the tearing emotion of the last few hours seemed to fall away from her like a somber, uncomfortable garment, which she had but to loosen to be rid of. She went back to that hour before Adèle had sent for her; and her senses kindled afresh in thinking of Robert's words, the pressure of his arms, and the feeling of his lips upon her own. She could picture at that moment no greater bliss on earth than possession of the beloved one. His expression of love had already given him to her in part. When she thought that he was there at hand, waiting for her, she grew numb with the intoxication of expectancy. It was so late; he should be asleep perhaps. She would awaken him with a kiss. She hoped he would be asleep that she might arouse him with her caresses.

Still, she remembered Adèle's voice whispering, "Think of the children; think of them." She meant to think of them, that determination had driven into her soul like a death wound—but not to-night. To-morrow would be time to think of everything.

Robert was not waiting for her in the little parlor. He was nowhere at hand. The house was empty. But he had scrawled on a piece of paper that lay in the lamplight:

"I love you. Good-by—because I love you."

Edna grew faint when she read the words. She went and sat on the sofa. Then she stretched herself out there, never uttering a sound. She did not sleep. She did not go to bed. The lamp sputtered and went out. She was still awake in the morning, when Celestine unlocked the kitchen door and came in to light the fire.

XXXIX

Victor, with hammer and nails and scraps of scantling,[4] was patching a corner of one of the galleries. Mariequita sat near by, dangling her legs, watching him work, and handing him nails from the tool-box. The sun was beating down upon them. The girl had covered her head with her apron folded into a square pad. They had been talking for an hour or more. She was never tired of hearing Victor describe the dinner at Mrs. Pontellier's. He exaggerated every detail, making it appear a veritable Lucullean[5] feast. The flowers were in tubs, he said. The champagne was quaffed from huge golden goblets. Venus rising from the foam[6] could have presented no more entrancing a spectacle than Mrs. Pontellier, blazing with beauty and diamonds at the head of the board, while the other women were all of them youthful houris[7] possessed of incomparable charms.

She got it into her head that Victor was in love with Mrs. Pontellier, and he gave her evasive answers, framed so as to confirm her belief. She grew sullen and cried a little, threatening to go off and leave him to his fine ladies. There were a dozen men crazy about her at the *Chênière*; and since it was the fashion to be in love with married people, why she could run away any time she liked to New Orleans with Célina's husband.

Célina's husband was a fool, a coward, and a pig, and to prove it to her, Victor intended to hammer his head into a jelly the next time he encountered him. This assurance was very consoling to Mariequita. She dried her eyes, and grew cheeful at the prospect.

They were still talking of the dinner and the allurements of city life when Mrs. Pontellier herself slipped around the corner of the house. The two youngsters stayed dumb with amazement before

4. A small piece of lumber.
5. After the first-century Roman general Lucius Licinius Lucullus, who was noted for his banquets.
6. Roman goddess of love and beauty, daughter of Jupiter and Dione, sprang from the foam at birth.
7. Virgin nymphs, everlastingly young and beautiful.

what they considered to be an apparition. But it was really she in flesh and blood, looking tired and a little travel-stained.

"I walked up from the wharf," she said, "and heard the hammering. I supposed it was you, mending the porch. It's a good thing. I was always tripping over those loose planks last summer. How dreary and deserted everything looks!"

It took Victor some little time to comprehend that she had come in Beaudelet's lugger, that she had come alone, and for no purpose but to rest.

"There's nothing fixed up yet, you see. I'll give you my room; it's the only place."

"Any corner will do," she assured him.

"And if you can stand Philomel's cooking," he went on, "though I might try to get her mother while you are here. Do you think she would come?" turning to Mariequita.

Mariequita thought that perhaps Philomel's mother might come for a few days, and money enough.

Beholding Mrs. Pontellier make her appearance, the girl had at once suspected a lovers' rendezvous. But Victor's astonishment was so genuine, and Mrs. Pontellier's indifference so apparent, that the disturbing notion did not lodge long in her brain. She contemplated with the greatest interest this woman who gave the most sumptuous dinners in America, and who had all the men in New Orleans at her feet.

"What time will you have dinner?" asked Edna. "I'm very hungry; but don't get anything extra."

"I'll have it ready in little or no time," he said, bustling and packing away his tools. "You may go to my room to brush up and rest yourself. Mariequita will show you."

"Thank you," said Edna. "But, do you know, I have a notion to go down to the beach and take a good wash and even a little swim, before dinner?"

"The water is too cold!" they both exclaimed. "Don't think of it."

"Well, I might go down and try—dip my toes in. Why, it seems to me the sun is hot enough to have warmed the very depths of the ocean. Could you get me a couple of towels? I'd better go right away, so as to be back in time. It would be a little too chilly if I waited till this afternoon."

Mariequita ran over to Victor's room, and returned with some towels, which she gave to Edna.

"I hope you have fish for dinner," said Edna, as she started to walk away; "but don't do anything extra if you haven't."

"Run and find Philomel's mother," Victor instructed the girl. "I'll go to the kitchen and see what I can do. By Gimminy! Women have no consideration! She might have sent me word."

Edna walked on down to the beach rather mechanically, not noticing anything special except that the sun was hot. She was not dwelling upon any particular train of thought. She had done all the thinking which was necessary after Robert went away, when she lay awake upon the sofa till morning.

She had said over and over to herself: "To-day it is Arobin; to-morrow it will be some one else. It makes no difference to me, it doesn't matter about Léonce Pontellier—but Raoul and Etienne!" She understood now clearly what she had meant long ago when she said to Adèle Ratignolle that she would give up the unessential, but she would never sacrifice herself for her children.

Despondency had come upon her there in the wakeful night, and had never lifted. There was no one thing in the world that she desired. There was no human being whom she wanted near her except Robert; and she even realized that the day would come when he, too, and the thought of him would melt out of her existence, leaving her alone. The children appeared before her like antagonists who had overcome her; who had overpowered her and sought to drag her into the soul's slavery for the rest of her days. But she knew a way to elude them. She was not thinking of these things when she walked down to the beach.

The water of the Gulf stretched out before her gleaming with the million lights of the sun. The voice of the sea is seductive, never ceasing, whispering, clamoring, murmuring, inviting the soul to wander in abysses of solitude. All along the white beach, up and down, there was no living thing in sight. A bird with a broken wing was beating the air above, reeling, fluttering, circling disabled down, down to the water.

Edna had found her old bathing suit still hanging, faded, upon its accustomed peg.

She put it on, leaving her clothing in the bath-house. But when she was there beside the sea, absolutely alone, she cast the unpleasant, pricking garments from her, and for the first time in her life she stood naked in the open air, at the mercy of the sun, the breeze that beat upon her, and the waves that invited her.

How strange and awful it seemed to stand naked under the sky! how delicious! She felt like some new-born creature, opening its eyes in a familiar world that it had never known.

The foamy wavelets curled up to her white feet, and coiled like serpents about her ankles. She walked out. The water was chill, but she walked on. The water was deep, but she lifted her white body and reached out with a long, sweeping stroke. The touch of the sea is sensuous, enfolding the body in its soft, close embrace.

She went on and on. She remembered the night she swam far out, and recalled the terror that seized her at the fear of being unable to regain the shore. She did not look back now, but went on and on, thinking of the blue-grass meadow that she had traversed when a little child, believing that it had no beginning and no end.

Her arms and legs were growing tired.

She thought of Léonce and the children. They were a part of her life. But they need not have thought that they could possess her, body and soul. How Mademoiselle Reisz would have laughed, perhaps sneered, if she knew! "And you call yourself an artist! What pretensions, Madame! The artist must possess the courageous soul that dares and defies."

Exhaustion was pressing upon and over-powering her.

"Good-by—because, I love you." He did not know; he did not understand. He would never understand. Perhaps Doctor Mandelet would have understood if she had seen him—but it was too late; the shore was far behind her, and her strength was gone.

She looked into the distance, and the old terror flamed up for an instant, then sank again. Edna heard her father's voice and her sister Margaret's. She heard the barking of an old dog that was chained to the sycamore tree. The spurs of the cavalry officer clanged as he walked across the porch. There was the hum of bees, and the musky odor of pinks filled the air.

1899

MARY E. WILKINS FREEMAN
1852–1930

Mary E. Wilkins Freeman, best known for her depiction of New England village life, was born on October 3, 1852, in Randolph, Massachusetts, a small town south of Boston. Mary was not a strong child, and two other Wilkins children died before they reached three years of age; the only other child, Anne, lived to be seventeen. Mary, as a result, may have been somewhat spoiled at home and at school, but her parents were orthodox Congregationalists and she was subject to a strict code of behavior. The constraints of religious belief and the effect of these constraints on character is, indeed, one of her chief subjects.

In 1867 Mary's father became part owner of a dry-goods store in Brattleboro, Vermont, where she graduated from high school. In 1870, she entered Mount Holyoke Female Seminary, which Emily Dickinson had attended two decades earlier. Like Dickinson, Wilkins left after a year because the school's pressure on all students to offer public testimony as to their Christian commitment was a strain on her health. She finished her formal education with a year at West Brattleboro Seminary, though the reading and discussion with her friend Evelyn Sawyer of Goethe, Emerson, Thoreau, Charles Dickens, William Makepeace Thackeray, Poe, Hawthorne, Harriet Beecher Stowe, and Sarah Orne Jewett was probably more important than her schoolwork in developing her literary taste.

After the death of her sister Anne and the failure of her father's business in 1876, Wilkins's family moved into the home of the Reverend Thomas Pickman Tyler, father of an early love of Mary's, where Mrs. Wilkins became housekeeper. Poverty was hard to bear for the Wilkinses, especially because their Puritan heritage led them to believe that poverty was a punishment for sin. Mrs. Wilkins died in 1880, her husband three years later. Mary was thus left alone at twenty-eight years of age with a legacy of less than one thousand dollars.

Fortunately, Wilkins had by this time begun to sell her poems and stories to such leading magazines of the day as *Harper's Bazaar*, and by the mid-1880s had a ready market for her work. As soon as she achieved a measure of economic independence she returned to her birthplace. Her early stories, most notably those gathered and published in *A Humble Romance* (1887), are set in the Vermont countryside, but the characters are amalgams of the people she knew as a youngster in Massachusetts and those she came to understand during her twenties in Vermont. As she put it in a preface to an edition of these stories published in Edinburgh, these characters are "studies of the descendants of the Massachusetts Bay colonists, in whom can still be seen traces of those features of will and conscience, so strong as to be almost exaggerations and deformities, which characterized their ancestors." More specifically, the title story dramatizes a theme Wilkins was to return to frequently: the potentiality for unpredictable revolt in ostensibly meek and downtrodden natures.

A New England Nun and Other Stories appeared in 1891; the quality of the stories is not as consistently high as in the earlier collection, but the volume does contain several of her best stories, most notably the title story and *The Revolt of "Mother,"* which treats the pervasive theme of psychic oppression and rebellion with particular dramatic success. It also offers an example of the way in which Wilkins's art raises her above the school of realism so widely practiced at the time. While she does provide a vivid sense of place, local dialect, and personality type, she also gives us in her best work an insight into the individual psychology and interior life produced when confining, inherited codes of village life are subjected to the pressure of a rapidly changing secular and urban world.

Wilkins continued to write for another three decades, steadily producing stories, plays, and a substantial number of novels, the best of which are *Pembroke* (1894) and *The Shoulders of Atlas* (1908). She married Dr. Charles Freeman in 1902 when she was forty-nine; after a few happy years, her husband's drinking turned into destructive alcoholism and he finally had to be institutionalized in 1920. When she was awarded the W. D. Howells medal for fiction by the American Academy of Arts and Letters in 1926, she had long since ceased producing first-rate work.

The Revolt of "Mother"[1]

"Father!"

"What is it?"

"What are them men diggin' over there in the field for?"

There was a sudden dropping and enlarging of the lower part of the old man's face, as if some heavy weight had settled therein; he shut his mouth tight, and went on harnessing the great bay mare. He hustled the collar on to her neck with a jerk.

"Father!"

The old man slapped the saddle upon the mare's back.

---

1. First published in *A New England Nun and Other Stories* (New York: Harper Brothers, 1891), the source of the present text.

"Look here, father, I want to know what them men are diggin'
over in the field for, an' I'm goin' to know."

"I wish you'd go into the house, mother, an' 'tend to your own
affairs," the old man said then. He ran his words together, and his
speech was almost as inarticulate as a growl.

But the woman understood; it was her most native tongue. "I
ain't goin' into the house till you tell me what them men are doin'
over there in the field," said she.

Then she stood waiting. She was a small woman, short and
straight-waisted like a child in her brown cotton gown. Her forehead was mild and benevolent between the smooth curves of gray
hair; there were meek downward lines about her nose and mouth;
but her eyes, fixed upon the old man, looked as if the meekness had
been the result of her own will, never of the will of another.

They were in the barn, standing before the wide open doors.
The spring air, full of the smell of growing grass and unseen blossoms, came in their faces. The deep yard in front was littered with
farm wagons and piles of wood; on the edges, close to the fence and
the house, the grass was a vivid green, and there were some dandelions.

The old man glanced doggedly at his wife as he tightened the
last buckles on the harness. She looked as immovable to him as
one of the rocks in his pasture-land, bound to the earth with generations of blackberry vines. He slapped the reins over the horse, and
started forth from the barn.

"*Father!*" said she.

The old man pulled up. "What is it?"

"I want to know what them men are diggin' over there in that
field for."

"They're diggin' a cellar, I s'pose, if you've got to know."

"A cellar for what?"

"A barn."

"A barn? You ain't goin' to build a barn over there where we was
goin' to have a house, father?"

The old man said not another word. He hurried the horse into
the farm wagon, and clattered out of the yard, jouncing as sturdily
on his seat as a boy.

The woman stood a moment looking after him, then she went
out of the barn across a corner of the yard to the house. The house,
standing at right angles with the great barn and a long reach of
sheds and out-buildings, was infinitesimal compared with them. It
was scarcely as commodious for people as the little boxes under the
barn eaves were for doves.

A pretty girl's face, pink and delicate as a flower, was looking
out of one of the house windows. She was watching three men who
were digging over in the field which bounded the yard near the road
line. She turned quietly when the woman entered.

"What are they digging for, mother?" said she. "Did he tell you?"

"They're diggin' for—a cellar for a new barn."

"Oh, mother, he ain't going to build another barn?"

"That's what he says."

A boy stood before the kitchen glass combing his hair. He combed slowly and painstakingly, arranging his brown hair in a smooth hillock over his forehead. He did not seem to pay any attention to the conversation.

"Sammy, did you know father was going to build a new barn?" asked the girl.

The boy combed assiduously.

"Sammy!"

He turned, and showed a face like his father's under his smooth crest of hair. "Yes, I s'pose I did," he said, reluctantly.

"How long have you known it?" asked his mother.

"'Bout three months, I guess."

"Why didn't you tell of it?"

"Didn't think 'twould do no good."

"I don't see what father wants another barn for," said the girl, in her sweet, slow voice. She turned again to the window, and stared out at the digging men in the field. Her tender, sweet face was full of a gentle distress. Her forehead was as bald and innocent as a baby's, with the light hair strained back from it in a row of curl-papers. She was quite large, but her soft curves did not look as if they covered muscles.

Her mother looked sternly at the boy. "Is he goin' to buy more cows?" said she.

The boy did not reply; he was tying his shoes.

"Sammy, I want you to tell me if he's going' to buy more cows."

"I s'pose he is."

"How many?"

"Four, I guess."

His mother said nothing more. She went up into the pantry, and there was a clatter of dishes. The boy got his cap from a nail behind the door, took an old arithmetic from the shelf, and started for school. He was lightly built, but clumsy. He went out of the yard with a curious spring in his hips. that made his loose home--made jacket tilt up in the rear.

The girl went to the sink, and began to wash the dishes that were piled up there. Her mother came promptly out of the pantry, and shoved her aside. "You wipe 'em," said she; "I'll wash. There's a good many this mornin'."

The mother plunged her hands vigorously into the water, the girl wiped the plates slowly and dreamily. "Mother," said she, "don't you think it's too bad father's going to build that new barn, much as we need a decent house to live in?"

Her mother scrubbed a dish fiercely. "You ain't found out yet we're women-folks, Nanny Penn," said she. "You ain't seen enough of men-folks yet to. One of these days you'll find it out, an' then you'll know that we know only what men-folks think we do, so far as any use of it goes, an' how we'd ought to reckon men-folks in with Providence, an' not complain of what they do any more than we do of the weather."

"I don't care; I don't believe George is anything like that, anyhow," said Nanny. Her delicate face flushed pink, her lips pouted softly, as if she were going to cry.

"You wait an' see. I guess George Eastman ain't no better than other men. You hadn't ought to judge father, though. He can't help it, 'cause he don't look at things jest the way we do. An' we've been pretty comfortable here, after all. The roof don't leak—ain't never but once—that's one thing. Father's kept it shingled right up."

"I do wish we had a parlor."

"I guess it won't hurt George Eastman any to come to see you in a nice clean kitchen. I guess a good many girls don't have as good a place as this. Nobody's ever heard me complain."

"I ain't complained either, mother."

"Well, I don't think you'd better, a good father an' a good home as you've got. S'pose your father made you go out an' work for your livin'? Lots of girls have to that ain't no stronger an' better able to than you be."

Sarah Penn washed the frying-pan with a conclusive air. She scrubbed the outside of it as faithfully as the inside. She was a masterly keeper of her box of a house. Her one living-room never seemed to have in it any of the dust which the friction of life with inanimate matter produces. She swept, and there seemed to be no dirt to go before the broom; she cleaned, and one could see no difference. She was like an artist so perfect that he has apparently no art. To-day she got out a mixing bowl and a board, and rolled some pies, and there was no more flour upon her than upon her daughter who was doing finer work. Nanny was to be married in the fall, and she was sewing on some white cambric and embroidery. She sewed industriously while her mother cooked, her soft milk-white hands and wrists showed whiter than her delicate work.

"We must have the stove moved out in the shed before long," said Mrs. Penn. "Talk about not havin' things, it's been a real blessin' to be able to put a stove up in that shed in hot weather. Father did one good thing when he fixed that stove-pipe out there."

Sarah Penn's face as she rolled her pies had that expression of meek vigor which might have characterized one of the New Testament saints. She was making mince-pies. Her husband, Adoniram Penn, liked them better than any other kind. She baked twice a week. Adoniram often liked a piece of pie between meals. She hurried this morning. It had been later than usual when she began, and she wanted to have a pie baked for dinner. However deep a resentment she might be forced to hold against her husband, she would never fail in sedulous attention to his wants.

Nobility of character manifests itself at loop-holes when it is not provided with large doors. Sarah Penn's showed itself to-day in flaky dishes of pastry. So she made the pies faithfully, while across the table she could see, when she glanced up from her work, the sight that rankled in her patient and steadfast soul—the digging of the cellar of the new barn in the place where Adoniram forty years ago had promised her their new house should stand.

The pies were done for dinner. Adoniram and Sammy were home a few minutes after twelve o'clock. The dinner was eaten with serious haste. There was never much conversation at the table in the Penn family. Adoniram asked a blessing, and they ate promptly, then rose up and went about their work.

Sammy went back to school, taking soft sly lopes out of the yard like a rabbit. He wanted a game of marbles before school, and feared his father would give him some chores to do. Adoniram hastened to the door and called after him, but he was out of sight.

"I don't see what you let him go for, mother," said he. "I wanted him to help me unload that wood."

Adoniram went to work out in the yard unloading wood from the wagon. Sarah put away the dinner dishes, while Nanny took down her curl-papers and changed her dress. She was going down to the store to buy some more embroidery and thread.

When Nanny was gone, Mrs. Penn went to the door. "Father!" she called.

"Well, what is it!"

"I want to see you jest a minute, father."

"I can't leave this wood nohow. I've got to git it unloaded an' go for a load of gravel afore two o'clock. Sammy had ought to helped me. You hadn't ought to let him go to school so early."

"I want to see you jest a minute."

"I tell ye I can't, nohow, mother."

"Father, you come here." Sarah Penn stood in the door like a queen; she held her head as if it bore a crown; there was that patience which makes authority royal in her voice. Adoniram went.

Mrs. Penn led the way into the kitchen, and pointed to a chair. "Sit down, father," said she; "I've got somethin' I want to say to you."

He sat down heavily; his face was quite stolid, but he looked at her with restive eyes. "Well, what is it, mother?"

"I want to know what you're buildin' that new barn for, father?"

"I ain't got nothin' to say about it."

"It can't be you think you need another barn?"

"I tell ye I ain't got nothin' to say about it, mother; an' I ain't goin' to say nothin'."

"Be you goin' to buy more cows?"

Adoniram did not reply; he shut his mouth tight.

"I know you be, as well as I want to. Now, father, look here"—Sarah Penn had not sat down; she stood before her husband in the humble fashion of a Scripture woman[2]—"I'm goin' to talk real plain to you; I never have sence I married you, but I'm goin' to now. I ain't never complained, an' I ain't goin' to complain now, but I'm goin' to talk plain. You see this room here, father; you look at it well. You see there ain't no carpet on the floor, an' you see the paper is all dirty, an' droppin' off the walls. We ain't had no new paper on it for ten year, an' then I put it on myself, an' it didn't cost but nine-pence a roll. You see this room, father; it's all the one I've had to work in an' eat in an' set in sence we was married. There ain't another woman in the whole town whose husband ain't got half the means you have but what's got better. It's all the room Nanny's got to have her company in; an' there ain't one of her mates but what's got better, an' their fathers not so able as hers is. It's all the room she'll have to be married in. What would you have thought, father, if we had had our weddin' in a room no better than this? I was married in my mother's parlor, with a carpet on the floor, an' stuffed furniture, an' a mahogany card-table. An' this is all the room my daughter will have to be married in. Look here, father!"

Sarah Penn went across the room as though it were a tragic stage. She flung open a door and disclosed a tiny bedroom, only large enough for a bed and bureau, with a path between. "There, father," said she—"there's all the room I've had to sleep in forty year. All my children were born there—the two that died, an' the two that's livin.' I was sick with a fever there."

She stepped to another door and opened it. It led into the small, ill-lighted pantry. "Here," said she, "is all the buttery[3] I've got—every place I've got for my dishes, to set away my victuals in, an' to keep my milk-pans in. Father, I've been takin' care of the milk of six cows in this place, an' now you're goin' to build a new barn, an' keep more cows, an' give me more to do in it."

She threw open another door. A narrow crooked flight of stairs wound upward from it. "There, father," said she, "I want you to look at the stairs that go up to them two unfinished chambers that are all the places our son an' daughter have had to sleep in all their lives. There ain't a prettier girl in town nor a more ladylike one than Nanny, an' that's the place she has to sleep in. It ain't so good as your horse's stall; it ain't so warm an' tight."

Sarah Penn went back and stood before her husband.

---

2. I.e., a woman, like Ruth, patient and obedient to her husband.
3. Pantry.

"Now, father," said she, "I want to know if you think you're doin' right an' accordin' to what you profess. Here, when we was married, forty year ago, you promised me faithful that we should have a new house built in that lot over in the field before the year was out. You said you had money enough, an' you wouldn't ask me to live in no such place as this. It is forty year now, an' you've been makin' more money, an' I've been savin' of it for you ever since, an' you ain't built no house yet. You've built sheds an' cow-houses an' one new barn, an' now you're goin' to build another. Father, I want to know if you think it's right. You're lodgin' your dumb beasts better than you are your own flesh an' blood. I want to know if you think it's right."

"I ain't got nothin' to say."

"You can't say nothin' without ownin' it ain't right, father. An' there's another thing—I ain't complained; I've got along forty year, an' I s'pose I should forty more, if it wa'n't for that—if we don't have another house. Nanny she can't live with us after she's married. She'll have to go somewheres else to live away from us, an' it don't seem as if I could have it so, noways, father. She wa'n't ever strong. She's got considerable color, but there wa'n't never any backbone to her. I've always took the heft of everything off her, an' she ain't fit to keep house an' do everything herself. She'll be all worn out inside of a year. Think of her doin' all the washin' an' ironin' an' bakin' with them soft white hands an' arms, an' sweepin'! I can't have it so, noways, father."

Mrs. Penn's face was burning; her mild eyes gleamed. She had pleaded her little cause like a Webster;[4] she had ranged from severity to pathos; but her opponent employed that obstinate silence which makes eloquence futile with mocking echoes. Adoniram arose clumsily.

"Father, ain't you got nothin' to say?" said Mrs. Penn.

"I've got to go off after that load of gravel. I can't stan' here talkin' all day."

"Father, won't you think it over, an' have a house built there instead of a barn?"

"I ain't got nothin' to say."

Adoniram shuffled out. Mrs. Penn went into her bedroom. When she came out, her eyes were red. She had a roll of unbleached cotton cloth. She spread it out on the kitchen table, and began cutting out some shirts for her husband. The men over in the field had a team to help them this afternoon; she could hear their halloos. She had a scanty pattern for the shirts; she had to plan and piece the sleeves.

Nanny came home with her embroidery, and sat down with her needlework. She had taken down her curl papers, and there was a soft roll of fair hair like an aureole over her forehead; her face was

4. I.e., like Daniel Webster (1782–1852), American statesman and celebrated orator.

as delicately fine and clear as porcelain. Suddenly she looked up, and the tender red flamed all over her face and neck. "Mother," said she.

"What say?"

"I've been thinking—I don't see how we're goin' to have any—wedding in this room. I'd be ashamed to have his folks come if we didn't have anybody else."

"Mebbe we can have some new paper before then; I can put it on. I guess you won't have no call to be ashamed of your belongin's."

"We might have the wedding in the new barn," said Nanny, with gentle pettishness. "Why, mother, what makes you look so?"

Mrs. Penn had started, and was staring at her with a curious expression. She turned again to her work, and spread out a pattern carefully on the cloth. "Nothin'," said she.

Presently Adoniram clattered out of the yard in his two-wheeled dump cart, standing as proudly upright as a Roman charioteer.[5] Mrs. Penn opened the door and stood there a minute looking out; the halloos of the men sounded louder.

It seemed to her all through the spring months that she heard nothing but the halloos and the noises of the saws and hammers. The new barn grew fast. It was a fine edifice for this little village. Men came on pleasant Sundays, in their meeting suits and clean shirt bosoms, and stood around it admiringly. Mrs. Penn did not speak of it, and Adoniram did not mention it to her, although sometimes, upon a return from inspecting it, he bore himself with injured dignity.

"It's a strange thing how your mother feels about the new barn," he said, confidentially, to Sammy one day.

Sammy only grunted after an odd fashion for a boy; he had learned it from his father.

The barn was all completed ready for use by the third week in July. Adoniram had planned to move his stock in on Wednesday; on Tuesday he received a letter which changed his plans. He came in with it early in the morning. "Sammy's been to the post-office," said he, "an' I've got a letter from Hiram." Hiram was Mrs. Penn's brother, who lived in Vermont.

"Well," said Mrs. Penn, "what does he say about the folks?"

"I guess they're all right. He says he thinks if I come up country right off there's a chance to buy jest the kind of a horse I want." He stared reflectively out of the window at the new barn.

Mrs. Penn was making pies. She went on clapping the rolling-pin into the crust, although she was very pale, and her heart beat loudly.

"I dun' know but what I'd better go," said Adoniram. "I hate to go off jest now, right in the midst of hayin', but the ten-acre lot's

5. Roman charioteers raced standing in their chariots.

cut, an' I guess Rufus an' the others can git along without me three or four days. I can't get a horse round here to suit me, nohow, an' I've got to have another for all the wood-haulin' in the fall. I told Hiram to watch out, an' if he got wind of a good horse to let me know. I guess I'd better go."

"I'll get out your clean shirt an' collar," said Mrs. Penn calmly.

She laid out Adoniram's Sunday suit and his clean clothes on the bed in the little bedroom. She got his shaving-water and razor ready. At last she buttoned on his collar and fastened his black cravat.

Adoniram never wore his collar and cravat except on extra occasions. He held his head high, with a rasped dignity. When he was all ready, with his coat and hat brushed, and a lunch of pie and cheese in a paper bag, he hesitated on the threshold of the door. He looked at his wife, and his manner was defiantly apologetic. "If them cows come to-day, Sammy can drive 'em into the new barn," said he; "an' when they bring the hay up, they can pitch it in there."

"Well," replied Mrs. Penn.

Adoniram set his shaven face ahead and started. When he had cleared the door-step, he turned and looked back with a kind of nervous solemnity. "I shall be back by Saturday if nothin' happens," said he.

"Do be careful, father," returned his wife.

She stood in the door with Nanny at her elbow and watched him out of sight. Her eyes had a strange, doubtful expression in them; her peaceful forehead was contracted. She went in, and about her baking again. Nanny sat sewing. Her wedding-day was drawing nearer, and she was getting pale and thin with her steady sewing. Her mother kept glancing at her.

"Have you got that pain in your side this mornin'?" she asked.

"A little."

Mrs. Penn's face, as she worked, changed, her perplexed forehead smoothed, her eyes were steady, her lips firmly set. She formed a maxim for herself, although incoherently with her unlettered thoughts. "Unsolicited opportunities are the guide posts of the Lord to the new roads of life," she repeated in effect, and she made up her mind to her course of action.

"S'posin' I *had* wrote to Hiram," she muttered once, when she was in the pantry—"s'posin' I had wrote, an' asked him if he knew of any horse? But I didn't, an' father's goin' wa'n't none of my doin'. It looks like a providence." Her voice rang out quite loud at the last.

"What you talkin' about, mother?" called Nanny.

"Nothin'."

Mrs. Penn hurried her baking; at eleven o'clock it was all done. The load of hay from the west field came slowly down the cart track, and drew up at the new barn. Mrs. Penn ran out. "Stop!" she screamed—"stop!"

The men stopped and looked; Sammy upreared from the top of the load, and stared at his mother.

"Stop!" she cried out again. "Don't you put the hay in that barn; put it in the old one."

"Why, he said to put it in here," returned one of the haymakers, wonderingly. He was a young man, a neighbor's son, whom Adoniram hired by the year to help on the farm.

"Don't you put the hay in the new barn; there's room enough in the old one, ain't there?" said Mrs. Penn.

"Room enough," returned the hired man, in his thick, rustic tones. "Didn't need the new barn, nohow, far as room's concerned. Well, I s'pose he changed his mind." He took hold of the horses' bridles.

Mrs. Penn went back to the house. Soon the kitchen windows were darkened, and a fragrance like warm honey came into the room.

Nanny laid down her work. "I thought father wanted them to put the hay into the new barn?" she said, wonderingly.

"It's all right," replied her mother.

Sammy slid down from the load of hay, and came in to see if dinner was ready.

"I ain't goin' to get a regular dinner to-day, as long as father's gone," said his mother. "I've let the fire go out. You can have some bread an' milk an' pie. I thought we could get along." She set out some bowls of milk, some bread, and a pie on the kitchen table. "You'd better eat your dinner now," said she. "You might jest as well get through with it. I want you to help me afterward."

Nanny and Sammy stared at each other. There was something strange in their mother's manner. Mrs. Penn did not eat anything herself. She went into the pantry, and they heard her moving dishes while they ate. Presently she came out with a pile of plates. She got the clothes-basket out of the shed, and packed them in it. Nanny and Sammy watched. She brought out cups and saucers, and put them in with the plates.

"What you goin' to do, mother?" inquired Nanny, in a timid voice. A sense of something unusual made her tremble, as if it were a ghost. Sammy rolled his eyes over his pie.

"You'll see what I'm going to do," replied Mrs. Penn. "If you're through, Nanny, I want you to go up-stairs an' pack up your things; an' I want you, Sammy, to help me take down the bed in the bedroom."

"Oh, mother, what for?" gasped Nanny.

"You'll see."

During the next few hours a feat was performed by this simple, pious New England mother which was equal in its way to Wolfe's storming of the Heights of Abraham.[6] It took no more genius and audacity of bravery for Wolfe to cheer his wondering soldiers up those steep precipices, under the sleeping eyes of the enemy, than for Sarah Penn, at the head of her children, to move all their little household goods into the new barn while her husband was away.

Nanny and Sammy followed their mother's instructions without a murmur; indeed, they were overawed. There is a certain uncanny and superhuman quality about all such purely original undertakings as their mother's was to them. Nanny went back and forth with her light loads, and Sammy tugged with sober energy.

At five o'clock in the afternoon the little house in which the Penns had lived for forty years had emptied itself into the new barn.

Every builder builds somewhat for unknown purposes, and is in a measure a prophet. The architect of Adoniram Penn's barn, while he designed it for the comfort of four-footed animals, had planned better than he knew for the comfort of humans. Sarah Penn saw at a glance its possibilities. Those great box-stalls, with quilts hung before them, would make better bedrooms than the one she had occupied for forty years, and there was a tight carriage-room. The harness room, with its chimney and shelves, would make a kitchen of her dreams. The great middle space would make a parlor, by and by, fit for a palace. Upstairs there was as much room as down. With partitions and windows, what a house would there be! Sarah looked at the row of stanchions[7] before the allotted space for cows, and reflected that she would have her front entry there.

At six o'clock the stove was up in the harness-room, the kettle was boiling, and the table set for tea. It looked almost as home-like as the abandoned house across the yard had ever done. The young hired man milked, and Sarah directed him calmly to bring the milk to the new barn. He came gaping, dropping little blots of foam from the brimming pails on the grass. Before the next morning he had spread the story of Adoniram Penn's wife moving into the new barn all over the little village. Men assembled in the store and talked it over, women with shawls over their heads scuttled into each other's houses before their work was done. Any deviation from the ordinary course of life in this quiet town was enough to stop all progress in it. Everybody paused to look at the staid, independent figure on the side track.[8] There was a difference of opinion with regard to her. Some held her to be insane; some, of a lawless and rebellious spirit.

Friday the minister went to see her. It was in the forenoon, and she was at the barn door shelling pease for dinner. She looked up

6. James Wolfe (1727–59), British General, led the arduous expedition to capture Quebec from the French. He died in his hour of victory on September 13, 1759, after he scaled the steep cliffs onto the Plains of Abraham near Quebec and defeated the French.
7. Upright supports which fit loosely around a cow's neck and limit the animal's forward and backward movement.
8. A short, side railroad track connected with the main track.

and returned his salutation with dignity, then she went on with her work. She did not invite him in. The saintly expression of her face remained fixed, but there was an angry flush over it.

The minister stood awkwardly before her, and talked. She handled the pease as if they were bullets. At last she looked up, and her eyes showed the spirit that her meek front had covered for a lifetime.

"There ain't no use talkin', Mr. Hersey," said she. "I've thought it all over an' over, an' I believe I'm doin' what's right. I've made it the subject of prayer, an' it's betwixt me an' the Lord an' Adoniram. There ain't no call for nobody else to worry about it."

"Well, of course, if you have brought it to the Lord in prayer, and feel satisfied that you are doing right, Mrs. Penn," said the minister, helplessly. His thin gray-bearded face was pathetic. He was a sickly man; his youthful confidence had cooled; he had to scourge himself up to some of his pastoral duties as relentlessly as a Catholic ascetic, and then he was prostrated by the smart.

"I think it's right jest as much as I think it was right for our forefathers to come over from the old country 'cause they didn't have what belonged to 'em," said Mrs. Penn. She arose. The barn threshold might have been Plymouth Rock from her bearing. "I don't doubt you mean well, Mr. Hersey," said she, "but there are things people hadn't ought to interfere with. I've been a member of the church for over forty year. I've got my own mind an' my own feet, an' I'm goin' to think my own thoughts an' go my own ways, an' nobody but the Lord is goin' to dictate to me unless I've a mind to have him. Won't you come in an' set down? How is Mis' Hersey?"

"She is well, I thank you," replied the minister. He added some more perplexed apologetic remarks; then he retreated.

He could expound the intricacies of every character study in the Scriptures, he was competent to grasp the Pilgrim Fathers and all historical innovators, but Sarah Penn was beyond him. He could deal with primal cases, but parallel ones worsted him. But, after all, although it was aside from his province, he wondered more how Adoniram Penn would deal with his wife than how the Lord would. Everybody shared the wonder. When Adoniram's four new cows arrived, Sarah ordered three to be put in the old barn, the other in the house shed where the cooking-stove had stood. That added to the excitement. It was whispered that all four cows were domiciled in the house.

Towards sunset on Saturday, when Adoniram was expected home, there was a knot of men in the road near the new barn. The hired man had milked, but he still hung around the premises. Sarah Penn had supper all ready. There was brown-bread and baked beans and a custard pie; it was the supper that Adoniram loved on a Saturday night. She had on a clean calico, and she bore herself imperturbably. Nanny and Sammy kept close at her heels. Their eyes were large, and Nanny was full of nervous tremors. Still there was to them more pleasant excitement than anything else. An inborn confidence in their mother over their father asserted itself.

Sammy looked out of the harness-room window. "There he is," he announced, in an awed whisper. He and Nanny peeped around the casing. Mrs. Penn kept on about her work. The children watched Adoniram leave the new horse standing in the drive while he went to the house door. It was fastened. Then he went around to the shed. That door was seldom locked, even when the family was away. The thought how her father would be confronted by the cow flashed upon Nanny. There was a hysterical sob in her throat. Adoniram emerged from the shed and stood looking about in a dazed fashion. His lips moved; he was saying something, but they could not hear what it was. The hired man was peeping around a corner of the old barn, but nobody saw him.

Adoniram took the new horse by the bridle and led him across the yard to the new barn. Nanny and Sammy slunk close to their mother. The barn doors rolled back, and there stood Adoniram, with the long mild face of the great Canadian farm horse looking over his shoulder.

Nanny kept behind her mother, but Sammy stepped suddenly forward, and stood in front of her.

Adoniram stared at the group. "What on airth you all down here for?" said he. "What's the matter over to the house?"

"We've come here to live, father," said Sammy. His shrill voice quavered out bravely.

"What"—Adoniram sniffed—"what is it smells like cookin?" said he. He stepped forward and looked in the open door of the harness-room. Then he turned to his wife. His old bristling face was pale and frightened. "What on airth does this mean, mother?" he gasped.

"You come in here, father," said Sarah. She led the way into the harness-room and shut the door. "Now, father," said she, "you needn't be scared. I ain't crazy. There ain't nothin' to be upset over. But we've come here to live, an' we're goin' to live here. We've got jest as good a right here as new horses an' cows. The house wa'n't fit for us to live in any longer, an' I made up my mind I wa'n't goin' to stay there. I've done my duty by you forty year, an' I'm goin' to do it now; but I'm goin' to live here. You've got to put in some windows and partitions; an' you'll have to buy some furniture."

"Why, mother!" the old man gasped.

"You'd better take your coat off an' get washed—there's the wash-basin—an' then we'll have supper."

"Why, mother!"

Sammy went past the window, leading the new horse to the old barn. The old man saw him, and shook his head speechlessly. He tried to take off his coat, but his arms seemed to lack the power. His wife helped him. She poured some water into the tin basin, and put in a piece of soap. She got the comb and brush, and smoothed his thin gray hair after he had washed. Then she put the beans, hot bread, and tea on the table. Sammy came in, and the family drew up. Adoniram sat looking dazedly at his plate, and they waited.

"Ain't you goin' to ask a blessin', father?" said Sarah.

And the old man bent his head and mumbled.

All through the meal he stopped eating at intervals, and stared furtively at his wife; but he ate well. The home food tasted good to him, and his old frame was too sturdily healthy to be affected by his mind. But after supper he went out, and sat down on the step of the smaller door at the right of the barn, through which he had meant his Jerseys to pass in stately file, but which Sarah designed for her front house door, and he leaned his head on his hands.

After supper dishes were cleared away and the milk-pans washed, Sarah went out to him. The twilight was deepening. There was a clear green glow in the sky. Before them stretched the smooth level of field; in the distance was a cluster of hay-stacks like the huts of a village; the air was very cool and calm and sweet. The landscape might have been an ideal one of peace.

Sarah bent over and touched her husband on one of his thin, sinewy shoulders. "Father!"

The old man's shoulders heaved: he was weeping.

"Why, don't do so, father," said Sarah.

"I'll put up the—partitions, an'—everything you—want, mother."

Sarah put her apron up to her face; she was overcome by her own triumph.

Adoniram was like a fortress whose walls had no active resistance, and went down the instant the right besieging tools were used. "Why, mother," he said, hoarsely, "I hadn't no idee you was so set on't as all this comes to."

1891

BOOKER T. WASHINGTON

1856?–1915

Between the end of the Civil War and the beginning of World War I, no one exercised more influence over the course of race relations in the United States than did Booker T. Washington. Washington lacked the personal dynamism and militancy of Frederick Douglass, and did not have the keen intellectual gifts and fierce independence of W. E. B. DuBois, but Washington was a shrewder politician than either and was able to institutionalize his power in such measure that the period from 1895 to 1915 is called by historians of black America the "Era of Booker T. Washington." No small part of that power he owed to his extraordinary rhetorical skill with written and spoken language.

Washington's exact birth date is uncertain, but as an adult he settled on April 5, 1856. His mother was a slave in Hale's Ford, Virginia; his father was a white man whose identity is unknown. As a boy, Booker had, like most slaves, only a first name, and it was not until he entered school that he adopted his stepfather's first name as his last name.

Washington's early life is a catalogue of deprivation and daily struggle. At the end of the war, he accompanied his mother to Malden, West Virginia, to join his stepfather, who had found work there in a salt furnace. There he attended makeshift schools in odd hours while he held jobs as a salt packer, coal miner, and houseboy, and thus began to satisfy his "intense longing" to learn to read and write. Several years later, his desire for learning still unsatisfied, he set out on a month-long journey by rail, by cart, and on foot for Hampton Normal and Agricultural Institute in Virginia, some 500 miles from Malden. The institute had been established by the American Missionary Association a few years earlier to train black teachers and to prepare students for agriculture and such trades as harness making. Washington earned his way at Hampton by serving as a janitor, and in three years graduated with honors and with a certificate to teach trade school. He had also learned, in the quasi-military atmosphere of the school, the Puritan work ethic and the virtues of cleanliness, thrift, and hard work that later would be so central to his life and educational philosophy.

In 1881, having taught in an experimental program for Indian students at Hampton with success, Washington was offered the position as first principal of what was to become Tuskegee Institute, a school established by the Alabama legislature to train black men and women in the agricultural and mechanical trades and for teaching. Tuskegee began with thirty students, but by practicing the Christian virtues and the simple, disciplined living he preached (and obliged others to follow), and by exercising his considerable powers as a conciliator and fund raiser, Washington soon established a thriving institution in rural Alabama.

It was not until 1895, however, that he emerged as a national figure as the result of a short address, reprinted below (Chapter XIV of *Up from Slavery*), to a crowd of 2,000 people at the Atlanta Exposition of 1895. Popularly known as the "Atlanta Compromise," the speech seemed to offer to trade black civil, social, and political rights for low-level economic opportunity and nonviolent relations with whites, an offer that appealed to the vast majority of southern blacks as well as to most whites in the North and the South. It is easy in retrospect to condemn Washington for his lack of principle and failure to assume a militant stance, but if one remembers that between 1885 and 1910, 3,500 blacks were lynched in America, and that most southern states had by this time disenfranchised blacks anyway, the attractiveness to most blacks of peaceful coexistence and the desire to have the opportunity for economic self-development are understandable. Even such militant black leaders as the editor T. Thomas Fortune and W. E. B. DuBois joined in praising the speech and in supporting the philosophy of conciliation that was its pragmatic basis; their opposition to Washington did not develop until several years later.

In the years following the Atlanta speech, Washington consolidated his position as the "Moses of his race." Nothing did more to create this mythic stature than his own brilliant, simple autobiography, *Up from Slavery*, a masterpiece of the genre. In these years, he was given an honorary degree by Harvard University, was invited to dine with President Theodore Roosevelt, was widely consulted on policy questions by white political and business leaders, effectively manipulated the black and white press, and controlled public and private patronage as it concerned blacks. He was, in short, a major power broker of his time, and the debate over his life and the book that reveals it is likely to continue.

From Up from Slavery[1]
Chapter XIV. The Atlanta Exposition Address

The Atlanta Exposition, at which I had been asked to make an address as a representative of the Negro race, as stated in the last chapter, was opened with a short address from Governor Bullock. After other interesting exercises, including an invocation from Bishop Nelson, of Georgia, a dedicatory ode by Albert Howell, Jr., and addresses by the President of the Exposition and Mrs. Joseph Thompson, the President of the Woman's Board, Governor Bullock introduced me with the words, "We have with us to-day a representative of Negro enterprise and Negro civilization."

When I arose to speak, there was considerable cheering, especially from the coloured people. As I remember it now, the thing that was uppermost in my mind was the desire to say something that would cement the friendship of the races and bring about hearty coöperation between them. So far as my outward surroundings were concerned, the only thing that I recall distinctly now is that when I got up, I saw thousands of eyes looking intently into my face. The following is the address which I delivered:—

Mr. President and Gentlemen of the Board of Directors and Citizens:
One-third of the population of the South is of the Negro race. No enterprise seeking the material, civil, or moral welfare of this section can disregard this element of our population and reach the highest success. I but convey to you, Mr. President and Directors, the sentiment of the masses of my race when I say that in no way have the value and manhood of the American Negro been more fittingly and generously recognized than by the managers of this magnificent Exposition at every stage of its progress. It is a recognition that will do more to cement the friendship of the two races than any occurrence since the dawn of our freedom.
Not only this, but the opportunity here afforded will awaken among us a new era of industrial progress. Ignorant and inexpe-

---

1. Originally published serially in *Outlook* from November 3, 1900, to February 23, 1901, *Up from Slavery* was first published in book form by Doubleday, Page and Company in 1901, the source of the present text.

rienced, it is not strange that in the first years of our new life we began at the top instead of at the bottom; that a seat in Congress or the state legislature was more sought than real estate or industrial skill; that the political convention or stump speaking had more attractions than starting a dairy farm or truck garden.

A ship lost at sea for many days suddenly sighted a friendly vessel. From the mast of the unfortunate vessel was seen a signal, "Water, water; we die of thirst!" The answer from the friendly vessel at once came back, "Cast down your bucket where you are." A second time the signal, "Water, water; send us water!" ran up from the distressed vessel, and was answered, "Cast down your bucket where you are." And a third and fourth signal for water was answered, "Cast down your bucket where you are." The captain of the distressed vessel, at last heeding the injunction, cast down his bucket, and it came up full of fresh, sparkling water from the mouth of the Amazon River. To those of my race who depend on bettering their condition in a foreign land or who underestimate the importance of cultivating friendly relations with the Southern white man, who is their next-door neighbour, I would say: "Cast down your bucket where you are"—cast it down in making friends in every manly way of the people of all races by whom we are surrounded.

Cast it down in agriculture, mechanics, in commerce, in domestic service, and in the professions. And in this connection it is well to bear in mind that whatever other sins the South may be called to bear, when it comes to business, pure and simple, it is in the South that the Negro is given a man's chance in the commercial world, and in nothing is this Exposition more eloquent than in emphasizing this chance. Our greatest danger is that in the great leap from slavery to freedom we may overlook the fact that the masses of us are to live by the productions of our hands, and fail to keep in mind that we shall prosper in proportion as we learn to dignify and glorify common labour and put brains and skill into the common occupations of life; shall prosper in proportion as we learn to draw the line between the superficial and the substantial, the ornamental gewgaws of life and the useful. No race can prosper till it learns that there is as much dignity in tilling a field as in writing a poem. It is at the bottom of life we must begin, and not at the top. Nor should we permit our grievances to overshadow our opportunities.

To those of the white race who look to the incoming of those of foreign birth and strange tongue and habits for the prosperity of the South, were I permitted I would repeat what I say to my own race, "Cast down your bucket where you are." Cast it down among the eight millions of Negroes whose habits you know, whose fidelity and love you have tested in days when to have proved treacherous meant the ruin of your firesides. Cast down your bucket among these people who have, without strikes and labour wars, tilled your fields, cleared your forests, builded your railroads and cities, and brought forth treasures from the bowels of the earth, and helped make possible this magnificent representation of the progress of the South. Casting down your bucket among my people, helping and encouraging them as you are doing on these grounds, and to education of head, hand, and heart, you will find that they will buy your surplus land, make blossom the waste places in your fields, and run your factories. While doing this, you can be sure in the future, as in the past, that you and your families will be surrounded by the most patient, faithful, law-abiding, and unresentful people that the world has seen. As we have proved our loyalty to you in the past, in nursing your children, watching by the sick-bed of your mothers and fathers, and often following them with tear-dimmed eyes to their graves, so in the future, in our humble way, we shall stand by you with a devotion that no foreigner can approach, ready to lay down our lives, if need be, in defence of yours, interlacing our industrial, commercial, civil, and religious life with yours in a way that shall make the interests of both races one. In all things that are purely social we can be as separate as the fingers, yet one as the hand in all things essential to mutual progress.

There is no defence or security for any of us except in the highest intelligence and development of all. If anywhere there are efforts tending to curtail the fullest growth of the Negro, let these efforts be turned into stimulating, encouraging, and making him the most useful and intelligent citizen. Effort or means so invested will pay a thousand per cent interest. These efforts will be twice blessed—"blessing him that gives and him that takes."[2]

There is no escape through law of man or God from the inevitable:—

> "The laws of changeless justice bind
> Oppressor with oppressed;
> And close as sin and suffering joined
> We march to fate abreast."[3]

Nearly sixteen millions of hands will aid you in pulling the load upward, or they will pull against you the load downward. We shall constitute one-third and more of the ignorance and crime of the South, or one-third its intelligence and progress; we shall contribute one-third to the business and industrial prosperity of the South, or we shall prove a veritable body of death, stagnating, depressing, retarding every effort to advance the body politic.

Gentlemen of the Exposition, as we present to you our humble effort at an exhibition of our progress, you must not expect overmuch. Starting thirty years ago with ownership here and there in a few quilts and pumpkins and chickens (gathered

2. "It blesseth him that gives and him that takes" (Shakespeare, *The Merchant of Venice*, 4.1.167).

3. John Greenleaf Whittier, *Song of Negro Boatmen*.

from miscellaneous sources), remember the path that has led from these to the invention and production of agricultural implements, buggies, steam-engines, newspapers, books, statuary, carving, paintings, the management of drugstores and banks, has not been trodden without contact with thorns and thistles. While we take pride in what we exhibit as a result of our independent efforts, we do not for a moment forget that our part in this exhibition would fall far short of your expectations but for the constant help that has come to our educational life, not only from the Southern states, but especially from Northern philanthropists, who have made their gifts a constant stream of blessing and encouragement.

The wisest among my race understand that the agitation of questions of social equality is the extremest folly, and that progress in the enjoyment of all the privileges that will come to us must be the result of severe and constant struggle rather than of artificial forcing. No race that has anything to contribute to the markets of the world is long in any degree ostracized. It is important and right that all privileges of the law be ours, but it is vastly more important that we be prepared for the exercise of these privileges. The opportunity to earn a dollar in a factory just now is worth infinitely more than the opportunity to spend a dollar in an opera-house.

In conclusion, may I repeat that nothing in thirty years has given us more hope and encouragement, and drawn us so near to you of the white race, as this opportunity offered by the Exposition; and here bending, as it were, over the altar that represents the results of the struggles of your race and mine, both starting practically empty-handed three decades ago, I pledge that in your effort to work out the great and intricate problem which God has laid at the doors of the South, you shall have at all times the patient, sympathetic help of my race; only let this be constantly in mind, that, while from representations in these buildings of the product of field, of forest, of mine, of factory, letters, and art, much good will come, yet far above and beyond material benefits will be that higher good, that, let us pray God, will come, in a blotting out of sectional differences and racial animosities and suspicions, in a determination to administer absolute justice, in a willing obedience among all classes to the mandates of law. This, coupled with our material prosperity, will bring into our beloved South a new heaven and a new earth.

The first thing that I remember, after I had finished speaking, was that Governor Bullock rushed across the platform and took me by the hand, and that others did the same. I received so many and such hearty congratulations that I found it difficult to get out of the building. I did not appreciate to any degree, however, the impression which my address seemed to have made, until the next morning, when I went into the business part of the city. As soon as I was recognized, I was surprised to find myself pointed out and surrounded by a crowd of men who wished to shake hands with me.

This was kept up on every street on to which I went, to an extent which embarrassed me so much that I went back to my boarding-place. The next morning I returned to Tuskegee. At the station in Atlanta, and at almost all of the stations at which the train stopped between the city and Tuskegee, I found a crowd of people anxious to shake hands with me.

The papers in all parts of the United States published the address in full, and for months afterward there were complimentary editorial references to it. Mr. Clark Howell, the editor of the Atlanta *Constitution*, telegraphed to a New York paper, among other words, the following, "I do not exaggerate when I say that Professor Booker T. Washington's address yesterday was one of the most notable speeches, both as to character and as to the warmth of its reception, ever delivered to a Southern audience. The address was a revelation. The whole speech is a platform upon which blacks and whites can stand with full justice to each other."

The Boston *Transcript* said editorially: "The speech of Booker T. Washington at the Atlanta Exposition, this week, seems to have dwarfed all the other proceedings and the Exposition itself. The sensation that it has caused in the press has never been equalled."

I very soon began receiving all kinds of propositions from lecture bureaus, and editors of magazines and papers, to take the lecture platform, and to write articles. One lecture bureau offered me fifty thousand dollars, or two hundred dollars a night and expenses, if I would place my services at its disposal for a given period. To all these communications I replied that my life-work was at Tuskegee; and that whenever I spoke it must be in the interests of the Tuskegee school and my race, and that I would enter into no arrangements that seemed to place a mere commercial value upon my services.

Some days after its delivery I sent a copy of my address to the President of the United States, the Hon. Grover Cleveland.[4] I received from him the following autograph reply:—

Gray Gables
Buzzard's Bay, Mass., October 6, 1895
Booker T. Washington, Esq.:

My Dear Sir: I thank you for sending me a copy of your address delivered at the Atlanta Exposition.

I thank you with much enthusiasm for making the address. I have read it with intense interest, and I think the Exposition would be fully justified if it did not do more than furnish the opportunity for its delivery. Your words cannot fail to delight and encourage all who wish well for your race; and if our coloured fellow-citizens do not from your utterances father new hope and form new determinations to gain every valuable

4. Grover Cleveland (1837–1908), 22nd (1885–89) and 24th (1893–97) President of the United States.

advantage offered them by their citizenship, it will be strange indeed. Yours very truly,

Grover Cleveland

Later I met Mr. Cleveland, for the first time, when, as President, he visited the Atlanta Exposition. At the request of myself and others he consented to spend an hour in the Negro Building, for the purpose of inspecting the Negro exhibit and of giving the coloured people in attendance an opportunity to shake hands with him. As soon as I met Mr. Cleveland I became impressed with his simplicity, greatness, and rugged honesty. I have met him many times since then, both at public functions and at his private residence in Princeton, and the more I see of him the more I admire him. When he visited the Negro Building in Atlanta he seemed to give himself up wholly, for that hour, to the coloured people. He seemed to be as careful to shake hands with some old coloured "auntie" clad partially in rags, and to take as much pleasure in doing so, as if he were greeting some millionaire. Many of the coloured people took advantage of the occasion to get him to write his name in a book or on a slip of paper. He was as careful and patient in doing this as if he were putting his signature to some great state document.

Mr. Cleveland has not only shown his friendship for me in many personal ways, but has always consented to do anything I have asked of him for our school. This he has done, whether it was to make a personal donation or to use his influence in securing the donations of others. Judging from my personal acquaintance with Mr. Cleveland, I do not believe that he is conscious of possessing any colour prejudice. He is too great for that. In my contact with people I find that, as a rule, it is only the little, narrow people who live for themselves, who never read good books, who do not travel, who never open up their souls in a way to permit them to come into contact with other souls—with the great outside world. No man whose vision is bounded by colour can come into contact with what is highest and best in the world. In meeting men, in many places, I have found that the happiest people are those who do the most for others; the most miserable are those who do the least. I have also found that few things, if any, are capable of making one so blind and narrow as race prejudice. I often say to our students, in the course of my talks to them on Sunday evenings in the chapel, that the longer I live and the more experience I have of the world, the more I am convinced that, after all, the one thing that is most worth living for—and dying for, if need be—is the opportunity of making some one else more happy and more useful.

The coloured people and the coloured newspapers at first seemed to be greatly pleased with the character of my Atlanta address, as well as with its reception. But after the first burst of enthusiasm began to die away, and the coloured people began reading the speech in cold type, some of them seemed to feel that they had been hypnotized. They seemed to feel that I had been too liberal in my remarks toward the Southern whites, and that I had not spoken out strongly enough for what they termed the "rights" of the race. For a while there was a reaction, so far as a certain element of my own race was concerned, but later these reactionary ones seemed to have been won over to my way of believing and acting.

While speaking of changes in public sentiment, I recall that about ten years after the school at Tuskegee was established, I had an experience that I shall never forget. Dr. Lyman Abbott, then the pastor of Plymouth Church, and also editor of the *Outlook* (then the *Christian Union*), asked me to write a letter for his paper giving my opinion of the exact condition, mental and moral of the coloured ministers in the South, as based upon my observations. I wrote the letter, giving the exact facts as I conceived them to be. The picture painted was a rather black one—or, since I am black, shall I say "white"? It could not be otherwise with a race but a few years out of slavery, a race which had not had time or opportunity to produce a competent ministry.

What I said soon reached every Negro minister in the country, I think, and the letters of condemnation which I received from them were not few. I think that for a year after the publication of this article every association and every conference or religious body of any kind, of my race, that met, did not fail before adjourning to pass a resolution condemning me, or calling upon me to retract or modify what I had said. Many of these organizations went so far in their resolutions as to advise parents to cease sending their children to Tuskegee. One association even appointed a "missionary" whose duty it was to warn the people against sending their children to Tuskegee. This missionary had a son in the school, and I noticed that, whatever the "missionary" might have said or done with regard to others, he was careful not to take his son away from the institution. Many of the coloured papers, especially those that were the organs of religious bodies, joined in the general chorus of condemnation or demands for retraction.

During the whole time of the excitement, and through all the criticism, I did not utter a word of explanation or retraction. I knew that I was right, and that time and the sober second thought of the people would vindicate me. It was not long before the bishops and other church leaders began to make a careful investigation of the conditions of the ministry, and they found out that I was right. In fact, the oldest and most influential bishop in one branch of the Methodist Church said that my words were far too mild. Very soon public sentiment began making itself felt, in demanding a purifying of the ministry. While this is not yet complete by any means, I think I may say, without egotism, and I have been told by many of our most influential ministers, that my words had much to do with starting a demand for the placing of a higher type of men in the pulpit. I have had the satisfaction of having many who once condemned me thank me heartily for my frank words.

The change of the attitude of the Negro ministry, so far as regards myself, is so complete that at the present time I have no warmer friends among any class than I have among the clergymen. The improvement in the character and life of the Negro ministers is one of the most gratifying evidences of the progress of the race. My experience with them, as well as other events in my life, convince me that the thing to do, when one feels sure that he has said or done the right thing, and is condemned, is to stand still and keep quiet. If he is right, time will show it.

In the midst of the discussion which was going on concerning my Atlanta speech, I received the letter which I give below, from Dr. Gilman, the President of Johns Hopkins University, who had been made chairman of the judges of award in connection with the Atlanta Exposition:—

Johns Hopkins University, Baltimore
President's Office, September 30, 1895
Dear Mr. Washington: Would it be agreeable to you to be one of the Judges of Award in the Department of Education at Atlanta? If so, I shall be glad to place your name upon the list. A line by telegraph will be welcomed. Yours very truly,
D. C. Gilman

I think I was even more surprised to receive this invitation than I had been to receive the invitation to speak at the opening of the Exposition. It was to be a part of my duty, as one of the jurors, to pass not only upon the exhibits of the coloured schools, but also upon those of the white schools. I accepted the position, and spent a month in Atlanta in performance of the duties which it entailed. The board of jurors was a large one, consisting in all of sixty members. It was about equally divided between Southern white people and Northern white people. Among them were college presidents, leading scientists and men of letters, and specialists in many subjects. When the group of jurors to which I was assigned met for organization, Mr. Thomas Nelson Page,[5] who was one of the number, moved that I be made secretary of that division, and the motion was unanimously adopted. Nearly half of our division were Southern people. In performing my duties in the inspection of the exhibits of white schools I was in every case treated with respect, and at the close of our labours I parted from my associates with regret.

I am often asked to express myself more freely than I do upon the political condition and the political future of my race. These

5. Thomas Nelson Page (1853–1922), American author and diplomat.

recollections of my experience in Atlanta give me the opportunity to do so briefly. My own belief is, although I have never before said so in so many words, that the time will come when the Negro in the South will be accorded all the political rights which his ability, character, and material possessions entitle him to. I think, though, that the opportunity to freely exercise such political rights will not come in any large degree through outside or artificial forcing, but will be accorded to the Negro by the Southern white people themselves, and that they will protect him in the exercise of those rights. Just as soon as the South gets over the old feeling that it is being forced by "foreigners," or "aliens," to do something which it does not want to do, I believe that the change in the direction that I have indicated is going to begin. In fact, there are indications that it is already beginning in a slight degree.

Let me illustrate my meaning. Suppose that some months before the opening of the Atlanta Exposition there had been a general demand from the press and public platform outside the South that a Negro be given a place on the opening programme, and that a Negro be placed upon the board of jurors of award. Would any such recognition of the race have taken place? I do not think so. The Atlanta officials went as far as they did because they felt it to be a pleasure, as well as a duty, to reward what they considered merit in the Negro race. Say what we will, there is something in human nature which we cannot blot out, which makes one man, in the end, recognize and reward merit in another, regardless of colour or race.

I believe it is the duty of the Negro—as the greater part of the race is already doing—to deport himself modestly in regard to political claims, depending upon the slow but sure influences that proceed from the possession of property, intelligence, and high character for the full recognition of his political rights. I think that the according of the full exercise of political rights is going to be a matter of natural, slow growth, not an over-night, gourd-vine affair. I do not believe that the Negro should cease voting, for a man cannot learn the exercise of self-government by ceasing to vote, any more than a boy can learn to swim by keeping out of the water, but I do believe that in his voting he should more and more be influenced by those of intelligence and character who are his next-door neighbours.

I know coloured men who, through the encouragement, help, and advice of Southern white people, have accumulated thousands of dollars' worth of property, but who, at the same time, would never think of going to those same persons for advice concerning the casting of their ballots. This, it seems to me, is unwise and unreasonable, and should cease. In saying this I do not mean that the Negro should truckle, or not vote from principle, for the instant he ceases to vote from principle he loses the confidence and respect of the Southern white man even.

I do not believe that any state should make a law that permits an ignorant and poverty-stricken white man to vote, and prevents a black man in the same condition from voting. Such a law is not only unjust, but it will react, as all unjust laws do, in time; for the effect of such a law is to encourage the Negro to secure education and property, and at the same time it encourages the white man to remain in ignorance and poverty. I believe that in time, through the operation of intelligence and friendly race relations, all cheating at the ballot-box in the South will cease. It will become apparent that the white man who begins by cheating a Negro out of his ballot soon learns to cheat a white man out of his, and that the man who does this ends his career of dishonesty by the theft of property or by some equally serious crime. In my opinion, the time will come when the South will encourage all of its citizens to vote. It will see that it pays better, from every standpoint, to have healthy, vigorous life than to have that political stagnation which always results when one-half of the population has no share and no interest in the Government.

As a rule, I believe in universal, free suffrage, but I believe that in the South we are confronted with peculiar conditions that justify the protection of the ballot in many of the states, for a while at least, either by an educational test, a property test, or by both combined; but whatever tests are required, they should be made to apply with equal and exact justice to both races.

1901

CHARLES W. CHESNUTT
1858–1932

Charles Waddell Chesnutt was born on June 20, 1858, in Cleveland, Ohio. His parents were born free Negroes from North Carolina; his father served in the Union Army and after the Civil War moved his family back to the South. Chesnutt was essentially self-taught but eventually became a teacher, school principal, newspaper reporter, accountant, court stenographer, and lawyer before he first achieved fame as a writer in 1887. In that year the *Atlantic Monthly* published *The Goophered Grapevine*. This was the first of what was to be a group of stories in the regional-dialect folktale tradition earlier brought to high art and national popularity by Joel Chandler Harris. Most readers of the story would have supposed that, like Harris, Chesnutt was white because the stories are framed in the language of an ostensibly superior and bemused white narrator. Chesnutt's Uncle Julius, though superficially like Harris's Uncle Remus, is in reality a wise old slave who has learned not only to survive but to use and defeat his supposed superiors through a mocking mask of ignorance. Chesnutt's contemporaries saw the picturesque stereotype of the old black man as an easygoing, shuffling retainer and took pleasure in the authenticity of the language, customs, and settings in these stories; only in recent years, however, have readers had the added satisfaction of perceiving the ironic drama played out between "master" and "slave."

With age and fame Chesnutt became more militant. Chesnutt was himself very light-skinned but had never tried to hide his racial identity; it was not until 1899, however, that he revealed himself to his readers as a black man. In that year the dialect stories set in rural North Carolina were gathered and published as *The Conjure Woman*. In addition, two other books appeared: a collection of nondialect, largely urban stories entitled *The Wife of His Youth and Other Stories of the Color Line* and a biography, the *Life of Frederick Douglass*. A number of his stories, written in the 1890s, dealt with the usually disastrous consequences of light-skinned Negroes attempting to pass as whites. In his first novel, *The House behind the Cedars* (1900), he continued this theme and added sharp attacks on the white South and on those black men who betrayed their racial inheritance. Chesnutt's next two novels, *The Marrow of Tradition* (1901) and *The Colonel's Dream* (1905), were even more blunt in their protest against the racial injustice of whites.

Chesnutt completed one more novel before his death, but could not find a publisher for it perhaps because the bitterness of the work is insufficiently converted into fiction. In 1928, he received the Spingarn Medal for his pioneering contribution to the literary depiction of the "life and struggle of Americans of Negro descent." In 1880, Chesnutt had recorded in his journal the desire to devote himself to writing because as a writer he could elevate both races by preparing them to recognize their common, admirable, and fallible humanity. By his own example over the next five decades as a man who protested the unfair treatment of any person regardless of skin color, Chesnutt realized his desire to an extent that we are only beginning to understand.

The Goophered Grapevine[1]

About ten years ago my wife was in poor health, and our family doctor, in whose skill and honesty I had implicit confidence, advised a change of climate. I was engaged in grape-culture in northern Ohio, and decided to look for a location suitable for carrying on the same business in some Southern State. I wrote to a cousin who had gone into the turpentine business in central North Carolina, and he assured me that no better place could be found in the South than the State and neighborhood in which he lived: climate and soil were all that could be asked for, and land could be bought for a mere song. A cordial invitation to visit him while I looked into the matter was accepted. We found the weather delightful at that season, the end of the summer, and were most hospitably entertained. Our host placed a horse and buggy at our

1. First published in the *Atlantic Monthly*, August, 1887—the source for the present text—this story was next published in book form in the collection *The Conjure Woman* (1899).

disposal, and himself acted as guide until I got somewhat familiar with the country.

I went several times to look at a place which I thought might suit me. It had been at one time a thriving plantation, but shiftless cultivation had well-nigh exhausted the soil. There had been a vineyard of some extent on the place, but it had not been attended to since the war, and had fallen into utter neglect. The vines—here partly supported by decayed and broken-down arbors, there twining themselves among the branches of the slender saplings which had sprung up among them—grew in wild and unpruned luxuriance, and the few scanty grapes which they bore were the undisputed prey of the first comer. The site was admirably adapted to grape-raising; the soil, with a little attention, could not have been better; and with the native grape, the luscious scuppernong, mainly to rely upon, I felt sure that I could introduce and cultivate successfully a number of other varieties.

One day I went over with my wife, to show her the place. We drove between the decayed gate-posts—the gate itself had long since disappeared—and up the straight, sandy lane to the open space where a dwelling-house had once stood. But the house had fallen a victim to the fortunes of war, and nothing remained of it except the brick pillars upon which the sills had rested. We alighted, and walked about the place for a while; but on Annie's complaining of weariness I led the way back to the yard, where a pine log, lying under a spreading elm, formed a shady though somewhat hard seat. One end of the log was already occupied by a venerable-looking colored man. He held on his knees a hat full of grapes, over which he was smacking his lips with great gusto, and a pile of grape-skins near him indicated that the performance was no new thing. He respectfully rose as we approached, and was moving away, when I begged him to keep his seat.

"Don't let us disturb you," I said. "There's plenty of room for us all."

He resumed his seat with somewhat of embarrassment.

"Do you live around here?" I asked, anxious to put him at his ease.

"Yas, suh. I lives des ober yander, behine de nex' san'-hill, on de Lumberton plank-road."

"Do you know anything about the time when this vineyard was cultivated?"

"Lawd bless yer, suh, I knows all about it. Dey ain' na'er a man in dis settlement w'at won' tell yer ole Julius McAdoo 'uz bawn an' raise' on dis yer same plantation. Is you de Norv'n gemman w'at's gwine ter buy de ole vimya'd?"

"I am looking at it," I replied; "but I don't know that I shall care to buy unless I can be reasonably sure of making something out of it."

"Well, suh, you is a stranger ter me, en I is a stranger ter you, en we is bofe strangers ter one anudder, but 'f I 'uz in yo' place, I would n' buy dis vimya'd."

"Why not?" I asked.

"Well, I dunner whe'r you b'lieves in cunj'in er not,—some er de w'ite folks don't, er says dey don't,—but de truf er de matter is dat dis yer old vimya'd is goophered."

"Is what?" I asked, not grasping the meaning of this unfamiliar word.

"Is goophered, cunju'd, bewitch'."

He imparted this information with such solemn earnestness, and with such an air of confidential mystery, that I felt somewhat interested, while Annie was evidently much impressed, and drew closer to me.

"How do you know it is bewitched?" I asked.

"I would n'spec' for you ter b'lieve me 'less you know all 'bout de fac's. But ef you en young miss dere doan' min' lis'n'in' ter a ole nigger run on a minute er two while you er restin,' I kin 'splain to yer how it all happen'."

We assured him that we would be glad to hear how it all happened, and he began to tell us. At first the current of his memory —or imagination—seemed somewhat sluggish; but as his embarrassment wore off, his language flowed more freely, and the story acquired perspective and coherence. As he became more and more absorbed in the narrative, his eyes assumed a dreamy expression, and he seemed to lose sight of his auditors, and to be living over again in monologue his life on the old plantation.

"Ole Mars Dugal' McAdoo bought dis place long many years befo' de wah, en I 'member well w'en he sot out all dis yer part er de plantation in scuppernon's. De vimes growed monst'us fas', en Mars Dugal' made a thousan gallon er scuppernon' wine eve'y year.

"Now, ef dey's an'thing a nigger lub, nex' ter 'possum, en chick'n, en watermillyums, it's scuppernon's. Dey ain' niffin dat kin stan' up side'n de scuppernon' for sweetness; sugar ain't a suckumstance ter scuppernon'. W'en de season is nigh 'bout ober, en de grapes begin ter swivel up des a little wid de wrinkles er ole age,—w'en de skin git sof' en brown,—den de scuppernon' make you smack yo' lip en roll yo' eye en wush fer mo'; so I reckon it ain' very 'stonishin' dat niggers lub scuppernon'.

"Dey wuz a sight er niggers in de naberhood er de vimya'd. Dere wuz ole Mars Henry Brayboy's niggers, en ole Mars Dunkin McLean's niggers, en Mars Dugal's own niggers; den dey wuz a settlement er free niggers en po' buckrahs[2] down by de Wim'l'ton Road, en Mars Dugal' had de only vimya'd in de naberhood. I reckon it ain't so much so nowadays, but befo' de wah, in slab'ry

---

2. "Buckrahs": regionalism meaning white men.

times, er nigger did n' mine goin' fi' er ten mile in a night, w'en dey wuz sump'n good ter eat at de yuther een.

"So atter a w'ile Mars Dugal' begin ter miss his scuppernon's. Co'se he 'cuse ' de niggers er it, but dey all 'nied it ter de las'. Mars Dugal' sot spring guns en steel traps, en he en de oberseah sot up nights once't er twice't, tel one night Mars Dugal'—he 'uz a monst'us keerless man—got his leg shot full er cow-peas. But somehow er nudder dey could n'nebber ketch none er de niggers. I dunner how it happen, but it happen des like I tell yer, en de grapes kep' on a-goin des de same.

"'But bimeby ole Mars Dugal' fix' up a plan ter stop it. Dey 'uz a cunjuh 'ooman livin' down mongs' de free niggers on de Wim'l'- ton Road, en all de darkies from Rockfish ter Beaver Crick wuz feared uv her. She could wuk de mos' powerfulles' kind er goopher, —could make people hab fits er rheumatiz, er make 'em des dwinel away en die; en dey say she went out ridin' de niggers at night, for she wuz a witch 'sides bein' a cunjuh 'ooman. Mars Dugal' hearn 'bout Aun' Peggy's doin's, en begun ter 'flect whe'r er no he could n'git her ter he'p him keep de niggers off'n de grapevines. One day in de spring er de year, ole miss pack' up a basket er chick'n en poun'-cake, en a bottle er scuppernon' wine, en Mars Dugal' tuk it in his buggy en driv ober ter Aun' Peggy's cabin. He tuk de basket in, en had a long talk wid Aun' Peggy. De nex' day Aun' Peggy come up ter de vimya'd. De niggers seed her slippin' 'roun', en day soon foun' out what she 'uz doin' dere. Mars Dugal' had hi'ed her ter goopher de grapevines. She sa'ntered 'roun mongs' de vimes, en tuk a leaf fum dis one, en a grape-hull fum dat one, en a grape-seed fum anudder one; en den a little twig fum here, en a little pinch er dirt fum dere—en put it all in a big black bottle, wid a snake's toof en a speckle' hen's gall en some ha'rs fum a black cat's tail, en den fill' de bottle wid scuppernon' wine. W'en she got de goopher all ready en fix', she tuk 'n went out in de woods en buried it under de root uv a red oak tree, en den come back en tole one er de niggers she done goopher de grapevines, en a'er a nigger w'at eat dem grapes 'ud be sho ter die inside'n twel' mont's.

"Atter dat de niggers let de scuppernons' lone, en Mars Dugal' didn' hab no'casion ter fine no mo' fault; en de season wuz mos' gone, w'en a strange gemman stop at de plantation one night ter see Mars Dugal' on some business; en his coachman, seein' de scuppernon's growin' so nice en sweet, slip 'roun behine de smoke- houses, en et all de scuppernon's he could hole. Nobody did n' notice it at de time, but dat night, on de way home, de gemman's hoss runned away en kill' de coachman. W'en we hearn de noos, Aun' Lucy, de cook, she up 'n say she seed de strange nigger eat'n er de scuppernon's behind de smoke-house; en den we knowed de goopher had b'en er wukkin. Den one er de nigger chilluns runned away fum de quarters one day, en got in de scuppernon's, en died de nex' week. W'ite folks say he die' er de fevah, but de niggers knowed it wuz de goopher. So you k'n be sho de darkies didn' hab much ter do wid dem scuppernon' vimes.

"W'en de scuppernon' season 'uz ober fer dat year, Mars Dugal' foun' he had made fifteen hund'ed gallon er wine; en one er de niggers hearn him laffin' wid de oberseah fit ter kill, en sayin' dem fifteen hund'ed gallon er wine wuz monst'us good intrus' on de ten dollars he laid out on de vimya'd. So I 'low ez he paid Aun' Peggy ten dollars fer to goopher de grapevimes.

"De goopher did'n wuk no mo' tel de nex' summer, w'en 'long to'ds de middle er de season one er de fiel' han's died; en ez dat lef' Mars Dugal' sho't er han's, he went off ter town fer ter buy anudder. He fotch de noo nigger home wid 'im. He wuz er ole nigger, er de color er a gingy-cake, en ball ez a hoss-apple on de top er his head. He wuz a peart ole nigger, do', en could do a big day's wuk.

"Now it happen dat one er de niggers on de nex' plantation, one er ole Mars Henry Brayboy's niggers, had runned away de day befo', en tuk ter de swamp, en ole Mars Dugal' en some er de yuther nabor w'ite folks had gone out wid dere guns en dere dogs fer ter he'p 'em hunt fer de nigger; en de han's on our own plantation wuz all so flusterated dat we fuhgot ter tell de noo han' 'bout de goopher on de scuppernon' vimes. Co'se he smell de grapes en see de vimes, an atter dahk de fus' thing he done wuz ter slip off ter de grapevimes 'dout sayin' nuffin ter nobody. Nex' mawnin' he tole some er de niggers 'bout de fine bait er scuppernon' he et de night befo'.

"W'en dey tole 'im 'bout de goopher on de grapevimes, he 'uz dat tarrified dat he turn pale, en look des like he gwine ter die right in his tracks. De oberseah come up en axed w'at 'uz de matter; en w'en dey tole 'im Henry be'n eatin' er de scuppernon's, en got de goopher on 'im, he gin Henry a big drink er w'iskey, en 'low dat de nex' rainy day he take 'im ober ter Aun' Peggy's, en see ef she wouldn' take de goopher off'n him, seein' ez he didn't know nuffin erbout it tel he done et de grapes.

"Sho nuff, it rain de nex' day, en de oberseah went ober ter Aun' Peggy's wid Henry. En Aun' Peggy say dat bein' ez Henry didn' know 'bout de goopher, en et de grapes in ign'ance er de quinseconces, she reckon she mought be able fer ter take de goopher off'n him. So she fotch out er bottle wid some cunjuh medicine in it, en po'd some out in a go'd fer Henry ter drink. He manage ter git it down; he say it tas'e like whiskey wid sump'n bitter in it. She 'lowed dat 'ud keep de goopher off'n him tel de spring; but w'en de sap begin' ter rise in de grapevimes he ha ter come en see her agin, en she tell him w'at e's ter do.

"Nex' spring, w'en de sap commence' ter rise in de scuppernon'

vime, Henry tuk a ham one night. Whar'd he git de ham? I doan
know; dey wa'nt no hams on de plantation 'cep'n w'at 'uz in de
smoke-house, but I never see Henry 'bout de smoke-house. But ez
I wuz a-sayin', he tuk de ham ober ter Aun' Peggy's; en Aun'
Peggy tole 'im dat w'en Mars Dugal' begin ter prune de grapevimes,
he mus' go en take 'n scrape off de sap whar it ooze out'n de cut een's
er de vimes, en 'n'int his ball head wid it; en ef he do dat once't a
year de goopher wouldn' wuk agin 'im long ez he done it. En bein
'ez he fotch her de ham, she fix' it so he kin eat all de scuppernon' he
want.

"So Henry 'n'int his head wid de sap out'n de big grapevime des
ha'f way 'twix' de quarters en de big house, en de goopher nebber
wuk agin him dat summer. But de beatenes' thing you eber see
happen ter Henry. Up ter dat time he wuz ez ball ez a sweeten'
'tater, but des ez soon ez de young leaves begun ter come out on de
grapevimes de ha'r begun ter grow out on Henry's head, en by de
middle er de summer he had de bigges' head er ha'r on de plantation. Befo' dat, Henry had tol'able good ha'r 'roun' de aidges, but
soon ez de young grapes begun ter come Henry's ha'r begun ter
quirl all up in little balls, des like dis yer reg'lar grapy ha'r, en by de
time de grapes got ripe his head look des like a bunch er grapes.
Combin' it did n' do no good; he wuk at it ha'f de night wid er Jim
Crow,[3] en think he git it straighten' out, but in de mawnin' de
grapes 'ud be dere des de same. So he gin it up, en tried ter keep de
grapes down by havin' his ha'r cut sho't.

"But dat wa'nt de quares' thing 'bout de goopher. When Henry
come ter de plantation, he wuz gittin' a little ole an stiff in de
j'ints. But dat summer he got des ez spray en libely ez any young
nigger on de plantation; fac' he got so biggity dat Mars Jackson, de
oberseah, ha' ter th'eaten ter whip 'im, ef he did n' stop cuttin' up
his didos en behave hisse'f. But de mos' cur'ouses' thing happen' in
de fall, when de sap begin ter go down in de grapevimes. Fus', when
de grapes 'uz gethered, de knots begun ter straighten out'n Henry's
h'ar; en w'en de leaves begin ter fall, Henry's ha'r begin ter drap
out; en w'en de vimes 'uz b'ar, Henry's head wuz baller'n it wuz in
de spring, en he begin ter git ole en stiff in de j'ints ag'in, en paid
no mo' tention ter de gals dyoin' er de whole winter. En nex'
spring, w'en he rub de sap on ag'in, he got young ag'in, en so soopl
en libely dat none er de young niggers on de plantation could n'
jump, ner dance, ner hoe ez much cotton ez Henry. But in de fall
er de year his grapes begun ter straighten out, en his j'ints ter git
stiff, en his ha'r drap off, en de rheumatiz begin ter wrastle wid 'im.

"Now, ef you'd a knowed ole Mars Dugal' McAdoo, you'd a
knowed dat it ha' ter be a mighty rainy day when he could n' fine
sump'n fer his niggers ter do, en it ha' ter be a mighty little hole he

---

3. "A small card, resembling a curry-comb in construction, and used by negroes in
the rural districts instead of a comb" [Chesnutt's note].

could n' crawl thoo, en ha' ter be a monst'us cloudy night w'en a dollar git by him in de dahkness; en w'en he see how Henry git young in de spring en ole in de fall, he 'lowed ter hisse'f ez how he could make mo' money outen Henry dan by wukkin' him in de cotton fiel'. 'Long de nex' spring, atter de sap commence' ter rise, en Henry 'n'int 'is head en commence fer ter git young en soopl, Mars Dugal' up'n tuk Henry ter town, en sole 'i fer fifteen hunder' dollars. Co'se de man w't bought Henry did n' know nuffin 'bout de goopher, en Mars Dugal' did n' see no 'casion fer ter tell 'im. Long to'ds de fall, w'en de sap went down, Henry begin ter git ole again same ez yuzhal, en his noo marster begin ter git skeered les'n he gwine ter lose his fifteen-hunder'-dollar nigger. He sent fer a mighty fine doctor, but de med'cine did n' 'pear ter do no good; de goopher had a good holt. Henry tole de doctor 'bout de goopher, but de doctor des laff at 'im.

"One day in de winter Mars Dugal' went ter town, en wuz santerin' 'long de Main Street, when who should he meet but Henry's noo marster. Dey said 'Hoddy,' en Mars Dugal' ax 'im ter hab a seegyar; en atter dey run on awhile 'bout de craps en de weather, Mars Dugal' ax 'im, sorter keerless, like ez ef he des thought of it, —

" 'How you like de nigger I sole you las' spring?'

"Henry's marster shuck his head en knock de ashes off'n his seegyar.

" 'Spec' I made a bad bahgin when I bought dat nigger. Henry done good wuk all de summer, but sence de fall set in he 'pears ter be sorter pinin' away. Dey ain' nuffin pertickler de matter wid 'im —leastways de doctor say so—'cep'n' a tech er de rheumatiz; but his ha'r is all fell out, en ef he don't pick up his strenk mighty soon, I spec' I'm gwine ter lose 'im.'

"Dey smoked on awhile, en bimeby ole mars say, 'Well, a bahgin's a bahgin, but you en me is good fren's, en I doan wan' ter see you lose all de money you paid fer dat digger; en ef w'at you say is so, en I ain't 'sputin' it, he ain't wuf much now. I spec's you wukked him too ha'd dis summer, er e'se de swamps down here don't agree wid de san'-hill nigger. So you des lemme know, en ef he gits any wusser I'll be willin' ter gib yer five hund'ed dollars fer 'im, en take my chances on his livin'.'

"Sho nuff, when Henry begun ter draw up wid de rheumatiz en it look like he gwine ter die fer sho, his noo marster sen' fer Mars Dugal', en Mars Dugal' gin him what he promus, en brung Henry home ag'in. He tuk good keer uv 'im dyoin' er de winter,—give 'im w'iskey ter rub his rheumatiz, en terbacker ter smoke, en all he want ter eat,—'caze a nigger w'at he could make a thousan' dollars a year off'n did n' grow on eve'y huckleberry bush.

"Nex' spring, w'en de sap ris en Henry's ha'r commence' ter sprout, Mars Dugal' sole 'im ag'in, down in Robeson County dis time; en he kep' dat sellin' business up fer five year er mo'. Henry nebber say nuffin 'bout de goopher ter his noo marsters, 'caze he knew he gwine ter be tuk good keer uv de nex' winter, w'en Mars Dugal' buy him back. En Mars Dugal' made 'nuff money off'n Henry ter buy anudder plantation ober on Beaver Crick.

"But long 'bout de een' er dat five year dey come a stranger ter stop at de plantation. De fus' day he 'us dere he went out wid Mars Dugal' en spent all de mawnin' lookin' ober de vimya'd, en atter dinner dey spent all de evenin' playin' kya'ds. De niggers soon 'skiver' dat he wuz a Yankee, en dat he come down ter Norf C'lina fer ter learn de w'ite folks how to raise grapes en make wine. He promus Mars Dugal' he cud make de grapevimes ba'r twice't ez many grapes, en dat de noo wine-press he wuz a-sellin' would make mo' d'n twice't ez many gallons er wine. En ole Mars Dugal' des drunk it all in, des 'peared ter be bewitched wid dat Yankee. W'en de darkies see dat Yankee runnin' 'roun de vimya'd en diggin' under de grapevines, dey shuk dere heads, en 'lowed dat dey feared Mars Dugal' losin' his min'. Mars Dugal' had all de dirt dug away fum under de roots er all de scuppernon' vimes, an' let 'em stan' dat away fer a week er mo'. Den dat Yankee made de niggers fix up a mixtry er lime en ashes en manyo,[4] en po' it roun' de roots er de grapevimes. Den he 'vise' Mars Dugal' fer ter trim de vimes close't, en Mars Dugal' tuck 'n done eve'ything de Yankee tole him ter do. Dyoin' all er dis time, mind yer, 'e wuz libbin' off'n de fat er de lan', at de big house, en playin' kyards wid Mars Dugal' eve'y night; en dey say Mars Dugal' los' mo'n a thousan' dollars dyoin' er de week dat Yankee wuz a runnin' de grapevimes.

"W'en de sap ris nex' spring, ole Henry 'n'inted his head ez yuzhal, en his ha'r commence' ter grow des de same ez it done eve'y year. De scuppernon' vimes growed monst's fas', en de leaves wuz greener en thicker dan dey eber be'n dyoin my remem'ance; en Henry's ha'r growed out thicker dan eber, en he 'peared ter git younger 'n younger, en soopler 'n soopler; en seein' ez he wuz sho't er han's dat spring, havin' tuk in consid'able noo groun', Mars Dugal' 'cluded he would n' sell Henry 'tel he git de crap in en de cotton chop'. So he kep' Henry on de plantation.

"But 'long 'bout time fer de grapes ter come on de scuppernon' vimes, dey 'peared ter come a change ober dem; de leaves wivered en swivel' up, en de young grapes turn' yaller, en bimeby eve'ybody on de plantation could see dat de whole vimya'd wuz dyin'. Mars Dugal' tuck'n water de vimes en done all he could, but 't wan' no use: dat Yankee done bus' de watermillyum. One time de vimes picked up a bit, en Mars Dugal' thought dey wuz gwine ter come out ag'in; but dat Yankee done dug too close unde' de roots, en

---

4. Mango, yam, or sweet potato; though there are differences among these starchy fruits or roots, the names are used interchangeably.

prune de branches too close ter de vime, en all dat lime en ashes done burn' de life outen de vimes, en dey des kep' a with'in' en a swivelin'.

"All dis time de goopher wuz a-wukkin'. W'en de vimes commence' ter wither, Henry commence' ter complain er his rheumatiz, en when de leaves begin ter dry up his ha'r commence' ter drap out. When de vimes fresh up a bit Henry 'ud git peart agin, en when de vimes wither agin Henry 'ud git ole agin, en des kep' gittin' mo' en mo' fitten fer nuffin; he des pined away, en fine'ly tuk ter his cabin; en when de big vime whar he got de sap ter 'n'int his head withered en turned yaller en died, Henry died too,—des went out sorter like a cannel. Dey did n't 'pear ter be nuffin de matter wid 'im, cep'n' de rheumatiz, but his strenk des dwinel' away, 'tel he did n' hab ernuff lef' ter draw his bref. De goopher had got de under holt, en th'owed Henry fer good en all dat time.

"Mars Dugal' tuk on might'ly 'bout losin' his vimes en his nigger in de same year; en he swo' dat ef he could git holt er dat Yankee he'd wear 'im ter a frazzle, en den chaw up de frazzle; en he'd done it, too, for Mars Dugal' 'uz a monst'us brash man w'en he once git started. He sot de vimya'd out ober agin, but it wuz th'ee er fo' year befo' de vimes got ter b'arin' any scuppernon's.

"W'en de wah broke out, Mars Dugal' raise' a comp'ny, en went off ter fight de Yankees. He say he wuz mighty glad dat wah come, en he des want ter kill a Yankee fer eve'y dollar he los' 'long er dat grape-raisin' Yankee. En I 'spec' he would a done it, too, ef de Yankees had n' s'picioned sump'n, en killed him fus'. Atter de s'render ole miss move' ter town, de niggers all scattered 'way fum de plantation, en de vimya'd ain' be'n cultervated sence."

"Is that story true?" asked Annie, doubtfully, but seriously, as the old man concluded his narrative.

"It's des ez true ez I'm a-settin' here, miss. Dey's a easy way ter prove it: I kin lead de way right ter Henry's grave ober yander in de plantation buryin'-groun'. En I tell yer w'at, marster, I would n' 'vise yer to buy dis yer ole vimya'd, 'caze de goopher's on it yit, en dey ain' no tellin' w'en it's gwine ter crap out."

"But I thought you said all the old vines died."

"Dey did 'pear ter die, but a few ov 'em come out ag'in, en is mixed in mongs' de yuthers. I ain' skeered ter eat de grapes, 'caze I knows de old vimes fum de noo ones; but wid strangers dey ain' no tellin' w'at might happen. I would n' 'vise yer ter buy dis vimya'd."

I bought the vineyard, nevertheless, and it has been for a long time in a thriving condition, and is referred to by the local press as a striking illustration of the opportunities open to Northern capital in the development of Southern industries. The luscious scuppernong holds first rank among our grapes, though we cultivate a great many other varieties, and our income from grapes packed and shipped to the Northern markets is quite considerable. I have not noticed any developments of the goopher in the vineyard, although I have a mild suspicion that our colored assistants do not suffer from want of grapes during the season.

I found, when I bought the vineyard, that Uncle Julius had occupied a cabin on the place for many years, and derived a respectable revenue from the neglected grapevines. This, doubtless, accounted for his advice to me not to buy the vineyard, though whether it inspired the goopher story I am unable to state. I believe, however, that the wages I pay him for his services are more than an equivalent for anything he lost by the sale of the vineyard.

1887, 1899

HAMLIN GARLAND
1860–1940

Hannibal Hamlin Garland, born in rural poverty, was self-educated and ambitious to better himself; he wished to leave behind the hard life he had known as a young man growing up on a succession of desolate Midwest farms from Wisconsin to the Dakotas. In 1884 he migrated to Boston where, after a period of loneliness and economic struggle, he was befriended by such influential literary figures as Oliver Wendell Holmes and William Dean Howells and began to earn a living as a teacher, lecturer, and writer. It was not until the late 1880s, however, after a visit to his family on their farm stirred him to try to describe the pain of their mean rural condition, that Garland gained public attention with the group of stories gathered in *Main-Travelled Roads* (1891). These rather pessimistic stories unsentimentally depicted the day-to-day lives of the farmers—and especially of their wives—who lived along this metaphorical "long and wearyful" byway. Often explicit, almost always implicit, in the stories is a strong reformist impulse: the meagerness of these silently heroic lives could be made more fruitful and loving, Garland believed, if the economic system was made more humane. This is the thesis of his most famous story, *Under the Lion's Paw*, which Garland read without fee before tax-reform groups across the land. He devoutly believed at this time that "if you would raise the standard of art in America you must raise the standard of living." Garland's conception of realism—he called it "veritism" in *Crumbling Idols* (1904)— entailed, as this story demonstrates, an allegiance to the accurate representation of outer surfaces, however grim, and inner truths, however somber. Garland was convinced that the deepest writer creates as a responsible and compassionate member of a social community whose end is justice.

Justice for Garland applied equally to women, and he was active in feminist reform movements, especially in this early period of his life. *Rose of Dutcher's Coolley* (1895), perhaps his best sustained fiction, tells the story of a farm girl's attempt to escape the physical drudgery and spiritual emptiness of farm life by going off to college and then becoming a writer in Chicago. Unable to attract an audience for unsentimentally realistic work of this kind, from 1896 to 1916 Garland turned out popular romantic adventure stories set in the Rocky Mountains. The best of them—*The Captain* of the Gray Horse Troop (1902), *Hesper* (1903), and *Cavanaugh, Forest Ranger* (1910)—contain realistic descriptions and a muted note of reformist propaganda, but they are in essence polite and romantic.

By the late 1890s Garland had begun to mine a vein that was eventually to be an important source of his literary capital through 1930, when he moved to California from New York. The vein was autobiography, and by general agreement *A Son of the Middle Border* (1917), *A Daughter of the Middle Border* (1921), *Trail-Makers of the Middle Border* (1928), and *Roadside Meetings* (1930) constitute a permanent contribution to American letters and history. Together with Garland's early work, in which he converts his anger over the oppressive condition of people he loved into powerful fiction, these works make uniquely available to us the rural life of common people of the upper Midwest in the second half of the nineteenth century.

Under the Lion's Paw[1]

I

It was the last of autumn and first day of winter coming together. All day long the ploughmen on their prairie farms had moved to and fro on their wide level fields through the falling snow, which melted as it fell, wetting them to the skin—all day, notwithstanding the frequent squalls of snow, the dripping, desolate clouds, and the muck of the furrows, black and tenacious as tar.

Under their dripping harnesses the horses swung to and fro silently, with that marvellous uncomplaining patience which marks the horse. All day the wild-geese, honking wildly, as they sprawled sidewise down the wind, seemed to be fleeing from an enemy behind, and with neck out-thrust and wings extended, sailed down the wind, soon lost to sight.

Yet the ploughman behind his plough, though the snow lay on his ragged great-coat, and the cold clinging mud rose on his heavy boots, fettering him like gyves, whistled in the very beard of the gale. As day passed, the snow, ceasing to melt, lay along the ploughed land, and lodged in the depth of the stubble, till on each slow round the last furrow stood out black and shining as jet between the ploughed land and the gray stubble.

When night began to fall, and the geese, flying low, began to alight invisibly in the near corn field, Stephen Council was still at work "finishing a land." He rode on his sulky-plough[2] when going with the wind, but walked when facing it. Sitting bent and cold but cheery under his slouch hat, he talked encouragingly to his weary four-in-hand.

"Come round there, boys!—round agin! We got t' finish this land. Come in there, Dan! *Stiddy*, Kate!—stiddy! None o' y'r tantrums, Kittie. It's purty tuff, but got a be did. *Tchk! tchk!* Step

1. This story first appeared in *Harper's Weekly*, Vol. 33, No. 1707 (September 7, 1889), the source of the present text.

2. Plow with wheels and a seat for the driver.

along, Pete! Don't let Kate git y'r single-tree[3] on the wheel. *Once more!*"

They seemed to know what he meant, and that this was the last round, for they worked with greater vigor than before.

"Once more, boys, an' sez I, oats an' a nice warm stall, an' sleep f'r all."

By the time the last furrow was turned on the land it was too dark to see the house, and the snow was changing to rain again. The tired and hungry man could see the light from the kitchen shining through the leafless hedge, and lifting a great shout, he yelled, "*Supper* f'r a half a dozen!"

It was nearly eight o'clock by the time he had finished his chores and started for supper. He was picking his way carefully through the mud, when the tall form of a man loomed up before him with a premonitory cough.

"Waddy ye want?" was the rather startled question of the farmer.

"Well, ye see," began the stranger, in a deprecating tone, "we'd like t' git in f'r the night. We've tried every house f'r the last two miles, but they hadn't any room f'r us. My wife's jest about sick, 'n' the children are cold and hungry—"

"Oh, y' want a stay all right, eh?"

"Yes, sir; it 'ud be a great accom—"

"Waal, I don't make it a practice t' turn anybuddy away hungry, not on sech nights as this. Drive right in. We 'ain't got much, but sech as it is—"

But the stranger had disappeared. And soon his steaming, weary team, with drooping heads and swinging single-trees, moved past the well on to the block beside the path. Council stood at the side of the "schooner" and helped the children out—two little half-sleeping children—and then a small woman with a babe in her arms.

"There ye go!" he shouted, jovially, to the children. "*Now* we're all right. Run right along to the house there, an' tell Mam' Council you wants umpthin' t' eat. Right this, way, Mis'—Keep right off t' the right there. I'll go an' git a lantern. Come," he said to the dazed and silent group at his side.

"Mother," he shouted, as he neared the fragrant and warmly lighted kitchen, "here are some wayfarers an' folks who need sumpthin' t' eat an' a place t' snooze," he ended, pushing them all in.

Mrs. Council, a large, jolly, rather coarse-looking woman, took the children in her arms. "Come right in, you little rabbits. 'Most asleep, hay? Now here's a drink o' milk f'r each o' ye. I'll have s'm' tea in a minute. Take off y'r things and set up t' the fire."

While she set the children to drinking milk, Council got out his

---

3. Pivoted swinging bar to which the traces of a harness are fastened and by which a vehicle or implement is drawn; also called whiffletree.

lantern and went out to the barn to help the stranger about his team, where his loud, hearty voice could be heard as it came and went between the hay-mow and the stalls.

The woman came to light as a small, timid, and discouraged-looking woman, but still pretty, in a thin and sorrowful way.

"Land sakes! An' you've travelled all the way from Clear Lake t'-day in this mud! Waal! waal! No wunder you're all tired out. Don't wait f'r the men, Mis'—" She hesitated, waiting for the name.

"Haskins."

"Mis' Haskins, set right up to the table an' take a good swig o' that tea, whilst I make y' s'm' toast. It's green tea, an' it's good. I tell Council as I git older I don't seem t' enjoy Young Hyson n'r gunpowder. I want the reel green tea, jest as it comes off'n the vines. Seems t' have more heart in it some way. Don't s'pose it has. Council says it's all in m' eye."

Going on in this easy way, she soon had the children filled with bread and milk and the woman thoroughly at home, eating some toast and sweet melon pickles, and sipping the tea.

"*See* the little rats!" she laughed at the children. "They're full as they can stick now, and they want to go to bed. Now don't git up, Mis' Haskins; set right where you are, an' let me look after 'em. I know all about young ones, though I *am* all alone now. Jane went an' married last fall. But, as I tell Council, it's lucky we keep our health. Set right *there*, Mis' Haskins; I won't have you stir a finger."

It was an unmeasured pleasure to sit there in the warm, homely kitchen, the jovial chatter of the housewife driving out and holding at bay the growl of the impotent, cheated wind.

The little woman's eyes filled with tears, which fell down upon the sleeping baby in her arms. The world was not so desolate and cold and hopeless, after all.

"Now I hope Council won't stop out there and talk politics all night. He's the greatest man to talk politics an' read the *Tribune*. How old is it?"

She broke off and peered down at the face of the babe.

"Two months 'n' five days," said the mother, with a mother's exactness.

"Ye don't say! I want t' know! The dear little pudzy-wudzy," she went on, stirring it up in the neighborhood of the ribs with her fat forefinger.

"Pooty tough on 'oo to go gallavant'n' 'cross lots this way."

"Yes, that's so; a man can't lift a mountain," said Council, entering the door. "Sarah, this is Mr. Haskins, from Kansas. He's been eat up 'n' drove out by grasshoppers."

"Glad t' see yeh! Pa, empty that wash-basin, 'n' give him a chance t' wash."

Haskins was a tall man, with a thin, gloomy face. His hair was a reddish brown, like his coat, and seemed equally faded by the wind and sun. And his sallow face, though hard and set, was pathetic somehow. You would have felt that he had suffered much by the line of his mouth showing under his thin yellow mustache.

"Hain't Ike got home yet, Sairy?"

"Hain't seen 'im."

"W-a-a-l, set right up, Mr. Haskins; wade right into what we've got; 'tain't much, but we manage t' live on it—least I do; *she* gits fat on it," laughed Council, pointing his thumb at his wife.

After supper, while the women put the children to bed, Haskins and Council talked on, seated near the huge cooking stove, the steam rising from their wet clothing. In the Western fashion Council told as much of his own life as he drew from his guest. He asked but few questions; but by-and-by the story of Haskins's struggles and defeat came out. The story was a terrible one, but he told it quietly, seated with his elbows on his knees, gazing most of the time at the hearth.

"I didn't like the looks of the country, anyhow," Haskins said, partly rising and glancing at his wife. "I was ust t' northern Ingyannie, where we hav' lots a timber 'n' lots a rain, 'n' I didn't like the looks o' that dry prairie. What galled me the worst was goin' s' far away acrosst so much fine land layin' all through here vacant."

"And the 'hoppers eat ye four years hand running, did they?"

"Eat! They wiped us out. They chawed everything that was green. They jest set around waitin' f'r us to die t' eat us too. My God! I ust t' dream of 'em sitt'n' 'round on the bedpost, six feet long, workin' their jaws. They eet the fork handles. They got worse 'n' worse, till they jest rolled on one another, piled up like snow in winter. Well, it ain't no use; if I was t' talk all winter I couldn't tell nawthin'. But all the while I couldn't help thinkin' of all that land back here that nobuddy was usin, that I ought a had 'stead o' bein' out there in that cussed country."

"Waal, why didn't ye stop an' settle here?" asked Ike, who had come in and was eating his supper.

"Fer the simple reason that you fellers wantid ten 'r fifteen dollars an acre fer the bare land, and I hadn't no money fer that kind o' thing."

"Yes, I do my own work," Mrs. Council was heard to say in the pause which followed. "I'm a-gettin' purty heavy t' be on m' laigs all day, but we can't afford t' hire, so I keep rackin' around somehow, like a foundered horse. S'lame—I tell Council he can't tell *how* lame I am, f'r I'm jest as lame in one laig as t'other." And the good soul laughed at the joke on herself as she took a handful of flour and dusted the biscuit board to keep the dough from sticking.

"Well, I hain't *never* been very strong," said Mrs. Haskins. "Our folks was Canadians an' small-boned, and then since my last child I hain't got up again fairly. I don't like t' complain—Tim has about all he can bear now—but they was days this week when I jest wanted to lay right down an' die."

"Waal, now, I'll tell ye," said Council, from his side of the stove, silencing everybody with his good-natured roar, "I'd go down and *see* Butler *anyway*, if I was you. I guess he'd let you have his place purty cheap; the farm's all run down. He's ben anxious t' let t' somebuddy next year. It 'ud be a good chance fer you. Anyhow, you go to bed, and sleep like a babe. I've got some ploughin' t' do anyhow, an' we'll see if somethin' can't be done about your case. Ike, you go out an' see if the horses is all right, an' I'll show the folks t' bed."

When the tired husband and wife were lying under the generous quilts of the spare bed, Haskins listened a moment to the wind in the eaves, and then said, with a slow and solemn tone,

"There are people in this world who are good enough t' be angels, an' only haff t' die to *be* angels."

II

Jim Butler was one of those men called in the West "land poor." Early in the history of Rock River he had come into the town and started in the grocery business in a small way, occupying a small building in a mean part of the town. At this period of his life he earned all he got, and was up early and late, sorting beans, working over butter, and carting his goods to and from the station. But a change came over him at the end of the second year, when he sold a lot of land for four times what he paid for it. From that time forward he believed in land speculation as the surest way of getting rich. Every cent he could save or spare from his trade he put into land at forced sale, or mortgages on land, which were "just as good as the wheat," he was accustomed to say.

Farm after farm fell into his hands, until he was recognized as one of the leading land-owners of the county. His mortgages were scattered all over Cedar County, and as they slowly but surely fell in, he sought usually to retain the former owner as tenant.

He was not ready to foreclose; indeed, he had the name of being one of the "easiest" men in the town. He let the debtor off again and again, extending the time whenever possible.

"I don't want y' land," he said. "All I'm after is the int'rest on my money—that's all. Now if y' want 'o stay on the farm, why, I'll give y' a good chance. I can't have the land layin' vacant." And in many cases the owner remained as tenant.

In the mean time he had sold his store; he couldn't spend time in it; he was mainly occupied now with sitting around town on rainy days, smoking and "gassin' with the boys," or in riding to and from his farms. In fishing-time he fished a good deal. Doc Grimes, Ben Ashley, and Cal Cheatham were his cronies on these fishing excursions or hunting trips in the time of chickens or partridges. In winter they went to northern Wisconsin to shoot deer.

In spite of all these signs of easy life, Butler persisted in saying he "hadn't money enough to pay taxes on his land," and was careful to convey the impression that he was poor in spite of his twenty farms. At one time he was said to be worth fifty thousand dollars, but land had been a little slow of sale of late, so that he was not worth so much. A fine farm, known as the Higley place, had fallen into his hands in the usual way the previous year, and he had not been able to find a tenant for it. Poor Higley, after working himself nearly to death on it, in the attempt to lift the mortgage, had gone off to Dakota, leaving the farm and his curse to Butler.

This was the farm which Council advised Haskins to apply for, and the next day Council hitched up his team and drove down-town to see Butler.

"You jest lem *me* do the talkin'," he said. "We'll find him wearin' out his pants on some salt barrel somewears; and if he thought you *wanted* a place, he'd sock it to you hot and heavy. You jest keep quiet; I'll fix 'im."

Butler was seated in Ben Ashley's store, telling "fish yarns," when Council sauntered in casually.

"Hello, But! lyin' agin, hay?"

"Hello, Steve! how goes it?"

"Oh, so-so. Too dang much rain these days. I thought it was goin' t' freeze up f'r good last night. Tight squeak if I git m' ploughin' done. How's farmin' with *you* these days?"

"Bad. Ploughin' ain't half done."

"It 'ud be a religious idee f'r you t' go out and take a hand y'rself."

"I don't haff to," said Butler, with a wink.

"Got anybody on the Higley place?"

"No. Know of anybody?"

"Waal, no; not eggsackly. I've got a relation back t' Michigan who's ben hot an' cold on the idee o' comin' West f'r some time. *Might* come if he could git a good lay-out. What do you talk on the farm?"

"Well, I d' know. I'll rent it on shares, or I'll rent it money rent."

"Waal, how much money, say?"

"Well, say ten per cent. on the price—$250."

"Waal, that ain't bad. Wait on 'im till 'e thrashes?"

Haskins listened eagerly to this important question, but Council was coolly eating a dried apple which he had speared out of a barrel with his knife. Butler studied him carefully.

"Well, knocks me out o' twenty-five dollars interest."

"My relation 'll need all he's got t' git his crops in," said Council, in the same indifferent way.

"Well, all right; say wait," concluded Butler.

"All right; this is the man. Haskins, this is Mr. Butler—no relation to Ben—the hardest-working man in Cedar County."

On the way home, Haskins said: "I ain't much better off. I'd like that farm; it's a good farm, but it's all run down, an' so 'm I. I could make a good farm of it if I had half a show. But I can't stock it n'r seed it."

"Waal, now, don't you worry," roared Council, in his ear. "We'll pull y' through somehow till next harvest. He's agreed t' hire it ploughed, an' you can earn a hundred dollars ploughin' an' y' c'n git the seed o' me, an' pay me back when y' can."

Haskins was silent with emotion, but at last he said, "I 'ain't got nothin' t live on."

"Now don't you worry 'bout that. You jest make your head-quarters at ol' Steve Council's. Mother 'll take a pile o' comfort in havin' y'r wife an' children 'round. Y'see Jane's married off lately, an' Ike's away a good 'eal, so we'll be darn glad t' have ye stop with us this winter. Nex' spring we'll see if y' can't git a start agin;" and he chirruped to the team, which sprang forward with the rumbling, clattering wagon.

"Say, looky here, Council, you can't do this. I never saw—" shouted Haskins in his neighbor's ear.

Council moved about uneasily in his seat, and stopped his stammering gratitude by saying: "Hold on now; don't make such a fuss over a little thing. When I see a man down, an' things all on top of 'im, I jest like t' kick 'em off an' help 'im up. That's the kind of religion I got, an' it's about the *only* kind."

They rode the rest of the way home in silence. And when the red light of the lamp shone out into the darkness of the cold and windy night, and he thought of this refuge for his children and wife, Haskins could have put his arm around the neck of his burly companion and squeezed him like a lover; but he contented himself with saying, "Steve Council, you'll git y'r pay f'r this some day."

"Don't want any pay. My religion ain't run on such business principles."

The wind was growing colder, and the ground was covered with a white frost, as they turned into the gate of the Council farm, and the children came rushing out, shouting, "Papa's come!" They hardly looked like the same children who had sat at the table the night before. Their torpidity under the influence of sunshine and Mother Council had given way to a sort of spasmodic cheerfulness, as insects in winter revive when laid on the hearth.

III

Haskins worked like a fiend, and his wife, like the heroic little woman that she was, bore also uncomplainingly the most terrible burdens. They rose early and toiled without intermission till the darkness fell on the plain, then tumbled into bed, every bone and muscle aching with fatigue, to rise with the sun the next morning to the same round of the same ferocity of labor.

The eldest boy, now nine years old, drove a team all through the spring, ploughing and seeding, milked the cows, and did chores innumerable, in most ways taking the place of a man; an infinitely pathetic but common figure—this boy—on the American farm, where there is no law against child labor. To see him in his coarse clothing, his huge boots, and his ragged cap, as he stogged with a pail of water from the well, or trudged in the cold and cheerless dawn out into the frosty field behind his team, gave the city-bred visitor a sharp pang of sympathetic pain. Yet Haskins loved his boy, and would have saved him from this if he could, but he could not.

By June the first year the result of such Herculean toil began to show on the farm. The yard was cleaned up and sown to grass, the garden ploughed and planted, and the house mended. Council had given them four of his cows.

"Take 'em an' run 'em on shares. I don't want a milk s' many. Ike's away s' much now, Sat'd'ys an' Sund'ys, I can't stand the bother anyhow."

Other men, seeing the confidence of Council in the new-comer, had sold him tools on time; and as he was really an able farmer, he soon had round him many evidences of his care and thrift. At the advice of Council he had taken the farm for three years, with the privilege of rerenting or buying at the end of the term.

"It's a good bargain, an' y' want 'o nail it," said Council. "If you have any kind ov a crop, you can pay half y'r debts, an' keep seed an' bread."

The new hope which now sprang up in the heart of Haskins and his wife grew great almost as a pain by the time the wide field of wheat began to wave and rustle and swirl in the winds of July. Day after day he would snatch a few moments after supper to go and look at it.

"Have ye seen the wheat t'-day, Nettie?" he asked one night as he rose from supper.

"No, Tim, I 'ain't had time."

"Well, take time now. Le's go look at it."

She threw an old hat on her head—Tommy's hat—and looking almost pretty in her thin sad way, went out with her husband to the hedge.

"Ain't it grand, Nettie? Just look at it."

It was grand. Level, russet here and there, heavy-headed, wide as a lake, and full of multitudinous whispers and gleams of health, it stretched away before the gazers like the fabled field of the cloth of gold.

"Oh, I think—I *hope* we'll have a good crop, Tim; and oh, how good the people have been to us!"

"Yes; I don't know where we'd be t'-day if it hadn't a ben f'r Council and his wife."

"They're the best people in the world," said the little woman, with a great sob of gratitude.

"We'll be into that field on Monday, sure," said Haskins, griping the rail on the fence as if already at the work of the harvest.

The harvest came bounteous, glorious, but the winds came and blew it into tangles, and the rain matted it here and there close to the ground, increasing the work of gathering it threefold.

Oh, how they toiled in those glorious days! Clothing dripping with sweat, arms aching, filled with briars, fingers raw and bleeding, backs broken with the weight of heavy bundles, Haskins and his man toiled on. Tommy drove the harvester while his father and a hired man bound on the machine. In this way they cut ten acres every day, and almost every night after supper, when the hand went to bed, Haskins returned to the field, shocking the bound grain in the light of the moon. Many a night he worked till he staggered with utter fatigue; worked till his anxious wife came out to call him in to rest and lunch.

At the same time she cooked for the men, took care of the children, washed and ironed, milked the cows at night, made the butter, and sometimes fed the horses and watered them while her husband kept at the shocking. No slave in the Roman galleys could have toiled so frightfully and lived, for this man *thought* himself a freeman, and that he was working for his wife and babes.

When he sank into his bed with a deep groan of relief, too tired to change his grimy, dripping clothing, he felt that he was getting nearer and nearer to a home of his own, and pushing the wolf of want a little further from his door.

There is no despair so deep as the despair of a homeless man or woman. To roam the roads of the country or the streets of the city, to feel there is no rood of ground on which the feet can rest, to halt weary and hungry outside lighted windows and hear laughter and song within—these are the hungers and rebellions that drive men to crime and women to shame.

It was the memory of this homelessness, and the fear of its coming again, that spurred Timothy Haskins and Nettie, his wife, to such ferocious labor during that first year.

IV

" 'M, yes; 'm, yes; first-rate," said Butler, as his eye took in the neat garden, the pigpen, and the well-filled barn-yard. "You're git'n' quite a stock around yer. Done well, eh?"

Haskins was showing Butler around the place. He had not seen it for a year, having spent the year in Washington and Boston with Ashley, his brother-in-law, who had been elected to Congress.

"Yes, I've laid out a good deal of money during the last three years. I've paid out three hundred dollars f'r fencin'."

"Um—h'm! I see, I see," said Butler, while Haskins went on.

"The kitchen there cost two hundred; the barn 'ain't cost much in money, but I've put a lot o' time on it. I've dug a new well, and I—"

"Yes, yes. I see! You've done well. Stalk worth a thousand dollars," said Butler, picking his teeth with a straw.

"About that," said Haskins, modestly. "We begin to feel 's if we wuz git'n' a home f'r ourselves; but we've worked hard. I tell ye we begin to feel it, Mr. Butler, and we're goin' t' begin t' ease up purty soon. We've been kind o' plannin' a trip back t' *her* folks after the fall ploughin's done."

"*Eggs*-actly!" said Butler, who was evidently thinking of something else. "I suppose you've kind o' kalklated on stayin' here three years more?"

"Well, yes. Fact is, I think I c'n buy the farm this fall, if you'll give me a reasonable show."

"Um—m! What do you call a reasonable show?"

"Waal; say a quarter down and three years' time."

Butler looked at the huge stacks of wheat which filled the yard, over which the chickens were fluttering and crawling, catching grasshoppers, and out of which the crickets were singing innumerably. He smiled in a peculiar way as he said, "Oh, I won't be hard on yeh. But what did you expect to pay f'r the place?"

"Why, about what you offered it for before, twenty-five hundred dollars, or *possibly* three thousand," he added, quickly, as he saw the owner shake his head.

"This farm is worth five thousand and five hundred dollars," said Butler, in a careless but decided voice.

"*What!*" almost shrieked the astounded Haskins. "What's that? Five thousand? Why, that's double what you offered it for three years ago."

"Of course; and it's worth it. It was all run down then; now it's in good shape. You've laid out fifteen hundred dollars in improvements, according to your own story."

"But *you* had nothin' t' do about that. It's my work an' my money."

"You bet it was; but it's my land."

"But what's to pay me for all?"

" 'Ain't you had the use of 'em?" replied Butler, smiling calmly into his face.

Haskins was like a man struck on the head with a sand-bag; he couldn't think, he stammered as he tried to say: "But—I never 'd git the use. You'd rob me. More'n that: you agreed—you promised that I could buy or rent at the end of three years at—"

"That's all right. But I didn't say I'd let you carry off the improvements, nor that I'd go on renting the farm at two-fifty. The land is doubled in value, it don't matter how; it don't enter into the question; an' now you can pay me five hundred dollars a year rent, or take it on your own terms at fifty-five hundred, or—git out."

He was turning away, when Haskins, the sweat pouring from his face, fronted him, saying again:

"But *you've* done nothing to make it so. You hain't added a cent. I put it all there myself, expectin' to buy. I worked an' sweat to improve it. I was workin' f'r myself an' babes."

"Well, why didn't you buy when I offered to sell? What y' kickin' about?"

"I'm kickin' about payin' you twice f'r my own things—my own fences, my own kitchen, my own garden."

Butler laughed. "You're too green t' eat, young feller. *Your* improvements! The law will sing another tune."

"But I trusted your word."

"Never trust anybody, my friend. Besides, I didn't promise not to do this thing. Why, man, don't look at me like that. Don't take me for a thief. It's the law. The reg'lar thing. Everybody does it."

"I don't care if they do. It's stealin' jest the same. You take three thousand dollars of my money. The work o' my hands and my wife's." He broke down at this point. He was not a strong man mentally. He could face hardship, ceaseless toil, but he could not face the cold and sneering face of Butler.

"But I don't take it," said Butler, coolly. "All you've got to do is to go on jest as you've been a-doin', or give me a thousand dollars down, and a mortgage at ten per cent on the rest."

Haskins sat down blindly on a bundle of oats near by, and with staring eyes and drooping head went over the situation. He was under the lion's paw. He felt a horrible numbness in his heart and limbs. He was hid in a mist, and there was no path out.

Butler walked about, looking at the huge stacks of grain, and pulling now and again a few handfuls out, shelling the heads in his hands and blowing the chaff away. He hummed a little tune as he did so. He had an accommodating air of waiting.

Haskins was in the midst of the terrible toil of the last year. He was walking again in the rain and the mud behind his plough, he felt the dust and dirt of the threshing. The ferocious husking-time, with its cutting wind and biting, clinging snows, lay hard upon him. Then he thought of his wife, how she had cheerfully cooked and baked, without holiday and without rest.

"Well, what do you think of it?" inquired the cool, mocking, insinuating voice of Butler.

"I think you're a thief and a liar," shouted Haskins, leaping up. "A black-hearted houn'!" Butler's smile maddened him; with a sudden leap he caught a fork in his hands, and whirled it in the air.

"You'll never rob another man, damn ye!" he grated through his teeth, a look of pitiless ferocity in his accusing eyes.

Butler shrank and quivered, expecting the blow; stood, held hypnotized by the eyes of the man he had a moment before despised—a man transformed into an avenging demon. But in the deadly hush between the lift of the weapon and its fall there came a gush of faint, childish laughter, and then across the range of his vision, far away and dim, he saw the sun-bright head of his baby girl, as, with the pretty tottering run of a two-year-old, she moved across the grass of the door-yard. His hands relaxed; the fork fell to the ground; his head lowered.

"Make out y'r deed an' morgige, an' git off'n my land, an' don't ye never cross my line again; if y' do, I'll kill ye."

Butler backed away from the man in wild haste, and climbing into his buggy with trembling limbs, drove off down the road, leaving Haskins seated dumbly on the sunny pile of sheaves, his head sunk into his hands.

1889   1891

EDITH WHARTON
1862–1937

Edith Wharton's patrician background, troubled marriage, and international social life are all of interest; above all else, however, she was a prolific and successful writer. She began to write as a very young woman, published some fifty varied volumes in her lifetime, and left a number of unpublished manuscripts and a voluminous correspondence at her death. *The House of Mirth* (1905), her second novel, was a best seller; another novel, *The Age of Innocence* (1920), won the Pulitzer Prize; in 1930 she was awarded the gold medal of the National Institute of Arts and Letters, the first woman to be so honored.

Edith Newbold Jones was born in New York City on January 24, 1862, into a patriarchal, monied, cultivated, and rather rigid family which, like others in its small circle, disdained and feared the drastic social, cultural, and economic changes brought on by post–Civil War expansionism. It is small wonder, then, that her work at its best deals with what she described as the tragic psychic and moral effects on its members of a frivolous society under pressure. She was educated by tutors and governesses, much of the time while the family resided in Europe. In 1885 she married the Bostonian Edward Wharton, a social equal thirteen years her senior. Though they lived together (in New York, Newport, Lenox, and Paris) for twenty-eight years, most of those years were unhappy because of the nervous illnesses they each suffered. That she did not seek a divorce until 1913 (on grounds of her husband's adultery) is more a tribute to what her biographer R. W. B. Lewis characterized as her "moral conservatism and her devotion to family ties and the sanctities of tradition" than to personal affection.

In 1905, with the publication of *The House of Mirth*, Wharton confirmed her unconventional choice of role as writer and immediately found a wide public. Though she was later to write about other subjects, she discovered in it her central settings, plots, and themes: the old aristocracy of New York in conflict with the nouveau riche, and the futile struggle of central characters trapped by social forces larger and individuals morally smaller than themselves. This same fundamental situation informs her most popular book, the novella *Ethan Frome* (1911), though this grim work is set in symbolically named Starkfield, Massachusetts, and the central character, a farmer, is emotionally cannibalized by two narrow, selfish countrywomen. In *The Custom of the Country* (1913), considered by many of her critics to be her most forceful and successful novel, she confronts the effects of cultural dislocation in the Gilded Age on a beautiful and rather vicious adventurer. In *Bunner Sisters*, composed in 1891–92 and first published in 1916, she once again works out her central theme of the trapped sensibility, this time in the context of genteel poverty. Grimmer than most commentators have allowed, this unsentimental story denies satisfaction to the sister who chooses renunciation as well as to the one who indulges her selfish, passionate nature.

There is general agreement that the rest of Wharton's literary career was less distinguished. Much of her best work seems to have been completed under pressure of great personal strain and crisis. In any case, after her divorce in 1913 her work, even when successful—as it surely was in the novel *The Age of Innocence* (1920), in a number of her stories, and in the charming reminiscence *A Backward Glance* (1934)—was softer and more nostalgic than her biting, satiric earlier writings. In these latter years, more and more of her time was given to the company of an impressive international circle of diplomats, artists, and intellectuals as various in age, personality, and interests as Henry James (whose style and person she admired greatly), Jean Cocteau, and Sinclair Lewis (who dedicated *Babbitt* to her). During the last thirty years of her life her periodic visits to America became more widely spaced; she died in August, 1937, in one of the two homes she maintained in France.

Bunner Sisters[1]

I

In the days when New York's traffic moved at the pace of the drooping horse-car, when society applauded Christine Nilsson at the Academy of Music and basked in the sunsets of the Hudson River School on the walls of the National Academy of Design, an inconspicuous shop with a single show-window was intimately and favourably known to the feminine population of the quarter bordering on Stuyvesant Square.[2]

---

1. This story, the first version of which was composed in 1891–92, was first printed in *Xingu and Other Stories* (Scribner, 1916), the source of the present text.
2. Christine Nilsson (1843–1921) was a celebrated Swedish opera singer who flourished in the 1860s; she appeared at the Academy of Music, at 14th Street and Irving Place, New York City's first opera house. The Hudson River school of painters, led by Thomas Cole (1801–48), was influenced by European Romanticism; the National Academy of Design, a society of painters, engravers, and sculptors, was founded in New York

It was a very small shop, in a shabby basement, in a side-street already doomed to decline; and from the miscellaneous display behind the window-pane, and the brevity of the sign surmounting it (merely "Bunner Sisters" in blotchy gold on a black ground) it would have been difficult for the uninitiated to guess the precise nature of the business carried on within. But that was of little consequence, since its fame was so purely local that the customers on whom its existence depended were amost congenitally aware of the exact range of "goods" to be found at Bunner Sisters'.

The house of which Bunner Sisters had annexed the basement was a private dwelling with a brick front, green shutters on weak hinges, and a dress-maker's sign in the window above the shop. On each side of its modest three stories stood higher buildings, with fronts of brown stone, cracked and blistered, cast-iron balconies and cat-haunted grass-patches behind twisted railings. These houses too had once been private, but now a cheap lunch-room filled the basement of one, while the other announced itself, above the knotty wistaria that clasped its central balcony, as the Mendoza Family Hotel. It was obvious from the chronic cluster of refuse-barrels at its area-gate and the blurred surface of its curtainless windows, that the families frequenting the Mendoza Hotel were not exacting in their tastes; though they doubtless indulged in as much fastidiousness as they could afford to pay for, and rather more than their landlord thought they had a right to express.

These three houses fairly exemplified the general character of the street, which, as it stretched eastward, rapidly fell from shabbiness to squalor, with an increasing frequency of projecting sign-boards, and of swinging doors that softly shut or opened at the touch of red-nosed men and pale little girls with broken jugs. The middle of the street was full of irregular depressions, well adapted to retain the long swirls of dust and straw and twisted paper that the wind drove up and down its sad untended length; and toward the end of the day, when traffic had been active, the fissured pavement formed a mosaic of coloured hand-bills, lids of tomato-cans, old shoes, cigar-stumps and banana skins, cemented together by a layer of mud, or veiled in a powdering of dust, as the state of the weather determined.

The sole refuge offered from the contemplation of this depressing waste was the sight of the Bunner Sisters' window. Its panes were always well-washed, and though their display of artificial flowers, bands of scalloped flannel, wire hat-frames, and jars of home-made preserves, had the undefinable greyish tinge of objects long preserved in the show-case of a museum, the window revealed a back-

---

City in 1828. Stuyvesant Square, part of the estate of the last Dutch Governor of New York, is found between 15th and 17th streets on either side of Second Avenue.

ground of orderly counters and white-washed walls in pleasant contrast to the adjoining dinginess.

The Bunner sisters were proud of the neatness of their shop and content with its humble prosperity. It was not what they had once imagined it would be, but though it presented but a shrunken image of their earlier ambitions it enabled them to pay their rent and keep themselves alive and out of debt; and it was long since their hopes had soared higher.

Now and then, however, among their greyer hours there came one not bright enough to be called sunny, but rather of the silvery twilight hue which sometimes ends a day of storm. It was such an hour that Ann Eliza, the elder of the firm, was soberly enjoying as she sat one January evening in the back room which served as bedroom, kitchen and parlour to herself and her sister Evelina. In the shop the blinds had been drawn down, the counters cleared and the wares in the window lightly covered with an old sheet; but the shop-door remained unlocked till Evelina, who had taken a parcel to the dyer's, should come back.

In the back room a kettle bubbled on the stove, and Ann Eliza had laid a cloth over one end of the centre table, and placed near the green-shaded sewing lamp two tea-cups, two plates, a sugar-bowl and a piece of pie. The rest of the room remained in a greenish shadow which discreetly veiled the outline of an old-fashioned mahogany bedstead surmounted by a chromo[3] of a young lady in a night-gown who clung with eloquently-rolling eyes to a crag described in illuminated letters as the Rock of Ages; and against the unshaded windows two rocking-chairs and a sewing-machine were silhouetted on the dusk.

Ann Eliza, her small and habitually anxious face smoothed to unusual serenity, and the streaks of pale hair on her veined temples shining glossily beneath the lamp, had seated herself at the table, and was tying up, with her usual fumbling deliberation, a knotty object wrapped in paper. Now and then, as she struggled with the string, which was too short, she fancied she heard the click of the shop-door, and paused to listen for her sister; then, as no one came, she straightened her spectacles and entered into renewed conflict with the parcel. In honour of some event of obvious importance, she had put on her double-dyed and triple-turned black silk. Age, while bestowing on this garment a *patine* worthy of a Renaissance bronze, had deprived it of whatever curves the wearer's pre-Raphaelite[4] figure had once been able to impress on it; but this stiffness of outline gave it an air of sacerdotal state which seemed to emphasize the importance of the occasion.

---

3. Inexpensive color lithographs.
4. The Pre-Raphaelites were a group of painters and poets who sought inspiration in Italian painting before Raphael (1483–1520).

Seen thus, in her sacramental black silk, a wisp of lace turned over the collar and fastened by a mosaic brooch, and her face smoothed into harmony with her apparel, Ann Eliza looked ten years younger than behind the counter, in the heat and burden of the day. It would have been as difficult to guess her approximate age as that of the black silk, for she had the same worn and glossy aspect as her dress; but a faint tinge of pink still lingered on her cheek-bones, like the reflection of sunset which sometimes colours the west long after the day is over.

When she had tied the parcel to her satisfaction, and laid it with furtive accuracy just opposite her sister's plate, she sat down, with an air of obviously-assumed indifference, in one of the rocking-chairs near the window; and a moment later the shop-door opened and Evelina entered.

The younger Bunner sister, who was a little taller than her elder, had a more pronounced nose, but a weaker slope of mouth and chin. She still permitted herself the frivolity of waving her pale hair, and its tight little ridges, stiff as the tresses of an Assyrian statue, were flattened under a dotted veil which ended at the tip of her cold-reddened nose. In her scant jacket and skirt of black cashmere she looked singularly nipped and faded; but it seemed possible that under happier conditions she might still warm into relative youth.

"Why, Ann Eliza," she exclaimed, in a thin voice pitched to chronic fretfulness, "what in the world you got your best silk on for?"

Ann Eliza had risen with a blush that made her steel-bowed spectacles incongruous.

"Why, Evelina, why shouldn't I, I sh'ld like to know? Ain't it your birthday, dear?" She put out her arms with the awkwardness of habitually repressed emotion.

Evelina, without seeming to notice the gesture, threw back the jacket from her narrow shoulders.

"Oh, pshaw," she said, less peevishly. "I guess we'd better give up birthdays. Much as we can do to keep Christmas nowadays."

"You hadn't oughter say that, Evelina. We ain't so badly off as all that. I guess you're cold and tired. Set down while I take the kettle off: it's right on the boil."

She pushed Evelina toward the table, keeping a sideward eye on her sister's listless movements, while her own hands were busy with the kettle. A moment later came the exclamation for which she waited.

"Why, Ann Eliza!" Evelina stood transfixed by the sight of the parcel beside her plate.

Ann Eliza, tremulously engaged in filling the teapot, lifted a look of hypocritical surprise.

"Sakes, Evelina! What's the matter?"

The younger sister had rapidly untied the string, and drawn from its wrappings a round nickel clock of the kind to be bought for a dollar-seventy-five.

"Oh, Ann Eliza, how could you?" She set the clock down, and the sisters exchanged agitated glances across the table.

"Well," the elder retorted, "*ain't* it your birthday?"

"Yes, but—"

"Well, and ain't you had to run round the corner to the Square every morning, rain or shine, to see what time it was, ever since we had to sell mother's watch last July? Ain't you, Evelina?"

"Yes, but—"

"There ain't any buts. We've always wanted a clock and now we've got one: that's all there is about it. Ain't she a beauty, Evelina?" Ann Eliza, putting back the kettle on the stove, leaned over her sister's shoulder to pass an approving hand over the circular rim of the clock. "Hear how loud she ticks. I was afraid you'd hear her soon as you come in."

"No. I wasn't thinking," murmured Evelina.

"Well, ain't you glad now?" Ann Eliza gently reproached her. The rebuke had no acerbity, for she knew that Evelina's seeming indifference was alive with unexpressed scruples.

"I'm real glad, sister; but you hadn't oughter. We could have got on well enough without."

"Evelina Bunner, just you sit down to your tea. I guess I know what I'd oughter and what I'd hadn't oughter just as well as you do —I'm old enough!"

"You're real good, Ann Eliza; but I know you've given up something you needed to get me this clock."

"What do I need, I'd like to know? Ain't I got a best black silk?" the elder sister said with a laugh full of nervous pleasure.

She poured out Evelina's tea, adding some condensed milk from the jug, and cutting for her the largest slice of pie; then she drew up her own chair to the table.

The two women ate in silence for a few moments before Evelina began to speak again. "The clock is perfectly lovely and I don't say it ain't a comfort to have it; but I hate to think what it must have cost you."

"No, it didn't, neither," Ann Eliza retorted. "I got it dirt cheap, if you want to know. And I paid for it out of a little extra work I did the other night on the machine for Mrs. Hawkins."

"The baby-waists?"

"Yes."

"There, I knew it! You swore to me you'd buy a new pair of shoes with that money."

"Well, and s'posin' I didn't want 'em—what then? I've patched up the old ones as good as new—and I do declare, Evelina Bunner, if you ask me another question you'll go and spoil all my pleasure."

"Very well, I won't," said the younger sister.

They continued to eat without farther words. Evelina yielded to her sister's entreaty that she should finish the pie, and poured out a second cup of tea, into which she put the last lump of sugar; and between them, on the table, the clock kept up its sociable tick.

"Where'd you get it, Ann Eliza?" asked Evelina, fascinated.

"Where'd you s'pose? Why, right round here, over across the Square, in the queerest little store you ever laid eyes on. I saw it in the window as I was passing, and I stepped right in and asked how much it was, and the store-keeper he was real pleasant about it. He was just the nicest man. I guess he's a German. I told him I couldn't give much, and he said, well, he knew what hard times was too. His name's Ramy—Herman Ramy: I saw it written up over the store. And he told me he used to work at Tiff'ny's,[5] oh, for years, in the clock-department, and three years ago he took sick with some kinder fever, and lost his place, and when he got well they'd engaged somebody else and didn't want him, and so he started this little store by himself. I guess he's real smart, and he spoke quite like an educated man—but he looks sick."

Evelina was listening with absorbed attention. In the narrow lives of the two sisters such an episode was not to be under-rated.

"What you say his name was?" she asked as Ann Eliza paused.

"Herman Ramy."

"How old is he?"

"Well, I couldn't exactly tell you, he looked so sick—but I don't b'lieve he's much over forty."

By this time the plates had been cleared and the teapot emptied, and the two sisters rose from the table. Ann Eliza, tying an apron over her black silk, carefully removed all traces of the meal; then, after washing the cups and plates, and putting them away in a cupboard, she drew her rocking-chair to the lamp and sat down to a heap of mending. Evelina, meanwhile, had been roaming about the room in search of an abiding-place for the clock. A rosewood what-not with ornamental fret-work hung on the wall beside the devout young lady in dishabille, and after much weighing of alternatives the sisters decided to dethrone a broken china vase filled with dried grasses which had long stood on the top shelf, and to put the clock in its place; the vase, after farther consideration, being relegated to a small table covered with blue and white bead-work, which held a Bible and prayer-book, and an illustrated copy of Longfellow's poems given as a school-prize to their father.

This change having been made, and the effect studied from every angle of the room, Evelina languidly put her pinking-machine[6] on the table, and sat down to the monotonous work of pinking a heap

---

5. Tiffany's, the fashionable jewelry firm.
6. Metal instrument for cutting or perforating designs on cloth, paper, or leather; flounces are strips of fabric attached to a garment by one edge.

of black silk flounces. The strips of stuff slid slowly to the floor at
her side, and the clock, from its commanding altitude, kept time
with the dispiriting click of the instrument under her fingers.

II

The purchase of Evelina's clock had been a more important event
in the life of Ann Eliza Bunner than her younger sister could divine.
In the first place, there had been the demoralizing satisfaction of
finding herself in possession of a sum of money which she need not
put into the common fund, but could spend as she chose, without
consulting Evelina, and then the excitement of her stealthy trips
abroad, undertaken on the rare occasions when she could trump up
a pretext for leaving the shop; since, as a rule, it was Evelina who
took the bundles to the dyer's, and delivered the purchases of those
among their customers who were too genteel to be seen carrying
home a bonnet or a bundle of pinking—so that, had it not been for
the excuse of having to see Mrs. Hawkins's teething baby, Ann
Eliza would hardly have known what motive to allege for deserting
her usual seat behind the counter.

The infrequency of her walks made them the chief events of her
life. The mere act of going out from the monastic quiet of the shop
into the tumult of the streets filled her with a subdued excitement
which grew too intense for pleasure as she was swallowed by the
engulfing roar of Broadway or Third Avenue, and began to do timid
battle with their incessant cross-currents of humanity. After a glance
or two into the great show-windows she usually allowed herself to
be swept back into the shelter of a side-street, and finally regained
her own roof in a state of breathless bewilderment and fatigue; but
gradually, as her nerves were soothed by the familiar quiet of the
little shop, and the click of Evelina's pinking-machine, certain
sights and sounds would detach themselves from the torrent along
which she had been swept, and she would devote the rest of the day
to a mental reconstruction of the different episodes of her walk, till
finally it took shape in her thought as a consecutive and highly-col-
oured experience, from which, for weeks afterwards, she would
detach some fragmentary recollection in the course of her long dialogues with her sister.

But when, to the unwanted excitement of going out, was added
the intenser interest of looking for a present for Evelina, Ann
Eliza's agitation, sharpened by concealment, actually preyed upon
her rest; and it was not till the present had been given, and she had
unbosomed herself of the experiences connected with its purchase,
that she could look back with anything like composure to that stirring moment of her life. From that day forward, however, she began
to take a certain tranquil pleasure in thinking of Mr. Ramy's small

shop, not unlike her own in its countrified obscurity, though the layer of dust which covered its counter and shelves made the comparison only superficially acceptable. Still, she did not judge the state of the shop severely, for Mr. Ramy had told her that he was alone in the world, and lone men, she was aware, did not know how to deal with dust. It gave her a good deal of occupation to wonder why he had never married, or if, on the other hand, he were a widower, and had lost all his dear little children; and she scarcely knew which alternative seemed to make him the more interesting. In either case, his life was assuredly a sad one; and she passed many hours in speculating on the manner in which he probably spent his evenings. She knew he lived at the back of his shop, for she had caught, on entering, a glimpse of a dingy room with a tumbled bed; and the pervading smell of cold fry suggested that he probably did his own cooking. She wondered if he did not often make his tea with water that had not boiled, and asked herself, almost jealously, who looked after the shop while he went to market. Then it occurred to her as likely that he bought his provisions at the same market as Evelina; and she was fascinated by the thought that he and her sister might constantly be meeting in total unconsciousness of the link between them. Whenever she reached this stage in her reflexions she lifted a furtive glance to the clock, whose loud staccato tick was becoming a part of her inmost being.

The seed sown by these long hours of meditation germinated at last in the secret wish to go to market some morning in Evelina's stead. As this purpose rose to the surface of Ann Eliza's thoughts she shrank back shyly from its contemplation. A plan so steeped in duplicity had never before taken shape in her crystalline soul. How was it possible for her to consider such a step? And, besides, (she did not possess sufficient logic to mark the downward trend of this "besides"), what excuse could she make that would not excite her sister's curiosity? From this second query it was an easy descent to the third: how soon could she manage to go?

It was Evelina herself, who furnished the necessary pretext by awaking with a sore throat on the day when she usually went to market. It was a Saturday, and as they always had their bit of steak on Sunday the expedition could not be postponed, and it seemed natural that Ann Eliza, as she tied an old stocking around Evelina's throat, should announce her intention of stepping round to the butcher's.

"Oh, Ann Eliza, they'll cheat you so," her sister wailed.

Ann Eliza brushed aside the imputation with a smile, and a few minutes later, having set the room to rights, and cast a last glance at the shop, she was tying on her bonnet with fumbling haste.

The morning was damp and cold, with a sky full of sulky clouds that would not make room for the sun, but as yet dropped only an occasional snow-flake. In the early light the street looked its mean-est and most neglected; but to Ann Eliza, never greatly troubled by any untidiness for which she was not responsible, it seemed to wear a singularly friendly aspect.

A few minutes' walk brought her to the market where Evelina made her purchases, and where, if he had any sense of topographi-cal fitness, Mr. Ramy must also deal.

Ann Eliza, making her way through the outskirts of potato-barrels and flabby fish, found no one in the shop but the gory-aproned butcher who stood in the background cutting chops.

As she approached him across the tessellation of fish-scales, blood and saw-dust, he laid aside his cleaver and not unsympathetically asked: "Sister sick?"

"Oh, not very—jest a cold," she answered, as guiltily as if Eveli-na's illness had been feigned. "We want a steak as usual, please—and my sister said you was to be sure to give me jest as good a cut as if it was her," she added with child-like candour.

"Oh, that's all right." The butcher picked up his weapon with a grin. "Your sister knows a cut as well as any of us," he remarked.

In another moment, Ann Eliza reflected, the steak would be cut and wrapped up, and no choice left her but to turn her disap-pointed steps toward home. She was too shy to try to delay the butcher by such conversational arts as she possessed, but the approach of a deaf old lady in an antiquated bonnet and mantle gave her her opportunity.

"Wait on her first, please," Ann Eliza whispered. "I ain't in any hurry."

The butcher advanced to his new customer, and Ann Eliza, palpi-tating in the back of the shop, saw that the old lady's hesitations between liver and pork chops were likely to be indefinitely pro-longed. They were still unresolved when she was interrupted by the entrance of a blowsy Irish girl with a basket on her arm. The new-comer caused a momentary diversion, and when she had departed the old lady, who was evidently as intolerant of interruption as a professional story-teller, insisted on returning to the beginning of her complicated order, and weighing anew, with an anxious appeal to the butcher's arbitration, the relative advantages of pork and liver. But even her hesitations, and the intrusion on them of two or three other customers, were of no avail, for Mr. Ramy was not among those who entered the shop; and at last Ann Eliza, ashamed of staying longer, reluctantly claimed her steak, and walked home through the thickening snow.

Even to her simple judgment the vanity of her hopes was plain, and in the clear light that disappointment turns upon our actions she wondered how she could have been foolish enough to suppose that, even if Mr. Ramy *did* go to that particular market, he would hit on the same day and hour as herself.

There followed a colourless week unmarked by farther incident. The old stocking cured Evelina's throat, and Mrs. Hawkins dropped in once or twice to talk of her baby's teeth; some new orders for pinking were received, and Evelina sold a bonnet to the lady with puffed sleeves. The lady with puffed sleeves—a resident of "the Square," whose name they had never learned, because she always carried her own parcels home—was the most distinguished and interesting figure on their horizon. She was youngish, she was elegant (as the title they had given her implied), and she had a sweet sad smile about which they had woven many histories; but even the news of her return to town—it was her first apparition that year—failed to arouse Ann Eliza's interest. All the small daily happenings which had once sufficed to fill the hours now appeared to her in their deadly insignificance; and for the first time in her long years of drudgery she rebelled at the dullness of her life. With Evelina such fits of discontent were habitual and openly proclaimed, and Ann Eliza still excused them as one of the prerogatives of youth. Besides, Evelina had not been intended by Providence to pine in such a narrow life: in the original plan of things, she had been meant to marry and have a baby, to wear silk on Sundays, and take a leading part in a Church circle. Hitherto opportunity had played her false; and for all her superior aspirations and carefully crimped hair she had remained as obscure and unsought as Ann Eliza. But the elder sister, who had long since accepted her own fate, had never accepted Evelina's. Once a pleasant young man who taught in Sunday-school had paid the younger Miss Bunner a few shy visits. That was years since, and he had speedily vanished from their view. Whether he had carried with him any of Evelina's illusions, Ann Eliza had never discovered; but his attentions had clad her sister in a halo of exquisite possibilities.

Ann Eliza, in those days, had never dreamed of allowing herself the luxury of self-pity; it seemed as much a personal right of Evelina's as her elaborately crinkled hair. But now she began to transfer to herself a portion of the sympathy she had so long bestowed on Evelina. She had at last recognized her right to set up some lost opportunities of her own; and once that dangerous precedent established, they began to crowd upon her memory.

It was at this stage of Ann Eliza's transformation that Evelina, looking up one evening from her work, said suddenly: "My! She's stopped."

Ann Eliza, raising her eyes from a brown merino seam, followed her sister's glance across the room. It was a Monday, and they always wound the clock on Sundays.

"Are you sure you wound her yesterday, Evelina?"

"Jest as sure as I live. She must be broke. I'll go and see."

Evelina laid down the hat she was trimming, and took the clock from its shelf.

"There—I knew it! She's wound jest as *tight*—what you suppose's happened to her, Ann Eliza?"

"I dunno, I'm sure," said the elder sister, wiping her spectacles
before proceeding to a close examination of the clock.

With anxiously bent heads the two women shook and turned it,
as though they were trying to revive a living thing, but it remained
unresponsive to their touch, and at length Evelina laid it down with
a sigh.

"Seems like somethin' *dead*, don't it, Ann Eliza? How still the
room is!"

"Yes, ain't it?"

"Well, I'll put her back where she belongs," Evelina continued,
in the tone of one about to perform the last offices for the departed.
"And I guess," she added, "you'll have to step round to Mr. Ramy's
to-morrow, and see if he can fix her."

Ann Eliza's face burned. "I—yes, I guess I'll have to," she stammered, stooping to pick up a spool of cotton which had rolled to the
floor. A sudden heart-throb stretched the seams of her flat alpaca[7]
bosom, and a pulse leapt to life in each of her temples.

That night, long after Evelina slept, Ann Eliza lay awake in the
unfamiliar silence, more acutely conscious of the nearness of the
crippled clock than when it had volubly told out the minutes. The
next morning she woke from a troubled dream of having carried it
to Mr. Ramy's, and found that he and his shop had vanished; and
all through the day's occupations the memory of this dream
oppressed her.

It had been agreed that Ann Eliza should take the clock to be
repaired as soon as they had dined; but while they were still at table
a weak-eyed little girl in a black apron stabbed with innumerable
pins burst in on them with the cry: "Oh, Miss Bunner, for mercy's
sake! Miss Mellins has been took again."

Miss Mellins was the dress-maker upstairs, and the weak-eyed
child one of her youthful apprentices.

Ann Eliza started from her seat. "I'll come at once. Quick, Evelina, the cordial!"

By this euphemistic name the sisters designated a bottle of cherry
brandy, the last of a dozen inherited from their grandmother, which
they kept locked in their cupboard against such emergencies. A
moment later, cordial in hand, Ann Eliza was hurrying upstairs
behind the weak-eyed child.

Miss Mellins's "turn" was sufficiently serious to detain Ann Eliza
for nearly two hours, and dusk had fallen when she took up the
depleted bottle of cordial and descended again to the shop. It was
empty, as usual, and Evelina sat at her pinking-machine in the back
room. Ann Eliza was still agitated by her efforts to restore the
dress-maker, but in spite of her preoccupation she was struck, as

7. Fine cloth made from the hair of the llama, domesticated in Peru.

soon as she entered, by the loud tick of the clock, which still stood on the shelf where she had left it.

"Why, she's going!" she gasped, before Evelina could question her about Miss Mellins. "Did she start up again by herself?"

"Oh, no; but I couldn't stand not knowing what time it was, I've got so accustomed to having her round; and just after you went upstairs Mrs. Hawkins dropped in, so I asked her to tend the store for a minute, and I clapped on my things and ran right round to Mr. Ramy's. It turned out there wasn't anything the matter with her—nothin' on'y a speck of dust in the works—and he fixed her for me in a minute and I brought her right back. Ain't it lovely to hear her going again? But tell me about Miss Mellins, quick!"

For a moment Ann Eliza found no words. Not till she learnt that she had missed her chance did she understand how many hopes had hung upon it. Even now she did not know why she had wanted so much to see the clock-maker again.

"I s'pose it's because nothing's ever happened to me," she thought, with a twinge of envy for the fate which gave Evelina every opportunity that came their way. "She had the Sunday-school teacher too," Ann Eliza murmured to herself; but she was well-trained in the arts of renunciation, and after a scarcely perceptible pause she plunged into a detailed description of the dress-maker's "turn."

Evelina, when her curiosity was roused, was an insatiable questioner, and it was supper-time before she had come to the end of her enquiries about Miss Mellins; but when the two sisters had seated themselves at their evening meal Ann Eliza at last found a chance to say: "So she on'y had a speck of dust in her."

Evelina understood at once that the reference was not to Miss Mellins. "Yes—at least he thinks so," she answered, helping herself as a matter of course to the first cup of tea.

"On'y to think!" murmured Ann Eliza.

"But he isn't *sure*," Evelina continued, absently pushing the teapot toward her sister. "It may be something wrong with the—I forget what he called it. Anyhow, he said he'd call round and see, day after to-morrow, after supper."

"Who said?" gasped Ann Eliza.

"Why, Mr. Ramy, of course. I think he's real nice, Ann Eliza. And I don't believe he's forty; but he *does* look sick. I guess he's pretty lonesome, all by himself in that store. He as much as told me so, and somehow"—Evelina paused and bridled—"I kinder thought that maybe his saying he'd call round about the clock was on'y just an excuse. He said it just as I was going out of the store. What you think, Ann Eliza?"

"Oh, I don't har'ly know." To save herself, Ann Eliza could produce nothing warmer.

"Well, I don't pretend to be smarter than other folks," said Evelina, putting a conscious hand to her hair, "but I guess Mr. Herman Ramy wouldn't be sorry to pass an evening here, 'stead of spending it all alone in that poky little place of his."

Her self-consciousness iritated Ann Eliza.

"I guess he's got plenty of friends of his own," she said, almost harshly.

"No, he ain't, either. He's got hardly any."

"Did he tell you that too?" Even to her own ears there was a faint sneer in the interrogation.

"Yes, he did," said Evelina, dropping her lids with a smile. "He seemed to be just crazy to talk to somebody—somebody agreeable, I mean. I think the man's unhappy, Ann Eliza."

"So do I," broke from the elder sister.

"He seems such an educated man, too. He was reading the paper when I went in. Ain't it sad to think of his being reduced to that little store, after being years at Tiff'ny's, and one of the head men in their clock-department?"

"He told you all that?"

"Why, yes. I think he'd a' told me everything ever happened to him if I'd had the time to stay and listen. I tell you he's dead lonely, Ann Eliza."

"Yes," said Ann Eliza.

III

Two days afterward, Ann Eliza noticed that Evelina, before they sat down to supper, pinned a crimson bow under her collar; and when the meal was finished the younger sister, who seldom concerned herself with the clearing of the table, set about with nervous haste to help Ann Eliza in the removal of the dishes.

"I hate to see food mussing about," she grumbled. "Ain't it hateful having to do everything in one room?"

"Oh, Evelina, I've always thought we was so comfortable," Ann Eliza protested.

"Well, so we are, comfortable enough; but I don't suppose there's any harm in my saying I wisht we had a parlour, is there? Anyway, we might manage to buy a screen to hide the bed."

Ann Eliza coloured. There was something vaguely embarrassing in Evelina's suggestion.

"I always think if we ask for more what we have may be taken from us," she ventured.

"Well, whoever took it wouldn't get much," Evelina retorted with a laugh as she swept up the table-cloth.

A few moments later the back room was in its usual flawless order and the two sisters had seated themselves near the lamp. Ann Eliza had taken up her sewing, and Evelina was preparing to make artificial flowers. The sisters usually relegated this more delicate business to the long leisure of the summer months; but to-night Evelina had brought out the box which lay all winter under the bed, and spread before her a bright array of muslin petals, yellow stamens and green corollas, and a tray of little implements curiously suggestive of the dental art. Ann Eliza made no remark on this unusual proceeding; perhaps she guessed why for that evening her sister had chosen a graceful task.

Presently a knock on the outer door made them look up; but Evelina, the first on her feet, said promptly: "Sit still. I'll see who it is."

Ann Eliza was glad to sit still: the baby's petticoat that she was stitching shook in her fingers.

"Sister, here's Mr. Ramy come to look at the clock," said Evelina, a moment later, in the high drawl she cultivated before strangers; and a shortish man with a pale bearded face and upturned coat-collar came stiffly into the room.

Ann Eliza let her work fall as she stood up. "You're very welcome, I'm sure, Mr. Ramy. It's real kind of you to call."

"Nod ad all, ma'am." A tendency to illustrate Grimm's law[8] in the interchange of his consonants betrayed the clock-maker's nationality, but he was evidently used to speaking English, or at least the particular branch of the vernacular with which the Bunner sisters were familiar. "I don't like to led any clock go out of my store without being sure it gives satisfaction," he added.

"Oh,—but we were satisfied," Ann Eliza assured him.

"But I wasn't, you see, ma'am," said Mr. Ramy looking slowly about the room, "nor I won't be, not till I see that clock's going all right."

"May I assist you off with your coat, Mr. Ramy?" Evelina interposed. She could never trust Ann Eliza to remember these opening ceremonies.

"Thank you, ma'am," he replied, and taking his thread-bare over-coat and shabby hat she laid them on a chair with the gesture she imagined the lady with the puffed sleeves might make use of on similar occasions. Ann Eliza's social sense was roused, and she felt that the next act of hospitality must be hers. "Won't you suit yourself to a seat?" she suggested. "My sister will reach down the clock; but I'm sure she's all right again. She's went beautiful ever since you fixed her."

"Dat's good," said Mr. Ramy. His lips parted in a smile which showed a row of yellowish teeth with one or two gaps in it; but in spite of this disclosure Ann Eliza thought his smile extremely pleasant: there was something wistful and conciliating in it which agreed with the pathos of his sunken cheeks and prominent eyes. As he took the clock from Evelina and bent toward the lamp, the light fell on his bulging forehead and wide skull thinly covered with gray-

8. The statement in historical linguistics which describes an important change in the pronunciation of consonants.

ish hair. His hands were pale and broad, with knotty joints and square finger-tips rimmed with grime; but his touch was as light as a woman's.

"Well, ladies, dat clock's all right," he pronounced.

"I'm sure we're very much obliged to you," said Evelina, throwing a glance at her sister.

"Oh,"Ann Eliza murmured, involuntarily answering the admonition. She selected a key from the bunch that hung at her waist with her cutting-out scissors, and fitting it into the lock of the cupboard, brought out the cherry brandy and three old-fashioned glasses engraved with vine wreaths.

"It's a very cold night," she said, "and maybe you'd like a sip of this cordial. It was made a great while ago by our grandmother."

"It looks fine," said Mr. Ramy bowing, and Ann Eliza filled the glasses. In her own and Evelina's she poured only a few drops, but she filled their guest's to the brim. "My sister and I seldom take wine," she explained.

With another bow, which included both his hostesses, Mr. Ramy drank off the cherry brandy and pronounced it excellent.

Evelina meanwhile, with an assumption of industry intended to put their guest at ease, had taken up her instruments and was twisting a rose-petal into shape.

"You make artificial flowers, I see, ma'am," said Mr. Ramy with interest. "It's very pretty work. I had a lady-vriend in Shermany dat used to make flowers." He put out a square finger-tip to touch the petal.

Evelina blushed a little. "You left Germany long ago, I suppose?"

"Dear me yes, a goot while ago. I was only ninedeen when I come to the States."

After this the conversation dragged on intermittently till Mr. Ramy, peering about the room with the short-sighted glance of his race, said with an air of interest: "You're pleasantly fixed here; it looks real cosy." The note of wistfulness in his voice was obscurely moving to Ann Eliza.

"Oh, we live very plainly," said Evelina, with an affectation of grandeur deeply impressive to her sister. "We have very simple tastes."

"You look real comfortable, anyhow," said Mr. Ramy. His bulging eyes seemed to muster the details of the scene with a gentle envy. "I wisht I had as good a store; but I guess no blace seems homelike when you're always alone in it."

For some minutes longer the conversation moved on at this desultory pace, and then Mr. Ramy, who had been obviously nerving himself for the difficult act of departure, took his leave with an abruptness which would have startled anyone used to the subtler gradations of intercourse. But to Ann Eliza and her sister there was nothing surprising in his abrupt retreat. The long-drawn agonies of preparing to leave, and the subsequent dumb plunge through the door, were so usual in their circle that they would have been as much embarrassed as Mr. Ramy if he had tried to put any fluency into his adieux.

After he had left both sisters remained silent for a while; then Evelina, laying aside her unfinished flower, said: "I'll go and lock up."

IV

Intolerably monotonous seemed now to the Bunner sisters the treadmill routine of the shop, colourless and long their evenings about the lamp, aimless their habitual interchange of words to the weary accompaniment of the sewing and pinking machines.

It was perhaps with the idea of relieving the tension of their mood that Evelina, the following Sunday, suggested inviting Miss Mellins to supper. The Bunner sisters were not in a position to be lavish of the humblest hospitality, but two or three times in the year they shared their evening meal with a friend; and Miss Mellins, still flushed with the importance of her "turn," seemed the most interesting guest they could invite.

As the three women seated themselves at the supper-table, embellished by the unwonted addition of pound cake and sweet pickles, the dress-maker's sharp swarthy person stood out vividly between the neutral-tinted sisters. Miss Mellins was a small woman with a glossy yellow face and a frizz of black hair bristling with imitation tortoise-shell pins. Her sleeves had a fashionable cut, and half a dozen metal bangles rattled on her wrists. Her voice rattled like her bangles as she poured forth a stream of anecdote and ejaculation; and her round black eyes jumped with acrobatic velocity from one face to another. Miss Mellins was always having or hearing of amazing adventures. She had surprised a burglar in her room at midnight (though how he got there, what he robbed her of, and by what means he escaped had never been quite clear to her auditors); she had been warned by anonymous letters that her grocer (a rejected suitor) was putting poison in her tea; she had a customer who was shadowed by detectives, and another (a very wealthy lady) who had been arrested in a department store for kleptomania; she had been present at a spiritualist seance where an old gentleman had died in a fit on seeing a materialization of his mother-in-law; she had escaped from two fires in her night-gown, and at the funeral of her first cousin the horses attached to the hearse had run away and smashed the coffin, precipitating her relative into an open man-hole before the eyes of his distracted family.

A sceptical observer might have explained Miss Mellins's proneness to adventure by the fact that she derived her chief mental nourishment from the *Police Gazette* and the *Fireside Weekly*; but her lot was cast in a circle where such insinuations were not likely to be heard, and where the title-role in blood-curdling drama had long been her recognized right.

"Yes," she was now saying, her emphatic eyes on Ann Eliza, "you may not believe it, Miss Bunner, and I don't know's I should myself if anybody else was to tell me, but over a year before ever I was born, my mother she went to see a gypsy fortune-teller that was exhibited in a tent on the Battery with the green-headed lady, though her father warned her not to—and what you s'pose she told her? Why, she told her these very words—says she: 'Your next child'll be a girl with jet-black curls, and she'll suffer from spasms.'"

"Mercy!" murmured Ann Eliza, a ripple of sympathy running down her spine.

"D'you ever have spasms before, Miss Mellins?" Evelina asked.

"Yes, ma'am," the dress-maker declared. "And where'd you suppose I had 'em? Why, at my cousin Emma McIntyre's wedding, her that married the apothecary over in Jersey City, though her mother appeared to her in a dream and told her she'd rue the day she done it, but as Emma said, she got more advice than she wanted from the living, and if she was to listen to spectres too she'd never be sure what she'd ought to do and what she'd oughtn't; but I will say her husband took to drink, and she never was the same woman after her fust baby—well, they had an elegant church wedding, and what you s'pose I saw as I was walkin' up the aisle with the wedding percession?"

"Well?" Ann Eliza whispered, forgetting to thread her needle.

"Why, a coffin, to be sure, right on the top step of the chancel —Emma's folks is 'piscopalians and she would have a church wedding, though *his* mother raised a terrible rumpus over it—well, there it set, right in front of where the minister stood that was going to marry 'em, a coffin, covered with a black velvet pall with a gold fringe, and a 'Gates Ajar'[9] in white camelias atop of it."

"Goodness," said Evelina, starting, "there's a knock!"

"Who can it be?" shuddered Ann Eliza, still under the spell of Miss Mellins's hallucination.

Evelina rose and lit a candle to guide her through the shop. They heard her turn the key of the outer door, and a gust of night air stirred the close atmosphere of the back room; then there was a sound of vivacious exclamations, and Evelina returned with Mr. Ramy.

Ann Eliza's heart rocked like a boat in a heavy sea, and the dress-maker's eyes, distended with curiosity, sprang eagerly from face to face.

"I just thought I'd call in again," said Mr. Ramy, evidently some-

9. A representation of the head of Saint Peter looking through the gates of heaven to symbolize the destination of the soul of the departed.

what disconcerted by the presence of Miss Mellins. "Just to see how the clock's behaving," he added with his hollow-cheeked smile.

"Oh, she's behaving beautiful," said Ann Eliza; "but we're real glad to see you all the same. Miss Mellins, let me make you acquainted with Mr. Ramy."

The dress-maker tossed back her head and dropped her lids in condescending recognition of the stranger's presence; and Mr. Ramy responded by an awkward bow. After the first moment of constraint a renewed sense of satisfaction filled the consciousness of the three women. The Bunner sisters were not sorry to let Miss Mellins see that they received an occasional evening visit, and Miss Mellins was clearly enchanted at the opportunity of pouring her latest tale into a new ear. As for Mr. Ramy, he adjusted himself to the situation with greater ease than might have been expected, and Evelina, who had been sorry that he should enter the room while the remains of supper still lingered on the table, blushed with pleasure at his good-humored offer to help her "glear away."

The table cleared, Ann Eliza suggested a game of cards; and it was after eleven o'clock when Mr. Ramy rose to take leave. His adieux were so much less abrupt than on the occasion of his first visit that Evelina was able to satisfy her sense of etiquette by escorting him, candle in hand, to the outer door; and as the two disappeared into the shop Miss Mellins playfully turned to Ann Eliza.

"Well, well, Miss Bunner," she murmured, jerking her chin in the direction of the retreating figures, "I'd no idea your sister was keeping company. On'y to think!"

Ann Eliza, roused from a state of dreamy beatitude, turned her timid eyes on the dress-maker.

"Oh, you're mistaken, Miss Mellins. We don't har'ly know Mr. Ramy."

Miss Mellins smiled incredulously. "You go 'long, Miss Bunner. I guess there'll be a wedding somewheres round here before spring, and I'll be real offended if I ain't asked to make the dress. I've always seen her in a gored satin with rooshings."[1]

Ann Eliza made no answer. She had grown very pale, and her eyes lingered searchingly on Evelina as the younger sister re-entered the room. Evelina's cheeks were pink, and her blue eyes glittered; but it seemed to Ann Eliza that the coquettish tilt of her head regrettably emphasized the weakness of her receding chin. It was the first time that Ann Eliza had ever seen a flaw in her sister's beauty, and her involuntary criticism startled her like a secret disloyalty.

That night, after the light had been put out, the elder sister knelt longer than usual at her prayers. In the silence of the darkened room she was offering up certain dreams and aspirations whose brief

1. I.e., satin trimming cut into tapering triangular form with gathering and pleated ribbons.

blossoming had lent a transient freshness to her days. She wondered now how she could ever have supposed that Mr. Ramy's visits had another cause than the one Miss Mellins suggested. Had not the sight of Evelina first inspired him with a sudden solicitude for the welfare of the clock? And what charms but Evelina's could have induced him to repeat his visit? Grief held up its torch to the frail fabric of Ann Eliza's illusions, and with a firm heart she watched them shrivel into ashes; then, rising from her knees full of the chill joy of renunciation, she laid a kiss on the crimping pins of the sleeping Evelina and crept under the bedspread at her side.

V

During the months that followed, Mr. Ramy visited the sisters with increasing frequency. It became his habit to call on them every Sunday evening, and occasionally during the week he would find an excuse for dropping in unannounced as they were settling down to their work beside the lamp. Ann Eliza noticed that Evelina now took the precaution of putting on her crimson bow every evening before supper, and that she had refurbished with a bit of carefully washed lace the black silk which they still called new because it had been bought a year after Ann Eliza's.

Mr. Ramy, as he grew more intimate, became less conversational, and after the sisters had blushingly accorded him the privilege of a pipe he began to permit himself long stretches of meditative silence that were not without charm to his hostesses. There was something at once fortifying and pacific in the sense of that tranquil male presence in an atmosphere which had so long quivered with little feminine doubts and distresses; and the sisters fell into the habit of saying to each other, in moments of uncertainty: "We'll ask Mr. Ramy when he comes," and of accepting his verdict, whatever it might be, with a fatalistic readiness that relieved them of all responsibility.

When Mr. Ramy drew the pipe from his mouth and became, in his turn, confidential, the acuteness of their sympathy grew almost painful to the sisters. With passionate participation they listened to the story of his early struggles in Germany, and of the long illness which had been the cause of his recent misfortunes. The name of the Mrs. Hochmüller (an old comrade's widow) who had nursed him through his fever was greeted with reverential sighs and an inward pang of envy whenever it recurred in his biographical monologues, and once when the sisters were alone Evelina called a responsive flush to Ann Eliza's brow by saying suddenly, without the mention of any name: "I wonder what she's like?"

One day toward spring Mr. Ramy, who had by this time become as much a part of their lives as the letter-carrier or the milkman, ventured the suggestion that the ladies should accompany him to an exhibition of stereopticon views which was to take place at Chickering Hall[2] on the following evening.

After their first breathless "Oh!" of pleasure there was a silence of mutual consultation, which Ann Eliza at last broke by saying: "You better go with Mr. Ramy, Evelina. I guess we don't both want to leave the store at night."

Evelina, with such protests as politeness demanded, acquiesced in this opinion, and spent the next day in trimming a white chip bonnet with forget-me-nots of her own making. Ann Eliza brought out her mosaic brooch, a cashmere scarf of their mother's was taken from its linen cerements, and thus adorned Evelina blushingly departed with Mr. Ramy, while the elder sister sat down in her place at the pinking-machine.

It seemed to Ann Eliza that she was alone for hours, and she was surprised, when she heard Evelina tap on the door, to find that the clock marked only half-past ten.

"It must have gone wrong again," she reflected as she rose to let her sister in.

The evening had been brilliantly interesting, and several striking stereopticon views of Berlin had afforded Mr. Ramy the opportunity of enlarging on the marvels of his native city.

"He said he'd love to show it all to me!" Evelina declared as Ann Eliza conned her glowing face. "Did you ever hear anything so silly? I didn't know which way to look."

Ann Eliza received this confidence with a sympathetic murmur.

"My bonnet *is* becoming, isn't it?" Evelina went on irrelevantly, smiling at her reflection in the cracked glass above the chest of drawers.

"You're jest lovely," said Ann Eliza.

Spring was making itself unmistakably known to the distrustful New Yorker by an increased harshness of wind and prevalence of dust, when one day Evelina entered the back room at supper-time with a cluster of jonquils in her hand.

"I was just that foolish," she answered Ann Eliza's wondering glance, "I couldn't help buyin' 'em. I felt as if I must have something pretty to look at right away."

"Oh, sister," said Ann Eliza, in trembling sympathy. She felt that special indulgence must be conceded to those in Evelina's state since she had had her own fleeting vision of such mysterious longings as the words betrayed.

Evelina, meanwhile, had taken the bundle of dried grasses out of the broken china vase, and was putting the jonquils in their place with touches that lingered down their smooth stems and blade-like leaves.

2. Chickering Hall, at Fifth Avenue and 18th Street, was a concert hall. Stereopticon views are created with a transparent slide projector, which gives the illusion of depth or dissolving views.

"Ain't they pretty?" she kept repeating as she gathered the flowers into a starry circle. "Seems as if spring was really here, don't it?"

Ann Eliza remembered that it was Mr. Ramy's evening.

When he came, the Teutonic eye for anything that blooms made him turn at once to the jonquils.

"Ain't dey pretty?" he said. "Seems like as if de spring was really here."

"Don't it?" Evelina exclaimed, thrilled by the coincidence of their thought. "It's just what I was saying to my sister."

Ann Eliza got up suddenly and moved away: she remembered that she had not wound the clock the day before. Evelina was sitting at the table; the jonquils rose slenderly between herself and Mr. Ramy.

"Oh," she murmured with vague eyes, "how I'd love to get away somewheres into the country this very minute—somewheres where it was green and quiet. Seems as if I couldn't stand the city another day." But Ann Eliza noticed that she was looking at Mr. Ramy, and not at the flowers.

"I guess we might go to Cendral Park some Sunday," their visitor suggested. "Do you ever go there, Miss Evelina?"

"No, we don't very often; leastways we ain't been for a good while." She sparkled at the prospect. "It would be lovely, wouldn't it, Ann Eliza?"

"Why, yes," said the elder sister, coming back to her seat.

"Well, why don't we go next Sunday?" Mr. Ramy continued. "And we'll invite Miss Mellins too—that'll make a gosy little party."

That night when Evelina undressed she took a jonquil from the vase and pressed it with a certain ostentation between the leaves of her prayer-book. Ann Eliza, covertly observing her, felt that Evelina was not sorry to be observed, and that her own acute consciousness of the act was somehow regarded as magnifying its significance.

The following Sunday broke blue and warm. The Bunner sisters were habitual church-goers, but for once they left their prayer-books on the what-not, and ten o'clock found them, gloved and bonneted, awaiting Miss Mellins's knock. Miss Mellins presently appeared in a glitter of jet sequins and spangles, with a tale of having seen a strange man prowling under her windows till he was called off at dawn by a confederate's whistle; and shortly afterward came Mr. Ramy, his hair brushed with more than usual care, his broad hands encased in gloves of olive-green kid.

The little party set out for the nearest street-car, and a flutter of mingled gratification and embarrassment stirred Ann Eliza's bosom when it was found that Mr. Ramy intended to pay their fares. Nor did he fail to live up to this opening liberality; for after guiding them through the Mall and the Ramble he led the way to a rustic restaurant where, also at his expense, they fared idyllically on milk and lemon-pie.

After this they resumed their walk, strolling on with the slowness of unaccustomed holiday-makers from one path to another— through budding shrubberies, past grass-banks sprinkled with lilac crocuses, and under rocks on which the forsythia lay like sudden sunshine. Everything about her seemed new and miraculously lovely to Ann Eliza; but she kept her feelings to herself, leaving it to Evelina to exclaim at the hepaticas under the shady ledges, and to Miss Mellins, less interested in the vegetable than in the human world, to remark significantly on the probable history of the persons they met. All the alleys were thronged with promenaders and obstructed by perambulators; and Miss Mellins's running commentary threw a glare of lurid possibilities over the placid family groups and their romping progeny.

Ann Eliza was in no mood for such interpretations of life; but, knowing that Miss Mellins had been invited for the sole purpose of keeping her company she continued to cling to the dress-maker's side, letting Mr. Ramy lead the way with Evelina. Miss Mellins, stimulated by the excitement of the occasion, grew more and more discursive, and her ceaseless talk, and the kaleidoscopic whirl of the crowd, were unspeakably bewildering to Ann Eliza. Her feet, accustomed to the slippered ease of the shop, ached with the unfamiliar effort of walking, and her ears with the din of the dress-maker's anecdotes; but every nerve in her was aware of Evelina's enjoyment, and she was determined that no weariness of hers should curtail it. Yet even her heroism shrank from the significant glances which Miss Mellins presently began to cast at the couple in front of them: Ann Eliza could bear to connive at Evelina's bliss, but not to acknowledge it to others.

At length Evelina's feet also failed her, and she turned to suggest that they ought to be going home. Her flushed face had grown pale with fatigue, but her eyes were radiant.

The return lived in Ann Eliza's memory with the persistence of an evil dream. The horse-cars were packed with the returning throng, and they had to let a dozen go by before they could push their way into one that was already crowded. Ann Eliza had never before felt so tired. Even Miss Mellins's flow of narrative ran dry, and they sat silent, wedged between a negro woman and a pock-marked man with a bandaged head, while the car rumbled slowly down a squalid avenue to their corner. Evelina and Mr. Ramy sat together in the forward part of the car, and Ann Eliza could catch only an occasional glimpse of the forget-me-not bonnet and the clock-maker's shiny coat-collar; but when the little party got out at their corner the crowd swept them together again, and they walked back in the effortless silence of tired children to the Bunner sisters' basement. As Miss Mellins and Mr. Ramy turned to go their various ways Evelina mustered a last display of smiles; but Ann Eliza crossed the threshold in silence, feeling the stillness of the little shop reach out to her like consoling arms.

That night she could not sleep; but as she lay cold and rigid at her sister's side, she suddenly felt the pressure of Evelina's arms, and heard her whisper: "Oh, Ann Eliza, warn't it heavenly?"

VI

For four days after their Sunday in the Park the Bunner sisters had no news of Mr. Ramy. At first neither one betrayed her disappointment and anxiety to the other; but on the fifth morning Evelina, always the first to yield to her feelings, said, as she turned from her untasted tea: "I thought you'd oughter take that money out by now, Ann Eliza."

Ann Eliza understood and reddened. The winter had been a fairly prosperous one for the sisters, and their slowly accumulated savings had now reached the handsome sum of two hundred dollars; but the satisfaction they might have felt in this unwonted opulence had been clouded by a suggestion of Miss Mellins's that there were dark rumours concerning the savings bank in which their funds were deposited. They knew Miss Mellins was given to vain alarms; but her words, by the sheer force of repetition, had so shaken Ann Eliza's peace that after long hours of midnight counsel the sisters had decided to advise with Mr. Ramy; and on Ann Eliza, as the head of the house, this duty had devolved. Mr. Ramy, when consulted, had not only confirmed the dress-maker's report, but had offered to find some safe investment which should give the sisters a higher rate of interest than the suspected savings bank; and Ann Eliza knew that Evelina alluded to the suggested transfer.

"Why, yes, to be sure," she agreed. "Mr. Ramy said if he was us he wouldn't want to leave his money there any longer'n he could help."

"It was over a week ago he said it," Evelina reminded her.

"I know; but he told me to wait till he'd found out for sure about that other investment; and we ain't seen him since then."

Ann Eliza's words released their secret fear. "I wonder what's happened to him," Evelina said. "You don't suppose he could be sick?"

"I was wondering too," Ann Eliza rejoined; and the sisters looked down at their plates.

"I should think you'd oughter do something about that money pretty soon," Evelina began again.

"Well, I know I'd oughter. What would you do if you was me?"

"If I was *you*," said her sister, with perceptible emphasis and a rising blush, "I'd go right round and see if Mr. Ramy was sick. *You* could."

The words pierced Ann Eliza like a blade. "Yes, that's so," she said.

"It would only seem friendly, if he really *is* sick. If I was you I'd go to-day," Evelina continued; and after dinner Ann Eliza went.

On the way she had to leave a parcel at the dyer's, and having performed that errand she turned toward Mr. Ramy's shop. Never before had she felt so old, so hopeless and humble. She knew she was bound on a love-errand of Evelina's, and the knowledge seemed to dry the last drop of young blood in her veins. It took from her, too, all her faded virginal shyness; and with a brisk composure she turned the handle of the clock-maker's door.

But as she entered her heart began to tremble, for she saw Mr. Ramy, his face hidden in his hands, sitting behind the counter in an attitude of strange dejection. At the click of the latch he looked up slowly, fixing a lustre-less stare on Ann Eliza. For a moment she thought he did not know her.

"Oh, you're sick!" she exclaimed; and the sound of her voice seemed to recall his wandering senses.

"Why, if it ain't Miss Bunner!" he said, in a low thick tone; but he made no attempt to move, and she noticed that his face was the colour of yellow ashes.

"You *are* sick," she persisted, emboldened by his evident need of help. "Mr. Ramy, it was real unfriendly of you not to let us know."

He continued to look at her with dull eyes. "I ain't been sick," he said. "Leastways not very: only one of my old turns." He spoke in a slow laboured way, as if he had difficulty in getting his words together.

"Rheumatism?" she ventured, seeing how unwillingly he seemed to move.

"Well—somethin' like, maybe. I couldn't hardly put a name to it."

"If it *was* anything like rheumatism, my grandmother used to make a tea—" Ann Eliza began: she had forgotten, in the warmth of the moment, that she had only come as Evelina's messenger.

At the mention of tea an expression of uncontrollable repugnance passed over Mr. Ramy's face. "Oh, I guess I'm getting on all right. I've just got a headache to-day."

Ann Eliza's courage dropped at the note of refusal in his voice.

"I'm sorry," she said gently. "My sister and me'd have been glad to do anything we could for you."

"Thank you kindly," said Mr. Ramy wearily; then, as she turned to the door, he added with an effort: "Maybe I'll step round to-morrow."

"We'll be real glad," Ann Eliza repeated. Her eyes were fixed on a dusty bronze clock in the window. She was unaware of looking at it at the time, but long afterward she remembered that it represented a Newfoundland dog with his paw on an open book.

When she reached home there was a purchaser in the shop, turning over hooks and eyes under Evelina's absent-minded supervision. Ann Eliza passed hastily into the back room, but in an instant she heard her sister at her side.

"Quick! I told her I was goin' to look for some smaller hooks—how is he?" Evelina gasped.

"He ain't been very well," said Ann Eliza slowly, her eyes on Evelina's eager face; "but he says he'll be sure to be round to-morrow night."

"He will? Are you telling me the truth?"

"Why, Evelina Bunner!"

"Oh, I don't care!" cried the younger recklessly, rushing back into the shop.

Ann Eliza stood burning with the shame of Evelina's self-exposure. She was shocked that, even to her, Evelina should lay bare the nakedness of her emotion; and she tried to turn her thoughts from it as though its recollection made her a sharer in her sister's debasement.

The next evening, Mr. Ramy reappeared, still somewhat sallow and red-lidded, but otherwise like his usual self. Ann Eliza consulted him about the investment he had recommended, and after it had been settled that he should attend to the matter for her he took up the illustrated volume of Longfellow—for, as the sisters had learned, his culture soared beyond the newspapers—and read aloud, with a fine confusion of consonants, the poem on "Maidenhood." Evelina lowered her lids while he read. It was a very beautiful evening, and Ann Eliza thought afterward how different life might have been with a companion who read poetry like Mr. Ramy.

VII

During the ensuing weeks Mr. Ramy, though his visits were as frequent as ever, did not seem to regain his usual spirits. He complained frequently of headache, but rejected Ann Eliza's tentatively proffered remedies, and seemed to shrink from any prolonged investigation of his symptoms. July had come, with a sudden ardour of heat, and one evening, as the three sat together by the open window in the back room, Evelina said: "I dunno what I wouldn't give, a night like this, for a breath of real country air."

"So would I," said Mr. Ramy, knocking the ashes from his pipe. "I'd like to be setting in an arbour dis very minute."

"Oh, wouldn't it be lovely?"

"I always think it's real cool here—we'd be heaps hotter up where Miss Mellins is," said Ann Eliza.

"Oh, I daresay—but we'd be heaps cooler somewhere else," her sister snapped: she was not infrequently exasperated by Ann Eliza's furtive attempts to mollify Providence.

A few days later Mr. Ramy appeared with a suggestion which

enchanted Evelina. He had gone the day before to see his friend, Mrs. Hochmüller, who lived in the outskirts of Hoboken, and Mrs. Hochmüller had proposed that on the following Sunday he should bring the Bunner sisters to spend the day with her.

"She's got a real garden, you know," Mr. Ramy explained, "wid trees and a real summer-house to set in; and hens and chickens too. And it's an elegant sail over on de ferry-boat."

The proposal drew no response from Ann Eliza. She was still oppressed by the recollection of her interminable Sunday in the Park; but, obedient to Evelina's imperious glance, she finally faltered out an acceptance.

The Sunday was a very hot one, and once on the ferry-boat Ann Eliza revived at the touch of the salt breeze, and the spectacle of the crowded waters; but when they reached the other shore, and stepped out on the dirty wharf, she began to ache with anticipated weariness. They got into a street-car, and were jolted from one mean street to another, till at length Mr. Ramy pulled the conductor's sleeve and they got out again; then they stood in the blazing sun, near the door of a crowded beer-saloon, waiting for another car to come; and that carried them out to a thinly settled district, past vacant lots and narrow brick houses standing in unsupported solitude, till they finally reached an almost rural region of scattered cottages and low wooden buildings that looked like village "stores." Here the car finally stopped of its own accord, and they walked along a rutty road, past a stone-cutter's yard with a high fence tapestried with theatrical advertisements, to a little red house with green blinds and a garden paling. Really, Mr. Ramy had not deceived them. Clumps of dielytra and day-lilies bloomed behind the paling, and a crooked elm hung romantically over the gable of the house.

At the gate Mrs. Hochmüller, a broad woman in brick-brown merino, met them with nods and smiles, while her daughter Linda, a flaxen-haired girl with mottled red cheeks and a sidelong stare, hovered inquisitively behind her. Mrs. Hochmüller, leading the way into the house, conducted the Bunner sisters the way to her bedroom. Here they were invited to spread out on a mountainous white feather-bed the cashmere mantles under which the solemnity of the occasion had compelled them to swelter, and when they had given their black silks the necessary twitch of readjustment, and Evelina had fluffed out her hair before a looking-glass framed in pink-shell work, their hostess led them to a stuffy parlour smelling of ginger-bread. After another ceremonial pause, broken by polite enquiries and shy ejaculations, they were shown into the kitchen, where the table was already spread with strange-looking spice-cakes and stewed fruits, and where they presently found themselves seated between Mrs. Hochmüller and Mr. Ramy, while the staring Linda bumped back and forth from the stove with steaming dishes.

To Ann Eliza the dinner seemed endless, and the rich fare

strangely unappetizing. She was abashed by the easy intimacy of her hostess's voice and eye. With Mr. Ramy, Mrs. Hochmüller was almost flippantly familiar, and it was only when Ann Eliza pictured her generous form bent above his sick-bed that she could forgive her for tersely addressing him as "Ramy." During one of the pauses of the meal Mrs. Hochmüller laid her knife and fork against the edges of her plate, and, fixing her eyes on the clock-maker's face, said accusingly: "You hat one of dem turns again, Ramy."

"I dunno as I had," he returned evasively.

Evelina glanced from one to the other. "Mr. Ramy *has* been sick," she said at length, as though to show that she also was in a position to speak with authority. "He's complained very frequently of headaches."

"Ho!—I know him," said Mrs. Hochmüller with a laugh, her eyes still on the clock-maker. "Ain't you ashamed of yourself, Ramy?"

Mr. Ramy, who was looking at his plate, said suddenly one word which the sisters could not understand; it sounded to Ann Eliza like "Shwike."[3]

Mrs. Hochmüller laughed again. "My, my," she said, "wouldn't you think he'd be ashamed to go and be sick and never dell me, me that nursed him troo dat awful fever?"

"Yes, I *should*," said Evelina, with a spirited glance at Ramy; but he was looking at the sausages that Linda had just put on the table.

When dinner was over Mrs. Hochmüller invited her guests to step out of the kitchen-door, and they found themselves in a green enclosure, half garden, half orchard. Grey hens followed by golden broods clucked under the twisted apple-boughs, a cat dozed on the edge of an old well, and from tree to tree ran the network of clothes-line that denoted Mrs. Hochmüller's calling. Beyond the apple trees stood a yellow summer-house festooned with scarlet runners; and below it, on the farther side of a rough fence, the land dipped down, holding a bit of woodland in its hollow. It was all strangely sweet and still on that hot Sunday afternoon, and as she moved across the grass under the apple-boughs Ann Eliza thought of quiet afternoons in church, and of the hymns her mother had sung to her when she was a baby.

Evelina was more restless. She wandered from the well to the summer-house and back, she tossed crumbs to the chickens and disturbed the cat with arch caresses; and at last she expressed a desire to go down into the wood.

"I guess you got to go round by the road, then," said Mrs. Hochmüller. "My Linda she goes troo a hole in de fence, but I guess you'd tear your dress if you was to dry."

"I'll help you," said Mr. Ramy; and guided by Linda the pair walked along the fence till they reached a narrow gap in its boards.

3. *Schweige* in German means "hush" or "be still."

Through this they disappeared, watched curiously in their descent by the grinning Linda, while Mrs. Hochmüller and Ann Eliza were left alone in the summer-house.

Mrs. Hochmüller looked at her guest with a confidential smile. "I guess dey'll be gone quite a while," she remarked, jerking her double chin toward the gap in the fence. "Folks like dat don't never remember about de dime." And she drew out her knitting.

Ann Eliza could think of nothing to say.

"Your sister she thinks a great lot of him, don't she?" her hostess continued.

Ann Eliza's cheeks grew hot. "Ain't you a teeny bit lonesome away out here sometimes?" she asked. "I should think you'd be scared nights, all alone with your daughter."

"Oh, no, I ain't," said Mrs. Hochmüller. "You see I take in washing—dat's my business—and it's a lot cheaper doing it out here dan in de city: where'd I get a drying-ground like dis in Hobucken? And den it's safer for Linda too; it geeps her outer de streets."

"Oh," said Ann Eliza, shrinking. She began to feel a distinct aversion for her hostess, and her eyes turned with involuntary annoyance to the square-backed form of Linda, still inquisitively suspended on the fence. It seemed to Ann Eliza that Evelina and her companion would never return from the wood; but they came at length, Mr. Ramy's brow pearled with perspiration, Evelina pink and conscious, a drooping bunch of ferns in her hand; and it was clear that, to her at least, the moments had been winged.

"D'you suppose they'll revive?" she asked, holding up the ferns; but Ann Eliza, rising at her approach, said stiffly: "We'd better be getting home, Evelina."

"Mercy me! Ain't you going to take your coffee first?" Mrs. Hochmüller protested; and Ann Eliza found to her dismay that another long gastronomic ceremony must intervene before politeness permitted them to leave. At length, however, they found themselves again on the ferry-boat. Water and sky were grey, with a dividing gleam of sunset that sent sleek opal waves in the boat's wake. The wind had a cool tarry breath, as though it had travelled over miles of shipping, and the hiss of the water about the paddles was as delicious as though it had been splashed into their tired faces.

Ann Eliza sat apart, looking away from the others. She had made up her mind that Mr. Ramy had proposed to Evelina in the wood, and she was silently preparing herself to receive her sister's confidence that evening.

But Evelina was apparently in no mood for confidences. When they reached home she put her faded ferns in water, and after supper, when she had laid aside her silk dress and the forget-me-not bonnet, she remained silently seated in her rocking-chair near the open window. It was long since Ann Eliza had seen her in so uncommunicative a mood.

The following Saturday Ann Eliza was sitting alone in the shop when the door opened and Mr. Ramy entered. He had never before called at that hour, and she wondered a little anxiously what had brought him.

"Has anything happened?" she asked, pushing aside the basketful of buttons she had been sorting.

"Not's I know of," said Mr. Ramy tranquilly. "But I always close up the store at two o'clock Saturdays at this season, so I thought I might as well call round and see you."

"I'm real glad, I'm sure," said Ann Eliza; "but Evelina's out."

"I know dat," Mr. Ramy answered. "I met her round de corner. She told me she got to go to dat new dyer's up in Fourty-eighth Street. She won't be back for a couple of hours, har'ly, will she?"

Ann Eliza looked at him with rising bewilderment. "No, I guess not," she answered; her instinctive hospitality prompting her to add: "Won't you set down jest the same?"

Mr. Ramy sat down on the stool beside the counter, and Ann Eliza returned to her place behind it.

"I can't leave the store," she explained.

"Well, I guess we're very well here." Ann Eliza had become suddenly aware that Mr. Ramy was looking at her with unusual intentness. Involuntarily her hand strayed to the thin streaks of hair on her temples, and thence descended to straighten the brooch beneath her collar.

"You're looking very well to-day, Miss Bunner," said Mr. Ramy, following her gesture with a smile.

"Oh," said Ann Eliza nervously. "I'm always well in health," she added.

"I guess you're healthier than your sister, even if you are less sizeable."

"Oh, I don't know. Evelina's a mite nervous sometimes, but she ain't a bit sickly."

"She eats heartier than you do; but that don't mean nothing," said Mr. Ramy.

Ann Eliza was silent. She could not follow the trend of his thought, and she did not care to commit herself farther about Evelina before she had ascertained if Mr. Ramy considered nervousness interesting or the reverse.

But Mr. Ramy spared her all farther indecision.

"Well, Miss Bunner," he said, drawing his stool closer to the counter, "I guess I might as well tell you fust as last what I come here for to-day. I want to get married."

Ann Eliza, in many a prayerful midnight hour, had sought to strengthen herself for the hearing of this avowal, but now that it had come she felt pitifully frightened and unprepared. Mr. Ramy was leaning with both elbows on the counter, and she noticed that his nails were clean and that he had brushed his hat; yet even these signs had not prepared her!

At last she heard herself say, with a dry throat in which her heart was hammering: "Mercy me, Mr. Ramy!"

"I want to get married," he repeated. "I'm too lonesome. It ain't good for a man to live all alone, and eat noding but cold meat every day."

"No," said Ann Eliza softly.

"And the dust fairly beats me."

"Oh, the dust—I know!"

Mr. Ramy stretched one of his blunt-fingered hands toward her. "I wisht you'd take me."

Still Ann Eliza did not understand. She rose hesitatingly from her seat, pushing aside the basket of buttons which lay between them; then she perceived that Mr. Ramy was trying to take her hand, and as their fingers met a flood of joy swept over her. Never afterward, though every other word of their interview was stamped on her memory beyond all possible forgetting, could she recall what he said while their hands touched; she only knew that she seemed to be floating on a summer sea, and that all its waves were in her ears.

"Me—me?" she gasped.

"I guess so," said her suitor placidly. "You suit me right down to the ground, Miss Bunner. Dat's the truth."

A woman passing along the street paused to look at the shop-window, and Ann Eliza half hoped she would come in; but after a desultory inspection she went on.

"Maybe you don't fancy me?" Mr. Ramy suggested, discountenanced by Ann Eliza's silence.

A word of assent was on her tongue, but her lips refused it. She must find some other way of telling him.

"I don't say that."

"Well, I always kinder thought we was suited to one another," Mr. Ramy continued, eased of his momentary doubt. "I always liked de quiet style—no fuss and airs, and not afraid of work." He spoke as though dispassionately cataloguing her charms.

Ann Eliza felt that she must make an end. "But, Mr. Ramy, you don't understand. I've never thought of marrying."

Mr. Ramy looked at her in surprise. "Why not?"

"Well, I don't know, har'ly." She moistened her twitching lips. "The fact is, I ain't as active as I look. Maybe I couldn't stand the care. I ain't as spry as Evelina—nor as young," she added, with a last great effort.

"But you do most of de work here, anyways," said her suitor doubtfully.

"Oh, well, that's because Evelina's busy outside; and where

there's only two women the work don't amount to much. Besides, I'm the oldest; I have to look after things," she hastened on, half pained that her simple ruse should so readily deceive him.

"Well, I guess you're active enough for me," he persisted. His calm determination began to frighten her; she trembled lest her own should be less staunch.

"No, no," she repeated, feeling the tears on her lashes. "I couldn't, Mr. Ramy, I couldn't marry. I'm so surprised. I always thought it was Evelina—always. And so did everybody else. She's so bright and pretty—it seemed so natural."

"Well, you was all mistaken," said Mr. Ramy obstinately.

"I'm so sorry."

He rose, pushing back his chair.

"You'd better think it over," he said, in the large tone of a man who feels he may safely wait.

"Oh, no, no. It ain't any sorter use, Mr. Ramy. I don't never mean to marry. I get tired so easily—I'd be afraid of the work. And I have such awful headaches." She paused, racking her brain for more convincing infirmities.

"Headaches, do you?" said Mr. Ramy, turning back.

"My, yes, awful ones, that I have to give right up to. Evelina has to do everything when I have one of them headaches. She has to bring me my tea in the mornings."

"Well, I'm sorry to hear it," said Mr. Ramy.

"Thank you kindly all the same," Ann Eliza murmured. "And please don't—don't—" She stopped suddenly, looking at him through her tears.

"Oh, that's all right," he answered. "Don't you fret, Miss Bunner. Folks have got to suit themselves." She thought his tone had grown more resigned since she had spoken of her headaches.

For some moments he stood looking at her with a hesitating eye, as though uncertain how to end their conversation; and at length she found courage to say (in the words of a novel she had once read): "I don't want this should make any difference between us."

"Oh, my, no," said Mr. Ramy, absently picking up his hat.

"You'll come in just the same?" she continued, nerving herself to the effort. "We'd miss you awfully if you didn't. Evelina, she—" She paused, torn between her desire to turn his thoughts to Evelina, and the dread of prematurely disclosing her sister's secret.

"Don't Miss Evelina have no headaches?" Mr. Ramy suddenly asked.

"My, no, never—well, not to speak of, anyway. She ain't had one for ages, and when Evelina *is* sick she won't never give in to it," Ann Eliza declared, making some hurried adjustments with her conscience.

"I wouldn't have thought that," said Mr. Ramy.

"I guess you don't know us as well as you thought you did."

"Well, no, that's so; maybe I don't. I'll wish you good day, Miss Bunner"; and Mr. Ramy moved toward the door.

"Good day, Mr. Ramy," Ann Eliza answered.

She felt unutterably thankful to be alone. She knew the crucial moment of her life had passed, and she was glad that she had not fallen below her own ideals. It had been a wonderful experience, full of undreamed-of fear and fascination; and in spite of the tears on her cheeks she was not sorry to have known it. Two facts, however, took the edge from its perfection: that it had happened in the shop, and that she had not had on her black silk.

She passed the next hour in a state of dreamy ecstasy. Something had entered into her life of which no subsequent empoverishment could rob it: she glowed with the same rich sense of possessorship that once, as a little girl, she had felt when her mother had given her a gold locket and she had sat up in bed in the dark to draw it from its hiding-place beneath her night-gown.

At length a dread of Evelina's return began to mingle with these musings. How could she meet her younger sister's eye without betraying what had happened? She felt as though a visible glory lay on her, and she was glad that dusk had fallen when Evelina entered. But her fears were superfluous. Evelina, always self-absorbed, had of late lost all interest in the simple happenings of the shop, and Ann Eliza, with mingled mortification and relief, perceived that she was in no danger of being cross-questioned as to the events of the afternoon. She was glad of this; yet there was a touch of humiliation in finding that the portentous secret in her bosom did not visibly shine forth. It struck her as dull, and even slightly absurd, of Evelina not to know at last that they were equals.

VIII

Mr. Ramy, after a decent interval, returned to the shop; and Ann Eliza, when they met, was unable to detect whether the emotions which seethed under her black alpaca found an echo in his bosom. Outwardly he made no sign. He lit his pipe as placidly as ever and seemed to relapse without effort into the unruffled intimacy of old. Yet to Ann Eliza's initiated eye a change became gradually perceptible. She saw that he was beginning to look at her sister as he had looked at her on that momentous afternoon: she even discerned a secret significance in the turn of his talk with Evelina. Once he asked her abruptly if she should like to travel, and Ann Eliza saw that the flush on Evelina's cheek was reflected from the same fire which had scorched her own.

So they drifted on through the sultry weeks of July. At that season the business of the little shop almost ceased, and one Saturday morning Mr. Ramy proposed that the sisters should lock up early and go with him for a sail down the bay in one of the Coney Island boats.

Ann Eliza saw the light in Evelina's eye and her resolve was instantly taken.

"I guess I won't go, thank you kindly; but I'm sure my sister will be happy to."

She was pained by the perfunctory phrase with which Evelina urged her to accompany them; and still more by Mr. Ramy's silence.

"No, I guess I won't go," she repeated, rather in answer to herself than to them. "It's dreadfully hot and I've got a kinder headache."

"Oh, well, I wouldn't then," said her sister hurriedly. "You'd better jest set here quietly and rest."

"Yes, I'll rest," Ann Eliza assented.

At two o'clock Mr. Ramy returned, and a moment later he and Evelina left the shop. Evelina had made herself another new bonnet for the occasion, a bonnet, Ann Eliza thought, almost too youthful in shape and colour. It was the first time it had ever occurred to her to criticize Evelina's taste, and she was frightened at the insidious change in her attitude toward her sister.

When Ann Eliza, in later days, looked back on that afternoon she felt that there had been something prophetic in the quality of its solitude; it seemed to distill the triple essence of loneliness in which all her after-life was to be lived. No purchasers came; not a hand fell on the door-latch; and the tick of the clock in the back room ironically emphasized the passing of the empty hours.

Evelina returned late and alone. Ann Eliza felt the coming crisis in the sound of her footstep, which wavered along as if not knowing on what it trod. The elder sister's affection had so passionately projected itself into her junior's fate that at such moments she seemed to be living two lives, her own and Evelina's; and her private longings shrank into silence at the sight of the other's hungry bliss. But it was evident that Evelina, never acutely alive to the emotional atmosphere about her, had no idea that her secret was suspected; and with an assumption of unconcern that would have made Ann Eliza smile if the pang had been less piercing, the younger sister prepared to confess herself.

"What are you so busy about?" she said impatiently, as Ann Eliza, beneath the gas-jet, fumbled for the matches. "Ain't you even got time to ask me if I'd had a pleasant day?"

Ann Eliza turned with a quiet smile. "I guess I don't have to. Seems to me it's pretty plain you have."

"Well, I don't know. I don't know *how* I feel—it's all so queer. I almost think I'd like to scream."

"I guess you're tired."

"No, I ain't. It's not that. But it all happened so suddenly, and the boat was so crowded I thought everybody'd hear what he was saying.—Ann Eliza," she broke out, "why on earth don't you ask me what I'm talking about?"

Ann Eliza, with a last effort of heroism, feigned a fond incomprehension.

"What *are* you?"

"Why, I'm engaged to be married—so there! Now it's out! And it happened right on the boat; only to think of it! Of course I wasn't exactly surprised—I've known right along he was going to sooner or later—on'y somehow I didn't think of its happening to-day. I thought he'd never get up his courage. He said he was so 'fraid I'd say no—that's what kep' him so long from asking me. Well, I ain't said yes *yet*—leastways I told him I'd have to think it over; but I guess he knows. Oh, Ann Eliza, I'm so happy!" She hid the blinding brightness of her face.

Ann Eliza, just then, would only let herself feel that she was glad. She drew down Evelina's hands and kissed her, and they held each other. When Evelina regained her voice she had a tale to tell which carried their vigil far into the night. Not a syllable, not a glance or gesture of Ramy's, was the elder sister spared; and with unconscious irony she found herself comparing the details of his proposal to her with those which Evelina was imparting with merciless prolixity.

The next few days were taken up with the embarrassed adjustment of their new relation to Mr. Ramy and to each other. Ann Eliza's ardour carried her to new heights of self-effacement, and she invented late duties in the shop in order to leave Evelina and her suitor longer alone in the back room. Later on, when she tried to remember the details of those first days, few came back to her: she knew only that she got up each morning with the sense of having to push the leaden hours up the same long steep of pain.

Mr. Ramy came daily now. Every evening he and his betrothed went out for a stroll around the Square, and when Evelina came in her cheeks were always pink. "He's kissed her under that tree at the corner, away from the lamp-post," Ann Eliza said to herself, with sudden insight into unconjectured things. On Sundays they usually went for the whole afternoon to the Central Park, and Ann Eliza, from her seat in the mortal hush of the back room, followed step by step their long slow beatific walk.

There had been, as yet, no allusion to their marriage, except that Evelina had once told her sister that Mr. Ramy wished them to invite Mrs. Hochmüller and Linda to the wedding. The mention of the laundress raised a half-forgotten fear in Ann Eliza, and she said in a tone of tentative appeal: "I guess if I was you I wouldn't want to be very great friends with Mrs. Hochmüller."

Evelina glanced at her compassionately. "I guess if you was me you'd want to do everything you could to please the man you loved.

It's lucky," she added with glacial irony, "that I'm not too grand for Herman's friends."

"Oh," Ann Eliza protested, "that ain't what I mean—and you know it ain't. Only somehow the day we saw her I didn't think she seemed like the kinder person you'd want for a friend."

"I guess a married woman's the best judge of such matters," Evelina replied, as though she already walked in the light of her future state.

Ann Eliza, after that, kept her own counsel. She saw that Evelina wanted her sympathy as little as her admonitions, and that already she counted for nothing in her sister's scheme of life. To Ann Eliza's idolatrous acceptance of the cruelties of fate this exclusion seemed both natural and just; but it caused her the most lively pain. She could not divest her love for Evelina of its passionate motherliness; no breath of reason could lower it to the cool temperature of sisterly affection.

She was then passing, as she thought, through the novitiate of her pain; preparing, in a hundred experimental ways, for the solitude awaiting her when Evelina left. It was true that it would be a tempered loneliness. They would not be far apart. Evelina would "run in" daily from the clock-maker's; they would doubtless take supper with her on Sundays. But already Ann Eliza guessed with what growing perfunctoriness her sister would fulfill these obligations; she even forsaw the day when, to get news of Evelina, she should have to lock the shop at nightfall and go herself to Mr. Ramy's door. But on that contingency she would not dwell. "They can come to me when they want to—they'll always find me here," she simply said to herself.

One evening Evelina came in flushed and agitated from her stroll around the Square. Ann Eliza saw at once that something had happened; but the new habit of reticence checked her question.

She had not long to wait. "Oh, Ann Eliza, on'y to think what he says—" (the pronoun stood exclusively for Mr. Ramy). "I declare I'm so upset I thought the people in the Square would notice me. Don't I look queer? He wants to get married right off—this very next week."

"Next week?"

"Yes. So's we can move out to St. Louis right away."

"Him and you—move out to St. Louis?"

"Well, I don't know as it would be natural for him to want to go out there without me," Evelina simpered. "But it's all so sudden I don't know what to think. He only got the letter this morning. *Do* I look queer, Ann Eliza?" Her eye was roving for the mirror.

"No, you don't," said Ann Eliza almost harshly.

"Well, it's a mercy," Evelina pursued with a tinge of disappointment. "It's a regular miracle I didn't faint right out there in the Square. Herman's so thoughtless—he just put the letter into my hand without a word. It's from a big firm out there—the Tiff'ny of St. Louis, he says it is—offering him a place in their clock-department. Seems they heard of him through a German friend of his that's settled out there. It's a splendid opening, and if he gives satisfaction they'll raise him at the end of the year."

She paused, flushed with the importance of the situation, which seemed to lift her once for all above the dull level of her former life.

"Then you'll have to go?" came at last from Ann Eliza.

Evelina stared. "You wouldn't have me interfere with his prospects, would you?"

"No—no. I only meant—has it got to be so soon?"

"Right away, I tell you—next week. Ain't it awful?" blushed the bride.

Well, this was what happened to mothers. They bore it, Ann Eliza mused; so why not she? Ah, but they had their own chance first; she had had no chance at all. And now this life which she had made her own was going from her forever; had gone, already, in the inner and deeper sense, and was soon to vanish in even its outward nearness, its surface-communion of voice and eye. At that moment even the thought of Evelina's happiness refused her its consolatory ray; or its light, if she saw it, was too remote to warm her. The thirst for a personal and inalienable tie, for pangs and problems of her own, was parching Ann Eliza's soul: it seemed to her that she could never again gather strength to look her loneliness in the face.

The trivial obligations of the moment came to her aid. Nursed in idleness her grief would have mastered her; but the needs of the shop and the back room, and the preparations for Evelina's marriage, kept the tyrant under.

Miss Mellins, true to her anticipations, had been called on to aid in the making of the wedding dress, and she and Ann Eliza were bending one evening over the breadths of pearl-grey cashmere which, in spite of the dress-maker's prophetic vision of gored satin, had been judged most suitable, when Evelina came into the room alone.

Ann Eliza had already had occasion to notice that it was a bad sign when Mr. Ramy left his affianced at the door. It generally meant that Evelina had something disturbing to communicate, and Ann Eliza's first glance told her that this time the news was grave.

Miss Mellins, who sat with her back to the door and her head bent over her sewing, started as Evelina came around to the opposite side of the table.

"Mercy, Miss Evelina! I declare I thought you was a ghost, the way you crep' in. I had a customer once up in Forty-ninth Street—a lovely young woman with a thirty-six bust and a waist you could ha' put into her wedding ring—and her husband, he crep' up behind her that way jest for a joke, and frightened her into a fit, and when she come to she was a raving maniac, and had to be taken to

Bloomingdale with two doctors and a nurse to hold her in the carriage, and a lovely baby on'y six weeks old—and there she is to this day, poor creature."

"I didn't mean to startle you," said Evelina.

She sat down on the nearest chair, and as the lamplight fell on her face Ann Eliza saw that she had been crying.

"You do look dead-beat," Miss Mellins resumed, after a pause of soul-probing scrutiny. "I guess Mr. Ramy lugs you round that Square too often. You'll walk your legs off if you ain't careful. Men don't never consider—they're all alike. Why, I had a cousin once that was engaged to a book-agent—"

"Maybe we'd better put away the work for to-night, Miss Mellins," Ann Eliza interposed. "I guess what Evelina wants is a good night's rest."

"That's so," assented the dress-maker. "Have you got the back breadths run together, Miss Bunner? Here's the sleeves. I'll pin 'em together." She drew a cluster of pins from her mouth, in which she seemed to secrete them as squirrels stow away nuts. "There," she said, rolling up her work, "you go right away to bed, Miss Evelina, and we'll set up a little later to-morrow night. I guess you're a mite nervous, ain't you? I know when my turn comes I'll be scared to death."

With this arch forecast she withdrew, and Ann Eliza, returning to the back room, found Evelina still listlessly seated by the table. True to her new policy of silence, the elder sister set about folding up the bridal dress; but suddenly Evelina said in a harsh unnatural voice: "There ain't any use in going on with that."

The folds slipped from Ann Eliza's hands.

"Evelina Bunner—what you mean?"

"Jest what I say. It's put off."

"Put off—what's put off?"

"Our getting married. He can't take me to St. Louis. He ain't got money enough." She brought the words out in the monotonous tone of a child reciting a lesson.

Ann Eliza picked up another breadth of cashmere and began to smooth it out. "I don't understand," she said at length.

"Well, it's plain enough. The journey's fearfully expensive, and we've got to have something left to start with when we get out there. We've counted up, and he ain't got the money to do it—that's all."

"But I thought he was going right into a splendid place."

"So he is; but the salary's pretty low the first year, and board's very high in St. Louis. He's jest got another letter from his German friend, and he's been figuring it out, and he's afraid to chance it. He'll have to go alone."

"But there's your money—have you forgotten that? The hundred dollars in the bank."

Evelina made an impatient movement. "Of course I ain't forgotten it. On'y it ain't enough. It would all have to go into buying furniture, and if he was took sick and lost his place again we wouldn't have a cent left. He says he's got to lay by another hundred dollars before he'll be willing to take me out there."

For a while Ann Eliza pondered this surprising statement; then she ventured: "Seems to me he might have thought of it before."

In an instant Evelina was aflame. "I guess he knows what's right as well as you or me. I'd sooner die than be a burden to him."

Ann Eliza made no answer. The clutch of an unformulated doubt had checked the words on her lips. She had meant, on the day of her sister's marriage, to give Evelina the other half of their common savings; but something warned her not to say so now.

The sisters undressed without farther words. After they had gone to bed, and the light had been put out, the sound of Evelina's weeping came to Ann Eliza in the darkness, but she lay motionless on her own side of the bed, out of contact with her sister's shaken body. Never had she felt so coldly remote from Evelina.

The hours of the night moved slowly, ticked off with wearisome insistence by the clock which had played so prominent a part in their lives. Evelina's sobs still stirred the bed at gradually lengthening intervals, till at length Ann Eliza thought she slept. But with the dawn the eyes of the sisters met, and Ann Eliza's courage failed her as she looked in Evelina's face.

She sat up in bed and put out a pleading hand.

"Don't cry so, dearie. Don't."

"Oh, I can't bear it, I can't bear it," Evelina moaned.

Ann Eliza stroked her quivering shoulder. "Don't, don't," she repeated. "If you take the other hundred, won't that be enough? I always meant to give it to you. On'y I didn't want to tell you till your wedding day."

IX

Evelina's marriage took place on the appointed day. It was celebrated in the evening, in the chantry[4] of the church which the sisters attended, and after it was over the few guests who had been present repaired to the Bunner Sisters' basement, where a wedding supper awaited them. Ann Eliza, aided by Miss Mellins and Mrs. Hawkins, and consciously supported by the sentimental interest of the whole street, had expended her utmost energy on the decoration of the shop and the back room. On the table a vase of white chrysanthemums stood between a dish of oranges and bananas and an iced wedding-cake wreathed with orange-blossoms of the bride's own making. Autumn leaves studded with paper roses festooned the what-not and the chromo of the Rock of Ages, and a wreath of yellow immortelles

---

4. A chapel for the chanting of masses.

was twined about the clock which Evelina revered as the mysterious agent of her happiness.

At the table sat Miss Mellins, profusely spangled and bangled, her head sewing-girl, a pale young thing who had helped with Evelina's outfit, Mr. and Mrs. Hawkins, with Johnny, their eldest boy, and Mrs. Hochmüller and her daughter.

Mrs. Hochmüller's large blonde personality seemed to pervade the room to the effacement of the less amply-proportioned guests. It was rendered more impressive by a dress of crimson poplin that stood out from her in organ-like folds; and Linda, whom Ann Eliza had remembered as an uncouth child with a sly look about the eyes, surprised her by a sudden blossoming into feminine grace such as sometimes follows on a gawky girlhood. The Hochmüllers, in fact, struck the dominant note in the entertainment. Besides them Evelina, unusually pale in her grey cashmere and white bonnet, looked like a faintly washed sketch beside a brilliant chromo; and Mr. Ramy, doomed to the traditional insignificance of the bridegroom's part, made no attempt to rise above his situation. Even Miss Mellins sparkled and jingled in vain in the shadow of Mrs. Hochmüller's crimson bulk; and Ann Eliza, with a sense of vague foreboding, saw that the wedding feast centred about the two guests she had most wished to exclude from it. What was said or done while they all sat about the table she never afterward recalled: the long hours remained in her memory as a whirl of high colours and loud voices, from which the pale presence of Evelina now and then emerged like a drowned face on a sunset-dabbled sea.

The next morning Mr. Ramy and his wife started for St. Louis, and Ann Eliza was left alone. Outwardly the first strain of parting was tempered by the arrival of Miss Mellins, Mrs. Hawkins and Johnny, who dropped in to help in the ungarlanding and tidying up of the back room. Ann Eliza was duly grateful for their kindness, but the "talking over" on which they had evidently counted was Dead Sea fruit[5] on her lips; and just beyond the familiar warmth of their presences she saw the form of Solitude at her door.

Ann Eliza was but a small person to harbour so great a guest, and a trembling sense of insufficiency possessed her. She had no high musings to offer to the new companion of her hearth. Every one of her thoughts had hitherto turned to Evelina and shaped itself in homely easy words; of the mighty speech of silence she knew not the earliest syllable.

Everything in the back room and the shop, on the second day after Evelina's going, seemed to have grown coldly unfamiliar. The whole aspect of the place had changed with the changed conditions of Ann Eliza's life. The first customer who opened the shop-door startled her like a ghost; and all night she lay tossing on her side

---

5. **Dead Sea fruit**, also called the apple of Sodom, is externally attractive but turns to smoke and ashes when plucked.

of the bed, sinking now and then into an uncertain doze from which she would suddenly wake to reach out her hand for Evelina. In the new silence surrounding her the walls and furniture found voice, frightening her at dusk and midnight with strange signs and stealthy whispers. Ghostly hands shook the window shutters or rattled at the outer latch, and once she grew cold at the sound of a step like Evelina's stealing through the dark shop to die out on the threshold. In time, of course, she found an explanation for these noises, telling herself that the bedstead was warping, that Miss Mellins trod heavily overhead, or that the thunder of passing beer-waggons shook the door-latch; but the hours leading up to these conclusions were fully of the floating terrors that harden into fixed foreboding. Worst of all were the solitary meals, when she absently continued to set aside the largest slice of pie for Evelina, and to let the tea grow cold while she waited for her sister to help herself to the first cup. Miss Mellins, coming in on one of these sad repasts, suggested the acquisition of a cat; but Ann Eliza shook her head. She had never been used to animals, and she felt the vague shrinking of the pious from creatures divided from her by the abyss of soullessness.

At length, after ten empty days, Evelina's first letter came.

"My dear Sister," she wrote, in her pinched Spencerian hand,[6] "it seems strange to be in this great City so far from home alone with him I have chosen for life, but marriage has its solemn duties which those who are not can never hope to understand, and happier perhaps for this reason, life for them has only simple tasks and pleasures, but those who must take thought for others must be prepared to do their duty in whatever station it has pleased the Almighty to call them. Not that I have cause to complain, my dear Husband is all love and devotion, but being absent all day at his business how can I help but feel lonesome at times, as the poet says it is hard for they that love to live apart, and I often wonder, my dear Sister, how you are getting along alone in the store, may you never experience the feelings of solitude I have underwent since I came here. We are boarding now, but soon expect to find rooms and change our place of Residence, then I shall have all the care of a household to bear, but such is the fate of those who join their Lot with others, they cannot hope to escape from the burdens of Life, nor would I ask it, I would not live alway, but while I live would always pray for strength to do my duty. This city is not near as large or handsome as New York, but had my lot been cast in a Wilderness I hope I should not repine, such never was my nature, and they who exchange their independence for the sweet name of Wife must be prepared to find all is not gold that glitters, nor I would not expect

6. A distinctively slanted form of handwriting.

like you to drift down the stream of Life unfettered and serene as a Summer cloud, such is not my fate, but come what may will always find in me a resigned and prayerful Spirit, and hoping this finds you as well as it leaves me, I remain, my dear Sister,

"Yours truly,
"Evelina B. Ramy"

Ann Eliza had always secretly admired the oratorical and impersonal tone of Evelina's letters; but the few she had previously read, having been addressed to schoolmates or distant relatives, had appeared in the light of literary compositions rather than as records of personal experience. Now she could not but wish that Evelina had laid aside her swelling periods[7] for a style more suited to the chronicling of homely incidents. She read the letter again and again, seeking for a clue to what her sister was really doing and thinking; but after each reading she emerged impressed but unenlightened from the labyrinth of Evelina's eloquence.

During the early winter she received two or three more letters of the same kind, each enclosing in its loose husk of rhetoric a smaller kernel of fact. By dint of patient interlinear study, Ann Eliza gathered from them that Evelina and her husband, after various costly experiments in boarding, had been reduced to a tenement-house flat; that living in St. Louis was more expensive than they had supposed, and that Mr. Ramy was kept out late at night (why, at a jeweller's, Ann Eliza wondered?) and found his position less satisfactory than he had been led to expect. Toward February the letters fell off; and finally they ceased to come.

At first Ann Eliza wrote, shyly but persistently, entreating for more frequent news; then, as one appeal after another was swallowed up in the mystery of Evelina's protracted silence, vague fears began to assail the elder sister. Perhaps Evelina was ill, and with no one to nurse her but a man who could not even make himself a cup of tea! Ann Eliza recalled the layer of dust in Mr. Ramy's shop, and pictures of domestic disorder mingled with the more poignant vision of her sister's illness. But surely if Evelina were ill Mr. Ramy would have written. He wrote a small neat hand, and epistolary communication was not an insuperable embarrassment to him. The too probable alternative was that both the unhappy pair had been prostrated by some disease which left them powerless to summon her—for summon her they surely would, Ann Eliza with unconscious cynicism reflected, if she or her small economies could be of use to them! The more she strained her eyes into the mystery, the darker it grew; and her lack of initiative, her inability to imagine what steps might be taken to trace the lost in distant places, left her benumbed and helpless.

7. A term from oratory, here applied to excessively long and formally constructed sentences.

At last there floated up from some depth of troubled memory the name of the firm of St. Louis jewellers by whom Mr. Ramy was employed. After much hesitation, and considerable effort, she addressed to them a timid request for news of her brother-in-law; and sooner than she could have hoped the answer reached her.

"Dear Madam,
    "In reply to yours of the 29th ult. we beg to state that the party you refer to was discharged from our employ a month ago. We are sorry we are unable to furnish you with his address.
                            "Yours respectfully,
                            "Ludwig and Hammerbusch"

Ann Eliza read and re-read the curt statement in a stupor of distress. She had lost her last trace of Evelina. All that night she lay awake, revolving the stupendous project of going to St. Louis in search of her sister; but though she pieced together her few financial possibilities with the ingenuity of a brain used to fitting odd scraps into patch-work quilts, she woke to the cold daylight fact that she could not raise the money for her fare. Her wedding gift to Evelina had left her without any resources beyond her daily earnings, and these had steadily dwindled as the winter passed. She had long since renounced her weekly visit to the butcher, and had reduced her other expenses to the narrowest measure; but the most systematic frugality had not enabled her to put by any money. In spite of her dogged efforts to maintain the prosperity of the little shop, her sister's absence had already told on its business. Now that Ann Eliza had to carry the bundles to the dyer's herself, the customers who called in her absence, finding the shop locked, too often went elsewhere. Moreover, after several stern but unavailing efforts, she had had to give up the trimming of bonnets, which in Evelina's hands had been the most lucrative as well as the most interesting part of the business. This change, to the passing female eye, robbed the shop window of its chief attraction; and when painful experience had convinced the regular customers of the Bunner Sisters of Ann Eliza's lack of millinery skill they began to lose faith in her ability to curl a feather or even "freshen up" a bunch of flowers. The time came when Ann Eliza had almost made up her mind to speak to the lady with puffed sleeves, who had always looked at her so kindly, and had once ordered a hat of Evelina. Perhaps the lady with puffed sleeves would be able to get her a little plain sewing to do; or she might recommend the shop to friends. Ann Eliza, with this possibility in view, rummaged out of a drawer the fly-blown remainder of the business cards which the sisters had ordered in the first flush of their commercial adventure; but when the lady with puffed sleeves finally appeared she was in deep mourning, and wore so sad a look that Ann Eliza dared not speak. She came in to buy some spools of black thread and silk, and in the doorway she turned back to say: "I am going away to-morrow for a long time. I hope you will have a pleasant winter." And the door shut on her.

One day not long after this it occurred to Ann Eliza to go to Hoboken in quest of Mrs. Hochmüller. Much as she shrank from pouring her distress into that particular ear, her anxiety had carried her beyond such reluctances; but when she began to think the matter over she was faced by a new difficulty. On the occasion of her only visit to Mrs. Hochmüller, she and Evelina had suffered themselves to be led there by Mr. Ramy; and Ann Eliza now perceived that she did not even know the name of the laundress's suburb, much less that of the street in which she lived. But she must have news of Evelina, and no obstacle was great enough to thwart her.

Though she longed to turn to some one for advice she disliked to expose her situation to Miss Mellins's searching eye, and at first she could think of no other confidant. Then she remembered Mrs. Hawkins, or rather her husband, who, though Ann Eliza had always thought him a dull uneducated man, was probably gifted with the mysterious masculine faculty of finding out people's addresses. It went hard with Ann Eliza to trust her secret even to the mild ear of Mrs. Hawkins, but at least she was spared the cross-examination to which the dress-maker would have subjected her. The accumulating pressure of domestic cares had so crushed in Mrs. Hawkins any curiosity concerning the affairs of others that she received her visitor's confidence with an almost masculine indifference, while she rocked her teething baby on one arm and with the other tried to check the acrobatic impulses of the next in age.

"My, my," she simply said as Ann Eliza ended. "Keep still now, Arthur: Miss Bunner don't want you to jump up and down on her foot to-day. And what are you gaping at, Johnny? Run right off and play," she added, turning sternly to her eldest, who, because he was the least naughty, usually bore the brunt of her wrath against the others.

"Well, perhaps Mr. Hawkins can help you," Mrs. Hawkins continued meditatively, while the children, after scattering at her bidding, returned to their previous pursuits like flies settling down on the spot from which an exasperated hand has swept them. "I'll send him right round the minute he comes in, and you can tell him the whole story. I wouldn't wonder but what he can find that Mrs. Hochmüller's address in the d'rectory. I know they've got one where he works."

"I'd be real thankful if he could," Ann Eliza murmured, rising from her seat with the factitious sense of lightness that comes from imparting a long-hidden dread.

X

Mr. Hawkins proved himself worthy of his wife's faith in his capacity. He learned from Ann Eliza as much as she could tell him about Mrs. Hochmüller and returned the next evening with a scrap of paper bearing her address, beneath which Johnny (the family scribe) had written in a large round hand the names of the streets that led there from the ferry.

Ann Eliza lay awake all that night, repeating over and over again the directions Mr. Hawkins had given her. He was a kind man, and she knew he would willingly have gone with her to Hoboken; indeed she read in his timid eye the half-formed intention of offering to accompany her—but on such an errand she preferred to go alone.

The next Sunday, accordingly, she set out early, and without much trouble found her way to the ferry. Nearly a year had passed since her previous visit to Mrs. Hochmüller, and a chilly April breeze smote her face as she stepped on the boat. Most of the passengers were huddled together in the cabin, and Ann Eliza shrank into its obscurest corner, shivering under the thin black mantle which had seemed so hot in July. She began to feel a little bewildered as she stepped ashore, but a paternal policeman put her into the right car, and as in a dream she found herself retracing the way to Mrs. Hochmüller's door. She had told the conductor the name of the street at which she wished to get out, and presently she stood in the biting wind at the corner near the beer-saloon, where the sun had once beat down on her so fiercely. At length an empty car appeared, its yellow flank emblazoned with the name of Mrs. Hochmüller's suburb, and Ann Eliza was presently jolting past the narrow brick houses islanded between vacant lots like giant piles in a desolate lagoon. When the car reached the end of its journey she got out and stood for some time trying to remember which turn Mr. Ramy had taken. She had just made up her mind to ask the car-driver when he shook the reins on the backs of his lean horses, and the car, still empty, jogged away toward Hoboken.

Ann Eliza, left alone by the roadside, began to move cautiously forward, looking about for a small red house with a gable overhung by an elm-tree; but everything about her seemed unfamiliar and forbidding. One or two surly looking men slouched past with inquisitive glances, and she could not make up her mind to stop and speak to them.

At length a tow-headed boy came out of a swinging door suggestive of illicit conviviality, and to him Ann Eliza ventured to confide her difficulty. The offer of five cents fired him with an instant willingness to lead her to Mrs. Hochmüller, and he was soon trotting past the stone-cutter's yard with Ann Eliza in his wake.

Another turn in the road brought them to the little red house, and having rewarded her guide, Ann Eliza unlatched the gate and walked up to the door. Her heart was beating violently, and she had to lean against the door-post to compose her twitching lips: she had not known till that moment how much it was going to hurt her to speak of Evelina to Mrs. Hochmüller. As her agitation subsided she began to notice how much the appearance of the house had changed. It was not only that winter had stripped the elm, and blackened the flower-borders: the house itself had a debased and deserted air. The window-panes were cracked and dirty, and one or two shutters swung dismally on loosened hinges.

She rang several times before the door was opened. At length an Irish woman with a shawl over her head and a baby in her arms appeared on the threshold, and glancing past her into the narrow passage Ann Eliza saw that Mrs. Hochmüller's neat abode had deteriorated as much within as without.

At the mention of the name the woman stared. "Mrs. who, did ye say?"

"Mrs. Hochmüller. This is surely her house?"

"No, it ain't neither," said the woman turning away.

"Oh, but wait, please," Ann Eliza entreated. "I can't be mistaken. I mean the Mrs. Hochmüller who takes in washing. I came out to see her last June."

"Oh, the Dutch washerwoman is it—her that used to live here? She's been gone two months and more. It's Mike McNulty lives here now. Whisht!" to the baby, who had squared his mouth for a howl.

Ann Eliza's knees grew weak. "Mrs. Hochmüller gone? But where has she gone? She must be somewhere round here. Can't you tell me?"

"Sure an' I can't," said the woman. "She wint away before iver we come."

"Dalia Geoghegan, will ye bring the choild in out av the cowld?" cried an irate voice from within.

"Please wait—oh, please wait," Ann Eliza insisted. "You see I must find Mrs. Hochmüller."

"Why don't ye go and look for her thin?'" the woman returned, slamming the door in her face.

She stood motionless on the door-step, dazed by the immensity of her disappointment; till a burst of loud voices inside the house drove her down the path and out of the gate.

Even then she could not grasp what had happened, and pausing in the road she looked back at the house, half hoping that Mrs. Hochmüller's once detested face might appear at one of the grimy windows.

She was roused by an icy wind that seemed to spring up suddenly from the desolate scene, piercing her thin dress like gauze; and turning away she began to retrace her steps. She thought of enquiring for Mrs. Hochmüller at some of the neighbouring houses, but their look was so unfriendly that she walked on without making up her mind at which door to ring. When she reached the horse-car terminus a car was just moving off toward Hoboken, and for nearly an hour she had to wait on the corner in the bitter wind. Her hands and feet were stiff with cold when the car at length loomed into sight again, and she thought of stopping somewhere on the way to the ferry for a cup of tea; but before the region of lunch-rooms was reached she had grown so sick and dizzy that the thought of food was repulsive. At length she found herself on the ferry-boat, in the soothing stuffiness of the crowded cabin; then came another interval of shivering on a street-corner, another long jolting journey in a "cross-town" car that smelt of damp straw and tobacco; and lastly, in the cold spring dusk, she unlocked her door and groped her way through the shop to her fireless bedroom.

The next morning Mrs. Hawkins, dropping in to hear the result of the trip, found Ann Eliza sitting behind the counter wrapped in an old shawl.

"Why, Miss Bunner, you're sick! You must have fever—your face is just as red!"

"It's nothing. I guess I caught cold yesterday on the ferry-boat," Ann Eliza acknowledged.

"And it's jest like a vault in here!" Mrs. Hawkins rebuked her. "Let me feel your hand—it's burning. Now, Miss Bunner, you've got to go right to bed this very minute."

"Oh, but I can't, Mrs. Hawkins." Ann Eliza attempted a wan smile. "You forget there ain't nobody but me to tend the store."

"I guess you won't tend it long neither, if you ain't careful," Mrs. Hawkins grimly rejoined. Beneath her placid exterior she cherished a morbid passion for disease and death, and the sight of Ann Eliza's suffering had roused her from her habitual indifference. "There ain't so many folks comes to the store anyhow," she went on with unconscious cruelty, "and I'll go right up and see if Miss Mellins can't spare one of her girls."

Ann Eliza, too weary to resist, allowed Mrs. Hawkins to put her to bed and make a cup of tea over the stove, while Miss Mellins, always good-naturedly responsive to any appeal for help, sent down the weak-eyed little girl to deal with hypothetical customers.

Ann Eliza, having so far abdicated her independence, sank into sudden apathy. As far as she could remember, it was the first time in her life that she had been taken care of instead of taking care, and there was a momentary relief in the surrender. She swallowed the tea like an obedient child, allowed a poultice to be applied to her aching chest and uttered no protest when a fire was kindled in the rarely used grate; but as Mrs. Hawkins bent over to "settle" her pillows she raised herself on her elbow to whisper: "Oh, Mrs. Hawkins, Mrs. Hochmüller warn't there." The tears rolled down her cheeks.

"She warn't there? Has she moved?"

"Over two months ago—and they don't know where she's gone. Oh what'll I do, Mrs. Hawkins?"

"There, there, Miss Bunner. You lay still and don't fret. I'll ask Mr. Hawkins soon as ever he comes home."

Ann Eliza murmured her gratitude, and Mrs. Hawkins, bending down, kissed her on the forehead. "Don't you fret," she repeated, in the voice with which she soothed her children.

For over a week Ann Eliza lay in bed, faithfully nursed by her two neighbours, while the weak-eyed child, and the pale sewing girl who had helped to finish Evelina's wedding dress, took turns in minding the shop. Every morning, when her friends appeared, Ann Eliza lifted her head to ask: "Is there a letter?" and at their gentle negative sank back in silence. Mrs. Hawkins, for several days, spoke no more of her promise to consult her husband as to the best way of tracing Mrs. Hochmüller; and dread of fresh disappointment kept Ann Eliza from bringing up the subject.

But the following Sunday evening, as she sat for the first time bolstered up in her rocking-chair near the stove, while Miss Mellins studied the *Police Gazette* beneath the lamp, there came a knock on the shop-door and Mr. Hawkins entered.

Ann Eliza's first glance at his plain friendly face showed her he had news to give, but though she no longer attempted to hide her anxiety from Miss Mellins, her lips trembled too much to let her speak.

"Good evening, Miss Bunner," said Mr. Hawkins in his dragging voice. "I've been over to Hoboken all day looking round for Mrs. Hochmüller."

"Oh, Mr. Hawkins—you *have?*"

"I made a thorough search, but I'm sorry to say it was no use. She's left Hoboken—moved clear away, and nobody seems to know where."

"It was real good of you, Mr. Hawkins." Ann Eliza's voice struggled up in a faint whisper through the submerging tide of her disappointment.

Mr. Hawkins, in his embarrassed sense of being the bringer of bad news, stood before her uncertainly; then he turned to go. "No trouble at all," he paused to assure her from the doorway.

She wanted to speak again, to detain him, to ask him to advise her; but the words caught in her throat and she lay back silent.

The next day she got up early, and dressed and bonneted herself with twitching fingers. She waited till the weak-eyed child appeared, and having laid on her minute instructions as to the care of the shop, she slipped out into the street. It had occurred to her in one of the weary watches of the previous night that she might go to Tiffany's and make enquiries about Ramy's past. Possibly in that way she might obtain some information that would suggest a new way of reaching Evelina. She was guiltily aware that Mrs. Hawkins and Miss Mellins would be angry with her for venturing out of doors, but she knew she should never feel any better till she had news of Evelina.

The morning air was sharp, and as she turned to face the wind she felt so weak and unsteady that she wondered if she should ever get as far as Union Square; but by walking very slowly, and standing still now and then when she could do so without being noticed, she found herself at last before the jeweller's great glass doors.

It was still so early that there were no purchasers in the shop, and she felt herself in the centre of innumerable unemployed eyes as she moved forward between long lines of show-cases glittering with diamonds and silver.

She was glancing about in the hope of finding the clock-department without having to approach one of the impressive gentlemen who paced the empty aisles, when she attracted the attention of one of the most impressive of the number.

The formidable benevolence with which he enquired what he could do for her made her almost despair of explaining herself; but she finally disentangled from a flurry of wrong beginnings the request to be shown to the clock-department.

The gentleman considered her thoughtfully. "May I ask what style of clock you are looking for? Would it be for a wedding-present, or—"

The irony of the allusion filled Ann Eliza's veins with sudden strength. "I don't want to buy a clock at all. I want to see the head of the department."

"Mr. Loomis?" His stare still weighed her—then he seemed to brush aside the problem she presented as beneath his notice. "Oh, certainly. Take the elevator to the second floor. Next aisle to the left." He waved her down the endless perspective of show-cases.

Ann Eliza followed the line of his lordly gesture, and a swift ascent brought her to a great hall full of the buzzing and booming of thousands of clocks. Whichever way she looked, clocks stretched away from her in glittering interminable vistas: clocks of all sizes and voices, from the bell-throated giant of the hallway to the chirping dressing-table toy; tall clocks of mahogany and brass with cathedral chimes; clocks of bronze, glass, porcelain, of every possible size, voice and configuration; and between their serried ranks, along the polished floor of the aisles, moved the languid forms of other gentlemanly floor-walkers, waiting for their duties to begin.

One of them soon approached, and Ann Eliza repeated her request. He received it affably.

"Mr. Loomis? Go right down to the office at the other end." He pointed to a kind of box of ground glass and highly polished panelling.

As she thanked him he turned to one of his companions and said something in which she caught the name of Mr. Loomis, and which was received with an appreciative chuckle. She suspected herself of being the object of the pleasantry, and straightened her thin shoulders under her mantle.

The door of the office stood open, and within sat a gray-bearded man at a desk. He looked up kindly, and again she asked for Mr. Loomis.

"I'm Mr. Loomis. What can I do for you?"

He was much less portentous than the others, though she guessed him to be above them in authority; and encouraged by his tone she seated herself on the edge of the chair he waved her to.

"I hope you'll excuse my troubling you, sir. I came to ask if you could tell me anything about Mr. Herman Ramy. He was employed here in the clock-department two or three years ago."

Mr. Loomis showed no recognition of the name.

"Ramy? When was he discharged?"

"I don't har'ly know. He was very sick, and when he got well his place had been filled. He married my sister last October and they went to St. Louis, I ain't had any news of them for over two months, and she's my only sister, and I'm most crazy worrying about her."

"I see." Mr. Loomis reflected. "In what capacity was Ramy employed here?" he asked after a moment.

"He——he told us that he was one of the heads of the clock department," Ann Eliza stammered, overswept by a sudden doubt.

"That was probably a slight exaggeration. But I can tell you about him by referring to our books. The name again?"

"Ramy—Herman Ramy."

There ensued a long silence, broken only by the flutter of leaves as Mr. Loomis turned over his ledgers. Presently he looked up, keeping his finger between the pages.

"Here it is—Herman Ramy. He was one of our ordinary workmen, and left us three years and a half ago last June."

"On account of sickness?" Ann Eliza faltered.

Mr. Loomis appeared to hesitate; then he said: "I see no mention of sickness." Ann Eliza felt his compassionate eyes on her again. "Perhaps I'd better tell you the truth. He was discharged for drug-taking. A capable workman, but we couldn't keep him straight. I'm sorry to have to tell you this, but it seems fairer, since you say you're anxious about your sister."

The polished sides of the office vanished from Ann Eliza's sight, and the cackle of the innumerable clocks came to her like the yell of waves in a storm. She tried to speak but could not; tried to get to her feet, but the floor was gone.

"I'm very sorry," Mr. Loomis repeated, closing the ledger. "I remember the man perfectly now. He used to disappear every now and then, and turn up again in a state that made him useless for days."

As she listened, Ann Eliza recalled the day when she had come on Mr. Ramy sitting in abject dejection behind his counter. She saw again the blurred unrecognizing eyes he had raised to her, the layer of dust over everything in the shop, and the green bronze clock in the window representing a Newfoundland dog with his paw on a book. She stood up slowly.

"Thank you. I'm sorry to have troubled you."

"It was no trouble. You say Ramy married your sister last October?"

"Yes, sir; and they went to St. Louis right afterward. I don't know how to find her. I thought maybe somebody here might know about him."

"Well, possibly some of the workmen might. Leave me your name and I'll send you word if I get on his track."

He handed her a pencil, and she wrote down her address; then she walked away blindly between the clocks.

XI

Mr. Loomis, true to his word, wrote a few days later that he had enquired in vain in the workshop for any news of Ramy; and as she folded this letter and laid it between the leaves of her Bible, Ann Eliza felt that her last hope was gone. Miss Mellins, of course, had long since suggested the mediation of the police, and cited from her favourite literature convincing instances of the supernatural ability of the Pinkerton detective; but Mr. Hawkins, when called in council, dashed this project by remarking that detectives cost something like twenty dollars a day; and a vague fear of the law, some half-formed vision of Evelina in the clutch of a blue-coated "officer," kept Ann Eliza from invoking the aid of the police.

After the arrival of Mr. Loomis's note the weeks followed each other uneventfully. Ann Eliza's cough clung to her till late in the spring, the reflection in her looking-glass grew more bent and meagre, and her forehead sloped back farther toward the twist of hair that was fastened above her parting by a comb of black India-rubber.

Toward spring a lady who was expecting a baby took up her abode at the Mendoza Family Hotel, and through the friendly intervention of Miss Mellins the making of some of the baby-clothes was entrusted to Ann Eliza. This eased her of anxiety for the immediate future; but she had to rouse herself to feel any sense of relief. Her personal welfare was what least concerned her. Sometimes she thought of giving up the shop altogether; and only the fear that, if she changed her address, Evelina might not be able to find her, kept her from carrying out this plan.

Since she had lost her last hope of tracing her sister, all the activ-

ities of her lonely imagination had been concentrated on the possibility of Evelina's coming back to her. The discovery of Ramy's
secret filled her with dreadful fears. In the solitude of the shop and
the back room she was tortured by vague pictures of Evelina's sufferings. What horrors might not be hidden beneath her silence?
Ann Eliza's great dread was that Miss Mellins should worm out of
her what she had learned from Mr. Loomis. She was sure Miss Mellins must have abominable things to tell about drug-fiends—things
she did not have the strength to hear. "Drug-fiend"—the very word
was Satanic: she could hear Miss Mellins roll it on her tongue. But
Ann Eliza's own imagination, left to itself, had begun to people the
long hours with evil visions. Sometimes, in the night, she thought she
heard herself called: the voice was her sister's, but faint with a
nameless terror. Her most peaceful moments were those in which she
managed to convince herself that Evelina was dead. She thought of
her then, mournfully but more calmly, as thrust away under the neglected mound of some unknown cemetery, where no headstone
marked her name, no mourner with flowers for another grave paused
in pity to lay a blossom on hers. But this vision did not often give
Ann Eliza its negative relief: and always, beneath its hazy lines,
lurked the dark conviction that Evelina was alive, in misery and
longing for her.

So the summer wore on. Ann Eliza was conscious that Mrs.
Hawkins and Miss Mellins were watching her with affectionate
anxiety, but the knowledge brought no comfort. She no longer
cared what they felt or thought about her. Her grief lay far beyond
touch of human healing, and after a while she became aware that
they knew they could not help her. They still came in as often as
their busy lives permitted, but their visits grew shorter, and Mrs.
Hawkins always brought Arthur or the baby, so that there should be
something to talk about, and some one whom she could scold.

The autumn came, and the winter. Business had fallen off
again, and but few purchasers came to the little shop in the basement. In January Ann Eliza pawned her mother's cashmere scarf,
her mosaic brooch, and the rosewood what-not on which the clock
had always stood; she would have sold the bedstead too, but for the
persistent vision of Evelina returning weak and weary, and not
knowing where to lay her head.

The winter passed in its turn, and March reappeared with its galaxies of yellow jonquils at the windy street corners, reminding Ann
Eliza of the spring day when Evelina had come home with a bunch
of jonquils in her hand. In spite of the flowers which lent such a premature brightness to the streets the month was fierce and stormy, and
Ann Eliza could get no warmth into her bones. Nevertheless, she
was insensibly beginning to take up the healing routine of life.
Little by little she had grown used to being alone, she had begun to
take a languid interest in the one or two new purchasers the season

had brought, and though the thought of Evelina was as poignant as ever, it was less persistently in the foreground of her mind.

Late one afternoon she was sitting behind the counter, wrapped in her shawl, and wondering how soon she might draw down the blinds and retreat into the comparative cosiness of the back room. She was not thinking of anything in particular, except perhaps in a hazy way of the lady with the puffed sleeves, who after her long eclipse had reappeared the day before in sleeves of a new cut, and bought some tape and needles. The lady still wore mourning, but she was evidently lightening it, and Ann Eliza saw in this the hope of future orders. The lady had left the shop about an hour before, walking away with her graceful step toward Fifth Avenue. She had wished Ann Eliza good day in her usual affable way, and Ann Eliza thought how odd it was that they should have been acquainted so long, and yet that she should not know the lady's name. From this consideration her mind wandered to the cut of the lady's new sleeves, and she was vexed with herself for not having noted it more carefully. She felt Miss Mellins might have liked to know about it. Ann Eliza's powers of observation had never been as keen as Evelina's, when the latter was not too self-absorbed to exert them. As Miss Mellins always said, Evelina could "take patterns with her eyes": she could have cut that new sleeve out of a folded newspaper in a trice! Musing on these things, Ann Eliza wished the lady would come back and give her another look at the sleeve. It was not unlikely that she might pass that way, for she certainly lived in or about the Square. Suddenly Ann Eliza remarked a small neat handkerchief on the counter: it must have dropped from the lady's purse, and she would probably come back to get it. Ann Eliza, pleased at the idea, sat on behind the counter and watched the darkening street. She always lit the gas as late as possible, keeping the box of matches at her elbow, so that if any one came she could apply a quick flame to the gas-jet. At length through the deepening dusk she distinguished a slim dark figure coming down the steps to the shop. With a little warmth of pleasure about her heart she reached up to light the gas. "I do believe I'll ask her name this time," she thought. She raised the flame to its full height, and saw her sister standing in the door.

There she was at last, the poor pale shade of Evelina, her thin face blanched of its faint pink, the stiff ripples gone from her hair, and a mantle shabbier than Ann Eliza's drawn about her narrow shoulders. The glare of the gas beat full on her as she stood and looked at Ann Eliza.

"Sister—oh, Evelina! I knowed you'd come!"

Ann Eliza had caught her close with a long moan of triumph. Vague words poured from her as she laid her cheek against Evelina's—trivial inarticulate endearments caught from Mrs. Hawkins's long discourses to her baby.

For a while Evelina let herself be passively held; then she drew back from her sister's clasp and looked about the shop. "I'm dead tired. Ain't there any fire?" she asked.

"Of course there is!" Ann Eliza, holding her hand fast, drew her into the back room. She did not want to ask any questions yet: she simply wanted to feel the emptiness of the room brimmed full again by the one presence that was warmth and light to her.

She knelt down before the grate, scraped some bits of coal and kindling from the bottom of the coal-scuttle, and drew one of the rocking-chairs up to the weak flame. "There—that'll blaze up in a minute," she said. She pressed Evelina down on the faded cushions of the rocking-chair, and, kneeling beside her, began to rub her hands.

"You're stone-cold, ain't you? Just sit still and warm yourself while I run and get the kettle. I've got something you always used to fancy for supper." She laid her hand on Evelina's shoulder. "Don't talk—oh, don't talk yet!" she implored. She wanted to keep that one frail second of happiness between herself and what she knew must come.

Evelina, without a word, bent over the fire, stretching her thin hands to the blaze and watching Ann Eliza fill the kettle and set the supper table. Her gaze had the dreamy fixity of a half-awakened child's.

Ann Eliza, with a smile of triumph, brought a slice of custard pie from the cupboard and put it by her sister's plate.

"You do like that, don't you? Miss Mellins sent it down to me this morning. She had her aunt from Brooklyn to dinner. Ain't it funny it just so happened?"

"I ain't hungry," said Evelina, rising to approach the table.

She sat down in her usual place, looked about her with the same wondering stare, and then, as of old, poured herself out the first cup of tea.

"Where's the what-not gone to?" she suddenly asked.

Ann Eliza set down the teapot and rose to get a spoon from the cupboard. With her back to the room she said: "The what-not? Why, you see, dearie, living here all alone by myself it only made one more thing to dust; so I sold it."

Evelina's eyes were still travelling about the familiar room. Though it was against all the traditions of the Bunner family to sell any household possession, she showed no surprise at her sister's answer.

"And the clock? The clock's gone too."

"Oh, I gave that away—I gave it to Mrs. Hawkins. She's kep' awake so nights with that last baby."

"I wish you'd never bought it," said Evelina harshly.

Ann Eliza's heart grew faint with fear. Without answering, she crossed over to her sister's seat and poured her out a second cup of tea. Then another thought struck her, and she went back to the cupboard and took out the cordial. In Evelina's absence considerable draughts had been drawn from it by invalid neighbours; but a glassful of the precious liquid still remained.

"Here, drink this right off—it'll warm you up quicker than anything," Ann Eliza said.

Evelina obeyed, and a slight spark of colour came into her cheeks. She turned to the custard pie and began to eat with a silent voracity distressing to watch. She did not even look to see what was left for Ann Eliza.

"I ain't hungry," she said at last as she laid down her fork. "I'm only so dead tired—that's the trouble."

"Then you better get right into bed. Here's my old plaid dressing-gown—you remember it, don't you?" Ann Eliza laughed, recalling Evelina's ironies on the subject of the antiquated garment. With trembling fingers she began to undo her sister's cloak. The dress beneath it told a tale of poverty that Ann Eliza dared not pause to note. She drew it gently off, and as it slipped from Evelina's shoulders it revealed a tiny black bag hanging on a ribbon about her neck. Evelina lifted her hand as though to screen the bag from Ann Eliza; and the elder sister, seeing the gesture, continued her task with lowered eyes. She undressed Evelina as quickly as she could, and wrapping her in the plaid dressing-gown put her to bed, and spread her own shawl and her sister's cloak above the blanket.

"Where's the old red comfortable?" Evelina asked, as she sank down on the pillow.

"The comfortable? Oh, it was so hot and heavy I never used it after you went—so I sold that too. I never could sleep under much clothes."

She became aware that her sister was looking at her more attentively.

"I guess you've been in trouble too," Evelina said.

"Me? In trouble? What do you mean, Evelina?"

"You've had to pawn the things, I suppose," Evelina continued in a weary unmoved tone. "Well, I've been through worse than that. I've been to hell and back."

"Oh, Evelina—don't say it, sister!" Ann Eliza implored, shrinking from the unholy word. She knelt down and began to rub her sister's feet beneath the bed-clothes.

"I've been to hell and back—if I *am* back," Evelina repeated. She lifted her head from the pillow and began to talk with a sudden feverish volubility. "It began right away, less than a month after we were married. I've been in hell all that time, Ann Eliza." She fixed her eyes with passionate intentness on Ann Eliza's face. "He took opium. I didn't find it out till long afterward—at first, when he acted so strange, I thought he drank. But it was worse, much worse than drinking."

"Oh, sister, don't say it—don't say it yet! It's so sweet just to have you here with me again."

"I must say it," Evelina insisted, her flushed face burning with a kind of bitter cruelty. "You don't know what life's like—you don't know anything about it—setting here safe all the while in this peaceful place."

"Oh, Evelina—why didn't you write and send for me if it was like that?"

"That's why I couldn't write. Didn't you guess I was ashamed?"

"How could you be? Ashamed to write to Ann Eliza?"

Evelina raised herself on her thin elbow, while Ann Eliza, bending over, drew a corner of the shawl about her shoulder.

"Do lay down again. You'll catch your death."

"My death? That don't frighten me! You don't know what I've been through." And sitting upright in the old mahogany bed, with flushed cheeks and chattering teeth, and Ann Eliza's trembling arm clasping the shawl about her neck, Evelina poured out her story. It was a tale of misery and humiliation so remote from the elder sister's innocent experiences that much of it was hardly intelligible to her. Evelina's dreadful familiarity with it all, her fluency about things which Ann Eliza half-guessed and quickly shuddered back from, seemed even more alien and terrible than the actual tale she told. It was one thing—and heaven knew it was bad enough!—to learn that one's sister's husband was a drug-fiend; it was another, and much worse thing, to learn from that sister's pallid lips what vileness lay behind the word.

Evelina, unconscious of any distress but her own, sat upright, shivering in Ann Eliza's hold, while she piled up, detail by detail, her dreary narrative.

"'The minute we got out there, and he found the job wasn't as good as he expected, he changed. At first I thought he was sick—I used to try to keep him home and nurse him. Then I saw it was something different. He used to go off for hours at a time, and when he came back his eyes kinder had a fog over them. Sometimes he didn't har'ly know me, and when he did he seemed to hate me. Once he hit me here." She touched her breast. "Do you remember, Ann Eliza, that time he didn't come to see us for a week—the time after we all went to Central Park together—and you and I thought he must be sick?"

Ann Eliza nodded.

"Well, that was the trouble—he'd been at it then. But nothing like as bad. After we'd been out there about a month he disappeared for a whole week. They took him back at the store, and gave him another chance; but the second time they discharged him, and he drifted round for ever so long before he could get another job. We spent all our money and had to move to a cheaper place. Then he got something to do, but they hardly paid him anything, and he didn't stay there long. When he found out about the baby—"

"The baby?" Ann Eliza faltered.

"It's dead—it only lived a day. When he found out about it, he got mad, and said he hadn't any money to pay doctors' bills, and I'd better write to you to help us. He had an idea you had money hidden away that I didn't know about." She turned to her sister with remorseful eyes. "It was him that made me get that hundred dollars out of you."

"Hush, hush. I always meant it for you anyhow."

"Yes, but I wouldn't have taken it if he hadn't been at me the whole time. He used to make me do just what he wanted. Well, when I said I wouldn't write to you for more money he said I'd better try and earn some myself. That was when he struck me. . . . Oh, you don't know what I'm talking about yet! . . . I tried to get work at a milliner's, but I was so sick I couldn't stay. I was sick all the time. I wisht I'd ha' died, Ann Eliza."

"No, no, Evelina."

"Yes, I do. It kept getting worse and worse. We pawned the furniture, and they turned us out because we couldn't pay the rent; and so then we went to board with Mrs. Hochmüller."

Ann Eliza pressed her closer to dissemble her own tremor. "Mrs. Hochmüller?"

"Didn't you know she was out there? She moved out a month after we did. She wasn't bad to me, and I think she tried to keep him straight—but Linda—"

"Linda?—"

"Well, when I kept getting worse, and he was always off, for days at a time, the doctor had me sent to a hospital."

"A hospital? Sister—sister!"

"It was better than being with him; and the doctors were real kind to me. After the baby was born I was very sick and had to stay there a good while. And one day when I was laying there Mrs. Hochmüller came in as white as a sheet, and told me him and Linda had gone off together and taken all her money. That's the last I ever saw of him." She broke off with a laugh and began to cough again.

Ann Eliza tried to persuade her to lie down and sleep, but the rest of her story had to be told before she could be soothed into consent. After the news of Ramy's flight she had had brain fever, and had been sent to another hospital where she stayed a long time—how long she couldn't remember. Dates and days meant nothing to her in the shapeless ruin of her life. When she left the hospital she found that Mrs. Hochmüller had gone too. She was penniless, and had no one to turn to. A lady visitor at the hospital was kind, and found her a place where she did housework; but she was so weak they couldn't keep her. Then she got a job as waitress in a down-town lunch-room, but one day she fainted while she was handing a dish, and that evening when they paid her they told her she needn't come again.

"After that I begged in the streets"—(Ann Eliza's grasp again grew tight)—"and one afternoon last week, when the matinées was coming out, I met a man with a pleasant face, something like Mr. Hawkins, and he stopped and asked me what the trouble was. I told him if he'd give me five dollars I'd have money enough to buy a ticket back to New York, and he took a good look at me and said, well, if that was what I wanted he'd go straight to the station with me and give me the five dollars there. So he did—and he bought the ticket, and put me in the cars."

Evelina sank back, her face a sallow wedge in the white cleft of the pillow. Ann Eliza leaned over her, and for a long time they held each other without speaking.

They were still clasped in this dumb embrace when there was a step in the shop and Ann Eliza, starting up, saw Miss Mellins in the doorway.

"My sakes, Miss Brunner! What in the land are you doing? Miss Evelina—Mrs. Ramy—it ain't you?"

Miss Mellins's eyes, bursting from their sockets, sprang from Evelina's pallid face to the disordered supper table and the heap of worn clothes on the floor; then they turned back to Ann Eliza, who had placed herself on the defensive between her sister and the dress-maker.

"My sister Evelina has come back—come back on a visit. She was taken sick in the cars on the way home—I guess she caught cold—so I made her go right to bed as soon as ever she got here."

Ann Eliza was surprised at the strength and steadiness of her voice. Fortified by its sound she went on, her eyes on Miss Mellins's baffled countenance: "Mr. Ramy has gone west on a trip—a trip connected with his business; and Evelina is going to stay with me till he comes back."

XII

What measure of belief her explanation of Evelina's return obtained in the small circle of her friends Ann Eliza did not pause to enquire. Though she could not remember ever having told a lie before, she adhered with rigid tenacity to the consequences of her first lapse from truth, and fortified her original statement with additional details whenever a questioner sought to take her unawares.

But other and more serious burdens lay on her startled conscience. For the first time in her life she dimly faced the awful problem of the inutility of self-sacrifice. Hitherto she had never thought of questioning the inherited principles which had guided her life. Self-effacement for the good of others had always seemed to her both natural and necessary; but then she had taken it for granted that it implied the securing of that good. Now she perceived that to refuse the gifts of life does not ensure their transmission to those for whom they have been surrendered; and her familiar heaven was unpeopled. She felt she could no longer trust in the goodness of God, and that if he was not good he was not God, and there was only a black abyss above the roof of Bunner Sisters.

But there was little time to brood upon such problems. The care of Evelina filled Ann Eliza's days and nights. The hastily summoned doctor had pronounced her to be suffering from pneumonia, and under his care the first stress of the disease was relieved. But her recovery was only partial, and long after the doctor's visits had ceased she continued to lie in bed, too weak to move, and seemingly indifferent to everything about her.

At length one evening, about six weeks after her return, she said to her sister: "I don't feel's if I'd ever get up again."

Ann Eliza turned from the kettle she was placing on the stove. She was startled by the echo the words woke in her own breast.

"Don't you talk like that, Evelina! I guess you're on'y tired out —and disheartened."

"Yes, I'm disheartened," Evelina murmured.

A few months earlier Ann Eliza would have met the confession with a word of pious admonition; now she accepted it in silence.

"Maybe you'll brighten up when your cough gets better," she suggested.

"Yes—or my cough'll get better when I brighten up," Evelina retorted with a touch of her old tartness.

"Does your cough keep on hurting you jest as much?"

"I don't see's there's much difference."

"Well, I guess I'll get the doctor to come round again," Ann Eliza said, trying for the matter-of-course tone in which one might speak of sending for the plumber or the gas-fitter.

"It ain't any use sending for the doctor—and who's going to pay him?"

"I am," answered the elder sister. "Here's your tea, and a mite of toast. Don't that tempt you?"

Already, in the watches of the night, Ann Eliza had been tormented by that same question—who was to pay the doctor?—and a few days before she had temporarily silenced it by borrowing twenty dollars of Miss Mellins. The transaction had cost her one of the bitterest struggles of her life. She had never borrowed a penny of any one before, and the possibility of having to do so had always been classed in her mind among those shameful extremities to which Providence does not let decent people come. But nowadays she no longer believed in the personal supervision of Providence; and had she been compelled to steal the money instead of borrowing it, she would have felt that her conscience was the only tribunal before which she had to answer. Nevertheless, the actual humiliation of having to ask for the money was no less bitter; and she could hardly hope that Miss Mellins would view the case with the same detachment as herself. Miss Mellins was very kind; but she not unnaturally felt that her kindness should be rewarded by according her the right to ask questions; and bit by bit Ann Eliza saw Evelina's miserable secret slipping into the dress-maker's possession.

When the doctor came she left him alone with Evelina, busying herself in the shop that she might have an opportunity of seeing him alone on his way out. To steady herself she began to sort a trayful of buttons, and when the doctor appeared she was reciting under her breath: "Twenty-four horn, two and a half cards fancy pearl. . . ." She saw at once that his look was grave.

He sat down on the chair beside the counter, and her mind travelled miles before he spoke.

"Miss Bunner, the best thing you can do is to let me get a bed for your sister at St. Luke's."

"The hospital?"

"Come now, you're above that sort of prejudice, aren't you?" The doctor spoke in the tone of one who coaxes a spoiled child. "I know how devoted you are—but Mrs. Ramy can be much better cared for there than here. You really haven't time to look after her and attend to your business as well. There'll be no expense, you understand—"

Ann Eliza made no answer. "You think my sister's going to be sick a good while, then?" she asked.

"Well, yes—possibly."

"You think she's very sick?"

"Well, yes. She's very sick."

His face had grown still graver; he sat there as though he had never known what it was to hurry.

Ann Eliza continued to separate the pearl and horn buttons. Suddenly she lifted her eyes and looked at him. "Is she going to die?"

The doctor laid a kindly hand on hers. "We never say that, Miss Bunner. Human skill works wonders—and at the hospital Mrs. Ramy would have every chance."

"What is it? What's she dying of?"

The doctor hesitated, seeking to substitute a popular phrase for the scientific terminology which rose to his lips.

"I want to know," Ann Eliza persisted.

"Yes, of course; I understand. Well, your sister has had a hard time lately, and there is a complication of causes, resulting in consumption—rapid consumption. At the hospital—"

"I'll keep her here," said Ann Eliza quietly.

After the doctor had gone she went on for some time sorting the buttons; then she slipped the tray into its place on a shelf behind the counter and went into the back room. She found Evelina propped upright against the pillows, a flush of agitation on her cheeks. Ann Eliza pulled up the shawl which had slipped from her sister's shoulders.

"'How long you've been! What's he been saying?"

"Oh, he went long ago—he on'y stopped to give me a prescription. I was sorting out that tray of buttons. Miss Mellins's girl got them all mixed up."

She felt Evelina's eyes upon her.

"He must have said something: what was it?"

"Why, he said you'd have to be careful—and stay in bed—and take this new medicine he's given you."

"Did he say I was going to get well?"

"Why, Evelina!"

"What's the use, Ann Eliza? You can't deceive me. I've just been up to look at myself in the glass; and I saw plenty of 'em in the hospital that looked like me. They didn't get well, and I ain't going to." Her head dropped back. "It don't much matter—I'm about tired. On'y there's one thing—Ann Eliza—"

The elder sister drew near to the bed.

"There's one thing I ain't told you. I didn't want to tell you yet because I was afraid you might be sorry—but if he says I'm going to die I've got to say it." She stopped to cough, and to Ann Eliza it now seemed as though every cough struck a minute from the hours remaining to her.

"Don't talk now—you're tired."

"I'll be tireder to-morrow, I guess. And I want you should know. Sit down close to me—there."

Ann Eliza sat down in silence, stroking her shrunken hand.

"I'm a Roman Catholic, Ann Eliza."

"Evelina—oh, Evelina Bunner! A Roman Catholic—*you*? Oh, Evelina, did *he* make you?"

Evelina shook her head. "I guess he didn't have no religion; he never spoke of it. But you see Mrs. Hochmüller was a Catholic, and so when I was sick she got the doctor to send me to a Roman Catholic hospital, and the sisters was so good to me there—and the priest used to come and talk to me; and the things he said kep' me from going crazy. He seemed to make everything easier."

"Oh, sister, how could you?" Ann Eliza wailed. She knew little of the Catholic religion except that "Papists" believed in it—in itself a sufficient indictment. Her spiritual rebellion had not freed her from the formal part of her religious belief, and apostasy had always seemed to her one of the sins from which the pure in mind avert their thoughts.

"And then when the baby was born," Evelina continued, "he christened it right away, so it could go to heaven; and after that, you see, I had to be a Catholic."

"I don't see—"

"Don't I have to be where the baby is? I couldn't ever ha' gone there if I hadn't been made a Catholic. Don't you understand that?"

Ann Eliza sat speechless, drawing her hand away. Once more she found herself shut out of Evelina's heart, an exile from her closest affections.

"I've got to go where the baby is," Evelina feverishly insisted.

Ann Eliza could think of nothing to say; she could only feel that Evelina was dying, and dying as a stranger in her arms. Ramy and the day-old baby had parted her forever from her sister.

Evelina began again. "If I get worse I want you to send for a priest. Miss Mellins'll know where to send—she's got an aunt that's a Catholic. Promise me faithful you will."

"I promise," said Ann Eliza.

After that they spoke no more of the matter; but Ann Eliza now understood that the little black bag about her sister's neck, which she had innocently taken for a memento of Ramy, was some kind of sacrilegious amulet, and her fingers shrank from its contact when she bathed and dressed Evelina. It seemed to her the diabolical instrument of their estrangement.

XIII

Spring had really come at last. There were leaves on the ailanthus-tree[8] that Evelina could see from her bed, gentle clouds floated over it in the blue, and now and then the cry of a flower-seller sounded from the street.

One day there was a shy knock on the back-room door, and Johnny Hawkins came in with two yellow jonquils in his fist. He was getting bigger and squarer, and his round freckled face was growing into a smaller copy of his father's. He walked up to Evelina and held out the flowers.

"They blew off the cart and the fellow said I could keep 'em. But you can have 'em," he announced.

Ann Eliza rose from her seat at the sewing-machine and tried to take the flowers from him.

"They ain't for you; they're for her," he sturdily objected; and Evelina held out her hand for the jonquils.

After Johnny had gone she lay and looked at them without speaking. Ann Eliza, who had gone back to the machine, bent her head over the seam she was stitching; the click, click, click of the machine sounded in her ear like the tick of Ramy's clock, and it seemed to her that life had gone backward, and that Evelina, radiant and foolish, had just come into the room with the yellow flowers in her hand.

When at last she ventured to look up, she saw that her sister's head had drooped against the pillow, and that she was sleeping quietly. Her relaxed hand still held the jonquils, but it was evident that

8. The ailanthus tree has bitter bark and ill-scented greenish blossoms.

they had awakened no memories; she had dozed off almost as soon as Johnny had given them to her. The discovery gave Ann Eliza a startled sense of the ruins that must be piled upon her past. "I don't believe I could have forgotten that day, though," she said to herself. But she was glad that Evelina had forgotten.

Evelina's disease moved on along the usual course, now lifting her on a brief wave of elation, now sinking her to new depths of weakness. There was little to be done, and the doctor came only at lengthening intervals. On his way out he always repeated his first friendly suggestion about sending Evelina to the hospital; and Ann Eliza always answered: "I guess we can manage."

The hours passed for her with the fierce rapidity that great joy or anguish lends them. She went through the days with a sternly smiling precision, but she hardly knew what was happening, and when night-fall released her from the shop, and she could carry her work to Evelina's bedside, the same sense of unreality accompanied her, and she still seemed to be accomplishing a task whose object had escaped her memory.

Once, when Evelina felt better, she expressed a desire to make some artificial flowers, and Ann Eliza, deluded by this awakening interest, got out the faded bundles of stems and petals and the little tools and spools of wire. But after a few minutes the work dropped from Evelina's hands and she said: "I'll wait till to-morrow."

She never again spoke of the flower-making, but one day, after watching Ann Eliza's laboured attempt to trim a spring hat for Mrs. Hawkins, she demanded impatiently that the hat should be brought to her, and in a trice had galvanized the lifeless bow and given the brim the twist it needed.

These were rare gleams; and more frequent were the days of speechless lassitude, when she lay for hours silently staring at the window, shaken only by the hard incessant cough that sounded to Ann Eliza like the hammering of nails into a coffin.

At length one morning Ann Eliza, starting up from the mattress at the foot of the bed, hastily called Miss Mellins down, and ran through the smoky dawn for the doctor. He came back with her and did what he could to give Evelina momentary relief; then he went away, promising to look in again before night. Miss Mellins, her head still covered with curl-papers, disappeared in his wake, and when the sisters were alone Evelina beckoned to Ann Eliza.

"You promised," she whispered, grasping her sister's arm; and Ann Eliza understood. She had not yet dared to tell Miss Mellins of Evelina's change of faith; it had seemed even more difficult than borrowing the money; but now it had to be done. She ran upstairs after the dress-maker and detained her on the landing.

"Miss Mellins, can you tell me where to send for a priest—a Roman Catholic priest?"

"A priest, Miss Bunner?"

"Yes. My sister became a Roman Catholic while she was away. They were kind to her in her sickness—and now she wants a priest." Ann Eliza faced Miss Mellins with unflinching eyes.

"My aunt Dugan'll know. I'll run right round to her the minute I get my papers off," the dress-maker promised; and Ann Eliza thanked her.

An hour or two later the priest appeared. Ann Eliza, who was watching, saw him coming down the steps to the shop-door and went to meet him. His expression was kind, but she shrank from his peculiar dress, and from his pale face with its bluish chin and enigmatic smile. Ann Eliza remained in the shop. Miss Mellins's girl had mixed the buttons again and she set herself to sort them. The priest stayed a long time with Evelina. When he again carried his enigmatic smile past the counter, and Ann Eliza rejoined her sister, Evelina was smiling with something of the same mystery; but she did not tell her secret.

After that it seemed to Ann Eliza that the shop and the back room no longer belonged to her. It was as though she were there on sufferance, indulgently tolerated by the unseen power which hovered over Evelina even in the absence of its minister. The priest came almost daily; and at last a day arrived when he was called to administer some rite of which Ann Eliza but dimly grasped the sacramental meaning. All she knew was that it meant that Evelina was going, and going, under this alien guidance, even farther from her than to the dark places of death.

When the priest came, with something covered in his hands, she crept into the shop, closing the door of the back room to leave him alone with Evelina.

It was a warm afternoon in May, and the crooked ailanthus-tree rooted in a fissure of the opposite pavement was a fountain of tender green. Women in light dresses passed with the languid step of spring; and presently there came a man with a hand-cart full of pansy and geranium plants who stopped outside the window, signalling to Ann Eliza to buy.

An hour went by before the door of the back room opened and the priest reappeared with that mysterious covered something in his hands. Ann Eliza had risen, drawing back as he passed. He had doubtless divined her antipathy, for he had hitherto only bowed in going in and out; but to-day he paused and looked at her compassionately.

"I have left your sister in a very beautiful state of mind," he said in a low voice like a woman's. "She is full of spiritual consolation."

Ann Eliza was silent, and he bowed and went out. She hastened back to Evelina's bed, and knelt down beside it. Evelina's eyes were very large and bright; she turned them on Ann Eliza with a look of inner illumination.

"I shall see the baby," she said; then her eyelids fell and she dozed.

The doctor came again at nightfall, administering some last palliatives; and after he had gone Ann Eliza, refusing to have her vigil shared by Miss Mellins or Mrs. Hawkins, sat down to keep watch alone.

It was a very quiet night. Evelina never spoke or opened her eyes, but in the still hour before dawn Ann Eliza saw that the restless hand outside the bed-clothes had stopped its twitching. She stooped over and felt no breath on her sister's lips.

The funeral took place three days later. Evelina was buried in Calvary Cemetery, the priest assuming the whole care of the necessary arrangements, while Ann Eliza, a passive spectator, beheld with stony indifference this last negation of her past.

A week afterward she stood in her bonnet and mantle in the doorway of the little shop. Its whole aspect had changed. Counter and shelves were bare, the window was stripped of its familiar miscellany of artificial flowers, note-paper, wire hat-frames, and limp garments from the dyer's; and against the glass pane of the doorway hung a sign: "This store to let."

Ann Eliza turned her eyes from the sign as she went out and locked the door behind her. Evelina's funeral had been very expensive, and Ann Eliza, having sold her stock-in-trade and the few articles of furniture that remained to her, was leaving the shop for the last time. She had not been able to buy any mourning, but Miss Mellins had sewed some crape on her old black mantle and bonnet, and having no gloves she slipped her bare hands under the folds of the mantle.

It was a beautiful morning, and the air was full of a warm sunshine that had coaxed open nearly every window in the street, and summoned to the window-sills the sickly plants nurtured indoors in winter. Ann Eliza's way lay westward, toward Broadway; but at the corner she paused and looked back down the familiar length of the street. Her eyes rested a moment on the blotched "Bunner Sisters" above the empty window of the shop; then they travelled on to the overflowing foliage of the Square, above which was the church tower with the dial that had marked the hours for the sisters before Ann Eliza had bought the nickel clock. She looked at it all as though it had been the scene of some unknown life, of which the vague report had reached her: she felt for herself the only remote pity that busy people accord to the misfortunes which come to them by hearsay.

She walked to Broadway and down to the office of the house-agent to whom she had entrusted the sub-letting of the shop. She left the key with one of his clerks, who took it from her as if it had been any one of a thousand others, and remarked that the weather looked as if spring was really coming; then she turned and began to move up the great thoroughfare, which was just beginning to wake to its multitudinous activities.

She walked less rapidly now, studying each shop window as she passed, but not with the desultory eye of enjoyment: the watchful fixity of her gaze overlooked everything but the object of its quest. At length she stopped before a small window wedged between two mammoth buildings, and displaying, behind its shining plate-glass festooned with muslin, a varied assortment of sofa-cushions, tea-cloths, pen-wipers, painted calendars and other specimens of feminine industry. In a corner of the window she had read, on a slip of paper pasted against the pane: "Wanted, a Saleslady," and after studying the display of fancy articles beneath it, she gave her mantle a twitch, straightened her shoulders and went in.

Behind a counter crowded with pin-cushions, watch-holders and other needle-work trifles, a plump young woman with smooth hair sat sewing bows of ribbon on a scrap basket. The little shop was about the size of the one on which Ann Eliza had just closed the door; and it looked as fresh and gay and thriving as she and Evelina had once dreamed of making Bunner Sisters. The friendly air of the place made her pluck up courage to speak.

"Saleslady? Yes, we do want one. Have you any one to recommend?" the young woman asked, not unkindly.

Ann Eliza hesitated, disconcerted by the unexpected question; and the other, cocking her head on one side to study the effect of the bow she had just sewed on the basket, continued: "We can't afford more than thirty dollars a month, but the work is light. She would be expected to do a little fancy sewing between times. We want a bright girl: stylish, and pleasant manners. You know what I mean. Not over thirty, anyhow; and nice-looking. Will you write down the name?"

Ann Eliza looked at her confusedly. She opened her lips to explain, and then, without speaking, turned toward the crisply-curtained door.

"Ain't you going to leave the *ad*-dress?" the young woman called out after her. Ann Eliza went out into the thronged street. The great city, under the fair spring sky, seemed to throb with the stir of innumerable beginnings. She walked on, looking for another shop window with a sign in it.

1891–92   1916

W. E. B. DUBOIS
1868–1963

William Edward Burghardt DuBois was born on February 23, 1868, in Great Barrington, Massachusetts. His childhood was happy, but with the approach of adolescence DuBois discovered that what made him different from his schoolmates was not so much his superior academic achievement as his brown skin. Looking back on his rejection by a white girl in grade school, "it dawned on me with a certain suddenness," DuBois wrote, "that I was * * * shut out from their world by a vast veil," a veil he claimed to have no desire to force his way behind. DuBois's entire career, nonetheless, may be understood as an attempt to lift that veil all over the world so that all races might see each other in the clear light of historical fact.

DuBois was educated at Fisk, Harvard, and the University of Berlin. His doctoral dissertation, *The Suppression of the African Slave Trade to the United States of America, 1638–1870*, was published as the first volume in the Harvard Historical Studies series. By the time DuBois completed his graduate studies his accomplishments were already considerable, but he could not secure an appointment at a major university. He taught first instead at Wilberforce College in Ohio, then a small, poor, provincial black college. There he offered Greek, Latin, German, and English—subjects far removed from his real interest in the relatively new field of sociology.

After spending a year at the University of Pennsylvania, where he produced his first major work, *The Philadelphia Negro*, DuBois moved to Atlanta University in 1897. There, over the next thirteen years, he produced a steady stream of important studies of Afro-American life. Dedicated to the rigorous, scholarly examination of the so-called Negro problem, DuBois soon had to face up to the violent emotional realities of the lives he proposed to study. On his way to present an appeal for reason in the case of a Negro accused of murder and rape, DuBois was met by the news that a lynch mob had dismembered and burned the black man at the stake and that "his knuckles were on exhibition at a grocery store." Though DuBois never ceased being a scholar, from this time on he became increasingly an activist and sought a wider audience for his writings.

DuBois first came to national attention with the publication of *The Souls of Black Folk* (1903). Several essay-chapters explore the implications of this extraordinary book's dramatic and prophetic announcement that "the problem of the Twentieth Century is the problem of the color line." The chapter which in particular caused a stir was the one which challenged—coolly and without rancor—the enormous authority and power that had accumulated in the hands of one black spokesman, Booker T. Washington. Washington had founded Tuskegee Institute in Alabama to train blacks in basic agricultural and mechanical skills, and had gained national prominence with his Atlanta Exposition speech in 1895. His address in effect accepted disenfranchisement and segregation and settled for a low level of education in exchange for white "toleration" and economic cooperation. Though DuBois had initially joined in the general approval of this "separate and unequal" philosophy, by the early 1900s he had begun to reject Washington's position, and with the publication of *Souls of Black Folk* his defiance of Washington amounted to a declaration of war. The almost immediate result of the controversy was to reinforce DuBois's innate radicalism and to make him become a leader in the Niagara Movement, a movement aggressively devoted to demanding for black people the same civil rights enjoyed by white Americans.

In 1910 DuBois left Atlanta for New York, where he served for the next quarter of a century as editor of *Crisis*, the organ of the newly formed NAACP, an organization he helped to create. Through this publication

DuBois reached an increasingly large audience—100,000 by 1919—with powerful messages which argued the need for black development and white enlightenment.

Frustrated by the lack of fundamental change and progress in the condition of black Americans, from 1920 on DuBois increasingly shifted his attention away from the attempt to reform race relations in America through research and political legislation, and toward the search for longer-range world-wide economic solutions to the international problems of inequity among the races. He began a steady movement toward Pan-African and socialist perspectives that led to his joining the Communist party of the United States in 1961 and, in the year of his death, becoming a citizen of Ghana. During these forty years he was extremely active as politician, organizer, and diplomat, and he also sustained his extraordinary productiveness as a powerful writer of poetry, fiction, autobiography, essays, and scholarly works. When, in his last major speech, Martin Luther King spoke of DuBois as "one of the most remarkable men of our time," he was uttering the verdict of history.

From The Souls of Black Folk
III. Of Mr. Booker T. Washington and Others[1]

From birth till death enslaved; in word, in deed, unmanned!
· · · · · · ·
Hereditary bondsmen! Know ye not
Who would be free themselves must strike the blow?
—BYRON

Easily the most striking thing in the history of the American Negro since 1876[3] is the ascendancy of Mr. Booker T. Washington. It began at the time when war memories and ideals were rapidly passing; a day of astonishing commercial development was dawning; a sense of doubt and hesitation overtook the freedmen's sons,—

1. *Of Mr. Booker T. Washington and Others* was first published in *Guardian*, July 27, 1902, and collected in *The Souls of Black Folk* (1903), which was otherwise a compilation of seven previously published and five unpublished essays. The source of the present text is the first book edition. Booker T. Washington (1856?–1915) founded and helped build with his own hands Tuskegee Institute, a black college in Alabama, and became a powerful leader of and spokesman for black Americans especially after his address at the Atlanta Exposition in 1895.
2. *Childe Harold's Pilgrimage*, Canto 11, 74.710, 76.720–21. The music is from the refrain of a Negro spiritual entitled *A Great Camp-Meetin' in de Promised Land* (also called *There's a Great Camp Meeting* and *Walk Together Children*). The words of the refrain set to this music are:

Going to mourn and never tire—
mourn and never tire, mourn and never tire.

3. Reconstruction effectively ended in 1876; federal troops were withdrawn from the South, and black political power was essentially destroyed.

then it was that his leading began. Mr. Washington came, with a simple definite programme, at the psychological moment when the nation was a little ashamed of having bestowed so much sentiment on Negroes, and was concentrating its energies on Dollars. His programme of industrial education, conciliation of the South, and submission and silence as to civil and political rights, was not wholly original; the Free Negroes from 1830 up to war-time had striven to build industrial schools, and the American Missionary Association had from the first taught various trades; and Price[4] and others had sought a way of honorable alliance with the best of the Southerners. But Mr. Washington first indissolubly linked these things; he put enthusiasm, unlimited energy, and perfect faith into this programme, and changed it from a by-path into a veritable Way of Life. And the tale of the methods by which he did this is a fascinating study of human life.

It startled the nation to hear a Negro advocating such a programme after many decades of bitter complaint; it startled and won the applause of the South, it interested and won the admiration of the North; and after a confused murmur of protest, it silenced if it did not convert the Negroes themselves.

To gain the sympathy and cooperation of the various elements comprising the white South was Mr. Washington's first task; and this, at the time Tuskegee was founded, seemed, for a black man, well-nigh impossible. And yet ten years later it was done in the word spoken at Atlanta: "In all things purely social we can be as separate as the five fingers, and yet one as the hand in all things essential to mutual progress." This "Atlanta Compromise"[5] is by all odds the most notable thing in Mr. Washington's career. The South interpreted it in different ways: the radicals received it as a complete surrender of the demand for civil and political equality; the conservatives, as a generously conceived working basis for mutual understanding. So both approved it, and to-day its author is certainly the most distinguished Southerner since Jefferson Davis, and the one with the largest personal following.

Next to this achievement comes Mr. Washington's work in gaining place and consideration in the North. Others less shrewd and tactful had formerly essayed to sit on these two stools and had fallen between them; but as Mr. Washington knew the heart of the South from birth and training, so by singular insight he intuitively grasped the spirit of the age which was dominating the North. And so thoroughly did he learn the speech and thought of triumphant commercialism, and the ideals of material prosperity, that the pic-

4. Thomas Frederick Price (1860–1919), American editor, missionary, Roman Catholic priest; one of the founders of the American Missionary Association.
5. In a speech at the Atlanta Exposition of 1895, Washington in effect traded political, civil, and social rights for Negroes for the promise of vocational training schools and jobs. His purpose was to reduce racial tension in the South while providing a stable black labor force whose skills would provide some hope for job security.

ture of a lone black boy poring over a French grammar amid the weeds and dirt of a neglected home soon seemed to him the acme of absurdities.[6] One wonders what Socrates and St. Francis of Assisi would say to this.

And yet this very singleness of vision and thorough oneness with his age is a mark of the successful man. It is as though Nature must needs make men narrow in order to give them force. So Mr. Washington's cult has gained unquestioning followers, his work has wonderfully prospered, his friends are legion, and his enemies are confounded. To-day he stands as the one recognized spokesman of his ten million fellows, and one of the most notable figures in a nation of seventy millions. One hesitates, therefore, to criticise a life which, beginning with so little, has done so much. And yet the time is come when one may speak in all sincerity and utter courtesy of the mistakes and shortcomings of Mr. Washington's career, as well as of his triumphs, without being thought captious or envious, and without forgetting that it is easier to do ill than well in the world.

The criticism that has hitherto met Mr. Washington has not always been of this broad character. In the South especially has he had to walk warily to avoid the harshest judgments,—and naturally so, for he is dealing with the one subject of deepest sensitiveness to that section. Twice—once when at the Chicago celebration of the Spanish-American War he alluded to the color-prejudice that is "eating away the vitals of the South," and once when he dined with President Roosevelt[7]—has the resulting Southern criticism been violent enough to threaten seriously his popularity. In the North the feeling has several times forced itself into words, that Mr. Washington's counsels of submission overlooked certain elements of true manhood, and that his educational programme was unnecessarily narrow. Usually, however, such criticism has not found open expression, although, too, the spiritual sons of the Abolitionists have not been prepared to acknowledge that the schools founded before Tuskegee, by men of broad ideals and self-sacrificing spirit, were wholly failures or worthy of ridicule. While, then, criticism has not failed to follow Mr. Washington, yet the prevailing public opinion of the land has been but too willing to deliver the solution of a wearisome problem into his hands, and say, "If that is all you and your race ask, take it."

Among his own people, however, Mr. Washington has encountered

6. In Washington's extremely popular *Up from Slavery: An Autobiography* (1901), Chapter VIII, "Teaching School in a Stable and a Hen-House," there is a passage on the absurdity of knowledge not practically useful:

In fact, one of the saddest things I saw during the month of travel which I have described was a young man, who had attended some high school,

sitting down in a one-room cabin, with grease on his clothing, filth all around him, and weeds in the yard and garden, engaged in studying French grammar.

7. Theodore Roosevelt (1858–1919), 26th President of the United States (1901–9). Washington's dining with him in 1901 caused a storm of criticism around the country.

the strongest and most lasting opposition, amounting at times to bitterness, and even to-day continuing strong and insistent even though largely silenced in outward expression by the public opinion of the nation. Some of this opposition is, of course, mere envy; the disappointment of displaced demagogues and the spite of narrow minds. But aside from this, there is among educated and thoughtful colored men in all parts of the land a feeling of deep regret, sorrow, and apprehension at the wide currency and ascendancy which some of Mr. Washington's theories have gained. These same men admire his sincerity of purpose, and are willing to forgive much to honest endeavor which is doing something worth the doing. They coöperate with Mr. Washington as far as they conscientiously can; and, indeed, it is no ordinary tribute to this man's tact and power that, steering as he must between so many diverse interests and opinions, he so largely retains the respect of all.

But the hushing of the criticism of honest opponents is a dangerous thing. It leads some of the best of the critics to unfortunate silence and paralysis of effort, and others to burst into speech so passionately and intemperately as to lose listeners. Honest and earnest criticism from those whose interests are most nearly touched,— criticism of writers by readers, of government by those governed, of leaders by those led,—this is the soul of democracy and the safeguard of modern society. If the best of the American Negroes receive by outer pressure a leader whom they had not recognized before, manifestly there is here a certain palpable gain. Yet there is also irreparable loss,—a loss of that peculiarly valuable education which a group receives when by search and criticism it finds and commissions its own leaders. The way in which this is done is at once the most elementary and the nicest problem of social growth. History is but the record of such group-leadership; and yet how infinitely changeful is its type and character! And of all types and kinds, what can be more instructive than the leadership of a group within a group? —that curious double movement where real progress may be negative and actual advance be relative retrogression. All this is the social student's inspiration and despair.

Now in the past the American Negro has had instructive experience in the choosing of group leaders, founding thus a peculiar dynasty which in the light of present conditions is worth while studying. When sticks and stones and beasts form the sole environment of a people, their attitude is largely one of determined opposition to and conquest of natural forces. But when to earth and brute is added an environment of men and ideas, then the attitude of the imprisoned group may take three main forms,—a feeling of revolt and revenge; an attempt to adjust all thought and action to the will of the greater group; or, finally, a determined effort at self-realization and self-development despite environing opinion. The influence of all of these attitudes at various times can be traced in the history of the American Negro, and in the evolution of his successive leaders.

Before 1750, while the fire of African freedom still burned in the veins of the slaves, there was in all leadership or attempted leadership but the one motive of revolt and revenge,—typified in the terrible Maroons, the Danish blacks, and Cato of Stono, and veiling all the Americans in fear of insurrection.[8] The liberalizing tendencies of the latter half of the eighteenth century brought, along with kindlier relations between black and white, thoughts of ultimate adjustment and assimilation. Such aspiration was especially voiced in the earnest songs of Phyllis, in the martyrdom of Attucks, the fighting of Salem and Poor, the intellectual accomplishments of Banneker and Derham, and the political demands of the Cuffes.[9]

Stern financial and social stress after the war cooled much of the previous humanitarian ardor. The disappointment and impatience of the Negroes at the persistence of slavery and serfdom voiced itself in two movements. The slaves in the South, aroused undoubtedly by vague rumors of the Haytian revolt, made three fierce attempts at insurrection,—in 1800 under Gabriel in Virginia, in 1822 under Vesey in Carolina, and in 1831 again in Virginia under the terrible Nat Turner.[1] In the Free States, on the other hand, a new and curious attempt at self-development was made. In Philadelphia and New York color-prescription led to a withdrawal of Negro communicants from white churches and the formation of a peculiar socio-religious institution among the Negroes known as the African Church,—an organization still living and controlling in its various branches over a million of men.

Walker's wild appeal[2] against the trend of the times showed how the world was changing after the coming of the cotton-gin. By 1830 slavery seemed hopelessly fastened on the South, and the

8. Maroons were fugitive Negro slaves from the West Indies and Guiana in the 17th and 18th centuries, or their descendants. Many of the slaves in the Danish West Indies revolted in 1733 because of the lack of sufficient food. Cato of Stono was the leader of the Stono, South Carolina, slave revolt of September 9, 1739, in which 25 whites were killed before the insurrection was put down.

9. Phyllis (or Phillis) Wheatley (c. 1753–84), black slave-poet. Crispus Attucks (c. 1723–70), the leader of the "Boston Massacre" against British troops, was killed in the massacre. Peter Salem (d. 1816), black patriot who killed Major Pitcairn in the battle of Bunker Hill. Salem Poor (1747–?), a black soldier who fought at Bunker Hill, Valley Forge, and White Plains. Benjamin Banneker (1731–1806), a black mathematician who also studied astronomy. James Derham (1762–?), the first recognized black physician in America; born a slave, he learned medicine from his physician master, bought his freedom

in 1783, and by 1788 was one of the foremost physicians of New Orleans. Paul Cuffe (1759–1817) organized to resettle free Negroes in African colonies; a champion of civil rights for free Negroes in Massachusetts, in 1815 he took 38 Negroes to Africa at his own expense.

1. Gabriel (1775?–1800) conspired to attack Richmond, Virginia, with 1,000 other slaves on August 30, 1800, but a storm forced a suspension of the mission and two slaves betrayed the conspiracy; on October 7 Gabriel and 15 others were hanged. Denmark Vesey (c. 1767–1822), a mulatto rebel, purchased his freedom in 1800; he led an unsuccessful uprising in 1822 and was hanged. Nat Turner (1800–31), a Negro slave, led the Southampton insurrection in 1831, during which 61 whites and over 100 slaves were killed or executed.

2. The "wild appeal" was a militant, inflammatory, eloquent antislavery pamphlet by David Walker (1785–1830), black leader.

slaves thoroughly cowed into submission. The free Negroes of the North, inspired by the mulatto immigrants from the West Indies, began to change the basis of their demands; they recognized the slavery of slaves, but insisted that they themselves were freemen, and sought assimilation and amalgamation with the nation on the same terms with other men. Thus, Forten and Purvis of Philadelphia, Shad of Wilmington, Du Bois of New Haven, Barbadoes of Boston, and others, strove singly and together as men, they said, not as slaves; as "people of color," not as "Negroes."[3] The trend of the times, however, refused them recognition save in individual and exceptional cases, considered them as one with all the despised blacks, and they soon found themselves striving to keep even the rights they formerly had of voting and working and moving as freemen. Schemes of migration and colonization arose among them; but these they refused to entertain, and they eventually turned to the Abolition movement as a final refuge.

Here, led by Remond, Nell, Wells-Brown, and Douglass, a new period of self-assertion and self-development dawned.[4] To be sure, ultimate freedom and assimilation was the ideal before the leaders, but the assertion of the manhood rights of the Negro by himself was the main reliance, and John Brown's raid was the extreme of its logic. After the war and emancipation, the great form of Frederick Douglass, the greatest of American Negro leaders, still led the host. Self-assertion, especially in political lines, was the main programme, and behind Douglass came Elliot, Bruce, and Langston, and the Reconstruction politicians, and, less conspicuous but of greater social significance Alexander Crummell and Bishop Daniel Payne.[5]

Then came the Revolution of 1876, the suppression of the Negro votes, the changing and shifting of ideals, and the seeking of new lights in the great night. Douglass, in his old age, still bravely

3. James Forten (1766–1842), black civic leader and philanthropist. Robert Purvis (1810–98), abolitionist, helped found the American Anti-Slavery Society in 1833 and was the president of the Underground Railway. Abraham Shadd, abolitionist, was on the first board of managers of the American Anti-Slavery Society, a delegate from Delaware for the first National Negro Convention (1830), and president of the third one in 1833. Alexander DuBois (1803–87), paternal grandfather of W. E. B. DuBois, helped form the Negro Episcopal Parish of St.ʹ Luke in 1847 and was the senior warden there. James G. Barbadoes was one of those present at the first National Negro Convention along with Forten, Purvis, Shadd, and others.
4. Charles Lenox Remond (1810–73), black leader. William Cooper Nell (1816–74), abolitionist, writer, and first Afro-American to hold office under the government of the United States (clerk in the post office); through his efforts equal school privileges were obtained for

black children in Boston. William Wells Brown (1816?–84), black writer, published *Clotel* in 1853, the first novel by a black American, and *The Escape* in 1858, the first play by an American Negro. Frederick Douglass (1817–95), abolitionist and orator, born a slave, was U.S. Minister to Haiti and U.S. Marshal of the District of Columbia.
5. Robert Brown Elliot (1842–84), black politician, graduate of Eton, South Carolina congressman in the U.S. House of Representatives. Blanche K. Bruce (1841–98), born a slave, first black man to serve a full term in the U.S. Senate (1875–81). John Mercer Langston (1829–97), congressman, lawyer, diplomat, educator, born a slave. Alexander Crummell (1819–98), clergyman of the Protestant Episcopal church, missionary in Liberia for 20 years and then in Washington, D.C. Daniel Alexander Payne (1811–93), Bishop of the African Methodist Episcopal church and president of Wilberforce University (1863–76).

stood for the ideals of his early manhood,—ultimate assimilation *through* self-assertion, and on no other terms. For a time Price arose as a new leader, destined, it seemed, not to give up, but to re-state the old ideals in a form less repugnant to the white South. But he passed away in his prime. Then came the new leader. Nearly all the former ones had become leaders by the silent suffrage of their fellows, had sought to lead their own people alone, and were usually, save Douglass, little known outside their race. But Booker T. Washington arose as essentially the leader not of one race but of two,—a compromiser between the South, the North, and the Negro. Naturally the Negroes resented, at first bitterly, signs of compromise which surrendered their civil and political rights, even though this was to be exchanged for larger chances of economic development. The rich and dominating North, however, was not only weary of the race problem, but was investing largely in Southern enterprises, and welcomed any method of peaceful coöperation. Thus, by national opinion, the Negroes began to recognize Mr. Washington's leadership; and the voice of criticism was hushed.

Mr. Washington represents in Negro thought the old attitude of adjustment and submission; but adjustment at such a peculiar time as to make his programme unique. This is an age of unusual economic development, and Mr. Washington's programme naturally takes an economic cast, becoming a gospel of Work and Money to such an extent as apparently almost completely to overshadow the higher aims of life. Moreover, this is an age when the more advanced races are coming in closer contact with the less developed races, and the race-feeling is therefore intensified; and Mr. Washington's programme practically accepts the alleged inferiority of the Negro races. Again, in our own land, the reaction from the sentiment of war time has given impetus to race-prejudice against Negroes, and Mr. Washington withdraws many of the high demands of Negroes as men and American citizens. In other periods of intensified prejudice all the Negro's tendency to self-assertion has been called forth; at this period a policy of submission is advocated. In the history of nearly all other races and peoples the doctrine preached at such crises has been that manly self-respect is worth more than lands and houses, and that a people who voluntarily surrender such respect, or cease striving for it, are not worth civilizing.

In answer to this, it has been claimed that the Negro can survive only through submission. Mr. Washington distinctly asks that black people give up, at least for the present, three things,—

First, political power,

Second, insistence on civil rights,

Third, higher education of Negro youth—

and concentrate all their energies on industrial education, the accumulation of wealth, and the conciliation of the South. This policy has been courageously and insistently advocated for over fifteen years, and has been triumphant for perhaps ten years. As a result of this tender of the palmbranch, what has been the return? In these years there have occurred:

1. The disfranchisement of the Negro.
2. The legal creation of a distinct status of civil inferiority for the Negro.
3. The steady withdrawal of aid from institutions for the higher training of the Negro.

These movements are not, to be sure, direct results of Mr. Washington's teachings; but his propaganda has, without a shadow of doubt, helped their speedier accomplishment. The question then comes: Is it possible, and probable, that nine millions of men can make effective progress in economic lines if they are deprived of political rights, made a servile caste, and allowed only the most meagre chance for developing their exceptional men? If history and reason give any distinct answer to these questions, it is an emphatic No. And Mr. Washington thus faces the triple paradox of his career:

1. He is striving nobly to make Negro artisans business men and property-owners; but it is utterly impossible, under modern competitive methods, for workingmen and property-owners to defend their rights and exist without the right of suffrage.
2. He insists on thrift and self-respect, but at the same time counsels a silent submission to civic inferiority such as is bound to sap the manhood of any race in the long run.
3. He advocates common-school[6] and industrial training, and depreciates institutions of higher learning; but neither the Negro common-schools, nor Tuskegee itself, could remain open a day were it not for teachers trained in Negro colleges, or trained by their graduates.

This triple paradox in Mr. Washington's position is the object of criticism by two classes of colored Americans. One class is spiritually descended from Toussaint the Savior,[7] through Gabriel, Vesey, and Turner, and they represent the attitude of revolt and revenge; they hate the white South blindly and distrust the white race generally, and so far as they agree on definite action, think that the Negro's only hope lies in emigration beyond the borders of the United States. And yet, by the irony of fate, nothing has more effectually made this programme seem hopeless than the recent course of the United States toward weaker and darker peoples in the West Indies, Hawaii, and the Philippines,—for where in the world may we go and be safe from lying and brute force?

The other class of Negroes who cannot agree with Mr. Washington has hitherto said little aloud. They deprecate the sight of scat-

6. A free public school offering courses at precollege level.
7. Pierre Dominique Toussaint, later called L'Ouverture (1743–1803), black Haitian leader of the slave insurrection which led eventually to Haitian independence even though Toussaint died in France as a result of Napoleon's treachery.

tered counsels, of internal disagreement; and especially they dislike making their just criticism of a useful and earnest man an excuse for a general discharge of venom from small-minded opponents. Nevertheless, the questions involved are so fundamental and serious that it is difficult to see how men like the Grimkes, Kelly Miller, J. W. E. Bowen,[8] and other representatives of this group, can much longer be silent. Such men feel in conscience bound to ask of this nation three things:

1. The right to vote.
2. Civic equality.
3. The education of youth according to ability.

They acknowledge Mr. Washington's invaluable service in counselling patience and courtesy in such demands; they do not ask that ignorant black men vote when ignorant whites are debarred, or that any reasonable restrictions in the suffrage should not be applied; they know that the low social level of the mass of the race is responsible for much discrimination against it, but they also know, and the nation knows, that relentless color-prejudice is more often a cause than a result of the Negro's degradation; they seek the abatement of this relic of barbarism, and not its systematic encouragement and pampering by all agencies of social power from the Associated Press to the Church of Christ. They advocate, with Mr. Washington, a broad system of Negro common schools supplemented by thorough industrial training; but they are surprised that a man of Mr. Washington's insight cannot see that no such educational system ever has rested or can rest on any other basis than that of the well-equipped college and university, and they insist that there is a demand for a few such institutions throughout the South to train the best of the Negro youth as teachers, professional men, and leaders.

This group of men honor Mr. Washington for his attitude of conciliation toward the white South; they accept the "Atlanta Compromise" in its broadest interpretation; they recognize, with him, many signs of promise, many men of high purpose and fair judgment, in this section; they know that no easy task has been laid upon a region already tottering under heavy burdens. But, nevertheless, they insist that the way to truth and right lies in straightforward honesty, not in indiscriminate flattery; in praising those of the South who do well and criticising uncompromisingly those who do ill; in taking advantage of the opportunities at hand and urging their fellows to do the same, but at the same time in remembering that only a firm adherence to their higher ideals and aspirations will ever keep those ideals within the realm of possibility. They do not expect that the free right to vote, to enjoy civic rights,

8. Archibad Grimké (1849–1930) and Francis Grimké (1850–1937), American civic leaders concerned with Negro affairs. Kelly Miller (1863–1939), dean of Howard University, lectured on the race problem. John Wesley Edward Bowen (1855–?), Methodist clergyman and educator, president of Gammon Theological Seminary of Atlanta.

and to be educated, will come in a moment; they do not expect to see the bias and prejudices of years disappear at the blast of a trumpet; but they are absolutely certain that the way for a people to gain their reasonable rights is not by voluntarily throwing them away and insisting that they do not want them; that the way for a people to gain respect is not by continually belittling and ridiculing themselves; that, on the contrary, Negroes must insist continually, in season and out of season, that voting is necessary to modern manhood, that color discrimination is barbarism, and that black boys need education as well as white boys.

In failing thus to state plainly and unequivocally the legitimate demands of their people, even at the cost of opposing an honored leader, the thinking classes of American Negroes would shirk a heavy responsibility,—a responsibility to themselves, a responsibility to the struggling masses, a responsibility to the darker races of men whose future depends so largely on this American experiment, but especially a responsibility to this nation,—this common Fatherland. It is wrong to encourage a man or a people in evil-doing; it is wrong to aid and abet a national crime simply because it is unpopular not to do so. The growing spirit of kindliness and reconciliation between the North and South after the frightful differences of a generation ago ought to be a source of deep congratulation to all, and especially to those whose mistreatment caused the war; but if that reconciliation is to be marked by the industrial slavery and civic death of those same black men, with permanent legislation into a position of inferiority, then those black men, if they are really men, are called upon by every consideration of patriotism and loyalty to oppose such a course by all civilized methods, even though such opposition involves disagreement with Mr. Booker T. Washington. We have no right to sit silently by while the inevitable seeds are sown for a harvest of disaster to our children, black and white.

First, it is the duty of black men to judge the South discriminatingly. The present generation of Southerners are not responsible for the past, and they should not be blindly hated or blamed for it. Furthermore, to no class is the indiscriminate endorsement of the recent course of the South toward Negroes more nauseating than to the best thought of the South. The South is not "solid"; it is a land in the ferment of social change, wherein forces of all kinds are fighting for supremacy; and to praise the ill the South is to-day perpetrating is just as wrong as to condemn the good. Discriminating and broad-minded criticism is what the South needs,—needs it for the sake of her own white sons and daughters, and for the insurance of robust, healthy mental and moral development.

To-day even the attitude of the Southern whites toward the blacks is not, as so many assume, in all cases the same; the ignorant Southerner hates the Negro, the workingmen fear his competition, the money-makers wish to use him as a laborer, some of the edu-

cated see a menace in his upward development, while others—
usually the sons of the masters—wish to help him to rise. National
opinion has enabled this last class to maintain the Negro common
schools, and to protect the Negro partially in property, life, and
limb. Through the pressure of the money-makers, the Negro is in
danger of being reduced to semi-slavery, especially in the country districts; the workingmen, and those of the educated who fear the Negro, have united to disfranchise him, and some have urged his
deportation; while the passions of the ignorant are easily aroused to
lynch and abuse any black man. To praise this intricate whirl of
thought and prejudice is nonsense; to inveigh indiscriminately against
"the South" is unjust; but to use the same breath in praising Governor Aycock, exposing Senator Morgan, arguing with Mr. Thomas
Nelson Page, and denouncing Senator Ben Tillman, is not only
sane, but the imperative duty of thinking black men.[9]

It would be unjust to Mr. Washington not to acknowledge that in
several instances he has opposed movements in the South which were
unjust to the Negro; he sent memorials to the Louisiana and Alabama
constitutional conventions, he has spoken against lynching, and in
other ways has openly or silently set his influence against sinister
schemes and unfortunate happenings. Notwithstanding this, it is
equally true to assert that on the whole the distinct impression left
by Mr. Washington's propaganda is, first, that the South is justified
in its present attitude toward the Negro because of the Negro's degradation; secondly, that the prime cause of the Negro's failure to
rise more quickly is his wrong education in the past; and, thirdly,
that his future rise depends primarily on his own efforts. Each of
these propositions is a dangerous half-truth. The supplementary
truths must never be lost sight of: first, slavery and race-prejudice
are potent if not sufficient causes of the Negro's position; second,
industrial and common-school training were necessarily slow in planting because they had to await the black teachers trained by higher
institutions,—it being extremely doubtful if any essentially different
development was possible, and certainly a Tuskegee was unthinkable
before 1880; and, third, while it is a great truth to say that the Negro
must strive and strive mightily to help himself, it is equally true that
unless his striving be not simply seconded, but rather aroused and

9. Charles Brantley Aycock (1859–1912),
Governor of North Carolina (1901–5).
Edwin Denison Morgan (1811–83), Governor of New York (1859–63), U.S. Senator (1863–69), voted with the minority
in President Johnson's veto of the Freedman's Bureau bill and for Johnson's
conviction. Thomas Nelson Page (1853–
1922), American novelist and diplomat,
did much to build up romantic legends
of the southern plantation. Benjamin
Ryan Tillman (1847–1918), Governor of
South Carolina (1890–94), U.S. Senator
(1895–1918), served as the chairman on
the committee on suffrage (during the
South Carolina constitutional convention) and framed the article providing
for an educational and property qualification for voting, thus eliminating the
Negro vote. He presented the views of
the southern extremists on the race question, justified lynching in cases of rape,
using force to disfranchise the Negro,
and advocated the repeal of the Fifteenth
Amendment.

encouraged, by the initiative of the richer and wiser environing group, he cannot hope for great success.

In his failure to realize and impress this last point, Mr. Washington is especially to be criticised. His doctrine has tended to make the whites, North and South, shift the burden of the Negro problem to the Negro's shoulders and stand aside as critical and rather pessimistic spectators; when in fact the burden belongs to the nation, and the hands of none of us are clean if we bend not our energies to righting these great wrongs.

The South ought to be led, by candid and honest criticism, to assert her better self and do her full duty to the race she has cruelly wronged and is still wronging. The North—her co-partner in guilt —cannot salve her conscience by plastering it with gold. We cannot settle this problem by diplomacy and suaveness, by "policy" alone. If worse come to worst, can the moral fibre of this country survive the slow throttling and murder of nine millions of men?

The black men of America have a duty to perform, a duty stern and delicate,—a forward movement to oppose a part of the work of their greatest leader. So far as Mr. Washington preaches Thrift, Patience, and Industrial Training for the masses, we must hold up his hands and strive with him, rejoicing in his honors and glorying in the strength of this Joshua called of God and of man to lead the headless host. But so far as Mr. Washington apologizes for injustice, North or South, does not rightly value the privilege and duty of voting, belittles the emasculating effects of caste distinctions, and opposes the higher training and ambition of our brighter minds,—so far as he, the South, or the Nation, does this,—we must unceasingly and firmly oppose them. By every civilized and peaceful method we must strive for the rights which the world accords to men, clinging unwaveringly to those great words which the sons of the Fathers would fain forget: "We hold these truths to be self-evident: That all men are created equal; that they are endowed by their Creator with certain unalienable rights; that among these are life, liberty, and the pursuit of happiness."

1902　　　　　　　　　　　　　　　　　　　　　　　1903

EMMA GOLDMAN
1869–1940

A rebellious child of Russian parents, Emma Goldman matured into one of America's most notorious social and political radicals and outspoken champions of labor at the turn of the century. Goldman's radicalization occurred gradually, but surely had its origins in her childhood. Born into a poor Russian Jewish family, she was raised by an embittered mother and an abusive father at the edges of an aggressively anti-Semitic society. Her school career was marred by conflicts with teachers, occasioned by her open flouting of their authority. Although she qualified for a place in the *Gymnasium* (or selective high school), she was prevented from entering by a teacher who regarded her as irreverent, immoral, and troublesome.

In her early teens she began associating with university students in Saint Petersburg, Russia, who introduced her to the antiauthoritarian principles of the Russian social philosopher Peter Kropotkin (1842–1921) and to such radical dramatists as Henrik Ibsen (1828–1906). So absorbed did she become with these ideas, that when her father, in keeping with the custom of the time, sought to match her in marriage, she refused, announcing that she would marry only for love's sake. In 1885, at sixteen, she emigrated to America with a half sister largely to escape her father's dominance.

Her idealist conception of "the land of opportunity and freedom" came into conflict with and was modified by reality soon after her arrival in Rochester, New York. She found new immigrants like herself exploited by America's economic and industrial system, and she quickly became a sharp critic of sweatshop conditions and ten- to twelve-hour working days. After several unhappy stints as a piece worker in clothing factories and a miserable marriage to an impotent factory companion, Goldman moved to New York in 1889. There she soon became an avid pupil of the well-known anarchist Johann Most and was inspired by Alexander ("Sasha") Berkman's fearless devotion to the cause. Before long she advanced to the front lines of the movement, but her first real political act ended disastrously when Berkman, now her lover, was imprisoned in 1892 following his attempt to assassinate industrialist Henry Clay Frick, a plot Goldman had helped to conceive.

In the following years, Goldman made numerous lecture tours around the country and abroad. She fought for voluntary motherhood, family limitation, and the use of contraceptives by women. Her open discussion of this last issue invited a prison term several years later. "Red Emma" as she was dubbed by the press, sparked considerable controversy over her notion of free love. She denounced marriage, claiming that it only created bondage to another person and to the institution of marriage itself. She preferred instead freely to give of herself to a man without legal bonds or religious vows.

When Berkman was paroled in 1906, he and Goldman co-edited the radical monthly journal *Mother Earth* (1906–17), which provided yet another platform for the advancement of their ideas, ideas which are perhaps most conveniently available in Goldman's collection, *Anarchism and Other Essays* (1911). Constantly hounded by the police, she became such a threat to the established order that the government rescinded her citizenship papers in 1908. Her freedom of movement ended when she was arrested in 1917 for her vehement opposition to conscription for World War I. After serving a two-year prison term she, Berkman, and other so-called political agitators were deported to Russia. She escaped to the West in 1919, living most of her last years in Saint-Tropez, France. *My Disillusionment with Russia* (1923) is a chronicle of her discontent with Soviet totalitarianism, but her bitterest criticism in the book is directed against Western liberals who ignored the even worse suppression of civil liberties in the Soviet Union.

Goldman thereafter earned her living by lecturing and from royalties earned by her autobiography *Living My Life* (1931). None of her other writings more successfully conveys her zest for life, her social and political passions, and her remarkable power with words. Indeed, no book of the time offers a more remarkably dramatic and vivid sense of what it was like to be a multiple "outsider": woman, Jew, immigrant, radical, and artist. Her lecture tours in Britain and Canada never ceased, but she was only once permitted to re-enter the United States for ninety days in 1934. Goldman died as she had lived. She suffered a stroke in 1940 in Canada, where she had gone to raise funds to combat General Franco during the Spanish Civil War.

From Living My Life[1]

From *Chapter III*

[*Most and Berkman offer me assistance · I meet Fedya · I, too loved beauty · Fedya objects to ugliness · Johann Most: preceptor · I dedicate myself to Most's happiness · I advocate free love · I am drawn to Sasha · I go to the opera with Most · I recall my first opera · Most proposes public speaking for me*]

* * *

The August heat was suffocating. Berkman[2] suggested a trip to the Battery[3] to cool off. I had not seen the harbour since my arrival in America. Its beauty gripped me again as on the memorable day. But the Statue of Liberty had ceased to be an alluring symbol. How childishly naïve I had been, how far I had advanced since that day!

We returned to our talk of the afternoon. My companion expressed doubt about my finding work as a dressmaker, having no connexion in the city. I replied that I would try a factory, one for corsets, gloves, or men's suits. He promised to inquire among the Jewish comrades who were in the needle trade. They would surely help find a job for me.

It was late in the evening when we parted. Berkman had told me little about himself, except that he had been expelled from the *Gymnasium*[4] for an anti-religious essay he had composed, and that he had left home for good. He had come to the United States in the belief that it was free and that here everyone had an equal chance in life. He knew better now. He had found exploitation

---

1. *Living My Life* was published by Alfred Knopf, New York, in 1931, the source of the present text. Since Goldman mentions many nonhistorical, personal friends and acquaintances, annotation is provided only for well-known figures. Chapters I and II record events in Emma's childhood, her arrival in America from Russia in 1885, her break with her husband of 10 months, and her subsequent encounters with leading anarchist figures in New York upon her return to the city in 1889.

2. Alexander Berkman (1870–1936), leading Polish-American anarchist, jailed for 14 years for his unsuccessful attempt to kill Henry Clay Frick in 1892. Until his death, he was Goldman's closest friend, lover, and strong supporter. Goldman refers to him throughout the book as Sasha.

3. Park on the southern tip of Manhattan island.

4. European secondary school with high entrance requirements.

more severe, and since the hanging of the Chicago anarchists[5] he had become convinced that America was as despotic as Russia.

"Lingg was right when he said: 'If you attack us with cannon, we will reply with dynamite.' Some day I will avenge our dead," he added with great earnestness. "I too! I too!" I cried; "their death gave me life. It now belongs to their memory—to their work." He gripped my arm until it hurt. "We are comrades. Let us be friends, too—let us work together." His intensity vibrated through me as I walked up the stairs to the Minkin flat.[6]

The following Friday, Berkman invited me to come to a Jewish lecture by Solotaroff[7] at 54 Orchard Street, on the East Side. In New Haven Solotaroff had impressed me as an exceptionally fine speaker, but now, after having heard Most,[8] his talk appeared flat to me, and his badly modulated voice affected me unpleasantly. His ardour, however, made up for much. I was too grateful for the warm reception he had given me on my first arrival in the city to allow myself any criticism of his lecture. Besides, everybody could not be an orator like Johann Most, I reflected. To me he was a man apart, the most remarkable in all the world.

After the meeting Berkman introduced me to a number of people, "all good active comrades," as he put it. "And here is my chum Fedya," he said, indicating a young man beside him; "he is also an anarchist, of course, but not so good as he should be."

The young chap was probably of the same age as Berkman, but not so strongly built, nor with the same aggressive manner about him. His features were rather delicate, with a sensitive mouth, while his eyes, though somewhat bulging, had a dreamy expression. He did not seem to mind in the least the banter of his friend. He smiled good-naturedly and suggested that we retire to Sachs's, "to give Sasha a chance to tell you what a good anarchist is."

Berkman did not wait till we reached the café. "A good anarchist," he began with deep conviction, "is one who lives only for the Cause and gives everything to it. My friend here"—he indicated Fedya—"is still too much of a *bourgeois* to realize that. He is a *mamenkin sin* (mother's spoilt darling), who even accepts money from home." He continued to explain why it was inconsistent for a

5. Goldman's political consciousness was radicalized in 1886 during the aftermath of the Haymarket riots in Chicago. During a demonstration for an eight-hour working day, a bomb was set off and 11 people were killed. Public opinion held the anarchists responsible, and a controversial trial of eight persons led to the conviction of all and the execution of four. Three persons were later pardoned by the Governor after it was established that no legal evidence implicated the anarchists in the terrorist act; the other member of the group had died in prison.
6. I.e., the apartment of Anna and Helen Minkin, where Goldman first stayed when she arrived in New York in 1889.
7. Young anarchist in New York. "East Side": an area of New York dominated by European immigrants who generated radical political activities because of their poverty and their intersection with many different cultural ideals and experiences.
8. Johann Most (1846–1906), German-American anarchist, widely admired leader of the American movement. A proponent of violence, he greatly influenced Emma Goldman's early political activities.

revolutionary to have anything to do with his *bourgeois* parents or relatives. His only reason for tolerating his friend Fedya's inconsistency, he added, was that he gave most of what he received from home to the movement. "If I'd let him, he'd spend all his money on useless things—'beautiful,' he calls them. Wouldn't you, Fedya?" He turned to his friend, patting him on the back affectionately.

The café was crowded, as usual, and filled with smoke and talk. For a little while my two escorts were much in demand, while I was greeted by several people I had met during the week. Finally we succeeded in capturing a table and ordered some coffee and cake. I became aware of Fedya watching me and studying my face. To hide my embarrassment I turned to Berkman. "Why should one not love beauty?" I asked; "flowers, for instance, music, the theatre—beautiful things?"

"I did not say one should not," Berkman replied; "I said it was wrong to spend money on such things when the movement is so much in need of it. It is inconsistent for an anarchist to enjoy luxuries when the people live in poverty."

"But beautiful things are not luxuries," I insisted; "they are necessaries. Life would be unbearable without them." Yet, at heart, I felt that Berkman was right. Revolutionists gave up even their lives —why not also beauty? Still the young artist struck a responsive chord in me. I, too, loved beauty. Our poverty-stricken life in Königsberg[9] had been made bearable to me only by the occasional outings with our teachers in the open. The forest, the moon casting its silvery shimmer on the fields, the green wreaths in our hair, the flowers we would pick—these made me forget for a time the sordid home surroundings. When Mother scolded me or when I had difficulties at school, a bunch of lilacs from our neighbour's garden or the sight of the colourful silks and velvets displayed in the shops would cause me to forget my sorrows and make the world seem beautiful and bright. Or the music I would on rare occasions be able to hear in Königsberg and, later, in St. Petersburg.[1] Should I have to forgo all that to be a good revolutionist, I wondered. Should I have the strength?

Before we parted that evening Fedya remarked that his friend had mentioned that I would like to see something of the city. He was free the next day and would be glad to show me some of the sights. "Are you also out of work, that you can afford the time?" I asked. "As you know from my friend, I am an artist," he replied, laughing. "Have you ever heard of artists working?" I flushed, having to admit that I had never met an artist before. "Artists are inspired people," I said, "everything comes easy to them." "Of course," Berkman retorted, "because the people work for them."

9. One of Emma's many resident towns;   1. Now Leningrad.
now called Kaliningrad.

His tone seemed too severe to me, and my sympathy went out to the artist boy. I turned to him and asked him to come for me the next day. But alone in my room, it was the uncompromising fervour of the "arrogant youngster," as I mentally called Berkman, that filled me with admiration.

The next day Fedya took me to Central Park. Along Fifth Avenue he pointed out the various mansions, naming their owners. I had read about those wealthy men, their affluence and extravagance, while the masses lived in poverty. I expressed my indignation at the contrast between those splendid palaces and the miserable tenements of the East Side. "Yes, it is a crime that the few should have all, the many nothing," the artist said. "My main objection," he continued, "is that they have such bad taste—those buildings are ugly." Berkman's attitude to beauty came to my mind. "You don't agree with your chum on the need and importance of beauty in one's life, do you?" I asked. "Indeed I do not. But, then, my friend is a revolutionist above everything else. I wish I could also be, but I am not." I liked his frankness and simplicity. He did not stir me as Berkman did when speaking of revolutionary ethics; Fedya awakened in me the mysterious yearning I used to feel in my childhood at sight of the sunset turning the Popelan meadows golden in its dying glow, as the sweet music of Petrushka's flute[2] did also.

The following week I went to the *Freiheit*[3] office. Several people were already there, busy addressing envelopes and folding the papers. Everybody talked. Johann Most was at his desk. I was assigned a place and given work. I marvelled at Most's capacity to go on writing in that hubbub. Several times I wanted to suggest that he was being disturbed, but I checked myself. After all, they must know whether he minded their chatter.

In the evening Most stopped writing and gruffly assailed the talkers as "toothless old women," "cackling geese," and other appellations I had hardly ever before heard in German. He snatched his large felt hat from the rack, called to me to come along, and walked out. I followed him and we went up on the Elevated.[4] "I'll take you to Terrace Garden," he said; "we can go into the theatre there if you like. They are giving *Der Zigeunerbaron*[5] tonight. Or we can sit in some corner, get food and drink, and talk." I replied that I did not care for light opera, that what I really wanted was to talk to him, or rather have him talk to me. "But not so violently as in the office," I added.

He selected the food and the wine. Their names were strange to me. The label on the bottle read: *Liebfrauenmilch*. "Milk of woman's love—what a lovely name!" I remarked. "For wine, yes,"

2. Goldman's father's stableboy with whom Emma was enchanted as a young girl.
3. "Freedom," a leading radical newspaper published in German by Johann Most.
4. Elevated railway in New York.
5. *The Gypsy Baron* (1885), operetta by Johann Strauss, Jr.

he retorted, "but not for woman's love. The one is always poetic—the other will never be anything but sordidly prosaic. It leaves a bad taste."

I had a feeling of guilt, as if I had made some bad break or had touched a sore spot. I told him I had never tasted any wine before, except the kind Mother made for Easter. Most shook with laughter, and I was near tears. He noticed my embarrassment and restrained himself. He poured out two glassfuls, saying: "*Prosit*,[6] my young, naïve lady," and drank his down at a gulp. Before I could drink half of mine, he had nearly finished the bottle and ordered another.

He became animated, witty, sparkling. There was no trace of the bitterness, of the hatred and defiance his oratory had breathed on the platform. Instead there sat next to me a transformed human being, no longer the repulsive caricature of the Rochester press[7] or the gruff creature of the office. He was a gracious host, an attentive and sympathetic friend. He made me tell him about myself and he grew thoughtful when he learned the motive that had decided me to break with my old life. He warned me to reflect carefully before taking the plunge. "The path of anarchism is steep and painful," he said; "so many have attempted to climb it and have fallen back. The price is exacting. Few men are ready to pay it, most women not at all. Louise Michel, Sophia Perovskaya—they were the great exceptions." Had I read about the Paris Commune[8] and about that marvellous Russian woman revolutionist? I had to admit ignorance. I had never heard the name of Louise Michel before, though I did know about the great Russian. "You shall read about their lives—they will inspire you," Most said.

I inquired whether the anarchist movement in America had no outstanding woman. "None at all, only stupids," he replied; "most of the girls come to the meetings to snatch up a man; then both vanish, like the silly fishermen at the lure of the Lorelei."[9] There was a roguish twinkle in his eye. He didn't believe much in woman's revolutionary zeal. But I, coming from Russia, might be different and he would help me. If I were really in earnest, I could find much work to do. "There is great need in our ranks of young, willing people—ardent ones, as you seem to be—and I have need of ardent friendship," he added with much feeling.

"You?" I questioned; "you have thousands in New York—all over the world. You are loved, you are idolized." "Yes, little girl, idolized by many, but loved by none. One can be very lonely among thousands—did you know that?" Something gripped my heart. I

6. "To good health!"
7. The press caricatured Most as a grotesque devil and frequently as a criminal.
8. Formed by French moderates and radicals in March, 1871, this diverse citizens' group opposed the French assembly, which acted in consort with the Germans and also sought to decentralize France by enlarging powers of the municipalities.
9. In German mythology, a siren who, by her singing, lured sailors to their death in the dangerous narrows of the Rhine.

wanted to take his hand, to tell him that I would be his friend. But I dared not speak out. —What could I give this man—I, a factory girl, uneducated; and he, the famous Johann Most, the leader of the masses, the man of magic tongue and powerful pen?

He promised to supply me with a list of books to read—the revolutionary poets, Freiligrath, Herwegh, Schiller, Heine, and Börne,[1] and our own literature, of course. It was almost daybreak when we left Terrace Garden. Most called a cab and we drove to the Minkin flat. At the door he lightly touched my hand. "Where did you get your silky blond hair?" he remarked; "and your blue eyes? You said you were Jewish." "At the pigs' market,"[2] I replied; "my father told me so." "You have a ready tongue, *mein Kind*."[3] He waited for me to unlock the door, then took my hand, looked deeply into my eyes, and said: "This was my first happy evening in a long while." A great gladness filled my being at his words. Slowly I climbed the stairs as the cab rolled away.

The next day, when Berkman called, I related to him my wonderful evening with Most. His face darkened. "Most has no right to squander money, to go to expensive restaurants, drink expensive wines," he said gravely; "he is spending the money contributed for the movement. He should be held to account. I myself will tell him."

"No, no, you mustn't," I cried. "I couldn't bear to be the cause of any affront to Most, who is giving so much. Is he not entitled to a little joy?"

Berkman persisted that I was too young in the movement, that I didn't know anything about revolutionary ethics or the meaning of revolutionary right and wrong. I admitted my ignorance, assured him I was willing to learn, to do anything, only not to have Most hurt. He walked out without bidding me good-bye.

I was greatly disturbed. The charm of Most was upon me. His remarkable gifts, his eagerness for life, for friendship, moved me deeply. And Berkman, too, appealed to me profoundly. His earnestness, his self-confidence, his youth—everything about him drew me with irresistible force. But I had the feeling that, of the two, Most was more of this earth.

When Fedya came to see me, he told me that he had already heard the story from Berkman. He was not surprised, he said; he knew how uncompromising our friend was and how hard he could be, but hardest towards himself. "It springs from his absorbing love of the people," Fedya added, "a love that will yet move him to great deeds."

1. Radical German poets: Ferdinand Freiligrath (1810–76), Georg Herwegh (1817–75), Friedrich von Schiller (1759–1805), Heinrich Heine (1797–1856), and Ludwig Börne (1786–1837).
2. Jews did not eat pork, and thus only gentiles frequented pig markets.
3. "My child."

For a whole week Berkman did not show up. When he came back again, it was to invite me for an outing in Prospect Park.[4] He liked it better than Central Park, he said, because it was less culti- vated, more natural. We walked about a great deal, admiring its rough beauty, and finally selected a lovely spot in which to eat the lunch I had brought with me.

We talked about my life in St. Petersburg and in Rochester. I told him of my marriage to Jacob Kershner and its failure. He wanted to know what books I had read on marriage and if it was their influence that had decided me to leave my husband. I had never read such works, but I had seen enough of the horrors of mar- ried life in my own home. Father's harsh treatment of Mother, the constant wrangles and bitter scenes that ended in Mother's fainting spells. I had also seen the debasing sordidness of the life of my mar- ried aunts and uncles, as well as in the homes of acquaintances in Rochester. Together with my own marital experiences they had con- vinced me that binding people for life was wrong. The constant proximity in the same house, the same room, the same bed, revolted me.

"If I ever I love a man again, I will give myself to him without being bound by the rabbi or the law," I declared, "and when that love dies, I will leave without permission."

My companion said he was glad to know that I felt that way. All true revolutionists had discarded marriage and were living in free- dom. That served to strengthen their love and helped them in their common task. He told me the story of Sophia Perovskaya and Zhel- yabov. They had been lovers, had worked in the same group, and together they elaborated the plan for the execution of Alexander II.[5] After the explosion of the bomb Perovskaya vanished. She was in hiding. She had every chance to escape, and her comrades begged her to do so. But she refused. She insisted that she must take the consequences, that she would share the fate of her comrades and die together with Zhelyabov. "Of course, it was wrong of her to be moved by personal sentiment," Berkman commented; "her love for the Cause should have urged her to live for other activities." Again I found myself disagreeing with him. I thought that it could not be wrong to die with one's beloved in a common act—it was beautiful, it was sublime. He retorted that I was too romantic and sentimental for a revolutionist, that the task before us was hard and we must become hard.

I wondered if the boy was really so hard, or was he merely trying to mask his tenderness, which I intuitively sensed in him. I felt myself drawn to him and I longed to throw my arms around him, but I was too shy.

4. City park in Brooklyn; Central Park is in Manhattan.
5. Russian Czar (1818–81), who elimi- nated serfdom and instituted other re- forms, but was assassinated by radical terrorists.

The day ended in a glowing sunset. Joy was in my heart. All the way home I sang German and Russian songs, *Veeyut, vitri, veeyut booyniy*,[6] being one of them. "That is my favourite song, Emma, *dorogaya* (dear)," he said. "I may call you that, may I not? And will you call me Sasha?" Our lips met in a spontaneous embrace.

I had begun to work in the corset factory where Helen Minkin was employed. But after a few weeks the strain became unbearable. I could hardly pull through the day; I suffered most from violent headaches. One evening I met a girl who told me of a silk waist factory that gave out work to be done at home. She would try to get me some, she promised. I knew it would be impossible to sew on a machine in the Minkin flat, it would be too disturbing for everybody. Furthermore, the girls' father had got on my nerves. He was a disagreeable person, never working, and living on his daughters. He seemed erotically fond of Anna,[7] fairly devouring her with his eyes. The most surprising was his strong dislike of Helen, which led to constant quarrelling. At last I decided to move out.

I found a room on Suffolk Street, not far from Sachs's café. It was small and half-dark, but the price was only three dollars a month, and I engaged it. There I began to work on silk waists. Occasionally I would also get some dresses to make for the girls I knew and their friends. The work was exhausting, but it freed me from the factory and its galling discipline. My earnings from the waists, once I acquired speed, were not less than in the shop.

Most had gone on a lecture tour. From time to time he would send me a few lines, witty and caustic comments on the people he was meeting, vitriolic denunciation of reporters who interviewed him and then wrote vilifying articles about him. Occasionally he would include in his letters the caricatures made of him, with his own marginal comments: "Behold the wife-killer!" or "Here's the man who eats little children."

The caricatures were more brutal and cruel than anything I had seen before. The loathing I had felt for the Rochester papers during the Chicago events[8] now turned into positive hatred for the entire American press. A wild thought took hold of me and I confided it to Sasha. "Don't you think one of the rotten newspaper offices should be blown up—editors, reporters, and all? That would teach the press a lesson." But Sasha shook his head and said that it would be useless. The press was only the hireling of capitalism. "We must strike at the root."

When Most returned from his tour, we all went to hear his report. He was more masterly, more witty and defiant against the system than on any previous occasion. He almost hypnotized me. I could not help going up after the lecture to tell him how splendid

6. "The winds are blowing, blowing stormily."

7. I.e., Anna Minkin.

8. I.e., the Haymarket riots of 1886.

his talk was. "Will you go with me to hear *Carmen*[9] Monday at the Metropolitan Opera House?" he whispered. He added that Monday was an awfully busy day because he had to keep his devils[1] supplied with copy, but that he would work ahead on Sunday if I would promise to come. "To the end of the world!" I replied impulsively.

We found the house sold out—no seats to be had at any price. We should have to stand. I knew that I was in for torture. Since childhood I had had trouble with the small toe of my left foot; new shoes used to cause me suffering for weeks, and I was wearing new shoes. But I was too ashamed to tell Most, afraid he would think me vain. I stood close to him, jammed in by a large crowd. My foot burned as if it were being held over a fire. But the first bar of the music, and the glorious singing, made me forget my agony. After the first act, when the lights went on, I found myself holding on to Most for dear life, my face distorted with pain. "What's the matter?" he asked. "I must get off my shoe," I panted, "or I shall scream out." Leaning against him, I bent down to loosen the buttons. The rest of the opera I heard supported by Most's arm, my shoe in my hand. I could not tell whether my rapture was due to the music of *Carmen* or the release from my shoe!

We left the Opera House arm in arm, I limping. We went to a café, and Most teased me about my vanity. But he was rather glad, he said, to find me so feminine, even if it was stupid to wear tight shoes. He was in a golden mood. He wanted to know if I had ever before heard an opera and asked me to tell him about it.

Till I was ten years of age I had never heard any music, except the plaintive flute of Petrushka, Father's stable-boy. The screeching of the violins at the Jewish weddings and the poundings of the piano at our singing lessons had always been hateful to me. When I heard the opera *Trovatore*[2] in Königsberg, I first realized the ecstasy music could create in me. My teacher may have been largely responsible for the electrifying effect of that experience: she had imbued me with the romance of her favourite German authors and had helped to rouse my imagination about the sad love of the Troubadour and Leonore. The tortuous suspense of the days before Mother gave her consent to my accompanying my teacher to the performance aggravated my tense expectancy. We reached the Opera a full hour before the beginning, myself in a cold sweat for fear we were late. Teacher, always in delicate health, could not keep up with my young legs and my frenzied haste to reach our places. I flew up to the top gallery, three steps at a time. The house was still empty and half-lit, and somewhat disappointing at first. As if by

9. Opera (1875) by Georges Bizet.
1. I.e., the *Freiheit* printers.
2. Opera (1852) by Giuseppe Verdi; the

main characters are Leonore and the Troubador.

magic, it soon became transformed. Quickly the place filled with a vast audience—women in silks and velvets of gorgeous hue, with glistening jewels on their bare necks and arms, the flood of light from the crystal chandeliers reflecting the colours of green, yellow, and amethyst. It was a fairyland more magnificent than any ever pictured in the stories I had read. I forgot the presence of my teacher, the mean surroundings of my home; half-hanging over the rail, I was lost in the enchanted world below. The orchestra broke into stirring tones, mysteriously rising from the darkened house. They sent tremors down my back and held me breathless by their swelling sounds. Leonore and the Troubadour made real my own romantic fancy of love. I lived with them, thrilled and intoxicated by their passionate song. Their tragedy was mine as well, and I felt their joy and sorrow as my own. The scene between the Troubadour and his mother, her plaintive song "*Ach, ich vergehe und sterbe hier,*" Troubadour's response in "*O, teuere Mutter,*"[3] filled me with deep woe and made my heart palpitate with compassionate sighs. The spell was broken by the loud clapping of hands and the new flood of light. I, too, clapped wildly, climbed on my bench, and shouted frantically for Leonore and the Troubadour, the hero and heroine of my fairy world. "Come along, come along," I heard my teacher say, tugging at my skirts. I followed in a daze, my body shaken with convulsive sobs, the music ringing in my ears. I had heard other operas in Königsberg and later in St. Petersburg, but the impression of *Trovatore* stood out for a long time as the most marvellous musical experience of my young life.

When I had finished relating this to Most, I noticed that his gaze was far away in the distance. He looked up as if from a dream. He had never heard, he remarked slowly, the stirrings of a child more dramatically told. I had great talent, he said, and I must begin soon to recite and speak in public. He would make me a great speaker—"to take my place when I am gone," he added.

I thought he was only making fun, or flattering me. He could not really believe that I could ever take his place or express his fire, his magic power. I did not want him to treat me that way—I wanted him to be a true comrade, frank and honest, without silly German compliments. Most grinned and emptied his glass to my "first public speech."

After that we went out together often. He opened up a new world to me, introduced me to music, books, the theatre. But his own rich personality meant far more to me—the alternating heights and depths of his spirit, his hatred of the capitalist system, his vision of a new society of beauty and joy for all.

Most became my idol. I worshipped him.

3. "Ah, I am wasting away and dying here"; "Oh, dear mother."

Chapter XVI[1]

[*Robert Reitzel, thunderous knight · A free spirit is
mowed down · Queen of the Anarchists · I visit my
"knight" · The church a hotbed of sin · I decide not
to mention the Congregational God— · —but am
forced to shock His creators*]

Three days later I arrived in Detroit. The lure of that city had
always been to me Robert Reitzel.[2] His wit and peerless pen had
fascinated me from the time I began to read his paper. His courageous defence of the Chicago martyrs and his bold effort to save
their lives had impressed him on my mind as an unflinching rebel
and fighter. The vision I had of him had become strengthened by
his stand in behalf of Sasha. While Most, knowing Sasha and his
revolutionary ardour, had calumniated him and disparaged his act,
Reitzel had gloried in the man and his *Attentat*. His article "*Im
Hochsummer fiel ein Schuss*"[3] was an exalted and moving tribute
to our brave boy. It brought Reitzel very close to me and made me
long to know him personally.

Almost five years had passed since I had first met the editor of
the *Armer Teufel*,[4] while he was visiting New York. The recollection of that experience now stood out vividly before me. It was late
one evening, while still at my sewing-machine, that I heard violent
knocking on the shutters of my window. "Let in the errant
knights!" boomed the bass of Justus. Beside him I saw a man
almost as tall and broad-shouldered as himself, whom I at once recognized as Robert Reitzel. Before I could greet him, he began to
upbraid me playfully. "A fine anarchist you are!" he thundered.
"You preach the need of leisure, and work longer than a galley-
slave. We have come to break your chains, and we are going to take
you with us if we have to use force. March! Little girl, get ready!
Come on out here, since you don't seem too anxious to invite us
into your virgin chamber." My unexpected visitors were standing in
full view of the street-lamp. Reitzel wore no hat. A shock of blond
hair, already considerably greyed, fell in confusion over his high
forehead. He looked big and strong, more youthful and vital than

1. Chapters IV through XV recount
Goldman's deepening friendships with
Berkman and Most, her first public lecture tours to promote the ideals of anarchism, and her efforts to help strikers
during the bloody Carnegie Strike of
1892 in Homestead, Pennsylvania. During this strike, her lover Berkman, attempted but failed to assassinate Henry
Clay Frick (1849–1919), acting head of
the Carnegie Steel Company who dealt
in a strong-handed fashion with the company's workers. She herself was imprisoned for one year in 1893 in Blackwell's
Island Penitentiary in New York for sug-

gesting to a Union Square audience that
it is the sacred right of man to take
bread when starving. In 1895 Goldman
traveled in England and Europe, where
she met with leading anarchists. In Vienna she earned degrees in midwifery
and nursing before returning to the
United States.
2. Robert Reitzel (1849–98), German-
American poet, editor, and critic.
3. "In the height of the summer, a shot
was heard."
4. *The Poor Devil*, a popular German
weekly newspaper of which Reitzel was
the editor.

Justus. He was holding on to the windowsill with both hands, his eyes inquisitively scrutinizing my face. "What's the verdict?" he exclaimed; "am I acceptable?" "Am I?" I questioned in return. "You have passed long ago," he replied, "and I have come to give you the prize, to offer myself as your knight."

Soon I was walking between the two men in the direction of Justus's place. There we were met by hilarious hurrahs and "*Hoch soll er leben*,"[5] and calls for more wine. Justus, with his usual graciousness, rolled up his sleeves, got behind the counter, and insisted on playing host. Robert gallantly offered his arm to lead me to the head of the table. As we walked up the aisle Justus intoned the wedding-march from *Lohengrin*.[6] The strains were taken up by the whole group of men, who had splendid voices.

Robert was the spirit of the gathering. His humour was more sparkling than the wine freely partaken of by all present. The amount he consumed transcended even Most's ability in that regard; and the more he imbibed, the more eloquent he grew. His stories, very colourful and amusing, came gushing like water from a brook. He was inexhaustible. Long after most of the others had caved in, my knight kept on singing and talking of life and love.

It was almost daybreak when, accompanied by Robert, I stepped into the street, clinging to his arm. A great longing possessed me to embrace the fascinating man at my side, so fine and beautiful in body and mind. I felt sure he was also strongly attracted to me; he had shown it all through the evening in his every glance and touch. As we walked along I could feel his agitation of passionate desire. Where could we go? The thought flitted through my mind, as in increasing excitement I walked close to him, waiting and madly hoping that he would make some suggestion.

"And Sasha?" he suddenly asked. "Do you hear often from our wonderful boy?" The spell was broken. I felt thrust back into the world of misery and strife. During the rest of the walk we talked of Sasha and his act, of Most's attitude and its dire effects. It was another Robert now; it was the rebel and fighter against injustice.

At my door he took me in his arms, with hot breath whispering: "I want you! Let's forget the ugliness of life." Gently I freed myself from his embrace. "Too late, my dear," I replied; "the mysterious voices of the night are silent, the dissonances of the day have begun." He understood. Gazing affectionately into my eyes, he said: "This is only the beginning of our friendship, my brave Emma. We will meet again soon in Detroit." I threw my window wide open and watched the rhythmic swing of his well-knit body until he disappeared round the corner. Then I went back to my life and to my machine.

A year later came the news of Reitzel's illness. He was suffering

5. "He ought to live it up."   6. Opera (1848) by Richard Wagner.

from spinal tuberculosis, which resulted in the paralysis of his lower extremities. He was bedridden, like Heine, whom he so greatly admired and whom in a certain measure he resembled in spirit and feeling. But even in his mattress-grave Robert could not be daunted. Every line he wrote was a clarion call to freedom and battle. From his sick-bed he had prevailed on the Central Labor Union of his city to invite me as speaker to that year's eleventh of November commemoration.[7] "Come a few days earlier," he had written me, "so that we can resume our friendship of the days when I was still young."

I arrived in Detroit late in the afternoon on the day of the scheduled meeting and was met by Martin Drescher, whose stirring poems had often appeared in the *Armer Teufel*. To my amusement and the astonishment of the crowd at the station, Drescher, tall and awkward, kneeled before me, holding out a bunch of red roses, and delivering himself of the following: "From your knight, my Queen, with his undying love." "And who may be the knight?" I queried. "Robert, of course! Who else would dare send his love to the Queen of the Anarchists?" The crowd laughed, but the man on his knees before me was not disturbed. To save him from catching a bad cold (there was snow on the ground) I held out my hand, saying: "Now, vassal, take me to my castle." Drescher got up, bowed low, gave me his arm, and solemnly led me to a cab. "To the Randolph Hotel," he commanded. On our arrival there, we found half a score of Robert's friends awaiting us. The owner himself was one of the *Armer Teufel* admirers. "My best room and wines are at your disposal," he announced. I knew it was Robert's thoughtfulness and friendship that had paved the way and secured for me and affection and hospitality of his circle.

Turner Hall was filled to the limit, the audience in tune with the spirit of the evening. The event was made more festive by the singing of a chorus of children and the masterly reading of a fine revolutionary poem by Martin Drescher. I was scheduled to speak in German. The impression on me of the Chicago tragedy had not paled with the passing years. That night it seemed more poignant, perhaps because of the nearness of Robert Reitzel, who had known, loved, and fought for our Chicago martyrs and who was himself now slowly dying. The memory of 1887 took living form, personifying their Calvary[8] and inspiring me to heights of exaltation, of hope and life springing from heroic death.

At the conclusion of the meeting I was called back to the platform to receive from the hands of a golden-haired maiden of five a huge bouquet of red carnations, too large for her wee body. I

---

7. After their conviction in September, the four Haymarket martyrs were hanged on November 11, 1887.

8. I.e., intense mental and physical suffering; the reference is to the hill outside Jerusalem where Jesus was crucified.

pressed the child to my heart and carried her off, bouquet and all.

Later in the evening I met Joe Labadie, a prominent individualist anarchist of picturesque appearance, who introduced to me the Reverend Dr. H. S. McCowan. Both expressed regret that I had not spoken in English. "I came especially to hear you," Dr. McCowan informed me, whereupon Joe, as everyone affectionately called Labadie, remarked: "Well, why don't you offer Miss Goldman your pulpit? Then you could hear our 'Red Emma'⁹ in English." "That's an idea!" the minister replied; "but Miss Goldman is opposed to churches; would you speak in one?" "In hell if need be," I said, "provided the Devil won't pull at my skirts." "All right," he exclaimed, "you shall speak in my church, and no one shall pull at your skirts or curtail a word of what you want to say." We agreed that my lecture should be on anarchism, it being a subject most people knew almost nothing about.

With the flowers my "knight" had sent me came also a note asking me to visit him any time after the meeting, since he would be awake. It seemed strange for a sick person to keep such late hours, but Drescher assured me that Robert felt best after sundown. His house was the last on the street, overlooking a large open space. "Luginsland,"¹ Robert had named it; it was all his eye had looked upon for the past three and a half years. His inner vision, though, keen and penetrating, wandered to distant lands and climes, bringing to him all the cultural wealth they contained. The bright light streaming through his bay window could be seen from afar; it reminded me of a lighthouse, with Robert Reitzel its keeper. Song and laughter sounded from the house. On entering Reitzel's room I found it filled with people; the smoke was so thick that it obscured Robert from view and blurred the faces of those present. His voice called out jovially: "Welcome to our sanctum! Welcome to the den of your adoring knight!" Robert, in a white shirt open wide at the neck, sat in bed propped up against a mountain of pillows. Except for the ashy colour of his face, the increased greyness of his hair, and his thin, transparent hands, there was no indication of his illness. His eyes alone spoke of the martyrdom he was suffering. Their care-free light was gone. With aching heart I put my arms around him, pressing his beautiful head to me. "So motherly?" he objected. "Aren't you going to kiss your knight?" "Of course," I stammered.

I had almost forgotten the others in the room, to whom Robert now began introducing me as the "Vestal of the Social Revolution." "Look at her!" he cried, "look at her; does she resemble the monster pictured by the press, the fury of a hetæra?² Behold her black dress and white collar, prim and proper, almost like a nun." He was making me embarrassed and self-conscious. "You are prais-

---

9. Nickname given by the press because of her political affiliations.
1. "Watchtower."

2. Cultivated ancient Greek courtesan often depicted in literature as tyrannical and conniving.

ing me as if I were a horse you wanted to sell," I finally objected. It did not dismay him in the least. "Didn't I say you are prim and proper?" he declared triumphantly; "you don't live up to your reputation. *Wein her*,"[3] he called; "let's drink to our Vestal!" The men surrounded Robert's bed, glasses in hand. He emptied his to the dregs and then flung it against the wall. "Emma is now one of us. Our pact is sealed; we will be true to her to our last breath!"

An account of the meeting and of my speech had preceded me to Reitzel, the manager of his paper having brought back a glowing report. When I mentioned McCowan's invitation, Robert was delighted. He knew the Reverend Doctor, whom he considered a rare exception in the "outfit of soul-savers." I told Robert about my friend in Blackwell's Island, the young priest, relating how fine and understanding he was. "A pity you met him in prison," Robert teased me, "else you might have found in him an ardent lover." I was sure I could not love a priest. "That's nonsense, my dear—love has no concern with ideas," he replied; "I have loved girls in every town and village and they were not remotely so interesting as your priest seems to be. Love has nothing to do with any ism, and you'll find it out when you grow older." In vain I insisted that I knew all about it. I was no child, being nearly twenty-nine. I was confident I should never fall in love with anyone who did not share my ideas.

The next morning I was awakened in my hotel by the announcement that a dozen reporters were waiting to interview me. They were eager for a story on my proposed speech in Dr. McCowan's church. They showed me the morning papers with the glaring headlines: "Emma shows mother instinct—free lover in a Detroit pulpit—Red Emma captures heart of McCowan—Congregational Church to be turned into hotbed of anarchy and free love."

For several succeeding days the front page of every paper in Detroit was filled with the impending desecration of the church and the portending ruin of the Congregation by "Red Emma." Reports about members' threatening to leave and committees' besieging poor Dr. McCowan followed one another. "It will mean his neck," I said to Reitzel when I saw him the day before the meeting, "and I'd hate to be the cause of it." But Robert held that the man knew what he was doing; it was only right for him to stick to his guns, if only to test his independence in the church. "At any rate, I must offer to withdraw," I suggested, "to give McCowan a chance to recall his invitation if he feels like it." A friend was dispatched to the minister, but he sent word that he would go through with his plan no matter what happened. "A church that refuses the right of expression to the most unpopular person or creed is no place for me," he said. "You must not mind the consequences to me."

In the Tabernacle the Reverend Dr. McCowan presided. In a

3. "Bring some wine."

short speech, which he read from a prepared text, he set forth his own position. He was not an anarchist, he declared; he had never given much thought to it and he really knew very little about it. It was for that reason that he had visited Turner Hall on the night of November 11. Unfortunately Emma Goldman had spoken in German, and when it was suggested that he might hear her in English in his own pulpit, he had accepted the idea at once. He felt that the members of his church would be glad to hear the woman who had for years been persecuted as a "social menace"; as good Christians, he thought, they would be charitable to her. He then turned over the pulpit to me.

I had decided to stick strictly to the economic side of anarchism and to avoid as far as possible matters of religion and sexual problems. I felt I owed it to the man who was making such a courageous stand. At least his congregation should have no cause to say that I had used the Tabernacle to attack their God or to undermine the sacred institution of marriage. I succeeded better than I had expected. My lecture, lasting an hour, was listened to without any interruption and was much applauded at the end. "We won!" Dr. McCowan whispered to me when I sat down.

He rejoiced too soon. The applause had barely died away when an elderly woman rose belligerently. "Mr. Chairman," she demanded, "does Miss Goldman believe in God or does she not?" She was followed by another. "Does the speaker favour killing off all rulers?" Then a small, emaciated man jumped to his feet and in a thin voice cried: "Miss Goldman! You're a believer in free love, aren't you? Now, wouldn't your system result in houses of prostitution at every lamp-post?"

"I shall have to answer these people straight from the shoulder," I remarked to the minister. "So be it," he replied.

"Ladies and gentlemen," I began, "I came here to avoid as much as possible treading on your corns. I had intended to deal only with the basic issue of economics that dictates our lives from the cradle to the grave, regardless of our religion or moral beliefs. I see now that it was a mistake. If one enters a battle, he cannot be squeamish about a few corns. Here, then, are my answers: I do not believe in God, because I believe in man. Whatever his mistakes, man has for thousands of years past been working to undo the botched job your God has made." The house went frantic. "Blasphemy! Heretic! Sinner!" the woman screamed. "Stop her! Throw her out!"

When order was restored, I continued: "As to killing rulers, it depends entirely on the position of the ruler. If it is the Russian Tsar, I most certainly believe in dispatching him to where he belongs. If the ruler is as ineffectual as an American president, it is hardly worth the effort. There are, however, some potentates I would kill by any and all means at my disposal. They are Ignorance, Superstition, and Bigotry—the most sinister and tyrannical rulers on earth. As for the gentleman who asked if free love would not build more houses of prostitution, my answer is: they will all be empty if the men of the future look like him."

There was instant pandemonium. In vain the chairman pounded for order. People jumped up on benches, waved their hats, shouted, and would not leave the church until the lights were turned out.

The next morning most of the papers reported the Tabernacle meeting as a disgraceful spectacle. There was general condemnation of the action of Dr. McCowan in permitting me to speak in the Tabernacle. Even the famous agnostic Robert Ingersoll[4] joined the chorus. "I think that all the anarchists are insane, Emma Goldman among the rest," he stated; "I also think that the Reverend Dr. McCowan is a generous man—not afraid. However, it is not commendable for a crazy man or woman to be invited to talk before any public assemblage." Dr. McCowan resigned from the church. "I'm going to a mining town," he told me; "I am sure the miners will appreciate my work much better." I was sure they would.

1931

---

4. Robert Ingersoll (1833–99), lawyer and noted agnostic who fought for rights of free speech and free press.

══════════════════════

FRANK NORRIS
1870–1902

Benjamin Franklin Norris was born in Chicago on March 5, 1870. Almost an exact contemporary of Stephen Crane, he too died virtually at the beginning of what might have been a hugely productive career. No one can say with confidence just what direction Norris's career would have taken, but there seems to be little doubt that he would have continued to strive to reconcile his concern to "reach down deep into the red, living heart of things" with his highly self-conscious cultivation of literary technique and attempt to create new forms. Nor is there any reason to doubt that Norris would have continued to pursue his defining ambition to write the Great American Novel in the form of the epic struggle between strong-willed individuals and the immutable forces of nature and society. These are the key and complementary tensions in the work he left behind, and both are revealed in the critical essay printed below.

Norris's father was a wealthy jeweler who took a keen interest in his son's aesthetic and intellectual development, taking him, at seventeen, to Europe to study painting. Norris lost interest in becoming a painter and in 1890 entered the University of California, where he read widely and was particularly struck by the theory and literary practice of the French novelist Émile Zola, who proposed that characters in fiction should be studied and depicted with the same objective attitude that characterized the chemist in his laboratory. By the time Norris crossed the country to enroll at Harvard in 1894, he had already completed and published the long chivalric poem

Yvernelle (1891) and had begun two novels, one of which, *Vandover and the Brute*, was not published until 1914.

Following his stay at Harvard, Norris worked as a journalist in the Boer War for the San Francisco *Chronicle* and *Collier's* before returning to America and a position on the *San Francisco Wave*. In 1898 he returned to the East Coast, published the adventure novel *Moran of the Lady Letty*, worked for the publisher Frank Doubleday in New York (where he read and enthusiastically recommended publication of Theodore Dreiser's *Sister Carrie*), and went to Cuba to cover the Spanish-American War for *McClure's Magazine*.

McTeague: A Story of San Francisco (1899), begun in 1894, is the story of the slow degeneration into madness and brutishness of several characters, and was Norris's first significant work; its frank treatment of greed, violence, and sexuality created a literary scandal. It was followed in 1900 by two lesser works, the sentimental, autobiographical romance *Blix* and *A Man's Woman*, an unsuccessful attempt to satisfy the growing audience for the sensational and sentimental.

The Octopus (1901), the title of which alludes metaphorically to the blindly greedy attempt of the railroad owners to squeeze out the ranchers who had developed the profitable wheat fields in southern California, is the first volume in what Norris conceived as a trilogy which would detail the growing of wheat, the drama of its sale and distribution, and the social and economic forces which condition its ultimate distribution around the world. This first volume is flawed—chiefly through its inconsistent conception of the source of responsibility for human action and its failure to integrate its three major plot lines—but many of its scenes are powerfully realized and it is impressive in the breadth and complexity of canvas it covers. *The Pit* (1903), the second volume, is set primarily in the Chicago stock exchange, and is a much weaker, more conventional work with an unbelievable happy ending. Before the final volume, tentatively entitled *The Wolf: A Story of Europe*, could be completed, Norris died of a ruptured appendix in 1902.

Norris's posthumously published critical essay, *The Responsibilities of the Novelist* (1903), argues that the novelist is responsible not to a coterie but to the broadest audience—"the people." The responsibility will be met, he asserts, only by writing about half-fabulous characters in the grip of elemental forces. Only in this way will fiction be universal. This essay, like his fiction, combines sentimental and romantic elements with strains of a severely deterministic view of human behavior.

A Plea for Romantic Fiction[1]

Let us at the start make a distinction. Observe that one speaks of Romanticism and not of sentimentalism. One claims that the latter is as distinct from the former as is that other form of art which is called Realism. Romance has been often put upon and overburdened by being forced to bear the onus of abuse that by right should fall to sentiment; but the two should be kept very distinct, for a very high and illustrious place will be claimed for Romance, while sentiment will be handed down the scullery[2] stairs.

1. This essay first appeared in the *Boston Evening Transcript*, December 18, 1901.   2. Room for coarse kitchen work.

Many people today are composing mere sentimentalism, and calling it and causing it to be called romance, so with those who are too busy to think much upon these subjects, but who none the less love honest literature, Romance too has fallen into disrepute. Consider now the cut-and-thrust stories. They are all labelled Romances, and it is very easy to get the impression that Romance must be an affair of cloaks and daggers, or moonlight and golden hair. But this is not so at all. The true Romance is a more serious business than this. It is not merely a conjurer's trick box, full of flimsy quackeries, tinsel and clap traps, meant only to amuse, and relying upon deception to do even that. Is it not something better than this? Can we not see in it an instrument, keen, finely tempered, flawless—an instrument with which we may go straight through the clothes and tissues and wrappings of flesh down deep into the red, living heart of things?

Is all this too subtle, too merely speculative and intrinsic, too *précieuse* and nice and "literary"? Devoutly one hopes the contrary. So much is made of so-called Romanticism in present day fiction, that the subject seems worthy of discussion, and a protest against the misuse of a really noble and honest formula of literature appears to be timely—misuse, that is, in the sense of limited use. Let us suppose for the moment that a Romance can be made out of the cut-and-thrust business. Good Heavens, are there no other things that are romantic, even in this—falsely, falsely called—humdrum world of today? Why should it be that so soon as the novelist addresses himself—seriously—to the consideration of contemporary life he must abandon Romance and take up that harsh, loveless, colorless, blunt tool called Realism?

Now, let us understand at once what is meant by Romance and what by Realism. Romance—I take it—is the kind of fiction that takes cognizance of variations from the type of normal life. Realism is the kind of fiction that confines itself to the type of normal life. According to this definition, then, Romance may even treat of the sordid, the unlovely—as for instance, the novels of M. Zola.[3] (Zola has been dubbed a Realist, but he is, on the contrary, the very head of the Romanticists.) Also, Realism, used as it sometimes is as a term of reproach, need not be in the remotest sense or degree offensive, but on the other hand respectable as a church and proper as a deacon—as, for instance, the novels of Mr. Howells.

The reason why one claims so much for Romance, and quarrels so pointedly with Realism, is that Realism stultifies itself. It notes only the surface of things. For it Beauty is not even skin-deep, but only a geometrical plane, without dimensions of depth, a mere outside. Realism is very excellent so far as it goes, but it goes no farther than the Realist himself can actually see, or actually hear. Realism is minute, it is the drama of a broken teacup, the tragedy of a walk

3. Émile Zola (1840–1902), French novelist and critic.

down the block, the excitement of an afternoon call, the adventure of an invitation to dinner. It is the visit to my neighbor's house, a formal visit, from which I may draw no conclusions. I see my neighbor and his friends—very, oh, such very! probable people—and that is all. Realism bows upon the doormat and goes away and says to me, as we link arms on the sidewalk: "That is life." And I say it is not. It is not, as you would very well see if you took Romance with you to call upon your neighbor.

Lately you have been taking Romance a weary journey across the water—ages and the flood of years—and haling her into the fubsy, musty, worm-eaten, moth-riddled, rust-corroded "Grandes Salles"[4] of the Middle Ages and the Renaissance, and she has found the drama of a bygone age for you there. But would you take her across the street to your neighbor's front parlor (with the bisque[5] fisher boy on the mantel and the photograph of Niagara Falls on glass hanging in the front window); would you introduce her there? Not you. Would you take a walk with her on Fifth avenue, or Beacon street, or Michigan avenue?[6] No indeed. Would you choose her for a companion of a morning spent in Wall Street, or an afternoon in the Waldorf-Astoria? You just guess you would not.

She would be out of place, you say, inappropriate. She might be awkward in my neighbor's front parlor, and knock over the little bisque fisher boy. Well, she might. If she did, you might find underneath the base of the statuette, hidden away, tucked away—what? God knows. But something which would be a complete revelation of my neighbor's secretest life.

So you think Romance would stop in the front parlor and discuss medicated flannels and mineral waters with the ladies? Not for more than five minutes. She would be off upstairs with you, prying, peeping, peering into the closets of the bedroom, into the nursery, into the sitting-room; yes, and into that little iron box screwed to the lower shelf of the closet in the library; and into those compartments and pigeon-holes of the *secrétaire*[7] in the study. She would find a heartache (may-be) between the pillows of the mistress's bed, and a memory carefully secreted in the master's deedbox. She would come upon a great hope amid the books and papers of the study table of the young man's room, and—perhaps—who knows —an affair, or, great heavens, an intrigue, in the scented ribbons and gloves and hairpins of the young lady's bureau. And she would pick here a little and there a little, making up a bag of hopes and fears, and a package of joys and sorrows—great ones, mind you— and then come down to the front door, and stepping out into the street, hand you the bags and package, and say to you—"That is Life!"

Romance does very well in the castles of the Middle Ages and

4. Great halls.
5. Pottery.

6. I.e., fashionable streets.
7. Writing table or desk.

the Renaissance chateaux, and she has the entrée there and is very well received. That is all well and good. But let us protest against limiting her to such places and such times. You will find her, I grant you, in the chatelaine's[8] chamber and the dungeon of the man-at-arms; but, if you choose to look for her, you will find her equally at home in the brownstone house on the corner and in the office building downtown. And this very day, in this very hour, she is sitting among the rags and wretchedness, the dirt and despair of the tenements of the East Side of New York.

"What?" I hear you say, "look for Romance—the lady of the silken robes and golden crown, our beautiful, chaste maiden of soft voice and gentle eyes—look for her among the vicious ruffians, male and female, of Allen street and Mulberry Bend?"[9] I tell you she is there, and to your shame be it said you will not know her in those surroundings. You, the aristocrats, who demand the fine linen and the purple in your fiction; you, the sensitive, the delicate, who will associate with your Romance only so long as she wears a silken gown. You will not follow her to the slums, for you believe that Romance should only amuse and entertain you, singing you sweet songs and touching the harp of silver strings with rosy-tipped fingers. If haply she should call to you from the squalor of a dive, or the awful degradation of a disorderly house, crying: "Look! listen! This, too, is life. These, too, are my children, look at them, know them and, knowing, help!" Should she call thus, you would stop your ears; you would avert your eyes, and you would answer, "Come from there, Romance. Your place is not there!" And you would make of her a harlequin, a tumbler, a sword dancer, when, as a matter of fact, she should be by right divine a teacher sent from God.

She will not always wear the robe of silk, the gold crown, the jeweled shoon, will not always sweep the silver harp. An iron note is hers if so she choose, and coarse garments, and stained hands; and, meeting her thus, it is for you to know her as she passes—know her for the same young queen of the blue mantle and lilies. She can teach you, if you will be humble to learn. Teach you by showing. God help you, if at last you take from Romance her mission of teaching, if you do not believe that she has a purpose, a nobler purpose and a mightier than mere amusement, mere entertainment. Let Realism do the entertaining with its meticulous presentation of teacups, rag carpets, wall paper and haircloth sofas, stopping with these, going no deeper than it sees, choosing the ordinary, the untroubled, the commonplace.

But to Romance belongs the wide world for range, and the unplumbed depths of the human heart, and the mystery of sex, and

---

8. Mistress of a château.
9. I.e., in the Italian quarter near the Bowery in New York City, a district that once had the reputation of being the most dangerous in the city.

the problems of life, and the black, unsearched penetralia of the soul of man. You, the indolent, must not always be amused. What matter the silken clothes, what matter the prince's houses? Romance, too, is a teacher, and if—throwing aside the purple—she wears the camel's hair and feeds upon the locusts, it is to cry aloud unto the people, "Prepare ye the way of the Lord; make straight his path."[1]

1901

1. Camel's hair and locusts were the raiment and food of John the Baptist. The quotation is from Matthew 3.3.

STEPHEN CRANE
1871–1900

Stephen Crane was born November 1, 1871, and died on June 5, 1900. By the age of twenty-eight he had published enough material to fill a dozen volumes of a collected edition and had lived a legendary life that has grown in complexity and interest to scholars and readers the more the facts have come to light. His family settled in America in the mid-seventeenth century. He himself was the son of a Methodist minister, but he systematically rejected religious and social traditions, identified with the urban poor, and "married" the mistress of one "of the better houses of ill-fame" in Jacksonville, Florida. Although he was temperamentally a gentle man, Crane was attracted to—even obsessed by—war and other forms of physical and psychic violence. He frequently lived the down-and-out life of a penniless artist; he was also ambitious and something of a snob; he was a poet and an impressionist: a journalist, a social critic and realist. In short, there is much about Crane's life and writing that is paradoxical; he is an original and not easy to be right about.

Crane once explained to an editor: "After all, I cannot help vanishing and disappearing and dissolving. It is my foremost trait." This distinctively restless, peripatetic quality of Crane's life began early. The last of fourteen children, Crane moved with his family at least three times before he entered school at age seven in the small town of Port Jervis, New York. His father died in 1880, and after a tentative return to Paterson the family settled in the coastal resort town of Asbury Park, New Jersey, three years later. The next five years, as his biographer and critic Edwin H. Cady has observed, "confirmed in the sensitive, vulnerable, fatherless preacher's kid his fate as isolato." Crane never took to schooling. At Syracuse University he distinguished himself as a baseball player but was unable to accept the routine of academic life and after one semester left with no intention of returning. He was not sure what he would do with himself, but by 1891 he had begun to write for newspapers, and he hungered for immersion in life of the kind that his early journalistic assignments caused him to witness at close hand.

New York City was the inevitable destination for a young man with literary ambitions and a desire to experience the fullness of life. A couple of jobs with New York newspapers proved abortive, and Crane spent much of the next two years shuttling between the seedy apartments of his artist friends and his brother Edmund's house in nearby Lake View, New Jersey. In these years of extreme privation, Crane developed his powers as an observer of psychological and social reality. Encouraged by the realist credo of Hamlin Garland, whom he had heard lecture in 1891, Crane wrote and then—after it had been rejected by several New York editors—published in 1893, at his own expense, a work he had begun while at Syracuse: *Maggie, A Girl of the Streets*. Though Garland admired the short novel, and the powerful literary arbiter William Dean Howells promoted Crane and his book (and continued to think it his best work), the book did not sell. The mass audience of the time sought from literature what *Maggie* denied: escape, distraction, and easy pleasure in romances which falsified and obscured the social, emotional, and moral nature of life.

Just why Crane turned next to the Civil War as a subject for *The Red Badge of Courage* is not clear. He may have wished to appeal to a popular audience and make some money; he later described the book as a "pot-boiler." Or he may have been compelled by a half-recognized need to test himself imaginatively by placing his young protagonist-counterpart in a psychological and philosophical pressure cooker. In any case, in 1893 Crane began his best-known work, *The Red Badge of Courage. An Episode of the American Civil War*, a novel which the present text, newly edited from manuscript, makes available for the first time as Crane originally conceived it. The narrative, which depicts the education of a young man in the context of struggle, is as old as Homer's *Odyssey* and is a dominant story-type in American literature from Benjamin Franklin through Melville, Hemingway, Malcolm X, and Saul Bellow. Until now, most criticism of *Red Badge* has either placed the novel within this tradition or has suggested that Crane treated the theme ironically. The present text, however, makes clear that Crane was not so much working within or against this tradition as he was departing sharply from it. That is, Crane is distinctively modern in conceiving personal identity as complex and ambiguous and in obliging his readers to judge for themselves the adequacy of Henry's responses to his experiences.

When *Red Badge* was first published as a syndicated newspaper story in December, 1894, Crane's fortunes began to improve. The same syndicate that took *Red Badge* assigned him early in 1895 as a roving reporter in the American West and Mexico, experience which would give him the material for several of his finest tales—*The Bride Comes to Yellow Sky* and *The Blue Hotel* among them. Early in 1895 an established New York publisher agreed to issue *Red Badge* in book form. In the spring of that year, *The Black Riders and Other Lines*, his first volume of poetry, was published. Predictably, Garland and Howells responded intelligently to Crane's spare, original, unflinchingly honest poetry, but it was too experimental in form and too unconventional in philosophic outlook to win wide acceptance. *The Red Badge of Courage* appeared in the fall as a book and became the first widely successful American work to be realistic in the modern way. It won Crane international acclaim at the age of twenty-four.

In all of his poetry, journalism, and fiction Crane clearly demonstrated his religious, social, and literary rebelliousness; his alienated, unconventional stance also led him to direct action. After challenging the New York police force on behalf of a prostitute who claimed harassment at its hands, Crane left the city in the winter of 1896–97 to cover the insurrection against

Spain in Cuba. On his way to Cuba he met Cora Howorth Taylor, the proprietress of the aptly named Hotel de Dream in Jacksonville, Florida, with whom he lived for the last three years of his life. On January 2, Crane's ship *The Commodore* sank off the coast of Florida. His report of this harrowing adventure was published a few days later in the New York *Press*. He promptly converted this event into *The Open Boat*. This story, like *Red Badge*, reveals Crane's characteristic subject matter—the physical, emotional, and intellectual responses of men under extreme pressure—and the dominant themes of nature's indifference to humanity's fate and the consequent need for compassionate collective action. In the late stories *The Open Boat* and *The Blue Hotel*, Crane achieved his mature style. In both of these works we can observe his tough-minded irony and his essential vision: a sympathetic but unflinching demand for courage, integrity, grace, and generosity in the face of a universe in which human beings, to quote from *The Blue Hotel*, are so many lice clinging "to a whirling, fire-smote, ice-locked, disease-stricken, space-lost bulb."

In the summer of 1897 Crane covered the Greco-Turkish War and later that year settled in England, where he made friends, most notably with the English writers Joseph Conrad, H. G. Wells, and Ford Maddox Hueffer (later Ford) and the American writers Henry James and Harold Frederic. The following year he covered the Spanish-American War for Joseph Pulitzer's New York *World*. When he wrote *The Red Badge of Courage*, he had never observed battle at firsthand, but his experiences during the Greco-Turkish and Spanish-American Wars confirmed his sense that he had recorded, with more than literal accuracy, the realities of battle.

In the last months of his life Crane's situation became desperate; he was suffering from tuberculosis and was hopelessly in debt. He wrote furiously in a doomed attempt to earn money, but the effort only worsened his health. In 1899 he drafted thirteen stories set in the fictional town Whilomville for *Harper's Magazine*, published his second volume of poetry, *War Is Kind*, the weak novel *Active Service*, and the American edition of *The Monster and Other Stories*. During a Christmas party that year Crane nearly died of a lung hemorrhage. Surviving only a few months, he somehow summoned the strength to write a series of nine articles on great battles and complete the first twenty-five chapters of the novel *The O'Ruddy*. In spite of Cora's hopes for a miraculous cure, and the generous assistance of Henry James and others, Crane died at Badenweiler, Germany, on June 5, 1900.

The Red Badge of Courage[1]
An Episode of the American Civil War

I

The cold passed reluctantly from the earth and the retiring fogs revealed an army stretched out on the hills, resting. As the land-

THE RED BADGE OF COURAGE by Stephen Crane, edited by Henry Binder. Copyright © 1979 by W. W. Norton & Company, Inc. Reprinted by permission of the editor and W. W. Norton & Company, Inc.

1. The text of *The Red Badge of Courage* printed here has been newly edited by Henry Binder for this anthology. It is based, as fully as possible, on Stephen Crane's manuscript.

The *Red Badge* that Crane wrote in manuscript differs considerably from the *Red Badge* first published in book form in October, 1895. In the book version, many phrases, sentences, long passages, and an entire chapter were omitted: the cuts were almost certainly suggested by

scape changed from brown to green the army awakened and began to tremble with eagerness at the noise of rumors. It cast its eyes upon the roads which were growing from long troughs of liquid mud to proper thoroughfares. A river, amber-tinted in the shadow of its banks, purled at the army's feet and at night when the stream had become of a sorrowful blackness one could see, across, the red eye-like gleam of hostile camp-fires set in the low brows of distant hills.

Once, a certain tall soldier developed virtues and went resolutely to wash a shirt. He came flying back from a brook waving his garment, banner-like. He was swelled with a tale he had heard from a reliable friend who had heard it from a truthful cavalryman who had heard it from his trust-worthy brother, one of the orderlies at division head-quarters. He adopted the important air of a herald in red and gold.

"We're goin' t' move t'morrah—sure," he said pompously to a group in the company street. "We're goin' 'way up th' river, cut across, an' come around in behint'em."

To his attentive audience he drew a loud and elaborate plan of a very brilliant campaign. When he had finished, the blue-clothed men scattered into small arguing groups between the rows of squat brown huts. A negro teamster who had been dancing upon a cracker-box with the hilarious encouragement of two-score soldiers, was deserted. He sat mournfully down. Smoke drifted lazily from a multitude of quaint chimneys.

"It's a lie—that's all it is. A thunderin' lie," said another private loudly. His smooth face was flushed and his hands were thrust sulkily into his trousers' pockets. He took the matter as an affront to him. "I don't believe th' derned ol' army's ever goin' t' move. We're set. I've got ready t' move eight times in th' last two weeks an' we aint moved yit."

The tall soldier felt called upon to defend the truth of a rumor he himself had introduced. He and the loud one came near to fighting over it.

Crane's editor with the intention of satisfying a wider contemporary audience with a simpler story. In the text that follows here, this material has been restored to present the novel in its original form and thus offer the modern reader what we know Crane wrote.

The surviving manuscript of *Red Badge* lacks some pages that cannot be fully recovered; however, three pages of an early draft of the novel supply closely equivalent text where the ending of Chapter X was deleted and for most of a page lost when Chapter XII was removed. By using these early draft pages, Crane's final manuscript can be reconstructed in all essentials with six short gaps that represent a loss of perhaps fewer than a thousand words with no interruption of the continuity of the story. Each gap is noted and described in a footnote.

In the manuscript, Crane began to change all of the proper names to descriptive phrases (for example, Henry Fleming became simply "the youth" and Jim Conklin became "the tall soldier"). He completed these changes for the published edition, and so in these instances the first edition readings have been adopted for the present text.

Crane's misspellings, which appear in the manuscript, have been corrected throughout; most of them involve inversions of i and e (as in "percieve" or "sieze") and Crane's use of "it's" for both the possessive pronoun and the contraction of "it is." Except for a handful of places where clarity can be served by a simple emendation, the manuscript punctuation has been carefully respected.

A corporal began to swear before the assemblage. He had just put a costly board floor in his house, he said. During the early spring he had refrained from adding extensively to the comfort of his environment because he had felt that the army might start on the march at any moment. Of late, however, he had been impressed that they were in a sort of eternal camp.

Many of the men engaged in a spirited debate. One out-lined in a peculiarly lucid manner all the plans of the commanding general. He was opposed by men who advocated that there were other plans of campaign. They clamored at each other, numbers making futile bids for the popular attention. The while, the soldier who had fetched the rumor bustled about with much importance. He was continually assailed by questions.

"What's up, Jim?"

"Th' army's goin' t' move."

"Ah, what yeh talkin' about? How yeh know it is?"

"Well, yeh kin b'lieve me er not—jest as yeh like. I don't care a hang. I tell yeh what I know an' yeh kin take it er leave it. Suit yerselves. It dont make no difference t' me."

There was much food for thought in the manner in which he replied. He came near to convincing them by disdaining to produce proofs. They grew much excited over it.

There was a youthful private who listened with eager ears to the words of the tall soldier and to the varied comments of his comrades. After receiving a fill of discussions concerning marches and attacks, he went to his hut and crawled through an intricate hole that served it as a door. He wished to be alone with some new thoughts that had lately come to him.

He lay down on a wide bunk that stretched across the end of the room. In the other end, cracker boxes were made to serve as furniture. They were grouped about the fire-place. A picture from an illustrated weekly was upon the log wall and three rifles were paralleled on pegs. Equipments hung on handy projections and some tin dishes lay upon a small pile of fire-wood. A folded tent was serving as a roof. The sun-light, without, beating upon it, made it glow a light yellow shade. A small window shot an oblique square of whiter light upon the cluttered floor. The smoke from the fire at times neglected the clay-chimney and wreathed into the room. And this flimsy chimney of clay and sticks made endless threats to set a-blaze the whole establishment.

The youth was in a little trance of astonishment. So they were at last going to fight. On the morrow perhaps there would be a battle and he would be in it. For a time, he was obliged to labor to make himself believe. He could not accept with assurance an omen that he was about to mingle in one of those great affairs of the earth.

He had of course dreamed of battles all of his life—of vague and bloody conflicts that had thrilled him with their sweep and fire. In visions, he had seen himself in many struggles. He had imagined peoples secure in the shadow of his eagle-eyed prowess. But awake he had regarded battles as crimson blotches on the pages of the past. He had put them as things of the bygone with his thought-images of heavy crowns and high castles. There was a portion of the world's history which he had regarded as the time of wars, but, it, he thought, had been long gone over the horizon and had disappeared forever.

From his home his youthful eyes had looked upon the war in his own country with distrust. It must be some sort of a play affair. He had long despaired of witnessing a Greek-like struggle. Such would be no more, he had said. Men were better, or, more timid. Secular and religious education had effaced the throat-grappling instinct, or, else, firm finance held in check the passions.

He had burned several times to enlist. Tales of great movements shook the land. They might not be distinctly Homeric, but there seemed to be much glory in them. He had read of marches, sieges, conflicts, and he had longed to see it all. His busy mind had drawn for him large pictures, extravagant in color, lurid with breathless deeds.

But his mother had discouraged him. She had affected to look with some contempt upon the quality of his war-ardor and patriotism. She could calmly seat herself and with no apparent difficulty give him many hundreds of reasons why he was of vastly more importance on the farm than on the field of battle. She had had certain ways of expression that told that her statements on the subject came from a deep conviction. Besides, on her side, was his belief that her ethical motive in the argument was impregnable.

At last, however, he had made firm rebellion against this yellow light thrown upon the color of his ambitions. The newspapers, the gossip of the village, his own picturings, had aroused him to an uncheckable degree. They were in truth fighting finely down there. Almost every day, the newspapers printed accounts of a decisive victory.

One night, as he lay in bed, the winds had carried to him the clangoring of the church-bell as some enthusiast jerked the rope frantically to tell the twisted news of a great battle. This voice of the people, rejoicing in the night, had made him shiver in a prolonged ecstasy of excitement. Later, he had gone down to his mother's room and had spoken thus: "Ma, I'm goin' t' enlist."

"Henry, don't you be a fool," his mother had replied. She had then covered her face with the quilt. There was an end to the matter for that night.

Nevertheless, the next morning, he had gone to a considerable town that was near his mother's farm and had enlisted in a company that was forming there. When he had returned home, his mother was milking the brindle cow. Four others stood waiting.

"Ma, I've enlisted," he had said to her diffidently.

There was a short silence. "Th' Lord's will be done, Henry," she had finally replied and had then continued to milk the brindle cow.

When he had stood in the door-way with his soldier's clothes on his back and with the light of excitement and expectancy in his eyes almost defeating the glow of regret for the home bonds, he had seen two tears leaving their hot trails on his mother's scarred cheeks.

Still, she had disappointed him by saying nothing whatever about returning with his shield or on it.[2] He had privately primed himself for a beautiful scene. He had prepared certain sentences which he thought could be used with touching effect. But her words destroyed his plans. She had doggedly peeled potatoes and addressed him as follows: "You watch out, Henry, an' take good keer of yerself in this here fightin' business—you watch out an' take good keer of yerself. Don't go a-thinkin' yeh kin lick th' hull rebel army at th' start, b'cause yeh can't. Yer jest one little feller 'mongst a hull lot 'a others an' yeh've got t' keep quiet an' do what they tell yeh. I know how you are, Henry.

"I've knet yeh eight pair a' socks, Henry, an' I've put in all yer best shirts, b'cause I want my boy t' be jest as warm an' comf'able as anybody in th' army. Whenever they git holes in 'em I want yeh t' send 'em right-away back t' me, so's I kin dern 'em.

"An' allus be keerful an' choose yer comp'ny. There's lots 'a bad men in the army, Henry. Th' army makes 'em wild an' they like nothin' better than th' job of leadin' off a young fellah like you—as aint never been away from home much an' has allus had a mother —an' a-learnin' 'im t' drink an' swear. Keep clear 'a them folks, Henry. I don't want yeh t' ever do anythin', Henry, that yeh would be shamed t' let me know about. Jest think as if I was a-watchin' yeh. If yeh keep that in yer mind allus, I guess yeh'll come out about right.

"Young fellers in th' army git awful keerless in their ways, Henry. They're away f'm home an' they don't have nobody t' look atter 'em. I'm 'feard fer yeh 'bout that. Yeh aint never been used t' doin' fer yerself. So yeh must keep writin' t' me how yer clothes are lastin'.

"Yeh must allus remember yer father, too, child, an' remember he never drunk a drop 'a licker in his life an' seldom swore a cross oath.

"I don't know what else t' tell yeh, Henry, exceptin' that yeh must never do no shirkin', child, on my account. If so be a time comes when yeh have t' be kilt or do a mean thing, why, Henry, don't think of anythin' 'cept what's right, b'cause there's many a

2. Traditionally, this is the best-known admonishment of a Spartan mother to a son leaving for war. It appears in Plutarch's *Moralia*: "Another as she handed her son his shield, exhorted him saying, 'Either this or upon this.'"

woman has to bear up 'ginst sech things these times an' th' Lord'ill take keer of us all. Don't fergit t' send yer socks t' me th' minute they git holes in'em an' here's a little bible I want yeh t' take along with yeh, Henry. I dont presume yeh'll be a'settin' readin' it all day long, child, ner nothin' like that. Many a time, yeh'll fergit yeh got it, I don't doubt. But there'll be many a time, too, Henry, when yeh'll be wantin' advice, boy, an' all like that, an' there'll be nobody round, p'rhaps, t' tell yeh things. Then if yeh take it out, boy, yeh'll find wisdom in it—wisdom in it, Henry—with little or no searchin'. Don't forgit about th' socks an' th' shirts, child, an' I've put a cup of blackberry jam with yer bundle b'cause I know yeh like it above all things. Good-bye, Henry. Watch out an' be a good boy."

He had of course been impatient under the ordeal of this speech. It had not been quite what he expected and he had borne it with an air of irritation. He departed feeling vague relief.

Still, when he had looked back from the gate, he had seen his mother kneeling among the potato-parings. Her brown face, up-raised, was stained with tears and her spare form was quivering. He bowed his head and went on, feeling suddenly ashamed of his purposes.

From his home, he had gone to the seminary[3] to bid adieu to many schoolmates. They had thronged about him with wonder and admiration. He had felt the gulf now between them and had swelled with calm pride. He and some of his fellows who had donned blue were quite over-whelmed with privileges for all of one afternoon and it had been a very delicious thing. They had strutted.

A certain light-haired girl had made vivacious fun at his martial-spirit but there was another and darker girl whom he had gazed at steadfastly and he thought she grew demure and sad at sight of his blue and brass. As he had walked down the path between the rows of oaks, he had turned his head and detected her at a window watching his departure. As he perceived her, she had immediately begun to stare up through the high tree branches at the sky. He had seen a good deal of flurry and haste as she changed her attitude. He often thought of it.

On the way to Washington, his spirit had soared. The regiment was fed and caressed at station after station until the youth had believed that he must be a hero. There was a lavish expenditure of bread and cold meats, coffee, and pickles and cheese. As he basked in the smiles of the girls and was patted and complimented by the old men, he had felt growing within him the strength to do mighty deeds of arms.

After complicated journeyings with many pauses, there had come months of monotonous life in a camp. He had had the belief that real war was a series of death-struggles with small time in between

3. An old-fashioned term for any school.

for sleep and meals but since his regiment had come to the field, the army had done little but sit still and try to keep warm.

He was brought then gradually back to his old ideas. Greek-like struggles would be no more. Men were better, or more timid. Secular and religious education had effaced the throat-grappling instinct or else firm finance held in check the passions.

He had grown to regard himself merely as a part of a vast blue demonstration. His province was to look out, as far as he could, for his personal comfort. For recreation, he could twiddle his thumbs and speculate on the thoughts which must agitate the minds of the generals. Also, he was drilled and drilled and reviewed, and drilled and drilled and reviewed.

The only foes he had seen were some pickets[4] along the river bank. They were a sun-tanned, philosophical lot who sometimes shot reflectively at the blue pickets. When reproached for this, afterwards, they usually expressed sorrow and swore by their gods that the guns had exploded without permission. The youth on guard duty one night, conversed across the stream with one. He was a slightly ragged man who spat skilfully between his shoes and possessed a great fund of bland and infantile assurance. The youth liked him personally.

"Yank," the other had informed him, "yer a right dum good feller." This sentiment, floating to him upon the still air, had made him temporarily regret war.

Various veterans had told him tales. Some talked of grey, be-whiskered hordes who were advancing, with relentless curses and chewing tobacco with unspeakable valor; tremendous bodies of fierce soldiery who were sweeping along like the Huns. Others spoke of tattered and eternally-hungry men who fired despondent powder. "They'll charge through hell's-fire an' brimstone t' git a holt on a haversack, an' sech stomachs aint a-lastin' long," he was told. From the stories, the youth imagined the red, live bones sticking out through slits in the faded uniforms.

Still he could not put a whole faith in veterans' tales, for recruits were their prey. They talked much of smoke, fire, and blood but he could not tell how much might be lies. They persistently yelled "Fresh fish," at him and were in no wise to be trusted.

However, he perceived now that it did not greatly matter what kind of soldiers he was going to fight, so long as they fought, which fact no one disputed. There was a more serious problem. He lay in his bunk pondering upon it. He tried to mathematically prove to himself that he would not run from a battle.

Previously, he had never felt obliged to wrestle too seriously with this question. In his life, he had taken certain things for granted, never challenging his belief in ultimate success and bothering little

4. Sentinels.

about means and roads. But here he was confronted with a thing of moment. It had suddenly appeared to him that perhaps in a battle he might run. He was forced to admit that as far as war was concerned he knew nothing of himself.

A sufficient time before, he would have allowed the problem to kick its heels at the outer portals of his mind but, now, he felt compelled to give serious attention to it.

A little panic-fear grew in his mind. As his imagination went forward to a fight, he saw hideous possibilities. He contemplated the lurking menaces of the future and failed in an effort to see himself standing stoutly in the midst of them. He re-called his visions of broken-bladed glory but in the shadow of the impending tumult, he suspected them to be impossible pictures.

He sprang from the bunk and began to pace nervously to and fro. "Good Lord, what's th' matter with me," he said aloud.

He felt that in this crisis his laws of life were useless. Whatever he had learned of himself was here of no avail. He was an unknown quantity. He saw that he would again be obliged to experiment as he had in early youth. He must accumulate information of himself and, meanwhile, he resolved to remain close upon his guard lest those qualities of which he knew nothing should everlastingly disgrace him. "Good Lord," he repeated in dismay.

After a time, the tall soldier slid dexterously through the hole. The loud private followed. They were wrangling.

"That's all right," said the tall soldier as he entered. He waved his hand expressively. "Yeh kin b'lieve me er not—jest as yeh like. All yeh got t' do is t' sit down an' wait as quiet as yeh kin. Then pretty soon yeh'll find out I was right."

His comrade grunted stubbornly. For a moment he seemed to be searching for a formidable reply. Finally he said: "Well, yeh don't know everythin' in th' world, do yeh?"

"Didn't say I knew everythin' in the world," retorted the other sharply. He began to stow various articles snugly into his knap-sack.

The youth, pausing in his nervous walk, looked down at the busy figure. "Goin' t' be a battle, sure, is there, Jim?" he asked.

"Of course there is," replied the tall soldier. "Of course there is. You jest wait 'til t'morrah an' you'll see one of th' bigges' battles ever was. You jest wait."

"Thunder," said the youth.

"Oh, you'll see fightin' this time, m' boy, what'll be reg'lar out-an'-out fightin'," added the tall soldier with the air of a man who is about to exhibit a battle for the benefit of his friends.

"Huh," said the loud one from a corner.

"Well," remarked the youth, "like as not this here story'll turn out jest like them others did."

"Not much it wont," replied the tall soldier exasperated. "Not much it wont. Didn't th' cavalry all start this mornin'?" He glared about him. No one denied his statement. "Th' cavalry started this mornin'," he continued. "They say there ain't hardly any cavalry left in camp. They're goin' t' Richmond or some place while we fight all th' Johnnies. It's some dodge like that. Th' reg'ment's got orders, too. A feller what seen'em go t' head-quarters told me a little while ago. An' they're raisin' blazes all over camp—anybody kin see that."

"Shucks," said the loud one.

The youth remained silent for a time. At last he spoke to the tall soldier. "Jim!"

"What?"

"How d' yeh think th' reg'ment'll do?"

"Oh, they'll fight all right, I guess, after they onct git inteh it," said the other with cold judgment. He made a fine use of the third person. "There's been heaps 'a fun poked at'em b'cause they're new, 'a course, an' all that, but they'll fight all right, I guess."

"Think any 'a th' boys'll run?" persisted the youth.

"Oh, there may a few of'em run but there's them kind in every reg'ment, 'specially when they first goes under fire," said the other in a tolerant way. " 'A course, it might happen that th' hull kit-an'-boodle might start an' run, if some big fightin' come first-off, an' then a'gin, they might stay an' fight like fun. But yeh cant bet on nothin'. A' course they aint never been under fire yit an' it aint likely they'll lick th' hull rebel army all-t'-onct th' first time, but I think they'll fight better than some, if worser than others. That's th' way I figger. They call th' reg'ment 'Fresh fish', an' everythin', but th' boys come a' good stock an' most 'a 'em'll fight like sin after —they—onct—git—shootin'," he added with a mighty emphasis on the four last words.

"Oh, you think you know—" began the loud soldier with scorn.

The other turned savagely upon him. They had a rapid altercation, in which they fastened upon each other various strange epithets.

The youth at last interrupted them. "Did yeh ever think yeh might run yerself, Jim?" he asked. On concluding the sentence he laughed as if he had meant to aim a joke. The loud soldier also giggled.

The tall private waved his hand. "Well," said he profoundly, "I've thought it might git too hot fer Jim Conklin in some 'a them scrimmages an' if a hull lot a' boys started an' run, why, I s'pose I'd start an' run. An' if I onct started t' run, I'd run like th' devil an' no mistake. But if everybody was a-standin' an' a-fightin', why, I'd stand an' fight. B'jiminy, I would. I'll bet on it."

"Huh," said the loud one.

The youth of this tale felt gratitude for these words of his comrade. He had feared that all of the untried men possessed a great and correct confidence. He now was, in a measure, re-assured.

II

The next morning, the youth discovered that his tall comrade had been the fast-flying messenger of a mistake. There was much scoffing at the latter by those who had yesterday been firm adherents of his views, and there was, even, a little sneering by men who had never believed the rumor. The tall one fought with a man from Chatfield Corners and beat him severely.

The youth felt however that his problem was in no wise lifted from him. There was, on the contrary, an irritating prolongation. The tale had created in him a great concern for himself. Now, with the new-born question in his mind he was compelled to sink back into his old place as part of a blue demonstration.

For days, he made ceaseless calculations, but they were all wondrously unsatisfactory. He found that he could establish nothing. He finally concluded that the only way to prove himself was to go into the blaze and then figuratively to watch his legs to discover their merits and faults. He reluctantly admitted that he could not sit still and, with a mental slate and pencil, derive an answer. To gain it, he must have blaze, blood and danger, even as a chemist requires this, that and the other. So, he fretted for an opportunity.

Meanwhile, he continually tried to measure himself by his comrades. The tall soldier, for one, gave him some assurance. This man's serene unconcern dealt him a measure of confidence for he had known him since childhood and from his intimate knowledge he did not see how he could be capable of anything that was beyond him, the youth. Still, he thought that his comrade might be mistaken about himself. Or, on the other hand, he might be a man heretofore doomed to peace and obscurity but, in reality, made to shine in war.

The youth would have liked to have discovered another who suspected himself. A sympathetic comparison of mental notes would have been a joy to him.

He occasionally tried to fathom a comrade with seductive sentences. He looked about to find men in the proper moods. All attempts failed to bring forth any statement which looked, in any way, like a confession to those doubts which he privately acknowledged in himself. He was afraid to make an open declaration of his concern because he dreaded to place some unscrupulous confidant upon the high plane of the unconfessed from which elevation he could be derided.

In regard to his companions, his mind wavered between two opinions, according to his mood. Sometimes, he inclined to believing them all heroes. In fact he usually admitted, in secret, the superior development of the higher qualities in others. He could conceive of men going very insignificantly about the world, bearing a load of courage, unseen, and although he had known many of his

comrades through boy-hood, he began to fear that his judgment of
them had been blind. Then, in other moments, he flouted these
theories and assured himself that his fellows were all privately wondering and quaking.

His emotions made him feel strange in the presence of men who
talked excitedly of a prospective battle as of a drama they were
about to witness with nothing but eagerness and curiosity apparent
in their faces. It was often that he suspected them to be liars.

He did not pass such thoughts without severe condemnation of
himself. He dinned reproaches, at times. He was convicted by himself of many shameful crimes against the gods of tradition.

In his great anxiety, his heart was continually clamoring at what
he considered to be the intolerable slowness of the generals. They
seemed content to perch tranquilly on the river bank and leave him
bowed down by the weight of a great problem. He wanted it settled
forthwith. He could not long bear such a load, he said. Sometimes,
his anger at the commanders reached an acute stage and he grumbled about the camp like a veteran.

One morning, however, he found himself in the ranks of his prepared regiment. The men were whispering speculations and recounting the old rumors. In the gloom before the break of the day, their
uniforms glowed a deep purple hue. From across the river the red
eyes were still peering. In the eastern sky, there was a yellow patch
like a rug laid for the feet of the coming sun. And against it, black
and pattern-like, loomed the gigantic figure of the colonel on a
gigantic horse.

From off in the darkness, came the trampling of feet. The youth
could occasionally see dark shadows that moved like monsters. The
regiment stood at rest for what seemed a long time. The youth grew
impatient. It was unendurable, the way these affairs were managed.
He wondered how long they were to be kept waiting.

As he looked all about him and pondered upon the mystic gloom,
he began to believe that at any moment the ominous distance
might be a-flare and the rolling crashes of an engagement come to
his ears. Staring, once, at the red eyes across the river, he conceived
them to be growing larger, as the orbs of a row of dragons, advancing. He turned toward the colonel and saw him lift his gigantic arm
and calmly stroke his moustache.

At last, he heard from along the road at the foot of the hill the
clatter of a horse's galloping hoofs. It must be the coming of orders.
He bended forward scarce breathing. The exciting clickety-click as it
grew louder and louder seemed to be beating upon his soul. Presently, a horseman with jangling equipment, drew rein before the
colonel of the regiment. The two held a short, sharp-worded conversation. The men in the foremost ranks craned their necks.

As the horseman wheeled his animal and galloped away, he
turned to shout over his shoulder. "Don't forget that box of cigars."

The colonel mumbled in reply. The youth wondered what a box of cigars had to do with war.

A moment later the regiment went swinging off into the darkness. It was now like one of those moving monsters wending with many feet. The air was heavy and cold with dew. A mass of wet grass, marched upon, rustled like silk.

There was an occasional flash and glimmer of steel from the backs of all these huge crawling reptiles. From the road, came creakings and grumblings as some surly guns were dragged away.

The men stumbled along still muttering speculations. There was a subdued debate. Once, a man fell down and as he reached for his rifle, a comrade, unseeing, trod upon his hand. He of the injured fingers swore bitterly and aloud. A low, tittering laugh went among his fellows.

Presently, they passed into a road-way and marched along with easy strides. A dark regiment moved before them, and, from behind, also, came the tinkle of equipments on the bodies of marching men.

The rushing yellow of the developing day went on behind their backs. When the sun-rays at last struck full and mellowingly upon the earth, the youth saw that the landscape was streaked with two long, thin, black columns which disappeared on the brow of a hill in front and rear-ward vanished in a wood. They were like two serpents crawling from the cavern of the night.

The river was not in view. The tall soldier burst out in praise of what he thought to be his powers of perception. "I told yeh so, didnt I? We're goin' up th' river, cut across, an' come around in behint'em."

"Huh," said the loud soldier.

Some of the tall one's companions cried with emphasis that they too had evolved the same thing and they congratulated themselves upon it. But there were others who said that the tall one's plan was not the true one at all. They persisted with other theories. There was a vigorous discussion.

The youth took no part in them. As he walked along in careless line, he was engaged with his own eternal debate. He could not hinder himself from dwelling upon it. He was despondent and sullen and threw shifting glances about him. He looked ahead often, expecting to hear from the advance the rattle of firing.

But the long serpents crawled slowly from hill to hill without bluster of smoke. A dun-colored cloud of dust floated away to the right. The sky over-head was of a fairy blue.

The youth studied the faces of his companions, ever on the watch to detect kindred emotions. He suffered disappointment. Some ardor of the air which was causing the veteran commands to move with glee, almost with song, had infected the new regiment. The men began to speak of victory as of a thing they knew. Also, the tall soldier received his vindication. They were certainly going to come around in behind the enemy. They expressed commiseration for that part of the army which had been left upon the river-bank felicitating themselves upon being a part of a blasting host.

The youth, considering himself as separated from the others, was saddened by the blithe and merry speeches that went from rank to rank. The company wags all made their best endeavors. The regiment tramped to the tune of laughter.

The loud soldier often convulsed whole files by his biting sarcasms aimed at the tall one.

And it was not long before all the men seemed to forget their mission. Whole brigades grinned in unison and regiments laughed.

A rather fat soldier attempted to pilfer a horse from a door-yard. He planned to load his knapsack upon it. He was escaping with his prize when a young girl rushed from the house and grabbed the animal's mane. There followed, a wrangle.

The observant regiment, standing at rest in the road-way, whooped at once and entered whole-souled upon the side of the maiden. The men became so engrossed in this affair that they entirely ceased to remember their own large war. They jeered the piratical private and called attention to various defects in his personal appearance. And they were wildly enthusiastic in support of the young girl.

"Gin' it to'im, Mary, 'gin it to'im."

"Don't let'im steal yer horse."

"Gin' him thunder."

To her from some distance came bold advice. "Hit him with a stick."

There were crows and cat-calls showered upon him when he retreated without the horse. The regiment rejoiced at his downfall. Loud and vociferous congratulations were showered upon the maiden who stood panting and regarding the troops with defiance.

At night-fall, the column broke into regimental pieces and the fragments went into the fields to camp. Tents sprang up like strange plants. Camp-fires, like red, peculiar blossoms, dotted the night.

The youth kept from intercourse with his companions as much as circumstances would allow him. In the evening, he wandered a few paces into the gloom. From this little distance, the many fires with the black forms of men passing to and fro before the crimson rays made weird and satanic effects.

He lay down in the grass. The blades pressed tenderly against his cheek. The moon had been lighted and was hung in a tree-top. The liquid stillness of the night, enveloping him, made him feel vast pity for himself. There was a caress in the soft winds. And the whole mood of the darkness, he thought, was one of sympathy for him in his distress.

He wished without reserve that he was at home again, making

the endless rounds, from the house to the barn, from the barn to the fields, from the fields to the barn, from the barn to the house. He remembered he had often cursed the brindle-cow and her mates, and had sometimes flung milking-stools. But from his present point of view, there was a halo of happiness about each of their heads and he would have sacrificed all the brass buttons on the continent to have been enabled to return to them. He told himself that he was not formed for a soldier. And he mused seriously upon the radical differences between himself and those men who were dodging, imp-like, around the fires.

As he mused thus, he heard the rustle of grass and, upon turning his head discovered, the loud soldier. He called out. "Oh, Wilson."

The latter approached and looked down. "Why, hello, Henry, is it you? What yeh doin' here?"

"Oh—thinkin'," said the youth.

The other sat down and carefully lighted his pipe. "You're gittin' blue, m' boy. You're lookin' thunderin' peek-ed. What th' dickens is wrong with yeh?"

"Oh—nothin'," said the youth.

The loud soldier launched then into the subject of the antici-pated fight. "Oh, we've got'em now." As he spoke his boyish face was wreathed in a gleeful smile and his voice had an exultant ring. "We've got'em now. At last by th' eternal thunders, we'll lick'em good."

"If th' truth was known," he added more soberly, "*they've* licked *us* about every clip up t' now, but this time—this time, we'll lick'em good."

"I thought yeh was objectin' t' this march a little while ago," said the youth coldly.

"Oh, it wasn't that," explained the other. "I don't mind mar-chin' if there's goin' t' be fightin' at th' end of it. What I hate is this gittin' moved here an' moved there with no good comin' of it, as far as I kin see, exceptin' sore feet an' damn' short rations."

"Well, Jim Conklin says we'll git a-plenty of fightin' this time."

"He's right fer once, I guess, 'though I can't see how it come. This time we're in for a big battle an' we've got th' best end of it certain-sure. Gee-rod, how we will thump'em."

He arose and began to pace to and fro excitedly. The thrill of his enthusiasm made him walk with an elastic step. He was sprightly, vigorous, fiery in his belief in success. He looked into the future with clear, proud eye. And he swore with the air of an old soldier.

The youth watched him for a moment in silence. When he finally spoke, his voice was as bitter as dregs. "Oh, you're goin' t' do great things, I s'pose."

The loud soldier blew a thoughtful cloud of smoke from his pipe. "Oh, I don't know," he remarked with dignity. "I don't know. I s'pose I'll do as well as th' rest. I'm goin' t' try like thunder." He evidently complimented himself upon the modesty of this statement.

"How d' yeh know yeh won't run when th' time comes?" asked the youth.

"Run?" said the loud one. "Run? Of course not." He laughed.

"Well," continued the youth, "lots of good-a-'nough men have thought they was goin' t' do great things before th' fight but when th' time come, they skedaddled."

"Oh, that's all true, I s'pose;" replied the other, "but I'm not goin' t' skedaddle. Th' man that bets on my runnin', will lose his money, that's all." He nodded confidently.

"Oh, shucks," said the youth. "Yeh aint th' bravest man in th' world, are yeh?"

"No, I aint," exclaimed the loud soldier indignantly. "An' I didnt say I was th' bravest man in th' world, neither. I said I was goin' t' do my share of fightin'—that's what I said. An' I am, too. Who are you, anyhow? You talk as if yeh thought yeh was Napolyon Bonypart." He glared at the youth for a moment and then strode away.

The youth called in a savage voice after his comrade. "Well, yeh needn't git mad about it." But the other continued on his way and made no reply.

He felt alone in space when his injured comrade had disappeared. His failure to discover any mite of resemblance in their view-points made him more miserable than before. No one seemed to be wrestling with such a terrific personal problem. He was a mental outcast.

He went slowly to his tent and stretched himself on a blanket by the side of the snoring tall soldier. In the darkness, he saw visions of a thousand-tongued fear that would babble at his back and cause him to flee while others were going coolly about their country's business. He admitted that he would not be able to cope with this monster. He felt that every nerve in his body would be an ear to hear the voices, while other men could remain stolid and deaf.

And as he sweated with the pain of these thoughts he could hear low, serene sentences. "I'll bid five." "Make it six." "Seven." "Seven goes."

He stared at the red, shivering reflection of a fire on the white wall of his tent until exhausted and ill from the monotony of his suffering he fell asleep.

III

When another night came, the columns changed to purple streaks, filed across two pontoon bridges. A glaring fire wine-tinted the waters of the river. Its rays, shining upon the moving masses of troops, brought forth here and there sudden gleams of silver or gold. Upon the other shore, a dark and mysterious range of hills was curved against the sky. The insect-voices of the night sang solemnly.

After this crossing, the youth assured himself that at any moment they might be suddenly and fearfully assaulted from the caves of the lowering woods. He kept his eyes watchfully upon the darkness.

But his regiment went unmolested to a camping-place and its soldiers slept the brave sleep of wearied men. In the morning they were routed out with early energy and hustled along a narrow road that led deep into the forest.

It was during this rapid march that the regiment lost many of the marks of a new command.

The men had begun to count the miles upon their fingers. And they grew tired. "Sore feet an' damned short rations, that's all," said the loud soldier. There was perspiration and grumbling. After a time, they began to shed their knapsacks. Some tossed them unconcernedly down; others hid them carefully, asserting their plans to return for them at some convenient time. Men extricated themselves from thick shirts. Presently, few carried anything but their necessary clothing, blankets, haversacks, canteens, and arms and ammunition. "Yeh kin now eat, drink, sleep an' shoot," said the tall soldier to the youth. "That's all yeh need. What d' yeh wanta do —carry a hotel?" There was sudden change from the ponderous infantry of theory to the light and speedy infantry of practise. The regiment, relieved of a burden, received a new impetus. But there was much loss of valuable knapsacks and, on the whole, very good shirts.

But the regiment was not yet veteran-like in appearance. Veteran regiments in this army were like to be very small aggregations of men. Once, when the command had first come to the field, some perambulating veterans, noting the length of their column, had accosted them thus: "Hay, fellers, what brigade is that?" And when the men had replied that they formed a regiment and not a brigade, the older soldiers had laughed and said: "Oh, Gawd!"[5]

Also, there was too great a similarity in the hats. The hats of a regiment should properly represent the history of head-gear for a period of years.

And, moreover, there were no letters of faded gold speaking from the colors. They were new and beautiful, and the color-bearer habitually oiled the pole.

Presently, the army again sat down to think. The odor of the peaceful pines was in the men's nostrils. The sound of monotonous axe-blows rang through the forest and the insects, nodding upon their perches, crooned like old women. The youth returned to his theory of a blue demonstration.

One grey dawn, however, he was kicked in the leg by the tall soldier and then before he was entirely awake, he found himself run-

---

5. A brigade usually comprises two or more regiments.

ning down a wood-road in the midst of men who were panting from the first effects of speed. His canteen banged rhythmically upon his thigh and his haversack bobbed softly. His musket bounced a trifle from his shoulder at each stride and made his cap feel uncertain upon his head.

He could hear the men whisper jerky sentences. "Say—what's all this—about?" "What th' thunder—we—skedaddlin' this way fer?" "Billie—keep off m' feet. Yeh run—like a cow." And the loud soldier's shrill voice could be heard: "What th' devil they in sech a hurry fer?"

The youth thought the damp fog of early morning moved from the rush of a great body of troops. From the distance, came a sudden spatter of firing.

He was bewildered. As he ran with his comrades, he strenuously tried to think but all he knew was that if he fell down, those coming behind would tread upon him. All his faculties seemed to be needed to guide him over and past obstructions. He felt carried along by a mob.

The sun spread disclosing rays and, one by one, regiments burst into view like armed men just born of the earth. The youth perceived that the time had come. He was about to be measured. For a moment he felt in the face of his great trial, like a babe. And the flesh over his heart seemed very thin. He seized time to look about him calculatingly.

But he instantly saw that it would be impossible for him to escape from the regiment. It enclosed him. And there were iron laws of tradition and law on four sides. He was in a moving box.

As he perceived this fact, it occurred to him that he had never wished to come to the war. He had not enlisted of his free will. He had been dragged by the merciless government. And now they were taking him out to be slaughtered!

The regiment slid down a bank and wallowed across a little stream. The mournful current moved slowly on and from the water, shaded black, some white bubble-eyes looked at the men.

As they climbed the hill on the further side artillery began to boom. Here the youth forgot many things as he felt a sudden impulse of curiosity. He scrambled up the bank with a speed that could not be exceeded by a blood-thirsty man.

He expected a battle-scene.

There were some little fields girted and squeezed by a forest. Spread over the grass and in among the tree-trunks, he could see knots and waving lines of skirmishers who were running hither and thither and firing at the landscape. A dark battle-line lay upon a sun-struck clearing that gleamed orange-color. A flag fluttered.

Other regiments floundered up the bank. The brigade was formed in line of battle and, after a pause, started slowly through the woods in the rear of the receding skirmishers who were continually melting into the scene to appear again further on. They were always busy as bees, deeply absorbed in their little combats.

The youth tried to observe everything. He did not use care to avoid trees and branches, and his forgotten feet were constantly knocking against stones or getting entangled in briars. He was aware that these battalions, with their commotions, were woven red and startling into the gentle fabric of softened greens and browns. It looked to be a wrong place for a battle-field.

The skirmishers in advance fascinated him. Their shots into thickets and at distant and prominent trees spoke to him of tragedies, hidden, mysterious, solemn.

Once, the line encountered the body of a dead soldier. He lay upon his back staring at the sky. He was dressed in an awkward suit of yellowish brown. The youth could see that the soles of his shoes had been worn to the thinnest of writing-paper and from a great rent in one, the dead foot projected piteously. And it was as if fate had betrayed the soldier. In death, it exposed to his enemies that poverty which in life he had perhaps concealed from his friends.

The ranks opened covertly to avoid the corpse. The invulnerable dead man forced a way for himself. The youth looked keenly at the ashen face. The wind raised the tawny beard. It moved as if a hand were stroking it. He vaguely desired to walk around and around the body and stare; the impulse of the living to try to read in dead eyes the answer to the Question.

During this march, the ardor which the youth had acquired when out of view of the field rapidly faded to nothing. His curiosity was quite easily satisfied. If an intense scene had caught him with its wild swing as he came to the top of the bank he might have gone roaring on. This advance upon nature was too calm. He had opportunity to reflect. He had time in which to wonder about himself and to attempt to probe his sensations.

Absurd ideas took hold upon him. He thought that he did not relish the landscape. It threatened him. A coldness swept over his back and it is true that his trousers felt to him that they were no fit for his legs at all.

A house, standing placidly in distant fields had to him an ominous look. The shadows of the woods were formidable. He was certain that in this vista there lurked fierce-eyed hosts. The swift thought came to him that the generals did not know what they were about. It was all a trap. Suddenly those close forests would bristle with rifle-barrels. Iron-like brigades would appear in the rear. They were all going to be sacrificed. The generals were stupids. The enemy would presently swallow the whole command. He glared about him, expecting to see the stealthy approach of his death.

He thought that he must break from the ranks and harangue his comrades. They must not all be killed like pigs. And he was sure it would come to pass unless they were informed of these dangers.

The generals were idiots to send them marching into a regular pen. There was but one pair of eyes in the corps. He would step forth and make a speech. Shrill and passionate words came to his lips.

The line, broken into moving fragments by the ground went calmly on through fields and woods. The youth looked at the men nearest him and saw, for the most part, expressions of deep interest as if they were investigating something that had fascinated them. One or two stepped with over-valiant airs as if they were already plunged into war. Others walked as upon thin ice. The greater part of the untested men appeared quiet and absorbed. They were going to look at war, the red animal, war, the blood-swollen god. And they were deeply engrossed in this march.

As he looked, the youth gripped his out-cry at his throat. He saw that even if the men were tottering with fear, they would laugh at his warning. They would jeer him and if practicable pelt him with missiles. Admitting that he might be wrong, a frenzied declamation of the kind would turn him into a worm.

He assumed, then, the demeanor of one who knows that he is doomed, alone, to unwritten responsibilities. He lagged, with tragic glances at the sky.

He was surprised, presently, by the young lieutenant of his company who began heartily to beat him with a sword, calling out in a loud and insolent voice. "Come, young man, get up into ranks there. No skulking'll do here." He mended his pace with suitable haste. And he hated the lieutenant, who had no appreciation of fine minds. He was a mere brute.

After a time, the brigade was halted in the cathedral-light of a forest. The busy skirmishers were still popping. Through the aisles of the wood could be seen the floating smoke from their rifles. Sometimes it went up in little balls, white and compact.

During this halt, many men in the regiment began erecting tiny hills in front of them. They used stones, sticks, earth and anything they thought might turn a bullet. Some built comparatively large ones while others seemed content with little ones.

This procedure caused a discussion among the men. Some wished to fight like duellists, believing it to be correct to stand erect and be, from their feet to their fore-heads, a mark. They said they scorned the devices of the cautious. But the others scoffed in reply and pointed to the veterans on the flanks who were digging at the ground like terriers. In a short time there was quite a barricade along the regimental front. Directly however they were ordered to withdraw from that place.

This astounded the youth. He forgot his stewing over the advance movement. "Well, then, what did they march us out here fer?" he demanded of the tall soldier. The latter with calm faith began a heavy explanation although he had been compelled to leave a little protection of stones and dirt to which he had devoted much care and skill.

When the regiment was aligned in another position each man's regard for his safety caused another line of small intrenchments. They ate their noon meal behind a third one. They were moved from this one also. They were marched from place to place with apparent aimlessness.

The youth had been taught that a man became another thing in a battle. He saw his salvation in such a change. Hence this waiting was an ordeal to him. He was in a fever of impatience. He considered that there was denoted a lack of purpose on the part of the generals. He began to complain to the tall soldier. "I can't stand this much longer," he cried. "I don't see what good it does t' make us wear out'r legs fer nothin'." He wished to return to camp, knowing that this affair was a blue demonstration; or, else, to go into a battle and discover that he had been a fool in his doubts and was in truth a man of traditional courage. The strain of present circumstances he felt to be intolerable.

The philosophical tall soldier measured a sandwich of cracker and pork and swallowed it in a nonchalant manner. "Oh, I s'pose we must go reconnoiterin' around th' kentry jest t' keep'em from gittin' too clost, or t' develope'm,[6] or somethin'."

"Huh," said the loud soldier.

"Well," cried the youth, still fidgeting, "I'd rather do anythin' 'most than go trampin' 'round th' kentry all day doin' no good t' nobody an' jest tirin' ourselves out."

"So would I," said the loud soldier. "It aint right. I tell yeh if anybody with any sense was a-runnin' this army, it—"

"Oh, shut up," roared the tall private. "Yeh little fool. Yeh little damn'-fool-cuss. Yeh aint had that there coat an' them pants on fer six months yit an' yit yeh talk as if—"

"Well, I wanta do some fightin' anyway," interrupted the other; "I didn't come here t' walk. I could 'a walked t' home, 'round an' 'round th' barn, if I jest wanted t' walk."

The tall one, red-faced, swallowed another sandwich as if taking poison in despair.

But, gradually, as he chewed, his face became again quiet and contented. He could not rage in fierce argument in the presence of such sandwiches. During his meals, he always wore an air of blissful contemplation of the food he had swallowed. His spirit seemed then to be communing with the viands.

He accepted new environment and circumstance with great coolness, eating from his haversack at every opportunity. On the march he went along with the stride of a hunter, objecting to neither gait nor distance. And he had not raised his voice when he had been

6. I.e., learn the enemy's strength and position.

ordered away from three little protective piles of earth and stone, each of which had been an engineering feat worthy of being made sacred to the name of his grandmother.

In the afternoon, the regiment went out over the same ground it had taken in the morning. The landscape then ceased to threaten the youth. He had been close to it and become familiar with it.

When, however, they began to pass into a new region, his old fears of stupidity and incompetence re-assailed him but this time he doggedly let them babble. He was occupied with his problem and in his desperation he concluded that the stupidity affair did not greatly matter.

Once he thought that he had concluded that it would be better to get killed directly and end his troubles. Regarding death thus out of the corner of his eye, he conceived it to be nothing but rest and he was filled with a momentary astonishment that he should have made an extraordinary commotion over the mere matter of getting killed. He would die; he would go to some place where he would be understood. It was useless to expect appreciation of his profound and fine senses from such men as the lieutenant. He must look to the grave for comprehension.

The unceasing skirmish-fire increased to a long clattering sound. With it was mingled faraway cheering. A battery spoke.

Directly, the youth could see the skirmishers running. They were pursued by the sound of musketry fire. After a time, the hot danger-ous flashes of the rifles were visible. Smoke-clouds went slowly and insolently across the fields, like observant phantoms. The din became crescendo like the roar of an oncoming train.

A brigade ahead of them and on the right went into action with a rending roar. It was as if it had exploded. And, thereafter, it lay stretched in the distance behind a long grey wall that one was obliged to look twice at to make sure that it was smoke.

The youth, forgetting his neat plan of getting killed, gazed spell-bound. His eyes grew wide and busy with the action of the scene. His mouth was a little ways open.

Of a sudden, he felt a heavy and sad hand laid upon his shoulder. Awakening from his trance of observation, he turned and beheld the loud soldier.

"It's m' first an' last battle, ol' boy," said the latter, with intense gloom. He was quite pale and his girlish lip was trembling.

"Eh?" murmured the youth in great astonishment.

"It's m' first an' last battle, ol' boy," continued the loud soldier. "Somethin' tells me—"

"What?"

"—I'm a gone coon this first time an'—an' I w-want yeh t' take these here things—t'—my—folks." He ended in a quavering sob of pity for himself. He handed the youth a little packet done up in a yellow envelope.

"Why, what th' devil—" began the youth again.

But the other gave him a glance as from the depths of a tomb, waved his limp hand in a prophetic manner and turned away.

IV

The brigade was halted in the fringe of a grove. The men crouched among the trees and pointed their restless guns out at the fields. They tried to look beyond the smoke.

Out of this haze they could see running men. Some shouted information, and gestured, as they hurried.

The men of the new regiment watched and listened eagerly, while their tongues ran on in the gossip of the battle. They mouthed rumors that had flown like birds out of the unknown.

"They say Perrey has been driven in with big loss."

"Yes, Carrott went t' th' hospital. He said he was sick. That smart lieutenant is commanding 'G' Company. Th' boys say they won't be under Carrott no more if they all have t' desert. They allus knew he was a—"

"Hannises' bat'try is took."

"It aint either. I saw Hannises' bat'try off on th' left not more'n fifteen minutes ago."

"Well—"

"Th' general, he ses he is goin' t' take th' hull command of th' 304th when we go inteh action an' then he ses we'll do sech fightin' as never another one reg'ment done."

"Th' boys of th' 47th, they took a hull string of rifle-pits."

"It wasn't the 47th a 'tall. It was th' 99th Vermont."

"There haint nobody took no rifle-pits. Th' 47th driv a lot a Johnnies from behint a fence."

"Well—"

"They say we're catchin' it over on th' left. They say th' enemy driv' our line inteh a devil of a swamp an' took Hannises' bat'try."

"No sech thing. Hannises' bat'try was 'long here 'bout a minute ago."

"That young Hasbrouck, he makes a good off'cer. He aint afraid 'a nothin'."

"I met one of th' 148th Maine boys an' he ses his brigade fit th' hull rebel army fer four hours over on th' turnpike-road an' killed about five thousand of'em. He ses one more sech fight as that an' th' war'll be over."

"Bill wasn't scared either. No, sir. It wasn't that. Bill aint a-gittin' scared easy. He was jest mad, that's what he was. When that feller trod on his hand, he up an' sed that he was willin' t' give his hand t' his country but he be dumbed if he was goin' t' have every dumb bushwhacker in th' kentry walkin' 'round on it. So he went t' th' hospital disregardless of th' fight. Three fingers was crunched.

Th' dern doctor wanted t' amputate'm an' Bill, he raised a heluva row, I hear. He's a funny feller."

"Hear that what th' ol' colonel ses, boys. He ses he'll shoot th' first man what'll turn an' run."

"He'd better try it. I'd like t' see him shoot at *me*."

"He wants t' look fer his *own*self. *He* don't wanta go 'round talkin' big."

"They say Perrey's division's a-givin'em thunder."

"Ed Williams over in Company A, he ses th' rebs'll all drop their guns an' run an' holler if we onct giv'em one good lickin'."

"Oh, thunder, Ed Williams, what does he know? Ever since he got shot at on picket, he's been runnin' th' war."

"Well, he—"

"Hear th' news, boys? Corkright's crushed th' hull rebel right an' captured two hull divisions. We'll be back in winter quarters by a short cut t'-morrah."

"I tell yeh I've been all over that there kentry where th' rebel right is an' it's th' nastiest part th' rebel line. It's all mussed up with hills an' little damn creeks. I'll bet m'shirt Corkright never harmed'em down there."

"Well he's a fighter an' if they could be licked, he'd lick'em."[7]

• • •

The din in front swelled to a tremendous chorus. The youth and his fellows were frozen to silence. They could see a flag that tossed in the smoke angrily. Near it were the blurred and agitated forms of troops. There came a turbulent stream of men across the fields. A battery, changing position at a frantic gallop, scattered the stragglers right and left.

A shell, screaming like a storm-banshee, went over the huddled heads of the reserves. It landed in the grove and, exploding redly, flung the brown earth. There was a little shower of pine needles.

Bullets began to whistle among the branches and nip at the trees. Twigs and leaves came sailing down. It was as if a thousand axes, wee and invisible, were being wielded. Many of the men were constantly dodging and ducking their heads.

The lieutenant of the youth's company was shot in the hand. He began to swear so wondrously that a nervous laugh went along the regimental line. The officer's profanity sounded conventional. It relieved the tightened senses of the new men. It was as if he had hit his fingers with a tack-hammer at home.

He held the wounded member carefully away from his side, so that the blood would not drip upon his trousers.

The captain of the company, tucking his sword under his arm, produced a handkerchief and began to bind with it the lieutenant's wound. And they had a dispute as to how the binding should be done.

The battle-flag in the distance jerked about madly. It seemed to be struggling to free itself from an agony. The billowing smoke was filled with horizontal flashes.

Men running swiftly emerged from it. They grew in numbers until it was seen that the whole command was fleeing. The flag suddenly sank down as if dying. Its motion, as it fell, was a gesture of despair.

Wild yells came from behind the walls of smoke. A sketch in gray and red dissolved into a mob-like body of men who galloped like wild horses.

The veteran regiments on the right and left of the 304th immediately began to jeer. With the passionate song of the bullets and the banshee shrieks of shells were mingled loud cat-calls and bits of facetious advice concerning places of safety.

But the new regiment was breathless with horror.

"Gawd! Saunders's got crushed!" whispered the man at the youth's elbow. They shrank back and crouched, as if compelled to await a flood.

The youth shot a swift glance along the blue ranks of the regiment. The profiles were motionless, carven. And afterward he remembered that the color-sergeant[8] was standing with his legs braced apart, as if he expected to be pushed to the ground.

The bellowing throng went whirling around the flank. Here and there were officers carried along on the stream like exasperated chips. They were striking about them with their swords and, with their left fists, punching every head they could reach. They cursed like highwaymen.

A mounted officer displayed the furious anger of a spoiled child. He raged with his head, his arms and his legs.

Another, the commander of the brigade, was galloping about, bawling. His hat was gone and his clothes were awry. He resembled a man who has come from bed to go to a fire.

The hoofs of his horse often threatened the heads of the running men, but they scampered with singular good fortune. In this rush, they were apparently all deaf and blind. They heeded not the largest and longest of the oaths that were thrown at them from all directions.

Frequently, over this tumult, could be heard the grim jokes of the critical veterans, but the retreating men apparently were not even conscious of the presence of an audience.

The battle-reflection that shone for an instant in the faces on the mad current made the youth feel that forceful hands from Heaven would not have been able to have held him in place if he could have got intelligent control of his legs.

8. I.e., the flag-bearer.

There was an appalling imprint upon these faces. The struggle in the smoke had pictured an exaggeration of itself on the bleached cheeks and in the eyes, wild with one desire.

The sight of this stampede exerted a flood-like force that seemed able to drag sticks and stones and men from the ground. They of the reserves had to hold on. They grew pale and firm, and red and quaking.

The youth achieved one little thought in the midst of this chaos. The composite monster which had caused the other troops to flee had not then appeared. He resolved to get a view of it, and then, he thought, he might, very likely, run better than the best of them.

V

There were moments of waiting. The youth thought of the village street at home before the arrival of the circus-parade on a day in the spring. He remembered how he had stood, a small thrillful boy, prepared to follow the dingy lady upon the white horse or the band in its faded chariot. He saw the yellow road, the lines of expectant people, and the sober houses. He particularly remembered an old fellow who used to sit upon a cracker-box in front of the store and feign to despise such exhibitions. A thousand details of color and form surged in his mind. The old fellow upon the cracker-box appeared in middle prominence.

Some one cried: "Here they come!"

There was rustling and muttering among the men. They displayed a feverish desire to have every possible cartridge ready to their hands. The boxes were pulled around into various positions and adjusted with great care. It was as if seven hundred new bonnets were being tried on.

The tall soldier having prepared his rifle, produced a red handkerchief of some kind. He was engaged in knotting it about his throat, with exquisite attention to its position, when the cry was repeated up and down the line in a muffled roar of sound. "Here they come! Here they come!" Gun-locks clicked.

Across the smoke-infested fields came a brown swarm of running men who were giving shrill yells. They came on stooping and swinging their rifles at all angles. A flag tilted forward sped near the front.

As he caught sight of them, the youth was momentarily startled by a thought that perhaps his gun was not loaded. He stood trying to rally his faltering intellect so that he might recollect the moment when he had loaded. But he could not.

A hatless general pulled his dripping horse to a stand near the colonel of the 304th. He shook his fist in the other's face. "You've got t' hold'em back," he shouted savagely. "You've got t' hold'em back."

In his agitation, the colonel began to stammer. "A-all r-right, general, all right, by Gawd. We-we'll do our—we-we'll d-d-do—do our best, general." The general made a passionate gesture and galloped away. The colonel perchance to relieve his feelings, began to scold like a wet parrot. The youth turning swiftly to make sure that the rear was unmolested, saw the commander regarding his men in a highly resentful manner as if he regretted, above everything, his association with them.

The man at the youth's elbow was mumbling as if to himself: "Oh, we're in for it, now. Oh, we're in for it now."

The captain of the company had been pacing excitedly to and fro in the rear. He coaxed in school-mistress fashion as to a congregation of boys with primers. His talk was an endless repetition. "Reserve your fire, boys—dont shoot 'til I tell you—save your fire—wait 'til they get close up—don't be damned fools—"

Perspiration streamed down the youth's face which was soiled like that of a weeping urchin. He frequently with a nervous movement wiped his eyes with his coat-sleeve. His mouth was still a little ways open.

He got the one glance at the foe-swarming field in front of him and instantly ceased to debate the question of his piece being loaded. Before he was ready to begin, before he had announced to himself that he was about to fight, he threw the obedient, well-balanced rifle into position and fired a first wild shot. Directly, he was working at his weapon like an automatic affair.

He suddenly lost concern for himself and forgot to look at a menacing fate. He became not a man but a member. He felt that something of which he was a part—a regiment, an army, a cause, or a country—was in a crisis. He was welded into a common personality which was dominated by a single desire. For moments, he could not flee no more than a little finger can commit a revolution from a hand.

If he had thought the regiment about to be annihilated perhaps he could have amputated himself from it. But its noise gave him assurance. The regiment was like a fire-work that, once ignited, proceeds superior to circumstances until its blazing vitality fades. It wheezed and banged with a mighty power. He pictured the ground before it as strewn with the discomfited.

There was a consciousness always of the presence of his comrades about him. He felt the subtle battle-brotherhood more potent even than the cause for which they were fighting. It was a mysterious fraternity, born of the smoke and danger of death.

He was at a task. He was like a carpenter who has made many boxes, making still another box, only there was furious haste in his movements. He, in his thoughts, was careering off in other places, even as the carpenter who as he works, whistles and thinks of his friend or his enemy, his home or a saloon. And these jolted dreams were never perfect to him afterward but remained a mass of blurred shapes.

Presently he began to feel the effects of the war-atmosphere—a blistering sweat, a sensation that his eye-balls were about to crack like hot stones. A burning roar filled his ears.

Following this came a red rage. He developed the acute exasperation of a pestered animal, a well-meaning cow worried by dogs. He had a mad feeling against his rifle which could only be used against one life at a time. He wished to rush forward and strangle with his fingers. He craved a power that would enable him to make a world-sweeping gesture and brush all back. His impotency appeared to him and made his rage into that of a driven beast.

Buried in the smoke of many rifles, his anger was directed not so much against the men whom he knew were rushing toward him, as against the swirling battle-phantoms who were choking him, stuffing their smoke-robes down his parched throat. He fought frantically for respite for his senses, for air, as a babe, being smothered, attacks the deadly blankets.

There was a blare of heated rage, mingled with a certain expression of intentness on all faces. Many of the men were making low-toned noises with their mouths and these subdued cheers, snarls, imprecations, prayers, made a wild, barbaric song that went as an under-current of sound, strange and chant-like, with the resounding chords of the war-march. The man at the youth's elbow was babbling. In it there was something soft and tender, like the monologue of a babe. The tall soldier was swearing in a loud voice. From his lips came a black procession of curious oaths. Of a sudden another broke out in a querulous way like a man who has mislaid his hat. "Well, why don't they support us? Why don't they send supports? Do they think—"

The youth in his battle-sleep, heard this as one who dozes, hears.

There was a singular absence of heroic poses. The men bending and surging in their haste and rage were in every impossible attitude. The steel ram-rods clanked and clanged with incessant din as the men pounded them feverishly into the hot rifle-barrels. The flaps of the cartridge-boxes were all unfastened, and flapped and bobbed idiotically with each movement. The rifles, once loaded, were jerked to the shoulder and fired without apparent aim into the smoke or at one of the blurred and shifting forms which upon the field before the regiment had been growing larger and larger like puppets under a magician's hand.

The officers, at their intervals, rearward, neglected to stand in picturesque attitudes. They were bobbing to and fro, roaring directions and encouragements. The dimensions of their howls were extraordinary. They expended their lungs with prodigal wills. And often they near stood upon their heads in their anxiety to observe the enemy on the other side of the tumbling smoke.

The lieutenant of the youth's company had encountered a soldier who had fled, screaming, at the first volley of his comrades. Behind the lines, these two were acting a little isolated scene. The man was blubbering and staring with sheep-like eyes at the lieutenant who had seized him by the collar and was pummeling him. He drove him back into the ranks with many blows. The soldier went mechanically, dully, with his animal-like eyes upon the officer. Perhaps there was to him a divinity expressed in the voice of the other, stern, hard, with no reflection of fear in it. He tried to re-load his gun but his shaking hands prevented. The lieutenant was obliged to assist him.

The men dropped here and there like bundles. The captain of the youth's company had been killed in an early part of the action. His body lay stretched out in the position of a tired man, resting, but upon his face there was an astonished and sorrowful look as if he thought some friend had done him an ill turn. The babbling man was grazed by a shot that made the blood stream widely down his face. He clapped both hands to his head. "Oh," he said and ran. Another grunted suddenly as if he had been struck by a club in the stomach. He sat down and gazed ruefully. In his eyes there was mute, indefinite reproach. Further up the line a man, standing behind a tree, had had his knee-joint splintered by a ball. Immediately, he had dropped his rifle and gripped the tree with both arms. And there he remained, clinging desperately, and crying for assistance that he might withdraw his hold upon the tree.

At last, an exultant yell went along the quivering line. The firing dwindled from an uproar to a last vindictive popping. As the smoke slowly eddied away, the youth saw that the charge had been repulsed. The enemy were scattered into reluctant groups. He saw a man climb to the top of the fence, straddle the rail and fire a parting shot. The waves had receded, leaving bits of dark debris upon the ground.

Some in the regiment began to whoop frenziedly. Many were silent. Apparently, they were trying to contemplate themselves.

After the fever had left his veins, the youth thought that at last he was going to suffocate. He became aware of the foul atmosphere in which he had been struggling. He was grimy and dripping like a laborer in a foundry. He grasped his canteen and took a long swallow of the warmed water.

A sentence with variations went up and down the line. "Well, we've helt'em back. We've helt'em back—derned if we haven't." The men said it blissfully, leering at each other with dirty smiles.

The youth turned to look behind him and off to the right and off to the left. He experienced the joy of a man who at last finds leisure in which to look about him.

Under foot, there were a few ghastly forms, motionless. They lay twisted in fantastic contortions. Arms were bended and heads were turned in incredible ways. It seemed that the dead men must have fallen from some great height to get into such positions. They looked to be dumped out upon the ground from the sky.

From a position in the rear of the grove a battery was throwing shells over it. The flash of the guns startled the youth at first. He thought they were aimed directly at him. Through the trees, he watched the black figures of the gunners as they worked swiftly and intently. Their labor seemed a complicated thing. He wondered how they could remember its formulae in the midst of confusion.

The guns squatted in a row like savage chiefs. They argued with abrupt violence. It was a grim pow-wow. Their busy servants ran hither and thither.

A small procession of wounded men were going drearily toward the rear. It was a flow of blood from the torn body of the brigade.

To the right and to the left were the dark lines of other troops. Far in front, he thought he could see lighter masses protruding in points from the forest. They were suggestive of unnumbered thousands.

Once he saw a tiny battery go dashing along the line of the horizon. The tiny riders were beating the tiny horses.

From a sloping hill came the sound of cheerings and clashes. Smoke welled slowly through the leaves.

Batteries were speaking with thunderous oratorical effort. Here and there were flags, the red in the stripes dominating. They splashed bits of warm color upon the dark lines of troops.

The youth felt the old thrill at the sight of the emblems. They were like beautiful birds strangely undaunted in a storm.

As he listened to the din from the hill side, to a deep, pulsating thunder that came from afar to the left, and to the lesser clamors which came from many directions, it occurred to him that they were fighting too, over there and over there and over there. Heretofore, he had supposed that all the battle was directly under his nose.

As he gazed around him, the youth felt a flash of astonishment at the blue pure sky and the sun-gleamings on the trees and fields. It was surprising that nature had gone tranquilly on with her golden processes in the midst of so much devilment.

VI

The youth awakened slowly. He came gradually back to a position from which he could regard himself. For moments, he had been scrutinizing his person in a dazed way as if he had never before seen himself. Then he picked up his cap from the ground. He wriggled in his jacket to make a more comfortable fit and, kneeling, re-laced his shoe. He thoughtfully mopped his reeking features.

So it was all over at last. The supreme trial had been passed. The red, formidable difficulties of war had been vanquished.

He went into an ecstasy of self-satisfaction. He had the most delightful sensations of his life. Standing as if apart from himself, he viewed the last scene. He perceived that the man who had fought thus was magnificent.

He felt that he was a fine fellow. He saw himself even with those ideals which he had considered as far beyond him. He smiled in deep gratification.

Upon his fellows, he beamed tenderness and good-will. "Gee, aint it hot, hay?" he said affably to a man who was polishing his streaming face with his coat-sleeve.

"You bet," said the other, grinning sociably. "I never seen sech dumb hotness." He sprawled out luxuriously on the ground. "Gee, yes! An' I hope we don't have no more fightin' 'til—'til a week from Monday."

There were some hand-shakings and deep speeches with men whose features only were familiar but with whom the youth now felt the bonds of tied hearts. He helped a cursing comrade to bind up a wound of the shin.

But, of a sudden, cries of amazement broke out along the ranks of the new regiment. "Here they come a'gin! Here they come a'gin!" The man who had sprawled upon the ground, started up and said: "Gosh!"

The youth turned quick eyes upon the field. He discerned forms begin to swell in masses out of a distant wood. He again saw the tilted flag, speeding forward.

The shells, which had ceased to trouble the regiment for a time, came swirling again and exploded in the grass or among the leaves of the trees. They looked to be strange war-flowers bursting into fierce bloom.

The men groaned. The lustre faded from their eyes. Their smudged countenances now expressed a profound dejection. They moved their stiffened bodies slowly and watched in sullen mood the frantic approach of the enemy. The slaves toiling in the temple of this god began to feel rebellion at his harsh tasks.

They fretted and complained each to each. "Oh, say, this is too much of a good thing. Why cant somebody send us supports."

"We aint never goin' t' stand this second bangin'. I didn't come here t' fight th' hull damn' rebel army."

There was one who raised a doleful cry. "I wish Bill Smithers had trod on my hand insteader me treddin' on his'n."

The sore joints of the regiment creaked as it painfully floundered into position to repulse.

The youth stared. Surely, he thought, this impossible thing was not about to happen. He waited as if he expected the enemy to suddenly stop, apologize and retire, bowing. It was all a mistake.

But the firing began somewhere on the regimental line and ripped along in both directions. The level sheets of flame developed great clouds of smoke that tumbled and tossed in the mild wind near the ground for a moment and then rolled through the ranks as through a grate. The clouds were tinged an earth-like yellow in the sun-rays and, in the shadow were a sorry blue. The flag was sometimes eaten and lost in this mass of vapor but more often it projected, sun-touched, resplendent.

Into the youth's eyes there came a look that one can see in the orbs of a jaded horse. His back was quivering with nervous weakness and the muscles of his arms felt numb and bloodless. His hands, too, seemed large and awkward as if he was wearing invisible mittens. And there was a great uncertainty about his knee-joints.

The words that comrades had uttered previous to the firing began to appear to him. "Oh, say, this is too much of a good thing." "What do they take us fer—why don't they send supports." "I didn't come here to fight th' hull damned rebel army."

He began to exaggerate the endurance, the skill, and the valor of those who were coming. Himself reeling from exhaustion, he was astonished beyond measure at such persistency. They must be machines of steel. It was very gloomy, struggling against such affairs, wound up, perhaps, to fight until sun-down.

He slowly lifted his rifle and catching a glimpse of the thick-spread field he blazed at a cantering cluster. He stopped then and began to peer as best he could through the smoke. He caught changing views of the ground covered with men who were all running like pursued imps, and yelling.

To the youth, it was an onslaught of redoubtable dragons. He became like the man who lost his legs at the approach of the red and green monster. He waited in a sort of a horrified, listening attitude. He seemed to shut his eyes and wait to be gobbled.

A man near him who up to this time had been working feverishly at his rifle, suddenly dropped it and ran with howls. A lad whose face had borne an expression of exalted courage, the majesty of he who dares give his life, was, at an instant smitten abject. He blanched like one who has come to the edge of a cliff at midnight and is suddenly made aware. There was a revelation. He too threw down his gun and fled. There was no shame in his face. He ran like a rabbit.

Others began to scamper away through the smoke. The youth turned his head, shaken from his trance, by this movement as if the regiment was leaving him behind. He saw the few fleeting forms.

He yelled then with fright and swung about. For a moment, in the great clamor, he was like a proverbial chicken. He lost the direction of safety. Destruction threatened him from all points.

Directly he began to speed toward the rear in great leaps. His rifle and cap were gone. His unbuttoned coat bulged in the wind. The flap of his cartridge-box bobbed wildly and his canteen, by its slender cord, swung out behind. On his face was all the horror of those things which he imagined.

The lieutenant sprang forward, bawling. The youth saw his features, wrathfully red, and saw him make a dab with his sword. His one thought of the incident was that the lieutenant was a peculiar creature, to feel interested in such matters upon this occasion.

He ran like a blind man. Two or three times he fell down. Once he knocked his shoulder so heavily against a tree that he went head-long.

Since he had turned his back upon the fight, his fears had been wondrously magnified. Death about to thrust him between the shoulder-blades was far more dreadful than death about to smite him between the eyes. When he thought of it later, he conceived the impression that it is better to view the appalling than to be merely within hearing. The noises of the battle were like stones; he believed himself liable to be crushed.

As he ran on, he mingled with others. He dimly saw men on his right and on his left, and he heard footsteps behind him. He thought that all the regiment was fleeing, pursued by these ominous crashes.

In his flight, the sound of these following footsteps gave him his one meagre relief. He felt vaguely that death must make a first choice of the men who were nearest; the initial morsels for the dragons would be, then, those who were following him. So he displayed the zeal of an insane sprinter in his purpose to keep them in the rear. There was a race.

As he, leading, went across a little field, he found himself in a region of shells. They hurtled over his head with long wild screams. As he heard them, he imagined them to have rows of cruel teeth that grinned at him. Once, one lit before him and the livid lightning of the explosion effectually barred his way in his chosen direction. He groveled on the ground and then springing up went careering off through some bushes.

He experienced a thrill of amazement when he came within view of a battery in action. The men there seemed to be in conventional moods, altogether unaware of the impending annihilation. The battery was disputing with a distant antagonist and the gunners were wrapped in admiration of their shooting. They were continually bending in coaxing postures over the guns. They seemed to be patting them on the back and encouraging them with words. The guns stolid and undaunted, spoke with dogged valor.

The precise gunners were coolly enthusiastic. They lifted their eyes every chance to the smoke-wreathed hillock from whence the hostile battery addressed them. The youth pitied them as he ran. Methodical idiots! Machine-like fools! The refined joy of planting shells in the midst of the other battery's formation would appear a little thing when the infantry came swooping out of the woods.

The face of a youthful rider who was jerking his frantic horse with an abandon of temper he might display in a placid barn-yard was impressed deep upon his mind. He knew that he looked upon a man who would presently be dead.

Too, he felt a pity for the guns, standing, six good comrades, in a bold row.

He saw a brigade going to the relief of its pestered fellows. He scrambled upon a wee hill and watched it sweeping finely, keeping formation in difficult places. The blue of the line was crusted with steel-color and the brilliant flags projected. Officers were shouting.

This sight, also, filled him with wonder. The brigade was hurrying briskly to be gulped into the infernal mouth of the war-god. What manner of men were they, anyhow. Ah, it was some wondrous breed. Or else they didnt comprehend—the fools.

A furious order caused commotion in the artillery. An officer on a bounding horse made maniacal motions with his arms. The teams went swinging up from the rear, the guns were whirled about, and the battery scampered away. The cannon with their noses poked slantingly at the ground grunted and grumbled like stout men, brave but with objections to hurry.

The youth went on, moderating his pace since he had left the place of noises.

Later, he came upon a general of division seated upon a horse that pricked its ears in an interested way at the battle. There was a great gleaming of yellow and patent-leather about the saddle and bridle. The quiet man, astride, looked mouse-colored upon such a splendid charger.

A jingling staff was galloping hither and thither. Sometimes the general was surrounded by horsemen and at other times he was quite alone. He looked to be much harassed. He had the appearance of a business man whose market is swinging up and down.

The youth went slinking around this spot. He went as near as he dared trying to over-hear words. Perhaps the general, unable to comprehend chaos might call upon him for information. And he could tell him. He knew all concerning it. Of a surety the force was in a fix and any fool could see that if they did not retreat while they had opportunity—why—

He felt that he would like to thrash the general, or, at least, approach and tell him in plain words exactly what he thought him to be. It was criminal to stay calmly in one spot and make no effort to stay destruction. He loitered in a fever of eagerness for the division-commander to apply to him.

As he warily moved about, he heard the general call out irritably. "Thompkins, go over an' see Taylor an' tell him not t' be in such all-fired hurry—tell him t' halt his brigade in th' edge of th' woods —tell him t' detach a reg'ment—say I think th' centre'll break if we don't help it out some—tell him t' hurry up."

A slim youth on a fine chestnut horse caught these swift words from the mouth of his superior. He made his horse bound into a gallop almost from a walk in his haste to go upon his mission. There was a cloud of dust.

A moment later, the youth saw the general bounce excitedly in his saddle.

"Yes—by Heavens—they have!" The officer leaned forward. His face was a-flame with excitement. "Yes, by Heavens, they've held'im! They've held'im."

He began to blithely roar at his staff. "We'll wallop'im now. We'll wallop'im now. We've got'em sure." He turned suddenly upon an aide. "Here—you—Jones—quick—ride after Thompkins— see Taylor—tell him t' go in—everlastingly—like blazes—anything."

As another officer sped his horse after the first messenger, the general beamed upon the earth like a sun. In his eyes was a desire to chant a paean.[9] He kept repeating: "They've held'em, by Heavens."

His excitement made his horse plunge and he merrily kicked and swore at it. He held a little carnival of joy on horseback.

VII

The youth cringed as if discovered at a crime. By heavens, they had won after all. The imbecile line had remained and become victors. He could hear cheering.

He lifted himself upon his toes and looked in the direction of the fight. A yellow fog lay wallowing on the tree-tops. From beneath it came the clatter of musketry. Hoarse cries told of an advance.

He turned away, amazed and angry. He felt that he had been wronged.

He had fled, he told himself, because annihilation approached. He had done a good part in saving himself who was a little piece of the army. He had considered the time, he said, to be one in which it was the duty of every little piece to rescue itself if possible. Later, the officers could fit the little pieces together again and make a battle-front. If none of the little pieces were wise enough to save themselves from the flurry of death at such a time, why, then, where would be the army? It was all plain that he had proceeded according to very correct and commendable rules. His actions had been sagacious things. They had been full of strategy. They were the work of a master's legs.

Thoughts of his comrades came to him. The brittle blue line had withstood the blows and won. He grew bitter over it. It seemed that the blind ignorance and stupidity of those little pieces had betrayed him. He had been overturned and crushed by their lack of sense in holding the position, when intelligent deliberation would have convinced them that it was impossible. He, the enlightened man who

9. A song of joy, triumph, praise.

looks afar in the dark, had fled because of his superior perceptions and knowledge. He felt a great anger against his comrades. He knew it could be proven that they had been fools.

He wondered what they would remark when later he appeared in camp. His mind heard howls of derision. Their density would not enable them to understand his sharper point of view.

He began to pity himself acutely. He was ill-used. He was trodden beneath the feet of an iron injustice. He had proceeded with wisdom and from the most righteous motives under Heaven's blue only to be frustrated by hateful circumstances.

A dull, animal-like rebellion against his fellows, war in the abstract, and fate, grew within him. He shambled along with bowed head, his brain in a tumult of agony and despair. When he looked loweringly up, quivering at each sound, his eyes had the expression of those of a criminal who thinks his guilt little and his punishment great and knows that he can find no words; who, through his suffering, thinks that he peers into the core of things and sees that the judgment of man is thistle-down in wind.

He went from the fields into a thick woods as if resolved to bury himself. He wished to get out of hearing of the crackling shots which were to him like voices.

The ground was cluttered with vines and bushes and the trees grew close and spread out like bouquets. He was obliged to force his way with much noise. The creepers, catching against his legs, cried out harshly as their sprays were torn from the barks of trees. The swishing saplings tried to make known his presence to the world. He could not conciliate the forest. As he made his way, it was always calling out protestations. When he separated embraces of trees and vines, the disturbed foliages waved their arms and turned their face-leaves toward him. He dreaded lest these noisy motions, and cries, should bring men to look at him. So, he went far, seeking dark and intricate places.

After a time, the sound of musketry grew faint and the cannon boomed in the distance. The sun, suddenly apparent, blazed among the trees. The insects were making rhythmical noises. They seemed to be grinding their teeth in unison. A wood-pecker stuck his impudent head around the side of a tree. A bird flew on light-hearted wing.

Off, was the rumble of death. It seemed now that nature had no ears.

This landscape gave him assurance. A fair field, holding life. It was the religion of peace. It would die if its timid eyes were compelled to see blood. He conceived nature to be a woman with a deep aversion to tragedy.

He threw a pine-cone at a jovial squirrel and he ran with chattering fear. High in a tree-top, he stopped and, poking his head cautiously from behind a branch, looked down with an air of trepidation.

The youth felt triumphant at this exhibition. There was the law, he said. Nature had given him a sign. The squirrel immediately upon recognizing a danger, had taken to his legs, without ado. He did not stand stolidly, baring his furry belly to the missile, and die with an upward glance at the sympathetic heavens. On the contrary, he had fled as fast as his legs could carry him. And he was but an ordinary squirrel too; doubtless, no philosopher of his race.

The youth wended, feeling that nature was of his mind. She reinforced his arguments with proofs that lived where the sun shone.

Once he found himself almost into a swamp. He was obliged to walk upon bog-tufts and watch his feet to keep from the oily mire. Pausing at one time to look about him, he saw out at some black water, a small animal pounce in and emerge directly with a silver-gleaming fish.

The youth went again into the deep thickets. The brushed branches made a noise that drowned the sounds of cannon. He walked on, going from obscurity into promises of a greater obscurity.

At length, he reached a place where the high, arching boughs made a chapel. He softly pushed the green doors aside and entered. Pine-needles were a gentle brown carpet. There was a religious half-light.

Near the threshold, he stopped horror-stricken at the sight of a thing.

He was being looked at by a dead man who was seated with his back against a column-like tree. The corpse was dressed in a uniform that once had been blue but was now faded to a melancholy shade of green. The eyes, staring at the youth, had changed to the dull hue to be seen on the side of a dead fish. The mouth was opened. Its red had changed to an appalling yellow. Over the grey skin of the face ran little ants. One was trundling some sort of a bundle along the upper lip.

The youth gave a shriek as he confronted the thing. He was, for moments, turned to stone before it. He remained staring into the liquid-looking eyes. The dead man and the living man exchanged a long look. Then, the youth cautiously put one hand behind him and brought it against a tree. Leaning upon this, retreated, step by step, with his face still toward the thing. He feared, that if he turned his back, the body might spring up and stealthily pursue him.

The branches, pushing against him, threatened to throw him over upon it. His unguided feet, too, caught aggravatingly in brambles. And, with it all, he received a subtle suggestion to touch the corpse. As he thought of his hand upon it, he shuddered profoundly.

At last, he burst the bonds which had fastened him to the spot and fled, unheeding the underbrush. He was pursued by a sight of the black ants swarming greedily upon the grey face and venturing horribly near to the eyes.

After a time, he paused and, breathless and panting, listened. He imagined some strange voice would come from the dead throat and squawk after him in horrible menaces.

The trees about the portal of the chapel moved sighingly in a soft wind. A sad silence was upon the little, guarding edifice.

Again the youth was in despair. Nature no longer condoled with him. There was nothing, then, after all, in that demonstration she gave—the frightened squirrel fleeing aloft from the missile.

He thought as he remembered the small animal capturing the fish and the greedy ants feeding upon the flesh of the dead soldier, that there was given another law which far-over-topped it—all life existing upon death, eating ravenously, stuffing itself with the hopes of the dead.

And nature's processes were obliged to hurry[1]

.   .   .

VIII

The trees began softly to sing a hymn of twilight. The burnished sun sank until slanted bronze rays struck the forest. There was a lull in the noises of insects as if they had bowed their beaks and were making a devotional pause. There was silence save for the chanted chorus of the trees.

Then, upon this stillness, there suddenly broke a tremendous clangor of sounds. A crimson roar came from the distance.

The youth stopped. He was transfixed by this terrific medley of all noises. It was as if worlds were being rended. There was the ripping sound of musketry and the breaking crash of the artillery.

His mind flew in all directions. He conceived the two armies to be at each other panther-fashion. He listened for a time. Then he began to run in the direction of the battle. He saw that it was an ironical thing for him to be running thus toward that which he had been at such pains to avoid. But he said, in substance, to himself that if the earth and the moon were about to clash, many persons would doubtless plan to get upon roofs to witness the collision.

As he ran, he became aware that the forest had stopped its music, as if at last becoming capable of hearing the foreign sounds. The trees hushed and stood motionless. Everything seemed to be listening to the crackle and clatter and ear-shaking thunder. The chorus pealed over the still earth.

It suddenly occurred to the youth that the fight in which he had

---

1. The single page that completes this chapter is missing from the manuscript with a loss of perhaps 80 words.

been, was, after all, but perfunctory popping. In the hearing of this present din, he was doubtful if he had seen real battle-scenes. This uproar explained a celestial battle; it was tumbling hordes a-struggle in the air.

Reflecting, he saw a sort of a humor in the point of view of himself and his fellows during the late encounter. They had taken themselves and the enemy very seriously and had imagined that they were deciding the war. Individuals must have supposed that they were cutting the letters of their names deep into everlasting tablets of brass or enshrining their reputations forever in the hearts of their countrymen, while, as to fact, the affair would appear in printed reports under a meek and immaterial title. But he saw that it was good, else, he said, in battle everyone would surely run save forlorn hopes and their ilk.

He went rapidly on. He wished to come to the edge of the forest that he might peer out.

As he hastened, there passed through his mind pictures of stupendous conflicts. His accumulated thought upon such subjects was used to form scenes. The noise was as the voice of an eloquent being, describing.

Sometimes, the brambles formed chains and tried to hold him back. Trees, confronting him, stretched out their arms and forbade him to pass. After its previous hostility, this new resistance of the forest filled him with a fine bitterness. It seemed that nature could not be quite ready to kill him.

But he obstinately took roundabout ways and presently he was where he could see long grey walls of vapor, where lay battle-lines. The voices of cannon shook him. The musketry sounded in long irregular surges that played havoc with his ears. He stood, regardant, for a moment. His eyes had an awe-struck expression. He gawked in the direction of the fight.

Presently, he proceeded again on his forward way. The battle was like the grinding of an immense and terrible machine to him. Its complexities and powers, its grim processes, fascinated him. He must go close and see it produce corpses.

He came to a fence and clambered over it. On the far side, the ground was littered with clothes and guns. A newspaper, folded up, lay in the dirt. A dead soldier was stretched with his face hidden in his arm. Further off, there was a group of four or five corpses, keeping mournful company. A hot sun had blazed upon the spot.

In this place, the youth felt that he was an invader. This forgotten part of the battle-ground was owned by the dead men, and he hurried, in the vague apprehension that one of the swollen and ghastly forms would rise and tell him to begone.

He came finally to a road from which he could see in the distance, dark and agitated bodies of troops, smoke-fringed. In the lane, was a blood-stained crowd streaming to the rear. The wounded men were cursing, groaning and wailing. In the air, always, was a mighty swell of sound that it seemed could sway the earth. With the courageous words of the artillery and the spiteful sentences of the musketry was mingled red cheers. And from this region of noises came the steady current of the maimed.

One of the wounded men had a shoeful of blood. He hopped like a school-boy in a game. He was laughing hysterically.

One was swearing that he had been shot in the arm, through the commanding general's mismanagement of the army.

One was marching with an air imitative of some sublime drum-major. Upon his features was an unholy mixture of merriment and agony. As he marched he sang a bit of doggerel in a high and quavering voice.

> "Sing a song 'a vic'try
> A pocketful 'a bullets
> Five an' twenty dead men
> Baked in a-pie."

Parts of the procession limped and staggered to this tune.

Another had the grey seal of death already upon his face. His lips were curled in hard lines and his teeth were clenched. His hands were bloody from where he had pressed them upon his wound. He seemed to be awaiting the moment when he should pitch headlong. He stalked like the spectre of a soldier, his eyes burning with the power of a stare into the unknown.

There were some who proceeded sullenly, full of anger at their wounds and ready to turn upon anything as an obscure cause.

An officer was carried along by two privates. He was peevish. "Don't joggle so, Johnson, yeh fool," he cried. "Think m'leg is made of iron? If yeh can't carry me decent, put me down an' let some one else do it."

He bellowed at the tottering crowd who blocked the quick march of his bearers. "Say, make way there, can't yeh? Make way, dickens take it all."

They sulkily parted and went to the roadsides. As he was carried past, they made pert remarks to him. When he raged in reply and threatened them, they told him to be damned.

The shoulder of one of the tramping bearers knocked heavily against the spectral soldier who was staring into the unknown.

The youth joined this crowd and marched along with it. The torn bodies expressed the awful machinery in which the men had been entangled.

Orderlies and couriers occasionally broke through the throng in the roadway, scattering wounded men right and left, galloping on, followed by howls. The melancholy march was continually disturbed by the messengers and sometimes by bustling batteries that came swinging and thumping down upon them, the officers shouting orders to clear the way.

There was a tattered man, fouled with dust, blood and powder-stain from hair to shoes who trudged quietly at the youth's side. He was listening with eagerness and much humility to the lurid descriptions of a bearded sergeant. His lean features wore an expression of awe and admiration. He was like a listener in a country-store to wondrous tales told among the sugar-barrels. He eyed the story-teller with unspeakable wonder. His mouth was a-gape in yokel fashion.

The sergeant, taking note of this, gave pause to his elaborate history while he administered a sardonic comment. "Be keerful, honey, you'll be a-ketchin' flies," he said.

The tattered man shrank back, abashed.

After a time, he began to sidle near to the youth and in a diffident way, try to make him a friend. His voice was gentle as a girl's voice and his eyes were pleading. The youth saw with surprise that the soldier had two wounds, one in the head, bound with a blood-soaked rag and the other in the arm, making that member dangle like a broken bough.

After they had walked together for some time, the tattered man mustered sufficient courage to speak. "Was pretty good fight, wa'n't it?" he timidly said. The youth, deep in thought, glanced up at the bloody and grim figure with its lamb-like eyes. "What?"

"Was pretty good fight, wa'n't it?"

"Yes," said the youth shortly. He quickened his pace.

But the other hobbled industriously after him. There was an air of apology in his manner but he evidently thought that he needed only to talk for a time and the youth would perceive that he was a good fellow.

"Was pretty good fight, wa'n't it?" he began in a small voice. And then he achieved the fortitude to continue. "Dern me if I ever see fellers fight so. Laws, how they did fight. I knowed th' boys'd lick when they onct got square at it. Th' boys aint had no fair chanct up t' now, but, this time, they showed what they was. I knowed it'd turn out this way. Yeh can't lick them boys. No sir. They're fighters, they be."

He breathed a deep breath of humble admiration. He had looked at the youth for encouragement several times. He received none, but, gradually he seemed to get absorbed in his subject.

"I was talkin' 'cross pickets with a boy from Georgie, onct, an' that boy, he ses: 'Your fellers'll all run like hell when they onct hearn a gun,' he ses. 'Mebbe they will,' I ses 'but I don't b'lieve none of it,' I ses, 'an' b'jiminy,' I ses back t'um, 'mebbe your fellers'll all run like hell when they onct hearn a gun,' I ses. He larfed.

"Well, they didn't run t'day, did they, hey? No, sir. They fit an' fit an' fit."

His homely face was suffused with a light of love for the army which was to him all things beautiful and powerful.

After a time, he turned to the youth. "Where yeh hit, ol' boy," he asked in a brotherly tone.

The youth felt instant panic at this question although at first its full import was not borne in upon him.

"What?" he asked.

"Where yeh hit?" repeated the tattered man.

"Why," began the youth, "I—I—that is—why—I—"

He turned away suddenly and slid through the crowd. His brow was heavily flushed, and his fingers were picking nervously at one of his buttons. He bended his head and fastened his eyes studiously upon the button as if it were a little problem.

The tattered man looked after him in astonishment.

IX

The youth fell back in the procession until the tattered soldier was not in sight. Then he started to walk on with others.

But he was amid wounds. The mob of men was bleeding. Because of the tattered soldier's question, he now felt that his shame could be viewed. He was continually casting side-long glances to see if the men were contemplating the letters of guilt he felt burned into his brow.

At times, he regarded the wounded soldiers in an envious way. He conceived persons with torn bodies to be peculiarly happy. He wished that he, too, had a wound, a little red badge of courage.

The spectral soldier was at his side like a stalking reproach. The man's eyes were still fixed in a stare into the unknown. His grey, appalling face had attracted attention in the crowd and men, slowing to his dreary pace, were walking with him. They were discussing his plight, questioning him and giving him advice. In a dogged way, he repelled them, signing to them to go on and leave him alone. The shadows of his face were deepening and his tight lips seemed holding in check the moan of great despair. There could be seen a certain stiffness in the movements of his body as if he were taking infinite care not to arouse the passions of his wounds. As he went on, he seemed always looking for a place, like one who goes to choose a grave.

Something in the gesture of the man as he waved the bloody and pitying soldiers away, made the youth start as if bitten. He yelled in horror. Tottering forward, he laid a quivering hand upon the man's arm. As the latter slowly turned his wax-like features toward him, the youth screamed.

"Gawd! Jim Conklin!"

The tall soldier made a little common-place smile. "Hello, Henry," he said.

The youth swayed on his legs and glared strangely. He stuttered and stammered. "Oh, Jim—oh, Jim—oh, Jim—"

The tall soldier held out his gory hand. There was a curious, red and black combination of new blood and old blood upon it. "Where yeh been, Henry?" he asked. He continued in a monotonous voice. "I thought mebbe yeh got keeled over. There's been thunder t' pay t'day. I was worryin' about it a good deal."

The youth still lamented. "Oh, Jim—oh, Jim—oh, Jim—"

"Yeh know," said the tall soldier, "I was out there." He made a careful gesture. "An', Lord, what a circus. An', b'jiminy, I got shot —I got shot. Yes, b'jiminy, I got shot." He reiterated this fact in a bewildered way as if he did not know how it came about.

The youth put forth anxious arms to assist him but the tall soldier went firmly on as if propelled. Since the youth's arrival as a guardian for his friend, the other wounded men had ceased to display much interest. They occupied themselves again in dragging their tragedies toward the rear.

Suddenly, as the two friends marched on, the tall soldier seemed to be over-come by a terror. His face turned to a semblance of grey paste. He clutched the youth's arm and looked all about him, as if dreading to be over-heard. Then he began to speak in a shaking whisper.

"I tell yeh what I'm 'fraid of, Henry—I'll tell yeh what I'm 'fraid of. I'm 'fraid I'll fall down—an' then yeh know—them damned artillery wagons—they like as not'll run over me. That's what I'm 'fraid of—"

The youth cried out to him hysterically. "I'll take keer of yeh, Jim! I'll take keer of yeh! I swear t' Gawd I will."

"Sure—will yeh, Henry?" the tall soldier beseeched.

"Yes—yes—I tell yeh—I'll take keer of yeh, Jim," protested the youth. He could not speak accurately because of the gulpings in his throat.

But the tall soldier continued to beg in a lowly way. He now hung babe-like to the youth's arm. His eyes rolled in the wildness of his terror. "I was allus a good friend t' yeh, wa'n't I, Henry? I've allus been pretty good feller, aint I? An' it aint much t' ask, is it? Jest t' pull me along outer th' road? I'd do it fer you, wouldn't I, Henry?"

He paused in piteous anxiety to await his friend's reply.

The youth had reached an anguish where the sobs scorched him. He strove to express his loyalty but he could only make fantastic gestures.

However, the tall soldier seemed suddenly to forget all those fears. He became again the grim, stalking spectre of a soldier. He went stonily forward. The youth wished his friend to lean upon him but the other always shook his head and strangely protested. "No —no—no—leave me be—leave me be—"

His look was fixed again upon the unknown. He moved with mysterious purpose. And all of the youth's offers he brushed aside. "No —no—leave me be—leave me be—"

The youth had to follow.

Presently the latter heard a voice talking softly near his shoulder. Turning he saw that it belonged to the tattered soldier. "Ye'd better take'im outa th' road, pardner. There's a bat'try comin' helitywhoop down th' road an' he'll git runned over. He's a goner anyhow in about five minutes—yeh kin see that. Ye'd better take 'im outa th' road. Where th' blazes does he git his stren'th from?"

"Lord knows," cried the youth. He was shaking his hands helplessly.

He ran forward, presently, and grasped the tall soldier by the arm. "Jim! Jim!" he coaxed, "come with me."

The tall soldier weakly tried to wrench himself free. "Huh," he said vacantly. He stared at the youth for a moment. At last he spoke as if dimly comprehending.

"Oh! Inteh th' fields? Oh!"

He started blindly through the grass.

The youth turned once to look at the lashing riders and jouncing guns of the battery. He was startled from this view by a shrill outcry from the tattered man.

"Gawd! He's runnin'!"

Turning his head swiftly, the youth saw his friend running in a staggering and stumbling way toward a little clump of bushes. His heart seemed to wrench itself almost free from his body at this sight. He made a noise of pain. He and the tattered man began a pursuit. There was a singular race.

When he over-took the tall soldier, he began to plead with all the words he could find. "Jim—Jim—what are yeh doin'—what makes yeh do this way—yeh'll hurt yerself."

The same purpose was in the tall soldier's face. He protested in a dulled way, keeping his eyes fastened on the mystic place of his intentions. "No—no—don't tech me—leave me be—leave me be—"

The youth, aghast and filled with wonder at the tall soldier, began quaveringly to question him. "Where yeh goin', Jim? What yeh thinkin' about? Where yeh goin'? Tell me, won't yeh, Jim?"

The tall soldier faced about as upon relentless pursuers. In his eyes, there was a great appeal. "Leave me be, can't yeh? Leave me be fer a minnit."

The youth recoiled. "Why, Jim," he said, in a dazed way, "what's th' matter with yeh?"

The tall soldier turned and, lurching dangerously, went on. The youth and the tattered soldier followed, sneaking as if whipped, feeling unable to face the stricken man if he should again confront them. They began to have thoughts of a solemn ceremony. There was something rite-like in these movements of the doomed soldier.

And there was a resemblance in him to a devotee of a mad religion, blood-sucking, muscle-wrenching, bone-crushing. They could not understand; they were awed and afraid. They hung back lest he have at command, a dreadful weapon.

At last, they saw him stop and stand motionless. Hastening up, they perceived that his face wore an expression telling that he had at last found the place for which he had struggled. His spare figure was erect; his bloody hands were quietly at his sides. He was waiting with patience for something that he had come to meet. He was at the rendezvous. They paused and stood, expectant.

There was a silence.

Finally, the chest of the doomed soldier began to heave with a strained motion. It increased in violence until it was as if an animal was within and was kicking and tumbling furiously to be free.

This spectacle of gradual strangulation made the youth writhe and once as his friend rolled his eyes, he saw something in them that made him sink wailing to the ground. He raised his voice in a last, supreme call.

"Jim—Jim—Jim—"

The tall soldier opened his lips and spoke. He made a gesture. "Leave me be—don't tech me—leave me be—"

There was another silence, while he waited.

Suddenly, his form stiffened and straightened. Then it was shaken by a prolonged ague. He stared into space. To the two watchers, there was a curious and profound dignity in the firm lines of his awful face.

He was invaded by a creeping strangeness that slowly enveloped him. For a moment, the tremor of his legs caused him to dance a sort of hideous horn-pipe. His arms beat wildly about his head in expression of imp-like enthusiasm.

His tall figure stretched itself to its full height. There was a slight rending sound. Then it began to swing forward, slow and straight, in the manner of a falling tree. A swift muscular contortion made the left shoulder strike the ground first.

The body seemed to bounce a little way from the earth. "Gawd," said the tattered soldier.

The youth had watched, spell-bound, this ceremony at the place of meeting. His face had been twisted into an expression of every agony he had imagined for his friend.

He now sprang to his feet and, going closer, gazed upon the paste-like face. The mouth was open and the teeth showed in a laugh.

As the flap of the blue jacket fell away from the body, he could see that the side looked as if it had been chewed by wolves.

The youth turned, with sudden, livid rage, toward the battle-field. He shook his fist. He seemed about to deliver a philippic.[2]

2. A bitter verbal attack.

"Hell—"

The red sun was pasted in the sky like a fierce wafer.

X

The tattered man stood musing.

"Well, he was reg'lar jim-dandy fer nerve, wa'n't he," said he finally in a little awe-struck voice. "A reg'lar jim-dandy." He thoughtfully poked one of the docile hands with his foot. "I wonner where he got'is stren'th from? I never seen a man do like that before. It was a funny thing. Well, he was a reg'lar jim-dandy."

The youth desired to screech out his grief. He was stabbed. But his tongue lay dead in the tomb of his mouth. He threw himself again upon the ground and began to brood.

The tattered man stood musing.

"Look-a-here, pardner," he said, after a time. He regarded the corpse as he spoke. "He's up an' gone, aint'e, an' we might as well begin t' look out fer ol' number one. This here thing is all over. He's up an' gone, aint'e? An' he's all right here. Nobody won't bother'im. An' I must say I aint enjoyin' any great health m'self these days."

The youth, awakened by the tattered soldier's tone, looked quickly up. He saw that he was swinging uncertainly on his legs and that his face had turned to a shade of blue.

"Good Lord," he cried, in fear, "you aint goin' t'—not you, too."

The tattered man waved his hand. "Nary die," he said. "All I want is some pea-soup an' a good bed. Some pea-soup," he repeated dreamfully.

The youth arose from the ground. "I wonder where he came from. I left him over there." He pointed. "An' now I find'im here. An' he was comin' from over there, too." He indicated a new direction. They both turned toward the body as if to ask of it a question.

"Well," at length spoke the tattered man, "there aint no use in our stayin' here an' tryin' t' ask him anything."

The youth nodded an assent, wearily. They both turned to gaze for a moment at the corpse.

The youth murmured something.

"Well, he was a jim-dandy, wa'n't'e?" said the tattered man as if in response.

They turned their backs upon it and started away. For a time, they stole softly, treading with their toes. It remained laughing there in the grass.

"I'm commencin' t' feel pretty bad," said the tattered man, suddenly breaking one of his little silences. "I'm commencin' t' feel pretty damn' bad."

The youth groaned. "Oh, Lord!" Was he to be the tortured witness of another grim encounter?

But his companion waved his hand re-assuringly. "Oh, I'm not goin' t' die yit. There too much dependin' on me fer me t' die yit. No, sir! Nary die! I *can't*! Ye'd oughta see th' swad a' chil'ren I've got, an' all like that."

The youth glancing at his companion could see by the shadow of a smile that he was making some kind of fun.

As they plodded on, the tattered soldier continued to talk. "Besides, if I died, I wouldn't die th' way that feller did. That was th' funniest thing. I'd jest flop down, I would. I never seen a feller die th' way that feller did.

"Yeh know, Tom Jamison, he lives next door t' me up home. He's a nice feller, he is, an' we was allus good friends. Smart, too. Smart as a steel trap. Well, when we was a-fightin' this afternoon, all-of-a-sudden, he begin t' rip up an' cuss an' beller at me. 'Yer shot, yeh blamed, infernal, tooty-tooty-tooty-too,' (he swear horrible) he ses t'me. I put up m' hand t' m' head an' when I looked at m' fingers, I seen, sure-'nough, I was shot. I give a holler an' begin t' run but b'fore I could git away, another one hit me in th' arm an' whirl' me clean 'round. I got dumb skeared when they was all a-shootin' b'hind me an' I run t' beat all, but I cotch it pretty bad. I've an idee I'd a' been fightin' yit, if t'wa'n't fer Tom Jamison."

Then he made a calm announcement. "There's two of'em—little ones—but they're beginnin' t' have fun with me now. I don't b'lieve I kin walk much furder."

They went slowly on in silence. "Yeh look pretty peek-ed yerself," said the tattered man at last. "I bet yeh've gota worser one than yeh think. Ye'd better take keer of yer hurt. It don't do t'let sech things go. It might be inside, mostly, an' them plays thunder. Where is it located?" But he continued his harangue without waiting for a reply. "I see a feller git hit plum in th' head when my reg-'ment was a-standin' at ease onct. An' everybody yelled out t' 'im: 'Hurt, John? Are yeh hurt much?' 'No,' ses he. He looked kinder surprised an' he went on tellin' 'em how he felt. He sed he didn't feel nothin'. But, by dad, th' first thing that feller knowed he was dead. Yes, he was. Dead—stone dead. So, yeh wanta watch out. Yeh might have some queer kind 'a hurt yerself. Yeh can't never tell. Where is your'n located?"

The youth had been wriggling since the introduction of this topic. He now gave a cry of exasperation and made a furious motion with his hand. "Oh, don't bother me," he said. He was enraged against the tattered man and could have strangled him. Was his companion ever to play such an intolerable part? Was he ever going to up-raise the ghost of shame on the stick of his curiosity?[3] He

3. Almost the only significant bit of re-writing (as opposed to cutting) that Crane did between the manuscript and the first edition was an alteration of these two sentences. They appear in the first edition as "His companions seemed ever to play intolerable parts. They were ever upraising the ghost of shame on the stick of their curiosity."

turned toward him as a man at bay. "Now, don't bother me," he repeated with desperate menace.

"Well, Lord knows I don't wanta bother anybody," said the tattered man. There was a little accent of despair in his voice as he replied. "Lord knows I've gota 'nough m'own t' tend to."

The youth, who had been holding a bitter debate with himself and casting glances of hate and contempt at the tattered man, here spoke in a hard voice. "Good-bye," he said.

The tattered man looked at him in gaping amazement. "Why— why, pardner, where yeh goin','" he asked unsteadily. The youth, looking at him, could see that he, too, like that other one, was beginning to act dumb and animal-like. His thoughts seemed to be floundering about in his head. "Now—now—look-a-here you Tom Jamison—now—I won't have this—this here won't do. Where— where yeh goin'?"

The youth pointed vaguely. "Over there," he replied.

"Well, now, look-a-here—now—" said the tattered man, rambling on in idiot-fashion. His head was hanging forward and his words were slurred. "This thing won't do, now, Tom Jamison. It won't do. I know yeh, yeh pig-headed devil. Yeh wanta go trompin' off with a bad hurt. It aint right—now—Tom Jamison—it aint. Yeh wanta leave me take keer of yeh, Tom Jamison. It aint—right —it aint—fer yeh t' go—trompin' off—with a bad hurt—it aint— aint—aint right—it aint."

In reply, the youth climbed a fence and started away. He could hear the tattered man bleating plaintively.

Once, he faced about angrily. "What?"

"Look-a-here, now, Tom Jamison—now—it aint—"

The youth went on. Turning at a distance he saw the tattered man wandering about helplessly in the fields.

He now thought that he wished he was dead. He believed that he envied those men whose bodies lay strewn over the grass of the fields and on the fallen leaves of the forest.

The simple questions of the tattered man had been knife-thrusts to him. They asserted a society that probes pitilessly at secrets until all is apparent. His late companion's chance persistency made him feel that he could not keep his crime concealed in his bosom. It was sure to be brought plain by one of those arrows which cloud the air and are constantly pricking, discovering, proclaiming those things which are willed to be forever hidden. He admitted that he could not defend himself against this agency. It was not within human vigilance.

Promptly, then, his old rebellious feelings returned. He thought the powers of fate had combined to heap misfortune upon him. He was an innocent victim.

He rebelled against the source of things, according to a law, perchance, that the most powerful shall receive the most blame.

War, he said bitterly to the sky, was a make-shift created because ordinary processes could not furnish deaths enough. Man had been born wary of the grey skeleton and had expended much of his intellect in erecting whatever safe-guards were possible, so that he had long been rather strongly intrenched behind the mass of his inventions. He kept an eye on his bath-tub, his fire-engine, his life-boat, and compelled . . .[4] To seduce her victims, nature had to formulate a beautiful excuse. She made glory. This made the men willing, anxious, in haste, to come and be killed.

And, with heavy humor, he thought of how nature must smile when she saw the men come running. They regarding war-fire and courage as holy things did not see that nature had placed them in hearts because virtuous indignation would not last through a black struggle. Men would grow tired of it. They would go home.

They must be inspired by some sentiment that they could call sacred and enshrine in their heart, something that would cause them to regard slaughter as fine and go at it cheerfully; something that could destroy all the bindings of loves and places that tie men's hearts. She made glory.

From his pinnacle of wisdom, he regarded the armies as large collections of dupes. Nature's dupes, who were killing each other to carry out some great scheme of life. They were under the impression that they were fighting for principles and honor and homes and various things.

Well, to be sure; they were.

Nature was miraculously skillful in concocting excuses, he thought, with a heavy, theatrical contempt. It could deck a hideous creature in enticing apparel.

When he saw how she, as a woman beckons, had cozened him out of his home and hoodwinked him into wielding a rifle, he went into a rage.

He turned in tupenny fury upon the high, tranquil sky. He would have like to have splashed it with a derisive paint.

And he was bitter that among all men, he should be the only one sufficiently wise to understand these things.

XI

He became aware that the furnace-roar of the battle was growing louder. Great brown clouds had floated to the still heights of air before him. The noise, too, was approaching. The woods filtered men and the fields became dotted.

As he rounded a hillock, he perceived that the road-way was now a crying mass of wagons, teams and men. From the heaving tangle issued exhortations, commands, imprecations. Fear was sweeping it

---

4. The four pages of Henry's thoughts that completed Chapter X in the manuscript are missing. Here the previous draft supplies the ending in its earlier form.

all along. The cracking whips bit and horses plunged and tugged. The white-topped wagons strained and stumbled in their exertions like fat sheep.

The youth felt comforted in a measure by this sight. They were all retreating. Perhaps, then, he was not so bad after all. He seated himself and watched the terror-stricken wagons. They fled like soft, ungainly animals. All the roarers and lashers served to help him to magnify the dangers and horrors of the engagement that he might try to prove to himself that the thing with which men could charge him was in truth a symmetrical act. There was an amount of pleasure to him in watching the wild march of this vindication.

Presently, the calm head of a forward-going column of infantry appeared in the road. It came swiftly on. Avoiding the obstructions gave it the sinuous movement of a serpent. The men at the head butted mules with their musket-stocks. They prodded teamsters, indifferent to all howls. The men forced their way through parts of the dense mass by strength. The blunt head of the column pushed. The raving teamsters swore many strange oaths.

The commands to make way had the ring of a great importance in them. The men were going forward to the heart of the din. They were to confront the eager rush of the enemy. They felt the pride of their onward movement when the remainder of the army seemed trying to dribble down this road. They tumbled teams about with a fine feeling that it was no matter so long as their column got to the front in time. This importance made their faces grave and stern. And the backs of the officers were very rigid.

As the youth looked at them, the black weight of his woe returned to him. He felt that he was regarding a procession of chosen beings. The separation was as great to him as if they had marched with weapons of flame and banners of sun-light. He could never be like them. He could have wept in his longings.

He searched about in his mind then for an adequate malediction for the indefinite cause, the thing upon which men turn the words of final blame. It—whatever it was—was responsible for him, he said. There lay the fault.

The haste of the column to reach the battle seemed to the forlorn young man to be something much finer than stout fighting. Heroes, he thought, could find excuses in that long seething lane. They could retire with perfect self-respect and make excuses to the stars.

He wondered what those men had eaten that they could be in such haste to force their way to grim chances of death. As he watched his envy grew until he thought that he wished to change lives with one of them. He would have like to have used a tremendous force, he said, throw off himself and become a better. Swift pictures of himself, apart, yet in himself came to him—a blue desperate figure leading lurid charges with one knee forward and a broken blade high—a blue, determined figure standing before a crimson and steel assault, getting calmly killed on a high place before the eyes of all. He thought of the magnificent pathos of his dead body.

These thoughts up-lifted him. He felt the quiver of war-desire. In his ears, he heard the ring of victory. He knew the frenzy of a rapid successful charge. The music of the trampling feet, the sharp voices, the clanking arms of the column near him made him soar on the red wings of war. For a few moments, he was sublime.

He thought that he was about to start fleetly for the front. Indeed, he saw a picture of himself, dust-stained, haggard, panting, flying to the front at the proper moment to seize and throttle the dark, leering witch of calamity.

Then the difficulties of the thing began to drag at him. He hesitated, balancing awkwardly on one foot.

He had no rifle; he could not fight with his hands, said he, resentfully to his plan. Well, rifles could be had for the picking. They were extraordinarily profuse.

Also, he continued, it would be a miracle if he found his regiment. Well, he could fight with any regiment.

He started forward slowly. He stepped as if he expected to tread upon some explosive thing. Doubts and he were struggling.

He would truly be a worm if any of his comrades should see him returning thus, the marks of his flight upon him. There was a reply that the intent fighters did not care for what happened rear-ward saving that no hostile bayonets appeared there. In the battle-blur his face would, in a way, be hidden like the face of a cowled man.

But then, he said, that his tireless fate would bring forth, when the strife lulled for a moment, a man to ask of him an explanation. In imagination he felt the scrutiny of his companions as he painfully labored through some lies.

Eventually, his courage expended itself upon these objections. The debates drained him of his fire.

He was not cast-down by this defeat of his plan, for, upon studying the affair carefully, he could not but admit that the objections were very formidable.

Furthermore, various ailments had begun to cry out. In their presence, he could not persist in flying high with the red wings of war; they rendered it almost impossible for him to see himself in a heroic light. He tumbled headlong.

He discovered that he had a scorching thirst. His face was so dry and grimy that he thought he could feel his skin crackle. Each bone of his body had an ache in it and seemingly threatened to break with each movement. His feet were like two sores. Also, his body was calling for food. It was more powerful than a direct hunger. There was a dull, weight-like feeling in his stomach and when he tried to walk, his head swayed and he tottered. He could not see with distinctness. Small patches of crimson mist floated before his vision.

While he had been tossed by many emotions, he had not been aware of ailments. Now they beset him and made clamor. As he was at last compelled to pay attention to them, his capacity for self-hate was multiplied. In despair, he declared that he was not like those others. He now conceded it to be impossible that he should ever become a hero. He was a craven loon. Those pictures of glory were piteous things. He groaned from his heart and went staggering off.

A certain moth-like quality within him kept him in the vicinity of the battle. He had a great desire to see, and to get news. He wished to know who was winning.

He told himself that, despite his unprecedented suffering, he had never lost his greed for a victory, yet, he said, in a half-apologetic manner to his conscience, he could not but know that a defeat for the army this time might mean many favorable things for him. The blows of the enemy would splinter regiments into fragments. Thus, many men of courage, he considered, would be obliged to desert the colors and scurry like chickens. He would appear as one of them. They would be sullen brothers in distress and he could then easily believe he had not run any further or faster than they. And if he himself could believe in his virtuous perfection, he conceived that there would be small trouble in convincing all others.

He said, as if in excuse for this hope, that previously the army had encountered great defeats and in a few months had shaken off all blood and tradition of them, emerging as bright and valiant as a new one; thrusting out of sight the memory of disaster and appearing with the valor and confidence of unconquered legions. The shrilling voices of the people at home would pipe dismally for a time but various generals were usually compelled to listen to these sad ditties. He of course felt no compunctions for proposing a general as a sacrifice. He could not tell who the chosen for the barbs might be, so he could centre no direct sympathy upon him. The people were afar and he did not conceive public opinion to be accurate at long range. It was quite probable they would hit the wrong man who after he had recovered from his amazement would perhaps spend the rest of his days in writing replies to the songs of his alleged failure. It would be very unfortunate, no doubt, but in this case, a general was of no consequence to the youth.

In a defeat there would be a roundabout vindication of himself. He thought it would prove, in a manner, that he had fled early because of his superior powers of perception. A serious prophet, upon predicting a flood, should be the first man to climb a tree. This would demonstrate that he was indeed a seer.

A moral vindication was regarded by the youth as a very important thing. Without salve, he could not, he thought, wear the sore badge of his dishonor through life. With his heart continually assuring him that he was despicable, he could not exist without making it, through his actions, apparent to all men.

If the army had gone gloriously on, he would be lost. If the din meant that now his army's flags were tilted forward he was a condemned wretch. He would be compelled to doom himself to isolation. If the men were advancing, their indifferent feet were trampling upon his chances for a successful life.

As these thoughts went rapidly through his mind, he turned upon them and tried to thrust them away. He denounced himself as a villain. He said that he was the most unutterably selfish man in existence. His mind pictured the soldiers who would place their defiant bodies before the spear of the yelling battle-fiend and as he saw their dripping corpses on an imagined field, he said that he was their murderer.

Again he thought that he wished he was dead. He believed that he envied a corpse. Thinking of the slain, he achieved a great contempt for some of them as if they were guilty for thus becoming lifeless. They might have been killed by lucky chances, he said, before they had had opportunities to flee or before they had been really tested. Yet they would receive laurels from tradition. He cried out bitterly that their crowns were stolen and their robes of glorious memories were shams. However, he still said that it was a great pity he was not as they.

A defeat of the army had suggested itself to him as a means of escape from the consequences of his fall. He considered, now, however, that it was useless to think of such a possibility. His education had been that success for that mighty blue machine was certain; that it would make victories as a contrivance turns out buttons. He presently discarded all his speculations in the other direction. He returned to the creed of soldiers.

When he perceived again that it was not possible for the army to be defeated, he tried to be-think him of a fine tale which he could take back to his regiment and with it turn the expected shafts of derision.

But, as he mortally feared these shafts, it became impossible for him to invent a tale which he felt he could trust. He experimented with many schemes but threw them aside one by one as flimsy. He was quick to see vulnerable places in them all.

Furthermore, he was much afraid that some arrow of scorn might lay him mentally low before he could raise his protecting tale.

He imagined the whole regiment saying: "Where's Henry Fleming? He run, didn't'e? Oh, my!" He recalled various persons who would be quite sure to leave him no peace about it. They would doubtless question him with sneers and laugh at his stammering hesitation. In the next engagement they would try to keep watch of him to discover when he would run.

Wherever he went in camp, he would encounter insolent and lingeringly-cruel stares. As he imagined himself passing near a crowd of comrades, he could hear some one say: "There he goes!"

Then, as if the heads were moved by one muscle, all the faces were turned toward him with wide, derisive grins. He seemed to hear some one make a humorous remark in a low tone. At it, the others all crowed and cackled. He was a slang-phrase.

XII

It was always clear to the youth that he was entirely different from other men; that his mind had been cast in a unique mold. Hence laws that might be just to the ordinary man, were, when applied to him, peculiar and galling outrages. Minds, he said, were not made all with one stamp and colored green. He was of no general pattern. It was not right to measure his acts by a world-wide standard. The laws of the world were wrong because through the vain spectacles of their makers, he appeared, with all men, as of a common size and of a green color. There was no justice on the earth when justice was meant. Men were too puny and prattling to know anything of it. If there was a justice, it must be in the hands of a God.

He regarded his sufferings as unprecedented. No man had ever achieved such misery. There was a melancholy grandeur in the isolation of his experiences. He saw that he was a speck raising his minute arms against all possible forces and fates which were swelling down upon him in black tempests. He could derive some consolation from viewing the sublimity of the odds.

As he went on, he began to feel that nature, for her part, would not blame him for his rebellion. He still distinctly felt that he was arrayed against the universe but he believed now that there was no malice in the vast breasts of his space-filling foes. It was merely law, not merciful to the individual; but just, to a system. Nature had provided the creations with various defenses and ways of escape that they might fight or flee, and she had limited dangers in powers of attack and pursuit that the things might resist or hide with a security proportionate to their strength and wisdom. It was cruel but it was war. Nature fought for her system; individuals fought for liberty to breathe. The animals had the privilege of using their legs and their brains. It was all the same old philosophy. He could not omit a small grunt of satisfaction as he saw with what brilliancy he had reasoned it out.

He now said that, if, as he supposed, his life was being relentlessly pursued, it was not his duty to bow to the approaching death. Nature did not expect submission. On the contrary, it was his business to kick and bite and give blows as a stripling in the hands of a murderer. The law was that he should fight. He would be saved according to the importance of his strength.

His egotism made him feel safe, for a time, from the iron hands.

It being in his mind that he had solved these matters, he eagerly applied his findings to the incident of his flight from the battle. It was not a fault, a shameful thing; it was an act obedient to a law. It was—

But he was aware that when he had erected a vindicating structure of great principles, it was the calm toes of tradition that kicked it all down about his ears. He immediately antagonized then this devotion to the by-gone; this universal adoration of the past. From the bitter pinnacle of his wisdom he saw that mankind not only worshipped the gods of the ashes but that the gods of the ashes were worshipped because they were the gods of the ashes. He perceived with anger the present state of affairs in its bearing upon his case. And he resolved to reform it all.

He had, presently, a feeling that he was the growing prophet of a world-reconstruction. Far down in the untouched depths of his being, among the hidden currents of his soul, he saw born a voice. He conceived a new world modelled by the pain of his life, and in which no old shadows fell blighting upon the temple of thought. And there were many personal advantages in it.[5]

∙ ∙ ∙

He thought for a time of piercing orations starting multitudes and of books wrung from his heart. In the gloom of his misery, his eyesight proclaimed that mankind were bowing to wrong and ridiculous idols. He said that if some all-powerful joker should take them away in the night, and leave only manufactured shadows falling upon the bended heads, mankind would go on counting the hollow beads of their progress until the shriveling of the fingers. He was a-blaze with desire to change. He saw himself, a sun-lit figure upon a peak, pointing with true and unchangeable gesture. "There!" And all men could see and no man would falter.

Gradually the idea grew upon him that the cattle which cluttered the earth, would, in their ignorance and calm faith in the next day, blunder stolidly on and he would be beating his fists against the brass of accepted things. A remarkable facility for abuse came to him then and in supreme disgust and rage, he railed. To him there was something terrible and awesome in these words spoken from his heart to his heart. He was very tragic.[6]

∙ ∙ ∙

He saw himself chasing a thought-phantom across the sky before the assembled eyes of mankind. He could say to them that it was an angel whose possession was existence perfected; they would declare it to be a greased pig. He had no desire to devote his life to proclaiming the angel, when he could plainly perceive that mankind

5. A page of manuscript is missing at this point, and the two subsequent paragraphs are recovered from an early draft page.

6. Since the early draft does not supply all of what appeared on the manuscript page missing here, approximately 80 words have been lost at this point.

would hold, from generation to generation, to the theory of the greased pig.

It would be pleasure to reform a docile race. But he saw that there were none and he did not intend to raise his voice against the hooting of continents.

Thus he abandoned the world to its devices. He felt that many men must have so abandoned it, but he saw how they could be reconciled to it and agree to accept the stone idols and the greased pigs, when they contemplated the opportunities for plunder.

For himself, however, he saw no salve, no reconciling opportunities. He was entangled in the errors. He began to rage anew against circumstances which he did not name and against processes of which he knew only the name. He felt that he was being grinded beneath stone feet which he despised. The detached bits of truth which formed the knowledge of the world could not save him. There was a dreadful, unwritten martyrdom in his state.

He made a little search for some thing upon which to concentrate the hate of his despair; he fumbled in his mangled intellect to find the Great Responsibility.

He again hit upon nature. He again saw her grim dogs upon his trail. They were unswerving, merciless and would overtake him at the appointed time. His mind pictured the death of Jim Conklin and in the scene, he saw the shadows of his fate. Dread words had been said from star to star. An event had been penned by the implacable forces.

He was of the unfit, then. He did not come into the scheme of further life. His tiny part had been done and he must go. There was no room for him. On all the vast lands there was not a foot-hold. He must be thrust out to make room for the more important.

Regarding himself as one of the unfit, he believed that nothing could exceed for misery, a perception of this fact. He thought that he measured with his falling heart, tossed in like a pebble by his supreme and awful foe, the most profound depths of pain. It was a barbarous process with affection for the man and the oak, and no sympathy for the rabbit and the weed. He thought of his own capacity for pity and there was an infinite irony in it.

He desired to revenge himself upon the universe. Feeling in his body all spears of pain, he would have capsized, if possible, the world and made chaos. Much cruelty lay in the fact that he was a babe.

Admitting that he was powerless and at the will of law, he yet planned to escape; menaced by fatality he schemed to avoid it. He thought of various places in the world where he imagined that he would be safe. He remembered hiding once in an empty flour-barrel that sat in his mother's pantry. His playmates, hunting the bandit-chief, had thundered on the barrel with their fierce sticks but he had lain snug and undetected. They had searched the house. He now created in thought a secure spot where an all-powerful eye would fail to perceive him; where an all-powerful stick would fail to bruise his life.

There was in him a creed of freedom which no contemplation of inexorable law could destroy. He saw himself living in watchfulness, frustrating the plans of the unchangeable, making of fate a fool. He had ways, he thought, of working out his[7]

* * *

XIII

The column that had butted stoutly at the obstacles in the road-way was barely out of the youth's sight before he saw dark waves of men come sweeping out of the woods and down through the fields. He knew at once that the steel fibres had been washed from their hearts. They were bursting from their coats and their equipments as from entanglements. They charged down upon him like terrified buffaloes.

Behind them, blue smoke curled and clouded above the tree-tops and through the thickets he could sometimes see a distant pink glare. The voices of the cannon were clamoring in interminable chorus.

The youth was horror-stricken. He stared in agony and amaze-ment. He forgot that he was engaged in combating the universe. He threw aside his mental pamphlets on the philosophy of the retreated and rules for the guidance of the doomed. He lost concern for himself.

The fight was lost. The dragons were coming with invincible strides. The army, helpless in the matted thickets, and blinded by the overhanging night, was going to be swallowed. War, the red animal, war, the blood-swollen god, would have bloated fill.

Within him, something bade to cry out. He had the impulse to make a rallying speech, to sing a battle-hymn but he could only get his tongue to call into the air: "Why—why—what—what's th' matter?"

Soon he was in the midst of them. They were leaping and scamp-ering all about him. Their blanched faces shone in the dusk. They seemed, for the most part, to be very burly men. The youth turned from one to another of them as they galloped along. His incoherent questions were lost. They were heedless of his appeals. They did not seem to see him.

They sometimes gabbled insanely. One huge man was asking of the sky: "Say, where de plank-road? Where de plank-road." It was as if he had lost a child. He wept in his pain and dismay.

Presently, men were running hither and thither, in all ways. The artillery booming, forward, rearward, and on the flanks made jumble

7. The final page of Chapter XII has been lost, and there is no indication of how much text appeared on that page.

of ideas of direction. Landmarks had vanished into the gathered gloom. The youth began to imagine that he had gotten into the centre of the tremendous quarrel and he could perceive no way out of it. From the mouths of the fleeing men came a thousand wild questions but no one made answers.

The youth, after rushing about and throwing interrogations at the heedless bands of retreating infantry, finally clutched a man by the arm. They swung around face to face.

"Why—why—" stammered the youth struggling with his balking tongue.

The man screamed. "Letgo me! Letgo me!" His face was livid and his eyes were rolling uncontrolled. He was heaving and panting. He still grasped his rifle, perhaps having forgotten to release his hold upon it. He tugged frantically and the youth being compelled to lean forward was dragged several paces.

"Letgo me! Letgo me!"

"Why—why—" stuttered the youth.

"Well, then—" bawled the man in a lurid rage. He adroitly and fiercely swung his rifle. It crushed upon the youth's head. The man ran on.

The youth's fingers had turned to paste upon the other's arm. The energy was smitten from his muscles. He saw the flaming wings of lightning flash before his vision. There was a deafening rumble of thunder within his head.

Suddenly his legs seemed to die. He sank writhing to the ground. He tried to arise. In his efforts against the numbing pain he was like a man wrestling with a creature of the air.

There was a sinister struggle.

Sometimes, he would achieve a position half-erect, battle with the air for a moment, and then fall again, grabbing at the grass. His face was of a clammy pallor. Deep groans were wrenched from him.

At last, with a twisting movement, he got upon his hands and knees and from thence, like a babe trying to walk, to his feet. Pressing his hands to his temples, he went lurching over the grass.

He fought an intense battle with his body. His dulled senses wished him to swoon and he opposed them stubbornly, his mind portraying unknown dangers and mutilations if he should fall upon the field. He went, tall soldier-fashion. He imagined secluded spots where he could fall and be unmolested. To reach one, he strove against the tide of his pain.

Once, he put his hand to the top of his head and timidly touched the wound. The scratching pain of the contact made him draw a long breath through his clenched teeth. His fingers were dabbled with blood. He regarded them with a fixed stare.

Around him, he could hear the grumble of jolted cannon as the scurrying horses were lashed toward the front. Once, a young officer on a be-splashed charger nearly ran him down. He turned and watched the mass of guns, men and horses sweeping in a wide curve toward a gap in a fence. The officer was making excited motions with a gauntleted hand. The guns followed the teams with an air of unwillingness—of being dragged by the heels.

Some officers of the scattered infantry were cursing and railing like fish-wives. Their scolding voices could be heard above the din. Into the unspeakable jumble in the road-way, rode a squadron of cavalry. The faded yellow of their facings shone bravely. There was a mighty altercation.

The artillery were assembling as if for a conference.

The blue haze of evening was upon the fields. The lines of forest were long purple shadows. One cloud lay along the western sky partly smothering the red.

As the youth left the scene behind him, he heard the guns suddenly roar out. He imagined them shaking in black rage. They belched and roared like brass devils guarding a gate. The soft air was filled with the tremendous remonstrance. With it came the shattering peal of opposing infantry. Turning to look behind him, he could see sheets of orange light illumine the shadowy distance. There were subtle and sudden lightnings in the far air. At times, he thought he could see heaving masses of men.

He hurried on in the dusk. The day had faded until he could barely distinguish place for his feet. The purple darkness was filled with men who lectured and jabbered. Sometimes, he could see them gesticulating against the blue and sombre sky. There seemed to be a great ruck of men and munitions spread about in the forest and in the fields. The little narrow road-way now lay, lifeless. There were over-turned wagons like sun-dried boulders. The bed of the former torrent was choked with the bodies of horses and splintered parts of war-machines.

It had come to pass that his wound pained him but little. He was afraid to move rapidly, however, for a dread of disturbing it. He held his head very still and took many precautions against stumbling. He was filled with anxiety and his face was pinched and drawn in anticipation of the pain of any sudden mistake of his feet in the gloom.

His thoughts, as he walked, fixed intently upon his hurt. There was a cool, liquid feeling about it and he imagined blood moving slowly down under his hair. His head seemed swollen to a size that made him think his neck to be inadequate.

The new silence of his wound made much worriment. The little, blistering voices of pain that had called out from his scalp, were, he thought, definite in their expression of danger. By them, he believed that he could measure his plight. But when they remained ominously silent, he became frightened and imagined terrible fingers that clutched into his brain.

Amidst it, he began to reflect upon various incidents and conditions of the past. He bethought him of certain meals his mother had cooked at home, in which those dishes of which he was particularly fond had occupied prominent positions. He saw the spread table. The pine walls of the kitchen were glowing in the warm light from the stove. Too, he remembered how he and his companions used to go from the school-house to the bank of a shaded pool. He saw his clothes in disorderly array upon the grass of the bank. He felt the swash of the fragrant water upon his body. The leaves of the over-hanging maple rustled with melody in the wind of youthful summer.

He was over-come presently by a dragging weariness. His head hung forward and his shoulders were stooped as if he were bearing a great bundle. His feet shuffled along the ground.

He held continuous arguments as to whether he should lie down and sleep at some near spot, or force himself on until he reached a certain haven. He often tried to dismiss the question but his body persisted in rebellion and his senses nagged at him like pampered babies.

At last, he heard a cheery voice near his shoulder. "Yeh seem t' be in a pretty bad way, boy?"

The youth did not look up but he assented with thick tongue. "Uh."

The owner of the cheery voice took him firmly by the arm. "Well," he said, with a round laugh, "I'm goin' your way. Th' hull gang is goin' your way. An' I guess I kin give yeh a lift." They began to walk like a drunken man and his friend.

As they went along, the man questioned the youth and assisted him with the replies like one manipulating the mind of a child. Sometimes he interjected anecdotes. "What reg'ment do yeh b'long teh? Eh? What's that? Th' 304th N'York? Why, what corps is that in? Oh, it is? Why, I thought they wasn't engaged t'-day—they're 'way over in th' centre. Oh, they was, eh? Well, pretty nearly everybody got their share 'a fightin' t'-day. By dad, I give myself up fer dead any number 'a times. There was shootin' here an' shootin' there, an' hollerin' here an' hollerin' there, in th' damn' darkness, until I couldn't tell t' save m' soul which side I was on. Sometimes I thought I was sure-'nough from Ohier an' other times I could 'a swore I was from th' bitter end of Florida. It was th' most mixed up dern thing I ever see. An' these here hull woods is a reg'lar mess. It'll be a miracle if we find our reg'ments t'-night. Pretty soon, though, we'll meet a-plenty of guards an' provost-guards an' one thing an' another. Ho, there they go with an off'cer, I guess. Look at his hand a-draggin'. He's got all th' war he wants, I bet. He won't be talkin' so big about his reputation an' all, when they go t' sawin' off his leg. Poor feller. My brother's got whiskers jest that color. How did yeh git 'way over here anyhow? Your reg'ment is a long way from here, aint it? Well, I guess we can find it. Yeh know, there was a boy killed in my comp'ny t'-day that I thought th' world an' all of. Jack was a nice feller. By ginger, it hurt like thunder t' see ol' Jack jest git knocked flat. We was a-standin' purty peaceable fer a spell, 'though there was men runnin' ev'ry way all 'round us, an' while we was a-standin' like that, 'long come a big fat feller. He began t' peck at Jack's elbow an' he ses: 'Say, where's th' road t' th' river?' An' Jack, he never paid no attention an' th' feller kept on a-peckin' at his elbow an' sayin': 'Say, where's th' road t' th' river?' Jack was a-lookin' ahead all th' time tryin' t' see th' Johnnies comin' through th' woods an' he never paid no attention t' this big fat feller fer a long time but at last he turned 'round an' he ses: 'Ah, go t' hell an' find th' road t' th' river.' An' jest then a shot slapped him bang on th' side th' head. He was a sergeant, too. Them was his last words. Thunder, I wish we was sure 'a findin' our reg'ments t'-night. It's goin' t' be long huntin'. But I guess we kin do it."

In the search which followed, the man of the cheery voice seemed, to the youth, to possess a wand of a magic kind. He threaded the mazes of the tangled forest with a strange fortune. In encounters with guards and patrols he displayed the keenness of a detective and the valor of a gamin.[8] Obstacles fell before him and became of assistance. The youth with his chin still on his breast stood woodenly by while his companion beat ways and means out of sullen things.

The forest seemed a vast hive of men buzzing about in frantic circles but the cheery man conducted the youth without mistakes, until at last he began to chuckle with glee and self-satisfaction. "Ah, there yeh are! See that fire!"

The youth nodded stupidly.

"Well, there's where your reg'ment is. An', now, good-bye, ol' boy, good luck t' yeh."

A warm and strong hand clasped the youth's languid fingers for an instant, and then he heard a cheerful and audacious whistling, as the man strided away. As he who so be-friended him was thus passing out of his life, it suddenly occurred to the youth that he had not once seen his face.

XIV

The youth went slowly toward the fire indicated by his departed friend. As he reeled, he bethought him of the welcome his comrades would give him. He had a conviction that he would soon feel in his sore heart the barbed missiles of ridicule. He had no strength to invent a tale; he would be a soft target.

He made vague plans to go off into the deeper darkness and hide, but they were all destroyed by the voices of exhaustion and pain

---

8. A neglected street urchin who has acquired an intuitive wisdom for survival.

from his body. His ailments, clamoring, forced him to seek the place of food and rest, at whatever cost.

He swung unsteadily toward the fire. He could see the forms of men throwing black shadows in the red light and as he went nearer, it became known to him in some way, that the ground was strewn with sleeping men.

Of a sudden, he confronted a black and monstrous figure. A rifle-barrel caught some glinting beams. "Halt—halt." He was dismayed for a moment but he presently thought that he recognized the nervous voice. As he stood tottering before the rifle-barrel, he called out: "Why, hello, Wilson, you—you here?"

The rifle was lowered to a position of caution and Wilson came slowly forward. He peered into the youth's face. "That you, Henry?"

"Yes, it's—it's me."

"Well, well, ol' boy," said the other, "by ginger, I'm glad t' see yeh. I give yeh up fer a goner. I thought yeh was dead sure-enough." There was husky emotion in his voice.

The youth found that now he could barely stand upon his feet. There was a sudden sinking of his forces. He thought he must hasten to produce his tale to protect him from the missiles already at the lips of his redoubtable comrade. So staggering before the loud soldier he began. "Yes, yes. I've—I've had an awful time. I've been all over. 'Way over on th' right. Ter'ble fightin' over there. I had an awful time. I got separated from th' reg'ment. Over on th' right, I got shot. In th' head. I never see sech fightin'. Awful time. I don't see how I could 'a got separated from th' reg'ment. I got shot, too."

His friend had stepped forward quickly. "What? Got shot? Why didn't yeh say so first? Poor ol' boy, we must—hol' on a minnit; what am I doin'. I'll call Simpson."

Another figure at that moment loomed in the gloom. They could see that it was the corporal. "Who yeh talkin' to, Wilson?" he demanded. His voice was anger-toned. "Who yeh talkin' to? Yer th' derndest sentinel—why—hello, Henry, you here? Why, I thought you was dead four hours ago. Great Jerusalem, they keep turnin' up every ten minutes or so. We thought we'd lost forty-two men by straight count but if they keep on a-comin' this way, we'll git th' comp'ny all back by mornin' yit—where was yeh?"

"Over on th' right. I got separated—" began the youth with considerable glibness.

But his friend had interrupted hastily. "Yes, an' he got shot in th' head an' he's in a fix an' we must see t' him right away." He rested his rifle in the hollow of his left arm and his right around the youth's shoulder.

"Gee, it must hurt like thunder," he said.

The youth leaned heavily upon his friend. "Yes, it hurts—hurts a good deal," he replied. There was a faltering in his voice.

"Oh," said the corporal. He linked his arm in the youth's and drew him forward. "Come on, Henry. I'll take keer 'a yeh."

As they went on together, the loud private called out after them. "Put'im t' sleep in my blanket, Simpson. An'—hol' on a minnit—here's my canteen. It's full 'a coffee. Look at his head by th' fire an' see how it looks. Maybe it's a pretty bad un. When I git relieved in a couple 'a minnits, I'll be over an' see t' him."

The youth's senses were so deadened that his friend's voice sounded from afar and he could scarcely feel the pressure of the corporal's arm. He submitted passively to the latter's directing strength. His head was in the old manner hanging forward upon his breast. His knees wobbled.

The corporal led him into the glare of the fire. "Now, Henry," he said, "let's have look at yer ol' head."

The youth sat down obediently and the corporal, laying down his rifle began to fumble in the bushy hair of his comrade. He was obliged to turn the other's head so that the full flush of the fire-light would beam upon it. He puckered his mouth with a critical air. He drew back his lips and whistled through his teeth when his fingers came in contact with the splashed blood and the rare wound.

"Ah, here we are," he said. He awkwardly made further investigations. "Jest as I thought," he added, presently. "Yeh've been grazed by a ball. It's raised a queer lump jest as if some feller had lammed yeh on th' head with a club. It stopped a-bleedin' long time ago. Th' most about it is that in th' mornin', yeh'll feel that a number-ten hat wouldn't fit yeh. An' your head'll be all het up an' feel as dry as burnt pork. An' yeh may git a lot 'a other sicknesses, too, by mornin'. Yeh can't never tell. Still, I don't much think so. It's jest a damn' good belt on th' head an' nothin' more. Now, you jest sit here an' don't move, while I go rout out th' relief. Then I'll send Wilson t' take keer 'a yeh."

The corporal went away. The youth remained on the ground like a parcel. He stared with a vacant look into the fire.

After a time, he aroused, for some part, and the things about him began to take form. He saw that ground in the deep shadows was cluttered with men, sprawling in every conceivable posture. Glancing narrowly into the more distant darkness, he caught occasional glimpses of visages that loomed pallid and ghostly, lit with a phosphorescent glow. These faces expressed in their lines the deep stupor of the tired soldiers. They made them appear like men drunk with wine. This bit of forest might have appeared to an ethereal wanderer as a scene of the result of some frightful debauch.

On the other side of the fire, the youth observed an officer asleep, seated bolt up-right with his back against a tree. There was something perilous in his position. Badgered by dreams, perhaps, he swayed with little bounces and starts like an old, toddy-stricken grandfather in a chimney corner. Dust and stains were upon his face. His lower jaw hung down as if lacking strength to assume its normal position. He was the picture of an exhausted soldier after a feast of war.

He had evidently gone to sleep with his sword in his arms. These two had slumbered in an embrace. But the weapon had been allowed, in time, to fall unheeded to the ground. The brass-mounted hilt lay in contact with some parts of the fire.

Within the gleam of rose and orange light from the burning sticks were other soldiers, snoring and heaving, or lying death-like in slumber. A few pairs of legs were stuck forth, rigid and straight. The shoes displayed the mud or dust of marches, and bits of rounded trousers, protruding from the blankets, showed rents and tears from hurried pitchings through the dense brambles.

The fire crackled musically. From it swelled light smoke. Overhead, the foliage moved softly. The leaves with their faces turned toward the blaze, were colored shifting hues of silver, often edged with red. Far off to the right, through a window in the forest could be seen a handful of stars laying, like glittering pebbles, on the black level of the night.

Occasionally, in this low-arched hall, a soldier would arouse and turn his body to a new position, the experience of his sleep having taught him of uneven and objectionable places upon the ground under him. Or, perhaps, he would lift himself to a sitting posture, blink at the fire for an unintelligent moment, throw a swift glance at his prostrate companion and then cuddle down again with a grunt of sleepy content.

The youth sat in a forlorn heap until his friend, the loud young soldier, came, swinging two canteens by their light strings. "Well, now, Henry, ol' boy," said the latter, "we'll have yeh fixed up in jest about a minnit."

He had the bustling ways of an amateur nurse. He fussed around the fire and stirred the sticks to brilliant exertions. He made his patient drink largely from the canteen that contained the coffee. It was to the youth a delicious draught. He tilted his head afar back and held the canteen long to his lips. The cool mixture went caressingly down his blistered throat. Having finished, he sighed with comfortable delight.

The loud young soldier watched his comrade with an air of satisfaction. He, later, produced an extensive handkerchief from his pocket. He folded it into a manner of bandage and soused water from the other canteen upon the middle of it. This crude arrangement he bound over the youth's head, tying the ends in a queer knot at the back of the neck.

"There," he said, moving off and surveying his deed, "yeh look like th' devil but I bet yeh feel better."

The youth looked at his friend with grateful eyes. Upon his aching and swelling head, the cold cloth was like a tender woman's hand.

"Yeh don't holler ner say nothin'," remarked his friend, approvingly. "I know I'm a blacksmith at takin' keer 'a sick folks an' yeh never squeaked. Yer a good un, Henry. Most 'a men would 'a been in th' hospital long ago. A shot in th' head aint foolin' business."

The youth made no reply but began to fumble with the buttons of his jacket.

"Well, come, now," continued his friend, "come on. I must put yeh t' bed an' see that yeh git a good night's rest."

The other got carefully erect and the loud young soldier led him among the sleeping forms lying in groups and rows. Presently he stooped and picked up his blankets. He spread the rubber one upon the ground and placed the woolen one about the youth's shoulders.

"There now," he said, "lie down an' git some sleep."

The youth with his manner of dog-like obedience got carefully down like a crone stooping. He stretched out with a murmur of relief and comfort. The ground felt like the softest couch.

But of a sudden, he ejaculated. "Hol' on a minnit. Where you goin' t' sleep?"

His friend waved his hand impatiently. "Right down there by yeh."

"Well, but hol' on a minnit," continued the youth. "What yeh goin' t' sleep in? I've got your—"

The loud young soldier snarled. "Shet up an' go on t' sleep. Don't be makin' a damn' fool 'a yerself," he said, severely.

After this reproof, the youth said no more. An exquisite drowsiness had spread through him. The warm comfort of the blanket enveloped him and made a gentle languor. His head fell forward on his crooked arm and his weighted lids went softly down over his eyes. Hearing a splatter of musketry from the distance, he wondered indifferently if those men sometimes slept. He gave a long sigh, snuggled down into his blanket and in a moment, was like his comrades.

XV

When the youth awoke, it seemed to him that he had been asleep for a thousand years and he felt sure that he opened his eyes upon an unexpected world. Grey mists were slowly shifting before the first efforts of the sun-rays. An impending splendor could be seen in the eastern sky. An icy dew had chilled his face and immediately upon arousing he curled further down into his blanket. He stared, for a while, at the leaves over-head, moving in a heraldic wind of the day.

The distance was splintering and blaring with the noise of fighting. There was in the sound, an expression of a deadly persistency as if it had not began and was not to cease.

About him, were the rows and groups of men that he had dimly seen the previous night. They were getting a last draught of sleep before the awakening. The gaunt, care-worn faces and dusty figures were made plain by this quaint light at the dawning but it dressed the skin of the men in corpse-like hues and made the tangled limbs appear pulseless and dead. The youth started up with a little cry when his eyes first swept over this motionless mass of men, thick spread upon the ground, pallid and in strange postures. His disordered mind interpreted the hall of the forest as a charnel place. He believed for an instant that he was in the house of the dead and he did not dare to move lest these corpses start up, squalling and squawking. In a second, however, he achieved his proper mind. He swore a complicated oath at himself. He saw that this sombre picture was not a fact of the present, but a mere prophecy.

He heard then the noise of a fire crackling briskly in the cold air and turning his head, he saw his friend pottering busily about a small blaze. A few other figures moved in the fog and he heard the hard cracking of axe-blows.

Suddenly, there was a hollow rumble of drums. A distant bugle sang faintly. Similar sounds, varying in strength, came from near and far over the forest. The bugles called to each other like brazen game-cocks. The near thunder of the regimental drums rolled.

The body of men in the woods rustled. There was a general uplifting of heads. A murmuring of voices broke upon the air. In it there was much bass of grumbling oaths. Strange gods were addressed in condemnation of the early hours necessary to correct war. An officer's peremptory tenor rang out and quickened the stiffened movement of the men. The tangled limbs unravelled. The corpse-hued faces were hidden behind fists that twisted slowly in eye-sockets. It was the soldier's bath.

The youth sat up and gave vent to an enormous yawn. "Thunder," he remarked, petulantly. He rubbed his eyes and then putting up his hand felt carefully of the bandage over his wound. His friend, perceiving him to be awake, came from the fire. "Well, Henry, ol' man, how do yeh feel this mornin'," he demanded.

The youth yawned again. Then he puckered his mouth to a bitter pucker. His head in truth felt precisely like a melon and there was an unpleasant sensation at his stomach.

"Oh, Lord, I feel pretty bad," he said.

"Thunder," exclaimed the other. "I hoped yed feel all right this mornin'. Let's see th' bandage—I guess it's slipped." He began to tinker at the wound in rather a clumsy way until suddenly the youth exploded.

"Gosh-dern it," he said in sharp irritation, "you're th' hangest man I ever see. You wear muffs on yer hands. Why in good-thun-deration can't yeh be more easy. I'd rather yed stand off an' throw guns at it. Now, go slow, an' don't act as if yeh was nailin' down carpet."

He glared with insolent command at his friend but the latter answered soothingly. "Well, well, come now, an' git some grub," he said. "Then, maybe, yeh'll feel better."

At the fire-side, the loud young soldier, watched over his com-rade's wants with tenderness and care. He was very busy, marshall-ing the little, black vagabonds of tin-cups and pouring into them the steaming, iron-colored mixture from a small and sooty tin-pail. He had some fresh meat which he roasted hurriedly upon a stick. He sat down then and contemplated the youth's attitute with glee.

The youth took note of a remarkable change in his comrade since those days of camp-life upon the river-bank. He seemed no more to be continually regarding the proportions of his personal prowess. He was not furious at small words that pricked his conceits. He was, no more, a loud young soldier.[9] There was about him now a fine reli-ance. He showed a quiet belief in his purposes and his abilities. And this inward confidence evidently enabled him to be indifferent to little words of other men aimed at him.

The youth reflected. He had been used to regarding his comrade as a blatant child with an audacity grown from his inexperience, thoughtless, head-strong, jealous, and filled with a tinsel courage. A swaggering babe accustomed to strut in his own door-yard. The youth wondered where had been born these new eyes; when his comrade had made the great discovery that there were many men who would refuse to be subjected by him. Apparently, the other had now climbed a peak of wisdom from which he could perceive himself as a very wee thing. And the youth saw that, ever after, it would be easier to live in his friend's neighborhood.

His comrade balanced his ebony coffee-cup on his knee. "Well, Henry," he said, "what d'yeh think th' chances are? D'yeh think we'll wallop'em?"

The youth considered for a moment. "Day-b'fore-yestirday," he finally replied with boldness, "yeh would 'a bet yed lick th' hull kit-an'-boodle all by yerself."

His friend looked a trifle amazed. "Would I?" he asked. He pon-dered. "Well, perhaps, I would," he decided at last. He stared humbly at the fire.

The youth was quite disconcerted at this surprising reception of his remarks. "Oh, no, yeh wouldn't either," he said, hastily trying to retrace.

9. This sentence originally appeared in the manuscript as "He was not a youth." In accord with the change indi-cated in Wilson, he is subsequently re-ferred to as "the youth's friend" or "his comrade" or "the friend."

But the other made a deprecatory gesture. "Oh, yeh needn't mind, Henry," he said. "I believe I was a pretty big fool in those days." He spoke as after a lapse of years.

There was a little pause.

"All th' off'cers say we've got th' rebs in a pretty tight box," said the friend, clearing his throat in a common-place way. "They all seem t' think we've got'em jest where we want'em."

"I don't know about that," the youth replied. "What I seen over on th' right makes me think it was th' other way about. From where I was, it looked as if we was gittin' a good poundin' yestirday."

"D'yeh think so?" enquired the friend. "I thought we handled 'em pretty rough yesterday."

"Not a bit," said the youth. "Why, lord, man, yeh didn't see nothin' 'a th' fight. Why—" Then a sudden thought came to him. "Oh! Jim Conklin's dead."

His friend started. "What? Is he? Jim Conklin?"

The youth spoke slowly. "Yep. He's dead. Shot in th' side."

"Yeh don't say so. Jim Conklin? . . . . Poor cuss."

All about them were other small fires surrounded by men with their little black utensils. From one of these, near, came sudden sharp voices in a row. It appeared that two light-footed soldiers had been teasing a huge bearded man, causing him to spill coffee upon his blue knees. The man had gone into a rage and had sworn comprehensively. Stung by his language, his tormentors had immediately bristled at him with a great show of resenting unjust oaths. Possibly there was going to be a fight.

The friend arose and went over to them making pacific motions with his arms. "Oh, here, now, boys, what's th' use?" he said. "We'll be at th' rebs in less'n an hour. What's th' good 'a fightin' 'mong ourselves."

One of the light-footed soldiers turned upon him red faced and violent. "Yeh needn't come around here with yer preachin'. I s'pose yeh don't approve 'a fightin' since Charley Morgan licked yeh but I don't see what business this here is 'a yours or anybody else."

"Well, it aint," said the friend mildly. "Still I hate t' see—"

There was a tangled argument.

"Well, he—" said the two, indicating their opponent with accusative fore-fingers.

The huge soldier was quite purple with rage. He pointed at the two soldiers with his great hand, extended claw-like. "Well, they—"

But during this argumentative time, the desire to deal blows seemed to pass, although they said much to each other. Finally the friend returned to his old seat. In a short while, the three antagonists could be seen together in an amiable bunch.

"Jimmie Rogers ses I'll have t' fight him after th' battle t'-day," announced the friend as he again seated himself. "He ses he don't allow no interferin' in his business. I hate t' see th' boys fightin' 'mong themselves."

The youth laughed. "Yer changed a good bit. Yeh aint at all like yeh was. I remember when you an' that Irish feller—" he stopped and laughed again.

"No, I didn't used t' be that way," said his friend, thoughtfully. "That's true 'nough."

"Well, I didn't mean—" began the youth.

The friend made another deprecatory gesture. "Oh, yeh needn't mind, Henry."

There was another little pause.

"Th' reg'ment lost over half th' men yestirday," remarked the friend, eventually. "I thought 'a course they was all dead but, laws, they kep a-comin' back last night until it seems, after all, we didnt lose but a few. They'd been scattered all over, wanderin' around in th' woods, fightin' with other reg'ments an' everything. Jest like you done."

"So?" said the youth.

He went into a brown mood. He thought with deep contempt of all his grapplings and tuggings with fate and the universe. It now was evident that a large proportion of the men of the regiment had been, if they chose, capable of the same quantity of condemnation of the world and could as righteously have taken arms against everything. He laughed.

He now rejoiced in a view of what he took to be the universal resemblance. He decided that he was not, as he had supposed, a unique man. There were many in his type. And he had believed that he was suffering new agonies and feeling new wrongs. On the contrary, they were old, all of them, they were born perhaps with the first life.

These thoughts took the element of grandeur from his experiences. Since many had had them there could be nothing fine about them. They were now ridiculous.

However, he yet considered himself to be below the standard of traditional man-hood. He felt abashed when confronting memories of some men he had seen.

These thoughts did not appear in his attitude. He now considered the fact of his having fled, as being buried. He was returned to his comrades and unimpeached. So despite the little shadow of his sin upon his mind, he felt his self-respect growing strong within him. His pride had almost recovered its balance and was about[1]

• • •

1. The final page of Chapter XV has been lost, and there is no indication of how much text appeared on that page. Henry probably recalls his desertion of the tattered man here which thwarts the "almost recovered" balance of his pride.

XVI

The regiment was standing at order-arms at the side of a lane, waiting for the command to march when suddenly the youth remembered the little packet enwrapped in a faded yellow envelope which the loud young soldier with lugubrious words had entrusted to him. It made him start. He uttered an exclamation and turned toward his comrade.

"Wilson!"

"What?"

His friend, at his side in the ranks, was thoughtfully staring down the road. From some cause, his expression was at that moment, very meek. The youth, regarding him with sidelong glances, felt impelled to change his purpose. "Oh, nothin'," he said.

His friend turned his head in some surprise. "Why, what was yeh goin' t' say."

"Oh, nothin'," repeated the youth.

He resolved not to deal the little blow. It was sufficient that the fact made him glad. It was not necessary to knock his friend on the head with the misguided packet.

He had been possessed of much fear of his friend for he saw how easily questionings could make holes in his feelings. Lately, he had assured himself that the altered comrade would not tantalize him with a persistent curiosity but he felt certain that during the first period of leisure his friend would ask him to relate his adventures of the previous day.

He now rejoiced in the possession of a small weapon with which he could prostrate his comrade at the first signs of a cross-examination. He was master. It would now be he who could laugh and shoot the shafts of derision.

The friend had, in a weak hour, spoken with sobs of his own death. He had delivered a melancholy oration previous to his funeral and had, doubtless, in the packet of letters, presented various keep-sakes to relatives. But he had not died, and thus he had delivered himself into the hands of the youth.

The latter felt immensely superior to his friend but he inclined to condescension. He adopted toward him an air of patronizing good-humor.

His self-pride was now entirely restored. In the shade of its flourishing growth, he stood with braced and self-confident legs, and since nothing could now be discovered, he did not shrink from an encounter with the eyes of judges, and allowed no thoughts of his own to keep him from an attitude of manfulness. He had performed his mistakes in the dark, so he was still a man.

Indeed, when he remembered his fortunes of yesterday, and looked at them from a distance he began to see something fine there. He had license to be pompous and veteran-like.

His panting agonies of the past he put out of his sight. The long tirades against nature he now believed to be foolish compositions born of his condition. He did not altogether repudiate them because he did not remember all that he had said. He was inclined to regard his past rebellions with an indulgent smile. They were all right in their hour, perhaps.

In the present, he declared to himself that it was only the doomed and the damned who roared with sincerity at nature. Few, but they, ever did it. A man with a full stomach and the respect of his fellows had no business to scold about anything that he might think to be wrong in the ways of the universe, or, even with the ways of society. Let the unfortunates rail; the others may play marbles.

Since he was comfortable and contented, he had no desire to set things straight. Indeed, he no more contended that they were not straight. How could they be crooked when he was restored to a requisite amount of happiness. There was a slowly developing conviction that in all his red speeches he had been ridiculously mistaken. Nature was a fine thing moving with a magnificent justice. The world was fair and wide and glorious. The sky was kind, and smiled tenderly, full of encouragement, upon him.

Some poets now received his scorn. Yesterday, in his misery, he had thought of certain persons who had written. Their remembered words, broken and detached, had come piece-meal to him. For these people he had then felt a glowing, brotherly regard. They had wandered in paths of pain and they had made pictures of the black landscape that others might enjoy it with them. He had, at that time, been sure that their wise, contemplating spirits had been in sympathy with him, had shed tears from the clouds. He had walked alone, but there had been pity, made before a reason for it.

But he was now, in a measure, a successful man and he could no longer tolerate in himself a spirit of fellowship for poets. He abandoned them. Their songs about black landscapes were of no importance to him since his new eyes said that his landscape was not black. People who called landscapes black were idiots.

He achieved a mighty scorn for such a snivelling race.

He felt that he was the child of the powers. Through the peace of his heart, he saw the earth to be a garden in which grew no weeds of agony. Or, perhaps, if there did grow a few, it was in obscure corners where no one was obliged to encounter them unless a ridiculous search was made. And, at any rate, they were tiny ones.

He returned to his old belief in the ultimate, astonishing success of his life. He, as usual, did not trouble about processes. It was ordained, because he was a fine creation. He saw plainly that he was the chosen of some gods. By fearful and wonderful roads he was to be led to a crown. He was, of course, satisfied that he deserved it.

He did not give a great deal of thought to these battles that lay directly before him. It was not essential that he should plan his ways in regard to them. He had been taught that many obligations of a life were easily avoided. The lessons of yesterday had been that retribution was a laggard and blind. With these facts before him he did not deem it necessary that he should become feverish over the possibilities of the ensuing twenty-four hours. He could leave much to chance. Beside, a faith in himself had secretly blossomed. There was a little flower of confidence growing within him. He was now a man of experience. He had been out among the dragons, he said, and he assured himself that they were not so hideous as he had imagined them. Also, they were inaccurate; they did not sting with precision. A stout heart often defied; and, defying, escaped.

And, furthermore, how could they kill him who was the chosen of gods and doomed to greatness.

He remembered how some of the men had run from the battle. As he re-called their terror-struck faces he felt a scorn for them. They had surely been more fleet and more wild than was absolutely necessary. They were weak mortals. As for himself, he had fled with discretion and dignity.

He was aroused from this reverie by his friend who having hitched about nervously and blinked at the trees for a time, suddenly coughed in an introductory way, and spoke.

"Fleming!"

"What?"

The friend put his hand up to his mouth and coughed again. He fidgeted in his jacket.

"Well," he gulped, at last, "I guess yeh might as well give me back them letters." Dark, prickling blood had flushed into his cheeks and brow.

"All right, Wilson," said the youth. He loosened two buttons of his coat, thrust in his hand and brought forth the packet. As he extended it to his friend, the latter's face was turned from him.

He had been slow in the act of producing the packet because during it he had been trying to invent a remarkable comment upon the affair. He could conjure nothing of sufficient point. He was compelled to allow his friend to escape unmolested with his packet. And for this he took unto himself considerable credit. It was a generous thing.

His friend at his side, seemed suffering great shame. As he contemplated him, the youth felt his heart grow more strong and stout. He had never been compelled to blush in such manner for his acts; he was an individual of extraordinary virtues.

He reflected, with condescending pity: "Too bad! Too bad! Th' poor devil, it makes him feel tough!"

After this incident, and as he reviewed the battle-pictures he had seen, he felt quite competent to return home and make the hearts of the people glow with stories of war. He could see himself in a room of warm tints telling tales to listeners. He could exhibit laurels. They were insignificant; still, in a district where laurels were infrequent, they might shine.

He saw his gaping audience picturing him as the central figure in blazing scenes. And he imagined the consternation and the ejaculations of his mother and the young lady at the seminary as they drank his recitals. Their vague feminine formula for beloved ones doing brave deeds on the field of battle without risk of life, would be destroyed.

XVII

A sputtering of musketry was always to be heard. Later, the cannon had entered the dispute. In the fog-filled air, their voices made a thudding sound. The reverberations were continual. This part of the world led a strange, battleful existence.

The youth's regiment was marched to relieve a command that had lain long in some damp trenches. The men took positions behind a curving line of rifle-pits that had been turned up, like a large furrow, along the line of woods. Before them was a level stretch, peopled with short, deformed stumps. From the woods beyond, came the dull popping of the skirmishers and pickets, firing in the fog. From the right came the noise of a terrific fracas.

The men cuddled behind the small embankment and sat in easy attitudes awaiting their turn. Many had their backs to the firing. The youth's friend lay down, buried his face in his arms, and almost instantly, it seemed, he was in a deep sleep.

The youth leaned his breast against the brown dirt and peered over at the woods and up and down the line. Curtains of trees interfered with his ways of vision. He could see the low line of trenches but for a short distance. A few idle flags were perched on the dirt-hills. Behind them were rows of dark bodies with a few heads sticking curiously over the top.

Always the noise of skirmishers came from the woods on the front and left, and the din on the right had grown to frightful proportions. The guns were roaring without an instant's pause for breath. It seemed that the cannon had come from all parts and were engaged in a stupendous wrangle. It became impossible to make a sentence heard.

The youth wished to launch a joke—a quotation from newspapers. He desired to say: "All quiet on the Rappahannock,"[2] but the guns refused to permit even a comment upon their up-roar. He never successfully concluded the sentence.

But at last, the guns stopped and among the men in the rifle-pits,

2. An echo of "All quiet along the Potomac," reputed to be a report sent to Washington, D.C., from the headquarters of General George McClellan while he was Commander of the Army of the Potomac in 1861–62. The northern public and newspapers were anxious for McClellan to take action and used the phrase sarcastically in attacking his reticence to launch an offensive.

rumors again flew, like birds, but they were now for the most part, black and croaking creatures who flapped their wings drearily near to the ground and refused to rise on any wings of hope. The men's faces grew doleful from the interpreting of many omens. Tales of hesitation and uncertainty on the part of those high in place and responsibility, came to their ears. Stories of disaster were borne in to their minds with many proofs. This din of musketry on the right, growing like a released genie of sound, expressed and emphasized the army's plight.

The men were disheartened and began to mutter. They made gestures expressive of the sentence: "Ah, what more can we do." And it could always be seen that they were bewildered by the alleged news and could not fully comprehend a defeat.

Before the grey mists had been totally obliterated by the sun-rays, the regiment was marching in a spread column that was retiring carefully through the woods. The disordered, hurrying lines of the enemy could sometimes be seen down through the groves and little fields. They were yelling, shrill and exultant.

At this sight, the youth forgot many personal matters and became greatly enraged. He exploded in loud sentence. "B'jiminy, we're generaled by a lot 'a lunkheads."

"More than one feller has said that t'-day," observed a man.

His friend, recently aroused, was still very drowsy. He looked behind him until his mind took in the meaning of the movement. Then he sighed. "Oh, well, I s'pose we got licked," he remarked, sadly.

The youth had a thought that it would not be handsome for him to freely condemn other men. He made an attempt to restrain himself but the words upon his tongue were too bitter. He presently began a long and intricate denunciation of the commander of the forces.

"Mebbe, it wa'n't all his fault—not all together. He did th' best he knowed. It's our luck t' git licked often," said his friend in a weary tone. He was trudging along with stooped shoulders and shifting eyes like a man who has been caned and kicked.

"Well, don't we fight like th' devil? Don't we do all that men kin?" demanded the youth loudly.

He was secretly dumb-founded at this sentiment when it came from his lips. For a moment his face lost its valor and he looked guiltily about him. But no one questioned his right to deal in such words, and, presently, he recovered his air of courage. He went on to repeat a statement he had heard going from group to group at the camp that morning. "Th' brigadier sed he never see a new reg-'ment fight th' way we fit yestirday, didnt he? An' we didn't no better than many another reg'ment, did we? Well, then, yeh can't say it's th' army's fault, kin yeh?"

In his reply, the friend's voice was stern. " 'A course not," he said. "No man dare say we don't fight like th' devil. No man will ever dare say it. Th' boys fight like hell-roosters. But still—still, we don't have no luck."

"Well, then, if we fight like th' devil an' don't ever whip, it must be th' general's fault," said the youth grandly and decisively. "An' I don't see no sense in fightin' an' fightin' an' fightin', yit allus losin' through some derned ol' lunkhead of a general."

A sarcastic man who was tramping at the youth's side, then spoke lazily. "Mebbe yeh think yeh fit th' hull battle yestirday, Flemin'," he remarked.

The speech pierced the youth. Inward, he was reduced to an abject pulp by these chance words. His legs quaked privately. He cast a frightened glance at the sarcastic man.

"Why, no," he hastened to say in a conciliatory voice, "I don't think I fit th' hull battle yestirday."

But the other seemed innocent of any deeper meaning. Apparently, he had no information. It was merely his habit. "Oh," he replied in the same tone of calm derision.

The youth, nevertheless, felt a threat. His mind shrank from going near to the danger and, thereafter, he was silent. The significance of the sarcastic man's words took from him all loud moods that would make him appear prominent. He became suddenly a modest man.

There was low-toned talk among the troops. The officers were impatient and snappy, their countenances clouded with the tales of misfortune. The troops, sifting through the forest, were sullen. In the youth's company once, a man's laugh rang out. A dozen soldiers turned their faces quickly toward him and frowned with vague displeasure.

The noise of firing dogged their foot-steps. Sometimes, it seemed to be driven a little way but it always returned again with increased insolence. The men muttered and cursed, throwing black looks in its direction.

In a clearer space, the troops were at last halted. Regiments and brigades, broken and detached through their encounters with thickets, grew together again and lines were faced toward the pursuing bark of the enemy's infantry.

This noise, following like the yelpings of eager, metallic hounds increased to a loud and joyous burst, and then, as the sun went serenely up the sky, throwing illuminating rays into the gloomy thickets, it broke forth into prolonged pealings. The woods began to crackle as if a-fire.

"Whoop-a-dadee," said a man, "here we are. Everybody fightin'. Blood an' destruction."

"I was willin' t' bet they'd attack as soon as th' sun got fairly up," savagely asserted the lieutenant who commanded the youth's company. He jerked without mercy at his little moustache. He strode to and fro with dark dignity in the rear of his men who were lying down behind whatever protection they had collected.

A battery had trundled into position in the rear and was thoughtfully shelling the distance. The regiment, unmolested as yet, awaited the moment when the grey shadows of the woods before them should be slashed by the lines of flame. There was much growling and swearing.

"Good Gawd," the youth grumbled, "we're allus bein' chased around like rats. It makes me sick. Nobody seems t' know where we go ner why we go. We jest git fired around from piller t' post an' git licked here an' git licked there an' nobody knows what it's done fer. It make a man feel like a damn' kitten in a bag. Now, I'd like t' know what th' eternal thunders we was marched inteh these here woods fer, anyhow, unless it was t' give th' rebs a reg'lar pot-shot at us. We came in here an' got our legs all tangled up in these here cussed briars an' then we begin t' fight an' th' rebs had an easy time of it. Don't tell Me it's jest luck. I know better. It's this derned ol' —"

The friend seemed jaded but he interrupted his comrade with a voice of calm confidence. "It'll turn out all right in th' end," he said.

"Oh, th' devil it will. You allus talk like a dog-hanged parson. Dont tell Me. I know—"

At this time, there was an interposition by the savage-minded lieutenant who was obliged to vent some of his inward dissatisfaction upon his men. "You boys shut right up. There no need 'a your wastin' your breath in long-winded arguments about this an' that an' th' other. You've been jawin' like a lot 'a old hens. All you've got t' do is to fight an' you'll get plenty 'a that t' do in about ten minutes. Less talkin' an' more fightin' is what's best fer you boys. I never saw sech gabbling jack-asses."

He paused, ready to pounce upon any man who might have the temerity to reply. No words being said, he resumed his dignified pacing.

"There's too much chin-music an' too little fightin' in this war, anyhow," he said to them, turning his head for a final remark.

The day had grown more white until the sun shed his full radiance upon the thronged forest. A sort of a gust of battle came sweeping toward that part of the line where lay the youth's regiment. The front shifted a trifle to meet it squarely. There was a wait. In this part of the field there passed slowly the intense moments that precede the tempest.

A single rifle flashed in a thicket before the regiment. In an instant, it was joined by many others. There was a mighty song of clashes and crashes that went sweeping through the woods. The guns in the rear, aroused and enraged by shells that had been thrown burr-like at them, suddenly involved themselves in a hideous altercation with another band of guns. The battle-roar settled to a rolling thunder which was a single, long explosion.

In the regiment, there was a peculiar kind of hesitation denoted in the attitudes of the men. They were worn, exhausted, having slept but little, and labored much. They rolled their eyes toward the advancing battle as they stood awaiting the shock. Some shrank and flinched. They stood as men tied to stakes.

XVIII

This advance of the enemy had seemed to the youth like a ruthless hunting. He began to fume with rage and exasperation. He beat his foot upon the ground and scowled with hate at the swirling smoke that was approaching like a phantom flood. There was a maddening quality in this seeming resolution of the foe to give him no rest, to give him no time to sit down and think. Yesterday, he had fought and had fled rapidly. There had been many adventures. For to-day he felt that he had earned opportunities for contemplative repose. He could have enjoyed portraying to uninitiated listeners various scenes at which he had been a witness, or, ably discussing the processes of war with other proven men. Too, it was important that he should have time for physical recuperation. He was sore and stiff from his experiences. He had received his fill of all exertions and he wished to rest.

But those other men seemed never to grow weary; they were fighting with their old speed. He had a wild hate for the relentless foe. Yesterday, when he had imagined the universe to be against him, he had hated it, little gods and big gods; to-day he hated the army of the foe with the same great hatred. He was not going to be badgered of his life like a kitten chased by boys, he said. It was not well to drive men into final corners; at those moments, they could all develop teeth and claws.

He leaned, and spoke into his friend's ear. He menaced the woods with a gesture. "If they keep on a-chasin' us, by Gawd, they wanta watch out. Can't stand *too* much."

The friend twisted his head and made a calm reply. "If they keep on a-chasin' us, they'll drive us all inteh th' river."

The youth cried out savagely at this statement. He crouched behind a little tree, with his eyes burning balefully and his teeth set in a cur-like snarl. The awkward bandage was still about his head and, upon it, over his wound there was a spot of dry blood. His hair was wondrously towsled and some straggling, moving locks hung over the cloth of the bandage down toward his forehead. His jacket and shirt were open at the neck and exposed his young, bronzed neck. There could be seen spasmodic gulpings at his throat.

His fingers twined nervously about his rifle. He wished that it was an engine of annihilating power. He felt that he and his companions were being taunted and derided from sincere convictions that they were poor and puny. His knowledge of his inability to take vengeance for it made his rage into a dark and stormy spectre that possessed him and made him dream of abominable cruelties. The tormentors were flies sucking insolently at his blood and he thought that he would have given his life for a revenge of seeing their faces in pitiful plights.

The winds of battle had swept all about the regiment until the one rifle, instantly followed by brothers, flashed in its front. A moment later, the regiment roared forth its sudden and valiant retort. A dense wall of smoke settled slowly down. It was furiously slit and slashed by the knife-like fire from the rifles.

To the youth, the fighters were like animals tossed for a death-struggle into a dark pit. There was a sensation that he and his fellows, at bay, were pushing back, always pushing fierce onslaughts of creatures who were slippery. Their beams of crimson seemed to get no purchase upon the bodies of their foes; the latter seemed to evade them with ease and come through, between, around and about, with unopposed skill.

When, in a dream, it occurred to the youth that his rifle was an impotent stick, he lost sense of everything but his hate, his desire to smash into pulp the glittering smile of victory which he could feel upon the faces of his enemies.

The blue, smoke-swallowed line curled and writhed like a snake, stepped upon. It swung its ends to and fro in an agony of fear and rage.

The youth was not conscious that he was erect upon his feet. He did not know the direction of the ground. Indeed, once he even lost the habit of balance and fell heavily. He was up again immediately. One thought went through the chaos of his brain at the time. He wondered if he had fallen because he had been shot. But the suspicion flew away at once. He did not think more of it.

He had taken up a first position behind the little tree with a direct determination to hold it against the world. He had not deemed it possible that his army could that day succeed and, from this, he felt the ability to fight harder. But the throng had surged in all ways until he lost directions and locations, save that he knew where lay the enemy.

The flames bit him and the hot smoke broiled his skin. His rifle-barrel grew so hot that, ordinarily, he could not have borne it upon his palms but he kept on stuffing cartridges into it and pounding them with his clanking, bending ram-rod. If he aimed at some changing form through the smoke, he pulled his trigger with a fierce grunt as if he were dealing a blow of the fist with all his strength.

When the enemy seemed falling back before him and his fellows, he went instantly forward, like a dog who seeing his foes lagging, turns and insists upon being pursued. And when he was compelled to retire again, he did it slowly, sullenly, taking steps of wrathful despair.

Once, he, in his intent hate, was almost alone and was firing when all those near him had ceased. He was so engrossed in his occupation that he was not aware of a lull.

He was re-called by a hoarse laugh and a sentence that came to his ears in a voice of contempt and amazement. "Yeh infernal fool, don't yeh know enough t' quit when there aint anything t' shoot at? Good Gawd!"

He turned then and pausing with his rifle thrown half into position, looked at the blue line of his comrades. During this moment of leisure, they seemed all to be engaged in staring with astonishment at him. They had become spectators. Turning to the front again, he saw, under the lifted smoke, a deserted ground.

He looked, bewildered, for a moment. Then there appeared upon the glazed vacancy of his eyes, a diamond-point of intelligence. "Oh," he said, comprehending.

He returned to his comrades and threw himself upon the ground. He sprawled like a man who has been thrashed. His flesh seemed strangely on fire and the sounds of the battle continued in his ears. He groped blindly for his canteen.

The lieutenant was crowing. He seemed drunk with fighting. He called out to the youth. "By heavens, if I had ten thousand wildcats like you, I could tear th' stomach outa this war in less'n a week." He puffed out his chest with large dignity as he said it.

Some of the men muttered and looked at the youth in awe-struck ways. It was plain that as he had gone on loading and firing and cursing without the proper intermission, they had found time to regard him. And they now looked upon him as a war-devil.

The friend came staggering to him. There was some fright and dismay in his voice. "Are yeh all right, Fleming? Do yeh feel all right? There aint nothin' th' matter with yeh, Henry, is there?"

"No," said the youth with difficulty. His throat seemed full of knobs and burrs.

These incidents made the youth ponder. It was revealed to him that he had been a barbarian, a beast. He had fought like a pagan who defends his religion. Regarding it, he saw that it was fine, wild and, in some ways, easy. He had been a tremendous figure, no doubt. By this struggle, he had over-come obstacles which he had admitted to be mountains. They had fallen like paper peaks and he was now what he called a hero. And he had not been aware of the process. He had slept and, awakening, found himself a knight.

He lay and basked in the occasional stares of his comrades. Their faces were varied in degree of blackness from the burned powder. Some were utterly smudged. They were reeking with perspiration and their breaths came hard and wheezing. And from these soiled expanses they peered at him.

"Hot work! Hot work!" cried the lieutenant deliriously. He walked up and down restless and eager. Sometimes, his voice could be heard in a wild, incomprehensible laugh.

When he had a particularly profound thought upon the science of war, he always unconsciously addressed himself to the youth.

There was some grim rejoicing by the men. "By thunder, I bet this army'll never see another new reg'ment like us."

"You bet!

> 'A dog, a woman, an' a walnut tree,
> Th' more yeh beat'em, th' better they be,'

That's like us."

"Lost a piler men, they did. If an ol' woman swep' up th' woods, she'd git a dust-pan full."

"Yes, an' if she'll come around ag'in in 'bout an hour she'll git a pile more."

The forest still bore its burden of clamor. From off under the trees came the rolling clatter of the musketry. Each distant thicket seemed a strange porcupine with quills of flame. A cloud of dark smoke as from smouldering ruins went up toward the sun now bright and gay in the blue, enamelled sky.

XIX

The ragged line had respite for some minutes but during its pause, the struggle in the forest became magnified until the trees seemed to quiver from the firing and the ground to shake from the rushings of the men. The voices of the cannon were mingled in a long and interminable row. It seemed difficult to live in such an atmosphere. The chests of the men strained for a bit of freshness and their throats craved water.

There was one, shot through the body, who raised a cry of bitter lamentation when came this lull. Perhaps, he had been calling out during the fighting also but at that time no one had heard him. But now the men turned at the woeful complaints of him upon the ground.

"Who is it? Who is it?"

"It's Jimmie Rogers! Jimmie Rogers."

When their eyes first encountered him there was a sudden halt as if they feared to go near. He was thrashing about in the grass, twisting his shuddering body into many strange postures. He was screaming loudly. This instant's hesitation seemed to fill him with a tremendous, fantastic contempt and he damned them in shrieked sentences.

The youth's friend had a geographical illusion concerning a stream and he obtained permission to go for some water. Immediately, canteens were showered upon him. "Fill mine, will yeh?" "Bring me some, too." "And me, too." He departed, ladened. The youth went with his friend, feeling a desire to throw his heated body into the stream and, soaking there, drink quarts.

They made a hurried search for the supposed stream but did not find it. "No water here," said the youth. They turned without delay and began to retrace their steps.

From their position as they again faced toward the place of the fighting, they could, of course, comprehend a greater amount of the battle than when their visions had been blurred by the hurlying smoke of the line. They could see dark stretches winding along the land and on one cleared space there was a row of guns making grey clouds which were filled with large flashes of orange-colored flame. Over some foliage they could see the roof of a house. One window, glowing a deep, murder-red, shone squarely through the leaves. From the edifice, a tall, leaning tower of smoke went far into the sky.

Looking over their own troops, they saw mixed masses slowly getting into regular form. The sun-light made twinkling points of the bright steel. To the rear, there was a glimpse of a distant road-way as it curved over a slope. It was crowded with retreating infantry. From all the interwoven forest arose the smoke and bluster of the battle. The air was always occupied by a blaring.

Near where they stood, shells were flip-flopping and hooting. Occasional bullets buzzed in the air and spanged into tree-trunks. Wounded men and other stragglers were slinking through the woods.

Looking down an aisle of the grove, the youth and his companion saw a jangling general and his staff almost ride upon a wounded man who was crawling on his hands and knees. The general reined strongly at his charger's opened and foamy mouth and guided it with dexterous horsemanship past the man. The latter scrambled in wild and torturing haste. His strength evidently failed him as he reached a place of safety. One of his arms suddenly weakened, and he fell, sliding over upon his back. He lay stretched out, breathing gently.

A moment later, the small, creaking cavalcade was directly in front of the two soldiers. Another officer, riding with the skilful abandon of a cow-boy, galloped his horse to a position directly before the general. The two unnoticed foot-soldiers made a little show of going on but they lingered near in the desire to over-hear the conversation. Perhaps, they thought, some great, inner historical things would be said.

The general, whom the boys knew as the commander of their division, looked at the other officer and spoke, coolly, as if he were criticising his clothes. "Th' enemy's formin' over there for another charge," he said. "It'll be directed against Whiterside, an' I fear they'll break through there unless we work like thunder t' stop them."

The other swore at his restive horse and then cleared his throat. He made a gesture toward his cap. "It'll be hell t' pay stoppin' them," he said, shortly.

"I presume so," remarked the general. Then he began to talk rapidly and in a lower tone. He frequently illustrated his words with a pointing finger. The two infantrymen could hear nothing until finally he asked: "What troops can you spare?"

The officer who rode like a cow-boy reflected for an instant. "Well," he said, "I had to order in th' 12th to help th' 76th an' I haven't really got any. But there's th' 304th. They fight like a lot 'a mule-drivers. I can spare them best of any."

The youth and his friend exchanged glances of astonishment.

The general spoke sharply. "Get'em ready then. I'll watch developments from here an' send you word when t' start them. It'll happen in five minutes."

As the other officer tossed his fingers toward his cap and, wheeling his horse, started away, the general called out to him in a sober voice: "I don't believe many of your mule-drivers will get back."

The other shouted something in reply. He smiled.

With scared faces, the youth and his companion, hurried back to the line.

These happenings had occupied an incredibly short time yet the youth felt that in them he had been made aged. New eyes were given to him. And the most startling thing was to learn suddenly that he was very insignificant. The officer spoke of the regiment as if he referred to a broom. Some part of the woods needed sweeping, perhaps, and he merely indicated a broom in a tone properly indifferent to its fate. It was war, no doubt, but it appeared strange.

As the two boys approached the line, the lieutenant perceived them and swelled with wrath. "Fleming—Wilson—how long does it take yeh t' git water, anyhow—where yeh been—"

But his oration ceased as he saw their eyes which were large with great tales. "We're goin' t' charge—we're goin' t' charge," cried the youth's friend, hastening with his news.

"Charge?" said the lieutenant. "Charge? Well, b'Gawd! Now, this is real fightin'." Over his soiled countenance there went a boastful smile. "Charge? Well, b'Gawd!"

A little group of soldiers surrounded the two youths. "Are we, sure-'nough? Well, I'll be derned. Charge? What fer? What at? Wilson, you're lyin'."

"I hope t' die," said the youth's friend, pitching his tones to the key of angry remonstrance. "Sure as shootin', I tell yeh."

And the youth spoke in reinforcement. "Not by a blame sight, he aint lyin'. We heard'em talkin'."

They caught sight of two mounted figures a short distance from them. One was the colonel of the regiment and the other was the officer who had received orders from the commander of the division.

They were gesticulating at each other. The youth's friend pointing at them, interpreted the scene.

One soldier had a final objection: "How could yeh hear'em talkin'," but the men, for a large part, nodded, admitting that previously the two friends had spoken truth.

They settled back into reposeful attitudes with airs of having accepted the matter. And they mused upon it, with a hundred varieties of expression. It was an engrossing thing to think about. Many tightened their belts carefully and hitched at their trousers.

A moment later, the officers began to bustle among the men, pushing them into a more compact mass and into a better alignment. They chased those that straggled and fumed at a few men who seemed to show by their attitudes, that they had decided to remain at that spot. They were like critical shepherds struggling with sheep.

Presently, the regiment seemed to draw itself up and heave a deep breath. None of the men's faces were mirrors of large thoughts. The soldiers were bended and stooped like sprinters before a signal. Many pairs of glinting eyes peered from the grimy faces toward the curtains of the deeper woods. They seemed to be engaged in deep calculations of time and distance.

They were surrounded by the noises of the monstrous altercation between the two armies. The world was fully interested in other matters. Apparently, the regiment had its small affair to itself.

The youth, turning, shot a quick, enquiring glance at his friend. The latter returned to him the same manner of look. They were the only ones who possessed an inner knowledge. "Mule-drivers—hell t' pay—don't believe many will get back." It was an ironical secret. Still, they saw no hesitation in each other's faces and they nodded a mute and unprotesting assent when a shaggy man near them said in a meek voice: "We'll git swallered."

XX

The youth stared at the land in front of him. Its foliages now seemed to veil powers and horrors. He was unaware of the machinery of orders that started the charge, although from the corners of his eyes, he saw an officer, who looked like a boy a-horseback, come galloping, waving his hat. Suddenly, he felt a straining and heaving among the men. The line fell slowly forward like a toppling wall and with a convulsive gasp that was intended for a cheer, the regiment began its journey. The youth was pushed and jostled for a moment before he understood the movement at all but directly he lunged ahead and began to run.

He fixed his eye upon a distant and prominent clump of trees where he had concluded the enemy were to be met, and he ran toward it as toward a goal. He had believed, throughout that it was mere question of getting over an unpleasant matter as quickly as possible and he ran desperately as if pursued for a murder. His face was drawn hard and tight with the stress of his endeavor. His eyes were fixed in a lurid glare. And with his soiled and disordered dress, his red and inflamed features surmounted by the dingy rag with its spot of blood, his wildly swinging rifle and banging accoutrements, he looked to be an insane soldier.

As the regiment swung from its position out into a cleared space, the woods and thickets before it, awakened. Yellow flames leaped toward it from many directions. The forest made a tremendous objection.

The line lurched straight for a moment. Then the right wing swung forward; it in turn was surpassed by the left. Afterward the centre careered to the front until the regiment was a wedge-shaped mass but an instant later, the opposition of the bushes, trees and uneven places on the ground split the command and scattered it into detached clusters.

The youth, light-footed, was unconsciously in advance. His eyes still kept note of the clump of trees. From all places near it the clannish yell of the enemy could be heard. The little flames of rifles leaped from it. The song of the bullets was in the air and shells snarled among the tree-tops. One tumbled directly into the middle of a hurrying group and exploded in crimson fury. There was an instant's spectacle of a man, almost over it, throwing up his hands to shield his eyes.

Other men, punched by bullets, fell in grotesque agonies. The regiment left a coherent trail of bodies.

They had passed into a clearer atmosphere. There was an effect like a revelation in the new appearance of the landscape. Some men working madly at a battery were plain to them and the opposing infantry's lines were defined by the grey walls and fringes of smoke.

It seemed to the youth that he saw everything. Each blade of the green grass was bold and clear. He thought that he was aware of every change in the thin, transparent vapor that floated idly in sheets. The brown or grey trunks of the trees showed each roughness of their surfaces. And the men of the regiment, with their starting eyes and sweating faces, running madly, or falling, as if thrown headlong, to queer, heaped-up corpses, all were comprehended. His mind took a mechanical but firm impression, so that, afterward, everything was pictured and explained to him, save why he himself was there.

But there was a frenzy made from this furious rush. The men, pitching forward insanely, had burst into cheerings, mob-like and barbaric, but tuned in strange keys that can arouse the dullard and the stoic. It made a mad enthusiasm that, it seemed, would be incapable of checking itself before granite and brass. There was the delirium that encounters despair and death, and is heedless and blind to the odds. It is a temporary but sublime absence of selfishness. And because it was of this order was the reason, perhaps, why the youth wondered, afterward, what reasons he could have had for being there.

Presently the straining pace ate up the energies of the men. As if by agreement, the leaders began to slacken their speed. The volleys directed against them had had a seeming wind-like effect. The regiment snorted and blew. Among some stolid trees it began to falter and hesitate. The men, staring intently, began to wait for some of the distant walls of smoke to move and disclose to them the scene. Since much of their strength and their breath had vanished, they returned to caution. They were become men again.

The youth had a vague belief that he had run miles and he thought, in a way, that he was now in some new and unknown land.

The moment the regiment ceased its advance, the protesting splutter of musketry became a steadied roar. Long and accurate fringes of smoke spread out. From the top of a small hill, came level belchings of yellow flame that caused an inhuman whistling in the air.

The men, halted, had opportunity to see some of their comrades dropping with moans and shrieks. A few lay under foot, still or wailing. And now for an instant the men stood, their rifles slack in their hands, and watched the regiment dwindle. They appeared dazed and stupid. This spectacle seemed to paralyze them, over-come them with a fatal fascination. They stared woodenly at the sights and, lowering their eyes, looked from face to face. It was a strange pause and a strange silence.

Then above the sounds of the outside commotion, arose the roar of the lieutenant. He strode suddenly forth, his infantile features black with rage.

"Come on, yeh fools," he bellowed. "Come on! Yeh can't stay here. Yeh must come on." He said more, but much of it could not be understood.

He started rapidly forward, with his head turned toward the men. "Come on," he was shouting. The men stared with blank and yokel-like eyes at him. He was obliged to halt and retrace his steps. He stood then with his back to the enemy and delivered gigantic curses into the faces of the men. His body vibrated from the weight and force of his imprecations. And he could string oaths with the facility of a maiden who strings beads.

The friend of the youth aroused. Lurching suddenly forward and dropping to his knees, he fired an angry shot at the persistent woods. This action awakened the men. They huddled no more like sheep. They seemed suddenly to bethink them of their weapons and at once commenced firing. Belabored by their officers they began to move forward. The regiment, involved like a cart involved in mud and muddle, started unevenly with many jolts and jerks. The men stopped, now, every few paces to fire and load, and in this manner moved slowly on from trees to trees.

The flaming opposition in their front grew with their advance until it seemed that all forward ways were barred by the thin leaping tongues and off to the right an ominous demonstration could sometimes be dimly discerned. The smoke, lately generated, was in confusing clouds that made it difficult for the regiment to proceed with intelligence. As he passed through each curling mass, the youth wondered what would confront him on the further side.

The command went painfully forward until an open space interposed between them and the lurid lines. Here, crouching and cowering behind some trees, the men clung with desperation as if threatened by a wave. They looked wild-eyed, and as if amazed, at this furious disturbance they had stirred. In the storm, there was an ironical expression of their importance. The faces of the men, too, showed a lack of a certain feeling of responsibility for being there. It was as if they had been driven. It was the dominant animal failing to remember in the supreme moments, the forceful causes of various superficial qualities. The whole affair seemed incomprehensible to many of them.

As they halted thus, the lieutenant again began to bellow profanely. Regardless of the vindictive threats of the bullets, he went about coaxing, berating and bedamning. His lips, that were habitually in a soft and child-like curve, were now writhed into unholy contortions. He swore by all possible deities.

Once, he grabbed the youth by the arm. "Come on, yeh lunkhead," he roared. "Come on. We'll all git killed if we stay here. We've on'y got t' go across that lot. An' then—" The remainder of his idea disappeared in a blue haze of curses.

The youth stretched forth his arm. "Cross there?" His mouth was puckered in doubt and awe.

"Cer'ly! Jest 'cross th' lot! We can't stay here," screamed the lieutenant. He poked his face close to the youth and waved his bandaged hand. "Come on!" Presently, he grappled with him as if for a wrestling bout. It was as if he planned to drag the youth by the ear on to the assault.

The private felt a sudden unspeakable indignation against his officer. He wrenched fiercely and shook him off.

"Come on yerself, then," he yelled. There was a bitter challenge in his voice.

They galloped together down the regimental front. The friend scrambled after them. In front of the colors, the three men began to bawl. "Come on! Come on!" They danced and gyrated like tortured savages.

The flag, obedient to these appeals, bended its glittering form and swept toward them. The men wavered in indecision for a moment and then with a long, wailful cry, the dilapidated regiment surged forward and began its new journey.

Over the field went the scurrying mass. It was a handful of men splattered into the faces of the enemy. Toward it instantly sprang the yellow tongues. A vast quantity of blue smoke hung before them. A mighty banging made ears valueless.

The youth ran like a madman to reach the woods before a bullet could discover him. He ducked his head low like a foot-ball player. In his haste, his eyes almost closed and the scene was a wild blur. Pulsating saliva stood at the corners of his mouth.

Within him, as he hurled himself forward, was born a love, a despairing fondness for this flag which was near him. It was a creation of beauty and invulnerability. It was a goddess, radiant, that bended its form with an imperious gesture to him. It was a woman, red and white, hating and loving, that called him with the voice of his hopes. Because no harm could come to it, he endowed it with power. He kept near as if it could be a saver of lives and an imploring cry went from his mind.

In the mad scramble, he was aware that the color-sergeant flinched suddenly as if struck by a bludgeon. He faltered and then became motionless, save for his quivering knees.

He made a spring and a clutch at the pole. At the same instant, his friend grabbed it from the other side. They jerked at it, stout and furious, but the color-sergeant was dead and the corpse would not relinquish its trust. For a moment, there was a grim encounter. The dead man, swinging with bended back seemed to be obstinately tugging, in ludicrous and awful ways for the possession of the flag.

It was past in an instant of time. They wrenched the flag furiously from the dead man, and, as they turned again, the corpse swayed forward with bowed head. One arm swung high and the curved hand fell with heavy protest on the friend's unheeding shoulder.

XXI

When the two youths turned with the flag, they saw that much of the regiment had crumbled away and the dejected remnant was coming slowly back. The men having hurled themselves in projectile-fashion, had presently expended their forces. They slowly retreated with their faces still toward the spluttering woods and their hot rifles still replying to the din. Several officers were giving orders, their voices keyed to screams.

"Where in hell yeh goin'?" the lieutenant was asking in a sarcastic howl. And a red-bearded officer, whose voice of triple brass could plainly be heard, was commanding: "Shoot in to'em! Shoot in to'em, Gawd damn their souls." There was a melee of speeches in which the men were ordered to do conflicting and impossible things.

The youth and his friend had a small scuffle over the flag. "Give it t' me." "No—let me keep it." Each felt satisfied with the other's possession of it but each felt bound to declare by an offer to carry the emblem, his willingness to further risk himself. The youth roughly pushed his friend away.

The regiment fell back to the stolid trees. There it halted for a moment to blaze at some dark forms that had begun to steal upon its track. Presently it resumed its march again curving among the tree-trunks. By the time the depleted regiment had again reached the first open space, they were receiving a fast and merciless fire. There seemed to be mobs all about them.

The greater part of the men, discouraged, their spirits worn by the turmoil, acted as if stunned. They accepted the pelting of the bullets with bowed and weary heads. It was of no purpose to strive against walls. It was of no use to batter themselves against granite. And from this consciousness that they had attempted to conquer an unconquerable thing, there seemed to arise a feeling that they had been betrayed. They glowered with bent brows but dangerously upon some of the officers, more particularly upon the red-bearded one with the voice of triple brass.

However, the rear of the regiment was fringed with men who continued to shoot irritably at the advancing foes. They seemed resolved to make every trouble. The lieutenant was perhaps the last man in the disordered mass. His forgotten back was toward the enemy. He had been shot in the arm. It hung straight and rigid. Occasionally he would cease to remember it and be about to emphasize an oath with a sweeping gesture. The multiplied pain caused him to swear with incredible power.

The youth went along with slipping, uncertain feet. He kept watchful eyes rear-ward. A scowl of mortification and rage was upon his face. He had thought of a fine revenge upon the officer who had referred to him and his fellows as mule-drivers. But he saw that it could not come to pass. His dreams had collapsed when the mule-drivers, dwindling rapidly, had wavered and hesitated on the little clearing and then had recoiled. And now the retreat of the mule-drivers was a march of shame to him.

A dagger-pointed gaze from without his blackened face was held toward the enemy but his greater hatred was riveted upon the man, who, not knowing him, had called him a mule-driver. When he knew that he and his comrades had failed to do anything in success-ful ways that might bring the little pangs of a kind of remorse upon the officer, the youth allowed the rage of the baffled to possess him. This cold officer upon a monument who dropped epithets uncon-cernedly down, would be finer as a dead man, he thought. So grievous did he think it that he could never possess the secret right to taunt truly in answer. He had pictured red letters of curious revenge. "We *are* mule-drivers, are we?" And now he was compelled to throw them away.

He presently wrapped his heart in the cloak of his pride and kept the flag erect. He harangued his fellows, pushing against their chests with his free hand. To those he knew well, he made frantic appeals, beseeching them by name. Between him and the lieutenant, scolding and near to losing his mind with rage, there was felt a subtle fellowship and equality. They supported each other in all manner of hoarse, howling protests.

But the regiment was a machine run-down. The two men babbled at a forceless thing. The soldiers who had heart to go slowly were continually shaken in their resolves by a knowledge that comrades were slipping with speed back to the lines. It was difficult to think of reputation when others were thinking of skins. Wounded men were left, crying, on this black journey.

The smoke-fringes and flames blustered always. The youth peering once through a sudden rift in a cloud, saw a brown mass of troops interwoven and magnified until they appeared to be thousands. A fierce-hued flag flashed before his vision.

Immediately, as if the up-lifting of the smoke had been pre-arranged, the discovered troops burst into a rasping yell and a hundred flames jetted toward the retreating band. A rolling, grey cloud again interposed as the regiment doggedly replied. The youth had to depend again upon his misused ears which were trembling and buzzing from the melee of musketry and yells.

The way seemed eternal. In the clouded haze, men became panic-stricken with the thought that the regiment had lost its path and was proceeding in a perilous direction. Once, the men who headed the wild procession turned and came pushing back against their comrades screaming that they were being fired upon from points which they had considered to be toward their own lines. At this cry, a hysterical fear and dismay beset the troops. A soldier who heretofore had been ambitious to make the regiment into a wise little band that would proceed calmly amid the huge-appearing difficulties, suddenly sank down and buried his face in his arms with an air of bowing to a doom. From another, a shrill lamentation rang out filled with profane allusions to a general. Men ran hither and thither seeking with their eyes, roads of escape. With serene regularity as if controlled by a schedule, bullets buffed into men.

The youth walked stolidly into the midst of the mob and with his flag in his hands, took a stand as if he expected an attempt to push him to the ground. He unconsciously assumed the attitude of the color-bearer in the fight of the preceding day. He passed over his brow a hand that trembled. His breath did not come freely. He was choking during this small wait for the crisis.

His friend came to him. "Well, Henry, I guess this is good-bye-John."

"Oh, shet up, yeh damn' fool," replied the youth and he would not look at the other.

The officers labored like politicians to beat the mass into a proper circle to face the menaces. The ground was uneven and torn. The men curled into depressions and fitted themselves snugly behind whatever would frustrate a bullet.

The youth noted with vague surprise that the lieutenant was standing mutely with his legs far apart and his sword held in the manner of a cane. The youth wondered what had happened to his vocal organs that he no more cursed.

There was something curious in this little intent pause of the lieutenant. He was like a babe which having wept its fill, raises its eyes and fixes upon a distant toy. He was engrossed in this contemplation, and the soft under-lip quivered from self-whispered words.

Some lazy and ignorant smoke curled slowly. The men, hiding from the bullets, waited anxiously for it to lift and disclose the plight of the regiment.

The silent ranks were suddenly thrilled by the eager voice of the lieutenant bawling out: "Here they come! Right onto us, b'Gawd." His further words were lost in a roar of wicked thunder from the men's rifles.

The youth's eyes had instantly turned in the direction indicated by the awakened and agitated lieutenant and he had seen the haze of treachery disclosing a body of soldiers of the enemy. They were so near that he could see their features. There was a recognition as he looked at the types of faces. He perceived with dim amazement that their uniforms were rather gay in effect, being light grey plentifully accented with a brilliant-hued facing. Too, the clothes seemed new.

These troops had apparently been going forward with caution, their rifles held in readiness, when the lieutenant had discovered them and their movement had been interrupted by the volley from the blue regiment. From the moment's glimpse, it was derived that they had been unaware of the proximity of their dark-suited foes, or, had mistaken the direction. Almost instantly, they were shut utterly from the youth's sight by the smoke from the energetic rifles of his companions. He strained his vision to learn the accomplishment of the volley but the smoke hung before him.

The two bodies of troops exchanged blows in the manner of a pair of boxers. The fast, angry firings went back and forth. The men in blue were intent with the despair of their circumstances and they seized upon the revenge to be had at close range. Their thunder swelled loud and valiant. Their curving front bristled with flashes and the place resounded with the clangor of their ram-rods. The youth ducked and dodged for a time and achieved a few unsatisfactory views of the enemy. There appeared to be many of them and they were replying swiftly. They seemed moving toward the blue regiment, step by step. He seated himself gloomily on the ground with his flag between his knees.

As he noted the vicious, wolf-like temper of his comrades, he had a sweet thought that if the enemy was about to swallow the regimental broom as a large prisoner, it could at least have the consolation of going down with bristles forward.

But the blows of the antagonist began to grow more weak. Fewer bullets ripped the air and finally when the men slackened to learn of the fight, they could see only dark, floating smoke. The regiment lay still and gazed. Presently, some chance whim came to the pestering blur and it began to coil heavily away. The men saw a ground vacant of fighters. It would have been an empty stage if it were not for a few corpses that lay thrown and twisted into fantastic shapes upon the sward.

At sight of this tableau, many of the men in blue sprang from behind their covers and made an ungainly dance of joy. Their eyes burned and a hoarse cheer of elation broke from their dry lips.

It had begun to seem to them that events were trying to prove that they were impotent. These little battles had evidently endeavored to demonstrate that the men could not fight well. When on the verge of submission to these opinions, the small duel had showed them that the proportions were not impossible, and by it they had revenged themselves upon their misgivings and upon the foe.

The impetus of enthusiasm was theirs again. They gazed about them with looks of uplifted pride, feeling new trust in the grim, always-confident weapons in their hands. And they were men.

XXII

Presently they knew that no firing threatened them. All ways seemed once more opened to them. The dusty blue lines of their friends were disclosed a short distance away. In the distance there were many colossal noises but in all this part of the field there was a sudden stillness.

They perceived that they were free. The depleted band drew a long breath of relief and gathered itself into a bunch to complete its trip.

In this last length of journey, the men began to show strange emotions. They hurried with nervous fear. Some who had been dark and unfaltering in the grimmest moments now could not conceal an anxiety that made them frantic. It was perhaps that they dreaded to be killed in insignificant ways after the times for proper military deaths had passed. Or, perhaps, they thought it would be too ironical to get killed at the portals of safety. With backward looks of perturbation, they hastened.

As they approached their own lines, there was some sarcasm exhibited on the part of a gaunt and bronzed regiment that lay resting in the shade of trees. Questions were wafted to them.

"Where th' hell yeh been?"

"What yeh comin' back fer?"

"Why didn't yeh stay there?"

"Was it warm out there, sonny?"

"Goin' home now, boys?"

One shouted in taunting mimicry. "Oh, mother, come quick an' look at th' sojers."

There was no reply from the bruised and battered regiment save that one man made broad-cast challenges to fist-fights and the red-bearded officer walked rather near and glared in great swashbuckler style at a tall captain in the other regiment. But the lieutenant suppressed the man who wished to fist-fight, and the tall captain, flushing at the little fanfare of the red-bearded one, was obliged to look intently at some trees.

The youth's tender flesh was deeply stung by these remarks. From under his creased brows, he glowered with hate at the mockers. He meditated upon a few revenges. Still, many in the regiment hung their heads in criminal fashion so that it came to pass that the men trudged with sudden heaviness as if they bore upon their bended shoulders the coffin of their honor. And the lieutenant recollecting himself began to mutter softly in black curses.

They turned, when they arrived at their old position, to regard the ground over which they had charged.

The youth, in this contemplation, was smitten with a large astonishment. He discovered that the distances, as compared with the brilliant measurings of his mind, were trivial and ridiculous. The stolid trees, where much had taken place, seemed incredibly near. The time, too, now that he reflected, he saw to have been short. He wondered at the number of emotions and events that had been crowded into such little spaces. Elfin thoughts must have exaggerated and enlarged everything, he said.

It seemed, then, that there was bitter justice in the speeches of the gaunt and bronzed veterans. He veiled a glance of disdain at his fellows who strewed the ground, choking with dust, red from perspiration, misty-eyed, dishevelled.

They were gulping at their canteens, fierce to wring every mite of water from them. And they polished at their swollen and watery features with coat-sleeves and bunches of grass.

However, to the youth there was a considerable joy in musing upon his performances during the charge. He had had very little time, previously, in which to appreciate himself, so that there was now much satisfaction in quietly thinking of his actions. He recalled bits of color that in the flurry, had stamped themselves unawares upon his engaged senses.

As the regiment lay heaving from its hot exertions, the officer who had named them as mule drivers came galloping along the line. He had lost his cap. His towsled hair streamed wildly and his face was dark with vexation and wrath. His temper was displayed with more clearness by the way in which he managed his horse. He jerked and wrenched savagely at his bridle, stopping the hard-breathing animal with a furious pull near the colonel of the regiment. He immediately exploded in reproaches which came unbidden to the ears of the men. They were suddenly alert, being always curious about black words between officers.

"Oh, thunder, MacChesnay, what an awful bull you made of this thing," began the officer. He attempted low tones but his indignation caused certain of the men to learn the sense of his words. "What an awful mess you made. Good Lord, man, you stopped about a hundred feet this side of a very pretty success. If your men had gone a hundred feet further you would have made a great charge, but as it is—what a lot of mud-diggers you've got anyway."

The men, listening with bated breath, now turned their curious eyes upon the colonel. They had a ragamuffin interest in this affair.

The colonel was seen to straighten his form and put one hand forth in oratorical fashion. He wore an injured air; it was as if a deacon had been accused of stealing. The men were wiggling in an ecstasy of excitement.

But, of a sudden, the colonel's manner changed from that of a deacon to that of a Frenchman. He shrugged his shoulders. "Oh, well, general, we went as far as we could," he said calmly.

"'As far as you could'? Did you, b'Gawd?" snorted the other. "Well, that wasn't very far, was it?" he added with a glance of cold contempt into the other's eyes. "Not very far, I think. You were intended to make a diversion in favor of Whiterside. How well you succeeded, your own ears can now tell you." He wheeled his horse and rode stiffly away.

The colonel, bidden to hear the jarring noises of an engagement in the woods to the left, broke out in vague damnations.

The lieutenant who had listened with an air of impotent rage to the interview spoke suddenly in firm and undaunted tones. "I don't care what a man is—whether he is a general, or what—if he says th' boys didn't put up a good fight out there, he's a damned fool."

"Lieutenant," began the colonel, severely, "this is my own affair and I'll trouble you—"

The lieutenant made an obedient gesture. "All right, colonel, all right," he said. He sat down with an air of being content with himself.

The news that the regiment had been reproached went along the line. For a time, the men were bewildered by it. "Good thunder," they ejaculated staring at the vanishing form of the general. They conceived it to be a huge mistake.

Presently, however, they began to believe that in truth their efforts had been called light. The youth could see this conviction weigh upon the entire regiment until the men were like cuffed and cursed animals but, withal, rebellious.

The friend, with a grievance in his eye, went to the youth. "I wonder what he does want," he said. "He must think we went out there an' played marbles. I never see sech a man."

The youth developed a tranquil philosophy for these moments of irritation. "Oh, well," he rejoined, "he probably didnt see nothin' of it at all an' got mad as blazes an' concluded we were a lot 'a sheep, jest b'cause we didnt do what he wanted done. It's a pity ol' Grandpa Henderson got killed yestirday—he'd a knowed we done our best an' fit good. It's jest our awful luck, that's what."

"I should say so," replied the friend. He seemed to be deeply wounded at an injustice. "I should say we did have awful luck. There's no fun in fightin' fer people when everything yeh do—no matter what—aint done right. I have a notion t' stay behind next time an' let'em take their ol' charge an' go t' th' devil with it."

The youth spoke soothingly to his comrade. "Well, we both done good. I'd like t' see th' fool what'd say we both didnt do as good as we could."

"'A course, we did," declared the friend stoutly. "An' I'd break th' feller's neck if he was as big as a church. But we're all right, anyhow, fer I heared one feller say that we two fit th' best in th' reg'ment an' they had a great argyment 'bout it. Another feller, 'a course, he had t' up an' say it was a lie—he seen all what was goin' on an' he never seen us from th' beginnin' t' th' end. An' a lot more struck in an' ses it wasn't a lie—we did fight like thunder, an' they give us quite a send-off. But this is what I can't stand—these everlastin' ol' soldiers, titterin' an' laughin', an' then that general, he's crazy."

The youth exclaimed with sudden exasperation. "He's a lunkhead. He makes me mad. I wish he'd come along next time. We'd show'im what—"

He ceased because several men had come hurrying up. Their faces expressed a bringing of great news.

"Oh, Flem, yeh jest oughta heard," cried one, eagerly.

"Heard what?" said the youth.

"Yeh jest oughta heard," repeated the other and he arranged himself to tell his tidings. The others made an excited circle. "Well, sir, th' colonel met your lieutenant right by us—it was damndest thing I ever heard—an' he ses, 'Ahem, ahem,' he ses, 'Mr. Hasbrouck,' he ses, 'by th' way, who was that lad what carried th' flag?' he ses. There, Flemin', what d' yeh think 'a that? 'Who was th' lad what carried th' flag?' he ses, an' th' lieutenant, he speaks up right away: 'That's Flemin', an' he's 'a jim-hickey,' he ses, right away. What? I say he did. 'A jim-hickey,' he ses—thos'r his

words. He did, too. I say, he did. If you kin tell this story better than
I kin, go ahead an' tell it. Well, then, keep yer mouth shet. Th' lieutenant, he ses: 'He's a jim-hickey,' an' th' colonel, he ses: 'Ahem,
ahem, he is indeed a very good man t' have, ahem. He kep th' flag
'way t' th' front. I saw'im. He's a good un,' ses th' colonel. 'You bet,'
ses th' lieutenant, 'he an' a feller named Wilson was at th' head 'a th'
charge, an' howlin' like Indians, all th' time,' he ses. 'Head 'a th'
charge all th' time,' he ses. 'A feller named Wilson,' he ses. There,
Wilson, m'boy, put that in a letter an' send it hum t' yer mother, hay?
'A feller named Wilson,' he ses. An' th' colonel, he ses: 'Were they,
indeed? Ahem, ahem. My sakes,' he ses. 'At th' head 'a th' reg-
'ment?' he ses. 'They were,' ses th' lieutenant. 'My sakes,' ses th'
colonel. He ses: 'Well, well, well,' he ses, 'those two babies?' 'They
were!' ses th' lieutenant. 'Well, well,' ses th' colonel, 'they deserve
t' be major-generals,' he ses. 'They deserve t' be major-generals.' "

The youth and his friend had said: "Huh!" "Yer lyin', Thompson." "Oh, go t' blazes." "He never sed it." "Oh, what a lie."
"Huh." But despite these youthful scoffings and embarrassments,
they knew that their faces were deeply flushing from thrills of pleasure. They exchanged a secret glance of joy and congratulation.

They speedily forgot many things. The past held no pictures of
error and disappointment. They were very happy and their hearts
swelled with grateful affection for the colonel and the lieutenant.

XXIII

When the woods again began to pour forth the dark-hued masses
of the enemy, the youth felt serene self-confidence. He smiled
briefly when he saw men dodge and duck at the long screechings of
shells that were thrown in giant handfuls over them. He stood,
erect and tranquil, watching the attack begin against a part of the
line that made a blue curve along the side of an adjacent hill. His
vision being unmolested by smoke from the rifles of his companions, he had opportunities to see parts of the hard fight. It was a
relief to perceive at last from whence came some of these noises
which had been roared into his ears.

Off a short way, he saw two regiments fighting a little separate
battle with two other regiments. It was in a cleared space, wearing a
set-apart look. They were blazing as if upon a wager, giving and
taking tremendous blows. The firings were incredibly fierce and
rapid. These intent regiments apparently were oblivious of all larger
purposes of war and were slugging each other as if at a matched
game.

In another direction, he saw a magnificent brigade going with the
evident intention of driving the enemy from a wood. They passed
in out of sight and presently there was a most, awe-inspiring racket
in the wood. The noise was unspeakable. Having stirred this prodigious up-roar and, apparently, finding it too prodigious, the brigade,

after a little time, came marching airily out again with its fine formation in no wise disturbed. There were no traces of speed in its
movements. The brigade was jaunty and seemed to point a proud
thumb at the yelling wood.

On a slope to the left, there was a long row of guns, gruff and
maddened, denouncing the enemy who down through the woods
were forming for another attack in the pitiless monotony of conflicts. The round, red discharges from the guns made a crimson flare
and a high, thick smoke. Occasional glimpses could be caught of
groups of the toiling artillerymen. In the rear of this row of guns
stood a house, calm and white, amid bursting shells. A congregation
of horses, tied to a long railing, were tugging frenziedly at their bridles. Men were running hither and thither.

The detached battle between the four regiments lasted for some
time. There chanced to be no interference and they settled their
dispute by themselves. They struck savagely and powerfully at each
other for a period of minutes and then the lighter-hued regiments
faltered and drew back, leaving the dark, blue lines, shouting. The
youth could see the two flags shaking and laughing amid the
smoke-remnants.

Presently, there was a stillness, pregnant with meaning. The blue
lines shifted and changed a trifle and stared expectantly at the silent
woods and fields before them. The hush was solemn and church-
like, save for a distant battery that, evidently unable to remain quiet
sent a faint rolling thunder over the ground. It irritated, like the
noises of unimpressed boys. The men imagined that it would prevent their perched ears from hearing the first words of the new
battle.

Of a sudden, the guns on the slope roared out a message of warning. A spluttering sound had begun in the woods. It swelled with
amazing speed to a profound clamor that involved the earth in
noises. The splitting crashes swept along the lines until an interminable roar was developed. To those in the midst of it, it became a
din fitted to the universe. It was the whirring and thumping of
gigantic machinery, complications among the smaller stars. The
youth's ears were filled cups. They were incapable of hearing more.

On an incline over which a road wound, he saw wild and desperate rushes of men. It was perpetually backward and forward in riotous surges. These parts of the opposing armies were two long
waves that pitched upon each other madly at dictated points. To
and fro, they swelled. Sometimes, one side by its yells and cheers
would proclaim decisive blows but, a moment later, the other side
would be all yells and cheers. Once, the youth saw a spray of light
forms go in hound-like leaps toward the waving blue lines. There
was much howling and presently it went away with a vast mouthful
of prisoners. Again, he saw a blue wave dash with such thunderous
force against a grey obstruction that it seemed to clear the earth of

it and leave nothing but trampled sod. And, always, in these swift and deadly rushes to and fro, the men screamed and yelled like maniacs.

Particular pieces of fence or secure positions behind collections of trees were wrangled over, as gold thrones or pearl bedsteads. There were desperate lunges at these chosen spots seemingly every instant and most of them were bandied like light toys between the contending forces. The youth could not tell from the battle-flags, flying like crimson foam in many directions, which color of cloth was winning.

His emaciated regiment bustled forth with undiminished fierceness when its time came. When assaulted again by bullets, the men burst out in a barbaric cry of rage and pain. They bended their heads in aims of intent hatred behind the projected hammers of their guns. Their ram-rods clanged loud with fury as their eager arms pounded the cartridges into the rifle-barrels. The front of the regiment was a smoke-wall penetrated by the flashing points of yellow and red.

Wallowing in the fight, they were in an astonishingly short time, re-smudged. They surpassed in stain and dirt all their previous appearances. Moving to and fro with strained exertion, jabbering the while, they were, with their swaying bodies, black faces and glowing eyes, like strange and ugly fiends jigging heavily in the smoke.

The lieutenant, returning from a tour after a bandage, produced from a hidden receptacle of his mind, new and portentous oaths suited to the emergency. Strings of expletives he swung lash-like over the backs of his men. And it was evident that his previous efforts had in no wise impaired his resources.

The youth, still the bearer of the colors, did not feel his idleness. He was deeply absorbed as a spectator. The crash and swing of the great drama made him lean forward, intent-eyed, his face working in small contortions. Sometimes, he prattled, words coming unconsciously from in him in grotesque exclamations. He did not know that he breathed; that the flag hung silently over him, so absorbed was he.

A formidable line of the enemy came within dangerous range. They could be seen plainly, tall, gaunt men with excited faces running with long strides toward a wandering fence.

At sight of this danger, the men suddenly ceased their cursing monotone. There was an instant of strained silence before they threw up their rifles and fired a plumping volley at the foes. There had been no order given; the men upon recognizing the menace, had immediately let drive their flock of bullets without waiting for word of command.

But the enemy were quick to gain the protection of the wandering line of fence. They slid down behind it with remarkable celerity and from this position, they began briskly to slice up the blue men.

These latter braced their energies for a great struggle. Often, white clenched teeth shone from the dusky faces. Many heads surged to and fro, floating upon a pale sea of smoke. Those behind the fence frequently shouted and yelped in taunts and gibe-like cries but the regiment maintained a stressed silence. Perhaps, at this new assault, the men re-called the fact that they had been named mud-diggers and it made their situation thrice bitter. They were breathlessly intent upon keeping the ground and thrusting away the rejoicing body of the enemy. They fought swiftly and with a despairing savageness denoted in their expressions.

The youth had resolved not to budge whatever should happen. Some arrows of scorn that had buried themselves in his heart, had generated strange and unspeakable hatreds. It was clear to him that his final and absolute revenge was to be achieved by his dead body lying, torn and gluttering, upon the field. This was to be a poignant retaliation upon the officer who had said "mule-driver," and, later, "mud-digger." For, in all the wild graspings of his mind for a unit responsible for his sufferings and commotions, he always seized upon the man who had dubbed him wrongly. And it was his idea, vaguely formulated, that his corpse would be for those eyes a great and salt reproach.

The regiment bled extravagantly. Grunting bundles of blue began to drop. The orderly-sergeant of the youth's company was shot through the cheeks. Its supports being injured, his jaw hung afar down, disclosing in the wide cavern of his mouth, a pulsing mass of blood and teeth. And, with it all, he made attempts to cry out. In his endeavor there was dreadful earnestness as if he conceived that one great shriek would make him well.

The youth saw him presently go rearward. His strength seemed in no wise impaired. He ran swiftly casting wild glances for succor.

Others fell down about the feet of their companions. Some of the wounded crawled out and away, but many lay still, their bodies twisted into impossible shapes.

The youth looked once for his friend. He saw a vehement young man, powder-smeared and frowsled, whom he knew to be him. The lieutenant, also, was unscathed in his position at the rear. He had continued to curse but it was now with the air of a man who was using his last box of oaths.

For the fire of the regiment had begun to wane and drip. The robust voice that had come strangely from the thin ranks, was growing rapidly weak.

XXIV

The colonel came running along back of the line. There were other officers following him. "We must charge'm," they shouted.

"We must charge'm." They cried with resentful voices, as if anticipating a rebellion against this plan by the men.

The youth, upon hearing the shouts, began to study the distance between him and the enemy. He made vague calculations. He saw that to be firm soldiers, they must go forward. It would be death to stay in the present place and, with all the circumstances, to go backward would exalt too many others. Their hope was to push the galling foes away from the fence.

He expected that his companions, weary and stiffened, would have to be driven to this assault but as he turned toward them, he perceived with a certain surprise that they were giving quick and unqualified expressions of assent. There was an ominous, clanging overture to the charge when the shafts of the bayonets rattled upon the rifle-barrels. At the yelled words of command, the soldiers sprang forward in eager leaps. There was new and unexpected force in the movement of the regiment. A knowledge of its faded and jaded condition made the charge appear like a paroxysm, a display of the strength that comes before a final feebleness. The men scampered in insane fever of haste, racing as if to achieve a sudden success before an exhilarating fluid should leave them. It was a blind and despairing rush by the collection of men in dusty and tattered blue, over a green sward and under a sapphire sky, toward a fence, dimly out-lined in smoke, from behind which spluttered the fierce rifles of enemies.

The youth kept the bright colors to the front. He was waving his free arm in furious circles, the while shrieking mad calls and appeals, urging on those that did not need to be urged. For, it seemed that the mob of blue men hurling themselves on the dangerous group of rifles were again grown suddenly wild with an enthusiasm of unselfishness. From the many firings starting toward them, it looked as if they would merely succeed in making a great sprinkling of corpses on the grass between their former position and the fence. But they were in a state of frenzy, perhaps because of forgotten vanities, and it made an exhibition of sublime recklessness. There was no obvious questionings, nor figurings, nor diagrams. There was, apparently, no considered loop-holes. It appeared that the swift wings of their desires would have shattered against the iron gates of the impossible.

He himself felt the daring spirit of a savage, religion-mad. He was capable of profound sacrifices, a tremendous death. He had no time for dissections but he knew that he thought of the bullets only as things that could prevent him from reaching the place of his endeavor. There were subtle flashings of joy within him, that thus should be his mind.

He strained all his strength. His eye-sight was shaken and dazzled by the tension of thought and muscle. He did not see anything excepting the mist of smoke gashed by the little knives of fire but he knew that in it lay the aged fence of a vanished farmer protecting the snuggled bodies of the grey men.

As he ran, a thought of the shock of contact gleamed in his mind. He expected a great concussion when the two bodies of troops crashed together. This became a part of his wild battle-madness. He could feel the onward swing of the regiment about him and he conceived of a thunderous, crushing blow that would prostrate the resistance and spread consternation and amazement for miles. The flying regiment was going to have a catapultian effect. This dream made him run faster among his comrades who were giving vent to hoarse and frantic cheers.

But presently he could see that many of the men in grey did not intend to abide the blow. The smoke, rolling, disclosed men who ran, their faces still turned. These grew to a crowd who retired stubbornly. Individuals wheeled frequently to send a bullet at the blue wave.

But at one part of the line there was a grim and obdurate group that made no movement to go. They were settled firmly down behind posts and rails. A flag, ruffled and fierce, waved over them and their rifles dinned fiercely.

The blue whirl of men got very near until it seemed that in truth there would be a close and frightful scuffle. There was an expressed disdain in the opposition of the little group, that changed the meaning of the cheers of the men in blue. They became yells of wrath, directed, personal. The cries of the two parties were now in sound an interchange of scathing insults.

They in blue showed their teeth; their eyes shone all white. They launched themselves as at the throats of those who stood resisting. The space between dwindled to an insignificant distance.

The youth had centred the gaze of his soul upon that other flag. Its possession would be high pride. It would express bloody minglings, near blows. He had a gigantic hatred for those who made great difficulties and complications. They caused it to be as a craved treasure of mythology, hung amid tasks and contrivances of danger.

He plunged like a mad horse at it. He was resolved it should not escape if wild blows and darings of blows could seize it. His own emblem, quivering and a-flare was winging toward the other. It seemed there would shortly be an encounter of strange beaks and claws, as of eagles.

The swirling body of blue men came to a sudden halt at close and disastrous range and roared a swift volley. The group in grey was split and broken by this fire but its riddled body still fought. The men in blue yelled again and rushed in upon it.

The youth, in his leapings, saw as through a mist, a picture of four or five men stretched upon the ground or writhing upon their knees with bowed heads as if they had been stricken by bolts from the sky. Tottering among them was the rival color-bearer whom the youth saw had been bitten vitally by the bullets of the last formidable volley. He perceived this man fighting a last struggle, the struggle of one whose legs are grasped by demons. It was a ghastly battle. Over his face was the bleach of death but set upon it was the dark and hard lines of determined purpose. With this grin of resolution, he hugged his precious flag to him and was stumbling and staggering in his design to go the way that led to safety for it.

But his wounds always made it seem that his feet were retarded, held, and he fought a grim fight as with invisible ghouls, fastened greedily upon his limbs.

Those in advance of the scampering blue men, howling cheers, leaped at the fence. The despair of the lost was in his eyes, as he glanced back at them.

The youth's friend went over the obstruction in a tumbling heap and sprang at the flag as a panther at prey. He pulled at it, and wrenching it free, swung up its red brilliancy with a mad cry of exultation even as the color-bearer, gasping, lurched over in a final throe and stiffening convulsively turned his dead face to the ground. There was much blood upon the grass-blades.

At the place of success there began more wild clamorings of cheers. The men gesticulated and bellowed in an ecstasy. When they spoke it was as if they considered their listener to be a mile away. What hats and caps were left to them, they often slung high in the air.

At one part of the line, four men had been swooped upon and they now sat as prisoners. Some blue men were about them in an eager and curious circle. The soldiers had trapped strange birds and there was an examination. A flurry of fast questions was in the air.

One of the prisoners was nursing a superficial wound in the foot. He cuddled it, baby-wise, but he looked up from it often to curse with an astonishing utter abandon straight at the noses of his captors. He consigned them to red regions; he called upon the pestilential wrath of strange gods. And with it all he was singularly free from recognition of the finer points of the conduct of prisoners-of-war. It was as if a clumsy clod had trod upon his tender toe and he conceived it to be his privilege, his duty, to use deep, resentful oaths.

Another, who was a boy in years, took his plight with great calmness and apparent good-nature. He conversed with the men in blue, studying their faces with his bright and keen eyes. They spoke of battles and conditions. There was an acute interest in all their faces during this exchange of view-points. It seemed a great satisfaction to hear voices from where all had been darkness and speculation.

The third captive sat with a morose countenance. He preserved a stoical and cold attitude. To all advances, he made one reply, without variation. "Ah, go t' hell."

The last of the four was always silent and, for the most part, kept his face turned in unmolested directions. From the views the youth received, he seemed to be in a state of absolute dejection. Shame was upon him and with it profound regret that he was perhaps no more to be counted in the ranks of his fellows. The youth could detect no expression that would allow him to believe that the other was giving a thought to his narrowed future, the pictured dungeons, perhaps, and starvations and brutalities, liable to the imagination. All to be seen was shame for captivity and regret for the right to antagonize.

After the men had celebrated sufficiently, they settled down behind the old rail fence, on the opposite side to the one from which their foes had been driven. A few shot perfunctorily at distant marks.

There was some long grass. The youth nestled in it and rested, making a convenient rail support the flag. His friend, jubilant and glorified, holding his treasure with vanity, came to him there. They sat side by side and congratulated each other.

XXV

The roarings that had stretched in a long line of sound across the face of the forest began to grow intermittent and weaker. The stentorian speeches of the artillery continued in some distant encounter but the crashes of the musketry had almost ceased. The youth and his friend, of a sudden looked up, feeling a deadened form of distress at the waning of these noises which had become a part of life. They could see changes going on among the troops. There were marchings this way and that way. A battery wheeled leisurely. On the crest of a small hill was the thick gleam of many departing muskets.

The youth arose. "Well, what now, I wonder," he said. By his tone, he seemed to be preparing to resent some new monstrosity in the way of dins and smashes. He shaded his eyes with his grimy hand and gazed over the field.

His friend also arose and stared. "I bet we're goin' t' git along outa this an' back over th' river," said he.

"Well, I swan," said the youth.

They waited, watching. Within a little while, the regiment received orders to retrace its way. The men got up grunting from the grass, regretting the soft reposes behind the rails. They jerked their stiffened legs and stretched their arms over their heads. One man swore as he rubbed his eyes. They all groaned. "Oh, Lord." They had as many objections to this change as they would have had to a proposal for a new battle.

They tramped slowly back over the field across which they had run in a mad scamper. The fence, deserted, resumed with its careening posts and disjointed bars, an air of quiet rural depravity. Beyond it, there lay spread a few corpses. Conspicuous, was the contorted body of the color-bearer in grey whose flag the youth's friend was now bearing away.

The regiment marched until it had joined its fellows. The re-formed brigade, in column, aimed through a wood at the road. Directly they were in a mass of dust-covered troops and were trudging along in a way parallel to the enemy's lines, as these had been defined by the previous turmoil.

They passed within view of the stolid white house and saw in front of it, groups of their comrades lying in wait behind a neat breastwork. A row of guns were booming at a distant enemy. Shells thrown in reply were raising clouds of dust and splinters. Horsemen dashed along the line of entrenchments.

As they passed near other commands, men of the dilapidated regiment procured the captured flag from the youth's friend and, tossing it high into the air cheered tumultuously as it turned, with apparent reluctance, slowly over and over.

At this point of its march, the division curved away from the field and went winding off in the direction of the river. When the significance of this movement had impressed itself upon the youth, he turned his head and looked over his shoulder toward the trampled and debris-strewed ground. He breathed a breath of new satisfaction. He finally nudged his friend. "Well, it's all over," he said to him.

His friend gazed backward. "B'Gawd, it is," he assented.

They mused.

For a time, the youth was obliged to reflect in a puzzled and uncertain way. His mind was under-going a subtle change. It took moments for his mind to cast off its battleful ways and resume its accustomed course of thought. Gradually his brain emerged from the clogged clouds and at last he was enabled to more closely comprehend himself and circumstance.

He understood then that the existence of shot and counter-shot was in the past. He had dwelt in a land of strange, squalling upheavals and had come forth. He had been where there was red of blood and black of passion, and he was escaped. His first thoughts were given to rejoicings at this fact.

Later, he began to study his deeds—his failures and his achievements. Thus fresh from scenes where many of his usual machines of reflection had been idle, from where he had proceeded sheep-like, he struggled to marshall all his acts.

At last, they marched before him clearly. From this present viewpoint, he was enabled to look upon them in spectator fashion and to criticise them with some correctness, for his new condition had already defeated certain sympathies.

His friend, too, seemed engaged with some retrospection for he suddenly gestured and said: "Good Lord!"

"What?" asked the youth.

"Good Lord!" repeated his friend. "Yeh know Jimmie Rogers? Well, he—gosh, when he was hurt I started t' git some water fer'im an', thunder, I aint seen'im from that time 'til this. I clean forgot what I—say, has anybody seen Jimmie Rogers?"

"Seen'im? No! He's dead," they told him.

His friend swore.

But the youth, regarding his procession of memory, felt gleeful and unregretting, for, in it, his public deeds were paraded in great and shining prominence. Those performances which had been witnessed by his fellows marched now in wide purple and gold, hiding various deflections. They went gaily, with music. It was pleasure to watch these things. He spent delightful minutes viewing the gilded images of memory.

He saw that he was good. He re-called with a thrill of joy the respectful comments of his fellows upon his conduct. He said to himself again the sentence of the insane lieutenant: "If I had ten thousand wild-cats like you, I could tear th' stomach outa this war in less'n a week." It was a little coronation.

Nevertheless, the ghost of his flight from the first engagement appeared to him and danced. Echoes of his terrible combat with the arrayed forces of the universe came to his ears. There were small shoutings in his brain about these matters. For a moment, he blushed, and the light of his soul flickered with shame.

However, he presently procured an explanation and an apology. He said that those tempestuous moments were of the wild mistakes and ravings of a novice who did not comprehend. He had been a mere man railing at a condition but now he was out of it and could see that it had been very proper and just. It had been necessary for him to swallow swords that he might have a better throat for grapes.[3] Fate had in truth, been kind to him; she had stabbed him with benign purpose and diligently cudgeled him for his own sake. In his rebellion, he had been very portentous, no doubt, and sincere, and anxious for humanity, but now that he stood safe, with no lack of blood, it was suddenly clear to him that he had been wrong not to kiss the knife and bow to the cudgel. He had foolishly squirmed.

But the sky would forget. It was true, he admitted, that in the world it was the habit to cry devil at persons who refused to trust what they could not trust, but he thought that perhaps the stars dealt differently. The imperturbable sun shines on insult and worship.

As the youth was thus fraternizing again with nature, a spectre of

---

3. This is probably one of the most striking of those passages where Crane introduces vestiges of Biblical imagery and ideas into Henry's thoughts. The relevant passage is: "And out of his mouth goeth a sharp sword, that with it he should smite the nations: and he shall rule them with a rod of iron: and he treadeth the winepress of the fierceness and wrath of Almighty God" (Revelation 19.15).

reproach came to him. There loomed the dogging memory of the tattered soldier, he, who gored by bullets and faint for blood, had fretted concerning an imagined wound in another, he, who had loaned his last of strength and intellect for the tall soldier, he who blind with weariness and pain, had been deserted in the field.

For an instant, a wretched chill of sweat was upon him at the thought that he might be detected in the thing. As it stood persistently before his vision, he gave vent to a cry of sharp irritation and agony.

His friend turned. "What's th' matter, Henry?" he demanded.

The youth's reply was an outburst of crimson oaths.

As he marched along the little branch-hung road-way among his prattling companions, this vision of cruelty brooded over him. It clung near him always and darkened his view of the deeds in purple and gold. Whichever way his thoughts turned, they were followed by the sombre phantom of the desertion in the fields. He looked stealthily at his companions feeling sure that they must discern in his face evidences of this pursuit. But they were plodding in ragged array, discussing with quick tongues, the accomplishment of the late battle.

"Oh, if a man should come up an' ask me, I'd say we got a dum good lickin'."

"Lickin'—in yer eye. We aint licked, sonny. We're goin' down here aways, swing aroun' an' come in behint'em."

"Oh, hush, with yer comin' in behint'em. I've seen all 'a that I wanta. Don't tell me about comin' in behint—"

"Bill Smithers, he ses he'd rather been in ten hunderd battles than been in that heluva hospital. He ses they got shootin' in th' night-time an' shells dropped plum among'em in th' hospital. He ses sech hollerin' he never see."

"Hasbrouck? He's th' best off'cer in this here reg'ment. He's a Whale."

"Didn't I tell yeh we'd come aroun' in behint'em? Didn't I tell yeh so? We—"

"Oh, shet yer mouth."

"You make me sick."

"G' home, yeh fool."

For a time, this pursuing recollection of the tattered man took all elation from the youth's veins. He saw his vivid error and he was afraid that it would stand before him all of his life. He took no share in the chatter of his comrades, nor did he look at them or know them, save when he felt sudden suspicion that they were seeing his thoughts and scrutinizing each detail of the scene with the tattered soldier.

Yet gradually he mustered force to put the sin at a distance. And then he regarded it with what he thought to be great calmness. At last, he concluded that he saw in it quaint uses. He exclaimed that

its importance in the aftertime would be great to him if it even succeeded in hindering the workings of his egotism. It would make a
sobering balance. It would become a good part of him. He would
have upon him often the consciousness of a great mistake. And he
would be taught to deal gently and with care. He would be a man.

This plan for the utilization of a sin did not give him complete
joy but it was the best sentiment he could formulate under the circumstances and when it was combined with his successes, or public
deeds, he knew that he was quite contented.

His eyes seemed to be opened to some new ways. He found that
he could look back upon the brass and bombast of his earlier gospels and see them truly. He was gleeful when he discovered that he
now despised them.

He was emerged from his struggles, with a large sympathy for the
machinery of the universe. With his new eyes, he could see that the
secret and open blows which were being dealt about the world with
such heavenly lavishness were in truth blessings. It was a deity
laying about him with the bludgeon of correction.

His loud mouth against these things had been lost as the storm
ceased. He would no more stand upon places high and false, and
denounce the distant planets. He beheld that he was tiny but not
inconsequent to the sun. In the space-wide whirl of events no grain
like him would be lost.

With this conviction came a store of assurance. He felt a quiet
manhood, non-assertive but of sturdy and strong blood. He knew
that he would no more quail before his guides wherever they should
point. He had been to touch the great death and found that, after
all, it was but the great death and was for others. He was a man.

So it came to pass that as he trudged from the place of blood and
wrath, his soul changed. He came from hot-ploughshares to prospects of clover tranquilly and it was as if hot-ploughshares were not.
Scars faded as flowers.

It rained. The procession of weary soldiers became a bedraggled
train, despondent and muttering, marching with churning effort, in
a trough of liquid brown mud under a low, wretched sky. Yet the
youth smiled, for he saw that the world was a world for him though
many discovered it to be made of oaths and walking-sticks.[4] He had
rid himself of the red sickness of battle. The sultry night-mare was
in the past. He had been an animal blistered and sweating in the
heat and pain of war. He turned now with a lover's thirst, to images
of tranquil skies, fresh meadows, cool brooks; an existence of soft
and eternal peace.

1893–94   1895, 1979

---

4. The world of war fever epitomized by
the Lieutenant of Henry's company. This
allusion was obscured, perhaps inadvertently, when Crane changed the mention
of the Lieutenant's sword as his "walk-
ing-stick" in Chapter XXI to a "cane."

The Open Boat[1]

A TALE INTENDED TO BE AFTER THE FACT. BEING THE EXPERIENCE OF FOUR MEN FROM THE SUNK STEAMER COMMODORE

I

None of them knew the color of the sky. Their eyes glanced level, and were fastened upon the waves that swept toward them. These waves were of the hue of slate, save for the tops, which were of foaming white, and all of the men knew the colors of the sea. The horizon narrowed and widened, and dipped and rose, and at all times its edge was jagged with waves that seemed thrust up in points like rocks.

Many a man ought to have a bath-tub larger than the boat which here rode upon the sea. These waves were most wrongfully and barbarously abrupt and tall, and each froth-top was a problem in small boat navigation.

The cook squatted in the bottom and looked with both eyes at the six inches of gunwale which separated him from the ocean. His sleeves were rolled over his fat forearms, and the two flaps of his unbuttoned vest dangled as he bent to bail out the boat. Often he said: "Gawd! That was a narrow clip." As he remarked it he invariably gazed eastward over the broken sea.

The oiler,[2] steering with one of the two oars in the boat, sometimes raised himself suddenly to keep clear of water that swirled in over the stern. It was a thin little oar and it seemed often ready to snap.

The correspondent, pulling at the other oar, watched the waves and wondered why he was there.

The injured captain, lying in the bow, was at this time buried in that profound dejection and indifference which comes, temporarily at least, to even the bravest and most enduring when, willy nilly, the firm fails, the army loses, the ship goes down. The mind of the master of a vessel is rooted deep in the timbers of her, though he command for a day or a decade, and this captain had on him the stern impression of a scene in the grays of dawn of seven turned faces, and later a stump of a top-mast with a white ball on it that

1. Crane sailed as a correspondent on the steamer *Commodore*, which on January 1, 1897, left Jacksonville, Florida, with munitions for the Cuban insurrectionists. Early on the morning of January 2, the steamer sank. With four others, Crane reached Daytona Beach in a 10-foot dinghy on the following morning. Under the title "Stephen Crane's Own Story" the New York *Press* carried the details of his nearly fatal experience on January 7. In June, 1897, he published his fictional account, *The Open Boat*, in *Scribner's Magazine*. The story gave the title to *The Open Boat and Other Tales of Adventure* (1898). The present text reprints that established for the University of Virginia edition of *The Works of Stephen Crane*, Vol. V, *Tales of Adventure* (1970).
2. One who oils machinery in the engine room of a ship.

slashed to and fro at the waves, went low and lower, and down.
Thereafter there was something strange in his voice. Although
steady, it was deep with mourning, and of a quality beyond oration
or tears.

"Keep'er a little more south, Billie," said he.

" 'A little more south,' sir," said the oiler in the stern.

A seat in this boat was not unlike a seat upon a bucking broncho,
and, by the same token, a broncho is not much smaller. The craft
pranced and reared, and plunged like an animal. As each wave
came, and she rose for it, she seemed like a horse making at a fence
outrageously high. The manner of her scramble over these walls of
water is a mystic thing, and, moreover, at the top of them were
ordinarily these problems in white water, the foam racing down
from the summit of each wave, requiring a new leap, and a leap
from the air. Then, after scornfully bumping a crest, she would
slide, and race, and splash down a long incline and arrive bobbing
and nodding in front of the next menace.

A singular disadvantage of the sea lies in the fact that after successfully surmounting one wave you discover that there is another
behind it just as important and just as nervously anxious to do
something effective in the way of swamping boats. In a ten-foot
dingey one can get an idea of the resources of the sea in the line of
waves that is not probable to the average experience, which is never
at sea in a dingey. As each slaty wall of water approached, it shut all
else from the view of the men in the boat, and it was not difficult
to imagine that this particular wave was the final outburst of the
ocean, the last effort of the grim water. There was a terrible grace in
the move of the waves, and they came in silence, save for the snarling of the crests.

In the wan light, the faces of the men must have been gray.
Their eyes must have glinted in strange ways as they gazed steadily
astern. Viewed from a balcony, the whole thing would doubtlessly
have been weirdly picturesque. But the men in the boat had no
time to see it, and if they had had leisure there were other things to
occupy their minds. The sun swung steadily up the sky, and they
knew it was broad day because the color of the sea changed from
slate to emerald-green, streaked with amber lights, and the foam
was like tumbling snow. The process of the breaking day was
unknown to them. They were aware only of this effect upon the
color of the waves that rolled toward them.

In disjointed sentences the cook and the correspondent argued as
to the difference between a life-saving station and a house of refuge.
The cook had said: "There's a house of refuge just north of the
Mosquito Inlet Light, and as soon as they see us, they'll come off in
their boat and pick us up."

"As soon as who see us?" said the correspondent.

"The crew," said the cook.

"Houses of refuge don't have crews," said the correspondent. "As I understand them, they are only places where clothes and grub are stored for the benefit of shipwrecked people. They don't carry crews."

"Oh, yes, they do," said the cook.

"No, they don't," said the correspondent.

"Well, we're not there yet, anyhow," said the oiler, in the stern.

"Well," said the cook, "perhaps it's not a house of refuge that I'm thinking of as being near Mosquito Inlet Light. Perhaps it's a life-saving station."

"We're not there yet," said the oiler, in the stern.

II

As the boat bounced from the top of each wave, the wind tore through the hair of the hatless men, and as the craft plopped her stern down again the spray slashed past them. The crest of each of these waves was a hill, from the top of which the men surveyed, for a moment, a broad tumultuous expanse, shining and wind-riven. It was probably splendid. It was probably glorious, this play of the free sea, wild with lights of emerald and white and amber.

"Bully good thing it's an on-shore wind," said the cook. "If not, where would we be? Wouldn't have a show."

"That's right," said the correspondent.

The busy oiler nodded his assent.

Then the captain, in the bow, chuckled in a way that expressed humor, contempt, tragedy, all in one. "Do you think we've got much of a show, now, boys?" said he.

Whereupon the three were silent, save for a trifle of hemming and hawing. To express any particular optimism at this time they felt to be childish and stupid, but they all doubtless possessed this sense of the situation in their mind. A young man thinks doggedly at such times. On the other hand, the ethics of their condition was decidedly against any open suggestion of hopelessness. So they were silent.

"Oh, well," said the captain, soothing his children, "we'll get ashore all right."

But there was that in his tone which made them think, so the oiler quoth: "Yes! If this wind holds!"

The cook was bailing. "Yes! If we don't catch hell in the surf."

Canton flannel[3] gulls flew near and far. Sometimes they sat down on the sea, near patches of brown sea-weed that rolled over the waves with a movement like carpets on a line in a gale. The birds sat comfortably in groups, and they were envied by some in the dingey, for the wrath of the sea was no more to them than it was to a covey of prairie chickens a thousand miles inland. Often they came very close and stared at the men with black bead-like eyes. At

3. Stout cotton fabric.

these times they were uncanny and sinister in their unblinking scrutiny, and the men hooted angrily at them, telling them to be gone. One came, and evidently decided to alight on the top of the captain's head. The bird flew parallel to the boat and did not circle, but made short sidelong jumps in the air in chicken-fashion. His black eyes were wistfully fixed upon the captain's head. "Ugly brute," said the oiler to the bird. "You look as if you were made with a jack-knife." The cook and the correspondent swore darkly at the creature. The captain naturally wished to knock it away with the end of the heavy painter, but he did not dare do it, because anything resembling an emphatic gesture would have capsized this freighted boat, and so with his open hand, the captain gently and carefully waved the gull away. After it had been discouraged from the pursuit the captain breathed easier on account of his hair, and others breathed easier because the bird struck their minds at this time as being somehow grewsome and ominous.

In the meantime the oiler and the correspondent rowed. And also they rowed.

They sat together in the same seat, and each rowed an oar. Then the oiler took both oars; then the correspondent took both oars; then the oiler; then the correspondent. They rowed and they rowed. The very ticklish part of the business was when the time came for the reclining one in the stern to take his turn at the oars. By the very last star of truth, it is easier to steal eggs from under a hen than it was to change seats in the dingey. First the man in the stern slid his hand along the thwart and moved with care, as if he were of Sèvres.[4] Then the man in the rowing seat slid his hand along the other thwart. It was all done with the most extraordinary care. As the two sidled past each other, the whole party kept watchful eyes on the coming wave, and the captain cried: "Look out now! Steady there!"

The brown mats of sea-weed that appeared from time to time were like islands, bits of earth. They were travelling, apparently, neither one way nor the other. They were, to all intents, stationary. They informed the men in the boat that it was making progress slowly toward the land.

The captain, rearing cautiously in the bow, after the dingey soared on a great swell, said that he had seen the light-house at Mosquito Inlet. Presently the cook remarked that he had seen it. The correspondent was at the oars, then, and for some reason he too wished to look at the light-house, but his back was toward the far shore and the waves were important, and for some time he could not seize an opportunity to turn his head. But at last there came a wave more gentle than the others, and when at the crest of it he swiftly scoured the western horizon.

"See it?" said the captain.

4. Fine, often ornately decorated, French porcelain.

"No," said the correspondent, slowly, "I didn't see anything."

"Look again," said the captain. He pointed. "It's exactly in that direction."

At the top of another wave, the correspondent did as he was bid, and this time his eyes chanced on a small still thing on the edge of the swaying horizon. It was precisely like the point of a pin. It took an anxious eye to find a light-house so tiny.

"Think we'll make it, Captain?"

"If this wind holds and the boat don't swamp, we can't do much else," said the captain.

The little boat, lifted by each towering sea, and splashed viciously by the crests, made progress that in the absence of sea-weed was not apparent to those in her. She seemed just a wee thing wallowing, miraculously, top-up, at the mercy of five oceans. Occasionally, a great spread of water, like white flames, swarmed into her.

"Bail her, cook," said the captain, serenely.

"All right, Captain," said the cheerful cook.

III

It would be difficult to describe the subtle brotherhood of men that was here established on the seas. No one said that it was so. No one mentioned it. But it dwelt in the boat, and each man felt it warm him. They were a captain, an oiler, a cook, and a correspondent, and they were friends, friends in a more curiously iron-bound degree than may be common. The hurt captain, lying against the water-jar in the bow, spoke always in a low voice and calmly, but he could never command a more ready and swiftly obedient crew than the motley three of the dingey. It was more than a mere recognition of what was best for the common safety. There was surely in it a quality that was personal and heartfelt. And after this devotion to the commander of the boat there was this comradeship that the correspondent, for instance, who had been taught to be cynical of men, knew even at the time was the best experience of his life. But no one said that it was so. No one mentioned it.

"I wish we had a sail," remarked the captain. "We might try my overcoat on the end of an oar and give you two boys a chance to rest." So the cook and the correspondent held the mast and spread wide the overcoat. The oiler steered, and the little boat made good way with her new rig. Sometimes the oiler had to scull sharply to keep a sea from breaking into the boat, but otherwise sailing was a success.

Meanwhile the light-house had been growing slowly larger. It had now almost assumed color, and appeared like a little gray shadow on the sky. The man at the oars could not be prevented from turning his head rather often to try for a glimpse of this little gray shadow.

At last, from the top of each wave the men in the tossing boat could see land. Even as the light-house was an upright shadow on the sky, this land seemed but a long black shadow on the sea. It certainly was thinner than paper. "We must be about opposite New Smyrna," said the cook, who had coasted this shore often in schooners. "Captain, by the way, I believe they abandoned that life-saving station there about a year ago."

"Did they?" said the captain.

The wind slowly died away. The cook and the correspondent were not now obliged to slave in order to hold high the oar. But the waves continued their old impetuous swooping at the dingey, and the little craft, no longer under way, struggled woundily over them. The oiler or the correspondent took the oars again.

Shipwrecks are *apropos* of nothing. If men could only train for them and have them occur when the men had reached pink condition, there would be less drowning at sea. Of the four in the dingey none had slept any time worth mentioning for two days and two nights previous to embarking in the dingey, and in the excitement of clambering about the deck of a foundering ship they had also forgotten to eat heartily.

For these reasons, and for others, neither the oiler nor the correspondent was fond of rowing at this time. The correspondent wondered ingenuously how in the name of all that was sane could there be people who thought it amusing to row a boat. It was not an amusement; it was a diabolical punishment, and even a genius of mental aberrations could never conclude that it was anything but a horror to the muscles and a crime against the back. He mentioned to the boat in general how the amusement of rowing struck him, and the weary-faced oiler smiled in full sympathy. Previously to the foundering, by the way, the oiler had worked double-watch in the engine-room of the ship.

"Take her easy, now, boys," said the captain. "Don't spend yourselves. If we have to run a surf you'll need all your strength, because we'll sure have to swim for it. Take your time."

Slowly the land arose from the sea. From a black line it became a line of black and a line of white—trees and sand. Finally, the captain said that he could make out a house on the shore. "That's the house of refuge, sure," said the cook. "They'll see us before long, and come out after us."

The distant light-house reared high. "The keeper ought to be able to make us out now, if he's looking through a glass," said the captain. "He'll notify the life-saving people."

"None of those other boats could have got ashore to give word of the wreck," said the oiler, in a low voice. "Else the life-boat would be out hunting us."

Slowly and beautifully the land loomed out of the sea. The wind came again. It had veered from the northeast to the southeast. Finally, a new sound struck the ears of the men in the boat. It was the low thunder of the surf on the shore. "We'll never be able to make the light-house now," said the captain. "Swing her head a little more north, Billie."

" 'A little more north,' sir," said the oiler.

Whereupon the little boat turned her nose once more down the wind, and all but the oarsman watched the shore grow. Under the influence of this expansion doubt and direful apprehension was leaving the minds of the men. The management of the boat was still most absorbing, but it could not prevent a quiet cheerfulness. In an hour, perhaps, they would be ashore.

Their back-bones had become thoroughly used to balancing in the boat and they now rode this wild colt of a dingey like circus men. The correspondent thought that he had been drenched to the skin, but happening to feel in the top pocket of his coat, he found therein eight cigars. Four of them were soaked with seawater; four were perfectly scatheless. After a search, somebody produced three dry matches, and thereupon the four waifs rode impudently in their little boat, and with an assurance of an impending rescue shining in their eyes, puffed at the big cigars and judged well and ill of all men. Everybody took a drink of water.

IV

"Cook," remarked the captain, "there don't seem to be any signs of life about your house of refuge."

"No," replied the cook. "Funny they don't see us!"

A broad stretch of lowly coast lay before the eyes of the men. It was of dunes topped with dark vegetation. The roar of the surf was plain, and sometimes they could see the white lip of a wave as it spun up the beach. A tiny house was blocked out black upon the sky. Southward, the slim light-house lifted its little gray length.

Tide, wind, and waves were swinging the dingey northward. "Funny they don't see us," said the men.

The surf's roar was here dulled, but its tone was, nevertheless, thunderous and mighty. As the boat swam over the great rollers, the men sat listening to this roar. "We'll swamp sure," said everybody.

It is fair to say here that there was not a life-saving station within twenty miles in either direction, but the men did not know this fact and in consequence they made dark and opprobrious remarks concerning the eyesight of the nation's life-savers. Four scowling men sat in the dingey and surpassed records in the invention of epithets.

"Funny they don't see us."

The light-heartedness of a former time had completely faded. To their sharpened minds it was easy to conjure pictures of all kinds of incompetency and blindness and, indeed, cowardice. There was the shore of the populous land, and it was bitter and bitter to them that from it came no sign.

"Well," said the captain, ultimately, "I suppose we'll have to make a try for ourselves. If we stay out here too long, we'll none of us have strength left to swim after the boat swamps."

And so the oiler, who was at the oars, turned the boat straight for the shore. There was a sudden tightening of muscles. There was some thinking.

"If we don't all get ashore—" said the captain. "If we don't all get ashore, I suppose you fellows know where to send news of my finish?"

They then briefly exchanged some addresses and admonitions. As for the reflections of the men, there was a great deal of rage in them. Perchance they might be formulated thus: "If I am going to be drowned—if I am going to be drowned—if I am going to be drowned, why, in the name of the seven mad gods who rule the sea, was I allowed to come thus far and contemplate sand and trees? Was I brought here merely to have my nose dragged away as I was about to nibble the sacred cheese of life? It is preposterous. If this old ninny-woman, Fate, cannot do better than this, she should be deprived of the management of men's fortunes. She is an old hen who knows not her intention. If she has decided to drown me, why did she not do it in the beginning and save me all this trouble. The whole affair is absurd. . . . But, no, she cannot mean to drown me. She dare not drown me. She cannot drown me. Not after all this work." Afterward the man might have had an impulse to shake his fist at the clouds. "Just you drown me, now, and then hear what I call you!"

The billows that came at this time were more formidable. They seemed always just about to break and roll over the little boat in a turmoil of foam. There was a preparatory and long growl in the speech of them. No mind unused to the sea would have concluded that the dingey could ascend these sheer heights in time. The shore was still afar. The oiler was a wily surfman. "Boys," he said, swiftly, "she won't live three minutes more and we're too far out to swim. Shall I take her to sea again, Captain?"

"Yes! Go ahead!" said the captain.

This oiler, by a series of quick miracles, and fast and steady oarsmanship, turned the boat in the middle of the surf and took her safely to sea again.

There was a considerable silence as the boat bumped over the furrowed sea to deeper water. Then somebody in gloom spoke. "Well, anyhow, they must have seen us from the shore by now."

The gulls went in slanting flight up the wind toward the gray desolate east. A squall, marked by dingy clouds, and clouds brick-red, like smoke from a burning building, appeared from the southeast.

"What do you think of those life-saving people? Ain't they peaches?"

"Funny they haven't seen us."

"Maybe they think we're out here for sport! Maybe they think we're fishin'. Maybe they think we're damned fools."

It was a long afternoon. A changed tide tried to force them southward, but wind and wave said northward. Far ahead, where coast-line, sea, and sky formed their mighty angle, there were little dots which seemed to indicate a city on the shore.

"St. Augustine?"

The captain shook his head. "Too near Mosquito Inlet."

And the oiler rowed, and then the correspondent rowed. Then the oiler rowed. It was a weary business. The human back can become the seat of more aches and pains than are registered in books for the composite anatomy of a regiment. It is a limited area, but it can become the theatre of innumerable muscular conflicts, tangles, wrenches, knots, and other comforts.

"Did you ever like to row, Billie?" asked the correspondent.

"No," said the oiler. "Hang it."

When one exchanged the rowing-seat for a place in the bottom of the boat, he suffered a bodily depression that caused him to be careless of everything save an obligation to wiggle one finger. There was cold sea-water swashing to and fro in the boat, and he lay in it. His head, pillowed on a thwart, was within an inch of the swirl of a wave crest, and sometimes a particularly obstreperous sea came inboard and drenched him once more. But these matters did not annoy him. It is almost certain that if the boat had capsized he would have tumbled comfortably out upon the ocean as if he felt sure that it was a great soft mattress.

"Look! There's a man on the shore!"

"Where?"

"There? See'im? See'im?"

"Yes, sure! He's walking along."

"Now he's stopped. Look! He's facing us!"

"He's waving at us!"

"So he is! By thunder!"

"Ah, now, we're all right! Now we're all right! There'll be a boat out here for us in half an hour."

"He's going on. He's running. He's going up to that house there."

The remote beach seemed lower than the sea, and it required a searching glance to discern the little black figure. The captain saw a floating stick and they rowed to it. A bath-towel was by some weird chance in the boat, and, tying this on the stick, the captain waved it. The oarsman did not dare turn his head, so he was obliged to ask questions.

"What's he doing now?"

"He's standing still again. He's looking, I think. . . . There he goes again. Toward the house. . . . Now he's stopped again."

"Is he waving at us?"

"No, not now! he was, though."

"Look! There comes another man!"

"He's running."

"Look at him go, would you."

"Why, he's on a bicycle. Now he's met the other man. They're both waving at us. Look!"

"There comes something up the beach."

"What the devil is that thing?"

"Why, it looks like a boat."

"Why, certainly it's a boat."

"No, it's on wheels."

"Yes, so it is. Well, that must be the life-boat. They drag them along shore on a wagon."

"That's the life-boat, sure."

"No, by——, it's—it's an omnibus."

"I tell you it's a life-boat."

"It is not! It's an omnibus. I can see it plain. See? One of those big hotel omnibuses."

"By thunder, you're right. It's an omnibus, sure as fate. What do you suppose they are doing with an omnibus? Maybe they are going around collecting the life-crew, hey?"

"That's it, likely. Look! There's a fellow waving a little black flag. He's standing on the steps of the omnibus. There come those other two fellows. Now they're all talking together. Look at the fellow with the flag. Maybe he ain't waving it!"

"That ain't a flag, is it? That's his coat. Why, certainly, that's his coat."

"So it is. It's his coat. He's taken it off and is waving it around his head. But would you look at him swing it!"

"Oh, say, there isn't any life-saving station there. That's just a winter resort hotel omnibus that has brought over some of the boarders to see us drown."

"What's that idiot with the coat mean? What's he signaling, anyhow?"

"It looks as if he were trying to tell us to go north. There must be a life-saving station up there."

"No! He thinks we're fishing. Just giving us a merry hand. See? Ah, there, Willie."

"Well, I wish I could make something out of those signals. What do you suppose he means?"

"He don't mean anything. He's just playing."

"Well, if he'd just signal us to try the surf again, or to go to sea and wait, or go north, or go south, or go to hell—there would be some reason in it. But look at him. He just stands there and keeps his coat revolving like a wheel. The ass!"

"There come more people."

"Now there's quite a mob. Look! Isn't that a boat?"

"Where? Oh, I see where you mean. No, that's no boat."

"That fellow is still waving his coat."

"He must think we like to see him do that. Why don't he quit it. It don't mean anything."

"I don't know. I think he is trying to make us go north. It must be that there's a life-saving station there somewhere."

"Say, he ain't tired yet. Look at 'im wave."

"Wonder how long he can keep that up. He's been revolving his coat ever since he caught sight of us. He's an idiot. Why aren't they getting men to bring a boat out. A fishing boat—one of those big yawls—could come out here all right. Why don't he do something?"

"Oh, it's all right, now."

"They'll have a boat out here for us in less than no time, now that they've seen us."

A faint yellow tone came into the sky over the low land. The shadows on the sea slowly deepened. The wind bore coldness with it, and the men began to shiver.

"Holy smoke!" said one, allowing his voice to express his impious mood, "if we keep on monkeying out here! If we've got to flounder out here all night!"

"Oh, we'll never have to stay here all night! Don't you worry. They've seen us now, and it won't be long before they'll come chasing out after us."

The shore grew dusky. The man waving a coat blended gradually into this gloom, and it swallowed in the same manner the omnibus and the group of people. The spray, when it dashed uproariously over the side, made the voyagers shrink and swear like men who were being branded.

"I'd like to catch the chump who waved the coat. I feel like soaking him one, just for luck."

"Why? What did he do?"

"Oh, nothing, but then he seemed so damned cheerful."

In the meantime the oiler rowed, and then the correspondent rowed, and then the oiler rowed. Gray-faced and bowed forward, they mechanically, turn by turn, plied the leaden oars. The form of the light-house had vanished from the southern horizon, but finally a pale star appeared, just lifting from the sea. The streaked saffron in the west passed before the all-merging darkness, and the sea to the east was black. The land had vanished, and was expressed only by the low and drear thunder of the surf.

"If I am going to be drowned—if I am going to be drowned—if I am going to be drowned, why, in the name of the seven mad gods who rule the sea, was I allowed to come thus far and contemplate sand and trees? Was I brought here merely to have my nose dragged away as I was about to nibble the sacred cheese of life?"

The patient captain, drooped over the water-jar, was sometimes obliged to speak to the oarsman.

"Keep her head up! Keep her head up!"

" 'Keep her head up,' sir." The voices were weary and low.

This was surely a quiet evening. All save the oarsman lay heavily and listlessly in the boat's bottom. As for him, his eyes were just capable of noting the tall black waves that swept forward in a most sinister silence, save for an occasional subdued growl of a crest.

The cook's head was on a thwart, and he looked without interest at the water under his nose. He was deep in other scenes. Finally he spoke. "Billie," he murmured, dreamfully, "what kind of pie do you like best?"

V

"Pie," said the oiler and the correspondent, agitatedly. "Don't talk about those things, blast you!"

"Well," said the cook, "I was just thinking about ham sandwiches, and——"

A night on the sea in an open boat is a long night. As darkness settled finally, the shine of the light, lifting from the sea in the south, changed to full gold. On the northern horizon a new light appeared, a small bluish gleam on the edge of the waters. These two lights were the furniture of the world. Otherwise there was nothing but waves.

Two men huddled in the stern, and distances were so magnificent in the dingey that the rower was enabled to keep his feet partly warmed by thrusting them under his companions. Their legs indeed extended far under the rowing-seat until they touched the feet of the captain forward. Sometimes, despite the efforts of the tired oarsman, a wave came piling into the boat, an icy wave of the night, and the chilling water soaked them anew. They would twist their bodies for a moment and groan, and sleep the dead sleep once more, while the water in the boat gurgled about them as the craft rocked.

The plan of the oiler and the correspondent was for one to row until he lost the ability, and then arouse the other from his sea-water couch in the bottom of the boat.

The oiler plied the oars until his head drooped forward, and the overpowering sleep blinded him. And he rowed yet afterward. Then he touched a man in the bottom of the boat, and called his name. "Will you spell me for a little while?" he said, meekly.

"Sure, Billie," said the correspondent, awakening and dragging himself to a sitting position. They exchanged places carefully, and the oiler, cuddling down in the sea-water at the cook's side, seemed to go to sleep instantly.

The particular violence of the sea had ceased. The waves came without snarling. The obligation of the man at the oars was to keep the boat headed so that the tilt of the rollers would not capsize her, and to preserve her from filling when the crests rushed past. The black waves were silent and hard to be seen in the darkness. Often one was almost upon the boat before the oarsman was aware.

In a low voice the correspondent addressed the captain. He was not sure that the captain was awake, although this iron man seemed to be always awake. "Captain, shall I keep her making for that light north, sir?"

The same steady voice answered him. "Yes. Keep it about two points off the port bow."

The cook had tied a life-belt around himself in order to get even the warmth which this clumsy cork contrivance could donate, and he seemed almost stove-like when a rower, whose teeth invariably chattered wildly as soon as he ceased his labor, dropped down to sleep.

The correspondent, as he rowed, looked down at the two men sleeping under foot. The cook's arm was around the oiler's shoulders, and, with their fragmentary clothing and haggard faces, they were the babes of the sea, a grotesque rendering of the old babes in the wood.

Later he must have grown stupid at his work, for suddenly there was a growling of water, and a crest came with a roar and a swash into the boat, and it was a wonder that it did not set the cook afloat in his life-belt. The cook continued to sleep, but the oiler sat up, blinking his eyes and shaking with the new cold.

"Oh, I'm awful sorry, Billie," said the correspondent, contritely.

"That's all right, old boy," said the oiler, and lay down again and was asleep.

Presently it seemed that even the captain dozed, and the correspondent thought that he was the one man afloat on all the oceans. The wind had a voice as it came over the waves, and it was sadder than the end.

There was a long, loud swishing astern of the boat, and a gleaming trail of phosphorescence, like blue flame, was furrowed on the black waters. It might have been made by a monstrous knife.

Then there came a stillness, while the correspondent breathed with the open mouth and looked at the sea.

Suddenly there was another swish and another long flash of bluish light, and this time it was alongside the boat, and might almost have been reached with an oar. The correspondent saw an enormous fin speed like a shadow through the water, hurling the crystalline spray and leaving the long glowing trail.

The correspondent looked over his shoulder at the captain. His face was hidden, and he seemed to be asleep. He looked at the babes of the sea. They certainly were asleep. So, being bereft of sympathy, he leaned a little way to one side and swore softly into the sea.

But the thing did not then leave the vicinity of the boat. Ahead or astern, on one side or the other, at intervals long or short, fled the long sparkling streak, and there was to be heard the whiroo of the dark fin. The speed and power of the thing was greatly to be admired. It cut the water like a gigantic and keen projectile.

The presence of this biding thing did not affect the man with the same horror that it would if he had been a picnicker. He simply looked at the sea dully and swore in an undertone.

Nevertheless, it is true that he did not wish to be alone with the thing. He wished one of his companions to awaken by chance and keep him company with it. But the captain hung motionless over the water-jar and the oiler and the cook in the bottom of the boat were plunged in slumber.

VI

"If I am going to be drowned—if I am going to be drowned—if I am going to be drowned, why, in the name of the seven mad gods who rule the sea, was I allowed to come thus far and contemplate sand and trees?"

During this dismal night, it may be remarked that a man would conclude that it was really the intention of the seven mad gods to drown him, despite the abominable injustice of it. For it was certainly an abominable injustice to drown a man who had worked so hard, so hard. The man felt it would be a crime most unnatural. Other people had drowned at sea since galleys swarmed with painted sails, but still——

When it occurs to a man that nature does not regard him as important, and that she feels she would not maim the universe by disposing of him, he at first wishes to throw bricks at the temple, and he hates deeply the fact that there are no bricks and no temples. Any visible expression of nature would surely be pelleted with his jeers.

Then, if there be no tangible thing to hoot he feels, perhaps, the desire to confront a personification and indulge in pleas, bowed to one knee, and with hands supplicant, saying: "Yes, but I love myself."

A high cold star on a winter's night is the word he feels that she says to him. Thereafter he knows the pathos of his situation.

The men in the dingey had not discussed these matters, but each had, no doubt, reflected upon them in silence and according to his mind. There was seldom any expression upon their faces save the general one of complete weariness. Speech was devoted to the business of the boat.

To chime the notes of his emotion, a verse mysteriously entered the correspondent's head. He had even forgotten that he had forgotten this verse, but it suddenly was in his mind.

> A soldier of the Legion lay dying in Algiers,
> There was lack of woman's nursing, there was dearth
>   of woman's tears;
> But a comrade stood beside him, and he took that
>   comrade's hand,
> And he said: "I never more shall see my own, my
>   native land."[5]

In his childhood, the correspondent had been made acquainted with the fact that a soldier of the Legion lay dying in Algiers, but he had never regarded it as important. Myriads of his school-fellows had informed him of the soldier's plight, but the dinning had naturally ended by making him perfectly indifferent. He had never considered it his affair that a soldier of the Legion lay dying in Algiers, nor had it appeared to him as a matter for sorrow. It was less to him than the breaking of a pencil's point.

Now, however, it quaintly came to him as a human, living thing. It was no longer merely a picture of a few throes in the breast of a poet, meanwhile drinking tea and warming his feet at the grate; it was an actuality—stern, mournful, and fine.

The correspondent plainly saw the soldier. He lay on the sand with his feet out straight and still. While his pale left hand was upon his chest in an attempt to thwart the going of his life, the blood came between his fingers. In the far Algerian distance, a city of low square forms was set against a sky that was faint with the last sunset hues. The correspondent, plying the oars and dreaming of the slow and slower movements of the lips of the soldier, was moved by a profound and perfectly impersonal comprehension. He was sorry for the soldier of the Legion who lay dying in Algiers.

The thing which had followed the boat and waited had evidently grown bored at the delay. There was no longer to be heard the slash of the cut-water, and there was no longer the flame of the long trail. The light in the north still glimmered, but it was apparently no nearer to the boat. Sometimes the boom of the surf rang in the correspondent's ears, and he turned the craft seaward then and rowed harder. Southward, some one had evidently built a watch-fire on the beach. It was too low and too far to be seen, but it made a shimmering, roseate reflection upon the bluff back of it, and this could be discerned from the boat. The wind came stronger, and sometimes a wave suddenly raged out like a mountain-cat and there was to be seen the sheen and sparkle of a broken crest.

The captain, in the bow, moved on his water-jar and sat erect.

5. The lines are incorrectly quoted from Caroline E. S. Norton's poem *Bingen on the Rhine* (1883).

"Pretty long night," he observed to the correspondent. He looked at the shore. "Those life-saving people take their time."

"Did you see that shark playing around?"

"Yes, I saw him. He was a big fellow, all right."

"Wish I had known you were awake."

Later the correspondent spoke into the bottom of the boat.

"Billie!" There was a slow and gradual disentanglement. "Billie, will you spell me?"

"Sure," said the oiler.

As soon as the correspondent touched the cold comfortable sea-water in the bottom of the boat, and had huddled close to the cook's life-belt he was deep in sleep, despite the fact that his teeth played all the popular airs. This sleep was so good to him that it was but a moment before he heard a voice call his name in a tone that demonstrated the last stages of exhaustion. "Will you spell me?"

"Sure, Billie."

The light in the north had mysteriously vanished, but the correspondent took his course from the wide-awake captain.

Later in the night they took the boat farther out to sea, and the captain directed the cook to take one oar at the stern and keep the boat facing the seas. He was to call out if he should hear the thunder of the surf. This plan enabled the oiler and the correspondent to get respite together. "We'll give those boys a chance to get into shape again," said the captain. They curled down and, after a few preliminary chatterings and trembles, slept once more the dead sleep. Neither knew they had bequeathed to the cook the company of another shark, or perhaps the same shark.

As the boat caroused on the waves, spray occasionally bumped over the side and gave them a fresh soaking, but this had no power to break their repose. The ominous slash of the wind and the water affected them as it would have affected mummies.

"Boys," said the cook, with the notes of every reluctance in his voice, "she's drifted in pretty close. I guess one of you had better take her to sea again." The correspondent, aroused, heard the crash of the toppled crests.

As he was rowing, the captain gave him some whiskey and water, and this steadied the chills out of him. "If I ever get ashore and anybody shows me even a photograph of an oar——"

At last there was a short conversation.

"Billie. . . . Billie, will you spell me?"

"Sure," said the oiler.

VII

When the correspondent again opened his eyes, the sea and the sky were each of the gray hue of the dawning. Later, carmine and gold was painted upon the waters. The morning appeared finally, in its splendor, with a sky of pure blue, and the sunlight flamed on the tips of the waves.

On the distant dunes were set many little black cottages, and a tall white wind-mill reared above them. No man, nor dog, nor bicycle appeared on the beach. The cottages might have formed a deserted village.

The voyagers scanned the shore. A conference was held in the boat. "Well," said the captain, "if no help is coming, we might better try a run through the surf right away. If we stay out here much longer we will be too weak to do anything for ourselves at all." The others silently acquiesced in this reasoning. The boat was headed for the beach. The correspondent wondered if none ever ascended the tall wind-tower, and if then they never looked seaward. This tower was a giant, standing with its back to the plight of the ants. It represented in a degree, to the correspondent, the serenity of nature amid the struggles of the individual—nature in the wind, and nature in the vision of men. She did not seem cruel to him then, nor beneficent, nor treacherous, nor wise. But she was indifferent, flatly indifferent. It is, perhaps, plausible that a man in this situation, impressed with the unconcern of the universe, should see the innumerable flaws of his life and have them taste wickedly in his mind and wish for another chance. A distinction between right and wrong seems absurdly clear to him, then, in this new ignorance of the grave-edge, and he understands that if he were given another opportunity he would mend his conduct and his words, and be better and brighter during an introduction, or at a tea.

"Now, boys," said the captain, "she is going to swamp sure. All we can do is to work her in as far as possible, and then when she swamps, pile out and scramble for the beach. Keep cool now, and don't jump until she swamps sure."

The oiler took the oars. Over his shoulders he scanned the surf. "Captain," he said, "I think I'd better bring her about, and keep her head-on to the seas and back her in."

"All right, Billie," said the captain. "Back her in." The oiler swung the boat then and, seated in the stern, the cook and the correspondent were obliged to look over their shoulders to contemplate the lonely and indifferent shore.

The monstrous inshore rollers heaved the boat high until the men were again enabled to see the white sheets of water scudding up the slanted beach. "We won't get in very close," said the captain. Each time a man could wrest his attention from the rollers, he turned his glance toward the shore, and in the expression of the eyes during this contemplation there was a singular quality. The correspondent, observing the others, knew that they were not afraid, but the full meaning of their glances was shrouded.

As for himself, he was too tired to grapple fundamentally with the fact. He tried to coerce his mind into thinking of it, but the mind was dominated at this time by the muscles, and the muscles said they did not care. It merely occurred to him that if he should drown it would be a shame.

There were no hurried words, no pallor, no plain agitation. The men simply looked at the shore. "Now, remember to get well clear of the boat when you jump," said the captain.

Seaward the crest of a roller suddenly fell with a thunderous crash, and the long white comber came roaring down upon the boat.

"Steady now," said the captain. The men were silent. They turned their eyes from the shore to the comber and waited. The boat slid up the incline, leaped at the furious top, bounced over it, and swung down the long back of the wave. Some water had been shipped and the cook bailed it out.

But the next crest crashed also. The tumbling boiling flood of white water caught the boat and whirled it almost perpendicular. Water swarmed in from all sides. The correspondent had his hands on the gunwale at this time, and when the water entered at that place he swiftly withdrew his fingers, as if he objected to wetting them.

The little boat, drunken with this weight of water, reeled and snuggled deeper into the sea.

"Bail her out, cook! Bail her out," said the captain.

"All right, Captain," said the cook.

"Now, boys, the next one will do for us, sure," said the oiler. "Mind to jump clear of the boat."

The third wave moved forward, huge, furious, implacable. It fairly swallowed the dingey, and almost simultaneously the men tumbled into the sea. A piece of life-belt had lain in the bottom of the boat, and as the correspondent went overboard he held this to his chest with his left hand.

The January water was icy, and he reflected immediately that it was colder than he had expected to find it off the coast of Florida. This appeared to his dazed mind as a fact important enough to be noted at the time. The coldness of the water was sad; it was tragic. This fact was somehow so mixed and confused with his opinion of his own situation that it seemed almost a proper reason for tears. The water was cold.

When he came to the surface he was conscious of little but the noisy water. Afterward he saw his companions in the sea. The oiler was ahead in the race. He was swimming strongly and rapidly. Off to the correspondent's left, the cook's great white and corked back bulged out of the water, and in the rear the captain was hanging with his one good hand to the keel of the overturned dingey.

There is a certain immovable quality to a shore, and the correspondent wondered at it amid the confusion of the sea.

It seemed also very attractive, but the correspondent knew that it was a long journey, and he paddled leisurely. The piece of life preserver lay under him, and sometimes he whirled down the incline of a wave as if he were on a hand-sled.

But finally he arrived at a place in the sea where travel was beset with difficulty. He did not pause swimming to inquire what manner of current had caught him, but there his progress ceased. The shore was set before him like a bit of scenery on a stage, and he looked at it and understood with his eyes each detail of it.

As the cook passed, much farther to the left, the captain was calling to him, "Turn over on your back, cook! Turn over on your back and use the oar."

"All right, sir." The cook turned on his back, and, paddling with an oar, went ahead as if he were a canoe.

Presently the boat also passed to the left of the correspondent with the captain clinging with one hand to the keel. He would have appeared like a man raising himself to look over a board fence, if it were not for the extraordinary gymnastics of the boat. The correspondent marvelled that the captain could still hold to it.

They passed on, nearer to shore—the oiler, the cook, the captain —and following them went the water-jar, bouncing gayly over the seas.

The correspondent remained in the grip of this strange new enemy—a current. The shore, with its white slope of sand and its green bluff, topped with little silent cottages, was spread like a picture before him. It was very near to him then, but he was impressed as one who in a gallery looks at a scene from Brittany or Holland.

He thought: "I am going to drown? Can it be possible? Can it be possible? Can it be possible?" Perhaps an individual must consider his own death to be the final phenomenon of nature.

But later a wave perhaps whirled him out of this small deadly current, for he found suddenly that he could again make progress toward the shore. Later still, he was aware that the captain, clinging with one hand to the keel of the dingey, had his face turned away from the shore and toward him, and was calling his name. "Come to the boat! Come to the boat!"

In his struggle to reach the captain and the boat, he reflected that when one gets properly wearied, drowning must really be a comfortable arrangement, a cessation of hostilities accompanied by a large degree of relief, and he was glad of it, for the main thing in his mind for some moments had been horror of the temporary agony. He did not wish to be hurt.

Presently he saw a man running along the shore. He was undressing with most remarkable speed. Coat, trousers, shirt, everything flew magically off him.

"Come to the boat," called the captain.

"All right, Captain." As the correspondent paddled, he saw the captain let himself down to bottom and leave the boat. Then the correspondent performed his one little marvel of the voyage. A large wave caught him and flung him with ease and supreme speed completely over the boat and far beyond it. It struck him even then as an event in gymnastics, and a true miracle of the sea. An overturned boat in the surf is not a plaything to a swimming man.

The correspondent arrived in water that reached only to his waist, but his condition did not enable him to stand for more than a moment. Each wave knocked him into a heap, and the under-tow pulled at him.

Then he saw the man who had been running and undressing, and undressing and running, come bounding into the water. He dragged ashore the cook, and then waded toward the captain, but the captain waved him away, and sent him to the correspondent. He was naked, naked as a tree in winter, but a halo was about his head, and he shone like a saint. He gave a strong pull, and a long drag, and a bully heave at the correspondent's hand. The correspondent, schooled in the minor formulæ, said: "Thanks, old man." But suddenly the man cried: "What's that?" He pointed a swift finger. The correspondent said: "Go."

In the shallows, face downward, lay the oiler. His forehead touched sand that was periodically, between each wave, clear of the sea.

The correspondent did not know all that transpired afterward. When he achieved safe ground he fell, striking the sand with each particular part of his body. It was as if he had dropped from a roof, but the thud was grateful to him.

It seems that instantly the beach was populated with men with blankets, clothes, and flasks, and women with coffee-pots and all the remedies sacred to their minds. The welcome of the land to the men from the sea was warm and generous, but a still and dripping shape was carried slowly up the beach, and the land's welcome for it could only be the different and sinister hospitality of the grave.

When it came night, the white waves paced to and fro in the moonlight, and the wind brought the sound of the great sea's voice to the men on shore, and they felt that they could then be interpreters.

1897, 1898

The Bride Comes to Yellow Sky[1]

I

The great Pullman was whirling onward with such dignity of motion that a glance from the window seemed simply to prove that the plains of Texas were pouring eastward. Vast flats of green grass,

1. The story was first published in February, 1898, in *McClure's Magazine* and in England in *Chapman's Magazine*. The present text reprints that established for the University of Virginia Edition of *The Works of Stephen Crane*, Vol. V, *Tales of Adventure* (1970).

dull-hued spaces of mesquite and cactus, little groups of frame houses, woods of light and tender trees, all were sweeping into the east, sweeping over the horizon, a precipice.

A newly married pair had boarded this coach at San Antonio. The man's face was reddened from many days in the wind and sun, and a direct result of his new black clothes was that his brick-colored hands were constantly performing in a most conscious fashion. From time to time he looked down respectfully at his attire. He sat with a hand on each knee, like a man waiting in a barber's shop. The glances he devoted to other passengers were furtive and shy.

The bride was not pretty, nor was she very young. She wore a dress of blue cashmere, with small reservations of velvet here and there and with steel buttons abounding. She continually twisted her head to regard her puff sleeves, very stiff, straight, and high. They embarrassed her. It was quite apparent that she had cooked, and that she expected to cook, dutifully. The blushes caused by the careless scrutiny of some passengers as she had entered the car were strange to see upon this plain, under-class countenance, which was drawn in placid, almost emotionless lines.

They were evidently very happy. "Ever been in a parlor-car before?" he asked, smiling with delight.

"No," she answered. "I never was. It's fine, ain't it?"

"Great! And then after a while we'll go forward to the diner and get a big lay-out. Finest meal in the world. Charge a dollar."

"Oh, do they?" cried the bride. "Charge a dollar? Why, that's too much—for us—ain't it, Jack?"

"Not this trip, anyhow," he answered bravely. "We're going to go the whole thing."

Later, he explained to her about the trains. "You see, it's a thousand miles from one end of Texas to the other, and this train runs right across it and never stops but four times." He had the pride of an owner. He pointed out to her the dazzling fittings of the coach, and in truth her eyes opened wider as she contemplated the sea-green figured velvet, the shining brass, silver, and glass, the wood that gleamed as darkly brilliant as the surface of a pool of oil. At one end a bronze figure sturdily held a support for a separated chamber and at convenient places on the ceiling were frescoes in olive and silver.

To the minds of the pair, their surroundings reflected the glory of their marriage that morning in San Antonio. This was the environment of their new estate, and the man's face in particular beamed with an elation that made him appear ridiculous to the negro porter. This individual at times surveyed them from afar with an amused and superior grin. On other occasions he bullied them with skill in ways that did not make it exactly plain to them that they were being bullied. He subtly used all the manners of the most unconquerable kind of snobbery. He oppressed them, but of this oppression they had small knowledge, and they speedily forgot that infrequently a number of travelers covered them with stares of derisive enjoyment. Historically there was supposed to be something infinitely humorous in their situation.

"We are due in Yellow Sky at 3.42," he said, looking tenderly into her eyes.

"Oh, are we?" she said, as if she had not been aware of it. To evince surprise at her husband's statement was part of her wifely amiability. She took from a pocket a little silver watch, and as she held it before her and stared at it with a frown of attention, the new husband's face shone.

"I bought it in San Anton' from a friend of mine," he told her gleefully.

"It's seventeen minutes past twelve," she said, looking up at him with a kind of shy and clumsy coquetry. A passenger, noting this play, grew excessively sardonic, and winked at himself in one of the numerous mirrors.

At last they went to the dining-car. Two rows of negro waiters in glowing white suits surveyed their entrance with the interest and also the equanimity of men who had been forewarned. The pair fell to the lot of a waiter who happened to feel pleasure in steering them through their meal. He viewed them with the manner of a fatherly pilot, his countenance radiant with benevolence. The patronage entwined with the ordinary deference was not plain to them. And yet as they returned to their coach they showed in their faces a sense of escape.

To the left, miles down a long purple slope, was a little ribbon of mist where moved the keening Rio Grande. The train was approaching it at an angle, and the apex was Yellow Sky. Presently it was apparent that as the distance from Yellow Sky grew shorter, the husband became commensurately restless. His brick-red hands were more insistent in their prominence. Occasionally he was even rather absent-minded and far-away when the bride leaned forward and addressed him.

As a matter of truth, Jack Potter was beginning to find the shadow of a deed weigh upon him like a leaden slab. He, the town marshal of Yellow Sky, a man known, liked, and feared in his corner, a prominent person, had gone to San Antonio to meet a girl he believed he loved, and there, after the usual prayers, had actually induced her to marry him, without consulting Yellow Sky for any part of the transaction. He was now bringing his bride before an innocent and unsuspecting community.

Of course, people in Yellow Sky married as it pleased them in accordance with a general custom; but such was Potter's thought of his duty to his friends, or of their idea of his duty, or of an unspoken form which does not control men in these matters, that he felt he was heinous. He had committed an extraordinary crime. Face to face with this girl in San Antonio, and spurred by his sharp impulse, he had gone headlong over all the social hedges. At San Antonio he was like a man hidden in the dark. A knife to sever any friendly duty, any form, was easy to his hand in that remote city. But the hour of Yellow Sky, the hour of daylight, was approaching.

He knew full well that his marriage was an important thing to his town. It could only be exceeded by the burning of the new hotel. His friends would not forgive him. Frequently he had reflected on the advisability of telling them by telegraph, but a new cowardice had been upon him. He feared to do it. And now the train was hurrying him toward a scene of amazement, glee, reproach. He glanced out of the window at the line of haze swinging slowly in toward the train.

Yellow Sky had a kind of brass band which played painfully to the delight of the populace. He laughed without heart as he thought of it. If the citizens could dream of his prospective arrival with his bride, they would parade the band at the station and escort them, amid cheers and laughing congratulations, to his adobe home.

He resolved that he would use all the devices of speed and plains-craft in making the journey from the station to his house. Once within that safe citadel, he could issue some sort of a vocal bulletin, and then not go among the citizens until they had time to wear off a little of their enthusiasm.

The bride looked anxiously at him. "What's worrying you, Jack?"

He laughed again. "I'm not worrying, girl. I'm only thinking of Yellow Sky."

She flushed in comprehension.

A sense of mutual guilt invaded their minds and developed a finer tenderness. They looked at each other with eyes softly aglow. But Potter often laughed the same nervous laugh. The flush upon the bride's face seemed quite permanent.

The traitor to the feelings of Yellow Sky narrowly watched the speeding landscape. "We're nearly there," he said.

Presently the porter came and announced the proximity of Potter's home. He held a brush in his hand and, with all his airy superiority gone, he brushed Potter's new clothes as the latter slowly turned this way and that way. Potter fumbled out a coin and gave it to the porter as he had seen others do. It was a heavy and muscle-bound business, as that of a man shoeing his first horse.

The porter took their bag, and as the train began to slow they moved forward to the hooded platform of the car. Presently the two engines and their long string of coaches rushed into the station of Yellow Sky.

"They have to take water here," said Potter, from a constricted throat and in mournful cadence as one announcing death. Before the train stopped his eye had swept the length of the platform, and he was glad and astonished to see there was none upon it but the station-agent, who, with a slightly hurried and anxious air, was walking toward the water-tanks. When the train had halted, the porter alighted first and placed in position a little temporary step.

"Come on, girl," said Potter hoarsely. As he helped her down they each laughed on a false note. He took the bag from the negro, and bade his wife cling to his arm. As they slunk rapidly away, his hang-dog glance perceived that they were unloading the two trunks, and also that the station-agent far ahead near the baggage-car had turned and was running toward him, making gestures. He laughed, and groaned as he laughed, when he noted the first effect of his marital bliss upon Yellow Sky. He gripped his wife's arm firmly to his side, and they fled. Behind them the porter stood chuckling fatuously.

II

The California Express on the Southern Railway was due at Yellow Sky in twenty-one minutes. There were six men at the bar of the Weary Gentleman saloon. One was a drummer[2] who talked a great deal and rapidly; three were Texans who did not care to talk at that time; and two were Mexican sheep-herders who did not talk as a general practice in the Weary Gentleman saloon. The bar-keeper's dog lay on the board-walk that crossed in front of the door. His head was on his paws, and he glanced drowsily here and there with the constant vigilance of a dog that is kicked on occasion. Across the sandy street were some vivid green grass plots, so wonderful in appearance amid the sands that burned near them in a blazing sun that they caused a doubt in the mind. They exactly resembled the grass mats used to represent lawns on the stage. At the cooler end of the railway station a man without a coat sat in a tilted chair and smoked his pipe. The fresh-cut bank of the Rio Grande circled near the town, and there could be seen beyond it a great plum-colored plain of mesquite.

Save for the busy drummer and his companions in the saloon, Yellow Sky was dozing. The new-comer leaned gracefully upon the bar, and recited many tales with the confidence of a bard who has come upon a new field.

"——and at the moment that the old man fell down stairs with the bureau in his arms, the old woman was coming up with two scuttles of coal, and, of course——"

The drummer's tale was interrupted by a young man who suddenly appeared in the open door. He cried: "Scratchy Wilson's drunk, and has turned loose with both hands." The two Mexicans at once set down their glasses and faded out of the rear entrance of the saloon.

2. A traveling salesman.

The drummer, innocent and jocular, answered: "All right, old man. S'pose he has. Come in and have a drink, anyhow."

But the information had made such an obvious cleft in every skull in the room that the drummer was obliged to see its importance. All had become instantly morose. "Say," said he, mystified, "what is this?" His three companions made the introductory gesture of eloquent speech, but the young man at the door forestalled them.

"It means, my friend," he answered, as he came into the saloon, "that for the next two hours this town won't be a health resort."

The bar-keeper went to the door and locked and barred it. Reaching out of the window, he pulled in heavy wooden shutters and barred them. Immediately a solemn, chapel-like gloom was upon the place. The drummer was looking from one to another.

"But say," he cried, "what is this, anyhow? You don't mean there is going to be a gun-fight?"

"Don't know whether there'll be a fight or not," answered one man grimly. "But there'll be some shootin'—some good shootin'."

The young man who had warned them waved his hand. "Oh, there'll be a fight fast enough, if anyone wants it. Anybody can get a fight out there in the street. There's a fight just waiting."

The drummer seemed to be swayed between the interest of a foreigner and a perception of personal danger.

"What did you say his name was?" he asked.

"Scratchy Wilson," they answered in chorus.

"And will he kill anybody? What are you going to do? Does this happen often? Does he rampage around like this once a week or so? Can he break in that door?"

"No, he can't break down that door," replied the bar-keeper. "He's tried it three times. But when he comes you'd better lay down on the floor, stranger. He's dead sure to shoot at it, and a bullet may come through."

Thereafter the drummer kept a strict eye upon the door. The time had not yet been called for him to hug the floor, but as a minor precaution he sidled near to the wall. "Will he kill anybody?" he said again.

The men laughed low and scornfully at the question.

"He's out to shoot, and he's out for trouble. Don't see any good in experimentin' with him."

"But what do you do in a case like this? What do you do?"

A man responded: "Why, he and Jack Potter——"

But, in chorus, the other men interrupted: "Jack Potter's in San Anton'."

"Well, who is he? What's he got to do with it?"

"Oh, he's the town marshal. He goes out and fights Scratchy when he gets on one of these tears."

"Wow," said the drummer, mopping his brow. "Nice job he's got."

The voices had toned away to mere whisperings. The drummer wished to ask further questions which were born of an increasing anxiety and bewilderment; but when he attempted them, the men merely looked at him in irritation and motioned him to remain silent. A tense waiting hush was upon them. In the deep shadows of the room their eyes shone as they listened for sounds from the street. One man made three gestures at the bar-keeper, and the latter, moving like a ghost, handed him a glass and a bottle. The man poured a full glass of whisky, and set down the bottle noise-lessly. He gulped the whisky in a swallow, and turned again toward the door in immovable silence. The drummer saw that the bar-keeper, without a sound, had taken a Winchester from beneath the bar. Later he saw this individual beckoning to him, so he tiptoed across the room.

"You better come with me back of the bar."

"No, thanks," said the drummer, perspiring. "I'd rather be where I can make a break for the back door."

Whereupon the man of bottles made a kindly but peremptory gesture. The drummer obeyed it, and finding himself seated on a box with his head below the level of the bar, balm was laid upon his soul at sight of various zinc and copper fittings that bore a resemblance to armor-plate. The bar-keeper took a seat comfortably upon an adjacent box.

"You see," he whispered, "this here Scratchy Wilson is a wonder with a gun—a perfect wonder—and when he goes on the war trail, we hunt our holes—naturally. He's about the last one of the old gang that used to hang out along the river here. He's a terror when he's drunk. When he's sober he's all right—kind of simple— wouldn't hurt a fly—nicest fellow in town. But when he's drunk— whoo!"

There were periods of stillness. "I wish Jack Potter was back from San Anton'," said the bar-keeper. "He shot Wilson up once—in the leg—and he would sail in and pull out the kinks in this thing."

Presently they heard from a distance the sound of a shot, fol-lowed by three wild yowls. It instantly removed a bond from the men in the darkened saloon. There was a shuffling of feet. They looked at each other. "Here he comes," they said.

III

A man in a maroon-colored flannel shirt, which had been pur-chased for purposes of decoration and made, principally, by some Jewish women on the east side of New York, rounded a corner and walked into the middle of the main street of Yellow Sky. In either hand the man held a long, heavy blue-black revolver. Often he

yelled, and these cries rang through a semblance of a deserted village, shrilly flying over the roofs in a volume that seemed to have
no relation to the ordinary vocal strength of a man. It was as if the
surrounding stillness formed the arch of a tomb over him. These
cries of ferocious challenge rang against walls of silence. And his
boots had red tops with gilded imprints, of the kind beloved in
winter by little sledding boys on the hillsides of New England.

The man's face flamed in a range begot of whisky. His eyes, rolling and yet keen for ambush, hunted the still door-ways and windows. He walked with the creeping movement of the midnight cat.
As it occurred to him, he roared menacing information. The long
revolvers in his hands were as easy as straws; they were moved with
an electric swiftness. The little fingers of each hand played sometimes in a musician's way. Plain from the low collar of the shirt, the
cords of his neck straightened and sank, straightened and sank, as
passion moved him. The only sounds were his terrible invitations.
The calm adobes preserved their demeanor at the passing of this
small thing in the middle of the street.

There was no offer of fight; no offer of fight. The man called to
the sky. There were no attractions. He bellowed and fumed and
swayed his revolvers here and everywhere.

The dog of the bar-keeper of the Weary Gentleman saloon had
not appreciated the advance of events. He yet lay dozing in front of
his master's door. At sight of the dog, the man paused and raised
his revolver humorously. At sight of the man, the dog sprang up
and walked diagonally away, with a sullen head and growling. The
man yelled, and the dog broke into a gallop. As it was about to
enter an alley, there was a loud noise, a whistling, and something
spat the ground directly before it. The dog screamed, and, wheeling
in terror, galloped headlong in a new direction. Again there was a
noise, a whistling, and sand was kicked viciously before it. Fear-
stricken, the dog turned and flurried like an animal in a pen. The
man stood laughing, his weapons at his hips.

Ultimately the man was attracted by the closed door of the
Weary Gentleman saloon. He went to it, and hammering with a
revolver, demanded drink.

The door remaining imperturbable, he picked a bit of paper from
the walk and nailed it to the framework with a knife. He then
turned his back contemptuously upon this popular resort, and walking to the opposite side of the street, and spinning there on his heel
quickly and lithely, fired at the bit of paper. He missed it by a half
inch. He swore at himself, and went away. Later, he comfortably
fusilladed the windows of his most intimate friend. The man was
playing with this town. It was a toy for him.

But still there was no offer of fight. The name of Jack Potter, his
ancient antagonist, entered his mind, and he concluded that it

would be a glad thing if he should go to Potter's house and by bombardment induce him to come out and fight. He moved in the direction of his desire, chanting Apache scalp-music.

When he arrived at it, Potter's house presented the same still, calm front as had the other adobes. Taking up a strategic position, the man howled a challenge. But this house regarded him as might a great stone god. It gave no sign. After a decent wait, the man howled further challenges, mingling with them wonderful epithets.

Presently there came the spectacle of a man churning himself into deepest rage over the immobility of a house. He fumed at it as the winter wind attacks a prairie cabin in the North. To the distance there should have gone the sound of a tumult like the fighting of two hundred Mexicans. As necessity bade him, he paused for breath or to reload his revolvers.

IV

Potter and his bride walked sheepishly and with speed. Sometimes they laughed together shamefacedly and low.

"Next corner, dear," he said finally.

They put forth the efforts of a pair walking bowed against a strong wind. Potter was about to raise a finger to point the first appearance of the new home when, as they circled the corner, they came face to face with a man in a maroon-colored shirt who was feverishly pushing cartridges into a large revolver. Upon the instant the man dropped this revolver to the ground, and, like lightning, whipped another from its holster. The second weapon was aimed at the bridegroom's chest.

There was a silence. Potter's mouth seemed to be merely a grave for his tongue. He exhibited an instinct to at once loosen his arm from the woman's grip, and he dropped the bag to the sand. As for the bride, her face had gone as yellow as old cloth. She was a slave to hideous rites gazing at the apparitional snake.

The two men faced each other at a distance of three paces. He of the revolver smiled with a new and quiet ferocity. "Tried to sneak up on me," he said. "Tried to sneak up on me!" His eyes grew more baleful. As Potter made a slight movement, the man thrust his revolver venomously forward. "No, don't you do it, Jack Potter. Don't you move a finger toward a gun just yet. Don't you move an eyelash. The time has come for me to settle with you, and I'm goin' to do it my own way and loaf along with no interferin'. So if you don't want a gun bent on you, just mind what I tell you."

Potter looked at his enemy. "I ain't got a gun on me, Scratchy," he said. "Honest, I ain't." He was stiffening and steadying, but yet somewhere at the back of his mind a vision of the Pullman floated, the sea-green figured velvet, the shining brass, silver, and glass, the wood that gleamed as darkly brilliant as the surface of a pool of oil

—all the glory of the marriage, the environment of the new estate. "You know I fight when it comes to fighting, Scratchy Wilson, but I ain't got a gun on me. You'll have to do all the shootin' yourself."

His enemy's face went livid. He stepped forward and lashed his weapon to and fro before Potter's chest. "Don't you tell me you ain't got no gun on you, you whelp. Don't tell me no lie like that. There ain't a man in Texas ever seen you without no gun. Don't take me for no kid." His eyes blazed with light, and his throat worked like a pump.

"I ain't takin' you for no kid," answered Potter. His heels had not moved an inch backward. "I'm takin' you for a —— fool. I tell you I ain't got a gun, and I ain't. If you're goin' to shoot me up, you better begin now. You'll never get a chance like this again."

So much enforced reasoning had told on Wilson's rage. He was calmer. "If you ain't got a gun, why ain't you got a gun?" he sneered. "Been to Sunday-school?"

"I ain't got a gun because I've just come from San Anton' with my wife. I'm married," said Potter. "And if I'd thought there was going to be any galoots like you prowling around when I brought my wife home, I'd had a gun, and don't you forget it."

"Married!" said Scratchy, not at all comprehending.

"Yes, married. I'm married," said Potter distinctly.

"Married?" said Scratchy. Seemingly for the first time he saw the drooping drowning woman at the other man's side. "No!" he said. He was like a creature allowed a glimpse of another world. He moved a pace backward, and his arm with the revolver dropped to his side. "Is this—is this the lady?" he asked.

"Yes, this is the lady," answered Potter.

There was another period of silence.

"Well," said Wilson at last, slowly, "I s'pose it's all off now."

"It's all off if you say so, Scratchy. You know I didn't make the trouble." Potter lifted his valise.

"Well, I 'low it's off, Jack," said Wilson. He was looking at the ground. "Married!" He was not a student of chivalry; it was merely that in the presence of this foreign condition he was a simple child of the earlier plains. He picked up his starboard revolver, and placing both weapons in their holsters, he went away. His feet made funnel-shaped tracks in the heavy sand.

1898

From THE BLACK RIDERS AND OTHER LINES[1]

I

Black riders came from the sea.
There was clang and clang of spear and shield,

1. These poems from *The Black Riders and Other Lines* (1895), together with their numbering, are reprinted from Joseph Katz's *The Poems of Stephen Crane* (1966).

And clash and clash of hoof and heel,
Wild shouts and the wave of hair
In the rush upon the wind: 5
Thus the ride of Sin.

27

A youth in apparel that glittered
Went to walk in a grim forest.
There he met an assassin
Attired all in garb of old days;
He, scowling through the thickets,   5
And dagger poised quivering,
Rushed upon the youth.
"Sir," said this latter,
"I am enchanted, believe me,
To die, thus,   10
In this medieval fashion,
According to the best legends;
Ah, what joy!"
Then took he the wound, smiling,
And died, content.   15

42

I walked in a desert.
And I cried:
"Ah, God, take me from this place!"
A voice said: "It is no desert."
I cried: "Well, but—   5
The sand, the heat, the vacant horizon."
A voice said: "It is no desert."

56

A man feared that he might find an assassin;
Another that he might find a victim.
One was more wise than the other.

From WAR IS KIND[1]

76

Do not weep, maiden, for war is kind.
Because your lover threw wild hands toward the sky
And the affrighted steed ran on alone,
Do not weep.
War is kind.   5

---

1. These poems from *War Is Kind* (1899) are reprinted from Joseph Katz's critical
edition of *The Poems of Stephen Crane* (1966).

Hoarse, booming drums of the regiment,
Little souls who thirst for fight,
These men were born to drill and die.
The unexplained glory flies above them,
Great is the Battle-God, great, and his Kingdom—   10
A field where a thousand corpses lie.

Do not weep, babe, for war is kind.
Because your father tumbled in the yellow trenches,
Raged at his breast, gulped and died,
Do not weep.   15
War is kind.

Swift blazing flag of the regiment,
Eagle with crest of red and gold,
These men were born to drill and die.
Point for them the virtue of slaughter,   20
Make plain to them the excellence of killing
And a field where a thousand corpses lie.

Mother whose heart hung humble as a button
On the bright splendid shroud of your son,
Do not weep.   25
War is kind.

1896   1899

83

Fast rode the knight
With spurs, hot and reeking
Ever waving an eager sword.
        "To save my lady!"
Fast rode the knight   5
And leaped from saddle to war.
Men of steel flickered and gleamed
Like riot of silver lights
And the gold of the knight's good banner
Still waved on a castle wall.   10

A horse
Blowing, staggering, bloody thing
Forgotten at foot of castle wall.
A horse
Dead at foot of castle wall.   15

1896   1899

87

A newspaper is a collection of half-injustices
Which, bawled by boys from mile to mile,
Spreads its curious opinion

To a million merciful and sneering men,
While families cuddle the joys of the fireside   5
When spurred by tale of dire lone agony.
A newspaper is a court
Where every one is kindly and unfairly tried
By a squalor of honest men.
A newspaper is a market   10
Where wisdom sells its freedom
And melons are crowned by the crowd.
A newspaper is a game
Where his error scores the player victory
While another's skill wins death.   15
A newspaper is a symbol;
It is fetless life's chronicle,
A collection of loud tales
Concentrating eternal stupidities,
That in remote ages lived unhaltered,   20
Roaming through a fenceless world.

                                                    1899

89

A slant of sun on dull brown walls
A forgotten sky of bashful blue.
Toward God a mighty hymn
A song of collisions and cries
Rumbling wheels, hoof-beats, bells,   5
Welcomes, farewells, love-calls, final moans,
Voices of joy, idiocy, warning, despair,
The unknown appeals of brutes,
The chanting of flowers
The screams of cut trees,   10
The senseless babble of hens and wise men—
A cluttered incoherency that says at the stars:
"Oh, God, save us."

1895   1899

96

A man said to the universe:
"Sir, I exist!"
"However," replied the universe,
"The fact has not created in me
A sense of obligation."

                                                    1899

From POSTHUMOUSLY PUBLISHED POEMS[1]

113

A man adrift on a slim spar
A horizon smaller than the rim of a bottle

1. The poem, first published in *The Bookman* for April, 1929, is reprinted from Joseph Katz's critical edition of *The Poems of Stephen Crane* (1966).

         Tented waves rearing lashy dark points
         The near whine of froth in circles.
                   God is cold.   5

         The incessant raise and swing of the sea
         And growl after growl of crest
         The sinkings, green, seething, endless
         The upheaval half-completed.
                   God is cold.   10

         The seas are in the hollow of The Hand;
         Oceans may be turned to a spray
         Raining down through the stars
         Because of a gesture of pity toward a babe.
         Oceans may become grey ashes,   15
         Die with a long moan and a roar
         Amid the tumult of the fishes
         And the cries of the ships,
         Because The Hand beckons the mice.

         A horizon smaller than a doomed assassin's cap,   20
         Inky, surging tumults
         A reeling, drunken sky and no sky
         A pale hand sliding from a polished spar.
                   God is cold.

         The puff of a coat imprisoning air: 25
         A face kissing the water-death
         A weary slow sway of a lost hand
         And the sea, the moving sea, the sea.
                   God is cold.

c. 1898   1929

THEODORE DREISER
1871–1945

Theodore Herman Albert Dreiser was born in Terre Haute, Indiana, on August 27, 1871, the twelfth of thirteen children. His gentle and devoted mother was illiterate; his German immigrant father was severe and distant. From the former he seems to have absorbed a quality of compassionate wonder; from the latter he seems to have inherited moral earnestness and the capacity to persist in the face of failure, disappointment, and despair.

Dreiser's childhood was decidedly unhappy. The large family moved from house to house in Indiana dogged by poverty, insecurity, and internal division. One of his brothers became a famous popular songwriter under the name of Paul Dresser, but other brothers and sisters drifted into drunkenness, promiscuity, and squalor. Dreiser as a youth was as ungainly, confused, shy, and full of vague yearnings as most of his fictional protagonists, male and female. In this as in many other ways, Dreiser's novels are direct projections of his inner life as well as careful transcriptions of his experiences.

From the age of fifteen Dreiser was essentially on his own, earning meager support from a variety of menial jobs. A high-school teacher staked him to a year at Indiana University in 1889, but Dreiser's education was to come from experience and from independent reading and thinking. This education began in 1892 when he wangled his first newspaper job with the Chicago *Globe*. Over the next decade as an itinerant journalist Dreiser slowly groped his way to authorship, testing what he knew from direct experience against what he was learning from reading Charles Darwin, Ernst Haeckel, Thomas Huxley, and Herbert Spencer, those late-nineteenth-century scientists and social scientists who lent support to the view that nature and society had no divine sanction.

Sister Carrie (1900), which traces the material rise of Carrie Meeber and the tragic decline of G. W. Hurstwood, was Dreiser's first novel. Because it depicted social transgressions by characters who felt no remorse and largely escaped punishment, and because it used "strong" language and used names of living persons, it was virtually suppressed by its publisher, who printed but refused to promote the book. Since its reissue in 1907 it has steadily risen in popularity and scholarly acceptance as one of the key works in the Dreiser canon. Indeed, though turn-of-the-century readers found Dreiser's point of view crude and immoral, his influence on the fiction of the first quarter of the century is perhaps greater than any other writer's. In this early period some of his best short fictions were written, among them *Nigger Jeff* and *Butcher Rogaum's Daughter*. The best of his short stories —like all of Dreiser's fiction—have the unusual power to compel our sympathy for and wonder over characters whose minds and inner life we never really enter. The lynching of Jeff Ingalls unfolds according to "some axiomatic, mathematical law" and against the incongruous backdrop of a "stillness of purest, summery-est, country-est quality." The events have the air of necessity of a Greek tragedy, a horrifying and moving spectacle.

In the first years of the century Dreiser suffered a breakdown. With the help of his brother Paul, however, he eventually recovered and by 1904 was on the way to several successful years as an editor, the last of them as editorial director of the Butterick Publishing Company. In 1910 he resigned to write *Jennie Gerhardt* (1911), the first of a long succession of books that marked his turn to writing as a full-time career.

In *The Financier* (1912), *The Titan* (1914), and *The Stoic* (not published until 1947) Dreiser shifted from the pathos of helpless protagonists to the power of those unusual individuals who assume dominant roles in business and society. The protagonist of this "Trilogy of Desire" (as Dreiser described it), Frank Cowperwood, is modeled after the Chicago speculator Charles T. Yerkes. These novels of the businessman as buccaneer introduced, even more explicitly than had *Sister Carrie*, the notion that men of high sexual energy were financially successful, a theme that is carried over into the rather weak autobiographical novel *The "Genius"* (1915).

The identification of potency with money is at the heart of Dreiser's greatest and most successful novel, *An American Tragedy* (1925). The center of this immense novel's thick texture of biographical circumstance, social fact, and industrial detail is a young man who acts as if the only way he can be truly fulfilled is by acquiring wealth—through marriage if necessary.

During the last two decades of his life Dreiser turned entirely away from fiction and toward political activism and polemical writing. He visited the Soviet Union in 1927 and published *Dreiser Looks at Russia* the following year. In the 1930s, like many other American intellectuals and writers, Dreiser was increasingly attracted by the philosophical program of the Communist party. Unable to believe in traditional religious credos, yet unable to give up his strong sense of justice, he continued to seek a way to reconcile his determinism with his compassionate sense of the mystery of life.

In his lifetime Dreiser was controversial as a man and as a writer. He was accused, with some justice by conventional standards, of being immoral in his personal behavior, a poor thinker, and a dangerous political radical; his style was said (by critics more than by fellow authors) to be ponderous and his narrative sense weak. As time has passed, however, Dreiser has become recognized as a profound and prescient critic of debased American values and as a powerful novelist.

Nigger Jeff[1]

The city editor was waiting for his good reporter, Eugene Davies. He had cut an item from one of the afternoon papers and laid it aside to give to Mr. Davies. Presently the reporter appeared.

It was one o'clock of a sunny, spring afternoon. Davies wore a new spring suit, a new hat and new shoes. In the lapel of his coat was a small bunch of violets. He was feeling exceedingly well and good-natured. The world seemed worth singing about.

"Read that, Davies," said the city editor, handing him the clipping. "I'll tell you what I want you to do afterward."

The reporter stood by the editorial chair and read:

"Pleasant Valley, Mo., April 16.

"A most dastardly crime has just been reported here. Jeff Ingalls, a negro, this morning assaulted Ada Whittier, the nineteen-year-old daughter of Morgan Whittier, a well-to-do farmer, whose home is four miles south of this place. A posse, headed by Sheriff Mathews, has started in pursuit. If he is caught, it is thought he will be lynched."

The reporter raised his eyes as he finished.

"You had better go out there, Davies," said the city editor. "It looks as if something might come of that. A lynching up here would be a big thing."

Davies smiled. He was always pleased to be sent out of town. It was a mark of appreciation. The city editor never sent any of the other boys on these big stories. What a nice ride he would have.

He found Pleasant Valley to be a small town, nestling between green slopes of low hills, with one small business corner and a rambling array of lanes. One or two merchants of St. Louis lived out here, but otherwise it was exceedingly rural. He took note of the whiteness of the little houses, the shimmering beauty of the little creek you had to cross in going from the depot. At the one main corner a few men were gathered about a typical village barroom.

1. Reprinted from *Ainslee's Magazine* (1901).

Davies headed for this as being the most apparent source of information.

In mingling with the company, he said nothing about his errand. He was very shy about mentioning that he was a newspaper man.

The whole company was craving excitement and wanted to see something come of the matter. They hadn't had such a chance to work up wrath and satisfy their animal propensities in years. It was a fine opportunity and such a righteous one.

He went away thinking that he had best find out for himself how the girl was. Accordingly he sought the old man that kept a stable in the village and procured a horse. No carriage was to be had. Davies was not an excellent rider, but he made a shift of it. The farm was not so very far away, and before long he knocked at the front door of the house, set back a hundred feet from the rough country road.

"I'm from the *Republic*," he said, with dignity. His position took very well with farmers. "How is Miss Whittier?"

"She's doing very well," said a tall, raw-boned woman. "Won't you come in? She's rather feverish, but the doctor says she'll be all right."

Davies acknowledged the invitation by entering. He was anxious to see the girl, but she was sleeping, and under the influence of an opiate.

"When did this happen?" he asked.

"About eight o'clock this morning," said the woman. "She started off to go over to our next neighbor here, Mr. Edmonds, and this negro met her. I didn't know anything about it until she came crying through the gate and dropped down in here."

"Were you the first one to meet her?" asked Davies.

"Yes, I was the only one," said Mrs. Whittier. "The men had gone out in the fields."

Davies listened to more of the details, and then rose to go. He was allowed to have a look at the girl, who was rather pretty. In the yard he met a country chap who had come over to hear the news. This man imparted more information.

"They're lookin' all around south of here," said the man, speaking of the crowd supposed to be in search. "I expect they'll make short work of him if they get him."

"Where does this negro live?" asked Davies.

"Oh, right down here a little way. You follow this road to the next crossing and turn to the right. It's a little log house that sits back off the road—something like this, only it's got a lot of chips scattered about."

Davies decided to go there, but changed his mind. It was getting late. He had better return to the village, he thought.

Accordingly, he rode back and put the horse in the hands of its owner. Then he went over to the principal corner. Much the same company was still present. He wondered what these people had been doing all the time. He decided to ingratiate himself by imparting a little information.

Just then a young fellow came galloping up.

"They've got him," he shouted, excitedly, "they've got him."

A chorus of "whos" and "wheres," with sundry other queries, greeted this information as the crowd gathered about the rider.

"Why, Mathews caught him up here at his own house. Says he'll shoot the first man that dares to try to take him away. He's taking him over to Clayton."

"Which way'd he go?" exclaimed the men.

" 'Cross Sellers' Lane," said the rider. "The boys think he's going to Baldwin."

"Whoopee," yelled one of the listeners. "Are you going, Sam?"

"You bet," said the latter. "Wait'll I get my horse."

Davies waited no longer. He saw the crowd would be off in a minute to catch up with the sheriff. There would be information in that quarter. He hastened after his horse.

"He's eating," said the man.

"I don't care," exclaimed Davies. "Turn him out. I'll give you a dollar more."

The man led the horse out, and the reporter mounted.

When he got back to the corner several of the men were already there. The young man who had brought the news had dashed off again.

Davies waited to see which road they would take. Then he did the riding of his life.

In an hour the company had come in sight of the sheriff, who, with two other men, was driving a wagon he had borrowed. He had a revolver in each hand and was sitting with his face toward the group, that trailed after at a respectful distance. Excited as every one was, there was no disposition to halt the progress of the law.

"He's in that wagon," Davies heard one man say. "Don't you see they've got him tied and laid down in there?"

Davies looked.

"We ought to take him away and hang him," said one of the young fellows who rode nearest the front.

"Where's old man Whittier?" asked one of the crowd, who felt that they needed a leader.

"He's out with the other crowd," was the reply.

"Somebody ought to go and tell him."

"Clark's gone," assured another, who hoped for the worst.

Davies rode among the company very much excited. He was astonished at the character of the crowd. It was largely impelled to its excited jaunt by curiosity and a desire to see what would happen.

There was not much daring in it. The men were afraid of the determined sheriff. They thought something ought to be done, but they did not feel like getting into trouble.

The sheriff, a sage, lusty, solemn man, contemplated the recent addition to these trailers with considerable feeling. He was determined to protect his man and avoid injustice. A mob should not have him if he had to shoot, and if he shot, he was going to empty both revolvers, and those of his companions. Finally, since the company thus added to did not dash upon him, he decided to scare them off. He thought he could do it since they trailed like calves.

"Stop a minute," he said to his driver.

The latter pulled up. So did the crowd behind. Then the sheriff stood over the prostrate body of the negro, who lay trembling in the jolting wagon bed and called back to the men.

"Go on away from here, you people," he said. "Go on, now. I won't have you foller after me."

"Give us the nigger," yelled one in a half-bantering, half-derisive tone of voice.

"I'll give you five minutes to go on back out of this road," returned the sheriff grimly. They were about a hundred feet apart. "If you don't, I'll clear you out."

"Give us the nigger!"

"I know you, Scott," answered the sheriff, recognizing the voice. "I'll arrest every last one of you to-morrow. Mark my word!"

The company listened in silence, the horses champing and twisting.

"We've got a right to follow," answered one of the men.

"I give you fair warning," said the sheriff, jumping from his wagon and leveling his pistols as he approached. "When I count five, I'll begin to shoot."

He was a serious and stalwart figure as he approached, and the crowd retreated.

"Get out o' this now," he yelled. "One, two——"

The company turned completely and retreated.

"We'll follow him when he gets farther on," said one of the men in explanation.

"He's got to do it," said another. "Let him get a little ahead."

The sheriff returned to his wagon and drove on. He knew that he would not be obeyed, and that safety lay in haste alone. If he could only make them lose track of him and get a good start it might be possible to get to Clayton and the strong county jail by morning.

Accordingly he whipped up his horses while keeping his grim lookout.

"He's going to Baldwin," said one of the company of which Davies was a member.

"Where is that?" asked Davies.

"Over west of here, about four miles."

The men lagged, hesitating what to do. They did not want to lose sight of him, and yet cowardice controlled them. They did not want to get into direct altercation with the law. It wasn't their place to hang the man, although he ought to be hanged and it would be a stirring and exciting thing if he were. Consequently, they desired to watch and be on hand—to get old Whittier and his son Jake if they could, who were out looking elsewhere. They wanted to see what the father and brother would do.

The quandary was solved by Dick Hewlitt, who suggested that they could get to Baldwin by going back to Pleasant Valley and taking the Sand River pike. It was a shorter cut than this. Maybe they could beat the sheriff there. Accordingly, while one or two remained to track the sheriff, the rest set off at a gallop to Pleasant Valley. It was nearly dusk when they got there and stopped for a few minutes at the corner store. Here they talked, and somehow the zest to follow departed; they were not certain now of going on. It was supper time. The fires of evening meals were marked by upcurling smoke. Evidently the sheriff had them worsted for to-night. Morg Whittier had not been found. Neither had Jake. Perhaps they had better eat. Two or three had already secretly fallen away.

They were telling the news to the one or two storekeepers, when Jake Whittier, the girl's brother, and several companions came riding up. They had been scouring the territory to the north of the town.

"The sheriff's got him," said one of the company. "He's taking him over to Baldwin in a wagon."

"Which way did he go?" asked young Jake, whose hardy figure, worn, hand-me-down clothes and rakish hat showed up picturesquely as he turned on his horse.

" 'Cross Sellers' Lane. You won't get him that way. Better take the short cut."

A babble of voices was making the little corner interesting. One told how he had been caught, another that the sheriff was defiant, a third that men were tracking him, until the chief points of the drama had been spoken, if not heard.

"Come on, boys," said Jake, jerking at the reins and heading up the pike. "I'll get the damn nigger."

Instantly suppers were forgotten. The whole customary order of the evening was neglected. The company started off on another exciting jaunt, up hill and down dale, through the lovely country that lay between Baldwin and Pleasant Valley.

Davies was very weary of his saddle. He wondered when he was to write his story. The night was exceedingly beautiful. Stars were already beginning to shine. Distant lamps twinkled like yellow eyes from the cottages in the valleys on the hillsides. The air was fresh

and tender. Some pea fowls were crying afar off and the east promised a golden moon.

Silently the assembled company trotted on—no more than a
score in all. It was too grim a pilgrimage for joking. Young Jake,
riding silently toward the front, looked as if he meant business. His
friends did not like to say anything to him, seeing that he was the
aggrieved. He was left alone.

After an hour's riding Baldwin came into view, lying in a shelter-
ing cup of low hills. Its lights were twinkling softly, and there was
an air of honest firesides and cheery suppers about it which
appealed to Davies in his hungry state. Still, he had no thought but
of carrying out his mission.

Once in the village they were greeted by calls of recognition.
Everybody knew what they had come for. The local storekeepers
and loungers followed the cavalcade up the street to the sheriff's
house, for the riders had now fallen into a solemn walk.

"You won't get him, boys," said Seavey, the young postmaster
and telegraph operator, as they passed his door. "Mathews says he's
sent him to Clayton."

At the first street corner they were joined by several men who
had followed the sheriff.

"He tried to give us the slip," they said, excitedly, "but he's got
the nigger in the house there, down in the cellar."

"How do you know?"

"I saw him bring him in this way. I think he is, anyhow."

A block from the sheriff's little white cottage the men parleyed.
They decided to go up and demand the negro.

"If he don't turn him out, we'll break in the door and take him,"
said Jake.

"That's right. We'll stand by you, Whittier."

A throng had gathered. The whole village was up in arms. The
one street was alive and running with people. Riders pranced up
and down, hallooing. A few shot off revolvers. Presently the mob
gathered about the sheriff's gate, and Jake stepped forward as
leader.

Their coming was not unexpected. Sheriff Mathews was ready for
them with a double-barreled Winchester. He had bolted the doors
and put the negro in the cellar, pending the arrival of the aid he
had telegraphed for to Clayton. The latter was cowering and chattering in the darkest corner of his dungeon against the cold, damp
earth, as he hearkened to the voices and the firing of the revolvers.
With wide, bulging eyes, he stared into the gloom.

Jake, the son and brother, took the precautionary method of calling to the sheriff.

"Hello, Mathews!"

"Eh, eh, eh," bellowed the crowd.

Suddenly the door flew open, and appearing first in the glow of the lamp came the double barrel of a Winchester, followed by the form of the sheriff, who held his gun ready for a quick throw to the shoulder. All except Jake fell back.

"We want that nigger," said Jake, deliberately.

"He isn't here," said the sheriff.

"Then what you got that gun for?" yelled a voice.

The sheriff made no answer.

"Better give him up, Mathews," called another, who was safe in the crowd, "or we'll come in and take him."

"Lookee here, gentlemen," said the sheriff, "I said the man wasn't here. I say it again. You couldn't have him if he was and you can't come in my house. Now, if you people don't want trouble, you'd better go on away."

"He's down in the cellar," yelled another.

The sheriff waved his gun slightly.

"Why don't you let us see?" said another.

"You'd better go away from here now," cautioned the sheriff.

The crowd continued to simmer and stew, while Jake stood out before. He was very pale and determined, but lacked initiative.

"He won't shoot. Why don't you go in, boys, and get him?"

"He won't, eh?" thought the sheriff. Then he said aloud: "The first man that comes inside that gate takes the consequences."

No one ventured near the gate. It seemed as if the planned assault must come to nothing.

"You'd better go away from here," cautioned the sheriff again. "You can't come in, it'll only mean bloodshed."

There was more chattering and jesting while the sheriff stood on guard. He said no more. Nor did he allow the banter, turmoil and lust for tragedy to disturb him. Only he kept his eye on Jake, on whose movements the crowd hung.

"I'll get him," said Jake, "before morning."

The truth was that he felt the weakness of the crowd. He was, to all intents and purposes, alone, for he did not inspire confidence.

Thus the minutes passed. It became a half hour and then an hour. With the extending time pedestrians dropped out and then horsemen. Some went up the street, several back to Pleasant Valley, more galloped about until there were very few left at the gate. It was plain that organization was lost. Finally Davies smiled and came away. He was sure he had a splendid story.

He began to look for something to eat, and hunted for the telegraph operator.

He found the operator first and told him he wanted to write a story and file it. The latter said there was a table in the little post-office and telegraph station which he could use. He got very much interested in Davies, and when he asked where he could get some-

thing to eat, said he would run across the street and tell the proprietor of the only boarding-house to fix him something which he could
eat as he wrote.

"You start your story," he said, "and I'll come back and see if I
can get the *Republic.*"

Davies sat down and started the account.

"Very obliging postmaster," he thought, but he had so often
encountered pleasant and obliging people on his rounds, that he
soon dropped that thought.

The food was brought and Davies wrote. By eight-thirty the
Republic answered an often-repeated call.

"Davies at Baldwin," ticked the postmaster, "get ready for quite
a story."

"Let 'er go," answered the operator in the *Republic*, who had
been expecting this dispatch.

Davies turned over page after page as the events of the day formulated themselves in his mind. He ate a little between whiles,
looking out through the small window before him, where afar off he
could see a lonely light twinkling in a hillside cottage. Not infrequently he stopped work to see if anything new was happening. The
operator also wandered about, waiting for an accumulation of pages
upon which he could work, but making sure to catch up with the
writer. The two became quite friendly.

Davies finished his dispatch with the caution that more might
follow, and was told by the city editor to watch it. Then he and the
postmaster sat down to talk.

About twelve o'clock the lights in all the village houses had vanished and the inhabitants had gone to bed. The man-hunters had
retired, and the night was left to its own sounds and murmurs,
when suddenly the faint beating of hoofs sounded out on the Sand
River Pike, which led away toward Pleasant Valley, back of the
post-office. The sheriff had not relaxed any of his vigilance. He was
not sleeping. There was no sleep for him until the county authorities should come to his aid.

"Here they come back again," exclaimed the postmaster.

"By George, you're right," said Davies.

There was a clattering of hoofs and grunting of saddle girths as a
large company of men dashed up the road and turned into the
narrow street of the village.

Instantly the place was astir again. Lights appeared in doorways,
and windows were thrown open. People were gazing out to see what
new movement was afoot. Davies saw that there was none of the
hip and hurrah business about this company such as had characterized the previous descent. There was grimness everywhere, and he
began to feel that this was the beginning of the end. He ran down
the street toward the sheriff's house, arriving a few moments after
the crowd, which was in part dismounted.

With the clear moon shining straight overhead, it was nearly as bright as day. Davies made out several of his companions of the afternoon and Jake, the son. There were many more, though, whom he did not know, and foremost among them an old man. He was strong, iron-gray and wore a full beard. He looked very much like a blacksmith.

While he was still looking, the old man went boldly forward to the little front porch of the house and knocked at the door. Some one lifted a curtain at the window and peeped out.

"Hello, in there," the old man cried, knocking again and much louder.

"What do you want?" said a voice.

"We want that nigger."

"Well, you can't have him. I've told you people once."

"Bring him out or we'll break down the door," said the old man.

"If you do, it's at your own risk. I'll give you three minutes to get off that porch."

"We want that nigger."

"If you don't get off that porch I'll fire through the door," said the voice, solemnly. "One, two——"

The old man backed cautiously away.

"Come out, Mathews," yelled the crowd. "You've got to give him up. We ain't going back without him."

Slowly the door opened, as if the individual within was very well satisfied as to his power to handle the mob. It revealed the tall form of Sheriff Mathews, armed with his Winchester. He looked around very stolidly and then addressed the old man as one would a friend.

"You can't have him, Morgan," he said, "it's against the law."

"Law or no law," said the old man, "I want that nigger."

"I can't let you have him, Morgan. It's against the law. You oughtn't to be coming around here at this time of night acting so."

"Well, we'll take him, then," said the old man, making a move.

The sheriff leveled his gun on the instant.

"Stand back, there," he shouted, noticing a movement on the part of the crowd. "I'll blow ye into kingdom come, sure as hell."

The crowd halted at this assurance.

The sheriff lowered his weapon as if he thought the danger were over.

"You all ought to be ashamed of yourselves," he said, softly, his voice sinking to a gentle, neighborly reproof, "tryin' to upset the law this way."

"The nigger didn't upset the law, did he?" asked one, derisively.

The sheriff made no answer.

"Give us that scoundrel, Mathews, you'd better do it," said the old man. "It'll save a heap of trouble."

"I'll not argue with you, Morgan. I said you couldn't have him, and you can't. If you want bloodshed, all right. But don't blame me. I'll kill the first man that tries to make a move this way."

He shifted his gun handily and waited. The crowd stood outside his little fence murmuring.

Presently the old man retired and spoke to several leaders.

There was more murmuring, and then he came back to the dead line.

"We don't want to cause trouble, Mathews," he began, explanatively, moving his hand oratorically, "but we think you ought to see that it won't do you any good to stand out. We think that——"

Davies was watching young Jake, the son, whose peculiar attitude attracted his attention. The latter was standing poised at the edge of the crowd, evidently seeking to remain unobserved. His eyes were on the sheriff, who was hearkening to the old man. Suddenly, when the sheriff seemed for a moment mollified and unsuspecting, he made a quick run for the porch. There was an intense movement all along the line, as the life and death of the deed became apparent. Quickly the sheriff drew his gun to his shoulder. He pressed both triggers at the same time, but not before Jake reached him. The latter knocked the gun barrel upward and fell upon his man. Both shots blazed out over the heads of the crowd in red puffs, and then followed a general onslaught. Men leaped the fence by tens, and crowded upon the little cottage. They swarmed on every side of the house, and crowded about the porch and the door, where four men were scuffling with the sheriff. The latter soon gave up, vowing vengeance. Torches were brought and a rope. A wagon drove up and was backed into the yard. Then began the calls for the negro.

The negro had been crouching in his corner in the cellar, trembling for his fate ever since the first attack. He had not dozed or lost consciousness during the intervening hours, but cowered there, wondering and praying. He was terrified lest the sheriff might not get him away in time. He was afraid that every sound meant a new assault. Now, however, he had begun to have the faintest glimmerings of hope when the new murmurs of contention arose. He heard the gallop of the horses' feet, voices of the men parleying, the ominous knock on the door.

At this sound, his body quaked and his teeth chattered. He began to quiver in each separate muscle and run cold. Already he saw the men at him, beating and kicking him.

"Before God, boss, I didn't mean to," he chattered, contemplating the chimera of his brain with startling eyes. "Oh, my God! boss, no, no. Oh, no, no."

He crowded closer to the wall. Another sound greeted his ears. It was the roar of a shotgun. He fell, groveling upon the floor, his nails digging in the earth.

"Oh, my Lawd, boss," he moaned, "oh, my Lawd, boss, don't kill me. I won't do it no mo'. I didn't go to do it. I didn't." His teeth were in the wet earth.

It was but now that the men were calling each other to the search. Five jumped to the outside entrance way of the low cellar, carrying a rope. Three others followed with their torches. They descended into the dark hole and looked cautiously about.

Suddenly, in the farthest corner, they espied him. In his agony, he had worked himself into a crouching position, as if he were about to spring. His hands were still in the earth. His eyes were rolling, his mouth foaming.

"Oh, my Lawd!" he was repeating monotonously, "oh, my Lawd!"

"Here he is. Pull him out, boys," cried several together.

The negro gave one yell of horror. He quite bounded as he did so, coming down with a dead chug on the earthen floor. Reason had forsaken him. He was a groveling, foaming brute. The last gleam of intelligence was that which notified him of the set eyes of his pursuers.

Davies was standing ten feet back when they began to reappear. He noted the heads of the torches, the disheveled appearance of the men, the scuffling and pulling. Then he clapped his hands over his mouth and worked his fingers convulsively, almost unconscious of what he was doing.

"Oh, my God," he whispered, his voice losing power.

The sickening sight was that of negro Jeff, foaming at the mouth, bloodshot in the eyes, his hands working convulsively, being dragged up the cellar steps, feet foremost. They had tied a rope about his waist and feet, and had hauled him out, leaving his head to hang and drag. The black face was distorted beyond all human semblance.

"Oh, my God!" said Davies again, biting his fingers unconsciously.

The crowd gathered about, more horror-stricken than gleeful at their own work. The negro was rudely bound and thrown like a sack of wheat into the wagon bed. Father and son mounted to drive, and the crowd took their horses. Wide-eyed and brain-racked, Davies ran for his own. He was so excited, he scarcely knew what he was doing.

Slowly the gloomy cavalcade took its way up the Sand River Pike. The moon was pouring down a wash of silvery light. The shadowy trees were stirring with a cool night wind. Davies hurried after and joined the silent, tramping throng.

"Are they going to hang him?" he asked.

"That's what they got him for," answered the man nearest him.

Davies dropped again into silence and tried to recover his nerves. The gloomy company seemed a terrible thing. He drew near the wagon and looked at the negro.

The latter seemed out of his senses. He was breathing heavily and groaning. His eyes were fixed and staring, his face and hands bleeding as if they had been scratched or trampled on. He was bundled up like limp wheat.

Davies could not stand it longer. He fell back, sick at heart, It seemed a ghastly, unmerciful way to do. Still, the company moved on and he followed, past fields lit white by the moon, under dark, silent groups of trees, through which the moonlight fell in patches, up hilltops and down into valleys, until at last the little stream came into view, sparkling like a molten flood of silver in the night. After a time the road drew close to the water and made for a wagon bridge, which could be seen a little way ahead. The company rode up to this and halted. Davies dismounted with the others. The wagon was driven up to the bridge and father and son got out.

Fully a score of men gathered about, and the negro was lifted from the wagon. Davies thought he could not stand it, and went down by the waterside slightly above the bridge. He could see long beams of iron sticking out over the water, where the bridge was braced.

The men fastened a rope to a beam and then he could see that they were fixing the other end around the negro's neck.

Finally the curious company stood back.

"Have you anything to say?" a voice demanded.

The negro only lolled and groaned, slobbering at the mouth. He was out of his mind.

Then came the concerted action of four men, a lifting of a black mass in the air, and then Davies saw the limp form plunge down and pull up with a creaking sound of rope. In the weak moonlight it seemed as if the body were struggling, but he could not tell. He watched, wide-mouthed and silent, and then the body ceased moving. He heard the company depart, but that did not seem important. Only the black mass swaying in the pale light, over the shiny water of the stream seemed wonderful.

He sat down upon the bank and gazed in silence. He was not afraid. Everything was summery and beautiful. The whole cavalcade disappeared, the moon sank. The light of morning began to show as tender lavender and gray in the east. Still he sat. Then came the roseate hue of day, to which the waters of the stream responded, the white pebbles shining beautifully at the bottom. Still the body hung black and limp, and now a light breeze sprang up and stirred it visibly. At last he arose and made his way back to Pleasant Valley.

Since his duties called him to another day's work here, he idled about, getting the details of what was to be done. He talked with citizens and officials, rode out to the injured girl's home, rode to Baldwin to see the sheriff. There was singular silence and placidity in that corner. The sheriff took his defeat as he did his danger, philosophically.

It was evening again before he remembered that he had not discovered whether the body had been removed. He had not heard why the negro came back or how he was caught. The little cabin was two miles away, but he decided to walk, the night was so springlike. Before he had traveled half way, the moon arose and stretched long shadows of budding trees across his path. It was not long before he came upon the cabin, set well back from the road and surrounded with a few scattered trees. The ground between the door and the road was open, and strewn with the scattered chips of a woodpile. The roof was sagged and the windows patched in places, but, for all that, it had the glow of a home. Through the front door, which stood open, the blaze of a fire shone, its yellow light filling the interior with golden fancies.

Davies stopped at the door and knocked, but received no answer. He looked in on the battered cane chairs and aged furniture with considerable interest.

A door in the rear room opened, and a little negro girl entered, carrying a battered tin lamp, without any chimney. She had not heard his knock, and started perceptibly at the sight of his figure in the doorway. Then she raised her smoking lamp above her head in order to see better and approached.

There was something comical about her unformed figure and loose gingham dress. Her black head was strongly emphasized by little pigtails of hair done up in white twine, which stood out all over her head. Her dark skin was made apparently more so by contrast with her white teeth and the whites of her eyes.

Davies looked at her for a moment and asked, "Is this where Ingalls lives?"

The girl nodded her head. She was exceedingly subdued, and looked as if she had been crying.

"Has the body been brought here?" he asked.

"Yes, suh," she answered, with a soft negro accent.

"When did they bring it home?"

"This moanin'."

"Are you his sister?"

"Yes, suh."

"Well, can you tell me how they caught him?" asked Davies, feeling slightly ashamed to intrude thus. "What did he come back for?"

"To see us," said the girl.

"Well, did he want anything? He didn't come just to see you, did he?"

"Yes, suh," said the girl, "he come to say good-by."

Her voice wavered.

"Didn't he know he might get caught?" asked Davies.

"Yes, suh, I think he did."

She still stood very quietly holding the poor battered lamp up, and looking down.

"Well, what did he have to say?" asked Davies.

"He said he wanted tuh see motha'. He was a-goin' away."

The girl seemed to regard Davies as an official of some sort, and he knew it.

"Can I have a look at the body?" he asked.

The girl did not answer, but started as if to lead the way.

"When is the funeral?" he asked.

"To-morrow."

The girl led him through several bare sheds of rooms to the furthermost one of the line. This last seemed a sort of storage shed for odds and ends. It had several windows, but they were bare of glass, and open to the moonlight, save for a few wooden boards nailed across from the outside. Davies had been wondering all the while at the lonely and forsaken air of the place. No one seemed about but this little girl. If they had colored neighbors, none thought it worth while to call.

Now, as he stepped into this cool, dark, exposed outer room, the desolation seemed complete. The body was there in the middle of the bare room, stretched upon an ironing board, which rested on a box and a chair, and covered with a white sheet. All the corners of the room were quite dark, and only in the middle were shining splotches of moonlight.

Davies came forward, but the girl left him, carrying her lamp. She did not seem able to remain. He lifted the sheet, for he could see well enough, and looked at the stiff, black form. The face was extremely distorted, even in death, and he could see where the rope had tightened. A bar of cool moonlight lay across the face and breast. He was still looking, thinking soon to restore the covering, when a sound, half sigh, half groan, reached his ears.

He started as if a ghost had touched him. His muscles tightened. Instantly his heart was hammering like mad in his chest. His first impression was that it came from the dead.

"Oo-o-ohh," came the sound again, this time whimpering, as if someone were crying.

He turned quickly, for now it seemed to come from the corner. Greatly disturbed, he hesitated, and then as his eyes strained he caught the shadow of something. It was in the extreme corner, huddled up, dark, almost indistinguishable—crouching against the cold walls.

"Oh, oh, oh," was repeated, even more plaintively than before.

Davies began to understand. He approached lightly. Then he made out an old black mammy, doubled up and weeping. She was in the very niche of the corner, her head sunk on her knees, her tears falling, her body rocking to and fro.

Davies drew silently back. Before such grief, his intrusion seemed cold and unwarranted. The sensation of tears came to his eyes. He covered the dead, and withdrew.

Out in the moonlight, he struck a pace, but soon stopped and looked back. The whole dreary cabin, with its one golden door, where the light was, seemed a pitiful thing. He swelled with feeling and pathos as he looked. The night, the tragedy, the grief, he saw it all.

"I'll get that in," he exclaimed, feelingly, "I'll get it all in."

1901

JACK LONDON
1876–1916

John Griffith London was born on January 12, 1876, the illegitimate son of W. H. Chaney, a talented and self-taught man who became an astrologer, and Flora Wellman, an eccentric woman from a wealthy Ohio family who was both a spiritualist and music teacher. London, who never saw his real father, took the name of his stepfather. He grew up in extreme poverty: from earliest youth he supported himself with menial and dangerous jobs, experiencing profoundly the struggle for survival that most other writers and intellectuals knew only from observation or books. By the time he was eighteen he had worked in a cannery and as an oyster pirate, seaman, jute-mill worker, and coal shoveler. After crossing much of the continent as a member of "Coxey's Army" (an organized group of unemployed who, following the panic of 1893, carried their call for economic reform to Washington, D.C.), he was jailed for thirty days for vagrancy. At this point he determined to educate himself in order to improve his own condition and that of others.

With an intellectual energy that matched his physical strength, London quickly completed high school and spent a semester reading prodigiously as a special student at the University of California. Temperament rather than logic led him to embrace the hopeful socialism of Marx on the one hand and the rather darker views of Nietzsche and Darwinism on the other. That is, London believed at the same time in the inevitable triumph of the working class and in the evolutionary necessity of the survival of the strongest individuals. London's sincere intellectual and personal involvement in the socialist movement is recorded in such novels and polemical works as *The People of the Abyss* (1903), *The Iron Heel* (1908), *The War of the Classes* (1905), and *Revolution* (1910); his competing, deeply felt commitment to the fundamental reality of the law of survival and the will to power is dramatized in his most popular novels, *The Call of the Wild* (1903) and *The Sea Wolf* (1904). Wolf Larsen, the ruthless, amoral protagonist of the latter book, best realizes the ideal of the "superman." The contradiction between these competing beliefs is most vividly projected in the patently autobiographical novel *Martin Eden* (1909), a central document for the London scholar.

London had been writing sporadically for five years, but his professional career began after he spent the winter of 1897–98 in the Klondike in a futile search for gold. Within two years, by the time he published his first collection of stories, *The Son of the Wolf* (1900), he was on his way to becoming the highest paid author of his time. By his twenty-seventh birthday *The Call of the Wild* had made him rich.

London frankly disliked his profession: he wrote for money, but he was also a methodical and careful craftsman who produced a minimum of 1,000 publishable words a day six days a week. He wrote on many subjects, from agronomy to penal reform, from astral projection to warfare. The most enduringly popular of his stories involved the primitive (and melodramatic) struggle of strong and weak individuals in the context of irresistible natural forces such as the wild sea or the arctic wastes. At a time when America's frontier was closing and President Theodore Roosevelt was urging the strenuous life, London adapted the physical ruggedness and psychological independence of Rudyard Kipling's heroes to the American experience in *The Call of the Wild*, *The Sea Wolf*, and *White Fang* (1906). Like his contemporaries Stephen Crane and Frank Norris (and like Hemingway a generation later), London was fascinated by the way violence tested and defined human character, though he was much more interested in ideas than Crane and less sentimental than Norris. Thus, in *The Law of Life*, the tribal patriarch's death is depicted as an illustration of the law that all living things die rather than in terms of the particular psychological state of the individual facing his end.

London continued to write until his death in 1916 from a "gastrointestinal type of uraemia," widely supposed to have been suicide. But the bulk of his best work had been done by 1910. He had written too much too fast, with too little concern for the stylistic and formal refinement and subtlety of characterization that rank high with critics. He had not, moreover, reconciled his contradictory views of man's nature and destiny. But London's stories of man in and against nature continue to be popular all over the world. In them, London strips everything down to the symbolic starkness of dream, to a primordial simplicity that has the strange and compelling power of ancient myth.

The Law of Life[1]

Old Koskoosh listened greedily. Though his sight had long since faded, his hearing was still acute, and the slightest sound penetrated to the glimmering intelligence which yet abode behind the withered forehead, but which no longer gazed forth upon the things of the world. Ah! that was Sit-cum-to-ha, shrilly anathematizing the dogs as she cuffed and beat them into the harnesses. Sit-cum-to-ha was his daughter's daughter, but she was too busy to waste a thought upon her broken grandfather, sitting alone there in the snow, forlorn and helpless. Camp must be broken. The long trail waited while the short day refused to linger. Life called her, and the duties of life, not death. And he was very close to death now.

The thought made the old man panicky for the moment, and he stretched forth a palsied hand which wandered tremblingly over the small heap of dry wood beside him. Reassured that it was indeed

1. This story was first printed in *Mc-Clure's Magazine*, Vol. 16 (March, 1901), and included in the collection *Children of the Frost* (1902); the present text is a reprint of the version in *McClure's*.

there, his hand returned to the shelter of his mangy furs, and he again fell to listening. The sulky crackling of half-frozen hides told him that the chief's moose-skin lodge had been struck, and even then was being rammed and jammed into portable compass. The chief was his son, stalwart and strong, head man of the tribesmen, and a mighty hunter. As the women toiled with the camp luggage, his voice rose, chiding them for their slowness. Old Koskoosh strained his ears. It was the last time he would hear that voice. There went Geehow's lodge! And Tusken's! Seven, eight, nine; only the Shaman's could be still standing. There! They were at work upon it now. He could hear the Shaman grunt as he piled it on the sled. A child whimpered, and a woman soothed it with soft, crooning gutturals. Little Koo-tee, the old man thought, a fretful child, and not over strong. It would die soon, perhaps, and they would burn a hole through the frozen tundra and pile rocks above to keep the wolverines away. Well, what did it matter? A few years at best, and as many an empty belly as a full one. And in the end, Death waited, ever-hungry and hungriest of them all.

What was that? Oh, the men lashing the sleds and drawing tight the thongs. He listened, who would listen no more. The whip-lashes snarled and bit among the dogs. Hear them whine! How they hated the work and the trail! They were off! Sled after sled churned slowly away into the silence. They were gone. They had passed out of his life, and he faced the last bitter hour alone. No. The snow crunched beneath a moccasin; a man stood beside him; upon his head a hand rested gently. His son was good to do this thing. He remembered other old men whose sons had not waited after the tribe. But his son had. He wandered away into the past, till the young man's voice brought him back.

"Is it well with you?" he asked.

And the old man answered, "It is well."

"There be wood beside you," the younger man continued, "and the fire burns bright. The morning is gray, and the cold has broken. It will snow presently. Even now is it snowing."

"Ay, even now is it snowing."

"The tribesmen hurry. Their bales are heavy, and their bellies flat with lack of feasting. The trail is long and they travel fast. I go now. It is well?"

"It is well. I am as a last year's leaf, clinging lightly to the stem. The first breath that blows, and I fall. My voice is become like an old woman's. My eyes no longer show me the way of my feet, and my feet are heavy, and I am tired. It is well."

He bowed his head in content till the last noise of the complaining snow had died away, and he knew his son was beyond recall. Then his hand crept out in haste to the wood. It alone stood betwixt him and the eternity which yawned in upon him. At last the measure of his life was a handful of faggots. One by one they would go to feed the fire, and just so, step by step, death would creep upon him. When the last stick had surrendered up its heat, the frost would begin to gather strength. First his feet would yield, then his hands; and the numbness would travel, slowly, from the extremities to the body. His head would fall forward upon his knees, and he would rest. It was easy. All men must die.

He did not complain. It was the way of life, and it was just. He had been born close to the earth, close to the earth had he lived, and the law thereof was not new to him. It was the law of all flesh. Nature was not kindly to the flesh. She had no concern for that concrete thing called the individual. Her interest lay in the species, the race. This was the deepest abstraction old Koskoosh's barbaric mind was capable of, but he grasped it firmly. He saw it exemplified in all life. The rise of the sap, the bursting greenness of the willow bud, the fall of the yellow leaf—in this alone was told the whole history. But one task did nature set the individual. Did he not perform it, he died. Did he perform it, it was all the same, he died. Nature did not care; there were plenty who were obedient, and it was only the obedience in this matter, not the obedient, which lived and lived always. The tribe of Koskoosh was very old. The old men he had known when a boy, had known old men before them. Therefore it was true that the tribe lived, that it stood for the obedience of all its members, way down into the forgotten past, whose very resting places were unremembered. They did not count; they were episodes. They had passed away like clouds from a summer sky. He also was an eipsode, and would pass away. Nature did not care. To life she set one task, gave one law. To perpetuate was the task of life, its law was death. A maiden was a good creature to look upon, full-breasted and strong, with spring to her step and light in her eyes. But her task was yet before her. The light in her eyes brightened, her step quickened, she was now bold with the young men, now timid, and she gave them of her own unrest. And ever she grew fairer and yet fairer to look upon, till some hunter, able no longer to withhold himself, took her to his lodge to cook and toil for him and to become the mother of his children. And with the coming of her offspring her looks left her. Her limbs dragged and shuffled, her eyes dimmed and bleared, and only the little children found joy against the withered cheek of the old squaw by the fire. Her task was done. But a little while, on the first pinch of famine or the first long trail, and she would be left, even as he had been left, in the snow, with a little pile of wood. Such was the law.

He placed a stick carefully upon the fire and resumed his meditations. It was the same everywhere, with all things. The mosquitos vanished with the first frost. The little tree-squirrel crawled away to die. When age settled upon the rabbit it became slow and heavy, and could no longer outfoot its enemies. Even the big bald-face grew clumsy and blind and quarrelsome, in the end to be dragged down by a handful of yelping huskies. He remembered how he had abandoned his own father on an upper reach of the Klondike one winter, the winter before the missionary came with his talk-books and his box of medicines. Many a time had Koskoosh smacked his lips over the recollection of that box, though now his mouth refused to moisten. The "painkiller" had been especially good. But the missionary was a bother after all, for he brought no meat into the camp, and he ate heartily, and the hunters grumbled. But he chilled his lungs on the divide by the Mayo, and the dogs afterwards nosed the stones away and fought over his bones.

Koskoosh placed another stick on the fire and harked back deeper into the past. There was the time of the Great Famine, when the old men crouched empty-bellied to the fire, and from their lips fell dim traditions of the ancient day when the Yukon ran wide open for three winters, and then lay frozen for three summers. He had lost his mother in that famine. In the summer the salmon run had failed, and the tribe looked forward to the winter and the coming of the caribou. Then the winter came, but with it there were no caribou. Never had the like been known, not even in the lives of the old men. But the caribou did not come, and it was the seventh year, and the rabbits had not replenished, and the dogs were naught but bundles of bones. And through the long darkness the children wailed and died, and the women, and the old men; and not one in ten of the tribe lived to meet the sun when it came back in the spring. That *was* a famine!

But he had seen times of plenty, too, when the meat spoiled on their hands, and the dogs were fat and worthless with over-eating— times when they let the game go unkilled, and the women were fertile, and the lodges were cluttered with sprawling men-children and women-children. Then it was the men became high-stomached, and revived ancient quarrels, and crossed the divides to the south to kill the Pellys, and to the west that they might sit by the dead fires of the Tananas. He remembered, when a boy, during a time of plenty, when he saw a moose pulled down by the wolves. Zing-ha lay with him in the snow and watched—Zing-ha, who later became the craftiest of hunters, and who, in the end, fell through an air-hole on the Yukon. They found him, a month afterward, just as he had crawled half-way out and frozen stiff to the ice.

But the moose. Zing-ha and he had gone out that day to play at hunting after the manner of their fathers. On the bed of the creek they struck the fresh track of a moose, and with it the tracks of many wolves. "An old one," Zing-ha, who was quicker at reading the sign, said—"an old one who cannot keep up with the herd. The wolves have cut him out from his brothers, and they will never leave him." And it was so. It was their way. By day and by night, never resting, snarling on his heels, snapping at his nose, they would stay by him to the end. How Zing-ha and he felt the blood-lust quicken! The finish would be a sight to see!

Eager-footed, they took the trail, and even he, Koskoosh, slow of sight and an unversed tracker, could have followed it blind, it was so wide. Hot were they on the heels of the chase, reading the grim tragedy, fresh-written, at every step. Now they came to where the moose had made a stand. Thrice the length of a grown man's body, in every direction, had the snow been stamped about and uptossed. In the midst were the deep impressions of the splay-hoofed game, and all about, everywhere, were the lighter footmarks of the wolves. Some, while their brothers harried the kill, had lain to one side and rested. The full-stretched impress of their bodies in the snow was as perfect as though made the moment before. One wolf had been caught in a wild lunge of the maddened victim and trampled to death. A few bones, well picked, bore witness.

Again, they ceased the uplift of their snowshoes at a second stand. Here the great animal had fought desperately. Twice had he been dragged down, as the snow attested, and twice had he shaken his assailants clear and gained footing once more. He had done his task long since, but none the less was life dear to him. Zing-ha said it was a strange thing, a moose once down to get free again; but this one certainly had. The Shaman would see signs and wonders in this when they told him.

And yet again, they came to where the moose had made to mount the bank and gain the timber. But his foes had laid on from behind, till he reared and fell back upon them, crushing two deep into the snow. It was plain the kill was at hand, for their brothers had left them untouched. Two more stands were hurried past, brief in time-length and very close together. The trail was red now, and the clean stride of the great beast had grown short and slovenly. Then they heard the first sounds of the battle—not the full-throated chorus of the chase, but the short, snappy bark which spoke of close quarters and teeth to flesh. Crawling up the wind, Zing-ha bellied it through the snow, and with him crept he, Koskoosh, who was to be chief of the tribesmen in the years to come. Together they shoved aside the under branches of a young spruce and peered forth. It was the end they saw.

The picture, like all of youth's impressions, was still strong with him, and his dim eyes watched the end played out as vividly as in that far-off time. Koskoosh marveled at this, for in the days which followed, when he was a leader of men and a head of councilors, he had done great deeds and made his name a curse in the mouths of the Pellys, to say naught of the strange white man he had killed, knife to knife, in open fight.

For long he pondered on the days of his youth, till the fire died down and the frost bit deeper. He replenished it with two sticks

this time, and gauged his grip on life by what remained. If Sit-cum-
to-ha had only remembered her grandfather, and gathered a larger
armful, his hours would have been longer. It would have been easy.
But she was ever a careless child, and honored not her ancestors
from the time the Beaver, son of the son of Zing-ha, first cast eyes
upon her. Well, what mattered it? Had he not done likewise in his
own quick youth? For a while he listened to the silence. Perhaps
the heart of his son might soften, and he would come back with the
dogs to take his old father on with the tribe to where the caribou
ran thick and the fat hung heavy upon them.

He strained his ears, his restless brain for the moment stilled.
Not a stir, nothing. He alone took breath in the midst of the great
silence. It was very lonely, Hark! What was that? A chill passed
over his body. The familiar, long-drawn howl broke the void, and it
was close at hand. Then on his darkened eyes was projected the
vision of the moose—the old bull moose—the torn flanks and
bloody sides, the riddled mane, and the great branching horns,
down low and tossing to the last. He saw the flashing forms of gray,
the gleaming eyes, the lolling tongues, the slavered fangs. And he
saw the inexorable circle close in till it became a dark point in the
midst of the stamped snow.

A cold muzzle thrust against his cheek, and at its touch his soul
leaped back to the present. His hand shot into the fire and dragged
out a burning faggot. Overcome for the nonce by his hereditary fear
of man, the brute retreated, raising a prolonged call to his brothers;
and greedily they answered, till a ring of crouching, jaw-slobbered
gray was stretched round about. The old man listened to the drawing in of this circle. He waved his brand wildly, and sniffs turned to
snarls; but the panting brutes refused to scatter. Now one wormed
his chest forward, dragging his haunches after, now a second, now a
third; but never a one drew back. Why should he cling to life? he
asked, and dropped the blazing stick into the snow. It sizzled and
went out. The circle grunted uneasily, but held its own. Again he
saw the last stand of the old bull moose, and Koskoosh dropped his
head wearily upon his knees. What did it matter after all? Was it
not the law of life?

                                                    1901, 1902

HENRY ADAMS
1838–1918

Henry Adams's great-grandfather John was second President of the United
States, his grandfather John Quincy was sixth President, and his father
Charles Francis was a distinguished political leader and diplomat. Despite
Henry's lifelong penchant for self-deprecation, his own achievements as

scholar, teacher, novelist, editor, and cultural historian are worthy of his eminent forebears, for they earn him an important place in American intellectual and literary history.

Adams was born in Boston, on Beacon Hill, and spent his happy childhood in the constant presence of renowned politicians, artists, and intellectuals; the index to his autobiography, *The Education of Henry Adams,* is virtually an *International Who Was Who* of the time. He was to claim that his studies at Harvard College of the 1850s prepared him neither for a career nor for the extraordinary intellectual, technological, and social transformations of the last half of the century, but the records reveal that he was a good student and his disparagement of his college experience should be understood as an example of Adams's persistent self-irony. After graduation, he studied and traveled in Europe before he returned to America in 1860 to become private secretary to his father, a position he held for nine years, first in Washington when the elder Adams was elected to Congress, then in London, where his father served as foreign minister during the Civil War years.

In 1870, after a brief career as a freelance journalist, he rather reluctantly accepted a position as assistant professor of medieval history at Harvard, doubting his own fitness for the position; he observed later that the entire educational system of the college was "fallacious from the beginning to the end," and that "the lecture-room was futile enough, but the faculty-room was worse." In the same period he undertook the editorship of the prestigious *North American Review,* using this position to criticize both of the major political parties in this period of uncontrolled expansion and widespread government corruption. He sardonically remarked of his two vocations that "a professor commonly became a pedagogue or a pedant; an editor an authority on advertising." By all accounts other than his own, however, he served the college and the journal well before he gave up both positions in the late 1870s in order to settle in Washington to devote full time to historical research.

Adams's new career as historian did not begin auspiciously. His biography (1879) of Albert Gallatin, Thomas Jefferson's Secretary of the Treasury, and his subsequent biography of the flamboyant Congressman John Randolph were successful neither with his professional colleagues nor with the public. The research in original documents Adams had undertaken in order to write these biographies, however, brought him to the grander subject of which they were a part: *The History of the United States of America during the Administrations of Thomas Jefferson and James Madison* (1889–91). The nine-volume work (which took almost nine years to complete) is still a standard account of this crucial period of transition from Old to New World dominance. During these years Adams also published two novels rich in social detail: *Democracy* in 1880, and *Esther* in 1884. Both novels stirred considerable interest when they were published and continue to attract readers who seek, in the first novel, a contemporary account of the corruption of government by business interests and, in the second, a representation of the effect of scientific thought on traditional religious belief.

Adams's life was profoundly changed by the suicide, in 1885, of his charming and seemingly contented wife, Marian Hooper. The publication of *The History* also left Adams physically drained and intellectually depleted. For a time it seemed that he would occupy himself with nothing more serious than travel to familiar places in Europe and to more exotic places in the Pacific and Middle East. But a trip to northern France in the summer of 1895 with Mrs. Henry Cabot Lodge, the wife of his friend the Senator from Massachusetts, stirred his intellectual curiosity and ignited his creative energies once again.

What most struck the world-weary Adams that summer was the severe and majestic harmony of the twelfth- and thirteenth-century Norman and Gothic cathedrals they visited, particularly the one at Chartres. *Mont-Saint-Michel and Chartres* (privately printed in 1904; published 1913) not only provided illuminating discussions of the literary and architectural monuments of the period but penetrated to the powerful spiritual forces that lay behind those achievements. Paradoxically, the insights which allowed Adams to represent what he considered a straight-line historical decline from this medieval unity to his own period of confusion and immanent disaster served to renew his own spirits and brought his mind and work to the attention of a wider public.

The Education of Henry Adams, begun as a kind of sequel to *Mont-Saint-Michel*, was privately printed early in 1907 and distributed to nearly one hundred friends and prominent personages mentioned in the text. In it, Adams rehearses his own miseducation by his family, by schools, and by his experience of various social institutions, ironically offers his own "failures" as a negative example to young men of the time, and describes the increasingly rapid collapse of Western culture in the era after the twelfth century, during which the Virgin Mary (the spiritually unifying) gave way to the Industrial Dynamo (the scientifically disunifying) as the object of man's worship.

The Virgin and the Dynamo were not presented simply as historical facts but to serve as symbols. In fact, *The Education* is primarily a literary, not a biographical or historical, work. This book, since it shows imaginatively how all the major intellectual, social, political, military, and economic issues and developments of Adams's day are interrelated, is now considered by many critics to be the one indispensable text for students seeking to understand the period between the Civil War and the First World War. The perspective taken by Adams in *The Education* used to seem excessively pessimistic; its final chapter (dated 1905) prophesied that the disintegrative forces unleashed by science threatened to effect the destruction of the world within a generation. This prophecy has not been borne out literally, but the sense of immanent global disaster has come to be widely shared. "Naturally," as Adams went on to observe in this chapter, "such an attitude of an umpire is apt to infuriate the spectators. Above all, it was profoundly unmoral, and tended to discourage effort. On the other hand, it tended to encourage foresight and to economize waste of mind. If this was not itself education, it pointed out the economies necessary for the education of the new American. There, the duty stopped."

The Education has grown in interest in recent years for two major reasons: for what it tells us about its complex, elusive, and paradoxical author, and for what it tells us about the technology-dominated, dehumanized world whose major power alignments, political and material, he foresaw so clearly. As a prophet, he was, as social analyst Daniel Bell observed, the first American writer who "caught a sense of the quickening change of pace that drives all our lives." As a historian of his own time, he was also, as historian Richard Hofstadter noted, "singular not only for the quality of his prose and the sophistication of his mind but also for the unparalleled mixture of his detachment and involvement." Adams, like many of us, was fascinated with the past, horrified by the present, and skeptical about the future; thus, more than half a century after his death, Adams and his most complex book speak with renewed pertinence to his dilemmas and ours.

From The Education of Henry Adams
Editor's Preface[1]

This volume, written in 1905 as a sequel to the same author's "Mont-Saint-Michel and Chartres," was privately printed, to the number of one hundred copies, in 1906, and sent to the persons interested, for their assent, correction, or suggestion. The idea of the two books was thus explained at the end of Chapter XXIX:—

"Any schoolboy could see that man as a force must be measured by motion from a fixed point. Psychology helped here by suggesting a unit—the point of history when man held the highest idea of himself as a unit in a unified universe. Eight or ten years of study had led Adams to think he might use the century 1150-1250, expressed in Amiens Cathedral and the Works of Thomas Aquinas, as the unit from which he might measure motion down to his own time, without assuming anything as true or untrue, except relation. The movement might be studied at once in philosophy and mechanics. Setting himself to the task, he began a volume which he mentally knew as 'Mont-Saint-Michel and Chartres: a Study of Thirteenth-Century Unity.' From that point he proposed to fix a position for himself, which he could label: "The Education of Henry Adams: a Study of Twentieth-Century Multiplicity.' With the help of these two points of relation, he hoped to project his lines forward and backward indefinitely, subject to correction from anyone who should know better."

The "Chartres" was finished and privately printed in 1904. The "Education" proved to be more difficult. The point on which the author failed to please himself, and could get no light from readers or friends, was the usual one of literary form. Probably he saw it in advance, for he used to say, half in jest, that his great ambition was to complete St. Augustine's "Confessions,"[2] but that St. Augustine,

1. The selections from *The Education* reprint Houghton Mifflin Company's Riverside Edition text established by Ernest Samuels. The notes to these selections are indebted to Samuels's annotation for that volume. This "Editor's Preface" was written by Adams in 1916; his friend Lodge simply agreed to have his name used. It rationalizes the process of composition of *The Education*, which actually grew out of the earlier book on Chartres. *The Education* was begun in 1903, essentially completed in 1905, and privately printed in 1907. Adams suffered

a cerebral thrombosis on April 24, 1912; his reference to midsummer, 1914, is to the beginning of World War I, which for Adams confirmed his worst views as to the eventual outcome of the force unleashed by science. Adams made a gift of the book's copyright to the Massachusetts Historical Society in 1918, the year of the first edition of the book for public sale.

2. Written c. 400, the *Confessions* is Augustine's account of his life and the events leading to his conversion to Christianity.

like a great artist, had worked from multiplicity to unity, while he, like a small one, had to reverse the method and work back from unity to multiplicity. The scheme became unmanageable as he approached his end.

Probably he was, in fact, trying only to work into it his favorite theory of history, which now fills the last three or four chapters of the "Education," and he could not satisfy himself with his workmanship. At all events, he was still pondering over the problem in 1910, when he tried to deal with it in another way which might be more intelligible to students. He printed a small volume called "A Letter to American Teachers," which he sent to his associates in the American Historical Association, hoping to provoke some response. Before he could satisfy himself even on this minor point, a severe illness in the spring of 1912 put an end to his literary activity forever.

The matter soon passed beyond his control. In 1913 the Institute of Architects published the "Mont-Saint-Michel and Chartres." Already the "Education" had become almost as well known, as the "Chartres," and was freely quoted by every book whose author requested it. The author could no longer withdraw either volume; he could no longer rewrite either, and he could not publish that which he thought unprepared and unfinished, although in his opinion the other was historically purposeless without its sequel. In the end, he preferred to leave the "Education" unpublished, avowedly incomplete, trusting that it might quietly fade from memory. According to his theory of history as explained in Chapters XXXIII and XXXIV, the teacher was at best helpless, and, in the immediate future, silence next to good temper was the mark of sense. After midsummer, 1914, the rule was made absolute.

The Massachusetts Historical Society has decided to publish the "Education" as it was printed in 1907, with only such marginal corrections as the author made, and it does this, not in opposition to the author's judgment, but only to put both volumes equally within reach of students who have occasion to consult them.

Henry Cabot Lodge

September, 1918

Preface

Jean Jacques Rousseau[1] began his famous "Confessions" by a vehement appeal to the Deity: "I have shown myself as I was; contemptible and vile when I was so; good, generous, sublime when I was so; I have unveiled my interior such as Thou thyself hast seen it, Eternal Father! Collect about me the innumerable swarm of my fellows; let them hear my confessions; let them groan at my unwor-

---

1. Jean Jacques Rousseau (1712–78), French philosopher who contended that man is good by nature and corrupted by the institutions of society. His *Confessions* was published posthumously. Adams's translation is apparently his own.

thiness; let them blush at my meannesses! Let each of them discover his heart in his turn at the foot of thy throne with the same sincerity; and then let any one of them tell thee if he dares: 'I was a better man!' "

Jean Jacques was a very great educator in the manner of the eighteenth century, and has been commonly thought to have had more influence than any other teacher of his time; but his peculiar method of improving human nature has not been universally admired. Most educators of the nineteenth century have declined to show themselves before their scholars as objects more vile or contemptible than necessary, and even the humblest teacher hides, if possible, the faults with which nature has generously embellished us all, as it did Jean Jacques, thinking, as most religious minds are apt to do, that the Eternal Father himself may not feel unmixed pleasure at our thrusting under his eyes chiefly the least agreeable details of his creation.

As an unfortunate result the twentieth century finds few recent guides to avoid, or to follow. American literature offers scarcely one working model for high education. The student must go back, beyond Jean Jacques, to Benjamin Franklin,[2] to find a model even of self-teaching. Except in the abandoned sphere of the dead languages, no one has discussed what part of education has, in his personal experience, turned out to be useful, and what not. This volume attempts to discuss it.

As educator, Jean Jacques was, in one respect, easily first; he erected a monument of warning against the Ego. Since his time, and largely thanks to him, the Ego has steadily tended to efface itself, and for purposes of model, to become a manikin on which the toilet[3] of education is to be draped in order to show the fit or misfit of the clothes. The object of study is the garment, not the figure. The tailor adapts the manikin as well as the clothes to his patron's wants. The tailor's object, in this volume, is to fit young men, in universities or elsewhere, to be men of the world, equipped for any emergency; and the garment offered to them is meant to show the faults of the patchwork fitted on their fathers.

At the utmost, the active-minded young man should ask of his teacher only mastery of his tools. The young man himself, the subject of education, is a certain form of energy; the object to be gained is economy of his force; the training is partly the clearing away of obstacles, partly the direct application of effort. Once acquired, the tools and models may be thrown away.

The manikin, therefore, has the same value as any other geometrical figure of three or more dimensions, which is used for the study of relation. For that purpose it cannot be spared; it is the only

---

2. Benjamin Franklin's *Autobiography* was first published in English in 1818; it was immediately popular and has be- come a classic.
3. Fashionable style of dress.

measure of motion, of proportion, of human condition; it must have the air of reality; must be taken for real; must be treated as though it had life. Who knows? Possibly it had![4]
February 16, 1907[5]

Chapter I. Quincy (1838–1848)

Under the shadow of Boston State House, turning its back on the house of John Hancock,[1] the little passage called Hancock Avenue runs, or ran, from Beacon Street, skirting the State House grounds, to Mount Vernon Street, on the summit of Beacon Hill; and there, in the third house below Mount Vernon Place, February 16, 1838, a child was born, and christened later by his uncle, the minister of the First Church after the tenets of Boston Unitarianism, as Henry Brooks Adams.

Had he been born in Jerusalem under the shadow of the Temple and circumcised in the Synagogue by his uncle the high priest, under the name of Israel Cohen, he would scarcely have been more distinctly branded, and not much more heavily handicapped in the races of the coming century, in running for such stakes as the century was to offer; but, on the other hand, the ordinary traveller, who does not enter the field of racing, finds advantage in being, so to speak, ticketed through life, with the safeguards of an old, established traffic. Safeguards are often irksome, but sometimes convenient, and if one needs them at all, one is apt to need them badly. A hundred years earlier, such safeguards as his would have secured any young man's success; and although in 1838 their value was not very great compared with what they would have had in 1738, yet the mere accident of starting a twentieth-century career from a nest of associations so colonial—so troglodytic—as the First Church, the Boston State House, Beacon Hill, John Hancock and John Adams, Mount Vernon Street and Quincy, all crowding on ten pounds of unconscious babyhood, was so queer as to offer a subject of curious speculation to the baby long after he had witnessed the solution. What could become of such a child of the seventeenth and eighteenth centuries, when he should wake up to find himself required to play the game of the twentieth? Had he been consulted, would he have cared to play the game at all, holding such cards as he held, and suspecting that the game was to be one of which neither he nor anyone else back to the beginning of time knew the rules or the risks or the stakes? He was not consulted and was not responsible, but had he been taken into the confidence of his parents, he would certainly have told them to change nothing as far as concerned him. He would have been astounded by his own luck. Probably no child,

4. Paraphrase of an observation by Ralph Waldo Emerson in his essay *Experience*: "Let us treat the men and women well; treat them as if they were real: perhaps they are."

5. Adams's 69th birthday.
1. John Hancock (1737–93), first signer of the Declaration of Independence and first Governor of the state of Massachusetts.

born in the year, held better cards than he. Whether life was an honest game of chance, or whether the cards were marked and forced, he could not refuse to play his excellent hand. He could never make the usual plea of irresponsibility. He accepted the situation as though he had been a party to it, and under the same circumstances would do it again, the more readily for knowing the exact values. To his life as a whole he was a consenting, contracting party and partner from the moment he was born to the moment he died. Only with that understanding—as a consciously assenting member in full partnership with the society of his age—had his education an interest to himself or to others.

As it happened, he never got to the point of playing the game at all; he lost himself in the study of it, watching the errors of the players; but this is the only interest in the story, which otherwise has no moral and little incident. A story of education—seventy years of it—the practical value remains to the end in doubt, like other values about which men have disputed since the birth of Cain and Abel; but the practical value of the universe has never been stated in dollars. Although everyone cannot be a Gargantua-Napoleon-Bismarck and walk off with the great bells of Notre Dame,[2] everyone must bear his own universe, and most persons are moderately interested in learning how their neighbors have managed to carry theirs.

This problem of education, started in 1838, went on for three years, while the baby grew, like other babies, unconsciously, as a vegetable, the outside world working as it never had worked before, to get his new universe ready for him. Often in old age he puzzled over the question whether, on the doctrine of chances, he was at liberty to accept himself or his world as an accident. No such accident had ever happened before in human experience. For him, alone, the old universe was thrown into the ash-heap and a new one created. He and his eighteenth-century, troglodytic Boston were suddenly cut apart—separated forever—in act if not in sentiment, by the opening of the Boston and Albany Railroad;[3] the appearance of the first Cunard steamers in the bay; and the telegraphic messages which carried from Baltimore to Washington the news that Henry Clay and James K. Polk were nominated for the Presidency. This was in May, 1844; he was six years old; his new world was ready for use, and only fragments of the old met his eyes.

Of all this that was being done to complicate his education, he knew only the color of yellow. He first found himself sitting on a yellow kitchen floor in strong sunlight. He was three years old when he took this earliest step in education; a lesson of color. The second

---

2. Gargantua's feat is recounted in Book I, Chapter XVII of Rabelais's *Gargantua and Pantagruel* (1552); Napoleon and Bismarck are famous military and political figures of 19th-century France and Germany respectively.
3. The section from Quincy to Boston was completed in 1846; regular transatlantic service by steamer began in 1840.

followed soon; a lesson of taste. On December 3, 1841, he developed scarlet fever. For several days he was as good as dead, reviving only under the careful nursing of his family. When he began to recover strength, about January 1, 1842, his hunger must have been stronger than any other pleasure or pain, for while in after life he retained not the faintest recollection of his illness, he remembered quite clearly his aunt entering the sickroom bearing in her hand a saucer with a baked apple.

The order of impressions retained by memory might naturally be that of color and taste, although one would rather suppose that the sense of pain would be first to educate. In fact, the third recollection of the child was that of discomfort. The moment he could be removed, he was bundled up in blankets and carried from the little house in Hancock Avenue to a larger one which his parents were to occupy for the rest of their lives in the neighboring Mount Vernon Street. The season was midwinter, January 10, 1842, and he never forgot his acute distress for want of air under his blankets, or the noises of moving furniture.

As a means of variation from a normal type, sickness in childhood ought to have a certain value not to be classed under any fitness or unfitness of natural selection; and especially scarlet fever affected boys seriously, both physically and in character, though they might through life puzzle themselves to decide whether it had fitted or unfitted them for success; but this fever of Henry Adams took greater and greater importance in his eyes, from the point of view of education, the longer he lived. At first, the effect was physical. He fell behind his brothers[4] two or three inches in height, and proportionally in bone and weight. His character and processes of mind seemed to share in this fining-down process of scale. He was not good in a fight, and his nerves were more delicate than boys' nerves ought to be. He exaggerated these weaknesses as he grew older. The habit of doubt; of distrusting his own judgment and of totally rejecting the judgment of the world; the tendency to regard every question as open; the hesitation to act except as a choice of evils; the shirking of responsibility; the love of line, form, quality; the horror of ennui; the passion for companionship and the antipathy to society—all these are well-known qualities of New England character in no way peculiar to individuals but in this instance they seemed to be stimulated by the fever, and Henry Adams could never make up his mind whether, on the whole, the change of character was morbid or healthy, good or bad for his purpose. His brothers were the type; he was the variation.

As far as the boy knew, the sickness did not affect him at all, and he grew up in excellent health, bodily and mental, taking life as it was given; accepting its local standards without a difficulty, and enjoying much of it as keenly as any other boy of his age. He

4. Charles Francis (1835–1915) and Brooks (1848–1927).

seemed to himself quite normal, and his companions seemed always
to think him so. Whatever was peculiar about him was education,
not character, and came to him, directly and indirectly, as the result
of that eighteenth-century inheritance which he took with his
name.

The atmosphere of education in which he lived was colonial, revolutionary, almost Cromwellian,[5] as though he were steeped, from
his greatest grandmother's birth, in the odor of political crime.
Resistance to something was the law of New England nature; the
boy looked out on the world with the instinct of resistance; for
numberless generations his predecessors had viewed the world
chiefly as a thing to be reformed, filled with evil forces to be abolished, and they saw no reason to suppose that they had wholly succeeded in the abolition; the duty was unchanged. That duty implied
not only resistance to evil, but hatred of it. Boys naturally look on
all force as an enemy, and generally find it so, but the New Englander, whether boy or man, in his long struggle with a stingy or
hostile universe, had learned also to love the pleasure of hating; his
joys were few.

Politics, as a practice, whatever its professions, had always been
the systematic organization of hatreds, and Massachusetts politics
had been as harsh as the climate. The chief charm of New England
was harshness of contrasts and extremes of sensibility—a cold that
froze the blood, and a heat that boiled it—so that the pleasure of
hating—oneself if no better victim offered—was not its rarest
amusement; but the charm was a true and natural child of the soil,
not a cultivated weed of the ancients. The violence of the contrast
was real and made the strongest motive of education. The double
exterior nature gave life its relative values. Winter and summer,
cold and heat, town and country, force and freedom, marked two
modes of life and thought, balanced like lobes of the brain. Town
was winter confinement, school, rule, discipline; straight, gloomy
streets, piled with six feet of snow in the middle; frosts that made
the snow sing under wheels or runners; thaws when the streets
became dangerous to cross; society of uncles, aunts, and cousins
who expected children to behave themselves, and who were not
always gratified; above all else, winter represented the desire to
escape and go free. Town was restraint, law, unity. Country, only
seven miles away, was liberty, diversity, outlawry, the endless delight
of mere sense impressions given by nature for nothing, and breathed
by boys without knowing it.

Boys are wild animals, rich in the treasures of sense, but the New
England boy had a wider range of emotions than boys of more eq-

---

5. Oliver Cromwell (1599–1658), dicta-
torial Lord Protector of England, deposed King Charles I in 1647, dispossessed the Irish, and provoked angry
struggles by the American colonists
against his rule.

uable climates. He felt his nature crudely, as it was meant. To the boy Henry Adams, summer was drunken. Among senses, smell was the strongest—smell of hot pine-woods and sweet-fern in the scorching summer noon; of new-mown hay; of ploughed earth; of box hedges; of peaches, lilacs, syringas; of stables, barns, cow-yards; of salt water and low tide on the marshes; nothing came amiss. Next to smell came taste, and the children knew the taste of everything they saw or touched, from pennyroyal and flagroot to the shell of a pignut and the letters of a spelling-book—the taste of A-B, AB, suddenly revived on the boy's tongue sixty years afterwards. Light, line, and color as sensual pleasures, came later and were as crude as the rest. The New England light is glare, and the atmosphere harshens color. The boy was a full man before he ever knew what was meant by atmosphere; his idea of pleasure in light was the blaze of a New England sun. His idea of color was a peony, with the dew of early morning on its petals. The intense blue of the sea, as he saw it a mile or two away, from the Quincy hills; the cumuli in a June afternoon sky; the strong reds and greens and purples of colored prints and children's picture-books, as the American colors then ran; these were ideals. The opposites or antipathies, were the cold grays of November evenings, and the thick, muddy thaws of Boston winter. With such standards, the Bostonian could not but develop a double nature. Life was a double thing. After a January blizzard, the boy who could look with pleasure into the violent snow-glare of the cold white sunshine, with its intense light and shade, scarcely knew what was meant by tone. He could reach it only by education.

Winter and summer, then, were two hostile lives, and bred two separate natures. Winter was always the effort to live; summer was tropical license. Whether the children rolled in the grass, or waded in the brook, or swam in the salt ocean, or sailed in the bay, or fished for smelts in the creeks, or netted minnows in the salt-marshes, or took to the pine-woods and the granite quarries, or chased muskrats and hunted snapping-turtles in the swamps, or mushrooms or nuts on the autumn hills, summer and country were always sensual living, while winter was always compulsory learning. Summer was the multiplicity of nature; winter was school.

The bearing of the two seasons on the education of Henry Adams was no fancy; it was the most decisive force he ever knew; it ran through life, and made the division between its perplexing, warring, irreconcilable problems, irreducible opposites, with growing emphasis to the last year of study. From earliest childhood the boy was accustomed to feel that, for him, life was double. Winter and summer, town and country, law and liberty, were hostile, and the man who pretended they were not, was in his eyes a schoolmaster —that is, a man employed to tell lies to little boys. Though Quincy was but two hours' walk from Beacon Hill,[6] it belonged in a different world. For two hundred years, every Adams, from father to son, had lived within sight of State Street,[7] and sometimes had lived in it, yet none had ever taken kindly to the town, or been taken kindly by it. The boy inherited his double nature. He knew as yet nothing about his great-grandfather, who had died a dozen years before his own birth: he took for granted that any great-grandfather of his must have always been good, and his enemies wicked; but he divined his great-grandfather's character from his own. Never for a moment did he connect the two ideas of Boston and John Adams; they were separate and antagonistic; the idea of John Adams went with Quincy. He knew his grandfather John Quincy Adams[8] only as an old man of seventy-five or eighty who was friendly and gentle with him, but except that he heard his grandfather always called "the President," and his grandmother "the Madam," he had no reason to suppose that his Adams grandfather differed in character from his Brooks grandfather who was equally kind and benevolent. He liked the Adams side best, but for no other reason than that it reminded him of the country, the summer, and the absence of restraint. Yet he felt also that Quincy was in a way inferior to Boston, and that socially Boston looked down on Quincy. The reason was clear enough even to a five-year-old child. Quincy had no Boston style. Little enough style had either; a simpler manner of life and thought could hardly exist, short of cave-dwelling. The flint-and-steel with which his grandfather Adams used to light his own fires in the early morning was still on the mantelpiece of his study. The idea of a livery or even a dress for servants, or of an evening toilette, was next to blasphemy. Bathrooms, water-supplies, lighting, heating, and the whole array of domestic comforts, were unknown at Quincy. Boston had already a bathroom, a water supply, a furnace, and gas. The superiority of Boston was evident, but a child liked it no better for that.

The magnificence of his grandfather Brooks's house in Pearl Street or South Street has long ago disappeared, but perhaps his country house at Medford may still remain to show what impressed the mind of a boy in 1845 with the idea of city splendor. The President's place at Quincy was the larger and older and far the more interesting of the two; but a boy felt at once its inferiority in fashion. It showed plainly enough its want of wealth. It smacked of colonial age, but not of Boston style or plush curtains. To the end of his life he never quite overcame the prejudice thus drawn in with his childish breath. He never could compel himself to care for nineteenth-century style. He was never able to adopt it, any more than his father or grandfather or great-grandfather had done. Not that he

---

6. Location of the State Capitol building; the political center of Boston and residential area of the oldest families.

7. The financial center of Boston.
8. John Quincy Adams (1767–1848), sixth President of the United States.

felt it as particularly hostile, for he reconciled himself to much that
was worse; but because, for some remote reason, he was born an
eighteenth-century child. The old house at Quincy was eighteenth
century. What style it had was in its Queen Anne mahogany panels
and its Louis Seize chairs and sofas. The panels belonged to an old
colonial Vassall[9] who built the house; the furniture had been
brought back from Paris in 1789 or 1801 or 1817, along with porcelain and books and much else of old diplomatic remnants; and neither of the two eighteenth-century styles—neither English Queen
Anne nor French Louis Seize—was comfortable for a boy, or for
anyone else. The dark mahogany had been painted white to suit
daily life in winter gloom. Nothing seemed to favor, for a child's
objects, the older forms. On the contrary, most boys, as well as
grown-up people, preferred the new, with good reason, and the
child felt himself distinctly at a disadvantage for the taste.

Nor had personal preference any share in his bias. The Brooks
grandfather was as amiable and as sympathetic as the Adams grandfather. Both were born in 1767, and both died in 1848. Both were
kind to children, and both belonged rather to the eighteenth than
to the nineteenth centuries. The child knew no difference between
them except that one was associated with winter and the other with
summer; one with Boston, the other with Quincy. Even with Medford, the association was hardly easier. Once as a very young boy he
was taken to pass a few days with his grandfather Brooks under
charge of his aunt, but became so violently homesick that within
twenty-four hours he was brought back in disgrace. Yet he could
not remember ever being seriously homesick again.

The attachment to Quincy was not altogether sentimental or
wholly sympathetic. Quincy was not a bed of thornless roses. Even
there the curse of Cain set its mark.[1] There as elsewhere a cruel
universe combined to crush a child. As though three or four vigorous brothers and sisters, with the best will, were not enough to
crush any child, everyone else conspired towards an education which
he hated. From cradle to grave this problem of running order
through chaos, direction through space, discipline through freedom,
unity through multiplicity, has always been, and must always be,
the task of education, as it is the moral of religion, philosophy, science, art, politics, and economy; but a boy's will is his life, and he
dies when it is broken, as the colt dies in harness, taking a new
nature in becoming tame. Rarely has the boy felt kindly towards his
tamers. Between him and his master has always been war. Henry
Adams never knew a boy of his generation to like a master, and the

9. "Queen Anne": an English architectural style of the early 18th century with
modified classical ornament. "Louis
Seize": intricate architecture and design
prevalent during the reign of Louis XVI,
King of France. Leonard Vassall sold
the house to John Adams, second President of the United States, in 1787.
1. According to Genesis 4.16, the Lord
condemned Cain to be a wanderer for
having killed his brother Abel. Adams
projects himself as both the "crushed"
Abel and the punished Cain.

task of remaining on friendly terms with one's own family, in such a relation, was never easy.

All the more singular it seemed afterwards to him that his first serious contact with the President should have been a struggle of will, in which the old man almost necessarily defeated the boy, but instead of leaving, as usual in such defeats, a lifelong sting, left rather an impression of as fair treatment as could be expected from a natural enemy. The boy met seldom with such restraint. He could not have been much more than six years old at the time—seven at the utmost—and his mother had taken him to Quincy for a long stay with the President during the summer. What became of the rest of the family he quite forgot; but he distinctly remembered standing at the house door one summer morning in a passionate outburst of rebellion against going to school. Naturally his mother was the immediate victim of his rage; that is what mothers are for, and boys also; but in this case the boy had his mother at unfair disadvantage, for she was a guest, and had no means of enforcing obedience. Henry showed a certain tactical ability by refusing to start, and he met all efforts at compulsion by successful, though too vehement protest. He was in fair way to win, and was holding his own, with sufficient energy, at the bottom of the long staircase which led up to the door of the President's library, when the door opened, and the old man slowly came down. Putting on his hat, he took the boy's hand without a word, and walked with him, paralyzed by awe, up the road to the town. After the first moments of consternation at this interference in a domestic dispute, the boy reflected that an old gentleman close on eighty would never trouble himself to walk near a mile on a hot summer morning over a shadeless road to take a boy to school, and that it would be strange if a lad imbued with the passion of freedom could not find a corner to dodge around, somewhere before reaching the school door. Then and always, the boy insisted that this reasoning justified his apparent submission; but the old man did not stop, and the boy saw all his strategical points turned, one after another, until he found himself seated inside the school, and obviously the centre of curious if not malevolent criticism. Not till then did the President release his hand and depart.

The point was that this act, contrary to the inalienable rights of boys, and nullifying the social compact, ought to have made him dislike his grandfather for life. He could not recall that it had this effect even for a moment. With a certain maturity of mind, the child must have recognized that the President, though a tool of tyranny, had done his disreputable work with a certain intelligence. He had shown no temper, no irritation, no personal feeling, and had made no display of force. Above all, he had held his tongue. During their long walk he had said nothing; he had uttered no syllable of revolting cant about the duty of obedience and the wickedness of resistance to law; he had shown no concern in the matter; hardly even a consciousness of the boy's existence. Probably his mind at that moment was actually troubling itself little about his grandson's iniquities, and much about the iniquities of President Polk,[2] but the boy could scarcely at that age feel the whole satisfaction of thinking that President Polk was to be the vicarious victim of his own sins, and he gave his grandfather credit for intelligent silence. For this forbearance he felt instinctive respect. He admitted force as a form of right; he admitted even temper, under protest; but the seeds of a moral education would at that moment have fallen on the stoniest soil in Quincy, which is, as everyone knows, the stoniest glacial and tidal drift known in any Puritan land.

Neither party to this momentary disagreement can have felt rancor, for during these three or four summers the old President's relations with the boy were friendly and almost intimate. Whether his older brothers and sisters were still more favored he failed to remember, but he was himself admitted to a sort of familiarity which, when in his turn he had reached old age, rather shocked him, for it must have sometimes tried the President's patience. He hung about the library; handled the books; deranged the papers; ransacked the drawers; searched the old purses and pocket-books for foreign coins; drew the sword-cane; snapped the travelling-pistols; upset everything in the corners, and penetrated the President's dressing-closet where a row of tumblers, inverted on the shelf, covered caterpillars which were supposed to become moths or butterflies, but never did. The Madam bore with fortitude the loss of the tumblers which her husband purloined for these hatcheries; but she made protest when he carried off her best cut-glass bowls to plant with acorns or peachstones that he might see the roots grow, but which, she said, he commonly forgot like the caterpillars.

At that time the President rode the hobby of tree-culture, and some fine old trees should still remain to witness it, unless they have been improved off the ground; but his was a restless mind, and although he took his hobbies seriously and would have been annoyed had his grandchild asked whether he was bored like an English duke, he probably cared more for the processes than for the results, so that his grandson was saddened by the sight and smell of peaches and pears, the best of their kind, which he brought up from the garden to rot on his shelves for seed. With the inherited virtues of his Puritan ancestors, the little boy Henry conscientiously brought up to him in his study the finest peaches he found in the garden, and ate only the less perfect. Naturally he ate more by way of compensation, but the act showed that he bore no grudge. As for his grandfather, it is even possible that he may have felt a certain self-reproach for his temporary rôle of schoolmaster—seeing that his

2. James K. Polk (1795–1849), 11th President, was detested for his proslavery sentiments and actions.

own career did not offer proof of the worldly advantages of docile obedience—for there still exists somewhere a little volume of critically edited Nursery Rhymes with the boy's name in full written in the President's trembling hand on the fly-leaf. Of course there was also the Bible, given to each child at birth, with the proper inscription in the President's hand on the fly-leaf; while their grandfather Brooks supplied the silver mugs.

So many Bibles and silver mugs had to be supplied, that a new house, or cottage, was built to hold them. It was "on the hill," five minutes' walk above "the old house," with a far view eastward over Quincy Bay, and northward over Boston. Till his twelfth year, the child passed his summers there, and his pleasures of childhood mostly centred in it. Of education he had as yet little to complain. Country schools were not very serious. Nothing stuck to the mind except home impressions, and the sharpest were those of kindred children; but as influences that warped a mind, none compared with the mere effect of the back of the President's bald head, as he sat in his pew on Sundays, in line with that of President Quincy,[3] who, though some ten years younger, seemed to children about the same age. Before railways entered the New England town, every parish church showed half-a-dozen of these leading citizens, with gray hair, who sat on the main aisle in the best pews, and had sat there, or in some equivalent dignity, since the time of St. Augustine, if not since the glacial epoch. It was unusual for boys to sit behind a President grandfather, and to read over his head the tablet in memory of a President great-grandfather, who had "pledged his life, his fortune, and his sacred honor" to secure the independence of his country and so forth; but boys naturally supposed, without much reasoning, that other boys had the equivalent of President grandfathers, and that churches would always go on, with the bald-headed leading citizens on the main aisle, and Presidents or their equivalents on the walls. The Irish gardener once said to the child: "You'll be thinkin' you'll be President too!" The casuality of the remark made so strong an impression on his mind that he never forgot it. He could not remember ever to have thought on the subject; to him, that there should be a doubt of his being President was a new idea. What had been would continue to be. He doubted neither about Presidents nor about Churches, and no one suggested at that time a doubt whether a system of society which had lasted since Adam would outlast one Adams more.

The Madam was a little more remote than the President, but more decorative. She stayed much in her own room with the Dutch tiles, looking out on her garden with the box walks, and seemed a fragile creature to a boy who sometimes brought her a note or a message, and took distinct pleasure in looking at her delicate face

---

3. Josiah Quincy (1772–1864), president of Harvard College 1829–45, was actually five years younger than John Quincy Adams.

under what seemed to him very becoming caps. He liked her refined figure; her gentle voice and manner; her vague effect of not belonging there, but to Washington or to Europe, like her furniture, and writing-desk with little glass doors above and little eighteenth-century volumes in old binding, labelled "Peregrine Pickle" or "Tom Jones" or "Hannah More."[4] Try as she might, the Madam could never be Bostonian, and it was her cross in life, but to the boy it was her charm. Even at that age, he felt drawn to it. The Madam's life had been in truth far from Boston. She was born in London in 1775, daughter of Joshua Johnson, an American merchant, brother of Governor Thomas Johnson of Maryland; and Catherine Nuth, of an English family in London. Driven from England by the Revolutionary War, Joshua Johnson took his family to Nantes,[5] where they remained till the peace. The girl Louisa Catherine was nearly ten years old when brought back to London, and her sense of nationality must have been confused; but the influence of the Johnsons and the services of Joshua obtained for him from President Washington the appointment of Consul in London on the organization of the Government in 1790. In 1794 President Washington appointed John Quincy Adams Minister to The Hague.[6] He was twenty-seven years old when he returned to London, and found the Consul's house a very agreeable haunt. Louisa was then twenty.

At that time, and long afterwards, the Consul's house, far more than the Minister's, was the centre of contact for travelling Americans, either official or other. The Legation was a shifting point, between 1785 and 1815; but the Consulate, far down in the City, near the Tower[7], was convenient and inviting; so inviting that it proved fatal to young Adams. Louisa was charming, like a Romney portrait,[8] but among her many charms that of being a New England woman was not one. The defect was serious. Her future mother-in-law, Abigail,[9] a famous New England woman whose authority over her turbulent husband, the second President, was hardly so great as that which she exercised over her son, the sixth to be, was troubled by the fear that Louisa might not be made of stuff stern enough, or brought up in conditions severe enough, to suit a New England climate, or to make an efficient wife for her paragon son, and Abigail was right on that point, as on most others where sound judgment was involved; but sound judgment is sometimes a source of weakness rather than of force, and John Quincy already had reason to think that his mother held sound judgments on the subject of daughters-in-law which human nature, since the fall of Eve,

---

4. Tobias Smollett's novel *Adventures of Peregrine Pickle* was published in 1751; Henry Fielding's novel *The History of Tom Jones* in 1749; Hannah More (1745–1833) was a popular English religious writer.
5. A city in France.
6. The Netherlands.

7. The Tower of London, on the east side of the city.
8. George Romney (1734–1802), English painter renowned for his portraits of aristocratic women.
9. Abigail Smith Adams (1744–1818) was famous as an advocate for women's rights and as a brilliant letter writer.

made Adams helpless to realize. Being three thousand miles away from his mother, and equally far in love, he married Louisa in London, July 26, 1797, and took her to Berlin to be the head of the United States Legation. During three or four exciting years, the young bride lived in Berlin; whether she was happy or not, whether she was content or not, whether she was socially successful or not, her descendants did not surely know; but in any case she could by no chance have become educated there for a life in Quincy or Boston. In 1801 the overthrow of the Federalist Party[1] drove her and her husband to America, and she became at last a member of the Quincy household, but by that time her children needed all her attention, and she remained there with occasional winters in Boston and Washington, till 1809. Her husband was made Senator in 1803, and in 1809 was appointed Minister to Russia. She went with him to St. Petersburg, taking her baby, Charles Francis, born in 1807; but broken-hearted at having to leave her two older boys behind. The life at St. Petersburg was hardly gay for her; they were far too poor to shine in that extravagant society; but she survived it, though her little girl baby did not, and in the winter of 1814-15, alone with the boy of seven years old, crossed Europe from St. Petersburg to Paris, in her travelling-carriage, passing through the armies, and reaching Paris in the *Cent Jours*[2] after Napoleon's return from Elba. Her husband next went to England as Minister, and she was for two years at the Court of the Regent.[3] In 1817 her husband came home to be Secretary of State, and she lived for eight years in F Street, doing her work of entertainer for President Monroe's administration. Next she lived four miserable years in the White House. When that chapter was closed in 1829, she had earned the right to be tired and delicate, but she still had fifteen years to serve as wife of a Member of the House, after her husband went back to Congress in 1833. Then it was that the little Henry, her grandson, first remembered her, from 1843 to 1848, sitting in her panelled room, at breakfast, with her heavy silver teapot and sugar-bowl and cream-jug, which still exist somewhere as an heirloom of the modern safety-vault. By that time she was seventy years old or more, and thoroughly weary of being beaten about a stormy world. To the boy she seemed singularly peaceful, a vision of silver gray, presiding over her old President and her Queen Anne mahogany; an exotic, like her Sèvres china; an object of deference to everyone, and of great affection to her son Charles; but hardly more Bostonian than she had been fifty years before, on her wedding-day, in the shadow of the Tower of London.

1. Republican Thomas Jefferson defeated President John Adams, a conservative Federalist, in a hard-fought election.
2. "One Hundred Days" of Napoleon's return to power, which ended with his defeat at Waterloo on June 18, 1815.
3. The Prince of Wales (1762–1830), later King George IV, ruled as Regent for nine years after his father became permanently insane in 1811.

Such a figure was even less fitted than that of her old husband, the President, to impress on a boy's mind the standards of the coming century. She was Louis Seize, like the furniture. The boy knew nothing of her interior life, which had been, as the venerable Abigail, long since at peace, foresaw, one of severe stress and little pure satisfaction. He never dreamed that from her might come some of those doubts and self-questionings, those hesitations, those rebellions against law and discipline, which marked more than one of her descendants; but he might even then have felt some vague instinctive suspicion that he was to inherit from her the seeds of the primal sin, the fall from grace, the curse of Abel, that he was not of pure New England stock, but half exotic. As a child of Quincy he was not a true Bostonian, but even as a child of Quincy he inherited a quarter taint of Maryland blood. Charles Francis, half Marylander by birth, had hardly seen Boston till he was ten years old, when his parents left him there at school in 1817, and he never forgot the experience. He was to be nearly as old as his mother had been in 1845, before he quite accepted Boston, or Boston quite accepted him.

A boy who began his education in these surroundings, with physical strength inferior to that of his brothers, and with a certain delicacy of mind and bone, ought rightly to have felt at home in the eighteenth century and should, in proper self-respect, have rebelled against the standards of the nineteenth. The atmosphere of his first ten years must have been very like that of his grandfather at the same age, from 1767 till 1776, barring the battle of Bunker Hill, and even as late as 1846, the battle of Bunker Hill remained actual. The tone of Boston society was colonial. The true Bostonian always knelt in self-abasement before the majesty of English standards; far from concealing it as a weakness, he was proud of it as his strength. The eighteenth century ruled society long after 1850. Perhaps the boy began to shake it off rather earlier than most of his mates.

Indeed this prehistoric stage of education ended rather abruptly with his tenth year. One winter morning he was conscious of a certain confusion in the house in Mount Vernon Street, and gathered, from such words as he could catch, that the President, who happened to be then staying there, on his way to Washington, had fallen and hurt himself. Then he heard the word paralysis. After that day he came to associate the word with the figure of his grandfather, in a tall-backed, invalid armchair, on one side of the spare bedroom fireplace, and one of his old friends, Dr. Parkman[4] or P. P. F. Degrand, on the other side, both dozing.

The end of this first, or ancestral and Revolutionary, chapter came on February 21, 1848—and the month of February brought

---

4. Dr. George Parkman (1790–1849); Peter P. F. Degrand (d. 1855), at one time a Philadelphia banker.

life and death as a family habit—when the eighteenth century, as an actual and living companion, vanished. If the scene on the floor of the House, when the old President fell, struck the still simple-minded American public with a sensation unusually dramatic, its effect on a ten-year-old boy, whose boy-life was fading away with the life of his grandfather, could not be slight. One had to pay for Revolutionary patriots; grandfathers and grandmothers; Presidents; diplomats; Queen Anne mahogany and Louis Seize chairs, as well as for Stuart[5] portraits. Such things warp young life. Americans commonly believed that they ruined it, and perhaps the practical common-sense of the American mind judged right. Many a boy might be ruined by much less than the emotions of the funeral service in the Quincy church, with its surroundings of national respect and family pride. By another dramatic chance it happened that the clergyman of the parish, Dr. Lunt,[6] was an unusual pulpit orator, the ideal of a somewhat austere intellectual type, such as the school of Buckminster and Channing[7] inherited from the old Congregational clergy. His extraordinarily refined appearance, his dignity of manner, his deeply cadenced voice, his remarkable English and his fine appreciation, gave to the funeral service a character that left an overwhelming impression on the boy's mind. He was to see many great functions—funerals and festivals—in after-life, till his only thought was to see no more, but he never again witnessed anything nearly so impressive to him as the last services at Quincy over the body of one President and the ashes of another.

The effect of the Quincy service was deepened by the official ceremony which afterwards took place in Faneuil Hall, when the boy was taken to hear his uncle, Edward Everett,[8] deliver a Eulogy. Like all Mr. Everett's orations, it was an admirable piece of oratory, such as only an admirable orator and scholar could create; too good for a ten-year-old boy to appreciate at its value; but already the boy knew that the dead President could not be in it, and had even learned why he would have been out of place there; for knowledge was beginning to come fast. The shadow of the War of 1812 still hung over State Street; the shadow of the Civil War to come had already begun to darken Faneuil Hall. No rhetoric could have reconciled Mr. Everett's audience to his subject. How could he say there, to an assemblage of Bostonians in the heart of mercantile Boston, that the only distinctive mark of all the Adamses, since old Sam Adams's father a hundred and fifty years before, had been their inherited quarrel with State Street, which had again and again

5. Gilbert Charles Stuart (1755–1828), American painter best known for his portraits of George Washington.
6. The Reverend William Parsons Lunt (1805–57).
7. Joseph Stevens Buckminster (1784–1812), Unitarian minister and distinguished founder of American Biblical scholarship; William Ellery Channing (1780–1842), leading Unitarian minister.
8. Edward Everett (1794–1865), Unitarian minister, congressman, diplomat, and president of Harvard College.

broken out into riot, bloodshed, personal feuds, foreign and civil war, wholesale banishments and confiscations, until the history of Florence was hardly more turbulent than that of Boston?[9] How could he whisper the word Hartford Convention[1] before the men who had made it? What would have been said had he suggested the chance of Secession and Civil War?

Thus already, at ten years old, the boy found himself standing face to face with a dilemma that might have puzzled an early Christian. What was he?—where was he going? Even then he felt that something was wrong, but he concluded that it must be Boston. Quincy had always been right, for Quincy represented a moral principle—the principle of resistance to Boston. His Adams ancestors must have been right, since they were always hostile to State Street. If State Street was wrong, Quincy must be right! Turn the dilemma as he pleased, he still came back on the eighteenth century and the law of Resistance; of Truth; of Duty, and of Freedom. He was a ten-year-old priest and politician. He could under no circumstances have guessed what the next fifty years had in store, and no one could teach him; but sometimes, in his old age, he wondered—and could never decide—whether the most clear and certain knowledge would have helped him. Supposing he had seen a New York stock-list of 1900, and had studied the statistics of railways, telegraphs, coal, and steel—would he have quitted his eighteenth-century, his ancestral prejudices, his abstract ideals, his semi-clerical training, and the rest, in order to perform an expiatory pilgrimage to State Street, and ask for the fatted calf of his grandfather Brooks and a clerkship in the Suffolk Bank?[2]

Sixty years afterwards he was still unable to make up his mind. Each course had its advantages, but the material advantages, looking back, seemed to lie wholly in State Street.

Chapter XIX. Chaos (1870)

One fine May afternoon in 1870 Adams drove again up St. James's Street wondering more than ever at the marvels of life. Nine years had passed since the historic entrance of May, 1861.[1] Outwardly London was the same. Outwardly Europe showed no great change. Palmerston and Russell were forgotten; but Disraeli

9. I.e., the Adamses of Quincy were idealists who stood for the unity of the United States in contrast to the materialists of mercantile Boston who were sectionalist in outlook; Quincy was antislavery, State Street proslavery. Throughout the Renaissance, Florence was plagued by conspiracies, political coups, and family feuds.
1. The Hartford Convention was the pro-English meeting called to oppose continuation of the War of 1812 and in support of the establishment of a New England federation outside the Union.
2. Luke 15.11–32 tells of the Prodigal Son, who was forgiven for wasting his inheritance and was welcomed home with a feast. Adams's grandfather Brooks was reportedly the wealthiest man in New England; the Suffolk Bank was the symbol of financial power in Boston.
1. Adams's father, Charles Francis Adams, was designated by President Lincoln as Minister to England in March, 1861, and arrived in London in May.

and Gladstone were still much alive.[2] One's friends were more than ever prominent. John Bright was in the Cabinet; W. E. Forster was about to enter it;[3] reform ran riot. Never had the sun of progress shone so fair. Evolution from lower to higher raged like an epidemic. Darwin[4] was the greatest of prophets in the most evolutionary of worlds. Gladstone had overthrown the Irish Church; was overthrowing the Irish landlords; was trying to pass an Education Act. Improvement, prosperity, power, were leaping and bounding over every country road. Even America, with her Erie scandals and Alabama Claims,[5] hardly made a discordant note.

At the Legation, Motley[6] ruled; the long Adams reign was forgotten; the rebellion had passed into history. In society no one cared to recall the years before the Prince of Wales.[7] The smart set had come to their own. Half the houses that Adams had frequented, from 1861 to 1865, were closed or closing in 1870. Death had ravaged one's circle of friends. Mrs. Milnes Gaskell and her sister Miss Charlotte Wynn were both dead, and Mr. James Milnes Gaskell was no longer in Parliament. That field of education seemed closed too.

One found oneself in a singular frame of mind—more eighteenth-century than ever—almost rococo—and unable to catch anywhere the cog-wheels of evolution. Experience ceased to educate. London taught less freely than of old. That one bad style was leading to another—that the older men were more amusing than the younger—that Lord Houghton's breakfast-table showed gaps hard to fill—that there were fewer men one wanted to meet—these, and a hundred more such remarks, helped little towards a quicker and more intelligent activity. For English reforms, Adams cared nothing. The reforms were themselves mediæval. The Education Bill of his friend W. E. Forster seemed to him a guaranty against all education he had use for.[8] He resented change. He would have kept the Pope in the Vatican and the Queen at Windsor Castle as historical monuments. He did not care to Americanize Europe. The

2. Henry John Temple Palmerston (1784–1865), English Prime Minister 1855–58, 1859–65; Lord John Russell (1792–1878), English statesman; Benjamin Disraeli (1804–81), English Prime Minister 1868, 1874–80; William Gladstone (1809–98), English Prime Minister 1868–74, 1880–1885, 1886, 1892–94.
3. John Bright (1811–89) British statesman and orator; W. E. Forster (1818–86), reformist English statesman.
4. Charles Robert Darwin (1809–82), English naturalist, formulated the theory of evolution by natural selection.
5. The Erie scandals involved the use of the Erie Railroad by the ruthless entrepreneurs Jay Gould and Jim Fisk as a pawn in the attempt to corner the gold market. They were prevented from accomplishing their aims only by the direct intervention of President Grant, who ordered the sale of government-owned gold. The Alabama Claims were successfully made by the United States against England because of her part in outfitting the Confederate ship *Alabama* during the Civil War. The point of this first paragraph is to suggest, ironically, that in spite of 10 years of suffering and destruction, the world behaved as if everything were improving steadily and surely.
6. John Lothrop Motley (1814–77), American historian, succeeded Adams's father as Minister to England in 1869; "rebellion": the Civil War.
7. The Prince of Wales, later Edward VII, was married in 1863.
8. Adams favored compulsory, secular, nondenominational, private education, as against the Education Act of 1870, which left standing the system of state-aided parochial elementary schools.

Bastille or the Ghetto[9] was a curiosity worth a great deal of money, if preserved; and so was a Bishop; so was Napoleon III.[1] The tourist was the great conservative who hated novelty and adored dirt. Adams came back to London without a thought of revolution or restlessness or reform. He wanted amusement, quiet, and gaiety.

Had he not been born in 1838 under the shadow of Boston State House, and been brought up in the Early Victorian epoch, he would have cast off his old skin, and made his court to Marlborough House,[2] in partnership with the American woman and the Jew banker. Common-sense dictated it; but Adams and his friends were unfashionable by some law of Anglo-Saxon custom—some innate atrophy of mind. Figuring himself as already a man of action, and rather far up towards the front, he had no idea of making a new effort or catching up with a new world. He saw nothing ahead of him. The world was never more calm. He wanted to talk with Ministers about the Alabama Claims, because he looked on the Claims as his own special creation, discussed between him and his father long before they had been discussed by Government; he wanted to make notes for his next year's articles; but he had not a thought that, within three months, his world was to be upset, and he under it. Frank Palgrave[3] came one day, more contentious, contemptuous, and paradoxical than ever, because Napoleon III seemed to be threatening war with Germany. Palgrave said that "Germany would beat France into scraps" if there was war. Adams thought not. The chances were always against catastrophes. No one else expected great changes in Europe. Palgrave was always extreme; his language was incautious—violent!

In this year of all years, Adams lost sight of education. Things began smoothly, and London glowed with the pleasant sense of familiarity and dinners. He sniffed with voluptuous delight the coal-smoke of Cheapside[4] and revelled in the architecture of Oxford Street. May Fair never shone so fair to Arthur Pendennis[5] as it did to the returned American. The country never smiled its velvet smile of trained and easy hostess as it did when he was so lucky as to be asked on a country visit. He loved it all—everything—had always loved it! He felt almost attached to the Royal Exchange.[6] He thought he owned the St. James's Club. He patronized the Legation.

The first shock came lightly, as though Nature were playing tricks

9. The Bastille was the infamous prison destroyed during the French Revolution in 1789; the Ghetto was the small, crowded section of major European cities where Jews had been required to live since the Middle Ages.
1. Louis Napoleon Bonaparte (1808–73), Emperor of France, nephew of Napoleon I.
2. The London residence of the Prince of Wales, where he lived a rather idle and profligate life attended by rich American women and supported by loans from Jewish bankers.
3. Francis Palgrave (1824–97), English poet and anthologist.
4. Cheapside and Oxford Street are important business streets in London.
5. The poet-dandy hero of William Makepeace Thackeray's novel of that name published in 1850.
6. The London Stock Exchange.

on her spoiled child, though she had thus far not exerted herself to spoil him. Reeve refused the Gold Conspiracy.[7] Adams had become used to the idea that he was free of the Quarterlies, and that his writing would be printed of course; but he was stunned by the reason of refusal. Reeve said it would bring half-a-dozen libel suits on him. One knew that the power of Erie[8] was almost as great in England as in America, but one was hardly prepared to find it controlling the Quarterlies. The English press professed to be shocked in 1870 by the Erie scandal, as it had professed in 1860 to be shocked by the scandal of slavery, but when invited to support those who were trying to abate these scandals, the English press said it was afraid. To Adams, Reeve's refusal seemed portentous. He and his brother and the *North American Review* were running greater risks every day, and no one thought of fear. That a notorious story, taken bodily from an official document, should scare the *Edinburgh Review* into silence for fear of Jay Gould and Jim Fisk, passed even Adams's experience of English eccentricity, though it was large.

He gladly set down Reeve's refusal of the Gold Conspiracy to respectability and editorial law, but when he sent the manuscript on to the *Quarterly*, the editor of the *Quarterly* also refused it. The literary standard of the two Quarterlies was not so high as to suggest that the article was illiterate beyond the power of an active and willing editor to redeem it. Adams had no choice but to realize that he had to deal in 1870 with the same old English character of 1860, and the same inability in himself to understand it. As usual, when an ally was needed, the American was driven into the arms of the radicals. Respectability, everywhere and always, turned its back the moment one asked to do it a favor. Called suddenly away from England, he despatched the article, at the last moment, to the *Westminster Review* and heard no more about it for nearly six months.

He had been some weeks in London when he received a telegram from his brother-in-law at the Bagni di Lucca[9] telling him that his sister[1] had been thrown from a cab and injured, and that he had better come on. He started that night, and reached the Bagni di Lucca on the second day. Tetanus had already set in.

The last lesson—the sum and term of education—began then. He had passed through thirty years of rather varied experience without having once felt the shell of custom broken. He had never seen Nature—only her surface—the sugar-coating that she shows to youth. Flung suddenly in his face, with the harsh brutality of

7. Henry Reeve (1813–95), editor of the *Edinburgh Review;* Adams's article on "The New York Gold Conspiracy" was published in the *Westminster Review* in October, 1870. The article tells of the attempt by Jay Gould and Jim Fisk to corner the gold market by using the Erie Railroad as a pawn.
8. I.e., the management of the Erie Railroad.
9. A famous mountain health resort in northwest Italy.
1. Louisa Catherine Kuhn (1831–70).

chance, the terror of the blow stayed by him thenceforth for life, until repetition made it more than the will could struggle with; more than he could call on himself to bear. He found his sister, a woman of forty, as gay and brilliant in the terrors of lockjaw as she had been in the careless fun of 1859, lying in bed in consequence of a miserable cab-accident that had bruised her foot. Hour by hour the muscles grew rigid, while the mind remained bright, until after ten days of fiendish torture she died in convulsions.

One had heard and read a great deal about death, and even seen a little of it, and knew by heart the thousand commonplaces of religion and poetry which seemed to deaden one's senses and veil the horror. Society being immortal, could put on immortality at will. Adams being mortal, felt only the mortality. Death took features altogether new to him, in these rich and sensuous surroundings. Nature enjoyed it, played with it, the horror added to her charm, she liked the torture, and smothered her victim with caresses. Never had one seen her so winning. The hot Italian summer brooded outside, over the market-place and the picturesque peasants, and, in the singular color of the Tuscan atmosphere, the hills and vineyards of the Apennines seemed bursting with midsummer blood. The sick-room itself glowed with the Italian joy of life; friends filled it; no harsh northern lights pierced the soft shadows; even the dying woman shared the sense of the Italian summer, the soft, velvet air, the humor, the courage, the sensual fulness of Nature and man. She faced death, as women mostly do, bravely and even gaily, racked slowly to unconsciousness, but yielding only to violence, as a soldier sabred in battle. For many thousands of years, on these hills and plains, Nature had gone on sabring men and women with the same air of sensual pleasure.

Impressions like these are not reasoned or catalogued in the mind; they are felt as part of violent emotion; and the mind that feels them is a different one from that which reasons; it is thought of a different power and a different person. The first serious consciousness of Nature's gesture—her attitude towards life—took form then as a phantasm, a nightmare, an insanity of force. For the first time, the stage-scenery of the senses collapsed; the human mind felt itself stripped naked, vibrating in a void of shapeless energies, with resistless mass, colliding, crushing, wasting, and destroying what these same energies had created and labored from eternity to perfect. Society became fantastic, a vision of pantomime with a mechanical motion; and its so-called thought merged in the mere sense of life, and pleasure in the sense. The usual anodynes of social medicine became evident artifice. Stoicism was perhaps the best; religion was the most human; but the idea that any personal deity could find pleasure or profit in torturing a poor woman, by accident, with a fiendish cruelty known to man only in perverted and insane temperaments, could not be held for a moment. For pure blasphemy, it made pure atheism a comfort. God might be, as the Church said, a Substance, but He could not be a Person.

With nerves strained for the first time beyond their power of tension, he slowly travelled northwards with his friends, and stopped for a few days at Ouchy[2] to recover his balance in a new world; for the fantastic mystery of coincidences had made the world, which he thought real, mimic and reproduce the distorted nightmare of his personal horror. He did not yet know it, and he was twenty years in finding it out; but he had need of all the beauty of the Lake below and of the Alps above, to restore the finite to its place. For the first time in his life, Mont Blanc for a moment looked to him what it was—a chaos of anarchic and purposeless forces—and he needed days of repose to see it clothe itself again with the illusions of his senses, the white purity of its snows, the splendor of its light, and the infinity of its heavenly peace. Nature was kind; Lake Geneva was beautiful beyond itself, and the Alps put on charms real as terrors; but man became chaotic, and before the illusions of Nature were wholly restored, the illusions of Europe suddenly vanished, leaving a new world to learn.

On July 4, all Europe had been in peace; on July 14, Europe was in full chaos of war.[3] One felt helpless and ignorant, but one might have been king or kaiser without feeling stronger to deal with the chaos. Mr. Gladstone was as much astounded as Adams; the Emperor Napoleon was nearly as stupefied as either, and Bismarck himself hardly knew how he did it. As education, the outbreak of the war was wholly lost on a man dealing with death hand-to-hand, who could not throw it aside to look at it across the Rhine. Only when he got up to Paris, he began to feel the approach of catastrophe. Providence set up no *affiches*[4] to announce the tragedy. Under one's eyes France cut herself adrift, and floated off, on an unknown stream, towards a less known ocean. Standing on the curb of the Boulevard, one could see as much as though one stood by the side of the Emperor or in command of an army corps. The effect was lurid. The public seemed to look on the war, as it had looked on the wars of Louis XIV and Francis I, as a branch of decorative art.[5] The French, like true artists, always regarded war as one of the fine arts. Louis XIV practised it; Napoleon I perfected it; and Napoleon III had till then pursued it in the same spirit with singular success. In Paris, in July, 1870, the war was brought out like an opera of Meyerbeer.[6] One felt oneself a supernumerary hired to fill the

2. The port of Lausanne on Lake Geneva in Switzerland.
3. In 1870 France declared war against Prussia; in January, 1871, France sued for peace.
4. Posters.
5. Louis XIV (1638–1715), King of France, fought the War of Revolution for Flanders and later became involved in the Third Dutch War over the same territory. Francis I (1494–1547), King of France, resumed the Italian Wars for possession of northern Italy and became involved in four wars to contest the supremacy of Spanish King Charles V, Holy Roman Emperor.
6. Giacomo Meyerbeer (1791–1864), German composer famed for elaborately staged operas.

scene. Every evening at the theatre the comedy was interrupted by order, and one stood up by order, to join in singing the *Marseillaise* to order. For nearly twenty years one had been forbidden to sing the *Marseillaise* under any circumstances, but at last regiment after regiment marched through the streets shouting "Marchons!" while the bystanders cared not enough to join. Patriotism seemed to have been brought out of the Government stores, and distributed by grammes *per capita*. One had seen one's own people dragged unwillingly into a war, and had watched one's own regiments march to the front without sign of enthusiasm; on the contrary, most serious, anxious, and conscious of the whole weight of the crisis; but in Paris everyone conspired to ignore the crisis, which everyone felt at hand. Here was education for the million, but the lesson was intricate. Superficially Napoleon and his Ministers and marshals were playing a game against Thiers and Gambetta.[7] A bystander knew almost as little as they did about the result. How could Adams prophesy that in another year or two, when he spoke of *his* Paris and its tastes, people would smile at his dotage?

As soon as he could, he fled to England and once more took refuge in the profound peace of Wenlock Abbey. Only the few remaining monks, undisturbed by the brutalities of Henry VIII— three or four young Englishmen—survived there, with Milnes Gaskell[8] acting as Prior. The August sun was warm; the calm of the Abbey was ten times secular; not a discordant sound—hardly a sound of any sort except the cawing of the ancient rookery at sunset —broke the stillness; and, after the excitement of the last month, one felt a palpable haze of peace brooding over the Edge and the Welsh Marches. Since the reign of *Pteraspis*,[9] nothing had greatly changed; nothing except the monks. Lying on the turf, the ground littered with newspapers, the monks studied the war correspondence. In one respect Adams had succeeded in educating himself; he had learned to follow a campaign.

While at Wenlock, he received a letter from President Eliot[1] inviting him to take an Assistant Professorship of History, to be created shortly at Harvard College. After waiting ten or a dozen years for some one to show consciousness of his existence, even a *Terebratula*[2] would be pleased and grateful for a compliment which implied that the new President of Harvard College wanted his help; but Adams knew nothing about history, and much less

7. Louis Adolphe Thiers (1797–1877) and Leon Gambetta (1838–82), French statesmen who led the Liberal opposition to Napoleon III's imperialistic policies.
8. Charles Milnes Gaskell (1842–1919), one of Adams's best English friends, represented Wenlock (Shropshire) in Parliament. The Abbey was not actually a religious institution at this time, and the terms "prior" and "monks" are merely literary.

9. A ganoid fish fossil characterizing the Silurian age of the Paleozoic era.
1. Charles William Eliot (1834–1926) became president of Harvard in 1869.
2. An ancient genus of brachiopods which Sir Charles Lyell had pointed out to Adams as an exception to Darwin's theory of evolution, because it had not changed since the beginning of geologic time.

about teaching, while he knew more than enough about Harvard College; and wrote at once to thank President Eliot, with much regret that the honor should be above his powers. His mind was full of other matters. The summer, from which he had expected only amusement and social relations with new people, had ended in the most intimate personal tragedy, and the most terrific political convulsion he had ever known or was likely to know. He had failed in every object of his trip. The Quarterlies had refused his best essay. He had made no acquaintances and hardly picked up the old ones. He sailed from Liverpool, on September 1, to begin again where he had started two years before, but with no longer a hope of attaching himself to a President or a party or a press. He was a free lance and no other career stood in sight or in mind. To that point education had brought him.

Yet he found, on reaching home, that he had not done quite so badly as he feared. His article on the Session[3] in the July *North American* had made a success. Though he could not quite see what partisan object it served, he heard with flattered astonishment that it had been reprinted by the Democratic National Committee and circulated as a campaign document by the hundred thousand copies. He was henceforth in opposition, do what he might; and a Massachusetts Democrat, say what he pleased; while his only reward or return for this partisan service consisted in being formally answered by Senator Timothy Howe, of Wisconsin, in a Republican campaign document, presumed to be also freely circulated, in which the Senator, besides refuting his opinions, did him the honor—most unusual and picturesque in a Senator's rhetoric—of likening him to a begonia.[4]

The begonia is, or then was, a plant of such senatorial qualities as to make the simile, in intention, most flattering. Far from charming in its refinement, the begonia was remarkable for curious and showy foliage; it was conspicuous; it seemed to have no useful purpose; and it insisted on standing always in the most prominent positions. Adams would have greatly liked to be a begonia in Washington, for this was rather his ideal of the successful statesman, and he thought about it still more when the *Westminster Review* for October brought him his article on the Gold Conspiracy, which was also instantly pirated on a great scale. Piratical he was himself henceforth driven to be, and he asked only to be pirated, for he was sure not to be paid; but the honors of piracy resemble the colors of the begonia; they are showy but not useful. Here was a *tour de force* he had never dreamed himself equal to performing: two long, dry, quarterly, thirty or forty page articles, appearing in quick succession,

3. This article on the congressional session of 1870 was a detailed exposé of governmental incompetence.
4. Senator Timothy Howe (1816–83) said that Adams belonged "to a family

in which statesmanship is preserved by propagation—something as color in the leaf of the Begonia" (*Wisconsin State Journal*, October 7, 1870).

and pirated for audiences running well into the hundred thousands; and not one person, man or woman, offering him so much as a congratulation, except to call him a begonia.

Had this been all, life might have gone on very happily as before, but the ways of America to a young person of literary and political tastes were such as the so-called evolution of civilized man had not before evolved. No sooner had Adams made at Washington what he modestly hoped was a sufficient success, than his whole family set on him to drag him away. For the first time since 1861 his father interposed; his mother entreated; and his brother Charles argued and urged that he should come to Harvard College. Charles had views of further joint operations in a new field. He said that Henry had done at Washington all he could possibly do; that his position there wanted solidity; that he was, after all, an adventurer; that a few years in Cambridge would give him personal weight; that his chief function was not to be that of teacher, but that of editing the *North American Review* which was to be coupled with the professorship, and would lead to the daily press. In short, that he needed the university more than the university needed him.

Henry knew the university well enough to know that the department of history was controlled by one of the most astute and ideal administrators in the world—Professor Gurney[5]—and that it was Gurney who had established the new professorship, and had cast his net over Adams to carry the double load of mediæval history and the *Review*. He could see no relation whatever between himself and a professorship. He sought education; he did not sell it. He knew no history; he knew only a few historians; his ignorance was mischievous because it was literary, accidental, indifferent. On the other hand he knew Gurney, and felt much influenced by his advice. One cannot take oneself quite seriously in such matters; it could not much affect the sum of solar energies whether one went on dancing with girls in Washington, or began talking to boys at Cambridge. The good people who thought it did matter had a sort of right to guide. One could not reject their advice; still less disregard their wishes.

The sum of the matter was that Henry went out to Cambridge and had a few words with President Eliot which seemed to him almost as American as the talk about diplomacy with his father ten years before.[6] "But, Mr. President," urged Adams, "I know nothing about Mediæval History." With the courteous manner and bland smile so familiar for the next generation of Americans, Mr. Eliot mildly but firmly replied, "If you will point out to me any one who

5. Ephraim Whitney Gurney (1829–86); Adams met his future wife, Marion Hooper (1843–85), at Gurney's house; they were married in 1872.
6. The reference is to his father's talk with President Lincoln in 1861 when the President appointed him Minister to Great Britain. Lincoln had assumed Adams would know what he should do and that he would accept the appointment out of a sense of duty.

knows more, Mr. Adams, I will appoint him." The answer was neither logical nor convincing, but Adams could not meet it without overstepping his privileges. He could not say that, under the circumstances, the appointment of any professor at all seemed to him unnecessary.

So, at twenty-four hours' notice, he broke his life in halves again in order to begin a new education, on lines he had not chosen, in subjects for which he cared less than nothing; in a place he did not love, and before a future which repelled. Thousands of men have to do the same thing, but his case was peculiar because he had no need to do it. He did it because his best and wisest friends urged it, and he never could make up his mind whether they were right or not. To him this kind of education was always false. For himself he had no doubts. He thought it a mistake; but his opinion did not prove that it was one, since, in all probability, whatever he did would be more or less a mistake. He had reached cross-roads of education which all led astray. What he could gain at Harvard College he did not know, but in any case it was nothing he wanted. What he lost at Washington he could partly see, but in any case it was not fortune. Grant's administration wrecked men by thousands, but profited few. Perhaps Mr. Fish[7] was the solitary exception. One might search the whole list of Congress, Judiciary, and Executive during the twenty-five years 1870 to 1895, and find little but damaged reputation. The period was poor in purpose and barren in results.

Henry Adams, if not the rose, lived as near it as any politician,[8] and knew, more or less, all the men in any way prominent at Washington, or knew all about them. Among them, in his opinion, the best equipped, the most active-minded, and most industrious was Abram Hewitt,[9] who sat in Congress for a dozen years, between 1874 and 1886, sometimes leading the House and always wielding influence second to none. With nobody did Adams form closer or longer relations than with Mr. Hewitt, whom he regarded as the most useful public man in Washington; and he was the more struck by Hewitt's saying, at the end of his laborious career as legislator, that he left behind him no permanent result except the Act consolidating the Surveys. Adams knew no other man who had done so much, unless Mr. Sherman's[1] legislation is accepted as an instance of success. Hewitt's nearest rival would probably have been Senator Pendleton[2] who stood father to civil service reform in 1882, an

7. Hamilton Fish (1808–93), Governor of New York, later Senator and Secretary of State (1869–77); he earned Adams's admiration because he maintained an honorable position in Grant's corrupt administration.
8. Allusion to a comment by the French author Benjamin Constant, "I am not the rose, but I have lived with her."
9. Abram Hewitt (1822–1903), reform-minded Congressman; he wrote the bill of 1879 consolidating geologic, geographic, and geodetic surveys of the West.
1. Senator John Sherman (1823–1900), author of the Sherman Antitrust Act of 1890.
2. Senator George Hunt Pendleton (1825–89), author of pioneering civil-service-reform legislation.

attempt to correct a vice that should never have been allowed to be born. These were the men who succeeded.

The press stood in much the same light. No editor, no political writer, and no public administrator achieved enough good reputation to preserve his memory for twenty years. A number of them achieved bad reputations, or damaged good ones that had been gained in the Civil War. On the whole, even for Senators, diplomats, and Cabinet officers, the period was wearisome and stale.

None of Adams's generation profited by public activity unless it were William C. Whitney,[3] and even he could not be induced to return to it. Such ambitions as these were out of one's reach, but supposing one tried for what was feasible, attached oneself closely to the Garfields, Arthurs, Frelinghuysens, Blaines, Bayards, or Whitneys, who happened to hold office;[4] and supposing one asked for the mission to Belgium or Portugal, and obtained it; supposing one served a term as Assistant Secretary or Chief of Bureau; or, finally, supposing one had gone as sub-editor on the *New York Tribune* or *Times*—how much more education would one have gained than by going to Harvard College? These questions seemed better worth an answer than most of the questions on examination papers at college or in the civil service; all the more because one never found an answer to them, then or afterwards, and because, to his mind, the value of American society altogether was mixed up with the value of Washington.

At first, the simple beginner, struggling with principles, wanted to throw off responsibility on the American people, whose bare and toiling shoulders had to carry the load of every social or political stupidity; but the American people had no more to do with it than with the customs of Peking. American character might perhaps account for it, but what accounted for American character? All Boston, all New England, and all respectable New York, including Charles Francis Adams the father and Charles Francis Adams the son, agreed that Washington was no place for a respectable young man. All Washington, including Presidents, Cabinet officers, Judiciary, Senators, Congressmen, and clerks, expressed the same opinion, and conspired to drive away every young man who happened to be there, or tried to approach. Not one young man of promise remained in the Government service. All drifted into opposition. The Government did not want them in Washington. Adams's case was perhaps the strongest because he thought he had done well. He was forced to guess it, since he knew no one who would have risked so extravagant a step as that of encouraging a young man in a liter-

3. William C. Whitney (1841–1904) helped break up the notorious Tweed ring in New York; after an honorable career in politics he became a successful businessman.
4. Chester Alan Arthur (1830–86), succeeded James A. Garfield (1831–81) in 1881 to become 21st President of the United States; Frederick Theodore Frelinghuysen (1817–85), James G. Blaine (1830–93), and Thomas Francis Bayard (1828–98) were all Secretaries of State in the late 19th century.

ary career, or even in a political one; society forbade it, as well as residence in a political capital; but Harvard College must have seen some hope for him, since it made him professor against his will; even the publishers and editors of the *North American Review* must have felt a certain amount of confidence in him, since they put the *Review* in his hands. After all, the *Review* was the first liter- ary power in America, even though it paid almost as little in gold as the United States Treasury. The degree of Harvard College might bear a value as ephemeral as the commission of a President of the United States; but the government of the college, measured by money alone, and patronage, was a matter of more importance than that of some branches of the national service. In social position, the college was the superior of them all put together. In knowledge, she could assert no superiority, since the Government made no claims, and prided itself on ignorance. The service of Harvard College was distinctly honorable; perhaps the most honorable in America; and if Harvard College thought Henry Adams worth employing at four dollars a day, why should Washington decline his services when he asked nothing? Why should he be dragged from a career he liked in a place he loved, into a career he detested, in a place and climate he shunned? Was it enough to satisfy him, that all America should call Washington barren and dangerous? What made Washington more dangerous than New York?

The American character showed singular limitations which some- times drove the student of civilized man to despair. Crushed by his own ignorance—lost in the darkness of his own gropings—the scholar finds himself jostled of a sudden by a crowd of men who seem to him ignorant that there is a thing called ignorance; who have forgotten how to amuse themselves; who cannot even under- stand that they are bored. The American thought of himself as a restless, pushing, energetic, ingenious person, always awake and trying to get ahead of his neighbors. Perhaps this idea of the national character might be correct for New York or Chicago; it was not correct for Washington. There the American showed him- self, four times in five, as a quiet, peaceful, shy figure, rather in the mould of Abraham Lincoln, somewhat sad, sometimes pathetic, once tragic; or like Grant, inarticulate, uncertain, distrustful of him- self, still more distrustful of others, and awed by money. That the American, by temperament, worked to excess, was true; work and whiskey were his stimulants; work was a form of vice; but he never cared much for money or power after he earned them. The amuse- ment of the pursuit was all the amusement he got from it; he had no use for wealth. Jim Fisk alone seemed to know what he wanted; Jay Gould never did. At Washington one met mostly such true Americans, but if one wanted to know them better, one went to study them in Europe. Bored, patient, helpless; pathetically depend- ent on his wife and daughters; indulgent to excess; mostly a modest, decent, excellent, valuable citizen; the American was to be met at every railway station in Europe, carefully explaining to every listener that the happiest day of his life would be the day he should land on the pier at New York. He was ashamed to be amused; his mind no longer answered to the stimulus of variety; he could not face a new thought. All his immense strength, his intense nervous energy, his keen analytic perceptions, were oriented in one direction, and he could not change it. Congress was full of such men; in the Senate, Sumner[5] was almost the only exception; in the Executive, Grant[6] and Boutwell were varieties of the type—political specimens—pathetic in their helplessness to do anything with power when it came to them. They knew not how to amuse themselves; they could not conceive how other people were amused. Work, whiskey, and cards were life. The atmosphere of political Washington was theirs—or was supposed by the outside world to be in their control—and this was the reason why the outside world judged that Washington was fatal even for a young man of thirty-two, who had passed through the whole variety of temptations, in every capital of Europe, for a dozen years; who never played cards, and who loathed whiskey.

Chapter XXV. The Dynamo and the Virgin (1900)

Until the Great Exposition of 1900[1] closed its doors in November, Adams haunted it, aching to absorb knowledge, and helpless to find it. He would have liked to know how much of it could have been grasped by the best-informed man in the world. While he was thus meditating chaos, Langley[2] came by, and showed it to him. At Langley's behest, the Exhibition dropped its superfluous rags and stripped itself to the skin, for Langley knew what to study, and why, and how; while Adams might as well have stood outside in the night, staring at the Milky Way. Yet Langley said nothing new, and taught nothing that one might not have learned from Lord Bacon,[3] three hundred years before; but though one should have known the "Advancement of Science" as well as one knew the "Comedy of Errors,"[4] the literary knowledge counted for nothing until some teacher should show how to apply it. Bacon took a vast deal of trouble in teaching King James I[5] and his subjects, American or other, towards the year 1620, that true science was the development or economy of forces; yet an elderly American in 1900 knew neither the formula nor the forces; or even so much as to say to himself that his historical business in the Exposition concerned

5. Charles Sumner (1811–74), U.S. Senator from Massachusetts and antislavery leader before, during, and after the Civil War.
6. Ulysses S. Grant (1822–85), 18th President of the United States; George S. Boutwell (1818–1905), Secretary of the Treasury under Grant, 1869–73.
1. The World's Fair held in Paris from April through November.

2. Samuel P. Langley (1834–1906), American astronomer and inventor, in 1896, of the first airplane to fly successfully.
3. Sir Francis Bacon (1561–1626), English natural philosopher, author of *The Advancement of Learning* (1605).
4. Early Shakespearean comedy (1594).
5. King of England 1603–25.

only the economies or developments of force since 1893, when he began the study at Chicago.[6]

Nothing in education is so astonishing as the amount of ignorance it accumulates in the form of inert facts. Adams had looked at most of the accumulations of art in the storehouses called Art Museums; yet he did not know how to look at the art exhibits of 1900. He had studied Karl Marx[7] and his doctrines of history with profound attention, yet he could not apply them at Paris. Langley, with the ease of a great master of experiment, threw out of the field every exhibit that did not reveal a new application of force, and naturally threw out, to begin with, almost the whole art exhibit. Equally, he ignored almost the whole industrial exhibit. He led his pupil directly to the forces. His chief interest was in new motors to make his airship feasible, and he taught Adams the astonishing complexities of the new Daimler[8] motor, and of the automobile, which, since 1893, had become a nightmare at a hundred kilometres an hour, almost as destructive as the electric tram which was only ten years older; and threatening to become as terrible as the locomotive steam-engine itself, which was almost exactly Adams's own age.

Then he showed his scholar the great hall of dynamos, and explained how little he knew about electricity or force of any kind, even of his own special sun, which spouted heat in inconceivable volume, but which, as far as he knew, might spout less or more, at any time, for all the certainty he felt in it. To him, the dynamo itself was but an ingenious channel for conveying somewhere the heat latent in a few tons of poor coal hidden in a dirty engine-house carefully kept out of sight; but to Adams the dynamo became a symbol of infinity. As he grew accustomed to the great gallery of machines, he began to feel the forty-foot dynamos as a moral force, much as the early Christians felt the Cross. The planet itself seemed less impressive, in its old-fashioned, deliberate, annual or daily revolution, than this huge wheel, revolving within arm's-length at some vertiginous speed, and barely murmuring—scarcely humming an audible warning to stand a hair's-breadth further for respect of power—while it would not wake the baby lying close against its frame. Before the end, one began to pray to it; inherited instinct taught the natural expression of man before silent and infinite force. Among the thousand symbols of ultimate energy, the dynamo was not so human as some, but it was the most expressive.

Yet the dynamo, next to the steam-engine, was the most familiar of exhibits. For Adams's objects its value lay chiefly in its occult

<hr>

6. The subject of Chapter XXII of the *Education*. The Chicago Exposition of 1893 first stimulated Adams's interest in the "economy of forces."

7. Karl Marx (1818–83), German social philosopher, architect of modern socialism and communism; formulated his theories on the principle of "dialectical materialism."

8. Gottlieb Daimler (1834–1900), German engineer, inventor of the high-speed internal combusion engine and an early developer of the automobile.

mechanism. Between the dynamo in the gallery of machines and the engine-house outside, the break of continuity amounted to abysmal fracture for a historian's objects. No more relation could he discover between the steam and the electric current than between the Cross and the cathedral. The forces were interchangeable if not reversible, but he could see only an absolute *fiat* in electricity as in faith. Langley could not help him. Indeed, Langley seemed to be worried by the same trouble, for he constantly repeated that the new forces were anarchical, and especially that he was not responsible for the new rays, that were little short of parricidal in their wicked spirit towards science. His own rays,[9] with which he had doubled the solar spectrum, were altogether harmless and beneficent; but Radium denied its God[1]—or, what was to Langley the same thing, denied the truths of his Science. The force was wholly new.

A historian who asked only to learn enough to be as futile as Langley or Kelvin,[2] made rapid progress under this teaching, and mixed himself up in the tangle of ideas until he achieved a sort of Paradise of ignorance vastly consoling to his fatigued senses. He wrapped himself in vibrations and rays which were new, and he would have hugged Marconi[3] and Branly had he met them, as he hugged the dynamo; while he lost his arithmetic in trying to figure out the equation between the discoveries and the economies of force. The economies, like the discoveries, were absolute, supersensual, occult; incapable of expression in horse-power. What mathematical equivalent could he suggest as the value of a Branly coherer? Frozen air, or the electric furnace, had some scale of measurement, no doubt, if somebody could invent a thermometer adequate to the purpose; but X-rays[4] had played no part whatever in man's consciousness, and the atom itself had figured only as a fiction of thought. In these seven years man had translated himself into a new universe which had no common scale of measurement with the old. He had entered a supersensual world, in which he could measure nothing except by chance collisions of movements imperceptible to his senses, perhaps even imperceptible to his instruments, but perceptible to each other, and so to some known ray at the end of the scale. Langley seemed prepared for anything, even for an indeterminable number of universes interfused—physics stark mad in metaphysics.

9. Langley had invented the bolometer, with which he was able to measure intensities of invisible heat rays in the infrared spectrum.
1. Since radium, first isolated by the Curies in 1898, underwent spontaneous transformation through radioactive emission, it did not fit prevailing scientific distinctions between matter and energy.
2. William Thomson, Baron Kelvin (1824–1907), English mathematician and physicist known especially for his work in thermodynamics and electrodynamics.
3. Guglielmo Marconi (1874–1937), Italian inventor of radio telegraphy in 1895; Édouard Branly (1844–1940), French physicist and inventor in 1890 of the Branly "coherer" for detecting radio waves.
4. Wilhelm Roentgen (1845–1923) discovered X-rays in 1895.

Historians undertake to arrange sequences,—called stories, or histories—assuming in silence a relation of cause and effect. These assumptions, hidden in the depths of dusty libraries, have been astounding, but commonly unconscious and childlike; so much so, that if any captious critic were to drag them to light, historians would probably reply, with one voice, that they had never supposed themselves required to know what they were talking about. Adams, for one, had toiled in vain to find out what he meant. He had even published a dozen volumes of American history for no other purpose than to satisfy himself whether, by the severest process of stating, with the least possible comment, such facts as seemed sure, in such order as seemed rigorously consequent, he could fix for a familiar moment a necessary sequence of human movement. The result had satisfied him as little as at Harvard College. Where he saw sequence, other men saw something quite different, and no one saw the same unit of measure. He cared little about his experiments and less about his statesmen, who seemed to him quite as ignorant as himself and, as a rule, no more honest; but he insisted on a relation of sequence, and if he could not reach it by one method, he would try as many methods as science knew. Satisfied that the sequence of men led to nothing and that the sequence of their society could lead no further, while the mere sequence of time was artificial, and the sequence of thought was chaos, he turned at last to the sequence of force; and thus it happened that, after ten years' pursuit, he found himself lying in the Gallery of Machines at the Great Exposition of 1900, with his historical neck broken by the sudden irruption of forces totally new.

Since no one else showed much concern, an elderly person without other cares had no need to betray alarm. The year 1900 was not the first to upset schoolmasters. Copernicus and Galileo had broken many professorial necks about 1600;[5] Columbus had stood the world on its head towards 1500; but the nearest approach to the revolution of 1900 was that of 310, when Constantine set up the Cross.[6] The rays that Langley disowned, as well as those which he fathered, were occult, supersensual, irrational; they were a revelation of mysterious energy like that of the Cross; they were what, in terms of mediæval science, were called immediate modes of the divine substance.

The historian was thus reduced to his last resources. Clearly if he was bound to reduce all these forces to a common value, this common value could have no measure but that of their attraction on his own mind. He must treat them as they had been felt; as con-

5. Copernicus (1473–1543), Polish astronomer, proved that the earth rotated around the sun and not vice versa; Galileo (1564–1642), Italian astronomer and developer of the refracting telescope, was condemned by the Inquisition for espousing Copernican heliocentric theory.
6. Constantine the Great (288?–337), Roman Emperor, issued the Edict of Milan in 313 proclaiming toleration of Christians, which paved the way for the ascendancy of Christianity.

vertible, reversible, interchangeable attractions on thought. He made up his mind to venture it; he would risk translating rays into faith. Such a reversible process would vastly amuse a chemist, but the chemist could not deny that he, or some of his fellow physicists, could feel the force of both. When Adams was a boy in Boston, the best chemist in the place had probably never heard of Venus except by way of scandal, or of the Virgin except as idolatry;[7] neither had he heard of dynamos or automobiles or radium; yet his mind was ready to feel the force of all, though the rays were unborn and the women were dead.

Here opened another totally new education, which promised to be by far the most hazardous of all. The knife-edge along which he must crawl, like Sir Lancelot in the twelfth century,[8] divided two kingdoms of force which had nothing in common but attraction. They were as different as a magnet is from gravitation, supposing one knew what a magnet was, or gravitation, or love. The force of the Virgin was still felt at Lourdes,[9] and seemed to be as potent as X-rays; but in America neither Venus nor Virgin ever had value as force—at most as sentiment. No American had ever been truly afraid of either.

This problem in dynamics gravely perplexed an American historian. The Woman had once been supreme; in France she still seemed potent, not merely as a sentiment, but as a force. Why was she unknown in America? For evidently America was ashamed of her, and she was ashamed of herself, otherwise they would not have strewn fig-leaves so profusely all over her.[1] When she was a true force, she was ignorant of fig-leaves, but the monthly-magazine-made American female had not a feature that would have been recognized by Adam. The trait was notorious, and often humorous, but anyone brought up among Puritans knew that sex was sin. In any previous age, sex was strength. Neither art nor beauty was needed. Everyone, even among Puritans, knew that neither Diana of the Ephesians[2] nor any of the Oriental goddesses was worshipped for her beauty. She was goddess because of her force; she was the animated dynamo; she was reproduction—the greatest and most mysterious of all energies; all she needed was to be fecund. Singularly enough, not one of Adams's many schools of education had ever drawn his attention to the opening lines of Lucretius,[3]

7. That is, the druggist knew of Venus only through selling medication for venereal disease; and since Boston was largely Protestant, he would only have heard of the Virgin as the object of idolatrous worship.
8. In Chrétien de Troyes's *Lancelot,* the hero was obliged to crawl across a bridge composed of a knife in order to enter a castle and rescue Guinevere.
9. A famous shrine in France known for its miraculous cures; the Virgin Mary was said to have appeared to a peasant girl there in 1858.
1. I.e., to conceal sexual organs and sensuality.
2. The shrine at Ephesus on the West Coast of Asia Minor was dedicated to Artemis, a virgin-goddess mother-figure.
3. Lucretius (c. 99–55 B.C.), in *On the Nature of Things,* I.21: "And since 'tis thou / Venus alone / Guidest the Cosmos." Trans. William Ellery Leonard.

though they were perhaps the finest in all Latin literature, where the poet invoked Venus exactly as Dante invoked the Virgin:—

"Quae quoniam rerum naturam *sola* gubernas."

The Venus of Epicurean philosophy survived in the Virgin of the Schools:—

"Donna, sei tanto grande, e tanto vali,
Che qual vuol grazia, e a te non ricorre,
Sua disianza vuol volar senz' ali."[4]

All this was to American thought as though it had never existed. The true American knew something of the facts, but nothing of the feelings; he read the letter, but he never felt the law. Before this historical chasm, a mind like that of Adams felt itself helpless; he turned from the Virgin to the Dynamo as though he were a Branly coherer. On one side, at the Louvre and at Chartres, as he knew by the record of work actually done and still before his eyes, was the highest energy ever known to man, the creator of four-fifths of his noblest art, exercising vastly more attraction over the human mind than all the steam-engines and dynamos ever dreamed of; and yet this energy was unknown to the American mind. An American Virgin would never dare command; an American Venus would never dare exist.

The question, which to any plain American of the nineteenth century seemed as remote as it did to Adams, drew him almost violently to study, once it was posed; and on this point Langleys were as useless as though they were Herbert Spencers[5] or dynamos. The idea survived only as art. There one turned as naturally as though the artist were himself a woman. Adams began to ponder, asking himself whether he knew of any American artist who had ever insisted on the power of sex, as every classic had always done; but he could think only of Walt Whitman; Bret Harte,[6] as far as the magazines would let him venture; and one or two painters, for the flesh-tones. All the rest had used sex for sentiment, never for force; to them, Eve was a tender flower, and Herodias[7] an unfeminine horror. American art, like the American language and American education, was as far as possible sexless.[8] Society regarded this vic-

4. The Virgin of the Schools is a reference to medieval scholastic philosophers. The lines from Dante translate:
Lady, thou art so great and hath such worth, that if there be who would have grace yet betaketh not himself to thee, his longing seeketh to fly without wings. (Dante, *Paradiso*, XXXIII, trans. Carlyle-Wicksteed)
5. Herbert Spencer (1820–93), English philosopher and popularizer of Darwinian evolutionary principles. Adams ironically suggests that Spencer's explanations were too general and abstract to explain this primal force.

6. Whitman's *Leaves of Grass* (1855) treated sex boldly and was much criticized on that account; Bret Harte (1836–1902) sympathetically portrayed prostitutes in such stories as *The Outcasts of Poker Flat*.
7. The wife of King Herod who collaborated with her daughter Salome in arranging the beheading of John the Baptist.
8. Just as the American language had no genders, American education was coeducational and in Adams's day entirely excluded sex as a subject from the curriculum.

tory over sex as its greatest triumph, and the historian readily admitted it, since the moral issue, for the moment, did not concern one who was studying the relations of unmoral force. He cared nothing for the sex of the dynamo until he could measure its energy.

Vaguely seeking a clue, he wandered through the art exhibit, and, in his stroll, stopped almost every day before St. Gaudens's[9] General Sherman, which had been given the central post of honor. St. Gaudens himself was in Paris, putting on the work his usual interminable last touches, and listening to the usual contradictory suggestions of brother sculptors. Of all the American artists who gave to American art whatever life it breathed in the seventies, St. Gaudens was perhaps the most sympathetic, but certainly the most inarticulate. General Grant or Don Cameron[1] had scarcely less instinct of rhetoric than he. All the others—the Hunts, Richardson, John La Farge, Stanford White[2]—were exuberant; only St. Gaudens could never discuss or dilate on an emotion, or suggest artistic arguments for giving to his work the forms that he felt. He never laid down the law, or affected the despot, or became brutalized like Whistler[3] by the brutalities of his world. He required no incense; he was no egoist; his simplicity of thought was excessive; he could not imitate, or give any form but his own to the creations of his hand. No one felt more strongly than he the strength of other men, but the idea that they could affect him never stirred an image in his mind.

This summer his health was poor and his spirits were low. For such a temper, Adams was not the best companion, since his own gaiety was not *folle*;[4] but he risked going now and then to the studio on Mont Parnasse to draw him out for a stroll in the Bois de Boulogne,[5] or dinner as pleased his moods, and in return St. Gaudens sometimes let Adams go about in his company.

Once St. Gaudens took him down to Amiens, with a party of Frenchmen, to see the cathedral. Not until they found themselves actually studying the sculpture of the western portal, did it dawn on Adams's mind that, for his purposes, St. Gaudens on that spot had more interest to him than the cathedral itself. Great men before great monuments express great truths, provided they are not taken too solemnly. Adams never tired of quoting the supreme phrase of his idol Gibbon, before the Gothic cathedrals: "I darted a contemptuous look on the stately monuments of superstition."[6] Even in the

9. Augustus Saint-Gaudens (1848–1907), American sculptor.
1. Senator James Donald Cameron (1833–1918), Secretary of War under President Grant, 1876.
2. William Morris Hunt (1824–79), noted painter, and his younger brother Richard Morris Hunt (1828–95), noted architect; Henry Hobson Richardson (1838–86), architect; John La Farge (1835–1910), muralist and maker of stained-glass windows; Stanford White (1853–1906), architect.
3. James Abbott McNeill Whistler (1834–1903), American painter and lithographer.
4. Excessive.
5. A large wooded park on the outskirts of Paris; "Mont Parnasse": a Paris Left Bank district frequented by artists and writers.
6. Apparently Adams's adaptation of a passage in Gibbon's French journal for February 21, 1763.

footnotes of his history, Gibbon had never inserted a bit of humor more human than this, and one would have paid largely for a photograph of the fat little historian, on the background of Notre Dame of Amiens, trying to persuade his readers—perhaps himself —that he was darting a contemptuous look on the stately monument, for which he felt in fact the respect which every man of his vast study and active mind always feels before objects worthy of it; but besides the humor, one felt also the relation. Gibbon ignored the Virgin, because in 1789 religious monuments were out of fashion. In 1900 his remark sounded fresh and simple as the green fields to ears that had heard a hundred years of other remarks, mostly no more fresh and certainly less simple. Without malice, one might find it more instructive than a whole lecture of Ruskin.[7] One sees what one brings, and at that moment Gibbon brought the French Revolution. Ruskin brought reaction against the Revolution. St. Gaudens had passed beyond all. He liked the stately monuments much more than he liked Gibbon or Ruskin; he loved their dignity; their unity; their scale; their lines; their lights and shadows; their decorative sculpture; but he was even less conscious than they of the force that created it all—the Virgin, the Woman—by whose genius "the stately monuments of superstition" were built, through which she was expressed. He would have seen more meaning in Isis[8] with the cow's horns, at Edfoo, who expressed the same thought. The art remained, but the energy was lost even upon the artist.

Yet in mind and person St. Gaudens was a survival of the 1500's; he bore the stamp of the Renaissance, and should have carried an image of the Virgin round his neck, or stuck in his hat, like Louis XI.[9] In mere time he was a lost soul that had strayed by chance into the twentieth century, and forgotten where it came from. He writhed and cursed at his ignorance, much as Adams did at his own, but in the opposite sense. St. Gaudens was a child of Benvenuto Cellini,[1] smothered in an American cradle. Adams was a quintessence of Boston, devoured by curiosity to think like Benvenuto. St. Gaudens's art was starved from birth, and Adams's instinct was blighted from babyhood. Each had but half of a nature, and when they came together before the Virgin of Amiens they ought both to have felt in her the force that made them one; but it was not so. To Adams she became more than ever a channel of force; to St. Gaudens she remained as before a channel of taste.

For a symbol of power, St. Gaudens instinctively preferred the horse, as was plain in his horse and Victory of the Sherman monu-

7. John Ruskin (1819–1900), English art critic and social reformer, famous for his highly imaginative interpretations of great works of the Italian Renaissance.
8. Egyptian earth-mother goddess; Adams visited Edfu, the site of the best-preserved temple in Egypt, in 1872–73 and in 1893.

9. A pious French King (1423–83) who often disguised himself as a pilgrim and wore an old felt hat decorated with the lead statuette of a saint.
1. Flamboyant Italian sculptor and goldsmith (1500–71), author of a famous autobiography.

ment. Doubtless Sherman also felt it so. The attitude was so American that, for at least forty years, Adams had never realized that any other could be in sound taste. How many years had he taken to admit a notion of what Michael Angelo and Rubens[2] were driving at? He could not say; but he knew that only since 1895 had he begun to feel the Virgin or Venus as force, and not everywhere even so. At Chartres—perhaps at Lourdes—possibly at Cnidos[3] if one could still find there the divinely naked Aphrodite of Praxiteles —but otherwise one must look for force to the goddesses of Indian mythology. The idea died out long ago in the German and English stock. St. Gaudens at Amiens was hardly less sensitive to the force of the female energy than Matthew Arnold at the Grande Chartreuse.[4] Neither of them felt goddesses as power—only as reflected emotion, human expression, beauty, purity, taste, scarcely even as sympathy. They felt a railway train as power; yet they, and all other artists, constantly complained that the power embodied in a railway train could never be embodied in art. All the steam in the world could not, like the Virgin, build Chartres.

Yet in mechanics, whatever the mechanicians might think, both energies acted as interchangeable forces on man, and by action on man all known force may be measured. Indeed, few men of science measured force in any other way. After once admitting that a straight line was the shortest distance between two points, no serious mathematician cared to deny anything that suited his convenience, and rejected no symbol, unproved or unproveable, that helped him to accomplish work. The symbol was force, as a compass-needle or a triangle was force, as the mechanist might prove by losing it, and nothing could be gained by ignoring their value. Symbol or energy, the Virgin had acted as the greatest force the Western world ever felt, and had drawn man's activities to herself more strongly than any other power, natural or super-natural, had ever done; the historian's business was to follow the track of the energy; to find where it came from and where it went to; its complex source and shifting channels; its values, equivalents, conversions. It could scarcely be more complex than radium; it could hardly be deflected, diverted, polarized, absorbed more perplexingly than other radiant matter. Adams knew nothing about any of them, but as a mathematical problem of influence on human progress, though all were occult, all reacted on his mind, and he rather inclined to think the Virgin easiest to handle.

The pursuit turned out to be long and tortuous, leading at last

2. Michelangelo Buonarroti (1475–1564), Italian sculptor, painter, architect, and poet of the High Renaissance. Peter Paul Rubens (1577–1640), 17th-century Flemish painter. Both are known for their exceptional renderings of the human body.
3. Cnidos or Cnidus is an ancient city in Asia Minor, site of the most famous of the statues of Aphrodite by Praxiteles (c. 370–330 B.C.); only a copy survives in the Vatican.
4. Matthew Arnold's (1822–88) poem *Stanzas from the Grande Chartreuse* invokes the Virgin Mary in mourning the loss of faith formerly held by ascetic Carthusian monks.

into the vast forests of scholastic science. From Zeno to Descartes, hand in hand with Thomas Aquinas, Montaigne, and Pascal,[5] one stumbled as stupidly as though one were still a German student of 1860. Only with the instinct of despair could one force one's self into this old thicket of ignorance after having been repulsed at a score of entrances more promising and more popular. Thus far, no path had led anywhere, unless perhaps to an exceedingly modest living. Forty-five years of study had proved to be quite futile for the pursuit of power; one controlled no more force in 1900 than in 1850, although the amount of force controlled by society had enormously increased. The secret of education still hid itself somewhere behind ignorance, and one fumbled over it as feebly as ever. In such labyrinths, the staff is a force almost more necessary than the legs; the pen becomes a sort of blind-man's dog, to keep him from falling into the gutters. The pen works for itself, and acts like a hand, modelling the plastic material over and over again to the form that suits it best. The form is never arbitrary, but is a sort of growth like crystallization, as any artist knows too well; for often the pencil or pen runs into side-paths and shapelessness, loses its relations, stops or is bogged. Then it has to return on its trail, and recover, if it can, its line of force. The result of a year's work depends more on what is struck out than on what is left in; on the sequence of the main lines of thought, than on their play or variety. Compelled once more to lean heavily on this support, Adams covered more thousands of pages with figures as formal as though they were algebra, laboriously striking out, altering, burning, experimenting, until the year had expired, the Exposition had long been closed, and winter drawing to its end, before he sailed from Cherbourg, on January 19, 1901, for home.

Chapter XXXIII. A Dynamic Theory of History (1904)

A dynamic theory, like most theories, begins by begging the question: it defines Progress as the development and economy of Forces. Further, it defines force as anything that does, or helps to do work. Man is a force; so is the sun; so is a mathematical point, though without dimensions or known existence.

Man commonly begs the question again by taking for granted that he captures the forces. A dynamic theory, assigning attractive force to opposing bodies in proportion to the law of mass, takes for granted that the forces of nature capture man. The sum of force attracts; the feeble atom or molecule called man is attracted; he suffers education or growth; he is the sum of the forces that attract

5. Probably Zeno of Citium (c. 366–264 B.C.), Greek philosopher; René Descartes (1596–1650), French philosopher; Thomas Aquinas (1225?–1274), Italian philosopher and theologian who is the subject of the last chapter of Adams's *Mont-Saint-Michel and Chartres*; Michel Eyquem de Montaigne (1533–92), French essayist and skeptical philosopher; Blaise Pascal (1623–62), French philosopher.

him; his body and his thought are alike their product; the movement of the forces controls the progress of his mind, since he can
know nothing but the motions which impinge on his senses, whose
sum makes education.

For convenience as an image, the theory may liken man to a
spider in its web, watching for chance prey. Forces of nature dance
like flies before the net, and the spider pounces on them when it
can; but it makes many fatal mistakes, though its theory of force is
sound. The spider-mind acquires a faculty of memory, and, with it,
a singular skill of analysis and synthesis, taking apart and putting
together in different relations the meshes of its trap. Man had in
the beginning no power of analysis or synthesis approaching that of
the spider, or even of the honey-bee; but he had acute sensibility to
the higher forces. Fire taught him secrets that no other animal
could learn; running water probably taught him even more, especially in his first lessons of mechanics; the animals helped to educate him, thrusting themselves into his hands merely for the sake of
their food, and carrying his burdens or supplying his clothing; the
grasses and grains were academies of study. With little or no effort
on his part, all these forces formed his thought, induced his action,
and even shaped his figure.

Long before history began, his education was complete, for the
record could not have been started until he had been taught to
record. The universe that had formed him took shape in his mind
as a reflection of his own unity, containing all forces except himself.
Either separately, or in groups, or as a whole, these forces never
ceased to act on him, enlarging his mind as they enlarged the surface foliage of a vegetable, and the mind needed only to respond, as
the forests did, to these attractions. Susceptibility to the highest
forces is the highest genius; selection between them is the highest
science; their mass is the highest educator. Man always made, and
still makes, grotesque blunders in selecting and measuring forces,
taken at random from the heap, but he never made a mistake in the
value he set on the whole, which he symbolized as unity and worshipped as God. To this day, his attitude towards it has never
changed, though science can no longer give to force a name.

Man's function as a force of nature was to assimilate other forces
as he assimilated food. He called it the love of power. He felt his
own feebleness, and he sought for an ass or a camel, a bow or a
sling, to widen his range of power, as he sought a fetish or a planet
in the world beyond. He cared little to know its immediate use, but
he could afford to throw nothing away which he could conceive to
have possible value in this or any other existence. He waited for the
object to teach him its use, or want of use, and the process was
slow. He may have gone on for hundreds of thousands of years,
waiting for Nature to tell him her secrets; and, to his rivals among
the monkeys, Nature has taught no more than at their start; but

certain lines of force were capable of acting on individual apes, and mechanically selecting types of race or sources of variation. The individual that responded or reacted to lines of new force then was possibly the same individual that reacts on it now, and his conception of the unity seems never to have changed in spite of the increasing diversity of forces; but the theory of variation is an affair of other science than history, and matters nothing to dynamics. The individual or the race would be educated on the same lines of illusion, which, according to Arthur Balfour[1], had not essentially varied down to the year 1900.

To the highest attractive energy, man gave the name of divine, and for its control he invented the science called Religion, a word which meant, and still means, cultivation of occult force whether in detail or mass. Unable to define Force as a unity, man symbolized it and pursued it, both in himself, and in the infinite, as philosophy and theology; the mind is itself the subtlest of all known forces, and its self-introspection necessarily created a science which had the singular value of lifting his education, at the start, to the finest, subtlest, and broadest training both in analysis and synthesis, so that, if language is a test, he must have reached his highest powers early in his history; while the mere motive remained as simple an appetite for power as the tribal greed which led him to trap an elephant. Hunger, whether for food or for the infinite, sets in motion multiplicity and infinity of thought, and the sure hope of gaining a share of infinite power in eternal life would lift most minds to effort.

He had reached this completeness five thousand years ago, and added nothing to his stock of known forces for a very long time. The mass of nature exercised on him so feeble an attraction that one can scarcely account for his apparent motion. Only a historian of very exceptional knowledge would venture to say at what date between 3000 B.C. and 1000 A.D., the momentum of Europe was greatest; but such progress as the world made consisted in economies of energy rather than in its development; it was proved in mathematics, measured by names like Archimedes, Aristarchus, Ptolemy, and Euclid;[2] or in Civil Law, measured by a number of names which Adams had begun life by failing to learn; or in coinage, which was most beautiful near its beginning, and most barbarous at its close;[3] or it was shown in roads, or the size of ships, or harbors; or by the use of metals, instruments, and writing; all of them econ-

---

1. **Arthur Balfour** (1848–1930), British philosopher and statesman, delivered a lecture in 1904, "On the Future of Science," which seriously questioned 19th-century notions of science and scientific progress.
2. **Archimedes** (c. 287–212 B.C.), Greek mathematician and inventor, famous for his work in geometry; Aristarchus (active c. 280–264 B.C.), Greek astronomer, proposed the heliocentric theory of the solar system; Claudius Ptolemaeus (27 B.C.–A.D. 48), Alexandrian astronomer, posited the geocentric theory; and Euclid (c. 300 B.C.), Alexandrian mathematician, presented Euclidean geometry in his book *The Elements*, still a standard text.
3. **Adams**, an amateur numismatist, added to his father's fine coin collection and later left it to the Massachusetts Historical Society.

omies of force, sometimes more forceful than the forces they helped; but the roads were still travelled by the horse, the ass, the camel, or the slave; the ships were still propelled by sails or oars; the lever, the spring, and the screw bounded the region of applied mechanics. Even the metals were old.

Much the same thing could be said of religious or supernatural forces. Down to the year 300[4] of the Christian era they were little changed, and in spite of Plato[5] and the sceptics were more apparently chaotic than ever. The experience of three thousand years had educated society to feel the vastness of Nature, and the infinity of her resources of power, but even this increase of attraction had not yet caused economies in its methods of pursuit.

There the Western world stood till the year A.D. 305, when the Emperor Diocletian[6] abdicated; and there it was that Adams broke down on the steps of Ara Coeli,[7] his path blocked by the scandalous failure of civilization at the moment it had achieved complete success. In the year 305 the empire had solved the problems of Europe more completely than they have ever been solved since. The Pax Romana,[8] the Civil Law, and Free Trade should, in four hundred years, have put Europe far in advance of the point reached by modern society in the four hundred years since 1500, when conditions were less simple.

The efforts to explain, or explain away, this scandal had been incessant, but none suited Adams unless it were the economic theory of adverse exchanges and exhaustion of minerals; but nations are not ruined beyond a certain point by adverse exchanges, and Rome had by no means exhausted her resources. On the contrary, the empire developed resources and energies quite astounding. No other four hundred years of history before A.D. 1800 knew anything like it; and although some of these developments, like the Civil Law, the roads, aqueducts, and harbors, were rather economies than force, yet in northwestern Europe alone the empire had developed three energies—France, England, and Germany—competent to master the world. The trouble seemed rather to be that the empire developed too much energy, and too fast.

A dynamic law requires that two masses—nature and man—must go on, reacting upon each other, without stop, as the sun and a comet react on each other, and that any appearance of stoppage is illusive. The theory seems to exact excess, rather than deficiency, of

4. Adams's approximate date for the victorious ascendance of Christianity over the Roman world.
5. Plato (427?–347 B.C.), Greek philosopher who postulated the realm of ideal forms and presented an outline of his ideal state in the *Republic*.
6. Diocletian (245–313), Roman Emperor who tried to renew the old Roman religion by ordering in 303 a general persecution of Christians.

7. "Altar of Heaven"; church in Rome built on the ancient foundations for the Roman temple of Juno where, according to legend, Augustus Caesar announced the birth of Christ.
8. "Peace" enforced throughout Europe and the Mediterranean by Rome. Civil law was codified for the entire Empire under the Byzantine Emperor Justinian (483–565). Free trade resulted from the uniform monetary system of the Empire.

action and reaction to account for the dissolution of the Roman Empire, which should, as a problem of mechanics, have been torn to pieces by acceleration. If the student means to try the experiment of framing a dynamic law, he must assign values to the forces of attraction that caused the trouble; and in this case he has them in plain evidence. With the relentless logic that stamped Roman thought, the empire, which had established unity on earth, could not help establishing unity in heaven. It was induced by its dynamic necessities to economize the gods.

The Church has never ceased to protest against the charge that Christianity ruined the empire,[9] and, with its usual force, has pointed out that its reforms alone saved the State. Any dynamic theory gladly admits it. All it asks is to find and follow the force that attracts. The Church points out this force in the Cross, and history needs only to follow it. The empire loudly asserted its motive. Good taste forbids saying that Constantine the Great[1] speculated as audaciously as a modern stock-broker on values of which he knew at the utmost only the volume; or that he merged all uncertain forces into a single trust, which he enormously over-capitalized, and forced on the market; but this is the substance of what Constantine himself said in his Edict of Milan in the year 313, which admitted Christianity into the Trust of State Religions. Regarded as an Act of Congress, it runs: "We have resolved to grant to Christians as well as all others the liberty to practise the religion they prefer, in order that whatever exists of divinity or celestial power may help and favor us and all who are under our government." The empire pursued power—not merely spiritual but physical—in the sense in which Constantine issued his army order the year before, at the battle of the Milvian Bridge: *In hoc signo vinces!*[2] using the Cross as a train of artillery, which, to his mind, it was. Society accepted it in the same character. Eighty years afterwards, Theodosius[3] marched against his rival Eugene with the Cross for physical champion; and Eugene raised the image of Hercules[4] to fight for the pagans; while society on both sides looked on, as though it were a boxing-match, to decide a final test of force between the divine powers. The Church was powerless to raise the ideal. What is now known as religion affected the mind of old society but little. The laity, the people, the million, almost to a man, bet on the gods as they bet on a horse.

9. Edward Gibbon advanced the idea in his classic *Decline and Fall of the Roman Empire* (1776–88).
1. Constantine the Great (288?–337), Roman Emperor sympathetic to Christianity, proclaimed the edict of toleration in 313 and was responsible for evolving the ecumenical council in the church.
2. "In this sign, you shall conquer."
3. Theodosius (346?–395), Roman Emperor of the East (379–95) and Emperor of the West (392–95). A devout Christian, he defeated the pagan Eugene, a puppet Emperor enthroned by the Frankish general Arbogast to thwart the gains of Christianity.
4. Classical hero famous for superhuman strength and courage; in the late Empire, he represented the cause of paganism.

No doubt the Church did all it could to purify the process, but society was almost wholly pagan in its point of view, and was drawn to the Cross because, in its system of physics, the Cross had absorbed all the old occult or fetish-power. The symbol represented the sum of nature—the Energy of modern science—and society believed it to be as real as X-rays; perhaps it was! The emperors used it like gunpowder in politics; the physicians used it like rays in medicine; the dying clung to it as the quintessence of force, to protect them from the forces of evil on their road to the next life.

Throughout these four centuries the empire knew that religion disturbed economy, for even the cost of heathen incense affected the exchanges; but no one could afford to buy or construct a costly and complicated machine when he could hire an occult force at trifling expense. Fetish-power was cheap and satisfactory, down to a certain point. Turgot[5] and Auguste Comte long ago fixed this stage of economy as a necessary phase of social education, and historians seem now to accept it as the only gain yet made towards scientific history. Great numbers of educated people—perhaps a majority— cling to the method still, and practise it more or less strictly; but, until quite recently, no other was known. The only occult power at man's disposal was fetish. Against it, no mechanical force could compete except within narrow limits.

Outside of occult or fetish-power, the Roman world was incredibly poor. It knew but one productive energy resembling a modern machine—the slave. No artificial force of serious value was applied to production or transportation, and when society developed itself so rapidly in political and social lines, it had no other means of keeping its economy on the same level than to extend its slave-system and its fetish-system to the utmost.

The result might have been stated in a mathematical formula as early as the time of Archimedes, six hundred years before Rome fell. The economic needs of a violently centralizing society forced the empire to enlarge its slave-system until the slave-system consumed itself and the empire too, leaving society no resource but further enlargement of its religious system in order to compensate for the losses and horrors of the failure. For a vicious circle, its mathematical completeness approached perfection. The dynamic law of attraction and reaction needed only a Newton[6] to fix it in algebraic form.

At last, in 410, Alaric[7] sacked Rome, and the slave-ridden, agricultural, uncommercial Western Empire—the poorer and less

5. Anne Robert Jacques Turgot (1727–81), French statesman and economist, asserted, "All epochs are fastened together by a sequence of causes and effects linking the condition of the world to all the conditions that have gone before it"; August Comte (1798–1857), French positivist philosopher, defined three phases of human knowledge—theological, metaphysical, and positive.

6. Sir Isaac Newton (1642–1727), English mathematician and physicist, formulated the law of universal gravitation.

7. Alaric (c. 370–410), Visigothic King who sacked Rome in 410.

Christianized half—went to pieces. Society, though terribly shocked by the horrors of Alaric's storm, felt still more deeply the disappointment in its new power, the Cross, which had failed to protect its Church. The outcry against the Cross became so loud among Christians that its literary champion, Bishop Augustine of Hippo[8] —a town between Algiers and Tunis—was led to write a famous treatise in defence of the Cross, familiar still to every scholar, in which he defended feebly the mechanical value of the symbol— arguing only that pagan symbols equally failed—but insisted on its spiritual value in the *Civitas Dei* which had taken the place of the *Civitas Romae*[9] in human interest. "Granted that we have lost all we had! Have we lost faith? Have we lost piety? Have we lost the wealth of the inner man who is rich before God? These are the wealth of Christians!" The *Civitas Dei*, in its turn, became the sum of attraction for the Western world, though it also showed the same weakness in mechanics that had wrecked the *Civitas Romae*. St. Augustine and his people perished at Hippo towards 430, leaving society in appearance dull to new attraction.

Yet the attraction remained constant. The delight of experimenting on occult force of every kind is such as to absorb all the free thought of the human race. The gods did their work; history has no quarrel with them; they led, educated, enlarged the mind; taught knowledge; betrayed ignorance; stimulated effort. So little is known about the mind—whether social, racial, sexual or heritable; whether material or spiritual; whether animal, vegetable or mineral—that history is inclined to avoid it altogether; but nothing forbids one to admit, for convenience, that it may assimilate food like the body, storing new force and growing, like a forest, with the storage. The brain has not yet revealed its mysterious mechanism of gray matter. Never has Nature offered it so violent a stimulant as when she opened to it the possibility of sharing infinite power in eternal life, and it might well need a thousand years of prolonged and intense experiment to prove the value of the motive. During these so-called Middle Ages, the Western mind reacted in many forms, on many sides, expressing its motives in modes, such as Romanesque and Gothic architecture, glass windows and mosaic walls, sculpture and poetry, war and love, which still affect some people as the noblest work of man, so that, even to-day, great masses of idle and ignorant tourists travel from far countries to look at Ravenna and San Marco, Palermo and Pisa, Assisi, Cordova, Chartres,[1] with vague notions about the force that created them, but with a certain sur-

8. St. Augustine (354–430), considered Christianity's most famous literary protagonist, wrote *The City of God (Civitas Dei)*, an ardent defense of Christianity against its pagan critics.
9. The Roman state during its control of the Empire.
1. Cities in Italy, Sicily, Spain, and France, respectively, famous for their outstanding Romanesque, Moorish, Gothic, and Christian art and architecture.

prise that a social mind of such singular energy and unity should still lurk in their shadows.

The tourist more rarely visits Constantinople or studies the architecture of Sancta Sofia,[2] but when he does, he is distinctly conscious of forces not quite the same. Justinian[3] has not the simplicity of Charlemagne. The Eastern Empire showed an activity and variety of forces that classical Europe had never possessed. The navy of Nicephoras Phocas[4] in the tenth century would have annihilated in half an hour any navy that Carthage or Athens or Rome ever set afloat. The dynamic scheme began by asserting rather recklessly that between the Pyramids (B.C. 3000), and the Cross (A.D. 300), no new force affected Western progress, and antiquarians may easily dispute the fact; but in any case the motive influence, old or new, which raised both Pyramids and Cross was the same attraction of power in a future life that raised the dome of Sancta Sofia and the Cathedral at Amiens, however much it was altered, enlarged, or removed to distance in space. Therefore, no single event has more puzzled historians than the sudden, unexplained appearance of at least two new natural forces[5] of the highest educational value in mechanics, for the first time within record of history. Literally, these two forces seemed to drop from the sky at the precise moment when the Cross on one side and the Crescent[6] on the other, proclaimed the complete triumph of the *Civitas Dei*. Had the Manichean doctrine[7] of Good and Evil as rival deities been orthodox, it would alone have accounted for this simultaneous victory of hostile powers.

Of the compass, as a step towards demonstration of the dynamic law, one may confidently say that it proved, better than any other force, the widening scope of the mind, since it widened immensely the range of contact between nature and thought. The compass educated. This must prove itself as needing no proof.

Of Greek fire[8] and gunpowder, the same thing cannot certainly be said, for they have the air of accidents due to the attraction of religious motives. They belong to the spiritual world; or to the doubtful ground of Magic which lay between Good and Evil. They were chemical forces, mostly explosives, which acted and still act as the most violent educators ever known to man, but they were justly

---

2. Pre-eminent masterpiece of Byzantine architecture (located in Istanbul) built in 532–37 by the Emperor Justinian.
3. Justinian (483–565), Byzantine Emperor, codified Roman civil law which unified the Empire, erected notable public works, and was actively involved in the theological disputes of his time.
4. Charlemagne (742?–814), Carolingian King of the Franks and Emperor of the Holy Roman Empire, extended and strengthened his empire through military victories, administrative prowess, and ed-

ucational and ecclesiastical reforms. Nicephoras II (912–969), Byzantine Emperor.
5. Adams refers to the introduction of the compass in navigation and gunpowder in warfare.
6. Religious symbol of Islam.
7. Manichean doctrine reflected a perpetual struggle between God's realm of light (good) and Satan's world of evil (dark).
8. Highly flammable chemical substance producing fire; used in naval warfare.

feared as diabolic, and whatever insolence man may have risked towards the milder teachers of his infancy, he was an abject pupil towards explosives. The Sieur de Joinville[9] left a record of the energy with which the relatively harmless Greek fire educated and enlarged the French mind in a single night in the year 1249,[1] when the crusaders were trying to advance on Cairo. The good king St. Louis and all his staff dropped on their knees at every fiery flame that flew by, praying—"God have pity on us!" and never had man more reason to call on his gods than they, for the battle of religion between Christian and Saracen was trifling compared with that of education between gunpowder and the Cross.

The fiction that society educated itself, or aimed at a conscious purpose, was upset by the compass and gunpowder which dragged and drove Europe at will through frightful bogs of learning. At first, the apparent lag for want of volume in the new energies lasted one or two centuries, which closed the great epochs of emotion by the Gothic cathedrals and scholastic theology. The moment had Greek beauty and more than Greek unity, but it was brief; and for another century or two, Western society seemed to float in space without apparent motion. Yet the attractive mass of nature's energy continued to attract, and education became more rapid than ever before. Society began to resist, but the individual showed greater and greater insistence, without realizing what he was doing. When the Crescent drove the Cross in ignominy from Constantinople in 1453,[2] Gutenberg[3] and Fust were printing their first Bible at Mainz under the impression that they were helping the Cross. When Columbus discovered the West Indies in 1492, the Church looked on it as a victory of the Cross. When Luther[4] and Calvin upset Europe half a century later, they were trying, like St. Augustine, to substitute the *Civitas Dei* for the *Civitas Romae*. When the Puritans set out for New England in 1620, they too were looking to found a *Civitas Dei* in State Street,[5] and when Bunyan made his Pilgrimage in 1678, he repeated St. Jerome.[6] Even when, after centuries of license, the Church reformed its discipline, and, to prove

9. Jean de Joinville (c. 1224–1317), French chronicler and biographer of Louis IX of France.
1. Egypt was attacked in 1249 during the Seventh Crusade, led by Louis IX (1214–70), King of France, but the expedition failed in 1250 when Louis was captured by the Arabs or Saracens.
2. Constantinople (now Istanbul) fell to the Ottoman Turks under Sultan Mohammed II (1430–81) on May 19, 1453.
3. Johann Gutenberg (1397–1468), German printer, the inventor of movable type. Fust (died c. 1466) was Gutenberg's printing partner.
4. Martin Luther (1483–1546) and John Calvin (1509–64), leaders of the Protestant Reformation.
5. Boston street, 19th-century hub of banking in the United States, the city being recognized as the financial center for the country.
6. John Bunyan (1628–88), author of *Pilgrim's Progress*. St. Jerome (c. 340–420), Church father who translated the Latin Bible (Vulgate) from the Greek. The parallel with Bunyan is a fanciful one, but Adams is perhaps suggesting that St. Jerome's spiritual efforts to render a correct Latin reading of the Bible resembled the later spiritual quest of Bunyan's hero who sought the "Celestial City" of true Christianity.

it, burned Giordano Bruno[7] in 1600, besides condemning Galileo in 1630—as science goes on repeating to us every day—it condemned anarchists, not atheists. None of the astronomers were irreligious men; all of them made a point of magnifying God through his works; a form of science which did their religion no credit. Neither Galileo nor Kepler,[8] neither Spinoza nor Descartes, neither Leibnitz nor Newton, any more than Constantine the Great—if so much—doubted Unity.[9] The utmost range of their heresies reached only its personality.

This persistence of thought-inertia is the leading idea of modern history. Except as reflected in himself, man has no reason for assuming unity in the universe, or an ultimate substance, or a prime-motor. The *a priori* insistence on this unity ended by fatiguing the more active—or reactive—minds; and Lord Bacon[1] tried to stop it. He urged society to lay aside the idea of evolving the universe from a thought, and to try evolving thought from the universe. The mind should observe and register forces—take them apart and put them together—without assuming unity at all. "Nature, to be commanded, must be obeyed." "The imagination must be given not wings but weights." As Galileo reversed the action of earth and sun, Bacon reversed the relation of thought to force. The mind was thenceforth to follow the movement of matter, and unity must be left to shift for itself.

The revolution in attitude seemed voluntary, but in fact was as mechanical as the fall of a feather. Man created nothing. After 1500, the speed of progress so rapidly surpassed man's gait as to alarm everyone, as though it were the acceleration of a falling body which the dynamic theory takes it to be. Lord Bacon was as much astonished by it as the Church was, and with reason. Suddenly society felt itself dragged into situations altogether new and anarchic—situations which it could not affect, but which painfully affected it. Instinct taught it that the universe in its thought must be in danger when its reflection lost itself in space. The danger was all the greater because men of science covered it with "larger synthesis,"[2] and poets called the undevout astronomer mad. Society knew better. Yet the telescope held it rigidly standing on its head;

7. Giordano Bruno (1548–1600), Italian philosopher, burned to death during the Inquisition for questioning Christian doctrines of transubstantiation and immaculate conception. Galileo Galilei (1564–1642), Italian astronomer; persecuted by the Inquisition for upholding Copernicus's heliocentric theory.
8. Johannes Kepler (1571–1630), German astronomer; Benedict Spinoza (1632–77), Dutch philosopher; René Descartes (1596–1650), French philosopher and mathematician; and Gottfried Wilhelm Leibnitz (1646–1716), German philosopher and mathematician.
9. Adams's expression for the theoretical disposition that the world is governed by an ordered structure rather than by chaos or multiplicity.
1. Francis Bacon (1561–1626), English statesman and natural philosopher.
2. Hegel's phrase from his theory of the dialectic in which he described the three phases of thought: thesis, antithesis, and synthesis, as building up through successive syntheses into a "larger synthesis," a more highly organized unity.

the microscope revealed a universe that defied the senses; gunpowder killed whole races that lagged behind; the compass coerced the most imbruted mariner to act on the impossible idea that the earth was round; the press drenched Europe with anarchism. Europe saw itself, violently resisting, wrenched into false positions, drawn along new lines as a fish that is caught on a hook; but unable to understand by what force it was controlled. The resistance was often bloody, sometimes humorous, always constant. Its contortions in the eighteenth century are best studied in the wit of Voltaire,[3] but all history and all philosophy from Montaigne and Pascal to Schopenhauer and Nietzsche deal with nothing else; and still, throughout it all, the Baconian law held good; thought did not evolve nature, but nature evolved thought. Not one considerable man of science dared face the stream of thought; and the whole number of those who acted, like Franklin, as electric conductors of the new forces from nature to man, down to the year 1800, did not exceed a few score, confined to a few towns in western Europe. Asia refused to be touched by the stream, and America, except for Franklin, stood outside.

Very slowly the accretion of these new forces, chemical and mechanical, grew in volume until they acquired sufficient mass to take the place of the old religious science, substituting their attraction for the attractions of the *Civitas Dei*, but the process remained the same. Nature, not mind, did the work that the sun does on the planets. Man depended more and more absolutely on forces other than his own, and on instruments which superseded his senses. Bacon foretold it: "Neither the naked hand nor the understanding, left to itself, can effect much. It is by instruments and helps that the work is done." Once done, the mind resumed its illusion, and society forgot its impotence; but no one better than Bacon knew its tricks, and for his true followers science always meant self-restraint, obedience, sensitiveness to impulse from without. "Non fingendum aut excogitandum sed inveniendum quid Natura faciat aut ferat."[4]

The success of this method staggers belief, and even today can be treated by history only as a miracle of growth, like the sports of nature. Evidently a new variety of mind had appeared. Certain men merely held out their hands—like Newton, watched

3. Pen name for François Marie Arouet (1694–1778), celebrated French satirist, religious skeptic, and advocate of freedom; Blaise Pascal (1623–62), French scientist and religious philosopher, stated that one must recognize the final necessity of faith to solve man's difficulties; Arthur Schopenhauer (1788–1860), German philosopher, who postulated the will, a nonrational and instinctual force which makes for never-ending conflict and tension in human affairs; Friedrich Nietzsche (1844–1900), German philosopher who extolled the creation of a superman to affirm life and the will to power.
4. "Not by supposition or thought but by inquiry learn what it is that nature might do or bring." From Bacon's *De Dignitate et Augmentis Scientiarum* (1623), the enlarged Latin version of his *Advancement of Learning* (1603).

an apple; like Franklin, flew a kite; like Watt,[5] played with a tea-kettle—and great forces of nature stuck to them as though she were playing ball. Governments did almost nothing but resist. Even gun-powder and ordnance, the great weapon of government, showed little development between 1400 and 1800. Society was hostile or indifferent, as Priestley and Jenner, and even Fulton,[6] with reason complained in the most advanced societies in the world, while its resistance became acute wherever the Church held control; until all mankind seemed to draw itself out in a long series of groups, dragged on by an attractive power in advance, which even the lead-ers obeyed without understanding, as the planets obeyed gravity, or the trees obeyed heat and light.

The influx of new force was nearly spontaneous. The reaction of mind on the mass of nature seemed not greater than that of a comet on the sun; and had the spontaneous influx of force stopped in Europe, society must have stood still, or gone backward, as in Asia or Africa. Then only economies of process would have counted as new force, and society would have been better pleased; for the idea that new force must be in itself a good is only an animal or vegetable instinct. As Nature developed her hidden energies, they tended to become destructive. Thought itself became tortured, suf-fering reluctantly, impatiently, painfully, the coercion of new method. Easy thought had always been movement of inertia, and mostly mere sentiment; but even the processes of mathematics measured feebly the needs of force.

The stupendous acceleration after 1800 ended in 1900 with the appearance of the new class of supersensual forces, before which the man of science stood at first as bewildered and helpless as, in the fourth century, a priest of Isis[7] before the Cross of Christ.

This, then, or something like this, would be a dynamic formula of history. Any schoolboy knows enough to object at once that it is the oldest and most universal of all theories. Church and State, the-ology and philosophy, have always preached it, differing only in the allotment of energy between nature and man. Whether the attrac-tive energy has been called God or Nature, the mechanism has been always the same, and history is not obliged to decide whether the Ultimate tends to a purpose or not, or whether ultimate energy is

---

5. James Watt (1736–1819), Scotsman who improved Newcomen's steam engine with a separate condensing chamber, in-sulation, and an air pump to bring steam into the engine.
6. All three men presented highly con-troversial inventions or modes of thought which led to their ridicule or rejection by society. Joseph Priestley's (1733–1804) unorthodox philosophical stance excluded him from Captain Cook's expe-dition to the South Seas; Edward Jen-ner's (1749–1823) vaccination against smallpox was described as dangerous and sacrilegious; and Robert Fulton's (1765–1815) unique steamboat, the *Clermont*, was nicknamed "Fulton's Folly."
7. The principal female deity in Egyp-tian mythology, symbolizing nature and worshiped throughout the Roman world as a goddess of the mysteries.

one or many. Everyone admits that the will is a free force, habitually decided by motives. No one denies that motives exist adequate
to decide the will; even though it may not always be conscious of
them. Science has proved that forces, sensible and occult, physical
and metaphysical, simple and complex, surround, traverse, vibrate,
rotate, repel, attract, without stop; that man's senses are conscious
of few, and only in a partial degree; but that, from the beginning of
organic existence, his consciousness has been induced, expanded,
trained in the lines of his sensitiveness; and that the rise of his faculties from a lower power to a higher, or from a narrower to a wider
field, may be due to the function of assimilating and storing outside
force or forces. There is nothing unscientific in the idea that,
beyond the lines of force felt by the senses, the universe may be—as
it has always been—either a supersensuous chaos or a divine unity,
which irresistibly attracts, and is either life or death to penetrate.
Thus far, religion, philosophy, and science seem to go hand in
hand. The schools begin their vital battle only there. In the earlier
stages of progress, the forces to be assimilated were simple and easy
to absorb, but, as the mind of man enlarged its range, it enlarged
the field of complexity, and must continue to do so, even into
chaos, until the reservoirs of sensuous or supersensuous energies are
exhausted, or cease to affect him, or until he succumbs to their
excess.

For past history, this way of grouping its sequences may answer
for a chart of relations, although any serious student would need to
invent another, to compare or correct its errors; but past history is
only a value of relation to the future, and this value is wholly one
of convenience, which can be tested only by experiment. Any law of
movement must include, to make it a convenience, some mechanical formula of acceleration.

                                                        1907, 1918

American Literature between the Wars
1914–1945

IN THE EARLY decades of the twentieth century the United States emerged as a major power whose actions in diplomacy, warfare, and political and economic affairs had profound and durable consequences on the international scene. There was a comparable accession of power in American writing which gave new urgency to the view of American culture set forth in 1870 in *Democratic Vistas* by Walt Whitman. There the poet issued a double challenge to the American imagination. On the one hand he celebrated the emergence of artists "commensurate with the people" and burdened them with the mission to remold society and to bring to their fulfillment the new eras in human history that he found incarnate in the American experiment. On the other hand he defined a profound crisis for the arts, itemizing the manifest deficiencies, the diseased corrosions of American civilization, which threatened increasingly to betray the high expectations it had aroused, and he warned that they might bring on a catastrophe comparable to the fate in hell of the "fabled damned." In the period encompassing two world wars and the Great Depression of 1929, ambitious missions for the arts comparable to those defined by Whitman, and comparably dire warnings agitated American writers, defining the confidence and boldness with which the best pursued their careers and sought recognition, but defining also the anxiety, even desperate urgency, with which most scrutinized their traditions and their contemporary environment as they weighed the chances for human fulfillment and sought to shape conditions that would enable them to fulfill their aspirations as artists.

They were the heirs of a provincial culture in the nineteenth century, located on the "circumference of civilization," as James wrote of Hawthorne's America, and, therefore, distant from the centers of power and taste in Europe. It was an America where literary pursuits and institutions were comparatively insecure in the experimental, still new society, and where writers with distinctive talents were partially alienated from the institutions and prevailing tastes of their environment. Those very insecurities and that alienation proved, however, in the late nineteenth and twentieth centuries, to be the very basis of the American tradition, a stimulus as much as a threat, and enabled American writers to play a leading role as innovators in the literary revolution that took shape in English and American letters during World War I. From the beginning Americans had been familiar with rootlessness, accelerated historical change, and cultural dislocations, and they were practiced, as Gertrude Stein noted, at coping with them, struggling to avoid the mere imitation of imported or established literary modes, striving to forge new ratios between form and substance in literary art, and seeking new ways to invigorate the language and establish contact with their audiences. The American tradition sustained the effort to confront and express the discontinuities and dislocations which were to be dominant characteristics of modern writing.

REASSESSMENT OF AMERICAN CULTURAL TRADITIONS

A reassessment of American cultural traditions was one of the major undertakings of creative writers and critics alike. Emerson's awareness that his traditions were in a state of flux and that an age of "transition" was a stimulus to creativity was heightened in the twentieth century. To see the epoch of World War I as "America's Coming of Age" (the title of Van Wyck Brooks's critical volume in 1915) aroused concern not only about the future but about the preceding stages, and the southern poet-critic Allen Tate later insisted that a period of transition was a stimulus to the imagination because diverging forms of behavior, conflicting values, or varied tastes and literary conventions were clearly juxtaposed, and they encouraged writers to compare and sift them. The exploration of their native past that the writers undertook reshaped it into a tradition more supportive of their efforts, more varied in its resources, and more firm in its orientation than had been the case earlier. They discovered the poetry of Emily Dickinson, first published in 1890 and issued piecemeal until the 1940s, and established her as one of the chief figures in American letters. They rediscovered Melville in the 1920s and reassessed Henry James in the 1930s, reargued the merits of Whitman and Mark Twain, and defined a durable importance for these writers that continued to be influential after World War II in American cultural circles and in the new British universities as well.

REGIONAL TRADITIONS

The New Englanders Thoreau, Emerson, and Hawthorne remained highly esteemed, and the poets Robinson and Frost paid tribute to their New England predecessors. But the long-dominant New England tradition more widely came under attack for the evasive gentility and prim idealism that it had encouraged. Aspects of the specifically Puritan tradition came under particularly intense scrutiny. It was attacked in the 1920s for its constraints and moral severity by the critic H. L. Mencken and others and for its reinforcement of the inhibiting complacencies of the middle-class "booboisie." But the subtleties of its contributions to American culture and its importance in defining the national character and America's "mission" were emphasized by Harvard historians and others in the 1930s and 1940s.

Groups and regions outside New England asserted their claims to recognition and importance, possibly because shifts in population and economic power were generating new energies there or because these subcultures—their familiar values and the mores of their communities—seemed threatened by industrialism and the increasing standardization of American life. Southern writers, although they broke away from the pieties of the plantation myth that dominated post–Civil War southern literature, explored their ties to an agrarian past that had been repudiated by the industrial North (as in the manifesto *I'll Take My Stand,* 1930); as critics, fiction writers, and poets they made the South the dominant regional force in national letters through the 1940s. Many midwestern writers were more apt than southerners to acknowledge the lure of the East Coast or foreign lands in the themes of their works. Sinclair Lewis and Sherwood Anderson subjected the small cities of Minnesota and Ohio and their commercial aspirations to scathing scrutiny; but their fiction, like F. Scott Fitzgerald's and Willa Cather's, was informed by a sense that a more wholesome past was slipping away and that regional traditions sanctioning innocence, simplicity, and dreams of enterprise and self-fulfillment were standards against which to measure the corrosions of contemporary society. For midwestern writers, even those who left the region in the course of their careers, Chicago became a center of ferment and stimulus. Asserting its prominence as an economic and cultural center, it was, as Carl Sandburg exclaims in his poem *Chicago,* a "tall bold slugger set vivid against the little soft cities." It provided writers with bohemian residential areas, literary salons, opportunities in journalism, and publishing outlets of international importance like Harriet Monroe's *Poetry, a Magazine of Verse* and Margaret Anderson's *The Little Review.*

New York City, however, remained the publishing center of the nation, and two neighborhoods there became important literary centers. In uptown Manhattan, Harlem, its fine avenues, its night spots featuring jazz music, as well as its congested slums, became the metropolitan center of black culture in the United States beginning in the earliest decades of the century, when rural black people were migrating by the thousands to urban centers and blacks in New York City, responding to the pressures of residential and economic segregation, completed the transformation of white suburban Harlem into a black ghetto. With heightened consciousness of their racial and community identity, black intellectuals launched in the 1920s the first important movement in black American literature, the "Harlem Renaissance," to strengthen the cultural traditions of their people and demonstrate their achievements to the white society that habitually ignored them. During the same decades, Greenwich Village in lower Manhattan, with its inexpensive tenements and relative isolation from the institutions of the native-born white middle-class, became the haven of literary and intellectual bohemians, prominent writers and intellectuals as well as "inglorious Miltons by the score, and Rodins, one to every floor," as the radical John Reed wrote mockingly in *The Day in Bohemia.* In the Village they found the freedom to pursue styles of living at odds with notions of propriety prevailing elsewhere, to circumvent the Prohibition laws against the sale of alcoholic beverages, and to experiment with radical political ideas and new literary forms.

THE CRISIS

The excitement of life in Harlem and in the Village (they became tourist attractions for other New Yorkers and outsiders alike) did much to set the tone for which "The Jazz Age" or "The Twenties" became famous. But the experimentation with radical ideas and new modes in the arts which marked the 1920s was not unique to the decade; it was an authentic response to a crisis in American culture that took shape earlier but was intensified during World War I (1914–18) and its aftermath, even though America's distance from the battlefields and relatively late entry into combat (1917) protected it from the worst consequences of a war which strained European economies, decimated their populations, and cut off the careers of countless young intellectuals. To many, like the novelists Hemingway and Dos Passos, who witnessed it, but to many more, like the pacifist philosopher John Dewey or the poet Ezra Pound, who did not, the war which President Woodrow Wilson proclaimed would "make the world safe for democracy" proved to be a senseless slaughter in the name of a "botched civilization." Postwar diplomacy, establishing the League of Nations on the shifting sands of power politics, seemed a futile and cynical charade.

The intellectuals' aroused concern as well as their imminent disenchantment quickened the efforts begun in the post–Civil War decades to scrutinize and challenge more forcefully the ideals of democracy and the institutions that presumably secured it, the institutions of industrial and finance capitalism which were becoming so dominant in all aspects of social and cultural life, and the institutions of the family and sexual codes that had been central in the structure of American values. Racial violence and industrial strife in the late war years and early 1920s, an aroused socialist movement, and scandalous corruption in league with official complacency during the presidency of William G. Harding intensified the challenge.

Late in the 1920s new jolts to American society extended the crisis into the 1930s and sharpened writers' sense of urgency about their mission. Open evasion of the Prohibition laws and illicit traffic in "bootleg" liquor were accompanied by the advent of gang warfare in major cities, marking a decay in private and public morals. Poverty spread through rural areas in the 1920s and 1930s, and the stock market crash of 1929 bankrupted individuals and institutions throughout the nation and sent shock waves through the economies of Europe, where fascist Italy and Nazi Germany were preparing the way for the outbreak of World War II in 1939. Industrial retrenchment and widespread unemployment during the Great Depression of the 1930s and the explosive violence of industrial strife between corporations and the labor force occasioned a major reorientation of American political and economic life under President Franklin D. Roosevelt's "New Deal," launched in 1933 to cope with the conditions which had reduced countless Americans to lives of unquiet desperation. To the crises of the 1920s and 1930s American writers responded by re-examining and redefining their distinctively American traditions and by treating social problems more explicitly in fiction and poetry as well as in literary journalism. They also looked to Europe for ideas, programs, and forms that could guide or implement their efforts.

AMERICA AND EUROPE

Though the poet William Carlos Williams and others, like James Fenimore Cooper in the early nineteenth century, warned against subservience to foreign models, Williams and most others responded nonetheless to major currents of thought and taste abroad. Indeed, Americans responded to European precedent with more confidence than before, rivaling while seeking to appropriate and adjust such models to their own purposes and determined to have a reciprocal impact abroad.

Marxism and Freudianism

Karl Marx's indictment of capitalism and his economic and historical theories, though familiar to such earlier American social critics as Thorstein Veblen, became widely influential in literary and intellectual circles after

1915. Interest in European radicalism, including anarchism and communism, was heightened by the outbreak in 1917 of the Russian Revolution, which held forth the hope of a strikingly new solution to social and political problems. Marxist thought infused the radicalism of Max Eastman and John Reed, editors of *The Masses* (at the time of its suppression in 1917 for opposition to the war) and of its successor, *The Liberator,* subsequently named *The New Masses,* which became the official journal of the American Communist party. These journals reinforced the critique of American society sustained by the conservative H. L. Mencken of *The American Mercury* and the liberal journalism of *The New Republic* and *The Nation.* And Marxist theory, along with radical organizations pursuing socialist aims, helped shape the careers of the critic Edmund Wilson and such fiction writers as Theodore Dreiser, John Dos Passos, Herbert Gold, and Richard Wright in the 1930s. Marxists and social critics informed by Marxist thought were among those in the 1930s, following the crash of 1929, who demanded that writers take direct cognizance of social and economic problems and enlist their writing in the cause of advancing social change or revolution. The suppression of dissent in Russia, demands for conformity within communist organizations in this country, and the alignment in 1939 of Stalinist Russia with Hitler's Germany disillusioned many intellectuals with communist-oriented radicalism; but Marxist theory continued to be influential in subsequent decades.

Freudianism, the theory and practice of psychoanalysis as defined by the Viennese doctor Sigmund Freud, was another Continental movement that penetrated deeply into American intellectual life. Psychoanalysis stressed the importance of the unconscious or the irrational in the human psyche; the dramas and dream symbols generated in the mind by mechanisms, psychological and social, of sexual repression; the pervasiveness of "discontents" that underlie all civilization; the ways in which psychic experience is masked or veiled by common language and the conscious operations of the mind; and the capacity of "depth psychology" to diagnose psychic illness and try, at least, to cure it. Freud found a readier acceptance in America (where he first lectured in 1909) than in Europe, and his theories, after becoming a fad in the journalism of the 1920s, inspired in subsequent decades a host of novels and such reinterpretations of American culture as Ludwig Lewisohn's *Expression in America* (1932). More significantly, psychoanalytic theory seemed to sanction quests for sexual liberation in actual behavior and disdain for established conventions which inhibited fulfillment of the self. Rival psychoanalysts, including Alfred Adler and Carl Jung, added new versions to the literature of psychoanalysis. By 1940 "the psychiatrist," the "archetypal symbol," and "the Oedipus complex" had become part of modern mythology, and both the mythology and the theories of psychoanalysis had infused literature as varied as the poems of Conrad Aiken, the plays of Eugene O'Neill, and most poetry and fiction that drew heavily on the subconscious implications of symbolic forms or probed the depths of psychic experience.

European Arts

Contemporary European movements in the arts also inspired new undertakings in American literature after 1914. In fiction the Irish novelist James Joyce perfected techniques of "realism" that rendered the surface textures of ordinary life while penetrating the hidden depths of psychological and social reality and, at the same time, radically altered novelistic conventions so as to accommodate patterns of classical myth, parodic manipulations of language, expressionistic effects, and allusive symbolic forms. Comparably innovative achievements in the music of Stravinsky, Hindemith, and Schoenberg (all of whom later emigrated to the United States) sounded cacophonous to large audiences but provocative to vanguard writers, and in 1913 a painting exhibition, the "Armory Show," which opened in New York City and traveled to Boston and Chicago, had a similar effect in introducing contemporary modes of painting. American painters advancing a bolder kind of "realism" than had prevailed in the nineteenth century (some were dubbed derisively the "Ash Can" school) were displayed alongside an immense selection representing the newest modes in European art. Particularly the explosively colorful Fauves and various forms of abstract painting from Europe, defying earlier conventions of representation and engaging in experiments with the basic elements of line, color, and the sheer medium of paint, shocked while intriguing thousands of viewers and sanctioned for vanguard writers new ways of treating their materials and more daring ways of dealing with their audiences. The emigration of European artists to the United States, which accelerated in the 1930s and 1940s, when totalitarian regimes abroad threatened the lives of Jews and radical dissidents, simply facilitated an exchange that was important in American culture from the 1920s on.

The Expatriates

Americans who chose to live abroad, by the very fact of their expatriation, presented a challenge to the American society they left and welcomed the stimulus of contemporary movements and cultural traditions in the countries where they resided. But expatriation, a common pattern in the cultural history of England and European countries since 1800, did not constitute a simple repudiation of American society, though it admittedly ran the risk of severance from familiar materials and a responsive audience, as the critic Van Wyck Brooks warned in his *Pilgrimage of Henry James* (1925). Instead, expatriation was an extension of America's traditions and part of the effort to redefine and strengthen them. Some expatriates settled abroad for frivolous reasons, and all benefited from the fact that living and publishing expenses were cheaper in other countries and that in France publication in English was not subject to censorship. But for earlier Americans, as for Donatello in Hawthorne's *The Marble Faun*, rootlessness was a condition which could eventually bring freedom and responsibility, and it was a condition with which they were familiar, whether they sought liberation and opportunities for their talent by moving into frontier territories and the West, by moving to cultural centers in the East, or by establishing residence in or near the capitals of England and Europe. American writers as diverse as James Fenimore Cooper, Nathaniel Hawthorne, and Henry James had lived for protracted periods of time outside the United States and had incorporated cosmopolitan perspectives in their writing. In the twentieth century some Americans decided to live in Europe early in their careers and stayed permanently; Gertrude Stein, T. S. Eliot, and Ezra Pound were the most famous examples. Others stayed for a protracted period (the poet Archibald MacLeish planned in advance a five-year stay in France) and then returned. The black novelist Richard Wright lived for the last fifteen years of his life in France. Hemingway spent years intermittently abroad, then returned to the edges of the United States to live on islands off Florida and Cuba. For most, the experience sharpened their sense of American identity and entailed choosing deliberately and selectively, like Emerson before them, those traditions, American or foreign, which would sustain their art. In the case of Pound and Eliot, they attained an importance on the London cultural scene comparable to that of the American expatriate painters Benjamin West and James McNeill Whistler in the nineteenth century, and they played leading roles, boldly and shrewdly, in the revolution of taste which established modern modes in Anglo-American literature.

MODERNISM

That revolution took shape in a convergence of tendencies in modern culture, accidental circumstance, and concerted effort on the part of influential writers, some politically conservative and some radical.

Imagism

It began to emerge after 1908 in the movement Imagism and the reaction of the English writer T. E. Hulme and his followers against amorphous abstraction, clichéd "poetic" diction, indulgent ornamentation, and monotonous regularity of meter in Victorian and Edwardian poetry. Ezra Pound issued an anthology of Imagist poems (*Des Imagistes,* 1914), and the American poet Amy Lowell, a propagandist for the movement, issued subsequent anthologies in 1915, 1916, and 1917. The 1915 Imagist "manifesto" warned against "sonorous" generalizations, "merely decorative" diction, and "old rhythms," and called instead for a poetic of the "exact word" and "common speech," "new rhythms," compression of statement, a "poetry that is hard and clear," and "free verse" as a "principle of liberty." The demand for precision and common speech was perfectly compatible with the experiments being worked out in prose at the same time by Gertrude Stein, and Pound defined the Imagists' aims more precisely. But the movement was soon superseded by others and by the more varied principles and practices of innovative writers in prose and verse that revealed the more ambitious aims and governing principles of Modernist writing.

Discontinuity and Fragmentation

One characteristic feature of Modernism is that it dramatizes discontinuity, the sense of disjunction and imminent severance from the past, while making determined efforts to appropriate the past, its values, and its artistic forms by incorporating them in new acts of creation. Pound's translations, the subtle echoes and quotations of earlier verse in Eliot's poems, William Carlos Williams's essays *In the American Grain,* or the disjunctive structure of Faulkner's fiction display in varied ways the urgency of this undertaking. A second characteristic is fragmentation: the sense that individual experience consists of severed or loosely connected pieces or moments, and that communities are atomized into individuals or groups that are antagonistic or distant from one another. The literature incorporates and expresses this fragmentation in varied ways—exposing it often in stunned repudiation or mordant satire, sometimes with a sense of futility verging on despair—while reaching beyond it toward possibilities of both self-integration and personal and social communion.

Language, Form, and Audience

A third feature of literary Modernism is its concern with language, all aspects of its medium, and the problematic relations between literature and its audiences. American writers had been anxious about these matters since the days of Cooper, Melville, and Whitman, but modern writers felt more intensely that the language prevailing in literary works was debilitated and needed resuscitation, that the conventions comprising their medium had become stale and needed either replacement or reworking, and that audiences had been numbed by the spread of minimal literacy and the impact of standardized journalism and cheapened tastes. Most significant writing in the twentieth century undertook to remake the language of literature, to experiment with new conventions of poetic structure and prose narration, and to establish new connections with audiences who needed to be prepared to respond to unfamiliar modes of writing.

Much poetry and popular fiction continued to cater to outmoded tastes and reading habits, and sensational journalism along with the diversions of movies and radio made it increasingly difficult for serious writers to reach large audiences, whose reading habits and preferences were not receptive to innovations. The most ambitious writers met the challenge by attacking the currently established foundations of writing in the attempt to reconstitute them. The variety of their strategies in this effort was striking, and their effects were of lasting importance. They found ways to capture the pace, tensions, and rhythms of urban life; they shaped the cadences of black dialect, of southern rhetoric, of colloquial speech as actually spoken into a medium for prose narration, for dialogue in fiction, and for lyric poetry. At times they abandoned or mocked conventions of punctuation and stanza form in verse; at other times they converted such conventions or the sonnet form to new uses. They wanted to extend the range of literature, to augment its resources and to perfect the techniques for controlling literary statement and the reactions of readers. For these purposes they exploited at times the irregularities of rhymeless free verse or the inconclusiveness of open form and improvisation, and relied at other times on tightly governed narrative form (as in Fitzgerald and Hemingway) or regular stanzas in verse. Some poets revived ancient or foreign stanza patterns (as did Pound in his early poems) or incorporated the forms of popular songs and ballads (as did Langston Hughes in his "blues"), often displaying the relish of sheer ingenuity which appeared also in the unique new stanza patterns devised by Marianne Moore. In fiction as well as in verse, writers drew on the complexities, and often the subtly implicit or subconscious effects, of symbolic forms so as to render them firmly functional rather than merely ornamental or clumsily imposed, as instruments. They adapted traditional epic conventions and seminal myths, ancient and modern, to enlarge the scale, define the ironies, or reveal and make persuasive the moral significance of their works.

Many of these strategies made for writing that was notably difficult to apprehend and appreciate and for writing that was in certain ways devious in its approach to its audiences because it ignored or violated familiar ways of revealing meaning and avoided certain sure ways of appealing to their expectations (pretty ornament, clichés, formulaic adventure plots, complacent optimism, overt moralizing, ingratiating addresses to "dear reader," and the like). Many modern productions in prose or verse are presented without overt solicitation of the reader's interest, emotions, or understanding and are difficult to apprehend because they are designed instead to have the vividness and discrete independence of a well-made artifact, the reality of an object. That objectivity is the work's claim on the reader's attention, and other appeals remain tacit or covert. Yet both the difficulty and the deviousness testify to the deliberateness with which the important writers of the period undertook to address their society. If modern society consisted not of one single audience but a "checkerboard" of different and separate audiences, as Henry James had discerned, one might hope for a response from some but not all audiences or make a variety of appeals designed to educate the audiences and create the taste for modern writing. Common to the strategies pursued by many vanguard writers was that of articulating or dramatizing the barrier between writer and audience by bluntly and explicitly assaulting the audience's expectations or by proceeding in seeming indifference to its needs, in either case catching and holding readers' attention by shocking them into a new alertness. Virtually new to American writing (though there were precedents in Melville and Twain) is the devious and sportive playfulness, the virtuoso posturing, the indulgent frivolity which in some poetry and fiction replaced the solemnity with which authors customarily had addressed their subjects and their readers.

THE INSTITUTIONALIZATION OF MODERNISM

Thanks to whatever luck and astuteness, the new modes gradually became dominant during the decades between the two wars, in part because leading writers campaigned for the new modes in countless journalistic essays and in critical essays of great subtlety and force, in part because they institutionalized their undertaking. Pound was the chief agent in these affairs, issuing manifestoes, serving on editorial boards, editing manuscripts, and goading publishers. Journals promoting the vanguard arts, the so-called "little magazines," multiplied on both sides of the ocean after 1912. Important writers became their editors or founded their own magazines as outlets for new creative productions and for their own critical essays. Pound's and Wyndham Lewis's *Blast* (1914–15) in London, *The Seven Arts* (1916–17) in New York City, *The Fugitive* (1922–25) in Memphis, Tennessee, and *The Dial* (1880–1929) in New York City were among the most important. *The Criterion* (1922–29), founded and edited by T. S. Eliot, was the most influential critical journal. Presses in London and Paris were pressed into service, and on one occasion two poets, Louis Zukovsky and William Carlos Williams, established a press (the short-lived Objectivist Press) which published Williams's own *Collected Poems*. Eliot became an important editor at Faber & Faber in London and the poet Allen Tate became poetry editor at Henry Holt in New York. In the theater, the Provincetown Players, founded in 1915, produced experimental plays by Edna St. Vincent Millay, E. E. Cummings, Sherwood Anderson, and landmark works by Eugene O'Neill which introduced expressionistic techniques (masks and symbolic forms to define subjective experience) into the American theater. Beginning with the poet-critic John Crowe Ransom at the end of World War I and with increasing frequency after 1930, prominent writers, including Allen Tate and the novelists Robert Penn Warren and Katherine Anne Porter, secured posts in colleges and universities which facilitated the acceptance of the new literature in academia and among younger generations of students. After 1940 established poets like E. E. Cummings and William Carlos Williams, along with Robert Frost and T. S. Eliot and, later, novelists, found new and widening audiences by recording their works on phonograph records for libraries and commercial companies and by giving public readings on countless campuses.

TRADITION AND REVOLUTION

The new modes of writing that became in these ways firmly established in the American literary tradition did not win acceptance without opposition. In the late 1950s Walter Allen and a number of other English critics who had been most appreciative of American achievements began to back away from the writing of Eliot's and Pound's generation, deploring the neglect of other English poets and claiming that the revolution in Anglo-American writing had been chiefly an American imposition on the English tradition. Before that, notable American literary historians, including Van Wyck Brooks, had called into question the validity of the new modes of writing, and the poet Archibald MacLeish, on returning from France in 1930, declared that poetry of his generation (including his own) had surrendered to pessimism, alienation, nostalgia, political conservatism, and the cry of individual isolation voiced so eloquently in Eliot's *The Waste Land*. He called for an extension of the revolution in aesthetics into a social revolution and for an art of "public speech" addressed, more directly than he thought his generation's had been, to social, economic, and moral issues. The new poetry and prose, however, had never ignored these issues, and political liberals, if not radicals, along with such notable conservatives as Pound and Eliot, had helped generate the literary revolution emerging in the early decades of the century. MacLeish's demands projected not so much a repudiation of the new literary modes as a renewed effort to extend them which had been part of the dynamics of American cultural history since the 1920s. The poet Hart Crane recognized astutely in 1930 that the literary revolution, by virtue of its very success, had created the problem of how to keep it from petrifying, how to sustain it as a tradition in new and continually varied creative effort. "Revolution flourishes still," he wrote in *Modern Poetry*, but "rather as a contemporary tradition. * * * It persists as a rapid momentum in certain groups or movements, but often in forms that are more constricting than liberating." A decade before, a poet, critic, and novelist who had helped launch the new movement, William Carlos Williams, charted the strategy that had, along with the efforts of expatriates, helped inaugurate the revolution in the first place and did the most to keep it a vital tradition, a sustaining force, for writers after World War II. Expatriate poets had betrayed the aims of Modernism by their undisguised use of foreign settings and the formal techniques of traditional verse, he declared in 1923, and he called for continually new experimentation that drew on specifically American settings and speech patterns, on the American environment and aspects of its traditions that the cosmopolitan writers had either obscured or ignored. However different his program, the impulses and traditions behind his demands were essentially the same that had impelled his antagonists to revamp tradition, to "make it new," as Pound had declared, and change the course of literary history. It was the full variety of American writers' achievements that transmitted to the post–World War II generation a strengthened and still generative literary tradition.

EZRA POUND
1885–1972

In 1908 Ezra Loomis Pound, a young scholar and poet, left his native
America for Venice and London, convinced that the authority of the arts
in America was unrecognized and insecure, and determined to reconstitute
the very foundations of literature and its sustaining civilization in the West.
His reception since 1930 has been complicated by his anti-Semitism, his
affiliation with fascist Italy during World War II, the charge of treason
brought against him by the United States, and the diagnosis of insanity
that resulted in the suspension of his trial and eventual dismissal of the
charge. But within six years after Pound's arrival in Europe in 1908, he had
become one of the dominant figures on the London literary scene. His
numerous critical and scholarly productions, his efforts on behalf of other
writers, the twelve volumes of verse that formed the basis for the collection
Personae issued in 1926, and the one hundred sixteen *Cantos* that he published between 1916 and 1969 made him the most important single figure,
with the most continuously sustained influence on other authors, in
Anglo-American poetry of the twentieth century.

He was born in Hailey, Idaho, to parents who had roots in New England
and upper New York State as well as in the West, and who settled, when
Pound was an infant, in a comfortable suburb near Philadelphia where his
father was employed by the Mint. His parents always maintained a genuine,
if often puzzled, interest in his career. He studied American history, the
ancient classics, and English literature at the University of Pennsylvania for
two years, then studied Old English and the Romance literatures at Hamilton College, where he graduated in 1905. He returned to Pennsylvania for
an M.A. (1906) preparatory to a career as a teacher and scholar of Romance
literatures. His dismissal from his first post at Wabash College in Indiana
(for innocuously offering shelter to a jobless burlesque queen) precipitated
his departure for Europe, but he never lost his ambition to teach nor his
sense of identification with his American origins. He taught in London at
the Regent Street Polytechnic in 1908–9, offering courses in Renaissance
and medieval literature while at the same time he was establishing his
reputation as a poet. His translations and scholarly studies of these materials
appeared as *The Spirit of Romance* in 1910; *A Lume Spento*, his first
volume of verse, was published in Venice in 1908, while *A Quinzaine for
This Yule* and *Personae* were published in London in 1908 and 1909. He
married Dorothy Shakespeare (who later bore him his only son) in 1914.
By then his zeal for teaching, combined, as T. S. Eliot remarked, with the
tactics of a "campaigner,"[1] was being channeled into his critical essays and
pronouncements advancing the cause of his own and others' poetic talents.

Although he remained an expatriate—lured by the dream of a world in
which cultural values would not be divorced from political and economic
structures as he found them to be in modern America—he became a conspicuously *American* expatriate, conscious of his American identity and

---

1. Introduction, *Literary Essays of Ezra Pound* (1954), p. xii.

using it strategically like Benjamin Franklin, Walt Whitman, and Benjamin West, the expatriate painter, before him. His memoir *Indiscretions* (1923) dwelt affectionately, if ironically, on his parents' gentility but underscored the Pounds' affiliations with the rough frontier of his lumberman grandfather in the West and the local notoriety of his mother's family in upper New York. (His father had had an Indian nurse; the Loomises had been known with some justification as horse thieves.) Sharing an obsession with his predecessors Cooper, Hawthorne, and Henry James, he had earlier noted that "Mrs. Columbia has no mysterious & shadowy past to make her interesting,"[2] and his compensatory sense of national identity became a consciously cultivated role, a willed Americanism as carefully defined and strenuously pursued as Whitman's, its characteristic signs showing in the boldness of his critical stance, his use of raw slang in his criticism (and obscenities in his letters), and his infusion of colloquialisms and slang into his poetry. Yet his role as an American expatriate included a willed cosmopolitanism that recalls Edgar Allan Poe: he is like Poe in his allegiance to exacting and extranational standards of taste, the bluntness with which he held writers accountable for lapses from such standards, and his determination to codify those standards, if not to redefine them from scratch, in an effort to reconstitute a literary tradition.

To that task Pound brought a rhetoric of revolutionary radicalism more strident than that of the contemporary Georgian poets who were calling for a literary "revolt" against the writers of the decadence, academicism in the arts, and Victorianism. Behind what T. S. Eliot later called "the revolution in taste and practice which [Pound] has brought about"[3] was an ambition as striking as Milton's in his striving for personal supremacy—Richard Aldington noted that Pound wanted to be "literary dictator of London"[4]—and in the mission he defined for the arts as the instrument for refounding civilization. Then as later in his career his tactics threatened to become mere petulance and bellicosity, and he enjoyed the delights of self-dramatization: for example, he wrote Harriet Monroe that "For one man I strike there are ten to strike back at me. I stand exposed."[5] Nevertheless, Pound's motives were genuine when scorning "the abominable dogbiscuit of Milton's rhetoric."[6] His literary criticism was part of a large-scale program to overhaul Anglo-American cultural traditions. (Characteristically, he came to terms with his traditions and predecessors by wrestling with them, as in the case of Whitman.)

Pound had, as he said, a "plymouth-rock conscience landed on a predilection for the arts,"[7] and his undertakings combined the fervor of a missionary with the enterprise of a colonizer. Essays such as *Patria Mia* (1912), *Prolegomena* (1912), and *Renaissance* (1914) constituted the "propaganda" that Pound thought necessary to launch a renaissance in American culture. Scholarship and the various arts should be partners in the search for models that were not to be imitated or plagiarized, but recreated, emulated, and surpassed. Poets were to break away from the poetics of "emotional slither," using "fewer painted adjectives" which impede "the shock and

2. Quoted by Alan Holder, *Three Voyagers in Search of Europe* (1965), p. 216.
3. *Literary Essays*, p. xii.
4. Quoted by Norman, *Ezra Pound* (1960), p. 273.
5. *Letters*, p. 13.
6. *Pavannes and Divisions* (1918), p. 247.
7. *Letters*, p. 12.

stroke" of authentic verse.[8] Poets should go "against the grain of contemporary taste," and writers were to be as boldly eclectic as Emerson wished, ranging through past and foreign cultures in their search for models or "instigations," he declared in *Renaissance*. They should ransack particular eras of history to uncover lost traditions, as Pound did in finding a "New Greece" in the culture of China. The arts could be subsidized by endowed, self-perpetuating trusts; these would free artists from the need to flatter an "ignorant" public or to meet the demands of commercial bureaucracies, which he scorned.

This design for cultural revolution governed Pound's almost incredible efforts on behalf of other artists, as well as the critical and scholarly activities he pursued in the decades before 1925. He was briefly the secretary and of a life-long friend of the Irish poet William Butler Yeats, a friend and sparring partner of William Carlos Williams, and promoted the music of the American composer George Antheil—Pound himself composed music. Pound was the first important reviewer to praise Frost's *A Boy's Will* in 1913 and recognized his "VURRY Amur'k'n" talent[9] before Frost was known on either side of the Atlantic. He was instrumental in getting Joyce's *Portrait of the Artist* published serially in *The Egoist*, and arranged for the publication of Marianne Moore's first book. He secured the appearance of Eliot's first published work in *Poetry*, and later, in one of the important instances of creative editing in the twentieth century, he suggested crucial inclusions and deletions in the manuscript of Eliot's *The Waste Land*. He championed the modernist sculpture of Gaudier-Brzeska, later killed in World War I, but Pound's *Memoir* (1916) of the sculptor was not only a personal tribute but a manifesto in Pound's critical campaign and an exploration of his own aesthetic principles.

While serving as foreign correspondent for Harriet Monroe's *Poetry* and editor of the anthology *Des Imagistes* (1913), Pound had joined Richard Aldington, Hilda Doolittle, and others in formulating the doctrines of Imagism, a movement advancing modernism in the arts which concentrated on reforming the medium of poetry. Pound endorsed the group's three main principles—the "direct treatment" of poetic subjects, elimination of merely ornamental or "superfluous" words, and rhythmical composition in the sequence of the supple "musical phrase" rather than in the "sequence of a metronome"—and Pound provided the title "Imagiste" for the group. But he also developed definitions of their aims that disclose his personal conception of the authority to be achieved by a new poetics. An image, he wrote in *A Few Don'ts by an Imagiste*, is "that which presents an intellectual and emotional complex in an instant of time," and he interpreted the term *complex* as a notably energized verbal experience that yields a "sudden liberation," expresses a "sense of freedom" and "sudden growth."[1] While he wanted *imagism* to mean "hard light, clear edges" in the textures of verse, and warned poets to "Go in fear of abstractions," his emphasis on the kinetic charge generated by verbal forms was the basis for his break with the Imagists and his launching (with the sculptors Jacob Epstein and Gaudier-Brzeska, the painter Wyndham Lewis, and others) of the movement Vorticism, whose theories dominated the short-lived magazine

---

8. *Literary Essays*, p. 12.   1. *Literary Essays*, pp. 4–5.
9. *Letters*, p. 114.

Blast in 1914–15. The principles of Vorticism remained central to Pound's poetic strategies, although he later used other vocabularies for defining them. Imagism, he felt, tended to produce visual and static patterns, while Vorticism called for forms that were both sculptural and generative of movement and power. Pound conceived the vortex as some generative "primary form"[2] that is prior to the specific forms in any art. In cultural history, a vortex is a period of shared ferment in the arts, or the channeling of effort and purpose that makes a city into a cultural capital. In poetry, an image is a "VORTEX," a "word beyond formulated language," "a radiant node or cluster * * * from which, and through which, and into which, ideas are constantly rushing."[3]

During these same years Pound was engaged in the study of Oriental literature, an interest evident in his own versions of Japanese *haiku* and translations from the Chinese in *Cathay* (1915) and *Lustra* (1916). The *haiku*, Pound declared, using his *In a Station of the Metro* as an example, provided a model of compression in verse; a "one-image poem" which renders "the precise instant when a thing outward and objective transforms itself, or darts into a thing inward and subjective,"[4] combining the graphic with the sense of motion and volatile discovery. Given the opportunity to study Ernest Fenollosa's manuscript of *The Chinese Written Character as a Medium of Poetry* (and to complete some translations Fenollosa left unfinished), Pound inferred that the condensed juxtapositions of Chinese ideograms embodied what in effect were events and actions, transferences of energy among words, with the graphic figures presenting, as Fenollosa said, "something of the character of a motion picture."[5] Pound's interest in Oriental culture, the "New Greece," extended to the Confucian ethics which pervades his *Cantos*, and the songs which he rendered freely in *The Classic Anthology Defined by Confucius* (1954). But, as in his earlier studies of Romance literature, his forays into scholarship (though judged deficient by specialized scholars) were inseparable from his campaigns in the critical arena and had provided by 1920 the basis for his "propaganda" and for the poetics he tirelessly sought to make authoritative in his generation.

In 1920 Pound abandoned England for Paris and the Continent, as scornful of what he thought literary London's backwardness as he had earlier been of New York's. He memorialized his departure in a "farewell to London," his early masterpiece *Hugh Selwyn Mauberley* (1920). By the time he had settled in Rapallo, Italy, in 1925, he had left behind the literary arenas of Europe's capitals and was dependent on publication and on his voluminous correspondence to effect his ends as a man of letters, devoting most of his creative effort to gathering materials and composing his long poem, the *Cantos*. Of the critical essays in *Make It New* (1934) and *Literary Essays* (1954), most date from 1920 and earlier. *The ABC of Reading* (1934) and *Polite Essays* (1937) continued his appraisals of literary traditions and of modern writing. His studies of Confucius confirmed Pound's conception of the poet's mission to renovate the language and bring about social and personal regeneration. Confucius also provided models of social order in the relation of the Chinese "Lord" to his community. In his continuing study of medieval culture he found the term *forma* which defined

---

2. *Blast*, I (January, 1914), 54.
3. *Gaudier-Brzeska* (1916), p. 92.
4. *Ibid.*, p. 103.

5. Quoted by Hugh Kenner, *The Pound Era* (1971), p. 289.

the basic, emergent "dynamic form," the generative shaping process that artists try to incarnate in the finished forms of particular works. His researches in history convinced him that there were crucial similarities among statesmen and art patrons of the Italian past (notably Sigismondo Malatesta), the Americans Thomas Jefferson and John Adams, and the fascist dictator Mussolini (an "artist" as well as a statesman, Pound insisted).[6] Pound's *Guide to Kulchur* (1938) contained some of his most perceptive notations on history and culture, but it displayed also something of the incoherence and hysteria that characterized much of his social program after 1930. His increasingly vicious denunciations of the Jews, vilification of America under Franklin D. Roosevelt, and corresponding endorsement of Italian fascism were justified in his eyes by the vastly simplified and obsessive notion that the root of all social evil and cultural disorder is "usury," and by his conviction that he was trying to awaken America to its true political and cultural tradition.

When the Italian government in World War II invited Pound to deliver radio broadcasts aimed at American troops, with no prescription as to content, he readily delivered the talks that resulted in his being charged by the United States with treason in 1943 (as well as provoking *Poetry* magazine's repudiation and the temporary deletion of his poetry from an anthology); he read from his *Cantos* over the air, abused President Roosevelt and the Jews, advocated monetary reform, and mocked the motives for America's entering and continuing the war. Taken into custody after the fall of Italy, Pound suffered deprivations and shattering humiliations during his imprisonment for months in an open-air cage, which are echoed in the humility and anguish of the *Pisan Cantos* (1948). He was returned to the United States in 1945 for trial, but his case was suspended when the court, accepting the report of a panel of psychiatrists, found Pound "insane and mentally unfit for trial."[7] He spent the years from 1946 to 1958 as a patient in St. Elizabeth's Hospital in Washington, D.C., receiving visits from his devoted wife and admirers, working on Confucius and the *Cantos*. The charge of treason was dropped in 1958 and Pound was released, to return to Italy, as the result of efforts on his behalf by lawyers, congressmen, and writers led by Archibald MacLeish. Pound spent the rest of his life in Europe, chiefly in Italy, cared for by his wife, the concert violinist Olga Rudge, who had been his long-time companion and bore him his only daughter, and his daughter, Mary, the Countess de Rachewiltz. He traveled occasionally to London and Paris, and he visited literary friends in a number of cities when he returned to the United States in 1969 to receive an honorary degree from Hamilton College. He continued to publish cantos and to receive visits from friends, although in his last years he withdrew into protracted periods of unbroken silence.

The award of the Bollingen Prize for poetry in 1948 by a committee of the Library of Congress to Pound's *Pisan Cantos* had touched off an explosive controversy that continues to color the critical reception of his writings, though his impact on poets continued to be immense in the 1960s and 1970s. Opinion was divided about the merits of Pound's poetry, the effect on it of his anti-Semitism, and the propriety of an award from a governmental agency to an alleged traitor. Pound received the Harriet Monroe

---

6. *Jefferson and/or Mussolini* (1935), p. 34.

7. Quoted by Noel Stock, *The Life of Ezra Pound* (1970), p. 418.

Award for poetry in 1962 and a prize from the Academy of American Poets in 1963. But just before his death in 1972, when a committee of the American Academy of Arts and Sciences nominated him for its Emerson-Thoreau Award, the Academy's governing board overruled its committee and did not award the prize. A remark Pound made to his biographer before his final departure for Italy captured both the imaginative daring and the tragedy always latent in his career: "When I talk it is like an explosion in an art museum, you have to hunt around for the pieces."[8]

THE POETRY THROUGH MAUBERLEY

Three things distinguish Ezra Pound's poetic productions through 1920: the refinements of the dramatic monologue that he developed from the models of Robert Browning; the translations and adaptations that were the proving ground for his many innovations and are among his finest achievements; and the meters and disciplined nuances of effect that both strengthen and refine the surface texture of his verse, fusing the cadences of spoken speech with those of music.

In Browning, the monologue is presented (in an ostensibly direct, prosaic idiom) as if spoken not by the poet but by a speaker resurrected from the past, whose words or thoughts define dramatically a situation in which he is involved; together the speaker and the context are objectively observed. In Pound's treatment the form becomes more personal, the figure from the past and the poet himself become intimately connected so that the figure becomes a mask for the poet's own voice, an instrument or "persona" through which both the speaker's voice and the poet's voice are presented. It becomes what Pound called a "dramatic lyric * * * the poetic part of a drama the rest of which (to me the prose part) is left to the reader's imagination or implied or set in a short note."[9] It becomes also, as in *Sestina: Altaforte*, a bold and complicated act of historical reconstruction, for Pound not only recaptures details of the speaker's life (usually a poet) but echoes or translates fragments of the documents in which the speaker's life is recorded, including images and lines from the speaker's poems. The "persona" became for Pound an important expressive form, no longer limited to dramatic monologues, and enabled him to express the various voices he assumed.

Pound's strategies of translation were an integral feature of his poetics, and while he has long been criticized for careless lapses and flagrant inaccuracies, his procedures have stimulated many of the best translators in the twentieth century while constituting a major resource for his own poetry. The process which Pound called "casting off * * * complete masks of the self in each poem" was part of his "search for the real" which he said he "continued in a long series of translations, which were but more elaborate masks."[1] With scrupulous attention to the original text, but recognizing that the lines are mere notations of the realities suggested by them, he devised equivalences in English that were neither their literal transcriptions nor irresponsible adaptations but creative works in their own right; they manage to recapture the essentials, formal contours, and effects of the original with astonishing fidelity. Pound's translations become "personae" themselves, and the illusion of a translation is often sustained in poems that are

8. Quoted by Norman, *Ezra Pound*, p. 457.
9. *Letters*, pp. 3–4.

1. "Vorticism," *Fortnightly Review*, 96 (September 1, 1914), 463–64.

not strictly translations at all. One brilliant instance of poetry where adaptive translation is basic to Pound's creative effort is the long poem *Homage to Sextus Propertius* (1917), in which he converted the Roman poet and certain of his texts into a persona through which Pound voices his disenchantment with imperial London and the war. Another is his early success *Sestina: Altaforte.* There Pound recreated the stanzaic form of his favorite Provençal poet, Arnaud Daniel, but attributed it to another troubadour who never used that form, Bertrand de Born, whose *Praise of War* is drawn on freely for attitudes, images, and rhetorical devices.

The "persona" was an enabling form through which Pound's voice found expression and by means of which he explored and appropriated his tradition, but it depended for its effectiveness on the achievement of a fully realized poetic surface, a surface that his disciplined meters and poetic line had achieved by the 1920s. Wary of "the borderline between forceful language and violent language,"[2] he could so control colloquial speech and the placement of alliterative "b" sounds as to etch graphically and powerfully the stark futility of World War I:

> There died a myriad,
> And of the best, among them,
> For an old bitch, gone in the teeth,
> For a botched civilization.

The " 'sculpture' of rhyme" and delicately suspended modulations of rhythm expose the affluent Mr. Nixon "In the cream gilded cabin of his steam yacht." What Pound later defined as his attempt "To break the pentameter" (Canto 81) is apparent in the frequency with which he avoids routine regularity in length of lines by breaking them with a caesura, and avoids the metronome's regularity of "hefty swats on alternate syllables" by subtle variations in cadence, modulations in tone, and nuances of rhyme in counterpoint with residual echoes. The discipline of his verse sustains ironies in *Hugh Selwyn Mauberley* that avoid the melodrama of obvious contrast and reversal, and it represents his extension of the resources of poetry to which T. S. Eliot and other modern poets have paid tribute.

THE CANTOS

Pound began to work intently on his epic poem the *Cantos* in 1915 and gathered the first collection of them (after rejecting and revising some of the originals) in *A Draft of XVI Cantos* (1925). From the start, the question of their merits—indeed of their precise nature—has agitated criticism, which now ranges from George P. Elliott's verdict that the series disintegrates into a disorderly "bundle of poetry and mutter" to Eva Hesse's celebration of them as a splendidly "open form" appropriate to the "pluralistic and relativistic mode of thinking" of his age.[3] The latest published collections, including *Section: Rock-Drill* (1956) and *Thrones* (1959), brought the collected number to 116 and marked the near-completion of one of the major undertakings of twentieth-century poets.

Statements by Pound himself help define the design that he hoped would emerge, including one when he speaks of his friend William Carlos Williams's habit of "yanking and hauling as much [material] as possible

2. *Letters*, p. 182.
3. George P. Elliott, *Ezra Pound: A Collection of Critical Essays* (1963), p. 152; Eva Hesse, *New Approaches to Ezra Pound* (1969), pp. 17, 46.

into some sort of order (or beauty), aware of it as both chaos and as potential";[4] in *Cantos* he said that they were a "rag-bag for the 'modern world' to stuff all its thought in."[5] It was an epic designed to appropriate history, a "poem including history,"[6] he declared, with three centers of attention: men of action (statesmen, warriors, bankers), documents and books, and creative genius, all presented in the idiom of anecdote and conversation:

> And men of unusual genius, books, arms,
> Both of ancient times and our own, in short, the usual subjects
> Of conversation between intelligent men. (Canto XI)

The vast stretches of history encompassed by the poem are presented not as a subject to be studied but as the realm of action and thought to be experienced that Emerson earlier had demanded in his essay *History*.

The historical materials so gathered and talked about are more important than is customary in poetry because they are "included" literally in the text, in fragmented phrases or long excerpts from literary works, biographies, letters, and business transactions, or in the form of the poet's personal memories of incident and information. On the basis of such materials it is possible to distinguish related groups of cantos within the larger sequence: the "Malatesta cantos," centering on the Renaissance soldier and patron Sigismondo Malatesta; the "American cantos," including the "John Adams cantos," featuring the statecraft of Presidents Jefferson, the Adamses, and Van Buren; the "Chinese History cantos;" and the "Pisan cantos," drawing on Pound's experience as a prisoner in the American detention camp. These categories, however, obscure the complicated juxtapositions and interconnections among them that fleetingly or recurringly emerge in the movement of the poem.

Singly and together, the *Cantos* are personae in which the voices of history intermingle with Pound's own in a shifting surface that is fluid and linear rather than agitated by dramatic conflict, and whose shape is an exploratory orientation toward form rather than a completion of fulfillment of a formal design. The various themes and values in the poem, with their often tenuous connections, are obscured by the "deliberate disconnectedness"[7] that R. P. Blackmur discerned as a controlling principle of the poem's movement. The *Cantos* do not display a new form so much as a new species of poetic statement in which the raw materials of historical data remain raw and often obscure while approaching the threshold of order, and the process of digesting history's meaning remains ruminative and partial while the poet seeks the full illumination of imaginative vision. At times there emerge moments of luminous beauty and lyric intensity that match the best of modern poetry. The poem's movement in the direction of these moments is quickened by such recurring symbols as the image of the city and the image of light; by such mythological figures as Aphrodite, the goddess of love, and Persephone, goddess of regeneration; and by the voices and figures of countless artists, from Homer, "blind as a bat," to Dante, Cavalcanti, and the troubadour poets, through Browning and Pound's American predecessors Whitman and Henry James, to such con-

4. *Polite Essays* (1966), p. 77.
5. *Lustra* (1917), p. 181.
6. *Selected Essays*, p. 86.

7. R. P. Blackmur, *Language as Gesture* (1952), p. 140.

temporaries as Eliot and Yeats. And the poem is governed by three archetypal quests which displace and dissolve into each other in the long series of metamorphoses that recreate them: Odysseus's journey across the sea and through the underworld in quest of home in Homer's epic; the exiled Dante's journey through hell and purgatory in search of the radiant light and angelic "thrones" which he finally glimpses in the paradise of the *Divine Comedy*; and the tragic search for an ideal social order or an imagined city, for the "stones of foundation" on which "to build the city of Dioce whose terraces are the color of stars" (Canto 74).[8]

Histrion[1]

No man hath dared to write this thing as yet,
And yet I know, how that the souls of all men great
At times pass through us,
And we are melted into them, and are not
Save reflexions of their souls.   5
Thus am I Dante for a space and am
One François Villon,[2] ballad-lord and thief,
Or am such holy ones I may not write
Lest blasphemy be writ against my name;
This for an instant and the flame is gone.   10

'Tis as in midmost us there glows a sphere
Translucent, molten gold, that is the "I"
And into this some form projects itself:
Christus, or John, or eke the Florentine;[3]
And as the clear space is not if a form's   15
Imposed thereon,
So cease we from all being for the time,
And these, the Masters of the Soul, live on.

1909

Cino[1]

Italian Campagna[2] 1309, the open road

Bah! I have sung women in three cities,
But it is all the same;
And I will sing of the sun.

Lips, words, and you snare them,
Dreams, words, and they are as jewels,   5

8. Deioces, legendary King of the Medes, whose terraces and golden tower, Ectaban, are described by the Greek historian Herodotus (480?–420? B.C.) in his *History* (1.98).
1. Actor.
2. Wandering, turbulent French poet (b. 1431).
3. "Eke": also; "Florentine": the poet Dante (1265–1321).
1. A dramatic monologue, its abrupt opening line and colloquial idiom are modeled on Browning. The speaker is Cino da Pistoia (1270–1336), noble-born lawyer, professor of jurisprudence, and poet whose verse was praised but whose inconstancy in love was criticized by Dante. In 1309 he was ambassador to Florence. Cino was banished for a time and traveled extensively. The "open road" in Pound's inscription echoes Whitman's *Song of the Open Road*.
2. Field.

Strange spells of old deity,
Ravens, nights, allurement:
And they are not;
Having become the souls of song.

Eyes, dreams, lips, and the night goes.   10
Being upon the road once more,
They are not.
Forgetful in their towers of our tuneing
Once for Wind-runeing[3]
They dream us-toward and   15
Sighing say, "Would Cino,
Passionate Cino, of the wrinkling eyes,
Gay Cino, of quick laughter,
Cino, of the dare, the jibe,
Frail Cino, strongest of his tribe   20
That tramp old ways beneath the sun-light,
Would Cino of the Luth[4] were here!"

Once, twice, a year—
Vaguely thus word they:

          "Cino?" "Oh, eh, Cino Polnesi[5]   25
          The singer is't you mean?"
          "Ah yes, passed once our way,
          A saucy fellow, but . . .
          (Oh they are all one these vagabonds),
          Peste! 'tis his own songs?   30
          Or some other's that he sings?
          But *you*, My Lord, how with your city?"

But you "My Lord," God's pity!
And[6] all I knew were out, My Lord, you
Were Lack-land Cino, e'en as I am,   35
O Sinistro.[7]

I have sung women in three cities.
But it is all one.
I will sing of the sun.
. . . eh? . . . they mostly had grey eyes,   40
But it is all one, I will sing of the sun.

          "'Pollo Phoibee, old tin pan, you
          Glory to Zeus' aegis-day;[8]
          Shield o' steel-blue, th' heaven o'er us
          Hath for boss[9] thy lustre gay!   45

---

3. Wind sounds as enchanting as runes, magical symbols in an ancient Teutonic alphabet.
4. Lute.
5. Dialect for Bolognese.
6. If.
7. Allusion to the "bar sinister," a sign in heraldry of illegitimacy.

8. "'Pollo Phoibee": Phoebus Apollo, Greek god of light and music, son of Zeus, ruler of the gods. "Aegis-day": time under special protection of Zeus's aegis (shield).
9. Knob at the center of a shield; in architecture, the decoration at the intersection of vault ribs in a ceiling.

'Pollo Phoibee, to our way-fare
Make thy laugh our wander-lied;
Bid thy 'fulgence bear away care.
Cloud and rain-tears pass they fleet!

Seeking e'er the new-laid rast-way[2]   55
To the gardens of the sun . . .

.   .   .   .

I have sung women in three cities
But it is all one.

I will sing of the white birds
In the blue waters of heaven,   55
The clouds that are spray to its sea.

1908

Famam Librosque Cano[1]

Your songs?
                    Oh! The little mothers
          Will sing them in the twilight,
And when the night
Shrinketh the kiss of the dawn   5
That loves and kills,
What times the swallow fills
Her note, the little rabbit folk
That some call children,
Such as are up and wide,   10
Will laugh your verses to each other,
Pulling on their shoes for the day's business,
Serious child business that the world
Laughs at, and grows stale;
Such is the tale   15
—Part of it—of thy song-life.

Mine?

          A book is known by them that read
          That same. Thy public in my screed
          Is listed. Well! Some score years hence   20
Behold mine audience,
          As we had seen him yesterday.

          Scrawny, be-spectacled, out at heels,
Such an one as the world feels
A sort of curse against its guzzling   25
And its age-lasting wallow for red greed
And yet; full speed
Though it should run for its own getting,

2. Gateway.
1. "I sing of fame and books," a recast-ing of the opening line of Virgil's *Aeneid*, "I sing of arms and the man."

Will turn aside to sneer at
'Cause he hath   30
No coin, no will to snatch the aftermath
Of Mammon[2]
Such an one as women draw away from
For the tobacco ashes scattered on his coat
And sith[3] his throat   35
Shows razor's unfamiliarity
And three days' beard;

Such an one picking a ragged
Backless copy from the stall,
Too cheap for cataloguing,   40
Loquitur,[4]

"Ah-eh! the strange rare name . . .
Ah-eh! He must be rare if even *I* have not . . ."
And lost mid-page
Such age   45
As his pardons the habit,
He analyses form and thought to see
How I 'scaped immortality.

1908

Sestina: Altaforte[1]

Loquitur: *En* Bertrans de Born[2]
Dante Alighieri put this man in hell for that he was a stirrer up of strife.
Eccovi![3]
Judge ye!
Have I dug him up again?
The scene is at his castle, Altaforte. "Papiols" is his jongleur.[4]
"The Leopard," the *device* of Richard Cœur de Lion.

I

Damn it all! all this our South stinks peace.
You whoreson dog, Papiols, come! Let's to music!

2. Demon of greed.
3. Since.
4. It is said.
1. Pound's early reputation in London literary circles was spread by reading aloud this poem, which crosses the drama of a Browningesque monologue on the intricate stanza pattern of a sestina and on a translation of *Praise of War* by the bloodthirsty Provençal poet Bertrand de Born (1140–1209?). The speaker earned a place in Dante's *Inferno* (Canto 28) for instigating strife between de Born's close friend Henry Plantagenet ("The Young King") and the latter's brother, Richard the Lionhearted. The sestina interested Pound for the intricacy of its stanza form, which calls for exact rhymes within the poem but not within any one stanza. In each successive stanza, the final word in the last line of the preceding stanza becomes the end word in the first line of the preceding becomes the rhyme word of the second line, the fifth becomes the third, the second becomes the fourth, the fourth becomes the fifth, and the third becomes the sixth. In the final stanza, which addresses the reader, all the rhyme words are supposed to be used. Pound deviated from the rhyme pattern in lines 21 and 22, used only four rhyme words in the "*envoi*," and moved the direct address to his listener into the opening stanza.
2. It is spoken by Lord Bertrand de Born.
3. Here you are!
4. Itinerant minstrel.

I have no life save when the swords clash.
But ah! when I see the standards gold, vair,[5] purple, opposing
And the broad fields beneath them turn crimson,   5
Then howl I my heart nigh mad with rejoicing.

II

In hot summer have I great rejoicing
When the tempests kill the earth's foul peace,
And the lightnings from black heav'n flash crimson,
And the fierce thunders roar me their music   10
And the winds shriek through the clouds mad, opposing,
And through all the riven skies God's swords clash.

III

Hell grant soon we hear again the swords clash!
And the shrill neighs of destriers[6] in battle rejoicing,
Spiked breast to spiked breast opposing!   15
Better one hour's stour[7] than a year's peace
With fat boards, bawds, wine and frail music!
Bah! there's no wine like the blood's crimson!

IV

And I love to see the sun rise blood-crimson.
And I watch his spears through the dark clash   20
And it fills all my heart with rejoicing
And pries wide my mouth with fast music
When I see him so scorn and defy peace,
His lone might 'gainst all darkness opposing.

V

The man who fears war and squats opposing   25
My words for stour, hath no blood of crimson
But is fit only to rot in womanish peace
Far from where worth's won and the swords clash
For the death of such sluts I go rejoicing;
Yea, I fill all the air with my music.   30

VI

Papiols, Papiols, to the music!
There's no sound like to swords swords opposing,
No cry like the battle's rejoicing
When our elbows and swords drip the crimson
And our charges 'gainst "The Leopard's" rush clash.   35
May God damn for ever all who cry "Peace!"

VII

And let the music of the swords make them crimson!
Hell grant soon we hear again the swords clash!
Hell blot black for alway the thought "Peace"!

                                                                   1909

---

5. Rows of shields, in alternating blue   6. War horses.
and silver, in heraldry.   7. Combat.

Erat Hora

"Thank you, whatever comes." And then she turned
    And, as the ray of sun on hanging flowers
Fades when the wind hath lifted them aside,
Went swiftly from me. Nay, whatever comes
One hour was sunlit and the most high gods   5
May not make boast of any better thing
Than to have watched that hour as it passed.

                                                 1911

To Whistler, American[1]

On the loan exhibit of his paintings at the Tate Gallery.

You also, our first great,
Had tried all ways;
Tested and pried and worked in many fashions,
And this much gives me heart to play the game.

Here is a part that's slight, and part gone wrong,   5
And much of little moment, and some few
Perfect as Dürer![2]
"In the Studio" and these two portraits,[3] if I had my choice!
And then these sketches in the mood of Greece?

You had your searches, your uncertainties,   10
And this is good to know—for us, I mean,
Who bear the brunt of our America
And try to wrench her impulse into art.

You were not always sure, not always set
To hiding night or tuning "symphonies";[4]   15
Had not one style from birth, but tried and pried
And stretched and tampered with the media.

You and Abe Lincoln from that mass of dolts
Show us there's chance at least of winning through.

                                         1912, 1949

Portrait d'une Femme[1]

Your mind and you are our Sargasso Sea,[2]
London has swept about you this score years

---

1. James Abbott McNeill Whistler (1834–1903), expatriate American painter.
2. Albrecht Dürer (1471–1528), German painter and engraver.
3. "Brown and Gold—de Race," "Grenat et Or—Le Petit Cardinal" ("Garnet and Gold—The Little Cardinal") [Pound's note]: titles and subjects of the portraits.
4. Whistler painted many night scenes and entitled many paintings "symphonies" to suggest their abstract or non-representational quality.
1. Portrait of a Lady.
2. Sea in the North Atlantic where boats were becalmed; named for its large masses of floating seaweed.

And bright ships left you this or that in fee:
Ideas, old gossip, oddments of all things,
Strange spars of knowledge and dimmed wares of price. 5
Great minds have sought you—lacking someone else.
You have been second always. Tragical?
No. You preferred it to the usual thing:
One dull man, dulling and uxorious,
One average mind—with one thought less, each year. 10
Oh, you are patient, I have seen you sit
Hours, where something might have floated up.
And now you pay one. Yes, you richly pay.
You are a person of some interest, one comes to you
And takes strange gain away: 15
Trophies fished up; some curious suggestion;
Fact that leads nowhere; and a tale or two,
Pregnant with mandrakes,[3] or with something else
That might prove useful and yet never proves,
That never fits a corner or shows use, 20
Or finds its hour upon the loom of days:
The tarnished, gaudy, wonderful old work;
Idols and ambergris and rare inlays,
These are your riches, your great store; and yet
For all this sea-hoard of deciduous things, 25
Strange woods half sodden, and new brighter stuff:
In the slow float of differing light and deep,
No! there is nothing! In the whole and all,
Nothing that's quite your own.
          Yet this is you. 30

               1912

A Virginal[1]

No, no! Go from me. I have left her lately.
I will not spoil my sheath with lesser brightness,
For my surrounding air hath a new lightness;
Slight are her arms, yet they have bound me straitly
And left me cloaked as with a gauze of aether; 5
As with sweet leaves; as with subtle clearness.
Oh, I have picked up magic in her nearness
To sheathe me half in half the things that sheathe her.
No, no! Go from me. I have still the flavour,
Soft as spring wind that's come from birchen bowers. 10
Green come the shoots, aye April in the branches,
As winter's wound with her sleight hand she staunches,

---

3. Herb, used as a cathartic; believed in legend to have human properties, to shriek when pinched, and to promote conception in women.

1. The title of this sonnet signifies a small spinet, a musical instrument popular in the 16th and 17th centuries.

Hath of the trees a likeness of the savour:
As white their bark, so white this lady's hours.

1912

Salutation the Second

You were praised, my books,
         because I had just come from the country;
I was twenty years behind the times
         so you found an audience ready.
I do not disown you,   5
         do not you disown your progeny.

Here they stand without quaint devices,
Here they are with nothing archaic about them.
Observe the irritation in general:

"Is this," they say, "the nonsense   10
         that we expect of poets?"
"Where is the Picturesque?"
         "Where is the vertigo of emotion?"
"No! his first work was the best."
         "Poor Dear! he has lost his illusions."   15

Go, little naked and impudent songs,
Go with a light foot!

1913, 1916

A Pact

I make a pact with you, Walt Whitman—
I have detested you long enough.
I come to you as a grown child
Who has had a pig-headed father;
I am old enough now to make friends.   5
It was you that broke the new wood,
Now is a time for carving.
We have one sap and one root—
Let there be commerce between us.

1913, 1916

The Rest

O helpless few in my country,
O remnant enslaved!

Artists broken against her,
A-stray, lost in the villages,
Mistrusted, spoken-against,   5

Lovers of beauty, starved,
Thwarted with systems,
Helpless against the control;

You who can not wear yourselves out
By persisting to successes,   10
You who can only speak,
Who can not steel yourselves into reiteration;

You of the finer sense,
Broken against false knowledge,
You who can know at first hand,   15
Hated, shut in, mistrusted:

Take thought:
I have weathered the storm,
I have beaten out my exile.

                                                    1913, 1916

In a Station of the Metro[1]

The apparition of these faces in the crowd;
Petals on a wet, black bough.

                                                    1913, 1916

L'Art, 1910

Green arsenic smeared on an egg-white cloth,
Crushed strawberries! Come, let us feast our eyes.

                                                    1914, 1916

The River-Merchant's Wife: A Letter[1]

While my hair was still cut straight across my forehead
I played about the front gate, pulling flowers.
You came by on bamboo stilts, playing horse,
You walked about my seat, playing with blue plums.

2. Paris subway.
1. Adaptation from the Chinese of Li Po (701–762), named Rihaku in Japanese. Pound found the material in the papers of Fenollosa and used Japanese paraphrases in making the translation with the result that the proper names are their Japanese equivalents. Among Pound's alterations are the substitution of blue for green (line 4), of August for October (line 23), and of the image of walking on bamboo stilts for that of riding a bamboo horse.

And we went on living in the village of Chokan:[2]   5
Two small people, without dislike or suspicion.
At fourteen I married My Lord you.
I never laughed, being bashful.
Lowering my head, I looked at the wall.
Called to, a thousand times, I never looked back.   10

At fifteen I stopped scowling,
I desired my dust to be mingled with yours
Forever and forever and forever.
Why should I climb the look out?

At sixteen you departed,   15
You went into far Ku-to-yen,[3] by the river of swirling eddies,
And you have been gone five months.
The monkeys make sorrowful noise overhead.

You dragged your feet when you went out.
By the gate now, the moss is grown, the different mosses   20
Too deep to clear them away!
The leaves fall early this autumn, in wind.
The paired butterflies are already yellow with August,
Over the grass in the West garden;
They hurt me. I grow older.   25
If you are coming down through the narrows of the river Kiang,
Please let me know beforehand,
And I will come out to meet you
          As far as Cho-fu-Sa.[4]

                                              By Rihaku
                                              1915

Villanelle: The Psychological Hour[1]

I had over-prepared the event,
          that much was ominous.
With middle-ageing care
          I had laid out just the right books.
I had almost turned down the pages.   5

          Beauty is so rare a thing.
          So few drink of my fountain.

So much barren regret,
So many hours wasted!
And now I watch, from the window,   10
          the rain, the wandering busses.

2. Suburb of Nanking.   Nanking.
3. An island several hundred miles up   1. Pound ignores the intricate stanza
the river Kiang.   pattern of the traditional villanelle.
4. Beach several hundred miles above

"Their little cosmos is shaken"—
　　　　the air is alive with that fact.
In their parts of the city
　　　　they are played on by diverse forces.　　　15
How do I know?
　　　　Oh, I know well enough.
For them there is something afoot.
　　　　As for me;
I had over-prepared the event—　　　　　　　　20

　　　Beauty is so rare a thing
　　　So few drink of my fountain.

Two friends: a breath of the forest . . .
Friends? Are people less friends
　　　　because one has just, at last, found them?　25
Twice they promised to come.

　　　"Between the night and morning?"[2]

Beauty would drink of my mind.
Youth would awhile forget
　　　　my youth is gone from me.　　　　　　　30
　　　　　　　　II
("Speak up! You have danced so stiffly?
　Someone admired your works,
　And said so frankly.

　"Did you talk like a fool,
　The first night?　　　　　　　　　　　　　35
　The second evening?"

"*But* they promised again:
　　　　'To-morrow at tea-time.'")
　　　　　　　　III
Now the third day is here—
　　　　no word from either;　　　　　　　　40
No word from her nor him,
Only another man's note:
　　　　"Dear Pound, I am leaving England."

　　　　　　　　　　　　　　1916

2. In *The People*, an uncollected poem published in 1916, William Butler Yeats complained of an "unmannerly town" that can ruin one's reputation "Between the night and the morning."

The Renaissance

'All criticism is an attempt to define the classic.'[1]

I

The Palette

No one wants the native American poet to be *au courant* with the literary affairs of Paris and London in order that he may make imitations of Paris and London models, but precisely in order that he shall not waste his lifetime making unconscious, or semi-conscious, imitations of French and English models thirty or forty or an hundred years old.

Chaucer is better than Crestien de Troyes,[2] and the Elizabethan playwrights are more interesting than the Pléïade,[3] because they went beyond their models.

The value of a capital or metropolis is that if a man in a capital cribs, quotes or imitates, someone else immediately lets the cat out of the bag and says what he is cribbing, quoting or imitating.

America has as yet no capital. The study of 'comparative literature' received that label about eighty years ago. It has existed for at least two thousand years. The best Latin poets knew Greek. The troubadours knew several jargons. Dante wrote in Italian, Latin and Provençal, and knew presumably other tongues, including a possible smattering of Hebrew.

I once met a very ancient Oxford 'head,' and in the middle of dinner he turned to me, saying: 'Ah—um, ah—poet. Ah, some one showed me a new poem the other day, the—ah—the *Hound of Heaven*.'[4]

I said, 'Well, what did you think of it?' and he answered, 'Couldn't be bothered to stop for every adjective!'

That enlightened opinion was based on a form of comparative literature called 'the classic education'.

The first step of a renaissance, or awakening, is the importation of models for painting, sculpture or writing. We have had many 'movements,' movements stimulated by 'comparison'. Flaminius and Amaltheus and the latinists of the quattrocentro and cinquecento[5] began a movement for enrichment which culminated in the Elizabethan stage, and which produced the French Pléïade. There was wastage and servile imitation. The first effect of the Greek learning was possibly bad. There was a deal of verbalism. We

1. Pound's summary of the main argument in *The Literary Influence of Academies* (*Essays in Criticism, First Series*, 1865) and *The Study of Poetry* (*Essays in Criticism, Second Series*, 1888) by the English Victorian poet and critic Matthew Arnold (1822–88).
2. French poet of the 12th century, author of romances about King Arthur's knights and about the quest for the Holy Grail. They are written in the courtly love tradition, which treats the abject love of devoted courtiers for virtuous

and haughty ladies.
3. Group of 16th-century French writers, including Pierre de Ronsard (1524–85), who substituted classical and Italian models for medieval ones.
4. Poem (1893) by the English poet Francis Thompson (1859–1907).
5. Italian terms in art history for the 14th and 15th centuries. Flaminius Raius (fl. 1577) and Heronymus Amaltheus (1506–74) were Renaissance poets who wrote verse in Latin.

find the decadence of this movement in Tasso and Ariosto and Milton.[6]

The romantic awakening dates from the production of *Ossian*.[7] The last century rediscovered the middle ages. It is possible that this century may find a new Greece in China. In the meantime we have come upon a new table of values. I can only compare this endeavour of criticism to the contemporary search for pure color in painting. We have come to some recognition of the fact that poets like Villon, Sappho and Catullus differ from poets like Milton, Tasso and Camoens, and that size is no more a criterion of writing than it is of painting.[8]

I suppose no two men will agree absolutely respecting 'pure color' or 'good color', but the modern painter recognizes the importance of the palette. One can but make out one's own spectrum or table. Let us choose: Homer, Sappho, Ibycus,[9] Theocritus'[1] idyl of the woman spinning with charmed wheel: Catullus, especially the *Collis O Heliconii.*[2] Not Virgil, especially not the Æneid, where he has no story worth telling, no sense of personality. His hero is a stick who would have contributed to *The New Statesman*.[3] He has a nice verbalism. Dante was right to respect him, for Dante had no Greek, and the Æneid would have stood out nobly against such literature as was available in the year 1300.

I should wish, for myself at least, a few *sirventes* of Bertran de Born, and a few strophes of Arnaut Daniel,[4] though one might learn from Dante himself all that one could learn from Arnaut: precision of statement, particularization. Still there is no tongue like the Provençal wherein to study the subsidiary arts of rhyme and rhyme-blending.

I should want also some further medieval song-book, containing a few more troubadour poems, especially one or two by Vidal and Marueil, six poems of Guido's, German songs out of Will Vesper's song book, and especially some by Walter von der Vogelweide.

I should want Dante of course, and the *Poema del Cid*,[5] and the *Sea-farer* and one passage out of *The Wanderer*.[6] In fact, some knowledge of the Anglo-Saxon fragments—not particularly the Beo-

---

6. Torquato Tasso (1544–95) and Lodovico Ariosto (1474–1533), Italian poets, and the English poet John Milton (1608–74), whose poetry and prose are infused with classical learning.

7. Epic poem, purporting to be by the mythical Irish bard Ossian, composed of Gaelic fragments and fabrications by the Scottish poet James Macpherson (1736–96).

8. The French poet François Villon (b. 1431) wrote lyrics, ballads, and light verse celebrating tricksters; the Greek poet Sappho (fl. 600 B.C.) wrote lyrics; the Roman poet Gaius Valerius Catullus (84?–54 B.C.) wrote satirical and erotic verse. Like Milton and Tasso, the Portuguese poet Luiz Vaz de Camoëns (1524–80) wrote epic poems.

9. Greek lyric poet of the sixth century B.C.

1. Greek poet of the third century B.C., author of pastoral idyls.

2. Opening line of Catullus's *Epithalamium of Julia and Manlius*, an invocation to Hymen, god of marriage, whose home was on Mount Helicon.

3. English journal, launched in 1913, emphasizing politics, economics, and public policy.

4. Provençal poets of the 12th century. *Sirventes* are Provençal medieval lyrics in couplets; strophes are sections of choral odes or, loosely, stanzas.

5. Spanish epic of the 12th century.

6. Old English poems copied in the Exeter Book (c. 975).

wulf—would prevent a man's sinking into contentment with a lot of wish-wash that passes for classic or 'standard' poetry.,

So far as the palette of sheer color is concerned, one could, at a pinch, do without nearly all the French poets save Villon. If a man knew Villon and the *Sea-farer* and Dante, and that one scrap of Ibycus, he would, I think, never be able to be content with a sort of pretentious and decorated verse which receives praise from those who had been instructed to like it, or with a certain sort of formal verbalism which is supposed to be good writing by those who have never read any French prose.

What one learns from other French poets, one might as readily learn from Voltaire and Stendhal and Flaubert. One is a fool, of course, if one forego the pleasure of Gautier, and Corbière and the Plêïade, but whether reading them will more discontent you with bad writing than would the reading of Mérimée, I do not know.[7]

A sound poetic training is nothing more than the science of being discontented.

After Villon, the next poet for an absolutely clear palette, is Heine.[8] It takes only a small amount of reading to disgust one, not with English poets, but with English standards. I can not make it too clear that this is not a destructive article. Let anyone drink any sort of liqueur that suits him. Let him enjoy the aroma as a unity, let him forget all that he has heard of technic, but let him not confuse enjoyment with criticism, constructive criticism, or preparation for writing. There is nothing like futurist abolition of past glories in this brief article. It does not preclude an enjoyment of Charles d'Orleans or Mark Alexander Boyd.[9] 'Fra bank to bank, fra wood to wood I rin.'

Since Lamb[1] and his contemporary critics everything has been based, and absurdly based, on the Elizabethans, who are a pastiche. They are 'neither very intense nor very accomplished.' (I leave Shakespeare out of this discussion and also the Greek dramatists.) Or let us say that Keats[2] very probably made the last profitable rehash of Elizabethanism. Or let us query the use of a twentieth century poet's trying to dig up what Sidney himself called 'Petrarch's long deceasèd woes'.[3]

Chaucer should be on every man's shelf. Milton is the worst sort

7. Pound lists important French prose stylists: the man of letters Voltaire (François Marie Arouet, 1694–1778); the novelists Stendhal (Marie Henri Beyle, 1783–1842), Gustave Flaubert (1821–80), and Prosper Mérimée (1803–70). Théophile Gautier (1811–72) wrote poetry and fiction and advocated "art for art's sake." Edouard Joachim Corbière (1845–75) infused poems about seafaring life with colloquial diction and irony. 8. Henrich Heine (1797–1856), German poet, critic, and journalist. 9. The French poet Charles d'Orléans (1391–1465) wrote delicate lyric verse; Mark Alexander Boyd (1563–1601) was a Scottish scholar and writer of Latin verse. 1. Charles Lamb, English essayist and critic (1775–1834). 2. John Keats (1795–1821), English Romantic poet. 3. From *Astrophel and Stella* (1591, 8.1.7) by the English statesman and poet Sir Philip Sidney (1554–86). Francesco Petrarca (Petrarch) (1304–74) was the Italian poet whose sonnets were models for much Renaissance verse.

of poison. He is a thorough-going decadent in the worst sense of the term. If he had stopped after writing the short poems one might respect him. The definite contribution in his later work consists in his developing the sonority of the English blank-verse paragraph. If poetry consisted in derivation from the Greek anthology one could not much improve on Drummond of Hawthornden's *Phoebus, Arise.*[4] Milton is certainly no better than Drummond. He makes his pastiche out of more people. He is bombast, of perhaps a very high order, but he is the worst possible food for a growing poet, save possibly Francis Thompson and Tasso.

Goethe[5] is perhaps the only one of the poets who tried to be colossi unsuccessfully, who does not breed noxious contentments. His lyrics are so fine, so unapproachable—I mean they are as good as Heine's and Von der Vogelweide's—but outside his lyrics he never comes off his perch. We are tired of men upon perches.[6]

Virgil is a man on a perch. All these writers of pseudo *épopée*[7] are people on perches. Homer and the author of the *Poema del Cid* are keen on their stories. Milton and Virgil are concerned with decorations and trappings, and they muck about with a moral. Dante is concerned with a *senso morale*,[8] which is totally different matter. He breeds discontentments. Milton does not breed discontentments, he only sets the neophyte trying to pile up noise and adjectives, as in these lines:

> Thus th' ichthyosaurus was dubbed combative . . .
> Captive he led with him Geography . . .
> Whom to encompass in th' exiguous bonds . . .[9]

There is no end to this leonine ramping.

It is possible that only Cavalcanti and Leopardi[1] can lift rhetoric into the realm of poetry. With them one never knows the border line. In Leopardi there is such sincerity, such fire of sombre pessimism, that one can not carp or much question his manner. I do not mean that one should copy the great poets whom I have named above—one does not copy colors on a palette. There is a difference between what one enjoys and what one takes as proof color.

I dare say it is, in this century, inexplicable how or why a man should try to hold up a standard of excellence to which he himself can not constantly attain. An acquaintance of mine deliberately says that mediocre poetry is worth writing. If mediocrities want immortality they must of course keep up some sort of cult of mediocrity; they must develop the habit of preserving Lewis Morris[2] and Co.

4. Poem by Sir William Drummond of Hawthornden (1585–1649), Scottish poet.
5. Johann Wolfgang von Goethe (1749–1832), German poet, dramatist, and novelist.
6. "Revision: Goethe did attempt to do an honest job of work *in his time.* E.P." [Pound's note].
7. Epic.
8. A moral sense, as distinct from a didactic moral.
9. Probably lines written by Pound in imitation of Milton.
1. For the Italian poet Guido Cavalcanti (c. 1250–1300), see Canto XXXVI, note 1. Giacomo Leopardi (1798–1837) is an Italian poet.
2. British poet (1833–1907).

The same crime is perpetrated in American schools by courses in
'American literature'. You might as well give courses in 'American
chemistry', neglecting all foreign discoveries. This is not patriotism.

No American poetry is of any use for the palette. Whitman is
the best of it, but he never pretended to have reached the goal. He
knew himself, and proclaimed himself 'a start in the right direction'. He never said, 'American poetry is to stay where I left it'; he
said it was to go on from where he started it.

The cult of Poe is an exotic introduced via Mallarmé and Arthur
Symons.[3] Poe's glory as an inventor of macabre subjects has been
shifted into a reputation for verse. The absurdity of the cult is well
gauged by Mallarmé's French translation—*Et le corbeau dit jamais
plus.*[4]

A care for American letters does not consist in breeding a contentment with what has been produced, but in setting a standard
for ambition. A decent artist weeps over a failure; a rotten artist
tries to palm it off as a masterpiece.

NOTE—I have not in this paper set out to give a whole history of
poetry. I have tried in a way to set forth a color-sense. I have said,
as it were, 'Such poets are pure red . . . pure green.' Knowledge of
them is of as much use to a poet as the finding of good color is to a
painter.

Undoubtedly pure color is to be found in Chinese poetry, when
we begin to know enough about it; indeed, a shadow of this perfection is already at hand in translations. Liu Ch'e, Chu Yuan, Chia
I,[5] and the great *vers libre*[6] writers before the Petrarchan age of Li
Po,[7] are a treasury to which the next century may look for as great
a stimulus as the renaissance had from the Greeks.

II

Whether from habit, or from profound intuition, or from sheer
national conceit, one is always looking to America for signs of a
'renaissance'. One is open-eyed to defects. I have heard passionate
nonentities rave about America's literary and artistic barrenness. I
have heard the greatest living American saying, with the measured
tones of deliberate curiosity, 'Strange how all taint of art or letters
seems to shun that continent . . . ah . . . ah, God knows there's
little enough here . . . ah . . .'[8]

And yet we look to the dawn; we count up our symptoms; year
in and year out we say we have this and that, we have so much, and
so much. Our best asset is a thing of the spirit. I have the ring of it
in a letter, now on my desk, from a good but little known poet,

3. Stéphane Mallarmé (1842–98), French
Symbolist poet, and Arthur Symons
(1865–1945), British critic and author of
The Symbolist Movement in Literature
(1899).
4. The translation of Poe's refrain in
The Raven reads literally: "And the

raven said nevermore."
5. Chinese poet and painter (d. 1375),
and two Chinese poets of the fourth and
second centuries B.C. respectively.
6. Free verse.
7. Chinese poet (701–762).
8. Possibly Henry James.

complaining of desperate loneliness, envying Synge[9] his material, to-wit, the Arran Islands and people, wishing me well with my exotics, and ending with a sort of defiance: 'For me nothing exists, *really exists*, outside America.'

That writer is not alone in his feeling, nor is he alone in his belief in tomorrow. That emotion and belief are our motive forces, and as to their application we can perhaps best serve it by taking stock of what we have, and devising practical measures. And we must do this without pride, and without parochialism; we have no one to cheat save ourselves. It is not a question of scaring someone else, but of making ourselves efficient. We must learn what we can from the past, we must learn what other nations have done successfully under similar circumstances, we must think how they did it.

We have, to begin with, architecture, the first of the arts to arrive, the most material, the least dependent on the inner need of the poor—for the arts are noble only as they meet the inner need of the poor. Bach is given to all men, Homer is given to all men: you need only the faculty of music or of patience to read or to hear. Painting and sculpture are given to all men in a particular place, to all who have money for travel.

And architecture comes first, being the finest branch of advertisement, advertisement of some god who has been successful, or of some emperor or of some business man—a material need, plus display. At any rate we have architecture, the only architecture of our time. I do not mean our copies of old buildings, lovely and lovable as they are; I mean our own creations, our office buildings like greater *campanili*,[1] and so on.

And we have, or we are beginning to have, collections. We have had at least one scholar in Ernest Fenollosa,[2] and one patron in Mr Freer.[3] I mean that these two men at least have worked as the great Italian researchers and collectors of the quattrocento worked and collected. But mostly America, from the White House to the gutter, is still dominated by a 'puritanical' hatred to what is beyond its understanding.

So it is to the fighting minority that I speak, to a minority that has been until now gradually forced out of the country. We have looked to the wrong powers. We have not sufficiently looked to ourselves. We have not defined the hostility or inertia that is against us. We have not recognized with any Voltairian clearness the nature of this opposition, and we have not realized to what an extent a renaissance is a thing made—a thing made by conscious propaganda.

9. John Millington Synge (1871–1909), Irish author of plays dealing with the Aran Isles off the west coast of Ireland.
1. Belltowers.
2. Ernest F. Fenollosa (1853–1908), American Orientalist and translator of Chinese poetry.
3. Charles L. Freer (1856–1919), American industrialist, collector of Whistler's paintings, donor of the Freer Gallery of Art in Washington, D.C.

The scholars of the quattrocento had just as stiff a stupidity and contentment and ignorance to contend with. It is in the biographies of Erasmus and Lorenzo Valla that we must find consolation.[4] They were willing to work at foundations. They did not give the crowd what it wanted. The middle ages had been a jumble. There may have been a charming diversity, but there was also the darkness of decentralization. There had been minute vortices at such castles as that of Savairic de Maleon, and later at the universities. But the *rinascimento*[5] began when Valla wrote in the preface of the *Elegantiae:* * * * '*Ibi namque Romanum imperium est, ubicunque Romana lingua dominatur.*'[6]

That is not 'the revival of classicism'. It is not a worship of corpses. It is an appreciation of the great Roman vortex, an understanding of, and an awakening to, the value of a capital, the value of centralization, in matters of knowledge and art, and of the interaction and stimulus of genius foregathered. *Ubicunque Romana lingua dominatur!*

That sense, that reawakening to the sense of the capital, resulted not in a single great vortex, such as Dante had dreamed of in his propaganda for a great central court, a peace tribunal, and in all his ghibelline[7] speculations; but it did result in the numerous vortices of the Italian cities, striving against each other not only in commerce but in the arts as well.

America has no natural capital. Washington is a political machine, I dare say a good enough one. If we are to have an art capital it also must be made by conscious effort. No city will make such effort on behalf of any other city. The city that plays for this glory will have to plot, deliberately to plot, for the gathering in of great artists, not merely as incidental lecturers but as residents. She will have to plot for the centralization of young artists. She will have to give them living conditions as comfortable as Paris has given since the days of Abelard.[8]

The universities can no longer remain divorced from contemporary intellectual activity. The press cannot longer remain divorced from the vitality and precision of an awakened university scholarship. Art and scholarship need not be wholly at loggerheads.

But above all there must be living conditions for artists; not merely for illustrators and magazine writers, not merely for commercial producers, catering to what they think 'the public' or 'their readers' desire.

Great art does not depend on the support of riches, but without

4. Two Renaissance humanists: Desiderius Erasmus (1466?–1536), Dutch scholar and Catholic religious reformer; and the Italian scholar Lorenzo Valla (1406–57).
5. Renaissance.
6. "For the Roman Empire extends wherever the Roman language reigns." Six lines deleted from Valla's *Elegantiae*

(*Elegancies of the Latin Language,* 1544), quoted by Pound, are a tribute to the civilizing influence of the Latin language.
7. Political faction in medieval and Renaissance Italy.
8. Peter Abelard (1079–1142), French philosopher.

such aid it will be individual, separate, and spasmodic; it will not group and become a great period. The individual artist will do fine work in corners, to be discovered after his death. Some good enough poet will be spoiled by trying to write stuff as vendible as bath-tubs; or another because, not willing or able to rely on his creative work, he had to make his mind didactic by preparing to be a professor of literature, or abstract by trying to be a professor of philosophy, or had to participate in some other fiasco. But for all that you will not be able to stop the great art, the true art, of the man of genius.

Great art does not depend upon comfort, it does not depend upon the support of riches. But a great age is brought about only with the aid of wealth, because a great age means the deliberate fostering of genius, the gathering-in and grouping and encouragement of artists.

In my final paper of this series, I shall put forth certain plans for improvement.

III

No, I am not such a fool as to believe that a man writes better for being well fed, or that he writes better for being hungry either. Hunger—some experience of it—is doubtless good for a man; it puts an edge on his style, and so does hard common sense. In the end I believe in hunger, because it is an experience, and no artist can have too many experiences. Prolonged hunger, intermittent hunger and anxiety, will of course break down a man's constitution, render him fussy and over-irritable, and in the end ruin his work or prevent its full development.

That nation is profoundly foolish which does not get the maximum of best work out of its artists. The artist is one of the few producers. He, the farmer and the artisan create wealth; the rest shift and consume it. The net value of good art to its place of residence has been computed in logarithms; I shall not go into the decimals. When there was talk of selling Holbein's[9] *Duchess of Milan* to an American, England bought the picture for three hundred and fifty thousand dollars. They figured that people came to London to see the picture, that the receipts of the community were worth more per annum than the interest on the money. People go where there are good works of art. Pictures and sculpture and architecture pay. Even literature and poetry pay, for where there is enough intelligence to produce and maintain good writing, there society is pleasant and the real estate values increase. Mr F. M. Hueffer[1] has said that the difference between London and other places is that 'No one lives in London merely for the sake of making money enough to live somewhere else.'

The real estate values, even in Newark, New Jersey, would go up

---

9. Hans Holbein the Younger (1497?–1543), German painter, resident in England in 1526–27 and 1532–43.
1. Ford Madox Hueffer (Ford Madox Ford, 1873–1939), British editor, expatriate, and novelist (*The Good Soldier*, 1915).

if Newark were capable of producing art, literature or the drama. In the quattrocento men went from one Italian city to another for reasons that were not solely commercial.

The question is not: Shall we try to keep up the arts?—but: How can we maintain the arts most efficiently? Paris can survive 1870 and 1914[2] because she is an intellectual and artistic vortex. She is that vortex not because she had a university in the middle ages— Cordova and Padua had also medieval universities. France recognizes the cash value of artists. They do not have to pay taxes save when covenient; they have a ministry of fine arts doing its semi-efficient best. Literary but inartistic England moves with a slow paw pushing occasional chunks of meat towards the favoured. England does as well as can be expected, considering that the management of such affairs is entrusted to men whose interests are wholly political and who have no sort of intuition or taste. That is to say, in England, if someone of good social position says that your work is 'really literary', and that you are not likely to attack the hereditary interests or criticise the Albert Memorial,[3] you can be reasonably sure of a pension. If your sales have suddenly slumped, you can also have 'royal bounty', provided that you respect the senile and decrepit and say a good word for Watts's pictures.[4]

The result is that France gets Rodin's[5] work when he is fifty instead of the day he began doing good work. England gets Rodin's work after it has gone to seed, and rejects the best work of Epstein[6] in his full vigor. England let half her last generation of poets die off, and pensioned such survivors as hadn't gone into something 'practical'.

But even this is enough to show that bourgeois France and stolid England recognize the cash value of art. I don't imagine that these sordid material considerations will weigh with my compatriots. America is a nation of idealists, as we all know; and they are going to support art for art's sake, because they love it, because they 'want the best', even in art. They want beauty; they can't get along without it. They are already tired of spurious literature.

They recognize that all great art, all good art, goes against the grain of contemporary taste. They want men who can stand out against it. They want to back such men and women to the limit. How are they to go about it? Subsidy? Oh, no. They don't want to pauperize artists!

Of course Swinburne was subsidized by his immediate forebears, and Shelley also; and Browning, the robust, the virile, was subsi-

---

2. The dates mark the outbreaks of the Franco-Prussian War and World War I respectively.
3. Monument in London honoring Prince Albert, husband of Queen Victoria.
4. George F. Watts (1817–1904), popular Victorian academic painter, awarded the Order of Merit in 1902.
5. Auguste Rodin (1840–1917), controversial French Romantic sculptor and precursor of modernism.
6. Sir Jacob Epstein (1880–1959), American-born sculptor who settled in London in 1905.

dized by his wife;[7] and even Dante and Villon did not escape the stigma of having received charities. Nevertheless it is undemocratic to believe that a man with money should give—horrible word!— *give* it, even though not all of it, to painters and poets.

They give it to sterile professors; to vacuous preachers of a sterilized form of Christianity; they support magazines whose set and avowed purpose is either to degrade letters or to prevent their natural development. Why in heaven's name shouldn't they back creators, as well as students of Quinet?[8] Why shouldn't they endow men whose studies are independent, put them on an equal footing with men whose scholarship is merely a pasteurized, Bostonized imitation of Leipzig?

How are they to go about it? Committees are notably stupid; they vote for mediocrity, their mind is the least common denominator. Even if there are a few intelligent members, the unintelligent members will be the ones with spare time, and they will get about trying to 'run the committee', trying to get in new members who will vote for their kind of inanity. *Et cetera, ad infinitum.*

There is one obvious way, which does not compel individuals to wait for an organization:

Private people can give stipends to individual artists. That is to say, you, Mr Rockefeller, you, Laird Andy of Skibo,[9] and the rest of you (I am not leaving you out, reader, because you have only one million or half of one); you can endow individuals for life just as you endow chairs in pedagogy and callisthenics. More than that, you can endow them with the right to name their successors. If they don't need the money they can pass it on, before their deaths, to younger artists in whom they believe.

For instance, you may begin by endowing Mr James Whitcomb Riley, Mr George Santayana, Mr Theodore Roosevelt, Mr Jack London, or anybody else you believe in.[1] And any artist will applaud you. Any artist would rather have a benefice conferred upon him by *one* of these men as an individual than by a committee of the 'forty leading luminaries of literature'. I take a hard case; I don't suppose for a moment that Mr Riley or Mr Roosevelt, Mr Santayana or Mr London wants money—in all probability they would one and all refuse it if offered; but none of them would refuse the right of allotting an income, sufficient to cover the bare necessities of life, to some active artist whom they believe in.

---

7. The British poets Algernon Charles Swinburne (1837–1909), Percy Bysshe Shelley (1792–1822), and Robert Browning (1812–89).
8. Edgar Quinet (1803–75), minor French academic philosopher, historian, and poet.
9. American financial magnates John D. Rockefeller (1839–1937) and Andrew Carnegie (1835–1919). The latter built the Castle of Skibo on an estate in northern Scotland. "Laird" is Scottish for "Lord."
1. Successful, eminent American men of letters. Theodore Roosevelt (1858–1919), historian and President of the United States (1901–8), was an ardent nationalist, advocate of a strong central government, founder of the Progressive party, and author of *The Naval War of 1812* (1882) and *The Winning of the West* (1889–96).

If you endow enough men, individuals of vivid and different personality, and make the endowment perpetual, to be handed down from artist to artist, you will have put the arts in a position to defy the subversive pressure of commercial advantage, and of the mediocre spirit which is the bane and hidden terror of democracy.

Democracies have fallen, they have always fallen, because humanity craves the outstanding personality. And hitherto no democracy has provided sufficient place for such an individuality. If you so endow sculptors and writers you will begin for America an age of awakening which will over-shadow the quattrocento; because our opportunity is greater than Leonardo's: we have more aliment, we have not one classic tradition to revivify, we have China and Egypt, and the unknown lands lying upon the roof of the world—Khotan, Kara-shar and Kan-su.[2]

So much for the individual opportunity—now for the civic. Any city which cares for its future can perfectly well start its vortex. It can found something between a graduate seminar and the usual 'Arts Club' made up of business men and of a few 'rather more than middle-aged artists who can afford to belong'.

I have set the individually endowed artist against the endowed professor or editor. I would set the endowment of such grouping of young artists parallel with the endowment, for one year or three, of scholars and fellows by our universities. Some hundreds of budding professors are so endowed, to say nothing of students of divinity.

There is no reason why students of the arts—not merely of painting but of all the arts—should not be so endowed, and so grouped: that is, as artists, not merely as followers of one segregated art. Such endowment would get them over the worst two or three years of their career, the years when their work can't possibly pay.

Scientists are so endowed. It is as futile to expect a poet to get the right words, or any sort of artists to do real work, with one eye on the public, as it would be to expect the experimenter in a chemical laboratory to advance the borders of science, if he have constantly to consider whether his atomic combinations are going to flatter popular belief, or suit the holders of monopolies in some over-expensive compound. The arts and sciences hang together. Any conception which does not see them in their interrelation belittles both. What is good for one is good for the other.

Has any one yet answered the query: why is it that in other times artists went on getting more and more powerful as they grew older, whereas now they decline after the first outburst, or at least after the first successes? Compare this with the steady growth of scientists.

The three main lines of attack, then, which I have proposed in this little series of articles, are as follows:

2. A town and river in Sinkiang province, a town in Sinkiang province, and a northwest province in China, respectively.

First, that we should develop a criticism of poetry based on world-poetry, on the work of maximum excellence. (It does not in the least matter whether this standard be that of my own predilections, or crochets or excesses. It matters very much that it be decided by men who have made a first-hand study of world-poetry, and who 'have had the tools in their hands'.)

Second, that there be definite subsidy of individual artists, writers, etc., such as will enable them to follow their highest ambitions without needing to conciliate the ignorant *en route*. (Even some of our stock-size magazine poets might produce something worth while if they could afford occasionally to keep quiet for six months or a year at a stretch.)

Third, there should be a foundation of such centres as I have described. There should be in America the '*gloire de cénacle*'.[3] Tariff laws should favor the creative author rather than the printer, but that matter is too long to be gone into.

In conclusion, the first of these matters must be fought out among the artists themselves. The second matter concerns not only the excessively rich, but the normally and moderately rich, who contribute to all sorts of less useful affairs: redundant universities, parsons, Y.M.C.A.'s, and the general encouragement of drab mediocrity. The third matter concerns millionaires, multimillionaires and municipalities.

When a civilization is vivid, it preserves and fosters all sorts of artists—painters, poets, sculptors, musicians, architects. When a civilization is dull and anemic it preserves a rabble of priests, sterile instructors, and repeaters of things second-hand. If literature is to reappear in America it must come through, but in spite of, the present commercial system of publication.

1915

Hugh Selwyn Mauberley[1]
(Life and Contacts)[2]

"Vocat aestus in umbram"[3]
—NEMESIANUS, *Ec. IV*

E. P. Ode pour l'election de Son Sepulchre[4]

For three years, out of key with his time,
He strove to resuscitate the dead art
Of poetry; to maintain "the sublime"
In the old sense. Wrong from the start—

3. "The splendor of cenacles," salons or groups for the discussion of literature and politics that flourished during the Romantic period.

1. This poem was published in 1920 when Pound was on the verge of leaving London and already at work on his more ambitious and innovative *Cantos*. Deftly ironic, the poem measures both the validity and the limitations of his aesthetic practices. At the same time he diagnosed

the ills of the social, economic, and cultural environment of England, which threatened to repress imaginative talent or channel it into trivial, escapist, and ineffectual forms. Pound declared that the poem was modeled partly on the technique of Henry James's prose fiction: it presents its subject through the medium of a character's mind or voice, a "center of consciousness" whose mind and standards are also part of the sub-

No, hardly, but seeing he had been born   5
In a half savage country, out of date;
Bent resolutely on wringing lilies from the acorn;
Capaneus;[5] trout for factitious bait;

Ἴδμεν γάρ τοι πάνθ᾽, ὅσ᾽ ἐνὶ Τροίῃ[6]
Caught in the unstopped ear;   10
Giving the rocks small lee-way
The chopped seas held him, therefore, that year.

His true Penelope[7] was Flaubert,[8]
He fished by obstinate isles;
Observed the elegance of Circe's[9] hair   15
Rather than the mottoes on sun-dials.

Unaffected by "the march of events,"
He passed from men's memory in *l'an trentiesme*
De son eage,[1] the case presents
No adjunct to the Muses' diadem.   20

II[2]

The age demanded an image
Of its accelerated grimace,

---

ject being treated and are exposed themselves to scrutiny and assessment. In *Hugh Selwyn Mauberley*, the first 13 lyrics are presented through "E.P.," a persona through which Pound expresses some of his own ambitions and tastes; cultural conditions in London and representative literary figures (some clearly opposed, some more closely linked to Pound's own aims and associations) are surveyed through the mind of "E.P.," and reactions to them are expressed in his voice, which verges on futility until it is quickened into passion in the "Envoi." In the next section, entitled "Mauberley" (I through "Medallion"), the persona of "E.P." is absorbed in his attention to the fictitious poet Mauberley, a second persona through whom Pound subtly mocks while simultaneously pursuing his own attempt to explore experience and resuscitate poetry in sculptured forms. Pound attempts by tender but pointed irony to exorcise the nostalgia, isolation, and cult of durable form that impels his own poetic practice but threatens to ennervate it and reduce it to an aesthete's "overblotted / Series / Of intermittences." By exaggerating these motives, Pound incorporates his own "profane protest" against them and triumphs over them in verse that culminates in the highly charged and durably sculptured, though still miniature, "Medallion."
2. Ironic echo of a conventional subtitle of literary biographies, "Life and Letters." In a subsequent edition of 1957, Pound reversed the sequence, claiming that "Contacts and Life" followed the "order of the subject matter." To the

American edition of *Personae* in 1926, Pound added the following note: "The sequence is so distinctly a farewell to London that the reader who chooses to regard this as an exclusively American edition may as well omit it and turn at once to page 205."
3. "The heat calls us into the shade," from the *Eclogues* (IV.38) of the third-century Carthaginian poet Nemesianus.
4. Adaptation of the title of an ode by Pierre de Ronsard (1524–85) *On the Selection of His Tomb* (*Odes*, IV.5.).
5. One of Seven against Thebes whom Zeus struck down by lightning for his rebellious defiance.
6. "For we know all the toils [endured] in wide Troy," part of the sirens' song to detain Odysseus in Homer's *Odyssey* (Book 12, 189). Odysseus stopped his comrades' ears with wax to prevent their succumbing to the lure.
7. Wife of Odysseus who remained faithful during his long absence but alternately enticed and held off the many suitors who sought to displace him.
8. Gustave Flaubert (1821–80), French novelist who cultivated form and stylistic precision.
9. Enchantress with whom Odysseus dallied for a year before returning home.
1. "The thirtieth year of his age," adapted from *The Testament* by the 15th-century French thief and poet François Villon. Since the turning point Pound had in mind was the publication of his *Lustra* in 1916, he later changed the line to "trentunieme" or "thirty–first" to conform to his age at that time.
2. The subtle ironies of this poem derive from three senses of the word *de-*

Something for the modern stage,
Not, at any rate, an Attic grace;

Not, not certainly, the obscure reveries   25
Of the inward gaze;
Better mendacities
Than the classics in paraphrase!

The "age demanded" chiefly a mould in plaster,
Made with no loss of time,   30
A prose kinema,³ not, not assuredly, alabaster
Or the "sculpture" of rhyme.

III

The tea-rose tea-gown, etc.
Supplants the mousseline of Cos,⁴
The pianola "replaces"   35
Sappho's barbitos.⁵

Christ follows Dionysus,⁶
Phallic and ambrosial
Made way for macerations;⁷
Caliban casts out Ariel.⁸   40

All things are a flowing,
Sage Heracleitus⁹ says;
But a tawdry cheapness
Shall outlast our days.

Even the Christian beauty   45
Defects—after Samothrace;¹
We see τὸ καλόν²
Decreed in the market place.

Faun's flesh is not to us,
Nor the saint's vision.   50
We have the press for wafer;
Franchise for circumcision.

---

manded: what the age wanted and liked, what by contrast it needed, and what it "asked for" in the sense of deserved to get. The poem defines the expectations that make it difficult for the modern poet to fulfill his public role, and also suggests the means that Pound characteristically tried to use: translations that go beyond mere paraphrase, forms with the force of prose and the movement of cinematic art, and the " 'sculpture' of rhyme."
3. Movement (Greek), and early spelling of *cinema*, motion pictures.
4. Gauzelike fabric for which the Aegean island Cos was famous.
5. Lyrelike instrument used by the Greek poetess Sappho (fl. 600 B.C.)
6. Greek god of fertility, regenerative

suffering, wine, and poetic inspiration; his worshipers were known for destructive frenzies and consuming ecstasies; his festivals included sexual rites, wine tasting, and dramatic performances.
7. Wasting, fasting. Pound compares Christian asceticism to Dionysian rites.
8. In Shakespeare's *Tempest*, Caliban is the earth-bound and rebellious slave of Prospero, ruler and magician; Ariel is the imaginative spirit whose assistance Prospero commandeers.
9. Greek philosopher (fl. 500 B.C.) who taught that all reality is flux or a "flowing."
1. North Aegean island, center of religious mystery cults, site of the famous statue *Winged Victory*.
2. The beautiful.

All men, in law, are equals.
Free of Pisistratus,[3]
We choose a knave or an eunuch   55
To rule over us.

O bright Apollo,
τίν' ἄνδρα, τίν' ἥρωα, τίνα θεόν,[4]
What god, man, or hero
Shall I place a tin wreath upon!   60

IV

These fought in any case,
and some believing,
                    pro domo,[5] in any case . . .

Some quick to arm,
some for adventure,   65
some from fear of weakness,
some from fear of censure,
some for love of slaughter, in imagination,
learning later . . .
some in fear, learning love of slaughter;   70

Died some, pro patria,
                    non "dulce" non "et decor"[6] . . .
walked eye-deep in hell
believing in old men's lies, then unbelieving
came home, home to a lie,   75
home to many deceits,
home to old lies and new infamy;
usury age-old and age-thick
and liars in public places.

Daring as never before, wastage as never before.   80
Young blood and high blood,
fair cheeks, and fine bodies;

fortitude as never before

frankness as never before,
disillusions as never told in the old days,   85
hysterias, trench confessions,
laughter out of dead bellies.

V

There died a myriad,
And of the best, among them,

3. Athenian tyrant and art patron (fl.
sixth century B.C.).
4. "What man, what hero, what god,"
Pound's version of Pindar's "What god,
what hero, what man shall we loudly
praise" (*Olympian Odes*, II.2).
5. "For the home," adapted from Cicero's *De Domo Sua*.
6. "For one's native land, not sweetly,
not gloriously," adapted from Horace,
"it is sweet and glorious to die for one's
fatherland" (*Odes*, III.ii.13).

For an old bitch gone in the teeth,   90
For a botched civilization,

Charm, smiling at the good mouth,
Quick eyes gone under earth's lid,

For two gross of broken statues,
For a few thousand battered books.   95

Yeux Glauques[7]

Gladstone was still respected,
When John Ruskin produced
"King's Treasuries"; Swinburne
And Rossetti still abused.

Foetid Buchanan lifted up his voice   100
When that faun's head of hers
Became a pastime for
Painters and adulterers.

The Burne-Jones cartons[8]
Have preserved her eyes;   105
Still, at the Tate, they teach
Cophetua to rhapsodize;

Thin like brook-water,
With a vacant gaze.
The English Rubaiyat was still-born[9]   110
In those days.

The thin, clear gaze, the same
Still darts out faun-like from the half-ruin'd face,
Questing and passive. . . .
"Ah, poor Jenny's case"[1] . . .   115

Bewildered that a world
Shows no surprise
At her last maquero's[2]
Adulteries.

---

7. The brilliant yellow-green eyes of Elizabeth Siddal, the seamstress who became the favorite model of the Pre-Raphaelite painters and later the wife of the painter and poet Dante Gabriel Rossetti (1828–82). She was the model for the beggar maid in *Cophetua and the Beggar Maid* (now hanging in the Tate Gallery, London), by Sir Edward Burne-Jones (1833–98). The Pre-Raphaelites, including the poet Algernon Swinburne (1837–1909), were attacked as "The Fleshly School of Poetry" by Robert W. Buchanan (1841–1901) in 1871, and were defended by the critic John Ruskin (1819–1900), whose *Sesame*

and Lilies (1865) contains a chapter entitled "Kings' Treasuries," calling for the diffusion of literature and the improvement of English tastes in the arts. William E. Gladstone (1809–98) was a politician and three times Prime Minister of Britain.
8. Drawings.
9. Edward Fitzgerald (1809–83) translated *The Rubáiyát of Omar Khayyám* in 1859, but it was not read ("stillborn") until discovered later by the Pre-Raphaelites.
1. Prostitute, heroine of a poem by Rossetti.
2. Or *magnereau*: sexual exploiter, pimp.

"Siena mi fe'; Disfecemi Maremma"[3]

Among the pickled foetuses and bottled bones,   120
Engaged in perfecting the catalogue,
I found the last scion of the
Senatorial families of Strasbourg, Monsieur Verog.[4]

For two hours he talked of Gallifet;[5]
Of Dowson; of the Rhymers' Club;   125
Told me how Johnson (Lionel) died
By falling from a high stool in a pub . . .

But showed no trace of alcohol
At the autopsy, privately performed—
Tissue preserved—the pure mind   130
Arose toward Newman[6] as the whiskey warmed.

Dowson found harlots cheaper than hotels;
Headlam for uplift; Image impartially imbued
With raptures for Bacchus, Terpsichore[7] and the Church.
So spoke the author of "The Dorian Mood,"   135

M. Verog, out of step with the decade,
Detached from his contemporaries,
Neglected by the young,
Because of these reveries.

Brennbaum

The sky-like limpid eyes,   140
The circular infant's face,
The stiffness from spats to collar
Never relaxing into grace;

The heavy memories of Horeb, Sinai and the forty
    years,[8]
Showed only when the daylight fell   145
Level across the face
Of Brennbaum "The Impeccable."

---

3. "Siena made me, Maremma unmade me," spoken by a Sienese woman, condemned by her husband to die in Maremma marshes for her infidelity, in Dante's *Purgatory* (V.134).
4. Victor Plarr (1863–1929), French poet (*In the Dorian Mood*, 1896) and raconteur from Strasbourg, later librarian of the Royal College of Surgeons and member of the Rhymer's Club. Other members: two Roman Catholic poets and heavy drinkers, Ernest Dowson (1867–1900), of whom Plarr published a memoir, and Lionel Johnson (1867–1902), whose *Poetical Works* Pound edited in 1915; the Reverend Stewart D. Headlam (1847–1924), forced to resign his curacy for lecturing on the dance to workingmen's clubs; and Selwyn Image (1849–1930), founder with Headlam of the Church and Stage Guild.
5. Marquis de Galliffet (1830–1909), French General at the battle of Sedan, which the French lost, in the Franco-Prussian War.
6. John Henry Newman (1801–90), editor and Roman Catholic convert and intellectual, later Cardinal.
7. Greek muse of the dance.
8. The children of Israel wandered in the wilderness for 40 years. Moses saw the burning bush at Horeb (Exodus 3.2); he received the Ten Commandments at Sinai (Exodus 19.20 ff.).

Mr. Nixon

In the cream gilded cabin of his steam yacht
Mr. Nixon advised me kindly, to advance with fewer
Dangers of delay. "Consider   150
    "Carefully the reviewer.

"I was as poor as you are;
"When I began I got, of course,
"Advance on royalties, fifty at first," said Mr. Nixon,
"Follow me, and take a column,   155
"Even if you have to work free.

"Butter reviewers. From fifty to three hundred
"I rose in eighteen months;
"The hardest nut I had to crack
"Was Dr. Dundas.   160

"I never mentioned a man but with the view
"Of selling my own works.
"The tip's a good one, as for literature
"It gives no man a sinecure.

"And no one knows, at sight, a masterpiece.   165
"And give up verse, my boy,
"There's nothing in it."

·   ·   ·   ·   ·   ·   ·   ·   ·   ·

Likewise a friend of Bloughram's once advised me:[9]
Don't kick against the pricks,[1]
Accept opinion. The "Nineties" tried your game   170
And died, there's nothing in it.

X

Beneath the sagging roof
The stylist has taken shelter,
Unpaid, uncelebrated,
At last from the world's welter   175

Nature receives him;
With a placid and uneducated mistress
He exercises his talents
And the soil meets his distress.

The haven from sophistications and contentions   180
Leaks through its thatch;
He offers succulent cooking;
The door has a creaking latch.

---

9. In Browning's *Bishop Bloughram's Apology*, the Bishop rationalized his doctrinal laxity.

1. Ironic echo of Christ's statement to Saul: "it is hard for thee to kick against the pricks" (Acts 9.5).

XI

"Conservatrix of Milésien"[2]
Habits of mind and feeling,   185
Possibly. But in Ealing[3]
With the most bank-clerky of Englishmen?

No, "Milésian" is an exaggeration.
No instinct has survived in her
Older than those her grandmother   190
Told her would fit her station.

XII

"Daphne with her thighs in bark
Stretches toward me her leafy hands,"[4]—
Subjectively. In the stuffed-satin drawing-room
I await The Lady Valentine's commands,   195

Knowing my coat has never been
Of precisely the fashion
To stimulate, in her,
A durable passion;

Doubtful, somewhat, of the value   200
Of well-gowned approbation
Of literary effort,
But never of The Lady Valentine's vocation:

Poetry, her border of ideas,
The edge, uncertain, but a means of blending   205
With other strata
Where the lower and higher have ending;

A hook to catch the Lady Jane's attention,
A modulation toward the theatre,
Also, in the case of revolution,   210
A possible friend and comforter.
   .   .   .   .

Conduct, on the other hand, the soul
"Which the highest cultures have nourished"[5]
To Fleet St. where
Dr. Johnson flourished;[6]   215

Beside this thoroughfare
The sale of half-hose has

2. I.e., conservator of the erotic indulgence for which the Ionian city of Miletus and Aristides' *Milesian Tales* (second century B.C.) were known.
3. London suburb.
4. The metamorphosis of the nymph Daphne into a laurel tree to escape the embrace of Apollo; Pound's lines are a translation of Théophile Gautier's version of Ovid's story in *Le Château de Souvenir*.
5. A translation of two lines from *Complainte de Pianos* by the short-lived French poet Jules Laforgue (1860–87).
6. Samuel Johnson (1709–84), journalist, poet, critic, and moral essayist, the reigning man of letters in late 18th-century London. "Fleet St.": newspaper publishing center in London.

Long since superseded the cultivation
Of Pierian roses.[7]

Envoi (1919)[8]

Go, dumb-born book,   220
Tell her that sang me once that song of Lawes:
Hadst thou but song
As thou hast subjects known.
Then were there cause in thee that should condone
Even my faults that heavy upon me lie,   225
And build her glories their longevity.

Tell her that sheds
Such treasure in the air,
Recking naught else but that her graces give
Life to the moment,   230
I would bid them live
As roses might, in magic amber laid,
Red overwrought with orange and all made
One substance and one colour
Braving time.   235

Tell her that goes
With song upon her lips
But sings not out the song, nor knows
The maker of it, some other mouth,
May be as fair as hers,   240
Might, in new ages, gain her worshippers,
When our two dusts with Waller's shall be laid,
Siftings on siftings in oblivion,
Till change hath broken down
All things save Beauty alone.   245

Mauberley
1920

"Vacuos exercet aera morsus."[9]

I

Turned from the "eau-forte
Par Jaquemart"[1]
To the strait head

---

7. Roses of Pieria, place near Mount Olympus where the Muses were worshiped.

8. This poem is modeled on the rhetoric and cadences of *Goe, Lovely Rose* by Edmund Waller (1606–87), whose poems were set to music by Henry Lawes (1596–1662). "E.P." first addresses his book and dispatches it with a message for the listener (to the poem) who once inspired him by singing Waller's song, then in line 222 breaks off to confess the limited powers of his poetry. The second stanza celebrates the beauty of the singer and listener, and offers to commemorate her in verse. The third warns of the incompleteness of her response and of the transience of all things but beauty. The concert singer whom Pound heard sing Lawes's and Waller's song was Raymonde Collignon.

9. "He snaps vacuously at the empty air," the vain effort of a dog in Ovid's *Metamorphoses* (VII.786) to bite an elusive monster attacking Thebes; both dog and monster are later turned to stone.

1. "Etching by Jacquemart," Jules Jacquemart, French graphic artist (1837–80).

Of Messalina:[2]

"His true Penelope   250
Was Flaubert,"[3]
And his tool
The engraver's.

Firmness,
Not the full smile,   255
His art, but an art
In profile;

Colourless
Pier Francesca,[4]
Pisanello[5] lacking the skill   260
To forge Achaia.[6]

II

"Qu'est ce qu'ils savent de l'amour, et qu'est ce qu'ils peuvent en comprendre?
  S'ils ne comprennent pas la poésie, s'ils ne sentent pas la musique, qu'est ce qu'ils peuvent comprendre de cette passion en comparison avec laquelle la rose est grossiè et le parfum des violettes un tonnere?"   —CAID ALI[7]

For three years, diabolus[8] in the scale,
He drank ambrosia,
All passes, ANANGKE[9] prevails,
Came end, at last, to that Arcadia.[1]   265

He had moved amid her phantasmagoria,
Amid her galaxies,
NUKTIS 'AGALMA[2]

·   ·   ·   ·   ·   ·   ·

Drifted . . . drifted precipitate,
Asking time to be rid of . . .   270
Of his bewilderment; to designate
His new found orchid. . . .

To be certain . . . certain . . .
(Amid aerial flowers) . . . time for arrangements—
Drifted on   275
To the final estrangement;

Unable in the supervening blankness
To sift TO AGATHON[3] from the chaff

2. Dissolute wife of the Roman Emperor Claudius (c. A.D. 8).
3. Quoted from line 13.
4. Piero della Francesca, Umbrian painter (1420?–92).
5. Vittore Pisano (1397?–1455?), Veronese painter and medalist who forged medallions based on Greek coins.
6. Southern Greece.
7. "What do they know of love, and what can they understand? If they do not understand poetry, if they do not respond to music, what can they under- stand of this passion in comparison to which the rose is gross and the perfume of violets a clap of thunder?" Caid Ali is a pseudonym of Pound.
8. The devil and, in music, the interval of the augmented fourth.
9. Necessity.
1. Greek mountain region thought of as an ideal rustic paradise.
2. "Night's jewel," a phrase from a celebration of the evening star in a pastoral by the Greek poet Bion (c. 100 B.C.).
3. The good.

Until he found his sieve . . .
Ultimately, his seismograph: 280

—Given that is his "fundamental passion,"
This urge to convey the relation
Of eye-lid and cheek-bone
By verbal manifestations;

To present the series   285
Of curious heads in medallion—

He had passed, inconscient, full gaze,
The wide-banded irides[4]
And botticellian sprays[5] implied
In their diastasis;[6]   290

Which anaethesis, noted a year late,
And weighed, revealed his great affect,
(Orchid), mandate
Of Eros,[7] a retrospect.

Mouths biting empty air,   295
The still stone dogs,
Caught in metamorphosis, were
Left him as epilogues.

"The Age Demanded"

VIDE[8] POEM II. PAGE 1056

For this agility chance found
Him of all men, unfit   300
As the red-beaked steeds of
The Cytheraean for a chain bit.[9]

The glow of porcelain
Brought no reforming sense
To his perception   305
Of the social inconsequence.

Thus, if her colour
Came against his gaze,
Tempered as if
It were through a perfect glaze   310

He made no immediate application
Of this to relation of the state
To the individual, the month was more temperate
Because this beauty had been.

---

4. Plural of *iris*: flowers and eyes.
5. Allusion to the Italian painter Sandro Botticelli (1444?–1510) and women carrying flowers in his painting *Primavera* ("Spring").
6. Separation.

7. Greek god of love, son of Aphrodite (Venus).
8. "Vide": see.
9. Doves harnessed to the chariot of Aphrodite, who first landed on the island of Cythera off the Laconian coast.

The coral isle, the lion-coloured sand   315
Burst in upon the porcelain revery:
Impetuous troubling
Of his imagery.

Mildness, amid the neo-Nietzschean[1] clatter,
His sense of graduations,   320
Quite out of place amid
Resistance to current exacerbations,

Invitation, mere invitation to perceptivity
Gradually led him to the isolation
Which these presents place   325
Under a more tolerant, perhaps, examination.

By constant elimination
The manifest universe
Yielded an armour
Against utter consternation,   330

A Minoan undulation,[2]
Seen, we admit, amid ambrosial circumstances
Strengthened him against
The discouraging doctrine of chances,

And his desire for survival,   335
Faint in the most strenuous moods,
Became an Olympian *apathein*[3]
In the presence of selected perceptions.

A pale gold, in the aforesaid pattern,
The unexpected palms   340
Destroying, certainly, the artist's urge,
Left him delighted with the imaginary
Audition of the phantasmal sea-surge,

Incapable of the least utterance or composition,
Emendation, conservation of the "better tradition,"   345
Refinement of medium, elimination of superfluities,
August attraction or concentration.

Nothing, in brief, but maudlin confession,
Irresponse to human aggression,
Amid the precipitation, down-float   350
Of insubstantial manna,
Lifting the faint susurrus

1. Ideas derived from Friedrich Wilhelm
Nietzsche (1844–1900), German philosopher. His paradoxical ethical and aesthetic theories, widely discussed at the
time, were a bold challenge to conventional ideas in England, Europe, and
America.

2. Stylistic feature of portrait sculptures
by the Cretan Scopas during the Minoan
period (2000–1500 B.C.), according to the
French archaeologist Salomon Reinach
(1858–1932) in his *Apollo* (1904).
3. The absence of feeling or indifference
of the Olympian gods to human affairs.

Of his subjective hosannah.

Ultimate affronts to
Human redundancies;   355

Non-esteem of self-styled "his betters"
Leading, as he well knew,
To his final
Exclusion from the world of letters.

IV

Scattered Moluccas[4]   360
Not knowing, day to day,
The first day's end, in the next noon;
The placid water
Unbroken by the Simoon;[5]

Thick foliage   365
Placid beneath warm suns,
Tawn fore-shores
Washed in the cobalt of oblivions;

Or through dawn-mist
The grey and rose   370
Of the juridical
Flamingoes;

A consciousness disjunct,
Being but this overblotted
Series   375
Of intermittences;

Coracle[6] of Pacific voyages,
The unforecasted beach;
Then on an oar
Read this: 380

"I was
And I no more exist;
Here drifted
An hedonist."

Medallion

Luini in porcelain![7]   385
The grand piano
Utters a profane
Protest with her clear soprano.

4. Spice Islands in the Malay Archipel-
ago.
5. Violent wind and sand storm of Near
Eastern deserts.

6. Small hide-covered wicker-frame boat
used by ancient Britons.
7. Bernardino Luini (1475?–1532?), Italian painter.

The sleek head emerges
From the gold-yellow frock   390
As Anadyomene[8] in the opening
Pages of Reinach.

Honey-red, closing the face-oval,
A basket-work of braids which seem as if they were
Spun in King Minos'[9] hall   395
From metal, or intractable amber;

The face-oval beneath the glaze,
Bright in its suave bounding-line, as,
Beneath half-watt rays,
The eyes turn topaz.   400

                                                          1920

From THE CANTOS
I[1]

And then went down to the ship,
Set keel to breakers, forth on the godly sea, and
We set up mast and sail on that swart ship,
Bore sheep aboard her, and our bodies also
Heavy with weeping, and winds from sternward   5
Bore us out onward with bellying canvas,
Circe's this craft, the trim-coifed goddess.[2]
Then sat we amidships, wind jamming the tiller,
Thus with stretched sail, we went over sea till day's end.
Sun to his slumber, shadows o'er all the ocean,   10
Came we then to the bounds of deepest water,
To the Kimmerian lands,[3] and peopled cities
Covered with close-webbed mist, unpierced ever
With glitter of sun-rays
Nor with stars stretched, nor looking back from heaven   15
Swartest night stretched over wretched men there.
The ocean flowing backward, came we then to the place
Aforesaid by Circe.
Here did they rites, Perimedes and Eurylochus,[4]
And drawing sword from my hip   20
I dug the ell-square pitkin;[5]
Poured we libations unto each the dead,
First mead and then sweet wine, water mixed with white flour.
Then prayed I many a prayer to the sickly death's-heads;
As set in Ithaca, sterile bulls of the best   25

---

8. Epithet of Aphrodite meaning foam-born. Reinach's *Apollo* included a reproduction of a head of Aphrodite.
9. Legendary King of Crete.
1. Lines 1–68 are an adaptation of Book 11 of Homer's *Odyssey*, which recounts Odysseus's voyage to Hades, the underworld of the dead.
2. Odysseus lived for a year with the enchantress Circe until he determined to return home to Ithaca. She instructed him to get directions for his trip home by first visiting the Theban prophet Tiresias in the underworld.
3. Mythical people living in a foggy region at the edge of the earth.
4. Two of Odysseus's companions.
5. Small pit, one ell on each side.

For sacrifice, heaping the pyre with goods,
A sheep to Tiresias only, black and a bell-sheep.[6]
Dark blood flowed in the fosse,[7]
Souls out of Erebus,[8] cadaverous dead, of brides
Of youths and of the old who had borne much;   30
Souls stained with recent tears, girls tender,
Men many, mauled with bronze lance heads,
Battle spoil, bearing yet dreory[9] arms,
These many crowded about me; with shouting,
Pallor upon me, cried to my men for more beasts;   35
Slaughtered the herds, sheep slain of bronze;
Poured ointment, cried to the gods,
To Pluto the strong, and praised Proserpine;[1]
Unsheathed the narrow sword,
I sat to keep off the impetuous impotent dead,   40
Till I should hear Tiresias.
But first Elpenor[2] came, our friend Elpenor,
Unburied, cast on the wide earth,
Limbs that we left in the house of Circe,
Unwept, unwrapped in sepulchre, since toils urged other.   45
Pitiful spirit. And I cried in hurried speech:
"Elpenor, how art thou come to this dark coast?
"Cam'st thou afoot, outstripping seamen?"
                    And he in heavy speech:
"Ill fate and abundant wine. I slept in Circe's ingle.[3]   50
"Going down the long ladder unguarded,
"I fell against the buttress,
"Shattered the nape-nerve, the soul sought Avernus.[4]
"But thou, O King, I bid remember me, unwept, unburied,
"Heap up mine arms, be tomb by sea-bord, and inscribed: 55
"A *man of no fortune, and with a name to come.*
"And set my oar up, that I swung mid fellows."

And Anticlea[5] came, whom I beat off, and then Tiresias Theban,
Holding his golden wand, knew me, and spoke first:
"A second time?[6] why? man of ill star,   60
"Facing the sunless dead and this joyless region?
"Stand from the fosse, leave me my bloody bever[7]
"For soothsay."
                    And I stepped back,
And he strong with the blood, said then; "Odysseus   65
"Shalt return through spiteful Neptune,[8] over dark seas,

6. The prophet Tiresias is likened to a sheep that leads the herd.
7. Ditch, trench.
8. Land of the dead, Hades.
9. Bloody.
1. Goddess of regeneration and wife of Pluto, god of the underworld.
2. Companion of Odysseus who fell to his death from the roof of Circe's house and was left unburied by his friends.
3. Corner, house.
4. Lake near Naples, the entrance to Hades.
5. Odysseus's mother. In the *Odyssey*, Odysseus weeps at the sight of her but obeys Circe's instructions to speak to no one until Tiresias has first drunk the libation of blood that will enable him to speak.
6. They met once before on earth.
7. Libation.
8. God of the sea, who was to delay Odysseus's return by a storm at sea.

"Lose all companions." And then Anticlea came.
Lie quite Divus. I mean, that is Andreas Divus,
In officina Wecheli, 1538, out of Homer.[9]
And he sailed, by Sirens and thence outward and away   70
And unto Circe.
　　　　　Venerandam,[1]
In the Cretan's phase, with the golden crown, Aphrodite,[2]
Cypri munimenta sortita est,[2] mirthful, oricalchi,[3] with golden
Girdles and breast bands, thou with dark eyelids   75
Bearing the golden bough of Argicida.[4] So that:

　　　　　　　　　　　　　　　　　　1925

XVII[1]

So that the vines burst from my fingers
And the bees weighted with pollen
More heavily in the vine-shoots:
chirr—chirr—chir-rikk—a purring sound,
And the birds sleepily in the branches.   5
　　　　　ZAGREUS! IO ZAGREUS.[2]
With the first pale-clear of the heaven
And the cities set in their hills,
And the goddess of the fair knees[3]
Moving there, with the oak-woods behind her,   10
The green slope, with white hounds
　　　leaping about her;

9. Pound acknowledges using the medieval Latin translation of Homer, produced in the workshop ("officina") of Wechel in Paris in 1538, by Andreas Divus.
1. "Commanding reverence," a phrase describing Aphrodite, the goddess of love, in the Latin translation of the second Homeric Hymn by Georgius Dartona Cretensis (the "Cretan").
2. "The fortresses of Cyprus were her appointed realm."
3. "Of copper," a reference to gifts presented to Aphrodite in the second Homeric Hymn.
4. Aeneas offered the Golden Bough to Proserpina before descending to the underworld. The Bough, usually associated with Diana, goddess of chastity, is here also associated with Aphrodite, goddess of love and slayer of the Greeks ("Argicida") during the Trojan War.
1. Canto 17 represents Pound's treatment of ancient myth and Renaissance history. Three sequences, as in a motion-picture montage, displace each other and interpenetrate in this canto: Ulysses' (Odysseus's) voyage through the Mediterranean in search of home in Ithaca, Jason's voyage to the island of Colchis in search of the Golden Fleece, and a ship's entrance into Venice. The poem suggests the imminence of dangers and corruption as the scene of beautiful

Mediterranean islands is translated into the lush and marble setting of mercantile Venice, but these premonitions are held in abeyance with the enchanting vitality and "Splendour" that dominate the verse. The poet evokes moments of tense excitement in ancient myth which immediately precede acts of violence. The epic quests become an experience of seing, a process of imaginative and sensory vision; the scenes emerge in their radiance without becoming static or fixed, and the poet's quest continues without settling into the finality of conclusion. Among the personae that Pound assumes, besides Ulysses and Jason, are Dionysus (Zagreus) the Greek god of wine, rebirth, and ecstasy; Actaeon, who enjoyed a glimpse of the goddess Diana bathing and was punished by being turned into a stag and torn apart by his hounds; and Hades (Pluto), god of the underworld, who loved Kore (Persephone, goddess of regeneration) and who kidnaped her from a meadow to make her queen of the lower regions but was later forced to allow her to return to earth in the spring for nine months each year.
2. "Zagreus. I am Zagreus!" A sacrificial god often identified in Greek myth with Dionysus (meaning "twice-born"), Zagreus was the offspring of Persephone (Koré) and Zeus; Zeus seduced her before she was kidnaped by Hades.
3. Diana, chaste goddess of the hunt.

And thence down to the creek's mouth, until evening,
Flat water before me,
        and the trees growing in water,   15
Marble trunks out of stillness,[4]
On past the palazzi,
        in the stillness,
The light now, not of the sun.
           Chrysophrase,[5]   20
And the water green clear, and blue clear;
On, to the great cliffs of amber.
            Between them,
Cave of Nerea,[6]
        she like a great shell curved,   25
And the boat drawn without sound,
Without odour of ship-work,
Nor bird-cry, nor any noise of wave moving,
Nor splash of porpoise, nor any noise of wave moving,
Within her cave, Nerea,   30
        she like a great shell curved
In the suavity of the rock,
        cliff green-gray in the far,
In the near, the gate-cliffs of amber,
And the wave   35
        green clear, and blue clear,
And the cave salt-white, and glare-purple,
        cool, porphyry smooth,
        the rock sea-worn.
No gull-cry, no sound of porpoise,   40
Sand as of malachite,[7] and no cold there,
        the light not of the sun.

Zagreus, feeding his panthers,
        the turf clear as on hills under light.
And under the almond-trees, gods,   45
        with them, *choros nympharum*.[8] Gods,
Hermes and Athene,[9]
        As shaft of compass,
Between them, trembled—
To the left is the place of fauns,   50
        sylva nympharum;[1]

4. The first glimpse of Venice. The marble façades and columns of its "palazzi" (palaces) are conceived as emerging from nature into art in accordance with the theories of the landscape painter and art critic Adrian Stokes (1854–1935), a friend of Pound in the late 1920s. Stokes (*The Stones of Rimini*, 1934, p. 19) stressed the affinity of Venetian arts with the salt sea, and the origin of marble from sunken forests and watery limestone: "Amid the sea Venice is built from the essence of the sea."
5. Apple-green precious stone.
6. Possibly the nymph Calypso, the temptress and death goddess who detained Ulysses for seven years in her island cave. She was the daughter of Atlas.
7. Green mineral.
8. Chorus of nymphs.
9. Athene (goddess of wisdom) and Hermes (messenger of the gods, patron of merchants and thieves) were Ulysses' protectors. Hermes freed Ulysses from the bonds of Calypso, and Athene calmed the waves for his final voyage home to Ithaca (Odyssey, Book 5).
1. Wood of the nymphs.

The low wood, moor-scrub,
    the doe, the young spotted deer,
    leap up through the broom-plants,
            as dry leaf amid yellow.   55
And by one cut of the hills,
    the great alley of Memnons.[2]
Beyond, sea, crests seen over dune
Night sea churning shingle,
To the left, the alley of cypress.   60
                A boat came,
One man holding her sail,
Guiding her with oar caught over gunwale, saying:
"   There, in the forest of marble,
"   the stone trees—out of water—   65
"   the arbours of stone—
"   marble leaf, over leaf,
"   silver, steel over steel,
"   silver beaks rising and crossing,
"   prow set against prow,   70
"   stone, ply over ply,
"   the gilt beams flare of an evening"
Borso, Carmagnola,[3] the men of craft, *i vitrei*,[4]
Thither, at one time, time after time,
And the waters richer than glass,   75
Bronze gold, the blaze over the silver,
Dye-pots in the torch-light,
The flash of wave under prows,
And the silver beaks rising and crossing.
        Stone trees, white and rose-white in the darkness, 80
Cypress there by the towers,
    Drift under hulls in the night.

       "In the gloom the gold
Gathers the light about it." . . .[5]

Now supine in burrow, half over-arched bramble, 85
One eye for the sea, through that peek-hole,
Gray light, with Athene.
Zothar[6] and her elephants, the gold loin-cloth,
The sistrum,[7] shaken, shaken,
       the cohorts of her dancers. 90
And Aletha, by bend of the shore,

2. Commander of Ethiopian troops in the defense of Troy, Memnon was called "son of dawn." His statue near Thebes, here likened to a row of cypress trees, reputedly issued a sound when dawn's light struck it.

3. Borse d'Este (1431–71) of Ferrara, patron of learning and unsuccessful peacemaker whose assassination was attempted in Venice; and Francesco Bussone da Carmagnola (1390?–1432), mercenary soldier, tried for treason in Venice and executed between two columns.

4. Glassmakers, craftsmen for whom Venice is famous.

5. "Quoted from an earlier Canto (#11) where 'about' reads 'against.' It is derived from a distich by Pindar" [Hugh Kenner's note].

6. Zothar and Aletha (below) are probably invented names.

7. An Egyptian metal rattle.

with her eyes seaward,
and in her hands sea-wrack
Salt-bright with the foam.
Koré⁸ through the bright meadow,   95
                with green-gray dust in the grass:
"For this hour, brother of Circe."⁹
Arm laid over my shoulder,
Saw the sun for three days, the sun fulvid,
As a lion lift over sand-plain;   100
                                and that day,
And for three days, and none after,
Splendour, as the splendour of Hermes,
And shipped thence
                                to the stone place,   105
Pale white, over water,
                known water,
And the white forest of marble, bent bough over bough,
The pleached arbour of stone,
Thither Borso, when they shot the barbed arrow at him,   110
And Carmagnola, between the two columns,
Sigismundo, after that wreck in Dalmatia.¹
Sunset like the grasshopper flying.

                                                                  1933

XXXVI¹

A lady asks me
        I speak in season
She seeks reason for an affect,² wild often
That is so proud he hath Love for a name
Who denys it can hear the truth now   5
Wherefore I speak to the present knowers
Having no hope that low-hearted
        Can bring sight to such reason

8. Persephone, goddess of regeneration and bride of Hades, ruler of the underworld of the dead.
9. "Circe": the enchantress who detained Ulysses for a year, then instructed him to consult Tiresias in the underworld to learn his route home, and told him how to enter the world of the dead through the Grove of Persephone. Her brother, Aetes, King of Colchis, maintained a cult of the sun (his father) on his island, and held possession of the Golden Fleece sought by Jason.
1. Sigismondo Malatesta (1417–68), Renaissance ruler of Rimini whom Pound admired; an art patron, antipapist, and builder of the Tempio Malatestiana in Rimini, he fought for Venice and other cities and in 1464 reached the Dalmatian coast in an unsuccessful crusade.
1. This canto is an example of Pound's historical reconstruction. Six of its seven stanzas are a highly adaptive translation of the love song *Donna me prega* ("A

Woman Asks Me") by the Florentine Guido Cavalcanti (c. 1250–1300), a friend of Dante whom Pound thought more "modern" in outlook. Pound began work on the poem around 1910, published a version in his essay on Cavalcanti in 1928, and reworked it extensively for inclusion in *A Draft of Eleven Cantos* (1934). A celebration of love, it follows a canto exposing the commercialism of "Mitteleuropa" and precedes one treating U.S. banking policies under President Van Buren. Pound admired Cavalcanti's revitalization of poetic tradition, his "struggle for clear definition" and the "obstreperous" independence of his mind. Though not guilty of the heresies he was suspected of, Cavalcanti came close to it; he questioned the "stupid authority" of received ideas, refused to "swallow" Aquinas whole, and rejected the "tyranny of the syllogism" in reasoning, stressing "experiment" or "natural demonstration" instead. While

Be there not natural demonstration
     I have no will to try proof-bringing[3]   10
Or say where it hath birth
What is its virtu[4] and power
Its being and every moving
Or delight whereby 'tis called "to love"
Or if man can show it to sight.   15

Where memory liveth,
     it takes its state
Formed like a diafan[5] from light on shade
Which shadow cometh of Mars and remaineth
Created, having a name sensate,   20
Custom of the soul,
     will from the heart;
Cometh from a seen form which being understood
Taketh locus and remaining in the intellect possible[6]
Wherein hath he neither weight nor still-standing,   25
Descendeth not by quality but shineth out
Himself his own effect unendingly
Not in delight but in the being aware
Nor can he leave his true likeness otherwhere.
He is not vertu but cometh of that perfection[7]   30
Which is so postulate not by the reason
But 'tis felt, I say.
Beyond salvation, holdeth his judging force
Deeming intention to be reason's peer and mate,
Poor in discernment, being thus weakness' friend   35
Often his power cometh on death in the end,[8]
Be it withstayed

---

he avoided the coded symbolism and "fancy snobbism" of intellectual fashions, he wrote an unabashedly difficult poem for an elite audience (*Selected Essays*, pp. 179, 158, 149, 181). Cavalcanti's six stanzas are intricately rhymed, densely obscure, and subject still to contradictory interpretations. In Pound's version, the technicalities of medieval philosophy and psychology remain opaquely abstruse and unexplained within Pound's lyric exploration of the relation between contemplative love and refined sexual passion, between the image of the beloved in a suitor's mind and the living object of his devotion, and between the beloved who inspires love and the lover who is enchanted, paralyzed, inflamed, and pierced by the intense light that sets them apart in their communion. As the stanzas proceed, the personified experience of Love, the mental image of the beloved, and the living embodiment of the lover's attention become intertwined and almost interchangeable. In Pound's seventh stanza, the celebration of love is poised against fragments that juxtapose angelic presences against a more earthy troubadour poet, question the sanctions of authority and the vulnerability of adventuresome speculation, and invoke a recurring theme of the *Cantos*, the sacred union of knowledge and sexual passion.

2. The kind of experience that is not a substance though it derives from substantial realities, as opposed to sheer abstractions and disembodied fancies.

3. Reasoning on the basis of syllogistic logic and argument.

4. Particular moral essence.

5. The diaphanous: the medium or screen though which light is made visible, as opposed to the shadow figured in the following line by Mars, who represents the opaque realm of sensuous ardor against which the light of love is screened.

6. Function of the mind in connection with sense and imaginative experience, as opposed to logic and reasoning.

7. Proper and essential function of anything, whether virtuous or not, as opposed to functions that are conducive specifically to virtue.

8. I.e., love often "dies" or is paralyzed when nature impedes it or it fails of its perfection, even though Love and nature are not by definition opposed to each other.

and so swinging counterweight.
Not that it were natural opposite, but only
Wry'd a bit from the perfect,   40
Let no man say love cometh from chance
Or hath not established lordship
Holding his power even though
             Memory hath him no more.

Cometh he to be   45
             when the will
From overplus
Twisteth out of natural measure,
Never adorned with rest Moveth he changing colour
Either to laugh or weep   50
Contorting the face with fear
             resteth but a little
Yet shall ye see of him That he is most often
With folk who deserve him
And his strange quality set sighs to move   55
Willing man look into that forméd trace in his mind
And with such uneasiness as rouseth the flame.
Unskilled can not from his image,
He himself moveth not, drawing all to his stillness,
Neither turneth about to seek his delight   60
Nor yet to seek out proving[9]
Be it so great or so small.

He draweth likeness and hue from like nature
So making pleasure more certain in seeming
Nor can stand hid in such nearness,   65
Beautys be darts tho' not savage
Skilled from such fear a man follows
Deserving spirit, that pierceth.
Nor is he known from his face
But taken in the white light that is allness   70
Toucheth his aim
Who heareth, seeth not form
But is led by its emanation.
Being divided,[1] set out from colour,
Disjunct in mid darkness   75
Grazeth the light, one moving by other,
Being divided, divided from all falsity
Worthy of trust
From him alone mercy proceedeth.

Go, song, surely thou mayest   80
Whither it please thee
For so art thou ornate[2] that thy reasons
Shall be praised from thy understanders,
             With others hast thou no will to make company.

9. Testing, demonstrating.   apart.
1. Pierced by the arrows of love, and set   2. Adorned and arranged.

"Called thrones, balascio or topaze"[3]   85
Eriugina[4] was not understood in his time
"which explains, perhaps, the delay in condemning him"
And they went looking for Manicheans[5]
And found, so far as I can make out, no Manicheans
So they dug for, and damned Scotus Eriugina   90
"Authority comes from right reason
                never the other way on"[6]
Hence the delay in condemning him
Aquinas[7] head down in a vacuum,
                Aristotle which way in a vacuum?   95
Sacrum, sacrum, inluminatio coitu[8]
Lo Sordels si fo di Mantovana[9]
                of a castle named Goito.
"Five castles!
"Five castles!"   100
        (king giv' him five castles)
"And what the hell do I know about dye-works?!"[1]
His Holiness has written a letter;
        "CHARLES the Mangy of Anjou. . . .
. . way you treat your men is a scandal. . . ."   105
Dilectis miles familiaris . . . castra Montis Odorisii
Montis Sancti Silvestri pallete et pile . . .
In partibus Thetis. . . . vineland
                        land tilled
                        the land incult   110
                        pratis nemoribus pascius
                        with legal jurisdiction[2]
his heirs of both sexes,
    . . . sold the damn lot six weeks later,
Sordellus de Godio.   115
            Quan ben m'albir e mon ric pensamen.[3]
                                        1928, 1934

3. Thrones are seats or foundations of power, and in Dante and medieval theology the term means a rank of angels radiating light in the brilliant hues of jewels in paradise. In Canto 88, Pound writes: "Belascio or Topaze, and not have it sqush,/'throne', [sic] something God can sit on without having it sqush."
4. Johannes Scotus Erigena (c. 815–877), translator, Neoplatonist, and theologian in the court of Charles the Bald. Suspected of heresy in his own day, his *De divisione naturae* ("On the Division of Nature") was condemned in 1225 and 1585 by the Roman Catholic Church.
5. Heretical sect deriving from doctrines of Manes (216?–276?), who believed in a basic dualism of good and evil.
6. Erigena, *De divisione naturae*, 1.69.
7. Thomas Aquinas (1225–74), Italian theologian who incorporated Aristotle's philosophy in treatises that provide a rational synthesis of Christian doctrine. Since 1870, his writings have been made the foundation of orthodoxy in the Roman Catholic Church.
8. "A sacred thing, sacred thing is the

knowledge of coition."
9. "The Sordellos are from Mantua." Sordello (c. 1180–1255) was an Italian troubadour poet and soldier born at Gioto near Mantua. He fled to Provence after a scandalous love affair. He served under Charles I, King of Naples and Sicily and Count of Anjou, whose treatment of his troops provoked the letter from the Pope quoted in this stanza.
1. An interjection, in a modern voice, alluding to Mantua's plans recounted in Canto 35 for securing a competitive advantage in the cloth trade.
2. Sordello was awarded five castles by King Charles in a document quoted in the text: "My beloved and familiar soldier * * * the castles of Monte Odoriso [and] Monte San Silvestro to have and to hold," including cultivated and uncultivated land, "meadows woodlands [and] pastures."
3. The closing line of the canto is the opening line of the sensuous third stanza of Sordello's *Third Canzone*: "When I consider well in my stately thought."

LXXXI[1]

Zeus lies in Ceres' bosom[2]
Taishan[3] is attended of loves
　　　　　under Cythera,[4] before sunrise
and he said: Hay aquí mucho catolicismo—
　　　(sounded catoli*th*ismo)
　　　　　y muy poco reli*H*ion"　　　　　　　　　　5
and he said: Yo creo que los reyes desparecen"
That was Padre José Elizondo[5]
　　　　　　　in 1906 and in 1917
or about 1917
　　　　　and Dolores said: Come pan, niño," eat bread, me lad[6] 10
Sargent[7] had painted her
　　　　　　before he descended
(i.e. if he descended
　　　　　but in those days he did thumb sketches,
impressions of the Velasquez in the Museo del Prado[8]　　　15
and books cost a peseta,[9]
　　　　　brass candlesticks in proportion,
hot wind came from the marshes
　　　and death-chill from the mountains.
And later Bowers[1] wrote: "but such hatred,　　　　　　20
　　　I had never conceived such"
and the London reds wouldn't show up his friends
　　　　　(i.e. friends of Franco[2]
working in London) and in Alcazar[3]
forty years gone, they said: go back to the station to eat　　25
you can sleep here for a peseta"
　　　　　goat bells tinkled all night

1. Written during Pound's imprisonment in the American detention camp near Pisa and published in 1948 as part of *The Pisan Cantos,* this poem is the most intimately personal of the entire series. In the opening section, the poet's memory ranges over scenes of beauty and acts of kindness he has known in foreign lands and during the Spanish Civil War, fragments of recollection that define a writer's alienation or expatriation and reveal his concerns about the routines of writing and the authenticity of emotion. Suddenly the memory of a wild rabbit and a drifting leaf bring home to him the extremity of his isolation. Then the "libretto" presents in parody an apotheosis of the poet's liberation and power, mocking the poem's unreality and questioning both its technical adequacy and its artificiality. With equal suddenness the appearance of two eyes transforms his vision and inspires a hymn to humility, love, and the integrity of his artistic vocation.
2. Zeus, ruler of the Greek gods on Mount Olympus, and Ceres, goddess of harvest and cornfields, conceived a child who is an important recurring figure in Pound's *Cantos*; Kore or Persephone, who was later carried off to Hades by the god of the underworld but then permitted to return to earth in the spring each year for nine months.
3. A sacred mountain, capped by shrines and temples, in Shantung province, China.
4. The Mediterranean island where Venus set foot after her birth from the sea.
5. Spanish priest who helped get Pound a copy of a Cavalcanti manuscript. His statements in Spanish may be translated: "Here there is very much Catholicism—but very little religion" and "I think that kings disappear."
6. Translation of the preceding Spanish.
7. The American expatriate painter (1856–1925). His subjects included Spanish figures and scenes. His later career was thought to decline by some critics.
8. The royal picture gallery in Madrid, Spain, which contains important works by the Spanish painter Diego Rodríguez de Silva y Velázquez (1599–1660).
9. Spanish coin.
1. Claude G. Bowers, American historian (1878–1958), author of books on Jefferson and Beveridge, and U.S. Ambassador to Spain during the Spanish Civil War.
2. Francisco Franco (1892–1975), fascist General and dictator of Spain.
3. City in central Spain.

and the hostess grinned: Eso es luto, *haw*!
mi marido es muerto
      (it is mourning, my husband is dead)[4]   30
when she gave me paper to write on
with a black border half an inch or more deep,
    say 5/8ths, of the locanda[5]
"We call *all* foreigners frenchies"
and the egg broke in Cabranez' pocket.   35
      thus making history. Basil[6] says
they beat drums for three days
till all the drumheads were busted
      (simple village fiesta)
and as for his life in the Canaries . . .   40
Possum[7] observed that the local   folk dance
was danced by the same dancers in divers localities
    in political welcome . . .
the technique of demonstration
      Cole studied that (not G.D.H., Horace)[8]   45
"You will find" said old André Spire,[9]
that every man on that board (Crédit Agricole)
has a brother-in-law
      "You the one, I the few"
    said John Adams   50
speaking of fears in the abstract
to his volatile friend Mr Jefferson[1]
(to break the pentameter, that was the first heave)[2]
or as Jo Bard[3] says: they never speak to each other,
if it is baker and concierge[4] visibly   55
    it is La Rouchefoucauld and de Maintenon audibly.[5]
"Te cavero le budelle"
        "La corata a te"[6]
In less than a geological epoch
      said Henry Mencken[7]   60

4. Translation of the preceding Spanish.
5. Inn.
6. Basil Bunting (b. 1900), British poet who lived in the Near East and in the Canary Islands off northern Africa. A follower of Pound, he formulated the principles of "objectivism" with the American poet Louis Zukovsky (b. 1904).
7. Familiar nickname of T. S. Eliot, who wrote *Old Possum's Book of Practical Cats* (1939).
8. Pound distinguishes between Horace Cole (b. 1874), English executive and writer on business topics, and George D. H. Cole (1880–1959), English economist and novelist.
9. French writer and Zionist (b. 1868), commenting on the board of directors of a French loan association.
1. In the correspondence between the two ex-Presidents, Adams declared that Thomas Jefferson feared the single executive as the chief danger in the American political system, while he himself feared the small class of the economi-

cally and socially powerful.
2. Pound claimed to have revolutionized English poetry by breaking away from iambic pentameter as the governing pattern for verse.
3. Joseph Bard (b. 1892), English essayist.
4. A doorkeeper, usually a woman, in French hotels or apartments.
5. François, Duc de la Rochefoucauld (1613–80), French author whose *Maximes* (1665) cultivated stylistic precision and dissected human pretensions; and Françoise d'Aubigné, Marquise de Maintenon (1635–1719). Born in prison to Protestant parents, she eventually became mistress to the French King Louis XIV (later in secret his second wife) and published a famous series of *Letters*, known for their elegance of style. The finesse of both writers contrasts to the bluntness of lines 57–58.
6. "I'll tear your guts out" and "And I yours."
7. H. L. Mencken (1880–1956), icono-

"Some cook, some do not cook
    some things cannot be altered"[8]
Ἴυγξ. . . . .'ἐμὸν ποτί δῶμα τὸν ἄνδρα[9]
What counts is the cultural level,
    thank Benin for this table ex packing box   65
      "doan yu tell no one I made it"
        from a mask fine as any in Frankfurt
"It'll get you offn th' groun'"[1]
        Light as the branch of Kuanon[2]
And at first disappointed with shoddy   70
the bare ram-shackle quais, but then saw the
high buggy wheels
        and was reconciled,
George Santayana[3] arriving in the port of Boston
and kept to the end of his life that faint *thethear*[4]   75
of the Spaniard
        as a grace quasi imperceptible
as did Muss[5] the *v* for *u* of Romagna
and said the grief was a full act
      repeated for each new condoleress   80
working up to a climax.
and George Horace said he wd/ "get Beveridge" (Senator)[6]
Beveridge wouldn't talk and he wouldn't write for the papers
but George got him by campin' in his hotel
and assailin' him at lunch breakfast an' dinner   85
      three articles
and my old man went on hoein' corn
    while George was a-tellin' him,
come across a vacant lot
      where you'd occasionally see a wild rabbit   90
or mebbe only a loose one
    AOI![7]
    a leaf in the current
        at my grates no Althea[8]

---

clastic journalist and editor of the *Smart Set* to whom Pound frequently sent and recommended manuscripts. He protested to Pound that mankind's economics cannot be changed in anything less than a geologic epoch (*Guide to Kulchur*, p. 182).
8. Mrs. Pound after her marriage stipulated that she would not cook.
9. In Theocritus's second *Idyll*, a nymph invokes a magical charm to attract her lover: "Little wheel [bring back that] man to my house."
1. A Negro prisoner made Pound a desk so that he no longer had to write on the ground, and his face is reminiscent of African masks. Benin is the name of a Nigerian tribe famous for its sculpture.
2. Japanese version of a Chinese goddess of mercy.
3. Santayana (1863–1952) was an expatriate poet and philosopher. Born in Spain but raised in Boston, he became a

professor of philosophy at Harvard, then left in 1912 to reside in Europe.
4. *Cecear*: the lisping pronunciation of *c* in Castilian Spanish.
5. Benito Mussolini (1883–1945), fascist dictator of Italy.
6. George Horace Lorimer (1868–1937), editor of the *Saturday Evening Post*, and Albert J. Beveridge (1862–1927), U.S. Senator, organizer of the Progressive party, and biographer of Chief Justice John Marshall.
7. A cry, of uncertain meaning, appearing repeatedly in the *Chanson de Roland* (12th century). His cry of anguish when Pound read this line aloud moved Mrs. Pound to tears.
8. The lover addressed by Richard Lovelace (1618–58), the English royalist who wrote a poem in prison entitled *To Althea from Prison,* imagining that she whispered to him at the "grates" of his window.

libretto[9]
Yet   95
Ere the season died a-cold
Borne upon a zephyr's shoulder
I rose through the aureate sky
              Lawes and Jenkyns guard thy rest
              Dolmetsch ever be thy guest,[1]   100
Has he tempered the viol's wood
To enforce both the grave and the acute?
Has he curved us the bowl of the lute?
              Lawes and Jenkyns guard thy rest
              Dolmetsch ever be thy guest   105
Hast 'ou fashioned so airy a mood
      To draw up leaf from the root?
   Hast 'ou found a cloud so light
      As seemed neither mist nor shade?

              Then resolve me, tell me aright   110
              If Waller sang or Dowland played.[2]

      Your eyen two wol sleye me sodenly
      I may the beauté of hem nat susteyne[3]

And for 180 years almost nothing.

Ed ascoltando al leggier mormorio[4]   115
      there came new subtlety of eyes into my tent,
where of spirit or hypostasis,[5]
      but what the blindfold hides
or at carneval
                     nor any pair showed anger   120
      Saw but the eyes and stance between the eyes,
colour, diastasis,[6]
      careless or unaware it had not the
   whole tent's room
nor was place for the full Εἰδὼς[7]   125
interpass, penetrate
      casting but shade beyond the other lights
         sky's clear
         night's sea
         green of the mountain pool   130
      shone from the unmasked eyes in half-mask's space.

---

9. Book or words of an opera.
1. Henry Lawes (1596–1662), English composer; John Jenkins (1592–1678), English composer of music for viol and organ, musician in the courts of Charles I and Charles II; Arnold Dolmetsch (1858–1940), French musician and instrument maker, advocate of the revival of pre-Baroque music.
2. Edmund Waller (1606–87), English poet; John Dowland (1563?–1626?),

English composer and lutist.
3. "Your two eyes will slay me suddenly/I cannot withstand their beauty," the opening lines of *Merciless Beauty* by the English poet Geoffrey Chaucer (1340?–1400).
4. "And listening to the light murmur."
5. Substance of divinity.
6. Separation.
7. Knowing.

What thou lovest well remains,
                    the rest is dross
What thou lov'st well shall not be reft from thee
What thou lov'st well is thy true heritage   135
Whose world, or mine or theirs
                    or is it of none?
First came the seen, then thus the palpable
        Elysium,[8] though it were in the halls of hell,
What thou lovest well is thy true heritage   140

The ant's a centaur in his dragon world.
Pull down thy vanity, it is not man
Made courage, or made order, or made grace,
        Pull down thy vanity, I say pull down.
Learn of the green world what can be thy place   145
In scaled invention or true artistry,
Pull down thy vanity,
                    Paquin[9] pull down!
The green casque[1] has outdone your elegance.

"Master thyself, then others shall thee beare"[2]   150
        Pull down thy vanity
Thou art a beaten dog beneath the hail,
A swollen magpie in a fitful sun,
Half black half white
Nor knowst'ou wing from tail   155
Pull down thy vanity
                    How mean thy hates
Fostered in falsity,
                    Pull down thy vanity,
Rathe[3] to destroy, niggard in charity,   160
Pull down thy vanity,
                    I say pull down.

But to have done instead of not doing
                    this is not vanity
To have, with decency, knocked   165
That a Blunt should open[4]
            To have gathered from the air a live tradition
or from a fine old eye the unconquered flame
This is not vanity.
            Here error is all in the not done,   170
all in the diffidence that faltered,

                                        1948

---

8. In Greek mythology, the heaven of
good or fortunate souls.
9. A Parisian dress designer.
1. A green helmet, like the head of some
insects. Also a hat.
2. A free rendering of line 13 in Chaucer's *Ballade of Good Counsel.*
3. Quick, ripe.

4. Wilfred S. Blunt (1840–1922), minor
British poet, an outspoken opponent of
British imperialism, admired by younger
writers for his independent mind. The
lines wittily echo Christ's injunction in
his Sermon on the Mount: "knock, and
it shall be opened unto you" (Matthew
7.7).

EDWIN ARLINGTON ROBINSON
1869–1935

The most important poet to launch his career between the generation of Whitman and Dickinson and the ascendency of Frost, Pound, and William Carlos Williams was a New Englander, Edwin Arlington Robinson. His lyrics gave a somber orientation to Emersonian Transcendentalism while probing the isolation of the psyche and the theme of tragic failure with an intensiveness comparable to Hawthorne's and Melville's. Compared to his major contemporaries, he had scarcely any influence on other writers, but he shared in the modern effort to appropriate for poetry the effects of good prose.

Robinson was raised in Gardiner, Maine, where cultivated friends undertook to encourage his vocation as a poet even though its cultural resources were limited and his family's misfortunes ruled out sustained support from his parents. His father's lumber business and land speculations were on the brink of failure even before his death in 1892 and the collapse of the family's holdings in 1893. His brothers' promise of success dissolved before his eyes (one, a physician, became addicted to drugs; the other, a businessman, to liquor), and after four exciting years and one postgraduate year in high school he drifted near despair as he tried to find a way to pursue his vocation as poet. The family managed to send him for two years to Harvard (1891–93) where Professor Charles Eliot Norton, among others, helped to widen his intellectual horizons. But he met with little success when he returned to Gardiner and began writing the miniature dramas and portraits (including *The House on the Hill* and *Richard Cory*) that were to identify "Tilbury Town" in his first published volumes. One source of encouragement was reading and conversation in the home of Mrs. Laura Richards, while another was instruction from the local poet Dr. Alanson T. Schumann, who set him to writing in the intricate traditional French forms popular among Pre-Raphaelite poets in England. It was in the 1890s that he discovered the meditative poetry of Wordsworth and the realistic verse of George Crabbe, along with the more recent verse of Whitman, Rudyard Kipling, and Thomas Hardy, the fiction of Hawthorne and James, the essays of Emerson. With his lifelong friend Harry de Forest Smith he read the classics and translated Sophocles. He published his first two volumes of verse at his own expense before moving from Gardiner to New York City; only when a group of Gardiner friends guaranteed the venture did he find a publisher for *Captain Craig* in 1902.

Robinson's first volume was brought to the attention of President Theodore Roosevelt, who secured him a position as customs inspector in New York from 1905 to 1909, but the poet's position remained desperate even after *The Town down the River* (1910) and *The Man against the Sky* (1916) had attracted a larger audience of readers and critics. Heavy drinking had long become a habit. He wrote fiction (which he destroyed) and plays (two of which were published) in an attempt to earn money and gain popularity. He lived in lonely rooms or in the studios and homes of friends, and was grateful for a small bequest in 1914 from a Gardiner friend, Hays Gardiner, and for the income from a trust established in 1917 by anonymous donors for his support. That support continued until 1922, when a measure of success followed the publication of *Avon's Harvest* and *Collected Poems* and the award of the first of his three Pulitzer Prizes. Robinson spent the rest of his life living in New York during the winter but did most of his writing in New England during the summers, which he spent after 1911 in New Hampshire at the MacDowell Colony, founded by Marian MacDowell, widow of the composer Edward MacDowell, for the support of American musicians, artists, and writers.

The deprivations of Robinson's personal experience, his reading in the Bible and in Eastern mysticism, and the Transcendental idealism of Emerson and idealistic philosophers whom he had studied at Harvard combined to form a secular religion which Robinson once called an "optimistic desperation."[1] This attitude underlies his longer narrative poems as well as his shorter poems; the grim residuum of affirmation is often figured in the images of a "Word" and "light." His poems, including his many brilliant sonnets, are characterized by austere diction, by somber wit in the tradition of Yankee humor, and by irony that is seldom subtle but is unrelieved, sustained, and consequently powerful. In his blank-verse narratives and notably in his short lyrics, traditional but simple verse forms are played unobtrusively against the momentum of long sentences and prolonged rhetorical questions which give his best poems the peculiar force of prose. Indeed, the late poet Conrad Aiken discerned, in Robinson's treatment of his painfully isolated characters, a novelistic focus on "relations and contacts" that are "always extraordinarily *conscious*" and thus comparable to the prose fiction of Henry James.[2]

After 1921 Robinson devoted his talents to long narrative poems, including a trilogy based on the Arthurian romances that he began in 1917 with *Merlin* and completed in 1927 with *Tristram*, a best seller which brought him his third Pulitzer Prize. These poems have not been as favorably received by critics as the earlier poems, even by such admirers of Robinson as the post-World War II poet Louis O. Coxe. *King Jasper*, which recounts the nemesis of a ruthless industrialist in a world he has repudiated, was published posthumously in 1935 and was prefaced by a tribute from his fellow New England poet Robert Frost.

George Crabbe[1]

Give him the darkest inch your shelf allows,
Hide him in lonely garrets, if you will,—
But his hard, human pulse is throbbing still
With the sure strength that fearless truth endows.
In spite of all fine science disavows,   5
Of his plain excellence and stubborn skill
There yet remains what fashion cannot kill,
Though years have thinned the laurel[2] from his brows.

1. Letter to Harry de Forest Smith in Charles T. Davis, ed., *Edwin Arlington Robinson: Selected Early Poems and Letters*, p. 210.
2. *Collected Criticism of Conrad Aiken* (1958), p. 342.
1. English physician, curate, and poet (1754–1832), known for his realistic narrative poems.
2. Evergreen shrub from which the ancient Romans wove wreaths for poetry prizes. Hence an emblem of poetic merit and public recognition.

Whether or not we read him, we can feel
From time to time the vigor of his name   10
Against us like a finger for the shame
And emptiness of what our souls reveal
In books that are as altars where we kneel
To consecrate the flicker, not the flame.

1896

The Sheaves

Where long the shadows of the wind had rolled,
Green wheat was yielding to the change assigned;
And as by some vast magic undivined
The world was turning slowly into gold.

Like nothing that was ever bought or sold   5
It waited there, the body and the mind;
And with a mighty meaning of a kind
That tells the more the more it is not told.

So in a land where all days are not fair,
Fair days went on till on another day   10
A thousand golden sheaves were lying there,
Shining and still, but not for long to stay—
As if a thousand girls with golden hair
Might rise from where they slept and go away.

1925

The House on the Hill[1]

They are all gone away,
   The House is shut and still,
There is nothing more to say.

Through broken walls and gray
   The winds blow bleak and shrill: 5
They are all gone away.

Nor is there one to-day
   To speak them good or ill:
There is nothing more to say.

Why is it then we stray   10
   Around the sunken sill?
They are all gone away,

And our poor fancy-play
   For them is wasted skill:

---

1. The form of the poem is that of the villanelle, a French form of 19 lines employing only two rhymes. A slightly different version was first published in the New York *Globe* in 1894.

There is nothing more to say.   15

There is ruin and decay
    In the House on the Hill:
They are all gone away,
There is nothing more to say.

                    1893, 1894, 1896

Richard Cory

Whenever Richard Cory went down town,
We people on the pavement looked at him:
He was a gentleman from sole to crown,
Clean favored, and imperially slim.

And he was always quietly arrayed,   5
And he was always human when he talked;
But still he fluttered pulses when he said,
"Good–morning," and he glittered when he walked.

And he was rich—yes, richer than a king—
And admirably schooled in every grace: 10
In fine, we thought that he was everything
To make us wish that we were in his place.

So on we worked, and waited for the light,
And went without the meat, and cursed the bread;
And Richard Cory, one calm summer night,   15
Went home and put a bullet through his head.

                    1896

The Clerks[1]

I did not think that I should find them there
When I came back again; but there they stood,
As in the days they dreamed of when young blood
Was in their cheeks and women called them fair.
Be sure, they met me with an ancient air,—   5
And yes, there was a shop-worn brotherhood
About them; but the men were just as good,
And just as human as they ever were.

And you that ache so much to be sublime,
And you that feed yourselves with your descent,   10
What comes of all your visions and your fears?
Poets and kings are but the clerks of Time,
Tiering the same dull webs of discontent,
Clipping the same sad alnage[2] of the years.

                    1896

1. First published in *The Boston Globe*, 1896.
2. A measurement of cloth.

Credo[1]

I cannot find my way: there is no star
In all the shrouded heavens anywhere;
And there is not a whisper in the air
Of any living voice but one so far
That I can hear it only as a bar   5
Of lost, imperial music, played when fair
And angel fingers wove, and unaware,
Dead leaves to garlands where no roses are.

No, there is not a glimmer, nor a call,
For one that welcomes, welcomes when he fears,   10
The black and awful chaos of the night;
For through it all—above, beyond it all—
I know the far-sent message of the years,
I feel the coming glory of the Light.

1896

On the Night of a Friend's Wedding

If ever I am old, and all alone,
I shall have killed one grief, at any rate;
For then, thank God, I shall not have to wait
Much longer for the sheaves that I have sown.
The devil only knows what I have done,   5
But here I am, and here are six or eight
Good friends, who most ingenuously prate
About my songs to such and such a one.

But everything is all askew to-night,—   10
As if the time were come, or almost come,
For their untenanted mirage of me
To lose itself and crumble out of sight,
Like a tall ship that floats above the foam
A little while, and then breaks utterly.

1896

Verlaine[2]

Why do you dig like long-clawed scavengers
To touch the covered corpse of him that fled
The uplands for the fens, and rioted
Like a sick satyr with doom's worshippers?
Come! let the grass grow there, and leave his verse   5
To tell the story of the life he led.
Let the man go: let the dead flesh be dead,
And let the worms be its biographers.

Song sloughs away the sin to find redress

1. A statement of belief (from the Latin, meaning "I believe").
2. Paul Verlaine (1844–96), the hard-drinking, violent, dissolute French Symbolist poet, companion of fellow poet Arthur Rimbaud (1854–91), who wrote *Une Saison en Enfer* (*A Season in Hell*). This sonnet was first published in *The Boston Evening Transcript* on the occasion of Verlaine's death.

In art's complete remembrance: nothing clings   10
For long but laurel to the stricken brow
That felt the Muse's finger; nothing less
Than hell's fulfilment of the end of things
Can blot the star that shines on Paris now.

                                        1896

Miniver Cheevy

Miniver Cheevy, child of scorn,
    Grew lean while he assailed the seasons;
He wept that he was ever born,
    And he had reasons.

Miniver loved the days of old   5
    When swords were bright and steeds were prancing;
The vision of a warrior bold
    Would set him dancing.

Miniver sighed for what was not,
    And dreamed, and rested from his labors;   10
He dreamed of Thebes and Camelot,
    And Priam's neighbors.[1]

Miniver mourned the ripe renown
    That made so many a name so fragrant;
He mourned Romance, now on the town,   15
    And Art, a vagrant.

Miniver loved the Medici,[2]
    Albeit he had never seen one;
He would have sinned incessantly
    Could he have been one.   20

Miniver cursed the commonplace
    And eyed a khaki suit with loathing;
He missed the mediaeval grace
    Of iron clothing.

Miniver scorned the gold he sought,   25
    But sore annoyed was he without it;
Miniver thought, and thought, and thought,
    And thought about it.
Miniver Cheevy, born too late,
    Scratched his head and kept on thinking;   30
Miniver coughed, and called it fate,
    And kept on drinking.

                                        1910

1. Thebes was an ancient city in Boeotia, rival of Athens and Sparta for supremacy in Greece and the setting of Sophocles' tragedies about Oedipus; Camelot is the legendary court of King Arthur and the Knights of the Round Table; the neighbors of King Priam in Homer's *Iliad* are his heroic compatriots in the doomed city of Troy.
2. Family of wealthy merchants, statesmen, and art patrons in Renaissance Florence.

Eros Turannos[1]

She fears him, and will always ask
 What fated her to choose him;
She meets in his engaging mask
 All reasons to refuse him;
But what she meets and what she fears   5
Are less than are the downward years,
Drawn slowly to the foamless weirs
 Of age, were she to lose him.

Between a blurred sagacity
 That once had power to sound him,   10
And Love, that will not let him be
 The Judas[2] that she found him,
Her pride assuages her almost,
As if it were alone the cost.—
He sees that he will not be lost,   15
 And waits and looks around him.

A sense of ocean and old trees
 Envelops and allures him;
Tradition, touching all he sees,
 Beguiles and reassures him;   20
And all her doubts of what he says
Are dimmed with what she knows of days—
Till even prejudice delays
 And fades, and she secures him.

The falling leaf inaugurates   25
 The reign of her confusion;
The pounding wave reverberates
 The dirge of her illusion;
And home, where passion lived and died,
Becomes a place where she can hide,   30
While all the town and harbor side
 Vibrate with her seclusion.

We tell you, tapping on our brows,
 The story as it should be,—
As if the story of a house   35
 Were told, or ever could be;
We'll have no kindly veil between
Her visions and those we have seen,—
As if we guessed what hers have been,
 Or what they are or would be.   40

Meanwhile we do no harm; for they
 That with a god have striven,
Not hearing much of what we say,

---

1. Greek for "Love, the King," an echo   *Oidipous Turranos* (*Oedipus the King*).
of the solemn title to Sophocles' tragedy   2. The disciple who betrayed Christ.

Take what the god has given;
Though like waves breaking it may be,   45
Or like a changed familiar tree,
Or like a stairway to the sea
    Where down the blind are driven.

                                    1913, 1916

Bewick Finzer

Time was when his half million drew
    The breath of six per cent;
But soon the worm of what-was-not
    Fed hard on his content;
And something crumbled in his brain   5
    When his half million went.

Time passed, and filled along with his
    The place of many more;
Time came, and hardly one of us
    Had credence to restore,   10
From what appeared one day, the man
    Whom we had known before.

The broken voice, the withered neck,
    The coat worn out with care,
The cleanliness of indigence,   15
    The brilliance of despair,
The fond imponderable dreams
    Of affluence,—all were there.

Poor Finzer, with his dreams and schemes,
    Fares hard now in the race,   20
With heart and eye that have a task
    When he looks in the face
Of one who might so easily
    Have been in Finzer's place.

He comes unfailing for the loan   25
    We give and then forget;
He comes, and probably for years
    Will he be coming yet,—
Familiar as an old mistake,
    And futile as regret.   30

                                          1916

The Man against the Sky

Between me and the sunset, like a dome
Against the glory of a world on fire,
Now burned a sudden hill,
Bleak, round, and high, by flame-lit height made higher,

With nothing on it for the flame to kill   5
Save one who moved and was alone up there
To loom before the chaos and the glare
As if he were the last god going home
Unto his last desire.

Dark, marvelous, and inscrutable he moved on   10
Till down the fiery distance he was gone,
Like one of those eternal, remote things
That range across a man's imaginings
When a sure music fills him and he knows
What he may say thereafter to few men,—   15
The touch of ages having wrought
An echo and a glimpse of what he thought
A phantom or a legend until then;
For whether lighted over ways that save,
Or lured from all repose,   20
If he go on too far to find a grave,
Mostly alone he goes.

Even he, who stood where I had found him,
On high with fire all round him,
Who moved along the molten west,   25
And over the round hill's crest
That seemed half ready with him to go down,
Flame–bitten and flame–cleft,
As if there were to be no lasting thing left
Of a nameless unimaginable town,—   30
Even he who climbed and vanished may have taken
Down to the perils of a depth not known,
From death defended though by men forsaken,
The bread that every man must eat alone;
He may have walked while others hardly dared   35
Look on to see him stand where many fell;
And upward out of that, as out of hell,
He may have sung and striven
To mount where more of him shall yet be given,
Bereft of all retreat,   40
To sevenfold, heat,—
As on a day when three in Dura shared
The furnace, and were spared
For glory by that king of Babylon
Who made himself so great that God, who heard   45
Covered him with long feathers, like a bird.[1]

Again, he may have gone down easily,
By comfortable altitudes, and found,

---

1. Three Jews (Shadrach, Meshach, and Abednego) refused to worship the idol erected on the plain of Dura by Nebuchadnezzar, King of Babylon, who condemned them to die in a "fiery furnace." They survived unscathed, and the King was converted to belief in the Hebrew God by their example. He was first punished by being reduced to a feathered animal, then restored by God to his kingdom (Daniel 3–4).

As always, underneath him solid ground
Whereon to be sufficient and to stand   50
Possessed already of the promised land,
Far stretched and fair to see:
A good sight, verily,
And one to make the eyes of her who bore him
Shine glad with hidden tears.   55
Why question of his ease of who before him,
In one place or another where they left
Their names as far behind them as their bones,
And yet by dint of slaughter toil and theft,
And shrewdly sharpened stones,   60
Carved hard the way for his ascendency
Through deserts of lost years?
Why trouble him now who sees and hears
No more than what his innocence requires,
And therefore to no other heights aspires   65
Than one at which he neither quails nor tires?
He may do more by seeing what he sees
Than others eager for iniquities;
He may, by seeing all things for the best,
Incite futurity to do the rest.   70

Or with an even likelihood,
He may have met with atrabilious[2] eyes
The fires of time on equal terms and passed
Indifferently down, until at last
His only kind of grandeur would have been,   75
Apparently, in being seen.
He may have had for evil or for good
No argument; he may have had no care
For what without himself went anywhere
To failure or to glory, and least of all   80
For such a stale, flamboyant miracle;
He may have been the prophet of an art
Immovable to old idolatries;
He may have been a player without a part,
Annoyed that even the sun should have the skies   85
For such a flaming way to advertise;
He may have been a painter sick at heart
With Nature's toiling for a new surprise;
He may have been a cynic, who now, for all
Of anything divine that his effete   90
Negation may have tasted,
Saw truth in his own image, rather small,
Forbore to fever the ephemeral,
Found any barren height a good retreat
From any swarming street,   95
And in the sun saw power superbly wasted;
And when the primitive old-fashioned stars
Came out again to shine on joys and wars

2. Bilious, melancholy, acrimonious.

More primitive, and all arrayed for doom,
He may have proved a world a sorry thing   100
In his imagining,
And life a lighted highway to the tomb.

Or, mounting with infirm unsearching tread,
His hopes to chaos led,
He may have stumbled up there from the past,   105
And with an aching strangeness viewed the last
Abysmal conflagration of his dreams,—
A flame where nothing seems
To burn but flame itself by nothing fed;
And while it all went out,   110
Not even the faint anodyne of doubt
May then have eased a painful going down
From pictured heights of power and lost renown,
Revealed at length to his outlived endeavor
Remote and unapproachable forever;   115
And at his heart there may have gnawed
Sick memories of a dead faith foiled and flawed
And long dishonored by the living death
Assigned alike by chance
To brutes and hierophants;[3]   120
And anguish fallen on those he loved around him
May once have dealt the last blow to confound him,
And so have left him as death leaves a child,
Who sees it all too near;
And he who knows no young way to forget   125
May struggle to the tomb unreconciled.
Whatever suns may rise or set
There may be nothing kinder for him here
Than shafts and agonies;
And under these   130
He may cry out and stay on horribly;
Or, seeing in death too small a thing to fear,
He may go forward like a stoic Roman
Where pangs and terrors in his pathway lie,—
Or, seizing the swift logic of a woman,   135
Curse God and die.[4]

Or maybe there, like many another one
Who might have stood aloft and looked ahead,
Black-drawn against wild red,
He may have built, unawed by fiery gules[5]   140
That in him no commotion stirred,
A living reason out of molecules
Why molecules occurred,
And one for smiling when he might have sighed
Had he seen far enough,   145

---

3. Priests who initiate devotees into sacred rites.
4. His wife gave Job this advice when

he was tested by God with boils (Job
2.9).
5. The color red.

And in the same inevitable stuff
Discovered an odd reason too for pride
In being what he must have been by laws
Infrangible and for no kind of cause.
Deterred by no confusion or surprise   150
He may have seen with his mechanic eyes
A world without a meaning, and had room,
Alone amid magnificence and doom,
To build himself an airy monument
That should, or fail him in his vague intent,   155
Outlast an accidental universe—
To call it nothing worse—
Or, by the burrowing guile
Of Time disintegrated and effaced,
Like once-remembered mighty trees go down   160
To ruin, of which by man may now be traced
No part sufficient even to be rotten,
And in the book of things that are forgotten
Is entered as a thing not quite worth while.
He may have been so great   165
That satraps would have shivered at his frown,
And all he prized alive may rule a state
No larger than a grave that holds a clown;
He may have been a master of his fate,
And of his atoms,—ready as another   170
In his emergence to exonerate
His father and his mother;
He may have been a captain of a host,
Self-eloquent and ripe for prodigies,
Doomed here to swell by dangerous degrees,   175
And then give up the ghost.
Nahum's great grasshoppers were such as these,[6]
Sun-scattered and soon lost.

Whatever the dark road he may have taken,
This man who stood on high   180
And faced alone the sky,
Whatever drove or lured or guided him,—
A vision answering a faith unshaken,
An easy trust assumed of easy trials,
A sick negation born of weak denials,   185
A crazed abhorrence of an old condition,
A blind attendance on a brief ambition,—
Whatever stayed him or derided him,
His way was even as ours;
And we, with all our wounds and all our powers,   190
Must each await alone at his own height
Another darkness or another light;
And there, of our poor self dominion reft,
If inference and reason shun

6. In Nahum 3.17, the Biblical prophet scornfully describes the proud captains of sinful Nineveh as oversized grasshoppers who disappear at sunrise.

Hell, Heaven, and Oblivion,   195
May thwarted will (perforce precarious,
But for our conservation better thus)
Have no misgiving left
Of doing yet what here we leave undone?
Or if unto the last of these we cleave,   200
Believing or protesting we believe
In such an idle and ephemeral
Florescence of the diabolical,—
If, robbed of two fond old enormities,
Our being had no onward auguries,   205
What then were this great love of ours to say
For launching other lives to voyage again
A little farther into time and pain,
A little faster in a futile chase
For a kingdom and a power and a Race   210
That would have still in sight
A manifest end of ashes and eternal night?
Is this the music of the toys we shake
So loud,—as if there might be no mistake
Somewhere in our indomitable will?   215
Are we no greater than the noise we make
Along one blind atomic pilgrimage
Whereon by crass chance billeted we go
Because our brains and bones and cartilage
Will have it so?   220
If this we say, then let us all be still
About our share in it, and live and die
More quietly thereby.

Where was he going, this man against the sky?
You know not, nor do I.   225
But this we know, if we know anything:
That we may laugh and fight and sing
And of our transience here make offering
To an orient Word[7] that will not be erased,
Or, save in incommunicable gleams   230
Too permanent for dreams,
Be found or known.
No tonic and ambitious irritant
Of increase or of want
Has made an otherwise insensate waste   235
Of ages overthrown
A ruthless, veiled, implacable foretaste
Of other ages that are still to be
Depleted and rewarded variously
Because a few, by fate's economy,   240
Shall seem to move the world the way it goes;

7. The origin of creation in John 1.1:
"In the beginning was the Word, and
the Word was with God, and the Word
was God." The term "orient" suggests
the East, the presumed location of the
original creation and the source of major
world religions.

No soft evangel of equality,
Safe-cradled in a communal repose
That huddles into death and may at last
Be covered well with equatorial snows—   245
And all for what, the devil only knows—
Will aggregate an inkling to confirm
The credit of a sage or of a worm,
Or tell us why one man in five
Should have a care to stay alive   250
While in his heart he feels no violence
Laid on his humor and intelligence
When infant Science makes a pleasant face
And waves again that hollow toy, the Race;
No planetary trap where souls are wrought   255
For nothing but the sake of being caught
And sent again to nothing will attune
Itself to any key of any reason
Why man should hunger through another season
To find out why 'twere better late than soon   260
To go away and let the sun and moon
And all the silly stars illuminate
A place for creeping things.
And those that root and trumpet and have wings,
And herd and ruminate,   265
Or dive and flash and poise in rivers and seas,
Or by their loyal tails in lofty trees
Hang screeching lewd victorious derision
Of man's immortal vision.

Shall we, because Eternity records   270
Too vast an answer for the time-born words
We spell, whereof so many are dead that once
In our capricious lexicons
Were so alive and final, hear no more
The Word itself, the living word   275
That none alive has ever heard
Or ever spelt,
And few have ever felt
Without the fears and old surrenderings
And terrors that began   280
When Death let fall a feather from his wings
And humbled the first man?
Because the weight of our humility,
Wherefrom we gain
A little wisdom and much pain,   285
Falls here too sore and there too tedious,
Are we in anguish or complacency,
Not looking far enough ahead
To see by what mad couriers we are led
Along the roads of the ridiculous,   290
To pity ourselves and laugh at faith
And while we curse life bear it?

And if we see the soul's dead end in death,
Are we to fear it?
What folly is here that has not yet a name   295
Unless we say outright that we are liars?
What have we seen beyond our sunset fires
That lights again the way by which we came?
Why pay we such a price, and one we give
So clamoringly, for each racked empty day   300
That leads one more last human hope away,
As quiet fiends would lead past our crazed eyes
Our children to an unseen sacrifice?
If after all that we have lived and thought,
All comes to Nought,—   305
If there be nothing after Now,
And we be nothing anyhow,
And we know that,—why live?
'Twere sure but weaklings' vain distress
To suffer dungeons where so many doors   310
Will open on the cold eternal shores
That look sheer down
To the dark tideless floods of Nothingness
Where all who know may drown.

1916

The Mill

The miller's wife had waited long,
    The tea was cold, the fire was dead;
And there might yet be nothing wrong
    In how he went and what he said:
"There are no millers any more,"   5
    Was all that she had heard him say;
And he had lingered at the door
    So long that it seemed yesterday.

Sick with fear that had no form
    She knew that she was there at last;   10
And in the mill there was a warm
    And mealy fragrance of the past.
What else there was would only seem
    To say again what he had meant;
And what was hanging from a beam   15
    Would not have heeded where she went.

And if she thought it followed her,
    She may have reasoned in the dark
That one way of the few there were
    Would hide her and would leave no mark: 20
Black water, smooth above the weir
    Like starry velvet in the night,
Though ruffled once, would soon appear
    The same as ever to the sight.

1920

Mr. Flood's Party

Old Eben Flood, climbing alone one night
Over the hill between the town below
And the forsaken upland hermitage
That held as much as he should ever know
On earth again of home, paused warily.   5
The road was his with not a native near;
And Eben, having leisure, said aloud,
For no man else in Tilbury Town[1] to hear:

"Well, Mr. Flood, we have the harvest moon
Again, and we may not have many more;   10
The bird is on the wing, the poet says,[2]
And you and I have said it here before.
Drink to the bird." He raised up to the light
The jug that he had gone so far to fill,
And answered huskily: "Well, Mr. Flood,   15
Since you propose it, I believe I will."

Alone, as if enduring to the end
A valiant armor of scarred hopes outworn,
He stood there in the middle of the road
Like Roland's ghost winding a silent horn.[3]   20
Below him, in the town among the trees,
Where friends of other days had honored him,
A phantom salutation of the dead
Rang thinly till old Eben's eyes were dim.

Then, as a mother lays her sleeping child   25
Down tenderly, fearing it may awake,
He set the jug down slowly at his feet
With trembling care, knowing that most things break;
And only when assured that on firm earth
It stood, as the uncertain lives of men   30
Assuredly did not, he paced away,
And with his hand extended paused again:

"Well, Mr. Flood, we have not met like this
In a long time; and many a change has come
To both of us, I fear, since last it was   35
We had a drop together. Welcome home!"
Convivially returning with himself,
Again he raised the jug up to the light;
And with an acquiescent quaver said:
"Well, Mr. Flood, if you insist, I might.   40

1. The fictive town named in a number of Robinson's poems, modeled on Gardiner, Maine.
2. Flood paraphrases lines 25–28 of the Persian poem *The Rubáiyát of Omar Khayyám* in the translation by the English poet Edward FitzGerald (1809–83): "Come, fill the Cup, and in the fire of Spring/Your Winter-garment of Repentance fling:/The Bird of Time has but a little way/To flutter and the Bird is on the Wing."
3. King Charlemagne's nephew, celebrated in the medieval *Chanson de Roland* (*Song of Roland*, c. 1000). Just before dying in the futile battle of Roncevalles (A.D. 778), he sounded his horn for help.

"Only a very little, Mr. Flood—
For auld lang syne.[4] No more, sir; that will do."
So, for the time, apparently it did,
And Eben evidently thought so too;
For soon amid the silver loneliness   45
Of night he lifted up his voice and sang,
Secure, with only two moons listening,
Until the whole harmonious landscape rang—

"For auld lang syne." The weary throat gave out,
The last word wavered, and the song was done.   50
He raised again the jug regretfully
And shook his head, and was again alone.
There was not much that was ahead of him,
And there was nothing in the town below—
Where strangers would have shut the many doors   55
That many friends had opened long ago.

                                                                                  1921

Haunted House

Here was a place where none would ever come
For shelter, save as we did from the rain.
We saw no ghost, yet once outside again
Each wondered why the other should be dumb;
For we had fronted nothing worse than gloom
And ruin, and to our vision it was plain
Where thrift, outshivering fear, had let remain
Some chairs that were like skeletons of home.

There were no trackless footsteps on the floor
Above us, and there were no sounds elsewhere.
But there was more than sound; and there was more
Than just an axe that once was in the air
Between us and the chimney, long before
Our time. So townsmen said who found her there.

                                                                                  1925

The Long Race

Up the old hill to the old house again
Where fifty years ago the friend was young
Who should be waiting somewhere there among
Old things that least remembered most remain,
He toiled on with a pleasure that was pain   5
To think how soon asunder would be flung
The curtain half a century had hung
Between the two ambitions they had slain.

4. Scottish meaning "for the days of
long ago," the title and refrain of a song
of comradeship and parting immortalized
by the Scottish poet Robert Burns
(1759–96).

They dredged an hour for words, and then were done.
"Good-bye! . . . You have the same old weather-vane—   10
Your little horse that's always on the run."
And all the way down back to the next train,
Down the old hill to the old road again,
It seemed as if the little horse had won.

1921

New England[1]

Here where the wind is always north-north-east
And children learn to walk on frozen toes,
Wonder begets an envy of all those
Who boil elsewhere with such a lyric yeast
Of love that you will hear them at a feast   5
Where demons would appeal for some repose,
Still clamoring where the chalice overflows
And crying wildest who have drunk the least.

Passion is here a soilure of the wits,
We're told, and Love a cross for them to bear;   10
Joy shivers in the corner where she knits
And Conscience always has the rocking-chair,
Cheerful as when she tortured into fits
The first cat that was ever killed by Care.

1920, 1925

1. When published in the *Gardiner Journal* in 1924, this sonnet was attacked by a local resident for misrepresenting the region. Robinson wrote his editor that the poem was "an oblique attack upon all those who are forever throwing dead cats at New England for its alleged emotional and moral frigidity." (Quoted by Emory Neff, *Edwin Arlington Robinson*, 1948, p. 221.)

ROBERT FROST
1874–1963

In 1915, when the expatriate Ezra Pound began writing his *Cantos* in London and T. S. Eliot took up residence there, the poet Robert Frost, who had sojourned in England with his family for three years, returned to the United States. Discouraged by his failure to get his poems published in this country, he had sold his New Hampshire farm and moved to England; within a month after arriving there, his first manuscript was accepted by a London publisher. Ezra Pound recommended his poems to American editors, and Frost's second volume, *North of Boston*, had received critical praise from Pound and other reviewers by the time Frost returned to America. Within the next two years an American publisher brought out his first two volumes and added a third, and Frost was chosen Phi Beta Kappa poet by two American colleges and elected to the National Institute of Arts and Letters. He was well on his way to becoming the most publicly honored and popular of America's first-rate poetic talents. For the next four decades he devoted his efforts to reaching a large audience that would support his writing, and to fashioning, consciously and deliberately, from literary tradition and from the regional materials of New England life and speech, the poetic idiom that is unmistakably his own.

Robert Lee Frost was born in 1874 in California, where his father, a disgruntled Yankee with sympathies for the Confederacy during the Civil War, went to pursue a career in journalism and nourished political ambitions. His father's occasional violent behavior toward his family scarred Frost's memories and heightened his apprehensions about vindictive and self-destructive impulses that became apparent in his own temperament. Frost's Scottish mother, who wrote poetry herself, introduced Frost to the writings of her fellow Scots, and to the poems of Wordsworth, Bryant, and Emerson; she introduced him also to the tradition of Christian piety that led in her own case from Presbyterianism to Unitarianism and finally to the New Jerusalem church of Emanuel Swedenborg (whose doctrines of symbolic correspondence had earlier fascinated Emerson). When Frost's father died in 1885 the family returned to New England, where Mrs. Frost taught in Massachusetts and New Hampshire schools, and Frost attended high school in Lawrence, Massachusetts, specializing in the classics. At his graduation in 1892 he was class poet and shared the post of valedictorian with Elinor White, whom he married three years later. Frost studied for a term at Dartmouth College, then taught intermittently in elementary schools and held jobs in mills and on local newspapers until enrolling as a special student at Harvard from 1897 to 1899, lured by the writings of the pragmatist William James. He took English courses but emphasized the Greek and Latin classics and philosophy, studying James's *Psychology* in one course and attending the philosopher George Santayana's lectures in another. After leaving Harvard he moved to a farm in Derry, New Hampshire, which his grandfather bought for him. These were years of hardship for the Frosts and their four children, and of personal anxieties for Frost himself that culminated in obsessions with suicide. But Frost also became intimate for the first time with the rural environment and with nature, and he wrote poetry, publishing some in such local papers as the Derry *Enterprise*. Particularly in the years 1906–7 he worked on some of the major poems that appeared later in *North of Boston* and *Mountain Interval* (1916). Frost left the farm in 1909 and taught in New Hampshire until he left for England in 1912.

When Frost chose to live in New England on his return in 1915 (he bought another farm in New Hampshire and began in 1917 the first of three teaching appointments at Amherst College), he committed himself consciously not only to a locale but to a tradition and to a poetic instrument that he was perfecting. Long before H. L. Mencken's *The American Language* had enforced Frost's "sense of national difference" between English and American idioms, the English poet Rudyard Kipling had warned that Frost seemed strange to readers from the "elder earth" of England because of his "alien speech."[1] Yet the differences in language habits, Frost insisted, enable members of one culture to entertain the speech of another with relish, recognizing in it the "freshness of a stranger." Moreover, he pointed out that such strangeness or "estrangement" that derives from the peculiarities of national or regional speech is essentially the same as the strangeness of images and other devices, the intriguing "word-shift by metaphor," that characterizes all poetry.[2] The settings and characteristic idiom of Frost's poems have had precisely that appeal (of refreshing strangeness and suggestiveness) for Americans living outside as well as inside New England, and his regionalism constitutes not a literalistic or photographic strategy for his poetry, but a metaphorical one. His settings, characters, and language are engagingly familiar but also intriguingly strange metaphors for experience and realities that are recognizable elsewhere.

The tradition which sanctioned such a strategy had many remote sources, including Wordsworth, the ancient classics, and the Bible, but the tradition in America led from such near contemporaries as Edwin Arlington Robinson and William James back to Thoreau and Emerson. Frost was as conscious of his predecessors as were Pound and Eliot or Crane and William Carlos Williams of theirs, though unlike them Frost was not troubled by discontinuities in his tradition and felt no impulse to reconstitute radically its foundations. He shaped that tradition cautiously to his own uses. He admired Thoreau's cranky independence (and his suspicion of professional reformers) rather than his belligerence, praising Thoreau's "declaration of independence" from the feverish "modern pace" and particularly the tough fiber of the prose with which Thoreau fronted life directly and articulated his convictions in *Walden*.[3] Chiefly he found his precedents in Emerson's combination of allusive meaning with simple diction and simple forms, his reliance, as Emerson said in *Monadnock*, on the speech actually spoken by the "Rude poets of the tavern hearth" (*On Emerson*, 1959).[4] It was by fashioning the cadences and phrasing of such colloquial New England speech into a poetic idiom that Frost appropriated to his own use the familiar conventions of nature poetry and the conventions of classical pastoral poetry.

In enunciating his principles Frost cautioned against the search always for "new ways to be new" in extreme experimentation, and he insisted that instead "We play the words as we find them" (*The Constant Symbol*, 1946).[5] His touchstones for poetry outside of literature were science and philosophy rather than the music or the modern arts that interested his bolder contemporary writers like Pound and Hart Crane; his derivations were more narrowly literary than theirs. Poets should accept and perfect the habitual meters of iambic verse (units of one accented and one unaccented syllables) since "iambic and loose iambic" meters are the only ones natural to English speech (*The Figure a Poem Makes*, 1939).[6] "All folk speech" is itself "musical," he insisted in 1915, and this resource could be converted into a poetic idiom by developing "the sound of sense."[7] By this he meant that discursive and intelligible meaning affected the total experience of a poem and that the poet should develop interconnections of sound and feeling with "sense" or meaning. Discursive and even didactic statement need not be eliminated but should be played against the sounds and tonal qualities of the idiom. Poetic effects are achieved when the cadences of actual speech and the rhythms of sequential thought are played off "against the rigidity of a limited meter," and when recognizable subjects and themes are treated so as to "steady us down."[8]

Such a fusion of meter with subject and theme, of sound with sense,

2. *Ibid.*, p. 77.
3. *Interviews with Robert Frost*, p. 146.
4. *Selected Prose*, p. 113.
5. *Ibid.*, p. 28.

6. *Ibid.*, pp. 17–18.
7. *Interviews*, p. 6.
8. *Selected Prose*, p. 18.

should also be dramatic, Frost claimed, for Emerson's prose had shown that "writing is unboring to the extent that it is dramatic." Frost insisted that the dramatic effect must penetrate even the sentences of a poem by rendering "the speaking tone of voice somehow entangled in the words and fastened to the page for the ear of the imagination."[9]

A poem so conceived becomes a symbol or "metaphor," which Frost defined as a way of "saying one thing in terms of another," an imaginative activity that yields the "pleasure of ulteriority" and grounds poetry on indirection, tangential or allusive implication, the "guardedness" of wry or tragic irony, and wily cunning.[1] It also founded poetry on disciplined, cautious restraint, for Frost conceived metaphor as something that "tamed" the "enthusiasm" it captured (*Education by Poetry*, 1931).[2] The poem becomes a careful, loving exploration of reality which is at the same time a defensive shield against its tragedies and perils, a "momentary stay against confusion."[3] In its confrontation with reality, which Frost, like William James, regarded as a hazard or trial, the poem is a "figure of the will braving alien entanglements"; it is an expression, however desperate or tentative, of what James called the will to believe. Frost once catalogued the important affirmations of belief from which poetry springs as "self-belief," "love-belief," "literary belief" (the belief in art), "God belief" (a "relation you enter into with Him to bring about the future"), and "national belief."[4]

Governed by these principles, Frost's idiom enabled him to create works of unmistakable beauty and power. The pointed wit of his animal fables, as well as the intensity of his best lyrics and the impact of his dramatic narratives, are enhanced by the suppleness with which he used a wide range of traditional conventions—rhymed couplets, rhyming quatrains, blank verse, and, brilliantly, the sonnet form. Yet the diction and cadences of colloquial speech are so deftly incorporated, the illusion of gestures and scene is so convincingly represented, the facts of nature and everyday occupations in rural New England are so tangibly recreated in the verse, that his poems are a much closer approximation of actuality than those of Wordsworth and Emerson or those of poets with comparable intentions, like Edward Thomas, whom Frost found congenial during his stay in England. At the same time the indirection or "ulteriority" of metaphor is generated by the "whispering" motion of a scythe in *Mowing*, by such images as the "tongue of bloom" in *The Tuft of Flowers*, or by such religious terms as "fall" in *After Apple-Picking* and "annunciation" in *West-Running Brook*. These poems metaphorically suggest dimensions of relevance beyond what is made explicit; they invite the reader to explore unspoken connections to the whispering of Frost's own poem, to the search for communion with God or nature, to the assessment of an apple picker's moral worth before death, or to the revelation of life's meaning in a New England brook.

Though Frost's allusiveness, like his resort to a rural setting removed from the urban world, ran the risk of evading pressing realities of his time, his best poems are somber, even terrifying, in rendering many anxieties that grip the modern imagination: apprehensions about the dissolution of marriages and families, the conformist standardization of urban civilization, the bleak isolation of an aging man, the imminence of death and extinction, the desperation with which abject men or women must "provide, provide"

9. *Ibid.*, pp. 114, 13–14.
1. *Selected Letters*, p. 299.
2. *Selected Prose*, p. 36.
3. *Ibid.*, p. 18.
4. *Ibid.*, pp. 25, 45.

in order to survive at all, the horror of a world in which nature's "design" is predatory if indeed any design governs nature at all.

His major poems (all written before 1930, and many of them appearing in his masterpiece *North of Boston* in 1914) are the dramatic monologues or dialogues, such as *A Servant to Servants* and *West-Running Brook*, and the dramatic narratives, including *Home Burial* and *The Witch of Coös*. Compressed in their impact and in the contraries of temperament and attitude they delineate, fully dramatized in speech and gesture, they are probing illuminations of such subjects as repressed passion and the ritualization of grief, and profoundly suggestive meditations on the human predicament.

Frost always gave first priority to his poetry, but his career as teacher, platform reader of his poems, and occasional lecturer was designed to support his writing and augment his audience as well as to stimulate an interest in poetry generally. His longest affiliation was with Amherst (1917–20, 1923–38, 1949), but he was also Poet in Residence at Michigan in the early 1920s, Norton Professor at Harvard in 1936, and Ticknor Fellow at Dartmouth College for six years in the 1940s. He was particularly attached after 1921 to the summer sessions of the Bread Loaf School of English and the Bread Loaf Writers Conference, which he helped to establish at Middlebury College in Vermont. His effectiveness in teaching—Socratic, anecdotal, folksy—was proverbial, but he sought arrangements that would leave much of the week, and much of the year, free for writing. By the time he had won four Pulitzer Prizes (the first in 1924 for *New Hampshire*, the last in 1943 for *A Witness Tree*) he was a public figure. The publication of two ambitious philosophical poems, *The Masque of Reason* and *The Masque of Mercy*, in 1945 and 1947, and *In the Clearing* in 1962 marked the end of his productive career. He received honorary degrees from both Oxford and Cambridge universities in 1957 when he was a "good-will ambassador" abroad for the Department of State, and he received the Emerson-Thoreau Medal of the American Academy of Arts and Sciences in the same year he was appointed Consultant in Poetry in the Library of Congress (1958). His most extraordinary honor, confirming his earlier hope that he "fitted, not into the nature of the Universe, but * * * into the nature of Americans—into their affections,"[5] was his selection by John F. Kennedy to read a poem at his presidential inauguration in 1961. (Though a long-time antagonist of liberal reform and of President Franklin D. Roosevelt's New Deal, Frost became an enthusiast for Kennedy.) A cold wind and blinding sun rendered his text unreadable, but Frost recited *The Gift Outright* from memory and later sent the President an expanded version of the "dedication" he had written for the occasion, in which he prophesied for America "The glory of a next Augustan age," a "golden age of poetry and power."

The Pasture

I'm going out to clean the pasture spring;
I'll only stop to rake the leaves away
(And wait to watch the water clear, I may):
I sha'n't be gone long.—You come too.

5. *Ibid.*, p. 102.

I'm going out to fetch the little calf   5
That's standing by the mother. It's so young
It totters when she licks it with her tongue.
I sha'n't be gone long.—You come too.

                                                    1913

Mowing

There was never a sound beside the wood but one,
And that was my long scythe whispering to the ground.
What was it it whispered? I knew not well myself;
Perhaps it was something about the heat of the sun,
Something, perhaps, about the lack of sound—   5
And that was why it whispered and did not speak.
It was no dream of the gift of idle hours,
Or easy gold at the hand of fay or elf:
Anything more than the truth would have seemed too weak
To the earnest love that laid the swale[1] in rows,   10
Not without feeble-pointed spikes of flowers
(Pale orchises), and scared a bright green snake.
The fact is the sweetest dream that labor knows.
My long scythe whispered and left the hay to make.

                                                    1913

The Tuft of Flowers

I went to turn the grass once after one
Who mowed it in the dew before the sun.

The dew was gone that made his blade so keen
Before I came to view the leveled scene.

I looked for him behind an isle of trees;   5
I listened for his whetstone on the breeze.

But he had gone his way, the grass all mown,
And I must be, as he had been,—alone,

'As all must be,' I said within my heart,
'Whether they work together or apart.'   10

But as I said it, swift there passed me by
On noiseless wing a bewildered butterfly,

Seeking with memories grown dim o'er night
Some resting flower of yesterday's delight.

And once I marked his flight go round and round,   15
As where some flower lay withering on the ground.

1. Grasses in a marshy meadow.

And then he flew as far as eye could see,
And then on tremulous wing came back to me.

I thought of questions that have no reply,
And would have turned to toss the grass to dry;   20

But he turned first, and led my eye to look
At a tall tuft of flowers beside a brook,

A leaping tongue of bloom the scythe had spared
Beside a reedy brook the scythe had bared.

The mower in the dew had loved them thus,   25
By leaving them to flourish, not for us,

Nor yet to draw one thought of ours to him,
But from sheer morning gladness at the brim.

The butterfly and I had lit upon,
Nevertheless, a message from the dawn,   30

That made me hear the wakening birds around,
And hear his long scythe whispering to the ground,

And feel a spirit kindred to my own;
So that henceforth I worked no more alone;

But glad with him, I worked as with his aid,   35
And weary, sought at noon with him the shade;

And dreaming, as it were, held brotherly speech
With one whose thought I had not hoped to reach.

'Men work together,' I told him from the heart,
'Whether they work together or apart.'   40
1906   1906, 1913

Mending Wall

Something there is that doesn't love a wall,
That sends the frozen-ground-swell under it,
And spills the upper boulders in the sun;
And makes gaps even two can pass abreast.
The work of hunters is another thing: 5
I have come after them and made repair
Where they have left not one stone on a stone,
But they would have the rabbit out of hiding,
To please the yelping dogs. The gaps I mean,
No one has seen them made or heard them made,   10
But at spring mending-time we find them there.
I let my neighbor know beyond the hill;
And on a day we meet to walk the line

And set the wall between us once again.
We keep the wall between us as we go.   15
To each the boulders that have fallen to each.
And some are loaves and some so nearly balls
We have to use a spell to make them balance:
'Stay where you are until our backs are turned!'
We wear our fingers rough with handling them.   20
Oh, just another kind of outdoor game,
One on a side. It comes to little more:
There where it is we do not need the wall:
He is all pine and I am apple orchard.
My apple trees will never get across   25
And eat the cones under his pines, I tell him.
He only says, 'Good fences make good neighbors.'
Spring is the mischief in me, and I wonder
If I could put a notion in his head:
'Why do they make good neighbors? Isn't it   30
Where there are cows? But here there are no cows.
Before I built a wall I'd ask to know
What I was walling in or walling out,
And to whom I was like to give offense.
Something there is that doesn't love a wall,   35
That wants it down.' I could say 'Elves' to him,
But it's not elves exactly, and I'd rather
He said it for himself. I see him there
Bringing a stone grasped firmly by the top
In each hand, like an old-stone savage armed.   40
He moves in darkness as it seems to me,
Not of woods only and the shade of trees.
He will not go behind his father's saying,
And he likes having thought of it so well
He says again, 'Good fences make good neighbors.'   45

                                                             1914

Home Burial[1]

He saw her from the bottom of the stairs
Before she saw him. She was starting down,
Looking back over her shoulder at some fear.
She took a doubtful step and then undid it
To raise herself and look again. He spoke   5
Advancing toward her: 'What is it you see
From up there always—for I want to know.'
She turned and sank upon her skirts at that,
And her face changed from terrified to dull.
He said to gain time: 'What is it you see.'   10

1. The title refers to the custom of burying members of the family on the home
property. Frost's biographer, Lawrance
Thompson (in *Robert Frost, the Early
Years*, p. 597) reports that the poem
commemorated the loss of a child and
the consequent marital difficulties of two
acquaintances, Mr. and Mrs. Nathaniel
Harvey, in 1895, and that the poem
draws on the grief of the Frosts after
the loss of their first child in 1900. Line
110 echoes Mrs. Frost's statement at the
time that "The world's evil."

Mounting until she cowered under him.
'I will find out now—you must tell me, dear.'
She, in her place, refused him any help
With the least stiffening of her neck and silence.
She let him look, sure that he wouldn't see,   15
Blind creature; and awhile he didn't see.
But at last he murmured, 'Oh,' and again, 'Oh.'

'What is it—what?' she said.

                          'Just that I see.'

'You don't,' she challenged. 'Tell me what it is.'   20

'The wonder is I didn't see at once.
I never noticed it from here before.
I must be wonted to it—that's the reason.
The little graveyard where my people are!
So small the window frames the whole of it.   25
Not so much larger than a bedroom, it is?
There are three stones of slate and one of marble,
Broad-shouldered little slabs there in the sunlight
On the sidehill. We haven't to mind *those*.
But I understand: it is not the stones,   30
But the child's mound—'

                    'Don't, don't, don't, don't,' she cried.

She withdrew shrinking from beneath his arm
That rested on the bannister, and slid downstairs;
And turned on him with such a daunting look,   35
He said twice over before he knew himself:
'Can't a man speak of his own child he's lost?'

'Not you! Oh, where's my hat? Oh, I don't need it!
I must get out of here. I must get air.
I don't know rightly whether any man can.'   40

'Amy! Don't go to someone else this time.
Listen to me. I won't come down the stairs.'
He sat and fixed his chin between his fists.
'There's something I should like to ask you, dear,'

'You don't know how ask it.'   45
                          'Help me, then.'

Her fingers moved the latch for all reply.

'My words are nearly always an offense.
I don't know how to speak of anything
So as to please you. But I might be taught   50
I should suppose. I can't say I see how.

A man must partly give up being a man
With women-folk. We could have some arrangement
By which I'd bind myself to keep hands off
Anything special you're a-mind to name. 55
Though I don't like such things 'twixt those that love.
Two that don't love can't live together without them.
But two that do can't live together with them.'
She moved the latch a little. 'Don't—don't go.
Don't carry it to someone else this time. 60
Tell me about it if it's something human.
Let me into your grief. I'm not so much
Unlike other folks as your standing there
Apart would make me out. Give me my chance.
I do think, though, you overdo it a little. 65
What was it brought you up to think it the thing
To take your mother-loss of a first child
So inconsolably—in the face of love.
You'd think his memory might be satisfied—'

'There you go sneering now!' 70

'I'm not, I'm not!
You make me angry. I'll come down to you.
God, what a woman! And it's come to this,
A man can't speak of his own child that's dead.'

'You can't because you don't know how to speak. 75
If you had any feelings, you that dug
With your own hand—how could you?—his little grave;
I saw you from that very window there,
Making the gravel leap and leap in air,
Leap up, like that, like that, and land so lightly 80
And roll back down the mound beside the hole.
I thought, Who is that man? I didn't know you.
And I crept down the stairs and up the stairs
To look again, and still your spade kept lifting.
Then you came in. I heard your rumbling voice 85
Out in the kitchen, and I don't know why,
But I went near to see with my own eyes.
You could sit there with the stains on your shoes
Of the fresh earth from your own baby's grave
And talk about your everyday concerns. 90
You had stood the spade up against the wall
Outside there in the entry, for I saw it.'

'I shall laugh the worst laugh I ever laughed.
I'm cursed. God, if I don't believe I'm cursed.'

'I can repeat the very words you were saying. 95
"Three foggy mornings and one rainy day
Will rot the best birch fence a man can build."
Think of it, talk like that at such a time!

What had how long it takes a birch to rot
To do with what was in the darkened parlor.   100
You *couldn't* care! The nearest friends can go
With anyone to death, comes so far short
They might as well not try to go at all.
No, from the time when one is sick to death,
One is alone, and he dies more alone.   105
Friends make pretense of following to the grave,
But before one is in it, their minds are turned
And making the best of their way back to life
And living people, and things they understand.
But the world's evil. I won't have grief so   110
If I can change it. Oh, I won't, I won't!'

'There, you have said it all and you feel better.
You won't go now. You're crying. Close the door.
The heart's gone out of it: why keep it up.
Amy! There's someone coming down the road!'   115

'You—oh, you think the talk is all. I must go—
Somewhere out of this house. How can I make you—'

'If—you—do!' She was opening the door wider.
'Where do you mean to go? First tell me that.
I'll follow and bring you back by force. I *will!*—'   120
1912–13   1914

The Black Cottage

We chanced in passing by that afternoon
To catch it in a sort of special picture
Among tar-banded ancient cherry trees,
Set well back from the road in rank lodged grass,
The little cottage we were speaking of,   5
A front with just a door between two windows,
Fresh painted by the shower a velvet black.
We paused, the minister and I, to look.
He made as if to hold it at arm's length
Or put the leaves aside that framed it in.   10
'Pretty,' he said. 'Come in. No one will care.'
The path was a vague parting in the grass
That led us to a weathered window-sill.
We pressed our faces to the pane. 'You see,' he said,
'Everything's as she left it when she died.   15
Her sons won't sell the house or the things in it.
They say they mean to come and summer here
Where they were boys. They haven't come this year.
They live so far away—one is out west—
It will be hard for them to keep their word.   20
Anyway they won't have the place disturbed.'
A buttoned hair-cloth lounge spread scrolling arms
Under a crayon portrait on the wall,

Done sadly from an old daguerreotype.[1]
'That was the father as he went to war.   25
She always, when she talked about the war,
Sooner or later came and leaned, half knelt
Against the lounge beside it, though I doubt
If such unlifelike lines kept power to stir
Anything in her after all the years.   30
He fell at Gettysburg or Fredericksburg,[2]
I ought to know—it makes a difference which:
Fredericksburg wasn't Gettysburg, of course.
But what I'm getting to is how forsaken
A little cottage this has always seemed;   35
Since she went more than ever, but before—
I don't mean altogether by the lives
That had gone out of it, the father first,
Then the two sons, till she was left alone.
(Nothing could draw her after those two sons.   40
She valued the considerate neglect
She had at some cost taught them after years.)
I mean by the world's having passed it by—
As we almost got by this afternoon.
It always seems to me a sort of mark   45
To measure how far fifty years have brought us.
Why not sit down if you are in no haste?
These doorsteps seldom have a visitor.
The warping boards pull out their own old nails
With none to tread and put them in their place.   50
She had her own idea of things, the old lady.
And she liked talk. She had seen Garrison
And Whittier,[3] and had her story of them.
One wasn't long in learning that she thought
Whatever else the Civil War was for,   55
It wasn't just to keep the States together,
Nor just to free the slaves, though it did both.
She wouldn't have believed those ends enough
To have given outright for them all she gave.
Her giving somehow touched the principle   60
That all men are created free and equal.
And to hear her quaint phrases—so removed
From the world's view today of all those things.
That's a hard mystery of Jefferson's.[4]
What did he mean? Of course the easy way   65
Is to decide it simply isn't true.
It may not be. I heard a fellow say so.
But never mind, the Welshman[5] got it planted

---

1. A type of 19th-century photograph, named for its French inventor, Louis J. M. Daguerre (1787–1851).
2. Sites of Civil War battles: Fredericksburg, Virginia, where Confederate troops defeated Union forces; and Gettysburg, Pennsylvania, where the North defeated the Confederacy.
3. The editor William Lloyd Garrison (1805–79) and the poet John Greenleaf Whittier (1807–92) were famous American abolitionists.
4. The principle, stated three lines above, that men are created free and equal.
5. Jefferson was of Welsh descent.

Where it will trouble us a thousand years.
Each age will have to reconsider it.   70
You couldn't tell her what the West was saying,
And what the South to her serene belief.
She had some art of hearing and yet not
Hearing the latter wisdom of the world.
White was the only race she ever knew.   75
Black she had scarcely seen, and yellow never.
But how could they be made so very unlike
By the same hand working in the same stuff?
She had supposed the war decided that.
What are you going to do with such a person?   80
Strange how such innocence gets its own way.
I shouldn't be surprised if in this world
It were the force that would at last prevail.
Do you know but for her there was a time
When to please younger members of the church,   85
Or rather say non-members in the church,
Whom we all have to think of nowadays,
I would have changed the Creed[6] a very little?
Not that she ever had to ask me not to;
It never got so far as that; but the bare thought   90
Of her old tremulous bonnet in the pew,
And of her half asleep was too much for me.
Why, I might wake her up and startle her.
It was the words "descended into Hades"[7]
That seemed too pagan to our liberal youth.   95
You know they suffered from a general onslaught.
And well, if they weren't true why keep right on
Saying them like the heathen? We could drop them.
Only—there was the bonnet in the pew.
Such a phrase couldn't have meant much to her.   100
But suppose she had missed it from the Creed
As a child misses the unsaid Good-night,
And falls asleep with heartache—how should *I* feel?
I'm just as glad she made me keep hands off,
For, dear me, why abandon a belief   105
Merely because it ceases to be true.
Cling to it long enough, and not a doubt
It will turn true again, for so it goes.
Most of the change we think we see in life
Is due to truths being in and out of favor.   110
As I sit here, and oftentimes, I wish
I could be monarch of a desert land
I could devote and dedicate forever
To the truths we keep coming back and back to.
So desert it would have to be, so walled   115
By mountain ranges half in summer snow,
No one would covet it or think it worth

6. The Apostles' Creed, recited in Protestant church services.
7. The Greek word for the land of the
dead or hell. The Creed states that
Christ descended into hell after his crucifixion and before his resurrection.

The pains of conquering to force change on.
Scattered oases where men dwelt, but mostly
Sand dunes held loosely in tamarisk[8]   120
Blown over and over themselves in idleness.
Sand grains should sugar in the natal dew
The babe born to the desert, the sand storm
Retard mid-waste my cowering caravans—
There are bees in this wall.' He struck the clapboards,   125
Fierce heads looked out; small bodies pivoted.
We rose to go. Sunset blazed on the windows.

1905–6   1914

A Servant to Servants

I didn't make you know how glad I was
To have you come and camp here on our land.
I promised myself to get down some day
And see the way you lived, but I don't know!
With a houseful of hungry men to feed   5
I guess you'd find. . . . It seems to me
I can't express my feelings any more
Than I can raise my voice or want to lift
My hand (oh, I can lift it when I have to).
Did ever you feel so? I hope you never.   10
It's got so I don't even know for sure
Whether I *am* glad, sorry, or anything.
There's nothing but a voice-like left inside
That seems to tell me how I ought to feel,
And would feel if I wasn't all gone wrong.   15
You take the lake. I look and look at it.
I see it's a fair, pretty sheet of water.
I stand and make myself repeat out loud
The advantages it has, so long and narrow,
Like a deep piece of some old running river   20
Cut short off at both ends. It lies five miles
Straight away through the mountain notch
From the sink window where I wash the plates,
And all our storms come up toward the house,
Drawing the slow waves whiter and whiter and whiter.   25
It took my mind off doughnuts and soda biscuit
To step outdoors and take the water dazzle
A sunny morning, or take the rising wind
About my face and body and through my wrapper,
When a storm threatened from the Dragon's Den,   30
And a cold chill shivered across the lake.
I see it's a fair, pretty sheet of water,
Our Willoughby! How did you hear of it?
I expect, though, everyone's heard of it.
In a book about ferns? Listen to that!   35
You let things more like feathers regulate

8. Near Eastern shrub planted as a wind- and sand-breaker in the desert.

Your going and coming. And you like it here?
I can see how you might. But I don't know!
It would be different if more people came,
For then there would be business. As it is,   40
The cottages Len built, sometimes we rent them,
Sometimes we don't. We've a good piece of shore
That ought to be worth something, and may yet.
But I don't count on it as much as Len.
He looks on the bright side of everything,   45
Including me. He thinks I'll be all right
With doctoring. But it's not medicine—
Lowe is the only doctor's dared to say so—
It's rest I want—there, I have said it out—
From cooking meals for hungry hired men   50
And washing dishes after them—from doing
Things over and over that just won't stay done.
By good rights I ought not to have so much
Put on me, but there seems no other way.
Len says one steady pull more ought to do it.   55
He says the best way out is always through,
And I agree to that, or in so far
As that I can see no way out but through—
Leastways for me—and then they'll be convinced.
It's not that Len don't want the best for me.   60
It was his plan our moving over in
Beside the lake from where that day I showed you
We used to live—ten miles from anywhere.
We didn't change without some sacrifice,
But Len went at it to make up the loss.   65
His work's a man's, of course, from sun to sun,
But he works when he works as hard as I do—
Though there's small profit in comparisons,
(Women and men will make them all the same.)
But work ain't all. Len undertakes too much.   70
He's into everything in town. This year
It's highways, and he's got too many men
Around him to look after that make waste.
They take advantage of him shamefully,
And proud, too, of themselves for doing so.   75
We have four here to board, great good-for-nothings,
Sprawling about the kitchen with their talk
While I fry their bacon. Much they care!
No more put out in what they do or say
Than if I wasn't in the room at all.   80
Coming and going all the time, they are:
I don't learn what their names are, let alone
Their characters, or whether they are safe
To have inside the house with doors unlocked.
I'm not afraid of them, though, if they're not   85
Afraid of me. There's two can play at that.
I have my fancies: it runs in the family.
My father's brother wasn't right. They kept him

Locked up for years back there at the old farm.
I've been away once—yes, I've been away.   90
The State Asylum. I was prejudiced;
I wouldn't have sent anyone of mine there;
You know the old idea—the only asylum
Was the poorhouse, and those who could afford,
Rather than send their folks to such a place,   95
Kept them at home; and it does seem more human.
But it's not so: the place is the asylum.
There they have every means proper to do with,
And you aren't darkening other people's lives—
Worse than no good to them, and they no good   100
To you in your condition; you can't know
Affection or the want of it in that state.
I've heard too much of the old-fashioned way.
My father's brother, he went mad quite young.
Some thought he had been bitten by a dog,   105
Because his violence took on the form
Of carrying his pillow in his teeth;
But it's more likely he was crossed in love,
Or so the story goes. It was some girl.
Anyway all he talked about was love.   110
They soon saw he would do someone a mischief
If he wa'n't kept strict watch of, and it ended
In father's building him a sort of cage,
Or room within a room, of hickory poles,
Like stanchions in the barn, from floor to ceiling,—   115
A narrow passage all the way around.
Anything they put in for furniture
He'd tear to pieces, even a bed to lie on.
So they made the place comfortable with straw,
Like a beast's stall, to ease their consciences.   120
Of course they had to feed him without dishes.
They tried to keep him clothed, but he paraded
With his clothes on his arm—all of his clothes.
Cruel—it sounds. I s'pose they did the best
They knew. And just when he was at the height,   125
Father and mother married, and mother came,
A bride, to help take care of such a creature,
And accommodate her young life to his.
That was what marrying father meant to her.
She had to lie and hear love things made dreadful   130
By his shouts in the night. He'd shout and shout
Until the strength was shouted out of him,
And his voice died down slowly from exhaustion.
He'd pull his bars apart like bow and bowstring,
And let them go and make them twang until   135
His hands had worn them smooth as any oxbow.[1]
And then he'd crow as if he thought that child's play
The only fun he had. I've heard them say, though,

---

1. U-shaped collar harnessing an ox to a yoke.

They found a way to put a stop to it.
He was before my time—I never saw him;   140
But the pen stayed exactly as it was
There in the upper chamber in the ell,
A sort of catch-all full of attic clutter.
I often think of the smooth hickory bars.
It got so I would say—you know, half fooling—   145
'It's time I took my turn upstairs in jail'—
Just as you will till it becomes a habit.
No wonder I was glad to get away.
Mind you, I waited till Len said the word.
I didn't want the blame if things went wrong.   150
I was glad though, no end, when we moved out,
And I looked to be happy, and I was,
As I said, for a while—but I don't know!
Somehow the change wore out like a prescription.
And there's more to it than just window-views   155
And living by a lake. I'm past such help—
Unless Len took the notion, which he won't,
And I won't ask him—it's not sure enough.
I s'pose I've got to go the road I'm going:
Other folks have to, and why shouldn't I?   160
I almost think if I could do like you,
Drop everything and live out on the ground—
But it might be, come night, I shouldn't like it,
Or a long rain. I should soon get enough,
And be glad of a good roof overhead.   165
I've lain awake thinking of you, I'll warrant,
More than you have yourself, some of these nights.
The wonder was the tents weren't snatched away
From over you as you lay in your beds.
I haven't courage for a risk like that.   170
Bless you, of course, you're keeping me from work,
But the thing of it is, I need to *be* kept.
There's work enough to do—there's always that;
But behind's behind. The worst that you can do
Is set me back a little more behind.   175
I sha'n't catch up in this world, anyway.
I'd *rather* you'd not go unless you must.

                                                          1914

After Apple-Picking

My long two-pointed ladder's sticking through a tree
Toward heaven still,
And there's a barrel that I didn't fill
Beside it, and there may be two or three
Apples I didn't pick upon some bough.   5
But I am done with apple-picking now.
Essence of winter sleep is on the night,
The scent of apples: I am drowsing off.
I cannot rub the strangeness from my sight

I got from looking through a pane of glass   10
I skimmed this morning from the drinking trough
And held against the world of hoary grass.
It melted, and I let it fall and break.
But I was well
Upon my way to sleep before it fell,   15
And I could tell
What form my dreaming was about to take.
Magnified apples appear and disappear,
Stem end and blossom end,
And every fleck of russet showing clear.   20
My instep arch not only keeps the ache,
It keeps the pressure of a ladder-round.
I feel the ladder sway as the boughs bend.
And I keep hearing from the cellar bin
The rumbling sound   25
Of load on load of apples coming in.
For I have had too much
Of apple-picking: I an overtired
Of the great harvest I myself desired.
There were ten thousand thousand fruit to touch,   30
Cherish in hand, lift down, and not let fall.
For all
That struck the earth,
No matter if not bruised or spiked with stubble,
Went surely to the cider-apple heap   35
As of no worth.
One can see what will trouble
This sleep of mine, whatever sleep it is.
Were he not gone,
The woodchuck could say whether it's like his   40
Long sleep, as I describe its coming on,
Or just some human sleep.

                                                                    1914

The Wood-Pile

Out walking in the frozen swamp one gray day,
I paused and said, 'I will turn back from here.
No, I will go on farther—and we shall see.'
The hard snow held me, save where now and then
One foot went through. The view was all in lines   5
Straight up and down of tall slim trees
Too much alike to mark or name a place by
So as to say for certain I was here
Or somewhere else: I was just far from home.
A small bird flew before me. He was careful   10
To put a tree between us when he lighted,
And say no word to tell me who he was
Who was so foolish as to think what *he* thought.
He thought that I was after him for a feather—

The white one in his tail; like one who takes   15
Everything said as personal to himself.
One flight out sideways would have undeceived him.
And then there was a pile of wood for which
I forgot him and let his little fear
Carry him off the way I might have gone,   20
Without so much as wishing him good-night.
He went behind it to make his last stand.
It was a cord of maple, cut and split
And piled—and measured, four by four by eight.
And not another like it could I see.   25
No runner tracks in this year's snow looped near it.
And it was older sure than this year's cutting,
Or even last year's or the year's before.
The wood was gray and the bark warping off it
And the pile somewhat sunken. Clematis   30
Had wound strings round and round it like a bundle.
What held it though on one side was a tree
Still growing, and on one a stake and prop,
These latter about to fall. I thought that only
Someone who lived in turning to fresh tasks   35
Could so forget his handiwork on which
He spent himself, the labor of his ax,
And leave it there far from a useful fireplace
To warm the frozen swamp as best it could
With the slow smokeless burning of decay.   40

                                                                1914

The Road Not Taken

Two roads diverged in a yellow wood,
And sorry I could not travel both
And be one traveler, long I stood
And looked down one as far as I could
To where it bent in the undergrowth;   5

Then took the other, as just as fair,
And having perhaps the better claim,
Because it was grassy and wanted wear;
Though as for that the passing there
Had worn them really about the same,   10

And both that morning equally lay
In leaves no step had trodden black.
Oh, I kept the first for another day!
Yet knowing how way leads on to way,
I doubted if I should ever come back.   15

I shall be telling this with a sigh
Somewhere ages and ages hence:
Two roads diverged in a wood, and I—

I took the one less traveled by,
And that has made all the difference.   20

                                                         1916

An Old Man's Winter Night

All out-of-doors looked darkly in at him
Through the thin frost, almost in separate stars,
That gathers on the pane in empty rooms.
What kept his eyes from giving back the gaze
Was the lamp tilted near them in his hand.   5
What kept him from remembering what it was
That brought him to that creaking room was age.
He stood with barrels round him—at a loss.
And having scared the cellar under him
In clomping here, he scared it once again   10
In clomping off;—and scared the outer night,
Which has its sounds, familiar, like the roar
Of trees and crack of branches, common things,
But nothing so like beating on a box.
A light he was to no one but himself   15
Where now he sat, concerned with he knew what,
A quiet light, and then not even that.
He consigned to the moon, such as she was,
So late-arising, to the broken moon
As better than the sun in any case   20
For such a charge, his snow upon the roof,
His icicles along the wall to keep;
And slept. The log that shifted with a jolt
Once in the stove, disturbed him and he shifted,
And eased his heavy breathing, but still slept.   25
One aged man—one man—can't keep a house,
A farm, a countryside, or if he can,
It's thus he does it of a winter night.

1906   1916

The Oven Bird

There is a singer everyone has heard,
Loud, a mid-summer and a mid-wood bird,
Who makes the solid tree trunks sound again.
He says that leaves are old and that for flowers
Mid-summer is to spring as one to ten.   5
He says the early petal-fall is past
When pear and cherry bloom went down in showers
On sunny days a moment overcast;
And comes that other fall we name the fall.
He says the highway dust is over all.   10
The bird would cease and be as other birds
But that he knows in singing not to sing.
The question that he frames in all but words
Is what to make of a diminished thing.

1906–7   1916

Birches

When I see birches bend to left and right
Across the lines of straighter darker trees,
I like to think some boy's been swinging them.
But swinging doesn't bend them down to stay
As ice-storms do. Often you must have seen them   5
Loaded with ice a sunny winter morning
After a rain. They click upon themselves
As the breeze rises, and turn many-colored
As the stir cracks and crazes their enamel.
Soon the sun's warmth makes them shed crystal shells   10
Shattering and avalanching on the snow-crust—
Such heaps of broken glass to sweep away
You'd think the inner dome of heaven had fallen.
They are dragged to the withered bracken by the load,
And they seem not to break; though once they are bowed   15
So low for long, they never right themselves:
You may see their trunks arching in the woods
Years afterwards, trailing their leaves on the ground
Like girls on hands and knees that throw their hair
Before them over their heads to dry in the sun.   20
But I was going to say when Truth broke in
With all her matter-of-fact about the ice-storm
I should prefer to have some boy bend them
As he went out and in to fetch the cows—
Some boy too far from town to learn baseball,   25
Whose only play was what he found himself,
Summer or winter, and could play alone.
One by one he subdued his father's trees
By riding them down over and over again
Until he took the stiffness out of them,   30
And not one but hung limp, not one was left
For him to conquer. He learned all there was
To learn about not launching out too soon
And so not carrying the tree away
Clear to the ground. He always kept his poise   35
To the top branches, climbing carefully
With the same pains you use to fill a cup
Up to the brim, and even above the brim.
Then he flung outward, feet first, with a swish,
Kicking his way down through the air to the ground.   40
So was I once myself a swinger of birches.
And so I dream of going back to be.
It's when I'm weary of considerations,
And life is too much like a pathless wood
Where your face burns and tickles with the cobwebs   45
Broken across it, and one eye is weeping
From a twig's having lashed across it open.
I'd like to get away from earth awhile
And then come back to it and begin over.
May no fate willfully misunderstand me   50

And half grant what I wish and snatch me away
Not to return. Earth's the right place for love:
I don't know where it's likely to go better.
I'd like to go by climbing a birch tree,
And climb black branches up a snow-white trunk   55
Toward heaven, till the tree could bear no more,
But dipped its top and set me down again.
That would be good both going and coming back.
One could do worse than be a swinger of birches.

1913–14   1916

The Cow in Apple Time

Something inspires the only cow of late
To make no more of a wall than an open gate,
And think no more of wall-builders than fools.
Her face is flecked with pomace[1] and she drools
A cider syrup. Having tasted fruit,   5
She scorns a pasture withering to the root.
She runs from tree to tree where lie and sweeten
The windfalls spiked with stubble and worm-eaten.
She leaves them bitten when she has to fly.
She bellows on a knoll against the sky.   10
Her udder shrivels and the milk goes dry.

1914, 1916

Range-Finding

The battle rent a cobweb diamond-strung
And cut a flower beside a ground bird's nest
Before it stained a single human breast.
The stricken flower bent double and so hung.
And still the bird revisited her young.   5
A butterfly its fall had dispossessed
A moment sought in air his flower of rest,
Then lightly stooped to it and fluttering clung.
On the bare upland pasture there had spread
O'ernight 'twixt mullein stalks a wheel of thread   10
And straining cables wet with silver dew.
A sudden passing bullet shook it dry.
The indwelling spider ran to greet the fly,
But finding nothing, sullenly withdrew.

1911   1916

'Out, Out—'[2]

The buzz saw snarled and rattled in the yard
And made dust and dropped stove-length sticks of wood,
Sweet-scented stuff when the breeze drew across it.

---

1. Apple pulp.
2. A quotation from Shakespeare's *Mac-*

beth (5.5.23–24): "Out, out, brief candle!
/Life's but a walking shadow."

And from there those that lifted eyes could count
Five mountain ranges one behind the other   5
Under the sunset far into Vermont.
And the saw snarled and rattled, snarled and rattled,
As it ran light, or had to bear a load.
And nothing happened: day was all but done.
Call it a day, I wish they might have said   10
To please the boy by giving him the half hour
That a boy counts so much when saved from work.
His sister stood beside them in her apron
To tell them 'Supper.' At the word, the saw,
As if to prove saws knew what supper meant,   15
Leaped out at the boy's hand, or seemed to leap—,
He must have given the hand. However it was,
Neither refused the meeting. But the hand!
The boy's first outcry was a rueful laugh,
As he swung toward them holding up the hand   20
Half in appeal, but half as if to keep
The life from spilling. Then the boy saw all—
Since he was old enough to know, big boy
Doing a man's work, though a child at heart—
He saw all spoiled. 'Don't let him cut my hand off—   25
The doctor, when he comes. Don't let him, sister!'
So. But the hand was gone already.
The doctor put him in the dark of ether.
He lay and puffed his lips out with his breath.
And then—the watcher at his pulse took fright.   30
No one believed. They listened at his heart.
Little—less—nothing!—and that ended it.
No more to build on there. And they, since they
Were not the one dead, turned to their affairs.

1916

The Ax-Helve

I've known ere now an interfering branch
Of alder catch my lifted ax behind me.
But that was in the woods, to hold my hand
From striking at another alder's roots,
And that was, as I say, an alder branch.   5
This was a man, Baptiste,[1] who stole one day
Behind me on the snow in my own yard
Where I was working at the chopping-block,
And cutting nothing not cut down already.
He caught my ax expertly on the rise.   10
When all my strength put forth was in his favor,
Held it a moment where it was, to calm me,
Then took it from me—and I let him take it.

---

1. The man's name in French means "baptized," and the line echoes Marc Antony's praise of Brutus in Shakespeare's *Julius Caesar* (5.5.73–75): "the elements/ So mix'd in him that Nature might stand up/ And say to all the world, 'This was a man!' "

I didn't know him well enough to know
What it was all about. There might be something   15
He had in mind to say to a bad neighbor
He might prefer to say to him disarmed.
But all he had to tell me in French-English
Was what he thought of—not me, but my ax,
Me only as I took my ax to heart.   20
It was the bad ax-helve someone had sold me—
'Made on machine,' he said, plowing the grain
With a thick thumbnail to show how it ran
Across the handle's long drawn serpentine,
Like the two strokes across a dollar sign.   25
'You give her one good crack, she's snap raght off,
Den where's your hax-ead flying t'rough de hair?'
Admitted; and yet, what was that to him?

'Come on my house and I put you one in
What's las' awhile—good hick'ry what's grow crooked.   30
De second growt' I cut myself—tough, tough!'

Something to sell? That wasn't how it sounded.

'Den when you say you come? It's cost you nothing.
Tonaght?'

       As well tonight as any night.

Beyond an over-warmth of kitchen stove   35
My welcome differed from no other welcome.
Baptiste knew best why I was where I was.
So long as he would leave enough unsaid,
I shouldn't mind his being overjoyed
(If overjoyed he was) at having got me   40
Where I must judge if what he knew about an ax
That not everybody else knew was to count
For nothing in the measure of a neighbor.
Hard if, though cast away for life with Yankees,
A Frenchman couldn't get his human rating!   45

Mrs. Baptiste came in and rocked a chair
That had as many motions as the world:
One back and forward, in and out of shadow,
That got her nowhere; one more gradual,
Sideways, that would have run her on the stove   50
In time, had she not realized her danger
And caught herself up bodily, chair and all,
And set herself back where she started from.
'She ain't spick too much Henglish—dat's too bad.'

I was afraid, in brightening first on me,   55
Then on Baptiste, as if she understood
What passed between us, she was only feigning,

Baptiste was anxious for her; but no more
Than for himself, so placed he couldn't hope
To keep his bargain of the morning with me   60
In time to keep me from suspecting him
Of really never having meant to keep it.

Needlessly soon he had his ax-helves out,
A quiverful to choose from, since he wished me
To have the best he had, or had to spare—   65
Not for me to ask which, when what he took
Had beauties he had to point me out at length
To insure their not being wasted on me.
He liked to have it slender as a whipstock,
Free from the least knot, equal to the strain   70
Of bending like a sword across the knee.
He showed me that the lines of a good helve
Were native to the grain before the knife
Expressed them, and its curves were no false curves
Put on it from without. And there its strength lay   75
For the hard work. He chafed its long white body
From end to end with his rough hand shut round it.
He tried it at the eye-hole in the ax-head.
'Hahn, hahn,' he mused, 'don't need much taking down.'
Baptiste knew how to make a short job long   80
For love of it, and yet not waste time either.

Do you know, what we talked about was knowledge?
Baptiste on his defense about the children
He kept from school, or did his best to keep—
Whatever school and children and our doubts   85
Of laid-on education had to do
With the curves of his ax-helves and his having
Used these unscrupulously to bring me
To see for once the inside of his house.
Was I desired in friendship, partly as someone   90
To leave it to, whether the right to hold
Such doubts of education should depend
Upon the education of those who held them?

But now he brushed his shavings from his knee
And stood the ax there on its horse's hoof,   95
Erect, but not without its waves, as when
The snake stood up for evil in the Garden,[2]—
Top-heavy with a heaviness his short,
Thick hand made light of, steel-blue chin drawn down
And in a little—a French touch in that.   100
Baptiste drew back and squinted at it, pleased;
'See how she's cock her head!'

1916   1917, 1923

The Witch of Coös[1]

I stayed the night for shelter at a farm
Behind the mountain, with a mother and son,
Two old-believers.[2] They did all the talking.

MOTHER. Folks think a witch who has familiar spirits
She could call up to pass a winter evening,   5
But won't, should be burned at the stake or something.
Summoning spirits isn't 'Button, button,
Who's got the button,' I would have them know.

SON. Mother can make a common table rear
And kick with two legs like an army mule.[3]   10

MOTHER. And when I've done it, what good have I done?
Rather than tip a table for you, let me
Tell you what Ralle the Sioux Control[4] once told me.
He said the dead had souls, but when I asked him
How could that be—I thought the dead were souls,   15
He broke my trance. Don't that make you suspicious
That there's something the dead are keeping back?
Yes, there's something the dead are keeping back.

SON. You wouldn't want to tell him what we have
Up attic, mother?   20

MOTHER. Bones—a skeleton.

SON. But the headboard of mother's bed is pushed
Against the attic door: the door is nailed.
It's harmless. Mother hears it in the night
Halting perplexed behind the barrier   25
Of door and headboard. Where it wants to get
Is back into the cellar where it came from.

MOTHER. We'll never let them, will we, son! We'll never!

SON. It left the cellar forty years ago
And carried itself like a pile of dishes   30
Up one flight from the cellar to the kitchen,
Another from the kitchen to the bedroom,
Another from the bedroom to the attic,
Right past both father and mother, and neither stopped it.
Father had gone upstairs; mother was downstairs.   35
I was a baby: I don't know where I was.

1. A county in northern New Hampshire.
2. Believers in traditional folklore and superstitions.
3. Mediums, supposedly in contact with supernatural spirits, claim to move furniture about during seances without exerting physical force.
4. In spiritualistic theory, a control is the agent who voices the utterances of the dead. American Indians were favorite controls at the turn of the 19th century.

MOTHER. The only fault my husband found with me—
I went to sleep before I went to bed,
Especially in winter when the bed
Might just as well be ice and the clothes snow.   40
The night the bones came up the cellar-stairs
Toffile had gone to bed alone and left me,
But left an open door to cool the room off
So as to sort of turn me out of it.
I was just coming to myself enough   45
To wonder where the cold was coming from,
When I heard Toffile upstairs in the bedroom
And thought I heard him downstairs in the cellar.
The board we had laid down to walk dry-shod on
When there was water in the cellar in spring   50
Struck the hard cellar bottom. And then someone
Began the stairs, two footsteps for each step,
The way a man with one leg and a crutch,
Or a little child, comes up. It was Toffile:
It wasn't anyone who could be there.   55
The bulkhead double-doors were double-locked
And swollen tight and buried under snow.
The cellar windows were banked up with sawdust
And swollen tight and buried under snow.
It was the bones. I knew them—and good reason.   60
My first impulse was to get to the knob
And hold the door. But the bones didn't try
The door; they halted helpless on the landing,
Waiting for things to happen in their favor.
The faintest restless rustling ran all through them.   65
I never could have done the thing I did
If the wish hadn't been too strong in me
To see how they were mounted for this walk.
I had a vision of them put together
Not like a man, but like a chandelier.   70
So suddenly I flung the door wide on him.
A moment he stood balancing with emotion,
And all but lost himself. (A tongue of fire
Flashed out and licked along his upper teeth.
Smoke rolled inside the sockets of his eyes.)   75
Then he came at me with one hand outstretched,
The way he did in life once; but this time
I struck the hand off brittle on the floor,
And fell back from him on the floor myself.
The finger-pieces slid in all directions.   80
(Where did I see one of those pieces lately?
Hand me my button-box—it must be there.)
I sat up on the floor and shouted, 'Toffile,
It's coming up to you.' It had its choice
Of the door to the cellar or the hall.   85
It took the hall door for the novelty,
And set off briskly for so slow a thing,
Still going every which way in the joints, though,

So that it looked like lightning or a scribble,
From the slap I had just now given its hand. 90
I listened till it almost climbed the stairs
From the hall to the only finished bedroom,
Before I got up to do anything;
Then ran and shouted, 'Shut the bedroom door,
Toffile, for my sake!' 'Company?' he said, 95
'Don't make me get up; I'm too warm in bed.'
So lying forward weakly on the handrail
I pushed myself upstairs, and in the light
(The kitchen had been dark) I had to own
I could see nothing. 'Toffile, I don't see it. 100
It's with us in the room though. It's the bones.'
'What bones?' 'The cellar bones—out of the grave.'
That made him throw his bare legs out of bed
And sit up by me and take hold of me.
I wanted to put out the light and see 105
If I could see it, or else mow the room,
With our arms at the level of our knees,
And bring the chalk-pile down. 'I'll tell you what—
It's looking for another door to try.
The uncommonly deep snow has made him think 110
Of his old song, *The Wild Colonial Boy*,
He always used to sing along the tote[5] road.
He's after an open door to get outdoors.
Let's trap him with an open door up attic.'
Toffile agreed to that, and sure enough, 115
Almost the moment he was given an opening,
The steps began to climb the attic stairs.
I heard them. Toffile didn't seem to hear them.
'Quick!' I slammed to the door and held the knob.
'Toffile, get nails.' I made him nail the door shut 120
And push the headboard of the bed against it.
Then we asked was there anything
Up attic that we'd ever want again.
The attic was less to us than the cellar.
If the bones liked the attic, let them have it. 125
Let them stay in the attic. When they sometimes
Come down the stairs at night and stand perplexed
Behind the door and headboard of the bed,
Brushing their chalky skull with chalky fingers,
With sounds like the dry rattling of a shutter, 130
That's what I sit up in the dark to say—
To no one any more since Toffile died.
Let them stay in the attic since they went there.
I promised Toffile to be cruel to them
For helping them be cruel once to him. 135

SON. We think they had a grave down in the cellar.

MOTHER. We know they had a grave down in the cellar.

5. Colloquial for hauling or carrying.

SON. We never could find out whose bones they were.

MOTHER. Yes, we could too, son. Tell the truth for once. 140
They were a man's his father killed for me.
I mean a man he killed instead of me.
The least I could do was to help dig their grave.
We were about it one night in the cellar.
Son knows the story: but 'twas not for him 145
To tell the truth, suppose the time had come.
Son looks surprised to see me end a lie
We'd kept all these years between ourselves
So as to have it ready for outsiders.
But tonight I don't care enough to lie—
I don't remember why I ever cared. 150
Toffile, if he were here, I don't believe
Could tell you why he ever cared himself. . . .

She hadn't found the finger-bone she wanted
Among the buttons poured out in her lap.
I verified the name next morning: Toffile. 155
The rural letter box said Toffile Lajway.

1923

Nothing Gold Can Stay

Nature's first green is gold,
Her hardest hue to hold.
Her early leaf's a flower;
But only so an hour.
Then leaf subsides to leaf. 5
So Eden sank to grief,
So dawn goes down to day.
Nothing gold can stay.

1923

The Runaway

Once when the snow of the year was beginning to fall,
We stopped by a mountain pasture to say, 'Whose colt?
A little Morgan[1] had one forefoot on the wall,
The other curled at his breast. He dipped his head
And snorted at us. And then he had to bolt. 5
We heard the miniature thunder where he fled,
And we saw him, or thought we saw him, dim and gray,
Like a shadow against the curtain of falling flakes.
'I think the little fellow's afraid of the snow.
He isn't winter-broken. It isn't play 10
With the little fellow at all. He's running away.
I doubt if even his mother could tell him, "Sakes,
It's only weather." He'd think she didn't know!

---

1. Breed of horse developed from the stallion Justin Morgan in Vermont in the 19th century.

Where is his mother? He can't be out alone.'
And now he comes again with clatter of stone,   15
And mounts the wall again with whited eyes
And all his tail that isn't hair up straight.
He shudders his coat as if to throw off flies.
'Whoever it is that leaves him out so late,
When other creatures have gone to stall and bin,   20
Ought to be told to come and take him in.'

1918, 1923

Stopping by Woods on a Snowy Evening

Whose woods these are I think I know.
His house is in the village though;
He will not see me stopping here
To watch his woods fill up with snow.

My little horse must think it queer   5
To stop without a farmhouse near
Between the woods and frozen lake
The darkest evening of the year.

He gives his harness bells a shake
To ask if there is some mistake.   10
The only other sound's the sweep
Of easy wind and downy flake.

The woods are lovely, dark and deep,
But I have promises to keep,
And miles to go before I sleep,   15
And miles to go before I sleep.

1923

A Brook in the City

The farmhouse lingers, though averse to square
With the new city street it has to wear
A number in. But what about the brook
That held the house as in an elbow-crook?
I ask as one who knew the brook, its strength   5
And impulse, having dipped a finger length
And made it leap my knuckle, having tossed
A flower to try its currents where they crossed.
The meadow grass could be cemented down
From growing under pavements of a town;   10
The apple trees be sent to hearth-stone flame.
Is water wood to serve a brook the same?
How else dispose of an immortal force
No longer needed? Staunch it at its source
With cinder loads dumped down? The brook was thrown   15
Deep in a sewer dungeon under stone
In fetid darkness still to live and run—

And all for nothing it had ever done
Except forget to go in fear perhaps.
No one would know except for ancient maps   20
That such a brook ran water. But I wonder
If from its being kept forever under
The thoughts may not have risen that so keep
This new-built city from both work and sleep.

1923

Spring Pools

These pools that, though in forests, still reflect
The total sky almost without defect,
And like the flowers beside them, chill and shiver,
Will like the flowers beside them soon be gone,
And yet not out by any brook or river,   5
But up by roots to bring dark foliage on.

The trees that have it in their pent-up buds
To darken nature and be summer woods—
Let them think twice before they use their powers
To blot out and drink up and sweep away   10
These flowery waters and these watery flowers
From snow that melted only yesterday.

1928

Acceptance

When the spent sun throws up its rays on cloud
And goes down burning into the gulf below,
No voice in nature is heard to cry aloud
At what has happened. Birds, at least, must know
It is the change to darkness in the sky.   5
Murmuring something quiet in her breast,
One bird begins to close a faded eye;
Or overtaken too far from his nest,
Hurrying low above the grove, some waif
Swoops just in time to his remembered tree.   10
At most he thinks or twitters softly, 'Safe!
Now let the night be dark for all of me.
Let the night be too dark for me to see
Into the future. Let what will be, be.'

1928

Once by the Pacific

The shattered water made a misty din.
Great waves looked over others coming in,
And thought of doing something to the shore
That water never did to land before.
The clouds were low and hairy in the skies,   5
Like locks blown forward in the gleam of eyes.

You could not tell, and yet it looked as if
The shore was lucky in being backed by cliff,
The cliff in being backed by continent;
It looked as if a night of dark intent   10
Was coming, and not only a night, an age.
Someone had better be prepareed for rage.
There would be more than ocean-water broken
Before God's last *Put out the Light* was spoken.[1]

                                        1928

West-Running Brook

'Fred, where is north?'
                        'North? North is there, my love.
The brook runs west.'
                        'West-running Brook then call it.'
(West-running Brook men call it to this day.)
'What does it think it's doing running west
When all the other country brooks flow east   5
To reach the ocean? It must be the brook
Can trust itself to go by contraries
The way I can with you—and you with me—
Because we're—we're—I don't know what we are.
What are we?'
                'Young or new?'
                                'We must be something.   10
We've said we two. Let's change that to we three.
As you and I are married to each other,
We'll both be married to the brook. We'll build
Our bridge across it, and the bridge shall be
Our arm thrown over it asleep beside it.   15
Look, look, it's waving to us with a wave
To let us know it hears me.'
                            'Why, my dear,
That wave's been standing off this jut of shore—'
(The black stream, catching on a sunken rock,
Flung backward on itself in one white wave,   20
And the white water rode the black forever,
Not gaining but not losing, like a bird
White feathers from the struggle of whose breast
Flecked the dark stream and flecked the darker pool
Below the point, and were at last driven wrinkled   25
In a white scarf against the far shore alders.)
'That wave's been standing off this jut of shore
Ever since rivers, I was going to say,
Were made in heaven. It wasn't waved to us.'

'It wasn't, yet it was. If not to you   30

1. Ironic reversal of God's creation of the world in Genesis 1.3: "And God said, Let there be light."

It was to me—in an annunciation.'[1]

'Oh, if you take it off to lady-land,
As't were the country of the Amazons[2]
We men must see you to the confines of
And leave you there, ourselves forbid to enter,—   35
It is your brook! I have no more to say.'

'Yes, you have, too. Go on. You thought of something.'

'Speaking of contraries, see how the brook
In that white wave runs counter to itself.
It is from that in water we were from   40
Long, long before we were from any creature.
Here we, in our impatience of the steps,
Get back to the beginning of beginnings,
The stream of everything that runs away.
Some say existence like a Pirouot   45
And Pirouette,[3] forever in one place,
Stands still and dances, but it runs away,
It seriously, sadly, runs away
To fill the abyss' void with emptiness.
It flows beside us in this water brook,   50
But it flows over us. It flows between us
To separate us for a panic moment.
It flows between us, over us, and *with* us.
And it is time, strength, tone, light, life, and love—
And even substance lapsing unsubstantial;   55
The universal cataract of death
That spends to nothingness—and unresisted,
Save by some strange resistance in itself,
Not just a swerving,[4] but a throwing back,
As if regret were in it and were sacred.   60
It has this throwing backward on itself
So that the fall of most of it is always
Raising a little, sending up a little.
Our life runs down in sending up the clock.
The brook runs down in sending up our life.   65
The sun runs down in sending up the brook.
And there is something sending up the sun.
It is this backward motion toward the source,
Against the stream, that most we see ourselves in,
The tribute of the current to the source.   70
It is from this in nature we are from.
It is most us.'

1. Act of announcing or proclaiming, usually in reference to the angel Gabriel's revelation to the Virgin Mary that she would give birth to Jesus Christ.
2. Legendary nation of women warriors.
3. Lovers in traditional French pantomime.
4. In the philosophical poem *De Rerum* *Natura* (*On the Nature of Things*) by the Roman Titus Lucretius Carus (96?–55? B.C.), the universe is explained as an endlessly descending flow of atoms, whose unpredictable swerving from a fixed course is the source of human volition.

'Today will be the day
You said so.'
        'No, today will be the day
You said the brook was called West-running Brook.'

'Today will be the day of what we both said.'   75
                               1928

A Drumlin[1] Woodchuck

One thing has a shelving bank,
Another a rotting plank,
To give it cozier skies
And make up for its lack of size.

My own strategic retreat   5
Is where two rocks almost meet,
And still more secure and snug,
A two-door burrow I dug.

With those in mind at my back
I can sit forth exposed to attack   10
As one who shrewdly pretends
That he and the world are friends.

All we who prefer to live
Have a little whistle we give,
And flash, at the least alarm   15
We dive down under the farm.

We allow some time for guile
And don't come out for a while
Either to eat or drink.
We take occasion to think.   20

And if after the hunt goes past
And the double-barreled blast
(Like war and pestilence
And the loss of common sense),

If I can with confidence say   25
That still for another day,
Or even another year,
I will be there for you, my dear,

It will be because, though small
As measured against the All,   30
I have been so instinctively thorough
About my crevice and burrow.
                            1936

---

1. A mound or hill formed by glacial action.

Departmental

An ant on the table cloth
Ran into a dormant moth
Of many times his size.
He showed not the least surprise.
His business wasn't with such.   5
He gave it scarcely a touch,
And was off on his duty run.
Yet if he encountered one
Of the hive's enquiry squad
Whose work is to find out God   10
And the nature of time and space,
He would put him onto the case.
Ants are a curious race;
One crossing with hurried tread
The body of one of their dead   15
Isn't given a moment's arrest—
Seems not even impressed.
But he no doubt reports to any
With whom he crosses antennae,
And they no doubt report   20
To the higher up at court.
Then word goes forth in Formic:[1]
'Death's come to Jerry McCormic,
Our selfless forager Jerry.
Will the special Janizary[2]   25
Whose office it is to bury
The dead of the commissary
Go bring him home to his people.
Lay him in state on a sepal.
Wrap him for shroud in a petal.   30
Embalm him with ichor of nettle.
This is the word of your Queen.'
And presently on the scene
Appears a solemn mortician;
And taking formal position   35
With feelers calmly atwiddle,
Seizes the dead by the middle,
And heaving him high in air,
Carries him out of there.
No one stands round to stare.   40
It is nobody else's affair.

It couldn't be called ungentle.
But how thoroughly departmental.

1936

Desert Places

Snow falling and night falling fast, oh, fast
In a field I looked into going past,

---

1. Acid emitted by ants. 2. Troop of Turkish infantry soldiers.

And the ground almost covered smooth in snow,
But a few weeds and stubble showing last.

The woods around it have it—it is theirs.   5
All animals are smothered in their lairs.
I am too absent-spirited to count;
The loneliness includes me unawares.

And lonely as it is that loneliness
Will be more lonely ere it will be less—   10
A blanker whiteness of benighted snow
With no expression, nothing to express.

They cannot scare me with their empty spaces
Between stars—on stars where no human race is.
I have it in me so much nearer home   15
To scare myself with my own desert places.

                                             1936

Design

I found a dimpled spider, fat and white,
On a white heal-all,[1] holding up a moth
Like a white piece of rigid satin cloth—
Assorted characters of death and blight
Mixed ready to begin the morning right,   5
Like the ingredients of a witches' broth—
A snow-drop spider, a flower like a froth,
And dead wings carried like a paper kite.

What had that flower to do with being white,
The wayside blue and innocent heal-all?   10
What brought the kindred spider to that height,
Then steered the white moth thither in the night?
What but design of darkness to appall?—
If design govern in a thing so small.

                                       1922, 1936

On a Bird Singing in Its Sleep

A bird half wakened in the lunar noon
Sang halfway through its little inborn tune.
Partly because it sang but once all night
And that from no especial bush's height;
Partly because it sang ventriloquist   5
And had the inspiration to desist
Almost before the prick of hostile ears,
It ventured less in peril than appears.
It could not have come down to us so far

1. An albino version of the common field flower *Prunella vulgaris*, whose hooded blossom is normally violet or blue, whose leaves are either toothed or toothless, and which was once widely used as a medicine.

Through the interstices of things ajar   10
On the long bead chain of repeated birth
To be a bird while we are men on earth
If singing out of sleep and dream that way
Had made it much more easily a prey.

                                                    1936

Provide, Provide[1]

The witch that came (the withered hag)
To wash the steps with pail and rag,
Was once the beauty Abishag,[2]

The picture pride of Hollywood.
Too many fall from great and good   5
For you to doubt the likelihood.

Die early and avoid the fate.
Or if predestined to die late,
Make up your mind to die in state.

Make the whole stock exchange your own!   10
If need be occupy a throne,
Where nobody can call *you* crone.

Some have relied on what they knew;
Others on being simple true.
What worked for them might work for you.   15

No memory of having starred
Atones for later disregard,
Or keeps the end from being hard.

Better to go down dignified
With boughten friendship at your side   20
Than none of all. Provide, provide!

                                                    1934, 1936

The Figure a Poem Makes[1]

Abstraction is an old story with the philosophers, but it has been like a new toy in the hands of the artists of our day. Why can't we have any one quality of poetry we choose by itself? We can have in thought. Then it will go hard if we can't in practice. Our lives for it.

Granted no one but a humanist much cares how sound a poem is

---

1. Frost's biographer, Lawrance Thompson, asserts that this poem was provoked by a strike of charwomen that some Harvard faculty members helped organize (*Robert Frost, the Years of Triumph*, p. 437).

2. A beautiful maiden brought to comfort King David in his old age (1 Kings 1.2–4).
1. This essay was published as an introduction to *The Collected Poems of Robert Frost* (1939).

if it is only *a* sound. The sound is the gold in the ore. Then we will have the sound out alone and dispense with the inessential. We do till we make the discovery that the object in writing poetry is to make all poems sound as different as possible from each other, and the resources for that of vowels, consonants, punctuation, syntax, words, sentences, meter are not enough. We need the help of context—meaning—subject matter. That is the greatest help towards variety. All that can be done with words is soon told. So also with meters—particularly in our language where there are virtually but two, strict iambic and loose iambic. The ancients with many were still poor if they depended on meters for all tune. It is painful to watch our sprung-rhythmists[2] straining at the point of omitting one short from a foot for relief from monotony. The possibilities for tune from the dramatic tones of meaning struck across the rigidity of a limited meter are endless. And we are back in poetry as merely one more art of having something to say, sound or unsound. Probably better if sound, because deeper and from wider experience.

Then there is this wildness whereof it is spoken. Granted again that it has an equal claim with sound to being a poem's better half. If it is a wild tune, it is a poem. Our problem then is, as modern abstractionists, to have the wildness pure; to be wild with nothing to be wild about. We bring up as aberrationists, giving way to undirected associations and kicking ourselves from one chance suggestion to another in all directions as of a hot afternoon in the life of a grasshopper. Theme alone can steady us down. Just as the first mystery was how a poem could have a tune in such a straightness as meter, so the second mystery is how a poem can have wildness and at the same time a subject that shall be fulfilled.

It should be of the pleasure of a poem itself to tell how it can. The figure a poem makes. It begins in delight and ends in wisdom. The figure is the same as for love. No one can really hold that the ecstasy should be static and stand still in one place. It begins in delight, it inclines to the impulse, it assumes direction with the first line laid down, it runs a course of lucky events, and ends in a clarification of life—not necessarily a great clarification, such as sects and cults are founded on, but in a momentary stay against confusion. It has denouement. It has an outcome that though unforeseen was predestined from the first image of the original mood—and indeed from the very mood. It is but a trick poem and no poem at all if the best of it was thought of first and saved for the last. It finds its own name as it goes and discovers the best waiting for it in some final phrase at once wise and sad—the happy-sad blend of the drinking song.

---

2. "Sprung rhythm" was a term invented by the English poet Gerard Manley Hopkins (1844–89) for his meters, which depended not on uniform units of syllables and accents, as in traditional verse, but on less regular and more intense compressions, derived from natural speech and from patterns of rhetorical effect.

No tears in the writer, no tears in the reader. No surprise for the writer, no surprise for the reader. For me the initial delight is in the surprise of remembering something I didn't know I knew. I am in a place, in a situation, as if I had materialized from cloud or risen out of the ground. There is a glad recognition of the long lost and the rest follows. Step by step the wonder of unexpected supply keeps growing. The impressions most useful to my purpose seem always those I was unaware of and so made no note of at the time when taken, and the conclusion is come to that like giants we are always hurling experience ahead of us to pave the future with against the day when we may want to strike a line of purpose across it for somewhere. The line will have the more charm for not being mechanically straight. We enjoy the straight crookedness of a good walking stick. Modern instruments of precision are being used to make things crooked as if by eye and hand in the old days.

I tell how there may be a better wildness of logic than of inconsequence. But the logic is backward, in retrospect, after the act. It must be more felt than seen ahead like prophecy. It must be a revelation, or a series of revelations, as much for the poet as for the reader. For it to be that there must have been the greatest freedom of the material to move about in it and to establish relations in it regardless of time and space, previous relation, and everything but affinity. We prate of freedom. We call our schools free because we are not free to stay away from them till we are sixteen years of age. I have given up my democratic prejudices and now willingly set the lower classes free to be completely taken care of by the upper classes. Political freedom is nothing to me. I bestow it right and left. All I would keep for myself is the freedom of my material—the condition of body and mind now and then to summon aptly from the vast chaos of all I have lived through.

Scholars and artists thrown together are often annoyed at the puzzle of where they differ. Both work from knowledge; but I suspect they differ most importantly in the way their knowledge is come by. Scholars get theirs with conscientious thoroughness along projected lines of logic; poets theirs cavalierly and as it happens in and out of books. They stick to nothing deliberately, but let what will stick to them like burrs where they walk in the fields. No acquirement is on assignment, or even self-assignment. Knowledge of the second kind is much more available in the wild free ways of wit and art. A schoolboy may be defined as one who can tell you what he knows in the order in which he learned it. The artist must value himself as he snatches a thing from some previous order in time and space into a new order with not so much as a ligature clinging to it of the old place where it was organic.

More than once I should have lost my soul to radicalism if it had been the originality it was mistaken for by its young converts.

Originality and initiative are what I ask for my country. For myself
the originality need be no more than the freshness of a poem run in
the way I have described: from delight to wisdom. The figure is the
same as for love. Like a piece of ice on a hot stove the poem must
ride on its own melting. A poem may be worked over once it is in
being, but may not be worried into being. Its most precious quality
will remain its having run itself and carried away the poet with it.
Read it a hundred times: it will forever keep its freshness as a metal
keeps its fragrance. It can never lose its sense of a meaning that
once unfolded by surprise as it went.

1939

The Silken Tent

> She is as in a field a silken tent
> At midday when a sunny summer breeze
> Has dried the dew and all its ropes relent,
> So that in guys[1] it gently sways at ease,
> And its supporting central cedar pole,⁣   5
> That is its pinnacle to heavenward
> And signifies the sureness of the soul,
> Seems to owe naught to any single cord,
> But strictly held by none, is loosely bound
> By countless silken ties of love and thought   10
> To everything on earth the compass round,
> And only by one's going slightly taut
> In the capriciousness of summer air
> Is of the slightest bondage made aware.

1942

The Most of It

> He thought he kept the universe alone;
> For all the voice in answer he could wake
> Was but the mocking echo of his own
> From some tree-hidden cliff across the lake.
> Some morning from the boulder-broken beach   5
> He would cry out on life, that what it wants
> Is not its own love back in copy speech,
> But counter-love, original response.
> And nothing ever came of what he cried
> Unless it was the embodiment that crashed   10
> In the cliff's talus[2] on the other side,
> And then in the far distant water splashed,
> But after a time allowed for it to swim,
> Instead of proving human when it neared
> And someone else additional to him,   15
> As a great buck it powerfully appeared,

---

1. Ropes holding an upright pole in position.

2. Sloping bank of rock fragments at the foot of a cliff.

Pushing the crumpled water up ahead,
And landed pouring like a waterfall,
And stumbled through the rocks with horny tread,
And forced the underbrush—and that was all.   20

                                                    1942

The Gift Outright[1]

The land was ours before we were the land's.
She was our land more than a hundred years
Before we were her people. She was ours
In Massachusetts, In Virginia,
But we were England's, still colonials,   5
Possessing what we still were unpossessed by,
Possessed by what we now no more possessed.
Something we were withholding made us weak
Until we found out that it was ourselves
We were withholding from our land of living,   10
And forthwith found salvation in surrender.
Such as we were we gave ourselves outright
(The deed of gift was many deeds of war)
To the land vaguely realizing westward,
But still unstoried, artless, unenhanced,   15
Such as she was, such as she would become.

                                                    1942

---

1. The poem recited by Frost at the inauguration of President John F. Kennedy in January, 1963.

CARL SANDBURG
1878–1967

In the three decades following the World's Fair of 1893, the city of Chicago became the center of a midwestern "renaissance" in the arts, a "vortex" (Ezra Pound's term) involving talents as diverse as the architect Frank Lloyd Wright, the novelists Theodore Dreiser, Henry Blake Fuller, and Robert Herrick, the radical journalist and novelist Floyd Dell, and the poet Edgar Lee Masters. Two new literary journals—*Poetry*, founded in 1912 by the poet Harriet Monroe, and *The Little Review*, founded by Margaret C. Anderson in 1914—soon had an international audience and made Chicago a center for the introduction of new writing on both sides of the Atlantic. One of the important poets discovered by *Poetry* magazine was Carl Sandburg, who became one of the most popularly read poets during the 1920s and 1930s.

Sandburg was the son of Swedish immigrants who settled in Galesburg, Illinois; his father was a machinist's blacksmith. Sandburg had irregular schooling and worked as an itinerant laborer and jack-of-all-trades in the Midwest before enlisting in the army during the Spanish-American War and serving as correspondent for the Galesburg *Evening Mail*. After the war he attended Lombard College, working for the fire department to support himself, but withdrew without a degree in 1902. He worked as advertising writer, roving reporter, and organizer for the Social Democratic party in Wisconsin, and he married the sister of famed photographer Edward Steichen in 1908. He served as secretary to the Socialist mayor of Milwaukee (1910–12) and wrote editorials for the Milwaukee *Leader* before moving to Chicago in 1913. He had published a pamphlet of poems privately in Galesburg in 1904, and *Poetry* magazine published his poem *Chicago* in 1914.

The poems that made Sandburg famous appeared in four volumes: *Chicago Poems* (1914), *Cornhuskers* (1918), *Smoke and Steel* (1920), and *Slabs of the Sunburnt West* (1922). With the precedent of Whitman behind them, they present a sweeping panorama of American life, encompassing prairie, eastern, and western landscapes as well as vignettes of the modern city. They celebrate, from the standpoint of a Populist radical, the lives of outcasts, the contributions of immigrants and common people to urban culture, and the occupations of those who have survived or been sacrificed in the rise of industrial civilization. Sandburg's language draws on the colorful diction of immigrants and the lingo of urban dwellers, but unvarnished directness of statement takes precedence over subtleties of imagery or rhythm in his verse, even in such poems as *Cool Tombs*, where the consistency of tone is impressive, or in *Flash Crimson*, where the techniques of symbolism are used. Sandburg avoided regular stanza patterns and traditional blank verse and wrote an utterly free verse, developing Whitman's long line but moderating its rhetorical impact and intensity, and composing what are often in effect prose paragraphs. As one who undertook as a spokesman for the common people to inscribe "public speech," he was proud late in his career to "favor simple poems for simple people."[1]

His most ambitious attempt to accomplish that aim was *The People, Yes* (1936), consisting of prose vignettes, anecdotes, and verse, which drew on his studies of American folksongs that preoccupied his attention after the publication of *The American Songbag* in 1927. Indeed, from 1918 on, other professional activities took precedence over his verse. He was a columnist, editorial writer, and feature writer on the *Chicago Daily News* from 1918 to 1933, and he published an account of *The Chicago Race Riots* in 1919. He published *The Rootabaga Stories* (for children) and two sequels between 1922 and 1930, and his biographies include *Steichen the Photographer* (1929) and *Mary Lincoln* (1932). His major work in prose was a monumental and celebratory biography of Abraham Lincoln, beginning with the two-volume *Prairie Years* in 1926 and culminating in *The War Years* (1939), a four-volume work which won the Pulitzer Prize in 1940.

Chicago

Hog Butcher for the World,
Tool Maker, Stacker of Wheat,
Player with Railroads and the Nation's Freight Handler;
Stormy, husky, brawling,
City of the Big Shoulders: 5

---

1. Introduction, *Complete Poems*, p. xxix.

They tell me you are wicked and I believe them, for I have seen
 your painted women under the gas lamps luring the farm boys.
And they tell me you are crooked and I answer: Yes, it is true I
 have seen the gunman kill and go free to kill again.
And they tell me you are brutal and my reply is: On the faces of
 women and children I have seen the marks of wanton hunger.
And having answered so I turn once more to those who sneer at this
 my city, and I give them back the sneer and say to them:
Come and show me another city with lifted head singing so proud
 to be alive and coarse and strong and cunning.   10
Flinging magnetic curses amid the toil of piling job on job, here is a
 tall bold slugger set vivid against the little soft cities;
Fierce as a dog with tongue lapping for action, cunning as a savage
 pitted against the wilderness,
  Bareheaded,
  Shoveling,
  Wrecking,   15
  Planning,
  Building, breaking, rebuilding,
Under the smoke, dust all over his mouth, laughing with white
 teeth,
Under the terrible burden of destiny laughing as a young man
 laughs,
Laughing even as an ignorant fighter laughs who has never lost a
 battle,   20
Bragging and laughing that under his wrist is the pulse, and under
 his ribs the heart of the people,
  Laughing!
Laughing the stormy, husky, brawling laughter of Youth, half-
 naked, sweating, proud to be Hog Butcher, Tool Maker, Stacker
 of Wheat, Player with railroads and Freight Handler to the
 Nation.

             1914, 1916

Halsted Street Car

  Come you, cartoonists,
  Hang on a strap with me here
  At seven o'clock in the morning
  On a Halsted street car.

    Take your pencils   5
    And draw these faces.

  Try with your pencils for these crooked faces,
  That pig-sticker[1] in one corner—his mouth—
  That overall factory girl—her loose cheeks.

    Find for your pencils   10
    A way to mark your memory
    Of tired empty faces.

1. Worker who cuts the throats of pigs in a slaughterhouse.

After their night's sleep,
In the moist dawn

And cool daybreak,   15
Faces
Tired of wishes,
Empty of dreams.

                                                    1916

Child of the Romans

The dago[1] shovelman sits by the railroad track
Eating a noon meal of bread and bologna.
   A train whirls by, and men and women at tables
   Alive with red roses and yellow jonquils,
   Eat steaks running with brown gravy,   5
   Strawberries and cream, eclairs and coffee.
The dago shovelman finishes the dry bread and bologna,
Washes it down with a dipper from the water-boy,
And goes back to the second half of a ten-hour day's work
Keeping the road-bed so the roses and jonquils   10
Shake hardly at all in the cut glass vases
Standing slender on the tables in the dining cars.

                                                    1916

Fog

The fog comes
on little cat feet.

It sits looking
over harbor and city
on silent haunches   5
and then moves on.

                                                    1916

Languages

There are no handles upon a language
Whereby men take hold of it
And mark it with signs for its remembrance.
It is a river, this language,
Once in a thousand years   5
Breaking a new course
Changing its way to the ocean.
It is mountain effluvia
Moving to valleys
And from nation to nation   10
Crossing borders and mixing.
Languages die like rivers.

1. An Italian (slang).

Words wrapped round your tongue today
And broken to shape of thought
Between your teeth and lips speaking   15
Now and today
Shall be faded hieroglyphics
Ten thousand years from now.
Sing—and singing—remember
Your song dies and changes   20
And is not here tomorrow
Any more than the wind
Blowing ten thousand years ago.

1916

Prairie Waters by Night

Chatter of birds two by two raises a night song joining a litany of
running water—sheer waters showing the russet of old stones
remembering many rains.

And the long willows drowse on the shoulders of the running water,
and sleep from much music; joined songs of day-end, feathery
throats and stony waters, in a choir chanting new psalms.

It is too much for the long willows when low laughter of a red
moon comes down; and the willows drowse and sleep on the
shoulders of the running water.

1918

Cool Tombs

When Abraham Lincoln was shoveled into the tombs, he forgot the
copperheads and the assassin . . . in the dust, in the cool
tombs.[1]

And Ulysses Grant lost all thought of con men and Wall Street,
cash and collateral turned ashes . . . in the dust, in the cool
tombs.[2]

Pocahontas' body, lovely as a poplar, sweet as a red haw in November or a pawpaw in May, did she wonder? does she remember?
. . . in the dust, in the cool tombs?[3]

Take any streetful of people buying clothes and groceries, cheering
a hero or throwing confetti and blowing tin horns . . . tell me
if the lovers are losers . . . tell me if any get more than the
lovers . . . in the dust . . . in the cool tombs.

1918

1. President Abraham Lincoln (1809–65)
was opposed by southern sympathizers in
the North, called Copperheads, and assassinated by John Wilkes Booth.
2. The second administration of President Ulysses S. Grant (1822–85) was
riddled with bribery and political corruption. After leaving office Grant was exploited in business and underwent bankruptcy.
3. Pocahontas (1595?–1617), daughter of
the Indian chief Powhatan, intervened to
save the life of Captain John Smith. The
red haw is a type of American hawthorn
tree; "pawpaw" is colloquial for the
fruit of the papaya tree.

Old Osawatomie[1]

John Brown's body under the morning stars.
Six feet of dust under the morning stars.
And a panorama[2] of war performs itself
Over the six-foot stage of circling armies.
Room for Gettysburg, Wilderness, Chickamauga,[3]   5
On a six-foot stage of dust.

                                        1918

Grass[4]

Pile the bodies high at Austerlitz and Waterloo.
Shovel them under and let me work—
                I am the grass; I cover all.

And pile them high at Gettysburg
And pile them high at Ypres and Verdun.   5
Shovel them under and let me work.
Two years, ten years, and passengers ask the conductor:
                What place is this?
                Where are we now?

                I am the grass.   10
                Let me work.

                                        1918

Pennsylvania

I have been in Pennsylvania,
In the Monongahela and the Hocking Valleys.[1]

In the blue Susquehanna
On a Saturday morning
I saw the mounted constabulary go by,   5
I saw boys playing marbles.
Spring and the hills laughed.

And in places
Along the Appalachian chain,
I saw steel arms handling coal and iron,   10
And I saw the white-cauliflower faces
Of miners' wives waiting for the men to come home
                from the day's work.

---

1. Settlement on the Osawatomie River in Kansas from which John Brown (1800–59) and his sons led a murderous assault on a proslavery settlement nearby in 1856.
2. A large painting displayed by unrolling it before the audience, popular in the 19th century.
3. Civil War battles.
4. The proper names in this poem are all famous battlefields in, respectively, the Napoleonic wars, the American Civil War, and World War I.
1. The Monongahela River joins the Ohio River at Pittsburgh, Pennsylvania, and the Hocking River in Ohio joins the Ohio River below Parkersburg, West Virginia; the Susquehanna River flows from New York to Maryland through east central Pennsylvania.

I made color studies in crimson and violet
Over the dust and domes of culm² at sunset.

1920

Manual System

Mary has a thingamajig clamped on her ears
And sits all day taking plugs out and sticking plugs in.
Flashes and flashes—voices and voices
            calling for ears to pour words in
Faces at the ends of wires asking for other faces   5
            at the ends of other wires:
All day taking plugs out and sticking plugs in,
Mary has a thingamajig clamped on her ears.

1920

Flash Crimson

I shall cry God to give me a broken foot.

I shall ask for a scar and a slashed nose.

I shall take the last and the worst.

I shall be eaten by gray creepers in a bunkhouse where no runners
    of the sun come and no dogs live.

And yet—of all "and yets" this is the bronze strongest—   5

I shall keep one thing better than all else; there is the blue steel of
    a great star of early evening in it; it lives longer than a broken
    foot or any scar.

The broken foot goes to a hole dug with a shovel or the bone of a
    nose may whiten on a hilltop—and yet—"and yet"—

There is one crimson pinch of ashes left after all; and none of the
    shifting winds that whip the grass and none of the pounding
    rains that beat the dust, know how to touch or find the flash of
    this crimson.

I cry God to give me a broken foot, a scar, or a lousy death.

I who have seen the flash of this crimson, I ask God for the last and
    worst.   10

1920

From The People, Yes

21

Who knows the people, the migratory harvest hands and berry pickers, the loan shark victims, the installment house wolves,

---

2. Piles of waste, the residue of mining operations.

The jugglers in sand and wood who smooth their hands along the
    mold that casts the frame of your motorcar engine,
The metal polishers, solderers, and paint-spray hands who put the
    final finish on the car,
The riveters and bolt-catchers, the cowboys of the air in the big
    city, the cowhands of the Great Plains, the ex-convicts, the
    bellhops, redcaps, lavatory men—
The union organizer with his list of those ready to join and those
    hesitating, the secret paid informers who report every move
    toward organizing,   5
The house-to-house canvassers, the doorbell ringers, the good-morn-
    ing-have-you-heard boys, the strike pickets, the strikebreakers,
    the hired sluggers, the ambulance crew, the ambulance chasers,
    the picture chasers, the meter readers, the oysterboat crews, the
    harborlight tenders—
        who knows the people?
Who knows this from pit to peak? The people, yes.

22

The people is a lighted believer and
    hoper—and this is to be held against
    them?
The panderers and cheaters are to have
    their way in trading on these lights   5
    of the people?
Not always, no, not always, for the people
    is a knower too.
With Johannson steel blocks[1] the people
    can measure itself as a knower   10
Knowing what it knows today with a deeper
    knowing than ever
Knowing in millionths and billionths of
    an inch
Knowing in the mystery of one automatic   15
    machine expertly shaping for your eyes
    another automatic machine
Knowing in traction, power-shafts, transmis-
    sion, twist drills, grinding, gears—
Knowing in the night air mail, the news-   20
    reel flicker, the broadcasts from Tokyo,
    Shanghai, Bombay and Somaliland—
The people a knower whose knowing
    grows by what it feeds on
The people wanting to know more, wanting.   25
The birds of the air and the fish of the sea
    leave off where man begins.

56

The sacred legion of the justborn—

1. A set of sliding steel blocks that ad-
here so closely together that they can be
used as an unusually accurate measuring device; invented by the Swedish engineer C. E. Johannsson.

how many thousands born this minute?
how many fallen for soon burial?
what are these deaths and replacements?
what is this endless shuttling of shadowlands   5
where the spent and done go marching into one
and from another arrive those crying Mama Mama?

In the people is the eternal child,
the wandering gypsy, the pioneer homeseeker,
the singer of home sweet home.   10

The people say and unsay,
put up and tear down
and put together again—
a builder, wrecker, and builder again—
this is the people.   15

* * *

96

Big oil tanks squat next to the railroad.
The shanties of the poor wear cinder coats.
The red and blue lights signal.
The control board tells the story.
Lights go on and off on a map.   5
Each light is a train gone by
Or a train soon heaving in.
    The big chutes grow cold.
    They stack up shadows.
    Their humps hold iron ore.   10
    This gang works hard.
    Some faces light up to hear:
    "We work today—
    what do you know about that?"

1936

WALLACE STEVENS
1879–1955

Wallace Stevens stood somewhat apart from the literary controversies that
engrossed Ezra Pound, T. S. Eliot, and William Carlos Williams. A lawyer
and insurance executive, he pursued a business career along with that of
poet until shortly before his death in 1955. By the end of World War II
he had produced a body of verse that distinguished him as one of the six or
seven major poets writing in English in the twentieth century. He gave
renewed strength to the Whitman tradition in American poetry by extending both the sensuous appeal of poetry and its capacity for abstract statement, celebrating the reality of the physical world and the poet's power to

shape that reality with his imagination, and affirming that "After the final no there comes a yes / And on that yes the future world depends."

Stevens was raised in Reading, Pennsylvania, the descendant of Pennsylvania farmers to whom he attributed his occasional grumpiness, stubbornness, and taciturnity. His father, a schoolteacher, attorney, and occasional poet, provided an impetus for both of Stevens's careers when his son graduated from public high school and left for Harvard in 1897. He instructed Stevens that the world offers success only to those who put "work and study" above "dreams," but also urged him to perfect his "power of painting pictures in words" and to "paint truth but not always in drab clothes."[1] Stevens later was to enjoy the sharp division between the practical and the imaginative activities, and made of it, along with the interraction between them, a structuring principle of his life. "After writing a poem," Stevens wrote in a comment on *To the One of Fictive Music*, it is "a good thing to walk around the block; after too much midnight, it is pleasant to hear the milkman, and yet, and this is the point of the poem, the imaginative world is the only real world after all."[2] Most of Stevens's associates at the Hartford insurance company where he worked were ignorant of his writing career, and for many years even his wife had little idea of his eminence as a poet.

During the three years he attended Harvard as a special student, Stevens published stories and verse in the *Harvard Advocate*, of which he became president, and in the *Harvard Monthly*. His verse then showed the influence of the English poets Keats, Tennyson, and Meredith, but he came to know personally the philosopher and poet George Santayana (for whom he wrote a moving elegy in 1952). Santayana's *Interpretations of Poetry and Religion* (1900), and later *Skepticism and Animal Faith* (1923), helped shape Stevens's belief that poetry, in a skeptical age, fulfills religion's office.

Stevens left Harvard in 1900 to pursue a literary career, but, having determined never to "make a petty struggle for existence—physical or literary"[3] he sought a well-paying job in journalism. He was a reporter on the New York *Tribune* but did not succeed, and he then followed his father's advice to enter the New York Law School. He was admitted to the bar in 1904, and after several unsuccessful years practicing law he joined the New York office of a bonding company in 1908. He married Elsie Moll in 1909. After a few years in New York City Stevens joined The Hartford Accident and Insurance Company and in 1916 moved with his wife to Hartford, Connecticut.

They made Hartford their lifetime home, and Stevens established the routines that enabled him to pursue two separate careers. He wrote his poems at night, on weekends, and during the summers, which his wife spent mostly in the country, where the air was better for her delicate health. Stevens traveled often on business, in the United States and Canada, but he never visited Europe. He enjoyed frequent vacations in Florida and business trips through the South; the contrast between its warm, lush climate and the austerity of chill New England became important in much of his poetry. His poems began to appear in the little magazines in 1914, notably in Harriet Monroe's *Poetry* and Alfred Kreymborg's *Others*, and his verse was published regularly until 1923. He also wrote

1. *Letters*, p. 14.   3. *Ibid.*, p. 34.
2. *Ibid.*, pp. 251–52.

three experimental one-act plays in 1915–17. During these years he joined occasionally in the activities of a circle of poets and artists in New York City, but he remained a peripheral figure at their gatherings. He became the friend of Monroe and Kreymborg, and a close professional friend of Williams and the poet Marianne Moore, with both of whom he kept up a friendly correspondence throughout his life. Yet the combination of his reticence and his business activities kept him removed from literary circles.

After the publication of his first volume of verse, *Harmonium*, in 1923, and the birth of his daughter Holly in 1924, Stevens's engrossment in family and business affairs kept him from writing for virtually six years. By the middle 1930s his economic situation was comfortable and secure (he became vice-president of his Hartford company in 1934), and his creative energies had revived early in the decade, prompted in part by widening recognition of *Harmonium*, which was reprinted in an expanded version in 1931. New volumes and major works appeared in swift succession: *Ideas of Order* in 1935, *Owl's Clover* in 1936, *The Man with the Blue Guitar* in 1937, *Parts of a World* in 1942, *Transport to Summer* in 1947, and *Auroras of Autumn* in 1950. On rare occasions he consented to give readings of his poems, and he wrote a few appreciations of his friends' poetry and lectured at Princeton, Mount Holyoke, Harvard, Yale, Columbia, and the English Institute in the Forties. A selection of these essays, *The Necessary Angel* (1951), pursued many tangents in exploring the central problem that had engaged Emerson and Whitman earlier: the role of the imagination in relation to reality, or the reality of poetry in relation to the reality outside it. In the "relentless contact" of their interaction, he believed, the imagination "enables us to perceive the normal in the abnormal, the opposite of chaos in chaos" and thus help persons to survive the conditions of modern life. The poet's role, though he speaks only to an elite, is "to help people to live their lives," Stevens declared. The poet can do this because he "gives to life the supreme fictions without which we are unable to conceive it" and creates "a world of poetry indistinguishable from the world in which we live, or, I ought to say, no doubt, from the world in which we shall come to live."[4]

Stevens's interest in the theory of poetry, though more pronounced in his essays and his later poetry, was never absent from his earlier productions. But what struck readers of the early poems was their sensuous surface and the poet's bravura effects, the flair, and at times the self-mockery of a virtuoso performance. Some, displaying the qualities of "water-colors, little statues,"[5] which he admired in the French symbolist Paul Verlaine or the American David Evans, were unusually refined in their nuances of tone; they led some readers to think him an aesthete without serious concern for the real world. Other poems flaunted dazzling, bold colors, elaborate apostrophes to readers or subjects, comic and at times self-deprecating mockery, or rhetorical acrobatics that led some critics to think him a posturing dandy. Yet the sensuous appeal of his verse displayed the "essential gaudiness" he thought important in all good poetry,[6] and his pose of dandy was a consciously assumed posture in his verse, adopted like Whitman's dandyism as a means of gaining freedom from solemn conventions of the past, so as to liberate the imagination. The comic antics of the speakers in many

4. *The Necessary Angel*, pp. 153, 30–31.　　6. *Ibid.*, p. 263.
5. *Letters*, p. 110.

poems were informed by the French philosopher Henri Bergson's theories of the comic, while the delight in self-dramatization and sheer performance sprang from energies that Stevens thought basic to imaginative activity; in one of his aphorisms he declared that "Authors are actors, books are theatres." His celebration of the senses and the physical world was part of a deliberate attempt to acknowledge the passing of traditional religious beliefs and, like Whitman, to confront a world in which irrationality, process, and change were the inescapable reality. One early masterpiece, *Peter Quince at the Clavier,* celebrates the beauty of the flesh that survives in memory only because it lives and dies in transitory moments. The long mock-epic *The Comedian as the Letter C* presents a comic version of the poet in the protagonist Crispin, who indulges in extravagant flights of the imagination while also undertaking a quasi-allegorical voyage across the Atlantic, to settle colonies in America; his grandiose dreams crumble in the face of the blunt practicalities he faces in the New World, but he finds in the prosaic conditions of everyday life, and in his domestic life with his four daughters, the potential for life and future fulfillments of the imagination.

To relish "gaiety of language," to arouse delight in "flawed words and stubborn sounds" for people living in the "imperfect" world which can be our only "paradise," was one of the chief aims of Stevens's early verse that remained a principle of his poetics throughout his career. Another aim, however, was to perfect an idiom for rendering astringently, without falsifying, the bareness of the social and natural environments he knew, or the sensations of futility and "nothingness." For either of these purposes he found formal technique, or intricate stanza patterns of the traditional kind that interested Ezra Pound, of little importance; "freedom regardless of form,"[7] he declared, was necessary for the poet. He wrote in blank verse, or devised simple stanzas, often of two unrhymed lines or three, and developed analogies with the arts of painting and music to achieve the effects of sensuous appeal and stark precision that he sought. His poems abound in allusions to singers, instrumental performers, and their musical instruments. Effects of color and precision of line comparable to those of the French painter Henri Matisse, or manipulations of perspective and abstract analytic precision comparable to those of Cubist painters, characterize many of his productions.

In his poems after 1931 Stevens incorporated, more often and directly than before, his theories of poetry and his conception of the heroic role for the poetic imagination. Some critics and poets thought that Stevens's later poetry suffered for becoming more abstractly theoretical and for focusing so intently on poetic theory. Others welcomed what they found to be deeper philosophical significance and Stevens's more direct concern with the aesthetic and moral issues—the relation of art to social realities and the relations of the self to the outer world—which have engrossed poets in the Romantic tradition since Wordsworth, Emerson, and Whitman. In any case he brought a serious and subtle imagination into play to define the "supreme fictions" that can become the ground for belief and commitment in the modern world, and he sustained a high level of achievement that was recognized in the award of the Bollingen Prize in 1950 and both the National Book Award and the Pulitzer prizes in the year of his death. In *The Man with the Blue Guitar* the creative imagination takes the form of

7. Quoted by Samuel F. Morse, *Wallace Stevens* (1970), p. 114.

a musician, drawn from a painting of Pablo Picasso. His improvisations define a poetics which is constantly changing and an art which alters reality outside it, for "Things as they are / Are changed upon the blue guitar." Yet those changes are part of the transformations occurring in reality itself. In *Notes toward a Supreme Fiction* he plays suggestively with the principal ideas around which his speculation about poetry is organized: that "It Must Be Abstract," "It Must Change," and "It Must Give Pleasure." He concludes with a tender tribute to a woman who, in his loving perception of her, becomes the "more than natural figure," the "irrational" or "more than rational distortion," "The Fiction that results from feeling." Even when searching through the "trash" of modernity in *Man on the Dump*, he discovers in the cacophony of grackles the vocation of the poet-priest and the materials for poetic stanzas. In *No Possum, No Sop, No Taters* he could face the "single emptiness of the bad" but find there "The last purity of the knowledge of good." As for Whitman, the prospect of death in Stevens's last poems could not obscure the "scrawny cry" which presaged the dawn of new life.

Sunday Morning[1]

I

Complacencies of the peignoir,[2] and late
Coffee and oranges in a sunny chair,
And the green freedom of a cockatoo
Upon a rug mingle to dissipate
The holy hush of ancient sacrifice.   5
She dreams a little, and she feels the dark
Encroachment of that old catastrophe,
As a calm darkens among water-lights.
The pungent oranges and bright, green wings
Seem things in some procession of the dead,   10
Winding across wide water, without sound.
The day is like wide water, without sound,

1. This, the poem that first brought Stevens to the attention of critics and other poets, is a religious meditation on death, on the conflicting but comparable claims of Christian and pagan rituals, and on the conflicting affirmations of supernatural values. The title suggests a pun on "Sunday": the day named for nature's "sun," and the day consecrated to the Christian "son" of God. Stevens declared in 1928 that it was "an expression of paganism, although, of course, I did not think I was expressing paganism when I wrote it" and that it is not simply a "woman's" but "anybody's meditation on religion and the meaning of life" (*Letters*, p. 250). Yet the poem, in its themes, setting, and structure, draws on Stevens's experience of the death in 1912 of his mother, a devout Christian. Stevens wrote his wife that his preoccupation with his mother's death would be "dissipated" by more pleasant surroundings and urged her to take pleasure in "sweet breaths, sweet fruits, sweet everything, make the most of it." His journal records his mother's last days in her bedroom, surrounded by the familiar rugs and furnishings she had arranged, enjoying "grape juice, orange juice, lemon and sugar," trying to collect her thoughts, resisting death but reiterating her faith in immortality; her faith could be considered just, Stevens declared, "if there be a God" (*Letters*, pp. 172–74). The poem counterpoints the dying woman's thoughts and the Christian claims voiced through her, and the responses of the poet's voice to her beliefs and the crisis of her death. It was first published in *Poetry* magazine in 1915; the editor Harriet Monroe printed only five of its eight stanzas, but arranged them in the order Stevens suggested when consenting to the deletions (I, VIII, IV, V, and VII); he restored the deletions and the original sequence in subsequent printings.
2. Loose dressing gown.

Stilled for the passing of her dreaming feet
Over the seas, to silent Palestine,
Dominion of the blood and sepulchre.[3]   15

II

Why should she give her bounty to the dead?
What is divinity if it can come
Only in silent shadows and in dreams?
Shall she not find in comforts of the sun,
In pungent fruit and bright, green wings, or else   20
In any balm or beauty of the earth,
Things to be cherished like the thought of heaven?
Divinity must live within herself:
Passions of rain, or moods in falling snow;
Grievings in loneliness, or unsubdued   25
Elations when the forest blooms; gusty
Emotions on wet roads on autumn nights;
All pleasures and all pains, remembering
The bough of summer and the winter branch.
These are the measures destined for her soul.   30

III

Jove[4] in the clouds had his inhuman birth.
No mother suckled him, no sweet land gave
Large-mannered motions to his mythy mind.
He moved among us, as a muttering king,
Magnificent, would move among his hinds,   35
Until our blood, commingling, virginal,
With heaven, brought such requital to desire
The very hinds[5] discerned it, in a star.
Shall our blood fail? Or shall it come to be
The blood of paradise? And shall the earth   40
Seem all of paradise that we shall know?
The sky will be much friendlier then than now,
A part of labor and a part of pain,
And next in glory to enduring love,
Not this dividing and indifferent blue.   45

IV

She says, "I am content when wakened birds,
Before they fly, test the reality
Of misty fields, by their sweet questionings;
But when the birds are gone, and their warm fields
Return no more, where, then, is paradise?"   50
There is not any haunt of prophecy,
Nor any old chimera[6] of the grave,
Neither the golden underground, nor isle
Melodious, where spirits gat them home,
Nor visionary south, nor cloudy palm   55
Remote on heaven's hill, that has endured

---

3. Palestine contains many sacred tombs
and was the scene of many blood sacrifices, including those of Jesus.
4. Roman name of Zeus, supreme god in
Greek and Roman mythology.
5. Farm servants. Possibly an allusion to
the shepherds who saw the star of Bethlehem that signaled the birth of Jesus.
6. Monster with lion's head, here an
image of fanciful beliefs in other worlds
and idealized realms.

As April's green endures; or will endure
Like her remembrance of awakened birds,
Or her desire for June and evening, tipped
By the consummation of the swallow's wings.   60

                              V
She says, "But in contentment I still feel
The need of some imperishable bliss."
Death is the mother of beauty;[7] hence from her,
Alone, shall come fulfilment to our dreams
And our desires. Although she strews the leaves   65
Of sure obliteration on our paths,
The path sick sorrow took, the many paths
Where triumph rang its brassy phrase, or love
Whispered a little out of tenderness,
She makes the willow shiver in the sun   70
For maidens who were wont to sit and gaze
Upon the grass, relinquished to their feet.
She causes boys to pile new plums and pears
On disregarded plate. The maidens taste
And stray impassioned in the littering leaves.[8]   75

                              VI
Is there no change of death in paradise?
Does ripe fruit never fall? Or do the boughs
Hang always heavy in that perfect sky,
Unchanging, yet so like our perishing earth,
With rivers like our own that seek for seas   80
They never find, the same receding shores
That never touch with inarticulate pang?
Why set the pear upon those river-banks
Or spice the shores with odors of the plum?
Alas, that they should wear our colors there,   85
The silken weavings of our afternoons,
And pick the strings of our insipid lutes!
Death is the mother of beauty, mystical,
Within whose burning bosom we devise
Our earthly mothers waiting, sleeplessly.   90

                              VII
Supple and turbulent, a ring of men
Shall chant in orgy on a summer morn
Their boisterous devotion to the sun,
Not as a god, but as a god might be,
Naked among them, like a savage source.   95
Their chant shall be a chant of paradise,
Out of their blood, returning to the sky;
And in their chant shall enter, voice by voice,

---

7. Stevens refers to "gentle, delicate death" in a letter about his mother's dying (*Selected Letters*, p. 174). Cf. the "delicious word death" in Whitman's *Out of the Cradle Endlessly Rocking*, line 168.
8. Stevens explained: "Plate is used in the sense of so-called family plate [silver-plated dinner service]. Disregarded refers to the disuse into which things fall that have been possessed for a long time. I mean, therefore, that death releases and renews. What the old have come to disregard, the young inherit and make use of" (*Selected Letters*, p. 183).

The windy lake wherein their lord delights,
The trees, like serafin,[9] and echoing hills,   100
That choir among themselves long afterward.
They shall know well the heavenly fellowship
Of men that perish and of summer morn.
And whence they came and whither they shall go
The dew upon their feet shall manifest.[1]   105

VIII

She hears, upon that water without sound,
A voice that cries, "The tomb in Palestine
Is not the porch of spirits lingering.
It is the grave of Jesus, where he lay."
We live in an old chaos[2] of the sun,   110
Or old dependency of day and night,
Or island solitude, unsponsored, free,
Of that wide water, inescapable.
Deer walk upon our mountains, and the quail
Whistle about us their spontaneous cries;   115
Sweet berries ripen in the wilderness;
And, in the isolation of the sky,
At evening, casual flocks of pigeons make
Ambiguous undulations as they sink,
Downward to darkness, on extended wings.[3]   120

                                              1915, 1923

Anecdote of the Jar

I placed a jar in Tennessee,
And round it was, upon a hill.
It made the slovenly wilderness
Surround that hill.

The wilderness rose up to it,   5
And sprawled around, no longer wild.
The jar was round upon the ground
And tall and of a port in air.

---

9. Seraphim, high-ranking angels or celestial beings.
1. Stevens explained: "Life is as fugitive as dew upon the feet of men dancing in dew" (*Selected Letters*, p. 250).
2. Unformed primordial matter; the origin or original god of creation according to the *Theogony* of the Greek poet Hesiod (fl. eighth century B.C.); a traditional term for fiery masses of elements, comparable to those in the sun.
3. Cf. Francis Higginson's description of the New England wilderness in *New England's Plantation*, 1630 (quoted in Perry Miller and T. H. Johnson, *The Puritans*, 1938, p. 125): "Here are * * * all manner of Berries and Fruits. In the winter time I have seen flocks of pidgeons and have eaten them. They doe fly from tree to tree as other birds doe; they are of all colors as ours are, but their wings and tayles are farr longer and therefore it is likely they fly swifter to escape the terrible Hawkes in this country." Cf. also the closing lines of the ode *To Autumn* by the English poet John Keats (1795–1821): "While barred clouds bloom the soft-dying day, / And touch the stubble-plains with rosey hue; / Then in a wailful choir the small gnats mourn / Among the river sallows, borne aloft / Or sinking as the light wind lives or dies; / And full-grown lambs loud bleat from hilly bourn; / Hedge-crickets sing; and now with treble soft / The red-breast whistles from a garden-croft; / And gathering swallows twitter in the skies."

It took dominion everywhere.
The jar was gray and bare.   10
It did not give of bird or bush,
Like nothing else in Tennessee.

1923

A High-toned Old Christian Woman

Poetry is the supreme fiction, madame.
Take the moral law and make a nave[1] of it
And from the nave build haunted heaven. Thus,
The conscience is converted into palms,
Like windy citherns[2] hankering for hymns.   5
We agree in principle. That's clear. But take
The opposing law and make a peristyle,[3]
And from the peristyle project a masque[4]
Beyond the planets. Thus, our bawdiness,
Unpurged by epitaph, indulged at last,   10
Is equally converted into palms,
Squiggling like saxophones. And palm for palm,
Madame, we are where we began. Allow,
Therefore, that in the planetary scene
Your disaffected flagellants,[5] well-stuffed,   15
Smacking their muzzy bellies in parade,
Proud of such novelties of the sublime,
Such tink and tank and tunk-a-tunk-tunk,
May, merely may, madame, whip from themselves
A jovial hullabaloo among the spheres.   20
This will make widows wince. But fictive things
Wink as they will. Wink most when widows wince.

1923

The Emperor of Ice-Cream[1]

Call the roller of big cigars,
The muscular one, and bid him whip
In kitchen cups concupiscent curds.[2]

1. Main body of a church building, especially the vaulted central portion of a Christian Gothic church.
2. Variation of "cittern," a pear-shaped guitar.
3. Colonnade surrounding a building, especially the cells or main chamber of an ancient Greek temple—an "opposing law" to a Christian church.
4. Spectacle or entertainment consisting of music, dancing, mime, and often poetry.
5. Religious devotees who whip themselves to intensify their fervor; "muzzy": sodden with drunkenness.
1. In 1945 Stevens remarked on the "singularity" of this poem: any poem "must have a peculiarity, as if it was the momentarily complete idiom of that which prompts it, even if what prompts it is the vaguest emotion." In 1933 he had written that it was his "favorite" and that he liked its combination of a "de-

liberately commonplace costume" with "the essential gaudiness of poetry." He said he remembered nothing of what prompted the poem other than his "state of mind": "This poem is an instance of letting myself go * * * . This represented what was in my mind at the moment, with the least possible manipulation" (*Letters*, pp. 500, 263–64). The poem's setting is a funeral or wake, an occasion when the living pay tribute to the dead and when commitments to life are juxtaposed against the face of death.
2. Stevens commented in 1945: "The words 'concupiscent curds' have no genealogy; they are merely expressive * * * . They express the concupiscence of life, but, by contrast with the things in relation to them in the poem, they express or accentuate life's destitution, and it is this that gives them something more than a cheap lustre" (*Letters*, p. 500).

Let the wenches dawdle in such dress
As they are used to wear, and let the boys   5
Bring flowers in last month's newspapers.
Let be be finale[3] of seem.
The only emperor is the emperor of ice-cream.

Take from the dresser of deal,[4]
Lacking the three glass knobs, that sheet   10
On which she embroidered fantails[5] once
And spread it so as to cover her face.
If her horny feet protrude, they come
To show how cold she is, and dumb.
Let the lamp[6] affix its beam.   15
The only emperor is the emperor of ice-cream.

                                                                1923

To the One of Fictive Music

Sister and mother and diviner love,
And of the sisterhood of the living dead
Most near, most clear, and of the clearest bloom,
And of the fragrant mothers the most dear
And queen, and of diviner love the day   5
And flame and summer and sweet fire, no thread
Of cloudy silver sprinkles in your gown
Its venom of renown, and on your head
No crown is simpler than the simple hair.

Now, of the music summoned by the birth   10
That separates us from the wind and sea,
Yet leaves us in them, until earth becomes,
By being so much of the things we are,
Gross effigy and simulacrum,[1] none
Gives motion to perfection more serene   15
Than yours, out of our imperfections wrought,
Most rare, or ever of more kindred air
In the laborious weaving that you wear.

For so retentive of themselves are men
That music is intensest which proclaims
The near, the clear, and vaunts the clearest bloom,   20
And of all vigils musing the obscure,

3. The concluding section of a musical composition, often including striking flourishes and virtuoso performances. Also: the final end, catastrophe. "Let be be finale of seem" suggests contrary readings: let being (actual existence) be consummated in a display of gaudy or brilliant illusions; let being put an end to mere appearances. Stevens claimed in 1939 that "the true sense of Let be be finale of seem is let being become the conclusion or denouement of appearing to be: in short, icecream is an absolute good. The poem is obviously not about icecream, but about being as distinguished from seeming to be" (*Letters*, p. 341).
4. Plain, unfinished wood.
5. Stevens explained that "the word fantails does not mean fans, but fantail pigeons * * *" (*Letters*, p. 340).
6. I.e., the light illuminating the corpse; also, the stark illumination of art.
1. Semblance, something having the form without the substance of a material object.

That apprehends the most which sees and names,
As in your name, an image that is sure,
Among the arrant[2] spices of the sun,   25
O bough and bush and scented vine, in whom
We give ourselves our likest issuance.

Yet not too like, yet not so like to be
Too near, too clear, saving a little to endow
Our feigning with the strange unlike, whence
      springs   30
The difference that heavenly pity brings.
For this, musician, in your girdle fixed
Bear other perfumes. On your pale head wear
A band entwining, set with fatal stones.
Unreal, give back to us what once you gave: 35
The imagination that we spurned and crave.

                                                       1923

The American Sublime

How does one stand
To behold the sublime,
To confront the mockers,
The mickey mockers
And plated pairs?[1]   5

When General Jackson
Posed for his statue[2]
He knew how one feels.
Shall a man go barefoot
Blinking and blank?   10

But how does one feel?
One grows used to the weather,
The landscape and that;
And the sublime comes down
To the spirit itself,   15

The spirit and space,
The empty spirit
In vacant space.
What wine does one drink?
What bread does one eat?[3]   20

                                                       1935

2. Confirmed, thoroughgoing; notorious.
1. Images opposed to the authentic sublime. "Mickey" is a pejorative slang
term for Irishman, while "mickey mockers" evokes the sentimental, tricky
Mickey Mouse in animated film cartoons. "Plated pairs": i.e., stereotyped
or identical objects, of ordinary material
but coated over with some more attractive surface, like silver plate.
2. In *The Noble Rider and the Sound of*
Words, Stevens described the statue of
General and President Andrew Jackson
(1767–1845) in Lafayette Square, Washington, D.C., by the sculptor Clark Mills
(1810–83). He associated it with inflated
eloquence and appeals to the complacency of a democratic society and to
fixed, stereotyped notions of the ideal.
3. "Wine" and "bread": familiar forms
of sustenance. Also the bread and wine
of Christian communion.

Dry Loaf[1]

It is equal to living in a tragic land
To live in a tragic time.
Regard now the sloping, mountainous rocks
And the river that batters its way over stones,
Regard the hovels of those that live in this land.   5

That was what I painted behind the loaf,
The rocks not even touched by snow,
The pines along the river and the dry men blown
Brown as the bread, thinking of birds
Flying from burning countries and brown sand
          shores,   10

Birds that came like dirty water in waves
Flowing above the rocks, flowing over the sky,
As if the sky was a current that bore them along,
Spreading them as waves spread flat on the shore,
One after another washing the mountains bare.   15

It was the battering of drums I heard
It was hunger, it was the hungry that cried
And the waves, the waves were soldiers moving,
Marching and marching in a tragic time
Below me, on the asphalt, under the trees.   20

It was soldiers went marching over the rocks
And still the birds came, came in watery flocks,
Because it was spring and the birds had to come.
No doubt that soldiers had to be marching
And that drums had to be rolling, rolling, rolling.   25

                                        1942

Of Modern Poetry

The poem of the mind in the act of finding
What will suffice. It has not always had
To find: the scene was set; it repeated what
Was in the script.
                    Then the theatre was changed   5
To something else. Its past was a souvenir.
It has to be living, to learn the speech of the place.
It has to face the men of the time and to meet
The women of the time. It has to think about war
And it has to find what will suffice. It has   10
To construct a new stage. It has to be on that stage
And, like an insatiable actor, slowly and
With meditation, speak words that in the ear,
In the delicatest ear of the mind, repeat,
Exactly, that which it wants to hear, at the sound   15

1. A loaf of bread, but also a mountain or hill in the shape of a loaf of bread.

Of which, an invisible audience listens,
Not to the play, but to itself, expressed
In an emotion as of two people, as of two
Emotions becoming one. The actor is
A metaphysician in the dark, twanging   20
An instrument, twanging a wiry string that gives
Sounds passing through sudden rightnesses, wholly
Containing the mind, below which it cannot descend,
Beyond which it has no will to rise.
                                   It must   25
Be the finding of a satisfaction, and may
Be of a man skating, a woman dancing, a woman
Combing. The poem of the act of the mind.

                                          1942

Asides on the Oboe

The prologues are over. It is a question, now,
Of final belief. So, say that final belief
Must be in a fiction. It is time to choose.

                    I

That obsolete fiction of the wide river in
An empty land;[1] the gods that Boucher killed;[2]   5
And the metal heroes that time granulates—
The philosophers' man alone still walks in dew,
Still by the sea-side mutters milky lines
Concerning an immaculate imagery.
If you say on the hautboy[3] man is not enough,   10
Can never stand as god, is ever wrong
In the end, however naked, tall, there is still
The impossible possible philosophers' man,
The man who has had the time to think enough,
The central man, the human globe, responsive   15
As a mirror with a voice, the man of glass,
Who in a million diamonds sums us up.[4]

                    II

He is the transparence of the place in which
He is and in his poems we find peace.
He sets this peddler's pie and cries in summer,   20
The glass man, cold and numbered, dewily cries,
"Thou art not August[5] unless I make thee so."
Clandestine steps upon imagined stairs
Climb through the night, because his cuckoos call.

1. I.e., the Christian Holy Land, with the river Jordan; also America, with the Mississippi River and other wide rivers. 2. Boucher could be Pierre Boucher (1622–1717), French explorer and Canadian settler; and Jonathan Boucher (1738–1804), Anglican clergyman and Loyalist during the American Revolution, author of *A View of the Causes and Consequences of the American Revolution* (1797); and François Boucher (1703–70), French decorative painter in the royal court of Louis XV. They represent, respectively, the displacement of native Indian gods and cultures; the rejection of the political "gods" of revolutionary America; and the trivialization of ancient mythologies in paintings of French court life. 3. Oboe. 4. Cf. Emerson's conception of the ideal poet in *The Poet* (1844): "He is a sovereign, and stands in the center." 5. I.e., the summer month, but also denoting nobility, magnificence.

III

One year, death and war prevented the jasmine scent   25
And the jasmine islands were bloody martyrdoms.
How was it then with the central man? Did we
Find peace? We found the sum of men. We found,
If we found the central evil, the central good.
We buried the fallen without jasmine crowns.   30
There was nothing he did not suffer, no; nor we.

It was not as if the jasmine ever returned.
But we and the diamond globe at last were one.
We had always been partly one. It was as we came
To see him, that we were wholly one, as we heard   35
Him chanting for those buried in their blood,
In the jasmine haunted forests, that we knew
The glass man, without external reference.

1940, 1942

The Motive for Metaphor

You like it under the trees in autumn,
Because everything is half dead.
The wind moves like a cripple among the leaves
And repeats words without meaning.

In the same way, you were happy in spring,   5
With the half colors of quarter-things,
The slightly brighter sky, the melting clouds,
The single bird, the obscure moon—

The obscure moon lighting an obscure world
Of things that would never be quite expressed,   10
Where you yourself were never quite yourself
And did not want nor have to be,

Desiring the exhilarations of changes:
The motive for metaphor, shrinking from
The weight of primary noon,   15
The A B C of being,

The ruddy temper, the hammer
Of red and blue, the hard sound—
Steel against intimation—the sharp flash,
The vital, arrogant, fatal, dominant X.   20

1947

Man Carrying Thing

The poem must resist the intelligence
Almost successfully. Illustration:

A brune[2] figure in winter evening resists
Identity. The thing he carries resists

The most necessitous sense. Accept them, then,   5
As secondary (parts not quite perceived

Of the obvious whole, uncertain particles
Of the certain solid, the primary free from doubt,

Things floating like the first hundred flakes of snow
Out of a storm we must endure all night,   10

Out of a storm of secondary things),
A horror of thoughts that suddenly are real.

We must endure our thoughts all night, until
The bright obvious stands motionless in cold.

1947

Questions Are Remarks

In the weed[1] of summer comes this green sprout why.
The sun aches and ails and then returns halloo
Upon the horizon amid adult enfantillages.[2]

Its fire fails to pierce the vision that beholds it,
Fails to destroy the antique acceptances,   5
Except that the grandson[3] sees it as it is,

Peter the voyant,[4] who says "Mother, what is that"—
The object that rises with so much rhetoric,
But not for him. His question is complete.

It is the question of what he is capable.   10
It is the extreme, the expert aetat.[5] 2.
He will never ride the red horse[6] she describes.

His question is complete because it contains
His utmost statement. It is his own array,
His own pageant and procession and display,   15

As far as nothingness permits . . . Hear him.
He does not say, "Mother, my mother, who are you,"
The way the drowsy, infant, old men do.

1950

2. French term intended to resist "intelligent" meaning. The adjective signifies a feminine figure with brown skin or hair. The noun signifies dusk.
1. Wild vegetation. Also garment (obs.).
2. Childishnesses.
3. The boy, Peter, though a mere grandson, and his elemental question, though a simple one, are the match for his grandiloquent grandsires and the age-old sun.
4. Clairvoyant, one who can see clearly.
5. Age (Latin abbreviation).
6. In ancient mythology, the god of the sun, Apollo, drives a fiery chariot across the sky.

The Hermitage at the Center

The leaves on the macadam make a noise—
How soft the grass on which the desired
Reclines in the temperature of heaven—

Like tales that were told the day before yesterday—
Sleek in a natural nakedness,   5
She attends the tintinnabula—[2]

And the wind sways like a great thing tottering—
Of birds called up by more than the sun,
Birds of more wit, that substitute—

Which suddenly is all dissolved and gone—   10
Their intelligible twittering
For unintelligible thought.

And yet this end and this begining are one,
And one last look at the ducks is a look
At lucent children round her in a ring.   15

1954

Not Ideas about the Thing
but the Thing Itself

At the earliest ending of winter,
In March, a scrawny cry from outside
Seemed like a sound in his mind.

He knew that he heard it,
A bird's cry, at daylight or before,   5
In the early March wind

The sun was rising at six,
No longer a battered panache[1] above snow . . .
It would have been outside.

It was not from the vast ventriloquism   10
Of sleep's faded papier-mâché[2] . . .
The sun was coming from outside.

That scrawny cry—it was
A chorister whose c[3] preceded the choir.
It was part of the colossal sun,   15

---

2. Jingling, tinkling sound as of bells. Cf. "the tintinabulation of the bells" in Edgar Allan Poe's poem *The Bells*.
1. Tuft, plume.
2. Paper pulp used for molding decora-
tive objects and imitations such as stage props and masks.
3. I.e., the note, middle C, sounded by a member of a choir which establishes the correct pitch.

Surrounded by its choral rings,
Still far away. It was like
A new knowledge of reality.

1954

From Adagia[1]

Authors are actors, books are theatres.

Literature is the better part of life. To this it seems inevitably necessary to add, provided life is the better part of literature.

Art, broadly, is the form of life or the sound or color of life. Considered as form (in the abstract) it is often indistinguishable from life itself.

Life is the reflection of literature.

Poetry is a means of redemption.

To a large extent, the problems of poets are the problems of painters, and poets must often turn to the literature of painting for a discussion of their own problems.

All poetry is experimental poetry.

Poetry must be irrational.

Poetry increases the feeling for reality.

One reads poetry with one's nerves.

The poet is the intermediary between people and the world in which they live and also, between people as between themselves; but not between people and some other world.

The final belief is to believe in a fiction, which you know to be a fiction, there being nothing else. The exquisite truth is to know that it is a friction and that you believe in it willingly.

The exquisite environment of fact. The final poem will be the poem of fact in the language of fact. But it will be the poem of fact not realized before.

To live in the world but outside of existing conceptions of it.

Poetry has to be something more than a conception of the mind. It has to be a revelation of nature. Conceptions are artificial. Perceptions are essential.

1. Adages (rare 17th-century spelling). Stevens's title suggests a comparison to "adagios" in the ballet: slow, graceful duets in which one dancer performs intricate and difficult movements. Collected in a notebook, his adagia were published in *Opus Posthumous* (1957). They contain some of his most compressed reflections on the interrelation of poetry and reality.

To read a poem should be an experience, like experiencing an act.

Money is a kind of poetry.

The poem is a nature created by the poet.

Religion is dependent on faith. But aesthetics is independent of faith. The relative positions of the two might be reversed. It is possible to establish aesthetics in the individual mind as immeasurably a greater thing than religion. Its present state is the result of the difficulty of establishing it except in the individual mind.

Perhaps there is a degree of perception at which what is real and what is imagined are one: a state of clairvoyant observation, accessible or possibly accessible to the poet or, say, the acutest poet.

The world is the only thing fit to think about.

All history is modern history.

The tongue is an eye.

God is a symbol for something that can as well take other forms, as, for example, the form of high poetry.

The body is the great poem.

Metaphor creates a new reality from which the original appears to be unreal.

Literature is based not on life but on propositions about life, of which this is one.

Life is a composite of the propositions about it.

A change of style is a change of subject.

The imagination consumes and exhausts some element of reality.

The poet is a god, or, the young poet is a god. The old poet is a tramp.

The poet represents the mind in the act of defending us against itself.

Every poem is a poem within a poem: the poem of the idea within the poem of the words.

On the death of some men the world reverts to ignorance.

Words are everything else in the world.

A poem need not have a meaning and like most things in nature often does not have.

Reality is not what it is. It consists of the many realities which it can be made into.

One's ignorance is one's chief asset.

The greatest piece of fiction: Greek mythology. Classical mythology but Greek above Latin.

Reality is a cliché from which we escape by metaphor. It is only *au pays de la métaphore qu'on est poète.*[2]

The degrees of metaphor. The absolute object slightly turned is a metaphor of the object.

Some objects are less susceptible to metaphor than others. The whole world is less susceptible to metaphor than a tea-cup is.

There is no such thing as a metaphor of a metaphor. One does not progress through metaphors. Thus reality is the indispensable element of each metaphor. When I say that man is a god it is very easy to see that if I also say that a god is something else, god has become reality.

Poetry seeks out the relation of men to facts.

The imagination is man's power over nature.

Imagination is the only genius.

The momentum of the mind is all toward abstraction.

The effect of the imagination on the works of artists is a different subject from that in which I am interested. In art its effect is the production of qualities: as strength (Pater, Michelangelo)[3] and its value is a question of the value of those qualities. In life it produces things and its value is a question of the value of those things as, for example, the value of works of art.

The imagination is the liberty of the mind and hence the liberty of reality.

Success as the result of industry is a peasant ideal.

In the long run the truth does not matter.

---

2. "It is only in the country of metaphor that one is a poet."
3. The English writer and aesthetician Walter Pater (1839–94) and Michelangelo Buonarroti (1475–1564), the Italian painter, scultptor, architect, and poet.

ELINOR WYLIE
1885–1928

Traditionalist, lyricist, metaphysical, romantic—all the many tags applied to Elinor Wylie's poetry have some measure of truth yet none of them defines the quintessential element of her work. A woman of great personal beauty and magnetism, fanatically proud, she combined aristocratic *hauteur* and bohemian flair with a poetic talent that dazzled both critics and the public. As Edmund Wilson wrote, "her submerged passion and her museum show-case culture are all characteristically American; her images of glass and bronze and gold * * * have the glitter of the world in which she has lived; they could have been cast in no other society than that of the American East."[1]

Elinor Hoyt was born into a prominent Philadelphia family and educated at exclusive schools. After a conventional enough beginning, a debut, marriage to an admiral's son, and the birth of a child, she scandalized her world in 1911 by eloping with a much older man, Horace Wylie, and fleeing to England to live.

She had begun to write poetry in her late teens (and some of her earliest verse was privately printed in 1912) but it was the volume *Nets to Catch the Wind* (1921) that caught the attention of critics and readers just after World War I. At the time of its publication, she and Wylie had returned to this country because of the war in 1916 and had married. They lived in the capital, where Wylie found a minor government position. In Washington, Elinor's brother, the painter Henry Martin Hoyt, brought Yale friends to visit, among them the writers Sinclair Lewis and William Rose Benét. Through their auspices, her poems began to appear in influential magazines of the period: *The Century, The Nation, Poetry, New Republic,* and *Vanity Fair.*

The critical acclaim that greeted *Nets to Catch the Wind* led her to move to New York City, where for the rest of her life she made her home, periodically escaping to Connecticut, to the English countryside she loved, or to the MacDowell Colony for artists and writers in New Hampshire. In 1923 she divorced Wylie, married William R. Benét, and worked for a time as poetry editor at *Vanity Fair. Jennifer Lorn,* the novel she had written at Benét's suggestion, was given an enthusiastic reception by Wilson and James Branch Cabell, among others, and in that same year, 1923, her second book of poetry, *Black Armour,* received even better reviews than had her first. Three more novels were to occupy her energies for the next several years and provided a steady income; *The Orphan Angel* was a Book-of-the-Month Club choice in 1926. Though she had been in precarious health since 1914, she spent her last years meeting the demands on her as a literary personage, writing poems, novels, and essays, collecting books and Shelley letters, buying Paris clothes, and enjoying the prominence that the writer Carl Van Doren likened to that of a "white queen."[2] She died suddenly of a stroke in 1928 on the very day she finished assembling her volume of poems *Angels and Earthly Creatures.*

1. *Shores of Light,* pp. 126–27.   2. *Three Worlds,* p. 221.

Her poetry at its best rises above her own declared intent, to make poems that are "enamelled snuffboxes," the products of "a small clean technique." But she stands charged, in her own words, with "gold and silver trickery,"[3] an overindulgence in elaborate imagery, and a glittering vocabulary that at times makes elegance the poem's only justification. In poems like *August* and *Wild Peaches*, however, the language beautifully bears the burden of the message. Her metrical facility, apt rhymes, and use of the traditional forms of sonnet and ballad were remarkable. Though her debts to such British poets as the romantic Shelley and the metaphysical poet John Donne are evident in such later poems as *The Lie*, *The Loving Cup*, and the sonnet sequence *One Person*, they derive from similarities of temperament and vocabulary rather than from deliberate imitation. Elinor Wylie won a distinctive place in an American tradition that has produced more impressive woman poets than has any other national tradition in the twentieth century, and she achieved her aim of writing "short lines, clean small stanzas, brilliant and compact."[4]

Beauty

Say not of Beauty she is good,
Or aught but beautiful,
Or sleek to doves' wings of the wood
Her wild wings of a gull.

Call her not wicked; that word's touch   5
Consumes her like a curse;
But love her not too much, too much,
For that is even worse.

O, she is neither good nor bad,
But innocent and wild!   10
Enshrine her and she dies, who had
The hard heart of a child.

         1921

August

Why should this Negro insolently stride
Down the red noonday on such noiseless feet?
Piled in his barrow, tawnier than wheat,
Lie heaps of smouldering daisies, sombre-eyed,
Their copper petals shrivelled up with pride,   5
Hot with a superfluity of heat,
Like a great brazier borne along the street
By captive leopards, black and burning pied.[1]

Are there no water-lilies, smooth as cream,
With long stems dripping crystal? Are there none   10
Like those white lilies, luminous and cool,

---

3. *Collected Prose*, pp. 873–76.   1. Mottled with two or more colors.
4. *Ibid.*, p. 873.

Plucked from some hemlock-darkened northern stream
By fair-haired swimmers, diving where the sun
Scarce warms the surface of the deepest pool?

1921

Wild Peaches

1

When the world turns completely upside down
You say we'll emigrate to the Eastern Shore
Aboard a river-boat from Baltimore;
We'll live among wild peach trees, miles from town,
You'll wear a coonskin cap, and I a gown   5
Homespun, dyed butternut's dark gold colour.
Lost, like your lotus-eating ancestor,
We'll swim in milk and honey till we drown.

The winter will be short, the summer long,
10The autumn amber-hued, sunny and hot,
Tasting of cider and of scuppernong;[1]
All seasons sweet, but autumn best of all.
The squirrels in their silver fur will fall
Like falling leaves, like fruit, before your shot.

2

The autumn frosts will lie upon the grass   15
Like bloom on grapes of purple-brown and gold.
The misted early mornings will be cold;
The little puddles will be roofed with glass.
The sun, which burns from copper into brass,
Melts these at noon, and makes the boys unfold   20
Their knitted mufflers; full as they can hold,
Fat pockets dribble chestnuts as they pass.

Peaches grow wild, and pigs can live in clover;
A barrel of salted herrings lasts a year;
The spring begins before the winter's over.   25
By February you may find the skins
Of garter snakes and water moccasins
Dwindled and harsh, dead-white and cloudy-clear.

3

When April pours the colours of a shell
Upon the hills, when every little creek   35
Is shot with silver from the Chesapeake
In shoals new-minted by the ocean swell,
When strawberries go begging, and the sleek
Blue plums lie open to the blackbird's beak,
We shall live well—we shall live very well.   30

The months between the cherries and the peaches
Are brimming cornucopias which spill

1. A sweet golden aromatic wine made from a native American grape.

Fruits red and purple, sombre-bloomed and black;
Then, down rich fields and frosty river beaches
We'll trample bright persimmons, while you kill   40
Bronze partridge, speckled quail, and canvasback.

4

Down to the Puritan marrow of my bones
There's something in this richness that I hate.
I love the look, austere, immaculate,
Of landscapes drawn in pearly monotones.   45
There's something in my very blood that owns
Bare hills, cold silver on a sky of slate,
A thread of water, churned to milky spate
Streaming through slanted pastures fenced with stones.
I love those skies, thin blue or snowy gray,   50
Those fields sparse-planted, rendering meagre sheaves;
That spring, briefer than apple-blossom's breath,
Summer, so much too beautiful to stay,
Swift autumn, like a bonfire of leaves,
And sleepy winter, like the sleep of death.   55

1921

Bronze Trumpets and Sea Water—
on Turning Latin into English

Alembics[1] turn to stranger things
Strange things, but never while we live
Shall magic turn this bronze that sings
To singing water in a sieve.

The trumpeters of Cæsar's guard   5
Salute his rigorous bastions
With ordered bruit;[2] the bronze is hard
Though there is silver in the bronze.

Our mutable tongue is like the sea,
Curled wave and shattering thunder-fit;   10
Dangle in strings of sand shall he
Who smooths the ripples out of it.

1921

Let No Charitable Hope

Now let no charitable hope
Confuse my mind with images
Of eagle and of antelope:
I am in nature none of these.

I was, being human, born alone;   5
In am, being woman, hard beset;

1. A distilling apparatus; the image is
here used to suggest the change of translation.
2. Noise, sound.

I live by squeezing from a stone
The little nourishment I get.

In masks outrageous and austere
The years go by in single file;[2]   10
But none has merited my fear,
And none has quite escaped my smile.

                                      1923

Parting Gift

I cannot give you the Metropolitan Tower;[1]
I cannot give you heaven;
Nor the nine Visigoth crowns in the Cluny Museum;[2]
Nor happiness, even.
But I can give you a very small purse   5
Made out of field-mouse skin,
With a painted picture of the universe
And seven blue tears therein.

I cannot give you the island of Capri;[3]
I cannot give you beauty;   10
Nor bake you marvellous crusty cherry pies
With love and duty.
But I can give you a very little locket
Made out of wildcat hide:
Put it into your left-hand pocket   15
And never look inside.

                                      1923

Speed the Parting——

I shall not sprinkle with dust
A creature so clearly lunar;
You must die—but of course you must—
And better later than sooner.
But if it should be in a year   5
That year itself must perish;
How dingy a thing is fear,
And sorrow, how dull to cherish!
And if it should be in a day
That day would be dark by evening,   10
But the morning might still be gay
And the noon have golden leavening.
And beauty's a moonlight grist
That comes to the mills of dying;
The silver grain may be missed   15

---

2. Reminiscent of Ralph W. Emerson's poem *Days*, lines 1–3: "Daughters of Time, the hypocritic Days, / Muffled and dumb like barefoot dervishes, / And marching single in an endless file. * * *"

1. New York City office building.
2. Treasures once displayed in the Paris museum.
3. Scenic isle in the Bay of Naples.

But there's no great good in crying.
Though luminous things are mould
They survive in a glance that crossed them,
And it's not very kind to scold
The empty air that has lost them.   20
The limpid blossom of youth
Turns into a poison berry;
Having perceived this truth
I shall not weep but be merry.
Therefore die when you please;   25
It's not very wise to worry;
I shall not shiver and freeze;
I shall not even be sorry.
Beautiful things are wild;
They are gone, and you go after;   30
Therefore I mean, my child,
To charm your going with laughter.
Love and pity are strong,
But wisdom is happily greater;
You will die, I suppose, before long.   35
Oh, worser sooner than later!

1928

From: One Person[1]

XII

In our content, before the autumn came
To shower sallow droppings on the mould,
Sometimes you have permitted me to fold
Your grief in swaddling-bands, and smile to name
Yourself my infant, with an infant's claim   5
To utmost adoration as of old,
Suckled with kindness, fondled from the cold,
And loved beyond philosophy or shame.

I dreamt I was the mother of a son
Who had deserved a manger for a crib;   10
Torn from your body, furbished from your rib,
I am the daughter of your skeleton,
Born of your bitter and excessive pain:
I shall not dream you are my child again.

XVI

I hereby swear that to uphold your house
I would lay my bones in quick destroying lime
Or turn my flesh to timber for all time;
Cut down my womanhood; lop off the boughs
Of that perpetual ecstasy that grows   5
From the heart's core; condemn it as a crime

---

1. A sonnet sequence.

If it be broader than a beam, or climb
Above the stature that your roof allows.

I am not the hearthstone nor the cornerstone
Within this noble fabric you have builded;   10
Not by my beauty was its cornice gilded;
Not on my courage were its arches thrown:
My lord, adjudge my strength, and set me where
I bear a little more than I can bear.

                                                    1929

Pretty Words

Poets make pets of pretty, docile words:
I love smooth words, like gold-enamelled fish
Which circle slowly with a silken swish,
And tender ones, like downy-feathered birds:
Words shy and dappled, deep-eyed deer in herds,   5
Come to my hand, and playful if I wish,
Or purring softly at a silver dish,
Blue Persian kittens, fed on cream and curds.

I love bright words, words up and singing early;
Words that are luminous in the dark, and sing;   10
Warm lazy words, white cattle under trees;
I love words opalescent, cool, and pearly,
Like midsummer moths, and honied words like bees,
Gilded and sticky, with a little sting.

                                                    1932

Sonnet

How many faults you might accuse me of
Are truth, and by my truthfulness admitted!
A fool, perhaps, how many caps had fitted,
How many motleys[1] clothed me like a glove.
Thriftless of gold and prodigal of love;   5
Fanatical in pride, and feather-witted
In the world's business; if your tongue had spitted
Such frailties, they were possible to prove.

But you have hit the invulnerable joint
In this poor armour patched from desperate fears; 10
This is the breastplate that you cannot pierce,
That turns and breaks your most malicious point;
This strict ascetic habit of control
That industry has woven for my soul.

                                                    1932

1. Many-colored cloth; jesters wore suits of motley.

HILDA DOOLITTLE (H. D.)
1886–1961

In January, 1913, Ezra Pound placed in *Poetry* magazine three poems by Hilda Doolittle and ordered that they be signed "H. D., Imagiste." Thus, simultaneously, Hilda Doolittle was "discovered," H. D. was invented, and the Imagist movement was proclaimed. The identification of H. D. with Imagism, persisting long beyond the life of the movement, has perhaps unfairly diminished the amount and limited the scope of critical attention to her work. She was, however, the most faithful adherent to the precepts of that "group of poets who, between 1912 and 1917, joined the reaction against the careless techniques and extra-poetic values of much nineteenth century verse."[1] The essential qualities of her poetry—its commitment to the precise word and to the presentation of hard and clear images, its creation of new rhythms to express new moods, its concentration—fulfill all the dictates of the Imagist Credo outlined by the contributors to the 1915 Imagist anthology.

The prevalence of classical and mythological settings in H. D.'s work and her borrowing of subjects and characters from ancient writers have led some readers unjustly to label her an escapist or "an inspired anachronism."[2] As her literary executor Norman Holmes Pearson comments, "She has been so praised as a kind of Greek publicity girl that people have forgotten that she writes the most intensely personal poems using Greek myth as a metaphor."[3] H. D.'s poems, like the Sapphic fragments of the ancient Greek poet Sappho upon which they sometimes are constructed, examine the problem of being a woman and a poet in a fragmented world. Her classical past is not simply an escapist alternative to modern life; its relation to the present is more intricate and symbiotic, like the relation of the partially erased earlier writing on a palimpsest to the new layer of words being inscribed.

Hilda Doolittle was born in Bethlehem, Pennsylvania, in 1886. Her father, a remote and forbidding figure to her, was a professor of mathematics and astronomy at Lehigh University and later at the University of Pennsylvania. H. D. attended local public and private schools and, in 1904, entered Bryn Mawr where she studied for two years before withdrawing because of poor health. Ezra Pound was a close friend and, according to William Carlos Williams, was in love with her. Williams, in his autobiography, remembers H. D. as a tall, carelessly dressed young woman with "a provocative indifference to rule and order which I liked."[4]

H. D. lived at home, reading mostly Greek and Latin literature and writing poetry, until in 1911 she went to Europe for what she thought would be a summer's visit. In London she renewed her friendship with Pound and was introduced into a circle of young poets who were experimenting in free

1. Stanley K. Coffman, Jr., *Imagism: A Chapter for the History of Modern Poetry* (Norman, Okla., 1951), p. 3.
2. Thomas Burnett Swann, *The Classical World of H. D.* (Lincoln, Neb., 1962), p. 3.

3. "Norman Holmes Pearson on H. D.: An Interview," *Contemporary Literature*, 10 (1969), 441.
4. William Carlos Williams, *The Autobiography of William Carlos Williams* (New York, 1948), p. 68.

verse and would soon refer to themselves as Imagists. One of these poets was Richard Aldington, whom H. D. married in 1913. They collaborated on some translations from the Greek, and, when he was called up for military service in 1916, H. D. assumed his position as literary editor of *The Egoist*. By the end of the war, the marriage had collapsed. In 1919, H. D. gave birth to a daughter and separated from Aldington. Both she and the infant were seriously ill, and H. D. credited their recovery to the spiritual and material assistance of Winifred Ellerman, a young admirer of her poetry who had become her friend and benefactress. In the next three years, H. D. and Miss Ellerman, who later wrote historical novels under the name of "Bryher," took trips to Greece, America, and Egypt. In 1923, H. D. settled in Switzerland where she spent most of the next thirty-eight years.

The settings of H. D.'s works of prose fiction—*Palimpsest* (1926), *Hedylus* (1928), and *Bid Me to Live* (1960)—range from ancient Rome and Greece to modern England and Egypt, but they are similar in theme and technique. Each of *Palimpsest's* three sections, and each of the other books, focuses meditatively on a sensitive woman's attempt to come to terms with herself and with a coarse and violent world. Like her long poem *Helen in Egypt* (1961), a dramatic monologue by Helen of Troy, the prose works are versions of spiritual autobiography.

H. D. chose to live in London during World War II. There she wrote her *Tribute to Freud* (1956), an account of her psychoanalysis by Freud in 1933 and 1934 and a re-creation of the self-portrait that emerged from it. She also wrote a trilogy of war poems—*The Walls Do Not Fall* (1944), *Tribute to the Angels* (1945), and *The Flowering of the Rod* (1946). These poems affirm the survival, even the strengthening, of the human spirit amid chaos and devastation. H. D. finally seeks a personal and universal mystic experience, but it is her language that both preserves her contact with the outside and provides "an inner region of defense."[5]

Oread[1]

Whirl up, sea—
whirl your pointed pines,
splash your great pines
on our rocks,
hurl your green over us,   5
cover us with your pools of fir.

1914, 1924

Heat[2]

O wind, rend open the heat,
cut apart the heat,
rend it to tatters.

---

5. Hilda Doolittle, "A Note on Poetry," in *The Oxford Anthology of American Literature,* ed. William Rose Benét and Norman Holmes Pearson (New York, 1938), p. 1288.

1. A nymph of mountains and hills.
2. In *Sea Garden* (1916) and *Collected Poems* (1925), *Heat* is published as the second part of a two-part poem called *Garden*.

Fruit cannot drop
through this thick air—   5
fruit cannot fall into heat
that presses up and blunts
the points of pears
and rounds the grapes.

Cut the heat—   10
plough through it,
turning it on either side
of your path.

                                                               1916

Leda[1]

Where the slow river
meets the tide,
a red swan lifts red wings
and darker beak,
and underneath the purple down   5
of his soft breast
uncurls his coral feet.

Through the deep purple
of the dying heat
of sun and mist,   10
the level ray of sun-beam
has caressed
the lily with dark breast,
and flecked with richer gold
its golden crest.   15

Where the slow lifting
of the tide,
floats into the river
and slowly drifts
among the reeds,   20
and lifts the yellow flags,
he floats
where tide and river meet.

Ah kingly kiss—
no more regret   25
nor old deep memories
to mar the bliss;
where the low sedge is thick,
the gold day-lily
outspreads and rests   30

1. In Greek mythology, Leda is the mor-   swan, rapes. Helen of Troy was born of
tal woman whom Zeus, in the guise of a   their union.

beneath soft fluttering
of red swan wings
and the warm quivering
of the red swan's breast.

1919, 1921

At Baia[2]

I should have thought
in a dream you would have brought
some lovely, perilous thing,
orchids piled in a great sheath,
as who would say (in a dream)   5
I send you this,
who left the blue veins
of your throat unkissed.

Why was it that your hands
(that never took mine)   10
your hands that I could see
drift over the orchid heads
so carefully,
your hands, so fragile, sure to lift
so gently, the fragile flower stuff—   15
ah, ah, how was it

You never sent (in a dream)
the very form, the very scent,
not heavy, not sensuous,
but perilous—perilous—   20
of orchids, piled in a great sheath,
and folded underneath on a bright scroll
some word:

Flower sent to flower;
for white hands, the lesser white,   25
less lovely of flower leaf,

or

Lover to lover, no kiss,
no touch, but forever and ever this.

1921

Heliodora[1]

He and I sought together,
over the spattered table,

2. An ancient Roman resort town.
1. Sixteen lines by Meleager, a poet of the first century B.C., in praise of his mistress Heliodora, comprise the nucleus of this poem. H. D. italicizes her trans- lations of Meleager's verse and constructs around them a poetry-composing contest between two admirers of a beautiful woman.

rhymes and flowers,
gifts for a name.

He said, among others,   5
I will bring
(and the phrase was just and good,
but not as good as mine,)
"the narcissus that loves the rain."

We strove for a name,   10
while the light of the lamps burnt thin
and the outer dawn came in,
a ghost, the last at the feast
or the first,
to sit within   15
with the two that remained
to quibble in flowers and verse
over a girl's name.

He said, "the rain, loving,"
I said, "the narcissus, drunk,   20
drunk with the rain."
Yet I had lost
for he said,
"the rose, the lover's gift,
is loved of love,"   25
he said it,
"loved of love;"
I waited, even as he spoke,
to see the room filled with a light,
as when in winter   30
the embers catch in a wind
when a room is dank;
so it would be filled, I thought,
our room with a light
when he said   35
(and he said it first,)
"the rose, the lover's delight,
is loved of love,"
but the light was the same.

Then he caught,   40
seeing the fire in my eyes,
my fire, my fever, perhaps,
for he leaned
with the purple wine
stained on his sleeve,   45
and said this:
"did you ever think
a girl's mouth
caught in a kiss,
is a lily that laughs?"   50

I had not.
I saw it now
as men must see it forever afterwards;
no poet could write again,
"the red-lily,   55
a girl's laugh caught in a kiss;"
it was his to pour in the vat
from which all poets dip and quaff,
for poets are brothers in this.

So I saw the fire in his eyes,   60
it was almost my fire,
(he was younger,)
I saw the face so white,
my heart beat,
it was almost my phrase;   65
I said, "surprise the muses,[2]
take them by surprise;
it is late,
rather it is dawn-rise,
those ladies sleep, the nine,   70
our own king's mistresses."

A name to rhyme,
flowers to bring to a name,
what was one girl faint and shy,
with eyes like the myrtle,   75
(I said: "her underlids
are rather like myrtle,")
to vie with the nine?

Let him take the name,
he had the rhymes,   80
"the rose, loved of love,
the lily, a mouth that laughs,"
he had the gift,
"the scented crocus,
the purple hyacinth,"   85
what was one girl to the nine?

He said:
"I will make her a wreath;"
he said:
"I will write it thus: 90

I will bring you the lily that laughs,
I will twine
with soft narcissus, the myrtle,
sweet crocus, white violet,
the purple hyacinth, and last,   95

---

2. Ancient Greek and Roman goddesses of the arts.

the rose, loved-of-love,
that these may drip on your hair
the less soft flowers,
may mingle sweet with the sweet
of Heliodora's locks,   100
myrrh³-curled."
(He wrote myrrh-curled,
I think, the first.)

I said:
"they sleep, the nine,"   105
when he shouted swift and passionate:
"*that* for the nine!
above the hills
the sun is about to wake,
and to-day white violets   110
shine beside white lilies
adrift on the mountain side;
to-day the narcissus opens
that loves the rain."

I watched him to the door,   115
catching his robe
as the wine-bowl crashed to the floor,
spilling a few wet lees,
(ah, his purple hyacinth!)
I saw him out of the door,   120
I thought:
there will never be a poet
in all the centuries after this,
who will dare write,
after my friend's verse,   125
"a girl's mouth
is a lily kissed."

1924

Helen¹

All Greece hates
the still eyes in the white face,
the lustre as of olives
where she stands,
and the white hands.   5

All Greece reviles
the wan face when she smiles,
hating it deeper still
when it grows wan and white,

---

3. An aromatic plant.
1. In Greek legend, the wife of Agamemnon whose abduction by the Trojan
prince Paris started the Trojan War. She
was the daughter of the god Zeus, the
product of his union, when disguised as
a swan, with the mortal woman Leda.

remembering past enchantments   10
and past ills.

Greece sees, unmoved,
God's daughter, born of love,
the beauty of cool feet
and slenderest knees,   15
could love indeed the maid,
only if she were laid,
white ash amid funereal cypresses.

                                                1924

Fragment 113

"Neither honey nor bee for me."
—SAPPHO[1]

Not honey,
not the plunder of the bee
from meadow or sand-flower
or mountain bush;
from winter-flower or shoot   5
born of the later heat:
not honey, not the sweet
stain on the lips and teeth:
not honey, not the deep
plunge of soft belly   10
and the clinging of the gold-edged
pollen-dusted feet;

though rapture blind my eyes,
and hunger crisp
dark and inert my mouth,   15
not honey, not the south,
not the tall stalk
of red twin-lilies,
nor light branch of fruit tree
caught in flexible light branch;   20
not honey, not the south;
ah flower of purple iris,
flower of white,
or of the iris, withering the grass—
for fleck of the sun's fire,   25
gathers such heat and power,
that shadow-print is light,
cast through the petals
of the yellow iris flower;

not iris—old desire—old passion—   30
old forgetfulness—old pain—
not this, nor any flower,

1. Greek woman lyric poet of Lesbos in the seventh century B.C.

but if you turn again,
seek strength of arm and throat,
touch as the god;   35
neglect the lyre-note;
knowing that you shall feel,
about the frame,
no trembling of the string
but heat, more passionate   40
of bone and the white shell
and fiery tempered steel.

                                                           1922

From The Walls Do Not Fall

1

An incident here and there,
and rails gone (for guns)
from your (and my) old town square:

mist and mist-grey, no color,
still the Luxor[1] bee, chick and hare   5
pursue unalterable purpose

in green, rose-red, lapis;
they continue to prophesy
from the stone papyrus:[2]

there, as here, ruin opens   10
the tomb, the temple; enter,
there as here, there are no doors:

the shrine lies open to the sky,
the rain falls, here, there
sand drifts; eternity endures: 15

ruin everywhere, yet as the fallen roof
leaves the sealed room
open to the air,

so, through our desolation,
thoughts stir, inspiration stalks us   20
through gloom:

unaware, Spirit announces the Presence;
shivering overtakes us,
as of old, Samuel:[3]

---

1. Site of temple and tombs at ancient Thebes in Egypt.
2. A plant of the Nile valley whose fiber was processed into scrolls by the ancient Egyptians, Greeks, and Romans.
3. A Biblical Hebrew judge and the first of the great prophets.

trembling at a known street-corner, 25
we know not nor are known;
the Pythian⁴ pronounces—we pass on

to another cellar, to another sliced wall
where poor utensils show
like rare objects in a museum; 30

Pompeii⁵ has nothing to teach us,
we know crack of volcanic fissure,
slow flow of terrible lava,

pressure on heart, lungs, the brain
about to burst its brittle case 35
(what the skull can endure!):

over us, Apocryphal fire,⁶
under us, the earth sway, dip of a floor,
slope of a pavement

where men roll, drunk 40
with a new bewilderment,
sorcery, bedevilment:

the bone-frame was made for
no such shock knit within terror,
yet the skeleton stood up to it: 45

the flesh? it was melted away,
the heart burnt out, dead ember,
tendons, muscles shattered, outer husk dismembered,

yet the frame held:
we passed the flame: we wonder 50
what saved us? what for?

1944

From Tribute to the Angels

4

Not in our time, O Lord,
the plowshare for the sword,

not in our time, the knife,
sated with life-blood and life,

to trim the barren vine; 5
no grape-leaf for the thorn,

4. Oracular priestess of Apollo at Delphi.
5. Ancient Roman city destroyed by the eruption of Mt. Vesuvius in A.D. 29.
6. The Apocrypha is a collection of quasi-scriptural books of doubtful authorship and authority. Hence, things that are apocryphal are untrustworthy or counterfeit. H. D. may be playing on the familiar idea of the apocalyptic fire that is prophesied to consume the earth in the Book of Revelation.

no vine-flower for the crown;
not in our time, O King,

the voice to quell the re-gathering,
thundering storm.   10

6

Never in Rome,
so many martyrs fell;

not in Jerusalem,
never in Thebes,[1]

so many stood and watched   5
chariot-wheels turning,

saw with their very eyes,
the battle of the Titans,[2]

saw Zeus' thunderbolts in action
and how, from giant hands,   10

the lightning shattered earth
and splintered sky, nor fled

to hide in caves,
but with unbroken will,

with unbowed head, watched   15
and though unaware, worshipped

and knew not that they worshipped
and that they were

that which they worshipped;
had they known, the fire   20

of strength, endurance, anger
in their hearts,

was part of that same fire
that in a candle on a candle-stick

or in a star,   25
is known as one of seven,

is named among the seven Angels,
Uriel.[3]

                                                         1945

1. Ancient Greek city and battle site.
2. Gods and goddesses of Greek mythology. They were overthrown in a 10-year
battle by Zeus, who thereby became
ruler of the Greek gods.
3. One of the Archangels, the angel of
fire or light.

From The Flowering of the Rod

3

In resurrection, there is confusion
if we start to argue; if we stand and stare,

we do not know where to go;
in resurrection, there is simple affirmation,

but do not delay to round up the others,   5
up and down the street; your going,

in a moment like this, is the best proof
that you know the way;

does the first wild-goose stop to explain
to the others? no—he is off;   10

they follow or not,
that is their affair;

does the first wild-goose care
whether the others follow or not?

I don't think so—he is so happy to be off—   15
he knows where he is going;

so we must be drawn or we must fly,
like the snow-geese of the Arctic circle,

to the Carolinas or to Florida,
or like those migratory flocks   20

who still (they say) hover
over the lost island, Atlantis;[1]

seeking what we once knew,
we know ultimately we will find

happiness; *today shalt thou be*   25
with me in Paradise.

1946

1. According to the ancients, a thriving island civilization that sank into the ocean.

MARIANNE MOORE
1887–1972

The "poet's poet" among those who rose to prominence toward the end of
World War I was a woman, Marianne Craig Moore. She produced a small
but unmistakably unique body of poems whose originality was greatly
admired by such contemporaries as Pound, Eliot, Stevens, and Williams,
and her radically inventive forms had an impact on Robert Lowell, Richard
Wilbur, and others of the generation who began writing after World War
II. For years an inconspicuous figure in the literary world, she was nevertheless among the finest of this century's American poets. In later years her
activities on behalf of the Ford Motor Company and the Brooklyn Dodgers

baseball team, along with her many literary honors, made her a charming footnote to the public scene.

She was born in 1887 to a devoutly Presbyterian family in Kirkwood, Missouri, near St. Louis. After her father suffered a business and personal collapse and abandoned the family, she moved with her mother in 1894 to Carlisle, Pennsylvania. She attended the Metzger Institute, where her mother taught, and in 1909 graduated from Bryn Mawr College, where she did better in biology than in literature but tried her hand at writing poetry and discovered the power of seventeenth-century English prose.

Moore took courses at the Carlisle Commercial College and traveled with her mother in England and France in 1911, then from 1911 to 1915 taught commercial subjects at the U.S. Indian School in Carlisle. Her verse was first published in 1915 and 1916 in *The Egoist* (London), *Poetry*, and *Others*, the magazine founded by Alfred Kreymborg to encourage experimental writing, and by the time her poems were appearing regularly in the journals she and her mother moved, first to New Jersey, and later to Brooklyn, to remain near her brother, who had been ordained a Presbyterian minister. (Throughout her life she remained exceptionally close to her mother and brother, whose judgment she often consulted when composing or revising her poems.) She was working as tutor and secretary in a girls' school and as a part-time assistant in a branch library, and attending parties with friends among the vanguard painters and writers associated with *Others*, when her first two books were published. Her jobs, she said in a later interview, had "hardened my muscle considerably, my mental approach to things."[1] Her *Poems* (1921) was brought out in London without her knowledge by two admirers, the writers Bryher (Mrs. Robert McAlmon) and Hilda Doolittle. *Observations* appeared in 1924 and received the Dial Award for that year.

Her tenure as editor of *The Dial* (1925–29) she described as five years of "compacted pleasantness" in an "atmosphere of excited triumph."[2] Her reviews commanded respect and her exacting standards inspired awe; she was criticized, however, for rejecting excerpts from James Joyce's *Finnegans Wake* on the grounds that its language and sexual allusions were offensive, and the alterations she insisted on in one of Hart Crane's poems provoked his exclamation that America's two most important literary journals (*The Dial* and Harriet Monroe's *Poetry*) were edited by "hysterical virgins."[3] She wrote virtually no verse until the magazine was disbanded in 1929 but resumed her poetic career with the publication of *Selected Poems* (1935). T. S. Eliot in his introduction declared that in her poetry "an original sensibility and alert intelligence and deep feeling have been engaged in maintaining the life of the English language."

One of the distinguishing features of her verse is its saturation "in the perfections of prose," as Eliot put it (introduction, 7), the qualities she admired in "prose stylists" from Xenophon, Francis Bacon, and Thomas Browne to Henry James and Ezra Pound.[4] Testifying to the impact of scientific language and procedures on her imagination, she declared that "Precision, economy of statement, logic employed to ends that are disinterested * * * liberate * * * the imagination, it seems to me."[5] Prose sources, as

1. Marianne Moore, *A Collection of Critical Essays*, p. 23.
2. "The Dial: A Retrospect," *Predilections* (1955), pp. 103, 105.
3. Hart Crane, *Letters*, p. 289.
4. "Interview," *Collection of Critical Essays*, pp. 30–31.
5. *Ibid.*, p. 23.

often as poetic ones, provide her materials, which she acknowledges candidly by putting quotation marks around excerpts from history books, reference works, and even travel brochures. The definiteness and solidity of prose, the momentum of its sentences and paragraphs, are incorporated in her verse to attain an "unbearable accuracy," a "precision" that has both "impact and exactitude, as with surgery," she declared.[6]

Her precision is combined with an emotional intensity and compressed drama that reveal Biblical prose and poetry to be one of the governing models for her verse. Precision, she wrote, derives from "diction that is virile because galvanized against inertia," and her stanza forms and versification are designed to achieve this galvanizing effect. She considered the stanza, not the line, to be the unit of poetry. Once words, "clustering like chromosomes," had shaped a stanza, she adjusted it and made subsequent stanzas conform to the first.[7] The results in such elaborately structured poems as *The Fish* or *Virginia Britannia* are numerous. The corresponding lines in all stanzas have the exact same number of syllables; rhymes occur in a strictly regular though unique sequence, even when they depend on unaccented syllables and words broken at the hyphen; concealed or interior and approximate rhymes contribute to a texture that is precise in tactile and auditory as well as visual detail, and also unbroken in the continuity of its syntax. Her poems become at once descriptive and meditative, analytic and emotional. The form provides an instrument for guiding and compressing emotion with exceptional control, and for focusing attention and shifting the focus of attention as the experience dramatized approaches its climax or the meditation on experience proceeds toward its conclusion. As she wrote in *The Past Is Present*, one of her many works which reflect on the nature of poetry, a necessary "expediency determines the form" but "Ecstasy affords the occasion."

Moore attained the height of her powers in *The Pangolin and other Verse* (1936) and in *What Are Years?* (1941) and *Nevertheless* (1944), which include poems written in disturbed response to World War II. She continued to write poems about animals which were none the less accurate in descriptive detail for being wide-ranging reflections on human experience, but the emotional depth and the scale of her meditations became more extensive, and her tone more elegiac. Her treatment of central themes—the search for freedom within restraint or the validity of familial love—becomes more troubled in such poems as *Bird-Witted* and *The Paper Nautilus*. Her most ambitious war poem, *In Distrust of Merits*, attempts to encompass the horrors of World War II and to find that the sacrifice of lives has been redeemed by a humane vision of racial tolerance and amity, but it confesses that the redemptive transformation has not yet been achieved.

Her most ambitious undertaking in later years was her translation of *The Fables of La Fontaine* (1954), but her original verse after 1956 became more perfunctory. *Hometown Piece for Messrs. Alston and Reese* had particular appeal for Brooklyn Dodger and other baseball fans (a fan herself, she once tossed in the ball to open the official season), and her topical poems frequently reflected the public life with which she became more involved after receiving the Bollingen, National Book, and Pulitzer awards for *Collected Poems* in 1951. One poem of 1963 was commissioned by the

Steuben Glass Corporation, and in 1955 she advised the Ford Motor Company, in a long, hilarious, and futile series of letters published in *The New Yorker*, on the name for a new car eventually named (by the company) for Edsel Ford. (Among countless suggestions Moore proposed "Utopian Turtletop" and "astranaut" [sic].) Although she disapproved of the explicit sexual elements in some postwar poetry, she appreciated the work of many younger poets.[8]

Her own place in the history of American poetry was well defined by the poet Randall Jarrell, who insisted in 1953 that she had "discovered both a new sort of subject (a queer many-headed one) and a new sort of connection and structure for it, so that she has widened the scope of poetry. * * *9

Except where indicated otherwise, selections are from *The Complete Poems of Marianne Moore* (1967).

The Past Is the Present[1]

If external action is effete
  and rhyme is outmoded,
    I shall revert to you,
Habakkuk,[2] as on a recent occasion I was goaded
      into doing by XY, who was speaking of unrhymed verse. 5
This man said—I think that I repeat
  his identical words:
    'Hebrew poetry is
prose with a sort of heightened consciousness.'[3] Ecstasy affords
    the occasion and expediency determines the form.   10

                    1915, 1924

To a Snail

If "compression is the first grace of style,"[4]
you have it. Contractility is a virtue
as modesty is a virtue.
It is not the acquisition of any one thing
that is able to adorn,   5
or the incidental quality that occurs
as a concomitant of something well said,
that we value in style,
but the principle that is hid:
in the absence of feet, "a method of conclusions";   10
"a knowledge of principles,"
in the curious phenomenon of your occipital horn.

                    1924

New York[1]

the savage's romance,
accreted where we need the space for commerce—

8. "The Way Our Poets Have Taken Since the War," *Marianne Moore Reader*, pp. 237–43.
9. *Poetry and the Age*, pp. 172–73.
1. Text and format are those of *Selected Poems* (1935).
2. A minor prophet, author of the Book of Habakkuk in the Old Testament.
3. "Dr. E. H. Kellogg in Bible class, Presbyterian Church, Carlisle, Pennsylvania" [Moore's note].
4. " 'The very first grace of style is that which comes from compression.' *Demetrius on Style* translated by W. Hamilton Fyfe. Heinemann, 1932" [Moore's note].
1. Text and format are those of *Selected Poems* (1935).

the centre of the wholesale fur trade,[2]
starred with tepees of ermine and peopled with foxes,
the long guard-hairs waving two inches beyond the body of   5
    the pelt;
the ground dotted with deer-skins—white with white spots,
'as satin needlework in a single colour may carry a varied
    pattern',[3]
and wilting eagle's-down compacted by the wind;   10
and picardels[4] of beaver-skin; white ones alert with snow.
It is a far cry from the 'queen full of jewels'
and the beau with the muff,
from the gilt coach shaped like a perfume-bottle,
to the conjunction of the Monongahela and the Allegheny,[5]   15
and the scholastic philosophy of the wilderness
to combat which one must stand outside and laugh
since to go in is to be lost.
It is not the dime-novel exterior,
Niagara Falls, the calico horses and the war-canoe;   20
it is not that 'if the fur is not finer than such as one sees others
    wear,
one would rather be without it'—[6]
that estimated in raw meat and berries, we could feed the
    universe;   25
it is not the atmosphere of ingenuity,
the otter, the beaver, the puma skins
without shooting-irons or dogs;
it is not the plunder,
but 'accessibility to experience'.[7]   30

1921, 1924

The Labours of Hercules,[1]

To popularize the mule, its neat exterior
expressing the principle of accommodation reduced to a minimum:
to persuade one of austere taste, proud in the possession of home
    and a musician—
that the piano is a free field for etching; that his 'charming tadpole
    notes'[2]

2. "In 1921 New York succeeded St. Louis as the centre of the wholesale fur trade" [Moore's note].
3. Miss Moore's note quotes from the *Literary Digest* (March 30, 1918), quoting from George Shiras in *Forest and Stream* (March, 1918), who reported on the capture of a newly born albino fawn: "During the earlier months this fawn had the usual row of white spots on back and sides, and although there was no difference between these and the body colour, they were conspicuous in the same way that satin needlework in a single colour may carry a varied pattern. * * * "
4. Collars or parts of garments made in the Renaissance by sewing together separate pieces or strips of material.

5. The Monongahela and Allegheny rivers join at Pittsburgh, Pennsylvania.
6. "Frank Alvah Parsons—*The Psychology of Dress* (Doubleday)—quotes Isabella, Duchess of Gonzago: 'I wish black cloth even if it cost ten ducats a yard. If it is only as good as that which I see other people wear, I had rather be without it' " [Moore's note].
7. "Henry James" [Moore's note].
1. In Greek and Roman mythology Hercules was a man of prodigious physical strength who was required to perform 12 seemingly impossible feats to absolve himself of the crime of killing his own family. The text and format are those of *Selected Poems* (1935).
2. " 'Charming tadpole notes.' *The London Spectator*" [Moore's note].

belong to the past when one had time to play them: 5
to persuade those self-wrought Midases[3] of brains
whose fourteen carat ignorance aspires to rise in value
till the sky is the limit,
that excessive conduct augurs disappointment,
that one must not borrow a long white beard and tie it on   10
and threaten with the scythe of time the casually curious:
to teach the bard with too elastic a selectiveness
that one detects creative power by its capacity to conquer one's
    detachment;
that while it may have more elasticity than logic,
it knows where it is going;   15
it flies along in a straight line like electricity,
depopulating areas that boast of their remoteness,
to prove to the high priests of caste
that snobbishness is a stupidity,
the best side out, of age-old toadyism,   20
kissing the feet of the man above,
kicking the face of the man below;
to teach the patron-saints-to-atheists, the Coliseum[4]
meet-me-alone-by-moonlight maudlin troubadour
that kickups for catstrings[5] are not life   25
nor yet appropriate to death—that we are sick of the earth,
sick of the pig-sty, wild geese and wild men;
to convince snake-charming controversialists
that it is one thing to change one's mind,
another to eradicate it—that one keeps on knowing   30
'that the Negro is not brutal,
that the Jew is not greedy,
that the Oriental is not immoral,
that the German is not a Hun.'[6]

                                         1924

A Grave[1]

Man looking into the sea,
taking the view from those who have as much right to it as you
    have to it yourself,
it is human nature to stand in the middle of a thing,
but you cannot stand in the middle of this;   5
the sea has nothing to give but a well excavated grave.
The firs stand in a procession, each with an emerald turkey-foot
    at the top,
reserved as their contours, saying nothing;
repression, however, is not the most obvious characteristic of   10
    the sea;

3. Midas, Phrygian King endowed by the god Dionysus with the power to turn anything he touched into gold; hence any fabulously wealthy person.
4. Amphitheater in Rome whose ruins are a popular spot for amatory rendezvous.

5. Flourishes on a lute, banjo, or stringed instrument.
6. Miss Moore's note attributes the quotation to "Reverend J. W. Darr, in a sermon."
1. Text and format are those of *Selected Poems* (1935).

the sea is a collector, quick to return a rapacious look.
There are others besides you who have worn that look—
whose expression is no longer a protest; the fish no longer
    investigate them   15
for their bones have not lasted:
men lower nets, unconscious of the fact that they are
    desecrating a grave,
and row quickly away—the blades of the oars
moving together like the feet of water-spiders as if there were   20
    no such thing as death.
The wrinkles progress upon themselves in a phalanx—beautiful
    under networks of foam,
and fade breathlessly while the sea rustles in and out of the
    seaweed;   25
the birds swim through the air at top speed, emitting cat-calls
    as heretofore—
the tortoise-shell scourges about the feet of the cliffs, in motion
    beneath them;
and the ocean, under the pulsation of lighthouses and noise of   30
    bell-buoys,
advances as usual, looking as if it were not that ocean in which
    dropped things are bound to sink—
in which if they turn and twist, it is neither with volition nor
    consciousness.   35

    1924

Poetry[1]

I, too, dislike it: there are things that are important beyond all
    this fiddle.
    Reading it, however, with a perfect contempt for it, one
        discovers in
it after all, a place for the genuine.   5
        Hands that can grasp, eyes
        that can dilate, hair that can rise
        if it must, these things are important not because a

high-sounding interpretation can be put upon them but because
    they are   10
useful. When they become so derivative as to become
    unintelligible,
    the same thing may be said for all of us, that we
        do not admire what
        we cannot understand: the bat   15
        holding on upside down or in quest of something to

eat, elephants pushing, a wild horse taking a roll, a tireless wolf
    under

1. First written in 1921 and published in *Poems* (1921) and in *Observations* (1924), this poem was frequently revised. In her *Complete Poems* (1967) Moore reduced it to its first two sentences but printed the longer version in her notes. The version printed here follows the text and format of *Selected Poems* (1935).

a tree, the immovable critic twitching his skin like a horse
    that feels a flea, the base-   20
ball fan, the statistician—
    nor is it valid
        to discriminate against 'business documents and

school-books';[2] all these phenomena are important. One must
    make a distinction   25
however: when dragged into prominence by half poets, the
    result is not poetry,
nor till the poets among us can be
    'literalists of
    the imagination'—[3]above   30
        insolence and triviality and can present

for inspection, imaginary gardens with real toads in them, shall
    we have
it. In the meantime, if you demand on the one hand,
the raw material of poetry in   35
    all its rawness and
    that which is on the other hand
        genuine, then you are interested in poetry.

                                      1921, 1935

Peter[1]

Strong and slippery, built for the midnight grass-party con-
    fronted by four cats,
he sleeps his time away—the detached first claw on the
    foreleg, which corresponds
to the thumb, retracted to its tip; the small tuft of fronds   5
    or katydid legs above each eye, still numbering the units in
    each group;
        the shadbones regularly set about the mouth, to droop
        or rise

2. "Diary of Tolstoy (Dutton), p. 84. 'Where the boundary between prose and poetry lies, I shall never be able to understand. The question is raised in manuals of style, yet the answer to it lies beyond me. Poetry is verse; prose is not verse. Or else poetry is everything with the exception of business documents and school books' " [Moore's note].
3. "Yeats: *Ideas of Good and Evil* (A. H. Bullen), p. 182. 'The limitation of his view was from the very intensity of his vision; he was a too literal realist of imagination, as others are of nature; and because he believed that the figures seen by the mind's eye, when exalted by inspiration, were "eternal existences," symbols of divine essences, he hated every grace of style that might obscure their lineaments' " [Moore's note].
1. This poem presents a woman's meditation on the masculine character, and a Protestant's meditation on Catholicism.

The cat's name "Peter" draws attention to his masculine gender and to religious issues that surface in the poem. Simon Peter, Christ's apostle and author of the First and Second Epistles, denied Christ three times to protect himself (Luke 23.56–62) but later as Bishop held the cathedral chair at Rome and founded the Roman Catholic Church, which requires celibacy of its priests and does not admit women to the priesthood. Miss Moore wryly drew attention to the issues of both personal and religious devotion in her note to the title: "Cat owned by Miss Magdalen Heuber and Miss Maria Weniger." The Virgin Mary and Mary Magdalen (one married, one not) were two women whose devotion to Christ, unlike Peter's, was unwavering. The poem first appeared in *Observations* (1929). The text and format printed here are those of *Selected Poems* (1935).

in unison like the porcupine's quills—motionless. He lets　10
　　himself be flat-
tened out by gravity, as it were a piece of seaweed tamed and
　　weakened by
exposure to the sun; compelled when extended, to lie
　　stationary. Sleep is the result of his delusion that one　15
　　must do as
　　well as one can for oneself; sleep—epitome of what is to

him as to the average person, the end of life. Demonstrate on
　　him how
the lady caught the dangerous southern snake,[2] placing a　20
　　forked stick on either
side of its innocuous neck; one need not try to stir
　　him up; his prune-shaped head and alligator eyes are not a
　　party to the
　　joke. Lifted and handled, he may be dangled like an eel　25
　　or set

up on the forearm like a mouse; his eyes bisected by pupils of a
　　pin's
width, are flickeringly exhibited, then covered up. May be?
　　I should say　30
might have been; when he has been got the better of in a
　　dream—as in a fight with nature or with cats— we all know
　　it. Profound sleep is
　　not with him a fixed illusion. Springing about with
　　froglike ac-　35

curacy, emitting jerky cries when taken in the hand, he is
　　himself
again; to sit caged by the rungs of a domestic chair would be
　　unprofit-
able—human. What is the good of hypocrisy? It　40
　　is permissible to choose one's employment, to abandon the
　　wire nail, the
　　roly-poly, when it shows signs of being no longer a
　　pleas-

ure, to score the adjacent magazine with a double line of
　　strokes.　45
　　　　He can
talk, but insolently says nothing. What of it? When one is
　　frank, one's very
presence is a compliment. It is clear that he can see
　　the virtue of naturalness, that he is one of those who do not
　　regard　50
　　the published fact as a surrender. As for the disposition

---

2. In Christian iconography, the Virgin Mary stamps out evil in the form of a snake.

invariably to affront, an animal with claws wants to have to use
  them; that eel-like extension of trunk into tail is not an
    accident. To   55
leap, to lengthen out, divide the air—to purloin, to pursue.
  To tell the hen: fly over the fence, go in the wrong way in
    your perturba-
      tion—this is life; to do less would be nothing but
      dishonesty.   60

c. 1921   1924, 1935

To Statecraft Embalmed

There is nothing to be said for you. Guard
your secret. Conceal it under your hard
  plumage, necromancer.
      O
bird,[1] whose tents were "awnings of Egyptian   5
yarn," shall Justice' faint zigzag inscription—
  leaning like a dancer—
    show
the pulse of its once vivid sovereignty?
You say not, and transmigrating from the   10
  sarcophagus, you wind
    snow
silence round us and with moribund talk,
half limping and half-ladyfied, you stalk
  about. Ibis, we find   15
    no
virtue in you—alive and yet so dumb.
Discreet behavior is not now the sum
  of statesmanlike good sense.
    Though   20
it were the incarnation of dead grace?
As if a death mask ever could replace
  life's faulty excellence!
    Slow
to remark the steep, too strict proportion   25
of your throne, you'll see the wrenched distortion
  of suicidal dreams
    go
staggering toward itself and with its bill
attack its own identity, until   30
  foe seems friend and friend seems
    foe.

                            1915, 1924

1. The ibis, a bird sacred in Egyptian mythology to the god Thoth, magician, inventor of numbers, creator through words, and the gods' scribe who recorded the merits of each soul when its heart was weighed in the scales. In the Egyptian Books of the Dead (illustrated papyrus books, buried with the dead, containing hymns and regulations for dead souls) he is portrayed with the head of an ibis.

The Fish

wade
through black jade.
   Of the crow-blue mussel shells, one keeps
   adjusting the ash heaps;
      opening and shutting itself like   5

an
injured fan.
   The barnacles which encrust the side
   of the wave, cannot hide
      there for the submerged shafts of the   10

sun,
split like spun
   glass, move themselves with spotlight swiftness
   into the crevices—
      in and out, illuminating   15

the
turquoise sea
   of bodies. The water drives a wedge
   of iron through the iron edge
      of the cliff; whereupon the stars,   20

pink
rice-grains, ink-
   bespattered jellyfish, crabs like green
   lilies, and submarine
      toadstools, slide each on the other.   25

All
external
   marks of abuse are present on this
   defiant edifice—
      all the physical features of   30

ac-
cident—lack
   of cornice, dynamite grooves, burns, and
   hatchet strokes, these things stand
      out on it; the chasm side is   35

dead.
Repeated
   evidence has proved that it can live
   on what can not revive
      its youth. The sea grows old in it.   40

1918, 1924

Sojourn in the Whale[1]

Trying to open locked doors with a sword, threading
    the points of needles, planting shade trees
    upside down; swallowed by the opaqueness of one whom
       the seas
love better than they love you, Ireland—   5

you have lived and lived on every kind of shortage.
    You have been compelled by hags to spin
    gold thread from straw and have heard men say: 'There is a
       feminine
temperament in direct contrast to   10

ours which makes her do these things. Circumscribed by a
    heritage of blindness and native
    incompetence, she will become wise and will be forced to
       give
in. Compelled by experience, she   15

will turn back; water seeks its own level:' and you
    have smiled. 'Water in motion is far
    from level.'[2] You have seen it, when obstacles happened to bar
the path, rise automatically.

                        1917, 1924

What Are Years?

    What is our innocence,
what is our guilt? All are
    naked, none is safe. And whence
is courage: the unanswered question,
the resolute doubt—   5
dumbly calling, deafly listening—that
in misfortune, even death,
    encourages others
    and in its defeat, stirs

    the soul to be strong? He   10
sees deep and is glad, who
    accedes to mortality
and in his imprisonment rises
upon himself as
the sea in a chasm, struggling to be   15
free and unable to be,
    in its surrendering
    finds its continuing.

1. An allusion to the Biblical story of Jonah, the prophet, who was swallowed by a whale as punishment for disobedience but then released after praying to Jehovah for help (Jonah 1–2). Text and format are those of *Selected Poems* (1935).
2. *"Literary Digest"* [Moore's note].

So he who strongly feels,
behaves. The very bird,   20
  grown taller as he sings, steels
his form straight up. Though he is captive,
his mighty singing
says, satisfaction is a lowly
  thing, how pure a thing is joy.   25
    This is mortality,
      this is eternity.

                                              1941

He 'Digesteth Harde Yron'[1]

Although the aepyornis
or roc[2] that lived in Madagascar, and
the moa are extinct,
the camel-sparrow, linked
  with them in size—the large sparrow   5
Xenophon saw walking by a stream[3]—was and is
a symbol of justice.[4]

This bird watches his chicks with
a maternal concentration—and he's
been mothering the eggs   10
at night six weeks—his legs
  their only weapon of defence.
He is swifter than a horse; he has a foot hard
as a hoof; the leopard

is not more suspicious. How   15
could he, prized for plumes and eggs and young, used
even as a riding-
beast, respect men hiding
  actor-like in ostrich-skins, with
the right hand making the neck move as if alive and   20
from a bag the left hand

strewing grain, that ostriches
might be decoyed and killed! Yes this is he
whose plume was anciently

---

1. The title is drawn from the statement that "The estrich [ostrich] digesteth harde yron to preserve his health" in the romance *Euphues* (1578) by the English author John Lyly (c. 1554–1606).
2. "Roc": large mythological Arabian bird; "moa": flightless ostrichlike New Zealand bird; "camel-sparrow": ostrich.
3. " 'Xenophon (*Anabasis*, I, 5, 2) reports many ostriches in the desert on the left . . . side of the middle Euphrates, on the way from North Syria to Babylonia.' George Jennison, *Animals for Show and Pleasure in Ancient Rome*" [Moore's note]. The *Anabasis* is an account of a Persian military expedition by the Athenian historian Xenophon (c. 430–c. 355 B.C.).
4. For the allusions to justice, men hiding in ostrich skins, and Leda's egg in lines 7, 17–18, and 31, Miss Moore's note cites "Berthold Laufer, 'Ostrich Egg-shell Cups from Mesopotamia,' *The Open Court*, May, 1926. 'An ostrich plume symbolized truth and justice, and was the emblem of the goddess Ma-at, the patron saint of judges. Her head is adorned with an ostrich feather, her eyes are closed . . . as Justice is blindfolded.' "

the plume of justice; he   25
    whose comic duckling head on its
great neck revolves with compass-needle nervousness
when he stands guard, in S-

    like foragings as he is
    preening the down on his leaden-skinned back.   30
The egg piously shown
as Leda's very own
    from which Castor and Pollux hatched,[5]
was an ostrich-egg. And what could have been more fit
for the Chinese lawn it   35

    grazed on as a gift to an
    emperor who admired strange birds, than this
one who builds his mud-made
nest in dust yet will wade
    in lake or sea till only the head shows.   40

            .   .   .   .   .   .

    Six hundred ostrich-brains served
    at one banquet,[6] the ostrich-plume-tipped tent
and desert spear, jewel-
gorgeous ugly egg-shell
    goblets,[7] eight pairs of ostriches   45
in harness,[8] dramatize a meaning always missed
by the externalist.

    The power of the visible
    is the invisible; as even where
no tree of freedom grows,   50
so-called brute courage knows.
    Heroism is exhausting, yet
it contradicts a greed that did not wisely spare
the harmless solitaire

    or great auk[9] in its grandeur;   55
    unsolicitude having swallowed up
all giant birds but an
alert gargantuan
    little-winged, magnificently speedy running-bird. This
    one   60
remaining rebel
is the sparrow-camel.

                                                              1941

5. In Greek mythology, the god Zeus in the guise of a swan fathered Castor, Pollux, and Helen of Troy on the Spartan Queen Leda.
6. "At a banquet given by Elagabalus . . . *Animals for Show and Pleasure in Ancient Rome*" [Moore's note].
7. "E.g., the painted ostrich-egg cup mounted in silver gilt by Elias Geier of Leipzig about 1589. Edward Wenham, 'Antiques in and about London,' *New York Sun*, May 22, 1937" [Moore's note].
8. "*Animals for Show and Pleasure in Ancient Rome*" [Moore's note].
9. Extinct flightless bird; the solitaire is an extinct flightless bird related to the dodo.

The Student[1]

"In America," began
the lecturer, "everyone must have a
degree. The French do not think that
all can have it, they don't say everyone
　　must go to college."[2] We　　　　　　　　　　5
incline to feel
　　that although it may be unnecessary

to know fifteen languages,
one degree is not too much. With us, a
school—like the singing tree of which　　　　　10
the leaves were mouths singing in concert[3]
　　is both a tree of knowledge
and of liberty—
　　seen in the unanimity of college

mottoes, *Lux et veritas*,　　　　　　　　　　15
*Christo et ecclesiae, Sapient
felici.*[4] It may be that we
have not knowledge, just opinions, that we
　　are undergraduates,
not students; we know　　　　　　　　　　　　20
　　we have been told with smiles, by expatriates

of whom we had asked "When will
your experiment be finished?" "Science
is never finished."[5] Secluded
from domestic strife, Jack Bookworm led a　　25
　　college life, says Goldsmith;[6]
and here also as
　　in France or Oxford, study is beset with

dangers—with bookworms, mildews,
and complaisancies. But someone in New　　　30
England has known enough to say
the student is patience personified,
　　is a variety

1. This poem first appeared in 1932 as the second in a three-part work entitled *Part of a Novel, Part of a Poem, Part of a Play*. Omitted from some later volumes, it was included as a separate poem in *What Are Years?* (1941) and, considerably revised, in *Complete Poems* (1967), the text reprinted here.
2. " '*Les Idéals de l'Education Française*,' lecture, December 3, 1931, by M. Auguste Desclos, Director-adjoint, Office National des Universités et Ecoles Françaises de Paris" [Moore's note].
3. " 'Each leaf was a mouth, and every leaf joined in concert.' *Arabian Nights*" [Moore's note].
4. "Light and Truth," "For Christ and the Church," "Fortunate Are the Learned." The first is the motto of Yale University; the second appeared on Harvard's seal from 1693 to 1935.
5. "Albert Einstein to an American student, *New York Times*" [Moore's note].
6. Moore's note refers readers to the character in *The Doubled Transformation* by the British writer Oliver Goldsmith (c. 1730–74).

of hero, "patient
of neglect and of reproach"—who can "hold by   35

himself."[7] You can't beat hens to
make them lay. Wolf's wool is the best of wool,
but it cannot be sheared because
the wolf will not comply.[8] With knowledge as
    with the wolf's surliness,   40
the student studies
    voluntarily, refusing to be less

than individual. He
"gives his opinion and then rests on it";[9]
he renders service when there is   45
no reward, and is too reclusive for
    some things to seem to touch
him, not because he
    has no feeling but because he has so much.

                                    1932, 1941

Bird-Witted[1]

With innocent wide penguin eyes, three
    large fledgling mockingbirds below
the pussy-willow tree,
    stand in a row,
wings touching, feebly solemn,   5
till they see
        their no longer larger
        mother bringing
something which will partially
feed one of them.   10

Toward the high-keyed intermittent squeak
    of broken carriage springs, made by
the three similar, meek-
    coated bird's-eye

<hr/>

7. "Emerson in *The American Scholar*: 'There can be no scholar without the heroic mind'; 'Let him hold by himself; . . . patient of neglect, patient of reproach" [Moore's note].
8. "Edmund Burke, November, 1781, in reply to Fox: 'There is excellent wool on the back of a wolf and therefore he must be sheared. . . . But will he comply?'" [Moore's note].
9. Moore's note quotes from the art critic Henry McBride, speaking of the appraisal of art works in the "*New York Sun*, December 12, 1931: 'Dr. Valentiner . . . has the typical reserve of the student. He does not enjoy the active battle of opinion that invariably rages when a decision is announced that can be weighed in great sums of money. He gives his opinion firmly and rests upon that.' "
1. Moore's note quotes the statement "If a boy be bird-witted" from *The Advancement of Learning* (1605), Book II, by Sir Francis Bacon (1561–1626), the English jurist, philosopher, and essayist. The poem, one of four originally published under the covering title of "Old Dominion" in *The Pangolin and Other Verse* (1936), was published separately in subsequent editions.

freckled forms she comes; and when   15
from the beak
    of one, the still living
    beetle has dropped
out, she picks it up and puts
it in again.   20

Standing in the shade till they have dressed
  their thickly filamented, pale
pussy-willow-surfaced
  coats, they spread tail
and wings, showing one by one,   25
the modest
    white stripe lengthwise on the
    tail and crosswise
underneath the wing, and the
accordion   30

is closed again. What delightful note
  with rapid unexpected flute
sounds leaping from the throat
  of the astute
grown bird, comes back to one from   35
the remote
    unenergetic sun-
    lit air before
the brood was here? How harsh
the bird's voice has become.   40

A piebald cat observing them,
  is slowly creeping toward the trim
trio on the tree stem.
  Unused to him
the three make room—uneasy   45
new problem.
    A dangling foot that missed
    its grasp, is raised
and finds the twig on which it
planned to perch. The   50

parent darting down, nerved by what chills
  the blood, and by hope rewarded—
of toil—since nothing fills
  squeaking unfed
mouths, wages deadly combat,   55
and half kills
    with bayonet beak and
    cruel wings, the
intellectual cautious-
ly creeping cat.   60

1936, 1941

Virginia Britannia[1]

Pale sand edges England's Old
Dominion. The air is soft, warm, hot
above the cedar-dotted emerald shore
    known to the redbird, the red-coated musketeer,
    the trumpet flower, the cavalier,   5
    the parson, and the wild parishioner. A deer-
track in a church-floor
    brick, and a fine pavement tomb with engraved top, remain.
The now tremendous vine-encompassed hackberry
    starred with the ivy flower,   10
        shades the church tower;
And a great sinner lyeth here under the sycamore.[2]

A fritillary[3] zigzags
    toward the chancel-shaded resting-place
of this unusual man and sinner who   15
    waits for a joyful resurrection. We-re-wo
co-mo-co's[4] fur crown could be no
    odder than we were, with ostrich, Latin motto,
and small gold horseshoe:[5]
    arms for an able sting-ray-hampered pioneer—   20
    painted as a Turk, it seems —continuously
        exciting Captain Smith
who, patient with
his inferiors, was a pugnacious equal, and to

Powhatan as unflattering   25

1. First published in *The Pangolin* (1936) as one of four poems under the covering title of "Old Dominion" (a familiar term for the state of Virginia), this poem is an elegiac meditation in the tradition of William Wordsworth's *Ode on the Intimations of Immortality.* It probes American colonial history to define the intersection of a derivative culture imported by the settlers with the more profusely luxuriant and vital civilization of the native Indians. It juxtaposes the odd decorum of an English lady against the oddity of an Indian princess, the injustice and aggressiveness of the emergent American civilization against the suppression of Indians and Negroes, the encroachment of enfeeblement and death against the resurgence of life in the song of a humble hedge sparrow which the poem celebrates at the conclusion.

Moore's note to the title refers readers generally to the *Historie of Travaile into Virginia Britannia* (1618) by William Strachey (fl. 1606–18), first Secretary of Virginia and resident in the colony at Jamestown from 1610 to 1611.

2. "Inscription in Jamestown churchyard: 'Here lyeth the body of Robert Sherwood who was born in the Parish of Whitechapel near London, a great sinner who waits for a joyful resurrection' " [Moore's note].

3. Small butterfly.

4. The capital of the Indian Powatan (d. 1618). "Of the Indians of a confederacy of about thirty tribes of Algonquins occupying Tidewater Virginia, Powatan was war chief or head werowance. He presented a deer-skin mantle—now in the Ashmolean [Museum in Oxford, England] to Captain Newport when crowned by him and Captain John Smith" [Moore's note]. Christopher Newport (d. 1617) captained the early voyages to Virginia. The adventurer Smith (1580–1631) campaigned against the Turks before his arrival in Virginia, his capture by Powatan, and his rescue by the Indian princess Pocahontas. He later served as Governor of the colony, helped explore New England, and published the *Generall Historie of Virginia* (1624) among other writings.

5. Moore's note: "As crest in Captain John Smith's coat of arms, the ostrich with a horseshoe in its beak—i.e. invincible digestion—reiterates the motto, *Vincre est vivere* [To conquer is to live]."

as grateful. Rare Indian, crowned by
Christopher Newport! The Old Dominion has
　　all-green box-sculptured grounds.
　　An almost English green surrounds
　　　them. Care has formed among un-English insect sounds,　30
the white wall-rose. As
　　thick as Daniel Boone's grapevine, the stem has wide spaced

　　　　　　　　　　　　　　　　　　　　　　　　　great
　　blunt alternating ostrich-skin warts that were thorns.
　　　Care has formed walls of yew　　　　　　　　　　35
　　　since Indians knew
the Fort Old Field and narrow tongue of land that Jamestown

　　　　　　　　　　　　　　　　　　　　　　　　　was.

　　Observe the terse Virginian,
　　the mettlesome gray one the drives the　　　　　　40
owl from tree to tree and imitates the call
　　　of whippoorwill or lark or katydid—the lead-
　　　gray lead-legged mockingbird with head
　　　held half away, and meditative eye as dead
as sculptured marble　　　　　　　　　　　　　45
　　　eye, alighting noiseless, musing in the semi-sun,
　　　　standing on tall thin legs as if he did not see,
　　　　　conspicuous, alone,
　　　　　on the stone-
topped table with lead cupids grouped to form the pedestal.　50

　　Narrow herringbone-laid bricks
　　a dusty pink beside the dwarf box-
bordered pansies, share the ivy-arbor shade
　　　with cemetery lace settees, one at each side,
　　　and with the bird: box-bordered tide-　　　　55
　　　water gigantic jet black pansies—splendor; pride—
not for a decade
　　　dressed, but for a day, in overpowering velvet; and
　　　gray-blue-Andalusian-cock-feather pale ones,[6]
　　　　ink-lined on the edge, fur-　　　　　　60
　　　　eyed, with ochre
on the cheek. The at first slow, saddle-horse quick cavalcade

　　of buckeye-burnished jumpers
　　and five-gaited mounts, the work-mule and
show-mule and witch-cross door and "strong sweet prison"[7]　65
　　　are a part of what has come about—in the Black
　　　idiom—from "advancin' back-
　　　wards in a circle"; from taking the Potomac
cowbird-like, and on
　　　the Chickahominy[8] establishing the Negro,　　70

---

6. Breed of chickens raised in Andalusia,　burg" [Moore's note].
a region in Spain.　　　　　　　　　8. River flowing near Jamestown.
7. "Of Middle Plantation, now Williams-

inadvertent ally and best enemy of tyranny. Rare
    unscent-
      ed, provident-
ly hot, too sweet, inconsistent flower bed! Old Dominion

flowers are curious. Some wilt   75
in daytime and some close at night. Some
have perfume; some have not. The scarlet much-quilled
    fruiting pomegranate, the African violet,
    fuchsia and camellia, none; yet
    the house-high glistening green magnolia's velvet-   80
textured flower is filled
    with anesthetic scent as inconsiderate as
    the gardenia's. Even the gardenia sprig's
      dark vein on greener
      leaf when seen   85
against the light, has not near it more small bees than the
                               frilled

silk substanceless faint flower of
the crape myrtle has. Odd Pamunkey[9]
princess, birdclaw-ear-ringed; with a pet raccoon   90
    from the Mattaponi[1] (what a bear!). Feminine
    odd Indian young lady! Odd thin-
    gauze-and-taffeta-dressed English one! Terrapin
meat and crested spoon
    feed the mistress of French plum-and-turquoise-piped
                                chaise-longue;   95
    of brass-knobbed slat front door, and everywhere open
    shaded house on Indian-
    named Virginian
streams in counties named for English lords. The rattlesnake
                               soon   100

said from our once dashingly
undiffident first flag, "Don't tread on
me"—tactless symbol of a new republic.
    Priorities were cradled in this region not
    noted for humility; spot   105
    that has high-singing frogs, cotton-mouth snakes and cot-
ton fields; a unique
    Lawrence pottery with loping wolf design; and too
    unvenomous terrapin in tepid greenness,
      idling near the sea-top;   110
      tobacco-crop
records on church walls; a Devil's Woodyard; and the one-brick-

thick serpentine wall built by
Jefferson.[2] Like strangler figs choking

---

9. Principal tribe in Powatan's Confederacy.
1. River in Virginia.

2. "The one-brick-thick wall designed by
Jefferson on the grounds of the University of Virginia" [Moore's note].

a banyan, not an explorer, no imperialist,   115
  not one of us, in taking what we
    pleased—in colonizing as the
      saying is—has been a synonym for mercy.
The redskin with the deer-
  fur crown,[3] famous for his cruelty, is not all brawn   120
  and animality. The outdoor tea-table,
    the mandolin-shaped big
      and little fig,
the silkworm-mulberry, the French mull dress with the Madeira-

vine-accompanied edge are,   125
  when compared with what the colonists
found here in tidewater Virginia, stark
    luxuries. The mere brown hedge sparrow, with reckless
      ardor, unable to suppress
        his satisfaction in man's trustworthy nearness,   130
even in the dark
  flutes his ecstatic burst of joy—the caraway seed-
spotted sparrow perched in the dew-drenched juniper
    beside the window ledge;
      this little hedge-   135
sparrow that wakes up seven minutes sooner than the lark.[4]

The live oak's darkening filigree
  of undulating boughs, the etched
solidity of a cypress indivisible
    from the now agèd English hackberry,
      become with lost identity,   140
        part of the ground, as sunset flames increasingly
against the leaf-chiselled
  blackening ridge of green; while clouds, expanding above
  the town's assertiveness, dwarf it, dwarf arrogance   145
    that can misunderstand
    importance; and
are to the child an intimation of what glory is.[5]

                  1936, 1941

The Paper Nautilus[1]

For authorities whose hopes
are shaped by mercenaries?
Writers entrapped by

3. "He [Arahatec] gave our Captaine his Crowne which was of Deare's hayre, Dyed redd.' *Travels and Works of Captain John Smith, President of Virginia and Admiral of New England, 1580–1631*; with an Introduction by A. G. Bradley. Arber's Reprints" [Moore's note].
4. "The British Empire Naturalists' Association has found that the hedge sparrow sings seven minutes earlier than the lark" [Moore's note].

5. In his *Ode: Intimations of Immortality from Recollections of Early Childhood* (1807), the English poet William Wordsworth voiced the fear that "the glory and the dream" known in childhood were irrevocably lost, but reaffirmed his faith that the adult, through recollection, can envision the "immortal sea" of his origin.
1. A fish, also named the Argonaut, related to the octopus. The female constructs an extremely fragile shell to serve as an

teatime fame and by
commuters' comforts? Not for these   5
    the paper nautilus
    constructs her thin glass shell.

    Giving her perishable
souvenir of hope, a dull
    white outside and smooth-   10
    edged inner surface
glossy as the sea, the watchful
    maker of it guards it
    day and night; she scarcely

    eats until the eggs are hatched.   15
Buried eightfold in her eight
    arms, for she is in
    a sense a devil-
fish, her glass ram's-horn-cradled freight
    is hid but is not crushed;   20
    as Hercules, bitten

    by a crab loyal to the hydra,[2]
was hindered to succeed,
    the intensively
    watched eggs coming from   25
the shell free it when they are freed—
    leaving its wasp-nest flaws
    of white on white, and close-

    laid Ionic chiton-folds[3]
like the lines in the mane of   30
    a Parthenon horse,[4]
    round which the arms had
wound themselves as if they knew love
    is the only fortress
    strong enough to trust to.   35

                                                                  1941

Nevertheless

    you've seen a strawberry
        that's had a struggle; yet
        was, where the fragments met,

---

egg case, which she carries on the surface
of the water, grasping it with two of her
eight arms which were once thought to
serve as sails.
2. In Greek mythology, the second of
Hercules' 12 labors required him to
subdue the Hydra, a many-headed monster. Attacked by a crab during the or-

deal, he crushed it with his foot.
3. Sleeved linen undergarment worn by
the ancient Greeks, named for the
Greeks in Ionia on the west coast of
Asia Minor.
4. A figure in the frieze of the Parthenon, the temple of Athena in Athens.

a hedgehog or a star-
    fish for the multitude   5
    of seeds. What better food

than apple seeds—the fruit
    within the fruit—locked in
    like counter-curved twin

hazelnuts? Frost that kills   10
    the little rubber-plant-
    leaves of *kok-saghyz*-stalks,[1] can't

harm the roots; they still grow
    in frozen ground. Once where
    there was a prickly-pear-   15

leaf clinging to barbed wire,
    a root shot down to grow
    in earth two feet below;

as carrots form mandrakes[2]
    or a ram's-horn root some-   20
    times. Victory won't come

to me unless I go
    to it; a grape tendril
    ties a knot in knots till

knotted thirty times,—so   25
    the bound twig that's under-
    gone and over-gone, can't stir.

The weak overcomes its
    menace, the strong over-
    comes itself. What is there   30

like fortitude! What sap
    went through that little thread
    to make the cherry red!

                      1944

Elephants[1]

Uplifted and waved till immobilized
wistaria-like, the opposing opposed
mouse-gray twined proboscises' trunk formed by two
trunks, fights itself to a spiraled inter-nosed

1. Russian dandelion.
2. Poisonous plants with a root thought
to resemble human form.
1. "Data used in these stanzas, from a
lecture-file entitled *Ceylon, the Wonder-
ous Isle* by Charles Brooke Elliott. And
Cicero, deploring the sacrifice of elephants in the Roman Games, said they
'aroused both pity and a feeling that the
elephant was somehow allied with man.'
George Jennison, *Animals for Show
and Pleasure in Ancient Rome*, p. 52"
[Moore's note].

deadlock of dyke-enforced massiveness. It's a   5
knock-down drag-out fight that asks no quarter? Just
a pastime, as when the trunk rains on itself
the pool siphoned up; or when—since each must

provide his forty-pound bough dinner—he broke
the leafy branches. These templars of the Tooth,[2]   10
these matched intensities, take master care of
master tools. One, sleeping with the calm of youth,

at full length in the half-dry sun-flecked stream-bed,
rests his hunting-horn-curled trunk on shallowed stone.
The sloping hollow of the sleeper's body   15
cradles the gently breathing eminence's prone

mahout,[3] asleep like a lifeless six-foot
frog, so feather light the elephant's stiff
ear's unconscious of the crossed feet's weight. And the
defenseless human thing sleeps as sound as if   20

incised with hard wrinkles, embossed with wide ears,
invincibly tusked, made safe by magic hairs!
As if, as if, it is all ifs; we are at
much unease. But magic's masterpiece is theirs—

Houdini's serenity quelling his fears.[4]   25
Elephant-ear-witnesses-to-be of hymns
and glorias, these ministrants all gray or
gray with white on legs or trunk, are a pilgrims'

pattern of revery not reverence—a
religious procession without any priests,   30
the centuries-old carefullest unrehearsed
play. Blessed by Buddha's Tooth, the obedient beasts

themselves as toothed temples blessing the street, see
the white elephant carry the cushion that
carries the casket that carries the Tooth.   35
Amenable to what, matched with him, are gnat

trustees, he does not step on them as the white-
canopied blue-cushioned Tooth is augustly
and slowly returned to the shrine. Though white is
the color of worship and of mourning, he   40

is not here to worship and he is too wise
to mourn—a life prisoner but reconciled.

2. Templars are associates or guards of temples. The "Sacred Tooth," presumably a relic of the Buddha, is enshrined in the Buddhist Temple of the Tooth at Kandy, Ceylon.

3. Elephant driver.
4. Erich Weiss ("Harry Houdini"), American magician (1874–1926), famous for daring escapes from confinement.

With trunk tucked up compactly—the elephant's
sign of defeat—he resisted, but is the child

of reason now. His straight trunk seems to say: when   45
what we hoped for came to nothing, we revived.
As loss could not ever alter Socrates'
tranquillity,⁵ equanimity's contrived

by the elephant. With the Socrates of
animals as with Sophocles the Bee,⁶ on whose   50
tombstone a hive was incised, sweetness tinctures
his gravity. His held-up foreleg for use

as a stair, to be climbed or descended with
the aid of his ear, expounds the brotherhood
of creatures to man the encroacher, by the   55
small word with the dot, meaning know—the verb bŭd.

These knowers "arouse the feeling that they are
allied to man" and can change roles with their trustees.
Hardship makes the soldier; then teachableness
makes him the philosopher—as Socrates,   60

prudently testing the suspicious thing, knew
the wisest is he who's not sure that he knows.
Who rides on a tiger can never dismount;
asleep on an elephant, that is repose.

                                                          1944

A Carriage from Sweden

They say there is a sweeter air
        where it was made, than we have here;
        a Hamlet's castle atmosphere.
At all events there is in Brooklyn
something that makes me feel at home.   5

No one may see this put-away
        museum-piece, this country cart
        that inner happiness made art;
and yet, in this city of freckled
integrity it is a vein   10

of resined straightness from north-wind
        hardened Sweden's once-opposed-to-
        compromise archipelago
of rocks. Washington and Gustavus
Adolphus,¹ forgive our decay.   15

---

5. Athenian philosopher (c. 470–399 B.C.).
Condemned to death for corrupting the
state with his questioning philosophy, he
willingly drank the poisonous hemlock.
6. The Greek tragic dramatist (496–406

B.C.).
1. Gustavus Adolphus III, autocratic
King of Sweden from 1771 until his
assassination in 1792, leader of a cultural
renaissance in Sweden.

Seats, dashboard and sides of smooth gourd-
        rind texture, a flowered step, swan-
        dart brake, and swirling crustacean-
tailed equine amphibious creatures
that garnish the axletree! What   20

a fine thing! What unannoying
        romance! And how beautiful, she
        with the natural stoop of the
snowy egret, gray-eyed and straight-haired,
for whom it should come to the door—   25

of whom it reminds me. The split
        pine fair hair, steady gannet-clear
        eyes and the pine-needled-path deer-
swift step; that is Sweden, land of the
free and the soil for a spruce tree—   30

vertical though a seedling—all
        needles: from a green trunk, green shelf
        on shelf fanning out by itself.
The deft white-stockinged dance in thick-soled
shoes! Denmark's sanctuaried Jews![2]   35

The puzzle-jugs and hand-spun rugs,
        the root-legged kracken[3] shaped like dogs,
        the hanging buttons and the frogs
that edge the Sunday jackets! Sweden,
you have a runner called the Deer, who   40

when he's won a race, likes to run
        more; you have the sun-right gable-
        ends due east and west, the table
spread as for a banquet; and the put-
in twin vest-pleats with a fish-fin   45

effect when you need none. Sweden,
        what makes the people dress that way
        and those who see you wish to stay?
The runner, not too tired to run more
at the end of the race? And that   50

cart, dolphin-graceful? A Dalen[4]
        lighthouse, self-lit?—responsive and
        responsible. I understand;
it's not pine-needle-paths that give spring
when they're run on, it's a Sweden   55

---

2. Denmark protected the Jews during
its occupation by Nazi Germany in
World War II.
3. Legendary sea monster, also spelled
"kracken."
4. Nihls Gustaf Dalén (1869–1937),
Swedish physicist and inventor of light-
house improvements.

of moated white castles—the bed
of white flowers densely grown in an S
meaning Sweden and stalwartness,
skill, and a surface that says
Made in Sweden: carts are my trade.   60

                                                    1944

The Mind Is an Enchanting Thing

is an enchanted thing
    like the glaze on a
katydid-wing
        subdivided by sun
            till the nettings are legion.   5
Like Gieseking playing Scarlatti;[1]

like the apteryx-awl
    as a beak, or the
kiwi's rain-shawl[2]
        of haired feathers, the mind   10
            feeling its way as though blind,
walks along with its eyes on the ground.

It has memory's ear
    that can hear without
having to hear.   15
        Like the gyroscope's fall,
            truly unequivocal
because trued by regnant certainty,

it is a power of
    strong enchantment. It   20
is like the dove-
        neck animated by
            sun; it is memory's eye;
it's conscientious inconsistency.

It tears off the veil; tears   25
    the temptation, the
mist the heart wears,
        from its eyes—if the heart
            has a face; it takes apart
dejection. It's fire in the dove-neck's   30

iridescence; in the
    inconsistencies

---

1. Walter Wilhelm Gieseking (1895–
1956), French-born German pianist,
known for his renditions of compositions
by the Italian composer Domenico Scarlatti (1685–1757).

2. Apteryx, a flightless New Zealand
bird, related to the kiwi, with a beak
shaped like an awl, a pointed tool for
punching holes in leather.

of Scarlatti.
    Unconfusion submits
      its confusion to proof; it's   35
not a Herod's oath that cannot change.[3]

                    1944

In Distrust of Merits

Strengthened to live, strengthened to die for
    medals and positioned victories?
They're fighting, fighting, fighting the blind
    man who thinks he sees—
who cannot see that the enslaver is   5
enslaved; the hater, harmed. O shining O
      firm star, O tumultuous
         ocean lashed till small things go
      as they will, the mountainous
        wave makes us who look, know   10

depth. Lost at sea before they fought! O
    star of David, star of Bethlehem,[1]
O black imperial lion
    of the Lord—emblem
of a risen world—be joined at last, be   15
joined. There is hate's crown beneath which all is
      death; there's love's without which none
        is king; the blessed deeds bless
      the halo. As contagion
        of sickness makes sickness,   20

contagion of trust can make trust. They're
    fighting in deserts and caves, one by
one, in battalions and squadrons;
    they're fighting that I
may yet recover from the disease, My   25
Self; some have it lightly; some will die. "Man's
      wolf to man" and we devour
        ourselves. The enemy could not
      have made a greater breach in our
        defenses. One pilot-   30

ing a blind man can escape him, but
    Job disheartened by false comfort[2] knew
that nothing can be so defeating
    as a blind man who
can see. O alive who are dead, who are   35
proud not to see, O small dust of the earth

---

3. Herod Antipas (d. A.D. 39), ruler of Judea under the Romans. He had John the Baptist beheaded in fulfillment of a promise to Salome (Mark 6.22–27).
1. The star of David is a symbol of Judaism, the star of Bethlehem of Christians.
2. When undergoing Jehovah's test of his fidelity, Job cursed the blindness of the friends who tried to comfort him.

that walks so arrogantly,
    trust begets power and faith is
an affectionate thing. We
    vow, we make this promise   40

to the fighting—it's a promise—"We'll
    never hate black, white, red, yellow, Jew,
Gentile, Untouchable."3 We are
    not competent to
make our vows. With set jaw they are fighting,   45
fighting, fighting—some we love whom we know,
    some we love but know not—that
        hearts may feel and not be numb.
    It cures me; or am I what
        I can't believe in? Some   50

in snow, some on crags, some in quicksands,
    little by little, much by much, they
are fighting fighting fighting that where
    there was death there may
be life. "When a man is prey to anger,   55
he is moved by outside things; when he holds
    his ground in patience patience
        patience, that is action or
    beauty," the soldier's defense
        and hardest armor for   60

the fight. The world's an orphans' home. Shall
    we never have peace without sorrow?
without pleas of the dying for
    help that won't come? O
quiet form upon the dust, I cannot   65
look and yet I must. If these great patient
    dyings—all these agonies
        and wound-bearings and bloodshed—
    can teach us how to live, these
        dyings were not wasted.   70

Hate-hardened heart, O heart of iron,
    iron is iron till it is rust.
There never was a war that was
    not inward; I must
fight till I have conquered in myself what   75
causes war, but I would not believe it.
    I inwardly did nothing.
        O Iscariot-like crime!4
    Beauty is everlasting
        and dust is for a time.   80

                 1944

---

3. Member of the lowest hereditary caste in India.   4. Judas Iscariot was the apostle who betrayed Jesus Christ.

Arthur Mitchell[2]

Slim dragonfly
too rapid for the eye
      to cage—
contagious gem of virtuosity—
make visible, mentality.   5
Your jewels of mobility

reveal
      and veil
         a peacock-tail.

                                                            1966

T. S. ELIOT
1888–1965

An expatriate American, Thomas Stearns Eliot, was for over two decades the most influential poet writing in English. Once he settled on a vocation, the brilliance of his verse as well as the persuasiveness of his criticism helped effect a major reorientation of the English literary tradition, secured his supremacy as a man of letters in London, and helped establish modernism as the dominant mode in Anglo-American poetry.

Eliot was raised in St. Louis, Missouri, the son of a successful, cultivated businessman and grandson of a New England Unitarian minister who founded Washington University. Eliot later testified to the good fortune of being born in St. Louis rather than in "Boston, or New York, or London," and to the lasting impress of childhood experience—memories of the Mississippi River, of seaside vacations on Cape Ann in Massachusetts, and of his family's earnest piety, the "Law of Public Service" that familial mores enforced and the respect it inculcated for "symbols of Religion, the Community and Education."[1] These cultural advantages and civic activities—notably his mother's philanthropic endeavors and her writing, including a verse drama about Savonarola which Eliot later published—identify the "Genteel Tradition" which had spread from the East to Midwestern cities during the nineteenth century.

Eliot attended Harvard for both undergraduate and graduate work (1906–10, 1911–14) where he came under the influence of the philosopher George Santayana and the humanist Irving Babbitt, and he began studying philosophy, the poets Donne and Dante, and the Elizabethan and Jacobean dramatists, who figured importantly later in his criticism. He published verse in college periodicals, but his discovery in 1908 of Arthur Symons's *The Symbolist Movement in Literature,* and through it the ironic poetry of Jules LaForgue and other French poets, had an immediate impact

---

2. Leading dancer with the New York City Center Ballet, founder of the Harlem Dance Theater. "Mr. Mitchell danced the role of Puck in Lincoln Kirstein's and George Balanchine's City Center production of *A Midsummer Night's Dream*" [Moore's note].
1. "American Literature and the American Language," *To Criticize the Critic,* 1965, pp. 44–45.

on the verse that he wrote later at Harvard and submitted for professional publication between 1915 and 1917. His graduate work, some of it pursued abroad, began to include social anthropology and to center on languages (notably Sanskrit) and philosophy; Eliot was at Oxford studying Greek philosophy at the outset of World War I, and he completed by 1916 a Harvard doctoral dissertation on the philosophy of F. H. Bradley, though wartime circumstances prevented his returning for the oral examination required for the degree.

The year 1915 marked a turning point in his career from the pursuit of philosophy as a profession (which his family hoped for) to the vocation of poet and man of letters. The publication of *The Love Song of J. Alfred Prufrock* in Chicago's *Poetry* magazine and of *Preludes* in London's *Blast* brought him professional attention as a poet, and Ezra Pound, who had facilitated publication of *Prufrock* and judged it "the best poem I have had or seen from an American," began to introduce in literary circles the young American who had "trained himself *and* modernized himself *on his own*."[2] At the same time Eliot decided to settle in England and married Vivian Haigh-Wood after a brief courtship and despite the stern misgivings of his parents. Though some friends thought her uninteresting, she was vivacious, took an interest in Eliot's poetry, and did some creative writing herself, but her mental health was fragile and deteriorated frequently before her death, in confinement, in 1947. The strains imposed on Eliot by her illnesses, and his anxieties about his responsibilities in their marriage, were a continual burden even after he abruptly arranged a separation from her in 1932.

After his marriage Eliot turned for support to teaching in London, then worked (1917–25) in the foreign department of Lloyd's Bank. There the daily routine, though demanding, provided a regimen less distracting than teaching from his writing.

Though most of Eliot's criticism before 1925 was written in the form of book reviews for money, and though virtually all of it was motivated by its bearing on the development of his own poetic techniques, it had a durable impact for several reasons in addition to the unmistakable astuteness of his essays. As an American expatriate Eliot cultivated assiduously an elegant manner and became well acquainted with the élite and vanguard intellectual circle, the Bloomsbury Group. Moreover, some of his criticism was published in such well-established journals as *The Athenaeum* and the *Times Literary Supplement*. As assistant editor of the *Egoist* (1917–19) and then founding editor of *The Criterion* (1922–39) he controlled subsidized journals that enabled him to circulate his own views regularly and exercise his predilections in selecting the writing of others. His persuasive style combined Olympian judiciousness with a wit more subtle, urbane learning with an earnestness more disciplined, than those of the Victorian Matthew Arnold on whose criticism Eliot to some extent modeled his own. His stance was at once more philosophical and more strictly literary than Pound's—less programmatic, promotional, and scrappy—and Eliot gave the effect of appraising and adjusting traditions rather than assaulting and appropriating them. Indeed Pound, recognizing that Eliot could not effectively operate as a "battering ram," urged him to "try a more oceanic and fluid method of sapping the foundations"[3] of the establishment culture. The

2. *Letters of Ezra Pound*, ed. D. D. Paige (1950), p. 40.   3. Quoted in Noel Stock, *The Life of Ezra Pound* (1970), p. 206.

essays gathered in *The Sacred Wood* (1920), notably *Tradition and the Individual Talent* and *Rhetoric and Poetic Drama,* and later in *Homage to Dryden* (1924) including *The Metaphysical Poets,* helped gain him an audience in some academic circles that preceded his impact as a poet.

The impact was unmistakable, however, after the publication of *Prufrock and Other Observations* (1917), *Gerontion* (1919), and *Poems* (1920). His urbanity, vivid dramatizations, subtle ironies, and symbolist techniques had already begun to inspire imitators when in 1921 he began work on *The Waste Land,* which he finished during convalescence in a Swiss sanatorium following a nervous collapse. Eliot made some alterations at his wife's suggestion, and major changes on the advice of Pound, before publishing it in 1922 in his own *Criterion,* then in America in the *Dial.* It won the Dial Award for that year, and for publication in book form Eliot added footnotes to expand the volume's size. The poem's learned allusions and unfamiliar structure antagonized some readers. Nevertheless by the time *Poems, 1909–1925* appeared in 1925 *The Waste Land* had presented the exciting challenge of a new poetic structure. Also it bequeathed to the Twenties a myth (recreated from archetypes Christian, Oriental, and primitive) about the deepening decay of Western civilization and the quest for regeneration. Both the poetic structure and the myth had reverberations among writers as diverse as the poet Hart Crane and the novelist William Faulkner.

In 1927 Eliot's assumption of British citizenship and confirmation in the Anglican Church focused professional attention on the point of view he defined in the preface to the collection of essays *For Lancelot Andrews* (1928): he was a "classicist in literature, royalist in politics, and anglo-catholic in religion." (He later regretted the label "classicist," which many critics thought had little application to his criticism and even less to his poetry.) Though Eliot never divorced literary study from social, cultural, or moral concerns, his criticism after 1925 became more emphatically social and cultural in its range, and more specifically Christian in its orientation. His power and influence were buttressed after 1925 by a position as editor and later director of the publishing firm Faber and Faber, which underwrote the expenses of the *Criterion.* Membership in discussion groups (the Chandos Group in the Thirties and the Moot from 1938 to 1947) kept him in touch with a variety of conservative intellectuals who shared Eliot's concern to diagnose the ills of Western civilization and, in Eliot's words, "to build a new structure in which democracy can live" (1928)[4] and to strengthen the authority of Christian principles. Though liberals and critics from the Left were disturbed by Eliot's sympathy with the authoritarian views of Charles Maurras and the *Action Française,* and by Eliot's emphasis on "order," "hierarchy," and racial homogeneity in his social thought, Eliot saw his position as opposed to secularism in fascism as well as in industrial capitalism and egalitarian democracy. In *After Strange Gods* (1934) he called for a combination of "orthodoxy" and "tradition" (an habitual "way of feeling and acting which characterizes a group through generations")[5] to combat the secularism and rival religions that prevailed among humanist critics and such writers as Pound and Yeats. In *The Idea of a Christian Society* (1940) he extended Coleridge's notion of a "clerisy" to define an "élite" of "superior intellectual and/or spiritual gifts," a "Community of

4. Quoted by Roger Kojecky, *T. S. Eliot's Social Criticism* (1971), p. 9.
5. P. 31.

Christians" composed of both Christian clergy and laity, who through example and persuasion would "form the conscious mind and the conscience of the nation."[6] In *Notes toward the Definition of Culture* (1949) he defined a fusion of religion and culture, operative at subconscious levels and sustained by family traditions and by "élites" affiliated with a "governing class," but insuring the interconnections among social groups across "a continuous gradation of cultural levels."[7]

To "cut across all the present stratifications of public taste—stratifications which are perhaps a sign of social disintegration," to write "for as large and miscellaneous an audience as possible,"[8] early became Eliot's aim, particularly in writing plays. He had discovered the power of myth to tap subconscious feelings which are the basis of poetic communication, and he had learned from literary anthropology the importance of ritual and rhythm to the communal theater among the ancients. The combination of sheer entertainment with poetry of a high order which he admired in Elizabethan drama, and the infectious rapport between Charlie Chaplin or music hall performers with their audiences, inspired Eliot to recreate the verse drama for the modern theater. In every collection after *Poems, 1909–1935* (1935) he always included the fragments of his first dramatic experiment, *Wanna Go Home, Baby?* 1926–27 (entitled *Sweeney Agonistes* after 1932). Like *The Rock* (1934), for which Eliot wrote the choruses, Eliot's first successful play was a ritual drama commissioned for a religious occasion (*Murder in the Cathedral*, presented in 1935 and later filmed). Later he sought to avoid the obvious trappings of dramatic verse for fear of arousing outdated expectations in a modern audience; he aimed to perfect a verse idiom derived instead from contemporary speech that would not sound like poetry but would operate unobtrusively on several levels at once, convey the play's musical pattern, and reveal the ritual substructure that lies beneath the surface. Myth, ritual, and dramatic conventions derived from ancient drama function more obviously in *The Family Reunion* (1939) than in later plays, but these patterns infuse the manor-house setting and contemporary idiom to reveal a drama of guilt and purgation. Likewise, in *The Cocktail Party* (1949), his most successful comedy of manners, they disclose the advent of sainthood and a makeshift search for salvation among sophisticated patients of a London psychiatrist. *The Confidential Clerk* (1953) presents the search for a Christian vocation. In *The Elder Statesman* (1959), written when Eliot was radiantly happy following his marriage to Valerie Fletcher in 1957, Sophocles' *Oedipus at Colonus* informs an aging statesman's discovery of divine forgiveness through his daughter's love.

Meditative poetry, however, not the verse drama, remained the basis for Eliot's reputation after 1925, and his poems commanded respect even though some readers were disappointed by the less innovative forms of his verse or its explicitly religious themes. While *The Hollow Men* (1925) in effect restated and intensified without resolving the dilemma of *The Waste Land* in its quest for regeneration, the poem was more liturgical in its motives. Yet it was the six devotional lyrics comprising *Ash Wednesday* (1930) that marked Eliot's conversion to Christianity, presenting the agonized incompletion of a doubt-ridden search for penitence and a prayer for

6. P. 43.
7. Pp. 45–47.

8. *The Use of Poetry and the Use of Criticism* (1933), pp. 152–53.

forgiveness. *Burnt Norton* (1934) was the first of four meditative poems which Eliot completed in the Forties and comprise his late masterpiece, *Four Quartets* (1943). In 1947 he received an honorary degree from Harvard, and in 1948 he was awarded the Order of Merit by the British crown and received the Nobel Prize for Literature.

ELIOT'S LITERARY CRITICISM

Eliot's essays concentrating on literary matters focused on two questions: the importance of tradition and the perennial need for reshaping it; and the resources of language as a means of objectifying states of feeling and achieving auditory effects in poetry.

Tradition, Eliot declared, gave the artist an "ideal order" which related his own productions to those of the past and served both to liberate and to discipline his talent. With a characteristic American feeling of alienation from cultural traditions, but with an equally typical disdain for automatically inheriting them, he insisted that tradition must be cultivated, indeed obtained "by great labor" (*Tradition and the Individual Talent*, 1919). In the active engagement between the past and present that Eliot defined, earlier and foreign works of art opened up perspectives and enlarged the poetic resources available to the poet, freeing him from dependence on his immediate predecessors. Correspondingly, the artist could reshape the tradition by his contributions to it and by revaluating it. Eliot's essays effect that revaluation, seeking to counteract the "dissociation of sensibility" (the severance of language from feeling) that he thought had occurred in the seventeenth century. He deplored the dominance of Milton (his elaborately baroque idiom) as well as the eccentricities of vision in the romantic poet William Blake and the amorphous sonorities of the Victorian Swinburne. He endorsed instead the conjunction of analytic intellect with passion in John Donne and the metaphysical poets, the "direct sensuous apprehension of thought," the "recreation of thought into feeling," that he aimed for in his own verse (*The Metaphysical Poets*, 1921). Although Eliot conceded, when reinterpreting the English tradition again in 1947, that enslavement to colloquial speech was dangerous and that poets now could learn from Milton's poetic structures, in earlier decades he had joined Pound in disparaging Milton and castigating the exhausted, attenuated language of the Victorian and Georgian periods and had voiced the need to incorporate the cadences of colloquial speech. The colloquial elements of Jacobean blank verse drama, and its rhetorical flexibility, made him assign it a higher priority in dramatic history than it had earlier enjoyed.

The meticulous attention to details of diction and rhetoric in poetry, for which Eliot's essays were famous, reinforced his efforts to reconstitute the language of poetry—the perennial task, as both Emerson and Thoreau had insisted, of the creative writer. Since the poet is both "more civilized" and "more *primitive*" than other men, his idiom must encompass the full range of intellect, learning, and conventionalized forms along with the energies of the subconscious mind. The poet should get "the whole weight of the history of the language behind his word" so that he can give "to the word a new life and to the language a new idiom."[9] Eliot sought to shape an idiom that embraced the full suggestiveness of the Symbolists along with the visual lucidity that he admired in Dante and the precision of the Imag-

9. Quoted by F. O. Matthiessen, *The Achievement of T. S. Eliot*, rev. ed. (1958), pp. 94, 83.

ists. Chiefly he wanted a language adequate to what he termed "the auditory imagination," a "feeling for syllable and rhythm, penetrating far below the conscious levels of thought and feeling," reaching "to the most primitive and forgotten" and fusing "the old and the obliterated and the trite, the current, and the new and surprising, the most ancient and the most civilized mentality."[1] Such a language would permit the enlargement and "concentration" of experience, the "fusion" under "pressure," entailed by a creative process in which the artist's mere "personality" is extinguished in a "continual self-sacrifice" to reveal objectively the genuinely intimate apprehensions of the self and create the new feelings enacted in art (*Tradition and the Individual Talent*).

ELIOT'S POETRY

The reorientation of response demanded of readers, once Eliot shifted from the late Victorian modes of his earliest verse under the impact of Jules Laforgue and the Symbolists, was a function chiefly of his ostensibly banal subjects; his subtle irony; his juxtaposition of unexpected images and seemingly discontinuous shifts in feeling without transitional passages or extended comment by the author; the mixture of erudition and common speech in his diction; and the emergence of mythological perspectives through often veiled allusion and sometimes faint echoes of the cadences of earlier poetry. The carefully controlled voice in *Preludes* yields not only the detachment of precise scrutiny but tender feeling as well. The mocking but deft caricature of *Sweeney among the Nightingales*, intensified by the regularity of stanza pattern, gradually evokes not only amusement but concern for the threatened protagonist; the culminating allusions to a convent and the mythological Agamemnon define the contrast in scale between Sweeney's sordid present and the heroic past but suggest also the imminent tragedy of their shared fate. Eliot's refinement of the dramatic monologue in *Prufrock* and *Gerontion* enabled him to project figures in whom objective observation and subjective response coexist; the speakers are symbolic figures in which the observed fragments of an outer world comprise a symbolic landscape but are indistinguishable from a mind's meditations, intimate responses, or fantasies. Eliot is able to define the pathos as well as the ineffectuality of Prufrock's alienation, revealing the aptness of Prufrock's recognitions while in the same allusions deftly mocking the disproportion with which Prufrock dramatizes his aspirations. Eliot's major poems manage to speak simultaneously in the "three voices of poetry" that Eliot defined in a lecture with that title in 1953: "the voice of the poet talking to himself— or nobody," the "voice of the poet addressing an audience," and the voice of "the poet when he attempts to create a dramatic character speaking in verse."[2]

In *The Waste Land*, Eliot's technique enabled him to create a poem that was not only intimate in feeling but virtually epic in scale which encompassed an impending crisis in all civilization and spoke to the disillusionment of readers in the Twenties. A shifting series of modern and ancient prophetic figures displace or dissolve into each other, intertwined with a series of merchants and commercial clerks, seducers, lovers, and married couples drawn from ancient mythology, Elizabethan history, and contemporary London. The poem reveals a landscape of sexual disorder and spiritual desolation and projects a desperate quest for regenera-

1. *Ibid.*, p. 81.   2. *On Poetry and Poets* (1957), p. 98.

tion that remains unfulfilled, though more clearly envisioned, at the end. Various legends, Christian as well as pagan, reinforce each other and are given focus by the legend of the Holy Grail and related Mediterranean fertility myths that Eliot studied in anthropological writings by Jessie Weston and James Frazer. Eliot's poem invokes in fragments the story of the dying god, the Fisher King, whose death or impotence brought desiccation to all vegetation and sterility to men and beasts in his kingdom. Lifebringing rain, sexual and spiritual regeneration, would be assured only if a knight ventured to the Chapel Perilous in the heart of the waste land and, after surviving a nightmarish temptation to despair, asked the proper ritual questions about the grail or cup (female) and the lance (male) harbored there. In Eliot's poem the sequences of bizarre images and estranged voices have the effect at once of cinematic montage and the developmental variations of musical composition. The final version, after Eliot pruned it severely in accordance with Pound's suggestions, is orchestrated in five separate lyrics which build with increasing intensity to an ambiguously portentous crisis (the planting of a corpse, the end of time, purgatorial fire, a drowning, the sound of thunder speaking in an untranslated foreign language), projecting the urgent need and possibility of regeneration but leaving the issue uncertain at the end.

In his later masterpiece, *Four Quartets*, Eliot also used a fivefold structure for each of the four poems that is even more suggestively modeled on musical form (possibly on Beethoven's late quartets), though the materials are openly personal and the themes are philosophical and finally religious. In each Quartet the first and fifth sections combine personal reminiscence (about childhood, his earlier career, or World War I experience) with philosophical meditation on history and "the point of the intersection of the timeless/With time" in the Christian Incarnation (*The Dry Salvages*). The second and fourth sections contain intense and highly formal lyrics. What is new to the *Quartets*, notably in parts of the second and third sections of each, are the passages of relatively discursive poetry of the kind Eliot had deliberately excluded from his earlier verse, providing transitions between more intense passages. Each Quartet contains a meditation on the function of language in art, the strains which "crack and sometimes break" the idiom of the poet (*Burnt Norton*) or conversely (in the concluding Quartet, *Little Gidding*) on the moments when "the old and the new," "the common word" and the "formal word," unite to become "the complete consort dancing together."

The Love Song of J. Alfred Prufrock[1]

S'io credessi che mia risposta fosse
a persona che mai tornasse al mondo,
questa fiamma staria senza più scosse.
Ma per ciò che giammai di questo fondo
non tornò vivo alcun, s'i'odo il vero,
senza tema d'infamia ti rispondo.[2]

Let us go then, you and I,
When the evening is spread out against the sky
Like a patient etherised upon a table;

---

1. Composed at Harvard, this dramatic monologue is a symbolist poem written in intermittently rhymed free verse. The title suggests an ironic contrast between a "love song" and a poem that proves to be about the absence of love, while the

Let us go, through certain half-deserted streets,
The muttering retreats   5
Of restless nights in one-night cheap hotels
And sawdust restaurants with oyster-shells:
Streets that follow like a tedious argument
Of insidious intent
To lead you to an overwhelming question. . .   10
Oh, do not ask, 'What is it?'
Let us go and make our visit.

In the room the women come and go
Talking of Michelangelo.

The yellow fog that rubs its back upon the window-panes,   15
The yellow smoke that rubs its muzzle on the window-panes,
Licked its tongue into the corners of the evening,
Lingered upon the pools that stand in drains,
Let fall upon its back the soot that falls from chimneys,
Slipped by the terrace, made a sudden leap,   20
And seeing that it was a soft October night,
Curled once about the house, and fell asleep.

And indeed there will be time[3]
For the yellow smoke that slides along the street
Rubbing its back upon the window-panes;   25
There will be time, there will be time
To prepare a face to meet the faces that you meet;
There will be time to murder and create,
And time for all the works and days[4] of hands
That lift and drop a question on your plate;   30
Time for you and time for me,
And time yet for a hundred indecisions,
And for a hundred visions and revisions,
Before the taking of a toast and tea.

In the room the women come and go   35
Talking of Michelangelo.

And indeed there will be time
To wonder, 'Do I dare?' and, 'Do I dare?'
Time to turn back and descend the stair,

---

speaker's name suggests an ironic contrast between his ordinary surname (that
of a St. Louis furniture dealer) and the
elegant convention of using the first initial
and middle name as a form of address,
in a world which includes Prufrock but
renders him profoundly alien in it.
2. "If I thought that my reply would be
to one who would ever return to the
world, this flame would stay without further movement; but since none has ever
returned alive from this depth, if what I
hear is true, I answer you without fear

of infamy" (Dante, *Inferno* XXVII, 61–
66). The speaker, Guido da Montefeltro,
consumed in his flame as punishment for
giving false counsel, confesses his shame
without fear of its being reported since
he believes Dante cannot return to earth.
3. An echo of Andrew Marvell's seductive plea in *To His Coy Mistress* (1681):
"Had we but world enough and time
* * *"
4. *Works and Days* is a didactic poem
about farming by the Greek poet Hesiod
(eighth century B.C.).

With a bald spot in the middle of my hair—   40
(They will say: 'How his hair is growing thin!')
My morning coat, my collar mounting firmly to the chin,
My necktie rich and modest, but asserted by a simple pin—
(They will say: 'But how his arms and legs are thin!')
Do I dare   45
Disturb the universe?
In a minute there is time
For decisions and revisions which a minute will reverse.

For I have known them all already, known them all—
Have known the evenings, mornings, afternoons,   50
I have measured out my life with coffee spoons;
I know the voices dying with a dying fall[5]
Beneath the music from a farther room.
    So how should I presume?

And I have known the eyes already, known them all—   55
The eyes that fix you in a formulated phrase,
And when I am formulated, sprawling on a pin,
When I am pinned and wriggling on the wall,
Then how should I begin
To spit out all the butt-ends of my days and ways?   60
    And how should I presume?

And I have known the arms already, known them all—
Arms that are braceleted and white and bare
(But in the lamplight, downed with light brown hair!)
Is it perfume from a dress   65
That makes me so digress?
Arms that lie along a table, or wrap about a shawl.
    And should I then presume?
    And how should I begin?

      .   .   .   .   .
Shall I say, I have gone at dusk through narrow streets   70
And watched the smoke that rises from the pipes
Of lonely men in shirt-sleeves, leaning out of windows? . . .

I should have been a pair of ragged claws
Scuttling across the floors of silent seas.[6]

      .   .   .   .   .
And the afternoon, the evening, sleeps so peacefully!   75
Smoothed by long fingers,
Asleep . . . tired . . . or it malingers,
Stretched on the floor, here beside you and me.
Should I, after tea and cakes and ices,
Have the strength to force the moment to its crisis?   80

5. Echo of Duke Orsino's self-indulgent
invocation of music in Shakespeare's
Twelfth Night (1.1.4): "If music be the
food of love, play on * * * That strain
again! It had a dying fall."

6. Cf. Hamlet's mocking of Polonius in
Shakespeare's *Hamlet* (1602), II.ii.205–6:
"you yourself, sir, should be old as I am,
if like a crab you could go backward."

But though I have wept and fasted, wept and prayed,
Though I have seen my head (grown slightly bald) brought in
    upon a platter,[7]
I am no prophet—and here's no great matter;
I have seen the moment of my greatness flicker,
And I have seen the eternal Footman hold my coat, and
    snicker,   85
And in short, I was afraid.

And would it have been worth it, after all,
After the cups, the marmalade, the tea,
Among the porcelain, among some talk of you and me,
Would it have been worth while,   90
To have bitten off the matter with a smile,
To have squeezed the universe into a ball
To roll it towards some overwhelming question,
To say: 'I am Lazarus,[8] come from the dead,
Come back to tell you all, I shall tell you all'—   95
If one, settling a pillow by her head,
    Should say: 'That is not what I meant at all.
    That is not it, at all.'

And would it have been worth it, after all,
Would it have been worth while,   100
After the sunsets and the dooryards and the sprinkled streets,
After the novels, after the teacups, after the skirts that trail along
    the floor—
And this, and so much more?—
It is impossible to say just what I mean!
But as if a magic lantern threw the nerves in patterns on a
    screen: 105
Would it have been worth while
If one, settling a pillow or throwing off a shawl,
And turning toward the window, should say:
    'That is not it at all,
    That is not what I meant, at all.'   110

    .   .   .   .   .

No! I am not Prince Hamlet, nor was meant to be;
Am an attendant lord, one that will do
To swell a progress,[9] start a scene or two,
Advise the prince; no doubt, an easy tool,
Deferential, glad to be of use,   115
Politic, cautious, and meticulous;
Full of high sentence,[1] but a bit obtuse;
At times, indeed, almost ridiculous—
Almost, at times, the Fool.

7. As did John the Baptist, beheaded by the temptress Salome, who presented his head to the spurned queen Herodias, in the story recounted in Mark 6.17–20, Matthew 14.3–11, and Oscar Wilde's play *Salome* (1894).
8. The resurrection of Lazarus is re-counted in Luke 16.19–31 and John 11.1–44.
9. A journey or procession made by royal courts and often portrayed on Elizabethan stages.
1. Opinions, sententiousness.

I grow old . . . I grow old . . .   120
I shall wear the bottoms of my trousers rolled.

Shall I part my hair behind? Do I dare to eat a peach?
I shall wear white flannel trousers, and walk upon the beach.
I have heard the mermaids singing, each to each.

I do not think that they will sing to me.   125

I have seen them riding seaward on the waves
Combing the white hair of the waves blown back
When the wind blows the water white and black.

We have lingered in the chambers of the sea
By sea-girls wreathed with seaweed red and brown   130
Till human voices wake us, and we drown.

1910–11   1915, 1917

From Preludes[2]

IV

His soul stretched tight across the skies
That fade behind a city block,
Or trampled by insistent feet
At four and five and six o'clock;
And short square fingers stuffing pipes,   5
And evening newspapers, and eyes
Assured of certain certainties,
The conscience of a blackened street
Impatient to assume the world.

I am moved by fancies that are curled   10
Around these images, and cling:
The notion of some infinitely gentle,
Infinitely suffering thing.

Wipe your hand across your mouth, and laugh;
The worlds revolve like ancient women   15
Gathering fuel in vacant lots.

1911   1915, 1917

Sweeney among the Nightingales[1]

ὤμοι, πέπληγμαι καιρίαν πληγὴν ἔσω.[2]

Apeneck Sweeney spreads his knees
Letting his arms hang down to laugh,

2. Written in Paris, this is the last of four poems treating the cityscape in a series of disjunctive images. Early drafts used, as titles, locations in Boston.

1. This poem, dramatizing a tragicomic conspiracy, is one in which Eliot disciplined his verse by employing a regular stanza pattern (rhyming quatrains), inspired by the *Emaux et Camées* (*Enamels and Cameos*, 1852) of the French writer Théophile Gautier (1811–72). The poem generates complex ironies and analogies between the imminent death of Sweeney in a grubby and nonheroic pres-

The zebra stripes along his jaw
Swelling to maculate[3] giraffe.

The circles of the stormy moon   5
Slide westward toward the River Plate,[4]
Death and the Raven drift above
And Sweeney guards the hornèd gate.[5]

Gloomy Orion and the Dog[6]
Are veiled; and hushed the shrunken seas;   10
The person in the Spanish cape
Tries to sit on Sweeney's knees

Slips and pulls the table cloth
Overturns a coffee-cup,
Reorganized upon the floor   15
She yawns and draws a stocking up;

The silent man in mocha brown
Sprawls at the window-sill and gapes;
The waiter brings in oranges
Bananas figs and hothouse grapes;   20

The silent vertebrate in brown
Contracts and concentrates, withdraws;
Rachel *née* Rabinovitch
Tears at the grapes with murderous paws;

She and the lady in the cape   25
Are suspect, thought to be in league;
Therefore the man with heavy eyes
Declines the gambit, shows fatigue,

Leaves the room and reappears
Outside the window, leaning in,   30
Branches of wistaria
Circumscribe a golden grin;

The host with someone indistinct
Converses at the door apart,

---

ent, the ritual sacrifice of Christ enacted
in a convent, the murder (by his wife
and her lover) of heroic Agamemnon in
Aeschylus's tragedy, and the tragedy of
the mythological Philomela. Raped by
her sister's brother, who then cut out her
tongue to prevent her identifying her at-
tacker, Philomela was transformed into a
nightingale whose song springs from the
violation she has suffered but cannot report.
2. Agamemnon's cry from within the
palace when he is murdered: "Alas, I
am struck a mortal blow within" (Aes-

chylus, *Agamemnon*, line 1343).
3. Blotched, stained.
4. Estuary between Argentina and Uru-
guay.
5. The gates of horn, in Hades; true
dreams pass through them to the upper
world.
6. Orion in mythology was a handsome
hunter, slain by Diana, then immortalized as a constellation of stars. The
"Dog" is the brilliant Dog Star, Sirius,
who in mythology sired the Sphinx and,
in Homer, was Orion's dog.

The nightingales are singing near   35
The Convent of the Sacred Heart,

And sang within the bloody wood
When Agamemnon cried aloud[7]
And let their liquid siftings fall
To stain the stiff dishonoured shroud.   40

1918, 1919

Tradition and the Individual Talent[1]

In English writing we seldom speak of tradition, though we occasionally apply its name in deploring its absence. We cannot refer to "the tradition" or to "a tradition"; at most, we employ the adjective in saying that the poetry of So-and-so is "traditional" or even "too traditional." Seldom, perhaps, does the word appear except in a phrase of censure. If otherwise, it is vaguely approbative, with the implication, as to the work approved, of some pleasing archaeological reconstruction. You can hardly make the word agreeable to English ears without this comfortable reference to the reassuring science of archaeology.

Certainly the word is not likely to appear in our appreciations of living or dead writers. Every nation, every race, has not only its own creative, but its own critical turn of mind; and is even more oblivious of the shortcomings and limitations of its critical habits than of those of its creative genius. We know, or think we know, from the enormous mass of critical writing that has appeared in the French language the critical method or habit of the French; we only conclude (we are such unconscious people) that the French are "more critical" than we, and sometimes even plume ourselves a little with the fact, as if the French were the less spontaneous. Perhaps they are; but we might remind ourselves that criticism is as inevitable as breathing, and that we should be none the worse for articulating what passes in our minds when we read a book and feel an emotion about it, for criticizing our own minds in their work of criticism. One of the facts that might come to light in this process is our tendency to insist, when we praise a poet, upon those aspects of his work in which he least resembles any one else. In these aspects or parts of his work we pretend to find what is individual, what is the peculiar essence of the man. We dwell with satisfaction upon the poet's difference from his predecessors, especially his immediate predecessors; we endeavour to find something that can be isolated in order to be enjoyed. Whereas if we approach a poet without this prejudice we shall often find that not only the best, but the most

7. The poem transfers Agamemnon's death to the woods where Philomela was ravished and to the "bloody wood" of Nemi where ancient priests were slain by their successors in the fertility rite described by James Frazer in *The Golden Bough*, Chapter 1.
1. From *The Sacred Wood* (1920), first published in the *Egoist* (1919).

individual parts of his work may be those in which the dead poets, his ancestors, assert their immortality most vigorously. And I do not mean the impressionable period of adolescence, but the period of full maturity.

Yet if the only form of tradition, of handing down, consisted in following the ways of the immediate generation before us in a blind or timid adherence to its successes, "tradition" should positively be discouraged. We have seen many such simple currents soon lost in the sand; and novelty is better than repetition. Tradition is a matter of much wider significance. It cannot be inherited, and if you want it you must obtain it by great labour. It involves, in the first place, the historical sense, which we may call nearly indispensable to any one who would continue to be a poet beyond his twenty-fifth year; and the historical sense involves a perception, not only of the past-ness of the past, but of its presence; the historical sense compels a man to write not merely with his own generation in his bones, but with a feeling that the whole of the literature of Europe from Homer and within it the whole of the literature of his own country has a simultaneous existence and composes a simultaneous order. This historical sense, which is a sense of the timeless as well as of the temporal and of the timeless and of the temporal together, is what makes a writer traditional. And it is at the same time what makes a writer most acutely conscious of his place in time, of his own con-temporaneity.

No poet, no artist of any art, has his complete meaning alone. His significance, his appreciation is the appreciation of his relation to the dead poets and artists. You cannot value him alone; you must set him, for contrast and comparison, among the dead. I mean this as a principle of aesthetic, not merely historical, criticism. The neces-sity that he shall conform, that he shall cohere, is not onesided; what happens when a new work of art is created is something that happens simultaneously to all the works of art which preceded it. The existing monuments form an ideal order among themselves, which is modified by the introduction of the new (the really new) work of art among them. The existing order is complete before the new work arrives; for order to persist after the supervention of nov-elty, the *whole* existing order must be, if ever so slightly, altered; and so the relations, proportions, values of each work of art toward the whole are readjusted; and this is conformity between the old and the new. Whoever has approved this idea of order, of the form of European, of English literature will not find it preposterous that the past should be altered by the present as much as the present is directed by the past. And the poet who is aware of this will be aware of great difficulties and responsibilities.

In a peculiar sense he will be aware also that he must inevitably be judged by the standards of the past. I say judged, not amputated, by them; not judged to be as good as, or worse or better than, the dead; and certainly not judged by the canons of dead critics. It is a judgment, a comparison, in which two things are measured by each other. To conform merely would be for the new work not really to conform at all; it would not be new, and would therefore not be a work of art. And we do not quite say that the new is more valuable because it fits in; but its fitting in is a test of its value—a test, it is true, which can only be slowly and cautiously applied, for we are none of us infallible judges of conformity. We say: it appears to conform, and is perhaps individual, or it appears individual, and may conform; but we are hardly likely to find that it is one and not the other.

To proceed to a more intelligible exposition of the relation of the poet to the past: he can neither take the past as a lump, an indiscriminate bolus,[2] nor can he form himself wholly on one or two private admirations, nor can he form himself wholly upon one preferred period. The first course is inadmissible, the second is an important experience of youth, and the third is a pleasant and highly desirable supplement. The poet must be very conscious of the main current, which does not at all flow invariably through the most distinguished reputations. He must be quite aware of the obvious fact that art never improves, but that the material of art is never quite the same. He must be aware that the mind of Europe—the mind of his own country—a mind which he learns in time to be much more important than his own private mind—is a mind which changes, and that this change is a development which abandons nothing *en route*, which does not superannuate either Shakespeare, or Homer, or the rock drawing of the Magdalenian[3] draughtsmen. That this development, refinement perhaps, complication certainly, is not, from the point of view of the artist, any improvement. Perhaps not even an improvement from the point of view of the psychologist or not to the extent which we imagine; perhaps only in the end based upon a complication in economics and machinery. But the difference between the present and the past is that the conscious present is an awareness of the past in a way and to an extent which the past's awareness of itself cannot show.

Some one said: "The dead writers are remote from us because we *know* so much more than they did." Precisely, and they are that which we know.

I am alive to a usual objection to what is clearly part of my programme for the *métier* of poetry. The objection is that the doctrine requires a ridiculous amount of erudition (pedantry), a claim which can be rejected by appeal to the lives of poets in any pantheon. It will even be affirmed that much learning deadens or perverts poetic sensibility. While, however, we persist in believing that a poet

2. Large pill.
3. The most advanced stage of European Paleolithic culture, named for La Made-

leine, France, where the drawings were discovered.

ought to know as much as will not encroach upon his necessary receptivity and necessary laziness, it is not desirable to confine knowledge to whatever can be put into a useful shape for examinations, drawing-rooms, or the still more pretentious modes of publicity. Some can absorb knowledge, the more tardy must sweat for it. Shakespeare acquired more essential history from Plutarch[4] than most men could from the whole British Museum. What is to be insisted upon is that the poet must develop or procure the consciousness of the past and that he should continue to develop this consciousness throughout his career.

What happens is a continual surrender of himself as he is at the moment to something which is more valuable. The progress of an artist is a continual self-sacrifice, a continual extinction of personality.

There remains to define this process of depersonalization and its relation to the sense of tradition. It is in this depersonalization that art may be said to approach the condition of science. I, therefore, invite you to consider, as a suggestive analogy, the action which takes place when a bit of finely filiated platinum is introduced into a chamber containing oxygen and sulphur dioxide.

II

Honest criticism and sensitive appreciation are directed not upon the poet but upon the poetry. If we attend to the confused cries of the newspaper critics and the *susurrus*[5] of popular repetition that follows, we shall hear the names of poets in great numbers; if we seek not Blue-book[6] knowledge but the enjoyment of poetry, and ask for a poem, we shall seldom find it. I have tried to point out the importance of the relation of the poem to other poems by other authors, and suggested the conception of poetry as a living whole of all the poetry that has ever been written. The other aspect of this Impersonal theory of poetry is the relation of the poem to its author. And I hinted, by an analogy, that the mind of the mature poet differs from that of the immature one not precisely in any valuation of "personality," not being necessarily more interesting, or having "more to say," but rather by being a more finely perfected medium in which special, or very varied, feelings are at liberty to enter into new combinations.

The analogy was that of the catalyst. When the two gases previously mentioned are mixed in the presence of a filament of platinum, they form sulphurous acid. This combination takes place only if the platinum is present; nevertheless the newly formed acid contains no trace of platinum, and the platinum itself is apparently unaffected; has remained inert, neutral, and unchanged. The mind

---

4. Greek biographer (first century A.D.) and Shakespeare's source for the plots of his Roman plays.

5. Latin for murmuring, buzzing.

6. Official British government publication.

of the poet is the shred of platinum. It may partly or exclusively operate upon the experience of the man himself; but, the more perfect the artist, the more completely separate in him will be the man who suffers and the mind which creates; the more perfectly will the mind digest and transmute the passions which are its material.

The experience, you will notice, the elements which enter the presence of the transforming catalyst, are of two kinds: emotions and feelings. The effect of a work of art upon the person who enjoys it is experience different in kind from any experience not of art. It may be formed out of one emotion, or may be a combination of several; and various feelings, inhering for the writer in particular words or phrases or images, may be added to compose the final result. Or great poetry may be made without the direct use of any emotion whatever: composed out of feelings solely. Canto XV of the *Inferno* (Brunetto Latini)[7] is a working up of the emotion evident in the situation; but the effect, though single as that of any work of art, is obtained by considerable complexity of detail. The last quatrain gives an image, a feeling attaching to an image, which "came," which did not develop simply out of what precedes, but which was probably in suspension in the poet's mind until the proper combination arrived for it to add itself to. The poet's mind is in fact a receptacle for seizing and storing up numberless feelings, phrases, images, which remain there until all the particles which can unite to form a new compound are present together.

If you compare several representative passages of the greatest poetry you see how great is the variety of types of combination, and also how completely any semi-ethical criterion of "sublimity" misses the mark. For it is not the "greatness," the intensity, of the emotions, the components, but the intensity of the artistic process, the pressure, so to speak, under which the fusion takes place, that counts. The episode of Paolo and Francesca[8] employs a definite emotion, but the intensity of the poetry is something quite different from whatever intensity in the supposed experience it may give the impression of. It is no more intense, furthermore, than Canto XXVI, the voyage of Ulysses,[9] which has not the direct dependence upon an emotion. Great variety is possible in the process of transmutation of emotion: the murder of Agamemnon,[1] or the agony of Othello,[2] gives an artistic effect apparently closer to a possible original than the scenes from Dante. In the *Agamemnon*, the artistic emotion approximates to the emotion of an actual spectator; in *Othello* to the emotion of the protagonist himself. But the differ-

7. The Florentine philosopher, one of Dante's masters (d. 1294?); Dante describes his eternal punishment in Hell for surrender to unnatural lusts but greets him with compassion.
8. Illicit lovers whose torment Dante pities in Canto V of the *Inferno*.
9. Ulysses, suffering in Hell for "false counseling," tells Dante of his last voyage in this Canto; the voyage, not found in Homer, is Dante's fabrication.
1. Agamemnon is murdered by his vengeful wife and her lover in Aeschylus's ancient Greek tragedy.
2. Othello's torment, when deciding to kill his wife, then suffering remorse for the deed afterward, in Shakespeare's tragedy.

ence between art and the event is always absolute; the combination which is the murder of Agamemnon is probably as complex as that which is the voyage of Ulysses. In either case there has been a fusion of elements. The ode of Keats[3] contains a number of feelings which have nothing particular to do with the nightingale, but which the nightingale, partly, perhaps, because of its attractive name, and partly because of its reputation, served to bring together.

The point of view which I am struggling to attack is perhaps related to the metaphysical theory of the substantial unity of the soul: for my meaning is, that the poet has, not a "personality" to express, but a particular medium, which is only a medium and not a personality, in which impressions and experiences combine in peculiar and unexpected ways. Impressions and experiences which are important for the man may take no place in the poetry, and those which become important in the poetry may play quite a negligible part in the man, the personality.

I will quote a passage which is unfamiliar enough to be regarded with fresh attention in the light—or darkness—of these observations:

> *And now methinks I could e'en chide myself*
> *For doating on her beauty, though her death*
> *Shall be revenged after no common action.*
> *Does the silkworm expend her yellow labours*
> *For thee? For thee does she undo herself?*
> *Are lordships sold to maintain ladyships*
> *For the poor benefit of a bewildering minute?*
> *Why does yon fellow falsify highways,*
> *And put his life between the judge's lips,*
> *To refine such a thing—keeps horse and men*
> *To beat their valours for her? . . .*[4]

In this passage (as is evident if it is taken in its context) there is a combination of positive and negative emotions: an intensely strong attraction toward beauty and an equally intense fascination by the ugliness which is contrasted with it and which destroys it. This balance of contrasted emotion is in the dramatic situation to which the speech is pertinent, but that situation alone is inadequate to it. This is, so to speak, the structural emotion, provided by the drama. But the whole effect, the dominant tone, is due to the fact that a number of floating feelings, having an affinity to this emotion by no means superficially evident, have combined with it to give us a new art emotion.

It is not in his personal emotions, the emotions provoked by particular events in his life, that the poet is in any way remarkable or interesting. His particular emotions may be simple, or crude, or flat.

---

3. *Ode to a Nightingale* by John Keats (1795–1821).   III.v.68–78, by Cyril Tourneur (1575?–1626).
4. From *The Revenger's Tragedy* (1607),

The emotion in his poetry will be a very complex thing, but not with the complexity of the emotions of people who have very complex or unusual emotions in life. One error, in fact, of eccentricity in poetry is to seek for new human emotions to express; and in this search for novelty in the wrong place it discovers the perverse. The business of the poet is not to find new emotions, but to use the ordinary ones and, in working them up into poetry, to express feelings which are not in actual emotions at all. And emotions which he has never experienced will serve his turn as well as those familiar to him. Consequently, we must believe that "emotion recollected in tranquillity"[5] is an inexact formula. For it is neither emotion, nor recolletcion, nor, without distortion of meaning, tranquillity. It is a concentration, and a new thing resulting from the concentration, of a very great number of experiences which to the practical and active person would not seem to be experiences at all; it is a concentration which does not happen consciously or of deliberation. These experiences are not "recollected," and they finally unite in an atmosphere which is "tranquil" only in that it is a passive attending upon the event. Of course this is not quite the whole story. There is a great deal, in the writing of poetry, which must be conscious and deliberate. In fact, the bad poet is usually unconscious where he ought to be conscious, and conscious where he ought to be unconscious. Both errors tend to make him "personal." Poetry is not a turning loose of emotion, but an escape from emotion; it is not the expression of personality, but an escape from personality. But, of course, only those who have personality and emotions know what it means to want to escape from these things.

III

ὁ δὲ νοῦς ἴσως θειότερόν τι καὶ ἀπαθές ἐστιν.[6]

This essay proposes to halt at the frontier of metaphysics or mysticism, and confine itself to such practical conclusions as can be applied by the responsible person interested in poetry. To divert interest from the poet to the poetry is a laudable aim: for it would conduce to a juster estimation of actual poetry, good and bad. There are many people who appreciate the expression of sincere emotion in verse, and there is a smaller number of people who can appreciate technical excellence. But very few know when there is an expression of *significant* emotion, emotion which has its life in the poem and not in the history of the poet. The emotion of art is impersonal. And the poet cannot reach this impersonality without surrendering himself wholly to the work to be done. And he is not likely to know what is to be done unless he lives in what is not

---

5. In his Preface to *Lyrical Ballads* (second edition, 1800), William Wordsworth (1770–1850) declared that "poetry takes its origin from emotion recollected in tranquility."

6. Aristotle, *De Anima* ("On the Soul"), I.4: "No doubt the mind is something divine and not subject to external impressions."

merely the present, but the present moment of the past, unless he is
conscious, not of what is dead, but of what is already living.

1919, 1920

Gerontion[1]

Thou hast nor youth nor age
But as it were an after dinner sleep
Dreaming of both.[2]

Here I am, an old man in a dry month,
Being read to by a boy, waiting for rain.
I was neither at the hot gates[3]
Nor fought in the warm rain
Nor knee deep in the salt marsh, heaving a cutlass,   5
Bitten by flies, fought.
My house is a decayed house,
And the Jew squats on the window sill, the owner,
Spawned in some estaminet[4] of Antwerp,
Blistered in Brussels, patched and peeled in London.[5]   10
The goat coughs at night in the field overhead;
Rocks, moss, stonecrop, iron, merds.[6]
The woman keeps the kitchen, makes tea,
Sneezes at evening, poking the peevish gutter.
              I an old man,   15
A dull head among windy spaces.

Signs are taken for wonders. 'We would see a sign!'[7]
The word within a word, unable to speak a word,
Swaddled with darkness. In the juvescence of the year
Came Christ the tiger   20

In depraved May,[8] dogwood and chestnut, flowering judas,
To be eaten, to be divided, to be drunk
Among whispers; by Mr. Silvero
With caressing hands, at Limoges
Who walked all night in the next room;   25
By Hakagawa, bowing among the Titians;
By Madame de Tornquist, in the dark room
Shifting the candles; Fräulein von Kulp

1. This dramatic monologue presents the re-examination of his life and a search for commitment on the part of an old man who, like the world he inhabits, has lost the passion for either sexual and human love or religious devotion. Eliot intended to reprint it as a prelude to *The Waste Land* until persuaded not to by Ezra Pound. The title is a coinage derived from the Greek word meaning "an old man."
2. Lines spoken by the wily Duke to prepare a young lover for death in Shakespeare's *Measure for Measure* (3.1.32–34).
3. A sexual image, and an allusion to Thermopylae, the mountain pass where the Spartans heroically defeated the Persians (480 B.C.).
4. Café.
5. Allusions to symptoms and cures for venereal disease.
6. Dung.
7. Echoes of the "signs and wonders" expected as testimony to Christ's divinity in John 4.48 and the demand "Master, we would see a sign from thee" in Matthew 12.38, the subject of a Nativity sermon by Bishop Lancelot Andrewes (1555–1626).
8. Cf. *The Education of Henry Adams* (1918), Chapter 18: the "passionate depravity that marked the Maryland May."

Who turned in the hall, one hand on the door.
   Vacant shuttles
Weave the wind. I have no ghosts,   30
An old man in a draughty house
Under a windy knob.[9]

After such knowledge, what forgiveness? Think now
History has many cunning passages, contrived corridors
And issues, deceives with whispering ambitions,   35
Guides us by vanities. Think now
She gives when our attention is distracted
And what she gives, gives with such supple confusions
That the giving famishes the craving. Gives too late
What's not believed in, or is still believed,   40
In memory only, reconsidered passion. Gives too soon
Into weak hands, what's thought can be dispensed with
Till the refusal propagates a fear. Think
Neither fear nor courage saves us. Unnatural vices
Are fathered by our heroism. Virtues   45
Are forced upon us by our impudent crimes.
These tears are shaken from the wrath-bearing tree.

The tiger springs in the new year. Us he devours. Think at
     last
We have not reached conclusion, when I
Stiffen in a rented house. Think at last   50
I have not made this show purposelessly
And it is not by any concitation[1]
Of the backward devils.
I would meet you upon this honestly.
I that was near your heart was removed therefrom   55
To lose beauty in terror, terror in inquisition.
I have lost my passion: why should I need to keep it
Since what is kept must be adulterated?
I have lost my sight, smell, hearing, taste and touch:[2]
How should I use them for your closer contact?   60

These with a thousand small deliberations
Protract the profit of their chilled delirium,
Excite the membrane, when the sense has cooled,
With pungent sauces, multiply variety
In a wilderness of mirrors. What will the spider do, 65
Suspend its operations, will the weevil

9. In lines 18–22, Gerontion imagines
Christ as a terrifying though enviably
powerful beast, like "the Lion of the
tribe of Judah" in Revelation 5.5, but he
recalls also that the springtime of
Christ's crucifixion was a time of betrayal and he renders the Christian
Word (message) as impenetrable and
impotent in a world which debases the
rites and gestures of Christian devotion.
Line 22 alludes to dividing and eating
the bread, and drinking the wine, in
Christian communion.
1. Stirring up, concerted action.
2. An echo of Henry Adams's statement
that civilization "has reached an age
when it can no longer depend, as in
childhood, on its taste, or smell, or
sight, or hearing, or memory" in *Mont-
Saint-Michel and Chartres* (1913), Chapter 8.

Delay? De Bailhache, Fresca, Mrs. Cammel, whirled[3]
Beyond the circuit of the shuddering Bear
In fractured atoms. Gull against the wind, in the windy straits
Of Belle Isle, or running on the Horn.   70
White feathers in the snow, the Gulf claims,
And an old man driven by the Trades[4]
To a sleepy corner.

                                    Tenants of the house,
Thoughts of a dry brain in a dry season.   75

                                                                      1920

The Metaphysical Poets[1]

By collecting these poems from the work of a generation more
often named than read, and more often read than profitably studied, Professor Grierson has rendered a service of some importance.
Certainly the reader will meet with many poems already preserved in
other anthologies, at the same time that he discovers poems such as
those of Aurelian Townshend or Lord Herbert of Cherbury here
included. But the function of such an anthology as this is neither
that of Professor Saintsbury's admirable edition of Caroline poets
nor that of the *Oxford Book of English Verse*. Mr. Grierson's book
is in itself a piece of criticism and a provocation of criticism; and
we think that he was right in including so many poems of Donne,
elsewhere (though not in many editions) accessible, as documents
in the case of "metaphysical poetry." The phrase has long done duty
as a term of abuse or as the label of a quaint and pleasant taste.
The question is to what extent the so-called metaphysicals formed a
school (in our own time we should say a "movement"), and how
far this so-called school or movement is a digression from the main
current.

Not only is it extremely difficult to define metaphysical poetry,
but difficult to decide what poets practise it and in which of their
verses. The poetry of Donne (to whom Marvell and Bishop King
are sometimes nearer than any of the other authors) is late Elizabethan, its feeling often very close to that of Chapman. The "courtly"
poetry is derivative from Jonson, who borrowed liberally from the
Latin; it expires in the next century with the sentiment and witti-
cism of Prior. There is finally the devotional verse of Herbert,
Vaughan, and Crashaw (echoed long after by Christina Rossetti
and Francis Thompson); Crashaw, sometimes more profound and
less sectarian than the others, has a quality which returns through

---

3. Unidentified persons whose fate, beyond the polestar in the constellation the
Bear, is compared to that of the gull
and Gerontion buffeted by the winds.
4. Trade winds.
1. First published in the *London Times
Literary Supplement*, this was a book review of a volume identified in Eliot's
note: "*Metaphysical Lyrics and Poems
of the Seventeenth Century: Donne to
Butler*. Selected and Edited, with an
Essay, by Herbert J. C. Grierson (Oxford: Clarendon Press. London: Milford)."

the Elizabethan period to the early Italians. It is difficult to find any precise use of metaphor, simile, or other conceit, which is common to all the poets and at the same time important enough as an element of style to isolate these poets as a group. Donne, and often Cowley, employ a device which is sometimes considered characteristically "metaphysical"; the elaboration (contrasted with the condensation) of a figure of speech to the farthest stage to which ingenuity can carry it. Thus Cowley develops the commonplace comparison of the world to a chess-board through long stanzas (*To Destiny*), and Donne, with more grace, in A *Valediction*,[2] the comparison of two lovers to a pair of compasses. But elsewhere we find, instead of the mere explication of the content of a comparison, a development by rapid association of thought which requires considerable agility on the part of the reader.

> On a round ball
> A workman that hath copies by, can lay
> An Europe, Afrique, and an Asia,
> And quickly make that, which was nothing, All,
> So doth each teare,
> Which thee doth weare,
> A globe, yea, world by that impression grow,
> Till they tears mixt with mine doe overflow
> This world, by waters sent from thee, my heaven dissolved so.[3]

Here we find at least two connexions which are not implicit in the first figure, but are forced upon it by the poet: from the geographer's globe to the tear, and the tear to the deluge. On the other hand, some of Donne's most successful and characteristic effects are secured by brief words and sudden contrasts:

> A bracelet of bright hair about the bone,[4]

where the most powerful effect is produced by the sudden contrast of associations of "bright hair" and of "bone." This telescoping of images and multiplied associations is characteristic of the phrase of some of the dramatists of the period which Donne knew: not to mention Shakespeare, it is frequent in Middleton, Webster, and Tourneur, and is one of the sources of the vitality of their language.

Johnson, who employed the term "metaphysical poets," apparently having Donne, Cleveland, and Cowley chiefly in mind, remarks of them that "the most heterogeneous ideas are yoked by violence together."[5] The force of this impeachment lies in the fail-

2. *A Valediction: Forbidding Mourning* by John Donne (1572–1631).
3. Donne's *A Valediction: Of Weeping*, lines 10–18.
4. *The Relique*, line 6.

5. In his *Lives of the Poets* (1779), Samuel Johnson (1709–84) published a *Life* of Abraham Cowley (1618–67), where the quotation appears as a definition of "wit."

ure of the conjunction, the fact that often the ideas are yoked but
not united; and if we are to judge of styles of poetry by their abuse,
enough examples may be found in Cleveland to justify Johnson's
condemnation. But a degree of heterogeneity of material compelled
into unity by the operation of the poet's mind is omnipresent in
poetry. We need not select for illustration such a line as:

> *Notre âme est un trois-mâts cherchant son Icarie;*[6]

we may find it in some of the best lines of Johnson himself (*The
Vanity of Human Wishes*):

> His fate was destined to a barren strand,
> A pretty fortress, and a dubious hand;
> He left a name at which the world grew pale,
> To point a moral, or adorn a tale.

where the effect is due to a contrast of ideas, different in degree but
the same in principle, as that which Johnson mildly reprehended.
And in one of the finest poems of the age (a poem which could not
have been written in any other age), the *Exequy* of Bishop King,
the extended comparison is used with perfect success: the idea and
the simile become one, in the passage in which the Bishop illustrates his impatience to see his dead wife, under the figure of a journey:

> Stay for me there; I will not faile
> To meet thee in that hollow Vale.
> And think not much of my delay;
> I am already on the way,
> And follow thee with all the speed
> Desire can make, or sorrows breed.
> Each minute is a short degree,
> And ev'ry houre a step towards thee.
> At night when I betake to rest,
> Next morn I rise nearer my West
> Of life, almost by eight houres sail,
> Than when sleep breath'd his drowsy gale. . . .
> But heark! My Pulse, like a soft Drum
> Beats my approach, tells Thee I come;
> And slow howere my marches be,
> I shall at last sit down by Thee.

(In the last few lines there is that effect of terror which is several
times attained by one of Bishop King's admirers, Edgar Poe.)

---

6. From *The Voyage* by the French poet
Charles Baudelaire (1821–67): "Our soul
is a three-masted ship searching for her
Icarie." Icarie js an imaginary utopia in
the novel by Étienne Cabet, *Voyage en
Icarie* (1840).

Again, we may justly take these quatrains from Lord Herbert's Ode,[7] stanzas which would, we think, be immediately pronounced to be of the metaphysical school:

> *So when from hence we shall be gone,*
>   *And be no more, nor you, nor I,*
>   *As one another's mystery,*
> *Each shall be both, yet both but one.*
>
> *This said, in her up-lifted face,*
>   *Her eyes, which did that beauty crown,*
>   *Were like two starrs, that having faln down,*
> *Look up again to find their place:*
>
> *While such a moveless silent peace*
>   *Did seize on their becalmed sense,*
>   *One would have thought some influence*
> *Their ravished spirits did possess.*

There is nothing in these lines (with the possible exception of the stars, a simile not at once grasped, but lovely and justified) which fits Johnson's general observations on the metaphysical poets in his essay on Cowley. A good deal resides in the richness of association which is at the same time borrowed from and given to the word "becalmed"; but the meaning is clear, the language simple and elegant. It is to be observed that the language of these poets is as a rule simple and pure; in the verse of George Herbert this simplicity is carried as far as it can go—a simplicity emulated without success by numerous modern poets. The *structure* of the sentences, on the other hand, is sometimes far from simple, but this is not a vice; it is a fidelity to thought and feeling. The effect, at its best, is far less artificial than that of an ode by Gray. And as this fidelity induces variety of thought and feeling, so it induces variety of music. We doubt whether, in the eighteenth century, could be found two poems in nominally the same metre, so dissimilar as Marvell's *Coy Mistress* and Crashaw's *Saint Teresa*; the one producing an effect of great speed by the use of short syllables, and the other an ecclesiastical solemnity by the use of long ones:

> *Love, thou art absolute sole lord*
> *Of life and death.*[8]

If so shrewd and sensitive (though so limited) a critic as Johnson failed to define metaphysical poetry by its faults, it is worth while to inquire whether we may not have more success by adopting the

---

7. *Ode upon a Question moved, whether Love should continue forever?* by Lord Herbert of Cherbury (1583–1648).

8. The opening lines of *A Hymn * * * to Saint Theresa* by Richard Crashaw (1612–49).

opposite method: by assuming that the poets of the seventeenth century (up to the Revolution)[9] were the direct and normal development of the precedent age; and, without prejudicing their case by the adjective "metaphysical," consider whether their virtue was not something permanently valuable, which subsequently disappeared, but ought not to have disappeared. Johnson has hit, perhaps by accident, on one of their peculiarities, when he observes that "their attempts were always analytic"; he would not agree that, after the dissociation, they put the material together again in a new unity.

It is certain that the dramatic verse of the later Elizabethan and early Jacobean poets expresses a degree of development of sensibility which is not found in any of the prose, good as it often is. If we except Marlowe, a man of prodigious intelligence, these dramatists were directly or indirectly (it is at least a tenable theory) affected by Montaigne. Even if we except also Jonson and Chapman, these two were notably erudite, and were notably men who incorporated their erudition into their sensibility: their mode of feeling was directly and freshly altered by their reading and thought. In Chapman especially there is a direct sensuous apprehension of thought, or a recreation of thought into feeling, which is exactly what we find in Donne:

> *in this one thing, all the discipline*
> *Of manners and of manhood is contained;*
> *A man to join himself with th' Universe*
> *In his main sway, and make in all things fit*
> *One with that All, and go on, round as it;*
> *Not plucking from the whole his wretched part,*
> *And into straits, or into nought revert,*
> *Wishing the complete Universe might be*
> *Subject to such a rag of it as he;*
> *But to consider great Necessity.*[1]

We compare this with some modern passage:

> *No, when the fight begins within himself,*
> *A man's worth something. God stoops o'er his head,*
> *Satan looks up between his feet—both tug—*
> *He's left, himself, i' the middle; the soul wakes*
> *And grows. Prolong that battle through his life!*[2]

It is perhaps somewhat less fair, though very tempting (as both poets are concerned with the perpetuation of love by offspring), to

9. The Revolution of 1688, when William and Mary replaced James II.
1. From *The Revenge of Bussy d'Ambois*, IV.i.137–46, by George Chapman (1559?–1634).
2. *Bishop Blougram's Apology*, lines 693–97, by Robert Browning (1812–89).

compare with the stanzas already quoted from Lord Herbert's Ode the following from Tennyson:

> *One walked between his wife and child,*
> *With measured footfall firm and mild,*
> *And now and then he gravely smiled.*
>> *The prudent partner of his blood*
>> *Leaned on him, faithful, gentle, good,*
>> *Wearing the rose of womanhood.*
> *And in their double love secure,*
> *The little maiden walked demure,*
> *Pacing with downward eyelids pure.*
>> *These three made unity so sweet,*
>> *My frozen heart began to beat,*
>> *Remembering its ancient heat.*[3]

The difference is not a simple difference of degree between poets. It is something which had happened to the mind of England between the time of Donne or Lord Herbert of Cherbury and the time of Tennyson and Browning; it is the difference between the intellectual poet and the reflective poet. Tennyson and Browning are poets, and they think; but they do not feel their thought as immediately as the odour of a rose. A thought to Donne was an experience; it modified his sensibility. When a poet's mind is perfectly equipped for its work, it is constantly amalgamating disparate experience; the ordinary man's experience is chaotic, irregular, fragmentary. The latter falls in love, or reads Spinoza, and these two experiences have nothing to do with each other, or with the noise of the typewriter or the smell of cooking; in the mind of the poet these experiences are always forming new wholes.

We may express the difference by the following theory: The poets of the seventeenth century, the successors of the dramatists of the sixteenth, possessed a mechanism of sensibility which could devour any kind of experience. They are simple, artificial, difficult, or fantastic, as their predecessors were; no less nor more than Dante, Guido Cavalcanti, Guinizelli, or Cino.[4] In the seventeenth century a dissociation of sensibility set in, from which we have never recovered; and this dissociation, as is natural, was aggravated by the influence of the two most powerful poets of the century, Milton and Dryden. Each of these men performed certain poetic functions so magnificently well that the magnitude of the effect concealed the absence of others. The language went on and in some respects improved; the best verse of Collins, Gray, Johnson, and even Goldsmith satisfies some of our fastidious demands better than

---

3. *The Two Voices*, lines 412–23, by Alfred Lord Tennyson (1808–92).
4. Cavalcanti, Guido Guinizelli, and Cino da Pistoia were 13th-century poets, masters or friends of Dante.

that of Donne or Marvell or King. But while the language became more refined, the feeling became more crude. The feeling, the sensibility, expressed in the *Country Churchyard* (to say nothing of Tennyson and Browning) is cruder than that in the *Coy Mistress*.

The second effect of the influence of Milton and Dryden followed from the first, and was therefore slow in manifestation. The sentimental age began early in the eighteenth century, and continued. The poets revolted against the ratiocinative, the descriptive; they thought and felt by fits, unbalanced; they reflected. In one or two passages of Shelley's *Triumph of Life*, in the second *Hyperion*, there are traces of a struggle toward unification of sensibility. But Keats and Shelley died, and Tennyson and Browning ruminated.

After this brief exposition of a theory—too brief, perhaps, to carry conviction—we may ask, what would have been the fate of the "metaphysical" had the current of poetry descended in a direct line from them, as it descended in a direct line to them? They would not, certainly, be classified as metaphysical. The possible interests of a poet are unlimited; the more intelligent he is the better; the more intelligent he is the more likely that he will have interests: our only condition is that he turn them into poetry, and not merely meditate on them poetically. A philosophical theory which has entered into poetry is established, for its truth or falsity in one sense ceases to matter, and its truth in another sense is proved. The poets in question have, like other poets, various faults. But they were, at best, engaged in the task of trying to find the verbal equivalent for states of mind and feeling. And this means both that they are more mature, and that they wear better, than later poets of certainly not less literary ability.

It is not a permanent necessity that poets should be interested in philosophy, or in any other subject. We can only say that it appears likely that poets in our civilization, as it exists at present, must be *difficult*. Our civilization comprehends great variety and complexity, and this variety and complexity, playing upon a refined sensibility, must produce various and complex results. The poet must become more and more comprehensive, more allusive, more indirect, in order to force, to dislocate if necessary, language into his meaning. (A brilliant and extreme statement of this view, with which it is not requisite to associate oneself, is that of M. Jean Epstein, *La Poésie d'aujourd'hui*.)[5] Hence we get something which looks very much like the conceit—we get, in fact, a method curiously similar to that of the "metaphysical poets," similar also in its use of obscure words and of simple phrasing.

> O géraniums diaphanes, guerroyeurs sortilèges,
> Sacrilèges monomanes!

5. "Poetry Today."

> *Emballages, dévergondages, douches! O pressoirs*
> *Des vendanges des grands soirs!*
> *Layettes aux abois,*
> *Thyrses au fond des bois!*
> *Relevailles, compresses et l'éternal potion,*
> *Transfusions, représailles,*
> *Angélus! n'en pouvoir plus*
> *De débâcles nuptiales! de débâcles nuptiales!*[6]

The same poet could write also simply:

> *Elle est bien loin, elle pleure,*
> *Le grand vent se lamente aussi . . .*[7]

Jules Laforgue, and Tristan Corbière[8] in many of his poems, are nearer to the "school of Donne" than any modern English poet. But poets more classical than they have the same essential quality of transmuting ideas into sensations, of transforming an observation into a state of mind.

> *Pour l'enfant, amoureux de cartes et d'estampes,*
> *L'univers est égal à son vaste appétit.*
> *Ah, que le monde est grand à la clarté des lampes!*
> *Aux yeux du souvenir que le monde est petit!*[9]

In French literature the great master of the seventeenth century—Racine—and the great master of the nineteenth—Baudelaire—are in some ways more like each other than they are like any one else. The greatest two masters of diction are also the greatest two psychologists, the most curious explorers of the soul. It is interesting to speculate whether it is not a misfortune that two of the greatest masters of diction in our language, Milton and Dryden, triumph with a dazzling disregard of the soul. If we continued to produce Miltons and Drydens it might not so much matter, but as things are it is a pity that English poetry has remained so incomplete. Those who object to the "artificiality" of Milton or Dryden sometimes tell us to "look into our hearts and write." But that is not looking deep enough; Racine or Donne looked into a good deal more than the heart. One must look into the cerebral cortex, the nervous system, and the digestive tracts.

6. From *Dernier vers X* (*Last Poems*, 1890) by Jules Laforgue (1860–87): "O transparent geraniums, soldiers' incantations, / Monomaniacal sacrileges! / Packing materials, shamelessness, shower baths! O wine presses / Of the vintages of grand evenings! / Hard-pressed baby linens, / Thyrsis in the depths of the woods! / Transfusions, reprisals, / Churchings, compresses and the eternal potion, / Angelus! To be worn out / by catastrophic marriages! catastrophic marriages!"
7. From *Sur une défunte* (*On a Dead Woman* in *Last Poems*): "She is far away, she weeps, / The great wind mourns also."
8. A French Symbolist poet (1845–75).
9. From Baudelaire's "The Voyage": "For the child, in love with maps and prints, / The universe is the equal of his vast appetite. / Ah, how big the world is by lamplight! / In the eyes of memory how the world is small!"

May we not conclude, then, that Donne, Crashaw, Vaughan, Herbert and Lord Herbert, Marvell, King, Cowley at his best, are in the direct current of English poetry, and that their faults should be reprimanded by this standard rather than coddled by antiquarian affection? They have been enough praised in terms which are implicit limitations because they are "metaphysical" or "witty," "quaint" or "obscure," though at their best they have not these attributes more than other serious poets. On the other hand, we must not reject the criticism of Johnson (a dangerous person to disagree with) without having mastered it, without having assimilated the Johnsonian canons of state. In reading the celebrated passage in his essay on Cowley we must remember that by wit he clearly means something more serious than we usually mean today; in his criticism of their versification we must remember in what a narrow discipline he was trained, but also how well trained; we must remember that Johnson tortures chiefly the chief offenders, Cowley and Cleveland. It would be a fruitful work, and one requiring a substantial book, to break up the classification of Johnson (for there has been none since) and exhibit these poets in all their difference of kind and of degree, from the massive music of Donne to the faint, pleasing tinkle of Aurelian Townshend—whose *Dialogue between a Pilgrim and Time* is one of the few regrettable omissions from the excellent anthology of Professor Grierson.

1921

The Waste Land[1]

'*Nam Sibyllam quidem Cumis ego ipse oculis meis vidi in ampulla pendere, et cum illi pueri dicerent: Σίβυλλα τί θέλεις: respondebat illa: ἀποθανεῖν θέλω.*'[2]

FOR EZRA POUND

il miglior fabbro.

I. The Burial of the Dead[3]

April is the cruellest month, breeding
Lilacs out of the dead land, mixing

1. The notes which Eliot provided for the first hard-cover edition of *The Waste Land* opened with his acknowledgment that "not only the title, but the plan and a good deal of the incidental symbolism of the poem were suggested by Miss Jessie L. Weston's book on the Grail Legend: *From Ritual to Romance*" (1920) and that he was indebted also to James G. Frazer's *The Golden Bough* (1890–1915), "especially the two volumes *Adonis, Attis, Osiris*," which deal with vegetation myths and fertility rites. Eliot's subsequent notes are incorporated in the present editor's footnotes.
2. A quotation from Petronius's *Satyricon* (first century A.D.) about the Sibyl

(prophetess) of Cumae, blessed with eternal life by Apollo but doomed to perpetual old age, who guided Aeneas through Hades in Virgil's *The Aeneid*: "For once I myself saw with my own eyes the Sibyl at Cumae hanging in a cage, and when the boys said to her 'Sibyl, what do you want?' she replied, 'I want to die.'" "*Il miglior fabbro*": "the better craftsman," the tribute in Dante's *Purgatorio* XXVI.117 to the Provençal poet Arnaut Daniel, here paid by Eliot to his friend Ezra Pound, whose editorial suggestions had contributed to the poem's elliptical structure and compression.
3. A phrase from the Anglican burial service.

Memory and desire, stirring
Dull roots with spring rain.
Winter kept us warm, covering   5
Earth in forgetful snow, feeding
A little life with dried tubers.
Summer surprised us, coming over the Starnbergersee[4]
With a shower of rain; we stopped in the colonnade,
And went on in sunlight, into the Hofgarten,[5]   10
And drank coffee, and talked for an hour.
Bin gar keine Russin, stamm' aus Litauen, echt deutsch.[6]
And when we were children, staying at the arch-duke's,
My cousin's, he took me out on a sled,
And I was frightened. He said, Marie,   15
Marie, hold on tight. And down we went.
In the mountains, there you feel free.
I read, much of the night, and go south in the winter.

What are the roots that clutch, what branches grow
Out of this stony rubbish? Son of man,[7]   20
You cannot say, or guess, for you know only
A heap of broken images, where the sun beats,
And the dead tree gives no shelter, the cricket no relief,[8]
And the dry stone no sound of water. Only
There is shadow under this red rock,[9]   25
(Come in under the shadow of this red rock),
And I will show you something different from either
Your shadow at morning striding behind you
Or your shadow at evening rising to meet you;
I will show you fear in a handful of dust.   30
          Frisch weht der Wind
          Der Heimat zu
          Mein Irisch Kind,
          Wo weilest du?[1]
'You gave me hyacinths first a year ago;   35
'They called me the hyacinth girl.'
—Yet when we came back, late, from the hyacinth garden,
Your arms full, and your hair wet, I could not
Speak, and my eyes failed, I was neither
Living nor dead, and I knew nothing,   40

4. A lake near Munich. Lines 8–16 were suggested by the Countess Marie Larisch's memoir, *My Past* (1913).
5. A public park in Munich, with cafés and a zoo.
6. "I am certainly not Russian; I come from Lithuania, a true German."
7. "Cf. Ezekiel II, i" [Eliot's note], where God addresses the prophet Ezekiel as "Son of man" and declares: "stand upon thy feet, and I will speak unto thee."
8. "Cf. Ecclesiastes XII,v" [Eliot's note], where the Preacher describes the bleakness of old age when "the grasshopper shall be a burden, and desire shall fail."

9. Cf. Isaiah 32.1–2 and the prophecy that the reign of the Messiah "shall be * * * as rivers of water in a dry place, as the shadow of a great rock in a weary land."
1. "V. [see] *Tristan und Isolde*, I, verses 5–8" [Eliot's note]. In Wagner's opera, a carefree sailor aboard Tristan's ship recalls his girlfriend in Ireland: "Fresh blows the wind to the homeland; my Irish child, where are you waiting?" The young boy Hyacinth, in Ovid's *Metamorphoses*, X, was beloved by Apollo but slain by a jealous rival. The Greeks celebrated his festival in May.

Looking into the heart of light, the silence.
Oed' und leer das Meer.[2]

Madame Sosostris,[3] famous clairvoyante,
Had a bad cold, nevertheless
Is known to be the wisest woman in Europe,   45
With a wicked pack of cards.[4] Here, said she,
Is your card, the drowned Phoenician Sailor,[5]
(Those are pearls that were his eyes.[6] Look!)
Here is Belladonna, the Lady of the Rocks,[7]
The lady of situations.   50
Here is the man with three staves,[8] and here the Wheel,
And here is the one-eyed merchant,[9] and this card,
Which is blank, is something he carries on his back,
Which I am forbidden to see. I do not find
The Hanged Man. Fear death by water.   55
I see crowds of people, walking round in a ring.
Thank you. If you see dear Mrs. Equitone,
Tell her I bring the horoscope myself:
One must be so careful these days.

Unreal City,[1]   60
Under the brown fog of a winter dawn,

2. In *Tristan* "III, verse 24" [Eliot's note] the dying Tristan, awaiting the ship that carries his beloved Isolde, is told that "Empty and barren is the sea."
3. Eliot derived the name from "Sesostris, the Sorceress of Ectabana," the pseudo-Egyptian name assumed by a woman who tells fortunes in Aldous Huxley's novel *Chrome Yellow* (1921). Sesostris was a 12th-dynasty Egyptian King.
4. The tarot deck of cards, once important in Eastern magic but now "fallen somewhat into disrepute, being principally used for purposes of divination," according to Weston's *From Ritual to Romance.* Its four suits are the recurring life symbols of the Grail legend: the cup, lance, sword, and dish. Eliot's note to this passage reads: "I am not familiar with the exact constitution of the Tarot pack of cards, from which I have obviously departed to suit my own convenience. The Hanged Man, a member of the traditional pack, fits my purpose in two ways: because he is associated in my mind with the Hanged God of Frazer, and because I associate him with the hooded figure in the passage of the disciples to Emmaus in Part V. The Phoenician Sailor and the Merchant appear later; also the 'crowds of people,' and Death by Water is executed in Part IV. The Man with Three Staves (an authentic member of the Tarot pack) I associate, quite arbitrarily, with the Fisher King himself."
5. The Phoenician Sailor is a symbolic figure which includes "Mr. Eugenides, the Smyrna merchant" in Part III and

"Phlebas the Phoenician" in Part IV. The ancient Phoenicians were sea-going merchants whose crews spread Egyptian fertility cults throughout the Mediterranean.
6. The line is a quotation from Ariel's song in Shakespeare's *The Tempest,* 1.2.398. Prince Ferdinand, disconsolate because he thinks his father had drowned in the storm, is consoled when Ariel sings of a miraculous "sea change" which has transformed disaster into "something rich and strange." Fears attendant on drowning, and the sea as an agent of purification and possible resurrection, are important elements throughout the poem.
7. Belladonna, literally meaning "beautiful lady," is the name of both the poisonous plant "nightshade" and a cosmetic. It suggests also the Christian "madonna" or Virgin Mary, particularly, in context, the painting *Madonna of the Rocks* by Leonardo da Vinci.
8. One tarot card, the Three Scepters, represents a successful merchant surveying his ships with three wands planted in the ground nearby. Another is associated with three phalli and the rebirth of the Egyptian god Osiris. The Wheel on another card is the Wheel of Fortune.
9. Later identified as "Mr. Eugenides," the figure is "one-eyed" because his activities are ominous and because he is shown in profile on the card.
1. "Cf. Baudelaire: 'Fourmillante cité, cité pleine de rêves, / Où le spectre en plein jour raccroche le passant" [Eliot's note]. The lines are quoted from *Les Sept Viellards (The Seven Old Men),*

A crowd flowed over London Bridge, so many,
I had not thought death had undone so many.[2]
Sighs, short and infrequent, were exhaled,[3]
And each man fixed his eyes before his feet.   65
Flowed up the hill and down King William Street,
To where Saint Mary Woolnoth kept the hours
With a dead sound on the final stroke of nine.[4]
There I saw one I knew, and stopped him, crying: 'Stetson!
'You who were with me in the ships at Mylae![5]   70
'That corpse you planted last year in your garden,
'Has it begun to sprout? Will it bloom this year?
'Or has the sudden frost disturbed its bed?
'O keep the Dog far hence, that's friend to men,
'Or with his nails he'll dig it up again![6]   75
'You! hypocrite lecteur!—mon semblable,—mon frère!'[7]

II. A Game of Chess[8]

The Chair she sat in, like a burnished throne,[9]
Glowed on the marble, where the glass
Held up by standards wrought with fruited vines
From which a golden Cupidon peeped out   80
(Another hid his eyes behind his wing)
Doubled the flames of sevenbranched candelabra
Reflecting light upon the table as

---

poem XCIII of *Les Fleurs du Mal* (*The Flowers of Evil*, 1857) by the French Symbolist Charles Baudelaire (1821–67), and may be translated: "Swarming city, city full of dreams, / Where the specter in broad daylight accosts the passerby."
2. "Cf. *Inferno* III, 55–57 * * * " [Eliot's note]. The note continues to quote Dante's lines, which may be translated: "So long a train of people, / That I should never have believed / That death had undone so many."
3. "Cf. *Inferno* IV, 25–27 * * * " [Eliot's note]. Dante describes, in Limbo, the virtuous but pagan dead who, living before Christ, could not achieve the hope of embracing the Christian God. The lines read: "Here, so far as I could tell by listening, / There was no lamentation except sighs, / Which caused the eternal air to tremble."
4. "A phenomenon which I have often noticed" [Eliot's note]. The church named is in the financial district of London, and the allusion is the first to suggest the Chapel Perilous of the Grail legend.
5. "Stetson" is the familiar name of a hat manufacturer; the battle of Mylae (260 B.C.) was a victory for Rome in her commercial war against Carthage.
6. Lines 71–75 present a grotesquely mocking image of the possible resurrection of a fertility god. "Cf. the dirge in Webster's *White Devil*" [Eliot's note]: in the play by John Webster (d. 1625), a crazed Renaissance Roman matron fears that the corpses of her decadent and murdered relatives might be disinterred: "But keep the wolf far thence, that's foe to men, / For with his nails he'll dig them up again." In echoing the lines Eliot altered "foe" to "friend" and the "wolf" to "Dog," invoking the brilliant Dog Star Sirius, whose rise in the heavens accompanied the flooding of the Nile and promised the return of fertility to Egypt.
7. "V. Baudelaire, Preface to *Fleurs du Mal*" [Eliot's note]. The last line of the introductory poem to *Les Fleurs du Mal*. "Au Lecteur" (To the Reader), may be translated: "Hypocrite reader!—my likeness—my brother!" It dramatizes the reader's and author's mutual involvement in the waste land.
8. Part II juxtaposes two contemporary settings—the first of elegant decadence. the second of lower-class vulgarity—in a bar or pub and interweaves echoes of the historical and literary past. The title suggests two plays by Thomas Middleton: *A Game of Chess* (1627), about a marriage of political expediency, and *Women Beware Women* (1657), containing a scene in which a mother-in-law is engrossed in a chess game while her daughter-in-law is seduced on a balcony onstage. Eliot's note to line 137 below refers readers to this play.
9. "Cf. *Antony and Cleopatra*, II, ii. 1. 190" [Eliot's note]. In Shakespeare's play, Enobarbus's description of Cleopatra's regal sensuous beauty begins: "The barge she sat in, like a burnish'd throne, / Burn'd on the water."

The glitter of her jewels rose to meet it,
From satin cases poured in rich profusion.   85
In vials of ivory and coloured glass
Unstoppered, lurked her strange synthetic perfumes,
Unguent, powdered, or liquid—troubled, confused
And drowned the sense in odours; stirred by the air
That freshened from the window, these ascended   90
In fattening the prolonged candle-flames,
Flung their smoke into the laquearia,[1]
Stirring the pattern on the coffered ceiling.
Huge sea-wood fed with copper
Burned green and orange, framed by the coloured stone,   95
In which sad light a carvèd dolphin swam.
Above the antique mantel was displayed
As though a window gave upon the sylvan scene[2]
The change of Philomel, by the barbarous king
So rudely forced; yet there the nightingale   100
Filled all the desert with inviolable voice
And still she cried, and still the world pursues,
'Jug Jug'[3] to dirty ears.
And other withered stumps of time
Were told upon the walls; staring forms   105
Leaned out, leaning, hushing the room enclosed.
Footsteps shuffled on the stair.
Under the firelight, under the brush, her hair
Spread out in fiery points
Glowed into words, then would be savagely still.   110

'My nerves are bad to-night. Yes, bad. Stay with me.[4]
'Speak to me. Why do you never speak. Speak.
    'What are you thinking of? What thinking? What?
'I never know what you are thinking. Think.'

I think we are in rats' alley[5]   115
Where the dead men lost their bones.

    'What is that noise?'

1. "Laqueaira. V. *Aeneid*, I, 726 * * * ."
Eliot quotes the passage containing
the term *laquearia* ("paneled ceiling")
and describing the banquet hall where
Queen Dido welcomed Aeneas to Carthage. It reads: "Blazing torches hang
from the gilded paneled ceiling, and
torches conquer the night with flames."
Aeneas became Dido's lover but abandoned her to continue his journey to
found Rome, and she committed suicide.
2. Eliot's notes for lines 98–99 refer the
reader to "Milton, *Paradise Lost*, IV,
140" for the phrase "sylvan scene" and
to "Ovid, *Metamorphoses*, VI, Philomela." The lines ironically splice the setting of Eve's temptation in the Garden
of Eden, first described through Satan's
eyes, with the rape of Philomela by her
sister's husband, King Tereus, and her
transformation into the nightingale.
Eliot's note for line 100 refers the reader
ahead to the nightingale's song as rendered in Part III, line 204, of his own
poem. The myth of Philomela suggests
the transformation of suffering into art.
3. The conventional rendering of the
nightingale's song in Elizabethan poetry.
4. Lines 111–138 may be read as an interior monologue, with the same person
speaking the quoted dialogue outright
while phrasing unspoken thoughts in the
intervening lines; or as a dialogue in
which a woman speaks the quoted remarks while her lover or husband responds silently in the intervening lines.
5. Eliot's note refers readers to "Part
III, 1.195."

The wind under the door.[6]
'What is that noise now? What is the wind doing?'
            Nothing again nothing.   120
                                        'Do
'You know nothing? Do you see nothing? Do you remember
'Nothing?'

            I remember
Those are pearls that were his eyes.   125
'Are you alive, or not? Is there nothing in your head?'
                                        But
O O O O that Shakespeherian Rag—
It's so elegant
So intelligent   130
'What shall I do now? What shall I do?'
'I shall rush out as I am, and walk the street
'With my hair down, so. What shall we do tomorrow?
'What shall we ever do?'
                        The hot water at ten.   135
And if it rains, a closed car at four.
And we shall play a game of chess,
Pressing lidless eyes and waiting for a knock upon the door.

When Lil's husband got demobbed,[7] I said—
I didn't mince my words, I said to her myself,   140
HURRY UP PLEASE ITS TIME[8]
Now Albert's coming back, make yourself a bit smart.
He'll want to know what you done with that money he gave
            you
To get yourself some teeth. He did, I was there.
You have them all out, Lil, and get a nice set,   145
He said, I swear, I can't bear to look at you.
And no more can't I, I said, and think of poor Albert,
He's been in the army four years, he wants a good time,
And if you don't give it him, there's others will, I said.
Oh is there, she said. Something o' that, I said.   150
Then I'll know who to thank, she said, and give me a straight
            look.
HURRY UP PLEASE ITS TIME
If you don't like it you can get on with it, I said.
Others can pick and choose if you can't.
But if Albert makes off, it won't be for lack of telling. 155
You ought to be ashamed, I said, to look so antique.
(And her only thirty-one.)
I can't help it, she said, pulling a long face,
It's them pills I took, to bring it off, she said.
(She's had five already, and nearly died of young George.) 160

6. "Cf. Webster: 'Is the wind in that door still?' " [Eliot's note]. In *The Devil's Law Case* (1623), III.ii.162, by John Webster (d. 1625), a Duke is cured of an infection by a wound intended to kill him; a surprised surgeon asks the quoted question meaning "Is he still alive?" 7. British slang for "demobilized," discharged from the army. 8. Routine call of British bartenders to clear the "pub" at closing time.

The chemist[9] said it would be all right, but I've never been
    the same.
You *are* a proper fool, I said.
Well, if Albert won't leave you alone, there it is, I said,
What you get married for if you don't want children?
HURRY UP PLEASE ITS TIME   165
Well, that Sunday Albert was home, they had a hot gammon,[1]
And they asked me in to dinner, to get the beauty of it hot—
HURRY UP PLEASE ITS TIME
HURRY UP PLEASE ITS TIME
Goonight Bill. Goonight Lou. Goonight May. Goonight.   170
Ta ta. Goodnight. Goonight.
Good night, ladies, good night, sweet ladies, good night,
    good night.[2]

III. The Fire Sermon[3]

The river's tent is broken; the last fingers of leaf
Clutch and sink into the wet bank. The wind
Crosses the brown land, unheard. The nymphs are departed. 175
Sweet Thames, run softly, till I end my song.[4]
The river bears no empty bottles, sandwich papers,
Silk handkerchiefs, cardboard boxes, cigarette ends
Or other testimony of summer nights. The nymphs are
    departed.
And their friends, the loitering heirs of City directors;   180
Departed, have left no addresses.
By the waters of Leman I sat down and wept . . .[5]
Sweet Thames, run softly till I end my song,
Sweet Thames, run softly, for I speak not loud or long.
But at my back in a cold blast I hear[6]   185
The rattle of the bones, and chuckle spread from ear to ear.

A rat crept softly through the vegetation
Dragging its slimy belly on the bank

---

9. Druggist.
1. Ham or bacon; in slang, "thigh."
2. A double echo of the popular song
*Good night ladies, we're going to leave
you now* and of mad Ophelia's pathetic
farewell before drowning herself in
Shakespeare's *Hamlet*, 4.5.72.
3. Eliot's notes to lines 307–9 of this
section identify two governing perspectives: "Buddha's Fire Sermon (which
corresponds in importance to the Sermon
on the Mount)" and "St. Augustine's
Confessions." The "collocation of these
two representatives of eastern and western asceticism, as the culmination of this
part of the poem, is not an accident."
Part III unfolds an increasingly drab
and ominous series of contemporary seductions and assignations, interwoven
with ironic evocations of the past, to define the lusts and sterile parodies of love
which Buddha's Fire Sermon denounces
as the "fire of passion," "the fire of
hatred," and "the fire of infatuation"

which consume the senses.
4. "V. Spenser, *Prothalamion*" [Eliot's
note]. The line is the refrain of the marriage song by Edmund Spenser (d.
1599), a pastoral celebration of marriage
set along the Thames River near London.
5. The phrasing recalls Psalms 137.1,
where the exiled Jews mourn for their
homeland: "By the rivers of Babylon,
there we sat down, yea, we wept, when
we remembered Zion." Lake Leman
is another name for Lake Geneva, location of the sanatorium where Eliot wrote
the bulk of *The Waste Land*. The
archaic term "leman," for illicit mistress,
led to the phrase "waters of leman" signifying lusts.
6. This line and line 196 below echo Andrew Marvell (1621–78), *To His Coy
Mistress*, lines 21–24: "But at my back I
always hear / Time's wingéd chariot
hurrying near, / And yonder all before
us lie / Deserts of vast eternity."

While I was fishing in the dull canal
On a winter evening round behind the gashouse   190
Musing upon the king my brother's wreck[7]
And on the king my father's death before him.
White bodies naked on the low damp ground
And bones cast in a little low dry garret,
Rattled by the rat's foot only, year to year.   195
But at my back from time to time I hear
The sound of horns and motors, which shall bring
Sweeney to Mrs. Porter in the spring.[8]
O the moon shone bright on Mrs. Porter
And on her daughter   200
They wash their feet in soda water[9]
Et O ces voix d'enfants, chantant dans la coupole![1]

Twit twit twit
Jug jug jug jug jug
So rudely forc'd.   205
Tereu[2]

Unreal City
Under the brown fog of a winter noon
Mr. Eugenides,[3] the Smyrna merchant
Unshaven, with a pocket full of currants   210
C.i.f.[4] London: documents at sight,
Asked me in demotic French
To luncheon at the Cannon Street Hotel
Followed by a weekend at the Metropole.[5]

7. "Cf. *The Tempest*, I, ii" [Eliot's note]. An allusion to Shakespeare's play, 1.2.389–90, where Prince Ferdinand, thinking his father dead, describes himself as "Sitting on a bank, / Weeping again the King my father's wreck."
8. "Cf. Day, *Parliament of Bees*: 'When of the sudden, listening, you shall hear, / A noise of horns and hunting, which shall bring / Actaeon to Diana in the spring, / Where all shall see her naked skin * * *'" [Eliot's note]. Actaeon was changed into a stag and hunted to death as punishment for seeing Diana, goddess of chastity, bathing. Eliot's parody of the poem by John Day (1574–c. 1640) suggests an analogy between Actaeon's deed and Sweeney's.
9. "I do not know the origin of the ballad from which these lines are taken: it was reported to me from Sydney, Australia" [Eliot's note]. The bawdy song, itself a parody of the American ballad *Little Redwing*, was popular among World War I troops. One decorous version follows: "O the moon shines bright on Mrs. Porter / And on the daughter / Of Mrs. Porter. / They wash their feet in soda water / And so they oughter / To keep them clean."

1. "V. Verlaine, *Parsifal*" [Eliot's note]. The last line of the sonnet *Parsifal* by the French Symbolist Paul Verlaine (1844–96) reads: "And O those children's voices singing in the cupola." In Wagner's opera, the feet of Parsifal, the questing knight, are washed before he enters the sanctuary of the Grail.
2. "Tereu" alludes to Tereus, the violator of Philomela, and like "jug" is a conventional Elizabethan term for the nightingale's songs.
3. The Turkish merchant's name suggests "well born" and the science of improving a species by selective breeding.
4. "The currants were quoted at a price 'carriage and insurance free to London'; and the Bill of Lading, etc. were to be handed to the buyer upon payment of the sight draft" [Eliot's note]. His second wife has corrected the phrase "carriage and insurance free" to read "cost, insurance and freight."
5. The Canon Street Hotel adjoins a London station frequented by Continental travelers. The Metropole, which Mr. Eugenides proposes for a probably lecherous weekend, is a luxury hotel in Brighton, England.

At the violet hour, when the eyes and back   215
Turn upward from the desk, when the human engine waits
Like a taxi throbbing waiting,
I Tiresias,[6] though blind, throbbing between two lives,
Old man with wrinkled female breasts, can see
At the violet hour, the evening hour that strives   220
Homeward, and brings the sailor home from sea,[7]
The typist home at teatime, clears her breakfast, lights
Her stove, and lays out food in tins.
Out of the window perilously spread
Her drying combinations touched by the sun's last rays,   225
On the divan are piled (at night her bed)
Stockings, slippers, camisoles, and stays.
I Tiresias, old man with wrinkled dugs
Perceived the scene, and foretold the rest—
I too awaited the expected guest.   230
He, the young man carbuncular, arrives,
A small house agent's clerk, with one bold stare,
One of the low on whom assurance sits
As a silk hat on a Bradford[8] millionaire.
The time is now propitious, as he guesses,   235
The meal is ended, she is bored and tired,
Endeavours to engage her in caresses
Which still are unreproved, if undesired.
Flushed and decided, he assaults at once;
Exploring hands encounter no defence;   240
His vanity requires no response,
And makes a welcome of indifference.
(And I Tiresias have foresuffered all
Enacted on this same divan or bed;

6. Eliot's note reads: "Tiresias, although a mere spectator and not indeed a 'character,' is yet the most important personage in the poem, uniting all the rest. Just as the one-eyed merchant, seller of currants, melts into the Phoenician Sailor, and the latter is not wholly distinct from Ferdinand Prince of Naples, so all the women are one woman, and the two sexes meet in Tiresias. What Tiresias *sees*, in fact, is the substance of the poem. The whole passage from Ovid is of great anthropological interest * * * ." The note quotes the Latin passage from Ovid's *Metamorphoses*, II, 421–43 which may be translated: "Jove, [very drunk] said jokingly to Juno: 'You women have greater pleasure in love than that enjoyed by men.' She denied it. So they decided to refer the question to wise Tiresias who knew love from both points of view. For once, with a blow of his staff, he had separated two huge snakes who were copulating in the forest, and miraculously was changed instantly from a man into a woman and remained so for seven years. In the eighth year he saw the snakes again and said: 'If a blow against you is so power-

ful that it changes the sex of the author of it, now I shall strike you again.' With these words he struck them, and his former shape and masculinity were restored. As referee in the sportive quarrel, he supported Jove's claim. Juno, overly upset by the decision, condemned the arbitrator to eternal blindness. But the all-powerful father (inasmuch as no god can undo what has been done by another god) gave him the power of prophecy, with this honor compensating him for the loss of sight."
7. "This may not appear as exact as Sappho's lines, but I had in mind the 'longshore' or 'dory' fisherman, who returns at nightfall" [Eliot's note]. Fragment CXLIX, by the Greek woman poet Sappho (fl. 600 B.C.), celebrates the Evening Star who "brings homeward all those / Scattered by the dawn, / The sheep to fold * * * / The children to their mother's side." A more familiar echo is "Home is the sailor, home from sea" in *Requiem* by the Scottish poet Robert Louis Stevenson (1850–94).
8. A Yorkshire, England, manufacturing town where quick fortunes were made during World War I.

I who have sat by Thebes below the wall[9]   245
And walked among the lowest of the dead.)
Bestows one final patronising kiss,
And gropes his way, finding the stairs unlit. .

She turns and looks a moment in the glass,
Hardly aware of her departed lover;   250
Her brain allows one half-formed thought to pass:
'Well now that's done: and I'm glad it's over.'
When lovely woman stoops to folly and
Paces about her room again, alone,
She smoothes her hair with automatic hand,   255
And puts a record on the gramophone.[1]

'This music crept by me upon the waters'[2]
And along the Strand, up Queen Victoria Street.
O City city, I can sometimes hear
Beside a public bar in Lower Thames Street,   260
The pleasant whining of a mandoline
And a clatter and a chatter from within
Where fishmen lounge at noon: where the walls
Of Magnus Martyr hold
Inexplicable splendour of Ionian white and gold.[3]   265

    The river sweats[4]
    Oil and tar
    The barges drift
    With the turning tide
    Red sails   270
    Wide
    To leeward, swing on the heavy spar.
    The barges wash
    Drifting logs
    Down Greenwich reach   275

9. Tiresias prophesied in the marketplace below the wall of Thebes, witnessed the tragedies of Oedipus and Creon in that city, and retained his prophetic powers in Hades.

1. Eliot's note refers to the novel *The Vicar of Wakefield* (1766) by Oliver Goldsmith (1728–74) and the song sung by Olivia when she revisits the scene of her seduction: "When lovely woman stoops to folly / And finds too late that men betray / What charm can soothe her melancholy, / What art can wash her guilt away? / The only art her guilt to cover, / To hide her shame from every eye, / To give repentance to her lover / And wring his bosom—is to die."

2. Eliot's note refers to Shakespeare's *The Tempest*, the scene where Ferdinand listens in wonder to Ariel's song telling of his father's miraculous "sea-change":

"This music crept by me on the waters, / Allaying both their fury and my passion / With its sweet air * * *" (1.2. 391–93).

3. "The interior of St. Magnus Martyr is to my mind one of the finest among [Christopher] Wren's interiors * * *" [Eliot's note].

4. "The Song of the (three) Thames-daughters begins here. From line 292 to 306 inclusive they speak in turn. V. *Götterdämmerung*, III, i: the Rhine-daughters" [Eliot's note]. A contemporary view of the Thames and the three songs which tell of passionless seductions are interwoven with a refrain (lines 277–78, 290–91) from the lament of the Rhine-maidens for the lost beauty of the Rhine River in the opera by Richard Wagner (1813–83), *Die Götterdämmerung* ("The Twilight of the Gods," 1876).

Past the Isle of Dogs.[5]
   Weialala leia
   Wallala leialala

Elizabeth and Leicester[6]
Beating oars   280
The stern was formed
A gilded shell
Red and gold
The brisk swell
Rippled both shores   285
Southwest wind
Carried down stream
The peal of bells
White towers
   Weialala leia   290
   Wallala leialala

'Trams and dusty trees.
Highbury bore me. Richmond and Kew
Undid me.[7] By Richmond I raised my knees
Supine on the floor of a narrow canoe.'   295

'My feet are at Moorgate,[8] and my heart
Under my feet. After the event
He wept. He promised "a new start."
I made no comment. What should I resent?'

'On Margate Sands.[9]   300
I can connect
Nothing with nothing.
The broken fingernails of dirty hands.
My people humble people who expect
Nothing.'   305
   la la

To Carthage then I came[1]

---

5. A peninsula in the Thames opposite Greenwich, a borough of London and the birthplace of Queen Elizabeth.

6. The love affair of Queen Elizabeth and the Earl of Leicester (Robert Dudley), though it transpired in courtly and beautiful settings, was fruitless and conducted with regard to diplomatic expediency. Eliot's note refers to the historian James A. Froude, "*Elizabeth*, Vol. I, ch. iv, letter of [Bishop] De Quadra [the ambassador] to Philip of Spain: 'In the afternoon we were in a barge, watching the games on the river. (The queen) was alone with Lord Robert and myself on the poop, when they began to talk nonsense, and went so far that Lord Robert at last said, as I was on the spot there was no reason why they should not be married if the queen pleased.' "

7. "Cf. *Purgatorio*, V, 133 ✳ ✳ ✳ " [Eliot's note]. Eliot quotes Dante's lines, which he parodied; they may be translated: "Remember me, who am La Pia. / Siena made me, Maremma undid me." Highbury is a London suburb, Richmond a London borough with park and boating facilities, and Kew an adjoining district containing the Kew Botanical Gardens.

8. An East London slum.

9. Resort on the Thames estuary.

1. "V. St. Augustine's *Confessions*: 'to Carthage then I came, where a cauldron of unholy loves sang all about mine ears' " [Eliot's note]. Augustine here recounts his licentious youth.

Burning burning burning burning[2]
O Lord Thou pluckest me out[3]
O Lord Thou pluckest   310

burning

IV. Death by Water[4]

Phlebas the Phoenician, a fortnight dead,
Forgot the cry of gulls, and the deep sea swell
And the profit and loss.
                    A current under sea   315
Picked his bones in whispers. As he rose and fell
He passed the stages of his age and youth
Entering the whirlpool.
                    Gentile or Jew
O you who turn the wheel and look to windward,   320
Consider Phlebas, who was once handsome and tall as you.

V. What the Thunder Said[5]

After the torchlight red on sweaty faces
After the frosty silence in the gardens
After the agony in stony places
The shouting and the crying   325
Prison and palace and reverberation
Of thunder of spring over distant mountains
He who was living is now dead
We who were living are now dying
With a little patience[6]   330

Here is no water but only rock
Rock and no water and the sandy road
The road winding above among the mountains
Which are mountains of rock without water
If there were water we should stop and drink   335

2. Eliot's note to lines 307–9 refers to "Buddha's Fire Sermon (which corresponds in importance to the Sermon on the Mount)" and "St. Augustine's Confessions." The "collocation of these two representatives of eastern and western asceticism, as the culmination of this part of the poem, is not an accident."
3. The line is from Augustine's *Confessions* and echoes also Zechariah 3.2, where Jehovah, rebuking Satan, calls the high priest Joshua "a brand plucked out of the fire."
4. This lyric section presents the fearsome "death by water" that Madame Sosostris warned against in line 55. Critics disagree as to whether Phlebas's death, in the context of the entire poem, is a catastrophe prefiguring annihilation, or a ritual sacrifice prefiguring rebirth.
5. "In the first part of Part V three themes are employed: the journey to Emmaus, the approach to the Chapel Perilous (see Miss Weston's book) and the present decay of eastern Europe" [Eliot's note]. During his disciples' journey to Emmaus, after his crucifixion and resurrection, Jesus walked alongside and conversed with them, but they thought him a stranger until he revealed his identity (Luke 24.13–34). This section interfuses (1) images of personal isolation and disintegration, social upheaval, and makeshift routine with (2) images of redemptive suffering, compassion, sacrificial ritual, and disciplined control.
6. The opening nine lines contain allusions to Christ's imprisonment and trial, to his agony in the garden of Gethsemane, and his crucifixion and burial in the garden of Golgotha; they suggest the imminent despair during the days between the crucifixion and the resurrection on Easter.

Amongst the rock one cannot stop or think
Sweat is dry and feet are in the sand
If there were only water amongst the rock
Dead mountain mouth of carious teeth that cannot spit
Here one can neither stand nor lie nor sit   340
There is not even silence in the mountains
But dry sterile thunder without rain
There is not even solitude in the mountains
But red sullen faces sneer and snarl
From doors of mudcracked houses   345
                             If there were water
    And no rock
    If there were rock
    And also water
    And water   350
    A spring
    A pool among the rock
    If there were the sound of water only
    Not the cicada[7]
    And dry grass singing   355
    But sound of water over a rock
    Where the hermit-thrush[8] sings in the pine trees
    Drip drop drip drop drop drop drop
    But there is no water

Who is the third who walks always beside you?[9]   360
When I count, there are only you and I together
But when I look ahead up the white road
There is always another one walking beside you
Gliding wrapt in a brown mantle, hooded
I do not know whether a man or a woman   365
—But who is that on the other side of you?

What is that sound high in the air[1]
Murmur of maternal lamentation
Who are those hooded hordes swarming
Over endless plains, stumbling in cracked earth   370

7. Grasshopper. Cf. line 23 and Ecclesiastes 12.5: "the grasshopper shall be a burden, and desire shall fail."
8. "This is * * * the hermit-thrush which I have heard in Quebec Province. Chapman says (*Handbook of Birds of Eastern North America*) 'it is most at home in secluded woodland and thickety retreats. * * * Its 'water dripping song' is justly celebrated" [Eliot's note].
9. "The following lines were stimulated by the account of one of the Antarctic expeditions (I forget which, but I think one of Shackleton's): it was related that the party of explorers, at the extremity of their strength, had the constant delusion that there was *one more member* than could actually be counted" [Eliot's

note]. The reminiscence is associated with Christ's unrecognized presence on the journey to Emmaus. (See introductory note to Part V.)
1. Eliot's note quotes a passage in German from *Blick ins Chaos* (1920) by Hermann Hesse (1877–1962), which may be translated: "Already half of Europe, already at least half of Eastern Europe, on the way to Chaos, drives drunk in sacred infatuation along the edge of the precipice, sings drunkenly, as though hymn-singing, as Dimitri Karamazov sang [in the novel *The Brothers Karamazov* (1882) by Feodor Dostoevsky (1821–81)]. The offended bourgeois laughs at the songs; the saint and the seer hear them with tears."

Ringed by the flat horizon only
What is the city over the mountains
Cracks and reforms and bursts in the violet air
Falling towers
Jerusalem Athens Alexandria   375
Vienna London
Unreal

A woman drew her long black hair out tight[2]
And fiddled whisper music on those strings
And bats with baby faces in the violet light   380
Whistled, and beat their wings
And crawled head downward down a blackened wall
And upside down in air were towers
Tolling reminiscent bells, that kept the hours
And voices singing out of empty cisterns and exhausted wells. 385

In this decayed hole among the mountains
In the faint moonlight, the grass is singing
Over the tumbled graves, about the chapel
There is the empty chapel, only the wind's home.
It has no windows, and the door swings,   390
Dry bones can harm no one.
Only a cock stood on the rooftree
Co co rico co co rico[3]
In a flash of lightning. Then a damp gust
Bringing rain   395

Ganga[4] was sunken, and the limp leaves
Waited for rain, while the black clouds
Gathered far distant, over Himavant.[5]
The jungle crouched, humped in silence.
Then spoke the thunder   400
DA[6]
Datta: what have we given?
My friend, blood shaking my heart
The awful daring of a moment's surrender
Which an age of prudence can never retract   405
By this, and this only, we have existed
Which is not to be found in our obituaries
Or in memories draped by the beneficient spider[7]

2. Lines 378–91 suggest the final temptation to despair as the questing knight encounters the Chapel Perilous in the Grail legend.
3. A cock's crow in folklore signaled the departure of ghosts (as in Shakespeare's *Hamlet*, 1.1.157 ff); in Matthew 26.34 and 74 a cock crowed, as Christ predicted, when Peter denied him three times.
4. The Indian river Ganges, sacred to Hindus and the scene of purgation and fertility ceremonies.
5. A mountain in the Himalayas.
6. " 'Datta, dayadhvam, damyata' (Give, sympathise, control). The fable of the

meaning of the Thunder is found in the *Brihadaranyaka—Upanishad*, 5, 1 * * *" [Eliot's note]. In the Hindu legend, the injunction of Prajapati (supreme diety) is "Da," which is interpreted in three different ways by gods, men, and demons, to mean "control ourselves," "give alms," and "have compassion." Prajapati assures them that when "the divine voice, The Thunder," repeats the syllable it means all three things and that therefore "one should practice * * * Self-Control, Alms-giving, and Compassion."
7. Eliot's note refers to *The White Devil*

Or under seals broken by the lean solicitor
In our empty rooms   410
DA
Dayadhvam: I have heard the key[8]
Turn in the door once and turn once only
We think of the key, each in his prison
Thinking of the key, each confirms a prison   415
Only at nightfall, aethereal rumours
Revive for a moment a broken Coriolanus[9]
DA
Damyata: The boat responded
Gaily, to the hand expert with sail and oar   420
The sea was calm, your heart would have responded
Gaily, when invited, beating obedient
To controlling hands

                    I sat upon the shore
Fishing,[1] with the arid plain behind me   425
Shall I at least set my lands in order?[2]
London Bridge is falling down falling down falling down
Poi s'ascose nel foco che gli affina[3]
Quando fiam uti chelidon[4]—O swallow swallow
Le Prince d'Aquitaine à la tour abolie[5]   430
These fragments I have shored against my ruins[6]
Why then Ile fit you. Hieronymo's mad againe.[7]

(1612) by the English playwright John Webster (d. 1625), V.vi: " * * * they'll remarry / Ere the worm pierce your winding-sheet, ere the spider / Make a thin curtain for your epitaphs."
8. "Cf. *Inferno*, XXXIII, 46 * * * " [Eliot's note]. At this point Ugolino recalls his imprisonment with his children, where they starved to death: "And I heard below the door of the horrible tower being locked up." Eliot's note continues: "Also F. H. Bradley, *Appearance and Reality*, p. 346. 'My external sensations are no less private to myself than are my thoughts or my feelings. In either case my experience falls within my own circle, a circle closed on the outside; and, with all its elements alike, every sphere is opaque to the others which surround it * * * . In brief, regarded as an existence which appears in a soul, the whole world for each is peculiar and private to that soul.' "
9. The Roman patrician Coriolanus defiantly chose self-exile when threatened with banishment by the leaders of the populace; he led enemy forces against Rome, then, persuaded by his family, he tried too late to reconcile the warring cities. He is the tragic protagonist in Shakespeare's *Coriolanus* (1608).
1. "V. Weston: *From Ritual to Romance*; chapter on the Fisher King" [Eliot's note].
2. Cf. Isaiah 38.1: "Thus saith the Lord, Set thine house in order: for thou shalt die, and not live."
3. Eliot's note to *Purgatorio*, XXVI, quotes in Italian the passage (lines 145–48) where the Provençal poet Arnaut Daniel, recalling his lusts, addresses Dante: "I pray you now, by the Goodness that guides you to the summit of this staircase, reflect in due season on my suffering." Then, in the line quoted in *The Waste Land*, "he hid himself in the fire that refines them."
4. Eliot's note refers to the *Pervigilium Veneris* ("The Vigil of Venus"), an anonymous Latin poem, and suggests a comparison with "Philomela in Parts II and III" of *The Waste Land*. The last stanzas of the *Pervigilium* recreate the myth of the nightingale in the image of a swallow, and the poet listening to the bird speaks the quoted line, "When shall I be as the swallow," and adds: "that I may cease to be silent." "O Swallow, Swallow" are the opening words of one of the songs interspersed in Tennyson's narrative poem *The Princess* (1847).
5. "V. Gerard de Nerval, Sonnet *El Desdichado*" [Eliot's note]. The line reads: "The Prince of Aquitaine in the ruined tower."
6. This line, like the invocation of the swallow in line 428, and the allusion to mad Hieronymo below, suggests the poet's attempt to come to terms with the waste land through his own verse.
7. Eliot's note refers to Thomas Kyd's

Datta. Dayadhvam. Damyata.
Shantih shantih shantih[8]

1921   1922

From FOUR QUARTETS
Burnt Norton[1]

τοῦ λόγον δ'ἐόντος ξυνοῦ ζώουσιν οἱ πολλοί
ὡς ἰδίαν ἔχοντες φρόνησιν.
I. p. 77. Fr. 2.
ὁδὸς ἄνω κάτω μία καὶ ὡυτή.
I. p. 89. Fr. 60.
—DIELS: *Die Fragmente der Vorsokratiker* (HERAKLEITOS)

I[2]

Time present and time past
Are both perhaps present in time future,
And time future contained in time past.
If all time is eternally present
All time is unredeemable.   5
What might have been is an abstraction
Remaining a perpetual possibility
Only in a world of speculation.
What might have been and what has been
Point to one end, which is always present.[3]   10

revenge play, *The Spanish Tragedy,* subtitled *Hieronymo's Mad Againe* (1594). In it Hieronymo is asked to write a court play and he answers "I'll fit you" in the double sense of "oblige" and "get even." He manages, though mad, to kill the murderers of his son by acting in the play and assigning parts appropriately, then commits suicide.

8. "Shantih. Repeated as here, a formal ending to an Upanishad [Vedic treatise, sacred Hindu text]. 'The peace which passeth understanding' is our equivalent to this word" [Eliot's note].

1. Eliot made *Burnt Norton,* though published originally as a separate poem, the basis and formal model for *East Coker* (1940), *The Dry Salvages* (1941), and *Little Gidding* (1942). Together they comprise *Four Quartets* (1943). Exploring the meaning of time in a search for its redemption, the *Quartets* seek to capture those rare moments when eternity "intersects" the temporal continuum, while treating also the relations between those moments and the flux of time. The series and each Quartet in it recapitulate the central theme through contrapuntal variations while moving gradually (through often tentative and enigmatic sequences) toward the explicit naming and more full revelation of its Christian content (the "Word" at the end of *Burnt Norton,* the "purgatorial fires" and "Annunciation" in subsequent Quartets, the coalescence of religious symbols at the end of *Little Gidding*). Central to its structure, and particularly in *Burnt Norton,* is the idea

of the Spanish mystic St. John of the Cross (1542–91) that the ascent of a soul to union with God is facilitated by memory and disciplined meditation but that meditation is superseded by a "dark night of the soul," a passive surrender of the will to God, an emptying of the senses and the self, a descent into darkness that is deepened paradoxically the nearer one approaches the light of God. The Greek epigraphs are from the pre-Socratic philosopher Heraclitus (540?–475 B.C.) and may be translated: "But although the Word is common to all, the majority of people live as though they had each an understanding peculiarly his own" and "The way up and the way down are one and the same."

2. Lines 1–10 introduce the theme of time abstractly and express skepticism about the redemption of time and the significance of a "might have been" in any but theoretical terms. The succeeding lines of Section I turn from abstraction to concrete memories, and the echoing words that accompany them, so as to explore childhood premonitions (glimpsed but not understood) of the sexual awakening and religious illumination that are figured in the rose garden and its empty pool that mysteriously fills with sunlight. Burnt Norton is a manor house in Gloucestershire, England. The opening lines echo Ecclesiastes 3.14–15: "That which hath been is now; and that which is to be hath already been."

3. In the double sense of "termination" and "purpose."

Footfalls echo in the memory
Down the passage which we did not take
Towards the door we never opened
Into the rose-garden.[4] My words echo
Thus, in your mind.
                                But to what purpose   15
Disturbing the dust on a bowl of rose-leaves
I do not know.
                        Other echoes
Inhabit the garden. Shall we follow?
Quick, said the bird, find them, find them,
Round the corner. Through the first gate,   20
Into our first world, shall we follow
The deception of the thrush? Into our first world.
There they were, dignified, invisible,
Moving without pressure, over the dead leaves,
In the autumn heat, through the vibrant air,   25
And the bird called, in response to
The unheard music hidden in the shrubbery,
And the unseen eyebeam crossed, for the roses
Had the look of flowers that are looked at.
There they were as our guests, accepted and accepting.   30
So we moved, and they, in a formal pattern,
Along the empty alley, into the box circle,[5]
To look down into the drained pool.
Dry the pool, dry concrete, brown edged,
And the pool was filled with water out of sunlight,   35
And the lotos[6] rose, quietly, quietly,
The surface glittered out of heart of light,[7]
And they were behind us, reflected in the pool.
Then a cloud passed, and the pool was empty.
Go, said the bird, for the leaves were full of children,   40
Hidden excitedly, containing laughter.
Go, go, go, said the bird: human kind
Cannot bear very much reality.
Time past and time future
What might have been and what has been   45
Point to one end, which is always present.

II[8]

Garlic and sapphires in the mud[9]
Clot the bedded axle-tree.
The trilling wire in the blood

4. The rose is a symbol of sexual and
spiritual love; in Christian traditions it is
associated with the harmony of religious
truth and with the Virgin Mary, her
bower being depicted often as a rose
garden.
5. Evergreen boxwood shrubs, planted
in a circle.
6. The lotus is a highly erotic symbol,
associated particularly with the goddess
Lakshmi in Hindu mythology.
7. An echo of Dante's *Paradiso*, XII.28–

29: "from out of the heart of one of
the new lights there moved a voice."
8. In this opening lyric, a turbulent and
paradoxical experience, compounding the
earthly and sensuous with the transcendent, leads to a state of being which is
neither static nor agitated but intensely
"still" in the double sense of "tranquil"
and "enduring." This state is imaged as
a dance.
9. Derived from line 10 of the sonnet by
the French Symbolist Stéphane Mallarmé

Sings below inveterate scars   50
Appeasing long forgotten wars.
The dance along the artery
The circulation of the lymph
Are figured in the drift of stars
Ascend to summer in the tree   55
We move above the moving tree
In light upon the figured leaf[1]
And hear upon the sodden floor
Below, the boarhound and the boar
Pursue their pattern as before   60
But reconciled among the stars.

At the still point of the turning world. Neither flesh nor
    fleshless;
Neither from nor towards; at the still point, there the dance
    is,
But neither arrest nor movement. And do not call it fixity,
Where past and future are gathered. Neither movement from
    nor towards,   65
Neither ascent nor decline. Except for the point, the still
    point,
There would be no dance, and there is only the dance.
I can only say, *there* we have been: but I cannot say where.
And I cannot say, how long, for that is to place it in time.

The inner freedom from the practical desire,   70
The release from action and suffering, release from the
    inner
And the outer compulsion, yet surrounded
By a grace of sense, a white light still and moving,
Erhebung[2] without motion, concentration
Without elimination, both a new world   75
And the old made explicit, understood
In the completion of its partial ecstasy,
The resolution of its partial horror.
Yet the enchainment of past and future
Woven in the weakness of the changing body,   80
Protects mankind from heaven and damnation
Which flesh cannot endure.
                              Time past and time future
Allow but a little consciousness.
To be conscious is not to be in time   85
But only in time can the moment in the rose-garden,
The moment in the arbour where the rain beat,
The moment in the draughty church at smokefall

(1842–98) "M'introduire dans ton his-
toire" ("To fit myself into your story").
Line 10 reads: "Tonnère et rubis aux
moyeux," or "Thunder and rubies at the
axles."
1. An echo of the description of death
in Tennyson's *In Memoriam* (1850),
XLIII.10–12: "So that still garden of the
souls / In many a figured leaf enrolls /
The total world since life began."
2. German for "exaltation."

Be remembered; involved with past and future.
Only through time time is conquered.   90

III[3]

Here is a place of disaffection
Time before and time after
In a dim light: neither daylight
Investing form with lucid stillness
Turning shadow into transient beauty   95
With slow rotation suggesting permanence
Nor darkness to purify the soul
Emptying the sensual with deprivation
Cleansing affection from the temporal.
Neither plenitude nor vacancy. Only a flicker   100
Over the strained time-ridden faces
Distracted from distraction by distraction
Filled with fancies and empty of meaning
Tumid apathy with no concentration
Men and bits of paper, whirled by the cold wind   105
That blows before and after time,
Wind in and out of unwholesome lungs
Time before and time after.
Eructation of unhealthy souls
Into the faded air, the torpid   110
Driven on the wind that sweeps the gloomy hills of London,
Hampstead and Clerkenwell, Campden and Putney,
Highgate, Primrose and Ludgate.[4] Not here
Not here the darkness, in this twittering world.

Descend lower, descend only   115
Into the world of perpetual solitude,
World not world, but that which is not world,
Internal darkness, deprivation
And destitution of all property,
Desiccation of the world of sense,   120
Evacuation of the world of fancy,
Inoperancy of the world of spirit;
This is the one way, and the other
Is the same, not in movement
But abstention from movement; while the world moves   125
In appetency, on its metalled ways
Of time past and time future.

IV[5]

Time and the bell have buried the day,
The black cloud carries the sun away.

3. This section presents first a descent into a subway, then a deeper descent into the darkness of the self.
4. Districts and neighborhoods in London.
5. This lyric is poised between anxious anticipation of night and death, and confidence in the eternity of the receding sunlight. The images evoke symbolic associations: the sunflower with light, the clematis (called "virgin's bower") with the Virgin Mary, the yew with death and immortality, the kingfisher with the Fisher King of the Grail legend, the light with Dante's vision of God in *Paradiso,* XXXIII.109–10.

Will the sunflower turn to us, will the clematis   130
Stray down, bend to us; tendril and spray
Clutch and cling?
Chill
Fingers of yew be curled
Down on us? After the kingfisher's wing   135
Has answered light to light, and is silent, the light is still
At the still point of the turning world.

V[6]

Words move, music moves
Only in time; but that which is only living
Can only die. Words, after speech, reach   140
Into the silence. Only by the form, the pattern,
Can words or music reach
The stillness, as a Chinese jar still
Moves perpetually in its stillness.
Not the stillness of the violin, while the note lasts,   145
Not that only, but the co-existence,
Or say that the end precedes the beginning,
And the end and the beginning were always there
Before the beginning and after the end.
And all is always now. Words strain,   150
Crack and sometimes break, under the burden,
Under the tension, slip, slide, perish,
Decay with imprecision, will not stay in place,
Will not stay still. Shrieking voices
Scolding, mocking, or merely chattering,   155
Always assail them. The Word in the desert[7]
Is most attacked by voices of temptation,
The crying shadow in the funeral dance,
The loud lament of the disconsolate chimera.[8]

The detail of the pattern is movement,   160
As in the figure of the ten stairs.[9]
Desire itself is movement
Not in itself desirable;
Love is itself unmoving,
Only the cause and end of movement,   165
Timeless, and undesiring
Except in the aspect of time
Caught in the form of limitation
Between un-being and being.

6. This section parallels the world's assaults on actual language with the temptation of the Christian Word in the wilderness, and celebrates the attempt of words and "pattern" in art to reach beyond themselves to the stillness of divine love and so capture the moment of revelation imaged in "the hidden laughter / Of children in the foliage."
7. An allusion to Christ's temptation in the wilderness, Luke 4.1–4.

8. A monster in Greek mythology, and a symbol of fantasies and delusions, slain by Bellerophon with the help of the winged horse Pegasus. Pegasus was a favorite of the Muses of the arts whom Bellerophon had tamed.
9. An allusion to St. John of the Cross's figure for the soul's ascent to God, "The Ten Degrees of the Mystical Ladder of Divine Love."

Sudden in a shaft of sunlight   170
Even while the dust moves
There rises the hidden laughter
Of children in the foliage
Quick, now, here, now always—
Ridiculous the waste sad time   175
Stretching before and after.

1934   1936, 1943

JOHN CROWE RANSOM
1888–1974

More than a decade before the Great Depression of the 1930s, when writers in significant numbers began teaching in American colleges and universities, the Southerner John Crowe Ransom accepted an appointment at Vanderbilt University, where he began writing poetry and criticism that soon established him as a leading exponent of southern agrarianism, the most influential of the "New Critics" writing in America, and the finest southern poet if his generation.

The son of a Methodist minister, Ransom was born in 1888 in Tennessee, was educated by his father until attending the Bowen School in Nashville, then studied philosophy and the Greek and Latin classics at Vanderbilt and later as a Rhodes Scholar at Oxford University in England. After teaching Latin in a preparatory school for a year, he began teaching English literature at Vanderbilt in 1914 and began writing poetry before leaving for service in the army. He was studying at Grenoble University in France when he finished his first book, *Poems without God*, which was published in 1919 just before his return to Vanderbilt and teaching. He remained at Vanderbilt until 1937 when he joined the faculty of Kenyon College in Ohio, where he founded in 1939 the influential *Kenyon Review* (which he continued to edit until his retirement in 1959) and launched in 1948 the Kenyon School of English (which became the School of Letters of Ohio University in 1951). Virtually all of his poems had been published by 1927 (in *Chills and Fever*, 1924, and *Two Gentlemen in Bonds*, 1927), and he added only five new poems to those he consented to reprint (he excluded *Poems without God* entirely), in *Selected Poems* (1945). But he revised his poems continuously, adding stanzas or deleting and altering lines, and readmitting some poems to revised editions of *Selected Poems* in 1963 and 1969, which were awarded respectively the Bollingen Prize for Poetry and the National Book Award.

Though literary criticism and cultural commentary took precedence over his poetry after 1927, the three pursuits were inseparably interwoven earlier in his career. At Vanderbilt Ransom became the center of a group known as The Fugitives which met fortnightly to discuss philosophy and to read their own verse; they included the poet Donald Davidson and later the poet Allen Tate and the poet and novelist Robert Penn Warren. In the group's journal, *The Fugitive*, published between 1922 and 1925, much of Ransom's best poetry appeared. The poems were conspicuous for their wit and learning but chiefly for the subtle irony which enabled Ransom to affirm traditional southern values without succumbing to sentimentality, and to combine sophisticated perspectives on human experience with the simplicity of ballad forms and children's stories. Ransom's versification and stanza patterns are more traditional than T. S. Eliot's, but approximate rhymes or an occasional rough rhyme and doubled rhyme ("Moo" and "set-to," "rogue" and "prologue," "clack clack") produce bizarre effects, give body to the texture of the verse, and strengthen both the impact and the irony of the poems. He called his irregular metric "accentual meter; that is to say, we just count the number of accented or stressed syllables in the line and let unstressed syllables take care of themselves. So that sometimes * * * you run over two or three, or maybe even four, unstressed syllables at once—which was against the rule of the old poets. * * *"[1] Ransom's conspicuously mixed diction—Latinate mixed with Old English terms, learned or abstruse terms fused with childlike colloquialisms, archaic terms or elegant usages joined with commonplaces—enable him to achieve the general aim that he defined in a letter to Allen Tate in 1927: "(1) I want to find the experience that is in the common actuals; (2) I want this experience to carry * * * the dearest possible values to which we have attached ourselves; (3) I want to face the disintegration or nullification of these values as calmly and religiously as possible."[2] The result (in *Captain Carpenter* or *Dog*, for instance) is often a parody or mockery of poetic conventions which does not repudiate their power but reinforces it with irony.

When treating his characteristic themes—mortality, the denial of the body by the intellect and codes of decorum, the consecration of the past, and the frustration of moral idealism—Ransom's verse displays many of the characteristics of such southern fiction as the noevls of William Faulkner or the stories of Flannery O'Connor: the repression of energy which breaks through the surface in bizarre gestures and explosive violence, the haunting presence of archetypal figures, redolent of a ghostly chivalric past but still vivid in the present, as in faded tapestries and cracked paintings. Ransom's idiom can also render complex psychological states and densely enigmatic philosophical speculation even when warning against what he regards as the mind's worst enemy, abstraction.

The habit of intellectual abstraction had been instilled in the modern mind, Ransom felt, by science and its attendant industrial technology which dominated culture in the North. Ransom championed instead a regionalism that asserted the primacy of the full sensibility and of a traditionalistic community with ties to the more leisurely pace, the social structures and amenities, and the Protestant religious myths of the South's agrarian past. Myths extolling subsistence farming and a life close to nature informed Ransom's contributions to the collaborative *I'll Take My Stand*, published by "Twelve Southerners" in 1930. The threat posed by science to religious myths in the Scopes trial of 1925 (which examined the right of a teacher to teach Darwinian evolutionary theories in the Tennessee schools) provoked Ransom to write *God without Thunder* (1930), in which he defended not the High Anglicanism of Eliot but the original orthodoxies of the evangelical denominations which comprised the "social solidar-

1. Quoted by Robert Buffington, *The Equilibrist*, 88.

2. Quoted by Louise Cowan, *The Fugitive Group*, 178.

ity of my own community."[3] Religious myths did more justice than narrowly rationalistic science, Ransom felt, to the dualities and complexities of the psyche, and the vitalities of the natural world.

Alternatives to science and abstraction were the basis not only of Ransom's conservative agrarianism but of his literary theory as well, which he developed in countless reviews and in two books: *The World's Body* (1938), a collection of essays on poetic strategy in works ranging from Shakespeare's sonnets to Eliot's *Murder in the Cathedral*, and *The New Criticism* (1941), essays on contemporary literary critics and questions of critical method. Ransom warned against not only the abstractions of science but those of "Platonic" idealists (or "monsters") who "worship universals, laws, Platonic ideas, reason, the 'immaterial' "[4] and he claimed for poetry a different and superior status as a means to knowledge. He claimed that poetry and, paradoxically, abstraction in art encompassed the particulars of actual experience, the concrete body of reality which eluded abstract modes of scientific and rational thought. While poetry aimed for the traditional fusion of a "moral effect with an aesthetic effect,"[5] the knowledge it contained was more extensive than philosophy because of the poem's texture of images, meters, and connotations; its texture could extend so far as to seem irrelevant to the poem's pattern (making for densely enigmatic poems), yet lead the reader into the full increment of knowledge that the poem made possible. Whatever the limitations of Ransom's critical theory, his method encouraged the close attention to details of poetic texts that distinguish them from other forms of discourse, an emphasis on verbal and formal features of poems rather than historical and philosophical contexts. He thereby defined the main aims of what came to be recognized as the "New Criticism" in American literary criticism. Kenyon College and its school of English became important centers for the encouragement of criticism and poetry—attracted by Ransom, the poet Robert Lowell transferred from Harvard to Kenyon—and the *Kenyon Review*, under Ransom's editorial direction, had a lasting impact on the younger ranks in academic circles and on the literary profession at large.

Dead Boy[1]

The little cousin is dead, by foul subtraction,
A green bough from Virginia's aged tree,
And none of the county kin like the transaction,
Nor some of the world of outer dark, like me.

A boy not beautiful, nor good, nor clever,   5
A black cloud full of storms too hot for keeping,
A sword beneath his mother's heart—yet never
Woman bewept her babe as this is weeping.

A pig with a pasty face, so I had said,
Squealing for cookies, kinned by poor pretense   10
With a noble house. But the little man quite dead,
I see the forebears' antique lineaments.

3. P. 327.
4. *The World's Body*, p. 225.
5. *Ibid.*, p. 57.

1. First published as a three-part sonnet sequence. The 1945 text is printed here.

The elder men have strode by the box of death
To the wide flag porch, and muttering low send round
The bruit[2] of the day. O friendly waste of breath!   15
Their hearts are hurt with a deep dynastic wound.

He was pale and little, the foolish neighbors say;
The first-fruits, saith the Preacher, the Lord hath taken;[3]
But this was the old tree's late branch wrenched away,
Grieving the sapless limbs, the shorn and shaken.   20

                                                    1920, 1927

Spectral Lovers

By night they haunted a thicket of April mist,
Out of that black ground suddenly come to birth,
Else angels lost in each other and fallen on earth.
Lovers they knew they were, but why unclasped, un-
     kissed?
Why should two lovers go frozen apart in fear?   5
And yet they were, they were.

Over the shredding of an April blossom
Scarcely her fingers touched him, quick with care,
Yet of evasions even she made a snare.
The heart was bold that clanged within her bosom,   10
The moment perfect, the time stopped for them,
Still her face turned from him.

Strong were the batteries[1] of the April night
And the stealthy emanations of the field;
Should the walls of her prison undefended yield   15
And open her treasure to the first clamorous knight?
"This is the mad moon, and shall I surrender all?
If he but ask it I shall."

And gesturing largely to the moon of Easter,
Mincing his steps and swishing the jubilant grass,   20
Beheading some field-flowers that had come to pass,
He had reduced his tributaries faster
Had not considerations pinched his heart
Unfitly for his art.

"Am I reeling with the sap of April like a drunkard?   25
Blessed is he that taketh this richest of cities;
But it is so stainless the sack were a thousand pities.
This is that marble fortress not to be conquered,
Lest its white peace in the black flame turn to tinder
And an unutterable cinder."   30

2. Rumor.
3. The preacher's text echoes "Thou
shalt not delay to offer the first of thy
ripe fruits * * * the first of thy sons shalt
thou give unto me" (Exodus 22.29).
1. Pun: acts of assault; military units;
clusters of vessels charged with power.

They passed me once in April, in the mist.
No other season is it when one walks and discovers
Two tall and wandering, like spectral lovers,
White in the season's moon-gold and amethyst,
Who touch their quick fingers fluttering like a bird   35
Whose songs shall never be heard.

1924

Bells for John Whiteside's Daughter

There was such speed in her little body,
And such lightness in her footfall,
It is no wonder her brown study[2]
Astonishes us all.

Her wars were bruited in our high window.   5
We looked among orchard trees and beyond,
Where she took arms against her shadow,
Or harried unto the pond

The lazy geese, like a snow cloud
Dripping their snow on the green grass,   10
Tricking and stopping, sleepy and proud,
Who cried in goose, Alas,

For the tireless heart within the little
Lady with rod that made them rise
From their noon apple-dreams and scuttle   15
Goose-fashion under the skies!

But now go the bells, and we are ready,
In one house we are sternly stopped
To say we are vexed at her brown study,
Lying so primly propped.   20

1924

Here Lies a Lady

Here lies a lady of beauty and high degree.
Of chills and fever she died, of fever and chills,
The delight of her husband, her aunt, an infant of three,
And of medicos[1] marveling sweetly on her ills.

For either she burned, and her confident eyes would blaze,   5
And her fingers fly in a manner to puzzle their heads—
What was she making? Why, nothing; she sat in a maze
Of old scraps of laces, snipped into curious shreds—

Or this would pass, and the light of her fire decline
Till she lay discouraged and cold, like a stalk white and blown,[10]

---

2. Reverie, somber musing.   1. Doctors (slang).

And would not open her eyes, to kisses, to wine;
The sixth of these states was her last; the cold settled down.

Sweet ladies, long may ye bloom, and toughly I hope ye may
    thole,[2]
But was she not lucky? In flowers and lace and mourning,
In love and great honor we bade God rest her soul   15
After six little spaces of chill, and six of burning.

                          1924

Philomela[1]

Procne, Philomela, and Itylus,
Your names are liquid, your improbable tale
Is recited in the classic numbers[2] of the nightingale.
Ah, but our numbers are not felicitous,
It goes not liquidly for us.   5

Perched on a Roman ilex, and duly apostrophized,[3]
The nightingale descanted[4] unto Ovid;
She has even appeared to the Teutons,[5] the swilled and
    gravid;
At Fontainebleau[6] it may be the bird was gallicized;
Never was she baptized.   10

To England came Philomela with her pain,
Fleeing the hawk her husband; querulous ghost,
She wanders when he sits heavy on his roost,
Utters herself in the original again,
The untranslatable refrain.   15

Not to these shores she came! this other Thrace,[7]
Environ barbarous to the royal Attic;
How could her delicate dirge run democratic,
Delivered in a cloudless boundless public place
To an inordinate race?   20

    I pernoctated[8] with the Oxford students once,

2. Endure (archaic).
1. This poem treats the traditional theme that the Western nations, notably America, are far removed from ancient Greek myth and sources of inspiration. It is based on two myths concerning the nightingale. The first, recounted by the Roman poet Ovid (43? B.C.–A.D. 17) in *Metamorphoses*, Book VI, tells of the Thracian King Tereus who married Procne from Athens in Attica but fell in love with her sister Philomela, whom he raped. To prevent her telling Procne of the crime, he cut out her tongue, but Philomela wove the message into a tapestry and Procne took revenge by killing her son Itys and tricking Tereus into eating him. Procne was later turned into a swallow, Tereus into a hoopoe or hawk, and Philomela into the nightingale. In the second myth, Aidon, planning to kill her nephew out of envy for her sister's large family, killed her own son Itylus by mistake and was transformed by Zeus into the nightingale.
2. Feet or meters of poetry.
3. Addressed or invoked.
4. Sang profusely.
5. Barbarian predecessors of the Germans, here described as flushed with drink and pregnant.
6. A 16th-century royal palace near Paris.
7. America.
8. Passed the night (as in a vigil, a metaphor for nightly discussions at Oxford University). The River Cher and Bagley Woods are near Oxford.

And in the quadrangles, in the cloisters, on the Cher,
Precociously knocked at antique doors ajar,
Fatuously touched the hems of the hierophants,[9]
Sick of my dissonance.   25

I went out to Bagley Wood, I climbed the hill;
Even the moon had slanted off in a twinkling,
I heard the sepulchral owl and a few bells tinkling,
There was no more villainous day to unfulfil,
The diuturnity[10] was still.   30

Up from the darkest wood where Philomela sat,
Her fairy numbers issued. What then ailed me?
My ears are called capacious but they failed me,
Her classics registered a little flat!
I rose, and venomously spat.   35

Philomela, Philomela, lover of song,
I am in despair if we may make us worthy,
A bantering breed sophistical and swarthy;
Unto more beautiful, persistently more young,
Thy fabulous provinces belong.   40

                                                   1924

Captain Carpenter[1]

Captain Carpenter rose up in his prime
Put on his pistols and went riding out
But had got wellnigh nowhere at that time
Till he fell in with ladies in a rout.

It was a pretty lady and all her train   5
That played with him so sweetly but before
An hour she'd taken a sword with all her main
And twined him of his nose for evermore.

Captain Carpenter mounted up one day
And rode straightway into a stranger rogue   10
That looked unchristian but be that as may
The Captain did not wait upon prologue.

But drew upon him out of his great heart
The other swung against him with a club
And cracked his two legs at the shinny part   15
And let him roll and stick like any tub.

9. Priests revealing mysteries in initia-
tory rites.
10. Long-enduring passage of time.
1. When reading from his own works,
Ransom declared: "There's an old hero
who dies with his boots on, so to speak,
and I've been asked if he could not have
represented the Old South. Or if he
could not have stood for the old-time
religion. But those ideas did not enter
my mind when I was composing the little ballad." (Quoted by Robert Buffington, *The Equilibrist*, p. 90.)

Captain Carpenter rode many a time
From male and female took he sundry harms
He met the wife of Satan crying "I'm
The she-wolf bids you shall bear no more arms."   20

Their strokes and counters whistled in the wind
I wish he had delivered half his blows
But where she should have made off like a hind
The bitch bit off his arms at the elbows.

And Captain Carpenter parted with his ears   25
To a black devil that used him in this wise
O Jesus ere his threescore and ten years
Another had plucked out his sweet blue eyes.

Captain Carpenter got up on his roan
And sallied from the gate in hell's despite   30
I heard him asking in the grimmest tone
If any enemy yet there was to fight?

"To any adversary it is fame
If he risk to be wounded by my tongue
Or burnt in two beneath my red heart's flame   35
Such are the perils he is cast among.

"But if he can he has a pretty choice
From an anatomy with little to lose
Whether he cut my tongue and take my voice
Or whether it be my round red heart he choose."   40

It was the neatest knave that ever was seen
Stepping in perfume from his lady's bower
Who at this word put in his merry mien
And fell on Captain Carpenter like a tower.

I would not knock old fellows in the dust   45
But there lay Captain Carpenter on his back
His weapons were the old heart in his bust
And a blade shook between rotten teeth alack.

The rogue in scarlet and grey soon knew his mind
He wished to get his trophy and depart   50
With gentle apology and touch refined
He pierced him and produced the Captain's heart.

God's mercy rest on Captain Carpenter now
I thought him Sirs an honest gentleman
Citizen husband soldier and scholar enow[2]   55
Let jangling kites[3] eat of him if they can.

_____

2. Enough (archaic).   3. Birds of prey.

But God's deep curses follow after those
That shore him of his goodly nose and ears
His legs and strong arms at the two elbows
And eyes that had not watered seventy years.   60

The curse of hell upon the sleek upstart
That got the Captain finally on his back
And took the red red vitals of his heart
And made the kites to whet their beaks clack clack.

                                                      1924

Old Mansion[1]

As an intruder I trudged with careful innocence
To mask in decency a meddlesome stare,
Passing the old house often on its eminence,
Exhaling my foreign weed[2] on its weighted air.

Here age seemed newly imaged for the historian   5
After his monstrous chateaux on the Loire,[3]
A beauty not for depicting by old vulgarian
Reiterations which gentle readers abhor.

Each time of seeing I absorbed some other feature
Of a house whose annals in no wise could be brief   10
Nor ignoble; for it expired as sweetly as Nature,
With her tinge of oxidation on autumn leaf.

It was a Southern manor. One need hardly imagine
Towers, white monoliths, or even ivied walls;
But sufficient state if its peacock *was* a pigeon;   15
Where no courts kept, but grave rites and funerals.

Indeed, not distant, possibly not external
To the property, were tombstones, where the catafalque
Had carried their dead; and projected a note too charnel
But for the honeysuckle on its intricate stalk.   20

Stability was the character of its rectangle
Whose line was seen in part and guessed in part
Through trees. Decay was the one of old brick and
        shingle.
Green blinds dragging frightened the watchful heart

To assert, "Your mansion, long and richly inhabited,   25

Its exits and entrances suiting the children of men,
Will not for ever be thus, O man, exhibited,
And one had best hurry to enter it if one can."

And at last, with my happier angel's own temerity,
Did I clang their brazen knocker against the door,   30
To beg their dole of a look, in simple charity,
Or crumbs of legend dropping from their great store.

But it came to nothing—and may so gross denial
Which has been deplored with a beating of the breast
Never shorten the tired historian, loyal   35
To acknowledge defeat and discover a new quest—

The old mistress was ill, and sent my dismissal
By one even more wrappered and lean and dark
Than that warped concierge and imperturbable vassal
Who bids you begone from her master's Gothic park.   40

Emphatically, the old house crumbled; the ruins
Would litter, as already the leaves, this petted sward;
And no annalist went in to the lords or the peons;[4]
The antiquary would finger the bits of shard.

But on retreating I saw myself in the token,   45
How loving from my foreign weed the feather curled
On the languid air; and I went with courage shaken
To dip, alas, into some unseemlier world.

                                              1924

Piazza[1] Piece

   —I am a gentleman in a dustcoat trying
To make you hear. Your ears are soft and small
And listen to an old man not at all,
They want the young men's whispering and sighing.
But see the roses on your trellis dying   5
And hear the spectral singing of the moon;
For I must have my lovely lady soon,
I am a gentleman in a dustcoat trying.

   —I am a lady young in beauty waiting
Until my truelove comes, and then we kiss.   10
But what grey man among the vines is this
Whose words are dry and faint as in a dream?
Back from my trellis, Sir, before I scream!
I am a lady young in beauty waiting.

                                          1925, 1927

---

4. Attendants or foot soldiers in India;   debtors in Mexico.
day laborers in Latin America; enslaved   1. Porch.

Janet Waking

Beautifully Janet slept
Till it was deeply morning. She woke then
And thought about her dainty-feathered hen,
To see how it had kept.

One kiss she gave her mother,   5
Only a small one gave she to her daddy
Who would have kissed each curl of his shining baby;
No kiss at all for her brother.

"Old Chucky, old Chucky!" she cried,
Running across the world upon the grass   10
To Chucky's house, and listening. But alas,
Her Chucky had died.

It was a transmogrifying[1] bee
Came droning down on Chucky's old bald head
And sat and put the poison. It scarcely bled,   15
But how exceedingly

And purply did the knot
Swell with the venom and communicate
Its rigor! Now the poor comb stood up straight
But Chucky did not.   20

So there was Janet
Kneeling on the wet grass, crying her brown hen
(Translated far beyond the daughters of men)
To rise and walk upon it.

                                                    1926, 1927

Two in August

Two that could not have lived their single lives
As can some husbands and wives
Did something strange: they tensed their vocal cords
And attacked each other with silences and words
Like catapulted stones and arrowed knives.   5

Dawn was not yet; night is for loving or sleeping,
Sweet dreams or safekeeping;
Yet he of the wide brows that were used to laurel[2]
And she, the famed for gentleness, must quarrel,
Furious both of them, and scared, and weeping.   10

---

1. Transforming by magic.
2. In Greek mythology, the nymph Daphne, to ward off Apollo's advances, begged to be turned into a laurel tree, and the laurel branch with which Apollo consoled himself became associated with the arts.

How sleepers groan, twitch, wake to such a mood
Is not well understood,
Nor why two entities grown almost one
Should rend and murder trying to get undone,
With individual tigers in their blood.   15

She in terror fled from the marriage chamber
Circuiting the dark rooms like a string of amber
Round and round and back,
And would not light one lamp against the black,
And heard the clock that clanged: Remember, Remember. 20

And he must tread barefooted the dim lawn,
Soon he was up and gone;
High in the trees the night-mastered birds were crying
With fear upon their tongues, no singing nor flying
Which are their lovely attitudes by dawn.   25

Whether those bird-cries were of heaven or hell
There is no way to tell;
In the long ditch of darkness the man walked
Under the hackberry trees where the birds talked
With words too sad and strange to syllable.   30

1927

Antique Harvesters[1]

(*Scene: Of the Mississippi the bank sinister, and of the Ohio the bank sinister.*[2])

Tawny are the leaves turned but they still hold,
And it is harvest; what shall this land produce?
A meager hill of kernels, a runnel of juice;
Declension looks from our land, it is old.
Therefore let us assemble, dry, grey, spare,   5
And mild as yellow air.

"I hear the croak of a raven's funeral wing."
The young men would be joying in the song
Of passionate birds; their memories are not long.
What is it thus rehearsed in sable? "Nothing."[3]   10
Trust not but the old endure, and shall be older
Than the scornful beholder.

We pluck the spindling ears and gather the corn.
One spot has special yield? "On this spot stood

---

1. Ransom revised many lines of this poem, eliminating the last stanza in 1927 but restoring it in 1945 and 1963. The 1945 text is printed here.
2. In heraldry, the left side of a shield, and, by association, ominous. The left banks of the Ohio and Mississippi rivers are the borders of the Old South.
3. Possibly an echo of the refrain "Nevermore" in *The Raven*, the poem by Edgar Allan Poe.

Heroes and drenched it with their only blood."   15
And talk meets talk, as echoes from the horn
Of the hunter—echoes are the old men's arts,
Ample are the chambers of their hearts.

Here come the hunters, keepers of a rite;
The horn, the hounds, the lank mares coursing by   20
Straddled with archetypes of chivalry;
And the fox, lovely ritualist, in flight
Offering his unearthly ghost to quarry;
And the fields, themselves to harry.

Resume, harvesters. The treasure is full bronze   25
Which you will garner for the Lady, and the moon
Could tinge it no yellower than does this noon;
But grey will quench it shortly—the field, men, stones.
Pluck fast, dreamers; prove as you amble slowly
Not less than men, not wholly.   30

Bare the arm, dainty youths, bend the knees
Under bronze burdens. And by an autumn tone
As by a grey, as by a green, you will have known
Your famous Lady's image; for so have these;
And if one say that easily will your hands   35
More prosper in other lands,

Angry as wasp-music be your cry then:
"Forsake the Proud Lady, of the heart of fire,
The look of snow, to the praise of a dwindled choir,
Song of degenerate specters that were men?   40
The sons of the fathers shall keep her, worthy of
What these have done in love."

True, it is said of our Lady, she ageth.
But see, if you peep shrewdly, she hath not stooped;
Take no thought of her servitors that have drooped,   45
For we are nothing; and if one talk of death—
Why, the ribs of the earth subsist frail as a breath
If but God wearieth.

                                                          1925, 1927

Dog[1]

Cock-a-doodle-doo the brass-lined rooster says,[2]
Brekekekex intones the fat Greek frog—[3]

1. The poem appeared in *Two Gentle-men in Bonds* (1927) in a section enti-tled "The Manliness of Man." The sev-enth stanza was removed from *Selected Poems* (1945) and subsequent editions. The 1927 version is printed here.
2. A weathervane.

3. The cacophonous song of the chorus of frogs in the ancient Greek comedy *The Frogs* by Aristophanes (445? B.C.–387? B.C.). The frogs sing to Hercules when he descends into Hades to rescue a tragic dramatist.

These fantasies do not terrify me as
The bow-wow-wow of dog.

I had a little doggie who used to sit and beg,　　　　5
A pretty little creature with tears in his eyes
And anomalous hand extended on his leg;
Housebroken was my Huendchen,[4] and so wise.

Booms the voice of a big dog like a bell.
But Fido sits at dusk on Madam's lap　　　　10
And, bored beyond his tongue's poor skill to tell,
Rehearses his pink paradigm, To yap.

However. Up the lane the tender bull
Proceeds unto his kine;[5] he yearns for them,
Whose eyes adore him and are beautiful;　　　　15
Love speeds him and no treason nor mayhem.

But, on arriving at the gap in the fence,
Behold! again the ubiquitous hairy dog,
Like a numerous army rattling the battlements
With shout, though it is but his monologue,　　　　20
With a lion's courage and a bee's virulence
Though he is but one dog.

Shrill is the fury of the proud red bull,
His knees quiver, and the honeysuckle vine
Expires with anguish as his voice, terrible,　　　　25
Cries, "What do you want of my twenty lady kine?"

Ah, nothing doubtless; yet his dog's fang is keen,
His dog's heart cannot suffer these marriage rites
Enacted in the dark if they are obscene;
Misogynist,[6] censorious of delights.　　　　30

Now the air trembles to the sorrowing Moo
Of twenty blameless ladies of the mead[7]
Fearing their lord's precarious set-to.
It is the sunset and the heavens bleed.

The hooves of the red bull slither the claybank　　　　35
And cut the green tendrils of the vine; his horn
Slices the young birch unto splinter and shank
But lunging leaves the bitch's boy untorn.

Across the red sky comes master, Hodge by name,
Upright, biped, tall-browed, and self-assured,　　　　40
In his hand a cudgel, in his cold eye a flame:
"Have I beat my dog so sore and he is not cured?"

4. German: doggie.　　　　6. Hater of women.
5. Cows (archaic).　　　　7. Meadow.

His stick and stone and curse rain on the brute
That pipped[8] his bull of gentle pedigree
Till the leonine smarts with pain and disrepute   45
And the bovine[9] weeps in the bosom of his family.

Old Hodge stays not his hand, but whips to kennel
The renegade. God's peace betide the souls
Of the pure in heart. But in the box that fennel
Grows round are two red eyes that stare like coals.   50

1925, 1927

The Equilibrists[1]

Full of her long white arms and milky skin
He had a thousand times remembered sin.
Alone in the press of people traveled he,
Minding her jacinth, and myrrh,[2] and ivory.

Mouth he remembered: the quaint orifice   5
From which came heat that flamed upon the kiss,
Till cold words came down spiral from the head,
Grey doves from the officious tower illsped.

Body: it was a white field ready for love,
On her body's field, with the gaunt tower above,   10
The lilies grew, beseeching him to take,
If he would pluck and wear them, bruise and break.

Eyes talking: Never mind the cruel words,
Embrace my flowers, but not embrace the swords.
But what they said, the doves came straightway flying   15
And unsaid: Honor, Honor, they came crying.

Importunate her doves. Too pure, too wise,
Clambering on his shoulder, saying, Arise,
Leave me now, and never let us meet,
Eternal distance now command thy feet.   20

Predicament indeed, which thus discovers
Honor among thieves, Honor between lovers.
O such a little word is Honor, they feel!
But the grey word is between them cold as steel.

At length I saw these lovers fully were come   25
Into their torture of equilibrium;
Dreadfully had forsworn each other, and yet
They were bound each to each, and they did not forget.

---

8. Marked with black spots (as in dice)
or peppered (as with shot).
9. Cowlike, here applied to the bull;
"leonine": lionlike, here applied to the
dog.
1. Tightrope walkers, acrobats.
2. Resin used in perfume, medicine, and
incense; "jacinth": reddish-orange gem.

And rigid as two painful stars, and twirled
About the clustered night their prison world,   30
They burned with fierce love always to come near,
But Honor beat them back and kept them clear.

Ah, the strict lovers, they are ruined now!
I cried in anger. But with puddled brow
Devising for those gibbeted and brave   35
Came I descanting:[3] Man, what would you have?

For spin your period out, and draw your breath,
A kinder saeculum[4] begins with Death.
Would you ascend to Heaven and bodiless dwell?
Or take your bodies honorless to Hell?   40

In Heaven you have heard no marriage is,[5]
No white flesh tinder to your lecheries,
Your male and female tissue sweetly shaped
Sublimed away, and furious blood escaped.

Great lovers lie in Hell, the stubborn ones   45
Infatuate of the flesh upon the bones;
Stuprate,[6] they rend each other when they kiss,
The pieces kiss again, no end to this.

But still I watched them spinning, orbited nice.
Their flames were not more radiant than their ice.   50
I dug in the quiet earth and wrought the tomb
And made these lines to memorize their doom:—

Epitaph

Equilibrists lie here; stranger, tread light;
Close, but untouching in each other's sight;
Mouldered the lips and ashy the tall skull,   55
Let them lie perilous and beautiful.

1925, 1927

Painted Head[1]

By dark severance the apparition head
Smiles from the air a capital on no
Column or a Platonic[2] perhaps head
On a canvas sky depending from nothing;

3. Singing in full praise; "puddled": stirred or concerned with in an untidy way; "Devising": bequeathing or imagining; "gibbeted": hung on a gallows.
4. Period of time.
5. "For in the resurrection they neither marry nor are given in marriage, but are as the angels of God in heaven" (Matthew 22.30).
6. Ravished. The allusion is to Paolo and Francesca, bodiless spirits damned in the torment of their illicit love in Dante's *Divine Comedy* (*Inferno*, V).

1. Originally published in 1934 and slightly revised in 1945 and 1963, the poem is printed here in its 1945 version. The painted head referred to in the title signifies the verbal portrait presented in the poem, and a painted figure on canvas. The poem suggests the danger of any figure's becoming totally abstract, but asserts that the abstractions of art have a tangible or visible body in their sensuous medium.
2. Ideal, abstract, as in the theory of the Greek philosopher Plato (427?–347 B.C.).

Stirs up an old illusion of grandeur   5
By tickling the instinct of heads to be
Absolute and to try decapitation
And to play truant from the body bush;

But too happy and beautiful for those sorts
Of head (homekeeping heads are happiest)   10
Discovers maybe thirty unwidowed years
Of not dishonoring the faithful stem;

Is nameless and has authored for the evil
Historian headhunters neither book
Nor state and is therefore distinct from tart   15
Heads with crowns and guilty gallery heads;

So that the extravagant device of art
Unhousing by abstraction this once head
Was capital irony by a loving hand
That knew the no treason of a head like this;   20

Makes repentance in an unlovely head
For having vinegarly traduced the flesh
Till, the hurt flesh recusing,[3] the hard egg
Is shrunken to its own deathlike surface;

And an image thus. The body bears the head   25
(So hardly one they terribly are two)
Feeds and obeys and unto please what end?
Not to the glory of tyrant head but to

The increase of body. Beauty is of body.
The flesh contouring shallowly on a head   30
Is a rock-garden needing body's love
And best bodiness to colorify

The big blue birds sitting and sea-shell flats
And caves, and on the iron acropolis[4]
To spread the hyacinthine hair and rear   35
The olive garden for the nightingales.

1934, 1945

Address to the Scholars of New England[1]
(Harvard Phi Beta Kappa poem, June 23, 1939)

When Sarah Pierrepont[2] let her spirit rage
Her love and scorn refused the bauble earth

---

3. Objecting.
4. The flesh contouring on a head needs the body's love; the edifices or the "iron" artifacts, buildings, of the acropolis (the citadel of an ancient Greek city) need natural birds, sea flats, and caves, so as to provide the sustenance for life and song.
1. Here the southern Protestant poet addresses the New England Puritan tradition: its fervent piety and its revolutionary idealism. He thinks the southern stu-

(Which took bloom even here, under the Bear)[3]
And groped for the Essence sitting in himself,
Subtle, I think, for a girl's unseasoned rage.   5

The late and sudden extravagance of soul[4]
By which they all were swollen exalted her
At seventeen years to Edwards' canopy,[5]
A match pleasing to any Heaven, had not
The twelve mortal labors[6] harassed her soul.   10

Thrifty and too proud were the sea-borne fathers
Who fetched the Pure Idea in a bound box
And fastened him in a steeple, to have his court
Shabby with an unkingly establishment
And Sabbath levees for the minion[7] fathers.   15

The majesty of Heaven has a great house,
And even if the Indian kingdom or the fox
Ran barking mad in a wide forest place,
They had his threshold, and you had the dream
Of property in him by a steepled house.   20

If once the entail[8] shall come on raffish sons,
Knife-wit scholar and merchant sharp in thumb,
With positive steel they'll pry into the steeple,
And blinking through the cracked ribs at the void
A judgment laughter rakes the cynic sons.   25

But like prevailing wind New England's honor
Carried, and teased small Southern boys in school,
Whose heads the temperate birds fleeing your winter
Construed for,[9] but the stiff heroes abashed
With their frozen fingers and unearthly honor.   30

Scared by the holy megrims[1] of those Pilgrims,
I thought the unhumbled and outcast and cold

---

dents lured to Harvard were more truly
the "heirs" of the divine and American
mission than the northern students, but
that the new generation of students, less
fanatical, are more apt than their predecessors to make "peace" with heaven
and with the earth they seek to subdue.
2. Wife of the Congregational minister
and theologian Jonathan Edwards
(1703–58), whose religious ecstasies Edwards observed minutely and thought
more genuine and intense than his own.
3. Though earthly values took root in
America, under the constellation of the
Bear in the northern sky, Sarah Pierrepont was devoted to the inner essence or
soul of her husband.
4. I.e., the religious revivals or waves of
religious enthusiasm, notably the "Great
Awakening," which swept through New

England in the 1730s and which Edwards's sermons and theology encouraged.
5. I.e., his bed.
6. A comparison of Mrs. Edwards's
labor pains to the 12 labors of Hercules
in Greek mythology. Mrs. Edwards bore
11 children.
7. Favorite children or servants; "levees": receptions, particularly those held
by royalty.
8. Inheritance.
9. Translated or interpreted favorably.
Nature's birds smiled upon southern
boys, but the New Englanders they
took for models, with their stern commitment to honor, confounded the
southerners.
1. Fancies, headaches, low spirits.

Were the rich Heirs[2] traveling incognito,
Bred too fine for the country's sweet produce
And but affecting that dog's life of pilgrims.   35

There used to be debate of soul and body,
The soul storming incontinent with shrew's tongue
Against what natural brilliance body had loved,
Even the green phases though deciduous
Of earth's zodiac homage to the body.   40

Plato, before Plotinus[3] gentled him,
Spoke the soul's part, and though its vice is known
We're in his shadow still, and it appears
Your founders most of all the nations held
By his scandal-mongering, and established him.   45

Perfect was the witch foundering in water,
The blasphemer that spraddled in the stocks,
The woman branded with her sin, the whales
Of ocean taken with a psalmer's sword,
The British tea infusing the bay's water.[4]   50

But they reared heads into the always clouds
And stooped to the event of war or bread,
The secular perforces and short speech
Being labors surlily done with the left hand,
The chief strength giddying with transcendent clouds.   55

The tangent Heavens mocked the fathers' strength,
And how the young sons know it, and study now
To take fresh conquest of the conquered earth,
But they're too strong for that,[5] you've seem them whip
The laggard will to deeds of lunatic strength.   60

To incline the powerful living unto peace
With Heaven is easier now, with Earth is hard,
Yet a rare metaphysic makes them one,
A gentle Majesty, whose myrtle and rain
Enforce the fathers' gravestones unto peace.   65

I saw the youngling bachelors of Harvard
Lit like torches, and scrambling to disperse
Like aimless firebrands pitiful to slake,
And if there's passion enough for half their flame,
Your wisdom has done this, sages of Harvard.   70

1939, 1945

2. The true heirs of the past are the outsiders committed to the body and to the earth.
3. Roman philosopher (205?–270) whose cosmology modified the philosophy of Plato.
4. The stanza asserts that tests for witchcraft, the punishments of sinners, the exploitation of whales as a holy mission, and the Revolutionary Boston Tea Party were examples of New England's strict idealism or perfectionism.
5. I.e., heaven's mockery.

ARCHIBALD MacLEISH
1892–

Archibald MacLeish is the only important American poet to hold high official positions in public affairs, and he based his career after 1930 on the attempt to reconcile modern modes of poetry, as defined by Eliot and Pound, with the demands of a public role for the poet that would accord with Emerson's and Whitman's conception of the poet's mission in a democracy.

MacLeish was born in Glencoe, an affluent Chicago suburb, attended Hotchkiss School, graduated from Yale in 1915, and acquired a Harvard law degree. He served in the artillery in France during World War I and practiced law in Boston from 1920 to 1923, but he had published a volume of verse as early as 1917, and in 1923 he dedicated himself to the writing of poetry, spending five years with his wife and children in Paris (an intentionally temporary stay), where he wrote the verse that appeared in *The Happy Marriage* (1924), *The Pot of Earth* (1925), *Streets on the Moon* (1926), and *The Hamlet of A. MacLeish* (1928). On his return, though conceding that "It is a strange thing—to be an American," he committed himself to his native land and to the American Dream (*American Letter* in *New Found Land*, 1930) and he did the research for *Conquistador* (1932), his epic on the Spanish conquest of Mexico for which he received the Pulitzer Prize. From 1930 to 1938 he was on the editorial board of *Fortune* magazine, writing articles on such subjects as advertising, financial magnates, skyscraper construction, and housing. During these years, increasingly concerned about the threat of fascist authoritarianism in Europe, he became committed to the liberal reforms of President Franklin Roosevelt's New Deal. His works exposing the Nazi threat include the radio plays *The Fall of the City* (1937) and *Air Raid* (1939), while *Speech to a Crowd* in *Public Speech* (1936) and *America Was Promises* (1939) take Americans to task for their failure to fulfill the American Dream.

Early in the 1930s MacLeish began to articulate a position that complicated critical reaction to his poems because it was so categorical and generalized in its formulation. He not only turned aside from his earlier works, notably *The Hamlet* and *Einstein*, because of their pessimism and their emphasis on the isolation of the intellectual, but he called into question the poetic revolution undertaken by Eliot and Pound, two of the poets on whom he modeled his own verse. Theirs had been a necessary but transitional revolution, he declared, which cleared the ground but dissolved in nostalgia for the past and failed to provide a basis for rebuilding the society of their time, for joining the poetic revolution to a revolution in social, political, and economic structures of the contemporary world. As an alternative to aestheticism and introversion in modern culture he pointed to the great poets of the past, including Chaucer, Shakespeare, Milton, and Dryden, who were concerned with public issues and wrote, he claimed, the poetry of "public speech." Attempting to distinguish his position from that of revolutionary Marxists, and from any narrowly partisan and ideological positions, he offered the contemporary German novelist Thomas Mann, Whitman, and Carl Sandburg as examples of the artistic mission he had in mind.

Most modern writers in America, he declared, in a highly controversial address of 1940 entitled *The Irresponsibles,* had failed to address themselves to the conditions that had produced fascism in Europe and brought on World War II.

Partly because MacLeish's rhetoric was so vague in its definition of "public issues" or "public speech" and in its attempt to distinguish between poetic celebration and partisan propaganda, partly because his pronouncements were so sweeping in their application, his position was vulnerable to critics of many persuasions. They were tempted to argue the pros and cons of his position and to ignore the fact that MacLeish continued to publish personal lyrics along with his own poetry of "public speech," or the fact that his poetry of "public speech" included some poems which have more sensitive effects and greater metrical interest than comparable works by Sandburg. None of MacLeish's works was profoundly original, but many were deft in their adaptation of current modes to his own purpose, and some of his poems on public issues (notably *Invocation to the Social Muse,* which aroused a heated controversy among critics) are more probing and complex in their attitudes and themes than MacLeish's theoretical positions would indicate.

MacLeish's prominence as a commentator on public issues led to a series of important public appointments in the 1940s. He served as Librarian of Congress from 1939 to 1944, Assistant Director of War Information, Assistant Secretary of State, and Chairman of the American Delegation to UNESCO. He resumed his writing career in 1948 with a long poem *Actfive,* a tribute to the stamina of the "human perishable heart" that shows the impact of Eliot's *Four Quartets* and Pound's *Cantos.* He held the prestigious Boylston Professorship of Rhetoric and Oratory at Harvard from 1949 to 1962, and along with volumes of commentary on literature and society he published two volumes of verse: *Collected Poems* in 1952, which won the Pulitzer and Bollingen prizes, along with the National Book Award, in 1953, and *Songs for Eve* in 1954. His poetic drama *J.B.* (1957), a Broadway success, was based on the Book of Job, and portrayed the hero's assertion of the self against the meaninglessness of existence. In the tragedy *Herakles* (1967) the hero's triumph is won at the cost of his children's lives. *The Wild Old Wicked Man, and Other Poems* (1968) contained additional lyrics, including touching tributes to his wife and to Ernest Hemingway.

Memorial Rain

FOR KENNETH MACLEISH,[1] 1894–1918

Ambassador Puser the ambassador
Reminds himself in French, felicitous tongue,
What these (young men no longer) lie here for
In rows that once, and somewhere else, were young. . .

All night in Brussels[2] the wind had tugged at my door: 5
I had heard the wind at my door and the trees strung
Taut, and to me who had never been before
In that country it was a strange wind, blowing

1. The poet's brother, killed in World War I.   2. Like Ghent and Waereghem below, a city in Belgium.

Steadily, stiffening the walls, the floor,
  The roof of my room. I had not slept for knowing 10
He too, dead, was a stranger in that land
  And felt beneath the earth in the wind's flowing
  A tightening of roots and would not understand,
Remembering lake winds in Illinois,
That strange wind. I had felt his bones in the sand 15
  Listening.

               . . . Reflects that these enjoy
Their country's gratitude, that deep repose,
That peace no pain can break, no hurt destroy,
That rest, that sleep . . . 20

                   At Ghent the wind rose.
There was a smell of rain and a heavy drag
Of wind in the hedges but not as the wind blows
  Over fresh water when the waves lag
Foaming and the willows huddle and it will rain: 25
  I felt him waiting.

               . . . Indicates the flag
Which (may he say) enisles in Flanders plain
This little field these happy, happy dead[3]
Have made America . . . 30

                  In the ripe grain
The wind coiled glistening, darted, fled,
Dragging its heavy body: at Waereghem
The wind coiled in the grass above his head:
  Waiting—listening . . . 35

              . . . Dedicates to them
This earth their bones have hallowed, this last gift
A Grateful country . . .

               Under the dry grass stem
The words are blurred, are thickened, the words sift 40
Confused by the rasp of the wind, by the thin grating
Of ants under the grass, the minute shift
And tumble of dusty sand separating
From dusty sand. The roots of the grass strain,
Tighten, the earth is rigid, waits—he is waiting— 45

And suddenly, and all at once, the rain!

The living scatter, they run into houses, the wind
Is trampled under the rain, shakes free, is again
Trampled. The rain gathers, running in thinned

---

3. Ironic echo of King Henry V's exhilarating exhortation to his troops before
the battle of Agincourt in Shakespeare's   *Henry V* (4.3.60): "We few, we happy
few, we band of brothers."

Spurts of water that ravel in the dry sand,   50
Seeping in the sand under the grass roots, seeping
Between cracked boards to the bones of a clenched hand:
The earth relaxes, loosens; he is sleeping,
He rests, he is quiet, he sleeps in a strange land.

1926

Ars Poetica[1]

A POEM should be palpable and mute
As a globed fruit

Dumb
As old medallions to the thumb

Silent as the sleeve-worn stone   5
Of casement ledges where the moss has grown—

A poem should be wordless
As the flight of birds

* * *

A poem should be motionless in time
As the moon climbs   10

Leaving, as the moon releases
Twig by twig the night-entangled trees,

Leaving, as the moon behind the winter leaves,
Memory by memory the mind—

A poem should be motionless in time   15
As the moon climbs

* * *

A poem should be equal to:
Not true

For all the history of grief
An empty doorway and a maple leaf   20

For love
The leaning grasses and two lights above the sea—

A poem should not mean
But be

1926

You, Andrew Marvell[2]

And here face down beneath the sun
And here upon earth's noonward height

---

1. *The Art of Poetry*, the Latin title assigned to a poem by the Roman poet
Horace (68–8 B.C.).

2. The title alludes to lines 21–22 from
To His Coy Mistress by the English poet
Andrew Marvell (1621–78): "But at my

To feel the always coming on
The always rising of the night:

To feel creep up the curving east   5
The earthly chill of dusk and slow
Upon those under lands the vast
And ever climbing shadow grow

And strange at Ecbatan the trees
Take leaf by leaf the evening strange   10
The flooding dark about their knees
The mountains over Persia change

And now at Kermanshah the gate
Dark empty and the withered grass
And through the twilight now the late   15
Few travelers in the westward pass

And Baghdad darken and the bridge
Across the silent river gone
And through Arabia the edge
Of evening widen and steal on   20

And deepen on Palmyra's street
The wheel rut in the ruined stone
And Lebanon fade out and Crete
High through the clouds and overblown

And over Sicily the air   25
Still flashing with the landward gulls
And loom and slowly disappear
The sails above the shadowy hulls

And Spain go under and the shore
Of Africa the gilded sand   30
And evening vanish and no more
The low pale light across that land

Nor now the long light on the sea:

And here face downward in the sun
To feel how swift how secretly   35
The shadow of the night comes on . . .

                                                            1930

Reproach to Dead Poets

You who have spoken words in the earth,
You who have broken the silence,
                                    utterers,

---

back I always hear / Time's wingéd   in lines 9, 13, 17, and 21 below are in
chariot hurrying near." The cities named   ancient Media, Persia, Iraq, and Syria.

Sayers in all lands to all peoples,
Writers in candle soot on the skins   5
Of rams for those who come after you,
                              voices
Echoed at night in the arched doors,
And at noon in the shadow of fig trees,
Hear me!   10
                    Were there not
Words?
Were there not words to tell with?
Were there not leaf sounds in the mouths
Of women from over-sea, and a call   15
Of birds on the lips of the children of strangers?
Were there not words in all languages—
In many tongues the same thing differently,
The name cried out, Thalassa!¹ the sea!
The Sea!   20
The sun and moon character representing
Brightness, the night sound of the wind for
Always, for ever and ever, the verb
Created after the speech of crickets—
                    Were there not words to tell with?   25
                              —to tell
What lands these are:
                    What are these
Lights through the night leaves and these voices
Crying among us as winds rise,   30

Or whence, of what race we are that dwell with them?
Were there not words to tell with,
                    you that have told
The kings' names and the hills remembered for battles?
                                                          1930

Immortal Autumn

I speak this poem now with grave and level voice
In praise of autumn, of the far-horn-winding fall.

I praise the flower-barren fields, the clouds, the tall
Unanswering branches where the wind makes sullen noise.

I praise the fall: it is the human season.   5
                              Now
No more the foreign sun does meddle at our earth,
Enforce the green and bring the fallow land to birth,
Nor winter yet weigh all with silence the pine bough,

But now in autumn with the black and outcast crows   10
Share we the spacious world: the whispering year is gone:

---

1. The sea (exclamation of Greek soldiers on reaching the Black Sea in the
Anabasis by the Athenian historian Xenophon, 430?–355? B.C.).

There is more room to live now: the once secret dawn
Comes late by daylight and the dark unguarded goes.

Between the mutinous brave burning of the leaves
And winter's covering of our hearts with his deep snow   15
We are alone: there are no evening birds: we know
The naked moon: the tame stars circle at our eaves.

It is the human season. On this sterile air
Do words outcarry breath: the sound goes on and on.
I hear a dead man's cry from autumn long since gone.   20

I cry to you beyond upon this bitter air.

                                                    1930

Tourist Death

FOR SYLVIA BEACH[1]

I promise you these days and an understanding
Of light in the twigs after sunfall.
                                Do you ask to descend
At dawn in a new world with wet on the pavements
And a yawning cat and the fresh odor of dew   5
And red geraniums under the station windows
And doors wide and brooms and sheets on the railing
And a whistling boy and the sun like shellac on the street?

Do you ask to embark at night at the third hour
Sliding away in the dark and the sails of the fishermen   10
Slack in the light of the lanterns and black seas
And the tide going down and the splash and drip of the hawser?

Do you ask something to happen as spring does
In a night in a small time and nothing the same again?
Life is neither a prize box nor a terminus.   15
Life is a haft that has fitted the palms of many,
Dark as the helved oak,
                        with sweat bitter,
Browned by numerous hands:
                                Death is the rest of it.   20
Death is the same bones and the trees nearer.
Death is a serious thing like the loam smell
Of the plowed earth in the fall.
                                Death is here:
Not in another place, not among strangers.   25
Death is under the moon here and the rain.
I promise you old signs and a recognition

1. American expatriate (1887–1962) owner of the Parisian bookstore Shakespeare & Co., which published James Joyce's *Ulysses* and was a gathering place of expatriate writers.

Of sun in the seething grass and the wind's rising.

Do you ask more?
            Do you ask to travel for ever?   30
                                                          1930

From Frescoes for Mr. Rockefeller's City[1]
Burying Ground by the Ties

Ayee! Ai! This is heavy earth on our shoulders:
There were none of us born to be buried in this earth:
Niggers we were, Portuguese, Magyars, Polacks:

We were born to another look of the sky certainly.
Now we lie here in the river pastures: 5
We lie in the mowings under the thick turf:

We hear the earth and the all-day rasp of the grasshoppers.
It was we laid the steel to this land from ocean to ocean:
It was we (if you know) put the U.P. through the passes

Bringing her down into Laramie full load,[2]   10
Eighteen mile on the granite anticlinal,[3]
Forty-three foot to the mile and the grade holding:

It was we did it: hunkies[4] of our kind.
It was we dug the caved-in holes for the cold water:
It was we built the gully spurs and the freight sidings: 15

Who would do it but we and the Irishmen bossing us?
It was all foreign-born men there were in this country:
It was Scotsmen, Englishmen, Chinese, Squareheads,[5] Aus-
        trians . . .

Ayee! but there's weight to the earth under it.
Not for this did we come out—to be lying here   20
Nameless under the ties in the clay cuts:

There's nothing good in the world but the rich will buy it:
Everything sticks to the grease of a gold note—
Even a continent—even a new sky!

1. *Frescoes for Mr. Rockefeller's City* was provoked by the controversy surrounding a mural, containing a portrait of the Communist Lenin, painted by the Mexican artist Diego Rivera, an avowed Communist, for the lobby of Radio City in New York City. The Rockefellers, who commissioned the work, paid the artist his fee of $21,000 for the unfinished mural, then had the mural destroyed. Each of the six poems is in effect a panel in a mural. We reprint the third and fourth poems. In the fifth MacLeish exposed exploitative empire builders while in the last he mocked Communist attempts to appropriate the American tradition.
2. The Union Pacific Railroad runs through Laramie, Wyoming.
3. A rock formation which complicates railroad bed construction.
4. Foreign-born, especially East European, laborer (slang).
5. Scandinavians (slang).

Do not pity us much for the strange grass over us: 25
We laid the steel to the stone stock of these mountains:
The place of our graves is marked by the telegraph poles!

It was not to lie in the bottoms we came out
And the trains going over us here in the dry hollows . . .

1933

Oil Painting of the Artist as the Artist

The plump Mr. Pl'f is washing his hands of America:
The plump Mr. Pl'f is in ochre with such hair:

America is in blue-black-grey-green-sandcolor.
America is a continent—many lands:

The plump Mr. Pl'f is washing his hands of America.   5
He is pictured at Pau[1] on the place and his eyes glaring:

He thinks of himself as an exile from all this,
As an émigré from his own time into history

(History being an empty house without owners
A practical man may get in by the privy stones: 10

The dead are excellent hosts, they have no objections,
And once in he can nail the knob[2] on the next one

Living the life of a classic in bad air
With himself for the Past and his face in the glass for Posterity).

The Cinquecento[3] is nothing at all like Nome   15
Or Natchez or Wounded Knee or the Shenandoah.

Your vulgarity, Tennessee: your violence, Texas:
The rocks under your fields Ohio, Connecticut:

Your clay Missouri your clay: you have driven him out.
You have shadowed his life Appalachians, purple mountains.   20

There is much too much of your flowing, Mississippi:
He prefers a tidier stream with a terrace for trippers and

Cypresses mentioned in Horace or Henry James:[4]
He prefers a country where everything carries the name of a

1. French winter resort.
2. Bolt the door.
3. The 15th century, a term for the Italian Renaissance at its height. It is compared to the American localities that follow: the frontier city of Nome, Alaska; the battle sites at Natchez, Mississippi, and Wounded Knee, South Dakota; and the Shenandoah River in Pennsylvania.
4. The Roman poet (68–8 B.C.) and the expatriate American novelist (1843–1916).

Countess or real king or an actual palace or   25
Something in Prose and the stock prices all in Italian.

There is more shade for an artist under a fig
Than under the whole rock range (he finds) of the Big Horns.[5]

1933

Cook County[6]

The northeast wind was the wind off the lake
Blowing the oak-leaves pale side out like
Aspen: blowing the sound of the surf far
Inland over the fences: blowing for
Miles over smell of the earth the lake smell in.   5

The southwest wind was thunder in afternoon.
You saw the wind first in the trumpet vine
And the green went white with the sky and the weather-vane
Whirled on the barn and the doors slammed all together.
After the rain in the grass we used to gather   10
Wind-fallen cold white apples.

                               The west
Wind was the August wind, the wind over waste
Valleys, over the waterless plains where still
Were skulls of the buffalo, where in the sand stale   15
Dung lay of wild cattle. The west wind blew
Day after day as the winds on the plains blow
Burning the grass, turning the leaves brown, filling
Noon with the bronze of cicadas, far out falling
Dark on the colorless water, the lake where not   20
Waves were nor movement.

                       The north wind was at night
When no leaves and the husk on the oak stirs
Only nor birds then. The north wind was stars
Over the whole sky and snow in the ways   25
And snow on the sand where in summer the water was . . .

1933

Invocation to the Social Muse

Señora,[1] it is true the Greeks are dead.

It is true also that we here are Americans:
That we use the machines: that a sight of the god is unusual:
That more people have more thoughts: that there are

Progress and science and tractors and revolutions and   5

Marx and the wars more antiseptic and murderous
And music in every home: there is also Hoover.[2]

Does the lady suggest we should write it out in The Word?
Does Madame recall our responsibilities? We are
Whores, Fräulein:[3] poets, Fräulein, are persons of   10

Known vocation following troops: they must sleep with
Stragglers from either prince and of both views.
The rules permit them to further the business of neither.

It is also strictly forbidden to mix in maneuvers.
Those that infringe are inflated with praise on the plazas—   15
Their bones are resultantly afterwards found under newspapers.

Preferring life with the sons to death with the fathers,
We also doubt on the record whether the sons
Will still be shouting around with the same huzzas—

For we hope Lady to live to lie with the youngest.   20
There are only a handful of things a man likes,
Generation to generation, hungry or

Well fed: the earth's one: life's
One: Mister Morgan[4] is not one.

There is nothing worse for our trade than to be in style.   25

He that goes naked goes further at last than another.
Wrap the bard in a flag or a school and they'll jimmy his
Door down and be thick in his bed—for a month:

(Who recalls the address now of the Imagists?)[5]
But the naked man has always his own nakedness.   30
People remember forever his live limbs.

They may drive him out of the camps but one will take him.
They may stop his tongue on his teeth with a rope's argu-
   ment—
He will lie in a house and be warm when they are shaking.

Besides, Tovarishch,[6] how to embrace an army?   35
How to take to one's chamber a million souls?
How to conceive in the name of a column of marchers?

The things of the poet are done to a man alone

2. Herbert C. Hoover (1874–1964), American President at the beginning of the Great Depression.
3. German for Miss.
4. John Pierpont Morgan (1837–1913), American banker and financier.
5. Group of American and British poets active around 1914 who called for precision in imagery and the elimination of needless ornament from poetry.
6. Russian for comrade, the conventional form of address among Russians since the Revolution.

As the things of love are done—or of death when he hears the
Step withdraw on the stair and the clock tick only.   40

Neither his class nor his kind nor his trade may come near him
There where he lies on his left arm and will die,
Nor his class nor his kind nor his trade when the blood is
        jeering

And his knee's in the soft of the bed where his love lies.

I remind you, Barinya,[7] the life of the poet is hard—   45
A hardy life with a boot as quick as a fiver:

Is it just to demand of us also to bear arms?

                                                                 1933

From Conquistador[1]

Dedication

*"O frati," dissi, "che per cento milia
Perigli siete giunti all' occidente"[2]*
—*The Divine Comedy*
Inferno, Canto xxvi, lines 112, 113

PROLOGUE

And the way goes on in the worn earth:

                              and we (others)—

What are the dead to us in our better fortune?
They have left us the roads made and the walls standing:

---

7. Russian for Baroness.
1. In *Conquistador*, a "personal epic" in 15 books plus a verse Prologue and a Preface, MacLeish turned from the myths of the Wasteland and Hamlet to the story of Spain's ruthless conquest of Mexico which had actually historical and direct ties to the founding of the United States. In a note MacLeish acknowledged painful memories and guilt in taking it for his subject, hoping that "the strength of my attachment to the country of Mexico may, to some extent, atone for my presumption, as an American, in writing of it." He "altered, transposed, and invented incidents" but relied heavily on the *True History of the Conquest of New Spain* by Bernál Díaz del Castillo (1492?–1581?), a soldier who boasted that his unlearned account was more true to the conquistadors' experience than more official versions (*Collected Poems*, p. 326). He is the persona of the poem, appearing at the end of the Prologue as the ghost of an aged man in Hades and summoned to speak by the narrator. Díaz's kaleidoscopic memories (centering on the suppression of a dissi-

dent faction by the leader Hernando Cortez, and finally the sacking of Montezuma's Aztec cities at Cholula and Tenochtitlan) comprise the remainder of the entire poem. The Narrator is likened to Dante encountering the epic poet Virgil in Hell in *The Divine Comedy*, and to Odysseus in Homer's *Odyssey* encountering in Hades the ghost of Elpenor, a dead comrade. The Narrator is pained to encounter the ghost, but he is irresistibly drawn to hear his message nevertheless. The Narrator's guilt-ridden encounter is MacLeish's means of launching his confrontation of the horrors of his past and his somber celebration of its exploits. The poem, which contains echoes of Virgil's epic, the *Aeneid*, and effects modeled on Pound's *Cantos*, is written in a three-line stanza derived from Dante's *terza rima*.
2. "O brothers," I said, "who through a hundred thousand perils have reached the West." Odysseus's exhortation to his comrades, encouraging them to continue their voyage home from Troy, as reported by Odysseus's ghost to Dante in hell.

They have left us the chairs in the rooms: 5
           what is there more of them—

Either their words in the stone or their graves in the land
Or the rusted tang in the turf-root where they fought—
Has truth against us?
          (And another man   10

Where the wild geese rise from Michigan the water
Veering the clay bluff: in another wind. . . .)

Surely the will of God in the earth alters:

Time done is dark as are sleep's thickets:
Dark is the past: none waking walk there: 15
Neither may live men of those waters drink:

And their speech they have left upon the coins to mock us:
And the weight of their skulls at our touch is a shuck's weight:
And their rains are dry and the sound of their leaves fallen:

(We that have still the sun and the green places)   20
And they care nothing for living men: and the honey of
Sun is slight in their teeth as a seed's taste—

What are the dead to us in the world's wonder?
Why (and again now) on their shadowy beaches
Pouring before them the slow painful blood   25

Do we return to force the truthful speech of them
Shrieking like snipe along their gusty sand
And stand: and as the dark ditch fills beseech them

(Reaching across the surf their fragile hands) to
Speak to us?   30
        as by that other ocean
The elder shadows to the sea-borne man[3]

Guarding the ram's flesh and the bloody dole. . . .
Speak to me Conquerors!
           But not as they!   35
Bring not those others with you whose new-closed

(O Brothers! Bones now in the witless rain!)
And weeping eyes remember living men:
(Not Anticlea! Not Elpenor's face!)[4]

---

3. Odysseus.
4. Anticlea was Odysseus's mother, Elpenor his companion, accidentally killed
on Circe's island; he was abandoned, unburied, by Odysseus and his crew. Odysseus encountered the two ghosts on his
trip through Hades.

Bring not among you hither the new dead—   40
Lest they should wake and the unwilling lids
Open and know me—and the not-known end!. . . .

And Sándoval[5] comes first and the Pálos[6] wind
Stirs in the young hair: and the smoky candle
Shudders the sick face and the fevered skin: 45

And still the dead feet come: and Alvarádo
Clear in that shadow as a faggot kindled:
The brave one: stupid: and the face he had

Shining with good looks: his skin pink:
His legs warped at the knee like the excellent horseman: 50
And gentleman's ways and the tail of the sword swinging:

And Olíd the good fighter: his face coarse:
His teeth clean as a dog's: the lip wrinkled:
Oléa—so do the winds follow unfortune—

And last and through the weak dead comes—the uncertain   55
Fingers before him on the sightless air—
An old man speaking:[7] and the wind-blown words

Blur and the mouth moves and before the staring
Eyes go shadows of that ancient time:
So does a man speak from the dream that bears his   60

Sleeping body with it and the cry
Comes from a great way off as over water—
As the sea-bell's that the veering wind divides:

(And the sound runs on the valleys of the water:)

And the light returns as in past time   65
                              as in evenings
Distant with yellow summer on the straw—

As the light in America comes: without leaves. . . .

The Fifteenth Book

Conquistador . . .

And we marched against them there in the next spring:

And we did the thing that time by the books and the science:

---

5. A conquistador who fought with Hernando Cortez in the conquest of Mexico. Alvarádo, Olíd, and Oléa in the lines following are others.
6. Pálos de la Frontéra, a Spanish port from which ships for the New World set out.
7. The conquistador Bernál Díaz del Castillo, who narrates the remainder of the poem.

And we burned the back towns and we cut the mulberries:
And their dykes were down and the pipes of their fountains dry:

And we laid them a Christian siege with the sun and the vultures: 5
And they kept us ninety and three days till they died of it:
And the whole action well conceived and conducted:

And they cared nothing for sieges on their side:
And the place stank to God and their dung was such as
Thin swine will pass for the winter flies and the   10

Whole city was grubbed for the roots and their guts were
Swollen with tree-bark: and we let them go:
And they crawled out by the soiled walls and the rubbish—

Three days they were there on the dykes going—
And the captains ill of the bad smell of that city   15
And the town gone—no stone to a stone of it—

And the whole thing was a very beautiful victory:
And we squared the streets like a city in old Spain
And we built barracks and shops: and the church conspicuous:

And those that had jeered at our youth (but the fashion
    changes:)   20
They came like nettles in dry slash: like beetles:
They ran on the new land like lice staining it:

They parcelled the bloody meadows: their late feet
Stood in the passes of harsh pain and of winter:
In the stale of the campments they culled herbs: they peeled the 25

Twigs of the birch and they stood at the hill-fights thinking:
They brought carts with their oak beds and their boards and the
Pots they had and the stale clothes and the stink of

Stewed grease in the gear and their wives before them
Sour and smelling of spent milk and their children: 30
They built their barns like the old cotes[8] under Córdova:

They raised the Spanish cities: the new hills
Showed as the old with the old walls and the tether of
Galled goats in the dung and the rock hidden. . . .

Old . . . an old man sickened and near death: 35
And the west is gone now: the west is the ocean sky. . . .
O day that brings the earth back bring again

That well-swept town those towers and that island. . . .

                                                                     1932

8. Sheds for animals; Cordova is a Spanish city.

EDNA ST. VINCENT MILLAY
1892–1950

Like the novelist F. Scott Fitzgerald, Edna St. Vincent Millay was a symbolic figure in the Twenties. She enjoyed an extraordinary popularity for heralding in verse the liberation of the woman. Fresh from Vassar College, a published poet and an aspiring actress, she took Greenwich Village in New York City by storm: countless readers could recite her famous quatrain:

> My candle burns at both its ends;
> It will not last the night;
> But ah, my foes, and oh, my friends—
> It gives a lovely light!

She was born in Maine, the eldest of three girls in a close family, raised by a mother who gave them books and music lessons despite the limited means her job as a practical nurse provided after her separation and divorce from their father. The landscape of coastal New England, her early musical training, and her mother's encouragement to pursue an artist's life all greatly influenced the young Millay.

She wrote poetry in high school for the school's literary publications and for children's magazines. Her prize poem *Renascence*, entered at her mother's behest in *The Lyric Year* contest in 1912, brought her to the attention of the literary world and favorably interested a patron, who sent her to Vassar (1913–17) after a semester at Barnard College.

At Vassar she studied languages, wrote songs and plays in verse, and began an acting career that took her to New York for roles with the Provincetown Playhouse and the Theatre Guild. Her first volume, *Renascence and Other Poems*, was published to critical acclaim in 1917. She numbered among her friends the novelist Floyd Dell, the critic Edmund Wilson, the poet John Peale Bishop, and the radical John Reed. Millay worked at a hectic pace, writing light magazine sketches (under the pseudonym Nancy Boyd) as well as poetry. She also wrote a verse play, *Aria da Capo*, which was published along with *A Few Figs from Thistles* in 1920. Fliply irreverent, cynical, gay, and candid in treating bodily love as a subject, she was the embodiment of the liberated woman of the 1920s, and she asserted a woman's right to speak as openly as men of erotic love.

Despite the appearance of a more serious volume, *Second April* (1921), it was difficult for Millay to shake her reputation as a wanton bohemian. Love affairs with Dell, Wilson, and the poet and lawyer Arthur D. Ficke, among others, drained her energies and took their toll. She went to Europe in 1921, ostensibly to write sketches for *Vanity Fair* but also to recover from a nervous breakdown, avoid the importunities of suitors, and sever her relation with Ficke.

She lived abroad from 1921 to 1923, nursed by her mother during the latter months of her stay. Her fourth book, *The Harp Weaver and Other Poems*, won the Pulitzer Prize in 1923. In that year she married Eugen Boissevain, a Dutch-American businessman who virtually gave up his career to care for and eventually nurse his poet-wife.

When returning to America they settled on an upstate New York farm, Steepletop, which was their home for the rest of Millay's life. There she retreated from the literary scene of New York City. She never wrote criticism or reviews, except for the early favorable notice of the poet Elinor Wylie's *Nets to Catch the Wind* (1922) and a preface to her own translation (with collaborator George Dillon) of Baudelaire's *Flowers of Evil* (1936). Yet she published seven more volumes of verse, traveled on reading tours, and broadcast the first poetry readings over national radio networks. Her love of music, drama, and poetry met in a libretto for an opera composed by Deems Taylor, *The King's Henchman*, successfully produced by the Metropolitan Opera in 1927.

Poor health and intermittent hospitalization did not keep her from active engagement with public issues of the time. She joined other writers and public figures in protesting the trial and execution of the anarchists Sacco and Vanzetti in 1927, for which she was jailed in Boston; her protest found expression in several poems in *The Buck in the Snow* (1928). The impending war in Europe and the rise of totalitarianism preoccupied her increasingly in the late 1930s. She devoted her talent to propaganda for the democratic cause, writing newspaper verse, radio plays, and speeches in an effort that depleted her strength and morale. She suffered a nervous collapse in 1944 and was only beginning to write again when her husband died in 1949. Millay lived a year longer in solitude and died after a heart attack in 1950.

By then her reputation was already in eclipse. Early extravagant praise had given way to measured approval in the late 1920s and then to deprecating dismissal of her later *Conversation at Midnight* (1937), *Make Bright the Arrows* (1940), and *The Murder of Lidice* (1942).

Controversial though her attitudes and subject matter were, her approach to poetry was unabashedly conventional. Her diction, and her preference for familiar forms, above all the sonnet, are an indication of how conservatively she practiced her art. She shares with New Englanders E. A. Robinson and Robert Frost an innately conservative temper and their delight in ordinary tasks and the familiar landscape. Too often archaisms, awkward inversions of subject and verb, and quaint locutions compromise her considerable skill in rendering ideas and emotions in a simple idiom and colloquial speech. Among her two hundred sonnets are several sonnet sequences on characteristic themes: *Fatal Interview* (1931) on the birth, duration, and death of love; *Sonnets from an Ungrafted Tree*, a psychological portrait of a New England woman; and *Epitaph for the Race of Man*, a bleak view of mankind's history. Her poems portraying the feelings of a modern woman in love are a landmark in the history of American taste.

Recuerdo[1]

We were very tired, we were very merry—
We had gone back and forth all night on the ferry.
It was bare and bright, and smelled like a stable—
But we looked into a fire, we leaned across a table,
We lay on a hill-top underneath the moon,   5
And the whistles kept blowing, and the dawn came soon.

1. Remembrance, souvenir.

We were very tired, we were very merry—
We had gone back and forth all night on the ferry;
And you ate an apple, and I ate a pear,
From a dozen of each we had bought somewhere;   10
And the sky went wan, and the wind came cold,
And the sun rose dripping, a bucketful of gold.

We were very tired, we were very merry,
We had gone back and forth all night on the ferry.
We hailed, "Good morrow, mother!" to a shawl-covered head, 15
And bought a morning paper, which neither of us read;
And she wept, "God bless you!" for the apples and pears,
And we gave her all our money but our subway fares.

                             1919, 1922

I Think I Should Have Loved You Presently

I think I should have loved you presently,
And given in earnest words I flung in jest;
And lifted honest eyes for you to see,
And caught your hand against my cheek and breast;
And all my pretty follies flung aside   5
That won you to me, and beneath your gaze,
Naked of reticence and shorn of pride,
Spread like a chart my little wicked ways.
I, that had been to you, had you remained,
But one more waking from a recurrent dream,   10
Cherish no less the certain stakes I gained,
And walk your memory's halls, austere, supreme,
A ghost in marble of a girl you knew
Who would have loved you in a day or two.

                             1920

Elegy before Death

There will be rose and rhododendron
   When you are dead and under ground;
Still will be heard from white syringas
   Heavy with bees, a sunny sound;

Still will the tamaracks be raining   5
   After the rain has ceased, and still
Will there be robins in the stubble,
   Grey sheep upon the warm green hill.

Spring will not ail nor autumn falter;
   Nothing will know that you are gone,—   10
Saving alone some sullen plough-land
   None but yourself sets foot upon;

Saving the may-weed and the pig-weed
   Nothing will know that you are dead,—

These, and perhaps a useless wagon   15
Standing beside some tumbled shed.

Oh, there will pass with your great passing
Little of beauty not your own,—
Only the light from common water,
Only the grace from simple stone!   20

1920, 1921

Loving You Less than Life, a Little Less

Loving you less than life, a little less
Than bitter-sweet upon a broken wall
Or brush-wood smoke in autumn, I confess
I cannot swear I love you not at all.
For there is that about you in this light—   5
A yellow darkness, sinister of rain—
Which sturdily recalls my stubborn sight
To dwell on you, and dwell on you again.
And I am made aware of many a week
I shall consume, remembering in what way   10
Your brown hair grows about your brow and cheek,
And what divine absurdities you say:
Till all the world, and I, and surely you,
Will know I love you, whether or not I do.

1920, 1923

Euclid Alone Has Looked on Beauty Bare

Euclid[1] alone has looked on Beauty bare.
Let all who prate of Beauty hold their peace,
And lay them prone upon the earth and cease
To ponder on themselves, the while they stare
At nothing, intricately drawn nowhere   5
In shapes of shifting lineage; let geese
Gabble and hiss, but heroes seek release
From dusty bondage into luminous air.
O blinding hour, O holy, terrible day,
When first the shaft into his vision shone   10
Of light anatomized! Euclid alone
Has looked on Beauty bare. Fortunate they
Who, though once only and then but far away,
Have heard her massive sandal set on stone.

1920, 1923

What Lips My Lips Have Kissed, and Where, and Why

What lips my lips have kissed, and where, and why,
I have forgotten, and what arms have lain

---

1. Greek mathematician (fl. c. 300 B.C.), author of *Elements*, a book on geometry.

Under my head till morning; but the rain
Is full of ghosts tonight, that tap and sigh
Upon the glass and listen for reply,   5
And in my heart there stirs a quiet pain
For unremembered lads that not again
Will turn to me at midnight with a cry.
Thus in the winter stands the lonely tree,
Nor knows what birds have vanished one by one,   10
Yet knows its boughs more silent than before:
I cannot say what loves have come and gone,
I only know that summer sang in me
A little while, that in me sings no more.

                                                  1922, 1923

Never May the Fruit Be Plucked

Never, never may the fruit be plucked from the bough
And gathered into barrels.
He that would eat of love must eat it where it hangs.
Though the branches bend like reeds,
Though the ripe fruit splash in the grass or wrinkle on the tree,   5
He that would eat of love may bear away with him
Only what his belly can hold,
Nothing in the apron,
Nothing in the pockets.
Never, never may the fruit be gathered from the bough   10
And harvested in barrels.
The winter of love is a cellar of empty bins,
In an orchard soft with rot.

                                                        1923

The Buck in the Snow

White sky, over the hemlocks bowed with snow,
Saw you not at the beginning of evening the antlered buck and
    his doe
Standing in the apple-orchard? I saw them. I saw them suddenly
    go,
Tails up, with long leaps lovely and slow,
Over the stone-wall into the wood of hemlocks bowed with snow.   5

Now lies he here, his wild blood scalding the snow.

How strange a thing is death, bringing to his knees, bringing to
    his antlers
The buck in the snow.
How strange a thing,—a mile away by now, it may be,
Under the heavy hemlocks that as the moments pass   10
Shift their loads a little, letting fall a feather of snow—
Life, looking out attentive from the eyes of the doe.

                                                        1928

From Fatal Interview[1]

xxx

Love is not all: it is not meat nor drink
Nor slumber nor a roof against the rain;
Nor yet a floating spar to men that sink
And rise and sink and rise and sink again;
Love can not fill the thickened lung with breath,   5
Nor clean the blood, nor set the fractured bone;
Yet many a man is making friends with death
Even as I speak, for lack of love alone.
It well may be that in a difficult hour,
Pinned down by pain and moaning for release,   10
Or nagged by want past resolution's power,
I might be driven to sell your love for peace,
Or trade the memory of this night for food.
It well may be. I do not think I would.

1931

xxxv

Clearly my ruined garden as it stood
Before the frost came on it I recall—
Stiff marigolds, and what a trunk of wood
The zinnia had, that was the first to fall;
These pale and oozy stalks, these hanging leaves   5
Nerveless and darkened, dripping in the sun,
Cannot gainsay me, though the spirit grieves
And wrings its hands at what the frost has done.
If in a widening silence you should guess
I read the moment with recording eyes,   10
Taking your love and all your loveliness
Into a listening body hushed of sighs . . .
Though summer's rife and the warm rose in season,
Rebuke me not: I have a winter reason.

1931

In the Grave No Flower[2]

Here dock and tare.
But there
No flower.

Here beggar-ticks, 'tis true;
Here the rank-smelling   5
Thorn-apple,—and who

---

1. Sonnets XXX and XXXV are from
Fatal Interview (1931), a sequence of 52
sonnets.
2. This poem is the second of a pair of
elegies to Millay's mother. The flowers
named in the poem are those of common
weeds.

Would plant this by his dwelling?
Here every manner of weed
To mock the faithful harrow:
Thistles, that feed   10
None but the finches; yarrow,
Blue vervain, yellow charlock; here
Bindweed, that chokes the struggling year;
Broad plantain and narrow.

But there no flower.   15

The rye is vexed and thinned,
The wheat comes limping home,
By vetch and whiteweed harried, and the sandy bloom
Of the sour-grass; here
Dandelions,—and the wind   20
Will blow them everywhere.

Save there.
There
No flower.

                                                         1934

Conscientious Objector

I shall die, but that is all that I shall do for Death.

I hear him leading his horse out of the stall; I hear the clatter on
    the barn-floor.
He is in haste; he has business in Cuba, business in the Balkans,
    many calls to make this morning.
But I will not hold the bridle while he cinches the girth.
And he may mount by himself: I will not give him a leg up.   5

Though he flick my shoulders with his whip, I will not tell him
    which way the fox ran.
With his hoof on my breast, I will not tell him where the black boy
    hides in the swamp.
I shall die, but that is all that I shall do for Death; I am not on his
    pay-roll.

I will not tell him the whereabouts of my friends nor of my ene-
    mies either.
Though he promise me much, I will not map him the route to any
    man's door.   10
Am I a spy in the land of the living, that I should deliver men to
    Death?
Brother, the password and the plans of our city are safe with me;
    never through me
Shall you be overcome.

                                                         1934

I Too beneath Your Moon, Almighty Sex

I too beneath your moon, almighty Sex,
Go forth at nightfall crying like a cat,
Leaving the lofty tower I laboured at
For birds to foul and boys and girls to vex
With tittering chalk; and you, and the long necks   5
Of neighbours sitting where their mothers sat
Are well aware of shadowy this and that
In me, that's neither noble nor complex.
Such as I am, however, I have brought
To what it is, this tower; it is my own;   10
Though it was reared To Beauty, it was wrought
From what I had to build with: honest bone
Is there, and anguish; pride; and burning thought;
And just is there, and nights not spent alone.

                              1936, 1939

The Snow Storm

No hawk hangs over in this air:
The urgent snow is everywhere.
The wing adroiter than a sail
Must lean away from such a gale,
Abandoning its straight intent,   5
Or else expose tough ligament
And tender flesh to what before
Meant dampened feathers, nothing more.

Forceless upon our backs there fall
Infrequent flakes hexagonal,   10
Devised in many a curious style
To charm our safety for a while,
Where close to earth like mice we go
Under the horizontal snow.

                              1939

Ragged Island

There, there where those black spruces crowd
To the edge of the precipitous cliff,
Above your boat, under the eastern wall of the island;
And no wave breaks; as if
All had been done, and long ago, that needed   5
Doing; and the cold tide, unimpeded
By shoal or shelving ledge, moves up and down,
Instead of in and out;
And there is no driftwood there, because there is no beach;
Clean cliff going down as deep as clear water can reach;   10

No driftwood, such as abounds on the roaring shingle,
To be hefted home, for fires in the kitchen stove;

Barrels, banged ashore about the boiling outer harbour;
Lobster-buoys, on the eel-grass of the sheltered cove:

There, thought unbraids itself, and the mind becomes
    single.   15
There you row with tranquil oars, and the ocean
Shows no scar from the cutting of your placid keel;
Care becomes senseless there; pride and promotion
Remote; you only look; you scarcely feel.

Even adventure, with its vital uses,   20
Is aimless ardour now; and thrift is waste.

Oh, to be there, under the silent spruces,
Where the wide, quiet evening darkens without haste
Over a sea with death acquainted, yet forever chaste.

1954

I Will Put Chaos into Fourteen Lines

I will put Chaos into fourteen lines
And keep him there; and let him thence escape
If he be lucky; let him twist, and ape
Flood, fire, and demon—his adroit designs
Will strain to nothing in the strict confines   5
Of this sweet Order, where, in pious rape,
I hold his essence and amorphous shape,
Till he with Order mingles and combines.
Past are the hours, the years, of our duress,
His arrogance, our awful servitude: 10
I have him. He is nothing more nor less
Than something simple not yet understood;
I shall not even force him to confess;
Or answer. I will only make him good.

1954

JEAN TOOMER
1894–1967

Jean Toomer's reputation rests on a single book, *Cane* (1923), whose position in the literature of the 1920s is unique. Writers and critics recognize it as one of the earliest productions of the "Harlem Renaissance," the movement launched by black intellectuals to gain a larger audience for black talent and provide outlets for the full range of cultural activities among American blacks. At the same time it was praised for making racial protest subordinate to the uninhibited celebration of human experience in the South. While it enforced a traditional myth about the blacks by portraying them as exotic primitives, it did so by experimenting with both verse and narrative forms in ways that were distinctly contemporary.

Toomer was born in Washington, D.C., the son of a Georgia Negro and grandson of a part-black acting Governor of Louisiana during Reconstruction. After graduating from public high school he took courses in a variety of fields at a number of colleges, including the University of Wisconsin and City College of New York, taught physical education in Wisconsin, and in 1921 was superintendent of a black rural school in Sparta, Georgia, his father's original home and the source of much of the material in *Cane*. During the 1920s he contributed to the black journals *Crisis* and *Opportunity* and to such vanguard journals edited by whites as the *Little Review* and *Broom*. Though he continued to write poems, novels, and plays that still exist in manuscript, he virtually disappeared from the literary scene after the mid-1920s because he could not find publishers for them. He became interested in Quaker pietism and in the mysticism of the Russian Georges I. Gurdjieff, studying his ideas at Fontainebleau in 1924 and returning to teach them in communities organized on Gurdjieffian principles. He married a white member of one of the communities in 1932, the writer Marjorie Latimer, but she died a year later after giving birth to their daughter. He later married another white woman, Marjorie Content, the daughter of a New York stockbroker. His only later volumes were *Portage Potential* (1932) and *Essentials* (1931), a collection of philosophical aphorisms.

Toomer lived at various times in the black community, at other times in the white, envisioning in a later poem (*Blue Meridian*, 1936) the emergence of a new state of being in which identities based on race, sex, or social class would be eliminated. Much earlier, in an autobiographical sketch submitted to the *Liberator* in 1922, Toomer had refused to accept identification exclusively as a black. While at that time he felt "deeper and deeper" ties with the Negro community as a professional writer, he was proud to claim seven national or ethnic strands ("French, Dutch, Welsh, Negro, German, Jewish, and Indian") and he insisted that "I am naturally and inevitably an American. I have strived for a spiritual fusion analogous to the fact of racial intermingling."[1] His treatment of racial injustice and the particularities of the blacks' experience in rural Georgia and Washington, D.C., was strikingly vivid, but his emphasis on their physical and psychic freedom —on the primitive and the exotic rather than the genteel and the respectable—seemed to many readers to "go below the surfaces of race"[2] in celebrating human vitality itself. The white writers Waldo Frank, Carl Van Vechten, and Sherwood Anderson, who undertook comparable subjects in their fiction, admired the simplicity, lyric intensity, and rhythm of Toomer's style. His abandonment of conventional narrative patterns, to intermingle lyric verse and impressionistic character sketches, constituted one of the distinctive experiments in the fiction of the 1920s.

From Cane[3]

Georgia Dusk

The sky, lazily disdaining to pursue
The setting sun, too indolent to hold

1. Quoted by Arna Bontemps, introduction to *Cane* (1969).
2. Waldo Frank, introduction to *Cane*

(1923).
3. Of the book's three sections, the first and last are Georgia scenes. *Fern* ap-

A lengthened tournament for flashing gold,
Passively darkens for night's barbecue,

A feast of moon and men and barking hounds, 5
An orgy for some genius of the South
With blood-hot eyes and cane-lipped scented mouth,
Surprised in making folk-songs from soul sounds.

The sawmill blows its whistle, buzz-saws stop,
And silence breaks the bud of knoll and hill, 10
Soft settling pollen where plowed lands fulfill
Their early promise of a bumper crop.

Smoke from the pyramidal sawdust pile
Curls up, blue ghosts of trees, tarrying low
Where only chips and stumps are left to show 15
The solid proof of former domicile.

Meanwhile, the men, with vestiges of pomp,
Race memories of king and caravan,
High-priests, an ostrich, and a juju-man,⁴
Go singing through the footpaths of the swamp. 20

Their voices rise . . the pine trees are guitars,
Strumming, pine-needles fall like sheets of rain . .
Their voices rise . . the chorus of the cane
Is caroling a vesper to the stars. .

O singers, resinous and soft your songs 25
Above the sacred whisper of the pines,
Give virgin lips to cornfield concubines,
Bring dreams of Christ to dusky cane-lipped throngs.

1923

Fern

Face flowed into her eyes. Flowed in soft cream foam and plaintive ripples, in such a way that wherever your glance may momentarily have rested, it immediately thereafter wavered in the direction of her eyes. The soft suggestion of down slightly darkened, like the shadow of a bird's wing might, the creamy brown color of her upper lip. Why, after noticing it, you sought her eyes, I cannot tell you. Her nose was aquiline, Semitic. If you have heard a Jewish cantor¹ sing, if he has touched you and made your own sorrow seem trivial when compared with his, you will know my feeling when I follow the curves of her profile, like mobile rivers, to their common delta.

pears in the first section, preceded immediately by the poem *Georgia Dusk*. The poem *Portrait in Georgia* appears in the first section immediately preceding a story of the lynching of a black woman's black lover by her white lover and his white cohorts. *Seventh Avenue* is the first sketch in the center section devoted to Washington, D.C., and Chicago.
4. West African tribesman who controls the magical fetish or charm "juju."
1. Male soloist who sings the Jewish liturgy.

They were strange eyes. In this, that they sought nothing—that is, nothing that was obvious and tangible and that one could see, and they gave the impression that nothing was to be denied. When a woman seeks, you will have observed, her eyes deny. Fern's eyes desired nothing that you could give her; there was no reason why they should withhold. Men saw her eyes and fooled themselves. Fern's eyes said to them that she was easy. When she was young, a few men took her, but got no joy from it. And then, once done, they felt bound to her (quite unlike their hit and run with other girls), felt as though it would take them a lifetime to fulfill an obligation which they could find no name for. They became attached to her, and hungered after finding the barest trace of what she might desire. As she grew up, new men who came to town felt as almost everyone did who ever saw her: that they would not be denied. Men were everlastingly bringing her their bodies. Something inside of her got tired of them, I guess, for I am certain that for the life of her she could not tell why or how she began to turn them off. A man in fever is no trifling thing to send away. They began to leave her, baffled and ashamed, yet vowing to themselves that some day they would do some fine thing for her: send her candy every week and not let her know whom it came from, watch out for her wedding-day and give her a magnificent something with no name on it, buy a house and deed it to her, rescue her from some unworthy fellow who had tricked her into marrying him. As you know, men are apt to idolize or fear that which they cannot understand, especially if it be a woman. She did not deny them, yet the fact was that they were denied. A sort of superstition crept into their consciousness of her being somehow above them. Being above them meant that she was not to be approached by anyone. She became a virgin. Now a virgin in a small southern town is by no means the usual thing, if you will believe me. That the sexes were made to mate is the practice of the South. Particularly, black folks were made to mate. And it is black folks whom I have been talking about thus far. What white men thought of Fern I can arrive at only by analogy. They let her alone.

Anyone, of course, could see her, could see her eyes. If you walked up the Dixie Pike most any time of day, you'd be most like to see her resting listless-like on the railing of her porch, back propped against a post, head tilted a little forward because there was a nail in the porch post just where her head came which for some reason or other she never took the trouble to pull out. Her eyes, if it were sunset, rested idly where the sun, molten and glorious, was pouring down between the fringe of pines. Or maybe they gazed at the gray cabin on the knoll from which an evening folk-song was coming. Perhaps they followed a cow that had been turned loose to roam and feed on cotton-stalks and corn leaves. Like as not they'd settle on some vague spot above the horizon, though hardly a trace of wistfulness would come to them. If it were dusk, then they'd wait for the search-light of the evening train which you could see miles up the track before it flared across the Dixie Pike, close to her home. Wherever they looked, you'd follow them and then waver back. Like her face, the whole countryside seemed to flow into her eyes. Flowed into them with the soft listless cadence of Georgia's South. A young Negro, once, was looking at her, spellbound, from the road. A white man passing in a buggy had to flick him with his whip if he was to get by without running him over. I first saw her on her porch. I was passing with a fellow whose crusty numbness (I was from the North and suspected of being prejudiced and stuck-up) was melting as he found me warm. I asked him who she was. "That's Fern," was all that I could get from him. Some folks already thought that I was given to nosing around; I let it go at that, so far as questions were concerned. But at first sight of her I felt as if I heard a Jewish cantor sing. As if his singing rose above the unheard chorus of a folk-song. And I felt bound to her. I too had my dreams: something I would do for her. I have knocked about from town to town too much not to know the futility of mere change of place. Besides, picture if you can, this cream-colored solitary girl sitting at a tenement window looking down on the indifferent throngs of Harlem. Better that she listen to folk-songs at dusk in Georgia, you would say, and so would I. Or, suppose she came up North and married. Even a doctor or a lawyer, say, one who would be sure to get along—that is, make money. You and I know, who have had experience in such things, that love is not a thing like prejudice which can be bettered by changes of town. Could men in Washington, Chicago, or New York, more than the men of Georgia, bring her something left vacant by the bestowal of their bodies? You and I who know men in these cities will have to say, they could not. See her out and out a prostitute along State Street in Chicago. See her move into a southern town where white men are more aggressive. See her become a white man's concubine. . . Something I must do for her. There was myself. What could I do for her? Talk, of course. Push back the fringe of pines upon new horizons. To what purpose? and what for? Her? Myself? Men in her case seem to lose their selfishness. I lost mine before I touched her. I ask you, friend (it makes no difference if you sit in the Pullman or the Jim Crow[2] as the train crosses her road), what thoughts would come to you—that is, after you'd finished with the thoughts that leap into men's minds at the sight of a pretty woman who will not deny them; what thoughts would come to you, had you seen her in a quick flash, keen and intuitively,

---

2. In the segregated South, black persons were required to sit in the "Jim Crow" section of railway cars and were not al-lowed as passengers in the first-class "Pullman" lounges or sleeping cars.

as she sat there on her porch when your train thundered by? Would you have got off at the next station and come back for her to take her where? Would you have completely forgotten her as soon as you reached Macon, Atlanta, Augusta, Pasadena, Madison, Chicago, Boston, or New Orleans? Would you tell your wife or sweetheart about a girl you saw? Your thoughts can help me, and I would like to know. Something I would do for her. . .

One evening I walked up the Pike on purpose, and stopped to say hello. Some of her family were about, but they moved away to make room for me. Damn if I knew how to begin. Would you? Mr. and Miss So-and-So, people, the weather, the crops, the new preacher, the frolic, the church benefit, rabbit and possum hunting, the new soft drink they had at old Pap's store, the schedule of the trains, what kind of town Macon was, Negro's migration north, bollweevils, syrup, the Bible—to all these things she gave a yassur or nassur, without further comment. I began to wonder if perhaps my own emotional sensibility had played one of its tricks on me. "Lets take a walk," I at last ventured. The suggestion, coming after so long an isolation, was novel enough, I guess, to surprise. But it wasnt that. Something told me that men before me had said just that as a prelude to the offering of their bodies. I tried to tell her with my eyes. I think she understood. The thing from her that made my throat catch, vanished. Its passing left her visible in a way I'd thought, but never seen. We walked down the Pike with people on all the porches gaping at us. "Doesnt it make you mad?" She meant the row of petty gossiping people. She meant the world. Through a canebrake that was ripe for cutting, the branch was reached. Under a sweet-gum tree, and where reddish leaves had dammed the creek a little, we sat down. Dusk, suggesting the almost imperceptible procession of giant trees, settled with a purple haze about the cane. I felt strange, as I always do in Georgia, particularly at dusk. I felt that things unseen to men were tangibly immediate. It would not have surprised me had I had vision. People have them in Georgia more often than you would suppose. A black woman once saw the mother of Christ and drew her in charcoal on the courthouse wall. . . When one is on the soil of one's ancestors, most anything can come to one. . . From force of habit, I suppose, I held Fern in my arms—that is, without at first noticing it. Then my mind came back to her. Her eyes, unusually weird and open, held me. Held God. He flowed in as I've seen the countryside flow in. Seen men. I must have done something—what, I dont know, in the confusion of my emotion. She sprang up. Rushed some distance from me. Fell to her knees, and began swaying, swaying. Her body was tortured with something it could not let out. Like boiling sap it flooded arms and fingers till she shook them as if they burned her. It found her throat, and spattered inarticulately in plaintive, convulsive sounds, mingled with calls to Christ Jesus. And then she sang, brokenly. A Jewish cantor singing with a broken voice. A child's voice, uncertain, or an old man's. Dusk hid her; I could hear only her song. It seemed to me as though she were pounding her head in anguish upon the ground. I rushed to her. She fainted in my arms.

There was talk about her fainting with me in the canefield. And I got one or two ugly looks from town men who'd set themselves up to protect her. In fact, there was talk of making me leave town. But they never did. They kept a watch-out for me, though. Shortly after, I came back North. From the train window I saw her as I crossed her road. Saw her on her porch, head tilted a little forward where the nail was, eyes vaguely focused on the sunset. Saw her face flow into them, the countryside and something that I call God, flowing into them. . . Nothing ever really happened. Nothing ever came to Fern, not even I. Something I would do for her. Some fine unnamed thing. . . And, friend, you? She is still living, I have reason to know. Her name, against the chance that you might happen down that way, is Fernie May Rosen.

Portrait in Georgia

Hair—braided chestnut,
    coiled like a lyncher's rope,
Eyes—fagots,
Lips—old scars, or the first red blisters,
Breath—the last sweet scent of cane,   5
And her slim body, white as the ash
    of black flesh after flame.

Seventh Street

Money burns the pocket, pocket hurts,
Bootleggers in silken shirts,
Ballooned, zooming Cadillacs,
Whizzing, whizzing down the street-car tracks.

Seventh Street is a bastard of Prohibition and the War.[1] A crude-boned, soft-skinned wedge of nigger life breathing its loafer air, jazz songs and love, thrusting unconscious rhythms, black reddish blood into the white and whitewashed wood of Washington. Stale soggy wood of Washington. Wedges rust in soggy wood. . . Split it! In two! Again! Shred it! . . the sun. Wedges are brilliant in the sun; ribbons of wet wood dry and blow away. Black reddish blood. Pouring for crude-boned soft-skinned life, who set you flowing? Blood suckers of the War would spin in a frenzy of dizzi-

1. World War I.

ness if they drank your blood. Prohibition would put a stop to it.
Who set you flowing? White and whitewash disappear in blood.
Who set you flowing? Flowing down the smooth asphalt of Seventh
Street, in shanties, brick office buildings, theaters, drug stores, restaurants, and cabarets? Eddying on the corners? Swirling like a
blood-red smoke up where the buzzards fly in heaven? God would
not dare to suck black red blood. A Nigger God! He would duck his
head in shame and call for the Judgment Day. Who set you
flowing?

> Money burns the pocket, pocket hurts,
> Bootleggers in silken shirts,
> Ballooned, zooming Cadillacs,
> Whizzing, whizzing down the street-car tracks.

1923

E. E. CUMMINGS
1894–1962

A remarkable talent, a flair for self-dramatization, and the accident of being
imprisoned in a French detention camp during World War I brought the
poet and painter Edward Estlin Cummings into prominence in the early
1920s. In the four ensuing decades he gave a striking redefinition to the tradition of New England individualism, helped invent what has since been
termed "pop art," and engaged a wondrously playful imagination in the
creation of ingenious poetic forms.

As a child in Cambridge, Massachusetts, where he was born, and later at
Harvard, he had the advantages of a favored son in a cultured family, whose
respect for the individual and concern for social ethics won Cummings's lasting devotion. (Two of his poems, *if there are any heavens my mother will*
(all by herself) have and my father moved through dooms of love, are
impassioned tributes to his parents.) His father, a Congregational minister,
taught English and later social ethics at Harvard. Encouraged by his parents, Cummings painted as a child, and he published poetry in college journals at Harvard while studying languages and the classics, taking sonnets as
his models (by Shakespeare, the Pre-Raphaelite Dante Gabriel Rossetti, and
the Harvard philosopher-poet George Santayana) along with the intricate
stanza forms of earlier English and Continental literature. By the time he
graduated from Harvard in 1915 (and received an M.A. in 1916), he had
discovered Ezra Pound's poetry and had made life-long friends with the
novelist John Dos Passos and with Scofield Thayer and James Sibley Watson, Jr., who were to assume control of *The Dial* and publish Cummings's
first poems in 1920. His graduation address ("The New Art") was a bold
endorsement of modern art—Stravinsky's music and the Cubists and Futur-
ists in painting.

In the famous Norton Harjes Ambulance Corps in France, he and his
friend Slater Brown aroused suspicion by their moustaches, their disdain for
the bureaucracy, and Brown's outspoken letters home (which censors thought
unpatriotic). Cummings was incarcerated along with his friend in October,

1917 in a French prison camp until letters from Cummings's father to U.S. officials and President Woodrow Wilson brought about his release three months later. Cummings's brilliantly surrealistic treatment of his experience, a celebration of the uniqueness of his fellow prisoners and a savage exposé of the French bureaucracy, was written at his father's urging and published as *The Enormous Room* in 1922. It made Cummings instantly famous.

Cummings lived in Paris from 1921 to 1923, and traveled frequently and regularly throughout his career, never disguising his enthusiasm for what was liberating in European culture but concluding (in pieces he wrote for *Vanity Fair* in 1925 and 1926) that America was more youthful and alive, that "France has happened more than she is happening whereas America is happening more than she has happened."[1] He was nothing less than appalled by Stalinist Russia, which he visited in 1931 and described in *Eimi* (1933), and he rendered the regimentation and deadness he found there in an image of the citizens dutifully lined up to pass by Lenin's tomb: "all toward All budgeshuffle:all Toward standwait. Isn'tish."[2] The America that excited him was divided between the family summer place in New Hampshire, which Cummings eventually inherited, and New York City, where he moved in 1918 and finally established himself in a Greenwich Village studio in 1924. He was still residing there with his third wife, an accomplished photographer, when he died in 1962.

There he pursued his "twin obsessions" of painting and writing,[3] painting during the day and writing at night. By carefully harboring his prizes, meager royalties and commissions, and the small income he received from his mother while she was alive, he managed to avoid the entanglements and routines of regular employment. His first volume of verse, *Tulips and Chimneys* (1923), was followed swiftly by two substantial volumes in 1925, the year he received the Dial Award, and *is 5* in 1926.

Cummings's verse displays a combination of Thoreau's controlled belligerency, the elitism of a privileged Bostonian, and the brash abandon of an uninhibited bohemian. He readily discerned in the modern environment a level of emotional deadness, conformity, barbarous warfare, intellectual abstractions, and clichés which he called a nonworld or "pseudoworld"[4] made up of "mostpeople" playing "impotent nongames of wrongright and rightwrong."[5] With a mixture of sardonic disdain, outright hatred, and earnest moral reproval he castigated that nonworld in mordantly sportive sonnets which caricatured it. Yet in the life around him Cummings also found sources of vitality and authenticity which he celebrated with refreshing candor in the lives of derelicts, unpretentious persons, lovers, his parents, and children, along with folk heroes, popular entertainers, and artists whose finesse as performers Cummings admired. His poems were designed to liberate the emotions and the imaginations of his readers by alternately (or simultaneously) shocking and exhilarating them, awakening them to their authentic selfhood as individuals and to a transformed world whose models are the process of birth and growth ("becoming") in nature, and the process of "making" in the arts. He conceived his poems as "competing" with the vitality of nature (its roses and "Niagara Falls"), surpassing "the 4th of

1. Quoted by Charles Norman, *The Magic-Maker*, p. 197.
2. Quoted by Cummings, *i: six nonlectures*, p. 101.
3. Quoted by Norman, *The Magic-Maker*, p. 251.
4. *i: six nonlectures*, p. 47.
5. Introduction, *Collected Poems* (1938).

July" in their celebration of independence, and rivaling the artifacts ("locomotives") that abound in industrial society (Foreword to *is 5*). His poems
became not statements but exuberant games played with the reader and
virtuoso performances by the writer.

Accordingly, Cummings's poetic forms, though less ambitious in their
attempt to reconstitute poetry than Eliot's and Pound's, Crane's, Stevens's,
or Williams's, are radically innovative and amount to more than the "pseudo-
experimental poetry" that the critic Yvor Winters judged his work to
be.[6] He clung to familiar themes and to the form of the sonnet, but he
perfected that form in many tender lyrics and overhauled it in other
instances, making it an unexpectedly effective instrument for satire and caricature. Shattering the conventions of syntax, punctuation, and typography,
Cummings (with the help of an expert typesetter and friend Samuel A.
Jacobs) devised poems that were as open-ended at beginning and conclusion as the processes of nature. These innovations converted print into
visual shape, anticipating the "composition by field" of Charles Olson and
such "concrete poets" as Aram Saroyan and Richard Kostelanetz. They also
converted nouns into verbs and words into motion of the kind he admired
as much in burlesque shows and the comic strip "Krazy Kat" as in the
cityscapes of the painter John Marin. Cummings could incorporate the
inflections of New England speech (in *rain or hail*), but more often he
adopted the lingo of the city streets, whether to expose the vulgarity of
anti-Semitism and the brutality of war, or to capture the energy and tenderness of urban life. Rivaling the intellectual abstractions he detested in the
life around him, he made a poetic vocabulary out of the most abstract components of the language (for instance the syllables "non" and "un," the
terms "it," "is," and "anyone") which enabled him to mock the unworld or
to create an alternative world of spontaneity and beauty. In many poems
Cummings boldly appropriated the clichés of public speech, popular culture, and advertising slogans, mocking their cheapness but capturing their
energy and the force of their reality in ways comparable to the paintings of
hamburgers, soup cans, and comic strips by "pop artists" of the 1960s.

Too often Cummings's ingenuities remain mere tricks and verbal puzzles,
and his career displayed little development in theme, social vision, or technical mastery, but he sustained a very high level of achievement throughout
his career in various genres. His first play, *Him*, an expressionistic work in
which an artist weighs the demands of art and love, was condemned by critics in 1927 but had an impact on John Dos Passos; he also wrote a scenario for a ballet based on *Uncle Tom's Cabin* entitled *Tom* (1935), and a
contemporary morality play entitled *Santa Claus* (1946). He had exhibited his paintings in 1919, but his first major show was in Cleveland
in 1931 at a time when he could find no publisher for his poems. Subsequent exhibitions in New York in the 1940s and 1950s coincided with the
revival of interest in his poetry occasioned by publication of his *Collected
Poems* in 1938. By the time he delivered his idiosyncratic Norton Lectures
at Harvard (published as *i: six nonlectures*, 1953) he was one of the most
popular of the established poets among college and high-school students. A
special citation by the National Book Award in 1955 and the award of the
Bollingen Prize in Poetry in 1957 were further testimony to the widening
recognition of this "proudhumble citizen of ecstasies."

6. *In Defense of Reason* (1947), p. 86.

Thy fingers make early flowers of

Thy fingers make early flowers of
all things.
thy hair mostly the hours love:
a smoothness which
sings,saying   5
(though love be a day)
do not fear,we will go amaying.

thy whitest feet crisply are straying.
Always
thy moist eyes are at kisses playing,   10
whose strangeness much
says;singing
(though love be a day)
for which girl art thou flowers bringing?

To be thy lips is a sweet thing   15
and small.
Death,Thee i call rich beyond wishing
if this thou catch,
else missing.
(though love be a day   20
and life be nothing,it shall not stop kissing).

                                                   1923

All in green went my love riding

All in green went my love riding
on a great horse of gold
into the silver dawn.

four lean hounds crouched low and smiling
the merry deer ran before.   5

Fleeter be they than dappled dreams
the swift sweet deer
the red rare deer.

Four red roebuck at a white water
the cruel bugle sang before.   10

Horn at hip went my love riding
riding the echo down
into the silver dawn.

four lean hounds crouched low and smiling
the level meadows ran before.   15

Softer be they than slippered sleep
the lean lithe deer
the fleet flown deer.

Four fleet does at a gold valley
the famished arrow sang before.   20

Bow at belt went my love riding
riding the mountain down
into the silver dawn.

four lean hounds crouched low and smiling
the sheer peaks ran before.   25

Paler be they than daunting death
the sleek slim deer
the tall tense deer.

Four tall stags at a green mountain
the lucky hunter sang before.   30

All in green went my love riding
on a great horse of gold
into the silver dawn.

four lean hounds crouched low and smiling
my heart fell dead before.   35

                                1916, 1923

in Just-

in Just-
spring   when the world is mud-
luscious the little
lame balloonman

whistles   far   and wee   5

and eddieandbill come
running from marbles and
piracies and it's
spring

when the world is puddle-wonderful   10

the queer
old balloonman whistles
far   and   wee
and bettyandisbel come dancing
from hop-scotch and jump-rope and   15

        it's
        spring
        and
            the

                goat-footed   20

        balloonMan   whistles
        far
        and
        wee

                                1920, 1923

O sweet spontaneous

O sweet spontaneous
earth how often have
the
doting

                fingers of   5
        prurient philosophers pinched
        and
        poked

        thee
        ,has the naughty thumb   10
        of science prodded
        thy

                beauty   .how
        often have religions taken
        thee upon their scraggy knees   15
        squeezing and

        buffeting thee that thou mightest conceive
        gods
                (but
        true   20

        to the incomparable
        couch of death thy
        rhythmic
        lover

                thou answerest   25

        them only with

                spring)

                                1920, 1923

Buffalo Bill 's[1]

Buffalo Bill 's
defunct
    who used to
    ride a watersmooth-silver
                 stallion   5
and break onetwothreefourfive pigeonsjustlikethat
                                   Jesus

he was a handsome man
                 and what i want to know is
how do you like your blueeyed boy   10
Mister Death

                                1920, 1923

the Cambridge ladies who live in furnished souls

the Cambridge ladies who live in furnished souls
are unbeautiful and have comfortable minds
(also,with the church's protestant blessings
daughters,unscented shapeless spirited)
they believe in Christ and Longfellow,[2] both dead,   5
are invariably interested in so many things—
at the present writing one still finds
delighted fingers knitting for the is it Poles?
perhaps.   While permanent faces coyly bandy
scandal of Mrs. N and Professor D   10
. . . . the Cambridge ladies do not care,above
Cambridge if sometimes in its box of
sky lavender and cornerless,the
moon rattles like a fragment of angry candy

                                  1923

when thou hast taken thy last applause,and when

when thou hast taken thy last applause,and when
the final curtain strikes the world away,
leaving to shadowy silence and dismay
that stage which shall not know thy smile again,
lingering a little while i see thee then   5
ponder the tinsel part they let thee play;
i see the large lips vivid,the face grey,
and silent smileless eyes of Magdalen.[3]
The lights have laughed their last;without,the street
darkling awaiteth her whose feet have trod   10

1. William F. Cody (1846–1917), American scout and Wild West showman.
2. Henry Wadsworth Longfellow (1807–82), American poet and professor of Romance languages at Harvard.
3. Mary Magdalen, prostitute converted by Jesus

the silly souls of men to golden dust:
she pauses on the lintel of defeat,
her heart breaks in a smile—and she is Lust . . . .

mine also,little painted poem of god

1923

it is at moments after i have dreamed

it is at moments after i have dreamed
of the rare entertainment of your eyes,
when(being fool to fancy)i have deemed

with your peculiar mouth my heart made wise;
at moments when the glassy darkness holds   5

the genuine apparition of your smile
(it was through tears always)and silence moulds
such strangeness as was mine a little while;

moments when my once more illustrious arms
are filled with fascination,when my breast   10
wears the intolerant brightness of your charms:

one pierced moment whiter than the rest

—turning from the tremendous lie of sleep
i watch the roses of the day grow deep.

1923

between the breasts

between the breasts
of bestial
Marj lie large
men who praise

Marj's cleancornered strokable   5
body   these men's
fingers toss trunks
shuffle sacks spin kegs they

curl
loving   10
around
beers

the world has
these men's hands but their
bodies big and boozing   15
belong to

Marj
the greenslim purse of whose
face opens
on a fatgold   20

grin
hooray
hoorah for the large
men who lie

between the breasts   25
of bestial Marj
for the strong men
who

sleep between the legs of Lil
                                                               1925

Spring is like a perhaps hand

Spring is like a perhaps hand
(which comes carefully
out of Nowhere)arranging
a window,into which people look(while
people stare   5
arranging and changing placing
carefully there a strange
thing and a known thing here)and

changing everything carefully

spring is like a perhaps   10
Hand in a window
(carefully to
and fro moving New and
Old things,while
people stare carefully   15
moving a perhaps
fraction of flower here placing
an inch of air there)and

without breaking anything.
                                                               1925

irreproachable ladies firmly lewd

irreproachable ladies firmly lewd
on dangerous slabs of tilting din whose
mouths distinctly walk
                         your smiles accuse

the dusk with an untimid svelte subdued   5
magic
        while in your eyes there lives
a green egyptian noise. ladies with whom time

feeds especially his immense lips

On whose deep nakedness death most believes,   10
perpetual girls marching to love

whose bodies kiss me with the square crime
of life . . . . Cecile,the oval shove
of hiding pleasure.   Alice,stinging quips
of flesh.   Loretta,cut the comedy   15
kid . . . .

            Fran Mag Glad Dorothy

                                                 1925

Picasso[1]

Picasso
you give us Things
which
bulge:grunting lungs pumped full of sharp thick mind

you make us shrill   5
presents always
shut in the sumptuous screech of
simplicity

(out of the
black unbunged   10
Something gushes vaguely a squeak of planes
or

between squeals of
Nothing grabbed with circular shrieking tightness
solid screams whisper.)   15
Lumberman of The Distinct

your brain's
axe only chops hugest inherent
Trees of Ego,from
whose living and biggest   20

bodies lopped
of every
prettiness

you hew form truly

                                                 1925

1. Pablo Picasso (1881–1973), Spanish painter and sculptor.

this is the garden:colours come and go

this is the garden:colours come and go,
frail azures fluttering from night's outer wing
strong silent greens serenely lingering,
absolute lights like baths of golden snow.
This is the garden:pursed lips do blow   5
upon cool flutes within wide glooms,and sing
(of harps celestial to the quivering string)
invisible faces hauntingly and slow.

This is the garden.   Time shall surely reap,
and on Death's blade lie many a flower curled,   10
in other lands where other songs be sung;
yet stand They here enraptured,as among
the slow deep trees perpetual of sleep
some silver-fingered fountain steals the world.

1925

Foreword to is 5

On the assumption that my technique is either complicated or original or both,the publishers have politely requested me to write an introduction to this book.

At least my theory of technique,if I have one,is very far from original;nor is it complicated.   I can express it in fifteen words,by quoting The Eternal Question And Immortal Answer of burlesk, viz. "Would you hit a woman with a child?—No,I'd hit her with a brick."   Like the burlesk comedian,I am abnormally fond of that precision which creates movement.

If a poet is anybody,he is somebody to whom things made matter very little—somebody who is obsessed by Making.   Like all obsessions,the Making obsession has disadvantages;for instance, my only interest in making money would be to make it.   Fortunately,however,I should prefer to make almost anything else, including locomotives and roses.   It is with roses and locomotives (not to mention acrobats Spring electricity Coney Island[1] the 4th of July the eyes of mice and Niagara Falls)that my "poems" are competing.

They are also competing with each other,with elephants,and with El Greco.[2]

Ineluctable preoccupation with The Verb gives a poet one priceless advantage:whereas nonmakers must content themselves with

---

1. Beach and amusement park in Brooklyn, New York.   2. Kyriakos Theotokopoulos, Cretan-born Spanish painter (1548?–1614?).

the merely undeniable fact that two times two is four,he rejoices in
a purely irresistible truth(to be found,in abbreviated costume,
upon the title page of the present volume).

1926

Poem,or Beauty Hurts Mr.Vinal

take it from me kiddo
believe me
my country,'tis of

you,land of the Cluett
Shirt Boston Garter and Spearmint   5
Girl With The Wrigley Eyes(of you
land of the Arrow Ide
and Earl &
Wilson
Collars)of you i   10
sing:land of Abraham Lincoln and Lydia E. Pinkham,[1]
land above all of Just Add Hot Water And Serve—
from every B.V.D.[2]

let freedom ring

amen.   i do however protest,anent the un   15
-spontaneous and otherwise scented merde which
greets one(Everywhere Why)as divine poesy per
that and this radically defunct periodical.   i would

suggest that certain ideas gestures
rhymes,like Gillette Razor Blades   20
having been used and reused
to the mystical moment of dullness emphatically are
Not To Be Resharpened.   (Case in point

if we are to believe these gently O sweetly
melancholy trillers amid the thrillers   25
these crepuscular[3] violinists among my and your
skyscrapers—Helen & Cleopatra[4] were Just Too Lovely,
The Snail's On The Thorn enter Morn and God's
In His andsoforth[5]

1. Lydia E. Pinkham (1819–83), manufacturer of a widely advertised patent
medicine.
2. Trade name of a brand of men's underwear. In this and other stanzas Cummings uses brand names and advertising
slogans.
3. Dimly lit, shadowy.
4. Two dangerously beautiful queens:
Helen, wife of Menelaus, whose abduction by Paris occasioned the Trojan War
in Homer's *Iliad*; Cleopatra (69–30 B.C.),

Queen of Egypt, Caesar's mistress, and
lover of the Roman general and triumvir
Marc Antony.
5. Parody of a song from *Pippa Passes*
(lines 223–28), a verse drama by the
English poet Robert Browning (1812–
89): "Morning's at seven; / The hillside's dew-pearled; / The lark's on the
wing; / The snail's on the thorn; /
God's in his heaven—/ All's right with
the world!"

do you get me?)according   30
to such supposedly indigenous
throstles[6] Art is O World O Life
a formula:example,Turn Your Shirttails Into
Drawers and If It Isn't An Eastman It Isn't A
Kodak therefore my friends let   35
us now sing each and all fortissimo A-
mer
i

ca,I
love,   40
You.   And there's a
hun-dred-mil-lion-oth-ers,like
all of you successfully if
delicately gelded(or spaded)[7]
gentlemen(and ladies)—pretty   45

littleliverpill-
hearted-Nujolneeding-[8]There's-A-Reason
americans(who tensetendoned and with
upward vacant eyes,painfully
perpetually crouched,quivering,upon the   50
sternly allotted sandpile
—how silently
emit a tiny violetflavoured nuisance:Odor?

ono.[9]
comes out like a ribbon lies flat on the brush   55

1922, 1926

Jimmie's got a goil

Jimmie's got a goil
            goil
                 goil,
                      Jimmie
's got a goil and   5
she coitnly can shimmie

when you see her shake
               shake
                   shake,
                      when   10
you see her shake a
shimmie how you wish that you was Jimmie.

6. European thrushes.
7. Common mispronunciation of "spayed," meaning a gelded or castrated female.
8. Allusions to two commercial laxatives, Carters' Little Liver Pills and Nujol.
9. Odorono, trade name of a deodorant.

Oh for such a gurl
        gurl
            gurl,   15
              oh
for such a gurl to
be a fellow's twistandtwirl

talk about your Sal-
         Sal-   20
            Sal-,
              talk
about your Salo
-mes[1] but gimmie Jimmie's gal.

1926

"next to of course god america i

"next to of course god america i
love you land of the pilgrims' and so forth oh
say can you see by the dawn's early my
country 'tis of centuries come and go
and are no more what of it we should worry   5
in every language even deafanddumb
thy sons acclaim your glorious name by gorry
by jingo by gee by gosh by gum
why talk of beauty what could be more beautiful than these heroic happy dead   10
who rushed like lions to the roaring slaughter
they did not stop to think they died instead
then shall the voice of liberty be mute?"

He spoke.   And drank rapidly a glass of water

1926

look at this)

look at this)
a 75^2 done
this nobody would
have believed
would they no   5
kidding this was my particular

pal
funny aint
it we was
buddies   10
i used to

---

1. Salome, sensual Biblical princess who danced before Herod Antipas in return for his promise to behead John the Bap- tist (Mark 6.22–27).
2. French 75, a piece of artillery used in World War I.

```
know
him lift the
poor cuss
tenderly this side up handle                                    15

with care
fragile
and send him home

to his old mother in
a new nice pine box                                            20

(collect
```
1926

come,gaze with me upon this dome

come,gaze with me upon this dome
of many coloured glass,[1]and see
his mother's pride,his father's joy,
unto whom duty whispers low

"thou must!" and who replies "I can!"[2]   5
—yon clean upstanding well dressed boy
that with his peers full oft hath quaffed
the wine of life and found it sweet—

a tear within his stern blue eye,
upon his firm white lips a smile,   10
one thought alone:to do or die
for God for country and for Yale

above his blond determined head
the sacred flag of truth unfurled,
in the bright heyday of his youth   15
the upper class American

unsullied stands,before the world:
with manly heart and conscience free,
upon the front steps of her home
by the high minded pure young girl   20

much kissed,by loving relatives
well fed,and fully photographed
the son of man[3] goes forth to war
with trumpets clap and syphillis

1926

1. From *Adonais* (1821), the elegy to the English poet John Keats by Percy Bysshe Shelley (1792–1822), LII, lines 462–63: "Life, like a dome of many-coloured glass, / Stains the white radiance of Eternity, / Until death tramples it to fragments."

2. Parody of Emerson's *Voluntaries*, iii, lines 13–14: "When Duty whispers low, Thou must, / The Youth replies I can." 3. The "Son of man" is one of Christ's frequent terms for himself—e.g., Matthew 24.27.

if there are any heavens my mother will
(all by herself) have

if there are any heavens my mother will(all by herself)have
one.   It will not be a pansy heaven nor
a fragile heaven of lilies-of-the-valley but
it will be a heaven of blackred roses

my father will be(deep like a rose   5
tall like a rose)

standing near my

swaying over her
(silent)
with eyes which are really petals and see   10

nothing with the face of a poet really which
is a flower and not a face with
hands
which whisper
This is my beloved my   15

                    (suddenly in sunlight
he will bow,

& the whole garden will bow)

                                   1931

he does not have to feel because he thinks

he does not have to feel because he thinks
(the thoughts of others,be it understood)
he does not have to think because he knows
(that anything is bad which you think good)

because he knows,he cannot understand   5
(why Jones don't pay me what he knows he owes)
because he cannot understand,he drinks
(and he drinks and he drinks and he drinks and)

not bald.   (Coughs.)   Two pale slippery small eyes

balanced upon one broken babypout   10
(pretty teeth wander into which and out
of)Life,dost Thou contain a marvel than
this death named Smith less strange?
                        Married and lies

afraid;aggressive and:American   15

                                   1935

r-p-o-p-h-e-s-s-a-g-r

                  r-p-o-p-h-e-s-s-a-g-r
          who
a)s w(e loo)k
upnowgath
       PPEGORHRASS   5
               eringint(o-
aThe):l
     eA
       !p:
S   a   10
             (r
rIvInG   .gRrEaPsPhOs)
                  to
rea(be)rran(com)gi(e)ngly
,grasshopper;   15
                1932, 1935

kumrads die because they're told)

kumrads die because they're told)
kumrads die before they're old
(kumrads aren't afraid to die
kumrads don't
and kumrads won't   5
believe in life)and death knows whie

(all good kumrads you can tell
by their altruistic smell
moscow pipes good kumrads dance)
kumrads enjoy   10
s.freud[1] knows whoy
the hope that you may mess your pance

every kumrad is a bit
of quite unmitigated hate
(travelling in a futile groove   15
god knows why)
and so do i
(because they are afraid to love

                1935

economic secu

economic secu
rity" is a cu
rious excu

1. Sigmund Freud (1856–1939), Austrian psychoanalyst.

```
se
(in                                                    5

use among pu
rposive pu
nks)¹for pu

tting the arse
before the torse²                                     10
```
                                                    1938

anyone lived in a pretty how town

anyone lived in a pretty how town
(with up so floating many bells down)
spring summer autumn winter
he sang his didn't he danced his did.

Women and men(both little and small)   5
cared for anyone not at all
they sowed their isn't they reaped their same
sun moon stars rain

children guessed(but only a few
and down they forgot as up they grew   10
autumn winter spring summer)
that noone loved him more by more

when by now and tree by leaf
she laughed his joy she cried his grief
bird by snow and stir by still   15
anyone's any was all to her

someones married their everyones
laughed their cryings and did their dance
(sleep wake hope and then)they
said their nevers they slept their dream   20

stars rain sun moon
(and only the snow can begin to explain
how children are apt to forget to remember
with up so floating many bells down)

one day anyone died i guess   25
(and noone stooped to kiss his face)
busy folk buried them side by side
little by little and was by was

---

1. Petty criminals, male prostitutes.
2. A play on the words "ass" and "torso," and on the expression "putting the cart before the horse," to suggest sodomy.

all by all and deep by deep
and more by more they dream their sleep   30
noone and anyone earth by april
wish by spirit and if by yes.

Women and men(both dong and ding)
summer autumn winter spring
reaped their sowing and went their came   35
sun moon stars rain

                                                           1940

my father moved through dooms of love

my father moved through dooms of love
through sames of am through haves of give,
singing each morning out of each night
my father moved through depths of height

this motionless forgetful where   5
turned at his glance to shining here;
that if(so timid air is firm)
under his eyes would stir and squirm

newly as from unburied which
floats the first who,his april touch   10
drove sleeping selves to swarm their fates
woke dreamers to their ghostly roots

and should some why completely weep
my father's fingers brought her sleep:
vainly no smallest voice might cry   15
for he could feel the mountains grow.

Lifting the valleys of the sea
my father moved through griefs of joy;
praised a forehead called the moon
singing desire into begin   20

joy was his song and joy so pure
a heart of star by him could steer
and pure so now and now so yes
the wrists of twilight would rejoice

keen as midsummer's keen beyond   25
conceiving mind of sun will stand,
so strictly(over utmost him
so hugely)stood my father's dream

his flesh was flesh his blood was blood:
no hungry man but wished him food;   30
no cripple wouldn't creep one mile
uphill to only see him smile.

Scorning the pomp of must and shall
my father moved through dooms of feel;
his anger was as right as rain   35
his pity was as green as grain

septembering arms of year extend
less humbly wealth to foe and friend
than he to foolish and to wise
offered immeasurable is   40

proudly and(by octobering flame
beckoned)as earth will downward climb,
so naked for immortal work
his shoulders marched against the dark

his sorrow was as true as bread: 45
no liar looked him in the head;
if every friend became his foe
he'd laugh and build a world with snow.

My father moved through theys of we,
singing each new leaf out of each tree   50
(and every child was sure that spring
danced when she heard my father sing)

then let men kill which cannot share,
let blood and flesh be mud and mire,
scheming imagine,passion willed,   55
freedom a drug that's bought and sold

giving to steal and cruel kind,
a heart to fear,to doubt a mind,
to differ a disease of same,
conform the pinnacle of am   60

though dull were all we taste as bright,
bitter all utterly things sweet,
maggoty minus and dumb death
all we inherit,all bequeath

and nothing quite so least as truth   65
—i say though hate were why men breathe—
because my father lived his soul
love is the whole and more than all

1940

a salesman is an it that stinks Excuse

a salesman is an it that stinks Excuse

Me whether it's president of the you were say
or a jennelman name misder finger isn't
important whether it's millions of other punks[1]
or just a handful absolutely doesn't   5
matter and whether it's in lonjewray[2]

or shrouds is immaterial it stinks

a salesman is an it that stinks to please

but whether to please itself or someone else
makes no more difference than if it sells   10
hate condoms education snakeoil vac
uumcleaners terror strawberries democ
ra(caveat emptor)[3]cy superfluous hair

or Think We've Met subhuman rights Before

                                                                    1944

pity this busy monster,manunkind

pity this busy monster,manunkind,

not.   Progress is a comfortable disease:
your victim(death and life safely beyond)

plays with the bigness of his littleness
—electrons deify one razorblade   5
into a mountainrange;lenses extend

unwish through curving wherewhen till unwish
returns on its unself.
                    A world of made
is not a world of born—pity poor flesh   10

and trees,poor stars and stones,but never this
fine specimen of hypermagical

ultraomnipotence.   We doctors know

a hopeless care if—listen:there's a hell
of a good universe next door;let's go   15

                                                                    1944

rain or hail

rain or hail
sam done
the best he kin
till they digged his hole

---

1. Petty criminals.
2. Lingerie, as pronounced in America.
3. A proverbial warning "the buyer beware."

                    :sam was a man   5

          stout as a bridge
          rugged as a bear
          slickern a weazel
          how be you

          (sun or snow)   10

          gone into what
          like all them kings
          you read about
          and on his sings

          a whippoorwill;   15

          heart was big
          as the world aint square
          with room for the devil
          and his angels too

          yes,sir   20

          what may be better
          or what may be worse
          and what may be clover
          clover clover

          (nobody'll know)   25

          sam was a man
          grinned his grin
          done his chores
          laid him down.

          Sleep well   30
                                                1944

all ignorance toboggans into know

all ignorance toboggans into know
and trudges up to ignorance again:
but winter's not forever,even snow
melts;and if spring should spoil the game,what then?

all history's a winter sport or three: 5
but were it five,i'd still insist that all
history is too small for even me;
for me and you,exceedingly too small.

Swoop(shrill collective myth)into thy grave
merely to toil the scale to shrillerness   10
per every madge and mabel dick and dave
—tomorrow is our permanent address

and there they'll scarcely find us(if they do,
we'll move away still further:into now

1944

so many selves(so many fiends and gods

so many selves(so many fiends and gods
each greedier than every)is a man
(so easily one in another hides;
yet man can,being all,escape from none)

so huge a tumult is the simplest wish: 5
so pitiless a massacre the hope
most innocent(so deep's the mind of flesh
and so awake what waking calls asleep)

so never is most lonely man alone
(his briefest breathing lives some planet's year,   10
his longest life's a heartbeat of some sun;
his least unmotion roams the youngest star)

—how should a fool that calls him "I" presume
to comprehend not numerable whom?

1950

when serpents bargain for the right to squirm

when serpents bargain for the right to squirm
and the sun strikes to gain a living wage—
when thorns regard their roses with alarm
and rainbows are insured against old age

when every thrush may sing no new moon in   5
if all screech-owls have not okayed his voice
—and any wave signs on the dotted line
or else an ocean is compelled to close

when the oak begs permission of the birch
to make an acorn—valleys accuse their   10
mountains of having altitude—and march
denounces april as a saboteur

then we'll believe in that incredible
unanimal mankind(and not until)

1950

why must itself up every of a park

why must itself up every of a park

anus stick some quote statue unquote to
prove that a hero equals any jerk
who was afraid to dare to answer "no"?

quote citizens unquote might otherwise   10
forget(to err is human;to forgive
divine)that if the quote state unquote says
"kill" killing is an act of christian love.

"Nothing" in 1944 AD

"can stand against the argument of mil   5
itary necessity"(generalissimo e)[1]
and echo answers "there is no appeal

from reason"(freud)[2]—you pays your money and
you doesn't take your choice. Ain't freedom grand

1950

this is a rubbish of human rind

this is a rubbish of human rind
with a photograph
clutched in the half
of a hand and the word
love underlined   5

this is a girl who died in her mind
with a warm thick scream
and a keen cold groan
while the gadgets purred
and the gangsters dined   10

this is a deaf dumb church and blind
with an if in its soul
and a hole in its life
where the young bell tolled
and the old vine twined   15

this is a dog of no known kind
with one white eye
and one black eye
and the eyes of his eyes
are as lost as you'll find   20

1950

1. General, later President, Dwight D.   psychologist and founder of psychoanal-
Eisenhower (1890–1969).   ysis.
2. Sigmund Freud (1856–1939), Austrian

when faces called flowers float out of the ground

when faces called flowers float out of the ground
and breathing is wishing and wishing is having—
but keeping is downward and doubting and never
—it's april(yes,april;my darling)it's spring!
yes the pretty birds frolic as spry as can fly   5
yes the little fish gambol as glad as can be
(yes the mountains are dancing together)

when every leaf opens without any sound
and wishing is having and having is giving—
but keeping is doting and nothing and nonsense   10
—alive;we're alive,dear:it's(kiss me now)spring!
now the pretty birds hover so she and so he
now the little fish quiver so you and so i
(now the mountains are dancing,the mountains)

when more than was lost has been found has been found 15
and having is giving and giving is living—
but keeping is darkness and winter and cringing
—it's spring(all our night comes day)o,it's spring!
all the pretty birds dive to the heart of the sky
all the little fish climb through the mind of the sea   20
(all the mountains are dancing;are dancing)

                                                                          1950

ALLEN TATE
1899–1979

John Orley Allen Tate was the twentieth century's most influential spokesman for the southern literary tradition, which his own criticism and poetry
immensely enriched. He was born in Kentucky in 1899 to a family with
considerable landowning and lumbering interests. His mother, an avid
reader and an occasional churchgoer, and his father, a freethinker with a
respect for learning, kept alive traditions of gentlemanly cultivation, though
his father virtually withdrew from social and family life after 1907 and his
series of business failures required the family to move often with consequent disruptions in the children's schooling. Tate attended a number of
public and private schools, nourishing an interest in the classics, before
enrolling at Vanderbilt University in 1919.

At Vanderbilt he and his roommate, the poet and novelist Robert Penn
Warren, were admitted as undergraduates to the Fugitives, the group of
older writers that was assembling around the professor and poet John
Crowe Ransom to discuss philosophy and comment on each others' creative
writing. In their journal, *The Fugitive*, were published Tate's first poems,
which caught the eye of the poet Hart Crane and led to a lasting, though
turbulent, friendship between the two poets. After graduating in 1923, Tate
helped edit *The Fugitive* until its demise in 1925.

Later he also served as editor on the literary journals *Hound and Horn* (1932–34) and *Sewanee Review* (1944–46) and in the publishing house of Henry Holt (1946–48), and after teaching in Princeton's Creative Arts Program (1939–42) he held the Chair of Poetry in the Library of Congress (1943–44). But his writing was his main occupation after he married novelist Caroline Gordon in 1924 and moved to New York City.

They lived with their daughter intermittently in the South, the North, and Europe while Tate pursued the careers of poet, biographer, and critic simultaneously. The careers were mutually reinforcing. *Mr. Pope and Other Poems* (1928), *Poems: 1928–1931* (1932), and *The Mediterranean and Other Poems* (1936) were the volumes that established his reputation as a poet, while *Stonewall Jackson* (1928) and *Jefferson Davis* (1929) were biographies in which he explored the history of the South, as in his only novel (*The Fathers*, 1938). In 1930 he joined with Ransom, Warren, Andrew Lytle, and others in a group that called themselves the Southern Agrarians to publish a collaborative venture, *I'll Take My Stand*, which advocated an agrarian, Jeffersonian tradition as an alternative to the industrial civilization dominant in the North. In Tate's *Reactionary Essays on Poetry and Ideas* (1936) and *Reason and Madness* (1941) he collected the essays and reviews in which he had made his contribution to what was called the New Criticism and explored the resources, for the modern writer, of southern literary culture.

Tate's strategy as an essayist was that of "attack," which he acknowledged along with the "toplofty" "snobbishness" of his tone,[1] as he fought against the prevailing habits in literary scholarship of relying on easy correspondences between biographical fact and creative writing, or between abstract ideas appearing outside poetry and their equivalents in poetic statement. Tate insisted that instead critics should give close attention to the complexities of imagery and emotion in the poetic text, and to the "tension"[2] within a poem which complicates literal meanings with the subtleties of figurative speech. He warned against a historical approach which made literature subordinate to mere abstraction and fact, while using himself (in brilliant essays on Poe and Emily Dickinson) "the historical imagination" or the method of "historical dramatization" which placed the critic "in history" so that he could "participate as a living imagination in a great work of literature."[3] The historical imagination, however, Tate found secondary to the "religious imagination" which was the strength of medieval Christianity and Dante,[4] and the two types of imagination enabled him to define the strength, and the incompleteness, of the Southern Agrarian tradition.

Its strength derived from its roots in the soil, a sense of a provincial or regional community of custom and purpose, and a sense that history is a troubled continuum of concrete events and tangible realities—of failed efforts, of shared wounds and aspirations—instead of an abstraction. The tradition's weakness derived from the fact that it substituted political and economic beliefs for "religious conviction."[5] The pre–Civil War world of Jefferson had known a harmony between the socioeconomic life and the moral life which made it a "traditional society,"[6] Tate believed, but the

---

1. *Essays of Four Decades*, pp. 616, 618.
2. "Tension in Poetry," *ibid.*, p. 64.
3. "Miss Emily and the Bibliographer," *ibid.*, pp. 151, 152.
4. "What Is a Traditional Society?"

ibid., p. 551.
5. "Religion and the Old South," *ibid.*, pp. 575–76.
6. "What Is a Traditional Society?" *ibid.*, p. 556.

American South had never found the "spiritual life"[7] which would insure a fully integrated tradition and community.

The complexities of Tate's view of history and tradition were matched by the density of his learned, often enigmatic, verse. His early poems seemed to himself a conventional amalgam of Baudelaire, E. A. Robinson, Pound, and others until his reading of T. S. Eliot gave a more firm orientation to his imagination. All his poems, he once claimed, were about "the suffering that comes from disbelief."[8] His poems that present a protagonist's engagement with the past dramatize also his sense of its incompleteness and his alienation from it.

Tate was converted to Roman Catholicism in 1950, the same year that marked his divorce from and remarriage to his first wife. In 1951 he accepted a tenured post at the University of Minnesota, where he taught until his retirement in 1968. His later years had seen new collections of his essays and poems and the publication of *The Swimmers and Other Selected Poems* in 1970. He traveled abroad as Fulbright lecturer and taught as visiting professor at Chicago, the University of North Carolina at Greensboro, and Vanderbilt. A member of both the American Academy of Arts and Letters and the American Academy of Arts and Sciences, he served as president of the National Institute of Arts and Letters in 1968. The Bollingen Prize for Poetry in 1956 and the Academy of American Poets Award in 1963 were among the public tributes to his writing. He married twice in Minnesota, and upon his retirement from the university he moved to Sewanee, Tennessee.

The selections below are from *Poems, 1922–1947*.

Mr. Pope

When Alexander Pope[1] strolled in the city
Strict was the glint of pearl and gold sedans.[2]
Ladies leaned out more out of fear than pity
For Pope's tight back[3] was rather a goat's than man's.

Often one thinks the urn should have more bones   5
Than skeletons provide for speedy dust,
The urn gets hollow, cobwebs brittle as stones
Weave to the funeral shell a frivolous rust.

And he who dribbled couplets like a snake
Coiled to a lithe precision in the sun   10
Is missing. The jar is empty; you may break
It only to find that Mr. Pope is gone.

What requisitions of a verity
Prompted the wit and rage between his teeth
One cannot say. Around a crooked tree   15
A moral climbs whose name should be a wreath.[4]

                1928

7. "Religion and the Old South," *ibid.*, p. 576.
8. Quoted by George Hemphill, *Allen Tate*, p. 19.
1. English poet (1688–1744) of the elegant and formal Augustan age. He was known for his scathing satires and for the precision of his rhymed couplets.
2. Sedan chairs.
3. Pope's body was severely deformed.
4. I.e., Pope's moral vision insinuates itself with a power comparable to that of

Message from Abroad

TO ANDREW LYTLE[1]

Paris, November 1929

*Their faces are bony and sharp but very red, although their ancestors
nearly two hundred years have dwelt by the miasmal banks of tidewaters
where malarial fever makes men gaunt and dosing with quinine shakes
them as with a palsy.*

—TRAVELLER TO AMERICA (1799)

I

What years of the other times, what centuries
Broken, divided up and claimed? A few
Here and there to the taste, in vigilance
Ceaseless, but now a little stale, to keep us
Fearless, not worried as the hare scurrying 5
Without memory . . .

Provence,

The Renascence, the age of Pericles,[2] each
A broad, rich-carpeted stair to pride
With manhood now the cost—they're easy to follow 10

For the ways taken are all notorious,
Lettered, sculptured, and rhymed;
Those others, incuriously complete, lost,
Not by poetry and statues timed,
Shattered by sunlight and the impartial sleet. 15
What years . . . What centuries . . .

Now only

The bent eaves and the windows cracked,
The thin grass picked by the wind,
Heaved by the mole; the hollow pine that 20
Screams in the latest storm—these,
These emblems of twilight have we seen at length,
And the man red-faced and tall seen, leaning
In the day of his strength
Not as a pine, but the stiff form 25
Against the west pillar,
Hearing the ox-cart in the street—
His shadow gliding, a long nigger
Gliding at his feet.

II

Wanderers to the east, wanderers west:
I followed the cold northern track, 30

Satan in the Garden of Eden and deserves the traditional accolade of poetry,
the laurel wreath.
1. Novelist, biographer, and essayist
(b. 1902), a contributor to the collaborative collection of essays in the Southern Agrarian *I'll Take My Stand* (1930).
2. Provence in southern France during
the Middle Ages, the Renaissance in

western Europe from the 14th to the
17th centuries, and the fifth century B.C.
in Athens under Pericles were rich in art
and literature, brought fame to individual artists, and established lasting traditions. Their example is enviable but
threatening to the 20th-century poet, who
seeks a new subject in the nameless
ancestors of his American past.

The sleet sprinkled the sea;
The dim foam mounted
The night, the ship mounted
The depths of night—   35
How absolute the sea!

With dawn came the gull to the crest,
Stared at the spray, fell asleep
Over the picked bones, the white face
Of the leaning man drowned deep;   40

The red-faced man, ceased wandering,
Never came to the boulevards
Nor covertly spat in the sawdust
Sunk in his collar
Shuffling the cards;   45

The man with the red face, the stiff back,
I cannot see in the rainfall
Down Saint-Michel by the quays,
At the corner the wind speaking
Destiny, the four ways.   50
                    III
I cannot see you
The incorruptibles,
Yours was a secret fate,
The stiff-backed liars, the dupes:
The universal blue   55
Of heaven rots,
Your anger is out of date—
What did you say mornings?
Evenings, what?
The bent eaves   60
On the cracked house,
That ghost of a hound. . . .
The man red-faced and tall
Will cast no shadow
From the province of the drowned.   65
                                                          1932

Last Days of Alice[1]

Alice grown lazy, mammoth but not fat,
Declines upon her lost and twilight age;
Above in the dozing leaves the grinning cat[2]
Quivers forever with his abstract rage:

1. The child heroine of *Alice's Adventures in Wonderland* (1865) and *Through the Looking Glass* (1872) by the English mathematician and writer Lewis Carroll (1832–98). Here grown old, she is denied the release into imaginative fantasy of Carroll's fictions and instead escapes into narcissism and sheer abstraction, lacking the vital strength of either evil or God's grace.
2. In *Alice's Adventures in Wonderland,* the grinning Cheshire cat alternately appears and fades from sight until only his grin remains.

Whatever light swayed on the perilous gate   5
Forever sways, nor will the arching grass,
Caught when the world clattered, undulate
In the deep suspension of the looking-glass.

Bright Alice! always pondering to gloze
The spoiled cruelty she had meant to say   10
Gazes learnedly down her airy nose
At nothing, nothing thinking all the day.

Turned absent-minded by infinity
She cannot move unless her double move,
The All-Alice of the world's entity   15
Smashed in the anger of her hopeless love,

Love for herself who, as an earthly twain,
Pouted to join her two in a sweet one;
No more the second lips to kiss in vain
The first she broke, plunged through the glass alone—   20

Alone to the weight of impassivity,
Incest of spirit, theorem of desire,
Without will as chalky cliffs by the sea,
Empty as the bodiless flesh of fire:

All space, that heaven is a dayless night,   25
A nightless day driven by perfect lust
For vacancy, in which her bored eyesight
Stares at the drowsy cubes of human dust.

—We too back to the world shall never pass
Through the shattered door, a dumb shade-harried
    crowd   30
Being all infinite, function depth and mass
Without figure, a mathematical shroud

Hurled at the air—blesséd without sin!
O God of our flesh, return us to Your wrath,
Let us be evil could we enter in   35
Your grace, and falter on the stony path!

                               1932

Mother and Son

Now all day long the man who is not dead
Hastens the dark with inattentive eyes,
The woman with white hand and erect head
Stares at the covers, leans for the son's replies
At last to her importunate womanhood—   5
Her hand of death laid on the living bed;
So lives the fierce compositor of blood.

She waits; he lies upon the bed of sin
Where greed, avarice, anger writhed and slept
Till to their silence they were gathered in: 10
There, fallen with time, his tall and bitter kin
Once fired the passions that were never kept
In the permanent heart, and there his mother lay
To bear him on the impenetrable day.

The falcon mother cannot will her hand   15
Up to the bed, nor break the manacle
His exile sets upon her harsh command
That he should say the time is beautiful—
Transfigured by her own possessing light:
The sick man craves the impalpable night.   20

Loosed betwixt eye and lid, the swimming beams
Of memory, blind school of cuttlefish,
Rise to the air, plunge to the cold streams—
Rising and plunging the half-forgotten wish
To tear his heart out in a slow disgrace   25
And freeze the hue of terror to her face.

Hate, misery, and fear beat off his heart
To the dry fury of the woman's mind;
The son, prone in his autumn, moves apart
A seed blown upon a returning wind.   30
O child, be vigilant till towards the south
On the flowered wall all the sweet afternoon,
The reaching sun, swift as the cottonmouth,[1]
Strikes at the black crucifix on her breast
Where the cold dusk comes suddenly to rest—   35
Mortality will speak the victor soon!

The dreary flies, lazy and casual,
Stick to the ceiling, buzz along the wall.
O heart, the spider shuffles from the mould
Weaving, between the pinks and grapes, his pall.   40
The bright wallpaper, imperishably old,
Uncurls and flutters, it will never fall.

                                                               1932

From Sonnets at Christmas

(1934)

I

This is the day His hour of life draws near,
Let me get ready from head to foot for it
Most handily with eyes to pick the year
For small feed to reward a feathered wit.

---

1. A poisonous snake.

Some men would see it an epiphany   5
At ease, at food and drink, others at chase
Yet I, stung lassitude, with ecstasy
Unspent argue the season's difficult case
So: Man, dull critter of enormous head,
What would he look at in the coiling sky?   10
But I must kneel again unto the Dead
While Christmas bells of paper white and red,
Figured with boys and girls split from a sled,
Ring out the silence I am nourished by.

                                                                    1936

The Ancestors

When the night's coming and the last light falls
A weak child among lost shadows on the floor,
It is your listening: pulse heeds the strain
Of fore and after, wind shivers the door.
What masterful delays commands the blood   5
Breaking its access to the living heart?
Consider this, the secret indecision,
Not rudeness of time but the systaltic² flood
Of ancient failure begging its new start:
The flickered pause between the day and night   10
(When the heart knows its informality)
The bones hear but the eyes will never see—
Punctilious abyss, the yawn of space
Come once a day to suffocate the sight.
There is no man on earth who can be free   15
Of this, the eldest in the latest crime.

                                                                    1936

Aeneas at Washington¹

I myself saw furious with blood
Neoptolemus, at his side the black Atridae,
Hecuba and the hundred daughters, Priam
Cut down, his filth drenching the holy fires.
In that extremity I bore me well,   5
A true gentleman, valorous in arms,
Disinterested and honourable. Then fled:
That was a time when civilization
Run by the few fell to the many, and
Crashed to the shout of men, the clang of arms: 10
Cold victualing I seized, I hoisted up

---

2. Contracting and dilating by turns. associated here with the tides.
1. Aeneas, hero of the epic *The Aeneid* by the Latin poet Virgil (70–19 B.C.), was a Trojan prince who rescued his father, carrying him on his back, from burning Troy, and after voyaging to Italy founded a new civilization at Rome. The opening lines are a translation of lines 499–502 of *The Aeneid*. The heroes whom Aeneas knew were Neoptolemus, the son of Hercules; the Atridae, the Greek generals Agamemnon and Menelaus; and Priam and Hecuba, King and Queen of defeated Troy.

The old man my father upon my back,
In the smoke made by sea for a new world
Saving little—a mind imperishable
If time is, a love of past things tenuous   15
As the hesitation of receding love.

(To the reduction of uncited littorals[2]
We brought chiefly the vigor of prophecy,
Our hunger breeding calculation
And fixed triumphs)   20

      I saw the thirsty dove
In the glowing fields of Troy, hemp ripening
And tawny corn, the thickening Blue Grass
All lying rich forever in the green sun.
I see all things apart, the towers that men   25
Contrive I too contrived long, long ago.
Now I demand little. The singular passion
Abides its object and consumes desire
In the circling shadow of its appetite.
There was a time when the young eyes were slow,   30
Their flame steady beyond the firstling fire,
I stood in the rain, far from home at nightfall
By the Potomac, the great Dome[3] lit the water,
The city my blood had built I knew no more
While the screech-owl whistled his new delight   35
Consecutively dark.

       Stuck in the wet mire
Four thousand leagues from the ninth buried city[4]
I thought of Troy, what we had built her for.

           1936

To the Lacedemonians[1]

*An old soldier on the night before the veterans' reunion talks partly
to himself, partly to imaginary comrades:*

  The people—people of my kind, my own
  People but strange with a white light
  In the face: the streets hard with motion
  And the hard eyes that look one way.
  Listen! the high whining tone   5
  Of the motors, I hear the dull commotion:
  I am come, a child in an old play.

  I am here with a secret in the night;

---

2. Regions bordering the sea.
3. The Capitol at Washington.
4. Troy, whose archaeological site contains the remains of nine cities.
1. Spartans. Sparta, an oligarchic Greek city-state, was victorious in the Peloponnesian War (431–404 B.C.) against Athens. It had fought with other Greek states against the Persians at the battle of Thermopylae (480 B.C.).

Because I am here the dead wear gray.

It is a privilege to be dead; for you   10
Cannot know what absence is nor seize
The ordour of pure distance until
From you, slowly dying in the head,
All sights and sounds of the moment, all
The life of sweet intimacy shall fall   15
Like a swift at dusk.

          Sheer time! Stroke of the heart
Towards retirement. . . .

         Gentlemen, my secret is
Damnation: where have they, the citizens, all   20
Come from? They were not born in my father's
House, nor in their fathers': on a street corner
By motion sired, not born; by rest dismayed.
The tempest will unwind—the hurricane
Consider, knowing its end, the headlong pace?   25
I have watched it and endured it, I have delayed
Judgment: it warn't in my time, by God, so
That the mere breed absorbed the generation!

Yet I, hollow head, do see but little;
Old man: no memory: aimless distractions.   30

I was a boy, I never knew cessation
Of the bright course of blood along the vein;
Moved, an old dog by me, to field and stream
In the speaking ease of the fall rain;
When I was a boy the light on the hills   35
Was there because I could see it, not because
Some special gift of God had put it there.

Men expect too much, do too little,
Put the contraption before the accomplishment,
Lack skill of the interior mind   40
To fashion dignity with shapes of air.
Luxury, yes—but not elegance!
Where have they come from?

        Go you tell them
That we their servants, well-trained, gray-coated   45
And haired (both foot and horse) or in
The grave, them obey . . . obey them,
What commands?[2]

        My father said

---

2. In his elegy to the Spartans who died defending Greece at Thermopylae, the Greek poet Simonides of Ceos (556?– 468? B.C.) wrote: "Stranger, carry the message to the Lacedemonians that we lie here, obeying their commands."

That everything but kin was less than kind.[3]   50
The young men like swine argue for a rind,
A flimsy shell to put their weakness in;
Will-less, ruled by what they cannot see;
Hunched like savages in a rotten tree
They wait for the thunder to speak: Union!   55
That joins their separate fear.

                       I fought
But did not care; a leg shot off at Bethel,[4]
Given up for dead; but knew neither shell-shock
Nor any self-indulgence. Well may war be   60
Terrible to those who have nothing to gain
For the illumination of the sense:
When the peace is a trade route, figures
For the budget, reduction of population,
Life grown sullen and immense   65
Lusts after immunity to pain.

There is no civilization without death;
There is now the wind for breath.

Waken, lords and ladies gay, we cried,
And marched to Cedar Run and Malvern Hill,[5]   70
Kinsmen and friends from Texas to the Tide—[6]
Vain chivalry of the personal will!

Waken, we shouted, lords and ladies gay,
We go to win the precincts of the light,
Unshadowing restriction of our day. . . .   75
Regard now, in the seventy years of night,

Them, the young men who watch us from the curbs:
They hold the glaze of wonder in their stare—
Our crooked backs, hands fetid as old herbs,
The tallow eyes, wax face, the foreign hair!   80

Soldiers, march! we shall not fight again
The Yankees with our guns well-aimed and rammed—
All are born Yankees of the race of men
And this, too, now the country of the damned:

Poor bodies crowding round us! The white face   85
Eyeless with eyesight only, the modern power—
Huddled sublimities of time and space,
They are the echoes of a raging tower
That reared its moment upon a gone land,
Pouring a long cold wrath into the mind—   90

3. Pun on "kind": (1) kindly, and (2) of the same type. Compare, in Shakespeare's *Hamlet* (1.2.64–65), the usurping King Claudius's address to his stepson as "my cousin Hamlet, and my son," and Hamlet's reply: "A little more than kin, and less than kind."
4. Big Bethel, Virginia, site of a Civil War battle in 1861.
5. Civil War battles in Virginia, 1862.
6. The Tidewater region of eastern Virginia.

Damned souls, running the way of sand
Into the destination of the wind!

1932, 1936

Ode to the Confederate Dead[1]

Row after row with strict impunity
The headstones yield their names to the element,
The wind whirrs without recollection;
In the riven troughs the splayed leaves
Pile up, of nature the casual sacrament   5
To the seasonal eternity of death;
Then driven by the fierce scrutiny
Of heaven to their election in the vast breath,
They sough the rumour of mortality.

Autumn is desolation in the plot   10
Of a thousand acres where these memories grow
From the inexhaustible bodies that are not
Dead, but feed the grass row after rich row.
Think of the autumns that have come and gone!—
Ambitious November with the humors of the year,   15
With a particular zeal for every slab,
Staining the uncomfortable angels that rot
On the slabs, a wing chipped here, an arm there:
The brute curiosity of an angel's stare
Turns you, like them, to stone,   20
Transforms the heaving air
Till plunged to a heavier world below
You shift your sea-space blindly
Heaving, turning like the blind crab.[2]
        Dazed by the wind, only the wind   25
        The leaves flying, plunge

You know who have waited by the wall
The twilight certainty of an animal,

1. Tate declared that this poem is governed by the myth of Narcissus, the youth in ancient Greek legend who was so enchanted by his own image in a pool that he leaped in to be joined to it and drowned. Tate claimed that the poem accordingly "is 'about' solipsism, a philosophical doctrine which says that we create the world in the act of perceiving it; or about Narcissism, or any other *ism* that denotes the failure of the human personality to function objectively in nature and society" ("Narcissus as Narcissus," *Essays of Four Decades*, pp. 595–96).
2. Tate's comment on the opening section: "Figure to yourself a man stopping at the gate of a Confederate graveyard on a late autumn afternoon. The leaves are falling; his first impressions bring him the 'rumor of mortality'; and the desolation barely allows him, at the be-

ginning of the second stanza, the conventionally heroic surmise that the dead will enrich the earth, 'where these memories grow.' From those quoted words to the end of that passage he pauses for a baroque meditation on the ravages of time, concluding with the figure of the 'blind crab.' This figure has mobility but no direction, energy but, from the human point of view, no purposeful world to use it in: in the entire poem there are only two explicit symbols for the locked-in ego; the crab is the first and less explicit symbol, * * * a planting of the idea that will become overt in its second instance—the jaguar towards the end. The crab is the first intimation of the nature of the moral conflict upon which the drama of the poem develops: the cut-off-ness of the modern 'intellectual man' from the world" (*ibid.*, p. 598).

Those midnight restitutions of the blood
You know—the immitigable pines, the smoky frieze   30
Of the sky, the sudden call: you know the rage,
The cold pool left by the mounting flood,
Of muted Zeno and Parmenides.[3]
You who have waited for the angry resolution
Of those desires that should be yours tomorrow,   35
You know the unimportant shrift of death
And praise the vision
And praise the arrogant circumstance
Of those who fall
Rank upon rank, hurried beyond decision—   40
Here by the sagging gate, stopped by the wall.[4]

    Seeing, seeing only the leaves
    Flying, plunge and expire

Turn your eyes to the immoderate past,
Turn to the inscrutable infantry rising   45
Demons out of the earth—they will not last.
Stonewall, Stonewall,[5] and the sunken fields of hemp,
Shiloh, Antietam, Malvern Hill, Bull Run.[6]
Lost in that orient of the thick-and-fast
You will curse the setting sun.   50

    Cursing only the leaves crying
    Like an old man in a storm

You hear the shout, the crazy hemlocks point
With troubled fingers to the silence which
Smothers you, a mummy, in time.   55

                 The hound bitch
Toothless and dying, in a musty cellar
Hears the wind only.

              Now that the salt of their blood

3. Greek philosophers of the fifth century B.C. who taught that the real universe is a unified, unchanging whole, and that the world of change and mere appearances is illusory and unknowable.
4. The above passage, Tate wrote, "states the other term of the conflict. It is the theme of heroism, not merely moral heroism, but heroism in the grand style, elevating even death from mere physical dissolution into a formal ritual: this heroism is a formal ebulliance of the human spirit in an entire society, not private, romantic illusion—something better than moral heroism, great as that may be, for moral heroism, being personal and individual, may be achieved by certain men in all ages, even ages of decadence. But the late Hart Crane * * * described the theme as the 'theme of chivalry, a tradition of excess (not literally excess, rather active faith) which

cannot be perpetuated in the fragmentary chaos of today * * * .' The structure then is the objective frame for the tension between the two themes, 'active faith' which has decayed, and the 'fragmentary chaos' which surrounds us * * * . In contemplating the heroic theme the man at the gate never quite commits himself to the illusion of its availability to him" ("Narcissus as Narcissus," p. 599).
5. The wall of the cemetery, and General Thomas Jonathan ("Stonewall") Jackson (1824–63), brilliant Confederate military strategist of the "Valley Campaign" and the second Battle of Bull Run during the Civil War, who was mortally wounded accidentally by his own forces at Chancellorsville.
6. Sites of Civil War battles, of which only the battles of Bull Run in 1861 and 1862 were Confederate victories.

Stiffens the saltier oblivion of the sea, 60
Seals the malignant purity of the flood,
What shall we who count our days and bow
Our heads with a commemorial woe
In the ribboned coats of grim felicity,
What shall we say of the bones, unclean, 65
Whose verdurous anonymity will grow?
The ragged arms, the ragged heads and eyes
Lost in these acres of the insane green?
The gray lean spiders come, they come and go;
In a tangle of willows without light 70
The singular screech-owl's tight
Invisible lyric seeds the mind
With the furious murmur of their chivalry.

    We shall say only the leaves
    Flying, plunge and expire 75

We shall say only the leaves whispering
In the improbable mist of nightfall
That flies on multiple wing;
Night is the beginning and the end
And in between the ends of distraction 80
Waits mute speculation, the patient curse
That stones the eyes, or like the jaguar leaps[7]
For his own image in a jungle pool, his victim.
What shall we say who have knowledge
Carried to the heart? Shall we take the act 85
To the grave? Shall we, more hopeful, set up the
    grave
In the house? The ravenous grave?

          Leave now
The shut gate and the decomposing wall:
The gentle serpent, green in the mulberry bush, 90
Riots with his tongue through the hush—
Sentinel of the grave who counts us all![8]

                    1928, 1937

The Eye

λαιδρὴ κορώνη, κῶς τὸ χεῖλος οὐκ ἀλγεῖς;
               —CALLIMACHUS[1]

TO E. E. CUMMINGS

I see the horses and the sad streets
Of my childhood in an agate eye

7. "This figure of the jaguar is the only explicit rendering of the Narcissus motif in the poem, but instead of a youth gazing into a pool, a predatory beast stares at a jungle stream, and leaps to devour himself" ("Narcissus as Narcissus," p. 607).
8. "The closing image, that of the serpent, is the ancient symbol of time, and I tried to give it the credibility of the commonplace by placing it in a mulberry bush—with the fait hope that the silkworm would somehow be implicit in it. But time is also death" (*ibid.*, pp. 600–1).
1. "Sad crow, why does your beak not ache?" from a poem by the North African Greek poet and critic of the third century B.C.

Roving, under the clean sheets,
Over a black hole in the sky.

The ill man becomes the child,   5
The evil man becomes the lover;
The natural man with evil roiled
Pulls down the sphereless sky for cover.

I see the gray heroes and the graves
Of my childhood in the nuclear eye—   10
Horizons spent in dun caves
Sucked down into the sinking sky.

The happy child becomes the man,
The elegant man becomes the mind,
The fathered gentleman who can   15
Perform quick feats of gentle kind.

I see the long field and the noon
Of my childhood in the carbolic eye,
Dissolving pupil of the moon
Seared from the raveled hole of the sky.   20

The nice ladies and gentlemen,
The teaser and the jelly-bean
Play cockalorum-and-the-hen,
When the cool afternoons pour green:

I see the father and the cooling cup   25
Of my childhood in the swallowing sky
Down, down, until down is up
And there is nothing in the eye,

Shut shutter of the mineral man
Who takes the fatherless dark to bed,   30
The acid sky to the brain-pan;
And calls the crows to peck his head.

                                                    1948

HART CRANE
1899–1932

In the course of a brief career that lasted scarcely fifteen years, Harold Hart
Crane aroused for his fellow writers some of the highest hopes and some of
the most gnawing fears about American culture and modernism in the arts.
Without either wide popularity or durable institutional affiliations to sus-

tain him, he devoted a tormented life to the perfection and then the exhaustion of an extraordinary talent, and bequeathed to his successors a body of brilliantly visionary poetry along with an image of tragic failure.

Crane was raised by parents whose marital turmoil and undisguised sexual incompatibility (leading to separations, reconciliations, and finally divorce in 1916) agitated Crane's affections from the age of eight and burdened him with what he called later, in *The Bridge*, the "curse of sundered parentage." He sought and welcomed the affection of his mother, and time and again had occasion to be grateful to her for the checks she sent him after he left home; though they quarreled at one point over an inheritance from his grandmother, Mrs. Crane in later years was proud of his reputation as a poet. Yet her needs for companionship and demands for affection were distracting throughout his life. His father, a successful candy manufacturer, introduced Crane to writers and gave some encouragement to Crane's poetic career, but he never genuinely understood his son's aspirations, continued to hope that he would follow a business career, and did not provide the regular support that Crane hoped for.

Crane attended high school in Cleveland, and at his parents' request made gestures toward preparing for college when he lived in New York City in 1917–18 and again in 1919 on an allowance from his father. But Crane, who had been painting since the age of eleven and had published a poem in *The Pagan* in 1916, quickly decided upon a literary career. He worked at his poetry and developed his aesthetic theories in conversations with the painter Carl Schmitt at his Stuyvesant Square studio, published *The Hive* in 1917, and became an unsalaried associate editor of *The Pagan* with the critic Gorham Munson, whose support and friendship were important throughout his early career. When Crane left New York for a job in his father's business in Cleveland in 1919, it was with the purpose of finding support for a literary career.

Protracted unemployment, a job in a bookstore, and a position with a direct-mail advertising house (writing copy for Sieberling Tires and the Fox Furnace Company) followed a dispute with his father in 1921. Crane applied himself assiduously to the work, convinced (he declared in 1919) that even "in an age of violent commercialism" an "artist's creation is bound to be largely interpretive of his environment" and that he "cannot remain aloof from the welters without losing the essential, imminent vitality of his vision." While he should avoid "smugness," he should count patiently on "America's great economic growth, eventually to complete a structure that will provide a quieter platform * * * for the artist and his audience."[1] Crane's career was complicated during these same years by increasingly frequent bouts of heavy drinking and by homosexual affairs— one an affair of passion in 1919 of the kind that later inspired some of his best poetry, others passionless encounters in the sexual underworld he sought out to his peril.

Crane's intellectual horizons widened significantly during his Cleveland years. Within a larger circle of acquaintances that included the composer Ernest Bloch, he became a close friend of the Swiss architect and painter William Lescaze and the painter William Sommer; he sustained a lively correspondence with associates he knew in New York like Gorham Munson, Sherwood Anderson, and other literary figures whose views he

1. Quoted by John Unterecker, *Voyager*, p. 156.

sought out and welcomed, including the poet and critic Allen Tate. His reading ranged from the cultural critics recommended by Anderson, Van Wyck Brooks, and Waldo Frank (whose *Our America* [1919] envisioned the transformation of industrial America) to the Continental writers Baudelaire, Dostoevsky, and Proust, who were recommended by Munson or Lescaze. His enthusiasms were diffuse, scattering in all the directions charted by contemporary criticism but including also the romantic poets; he scorned Milton and Tennyson among others, he wrote in 1921, adding that "I *do* run joyfully toward Messrs. Poe, Shakespeare, Keats, Shelley, Coleridge, John Donne!!!, John Webster!!! Marlowe, Baudelaire, Laforgue, Dante, Cavalcanti, Li Po, and a host of others."[2] He responded early to Pound, William Carlos Williams, Marianne Moore, and notably Wallace Stevens, but he had been steeped in T. S. Eliot since 1919 and Eliot represented the most stimulating challenge. Eliot's achievement, Crane wrote, threatened to become an "absolute impasse" but Crane felt that he had "discovered a safe tangent to strike which, if I can possibly explain the position, goes *through* [Eliot] toward a different goal." After "having absorbed him enough we can trust ourselves as never before," Crane said, adding that "I * * * would like to leave a few of his 'negations' behind me, risk the realm of the obvious more, in quest of new sensations * * * ."[3]

It was in Ohio that Crane produced his first distinctive poems and moreover established the basis for his subsequent career. *My Grandmother's Love Letters,* the first poem for which he was paid, appeared in the *Dial* in 1920, *Chaplinesque* in the *Gargoyle* in 1921, and *Praise for an Urn* in the *Dial* in 1922. By 1923 he had finished his first masterpiece, *For the Marriage of Faustus and Helen,* and composed the first versions of two poems which were to be incorporated in his second masterpiece, *Voyages* (1926). He published one of the latter in Gorham Munson's *Secession* in 1923, entitling it *Poster* because he conceived it as approaching "the 'advertisement' form."[4] He acknowledged to Munson that he was discovering his affinities with Whitman, that he thought himself potentially "the Pindar for the dawn of the machine age," and that he was "ruminating" on the epic and "mystical synthesis of America" that was to be his major undertaking, *The Bridge.*[5]

In 1923 Crane settled on New York City as the most stimulating environment for a writer. Between 1923 and 1927 he wrote the best, indeed most, of his poetry, completing the love poem *Voyages* in 1924, then publishing his first collection, *White Buildings,* and writing ten of the fifteen poems that were to comprise *The Bridge* in the single year 1926. He held intermittent jobs, but he was enabled to pursue his career chiefly by funds sent by his parents, by the generosity of friends with whom he stayed for protracted periods, by sizable grants from the banker and patron Otto Kahn which Crane requested when his needs were most desperate—and by his own strong commitment to an increasingly desperate visionary poetics. He had been inspired by P. D. Ouspensky's *Tertium Organum* (tr. 1922), which had attributed a higher state of consciousness to poets than to ordinary men; but he was influenced more directly by the rhetorical intensity of Melville and the Jacobean dramatists, and the poetry of Whitman and William Blake to undertake a "complete reversal of direction" from the pessi-

2. *Letters,* p. 67.   4. *Ibid.,* p. 99.
3. *Ibid.,* p. 90.   5. *Ibid.,* pp. 128–29.

mism of Eliot (he wrote in 1923) and to aim for "a more positive, or (if [I] must put it so in a skeptical age) ecstatic goal." The "modern artist," he wrote, in order to get composers like "Strauss, Ravel, Scriabin, and Bloch into *words*," must "*ransack* the vocabularies of Shakespeare, Jonson, Webster * * * and add our scientific, street and counter, and psychological terms * * * "; he "needs gigantic assimilative capacities, emotion,—and the greatest of all—*vision*."[6] The "full contemporary function" of modern poetry embraced the imperative to "absorb the machine, i.e., *acclimatize* it as naturally and casually as trees * * * castles and all other human associations of the past" (*Of Modern Poetry*, 1929).[7] This Crane himself undertook to do through images of machines and patterns of motion in the poems derived from technological symbols like the Brooklyn Bridge, aircraft, and subway trains.

In New York as in Cleveland, Crane pursued an "ecstatic goal" in poetry under the stimulus of wine and recorded phonograph music to help generate the production of his first drafts, which he later worked over assiduously. His diction became more abstract, his verse more compressed, his poems consequently more abstruse. He aimed—and this has been of increasing interest to poets after World War II—for a visionary poetry he called "absolute" (*General Aims and Theories*, 1925) in which a poem had "an orbit or predetermined direction of its own" and gave the reader a "single, new *word*, never before spoken and impossible to actually enunciate, but self-evident as an active principle in the reader's consciousness henceforward." Whether employing traditional stanza patterns or free verse, he relied at once on the abstract associations and sensuous impingements of words, drawing on "the implicit emotional dynamics of the materials used" and selecting his terms and images "less for their logical (literal) significance than for their associational meanings." The "entire construction of the poem," he insisted, builds on the " 'logic of metaphor,' which antedates our so-called pure logic, and which is the genetic basis of all speech, hence consciousness and thought-extension."[8]

Plans for *The Bridge* that Crane had been nurturing since 1923 began to be realized early in 1926 when he finished *Atlantis*, its exhilarating concluding lyric. He explained to his patron Otto Kahn in 1927 that his poetic "symphony with an epic theme" was to encompass "the Myth of America" on a scale comparable to Virgil's *Aeneid*, and he had explained to Gorham Munson in 1923 that in it "History and fact, location, etc., all have to be transfigured into abstract form that would almost function independently of its subject matter."[9] The poem's materials included the full panorama of America's history from geological eras to contemporary suburbia and urban New York, and such figures from history and legend as Columbus, Rip Van Winkle, Pocahontas, Whitman, and Poe who define the aspirations, anxieties, and tragedies that have shaped the myth of America. Crane's governing symbol was drawn from Brooklyn Bridge, which epitomized the reconciliation of technological civilization with art, spanned the full range of human possibility, and imaged the communion of love. The "very idea of a bridge," he wrote to the critic Waldo Frank in 1926, depends on "spiritual convictions" and accomplishes in fact an "act of faith" and an act of "communication."[1] One thrust of the poem is to celebrate those values as

6. *Ibid.*, pp. 114–15, 129.
7. *Complete Poems and Selected Letters and Prose*, p. 262.
8. *Ibid.*, pp. 220–21.
9. *Letters*, pp. 305, 309.
1. *Ibid.*, p. 124.

incarnate in the *Bridge* and to embody in the poem's movement a personal commitment to those values. Nevertheless the poem was animated also by Crane's fears about the validity of the myth and the forces of disintegration in modern life which threatened its fulfillment, to anxieties about his own career and talent that made it difficult for him to complete the poem, and by apprehensions that his willed commitment to the celebration of the vision was false. The "forms, materials, dynamics" on which his commitment depended "are simply non-existent in the [contemporary] world," he added in the letter to Frank, and "I may amuse and * * * flatter myself as much as I please—but I am only evading a recognition and playing Don Quixote in an immorally conscious way. * * * The bridge as a symbol today has no significance beyond an economical approach to shorter hours, quicker lunches, behaviorism and toothpicks."[2] Impelled by such recognitions, Crane's poem became not only a willed celebration of the myth but a quest for the self-transformation that would validate his commitment to the vision, a quest that is challenged frequently in the poem by imminent disenchantment or disillusion.

Crane did not finish *The Bridge* until 1930, when it was published first in Paris and then in New York, after years troubled by family problems, self-doubts about his capacities as a poet, and by extremities of debauchery which continued when he traveled abroad in 1928 and 1929. Although he received *Poetry* magazine's Levinson Award for *The Bridge*, reviews of the poem were not highly favorable, and Crane was held up by the critics Allen Tate and Yvor Winters as an object lesson in the excesses attributed to romanticism. He received a Guggenheim fellowship in 1930 and went to Mexico in hope of salvaging his talent. He produced some poems, including *The Broken Tower*, and was living happily with Peggy Baird Cowley, the divorced wife of the critic Malcolm Cowley, and talking of marriage. But the violence of his drinking bouts and the sordidness of his homosexual dissipations were conspicuous to the novelist Katherine Anne Porter and other friends in Mexico. Before his death he had completed arranging a volume to be entitled *Key West*. In 1932 he jumped to his death from the deck of the ship carrying him to New York City. In the eyes of the poet Karl Shapiro, Crane died a "wasted death," an object lesson in the folly of total commitment to poetry (*Essay on Rime*, 1945). To the poet Robert Lowell in *Words for Hart Crane* (1958), Crane died in defiance of a world which did not reward his talent.

Legend[1]

As silent as a mirror is believed
Realities plunge in silence by . . .

I am not ready for repentance;
Nor to match regrets. For the moth
Bends no more than the still   5
Imploring flame. And tremorous

2. *Ibid.*, p. 261.
1. The poems *Legend* through *Voyages VI* are presented in the sequence Crane determined for them in *White Buildings* (1926); the arrangement was designed to make the poems more accessible to the reader. The title *White Buildings* is drawn from a recurring motif in the surrealistic paintings of Giorgio de Chirico (b. 1888).

In the white falling flakes
Kisses are,—
The only worth all granting.

It is to be learned—   10
This cleaving and this burning,
But only by the one who
Spends out himself again.

Twice and twice
(Again the smoking souvenir,   15
Bleeding eidolon!)² and yet again.
Until the bright logic is won
Unwhispering as a mirror
Is believed.

Then, drop by caustic drop, a perfect cry   20
Shall string some constant harmony,—
Relentless caper for all those who step
The legend of their youth into the noon.

1925   1926

Black Tambourine¹

The interests of a black man in a cellar
Mark tardy judgment on the world's closed door.
Gnats toss in the shadow of a bottle,
And a roach spans a crevice in the floor.

Æsop,² driven to pondering, found   5
Heaven with the tortoise and the hare;
Fox brush and sow ear top his grave
And mingling incantations on the air.

The black man, forlorn in the cellar,
Wanders in some mid-kingdom, dark, that lies,   10
Between his tambourine, stuck on the wall,
And, in Africa, a carcass quick with flies.

1921   1921, 1926

---

2. Specter, phantom.
1. Crane claimed in letters to Sherwood
Anderson and Gorham Munson (*Letters*,
pp. 77, 58) that his aim in this poem
was to create a "form that is so thorough and intense as to dye the words
themselves with a peculiarity of meaning,
slightly different maybe from the ordinary definition of them separate from
the poem," that he had gone back to
"rime and rhythm" so as to avoid the
disorder of Dada art, and that "the
poem is * * * a bundle of insinuations,
suggestions, bearing on the Negro's place
somewhere between man and beast. That
is why Aesop is brought in, etc.—the
popular conception of Negro romance,
the tambourine on the wall. The value of
the poem is only, to me, in what a
painter would call its 'tactile' quality,
—an entirely aesthetic feature. A propagandist for either side of the Negro
question could find anything he wanted
to in it. My only declaration is that I
find the Negro (in the popular mind)
sentimentally or brutally 'placed' in this
midkingdom, etc."
2. Greek author of *Fables* (fl. 620–560
B.C.) and a freed slave.

My Grandmother's Love Letters

There are no stars to-night
But those of memory.
Yet how much room for memory there is
In the loose girdle of soft rain.

There is even room enough   5
For the letters of my mother's mother,
Elizabeth,
That have been pressed so long
Into a corner of the roof
That they are brown and soft,   10
And liable to melt as snow.

Over the greatness of such space
Steps must be gentle.
It is all hung by an invisible white hair.
It trembles as birch limbs webbing the air.   15

And I ask myself:

"Are your fingers long enough to play
Old keys that are but echoes:
Is the silence strong enough
To carry back the music to its source   20
And back to you again
As though to her?"

Yet I would lead my grandmother by the hand
Through much of what she would not understand;
And so I stumble. And the rain continues on the roof   25
With such a sound of gently pitying laughter.

1919   1920

Chaplinesque[1]

We make our meek adjustments,
Contented with such random consolations
As the wind deposits
In slithered and too ample pockets.

For we can still love the world, who find   5

---

1. Crane wrote in letters of his excitement at seeing Charles Chaplin's film *The Kid* (1921) and said that he aimed "to put in words some of the Chaplin pantomime, so beautiful, and so full of eloquence, and so modern." The film "made me feel myself, as a poet, as being 'in the same boat' with him," Crane wrote; "Poetry, the human feelings, 'the kitten,' is so crowded out of the humdrum, rushing, mechanical scramble of today that the man who would preserve them must duck and camouflage for dear life to keep them or keep himself from annihilation. * * * I have tried to express these 'social sympathies' in words corresponding somewhat to the antics of the actor" (*Letters*, p. 68).

A famished kitten[2] on the step, and know
Recesses for it from the fury of the street
Or warm torn elbow coverts.

We will sidestep, and to the final smirk
Dally the doom of that inevitable thumb   10
That slowly chafes its puckered index toward us,
Facing the dull squint with what innocence
And what surprise!

And yet these fine collapses are not lies
More than the pirouettes of any pliant cane;   15
Our obsequies[3] are, in a way, no enterprise.
We can evade you, and all else but the heart:
What blame to us if the heart live on.

The game enforces smirks; but we have seen
The moon in lonely alleys make   20
A grail of laughter of an empty ash can,
And through all sound of gaiety and quest
Have heard a kitten in the wilderness.

                                                          1921, 1926

Repose of Rivers[1]

The willows carried a slow sound,
A sarabande the wind mowed on the mead.
I could never remember
That seething, steady leveling of the marshes
Till age had brought me to the sea.   5

Flags, weeds. And remembrance of steep alcoves
Where cypresses shared the noon's
Tyranny; they drew me into hades almost.
And mammoth turtles climbing sulphur dreams
Yielded, while sun-silt rippled them   10
Asunder . . .

How much I would have bartered! the black gorge
And all the singular nestings in the hills
Where beavers learn stitch and tooth.

---

2. Crane declared in a letter that he
meant to capture in the image of the kitten the "notion of some infinitely gentle
/ Infinitely suffering thing" from T. S.
Eliot's fourth *Prelude*, lines 12–13 (*Letters*, p. 66).
3. In the double sense of "funeral rites"
and "obsequiousness" or cagey deference
to threatening superiors. Crane suggests
that side-stepping evasions displayed in
Chaplin's gestures are not premonitions of
death or tragic failure but that they are
justifiable defenses in the name of survival and tender feeling.
1. A companion piece to *O Carib Isle!*
In this poem Crane remembers two moments, both of which aroused and at the
same time threatened to immobilize his
imaginative power: an occasion in early
manhood when he entered a marshy pond
surrounded by willows; and a more recent occasion in the hurricane-swept
Caribbean.

The pond I entered once and quickly fled—   15
I remember now its singing willow rim.

And finally, in that memory all things nurse;
After the city that I finally passed
With scalding unguents spread and smoking darts
The monsoon cut across the delta   20
At gulf gates . . . There, beyond the dykes

I heard wind flaking sapphire, like this summer,
And willows could not hold more steady sound.

                                                    1926

Possessions[1]

Witness now this trust! the rain
That steals softly direction
And the key, ready to hand—sifting
One moment in sacrifice (the direst)
Through a thousand nights the flesh   5
Assaults outright for bolts[2] that linger
Hidden,—O undirected as the sky
That through its black foam has no eyes
For this fixed stone of lust . . .

Accumulate such moments to an hour: 10
Account the total of this trembling tabulation.
I know the screen, the distant flying taps
And stabbing medley that sways—
And the mercy, feminine, that stays
As though prepared.   15

And I, entering, take up the stone
As quiet as you can make a man . . .
In Bleecker Street,[3] still trenchant in a void,
Wounded by apprehensions out of speech,
I hold it up against a disk of light—   20
I, turning, turning on smoked forking spires,
The city's stubborn lives, desires.

Tossed on these horns, who bleeding dies,
Lacks all but piteous admissions to be spilt
Upon the page whose blind sum finally burns   25
Record of rage and partial appetites.

1. This poem presents the re-enactment of a passion that the poet recognizes as destructive and "partial"; a tortured examination of the experience afterward, turning it over in the imagination, finding it typical of lives in his city, until it becomes a burning record of the passion on the poem's page; and an attempt to envision a tempestuous passion which will purge the stones of lust, transforming them into valid passion.
2. The image of bolts suggests the entrances to passion that the speaker must unlock, and also the hidden fires (like lightning) in the storm of passion.
3. Street in New York City.

The pure possession, the inclusive cloud
Whose heart is fire shall come,—the white wind rase
All but bright stones wherein our smiling plays.

1923, 1926

Lachrymae Christi[1]

Whitely, while benzine[2]
Rinsings from the moon
Dissolve all but the windows of the mills
(Inside the sure machinery
Is still   5
And curdled[3] only where a sill
Sluices its one unyielding smile)

Immaculate venom binds
The fox's teeth, and swart
Thorns freshen on the year's   10
First blood. From flanks unfended,
Twanged red perfidies of spring
Are trillion on the hill.

And the nights opening
Chant pyramids,—   15
Anoint with innocence,—recall
To music and retrieve what perjuries
Had galvanized[4] the eyes.

While chime
Beneath and all around   20
Distilling clemencies,—worms'[5]
Inaudible whistle, tunneling
Not penitence
But song, as these
Perpetual fountains, vines,—   25

Thy Nazarene[6] and tinder eyes.
(Let[7] sphinxes from the ripe

1. The first version of this poem, begun early in 1924, was enclosed in a letter to Waldo Frank in which Crane wrote of his encouragement at the prospect of a new job in advertising, his excitement at having begun *The Bridge*, and his passionate love for Emil Opffer, Jr., a merchant seaman with whom he soon established residence. The poem celebrates a tortured process of redemption: the transfiguration of an industrial factory, the revitalization of the speaker's sexual passion and the reawakening of his powers of expression, and the rebirth of nature in springtime. The title ("Tears of Christ") is the name of an Italian wine, frequently used as communion wine. The poem is built on paradoxes: the redemptive process is conceived as being both natural and supernatural, Christian and pagan, violently destructive and life-giving, agonizing and ecstatic.
2. A poisonous cleaning fluid.
3. In the sense of "reduced to its richest essence."
4. Both coated over and charged with energy.
5. A punning allusion to earthworms and gears of machinery.
6. From the town of Nazareth: Jesus.
7. A verb in the sense of "may." The stanza in parenthesis is a silent prayer in

Borage[8] of death have cleared my tongue
Once and again; vermin and rod
No longer bind. Some sentient cloud   30
Of tears flocks through the tendoned loam:
Betrayed stones slowly speak.)

Names peeling from Thine eyes
And their undimming lattices of flame,
Spell out in palm and pain   35
Compulsion of the year, O Nazarene.

Lean long from sable, slender boughs,
Unstanched and luminous. And as the nights
Strike from Thee perfect spheres,
Lift up in lilac-emerald breath the grail   40
Of earth again—

                Thy face
From charred and riven stakes, O
Dionysus,[9] Thy
Unmangled target smile.   45

1924–25   1926

For the Marriage of Faustus and Helen[1]

> *"And so we may arrive by Talmud skill*
> *And profane Greek to raise the building up*
> *Of Helen's house against the Ismaelite,*
> *King of Thogarma, and his habergeons*
> *Brimstony, blue and fiery; and the force*
> *Of King Abaddon, and the beast of Cittim;*
> *Which Rabbi David Kimchi, Onkelos,*
> *And Aben Ezra do interpret Rome."*
> —THE ALCHEMIST[2]

I

The mind has shown itself at times
Too much the baked and labeled dough
Divided by accepted multitudes.
Across the stacked partitions of the day—
Across the memoranda, baseball scores,   5

---

which the speaker begs that his powers of speech be cleansed while imagining that they have been revitalized already; the process of renewal must be repeated "once and again," but the cleansing process begins even before he finishes the prayer.

8. An herb used to flavor salads and claret punch and believed to cure melancholy and to quiet lunatics.

9. Greek god, inventor of wine, and the center of mystery cults, whose metamorphoses and sacrifice were associated with the rebirth of spring. His rites were characterized by intoxication, religious frenzy, madness, and orgiastic indulgence, while his spring festival in Athens

was the occasion for the production of new tragedies and comedies.

1. This poem established Crane's reputation as a major poet. The title alludes to the learned Renaissance magician who bartered his soul to the devil in return for limitless power, and to the beautiful woman he longed to possess, the wife of the Greek King Menelaus whose abduction by the Trojan Paris brought on war and the fall of Troy. Crane's *Letters* (pp. 120–21) explain that Faustus is intended as "the symbol of myself, the poetic or imaginative man * * * ," and Helen as a symbol of an "abstract 'sense of beauty * * *'." Helen's beauty, however, remains inseparable from her sen-

The stenographic smiles and stock quotations
Smutty wings flash out equivocations.

The mind is brushed by sparrow wings;
Numbers, rebuffed by asphalt, crowd
The margins of the day, accent the curbs,   10
Convoying divers dawns on every corner
To druggist, barber and tobacconist,
Until the graduate opacities of evening
Take them away as suddenly to somewhere
Virginal perhaps, less fragmentary, cool.   15

> *There is the world dimensional for*
> *those untwisted by the love of things*
> *irreconcilable . . .*

And yet, suppose some evening I forgot
The fare and transfer, yet got by that way   20
Without recall,—lost yet poised in traffic.
Then I might find your eyes across an aisle,
Still flickering with those prefigurations—
Prodigal, yet uncontested now,
Half-riant before the jerky window frame.   25

There is some way, I think, to touch
Those hands of yours that count the nights
Stippled³ with pink and green advertisements.
And now, before its arteries turn dark
I would have you meet this bartered blood.   30
Imminent in his dream, none better knows
The white wafer cheek of love, or offers words
Lightly as moonlight on the eaves meets snow.

Reflective conversion of all things
At your deep blush, when ecstasies thread   35

suality and body, and Crane sought to suggest the gradations from the everyday world of commerce and conventionality "into the abstract." The poem celebrates the attainment of an abstract beauty beyond words through sensuous ecstasy, a hazardous but redemptive commitment of the imagination to passion. Part I scans the everyday, equivocal "world dimensional" to find "prefigurations" merely, though tantalizing glimpses, of Helen's beauty. Crane termed Part I the "EVOCATION of beauty." He called Part II "the DANCE and sensual culmination," and sought an idiom for the "transposition of Jazz into words." It presents the beginnings of the poet's achievement of beauty, in a surrender to the siren song in the grooves of phonograph records, then the poet's and his partner's abandonment to illicit passion. Part III Crane termed "the ecstasy"

which "begins with *catharsis*, the acceptance of tragedy through destruction (The Fall of Troy, etc., also in it)." In it two passionate lovers are imaged as warplanes which bring purgative destruction to the everyday world and bring themselves to unexpected heights where, like thieves and the conquerors of cities, they apprehend Helen's awesome beauty and return to celebrate it.
2. The lines are from the Elizabethan playwright Ben Jonson's *The Alchemist* (1610); IV.v.30–37. They are spoken by a prostitute whose comic pretense to learning and religious zeal is part of an elaborate effort to trick a lustful gentleman.
3. Engraved or painted in dots, as in "pointillist" paintings or in printed reproductions of paintings in newspapers and books.

The limbs and belly, when rainbows spread
Impinging on the throat and sides . . .
Inevitable, the body of the world
Weeps in inventive dust for the hiatus
That winks above it, bluet in your breasts.   40

The earth may glide diaphanous to death;
But if I lift my arms it is to bend
To you who turned away once, Helen, knowing
The press of troubled hands, too alternate
With steel and soil to hold you endlessly.   45
I meet you, therefore, in that eventual flame

You found in final chains, no captive then—
Beyond their million brittle, bloodshot eyes;
White, through white cities passed on to assume
That world which comes to each of us alone.   50

Accept a lone eye riveted to your plane,
Bent axle of devotion along companion ways
That beat, continuous, to hourless days—
One inconspicuous, glowing orb of praise.

II

Brazen hynotics glitter here;   55
Glee shifts from foot to foot,
Magnetic to their tremolo.
This crashing opéra bouffe,
Blest excursion! this ricochet
From roof to roof—   60
Know, Olympians, we are breathless
While nigger cupids scour the stars!

A thousand light shrugs balance us
Through snarling hails of melody.
White shadows slip across the floor   65
Splayed like cards from a loose hand;
Rhythmic ellipses lead into canters
Until somewhere a rooster banters.

Greet naïvely—yet intrepidly
New soothings, new amazements   70
That cornets introduce at every turn—
And you may fall downstairs with me
With perfect grace and equanimity.
Or, plaintively scud past shores
Where, by strange harmonic laws   75
All relatives, serene and cool,
Sit rocked in patent armchairs.

O, I have known metallic paradises
Where cuckoos clucked to finches

Above the deft catastrophes of drums.   80
While titters hailed the groans of death
Beneath gyrating awnings I have seen
The incunabula[4] of the divine grotesque.
This music has a reassuring way.

The siren of the springs of guilty song—   85
Let us take her on the incandescent wax
Striated with nuances, nervosities
That we are heir to: she is still so young,
We cannot frown upon her as she smiles,
Dipping here in this cultivated storm   90
Among slim skaters of the gardened skies.

III

Capped arbiter of beauty in this street
That narrows darkly into motor dawn,—
You, here beside me, delicate ambassador
Of intricate slain numbers that arise
In whispers, naked of steel;   95
                       religious gunman!
Who faithfully, yourself, will fall too soon,
And in other ways than as the wind settles
On the sixteen thrifty bridges of the city:
Let us unbind our throats of fear and pity.   100

                                We even,
Who drove speediest destruction
In corymbulous[5] formations of mechanics,—
Who hurried the hill breezes, spouting malice
Plangent over meadows, and looked down   105
On rifts of torn and empty houses
Like old women with teeth unjubilant
That waited faintly, briefly and in vain:

We know, eternal gunman, our flesh remembers
The tensile boughs, the nimble blue plateaus,   110
The mounted, yielding cities of the air!

That saddled sky that shook down vertical
Repeated play of fire—no hypogeum[6]
Of wave or rock was good against one hour.
We did not ask for that, but have survived,   115
And will persist to speak again before
All stubble streets that have not curved
To memory, or known the ominous lifted arm
That lowers down the arc of Helen's brow
To saturate with blessing and dismay.   120

---

4. Beginnings of anything; early printed books.
5. Clustering of flowers or fruit around a stem. Possibly an image of machine-gun fire, or of a formation of aircraft.
6. Underground vault, basement refuge.

A goose, tobacco and cologne—[7]
Three winged and gold-shod prophecies of heaven,
The lavish heart shall always have to leaven
And spread with bells and voices, and atone
The abating shadows of our conscript dust.   125

Anchises'[8] navel, dripping of the sea,—
The hands Erasmus[9] dipped in gleaming tides,
Gathered the voltage of blown blood and vine;
Delve upward for the new and scattered wine,[10]
O brother-thief of time, that we recall.   130
Laugh out the meager penance of their days
Who dare not share with us the breath released,
The substance drilled and spent beyond repair
For golden, or the shadow of gold hair.

Distinctly praise the years, whose volatile   135
Blamed bleeding hands extend and thresh the height
The imagination spans beyond despair,
Outpacing bargain, vocable and prayer.

1922–23   1923, 1926

At Melville's Tomb[1]

Often beneath the wave, wide from this ledge
The dice of drowned men's bones he saw bequeath
An embassy. Their numbers as he watched,
Beat on the dusty shore and were obscured.[2]

7. Crane had read of a thief who was arrested for stealing these items. Crane uses them to suggest souvenirs of passion and beauty that are bizarre tokens merely, though nonetheless cherished, of the stolen hour.
8. Trojan lover of the god Aphrodite (born from the sea), and father of Aeneas, whom Aeneas rescued from burning Troy before leaving on the journey that eventuated in the founding of Rome, in the epic *Aeneid* by the Roman poet Virgil (c. 70–19 B.C.).
9. Desiderius Erasmus (1466–1536), humanist scholar, Catholic reformer, translator of the Bible and ancient classics.
10. Crane exalts the "cities of the air" and the "new wine" of his vision even above the fruitfulness and power he associates with Anchises and Erasmus and with the sea.
1. This poem was published in *Poetry* magazine only after Crane provided the editor, Harriet Monroe, with a detailed explanation of its images. His letter, and Monroe's inquiries and comments, were published with the poem. Crane's letter (*Complete Poems and Selected Letters and Prose*, pp. 234–40) insisted that poetry, like his and that written by Eliot and William Blake, derives from an "emotional dynamics," a "dynamics of metaphor," that is distinct from the "rationalized definitions" used in science

and everyday experience; that poetry, exploiting the "illogical impingements of the connotations of words on the consciousness," depends on "something like short-hand" as a "connective agent" when the poet explores "fresh concepts, more inclusive evaluations" than those already worked out by his predecessors. Crane's detailed comments in the letter are incorporated in the notes below. The poem is a tribute to one of Crane's most admired American predecessors, Herman Melville, and evokes Melville's treatment of the horrors and mystery of the sea in such works as *Moby-Dick* (1851). The poem celebrates Melville's confrontation of extinction and the translation of death's enigmatic meaning into a silent hymn of reconciliation that makes life sacred.
2. "Dice bequeath an embassy, in the first place, by being ground (in this connection only, of course) in little cubes from the bones of drowned men by the action of the sea, and are finally thrown up on the sand, having 'numbers' but no identification. These being the bones of dead men who never completed their voyage, it seems legitimate to refer to them as the only surviving evidence of certain messages undelivered, mute evidence of certain things * * * . Dice as a symbol of chance and circumstance is also implied" [Crane's note].

And wrecks passed without sound of bells,   5
The calyx of death's bounty giving back
A scattered chapter, livid hieroglyph,
The portent wound in corridors of shells.[3]

Then in the circuit calm of one vast coil,
Its lashings charmed and malice reconciled,   10
Frosted eyes there were that lifted altars;[4]
And silent answers crept across the stars.

Compass, quadrant and sextant contrive
No farther tides[5] . . . High in the azure steeps
Monody shall not wake the mariner.   15
This fabulous shadow only the sea keeps.

1925–26   1926

Voyages[1]

I

Above the fresh ruffles[2] of the surf
Bright striped urchins flay each other with sand.
They have contrived a conquest for shell shucks,
And their fingers crumble fragments of baked weed
Gaily digging and scattering.   5

And in answer to their treble interjections

3. "This calyx refers in a double ironic sense both to a cornucopia and the vortex made by a sinking vessel. As soon as the water has closed over a ship this whirlpool sends up broken spars, wreckage, etc., which can be alluded to as livid *hieroglyphs,* making a *scattered chapter* so far as any complete record of the recent ship and crew is concerned. In fact, about as much definite knowledge might come from all this as anyone might gain from the roar of his own veins, which is easily heard (haven't you ever done it?) by holding a shell close to one's ear" [Crane's note]. A calyx is a whorl of leaves forming the outer casing of the bud of a plant.
4. "Refers simply to a conviction that a man, not knowing perhaps a definite god yet being endowed with a reverence for deity—such a man naturally postulates a deity somehow, and the altar of that deity by the very *action* of the eyes *lifted* in searching" [Crane's note].
5. "Hasn't it often occurred that instruments originally invented for record and computation have inadvertently so extended the concepts of the entity they were invented to measure (concepts of space, etc.) in the mind and imagination that employed them, that they may metaphorically be said to have extended the original boundaries of the entity measured? This little bit of 'relativity' ought not to be discredited in poetry now that

scientists are proceeding to measure the universe on principles of pure *ratio,* quote as metaphorical, so far as previous standards of scientific methods extended, as some of the axioms in *Job*" [Crane's note].
1. Crane composed this suite of love poems in 1924 and 1925, revising two earlier poems (*Poster* and *Belle Isle*) which became sections I and VI of *Voyages.* The lover with whom he was living was Emil Opffer, Jr., a merchant seaman; the facts that his knowledge of the sea and exotic islands exceeded Crane's, and that he was separated from Crane while on sea duty, contributed a dynamic to the poem: images of the *consummation* of passion blend with images of the *anticipation* of its ecstasies and its treacheries, and with fears of its dissolution. Crane presents love as a time-bound passion, tormenting as well as exhilarating, a communion that affords ecstasy and beauty or imaginative vision but also portends the dissolution of passion and death. The poem's central symbol is the sea. Its motion charts the course of the lovers' passion. The sea also images the art which the passion inspired (the "snowy sentences," the "transmemberment of song," Crane's own poem), and the transcendent vision, which lies beyond the poet's experience and expressive power.
2. Cloth gathered in ripples, and also

The sun beats lightning on the waves,
The waves fold thunder on the sand;
And could they hear me I would tell them:

O brilliant kids, frisk with your dog,   10
Fondle your shells and sticks, bleached
By time and the elements; but there is a line
You must not cross nor ever trust beyond it
Spry cordage[3] of your bodies to caresses
Too lichen-faithful from too wide a breast.   15
The bottom of the sea is cruel.

1921–23   1923, 1926

II

—And yet this great wink of eternity,
Of rimless floods, unfettered leewardings,
Samite[4] sheeted and processioned where
Her undinal[5] vast belly moonward bends,   20
Laughing the wrapt inflections of our love;

Take this Sea, whose diapason[6] knells
On scrolls of silver snowy sentences,
The sceptred terror of whose sessions rends
As her demeanors notion well or ill,   25
All but the pieties of lovers' hands.

And onward, as bells off San Salvador
Salute the crocus lustres of the stars,
In these poinsettia meadows of her tides,—
Adagios of islands,[7] O my Prodigal,   30
Complete the dark confessions her veins spell.

Mark how her turning shoulders wind the hours,
And hasten while her penniless rich palms
Pass superscription of bent foam and wave,—
Hasten, while they are true,—sleep, death, desire,   35
Close round one instant in one floating flower.

Bind us in time, O Seasons clear, and awe.
O minstrel galleons of Carib fire,
Bequeath us to no earthly shore until

the rhythms of drum beats. Musical images recur in *Voyages*.
3. Rigging of ships, associated here with lovers' bodies.
4. Medieval gold-threaded silk cloth.
5. Alluding to Undine, a water nymph capable of becoming human through love.
6. Melody or harmony in music.
7. Crane explained that "adagios of islands" refers "to the motion of a boat through islands clustered thickly, the rhythm of the motion, etc. And it seems a much more direct and creative statement than any more logical employment of words such as 'coasting slowly through the islands.' besides ushering in a whole world of music." ("General Aims and Theories," *Complete Poems and Selected Letters and Prose*, p. 221.) Like the "insular Tahiti" invoked in Melville's *Moby-Dick* (Chapter 58), islands function in Crane's poem as an image of serene joy surrounded by tempestuous, dangerous seas.

Is answered in the vortex of our grave   40
The seal's wide spindrift[8] gaze toward paradise.

1924   1926

III

Infinite consanguinity it bears—
This tendered theme of you that light
Retrieves from sea plains where the sky
Resigns a breast that every wave enthrones;   45
While ribboned water lanes I wind
Are laved and scattered with no stroke
Wide from your side, whereto this hour
The sea lifts, also, reliquary hands.

And so, admitted through black swollen gates   50
That must arrest all distance otherwise,—
Past whirling pillars and lithe pediments,
Light wrestling there incessantly with light,
Star kissing star through wave on wave unto
Your body rocking!   55
                    and where death, if shed,
Presumes no carnage, but this single change,—
Upon the steep floor flung down from dawn to dawn
The silken skilled transmemberment[9] of song;   60

Permit me voyage, love, into your hands . . .

1924   1926

IV[1]

Whose counted smile of hours and days, suppose
I know as spectrum of the sea and pledge
Vastly now parting gulf on gulf of wings
Whose circles bridge, I know, (from palms to the
      severe   65
Chilled albatross's white immutability)
No stream of greater love advancing now
Than, singing, this mortality alone
Through clay aflow immortally to you.

All fragrance irrefragibly,[2] and claim   70
Madly meeting logically in this hour
And region that is ours to wreathe again,

---

8. Sea foam. The suggestions of "drift-ing" and "spinning" define Crane's conception of the currents and intensity of passion.
9. The lines relate the consummation of love to the miraculous "sea-change" of death into life celebrated in Shakespeare's *The Tempest* (1.2.400) and to the creation of art. "Transmemberment" is a coinage of Crane's, suggesting the fragmentation, dismemberment, or suffering he associated with both love and imaginative creation, and the transmutation or transformation that love and poetry bring about.
1. This section emphasizes the anticipations of love: the "pledge" that can span distances and absences, the promise that portends fulfillment in the immediate future but also foresees the "islands" of more remote consummations.
2. Either a misspelling or a coinage of Crane's. "Irrefragable" means undisputed; "irrefrangible" means incapable of being refracted.

Portending eyes and lips and making told
The chancel port and portion of our June—

Shall they not stem and close in our own steps   75
Bright staves of flowers and quills to-day as I
Must first be lost in fatal tides to tell?

In signature of the incarnate word
The harbor shoulders to resign in mingling
Mutual blood, transpiring as foreknown   80
And widening noon within your breast for gathering
All bright insinuations that my years have caught
For islands where must lead inviolably
Blue latitudes and levels of your eyes,—

In this expectant, still exclaim receive   85
The secret oar and petals of all love.

1924   1926

V³

Meticulous, past midnight in clear rime,
Infrangible and lonely, smooth as though cast
Together in one merciless white blade—
The bay estuaries fleck the hard sky limits.   90

—As if too brittle or too clear to touch!
The cables of our sleep so swiftly filed,
Already hang, shred ends from remembered stars.
One frozen trackless smile . . . What words
Can strangle this deaf moonlight? For we   95

Are overtaken. Now no cry, no sword
Can fasten or deflect this tidal wedge,
Slow tyranny of moonlight, moonlight loved
And changed . . . "There's

Nothing like this in the world," you say,   100
Knowing I cannot touch your hand and look
Too, into that godless cleft of sky
Where nothing turns but dead sands flashing.

"—And never to quite understand!" No,
In all the argosy of your bright hair I dreamed   105
Nothing so flagless as this piracy.

                          But now
Draw in your head, alone and too tall here.
Your eyes already in the slant of drifting foam;

---

3. This section emphasizes the tranquility following love's consummation, the poet's premonition of its dissolution, and his recognition that his lover has insights beyond his own.

Your breath sealed by the ghosts I do not know:⁣ 110
Draw in your head and sleep the long way home.

1924⁣ 1926

VI⁴

Where icy and bright dungeons lift
Of swimmers their lost morning eyes,
And ocean rivers, churning, shift
Green borders under stranger skies,⁣ 115

Steadily as a shell secretes
Its beating leagues of monotone,
Or as many waters trough the sun's
Red kelson⁵ past the cape's wet stone;

O rivers mingling toward the sky⁣ 120
And harbor of the phoenix' breast—
My eyes pressed black against the prow,
—Thy derelict and blinded guest

Waiting, afire, what name, unspoke,
I cannot claim: let thy waves rear⁣ 125
More savage than the death of kings,⁶
Some splintered garland for the seer.

Beyond siroccos harvesting
The solstice thunders, crept away,
Like a cliff swinging or a sail⁣ 130
Flung into April's inmost day—

Creation's blithe and petalled word
To the lounged goddess when she rose⁷
Conceding dialogue with eyes
That smile unsearchable repose—⁣ 135

Still fervid covenant, Belle Isle,⁸
—Unfolded floating dais before
Which rainbows twine continual hair—
Belle Isle, white echo of the oar!

The imaged Word, it is, that holds⁣ 140
Hushed willows anchored in its glow.
It is the unbetrayable reply
Whose accent no farewell can know.

1921–25⁣ 1923, 1926

4. This section celebrates the endurance of love, transcending death and the wreck of love, as imaged even in the "icy" Belle Isle and in the "imaged Word" of poetry.
5. Timber of a ship joining the ribs to the keel.
6. Richard II calls for tales of the "sad death of kings" in Shakespeare's play (3.3.156).
7. Possibly Aphrodite (Venus), goddess of love, who was born of the foam of the sea; possibly Eos, goddess of dawn, the lover of Orion who restored his blinded eyes to sight.
8. An island off Labrador southeast of Cape St. Charles.

The Bridge   This poem presents a heroic quest, subjective or personal in its intensity but epic in its panoramic scale, for the renewal of the self and the discovery of a coherent world in which the debasements and cleavages of modern society could be transformed. The poem's recurring symbols include: the sea, not only as a setting for pioneering adventure but as the source of natural vitality, the depths of the psyche, and the renewal of life through death; a woman, associated particularly with the earth and the American continent, and presented in such figures as the Virgin Mary and the legendary Indian princess Pocahontas; and a series of predecessors who guide the poet's quest, including Columbus, Rip Van Winkle, and the American writers Poe and Whitman. The poem's governing symbol is the Brooklyn Bridge, a triumph of industrial technology and aesthetic form when it was completed in 1883 and the dominant feature of the urban landscape from Crane's apartment window in Brooklyn. Though he came to believe while writing the poem that the values represented by the Bridge no longer prevailed in modern America, he felt that the "very idea of a bridge * * * is a form peculiarly dependent on * * * spiritual convictions. It is an act of faith besides being a communication." Also it represented love, the "ecstasy of walking hand in hand across the most beautiful bridge of the world, the cables enclosing us and pulling us upward in such a dance as I have never walked and never can walk with another" (*Letters*, pp. 261, 181). The symbol represented, however, not the full achievement of spiritual values, communication in art, and love, but the process of seeking these values, the act of bridging or spanning, through time and space, the full range of American history and the entire spectrum of consciousness from the subconscious to the visionary imagination. As a symbol-in-process the Bridge encompasses Crane's poem itself and becomes closely associated with the other symbols that appear fleetingly or emphatically in the poem, becoming a sacred altar and as Crane claimed "a tremendous harp" as he tried to "induce the same feelings of elation, etc.—like being carried forward and upward simultaneously—both in imagery, rhythm, and repetition, that one experiences in walking across my beloved Brooklyn Bridge" (*ibid.*, p. 232). At the end the quest terminates not in the attainment of its goal but in visionary prefigurations of its fulfillment.

    Crane conceived the arrangement of the separate lyrics as symphonic rather than chronological. The poem's form, dependent on thematic juxtapositions and the "logic of metaphor," is based on two intersecting axes of movement. Along a horizontal axis the poet's quest moves westward in imagination from Brooklyn to the prairie heartland and the gold-rush mining camps, then turns eastward again (in *Indiana*) and returns to Brooklyn as his disillusionment mounts and he faces the final crisis of *The Tunnel*. Along the same axis the quest moves backward in time through the era of discovery to the past of the Indians and the prehistory of geological eras, then returns through the era of the clipper ships and Whitman to the crisis of modern culture. Along a vertical axis the poet's quest moves upward in response to his hopes and exaltations, or downward in response to his disillusionment and the desperation of his final descent beneath time and consciousness into the sea at the end of *The Tunnel*. The separate lyrics are varied in their stanzaic forms, but the several patterns of movement operate simultaneously in them and often intersect, defining the structure of the individual poems as well as the structure of the entire epic.

THE BRIDGE

From going to and fro in the earth,
and from walking up and down in it.
—THE BOOK OF JOB[1]

To Brooklyn Bridge

How many dawns, chill from his rippling rest
The seagull's wings shall dip and pivot him,
Shedding white rings of tumult, building high
Over the chained bay waters Liberty—

Then, with inviolate curve, forsake our eyes   5
As apparitional as sails that cross
Some page of figures to be filed away;
—Till elevators drop us from our day . . .

I think of cinemas, panoramic sleights
With multitudes bent toward some flashing scene   10
Never disclosed, but hastened to again,
Foretold to other eyes on the same screen;

And Thee, across the harbor, silver-paced
As though the sun took step of thee, yet left
Some motion ever unspent in thy stride,—   15
Implicitly thy freedom staying thee!

Out of some subway scuttle, cell or loft
A bedlamite[2] speeds to thy parapets,
Tilting there momently, shrill shirt ballooning,
A jest falls from the speechless caravan.   20

Down Wall, from girder into street noon leaks,
A rip-tooth of the sky's acetylene;
All afternoon the cloud-flown derricks turn . . .
Thy cables breathe the North Atlantic still.

And obscure as that heaven of the Jews,   25
Thy guerdon . . . Accolade thou dost bestow
Of anonymity time cannot raise:
Vibrant reprieve and pardon thou dost show.

O harp and altar, of the fury fused,
(How could mere toil align thy choiring strings!)   30
Terrific threshold of the prophet's pledge,
Prayer of pariah, and the lover's cry,—

Again the traffic lights that skim thy swift
Unfractioned idiom, immaculate sigh of stars,

1. The formal pattern of the poem is
suggested by this quotation from *Job*,
which gives Satan's answer to Jehovah
when asked where he has been (1.7).
2. Madman, inmate of a hospital for the
insane.

Beading thy path—condense eternity: 35
And we have seen night lifted in thine arms.

Under thy shadow by the piers I waited;
Only in darkness is thy shadow clear.
The City's fiery parcels all undone,
Already snow submerges an iron year . . .   40

O Sleepless as the river under thee,
Vaulting the sea, the prairies' dreaming sod,
Unto us lowliest sometime sweep, descend
And of the curveship lend a myth to God.

1926   1927, 1930

I. Ave Maria[3]

Venient annis, saecula seris,
Quibus Oceanus vincula rerum
Laxet et ingens pateat tellus
Tiphysque novos detegat orbes
Nec sit terris ultima Thule.
—SENECA[4]

Columbus, alone, gazing toward Spain, invokes the presence of two faithful partisans of his quest . . .

Be with me, Luis de San Angel,[5] now—
Witness before the tides can wrest away
The word I bring, O you who reined my suit
Into the Queen's great heart that doubtful day;
For I have seen now what no perjured breath   5
Of clown nor sage can riddle or gainsay;—
To you, too, Juan Perez, whose counsel fear
And greed adjourned,—I bring you back Cathay!

Here waves climb into dusk on gleaming mail;
Invisible valves of the sea,—locks, tendons   10
Crested and creeping, troughing corridors
That fall back yawning to another plunge.
Slowly the sun's red caravel drops light
Once more behind us. . . . It is morning there—

3. This poem presents the test of Columbus's faith and his impassioned prayer to God for safe return to Spain at a time in 1493 when he had discovered the New World but still thought it the India or Cathay (China) of his dreams and was returning from the first voyage to report his discovery to the court of Ferdinand and Isabella; at the time his two surviving ships, the *Niña* and the *Pinta*, were threatened by a violent storm off the Azores. Crane insisted (*Letters*, p. 232) that "Cathay" was an ideal of spiritual knowledge for Columbus, as contrasted to the worldly hope for gold on King Ferdinand's part. "Ave Maria" ("Hail Mary") is the traditional invocation of the Virgin Mary in Roman Catholic devotionals. Crane drew on Columbus's "Journal" (summarized in William Carlos Williams's *In the American Grain* [1925]) for the account of preserving the records of the voyage in a barrel in case of shipwreck.
4. A passage from the Roman dramatist Seneca's tragedy *Medea*, which celebrates the heroism of Jason and the Argonauts in surviving the challenge of the sea and founding new nations: "A time will come in distant years when Ocean will loosen the bonds of things and the whole earth's surface will be open to view, and Tethys [Jason's steersman] will discover new worlds; Thule will no longer be the outermost limit of the world." Columbus's son believed that "this prophecy was fulfilled by my father * * * in the year 1492."
5. A collector of church revenues and, with Queen Isabella's confessor Juan Perez in line 7, a Franciscan prior, one of Columbus's advocates in the Spanish court.

O where our Indian emperies lie revealed,   15
Yet lost, all, let this keel one instant yield!

I thought of Genoa;[6] and this truth, now proved,
That made me exile in her streets, stood me
More absolute than ever—biding the moon
Till dawn should clear that dim frontier, first seen   20
—The Chan's[7] great continent. . . . Then faith, not
    fear
Nigh surged me witless. . . . Hearing the surf near—
I, wonder-breathing, kept the watch,—saw
The first palm chevron the first lighted hill.

And lowered. And they came out to us crying,   25
"The Great White Birds!" (O Madre María,[8] still
One ship of these thou grantest safe returning;
Assure us through thy mantle's ageless blue!)
And record of more, floating in a casque,[9]
Was tumbled from us under bare poles scudding;   30
And later hurricanes may claim more pawn. . . .
For here between two worlds, another, harsh,

This third, of water, tests the word; lo, here
Bewilderment and mutiny heap whelming
Laughter, and shadow cuts sleep from the heart   35
Almost as though the Moor's flung scimitar
Found more than flesh to fathom in its fall.
Yet under tempest-lash and surfeitings
Some inmost sob, half-heard, dissuades the abyss,
Merges the wind in measure to the waves,   40

Series on series, infinite,—till eyes
Starved wide on blackened tides, accrete—enclose
This turning rondure whole,[1] this crescent ring
Sun-cusped and zoned with modulated fire
Like pearls that whisper through the Doge's[2] hands   45
—Yet no delirium of jewels! O Fernando,
Take of that eastern shore, this western sea,
Yet yield thy God's, thy Virgin's charity!

—Rush down the plenitude, and you shall see
Isaiah counting famine on this lee![3]   50

·   ·   ·

An herb, a stray branch among salty teeth,
The jellied weeds that drag the shore,—perhaps

6. Italian city, Columbus's birthplace.
7. Khan, title of ruler in the Middle East and China.
8. "O Mother Mary," mother of Jesus.
9. Cask, barrel.
1. An echo of Whitman's apostrophe to the world in *Passage to India* (5.1.1): "O vast Rondure, swimming in space." Whitman invokes Columbus as a "visionary" and "History's type of courage,

action, faith" in stanzas 3 and 6.
2. Ruler of Venice, center of trade with the Orient until supplanted by Atlantic ports after the discovery of America; the Doge offered a jeweled ring in an annual ceremonial marriage with the sea.
3. Loosely paraphrases the Biblical prophet Isaiah's warning of what would be God's punishment for placing material above spiritual values.

Tomorrow's moon will grant us Saltes Bar—
Palos again,[4]—a land cleared of long war.
Some Angelus environs the cordage tree;[5]   55
Dark waters onward shake the dark prow free.

.   .   .

O Thou who sleepest on Thyself,[6] apart
Like ocean athwart lanes of death and birth,
And all the eddying breath between dost search
Cruelly with love thy parable of man,—   60
Inquisitor! incognizable Word
Of Eden and the enchained Sepulchre,
Into thy steep savannahs, burning blue,
Utter to loneliness the sail is true.

Who grindest oar, and arguing the mast   65
Subscribest holocaust of ships, O Thou
Within whose primal scan consummately
The glistening seignories of Ganges swim;—
Who sendest greeting by the corposant,[7]
And Teneriffe's garnet—flamed it in a cloud,   70
Urging through night our passage to the Chan;—
Te Deum laudamus,[8] for thy teeming span!

Of all that amplitude that time explores,
A needle in the sight, suspended north,—
Yielding by inference and discard, faith   75
And true appointment from the hidden shoal:
This disposition that thy night relates
From Moon to Saturn in one sapphire wheel:
The orbic wake of thy once whirling feet,
Elohim, still I hear thy sounding heel!   80

White toil of heaven's cordons, mustering
In holy rings all sails charged to the far
Hushed gleaming fields and pendant seething wheat
Of knowledge,—round thy brows unhooded now
—The kindled Crown! acceded of the poles   85
And biassed by full sails, meridians reel
Thy purpose—still one shore beyond desire!
The sea's green crying towers a-sway, Beyond
And kingdoms
                    naked in the   90
                              trembling heart—
          Te Deum laudamus
                         O Thou Hand of Fire

1926   1927, 1930

4. Spanish port to which Columbus returned in 1493.
5. Columbus hears in the rigging the sounds of the Angelus Dominus, the devotional he had ordered to be sung by the crew in thanksgiving.
6. This introduces a prayer to God (in Hebrew, Elohim), whose tempest and

"Hand of Fire" test Columbus' quest but eventually guarantee it.
7. A glowing ball of fire which, like the "garnet" glow of the volcano on Teneriffe Island, Columbus, in his journal, reported seeing.
8. "O Lord we praise Thee," from the Roman Catholic daily morning prayer.

II. Powhatan's Daughter[9]

*"—Pocahuntus, a well-featured but wanton yong girle . . . of the age
of eleven or twelve years, get the boyes forth with her into the market
place, and make them wheele, falling on their hands, turning their heels
upwards, whom she would followe, and wheele so herself, naked as she
was, all the fort over."*

The Harbor Dawn

<table>
<tr><td>400 years
and more
. . . or is it
from the
soundless
shore of
sleep that
time</td><td>Insistently through sleep—a tide of voices—
They meet you listening midway in your dream,
The long, tired sounds, fog-insulated noises:
Gongs in white surplices, beshrouded wails,
Far strum of fog horns . . . signals dispersed in veils.</td><td>5</td></tr>
</table>

And then a truck will lumber past the wharves
As winch engines begin throbbing on some deck;
Or a drunken stevedore's howl and thud below
Comes echoing alley-upward[1] through dim snow.

And if they take your sleep away sometimes   10
They give it back again. Soft sleeves of sound
Attend the darkling harbor, the pillowed bay;
Somewhere out there in blankness steam

Spills into steam, and wanders, washed away
—Flurried by keen fifings, eddied   15
Among distant chiming buoys—adrift. The sky,
Cool feathery fold, suspends, distills
This wavering slumber. . . . Slowly—
Immemorially the window, the half-covered chair
Ask nothing but this sheath of pallid air.   20

<table>
<tr><td>recalls you
to your
love, there
in a wak-
ing dream
to merge
your seed</td><td>And you beside me, blessèd now while sirens
Sing to us, stealthily weave us into day—
Serenely now, before day claims our eyes
Your cool arms murmurously about me lay.</td><td></td></tr>
</table>

While myriad snowy hands are clustering at the
    panes—   25

    your hands within my hands are deeds;
    my tongue upon your throat—singing
    arms close; eyes wide, undoubtful
        dark
        drink the dawn—   30
  a forest shudders in your hair!

9. Pocahontas, the legendary figure whom Crane associated with the American "continent," a "nature symbol" comparable to the "traditional Hertha of ancient Teutonic mythology." In this section the sights and sounds of modernity are displaced first by fleeting glimpses, then persistent memories, of the past, yielding finally a deep communion with the "River of Time" and revealing something vital, tragic, and sacred in the mythic past. The epigraph is from William Strachey, *History of Travaile into Virginia Britannica* (1615).
1. A pun which translates the slang expression meaning "hoist up" popularized by the comic strip character Alley Oop.

*—with
whom?*

The window goes blond slowly. Frostily clears.
From Cyclopean[2] towers across Manhattan waters
—Two—three bright window-eyes aglitter, disk
The sun, released—aloft with cold gulls hither.   35

*Who is the
woman
with us in
the dawn?
. . . whose
is the flesh
our feet
have moved
upon?*

The fog leans one last moment on the sill.
Under the mistletoe of dreams, a star—
As though to join us at some distant hill—
Turns in the waking west and goes to sleep.
1926   1927, 1930

Van Winkle[3]

*Streets
spread past
store and
factory—
sped by
sunlight
and her
smile . . .*

Macadam, gun-grey as the tunny's[4] belt,
Leaps from Far Rockaway to Golden Gate:[5]
Listen! the miles a hurdy-gurdy grinds—
Down gold arpeggios mile on mile unwinds.

Times earlier, when you hurried off to school,   5
—It is the same hour though a later day—
You walked with Pizarro in a copybook,
And Cortes rode up, reining tautly in—
Firmly as coffee grips the taste,—and away!

There was Priscilla's cheek close in the wind,   10
And Captain Smith, all beard and certainty,
And Rip Van Winkle bowing by the way,—

*Like Mem-
ory, she is
time's
truant, shall
take you
by the
hand . . .*

"Is this Sleepy Hollow,[6] friend—?" And he—

And Rip forgot the office hours,
              and he forgot the pay;   15
Van Winkle sweeps a tenement
              way down on Avenue A,—

The grind-organ says . . . Remember, remember
The cinder pile at the end of the backyard
Where we stoned the family of young   20
Garter snakes under . . . And the monoplanes
We launched—with paper wings and twisted
Rubber bands . . . Recall—recall
              the rapid tongues

2. Cyclops was a one-eyed giant who threatened Ulysses' epic quest in Homer's *Odyssey.*
3. Rip Van Winkle in Washington Irving's tale is the Dutch settler in New York who sleeps for 20 years in the Catskill Mountains, then awakes after the Revolutionary War to find himself an alien in the new America he cannot understand. Crane presents him as his guide on a journey into the past through remembered schoolbook accounts of the Spanish conquistadors Francisco Pizarro (1485–1547) and Hernando Cortez (1471–1541), Priscilla Alden who was courted by Miles Standish in Longfellow's *The Courtship of Miles Standish* (1858), Captain John Smith (1580–1631), the Virginia colonist whose life was reportedly saved by the Indian princess Pocahontas (1595–1617), and personal recollections of incidents from the poet's childhood.
4. Tuna.
5. I.e., a Long Island beach to San Francisco Bay.
6. Hometown of Dutch settlers in Irving's *The Legend of Sleepy Hollow* (1820).

That flittered from under the ash heap day   25
After day whenever your stick discovered
Some sunning inch of unsuspecting fibre—
It flashed back at your thrust, as clean as fire.

And Rip was slowly made aware
      that he, Van Winkle, was not here   30
nor there. He woke and swore he'd seen Broadway
    a Catskill daisy chain in May—

So memory, that strikes a rhyme out of a box,
Or splits a random smell of flowers through glass—
Is it the whip stripped from the lilac tree   35
One day in spring my father took to me,
Or is it the Sabbatical, unconscious smile
My mother almost brought me once from church
And once only, as I recall—?

It flickered through the snow screen, blindly   40
It forsook her at the doorway, it was gone
Before I had left the window. It
Did not return with the kiss in the hall.

Macadam, gun-grey as the tunny's belt,
Leaps from Far Rockaway to Golden Gate. . . .   45
Keep hold of that nickel for car-change, Rip,—
Have you got your *"Times"*—?
And hurry along, Van Winkle—it's getting late!

1927   1927, 1930

The River[7]

. . . and
past the
din and
slogans of
the year—

Stick your patent name on a signboard
brother—all over—going west—young man
Tintex—Japalac—Certain-teed Overalls ads[8]
and land sakes! under the new playbill ripped
in the guaranteed corner—see Bert Williams[9] what?   5
Minstrels when you steal a chicken just
save me the wing for if it isn't
Erie it ain't for miles around a
Mazda—and the telegraphic night coming on Thomas

7. Crane wrote to Mrs. T. W. Simpson (*Letters*, p. 303): "I'm trying in this part of the poem to chart the pioneer experience of our forefathers—and to tell the story backwards * * * on the 'backs' of hoboes. These hoboes are simply 'psychological ponies' to carry the reader across the country and back to the Mississippi, which you will notice is described as a great River of Time. I also unlatch the door to the pure Indian world which opens out in 'The Dance' section, so the reader is gradually led back in time to the pure savage world, while existing at the same time in the present." The poem probes beneath the surface excitements and tawdry debasements of modern commercial life to reveal deep continuities with folk culture and the pagan past. In the opening lines the image of a subway is translated into an image of a luxury express train, The Twentieth Century Limited, traveling from New York City to Chicago.
8. Advertising slogans: trade names of a dye, a varnish, and a brand of overalls.
9. Egbert A. Williams (1876–1922), popular, talented black minstrel show entertainer.

a Ediford[1]—and whistling down the tracks   10
a headlight rushing with the sound—can you
imagine—while an EXPRESS makes time like
SCIENCE—COMMERCE and the HOLYGHOST
RADIO ROARS IN EVERY HOME WE HAVE THE NORTHPOLE
WALLSTREET AND VIRGINBIRTH WITHOUT STONES OR   15
WIRES OR EVEN RUNning brooks connecting ears
and no more sermons windows flashing roar
breathtaking—as you like it . . . eh?[2]

                        So the 20th Century—so
whizzed the Limited—roared by and left   20
three men, still hungry on the tracks, ploddingly
watching the tail lights wizen and converge, slipping gimleted and nearly out of sight.

   .   .   .   .   .

The last bear, shot drinking in the Dakotas
Loped under wires that span the mountain stream.   25
Keen instruments,[3] strung to a vast precision
to those Bind town to town and dream to ticking dream.
whose ad- But some men take their liquor slow—and count
dresses are —Though they'll confess no rosary nor clue—
never near The river's minute by the far brook's year.   30
Under a world of whistles, wires and steam
Caboose-like they go ruminating through
Ohio, Indiana—blind baggage—
To Cheyenne tagging . . . Maybe Kalamazoo.

Time's rendings, time's blendings they construe   35
As final reckonings of fire and snow;
Strange bird-wit, like the elemental gist
Of unwalled winds they offer, singing low
My Old Kentucky Home and *Casey Jones,*
Some Sunny Day. I heard a road-gang chanting so.   40
And afterwards, who had a colt's eyes—one said,
"Jesus! Oh I remember watermelon days!" And sped
High in a cloud of merriment, recalled
"—And when my Aunt Sally Simpson smiled," he
    drawled—
"It was almost Louisiana, long ago."   45
"There's no place like Booneville though, Buddy,"
One said, excising a last burr from his vest,
"—For early trouting." Then peering in the can,
"—But I kept on the tracks." Possessed, resigned,
He trod the fire down pensively and grinned,   50
Spreading dry shingles of a beard. . . .

1. A mocking reference to Thomas A. Edison (1847–1931), inventor of the electric light bulb (trade name "Mazda"), and Henry Ford (1863–1947), automobile manufacturer.
2. An echo of Shakespeare's *As You Like It* (2.1.16–17): "books in the running brooks / Sermons in stones."
3. The telephone and telegraph.

                                                   Behind
My father's cannery works I used to see
Rail-squatters ranged in nomad raillery,
The ancient men—wifeless or runaway
Hobo-trekkers that forever search   55
An empire wilderness of freight and rails.
Each seemed a child, like me, on a loose perch,
Holding to childhood like some termless play.
John, Jake or Charley, hopping the slow freight
—Memphis to Tallahassee—riding the rods,   60
Blind fists of nothing, humpty-dumpty clods.

Yet they touch something like a key perhaps.
From pole to pole across the hills, the states
—They know a body under the wide rain;
Youngsters with eyes like fjords, old reprobates   65
With racetrack jargon,—dotting immensity
They lurk across her, knowing her yonder breast
Snow-silvered, sumac-stained or smoky blue—
Is past the valley-sleepers, south or west.
—As I have trod the rumorous midnights, too,   70

And past the circuit of the lamp's thin flame
(O Nights that brought me to her body bare!)
Have dreamed beyond the print that bound her name.
Trains sounding the long blizzards out—I heard
Wail into distances I knew were hers.   75
Papooses crying on the wind's long mane
Screamed redskin dynasties that fled the brain,
—Dead echoes! But I knew her body there,
Time like a serpent down her shoulder, dark,
And space, an eaglet's wing, laid on her hair.[4]   80

Under the Ozarks, domed by Iron Mountain,
The old gods of the rain lie wrapped in pools
Where eyeless fish curvet a sunken fountain
And re-descend with corn from querulous crows.
Such pilferings make up their timeless eatage,   85
Propitiate them for their timber torn
By iron, iron—always the iron dealt cleavage!
They doze now, below axe and powder horn.
And Pullman breakfasters glide glistening steel
From tunnel into field—iron strides the dew—   90
Straddles the hill, a dance of wheel on wheel.
You have a half-hour's wait at Siskiyou,
Or stay the night and take the next train through.
Southward, near Cairo passing, you can see
The Ohio merging,—borne down Tennessee;   95
And if it's summer and the sun's in dusk

*but who
have
touched
her, know-
ing her
without
name*

*nor the
myths of
her
fathers . . .*

---

4. Feathered headdresses and serpents
are familiar tokens of Indian culture.
William Strachey reported that 17th-
century Indians wore small live snakes
as earrings.

Maybe the breeze will lift the River's musk
—As though the waters breathed that you might know
Memphis Johnny, Steamboat Bill, Missouri Joe.
Oh, lean from the window, if the train slows down,   100
As though you touched hands with some ancient
        clown,
—A little while gaze absently below
And hum *Deep River* with them while they go.

Yes, turn again and sniff once more—look see,
O Sheriff, Brakeman and Authority—   105
Hitch up your pants and crunch another quid,[5]
For you, too, feed the River timelessly.
And few evade full measure of their fate;
Always they smile out eerily what they seem.
I could believe he joked at heaven's gate—   110
Dan Midland—jolted from the cold brake-beam.[6]

Down, down—born pioneers in time's despite,
Grimed tributaries to an ancient flow—
They win no frontier by their wayward plight,
But drift in stillness, as from Jordan's[7] brow.   115

You will not hear it as the sea; even stone
Is not more hushed by gravity . . . But slow,
As loth to take more tribute—sliding prone
Like one whose eyes were buried long ago
The River, spreading, flows—and spends your dream.   120
What are you, lost within this tideless spell?
You are your father's father, and the stream—
A liquid theme that floating niggers swell.

Damp tonnage and alluvial march of days—
Nights turbid, vascular with silted shale   125
And roots surrendered down of moraine clays:
The Mississippi drinks the farthest dale.

O quarrying passion, undertowed sunlight!
The basalt surface drags a jungle grace
Ochreous and lynx-barred in lengthening might;   130
Patience! and you shall reach the biding place!

Over De Soto's bones the freighted floors
Throb past the City storied of three thrones.[8]

5. Chunk of chewing tobacco.
6. Structure on a railroad car where hoboes ride; Dan Midland was a legendary hobo who fell to his death from a train.
7. Palestinian river, celebrated in Negro spirituals as the boundary between earth and heaven.
8. New Orleans, at various times under Spanish, French, and English rule. The body of the Spanish explorer Hernando de Soto (1500–42) was secretly committed to the Mississippi River so that hostile Indians would continue to believe in his divinity. In 1862 Admiral David G. Farragut (1801–70) led a Union fleet up the Mississippi from the Gulf and captured New Orleans. "Ironsides" is a term for warships, whether or not ironclad.

Down two more turns the Mississippi pours
(Anon tall ironsides up from salt lagoons)   135

And flows within itself, heaps itself free.
All fades but one thin skyline 'round . . . Ahead
No embrace opens but the stinging sea;
The River lifts itself from its long bed,

Poised wholly on its dream, a mustard glow   140
Tortured with history, its one will—flow!
—The Passion spreads in wide tongues, choked and
    slow,
Meeting the Gulf, hosannas silently below.

1926   1930

The Dance[9]

*Then you
shall see
her truly—
your blood
remember-
ing its first
invasion of
her secrecy,
its first
encounters
with her
kin, her
chieftain
lover . . .
his shade
that haunts
the lakes
and hills*

The swift red flesh, a winter king—
Who squired the glacier woman down the sky?
She ran the neighing canyons all the spring;
She spouted arms; she rose with maize—to die.

And in the autumn drouth, whose burnished hands   5
With mineral wariness found out the stone
Where prayers, forgotten, streamed mesa sands?
He holds the twilight's dim, perpetual throne.

Mythical brows we saw retiring—loth,
Disturbed and destined, into denser green.   10
Greeting they sped us, on the arrow's oath:
Now lie incorrigibly what years between . . .

There was a bed of leaves, and broken play;
There was a veil upon you, Pocahontas, bride—
O Princess whose brown lap was virgin May;   15
And bridal flanks and eyes hid tawny pride.

I left the village for dogwood. By the canoe
Tugging below the mill-race, I could see
Your hair's keen crescent running, and the blue
First moth of evening take wing stealthily.   20

What laughing chains the water wove and threw!
I learned to catch the trout's moon whisper; I
Drifted how many hours I never knew,
But, watching, saw that fleet young crescent die,—
And one star, swinging, take its place, alone,   25

9. This section presents Crane's imaginary consummation of his adventure
westward and quest into the past. Crane
intended to become "identified with the
Indian and his world before it is over.
* * * Pocahontas (the continent) is the
common basis of our meeting, she survives the extinction of the Indian, who
finally, after being assumed into the elements of nature * * * persists only as a
kind of 'eye' in the sky, or a star
* * *" (*Letters*, p. 307).

Cupped in the larches of the mountain pass—
Until, immortally, it bled into the dawn.
I left my sleek boat nibbling margin grass . . .

I took the portage climb, then chose
A further valley-shed; I could not stop.   30
Feet nozzled wat'ry webs of upper flows;
One white veil gusted from the very top.

O Appalachian Spring! I gained the ledge;
Steep, inaccessible smile that eastward bends
And northward reaches in that violet wedge   35
Of Adirondacks!—wisped of azure wands,

Over how many bluffs, tarns, streams I sped!
—And knew myself within some boding shade:—
Grey tepees tufting the blue knolls ahead,
Smoke swirling through the yellow chestnut glade . . .   40

A distant cloud, a thunder-bud—it grew,
That blanket of the skies: the padded foot
Within,—I heard it; 'til its rhythm drew,
—Siphoned the black pool from the heart's hot root!

A cyclone threshes in the turbine crest,   45
Swooping in eagle feathers down your back;
Know, Maquokeeta,[1] greeting; know death's best;
—Fall, Sachem, strictly as the tamarack!

A birch kneels. All her whistling fingers fly.
The oak grove circles in a crash of leaves;   50
The long moan of a dance is in the sky.
Dance, Maquokeeta: Pocahontas grieves . . .

And every tendon scurries toward the twangs
Of lightning deltaed down your saber hair.
Now snaps the flint in every tooth; red fangs   55
And splay tongues thinly busy the blue air . . .

Dance, Maquokeeta! snake that lives before,
That casts his pelt, and lives beyond![2] Sprout, horn!
Spark, tooth! Medicine-man, relent, restore—
Lie to us,—dance us back the tribal morn!   60

Spears and assemblies: black drums thrusting on—
O yelling battlements,—I, too, was liege
To rainbows currying each pulsant bone:
Surpassed the circumstance, danced out the siege!

And buzzard-circleted, screamed from the stake;   65
I could not pick the arrows from my side.

---

1. The name of an Indian cab-driver who told Crane it meant "Big River" and signified a god whose rains refreshed the plains. "Sachem" (Algonquin): chief.

2. The snake is an archetypal symbol of time, and shedding its skin is a symbol of time's renewal.

Wrapped in that fire, I saw more escorts wake—
Flickering, spring up the hill groins like a tide.

I heard the hush of lava wrestling your arms,
And stag teeth foam about the raven throat;   70
Flame cataracts of heaven in seething swarms
Fed down your anklets to the sunset's moat.

O, like the lizard in the furious noon,
That drops his legs and colors in the sun,
—And laughs, pure serpent, Time itself, and moon   75
Of his own fate, I saw thy change begun!

And saw thee dive to kiss that destiny
Like one white meteor, sacrosanct and blent
At last with all that's consummate and free
There, where the first and last gods keep thy tent.   80

. . .

Thewed of the levin,[3] thunder-shod and lean,
Lo, through what infinite seasons dost thou gaze—
Across what bivouacs of thine angered slain,
And see'st thy bride immortal in the maize!

Totem and fire-gall, slumbering pyramid—[4]   85
Though other calendars now stack the sky,
Thy freedom is her largesse, Prince, and hid
On paths thou knewest best to claim her by.

High unto Labrador the sun strikes free
Her speechless dream of snow, and stirred again,   90
She is the torrent and the singing tree;
And she is virgin to the last of men . . .

West, west and south! winds over Cumberland
And winds across the llano[5] grass resume
Her hair's warm sibilance. Her breasts are fanned   95
O stream by slope and vineyard—into bloom!

And when the caribou slant down for salt
Do arrows thirst and leap? Do antlers shine
Alert, star-triggered in the listening vault
Of dusk?—And are her perfect brows to thine?   100

We danced, O Brave, we danced beyond their farms,
In cobalt desert closures made our vows . . .
Now is the strong prayer folded in thine arms,
The serpent with the eagle in the boughs.

1926   1927, 1930

3. Lightning.
4. Suggests the smoldering volcano Popocatepetl near Mexico City, and the
huge pyramids of the Mayans, used for
sacrificial ceremonies and the astronomi-
cal measurement of time. "Fire-gall":
charred ashes, like the excrescence made
by insects on a tree.
5. Treeless plain.

Indiana

... *and
read her in
a mother's
farewell
gaze.*

The morning glory, climbing the morning long
    Over the lintel on its wiry vine,
Closes before the dusk, furls in its song
      As I close mine . . .

And bison thunder rends my dreams no more   5
    As once my womb was torn, my boy, when you
Yielded your first cry at the prairie's door . . .
      Your father knew

Then, though we'd buried him behind us, far
    Back on the gold trail—then his lost bones
      stirred . . .   10
But you who drop the scythe to grasp the oar
    Knew not, nor heard.

How we, too, Prodigal, once rode off, too—
    Waved Seminary Hill a gay good-bye . . .
We found God lavish there in Colorado   15
      But passing sly.

The pebbles sang, the firecat slunk away
    And glistening through the sluggard freshets came
In golden syllables loosed from the clay
      His gleaming name.   20

A dream called Eldorado[6] was his town,
    It rose up shambling in the nuggets' wake,
It had no charter but a promised crown
      Of claims to stake.

But we,—too late, too early, howsoever—   25
    Won nothing out of fifty-nine[7]—those years—
But gilded promise, yielded to us never,
      And barren tears . . .

The long trail back! I huddled in the shade
    Of wagon-tenting looked out once and saw   30
Bent westward, passing on a stumbling jade
      A homeless squaw—

Perhaps a halfbreed. On her slender back
    She cradled a babe's body, riding without rein.
Her eyes, strange for an Indian's, were not black   35
      But sharp with pain

And like twin stars. They seemed to shun the gaze

---

6. The mythical kingdom of gold which the Spanish searched for in America.
7. The second gold rush (1859) which lured the pioneer family to the mine-fields of Colorado. "Jade" (below): worn-out horse.

Of all our silent men—the long team line—
Until she saw me—when their violet haze
Lit with love shine . . .   40

I held you up—I suddenly the bolder,
Knew that mere words could not have brought us
nearer.
She nodded—and that smile across her shoulder
Will still endear her

As long as Jim, your father's memory, is warm.   45
Yes, Larry, now you're going to sea, remember
You were the first—before Ned and this farm,—
First-born, remember—

And since then—all that's left to me of Jim
Whose folks, like mine, came out of Arrowhead.   50
And you're the only one with eyes like him—
Kentucky bred!

I'm standing still, I'm old, I'm half of stone!
Oh, hold me in those eyes' engaging blue;
There's where the stubborn years gleam and atone,—   55
Where gold is true!

Down the dim turnpike to the river's edge—
Perhaps I'll hear the mare's hoofs to the ford . . .
Write me from Rio[8] . . . and you'll keep your pledge;
I know your word!   60

Come back to Indiana—not too late!
(Or will you be a ranger to the end?)
Good-bye . . . Good-bye . . . oh, I shall always wait
You, Larry, traveller—
                              stranger,   65
                                        son,
                                                —my friend—

1929   1930

III. Cutty Sark[9]

O, the navies old and oaken,
O, the Temeraire no more!
—MELVILLE[1]

I met a man in South Street, tall—
a nervous shark tooth swung on his chain.
His eyes pressed through green grass

8. Rio de Janeiro, Brazil, an expected
port of call for the son, Larry, who is
going to sea.
9. The title is the brand name of a
Scotch whiskey and the name of a clipper
ship famous in the tea trade.

1. Closing lines of Herman Melville's
Temeraire in (*Battle-Pieces*, 1866), a
poem celebrating a famous British warship and those wooden warships rendered obsolete by ironclads.

—green glasses, or bar lights made them
so—   5
   shine—
         GREEN—
             eyes—
stepped out—forgot to look at you
or left you several blocks away—   10

in the nickel-in-the-slot piano jogged
"Stamboul Nights"—weaving somebody's nickel—
     sang—

     O Stamboul Rose—*dreams weave the rose!..*

      Murmurs of Leviathan[2] he spoke,
      and rum was Plato in our heads . . .   15

"It's S.S. *Ala*—Antwerp—now remember kid
to put me out at three she sails on time.
I'm not much good at time any more keep
weakeyed watches sometimes snooze—" his bony hands
got to beating time . . . "A whaler once—   20
I ought to keep time and get over it—I'm a
Democrat—I know what time it is—No
I don't want to know what time it is—that
damned white Arctic killed my time . . ."[3]

     O Stamboul Rose—*drums weave—*   25

"I ran a donkey engine down there on the Canal
in Panama—got tired of that—
then Yucatan selling kitchenware—beads—
have you seen Popocatepetl[4]—birdless mouth
with ashes sifting down—?
           and then the coast again . . ."   30

    Rose of Stamboul O coral Queen—
    teased remnants of the skeletons of cities—
    and galleries, galleries of watergutted lava
    snarling stone—green—drums—drown

Sing!   35
"—that spiracle!" he shot a finger out the door . . .
"O life's a geyser—beautiful—my lungs—
No—I can't live on land—!"

I saw the frontiers gleaming of his mind;

2. Sea monster in the Bible; here the awesome, mysterious white whale in Melville's *Moby-Dick* (1851).
3. Possibly an allusion to the mysterious catastrophe that befalls the protagonist in Poe's novel, the *Narrative of Arthur Gordon Pym* (1838).
4. Volcano near Mexico City.

or are there frontiers—running sands sometimes   40
running sands—somewhere—sands running . . .
Or they may start some white machine that sings.
Then you may laugh and dance the axletree—
steel—silver—kick the traces—and know—

> ATLANTIS[5] ROSE *drums wreathe the rose,*   45
> *the star floats burning in a gulf of tears*
> *and sleep another thousand—*

                              interminably
long since somebody's nickel—stopped—
playing—   50

A wind worried those wicker-neat lapels, the
swinging summer entrances to cooler hells . . .
Outside a wharf truck nearly ran him down
—he lunged up Bowery way while the dawn
was putting the Statue of Liberty out—that   55
torch of hers you know—

I started walking home across the Bridge . . .

                    .   .   .   .   .   .

Blithe Yankee vanities, turreted sprites, winged
                              British repartees, skil-
ful savage sea-girls
that bloomed in the spring—Heave, weave   60
those bright designs in the trade winds drive . . .

> *Sweet opium and tea, Yo-ho!*
> *Pennies for porpoises that bank the keel!*
> *Fins whip the breeze around Japan!*

Bright skysails ticketing the Line, wink round the
          Horn   65
to Frisco, Melbourne . . .
                    Pennants, parabolas—
clipper dreams indelible and ranging,
baronial white on lucky blue!

> Perennial-*Cutty*-trophied-*Sark!*

Thermopylae, Black Prince, Flying Cloud through
          Sunda[6]   70
—scarfed of foam, their bellies veered green espla-
          nades,
locked in wind-humors, ran their eastings down;

---

5. Mythical island in the Atlantic described in Plato's *Timaeus*. The ancients
believed that it sank into the sea as punishment for its sins and might rise again.
6. A bay in the Java Sea. The italicized
names are those of clipper ships.

at Java Head freshened the nip
(sweet opium and tea!)
and turned and left us on the lee . . .

Buntlines tusseling (91 days, 20 hours and anchored!)   75
                              Rainbow, Leander[7]
(last trip a tragedy)—where can you be
Nimbus? and you rivals two—

        a long tack keeping—
                                    Taeping?
                                    Ariel?[8]   80

1926   1927, 1930

IV. Cape Hatteras[9]

The seas all crossed,
weathered the capes, the voyage done . . .
        —WALT WHITMAN

Imponderable the dinosaur
        sinks slow,
                the mammoth saurian
                        ghoul, the eastern
                                Cape . . .
While rises in the west the coastwise range,   5
                slowly the hushed land—
Combustion at the astral core—the dorsal change
Of energy—convulsive shift of sand . . .
But we, who round the capes, the promontories
Where strange tongues vary messages of surf   10
Below grey citadels, repeating to the stars
The ancient names—return home to our own
Hearths, there to eat an apple and recall
The songs that gypsies dealt us at Marseille
Or how the priests walked—slowly through Bombay—   15
Or to read you, Walt,—knowing us in thrall

To that deep wonderment, our native clay
Whose depth of red, eternal flesh of Pocahontas—
Those continental folded aeons, surcharged
With sweetness below derricks, chimneys, tunnels—   20

7. The *Leander* was named for the mythological hero who drowned swimming
the Hellespont to reach his lover.
8. *Taeping* and *Ariel* were rival ships in
the tea trade, the latter named for the
spirit who sings of a "sea-change" of
death into life in Shakespeare's *The
Tempest* (1.2.400).
9. This poem centers on two symbolic
figures: (1) The airplane, first successfully flown by the Wright Brothers at
Kitty Hawk, North Carolina, on Cape
Hatteras, represents man's power and
adventuresome aspirations that have be-

come imperialistic and destructive in an
urban and commercial world; the plane
plunges (like the Indian Maquokeeta
earlier) in a fatal crash but is blessed by
the poet. (2) The poet Walt Whitman
(a "Lounger" and "Saunterer" on the
open road, the beaches of Long Island,
and the streets of Manhattan) mourned
the dead of the Civil War; his "span of
consciousness" encompassed death and a
redeeming vision of human destiny. The
epigraph is from Whitman's *Passage to
India.*

Is veined by all that time has really pledged us . . .
And from above, thin squeaks of radio static,
The captured fume of space foams in our ears—
What whisperings of far watches on the main
Relapsing into silence, while time clears   25
Our lenses, lifts a focus, resurrects
A periscope to glimpse what joys or pain
Our eyes can share or answer—then deflects
Us, shunting to a labyrinth submersed
Where each sees only his dim past reversed . . .   30

But that star-glistered salver of infinity,
The circle, blind crucible of endless space,
Is sluiced by motion,—subjugated never.[1]
Adam and Adam's answer in the forest
Left Hesperus[2] mirrored in the lucid pool.   35
Now the eagle dominates our days, is jurist
Of the ambiguous cloud. We know the strident rule
Of wings imperious . . . Space, instantaneous,
Flickers a moment, consumes us in its smile:
A flash over the horizon—shifting gears—   40
And we have laughter, or more sudden tears.
Dream cancels dream in this new realm of fact
From which we wake into the dream of act;
Seeing himself an atom in a shroud—
Man hears himself an engine in a cloud!   45

"—Recorders ages hence"[3]—ah, syllables of faith!
Walt, tell me, Walt Whitman, if infinity
Be still the same as when you walked the beach
Near Paumanok—your lone patrol—and heard the
    wraith
Through surf, its bird note there a long time   50
    falling . . .[4]
For you, the panoramas and this breed of towers,
Of you—the theme that's statured in the cliff.
O Saunterer on free ways still ahead!
Not this our empire yet, but labyrinth
Wherein your eyes, like the Great Navigator's[5] without
    ship,   55
Gleam from the great stones of each prison crypt
Of canyoned traffic . . . Confronting the Exchange,
Surviving in a world of stocks,—they also range
Across the hills where second timber strays
Back over Connecticut farms, abandoned pastures,—   60
Sea eyes and tidal, undenying, bright with myth!

1. A plane introduces motion into the
infinite reaches of the sky but does not
subjugate it.
2. The evening star.
3. Title and first line of a poem by
Whitman.

4. Allusions to the bird's song of love
and death rising above the surf in
Whitman's *Out of the Cradle Endlessly
Rocking.* Paumanok is an Indian name,
Whitman's favorite, for Long Island.
5. Christopher Columbus.

The nasal whine of power whips a new universe . . .
Where spouting pillars spoor the evening sky,
Under the looming stacks of the gigantic power house
Stars prick the eyes with sharp ammoniac proverbs,   65
New verities, new inklings in the velvet hummed
Of dynamos, where hearing's leash is strummed . . .
Power's script,—wound, bobbin-bound, refined—
Is stropped to the slap of belts on booming spools,
        spurred
Into the bulging bouillon, harnessed jelly of the stars.   70
Towards what? The forked crash of split thunder parts
Our hearing momentwise; but fast in whirling arma-
        tures
As bright as frogs' eyes, giggling in the girth
Of steely gizzards—axle-bound, confined
In coiled precision, bunched in mutual glee   75
The bearings glint,—O murmurless and shined
In oilrinsed circles of blind ecstasy!

Stars scribble on our eyes the frosty sagas,
The gleaming cantos of unvanquished space . . .
O sinewy silver biplane, nudging the wind's withers!   80
There, from Kill Devils Hill at Kitty Hawk
Two brothers in their twinship left the dune;
Warping the gale, the Wright windwrestlers veered
Capeward, then blading the wind's flank, banked and
        spun
What ciphers risen from prophetic script,   85
What marathons new-set between the stars!
The soul, by naphtha fledged into new reaches
Already knows the closer clasp of Mars,—
New latitudes, unknotting, soon give place
To what fierce schedules, rife of doom apace!   90

Behold the dragon's covey—amphibian, ubiquitous
To hedge the seaboard, wrap the headland, ride
The blue's cloud-templed districts unto ether . . .
While Iliads glimmer through eyes raised in pride[6]
Hell's belt springs wider into heaven's plumed side.   95
O bright circumferences, heights employed to fly
War's fiery kennel masked in downy offings,—
This tournament of space, the threshed and chiselled
        height,
Is baited by marauding circles, bludgeon flail
Of rancorous grenades whose screaming petals carve us   100
Wounds that we wrap with theorems sharp as hail!

Wheeled swiftly, wings emerge from larval-silver
        hangars.

---

6. Modern onlookers perceive a grandeur   the exalted poetry in Homer's epic *The*
in the flight of planes and in aerial war-   *Iliad.*
fare comparable to the heroic feats and

Taut motors surge, space-gnawing, into flight;
Through sparkling visibility, outspread, unsleeping,
Wings clip the last peripheries of light . . .   105
Tellurian[7] wind-sleuths on dawn patrol,
Each plane a hurtling javelin of winged ordnance,
Bristle the heights above a screeching gale to hover;
Surely no eye that Sunward Escadrille[8] can cover!
There, meaningful, fledged as the Pleiades[9]   110
With razor sheen they zoom each rapid helix!
Up-chartered choristers of their own speeding
They, cavalcade on escapade, shear Cumulus—
Lay siege and hurdle Cirrus down the skies![1]
While Cetus[2]-like, O thou Dirigible, enormous Lounger   115
Of pendulous auroral beaches,—satellited wide
By convoy planes, moonferrets that rejoin thee
On fleeing balconies as thou dost glide,
—Hast splintered space!

                  Low, shadowed of the Cape,   120
Regard the moving turrets! From grey decks
See scouting griffons[3] rise through gaseous crepe
Hung low . . . until a conch of thunder answers
Cloud-belfries, banging, while searchlights, like
    fencers,
Slit the sky's pancreas of foaming anthracite   125
Toward thee, O Corsair of the typhoon,—pilot, hear!
Thine eyes bicarbonated white by speed, O Skygak,[4] see
How from thy path above the levin's lance
Thou sowest doom thou hast nor time nor chance
To reckon—as thy stilly eyes partake   130
What alcohol of space . . . ! Remember, Falcon-Ace,
Thou hast there in thy wrist a Sanskrit charge
To conjugate infinity's dim marge—[5]
Anew . . . !

        But first, here at this height receive   135
The benediction of the shell's deep, sure reprieve!
Lead-perforated fuselage, escutcheoned wings
Lift agonized quittance, tilting from the invisible brink
Now eagle-bright, now
                 quarry-hid, twist-   140
                       -ing, sink with
Enormous repercussive list-
                 -ings down
    Giddily spiralled
            gauntlets, upturned, unlooping   145

7. Inhabiting the earth.
8. French for air squadron.
9. Name of a constellation of stars.
1. Cumulus and cirrus are types of cloud.
2. The Whale, a constellation of stars.
3. A breed of dogs, here a dog fight between aircraft in "War's fiery kennel"
(line 97).
4. Stunt pilot.
5. I.e., a moral responsibility, as if written in the sacred Sanskrit language of India, to devote his power to spiritual explorations.

In guerrilla sleights, trapped in combustion gyr-
Ing, dance the curdled depth
                          down whizzing
Zodiacs, dashed
                    (now nearing fast the Cape!)   150
                          down gravitation's
                             vortex into crashed
. . . . dispersion . . . into mashed and shapeless de-
     bris. . . .
By Hatteras bunched the beached heap of high
     bravery!

            .   .   .   .   .   .

The stars have grooved our eyes with old persuasions   155
Of love and hatred, birth,—surcease of nations . . .
But who has held the heights more sure than thou,
O Walt!—Ascensions of thee hover in me now
As thou at junctions elegiac, there, of speed
With vast eternity, dost wield the rebound seed!   160
The competent loam, the probable grass,—travail
Of tides awash the pedestal of Everest, fail
Not less than thou in pure impulse inbred
To answer deepest soundings! O, upward from the
     dead
Thou bringest tally, and a pact, new bound   165
Of living brotherhood!

                    Thou, there beyond—
Glacial sierras and the flight of ravens,
Hermetically past condor zones, through zenith havens
Past where the albatross has offered up   170
His last wing-pulse, and downcast as a cup
That's drained, is shivered back to earth—thy wand
Has beat a song, O Walt,—there and beyond!
And this, thine other hand, upon my heart
Is plummet ushered of those tears that start   175
What memories of vigils, bloody, by that Cape,—
Ghoul-mound of man's perversity at balk
And fraternal massacre! Thou, pallid there as chalk,
Hast kept of wounds, O Mourner, all that sum
That then from Appomattox stretched to Somme![6]   180

Cowslip and shad-blow, flaked like tethered foam
Around bared teeth of stallions, bloomed that spring
When first I read thy lines, rife as the loam
Of prairies, yet like breakers cliffward leaping!
O, early following thee, I searched the hill   185
Blue-writ and odor-firm with violets, 'til
With June the mountain laurel broke through green

<hr>

6. Allusions to Whitman's elegiac Civil War poems, to the site of the Union victory over the Confederacy, and to the World War I battleground in France.

And filled the forest with what clustrous sheen!
Potomac lilies,—then the Pontiac rose,
And Klondike edelweiss of occult snows!   190
White banks of moonlight came descending valleys—
How speechful on oak-vizored palisades,
As vibrantly I following down Sequoia alleys
Heard thunder's eloquence through green arcades
Set trumpets breathing in each clump and grass tuft—
   'til   195
Gold autumn, captured, crowned the trembling hill!

Panis Angelicus![7] Eyes tranquil with the blaze
Of love's own diametric gaze, of love's amaze!
Not greatest, thou,—not first, nor last,—but near
And onward yielding past my utmost year.   200
Familiar, thou, as mendicants in public places;
Evasive—too—as dayspring's spreading arc to trace
   is:—
Our Meistersinger,[8] thou set breath in steel;
And it was thou who on the boldest heel
Stood up and flung the span on even wing   205
Of that great Bridge, our Myth, whereof I sing!

Years of the Modern! Propulsions toward what capes?
But thou, *Panis Angelicus*, hast thou not seen
And passed that Barrier that none escapes—
But knows it leastwise as death-strife?—O, something   210
   green,
Beyond all sesames of science was thy choice
Wherewith to bind us throbbing with one voice,
New integers of Roman, Viking, Celt—
Thou, Vedic Caesar,[9] to the greensward[1] knelt!

And now, as launched in abysmal cupolas of space,   215
Toward endless terminals, Easters of speeding light—
Vast engines outward veering with seraphic grace
On clarion cylinders pass out of sight
To course that span of consciousness thou'st named
The Open Road[2]—thy vision is reclaimed!   220
What heritage thou'st signalled to our hands!

And see! the rainbow's arch—how shimmeringly stands
Above the Cape's ghoul-mound, O joyous seer!
Recorders ages hence, yes, they shall hear
In their own veins uncancelled thy sure tread   225
And read thee by the aureole 'round thy head

---

7. "Bread of angels," the invocation in a
Christian hymn.
8. "Mastersinger," the highest rank in
the medieval German guild of poets and
singers.
9. Combines the secular power of Caesar
in the West with the Sanskrit term for
sacred lore.
1. Grass lawn, an allusion to Whitman's
book *Leaves of Grass* and the central
symbol in *Song of Myself*.
2. Central image in Whitman's *Song of
the Open Road*.

Of pasture-shine, *Panis Angelicus!*

> yes, Walt,

Afoot again, and onward without halt,—
Not soon, nor suddenly,—no, never to let go
>> My hand   230
>>> in yours,
>>>> Walt Whitman—

>>>>> so—

1929   1930

V. Three Songs

The one Sestos, the other Abydos hight.[3]
—MARLOWE

Southern Cross[4]

I wanted you, nameless Woman of the South,
No wraith, but utterly—as still more alone
The Southern Cross takes night
And lifts her girdles from her, one by one—
High, cool,   5
>> wide from the slowly smoldering fire
Of lower heavens,—
>>> vaporous scars!

Eve! Magdalene!
>> or Mary, you?

Whatever call—falls vainly on the wave.   10
O simian Venus, homeless Eve,
Unwedded, stumbling gardenless to grieve
Windswept guitars on lonely decks forever;
Finally to answer all within one grave!

And this long wake of phosphor,   15
>> iridescent
Furrow of all our travel—trailed derision!
Eyes crumble at its kiss. Its long-drawn spell
Incites a yell. Slid on that backward vision
The mind is churned to spittle, whispering hell.   20

I wanted you . . . The embers of the Cross
Climbed by aslant and huddling aromatically.
It is blood to remember; it is fire
To stammer back . . . It is
God—your namelessness. And the wash—   25

---

3. From *Hero and Leander* (1598) by the English poet Christopher Marlowe (1564–93), giving the names of the banks at the mouth of the Hellespont where Leander drowned.
4. The title alludes to the constellation of stars visible in the southern hemisphere, identified with the central figure of a woman who embraces the Biblical Eve, Mary Magdalene (the prostitute who became a devoted follower of Jesus), and the Virgin Mary.

All night the water combed you with black
Insolence. You crept out simmering, accomplished.
Water rattled that stinging coil, your
Rehearsed hair—docile, alas, from many arms.
Yes, Eve—wraith of my unloved seed!   30

The Cross, a phantom, buckled—dropped below the
     dawn.
Light drowned the lithic trillions of your spawn.

1926   1927, 1930

*National Winter Garden*⁵

Outspoken buttocks in pink beads
Invite the necessary cloudy clinch
Of bandy eyes. . . . No extra mufflings here:
The world's one flagrant, sweating cinch.

And while legs waken salads in the brain   5
You pick your blonde out neatly through the smoke.
Always you wait for someone else though, always—
(Then rush the nearest exit through the smoke).

Always and last, before the final ring
When all the fireworks blare, begins   10
A tom-tom scrimmage with a somewhere violin,
Some cheapest echo of them all—begins.

And shall we call her whiter than the snow?
Sprayed first with ruby, then with emerald sheen—
Least tearful and least glad (who knows her smile?)   15
A caught slide shows her sandstone grey between.

Her eyes exist in swivellings of her teats,
Pearls whip her hips, a drench of whirling strands.
Her silly snake rings begin to mount, surmount
Each other—turquoise fakes on tinselled hands.   20

We wait that writing pool, her pearls collapsed,
—All but her belly buried in the floor;
And the lewd trounce of a final muted beat!
We flee her spasm through a fleshless door. . . .

Yet, to the empty trapeze of your flesh,   25
O Magdalene, each comes back to die alone.
Then you, the burlesque of our lust—and faith,
Lug us back lifeward—bone by infant bone.

1926   1927, 1930

---

5. A New York burlesque theater.

Virginia

O rain at seven,
Pay-check at eleven—
Keep smiling the boss away,
Mary (what are you going to do?)
Gone seven—gone eleven,   5
And I'm still waiting you—

O blue-eyed Mary with the claret scarf,
Saturday Mary, mine!

It's high carillon
From the popcorn bells!   10
Pigeons by the million—
And Spring in Prince Street[6]
Where green figs gleam
By oyster shells!

O Mary, leaning from the high wheat tower,   15
Let down your golden hair!

High in the noon of May
On cornices of daffodils
The slender violets stray.
Crap-shooting gangs in Bleecker reign,   20
Peonies with pony manes—
Forget-me-nots at windowpanes:

Out of the way-up nickel-dime tower shine,
Cathedral Mary,
shine!—   25

1926   1927, 1930

VI. Quaker Hill[7]

*I see only the ideal. But no
ideals have ever been fully
successful on this earth.*
—ISADORA DUNCAN[8]

*The gentian weaves her fringes,
The maple's loom is red.*
—EMILY DICKINSON[9]

Perspective never withers from their eyes;
They keep that docile edict of the Spring

6. Prince and Bleecker (line 20) are streets in lower Manhattan.
7. The last poem in *The Bridge* to be conceived and finished, *Quaker Hill* takes its title from a New York resort near Pawling, the former site of a Quaker meetinghouse, where Crane lived intermittently between 1925 and 1930.
8. Isadora Duncan (1878–1927), the talented dancer and messianic promoter of the art of the dance. Her personal conduct and seminudity on stage shocked audiences in America, and her dream of achieving social transformation through the dance came to a tragic end in an accident in 1927. Crane had applauded her performance in Cleveland in 1922 when she urged a booing audience to read Whitman's poems.
9. The opening lines of a Dickinson poem about death.

That blends March with August Antarctic skies:
These are but cows that see no other thing
Than grass and snow, and their own inner being   5
Through the rich halo that they do not trouble
Even to cast upon the seasons fleeting
Though they should thin and die on last year's stubble.

And they are awkward, ponderous and uncoy . . .
While we who press the cider mill, regarding them—   10
We, who with pledges taste the bright annoy
Of friendship's acid wine, retarding phlegm,
Shifting reprisals ('til who shall tell us when
The jest is too sharp to be kindly?) boast
Much of our store of faith in other men   15
Who would, ourselves, stalk down the merriest ghost.

Above them old Mizzentop,[1] palatial white
Hostelry—floor by floor to cinquefoil[2] dormer
Portholes the ceilings stack their stoic height.
Long tiers of windows staring out toward former   20
Faces—loose panes crown the hill and gleam
At sunset with a silent, cobwebbed patience . . .
See them, like eyes that still uphold some dream
Through mapled vistas, cancelled reservations!

High from the central cupola, they say   25
One's glance could cross the borders of three states;
But I have seen death's stare in slow survey
From four horizons that no one relates . . .
Weekenders avid of their turf-won scores,
Here three hours from the semaphores, the Czars   30
Of golf, by twos and threes in plaid plusfours
Alight with sticks abristle and cigars.

This was the Promised Land, and still it is
To the persuasive suburban land agent
In bootleg roadhouses where the gin fizz   35
Bubbles in time to Hollywood's new love-nest pageant.
Fresh from the radio in the old Meeting House
(Now the New Avalon Hotel) volcanoes roar
A welcome to highsteppers that no mouse
Who saw the Friends there ever heard before.   40

What cunning neighbors history has in fine!
The woodlouse mortgages the ancient deal
Table that Powitzky buys for only nine-
Ty-five at Adams' auction,—eats the seal,
The spinster polish of antiquity . . .   45
Who holds the lease on time and on disgrace?

1. An abandoned hotel; the name means   2. Ornamental five-sectioned window.
the aftermast of a ship.

What eats the pattern with ubiquity?
Where are my kinsmen and the patriarch race?

The resigned factions of the dead preside.
Dead rangers bled their comfort on the snow;   50
But I must ask slain Iroquois to guide
Me farther than scalped Yankees knew to go:
Shoulder the curse of sundered parentage,[3]
Wait for the postman driving from Birch Hill
With birthright by blackmail,[4] the arrant page   55
That unfolds a new destiny to fill. . . .

So, must we from the hawk's far stemming view,
Must we descend as worm's eye to construe
Our love of all we touch, and take it to the Gate
As humbly as a guest who knows himself too late,   60
His news already told? Yes, while the heart is wrung,
Arise—yes, take this sheaf of dust upon your tongue!
In one last angelus lift throbbing throat—
Listen, transmuting silence with that stilly note

Of pain that Emily, that Isadora knew!   65
While high from dim elm-chancels hung with dew,
That triple-noted clause of moonlight—
Yes, whip-poor-will, unhusks the heart of fright,
Breaks us and saves, yes, breaks the heart, yet yields
That patience that is armour and that shields   70
Love from despair—when love foresees the end—
Leaf after autumnal leaf
             break off,
                    descend—
                          descend—   75

1929   1930

VII. The Tunnel[5]

*To Find the Western path
Right thro' the Gates of Wrath.*
        —BLAKE[6]

Performances, assortments, résumés—
Up Times Square to Columbus Circle lights
Channel the congresses, nightly sessions,
Refractions of the thousand theatres, faces—
Mysterious kitchens. . . . You shall search them all.   5

3. An allusion to Crane's parents' divorce and an image of the "cleavage" between America's present and its past.
4. An allusion to Crane's dispute with his mother over his claim to an inheritance ("birthright") from his grandmother.
5. *The Tunnel*, representing the epic convention of a descent into hell, renders the poet's descent into a subway and the interior of his mind, followed by the resurgence of desperate hope when he emerges to see the Bridge and the East River leading to the distant sea.
6. The opening lines of *Morning*, by the visionary English poet William Blake (1757–1827), which foresees the return of dawn and the triumph of love after facing the crisis which tests it.

Someday by heart you'll learn each famous sight
And watch the curtain lift in hell's despite;
You'll find the garden in the third act dead,
Finger your knees—and wish yourself in bed
With tabloid crime-sheets perched in easy sight.   10

> Then let you reach your hat
> and go.
> As usual, let you—also
> walking down—exclaim
> to twelve upward leaving   15
> a subscription praise
> for what time slays.

Or can't you quite make up your mind to ride;
A walk is better underneath the L[7] a brisk
Ten blocks or so before? But you find yourself   20
Preparing penguin flexions of the arms,—
As usual you will meet the scuttle yawn:
The subway yawns the quickest promise home.

Be minimum, then, to swim the hiving swarms
Out of the Square, the Circle burning bright—[8]   25
Avoid the glass doors gyring at your right,
Where boxed alone a second, eyes take fright
—Quite unprepared rush naked back to light:
And down beside the turnstile press the coin
Into the slot. The gongs already rattle.   30

> And so
> of cities you bespeak
> subways, rivered under streets
> and rivers. . . . In the car
> the overtone of motion   35
> underground, the monotone
> of motion is the sound
> of other faces, also underground—

"Let's have a pencil Jimmy—living now
at Floral Park   40
Flatbush—on the fourth of July—
like a pigeon's muddy dream—potatoes
to dig in the field—travlin the town—too—
night after night—the Culver line—the
girls all shaping up—it used to be—"   45

Our tongues recant like beaten weather vanes.
This answer lives like verdigris,[9] like hair

7. Abbreviation: elevated railway.
8. An echo of Blake's poem *The Tiger*: "Tiger! Tiger! burning bright / In the forests of the night, / What immortal hand or eye / Could frame thy fearful symmetry?" Also the lighted sign indicating a subway station.
9. Green coating or stain on copper.

Beyond extinction, surcease of the bone;
And repetition freezes—"What

"what do you want? getting weak on the links?   50
fandaddle daddy don't ask for change—IS THIS
FOURTEENTH? it's half past six she said—if
you don't like my gate why did you
swing on it, why *didja*
swing on it   55
anyhow—"

        And somehow anyhow swing—

The phonographs of hades in the brain
Are tunnels that re-wind themselves, and love
A burnt match skating in a urinal—   60
Somewhere above Fourteenth TAKE THE EXPRESS
To brush some new presentiment of pain—

"But I want service in this office SERVICE
I said—after
the show she cried a little afterwards but—"   65

Whose head is swinging from the swollen strap?[1]
Whose body smokes along the bitten rails,
Bursts from a smoldering bundle far behind
In back forks of the chasms of the brain,—
Puffs from a riven stump far out behind   70
In interborough fissures of the mind . . . ?

And why do I often meet your visage here,
Your eyes like agate lanterns—on and on
Below the toothpaste and the dandruff ads?
—And did their riding eyes right through your side,   75
And did their eyes like unwashed platters ride?
And Death, aloft,—gigantically down
Probing through you—toward me, O evermore![2]
And when they dragged your retching flesh,
Your trembling hands that night through Baltimore—   80
That last night on the ballot rounds, did you
Shaking, did you deny the ticket, Poe?

For Gravesend Manor change at Chambers Street.
The platform hurries along to a dead stop.

The intent escalator lifts a serenade   85
Stilly

1. The images of disfigurement and violent death in this section introduce the
tortured figure and haunted imagination
of Edgar Allan Poe. He died in Baltimore in 1849, reputedly of brutal mistreatment while drunk at the hands of a
political gang who wanted him to cast
multiple ballots illegally for their
"ticket."
2. Echoes of the line "Death looks gigantically down" in *The City in the Sea*,
and of the refrain "Nevermore" in *The
Raven*, by Poe.

Of shoes, umbrellas, each eye attending its shoe, then
Bolting outright somewhere above where streets
Burst suddenly in rain. . . . The gongs recur:
Elbows and levers, guard and hissing door.
Thunder is galvothermic[3] here below. . . . The car   90
Wheels off. The train rounds, bending to a scream,
Taking the final level for the dive
Under the river—
And somewhat emptier than before,   95
Demented, for a hitching second, humps; then
Lets go. . . . Toward corners of the floor
Newspapers wing, revolve and wing.
Blank windows gargle signals through the roar.

And does the Daemon take you home, also,   100
Wop washerwoman, with the bandaged hair?
After the corridors are swept, the cuspidors—
The gaunt sky-barracks cleanly now, and bare,
O Genoese,[4] do you bring mother eyes and hands
Back home to children and to golden hair?   105

Daemon, demurring and eventful yawn!
Whose hideous laughter is a bellows mirth
—Or the muffled slaughter of a day in birth—
O cruelly to inoculate the brinking dawn
With antennae toward worlds that glow and sink;—   110
To spoon us out more liquid than the dim
Locution of the eldest star, and pack
The conscience navelled in the plunging wind,
Umbilical to call—and straightway die!

O caught like pennies beneath soot and steam,   115
Kiss of our agony thou gatherest;
Condensed, thou takest all—shrill ganglia
Impassioned with some song we fail to keep.
And yet, like Lazarus,[5] to feel the slope,
The sod and billow breaking,—lifting ground,   120
—A sound of waters bending astride the sky
Unceasing with some Word that will not die . . .!

  .   .   .   .

A tugboat, wheezing wreaths of steam,
Lunged past, with one galvanic blare stove up the
    River.
I counted the echoes assembling, one after one,   125
Searching, thumbing the midnight on the piers.
Lights, coasting, left the oily tympanum of waters;
The blackness somewhere gouged glass on a sky.

---

3. I.e., galvanothermic, producing heat
by electricity.
4. The Italian-American mother is called
Genoese to recall Genoa, Italy, the
birthplace of Columbus.
5. Lazarus was resurrected from the
grave by Jesus in John 11.43–44.

And this thy harbor, O my City, I have driven under,
Tossed from the coil of ticking towers. . . .   130
    Tomorrow,
And to be. . . . Here by the River that is East—
Here at the waters' edge the hands drop memory;
Shadowless in that abyss they unaccounting lie.
How far away the star has pooled the sea—   135
Or shall the hands be drawn away, to die?

Kiss of our agony Thou gatherest,
          O Hand of Fire
              gatherest —

1926   1927, 1930

VIII. Atlantis[6]

*Music is then the knowledge of that which relates to love in harmony and
system.*
                                      —PLATO[7]

Through the bound cable strands, the arching path
Upward, veering with light, the flight of strings,—
Taut miles of shuttling moonlight syncopate
The whispered rush, telepathy of wires.
Up the index of night, granite and steel—   5
Transparent meshes—fleckless the gleaming staves—
Sibylline[8] voices flicker, waveringly stream
As though a god were issue of the strings. . . .

And through that cordage, threading with its call
One arc synoptic of all tides below—   10
Their labyrinthine mouths of history
Pouring reply as though all ships at sea
Complighted in one vibrant breath made cry,—
"Make thy love sure—to weave whose song we ply!"
—From black embankments, moveless soundings   15
    hailed,
So seven oceans answer from their dream.

And on, obliquely up bright carrier bars
New octaves trestle the twin monoliths
Beyond whose frosted capes the moon bequeaths
Two worlds of sleep (O arching strands of song!)—   20
Onward and up the crystal-flooded aisle
White tempest nets file upward, upward ring
With silver terraces the humming spars,
The loft of vision, palladium helm of stars.

---

6. In this section, the first that Crane wrote, the poet imagines the perfect unison of his song with the vision incarnate in *The Bridge*, celebrates the fusion of the sacred and the aesthetic which spans the seas and eras of history, and envisions the yet incomplete fulfillment of his quest.
7. From Plato's *Republic* (III, 403).
8. Enigmatic, prophetic; issuing from ancient oracles, sibyls.

Sheerly the eyes, like seagulls stung with rime—   25
Slit and propelled by glistening fins of light—
Pick biting way up towering looms that press
Sidelong with flight of blade on tendon blade
—Tomorrows into yesteryear—and link
What cipher-script of time no traveller reads   30
But who, through smoking pyres of love and death,
Searches the timeless laugh of mythic spears.

Like hails, farewells—up planet-sequined heights
Some trillion whispering hammers glimmer Tyre:[9]
Serenely, sharply up the long anvil cry   35
Of inchling æons silence rivets Troy.
And you, aloft there—Jason![1] hesting Shout!
Still wrapping harness to the swarming air!
Silvery the rushing wake, surpassing call,
Beams yelling Æolus![2] splintered in the straits!   40

From gulfs unfolding, terrible of drums,
Tall Vision-of-the-Voyage, tensely spare—
Bridge, lifting night to cycloramic crest
Of deepest day—O Choir, translating time
Into what multitudinous Verb the suns   45
And synergy of waters ever fuse, recast
In myriad syllables,—Psalm of Cathay!
O Love, thy white, pervasive Paradigm . . .!

We left the haven hanging in the night—
Sheened harbor lanterns backward fled the keel.   50
Pacific here at time's end, bearing corn,—
Eyes stammer through the pangs of dust and steel.
And still the circular, indubitable frieze
Of heaven's meditation, yoking wave
To kneeling wave, one song devoutly binds—   55
The vernal strophe chimes from deathless strings!

O Thou steeled Cognizance whose leap commits
The agile precincts of the lark's return;
Within whose lariat sweep encinctured sing
In single chrysalis the many twain,—   60
Of stars Thou art the stitch and stallion glow
And like an organ, Thou, with sound of doom—
Sight, sound and flesh Thou leadest from time's realm
As love strikes clear direction for the helm.

Swift peal of secular light, intrinsic Myth   65
Whose fell unshadow is death's utter wound,—
O River-throated—iridescently upborne
Through the bright drench and fabric of our veins;

9. Ancient Phoenician sea-going city.   search for the Golden Fleece.
1. Leader of the Greek Argonauts in the   2. Keeper of the winds in Homer's epics.

With white escarpments swinging into light,
Sustained in tears the cities are endowed   70
And justified conclamant with ripe fields
Revolving through their harvests in sweet torment.

Forever Deity's glittering Pledge, O Thou
Whose canticle fresh chemistry assigns
To wrapt inception and beatitude,—   75
Always through blinding cables, to our joy,
Of thy white seizure springs the prophecy:
Always through spiring cordage, pyramids
Of silver sequel, Deity's young name
Kinetic of white choiring wings . . . ascends.   80

Migrations that must needs void memory,
Inventions that cobblestone the heart,—
Unspeakable Thou Bridge to Thee, O Love.
Thy pardon for this history, whitest Flower,
O Answerer of all,—Anemone,[3]—   85
Now while thy petals spend the suns about us, hold—
(O Thou whose radiance doth inherit me)
Atlantis,—hold thy floating singer late!

So to thine Everpresence, beyond time,
Like spears ensanguined of one tolling star   90
That bleeds infinity—the orphic[4] strings,
Sidereal phalanxes, leap and converge:
—One Song, one Bridge of Fire! Is it Cathay,
Now pity steeps the grass and rainbows ring
The serpent with the eagle in the leaves . . .?   95
Whispers antiphonal in azure swing.

1926   1930

A Name for All

Moonmoth and grasshopper that flee our page
And still wing on, untarnished of the name
We pinion to your bodies to assuage
Our envy of your freedom—we must maim

Because we are usurpers, and chagrined—   5
And take the wing and scar it in the hand.
Names we have, even, to clap on the wind;
But we must die, as you, to understand.

3. Flower. At the end of the strife-torn love affair of the god Venus and Adonis in Greek mythology, the white anemone sprang from her tears, the red from Adonis's blood.
4. Prophetic and enchanting, so named from the mythological poet and musician Orpheus, whose lyre or harp could charm even animals and the powers of hell. Even after his brutal murder by the Maenads, his severed head kept singing as it floated down the river.

I dreamed that all men dropped their names, and sang
As only they can praise, who build their days   10
With fin and hoof, with wing and sweetened fang
Struck free and holy in one Name always.

1928   1929, 1933

O Carib Isle[1]

The tarantula rattling at the lily's foot
Across the feet of the dead, laid in white sand
Near the coral beach—nor zigzag fiddle crabs
Side-stilting from the path (that shift, subvert
And anagrammatize your name)—No, nothing here   5
Below the palsy that one eucalyptus lifts
In wrinkled shadows—mourns.
                              And yet suppose
I count these nacreous frames of tropic death,
Brutal necklaces of shells around each grave   10
Squared off so carefully. Then

To the white sand I may speak a name, fertile
Albeit in a stranger tongue. Tree names, flower names
Deliberate, gainsay death's brittle crypt. Meanwhile
The wind that knots itself in one great death—   15
Coils and withdraws. So syllables want breath.

But where is the Captain of this doubloon isle
Without a turnstile? Who but catchword crabs
Patrols the dry groins of the underbrush?
What man, or What   20
Is Commissioner of mildew throughout the ambushed
    senses?
His Carib mathematics web the eyes' baked lenses!

Under the poinciana, of a noon or afternoon
Let fiery blossoms clot the light, render my ghost
Sieved upward, white and black along the air   25
Until it meets the blue's comedian host.

Let not the pilgrim see himself again
For slow evisceration bound like those huge terrapin[2]
Each daybreak on the wharf, their brine-caked eyes;

---

1. This poem was written at the same time as *Repose of Rivers*. Its original title, *Kidd's Cove*, alluded to the pirate Captain William Kidd (c. 1645–1701), who reputedly buried treasure in the Caribbean Islands. The poem opens with a scene of death and isolated graves (on a hurricane-swept Caribbean island) which Crane in later stanzas imagines his own. He tries to transfigure the deaths in a commemorative requiem of names and images, and partially succeeds, only to recognize that his power subsides and that Satan-sponsored shells are the sole relics of the life and inspiration.
2. Tortoises. Melville described them in *The Encantadas* (1856) and reported the sailors' superstition that evil officers were transformed into tortoises.

—Spiked, overturned; such thunder in their strain!   30
And clenched beaks coughing for the surge again!

Slagged[3] of the hurricane—I, cast within its flow,
Congeal by afternoons here, satin and vacant.
You have given me the shell, Satan,—carbonic amulet
Sere of the sun exploded in the sea.   35
1926   1927, 1933

3. I.e., cast off as a by-product in the process of refining ore.

LANGSTON HUGHES
1902–1967

Of the writers who contributed to the "Harlem Renaissance" in the 1920s,
the one with the most durable and varied talent was Langston Hughes, who
first gained public attention as the "busboy poet" and later was known as
the Poet Laureate of Harlem. He introduced the rhythms of jazz and the
blues into his lyric verse, developed subjects from Negro life and racial
themes, and contributed to the strengthening of black consciousness and
racial pride that was the Harlem Renaissance's legacy to the more militant
decades of the '50s and '60s.

James Langston Hughes was born in Joplin, Missouri, to parents who
soon separated. His principal home before 1914 was with his maternal
grandmother. But he lived intermittently with his mother (who wrote
poems occasionally, insisted on an integrated school for her son, and took
him to the theater) and briefly with his father, who had developed contempt for Negroes who accepted their lot in the United States and had
moved to a ranch in Mexico. Hughes learned German and Spanish at the
instigation of his father and began to write poetry while living with him in
Mexico after graduating from high school in 1920, and his father financed
his one unsuccessful year at Columbia University in 1921–22. Yet before
leaving Mexico for Columbia, Hughes had been brought to the verge of suicide and to an intense hatred for his father which never healed.

His intellectual awakening had begun earlier at high school in Cleveland
while living with his mother and stepfather. The famous Karamu settlement house, social occasions at the home of a high school teacher (Helen
M. Chesnutt, daughter of the black novelist Charles W. Chesnutt), the enthusiasm of another teacher, Miss Ethel Weimer, for Shakespeare and Carl
Sandburg, and the racial consciousness heightened by personal experience
and his reading in the Negro journal *The Crisis*—all helped to stimulate
the imagination of the young poet. *The Crisis* published his early poems
sporadically during the two years (1923–24) when he shipped out as a merchant seaman, traveled in Africa and the Mediterranean, and worked for a
while in a Paris nightclub. It was there that Dr. Alain Locke, chief black
proponent of the "Harlem Renaissance," met him and arranged to include
eleven poems in his important anthology, *The New Negro* (1925). On
returning to the States, Hughes was working as busboy in a Washington,
D.C., hotel when he ventured to show some poems to the white poet

Vachel Lindsay, who included them in a public reading that night and brought Hughes to the attention of the local press. He was by then familiar with the leaders of the "Harlem Renaissance," and one of its principal white supporters, the novelist Carl Van Vechten, was instrumental in securing publication of Hughes's first volume, *The Weary Blues*, in 1926.

Hughes was enrolled in Lincoln University, supported by grants from the white philanthropist Mrs. Amy Spingarn, when his second volume appeared (*Fine Clothes to the Jew*, 1927) and he had completed an extensive tour of the South, reading his poems, by the time he graduated from Lincoln in 1929. Grants from a white patron, Mrs. Rufus O. Mason, enabled him to live in New York after 1928, but he terminated the arrangement in 1930 shortly after completing his first novel, *Not Without Laughter*, which won the Harmon Gold Award for Literature. From then on he attempted to live on his earnings as a writer. He conducted a long reading tour in the South in 1931, reaching countless communities despite the fact that his protest poems were controversial among Negroes at Hampton Institute and that his reading at the University of North Carolina aroused the animosities of whites and so ruled out later appearances on other white campuses. He toured Russia, writing on Asia and race relations for Moscow journals. His friendship there with the novelist Arthur Koestler and his discovery of the short stories of the English novelist D. H. Lawrence revived his interest in fiction, and shortly after his return in 1933 appeared his first volume of short stories, *The Ways of White Folks* (1934).

Hughes's various literary activities were prodigious during the '30s and later decades. He engaged in radical protest in California and submitted a speech to the leftist First American Writer's Conference in New York City in 1935. In that year an earlier play, *The Mulatto*, appeared on Broadway. He covered the Spanish Civil War for the Baltimore *Afro-American* in 1937. He founded black theaters in Harlem, Los Angeles, and Chicago, published numerous anthologies of Negro writing and histories of eminent Negroes, wrote two autobiographical volumes (*The Big Sea*, 1940, and *I Wonder as I Wander*, 1956), turned his play *Troubled Island* into the libretto for an opera by the black composer William Grant Still (1949), and collaborated on the script for a Hollywood film. In 1943 he began a series of newspaper sketches centering on an engagingly comic urban Negro named Jesse B. Semple which became very popular and were collected in four volumes. The vignettes are a vivid reflection of life in Negro urban communities and present pointed comment on public affairs and the injustices of white racism. Besides the many volumes of his own verse, including *Montage of a Dream Deferred* (1951), he published translations of the Spanish playwright Federico García Lorca's *Blood Wedding* (1951) and the poems of the Chilean poet Gabriela Mistral (1957).

Hughes's poetry, liberated by the example of Sandburg's free verse forms, aimed from the start for utter directness and simplicity, not only in poems like *To a Little Lover-Lass, Dead*, which have no racial content and do not employ the distinctive diction and cadences of Negro idioms, but also in the "90 percent" of his work which he said attempts to "explain and illuminate the Negro condition in America." (Quoted by James Emanuel, *Langston Hughes*, p. 68.) While Hughes never militantly repudiated cooperation with the white community, the poems which protest against white racism are boldly direct.

Simple stanza patterns and strict rhyme schemes derived from blues songs enabled him to capture the ambience of the setting as well as the rhythms of jazz music. At his best, in *Love*, a direct allusion to a Negro folk hero charges a celebration of all human love with paradox and tragic feeling.

The Negro Speaks of Rivers

I've known rivers:
I've known rivers ancient as the world and older than the
     flow of human blood in human veins.

My soul has grown deep like the rivers.

I bathed in the Euphrates[1] when dawns were young.   5
I built my hut near the Congo and it lulled me to sleep.
I looked upon the Nile and raised the pyramids above it.
I heard the singing of the Mississippi when Abe Lincoln
     went down to New Orleans, and I've seen its muddy
     bosom turn all golden in the sunset.   10

I've known rivers:
Ancient, dusky rivers.

My soul has grown deep like the rivers.

1920   1921, 1926

Mother to Son

Well, son, I'll tell you:
Life for me ain't been no crystal stair.
It's had tacks in it,
And splinters,
And boards torn up,   5
And places with no carpet on the floor—
Bare.
But all the time
I'se been a-climbin' on,
And reachin' landin's,   10
And turnin' corners,
And sometimes goin' in the dark
Where there ain't been no light.
So boy, don't you turn back.
Don't you set down on the steps   15
'Cause you finds it's kinder hard.
Don't you fall now—
For I'se still goin', honey,
I'se still climbin',
And life for me ain't been no crystal stair.   20

                                     1922, 1926

1. The Euphrates River, cradle of ancient Babylonian civilization, flows from Turkey through Syria and Iraq; the Congo flows from the Republic of the Congo in central Africa into the Atlantic Ocean; the Nile, site of ancient Egyptian civilization, empties into the Mediterranean Sea.

The South

The lazy, laughing South
With blood on its mouth.
The sunny-faced South,
    Beast-strong,
    Idiot-brained.   5
The child-minded South
Scratching in the dead fire's ashes
For a Negro's bones.
    Cotton and the moon,
    Warmth, earth, warmth,   10
    The sky, the sun, the stars,
    The magnolia-scented South.
Beautiful, like a woman,
Seductive as a dark-eyed whore,
    Passionate, cruel,   15
    Honey-lipped, syphilitic—
    That is the South.
And I, who am black, would love her
But she spits in my face.
And I, who am black,   20
Would give her many rare gifts
But she turns her back upon me.
    So now I seek the North—
    The cold-faced North,
    For she, they say,   25
    Is a kinder mistress,
And in her house my children
May escape the spell of the South.

                          1922, 1926

Dream Variations

To fling my arms wide
In some place of the sun,
To whirl and to dance
Till the white day is done.
Then rest at cool evening   5
Beneath a tall tree
While night comes on gently,
    Dark like me—
That is my dream!

To fling my arms wide   10
In the face of the sun,
Dance! Whirl! Whirl!
Till the quick day is done.
Rest at pale evening . . .
A tall, slim tree . . .   15
Night coming tenderly
    Black like me.

1922   1924, 1926

To a Little Lover-Lass, Dead

She
Who searched for lovers
In the night
Has gone the quiet way
Into the still,   5
Dark land of death
Beyond the rim of day.

Now like a little lonely waif
She walks
An endless street   10
And gives her kiss to nothingness.
Would God his lips were sweet!

                                                     1926

Soledad[1]

A Cuban Portrait

The shadows
Of too many nights of love
Have fallen beneath your eyes.
Your eyes,
So full of pain and passion,   5
So full of lies.
So full of pain and passion,
Soledad,
So deeply scarred,
So still with silent cries.   10

                                                     1926

Mulatto

I am your son, white man!

Georgia dusk
And the turpentine woods.
One of the pillars of the temple fell.

   You are my son!   5
   Like hell!

The moon over the turpentine woods.
The Southern night
Full of stars,
Great big yellow stars.   10
   What's a body but a toy?
   Juicy bodies

---

1. Spanish for solitude, loneliness, state of being orphaned.

Of nigger wenches
Blue black
Against black fences.   15
O, you little bastard boy,
What's a body but a toy?
The scent of pine wood stings the soft night air.
  What's the body of your mother?
Silver moonlight everywhere.   20
  What's the body of your mother?
Sharp pine scent in the evening air.
      A nigger night,
      A nigger joy,
      A little yellow   25
      Bastard boy.

  Naw, you ain't my brother.
  Niggers ain't my brother.

  Not ever.
  Niggers ain't my brother.   30

The Southern night is full of stars,
Great big yellow stars.
      O, sweet as earth,
      Dusk dark bodies
      Give sweet birth   35
To little yellow bastard boys.

  Git on back there in the night,
  You ain't white.

The bright stars scatter everywhere.
Pine wood scent in the evening air.   40
      A nigger night,
      A nigger joy.

  I am your son, white man!

      A little yellow
      Bastard boy.   45

                                                           1927

Song for a Dark Girl

Way Down South in Dixie[1]
  (Break the heart of me)
They hung my black young lover
  To a cross roads tree.

---

1. This ironic refrain is the last line of *Dixie*, the popular minstrel song, probably composed by Daniel D. Emmett (1815–1904), which became the rallying cry of southern patriotism during and after the Civil War.

Way Down South in Dixie   5
   (Bruised body high in air)
I asked the white Lord Jesus
   What was the use of prayer.

Way Down South in Dixie
   (Break the heart of me)   10
Love is a naked shadow
   On a gnarled and naked tree.

                    1927

Young Gal's Blues

I'm gonna walk to the graveyard
'Hind ma friend Miss Cora Lee.
Gonna walk to the graveyard
'Hind ma dear friend Cora Lee
Cause when I'm dead some   5
Body'll have to walk behind me.

I'm goin' to the po' house
To see ma old Aunt Clew.
Goin' to the po' house
To see ma old Aunt Clew.   10
When I'm old an' ugly
I'll want to see somebody, too.

The po' house is lonely
An' the grave is cold.
O, the po' house is lonely,   15
The graveyard grave is cold.
But I'd rather be dead than
To be ugly an' old.

When love is gone what
Can a young gal do?   20
When love is gone, O,
What can a young gal do?
Keep on a-lovin' me, daddy,
Cause I don't want to be blue.

                    1927

Morning After

I was so sick last night I
Didn't hardly know my mind.
So sick last night I
Didn't know my mind.
I drunk some bad licker that   5
Almost made me blind.

Had a dream last night I
Thought I was in hell.
I drempt last night I
Thought I was in hell.   10
Woke up and looked around me—
Babe, your mouth was open like a well.

I said, Baby! Baby!
Please don't snore so loud.
Baby! Please!   15
Please don't snore so loud.
You jest a little bit o' woman but you
Sound like a great big crowd.

1942

Love

Love is a wild wonder
And stars that sing,
Rocks that burst asunder
And mountains that take wing.

John Henry[1] with his hammer   5
Makes a little spark.
That little spark is love
Dying in the dark.

1942

Uncle Tom[2]

Within—
The beaten pride.
Without—
The grinning face,
The low, obsequious,   5
Double bow,
The sly and servile grace
Of one the white folks
Long ago
Taught well   10
To know his
Place.

1944

Vagabonds

We are the desperate
Who do not care,

---

1. **Legendary black hero, celebrated in** ballads and tall tales for driving steel in competition with a steam drill; he outpaced the drill but died from the effort "with the hammer in his hand."
2. **The name of the central Negro char**acter in the antislavery novel *Uncle Tom's Cabin*, by Harriet Beecher Stowe (1811–96), which has since come to signify a Negro who accepts domination by whites and masks his resentment or his attempts to circumvent it.

The hungry
Who have nowhere
To eat,   5
No place to sleep,
The tearless
Who cannot
Weep.

1941, 1947

Trumpet Player

The Negro
With the trumpet at his lips
Has dark moons of weariness
Beneath his eyes
Where the smoldering memory   5
Of slave ships
Blazed to the crack of whips
About his thighs.

The Negro
With the trumpet at his lips   10
Has a head of vibrant hair
Tamed down,
Patent-leathered now
Until it gleams
Like jet—   15
Were jet a crown.

The music
From the trumpet at his lips
Is honey
Mixed with liquid fire.   20
The rhythm
From the trumpet at his lips
Is ecstasy
Distilled from old desire—

Desire   25
That is longing for the moon
Where the moonlight's but a spotlight
In his eyes,
Desire
That is longing for the sea   30
Where the sea's a bar-glass
Sucker size.

The Negro
With the trumpet at his lips
Whose jacket   35
Has a *fine* one-button roll,

Does not know
Upon what riff the music slips
Its hypodermic needle
To his soul—   40

But softly
As the tune comes from his throat
Trouble
Mellows to a golden note.

                                                                    1947

Dear Dr. Butts[1]

"Do you know what has happened to me?" said Semple.

"No."

"I'm out of a job."

"That's tough. How did that come about?"

"Laid off—they're converting again. And right now, just when I
am planning to get married this spring, they have to go changing
from civilian production to war contracts, installing new machinery.
Manager says it might take two months, might take three or four.
They'll send us mens notices. If it takes four months, that's up to
June, which is no good for my plans. To get married a man needs
money. To stay married he needs more money. And where am I? As
usual, behind the eight-ball."

"You can find another job meanwhile, no doubt."

"That ain't easy. And if I do, they liable not to pay much. Jobs
that pay good money nowadays are scarce as hen's teeth. But Joyce
says she do not care. She is going to marry me, come June, anyhow
—even if she has to pay for it herself. Joyce says since I paid for
the divorce, she can pay for the wedding. But I do not want her to
do that."

"Naturally not, but maybe you can curtail your plans somewhat
and not have so big a wedding. Wedlock does not require an elaborate ceremony."

"I do not care if we don't have none, just so we get locked. But
you know how womens is. Joyce has waited an extra year for her
great day. Now here I am broke as a busted bank."

"How're you keeping up with your expenses?"

"I ain't. And I don't drop by Joyce's every night like I did when
I was working. I'm embarrassed. Then she didn't have to ask me to
eat. Now she does. In fact, she insists. She says, 'You got to eat
somewheres. I enjoy your company. Eat with me.' I do, if I'm there
when she extends the invitation. But I don't go looking for it. I

1. This sketch, featuring Hughes's folk
hero Jesse B. Semple, appeared in the
second collection of the Semple stories,
Semple Takes a Wife (1953). The combination of shrewd performing and candor
in Semple's monologues recalls the best
in traditional Negro humor, urban dialect sketches like Finley P. Dunne's "Mr.
Dooley" series, and at times the controlled exaggerations of the frontier tall
tale.

just sets home and broods, man, and looks at my four walls, which gives me plenty of time to think. And do you know what I been thinking about lately?"

"Finding work, I presume."

"Besides that?"

"No. I don't know what you've been thinking about."

"Negro leaders, and how they're talking about how great democracy is—and me out of a job. Also how there is so many leaders I don't know that white folks know about, because they are always in the white papers. Yet *I'm* the one they are supposed to be leading. Now, you take that little short leader named Dr. Butts, I do not know him, except in name only. If he ever made a speech in Harlem it were not well advertised. From what I reads, he teaches at a white college in Massachusetts, stays at the Commodore[2] when he's in New York, and ain't lived in Harlem for ten years. Yet he's leading me. He's an article writer, but he does not write in colored papers. But lately the colored papers taken to reprinting parts of what he writes—otherwise I would have never seen it. Anyhow, with all this time on my hands these days, I writ him a letter last night. Here, read it."

Harlem, U.S.A.

Dear Dr. Butts,   One Cold February Day

I seen last week in the colored papers where you have writ an article for The New York Times *in which you say America is the greatest country in the world for the Negro race and Democracy the greatest kind of government for all, but it would be better if there was equal education for colored folks in the South, and if everybody could vote, and if there were not Jim Crow[3] in the army, also if the churches was not divided up into white churches and colored churches, and if Negroes did not have to ride on the back seats of busses South of Washington.*

Now, all this later part of your article is hanging onto your but. You start off talking about how great American democracy is, then you but it all over the place. In fact, the but end of your see-saw is so far down on the ground I do not believe the other end can ever pull it up. So me myself, I would not write no article for no New York Times if I had to put in so many buts. I reckon maybe you come by it naturally, though, that being your name, dear Dr. Butts.

I hear tell that you are a race leader, but I do not know who you lead because I have not heard tell of you before and I have not laid eyes on you. But if you are leading me, make me know it, *because I do not read the* New York Times *very often, less I happen to pick*

2. A large commercial hotel in central Manhattan, far from Harlem.
3. Term derived from a dancing comic figure in Negro minstrel shows and a song introduced in 1830 by Thomas Rice (1808–60), now a metaphor for segregation and discriminatory practices against Negroes in the United States.

up a copy blowing around in the subway, so I did not know you were my leader. But since you are my leader, lead on, and see if I will follow behind your but—because there is more behind that but than there is in front of it.

Dr. Butts, I am glad to read that you writ an article in The New York Times, *but also* sometime I wish you would write one in the colored papers and let me know how to get out from behind all these buts *that are staring me in the face. I know America is a great country but—and it is that but that has been keeping me where I is all these years. I can't get over it, I can't get under it, and I can't get around it, so what am I supposed to do? If you are leading me, lemme see. Because we have too many colored leaders now that nobody knows until they get from the white papers to the colored papers and from the colored papers to me who has never seen hair nor hide of you. Dear Dr. Butts, are you hiding from me—and leading me, too?*

From the way you write, a man would think my race problem was made out of nothing but buts. But *this,* but *that,* and, yes, there is Jim Crow in Georgia but—. America admits they bomb folks in Florida—but Hitler gassed the Jews. Mississippi is bad— but Russia is worse. Detroit slums are awful—but compared to the slums in India, Detroit's Paradise Valley is Paradise.

Dear Dr. Butts, Hitler is dead. I don't live in Russia. India is across the Pacific Ocean. And I do not hope to see Paradise no time soon. I am nowhere near some of them foreign countries you are talking about being so bad. I am here! And you know as well as I do, Mississippi is hell. There ain't no *but* in the world can make it out different. They tell me when Nazis gas you, you die slow. But when they put a bomb under you like in Florida, you don't have time to say your prayers. As for Detroit, there is as much difference between Paradise Valley and Paradise as there is between heaven and Harlem. I don't know nothing about India, but I been in Washington, D.C. If you think there ain't slums there, just take your *but* up Seventh Street late some night, and see if you still got it by the time you get to Howard University.

I should not have to be telling you these things. You are colored just like me. To put a *but* after all this Jim Crow fly-papering around our feet is just like telling a hungry man, "But Mr. Rockefeller has got plenty to eat." It's just like telling a joker with no overcoat in the winter time, "But you will be hot next summer." The fellow is liable to haul off and say, "I am hot now!" And bop you over your head.

Are you in your right mind, dear Dr. Butts? Or are you just writing? Do you really think a new day is dawning? Do you really think Christians are having a change of heart? I can see you now taking your pen in hand to write, "But just last year the Southern Denom-

*inations of Hell-Fired Salvation resolved to work toward Brother-
hood." In fact, that is what you already writ. Do you think Brotherhood means colored to them Southerners?*

*Do you reckon they will recognize you for a brother, Dr. Butts,
since you done had your picture taken in the Grand Ballroom of
the Waldorf-Astoria[4] shaking hands at some kind of meeting with
five hundred white big-shots and five Negroes, all five of them
Negro leaders, so it said underneath the picture? I did not know
any of them Negro leaders by sight, neither by name, but since it
says in the white papers that they are leaders, I reckon they are.
Anyhow, I take my pen in hand to write you this letter to ask you
to make yourself clear to me. When you answer me, do not write
no "so-and-so-and-so but—." I will not take but for an answer.
Negroes have been looking at Democracy's but too long. What we
want to know is how to get rid of that but.*

Do you dig me, dear Dr. Butts?

Sincerely very truly,
JESSE B. SEMPLE
1953

Central High[1]

I had no sooner graduated from grammar school in Lincoln than
we moved from Illinois to Cleveland. My step-father sent for us. He
was working in a steel mill during the war, and making lots of
money. But it was hard work, and he never looked the same afterwards. Every day he worked several hours overtime, because they
paid well for overtime. But after a while, he couldn't stand the heat
of the furnaces, so he got a job as caretaker of a theater building,
and after that as janitor of an apartment house.

Rents were very high for colored people in Cleveland, and the
Negro district was extremely crowded, because of the great migration. It was difficult to find a place to live. We always lived, during
my high school years, either in an attic or a basement, and paid
quite a lot for such inconvenient quarters. White people on the east
side of the city were moving out of their frame houses and renting
them to Negroes at double and triple the rents they could receive
from others. An eight-room house with one bath would be cut up
into apartments and five or six families crowded into it, each two-
room kitchenette apartment renting for what the whole house had
rented for before.

But Negroes were coming in in a great dark tide from the South,
and they had to have some place to live. Sheds and garages and
store fronts were turned into living quarters. As always, the white
neighborhoods resented Negroes moving closer and closer—but
when the whites did give way, they gave way at very profitable rent-

4. Swank hotel on Park Avenue in Manhattan, far from Harlem.
1. A chapter from *The Big Sea* (1940),
the first of Hughes's autobiographical
volumes.

als. So most of the colored people's wages went for rent. The land-lords and the banks made it difficult for them to buy houses, so they had to pay the exorbitant rents required. When my step-father quit the steel mill job, my mother went out to work in service to help him meet expenses. She paid a woman four dollars a week to take care of my little brother while she worked as a maid.

I went to Central High School in Cleveland. We had a magazine called the *Belfry Owl*. I wrote poems for the *Belfry Owl*. We had some wise and very good teachers, Miss Roberts and Miss Weimer in English, Miss Chesnutt, who was the daughter of the famous colored writer, Charles W. Chesnutt,[2] and Mr. Hitchcock, who taught geometry with humor, and Mr. Ozanne, who spread the whole world before us in his history classes. Also Clara Dieke, who painted beautiful pictures and who taught us a great deal about many things that are useful to know—about law and order in art and life, and about sticking to a thing until it is done.

Ethel Weimer discovered Carl Sandburg for me. Although I had read of Carl Sandburg before—in an article, I think, in the *Kansas City Star* about how bad free verse was—I didn't really know him until Miss Weimer in second-year English brought him, as well as Amy Lowell, Vachel Lindsay, and Edgar Lee Masters, to us. Then I began to try to write like Carl Sandburg.[3]

Little Negro dialect poems like Paul Lawrence Dunbar's[4] and poems without rhyme like Sandburg's were the first real poems I tried to write. I wrote about love, about the steel mills where my step-father worked, the slums where we lived, and the brown girls from the South, prancing up and down Central Avenue on a spring day.

One of the first of my high school poems went like this:

> *Just because I loves you—*
> *That's de reason why*
> *My soul is full of color*
> *Like de wings of a butterfly.*

> *Just because I loves you*
> *That's de reason why*
> *My heart's a fluttering aspen leaf*
> *When you pass by.*

I was fourteen then. And another of the poems was this about the mills:

2. Negro writer (1858–1932), author of *The Conjure Woman* (dialect stories, 1899), a biography of the black aboli-tionist Frederick Douglass, and several novels.
3. The white American poets listed are Amy Lowell (1874–1925), Boston Ima-gist poet; Vachel Lindsay (1879–1931), who later helped Hughes by reading his poems to an audience in Washington, D.C.; Edgar Lee Masters (1869–1950), author of *Spoon-River Anthology* (1915); and Carl Sandburg (1878–1967), author of *Chicago Poems* (1916).
4. American Negro poet (1872–1906).

The mills
That grind and grind,
That grind out steel
And grind away the lives
Of men—
In the sunset their stacks
Are great black silhouettes
Against the sky.
In the dawn
They belch red fire.
The mills—
Grinding new steel,
Old men.

And about Carl Sandburg, my guiding star, I wrote:

Carl Sandburg's poems
Fall on the white pages of his books
Like blood-clots of song
From the wounds of humanity.
I know a lover of life sings
When Carl Sandburg sings.
I know a lover of all the living
Sings then.

Central was the high school of students of foreign-born parents —until the Negroes came. It is an old high school with many famous graduates. It used to be long ago the high school of the aristocrats, until the aristocrats moved farther out. Then poor whites and foreign-born took over the district. Then during the war, the Negroes came. Now Central is almost entirely a Negro school in the heart of Cleveland's vast Negro quarter.

When I was there, it was very nearly entirely a foreign-born school, with a new native white and colored American students mixed in. By foreign, I mean children of foreign-born parents. Although some of the students themselves had been born in Poland or Russia, Hungary or Italy. And most were Catholic or Jewish.

Although we got on very well, whenever class elections would come up, there was a distinct Jewish-Gentile division among my classmates. That was perhaps why I held many class and club offices in high school, because often when there was a religious deadlock, a Negro student would win the election. They would compromise on a Negro, feeling, I suppose, that a Negro was neither Jew nor Gentile!

I wore a sweater covered with club pins most of the time. I was on the track team, and for two seasons, my relay team won the city-wide championships. I was a lieutenant in the military training corps. Once or twice I was on the monthly honor roll for scholarship. And when we were graduated, Class of '20, I edited the Year Book.

My best pal in high school was a Polish boy named Sartur Andrzejewski. His parents lived in the steel mill district. His mother cooked wonderful cabbage in sweetened vinegar. His rosy-cheeked sisters were named Regina and Sabina. And the whole family had about them a quaint and kindly foreign air, bubbling with hospitality. They were devout Catholics, who lived well and were very jolly.

I had lots of Jewish friends, too, boys named Nathan and Sidney and Herman, and girls named Sonya and Bess and Leah. I went to my first symphony concert with a Jewish girl—for these children of foreign-born parents were more democratic than native white Americans, and less anti-Negro. They lent me *The Gadfly* and *Jean Christophe*[5] to read, and copies of the *Liberator* and the *Socialist Call*.[6] They were almost all interested in more than basketball and the glee club. They took me to hear Eugene Debs.[7] And when the Russian Revolution broke out, our school almost held a celebration.

Since it was during the war, and Americanism was being stressed, many of our students, including myself, were then called down to the principal's office and questioned about our belief in Americanism. Police went to some of the parents' homes and took all their books away. After that, the principal organized an Americanism Club in our school, and, I reckon, because of the customary split between Jews and Gentiles, I was elected president. But the club didn't last long, because we were never quite clear about what we were supposed to do. Or why. Except that none of us wanted Eugene Debs locked up. But the principal didn't seem to feel that Debs fell within the scope of our club. So the faculty let the club die.

Four years at Central High School taught me many invaluable things. From Miss Dieke, who instructed in painting and lettering and ceramics, I learnt that the only way to get a thing done is to start to do it, then keep on doing it, and finally you'll finish it, even if in the beginning you think you can't do it at all. From Miss Weimer I learnt that there are ways of saying or doing things, which may not be the currently approved ways, yet that can be very true and beautiful ways, that people will come to recognize as such in due time. In 1916, the critics said Carl Sandburg was no good as a poet, and free verse was no good. Nobody says that today—yet 1916 is not a lifetime ago.

From the students I learnt that Europe was not so far away, and

5. Novels by the Russian novelist Ethel Voynich (1864–1960) and the French writer Romain Rolland (1868–1944).
6. American radical journals.

7. American trade unionist (1855–1926), pacifist, and Socialist candidate for the presidency in 1920.

that when Lenin[8] took power in Russia, something happened in the slums of Woodlawn Avenue that the teachers couldn't tell us about, and that our principal didn't want us to know. From the students I learnt, too, that lots of painful words can be flung at people that aren't *nigger.* *Kike* was one; *spick,* and *hunky,* others.[9]

But I soon realized that the kikes and the spicks and the hunkies —scorned though they might be by the pure Americans—all had it on the niggers in one thing. Summer time came and they could get jobs quickly. For even during the war, when help was badly needed, lots of employers would *not* hire Negroes. A colored boy had to search and search for a job.

My first summer vacation from high school, I ran a dumb-waiter at Halle's, a big department store. The dumb-waiter carried stock from the stock room to the various departments of the store. I was continually amazed at trays of perfume that cost fifty dollars a bottle, ladies' lace collars at twenty-five, and useless little gadgets like gold cigarette lighters that were worth more than six months' rent on the house where we lived. Yet some people could afford to buy such things without a thought. And did buy them.

The second summer vacation I went to join my mother in Chicago. Dad and my mother were separated again, and she was working as cook for a lady who owned a millinery shop in the Loop,[1] a very fashionable shop where society leaders came by appointment and hats were designed to order. I became a delivery boy for that shop. It was a terrifically hot summer, and we lived on the crowded Chicago South Side in a house next to the elevated. The thunder of the trains kept us awake at night. We could afford only one small room for my mother, my little brother, and me.

South State Street was in its glory then, a teeming Negro street with crowded theaters, restaurants, and cabarets. And excitement from noon to noon. Midnight was like day. The street was full of workers and gamblers, prostitutes and pimps, church folks and sinners. The tenements on either side were very congested. For neither love nor money could you find a decent place to live. Profiteers, thugs, and gangsters were coming into their own. The first Sunday I was in town, I went out walking alone to see what the city looked like. I wandered too far outside the Negro district, over beyond Wentworth, and was set upon and beaten by a group of white boys, who said they didn't allow niggers in that neighborhood. I came home with both eyes blacked and a swollen jaw. That was the summer before the Chicago riots.

I managed to save a little money, so I went back to high school in Cleveland, leaving my mother in Chicago. I couldn't afford to eat in a restaurant, and the only thing I knew how to cook myself

---

8. Nikolai Lenin (1870–1924), Russian Soviet leader and President (1917–24).
9. Pejorative slang terms for, respectively, a Negro, Jew, Spaniard, and Hun- garian or central European in the U.S.
1. Area in central Chicago surrounded by tracks of the elevated railway.

in the kitchen of the house where I roomed was rice, which I boiled to a paste. Rice and hot dogs, rice and hot dogs, every night for dinner. Then I read myself to sleep.

I was reading Schopenhauer and Nietzsche, and Edna Ferber and Dreiser, and de Maupassant in French.[2] I never will forget the thrill of first understanding the French of de Maupassant. The soft snow was falling through one of his stories in the little book we used in school, and that I had worked over so long, before I really felt the snow falling there. Then all of a sudden one night the beauty and the meaning of the words in which he made the snow fall, came to me. I think it was de Maupassant who made me really want to be a writer and write stories about Negroes, so true that people in faraway lands would read them—even after I was dead.

But I did not dare write stories yet, although poems came to me now spontaneously, from somewhere inside. But there were no stories in my mind. I put the poems down quickly on anything I had at hand when they came into my head, and later I copied them in a notebook. But I began to be afraid to show my poems to anybody, because they had become very serious and very much a part of me. And I was afraid other people might not like them or understand them.

However, I sent some away to a big magazine in New York, where nobody knew me. And the big magazine sent them right back with a printed rejection slip. Then I sent them to one magazine after another—and they always came back promptly. But once Floyd Dell[3] wrote an encouraging word across one of the rejection slips from the *Liberator*.

1940

Making Poetry Pay[1]

By midwinter I had worked out a public routine of reading my poetry that almost never failed to provoke, after each poem, some sort of audible audience response—laughter, applause, a grunt, a groan, a sigh, or an "Amen!" I began my programs quite simply by telling where I was born in Missouri, that I grew up in Kansas in the geographical heart of the country, and was, therefore very American, that I belonged to a family that was always moving; and I told something of my early travels about the Midwest and how, at fourteen, in Lincoln, Illinois, I was elected Class Poet for the eighthgrade graduating exercises, and from then on I kept writing poetry.

After this biographical introduction I would read to my audiences the first of my poems, written in high school, and show how my

2. The German philosophers Arthur Schopenhauer (1788–1860) and Friedrich Wilhelm Nietzsche (1844–1900); the American novelists Edna Ferber (1887–1968) and Theodore Dreiser (1871–1946); the French novelist and short-story writer Guy de Maupassant (1850–93).
3. Chicago novelist and radical journalist (b. 1887), editor of *The Liberator*.
1. A chapter from Hughes's autobiographical *I Wonder as I Wander* (1956).

poetry had changed over the years. To start my reading, I usually selected some verses written when I was about fifteen:

> I had my clothes cleaned
> Just like new.
> I put 'em on but
> I still feels blue.
>
> I bought a new hat,
> Sho is fine,
> But I wish I had back that
> Old gal o' mine.
>
> I got new shoes,
> They don't hurt my feet,
> But I ain't got nobody
> To call me sweet.

Then I would say, "That's a sad poem, isn't it?" Everybody would laugh. Then I would read some of my jazz poems so my listeners could laugh more. I wanted them to laugh a lot early in the program, so that later in the evening they would not laugh when I read poems like "Porter":

> I must say,
> Yes, sir,
> To you all the time.
> Yes, sir!
> Yes, sir!
>
> All my days
> Climbing up a great big mountain
> Of yes, sirs!
> Rich old white man
> Owns the world.
> Gimme yo' shoes to shine.
>
> Yes, sir, boss!
> Yes, sir!

By the time I reached this point in the program my nonliterary listeners would be ready to think in terms of their own problems. Then I read poems about women domestics, workers on the Florida roads, poor black students wanting to shatter the darkness of ignorance and prejudice, and one about the sharecroppers of Mississippi:

Just a herd of Negroes
Driven to the field,
Plowing, planting, hoeing,
To make the cotton yield.

When the cotton's picked
And the work is done,
Boss man takes the money
And you get none.

Just a herd of Negroes
Driven to the field.
Plowing, planting, hoeing,
To make the cotton yield.

Many of my verses were documentary, journalistic and topical.
All across the South in that winter I read my poems about the
plight of the Scottsboro boys.[2]

Justice is a blind goddess.
To this we blacks are wise:
Her bandage hides two festering sores
That once perhaps were eyes.

Usually people were deeply attentive. But if at some point in the
program my audience became restless—as audiences sometimes will,
no matter what a speaker is saying—or if I looked down from the
platform and noticed someone about to go to sleep, I would pull
out my ace in the hole, a poem called "Cross." This poem, delivered dramatically, I had learned, would make anybody, white or
black, sit up and take notice. It is a poem about miscegenation—a
very provocative subject in the South. The first line—intended to
awaken all sleepers—I would read in a loud voice:

My old man's a white old man. . . .

And this would usually arouse any who dozed. Then I would pause
before continuing in a more subdued tone:

My old mother's black.

Then in a low, sad, thoughtful tragic vein:

2. Nine Negro boys, accused on dubious
grounds of raping two white prostitutes
near Scottsboro, Alabama, and sentenced
to die in 1931. After years of public protest and two Supreme Court reviews in
1932 and 1935, the death sentences were
reduced to equivalents of life imprisonment for four of the defendants, and the
charge of rape was dropped against the
other five.

But if ever I cursed my white old man
I take my curses back.

If ever I cursed my black old mother
And wished she were in hell,
I'm sorry for that evil wish
And now I wish her well.

My old man died in a fine big house,
My ma died in a shack.
I wonder where I'm gonna die,
Being neither white nor black.

Here I would let my voice trail off into a lonely silence. Then I would stand quite still for a long time, because I knew I had the complete attention of my listeners again.

Usually after a résumé of the racial situation in our country, with an optimistic listing of past achievements on the part of Negroes, and future possibilities, I would end the evening with:

I, too, sing America.

I am the darker brother.
They send me
To eat in the kitchen
When company comes,
But I laugh,
And eat well,
And grow strong.

Tomorrow
I'll sit at the table
When company comes.
Nobody'll dare
Say to me,
"Eat in the kitchen,"
Then.

Besides,
They'll see
How beautiful I am
And be ashamed.

I, too, am America.

1956

COUNTEE CULLEN
1903–1946

In the mid-1920s the "Harlem Renaissance" took form around the efforts of intellectual leaders in the black community to find outlets for black talent, secure a wider audience for their productions, convince the white world that Negroes could meet high standards of performance, and foster the ambitions of black intellectuals who were stirred by the migration of blacks into the urban North and were confident that Harlem in New York City was becoming a cultural capital for their race. Black sociologists and historians, as well as artists and writers, took part. The poet Countee Cullen was one involved in the Harlem Renaissance who felt most sensitively the dilemma of responding to the then traditional standards for poetic excellence while also expressing the distinctive experience of Afro-Americans.

Raised in New York City, Countee Porter Cullen was the adopted son of a Methodist minister whose household provided him with a secure and conventional childhood. He attended New York public schools and traveled with his father in Europe before entering New York University, where he won a Witter Bynner Poetry Prize for verse and election to Phi Beta Kappa on graduating in 1925. After acquiring a master's degree at Harvard in 1926, he began a career as teacher in the New York public schools which continued until his death. He was an assistant editor of *Opportunity: Journal of Negro Life* for a brief time, and his short-lived marriage to the daughter of the black historian W. E. B. DuBois ended in divorce.

Cullen's first book of verse, *Color* (1925), published when he was only twenty-two, won a Harmon Gold Award in that year and established his reputation. Other volumes followed swiftly—*Copper Sun* in 1927 and *The Ballad of the Brown Girl* in 1928. He received a Guggenheim Fellowship to complete *The Black Christ* (1929) and he published his only novel, *One Way to Heaven*, in 1932. His *The Medea and Some Poems* (1935) includes a translation of Euripides' tragedy *Medea*. His later works include *The Lost Zoo* (1940), *My Nine Lives and How I Lost Them* (1942), and the posthumous selection of his verse, *On These I Stand* (1947). Shortly before his death he collaborated with the black writer Arna Bontemps on a musical version of a novel by Bontemps that was produced as *St. Louis Woman* in 1946.

Cullen's anthology of Negro poetry, *Caroling Dusk* (1927), was an important production of the Harlem Renaissance, but in his introduction, Cullen made it clear that the traditions of English poetry, rather than Negro dialect or racial militancy, should provide the idiom for black verse, and despite the challenge of some fellow black writers he held to his position even when giving voice, sometimes with wry wit, to racial themes. He stood apart from the innovations of contemporary poets and held to the English poets John Keats, Percy Bysshe Shelley, and A. E. Housman as models for his verse, which time and again reveals the authentic pathos, the bewildered anguish, and the muted resignation of a voice which seeks response and recognition.

Yet Do I Marvel

I doubt not God is good, well-meaning, kind,
And did He stoop to quibble could tell why
The little buried mole continues blind,
Why flesh that mirrors Him must some day die,
Make plain the reason tortured Tantalus[1]   5
Is baited by the fickle fruit, declare
If merely brute caprice dooms Sisyphus
To struggle up a never-ending stair.
Inscrutable His ways are, and immune
To catechism by a mind too strewn   10
With petty cares to slightly understand
What awful brain compels His awful hand.
Yet do I marvel at this curious thing:
To make a poet black, and bid him sing!

                                                             1925

Incident

Once riding in old Baltimore,
    Heart-filled, head-filled with glee,
I saw a Baltimorean
    Keep looking straight at me.

Now I was eight and very small,   5
    And he was no whit bigger,
And so I smiled, but he poked out
    His tongue, and called me, "Nigger."

I saw the whole of Baltimore
    From May until December;   10
Of all the things that happened there
    That's all that I remember.

                                                             1925

To John Keats, Poet at Spring Time[2]

I cannot hold my peace, John Keats;
There never was a spring like this;
It is an echo, that repeats
My last year's song and next year's bliss.
I know, in spite of all men say   5
Of Beauty, you have felt her most.
Yea, even in your grave her way
Is laid. Poor, troubled, lyric ghost,
Spring never was so fair and dear
As Beauty makes her seem this year.   10

1. Tantalus, and Sisyphus in line 7 below, are figures in Greek mythology who were punished in Hades for crimes committed on earth. Tantalus's punishment was to be offered food and water that was then instantly snatched away. Sisyphus's torment was to roll a heavy stone to the top of a hill and, after it rolled back down, to repeat the ordeal perpetually.
2. The English Romantic poet (1795–1821). "Spring, 1924" [Cullen's note].

I cannot hold my peace, John Keats,
I am as helpless in the toil
Of Spring as any lamb that bleats
To feel the solid earth recoil
Beneath his puny legs. Spring beats   15
Her tocsin call to those who love her,
And lo! the dogwood petals cover
Her breast with drifts of snow, and sleek
White gulls fly screaming to her, and hover
About her shoulders, and kiss her cheek,   20
While white and purple lilacs muster
A strength that bears them to a cluster
Of color and odor; for her sake
All things that slept are now awake.

And you and I, shall we lie still,   25
John Keats, while Beauty summons us?
Somehow I feel your sensitive will
Is pulsing up some tremulous
Sap road of a maple tree, whose leaves
Grow music as they grow, since your   30
Wild voice is in them, a harp that grieves
For life that opens death's dark door.
Though dust, your fingers still can push
The Vision Splendid to a birth,
Though now they work as grass in the hush   35
Of the night on the broad sweet page of the earth.

"John Keats is dead," they say, but I
Who hear your full insistent cry
In bud and blossom, leaf and tree,
Know John Keats still writes poetry.   40
And while my head is earthward bowed
To read new life sprung from your shroud,
Folks seeing me must think it strange
That merely spring should so derange
My mind. They do not know that you,   45
John Keats, keep revel with me, too.

                                                        1925

Heritage

What is Africa to me:
Copper sun or scarlet sea,
Jungle star or jungle track,
Strong bronzed men, or regal black
Women from whose loins I sprang   5
When the birds of Eden sang?
One three centuries removed
From the scenes his fathers loved,
Spicy grove, cinnamon tree,
What is Africa to me?   10

So I lie, who all day long
Want no sound except the song
Sung by wild barbaric birds
Goading massive jungle herds,
Juggernauts[1] of flesh that pass   15
Trampling tall defiant grass
Where young forest lovers lie,
Plighting troth beneath the sky.
So I lie, who always hear,
Though I cram against my ear   20
Both my thumbs, and keep them there,
Great drums throbbing through the air.
So I lie, whose fount of pride,
Dear distress, and joy allied,
Is my somber flesh and skin,   25
With the dark blood dammed within
Like great pulsing tides of wine
That, I fear, must burst the fine
Channels of the chafing net
Where they surge and foam and fret.   30

Africa? A book one thumbs
Listlessly, till slumber comes.
Unremembered are her bats
Circling through the night, her cats
Crouching in the river reeds,   35
Stalking gentle flesh that feeds
By the river brink; no more
Does the bugle-throated roar
Cry that monarch claws have leapt
From the scabbards where they slept.   40
Silver snakes that once a year
Doff the lovely coats you wear,
Seek no covert in your fear
Lest a mortal eye should see;
What's your nakedness to me?   45
Here no leprous flowers rear
Fierce corollas[2] in the air;
Here no bodies sleek and wet,
Dripping mingled rain and sweat,
Tread the savage measures of   50
Jungle boys and girls in love.
What is last year's snow to me,[3]
Last year's anything? The tree
Budding yearly must forget
How its past arose or set—   55
Bough and blossom, flower, fruit,

1. In a Hindu festival, the juggernaut is a sacred idol dragged on a huge car in the path of which devotees were believed to throw themselves. Hence, any power demanding blind sacrifice, here spliced with the image of elephants.

2. The whorl of petals forming the inner envelope of a flower.
3. An echo of the lament "Where are the snows of yesteryear?" from the poem *Grand Testament* by the 15th-century French poet François Villon.

Even what shy bird with mute
Wonder at her travail there,
Meekly labored in its hair.
One three centuries removed   60
From the scenes his fathers loved,
Spicy grove, cinnamon tree,
What is Africa to me?

So I lie, who find no peace
Night or day, no slight release   65
From the unremittant beat
Made by cruel padded feet
Walking through my body's street.
Up and down they go, and back,
Treading out a jungle track.   70
So I lie, who never quite
Safely sleep from rain at night—
I can never rest at all
When the rain begins to fall;
Like a soul gone mad with pain   75
I must match its weird refrain;
Ever must I twist and squirm,
Writhing like a baited worm,
While its primal measures drip
Through my body, crying, "Strip!   80
Doff this new exuberance.
Come and dance the Lover's Dance!"
In an old remembered way
Rain works on me night and day.

Quaint, outlandish heathen gods   85
Black men fashion out of rods,
Clay, and brittle bits of stone,
In a likeness like their own,
My conversion came high-priced;
I belong to Jesus Christ,   90
Preacher of humility;
Heathen gods are naught to me.

Father, Son, and Holy Ghost,
So I make an idle boast;
Jesus of the twice-turned cheek[4]   95
Lamb of God, although I speak
With my mouth thus, in my heart
Do I play a double part.
Ever at Thy glowing altar
Must my heart grow sick and falter,   100
Wishing He I served were black,
Thinking then it would not lack

---

4. In his Sermon on the Mount (Matthew 5.39), Jesus declared that a good man, when struck on one cheek, should turn the other cheek rather than strike back.

Precedent of pain to guide it,
Let who would or might deride it;
Surely then this flesh would know   105
Yours had borne a kindred woe.
Lord, I fashion dark gods, too,
Daring even to give You
Dark despairing features where,
Crowned with dark rebellious hair,   110
Patience wavers just so much as
Mortal grief compels, while touches
Quick and hot, of anger, rise
To smitten cheek and weary eyes.
Lord, forgive me if my need   115
Sometimes shapes a human creed.
All day long and all night through,
One thing only must I do:
Quench my pride and cool my blood,
Lest I perish in the flood.   120
Lest a hidden ember set
Timber that I thought was wet
Burning like the dryest flax,
Melting like the merest wax,
Lest the grave restore its dead.   125
Not yet has my heart or head
In the least way realized
They and I are civilized.

                                        1925

From the Dark Tower

We shall not always plant while others reap
The golden increment of bursting fruit,
Not always countenance, abject and mute,
That lesser men should hold their brothers cheap;
Not everlastingly while others sleep   5
Shall we beguile their limbs with mellow flute,
Not always bend to some more subtle brute;
We were not made eternally to weep.

The night whose sable breast relieves the stark,
White stars is no less lovely being dark,   10
And there are buds that cannot bloom at all
In light, but crumple, piteous, and fall;
So in the dark we hide the heart that bleeds,
And wait, and tend our agonizing seeds.

                                        1927

Uncle Jim

"White folks is white," says uncle Jim;
"A platitude," I sneer;

And then I tell him so is milk,
And the froth upon his beer.

His heart walled up with bitterness,   5
He smokes his pungent pipe,
And nods at me as if to say,
"Young fool, you'll soon be ripe!"

I have a friend who eats his heart
Away with grief of mine,   10
Who drinks my joy as tipplers drain
Deep goblets filled with wine.

I wonder why here at his side,
Face-in-the-grass with him,
My mind should stray the Grecian urn[1]   15
To muse on uncle Jim.

1927

1. An allusion to *Ode on a Grecian Urn* by the British Romantic poet John Keats (1795–1821).

WILLIAM CARLOS WILLIAMS
1883–1963

The writer who did most to sponsor younger American poets after World War II was William Carlos Williams, whose own career spanned six decades during which he combined the careers of poet and pediatrician. He became, with Hart Crane, the leading exponent of a Whitman tradition in American letters. To an already long list of poems, critical essays, plays, and fiction, Williams added in the 1940s, 1950s, and 1960s an epic poem, *Paterson,* and a body of love poems that are among the major achievements of twentieth-century American poetry.

Williams was born in 1883 near Paterson in Rutherford, New Jersey, which he made his lifelong home. His immigrant parents—a "too English" father and a Puerto Rican mother who had studied painting in Paris—early exposed him to European culture, but his "mixed ancestry" made him feel the more deeply that America was his only home and that it was his "first business in life to possess it" (*Selected Letters,* pp. 127, 185). He attended schools in Switzerland and Paris as well as local schools, and he went directly from the Horace Mann High School into medical school at the University of Pennsylvania, where he became friends with Ezra Pound, the poet Hilda Doolittle, and the painter Charles Demuth. He graduated in 1906, interned in New York City, and after postgraduate work in pediatrics at Leipzig, Germany, he returned to Rutherford, married Florence Herman, and began his medical practice. Except during European travels in 1924 and 1927, he pursued his medical career full time until the middle 1950s when, following a series of strokes, he turned over his practice to one of his sons. He accomplished his writing at night and between professional appointments, "determined to be a poet," as he wrote later, and convinced that "only medicine, a job I enjoyed, would make it possible for me to live and write as I wanted to * * * " (*Autobiography*, p. 51). His professional career involved him in community activities (mosquito control, medical inspection of schools), brought him directly into the lives of patients with various racial and social backgrounds, and strengthened the respect for sheer physical life, the vitality of the body, that characterizes his poetry.

Williams published his first book, *Poems*, privately in 1909, but it was *The Tempers* (published with Ezra Pound's help in 1913) that first revealed the impact of Pound's verse as well as Williams's struggle to respond to modern modes of poetry while yet developing for himself a distinctly individual voice. At gatherings of vanguard painters and writers in New York City and Grantwood, New Jersey, he became familiar with the painters Francis Picabia and Marcel Duchamp, the poets Marianne Moore and Wallace Stevens, the critic Kenneth Burke. Though he was increasingly suspicious of Pound's expatriation and cultivation of traditional verse forms, Williams endorsed Pound's principles of "imagism"; he kept up an argumentative correspondence with him that remained frequent through the Twenties. He had read Whitman enthusiastically during high school and medical school, and while by 1917 Williams had become critical of Whitman's formlessness, as he saw it, he developed a conception of the poet's role that reaffirmed Whitman's celebration of the body and his views on the liberation of feeling, the authenticity of native materials for poetry, and the poet's crucial mission in a democratic society. By the time he published his manifesto "Prologue to *Kora in Hell*" (1920), essays in the magazine *Contact*, which he edited with Robert McAlmon (1920–23), the poems and prose statements in *Spring and All* (1923), and the historical essays *In the American Grain* (1925), Williams had differentiated his program from that of the expatriates and defined a tradition grounded on his own cranky rebelliousness and the elemental realities of the American scene.

Since new life is always "subversive of life as it was the moment before," Williams declared, poetry should be impelled by the same energy of "disestablishment, something in the nature of an impalpable revolution * * * "; poetry is "a rival government always in opposition to its cruder replicas" (*Selected Letters*, pp. 23–24; *Selected Essays*, p. 180). The expatriates had fled from that "immediate contact with the world" on which original writing depends, with the result that even Eliot's "exquisite work" was a "rehash" and Pound's early poems were "paraphrases" (*Spring and All*)— the work of men "content with the connotations of their masters" ("Prologue to *Kora in Hell*"). *The Waste Land* was a "catastrophe" for American letters that confirmed Williams in his commitment to Whitman (*Autobiography*, p. 146). Williams called for a confrontation with immediate reality, even the "filth" and "ignorance" of the present, and denounced in his antagonists their use of explicit metaphor, "crude symbolism," "strained associations," and "complicated ritualistic forms designed to separate the work from reality" (*Spring and All*). The phrase "no ideas but in things" recurs in Williams's poetry and prose; meanings should be found only in actual things, and universality could be found only in the concrete particulars of the locality. The figures Williams most admired in his study of the American past had, like Poe, a direct sense of their *"new locality"* and the determination to "clear the GROUND" for a new beginning; like the French Jesuit missionary Sebastian Rasles, they had the nerve "to MARRY—to touch" the reality around them (*In the American Grain*, pp. 216, 121).

To make this contact possible in poetry—to confront the "cruder," elemental realities and "the primitive profundity of the personality" (*Selected Letters*, p. 226; *How to Write*, Wagner, *The Poems of William Carlos Williams*, p. 145)—Williams insisted throughout his career that American poets should rely on the diction and cadences of the distinctively American language; they should derive their rhythms and measures from American speech as actually spoken whose very "instability" made it exceptionally receptive to "innovation" (*The Poem as a Field of Action*, 1948). But the poet, Williams insisted, could not simply record that speech or "copy" reality. He must assault conventional ways of perceiving the world and the conventional language patterns for expressing it. To gain access to elemental realities he must destroy these conventions as part of the creative "process of ordering" which produces inventive "imitations," not copies, and distinctly new poetic forms; destruction and creation are simultaneous (*Autobiography*, p. 241; *Selected Essays*, pp. 121, 288). The imagination's exposure to reality in each poem is contingent on the creation of a new, striking, and flexible poetic form which Williams called a "structure" and, later, a "mutation" (*Against the Weather*, 1930, *Selected Essays*, p. 208).

Accordingly Williams's poems intentionally disorient readers by avoiding traditional rhyme or stanza and line patterns, presenting an unsettling mixture of attitudes or tones (as at the opening of Section III, Book II, of *Paterson*), or offering a rough jumble of images and allusions which prepares the reader for the unusual perception or emotion that is created by the poem (as in *Portrait of a Lady*). The objects, figures, and emotions are revealed with exceptional clarity, while the poem is exposed with equal candor as an artifact or structure. The conjunction of "thighs" and "appletrees" in *Portrait of a Lady*, for instance, appears simultaneously as a revealed fact and a mockingly arbitrary, painted arrangement. In Williams's characteristic style, the line breaks do not coincide regularly or easily with the phrasing or syntax of the language. The effect of this ostensible fragmentation is to induce the reader to focus with unusual intentness on concrete objects, phases of emotion and movement, specific aspects of the subject, and particulars of the poem's language and rhythm, while drawing attention at the same time to the discrete lines and the artifice of their sequence which articulate the poem's structure.

The language of painting, as well as American speech, provided Williams with a means of circumventing the traditional conventions of poetry. The transformation of his poetics that culminated in *Sour Grapes* (1921) and *Spring and All* was inspired in part by the excitement of the Armory Show of 1913, which introduced modern modes of European painting to a shocked public in New York City, and Williams not only admired such Europeans as Duchamp, the Dadaist Picabia, and the Cubist Juan Gris, but numbered the Expressionist Marsden Hartley and the "Precisionists" Charles Demuth and Charles Sheeler among his friends. He found models for the clarity and vividness of his own poems in the analytic abstractions and the fragmentation of objects in Cubism, in the precise linear outlines of Demuth's watercolors of flowers, and in the Precisionists' combination of objective realism with geometric abstraction.

The objectification of perception and feeling became more pronounced in Williams's poems of the 1930s, when his poetry became one of the models for the movement "Objectivism" which he helped to sponsor and whose Objectivist Press published his *Collected Poems, 1921–1931* in 1934. Although *The Yachts* and other excellent poems appeared in the 1930s, much of Williams's creative effort went into prose fiction. He had published *The Great American Novel* in 1923 (an autobiographical, Joycean treatment of the writer) and *A Voyage to Pagany* (an autobiographical pilgrimage abroad which explores the contrast between European and American cultures) in 1928. The prose is more spare in his collections of short stories, *The Edge of the Knife* (1932) and *Life along the Passaic River* (1938), which treat the bleakness and heroisms, at times comic, in the lives of immigrants, adolescents, and various professional people during the Depression. The novels *White Mule* (1937) and its sequel *In the Money* (1940) treat the immigrant's search for a community, and then success, in an America dominated by business.

Williams's political activities during the 1930s and 1940s included a commitment to the Democratic party, membership in his local social club (The Fortnightly) and in several societies of the American Social Credit movement, affiliation with such leftist causes as the "Open Letter of the Friends of the Soviet Union" calling for cooperation with Stalinist Russia (1939), and membership in the Cooperative Consumers' Society of Bergen County whose presidency he accepted in 1942. Some of these activities marked him a "fellow traveler" in the eyes of conservative opponents, despite Williams's repudiations of authoritarianism and his commitment to libertarian democracy, and he was deprived of the post of Consultant in Poetry at the Library of Congress which had been offered to him in 1948 and which he planned to take up when his health and medical practice permitted in 1952.

The completion of Williams's epic *Paterson* (Book I in 1946, subsequent volumes in 1948, 1949, 1951, and 1958), signaled a resurgence in his career as poet which was all the more remarkable for the series of heart attacks which began in 1948 and eventually made it difficult physically to write. Born in *"local pride,"* conceived as *"a confession . . . a reply to Greek and Latin with the bare hands"* (Book I), and intended to "lift an environment to expression" (*Selected Letters*, p. 286), the poem celebrated the search for a community and imaginative expression in the modern city. It seemed chaotic to many readers, including such admirers as the poet Randall Jarrell, but was praised as a major undertaking of the twentieth century by other poets; Robert Lowell, for instance, called it "our *Leaves of Grass*" (Miller, *William Carlos Williams: A Collection of Critical Essays*, p. 158). Book IV (originally the final book) concluded with the protagonist, like the epic hero Odysseus, returning to his native land; he returned to the state of New Jersey where Whitman and later Allen Ginsberg (born in Paterson) made their home. A letter from Ginsberg incorporated in the poem testifies that "at least one actual citizen in your community," Ginsberg himself, "has inherited your experience in his struggle to love and know a world-city, through your work. * * *"

Williams's unabashed candor, the directness of his style, and his openness to formal innovation found a larger audience in postwar generations whose poets he inspired, as in the cases of Allen Ginsberg, Denise Levertov,

Charles Olson, and Robert Creeley. While he had earlier received the Dial Award (1926) and other honors, his talks and readings on college campuses and such awards as the National Book Award (1950), the Bollingen Award (1953), and the Pulitzer Prize (1962) testified to wider recognition during his later career.

Williams's critical attacks on his antagonists and his defense of his own poetic aims became more moderate, and he devoted renewed effort to exploring the resources of American speech and perfecting the verse form that first appeared in *Paterson* II (Section iii) and which Williams called the "variable foot" and the "triadic line." He believed that he had found in the cadences of the American idiom a new "measure"; it was more regular than free verse (which he thought unstructured or formless), yet more resilient than the "Euclidian" metrics that traditional verse depended on. A "relative order," rather than absolute or fixed order, "is operative elsewhere in our lives," he declared, and the "variable foot," with no fixed number of units, was a "*relatively* stable foot, not a rigid one." This would bring the necessary "discipline" to verse that Whitman neglected, though Whitman had been correct in "breaking [the] bounds" of traditional metrics (*On Measure, Selected Essays*, pp. 337–40). To construct the "triadic line" Williams arranged relatively short feet, of uneven length, in gradually descending steps across the page, establishing a musical pace, as he wrote the poet Richard Eberhart, that gives weight to silent pauses as well as to the words, and accords an even time interval to each of the segments (*Selected Letters*, pp. 326–27). Williams did not always use the triadic line in his later verse, and he frequently allowed himself the license of employing units of two and four feet instead of three. But the triadic form, as used in *The Sparrow*, for instance, achieved the same precision of notation which had characterized his earlier verse, while in such works as *Daphne and Virginia* the form sustained a more meditative tone and resilient line that combined fluency with intense compression: "IN OUR FAMILY we stammer unless, / half mad, / we come to speech at last   ."

Besides *Paterson*, Williams's late verse is distinguished particularly by the long love poems in *Desert Music and Other Poems* (1954) and *Journey to Love* (1955), which were gathered with later poems in *Pictures from Brueghel* (1962). In them and notably in *Asphodel, That Greeny Flower*, he examines with the tender but probing candor of an aging man the deviousness and authenticity of passion, the pained intricacies and redemptive power of marital and familial love, and their integral connection with the dance of life and the reality of poetry to which he consecrated his art.

Overture to a Dance of Locomotives

I[1]

Men with picked voices chant the names
of cities in a huge gallery: promises
that pull through descending stairways
to a deep rumbling.

       The rubbing feet   5
of those coming to be carried quicken a

---

1. "I" suggests an overture or beginning. There are no other parts to the poem.

grey pavement into soft light that rocks
to and fro, under the domed ceiling,
across and across from pale
earthcolored walls of bare limestone.   10

Covertly the hands of a great clock
go round and round! Were they to
move quickly and at once the whole
secret would be out and the shuffling
of all ants be done forever.   15

A leaning pyramid of sunlight, narrowing
out at a high window, moves by the clock;
discordant hands straining out from
a center: inevitable postures infinitely
repeated—   20

two—twofour—twoeight!

Porters in red hats run on narrow platforms.

This way ma'am!
          —important not to take
the wrong train!   25
            Lights from the concrete
ceiling hang crooked but—
              Poised horizontal
on glittering parallels the dingy cylinders
packed with a warm glow—inviting entry—   30
pull against the hour. But brakes can
hold a fixed posture till—
            The whistle!

Not twoeight. Not twofour. Two!

Gliding windows. Colored cooks sweating   35
in a small kitchen. Taillights—
In time: twofour!
In time: twoeight!

—rivers are tunneled: trestles
cross oozy swampland: wheels repeating   40
the same gesture remain relatively
stationary: rails forever parallel
return on themselves infinitely.
           The dance is sure.

c. 1913   1921

Portrait of a Lady

Your thighs are appletrees
whose blossoms touch the sky.

Which sky? The sky
where Watteau[1] hung a lady's
slipper. Your knees   5
are a southern breeze—or
a gust of snow. Agh! what
sort of man was Fragonard?[2]
—as if that answered
anything. Ah, yes—below   10
the knees, since the tune
drops that way, it is
one of those white summer days,
the tall grass of your ankles
flickers upon the shore—   15
Which shore?—
the sand clings to my lips—
Which shore?
Agh, petals maybe. How
should I know?   20
Which shore? Which shore?
I said petals from an appletree.

1915   1913

Willow Poem

It is a willow when summer is over,
a willow by the river
from which no leaf has fallen nor
bitten by the sun
turned orange or crimson.   5
The leaves cling and grow paler,
swing and grow paler
over the swirling waters of the river
as if loath to let go,
they are so cool, so drunk with
the swirl of the wind and of the river—
oblivious to winter,
the last to let go and fall   10
into the water and on the ground.

1921

Queen-Ann's-Lace[1]

Her body is not so white as
anemone petals nor so smooth—nor
so remote a thing. It is a field

---

1. Jean Antoine Watteau (1684–1721), French Rococo artist. He painted sensuous, refined love scenes, with elegantly dressed lovers in idealized rustic settings.
2. Jean Honoré Fragonard (1732–1806), French painter, depicted fashionable lovers in paintings more wittily and openly erotic than Watteau's. Fragonard's *The Swing* depicts a girl who has kicked her slipper into the air.
1. The common field flower (wild carrot), whose wide white flower is composed of a multitude of minute blossoms, each with a dark spot at the center, joined to the stalk by fibrous stems.

of the wild carrot taking
the field by force; the grass   5
does not raise above it.
Here is no question of whiteness,
white as can be, with a purple mole
at the center of each flower.
Each flower is a hand's span   10
of her whiteness. Wherever
his hand has lain there is
a tiny purple blemish. Each part
is a blossom under his touch
to which the fibres of her being   15
stem one by one, each to its end,
until the whole field is a
white desire, empty, a single stem,
a cluster, flower by flower,
a pious wish to whiteness gone over—   20
or nothing.

1921

The Widow's Lament in Springtime

Sorrow is my own yard
where the new grass
flames as it has flamed
often before but not
with the cold fire   5
that closes round me this year.
Thirtyfive years
I lived with my husband.
The plumtree is white today
with masses of flowers.   10
Masses of flowers
load the cherry branches
and color some bushes
yellow and some red
but the grief in my heart   15
is stronger than they
for though they were my joy
formerly, today I notice them
and turned away forgetting.
Today my son told me   20
that in the meadows,
at the edge of the heavy woods
in the distance, he saw
trees of white flowers.
I feel that I would like   25
to go there
and fall into those flowers
and sink into the marsh near them.

1921

Spring and All[1]

By the road to the contagious hospital[2]
under the surge of the blue
mottled clouds driven from the
northeast—a cold wind. Beyond, the
waste of broad, muddy fields   5
brown with dried weeds, standing and fallen

patches of standing water
the scattering of tall trees

All along the road the reddish
purplish, forked, upstanding, twiggy   10
stuff of bushes and small trees
with dead, brown leaves under them
leafless vines—

Lifeless in appearance, sluggish
dazed spring approaches—   15

They enter the new world naked,
cold, uncertain of all
save that they enter. All about them
the familiar wind—

Now the grass, tomorrow   20
the stiff curl of wildcarrot leaf
One by one objects are defined—
It quickens: clarity, outline of leaf

But now the stark dignity of
entrance—Still, the profound change   25
has come upon them: rooted, they
grip down and begin to awaken

                                                                        1923

Shoot It Jimmy!

Our orchestra
is the cat's nuts—

Banjo jazz
with a nickelplated

amplifier to   5
soothe

the savage beast—

---

1. In *Spring and All* (as originally published, 1923), prose statements were interspersed through the poems and the
poems were identified by roman numerals. Williams added titles later and used
the volume's title for the opening poem.
2. A hospital for treating contagious diseases.

Get the rhythm

That sheet stuff
's a lot a cheese.   10

Man
gimme the key

and lemme loose—
I make 'em crazy

with my harmonies—   15
Shoot it Jimmy

Nobody
Nobody else

but me—
They can't copy it   20

1923

To Elsie

The pure products of America[1]
go crazy—
mountain folk from Kentucky

or the ribbed north end of
Jersey   5
with its isolate lakes and

valleys, its deaf-mutes, thieves
old names
and promiscuity between

devil-may-care men who have taken   10
to railroading
out of sheer lust of adventure—

and young slatterns, bathed
in filth
from Monday to Saturday   15

to be tricked out that night
with gauds

---

1. What Williams calls "pure products of America" are those whose descent is through generations of inbreeding in isolated communities; they are "pure" because unmixed with later American strains, but also because racial mixture is the essence of the American "melting pot." Elsie herself is descended from the "Jackson Whites" who lived in northern New Jersey. The Whites were offspring of Indians, Hessian deserters during the Revolutionary War, escaped Negro slaves, and white women imported (reputedly by a person named Jackson) as sexual companions for British troops.

from imaginations which have no

peasant traditions to give them
character   20
but flutter and flaunt

sheer rags—succumbing without
emotion
save numbed terror

under some hedge of choke-cherry   25
or viburnum—
which they cannot express—

Unless it be that marriage
perhaps
with a dash of Indian blood   30

will throw up a girl so desolate
so hemmed round
with disease or murder

that she'll be rescued by an
agent—   35
reared by the state and

sent out at fifteen to work in
some hard-pressed
house in the suburbs—

some doctor's family, some Elsie—   40
voluptuous water
expressing with broken

brain the truth about us—
her great
ungainly hips and flopping breasts   45

addressed to cheap
jewelry
and rich young men with fine eyes

as if the earth under our feet
were   50
an excrement of some sky

and we degraded prisoners
destined
to hunger until we eat filth

while the imagination strains   55

after deer
going by fields of goldenrod in

the stifling heat of September
Somehow
it seems to destroy us   60

It is only in isolate flecks that
something
is given off

No one
to witness   65
and adjust, no one to drive the car

                                                        1923

The Red Wheelbarrow

so much depends
upon

a red wheel
barrow

glazed with rain   5
water

beside the white
chickens.

                                                        1923

From In the American Grain[1]
Sir Walter Raleigh

Of the pursuit of beauty and the husk that remains, perversions
and mistakes, while the true form escapes in the wind, sing O
Muse;[2] of Raleigh, beloved by majesty, plunging his lust into the
body of a new world—and the deaths, misfortunes, counter coups,

1. *In the American Grain* (1925) is Williams's attempt to define the historical origins of American culture and to reveal its capacity for renewal or revitalization. In it he treats a number of historical characters (among them the Puritan preacher Cotton Mather and the Jesuit missionary Sebastian Rasles, the explorer Cortez and the Aztec Indian Montezuma, the frontiersman Daniel Boone and Abraham Lincoln) in a highly personal and imaginative way; he associates himself closely with figures of the past, introduces dialogues with other commentators, paraphrases closely the narrative sources he draws on, and emphasizes the symbolic or mythological dimensions of the historical figures. He contrasts the figures who encourage loving contact with the vitalities of the natural environment and the new society, to those figures who evade such contact or repress its liberating energies. His recurring image of society—the new world, or Elizabethan England—is the body of a woman. In Sir Walter Raleigh (1552–1618), the writer and adventurer and favorite courtier of Queen Elizabeth, Williams presented a hero who represented both the ardor to beget settlements on the body of his Queen and the new land (Virginia) that he named for her, and the failure to bring that effort to full fruition.

2. Williams is imitating a traditional panegyric to heroic figures, an elaborately laudatory discourse with an invocation to the Muse for inspiration.

which swelled back to certify that ardor with defeat.[3] Sing! and let the rumor of these things make the timid more timid and the brave desperate, careless of monuments which celebrate the subtle conversions of sense and let truth go unrecognized. Sing! and make known Raleigh, who would found colonies; his England become a mouthful of smoke sucked from the embers of a burnt weed.[4] And if the nations, well founded on a million hindrances, taxes, laws and laws to annul laws must have a monument, let it be here implied: this undersong, this worm armed to gnaw away lies and to release—Raleigh: if it so please the immortal gods.

Sing of his wisdom, O Muse: The truth is that all nations, how remote soever, being all reasonable creatures, and enjoying one and the same imagination and fantasy, have devised, according to their means and materials, the same things.

They all have lighted on the invention of bows and arrows; all have targets and wooden swords, all have instruments to encourage them to fight, all that have corn beat it in mortars and make cakes, baking them upon slate stones; all devised laws without any grounds had from the scriptures or from Aristotle's Politick,[5] whereby they are governed; all that dwell near their enemies impale[6] their villages, to save themselves from surprise. Yea, besides the same inventions, all have the same natural impulsions; they follow nature in the choice of many wives; and there are among them which, out of a kind of wolfish ferocity, eat man's flesh; yea, most of them believe in a second life, and they are all of them idolators in one kind or another.——

These things, still chewing, he chewed out. And as an atheist, with Marlow, they would have burned him.[7] It was his style! To the sea, then! mixed with soundest sense—on selling cannon to one's enemies.

But through all else, O Muse, say that he penetrated to the Queen!

Sing! O muse and say, he was too mad in love, too clear, too desperate for her to trust upon great councils. He was not England, as she was. She held him, but she was too shrewd a woman not to know she held him as a woman, she, the Queen; which left an element. Say that he was made and cracked by majesty, knew that devotion, tasted that wisdom and became too wise—and she all eyes and wit looking through until her man, her Raleigh became thin, light, a spirit. He was the whetter, the life giver through the Queen —but wounded cruelly. In this desperate condition, willless,

3. Raleigh organized and outfitted three settlements in Virginia, but the colonists either returned to England or perished; Raleigh himself never went to Virginia.
4. Raleigh's adventurers introduced tobacco into England in 1586; Raleigh himself smoked regularly and spread the fad throughout the English court.
5. The Bible and the treatise on politics by the ancient Greek philosopher Aristotle (384–322 B.C.) were authoritative sources for principles of government in Western Europe.
6. Fortify with spikes or paling.
7. Like the English playwright Christopher Marlowe (1564–93), Raleigh was thought to be an atheist.

inspired, the tool of a woman, flaming, falling, being lifted up, robbed of himself to feed her, caught, dispatched, starting, held again, giving yet seeking round the circle for an outlet: this was, herself; but what, O Muse, of Raleigh, that proud man?

Say, first, he was the breath of the Queen—for a few years; say, too, that he had traveled much before he knew her, that he had seen the tropics and explored the Orinoco River for a hundred miles. Then say, O Muse, that now he saw himself afar, that he became—America! that he conceived a voyage from perfection to find—an England new again; to found a colony; the outward thrust, to seek. But it turned out to be a voyage on the body of his Queen: England, Elizabeth—Virginia!

He sent out colonists, she would not let him go himself; nothing succeeded. It was a venture in the crook of a lady's finger, pointing, then curving in. Virginia? It was the nail upon that finger. O Raleigh! nowhere, everywhere—and nothing. Declare, O Muse, impartially, how he had gone with the English fleet to strike at Spain and how she called him back—Sire, do you not know, you!? These women are my person. What have you dared to do? How have you dared, without my order, to possess yourself of what is mine? Marry this woman![8]

Sing, O Muse, with an easy voice, how she, Elizabeth, she England, she the Queen—deserted him; Raleign for Leicester, Essex now for Raleigh;[9] she Spencer whom he friended, she "The Faery Queen,"[1] she Guiana,[2] she Virginia, she atheist, she "my dear friend Marlow," she rents, rewards, honors, influence, reputation, she "the fundamental laws of human knowledge," she prison, she tobacco, the introduction of potatoes to the Irish soil:[3] It is the body of the Queen stirred by that plough—now all withdrawn.

O Muse, in that still pasture where you dwell amid the hardly noticed sounds of water falling and the little cries of crickets and small birds, sing of Virginia floating off: the broken chips of Raleigh: the Queen is dead.

O Virginia! who will gather you again as Raleigh had you gathered? science, wisdom, love, despair. O America, the deathplace of his son![4] It is Raleigh, anti-tropical. It is the cold north, flaring up in ice again.

---

8. Raleigh courted, seduced, and subsequently married Elizabeth Throckmorton, a young woman in Queen Elizabeth's court. The Queen, displeased, imprisoned him for a time in the Tower of London.
9. The Earls of Leicester and Essex, like Raleigh, were influential members of the Queen's court and rivals for her favor.
1. Raleigh was a friend of the poet Edmund Spenser (1552–99), wrote a poem in praise of him, and introduced him to Queen Elizabeth. Spenser included a tribute to the Queen in his allegorical poem, *The Faerie Queene* (1590–96).
2. Raleigh led two expeditions to Guiana

in South America and published an account of the first, *The Discovery of the Large, Rich, and Beautiful Empire of Guiana* (1596). His second expedition (1616) in search of gold ended in failure.
3. Raleigh commanded English troops in the ruthless suppression of Irish rebels (1580–81). He launched a settlement of Englishmen in Munster, Ireland, in 1584, and introduced the cultivation of the potato.
4. Raleigh's son accompanied him on his second expedition to Guiana and was killed.

What might he have known, what seen, O Muse?—Shoal water where we smelt so sweet and so strong a smell, as if we had been in the midst of some delicate garden; and keeping good watch and keeping but slack sail—we arrived upon the coast; a land so full of grapes as the very beating and surge of the sea overflow them, such plenty, as well there as in all places else, on the sand and on the green soil on the hills, as well as every little shrub, as also climbing towards the tops of high cedars, that in all the world I think a like abundance is not to be found. And from below the hill such a flock of cranes, mostly white, arose with such a cry as if an army of men had shouted all together.—He might have seen the brother of the king, Granganimo, with copper cap, whose wife, comely and bashful, might have come aboard the ship, her brows bound with white coral; or running out to meet them very cheerfully, at Roanoak, plucked off his socks and washed his feet in warm water. A people gentle, loving, faithful, void of all guile and treason. Earthen pots, large, white and sweet and wooden platters of sweet timber.[5]

Sing, O Muse and say, there is a spirit that is seeking through America for Raleigh: in the earth, the air, the waters, up and down, for Raleigh, that lost man: seer who failed, planter who never planted, poet whose works are questioned, leader without command, favorite deposed—but one who yet gave title for his Queen, his England, to a coast he never saw but grazed alone with genius.

Question him in hell, O Muse, where he has gone, and when there is an answer, sing and make clear the reasons that he gave for that last blow. Why did he send his son into that tropic jungle and not go himself, upon so dangerous an errand? And when the boy had died why not die too? Why England again and force the new King to keep his promise and behead him?[6]

1925

The Wind Increases

The harried
earth is swept
                    The trees
the tulip's bright
            tips   5
                    sidle and

    toss—

---

5. This paragraph summarizes and closely paraphrases passages in *The First Voyage Made to the Coast of America* (1584), a report on the settlement of Virginia sent to Raleigh by Captain Arthur Barlowe, reprinted by Henry S. Burrage in *Early English and French Voyages* (1906), pp. 228–29, 232, 235–37. The Indian Granganimo died in 1585.
6. After the death of Queen Elizabeth and the accession of King James I, Raleigh was suspected of disloyalty to the King, and was imprisoned for treason in 1603. He was released, though not pardoned, in 1616 to permit his expedition to Guiana, on the condition that he not attack the Spanish there. His forces disobeyed that injunction, and on Raleigh's return to London he was executed under the original charge of treason in 1618.

       Loose your love
to flow

Blow!   10

Good Christ what is
a poet—if any
            exists?

a man
whose words will   15
      bite
           their way
home—being actual

having the form
           of motion   20

At each twigtip

new

upon the tortured
body of thought

        gripping   25
the ground

a way
      to the last leaftip

1928   1934

Death

He's dead
the dog won't have to
sleep on his potatoes
any more to keep them
from freezing   5

he's dead
the old bastard—
He's a bastard because

there's nothing
legitimate in him any   10
more
      he's dead
He's sick-dead

      he's

a godforsaken curio   15
without
any breath in it

He's nothing at all
        he's dead
shrunken up to skin   20

        Put his head on
one chair and his
feet on another and
he'll lie there
like an acrobat—   25

Love's beaten. He
beat it. That's why
he's insufferable—

        because
he's here needing a   30
shave and making love
an inside howl
of anguish and defeat—

He's come out of the man
and he's let   35
the man go—
                the liar

Dead
        his eyes
rolled up out of   40
the light—a mockery

                                which
love cannot touch—

just bury it
and hide its face   45
for shame.

1928   1934

The Botticellian Trees[1]

        The alphabet of
        the trees

        is fading in the
        song of the leaves

1. An allusion to the painting *Primavera* ("Spring") by the Italian Sandro Botti-celli (1444–1510).

the crossing
bars of the thin   5

letters that spelled
winter

and the cold
have been illumined   10

with
pointed green

by the rain and sun—
The strict simple

principles of   15
straight branches

are being modified
by pinched-out

ifs of color, devout
conditions   20

the smiles of love—
. . . . . .

until the stript
sentences

move as a woman's
limbs under cloth   30

and praise from secrecy
quick with desire

love's ascendancy
in summer—

In summer the song   25
sings itself

above the muffled words—

1928   1934

The Yachts

contend in a sea which the land partly encloses
shielding them from the too-heavy blows
of an ungoverned ocean which when it chooses

tortures the biggest hulls, the best man knows

to pit against its beatings, and sinks them pitilessly.   5
Mothlike in mists, scintillant in the minute

brilliance of cloudless days, with broad bellying sails
they glide to the wind tossing green water
from their sharp prows while over them the crew crawls

ant-like, solicitously grooming them, releasing,   10
making fast as they turn, lean far over and having
caught the wind again, side by side, head for the mark.

In a well guarded arena of open water surrounded by
lesser and greater craft which, sycophant, lumbering
and flittering follow them, they appear youthful, rare   15

as the light of a happy eye, live with the grace
of all that in the mind is feckless, free and
naturally to be desired. Now the sea which holds them

is moody, lapping their glossy sides, as if feeling
for some slightest flaw but fails completely.   20
Today no race. Then the wind comes again. The yachts

move, jockeying for a start, the signal is set and they
are off. Now the waves strike at them but they are too
well made, they slip through, though they take in canvas.

Arms with hands grasping seek to clutch at the prows.   25
Bodies thrown recklessly in the way are cut aside.
It is a sea of faces about them in agony, in despair

until the horror of the race dawns staggering the mind,
the whole sea become an entanglement of watery bodies
lost to the world bearing what they cannot hold. Broken,   30

beaten, desolate, reaching from the dead to be taken up
they cry out, failing, failing! their cries rising
in waves still as the skillful yachts pass over.[1]

1935

The Dead Baby

Sweep the house
    under the feet of the curious
    holiday seekers—
sweep under the table and the bed
    the baby is dead—   5

---

1. An ironic echo of the Jewish feast of Passover, commemorating the occasion when Jewish infants were saved from the plague in Exodus 11–12. Jeho-vah exempted or "passed over" the children of Jews when he inflicted death on the firstborn Egyptian infants.

The mother's eyes were she sits
   by the window, unconsoled—
have purple bags under them
   the father—
tall, wellspoken, pitiful   10
   is the abler of these two—

Sweep the house clean
   here is one who has gone up
   (though problematically)
to heaven, blindly   15
   by force of the facts—
a clean sweep
   is one way of expressing it—

Hurry up! any minute
   they will be bringing it   20
   from the hospital—
a white model of our lives
   a curiosity—
surrounded by fresh flowers

1935

Classic Scene

A power-house
in the shape of
a red brick chair
90 feet high

on the seat of which   5
sit the figures
of two metal
stacks—aluminum—

commanding an area
of squalid shacks   10
side by side—
from one of which

buff smoke
streams while under
a grey sky   15
the other remains

passive today—

1938

The Term

A rumpled sheet
of brown paper
about the length

and apparent bulk
of a man was   5
rolling with the

wind slowly over
and over in
the street as

a car drove down   10
upon it and
crushed it to

the ground. Unlike
a man it rose
again rolling   15

with the wind over
and over to be as
it was before.

1938

The Dance

In Breughel's great picture, The Kermess,[1]
the dancers go round, they go round and
around, the squeal and the blare and the
tweedle of bagpipes, a bugle and fiddles   5
tipping their bellies (round as the thick-
sided glasses whose wash they impound)
their hips and their bellies off balance
to turn them. Kicking and rolling about
the Fair Grounds, swinging their butts, those   10
shanks must be sound to bear up under such
rollicking measures, prance as they dance
in Breughel's great picture, The Kermess.

1944

Burning the Christmas Greens

Their time past, pulled down
cracked and flung to the fire
—go up in a roar

All recognition lost, burnt clean
clean in the flame, the green   5
dispersed, a living red,
flame red, red as blood wakes
on the ash—

and ebbs to a steady burning

1. *The Wedding Dance* by the Flemish painter Peter Breughel the Elder (c. 1525–69).

the rekindled bed become   10
a landscape of flame

At the winter's midnight
we went to the trees, the coarse
holly, the balsam and
the hemlock for their green   15

At the thick of the dark
the moment of the cold's
deepest plunge we brought branches
cut from the green trees

to fill our need, and over   20
doorways, about paper Christmas
bells covered with tinfoil
and fastened by red ribbons

we stuck the green prongs
in the windows hung   25
woven wreaths and above pictures
the living green. On the

mantle we built a green forest
and among those hemlock
sprays put a herd of small   30
white deer as if they

were walking there. All this!
and it seemed gentle and good
to us. Their time past,
relief! The room bare. We   35

stuffed the dead grate
with them upon the half burnt out
log's smoldering eye, opening
red and closing under them

and we stood there looking down.   40
Green is a solace
a promise of peace, a fort
against the cold (though we

did not say so) a challenge
above the snow's   45
hard shell. Green (we might
have said) that, where

small birds hide and dodge

and lift their plaintive
rallying cries, blocks for them   50
and knocks down

the unseeing bullets of
the storm. Green spruce boughs
pulled down by a weight of
snow—Transformed!   55

Violence leaped and appeared.
Recreant! roared to life
as the flame rose through and
our eyes recoiled from it.

In the jagged flames green   60
to red, instant and alive. Green!
those sure abutments . . . Gone!
lost to mind

and quick in the contracting
tunnel of the grate   65
appeared a world! Black
mountains, black and red—as

yet uncolored—and ash white,
an infant landscape of shimmering
ash and flame and we, in   70
that instant, lost,

breathless to be witnesses,
as if we stood
ourselves refreshed among
the shining fauna of that fire.   75

                                        1944

The Well Disciplined Bargeman

The shadow does not move. It is the water moves,
running out. A monolith of sand on a passing barge,
riding the swift water, makes that its fellow.

Standing upon the load the well disciplined bargeman
rakes it carefully, smooth on top with nicely squared   5
edges to conform to the barge outlines—ritually: sand.

All about him the silver water, fish-swift, races
under the Presence. Whatever there is else is moving.
The restless gulls, unlike companionable pigeons,

taking their cue from the ruffled water, dip and circle   10

avidly into the gale. Only the bargeman raking
upon his barge remains, like the shadow, sleeping

1948

Lear[1]

When the world takes over for us
and the storm in the trees
replaces our brittle consciences
(like ships, female to all seas)
when the few last yellow leaves   5
stand out like flags on tossed ships
at anchor—our minds are rested

Yesterday we sweated and dreamed
or sweated in our dreams walking
at a loss through the bulk of figures   10
that appeared solid, men or women,
but as we approached down the paved
corridor, melted—Was it I?—like
smoke from bonfires blowing away

Today the storm, inescapable, has   15
taken the scene and we return
our hearts to it, however made, made
wives by it and though we secure
ourselves for a dry skin from the drench
of its passionate approaches we   20
yield and are made quiet by its fury

Pitiful Lear, not even you could
outshout the storm—to make a fool
cry! Wife to its power might you not
better have yielded sooner? as on ships   25
facing the seas were carried once
the figures of women at repose to
signify the strength of the waves' lash.

1948

The Poem as a Field of Action

Talk given at the University of Washington, 1948

Let's begin by quoting Mr. Auden[1]—(from *The Orators*):
"Need I remind you that you're no longer living in ancient Egypt?"

I'm going to say one thing to you—for a week! And I hope to
God when I'm through that I've succeeded in making you under-

---

1. The aging King whose madness
reaches its height during a storm on the
heath in Shakespeare's tragedy *King
Lear* (1606).

1. The English poet W. H. Auden (1907–
73), in a prose section of *The Orators*,
Book I (1).

stand me. It concerns the poem as a field of action, at what pitch the battle is today and what may come of it.

As Freud[2] says bitterly in the first chapter of his *The Interpretation of Dreams*, speaking of the early opposition to his theory:

> —the aversion of scientific men to
> learning something new

we shall learn that is a characteristic quite as pronounced in literature—where they will *copy* "the new"—but the tiresome repetition of this "new," now twenty years old, disfigures every journal: I said a field of action. I can see why so many wish rather, avoiding thought, to return to the classic front of orthodox acceptance. As Anatole France put it in Freud's time, *"Les savants ne sont pas curieux."*[3]

It is next to impossible to bring over the quantitative[4] Greek and Latin texts into our language. But does anyone ever ask *why* a Latin line in translation tends to break in half in our language? *Why* it cannot be maintained in its character, its quantitative character as against our accented verse? Have *all* the equivalents been exhausted or even tried? I doubt it.

I offer you then an initiation, what seems and what is actually only a half-baked proposal—since I cannot follow it up with proofs or even *final* examples—but I do it with at least my eyes open—for what I myself may get out of it by presenting it as well as I can to you.

I propose sweeping changes from top to bottom of the poetic structure. I said structure. So now you are beginning to get the drift of my theme. I say we are *through* with the iambic pentameter as presently conceived, at least for dramatic verse; through with the measured quatrain, the staid concatenations of sounds in the usual stanza, the sonnet. More has been done than you think about this though not yet been specifically named for what it is. I believe something can be said. Perhaps all that I can do here is to call attention to it: a revolution in the conception of the poetic foot—pointing out the evidence of something that has been going on for a long time.

At this point it might be profitable (since it would bring me back to my subject from a new point of view) to turn aside for a brief, very brief discussion (since it is not in the direct path of my essay) of the materials—that is to say, the subject matter of the poem. In this let me accept all the help I can get from Freud's theory of the dream—as a fulfillment of the wish—which I accept here holus-bolus.[5] The poem is a dream, a daydream of wish fulfillment but

2. Sigmund Freud (1856–1939), founder of psychoanalysis.
3. Jacques A. F. Thibault, French critic and novelist (1844–1924): "The men of learning have no curiosity."
4. Poetry whose lines are determined by the number of syllables rather than the pattern of accents.
5. The whole pill.

not by any means because of that a field of action and purposive action of a high order because of that.

It has had in the past a varying subject matter—almost one might say a progressively varying choice of subject matter as you shall see—I must stress here that we are talking of the *recent* past.

And let me remind you here to keep in your minds the term reality as contrasted with phantasy and to tell you that the *subject matter* of the poem is always phantasy—what is wished for, realized in the "dream" of the poem—but that the structure confronts something else.

We may mention Poe's dreams in a pioneer society, his dreams of gentleness and bliss—also, by the way, his professional interest in meter and his very successful experiments with form. Yeats's subject matter of faery. Shakespeare—the butcher's son dreaming of Caesar and Wolsey.[6] No need to go on through Keats, Shelley to Tennyson. It is all, the subject matter, a wish for aristocratic attainment —a "spiritual" bureaucracy of the "soul" or what you will.

There was then a subject matter that was "poetic" and in many minds that is still poetry—and exclusively so—the "beautiful" or pious (and so beautiful) wish expressed in beautiful language—a dream. That is still poetry: full stop. Well, that was the world to be desired and the poets merely expressed a general wish and so were useful each in his day.

But with the industrial revolution, and steadily since then, a new spirit—a new *Zeitgeist*[7] has possessed the world, and as a consequence new values have replaced the old, aristocratic concepts— which had a pretty seamy side if you looked at them like a Christian. A new subject matter began to be manifest. It began to be noticed that there could be a new subject matter and that that was not in fact the poem at all. Briefly then, money talks, and the poet, the modern poet has admitted new subject matter to his dreams— that is, the serious poet has admitted the whole armamentarium of the industrial age to his poems—

Look at Mr. Auden's earlier poems as an example, with their ruined industrial background of waste and destruction. But even that is passing and becoming old-fashioned with the new physics taking its place. All this is a subject in itself and a fascinating one which I regret to leave, I am sorry to say, for a more pressing one.

Remember we are still in the world of fancy if perhaps disguised but still a world of wish-fulfillment in dreams. The poet was not an owner, he was not a money man—he was still only a poet; a wisher; a word man. The best of all to my way of thinking! Words are the

---

6. The Irish poet William Butler Yeats (1865–1939) wrote *Fairy and Folk Tales of the Irish Peasantry* (1888). For William Shakespeare (1564–1616), reputedly the son of a butcher, two examples of worldly success were Julius Caesar, the Roman general and consul (100–44 B.C.); and Thomas Wolsey (1471–1530), church bureaucrat, later Archbishop of York and Lord Chancellor under Henry VII of England.

7. Spirit of the age.

keys that unlock the mind. But is that all of poetry? Certainly not —no more so than the material of dreams was phantasy to Dr. Sigmund Freud.

There is something else. Something if you will listen to many, something permanent and sacrosanct. The one thing that the poet has not wanted to change, the one thing he has clung to in his dream—unwilling to let go—the place where the time-lag is still adamant—is structure. Here we are unmovable. But here is precisely where we come into contact with reality. Reluctant, we waken from our dreams. And what is reality? How do we know reality? The only reality that we can know is MEASURE.

Now to return to our subject—the structure of the poem. Everything in the social, economic complex of the world at any time-sector ties in together—

(Quote Wilson on Proust—modern physics, etc.)[8]

But it might at this time be a good thing to take up first what is spoken of as free verse.

How can we accept Einstein's[9] theory of relativity, affecting our very conception of the heavens about us of which poets write so much, without incorporating its essential fact—the relativity of measurements—into our own category of activity: the poem. Do we think we stand outside the universe? Or that the Church of England does? Relativity applies to everything, like love, if it applies to anything in the world.

What, by this approach I am trying to sketch, what we are trying to do is not only to disengage the elements of a measure but to seek (what we believe is there) a new measure or a new way of measuring that will be commensurate with the social, economic world in which we are living as contrasted with the past. It is in many ways a different world from the past calling for a different measure.

According to this conception there is no such thing as "free verse" and so I insist. Imagism was not structural: that was the reason for its disappearance.

The impression I give is that we are about to make some discoveries. That they will be far-reaching in their effects.—This will depend on many things. My address (toward the task) is all that concerns me now: That we do approach a change.

What is it? I make a clear and definite statement—that it lies in the structure of the verse. That it may possibly lie elsewhere I do not for a moment deny or care—I have here to defend that only and that is my theme.

I hope you will pardon my deliberation, for I wish again to enter a short by-path: It may be said that I wish to destroy the past. It is

---

8. Williams's note to himself to read from the chapter on the French novelist Marcel Proust (1871–1922) in *Axel's Castle* (1931) by the American literary critic Edmund Wilson (1895–1972).
9. Albert Einstein (1879–1955), German-born physicist.

precisely a service to tradition, honoring it and serving it that is envisioned and intended by my attack, and not disfigurement—confirming and *enlarging* its application.

Set the overall proposal of an enlarged technical means—in order to liberate the possibilities of depicting reality in a modern world that has seen more if not felt more than in the past—in order to be *able* to feel more (for we know we feel less, or surmise that we do. Vocabulary opens the mind to feeling). But modern in that by psychology and all its dependencies we *know*, for we have learned that to feel more we have to have, in our day, the means to feel *with*—the tokens, the apparatus. We are lacking in the means—the appropriate paraphernalia, just as modern use of the products of chemistry for *refinement* must have means which the past lacked. Our poems are not subtly enough made, the structure, the staid manner of the poem cannot let our feelings through.

(Note: Then show (in what detail I can) what we may do to achieve this end by a review of early twentieth-century literary accomplishments. Work done.)

We seek profusion, the Mass—heterogeneous—ill-assorted—quite breathless—grasping at all kinds of things—as if—like Audubon[1] shooting some little bird, really only to look at it the better.

If any one man's work lacks the distinction to be expected from the finished artist, we might well think of the *profusion* of a Rabelais[2]—as against a limited output. It is as though for the moment we should be profuse, we Americans; we need to build up a mass, a congolomerate maybe, containing few gems but bits of them—Brazilian brilliants—that shine of themselves, uncut as they are.

Now when Mr. Eliot came along he had a choice: 1. Join the crowd, adding his blackbird's voice to the flock, contributing to the conglomerate (or working over it for his selections) or 2. To go where there was already a mass of more ready distinction (to turn his back on the first), already an established literature in what to him was the same language (?) an already established place in world literature—a short cut, in short.

Stop a minute to emphasize our own position: It is *not* that of Mr. Eliot. We are making a modern bolus: That is our somewhat undistinguished burden; profusion, as, we must add in all fairness, against his distinction. His is a few poems beautifully phrased—in his longest effort thirty-five quotations in seven languages. We, let us say, are the Sermons of Launcelot Andrewes from which (in time) some selector will pick *one* phrase. Or say, the *Upanishad*

1. John J. Audubon (1785–1851), American painter and naturalist, author of *Birds of America* (1827–38).
2. François Rabelais (1494–1553), French physician and writer, author of the sprawling, ribald, irreverent *Gargantua* (1534).

that will contribute a single word![3] There are summative geniuses like that—they shine. We must value them—the extractors of genius—for what they do: extract. But they are there; we are here. It is not possible for us to imitate them. We are in a different phase—a new language—we are making the mass in which some other later Eliot will dig. We must *see* our opportunity and increase the hoard others will find to use. We must find our *pride* in *that*. We must have the pride, the humility and the thrill in the making. (Tell the story of Bramante[4] and the building of the dome of the Duomo[5] in Florence.)

The clearness we must have is first the clarity of knowing what we are doing—what we may do: Make anew—a reexamination of the means—on a fresh—basis. Not at *this* time an analysis so much as an accumulation. You couldn't expect us to be as prominent (as *read* in particular achievements—outstanding single poems). We're not doing the same thing. We're not putting the rose, the single rose, in the little glass vase in the window—we're digging a hole for the tree—and as we dig have disappeared in it.

(Note: Pound's story of my being interested in the loam whereas he wanted the finished product.)

(Note: Read Bridges—two short pieces in the anthology: 1. The Child 2. Snow.)[6]

We begin to pick up what so far is little more than a feeling (a feeling entirely foreign to a Mr. E. or a Mr. P.[7]—though less to them than to some others) that something is taking place in the accepted prosody or ought to be taking place. (Of course we have had Whitman—but he is a difficult subject—prosodically and I do not want to get off into that now.) It is similar to what must have been the early feelings of Einstein toward the laws of Isaac Newton in physics. Thus from being fixed, our prosodic values should rightly be seen as only relatively true. Einstein had the speed of light as a constant—his only constant—What have we? Perhaps our concept of musical time. I think so. But don't let us close down on that either at least for the moment.

In any case we as loose, disassociated (linguistically), yawping speakers of a new language,[8] are privileged (I guess) to sense and so to seek to discover that possible thing which is disturbing the metrical table of values—as unknown elements would disturb Mendelyeev's[9] table of the periodicity of atomic weights and so lead to discoveries.

3. The *Upanishad*, sacred Hindu treatises of India, and the sermons of Bishop Lancelot Andrewes (1555–1626) were drawn on by T. S. Eliot in his poetry.
4. Donato Bramante (1444–1514), Italian architect of St. Peter's Basilica in Rome.
5. Cathedral.
6. Poems by the English poet Robert Bridges (1844–1930).
7. T. S. Eliot and Ezra Pound.
8. Cf. Whitman, "I sound my barbaric yawp over the roofs of the world" (*Song of Myself*, 52, line 1353).
9. Dmitri Mendelyeev (1834–1907), Russian chemist.

And we had better get on the job and make our discoveries or, quietly, someone else will make them for us—covertly and without acknowledgment—(one acknowledges one's indebtedness in one's notes only to dead writers—preferably long dead!).

We wish to find an objective way at least of looking at verse and to redefine its elements; this I say is the theme (the radium) that underlies Bridges' experiments as it is the yeast animating Whitman and all the "moderns."

That the very project itself, quite apart from its solutions, is not yet raised to consciousness, to a clear statement of purpose, is our fault. (Note: the little Mag: Variegations)[1] But one thing, a semi-conscious sense of a rending discovery to be made is becoming apparent. For one great thing about "the bomb" is the awakened sense it gives us that catastrophic (but why?) alterations are also possible in the human *mind*, in art, in the arts. . . . We are too cowed by our fear to realize it fully. But it is *possible*. That is what we mean. This isn't optimism, it is chemistry: Or better, physics.

It appears, it disappears, a sheen of it comes up, when, as its shattering implications affront us, all the gnomes hurry to cover up its traces.

Note: *Proust*: (Wilson) He has supplied for the first time in literature an equivalent on the full scale for the new theory of modern physics—I mention this merely to show a possible relationship—between a style and a natural science—intelligently considered.

Now for an entirely new issue: Mr. Auden is an interesting case —in fact he presents to me a deciding issue. His poems are phenomenally worth studying in the context of this theme.

There is no modern poet so agile—so impressive in the use of the poetic means. He can do anything—except one thing. He came to America and became a citizen of this country. He is truly, I should say, learned. Now Mr. Auden didn't come here for nothing or, if you know Auden, without a deep-seated conviction that he *had* to come. Don't put it down to any of the superficial things that might first occur to you—that he hates England, etc. He came here because of a crisis in his career—his career as a writer, as a poet particularly I should say. Mr. Auden may disagree with me in some of this but he will not disagree, I think, when I say he is a writer to whom writing is his life, his very breath which, as he or any man goes on, in the end absorbs *all* his breath.

Auden might have gone to France or to Italy or to South America or following Rimbaud[2] to Ceylon or Timbuctoo. No! He came to the United States and became a citizen. Now the crisis, the only crisis which could drive a man, a distinguished poet, to

1. Title of a literary magazine.
2. Arthur Rimbaud (1854–91), French Symbolist poet.

that would be that he had come to an end of some sort in his poetic means—something that England could no longer supply, and that he came here implicitly to find an answer—in another language. As yet I see no evidence that he has found it. I wonder why? Mind you, this is one of the cleverest, most skilled poets of our age and one of the most versatile and prolific. He can do anything.

But when he writes an ode to a successful soccer season for his school, as Pindar wrote them for the Olympic heroes of his day—it is in a classic meter so successful in spite of the subject, which you might think trivial, that it becomes a serious poem. And a bad sign to me is always a religious or social tinge beginning to creep into a poet's work. You can put it down as a general rule that when a poet, in the broadest sense, begins to devote himself to the *subject matter* of his poems, *genre*, he has come to an end of his poetic means.

What does all this signify? That Auden came here to find a new way of writing—for it looked as if this were the place where one might reasonably expect to find that instability in the language where innovation would be at home. Remember even Mr. Eliot once said that no poetic drama could any longer be written in the iambic pentameter, but that perhaps jazz might offer a suggestion. He even wrote something about "My Baby,"[3] but it can't have been very successful for we seldom hear any more of it.

I wish I could enlist Auden in an attack, a basic attack upon the whole realm of structure in the poem. I have tried but without success so far. I think that's what he came here looking for, I think he has failed to find it (it may be constitutional with him). I think we have disappointed him. Perhaps he has disappointed himself. I am sure the attack must be concentrated on the *rigidity of the poetic foot.*

This began as a basic criticism of Auden's poems—as a reason for his coming to America, and has at least served me as an illustration for the *theory* upon which I am speaking.

Look at his poems with this in view—his very skill seems to defeat him. It need not continue to do so in my opinion.

Mr. Eliot, meanwhile, has written his *Quartets.* He is a very subtle creator—who knows how to squeeze the last ounce of force out of his material. He has done a good job here though when he speaks of developing a new manner of writing, new manners following new manners only to be spent as soon as that particular piece of writing has been accomplished—I do not think he quite knows what he is about.

But in spite of everything and completely discounting his subject matter, his *genre*, Eliot's experiments in the *Quartets* though limited, show him to be more American in the sense I seek than, sad

---

3. T. S. Eliot's unfinished verse drama, *Wanna Go Home, Baby*, better known as *Sweeney Agonistes* (1926–27).

to relate, Auden, with his English ears and the best will in the world, will ever be able to be.

It may be the tragedy of a situation whose ramifications we are for the moment unable to trace: That the American gone over to England might make the contribution (or assist in it) which the Englishman come to America to find it and with the best will in the world, is unable to make.

Thus the Gallicized American, D'A——, according to Edmund Wilson in *Axel's Castle*, with the iambic pentameter in his brain, was able, at the beginning of the symbolist movement in Paris to break the French from their six-syllable line in a way they had of themselves never been able to do.[4] There is Ezra Pound also to be thought of—another entire thesis—in this respect. I see that I am outlining a year's or at least a semester's series of lectures as I go along.

Now we come to the question of the origin of our discoveries. Where else can what we are seeking arise from but speech? From speech, from American speech as distinct from English speech, or presumably so, if what I say above is correct. In any case (since we have no body of poems comparable to the English) from what we *hear* in America. Not, that is, from a study of the classics, not even the American "Classics"—the *dead* classics which—may I remind you, we have *never heard* as living speech. No one has or can *hear* them as they were written any more than we can *hear* Greek today.

I say this once again to emphasize what I have often said—that we here must *listen* to the language for the discoveries we hope to make. This is not the same as the hierarchic or tapeworm mode of making additions to the total poetic body: the mode of the schools. This will come up again elsewhere.

That being so, what I have presumed but not proven, concerning Auden's work, can we not say that there are many more *hints* toward literary composition in the American language than in English—where they are inhibited by classicism and "good taste." (Note the French word *tête*,[5] its derivation from "pot.") I'd put it much stronger, but let's not be diverted at this point, there are too many more important things pressing for attention.

In the first place, we have to say, following H. L. Mencken's *The American Language*,[6] which American language? Since Mencken pointed out that the American student (the *formative* years—very important) is bilingual, he speaks English in the classroom but his own tongue outside of it.

We mean, then, American—the language Mr. Eliot and Mr. Pound carried to Europe *in their ears*—willy-nilly—when they left here for their adventures and which presumably Mr. Auden came

---

4. Wilson wrote this, in *Axel's Castle* ("Symbolism"), of François Vielé-Griffin (1864–1937), Virginia-born expatriate and author of the Symbolist poem *Che-* *vauchée d'Yeldis*.
5. Head.
6. Henry L. Mencken (1880–1956), American editor and critic.

here to find—perhaps too late. A language full of those hints toward newness of which I have been speaking. I am not interested in the history but these things offer a point worth making, a rich opportunity for development lies before us at this point.

I said "hints toward composition." This does not mean realism in the language. What it does mean, I think, is ways of managing the language, new ways. Primarily it means to me opportunity to expand the structure, the basis, the actual making of the poem.

It is a chance to attack the language of the poem seriously. For to us our language is serious in a way that English is not. Just as to them English is serious—too serious—in a way no dialect could be. But the dialect is the mobile phase, the changing phase, the productive phase—as their languages were to Chaucer, Shakespeare, Dante, Rabelais in their day.

It is there, in the mouths of the living, that the language is changing and giving new means for expanded possibilities in literary expression and, I add, basic structure—the most important of all.

To the English, English is England: "History is England," yodels Mr. Eliot.[7] To us this is not so, not so *if* we prove it by writing a poem built to refute it—otherwise he wins!! But that leads to mere controversy. For us rehash of rehash of hash of rehash is *not* the business.

A whole semester of studies is implicit here. Perhaps a whole course of post-graduate studies—with theses—extending into a life's work!! But before I extol too much and advocate the experimental method, let me emphasize that, like God's creation, the objective is not experimentation but *man*. In our case, poems! There were enough experiments it seems, from what natural history shows, in that first instance but that was not the culmination. The poem is what we are after.

And again let me emphasize that this is something that has been going on, unrecognized for years—here *and* in England. What we are at is to try to discover and isolate and *use* the underlying element or principle motivating this change which is trying to speak outright. Do you not see now why I have been inveighing against the sonnet all these years? And why it has been so violently defended? Because it is a form which does not admit of the slightest structural change in its composition.

1948

Paterson Williams published his personal epic in four Books between 1946 and 1951, then in 1958 added Book V, which recommences the entire work. The poem is his challenge to the expatriates, "the cults and the kind of thought that destroyed Pound and made what it has made of Eliot" (*Selected Letters*, p. 214), and it is his most ambitious attempt to

7. Eliot wrote that "History is now and England" in *Four Quartets* (1943), "Little Gidding," V, line 24.

fulfill Whitman's dream of forging a distinctly American poetics from native materials. It is like other personal epics (Crane's *The Bridge*, Eliot's *The Waste Land* or *Four Quartets*, and Pound's *Cantos*) in combining a panoramic scale with minute notation and direct or intimately personal statement. Yet its strategy of disjunction or discontinuity is more extreme, it incorporates actual letters and other prose documents along with verse in its montage, and its local setting in Paterson, New Jersey, with the history and legends particular to the region, is less widely familiar.

The poem undertakes to front directly the raw, "elemental" realities of modern urban America—including the disorder, antagonisms, and cleavages that the work encompasses in the metaphor of "divorce." Simultaneously it searches in those same realities for the "deeper implications" of democratic culture and the redeeming language that would reconcile learning with experience, the male with the female, the present with its past, urban civilization with nature, the poet with his community—the integrations that the poem embraces in the metaphor of "marriage" (*Selected Letters*, pp. 226–27). The work's prose passages are incorporated because Williams was convinced that there is "an *identity* between prose and verse" (*Selected Letters*, p. 265) and actual prose not only records the facts that the poet draws on but contains the idiomatic resources of language which are the matrix of the poet's speech. The work presents from time to time partial fulfillments of its quest, but Williams once called his poem "the impossible poem *Paterson*" (*Selected Letters*, p. 230) not only because he acknowledged the persistence of disorder in his world and flaws in his poem, but because he thought that poetry, like life, must generate disorder and destructive violence as part of the creative process. It must repeatedly disorient readers (as at the opening of Section iii, Book II) and descend or fall into disintegrations of experience (as anticipated in lines 18–44 of Section iii, Book II) so as to make possible the liberation of new life and the creation of new speech. The work repeatedly begins again; instead of achieving the products of order it enacts and re-enacts the "process of ordering" itself (*Selected Essays*, p. 188).

Three central figures dominate the poem. One is "a man like a city," sometimes alienated from his city but often identified with it, who is presented as a sleeping giant, a dog sniffing about his habitat, the city Paterson, and "Dr. P.," a physician and poet who is a surrogate for Williams. The second is a woman who has numerous incarnations: the park in the vicinity of Paterson with her head at Garret Mountain (the "female to the city / —upon whose body Paterson instructs his thoughts" in Section i, Book II), and the woman poet whose letters (signed "C" or "Cress") appear frequently. The third figure is the Passaic River and its falls, an image of currents in the mind, of natural power and the source of industrial power, of the marriage bed, and of a roaring, confusing "language" which the poet must decipher and harness as the matrix of his own redeeming speech. Among the public figures who appear in the poem are the French physicist Eve Curie, who extracted the "radiant gist" of radium from its crude ore, and Alexander Hamilton, first Secretary of the Treasury and author of a plan for harnessing the power of the falls to create a manufacturing conglomerate at Paterson. Most notable, however, are figures from local legend whose exploits dramatize the risks and daring of the poet's quest: a young wife who drowned at the falls; and the professional daredevil Sam Patch (d. 1829) who successfully leaped into the Passaic from the falls but later died, after making a speech, when leaping from the falls of the Genesee River in New York.

In Book II, Section iii, Dr. P. leaves Garrett Mountain Park and strolls toward the falls, ruminating on an evangelist's sermon he has just heard and on the ugly fragmentation of the world around him, and accepting the challenge to descend to the elemental "base" of experience which revives an earlier vision of the "summits" he would like to attain. The section is a response to the letter from "Cress" which begins at the end of Section ii and which is continued as a challenge to Dr. P. at the end of Section iii. The forty-four lines beginning "The descent beckons" mark Williams's discovery of the new form (the "triadic line" with the "variable foot") that he used often in his poetry after 1954. He published the lines as a separate poem, *The Descent*, in *The Desert Music* (1954).

From PATERSON
Book II, Sunday in the Park
From *Section ii*

Whatever your reasons were for that note of yours and for your indifferent evasion of my letters just previous to that note—the one thing that I still wish more than any other is that I could see you. It's tied up with even more than I've said here. And more importantly, it is the one impulse I have that breaks through that film, that crust, which has gathered there so fatally between my true self and that which can make only mechanical gestures of living. But even if you should grant it, I wouldn't want to see you unless with some little warmth of friendliness and friendship on your part. * * * I have been feeling (with that feeling increasingly stronger) that I shall never again be able to recapture any sense of my own personal identity (without which I cannot write, of course—but in itself far more important than the writing) until I can recapture some faith in the reality of my own thoughts and ideas and problems which were turned into dry sand by your attitude toward those letters and by that note of yours later. That is why I cannot throw off my desire to see you—not impersonally, but in the most personal ways, since I could never have written you at all in a completely impersonal fashion.

From *Section iii*

Look for the nul[1]
defeats it all

the N of all
equations   .

that rock, the blank   5
that holds them up

---

1. Utter insignificance, nothingness, non-existence. "Look for" implies both "seek" and "watch out for" or "guard against."

which pulled away—
the rock's

their fall. Look
for that nul   10

that's past all
seeing

the death of all
that's past

all being   .   15

But Spring shall come and flowers will bloom
and man must chatter of his doom   .   .

The descent beckons
                as the ascent beckoned
                                Memory is a kind   20
of accomplishment
                a sort of renewal
                                        even
an initiation, since the spaces it opens are new
places   25
                inhabited by hordes
                                heretofore unrealized,
of new kinds—
                since their movements
                                are towards new objectives   30
(even though formerly they were abandoned)

No defeat is made up entirely of defeat—since
the world it opens is always a place
                formerly
                                unsuspected. A   35
world lost,
                a world unsuspected
                                beckons to new places
and no whiteness (lost) is so white as the memory
of whiteness   .   40

With evening, love wakens
                though its shadows
                                which are alive by reason
of the sun shining—
                grow sleepy now and drop away   45
                                from desire   .

Love without shadows stirs now
                beginning to waken
                                as night

advances.   50
The descent
                    made up of despairs
                        and without accomplishment
realizes a new awakening   :
                                which is a reversal   55
of despair.

            For what we cannot accomplish, what
is denied to love,
            what we have lost in the anticipation—
                                a descent follows,   60
endless and indestructible   .

Listen!—

the pouring water!
                    The dogs and trees
conspire to invent   65
a world—gone!

Bow, wow! A
departing car scatters gravel as it
picks up speed!

Outworn! *le pauvre petit ministre*[2]   70
did his best, they cry,
but though he sweat for all his worth
no poet has come   .

Bow, wow! Bow, wow!

Variously the dogs barked, the trees   75
stuck their fingers to their noses. No
poet has come, no poet has come.

—soon no one in the park but
guilty lovers and stray dogs   .

                                Unleashed!   80

Alone, watching the May moon above the
trees   .

At nine o'clock the park closes. You
must be out of the lake, dressed, in
your cars and going: they change into   85
their street clothes in the back seats
and move out among the trees   .

---

2. "The poor little minister"—the itin-   effectual open-air sermon Dr. P. heard
erant preacher, Klaus Ehrens, whose in-   in II.ii.

The "great beast"[3] all removed
before the plunging night, the crickets'
black wings and hylas wake   .   90

Missing was the thing Jim had found in Marx and Veblen and
Adam Smith and Darwin—the dignified sound of a great, calm bell
tolling the morning of a new age   .   .   .   instead, the
slow complaining of a door loose on its hinges.[4]

                    Faitoute,[5] conscious by moments,
rouses by moments, rejects him finally
and strolls off   .

                    That the poem,
the most perfect rock and temple, the highest   95
falls, in clouds of gauzy spray, should be
so rivaled   .   that the poet,
in disgrace, should borrow from erudition (to
unslave the mind): railing at the vocabulary
(borrowing from those he hates, to his own   100
disfranchisement)   .

—discounting his failures   .
seeks to induce his bones to rise into a scene,
his dry bones,[6] above the scene, (they will not)
illuminating it within itself, out of itself   105
to form the colors, in the terms of some
back street, so that the history may escape
the panders

    .   .   accomplish the inevitable
poor, the invisible, thrashing, breeding   110
    .   debased city[7]

Love is no comforter, rather a nail in the
skull

    .   reversed in the mirror of its
own squalor, debased by the divorce from learning,   115
its garbage on the curbs, its legislators

3. I.e., the populace, used in a letter by
Alexander Hamilton (1757–1804).
4. The German Karl Marx (1818–83),
the American Thorstein B. Veblen
(1857–1929), and the Scotsman Adam
Smith (1723–90) are important economists and authors respectively of *Das
Kapital* (1867), *The Theory of the Lei-*
sure Class (1899), and *The Wealth of*
Nations (1776); the English biologist
Charles R. Darwin (1809–82) presented
his theory of evolution in *The Origin of*
Species (1859).
5. Faitoute, meaning "does everything,"
is identified in Book I as Dr. P.'s middle

name; here he rejects the preacher's sermon as a rival, inferior "poem."
6. An image of the community's rebirth,
drawn from the resurrection of "dry
bones" to form an army and a reunited
Israel in Ezekiel 37.
7. The preceding 18 lines have restated
the poet's ambition to articulate the
modern city, and rival in the poem's
perfection the actuality of its environment, even if he must resort to vocabularies, learning, and precedents that he
disdains and that traditionalists like Eliot
and Pound rely on more heavily.

under the garbage, uninstructed, incapable of
self instruction   .

        a thwarting, an avulsion   :

—flowers uprooted, Columbine, yellow and red,   120
strewn upon the path; dogwoods in full flower,
the trees dismembered; its women
shallow, its men steadfastly refusing—at
the best   .

            The language   .   words   125
without style! whose scholars (there are none)
        or dangling, about whom
the water weaves its strands encasing them
in a sort of thick lacquer, lodged
under its flow   .   130

            Caught (in mind)
beside the water he looks down, listens!
But discovers, still, no syllable in the confused
uproar: missing the sense (though he tries)
untaught but listening, shakes with the intensity   135
of his listening   .

Only the thought of the stream comforts him,
its terrifying plunge, inviting marriage—and
a wreath of fur   .

And She[8]   —   140
        Stones invent nothing, only a man invents.
        What answer the waterfall? filling
        the basin by the snag-toothed stones?

And He   —
        Clearly, it is the new, uninterpreted, that   145
        remoulds the old, pouring down   .

And she   —
        It has not been enacted in our day!

                    Le
pauvre petit ministre, swinging his arms, drowns   150
under the indifferent fragrance of the bass-wood
trees   .

*My feelings about you now are those of anger and indignation; and
they enable me to tell you a lot of things straight from the shoulder, without my usual tongue tied round-aboutness.*
    You might as well take all your own literature and everyone else's

8. The female principle, passive but energized, necessary to poetic creation.

and toss it into one of those big garbage trucks of the Sanitation
Department, so long as the people with the top-cream minds and
the "finer" sensibilities use those minds and sensibilities not to
make themselves more humane human beings than the average
person, but merely as means of ducking responsibility toward a
better understanding of their fellow men, except theoretically—
which doesn't mean a God damned thing.

    .   and there go the Evangels! (their organ
loaded into the rear of a light truck) scooting   155
down-hill   .   the children
are at least getting a kick out of *this!*

His anger mounts. He is chilled to the bone.
As there appears a dwarf, hideously deformed—[9]
he sees squirming roots trampled   160
under the foliage of his mind by the holiday
crowds as by the feet of the straining
minister. From his eyes sparrows start and
sing. His ears are toadstools, his fingers have
begun to sprout leaves (his voice is drowned   165
under the falls)   .

Poet, poet! sing your song, quickly! or
not insects but pulpy weeds will blot out
your kind.
        He all but falls   .   .

And She —   170
Marry us! Marry us!
        Or! be dragged down, dragged
under and lost

She[1] was married with empty words:

           better to   175
         stumble at
            the edge
             to fall
              fall
             and be   180

            —divorced
from the insistence of place—
          from knowledge,
from learning—the terms
foreign, conveying no immediacy, pouring down.   185

9. Peter Van Winkle, a dwarf with an
enormous head who was kept in a cradle
and regarded as a "wonder" by residents
and visitors in Paterson during the Revolution.

1. Mrs. Sarah Cumming, bride of the
Reverend Hopper Cumming, whose accidental drowning, or possibly suicide, at
the falls in 1812 is a recurring image in
Paterson.

—divorced

from time (no invention more), bald as an
egg   .

      and leaped (or fell) without a
language, tongue-tied   190
      the language worn out   .

The dwarf lived there, close to the waterfall—
saved by his protective coloring.

Go home. Write. Compose   .

Ha!   195

Be reconciled, poet, with your world, it is
the only truth!

Ha!

—the language is worn out.

And She —   200

      You have abandoned me!

      —at the magic sound of the stream
      she threw herself upon the bed—
      a pitiful gesture! lost among the words:
      Invent (if you can) discover or   205
      nothing is clear—will surmount
      the drumming in your head. There will be
      nothing clear, nothing clear   .

      He fled pursued by the roar.

Seventy-five of the world's leading scholars, poets and philoso-
phers gathered at Princeton last week   .   .   .   2

      Faitoute ground his heel   210
hard down on the stone:

Sunny today, with the highest temperature near 80 degrees; mod-
erate southerly winds. Partly cloudy and continued warm tomorrow,
with moderate southerly winds.

      Her belly   .   her belly is like
      a cloud   .   a cloud
             at evening   .

---

2. A newspaper account, probably of a
conference held in 1945–46 to commemorate the bicentennial of Princeton
University.

His mind would reawaken: 215
He
   Me with my pants, coat and vest still on!
She
   And me still in my galoshes!

—the descent follows the ascent—to wisdom   220
as to despair.
A man is under the crassest necessity
to break down the pinnacles of his moods
fearlessly —
to the bases; base! to the screaming dregs,   225
to have known the clean air   .

From that base, unabashed, to regain
the sun kissed summits of love!

                   —obscurely
in to scribble   .   and a war won!   230

—saying over to himself a song written
previously   .   inclines to believe
he sees, in the structure, something
                   of interest:

On this most voluptuous night of the year   235
the term of the moon is yellow with no light
the air's soft, the night bird has
only one note, the cherry tree in bloom

makes a blurr on the woods, its perfume
no more than half guessed moves in the mind.   240
No insect is yet awake, leaves are few.
In the arching trees there is no sleep.

The blood is still and indifferent, the face
does not ache nor sweat soil nor the
mouth thirst. Now love might enjoy its play   245
and nothing disturb the full octave of its run.

Her belly   .   her belly is like a white cloud   .   a
white cloud at evening   .   before the shuddering night!

*My attitude toward woman's wretched position in society and my
ideas about all the changes necessary there, were interesting to you,
weren't they, in so far as they made for literature? That my particular emotional orientation, in wrenching myself free from patterned
standardized feminine feelings, enabled me to do some passably
good work with poetry—all that was fine, wasn't it—something for*

you to sit up and take notice of! And you saw in one of my first letters to you (the one you had wanted to make use of, then, in the Introduction to your Paterson) an indication that my thoughts were to be taken seriously, because that too could be turned by you into literature, as something disconnected from life.

But when my actual personal life crept in, stamped all over with the very same attitudes and sensibilities and preoccupations that you found quite admirable as literature—that was an entirely different matter, wasn't it? No longer admirable, but, on the contrary, deplorable, annoying, stupid, or in some other way unpardonable; because those very ideas and feelings which make one a writer with some kind of new vision, are often the very same ones which, in living itself, make one clumsy, awkward, absurd, ungrateful, confidential where most people are reticent, and reticent where one should be confidential, and which cause one, all too often, to step on the toes of other people's sensitive egos as a result of one's stumbling earnestness or honesty carried too far. And that they are the very same ones—that's important, something to be remembered at all times, especially by writers like yourself who are so sheltered from life in the raw by the glass-walled conditions of their own safe lives.

Only my writing (when I write) is myself: only that is the real me in any essential way. Not because I bring to literature and to life two different inconsistent sets of values, as you do. No, I don't do that; and I feel that when anyone does do it, literature is turned into just so much intellectual excrement fit for the same stinking hole as any other kind.

But in writing (as in all forms of creative art) one derives one's unity of being and one's freedom to be one's self, from one's relationship to those particular externals (language, clay, paints, et cetera) over which one has complete control and the shaping of which lies entirely in one's own power; whereas in living, one's shaping of the externals involved there (of one's friendships, the structure of society, et cetera) is no longer entirely within one's own power but requires the cooperation and the understanding and the humanity of others in order to bring out what is best and most real in one's self.

That's why all that fine talk of yours about woman's need to "sail free in her own element" as a poet, becomes nothing but empty rhetoric in the light of your behavior towards me. No woman will ever be able to do that, completely, until she is able first to "sail free in her own element" in living itself—which means in her relationships with men even before she can do so in her relationships with other women. The members of any underprivileged class distrust and hate the "outsider" who is one of them, and women therefore—women in general—will never be content with their lot until the light seeps down to them, not from one of their own, but *from the eyes of changed male attitudes toward them—so that in the mean time, the problems and the awareness of a woman like myself are looked upon even more unsympathetically by other women than by men.*

And that, my dear doctor, is another reason why I needed of you a very different kind of friendship from the one you offered me.

I still don't know of course the specific thing that caused the cooling of your friendliness toward me. But I do know that if you were going to bother with me at all, there were only two things for you to have considered: (1) that I was, as I still am, a woman dying of loneliness—yes, really dying of it almost in the same way that people die slowly of cancer or consumption or any other such disease (and with all my efficiency in the practical world continually undermined by that loneliness); and (2) that I needed desperately, and still do, some ways and means of leading a writer's life, either by securing some sort of writer's job (or any other job having to do with my cultural interests) or else through some kind of literary journalism such as the book reviews—because only in work and jobs of that kind, can I turn into assets what are liabilities for me in jobs of a different kind.

Those were the two problems of mine that you continually and almost deliberately placed in the background of your attempts to help me. And yet they were, and remain, much greater than whether or not I get my poetry published. I didn't need the publication *of my poetry with your name lent to it, in order to go on writing poetry, half as much as I needed your friendship in other ways (the very ways you ignored) in order to write it. I couldn't, for that reason, have brought the kind of responsiveness and appreciation that you expected of me (not with any real honesty) to the kind of help from you which I needed so much less than the kind you withheld.*

Your whole relationship with me amounted to pretty much the same thing as your trying to come to the aid of a patient suffering from pneumonia by handing her a box of aspirin or Grove's cold pills and a glass of hot lemonade. I couldn't tell you that outright. And how were you, a man of letters, to have realized it when the imagination, so quick to assert itself most powerfully in the creation of a piece of literature, seems to have no power at all in enabling writers in your circumstances to fully understand the maladjustment and impotencies of a woman in my position?

When you wrote to me up in W. about that possible censor job, it seemed a very simple matter to you, didn't it, for me to make all the necessary inquiries about the job, arrange for the necessary interviews, start work (if I was hired) with all the necessary living conditions for holding down such a job, and thus find my life all straightened out in its practical aspects, at least—as if by magic?

But it's never so simple as that to get on one's feet even in the most ordinary practical ways, for anyone on my side of the railway tracks—which isn't your side, nor the side of your great admirer, Miss Fleming, nor even the side of those well cared for people like S. T. and S. S. who've spent most of their lives with some Clara or some Jeanne to look after them even when they themselves have been flat broke.

A completely down and out person with months of stripped, bare hardship behind him needs all kinds of things to even get himself in shape for looking for a respectable, important white-collar job. And then he needs ample funds for eating and sleeping and keeping up appearances (especially the latter) while going around for various interviews involved. And even if and when a job of that kind is obtained, he still needs the eating and the sleeping and the carfares and the keeping up of appearances and what not, waiting for his first pay check and even perhaps for the second pay check since the first one might have to go almost entirely for back rent or something else of that sort.

And all that takes a hell of a lot of money (especially for a woman)—a lot more than ten dollars or twenty five dollars. Or else it takes the kind of very close friends at whose apartment one is quite welcome to stay for a month or two, and whose typewriter one can use in getting off some of the required letters asking for interviews, and whose electric iron one can use in keeping one's clothes pressed, et cetera—the kind of close friends that I don't have and never have had, for reasons which you know.

Naturally, I couldn't turn to you, a stranger, for any such practical help on so large a scale; and it was stupid of me to have minimized the extent of help I needed when I asked you for that first money-order that got stolen and later for the second twenty five dollars—stupid because it was misleading. But the different kind of help I asked for, finally (and which you placed in the background) would have been an adequate substitute, because I could have carried out those plans which I mentioned to you in the late fall (the book reviews, supplemented by almost any kind of part-time job, and later some articles, and maybe a month at Yaddo this summer) without what it takes to get on one's feet in other very different ways. And the, eventually, the very fact that my name had appeared here and there in the book review sections of a few publications (I'd prefer not to use poetry that way) would have enabled me to obtain certain kinds of jobs (such as an O. W. I. job for instance) without all that red tape which affects only obscure, unknown people.

The anger and the indignation which I feel towards you now has served to pierce through the rough ice of that congealment which my creative faculties began to suffer from as a result of that last note from you. I find myself thinking and feeling in terms of poetry

again. But over and against that is the fact that I'm even more lack-
ing in anchorage of any kind than when I first got to know you. My
loneliness is a million fathoms deeper, and my physical energies
even more seriously sapped by it; and my economic situation is
naturally worse, with living costs so terribly high now, and with my
contact with your friend Miss X having come off so badly.

    However, she may have had another reason for paying no atten-
tion to that note of mine—perhaps the reason of having found out
that your friendliness toward me had cooled—which would have
made a difference to her, I suppose, since she is such a great
"admirer" of yours. But I don't know. That I'm in the dark about,
too; and when I went up to the "Times" last week, to try, on my
own, to get some of their fiction reviews (the "Times" publishes so
many of those), nothing came of that either. And it's writing that I
want to do—not operating a machine or a lathe, because with liter-
ature more and more tied up with the social problems and social
progress (for me, in my way of thinking) any contribution I might
be able to make to the welfare of humanity (in wartime or peace-
time) would have to be as a writer, and not as a factory worker.

    When I was very young, ridiculously young (of school-girl age)
for a critical role, with my mind not at all developed and all my
ideas in a state of first-week embryonic formlessness, I was able to
obtain book-reviews from any number of magazines without any dif-
ficulty—and all of them books by writers of accepted importance
(such as Cummings, Babette Deutsch, H. D.) whereas now when
my ideas have matured, and when I really have something to say, I
can get no work of that kind at all. And why is that? It's because in
all those intervening years, I have been forced, as a woman not con-
tent with woman's position in the world, to do a lot of pioneer
living which writers of your sex and with your particular social back-
ground do not have thrust upon them, and which the members of
my own sex frown upon (for reasons I've already referred to)—so
that at the very moment when I wanted to return to writing from
living (with my ideas clarified and enriched by living) there I was
(and still am)—because of that living—completely in exile socially.

    I glossed over and treated very lightly (in my first conversation
with you) those literary activities of my early girlhood, because the
work in itself was not much better than that which any talented
college freshman or precocious prep-school senior contributes to her
school paper. But, after all, that work, instead of appearing in a
school paper where it belonged, was taken so seriously by editors of
the acceptably important literary publications of that time, that I
was able to average as much as $15 a week, very easily, from it.
And I go into that now and stress it here; because you can better
imagine, in the light of that, just how I feel in realizing that on the
basis of just a few superficials (such as possessing a lot of appeal-
ingly youthful sex-appeal and getting in with the right set) I was

able to maintain my personal identity as a writer in my relationship to the world, whereas now I am cut off from doing so because it was necessary for me in my living, to strip myself of those superficials.

You've never had to live, Dr. P—not in any of the by-ways and dark underground passages where life so often has to be tested. The very circumstances of your birth and social background provided you with an escape from life in the raw; and you confuse that protection from life with an inability to live—*and are thus able to regard literature as nothing more than a desperate last extremity resulting from that illusionary inability to live. (I've been looking at some of your autobiographical works, as this indicates.)*

But living (unsafe living, I mean) isn't something one just sits back and decides about. It happens to one, in a small way, like measles; or in a big way, like a leaking boat or an earthquake. Or else it doesn't happen. And when it does, then one must bring, as I must, one's life to literature; and when it doesn't then one brings to life (as you do) purely literary sympathies and understandings, the insights and humanity of words on paper only—and also, alas, the ego of the literary man which most likely played an important part in the change of your attitude toward me. That literary man's ego wanted to help me in such a way, I think, that my own achievements might serve as a flower in his buttonhole, if that kind of help had been enough to make me bloom.

But I have no blossoms to bring to any man in the way of either love or friendship. That's one of the reasons why I didn't want that introduction to my poems. And I'm not wanting to be nasty or sarcastic in the last lines of this letter. On the contrary a feeling of profound sadness has replaced now the anger and the indignation with which I started to write all this. I wanted your friendship more than I ever wanted anything else (yes, more, and I've wanted other things badly) I wanted it desperately, not because I have a single thing with which to adorn any man's pride—but just because I haven't.

Yes, the anger which I imagined myself to feel on all the previous pages, was false. I am too unhappy and too lonely to be angry; and if some of the things to which I have called your attention here should cause any change of heart in you regarding me, that would be just about the only thing I can conceive of as occurring in my life right now.   *La votre*
                                                                        C.[3]

P.S. That I'm back here at 21 Pine Street causes me to add that that mystery as to who forged the "Cress" on that money order and

---

3. "Yours, C." the signature assigned to Cressida by Geoffrey Chaucer (c. 1340–1400) in *Troilus and Criseyde* (Book V, line 1631); the signature was admired by Williams for its suggestion of "a metropolitan softness of tone" in Cressida (*Selected Letters*, p. 233).

also took one of Brown's checks (though his was not cashed, and therefore replaced later) never did get cleared up. And the janitor who was here at the time, is dead now. I don't think it was he took any of the money. But still I was rather glad that the postoffice didn't follow it through because just in case Bob did have anything to do with it, he would have gotten into serious trouble—which I shouldn't have welcomed, because he was one of those miserably underpaid negroes and an awfully decent human being in lots of ways. But now I wish it had been followed through after he died (which was over two months ago) because the crooks may have been those low vile upstate farm people whose year-round exploitation of down and out farm help ought to be brought to light in some fashion, and because if they did steal the money order and were arrested for it, that in itself would have brought to the attention of the proper authorities all their other illegal activities as well: And yet that kind of justice doesn't interest me greatly. What's at the root of this or that crime or antisocial act, both psychologically and environmentally, always interests me more. But as I make that last statement, I'm reminded of how much I'd like to do a lot of things with people *in some prose—some stories, maybe a novel. I can't tell you how much I want the living which I need in order to write. And I simply can't achieve them entirely alone. I don't even possess a typewriter now, nor have even a rented one—and I can't think properly except on a typewriter. I can do poetry (though only the first draft) in long-hand, and letters. But for any prose writing, other than letters, I can't do any work without a typewriter. But that of course is the least of my problems—the typewriter; at least the easiest to do something about.* C.

Dr. P.:

This is the simplest, most outright letter I've ever written to you; and you ought to read it all the way through, and carefully, because it's about you, as a writer, and about the ideas regarding women that you expressed in your article on A. N.,[4] and because in regard to myself, it contains certain information which I did not think it necessary to give you before, and which I do think now you ought to have. And if my anger in the beginning makes you too angry to go on from there—well, that anger of mine isn't there in the last part, now as I attach this post-script. C.

And if you don't feel like reading it even for those reasons, will you then do so, please, *merely out of fairness to me—much time and much thought and much unhappiness having gone into those pages.*

1948

---

4. The American woman author Anaïs Nin (1903–77).

To Daphne[1] and Virginia

THE SMELL OF the heat is boxwood
    when rousing us
        a movement of the air
stirs our thoughts
    that had no life in them   5
        to a life, a life in which
two women agonize:
    to live and to breathe is no less.
        Two young women.
The box odor   10
    is the odor of that of which
        partaking separately,
each to herself
    I partake also
        .   .   separately.   15

BE PATIENT THAT I address you in a poem,
    there is no other
        fit medium.
The mind
    lives there. It is uncertain,   20
        can trick us and leave us
agonized. But for resources
    what can equal it?
        There is nothing. We
should be lost   25
    without its wings to
        fly off upon.

THE MIND IS the cause of our distresses
    but of it we can build anew.
        Oh something more than   30
it flies off to:
    a woman's world,
        of crossed sticks, stopping
thought. A new world
    is only a new mind.   35
        And the mind and the poem
are all apiece.
    Two young women
        to be snared,
odor of box,   40
    to bind and hold them
        for the mind's labors.

---

1. In Greek mythology, the water nymph who frustrated two lovers. The first, Leucippus, a mortal, disguised as a woman, intruded on Daphne and the other nymphs who were bathing; his rival, the god Apollo, warned them and the nymphs tore Leucippus apart. To evade the advances of Apollo, the second lover, Daphne begged to be turned into a laurel tree, and the laurel wreath with which Apollo consoled himself became associated with the arts.

ALL WOMEN ARE fated similarly
    facing men
        and there is always   45
another, such as I,
    who loves them,
        loves all women, but
finds himself, touching them,
    like other men,   50
        often confused.

I HAVE TWO sons,
    the husbands of these women,
        who live also
in a world of love,   55
    apart.
        Shall this odor of box in
        the heat
not also touch them
    fronting a world of women   60
        from which they are
debarred
    by the very scents which draw them on
        against easy access?

IN OUR FAMILY we stammer unless,   65
    half mad,
        we come to speech at last

AND I AM not
    a young man.
        My love encumbers me.   70
It is a love
    less than
        a young man's love but,
like this box odor
    more penetrant, infinitely   75
        more penetrant,
in that sense not to be resisted.

THERE IS, IN the hard
    give and take
        of a man's life with   80
        a woman
a thing which is not the stress itself
    but beyond
        and above
that,   85
    something that wants to rise
        and shake itself
free. We are not chickadees

on a bare limb
    with a worm in the mouth.   90
The worm is in our brains
   and concerns them
     and not food for our
offspring, wants to disrupt
   our thought   95
     and throw it
to the newspapers
   or anywhere.
     There is, in short,
a counter stress,   100
   born of the sexual shock,
    which survives it
consonant with the moon,
   to keep its own mind.
     There is, of course,   105
more.
   Women
    are not alone
in that. At least
   while this healing odor is abroad   110
    one can write a poem.

STAYING HERE in the country
   on an old farm
    we eat our breakfasts
on a balcony under an elm.   115
   The shrubs below us
    are neglected. And
there, penned in,
   or he would eat the garden,
    lives a pet goose who   120
tilts his head
   sidewise
    and looks up at us,
a very quiet old fellow
   who writes no poems.   125
    Fine mornings we sit there
while birds
   come and go.
    A pair of robins
is building a nest   .   130
   for the second time
    this season. Men
against their reason
   speak of love, sometimes,
    when they are old. It is   135
all they can do   .
   or watch a heavy goose

who waddles, slopping
            noisily in the mud of
his pool.   140

                                                            1954

The Ivy Crown[1]

The whole process is a lie,
            unless,
                        crowned by excess,
it break forcefully,
            one way or another,   5
                        from its confinement—
or find a deeper well.
            Anthony and Cleopatra[2]
                        were right;
they have shown   10
            the way. I love you
                        or I do not live
at all.
Daffodil time
            is past. This is   15
                        summer, summer!
the heart says,
            and not even the full of it.
                        no doubts
are permitted—   20
            though they will come
                        and may
before our time
            overwhelm us.
                        We are only mortal   25
but being mortal
            can defy our fate.
                        We may
by an outside chance
            even win! We do not   30
                        look to see
jonquils and violets
            come again
                        but there are,
still,   35
            the roses!
Romance has no part in it.
            The business of love is
                        cruelty which,

---

1. Ivy crowns are associated traditionally
with awards for victory and honor. Ivy
was sacred to Dionysus, the ancient
Greek god of wine, ecstasy, sacrifice, regeneration, and poetic inspiration.

2. The Roman warrior Marc Anthony
(c. 83–30 B.C.) and the Egyptian Queen
(69–30 B.C.). Their passionate, tempestuous love affair and eventual suicides
are recounted in Shakespeare's tragedy
Anthony and Cleopatra (1608).

by our wills,
        we transform
                to live together.   40
It has its seasons,
        for and against,
                whatever the heart   45
fumbles in the dark
        to assert
                toward the end of May.
Just as the nature of briars
        is to tear flesh,   50
                I have proceeded
through them.
        Keep
                the briars out,
they say.   55
        You cannot live
                and keep free of
briars.
Children pick flowers.
        Let them.   60
                Though having them
in hand they have
        no further use for them
                but leave them crumpled
at the curb's edge.   65
At our age the imagination
        across the sorry facts
                lifts us
to make roses
        stand before thorns.   70
                Sure
love is cruel,
        and selfish
                and totally obtuse—
at least, blinded by the light,   75
        young love is.
                But we are older,
I to love
        and you to be loved,
                we have,   80
no matter how,
        by our wills survived
                to keep
the jeweled prize
        always   85
                at our finger tips.
We will it so
        and so it is
                past all accident.

1955

The Sparrow
TO MY FATHER

This sparrow
        who comes to sit at my window
                is a poetic truth
more than a natural one.
        His voice,
                his movements,
his habits—
        how he loves to
                flutter his wings
in the dust—
        all attest it;
                granted, he does it
to rid himself of lice
        but the relief he feels
                makes him
cry out lustily—
        which is a trait
                more related to music
than otherwise.
        Wherever he finds himself
                in early spring,
on back streets
        or beside palaces,
                he carries on
unaffectedly
        his amours.
                It begins in the egg,
his sex genders it:
        What is more pretentiously
                useless
or about which
        we more pride ourselves?
                It leads as often as not
to our undoing.
        The cockerel, the crow
                with their challenging voices
cannot surpass
        the insistence
                of his cheep!
Once
        at El Paso
                toward evening,
I saw—and heard!—
        ten thousand sparrows
                who had come in from
the desert
        to roost. They filled the trees
                of a small park. Men fled

(with ears ringing!)
   from their droppings,   50
     leaving the premises
to the alligators
   who inhabit
     the fountain. His image
is familiar   55
   as that of the aristocratic
    Unicorn,[1] a pity
there are not more oats eaten
   now-a-days
     to make living easier 60
for him.[2]
   At that,
     his small size,
keen eyes,
   serviceable beak   65
     and general truculence
assure his survival—
   to say nothing
    of his innumerable
brood.   70
   Even the Japanese
    know him
and have painted him
   sympathetically,
     with profound insight 75
into his minor
   characteristics.
     Nothing even remotely
subtle
   about his lovemaking.   80
    He crouches
before the female,
   drags his wings,
    waltzing,
throws back his head   85
   and simply—
    yells! The din
is terrific.
   The way he swipes his bill
    across a plank   90
to clean it,
   is decisive.
     So with everything
he does. His coppery
   eyebrows   95
    give him the air

1. A mythological creature, horse-like, with a long horn growing from its forehead.
2. Before the introduction of the auto-mobile, when horses were the common mode of transportation, a major source of food for the sparrows was the par-tially digested oat kernels left in the horse droppings.

of being always
      a winner—and yet
           I saw once,
the female of his species   100
      clinging determinedly
           to the edge of
a waterpipe,
      catch him
           by his crown-feathers   105
to hold him
      silent,
           subdued,
hanging above the city streets
      until   110
           she was through with him.
What was the use
      of that?
           She hung there
herself,   115
      puzzled at her success.
           I laughed heartily.
Practical to the end,
      it is the poem
           of his existence   120
that trumphed
      finally;
           a wisp of feathers
flattened to the pavement,
      wings spread symmetrically   125
           as if in flight,
the head gone,
      the black escutcheon
           undecipherable,
an effigy of a sparrow,   130
      a dried wafer only,
           left to say
and it says it
      without offense,
           beautifully;   135
This was I,
      a sparrow.
           I did my best;
farewell.

                              1955

The Lady Speaks

A storm raged among the live oaks
      while my husband and I
           sat in the semi-dark
listening!

We watched from the windows   5
          the lights off
saw the moss
          whipped upright
                by the wind's force.
Two candles we had lit   10
          side by side
                before us
so solidly had our house been built
          kept their tall flames
                unmoved.   15
May it be so
          when a storm sends the moss
                whipping
back and forth
          upright   20
                above my head
like flames in the final
          fury.

                                    1955

The Dance

When the snow falls the flakes
spin upon the long axis
that concerns them most intimately
two and two to make a dance

the mind dances with itself,   5
taking you by the hand,
your lover follows
there are always two,

yourself and the other,
the point of your shoe setting the pace,   10
if you break away and run
the dance is over

Breathlessly you will take
another partner
better or worse who will keep   15
at your side, at your stops

whirls and glides until he too
leaves off
on his way down as if
there were another direction   20

gayer, more carefree
spinning face to face but always down
with each other secure
only in each other's arms

But only the dance is sure!   25
make it your own.
Who can tell
what is to come of it?

in the woods of your
own nature whatever   30
twig interposes, and bare twigs
have an actuality of their own

this flurry of the storm
that holds us,
plays with us and discards us   35
dancing, dancing as may be credible.

1962

WILLA CATHER

1873–1947

When she was ten, Willa Sibert Cather's family moved from a Virginia farm to the Nebraska prairie, where their fertile land was surrounded by less good soil that was tilled by Scandinavian, French, and Bohemian families who had recently immigrated to the United States. Her father abandoned farming after one year to become a mortgage and loan broker in Red Cloud, a small town where the immigrant farmers' daughters sought jobs as servants and where middle-class families of European extraction—a German music teacher, an English tutor in Latin and Greek, a couple who spoke both German and French and encouraged Cather to use their large library—exposed her to European culture. That process continued when she attended the University of Nebraska, 1891–95, where sophisticated residents of Lincoln brought her in touch with French writing and with the literary and musical world of the eastern seaboard. In the harsh beauty of the prairie landscape, the desperate struggles of immigrant families to survive, and the quest for cultural refinement in the American environment, Cather was to find the materials for the moving and evocative fiction that marked her career.

While in college Cather began publishing stories whose explosive violence and brutal ironies match those in the fiction of Hamlin Garland and Stephen Crane. She also wrote columns and theater reviews for the *Nebraska Journal*; taking the firm stand of one determined to show easterners that the Midwest has high standards, she became known to traveling theatrical troupes as the "meat axe young girl."[1]

She moved to Pittsburgh in 1896 to take an editorial position on a family magazine but after five successful years turned to teaching English in high school, where the predictable routines left time for writing. Then in 1906 she accepted the managing editorship of the famed *McClure's*

1. Quoted by Edward K. Brown and Leon Edel, *Willa Cather* (1953), p. 68.

Magazine in New York City. She had made three trips to Europe by 1912, when she concluded her successful journalistic career to devote her full time to writing.

She had published a volume of verse in 1903 (*April Twilights*), but the first works to attract critical attention were a collection of stories, *The Troll Garden* (1905), and the novel *Alexander's Bridge* (1912). The stories, comparable in theme to those of Henry James, recount the lives of sensitive persons or artists who, after leaving small towns in the West, return in defeat to the communities that do not appreciate their talents, or tell of successful artists, moving in pleasant middle-class or cosmopolitan circles, whose talents are mediocre. In the novel an engineer's bridge, flawed in its design, collapses beneath him before he can correct the flaw or warn workers of its danger. His talent has been corroded by success, and social diversions keep him from the construction site, while the design has been compromised by the budget and specifications of those who commissioned the structure.

It was her next three novels, however, which drew most deeply on her experience of the pioneering West, that established her position on the literary scene. Her confession in 1912 that whenever she returned to the prairie she had an obsessive fear that death might overtake her in a cornfield[2] testifies to the strength of the fascination which the material held for her. The novels celebrate courageous heroines whose success is won from tragic circumstances. In *O Pioneers!* (1913) a young engraver returns to the Nebraska prairie from the Alaska mining frontier to marry a Swedish farm girl who has found the stamina to succeed in farming and who has the requisite "imagination" to hold to the "idea" of the pioneer dream and to find her medium of expression in the land itself, creating "order" and symmetry in the "fine arrangement manifest all over the great farm"; her heroism is to accept her life and a husband in the light of that vision. In *Song of the Lark* (1915) an aspiring concert singer finds encouragement but no personal or professional fulfillment in her Colorado home or in Chicago, where she is sent for voice training. Finally, on a visit to Arizona, bathing in a stream near the ruins of cliff-dwelling Indians, she finds the sanction for her vocation as artist in the "ritualistic" atmosphere of the canyon, which reveals a "continuity of life, that reached back into the old time." In *My Antonia* (1918), the personal memoir of a Harvard-educated man focuses on the story of another frontier heroine who survives the bleakness of life on her defeated father's farm, the drudgery of a serving girl's life, and betrayal by a faithless lover, to find satisfaction as wife and mother on a Nebraska farm, becoming a "rich mine of life, like the founders of early races."

These novels attracted favorable critical attention, but her bleak war novel entitled *One of Ours* (1922), though it received the Pulitzer Prize, was not well received. Indeed its completion coincided with a crisis in her personal and professional life. Poor health, dissatisfaction with her publisher's promotion of her books, and distress over the increasing standardization of a machine-dominated society lay behind her later statement that "the world broke in two in 1922 or thereabouts."[3] In 1920 she gave the manuscript of her war novel to a new publisher, who brought it out along with a collection of earlier tales and helped increase her income to

2. *Ibid.*, p. 164.   3. *Not under Forty*, p. v.

$19,000 in 1923. And in 1922 Cather returned to Red Cloud to be confirmed in the Protestant Episcopal Church. From 1922 on the dominant themes of her fiction were the need for sustaining illusions in the face of corrosive contemporary values, the perils of success, the importance of ritualistic religion, and the nostalgic evocation of the remote American past.

In her masterful *A Lost Lady* (1923) the young Niel Herbert learns that the gracious world of Captain Forrester and his wife Marian has been undermined, and the wife corrupted, by a profiteering lawyer. But he celebrates nevertheless Marian's stubborn courage in her later years, her refined manners, and her "power of suggesting things much lovelier than herself," while celebrating also the captain's commitment to the "mirage" of the West, the "dreams" of "courteous" and "great-hearted adventurers" who settled the land and built the railways. In *The Professor's House*, Godfrey St. John is brought to the point of suicide at the age of fifty-two by his wife's luxurious tastes, the recognition that his career lies behind him, and his guilt at living off the income of a young physicist who was killed in the war. But he is saved by a devout Roman Catholic seamstress, and he lives to publish the memoir of a young friend to which the central section of the book is devoted. The memoir tells of the young man's discovery of the ruins of a cliff-dwellers' civilization that is an image of an ancient "world above the world" suggesting symmetry, order, and "eternal repose." Cather's nostalgia is even more pronounced, though sensitively evoked, in *Death Comes for the Archbishop*, an account of two well-bred European priests who test and renew their vocation while bringing Roman Catholicism to New Mexico, and in *Shadows on the Rock* (1931), where seventeenth-century Quebec, sustaining a civilized world of "twilight and miracles," confronts the wilderness forests and provides a setting for the marriage of the fur trader Pierre Charron, who combines the "good manners of the Old World" with "the dash and daring of the new."

In these last two works Cather sought consciously to emulate the loosely structured narrations of legend and the effects of "pictures remembered rather than experienced."[4] But in all her writings she avoided the cataloguing of realistic detail which she associated with journalism or realism and strove to work "by suggestion rather than by enumeration" in ways she associated at once with "modern painting," with the fastidious reserve of Hawthorne's *Scarlet Letter*, and with the delicacy of Sarah Orne Jewett's local-color fiction.[5] She is best remembered for the lucidity of her style, the sensitivity with which she rendered the prairie landscape, and the insight with which she treated the struggles of immigrant heroines and persons of culture and refinement to discover their vocations in the West.

Neighbour Rosicky[1]

I

When Doctor Burleigh told neighbour Rosicky he had a bad heart, Rosicky protested.

---

4. *Willa Cather on Writing*, pp. 9, 15.
5. *Not under Forty*, pp. 48–49, 84.

1. From *Obscure Destinies* (1932), pp. 7–62.

'So? No, I guess my heart was always pretty good. I got a little asthma, maybe. Just a awful short breath when I was pitchin' hay last summer, dat's all.'

'Well, now, Rosicky, if you know more about it than I do, what did you come to me for? It's your heart that makes you short of breath, I tell you. You're sixty-five years old, and you've always worked hard, and your heart's tired. You've got to be careful from now on, and you can't do heavy work any more. You've got five boys at home to do it for you.'

The old farmer looked up at the doctor with a gleam of amusement in his queer, triangular-shaped eyes. His eyes were large and lively, but the lids were caught up in the middle in a curious way, so that they formed a triangle. He did not look like a sick man. His brown face was creased but not wrinkled, he had a ruddy colour in his smooth-shaven cheeks and in his lips, under his long brown moustache. His hair was thin and ragged around his ears, but very little grey. His forehead, naturally high and crossed by deep parallel lines, now ran all the way up to his pointed crown. Rosicky's face had the habit of looking interested—suggested a contented disposition and a reflective quality that was gay rather than grave. This gave him a certain detachment, the easy manner of an onlooker and observer.

'Well, I guess you ain't got no pills fur a bad heart, Doctor Ed. I guess the only thing is fur me to git me a new one.'

Doctor Burleigh swung round in his desk chair and frowned at the old farmer.

'I think if I were you I'd take a little care of the old one, Rosicky.'

Rosicky shrugged. 'Maybe I don't know how. I expect you mean fur me not to drink my coffee no more.'

'I wouldn't, in your place. But you will do as you choose about that. I've never yet been able to separate a Bohemian[2] from his coffee or his pipe. I've quit trying. But the sure thing is you've got to cut out farm work. You can feed the stock and do chores about the barn, but you can't do anything in the fields that makes you short of breath.'

'How about shelling corn?'

'Of course not!'

Rosicky considered with puckered brows.

'I can't make my heart go no longer'n it wants to, can I, Doctor Ed?'

'I think it's good for five or six years yet, maybe more, if you'll take the strain off it. Sit around the house and help Mary. If I had a good wife like yours, I'd want to stay around the house.'

His patient chuckled. 'It ain't no place fur a man. I don't like

2. Native of Bohemia, a region in western Czechoslovakia.

no old man hanging round the kitchen too much. An' my wife, she's a awful hard worker her own self.'

'That's it; you can help her a little. My Lord, Rosicky, you are one of the few men I know who has a family he can get some comfort out of; happy dispositions, never quarrel among themselves, and they treat you right. I want to see you live a few years and enjoy them.'

'Oh, they're good kids, all right.' Rosicky assented.

The doctor wrote him a prescription and asked him how his oldest son, Rudolph, who had married in the spring, was getting on. Rudolph had struck out for himself, on rented land. 'And how's Polly? I was afraid Mary mightn't like an American daughter-in-law, but it seems to be working out all right.'

'Yes, she's a fine girl. Dat widder woman bring her daughters up very nice. Polly got lots of spunk, an' she got some style, too. Da's nice, for young folks to have some style.' Rosicky inclined his head gallantly. His voice and his twinkly smile were an affectionate compliment to his daughter-in-law.

'It looks like a storm, and you'd better be getting home before it comes. In town in the car?' Doctor Burleigh rose.

'No, I'm in de wagon. When you got five boys, you ain't got much chance to ride round in de Ford. I ain't much for cars, noway.'

'Well, it's a good road out to your place; but I don't want you bumping around in a wagon much. And never again on a hay-rake, remember!'

Rosicky placed the doctor's fee delicately behind the desk-telephone, looking the other way, as if this were an absent-minded gesture. He put on his plush cap and his corduroy jacket with a sheepskin collar, and went out.

The doctor picked up his stethoscope and frowned at it as if he were seriously annoyed with the instrument. He wished it had been telling tales about some other man's heart, some old man who didn't look the doctor in the eye so knowingly, or hold out such a warm brown hand when he said good-bye. Doctor Burleigh had been a poor boy in the country before he went away to medical school; he had known Rosicky almost ever since he could remember, and he had a deep affection for Mrs. Rosicky.

Only last winter he had had such a good breakfast at Rosicky's, and that when he needed it. He had been out all night on a long, hard confinement case at Tom Marshall's—a big rich farm where there was plenty of stock and plenty of feed and a great deal of expensive farm machinery of the newest model, and no comfort whatever. The woman had too many children and too much work, and she was no manager. When the baby was born at last, and handed over to the assisting neighbour woman, and the mother was properly attended to, Burleigh refused any breakfast in that slovenly house, and drove his buggy—the snow was too deep for a car —eight miles to Anton Rosicky's place. He didn't know another farm-house where a man could get such a warm welcome, and such good strong coffee with rich cream. No wonder the old chap didn't want to give up his coffee!

He had driven in just when the boys had come back from the barn and were washing up for breakfast. The long table, covered with a bright oilcloth, was set out with dishes waiting for them, and the warm kitchen was full of the smell of coffee and hot biscuit and sausage. Five big handsome boys, running from twenty to twelve, all with what Burleigh called natural good manners—they hadn't a bit of the painful self-consciousness he himself had to struggle with when he was a lad. One ran to put his horse away, another helped him off with his fur coat and hung it up, and Josephine, the youngest child and the only daughter, quickly set another place under her mother's direction.

With Mary, to feed creatures was the natural expression of affection—her chickens, the calves, her big hungry boys. It was a rare pleasure to feed a young man whom she seldom saw and of whom she was as proud as if he belonged to her. Some country house-keepers would have stopped to spread a white cloth over the oil-cloth, to change the thick cups and plates for their best china, and the wooden-handled knives for plated ones. But not Mary.

'You must take us as you find us, Doctor Ed. I'd be glad to put out my good things for you if you was expected, but I'm glad to get you any way at all.'

He knew she was glad—she threw back her head and spoke out as if she were announcing him to the whole prairie. Rosicky hadn't said anything at all; he merely smiled his twinkling smile, put some more coal on the fire, and went into his own room to pour the doctor a little drink in a medicine glass. When they were all seated, he watched his wife's face from his end of the table and spoke to her in Czech. Then, with the instinct of politeness which seldom failed him, he turned to the doctor and said slyly: 'I was just tellin' her not to ask you no questions about Mrs. Marshall till you eat some breakfast. My wife, she's terrible fur to ask questions.'

The boys laughed, and so did Mary. She watched the doctor devour her biscuit and sausage, too much excited to eat anything herself. She drank her coffee and sat taking in everything about her visitor. She had known him when he was a poor country boy, and was boastfully proud of his success, always saying: 'What do people go to Omaha for, to see a doctor, when we got the best one in the State right here?' If Mary liked people at all, she felt physical pleasure in the sight of them, personal exultation in any good fortune that came to them. Burleigh didn't know many women like that, but he knew she was like that.

When his hunger was satisfied, he did, of course, have to tell them about Mrs. Marshall, and he noticed what a friendly interest the boys took in the matter.

Rudolph, the oldest one (he was still living at home then), said: 'The last time I was over there, she was lifting them big heavy milk-cans, and I knew she ought not to be doing it.'

'Yes, Rudolph told me about that when he come home, and I said it wasn't right,' Mary put in warmly. 'It was all right for me to do them things up to the last, for I was terrible strong, but that woman's weakly. And do you think she'll be able to nurse it, Ed?' She sometimes forgot to give him the title she was so proud of. 'And to think of your being up all night and then not able to get a decent breakfast! I don't know what's the matter with such people.'

'Why, mother,' said one of the boys, 'if Doctor Ed had got breakfast there, we wouldn't have him here. So you ought to be glad.'

'He knows I'm glad to have him, John, any time. But I'm sorry for that poor woman, how bad she'll feel the doctor had to go away in the cold without his breakfast.'

'I wish I had been in practice when these were getting born.' The doctor looked down the row of close-clipped heads. 'I missed some good breakfasts by not being.'

The boys begin to laugh at their mother because she flushed so red, but she stood her ground and threw up her head. 'I don't care, you wouldn't have got away from this house without breakfast. No doctor ever did. I'd have had something ready fixed that Anton could warm up for you.'

The boys laughed harder than ever, and exclaimed at her: 'I'll bet you would!' 'She would, that!'

'Father, did you get breakfast for the doctor when we were born?'

'Yes, and he used to bring me my breakfast, too, mighty nice. I was always awful hungry!' Mary admitted with a guilty laugh.

While the boys were getting the doctor's horse, he went to the window to examine the house plants.

'What do you do to your geraniums to keep them blooming all winter, Mary? I never pass this house that from the road I don't see your windows full of flowers.'

She snapped off a dark red one, and a ruffled new green leaf, and put them in his buttonhole. 'There, that looks better. You look too solemn for a young man, Ed. Why don't you git married? I'm worried about you. Settin' at breakfast, I looked at you real hard, and I seen you've got some grey hairs already.'

'Oh, yes! They're coming. Maybe they'd come faster if I married.'

'Don't talk so. You'll ruin your health eating at the hotel. I could send your wife a nice loaf of nut bread, if you only had one.

I don't like to see a young man getting grey. I'll tell you something, Ed; you make some strong black tea and keep it handy in a bowl, and every morning just brush it into your hair, an' it'll keep the grey from showin' much. That's the way I do!'

Sometimes the doctor heard the gossipers in the drugstore wondering why Rosicky didn't get on faster. He was industrious, and so were his boys, but they were rather free and easy, weren't pushers, and they didn't always show good judgment. They were comfortable, they were out of debt, but they didn't get much ahead. Maybe, Doctor Burleigh reflected, people as generous and warm-hearted and affectionate as the Rosickys never got ahead much; maybe you could not enjoy your life and put it into the bank, too.

II

When Rosicky left Doctor Burleigh's office, he went into the farm-implement store to light his pipe and put on his glasses and read over the list Mary had given him. Then he went into the general merchandise place next door and stood about until the pretty girl with the plucked eyebrows, who always waited on him, was free. Those eyebrows, two thin India-ink strokes, amused him, because he remembered how they used to be. Rosicky always prolonged his shopping by a little joking; the girl knew the old fellow admired her, and she liked to chaff with him.

'Seems to me about every other week you buy ticking, Mr. Rosicky, and always the best quality,' she remarked as she measured off the heavy bolt with red stripes.

'You see, my wife is always makin' goose-fedder pillows, an' de thin stuff don't hold in dem little down-fedders.'

'You must have lots of pillows at your home.'

'Sure. She makes quilts of dem, too. We sleeps easy. Now she's makin' a fedder quilt for my son's wife. You know Polly, that married my Rudolph. How much my bill, Miss Pearl?'

'Eight eighty-five.'

'Chust make it nine, and put in some candy fur de women.'

'As usual. I never did see a man buy so much candy for his wife. First thing you know, she'll be getting too fat.'

'I'd like dat. I ain't much fur all dem slim women like what de style is now.'

'That's one for me, I suppose, Mr. Bohunk!' Pearl sniffed and elevated her India-ink strokes.

When Rosicky went out to his wagon, it was beginning to snow —the first snow of the season, and he was glad to see it. He rattled out of town and along the highway through a wonderfully rich stretch of country, the finest farms in the county. He admired this High Prairie, as it was called, and always liked to drive through it.

His own place lay in a rougher territory, where there was some clay in the soil and it was not so productive. When he bought his land, he hadn't the money to buy on High Prairie; so he told his boys, when they grumbled, that if their land hadn't some clay in it, they wouldn't own it at all. All the same, he enjoyed looking at these fine farms, as he enjoyed looking at a prize bull

After he had gone eight miles, he came to the graveyard, which lay just at the edge of his own hay-land. There he stopped his horses and sat still on his wagon seat, looking about at the snow-fall. Over yonder on the hill he could see his own house, crouching low, with the clump of orchard behind and the windmill before, and all down the gentle hill-slope the rows of pale gold cornstalks stood out against the white field. The snow was falling over the cornfield and the pasture and the hay-land, steadily, with very little wind—a nice dry snow. The graveyard had only a light wire fence about it and was all overgrown with long red grass. The fine snow, settling into this red grass and upon the few little evergreens and the headstones, looked very pretty.

It was a nice graveyard, Rosicky reflected, sort of snug and home-like, not cramped or mournful—a big sweep all round it. A man could lie down in the long grass and see the complete arch of the sky over him, hear the wagons go by; in summer the mowing-machine rattled right up to the wire fence. And it was so near home. Over there across the cornstalks his own roof and windmill looked so good to him that he promised himself to mind the doctor and take care of himself. He was awful fond of his place, he ad-mitted. He wasn't anxious to leave it. And it was a comfort to think that he would never have to go farther than the edge of his own hayfield. The snow, falling over his barnyard and the graveyard, seemed to draw things together like. And they were all old neigh-bours in the graveyard, most of them friends; there was nothing to feel awkward or embarrassed about. Embarrassment was the most disagreeable feeling Rosicky knew. He didn't often have it—only with certain people whom he didn't understand at all.

Well, it was a nice snowstorm; a fine sight to see the snow falling so quietly and graciously over so much open country. On his cap and shoulders, on the horses' backs and manes, light, delicate, mysterious it fell; and with it a dry cool fragrance was released into the air. It meant rest for vegetation and men and beast, for the ground itself; a season of long nights for sleep, leisurely break-fasts, peace by the fire. This and much more went through Rosicky's mind, but he merely told himself that winter was coming, clucked to his horses, and drove on.

When he reached home, John, the youngest boy, ran out to put away his team for him, and he met Mary coming up from the out-side cellar with her apron full of carrots. They went into the house together. On the table, covered with oilcloth figured with clusters of blue grapes, a place was set, and he smelled hot coffeecake of some kind. Anton never lunched in town; he thought that extravagant, and anyhow he didn't like the food. So Mary always had something ready for him when he got home.

After he was settled in his chair, stirring his coffee in a big cup, Mary took out of the oven a pan of *kolache* stuffed with apricots, examined them anxiously to see whether they had got too dry, put them beside his plate, and then sat down opposite him.

Rosicky asked her in Czech if she wasn't going to have any coffee.

She replied in English, as being somehow the right language for transacting business: 'Now what did Doctor Ed say, Anton? You tell me just what.'

'He said I was to tell you some compliments, but I forgot 'em.' Rosicky's eyes twinkled.

'About you, I mean. What did he say about your asthma?'

'He says I ain't got no asthma.' Rosicky took one of the little rolls in his broad brown fingers. The thickened nail of his right thumb told the story of his past.

'Well, what is the matter? And don't try to put me off.'

'He don't say nothing much, only I'm a little older, and my heart ain't so good like it used to be.'

Mary started and brushed her hair back from her temples with both hands as if she were a little out of her mind. From the way she glared, she might have been in a rage with him.

'He says there's something the matter with your heart? Doctor Ed says so?'

'Now don't yell at me like I was a hog in de garden, Mary. You know I always did like to hear a woman talk soft. He didn't say anything de matter wid my heart, only it ain't so young like it used to be, an' he tell me not to pitch hay or run de corn-sheller.'

Mary wanted to jump up, but she sat still. She admired the way he never under any circumstances raised his voice or spoke roughly. He was city-bred, and she was country-bred; she often said she wanted her boys to have their papa's nice ways.

'You never have no pain there, do you? It's your breathing and your stomach that's been wrong. I wouldn't believe nobody but Doctor Ed about it. I guess I'll go see him myself. Didn't he give you no advice?'

'Chust to take it easy like, an' stay round de house dis winter. I guess you got some carpenter work for me to do. I kin make some new shelves for you, and I want dis long time to build a closet in de boys' room and make dem two little fellers keep dere clo'es hung up.'

Rosicky drank his coffee from time to time, while he considered. His moustache was of the soft long variety and came down over his mouth like the teeth of a buggy rake over a bundle of hay. Each time he put down his cup, he ran his blue handkerchief over his lips. When he took a drink of water, he managed very neatly with the back of his hand.

Mary sat watching him intently, trying to find any change in his face. It is hard to see anyone who has become like your own body to you. Yes, his hair had got thin, and his high forehead had deep lines running from left to right. But his neck, always clean-shaved except in the busiest seasons, was not loose or baggy. It was burned a dark reddish brown, and there were deep creases in it, but it looked firm and full of blood. His cheeks had a good colour. On either side of his mouth there was a half-moon down the length of his cheek, not wrinkles, but two lines that had come there from his habitual expression. He was shorter and broader than when she married him; his back had grown broad and curved, a good deal like the shell of an old turtle, and his arms and legs were short.

He was fifteen years older than Mary, but she had hardly ever thought about it before. He was her man, and the kind of man she liked. She was rough, and he was gentle—city-bred, as she always said. They had been shipmates on a rough voyage and had stood by each other in trying times. Life had gone well with them because, at bottom, they had the same ideas about life. They agreed, without discussion, as to what was most important and what was secondary. They didn't often exchange opinions, even in Czech—it was as if they had thought the same thought together. A good deal had to be sacrificed and thrown overboard in a hard life like theirs, and they had never disagreed as to the things that could go. It had been a hard life, and a soft life, too. There wasn't anything brutal in the short, broad-backed man with the three-cornered eyes and the forehead that went on to the top of his skull. He was a city man, a gentle man, and though he had married a rough farm girl, he had never touched her without gentleness.

They had been at one accord not to hurry through life, not to be always skimping and saving. They saw their neighbours buy more land and feed more stock than they did, without discontent. Once when the creamery agent came to the Rosickys to persuade them to sell him their cream, he told them how much money the Fasslers, their nearest neighbours, had made on their cream last year.

'Yes,' said Mary, 'and look at them Fassler children! Pale, pinched little things, they look like skimmed milk. I had rather put some colour into my children's faces than put money into the bank.'

The agent shrugged and turned to Anton.

'I guess we'll do like she says,' said Rosicky.

III

Mary very soon got into town to see Doctor Ed, and then she had a talk with her boys and set a guard over Rosicky. Even John, the youngest, had his father on his mind. If Rosicky went to throw hay down from the loft, one of the boys ran up the ladder and took the fork from him. He sometimes complained that though he was getting to be an old man, he wasn't an old woman yet.

That winter he stayed in the house in the afternoons and carpentered, or sat in the chair between the window full of plants and the wooden bench where the two pails of drinking-water stood. This spot was called 'Father's corner,' though it was not a corner at all. He had a shelf there, where he kept his Bohemian papers and his pipes and tobacco, and his shears and needles and thread and tailor's thimble. Having been a tailor in his youth, he couldn't bear to see a woman patching at his clothes, or at the boys'. He liked tailoring, and always patched all the overalls and jackets and work shirts. Occasionally he made over a pair of pants one of the older boys had outgrown, for the little fellow.

While he sewed, he let his mind run back over his life. He had a good deal to remember, really; life in three countries. The only part of his youth he didn't like to remember was the two years he had spent in London, in Cheapside, working for a German tailor who was wretchedly poor. Those days, when he was nearly always hungry, when his clothes were dropping off him for dirt, and the sound of a strange language kept him in continual bewilderment, had left a sore spot in his mind that wouldn't bear touching.

He was twenty when he landed at Castle Garden in New York, and he had a protector who got him work in a tailor shop in Vesey Street, down near the Washington Market. He looked upon that part of his life as very happy. He became a good workman, he was industrious, and his wages were increased from time to time. He minded his own business and envied nobody's good fortune. He went to night school and learned to read English. He often did overtime work and was well paid for it, but somehow he never saved anything. He couldn't refuse a loan to a friend, and he was self-indulgent. He liked a good dinner, and a little went for beer, a little for tobacco; a good deal went to the girls. He often stood through an opera on Saturday nights; he could get standing-room for a dollar. Those were the great days of opera in New York, and it gave a fellow something to think about for the rest of the week. Rosicky had a quick ear, and a childish love of all the stage splendour; the scenery, the costumes, the ballet. He usually went with a chum, and after the performance they had beer, and maybe some oysters, somewhere. It was a fine life; for the first five years or so it satisfied him completely. He was never hungry or cold or dirty, and everything amused him: a fire, a dog fight, a parade, a storm, a ferry ride. He thought New York the finest, richest, friendliest city in the world.

Moreover, he had what he called a happy home life. Very near the tailor shop was a small furniture factory, where an old Austrian,

Loeffler, employed a few skilled men and made unusual furniture, most of it to order, for the rich German housewives uptown. The top floor of Loeffler's five-story factory was a loft, where he kept his choice lumber and stored the old pieces of furniture left on his hands. One of the young workmen he employed was a Czech, and he and Rosicky became fast friends. They persuaded Loeffler to let them have a sleeping-room in one corner of the loft. They bought good beds and bedding and had their pick of the furniture kept up there. The loft was low-pitched, but light and airy, full of windows, and good-smelling by reason of the fine lumber put up there to season. Old Loeffler used to go down to the docks and buy wood from South America and the East from the sea captains. The young men were as foolish about their house as a bridal pair. Zichec, the young cabinet-maker, devised every sort of convenience, and Rosicky kept their clothes in order. At night and on Sundays, when the quiver of machinery underneath was still, it was the quietest place in the world, and on summer nights all the sea winds blew in. Zichec often practised on his flute in the evening. They were both fond of music and went to the opera together. Rosicky thought he wanted to live like that forever.

But as the years passed, all alike, he began to get a little restless. When spring came round, he would begin to feel fretted, and he got to drinking. He was likely to drink too much of a Saturday night. On Sunday he was languid and heavy, getting over his spree. On Monday he plunged into work again. So he never had time to figure out what ailed him, although he knew something did. When the grass turned green in Park Place, and the lilac hedge at the back of Trinity churchyard put out its blossoms, he was tormented by a longing to run away. That was why he drank too much; to get a temporary illusion of freedom and wide horizons.

Rosicky, the old Rosicky, could remember as if it were yesterday the day when the young Rosicky found out what was the matter with him. It was on a Fourth-of-July afternoon, and he was sitting in Park Place in the sun. The lower part of New York was empty. Wall Street, Liberty Street, Broadway, all empty. So much stone and asphalt with nothing going on, so many empty windows. The emptiness was intense, like the stillness in a great factory when the machinery stops and the belts and bands cease running. It was too great a change, it took all the strength out of one. Those blank buildings, without the stream of life pouring through them, were like empty jails. It struck young Rosicky that this was the trouble with big cities; they built you in from the earth itself, cemented you away from any contact with the ground. You lived in an unnatural world, like the fish in an aquarium, who were probably much more comfortable than they ever were in the sea.

On that very day he began to think seriously about the articles he had read in the Bohemian papers, describing prosperous Czech farming communities in the West. He believed he would like to go out there as a farm-hand; it was hardly possible that he could ever have land of his own. His people had always been workmen; his father and grandfather had worked in shops. His mother's parents had lived in the country, but they rented their farm and had a hard time to get along. Nobody in his family had ever owned any land—that belonged to a different station of life altogether. Anton's mother died when he was little, and he was sent into the country to her parents. He stayed with them until he was twelve, and formed those ties with the earth and the farm animals and growing things which are never made at all unless they are made early. After his grandfather died, he went back to live with his father and stepmother, but she was very hard on him, and his father helped him to get passage to London.

After that Fourth-of-July day in Park Place, the desire to return to the country never left him. To work on another man's farm would be all he asked; to see the sun rise and set and to plant things and watch them grow. He was a very simple man. He was like a tree that has not many roots, but one tap-root that goes down deep. He subscribed for a Bohemian paper printed in Chicago, then for one printed in Omaha. His mind got farther and farther west. He began to save a little money to buy his liberty. When he was thirty-five, there was a great meeting in New York of Bohemian athletic societies, and Rosicky left the tailor shop and went home with the Omaha delegates to try his fortune in another part of the world.

IV

Perhaps the fact that his own youth was well over before he began to have a family was one reason why Rosicky was so fond of his boys. He had almost a grandfather's indulgence for them. He had never had to worry about any of them—except, just now, a little about Rudolph.

On Saturday night the boys always piled into the Ford, took little Josephine, and went to town to the moving-picture show. One Saturday morning they were talking at the breakfast table about starting early that evening, so that they would have an hour or so to see the Christmas things in the stores before the show began. Rosicky looked down the table.

'I hope you boys ain't disappointed, but I want you to let me have de car to-night. Maybe some of you can go in with the neighbours.'

Their faces fell. They worked hard all the week, and they were still like children. A new jack-knife or a box of candy pleased the older ones as much as the little fellow.

'If you and mother are going to town,' Frank said, 'maybe you could take a couple of us along with you, anyway.'

'No, I want to take de car down to Rudolph's, and let him an' Polly go in to de show. She don't git into town enough, an' I'm afraid she's gittin' lonesome, an' he can't afford no car yet.'

That settled it. The boys were a good deal dashed. Their father took another piece of apple-cake and went on: 'Maybe next Saturday night de two little fellers can go along wid dem.'

'Oh, is Rudolph going to have the car every Saturday night?'

Rosicky did not reply at once; then he began to speak seriously: 'Listen, boys; Polly ain't lookin' so good. I don't like to see nobody lookin' sad. It comes hard fur a town girl to be a farmer's wife. I don't want no trouble to start in Rudolph's family. When it starts, it ain't so easy to stop. An American girl don't git used to our ways all at once. I like to tell Polly she and Rudolph can have the car every Saturday night till after New Year's, if it's all right with you boys.'

'Sure, it's all right, papa,' Mary cut in. 'And it's good you thought about that. Town girls is used to more than country girls. I lay awake nights, scared she'll make Rudolph discontented with the farm.'

The boys put as good a face on it as they could. They surely looked forward to their Saturday nights in town. That evening Rosicky drove the car the half-mile down to Rudolph's new, bare little house.

Polly was in a short-sleeved gingham dress, clearing away the supper dishes. She was a trim, slim little thing, with blue eyes and shingled yellow hair, and her eyebrows were reduced to a mere brush-stroke, like Miss Pearl's.

'Good-evening, Mr. Rosicky. Rudolph's at the barn, I guess.' She never called him father, or Mary mother. She was sensitive about having married a foreigner. She never in the world would have done it if Rudolph hadn't been such a handsome, persuasive fellow and such a gallant lover. He had graduated in her class in the high school in town, and their friendship began in the ninth grade.

Rosicky went in, though he wasn't exactly asked. 'My boys ain't going' to town to-night, an' I brought de car over fur you two to go in de picture show.'

Polly, carrying dishes to the sink, looked over her shoulder at him. 'Thank you. But I'm late with my work to-night, and pretty tired. Maybe Rudolph would like to go in with you.'

'Oh, I don't go to de shows! I'm too old-fashioned. You won't feel so tired after you ride in de air a ways. It's a nice clear night, an' it ain't cold. You go an' fix yourself up, Polly, an' I'll wash de dishes an' leave everything nice fur you.'

Polly blushed and tossed her bob. 'I couldn't let you do that, Mr. Rosicky. I wouldn't think of it.'

Rosicky said nothing. He found a bib apron on a nail behind the kitchen door. He slipped it over his head and then took Polly by her two elbows and pushed her gently toward the door of her own room. 'I washed up de kitchen many times for my wife, when de babies was sick or somethin.' You go an' make yourself look nice. I like you to look prettier'n any of dem town girls when you go in. De young folks must have some fun, an' I'm goin' to look out fur you, Polly.'

That kind, reassuring grip on her elbows, the old man's funny bright eyes, made Polly want to drop her head on his shoulder for a second. She restrained herself, but she lingered in his grasp at the door of her room, murmuring tearfully: 'You always lived in the city when you were young, didn't you? Don't you ever get lonesome out here?'

As she turned round to him, her hand fell naturally into his, and he stood holding it and smiling into her face with his peculiar, knowing, indulgent smile without a shadow of reproach in it. 'Dem big cities is all right fur de rich, but dey is terrible hard fur de poor.'

'I don't know. Sometimes I think I'd like to take a chance. You lived in New York, didn't you?'

'An' London. Da's bigger still. I learned my trade dere. Here's Rudolph comin', you better hurry.'

'Will you tell me about London sometime?'

'Maybe. Only I ain't no talker, Polly. Run an' dress yourself up.'

The bedroom door closed ·behind her, and Rudolph came in from the outside, looking anxious. He had seen the car and was sorry any of his family should come just then. Supper hadn't been a very pleasant occasion. Halting in the doorway, he saw his father in a kitchen apron, carrying dishes to the sink. He flushed crimson and something flashed in his eye. Rosicky held up a warning finger.

'I brought de car over fur you an' Polly to go to de picture show, an' I made her let me finish here so you won't be late. You go put on a clean shirt, quick!'

'But don't the boys want the car, father?'

'Not to-night dey don't.' Rosicky fumbled under his apron and found his pants pocket. He took out a silver dollar and said in a hurried whisper: 'You go an' buy dat girl some ice cream an' candy to-night, like you was courtin'. She's awful good friends wid me.'

Rudolph was very short of cash, but he took the money as if it hurt him. There has been a crop failure all over the county. He had more than once been sorry he'd married this year.

In a few minutes the young people came out, looking clean and a little stiff. Rosicky hurried them off, and then he took his own time with the dishes. He scoured the pots and pans and put away the milk and swept the kitchen. He put some coal in the stove and shut off the draughts, so the place would be warm for them when they got home late at night. Then he sat down and had a pipe and listened to the clock tick.

Generally speaking, marrying an American girl was certainly a risk. A Czech should marry a Czech. It was lucky that Polly was the daughter of a poor widow woman; Rudolph was proud, and if she had a prosperous family to throw up at him, they could never make it go. Polly was one of four sisters, and they all worked; one was book-keeper in the bank, one taught music, and Polly and her younger sister had been clerks, like Miss Pearl. All four of them were musical, had pretty voices, and sang in the Methodist choir, which the eldest sister directed.

Polly missed the sociability of a store position. She missed the choir, and the company of her sisters. She didn't dislike housework, but she disliked so much of it. Rosicky was a little anxious about this pair. He was afraid Polly would grow so discontented that Rudy would quit the farm and take a factory job in Omaha. He had worked for a winter up there, two years ago, to get money to marry on. He had done very well, and they would always take him back at the stockyards. But to Rosicky that meant the end of everything for his son. To be a landless man was to be a wage-earner, a slave, all your life; to have nothing, to be nothing.

Rosicky thought he would come over and do a little carpentering for Polly after the New Year. He guessed she needed jollying. Rudolph was a serious sort of chap, serious in love and serious about his work.

Rosicky shook out his pipe and walked home across the fields. Ahead of him the lamplight shone from his kitchen windows. Suppose he were still in a tailor shop on Vesey Street, with a bunch of pale, narrow-chested sons working on machines, all coming home tired and sullen to eat supper in a kitchen that was a parlour also; with another crowded, angry family quarrelling just across the dumb-waiter shaft, and squeaking pulleys at the windows where dirty washings hung on dirty lines above a court full of old brooms and mops and ash-cans . . .

He stopped by the windmill to look up at the frosty winter stars and draw a long breath before he went inside. That kitchen with the shining windows was dear to him; but the sleeping fields and bright stars and the noble darkness were dearer still.

V

On the day before Christmas the weather set in very cold; no snow, but a bitter, biting wind that whistled and sang over the flat land and lashed one's face like fine wires. There was baking going on in the Rosicky kitchen all day, and Rosicky sat inside, making over a coat that Albert had outgrown into an overcoat for John. Mary had a big red geranium in bloom for Christmas, and a row of Jerusalem cherry trees, full of berries. It was the first year she had ever grown these; Doctor Ed brought her the seeds from Omaha when he went to some medical convention. They reminded Rosicky of plants he had seen in England; and all afternoon, as he stitched, he sat thinking about those two years in London, which his mind usually shrank from even after all this while.

He was a lad of eighteen when he dropped down into London, with no money and no connexions except the address of a cousin who was supposed to be working at a confectioner's. When he went to the pastry shop, however, he found that the cousin had gone to America. Anton tramped the streets for several days, sleeping in doorways and on the Embankment, until he was in utter despair. He knew no English, and the sound of the strange language all about him confused him. By chance he met a poor German tailor who had learned his trade in Vienna, and could speak a little Czech. This tailor, Lifschnitz, kept a repair shop in a Cheapside basement, underneath a cobbler. He didn't much need an apprentice, but he was sorry for the boy and took him in for no wages but his keep and what he could pick up. The pickings were supposed to be coppers given you when you took work home to a customer. But most of the customers called for their clothes themselves, and the coppers that came Anton's way were very few. He had, however, a place to sleep. The tailor's family lived upstairs in three rooms; a kitchen, a bedroom, where Lifschnitz and his wife and five children slept, and a living-room. Two corners of this living room were curtained off for lodgers; in one Rosicky slept on an old horsehair sofa, with a feather quilt to wrap himself in. The other corner was rented to a wretched, dirty boy, who was studying the violin. He actually practised there. Rosicky was dirty, too. There was no way to be anything else. Mrs. Lifschnitz got the water she cooked and washed with from a pump in a brick court, four flights down. There were bugs in the place, and multitudes of fleas, though the poor woman did the best she could. Rosicky knew she often went empty to give another potato or a spoonful of dripping to the two hungry, sad-eyed boys who lodged with her. He used to think he would never get out of there, never get a clean shirt to his back again. What would he do, he wondered, when his clothes actually dropped to pieces and the worn cloth wouldn't hold patches any longer?

It was still early when the old farmer put aside his sewing and his recollections. The sky had been a dark grey all day, with not a gleam of sun, and the light failed at four o'clock. He went to shave and change his shirt while the turkey was roasting. Rudolph and Polly were coming over for supper.

After supper they sat round in the kitchen, and the younger boys were saying how sorry they were it hadn't snowed. Everybody was sorry. They wanted a deep snow that would lie long and keep the wheat warm, and leave the ground soaked when it melted.

'Yes, sir!' Rudolph broke out fiercely; 'if we have another dry year like last year, there's going to be hard times in this country.'

Rosicky filled his pipe. 'You boys don't know what hard times is. You don't owe nobody, you got plenty to eat an' keep warm, an' plenty water to keep clean. When you got them, you can't have it very hard.'

Rudolph frowned, opened and shut his big right hand, and dropped it clenched upon his knee. 'I've got to have a good deal more than that, father, or I'll quit this farming gamble. I can always make good wages railroading, or at the packing-house, and be sure of my money.'

'Maybe so,' his father answered dryly.

Mary, who had just come in from the pantry and was wiping her hands on the roller towel, thought Rudy and his father were getting too serious. She brought her darning-basket and sat down in the middle of the group.

'I ain't much afraid of hard times, Rudy,' she said heartily. 'We've had a plenty, but we've always come through. Your father wouldn't never take nothing very hard, not even hard times. I got a mind to tell you a story on him. Maybe you boys can't hardly remember the year we had that terrible hot wind, that burned everything up on the Fourth of July? All the corn an' the gardens. An' that was in the days when we didn't have alfalfa yet— I guess it wasn't invented.

'Well, that very day your father was out cultivatin' corn, and I was here in the kitchen makin' plum preserves. We had bushels of plums that year. I noticed it was terrible hot, but it's always hot in the kitchen when you're preservin', an' I was too busy with my plums to mind. Anton come in from the field about three o'clock, an' I asked him what was the matter.

' "Nothin'," he says, "but it's pretty hot, an' I think I won't work no more to-day." He stood round for a few minutes, an' then he says: "Ain't you near through? I want you should git up a nice supper for us to-night. It's Fourth of July."

'I told him to git along, that I was right in the middle of preservin', but the plums would taste good on hot biscuit. "I'm goin' to have fried chicken, too," he says, and he went off an' killed a couple. You three oldest boys was little fellers, playin' round outside, real hot an' sweaty, an' your father took you to the horse tank down by the windmill an' took off your clothes an' put you in. Them two box-elder trees were little then, but they made shade over the tank. Then he took off all his own clothes, an' got in with you. While he was playin' in the water with you, the Methodist preacher drove into our place to say how all the neighbours was goin' to meet at the schoolhouse that night, to pray for rain. He drove right to the windmill, of course, and there was your father and you there with no clothes on. I was in the kitchen door, an' I had to laugh, for the preacher acted like he ain't never seen a naked man before. He surely was embarrassed, an' your father couldn't git to his clothes; they was all hangin' up on the windmill to let the sweat dry out of 'em. So he laid in the tank where he was, an' put one of you boys on top of him to cover him up a little, an' talked to the preacher.

'When you got through playin' in the water, he put clean clothes on you and a clean shirt on himself, and by that time I'd begun to get supper. He says: "It's too hot in here to eat comfortable. Let's have a picnic in the orchard. We'll eat our supper behind the mulberry hedge, under them linden trees."

'So he carried our supper down, an' a bottle of my wild-grape wine, an' everything tasted good, I can tell you. The wind got cooler as the sun was goin' down, and it turned out pleasant, only I noticed how the leaves was curled up on the linden trees. That made me think, an' I asked your father if that hot wind all day hadn't been terrible hard on the gardens an' the corn.

' "Corn," he says, "there ain't no corn."

' "What you talkin' about?" I said. "Ain't we got forty acres?"

' "We ain't got an ear," he says, "nor nobody else ain't got none. All the corn in this country was cooked by three o'clock today, like you'd roasted it in an oven."

' "You mean you won't get no crop at all?" I asked him. I couldn't believe it, after he'd worked so hard.

' "No crop this year," he says. "That's why we're havin' a picnic. We might as well enjoy what we got."

'An' that's how your father behaved, when all the neighbours was so discouraged they couldn't look you in the face. An' we enjoyed ourselves that year, poor as we was, an' our neighbours wasn't a bit better off for bein' miserable. Some of 'em grieved till they got poor digestions and couldn't relish what they did have.'

The younger boys said they thought their father had the best of it. But Rudolph was thinking that, all the same, the neighbours had managed to get ahead more, in the fifteen years since that time. There must be something wrong about his father's way of doing things. He wished he knew what was going on in the back of Polly's mind. He knew she liked his father, but he knew, too, that she was afraid of something. When his mother sent over coffee-cake or prune tarts or a loaf of fresh bread, Polly seemed to regard them with a certain suspicion. When she observed to him that his brothers had nice manners, her tone implied that it was remarkable they should have. With his mother she was stiff and on her guard. Mary's hearty frankness and gusts of good humour irritated her. Polly was afraid of being unusual or conspicuous in any way, of being 'ordinary,' as she said!

When Mary had finished her story, Rosicky laid aside his pipe.

'You boys like me to tell you about some of dem hard times I been through in London?' Warmly encouraged, he sat rubbing his forehead along the deep creases. It was bothersome to tell a long story in English (he nearly always talked to the boys in Czech), but he wanted Polly to hear this one.

'Well, you know about dat tailor shop I worked in in London? I had one Christmas dere I ain't never forgot. Times was awful bad before Christmas; de boss ain't got much work, an' have it awful hard to pay his rent. It ain't so much fun, bein' poor in a big city like London, I'll say! All de windows is full of good t'ings to eat, an' all de pushcarts in de streets is full, an' you smell 'em all de time, an' you ain't got no money—not a damn bit. I didn't mind de cold so much, though I didn't have no overcoat, chust a short jacket I'd outgrowed so it wouldn't meet on me, an' my hands was chapped raw. But I always had a good appetite, like you all know, an' de sight of dem pork pies in de windows was awful fur me!

'Day before Christmas was terribly foggy dat year, an' dat fog gits into your bones and makes you all damp like. Mrs. Lifschnitz didn't give us nothin' but a little bread an' drippin' for supper, because she was savin' to try for to give us a good dinner on Christmas Day. After supper de boss say I go an' enjoy myself, so I went into de streets to listen to de Christmas singers. Dey sing old songs an' make very nice music, an' I run round after dem a good ways, till I got awful hungry. I t'ink maybe if I go home, I can sleep till morning an' forgit my belly.

'I went into my corner real quiet, and roll up in my fedder quilt. But I ain't got my head down, till I smell somet'ing good. Seem like it git stronger an' stronger, an' I can't git to sleep noway. I can't understand dat smell. Dere was a gas light in a hall across de court, dat always shine in at my window a little. I got up an' look round. I got a little wooden box in my corner fur a stool, 'cause I ain't got no chair. I picks up dat box, and under it dere is a roast goose on a platter! I can't believe my eyes. I carry it to de window where de light comes in, an' touch it and smell it to find out, an' den I taste it to be sure. I say, I will eat chust one little bite of dat goose, so I can go to sleep, and to-morrow I won't eat none at all. But I tell you, boys, when I stop, one half of dat goose was gone!'

The narrator bowed his head, and the boys shouted. But little Josephine slipped behind his chair and kissed him on the neck beneath his ear.

'Poor little papa, I don't want him to be hungry!'

'Da's long ago, child. I ain't never been hungry since I had your mudder to cook fur me.'

'Go on and tell us the rest, please,' said Polly.

'Well, when I come to realize what I done, of course, I felt terrible. I felt better in de stomach, but very bad in de heart. I set on my bed wid dat platter on my knees, an' it all come to me; how hard dat poor woman save to buy dat goose, and how she get some neighbour to cook it dat got more fire, an' how she put it in my corner to keep it away from dem hungry children. Dere was a old carpet hung up to shut my corner off, an' de children wasn't allowed to go in dere. An' I know she put it in my corner because she trust me more'n she did de violin boy. I can't stand it to face her after I spoil de Christmas. So I put on my shoes and go out into de city. I tell myself I better throw myself in de river; but I guess I ain't dat kind of a boy.

'It was after twelve o'clock, an' terrible cold, an' I start out to walk about London all night. I walk along de river awhile, but dey was lots of drunks all along; men, and women too. I chust move along to keep away from de police. I git onto de Strand, an' den over to New Oxford Street, where dere was a big German restaurant on de ground floor, wid big windows all fixed up fine, an' I could see de people havin' parties inside. While I was lookin' in, two men and two ladies come out, laughin' and talkin' and feelin' happy about all dey been eatin' an' drinkin', and dey was speakin' Czech—not like de Austrians, but like de home folks talk it.

'I guess I went crazy, an' I done what I ain't never done before nor since. I went right up to dem gay people an' begun to beg dem: "Fellow countrymen, for God's sake give me money enough to buy a goose!"

'Dey laugh, of course, but de ladies speak awful kind to me, an' dey take me back into de restaurant and give me hot coffee and cakes, an' make me tell all about how I happened to come to London, an' what I was doin' dere. Dey take my name and where I work down on paper, an' both of dem ladies give me ten shillings.

'De big market at Covent Garden[3] ain't very far away, an' by dat time it was open. I go dere an' buy a big goose an' some pork pies, an' potatoes and onions, an' cakes an' oranges fur de children—all I could carry! When I git home, everybody is still asleep. I pile all I bought on de kitchen table, an' go in an' lay down on my bed, an I ain't waken up till I hear dat woman scream when she come out into her kitchen. My goodness, but she was surprise'! She laugh an' cry at de same time, an' hug me and waken all de children. She ain't stop fur no breakfast; she git de Christmas dinner ready dat morning, and we all sit down an' eat all we can hold. I ain't never seen dat violin boy have all he can hold before.

'Two-t'ree days after dat, de two men come to hunt me up, an' dey ask my boss, and he give me a good report an' tell dem I was a steady boy all right. One of dem Bohemians was very smart an'

---

3. Square in London, site of a famous flower and vegetable market and of the Covent Garden opera house.

run a Bohemian newspaper in New York, an' de odder was a rich man, in de importing business, an' dey been travelling togedder. Dey told me how t'ings was easier in New York, an' offered to pay my passage when dey was goin' home soon on a boat. My boss say to me: "You go. You ain't got no chance here, an' I like to see you git ahead, fur you always been a good boy to my woman, and fur dat fine Christmas dinner you give us all." An' da's how I got to New York.'

That night when Rudolph and Polly, arm in arm, were running home across the fields with the bitter wind at their backs, his heart leaped for joy when she said she thought they might have his family come over for supper on New Year's Eve. 'Let's get up a nice supper, and not let your mother help at all; make her be company for once.'

'That would be lovely of you, Polly,' he said humbly. He was a very simple, modest boy, and he, too, felt vaguely that Polly and her sisters were more experienced and worldly than his people.

VI

The winter turned out badly for farmers. It was bitterly cold, and after the first light snows before Christmas there was no snow at all—and no rain. March was as bitter as February. On those days when the wind fairly punished the country, Rosicky sat by his window. In the fall he and the boys had put in a big wheat planting, and now the seed had frozen in the ground. All that land would have to be ploughed up and planted over again, planted in corn. It had happened before, but he was younger then, and he never worried about what had to be. He was sure of himself and of Mary; he knew they could bear what they had to bear, that they would always pull through somehow. But he was not so sure about the young ones, and he felt troubled because Rudolph and Polly were having such a hard start.

Sitting beside his flowering window while the panes rattled and the wind blew in under the door, Rosicky gave himself to reflection as he had not done since those Sundays in the loft of the furniture factory in New York, long ago. Then he was trying to find what he wanted in life for himself; now he was trying to find what he wanted for his boys, and why it was he so hungered to feel sure they would be here, working this very land, after he was gone.

They would have to work hard on the farm, and probably they would never do much more than make a living. But if he could think of them as staying here on the land, he wouldn't have to fear any great unkindness for them. Hardships, certainly; it was a hardship to have the wheat freeze in the ground when seed was so high; and to have to sell your stock because you had no feed. But there would be other years when everything came along right, and you caught up. And what you had was your own. You didn't have to choose between bosses and strikers, and go wrong either way. You didn't have to do with dishonest and cruel people. They were the only things in his experience he had found terrifying and horrible; the look in the eyes of a dishonest and crafty man, of a scheming and rapacious woman.

In the country, if you had a mean neighbour, you could keep off his land and make him keep off yours. But in the city, all the foulness and misery and brutality of your neighbours was part of your life. The worst things he had come upon in his journey through the world were human—depraved and poisonous specimens of man. To this day he could recall certain terrible faces in the London streets. There were mean people everywhere, to be sure, even in their own country town here. But they weren't tempered, hardened, sharpened, like the treacherous people in cities who live by grinding or cheating or poisoning their fellow men. He had helped to bury two of his fellow workmen in the tailoring trade, and he was distrustful of the organized industries that see one out of the world in big cities. Here, if you were sick, you had Doctor Ed to look after you; and if you died, fat Mr. Haycock, the kindest man in the world, buried you.

It seemed to Rosicky that for good, honest boys like his, the worst they could do on the farm was better than the best they would be likely to do in the city. If he'd had a mean boy, now, one who was crooked and sharp and tried to put anything over on his brothers, then town would be the place for him. But he had no such boy. As for Rudolph, the discontented one, he would give the shirt off his back to anyone who touched his heart. What Rosicky really hoped for his boys was that they could get through the world without ever knowing much about the cruelty of human beings. 'Their mother and me ain't prepared them for that,' he sometimes said to himself.

These thoughts brought him back to a grateful consideration of his own case. What an escape he had had, to be sure! He, too, in his time, had had to take money for repair work from the hand of a hungry child who let it go so wistfully; because it was money due his boss. And now, in all these years, he had never had to take a cent from anyone in bitter need—never had to look at the face of a woman become like a wolf's from struggle and famine. When he thought of these things, Rosicky would put on his cap and jacket and slip down to the barn and give his work-horses a little extra oats, letting them eat it out of his hand in their slobbery fashion. It was his way of expressing what he felt, and made him chuckle with pleasure.

The spring came warm, with blue skies—but dry, dry as bone. The boys began ploughing up the wheatfields to plant them over in corn. Rosicky would stand at the fence corner and watch them, and the earth was so dry it blew up in clouds of brown dust that hid the horses and the sulky plough and the driver. It was a bad outlook.

The big alfalfa-field that lay between the homeplace and Rudolph's came up green, but Rosicky was worried because during that open windy winter a great many Russian thistle plants had blown in there and lodged. He kept asking the boys to rake them out; he was afraid their seed would root and 'take the alfalfa.' Rudolph said that was nonsense. The boys were working so hard planting corn, their father felt he couldn't insist about the thistles, but he set great store by that big alfalfa-field. It was a feed you could depend on—and there was some deeper reason, vague, but strong. The peculiar green of that clover woke early memories in old Rosicky, went back to something in his childhood in the Old World. When he was a little boy, he had played in fields of that strong blue-green colour.

One morning, when Rudolph had gone to town in the car, leaving a work-team idle in his barn, Rosicky went over to his son's place, put the horses to the buggy rake, and set about quietly raking up those thistles. He behaved with guilty caution, and rather enjoyed stealing a march on Doctor Ed, who was just then taking his first vacation in seven years of practice and was attending a clinic in Chicago. Rosicky got the thistles raked up, but did not stop to burn them. That would take some time, and his breath was pretty short, so he thought he had better get the horses back to the barn.

He got them into the barn and to their stalls, but the pain had come on so sharp in his chest that he didn't try to take the harness off. He started for the house, bending lower with every step. The cramp in his chest was shutting him up like a jack-knife. When he reached the windmill, he swayed and caught at the ladder. He saw Polly coming down the hill, running with the swiftness of a slim greyhound. In a flash she had her shoulder under his armpit.

'Lean on me, father, hard! Don't be afraid. We can get to the house all right.'

Somehow they did, though Rosicky became blind with pain; he could keep on his legs, but he couldn't steer his course. The next thing he was conscious of was lying on Polly's bed, and Polly bending over him wringing out bath-towels in hot water and putting them on his chest. She stopped only to throw coal into the stove, and she kept the tea-kettle and the black pot going. She put these hot applications on him for nearly an hour, she told him afterward, and all that time he was drawn up stiff and blue, with the sweat pouring off him.

As the pain gradually loosed its grip, the stiffness went out of his jaws, the black circles round his eyes disappeared, and a little of his natural colour came back. When his daughter-in-law buttoned his shirt over his chest at last, he sighed.

'Da's fine, de way I feel now, Polly. It was a awful bad spell, an' I was so sorry it all come on you like it did.'

Polly was flushed and excited. 'Is the pain really gone? Can I leave you long enough to telephone over to your place?'

Rosicky's eyelids fluttered. 'Don't telephone, Polly. It ain't no use to scare my wife. It's nice and quiet here, an' if I ain't too much trouble to you, just let me lay still till I feel like myself. I ain't got no pain now. It's nice here.'

Polly bent over him and wiped the moisture from his face. 'Oh, I'm so glad it's over!' she broke out impulsively. 'It just broke my heart to see you suffer so, father.'

Rosicky motioned her to sit down on the chair where the teakettle had been, and looked up at her with that lively affectionate gleam in his eyes. 'You was awful good to me, I won't never forget dat. I hate it to be sick on you like dis. Down at de barn I say to myself, dat young girl ain't had much experience in sickness, I don't want to scare her, an' maybe she's got a baby comin' or somet'ing.'

Polly took his hand. He was looking at her so intently and affectionately and confidingly; his eyes seemed to caress her face, to regard it with pleasure. She frowned with her funny streaks of eyebrows, and then smiled back at him.

'I guess maybe there is something of that kind going to happen. But I haven't told anyone yet, not my mother or Rudolph. You'll be the first to know.'

His hand pressed hers. She noticed that it was warm again. The twinkle in his yellow-brown eyes seemed to come nearer.

'I like mighty well to see dat little child, Polly,' was all he said. Then he closed his eyes and lay half-smiling. But Polly sat still, thinking hard. She had a sudden feeling that nobody in the world, not her mother, not Rudolph, or anyone, really loved her as much as old Rosicky did. It perplexed her. She sat frowning and trying to puzzle it out. It was as if Rosicky had a special gift for loving people, something that was like an ear for music or an eye for colour. It was quiet, unobtrusive; it was merely there. You saw it in his eyes—perhaps that was why they were merry. You felt it in his hands, too. After he dropped off to sleep, she sat holding his warm, broad, flexible brown hand. She had never seen another in the least like it. She wondered if it wasn't a kind of gipsy hand, it was so alive and quick and light in its communications—very strange in a farmer. Nearly all the farmers she knew had huge lumps of fists, like mauls, or they were knotty and bony and uncomfortable-looking, with stiff fingers. But Rosicky's hand was like quicksilver, flexible, muscular, about the colour of a pale cigar, with deep, deep creases across the palm. It wasn't nervous, it wasn't a stupid lump; it was a warm brown human hand, with some cleverness in it, a great deal of generosity, and something else which Polly could only call 'gipsy-like'—something nimble and lively and sure, in the way that animals are.

Polly remembered that hour long afterward; it had been like an awakening to her. It seemed to her that she had never learned so much about life from anything as from old Rosicky's hand. It brought her to herself; it communicated some direct and untranslatable message.

When she heard Rudolph coming in the car, she ran out to meet him.

'Oh, Rudy, your father's been awful sick! He raked up those thistles he's been worrying about, and afterward he could hardly get to the house. He suffered so I was afraid he was going to die.'

Rudolph jumped to the ground. 'Where is he now?'

'On the bed. He's asleep. I was terribly scared, because, you know, I'm so fond of your father.' She slipped her arm through his and they went into the house.

That afternoon they took Rosicky home and put him to bed, though he protested that he was quite well again.

The next morning he got up and dressed and sat down to breakfast with his family. He told Mary that his coffee tasted better than usual to him, and he warned the boys not to bear any tales to Doctor Ed when he got home. After breakfast he sat down by his window to do some patching and asked Mary to thread several needles for him before she went to feed her chickens—her eyes were better than his, and her hands steadier. He lit his pipe and took up John's overalls. Mary had been watching him anxiously all morning, and as she went out of the door with her bucket of scraps, she saw that he was smiling. He was thinking, indeed, about Polly, and how he might never have known what a tender heart she had if he hadn't got sick over there. Girls nowadays didn't wear their hearts on their sleeves. But now he knew Polly would make a fine woman after the foolishness wore off. Either a woman had that sweetness at her heart or she hadn't. You couldn't always tell by the look of them; but if they had that, everything came out right in the end.

After he had taken a few stitches, the cramp began in his chest, like yesterday. He put his pipe cautiously down on the window-sill and bent over to ease the pull. No use—he had better try to get to his bed if he could. He rose and groped his way across the familiar floor, which was rising and falling like the deck of a ship. At the door he fell. When Mary came in, she found him lying there, and the moment she touched him she knew that he was gone.

Doctor Ed was away when Rosicky died, and for the first few weeks after he got home he was hard-driven. Every day he said to himself that he must get out to see that family that had lost their father. One soft, warm moonlight night in early summer he started for the farm. His mind was on other things, and not until his road ran by the graveyard did he realize that Rosicky wasn't over there on the hill where the red lamplight shone, but here, in the moonlight. He stopped his car, shut off the engine, and sat there for a while.

A sudden hush had fallen on his soul. Everything here seemed strangely moving and significant, though signifying what, he did not know. Close by the wire fence stood Rosicky's mowing-machine, where one of the boys had been cutting hay that afternoon; his own work-horses had been going up and down there. The new-cut hay perfumed all the night air. The moonlight silvered the long, billowy grass that grew over the graves and hid the fence; the few little evergreens stood out black in it, like shadows in a pool. The sky was very blue and soft, the stars rather faint because the moon was full.

For the first time it struck Doctor Ed that this was really a beautiful graveyard. He thought of city cemeteries; acres of shrubbery and heavy stone, so arranged and lonely and unlike anything in the living world. Cities of the dead, indeed; cities of the forgotten, of the 'put away.' But this was open and free, this little square of long grass which the wind forever stirred. Nothing but the sky overhead, and the many-coloured fields running on until they met that sky. The horses worked here in summer; the neighbours passed on their way to town; and over yonder, in the cornfield, Rosicky's own cattle would be eating fodder as winter came on. Nothing could be more undeathlike than this place; nothing could be more right for a man who had helped to do the work of great cities and had always longed for the open country and had got to it at last. Rosicky's life seemed to him complete and beautiful.

1928, 1932

GERTRUDE STEIN
1874–1946

The first important Jewish writer in America, and one of its most famous expatriates, was Gertrude Stein, whose witty conversation, continuous experimentation in writing, and widening fame as an eccentric "personality" have assured her a place in literary history. Although most of her poetry is indecipherable, and much of her later prose is a combination of the patently obvious and the abstruse, she produced in *Melanctha* an unmistakable masterpiece. She also contributed to the remaking of literary language that was the joint undertaking of Pound, Eliot, Hemingway, and other major writers of the twentieth century.

The "Mother Goose of Montparnasse," as she was dubbed by an admirer who was amused by her service to younger writers in Paris,[1] was born in Allegheny, Pennsylvania. Her well-to-do German-Jewish family was bourgeois and unintellectual but distinctly unconventional. The Stein grandparents emigrated from Germany to the United States before the Civil War and were well established in business in Baltimore at the time of her birth. She was the youngest child of seven and had an unusually close relationship with Leo, an older brother.

The Stein family lived abroad in Austria and France from 1875 to 1879, so her first spoken language was German, then French, though she later wrote that "there is for me only one language and that is English."[2] Upon the family's return to the United States in 1879 they moved to California, where the five surviving children attended intermittently the Oakland schools. Her mother, for whom Gertrude seemed to have little affection, and her father, whom she portrayed as a capricious tyrant, died during her adolescence. With income from the sale of the family business (a San Francisco railway), the young Steins were free to live where and as they chose. "Thus our life without a father began a very pleasant one."[3]

When Leo transferred from Berkeley to Harvard in 1892, Gertrude followed him, and though she lacked a high-school diploma she was admitted to Harvard's Annex for women, now Radcliffe College, as a special student in 1893. There she studied under the philosophers Josiah Royce and George Santayana and the psychologist and philosopher William James. In James's laboratory she undertook research on the role of repetition in memory. This research led to the publication, with other graduate students, of several articles in 1896. James encouraged her to pursue studies in psychology and philosophy, but her brother Leo decided to study biology at Johns Hopkins and Gertrude followed him there, enrolling in the medical school.

The Steins had a wide circle of friends in Baltimore, including the art patrons the Cone sisters: Dr. Claribel, one of the first women to earn a Hopkins medical degree, and Etta, who became Stein's secretary later in Paris and typed the manuscript of Stein's first important work, *Three Lives* (1909). After two years of creditable work in medical school, Stein seems deliberately to have failed, whether because, as she claimed, she became bored by medical study, because Leo was abandoning Baltimore and biology for aesthetics and Europe, or because she was becoming involved in a triangular love affair with two women (documented in a novel written in 1903 and published posthumously as *Q.E.D.* or *Things As They Are*, 1950). In any case she moved in 1902 to Paris, where the Steins began to accumulate their famous collection of Postimpressionist paintings. Though Leo usually took the lead in determining their purchases of paintings and theorizing about visual aesthetics, Gertrude led in the discovery of Picasso.

In Paris Stein launched her major experiments in writing. She finished *Three Lives* in 1905 and in 1908 finished *The Making of Americans* (1925), a long work that converts the history of her family and friends into a discontinuous and convoluted narration. While working on these manuscripts, as she explained later in a number of lectures, she developed the techniques which distinguish her prose. Impressed by what she had learned from William James and her own studies about the fluidity of the "stream"

---

1. William Gass, introduction to *The Geographical History of America* (New York: Vintage), p. 20.

2. *Autobiography of Alice B. Toklas*, p. 20.

3. *Everybody's Autobiography*, p. 142.

of consciousness and the importance of memory to perception, sequential thinking, and feeling, she felt that repetitions or recurrences in speech were what expressed the "bottom nature" of an individual's identity and experience.[4] Yet such recurrences were not sheer or exact repetitions but slight shifts in emphasis or "insistence" as she called it, likening it to what "William James calls the Will to Live."[5] A sequence of recurring phrases or "insistences" defines a process of "beginning again and again" and extends a "prolonged present" into the "continuous present" that characterizes her prose.[6]

Moreover, she felt that the variety of differing perspectives on a person, which are defined by the recurring feelings and reactions of others, creates a process of "composition" in experience as it is lived as well as in writing, so that the "subtle variations" of "insistence" reveal the "complete rhythm of a personality," as it is "coming clear into ordered recognition."[7] The result in the three short novels, *Three Lives*, is that the writing captures without condescension the simplicity and integrity of two white immigrant serving women and black Melanctha Herbert. The tensions among domestic propriety, sensuousness, and self-recognition that agitated Stein's own affairs she located in the experience of a black woman, and *Melanctha* is a landmark in the sensitive treatment by a white writer of a black character, while converting the halting and echoing phrasing of colloquial speech into the cadences of music. The book failed to find a commercial publisher and was published in 1909 at the author's expense.

In 1909 Alice B. Toklas, who was to become Gertrude Stein's lover and life-long companion, joined the household to serve as housekeeper, typist, and editor. Within several years friction in the household and differences of opinion about painting between the two Steins led to Leo's withdrawal, after dividing the painting collection with his sister. Gertrude's home and salon at 22 rue de Fleurus continued to be the mecca of expatriate writers and artists interested in vanguard movements in the arts.

After 1909 the fascination of her experiments with language and writing, and the success with which she made her eccentricities and the force of her personality the center of attention at her salon, made her an important catalyst in literary circles and eventually turned her into a public figure with a wide audience. If she did not have the generative influence on Sherwood Anderson and Ernest Hemingway that she claimed, she nonetheless read and commented on their work; and she encouraged the development of their distinctive styles by her emphasis on precise observation, simplicity of statement, deliberate construction, and the basic elements of sheer language. Her own writing after 1909 undertook to achieve in verbal language the effects of abstract or nonrepresentational painting. *Tender Buttons* (1914) consisted of word pictures or collages, arranged under the headings of "Objects," "Food," and "Rooms," with no coherent syntax or paraphrasable meaning; the nonsensical splicing of discrete words and phrases creates an often witty and teasing sequence in which the effect of spoken speech, and the play of color and visual form, are heightened. Her experiments with the time sense in narration and with the elimination of punctuation and the construction of paragraphs continued in collections of stories and plays,

4. *Ibid.*, p. 231.
5. "Portraits and Repetition," *Lectures in America*, p. 169.
6. "Composition as Explanation," *What*

Are Masterpieces?, pp. 29, 31.
7. "The Gradual Making of Americans," *Lectures in America*, pp. 140, 147.

and she promoted her theories while explaining them in lectures at Oxford and Cambridge in 1926 and a wildly successful lecture tour of the United States in 1934. (*Composition as Explanation*, 1926, *Narration*, 1935, and the *Geographical History of America*, 1936, are the fruits of these lectures, and *Everybody's Autobiography*, 1937, is an account of her American lecture tour.)

Her fame became notoriety with the publication of the best seller *The Autobiography of Alice B. Toklas* (1933), in which Stein, in the guise of her companion, assembled her views of writing and artists in the twentieth century. Her claims to importance and her questionable judgments of painting were attacked by prominent painters in a special supplement of the magazine *Transition* entitled "Testimony against Gertrude Stein" (1935), and the writers Katherine Anne Porter and Hemingway were among those who acknowledged her early experiments but later denigrated the extent and nature of her influence.

Among her popular successes were the opera *Four Saints in Three Acts* (1934) with music by Virgil Thompson, and accounts of her years during World War II in occupied France. Her exhilaration upon becoming acquainted with hundreds of American troops who flocked to see her and enjoyed her hospitality after the liberation of France is recorded in *Wars I Have Seen* (1945) and *Brewsie and Willie* (1946). The war years and her anxieties about the fate of Western civilization had made her acutely conscious of that identity as an American which she had insisted on during her long years of expatriation. She died in Paris after an operation for cancer in 1946.

From Melanctha[1]

[*Conclusion*]

Melanctha Herbert began to feel she must begin again to look and see if she could find what it was she had always wanted. Now Rose Johnson could no longer help her.

And so Melanctha Herbert began once more to wander and with men Rose never thought it was right she should be with.

One day Melanctha had been very busy with the different kinds of ways she wandered. It was a pleasant late afternoon at the end of a long summer. Melanctha was walking along, and she was free and excited. Melanctha had just parted from a white man and she had a bunch of flowers he had left with her. A young buck, a mulatto, passed by and snatched them from her. "It certainly is real sweet in you sister, to be giving me them pretty flowers," he said to her.

"I don't see no way it can make them sweeter to have with you," said Melanctha. "What one man gives, another man had certainly

1. *Melanctha* is one of *Three Lives* (1909) in which Stein examines the relation of suffering and dependency in the lives of three serving women. Melanctha Herbert, a promiscuous black woman, has sought security and affection with two friends: Jeff Campbell, her lover and a physician, whose concern for "reg-ular living" has proved to be incompatible with Melanctha's willingness to drift while seeking satisfaction; and Rose Johnson, who, since her recent marriage to Sam, welcomes Melanctha's help as a servant but does not wish to live with her.

just as much good right to be taking." "Keep your old flowers then, I certainly don't never want to have them." Melanctha Herbert laughed at him and took them. "No, I didn't nohow think you really did want to have them. Thank you kindly mister, for them. I certainly always do admire to see a man always so kind of real polite to people." The man laughed, "You ain't nobody's fool I can say for you, but you certainly are a damned pretty kind of girl, now I look at you. Want men to be polite to you? All right, I can love you, that's real polite now, want to see me try it." "I certainly ain't got no time this evening just only left to thank you. I certainly got to be real busy now, but I certainly always will admire to see you." The man tried to catch and stop her, Melanctha Herbert laughed and dodged so that he could not touch her. Melanctha went quickly down a side street near her and so the man for that time lost her.

For some days Melanctha did not see any more of her mulatto. One day Melanctha was with a white man and they saw him. The white man stopped to speak to him. Afterwards Melanctha left the white man and she then soon met him. Melanctha stopped to talk to him. Melanctha Herbert soon began to like him.

Jem Richards, the new man Melanctha had begun to know now, was a dashing kind of fellow, who had to do with fine horses and with racing. Sometimes Jem Richards would be betting and would be good and lucky, and be making lots of money. Sometimes Jem would be betting badly, and then he would not be having any money.

Jem Richards was a straight man. Jem Richards always knew that by and by he would win again and pay it, and so Jem mostly did win again, and then he always paid it.

Jem Richards was a man other men always trusted. Men gave him money when he lost all his, for they all knew Jem Richards would win again, and when he did win they knew, and they were right, that he would pay it.

Melanctha Herbert all her life had always loved to be with horses. Melanctha liked it that Jem knew all about fine horses. He was a reckless man was Jem Richards. He knew how to win out, and always all her life, Melanctha Herbert loved successful power.

Melanctha Herbert always liked Jem Richards better. Things soon began to be very strong between them.

Jem was more game even than Melanctha. Jem always had known what it was to have real wisdom. Jem had always all his life been understanding.

Jem Richards made Melanctha Herbert come fast with him. He never gave her any time with waiting. Soon Melanctha always had Jem with her. Melanctha did not want anything better. Now in Jem Richards, Melanctha found everything she had ever needed to content her.

Melanctha was now less and less with Rose Johnson. Rose did

not think much of the way Melanctha now was going. Jem
Richards was all right, only Melanctha never had no sense of the
right kind of way she should be doing. Rose often was telling Sam
now, she did not like the fast way Melanctha was going. Rose told
it to Sam, and to all the girls and men, when she saw them. But
Rose was nothing just then to Melanctha. Melanctha Herbert now
only needed Jem Richards to be with her.

And things were always getting stronger between Jem Richards
and Melanctha Herbert. Jem Richards began to talk now as if he
wanted to get married to her. Jem was deep in his love now for her.
And as for Melanctha, Jem was all the world now to her. And so
Jem gave her a ring, like white folks, to show he was engaged to
her, and would by and by be married to her. And Melanctha was
filled full with joy to have Jem so good to her.

Melanctha always loved to go with Jem to the races. Jem had
been lucky lately with his betting, and he had a swell turn-out to
drive in, and Melanctha looked very handsome there beside him.

Melanctha was very proud to have Jem Richards want her.
Melanctha loved it the way Jem knew how to do it. Melanctha
loved Jem and loved that he should want her. She loved it too, that
he wanted to be married to her. Jem Richards was a straight decent
man, whom other men always looked up to and trusted. Melanctha
needed badly a man to content her.

Melanctha's joy made her foolish. Melanctha told everybody
about how Jem Richards, that swell man who owned all those fine
horses and was so game, nothing ever scared him, was engaged to be
married to her, and that was the ring he gave her.

Melanctha let out her joy very often to Rose Johnson. Melanctha
had begun again now to go there.

Melanctha's love for Jem made her foolish. Melanctha had to
have some one always now to talk to and so she went often to Rose
Johnson.

Melanctha put all herself into Jem Richards. She was mad and
foolish in the joy she had there.

Rose never liked the way Melanctha did it. "No Sam I don't say
never Melanctha ain't engaged to Jem Richards the way she always
says it, and Jem he is all right for that kind of a man he is, though
he do think himself so smart and like he owns the earth and everything he can get with it, and he sure gave Melanctha a ring like he
really meant he should be married right soon with it, only Sam, I
don't ever like it the way Melanctha is going. When she is engaged
to him Sam, she ain't not right to take on so excited. That ain't no
decent kind of a way a girl ever should be acting. There ain't no
kind of a man going stand that, not like I knows men Sam, and I
sure does know them. I knows them white and I knows them
colored, for I was raised by white folks, and they don't none of

them like a girl to act so. That's all right to be so when you is just
only loving, but it ain't no ways right to be acting so when you is
engaged to him, and when he says, all right he get really regularly
married to you. You see Sam I am right like I am always and I
knows it. Jem Richards, he ain't going to the last to get real married, not if I knows it right, the way Melanctha now is acting to
him. Rings or anything ain't nothing to them, and they don't never
do no good for them, when a girl acts foolish like Melanctha always
now is acting. I certainly will be right sorry Sam, if Melanctha has
real bad trouble come now to her, but I certainly don't no ways like
it Sam the kind of way Melanctha is acting to him. I don't never
say nothing to her Sam. I just listens to what she is saying always,
and I thinks it out like I am telling to you Sam but I don't never
say nothing no more now to Melanctha. Melanctha didn't say nothing to me about that Jem Richards till she was all like finished with
him, and I never did like it Sam, much, the way she was acting, not
coming here never when she first ran with those men and met him.
And I didn't never say nothing to her, Sam, about it, and it ain't
nothing ever to me, only I don't never no more want to say nothing
to her, so I just listens to what she got to tell like she wants it. No
Sam, I don't never want to say nothing to her. Melanctha just got
to go her own way, not as I want to see her have bad trouble ever
come hard to her, only it ain't in me never Sam, after Melanctha
did so, ever to say nothing more to her how she should be acting.
You just see Sam like I tell you, what way Jem Richards will act to
her, you see Sam I just am right like I always am when I knows it."

Melanctha Herbert never thought she could ever again be in
trouble. Melanctha's joy had made her foolish.

And now Jem Richards had some bad trouble with his betting.
Melanctha sometimes felt now when she was with him that there
was something wrong inside him. Melanctha knew he had had trouble with his betting but Melanctha never felt that that could make
any difference to them.

Melanctha once had told Jem, sure he knew she always would
love to be with him, if he was in jail or only just a beggar. Now
Melanctha said to him, "Sure you know Jem that it don't never
make any kind of difference you're having any kind of trouble, you
just try me Jem and be game, don't look so worried to me. Jem sure
I know you love me like I love you always, and its all I ever could
be wanting Jem to me, just your wanting me always to be with you.
I get married Jem to you soon ever as you can want me, if you once
say it Jem to me. It ain't nothing to me ever, anything like having
any money Jem, why you look so worried to me."

Melanctha Herbert's love had surely made her mad and foolish.
She thrust it always deep into Jem Richards and now that he had
trouble with his betting, Jem had no way that he ever wanted to be

made to feel it. Jem Richards never could want to marry any girl while he had trouble. That was no way a man like him should do it. Melanctha's love had made her mad and foolish, she should be silent now and let him do it. Jem Richards was not a kind of man to want a woman to be strong to him, when he was in trouble with his betting. That was not the kind of a time when a man like him needed to have it.

Melanctha needed so badly to have it, this love which she had always wanted, she did not know what she should do to save it. Melanctha saw now, Jem Richards always had something wrong inside him. Melanctha soon dared not ask him. Jem was busy now, he had to sell things and see men to raise money. Jem could not meet Melanctha now so often.

It was lucky for Melanctha Herbert that Rose Johnson was coming now to have her baby. It had always been understood between them, Rose should come and stay then in the house where Melanctha lived with an old colored woman, so that Rose could have the Doctor from the hospital near by to help her, and Melanctha there to take care of her the way Melanctha always used to do it.

Melanctha was very good now to Rose Johnson. Melanctha did everything that any woman could, she tended Rose, and she was patient, submissive, soothing and untiring, while the sullen, childish, cowardly, black Rosie grumbled, and fussed, and howled, and made herself to be an abomination and like a simple beast.

All this time Melanctha was always being every now and then with Jem Richards. Melanctha was beginning to be stronger with Jem Richards. Melanctha was never so strong and sweet and in her nature as when she was deep in trouble, when she was fighting so with all she had, she could not do any foolish thing with her nature.

Always now Melanctha Herbert came back again to be nearer to Rose Johnson. Always now Melanctha would tell all about her troubles to Rose Johnson. Rose had begun now a little again to advise her.

Melanctha always told Rose now about the talks she had with Jem Richards, talks where they neither of them liked very well what the other one was saying. Melanctha did not know what it was Jem Richards wanted. All Melanctha knew was, he did not like it when she wanted to be good friends and get really married, and then when Melanctha would say, "all right, I never wear your ring no more Jem, we ain't not any more to meet ever like we ever going to get really regular married," then Jem did not like it either. What was it Jem Richards really wanted?

Melanctha stopped wearing Jem's ring on her finger. Poor Melanctha, she wore it on a string she tied around her neck so that she could always feel it, but Melanctha was strong now with Jem Richards, and he never saw it. And sometimes Jem seemed to be awful sorry for it, and sometimes he seemed kind of glad of it. Melanctha never could make out really what it was Jem Richards wanted.

There was no other woman yet to Jem, that Melanctha knew, and so she always trusted that Jem would come back to her, deep in his love, the way once he had had it and had made all the world like she once had never believed anybody could really make it. But Jem Richards was more game than Melanctha Herbert. He knew how to fight to win out, better. Melanctha really had already lost it, in not keeping quiet and waiting for Jem to do it.

Jem Richards was not yet having better luck in his betting. He never before had had such a long time without some good coming to him in his betting. Sometimes Jem talked as if he wanted to go off on a trip somewhere and try some other place for luck with his betting. Jem Richards never talked as if he wanted to take Melanctha with him.

And so Melanctha sometimes was really trusting, and sometimes she was all sick inside her with her doubting. What was it Jem really wanted to do with her? He did not have any other woman, in that Melanctha could be really trusting, and when she said no to him, no she never would come near him, now he did not want to have her, then Jem would change and swear, yes sure he did want her, now and always right here near him, but he never now any more said he wanted to be married soon to her. But then Jem Richards never would marry a girl, he said that very often, when he was in this kind of trouble, and now he did not see any way he could get out of his trouble. But Melanctha ought to wear his ring, sure she knew he never had loved any kind of woman like he loved her. Melanctha would wear the ring a little while, and then they would have some more trouble, and then she would say to him, no she certainly never would any more wear anything he gave her, and then she would wear it on the string so nobody could see it but she could always feel it on her.

Poor Melanctha, surely her love had made her mad and foolish.

And now Melanctha needed always more and more to be with Rose Johnson, and Rose had commenced again to advise her, but Rose could not help her. There was no way now that anybody could advise her. The time when Melanctha could have changed it with Jem Richards was now all past for her. Rose knew it, and Melanctha too, she knew it, and it almost killed her to let herself believe it.

The only comfort Melanctha ever had now was waiting on Rose till she was so tired she could hardly stand it. Always Melanctha did everything Rose ever wanted. Sam Johnson began now to be very gentle and a little tender to Melanctha. She was so good to Rose and Sam was so glad to have her there to help Rose and to do things and to be a comfort to her.

Rose had a hard time to bring her baby to its birth and Melanctha did everything that any woman could.

The baby though it was healthy after it was born did not live long. Rose Johnson was careless and negligent and selfish and when Melanctha had to leave for a few days the baby died. Rose Johnson had liked her baby well enough and perhaps she just forgot it for a while, anyway the child was dead and Rose and Sam were very sorry, but then these things came so often in the negro world in Bridgepoint that they neither of them thought about it very long. When Rose had become strong again she went back to her house with Sam. And Sam Johnson was always now very gentle and kind and good to Melanctha who had been so good to Rose in her bad trouble.

Melanctha Herbert's troubles with Jem Richards were never getting any better. Jem always now had less and less time to be with her. When Jem was with Melanctha now he was good enough to her. Jem Richards was worried with his betting. Never since Jem had first begun to make a living had he ever had so much trouble for such a long time together with his betting. Jem Richards was good enough now to Melanctha but he had not much strength to give her. Melanctha could never any more now make him quarrel with her. Melanctha never now could complain of his treatment of her, for surely, he said it always by his actions to her, surely she must know how a man was when he had trouble on his mind with trying to make things go a little better.

Sometimes Jem and Melanctha had long talks when they neither of them liked very well what the other one was saying, but mostly now Melanctha could not make Jem Richards quarrel with her, and more and more, Melanctha could not find any way to make it right to blame him for the trouble she now always had inside her. Jem was good to her, and she knew, for he told her, that he had trouble all the time now with his betting. Melanctha knew very well that for her it was all wrong inside Jem Richards, but Melanctha had now no way that she could really reach him.

Things between Melanctha and Jem Richards were now never getting any better. Melanctha now more and more needed to be with Rose Johnson. Rose still liked to have Melanctha come to her house and do things for her, and Rose liked to grumble to her and to scold her and to tell Melanctha what was the way Melanctha always should be doing so she could make things come out better and not always be so much in trouble. Sam Johnson in these days was always very good and gentle to Melanctha. Sam was now beginning to be very sorry for her.

Jem Richards never made things any better for Melanctha. Often

Jem would talk so as to make Melanctha almost certain that he never any more wanted to have her. Then Melanctha would get very blue, and she would say to Rose, sure she would kill herself, for that certainly now was the best way she could do.

Rose Johnson never saw it the least bit that way. "I don't see Melanctha why you should talk like you would kill yourself just because you're blue. I'd never kill myself Melanctha cause I was blue. I'd maybe kill somebody else but I'd never kill myself. If I ever killed myself, Melanctha it'd be by accident and if I ever killed myself by accident, Melanctha, I'd be awful sorry. And that certainly is the way you should feel it Melanctha, now you hear me, not just talking foolish like you always do. It certainly is only your way just always being foolish makes you all that trouble to come to you always now, Melanctha, and I certainly right well knows that. You certainly never can learn no way Melanctha ever with all I certainly been telling to you, ever since I know you good, that it ain't never no way like you do always is the right way you be acting ever and talking, the way I certainly always have seen you do so Melanctha always. I certainly am right Melanctha about them ways you have to do it, and I knows it; but you certainly never can noways learn to act right Melanctha, I certainly do know that, I certainly do my best Melanctha to help you with it only you certainly never do act right Melanctha, not to nobody ever, I can see it. You never act right by me Melanctha no more than by everybody. I never say nothing to you Melanctha when you do so, for I certainly never do like it when I just got to say it to you, but you just certainly done with that Jem Richards you always say wanted real bad to be married to you, just like I always said to Sam you certainly was going to do it. And I certainly am real kind of sorry like for you Melanctha, but you certainly had ought to have come to see me to talk to you, when you first was engaged to him so I could show you, and now you got all this trouble come to you Melanctha like I certainly know you always catch it. It certainly ain't never Melanctha I ain't real sorry to see trouble come so hard to you, but I certainly can see Melanctha it all is always just the way you always be having it in you not never to do right. And now you always talk like you just kill yourself because you are so blue, that certainly never is Melanctha, no kind of a way for any decent kind of a girl to do."

Rose had begun to be strong now to scold Melanctha and she was impatient very often with her, but Rose could now never any more to be a help to her. Melanctha Herbert never could know now what it was right she should do. Melanctha always wanted to have Jem Richards with her and now he never seemed to want her, and what could Melanctha do. Surely she was right now when she said she would just kill herself, for that was the only way now she could do.

Sam Johnson always, more and more, was good and gentle to Melanctha. Poor Melanctha, she was so good and sweet to do anything anybody ever wanted, and Melanctha always liked it if she could have peace and quiet, and always she could only find new ways to be in trouble. Sam often said this now to Rose about Melanctha.

"I certainly don't never want Sam to say bad things about Melanctha, for she certainly always do have most awful kind of trouble come hard to her, but I never can say I like it real right Sam the way Melanctha always has to do it. Its now just the same with her like it is always she has got to do it, now the way she is with that Jem Richards. Her certainly now don't never want to have her but Melanctha she ain't got no right kind of spirit. No Sam I don't never like the way any more Melanctha is acting to him, and then Sam, she ain't never real right honest, the way she always should do it. She certainly just don't kind of never Sam tell right what way she is doing with it. I don't never like to say nothing Sam no more to her about the way she always has to be acting. She always say, yes all right Rose, I do the way you say it, and then Sam she don't never noways do it. She certainly is right sweet and good, Sam, is Melanctha, nobody ever can hear me say she ain't always ready to do things for everybody any way she ever can see to do it, only Sam some ways she never does act real right ever, and some ways, Sam, she ain't ever real honest with it. And Sam sometimes I hear awful kind of things she been doing, some girls know about her how she does it, and sometimes they tell me what kind of ways she has to do it, and Sam it certainly do seem to me like more and more I certainly am awful afraid Melanctha never will come to any good. And then Sam, sometimes, you hear it, she always talk like she kill herself all the time she is so blue, and Sam that certainly never is no kind of way any decent girl ever had ought to do. You see Sam, how I am right like I always is when I knows it. You just be careful, Sam, now you hear me, you be careful Sam sure, I tell you, Melanctha more and more I see her I certainly do feel Melanctha no way is really honest. You be careful, Sam now, like I tell you, for I knows it, now you hear to me, Sam, what I tell you, for I certainly always is right, Sam, when I knows it."

At first Sam tried a little to defend Melanctha, and Sam always was good and gentle to her, and Sam liked the ways Melanctha had to be quiet to him, and to always listen as if she was learning, when she was there and heard him talking, and then Sam liked the sweet way she always did everything so nicely for him; but Sam never liked to fight with anybody ever, and surely Rose knew best about Melanctha and anyway Sam never did really care much about Melanctha. Her mystery never had had any interest for him. Sam liked it that she was sweet to him and that she always did everything Rose ever wanted that she should be doing, but Melanctha never could be important to him. All Sam ever wanted was to have a little house and to live regular and to work hard and to come home to his dinner, when he was tired with his working and by and by he wanted to have some children all his own to be good to, and so Sam was real sorry for Melanctha, she was so good and so sweet always to them, and Jem Richards was a bad man to behave so to her, but that was always the way a girl got it when she liked that kind of a fast fellow. Anyhow Melanctha was Rose's friend, and Sam never cared to have anything to do with the kind of trouble always came to women, when they wanted to have men, who never could know how to behave good and steady to their women.

And so Sam never said much to Rose about Melanctha. Sam was always very gentle to her, but now he began less and less to see her. Soon Melanctha never came any more to the house to see Rose and Sam never asked Rose anything about her.

Melanctha Herbert was beginning now to come less and less to the house to be with Rose Johnson. This was because Rose seemed always less and less now to want her, and Rose would not let Melanctha now do things for her. Melanctha was always humble to her and Melanctha always wanted in every way she could to do things for her. Rose said no, she guessed she do that herself like she likes to have it better. Melanctha is real good to stay so long to help her, but Rose guessed perhaps Melanctha better go home now, Rose don't need nobody to help her now, she is feeling real strong, not like just after she had all that trouble with the baby, and then Sam, when he comes home for his dinner he likes it when Rose is all alone there just to give him his dinner. Sam always is so tired now, like he always is in the summer, so many people always on the steamer, and they make so much work so Sam is real tired now, and he likes just to eat his dinner and never have people in the house to be a trouble to him.

Each day Rose treated Melanctha more and more as if she never wanted Melanctha any more to come there to the house to see her. Melanctha dared not ask Rose why she acted in this way to her. Melanctha badly needed to have Rose always there to save her. Melanctha wanted badly to cling to her and Rose had always been so solid for her. Melanctha did not dare to ask Rose if she now no longer wanted her to come and see her.

Melanctha now never any more had Sam to be gentle to her. Rose always sent Melanctha away from her before it was time for Sam to come home to her. One day Melanctha had stayed a little longer, for Rose that day had been good to let Melanctha begin to do things for her. Melanctha then left her and Melanctha met Sam Johnson who stopped a minute to speak kindly to her.

The next day Rose Johnson would not let Melanctha come in to her. Rose stood on the steps, and there she told Melanctha what she thought now of her.

"I guess Melanctha it certainly ain't no ways right for you to come here no more just to see me. I certainly don't Melanctha no ways like to be a trouble to you. I certainly think Melanctha I get along better now when I don't have nobody like you are, always here to help me, and Sam he do so good now with his working, he pay a little girl something to come every day to help me. I certainly do think Melanctha I don't never want you no more to come here just to see me." "Why Rose, what I ever done to you, I certainly don't think you is right Rose to be so bad now to me." "I certainly don't no ways Melanctha Herbert think you got any right ever to be complaining the way I been acting to you. I certainly never do think Melanctha Herbert, you hear to me, nobody ever been more patient to you than I always been to like you, only Melanctha, I hear more things now so awful bad about you, everybody always is telling to me what kind of a way you always have been doing so much, and me always so good to you, and you never no ways, knowing how to be honest to me. No Melanctha it ain't ever in me, not to want you to have good luck come to you, and I like it real well Melanctha when you some time learn how to act the way it is decent and right for a girl to be doing, but I don't no ways ever like it the kind of things everybody tell me now about you. No Melanctha, I can't never any more trust you. I certainly am real sorry to have never any more to see you, but there ain't no other way, I ever can be acting to you. That's all I ever got any more to say to you now Melanctha." "But Rose, deed; I certainly don't know, no more than the dead, nothing I ever done to make you act so to me. Anybody say anything bad about me Rose, to you, they just a pack of liars to you, they certainly is Rose, I tell you true. I certainly never done nothing I ever been ashamed to tell you. Why you act so bad to me Rose. Sam he certainly don't think ever like you do, and Rose I always do everything I can, you ever want me to do for you." "It ain't never no use standing there talking, Melanctha Herbert. I just can tell it to you, and Sam, he don't know nothing about women ever the way they can be acting. I certainly am very sorry Melanctha, to have to act so now to you, but I certainly can't do no other way with you, when you do things always so bad, and everybody is talking so about you. It ain't no use to you to stand there and say it different to me Melanctha. I certainly am always right Melanctha Herbert, the way I certainly always have been when I knows it, to you. No Melanctha, it just is, you never can have no kind of a way to act right, the way a decent girl has to do, and I done my best always to be telling it to you Melanctha Herbert, but it don't never do no good to tell nobody how to act right; they certainly never can learn when they ain't got no sense right to know it, and you never have no sense right Melanctha to be honest, and I ain't never wishing no harm to you ever Melanctha Herbert, only I don't never want any more to see you come here. I just say to you now, like I always been saying to you, you don't know never the right way, any kind of decent girl has to be acting, and so Melanctha Herbert, me and Sam, we don't never any more want you to be setting your foot in my house here Melanctha Herbert, I just tell you. And so you just go along now, Melanctha Herbert, you hear me, and I don't never wish no harm to come to you."

Rose Johnson went into her house and closed the door behind her. Melanctha stood like one dazed, she did not know how to bear this blow that almost killed her. Slowly then Melanctha went away without even turning to look behind her.

Melanctha Herbert was all sore and bruised inside her. Melanctha had needed Rose always to believe her, Melanctha needed Rose always to let her cling to her, Melanctha wanted badly to have somebody who could make her always feel a little safe inside her, and now Rose had sent her from her. Melanctha wanted Rose more than she had ever wanted all the others. Rose always was so simple, solid, decent, for her. And now Rose had cast her from her. Melanctha was lost, and all the world went whirling in a mad weary dance around her.

Melanctha Herbert never had any strength alone ever to feel safe inside her. And now Rose Johnson had cast her from her, and Melanctha could never any more be near her. Melanctha Herbert knew now, way inside her, that she was lost, and nothing any more could ever help her.

Melanctha went that night to meet Jem Richards who had promised to be at the old place to meet her. Jem Richards was absent in his manner to her. By and by he began to talk to her, about the trip he was going to take soon, to see if he could get some luck back in his betting. Melanctha trembled, was Jem too now going to leave her. Jem Richards talked some more then to her, about the bad luck he always had now, and how he needed to go away to see if he could make it come out any better.

Then Jem stopped, and then he looked straight at Melanctha.

"Tell me Melanctha right and true, you don't care really nothing more about me now Melanctha," he said to her.

"Why you ask me that, Jem Richards," said Melanctha.

"Why I ask you that Melanctha, God Almighty, because I just don't give a damn now for you any more Melanctha. That the reason I was asking."

Melanctha never could have for this an answer. Jem Richards waited and then he went away and left her.

Melanctha Herbert never again saw Jem Richards. Melanctha never again saw Rose Johnson, and it was hard to Melanctha never any more to see her. Rose Johnson had worked in to be the deepest of all Melanctha's emotions.

"No, I don't never see Melanctha Herbert no more now," Rose

would say to anybody who asked her about Melanctha. "No, Melanctha she never comes here no more now, after we had all that trouble with her acting so bad with them kind of men she liked so much to be with. She don't never come to no good Melanctha Herbert don't, and me and Sam don't want no more to see her. She didn't do right ever the way I told her. Melanctha just wouldn't, and I always said it to her, if she don't be more kind of careful, the way she always had to be acting, I never did want no more she should come here in my house no more to see me. I ain't no ways ever against any girl having any kind of a way, to have a good time like she wants it, but not that kind of a way Melanctha always had to do it. I expect some day Melanctha kill herself, when she act so bad like she do always, and then she get so awful blue. Melanctha always says that's the only way she ever can think it a easy way for her to do. No, I always am real sorry for Melanctha, she never was no just common kind of nigger, but she don't never know not with all the time I always was telling it to her, no she never no way could learn, what was the right way she should do. I certainly don't never want no kind of harm to come bad to Melanctha, but I certainly do think she will most kill herself some time, the way she always say it would be easy way for her to do. I never see nobody ever could be so awful blue."

But Melanctha Herbert never really killed herself because she was so blue, though often she thought this would be really the best way for her to do. Melanctha never killed herself, she only got a bad fever and went into the hospital where they took good care of her and cured her.

When Melanctha was well again, she took a place and began to work and to live regular. Then Melanctha got very sick again, she began to cough and sweat and be so weak she could not stand to do her work.

Melanctha went back to the hospital, and there the Doctor told her she had the consumption, and before long she would surely die. They sent her where she would be taken care of, a home for poor consumptives, and there Melanctha stayed until she died.

1905   1909

From Portraits and Repetition[1]

In Composition As Explanation[2] I said nothing changes from generation to generation except the composition in which we live and the composition in which we live makes the art which we see and hear. I said in Lucy Church Amiably[3] that women and children change, I said if men have not changed women and children have. But it really is of no importance even if this is true. The thing

1. Published in *Lectures in America* (1935).
2. Lecture delivered at Cambridge and Oxford universities and published in 1926.
3. Stein's novel (1930).

that is important is the way that portraits of men and women and children are written, by written I mean made. And by made I mean felt. Portraits of men and women and children are differently felt in every generation and by a generation one means any period of time. One does mean any period of time by a generation. A generation can be anywhere from two years to a hundred years. What was it somebody said that the only thing God could not do was to make a two year old mule in a minute. But the strange thing about the realization of existence is that like a train moving there is no real realization of it moving if it does not move against something and so that is what a generation does it shows that moving is existing. So then there are generations and in a way that too is not important because, and this thing is a thing to know, if and we in America have tried to make this thing a real thing, if the movement, that is any movement, is lively enough, perhaps it is possible to know that it is moving even if it is not moving against anything. And so in a way the American way has been not to need that generations are existing. If this were really true and perhaps it is really true then really and truly there is a new way of making portraits of men and women and children. And I, I in my way have tried to do this thing.

It is true that generations are not of necessity existing that is to say if the actual movement within a thing is alive enough. A motor goes inside of an automobile and the car goes. In short this generation has conceived an intensity of movement so great that it has not to be seen against something else to be known, and therefore, this generation does not connect itself with anything, that is what makes this generation what it is and that is why it is American, and this is very important in connection with portraits of anything. I say portraits and not description and I will gradually explain why. Then also there is the important question of repetition and is there any such thing. Is there repetition or is there insistence. I am inclined to believe there is no such thing as repetition. And really how can there be. This is a thing about which I want you to think before I go on telling about portraits of anything. Think about all the detective stories everybody reads. The kind of crime is the same, and the idea of the story is very often the same, take for example a man like Wallace, he always has the same theme, take a man like Fletcher he always has the same theme,[4] take any American ones, they too always have the scene, the same scene, the kind of invention that is necessary to make a general scheme is very limited in everybody's experience, every time one of the hundreds of times a newspaper man makes fun of my writing and of my repetition he always has the same theme, always having the same theme, that is, if you like, repetition, that is if you like the repeating that is the same thing,

4. Probably Edgar Wallace (1875–1932), English writer of popular fiction, and   John Gould Fletcher (1886–1950), American poet.

but once started expressing this thing, expressing any thing there can be no repetition because the essence of that expression is insistence, and if you insist you must each time use emphasis and if you use emphasis it is not possible while anybody is alive that they should use exactly the same emphasis. And so let us think seriously of the difference between repetition and insistence.

Anybody can be interested in a story of a crime because no matter how often the witnesses tell the same story the insistence is different. That is what makes life that the insistence is different, no matter how often you tell the same story if there is anything alive in the telling the emphasis is different. It has to be, anybody can know that.

It is very like a frog hopping he cannot ever hop exactly the same distance or the same way of hopping at every hop. A bird's singing is perhaps the nearest thing to repetition but if you listen they too vary their insistence. That is the human expression saying the same thing and in insisting and we all insist varying the emphasising.

I remember very well first beginning to be conscious of this thing. I became conscious of these things, I suppose anybody does when they first really know that the stars are worlds and that everything is moving, that is the first conscious feeling of necessary repetition, and it comes to one and it is very disconcerting. Then the second thing is when you first realize the history of various civilizations, that have been on this earth, that too makes one realize repetition and at the same time the difference of insistence. Each civilization insisted in its own way before it went away. I remember the first time I really realized this in this way was from reading a book we had at home of the excavations of Nineveh, but these emotions although they tell one so much and one really never forgets them, after all are not in one's daily living, they are like the books of Jules Verne terribly real terribly near but still not here. When I first really realized the inevitable repetition in human expression that was not repetition but insistence when I first began to be really conscious of it was when at about seventeen years of age, I left the more or less internal and solitary and concentrated life I led in California and came to Baltimore and lived with a lot of my relations and principally with a whole group of very lively little aunts who had to know anything.

If they had to know anything and anybody does they naturally had to say and hear it often, anybody does, and as there were ten and eleven of them they did have to say and hear said whatever was said and any one not hearing what it was they said had to come in to hear what had been said. That inevitably made everything said often. I began then to consciously listen to what anybody was saying and what they did say while they were saying what they were saying. This was not yet the beginning of writing but it was the beginning of knowing what there was that made there be no repetition. No matter how often what happened had happened any time any one told anything there was no repetition. This is what William James calls the Will to Live.[5] If not nobody would live.

And so I began to find out then by listening the difference between repetition and insisting and it is a very important thing to know. You listen as you know.

Then there is another thing that also has something to do with repeating.

When all these eleven little aunts were listening as they were talking gradually some one of them was no longer listening. When this happened it might be that the time had come that any one or one of them was beginning repeating, that is was ceasing to be insisting or else perhaps it might be that the attention of one of some one of them had been worn out by adding something. What is the difference. Nothing makes any difference as long as some one is listening while they are talking.

That is what I gradually began to know.

Nothing makes any difference as long as some one is listening while they are talking. If the same person does the talking and the listening why so much the better there is just by so much the greater concentration. One may really indeed say that that is the essence of genius, of being most intensely alive, that is being one who is at the same time talking and listening. It is really that that makes one a genius. And it is necessary if you are to be really and truly alive it is necessary to be at once talking and listening, doing both things, not as if there were one thing, not as if they were two things, but doing them, well if you like, like the motor going inside and the car moving, they are part of the same thing.

I said in the beginning of saying this thing that if it were possible that a movement were lively enough it would exist so completely that it would not be necessary to see it moving against anything to know that it is moving. This is what we mean by life and in my way I have tried to make portraits of this thing always have tried always may try to make portraits of this thing.

If this existence is this thing is actually existing there can be no repetition. There is only repetition when there are descriptions being given of these things not when the things themselves are actually existing and this is therefore how my portrait writing began.

So we have now, a movement lively enough to be a thing in itself moving, it does not have to move against anything to know that it is moving, it does not need that there are generations existing.

Then we have insistence insistence that in its emphasis can never be repeating, because insistence is always alive and if it is alive it is never saying anything in the same way because emphasis can never

5. In *The Will to Believe and Other Essays in Popular Philosophy* (1897).

be the same not even when it is most the same that is when it has been taught.

How do you like what you have.

This is a question that anybody can ask anybody. Ask it.

In asking it I began to make portraits of anybody.

How do you like what you have is one way of having an important thing to ask of any one.

That is essentially the portrait of any one, one portrait of any one.

I began to think about portraits of any one.

If they are themselves inside them what are they and what has it to do with what they do.

And does it make any difference what they do or how they do it, does it make any difference what they say or how they say it. Must they be in relation with any one or with anything in order to be one of whom one can make a portrait. I began to think a great deal about all these things.

Anybody can be interested in what anybody does but does that make any difference, is it all important.

Anybody can be interested in what anybody says, but does that make any difference, is it at all important.

I began to wonder about all that.

I began to wonder what it was that I wanted to have as a portrait, what there is that was to be the portrait.

I do not wonder so much now about that. I do not wonder about that at all any more. Now I wonder about other things, I wonder if what has been done makes any difference.

I wonder now if it is necessary to stand still to live if it is not necessary to stand still to live, and if it is if that is not perhaps to be a new way to write a novel. I wonder if you know what I mean. I do not quite know whether I do myself. I will not know until I have written that novel.

* * *

1935

From Wars I Have Seen[1]

[*They Were Americans God Bless Them*]

* * * I said in a loud voice are there any Americans here and three men stood up and they were Americans God bless them and were we pleased. We held each other's hands and we patted each

1. *Wars I Have Seen* is drawn from a journal Stein kept from the spring of 1943 through the fall of 1944 and the liberation of France. She first discounted the seriousness of the war and the threat of Hitler. But even after recognizing them, she decided to remain, with her companion Alice Toklas, in Bilignin and, later, Culoz in southeastern France, near the towns Belley, Chambéry, Aix-les-Bains, and Voiron, mentioned in the excerpt printed below. Protected by friendly officials and villagers, they lived in semiretirement as a precaution against deportation as enemies of the Third Reich or later apprehension by German troops.

other and we sat down together and I told them who we were, and they knew, I always take it for granted that people will know who I am and at the same time at the last moment I kind of doubt, but they knew of course they knew, they were lieutenant Walter E. Oleson 120th Engineers and private Edward Landry and Walter Hartze, and they belonged to the Thunderbirds and how we talked and how we patted each other in the good American way, and I had to know where they came from and where they were going and where they were born. In the last war we had come across our first American soldiers and it had been nice but nothing like this, after almost two years of not a word with America, there they were, all three of them. Then we went to look at their car the jeep, and I had expected it to be much smaller but it was quite big and they said did I want a ride and I said you bet I wanted a ride and we all climbed in and there I was riding in an American army car driven by an American soldier. Everybody was so excited.

Then we all said good-bye and we did hope to see them again, and then we went on with our shopping, then suddenly everybody got excited army trucks filled with soldiers were coming along but not Americans, this was the French army in American cars and they were happy and we were happy and tired and happy and then we saw two who looked like Americans in a car standing alone and I went over and said are you Americans and they said sure, and by that time I was confident and I said I was Gertrude Stein and did they want to come back with us and spend the night. They said well yes they thought that the war could get along without them for a few hours so they came, Alice Toklas got into the car with the driver and the colonel came with me, oh a joyous moment and we all drove home and the village was wild with excitement and they all wanted to shake the colonel's hand and at last we got into the house, and were we excited. Here were the first Americans actually in the house with us, impossible to believe that only three weeks before the Germans had been in the village still and feeling themselves masters, it was wonderful. Lieutenant Colonel William O. Perry Headquarters 47th Infantry Division and private John Schmaltz, wonderful that is all I can say about it wonderful, and I said you are going to sleep in beds where German officers slept six weeks ago, wonderful my gracious perfectly wonderful.

How we talked that night, they just brought all America to us every bit of it, they came from Colorado, lovely Colorado, I do not know Colorado but that is the way I felt about it lovely Colorado and then everybody was tired out and they gave us nice American specialties and my were we happy, we were, completely and truly happy and completely and entirely worn out with emotion. The next morning while they breakfasted we talked some more and we patted each other and then kissed each other and then they went away. Just as we were sitting down to lunch, in came four more

Americans this time war correspondents, our emotions were not yet exhausted nor our capacity to talk, how we talked and talked and where they were born was music to the ears Baltimore and Washington D. C. and Detroit and Chicago, it is all music to the ears so long long long away from the names of the places where they were born. Well they have asked me to go with them to Voiron to broadcast with them to America next Sunday and I am going and the war is over and this certainly this is the last war to remember.

Epilogue

Write about us they all said a little sadly, and write about them I will. They all said good-bye Gerty as the train pulled out and then they said, well we will see you in America, and then they said we will stop on our way back, and then they said we will see you in California and then one said, you got to get to New York first.

It is pretty wonderful and pretty awful to have been intimate and friendly and proud of two American armies in France apart only by twenty-seven years. It is wonderful and if I could live twenty-seven more years could I see them here again. No I do not think so, maybe in other places but not here.

In the beginning when the Americans were here we had officers and their companion drivers. They were companion drivers, companions and drivers drivers and companions. The French revolution said, liberty brotherhood and equality, well they said it and we are it, bless us.

Of course the driver is a little prouder when it is a colonel than when it is a lieutenant or captain, well just a little. The first one was Lieutenant-Colonel Peary of Colorado, he came with me in the taxi from Belley and Miss Toklas went with Jake in the jeep, his name was not Jake but the colonel called him Jake because he used, while sitting in the jeep waiting, to sign his name as autograph for the French who crowded around him and wanted it, just like a film star, so the colonel called him Jake.

Well Miss Toklas asked him if the other one was a soldier like himself, they were our first Americans and we did not know how to tell one from the other as on the outside they all look alike particularly when their outside jacket is buttoned up, Miss Toklas asked him and he said with contentment oh he is a lieutenant colonel.

After that we had lots of officers and finally I met three majors in Aix-les-Bains. I said well it's all right, but now we have had everything from a second lieutenant to a full colonel and indeed several specimens of each now I want a general. The majors at least one of them said I think I can get you one. Would you like General Patch. Would I, I said, well I guess I would. If, said he, you write him a note I am sure he would come. He gave me an old card, I had already given him my autograph on a piece of French paper money, it is hard to write on French paper money but I finally did get the habit, so I wrote the note to General Patch and of course we thought it all a joke but not at all. About ten days later, came the personal secretary of General Patch with a nice driver from Arkansas who said modestly he always drove the general, and they brought me a charming letter from the general saying he would be coming along very soon, to eat the chicken dinner I had offered him. The secretary said that the general would be coming along in about two weeks. When that time came heavy fighting began in the Vosges mountains, the general's headquarters moved away from our region, and now we are still waiting, but he surely will come, he said he would and he will.

Gradually as the joy and excitement of really having Americans here really having them here began to settle a little I began to realise that Americans converse much more than they did, American men in those other days, the days before these days did not converse. How well I remember in the last war seeing four or five of them at a table at a hotel and one man would sort of drone along monologuing about what he had or had not done and the others solemnly and quietly eating and drinking and never saying a word. And seeing the soldiers stand at a corner or be seated somewhere and there they were and minutes hours passed and they never said a word, and then one would get up and leave and the others got up and left and that was that. No this army was not like that, this army conversed, it talked it listened, and each one of them had something to say no this army was not like that other army. People do not change no they don't, when I was in America after almost thirty years of absence they asked me if I did not find Americans changed and I said no what could they change to except to be American and anyway I could have gone to school with any of them they were just like the ones I went to school with and now they are still American but they can converse and they are interesting when they talk. The older Americans always told stories that was about all there was to their talking but these don't tell stories they converse and what they say is interesting and what they hear interests them and that does make them different not really different God bless them but just the same they are not quite the same.

We did not talk about that then. We had too much to tell and they had too much to tell to spend any time conversing about conversation. What we always wanted to know was the state they came from and what they did before they came over here. One said that he was born on a race track and worked in a night club. Another was the golf champion of Mississippi, but what we wanted most was to hear them say the name of the state in which they were born and the names of the other states where they had lived.

After every war, there have only been two like that but I do not think that just to say after the other war makes it feel as it does, no I do mean after every war, it feels like that, after every war when I talk and listen to all our army, it feels like that too, the thing I like most are the names of all the states of the United States. They make music and they are poetry, you do not have to recite them all but you just say any one two three four or five of them and you will see they make music and they make poetry.

After the last war I wanted to write a long book or a poem, I never did either but I wanted to, about how Kansas differed from Iowa and Iowa from Illinois and Illinois from Ohio, and Mississippi from Louisiana and Louisiana from Tennessee and Tennessee from Kentucky, and all the rest from all the rest, it would be most exciting, because each one of them does so completely differ from all the rest including their neighbors. And when you think how ruled the lines are of the states, no natural boundaries of mountains or rivers but just ruled out with a ruler to make lines and angles and all the same each one of the states has its own character, its own accent, just like provinces in France which are so ancient. It does not take long to make one state different from another state not so very long, they are all just as American as that but they are all so different one from the other Dakota and Wyoming and Texas and Oklahoma. Well any one you like. I like them all.

After all every one is as their land is, as the climate is, as the mountains and the rivers or their oceans are as the wind and rain and snow and ice and heat and moisture is, they just are and that makes them have their way to eat their way to drink their way to act their way to think and their way to be subtle, and even if the lines of demarcation are only made with a ruler after all what is inside those right angles is different from those on the outside of those right angles, any American knows that.

It is just that, I do not know why but Arkansas touched me particularly, anything touches me particularly now that is American. There is something in this native land business and you cannot get away from it, in peace time you do not seem to notice it much particularly when you live in foreign parts but when there is a war and you are all alone and completely cut off from knowing about your country well then there it is, your native land is your native land, it certainly is.

After all the excitement of all the jeeps and all the officers and all the drivers was over we were quiet a little while and we wondered are they all gone will we not see them again, and then Culoz which is a small town but a railroad center began to have them and we began to have them.

Troop trains began to pass through the station on their way to the front.

I was coming home from a walk and an F. F. I.[2] said to me there is a train of your compatriots standing at a siding just below, I

2. I.e., a member of the Free French of the Interior, the "resistance" forces who waged guerrilla warfare against the Germans in occupied France.

imagine it would please you to see them, thank you I said it will and I went quickly. There they were strolling along and standing about and I said Hello to the first group and they said Hello and I said I am an American and they laughed and said so were they and how did I happen to get caught here and I told them how I had passed the war here, and they wanted to know if there was snow on the mountains in winter and there was a large group of them and I told them who I was thinking some one of them might have heard of me but lots of them had and they crowded around and we talked and we talked. It was the first time I had been with a real lot of honest to God infantry and they said they were just that. We began to talk states and they wanted to know about our life under the Germans and I told them and they were interested, and they told me about where they had been and what they thought of the people they had seen and then they wanted autographs and they gave me pieces of money to write on, and one Pole who was the most extravagant gave me a hundred franc bill to sign for him, funny that a Pole should have been the most wasteful of his money, perhaps he was only going to spend it anyway, and one of them told me that they knew about me because they study my poems along with other American poetry in the public schools and that did please me immensely it most certainly did and then I left and they left.

I came away meditating yes they were American boys but they had a poise and completely lacked the provincialism which did characterise the last American army, they talked and they listened and they had a sureness, they were quite certain of themselves, they had no doubts or uncertainties and they had not to make any explanations. The last army was rather given to explaining, oh just anything, they were given to explaining, these did not explain, they were just conversational.

Then more troop trains came along and we took apples down to them and we talked to them and they talked to us and I was getting more impressed with their being different, they knew where they were and what they were and why they were, yes they did, they had poise and not any of them was ever drunk, not a bit, it was most exciting that they were like that.

The last American army used to ask questions, why do the French people put walls around their houses what are they afraid of what do they want to hide. Why do they want to stay and work this ground when there is so much better land to find. This army does not ask questions like that, they consider that people have their habits and their ways of living, some you can get along with and others you can't, but they all are perfectly reasonable for the people who use them. That is the great change in the Americans, they are interested, they are observant, they are accustomed to various types of people and ways of being, they have plenty of curiosity, but not any criticism, that is the new army. It was all very exciting.

Then one day down at the station, it was raining, I saw three American soldiers standing, I said hello what are you doing, why we just came here, they said, to stay a few days. I laughed. Is it A. W. O. L.[3] I said or do you call it something else now, well no they said we still call it that. And said I what are you going to do, just stay a few days they said. Come along I said, even if you are A. W. O. L. you will have to be given some tea and cake so come along. They came. One from Detroit, one little one from Tennessee, one big young one from New Jersey. We talked, it seemed somehow more like that old army, their being A. W. O. L. and deciding to stay here a few days. They came back with me, and we talked. They were interested, Tennessee said honestly he was tired of ten inch shells, he just had had enough of ten inch shells. The other two seemed to be just tired, they were not particular what they were tired of, they were just tired. We talked and then in talking to them I began to realise that men from the South seemed to be quite often men who had been orphans since they were children, the men from Tennessee and from Arkansas seemed to tend to be orphans from very young, they were members of large families and the large family once having been made, they promptly became orphans, I also began to realise that there were lots of pure American families where there were lots of brothers and sisters. The last army seven to eleven in a family was rare, but now it seemed to be quite common. Not emigrant families but pure American families. I was very much interested. And now the difference between the old army and the new began to be so real to me that I began to ask the American army about it. In the meanwhile the three A. W. O. L.s after moving into the village and then moving out and then moving in again did finally move out. They came to see us before they left, they did not say where they were going and they said it had been a pleasure to know us.

In the meanwhile, five M. P.s[4] had come to stay in the station to watch the stuff on the trains and see that it did not get stolen, and with these we got to be very good friends, and they were the first ones with whom I began to talk about the difference between the last army and this army. Why is it, I said.

They said, yes we know we are different, and I said and how did you find it out. From what we heard about the other army, that made us know we were very different, I said there is no doubt about that, you don't drink much I said, no we don't and we have our money they said, we don't want to go home and when we get there not have any money, we want to have a thousand dollars or so at

---

3. "Absent Without Official Leave," the charge registered against American military personnel who failed to report for duty.

4. Military police.

least to be able to look around and to find out what we really want to do. (Even the three A. W. O. L.s felt like that about money.) Well I explained what one used to complain of about American men was that as they grew older they did not grow more interesting, they grew duller. When I made that lecture tour in '35 to the American universities I used to say to them, now all sorts of things interest you but what will happen to you five years hence when you are working at some job will things interest you or will you just get dull. Yes said one of the soldiers yes but you see the depression made them know that a job was not all there was to it as mostly there was no job, and if there was it was any kind of job not the kind of job they had expected it to be, you would see a college man digging on the road doing anything and so we all came to find out you might just as well be interested in anything since anyway your job might not be a job and if it was well then it was not the kind of a job it might have been. Yes that did a lot, they all said, it certainly did do a lot.

Yes said one of the younger ones even if you were only kids during the depression you got to feel that way about it. Anyway they all agreed the depression had a lot to do with it.

There is one thing in which this army is not different from that other army that is in being generous and sweet and particularly kind to children.

They are sweet and kind and considerate all of them, how they do think about what you need and what will please you, they did then that other army and they do now this army.

When our M. P.s had got settled completely in their box car I used to go down to see them, and one day one of the mothers in the town told me that her nine year old daughter had been praying every single day that she might see an American soldier and she never had and now the mother was beginning to be afraid that the child would lose faith in prayer. I said I would take her down to see the American soldiers and we went. Naturally they were sweet and each one of them thought of something to give her, candies chewing gum, one of them gave her one of the U. S. badges they wear on their caps and one gave her a medal that the Pope had blessed in Rome and given to the American soldiers. And she was so happy, she sang them all the old French songs, Claire de la Lune, The Good King Dagobert and On the Bridge of Avignon.

Then as we were going home I said to her, about that chewing gum you must chew it but be careful not to swallow it. Oh yes I know she said. How do you know that I asked oh she said because when there was the last war my mother was a little girl and the American soldiers gave her chewing gum and all through this war my mother used to tell us about it, and she gave a rapturous sigh and said and now I have it.

More Americans came to stay at Culoz station, this time railroad workers and it became natural to have them there, natural for them and natural for us. They used all of them to want to know how we managed to escape the Germans and gradually with their asking and with the news that in the month of August the Gestapo[5] had been in my apartment in Paris to look at everything, naturally I began to have what you might call a posthumous fear. I was quite frightened. All the time the Germans were here we were so busy trying to live through each day that except once in a while when something happened you did not know about being frightened, but now somehow with the American soldiers questions and hearing what had been happening to others, of course one knew it but now one had time to feel it and so I was quite frightened, now that there was nothing dangerous and the whole American army between us and danger. One is like that.

As I say we were getting used to having Americans here and they were getting used to being here.

In the early days when the American army was first passing by, in jeeps and trucks the Americans used to say to me but they do not seem to get used to us, we have been right here over a week and they get just as excited when they see us as if they had never seen us before. You do not understand, I said to them you see every time they see you it makes them know it is not a dream that it is true that the Germans are gone and that you are here that you are here and that the Germans are gone. Every time they see you it is a new proof, a new proof that it is all true really true that the Germans are really truly completely and entirely gone, gone gone.

Yes even now when it has become so natural to see them here there are moments when it is hard to believe it. Yes of course they are really here.

Just this evening I saw a nun who had come over from Aix-les-Bains to see some sisters here, she had been in a convent in Connecticut. She said to me you know I just saw some American soldiers in the square and I just had to speak to them I just had to.

That is the way we all were we just had to.

So there were more Americans here and naturally we talked a lot, and one day one of them Ernest Humphrey from Tennessee was here and a French friend was here, he had known the American army of '17 and he too was struck with the poise and the conversation of this army. He asked him lots of questions, about what Americans feel about France about the French country and about French girls and about American men, and said my friend after Humphrey left, they are different now, they are so easy to converse with, the last army was easy to get along with but this army is easy to converse with and as French people do believe that conversation is the finest part of civilisation, naturally what he said meant a great deal.

5. German secret police.

Is it, said the Frenchman, the cinema that has taught them to be such men of the world, to be sure it has not much effect on our young men he added.

I asked so many of them about it, we had long talks about it, they all agreed that the depression had a lot to do with it, it made people stay at home because they had no money to go out with, all the same said some of them that military service that they did before we came into the war had something to do with it, it kind of sobered everybody up, kind of made them feel what it was to get ready. Some of them said the radio had a lot to do with it, they got the habit of listening to information, and then the quizzes that the radio used to give kind of made them feel that it was no use just being ignorant, and then some of them said crossword puzzles had a lot to do with it.

The conclusion that one came to was that it had happened the American men had at last come to be interested and to be interesting and conversational, and it was mighty interesting to see and hear it. Naturally we exchanged books a lot, I have all kinds here and they gave me what they had, two I enjoyed immensely, Ernie Pyle, Here Is Your War, and Helen McInnes, Assignment in Brittany,[6] some of the boys passing through on the train gave me the one and the railroad boys at Chambery gave me the other, the house here is filled with English books that I have been buying as I could through the war and other odds and ends, I was interested that they were a bit tired of detectives,[7] I like them as much as ever but that is because I am so much older and they do like Westerns and then they like adventures, and any longish American novel. They do not care for English ones, they say they can't seem to get into them. They also gave me a book on Head Hunters in the Solomon Islands which they all read. Well of course they did in the last war give me The Trail of the Lonesome Pine,[8] they did not read much not those we knew. Undoubtedly the depression had a lot to do with that, a lot.

They asked me in Lyon[9] to go and speak to the French on the radio. When I was there I saw lots of Americans on the streets but as I was in cars I could not speak to them but one evening I wandered out on foot and in a school near by I found a number of them. Naturally well just so naturally we talked, they were glad to see me and I was glad to see them, there were about thirty of them and we told each other a lot. One who had been a schoolteacher in North Carolina walked home with me and we interested each other very much. He said I was quite right about the difference between the two armies, he said he had noticed it before he had left home but now he was sure. We said we would meet again but in a war it

6. Popular journalistic works, published in 1943 and 1942, by Ernie Pyle (1900–45) and Helen McInnes (b. 1907).
7. Detective stories.
8. Sentimental romance about the Kentucky mountain region, published in 1908 by John W. Fox (1863–1919).
9. Large city in southeastern France.

is always difficult to meet again, very often not possible. I do hope that we will meet again.

Of course one has to remember that many in fact most of these soldiers have not been home for almost two years. It is a long time a very long time.

When I got back from Lyon the Americans here in Culoz wanted to know what I had talked about in Lyon, I said I had been telling French people what Americans are and they said what are they, and I said this is what I told them and so I told them. They were interested.

I said that I had begun by saying that after all to-day, America was the oldest country in the world and the reason why was that she was the first country to enter into the twentieth century. She had her birthday of the twentieth century when the other countries were still all either in the nineteenth century or still further back in other centuries, now all the countries except Germany, are trying to be in the twentieth century, so that considering the world as twentieth century America is the oldest as she came into the twentieth century in the eighties before any other country had any idea what the twentieth century was going to be. And now what is the twentieth century that America discovered. The twentieth century is a century that found out that the cheapest articles should be made of the very best material. The nineteenth century believed that the best material should be only used in expensive objects and that cheap things should be made of cheap material. The Americans knew that if you wanted to make a lot of things that is things that will sell cheap you had to make them of the best material otherwise you could not turn them out fast enough, that is series manufacture because cheap material could not stand the strain. So America began to live in the twentieth century in the eighties with the Ford car and all the other series manufacturing.

And so America is at the present moment the oldest country in the world because she had her twentieth century birthday in the eighteen eighties, long before any other country had their twentieth century birthday.

There is one thing one has to remember about America, it had a certain difficulty in proving itself American which no other nation has ever had.

After all anybody is as their land and air is. Anybody is as the sky is low or high. Anybody is as there is wind or no wind there. That is what makes a people, makes their kind of looks, their kind of thinking, their subtlety and their stupidity, and their eating and their drinking and their language.

I was much taken with what one American soldier said when he was in England. He said we did not get along at all with the English until they finally did get it into their heads that we were not cousins, but foreigners, once they really got that, there was no more trouble.

The trouble of course is or was that by the time America became itself everybody or very nearly everybody could read and write and so the language which would naturally have changed as Latin languages changed to suit each country, French, Italian and Spanish, Saxon countries England and Germany, Slav countries etcetera, America as everybody knew how to read and write the language instead of changing as it did in countries where nobody knew how to read and write while the language was being formed, the American language instead of changing remained English, long after the Americans in their nature their habits their feelings their pleasures and their pains had nothing to do with England.

So the only way the Americans could change their language was by choosing words which they liked better than other words, by putting words next to each other in a different way than the English way, by shoving the language around until at last now the job is done, we use the same words as the English do but the words say an entirely different thing.

Yes in that sense Americans have changed, I think of the Americans of the last war, they had their language but they were not yet in possession of it, and the children of the depression as that generation called itself it was beginning to possess its language but it was still struggling but now the job is done, the G. I. Joes[1] have this language that is theirs, they do not have to worry about it, they dominate their language and in dominating their language which is now all theirs they have ceased to be adolescents and have become men.

When I was in America in '34 they asked me if I did not find Americans changed. I said no what could they change to, just to become more American. No I said I could have gone to school with any of them.

But all the same yes that is what they have changed to they have become more American all American, and the G. I. Joes show it and know it, God bless them.

1945

1. World War II slang for "soldier" ("G.I.": government issue—i.e., equipment issued to soldiers by the army).

SHERWOOD ANDERSON
1876–1941

Sherwood Anderson brought simultaneously the instincts of a naïf and the earnestness of a devotee to bear on the craft of writing and became one of the important catalysts in the literary world of the 1920s, stimulating other prose writers to achievements beyond his own. He also produced in *Winesburg, Ohio*, one of the masterpieces of American prose fiction.

He was born in southern Ohio near the Kentucky border, the third of seven children in a family that drifted north through small Ohio towns as his father turned from harness-making to odd jobs and sign-painting. In 1894 they settled in Clyde. His memories of that rural town were to provide the setting for *Winesburg*. His memories of his mother's stamina and tenderness, and of his father's wanderlust, his boozing, and facility as a storyteller, were to appear, altered and magnified, in his three volumes of highly imaginative autobiography: *A Story-Teller's Story* (1924), *Tar* (1926), and *Sherwood Anderson's Memoirs* (1942).

His family's migration and his jobs as farm hand, stableboy, and worker in a bicycle factory made for irregular schooling, and he dropped out of high school before graduating. In 1896 he followed his older brother Karl (a painter) to Chicago, and after serving briefly in Cuba during the Spanish-American War he went with his brother to Springfield, Ohio, where he enrolled for a year in Wittenberg Academy and became acquainted with the editors, artists, and advertising men at Crowell Publishing Company, where his brother was employed. The offer of a job as advertising copywriter in 1900 took him to Chicago, where he wrote promotional articles for a house journal extolling the virtues of business enterprise. He married the first of his four wives in 1904, the daughter of a well-to-do Ohio merchant, and in 1906 moved to Ohio, where he managed a mail-order business and two paint firms, living the life of a successful businessman but writing fiction in secret and finding that his business career and his writing craft were increasingly incompatible.

In 1912 he suddenly disappeared for several days, reappeared in Cleveland in a state of nervous collapse, and after a quick recovery made the partial break with the business world that he later dramatized repeatedly in his autobiographical essays and memoirs. He returned temporarily to his advertising job in Chicago but took with him the drafts of two novels and other manuscripts. Advertising had earlier seemed to nourish his facility with words, but he now became acquainted with the serious writers of the Chicago "renaissance," including Floyd Dell, Carl Sandburg, and Theodore Dreiser, who encouraged his serious ambitions. His reading earlier had included such figures as Poe, Whitman, and Twain, the British poets Keats and Browning, the English novelists Arnold Bennett and Thomas Hardy, and the English writer of character sketches George Borrow. Now his reading extended to D. H. Lawrence, Sigmund Freud, the Russian novelist Turgenev, and Gertrude Stein, whose *Three Lives* he had read in 1909 but whose experimental *Tender Buttons* was an exciting discovery in 1914. His first major publication was *Windy McPherson's Son* (1916), the story of a man who flees a small Iowa town to engage in a futile search for life's meaning first as a businessman, then as a vagabond among the common people, finally as father to three adopted children. Anderson's next novel was *Marching Men* (1917), whose protagonist, a charismatic lawyer, combats the dehumanization of an industrial society by organizing its masses into phalanxes which threaten their further dehumanization.

Anderson had started writing the tales that were to comprise *Winesburg*,

Ohio in 1916, and some had appeared in journals between 1916 and 1918 before they were gathered in 1919 to form the loosely but suggestively related group of stories that have the integral coherence of a novel. His models were the comparably related sketches in Turgenev's *Sportsman's Sketches* (1852) and Edgar Lee Masters's collection of elegiac portraits in verse, *Spoon River Anthology* (1915). But Anderson's volume is unique. Each character is a "grotesque" whose conduct and usually fumbling attempts at communication are warped versions of some reality or "truth," whose realization is never achieved in the life of the community. The pathos of the inhabitants' isolation and quest for fulfillment is given focus by the maturing consciousness of the young reporter and future writer, George Willard, who discovers his ties to the community in the process of deciding to leave it. The groping attempts of the townspeople to articulate their feelings and communicate with others—the repressed yearnings and obsessions which surface fleetingly or explosively from the depths of their experience—are surrealistic or expressionistic in their effects. And these effects are captured by the narrative's simple but bold imagery (like the twisted apples in "Paper Pills") and the stylization of Anderson's prose, which becomes a species of elegiac poetry. The simple vernacular diction and the declarative sentence structure, the repetition of words and phrases, the recurring restatements of ideals and feelings have at once the power of colloquial speech that Anderson admired in Twain and the "pure and beautiful prose" that he found exemplified in Gertrude Stein.[1]

Anderson's best writing in *Winesburg* was matched only by his short stories (collected in *The Triumph of the Egg*, 1921; *Horses and Men*, 1923; and *Death in the Woods and Other Stories*, 1933) and, to a lesser extent, by the novel *Poor White* (1920), the story of an inventor who brings industrialism to a rural town only to find that it blights the community and that his business success is no answer to his alienation from his fellows. Though each contained some impressive sections, the two novels about sexuality, *Many Marriages* (1923) and *Beyond Desire* (1932), and *Kit Brandon* (1936) were neither critical nor popular successes. Anderson published a volume of rhapsodic free verse (*Mid-American Chants*, 1918), a volume of prose poems (*A New Testament*, 1927), four plays (*Winesburg and Others*, 1937), as well as collections of essays on social issues (*Perhaps Women*, 1931, and *Puzzled America*, 1935) and essays on literary figures (*No Swank*, 1934). But his chief importance in the 1920s and afterward, as the reputation of his fiction declined, was the series of autobiographical volumes that centered on his own professional career and his attempt to define the writer's vocation in America and on his impact on other writers. He had met Hemingway in Europe in 1921 and had helped secure publication of *In Our Time* in the United States. And while Hemingway later mocked Anderson's style and cult of the primitive in *Torrents of Spring*, he had been inspired by the "simplification"[2] of Anderson's prose to make his own, similar break from the more elaborate conventions of earlier fiction. Anderson's treatment of violence and his "grotesques" provided models for Nathanael West in the 1930s. During two periods, in 1922–23 and 1924–25, Anderson had known William Faulkner in New Orleans and had shared an

1. "Gertrude Stein," *No Swank* (1934), p. 82.
2. *Hello, Towns* (1929), p. 325.

apartment with him. Faulkner later testified that Anderson's encouragement, and his example, had enabled him to see that he could rely on the uniqueness of his own talent as a writer and on the milieu of his own native region for material.[3]

Anderson's own search for roots in his native land was never satisfied. He moved with his third wife to Virginia in 1927 and bought two local newspapers to bond his attachment to the region. He published editorials from the papers in *Hello, Towns* (1929). His concern with the dislocations of modern industrialism led to his involvement in leftist political activity in the early 1930s, and his interest in public issues continued until 1941, when he died on a good-will mission to South America for the State Department.

From WINESBURG, OHIO
The Book of the Grotesque

The writer, an old man with a white mustache, had some difficulty in getting into bed. The windows of the house in which he lived were high and he wanted to look at the trees when he awoke in the morning. A carpenter came to fix the bed so that it would be on a level with the window.

Quite a fuss was made about the matter. The carpenter, who had been a soldier in the Civil War, came into the writer's room and sat down to talk of building a platform for the purpose of raising the bed. The writer had cigars lying about and the carpenter smoked.

For a time the two men talked of the raising of the bed and then they talked of other things. The soldier got on the subject of the war. The writer, in fact, led him to that subject. The carpenter had once been a prisoner in Andersonville prison[1] and had lost a brother. The brother had died of starvation, and whenever the carpenter got upon that subject he cried. He, like the old writer, had a white mustache, and when he cried he puckered up his lips and the mustache bobbed up and down. The weeping old man with the cigar in his mouth was ludicrous. The plan the writer had for the raising of his bed was forgotten and later the carpenter did it in his own way and the writer, who was past sixty, had to help himself with a chair when he went to bed at night.

In his bed the writer rolled over on his side and lay quite still. For years he had been beset with notions concerning his heart. He was a hard smoker and his heart fluttered. The idea had got into his mind that he would some time die unexpectedly and always when he got into bed he thought of that. It did not alarm him.

3. "Sherwood Anderson: An Appreciation," *Atlantic Monthly*, 1953, p. 29.

1. Notorious Confederate prison in Georgia during the Civil War.

The effect in fact was quite a special thing and not easily explained. It made him more alive, there in bed, than at any other time. Perfectly still he lay and his body was old and not of much use any more, but something inside him was altogether young. He was like a pregnant woman, only that the thing inside him was not a baby but a youth. No, it wasn't a youth, it was a woman, young, and wearing a coat of mail like a knight. It is absurd, you see, to try to tell what was inside the old writer as he lay on his high bed and listened to the fluttering of his heart. The thing to get at is what the writer, or the young thing within the writer, was thinking about.

The old writer, like all of the people in the world, had got, during his long life, a great many notions in his head. He had once been quite handsome and a number of women had been in love with him. And then, of course, he had known people, many people, known them in a peculiarly intimate way that was different from the way in which you and I know people. At least that is what the writer thought and the thought pleased him. Why quarrel with an old man concerning his thoughts?

In the bed the writer had a dream that was not a dream. As he grew somewhat sleepy but was still conscious, figures began to appear before his eyes. He imagined the young indescribable thing within himself was driving a long procession of figures before his eyes.

You see the interest in all this lies in the figures that went before the eyes of the writer. They were all grotesques. All of the men and women the writer had ever known had become grotesques.

The grotesques were not all horrible. Some were amusing, some almost beautiful, and one, a woman all drawn out of shape, hurt the old man by her grotesqueness. When she passed he made a noise like a small dog whimpering. Had you come into the room you might have supposed the old man had unpleasant dreams or perhaps indigestion.

For an hour the procession of grotesques passed before the eyes of the old man, and then, although it was a painful thing to do, he crept out of bed and began to write. Some one of the grotesques had made a deep impression on his mind and he wanted to describe it.

At his desk the writer worked for an hour. In the end he wrote a book which he called "The Book of the Grotesque." It was never published, but I saw it once and it made an indelible impression on my mind. The book had one central thought that is very strange and has always remained with me. By remembering it I have been able to understand many people and things that I was never able to understand before. The thought was involved but a simple statement of it would be something like this:

That in the beginning when the world was young there were a

great many thoughts but no such thing as a truth. Man made the truths himself and each truth was a composite of a great many vague thoughts. All about in the world were the truths and they were all beautiful.

The old man had listed hundreds of the truths in his book. I will not try to tell you of all of them. There was the truth of virginity and the truth of passion, the truth of wealth and of poverty, of thrift and of profligacy, of carelessness and abandon. Hundreds and hundreds were the truths and they were all beautiful.

And then the people came along. Each as he appeared snatched up one of the truths and some who were quite strong snatched up a dozen of them.

It was the truths that made the people grotesques. The old man had quite an elaborate theory concerning the matter. It was his notion that the moment one of the people took one of the truths to himself, called it his truth, and tried to live his life by it, he came a grotesque and the truth he embraced became a falsehood.

You can see for yourself how the old man, who had spent all of his life writing and was filled with words, would write hundreds of pages concerning this matter. The subject would become so big in his mind that he himself would be in danger of becoming a grotesque. He didn't, I suppose, for the same reason that he never published the book. It was the young thing inside him that saved the old man.

Concerning the old carpenter who fixed the bed for the writer, I only mentioned him because he, like many of what are called very common people, became the nearest thing to what is understandable and lovable of all the grotesques in the writer's book.

Paper Pills

He was an old man with a white beard and huge nose and hands. Long before the time during which we will know him, he was a doctor and drove a jaded white horse from house to house through the streets of Winesburg. Later he married a girl who had money. She had been left a large fertile farm when her father died. The girl was quiet, tall, and dark, and to many people she seemed very beautiful. Everyone in Winesburg wondered why she married the doctor. Within a year after the marriage she died.

The knuckles of the doctor's hand were extraordinarily large. When the hands were closed they looked like clusters of unpainted wooden balls as large as walnuts fastened together by steel rods. He smoked a cob pipe and after his wife's death sat all day in his empty office close by a window that was covered with cobwebs. He never opened the window. Once on a hot day in August he tried but found it stuck fast and after that he forgot all about it.

Winesburg had forgotten the old man, but in Doctor Reefy

there were the seeds of something very fine. Alone in his musty office in the Heffner Block above the Paris Dry Goods Company's Store, he worked ceaselessly, building up something that he himself destroyed. Little pyramids of truth he erected and after erecting knocked them down again that he might have the truths to erect other pyramids.

Doctor Reefy was a tall man who had worn one suit of clothes for ten years. It was frayed at the sleeves and little holes had appeared at the knees and elbows. In the office he wore also a linen duster with huge pockets into which he continually stuffed scraps of paper. After some weeks the scraps of paper became little hard round balls, and when the pockets were filled he dumped them out upon the floor. For ten years he had but one friend, another old man named John Spaniard who owned a tree nursery. Sometimes, in a playful mood, old Doctor Reefy took from his pockets a handful of the paper balls and threw them at the nursery man. "That is to confound you, you blithering old sentimentalist," he cried, shaking with laughter.

The story of Doctor Reefy and his courtship of the tall dark girl who became his wife and left her money to him is a very curious story. It is delicious, like the twisted little apples that grow in the orchards of Winesburg. In the fall one walks in the orchards and the ground is hard with frost underfoot. The apples have been taken from the trees by the pickers. They have been put in barrels and shipped to the cities where they will be eaten in apartments that are filled with books, magazines, furniture, and people. On the trees are only a few gnarled apples that the pickers have rejected. They look like the knuckles of Doctor Reefy's hands. One nibbles at them and they are delicious. Into a little round place at the side of the apple has been gathered all of its sweetness. One runs from tree to tree over the frosted ground picking the gnarled, twisted apples and filling his pockets with them. Only the few know the sweetness of the twisted apples.

The girl and Doctor Reefy began their courtship on a summer afternoon. He was forty-five then and already he had begun the practice of filling his pockets with the scraps of paper that became hard balls and were thrown away. The habit had been formed as he sat in his buggy behind the jaded grey horse and went slowly along country roads. On the papers were written thoughts, ends of thoughts, beginnings of thoughts.

One by one the mind of Doctor Reefy had made the thoughts. Out of many of them he formed a truth that arose gigantic in his mind. The truth clouded the world. It became terrible and then faded away and the little thoughts began again.

The tall dark girl came to see Doctor Reefy because she was in the family way and had become frightened. She was in that condition because of a series of circumstances also curious.

The death of her father and mother and the rich acres of land that had come down to her had set a train of suitors on her heels. For two years she saw suitors almost every evening. Except two they were all alike. They talked to her of passion and there was a strained eager quality in their voices and in their eyes when they looked at her. The two who were different were much unlike each other. One of them, a slender young man with white hands, the son of a jeweler in Winesburg, talked continually of virginity. When he was with her he was never off the subject. The other, a black-haired boy with large ears, said nothing at all but always managed to get her into the darkness where he began to kiss her.

For a time the tall dark girl thought she would marry the jeweler's son. For hours she sat in silence listening as he talked to her and then she began to be afraid of something. Beneath his talk of virginity she began to think there was a lust greater than in all the others. At times it seemed to her that as he talked he was holding her body in his hands. She imagined him turning it slowly about in the white hands and staring at it. At night she dreamed that he had bitten into her body and that his jaws were dripping. She had the dream three times, then she became in the family way to the one who said nothing at all but who in the moment of his passion actually did bite her shoulder so that for days the marks of his teeth showed.

After the tall dark girl came to know Doctor Reefy it seemed to her that she never wanted to leave him again. She went into his office one morning and without her saying anything he seemed to know what had happened to her.

In the office of the doctor there was a woman, the wife of the man who kept the bookstore in Winesburg. Like all old-fashioned country practitioners, Doctor Reefy pulled teeth, and the woman who waited held a handkerchief to her teeth and groaned. Her husband was with her and when the tooth was taken out they both screamed and blood ran down on the woman's white dress. The tall dark girl did not pay any attention. When the woman and the man had gone the doctor smiled. "I will take you driving into the country with me," he said.

For several weeks the tall dark girl and the doctor were together almost every day. The condition that had brought her to him passed in an illness, but she was like one who has discovered the sweetness of the twisted apples, she could not get her mind fixed again upon the round perfect fruit that is eaten in the city apartments. In the fall after the beginning of her acquaintanceship with him she married Doctor Reefy and in the following spring she died. During the winter he read to her all of the odds and ends of thoughts he had scribbled on the bits of paper. After he had read them he laughed and stuffed them away in his pockets to become round hard balls.

Mother

Elizabeth Willard, the mother of George Willard, was tall and gaunt and her face was marked with smallpox scars. Although she was but forty-five, some obscure disease had taken the fire out of her figure. Listlessly she went about the disorderly old hotel looking at the faded wall-paper and the ragged carpets and, when she was able to be about, doing the work of a chambermaid among beds soiled by the slumbers of fat traveling men. Her husband, Tom Willard, a slender, graceful man with square shoulders, a quick military step, and a black mustache, trained to turn sharply up at the ends, tried to put the wife out of his mind. The presence of the tall ghostly figure, moving slowly through the halls, he took as a reproach to himself. When he thought of her he grew angry and swore. The hotel was unprofitable and forever on the edge of failure and he wished himself out of it. He thought of the old house and the woman who lived there with him as things defeated and done for. The hotel in which he had begun life so hopefully was now a mere ghost of what a hotel should be. As he went spruce and businesslike through the streets of Winesburg, he sometimes stopped and turned quickly about as though fearing that the spirit of the hotel and of the woman would follow him even into the streets. "Damn such a life, damn it!" he sputtered aimlessly.

Tom Willard had a passion for village politics and for years had been the leading Democrat in a strongly Republican community. Some day, he told himself, the tide of things political will turn in my favor and the years of ineffectual service count big in the bestowal of rewards. He dreamed of going to Congress and even of becoming governor. Once when a younger member of the party arose at a political conference and began to boast of his faithful service, Tom Willard grew white with fury. "Shut up, you," he roared, glaring about. "What do you know of service? What are you but a boy? Look at what I've done here! I was a Democrat here in Winesburg when it was a crime to be a Democrat. In the old days they fairly hunted us with guns."

Between Elizabeth and her one son George there was a deep unexpressed bond of sympathy, based on a girlhood dream that had long ago died. In the son's presence she was timid and reserved, but sometimes while he hurried about town intent upon his duties as a reporter, she went into his room and closing the door knelt by a little desk, made of a kitchen table, that sat near a window. In the room by the desk she went through a ceremony that was half a prayer, half a demand, addressed to the skies. In the boyish figure she yearned to see something half forgotten that had once been a part of herself recreated. The prayer concerned that. "Even though I die, I will in some way keep defeat from you," she cried, and so deep was her determination that her whole body shook. Her eyes glowed and she clenched her fists. "If I am dead and see him becoming a meaningless drab figure like myself, I will come back," she declared. "I ask God now to give me that privilege. I demand it. I will pay for it. God may beat me with his fists. I will take any blow that may befall if but this my boy be allowed to express something for us both." Pausing uncertainly, the woman stared about the boy's room. "And do not let him become smart and successful either," she added vaguely.

The communion between George Willard and his mother was outwardly a formal thing without meaning. When she was ill and sat by the window in her room he sometimes went in the evening to make her a visit. They sat by a window that looked over the roof of a small frame building into Main Street. By turning their heads they could see, through another window, along an alleyway that ran behind the Main Street stores and into the back door of Abner Groff's bakery. Sometimes as they sat thus a picture of village life presented itself to them. At the back door of his shop appeared Abner Groff with a stick or an empty milk bottle in his hand. For a long time there was a feud between the baker and a grey cat that belonged to Sylvester West, the druggist. The boy and his mother saw the cat creep into the door of the bakery and presently emerge followed by the baker who swore and waved his arms about. The baker's eyes were small and red and his black hair and beard were filled with flour dust. Sometimes he was so angry that, although the cat had disappeared, he hurled sticks, bits of broken glass, and even some of the tools of his trade about. Once he broke a window at the back of Sinning's Hardware Store. In the alley the grey cat crouched behind barrels filled with torn paper and broken bottles above which flew a black swarm of flies. Once when she was alone, and after watching a prolonged and ineffectual outburst on the part of the baker, Elizabeth Willard put her head down on her long white hands and wept. After that she did not look along the alleyway any more, but tried to forget the contest between the bearded man and the cat. It seemed like a rehearsal of her own life, terrible in its vividness.

In the evening when the son sat in the room with his mother, the silence made them both feel awkward. Darkness came on and the evening train came in at the station. In the street below feet tramped up and down upon a board sidewalk. In the station yard, after the evening train had gone, there was a heavy silence. Perhaps Skinner Leason, the express agent, moved a truck the length of the station platform. Over on Main Street sounded a man's voice, laughing. The door of the express office banged. George Willard arose and crossing the room fumbled for the doorknob. Sometimes he knocked against a chair, making it scrape along the floor. By the window sat the sick woman, perfectly still, listless. Her long hands, white and bloodless, could be seen drooping over the ends of the arms of the chair. "I think you had better be out among the boys. You are too much indoors," she said, striving to relieve the embarrassment of the departure. "I thought I would take a walk," replied George Willard, who felt awkward and confused.

One evening in July, when the transient guests who made the New Willard House their temporary homes had become scarce, and the hallways, lighted only by kerosene lamps turned low, were plunged in gloom, Elizabeth Willard had an adventure. She had been ill in bed for several days and her son had not come to visit her. She was alarmed. The feeble blaze of life that remained in her body was blown into a flame by her anxiety and she crept out of bed, dressed and hurried along the hallway toward her son's room, shaking with exaggerated fears. As she went along she steadied herself with her hand, slipped along the papered walls of the hall and breathed with difficulty. The air whistled through her teeth. As she hurried forward she thought how foolish she was. "He is concerned with boyish affairs," she told herself. "Perhaps he has now begun to walk about in the evening with girls."

Elizabeth Willard had a dread of being seen by guests in the hotel that had once belonged to her father and the ownership of which still stood recorded in her name in the county courthouse. The hotel was continually losing patronage because of its shabbiness and she thought of herself as also shabby. Her own room was in an obscure corner and when she felt able to work she voluntarily worked among the beds, preferring the labor that could be done when the guests were abroad seeking trade among the merchants of Winesburg.

By the door of her son's room the mother knelt upon the floor and listened for some sound from within. When she heard the boy moving about and talking in low tones a smile came to her lips. George Willard had a habit of talking aloud to himself and to hear him doing so had always given his mother a peculiar pleasure. The habit in him, she felt, strengthened the secret bond that existed between them. A thousand times she had whispered to herself of the matter. "He is groping about, trying to find himself," she thought. "He is not a dull clod, all words and smartness. Within him there is a secret something that is striving to grow. It is the thing I let be killed in myself."

In the darkness in the hallway by the door the sick woman arose and started again toward her own room. She was afraid that the door would open and the boy come upon her. When she had reached a safe distance and was about to turn a corner into a second hallway she stopped and bracing herself with her hands waited, thinking to shake off a trembling fit of weakness that had come upon her. The presence of the boy in the room had made her happy. In her bed, during the long hours alone, the little fears that had visited her had become giants. Now they were all gone.

"When I get back to my room I shall sleep," she murmured gratefully.

But Elizabeth Willard was not to return to her bed and sleep. As she stood trembling in the darkness the door of her son's room opened and the boy's father, Tom Willard, stepped out. In the light that streamed out at the door he stood with the knob in his hand and talked. What he said infuriated the woman.

Tom Willard was ambitious for his son. He had always thought of himself as a successful man, although nothing he had ever done had turned out successfully. However, when he was out of sight of the New Willard House and had no fear of coming upon his wife, he swaggered and began to dramatize himself as one of the chief men of the town. He wanted his son to succeed. He it was who had secured for the boy the position on the *Winesburg Eagle*. Now, with a ring of earnestness in his voice, he was advising concerning some course of conduct. "I tell you what, George, you've got to wake up," he said sharply. "Will Henderson has spoken to me three times concerning the matter. He says you go along for hours not hearing when you are spoken to and acting like a gawky girl. What ails you?" Tom Willard laughed good-naturedly. "Well, I guess you'll get over it," he said. "I told Will that. You're not a fool and you're not a woman. You're Tom Willard's son and you'll wake up. I'm not afraid. What you say clears things up. If being a newspaper man had put the notion of becoming a writer into your mind that's all right. Only I guess you'll have to wake up to do that too, eh?"

Tom Willard went briskly along the hallway and down a flight of stairs to the office. The woman in the darkness could hear him laughing and talking with a guest who was striving to wear away a dull evening by dozing in a chair by the office door. She returned to the door of her son's room. The weakness had passed from her body as by a miracle and she stepped boldly along. A thousand ideas raced through her head. When she heard the scraping of a chair and the sound of a pen scratching upon paper, she again turned and went back along the hallway to her own room.

A definite determination had come into the mind of the defeated wife of the Winesburg Hotel keeper. The determination was the result of long years of quiet and rather ineffectual thinking. "Now," she told herself, "I will act. There is something threatening my boy and I will ward it off." The fact that the conversation between Tom Willard and his son had been rather quiet and natural, as though an understanding existed between them, maddened her. Although for years she had hated her husband, her hatred had always before been a quite impersonal thing. He had been merely a part of something else that she hated. Now, and by the few words at the door, he had become the thing personified. In the darkness of her own room she clenched her fists and glared about. Going to a cloth bag that hung on a nail by the wall she took out a long pair of sewing scissors and held them in her hand like a dagger. "I will stab him." she said aloud. "He has chosen to be the voice of evil and I will kill him. When I have killed him something will snap within myself and I will die also. It will be a release for all of us."

In her girlhood and before her marriage with Tom Willard, Elizabeth had borne a somewhat shaky reputation in Winesburg. For years she had been what is called "stage-struck" and had paraded through the streets with traveling men guests at her father's hotel, wearing loud clothes and urging them to tell her of life in the cities out of which they had come. Once she startled the town by putting on men's clothes and riding a bicycle down Main Street.

In her own mind the tall girl had been in those days much confused. A great restlessness was in her and it expressed itself in two ways. First there was an uneasy desire for change, for some big definite movement to her life. It was this feeling that had turned her mind to the stage. She dreamed of joining some company and wandering over the world, seeing always new faces and giving something out of herself to all people. Sometimes at night she was quite beside herself with the thought, but when she tried to talk of the matter to the members of the theatrical companies that came to Winesburg and stopped at her father's hotel, she got nowhere. They did not seem to know what she meant, or if she did get something of her passion expressed, they only laughed. "It's not like that," they said. "It's as dull and uninteresting as this here. Nothing comes of it."

With the traveling men when she walked about with them, and later with Tom Willard, it was quite different. Always they seemed to understand and sympathize with her. On the side streets of the village, in the darkness under the trees, they took hold of her hand and she thought that something unexpressed in herself came forth and became a part of an unexpressed something in them.

And then there was the second expression of her restlessness. When that came she felt for a time released and happy. She did not blame the men who walked with her and later did not blame Tom Willard. It was always the same, beginning with kisses and ending, after strange wild emotions, with peace and then sobbing repentance. When she sobbed she put her hand upon the face of the man and had always the same thought. Even though he were large and bearded she thought he had become suddenly a little boy. She wondered why he did not sob also.

In her room, tucked away in a corner of the old Willard House, Elizabeth Willard lighted a lamp and put it on a dressing table that stood by the door. A thought had come into her mind and she went to a closet and brought out a small square box and set it on the table. The box contained material for make-up and had been left with other things by a theatrical company that had once been stranded in Winesburg. Elizabeth Willard had decided that she would be beautiful. Her hair was still black and there was a great mass of it braided and coiled about her head. The scene that was to take place in the office below began to grow in her mind. No ghostly worn-out figure should confront Tom Willard, but something quite unexpected and startling. Tall and with dusky cheeks and hair that fell in a mass from her shoulders, a figure should come striding down the stairway before the startled loungers in the hotel office. The figure would be silent— it would be swift and terrible. As a tigress whose cub had been threatened would she appear, coming out of the shadows, stealing noiselessly along and holding the long wicked scissors in her hand.

With a little broken sob in her throat, Elizabeth Willard blew out the light that stood upon the table and stood weak and trembling in the darkness. The strength that had been as a miracle in her body left and she half reeled across the floor, clutching at the back of the chair in which she had spent so many long days staring out over the tin roofs into the main street of Winesburg. In the hallway there was the sound of footsteps and George Willard came in at the door. Sitting in a chair beside his mother he began to talk. "I'm going to get out of here," he said. "I don't know where I shall go or what I shall do but I am going away."

The woman in the chair waited and trembled. An impulse came to her. "I suppose you had better wake up," she said. "You think that? You will go to the city and make money, eh? It will be better for you, you think, to be a business man, to be brisk and smart and alive?" She waited and trembled.

The son shook his head. "I suppose I can't make you understand, but oh, I wish I could," he said earnestly. "I can't even talk to father about it. I don't try. There isn't any use. I don't know what I shall do. I just want to go away and look at people and think."

Silence fell upon the room where the boy and woman sat together. Again, as on the other evenings, they were embarrassed. After a time the boy tried again to talk. "I suppose it won't be for a year or two but I've been thinking about it," he said, rising and going toward the door. "Something father said makes it sure that I shall have to go away." He fumbled with the door knob. In the room the silence became unbearable to the woman. She wanted to cry out with joy because of the words that had come from the lips of her son, but the expression of joy had become impossible to her. "I think you had better go out among the boys. You are too much indoors," she said. "I thought I would go for a little walk," replied the son stepping awkwardly out of the room and closing the door.

Departure

Young George Willard got out of bed at four in the morning. It was April and the young tree leaves were just coming out of their buds. The trees along the residence streets in Winesburg are maple and the seeds are winged. When the wind blows they whirl crazily about, filling the air and making a carpet underfoot.

George came down stairs into the hotel office carrying a brown leather bag. His trunk was packed for departure. Since two o'clock he had been awake thinking of the journey he was about to take and wondering what he would find at the end of his journey. The boy who slept in the hotel office lay on a cot by the door. His mouth was open and he snored lustily. George crept past the cot and went out into the silent deserted main street. The east was pink with the dawn and long streaks of light climbed into the sky where a few stars still shone.

Beyond the last house on Trunion Pike in Winesburg there is a great stretch of open fields. The fields are owned by farmers who live in town and drive homeward at evening along Trunion Pike in light creaking wagons. In the fields are planted berries and small fruits. In the late afternoon in the hot summers when the road and the fields are covered with dust, a smoky haze lies over the great flat basin of land. To look across it is like looking out across the sea. In the spring when the land is green the effect is somewhat different. The land becomes a wide green billiard table on which tiny human insects toil up and down.

All through his boyhood and young manhood George Willard had been in the habit of walking on Trunion Pike. He had been in the midst of the great open place on winter nights when it was covered with snow and only the moon looked down at him; he had been there in the fall when bleak winds blew and on summer evenings when the air vibrated with the song of insects. On the April morning he wanted to go there again, to walk again in the silence. He did walk to where the road dipped down by a little stream two miles from town and then turned and walked silently back again. When he got to Main Street clerks were sweeping the sidewalks before the stores. "Hey, you George. How does it feel to be going away?" they asked.

The west bound train leaves Winesburg at seven forty-five in the morning. Tom Little is conductor. His train runs from Cleveland to where it connects with a great trunk line railroad with terminals in Chicago and New York. Tom has what in railroad circles is called an "easy run." Every evening he returned to his family. In the fall and spring he spends his Sundays fishing in Lake Erie. He has a round red face and small blue eyes. He knows the people in the towns along his railroad better than a city man knows the people who live in his apartment building.

George came down the little incline from the New Willard House at seven o'clock. Tom Willard carried his bag. The son had become taller than the father.

On the station platform everyone shook the young man's hand. More than a dozen people waited about. Then they talked of their own affairs. Even Will Henderson, who was lazy and often slept until nine, had got out of bed. George was embarrassed. Gertrude Wilmot, a tall thin woman of fifty who worked in the Winesburg post office, came along the station platform. She had never before paid any attention to George. Now she stopped and put out her hand. In two words she voiced what everyone felt. "Good luck," she said sharply and then turning went on her way.

When the train came into the station George felt relieved. He scampered hurriedly aboard. Helen White[2] came running along Main Street hoping to have a parting word with him, but he had found a seat and did not see her. When the train started Tom Little punched his ticket, grinned and, although he knew George well and knew on what adventure he was just setting out, made no comment. Tom had seen a thousand George Willards go out of their towns to the city. It was a commonplace enough incident with him. In the smoking car there was a man who had just invited Tom to go on a fishing trip to Sandusky Bay. He wanted to accept the invitation and talk over details.

George glanced up and down the car to be sure no one was looking then took out his pocketbook and counted his money. His mind was occupied with a desire not to appear green. Almost the last words his father had said to him concerned the matter of his behavior when he got to the city. "Be a sharp one," Tom Willard had said. "Keep your eyes on your money. Be awake. That's the ticket. Don't let any one think you're a greenhorn."

After George counted his money he looked out of the window and was surprised to see that the train was still in Winesburg.

The young man, going out of his town to meet the adventure of life, began to think but he did not think of anything very big or dramatic. Things like his mother's death, his departure from Winesburg, the uncertainty of his future life in the city, the serious and larger aspects of his life did not come into his mind.

He thought of little things—Turk Smollet wheeling boards through the main street of his town in the morning, a tall woman, beautifully gowned, who had once stayed over night at his father's hotel, Butch Wheeler the lamp lighter of Winesburg hurrying through the streets on a summer evening and holding a torch in his hand, Helen White standing by a window in the Winesburg post office and putting a stamp on an envelope.

The young man's mind was carried away by his growing passion for dreams. One looking at him would not have thought him par-

2. George Willard's girl friend, daughter of a Winesburg banker.

ticularly sharp. With the recollection of little things occupying his mind he closed his eyes and leaned back in the car seat. He stayed that way for a long time and when he aroused himself and again looked out of the car window the town of Winesburg had disappeared and his life there had become but a background on which to paint the dreams of his manhood.

1919

From A Story-Teller's Story[1]

Book I, Note 1

In all of the towns and over the wide countrysides of my own Mid-American boyhood there was no such thing as poverty, as I myself saw it and knew it later in our great American industrial towns and cities.

My own family was poor but of what did our poverty consist? My father, a ruined dandy from the South,[2] had been reduced to keeping a small harness repair shop and, when that failed, he became ostensibly a house and barn painter. However, he did not call himself a house painter. The idea was not flashy enough for him. He called himself a "sign writer." The day of universal advertising had not yet come and there was but little sign writing to do in our town but still he stuck out bravely for the higher life. At any time he would let go by the board the privilege of painting Alf Mann, the butcher's, house (it would have kept him busily at work for a month) in order to have a go at lettering signs on fences along country roads for Alf Granger the baker.

There was your true pilgrimage abroad, out into the land. Father engaged a horse and a spring wagon and took the three older of his sons with him. My older brother and the one next younger than myself were, from the first, adept at sign writing, while both father and myself were helpless with a brush in our hands. And so I drove the horse and father supervised the whole affair. He had a natural boyish love for the supervision of affairs and the picking out of a particular fence on a particular road became to him as important a matter as the selection of a site for a city, or the fortification that was to defend it.

And then the farmer, who owned the fence, had to be consulted and if he refused his consent the joy of the situation became intensified. We drove off up the road and turned into a wood

---

1. The selection is Note 1 from Book I, the opening of Anderson's *A Story-Teller's Story* (1924), the first of three memoirs in which Anderson treated the facts of his life very freely so as to authenticate the legends with which he embroidered his biography. It was written in 1922 at the time when Anderson was leaving Chicago and his second wife to move to New York City. In the first section Anderson drew on childhood memories to define the emergence of his vocation as a writer.
2. Irwin McLain Anderson (b. 1845) was born in southern Ohio and resided there until after the Civil War, when he moved to northern Ohio. He served in an Ohio unit of the Union forces in the Civil War.

and the farmer went back to his work of cultivating corn. We watched and waited, our boyish hearts beating madly. It was a summer day and in the small wood, in which we were concealed, we all sat on a fallen log in silence. Birds flew overhead and a squirrel chattered. What a delicate tinge of romance spread over our common-place-enough business!

Father was made for romance. For him there was no such thing as a fact. It had fallen out that he, never having had the glorious opportunity to fret his little hour upon a greater stage, was intent on fretting his hour, as best he could, in a money-saving prosperous corn-shipping cabbage-raising Ohio village.

He magnified the danger of our situation. "He might have a shotgun," he said, pointing to where, in the distance, the farmer was again at work. As we waited in the wood he sometimes told us a story of the Civil War and how he, with a companion, had crept for days and nights through an enemy country at the risk of their lives. "We were carrying messages," he said raising his eyebrows and throwing out his hands. By the gesture there was something implied. "Well it was an affair of life or death. Why speak of the matter? My country needed me and I and my intrepid companion had been selected because we were the bravest men in the army," the raised eyebrows were saying.

And so with their paint pot and brushes in their hands my two brothers presently crept out of the wood and ran crouching through cornfields and got into the dusty road. Quickly and with mad haste they dabbed the name of Alf Granger on the fence with the declaration that he baked the best bread in the State of Ohio and when they returned to us we all got back into the spring wagon and drove back along the road past the sign. Father commanded me to stop the horse. "Look," he said frowning savagely at my two brothers, "your N is wrong. You are being careless again with your B's. Good gracious, will I never teach you two to handle a brush?"

If our family was poor of what did our poverty consist? If our clothes were torn the torn places only let in the sun and wind. In the winter we had no overcoats but that only meant we ran rather than loitered. Those who are to follow the arts should have a training in what is called poverty. Given a comfortable, middle-class start in life, the artist is almost sure to end up by becoming a bellyacher, constantly complaining because the public does not rush forward at once to proclaim him.

The boy who has no warm overcoat throws back his head and runs through the streets, past houses where smoke goes up into a clear cold sky, across vacant lots, through fields. The sky clouds and snow comes and the bare hands are cold and chapped. They are raw and red but at night, before the boy sleeps, his mother will come with melted fat and rub it over the raw places.

The warm fat is soothing. The touch of a mother's fingers is soothing. Well, you see, with us, we were all of us, mother father and the children, in some way outlaws in our native place and that thought was soothing to a boy. It is a soothing thought in all my memories of my boyhood. Only recently one connected with my family said to me, "You must remember, now that you are an author, you have a respectable place in the world to maintain," and for a moment my heart swelled with pride in the thought.

And then I went out of the presence of the cautious one to associate with many other respectables, and into my mind flashed thoughts of the sweetness I have seen shining in the eyes of others, of waiters, horsemen, thieves, gamblers, women, driven by poverty to the outer rim of society. Where were the respectables among those who had been kindest and sweetest to me?

Whatever may be said in this matter and I admit my feet have slipped many times toward solid respectability, we of our family were not too respectable then.

For one thing father never paid his rent and so we were always living in haunted houses. Never was such a family to take the haunt out of a house. Old women riding white horses, dead men screaming, groans, cries—all were quieted when we came to live in a haunted house; and how often, because of this talent—inherent in my family—we lived for months, scot-free, in a fairly comfortable house, while at the same time conferring a benefit on the property owner. It is a system—I recommend it to poets with large families.

There were not enough bed clothes so three boys slept in one bed and there was a window, that in summer looked out upon fields but in winter had been painted by the hand of the frost king so that moonlight came softly and dimly into the room. It was no doubt the fact that there were three of us in one bed that drove away all fear of the haunts.

Mother was tall and slender and had once been beautiful. She had been a bound girl in a farmer's family when she married father, the improvident young dandy. There was Italian blood in her veins and her origin was something of a mystery.[3] Perhaps we never cared to solve it—wanted it to remain a mystery. It is so wonderfully comforting to think of one's mother as a dark beautiful and somewhat mysterious woman. I later saw her mother—my own grandmother—but that is another story.

She the dark evil old woman with the broad hips and the great breasts of a peasant, and with the glowing hate shining out of her one eye, would be worth a book in herself. It was said she had shuffled off four husbands and when I knew her—although she was old—she looked not unwilling to tackle another. Some day

3. There is no evidence that Emma Smith Anderson (b. 1851) had been a "bound girl" (i.e., a young woman contracted for service), or had Italian lineage.

perhaps I shall tell the tale of the old woman and the tramp who tried to rob the farm house when she was staying alone—and of how she, after beating him into submission with her old fists, got drunk with him over a barrel of hard cider in a shed, and of how the two went singing off together down the road—but not now.

Our own mother had eyes that were like pools lying in deep shadows at the edge of a wood but when she grew angry and fell into one of her deep silences lights danced in the pools. When she spoke her words were filled with strange wisdom (how sharply yet I remember certain comments of hers—on life—on your neighbors)—but often she commanded all of us by the strength of her silences.

She came into the bedroom where three boys lay on one bed, carrying in one hand a small kerosene lamp and in the other a dish in which was warm melted fat.

There were three boys in one bed, two of them almost of the same size. The third was then a small silent fellow. Later his life was to be very strange. He was one who could not fit himself into the social scheme and, until he was a grown man, he stayed about, living sometimes with one, sometimes with another of his brothers, always reading books, dreaming, quarreling with no one.

He, the youngest of the three, looked out at life always as from a great distance. He was of the stuff of which poets are made. What instinctive wisdom in him! All loved him but no one could help him in the difficult business of living his life and when, on summer evenings, as the three lay in the bed, the two older boys fought or made great plans for their lives, he lay beside them in silence—but sometimes he spoke and his words came always as from a far place. We were perhaps discussing the wonders of life. "Well," he said, "it is so and so. There will be no more babies but the new babies do not come as you say. I know how they come. They come the same way you grow corn. Father plants seed in the earth and mother is the earth in which the seed grows."

I am thinking of my younger brother after he had grown a little older—I am thinking of him grown into a man and become habitually silent like mother—I am thinking of him as he was just before he mysteriously disappeared out of our lives and never came back.

Now however he is in bed with the other brother and myself. An older brother, he who crept through the cornfields to paint the name of Alf Granger on the fence, had already gone from our lives. He had a talent for drawing and a drunken half-insane cutter of stones for graveyards has taken him away from our town to another town, where he is already sitting at a desk drawing designs for gravestones. A dove descends out of the sky and holds a leaf in its bill. There is an angel clinging to a rock in the midst of a storm at sea.

> Rock of ages, cleft for me,
> Let me hide myself in Thee.[4]

The three boys are in the bed in the room and there is not enough bed clothing. Father's overcoat, now too old to be worn, is thrown over the foot of the bed and the three boys have been permitted to undress downstairs, in the kitchen of the house, by the kitchen stove.

The oldest of the boys remaining at home (that is myself) must undress first and must arrange his clothes neatly on a kitchen chair. Mother does not scold about such a trifling matter. She stands silently looking and the boy does as he has been told. There is something of my grandmother in a certain look that can come into her eyes. "Well, you'd better," it says. How unsuccessfully I have tried all my life to cultivate just that look.

And now the boy has undressed and must run, in his white flannel nightgown, bare-footed, through the cold house, past frosted windows, up a flight of stairs and, with a flying leap, into the bed. The flannel nightgown has been worn almost threadbare by the older brother—now gone out into the world—before it has come down to him who wears it now.

He is the oldest of the brothers at home and must take the first plunge into the icy bed but soon the others come running. They are lying like little puppies in the bed, but as they grow warmer the two older boys begin to fight. There is a contest. The point is not to be compelled to lie on the outside where the covers may come off in the night. Blows are struck and tense young bodies are interwined. "It's your turn tonight! No it's yours! You're a liar! Take that! Well, then, take that! I'll show you!"

The youngest brother of the three has already taken one of the two outside positions. It is his fate. He is not strong enough to fight with either of the other two and perhaps he does not care for fighting. He lies silently in the cold, in the darkness, while the fight between the other two goes on and on. They are of almost equal strength and the fight might possibly last for an hour.

But there is now the sound of the mother's footsteps on the stairs and that is the end of the struggle. Now—at this moment—the boy who has the coveted position may keep it. That is an understood thing.

The mother puts the kerosene lamp on a little table by the bed and beside it the dish of warm comforting melted fat. One by one six hands are thrust out to her.

There is a caress in her long toil-hardened fingers.

4. Opening lines from a Methodist hymn composed by Thomas Hastings (1784–1872) with words by Augustus Montague Toplady (1740–78).

In the night and in the dim light of the lamp her dark eyes are like luminous pools.

The fat, in the little cracked china dish, is warm and soothing to burning itching hands. For an hour she has had the dish sitting at the back of the kitchen stove in the little frame house far out at the edge of the town.

The strange silent mother! She is making love to her sons but there are no words for her love. There are no kisses, no caresses.

The rubbing of the warm fat into the cracked hands of her sons is a caress. The light that now shines in her eyes is a caress.

The silent woman has left deep traces of herself in one of her sons. He is the one now lying stilly in the bed with his two noisy brothers. What has happened in the life of the mother? In herself, in her own physical self, even the two quarreling fighting sons feel that nothing can matter too much. If her husband, the father of the boys, is a no-account and cannot bring money home —the money that would feed and clothe her children in comfort—one feels it does not matter too much. If she herself, the proud quiet one, must humiliate herself, washing—for the sake of the few dimes it may bring in—the soiled clothes of her neighbors, one knows it does not matter too much.

And yet there is no Christian forbearance in her. She speaks sometimes, as she sits on the edge of the bed in the lamplight rubbing the warm fat into the cracked frost-bitten hands of her children, and there is often a kind of smoldering fire in her words.

One of the boys in the bed has had a fight with the son of a neighbor. He, the third son of the family, has taken a hatchet out of the neighbor boy's hands. We had been cramming ourselves with the contents of a book, *The Last of the Mohicans*,[5] and the neighbor boy, whose father is the town shoemaker, had had the hatchet given him as a Christmas present. He would not let it go out of his hands, and so my brother, the determined one, has snatched it away.

The struggle took place in a little grove a half mile from the house. "Le Renard Subtil,"[6] cries my brother jerking the hatchet out of the neighbor boy's hand. The neighbor boy did not want to be the villain—"Le Renard Subtil."

And so he went crying off toward his home, on the farther side of the field. He lived in a yellow house just beyond our own and near the end of the street at the edge of the town.

My brother now had possession of the hatchet and paid no more attention to him, but I went to stand by a fence and watch him go.

It is because I am a white man and understand the whites bet-

5. Romance in *The Leatherstocking Tales* by James Fenimore Cooper, published in 1826.

6. French name, "Subtle Fox," for Magua, a villainous Huron Indian in *The Last of the Mohicans*.

ter than he. I am Hawk-eye the scout, "La Longue Carabine,"[7] and as I stand by the fence *La Longue Carabine* is lying across the crook of my arm. It is represented by a stick. "I could pick him off from here, shall I do it?" I ask, speaking to my brother, with whom I fight viciously every night after we have got into bed, but who, during the day, is my sworn comrade in arms.

Uncas—"Le Cerf Agile"[8]—pays no attention to my words and I rest the stick over the fence, half-determined to pick off the neighbor boy but at the last withholding my fire. "He is a little pig, never to let a fellow take his hatchet. Uncas was right to snatch it out of his hand."

As I withhold my fire and the boy goes unscathed and crying across the snow-covered field I feel very magnanimous—as at any moment I could have dropped him like a deer in flight—and then I see him go crying into his mother's house. Uncas has, in fact, cuffed him a couple of times in the face. But was it not justified? "Dare a dirty Huron, a squaw man, dare such a one question the authority of a Delaware? Ugh!"

And now Le Renard Subtil has gone into his mother's house and has blabbed on us and I tell Uncas the news but, with the impenetrable stoicism of a true savage, he pays no attention. He is as one sitting by the council fire. Are words to be wasted on a dog of a Huron?

And now Le Cerf Agile has an idea. Drawing a line in the snow he stands some fifty feet from the largest of the trees in the grove and hurls the hatchet through the air.

What a determined fellow! I am of the pale-face race myself and shall always depend for my execution upon *La Longue Carabine*, but Uncas is of another breed. Is there not painted on his breast a crawling tortoise? In ink I have traced it there myself, from a drawing he has made.

During the short winter afternoon the hatchet will be thrown not once but a hundred, perhaps two hundred times. It whirls through the air. The thing is to so throw the hatchet that, at the end of its flight, the blade goes, just so, firmly into the soft bark of the tree. And it must enter the bark of the tree at just a particular spot.

The matter is of infinite importance. Has not Uncas, "The Last of the Mohicans," broad shoulders? He will later be a strong man. Now is the time to acquire infinite skill.

He has measured carefully the spot on the body of the tree where the blade of the hatchet must enter—with a soft chug, deep into the yielding bark. There is a tall warrior, a hated Huron,

---

7. French name, "Long Rifle," for the white frontiersman Hawkeye (also known as Natty Bumppo) in *The Last of the Mohicans*.
8. French name, "Agile Stag" (or

"Deer"), for Uncas, son of the chief Chingachgook, a friendly Delaware Indian and last of the Mohicans in Cooper's romance.

standing by the tree and young Uncas has measured carefully so that he knows just where the top of the warrior's head should come. An idea has come to him. He will just scalp the unsuspecting warrior with the blade of the tomahawk, and has he, Uncas, not crept for many weary miles through the forest, going without food, eating snow for his drink? A skulking Huron has dared creep into the hunting grounds of the Delawares and has learned the winter abiding place of our tribe. Dare we let him go back to his squaw-loving people, bearing such knowledge? Uncas will show him!

He, Uncas, is absorbed in the problem before him and has not deigned to look off across the fields to where the neighbor boy has gone crying to his mother. Le Renard Subtil will be heard from again but for the present is forgotten. The foot must be advanced just so. The arm must be drawn back just so. When one hurls the hatchet the body must be swung forward just so. An absolute silence must be maintained. The skulking Huron, who has dared come into our hunting grounds, is unaware of the presence of the young Uncas. Is he, Uncas, not one whose feet leave no traces in the morning dew?

Deep within the breasts of my brother and myself there is a resentment that we were born out of our time. By what a narrow margin in the scroll of time have we missed the great adventure! Two, three, at the most a dozen generations earlier, and we might so well have been born in the virgin forest itself. On the very ground where we now stand Indians have indeed stalked each other in the forest, and how often Uncas and myself have discussed the matter. As for our father, we dismiss him half-contemptuously. He is born to be a dandy of the cities and has turned out to be a village house painter, in the dwelling places of the pale faces. The devil, with luck he might have turned out to be an actor, or a writer, or some such scum of earth, but never could he have been a warrior. Why had not our mother, who might have been such a splendid Indian princess, the daughter of a great chief, why had she also not been born a few generations earlier? She had just the silent stoicism needed for the wife of a great warrior. A deep injustice had been done us and something of the feeling of that injustice was in the stern face of Uncas as he crept each time to the line he had marked out in the snow and sent the hatchet hurtling through the air.

The two boys, filled with scorn of their parentage, on the father's side, are in a little grove of trees at the edge of an Ohio town. In later days the father—also born out of his place and time—will come to mean more to them, but now he has little but their contempt. Now Uncas is determined—absorbed—and I, who have so little of his persistence, am impressed by his silent determination. It makes me a little uncomfortable for, since he has snatched the hatchet out of the neighbor boy's hand saying, "Go on home, cry-baby," no word has passed his lips. There is but a small grunting sound when the hatchet is hurled and a scowl on his face when it misses the mark.

And Le Renard Subtil has gone home and blabbed to his mother who in turn has thrown a shawl over her head and has gone to our house, no doubt to blab, in her turn, to our mother. La Longue Carabine, being a pale-face, is a little intent on disturbing the aim of Le Cerf Agile. "We'll catch hell," he says, looking at the hatchet thrower who has not so far unbent from the natural dignity of the Indian as to reply. He grunts and, taking his place solemnly at the line, poises his body. There is the quick abrupt swing forward of the body. What a shame Uncas did not later become a professional baseball player. He might have made his mark in the world. The hatchet sings through the air. Well it has struck sideways. The Huron is injured but not fatally. Uncas goes and sets him upright again. He has marked the place where the Huron warrior's head should be by pressing a ball of snow into the wrinkled bark of the tree and has indicated the dog's body by a dead branch.

And so Hawk-eye the scout—La Longue Carabine—has gone creeping off among the trees, to see if there are any more Hurons lurking about, and has come upon a great buck, pawing the snow and feeding on dry grass, at the edge of a small creek. Up goes *La Longue Carabine* and the buck pitches forward, dead, on the ice. Hawk-eye runs forward and swiftly passes his hunting knife across the neck of the buck. It will not do to build a fire, now that there are Hurons lurking in the hunting ground of the Delawares, so Uncas and he must feed upon raw meat. Well, the hunter's life for the hunter! What must be must be! Hawk-eye cuts several great steaks from the carcass of the buck and makes his way slowly and cautiously back to Uncas. As he approaches he three times imitates the call of a catbird and an answering call comes from the lip of Le Cerf Agile.

"Aha. The night is coming on," Uncas now says, having at last laid the Huron low. "Now that the dirty lover of squaws is dead we may build a fire and feast. Cook the venison ere the night falls. When darkness has come we must show no fire. Do not make much smoke—big fires for the pale-faces but little fires for us Indians."

Uncas stands for a moment, gnawing the bone of the buck, and then of a sudden becomes still and alert. "Aha. I thought so," he says and goes back again to where he has drawn the mark in the snow. "Go," he says, "see how many come."

And now Hawk-eye must creep through the thick forests, climb mountains, leap canyons. Word has come that Le Renard Subtil but feigned when he went off, crying across the field—fools that we were! While we have been in the forest he has crept into the very teepee of our people and has stolen the princess, the mother of Uncas. And now Le Renard Subtil, with subtle daring, drags the stoical princess right across the path of her warrior son. In one moment from a great height Hawk-eye draws the faithful Deer Killer to his shoulder and fires and at the same moment the tomahawk of Uncas sinks itself in the skull of the Huron dog.

"Le Renard Subtil had drunk firewater and was reckless," says Uncas, as the two boys go homeward in the dusk.

The older of the two boys, now homeward bound, is somewhat afraid but Uncas is filled with pride. As they go homeward in the gathering darkness and come to the house, where lives Le Renard Subtil, to which he has gone crying but a few hours before, an idea comes to him. Uncas creeps in the darkness, half way between the house and the picket fence in front and, balancing the hatchet in his hand, hurls it proudly. Well for the neighbor's family that no one came to the door at that moment for Uncas' long afternoon of practising has got results. The hatchet flies through the air and sinks itself fairly and deeply into the door panel as Uncas and Hawk-eye run away home.

And now they are in the bed and the mother is rubbing the warm grease into their chapped hands. Her own hands are rough but how gentle they are. She is thinking of her sons, of the one already gone out into the world and most of all, at the moment, of Uncas.

There is something direct brutal and fine in the nature of Uncas. It is not quite an accident that in our games he is always the Indian while I am the despised white, the pale-face. It is permitted me to heal my misfortune, a little, by being, not a store-keeper or a fur trader, but that man nearest the Indian's nature of all the pale-faces who ever lived on our continent, La Longue Carabine, but I cannot be an Indian and least of all an Indian of the tribe of the Delawares. I am not persistent patient and determined enough. As for Uncas, one may coax and wheedle him along any road, and I am always clinging to that slight sense of leadership, that my additional fifteen months of living gives me, by coaxing and wheedling, but one may not drive Uncas. To attempt driving him is but to arouse a stubbornness and obstinacy that is limitless. Having told a lie to mother or father, he will stick to the lie to the death while I—well, perhaps there is in me something of the dog-like, the squaw-man, the pale-face—the very spirit of Le Renard Subtil—if the bitter truth must be told. In all my after years I shall have to struggle against a tendency toward slickness and plausibility in myself. I am the tale teller, the man who sits by the fire waiting for listeners, the man whose life must be led in the world of his fancies—I am the one destined to follow the little crooked words of men's speech through the uncharted paths of the forests of fancy. What my father should have been I am to become. Through long years of the baffling uncertainty, that only such men as myself can ever know, I am to creep with trembling steps forward in a strange land, following the little words, striving to learn all of the ways of the ever-changing words, the smooth lying little words, the hard jagged cutting words, the round melodious healing words. All of the words I am in the end to come to know a little and to attempt to use for my purpose have, at the same time, the power in them to both heal and destroy. How often am I to be made sick by words, how often am I to be healed by words, before I can come at all near to man's estate.

And so as I lie in the bed putting out my chapped hands to the healing touch of mother's hands I do not look at her. Already I am often too conscious of my own inner thoughts to look directly at people and now, although I am not the one who has cuffed the neighbor boy and jerked the hatchet out of his hands, I am nevertheless busily at work borrowing the troubles of Uncas. I cannot let what is to be be, but must push forward striving to change all by the power of words. I dare not thrust my words forward in the presence of mother but they are busily getting themselves said inside myself.

There is a consciousness of Uncas also within me. Another curse that is to lie heavily on me all through my life has its grip on me. I am not one to be satisfied to act for myself, think for myself, feel for myself—but must also attempt to think and feel for Uncas.

At the moment slick plausible excuses for what has happened during the afternoon are rising to my lips, struggling for expression. I am not satisfied with being myself and letting things take their course but must be inside the very body of Uncas, striving to fill his stout young body with the questioning soul of myself.

As I write this I am remembering that my father, like myself, could never be singly himself but must always be a playing some role, everlasting-strutting on the stage of life in some part not his own. Was there a role of his own to be played? That I do not know and I fancy he never knew but I remember that he once took it into his head to enact the role of the stern and unyielding parent to Uncas and what came of it.

The little tragic comedy took place in the woodshed back of one of the innumerable houses to which we were always moving—when some absurd landlord took it into his head that he should have some rent for the house we occupied—and Uncas had just beaten with his fists a neighbor boy who had tried to run away with a baseball bat belonging to us. Uncas had retrieved the bat and had brought it proudly home and father, who happened along the street at that moment, had got the notion fixed in his mind that the bat belonged, not to us, but to the neighbor boy. Uncas tried to explain but father, having taken up the role of the just man, must needs play it out to the bitter end. He demanded that Uncas return the bat into the hands of the boy from whom he had just ravaged it and Uncas, growing white and silent, ran home and hid himself in the woodshed where father quickly found him out.

"I won't," declared Uncas, "the bat's ours"; and then father—fool that he was for ever allowing himself to get into such an undignified position—began to beat him with a switch he had cut from a tree at the front of the house. As the beating did no good and Uncas only took it unmoved, father, as always happened with him, lost his head.

And so there was the boy, white with the sense of the injustice being done, and no doubt father also began to feel that he had put his foot into a trap. He grew furious and picking up a large stick of wood from a woodpile in the shed threatened to hit Uncas with it.

What a moment! I had run to the back of the shed and had thrown myself on the ground where I could look through a crack and, as long as I live, I shall never forget the next few moments—with the man and the boy, both white, looking at each other—and, that night in the bed later, when mother was rubbing my chapped hands and when I knew there was something to be settled between her and Uncas, that picture danced like a crazy ghost in my fancy.

I trembled at the thought of what might happen, at the thought of what had happened that day in the shed.

Father had stood—I shall never know how long—with the heavy stick upraised, looking into the eyes of his son, and the son had stared, with a fixed determined stare, back into the eyes of his father.

At the moment I had thought that—boy as I was—I understood how such a strange unaccountable thing as a murder could happen. Thoughts did not form themselves definitely in my mind but, after that moment, I knew that it was always the weak, frightened by their own weakness, who kill the strong, and perhaps I also knew myself for one of the weak ones of the world. At the moment, as father stood with the stick upraised, glaring at Uncas, my own sympathies (if my own fancy has not tricked me again) were with father. My heart ached for him.

He was saved by mother. She came to the door of the shed and stood looking at him and his eyes wavered, and then he threw the stick back upon the pile from which he had taken it and went silently away. I remembered that he tramped off to Main Street and that, later in the evening when he came back to the house, he was drunk and went drunken to bed. The trick of drunkenness

had saved him from the ordeal of looking into the eyes of Uncas
or mother, as so often words have later saved me from meeting
fairly some absurd position into which I have got myself.

And so there was I now, in the bed and up to one of father's
tricks—upstart that I was, dog of a Huron myself, I was trembling
for mother and for Uncas—two people very well able to take care
of themselves.

Mother dropped my hand and took the outstretched hand of
my brother.

"What happened?" she asked.

And Uncas told her, fairly and squarely. "He was a cry-baby
and a big calf and I wolloped him one. I wanted the hatchet and
so I took it—that's what I did. I banged him one on the nose and
jerked it out of his hand."

Mother laughed—a queer unmirthful little laugh. It was the
kind of laugh that hurts. There was irony in it and that got to
Uncas at once. "It doesn't take much of a fellow to snatch a
hatchet out of the hands of a cry-baby," she said.

That was all. She kept on rubbing his hands and now it was my
eyes, and not the eyes of Uncas, that could look directly into our
mother's eyes.

Perhaps it was in that moment, and not in the moment when
I lay on the ground peeking through the crack into the shed, that
the first dim traces of understanding of all such fellows as father
and myself came to me. I looked at mother with adoration in my
own eyes, and when she had taken the kerosene lamp and had gone
away, and when we boys were all again curled quietly like sleeping
puppies in the bed, I cried a little as I am sure father must have
cried sometimes when there was no one about. Perhaps his getting
drunk, as he did on all possible occasions, was a way of crying too.

And I cried also I suppose because in Uncas and mother there
was a kind of directness and simplicity that father and all fellows
who, like myself, are of the same breed with him, could never
quite achieve.

1924

KATHERINE ANNE PORTER
1890–

One of the finest stylists among important American writers of fiction is
Katherine Anne Porter, who is acutely conscious of her southern origins.
She herself has declared that she was "the grandchild of a Lost War,"
born in Indian Creek, Texas, into a family that was conscious of former
wealth and position in the older South of Louisiana and Kentucky.[1]

1. "Portrait: Old South," *The Days Before*, p. 155.

Little is known about her life, and it is uncertain whether she was raised in early childhood as a Roman Catholic or a Methodist. She was brought up by her paternal grandmother after her mother's death in 1892. Like her fictional surrogate Miranda in *Old Mortality* and other stories, she was educated in convent schools where she received a "fragmentary, but strangely useless and ornamental education."[2] She eloped from such a school when about sixteen and subsequently was married to and divorced from Eugene Pressly, a foreign-service officer, and Albert Erskine, an editor of the *Southern Review*. As she candidly explained, "They couldn't live with me because I was a writer, and, now as then, writing took first place."[3] She worked on newspapers in Texas, Denver, and Chicago before and during World War I and lived between 1918 and 1921 in Mexico, where she studied art and became involved in left-wing politics. (She has declared recently that "my political thinking was the lamentable 'political illiteracy' of a liberal idealist—we might say a species of Jeffersonian.")[4] She returned to Mexico on a Guggenheim fellowship in 1931, then journeyed to Europe, residing in Switzerland, France, and Germany until returning permanently to the States in 1937.

Her first short story (*Maria Concepcion*) had been published in 1922, and her first collections of stories and short novels, *Flowering Judas* and *Noon Wine*, in 1930 and 1937. These gained her a secure reputation among critics that was sustained by *Pale Horse, Pale Rider* (1939) and *The Leaning Tower* (1944). But it was not until 1962 that she gained a large audience with the publication of her first and only novel, *The Ship of Fools*. Though it received mixed reviews, its account of cosmopolitan passengers traveling from Mexico to Germany at the onset of Hitler's Nazi regime was widely read, and it formed the basis of a popular Hollywood film. She did some screen writing for MGM in 1948–50, and after 1950 she lectured frequently and gave public readings from her works. She was the Fulbright Professor at Liège, Belgium, in 1945 and succeeded William Faulkner as Writer in Residence at the University of Virginia in 1958. A selection of her reviews, essays, and translations, *The Days Before*, appeared in 1952. Her *Collected Stories* (1965) brought both the National Book Award and the Pulitzer Prize in 1966, as well as election to the American Academy of Letters. In 1967 she won the Gold Medal for Fiction of the National Institute of Arts and Letters to which she had been elected in 1941. She now lives, in delicate health and semiretirement, near Washington, D.C.

The power and subtlety of Porter's fiction were acclaimed by critics and fellow writers from the 1930s on, despite the fact that her output consists of only one full-length novel and a mere twenty-seven stories and short novels. Her prose, with its spare use of figures of speech and its deceptive simplicity, displays what the critic Edmund Wilson called a "purity and precision almost unique in contemporary American fiction."[5] While some tales deal with Irish immigrants, a larger and more powerful number deal with cultural conflict and revolutionary ferment in Mexico, exploring the Indian's half-Christian, half-pagan world of primitive emotion (in *Maria Concepcion*) or the reactions of North Americans to the

2. *Ibid.*, p. 159.
3. *The Never Ending Wrong*, p. 13.
4. *Baltimore Evening Sun*, Feb. 28, 1969.
5. Edmund Wilson, *Classics and Commercials*, p. 219.

exotic in Spanish America (in *Flowering Judas and Hacienda*). The most
clearly autobiographical stories center on the stresses of marriage, the
family pieties and social proprieties that have been important in southern
fiction, and the growing up of the young girl Miranda in *Old Mortality*.
The precision with which Porter captures the nuances of anger, fear, and
wounded pathos when people encounter death or the death of cherished
dreams mark *Pale Horse, Pale Rider* and *The Jilting of Granny Weatherall* as masterful pieces of short fiction. *The Jilting of Granny Weatherall*
is reprinted from *The Collected Stories of Katherine Anne Porter*.

The Jilting of Granny Weatherall

She flicked her wrist neatly out of Doctor Harry's pudgy careful
fingers and pulled the sheet up to her chin. The brat ought to be in
knee breeches. Doctoring around the country with spectacles on
his nose! "Get along now, take your schoolbooks and go. There's
nothing wrong with me."

Doctor Harry spread a warm paw like a cushion on her forehead where the forked green vein danced and made her eyelids
twitch. "Now, now, be a good girl, and we'll have you up in no
time."

"That's no way to speak to a woman nearly eighty years old just
because she's down. I'd have you respect your elders, young man."

"Well, Missy, excuse me." Doctor Harry patted her cheek. "But
I've got to warn you, haven't I? You're a marvel, but you must be
careful or you're going to be good and sorry."

"Don't tell me what I'm going to be. I'm on my feet now,
morally speaking. It's Cornelia. I had to go to bed to get rid of
her."

Her bones felt loose, and floated around in her skin, and Doctor
Harry floated like a balloon around the foot of the bed. He floated
and pulled down his waistcoat and swung his glasses on a cord.
"Well, stay where you are, it certainly can't hurt you."

"Get along and doctor your sick," said Granny Weatherall.
"Leave a well woman alone. I'll call for you when I want you.
. . . Where were you forty years ago when I pulled through
milk-leg[1] and double pneumonia? You weren't even born. Don't
let Cornelia lead you on," she shouted, because Doctor Harry
appeared to float up to the ceiling and out. "I pay my own bills,
and I don't throw my money away on nonsense!"

She meant to wave good-bye, but it was too much trouble. Her
eyes closed of themselves, it was like a dark curtain drawn around
the bed. The pillow rose and floated under her, pleasant as a hammock in a light wind. She listened to the leaves rustling outside the
window. No, somebody was swishing newspapers: no, Cornelia
and Doctor Harry were whispering together. She leaped broad
awake, thinking they whispered in her ear.

1. Swelling of the legs after childbirth.

"She was never like this, *never* like this!" "Well, what can we expect?" "Yes, eighty years old. . . ."

Well, and what if she was? She still had ears. It was like Cornelia to whisper around doors. She always kept things secret in such a public way. She was always being tactful and kind. Cornelia was dutiful; that was the trouble with her. Dutiful and good: "So good and dutiful," said Granny, "that I'd like to spank her." She saw herself spanking Cornelia and making a fine job of it.

"What'd you say, Mother?"

Granny felt her face tying up in hard knots.

"Can't a body think, I'd like to know?"

"I thought you might want something."

"I do. I want a lot of things. First off, go away and don't whisper."

She lay and drowsed, hoping in her sleep that the children would keep out and let her rest a minute. It had been a long day. Not that she was tired. It was always pleasant to snatch a minute now and then. There was always so much to be done, let me see: tomorrow.

Tomorrow was far away and there was nothing to trouble about. Things were finished somehow when the time came; thank God there was always a little margin over for peace: then a person could spread out the plan of life and tuck in the edges orderly. It was good to have everything clean and folded away, with the hair brushes and tonic bottles sitting straight on the white embroidered linen: the day started without fuss and the pantry shelves laid out with rows of jelly glasses and brown jugs and white stone-china jars with blue whirligigs and words painted on them: coffee, tea, sugar, ginger, cinnamon, allspice: and the bronze clock with the lion on top nicely dusted off. The dust that lion could collect in twenty-four hours! The box in the attic with all those letters tied up, well, she'd have to go through that tomorrow. All those letters —George's letters and John's letters and her letters to them both —lying around for the children to find afterwards made her uneasy. Yes, that would be tomorrow's business. No use to let them know how silly she had been once.

While she was rummaging around she found death in her mind and it felt clammy and unfamiliar. She had spent so much time preparing for death there was no need for bringing it up again. Let it take care of itself now. When she was sixty she had felt very old, finished, and went around making farewell trips to see her children and grandchildren, with a secret in her mind: This is the very last of your mother, children! Then she made her will and came down with a long fever. That was all just a notion like a lot of other things, but it was lucky too, for she had once for all got over the idea of dying for a long time. Now she couldn't be worried. She hoped she had better sense now. Her father had lived to be one hundred and two years old and had drunk a noggin of strong hot toddy on his last birthday. He told the reporters it was his daily habit, and he owed his long life to that. He had made quite a scandal and was very pleased about it. She believed she'd just plague Cornelia a little.

"Cornelia! Cornelia!" No footsteps, but a sudden hand on her cheek. "Bless you, where have you been?"

"Here, Mother."

"Well, Cornelia, I want a noggin of hot toddy."

"Are you cold, darling?"

"I'm chilly, Cornelia. Lying in bed stops the circulation. I must have told you that a thousand times."

Well, she could just hear Cornelia telling her husband that Mother was getting a little childish and they'd have to humor her. The thing that most annoyed her was that Cornelia thought she was deaf, dumb, and blind. Little hasty glances and tiny gestures tossed around her and over her head saying, "Don't cross her, let her have her way, she's eighty years old," and she sitting there as if she lived in a thin glass cage. Sometimes Granny almost made up her mind to pack up and move back to her own house where nobody could remind her every minute that she was old. Wait, wait, Cornelia, till your own children whisper behind your back!

In her day she had kept a better house and had got more work done. She wasn't too old yet for Lydia to be driving eighty miles for advice when one of the children jumped the track, and Jimmy still dropped in and talked things over: "Now, Mammy, you've a good business head, I want to know what you think of this? . . ." Old. Cornelia couldn't change the furniture around without asking. Little things, little things! They had been so sweet when they were little. Granny wished the old days were back again with the children young and everything to be done over. It had been a hard pull, but not too much for her. When she thought of all the food she had cooked, and all the clothes she had cut and sewed, and all the gardens she had made—well, the children showed it. There they were, made out of her, and they couldn't get away from that. Sometimes she wanted to see John again and point to them and say, Well, I didn't do so badly, did I? But that would have to wait. That was for tomorrow. She used to think of him as a man, but now all the children were older than their father, and he would be a child beside her if she saw him now. It seemed strange and there was something wrong in the idea. Why, he couldn't possibly recognize her. She had fenced in a hundred acres once, digging the post holes herself and clamping the wires with just a negro boy to help. That changed a woman. John would be looking for a young woman with the peaked Spanish comb in her hair and the painted fan. Digging post holes changed a woman. Riding country roads in the winter when women had their babies was another thing: sitting up nights with sick horses and sick negroes and sick children and hardly ever losing one. John, I hardly ever lost one of them! John would see that in a minute, that would be something he could understand, she wouldn't have to explain anything!

It made her feel like rolling up her sleeves and putting the whole place to rights again. No matter if Cornelia was determined to be everywhere at once, there were a great many things left undone on this place. She would start tomorrow and do them. It was good to be strong enough for everything, even if all you made melted and changed and slipped under your hands, so that by the time you finished you almost forgot what you were working for. What was it I set out to do? she asked herself intently, but she could not remember. A fog rose over the valley, she saw it marching across the creek swallowing the trees and moving up the hill like an army of ghosts. Soon it would be at the near edge of the orchard, and then it was time to go in and light the lamps. Come in, children, don't stay out in the night air.

Lighting the lamps had been beautiful. The children huddled up to her and breathed like little calves waiting at the bars in the twilight. Their eyes followed the match and watched the flame rise and settle in a blue curve, then they moved away from her. The lamp was lit, they didn't have to be scared and hang on to mother any more. Never, never, never more. God, for all my life I thank Thee. Without Thee, my God, I could never have done it. Hail, Mary, full of grace.

I want you to pick all the fruit this year and see that nothing is wasted. There's always someone who can use it. Don't let good things rot for want of using. You waste life when you waste good food. Don't let things get lost. It's bitter to lose things. Now, don't let me get to thinking, not when I am tired and taking a little nap before supper. . . .

The pillow rose about her shoulders and pressed against her heart and the memory was being squeezed out of it: oh, push down the pillow, somebody: it would smother her if she tried to hold it. Such a fresh breeze blowing and such a green day with no threats in it. But he had not come, just the same. What does a woman do when she has put on the white veil and set out the white cake for a man and he doesn't come? She tried to remember. No, I swear he never harmed me but in that. He never harmed me but in that . . . and what if he did? There was the day, the day, but a whirl of dark smoke rose and covered it, crept up and over into the bright field where everything was planted so carefully in orderly rows. That was hell, she knew hell when she saw it. For sixty years she had prayed against remembering him and against losing her soul in the deep pit of hell, and now the two things were mingled in one and the thought of him was a smoky cloud from hell that moved and crept in her head when she had just got rid of

Doctor Harry and was trying to rest a minute. Wounded vanity, Ellen, said a sharp voice in the top of her mind. Don't let your wounded vanity get the upper hand of you. Plenty of girls get jilted. You were jilted, weren't you? Then stand up to it. Her eyelids wavered and let in streamers of blue-gray light like tissue paper over her eyes. She must get up and pull the shades down or she'd never sleep. She was in bed again and the shades were not down. How could that happen? Better turn over, hide from the light, sleeping in the light gave you nightmares. "Mother, how do you feel now?" and a stinging wetness on her forehead. But I don't like having my face washed in cold water!

Hapsy? George? Lydia? Jimmy? No, Cornelia, and her features were swollen and full of little puddles. "They're coming, darling, they'll all be here soon." Go wash your face, child, you look funny.

Instead of obeying, Cornelia knelt down and put her head on the pillow. She seemed to be talking but there was no sound. "Well, are you tongue-tied? Whose birthday is it? Are you going to give a party?"

Cornelia's mouth moved urgently in strange shapes. "Don't do that, you bother me, daughter."

"Oh, no, Mother. Oh, no. . . ."

Nonsense. It was strange about children. They disputed your every word. "No what, Cornelia?"

"Here's Doctor Harry."

"I won't see that boy again. He just left five minutes ago."

"That was this morning, Mother. It's night now. Here's the nurse."

"This is Doctor Harry, Mrs. Weatherall. I never saw you look so young and happy!"

"Ah, I'll never be young again—but I'd be happy if they'd let me lie in peace and get rested."

She thought she spoke up loudly, but no one answered. A warm weight on her forehead, a warm bracelet on her wrist, and a breeze went on whispering, trying to tell her something. A shuffle of leaves in the everlasting hand of God, He blew on them and they danced and rattled. "Mother, don't mind, we're going to give you a little hypodermic." "Look here, daughter, how do ants get in this bed? I saw sugar ants yesterday." Did you send for Hapsy too?

It was Hapsy she really wanted. She had to go a long way back through a great many rooms to find Hapsy standing with a baby on her arm. She seemed to herself to be Hapsy also, and the baby on Hapsy's arm was Hapsy and himself and herself, all at once, and there was no surprise in the meeting. Then Hapsy melted from within and turned flimsy as gray gauze and the baby was a gauzy shadow, and Hapsy came up close and said, "I thought you'd never come," and looked at her very searchingly and said, "You haven't changed a bit!" They leaned forward to kiss, when Cornelia began whispering from a long way off, "Oh, is there anything you want to tell me? Is there anything I can do for you?"

Yes, she had changed her mind after sixty years and she would like to see George. I want you to find George. Find him and be sure to tell him I forgot him. I want him to know I had my husband just the same and my children and my house like any other woman. A good house too and a good husband that I loved and fine children out of him. Better than I hoped for even. Tell him I was given back everything he took away and more. Oh, no, oh, God, no, there was something else besides the house and the man and the children. Oh, surely they were not all? What was it? Something not given back. . . . Her breath crowded down under her ribs and grew into a monstrous frightening shape with cutting edges; it bored up into her head, and the agony was unbelievable: Yes, John, get the Doctor now, no more talk, my time has come.

When this one was born it should be the last. The last. It should have been born first, for it was the one she had truly wanted. Everything came in good time. Nothing left out, left over. She was strong, in three days she would be as well as ever. Better. A woman needed milk in her to have her full health.

"Mother, do you hear me?"

"I've been telling you—"

"Mother, Father Connolly's here."

"I went to Holy Communion only last week. Tell him I'm not so sinful as all that."

"Father just wants to speak to you."

He could speak as much as he pleased. It was like him to drop in and inquire about her soul as if it were a teething baby, and then stay on for a cup of tea and a round of cards and gossip. He always had a funny story of some sort, usually about an Irishman who made his little mistakes and confessed them, and the point lay in some absurd thing he would blurt out in the confessional showing his struggles between native piety and original sin. Granny felt easy about her soul. Cornelia, where are your manners? Give Father Connolly a chair. She had her secret comfortable understanding with a few favorite saints who cleared a straight road to God for her. All as surely signed and sealed as the papers for the new Forty Acres. Forever . . . heirs and assigns[2] forever. Since the day the wedding cake was not cut, but thrown out and wasted. The whole bottom dropped out of the world, and there she was blind and sweating with nothing under her feet and the walls falling away. His hand had caught her under the breast, she had not fallen, there was the freshly polished floor with the green rug on it, just as before. He had cursed like a sailor's parrot and said, "I'll kill him for you." Don't lay a hand on him, for my sake leave

---

2. Legal term for those persons charged with carrying out the provisions of a will.

something to God. "Now, Ellen, you must believe what I tell you. . . ."

So there was nothing, nothing to worry about any more, except sometimes in the night one of the children screamed in a nightmare, and they both hustled out shaking and hunting for the matches and calling, "There, wait a minute, here we are!" John, get the doctor now. Hapsy's time has come. But there was Hapsy standing by the bed in a white cap. "Cornelia, tell Hapsy to take off her cap. I can't see her plain."

Her eyes opened very wide and the room stood out like a picture she had seen somewhere. Dark colors with the shadows rising towards the ceiling in long angles. The tall black dresser gleamed with nothing on it but John's picture, enlarged from a little one, with John's eyes very black when they should have been blue. You never saw him, so how do you know how he looked? But the man insisted the copy was perfect, it was very rich and handsome. For a picture, yes, but it's not my husband. The table by the bed had a linen cover and a candle and a crucifix. The light was blue from Cornelia's silk lampshades. No sort of light at all, just frippery. You had to live forty years with kerosene lamps to appreciate honest electricity. She felt very strong and she saw Doctor Harry with a rosy nimbus[3] around him.

"You look like a saint, Doctor Harry, and I vow that's as near as you'll ever come to it."

"She's saying something."

"I heard you, Cornelia. What's all this carrying-on?"

"Father Connolly's saying—"

Cornelia's voice staggered and bumped like a cart in a bad road. It rounded corners and turned back again and arrived nowhere. Granny stepped up in the cart very lightly and reached for the reins, but a man sat beside her and she knew him by his hands, driving the cart. She did not look in his face, for she knew without seeing, but looked instead down the road where the trees leaned over and bowed to each other and a thousand birds were singing a Mass. She felt like singing too, but she put her hand in the bosom of her dress and pulled out a rosary, and Father Connolly murmured Latin in a very solemn voice and tickled her feet. My God, will you stop that nonsense? I'm a married woman. What if he did run away and leave me to face the priest by myself? I found another a whole world better. I wouldn't have exchanged my husband for anybody except St. Michael himself, and you may tell him that for me with a thank you in the bargain.

Light flashed on her closed eyelids, and a deep roaring shook her. Cornelia, is that lightning? I hear thunder. There's going to be a storm. Close all the windows. Call the children in. . . .

"Mother, here we are, all of us." "Is that you, Hapsy?" "Oh, no,

3. Bright halo around or over the head.

I'm Lydia. We drove as fast as we could." Their faces drifted above her, drifted away. The rosary fell out of her hands and Lydia put it back. Jimmy tried to help, their hands fumbled together, and Granny closed two fingers around Jimmy's thumb. Beads wouldn't do, it must be something alive. She was so amazed her thoughts ran round and round. So, my dear Lord, this is my death and I wasn't even thinking about it. My children have come to see me die. But I can't, it's not time. Oh, I always hated surprises. I wanted to give Cornelia the amethyst set—Cornelia, you're to have the amethyst set, but Hapsy's to wear it when she wants, and, Doctor Harry, do shut up. Nobody sent for you. Oh, my dear Lord, do wait a minute. I meant to do something about the Forty Acres, Jimmy doesn't need it and Lydia will later on, with that worthless husband of hers. I meant to finish the altar cloth and send six bottles of wine to Sister Borgia for her dyspepsia.[4] I want to send six bottles of wine to Sister Borgia, Father Connolly, now don't let me forget.

Cornelia's voice made short turns and tilted over and crashed. "Oh, Mother, oh, Mother, oh, Mother. . . ."

"I'm not going Cornelia. I'm taken by surprise. I can't go."

You'll see Hapsy again. What about her? "I thought you'd never come." Granny made a long journey outward, looking for Hapsy. What if I don't find her? What then? Her heart sank down and down, there was no bottom to death, she couldn't come to the end of it. The blue light from Cornelia's lampshade drew into a tiny point in the center of her brain, it flickered and winked like an eye, quietly it fluttered and dwindled. Granny lay curled down within herself, amazed and watchful, staring at the point of light that was herself; her body was now only a deeper mass of shadow in an endless darkness and this darkness would curl around the light and swallow it up. God, give a sign!

For the second time there was no sign. Again no bridegroom and the priest in the house. She could not remember any other sorrow because this grief wiped them all away. Oh, no, there's nothing more cruel than this—I'll never forgive it. She stretched herself with a deep breath and blew out the light.

1930

---

4. Indigestion.

===

JOHN DOS PASSOS
1896–1970

Some of the most ambitious experiments in twentieth-century American fiction were those of John Dos Passos. In decades when many contemporary writers were concentrating on specific regions, perfecting shorter forms of fiction, or fashioning novels designed for the intensive scrutiny of characters and institutions, Dos Passos was impelled by an aroused social conscience to survey modern American society in its larger contours and to create panoramic forms that could accommodate the multiplicity of historical currents, characters, and events on so large a scene.

Born in Chicago, John Roderigo Dos Passos was raised by parents who lived apart but provided him with the advantages of travel in Europe and private schooling in England and at Choate in Connecticut. His father (who refused to acknowledge his son until 1916) was of Portuguese descent, a well-to-do lawyer who wrote a book on America's rise to dominance in the twentieth century. In 1916 Dos Passos graduated with honors from Harvard, where he was introduced to the incisive critiques of capitalistic society by the sociologist Thorstein Veblen and to such progenitors of modernism in literature as Walter Pater and James Joyce. He also wrote verse and published reviews in the *Advocate*, among them commentaries on the new poetry of Pound and Eliot and on the radical John Reed's *Insurgent Mexico*. He followed his father's wishes in beginning the study of architecture in Spain in 1916, but in 1917 he joined the famous Morton-Harjes volunteer ambulance corps, serving in France and Italy, and later became a medical corpsman in the U.S. Army. Much of the next ten years he spent as a free-lance journalist, traveling in Spain and Europe and serving with the Near East relief mission. In 1926 he joined the executive board of the Communist *New Masses*.

By that time Dos Passos's particular kind of radicalism was finding expression both in political action and in a variety of literary productions. In 1922 a volume of poems, *A Pushcart at the Curb*, appeared along with *Rosinante to the Road Again*, in which essays on Spanish culture and a dialogue between two travelers define Dos Passos's growing dissatisfaction with existing institutions in modern America and his attempt to identify with the masses. Two plays, expressionistic in technique, *The Garbage Man* and *Airways, Inc.*, appeared between 1925 and 1928, and a second travel book, *Orient Express* (1927), deplored the encroachment of American technological civilization on the ancient worlds of the Near East. But it was his fiction that secured his reputation. *One Man's Initiation—1917* (1920) consists of vignettes describing the impact of World War I on France and on an imaginative young American who serves in the ambulance corps. The more bluntly powerful *Three Soldiers* turns World War I and the U.S. Army into images of a repressive, mechanized society that grinds under an optical worker from San Francisco, a farm boy from Indiana, and a Harvard-educated composer named Andrews who rebels, then escapes from a labor battalion with the help of an anarchist and deserts the army so as to write music in Paris. At the end he is working on a composition entitled *The Soul and Body of John Brown*, the fanatical abolitionist who led the attack on slave-owning society in 1859 at Harpers Ferry and whom Andrews calls "the madman who wanted to free people." A comparable combination of explosive protest with a sense of futility governs the brilliant *Manhattan Transfer* (1925) in which Dos Passos devised kaleidoscopic techniques to render the contemporary urban scene: swiftly shifting episodes of crime and violence shatter the illusions of opportunity that entice the reporter Jimmy Herf; a roller coaster, a nickelodeon, and revolving doors provide a phantasmagoric imagery for the energetic but aimless society which threatens to stifle all individuality.

Between 1926 and 1936 Dos Passos's disgust with the institutions of American capitalism and the mechanization of life was intensified to the point of hatred, but it was complicated by the profound distrust of all institutions and all power that he displayed even while seeking to exert power as a writer and activist. He was aroused by industrial strikes and the efforts to suppress them, by the onset of the Great Depression, and notably by the prolonged trial and subsequent execution in 1927 of the two immigrant anarchists Sacco and Vanzetti, which to him and many other intellectuals seemed a gross miscarriage of justice perpetrated by the American establishment. He wrote for Communist journals, served on committees to aid political prisoners and strikers sponsored by the Communist party, and publicly supported Communist candidates in the 1932 elections, but he never joined the Communist party. He insisted that editors of Communist journals allow room for dissent, that the struggle against oppression be conducted as humanely as possible, and that he preferred the looser affiliation of a fellow traveler or "scavenger and campfollower."[1] Soon after Communists broke up a rally of Socialists in Madison Square Garden in 1934, Dos Passos withdrew from Communist front activities and supported Franklin D. Roosevelt for President in 1936.

His masterpiece, gathered as the trilogy *U.S.A.* in 1937, consists of three novels that were published between 1930 and 1936: *The 42nd Parallel*, *1919*, and *The Big Money*. Its span encompasses the decades before World War I to 1936; its geography extends from Seattle, San Francisco, Hollywood, and Mexico to Chicago, New York, Miami, and France; its social settings include the union offices of the International Workers of the World, the public relations office and the affluent circle of the magnate J. Ward Moorehouse, the airplane factory of Charlie Anderson, the tinsel world of the film actress Margo Dowling, and the strike headquarters of radical organizers in Pennsylvania and New Jersey. The cast of characters includes eleven major figures whose private and public lives intersect or diverge, terminating often in obscurity, accidental death, or suicide. Three of their careers are typical. Charlie Anderson, a Dakota farm boy and later a Socialist, joins the ambulance corps and returns from World War I to found an airplane factory, sells out to a large Detroit firm and marries an heiress, then spends out his life in unsuccessful business deals until killed in an auto crash. Ben Compton, a Brooklyn construction worker, union organizer, and Communist party member, is eventually expelled from the party for deviation from party policy. Mary French, a liberal college graduate and Communist supporter though never a member of the party, is shattered when her Communist lover deserts her and when another Communist co-worker is shot by strike breakers in the Pennsylvania mining camps. The trilogy closes with a panoramic view that contrasts a well-fed but airsick executive on a transcontinental plane with a hungry, valueless vagabond bypassed by speeding traffic on the highway below. The effect is to underscore the bleak declarations earlier in the triology that all individuals have been rendered "foreigners" by modern society, that America stands "defeated," sharply divided into "two nations."

The trilogy is sustained by a style as harshly blunt, as driven, as energized and machinelike as the powers and conflicts it depicts, and the vast scale of the fictive action is extended by three structural devices that Dos Passos used in later fiction. One he called the "Newsreel," a collage

1. Quoted by Granville Hicks in Andrew   *Critical Essays*, p. 23.
Hook, ed., *Dos Passos: A Collection of*

of newspaper excerpts and headlines, snatches of popular songs, and quotations from official oratory and reports, which, scattered through the
narrative, establish a public context for the themes and incidents of the
fiction. The second he called the "Camera Eye," a sequence of impressionistic fragments, emotional and subjective, in effect lyrical or elegiac,
giving an interval of submerged response to the issues and conflicts that
appear in the narrative and in the public world. The third is the series
of brilliantly concise biographies of historical personages that are interspersed throughout each volume, from the labor leader Eugene Debs,
to such figures as the dancer Isadora Duncan and the film star Rudolph
Valentino, the politicians Robert La Follette and Woodrow Wilson, the
inventors Thomas Edison and the Wright Brothers, the financier J. P.
Morgan, the sociologist Thorstein Veblen, the architect Frank Lloyd
Wright. The biographies measure the cost of success—or of failure—in
American life. And they give particular point to Dos Passos's hope that
by "writing straight," instead of either overtly preaching or cranking out
prose as mechanical as the machine civilization he detested, a writer
could become an "architect of history."[2]

A historical point of view—non-Marxist and increasingly patriotic—
proved to be the governing perspective of Dos Passos's career in later decades. His concern for personal liberty, and his fear of encroaching institutions and concentrations of power, shifted its base to the right; his
antagonists became the Washington bureaucracy, the labor unions, and the
Communists; his sanctions for his position became increasingly the remote
past of Jeffersonianism; his castigation of the present and warnings about
the future became more shrill. He went to Spain during the Spanish
Civil War but returned in protest against Communist interference with
the Loyalist cause, and continued a prolific career. Following the death
of his first wife in an auto accident, he remarried and lived with his wife
and daughter in the vicinity of Washington and Baltimore. He published
two volumes of reports on World War II (*State of the Nation*, 1944,
and *Tour of Duty*, 1946), a number of historical works (including *The
Heart and Head of Thomas Jefferson*, 1954, and *The Men Who Made
the Nation*, 1957), and a series of increasingly bitter novels. The three
comprising the trilogy *District of Columbia* (1952) deal with the amatory
and political entanglements of characters involved in the Spanish war, the
Huey Long regime in Louisiana, and the Washington bureaucracy under
the New Deal. In *Midcentury* (1961) Dos Passos returned to the format
of *U.S.A.*, but it serves only to mask a hopeless denunciation of power
struggles among financiers and labor leaders.

From U.S.A.
The Big Money[1]
Newsreel LXVIII

WALL STREET STUNNED

*This is not Thirty-eight, but it's old Ninety-seven
You must put her in Center on time*[2]

2. *Occasions and Protests*, pp. 7–8.
1. The following selections are the concluding sections of *The Big Money*
(1936), the last novel in the trilogy

U.S.A.
2. The engineer of the locomotive
Ninety-seven was the legendary Casey
Jones, who died in a head-on collision

MARKET SURE TO RECOVER FROM SLUMP
Decline in Contracts
POLICE TURN MACHINE GUNS ON COLORADO MINE STRIKERS
KILL 5 WOUND 40

sympathizers appeared on the scene just as thousands of office
workers were pouring out of the buildings at the lunch hour. As
they raised their placard high and started an indefinite march
from one side to the other, they were jeered and hooted not only
by the office workers but also by workmen on a building under
construction

NEW METHODS OF SELLING SEEN
Rescue Crews Try To Upend Ill-fated Craft While Waiting
For Pontoons

He looked 'round an' said to his black greasy fireman
Jus' shovel in a little more coal
And when we cross that White Oak Mountain
You can watch your Ninety-seven roll

I find your column interesting and need advice. I have saved
four thousand dollars which I want to invest for a better income.
Do you think I might buy stocks?

POLICE KILLER FLICKS CIGARETTE AS HE
GOES TREMBLING TO DOOM
PLAY AGENCIES IN RING OF SLAVE GIRL MARTS
Maker of Love Disbarred as Lawyer

Oh the right wing clothesmakers
And the Socialist fakers
They make by the workers . . .
Double cross

They preach Social-ism
But practice Fasc-ism
To keep capitalism
By the boss[3]

MOSCOW CONGRESS OUSTS OPPOSITION[4]

It's a mighty rough road from Lynchburg to Danville
An' a line on a three mile grade
It was on that grade he lost his average
An' you see what a jump he made

MILL THUGS IN MURDER RAID

here is the most dangerous example of how at the decisive
moment the bourgeois ideology liquidates class solidarity and
turns a friend of the workingclass of yesterday into a most miserable propagandist for imperialism today

---

when he tried to get his train to San
Francisco on time. Excerpts from the
ballad celebrating Jones are interspersed
in this "Newsreel."
3. Excerpts from this labor-union protest
song are also interspersed in this "Newsreel."
4. Probably the Seventh Congress of
the Third International held in Moscow
in 1935.

RED PICKETS FINED FOR PROTEST HERE

We leave our home in the morning
We kiss our children goodby

OFFICIALS STILL HOPE FOR RESCUE OF MEN

He was goin' downgrade makin' ninety miles an hour
When his whistle broke into a scream
He was found in the wreck with his hand on the throttle
An' was scalded to death with the steam

RADICALS FIGHT WITH CHAIRS AT UNITY MEETING
PATROLMEN PROTECT REDS
U.S. CHAMBER OF COMMERCE URGES CONFIDENCE
REAL VALUES UNHARMED

While we slave for the bosses
Our children scream an' cry
But when we draw our money
Our grocery bills to pay

PRESIDENT SEES PROSPERITY NEAR

Not a cent to spend for clothing
Not a cent to lay away

STEAMROLLER IN ACTION AGAINST MILITANTS
MINERS BATTLE SCABS

But we cannot buy for our children
Our wages are too low
Now listen to me you workers
Both you women and men
Let us win for them the victory
I'm sure it ain't no sin

CARILLON PEALS IN SINGING TOWER[5]

the President declared it was impossible to view the increased advantages for the many without smiling at those who a short time ago expressed so much fear lest our country might come under the control of a few individuals of great wealth

HAPPY CROWDS THRONG CEREMONY

on a tiny island nestling like a green jewel in the lake that mirrors the singing tower, the President today participated in the dedication of a bird sanctuary and its pealing carillon, fulfilling the dream of an immigrant boy

The Camera Eye (51)

at the head of the valley in the dark of the hills on the broken floor of a lurchedover cabin a man halfsits halflies propped up by an old woman two wrinkled girls that might be young   chunks of coal flare in the hearth flicker in his face white and sagging as

---

5. The Singing Tower was erected in Florida as a monument to Edward W. Bok (1863–1930), Dutch-born editor and philanthropist, who is buried at its base. President Calvin Coolidge spoke at its dedication in 1929.

dough   blacken the cavedin mouth the taut throat the belly
swelled enormous with the wound he got working on the mine-
tipple[6]   the barefoot girl brings him a tincup of water   the
woman wipes sweat off his streaming face with a dirty denim
sleeve   the firelight flares in his eyes stretched big with fever
in the women's scared eyes and in the blanched faces of the
foreigners
     without help in the valley hemmed by dark strike-silent hills
the man will die (my father died we know what it is like to see
a man die) the women will lay him out on the rickety cot the
miners will bury him

     in the jail it's light too hot the steamheat hisses we talk through
the greenpainted iron bars to a tall white mustachioed old man
some smiling miners in shirtsleeves a boy   faces white from mining have already the tallowy look of jailfaces
     foreigners what can we say to the dead?   foreigners what
can we say to the jailed?   the representative of the political
party talks fast through the bars join up with us and no other
union we'll send you tobacco candy solidarity our lawyers will write
briefs speakers will shout your names at meetings they'll carry
your names on cardboard on picketlines   the men in jail shrug
their shoulders smile thinly our eyes look in their eyes through the
bars   what can I say?   (in another continent I have seen the
faces looking out through the barred basement windows behind
the ragged sentry's boots I have seen before day the straggling
footsore prisoners herded through the streets limping between
bayonets   heard the volley
     I have seen the dead lying out in those distant deeper valleys)
     what can we say to the jailed?

     in the law's office we stand against the wall the law is a big
man with eyes angry in a big pumpkinface   who sits and stares
at us meddling foreigners through the door the deputies crane
with their guns   they stand guard at the mines   they
blockade the miners' soupkitchens they've cut off the road up the
valley   the hiredmen with guns stand ready to shoot (they have
made us foreigners in the land where we were born they are the
conquering army that has filtered into the country unnoticed they
have taken the hilltops by stealth they levy toll they stand at the
minehead   they stand at the polls   they stand by when the
bailiffs carry the furniture of the family evicted from the city tenement out on the sidewalk they are there when the bankers foreclose
on a farm they are ambushed and ready to shoot down the strikers

---

6. The apparatus at a coal mine which tips cars at an angle to unload the coal.

marching behind the flag up the switchback road to the mine
those that the guns spare they jail)

the law stares across the desk out of angry eyes his face reddens
in splotches like a gobbler's neck with the strut of the power of
submachineguns sawedoffshotguns teargas and vomitinggas the
power that can feed you or leave you to starve

sits easy at his desk his back is covered he feels strong behind
him he feels the prosecutingattorney the judge an owner himself
the political boss the minesuperintendent the board of directors
the president of the utility the manipulator of the holding-
company

he lifts his hand towards the telephone
the deputies crowd in the door
we have only words against

Power Superpower

In eighteen eighty when Thomas Edison's[7] agent was hooking
up the first telephone in London, he put an ad in the paper for
a secretary and stenographer. The eager young cockney with sprouting muttonchop whiskers who answered it[8]

had recently lost his job as officeboy. In his spare time he had
been learning shorthand and bookkeeping and taking dictation
from the editor of the English *Vanity Fair* at night and jotting
down the speeches in Parliament for the papers. He came of temperance smallshopkeeper stock; already he was butting his bullet-
head against the harsh structure of caste that doomed boys of his
class to a life of alpaca jackets, penmanship, subordination. To
get a job with an American firm was to put a foot on the rung of
a ladder that led up into the blue.

He did his best to make himself indispensable; they let him
operate the switchboard for the first half-hour when the telephone
service was opened. Edison noticed his weekly reports on the
electrical situation in England

and sent for him to be his personal secretary.

Samuel Insull landed in America on a raw March day in eighty-
one. Immediately he was taken out to Menlo Park, shown about
the little group of laboratories, saw the strings of electriclightbulbs
shining at intervals across the snowy lots, all lit from the world's
first central electric station. Edison put him right to work and he
wasn't through till midnight. Next morning at six he was on the
job; Edison had no use for any nonsense about hours or vacations.
Insull worked from that time on until he was seventy without a

---

7. Thomas A. Edison (1847–1931), inventor of the phonograph whose engineering and entrepreneurial skills paved
the way for the commercial development of the electric light and the organization of the motion-picture industry. His laboratory was at Menlo Park,
New Jersey.
8. Samuel Insull (1859–1938), British-
born American utilities executive.

break; no nonsense about hours or vacations. Electric power turned the ladder into an elevator.

Young Insull made himself indispensable to Edison and took more and more charge of Edison's business deals. He was tireless, ruthless, reliable as the tides, Edison used to say, and fiercely determined to rise.

In ninetytwo he induced Edison to send him to Chicago and put him in as President of the Chicago Edison Company. Now he was on his own. *My engineering,* he said once in a speech, when he was sufficiently czar of Chicago to allow himself the luxury of plain speaking, *has been largely concerned with engineering all I could out of the dollar.*

He was a stiffly arrogant redfaced man with a closecropped mustache; he lived on Lake Shore Drive and was at the office at 7:10 every morning. It took him fifteen years to merge the five electrical companies into the Commonwealth Edison Company. *Very early I discovered that the first essential, as in other public utility business, was that it should be operated as a monopoly.*

When his power was firm in electricity he captured gas, spread out into the surrounding townships in northern Illinois. When politicians got in his way, he bought them, when laborleaders got in his way he bought them. Incredibly his power grew. He was scornful of bankers, lawyers were his hired men. He put his own lawyer in as corporation counsel and through him ran Chicago. When he found to his amazement that there were men (even a couple of young lawyers, Richberg and Ickes)[9] in Chicago that he couldn't buy, he decided he'd better put on a show for the public;

> Big Bill Thompson, the Builder:[1]
> *punch King George in the nose,*
> the hunt for the treeclimbing fish,
> the Chicago Opera.

It was too easy; the public had money, there was one of them born every minute,[2] with the founding of Middlewest Utilities in nineteen twelve Insull began to use the public's money to spread his empire. His companies began to have open stockholders' meetings, to ballyhoo service, the small investor could sit there all day hearing the bigwigs talk. It's fun to be fooled. Companyunions hypnotized his employees; everybody had to buy stock in his com-

9. Donald R. Richberg (1881–1960), Washington bureaucrat and leading architect of President Franklin D. Roosevelt's New Deal; Harold L. Ickes (1874–1952), Progressive party politician, Secretary of Labor and director of the Public Works Administration under President Roosevelt.
1. William H. Thompson (1868–1944), flamboyant politician, self-styled "the Builder," repeatedly Mayor of Chicago between 1915 and 1930, fanatical anglophobe.
2. "There's a sucker born every minute": a proverbial saying of Phineas T. Barnum (1810–91), the American circus impresario and showman.

panies, employees had to go out and sell stock, officeboys, linemen, trolleyconductors. Even Owen D. Young[3] was afraid of him. *My experience is that the greatest aid in the efficiency of labor is a long line of men waiting at the gate.*

War shut up the progressives (no more nonsense about trust-busting, controlling monopoly, the public good) and raised Samuel Insull to the peak.

He was head of the Illinois State Council of Defense. *Now,* he said delightedly, *I can do anything I like.* With it came the perpetual spotlight, the purple taste of empire. If anybody didn't like what Samuel Insull did he was a traitor. Chicago damn well kept its mouth shut.

The Insull companies spread and merged put competitors out of business until Samuel Insull and his stooge brother Martin controlled through the leverage of holdingcompanies and directorates and blocks of minority stock.

light and power, coalmines and tractioncompanies

in Illinois, Michigan, the Dakotas, Nebraska, Arkansas, Oklahoma, Missouri, Maine, Kansas, Wisconsin, Virginia, Ohio, North Carolina, Indiana, New York, New Jersey, Texas, in Canada, in Louisiana, in Georgia, in Florida and Alabama.

(It has been figured out that one dollar in Middle West Utilities controlled seventeen hundred and fifty dollars invested by the public in the subsidiary companies that actually did the work of producing electricity. With the delicate lever of a voting trust controlling the stock of the two top holdingcompanies he controlled a twelfth of the power output of America.)

Samuel Insull began to think he owned all that the way a man owns the roll of bills in his back pocket.

Always he'd been scornful of bankers. He owned quite a few in Chicago. But the New York bankers were laying for him; they felt he was a bounder, whispered that this financial structure was unsound. Fingers itched to grasp the lever that so delicately moved this enormous power over lives,

superpower, Insull liked to call it.

A certain Cyrus S. Eaton[4] of Cleveland, an exBaptistminister, was the David that brought down this Goliath. Whether it was so or not he made Insull believe that Wall Street was behind him.

He started buying stock in the three Chicago utilities. Insull in a panic for fear he'd lose his control went into the market to buy against him. Finally the Reverend Eaton let himself be bought

---

3. Owen D. Young (1874–1962), lawyer and financier, organizer of R.C.A. in 1919, and head of General Electric Corporation in 1922.

4. Cyrus S. Eaton (b. 1883), Canadian-born financier, utilities magnate, founder of Republic Steel.

out, shaking down the old man for a profit of twenty million dollars.

The stockmarket crash.

Paper values were slipping. Insull's companies were intertwined in a tangle that no bookkeeper has ever been able to unravel.

The gas hissed out of the torn balloon. Insull threw away his imperial pride and went on his knees to the bankers.

The bankers had him where they wanted him. To save the face of the tottering czar he was made a receiver of his own concerns. But the old man couldn't get out of his head the illusion that the money was all his. When it was discovered that he was using the stockholders' funds to pay off his brothers' brokerage accounts it was too thick even for a federal judge. Insull was forced to resign.

He held directorates in eightyfive companies, he was chairman of sixtyfive, president of eleven: it took him three hours to sign his resignations.

As a reward for his services to monopoly his companies chipped in on a pension of eighteen thousand a year. But the public was shouting for criminal prosecution. When the handouts stopped newspapers and politicians turned on him. Revolt against the moneymanipulators was in the air. Samuel Insull got the wind up and ran off to Canada with his wife.

Extradition proceedings. He fled to Paris. When the authorities began to close in on him there he slipped away to Italy, took a plane to Tirana, another to Saloniki and then the train to Athens. There the old fox went to earth. Money talked as sweetly in Athens as it had in Chicago in the old days.

The American ambassador tried to extradite him. Insull hired a chorus of Hellenic lawyers and politicos and sat drinking coffee in the lobby of the Grande Bretagne, while they proceeded to tie up the ambassador in a snarl of chicanery as complicated as the bookkeeping of his holdingcompanies. The successors of Demosthenes[5] were delighted. The ancestral itch in many a Hellenic palm was temporarily assuaged. Samuel Insull settled down cozily in Athens, was stirred by the sight of the Parthenon, watched the goats feeding on the Pentelic slopes, visited the Areopagus, admired marble fragments ascribed to Phidias, talked with the local bankers about reorganizing the public utilities of Greece, was said to be promoting Macedonian lignite. He was the toast of the Athenians; Mme. Kouryoumdjouglou the vivacious wife of a Bagdad datemerchant devoted herself to his comfort. When the first effort

---

5. Famed Athenian orator of the fifth century B.C. References in the succeeding lines are to sites in or near Athens (the Temple of Athens, the slopes of Mount Pentelicus, and the hill Areopagus after which a quasi-judicial elite tribunal was named) and to Phidias, a famous fifth-century-B.C. Athenian sculptor.

at extradition failed, the old gentleman declared in the courtroom, as he struggled out from the embraces of his four lawyers: *Greece is a small but great country.*

The idyll was interrupted when the Roosevelt Administration began to put the heat on the Greek foreign office. Government lawyers in Chicago were accumulating truckloads of evidence and chalking up more and more drastic indictments.

Finally after many a postponement (he had hired physicians as well as lawyers, they cried to high heaven that it would kill him to leave the genial climate of the Attic plain),

he was ordered to leave Greece as an undesirable alien to the great indignation of Balkan society and of Mme. Kouryoumdjouglou.

He hired the *Maiotis* a small and grubby Greek freighter and panicked the foreignnews services by slipping off for an unknown destination.

It was rumored that the new Odysseus was bound for Aden, for the islands of the South Seas, that he'd been invited to Persia. After a few days he turned up rather seasick in the Bosporus on his way, it was said, to Rumania where Madame Kouryoumdjouglou had advised him to put himself under the protection of her friend la Lupescu.[6]

At the request of the American ambassador the Turks were delighted to drag him off the Greek freighter and place him in a not at all comfortable jail. Again money had been mysteriously wafted from England, the healing balm began to flow, lawyers were hired, interpreters expostulated, doctors made diagnoses;

but Angora[7] was boss

and Insull was shipped off to Smyrna to be turned over to the assistant federal districtattorney who had come all that way to arrest him.

The Turks wouldn't even let Mme. Kouryoumdjouglou, on her way back from making arrangements in Bucharest, go ashore to speak to him. In a scuffle with the officials on the steamboat the poor lady was pushed overboard

and with difficulty fished out of the Bosporus.

Once he was cornered the old man let himself tamely be taken home on the *Exilona*, started writing his memoirs, made himself agreeable to his fellow passengers, was taken off at Sandy Hook and rushed to Chicago to be arraigned.

In Chicago the government spitefully kept him a couple of nights in jail; men he'd never known, so the newspapers said, stepped forward to go on his twohundredandfiftythousanddollar bail. He was moved to a hospital that he himself had endowed.

6. Madame Magda Lupescu (b. 1902), Rumanian adventuress, the "Cleopatra of the Near East," mistress of King Carol II of Rumania.
7. City in central Turkey.

Solidarity. The leading businessmen in Chicago were photographed visiting him there. Henry Ford[8] paid a call.

The trial was very beautiful. The prosecution got bogged in finance technicalities. The judge was not unfriendly. The Insulls stole the show.

They were folks, they smiled at reporters, they posed for photographers, they went down to the courtroom by bus. Investors might have been ruined but so, they allowed it to be known, were the Insulls; the captain had gone down with the ship.

Old Samuel Insull rambled amiably on the stand, told his lifestory: from officeboy to powermagnate, his struggle to make good, his love for his home and the kiddies. He didn't deny he'd made mistakes; who hadn't, but they were honest errors. Samuel Insull wept. Brother Martin wept. The lawyers wept. With voices choked with emotion headliners of Chicago business told from the witnessstand how much Insull had done for business in Chicago. There wasn't a dry eye in the jury.

Finally driven to the wall by the prosecutingattorney Samuel Insull blurted out that yes, he had made an error of some ten million dollars in accounting but that it had been an honest error.

Verdict: Not Guilty.

Smiling through their tears the happy Insulls went to their towncar amid the cheers of the crowd. Thousands of ruined investors, at least so the newspapers said, who had lost their life savings sat crying over the home editions at the thought of how Mr. Insull had suffered. The bankers were happy, the bankers had moved in on the properties.

In an odor of sanctity the deposed monarch of superpower, the officeboy who made good, enjoys his declining years spending the pension of twenty-one hundred a year that the directors of his old companies dutifully restored to him. *After fifty years of work,* he said, *my job is gone.*

Mary French

Mary French had to stay late at the office and couldn't get to the hall until the meeting was almost over. There were no seats left so she stood in the back. So many people were standing in front of her that she couldn't see Don, she could only hear his ringing harsh voice and feel the tense attention in the silence during his pauses. When a roar of applause answered his last words and the hall filled suddenly with voices and the scrape and shuffle of feet she ran out ahead of the crowd and up the alley to the back door. Don was just coming out of the black sheetiron door talking over his shoulder as he came to two of the miners' delegates. He stopped a second to hold the door open for them with a long arm. His face had the flushed smile, there was the shine in

---

8. Henry Ford (1863–1947), American automobile magnate.

his eye he often had after speaking, the look, Mary used to tell
herself, of a man who had just come from a date with his best girl.
It was some time before Don saw her in the group that gathered
round him in the alley. Without looking at her he swept her along
with the men he was talking to and walked them fast towards the
corner of the street. Eyes looked after them as they went from
the groups of furworkers and garmentworkers that dotted the pavement in front of the hall. Mary tingled with the feeling of warm
ownership in the looks of the workers as their eyes followed Don
Stevens down the street.

It wasn't until they were seated in a small lunchroom under
the el that Don turned to Mary and squeezed her hand. "Tired?"
She nodded. "Aren't you, Don?" He laughed and drawled, "No,
I'm not tired. I'm hungry."

"Comrade French, I thought we'd detailed you to see that
Comrade Stevens ate regular," said Rudy Goldfarb with a flash of
teeth out of a dark Italianlooking face.

"He won't ever eat anything when he's going to speak," Mary
said.

"I make up for it afterwards," said Don. "Say, Mary, I hope
you have some change. I don't think I've got a cent on me."
Mary nodded, smiling. "Mother came across again," she whispered.

"Money," broke in Steve Mestrovich. "We got to have money
or else we're licked." "The truck got off today," said Mary. "That's
why I was so late getting to the meeting." Mestrovich passed the
grimed bulk of his hand across his puttycolored face that had a
sharply turnedup nose peppered with black pores. "If cossack[9]
don't git him."

"Eddy Spellman's a smart kid. He gets through like a shadow.
I don't know how he does it."

"You don't know what them clothes means to women and kids
and . . . listen, Miss French, don't hold back nothin' because too
raggedy. Ain't nothin' so ragged like what our little kids got on
their backs."

"Eddy's taking five cases of condensed milk. We'll have more
as soon as he comes back."

"Say, Mary," said Don suddenly, looking up from his plate of
soup, "how about calling up Sylvia? I forgot to ask how much we
collected at the meeting." Young Goldfarb got to his feet. "I'll
call. You look tired, Comrade French. . . . Anybody got a nickel?"

"Here, I got nickel," said Mestrovich. He threw back his head
and laughed. "Damn funny . . . miner with nickel. Down our way
miner got nickel put in frame send Meester Carnegie Museum
. . . very rare." He got up roaring laughter and put on his black
longvisored miner's cap. "Goodnight, comrade, I walk Brooklyn.

9. Cavalryman in the armies of czar-   and strikebreakers.
ist Russia, here applied to the deputies

Reliefcommittee nine o'clock . . . right, Miss French?" As he strode out of the lunchroom the heavy tread of his black boots made the sugarbowls jingle on the tables. "Oh, Lord," said Mary, with tears suddenly coming to her eyes. "That was his last nickel."

Goldfarb came back saying that the collection hadn't been so good. Sixtynine dollars and some pledges. "Christmas time coming on . . . you know. Everybody's always broke at Christmas." "Henderson made a lousy speech," grumbled Don. "He's more of a socialfascist[1] every day."

Mary sat there feeling the tiredness in every bone of her body waiting until Don got ready to go home. She was too sleepy to follow what they were talking about but every now and then the words centralcommittee, expulsions, oppositionists, splitters rasped in her ears. Then Don was tapping her on the shoulder and she was waking up and walking beside him through the dark streets.

"It's funny, Don," she was saying, "I always go to sleep when you talk about party discipline. I guess it's because I don't want to hear about it." "No use being sentimental about it," said Don savagely. "But is it sentimental to be more interested in saving the miners' unions?" she said, suddenly feeling wide awake again. "Of course that's what we all believe but we have to follow the party line. A lot of those boys . . . Goldfarb's one of them . . . Ben Compton's another . . . think this is a debatingsociety. If they're not very careful indeed they'll find themselves out on their ear. . . . You just watch."

Once they'd staggered up the five flights to their dingy little apartment where Mary had always planned to put up curtains but had never had time, Don suddenly caved in with fatigue and threw himself on the couch and fell asleep without taking off his clothes. Mary tried to rouse him but gave it up. She unlaced his shoes for him and threw a blanket over him and got into bed herself and tried to sleep.

She was staring wide awake, she was counting old pairs of trousers, torn suits of woolly underwear, old armyshirts with the sleeves cut off, socks with holes in them that didn't match. She was seeing the rickety children with puffy bellies showing through their rags, the scrawny women with uncombed hair and hands distorted with work, the boys with their heads battered and bleeding from the clubs of the Coal and Iron Police, the photograph of a miner's body shot through with machinegun bullets. She got up and took two or three swigs from a bottle of gin she kept in the medicinecloset in the bathroom. The gin burned her throat. Coughing she went back to bed and went off into a hot dreamless sleep.

Towards morning Don woke her getting into the bed. He kissed her. "Darling, I've set the alarm for seven. . . . Be sure to

1. Communists regarded non-Marxist Socialists and Fascists as their enemies; the term "social fascist" was applied loosely to supporters of President Franklin D. Roosevelt's New Deal.

get me up. I've got a very important committeemeeting. . . . Be
sure and do it." He went off to sleep again right away like a child.
She lay beside his bigboned lanky body, listening to his regular
breathing, feeling happy and safe there in the bed with him.

Eddy Spellman got through with his truck again and distributed
his stuff to several striking locals U.M.W.[2] in the Pittsburgh district, although he had a narrow squeak when the deputies tried
to ambush him near Greensburg. They'd have nabbed him if a guy
he knew who was a bootlegger[3] hadn't tipped him off. The same
bootlegger helped him out when he skidded into a snowdrift on
the hill going down into Johnstown on the way back. He was
laughing about it as he helped Mary pack up the new shipment.
"He wanted to give me some liquor. . . . He's a good feller, do
you know it, Miss Mary? . . . Tough kinder . . that racket hardens
a feller up . . . but a prince when you know him. . . . 'Hell, no,
Ed,' his name's Eddy too, I says to him when he tries to slip me
a pint, 'I ain't going' to take a drink until after the revolution and
then I'll be ridin' so high I won't need to.' " Mary laughed. "I
guess we all ought to do that, Eddy. . . . But I feel so tired and
discouraged at night sometimes." "Sure," said Eddy, turning
serious. "It gits you down thinkin' how they got all the guns an'
all the money an' we ain't got nothin'."

"One thing you're going to have, Comrade Spellman, is a pair
of warm gloves and a good overcoat before you make the next
trip."

His freckled face turned red to the roots of his red hair. "Honest,
Miss Mary, I don't git cold. To tell the truth the motor heats up
so much in that old pile of junk it keeps me warm in the coldest weather. . . . After the next trip we got to put a new clutch
in her and that'll take more jack than we kin spare from the milk.
. . . I tell you things are bad up there in the coalfields this winter."

"But those miners have got such wonderful spirit," said Mary.

"The trouble is, Miss Mary, you kin only keep your spirit up
a certain length of time on an empty stumick."

That evening Don came by to the office to get Mary for supper.
He was very cheerful and his gaunt bony face had more color in it
than usual. "Well, little girl, what would you think of moving up
to Pittsburgh? After the plenum[4] I may go out to do some organizing in western Pennsylvania and Ohio. Mestrovich says they need
somebody to pep 'em up a little." Eddy Spellman looked up from
the bale of clothes he was tying up. "Take it from me, Comrade
Stevens, they sure do."

Mary felt a chill go through her. Don must have noticed the
pallor spreading over her face. "We won't take any risks," he

---

2. United Mine Workers, an industrial
union and the more aggressive of the
two major American labor unions in
the 1930s.

3. One who manufactures or distributes
liquor illegally.
4. Meeting of the full committee.

added hurriedly. "Those miners take good care of a feller, don't they, Eddy?" "They sure do. . . . Wherever the locals is strong you'll be safer than you are right here in New York." "Anyway," said Mary, her throat tight and dry, "if you've got to go you've got to go."

"You two go out an' eat," said Eddy. "I'll finish up . . . I'm bunkin' here anyway. Saves the price of a flop. . . . You feed Miss Mary up good, Comrade Stevens. We don't want her gettin' sick. . . . If all the real partymembers worked like she does we'd have . . . hell, we'd have the finest kind of a revolution by the spring of the year."

They went out laughing, and walked down to Bleecker Street and settled happily at a table in an Italian restaurant and ordered up the seventyfivecent dinner and a bottle of wine. "You've got a great admirer in Eddy," Don said, smiling at her across the table.

A couple of weeks later Mary came home one icy winter evening to find Don busy packing his grip. She couldn't help letting out a cry, her nerves were getting harder and harder to control. "Oh, Don, it's not Pittsburgh yet?" Don shook his head and went on packing. When he had closed up his wicker suitcase he came over to her and put his arm round her shoulder. "I've got to go across to the other side with . . . you know who . . . essential party business."

"Oh, Don, I'd love to go too. I've never been to Russia or anywhere." "I'll only be gone a month. We're sailing at midnight . . . and Mary darling . . . if anybody asks after me I'm in Pittsburgh, see?" Mary started to cry. "I'll have to say I don't know where you are . . . I know I can't ever get away with a lie." "Mary dear, it'll just be a few days . . . don't be a little silly." Mary smiled through her tears. "But I am . . I'm an awful little silly." He kissed her and patted her gently on the back. Then he picked up his suitcase and hurried out of the room with a big checked cap pulled down over his eyes.

Mary walked up and down the narrow room with her lips twitching, fighting to keep down the hysterical sobs. To give herself something to do she began to plan how she could fix up the apartment so that it wouldn't look so dreary when Don came back. She pulled out the couch and pushed it across the window like a windowseat. Then she pulled the table out in front of it and grouped the chairs round the table. She made up her mind she'd paint the woodwork white and get turkeyred for the curtains.

Next morning she was in the middle of drinking her coffee out of a racked cup without a saucer, feeling bitterly lonely in the empty apartment when the telephone rang. At first she didn't recognize whose voice it was. She was confused and kept stammering, "Who is it, please?" into the receiver. "But, Mary," the voice was saying in an exasperated tone, "you must know who I

am. It's Ben Compton . . . bee ee enn . . . Ben. I've got to see
you about something. Where could I meet you? Not at your
place." Mary tried to keep her voice from sounding stiff and chilly.
"I've got to be uptown today. I've got to have lunch with a woman
who may give some money to the miners. It's a horrible waste of
time but I can't help it. She won't give a cent unless I listen to
her sad story. How about meeting me in front of the Public
Library at two thirty?" "Better say inside. . . . It's about zero out
today. I just got up out of bed from the flu."

Mary hardly knew Ben he looked so much older. There was grey
in the hair spilling out untidily from under his cap. He stooped
and peered into her face querulously through his thick glasses. He
didn't shake hands. "Well, I might as well tell you . . . you'll
know it soon enough if you don't know it already . . . I've been
expelled from the party . . . oppositionist . . . exceptionalism . . .
a lot of nonsense. . . . Well, that doesn't matter, I'm still a revolutionist . . . I'll continue to work outside of the party."

"Oh, Ben, I'm so sorry," was all Mary could find to say. "You
know I don't know anything except what I read in the *Daily.*[5] It
all seems too terrible to me." "Let's go out, that guard's watching
us." Outside Ben began to shiver from the cold. His wrists stuck
out red from his frayed green overcoat with sleeves much too short
for his long arms. "Oh, where can we go?" Mary kept saying.

Finally they went down into a basement automat and sat talking in low voices over a cup of coffee. "I didn't want to go to your
place because I didn't want to meet Stevens. . . . Stevens and me
have never been friends, you know that. . . . Now he's in with the
comintern[6] crowd. He'll make the centralcommittee when they've
cleaned out all the brains."

"But, Ben, people can have differences of opinion and still . . ."

"A party of yesmen . . . that'll be great. . . . But, Mary, I had
to see you . . . I feel so lonely suddenly . . . you know, cut off
from everything. . . . You know if we hadn't been fools we'd
have had that baby that time . . . we'd still love each other. . . .
Mary, you were very lovely to me when I first got out of jail. . . .
Say, where's your friend Ada, the musician who had that fancy
apartment?"

"Oh, she's as silly as ever . . . running around with some fool
violinist or other."

"I've always liked music. . . . I ought to have kept you, Mary."

"A lot of water's run under the bridge since then," said Mary
coldly.

"Are you happy with Stevens? I haven't any right to ask."

"But, Ben, what's the use of raking all this old stuff up?"

"You see, often a young guy thinks, I'll sacrifice everything, and then when he is cut off all that side of his life, he's not as good as he was, do you see? For the first time in my life I have no contact. I thought maybe you could get me in on reliefwork somehow. The discipline isn't so strict in the relief organizations."

"I don't think they want any disrupting influences in the I.L.D.," said Mary.

"So I'm a disrupter to you too. . . . All right, in the end the workingclass will judge between us."

"Let's not talk about it, Ben."

"I'd like you to put it up to Stevens and ask him to sound out the proper quarters . . . that's not much to ask, is it?"

"But Don's not here at present." Before she could catch herself she'd blurted it out.

Ben looked her in the eye with a sudden sharp look.

"He hasn't by any chance sailed for Moscow with certain other comrades?"

"He's gone to Pittsburgh on secret partywork and for God's sake shut up about it. You just got hold of me to pump me." She got to her feet, her face flaming. "Well, goodby, Mr. Compton. . . . You don't happen to be a stoolpigeon as well as a disrupter, do you?"

Ben Compton's face broke in pieces suddenly the way a child's face does when it is just going to bawl. He sat there staring at her, senselessly scraping the spoon round and round in the empty coffeemug. She was halfway up the stairs when on an impulse she went back and stood for a second looking down at his bowed head. "Ben," she said in a gentler voice, "I shouldn't have said that . . . without proof. . . . I don't believe it." Ben Compton didn't look up. She went up the stairs again out into the stinging wind and hurried down Fortysecond Street in the afternoon crowd and took the subway down to Union Square.

The last day of the year Mary French got a telegram at the office from Ada Cohn. PLEASE PLEASE COMMUNICATE YOUR MOTHER IN TOWN AT PLAZA SAILING SOON WANTS TO SEE YOU DOESNT KNOW ADDRESS WHAT SHALL I TELL HER. Newyearsday there wasn't much doing at the office. Mary was the only one who had turned up, so in the middle of the morning she called up the Plaza and asked for Mrs. French. No such party staying there. Next she called up Ada. Ada talked and talked about how Mary's mother had married again, a Judge Blake, a very prominent man, a retired federal circuit judge, such an attractive man with a white vandyke beard and Ada had to see Mary and Mrs. Blake had been so sweet to her and they'd asked her to dinner at the Plaza and wanted to know all about Mary and that she'd had to admit that she never saw her although she was her best friend and she'd been to a newyearseve party and had such a headache she couldn't practice and she'd invited some lovely people in that afternoon and wouldn't Mary come, she'd be sure to like them.

Mary almost hung up on her, Ada sounded so silly, but she said she'd call her back right away after she'd talked to her mother. It ended by her going home and getting her best dress on and going uptown to the Plaza to see Judge and Mrs. Blake. She tried to find some place she could get her hair curled because she knew the first thing her mother would say was that she looked a fright, but everything was closed on account of its being newyearsday.

Judge and Mrs. Blake were getting ready to have lunch in a big private drawingroom on the corner looking out over the humped snowy hills of the park bristly with bare branches and interwoven with fastmoving shining streams of traffic. Mary's mother didn't look as if she'd aged a day, she was dressed in darkgreen and really looked stunning with a little white ruffle round her neck sitting there so at her ease, with rings on her fingers that sparkled in the grey winter light that came in through the big windows. The judge had a soft caressing voice. He talked elaborately about the prodigal daughter and the fatted calf until her mother broke in to say that they were going to Europe on a spree; they'd both of them made big killings on the stockexchange on the same day and they felt they owed themselves a little rest and relaxation. And she went on about how worried she'd been because all her letters had been returned from Mary's last address and that she'd written Ada again and again and Ada had always said Mary was in Pittsburgh or Fall River or some horrible place doing social work and that she felt it was about time she gave up doing everything for the poor and unfortunate and devoted a little attention to her own kith and kin.

"I hear you are a very dreadful young lady, Mary, my dear," said the judge, blandly, ladling some creamofcelery soup into her plate. "I hope you didn't bring any bombs with you." They both seemed to think that that was a splendid joke and laughed and laughed. "But to be serious," went on the judge, "I know that social inequality is a very dreadful thing and a blot on the fair name of American democracy. But as we get older, my dear, we learn to live and let live, that we have to take the bad with the good a little."

"Mary dear, why don't you go abroad with Ada Cohn and have a nice rest? . . . I'll find the money for the trip. I know it'll do you good. . . . You know I've never approved of your friendship with Ada Cohn. Out home we are probably a little oldfashioned about those things. Here she seems to be accepted everywhere. In fact she seems to know all the prominent musical people. Of course how good a musician she is herself I'm not in a position to judge."

"Hilda dear," said the judge, "Ada Cohn has a heart of gold. I find her a very sweet little girl. Her father was a very distinguished lawyer. You know we decided we'd lay aside our prejudices a little . . . didn't we, dear?"

"The judge is reforming me," laughed Mary's mother coyly.

Mary was so nervous she felt she was going to scream. The heavy buttery food, the suave attentions of the waiter and the fatherly geniality of the judge made her almost gag. "Look, Mother," she said, "if you really have a little money to spare you might let me have something for our milkfund. After all miners' children aren't guilty of anything."

"My dear, I've already made substantial contributions to the Red Cross. . . . After all, we've had a miners' strike out in Colorado on our hands much worse than in Pennsylvania. . . . I've always felt, Mary dear, that if you were interested in labor conditions the place for you was home in Colorado Springs. If you must study that sort of thing there was never any need to come East for it."

"Even the I.W.W. has reared its ugly head again," said the judge.

"I don't happen to approve of the tactics of the I.W.W.," said Mary stiffly.

"I should hope not," said her mother.

"But, Mother, don't you think you could let me have a couple of hundred dollars?"

"To spend on these dreadful agitators, they may not be I Won't Works but they're just as bad."

"I'll promise that every cent goes into milk for the babies."

"But that's just handing the miners over to these miserable Russian agitators. Naturally if they can give milk to the children it makes them popular, puts them in a position where they can mislead these poor miserable foreigners worse than ever." The judge leaned forward across the table and put his blueveined hand in its white starched cuff on Mary's mother's hand. "It's not that we lack sympathy with the plight of the miners' women and children, or that we don't understand the dreadful conditions of the whole mining industry . . . we know altogether too much about that, don't we, Hilda? But . . ."

Mary suddenly found that she'd folded her napkin and gotten trembling to her feet. "I don't see any reason for further prolonging this interview, that must be painful to you, Mother, as it is to me. . . ."

"Perhaps I can arbitrate," said the judge, smiling, getting to his feet with his napkin in his hand.

Mary felt a desperate tight feeling like a metal ring round her head. "I've got to go, Mother . . . I don't feel very well today. Have a nice trip. . . . I don't want to argue." Before they could

7. International Workers of the World, a labor organization committed to world revolution and general strikes, active during World War I and the 1920s.

stop her she was off down the hall and on her way down in the elevator.

Mary felt so upset she had to talk to somebody so she went to a telephone booth and called up Ada. Ada's voice was full of sobs, she said something dreadful had happened and that she'd called off her party and that Mary must come up to see her immediately. Even before Ada opened the door of the apartment on Madison Avenue Mary got a whiff of the Forêt Vierge[8] perfume Ada had taken to using when she first came to New York. Ada opened the door wearing a green and pink flowered silk wrapper with all sorts of little tassels hanging from it. She fell on Mary's neck. Her eyes were red and she sniffed as she talked. "Why, what's the matter, Ada?" asked Mary coolly. "Darling, I've just had the most dreadful row with Hjalmar. We have parted forever. . . . Of course I had to call off the party because I was giving it for him."

"Who's Hjalmar?"

"He's somebody very beautiful . . . and very hateful. . . . But let's talk about you, Mary darling . . . I do hope you've made it up with your brother and Judge Blake."

"I just walked out. . . . What's the use of arguing? They're on one side of the barricades and I'm on the other."

Ada strode up and down the room. "Oh, I hate talk like that. . . . It makes me feel awful. . . . At least you'll have a drink. . . . I've got to drink, I've been too nervous to practice all day."

Mary stayed all afternoon at Ada's drinking ginrickeys and eating the sandwiches and little cakes that had been laid out in the kitchenette for the party and talking about old times and Ada's unhappy loveaffair. Ada made Mary read all his letters and Mary said he was a damn fool and good riddance. Then Ada cried and Mary told her she ought to be ashamed of herself, she didn't know what real misery was. Ada was very meek about it and went to her desk and wrote out a check in a shaky hand for a hundred dollars for the miners' milkfund. Ada had some supper sent up for them from the uptown Longchamps and declared she'd spent the happiest afternoon in years. She made Mary promise to come to her concert in the small hall at the Aeolian the following week. When Mary was going Ada made her take a couple of dollars for a taxi. They were both reeling a little in the hall waiting for the elevator. "We've just gotten to be a pair of old topers," said Ada gaily. It was a good thing Mary had decided to take a taxi because she found it hard to stand on her feet.

That winter the situation of the miners in the Pittsburgh district got worse and worse. Evictions began. Families with little children were living in tents and in broken-down unheated tarpaper barracks. Mary lived in a feeling of nightmare, writing letters, mimeographing appeals, making speeches at meetings of cloth-

8. Virgin Forest, the name of a French perfume.

ing and fur workers, canvassing wealthy liberals. The money that
came in was never enough. She took no salary for her work so she
had to get Ada to lend her money to pay her rent. She was thin
and haggard and coughed all the time. Too many cigarettes, she'd
explain. Eddy Spellman and Rudy Goldfarb worried about her.
She could see they'd decided she wasn't eating enough because
she was all the time finding on the corner of her desk a paper
bag of sandwiches or a carton of coffee that one of them had
brought in. Once Eddy brought her a big package of smearcase[9] that
his mother had made up home near Scranton. She couldn't eat
it; she felt guilty every time she saw it sprouting green mold in
the icebox that had no ice in it because she'd given up cooking
now that Don was away.

One evening Rudy came into the office with smiles all over his
face. Eddy was leaning over packing the old clothes into bales as
usual for his next trip. Rudy gave him a light kick in the seat
of the pants. "Hay you, Trotzkyite,"[1] said Eddy, jumping at him
and pulling out his necktie. "Smile when you say that," said Rudy,
pummeling him. They were all laughing. Mary felt like an oldmaid
schoolteacher watching the boys roughhousing in front of her desk.
"Meeting comes to order," she said. "They tried to hang it on
me but they couldn't," said Rudy, panting, straightening his necktie and his mussed hair. "But what I was going to say, Comrade
French, was that I thought you might like to know that a certain
comrade is getting in on the *Aquitania* tomorrow . . . tourist class."
"Rudy, are you sure?" "Saw the cable."

Mary got to the dock too early and had to wait two hours.
She tried to read the afternoon papers but her eyes wouldn't follow
the print. It was too hot in the receptionroom and too cold outside. She fidgeted around miserably until at last she saw the enormous black sheetiron wall sliding with its rows of lighted portholes
past the opening in the wharfbuilding. Her hands and feet were
icy. Her whole body ached to feel his arms around her, for the
rasp of his deep voice in her ears. All the time a vague worry
flitted in the back of her head because she hadn't had a letter
from him while he'd been away.

Suddenly there he was coming down the gangplank alone, with
the old wicker suitcase in his hand. He had on a new belted German raincoat but the same checked cap. She was face to face
with him. He gave her a little hug but he didn't kiss her. There
was something odd in his voice. "Hello, Mary . . . I didn't expect to
find you here. . . . I don't want to be noticed, you know." His
voice had a low furtive sound in her ears. He was nervously
changing his suitcase from one hand to the other. "See you in a

9. Cottage cheese.
1. Follower of Leon Trotsky (1877–
1940), Russian Communist leader exiled
from Russia in 1928 for upholding the
aims of international communism
against the nationalistic policies of
Joseph Stalin.

few days . . . I'm going to be pretty busy." She turned without a word and ran down the wharf. She hurried breathless along the crosstown street to the Ninth Avenue el. When she opened her door the new turkeyred curtains were like a blow from a whip in her face.

She couldn't go back to the office. She couldn't bear the thought of facing the boys and the people she knew, the people who had known them together. She called up and said she had a bad case of grippe and would have to stay in bed a couple of days. She stayed all day in the blank misery of the narrow rooms. Towards evening she dozed off to sleep on the couch. She woke up with a start thinking she heard a step in the hall outside. It wasn't Don, the steps went on up the next flight. After that she didn't sleep any more.

The next morning the phone woke her just when she settled herself in bed to drowse a little. It was Sylvia Goldstein saying she was sorry Mary had the grippe and asking if there was anything she could do. Oh, no, she was fine, she was just going to stay in bed all day, Mary answered in a dead voice. "Well, I suppose you knew all the time about Comrade Stevens and Comrade Lichfield . . . you two were always so close . . . they were married in Moscow . . . she's an English comrade . . . she spoke at the big meeting at the Bronx Casino last night . . . she's got a great shock of red hair . . . stunning but some of the girls think it's dyed. Lots of the comrades didn't know you and Comrade Stevens had broken up . . . isn't it sad things like that have to happen in the movement?" "Oh, that was a long time ago. . . . Goodby, Sylvia," said Mary harshly and hung up. She called up a bootlegger she knew and told him to send her up a bottle of gin.

The next afternoon there was a light rap on the door and when Mary opened it a crack there was Ada wreathed in silver fox and breathing out a great gust of Forêt Vierge. "Oh, Mary darling, I knew something was the matter. . . . You know sometimes I'm quite psychic. And when you didn't come to my concert, first I was mad but then I said to myself I know the poor darling's sick. So I just went right down to your office. There was the handsomest boy there and I just made him tell me where you lived. He said you were sick with the grippe and so I came right over. My dear, why aren't you in bed? You look a sight."

"I'm all right," mumbled Mary numbly, pushing the stringy hair off her face. "I been . . . making plans . . . about how we can handle this relief situation better."

"Well, you're just coming up right away to my spare bedroom and let me pet you up a little. . . . I don't believe it's grippe, I think it's overwork. . . . If you're not careful you'll be having a nervous breakdown." "Maybe sumpen like that." Mary couldn't articulate her words. She didn't seem to have any will of her own any more; she did everything Ada told her. When she was settled in Ada's clean lavendersmelling spare bed they sent out for some barbital and it put her to sleep. Mary stayed there several days eating the meals Ada's maid brought her, drinking all the drinks Ada would give her, listening to the continual scrape of violin practice that came from the other room all morning. But at night she couldn't sleep without filling herself up with dope. She didn't seem to have any will left. It would take her a half an hour to decide to get up to go to the toilet.

After she'd been at Ada's a week she began to feel she ought to go home. She began to be impatient of Ada's sly references to unhappy loveaffairs and broken hearts and the beauty of abnegation and would snap Ada's head off whenever she started it. "That's fine," Ada would say. "You are getting your meanness back." For some time Ada had been bringing up the subject of somebody she knew who's been crazy about Mary for years and who was dying to see her again. Finally Mary gave in and said she would go to a cocktail party at Eveline Johnson's where Ada said she knew he'd be. "And Eveline gives the most wonderful parties. I don't know how she does it because she never has any money, but all the most interesting people in New York will be there. They always are. Radicals too, you know. Eveline can't live without her little group of reds."

Mary wore one of Ada's dresses that didn't fit her very well and went out in the morning to have her hair curled at Saks's where Ada always had hers curled. They had some cocktails at Ada's place before they went. At the last minute Mary said she couldn't go because she'd finally got it out of Ada that it was George Barrow who was going to be at the party. Ada made Mary drink another cocktail and a reckless feeling came over her and she said all right, let's get a move on.

There was a smiling colored maid in a fancy lace cap and apron at the door of the house who took them down the hall to a bedroom full of coats and furs where they were to take off their wraps. As Ada was doing her face at the dressingtable Mary whispered in her ear, "Just think what our reliefcommittee could do with the money that woman wastes on senseless entertaining." "But she's a darling," Ada whispered back excitedly. "Honestly, you'll like her." The door had opened behind their backs letting in a racketing gust of voices, laughs, tinkle of glasses, a whiff of perfume and toast and cigarettesmoke and gin. "Oh, Ada," came a ringing voice. "Eveline darling, how lovely you look. . . . This is Mary French, you know I said I'd bring her. . . . She's my oldest friend." Mary found herself shaking hands with a tall slender woman in a pearlgrey dress. Her face was very white and her lips were very red and her long large eyes were exaggerated with mascara. "So nice of you to come," Eveline Johnson said and sat down suddenly among the furs and wraps on the bed. "It sounds like a lovely party," cried Ada.

"I hate parties. I don't know why I give them," said Eveline Johnson. "Well, I guess I've got to go back to the menagerie. . . . Oh, Ada, I'm so tired."

Mary found herself studying the harsh desperate lines under the makeup round Mrs. Johnson's mouth and the strained tenseness of the cords of her neck. Their silly life tells on them, she was saying to herself.

"What about the play?" Ada was asking. "I was so excited when I heard about it."

"Oh, that's ancient history now," said Eveline Johnson sharply. "I'm working on a plan to bring over the ballet . . . turn it into something American. . . . I'll tell you about it some time."

"Oh, Eveline, did the screenstar come?"[2] asked Ada, giggling.

"Oh, yes, they always come." Eveline Johnson sighed. "She's beautiful. . . . You must meet her."

"Of course anybody in the world would come to your parties, Eveline."

"I don't know why they should . . . they seem just too boring to me." Eveline Johnson was ushering them through some sliding doors into a highceilinged room dusky from shaded lights and cigarettesmoke where they were swallowed up in a jam of well-dressed people talking and making faces and tossing their heads over cocktail glasses. There seemed no place to stand so Mary sat down at the end of a couch beside a little marbletopped table. The other people on the couch were jabbering away among themselves and paid no attention to her. Ada and the hostess had disappeared behind a wall of men's suits and afternoongowns.

Mary had had time to smoke an entire cigarette before Ada came back followed by George Barrow, whose thin face looked flushed and whose adamsapple stuck out further than ever over his collar. He had a cocktail in each hand. "Well well well, little Mary French, after all these years," he was saying with a kind of forced jollity. "If you knew the trouble we'd had getting these through the crush."

"Hello, George," said Mary casually. She took the cocktail he handed her and drank it off. After the other drinks she'd had it made her head spin. Somehow George and Ada managed to squeeze themselves in on the couch on either side of Mary. "I want to hear all about the coalstrike," George was saying, knitting his brows. "Too bad the insurgent locals had to choose a moment when a strike played right into the operators' hands." Mary got angry. "That's just the sort of remark I'd expect from a man of

2. **Margo Dowling,** a prominent character in *U.S.A.*

your sort. If we waited for a favorable moment there wouldn't be any strikes. . . . There never is any favorable moment for the workers."

"What sort of a man is a man of my sort?" said George Barrow with fake humility, so Mary thought. "That's what I often ask myself." "Oh, I don't want to argue . . . I'm sick and tired of arguing. . . . Get me another cocktail, George."

He got up obediently and started threading his way across the room. "Now, Mary, don't row with poor George. . . . He's so sweet. . . . Do you know, Margo Dowling really is here . . . and her husband and Rodney Cathcart . . . they're always together. They're on their way to the Riviera," Ada talked into her ear in a loud stage whisper. "I'm sick of seeing movie actors on the screen," said Mary, "I don't want to see them in real life."

Ada had slipped away. George was back with two more cocktails and a plate of cold salmon and cucumbers. She wouldn't eat anything. "Don't you think you'd better, with all the drinks?" She shook her head. "Well, I'll eat it myself. . . . You know, Mary," he went on, "I often wonder these days if I wouldn't have been a happier man if I'd just stayed all my life an expressagent in South Chicago and married some nice workinggirl and had a flock of kids. . . . I'd be a wealthier and a happier man today if I'd gone into business even." "Well, you don't look so badly off," said Mary. "You know it hurts me to be attacked as a laborfaker by you reds. . . . I may believe in compromise but I've gained some very substantial dollarsandcents victories. . . . What you communists won't see is that there are sometimes two sides to a case."

"I'm not a partymember," said Mary.

"I know . . . but you work with them. . . . Why should you think you know better what's good for the miners than their own tried and true leaders?" "If the miners ever had a chance to vote in their unions you'd find out how much they trust your sellout crowd."

George Barrow shook his head. "Mary, Mary . . . just the same headstrong warmhearted girl."

"Rubbish, I haven't any feelings at all any more. I've seen how it works in the field. . . . It doesn't take a good heart to know which end of a riotgun's pointed at you."

"Mary, I'm a very unhappy man."

"Get me another cocktail, George."

Mary had time to smoke two cigarettes before George came back. The nodding jabbering faces, the dresses, the gestures with hands floated in a smoky haze before her eyes. The crowd was beginning to thin a little when George came back all flushed and smiling. "Well, I had the pleasure of exchanging a few words with Miss Dowling, she was most charming. . . . But do you know what Red Haines tells me? I wonder if it's true. . . . It seems she's through; it seems that she's no good for talkingpictures . . . voice sounds like the croaking of an old crow over the loudspeaker," he giggled a little drunkenly. "There she is now, she's just leaving."

A hush had fallen over the room. Through the dizzy swirl of cigarettesmoke Mary saw a small woman with blue eyelids and features regular as those of a porcelain doll under a mass of pale-blond hair turn for a second to smile at somebody before she went out through the sliding doors. She had on a yellow dress and a lot of big sapphires. A tall bronzefaced actor and a bowlegged sallowfaced little man followed her out, and Eveline Johnson talking and talking in her breathless hectic way swept after them.

Mary was looking at it all through a humming haze like seeing a play from way up in a smoky balcony. Ada came and stood in front of her rolling her eyes and opening her mouth wide when she talked. "Oh, isn't it a wonderful party. . . . I met her. She had the loveliest manners . . . I don't know why, I expected her to be kinda tough. They say she came from the gutter."

"Not at all," said George. "Her people were Spaniards of noble birth who lived in Cuba."

"Ada, I want to go home," said Mary.

"Just a minute . . . I haven't had a chance to talk to dear Eveline. . . . She looks awfully tired and nervous today, poor dear." A lily-pale young man brushed past them laughing over his shoulder at an older woman covered with silver lamé who followed him, her scrawny neck, wattled under the powder, thrust out and her hooknose quivering and eyes bulging over illconcealed pouches.

"Ada, I want to go home."

"I thought you and I and George might have dinner together." Mary was seeing blurred faces getting big as they came towards her, changing shape as they went past, fading into the gloom like fish opening and closing their mouths in an aquarium.

"How about it? Miss Cohn, have you seen Charles Edward Holden around? He's usually quite a feature of Eveline's parties." Mary hated George Barrow's doggy pop-eyed look when he talked. "Now there's a sound intelligent fellow for you. I can talk to him all night."

Ada narrowed her eyes as she leaned over and whispered shrilly in George Barrow's ear. "He's engaged to be married to somebody else. Eveline's cut up about it. She's just living on her nerve."

"George, if we've got to stay . . ." Mary said, "get me another cocktail."

A broadfaced woman in spangles with very red cheeks who was sitting on the couch beside Mary leaned across and said in a stage whisper, "Isn't it dreadful? . . . You know I think it's most ungrateful of Holdy after all Eveline's done for him . . . in a social

way . . . since she took him up . . . now he's accepted anywhere.
I know the girl . . . a little bitch if there ever was one . . . not
even wealthy."

"Shush," said Ada. "Here's Eveline now. . . . Well, Eveline
dear, the captains and the kings depart. Soon there'll be nothing but
us smallfry left."

"She didn't seem awful bright to me," said Eveline, dropping
into a chair beside them. "Let me get you a drink, Eveline dear,"
said Ada. Eveline shook her head. "What you need, Eveline, my
dear," said the broadfaced woman, leaning across the couch again,
". . . is a good trip abroad. New York's impossible after January . . .
I shan't attempt to stay. . . . It would just mean a nervous breakdown if I did."

"I thought maybe I might go to Morocco sometime if I could
scrape up the cash," said Eveline.

"Try Tunis, my dear. Tunis is divine."

After she'd drunk the cocktail Barrow brought Mary sat there
seeing faces, hearing voices in a blank hateful haze. It took all her
attention not to teeter on the edge of the couch. "I really must
go." She had hold of George's arm crossing the room. She could
walk very well but she couldn't talk very well. In the bedroom
Ada was helping her on with her coat. Eveline Johnson was there
with her big hazel eyes and her teasing singsong voice. "Oh, Ada,
it was sweet of you to come. I'm afraid it was just too boring. . . .
Oh, Miss French, I so wanted to talk to you about the miners . . .
I never get a chance to talk about things I'm really interested in
any more. Do you know, Ada, I don't think I'll ever do this again.
. . . It's just too boring." She put her long hand to her temple
and rubbed the fingers slowly across her forehead. "Oh, Ada, I
hope they go home soon. . . . I've got such a headache."

"Oughtn't you to take something for it?"

"I will. I've got a wonderful painkiller. Ask me up next time
you play Bach, Ada . . . I'd like that. You know it does seem too
silly to spend your life filling up rooms with illassorted people who
really hate each other." Eveline Johnson followed them all the
way down the hall to the front door as if she didn't want to let
them go. She stood in her thin dress in the gust of cold wind that
came from the open door while George went to the corner to get
a cab. "Eveline, go back in, you'll catch your death," said Ada.
"Well, goodby . . . you were darlings to come." As the door closed
slowly behind her Mary watched Eveline Johnson's narrow shoulders. She was shivering as she walked back down the hall.

Mary reeled, suddenly feeling drunk in the cold air and Ada
put her arm round her to steady her. "Oh, Mary," Ada said in
her ear, "I wish everybody wasn't so unhappy."

"It's the waste," Mary cried out savagely, suddenly able to articulate. Ada and George Barrow were helping her into the cab. "The food they waste and the money they waste while our people starve in tarpaper barracks." "The contradictions of capitalism," said George Barrow with a knowing leer. "How about a bite to eat?"

"Take me home first. No, not to Ada's," Mary almost yelled. "I'm sick of this parasite life. I'm going back to the office tomorrow. . . . I've got to call up tonight to see if they got in all right with that load of condensed milk. . . ." She picked up Ada's hand, suddenly feeling like old times again, and squeezed it. "Ada, you've been sweet, honestly you've saved my life."

"Ada's the perfect cure for hysterical people like us," said George Barrow. The taxi had stopped beside the row of garbagecans in front of the house where Mary lived. "No, I can walk up alone," she said harshly and angrily again. "It's just that being tiredout a drink makes me feel funny. Goodnight. I'll get my bag at your place tomorrow." Ada and Barrow went off in the taxicab with their heads together chatting and laughing. They've forgotten me already, thought Mary as she made her way up the stairs. She made the stairs all right but had some trouble getting the key in the lock. When the door finally would open she went straight to the couch in the front room and lay down and fell heavily asleep.

In the morning she felt more rested than she had in years. She got up early and ate a big breakfast with bacon and eggs at Childs on the way to the office. Rudy Goldfarb was already there, sitting at her desk.

He got up and stared at her without speaking for a moment. His eyes were red and bloodshot and his usually sleek black hair was all over his forehead. "What's the matter, Rudy?"

"Comrade French, they got Eddy."

"You mean they arrested him."

"Arrested him nothing, they shot him."

"They killed him." Mary felt a wave of nausea rising in her. The room started to spin around. She clenched her fists and the room fell into place again. Rudy was telling her how some miners had found the truck wrecked in a ditch. At first they thought that it had been an accident but when they picked up Eddy Spellman he had a bullet-hole through his temple.

"We've got to have a protest meeting . . . do they know about it over at the Party?"

"Sure, they're trying to get Madison Square Garden. But, Comrade French, he was one hell of a swell kid." Mary was shaking all over. The phone rang. Rudy answered it. "Comrade French, they want you over there right away. They want you to be secretary of the committee for the protest meeting." Mary let herself drop into the chair at her desk for a moment and began noting down the names of organizations to be notified. Suddenly she looked up and looked Rudy straight in the eye. "Do you know what we've got to do . . . we've got to move the reliefcommittee to Pittsburgh. I knew all along we ought to have been in Pittsburgh."

"Risky business."

"We ought to have been in Pittsburgh all along," Mary said firmly and quietly.

The phone rang again.

"It's somebody for you, Comrade French."

As soon as the receiver touched Mary's ear there was Ada talking and talking. At first Mary couldn't make out what it was about. "But, Mary darling, haven't you read the papers?" "No, I said I hadn't. You mean about Eddy Spellman?" "No, darling, it's too awful, you remember we were just there yesterday for a cocktail party . . . you must remember, Eveline Johnson, it's so awful. I've sent out and got all the papers. Of course the tabloids all say it's suicide." "Ada, I don't understand." "But, Mary, I'm trying to tell you . . . I'm so upset I can't talk . . . she was such a lovely woman, so talented, an artist really. . . . Well, when the maid got there this morning she found her dead in her bed and we were just there twelve hours before. It gives me the horrors. Some of the papers say it was an overdose of a sleeping medicine. She couldn't have meant to do it. If we'd only known we might have been able to do something, you know she said she had a headache. Don't you think you could come up, I can't stay here alone I feel so terrible." "Ada, I can't. . . . Something very serious has happened in Pennsylvania. I have a great deal of work to do organizing a protest. Goodbye, Ada." Mary hung up, frowning.

"Say, Rudy, if Ada Cohn calls up again tell her I'm out of the office. . . . I have too much to do to spend my time taking care of hysterical women a day like this." She put on her hat, collected her papers, and hurried over to the meeting of the committee.

Vag

The young man waits at the edge of the concrete, with one hand he grips a rubbed suitcase of phony leather, the other hand almost making a fist, thumb up

that moves in ever so slight an arc when a car slithers past, a truck roars clatters; the wind of cars passing ruffles his hair, slaps grit in his face.

Head swims, hunger has twisted the belly tight,

he has skinned a heel through the torn sock, feet ache in the broken shoes, under the threadbare suit carefully brushed off with the hand, the torn drawers have a crummy feel, the feel of having slept in your clothes; in the nostrils lingers the staleness of discouraged carcasses crowded into a transient camp, the carbolic stench of the jail, on the taut cheeks the shamed flush from the boring eyes of cops and deputies, railroadbulls (they eat three squares a day, they are buttoned into wellmade clothes, they have wives to sleep with, kids to play with after supper, they work for the big men who buy their way, they stick their chests out with the sureness of power behind their backs). Git the hell out, scram. Know what's good for you, you'll make yourself scarce. Gittin' tough, eh? Think you kin take it, eh?

The punch in the jaw, the slam on the head with the nightstick, the wrist grabbed and twisted behind the back, the big knee brought up sharp into the crotch,

the walk out of town with sore feet to stand and wait at the edge of the hissing speeding string of cars where the reek of ether and lead and gas melts into the silent grassy smell of the earth.

Eyes black with want seek out the eyes of the drivers, a hitch, a hundred miles down the road.

Overhead in the blue a plane drones. Eyes follow the silver Douglas that flashes once in the sun and bores its smooth way out of sight into the blue.

(The transcontinental passengers sit pretty, big men with bankaccounts, highlypaid jobs, who are saluted by doormen; telephonegirls say goodmorning to them. Last night after a fine dinner, drinks with friends, they left Newark. Roar of climbing motors slanting up into the inky haze. Lights drop away. An hour staring along a silvery wing at a big lonesome moon hurrying west through curdling scum. Beacons flash in a line across Ohio.

At Cleveland the plane drops banking in a smooth spiral, the string of lights along the lake swings in a circle. Climbing roar of the motors again; slumped in the soft seat drowsing through the flat moonlight night.

Chi. A glimpse of the dipper. Another spiral swoop from cool into hot air thick with dust and the reek of burnt prairies.

Beyond the Mississippi dawn creeps up behind through the murk over the great plains. Puddles of mist go white in the Iowa hills, farms, fences, silos, steel glint from a river. The blinking eyes of the beacons reddening into day. Watercourses vein the eroded hills.

Omaha. Great cumulus clouds, from coppery churning to creamy to silvery white, trail brown skirts of rain over the hot plains. Red and yellow badlands, tiny horned shapes of cattle.

Cheyenne. The cool high air smells of sweetgrass.

The tightbaled clouds to westward burst and scatter in tatters over the strawcolored hills. Indigo mountains jut rimrock. The plane breasts a huge crumbling cloudbank and toboggans over bumpy air across green and crimson slopes into the sunny dazzle of Salt Lake.

The transcontinental passenger thinks contracts, profits, vacationtrips, mighty continent between Atlantic and Pacific, power, wires humming dollars, cities jammed, hills empty, the indiantrail leading into the wagonroad, the macadamed pike, the concrete skyway; trains, planes: history the billiondollar speedup,

and in the bumpy air over the desert ranges towards Las Vegas
sickens and vomits into the carton container the steak and mushrooms he ate in New York. No matter, silver in the pocket, greenbacks in the wallets, drafts, certified checks, plenty restaurants in
L.A.)

The young man waits on the side of the road; the plane has gone;
thumb moves in a small arc when a car tears hissing past. Eyes
seek the driver's eyes. A hundred miles down the road. Head swims,
belly tightens, wants crawl over his skin like ants:

went to school, books said opportunity, ads promised speed, own
your home, shine bigger than your neighbor, the radiocrooner
whispered girls, ghosts of platinum girls coaxed from the screen,
millions in winnings were chalked up on the boards in the offices,
paychecks were for hands willing to work, the cleared desk of an
executive with three telephones on it;

waits with swimming head, needs knot the belly, idle hands numb,
beside the speeding traffic.

A hundred miles down the road.

1936, 1937

F. SCOTT FITZGERALD
1896–1940

In Fitzgerald's essay *The Crack-Up*, where he traces the process of emotional disintegration that followed his spectacular early success as a
writer and moneymaker, he declares that "the test of a first-rate intelligence is the ability to hold two opposed ideas in the mind at the same
time, and still retain the ability to function."[1] Fitzgerald's own career
may be viewed as a series of struggles to achieve this ideal convergence
of intellectual tension and productive capacity. His work at its best sustains the tensions that his personal life finally buckled under: his dual roles
as representative and critic of the decade he labeled "The Jazz Age"; his
fascination with wealth, along with his horror at the "vast carelessness"
and varieties of dehumanization which afflict its possessors; his romantic
idealization of sexual love along with his suspicion of its economic under-
pinnings and its risks of self-destruction. As the critic Lionel Trilling
remarked, Fitzgerald's success lies less in his narrative power than in the
delicate and elegant "voice of his prose,"[2] which rarely loses its irony
in his involvement and never sacrifices its sympathy in his detachment.

Francis Scott Key Fitzgerald was born in St. Paul, Minnesota, in 1896.
His father never attained the social status of his maternal ancestors—
southern landowners and legislators from the early colonial period—but
he retained their upper-class manners despite numerous commercial failures. His mother, the daughter of a prosperous Irish immigrant, was a
dominant and eccentric woman whose devotion to her only son grew
more fervent as the family moved from apartment to apartment and city

1. *The Crack-Up*, p. 69.   2. *The Liberal Imagination*, p. 253.

to city in order to keep marginally solvent. At fifteen Fitzgerald was sent
to a Catholic boarding school in New Jersey (an aunt paid the tuition
in the hope of gaining a more disciplined and pious nephew); two years
later he enrolled at Princeton. There, he helped write and produce the
Triangle Club's annual musical comedies and participated on or behind
stage in campus theatricals, and wrote for the college literary magazines.
Friendships with campus intellectuals—Professor Christian Gauss, Edmund Wilson, and John Peale Bishop, who later became prominent as
critic and poet—nourished his ambition to become a writer. But neglect
of academic study disqualified him from extracurricular activities, and he
left college in 1917 to accept an army commission.

Stationed near Montgomery, Alabama, he fell in love with Zelda Sayre,
a talented, high-spirited beauty. Enshrined in his idealizing imagination,
she seemed entitled to the luxurious and romantic life they both desired;
after their engagement her demands for his financial and professional
success made for a protracted and tempestuous courtship. After his discharge from the army in 1919 Fitzgerald went to New York—the "land
of ambition and success," he called it[3]—to make a fortune. He made
less than that at his job with an advertising agency; his long-distance
engagement became strained and Zelda soon broke it off. Fitzgerald
then quit his job and returned to St. Paul to finish a novel entitled *The
Romantic Egoist* which he had begun in college and had worked on in
army training camps, the story of a flamboyant young man's coming of
age at Princeton. It was published in 1920 as *This Side of Paradise*, and
one week later, while the book's sales skyrocketed, Fitzgerald and Zelda
Sayre were married.

This Side of Paradise sold forty thousand copies in its first year and
Fitzgerald became a hero of popular culture. He looked back in the
1930s on his early success as an illusion-ridden period in his life when
success came inexplicably but tempted him to believe in his personal
destiny and enticed him to play a role, for which he was not equipped, as
"spokesman" for his time and "its typical product."[4] Yet Fitzgerald was
better equipped than he recognized to represent his age and his profession. The monetary success of his first novel had enabled him to ransom
his fairy princess and to re-create his life in the shape of his fantasy, producing in his personal experience a precarious and highly charged union
of material success and idealization. This union of the material and the
ideal corresponded to the quest for material affluence, excitement, and
intellectual liberation that emerged among the privileged young in the
1920s. At the same time the tension between the monetary and the ideal,
and Fitzgerald's scrupulously ambivalent treatment of it in such works
as *The Rich Boy*, placed his fiction in line with that recurring theme in
such earlier writers as Melville, Hawthorne, and Henry James and lent
his writing an historical significance beyond its value as a document of
the Twenties. The hero of one masterpiece, Jay Gatsby, is a wealthy
gangster who longs to win a sweetheart in the glamorous upper-class
society of Long Island, but he is also a midwestern boy who is enchanted,
like Benjamin Franklin earlier, by the American dream of success and
recognition; he is a person whose identity is created by his ideal "Platonic

3. Quoted by Arthur Mizener, *The Far
Side of Paradise*, p. 86.

4. "My Lost City," *The Crack-Up*, p.
27.

conception of himself" and whose beloved seems an incarnation of his "unutterable visions."[5] His tragic career is not only a phenomenon of the Jazz Age but a haunting version of America's history and Fitzgerald's own life. Gatsby's illusions render him vulnerable to delusion and the disdain of others, but they give him a dignity and pathos that is not matched in the fashionably wealthy society, feckless and deceptively elegant, that excludes him.

The Fitzgeralds lived extravagantly in New York City, in St. Paul, and on Long Island, spending money faster than two collections of short stories (*Flappers and Philosophers*, 1921, and *Tales of the Jazz Age*, 1922) and his second novel (*The Beautiful and Damned*, 1922) could earn it. For two and a half years after 1924 the Fitzgeralds lived in Europe among such expatriated Americans as Hemingway, Gertrude Stein, and Ezra Pound. During this time *The Great Gatsby* appeared (1925) and in 1926 he published *All the Sad Young Men*, which, along with his last volume of stories, *Taps at Reveille* (1935), contains his best short fiction. The market for short fiction was a lucrative one, and throughout the Twenties and Thirties Fitzgerald often allowed the prospect of easy money to seduce him into writing substandard stories. This practice gradually eroded his self-esteem and contributed to his subsequent bouts of despair and profligacy.

In December, 1926, the family returned to the United States. Fitzgerald stopped briefly in Hollywood to fulfill his first assignment as a screen writer. Then he settled with Zelda and their daughter, Scottie, near Wilmington, Delaware, where financial problems, Fitzgerald's alcoholism, and Zelda's frustrated artistic ambitions dominated their lives. (She was a writer whose talent Fitzgerald denigrated and discouraged, and in 1928 she became obsessed with a belated desire to become a ballerina). Back in Europe in 1930, Zelda suffered the first in a series of breakdowns which necessitated her residence in mental institutions for most of the remaining seventeen years of her life. Fitzgerald returned permanently to the United States in 1931, establishing residence eventually in the vicinity of Baltimore to be near Zelda's hospitals. In 1934 he published his second masterpiece, *Tender Is the Night*, which traces the decline of a young American psychiatrist whose personal energies are sapped, and his professional career corroded, by his marriage to a beautiful and wealthy patient. The protagonist's attempt to salvage the rituals of domestic harmony and social affability in a community of expatriates on the French Riviera is an elegy to values that are vanishing in his society.

In 1937, after several alcoholic and infirm years, when his income from writing all but disappeared, Fitzgerald went to work regularly as a screen-writer in Hollywood. His salaries enabled him to recoup his finances and provide for the education of his daughter, and, bolstered by a love affair with the journalist Sheilah Graham, he hoped to revive his career as a writer of fiction. He died of a heart attack at the age of forty-four in New York, leaving unfinished his novel about a self-made mogul of the film industry, *The Last Tycoon*.

The posthumous publication of *The Last Tycoon* in 1941, and of the collection of essays and miscellanies, *The Crack-Up* (edited by his friend Edmund Wilson), in 1945, revived critical interest in Fitzgerald and

5. *The Great Gatsby*, pp. 99, 112.

secured his reputation as a celebrant, and a diagnostician, of twentieth-century manners and morals. As he learned to discipline the self-indulgence and extravagance of his early novels, he achieved a firmness of narrative structure that he modeled on the fiction of the British novelist Joseph Conrad and that of Henry James: intelligent and wary, but sensitive and sympathetic, observers (like the narrator in *The Rich Boy*) enable him to focus on the fascinating behavior of his protagonists and the enchanting surfaces of their worlds, while exposing beneath them the ambiguous motives, the violence that threatens, the affluence that paralyzes while seeming to release affection, the presumption to dominate that makes one incapable of love.

The Rich Boy is printed from *All the Sad Young Men*. *The Crack-Up, Handle with Care, Pasting It Together,* and *Early Success* are from *The Crack-Up*.

The Rich Boy

Begin with an individual, and before you know it you find that you have created a type; begin with a type, and you find that you have created—nothing. That is because we are all queer fish, queerer behind our faces and voices than we want any one to know or than we know ourselves. When I hear a man proclaiming himself an "average, honest, open fellow," I feel pretty sure that he has some definite and perhaps terrible abnormality which he has agreed to conceal—and his protestation of being average and honest and open is his way of reminding himself of his misprision.

There are no types, no plurals. There is a rich boy, and this is his and not his brothers' story. All my life I have lived among his brothers but this one has been my friend. Besides, if I wrote about his brothers I should have to begin by attacking all the lies that the poor have told about the rich and the rich have told about themselves—such a wild structure they have erected that when we pick up a book about the rich, some instinct prepares us for un-reality. Even the intelligent and impassioned reporters of life have made the country of the rich as unreal as fairy-land.

Let me tell you about the very rich. They are different from you and me. They possess and enjoy early, and it does something to them, makes them soft where we are hard, and cynical where we are trustful, in a way that, unless you were born rich, it is very difficult to understand. They think, deep in their hearts, that they are better than we are because we had to discover the compensations and refuges of life for ourselves. Even when they enter deep into our world or sink below us, they still think that they are better than we are. They are different. The only way I can describe young Anson Hunter is to approach him as if he were a foreigner and cling stubbornly to my point of view. If I accept his for a moment I am lost—I have nothing to show but a preposterous movie.

II

Anson was the eldest of six children who would some day divide a fortune of fifteen million dollars, and he reached the age of reason—is it seven?—at the beginning of the century when daring young women were already gliding along Fifth Avenue in electric "mobiles." In those days he and his brother had an English governess who spoke the language very clearly and crisply and well, so that the two boys grew to speak as she did—their words and sentences were all crisp and clear and not run together as ours are. They didn't talk exactly like English children but acquired an accent that is peculiar to fashionable people in the city of New York.

In the summer the six children were moved from the house on 71st Street to a big estate in northern Connecticut. It was not a fashionable locality—Anson's father wanted to delay as long as possible his children's knowledge of that side of life. He was a man somewhat superior to his class, which composed New York society, and to his period, which was the snobbish and formalized vulgarity of the Gilded Age,[1] and he wanted his sons to learn habits of concentration and have sound constitutions and grow up into right-living and successful men. He and his wife kept an eye on them as well as they were able until the two older boys went away to school, but in huge establishments this is difficult—it was much simpler in the series of small and medium-sized houses in which my own youth was spent—I was never far out of the reach of my mother's voice, of the sense of her presence, her approval or disapproval.

Anson's first sense of his superiority came to him when he realized the half-grudging American deference that was paid to him in the Connecticut village. The parents of the boys he played with always inquired after his father and mother, and were vaguely excited when their own children were asked to the Hunters' house. He accepted this as the natural state of things, and a sort of impatience with all groups of which he was not the centre—in money, in position, in authority—remained with him for the rest of his life. He disdained to struggle with other boys for precedence—he expected it to be given him freely, and when it wasn't he withdrew into his family. His family was sufficient, for in the East money is still a somewhat feudal thing, a clan-forming thing. In the snobbish West, money separates families to form "sets."

At eighteen, when he went to New Haven, Anson was tall and thick-set, with a clear complexion and a healthy color from the ordered life he had led in school. His hair was yellow and grew

1. Era of economic expansion and political corruption following the Civil War, named from Mark Twain's and Charles Dudley Warner's novel *The Gilded Age* (1873).

in a funny way on his head, his nose was beaked—these two things kept him from being handsome—but he had a confident charm and a certain brusque style, and the upper-class men who passed him on the street knew without being told that he was a rich boy and had gone to one of the best schools. Nevertheless, his very superiority kept him from being a success in college—the independence was mistaken for egotism, and the refusal to accept Yale standards with the proper awe seemed to belittle all those who had. So, long before he graduated, he began to shift the centre of his life to New York.

He was at home in New York—there was his own house with "the kind of servants you can't get any more"—and his own family, of which, because of his good humor and a certain ability to make things go, he was rapidly becoming the centre, and the débutante parties, and the correct manly world of the men's clubs, and the occasional wild spree with the gallant girls whom New Haven only knew from the fifth row.[2] His aspirations were conventional enough—they included even the irreproachable shadow he would some day marry, but they differed from the aspirations of the majority of young men in that there was no mist over them, none of that quality which is variously known as "idealism" or "illusion." Anson accepted without reservation the world of high finance and high extravagance, of divorce and dissipation, of snobbery and of privilege. Most of our lives end as a compromise—it was as a compromise that his life began.

He and I first met in the late summer of 1917 when he was just out of Yale, and, like the rest of us, was swept up into the systematized hysteria of the war. In the blue-green uniform of the naval aviation he came down to Pensacola, where the hotel orchestras played "I'm sorry, dear," and we young officers danced with the girls. Every one liked him, and though he ran with the drinkers and wasn't an especially good pilot, even the instructors treated him with a certain respect. He was always having long talks with them in his confident, logical voice—talks which ended by his getting himself, or, more frequently, another officer, out of some impending trouble. He was convivial, bawdy, robustly avid for pleasure, and we were all surprised when he fell in love with a conservative and rather proper girl.

Her name was Paula Legendre, a dark, serious beauty from somewhere in California. Her family kept a winter residence just outside of town, and in spite of her primness she was enormously popular; there is a large class of men whose egotism can't endure humor in a woman. But Anson wasn't that sort, and I couldn't understand the attraction of her "sincerity"—that was the thing to say about her—for his keen and somewhat sardonic mind.

---

2. I.e., chorus girls or performers in burlesque theaters.

Nevertheless, they fell in love—and on her terms. He no longer joined the twilight gathering at the De Sota bar, and whenever they were seen together they were engaged in a long, serious dialogue, which must have gone on several weeks. Long afterward he told me that it was not about anything in particular but was composed on both sides of immature and even meaningless statements—the emotional content that gradually came to fill it grew up not out of the words but out of its enormous seriousness. It was a sort of hypnosis. Often it was interrupted, giving way to that emasculated humor we call fun; when they were alone it was resumed again, solemn, low-keyed, and pitched so as to give each other a sense of unity in feeling and thought. They came to resent any interruptions of it, to be unresponsive to facetiousness about life, even to the mild cynicism of their contemporaries. They were only happy when the dialogue was going on, and its seriousness bathed them like the amber glow of an open fire. Toward the end there came an interruption they did not resent—it began to be interrupted by passion.

Oddly enough, Anson was as engrossed in the dialogue as she was and as profoundly affected by it, yet at the same time aware that on his side much was insincere, and on hers much was merely simple. At first, too, he despised her emotional simplicity as well, but with his love her nature deepened and blossomed, and he could despise it no longer. He felt that if he could enter into Paula's warm safe life he would be happy. The long preparation of the dialogue removed any constraint—he taught her some of what he had learned from more adventurous women, and she responded with a rapt holy intensity. One evening after a dance they agreed to marry, and he wrote a long letter about her to his mother. The next day Paula told him that she was rich, that she had a personal fortune of nearly a million dollars.

III

It was exactly as if they could say "Neither of us has anything: we shall be poor together"—just as delightful that they should be rich instead. It gave them the same communion of adventure. Yet when Anson got leave in April, and Paula and her mother accompanied him North, she was impressed with the standing of his family in New York and with the scale on which they lived. Alone with Anson for the first time in the rooms where he had played as a boy, she was filled with a comfortable emotion, as though she were pre-eminently safe and taken care of. The pictures of Anson in a skull cap at his first school, of Anson on horseback with the sweetheart of a mysterious forgotten summer, of Anson in a gay group of ushers and bridesmaid at a wedding, made her jealous of his life apart from her in the past, and so completely did his **authoritative person** seem to sum up and typify these possessions of his that she was inspired with the idea of being married immediately and returning to Pensacola as his wife.

But an immediate marriage wasn't discussed—even the engagement was to be secret until after the war. When she realized that only two days of his leave remained, her dissatisfaction crystallized in the intention of making him as unwilling to wait as she was. They were driving to the country for dinner and she determined to force the issue that night.

Now a cousin of Paula's was staying with them at the Ritz,[3] a severe, bitter girl who loved Paula but was somewhat jealous of her impressive engagement, and as Paula was late in dressing, the cousin, who wasn't going to the party, received Anson in the parlor of the suite.

Anson had met friends at five o'clock and drunk freely and indiscreetly with them for an hour. He left the Yale Club at a proper time, and his mother's chauffeur drove him to the Ritz, but his usual capacity was not in evidence, and the impact of the steam-heated sitting-room made him suddenly dizzy. He knew it, and he was both amused and sorry.

Paula's cousin was twenty-five, but she was exceptionally naïve, and at first failed to realize what was up. She had never met Anson before, and she was surprised when he mumbled strange information and nearly fell off his chair, but until Paula appeared it didn't occur to her that what she had taken for the odor of a dry-cleaned uniform was really whiskey. But Paula understood as soon as she appeared; her only thought was to get Anson away before her mother saw him, and at the look in her eyes the cousin understood too.

When Paula and Anson descended to the limousine they found two men inside, both asleep; they were the men with whom he had been drinking at the Yale Club, and they were also going to the party. He had entirely forgotten their presence in the car. On the way to Hempstead[4] they awoke and sang. Some of the songs were rough, and though Paula tried to reconcile herself to the fact that Anson had few verbal inhibitions, her lips tightened with shame and distaste.

Back at the hotel the cousin, confused and agitated, considered the incident, and then walked into Mrs. Legendre's bedroom, saying: "Isn't he funny?"

"Who is funny?"

"Why—Mr. Hunter. He seemed so funny."

Mrs. Legendre looked at her sharply.

"How is he funny?"

"Why, he said he was French. I didn't know he was French."

"That's absurd. You must have misunderstood." She smiled: "It was a joke."

The cousin shook her head stubbornly.

---

3. Swank hotel in New York City.   4. Town on Long Island.

"No. He said he was brought up in France. He said he couldn't speak any English, and that's why he couldn't talk to me. And he couldn't!"

Mrs. Legendre looked away with impatience just as the cousin added thoughtfully, "Perhaps it was because he was so drunk," and walked out of the room.

This curious report was true. Anson, finding his voice thick and uncontrollable, had taken the unusual refuge of announcing that he spoke no English. Years afterward he used to tell that part of the story, and he invariably communicated the uproarious laughter which the memory aroused in him.

Five times in the next hour Mrs. Legendre tried to get Hempstead on the phone. When she succeeded, there was a ten-minute delay before she heard Paula's voice on the wire.

"Cousin Jo told me Anson was intoxicated."

"Oh, no. . . ."

"Oh, yes. Cousin Jo says he was intoxicated. He told her he was French, and fell off his chair and behaved as if he was very intoxicated. I don't want you to come home with him."

"Mother, he's all right! Please don't worry about ———"

"But I do worry. I think it's dreadful. I want you to promise me not to come home with him."

"I'll take care of it, mother. . . ."

"I don't want you to come home with him."

"All right, mother. Good-by."

"Be sure now, Paula. Ask some one to bring you."

Deliberately Paula took the receiver from her ear and hung it up. Her face was flushed with helpless annoyance. Anson was stretched asleep out in a bedroom up-stairs, while the dinner-party below was proceeding lamely toward conclusion.

The hour's drive had sobered him somewhat—his arrival was merely hilarious—and Paula hoped that the evening was not spoiled, after all, but two imprudent cocktails before dinner completed the disaster. He talked boisterously and somewhat offensively to the party at large for fifteen minutes, and then slid silently under the table; like a man in an old print—but, unlike an old print, it was rather horrible without being at all quaint. None of the young girls present remarked upon the incident—it seemed to merit only silence. His uncle and two other men carried him up-stairs, and it was just after this that Paula was called to the phone.

An hour later Anson awoke in a fog of nervous agony, through which he perceived after a moment the figure of his uncle Robert standing by the door.

". . . I said are you better?"

"What?"

"Do you feel better, old man?"

"Terrible," said Anson.

"I'm going to try you on another bromo-seltzer. If you can hold it down, it'll do you good to sleep."

With an effort Anson slid his legs from the bed and stood up.

"I'm all right," he said dully.

"Take it easy."

"I thin' if you gave me a glassbrandy I could go down-stairs."

"Oh, no——"

"Yes, that's the only thin'. I'm all right now. . . . I suppose I'm in Dutch[5] dow' there."

"They know you're a little under the weather," said his uncle deprecatingly. "But don't worry about it. Schuyler didn't even get here. He passed away in the locker-room over at the Links."[6]

Indifferent to any opinion, except Paula's, Anson was nevertheless determined to save the débris of the evening, but when after a cold bath he made his appearance most of the party had already left. Paula got up immediately to go home.

In the limousine the old serious dialogue began. She had known that he drank, she admitted, but she had never expected anything like this—it seemed to her that perhaps they were not suited to each other, after all. Their ideas about life were too different, and so forth. When she finished speaking, Anson spoke in turn, very soberly. Then Paula said she'd have to think it over; she wouldn't decide to-night; she was not angry but she was terribly sorry. Nor would she let him come into the hotel with her, but just before she got out of the car she leaned and kissed him unhappily on the cheek.

The next afternoon Anson had a long talk with Mrs. Legendre while Paula sat listening in silence. It was agreed that Paula was to brood over the incident for a proper period and then, if mother and daughter thought it best, they would follow Anson to Pensacola. On his part he apologized with sincerity and dignity—that was all; with every card in her hand Mrs. Legendre was unable to establish any advantage over him. He made no promises, showed no humility, only delivered a few serious comments on life which brought him off with rather a moral superiority at the end. When they came South three weeks later, neither Anson in his satisfaction nor Paula in her relief at the reunion realized that the psychological moment had passed forever.

IV

He dominated and attracted her, and at the same time filled her with anxiety. Confused by his mixture of solidity and self-indulgence, of sentiment and cynicism—incongruities which her gentle mind was unable to resolve—Paula grew to think of him as two alternating personalities. When she saw him alone, or at a formal party, or with his casual inferiors, she felt a tremendous

5. Slang: in trouble.   6. Golf course.

pride in his strong, attractive presence, the paternal, understanding stature of his mind. In other company she became uneasy when what had been a fine imperviousness to mere gentility showed its other face. The other face was gross, humorous, reckless of everything but pleasure. It startled her mind temporarily away from him, even led her into a short covert experiment with an old beau, but it was no use—after four months of Anson's enveloping vitality there was an anæmic pallor in all other men.

In July he was ordered abroad, and their tenderness and desire reached a crescendo. Paula considered a last-minute marriage—decided against it only because there were always cocktails on his breath now, but the parting itself made her physically ill with grief. After his departure she wrote him long letters of regret for the days of love they had missed by waiting. In August Anson's plane slipped down into the North Sea. He was pulled onto a destroyer after a night in the water and sent to hospital with pneumonia; the armistice was signed before he was finally sent home.

Then, with every opportunity given back to them, with no material obstacle to overcome, the secret weavings of their temperaments came between them, drying up their kisses and their tears, making their voices less loud to one another, muffling the intimate chatter of their hearts until the old communcation was only possible by letters, from far away. One afternoon a society reporter waited for two hours in the Hunters' house for a confirmation of their engagement. Anson denied it; nevertheless an early issue carried the report as a leading paragraph—they were "constantly seen together at Southampton, Hot Springs, and Tuxedo Park."[7] But the serious dialogue had turned a corner into a long-sustained quarrel, and the affair was almost played out. Anson got drunk flagrantly and missed an engagement with her, whereupon Paula made certain behavioristic demands. His despair was helpless before his pride and his knowledge of himself; the engagement was definitely broken.

"Dearest," said their letters now, "Dearest, Dearest, when I wake up in the middle of the night and realize that after all it was not to be, I feel that I want to die. I can't go on living any more. Perhaps when we meet this summer we may talk things over and decide differently—we were so excited and sad that day, and I don't feel that I can live all my life without you. You speak of other people. Don't you know there are no other people for me, but only you. . . ."

But as Paula drifted here and there around the East she would sometimes mention her gaieties to make him wonder. Anson was too acute to wonder. When he saw a man's name in her letters he felt more sure of her and a little disdainful—he was always

---

7. A wealthy Long Island suburb, an Arkansas resort, and a resort near New York City, respectively.

superior to such things. But he still hoped that they would some day marry.

Meanwhile he plunged vigorously into all the movement and glitter of post-bellum[8] New York, entering a brokerage house, joining half a dozen clubs, dancing late, and moving in three worlds—his own world, the world of young Yale graduates, and that section of the half-world which rests one end on Broadway. But there was always a thorough and infractible eight hours devoted to his work in Wall Street, where the combination of his influential family connection, his sharp intelligence, and his abundance of sheer physical energy brought him almost immediately forward. He had one of those invaluable minds with partitions in it; sometimes he appeared at his office refreshed by less than an hour's sleep, but such occurrences were rare. So early as 1920 his income in salary and commissions exceeded twelve thousand dollars.

As the Yale tradition slipped into the past he became more and more of a popular figure among his classmates in New York, more popular than he had ever been in college. He lived in a great house, and had the means of introducing young men into other great houses. Moreover, his life already seemed secure, while theirs, for the most part, had arrived again at precarious beginnings. They commenced to turn to him for amusement and escape, and Anson responded readily, taking pleasure in helping people and arranging their affairs.

There were no men in Paula's letters now, but a note of tenderness ran through them that had not been there before. From several sources he heard that she had "a heavy beau,"[9] Lowell Thayer, a Bostonian of wealth and position, and though he was sure she still loved him, it made him uneasy to think that he might lose her, after all. Save for one unsatisfactory day she had not been in New York for almost five months, and as the rumors multiplied he became increasingly anxious to see her. In February he took his vacation and went down to Florida.

Palm Beach sprawled plump and opulent between the sparkling sapphire of Lake Worth, flawed here and there by house-boats at anchor, and the great turquoise bar of the Atlantic Ocean. The huge bulks of the Breakers and the Royal Poinciana[1] rose as twin paunches from the bright level of the sand, and around them clustered the Dancing Glade, Bradley's House of Chance, and a dozen modistes and milliners with goods at triple prices from New York. Upon the trellissed veranda of the Breakers two hundred women stepped right, stepped left, wheeled, and slid in that then celebrated calisthenic known as the double-shuffle, while in half-time to the music two thousand bracelets clicked up and down on two hundred arms.

---

8. Postwar, after World War I.
9. A very attentive boyfriend.

1. Swank hotels in Palm Beach, Florida.

At the Everglades Club after dark Paula and Lowell Thayer and Anson and a casual fourth played bridge with hot cards. It seemed to Anson that her kind, serious face was wan and tired—she had been around now for four, five, years. He had known her for three.

"Two spades."

"Cigarette? . . . Oh, I beg your pardon. By me."

"By."

"I'll double three spades."

There were a dozen tables of bridge in the room, which was filling up with smoke. Anson's eyes met Paula's, held them persistently even when Thayer's glance fell between them. . . .

"What was bid?" he asked abstractedly.

"Rose of Washington Square"

sang the young people in the corners:

*"I'm withering there
In basement air———"*

The smoke banked like fog, and the opening of a door filled the room with blown swirls of ectoplasm. Little Bright Eyes streaked past the tables seeking Mr. Conan Doyle among the Englishmen who were posing as Englishmen about the lobby.[2]

"You could cut it with a knife."

". . . cut it with a knife."

". . . a knife."

At the end of the rubber Paula suddenly got up and spoke to Anson in a tense, low voice. With scarcely a glance at Lowell Thayer, they walked out the door and descended a long flight of stone steps—in a moment they were walking hand in hand along the moonlit beach.

"Darling, darling. . . ." They embraced recklessly, passionately, in a shadow. . . . Then Paula drew back her face to let his lips say what she wanted to hear—she could feel the words forming as they kissed again. . . . Again she broke away, listening, but as he pulled her close once more she realized that he had said nothing—only *"Darling! Darling!"* in that deep, sad whisper that always made her cry. Humbly, obediently, her emotions yielded to him and the tears streamed down her face, but her heart kept on crying: "Ask me—oh, Anson, dearest, ask me!"

"Paula. . . . *Paula!*"

The words wrung her heart like hands, and Anson, feeling her tremble, knew that emotion was enough. He need say no more, commit their destinies to no practical enigma. Why should he,

2. To the narrator, the silly girl (Little Miss Bright Eyes) who seeks out the posturing Englishmen in the smoke-filled room resembles a character surrounded by the effusions (ectoplasm) of a spir- itualistic medium in a mystery thriller by A. Conan Doyle (1859–1930), British author of Sherlock Holmes mystery stories.

when he might hold her so, biding his own time, for another year—forever? He was considering them both, her more than himself. For a moment, when she said suddenly that she must go back to her hotel, he hesitated, thinking, first, "This is the moment, after all," and then: "No, let it wait—she is mine. . . ."

He had forgotten that Paula too was worn away inside with the strain of three years. Her mood passed forever in the night.

He went back to New York next morning filled with a certain restless dissatisfaction. Late in April, without warning, he received a telegram from Bar Harbor in which Paula told him that she was engaged to Lowell Thayer, and that they would be married immediately in Boston. What he never really believed could happen had happened at last.

Anson filled himself with whiskey that morning, and going to the office, carried on his work without a break—rather with a fear if what would happen if he stopped. In the evening he went out as usual, saying nothing of what had occurred; he was cordial, humorous, unabstracted. But one thing he could not help—for three days, in any place, in any company, he would suddenly bend his head into his hands and cry like a child.

V

In 1922 when Anson went abroad with the junior partner to investigate some London loans, the journey intimated that he was to be taken into the firm. He was twenty-seven now, a little heavy without being definitely stout, and with a manner older than his years. Old people and young people liked him and trusted him, and mothers felt safe when their daughters were in his charge, for he had a way, when he came into a room, of putting himself on a footing with the oldest and most conservative people there. "You and I," he seemed to say, "we're solid. We understand."

He had an instinctive and rather charitable knowledge of the weaknesses of men and women, and, like a priest, it made him the more concerned for the maintenance of outward forms. It was typical of him that every Sunday morning he taught in a fashionable Episcopal Sunday-school—even though a cold shower and a quick change into a cutaway coat were all that separated him from the wild night before.

After his father's death he was the practical head of his family, and, in effect, guided the destinies of the younger children. Through a complication his authority did not extend to his father's estate, which was administrated by his Uncle Robert, who was the horsey member of the family, a good-natured, hard-drinking member of that set which centres about Wheatley Hills.

Uncle Robert and his wife, Edna, had been great friends of Anson's youth, and the former was disappointed when his nephew's superiority failed to take a horsey form. He backed him for a city club which was the most difficult in America to enter—one could only join if one's family had "helped to build up New York" (or, in other words, were rich before 1880)—and when Anson, after his election, neglected it for the Yale Club, Uncle Robert gave him a little talk on the subject. But when on top of that Anson declined to enter Robert Hunter's own conservative and somewhat neglected brokerage house, his manner grew cooler. Like a primary teacher who has taught all he knew, he slipped out of Anson's life.

There were so many friends in Anson's life—scarcely one for whom he had not done some unusual kindness and scarcely one whom he did not occasionally embarrass by his bursts of rough conversation or his habit of getting drunk whenever and however he liked. It annoyed him when any one else blundered in that regard—about his own lapses he was always humorous. Odd things happened to him and he told them with infectious laughter.

I was working in New York that spring, and I used to lunch with him at the Yale Club, which my university was sharing until the completion of our own. I had read of Paula's marriage, and one afternoon, when I asked him about her, something moved him to tell me the story. After that he frequently invited me to family dinners at his house and behaved as though there was a special relation between us, as though with his confidence a little of that consuming memory had passed into me.

I found that despite the trusting mothers, his attitude toward girls was not indiscriminately protective. It was up to the girl—if she showed an inclination toward looseness, she must take care of herself, even with him.

"Life," he would explain sometimes, "has made a cynic of me."

By life he meant Paula. Sometimes, especially when he was drinking, it became a little twisted in his mind, and he thought that she had callously thrown him over.

This "cynicism," or rather his realization that naturally fast girls were not worth sparing, led to his affair with Dolly Karger. It wasn't his only affair in those years, but it came nearest to touching him deeply, and it had a profound effect upon his attitude toward life.

Dolly was the daughter of a notorious "publicist"[3] who had married into society. She herself grew up into the Junior League, came out at the Plaza, and went to the Assembly;[4] and only a few old families like the Hunters could question whether or not she "belonged," for her picture was often in the papers, and she had more enviable attention than many girls who undoubtedly did. She was dark-haired, with carmine lips and a high, lovely color, which

3. Public relations agent.
4. Annual dance for debutantes; "Junior League": organization of socialite women for charitable work and social diversion; "Plaza": New York City hotel, location of many socialite "coming out" parties.

she concealed under pinkish-gray powder all through the first year out, because high color was unfashionable—Victorian-pale was the thing to be. She wore black, severe suits and stood with her hands in her pockets leaning a little forward, with a humorous restraint on her face. She danced exquisitely—better than anything she liked to dance—better than anything except making love. Since she was ten she had always been in love, and, usually, with some boy who didn't respond to her. Those who did—and there were many— bored her after a brief encounter, but for her failures she reserved the warmest spot in her heart. When she met them she would always try once more—sometimes she succeeded, more often she failed.

It never occurred to this gypsy of the unattainable that there was a certain resemblance in those who refused to love her—they shared a hard intuition that saw through to her weakness, not a weakness of emotion but a weakness of rudder. Anson perceived this when he first met her, less than a month after Paula's marriage. He was drinking rather heavily, and he pretended for a week that he was falling in love with her. Then he dropped her abruptly and forgot—immediately he took up the commanding position in her heart.

Like so many girls of that day Dolly was slackly and indiscreetly wild. The unconventionality of a slightly older generation had been simply one facet of a post-war movement to discredit obsolete manners—Dolly's was both older and shabbier, and she saw in Anson the two extremes which the emotionally shiftless woman seeks, an abandon to indulgence alternating with a protective strength. In his character she felt both the sybarite and the solid rock, and these two satisfied every need of her nature.

She felt that it was going to be difficult, but she mistook the reason—she thought that Anson and his family expected a more spectacular marriage, but she guessed immediately that her advantage lay in his tendency to drink.

They met at the large débutante dances, but as her infatuation increased they managed to be more and more together. Like most mothers, Mrs. Karger believed that Anson was exceptionally reliable, so she allowed Dolly to go with him to distant country clubs and suburban houses without inquiring closely into their activities or questioning her explanations when they came in late. At first these explanations might have been accurate, but Dolly's worldly ideas of capturing Anson were soon engulfed in the rising sweep of her emotion. Kisses in the back of taxis and motor-cars were no longer enough; they did a curious thing:

They dropped out of their world for a while and made another world just beneath it where Anson's tippling and Dolly's irregular hours would be less noticed and commented on. It was composed, this world, of varying elements—several of Anson's Yale friends and their wives, two or three young brokers and bond salesmen and a handful of unattached men, fresh from college, with money and a propensity to dissipation. What this world lacked in spaciousness and scale it made up for by allowing them a liberty that it scarcely permitted itself. Moreover it centred around them and permitted Dolly the pleasure of a faint condescension—a pleasure which Anson, whose whole life was a condescension from the certitudes of his childhood, was unable to share.

He was not in love with her, and in the long feverish winter of their affair he frequently told her so. In the spring he was weary— he wanted to renew his life at some other source—moreover, he saw that either he must break with her now or accept the responsibility of a definite seduction. Her family's encouraging attitude precipitated his decision—one evening when Mr. Karger knocked discreetly at the library door to announce that he had left a bottle of old brandy in the dining-room, Anson felt that life was hemming him in. That night he wrote her a short letter in which he told her that he was going on his vacation, and that in view of all the circumstances they had better meet no more.

It was June. His family had closed up the house and gone to the country, so he was living temporarily at the Yale Club. I had heard about his affair with Dolly as it developed—accounts salted with humor, for he despised unstable women, and granted them no place in the social edifice in which he believed—and when he told me that night that he was definitely breaking with her I was glad. I had seen Dolly here and there, and each time with a feeling of pity at the hopelessness of her struggle, and of shame at knowing so much about her that I had no right to know. She was what is known as "a pretty little thing," but there was a certain recklessness which rather fascinated me. Her dedication to the goddess of waste would have been less obvious had she been less spirited—she would most certainly throw herself away, but I was glad when I heard that the sacrifice would not be consummated in my sight.

Anson was going to leave the letter of farewell at her house next morning. It was one of the few houses left open in the Fifth Avenue district, and he knew that the Kargers, acting upon erroneous information from Dolly, had foregone a trip abroad to give their daughter her chance. As he stepped out the door of the Yale Club into Madison Avenue the postman passed him, and he followed back inside. The first letter that caught his eye was in Dolly's hand.

He knew what it would be—a lonely and tragic monologue, full of the reproaches he knew, the invoked memories, the "I wonder if's"—all the immemorial intimacies that he had communicated to

Paula Legendre in what seemed another age. Thumbing over some bills, he brought it on top again and opened it. To his surprise it was a short, somewhat formal note, which said that Dolly would be unable to go to the country with him for the week-end, because Perry Hull from Chicago had unexpectedly come to town. It added that Anson had brought this on himself: "—if I felt that you loved me as I love you I would go with you at any time, any place, but Perry is *so* nice, and he so much wants me to marry him——"

Anson smiled contemptuously—he had had experience with such decoy epistles. Moreover, he knew how Dolly had labored over this plan, probably sent for the faithful Perry and calculated the time of his arrival—even labored over the note so that it would make him jealous without driving him away. Like most compromises, it had neither force nor vitality but only a timorous despair.

Suddenly he was angry. He sat down in the lobby and read it again. Then he went to the phone, called Dolly and told her in his clear, compelling voice that he had received her note and would call for her at five o'clock as they had previously planned. Scarcely waiting for the pretended uncertainty of her "Perhaps I can see you for an hour," he hung up the receiver and went down to his office. On the way he tore his own letter into bits and dropped it in the street.

He was not jealous—she meant nothing to him—but at her pathetic ruse everything stubborn and self-indulgent in him came to the surface. It was a presumption from a mental inferior and it could not be overlooked. If she wanted to know to whom she belonged she would see.

He was on the door-step at quarter past five. Dolly was dressed for the street, and he listened in silence to the paragraph of "I can only see you for an hour," which she had begun on the phone.

"Put on your hat, Dolly," he said, "we'll take a walk."

They strolled up Madison Avenue and over to Fifth while Anson's shirt dampened upon his portly body in the deep heat. He talked little, scolding her, making no love to her, but before they had walked six blocks she was his again, apologizing for the note, offering not to see Perry at all as an atonement, offering anything. She thought that he had come because he was beginning to love her.

"I'm hot," he said when they reached 71st Street. "This is a winter suit. If I stop by the house and change, would you mind waiting for me down-stairs? I'll only be a minute."

She was happy; the intimacy of his being hot, of any physical fact about him, thrilled her. When they came to the iron-grated door and Anson took out his key she experienced a sort of delight.

Down-stairs it was dark, and after he ascended in the lift Dolly raised a curtain and looked out through opaque lace at the houses over the way. She heard the lift machinery stop, and with the notion of teasing him pressed the button that brought it down. Then on what was more than an impulse she got into it and sent it up to what she guessed was his floor.

"Anson," she called, laughing a little.

"Just a minute," he answered from his bedroom . . . then after a brief delay: "Now you can come in."

He had changed and was buttoning his vest. "This is my room," he said lightly. "How do you like it?"

She caught sight of Paula's picture on the wall and stared at it in fascination, just as Paula had stared at the pictures of Anson's childish sweethearts five years before. She knew something about Paula—sometimes she tortured herself with fragments of the story.

Suddenly she came close to Anson, raising her arms. They embraced. Outside the area window a soft artificial twilight already hovered, though the sun was still bright on a back roof across the way. In half an hour the room would be quite dark. The uncalculated opportunity overwhelmed them, made them both breathless, and they clung more closely. It was eminent, inevitable. Still holding one another, they raised their heads—their eyes fell together upon Paula's picture, staring down at them from the wall.

Suddenly Anson dropped his arms, and sitting down at his desk tried the drawer with a bunch of keys.

"Like a drink?" he asked in a gruff voice.

"No, Anson."

He poured himself half a tumbler of whiskey, swallowed it, and then opened the door into the hall.

"Come on," he said.

Dolly hesitated.

"Anson—I'm going to the country with you tonight, after all. You understand that, don't you?"

"Of course," he answered brusquely.

In Dolly's car they rode on to Long Island, closer in their emotions than they had ever been before. They knew what would happen—not with Paula's face to remind them that something was lacking, but when they were alone in the still, hot Long Island night they did not care.

The estate in Port Washington[5] where they were to spend the week-end belonged to a cousin of Anson's who had married a Montana copper operator. An interminable drive began at the lodge and twisted under imported poplar saplings toward a huge, pink, Spanish house. Anson had often visited there before.

After dinner they danced at the Linx Club. About midnight

5. Town on Long Island.

Anson assured himself that his cousins would not leave before two —then he explained that Dolly was tired; he would take her home and return to the dance later. Trembling a little with excitement, they got into a borrowed car together and drove to Port Washington. As they reached the lodge he stopped and spoke to the night-watchman.

"When are you making a round, Carl?"

"Right away."

"Then you'll be here till everybody's in?"

"Yes, sir."

"All right. Listen: if any automobile, no matter whose it is, turns in at this gate, I want you to phone the house immediately." He put a five-dollar bill into Carl's hand. "Is that clear?"

"Yes, Mr. Anson." Being of the Old World, he neither winked nor smiled. Yet Dolly sat with her face turned slightly away.

Anson had a key. Once inside he poured a drink for both of them—Dolly left hers untouched—then he ascertained definitely the location of the phone, and found that it was within easy hearing distance of their rooms, both of which were on the first floor.

Five minutes later he knocked at the door of Dolly's room.

"Anson?" He went in, closing the door behind him. She was in bed, leaning up anxiously with elbows on the pillow; sitting beside her he took her in his arms.

"Anson, darling."

He didn't answer.

"Anson. . . . Anson! I love you. . . . Say you love me. Say it now—can't you say it now? Even if you don't mean it?"

He did not listen. Over her head he perceived that the picture of Paula was hanging here upon this wall.

He got up and went close to it. The frame gleamed faintly with thrice-reflected moonlight—within was a blurred shadow of a face that he saw he did not know. Almost sobbing, he turned around and stared with abomination at the little figure on the bed.

"This is all foolishness," he said thickly. "I don't know what I was thinking about. I don't love you and you'd better wait for somebody that loves you. I don't love you a bit, can't you understand?"

His voice broke, and he went hurriedly out. Back in the salon he was pouring himself a drink with uneasy fingers, when the front door opened suddenly, and his cousin came in.

"Why, Anson, I hear Dolly's sick," she began solicitously. "I hear she's sick. . . ."

"It was nothing," he interrupted, raising his voice so that it would carry into Dolly's room. "She was a little tired. She went to bed."

For a long time afterward Anson believed that a protective God sometimes interfered in human affairs. But Dolly Karger, lying awake and staring at the ceiling, never again believed in anything at all.

VI

When Dolly married during the following autumn, Anson was in London on business. Like Paula's marriage, it was sudden, but it affected him in a different way. At first he felt that it was funny, and had an inclination to laugh when he thought of it. Later it depressed him—it made him feel old.

There was something repetitive about it—why, Paula and Dolly had belonged to different generations. He had a foretaste of the sensation of a man of forty who hears that the daughter of an old flame has married. He wired congratulations and, as was not the case with Paula, they were sincere—he had never really hoped that Paula would be happy.

When he returned to New York, he was made a partner in the firm, and, as his responsibilities increased, he had less time on his hands. The refusal of a life-insurance company to issue him a policy made such an impression on him that he stopped drinking for a year, and claimed that he felt better physically, though I think he missed the convivial recounting of those Celliniesque adventures[6] which, in his early twenties, had played such a part of his life. But he never abandoned the Yale Club. He was a figure there, a personality, and the tendency of his class, who were now seven years out of college, to drift away to more sober haunts was checked by his presence.

His day was never too full nor his mind too weary to give any sort of aid to any one who asked it. What had been done at first through pride and superiority had become a habit and a passion. And there was always something—a younger brother in trouble at New Haven, a quarrel to be patched up between a friend and his wife, a position to be found for this man, an investment for that. But his specialty was the solving of problems for young married people. Young married people fascinated him and their apartments were almost sacred to him—he knew the story of their love-affair, advised them where to live and how, and remembered their babies' names. Toward young wives his attitude was circumspect: he never abused the trust which their husbands—strangely enough in view of his unconcealed irregularities—invariable reposed in him.

He came to take a vicarious pleasure in happy marriages, and to be inspired to an almost equally pleasant melancholy by those that went astray. Not a season passed that he did not witness the collapse of an affair that perhaps he himself had fathered. When

---

6. Amatory adventures like those of Benvenuto Cellini (1500–71), Italian sculptor and a legendary lover.

Paula was divorced and almost immediately remarried to another

Bostonian, he talked about her to me all one afternoon. He would never love any one as he had loved Paula, but he insisted that he no longer cared.

"I'll never marry," he came to say; "I've seen too much of it, and I know a happy marriage is a very rare thing. Besides, I'm too old."

But he did believe in marriage. Like all men who spring from a happy and successful marriage, he believed in it passionately— nothing he had seen would change his belief, his cynicism dissolved upon it like air. But he did really believe he was too old. At twenty-eight he began to accept with equanimity the prospect of marrying without romantic love; he resolutely chose a New York girl of his own class, pretty, intelligent, congenial, above reproach— and set about falling in love with her. The things he had said to Paula with sincerity, to other girls with grace, he could no longer say at all without smiling, or with the force necessary to convince.

"When I'm forty," he told his friends, "I'll be ripe. I'll fall for some chorus girl like the rest."

Nevertheless, he persisted in his attempt. His mother wanted to see him married, and he could now well afford it—he had a seat on the Stock Exchange, and his earned income came to twenty-five thousand a year. The idea was agreeable: when his friends— he spent most of his time with the set he and Dolly had evolved— closed themselves in behind domestic doors at night, he no longer rejoiced in his freedom. He even wondered if he should have married Dolly. Not even Paula had loved him more, and he was learning the rarity, in a single life, of encountering true emotion.

Just as this mood began to creep over him a disquieting story reached his ear. His aunt Edna, a woman just this side of forty, was carrying on an open intrigue with a dissolute, hard-drinking young man named Cary Sloane. Every one knew of it except Anson's Uncle Robert, who for fifteen years had talked long in clubs and taken his wife for granted.

Anson heard the story again and again with increasing annoyance. Something of his old feeling for his uncle came back to him, a feeling that was more than personal, a reversion toward that family solidarity on which he had based his pride. His intuition singled out the essential point of the affair, which was that his uncle shouldn't be hurt. It was his first experiment in unsolicited meddling, but with his knowledge of Edna's character he felt that he could handle the matter better than a district judge or his uncle.

His uncle was in Hot Springs. Anson traced down the sources of the scandal so that there should be no possibility of mistake and then he called Edna and asked her to lunch with him at the Plaza next day. Something in his tone must have frightened her, for she was reluctant, but he insisted, putting off the date until she had no excuse for refusing.

She met him at the appointed time in the Plaza lobby, a lovely, faded, gray-eyed blonde in a coat of Russian sable. Five great rings, cold with diamonds and emeralds, sparkled on her slender hands. It occurred to Anson that it was his father's intelligence and not his uncle's that had earned the fur and the stones, the rich brilliance that buoyed up her passing beauty.

Though Edna scented his hostility, she was unprepared for the directness of his approach.

"Edna, I'm astonished at the way you've been acting," he said in a strong, frank voice. "At first I couldn't believe it."

"Believe what?" she demanded sharply.

"You needn't pretend with me, Edna. I'm talking about Cary Sloane. Aside from any other consideration, I didn't think you could treat Uncle Robert——"

"Now look here, Anson——" she began angrily, but his peremptory voice broke through hers:

"——and your children in such a way. You've been married eighteen years, and you're old enough to know better."

"You can't talk to me like that! You——"

"Yes, I can. Uncle Robert has always been my best friend." He was tremendously moved. He felt a real distress about his uncle, about his three young cousins.

Edna stood up, leaving her crab-flake cocktail untasted.

"This is the silliest thing——"

"Very well, if you won't listen to me I'll go to Uncle Robert and tell him the whole story—he's bound to hear it sooner or later. And afterward I'll go to old Moses Sloane."

Edna faltered back into her chair.

"Don't talk so loud," she begged him. Her eyes blurred with tears. "You have no idea how your voice carries. You might have chosen a less public place to make all these crazy accusations."

He didn't answer.

"Oh, you never liked me, I know," she went on. "You're just taking advantage of some silly gossip to try and break up the only interesting friendship I've ever had. What did I ever do to make you hate me so?"

Still Anson waited. There would be the appeal to his chivalry, then to his pity, finally to his superior sophistication—when he had shouldered his way through all these there would be admissions, and he could come to grips with her. By being silent, by being impervious, by returning constantly to his main weapon, which was his own true emotion, he bullied her into frantic despair as the luncheon hour slipped away. At two o'clock she took out a mirror and a handkerchief, shined away the marks of her tears and powdered the slight hollows where they had lain. She had agreed to meet him at her own house at five.

When he arrived she was stretched on a *chaise-longue*⁷ which was covered with cretonne for the summer, and the tears he had called up at luncheon seemed still to be standing in her eyes. Then he was aware of Cary Sloane's dark anxious presence upon the cold hearth.

"What's this idea of yours?" broke out Sloane immediately. "I understand you invited Edna to lunch and then threatened her on the basis of some cheap scandal."

Anson sat down.

"I have no reason to think it's only scandal."

"I hear you're going to take it to Robert Hunter, and to my father."

Anson nodded.

"Either you break it off—or I will," he said.

"What God damned business is it of yours, Hunter?"

"Don't lose your temper, Cary," said Edna nervously. "It's only a question of showing him how absurd——"

"For one thing, it's my name that's being handed around," interrupted Anson. "That's all that concerns you, Cary."

"Edna isn't a member of your family."

"She most certainly is!" His anger mounted. "Why—she owes this house and the rings on her fingers to my father's brains. When Uncle Robert married her she didn't have a penny."

They all looked at the rings as if they had a significant bearing on the situation. Edna made a gesture to take them from her hand.

"I guess they're not the only rings in the world," said Sloane.

"Oh, this is absurd," cried Edna. "Anson, will you listen to me? I've found out how the silly story started. It was a maid I discharged who went right to the Chilicheffs—all these Russians pump things out of their servants and then put a false meaning on them." She brought down her fist angrily on the table: "And after Tom lent them the limousine for a whole month when we were South last winter——"

"Do you see?" demanded Sloane eagerly. "This maid got hold of the wrong end of the thing. She knew that Edna and I were friends, and she carried it to the Chilicheffs. In Russia they assume that if a man and a woman——"

He enlarged the theme to a disquisition upon social relations in the Caucasus.

"If that's the case it better be explained to Uncle Robert," said Anson dryly, "so that when the rumors do reach him he'll know they're not true."

Adopting the method he had followed with Edna at luncheon he let them explain it all away. He knew that they were guilty and

---

7. Reclining lounge chair.

that presently they would cross the line from explanation into justification and convict themselves more definitely than he could ever do. By seven they had taken the desperate step of telling him the truth—Robert Hunter's neglect, Edna's empty life, the casual dalliance that had flamed up into passion—but like so many true stories it had the misfortune of being old, and its enfeebled body beat helplessly against the armor of Anson's will. The threat to go to Sloane's father sealed their helplessness, for the latter, a retired cotton broker out of Alabama, was a notorious fundamentalist who controlled his son by a rigid allowance and the promise that at his next vagary the allowance would stop forever.

They dined at a small French restaurant, and the discussion continued—at one time Sloane resorted to physical threats, a little later they were both imploring him to give them time. But Anson was obdurate. He saw that Edna was breaking up, and that her spirit must not be refreshed by any renewal of their passion.

At two o'clock in a small night-club on 53d Street, Edna's nerves suddenly collapsed, and she cried to go home. Sloane had been drinking heavily all evening, and he was faintly maudlin, leaning on the table and weeping a little with his face in his hands. Quickly Anson gave them his terms. Sloane was to leave town for six months, and he must be gone within forty-eight hours. When he returned there was to be no resumption of the affair, but at the end of a year Edna might, if she wished, tell Robert Hunter that she wanted a divorce and go about it in the usual way.

He paused, gaining confidence from their faces for his final word.

"Or there's another thing you can do," he said slowly, "if Edna wants to leave her children, there's nothing I can do to prevent your running off together."

"I want to go home!" cried Edna again. "Oh, haven't you done enough to us for one day?"

Outside it was dark, save for a blurred glow from Sixth Avenue down the street. In that light those two who had been lovers looked for the last time into each other's tragic faces, realizing that between them there was not enough youth and strength to avert their eternal parting. Sloane walked suddenly off down the street and Anson tapped a dozing taxi-driver on the arm.

It was almost four; there was a patient flow of cleaning water along the ghostly pavement of Fifth Avenue, and the shadows of two night women[8] flitted over the dark façade of St. Thomas's church. Then the desolate shrubbery of Central Park where Anson had often played as a child, and the mounting numbers, significant as names, of the marching streets. This was his city, he thought, where his name had flourished through five generations. No change could alter the permanence of its place here, for change itself was

8. Prostitutes.

the essential substratum by which he and those of his name identified themselves with the spirit of New York. Resourcefulness and a powerful will—for his threats in weaker hands would have been less than nothing—had beaten the gathering dust from his uncle's name, from the name of his family, from even this shivering figure that sat beside him in the car.

Cary Sloane's body was found next morning on the lower shelf of a pillar of Queensboro Bridge. In the darkness and in his excitement he had thought that it was the water flowing black beneath him, but in less than a second it made no possible difference—unless he had planned to think one last thought of Edna, and call out her name as he struggled feebly in the water.

VII

Anson never blamed himself for his part in this affair—the situation which brought it about had not been of his making. But the just suffer with the unjust, and he found that his oldest and somehow his most precious friendship was over. He never knew what distorted story Edna told, but he was welcome in his uncle's house no longer.

Just before Christmas Mrs. Hunter retired to a select Episcopal heaven, and Anson became the responsible head of his family. An unmarried aunt who had lived with them for years ran the house, and attempted with helpless inefficiency to chaperone the younger girls. All the children were less self-reliant than Anson, more conventional both in their virtues and in their shortcomings. Mrs. Hunter's death had postponed the début of one daughter and the wedding of another. Also it had taken something deeply material from all of them, for with her passing the quiet, expensive superiority of the Hunters came to an end.

For one thing, the estate, considerably diminished by two inheritance taxes and soon to be divided among six children, was not a notable fortune any more. Anson saw a tendency in his youngest sisters to speak rather respectfully of families that hadn't "existed" twenty years ago. His own feeling of precedence was not echoed in them—sometimes they were conventionally snobbish, that was all. For another thing, this was the last summer they would spend on the Connecticut estate; the clamor against it was too loud: "Who wants to waste the best months of the year shut up in that dead old town?" Reluctantly he yielded—the house would go into the market in the fall, and next summer they would rent a smaller place in Westchester County. It was a step down from the expensive simplicity of his father's idea, and, while he sympathized with the revolt, it also annoyed him; during his mother's lifetime he had gone up there at least every other week-end—even in the gayest summers.

Yet he himself was part of this change, and his strong instinct for life had turned him in his twenties from the hollow obsequies of that abortive leisure class. He did not see this clearly—he still felt that there was a norm, a standard of society. But there was no norm, it was doubtful if there had ever been a true norm in New York. The few who still paid and fought to enter a particular set succeeded only to find that as a society it scarcely functioned—or, what was more alarming, that the Bohemia from which they fled sat above them at table.[9]

At twenty-nine Anson's chief concern was his own growing loneliness. He was sure now that he would never marry. The number of weddings at which he had officiated as best man or usher was past all counting—there was a drawer at home that bulged with the official neckties of this or that wedding-party, neckties standing for romances that had not endured a year, for couples who had passed completely from his life. Scarf-pins, gold pencils, cuff-buttons, presents from a generation of grooms had passed through his jewel-box and been lost—and with every ceremony he was less and less able to imagine himself in the groom's place. Under his hearty good-will toward all those marriages there was despair about his own.

And as he neared thirty he became not a little depressed at the inroads that marriage, especially lately, had made upon his friendships. Groups of people had a disconcerting tendency to dissolve and disappear. The men from his own college—and it was upon them he had expended the most time and affection—were the most elusive of all. Most of them were drawn deep into domesticity, two were dead, one lived abroad, one was in Hollywood writing continuities for pictures that Anson went faithfully to see. Most of them, however, were permanent commuters with an intricate family life centring around some suburban country club, and it was from these that he felt his estrangement most keenly.

In the early days of their married life they had all needed him; he gave them advice about their slim finances, he exorcised their doubts about the advisability of bringing a baby into two rooms and a bath, especially he stood for the great world outside. But now their financial troubles were in the past and the fearfully expected child had evolved into an absorbing family. They were always glad to see old Anson, but they dressed up for him and tried to impress him with their present importance, and kept their troubles to themselves. They needed him no longer.

A few weeks before his thirtieth birthday the last of his early and intimate friends was married. Anson acted in his usual rôle of best man, gave his usual silver tea-service, and went down to the usual *Homeric*[1] to say good-by. It was a hot Friday afternoon in May, and as he walked from the pier he realized that Saturday closing had begun and he was free until Monday morning.

"Go where?" he asked himself.

The Yale Club, of course; bridge until dinner, then four or five raw cocktails in somebody's room and a pleasant confused evening. He regretted that this afternoon's groom wouldn't be along —they had always been able to cram so much into such nights: they knew how to attach women and how to get rid of them, how much consideration any girl deserved from their intelligent hedonism. A party was an adjusted thing—you took certain girls to certain places and spent just so much on their amusement; you drank a little, not much, more than you ought to drink, and at a certain time in the morning you stood up and said you were going home. You avoided college boys, sponges, future engagements, fights, sentiment, and indiscretions. That was the way it was done. All the rest was dissipation.

In the morning you were never violently sorry—you made no resolutions, but if you had overdone it and your heart was slightly out of order, you went on the wagon for a few days without saying anything about it, and waited until an accumulation of nervous boredom projected you into another party.

The lobby of the Yale Club was unpopulated. In the bar three very young alumni looked up at him, momentarily and without curiosity.

"Hello there, Oscar," he said to the bartender. "Mr. Cahill been around this afternoon?"

"Mr. Cahill's gone to New Haven."

"Oh . . . that so?"

"Gone to the ball game. Lot of men gone up."

Anson looked once again into the lobby, considered for a moment, and then walked out and over to Fifth Avenue. From the broad window of one of his clubs—one that he had scarcely visited in five years—a gray man with watery eyes stared down at him. Anson looked quickly away—that figure sitting in vacant resignation, in supercilious solitude, depressed him. He stopped and, retracing his steps, started over 47th Street toward Teak Warden's apartment. Teak and his wife had once been his most familiar friends—it was a household where he and Dolly Karger had been used to go in the days of their affair. But Teak had taken to drink, and his wife had remarked publicly that Anson was a bad influence on him. The remark reached Anson in an exaggerated form—when it was finally cleared up, the delicate spell of intimacy was broken, never to be renewed.

"Is Mr. Warden at home?" he inquired.

"They've gone to the country."

The fact unexpectedly cut at him. They were gone to the country and he hadn't known. Two years before he would have known the date, the hour, come up at the last moment for a final drink, and planned his first visit to them. Now they had gone without a word.

Anson looked at his watch and considered a weekend with his family, but the only train was a local that would jolt through the aggressive heat for three hours. And to-morrow in the country, and Sunday—he was in no mood for porch-bridge with polite undergraduates, and dancing after dinner at a rural roadhouse, a diminutive of gaiety which his father had estimated too well.

"Oh, no," he said to himself. . . . "No."

He was a dignified, impressive young man, rather stout now, but otherwise unmarked by dissipation. He could have been cast for a pillar of something—at times you were sure it was not society, at others nothing else—for the law, for the church. He stood for a few minutes motionless on the sidewalk in front of a 47th Street apartment-house; for almost the first time in his life he had nothing whatever to do.

Then he began to walk briskly up Fifth Avenue, as if he had just been reminded of an important engagement there. The necessity of dissimulation is one of the few characteristics that we share with dogs, and I think of Anson on that day as some well-bred specimen who had been disappointed at a familiar back door. He was going to see Nick, once a fashionable bartender in demand at all private dances, and now employed in cooling non-alcoholic champagne among the labyrinthine cellars of the Plaza Hotel.

"Nick," he said, "what's happened to everything?"

"Dead," Nick said.

"Make me a whiskey sour." Anson handed a pint bottle over the counter.[2] "Nick, the girls are different; I had a little girl in Brooklyn and she got married last week without letting me know."

"That a fact? Ha-ha-ha," responded Nick diplomatically. "Slipped it over on you."

"Absolutely," said Anson. "And I was out with her the night before."

"Ha-ha-ha," said Nick, "ha-ha-ha!"

"Do you remember the wedding, Nick, in Hot Springs where I had the waiters and the musicians singing 'God save the King'?"

"Now where was that, Mr. Hunter?" Nick concentrated doubtfully. "Seems to me that was——"

"Next time they were back for more, and I began to wonder how much I'd paid them," continued Anson.

"—seems to me that was at Mr. Trenholm's wedding."

2. From 1919 to 1933, a federal "Prohibition" law and a constitutional amendment prohibited the manufacture and sale of intoxicating alcoholic beverages. Violation of the law was widespread; individuals secured contraband or "bootleg" liquor from illegal distillers or stores and brought it with them to bars and parties.

"Don't know him," said Anson decisively. He was offended that a strange name should intrude upon his reminiscences; Nick perceived this.

"Naw—aw—" he admitted, "I ought to know that. It was one of *your* crowd—Brakins . . . . Baker——"

"Bicker Baker," said Anson responsively. "They put me in a hearse after it was over and covered me up with flowers and drove me away."

"Ha-ha-ha," said Nick. "Ha-ha-ha."

Nick's simulation of the old family servant paled presently and Anson went up-stairs to the lobby. He looked around—his eyes met the glance of an unfamiliar clerk at the desk, then fell upon a flower from the morning's marriage hesitating in the mouth of a brass cuspidor. He went out and walked slowly toward the blood-red sun over Columbus Circle. Suddenly he turned around and, retracing his steps to the Plaza, immured himself in a telephone-booth.

Later he said that he tried to get me three times that afternoon, that he tried every one who might be in New York—men and girls he had not seen for years, an artist's model of his college days whose faded number was still in his address book—Central[3] told him that even the exchange existed no longer. At length his quest roved into the country, and he held brief disappointing conversations with emphatic butlers and maids. So-and-so was out, riding, swimming, playing golf, sailed to Europe last week. Who shall I say phoned?

It was intolerable that he should pass the evening alone—the private reckonings which one plans for a moment of leisure lose every charm when the solitude is enforced. There were always women of a sort, but the ones he knew had temporarily vanished, and to pass a New York evening in the hired company of a stranger never occurred to him—he would have considered that that was something shameful and secret, the diversion of a travelling salesman in a strange town.

Anson paid the telephone bill—the girl tried unsuccessfully to joke with him about its size—and for the second time that afternoon started to leave the Plaza and go he knew not where. Near the revolving door the figure of a woman, obviously with child, stood sideways to the light—a sheer beige cape fluttered at her shoulders when the door turned and, each time, she looked impatiently toward it as if she were weary of waiting. At the first sight of her a strong nervous thrill of familiarity went over him, but not until he was within five feet of her did he realize that it was Paula.

"Why, Anson Hunter!"

His heart turned over.

"Why, Paula——"

"Why, this is wonderful. I can't believe it, *Anson!*"

3. Telephone operator.

She took both his hands, and he saw in the freedom of the gesture that the memory of him had lost poignancy to her. But not to him—he felt that old mood that she evoked in him stealing over his brain, that gentleness with which he had always met her optimism as if afraid to mar its surface.

"We're at Rye for the summer. Pete had to come East on business—you know of course I'm Mrs. Peter Hagerty now—so we brought the children and took a house. You've got to come out and see us."

"Can I?" he asked directly. "When?"

"When you like. Here's Pete." The revolving door functioned, giving up a fine tall man of thirty with a tanned face and a trim mustache. His immaculate fitness made a sharp contrast with Anson's increasing bulk, which was obvious under the faintly tight cut-away coat.

"You oughtn't to be standing," said Hagerty to his wife. "Let's sit down here." He indicated lobby chairs, but Paula hesitated.

"I've got to go right home," she said. "Anson, why don't you— why don't you come out and have dinner with us to-night? We're just getting settled, but if you can stand that——"

Hagerty confirmed the invitation cordially.

"Come out for the night."

Their car waited in front of the hotel, and Paula with a tired gesture sank back against silk cushions in the corner.

"There's so much I want to talk to you about," she said, "it seems hopeless."

"I want to hear about you."

"Well"—she smiled at Hagerty—"that would take a long time too. I have three children—by my first marriage. The oldest is five, then four, then three." She smiled again. "I didn't waste much time having them, did I?"

"Boys?"

"A boy and two girls. Then—oh, a lot of things happened, and I got a divorce in Paris a year ago and married Pete. That's all— except that I'm awfully happy."

In Rye they drove up to a large house near the Beach Club, from which there issued presently three dark, slim children who broke from an English governess and approached them with an esoteric cry. Abstractedly and with difficulty Paula took each one into her arms, a caress which they accepted stiffly, as they had evidently been told not to bump into Mummy. Even against their fresh faces Paula's skin showed scarcely any weariness—for all her physical languor she seemed younger than when he had last seen her at Palm Beach seven years ago.

At dinner she was preoccupied, and afterward, during the homage to the radio, she lay with closed eyes on the sofa, until Anson wondered if his presence at this time were not an intrusion. But at nine o'clock, when Hagerty rose and said pleasantly that he was going to leave them by themselves for a while, she began to talk slowly about herself and the past.

"My first baby," she said—"the one we call Darling, the biggest little girl—I wanted to die when I knew I was going to have her, because Lowell was like a stranger to me. It didn't seem as though she could be my own. I wrote you a letter and tore it up. Oh, you were so bad to me, Anson."

It was the dialogue again, rising and falling. Anson felt a sudden quickening of memory.

"Weren't you engaged once?" she asked—"a girl named Dolly something?"

"I wasn't ever engaged. I tried to be engaged, but I never loved anybody but you, Paula."

"Oh," she said. Then after a moment: "This baby is the first one I ever really wanted. You see, I'm in love now—at last."

He didn't answer, shocked at the treachery of her remembrance. She must have seen that the "at last" bruised him, for she continued:

"I was infatuated with you, Anson—you could make me do anything you liked. But we wouldn't have been happy. I'm not smart enough for you. I don't like things to be complicated like you do." She paused. "You'll never settle down," she said.

The phrase struck at him from behind—it was an accusation that of all accusations he had never merited.

"I could settle down if women were different," he said. "If I didn't understand so much about them, if women didn't spoil you for other women, if they had only a little pride. If I could go to sleep for a while and wake up into a home that was really mine— why, that's what I'm made for, Paula, that's what women have seen in me and liked in me. It's only that I can't get through the preliminaries any more."

Hagerty came in a little before eleven; after a whiskey Paula stood up and announced that she was going to bed. She went over and stood by her husband.

"Where did you go, dearest?" she demanded.

"I had a drink with Ed Saunders."

"I was worried. I thought maybe you'd run away."

She rested her head against his coat.

"He's sweet, isn't he, Anson?" she demanded.

"Absolutely," said Anson, laughing.

She raised her face to her husband.

"Well, I'm ready," she said. She turned to Anson: "Do you want to see our family gymnastic stunt?"

"Yes," he said in an interested voice.

"All right. Here we go!"

Hagerty picked her up easily in his arms.

"This is called the family acrobatic stunt," said Paula. "He carries me up-stairs. Isn't it sweet of him?"

"Yes," said Anson.

Hagerty bent his head slightly until his face touched Paula's.

"And I love him," she said. "I've just been telling you, haven't I, Anson?"

"Yes," he said.

"He's the dearest thing that ever lived in this world; aren't you, darling? . . . Well, good night. Here we go. Isn't he strong?"

"Yes," Anson said.

"You'll find a pair of Pete's pajamas laid out for you. Sweet dreams—see you at breakfast."

"Yes," Anson said.

VIII

The older members of the firm insisted that Anson should go abroad for the summer. He had scarcely had a vacation in seven years, they said. He was stale and needed a change. Anson resisted.

"If I go," he declared, "I won't come back any more."

"That's absurd, old man. You'll be back in three months with all this depression gone. Fit as ever."

"No." He shook his head stubbornly. "If I stop, I won't go back to work. If I stop, that means I've given up—I'm through."

"We'll take a chance on that. Stay six months if you like—we're not afraid you'll leave us. Why, you'd be miserable if you didn't work."

They arranged his passage for him. They liked Anson—every one liked Anson—and the change that had been coming over him cast a sort of pall over the office. The enthusiasm that had invariably signalled up business, the consideration toward his equals and his inferiors, the lift of his vital presence—within the past four months his intense nervousness had melted down these qualities into the fussy pessimism of a man of forty. On every transaction in which he was involved he acted as a drag and a strain.

"If I go I'll never come back," he said.

Three days before he sailed Paula Legendre Hagerty died in childbirth. I was with him a great deal then, for we were crossing together, but for the first time in our friendship he told me not a word of how he felt, nor did I see the slightest sign of emotion. His chief preoccupation was with the fact that he was thirty years old— he would turn the conversation to the point where he could remind you of it and then fall silent, as if he assumed that the statement would start a chain of thought sufficient to itself. Like his partners, I was amazed at the change in him, and I was glad when the *Paris* moved off into the wet space between the worlds, leaving his principality behind.

"How about a drink?" he suggested.

We walked into the bar with that defiant feeling that characterizes the day of departure and ordered four Martinis. After one cocktail a change came over him—he suddenly reached across and slapped my knee with the first joviality I had seen him exhibit for months.

"Did you see that girl in the red tam?" he demanded, "the one with the high color who had the two police dogs down to bid her good-by."

"She's pretty," I agreed.

"I looked her up in the purser's office and found out that she's alone. I'm going down to see the steward in a few minutes. We'll have dinner with her to-night."

After a while he left me, and within an hour he was walking up and down the deck with her, talking to her in his strong, clear voice. Her red tam was a bright spot of color against the steel-green sea, and from time to time she looked up with a flashing bob of her head, and smiled with amusement and interest, and anticipation. At dinner we had champagne, and were very joyous—afterward Anson ran the pool[4] with infectious gusto, and several people who had seen me with him asked me his name. He and the girl were talking and laughing together on a lounge in the bar when I went to bed.

I saw less of him on the trip than I had hoped. He wanted to arrange a foursome, but there was no one available, so I saw him only at meals. Sometimes, though, he would have a cocktail in the bar, and he told me about the girl in the red tam, and his adventures with her, making them all bizarre and amusing, as he had a way of doing, and I was glad that he was himself again, or at least the self that I knew, and with which I felt at home. I don't think he was ever happy unless some one was in love with him, responding to him like filings to a magnet, helping him to explain himself, promising him something. What it was I do not know. Perhaps they promised that there would always be women in the world who would spend their brightest, freshest, rarest hours to nurse and protect that superiority he cherished in his heart.

1926

From THE CRACK-UP
The Crack-Up

February, 1936

Of course all life is a process of breaking down, but the blows that do the dramatic side of the work—the big sudden blows that come, or seem to come, from outside—the ones you remember and blame things on and, in moments of weakness, tell your friends about, don't show their effect all at once. There is another sort of blow that comes from within—that you don't feel until it's too late to do anything about it, until you realize with finality that in some

4. Betting game organized for guests aboard ship.

regard you will never be as good a man again. The first sort of breakage seems to happen quick—the second kind happens almost without your knowing it but is realized suddenly indeed.

Before I go on with this short history, let me make a general observation—the test of a first-rate intelligence is the ability to hold two opposed ideas in the mind at the same time, and still retain the ability to function. One should, for example, be able to see that things are hopeless and yet be determined to make them otherwise. This philosophy fitted on to my early adult life, when I saw the improbable, the implausible, often the "impossible," come true. Life was something you dominated if you were any good. Life yielded easily to intelligence and effort, or to what proportion could be mustered of both. It seemed a romantic business to be a successful literary man—you were not ever going to be as famous as a movie star but what note you had was probably longer-lived—you were never going to have the power of a man of strong political or religious convictions but you were certainly more independent. Of course within the practice of your trade you were forever unsatisfied—but I, for one, would not have chosen any other.

As the twenties passed, with my own twenties marching a little ahead of them, my two juvenile regrets—at not being big enough (or good enough) to play football in college, and at not getting overseas during the war—resolved themselves into childish waking dreams of imaginary heroism that were good enough to go to sleep on in restless nights. The big problems of life seemed to solve themselves, and if the business of fixing them was difficult, it made one too tired to think of more general problems.

Life, ten years ago, was largely a personal matter. I must hold in balance the sense of the futility of effort and the sense of the necessity to struggle; the conviction of the inevitability of failure and still the determination to "succeed"—and, more than these, the contradiction between the dead hand of the past and the high intentions of the future. If I could do this through the common ills—domestic, professional and personal—then the ego would continue as an arrow shot from nothingness to nothingness with such force that only gravity would bring it to earth at last.

For seventeen years, with a year of deliberate loafing and resting out in the center—things went on like that, with a new chore only a nice prospect for the next day. I was living hard, too, but: "Up to forty-nine it'll be all right," I said. "I can count on that. For a man who's lived as I have, that's all you could ask."

—And then, ten years this side of forty-nine, I suddenly realized that I had prematurely cracked.

II

Now a man can crack in many ways—can crack in the head—in which case the power of decision is taken from you by others! or in the body, when one can but submit to the white hospital world; or in the nerves. William Seabrook[1] in an unsympathetic book tells, with some pride and a movie ending, of how he became a public charge. What led to his alcoholism or was bound up with it, was a collapse of his nervous system. Though the present writer was not so entangled—having at the time not tasted so much as a glass of beer for six months—it was his nervous reflexes that were giving way—too much anger and too many tears.

Moreover, to go back to my thesis that life has a varying offensive, the realization of having cracked was not simultaneous with a blow, but with a reprieve.

Not long before, I had sat in the office of a great doctor and listened to a grave sentence. With what, in retrospect, seems some equanimity, I had gone on about my affairs in the city where I was then living, not caring much, not thinking how much had been left undone, or what would become of this and that responsibility, like people do in books; I was well insured and anyhow I had been only a mediocre caretaker of most of the things left in my hands, even of my talent.

But I had a strong sudden instinct that I must be alone. I didn't want to see any people at all. I had seen so many people all my life —I was an average mixer, but more than average in a tendency to identify myself, my ideas, my destiny, with those of all classes that I came in contact with. I was always saving or being saved—in a single morning I would go through the emotions ascribable to Wellington at Waterloo.[2] I lived in a world of inscrutable hostiles and inalienable friends and supporters.

But now I wanted to be absolutely alone and so arranged a certain insulation from ordinary cares.

It was not an unhappy time. I went away and there were fewer people. I found I was good-and-tired. I could lie around and was glad to, sleeping or dozing sometimes twenty hours a day and in the intervals trying resolutely not to think—instead I made lists— made lists and tore them up, hundreds of lists: of cavalry leaders and football players and cities, and popular tunes and pitchers, and happy times, and hobbies and houses lived in and how many suits since I left the army and how many pairs of shoes (I didn't count the suit I bought in Sorrento that shrunk, nor the pumps and dress shirt and collar that I carried around for years and never wore, because the pumps got damp and grainy and the shirt and collar got yellow and starch-rotted). And lists of women I'd liked, and of the times I had let myself be snubbed by people who had not been my betters in character or ability.

—And then suddenly, surprisingly, I got better.

1. Author of *Asylum* (1935), an account of his drift into alcoholism.
2. Arthur W. Wellington, British General, victor over Napoleon at the Battle of Waterloo (1815).

—And cracked like an old plate as soon as I heard the news.

That is the real end of this story. What was to be done about it will have to rest in what used to be called the "womb of time." Suffice it to say that after about an hour of solitary pillow-hugging, I began to realize that for two years my life had been a drawing on resources that I did not possess, that I had been mortgaging myself physically and spiritually up to the hilt. What was the small gift of life given back in comparison to that?—when there had once been a pride of direction and a confidence in enduring independence.

I realized that in those two years, in order to preserve something —an inner hush maybe, maybe not—I had weaned myself from all the things I used to love—that every act of life from the morning tooth-brush to the friend at dinner had become an effort. I saw that for a long time I had not liked people and things, but only followed the rickety old pretense of liking. I saw that even my love for those closest to me was become only an attempt to love, that my casual relations—with an editor, a tobacco seller, the child of a friend, were only what I remembered I *should* do, from other days. All in the same month I became bitter about such things as the sound of the radio, the advertisements in the magazines, the screech of tracks, the dead silence of the country—contemptuous at human softness, immediately (if secretively) quarrelsome toward hardness—hating the night when I couldn't sleep and hating the day because it went toward night. I slept on the heart side now because I knew that the sooner I could tire that out, even a little, the sooner would come that blessed hour of nightmare which, like a catharsis, would enable me to better meet the new day.

There were certain spots, certain faces I could look at. Like most Middle Westerners, I have never had any but the vaguest race prejudices—I always had a secret yen for the lovely Scandinavian blondes who sat on porches in St. Paul but hadn't emerged enough economically to be part of what was then society. They were too nice to be "chickens" and too quickly off the farmlands to seize a place in the sun, but I remember going round blocks to catch a single glimpse of shining hair—the bright shock of a girl I'd never know. This is urban, unpopular talk. It strays afield from the fact that in these latter days I couldn't stand the sight of Celts, English, Politicians, Strangers, Virginians, Negroes (light or dark), Hunting People, or retail clerks, and middlemen in general, all writers (I avoided writers very carefully because they can perpetuate trouble as no one else can)—and all the classes as classes and most of them as members of their class . . .

Trying to cling to something, I liked doctors and girl children up to the age of about thirteen and well-brought-up boy children from about eight years old on. I could have peace and happiness with these few categories of people. I forgot to add that I liked old men

—men over seventy, sometimes over sixty if their faces looked seasoned. I liked Katharine Hepburn's[3] face on the screen, no matter what was said about her pretentiousness, and Miriam Hopkins'[4] face, and old friends if I only saw them once a year and could remember their ghosts.

All rather inhuman and undernourished, isn't it? Well, that, children, is the true sign of cracking up.

It is not a pretty picture. Inevitably it was carted here and there within its frame and exposed to various critics. One of them can only be described as a person whose life makes other people's lives seem like death—even this time when she was cast in the usually unappealing role of Job's comforter.[5] In spite of the fact that this story is over, let me append our conversation as a sort of postscript:

"Instead of being so sorry for yourself, listen—" she said. (She always says "Listen," because she thinks while she talks—*really* thinks.) So she said: "Listen. Suppose this wasn't a crack in you—suppose it was a crack in the Grand Canyon."

"The crack's in me," I said heroically.

"Listen! The world only exists in your eyes—your conception of it. You can make it as big or as small as you want to. And you're trying to be a little puny individual. By God, if I ever cracked, I'd try to make the world crack with me. Listen! The world only exists through your apprehension of it, and so it's much better to say that it's not you that's cracked—it's the Grand Canyon."

"Baby et up all her Spinoza?"[6]

"I don't know anything about Spinoza. I know—" She spoke, then, of old woes of her own, that seemed, in the telling, to have been more dolorous than mine, and how she had met them, over-ridden them, beaten them.

I felt a certain reaction to what she said, but I am a slow-thinking man, and it occurred to me simultaneously that of all natural forces, vitality is the incommunicable one. In days when juice came into one as an article without duty, one tried to distribute it—but always without success; to further mix metaphors, vitality never "takes." You have it or you haven't it, like health or brown eyes or honor or a baritone voice. I might have asked some of it from her, neatly wrapped and ready for home cooking and digestion, but I could never have got it—not if I'd waited around for a thousand hours with the tin cup of self-pity. I could walk from her door, holding myself very carefully like cracked crockery, and go away into the world of bitterness, where I was making a home with such materials as are found there—and quote to myself after I left her door:

3. Film star (b. 1909).
4. Film star (b. 1902).
5. In the Bible, God tests Job's faith by inflicting on him a series of painful and humiliating punishments. Three friends try vainly to comfort him by explaining or rationalizing God's acts.

6. Fitzgerald answers in mocking baby-talk, substituting for "spinach" the name of Baruch Spinoza (1632–77), the Jewish heretical philosopher and rationalist, for whom God was an impersonal principal of order in the universe.

*"Ye are the salt of the earth. But if the salt hath lost its savour,
wherewith shall it be salted?"*
  Matthew 5-13.

Handle with Care

March, 1936

In a previous article this writer told about his realization that
what he had before him was not the dish that he had ordered for
his forties. In fact—since he and the dish were one, he described
himself as a cracked plate, the kind that one wonders whether it is
worth preserving. Your editor thought that the article suggested too
many aspects without regarding them closely, and probably many
readers felt the same way—and there are always those to whom all
self-revelation is contemptible, unless it ends with a noble thanks
to the gods for the Unconquerable Soul.

But I had been thanking the gods too long, and thanking them
for nothing. I wanted to put a lament into my record, without even
the background of the Euganean Hills[7] to give it color. There
weren't any Euganean hills that I could see.

Sometimes, though, the cracked plate has to be retained in the
pantry, has to be kept in service as a household necessity. It can
never again be warmed on the stove nor shuffled with the other
plates in the dishpan; it will not be brought out for company, but it
will do to hold crackers late at night or to go into the ice box under
left-overs . . .

Hence this sequel—a cracked plate's further history.

Now the standard cure for one who is sunk is to consider those
in actual destitution or physical suffering—this is an all-weather
beatitude for gloom in general and fairly salutory day-time advice
for everyone. But at three o'clock in the morning, a forgotten package has the same tragic importance as a death sentence, and the
cure doesn't work—and in a real dark night of the soul it is always
three o'clock in the morning, day after day. At that hour the tendency is to refuse to face things as long as possible by retiring into
an infantile dream—but one is continually startled out of this by
various contacts with the world. One meets these occasions as
quickly and carelessly as possible and retires once more back into
the dream, hoping that things will adjust themselves by some great
material or spiritual bonanza. But as the withdrawal persists there
is less and less chance of the bonanza—one is not waiting for the
fade-out of a single sorrow, but rather being an unwilling witness
of an execution, the disintegration of one's own personality . . .

Unless madness or drugs or drink come into it, this phase comes
to a dead-end, eventually, and is succeeded by a vacuous quiet. In
this you can try to estimate what has been sheared away and what is

7. Hills near Verona, Italy, the home of
the Latin poet Catullus (84?–54? B.C.),
who wrote a famous lament, *Farewell
to My Brother* (*Ave Atque Vale*).

left. Only when this quiet came to me, did I realize that I had gone through two parallel experiences.

The first time was twenty years ago, when I left Princeton in junior year with a complaint diagnosed as malaria. It transpired, through an X-ray taken a dozen years later, that it had been tuberculosis—a mild case, and after a few months of rest I went back to college. But I had lost certain offices, the chief one was the presidency of the Triangle Club, a musical comedy idea, and also I dropped back a class. To me college would never be the same. There were to be no badges of pride, no medals, after all. It seemed on one March afternoon that I had lost every single thing I wanted— and that night was the first time that I hunted down the spectre of womanhood that, for a little while, makes everything else seem unimportant.

Years later I realized that my failure as a big shot in college was all right—instead of serving on committees, I took a beating on English poetry; when I got the idea of what it was all about, I set about learning how to write. On Shaw's[8] principle that "If you don't get what you like, you better like what you get," it was a lucky break—at the moment it was a harsh and bitter business to know that my career as a leader of men was over.

Since that day I have not been able to fire a bad servant, and I am astonished and impressed by people who can. Some old desire for personal dominance was broken and gone. Life around me was a solemn dream, and I lived on the letters I wrote to a girl in another city. A man does not recover from such jolts—he becomes a different person and, eventually, the new person finds new things to care about.

The other episode parallel to my current situation took place after the war, when I had again over-extended my flank. It was one of those tragic loves doomed for lack of money, and one day the girl closed it out on the basis of common sense. During a long summer of despair I wrote a novel instead of letters, so it came out all right, but it came out all right for a different person. The man with the jingle of money in his pocket who married the girl a year later would always cherish an abiding distrust, an animosity, toward the leisure class—not the conviction of a revolutionist but the smouldering hatred of a peasant. In the years since then I have never been able to stop wondering where my friends' money came from, nor to stop thinking that at one time a sort of *droit de seigneur*[9] might have been exercised to give one of them my girl.

For sixteen years I lived pretty much as this latter person, distrusting the rich, yet working for money with which to share

8. George Bernard Shaw (1856–1950), British dramatist.
9. The "right of the lord" in feudal custom was later believed to give a feudal lord a claim to the sexual favors of any bride in his domain on her wedding night; it originally sanctioned abstinence on the wedding night in deference to the "right of God" to the bride's devotion.

their mobility and the grace that some of them brought into their lives. During this time I had plenty of the usual horses shot from under me—I remember some of their names—*Punctured Pride, Thwarted Expectation, Faithless, Show-off, Hard Hit, Never Again.* And after awhile I wasn't twenty-five, then not even thirty-five, and nothing was quite as good. But in all these years I don't remember a moment of discouragement. I saw honest men through moods of suicidal gloom—some of them gave up and died; others adjusted themselves and went on to a larger success than mine; but my morale never sank below the level of self-disgust when I had put on some unsightly personal show. Trouble has no necessary connection with discouragement—discouragement has a germ of its own, as different from trouble as arthritis is different from a stiff joint.

When a new sky cut off the sun last spring, I didn't at first relate it to what had happened fifteen or twenty years ago. Only gradually did a certain family resemblance come through—an over-extension of the flank, a burning of the candle at both ends; a call upon physical resources that I did not command, like a man over-drawing at his bank. In its impact this blow was more violent than the other two but it was the same in kind—a feeling that I was standing at twilight on a deserted range, with an empty rifle in my hands and the targets down. No problem set—simply a silence with only the sound of my own breathing.

In this silence there was a vast irresponsibility toward every obligation, a deflation of all my values. A passionate belief in order, a disregard of motives or consequences in favor of guess work and prophecy, a feeling that craft and industry would have a place in any world—one by one, these and other convictions were swept away. I saw that the novel, which at my maturity was the strongest and supplest medium for conveying thought and emotion from one human being to another, was becoming subordinated to a mechanical and communal art that, whether in the hands of Hollywood merchants or Russian idealists, was capable of reflecting only the tritest thought, the most obvious emotion. It was an art in which words were subordinate to images, where personality was worn down to the inevitable low gear of collaboration. As long past as 1930, I had a hunch that the talkies would make even the best selling novelist as archaic as silent pictures. People still read, if only Professor Canby's book of the month[1]—curious children nosed at the slime of Mr. Tiffany Thayer[2] in the drugstore libraries—but there was a rankling indignity, that to me had become almost an obsession, in seeing the power of the written word subordinated to another power, a more glittering, a grosser power . . .

I set that down as an example of what haunted me during the

1. Henry Seidel Canby (1878–1961), American literary scholar, popularizer, and founder of The Book-of-the-Month Club.

2. American screenwriter and author of pulp fiction (1902–50).

long night—this was something I could neither accept nor struggle against, something which tended to make my efforts obsolescent, as the chain stores have crippled the small merchant, an exterior force, unbeatable—

(I have the sense of lecturing now, looking at a watch on the desk before me and seeing how many more minutes—).

Well, when I had reached this period of silence, I was forced into a measure that no one ever adopts voluntarily: I was impelled to think. God, was it difficult! The moving about of great secret trunks. In the first exhausted halt, I wondered whether I had ever thought. After a long time I came to these conclusions, just as I write them here:

(1) That I had done very little thinking, save within the problems of my craft. For twenty years a certain man had been my intellectual conscience. That was Edmund Wilson.[3]

(2) That another man represented my sense of the "good life," though I saw him once in a decade, and since then he might have been hung. He is in the fur business in the Northwest and wouldn't like his name set down here. But in difficult situations I had tried to think what *he* would have thought, how *he* would have acted.

(3) That a third contemporary had been an artistic conscience to me—I had not imitated his infectious style, because my own style, such as it is, was formed before he published anything, but there was an awful pull toward him when I was on a spot.

(4) That a fourth man had come to dictate my relations with other people when these relations were successful: how to do, what to say. How to make people at least momentarily happy (in opposition to Mrs. Post's[4] theories of how to make everyone thoroughly uncomfortable with a sort of systematized vulgarity). This always confused me and made me want to go out and get drunk, but this man had seen the game, analyzed it and beaten it, and his word was good enough for me.

(5) That my political conscience had scarcely existed for ten years save as an element of irony in my stuff. When I became again concerned with the system I should function under, it was a man much younger than myself who brought it to me, with a mixture of passion and fresh air.

So there was not an "I" any more—not a basis on which I could organize my self-respect—save my limitless capacity for toil that it seemed I possessed no more. It was strange to have no self—to be like a little boy left alone in a big house, who knew that now he could do anything he wanted to do, but found that there was nothing that he wanted to do—

(The watch is past the hour and I have barely reached my thesis. I have some doubts as to whether this is of general interest, but if anyone wants more, there is plenty left, and your editor

3. Prominent literary critic and friend of Fitzgerald at Princeton (1895–1972).   4. Emily Post (1873–1960), American writer on etiquette.

will tell me. If you've had enough, say so—but not too loud, because I have the feeling that someone, I'm not sure who, is sound asleep—someone who could have helped me to keep my shop open. It wasn't Lenin,[5] and it wasn't God.)

Pasting It Together

April, 1936

I have spoken in these pages of how an exceptionally optimistic young man experienced a crack-up of all values, a crack-up that he scarcely knew of until long after it occurred. I told of the succeeding period of desolation and of the necessity of going on, but without benefit of Henley's[6] familiar heroics, "my head is bloody but unbowed." For a check-up of my spiritual liabilities indicated that I had no particular head to be bowed or unbowed. Once I had had a heart but that was about all I was sure of.

This was at least a starting place out of the morass in which I floundered: "I felt—therefore I was." At one time or another there had been many people who had leaned on me, come to me in difficulties or written me from afar, believed implicitly in my advice and my attitude toward life. The dullest platitude monger or the most unscrupulous Rasputin who can influence the destinies of many people must have some individuality, so the question became one of finding why and where I had changed, where was the leak through which, unknown to myself, my enthusiasm and my vitality had been steadily and prematurely trickling away.

One harassed and despairing night I packed a brief case and went off a thousand miles to think it over. I took a dollar room in a drab little town where I knew no one and sunk all the money I had with me in a stock of potted meat, crackers and apples. But don't let me suggest that the change from a rather overstuffed world to a comparative asceticism was any Research Magnificent— I only wanted absolute quiet to think out why I had developed a sad attitude toward sadness, a melancholy attitude toward melancholy and a tragic attitude toward tragedy—*why I had become identified with the objects of my horror or compassion.*

Does this seem a fine distinction? It isn't: identification such as this spells the death of accomplishment. It is something like this that keeps insane people from working. Lenin did not willingly endure the sufferings of his proletariat, nor Washington of his troops, nor Dickens of his London poor. And when Tolstoy[7] tried some such merging of himself with the objects of his attention, it was a fake and a failure. I mention these because they are the men best known to us all.

---

5. Nikolai Lenin (1870–1924), Russian revolutionist and Soviet President.
6. William E. Henley (1849–1903), British writer, author of the poem *Invictus* from which Fitzgerald quotes line 8.

7. The American General and President, George Washington (1732–99); the British novelist Charles Dickens (1812–70); and the Russian novelist Leo Tolstoy (1828–1910).

It was dangerous mist. When Wordsworth decided that "there had passed away a glory from the earth,"[8] he felt no compulsion to pass away with it, and the Fiery Particle Keats[9] never ceased his struggle against t. b. nor in his last moments relinquished his hope of being among the English poets.

My self-immolation was something sodden-dark. It was very distinctly not modern—yet I saw it in others, saw it in a dozen men of honor and industry since the war. (I heard you, but that's too easy—there were Marxians among these men.) I had stood by while one famous contemporary of mine played with the idea of the Big Out for half a year; I had watched when another, equally eminent, spent months in an asylum unable to endure any contact with his fellow men. And of those who had given up and passed on I could list a score.

This led me to the idea that the ones who had survived had made some sort of clean break. This is a big word and is no parallel to a jail-break when one is probably headed for a new jail or will be forced back to the old one. The famous "Escape" or "run away from it all" is an excursion in a trap even if the trap includes the south seas, which are only for those who want to paint them or sail them. A clean break is something you cannot come back from; that is irretrievable because it makes the past cease to exist. So, since I could no longer fulfill the obligations that life had set for me or that I had set for myself, why not slay the empty shell who had been posturing at it for four years? I must continue to be a writer because that was my only way of life, but I would cease any attempts to be a person—to be kind, just or generous. There were plenty of counterfeit coins around that would pass instead of these and I knew where I could get them at a nickel on the dollar. In thirty-nine years an observant eye has learned to detect where the milk is watered and the sugar is sanded, the rhinestone passed for diamond and the stucco for stone. There was to be no more giving of myself—all giving was to be outlawed henceforth under a new name, and that name was Waste.

The decision made me rather exuberant, like anything that is both real and new. As a sort of beginning there was a whole shaft of letters to be tipped into the waste basket when I went home, letters that wanted something for nothing—to read this man's manuscript, market this man's poem, speak free on the radio, indite notes of introduction, give this interview, help with the plot of this play, with this domestic situation, perform this act of thoughtfulness or charity.

The conjuror's hat was empty. To draw things out of it had long been a sort of sleight of hand, and now, to change the meta-

---

8. *Intimations of Immortality*, line 18 (spelling modernized), by William Wordsworth (1770–1850), English poet.   9. John Keats (1795–1821), English poet, who died of tuberculosis ("t.b.").

phor, I was off the dispensing end of the relief roll forever.

The heady villainous feeling continued.

I felt like the beady-eyed men I used to see on the commuting train from Great Neck fifteen years back—men who didn't care whether the world tumbled into chaos tomorrow if it spared their houses. I was one with them now, one with the smooth articles who said:

"I'm sorry but business is business." Or:

"You ought to have thought of that before you got into this trouble." Or:

"I'm not the person to see about that."

And a smile—ah, I would get me a smile. I'm still working on that smile. It is to combine the best qualities of a hotel manager, an experienced old social weasel, a headmaster on visitors' day, a colored elevator man, a pansy pulling a profile, a producer getting stuff at half its market value, a trained nurse coming on a new job, a body-vender in her first rotogravure, a hopeful extra swept near the camera, a ballet dancer with an infected toe, and of course the great beam of loving kindness common to all those from Washington to Beverly Hills who must exist by virtue of the contorted pan.

The voice too—I am working with a teacher on the voice. When I have perfected it the larynx will show no ring of conviction except the conviction of the person I am talking to. Since it will be largely called upon for the elicitation of the word "Yes," my teacher (a lawyer) and I are concentrating on that, but in extra hours. I am learning to bring into it that polite acerbity that makes people feel that far from being welcome they are not even tolerated and are under continual and scathing analysis at every moment. These times will of course not coincide with the smile. This will be reserved exclusively for those from whom I have nothing to gain, old worn-out people or young struggling people. They won't mind—what the hell, they get it most of the time anyhow.

But enough. It is not a matter of levity. If you are young and you should write asking to see me and learn how to be a sombre literary man writing pieces upon the state of emotional exhaustion that often overtakes writers in their prime—if you should be so young and so fatuous as to do this, I would not do so much as acknowledge your letter, unless you were related to someone very rich and important indeed. And if you were dying of starvation outside my window, I would go out quickly and give you the smile and the voice (if no longer the hand) and stick around till somebody raised a nickel to phone for the ambulance, that is if I thought there would be any copy in it for me.

I have now at last become a writer only. The man I had persistently tried to be became such a burden that I have "cut him loose" with as little compunction as a Negro lady cuts loose a rival on Saturday night. Let the good people function as such—let the overworked doctors die in harness, with one week's "vacation" a year that they can devote to straightening out their family affairs, and let the underworked doctors scramble for cases at one dollar a throw; let the soldiers be killed and enter immediately into the Valhalla[1] of their profession. That is their contract with the gods. A writer need have no such ideals unless he makes them for himself, and this one has quit. The old dream of being an entire man in the Goethe-Byron-Shaw tradition,[2] with an opulent American touch, a sort of combination of J. P. Morgan, Topham Beauclerk and St. Francis of Assisi,[3] has been relegated to the junk heap of the shoulder pads worn for one day on the Princeton freshman football field and the overseas cap never worn overseas.

So what? This is what I think now: that the natural state of the sentient adult is a qualified unhappiness. I think also that in an adult the desire to be finer in grain than you are, "a constant striving" (as those people say who gain their bread by saying it) only adds to this unhappiness in the end—that end that comes to our youth and hope. My own happiness in the past often approached such an ecstacy that I could not share it even with the person dearest to me but had to walk it away in quiet streets and lanes with only fragments of it to distil into little lines in books —and I think that my happiness, or talent for self-delusion or what you will, was an exception. It was not the natural thing but the unnatural—unnatural as the Boom; and my recent experience parallels the wave of despair that swept the nation when the Boom was over.

I shall manage to live with the new dispensation, though it has taken some months to be certain of the fact. And just as the laughing stoicism which has enabled the American Negro to endure the intolerable conditions of his existence has cost him his sense of the truth—so in my case there is a price to pay. I do not any longer like the postman, nor the grocer, nor the editor, nor the cousin's husband, and he in turn will come to dislike me, so that life will never be very pleasant again, and the sign *Cave Canem*[4] is hung permanently just above my door. I will try to be a correct animal though, and if you throw me a bone with enough meat on it I may even lick your hand.

---

1. In Norse legend, Odin's hall to which warriors returned to feast with the gods.
2. Johann Wolfgang von Goethe (1749–1832), German writer, George Gordon, Lord Byron (1788–1824), English poet, and Bernard Shaw, the English dramatist, believed that an author's writing should be part of a larger career as citizen.
3. The American financier (1837–1913); an 18th-century wit, conversationalist, and collector (1739–80); and the Italian monk (1182–1226), respectively.
4. "Beware of the Dog," the Latin motto ascribed to the Athenian philosopher Diogenes (fourth century B.C.), exponent of the philosophy of "cynicism." He was believed to have been killed by a dog bite, so the statue of a dog surmounted his tomb.

Early Success

October, 1937

Seventeen years ago this month I quit work or, if you prefer, I retired from business. I was through—let the Street Railway Advertising Company carry along under its own power. I retired, not on my profits, but on my liabilities, which included debts, despair, and a broken engagement and crept home to St. Paul to "finish a novel."

That novel, begun in a training camp late in the war, was my ace in the hole. I had put it aside when I got a job in New York, but I was as constantly aware of it as of the shoe with cardboard in the sole, during all one desolate spring. It was like the fox and goose and the bag of beans. If I stopped working to finish the novel, I lost the girl.

So I struggled on in a business I detested and all the confidence I had garnered at Princeton and in a haughty career as the army's worst aide-de-camp melted gradually away. Lost and forgotten, I walked quickly from certain places—from the pawn shop where one left the field glasses, from prosperous friends whom one met when wearing the suit from before the war—from restaurants after tipping with the last nickel, from busy cheerful offices that were saving the jobs for their own boys from the war.

Even having a first story accepted had not proved very exciting. Dutch Mount and I sat across from each other in a car-card slogan advertising office, and the same mail brought each of us an acceptance from the same magazine—the old *Smart Set*.[1]

"My check was thirty—how much was yours?"

"Thirty-five."

The real blight, however, was that my story had been written in college two years before, and a dozen new ones hadn't even drawn a personal letter. The implication was that I was on the downgrade at twenty-two. I spent the thirty dollars on a magenta feather fan for a girl in Alabama.

My friends who were not in love or who had waiting arrangements with "sensible" girls, braced themselves patiently for a long pull. Not I—I was in love with a whirlwind and I must spin a net big enough to catch it out of my head, a head full of trickling nickels and sliding dimes, the incessant music box of the poor. It couldn't be done like that, so when the girl threw me over I went home and finished my novel. And then, suddenly, everything changed, and this article is about that first wild wind of success and the delicious mist it brings with it. It is a short and precious

---

1. Sophisticated literary journal, founded in 1890 and edited from 1914 to 1924 jointly by Henry L. Mencken and George Jean Nathan, who introduced the early writing of Eugene O'Neill, Fitzgerald, and others. Bought in 1924 by William Randolph Hearst, the "new" *Smart Set* became conventional.

time—for when the mist rises in a few weeks, or a few months, one finds that the very best is over.

It began to happen in the autumn of 1919 when I was an empty bucket, so mentally blunted with the summer's writing that I'd taken a job repairing car roofs at the Northern Pacific[2] shops. Then the postman rang, and that day I quit work and ran along the streets, stopping automobiles to tell friends and acquaintances about it—my novel *This Side of Paradise* was accepted for publication. That week the postman rang and rang, and I paid off my terrible small debts, bought a suit, and woke up every morning with a world of ineffable toploftiness and promise.

While I waited for the novel to appear, the metamorphosis of amateur into professional began to take place—a sort of stitching together of your whole life into a pattern of work, so that the end of one job is automatically the beginning of another. I had been an amateur before; in October, when I strolled with a girl among the stones of a southern graveyard, I was a professional and my enchantment with certain things that she felt and said was already paced by an anxiety to set them down in a story—it was called *The Ice Palace* and it was published later. Similarly, during Christmas week in St. Paul, there was a night when I had stayed home from two dances to work on a story. Three friends called up during the evening to tell me I had missed some rare doings: a well-known man-about-town had disguised himself as a camel and, with a taxi-driver as the rear half, managed to attend the wrong party. Aghast with myself for not being there, I spent the next day trying to collect the fragments of the story.

"Well, all I can say is it was funny when it happened." "No, I don't know where he got the taxi-man." "You'd have to know him well to understand how funny it was."

In despair I said:

"Well, I can't seem to find out exactly what happened but I'm going to write about it as if it was ten times funnier than anything you've said." So I wrote it, in twenty-two consecutive hours, and wrote it "funny," simply because I was so emphatically told it was funny. *The Camel's Back* was published and still crops up in the humorous anthologies.

With the end of the winter set in another pleasant pumped-dry period, and, while I took a little time off, a fresh picture of life in America began to form before my eyes. The uncertainties of 1919 were over—there seemed little doubt about what was going to happen—America was going on the greatest, gaudiest spree in history and there was going to be plenty to tell about it. The whole golden boom was in the air—its splendid generosities, its outrageous corruptions and the tortuous death struggle of the old America in prohibition. All the stories that came into my head had a touch of

2. Railway.

disaster in them—the lovely young creatures in my novels went to ruin, the diamond mountains of my short stories blew up, my millionaires were as beautiful and damned as Thomas Hardy's[3] peasants. In life these things hadn't happened yet, but I was pretty sure living wasn't the reckless, careless business these people thought— this generation just younger than me.

For my point of vantage was the dividing line between the two generations, and there I sat—somewhat self-consciously. When my first big mail came in—hundreds and hundreds of letters on a story about a girl who bobbed her hair—it seemed rather absurd that they should come to me about it. On the other hand, for a shy man it was nice to be somebody except oneself again: to be "the Author" as one had been "the Lieutenant." Of course one wasn't really an author any more than one had been an army officer, but nobody seemed to guess behind the false face.

All in three days I got married and the presses were pounding out *This Side of Paradise* like they pound out extras in the movies.

With its publication I had reached a stage of manic depressive insanity. Rage and bliss alternated hour by hour. A lot of people thought it was a fake, and perhaps it was, and a lot of others thought it was a lie, which it was not. In a daze I gave out an interview—I told what a great writer I was and how I'd achieved the heights. Heywood Broun,[4] who was on my trail, simply quoted it with the comment that I seemed to be a very self-satisfied young man, and for some days I was notably poor company. I invited him to lunch and in a kindly way told him that it was too bad he had let his life slide away without accomplishing anything. He had just turned thirty and it was about then that I wrote a line which certain people will not let me forget: "She was a faded but still lovely woman of twenty-seven."

In a daze I told the Scribner Company[5] that I didn't expect my novel to sell more than twenty thousand copies and when the laughter died away I was told that a sale of five thousand was excellent for a first novel. I think it was a week after publication that it passed the twenty thousand mark, but I took myself so seriously that I didn't even think it was funny.

These weeks in the clouds ended abruptly a week later when Princeton turned on the book—not undergraduate Princeton but the black mass of faculty and alumni. There was a kind but reproachful letter from President Hibben,[6] and a room full of classmates who suddenly turned on me with condemnation. We had been part of a rather gay party staged conspicuously in Harvey Firestone's car of robin's-egg blue, and in the course of it I got an accidental black eye trying to stop a fight. This was magnified

3. British novelist (1840–1928).
4. American journalist, critic, and novelist (1888–1939).
5. Fitzgerald's publisher.

6. John G. Hibben (1861–1933), philosopher and clergyman, president of Princeton University (1912–32).

into an orgy and in spite of a delegation of undergraduates who went to the board of Governors, I was suspended from my club for a couple of months. The *Alumni Weekly* got after my book and only Dean Gauss[7] had a good word to say for me. The unctuousness and hypocrisy of the proceedings was exasperating and for seven years I didn't go to Princeton. Then a magazine asked me for an article about it and when I started to write it, I found I really loved the place and that the experience of one week was a small item in the total budget. But on that day in 1920 most of the joy went out of my success.

But one was now a professional—and the new world couldn't possibly be presented without bumping the old out of the way. One gradually developed a protective hardness against both praise and blame. Too often people liked your things for the wrong reasons or people liked them whose dislike would be a compliment. No decent career was ever founded on a public and one learned to go ahead without precedents and without fear. Counting the bag, I found that in 1919 I had made $800 by writing, that in 1920 I had made $18,000, stories, picture rights and book. My story price had gone from $30 to $1,000. That's a small price to what was paid later in the Boom, but what it sounded like to me couldn't be exaggerated.

The dream had been early realized and the realization carried with it a certain bonus and a certain burden. Premature success gives one an almost mystical conception of destiny as opposed to will power—at its worst the Napoleonic delusion. The man who arrives young believes that he exercises his will because his star is shining. The man who only asserts himself at thirty has a balanced idea of what will power and fate have each contributed, the one who gets there at forty is liable to put the emphasis on will alone. This comes out when the storms strike your craft.

The compensation of a very early success is a conviction that life is a romantic matter. In the best sense one stays young. When the primary objects of love and money could be taken for granted and a shaky eminence had lost its fascination, I had fair years to waste, years that I can't honestly regret, in seeking the eternal Carnival by the Sea. Once in the middle twenties I was driving along the High Corniche Road through the twilight with the whole French Riviera twinkling on the sea below. As far ahead as I could see was Monte Carlo, and though it was out of season and there were no Grand Dukes left to gamble and E. Phillips Oppenheim[8] was a fat industrious man in my hotel, who lived in a bathrobe— the very name was so incorrigibly enchanting that I could only stop the car and like the Chinese whisper: "Ah me! Ah me!" It was not Monte Carlo I was looking at. It was back into the mind

---

7. Christian Gauss (1878–1951), professor of romance languages, later Dean of
the College, at Princeton, mentor to

campus writers.
8. English novelist (1866–1946).

of the young man with cardboard soles who had walked the streets of New York. I was him again—for an instant I had the good fortune to share his dreams, I who had no more dreams of my own. And there are still times when I creep up on him, surprise him on an autumn morning in New York or a spring night in Carolina when it is so quiet that you can hear a dog barking in the next county. But never again as during that all too short period when he and I were one person, when the fulfilled future and the wistful past were mingled in a single gorgeous moment—when life was literally a dream.

1945

ERNEST HEMINGWAY
1899–1961

By the time he was twenty-four, when he published his first book in Paris, Ernest Hemingway possessed much of the raw material out of which he would fashion a forty-year literary career and a durable personal myth. He had spent his boyhood shuttling with his family between a comfortable Chicago suburb and a remnant of the earlier frontier in the backwoods of northern Michigan. From his experience as a contestant in the academic and athletic competitions of his high school, and from his exposure as hunter and fisherman to the landscape and primitive society of the Michigan woods, emerged a set of values stressing a cult of elemental experience, courage, and masculine prowess like those of a frontiersman, along with the habit of comparing the social codes of different environments, that were displayed in Hemingway's own later conduct and that of his fictional heroes.

When he served with the ambulance corps in Italy in World War I, both his legs were shattered by Austrian shrapnel while he was rescuing a wounded Italian soldier; he had accepted baptism by a Roman Catholic priest in a battlefield hospital, suffered the pain of the wound and the surgery afterward, and had survived. The reality of war, the imminence of death, and desperate commitments to survival haunted his fiction throughout his career.

Finally, as a newspaperman and then as an expatriate writer in Paris, he had honed his prose style on the principles of the best journalism and on the example of such contemporaries as Sherwood Anderson and Hemingway's fellow expatriates, Gertrude Stein and Ezra Pound. Within a decade Hemingway's style was internationally famous. Moreover, the desperate necessity for style, both in actual conduct and in writing, as a triumph over meaningless death or a shield against the disintegration of one's values and talent, had become one of his central themes in fiction, along with the quest by expatriates for rituals of commitment to vocations and actions that would constitute a stoic heroism.

Ernest Miller Hemingway was born in Oak Park, Illinois. His mother taught music, directed the choir in the Congregational church where Hemingway was confirmed in 1911, and took her six children frequently to painting exhibitions, concerts, and plays. His father was a successful physician with a relish for hunting, fishing, cooking, and taxidermy. The Hemingways spent summers at their cottage in northern Michigan. Alone, with his father, or with some Ottawa Indian children from a nearby settlement, Hemingway explored the surrounding woods. Dr. Hemingway initiated his son into the rituals of the sportsman.

In Oak Park, Hemingway was a sociable and competitive suburban youth. He learned to box, played on several high school athletic teams ("At Oak Park if you could play football you had to play it"),[1] joined civic and debating societies, and played the cello in the high school orchestra ("I played it worse than anyone on earth").[2] He also wrote regularly for the school's newspaper and literary magazine.

Hemingway refused to attend college, and, beginning to break away from the family circle whose pressures and stern piety seemed constricting, he got a job as cub reporter on the Kansas City *Star*. His assignments familiarized him with the violence and the seamy side of the city. The newspaper's style sheet instructed reporters to "Avoid the use of adjectives, especially such extravagant ones as *splendid, gorgeous, grand, magnificent*, etc.," and enjoined "short sentences," "short first paragraphs," and "vigorous English"; Hemingway later called these "the best rules I ever learned for the business of writing."[3] Though an eye defect kept him from enlisting in the army, Hemingway joined the ambulance corps in 1918 and was wounded after three weeks of active duty. He recuperated for six months and shipped home in 1919 to a hero's welcome. In 1921, after two years of loafing and sporadic journalism for *The Toronto Star*, he married Hadley Richardson and took her to live in Paris.

There he set out to bring his writing up to his own high standards of proficiency. He sent articles to Toronto journals, and he covered the Greco-Turkish war in Constantinople in 1922, but he made more exacting demands of his writing than those required for journalism. He said later that mere "timeliness" was a crutch on which newspaper writing could rely to secure emotional effect, but he recalled that in the early 1920s, in his creative writing, he was aiming for "the real thing, the sequence of motion and fact that made the motion and which would be as valid in a year or in ten years, or, with luck * * * always. * * *"[4] He traveled with Hadley in Spain, Italy, and Switzerland and shared the excitement of postwar Paris with artists, adventurers, and intellectuals, many of them British or American expatriates, whose common bond was a bitter disillusionment with traditional institutions, vague ideologies, hypocritical values, and hackneyed, imprecise language. He responded to the writing of his contemporaries, as to those of such predecessors as Turgenev or Conrad, with the canniness and at times the aggressiveness of an equal contestant or rival, and he sought models for his writing also in the paintings of such artists as Cézanne and Goya. *A Moveable Feast* (1964), containing mordant recollections of F. Scott Fitzgerald and Gertrude Stein among others, is Hemingway's nostalgic memoir of his early years in Paris.

Hemingway's first book, *Three Stories and Ten Poems*, was published in Paris in 1923, but it was his next volumes that secured his critical

1. Quoted by Charles Fenton, *The Apprenticeship of Ernest Hemingway*, p. 7.
2. George Plimpton, "Interview with Hemingway," in *Hemingway and His* *Critics*, ed. Carlos Baker, p. 28.
3. Quoted by Fenton, *The Apprenticeship of Ernest Hemingway*, pp. 31–34.
4. *Death in the Afternoon*, p. 2.

reputation and after 1929 brought him financial security. *In Our Time*, published first in Paris and then, thanks to efforts by Fitzgerald and Sherwood Anderson, published in an enlarged edition in America in 1925, traced in separate, but thematically related, short stories the growth of a youth called Nick Adams from his childhood in the Michigan woods to his return as a war veteran. Interspersed in the sequence are brief prose sketches or vignettes—including a hanging in Kansas City, a massacre in Turkey, the culmination of a bullfight in Spain—which underscore the violence and imminent tragedy that are manifest in Nick's world. Both the stories and the vignettes display the compressed irony and the understatement that characterize Hemingway's style. In 1926 appeared *The Torrents of Spring*, a savage parody of primitivistic attitudes and styles that Hemingway attributed to Sherwood Anderson, and his first and best novel, *The Sun Also Rises*. The novel's protagonist is Jake Barnes, a writer rendered impotent by a war wound, who tries to bring some measure of order to the lives of his expatriate friends in Paris and finds the epitome of courage and honor, finally, in the figure of a young bullfighter in Spain. A collection of stories, *Men without Women*, appeared in 1927. The novel *A Farewell to Arms* (1929) wrote the epitaph to a decade in its story of the tragic love affair of a wounded American lieutenant who falls in love with his British nurse and deserts the army, making "a separate peace," to flee with her to Switzerland. Their brief idyll ends when she dies in childbirth.

Hemingway's cult of athletic prowess and masculinity, his unending quest for adventure abroad and his exploits as a war correspondent in the Spanish Civil War and later in World War II, and his contributions to popular magazines made him a conspicuous public figure whose image threatened to distract readers (and to divert Hemingway himself) from his devotion to the writer's craft. He married four times and lived or traveled abroad for much of his life, even after settling in locations on the edge of America where he enjoyed frequent reunions with his three sons, first at Key West, then on the island of Bimini off Miami, later in Cuba, and finally in the American West at Ketchum, Idaho. Yet Hemingway's writings make clear that his expatriation and various threats to his vocation were precisely the material with which his imagination worked.

His tribute to Spanish culture, *Death in the Afternoon* (1932), centers on the "tragedy and ritual"[5] of the bullfight where Hemingway found an art comparable to the art of writing he wanted to perfect. The co-presence of "life and death" in the bullring, the imminence of "violent death" as "one of the simplest things of all and the most fundamental," is the elemental reality he wanted to test his feelings and his writing against.[6] The feelings aroused were more intense because grounded in bodily sensations. The bullfighter not only confronted mortal danger but, through his stylized ritual performance, "increased" and "created" the danger to his body,[7] and the ritual which thus threatened his survival also permitted him to triumph by achieving the grace and power of the matador Romero whom Hemingway had celebrated in his first novel. Such is the disciplined heroism of the bullfighters and other heroes, even those who are

5. *Ibid.*, p. 9.
6. *Ibid.*, p. 2.
7. *Ibid.*, pp. 16, 21.

defeated, in the early fiction and in Hemingway's second collection of stories (*Winner Take Nothing*, 1933).

The writer's struggle to survive, against the threats to his talent of genteel traditions in America, success, money, and domestic entanglements, is central in Hemingway's account of his safari in Africa, *The Green Hills of Africa* (1935). There he asserts a connection between big game hunting and writing, and he defines his expatriation as a continuation of the settlement of America and the movement west, claiming that "I would go, now, somewhere else as we had always had the right to go somewhere else and as we had always done."[8] The attempt by a mortally wounded American writer, on safari in Africa, to redeem his imagination from the corrosions of wealth and domestic strife is the subject of the brilliant short story *The Snows of Kilimanjaro* (1936).

Since the early 1930s Hemingway's leftist friends and critics had condemned his abstention from political affiliations and his avoidance of overtly political themes in his fiction; these were deliberate strategies in keeping with Hemingway's feeling that "anyone is cheating who takes politics as a way out" from the writer's responsibility "to write straight honest prose on human beings."[9] His next novels, while they treated more openly the theme of social solidarity, kept to Hemingway's characteristic pattern of a lonely, individualized heroism. *To Have and Have Not* (1937) experiments with narrative structure to encompass the economic hardships and cruel ironies in the life of a desperate Florida boatman who takes to smuggling during the Depression.

It culminates in the dying hero's recognition that "one man alone ain't got no bloody f - - - ing chance,"[1] but it articulates no political or social alternative to his plight. *For Whom the Bell Tolls* (1940) takes Madrid and the mountain areas of Spain during the Spanish Civil War for its canvas, and for its hero a Montana Spanish instructor who fights with a guerrilla band in the Loyalist cause, carrying out his military mission even after it proves to be absurdly futile and, while mortally wounded, mustering the strength to protect the escape of the Spanish girl with whom he has fallen in love. Yet his vaguely Jeffersonian principles have little to do with his commitment to the cause of anti-Fascism, and his experience in Madrid exposes the political machinations of Spanish and Communist politicians who have betrayed the cause. His heroism constitutes a commitment to personal responsibility and intimate love in the face of a lost gamble in a losing game.

"You are all a lost generation," Gertrude Stein had once told the young Hemingway.[2] And the concept of loss informs everything he wrote, though Hemingway's heroes seek ways to minimize the loss and to find the dignity of bravery and disciplined commitment even in defeat. Like Jake Barnes in *The Sun Also Rises*, making a staunch commitment to playing an unwinnable game properly, they care less about understanding the world than about the desperate and pragmatic need to learn "how to live in it."[3]

The requirements for playing properly—a view of the field uncluttered by delusions, and close attention to the game's technicalities—are

---

8. P. 192.
9. *By-Line: Ernest Hemingway*, ed. William White, p. 183.
1. P. 225.

2. Quoted as an epigraph to *The Sun Also Rises*.
3. *Ibid.*, p. 148.

Hemingway's stylistic requirements for his art in seeking the "discipline" that enables the imagination to "survive."[4] With such models as Biblical prose, the painter Van Gogh, the fiction of Stendhal, and, among Americans, the "good writers" Henry James, Stephen Crane, and Mark Twain,[5] he forged the discipline that amounted to a poetics of prose. "All our words from loose using have lost their edge," he charged.[6] A writer could restore that edge by using words sparingly, savoring each word as one savors good wine, and by making sentences that minutely render physical reality and physical sensation so as to capture their particularity. If a writer's prose were transparently simple and honest, Hemingway felt, he could leave his meaning implicit and the reader would discern it and even help provide it: "I always try to write on the principle of the iceberg. There is seven eighths of it under water for every part that shows."[7] Accordingly Hemingway's seemingly matter-of-fact, laconic statements are highly stylized sentences that can incorporate the rhythms and diction of colloquial speech along with archaic inversions of sentence structure and parodies of Gertrude Stein's or the Bible's prose. Their simplicity, like Twain's in *Huckleberry Finn*, assigns a priority to feeling over thought and to action over comment. The result is that Hemingway can suggest, through oblique implication, compressed irony, or understatement, a sense of moral urgency along with a considerable range and astonishing intensity of feeling, while rendering outward actions and scenes with a vividness seldom matched. His prose style had an immense impact on contemporary and younger writers in France and Italy as well as in England and America.

For Whom the Bell Tolls, though widely popular, marked the beginning of a decline in Hemingway's work, for the language had lost some of its edge and the book indulged in some self-conscious meditation and sentiment that Hemingway earlier kept better controlled. His wartime love idyll, *Across the River and into the Trees* (1950), elicited boredom and even scorn. Only the novella *The Old Man and the Sea* (1952), which reached a mass audience through *Life* magazine, *The Moveable Feast* (1964), and parts of the posthumous novel *Islands in the Stream* (1970) approached the quality of his earlier work. *The Old Man and the Sea* won the Pulitzer Prize in 1953 and occasioned the award of the Nobel Prize a year later. But for several years Hemingway suffered from physical ailments, and his emotional breakdowns that required clinical treatment were the sign of his despair that he could no longer write consistently and well. In July, 1961, in Ketchum, Idaho, following his father's example, he used a gun to take his own life.

Big Two-Hearted River
Part I[1]

The train went on up the track out of sight, around one of the hills of burnt timber. Nick sat down on the bundle of canvas and bedding the baggage man had pitched out of the door of the bag-

4. *The Green Hills of Africa*, p. 23.
5. *Ibid.*, p. 19.
6. *Ibid.*, p. 71.
7. George Plimpton, "Interview with Hemingway," in *Hemingway and His Critics*, ed. Carlos Baker, p. 34.

1. "Big Two-Hearted River" is the concluding story in *In Our Time*. In it Nick Adams returns from the ravage of World War I to the northern Michigan he had known as a child and younger man. Alone and in virtual silence, he seeks

gage car. There was no town, nothing but the rails and the burned-over country. The thirteen saloons that had lined the one street of Seney had not left a trace. The foundations of the Mansion House hotel stuck up above the ground. The stone was chipped and split by the fire. It was all that was left of the town of Seney. Even the surface had been burned off the ground.

Nick looked at the burned-over stretch of hillside, where he had expected to find the scattered houses of the town and then walked down the railroad track to the bridge over the river. The river was there. It swirled against the log spiles of the bridge. Nick looked down into the clear, brown water, colored from the pebbly bottom, and watched the trout keeping themselves steady in the current with wavering fins. As he watched them they changed their positions by quick angles, only to hold steady in the fast water again. Nick watched them a long time.

He watched them holding themselves with their noses into the current, many trout in deep, fast moving water, slightly distorted as he watched far down through the glassy convex surface of the pool, its surface pushing and swelling smooth against the resistance of the log-driven piles of the bridge. At the bottom of the pool were the big trout. Nick did not see them at first. Then he saw them at the bottom of the pool, big trout looking to hold themselves on the gravel bottom in a varying mist of gravel and sand, raised in spurts by the current.

Nick looked down into the pool from the bridge. It was a hot day. A kingfisher flew up the stream. It was a long time since Nick had looked into a stream and seen trout. They were very satisfactory. As the shadow of the kingfisher moved up the stream, a big trout shot upstream in a long angle, only his shadow marking the angle, then lost his shadow as he came through the surface of the water, caught the sun, and then, as he went back into the stream under the surface, his shadow seemed to float down the stream with the current, unresisting, to his post under the bridge where he tightened facing up into the current.

Nick's heart tightened as the trout moved. He felt all the old feeling.

He turned and looked down the stream. It stretched away, pebbly-bottomed with shallows and big boulders and a deep pool as it curved away around the foot of a bluff.

Nick walked back up the ties to where his pack lay in the cinders beside the railway track. He was happy. He adjusted the pack

---

to construct for himself a substitute for home and, through the ritual of fishing, to renew his contact with nature's vitality, discipline his feelings, bring order to the violence his sport entails, and find in the experience an alternative to the desiccation of the "burned over" area around him and the imminent trag-edy he may encounter in the future. The story is preceded by a vignette describing the death of a matador. The two parts are separated by a vignette describing the hanging of a criminal in Kansas City. The story is followed by a vignette describing an exiled King.

harness around the bundle, pulling straps tight, slung the pack on his back, got his arms through the shoulder straps and took some of the pull off his shoulders by leaning his forehead against the wide band of the tump-line. Still, it was too heavy. It was much too heavy. He had his leather rod-case in his hand and leaning forward to keep the weight of the pack high on his shoulders he walked along the road that paralleled the railway track, leaving the burned town behind in the heat, and then turned off around a hill with a high, fire-scarred hill on either side onto a road that went back into the country. He walked along the road feeling the ache from the pull of the heavy pack. The road climbed steadily. It was hard work walking up-hill. His muscles ached and the day was hot, but Nick felt happy. He felt he had left everything behind, the need for thinking, the need to write, other needs. It was all back of him.

From the time he had gotten down off the train and the baggage man had thrown his pack out of the open car door things had been different. Seney was burned, the country was burned over and changed, but it did not matter. It could not all be burned. He knew that. He hiked along the road, sweating in the sun, climbing to cross the range of hills that separated the railway from the pine plains.

The road ran on, dipping occasionally, but always climbing. Nick went on up. Finally the road after going parallel to the burnt hillside reached the top. Nick leaned against a stump and slipped out of the pack harness. Ahead of him, as far as he could see, was the pine plain. The burned country stopped off at the left with the range of hills. On ahead islands of dark pine trees rose out of the plain. Far off to the left was the line of the river. Nick followed it with his eye and caught glints of the water in the sun.

There was nothing but the pine plain ahead of him, until the far blue hills that marked the Lake Superior height of land. He could hardly see them, faint and far away in the heat-light over the plain. If he looked too steadily they were gone. But if he only half-looked they were there, the far off hills of the height of land.

Nick sat down against the charred stump and smoked a cigarette. His pack balanced on the top of the stump, harness holding ready, a hollow molded in it from his back. Nick sat smoking, looking out over the country. He did not need to get his map out. He knew where he was from the position of the river.

As he smoked, his legs stretched out in front of him, he noticed a grasshopper walk along the ground and up onto his woolen sock. The grasshopper was black. As he had walked along the road, climbing, he had started many grasshoppers from the dust. They were all black. They were not the big grasshoppers with yellow and black or red and black wings whirring out from their black wing sheathing as they fly up. These were just ordinary hoppers, but all a sooty black in color. Nick had wondered about them as he walked, without really thinking about them. Now, as he watched the black hopper that was nibbling at the wool of his sock with its fourway lip, he realized that they had all turned black from living in the burned-over land. He realized that the fire must have come the year before, but the grasshoppers were all black now. He wondered how long they would stay that way.

Carefully he reached his hand down and took hold of the hopper by the wings. He turned him up, all his legs walking in the air, and looked at his jointed belly. Yes, it was black too, iridescent where the back and head were dusty.

"Go on, hopper," Nick said, speaking out loud for the first time, "Fly away somewhere."

He tossed the grasshopper up into the air and watched him sail away to a charcoal stump across the road.

Nick stood up. He leaned his back against the weight of his pack where it rested upright on the stump and got his arms through the shoulder straps. He stood with the pack on his back on the brow of the hill looking out across the country, toward the distant river and then struck down the hillside away from the road. Underfoot the ground was good walking. Two hundred yards down the hillside the fire line stopped. Then it was sweet fern, growing ankle high, to walk through, and clumps of jack pines; a long undulating country with frequent rises and descents, sandy underfoot and the country alive again.

Nick kept his direction by the sun. He knew where he wanted to strike the river and he kept on through the pine plain, mounting small rises to see other rises ahead of him and sometimes from the top of a rise a great solid island of pines off to his right or his left. He broke off some sprigs of the heathery sweet fern, and put them under his pack straps. The chafing crushed it and he smelled it as he walked.

He was tired and very hot, walking across the uneven, shadeless pine plain. At any time he knew he could strike the river by turning off to his left. It could not be more than a mile away. But he kept on toward the north to hit the river as far upstream as he could go in one day's walking.

For some time as he walked Nick had been in sight of one of the big islands of pine standing out above the rolling high ground he was crossing. He dipped down and then as he came slowly up to the crest of the ridge he turned and made toward the pine trees.

There was no underbrush in the island of pine trees. The trunks of the trees went straight up or slanted toward each other. The trunks were straight and brown without branches. The branches were high above. Some interlocked to make a solid shadow on the brown forest floor. Around the grove of trees was a bare space. It was brown and soft underfoot as Nick walked on it. This was the over-lapping of the pine needle floor, extending out beyond the width of the high branches. The trees had grown tall and the branches moved high, leaving in the sun this bare space they had once covered with shadow. Sharp at the edge of this extension of the forest floor commenced the sweet fern.

Nick slipped off his pack and lay down in the shade. He lay on his back and looked up into the pine trees. His neck and back and the small of his back rested as he stretched. The earth felt good against his back. He looked up at the sky, through the branches, and then shut his eyes. He opened them and looked up again. There was a wind high up in the branches. He shut his eyes again and went to sleep.

Nick woke stiff and cramped. The sun was nearly down. His pack was heavy and the straps painful as he lifted it on. He leaned over with the pack on and picked up the leather rod-case and started out from the pine trees across the sweet fern swale, toward the river. He knew it could not be more than a mile.

He came down a hillside covered with stumps into a meadow. At the edge of the meadow flowed the river. Nick was glad to get to the river. He walked upstream through the meadow. His trousers were soaked with the dew as he walked. After the hot day, the dew had come quickly and heavily. The river made no sound. It was too fast and smooth. At the edge of the meadow, before he mounted to a piece of high ground to make camp, Nick looked down the river at the trout rising. They were rising to insects come from the swamp on the other side of the stream when the sun went down. The trout jumped out of water to take them. While Nick walked through the little stretch of meadow alongside the stream, trout had jumped high out of water. Now as he looked down the river, the insects must be settling on the surface, for the trout were feeding steadily all down the stream. As far down the long stretch as he could see, the trout were rising, making circles all down the surface of the water, as though it were starting to rain.

The ground rose, wooded and sandy, to overlook the meadow, the stretch of river and the swamp. Nick dropped his pack and rod-case and looked for a level piece of ground. He was very hungry and he wanted to make his camp before he cooked. Between two jack pines, the ground was quite level. He took the ax out of the pack and chopped out two projecting roots. That leveled a piece of ground large enough to sleep on. He smoothed out the sandy soil with his hand and pulled all the sweet fern bushes by their roots. His hands smelled good from the sweet fern. He smoothed the uprooted earth. He did not want anything making lumps under the blankets. When he had the ground smooth, he spread his three blankets. One he folded double, next to the ground. The other two he spread on top.

With the ax he slit off a bright slab of pine from one of the stumps and split it into pegs for the tent. He wanted them long and solid to hold in the ground. With the tent unpacked and spread on the ground, the pack, leaning against a jackpine, looked much smaller. Nick tied the rope that served the tent for a ridge-pole to the trunk of one of the pine trees and pulled the tent up off the ground with the other end of the rope and tied it to the other pine. The tent hung on the rope like a canvas blanket on a clothes line. Nick poked a pole he had cut up under the back peak of the canvas and then made it a tent by pegging out the sides. He pegged the sides out taut and drove the pegs deep, hitting them down into the ground with the flat of the ax until the rope loops were buried and the canvas was drum tight.

Across the open mouth of the tent Nick fixed cheese cloth to keep out mosquitoes. He crawled inside under the mosquito bar with various things from the pack to put at the head of the bed under the slant of the canvas. Inside the tent the light came through the brown canvas. It smelled pleasantly of canvas. Already there was something mysterious and homelike. Nick was happy as he crawled inside the tent. He had not been unhappy all day. This was different though. Now things were done. There had been this to do. Now it was done. It had been a hard trip. He was very tired. That was done. He had made his camp. He was settled. Nothing could touch him. It was a good place to camp. He was there, in the good place. He was in his home where he had made it. Now he was hungry.

He came out, crawling under the cheese cloth. It was quite dark outside. It was lighter in the tent.

Nick went over to the pack and found, with his fingers, a long nail in a paper sack of nails, in the bottom of the pack. He drove it into the pine tree, holding it close and hitting it gently with the flat of the ax. He hung the pack up on the nail. All his supplies were in the pack. They were off the ground and sheltered now.

Nick was hungry. He did not believe he had ever been hungrier. He opened and emptied a can of pork and beans and a can of spaghetti into the frying pan.

"I've got a right to eat this kind of stuff, if I'm willing to carry it," Nick said. His voice sounded strange in the darkening woods. He did not speak again.

He started a fire with some chunks of pine he got with the ax from a stump. Over the fire he stuck a wire grill, pushing the four legs down into the ground with his boot. Nick put the frying pan on the grill over the flames. He was hungrier. The beans and spaghetti warmed. Nick stirred them and mixed them together. They began to bubble, making little bubbles that rose with difficulty to the surface. There was a good smell. Nick got out a bottle of tomato catchup and cut four slices of bread. The little bubbles were coming faster now. Nick sat down beside the fire and lifted the frying pan off. He poured about half the contents out into the tin plate. It spread slowly on the plate. Nick knew it was too hot. He poured on some tomato catchup. He knew the beans and spaghetti were still too hot. He looked at the fire, then at the tent, he was not going to spoil it all by burning his tongue. For years he had never enjoyed fried bananas because he had never been able to wait for them to cool. His tongue was very sensitive. He was very hungry. Across the river in the swamp, in the almost dark, he saw a mist rising. He looked at the tent once more. All right. He took a full spoonful from the plate.

"Chrise," Nick said, "Geezus Chrise," he said happily.

He ate the whole plateful before he remembered the bread. Nick finished the second plateful with the bread, mopping the plate shiny. He had not eaten since a cup of coffee and a ham sandwich in the station restaurant at St. Ignace. It had been a very fine experience. He had been that hungry before, but had not been able to satisfy it. He could have made camp hours before if he had wanted to. There were plenty of good places to camp on the river. But this was good.

Nick tucked two big chips of pine under the grill. The fire flared up. He had forgotten to get water for the coffee. Out of the pack he got a folding canvas bucket and walked down the hill, across the edge of the meadow, to the stream. The other bank was in the white mist. The grass was wet and cold as he knelt on the bank and dipped the canvas bucket into the stream. It bellied and pulled hard in the current. The water was ice cold. Nick rinsed the bucket and carried it full up to the camp. Up away from the stream it was not so cold.

Nick drove another big nail and hung up the bucket full of water. He dipped the coffee pot half full, put some more chips under the grill onto the fire and put the pot on. He could not remember which way he made coffee. He could remember an argument about it with Hopkins, but not which side he had taken. He decided to bring it to a boil. He remembered now that was Hopkins's way. He had once argued about everything with Hopkins. While he waited for the coffee to boil, he opened a small can of apricots. He liked to open cans. He emptied the can of apricots out into a tin cup. While he watched the coffee on the fire, he drank the juice syrup of the apricots, carefully at first to keep from spilling, then meditatively, sucking the apricots down. They were better than fresh apricots.

The coffee boiled as he watched. The lid came up and coffee and grounds ran down the side of the pot. Nick took it off the grill. It was a triumph for Hopkins. He put sugar in the empty apricot cup and poured some of the coffee out to cool. It was too

hot to pour and he used his hat to hold the handle of the coffee
pot. He would not let it steep in the pot at all. Not the first cup.
It should be straight Hopkins all the way. Hop deserved that. He
was a very serious coffee maker. He was the most serious man
Nick had ever known. Not heavy, serious. That was a long time
ago. Hopkins spoke without moving his lips. He had played polo.
He made made millions of dollars in Texas. He had borrowed car-
fare to go to Chicago, when the wire came that his first big well
had come in. He could have wired for money. That would have
been too slow. They called Hop's girl the Blonde Venus. Hop did
not mind because she was not his real girl. Hopkins said very
confidently that none of them would make fun of his real girl. He
was right. Hopkins went away when the telegram came. That was
on the Black River. It took eight days for the telegram to reach
him. Hopkins gave away his .22 caliber Colt automatic pistol to
Nick. He gave his camera to Bill. It was to remember him always
by. They were all going fishing again next summer. The Hop Head
was rich. He would get a yacht and they would all cruise along
the north shore of Lake Superior. He was excited but serious. They
said good-bye and all felt bad. It broke up the trip. They never saw
Hopkins again. That was a long time ago on the Black River.

Nick drank the coffee, the coffee according to Hopkins. The
coffee was bitter. Nick laughed. It made a good ending to the
story. His mind was starting to work. He knew he could choke it
because he was tired enough. He spilled the coffee out of the pot
and shook the grounds loose into the fire. He lit a cigarette and
went inside the tent. He took off his shoes and trousers, sitting
on the blankets, rolled the shoes up inside the trousers for a pillow
and got in between the blankets.

Out through the front of the tent he watched the glow of the
fire, when the night wind blew on it. It was a quiet night. The
swamp was perfectly quiet. Nick stretched under the blanket comfortably. A mosquito hummed close to his ear. Nick sat up and
lit a match. The mosquito was on the canvas, over his head.
Nick moved the match quickly up to it. The mosquito made a
satisfactory hiss in the flame. The match went out. Nick lay down
again under the blankets. He turned on his side and shut his
eyes. He was sleepy. He felt sleep coming. He curled up under
the blanket and went to sleep.

Big Two-Hearted River
Part II

In the morning the sun was up and the tent was starting to get
hot. Nick crawled out under the mosquito netting stretched across
the mouth of the tent, to look at the morning. The grass was wet
on his hands as he came out. He held his trousers and his shoes in

his hands. The sun was just up over the hill. There was the meadow, the river and the swamp. There were birch trees in the green of the swamp on the other side of the river.

The river was clear and smoothly fast in the early morning. Down about two hundred yards were three logs all the way across the stream. They made the water smooth and deep above them. As Nick watched, a mink crossed the river on the logs and went into the swamp. Nick was excited. He was excited by the early morning and the river. He was really too hurried to eat breakfast, but he knew he must. He built a little fire and put on the coffee pot. While the water was heating in the pot he took an empty bottle and went down over the edge of the high ground to the meadow. The meadow was wet with dew and Nick wanted to catch grasshoppers for bait before the sun dried the grass. He found plenty of good grasshoppers. They were at the base of the grass stems. Sometimes they clung to a grass stem. They were cold and wet with the dew, and could not jump until the sun warmed them. Nick picked them up, taking only the medium sized brown ones, and put them into the bottle. He turned over a log and just under the shelter of the edge were several hundred hoppers. It was a grasshopper lodging house. Nick put about fifty of the medium browns into the bottle. While he was picking up the hoppers the others warmed in the sun and commenced to hop away. They flew when they hopped. At first they made one flight and stayed stiff when they landed, as though they were dead.

Nick knew that by the time he was through with breakfast they would be as lively as ever. Without dew in the grass it would take him all day to catch a bottle full of good grasshoppers and he would have to crush many of them, slamming at them with his hat. He washed his hands at the stream. He was excited to be near it. Then he walked up to the tent. The hoppers were already jumping stiffly in the grass. In the bottle, warmed by the sun, they were jumping in a mass. Nick put in a pine stick as a cork. It plugged the mouth of the bottle enough, so the hoppers could not get out and left plenty of air passage.

He had rolled the log back and knew he could get grasshoppers there every morning.

Nick laid the bottle full of jumping grasshoppers against a pine trunk. Rapidly he mixed some buckwheat flour with water and stirred it smooth, one cup of flour, one cup of water. He put a handful of coffee in the pot and dipped a lump of grease out of a can and slid it sputtering across the hot skillet. On the smoking skillet he poured smoothly the buckwheat batter. It spread like lava, the grease spitting sharply. Around the edges the buckwheat cake began to firm, then brown, then crisp. The surface was bubbling slowly to porousness. Nick pushed under the browned under surface with a fresh pine chip. He shook the skillet sideways and the cake was loose on the surface. I won't try and flop it, he thought. He slid the chip of clean wood all the way under the cake, and flopped it over onto its face. It sputtered in the pan.

When it was cooked Nick greased the skillet. He used all the batter. It made another big flapjack and one smaller one.

Nick ate a big flapjack and a smaller one, covered with apple butter. He put apple butter on the third cake, folded it over twice, wrapped it in oiled paper and put it in his shirt pocket. He put the apple butter jar back in the pack and cut bread for two sandwiches.

In the pack he found a big onion. He sliced it in two and peeled the silky outer skin. Then he cut one half into slices and made onion sandwiches. He wrapped them in oiled paper and buttoned them in the other pocket of his khaki shirt. He turned the skillet upside down on the grill, drank the coffee, sweetened and yellow brown with the condensed milk in it, and tidied up the camp. It was a nice little camp.

Nick took his fly rod out of the leather rod-case, jointed it, and shoved the rod-case back into the tent. He put on the reel and threaded the line through the guides. He had to hold it from hand to hand, as he threaded it, or it would slip back through its own weight. It was a heavy, double tapered fly line. Nick had paid eight dollars for it a long time ago. It was made heavy to lift back in the air and come forward flat and heavy and straight to make it possible to cast a fly which has no weight. Nick opened the aluminum leader box. The leaders were coiled between the damp flannel pads. Nick had wet the pads at the water cooler on the train up to St. Ignace. In the damp pads the gut leaders had softened and Nick unrolled one and tied it by a loop at the end to the heavy fly line. He fastened a hook on the end of the leader. It was a small hook; very thin and springy.

Nick took it from his hook book, sitting with the rod across his lap. He tested the knot and the spring of the rod by pulling the line taut. It was a good feeling. He was careful not to let the hook bite into his finger.

He started down to the stream, holding his rod, the bottle of grasshoppers hung from his neck by a thong tied in half hitches around the neck of the bottle. His landing net hung by a hook from his belt. Over his shoulder was a long flour sack tied at each corner into an ear. The cord went over his shoulder. The sack flapped against his legs.

Nick felt awkward and professionally happy with all his equipment hanging from him. The grasshopper bottle swung against his chest. In his shirt the breast pockets bulged against him with the lunch and his fly book.

He stepped into the stream. It was a shock. His trousers clung tight to his legs. His shoes felt the gravel. The water was a rising cold shock.

Rushing, the current sucked against his legs. Where he stepped in, the water was over his knees. He waded with the current. The gravel slid under his shoes. He looked down at the swirl of water below each leg and tipped up the bottle to get a grasshopper.

The first grasshopper gave a jump in the neck of the bottle and went out into the water. He was sucked under in the whirl by Nick's right leg and came to the surface a little way down stream. He floated rapidly, kicking. In a quick circle, breaking the smooth surface of the water, he disappeared. A trout had taken him.

Another hopper poked his head out of the bottle. His antennæ wavered. He was getting his front legs out of the bottle to jump. Nick took him by the head and held him while he threaded the slim hook under his chin, down through his thorax and into the last segments of his abdomen. The grasshopper took hold of the hook with his front feet, spitting tobacco juice on it. Nick dropped him into the water.

Holding the rod in his right hand he let out line against the pull of the grasshopper in the current. He stripped off line from the reel with his left hand and let it run free. He could see the hopper in the little waves of the current. It went out of sight.

There was a tug on the line. Nick pulled against the taut line. It was his first strike. Holding the now living rod across the current, he brought in the line with his left hand. The rod bent in jerks, the trout pumping against the current. Nick knew it was a small one. He lifted the rod straight up in the air. It bowed with the pull.

He saw the trout in the water jerking with his head and body against the shifting tangent of the line in the stream.

Nick took the line in his left hand and pulled the trout, thumping tiredly against the current, to the surface. His back was mottled the clear, water-over-gravel color, his side flashing in the sun. The rod under his right arm, Nick stooped, dipping his right hand into the current. He held the trout, never still, with his moist right hand, while he unhooked the barb from his mouth, then dropped him back into the stream.

He hung unsteadily in the current, then settled to the bottom beside a stone. Nick reached down his hand to touch him, his arm to the elbow under water. The trout was steady in the moving stream, resting on the gravel, beside a stone. As Nick's fingers touched him, touched his smooth, cool, underwater feeling he was gone, gone in a shadow across the bottom of the stream.

He's all right, Nick thought. He was only tired.

He had wet his hand before he touched the trout, so he would not disturb the delicate mucus that covered him. If a trout was touched with a dry hand, a white fungus attacked the unprotected spot. Years before when he had fished crowded streams, with fly fishermen ahead of him and behind him, Nick had again and again come on dead trout, furry with white fungus, drifted against a rock, or floating belly up in some pool. Nick did not like to fish with other men on the river. Unless they were of your party, they spoiled it.

He wallowed down the stream, above his knees in the current, through the fifty yards of shallow water above the pile of logs that crossed the stream. He did not rebait his hook and held it in his hand as he waded. He was certain he could catch small trout in the shallows, but he did not want them. There would be no big trout in the shallows this time of day.

Now the water deepened up his thighs sharply and coldly. Ahead was the smooth dammed-back flood of water above the logs. The water was smooth and dark; on the left, the lower edge of the meadow; on the right the swamp.

Nick leaned back against the current and took a hopper from the bottle. He threaded the hopper on the hook and spat on him for good luck. Then he pulled several yards of line from the reel and tossed the hopper out ahead onto the fast, dark water. It floated down towards the logs, then the weight of the line pulled the bait under the surface. Nick held the rod in his right hand, letting the line run out through his fingers.

There was a long tug. Nick struck and the rod came alive and dangerous, bent double, the line tightening, coming out of water, tightening, all in a heavy, dangerous, steady pull. Nick felt the moment when the leader would break if the strain increased and let the line go.

The reel ratcheted into a mechanical shriek as the line went out in a rush. Too fast. Nick could not check it, the line rushing out, the reel note rising as the line ran out.

With the core of the reel showing, his heart feeling stopped with the excitement, leaning back against the current that mounted icily his thighs, Nick thumbed the reel hard with his left hand. It was awkward getting his thumb inside the fly reel frame.

As he put on pressure the line tightened into sudden hardness and beyond the logs a huge trout went high out of water. As he jumped, Nick lowered the tip of the rod. But he felt, as he dropped the tip to ease the strain, the moment when the strain was too great; the hardness too tight. Of course, the leader had broken. There was no mistaking the feeling when all spring left the line and it became dry and hard. Then it went slack.

His mouth dry, his heart down, Nick reeled in. He had never seen so big a trout. There was a heaviness, a power not to be held, and then the bulk of him, as he jumped. He looked as broad as a salmon.

Nick's hand was shaky. He reeled in slowly. The thrill had been too much. He felt, vaguely, a little sick, as though it would be better to sit down.

The leader had broken where the hook was tied to it. Nick took it in his hand. He thought of the trout somewhere on the bottom, holding himself steady over the gravel, far down below the light, under the logs, with the hook in his jaw. Nick knew the trout's teeth would cut through the snell of the hook. The hook would imbed itself in his jaw. He'd bet the trout was angry. Anything that size would be angry. That was a trout. He had been solidly hooked. Solid as a rock. He felt like a rock, too, before he started off. By God, he was a big one. By God, he was the biggest one I ever heard of.

Nick climbed out onto the meadow and stood, water running down his trousers and out of his shoes, his shoes squlchy. He went over and sat on the logs. He did not want to rush his sensations any.

He wriggled his toes in the water, in his shoes, and got out a cigarette from his breast pocket. He lit it and tossed the match into the fast water below the logs. A tiny trout rose at the match, as it swung around in the fast current. Nick laughed. He would finish the cigarette.

He sat on the logs, smoking, drying in the sun, the sun warm on his back, the river shallow ahead entering the woods, curving into the woods, shallows, light glittering, big water-smooth rocks, cedars along the bank and white birches, the logs warm in the sun, smooth to sit on, without bark, gray to the touch; slowly the feeling of disappointment left him. It went away slowly, the feeling of disappointment that came sharply after the thrill that made his shoulders ache. It was all right now. His rod lying out on the logs, Nick tied a new hook on the leader, pulling the gut tight until it grimped into itself in a hard knot.

He baited up, then picked up the rod and walked to the far end of the logs to get into the water, where it was not too deep. Under and beyond the logs was a deep pool. Nick walked around the shallow shelf near the swamp shore until he came out on the shallow bed of the stream.

On the left, where the meadow ended and the woods began, a great elm tree was uprooted. Gone over in a storm, it lay back into the woods, its roots clotted with dirt, grass growing in them, rising a solid bank beside the stream. The river cut to the edge of the uprooted tree. From where Nick stood he could see deep channels, like ruts, cut in the shallow bed of the stream by the flow of the current. Pebbly where he stood and pebbly and full of boulders beyond; where it curved near the tree roots, the bed of the stream was marly and between the ruts of deep water green weed fronds swung in the current.

Nick swung the rod back over his shoulder and forward, and

the line, curving forward, laid the grasshopper down on one of the deep channels in the weeds. A trout struck and Nick hooked him.

Holding the rod far out toward the uprooted tree and sloshing backward in the current, Nick worked the trout, plunging, the rod bending alive, out of the danger of the weeds into the open river. Holding the rod, pumping alive against the current, Nick brought the trout in. He rushed, but always came, the spring of the rod yielding to the rushes, sometimes jerking under water, but always bringing him in. Nick eased downstream with the rushes. The rod above his head he led the trout over the net, then lifted.

The trout hung heavy in the net, mottled trout back and silver sides in the meshes. Nick unhooked him; heavy sides, good to hold, big undershot jaw, and slipped him, heaving and big sliding, into the long sack that hung from his shoulders in the water.

Nick spread the mouth of the sack against the current and it filled, heavy with water. He held it up, the bottom in the stream, and the water poured out through the sides. Inside at the bottom was the big trout, alive in the water.

Nick moved downstream. The sack out ahead of him, sunk, heavy in the water, pulling from his shoulders.

It was getting hot, the sun hot on the back of his neck.

Nick had one good trout. He did not care about getting many trout. Now the stream was shallow and wide. There were trees along both banks. The trees of the left bank made short shadows on the current in the forenoon sun. Nick knew there were trout in each shadow. In the afternoon, after the sun had crossed toward the hills, the trout would be in the cool shadows on the other side of the stream.

The very biggest ones would lie up close to the bank. You could always pick them up there on the Black. When the sun was down they all moved out into the current. Just when the sun made the water blinding in the glare before it went down, you were liable to strike a big trout anywhere in the current. It was almost impossible to fish then, the surface of the water was blinding as a mirror in the sun. Of course, you could fish upstream, but in a stream like the Black, or this, you had to wallow against the current and in a deep place, the water piled up on you. It was no fun to fish upstream with this much current.

Nick moved along through the shallow stretch watching the banks for deep holes. A beech tree grew close beside the river, so that the branches hung down into the water. The stream went back in under the leaves. There were always trout in a place like that.

Nick did not care about fishing that hole. He was sure he would get hooked in the branches.

It looked deep though. He dropped the grasshopper so the current took it under water, back in under the overhanging branch.

The line pulled hard and Nick struck. The trout threshed heavily, half out of water in the leaves and branches. The line was caught. Nick pulled hard and the trout was off. He reeled in and holding the hook in his hand, walked down the stream.

Ahead, close to the left bank, was a big log. Nick saw it was hollow; pointing up river the current entered it smoothly, only a little ripple spread each side of the log. The water was deepening. The top of the hollow log was gray and dry. It was partly in the shadow.

Nick took the cork out of the grasshopper bottle and a hopper clung to it. He picked him off, hooked him and tossed him out. He held the rod far out so that the hopper on the water moved into the current flowing into the hollow log. Nick lowered the rod and the hopper floated in. There was a heavy strike. Nick swung the rod against the pull. It felt as though he were hooked into the log itself, except for the live feeling.

He tried to force the fish out into the current. It came, heavily.

The line went slack and Nick thought the trout was gone. Then he saw him, very near, in the current, shaking his head, trying to get the hook out. His mouth was clamped shut. He was fighting the hook in the clear flowing current.

Looping in the line with his left hand, Nick swung the rod to make the line taut and tried to lead the trout toward the net, but he was gone, out of sight, the line pumping. Nick fought him against the current, letting him thump in the water against the spring of the rod. He shifted the rod to his left hand, worked the trout upstream, holding his weight, fighting on the rod, and then let him down into the net. He lifted him clear of the water, a heavy half circle in the net, the net dripping, unhooked him and slid him into the sack.

He spread the mouth of the sack and looked down in at the two big trout alive in the water.

Through the deepening water, Nick waded over to the hollow log. He took the sack off, over his head, the trout flopping as it came out of water, and hung it so the trout were deep in the water. Then he pulled himself up on the log and sat, the water from his trousers and boots running down into the stream. He laid his rod down, moved along to the shady end of the log and took the sandwiches out of his pocket. He dipped the sandwiches in the cold water. The current carried away the crumbs. He ate the sandwiches and dipped his hat full of water to drink, the water running out through his hat just ahead of his drinking.

It was cool in the shade, sitting on the log. He took a cigarette out and struck a match to light it. The match sunk into the gray wood, making a tiny furrow. Nick leaned over the side of the log, found a hard place and lit the match. He sat smoking and watching the river.

Ahead the river narrowed and went into a swamp. The river became smooth and deep and the swamp looked solid with cedar trees, their trunks close together, their branches solid. It would not be possible to walk through a swamp like that. The branches grew so low. You would have to keep almost level with the ground to move at all. You could not crash through the branches. That must be why the animals that lived in swamps were built the way they were, Nick thought.

He wished he had brought something to read. He felt like reading. He did not feel like going on into the swamp. He looked down the river. A big cedar slanted all the way across the stream. Beyond that the river went into the swamp.

Nick did not want to go in there now. He felt a reaction against deep wading with the water deepening up under his armpits, to hook big trout in places impossible to land them. In the swamp the banks were bare, the big cedars came together overhead, the sun did not come through, except in patches; in the fast deep water, in the half light, the fishing would be tragic. In the swamp fishing was a tragic adventure. Nick did not want it. He did not want to go down the stream any further today.

He took out his knife, opened it and stuck it in the log. Then he pulled up the sack, reached into it and brought out one of the trout. Holding him near the tail, hard to hold, alive, in his hand, he whacked him against the log. The trout quivered, rigid. Nick laid him on the log in the shade and broke the neck of the other fish the same way. He laid them side by side on the log. They were fine trout.

Nick cleaned them, slitting them from the vent to the tip of the jaw. All the insides and the gills and tongue came out in one piece. They were both males; long gray-white strips of milt, smooth and clean. All the insides clean and compact, coming out all together. Nick tossed the offal ashore for the minks to find.

He washed the trout in the stream. When he held them back up in the water they looked like live fish. Their color was not gone yet. He washed his hands and dried them on the log. Then he laid the trout on the sack spread out on the log, rolled them up in it, tied the bundle and put it in the landing net. His knife was still standing, blade stuck in the log. He cleaned it on the wood and put it in his pocket.

Nick stood up on the log, holding his rod, the landing net hanging heavy, then stepped into the water and splashed ashore. He climbed the bank and cut up into the woods, toward the high ground. He was going back to camp. He looked back. The river just showed through the trees. There were plenty of days coming when he could fish the swamp.

1923, 1925

JOHN STEINBECK
1902–1968

California-born and Stanford-educated, John Steinbeck gained prominence during the Great Depression of the 1930s as a novelist who combined themes of social protest with a benign view of human nature and a biological interpretation of human experience, a combination that gained him wide popularity and provided the basis for a career not only in fiction but also in journalism, the theater, and films.

John Ernst Steinbeck, Jr., was born in 1902 in the Salinas Valley, whose scenery, agricultural workers, and ne'er-do-well *paisanos* appear frequently in his fiction. His father was treasurer of Monterey County, and his mother was a former schoolteacher. Their library introduced him early to such standard authors as Milton, Dostoevsky, Flaubert, George Eliot, and Thomas Hardy. He was a contributor to the school newspaper, a varsity athlete, and president of his graduating class in high school, and he attended Stanford University sporadically between 1920 and 1925, majoring in English, but never finished the degree. He worked on ranches and on a road gang before trying futilely to establish himself as a writer during a brief stay in New York City in 1926, and he worked in a California fish hatchery and camped in the Sierras before publishing his first novel, *Cup of Gold*, in 1929. In those years he read D. H. Lawrence, Willa Cather, Sherwood Anderson, and particularly the novelist James Branch Cabell and Hemingway with enthusiasm, but his perennial interests were in the classics of Continental literature and the ancient historians.

In 1930 he married and moved to Pacific Grove, California, where his father provided a house and small allowance to support him. Two unsuccessful novels treating the enchantment of the American Dream and the cost of pursuing it (*The Pastures of Heaven*, 1932, and *To a God Unknown*, 1933) preceded his first successes, *Tortilla Flat* in 1935 and *In Dubious Battle* in 1936. The first was an episodic, warmly humorous treatment of a band of *paisanos* (a mixture of Spanish, Indian, and Caucasian strands). Their picturesque and shiftless ways, naïve affection for their church, mystical appreciation of nature, and loyalty to their band are given the air of legend and likened to the tales of King Arthur's Round Table. The second deals with a strike among fruit pickers, its defeat by the landowners with their vigilantes, and the efforts of Communist organizers first to organize the strike and then to exploit the workers.

Both these novels reveal the quasi-mystical appreciation of the land that characterizes Steinbeck's fiction and the theories of biological organicism and "group man" that accompany it. His interest in biology had been fired by a lasting friendship with Dr. Edward F. Ricketts, a marine biologist with whom he collaborated on an account of a marine expedition, *The Sea of Cortez* (1941). Steinbeck's conviction was that one should first accept life for what it is, not try to explain it by teleological or cause-and-effect reasoning; one should amiably admire the interrelations among organic species and particularly the "mystery" of each organism's membership in a larger organism, a "colony" or group that is greater than the sum of its components.[1] The governing view in *In Dubious Battle* is that of the sanitation doctor in the workers' camp who likes to observe, sympathetically but with detachment, the "group-men" in the strikers' ranks, each a "cell in an organism" who is "not at all like single men" because he is part of a larger entity, the group. Accordingly, the political or economic conflict in the book, though sharply dramatized, rests not so much on critical scrutiny as on wonder at the social organisms in their struggle upon the land. The same affectionate wonder at the waste of human effort and the dignity of human striving governs Steinbeck's masterpiece and most popular novel, *The Grapes of Wrath*, which won the Pulitzer Prize in 1939. Steinbeck lived and traveled with displaced migrant farmers before writing the story of the Joad family's expulsion from the Oklahoma farm by agricultural combines and bankers, their hegira to California on Route 66 in search of land and opportunity, and the persistence of their hopes when denied jobs by exploitative California landowners, even though the family is breaking up and the outcome of the radicalism to which Joad turns is uncertain. Their journey and their lives are made part of an epic quest and destiny.

An earlier and very popular success, *Of Mice and Men* (1937), revealed a facility that Steinbeck was to display often for writing in interchangeable literary forms. Conceived originally as a play, it was first written as a narrative recounting the tragic comradeship of two ranch hands; then Steinbeck wrote a dramatic version which was a Broadway hit late in the same year. *The Moon Is Down* (about Norwegian resistance to Nazi occupation) appeared almost simultaneously in novelette and dramatic versions in 1942, and the play version of *Burning Bright* (1950) was produced even before the novelette appeared. Later *Sweet Thursday* (1954) was written with the theater in mind at the start. The narratives had the sparseness of a script or scenario, reflecting the talent that Steinbeck employed on such films as the documentary about Mexico, *The Forgotten Village* (1941), and the film based on his own story, *The Red Pony* (1948).

Steinbeck's versatility extended to wartime propaganda (*Bombs Away*, 1942) and to fiction in a variety of forms that after World War II became more sentimental and at times more openly allegorical. In 1950 Steinbeck married Elaine Scott, his third wife, and moved to New York City, where he lived with his wife and son. Neither *The Wayward Bus* in 1947 (testing civilization's power to survive) nor *East of Eden* in 1952 (the history of a family that migrated to the Salinas Valley with parallels to the Biblical story of Cain and Abel) was well received. Nevertheless *Cannery Row* (1945), celebrating the hedonistic virtues of Monterey dockside bums, sustained Steinbeck's wide popularity, as did the tragic parable *The Pearl* (1947) and the travel account *Travels with Charlie in Search of America*, which occasioned the award of the Nobel Prize in 1952. The prize, though its award to Steinbeck was widely criticized by American commentators, testified to the high regard in which Steinbeck's writings had been held since the 1930s in Scandinavia, Russia, and France.

---

1. *The Sea of Cortez*, p. 165.

From The Grapes of Wrath[1]

Chapter Twenty-three

The migrant people, scuttling for work, scrabbling to live, looked always for pleasure, dug for pleasure, manufactured pleasure, and they were hungry for amusement. Sometimes amusement lay in speech, and they climbed up their lives with jokes. And it came about in the camps along the road, on the ditch banks beside the streams, under the sycamores, that the story teller grew into being, so that the people gathered in the low firelight to hear the gifted ones. And they listened while the tales were told, and their participation made the stories great.

I was a recruit against Geronimo—[2]

And the people listened, and their quiet eyes reflected the dying fire.

Them Injuns was cute—slick as snakes, an' quiet when they wanted. Could go through dry leaves, an' make no rustle. Try to do that sometime.

And the people listened and remembered the crash of dry leaves under their feet.

Come the change of season an' the clouds up. Wrong time. Ever hear of the army doing anything right? Give the army ten chances, an' they'll stumble along. Took three regiments to kill a hundred braves—always.

And the people listened, and their faces were quiet with listening. The story tellers, gathering attention into their tales, spoke in great

1. The title is from a line in *The Battle Hymn of the Republic*: "He [God] is trampling out the vintage where the grapes of wrath are stored." The novel celebrates the trek to California of the Joad family: Ma and Pa, their oldest son Tom (paroled from prison where he was serving a manslaughter sentence), the younger children Al, Ruthie, and Winfield, the pregnant, husbandless daughter Rose of Sharon and her boy friend Connie, and their grandparents. Forced off their tenant farms in the Oklahoma Dust Bowl and enticed by ads for farm workers in the Promised Land of California, they make the journey across Route 66 in their ramshackle truck to California. There, except for a temporary stay in a comfortable government camp, they are scorned as "Okies," hounded out of towns by sheriffs, and repelled by rival workers, exploited by labor contractors, driven to the verge of starvation. Caught up in a strike while picking cotton, Tom commits murder and goes off to become a labor organizer, Rose of Sharon gives birth to a stillborn child, and the family breaks up. Its hopes are sustained nevertheless by Ma's conviction that "We're the people

—we go on," Tom's assurance that he will live in the "hungry people's" struggle to "eat the stuff they raise an' live in the houses they build," and the Preacher Casy's tribute to the enduring "holiness" of people working together. The narrative and the characters are given an epic dimension by Steinbeck's lyric and celebratory prose, with its at-times Biblical rhetoric and rhythms, and by chapters interspersed through the narration as interludes; the interludes do not relate directly to the Joads but extend the scope of the novel by treating social and economic issues or portraying incidents and occasions that are typical of the human experience that the Joads share. The following selections discuss the people's relish of diversion and entertainment, narrate an attempt by outsiders to break up a dance at the government camp where the Joads are living, and lament an economic system that permits simultaneous human starvation and waste of the fruits of nature.

2. Geronimo (1829–1909), Apache chief who led his tribe in the Apache wars of the 1880s, was captured in Mexico in 1886, and later became a farmer and stock raiser in Oklahoma.

rhythms, spoke in great words because the tales were great, and the listeners became great through them.

They was a brave on a ridge, against the sun. Knowed he stood out. Spread his arms an' stood. Naked as morning, an' against the sun. Maybe he was crazy. I don't know. Stood there, arms spread out; like a cross he looked. Four hundred yards. An' the men— well, they raised their sights an' they felt the wind with their fingers; an' then they jus' lay there an' couldn't shoot. Maybe that Injun knowed somepin. Knowed we couldn' shoot. Jes' laid there with the rifles cocked, an didn' even put 'em to our shoulders. Lookin' at him. Head-band, one feather. Could see it, an' naked as the sun. Long time we laid there an' looked, an' he never moved. An' then the captain got mad. "Shoot, you crazy bastards, shoot!" he yells. An' we jus' laid there. "I'll give you to a five-count, an' then mark you down," the captain says. Well, sir—we put up our rifles slow, an' ever' man hoped somebody'd shoot first. I ain't never been so sad in my life. An' I laid my sights on his belly, 'cause you can't stop a Injun no other place—an'—then. Well, he jest plunked down an' rolled. An' we went up. An' he wasn' big—he'd looked so grand—up there. All tore to pieces an' little. Ever see a cock pheasant, stiff and beautiful, ever' feather drawed an' painted, an' even his eyes drawed in pretty? An' bang; You pick him up—bloody an' twisted, an' you spoiled somepin better'n you; an' eatin' him don't never make it up to you, 'cause you spoiled somepin in yaself, an' you can't never fix it up.

And the people nodded, and perhaps the fire spurted a little light and showed their eyes looking in on themselves.

Against the sun, with his arms out. An' he looked big—as God.

And perhaps a man balanced twenty cents between food and pleasure, and he went to a movie in Marysville or Tulare, in Ceres or Mountain View. And he came back to the ditch camp with his memory crowded. And he told how it was:

They was this rich fella, an' he makes like he's poor, an' they's this rich girl, an' she purtends like she's poor too, an' they meet in a hamburg' stan'.

Why?

I don't know why—that's how it was.

Why'd they purtend like they's poor?

Well, they're tired of bein' rich.

Horseshit!

You want to hear this, or not?

Well, go on then. Sure, I wanta hear it, but if I was rich, if I was rich I'd git so many pork chops—I'd cord 'em up aroun' me like wood, an' I'd eat my way out. Go on.

Well, they each think the other one's poor. An' they git arrested an' they git in jail, an' they don' git out 'cause the other one'd find out the first one is rich. An' the jail keeper, he's mean to 'em 'cause he thinks they're poor. Oughta see how he looks when he finds out. Jes' nearly faints, that's all.

What they git in jail for?

Well, they git caught at some kind a radical meetin' but they ain't radicals. They jes' happen to be there. An' they don't each one wanta marry fur money, ya see.

So the sons-of-bitches start lyin' to each other right off.

Well, in the pitcher it was like they was doin' good. They're nice to people, you see.

I was to a show oncet that was me, an' more'n me; an' my life, an' more'n my life, so ever'thing was bigger.

Well, I git enough sorrow. I like to git away from it.

Sure—if you can believe it.

So they got married, an' then they foun' out, an' all them people that's treated 'em mean. They was a fella had been uppity, an' he nearly fainted when this fella come in with a plug hat on. Jes' nearly fainted. An' they was a newsreel with them German soldiers kickin' up their feet[3]—funny as hell.

And always, if he had a little money, a man could get drunk. The hard edges gone, and the warmth. Then there was no loneliness, for a man could people his brain with friends, and he could find his enemies and destroy them. Sitting in a ditch, the earth grew soft under him. Failures dulled and the future was no threat. And hunger did not skulk about, but the world was soft and easy, and a man could reach the place he started for. The stars came down wonderfully close and the sky was soft. Death was a friend, and sleep was death's brother. The old times came back—a girl with pretty feet, who danced one time at home—a horse—a long time ago. A horse and a saddle. And the leather was carved. When was that? Ought to find a girl to talk to. That's nice. Might lay with her, too. But warm here. And the stars down so close, and sadness and pleasure so close together, really the same thing. Like to stay drunk all the time. Who says it's bad? Who dares to say it's bad? Preachers—but they got their own kinda drunkeness. Thin, barren women, but they're too miserable to know. Reformers—but they don't bite deep enough into living to know. No—the stars are close and dear and I have joined the brotherhood of the worlds. And everything's holy—everything, even me.

A harmonica is easy to carry. Take it out of your hip pocket, knock it against your palm to shake out the dirt and pocket fuzz and bits of tobacco. Now it's ready. You can do anything with a harmonica: thin reedy single tone, or chords, or melody with rhythm chords. You can mold the music with curved hands, making it wail and cry like bagpipes, making it full and round like an organ,

3. The "goose step" of marching German troops.

making it as sharp and bitter as the reed pipes of the hills. And you can play and put it back in your pocket. It is always with you, always in your pocket. And as you play, you learn new tricks, new ways to mold the tone with your hands, to pinch the tone with your lips, and no one teaches you. You feel around—sometimes alone in the shade at noon, sometimes in the tent door after supper when the women are washing up. Your foot taps gently on the ground. Your eyebrows rise and fall in rhythm. And if you lose it or break it, why, it's no great loss. You can buy another for a quarter.

A guitar is more precious. Must learn this thing. Fingers of the left hand must have callus caps. Thumb of the right hand a horn of callus. Stretch the left-hand fingers, stretch them like a spider's legs to get the hard pads on the frets.

This was my father's box. Wasn't no bigger'n a bug first time he give me C chord. An' when I learned as good as him, he hardly never played no more. Used to set in the door, an' listen an' tap his foot. I'm tryin' for a break, an' he'd scowl mean till I get her, an' then he'd settle back easy, an' he'd nod. "Play," he'd say. "Play nice." It's a good box. See how the head is wore. They's many a million songs wore down that wood an' scooped her out. Some day she'll cave in like a egg. But you can't patch her nor worry her no way or she'll lose tone. Play her in the evening, an' they's a harmonica player in the nex' tent. Makes it pretty nice together.

The fiddle is rare, hard to learn. No frets, no teacher.

Jes' listen to a ol' man an' try to pick it up. Won't tell how to double.[4] Says it's a secret. But I watched. Here's how he done it.

Shrill as a wind, the fiddle, quick and nervous and shrill.

She ain't much of a fiddle. Give two dollars for her. Fella says they's fiddles four hundred years old, and they git mellow like whisky. Says they'll cost fifty-sixty thousan' dollars. I don't know. Soun's like a lie. Harsh ol' bastard, ain't she? Wanta dance? I'll rub up the bow with plenty rosin. Man! Then she'll squawk. Hear her a mile.

These three in the evening, harmonica and fiddle and guitar. Playing a reel and tapping out the tune, and the big deep strings of the guitar beating like a heart, and the harmonica's sharp chords and the skirl and squeal of the fiddle. People have to move close. They can't help it. "Chicken Reel" now, and the feet tap and a young lean buck takes three quick steps, and his arms hang limp. The square closes up and the dancing starts, feet on the bare ground, beating dull, strike with your heels. Hands 'round and swing. Hair falls down, and panting breaths. Lean to the side now.

Look at that Texas boy, long legs loose, taps four times for ever' damn step. Never seen a boy swing aroun' like that. Look at him swing that Cherokee girl, red in her cheeks an' her toe points out. Look at her pant, look at her heave. Think she's tired? Think she's

---

4. To play two strings simultaneously on a violin.

winded? Well, she ain't. Texas boy got his hair in his eyes, mouth's wide open, can't get air, but he pats four times for ever' darn step, an' he'll keep a-going' with the Cherokee girl.

The fiddle squeaks and the guitar bongs. Mouth-organ man is red in the face. Texas boy and the Cherokee girl, pantin' like dogs an' a-beatin' the groun'. Ol' folks stan' a-pattin' their han's. Smilin' a little, tappin' their feet.

Back home—in the schoolhouse, it was. The big moon sailed off to the westward. An' we walked, him an' me—a little ways. Didn' talk 'cause our throats was choked up. Didn't talk none at all. An' purty soon they was a haycock. Went right to it and laid down there. Seein' the Texas boy an' that girl a-steppin' away into the dark—think nobody seen 'em go. Oh God! I wisht I was a-goin' with that Texas boy. Moon'll be up 'fore long. I seen that girl's ol' man move out to stop 'em, an' then he didn'. He knowed. Might as well stop the fall from comin', and might as well stop the sap from movin' in the trees. An' the moon'll be up 'fore long.

Play more—play the story songs—"As I Walked through the Streets of Laredo."

The fire's gone down. Be a shame to build her up. Little ol' moon'll be up 'fore long.

Beside an irrigation ditch a preacher labored and the people cried. And the preacher paced like a tiger, whipping the people with his voice, and they groveled and whined on the ground. He calculated them, gauged them, played on them, and when they were all squirming on the ground he stooped down and of his great strength he picked each one up in is arms and shouted, Take 'em, Christ! and threw each one in the water. And when they were all in, waist deep in the water, and looking with frightened eyes at the master, he knelt down on the bank and he prayed for them; and he prayed that all men and women might grovel and whine on the ground. Men and women, dripping, clothes sticking tight, watched; then gurgling and sloshing in their shoes they walked back to the camp, to the tents, and they talked softly in wonder:

We been saved, they said. We're washed white as snow. We won't never sin again.

And the children, frightened and wet, whispered together:

We been saved. We won't sin no more.

Wisht I knowed what all the sins was, so I could do 'em.

The migrant people looked humbly for pleasure on the roads.

Chapter Twenty-four

On Saturday morning the wash tubs were crowded. The women washed dresses, pink ginghams and flowered cottons, and they hung them in the sun and stretched the cloth to smooth it. When afternoon came the whole camp quickened and the people grew excited. The children caught the fever and were more noisy than usual. About mid-afternoon child bathing began, and as each child was caught, subdued, and washed, the noise on the playground gradually subsided. Before five, the children were scrubbed and warned about getting dirty again; and they walked about, stiff in clean clothes, miserable with carefulness.

At the big open-air dance platform a committee was busy. Every bit of electric wire had been requisitioned. The city dump had been visited for wire, every tool box had contributed friction tape. And now the patched, spliced wire was strung out to the dance floor, with bottle necks as insulators. This night the floor would be lighted for the first time. By six o'clock the men were back from work or from looking for work, and a new wave of bathing started. By seven, dinners were over, men had on their best clothes: freshly washed overalls, clean blue shirts, sometimes the decent blacks. The girls were ready in their print dresses, stretched and clean, their hair braided and ribboned. The worried women watched the families and cleaned up the evening dishes. On the platform the string band practiced, surrounded by a double wall of children. The people were intent and excited.

In the tent of Ezra Huston, chairman, the Central Committee of five men went into meeting. Huston, a tall spare man, wind-blackened, with eyes like little blades, spoke to his committee, one man from each sanitary unit.

"It's goddamn lucky we got the word they was gonna try to bust up the dance!" he said.

The tubby little representative from Unit Three spoke up. "I think we oughta squash the hell out of 'em, an' show 'em."

"No," said Huston. "That's what they want. No, sir. If they can git a fight goin', then they can run in the cops an' say we ain't orderly. They tried it before—other places." He turned to the sad dark boy from Unit Two. "Got the fellas together to go roun' the fences an' see nobody sneaks in?"

The sad boy nodded. "Yeah! Twelve. Tol' em not to hit nobody. Jes' push 'em out ag'in."

Huston said, "Will you go out an' find Willie Eaton? He's chairman a the entertainment, ain't he?"

"Yeah."

"Well, tell 'im we wanta see 'im."

The boy went out, and he returned in a moment with a stringy Texas man. Willie Eaton had a long fragile jaw and dust-colored hair. His arms and legs were long and loose, and he had the gray sunburned eyes of the Panhandle. He stood in the tent, grinning, and his hands pivoted restlessly on his wrists.

Huston said, "You heard about tonight?"

Willie grinned. "Yeah!"

"Did anything 'bout it?"

"Yeah!"

"Tell what you done."

Willie Eaton grinned happily. "Well, sir, ordinary ent'tainment committee is five. I got twenty more—all good strong boys. They're a-gonna be a-dancin' an a-keepin' their eyes open an' their ears open. First sign—any talk or argament, they close in tight. Worked her out purty nice. Can't even see nothing. Kinda move out, an' the fella will go out with 'em."

"Tell 'em they ain't to hurt the fellas."

Willie laughed gleefully. "I tol' 'em," he said.

"Well, tell 'em so they know."

"They know. Got five men out to the gate lookin' over the folks that comes in. Try to spot 'em 'fore they git started."

Huston stood up. His steel-colored eyes were stern. "Now you look here, Willie. We don't want them fellas hurt. They's gonna be deputies out by the front gate. If you blood 'em up, why—them deputies'll git you."

"Got that there figgered out," said Willie. "Take 'em out the back way, into the fiel'. Some a the boys'll see they git on their way."

"Well, it soun's awright," Huston said worriedly. "But don't you let nothin happen, Willie. You're responsible. Don' you hurt them fellas. Don' you use no stick nor no knife or arn, or nothing like that."

"No, sir," said Willie. "We won't mark 'em."

Huston was suspicious. "I wisht I knowed I could trus' you, Willie. If you got to sock 'em, sock 'em where they won't bleed."

"Yes, sir!" said Willie.

"You sure of the fellas you picked?"

"Yes, sir."

"Awright. An' if she gits outa han', I'll be in the right-han' corner, this way on the dance floor."

Willie saluted in mockery and went out.

Huston said, "I dunno. I jes' hope Willie's boys don't kill nobody. What the hell the deputies want to hurt the camp for? Why can't they let us be?"

The sad boy from Unit Two said, "I lived out at Sunlan' Lan' an' Cattle Company's place. Honest to God, they got a cop for ever' ten people. Got one water faucet for 'bout two hundred people."

The tubby man said, "Jesus, God, Jeremy. You ain't got to tell me. I was there. They got a block of shacks—thirty-five of 'em in a row, an' fifteen deep. An' they got ten crappers for the whole shebang. An', Christ, you could smell 'em a mile. One of them deputies give me the lowdown. We was settin' aroun', an' he says, 'Them goddamn gov'ment camps,' he says. 'Give people hot water, an' they gonna want hot water. Give 'em flush toilets, an' they gonna want 'em.' He says, 'You give them goddamn Okies stuff like that an' they'll want 'em.' An' he says, 'They hol' red meetin's[5] in them gov'ment camps. All figgerin' how to git on relief,' he says."

Huston asked, "Didn' nobody sock him?"

"No. They was a little fella, an' he says, 'What you mean, relief?'

" 'I mean relief—what us taxpayers puts in an' you goddamn Okies takes out.'

" 'We pay sales tax an' gas tax an' tobacco tax,' this little guy says. An' he says, 'Farmers get four cents a cotton poun' from the gov'ment—ain't that relief?' An' he says, 'Railroads an' shippin' companies draws subsidies—ain't that relief?'

" 'They're doin' stuff got to be done,' this deputy says.

" 'Well,' the little guy says, 'how'd your goddamn crops get picked if it wasn't for us?' " The tubby man looked around.

"What'd the deputy say?" Huston asked.

"Well, the deputy got mad. An' he says, 'You goddamn reds is all the time stirrin' up trouble,' he says. 'You better come along with me.' So he takes this little guy in, an' they give him sixty days in jail for vagrancy."

"How'd they do that if he had a job?" asked Timothy Wallace.

The tubby man laughed. "You know better'n that," he said. "You know a vagrant is anybody a cop don't like. An' that's why they hate this here camp. No cops can get in. This here's United States, not California."

Huston sighed. "Wisht we could stay here. Got to be goin' 'fore long. I like this here. Folks gits along nice; an', God Awmighty, why can't they let us do it 'stead of keepin' us miserable an' puttin' us in jail? I swear to God they gonna push us into fightin' if they don't quit a-worryin' us." Then he calmed his voice. "We jes' got to keep peaceful," he reminded himself. "The committee got no right to fly off'n the handle."

The tubby man from Unit Three said, "Anybody that thinks this committee got all cheese an' crackers ought to jes' try her. They was a fight in my unit today—women. Got to callin' names, an' then got to throwin' garbage. Ladies' Committee couldn' handle it, an' they come to me. Want me to bring the fight in this here committee. I tol' 'em they got to handle women trouble theirselves. This here committee ain't gonna mess with no garbage fights."

Huston nodded. "You done good," he said.

And now the dusk was falling, and as the darkness deepened the practicing of the string band seemed to grow louder. The lights flashed on and two men inspected the patched wire to the dance floor. The children crowded thickly about the musicians. A boy with a guitar sang the "Down Home Blues," chording delicately for himself, and on his second chorus three harmonicas and a fiddle

5. Radical meetings, supposedly organized by the "reds" (Communists).

joined him. From the tents the people streamed toward the platform, men in their clean blue denim and women in their ginghams.
They came near to the platform and then stood quietly waiting,
their faces bright and intent under the light.

Around the reservation there was a high wire fence, and along
the fence, at intervals of fifty feet, the guards sat in the grass and
waited.

Now the cars of the guests began to arrive, small farmers and
their families, migrants from other camps. And as each guest came
through the gate he mentioned the name of the camper who had
invited him.

The string band took a reel tune up and played loudly, for they
were not practicing any more. In front of their tents the Jesus-lovers
sat and watched, their faces hard and contemptuous. They did not
speak to one another, they watched for sin, and their faces condemned the whole proceeding.

At the Joad tent Ruthie and Winfield had bolted what little
dinner they had, and then they started for the platform. Ma called
them back, held up their faces with a hand under each chin, and
looked into their nostrils, pulled their ears and looked inside, and
sent them to the sanitary unit to wash their hands once more. They
dodged around the back of the building and bolted for the platform, to stand among the children, close-packed about the band.

Al finished his dinner and spent half an hour shaving with Tom's
razor. Al had a tight-fitting wool suit and a striped shirt, and he
bathed and washed and combed his straight hair back. And when
the washroom was vacant for a moment, he smiled engagingly at
himself in the mirror, and he turned and tried to see himself in profile when he smiled. He slipped his purple arm-bands on and put on
his tight coat. And he rubbed up his yellow shoes with a piece of
toilet paper. A late bather came in, and Al hurried out and walked
recklessly toward the platform, his eye peeled for girls. Near the
dance floor he saw a pretty blond girl sitting in front of a tent. He
sidled near and threw open his coat to show his shirt.

"Gonna dance tonight?" he asked.

The girl looked away and did not answer.

"Can't a fella pass a word with you? How 'bout you an' me
dancin'?" And he said nonchalantly, "I can waltz."

The girl raised her eyes shyly, and she said, "That ain't nothin'
—anybody can waltz."

"Not like me," said Al. The music surged, and he tapped one
foot in time. "Come on," he said.

A very fat woman poked her head out of the tent and scowled at
him. "You git along," she said fiercely. "This here girl's spoke for.
She's a-gonna be married, an' her man's a-comin' for her."

Al winked rakishly at the girl, and he tripped on, striking his feet
to the music and swaying his shoulders and swinging his arms. And

the girl looked after him intently.

Pa put down his plate and stood up. "Come on, John," he said; and he explained to Ma, "We're a-gonna talk to some fellas about gettin' work." And Pa and Uncle John walked toward the manager's house.

Tom worked a piece of store bread into the stew gravy on his plate and ate the bread. He handed his plate to Ma, and she put it in the bucket of hot water and washed it and handed it to Rose of Sharon to wipe. "Ain't you goin' to the dance?" Ma asked.

"Sure," said Tom. "I'm on a committee. We're gonna entertain some fellas."

"Already on a committee?" Ma said. "I guess it's 'cause you got work."

Rose of Sharon turned to put the dish away. Tom pointed at her. "My God, she's a-gettin' big," he said.

Rose of Sharon blushed and took another dish from Ma. "Sure she is," Ma said.

"An' she's gettin' prettier," said Tom.

The girl blushed more deeply and hung her head. "You stop it," she said, softly.

" 'Course she is," said Ma. "Girl with a baby always gets prettier."

Tom laughed. "If she keeps a-swellin' like this, she gonna need a wheelbarra to carry it."

"Now you stop," Rose of Sharon said, and she went inside the tent, out of sight.

Ma chuckled, "You shouldn' ought to worry her."

"She likes it," said Tom.

"I know she likes it, but it worries her, too. And she's a-mournin' for Connie."

"Well, she might's well give him up. He's prob'ly studyin' to be President of the United States by now."

"Don't worry her," Ma said. "She ain't got no easy row to hoe."

Willie Eaton moved near, and he grinned and said, "You Tom Joad?"

"Yeah."

"Well, I'm Chairman the Entertainment Committee. We gonna need you. Fella tol' me 'bout you."

"Sure, I'll play with you," said Tom. "This here's Ma."

"Howdy," said Willie.

"Glad to meet ya."

Willie said, "Gonna put you on the gate to start, an' then on the floor. Want ya to look over the guys when they come in, an' try to spot 'em. You'll be with another fella. Then later I want ya to dance an' watch."

"Yeah! I can do that awright," said Tom.

Ma said apprehensively, "They ain't no trouble?"

"No, ma'am," Willie said. "They ain't gonna be no trouble."

"None at all," said Tom. "Well, I'll come 'long. See you at the dance, Ma." The two young men walked quickly away toward the main gate.

Ma piled the washed dishes on a box. "Come on out," she called, and when there was no answer, "Rosasharn, you come out."

The girl stepped from the tent, and she went on with the dish-wiping.

"Tom was on'y jollyin' ya."

"I know. I didn't mind; on'y I hate to have folks look at me."

"Ain't no way to he'p that. Folks gonna look. But it makes folks happy to see a girl in a fambly way—makes folks sort of giggly an' happy. Ain't you a-goin' to the dance?"

"I was—but I don' know. I wisht Connie was here." Her voice rose. "Ma, I wisht he was here. I can't hardly stan' it."

Ma looked closely at her. "I know," she said. "But, Rosasharn—don' shame your folks."

"I don' aim to, Ma."

"Well, don't you shame us. We got too much on us now, without no shame."

The girl's lip quivered. "I—I ain' goin' to the dance. I couldn'—Ma—he'p me!" She sat down and buried her head in her arms.

Ma wiped her hands on the dish towel and she squatted down in front of her daughter, and she put her two hands on Rose of Sharon's hair. "You're a good girl," she said. "You always was a good girl. I'll take care a you. Don't you fret." She put an interest in her tone. "Know what you an' me's gonna do? We're a-goin' to that dance, an' we're a-gonna set there an' watch. If anybody says to come dance—why, I'll say you ain't strong enough. I'll say you're poorly. An' you can hear the music an' all like that."

Rose of Sharon raised her head. "You won't let me dance?"

"No, I won't."

"An don' let nobody touch me."

"No, I won't."

The girl sighed. She said desperately, "I don' know what I'm a-gonna do, Ma. I jus' don' know. I don' know."

Ma patted her knee. "Look," she said. "Look here at me. I'm a-gonna tell ya. In a little while it ain't gonna be so bad. In a little while. An' that's true. Now come on. We'll go get washed up, an' we'll put on our nice dress an' we'll set by the dance." She led Rose of Sharon toward the sanitary unit.

Pa and Uncle John squatted with a group of men by the porch of the office. "We nearly got work today," Pa said. "We was jus' a few minutes late. They awready got two fellas. An', well, sir, it was a funny thing. They's a straw boss there, an' he says, 'We jus' got some two-bit men. 'Course we could use twenty-cent men. We can use a lot a twenty-cent men. You go to your camp an' say we'll put a lot a fellas on for twenty cents.' "

The squatting men moved nervously. A broad-shouldered man, his face completely in the shadow of a black hat, spatted his knee with his palm. "I know it, goddamn it!" he cried. "An' they'll git men. They'll git hungry men. You can't feed your fam'ly on twenty cents an hour, but you'll take anything. They got you goin' an' comin'. They jes' auction a job off. Jesus Christ, pretty soon they're gonna make us pay to work."

"We would of took her," Pa said. "We ain't had no job. We sure would a took her, but they was them guys in there, an' the way they looked, we was scairt to take her."

Black Hat said, "Get crazy thinkin'! I been workin' for a fella, an' he can't pick his crop. Cost more jes' to pick her than he can git for her, an' he don' know what to do."

"Seems to me—" Pa stopped. The circle was silent for him. "Well—I jus' thought, if a fella had a acre. Well, my woman she could raise a little truck an' a couple pigs an' some chickens. An' us men could get out an' find work, an' then go back. Kids could maybe go to school. Never seen sech schools as out here."

"Our kids ain't happy in them schools," Black Hat said.

"Why not? They're pretty nice, them schools."

"Well, a raggedy kid with no shoes, an' them other kids with socks on, an' nice pants, an' them a-yellin' 'Okie.' My boy went to school. Had a fight evr' day. Done good, too. Tough little bastard. Ever' day he got to fight. Come home with his clothes tore an' his nose bloody. An' his ma'd whale him. Made her stop that. No need ever'body beatin' the hell outa him, poor little fella. Jesus! He give some a them kids a goin'-over, though—them nice-pants sons-a-bitches. I dunno. I dunno."

Pa demanded, "Well, what the hell am I gonna do? We're outa money. One of my boys got a short job, but that won't feed us. I'm a-gonna go an' take twenty cents. I got to."

Black Hat raised his head, and his bristled chin showed in the light, and his stringy neck where the whiskers lay flat like fur. "Yeah!" he said bitterly. "You'll do that. An' I'm a two-bit man. You'll take my job for twenty cents. An' then I'll git hungry an' I'll take my job back for fifteen. Yeah! You go right on an' do her."

"Well, what the hell can I do?" Pa demanded. "I can't starve so's you can get two bits."

Black Hat dipped his head again, and his chin went into the shadow. "I dunno," he said. "I jes' dunno. It's bad enough to work twelve hours a day an' come out jes' a little bit hungry, but we got to figure all a time, too. My kid ain't gettin' enough to eat. I can't think all the time, goddamn it! It drives a man crazy." The circle of men shifted their feet nervously.

Tom stood at the gate and watched the people coming in to the dance. A floodlight shone down into their faces. Willie Eaton said, "Jes' keep your eyes open. I'm sendin' Jule Vitela over. He's half Cherokee. Nice fella. Keep your eyes open. An' see if you can pick out the ones."

"O.K.," said Tom. He watched the farm families come in, the girls with braided hair and the boys polished for the dance. Jule came and stood beside him.

"I'm with you," he said.

Tom looked at the hawk nose and the high brown cheek bones and the slender receding chin. "They says you're half Injun. You look all Injun to me."

"No," said Jule. "Jes' half. Wisht I was a full-blood. I'd have my lan' on the reservation. Them full-bloods got it pretty nice, some of 'em."

"Look a them people," Tom said.

The guests were moving in through the gateway, families from the farms, migrants from the ditch camps. Children straining to be free and quiet parents holding them back.

Jule said, "These here dances done funny things. Our people got nothing, but jes' because they can ast their frien's to come here to the dance, sets 'em up an' makes 'em proud. An' the folks respects 'em 'count of these here dances. Fella got a little place where I was a-workin'. He come to a dance here. I ast him myself, an' he come. Says we got the only decent dance in the county, where a man can take his girls an' his wife. Hey! Look."

Three young men were coming through the gate—young working men in jeans. They walked close together. The guard at the gate questioned them, and they answered and passed through.

"Look at 'em careful," Jule said. He moved to the guard. "Who ast them three?" he asked.

"Fella named Jackson, Unit Four."

Jule came back to Tom. "I think them's our fellas."

"How ya know?"

"I dunno how. Jes' got a feelin'. They're kinda scared. Foller 'em an' tell Willie to look 'em over, an' tell Willie to check with Jackson, Unit Four. Get him to see if they're all right. I'll stay here."

Tom strolled after the three young men. They moved toward the dance floor and took their positions quietly on the edge of the crowd. Tom saw Willie near the band and signaled him.

"What cha want?" Willie asked.

"Them three—see—there?"

"Yeah."

"They say a fella name' Jackson, Unit Four, ast 'em."

Willie craned his neck and saw Huston and called him over. "Them three fellas," he said. "We better get Jackson, Unit Four, an' see if he ast 'em."

Huston turned on his heel and walked away; and in a few moments he was back with a lean and bony Kansan. "This here's Jackson," Huston said. "Look, Jackson, see them three young fellas —?"

"Yeah."

"Well, did you ast 'em?"

"No."

"Ever see 'em before?"

Jackson peered at them. "Sure. Worked at Gregorio's with 'em."

"So they knowed your name."

"Sure. I worked right beside 'em."

"Awright," Huston said. "Don't you go near 'em. We ain't gonna th'ow 'em out if they're nice. Thanks, Mr. Jackson."

"Good work," he said to Tom. "I guess them's the fellas."

"Jule picked 'em out," said Tom.

"Hell, no wonder," said Willie. "His Injun blood smelled 'em. Well, I'll point 'em out to the boys."

A sixteen-year-old boy came running through the crowd. He stopped, panting, in front of Huston. "Mista Huston," he said. "I been like you said. They's a car with six men parked down by the euc'lyptus trees, an' they's one with four men up the north-side road. I ast 'em for a match. They got guns. I seen 'em."

Huston's eyes grew hard and cruel. "Willie," he said, "you sure you got ever'thing ready?"

Willie grinned happily. "Sure have, Mr. Huston. Ain't gonna be no trouble."

"Well, don't hurt 'em. 'Member now. If you kin, quiet an' nice, I kinda like to see 'em. Be in my tent."

"I'll see what we kin do," said Willie.

Dancing had not formally started, but now Willie climbed onto the platform. "Choose up your squares," he called. The music stopped. Boys and girls, young men and women, ran about until eight squares were ready on the big floor, ready and waiting. The girls held their hands in front of them and squirmed their fingers. The boys tapped their feet restlessly. Around the floor the old folks sat, smiling slightly, holding the children back from the floor. And in the distance the Jesus-lovers sat with hard condemning faces and watched the sin.

Ma and Rose of Sharon sat on a bench and watched. And as each boy asked Rose of Sharon as partner, Ma said, "No, she ain't well." And Rose of Sharon blushed and her eyes were bright.

The caller stepped to the middle of the floor and held up his hands. "All ready? Then let her go!"

The music snarled out "Chicken Reel," shrill and clear, fiddle skirling, harmonicas nasal and sharp, and the guitars booming on the bass strings. The caller named the turns, the squares moved. And they danced forward and back, hands 'round, swing your lady.

The caller, in a frenzy, tapped his feet, strutted back and forth, went through the figures as he called them.

"Swing your ladies an' a dol ce do. Join han's roun' an' away we go." The music rose and fell, and the moving shoes beating in time on the platform sounded like drums. "Swing to the right an' a swing to lef'; break, now—break—back to—back," the caller sang the high vibrant montone. Now the girls' hair lost the careful combing. Now perspiration stood out on the foreheads of the boys. Now the experts showed the tricky inter-steps. And the old people on the edge of the floor took up the rhythm, patted their hands softly, and tapped their feet; and they smiled gently and then caught one another's eyes and nodded.

Ma leaned her head close to Rose of Sharon's ear. "Maybe you wouldn't think it, but your Pa was as nice a dancer as I ever seen, when he was young." And Ma smiled. "Makes me think of ol' times," she said. And on the faces of the watchers the smiles were of old times.

"Up near Muskogee twenty years ago, they was a blin' man with a fiddle—"

"I seen a fella oncet could slap his heels four times in one jump."

"Swedes up in Dakota—know what they do sometimes? Put pepper on the floor. Gits up the ladies' skirts an' makes 'em purty lively—lively as a filly in season. Swedes do that sometimes."

In the distance, the Jesus-lovers watched their restive children. "Look on sin," they said. "Them folks is ridin' to hell on a poker. It's a shame the godly got to see it." And their children were silent and nervous.

"One more roun' an' then a little res'," the caller chanted. "Hit her hard, 'cause we're gonna stop soon." And the girls were damp and flushed, and they danced with open mouths and serious reverent faces, and the boys flung back their long hair and pranced, pointed their toes, and clicked their heels. In and out the squares moved, crossing, backing, whirling, and the music shrilled.

Then suddenly it stopped. The dancers stood still, panting with fatigue. And the children broke from restraint, dashed on the floor, chased one another madly, ran, slid, stole caps, and pulled hair. The dancers sat down, fanning themselves with their hands. The members of the band got up and stretched themselves and sat down again. And the guitar players worked softly over their strings.

Now Willie called, "Choose again for another square, if you can." The dancers scrambled to their feet and new dancers plunged forward for partners. Tom stood near the three young men. He saw them force their way through, out on the floor, toward one of the forming squares. He waved his hand at Willie, and Willie spoke to the fiddler. The fiddler squawked his bow across the strings. Twenty young men lounged slowly across the floor. The three reached the square. And one of them said, "I'll dance with this here."

A blond boy looked up in astonishment. "She's my partner."

"Listen, you little son-of-a-bitch—"

Off in the darkness a shrill whistle sounded. The three were walled in now. And each one felt the grip of hands. And then the wall of men moved slowly off the platform.

Willie yelped, "Le's go!" The music shrilled out, the caller intoned the figures, the feet thudded on the platform.

A touring car drove to the entrance. The driver called, "Open up. We hear you got a riot."

The guard kept his position. "We got no riot. Listen to that music. Who are you?"

"Deputy sheriffs."

"Got a warrant?"

"We don't need a warrant if there's a riot."

"Well, we got no riots here," said the gate guard.

The men in the car listened to the music and the sound of the caller, and then the car pulled slowly away and parked in a cross-road and waited.

In the moving squad each of the three young men was pinioned, and a hand was over each mouth. When they reached the darkness the group opened up.

Tom said, "That sure was did nice." He held both arms of his victim from behind.

Willie ran over to them from the dance floor. "Nice work," he said. "On'y need six now. Huston wants to see these here fellers."

Huston himself emerged from the darkness. "These the ones?"

"Sure," said Jule. "Went right up an' started it. But they didn' even swing once."

"Let's look at 'em." The prisoners were swung around to face him. Their heads were down. Huston put a flashlight beam in each sullen face. "What did you wanta do it for?" he asked. There was no answer. "Who the hell tol' you to do it?"

"Goddarn it, we didn't do nothing. We was jes' gonna dance."

"No, you wasn't," Jule said. "You was gonna sock that kid."

Tom said, "Mr. Huston, jus' when these here fellas moved in, somebody give a whistle."

"Yeah, I know! The cops come right to the gate." He turned back. "We ain't gonna hurt you. Now who tol' you to come bus' up our dance?" He waited for a reply. "You're our own folks," Huston said sadly. "You belong with us. How'd you happen to come? We know all about it," he added.

"Well, goddamn it, a fella got to eat."

"Well, who sent you? Who paid you to come?"

"We ain't been paid."

"An' you ain't gonna be. No fight, no pay. Ain't that right?"

One of the pinioned men said, "Do what you want. We ain't gonna tell nothing."

Huston's head sank down for a moment, and then he said softly, "O.K. Don't tell. But looka here. Don't knife your own folks. We're trying to get along, havin' fun an' keepin' order. Don't tear all that down. Jes' think about it. You're jes' harmin' yourself.

"Awright, boys, put 'em over the back fence. An' don't hurt 'em. They don't know what they're doin'."

The squad moved slowly toward the rear of the camp, and Huston looked after them.

Jule said, "Le's jes' take one good kick at 'em."

"No, you don't!" Willie cried. "I said we wouldn'."

"Jes' one nice little kick," Jule pleaded. "Jes' loft 'em over the fence."

"No, sir," Willie insisted.

"Listen, you," he said, "we're lettin' you off this time. But you take back the word. If'n ever this here happens again, we'll jes' natcherally kick the hell outa whoever comes; we'll bust ever' bone in their body. Now you tell your boys that. Huston says you're our kinda folks—maybe. I'd hate to think it."

They neared the fence. Two of the seated guards stood up and moved over. "Got some fellas goin' home early," said Willie. The three men climbed over the fence and disappeared into the darkness.

And the squad moved quickly back toward the dance floor. And the music of "Ol' Dan Tucker" skirled and whined from the string band.

Over near the office the men still squatted and talked, and the shrill music came to them.

Pa said, "They's change a-comin'. I don' know what. Maybe we won't live to see her. But she's a-comin'. They's a res'less feelin'. Fella can't figger nothin' out, he's so nervous."

And Black Hat lifted his head up again, and the light fell on his bristly whiskers. He gathered some little rocks from the ground and shot them like marbles, with his thumb. "I don' know. She's a-comin' awright, like you say. Fella tol' me what happened in Akron, Ohio. Rubber companies. They got mountain people in 'cause they'd work cheap. An' these here mountain people up an' joined the union. Well, sir, hell jes' popped. All them storekeepers and legioners an' people like that, they get drillin' and yellin', 'Red!' An' they're gonna run the union right outa Akron. Preachers git a-preachin' about it, an' papers a-yowlin', an' they's pick handles put out by the rubber companies, an' they're a buyin' gas. Jesus, you'd think them mountain boys was reg'lar devils!" He stopped and found some more rocks to shoot. "Well, sir—it was las' March, an' one Sunday five thousan' of them mountain men had a turkey shoot outside a town. Five thousan' of 'em jes' marched through town with their rifles. An' they had their turkey shoot, an' then they marched back. An' that's all they done. Well sir, they ain't been no trouble sence then. These here citizens committees give back the pick handles, an' the storekeepers keep their stores, an' nobody been clubbed nor tarred an' feathered, an' nobody been killed." There was a long silence, and then Black Hat said, "They're gettin' purty mean out here. Burned that camp an' beat up folks. I been thinkin'. All our folks got guns. I been thinkin' maybe we ought to git up a turkey shootin' club an' have meetin's ever' Sunday."

The men looked up at him, and then down at the ground, and their feet moved restlessly and they shifted their weight from one leg to the other.

Chapter Twenty-five

The spring is beautiful in California. Valleys in which the fruit blossoms are fragrant pink and white waters in a shallow sea. Then the first tendrils of the grapes, swelling from the old gnarled vines, cascade down to cover the trunks. The full green hills are round and soft as breasts. And on the level vegetable lands are the mile-long rows of pale green lettuce and the spindly little cauliflowers, the gray-green unearthly artichoke plants.

And then the leaves break out on the trees, and the petals drop from the fruit trees and carpet the earth with pink and white. The centers of the blossoms swell and grow and color: cherries and apples, peaches and pears, figs which close the flower in the fruit. All California quickens with produce, and the fruit grows heavy, and the limbs bend gradually under the fruit so that little crutches must be placed under them to support the weight.

Behind the fruitfulness are men of understanding and knowledge and skill, men who experiment with seed, endlessly developing the techniques for greater crops of plants whose roots will resist the million enemies of the earth: the molds, the insects, the rusts, the blights. These men work carefully and endlessly to perfect the seed, the roots. And there are the men of chemistry who spray the trees against pests, who sulphur the grapes, who cut out disease and rots, mildews and sicknesses. Doctors of preventive medicine, men at the borders who look for fruit flies, for Japanese beetle, men who quarantine the sick trees and root them out and burn them, men of knowledge. The men who graft the young trees, the little vines, are the cleverest of all, for theirs is a surgeon's job, as tender and delicate; and these men must have surgeons' hands and surgeons' hearts to slit the bark, to place the grafts, to bind the wounds and cover them from the air. These are great men.

Along the rows, the cultivators move, tearing the spring grass and turning it under to make a fertile earth, breaking the ground to hold the water up near the surface, ridging the ground in little pools for the irrigation, destroying the weed roots that may drink the water away from the trees.

And all the time the fruit swells and the flowers break out in long clusters on the vines. And in the growing year the warmth grows and the leaves turn dark green. The prunes lengthen like little green bird's eggs, and the limbs sag down against the crutches under the weight. And the hard little pears take shape, and the beginning of the fuzz comes out on the peaches. Grape blossoms shed their tiny petals and the hard little beads become green buttons, and the buttons grow heavy. The men who work in the fields, the owners of the little orchards, watch and calculate. The year is heavy with produce. And men are proud, for of their knowledge they can make the year heavy. They have transformed the world with their knowledge. The short, lean wheat has been made big and productive. Little sour apples have grown large and sweet, and that old grape that grew among the trees and fed the birds its tiny fruit has mothered a thousand varieties, red and black, green and pale pink, purple and yellow; and each variety with its own flavor. The men who work in the experimental farms have made new fruits: nectarines and forty kinds of plums, walnuts with paper shells. And always they work, selecting, grafting, changing, driving themselves, driving the earth to produce.

And first the cherries ripen. Cent and a half a pound. Hell, we can't pick 'em for that. Black cherries and red cherries, full and sweet, and the birds eat half of each cherry and the yellowjackets buzz into the holes the birds made. And on the ground the seeds drop and dry with black shreds hanging from them.

The purple prunes soften and sweeten. My God, we can't pick them and dry and sulphur them. We can't pay wages, no matter what wages. And the purple prunes carpet the ground. And first the skins wrinkle a little and swarms of flies come to feast, and the valley is filled with the odor of sweet decay. The meat turns dark and the crop shrivels on the ground.

And the pears grow yellow and soft. Five dollars a ton. Five dollars for forty-fifty-pound boxes; trees pruned and sprayed, orchards cultivated—pick the fruit, put it in boxes, load the trucks, deliver the fruit to the cannery—forty boxes for five dollars. We can't do it. And the yellow fruit falls heavily to the ground and splashes on the ground. The yellowjackets dig into the soft meat, and there is a smell of ferment and rot.

Then the grapes—we can't make good wine. People can't buy good wine. Rip the grapes from the vines, good grapes, rotten grapes, wasp-stung grapes. Press stems, press dirt and rot.

But there's mildew and formic acid in the vats.

Add sulphur and tannic acid.

The smell from the ferment is not the rich odor of wine, but the smell of decay and chemicals.

Oh, well. It has alcohol in it, anyway. They can get drunk.

The little farmers watched debt creep up on them like the tide.

They sprayed the trees and sold no crop, they pruned and grafted and could not pick the crop. And the men of knowledge have worked, have considered, and the fruit is rotting on the ground, and the decaying mash in the wine vats is poisoning the air. And taste the wine—no grape flavor at all, just sulphur and tannic acid and alcohol.

This little orchard will be a part of a great holding next year, for the debt will have choked the owner.

This vineyard will belong to the bank. Only the great owners can survive, for they own the canneries too. And four pears peeled and cut in half, cooked and canned, still cost fifteen cents. And the canned pears do not spoil. They will last for years.

The decay spread over the State, and the sweet smell is a great sorrow on the land. Men who can graft the trees and make the seed fertile and big can find no way to let the hungry people eat their produce. Men who have created new fruits in the world cannot create a system whereby their fruits may be eaten. And the failure hangs over the State like a great sorrow.

The works of the roots of the vines, of the trees, must be destroyed to keep up the price, and this is the saddest, bitterest thing of all. Carloads of oranges dumped on the ground. The people came for miles to take the fruit, but this could not be. How would they buy oranges at twenty cents a dozen if they could drive out and pick them up? And men with hoses squirt kerosene on the oranges, and they are angry at the crime, angry at the people who have come to take the fruit. A million people hungry, needing the fruit—and kerosene sprayed over the golden mountains.

And the smell of rot fills the country.

Burn coffee for fuel in the ships. Burn corn to keep warm, it makes a hot fire. Dump potatoes in the rivers and place guards along the banks to keep the hungry people from fishing them out. Slaughter the pigs and bury them, and let the putrescence drip down into the earth.

There is a crime here that goes beyond denunciation. There is a sorrow here that weeping cannot symbolize. There is a failure here that topples all our success. The fertile earth, the straight tree rows, the sturdy trunks, and the ripe fruit. And children dying of pellagra must die because a profit cannot be taken from an orange. And coroners must fill in the certificates—died of malnutrition—because the food must rot, must be forced to rot.

The people come with nets to fish for potatoes in the river, and the guards hold them back; they come in rattling cars to get the dumped oranges, but the kerosene is sprayed. And they stand still and watch the potatoes float by, listen to the screaming pigs being killed in a ditch and covered with quicklime, watch the mountains of oranges slop down to a putrefying ooze; and in the eyes of the people there is the failure; and in the eyes of the hungry there is a growing wrath. In the souls of the people the grapes of wrath are filling and growing heavy, growing heavy for the vintage.

1939

NATHANAEL WEST
1903–1940

A fatal automobile accident in 1940 took the life of Nathanael West and his bride of eight months, and thus cut short the career, begun less than a decade earlier, of America's first important Jewish novelist and one of its most radical writers. His was one of the most bizarre careers in the history of American letters.

West was born Nathan Weinstein, the son of Jewish immigrants from Russia. In 1925, before beginning his first novel, he changed his name, relishing the Biblical derivation of "Nathanael" (meaning "gift of God") but trying to screen the Jewish identity that, despite his fondness for his family, had embarrassed him since college days at Brown University. He was particularly close to the younger of his two sisters and to his father, a prosperous New York contractor, though he rebelled early against pressures to conform to middle-class educational and career patterns.

He read avidly even in his preteen years, encouraged by his family's devotion to learning and by their gifts of books—Shakespeare, Thomas Hardy, and the Continental classics. But he neglected his academic work in public school and left high school without graduating. He gained admission to Tufts College (from which he quickly flunked out), and then to Brown University, by forging admissions records. At Brown (1922–24) he began to cultivate the dress and manner of the gentile Ivy League elite, but also he took seriously his studies in literature, philosophy, and history, and he edited the campus literary magazine. Moreover, he read the literature of medieval Catholicism and that of the sixteenth-century aesthetic movement, the French Symbolists, contemporary Dadaists, and James Joyce, who nourished his taste for the surreal and the fantastic. He also read the vanguard contemporary American writers Gertrude Stein, Sherwood Anderson, and Hemingway, and the poets Pound, E. E. Cummings, Wallace Stevens, and William Carlos Williams. Though he worked at times on construction jobs and his family hoped he would enter business or a conventional profession after graduating from Brown, he persuaded his father and an uncle to underwrite two years in Paris (1926–27). There he sustained his virtually compulsive devotion to literature while working on his first short novel, *The Dream Life of Balso Snell* (1931), a garish comic fantasy exposing the pretensions of artists and the decadence of modern life.

West's efforts to support a literary career were based on a series of expedients. For intervals between 1927 and 1932 he worked as a night clerk in two New York City hotels, where he could read while on duty, gather material for his fiction by surreptitiously opening the residents' mail, and fraudulently secure rooms at little or no cost for his literary friends. From

1933 until his death he worked in Hollywood on a series of routine scripts for inconsequential films to earn money that would enable him to continue his serious writing. He was co-editor of the literary journal *Contact* with William Carlos Williams in 1932, and he edited the magazine *Americana* briefly in 1933. After 1933 he took part in political controversy as a Communist sympathizer, though he never joined the party or made political ideology programmatic in his fiction.

West's four novels brought the Gothic novel (fiction marked by terror and compulsive fascination with forbidden and decadent themes) to a new pitch of intensity, and brought the comic grotesque to new heights of absurdity and inventiveness. He worked (as in *The Day of the Locust*) by parodying or caricaturing the themes and effects of masterpieces in literature and painting, to portray a world in which violence, utterly repulsive tastes, and shallow fantasies are outrageously grotesque but inescapably real, crying out for redemption but finding none. (*The Dream Life of Balso Snell* takes place inside the Trojan horse of ancient legend, which the poet Snell enters via the rectum.) In one masterpiece, *Miss Lonelyhearts*, the male author of an advice-to-the-lovelorn column in a newspaper is consumed by his sympathy for his correspondents, whose lives are a nightmare of vulgarity and bizarre disasters. He is a "priest of our time who has a religious experience" comparable, West declared, to cases analyzed by William James in *Varieties of Religious Experience*.[1] Yet his imitation of Christ's compassion proves to be as sterile as the lives of the victims he would help. In *A Cool Million* (1934), a jailhouse, a museum, and Wu Fong's whorehouse provide the setting for West's mockery of the Horatio Alger success myth, which he shows to be fraudulent but ineradicable in an America whose vulgarities and fantasies are the seedbed of fascism. West's last novel, *The Day of the Locust* (1939), found the fantasies and the realties of Hollywood to be indistinguishable in their fraudulence, and haunting as a portent of annihilation. West's works are, as he once declared, "lyric novels" constructed "according to Poe's definition of a lyric poem,"[2] and part of their bleak horror, as West recognized, is that "there is nothing to root for in my work and what is even worse, no rooters."[3]

During his brief lifetime West's fiction gained some favorable critical attention in America but earned scarcely a penny and found very few readers. In the aftermath of World War II, however, the publication of his works in Britain and France attracted favorable attention from both writers and critics, and paperback editions gained him hundreds of thousands of readers in the United States. West brought Biblical visions of national destiny and apocalypse, which had earlier shaped the imaginations of New England Puritans and of Hawthorne and Melville, into an explosive confrontation with the facts of modern life, a confrontation which had vivid meaning after the horrors of World War II. His combination of the agonized conscience with the comic had much in common with the fiction of such Jewish writers as Bernard Malamud and Saul Bellow who flourished after the war, and his parodic and grotesque effects proved to be in the vanguard of the later fiction of John Barth, Thomas Pynchon, and Joseph Heller.

1. "Some Notes on Miss Lonelyhearts," *Contempo*, 3 (May 15, 1933), 1–2.
2. *Ibid.*, 1.
3. Letter to George Milburn, quoted by Richard B. Lehman, introduction to *The Day of the Locust* (1950), p. xx.

From The Day of the Locust[1]

Chapter Eighteen

Faye moved out of the San Berdoo the day after the funeral. Tod didn't know where she had gone and was getting up the courage to call Mrs. Jenning[2] when he saw her from the window of his office. She was dressed in the costume of a Napoleonic vivandière.[3] By the time he got the window open, she had almost turned the corner of the building. He shouted for her to wait. She waved, but when he got downstairs she was gone.

From her dress, he was sure that she was working in the picture called "Waterloo."[4] He asked a studio policeman where the company was shooting and was told on the back lot. He started toward it at once. A platoon of cuirassiers,[5] big men mounted on gigantic horses, went by. He knew that they must be headed for the same set and followed them. They broke into a gallop and he was soon outdistanced.

The sun was very hot. His eyes and throat were choked with the dust thrown up by the horses' hooves and his head throbbed. The only bit of shade he could find was under an ocean liner made of painted canvas with real lifeboats hanging from its davits. He stood in its narrow shadow for a while then went on toward a great forty-foot papier mâché[6] sphinx that loomed up in the distance. He had to cross a desert to reach it, a desert that was continually being made larger by a fleet of trucks dumping white sand. He had gone only a few feet when a man with a megaphone ordered him off.

He skirted the desert, making a wide turn to the right, and came to a Western street with a plank sidewalk. On the porch of the "Last Chance Saloon" was a rocking chair. He sat down on it and lit a cigarette.

From there he could see a jungle compound with a water buffalo

---

1. The title derives from the accounts in Exodus 10.4–15 of Jehovah's laying waste to Egypt by a plague of locusts, and the prophecy in the apocalyptic Book of Revelation 9.3–10 of locusts sent by God to destroy those not sealed in his faith. The novel (originally entitled, *The Cheated*) depicts an assortment of characters who seek the Promised Land in Los Angeles, California. The cast includes Tod Hackett, a graduate of Yale's school of fine art, now in training as a costume and set designer and planning a mammoth painting entitled *The Burning of Los Angeles;* Harry Greener, a broken-down vaudevillian who peddles silver polish until he dies; his daughter Faye, a would-be film actress who enters a callhouse for prostitutes to earn the expenses of her father's funeral, then moves into the house of a reclusive eccentric, Homer Simpson; and Simpson, a painfully inarticulate Iowa bookkeeper residing in California to recover from pneumonia. The novel ends when a crowd riots at a Hollywood film premier, enflamed because Homer Simpson, gone berserk, has trampled child actor Adore Loomis to death. We reprint two chapters in which Tod witnesses a disaster on the set of the film *Waterloo*, then turns to encounter Adore Loomis and his mother.

2. Proprietress of the callhouse where Faye works.

3. Woman accompanying French troops to sell provisions and liquor.

4. Battle of Waterloo in Belgium where the British, under General Wellington, and their allies defeated the French under Napoleon in 1815.

5. Cavalry soldiers wearing armored breastplates.

6. Substance made by mixing paper pulp and glue, which hardens after being shaped in molds.

tethered to the side of a conical grass hut. Every few seconds the animal groaned musically. Suddenly an Arab charged by on a white stallion. He shouted at the man, but got no answer. A little while later he saw a truck with a load of snow and several malamute dogs. He shouted again. The driver shouted something back, but didn't stop.

Throwing away his cigarette, he went through the swinging doors of the saloon. There was no back to the building and he found himself in a Paris street. He followed it to its end, coming out in a Romanesque[7] courtyard. He heard voices a short distance away and went toward them. On a lawn of fiber, a group of men and women in riding costume were picnicking. They were eating cardboard food in front of a cellophane waterfall. He started toward them to ask his way, but was stopped by a man who scowled and held up a sign— "Quiet, Please, We're Shooting." When Tod took another step forward, the man shook his fist threateningly.

Next he came to a small pond with large celluloid swans floating on it. Across one end was a bridge with a sign that read, "To Kamp Komfit." He crossed the bridge and followed a little path that ended at a Greek temple dedicated to Eros.[8] The god himself lay face downward in a pile of old newspapers and bottles.

From the steps of the temple, he could see in the distance a road lined with Lombardy poplars. It was the one on which he had lost the cuirassiers. He pushed his way through a tangle of briars, old flats and iron junk, skirting the skeleton of a Zeppelin, a bamboo stockade, an adobe fort, the wooden horse of Troy, a flight of baroque palace stairs that started in a bed of weeds and ended against the branches of an oak, part of the Fourteenth Street elevated station, a Dutch windmill, the bones of a dinosaur, the upper half of the Merrimac,[9] a corner of a Mayan temple, until he finally reached the road.

He was out of breath. He sat down under one of the poplars on a rock made of brown plaster and took off his jacket. There was a cool breeze blowing and he soon felt more comfortable.

He had lately begun to think not only of Goya and Daumier but also of certain Italian artists of the seventeenth and eighteenth centuries,[1] of Salvator Rosa, Francesco Guardi and Monsu Desiderio, the painters of Decay and Mystery. Looking downhill now, he could see compositions that might have actually been arranged

---

7. European architectural style prevailing between the Roman and Gothic periods, c. 775–1200.
8. Greek god of love.
9. I.e., a model of the *Merrimack*, warship salvaged and armored by the Confederacy during the Civil War, defeated by the Union's ironclad *Monitor* in the battle of Hampton Roads, 1862, later burned and abandoned.
1. Painters of the fantastic and grotesque: Francisco José de Goya y Lu-

cientes (1746–1828), Spanish painter and graphic artist who recorded the horrors of the Napoleonic wars in *The Disasters of War* (1810–14); Honoré Daumier (1808–79), French caricaturist and painter; Salvator Rosa (1615–73), Italian painter of wild landscapes; Francesco Guardi (1712–93), Venetian painter; "Monsu Desiderio," the name used by several minor 17th-century painters of architectural fantasies.

from the Calabrian[2] work of Rosa. There were partially demolished buildings and broken monuments, half-hidden by great, tortured trees, whose exposed roots writhed dramatically in the arid ground, and by shrubs that carried, not flowers or berries, but armories of spikes, hooks and swords.

For Guardi and Desiderio there were bridges which bridged nothing, sculpture in trees, palaces that seemed of marble until a whole stone portico began to flap in the light breeze. And there were figures as well. A hundred yards from where Tod was sitting a man in a derby hat leaned drowsily against the gilded poop of a Venetian barque and peeled an apple. Still farther on, a charwoman on a stepladder was scrubbing with soap and water the face of a Buddha thirty feet high.

He left the road and climbed across the spine of the hill to look down on the other side. From there he could see a ten-acre field of cockleburs spotted with clumps of sunflowers and wild gum. In the center of the field was a gigantic pile of sets, flats and props. While he watched, a ten-ton truck added another load to it. This was the final dumping ground. He thought of Janvier's "Sargasso Sea."[3] Just as that imaginary body of water was a history of civilization in the form of a marine junkyard, the studio lot was one in the form of a dream dump. A Sargasso of the imagination! And the dump grew continually, for there wasn't a dream afloat somewhere which wouldn't sooner or later turn up on it, having first been made photographic by plaster, canvas, lath and paint. Many boats sink and never reach the Sargasso, but no dream ever entirely disappears. Somewhere it troubles some unfortunate person and some day, when that person has been sufficiently troubled, it will be reproduced on the lot.

When he saw a red glare in the sky and heard the rumble of cannon, he knew it must be Waterloo. From around a bend in the road trotted several cavalry regiments. They wore casques and chest armor of black cardboard and carried long horse pistols in their saddle holsters. They were Victor Hugo's[4] soldiers. He had worked on some of the drawings for their uniforms himself, following carefully the descriptions in "Les Miserables."

He went in the direction they took. Before long he was passed by the men of Lefebvre-Desnouttes,[5] followed by a regiment of gendarmes d'élite, several companies of chasseurs of the guard and a flying detachment of Rimbaud's lancers.

They must be moving up for the disastrous attack on La Haite

2. Pertaining to Calabria, department in southern Italy.
3. The Sargasso Sea is a large region of relatively still water in the middle of the North Atlantic where seaweed and debris accumulate.
4. French poet, dramatist, and novelist (1802–85), whose novel *Les Miserables* (1862) contains a description of the Bat-

tle of Waterloo.
5. Names in this and the following paragraphs, except fictitious names, identify military commanders and their units. "Gendarmes d'élite": elite cavalry troops; "chasseurs": fast-moving cavalry or infantry troops; "lancers": cavalrymen armed with lances.

Santée. He hadn't read the scenario and wondered if it had rained yesterday. Would Grouchy or Bulcher arrive? Grotenstein, the producer, might have changed it.

The sound of cannon was becoming louder all the time and the red fan in the sky more intense. He could smell the sweet, pungent odor of blank powder. It might be over before he could get there. He started to run. When he topped a rise after a sharp bend in the road, he found a great plain below him covered with early nineteenth-century troops, wearing all the gay and elaborate uniforms that used to please him so much when he was a child and spent long hours looking at the soldiers in an old dictionary. At the far end of the field, he could see an enormous hump around which the English and their allies were gathered. It was Mont St. Jean and they were getting ready to defend it gallantly. It wasn't quite finished, however, and swarmed with grips, property men, set dressers, carpenters and painters.

Tod stood near a eucalyptus tree to watch, concealing himself behind a sign that read, " 'Waterloo'—A Charles H. Grotenstein Production." Nearby a youth in a carefully torn horse guard's uniform was being rehearsed in his lines by one of the assistant directors.

"Vive L'Empereur!"[6] the young man shouted, then clutched his breast and fell forward dead. The assistant director was a hard man to please and made him do it over and over again.

In the center of the plain, the battle was going ahead briskly. Things looked tough for the British and their allies. The Prince of Orange commanding the center, Hill the right and Picton the left wing, were being pressed hard by the veteran French. The desperate and intrepid Prince was in an especially bad spot. Tod heard him cry hoarsely above the din of battle, shouting to the Hollande-Belgians, "Nassau! Brunswick! Never retreat!" Nevertheless, the retreat began. Hill, too, fell back. The French killed General Picton with a ball through the head and he returned to his dressing room. Alten was put to the sword and also retired. The colors of the Lunenberg battalion, borne by a prince of the family of Deux-Ponts, were captured by a famous child star in the uniform of a Parisian drummer boy. The Scotch Greys were destroyed and went to change into another uniform. Ponsonby's heavy dragoons were also cut to ribbons. Mr. Grotenstein would have a large bill to pay at the Western Costume Company.

Neither Napoleon nor Wellington was to be seen. In Wellington's absence, one of the assistant directors, a Mr. Crane, was in command of the allies. He reinforced his center with one of Chasse's brigades and one of Wincke's. He supported these with infantry from Brunswick, Welsh foot, Devon yeomanry and Hanoverian light horse with oblong leather caps and flowing plumes of horsehair.

6. "Long live the Emperor."

For the French, a man in a checked cap ordered Milhaud's cuirassiers to carry Mont St. Jean. With their sabers in their teeth and their pistols in their hands, they charged. It was a fearful sight.

The man in the checked cap was making a fatal error. Mont St. Jean was unfinished. The paint was not yet dry and all the struts were not in place. Because of the thickness of the cannon smoke, he had failed to see that the hill was still being worked on by property men, grips and carpenters.

It was the classic mistake, Tod realized, the same one Napoleon had made. Then it had been wrong for a different reason. The Emperor had ordered the cuirassiers to charge Mont St. Jean not knowing that a deep ditch was hidden at its foot to trap his heavy cavalry. The result had been disaster for the French; the beginning of the end.

This time the same mistake had a different outcome. Waterloo, instead of being the end of the Grand Army, resulted in a draw. Neither side won, and it would have to be fought over again the next day. Big losses, however, were sustained by the insurance company in workmen's compensation. The man in the checked cap was sent to the dog house by Mr. Grotenstein just as Napoleon was sent to St. Helena.[7]

When the front rank of Milhaud's heavy division started up the slope of Mont St. Jean, the hill collapsed. The noise was terrific. Nails screamed with agony as they pulled out of joists. The sound of ripping canvas was like that of little children whimpering. Lath and scantling snapped as though they were brittle bones. The whole hill folded like an enormous umbrella and covered Napoleon's army with painted cloth.

It turned into a rout. The victors of Bersina, Leipsic, Austerlitz,[8] fled like schoolboys who had broken a pane of glass. "Sauve qui peut!"[9] they cried, or, rather, "Scram!"

The armies of England and her allies were too deep in scenery to flee. They had to wait for the carpenters and ambulances to come up. The men of the gallant Seventy-Fifth Highlanders were lifted out of the wreck with block and tackle. They were carted off by the stretcher-bearers, still clinging bravely to their claymores.[10]

Chapter Nineteen

Tod got a lift back to his office in a studio car. He had to ride on the running board because the seats were occupied by two Walloon grenadiers and four Swabian foot.[1] One of the infantrymen had a broken leg, the other extras were only scratched and bruised. They were quite happy about their wounds. They were certain to receive several extra days' pay, and the man with the broken leg thought he might get as much as five hundred dollars.

7. Island in the Mediterranean to which Napoleon was exiled from 1815 to 1821.
8. Sites of Napoleon's victories.
9. "Every man for himself."

10. Large two-edged Scottish sword.
1. Soldiers from regions in southern Belgium and southwestern Germany, respectively.

When Tod arrived at his office, he found Faye waiting to see him. She hadn't been in the battle. At the last moment, the director had decided not to use any vivandières.

To his surprise, she greeted him with warm friendliness. Nevertheless, he tried to apologize for his behavior in the funeral parlor. He had hardly started before she interrupted him. She wasn't angry, but grateful for his lecture on venereal disease. It had brought her to her senses.

She had still another surprise for him. She was living in Homer Simpson's house. The arrangement was a business one. Homer had agreed to board and dress her until she became a star. They were keeping a record of every cent he spent and as soon as she clicked in pictures, she would pay him back with six per cent interest. To make it absolutely legal, they were going to have a lawyer draw up a contract.

She pressed Tod for an opinion and he said it was a splendid idea. She thanked him and invited him to dinner for the next night.

After she had gone, he wondered what living with her would do to Homer. He thought it might straighten him out. He fooled himself into believing this with an image, as though a man were a piece of iron to be heated and then straightened with hammer blows. He should have known better, for if anyone ever lacked malleability Homer did.

He continued to make this mistake when he had dinner with them. Faye seemed very happy, talking about charge accounts and stupid sales clerks. Homer had a flower in his buttonhole, wore carpet slippers and beamed at her continually.

After they had eaten, while Homer was in the kitchen washing dishes, Tod got her to tell him what they did with themselves all day. She said that they lived quietly and that she was glad because she was tired of excitement. All she wanted was a career. Homer did the housework and she was getting a real rest. Daddy's long sickness had tired her out completely. Homer liked to do housework and anyway he wouldn't let her go into the kitchen because of her hands.

"Protecting his investment," Tod said.

"Yes," she replied seriously, "they have to be beautiful."

They had breakfast around ten, she went on. Homer brought it to her in bed. He took a housekeeping magazine and fixed the tray like the pictures in it. While she bathed and dressed, he cleaned the house. Then they went downtown to the stores and she bought all sorts of things, mostly clothes. They didn't eat lunch on account of her figure, but usually had dinner out and went to the movies.

"Then, ice cream sodas," Homer finished for her, as he came out of the kitchen.

Faye laughed and excused herself. They were going to a picture and she wanted to change her dress. When she had left, Homer suggested that they get some air in the patio. He made Tod take the deck chair while he sat on an upturned orange crate.

If he had been careful and had acted decently, Tod could't help thinking, she might be living with him. He was at least better looking than Homer. But then there was her other prerequisite. Homer had an income and lived in a house, while he earned thirty dollars a week and lived in a furnished room.

The happy grin on Homer's face made him feel ashamed of himself. He was being unfair. Homer was a humble, grateful man who would never laugh at her, who was incapable of laughing at anything. Because of this great quality, she could live with him on what she considered a much higher plane.

"What's the matter?" Homer asked softly, laying one of his heavy hands on Tod's knee.

"Nothing. Why?"

Tod moved so that the hand slipped off.

"You were making faces."

"I was thinking of something."

"Oh," Homer said sympathetically.

Tod couldn't resist asking an ugly question.

"When are you two getting married?"

Homer looked hurt.

"Didn't Faye tell about us?"

"Yes, sort of."

"It's a business arrangement."

"Yes?"

To make Tod believe it, he poured out a long disjointed argument, the one he must have used on himself. He even went further than the business part and claimed that they were doing it for poor Harry's sake. Faye had nothing left in the world except her career and she must succeed for her daddy's sake. The reason she wasn't a star was because she didn't have the right clothes. He had money and believed in her talent, so it was only natural for them to enter into a business arrangement. Did Tod know a good lawyer?

It was a rhetorical question, but would become a real one, painfully insistent, if Tod smiled. He frowned. That was wrong, too.

"We must see a lawyer this week and have papers drawn up."

His eagerness was pathetic. Tod wanted to help him, but didn't know what to say. He was still fumbling for an answer when they heard a woman shouting from the hill behind the garage.

"Adore! Adore!"

She had a high soprano voice, very clear and pure.

"What a funny name," Tod said, glad to change the subject.

"Maybe it's a foreigner," Homer said.

The woman came into the yard from around the corner of the garage. She was eager and plump and very American.

"Have you seen my little boy?" she asked, making a gesture of helplessness. "Adore's such a wanderer."

Homer surprised Tod by standing up and smiling at the woman. Faye had certainly helped his timidity.

"Is your son lost?" Homer said.

"Oh, no—just hiding to tease me."

She held out her hand.

"We're neighbors. I'm Maybelle Loomis."

"Glad to know you, ma'am. I'm Homer Simpson and this is Mr. Hackett."

Tod also shook hands with her.

"Have you been living here long?" she asked.

"No. I've just come from the East," Homer said.

"Oh, have you? I've been here ever since Mr. Loomis passed on six years ago. I'm an old settler."

"You like it then?" Tod asked.

"Like California?" she laughed at the idea that anyone might not like it. "Why, it's a paradise on earth!"

"Yes," Homer agreed gravely.

"And anyway," she went on, "I have to live here on account of Adore."

"Is he sick?"

"Oh, no. On account of his career. His agent calls him the biggest little attraction in Hollywood."

She spoke so vehemently that Homer flinched.

"He's in the movies?" Tod asked.

"I'll say," she snapped.

Homer tried to placate her.

"That's very nice."

"If it weren't for favoritism," she said bitterly, "he'd be a star. It ain't talent. It's pull. What's Shirley Temple[2] got that he ain't got?"

"Why, I don't know," Homer mumbled.

She ignored this and let out a fearful bellow.

"Adore! Adore!"

Tod had seen her kind around the studio. She was one of that army of women who drag their children from casting office to casting office and sit for hours, weeks, months, waiting for a chance to show what Junior can do. Some of them are very poor, but no matter how poor, they always manage to scrape together enough money, often by making great sacrifices, to send their children to one of the innumerable talent schools.

"Adore!" she yelled once more, then laughed and became a friendly housewife again, a chubby little person with dimples in her fat cheeks and fat elbows.

"Have you any children, Mr. Simpson?" she asked.

2. Shirley Temple (b. 1928), popular tap-dancing child star in saccharine movies.

"No," he replied, blushing.

"You're lucky—they're a nuisance."

She laughed to show that she didn't really mean it and called her child again.

"Adore . . . Oh, Adore . . ."

Her next question surprised them both.

"Who do you follow?"

"What?" said Tod.

"I mean—in the Search for Health, along the Road of Life?"

They both gaped at her.

"I'm a raw-foodist, myself," she said. "Dr. Pierce is our leader. You must have seen his ads—'Know-All Pierce-All.' "

"Oh, yes," Tod said, "you're vegetarians."

She laughed at his ignorance.

"Far from it. We're much stricter. Vegetarians eat cooked vegetables. We eat only raw ones. Death comes from eating dead things."

Neither Tod nor Homer found anything to say.

"Adore," she began again. "Adore . . ."

This time there was an answer from around the corner of the garage.

"Here I am, mama."

A minute later, a little boy appeared dragging behind him a small sailboat on wheels. He was about eight years old, with a pale, peaked face and a large, troubled forehead. He had great staring eyes. His eyebrows had been plucked and shaped carefully. Except for his Buster Brown collar,[3] he was dressed like a man, in long trousers, vest and jacket.

He tried to kiss his mother, but she fended him off and pulled at his clothes, straightening and arranging them with savage little tugs.

"Adore," she said sternly, "I want you to meet Mr. Simpson, our neighbor."

Turning like a soldier at the command of a drill sergeant, he walked up to Homer and grasped his hand.

"A pleasure, sir," he said, bowing stiffly with his heels together.

"That's the way they do it in Europe," Mrs. Loomis beamed. "Isn't he cute?"

"What a pretty sailboat!" Homer said, trying to be friendly.

Both mother and son ignored his comment. She pointed to Tod, and the child repeated his bow and heel-click.

"Well, we've got to go," she said.

Tod watched the child, who was standing a little to one side of his mother and making faces at Homer. He rolled his eyes back in his head so that only the whites showed and twisted his lips in a snarl.

---

3. Round wide collar on jackets of small boys, named for the figure in advertise-   ments for Buster Brown shoes.

Mrs. Loomis noticed Tod's glance and turned sharply. When she saw what Adore was doing, she yanked him by the arm, jerking him clear off the ground.

"Adore!" she yelled.

To Tod she said apologetically, "He thinks he's the Frankenstein monster."

She picked the boy up, hugging and kissing him ardently. Then she set him down again and fixed his rumpled clothing.

"Won't Adore sing something for us?" Tod asked.

"No," the little boy said sharply.

"Adore," his mother scolded, "sing at once."

"That's all right, if he doesn't feel like it," Homer said.

But Mrs. Loomis was determined to have him sing. She could never permit him to refuse an audience.

"Sing, Adore," she repeated with quiet menace. "Sing 'Mama Doan Wan' No Peas.' "

His shoulders twitched as though they already felt the strap. He tilted his straw sailor over one eye, buttoned up his jacket and did a little strut, then began:

> *"Mama doan wan' no peas,*
> *An' rice, an' cocoanut oil,*
> *Just a bottle of brandy handy all the day.*
> *Mama doan wan' no peas,*
> *Mama doan wan' no cocoanut oil."*

His singing voice was deep and rough and he used the broken groan of the blues singer quite expertly. He moved his body only a little, against rather than in time with the music. The gestures he made with his hands were extremely suggestive.

> *"Mama doan wan't no gin,*
> *Because gin do make her sin,*
> *Mama doan wan' no glass of gin,*
> *Because it boun' to make her sin,*
> *An' keep her hot and bothered all the day."*

He seemed to know what the words meant, or at least his body and his voice seemed to know. When he came to the final chorus, his buttocks writhed and his voice carried a top-heavy load of sexual pain.

Tod and Homer applauded. Adore grabbed the string of his sailboat and circled the yard. He was imitating a tugboat. He tooted several times, then ran off.

"He's just a baby," Mrs. Loomis said proudly, "but he's got loads of talent."

Tod and Homer agreed.

She saw that he was gone again and left hurriedly. They could hear her calling in the brush back of the garage.

"Adore! Adore . . ."

"That's a funny woman," Tod said.

Homer sighed.

"I guess it's hard to get a start in pictures. But Faye is awfully pretty."

Tod agreed. She appeared a moment later in a new flower print dress and picture hat and it was his turn to sigh. She was much more than pretty. She posed, quivering and balanced, on the doorstep and looked down at the two men in the patio. She was smiling, a subtle half-smile uncontaminated by thought. She looked just born, everything moist and fresh, volatile and perfumed. Tod suddenly became very conscious of his dull, insensitive feet bound in dead skin and of his hands, sticky and thick, holding a heavy, rough felt hat.

He tried to get out of going to the pictures with them, but couldn't. Sitting next to her in the dark proved the ordeal he expected it to be. Her self-sufficiency made him squirm and the desire to break its smooth surface with a blow, or at least a sudden obscene gesture, became irresistible.

He began to wonder if he himself didn't suffer from the ingrained, morbid apathy he liked to draw in others. Maybe he could only be galvanized into sensibility and that was why he was chasing Faye.

He left hurriedly, without saying good-bye. He had decided to stop running after her. It was an easy decision to make, but a hard one to carry out. In order to manage it, he fell back on one of the oldest tricks in the very full bag of the intellectual. After all, he told himself, he had drawn her enough times. He shut the portfolio that held the drawings he had made of her, tied it with a string, and put it away in his trunk.

It was a childish trick, hardly worthy of a primitive witch doctor, yet it worked. He was able to avoid her for several months. During this time, he took his pad and pencils on a continuous hunt for other models. He spent his nights at the different Hollywood churches, drawing the worshipers. He visited the "Church of Christ, Physical" where holiness was attained through the constant use of chestweights and spring grips; the "Church Invisible" where fortunes were told and the dead made to find lost objects; the "Tabernacle of the Third Coming" where a woman in male clothing preached the "Crusade Against Salt"; and the "Temple Moderne" under whose glass and chromium roof "Brain-Breathing, the Secret of the Aztecs" was taught.

As he watched these people writhe on the hard seats of their churches, he thought of how well Alessandro Magnasco[4] would

4. Italian painter (1667–1749) of menacing landscapes.

dramatize the contrast between their drained-out, feeble bodies and their wild, disordered minds. He would not satirize them as Hogarth[5] or Daumier might, nor would he pity them. He would paint their fury with respect, appreciating its awful, anarchic power and aware that they had it in them to destroy civilization.

One Friday night in the "Tabernacle of the Third Coming," a man near Tod stood up to speak. Although his name most likely was Thompson or Johnson and his home town Sioux City, he had the same countersunk eyes, like the heads of burnished spikes, that a monk by Magnasco might have. He was probably just in from one of the colonies in the desert near Soboba Hot Springs where he had been conning over his soul on a diet of raw fruit and nuts. He was very angry. The message he had brought to the city was one that an illiterate anchorite might have given decadent Rome. It was a crazy jumble of dietary rules, economics and Biblical threats. He claimed to have seen the Tiger of Wrath stalking the walls of the citadel and the Jackal of Lust skulking in the shrubbery, and he connected these omens with "thirty dollars every Thursday" and meat eating.

Tod didn't laugh at the man's rhetoric. He knew it was unimportant. What mattered were his messianic rage and the emotional response of his hearers. They sprang to their feet, shaking their fists and shouting. On the altar someone began to beat a bass drum and soon the entire congregation was singing "Onward Christian Soldiers."

1939

5. William Hogarth (1697–1764), English satirical painter and graphic artist, and Honoré Daumier (1808–79), French caricaturist and painter.

RICHARD WRIGHT

1908–1960

Richard Wright—a black novelist, for ten years a member of the Communist party, and later an expatriate—was the first Negro writer to reach a large white audience with a militant attack on racism in America. His explosively powerful novel *Native Son* and his autobiographical volume *Black Boy* (1945) achieved immediate success and established him as the most important Negro writer before Ralph Ellison and James Baldwin.

The cruel debasements that Wright suffered as a black child in a dominantly white America find no full equivalents in the biographies of other American writers. Wright's father, an impoverished sharecropper on a Mississippi farm, abandoned his family when Wright was five, and his mother struggled as a housemaid to support the family until she was incapacitated when Wright was twelve. Wright was raised by a series of relatives in Jackson, Mississippi, and Memphis, Tennessee. His schooling was irregular (though he was valedictorian when he graduated from ninth grade in Memphis in 1925), and his grandmother's fervent evangelism ruled out children's games and forbade all but religious reading. His mother demanded his obedience to the codes of white supremacy, enforcing them with exceedingly harsh punishment when he violated them. Left to his own devices during the day when his relatives were working, he was introduced to hard liquor at the age of six and experienced the ruthlessness and desperation of ghetto street life. His autobiography records vividly the shock with which he learned that an uncle had been shot by whites who coveted his thriving liquor business, the vulgar contempt with which Wright was treated by white prostitutes and their customers when he worked as a hall boy in a disreputable hotel, his initiation into deceit and theft. Long before Wright decided to leave the South at the age of seventeen and follow his Aunt Maggie Wilson to Chicago, he had known the vehement feelings that were to impel his fiction: the "dread of white people [that] now came to live permanently in my feelings and imagination," the consciousness that "a white censor was standing over me," the "sustained expectation of violence," the fear that "Negroes had never been allowed to catch the full Western civilization, that they lived somehow in it but not of it."[1] In retrospect he felt so alienated that, unlike some other Negroes who found tenderness and sustaining strength within the black community, he found that his "life at home had cut me off, not only from white people but from Negroes as well" and he wondered if such qualities as "tenderness, love, honor, [and] loyalty," instead of being "native with man," must be "fostered, won, struggled and suffered for, preserved in ritual from one generation to another."[2] The only thing that had bolstered his identity and his hopes was reading, which he managed to do despite the censorious restrictions of his mother and grandmother and the refusal of southern libraries to grant him access to books. While working as an errand boy for an optical company in Memphis, he persuaded a white employee to lend him his library card so that he might surreptitiously charge books and forged the white man's name to a note to the librarian reading *"Will you please let this nigger boy * * * have some books by* [the critic] *H. L. Mencken?"*[3] When Wright left Memphis for Chicago in 1927 he had discovered Mencken's prefaces. Dreiser's *Sister Carrie* and *Jennie Gerhardt*, and the fiction by Sherwood Anderson and Sinclair Lewis that he thought "defensively critical of the straitened American environment." He wrote one story at the age of fifteen and published it in a Memphis Negro publication. He declared later that "it had been only through books—at best, no more than vicarious cultural transfusions—that I had managed to keep myself alive" and that it had been "my accidental reading of fiction and literary criticism that had evoked in me vague glimpses of life's possibilities."[4]

In Chicago Wright worked as a porter, burial-insurance salesman, and postal clerk before going on relief during the Depression and joining the WPA Writers Project, first as a writer of guidebooks, then as a director of the Federal Negro Theater. He steeped himself in the writings of the urban sociologists at the University of Chicago at the time when he was exploring Marxist theory, and Mrs. Mary Wirth, wife of Professor Louis Wirth, who had helped get him a job with the federal Writers Project, encouraged him in his writing. He joined the leftist John Reed Club in 1932 and published poems in its journal *Left Front*. Shortly afterward he joined the Communist

---

1. *Black Boy*, pp. 64, 225, 171, 33.   3. *Ibid.*, p. 216.
2. *Ibid.*, pp. 187, 33.   4. *Ibid.*, pp. 226–27.

party, whose journals published his poems and essays. Wright drew on the experience of fellow black party members for his first work of fiction, *Uncle Tom's Children* (1938), a collection of short novels, including *Long Black Song*. The tales, which won first prize in a WPA competition, treat the southern black's entanglement in the values of a white society that he or she takes for models of achievement, the violence inflicted on those blacks who defy the codes of white supremacy, and, in *Fire and Cloud*, a black preacher's commitment to a protest demonstration organized by Communists.

Wright moved to New York City in 1937 to become Harlem editor of the *Daily Worker*. His "legman" in the office was the future novelist Ralph Ellison, a musician and sculptor whom Wright persuaded to take up writing. While Wright continued to take part in Communist affairs until his break with the party in 1942, he found himself increasingly at odds with party policies that sought to constrain the artist's freedom and that subordinated black protests against racial injustice to the aims of Communist revolution. When Wright published *Native Son* in 1940 it shocked party members as well as non-Marxist middle-class readers, both black and white, because its criminal black hero, Bigger Thomas, is never fully understood by the Communist lawyer who defends him in court, nor by the blacks, nor by the whites who find in his baffled rage the threat of rape and a challenge to their power structure. Bigger's crimes—the accidental killing of the liberal white daughter of a wealthy slum landlord, his attempt to bury the evidence of that offense, the rape and intentional murder later of a black girl friend who might betray him—have the effect of exposing the combination of exploitative capitalism and condescending charity toward Negroes that traps him, but they also enable him to discover his identity and to attain the dignity of one who in puzzling over "why all the killing was" begins "to feel what I wanted, what I am." The book, Wright's first novel, won him the Spingarn Award of the National Association for the Advancement of Colored People and, along with his autobiographical *Black Boy* (1945), brought him financial security and international fame.

Wright's first marriage, to a white dancer in 1940, was short-lived. But in 1941 he married Ellen Poplar, another white woman and a fellow party worker who remained with Wright when he broke with the Communists in 1942 and who bore him two daughters. In 1947 they moved permanently to France, where Wright became an outspoken anti-Communist, an advisor to African diplomats, a frequent lecturer, the familiar friend of Gertrude Stein and of the Marxist Existentialist philosopher Sartre and other French intellectuals who admired Wright's work and introduced him to the writings of contemporary philosophers. The sense of alienation that was pronounced in Bigger Thomas became more central to his vision and governed both the fiction that he resumed writing in the 1950s and the nonfiction that increasingly preoccupied him. But his later writings seldom achieved the impact of his earlier works. In collections of travelogues and political essays (*Black Power*, 1954; *The Color Curtain*, 1956; *Pagan Spain*, 1957; and *White Man, Listen!*, 1957) he tried to affect the policies of the developing nations in Asia and Africa, asserting the advantages of a hybrid, Westernized "Asian-African elite."[5] But none of the developing nations would accept the repudiation of native traditions, their "ancestor-worshiping attitudes,"[6] that Wright's program seemed to call for. Neither *The Outsider*

---

5. *White Man, Listen!*, p. 65.   6. *Ibid.*, p. 133.

(1953) nor *The Long Dream* (1958), set in Mississippi, has the power of
Black Boy or Wright's best fiction with a southern setting. Of the stories
published posthumously in *Eight Men* (1961), only the brilliant *The Man
Who Lived Underground*, written in 1942, has the power of his best writing.

That power derives from Wright's combination of bluntly direct narration with surrealistic or expressionistic gestures and imagery which reveal
the explosive pressures beneath the façades of order in his world, and the
intensity of obsessive fantasies which motivate his characters and challenge
their capacity to articulate their feelings in word or deed. The stock situations and responses in *Long Black Song* render luridly the mechanisms of
racial oppression and enraged protest in the South of Sarah and Silas, while
such refrains as "the long hope of white bright days and the deep desire of
dark black nights" suggest the reality of forces that threaten or invigorate
the lives of the characters. Though both the later black novelists James
Baldwin and Ralph Ellison questioned Wright's resort to melodrama and
the explicitness of protest in his fiction, Wright's example paved the way
for the flourishing of black writing in subsequent decades and, in Ellison's
words, "converted the American Negro impulse toward self-annihilation and
'going-underground' into a will to confront the world * * * and throw his
findings unashamedly into the guilty conscience of America."[7]

Long Black Song

I

> *Go t sleep, baby*
> *Papas gone t town*
> *Go t sleep, baby*
> *The suns goin down*
> *Go t sleep, baby*
> *Yo candys in the sack*
> *Go t sleep, baby*
> *Papas comin back . . .*

Over and over she crooned, and at each lull of her voice she
rocked the wooden cradle with a bare black foot. But the baby
squalled louder, its wail drowning out the song. She stopped and
stood over the cradle, wondering what was bothering it, if its stomach hurt. She felt the diaper; it was dry. She lifted it up and patted
its back. Still it cried, longer and louder. She put it back into the
cradle and dangled a string of red beads before its eyes. The little
black fingers clawed them away. She bent over, frowning, murmuring: "Whuts the mattah, chile? Yuh wan some watah?" She held
a dripping gourd to the black lips, but the baby turned its head
and kicked its legs. She stood a moment, perplexed. Whuts wrong
wid that chile? She ain never carried on like this this tima day.
She picked it up and went to the open door. "See the sun, baby?"
she asked, pointing to a big ball of red dying between the branches

7. "Richard Wright's Blues," *Shadow and Act*, p. 94.

of trees. The baby pulled back and strained its round black arms and legs against her stomach and shoulders. She knew it was tired; she could tell by the halting way it opened its mouth to draw in air. She sat on a wooden stool, unbuttoned the front of her dress, brought the baby closer and offered it a black teat.

"Don baby wan suppah?" It pulled away and went limp, crying softly, piteously, as though it would never stop. Then it pushed its fingers against her breasts and wailed. Lawd, chile, what yuh wan? Yo ma cant hep yuh less she knows whut yuh wan. Tears gushed; four white teeth flashed in red gums; the little chest heaved up and down and round black fingers stretched floorward. Lawd, chile, whuts wrong wid yuh? She stooped slowly, allowing her body to be guided by the downward tug. As soon as the little fingers touched the floor the wail quieted into a broken sniffle. She turned the baby loose and watched it crawl toward a corner. She followed and saw the little fingers reach for the tail-end of an old eight-day clock. "Yuh wan tha ol clock?" She dragged the clock into the center of the floor. The baby crawled after it, calling, "Ahh!" Then it raised its hands and beat on the top of the clock Bink! Bink! Bink! "Naw, yuhll hurt yo hans!" She held the baby and looked around. It cried and struggled. "Wait, baby!" She fetched a small stick from the top of a rickety dresser. "Here," she said, closing the little fingers about it. "Beat wid this, see?" She heard each blow landing squarely on top of the clock. Bang! Bang! Bang! And with each bang the baby smiled and said, "Ahh!" Mabbe thall keep yuh quiet erwhile. Mabbe Ah kin git some res now. She stood in the doorway. Lawd, tha chiles a pain! She mus be teethin. Er something . . .

She wiped sweat from her forehead with the bottom of her dress and looked out over the green fields rolling up the hillsides. She sighed, fighting a feeling of loneliness. Lawd, its sho hard t pass the days wid Silas gone. Been mos a week now since he took the wagon outta here. Hope ain nothin wrong. He must be buyin a heapa stuff there in Colwatah t be stayin all this time. Yes; maybe Silas would remember and bring that five-yard piece of red calico she wanted. Oh, Lawd! Ah *hope* he don fergit it!

She saw green fields wrapped in the thickening gloam. It was as if they had left the earth, those fields, and were floating slowly skyward. The afterglow lingered, red, dying, somehow tenderly sad. And far away, in front of her, earth and sky met in a soft swoon of shadow. A cricket chirped, sharp and lonely; and it seemed she could hear it chirping long after it had stopped. Silas oughta c mon soon. Ahm tireda staying here by mahsef.

Loneliness ached in her. She swallowed, hearing Bang! Bang! Bang! Tom been gone t war mos a year now. N tha ol wars over n we ain heard nothin yit. Lawd, don let Tom be dead! She frowned into the gloam and wondered about that awful war so far away. They said it was over now. Yeah, Gawd had t stop em fo they killed everybody. She felt that merely to go so far away from home was a kind of death in itself. Just to go that far away was to be killed. Nothing good could come from men going miles across the sea to fight. N how come they wanna kill each other? How come they wanna make blood? Killing was not what men ought to do. Shucks! she thought.

She sighed, thinking of Tom, hearing Bang! Bang! Bang! She saw Tom, saw his big black smiling face; her eyes went dreamily blank, drinking in the red afterglow. Yes, God; it could have been Tom instead of Silas who was having her now. Yes; it could have been Tom she was loving. She smiled and asked herself, Lawd, Ah wondah how would it been wid Tom? Against the plush sky she saw a white bright day and a green cornfield and she saw Tom walking in his overalls and she was with Tom and he had his arm about her waist. She remembered how weak she had felt feeling his fingers sinking into the flesh of her hips. Her knees had trembled and she had had a hard time trying to stand up and not just sink right there to the ground. Yes; that was what Tom had wanted her to do. But she had held Tom up and he had held her up; they had held each other up to keep from slipping to the ground there in the green cornfield. Lawd! Her breath went and she passed her tongue over her lips. But that was not as exciting as that winter evening when the grey skies were sleeping and she and Tom were coming home from church down dark Lover's Lane. She felt the tips of her teats tingling and touching the front of her dress as she remembered how he had crushed her against him and hurt her. She had closed her eyes and was smelling the acrid scent of dry October leaves and had gone weak in his arms and had felt she could not breathe any more and had torn away and run, run home. And the sweet ache which had frightened her then was stealing back to her loins now with the silence and the cricket calls and the red afterglow and Bang! Bang! Bang! Lawd, Ah wondah how would it been wid Tom?

She stepped out on the porch and leaned against the wall of the house. Sky sang a red song. Fields whispered a green prayer. And song and prayer were dying in silence and shadow. Never in all her life had she been so much alone as she was now. Days were never so long as these days; and nights were never so empty as these nights. She jerked her head impatiently, hearing Bang! Bang! Bang! Shucks! she thought. When Tom had gone something had ebbed so slowly that at first she had not noticed it. Now she felt all of it as though the feeling had no bottom. She tried to think just how it had happened. Yes; there had been all her life the long hope of white bright days and the deep desire of dark black nights and then Tom had gone. Bang! Bang! Bang! There had been laughter and eating and singing and the long gladness of green cornfields in summer. There had been cooking and sewing and sweeping and the deep dream of sleeping grey skies in winter. Always it had been like that and she had been happy. But no more. The happiness of those days and nights, of those green cornfields and grey skies had started to go from her when Tom had gone to war. His leaving had left an empty black hole in her heart, a black hole that Silas had come in and filled. But not quite. Silas had not quite filled that hole. No; days and nights were not as they were before.

She lifted her chin, listening. She had heard something, a dull throb like she had heard that day Silas had called her outdoors to look at the airplane. Her eyes swept the sky. But there was no plane. Mabbe its behin the house? She stepped into the yard and looked upward through paling light. There were only a few big wet stars trembling in the east. Then she heard the throb again. She turned, looking up and down the road. The throb grew louder, droning; and she heard Bang! Bang! Bang! There! A car! Wondah whuts a car doin coming out here? A black car was winding over a dusty road, coming toward her. Mabbe some white mans bringing Silas home wida loada goods? But, Lawd, Ah *hope* its no trouble! The car stopped in front of the house and a white man got out. Wondah whut he wans? She looked at the car, but could not see Silas. The white man was young; he wore a straw hat and had no coat. He walked toward her with a huge black package under his arm.

"Well, howre yuh today, Aunty?"

"Ahm well. How yuh?"

"Oh, so-so. Its sure hot today, hunh?"

She brushed her hand across her forehead and sighed.

"Yeah; it is kinda warm."

"You busy?"

"Naw, Ah ain doin nothin."

"Ive got something to show you. Can I sit here, on your porch?"

"Ah reckon so. But, Mistah, Ah ain got no money."

"Haven't you sold your cotton yet?"

"Silas gone t town wid it now."

"Whens he coming back?"

"Ah don know. Ahm waitin fer im."

She saw the white man take out a handkerchief and mop his face. Bang! Bang! Bang! He turned his head and looked through the open doorway, into the front room.

"Whats all that going on in there?"

She laughed

"Aw, thas just Ruth."

"Whats she doing?"

"She beatin tha ol clock."

"Beating a *clock*?"

She laughed again.

"She wouldn't go t sleep so Ah give her tha ol clock t play wid."

The white man got up and went to the front door; he stood a

moment looking at the black baby hammering on the clock. Bang! Bang! Bang!

"But why let her tear your clock up?"

"It ain no good."

"You could have it fixed."

"We ain got no money to be fixin' no clocks."

"Haven't you got a clock?"

"Naw."

"But how do you keep time?"

"We git erlong widout time."

"But how do you know when to get up in the morning?"

"We jus git up, thas all."

"But how do you know what time it is when you get up?"

"We git up wid the sun."

"And at night, how do you tell when its night?"

"It gits dark when the sun goes down."

"Haven't you ever had a clock?"

She laughed and turned her face toward the silent fields. "Mistah, we don need no clock."

"Well, this beats everything! I don't see how in the world anybody can live without time."

"We just don need no time, Mistah."

The white man laughed and shook his head; she laughed and looked at him. The white man was funny. Jus like lil boy. Astin how do Ah know when t git up in the mawnin! She laughed again and mused on the baby, hearing Bang! Bang! Bang! She could hear the white man breathing at her side; she felt his eyes on her face. She looked at him; she saw he was looking at her breasts. Hes jus lika lil boy. Acks like he cant understand *nothin!*

"But you need a clock," the white man insisted. "Thats what Im out here for. I'm selling clocks and graphophones.[1] The clocks are made right into the graphophones, a nice sort of combination, hunh? You can have music and time all at once. Ill show you . . ."

"Mistah, we don need no clock!"

"You dont have to buy it. It wont cost you anything just to look."

He unpacked the big black box. She saw the strands of his auburn hair glinting in the afterglow. His back bulged against his white shirt as he stooped. He pulled out a square brown graphophone. She bent forward, looking. Lawd, but its pretty! She saw the face of a clock under the horn of the graphophone. The gilt on the corners sparkled. The color in the wood glowed softly. It reminded her of the light she saw sometimes in the baby's eyes. Slowly she slid a finger over a beveled edge; she wanted to take the box into her arms and kiss it.

---

1. Gramophones, record-playing machines.

"Its eight o'clock," he said.

"Yeah?"

"It only costs fifty dollars. And you dont have to pay for it all at once. Just five dollars down and five dollars a month."

She smiled. The white man was just like a little boy. Jus like a chile. She saw him grinding the handle of the box.

There was a sharp, scratching noise; then she moved nervously, her body caught in the ringing coils of music.

When the trumpet of the Lord shall sound . . .

She rose on circling waves of white bright days and dark black nights.

. . . and time shall be no more . . .

Higher and higher she mounted.

And the morning breaks . . .

Earth fell far behind, forgotten.

. . . eternal, bright and fair . . .

Echo after echo sounded.

When the saved of the earth shall gather . . .

Her blood surged like the long gladness of summer.

. . . over the other shore . . .

Her blood ebbed like the deep dream of sleep in winter.

And when the roll is called up yonder . . .

She gave up, holding her breath.

I'll be there . . .

A lump filled her throat. She leaned her back against a post, trembling, feeling the rise and fall of days and nights, of summer and winter; surging, ebbing, leaping about her, beyond her, far out the fields to where earth and sky lay folded in darkness. She wanted to lie down and sleep, or else leap up and shout. When the music stopped she felt herself coming back, being let down slowly. She sighed. It was dark now. She looked into the doorway. The baby was sleeping on the floor. Ah gotta git up n put tha chile t bed, she thought.

"Wasnt that pretty?"

"It wuz pretty, awright."

"When do you think your husbands coming back?"

"Ah don know, Mistah."

She went into the room and put the baby into the cradle. She stood again in the doorway and looked at the shadowy box that had lifted her up and carried her away. Crickets called. The dark sky had swallowed up the earth, and more stars were hanging, clustered, burning. She heard the white man sigh. His face was lost in shadow. She saw him rub his palms over his forehead. Hes just lika lil boy.

"Id like to see your husband tonight," he said. "I've got to be in Lilydale at six o'clock in the morning and I wont be back through here soon. I got to pick up my buddy over there and we're heading North."

She smiled into the darkness. He was just like a little boy. A little boy selling clocks.

"Yuh sell them things alla time?" she asked.

"Just for the summer," he said. "I go to school in winter. If I can make enough money out of this Ill go to Chicago to school this fall . . ."

"Whut yuh gonna be?"

"*Be?* What do you mean?"

"Whut yuh goin to school fer?"

"Im studying science."

"Whuts tha?"

"Oh, er . . ." He looked at her. "Its about why things are as they are."

"Why things is as they *is*?"

"Well, its something like that."

"How come yuh wanna study tha?"

"Oh, you wouldnt understand."

She sighed.

"Naw, Ah guess Ah wouldnt."

"Well, I reckon Ill be getting along," said the white man. "Can I have a drink of water?"

"Sho. But we ain got nothin but well-watah, n yuhll have t come n git."

"Thats all right."

She slid off the porch and walked over the ground with bare feet. She heard the shoes of the white man behind her, falling to the earth in soft whispers. It was dark now. She led him to the well, groped her way, caught the bucket and let it down with a rope; she heard a splash and the bucket grew heavy. She drew it up, pulling against its weight, throwing one hand over the other, feeling the cool wet of the rope on her palms.

"Ah don git watah outa here much," she said, a little out of breath. "Silas gits the watah mos of the time. This buckets too heavy fer me."

"Oh, wait! Ill help!"

His shoulder touched hers. In the darkness she felt his warm hands fumbling for the rope.

"Where is it?"

"Here."

She extended the rope through the darkness. His fingers touched her breasts.

"Oh!"

She said it in spite of herself. He would think she was thinking about that. And he was a white man. She was sorry she had said that.

"Wheres the gourd?" he asked. "Gee, its dark!"

She stepped back and tried to see him.

"Here."

"I cant see!" he said, laughing.

Again she felt his fingers on the tips of her breasts. She backed away, saying nothing this time. She thrust the gourd out from her. Warm fingers met her cold hands. He had the gourd. She heard him drink; it was the faint, soft music of water going down a dry throat, the music of water in a silent night. He sighed and drank again.

"I was thirsty," he said. "I hadnt had any water since noon."

She knew he was standing in front of her; she could not see him, but she felt him. She heard the gourd rest against the wall of the well. She turned, then felt his hands full on her breasts. She struggled back.

"Naw Mistah!"

"Im not going to hurt you!"

White arms were about her, tightly. She was still. But hes a *white* man. A *white* man. She felt his breath coming hot on her neck and where his hands held her breasts the flesh seemed to knot. She was rigid, poised; she swayed backward, then forward. She caught his shoulders and pushed.

"Naw, naw . . . Mistah, Ah cant do that!"

She jerked away. He caught her hand.

"Please . . ."

"Lemme go!"

She tried to pull her hand out of his and felt his fingers tighten. She pulled harder, and for a moment they were balanced, one against the other. Then he was at her side again, his arms about her.

"I wont hurt you! I wont hurt you . . ."

She leaned backward and tried to dodge his face. Her breasts were full against him; she gasped, feeling the full length of his body. She held her head far to one side; she knew he was seeking her mouth. His hands were on her breasts again. A wave of warm blood swept into her stomach and loins. She felt his lips touching her throat and where he kissed it burned.

"Naw, naw . . ."

Her eyes were full of the wet stars and they blurred, silver and blue. Her knees were loose and she heard her own breathing; she was trying to keep from falling. But hes a *white* man! A *white* man! Naw! Naw! And still she would not let him have her lips; she kept her face away. Her breasts hurt where they were crushed against him and each time she caught her breath she held it and while she held it it seemed that if she would let it go it would kill her. Her knees were pressed hard against his and she clutched the upper parts of his arms, trying to hold on. Her loins ached. She felt her body sliding.

"Gawd . . ."

He helped her up. She could not see the stars now; her eyes were full of the feeling that surged over her body each time she caught her breath. He held her close, breathing into her ear; she straightened, rigidly, feeling that she had to straighten or die. And then her lips felt his and she held her breath and dreaded ever to breathe again for fear of the feeling that would sweep down over her limbs. She held tightly, hearing a mountain tide of blood beating against her throat and temples. Then she gripped him, tore her face away, emptied her lungs in one long despairing gasp and went limp. She felt his hand; she was still, taut, feeling his hand, then his fingers. The muscles in her legs flexed and she bit her lips and pushed her toes deep into the wet dust by the side of the well and tried to wait and tried to wait until she could wait no longer. She whirled away from him and a streak of silver and blue swept across her blood. The wet ground cooled her palms and knee-caps. She stumbled up and ran, blindly, her toes flicking warm, dry dust. Her numbed fingers grabbed at a rusty nail in the post at the porch and she pushed ahead of hands that held her breasts. Her fingers found the door-facing; she moved into the darkened room, her hands before her. She touched the cradle and turned till her knees hit the bed. She went over, face down, her fingers trembling in the crumpled folds of his shirt. She moved and moved again and again, trying to keep ahead of the warm flood of blood that sought to catch her. A liquid metal covered her and she rode on the curve of white bright days and dark black nights and the surge of the long gladness of summer and the ebb of the deep dream of sleep in winter till a high red wave of hotness drowned her in a deluge of silver and blue and boiled her blood and blistered her flesh *bangbangbang* . . .

II

"Yuh bettah go," she said.

She felt him standing by the side of the bed, in the dark. She heard him clear his throat. His belt-buckle tinkled.

"Im leaving that clock and graphophone," he said.

She said nothing. In her mind she saw the box glowing softly, like the light in the baby's eyes. She stretched out her legs and relaxed.

"You can have it for forty instead of fifty. Ill be by early in the morning to see if your husbands in."

She said nothing. She felt the hot skin of her body growing steadily cooler.

"Do you think hell pay ten on it? Hell only owe thirty then."

She pushed her toes deep into the quilt, feeling a night wind blowing through the door. Her palms rested lightly on top of her breasts.

"Do you think hell pay ten on it?"

"Hunh?"

"Hell pay ten, wont he?"

"Ah don know," she whispered.

She heard his shoe hit against a wall; footsteps echoed on the wooden porch. She started nervously when she heard the roar of his car; she followed the throb of the motor till she heard it when she could hear it no more, followed it till she heard it roaring faintly in her ears in the dark and silent room. Her hands moved on her breasts and she was conscious of herself, all over; she felt the weight of her body resting heavily on shucks. She felt the presence of fields lying out there covered with night. She turned over slowly and lay on her stomach, her hands tucked under her. From somewhere came a creaking noise. She sat upright, feeling fear. The wind sighed. Crickets called. She lay down again, hearing shucks rustle. Her eyes looked straight up in the darkness and her blood sogged. She had lain a long time, full of a vast peace, when a far away tinkle made her feel the bed again. The tinkle came through the night; she listened, knowing that soon she would hear the rattle of Silas' wagon. Even then she tried to fight off the sounds of Silas' coming, even then she wanted to feel the peace of night filling her again; but the tinkle grew louder and she heard the jangle of a wagon and the quick trot of horses. Thas Silas! She gave up and waited. She heard horses neighing. Out of the window bare feet whispered in the dust, then crossed the porch, echoing in soft booms. She closed her eyes and saw Silas come into the room in his dirty overalls as she had seen him come in a thousand times before.

"Yuh sleep, Sarah?"

She did not answer. Feet walking across the floor and a match scratched. She opened her eyes and saw Silas standing over her with a lighted lamp. His hat was pushed far back on his head and he was laughing.

"Ah reckon yuh thought Ah waznt never comin back, hunh? Cant yuh wake up? See, Ah got that red cloth yuh wanted . . ." He laughed again and threw the red cloth on the mantel.

"Yuh hongry?" she asked.

"Naw, Ah kin make out till mawnin." Shucks rustled as he sat on the edge of the bed. "Ah got two hundred n fifty fer mah cotton."

"Two hundred n fifty?"

"Nothin different! N guess whut Ah done?"

"Whut?"

"Ah bought ten mo acres o lan. Got em from ol man Burgess. Paid im a hundred n fifty dollahs down. Ahll pay the rest next year ef things go erlong awright. Ahma have t git a man t hep me nex spring . . ."

"Yuh mean hire somebody?"

"Sho, hire somebody! Whut yuh think? Ain tha the way the white folks do? Ef yuhs gonna git anywheres yuhs gotta do just like they do." He paused. "Whut yuh been doin since Ah been gone?"

"Nothin. Cookin, cleanin, n . . ."

"How Ruth?"

"She awright." She lifted her head. "Silas, yuh git any lettahs?"

"Naw. But Ah heard Tom wuz in town."

"In *town?*"

She sat straight up.

"Yeah, thas whut the folks wuz sayin at the sto."

"Back from the war?"

"Ah ast erroun t see ef Ah could fin im. But Ah couldnt."

"Lawd, Ah wish hed c mon home."

"Them white folks shos glad the wars over. But things wuz kinda bad there in town. Everywhere Ah looked wuznt nothin but black n white soljers. N them white folks beat up a black soljer yestiddy. He was jus in from France. Wuz still wearin his soljers suit. They claimed he sassed a white woman . . ."

"Who wuz he?"

"Ah don know. Never saw im befo."

"Yuh see An Peel?"

"Naw."

"Silas!" she said reprovingly.

"Aw, Sarah, Ah jus couldnt git out there."

"Whut else yuh bring sides the cloth?"

"Ah got yuh some high-top shoes." He turned and looked at her in the dim light of the lamp. "Woman, ain yuh glad Ah bought yuh some shoes n cloth?" He laughed and lifted his feet to the bed. "Lawd, Sarah, yuhs sho sleepy, ain yuh?"

"Bettah put tha lamp out, Silas . . ."

"Aw . . ." He swung out of the bed and stood still for a moment. She watched him, then turned her face to the wall.

"Whuts that by the windah?" he asked.

She saw him bending over and touching the graphophone with his fingers.

"Thasa graphophone."

"Where yuh git it from?"

"A man lef it here."

"When he bring it?"

"Today."

"But how come he t leave it?"

"He says hell be out here in the mawnin t see ef yuh wans t buy it."

He was on his knees, feeling the wood and looking at the gilt on the edges of the box. He stood up and looked at her.

"Yuh ain never said yuh wanted one of these things."

She said nothin.

"Where wuz the man from?"

"Ah don know."

"He white?"

"Yeah."

He put the lamp back on the mantle. As he lifted the globe to blow out the flame, his hand paused.

"Whos hats this?"

She raised herself and looked. A straw hat lay bottom upwards on the edge of the mantel. Silas picked it up and looked back to the bed, to Sarah.

"Ah guess its the white mans. He must a lef it . . ."

"Whut he doin *in our room*?"

"He wuz talkin t me bout that graphophone."

She watched him go to the window and stoop again to the box. He picked it up, fumbled with the price-tag and took the box to the light.

"Whut this thing cos?"

"Forty dollahs."

"But its marked fifty here."

"Oh, Ah means he said fifty . . ."

"Yuh lyin t me!"

"Silas!"

He heaved the box out of the front door; there was a smashing, tinkling noise as it bounded off the front porch and hit the ground. "Whut in hell yuh lie t me fer?"

"Yuh broke the box!"

"Ahma break yo Gawddam neck ef yuh don stop lyin t me!"

"Silas, Ah ain lied t yuh!"

He was standing by the bed with the lamp trembling in his hand. She stood on the other side, between the bed and the wall.

"How come yuh tell me that thing cos *forty* dollahs when it cos *fifty*?"

"Thas whut he tol me."

"How come he take *ten* dollars off fer yuh?"

"He ain took nothin off fer me, Silas!"

"Yuh lyin t me! N yuh lied t me bout Tom, too!"

She stood with her back to the wall, her lips parted, looking at him silently, steadily. Their eyes held for a moment. Silas looked down, as though he were about to believe her. Then he stiffened.

"Whos this?" he asked, picking up a short, yellow pencil from the crumpled quilt.

She said nothing. He started toward her.

"Yuh wan me t take mah raw-hide whip n make yuh talk?"

"Naw, naw, Silas! Yuh wrong! He wuz figgerin wid tha pencil!"

He was silent a moment, his eyes searching her face.

"Gawddam yo black soul t hell, don yuh try lyin t me! Ef yuh start layin wid white men Ahll hosswhip yuh t a incha yo life. Shos theres a Gawd in Heaven Ah will! From sunup t sundown Ah works mah guts out t pay them white trash bastards whut Ah owe em, n then Ah comes n fins they been in mah house! Ah cant go into their houses, n yuh know Gawddam well Ah cant! They don have no mercy on no black folks; wes jus like dirt under their feet! Fer ten years Ah slaves lika dog t git mah farm free, givin ever penny Ah kin t em, n then Ah comes n fins they been in mah house . . ." He was speechless with outrage. "If yuh wans t eat at mah table yuhs gonna keep them white trash bastards out, yuh hear? Tha white ape kin come n git tha damn box n Ah ain gonna pay im a cent! He had no bisness leavin it here, n yuh had no bisness lettin im! Ahma tell tha sonofabitch something when he comes out here in the mawnin, so hep me Gawd! Now git back in tha bed!"

She slipped beneath the quilt and lay still, her face turned to the wall. Her heart thumped slowly and heavily. She heard him walk across the floor in his bare feet. She heard the bottom of the lamp as it rested on the mantel. She stiffened when the room darkened. Feet whispered across the floor again. The shucks rustled from Silas' weight as he sat on the edge of the bed. She was still, breathing softly. Silas was mumbling. She felt sorry for him. In the darkness it seemed that she could see the hurt look on his black face. The crow of a rooster came from far away, came so faintly that it seemed she had not heard it. The bed sank and the shucks cried out in dry whispers; she knew Silas had stretched out. She heard him sigh. Then she jumped because he jumped. She could feel the tenseness of his body; she knew he was sitting bolt upright. She felt his hands fumbling jerkily under the quilt. Then the bed heaved amid a wild shout of shucks and Silas' feet hit the floor with a loud boom. She snatched herself to her elbows, straining her eyes in the dark, wondering what was wrong now. Silas was moving about, cursing under his breath.

"Don wake Ruth up!" she whispered.

"Ef yuh say one mo word t me Ahma slap yuh inter a black spasm!"

She grabbed her dress, got up and stood by the bed, the tips of her fingers touching the wall behind her. A match flared in yellow flame; Silas' face was caught in a circle of light. He was looking downward, staring intently at a white wad of cloth balled in his hand. His black cheeks were hard, set; his lips were tightly pursed. She looked closer; she saw that the white cloth was a man's handkerchief. Silas' fingers loosened; she heard the handkerchief hit the floor softly, damply. The match went out.

"Yuh little bitch!"

Her knees gave. Fear oozed from her throat to her stomach. She moved in the dark toward the door, struggling with the dress, jamming it over her head. She heard the thick skin of Silas' feet swish across the wooden planks.

"Ah got mah raw-hide whip n Ahm takin yuh t the barn!"

She ran on tiptoe to the porch and paused, thinking of the baby. She shrank as something whined through the air. A red streak of pain cut across the small of her back and burned its way into her body, deeply.

"Silas!" she screamed.

She grabbed for the post and fell in dust. She screamed again and crawled out of reach.

"Git t the barn, Gawddammit!"

She scrambled up and ran through the dark, hearing the baby cry. Behind her leather thongs hummed and feet whispered swiftly over the dusty ground.

"C mere, yuh bitch! C mere, Ah say!"

She ran to the road and stopped. She wanted to go back and get the baby, but she dared not. Not as long as Silas had that whip. She stiffened, feeling that he was near.

"Yuh just as well c mon back n git yo beatin!"

She ran again, slowing now and then to listen. If she only knew where he was she would slip back into the house and get the baby and walk all the way to Aunt Peel's.

"Yuh ain comin back in mah house till Ah beat yuh!"

She was sorry for the anger she knew he had out there in the field. She had a bewildering impulse to go to him and ask him not to be angry; she wanted to tell him that there was nothing to be angry about; that what she had done did not matter; that she was sorry; that after all she was his wife and still loved him. But there was no way she could do that now; if she went to him he would whip her as she had seen him whip a horse.

"Sarah! Sarah!"

His voice came from far away. Ahm goin git Ruth. Back through dust she sped, going on her toes, holding her breath.

"Saaaarah!"

From far off his voice floated over the fields. She ran into the house and caught the baby in her arms. Again she sped through dust on her toes. She did not stop till she was so far away that his voice sounded like a faint echo falling from the sky. She looked up; the stars were paling a little. Mus be gittin near mawnin. She walked now, letting her feet sink softly into the cool dust. The baby was sleeping; she could feel the little chest swelling against her arm. She looked up again; the sky was solid black. Its gittin near mawnin. Ahma take Ruth t An Peels. N mabbe Ahll fin Tom . . . But she could not walk all that distance in the dark. Not now. Her legs were tired. For a moment a memory of surge and ebb rose in her blood; she felt her legs straining, upward. She sighed. Yes, she would go to the sloping hillside back of the garden and wait until morning. Then she would slip away. She stopped, listened. She heard a faint, rattling noise. She imagined Silas' kicking or throwing the smashed graphophone. Hes mad! Hes sho mad! Aw, Lawd! . . . She stopped stock still, squeezing the baby till it whimpered. What would happen when that white man came out in the morning? She had forgotten him. She would have to head him off and tell him. Yeah, cause Silas jus mad ernuff t kill! Lawd, hes mad ernuff t kill!

III

She circled the house widely, climbing a slope, groping her way, holding the baby high in her arms. After awhile she stopped and wondered where on the slope she was. She remembered there was an elm tree near the edge; if she could find it she would know. She groped farther, feeling with her feet. Ahm gittin los! And she did not want to fall with the baby. Ahma stop here, she thought. When morning came she would see the car of the white man from this hill and she would run down the road and tell him to go back; and then there would be no killing. Dimly she saw in her mind a picture of men killing and being killed. White men killed the black and black men killed the white. White men killed the black men because they could, and the black men killed the white men to keep from being killed. And killing was blood. Lawd, Ah wish Tom wuz here. She shuddered, sat on the ground and watched the sky for signs of morning. Mabbe Ah oughta walk on down the road? Naw . . . Her legs were tired. Again she felt her body straining. Then she saw Silas holding the white man's handkerchief. She heard it hit the floor, softly, damply. She was sorry for what she had done. Silas was as good to her as any black man could be to a black woman. Most of the black women worked in the fields as croppers.[2] But Silas had given her her own home, and that was more than many others had done for their women. Yes, she knew how Silas felt. Always he had said he was as good as any white man. He had worked hard and saved his money and bought a farm so he could

2. Tenant farmers whose only pay is the share of the crop they raise.

grow his own crops like white men. Silas hates white folks! Lawd, he sho hates em!

The baby whimpered. She unbuttoned her dress and nursed her in the dark. She looked toward the east. There! A tinge of grey hovered. It wont be long now. She could see ghostly outlines of trees. Soon she would see the elm, and by the elm she would sit till it was light enough to see the road.

The baby slept. Far off a rooster crowed. Sky deepened. She rose and walked slowly down a narrow, curving path and came to the elm tree. Standing on the edge of a slope, she saw a dark smudge in a sea of shifting shadows. That was her home. Wondah how come Silas didn't light the lamp? She shifted the baby from her right hip to her left, sighed, struggled against sleep. She sat on the ground again, caught the baby close and leaned against the trunk of a tree. Her eye-lids drooped and it seemed that a hard, cold hand caught hold of her right leg or was it her left leg—she did not know which —and began to drag her over a rough litter of shucks and when she strained to see who it was that was pulling her no one was in sight but far ahead was darkness and it seemed that out of the darkness some force came and pulled her like a magnet and she went sliding along over a rough bed of screeching shucks and it seemed that a wild fear made her want to scream but when she opened her mouth to scream she could not scream and she felt she was coming to a wide black hole and again she made ready to scream and then it was too late for she was already over the wide black hole falling falling falling . . .

She awakened with a start and blinked her eyes in the sunshine. She found she was clutching the baby so hard that it had begun to cry. She got to her feet, trembling from fright of the dream, remembering Silas and the white man and Silas' running her out of the house and the white man's coming. Silas was standing in the front yard; she caught her breath. Yes, she had to go and head that white man off! Naw! She could not do that, not with Silas standing there with that whip in his hand. If she tried to climb any of those slopes he would see her surely. And Silas would never forgive her for something like that. If it were anybody but a white man it would be different.

Then, while standing there on the edge of the slope looking wonderingly at Silas striking the whip against his overall-leg—and then, while standing there looking—she froze. There came from the hills a distant throb. Lawd! The baby whimpered. She loosened her arms. The throb grew louder, droning. Hes comin fas! She wanted to run to Silas and beg him not to bother the white man. But he had that whip in his hand. She should not have done what she had done last night. This was all her fault. Lawd, ef anything happens t im its mah blame . . . Her eyes watched a black car speed over the crest of a hill. She should have been out there on the road instead of sleeping here by the tree. But it was too late now. Silas was standing in the yard; she saw him turn with a nervous jerk and sit on the edge of the porch. He was holding the whip stiffly. The car came to a stop. A door swung open. A white man got out. *Thas im!* She saw another white man in the front seat of the car. *N thats his buddy . . .* The white man who had gotten out walked over the ground, going to Silas. They faced each other, the white man standing up and Silas sitting down; like two toy men they faced each other. She saw Silas point the whip to the smashed graphophone. The white man looked down and took a quick step backward. The white man's shoulders were bent and he shook his head from left to right. Then Silas got up and they faced each other again; like two dolls, a white doll and a black doll, they faced each other in the valley below. The white man pointed his finger into Silas' face. Then Silas' right arm went up; the whip flashed. The white man turned, bending, flinging his hands to shield his head. Silas' arm rose and fell, rose and fell. She saw the white man crawling in dust, trying to get out of reach. She screamed when she saw the other white man get out of the car and run to Silas. Then all three were on the ground, rolling in dust, grappling for the whip. She clutched the baby and ran. *Lawd!* Then she stopped, her mouth hanging open. Silas had broken loose and was running toward the house. She knew he was going for his gun.

"Silas!"

Running, she stumbled and fell. The baby rolled in the dust and bawled. She grabbed it up and ran again. The white men were scrambling for their car. She reached level ground, running. *Hell be killed!* Then again she stopped. Silas was on the front porch, aiming a rifle. One of the white men was climbing into the car. The other was standing, waving his arms, shouting at Silas. She tried to scream, but choked; and she could not scream till she heard a shot ring out.

"Silas!"

One of the white men was on the ground. The other was in the car. Silas was aiming again. The car started, running in a cloud of dust. She fell to her knees and hugged the baby close. She heard another shot, but the car was roaring over the top of the southern hill. Fear was gone now. Down the slope she ran. Silas was standing on the porch, holding his gun and looking at the fleeing car. Then she saw him go to the white man lying in dust and stoop over him. He caught one of the man's legs and dragged the body into the middle of the road. Then he turned and came slowly back to the house. She ran, holding the baby, and fell at his feet.

"Silas!"

IV

"Git up, Sarah!"

His voice was hard and cold. She lifted her eyes and saw blurred

black feet. She wiped tears away with dusty fingers and pulled up.
Something took speech from her and she stood with bowed shoulders. Silas was standing still, mute; the look on his face condemned
her. It was as though he had gone far off and had stayed a long
time and had come back changed even while she was standing there
in the sunshine before him. She wanted to say something, to give
herself. She cried.

"Git the chile up, Sarah!"

She lifted the baby and stood waiting for him to speak, to tell
her something to change all this. But he said nothing. He walked
toward the house. She followed. As she attempted to go in, he
blocked the way. She jumped to one side as he threw the red cloth
outdoors to the ground. The new shoes came next. Then Silas
heaved the baby's cradle. It hit the porch and a rocker splintered;
the cradle swayed for a second, then fell to the ground, lifting a
cloud of brown dust against the sun. All of her clothes and the
baby's clothes were thrown out.

"Silas!"

She cried, seeing blurred objects sailing through the air and hearing them hit softly in the dust.

"Git yo things n go!"

"Silas!"

"Ain no use yuh saying *nothin* now!"

"But theyll kill yuh!"

"There ain nothin Ah kin do. N there ain nothin yuh kin do.
Yuh done done too Gawddam much awready. Git yo things n go!"

"Theyll kill yuh, Silas!"

He pushed her off the porch.

"GIT YO THINGS N GO T AN PEELS!"

"Les *both* go, Silas!"

"Ahm stayin here till they come back!"

She grabbed his arm and he slapped her hand away. She dropped
to the edge of the porch and sat looking at the ground.

"Go way," she said quietly. "Go way fo they comes. Ah didnt
mean no harm . . ."

"Go way fer whut?"

"Theyll *kill* yuh . . ."

"It don make no difference." He looked out over the sunfilled
fields. "Fer ten years Ah slaved mah life out t git mah farm free
. . ." His voice broke off. His lips moved as though a thousand words
were spilling silently out of his mouth, as though he did not have
breath enough to give them sound. He looked to the sky, and then
back to the dust. "Now, its all gone. *Gone* . . . Ef Ah run erway,
Ah ain got nothin. Ef Ah stay n fight, Ah ain got nothin. It dont
make no difference which way Ah go. Gawd! Gawd, Ah wish all
them white folks wuz dead! *Dead*, Ah tell yuh! Ah wish Gawd
would kill em *all!*"

She watched him run a few steps and stop. His throat swelled. He lifted his hands to his face; his fingers trembled. Then he bent to the ground and cried. She touched his shoulders.

"Silas!"

He stood up. She saw he was staring at the white man's body lying in the dust in the middle of the road. She watched him walk over to it. He began to talk to no one in particular; he simply stood over the dead white man and talked out of his life, out of a deep and final sense that now it was all over and nothing could make any difference.

"The white folks ain never gimme a chance! They ain never give no black man a chance! There ain nothin in yo whole life yuh kin keep from em! They take yo lan! They take yo freedom! They take yo women! N then they take yo life!" He turned to her, screaming. "N then Ah gits stabbed in the back by mah own blood! When mah eyes is on the white folks to keep em from killin me, mah own blood trips me up!" He knelt in the dust again and sobbed; after a bit he looked to the sky, his face wet with tears. "Ahm gonna be hard like they is! So hep me, Gawd, Ah'm gonna be *hard!* When they come fer me Ahm gonna *be here!* N when they git me outta here theys gonna *know* Ahm gone! Ef Gawd lets me live Ahm gonna make 'em *feel it!*" He stopped and tried to get his breath. "But, Lawd, Ah don wanna be this way! I don mean nothin! Yuh die ef yuh fight! Yuh die ef yuh don fight! Either way yuh die n it don mean nothin . . ."

He was lying flat on the ground, the side of his face deep in dust. Sarah stood nursing the baby with eyes black and stony. Silas pulled up slowly and stood again on the porch.

"Git on t An Peels, Sarah!"

A dull roar came from the south. They both turned. A long streak of brown dust was weaving down the hillside.

"Silas!"

"Go on cross the fiels, Sarah!"

"We kin *both* go! Git the hosses!"

He pushed her off the porch, grabbed her hand, and led her to the rear of the house, past the well, to where a path led up a slope to the elm tree.

"Silas!"

"Yuh git on fo they ketch yuh too!"

Blind from tears, she went across the swaying fields, stumbling over blurred grass. It ain no use! She knew it was now too late to make him change his mind. The calves of her legs knotted. Suddenly her throat tightened, aching. She stopped, closed her eyes and tried to stem a flood of sorrow that drenched her. Yes, killing of white men by black men and killing of black men by white men went on in spite of the hope of white bright days and the desire of dark black nights and the long gladness of green cornfields in

summer and the deep dream of sleepy grey skies in winter. And
when killing started it went on, like a river flowing. Oh, she felt
sorry for Silas! Silas. . . . He was following that long river of blood.
Lawd, how come he wans t stay there like tha? And he did not want
to die; she knew he hated dying by the way he talked of it. Yet he
followed the old river of blood, knowing that it meant nothing. He
followed it, cursing and whimpering. But he followed it. She stared
before her at the dry, dusty grass. Somehow, men, black men and
white men, land and houses, green cornfields and grey skies, gladness and dreams, were all a part of that which made life good. Yes,
somehow, they were linked, like the spokes in a spinning wheel. She
felt they were. She knew they were. She felt it when she breathed
and knew it when she looked. But she could not say how; she could
not put her finger on it and when she thought hard about it it
became all mixed up, like milk spilling suddenly. Or else it knotted
in her throat and chest in a hard, aching lump, like the one she felt
now. She touched her face to the baby's face and cried again.

There was a loud blare of auto horns. The growing roar made her
turn round. Silas was standing, seemingly unafraid, leaning against a
post of the porch. The long line of cars came speeding in clouds of
dust. Silas moved toward the door and went in. Sarah ran down the
slope a piece, coming again to the elm tree. Her breath was slow
and hard. The cars stopped in front of the house. There was a
steady drone of motors and drifting clouds of dust. For a moment
she could not see what was happening. Then on all sides white men
with pistols and rifles swarmed over the fields. She dropped to her
knees, unable to take her eyes away, unable, it seemed, to breathe.
A shot rang out. A white man fell, rolling over, face downward.

"Hes gotta gun!"

"Git back!"

"Lay down!"

The white men ran back and crouched behind cars. Three more
shots came from the house. She looked, her head and eyes aching.
She rested the baby in her lap and shut her eyes. Her knees sank
into the dust. More shots came, but it was no use looking now. She
knew it all by heart. She could feel it happening even before it happened. There were men killing and being killed. Then she jerked
up, being compelled to look.

"Burn the bastard out!"

"Set the sonofabitch on fire!"

"Cook the coon!"

"Smoke im out!"

She saw two white men on all fours creeping past the well. One
carried a gun and the other a red tin can. When they reached the
back steps the one with the tin can crept under the house and crept
out again. Then both rose and ran. Shots. One fell. A yell went up.

A yellow tongue of fire licked out from under the back steps.

"Burn the nigger!"

"C mon out, nigger, n git yos!"

She watched from the hill-slope; the back steps blazed. The white men fired a steady stream of bullets. Black smoke spiraled upward in the sunshine. Shots came from the house. The white men crouched out of sight, behind their cars.

"Make up your mind, nigger!"

"C mon out er burn, yuh black bastard!"

"Yuh think yuhre white now, nigger?"

The shack blazed, flanked on all sides by whirling smoke filled with flying sparks. She heard the distant hiss of flames. White men were crawling on their stomachs. Now and then they stopped, aimed, and fired into the bulging smoke. She looked with a tense numbness; she looked, waiting for Silas to scream, or run out. But the house crackled and blazed, spouting yellow plumes to the blue sky. The white men shot again, sending a hail of bullets into the furious pillars of smoke. And still she could not see Silas running out, or hear his voice calling. Then she jumped, standing. There was a loud crash; the roof caved in. A black chimney loomed amid crumbling wood. Flames roared and black smoke billowed, hiding the house. The white men stood up, no longer afraid. Again she waited for Silas, waited to see him fight his way out, waited to hear his call. Then she breathed a long, slow breath, emptying her lungs. She knew now. Silas had killed as many as he could and stayed on to burn, had stayed without a murmur. She filled her lungs with a quick gasp as the walls fell in; the house was hidden by eager plumes of red. She turned and ran with the baby in her arms, ran blindly across the fields, crying, "Naw, Gawd!"

1938

EUDORA WELTY

1909–

Eudora Welty's three volumes of short stories, seven novels, several essays on the art of fiction, and an album of photographs identify not only an important talent among American women but a leading figure in the literature of the South.

Welty was born in Jackson, Mississippi, to parents who had come from the North, and was raised in comfortable circumstances (her father headed an insurance company). She attended Mississippi State College for Women, graduated from the University of Wisconsin in 1929, and then went to New York for a course in advertising at Columbia University's Business School. Returning home to a depression-blighted South, she worked as a radio continuity writer and society editor before traveling throughout the state of Mississippi for the Works Progress Administration, taking photographs and interviewing local residents. Those travels are reflected in her fiction and also in a book of her photographs published in 1971, *One Time and Place*.

In 1941 Katherine Anne Porter wrote a warm introduction to *A Curtain of Green and Other Stories*, hailing the arrival of yet another gifted southern fiction writer. From then on her productions were greeted with comparable acclaim. During the next decades her stories were published in leading national journals, *Southern Review* and *Sewanee Review* as well as *Atlantic Monthly* and *The New Yorker*, and her writing was praised by the critic John Crowe Ransom and the novelist Robert Penn Warren. Even a less favorable judge, Diana Trilling, was struck by the emotional impact of Welty's fiction.

Her first collection included the famous *Why I Live at the P.O.* and *Death of a Traveling Salesman*, her first story which had appeared in 1936, and the book introduced many of the characters and themes that make up her unique fictional world: the fulfillment of marriage; the satisfactions and the constraints of domestic rituals; the involuted, extended southern families; the physically handicapped, mentally retarded, or unstable kinfolk; the more somber undercurrents of death, violence, and degradation that characterize so much southern fiction. They emerge in highly charged descriptions of delta- or hill-country communities, and they are treated with a gentle tolerance of human foibles and with an antic humor that has characterized the literature of the Southwest since Mark Twain.

Her next book, *The Robber Bridegroom* (1942), was an extended fantasy, a folk tale mixing elements of Grimm's fairy tales and W. B. Yeats's Celtic tales with those of ancient classical myths, and treating the materials with the bizarre exaggerations of American frontier humor and the "tall tale." Set in the Natchez Trace country of Mississippi in the eighteenth century, its fantastic trappings (ghosts, talking heads, Indians and outlaws, magic potions) are grounded in the reality of that time and place. At its center is a quietly poignant tale of self-deception, self-discovery, and the ambiguity of love.

Her characters' search for identity, rather than plot or character development, provides the structure for her best work, along with a strong sense of place. Though Welty has refused the label of regionalist, she once wrote that "like a good many other writers, I am myself touched off by place, the place where I am and the place I know." Indeed "location is the ground-conductor of all the currents of emotion and belief and moral conviction that charge out from the story in its course." While "it is through place that we put out roots," yet "where these roots reach toward * * * is the deep running vein * * * that feeds and is fed by human understanding."[1] Her stories are evocative of season and soil, the topography and atmosphere of her Mississippi.

Welty's contention that character is brought out by a strong sense of place is borne out by the striking gallery of amiably eccentric characters who inhabit her fiction: the wizened, club-footed old black forced to play *Keela the Outcast Indian Maiden* in a freak show; hotelkeeper Edna Earle, the garrulous chronicler of *The Ponder Heart* (1954), and her dim-witted

1. "Place in Fiction," *Three Papers on Fiction* (1962).

Uncle Daniel Ponder, whose weakness is to go on "giving away" sprees. Other memorable characters are the strong, not overly bright, young heroes of *The Wide Net* (1943) and *Losing Battles* (1970), as well as the vulgar yet touchingly vulnerable "common" women of *Going to Naples* and *The Optimist's Daughter* (1972).

An overabundance of metaphor and strained similes, which the novelist Robert Penn Warren complained about in her early fiction, is less evident in her later writing. The profusion of metaphor may have been encouraged by her acknowledged models, Virginia Woolf, Katherine Mansfield, and William Faulkner, who in any case sanctioned her deliberate strategy of baffling or mystifying her readers, a strategy that was conspicuous in *The Burning* and the title story of *The Bride of the Innisfallen* (1955). Welty herself has written that "fine story writers seem to be in a sense obstructionists."[2]

Her narratives unfold on the principle of varied repetitions or reiterations that have, Welty has claimed, the function of a deliberate double exposure in photography. Hers is a distinctly visual imagination; scenes seem composed as by a camera frame, with carefully delineated foregrounds and backgrounds and a strong play of light and shade on surface detail. One of the functions of "place," she wrote, "is to focus the gigantic, voracious eye of genius and bring its gaze to a point."[3]

Since her early success in securing publication and gaining recognition, Welty has had an uninterrupted career and has received many of the major awards for fiction, including most recently the Howells Gold Medal for Fiction of the Academy of Arts and Letters (1955), and a term as Honorary Consultant at the Library of Congress (1958–61). She has held Guggenheim fellowships and lectureships at Cambridge University (1955) and Smith College (1952). But she has avoided the role of a public literary figure, returning always to the Mississippi which she celebrates in her fiction.

Why I Live at the P.O.[1]

I was getting along fine with Mama, Papa-Daddy and Uncle Rondo until my sister Stella-Rondo just separated from her husband and came back home again. Mr. Whitaker! Of course I went with Mr. Whitaker first, when he first appeared here in China Grove, taking "Pose Yourself" photos, and Stella-Rondo broke us up. Told him I was one-sided. Bigger on one side than the other, which is a deliberate, calculated falsehood: I'm the same. Stella-Rondo is exactly twelve months to the day younger than I am and for that reason she's spoiled.

She's always had anything in the world she wanted and then she'd throw it away. Papa-Daddy gave her this gorgeous Add-a-Pearl necklace when she was eight years old and she threw it away playing baseball when she was nine, with only two pearls.

So as soon as she got married and moved away from home the first thing she did was separate! From Mr. Whitaker! This photographer with the popeyes she said she trusted. Came home from one

---

2. *Three Essays.*   1. "P.O.": post office.
3. "Place in Fiction," *Three Essays.*

of those towns up in Illinois and to our complete surprise brought this child of two.

Mama said she like to made her drop dead for a second. "Here you had this marvelous blonde child and never so much as wrote your mother a word about it," says Mama. "I'm thoroughly ashamed of you." But of course she wasn't.

Stella-Rondo just calmly takes off this *hat*, I wish you could see it. She says, "Why, Mama, Shirley-T.'s adopted, I can prove it."

"How?" says Mama, but all I says was, "H'm!" There I was over the hot stove, trying to stretch two chickens over five people and a completely unexpected child into the bargain, without one moment's notice.

"What do you mean—'H'm!'?" says Stella-Rondo, and Mama says, "I heard that, Sister."

I said that oh, I didn't mean a thing, only that whoever Shirley-T. was, she was the spit-image of Papa-Daddy if he'd cut off his beard, which of course he'd never do in the world. Papa-Daddy's Mama's papa and sulks.

Stella-Rondo got furious! She said, "Sister, I don't need to tell you you got a lot of nerve and always did have and I'll thank you to make no future reference to my adopted child whatsoever."

"Very well," I said. "Very well, very well. Of course I noticed at once she looks like Mr. Whitaker's side too. That frown. She looks like a cross between Mr. Whitaker and Papa-Daddy."

"Well, all I can say is she isn't."

"She looks exactly like Shirley Temple[2] to me," says Mama, but Shirley-T. just ran away from her.

So the first thing Stella-Rondo did at the table was turn Papa-Daddy against me.

"Papa-Daddy," she says. He was trying to cut up his meat. "Papa-Daddy!" I was taken completely by surprise. Papa-Daddy is about a million years old and's got this long-long beard. "Papa-Daddy, Sister says she fails to understand why you don't cut off your beard."

So Papa-Daddy l-a-y-s down his knife and fork! He's real rich. Mama says he is, he says he isn't. So he says, "Have I heard correctly? You don't understand why I don't cut off my beard?"

"Why," I says, "Papa-Daddy, of course I understand, I did not say any such of a thing, the idea!"

He says, "Hussy!"

I says, "Papa-Daddy, you know I wouldn't any more want you to cut off your beard than the man in the moon. It was the farthest thing from my mind! Stella-Rondo sat there and made that up while she was eating breast of chicken."

But he says, "So the postmistress fails to understand why I don't cut off my beard. Which job I got you through my influence with

---

2. Shirley Temple (b. 1928), tap-dancing child star in saccharine motion pictures.

the government. 'Bird's nest'—is that what you call it?"

Not that it isn't the next to smallest P.O. in the entire state of Mississippi.

I says, "Oh, Papa-Daddy," I says, "I didn't say any such of a thing, I never dreamed it was a bird's nest, I have always been grateful though this is the next to smallest P.O. in the state of Mississippi, and I do not enjoy being referred to as a hussy by my own grandfather."

But Stella-Rondo says, "Yes, you did say it too. Anybody in the world could of heard you, that had ears."

"Stop right there," says Mama, looking at *me*.

So I pulled my napkin straight back through the napkin ring and left the table.

As soon as I was out of the room Mama says, "Call her back, or she'll starve to death," but Papa-Daddy says, "This is the beard I started growing on the Coast when I was fifteen years old." He would of gone on till nightfall if Shirley-T. hadn't lost the Milky Way she ate in Cairo.

So Papa-Daddy says, "I am going out and lie in the hammock, and you can all sit here and remember my words: I'll never cut off my beard as long as I live, even one inch, and I don't appreciate it in you at all." Passed right by me in the hall and went straight out and got in the hammock.

It would be a holiday. It wasn't five minutes before Uncle Rondo suddenly appeared in the hall in one of Stella-Rondo's flesh-colored kimonos, all cut on the bias, like something Mr. Whitaker probably thought was gorgeous.

"Uncle Rondo!" I says. "I didn't know who that was! Where are you going?"

"Sister," he says, "get out of my way, I'm poisoned."

"If you're poisoned stay away from Papa-Daddy," I says. "Keep out of the hammock. Papa-Daddy will certainly beat you on the head if you come within forty miles of him. He thinks I deliberately said he ought to cut off his beard after he got me the P.O., and I've told him and told him and told him, and he acts like he just don't hear me. Papa-Daddy must of gone stone deaf."

"He picked a fine day to do it then," says Uncle Rondo, and before you could say "Jack Robinson" flew out in the yard.

What he'd really done, he'd drunk another bottle of that prescription. He does it every single Fourth of July as sure as shooting, and it's horribly expensive. Then he falls over in the hammock and snores. So he insisted on zigzagging right on out to the hammock, looking like a half-wit.

Papa-Daddy woke up with this horrible yell and right there without moving an inch he tried to turn Uncle Rondo against me. I heard every word he said. Oh, he told Uncle Rondo I didn't learn to read till I was eight years old and he didn't see how in the world

I ever got the mail put up at the P.O., much less read it all, and he said if Uncle Rondo could only fathom the lengths he had gone to to get me that job! And he said on the other hand he thought Stella-Rondo had a brilliant mind and deserved credit for getting out of town. All the time he was just lying there swinging as pretty as you please and looping out his beard, and poor Uncle Rondo was *pleading* with him to slow down the hammock, it was making him as dizzy as a witch to watch it. But that's what Papa-Daddy likes about a hammock. So Uncle Rondo was too dizzy to get turned against me for the time being. He's Mama's only brother and is a good case of a one-track mind. Ask anybody. A certified pharmacist.

Just then I heard Stella-Rondo raising the upstairs window. While she was married she got this peculiar idea that it's cooler with the windows shut and locked. So she has to raise the window before she can make a soul hear her outdoors.

So she raises the window and says, "*Oh!*" You would have thought she was mortally wounded.

Uncle Rondo and Papa-Daddy didn't even look up, but kept right on with what they were doing. I had to laugh.

I flew up the stairs and threw the door open! I says, "What in the wide world's the matter, Stella-Rondo? You mortally wounded?"

"No," she says, "I am not mortally wounded but I wish you would do me the favor of looking out that window there and telling me what you see."

So I shade my eyes and look out the window.

"I see the front yard," I says.

"Don't you see any human beings?" she says.

"I see Uncle Rondo trying to run Papa-Daddy out of the hammock," I says. "Nothing more. Naturally, it's so suffocating-hot in the house, with all the windows shut and locked, everybody who cares to stay in their right mind will have to go out and get in the hammock before the Fourth of July is over."

"Don't you notice anything different about Uncle Rondo?" asks Stella-Rondo.

"Why, no, except he's got on some terrible-looking flesh-colored contraption I wouldn't be found dead in, is all I can see," I says.

"Never mind, you won't be found dead in it, because it happens to be part of my trousseau, and Mr. Whitaker took several dozen photographs of me in it," says Stella-Rondo. "What on earth could Uncle Rondo *mean* by wearing part of my trousseau out in the broad open daylight without saying so much as 'Kiss my foot,' *knowing* I only got home this morning after my separation and hung my negligee up on the bathroom door, just as nervous as I could be?"

"I'm sure I don't know, and what do you expect me to do about it?" I says. "Jump out the window?"

"No, I expect nothing of the kind. I simply declare that Uncle Rondo looks like a fool in it, that's all," she says. "It makes me sick to my stomach."

"Well, he looks as good as he can," I says. "As good as anybody in reason could." I stood up for Uncle Rondo, please remember. And I said to Stella-Rondo, "I think I would do well not to criticize so freely if I were you and came home with a two-year-old child I had never said a word about, and no explanation whatever about my separation."

"I asked you the instant I entered this house not to refer one more time to my adopted child, and you gave me your word of honor you would not," was all Stella-Rondo would say, and started pulling out every one of her eyebrows with some cheap Kress tweezers.

So I merely slammed the door behind me and went down and made some green-tomato pickle. Somebody had to do it. Of course Mama had turned both the niggers loose; she always said no earthly power could hold one anyway on the Fourth of July, so she wouldn't even try. It turned out that Jaypan fell in the lake and came within a very narrow limit of drowning.

So Mama trots in. Lifts up the lid and says, "H'm! Not very good for your Uncle Rondo in his precarious condition, I must say. Or poor little adopted Shirley-T. Shame on you!"

That made me tired. I says, "Well, Stella-Rondo had better thank her lucky stars it was her instead of me came trotting in with that very peculiar-looking child. Now if it had been me that trotted in from Illinois and brought a peculiar-looking child of two, I shudder to think of the reception I'd of got, much less controlled the diet of an entire family."

"But you must remember, Sister, that you were never married to Mr. Whitaker in the first place and didn't go up to Illinois to live," says Mama, shaking a spoon in my face. "If you had I would of been just as overjoyed to see you and your little adopted girl as I was to see Stella-Rondo, when you wound up with your separation and came on back home."

"You would not," I says.

"Don't contradict me, I would," says Mama.

But I said she couldn't convince me though she talked till she was blue in the face. Then I said, "Besides, you know as well as I do that that child is not adopted."

"She most certainly is adopted," says Mama, stiff as a poker.

I says, "Why Mama, Stella-Rondo had her just as sure as anything in this world, and just too stuck up to admit it."

"Why, Sister," said Mama. "Here I thought we were going to have a pleasant Fourth of July, and you start right out not believing a word your own baby sister tells you!"

"Just like Cousin Annie Flo. Went to her grave denying the facts of life," I remind Mama.

"I told you if you ever mentioned Annie Flo's name I'd slap your face," says Mama, and slaps my face.

"All right, you wait and see," I says.

"I," says Mama, "I prefer to take my children's word for anything when it's humanly possible." You ought to see Mama, she weighs two hundred pounds and has real tiny feet.

Just then something perfectly horrible occurred to me.

"Mama," I says, "can that child talk?" I simply had to whisper! "Mama, I wonder if that child can be—you know—in any way? Do you realize," I says, "that she hasn't spoken one single, solitary word to a human being up to this minute? This is the way she looks," I says, and I looked like this.

Well, Mama and I just stood there and stared at each other. It was horrible!

"I remember well that Joe Whitaker frequently drank like a fish," says Mama. "I believed to my soul he drank *chemicals*." And without another word she marches to the foot of the stairs and calls Stella-Rondo.

"Stella-Rondo? O-o-o-o-o! Stella-Rondo!"

"What?" says Stella-Rondo from upstairs. Not even the grace to get up off the bed.

"Can that child of yours talk?" asks Mama.

Stella-Rondo says, "Can she what?"

"Talk! Talk!" says Mama. "Burdyburdyburdyburdy!"

So Stella-Rondo yells back, "Who says she can't talk?"

"Sister says so," says Mama.

"You didn't have to tell me, I know whose word of honor don't mean a thing in this house," says Stella-Rondo.

And in a minute the loudest Yankee voice I ever heard in my life yells out, "OE'm Pop-OE the Sailor-r-r-r Ma-a-an!"[3] and then somebody jumps up and down in the upstairs hall. In another second the house would of fallen down.

"Not only talks, she can tap-dance!" calls Stella-Rondo. "Which is more than some people I won't name can do."

"Why, the little precious darling thing!" Mama says, so surprised. "Just as smart as she can be!" Starts talking baby talk right there. Then she turns on me. "Sister, you ought to be thoroughly ashamed! Run upstairs this instant and apologize to Stella-Rondo and Shirley-T."

"Apologize for what?" I says. "I merely wondered if the child was normal, that's all. Now that she's proved she is, why, I have nothing further to say."

But Mama just turned on her heel and flew out, furious. She ran right upstairs and hugged the baby. She believed it was adopted. Stella-Rondo hadn't done a thing but turn her against me from upstairs while I stood there helpless over the hot stove. So that made Mama, Papa-Daddy and the baby all on Stella-Rondo's side.

Next, Uncle Rondo.

I must say that Uncle Rondo has been marvelous to me at various times in the past and I was completely unprepared to be made to jump out of my skin, the way it turned out. Once Stella-Rondo did something perfectly horrible to him—broke a chain letter from Flanders Field[4]—and he took the radio back he had given her and gave it to me. Stella-Rondo was furious! For six months we all had to call her Stella instead of Stella-Rondo, or she wouldn't answer. I always thought Uncle Rondo had all the brains of the entire family. Another time he sent me to Mammoth Cave, with all expenses paid.

But this would be the day he was drinking that prescription, the Fourth of July.

So at supper Stella-Rondo speaks up and says she thinks Uncle Rondo ought to try to eat a little something. So finally Uncle Rondo said he would try a little cold biscuits and ketchup, but that was all. So *she* brought it to him.

"Do you think it wise to disport with ketchup in Stella-Rondo's flesh-colored kimono?" I says. Trying to be considerate! If Stella-Rondo couldn't watch out for her trousseau, somebody had to.

"Any objections?" asks Uncle Rondo, just about to pour out all the ketchup.

"Don't mind what she says, Uncle Rondo," says Stella-Rondo. "Sister has been devoting this solid afternoon to sneering out my bedroom window at the way you look."

"What's that?" says Uncle Rondo. Uncle Rondo has got the most terrible temper in the world. Anything is liable to make him tear the house down if it comes at the wrong time.

So Stella-Rondo says, "Sister says, 'Uncle Rondo certainly does look like a fool in that pink kimono!'"

Do you remember who it was really said that?

Uncle Rondo spills out all the ketchup and jumps out of his chair and tears off the kimono and throws it down on the dirty floor and puts his foot on it. It had to be sent all the way to Jackson to the cleaners and re-pleated.

"So that's your opinion of your Uncle Rondo, is it?" he says. "I look like a fool, do I? Well, that's the last straw. A whole day in this house with nothing to do, and then to hear you come out with a remark like that behind my back!"

"I didn't say any such of a thing, Uncle Rondo," I says, "and I'm not saying who did, either. Why, I think you look all right. Just try to take care of yourself and not talk and eat at the same time," I says. "I think you better go lie down."

"Lie down my foot," says Uncle Rondo. I ought to of known by

4. World War I battle site and military cemetery.

that he was fixing to do something perfectly horrible.

So he didn't do anything that night in the precarious state he was in—just played Casino[5] with Mama and Stella-Rondo and Shirley-T. and gave Shirley-T. a nickel with a head on both sides. It tickled her nearly to death, and she called him "Papa." But at 6:30 A.M. the next morning, he threw a whole five-cent package of some unsold one-inch firecrackers from the store as hard as he could into my bedroom and they every one went off. Not one bad one in the string. Anybody else, there'd be one that wouldn't go off.

Well, I'm just terribly susceptible to noise of any kind, the doctor has always told me I was the most sensitive person he had ever seen in his whole life, and I was simply prostrated. I couldn't eat! People tell me they heard it as far as the cemetery, and old Aunt Jep Peterson, that had been holding her own so good, thought it was Judgment Day and she was going to meet her whole family. It's usually so quiet here.

And I'll tell you it didn't take me any longer than a minute to make up my mind what to do. There I was with the whole entire house on Stella-Rondo's side and turned against me. If I have anything at all I have pride.

So I just decided I'd go straight down to the P.O. There's plenty of room there in the back, I says to myself.

Well! I made no bones about letting the family catch on to what I was up to. I didn't try to conceal it.

The first thing they knew, I marched in where they were all playing Old Maid[6] and pulled the electric oscillating fan out by the plug, and everything got real hot. Next I snatched the pillow I'd done the needlepoint on right off the davenport from behind Papa-Daddy. He went "Ugh!" I beat Stella-Rondo up the stairs and finally found my charm bracelet in her bureau drawer under a picture of Nelson Eddy.[7]

"So that's the way the land lies," says Uncle Rondo. There he was, piecing on the ham. "Well, Sister, I'll be glad to donate my army cot if you got any place to set it up, providing you'll leave right this minute and let me get some peace." Uncle Rondo was in France.

"Thank you kindly for the cot and 'peace' is hardly the word I would select if I had to resort to firecrackers at 6:30 A.M. in a young girl's bedroom," I says back to him. "And as to where I intend to go, you seem to forget my position as postmistress of China Grove, Mississippi," I says. "I've always got the P.O."

Well, that made them all sit up and take notice.

I went out front and started digging up some four-o'clocks to plant around the P.O.

"Ah-ah-ah!" says Mama, raising the window. "Those happen to

---

5. Card game.
6. Card game.

7. Nelson Eddy (1901–67), singing star in movie operettas.

be my four-o'clocks. Everything planted in that star is mine. I've never known you to make anything grow in your life."

"Very well," I says. "But I take the fern. Even you, Mama, can't stand there and deny that I'm the one watered that fern. And I happen to know where I can send in a box top and get a packet of one thousand mixed seeds, no two the same kind, free."

"Oh, where?" Mama wants to know.

But I says, "Too late. You 'tend to your house, and I'll 'tend to mine. You hear things like that all the time if you know how to listen to the radio. Perfectly marvelous offers. Get anything you want free."

So I hope to tell you I marched in and got that radio, and they could of all bit a nail in two, especially Stella-Rondo, that it used to belong to, and she well knew she couldn't get it back, I'd sue for it like a shot. And I very politely took the sewing-machine motor I helped pay the most on to give Mama for Christmas back in 1929, and a good big calendar, with the first-aid remedies on it. The thermometer and the Hawaiian ukulele certainly were rightfully mine, and I stood on the step-ladder and got all my watermelon-rind preserves and every fruit and vegetable I'd put up, every jar. Then I began to pull the tacks out of the bluebird wall vases on the archway to the dining room.

"Who told you you could have those, Miss Priss?" says Mama, fanning as hard as she could.

"I bought 'em and I'll keep track of 'em," I says. "I'll tack 'em up and I'll keep track of 'em," I says. "I'll tack 'em up one on each side the postoffice window, and you can see 'em when you come to ask me for your mail, if you're so dead to see 'em."

"Not I! I'll never darken the door to that post office again if I live to be a hundred," Mama says. "Ungrateful child! After all the money we spent on you at the Normal."[8]

"Me either," says Stella-Rondo. "You just let my mail lie there and *rot*, for all I care. I'll never come and relieve you of a single, solitary piece."

"I should worry," I says. "And who you think's going to sit down and write you all those big fat letters and postcards, by the way? Mr. Whitaker? Just because he was the only man ever dropped down in China Grove and you got him—unfairly—is he going to sit down and write you a lengthy correspondence after you come home giving no rhyme nor reason whatsoever for your separation and no explanation for the presence of that child? I may not have your brilliant mind, but I fail to see it."

So Mama says, "Sister, I've told you a thousand times that Stella-Rondo simply got homesick, and this child is far too big to be hers," and she says, "Now, why don't you all just sit down and play Casino?"

8. Normal School, teachers' college.

Then Shirley-T. sticks out her tongue at me in this perfectly horrible way. She has no more manners than the man in the moon. I told her she was going to cross her eyes like that some day and they'd stick.

"It's too late to stop me now," I says. "You should have tried that yesterday. I'm going to the P.O. and the only way you can possibly see me is to visit me there."

So Papa-Daddy says, "You'll never catch me setting foot in that post office, even if I should take a notion into my head to write a letter some place." He says, "I won't have you reachin' out of that little old window with a pair of shears and cuttin' off any beard of mine. I'm too smart for you!"

"We all are," says Stella-Rondo.

But I said, "If you're so smart, where's Mr. Whitaker?"

So then Uncle Rondo says, "I'll thank you from now on to stop reading all the orders I get on postcards and telling everybody in China Grove what you think is the matter with them," but I says, "I draw my own conclusions and will continue in the future to draw them." I says, "If people want to write their inmost secrets on penny postcards, there's nothing in the wide world you can do about it, Uncle Rondo."

"And if you think we'll ever *write* another postcard you're sadly mistaken," says Mama.

"Cutting off your nose to spite your face then," I says. "But if you're all determined to have no more to do with the U.S. mail, think of this: What will Stella-Rondo do now, if she wants to tell Mr. Whitaker to come after her?"

"Wah!" says Stella-Rondo. I knew she'd cry. She had a conniption fit right there in the kitchen.

"It will be interesting to see how long she holds out," I says. "And now—I am leaving."

"Good-bye," says Uncle Rondo.

"Oh, I declare," says Mama, "to think a family of mine should quarrel on the Fourth of July, or the day after, over Stella-Rondo leaving old Mr. Whitaker and having the sweetest little adopted child! It looks like we'd all be glad!"

"Wah!" says Stella-Rondo, and has a fresh conniption fit.

"*He* left *her*—you mark my words," I says. "That's Mr. Whitaker. I know Mr. Whitaker. After all, I knew him first. I said from the beginning he'd up and leave her. I foretold every single thing that's happened."

"Where did he go?" asks Mama.

"Probably to the North Pole, if he knows what's good for him," I says.

But Stella-Rondo just bawled and wouldn't say another word. She flew to her room and slammed the door.

"Now look what you've gone and done, Sister," says Mama.

"You go apologize."

"I haven't got time, I'm leaving," I says.

"Well, what are you waiting around for?" asks Uncle Rondo.

So I just picked up the kitchen clock and marched off, without saying "Kiss my foot" or anything, and never did tell Stella-Rondo goodbye.

There was a nigger girl going along on a little wagon right in front.

"Nigger girl," I says, "come help me haul these things down the hill, I'm going to live in the post office."

Took her nine trips in her express wagon. Uncle Rondo came out on the porch and threw her a nickel.

And that's the last I've laid eyes on any of my family or my family laid eyes on me for five solid days and nights. Stella-Rondo may be telling the most horrible tales in the world about Mr. Whitaker, but I haven't heard them. As I tell everybody, I draw my own conclusions.

But oh, I like it here. It's ideal, as I've been saying. You see, I've got everything cater-cornered, the way I like it. Hear the radio? All the war news. Radio, sewing machine, book ends, ironing board and that great big piano lamp—peace, that's what I like. Butter-bean vines planted all along the front where the strings are.

Of course, there's not much mail. My family are naturally the main people in China Grove, and if they prefer to vanish from the face of the earth, for all the mail they get or the mail they write, why, I'm not going to open my mouth. Some of the folks here in town are taking up for me and some turned against me. I know which is which. There are always people who will quit buying stamps just to get on the right side of Papa-Daddy.

But here I am, and here I'll stay. I want the world to know I'm happy.

And if Stella-Rondo should come to me this minute, on bended knees, and *attempt* to explain the incidents of her life with Mr. Whitaker, I'd simply put my fingers in both my ears and refuse to listen.

1941

WILLIAM FAULKNER
1897–1962

The most imposing body of fiction written by an American after World War I consisted of the novels and tales of a southerner from Mississippi, William Faulkner. His brilliantly inventive fiction drew admiration from a growing number of writers and critics in America and France after 1929 during decades when wider audiences disdained him. Many readers were offended by his sensationalism; others were baffled by the density and intricacies of his style. In 1944, scarcely any of his works was in print. After World War II, however, larger audiences in Europe and America responded to the power of his prose. They were gripped by Faulkner's devotion to traditional values in a world of crisis which threatened them, and by the anguish and boldness with which he himself challenged those values, recognizing the need to redefine and reaffirm them.

William Cuthbert Falkner was born near Oxford, Mississippi, where he was raised and in which he later made his permanent home. His family had figured prominently in the history of the region, whose habit of violence, codes of honor, cult of white social status and racial solidarity, and entrepreneurial ambitions provided Faulkner with material for his fiction. His great-grandfather had fought as a colonel in the Civil War and returned to pursue a career as lawyer, railroad financier, civic benefactor, politician, and novelist. (Faulkner is thought to have added the "u" to the spelling of his family name "Falkner" so as to avoid confusion with his novel-writing great-grandfather.) The Colonel had written two novels and a play, run for the state legislature, and helped found the thriving Gulf and Chicago Railroad before being shot dead by an envious political rival and business partner in 1889. Faulkner's father worked for the family railroad until it was sold in 1902, then bought and operated a livery stable and a hardware store, and became business manager of the University of Mississippi at the end of World War I.

Faulkner attended grammar school and two years of high school in Oxford. The only attraction for him at high school was football, and the temptations of hunting, drinking parties, and other diversions continued to be strong after he dropped out in 1915; the family saw to it that he took a clerical job in his grandfather's bank. He had begun drawing early in school, and was trying his hand at writing as early as the sixth grade, but his frequent truancy was a clear sign that academic work was neither stimulating nor disciplining his mind. He found Melville's *Moby-Dick*, Shakespeare's plays, and the novels of Fielding and Conrad elsewhere, notably in his grandfather's library.

The most durable influence on his reading was a slightly older friend, Phil Stone, who encouraged his ambition to be a writer. Educated at Mississippi and Yale, Stone shared Faulkner's interest in regional history and made available to him his family's large library. Faulkner read in the ancient classics, began to teach himself French, and discovered Balzac's novels under Stone's tutelage. In 1918 when his sweetheart decided to marry another young man, Faulkner went for a year to New Haven where Stone was in law school, working for a time as a clerk in an arms factory but continuing his writing and his discussions of literature with Stone. When Faulkner became eligible for military service, he enlisted in the Royal Air Force in Canada and was trained as a pilot, but he returned to Oxford at the end of the war and resumed his writing. Stone, by then a practicing lawyer, began to play a more active role in Faulkner's career; he entered into negotiations with publishers, criticized manuscripts, helped to finance his friend's first published volume, and eventually wrote biographical sketches of Faulkner to bring the author to the attention of critics and readers. Though Faulkner studied languages and English literature for over a year as a special student at the University of Mississippi, worked in a bookstore for a short time in New York City in 1920, worked briefly (and with marked inefficiency) as university postmaster in Oxford, and held jobs as a skilled carpenter and housepainter, his chosen vocation after 1920 was writing.

His first published works were poems. Many drew on the conventions of Shakespearean and pastoral poetry, and Victorian or Edwardian modes of Swinburne and A. E. Housman, while others echoed Yeats, T. S. Eliot, and the French Symbolists Mallarmé and Verlaine. He subsequently published two volumes of verse, *The Marble Faun* (1924) and *A Green Bough* (1931). Faulkner also experimented with plays written for the university's dramatic association. His first published short story (an account of the misadventures of an RAF pilot) appeared in *The Mississippian* in 1920, and he wrote other short fiction in the early 1920s.

By 1924, when *The Double Dealer*, a new literary magazine, accepted the second of his early poems, Faulkner's literary horizons were widening and he spent much of 1925 living in New Orleans, where *The Double Dealer* and the *Times Picayune* published his verse, articles, and the sketches later collected as *New Orleans Sketches* (1968). A thriving literary colony in New Orleans drew Faulkner into the discussion of Freud's psychology, James Joyce's vanguard fiction, and the anthropology of Sir James Frazer's *Golden Bough*. At the center of the colony was the fiction writer Sherwood Anderson, with whom Faulkner became closely acquainted. Personal relations between them became distant after Faulkner collaborated in a parody of Anderson's prose style (*Sherwood Anderson and Other Famous Creoles*, 1926). But the two writers developed some ideas for fiction together, and it was Anderson, Faulkner later testified, who encouraged him to develop his own style as a writer and to draw on his native region for material. Though he had not read it, Anderson recommended to his own publisher the novel that Faulkner wrote in New Orleans, the story of a dying air force veteran entitled *Soldier's Pay* (1926). Faulkner left New Orleans in 1925 for Europe, where he visited museums and took long hiking tours through Italy, France, and England, and visited New Orleans again briefly before settling in Mississippi in 1926.

During the next four years, with time out for odd jobs, hunting expeditions, escapades in Memphis, vacations on the Gulf beaches, and politicking in the unsuccessful political campaigns of his brother John, he finished the work that brought the first phase of his career to its culmination. In 1927 appeared his second novel, *Mosquitoes*, a mocking and at times surrealistic treatment of New Orleans intellectuals and the "jazz age" mores of their wealthy acquaintances aboard a yacht in the Mississippi River basin. Two years later he published *Sartoris*. Its account of a wounded veteran's return home in 1919, his marriage and death, focuses on the interconnections between a prominent southern family and the local community later named Yoknapatawpha County that became legendary in Faulkner's mature fiction. In the same year he finished two of his most ambitious and radically inventive works, which caught the attention of Jean-Paul Sartre in France and other leading critics and charted the main directions of his later writing. *The Sound and the Fury* (1929), Faulkner's favorite among his novels, is the tragic account of a disintegrating southern "aristocratic" family, its vestiges of starved and warped affection, kept perilously intact by its charade of family honor and the ministrations of loyal Negro servants. Of its four chapters, one is narrated through the mind of a thirty-three-year-old idiot, another through the mind of his brother at Harvard who is on the verge of suicide. *As I Lay Dying* (1930), grotesquely comic and grimly tragic at the same time (and written, Faulkner claimed, without revision during six weeks when he worked a night shift in the university power plant), recounts the desperate struggle of a family of "poor whites" to get the mother's body to her home town for proper burial while pursuing their own mundane objectives in the city: an abortion, the purchase of some false teeth, the acquisition of a new wife. Each chapter (one of them only one sentence long) is the "interior monologue" of one of the characters.

In 1929 Faulkner married Mrs. Estelle Franklin, his former sweetheart, who had divorced her first husband and returned with her two children to live in Oxford. They purchased a pillared mansion, Rowan Oak, in 1930, where their own daughter was born in 1933, and made it their permanent home.

While Faulkner's fiction had begun to attract favorable attention, and he was able to sell some stories to national magazines after 1930, it was often refused publication, and his earnings from writing were not enough to support his immediate family and the relatives who were dependent on him. One expedient he turned to was sensationalism in the novel *Sanctuary* (1931); it was written to sell, he acknowledged, but he revised it extensively to meet the high standards of his best writing. It is the story of an arsonist, gangster, and murderer and the college girl he corrupts, who together betray a bootlegger and his devoted common-law wife. The book brought brief notoriety but not lasting success. A second expedient was to write for the films. He regarded this work as distinctly separate from his writing career, but from 1932 to 1936, 1942 to 1945, and again in 1951 and 1954, he spent some time each year in Hollywood or writing on contract for various movie studios.

During the same years he published the brilliant and inventive novels that were to bring him international recognition. *Light in August* (1932) enclosed an explosive drama, about a white but allegedly Negro murderer and his subsequent lynching, within an amusing pastoral idyl about a pregnant girl journeying from Alabama to Mississippi in search of the father of her child. *Absalom, Absalom!* (1936) was at once a tour de force of historical reconstruction and a lyric tragedy; it probed the incestuous love, the fear of miscegenation, and the dream of founding a dynasty in a Mississippi plantation owner's family, and it celebrated the agony of a Mississippi community during and after the Civil War that could neither achieve, nor purge and purify, its flawed ambitions. *Wild Palms* (1939) ingeniously spliced two stories (one of them *Old Man*, below) in a counterpoint of alternating chapters. At the outbreak of World War II Faulkner published two of his most impressive works, each composed of separate but related stories he had been working on since the early Thirties. *The Hamlet* (1940), riotously comic and horrifying at the same time, describes a southern community's attempt to cope with the rise to prominence of a proliferating family of "poor whites" named Snopes. *Go Down, Moses* (1942). comic at times but elegiac in tone, explores the interconnections over generations between two branches of the McCaslin family in Yoknapatawpha County, the white branch epitomized by Ike McCaslin, who relinquishes his inheritance in an effort to atone for racial injustice, the black branch epitomized by Lucas Beauchamp, who insists on his claim to his rights and the family tradition.

The publication of the anthology *The Portable Faulkner* in 1946, edited by Malcolm Cowley, helped to enlarge the American audience for Faulkner's works and marked a new era in his critical esteem. Elected to the National Institute of Arts and Letters in 1939 and to the American Academy of Arts and Letters in 1948, he received in the next three years the American Academy's Howells Award for American Fiction, the National Book Award, and the Nobel Prize for Literature. Though he consistently kept his distance from literary circles, in his later years he appeared often on college campuses to lecture, read from his works, or confer with students and faculty members about the literary profession. He was writer in residence at the University of Virginia in 1957–58 and joined the faculty in 1960, and he conducted seminars in Japan, Greece, and Venezuela under the auspices of the U.S. State Department.

Faulkner commented publicly on race relations during the struggle to desegregate public schools in the South. He acknowledged the rightful claims, the stamina, and the human dignity of the blacks, and he deplored the brutality and injustice inflicted on them, but he warned against federal interference in southern affairs, begged time for the gradual solution of racial problems, and on occasion belligerently defended the desire of southern whites to work out their own solutions to racial conflict. His fiction, not his public pronouncements, remained the most sensitive register of his anguished recognition of the power and human capacities of the black people. There he had "explored," in the words of the black novelist Ralph Ellison, "perhaps more successfully than anyone else, white or black, certain forms of Negro humanity." In portraying American Negroes he "had been more willing perhaps than any other artist to start with the stereotype, accept it as true, and then seek out the human truth which it hides."[1]

Faulkner's major productions after World War II were *The Fable* (1954), an allegorical story about a World War I general and a corporal who is his illegitimate son, and two chronicles which, with the earlier *The Hamlet*, comprise a trilogy of the Snopes clan: *The Town* (1957) and *The Mansion* (1959). Just before his death from a heart attack in 1962, Faulkter dedicated to his grandsons *The Rievers*, a comic and nostalgic recapitulation of episodes from his own life and from his earlier fiction.

When speaking in public of his literary themes and methods, Faulkner often took the stance of a devoted but amateur craftsman, likening his use of religious symbols to the selection of an ax by a woodsman, speaking as a farmer or carpenter who stumbled upon significant Biblical images while looking "for a tool that will make a better chicken-house."[2] Such ostensibly deprecating remarks reveal both the boldness with which he improvised and the deliberateness with which he "built" or composed his fiction. The sequence of sections or chapters of his stories does not follow the chronology of the events they recount; rather, the narration is deliberately constructed to defy and fracture chronology, intriguing readers by puzzling them until gradually they apprehend, or are suddenly shocked into recognizing, what has been going on and what its significance is. (In *Old Man*, the account of the convict's deeds on the flooded Mississippi is spliced with incidents that take place afterward in the prison where he tells about his

1. Ellison, *Shadow and Act* (Vintage),   2. *Faulkner in the University*, p. 68.
pp. 30, 43.

seven weeks' adventure, and information about his earlier life is scattered in the opening and closing pages of the story.) The narrative tries to encompass complexities in the course of history, or different rhythms and phases in the flow of time and in the consciousness of time, that lie beneath the surface of chronology.

The violation of chronology in the narrative structure is matched by a violation of everyday language habits in Faulkner's prose style. He assaults outright, or strains to the utmost, the conventions of grammar and syntax, so as to achieve a number of effects: to channel energies emerging in the past and extending into the future in a "long sentence" that gets a character's "past and possibly his future into the instant in which he does something * * *";[3] to achieve a level of lyric, even rhapsodic, intensity appropriate to the feelings of rage or longing or astonishment being evoked, and to the sense of urgency he wanted to arouse in readers; and to convert prose into quickened and fluid movement. Though he was fearful that language might not be capable of sustaining the burdens of expression that he assigned it—that, as one character says in *As I Lay Dying*, words could merely "say at" reality and always miss or distort it—that fear simply gave urgency to Faulkner's early conviction that the "earthy strength" of the English language as spoken in America could provide a substitute for the richer literary traditions it lacked.[4] Faulkner's incorporation in his style of the diction and cadences of American colloquial speech, along with his overtly rhetorical intensity and elaboration, provide links to two of the books he thought best in American literature, Twain's *Huckleberry Finn* and (his favorite) Melville's *Moby-Dick*.

Faulkner's literary form is distinctly appropriate to the sense of desperate urgency with which he confronts the world he envisions. The contortions into which he twists his materials (which he defended as the "artist's prerogative * * * to underline, to blow up facts, distort facts in order to state a truth")[5] and the sensationalism of his themes and formal effects (which he admitted was a "betrayal" of a writer's "vocation" unless subordinated to the governing purposes of his story)[6] define Faulkner's world. It is a world in which "despair" and "doom" are recurring motifs because social and moral orders prove to be founded on racial exploitation and violence; civil wars, macabre murders, suicides, labor pains, and flood waters on the rampage are its characteristic events; social and moral traditions are threatened with enervation and perversion, and human destiny is faced with the alternatives of annihilation or apocalypse. In a world threatened late in his life by the portent of the atomic bomb, Faulkner declared at his daughter's college graduation (in the speech printed below) that only a revolution accomplished within the textures of everyday life could save mankind from extinction. Such an immanent and ultimate crisis had been the central challenge in all his fiction, where the remnants of an upper-class family are located perilously on the "ultimate edge" of the earth in *The Sound and the Fury*, or where the frantic members of a poor white family in *As I Lay Dying* struggle to keep standing in a crisis "where the motion of wasted world accelerates, just before the final precipice," or where a defeated South in *Absalom, Absalom!* tries to salvage new life from the despair of defeat, to "salvage something anyway of the old lost enchantment of the

3. *Ibid.*, p. 84.
4. *Early Prose and Poetry*, pp. 87, 96.
5. *Faulkner in the University*, p. 282.
6. *Ibid.*, p. 49.

heart." Faulkner's characters fail to cleanse their world of guilt, to escape completely from its paralysis, or to achieve lasting solutions to its problems, but some (like the Tall Convict in *Old Man*) have the desperate courage to try. Their often bizarre heroism signals the urgency of the challenge life presents to human values, and their suffering reveals the need for reconstituting those values and prefigures the transformation their world seeks. The mission for young writers that Faulkner defined in the Nobel Prize speech of 1950 was to remind readers "of the courage and honor and hope and pride and compassion and pity and sacrifice which have been the glory of [mankind's] past" so as to enable men and women not only to "endure" the crisis of life but to "prevail."[7]

From Mosquitoes[1]
From *The Second Day*
From NINE O'CLOCK

It was a sleazy scrap of slightly soiled applegreen crêpe and its principal purpose seemed to be that of indicating vaguely the shape of Jenny's[2] behind, as she danced, caressing the twin soft points of her thighs with the lingering sterility of an aged lover. It looked as if she might have slept in it recently, and there was also a small hat of pale straw, of no particular shape, ribboned.

Jenny slid about in Mr. Talliaferro's[3] embrace with placid skill. She and Pete had just quarreled bitterly. Pete had, that is. Jenny's bovine troubling placidity had merely dissolved into tears, causing her eyes to be more ineffable than ever, and she had gone calmly about what she had intended all the time: to have as much fun as she could, as long as she was here. Pete couldn't walk out on her: all he could do would be to fuss at her or sulk, or maybe hit her. He had done that once, thereby voluntarily making himself her bond slave. She had rather liked it. . . .

Beyond lights, beyond the sound of the victrola, water was a minor ceaseless sound in the darkness; above, vague drowsy stars. Jenny danced on placidly, untroubled by Mr. Talliaferro's endless flow of soft words against her neck, hardly conscious of his hand sliding a small concentric circle at the small of her back.

"She looks kind of nice, don't she?" Fairchild[4] said to his companion as they stood at the head of the companionway,[5] come up for air. "Kind of soft and stupid and young, you know. Passive, and at

7. *Essays, Speeches, & Public Letters*, p. 120.
1. *Mosquitoes* (1927) satirizes Louisiana intellectuals and socialites who have been invited to a house party aboard the yacht of Mrs. Maurier, a New Orleans matron and would-be patron of the arts. During much of the novel the yacht has run aground in Lake Pontchartrain. Faulkner depicts social manners in the mode of F. Scott Fitzgerald's early fiction, and treats ideas (notably about sex, language, and the creative arts) in the serious but sportive manner of the British novelist Aldous Huxley, yet he moves beyond such influences in his experiment with stylistic and structural devices.
2. A "flagrantly young" flirtatious woman, the girl friend of Pete.
3. A sexless widower and dilettante, a wholesale buyer of women's clothing for a department store.
4. Dawson Fairchild, a novelist from Ohio, modeled on Faulkner's friend and fellow novelist Sherwood Anderson.
5. Stairway between decks aboard ship.

the same time troubling, challenging." He watched them for a time, then he added: "Now, there goes the Great Illusion, par excellence."

"What's Talliaferro's trouble?" asked the Semitic man.[6]

"The illusion that you can seduce women. Which you can't. They just elect you."

"And then, God help you," the other added.

"And with words, at that," Fairchild continued. "With words," he repeated savagely.

"Well, why not with words? One thing gets along with women as well as another. And you are a funny sort to disparage words; you, a member of that species all of whose actions are controlled by words. It's the word that overturns thrones and political parties and instigates vice crusades, not things: the Thing is merely the symbol for the Word. And more than that, think what a devil of a fix you and I'd be in were it not for words, were we to lose our faith in words. I'd have nothing to do all day long, and you'd have to work or starve to death." He was silent for a while. Jenny yet slid and poised, pleasuring her soft young placidity. "And, after all, his illusion is just as nourishing as your. Or mine, either."

"I know: but yours or mine ain't quite so ridiculous as his is."

"How do you know they aren't?" Fairchild had no reply, and the other continued: "After all, it doesn't make any difference what you believe. Man is not only nourished by convictions, he is nourished by any conviction. Whatever you believe, you'll always annoy some one, but you yourself will follow and bleed and die for it in the face of law, hell or high water. And those who die for causes will perish for any cause, the more tawdry it is, the quicker they flock to it. And be quite happy at it, too. It's a provision of providence to keep their time occupied." He sucked at his cigar, but it was dead.

"Do you know who is the happiest man in the world today? Mussolini,[7] of course. And do you know who are next? The poor devils he will get killed with his Cæsar illusion.[8] Don't pity them, however: were it not Mussolini and his illusion it would be some one else and his cause. I believe it is some grand cosmic scheme for fertilizing the earth. And it could be so much worse," he added. "Who knows? They might all migrate to America and fall into the hands of Henry Ford.[9]

"So don't you go around feeling superior to Talliaferro. I think his present illusion and its object are rather charming, almost as charming as the consummation of it would be—which is more than you can say for yours." He held a match to his cigar. His sucking, intent face came abruptly out of the darkness, and as abruptly van-

---

6. Julius, a New Orleans intellectual and editor.

7. Benito Mussolini (1883–1945), Italian Premier and dictator.

8. Illusion of being Cæsar Augustus (63 B.C.–A D. 14), Roman General and Emperor.

9. American automobile magnate (1863–1947) whose automobiles threatened to become a tyranny comparable to Mussolini's or Caesar's.

ished again. He flipped the match toward the rail. "And so do you, you poor emotional eunuch; so do you, despite that bastard of a surgeon and a stenographer which you call your soul, so do you remember with regret kissing in the dark and all the tender and sweet stupidity of young flesh."

"Hell," said Fairchild, "let's have another drink."

From *The Third Day*

FOUR O'CLOCK

He[1] strode on in the dust, along the endless shimmering road between pines like fixed explosions on the afternoon. The afternoon was an endless unbearable brightness. Their shapeless, merged shadow moved on: two steps more and he would tread upon it and through it as he did the sparse shadows of pines, but it moved on just ahead of him between the faded forgotten ruts, keeping its distance effortlessly in the uneven dust. The dust was fine as powder and unbroken; only an occasional hoofprint, a fading ghost of a forgotten passage. Above, the metallic implacable sky resting upon his bowed neck and her lax, damp weight upon his back and her cheek against his neck, rubbing monotonously against it. Thin fire darted upon him constantly. He strode on.

The dusty road swam into his vision, passed beneath his feet and so behind like an endless ribbon. He found that his mouth was open, drooling, though no moisture came, and his gums took a thin dry texture like cigarette paper. He closed his mouth, trying to moisten his gums.

Trees without tops passed him, marched up abreast of him, topless, and fell behind; the rank roadside grass approached and became monstrous and separate, blade by blade: lizards hissed in it sibilantly ere it faded behind him. Thin unseen fire darted upon him but he didn't even feel it, for in his shoulders and arms there was no longer any sensation at all save that of her lax weight upon his back and the brass sky resting against his neck and her moist cheek rubbing against his neck monotonously. He found that his mouth was open again and he closed it.

"That's far enough," she said, presently rousing. "Let me down." Their merged shadow blended at intervals with the shadows of the tall topless trees, but beyond the shadow of the trees their blended shadow appeared again, two paces ahead of him. And the road went on ahead of him shimmering and blistered and whiter than salt. "Put me down, David," she repeated.

"No," he said between his dry, rough teeth, above the remote, imperturbable tramping of his heart, "not tired." His heart made a

---

1. David, the yacht's steward, who has consented to swim ashore with Mrs. Maurier's niece Pat, a young, teasingly flirtatious woman in search of adventure. Because her feet are sore after their struggle through a swamp, David is carrying her on his back.

remote sound. Each beat seemed to be somewhere in his head, just behind his eyes; each beat was a red tide that temporarily obscured his vision. But it always ended, then another dull surge blinded him for a moment. But remote, like a tramping of soldiers in red uniforms stepping endlessly across the door of a room where he was, where he crouched trying to look out the door. It was a dull, heavy sound, like a steamer's engines, and he found that he was thinking of water, of a blue monotony of seas. It was a red sound, just back of his eyes.

The road came on, an endless blistering ribbon between worn ruts where nothing had passed for a long time. The sea makes a swishing sound in your ears. Regular. Swish. Swish. Not against your eyes, though. Not against the backs of your eyes. The shadow came out of a blotch of larger shadows cast by trees that had no tops. Two steps more. No, three steps now. Three steps. Getting to be afternoon, getting to be later than it was once. Three steps, then. All right. Man walks on his hind legs; a man can take three steps, a monkey can take three steps, but there is water in a monkey's cage, in a pan. Three steps. All right. One. Two. Three. Gone. Gone. Gone. It's a red sound. Not behind your eyes. Sea. See. Sea. See. You're in a cave, you're in a cave of dark sound, the sound of the sea is outside the cave. Sea. See. See. See. Not when they keep stepping in front of the door.

There was another sound in his ears now, a faint annoying sound, and the weight on his back was shifting of its own volition, thrusting him downward toward the blistering, blanched dust in which he walked, took three steps a man can take three steps and he staggered, trying to shift his numb arms and get a new grip. His mouth was open again and when he tried to shut it, it made a dry, hissing sound. One. Two. Three. One. Two. Three.

"Let me down, I tell you," she repeated, thrusting herself backward. "Look, there's a signboard. Let me down, I tell you. I can walk now."

She thrust herself away from him, twisting her legs from his grasp and forcing him down, and he stumbled and went to his knees. Her feet touched the ground and still astride of his body she braced herself and held him partially up by his shoulders. He stopped at last, on all fours like a beast, his head hanging between his shoulders; and kneeling beside him in the dust she slid her hand under his forehead to lessen the tension on his neck and raised her eyes to the signboard. Mandeville. Fourteen miles, and a crude finger pointing in the direction from which they had come. The front of her dress was damp, blotched darkly with his sweat.

After the women had hovered Jenny's draggled helplessness below decks[2] Fairchild removed his hat and mopped his face, looking

2. Jenny and Talliaferro had fallen overboard.

about upon his fatuous Frankenstein with a sort of childlike astonishment. Then his gaze came to rest on Mr. Talliaferro's haggard damp despair and he laughed and laughed.

"Laugh you may," the Semitic man told him, "but much more of this sort of humor and you'll be doing your laughing ashore. I think now, if Talliaferro'd start an active protest with you as its immediate object, that we'd all be inclined to support him." Mr. Talliaferro dripped forlornly: an utter and hopeless dejection. The Semitic man looked at him, then he too looked about at the others and upon the now peaceful scene of their recent activities. "One certainly pays a price for art," he murmured, "one really does."

"Talliaferro's the only one who has suffered any actual damage," Fairchild protested. "And I'm just going to buy him off now. Come on, Talliaferro, we can fix you up."

"That won't be sufficient," the Semitic man said, still ominous. "The rest of us have been assailed enough in our vanities to rise from principle."

"Well, then, if I have to, I'll buy you all off," Fairchild answered. He led the way toward the stairs. But he halted again and looked back at them. "Where's Gordon?"[3] he asked. Nobody knew. "Well, no matter. He knows where to come." He went on. "After all," he said, "there are compensations for art, ain't there?"

The Semitic man admitted that there were. "Though," he added, "it's a high price to pay for whisky." He descended in his turn. "Yes, we really must get something out of it. We spend enough time on it and suffer enough moral and mental turmoil because of it."

"Sure," Fairchild agreed. "The ones that produce it get a lot from it. They get the boon of keeping their time pretty well filled. And that's a whole lot to expect in this world," he said profoundly, fumbling at his door. It opened at last and he said: "Oh, here you are. Say, you just missed it."

Major Ayers,[4] his neglected tumbler beside him and clutching a book, came up for air when they entered, festooned yet with a kind of affable bewilderment. "Missed what?" he repeated.

They all began to tell him about it at once, producing Mr. Talliaferro as evidence from where he lurked unhappily in their midst, for Major Ayers' inspection and commiseration; and still telling him about it they found seats while Fairchild again assumed the ritual of his hidden suitcase. Major Ayers already had the chair, but the Semitic man attempted the book anyway. "What have you got there?" he asked.

Major Ayers' hearty bewilderment descended upon him again. "I was passing the time," he explained quickly. He stared at the book. "It's quite strange," he said. Then he added: "I mean, the way . . .

The way they get their books up nowadays. I like the way they get their books up. Jolly, with colors, y'know. But I—" He considered a moment. "I rather lost the habit of reading at Sandhurst,"[5] he explained in a burst of confidence. "And then, on active service constantly . . ."

"War is bad," the Semitic man agreed. "What were you reading?"

"I rather lost the habit of reading at Sandhurst," Major Ayers explained again. He raised the book again.

Fairchild opened a fresh bottle. "Somebody'll have to dig up some more glasses. Mark,[6] see if you can slip back to the kitchen and get one or two more. Let's see the book," he said reaching his hand. The Semitic man forestalled him.

"You go ahead and give us some whisky. I'd rather forget my grief that way, just now."

"But look," Fairchild insisted. The other fended him off.

"Give us some whisky, I tell you," he repeated. "Here's Mark with the glasses. What we need in this country is protection from artists. They even want to annoy us with each other's stuff."

"Go ahead," Fairchild replied equably, "have your joke. You know my opinion of smartness." He passed glasses among them.

"He can't mean that," the Semitic man said. "Just because the *New Republic*[7] gives him hell—"

"But the *Dial* once bought a story of him," Mark Frost said with hollow envy.

"And what a fate for a man in all the lusty pride of his Ohio valley masculinity: immolation in a home for old young ladies of either sex. . . . That atmosphere was too rare for him. Eh, Dawson?"

Fairchild laughed. "Well, I ain't much of an Alpinist.[8] What do you want to be in there for, Mark?"

"It would suit Mark exactly," the Semitic man said, "that vague polite fury of the intellect in which they function. What I can't see is how Mark has managed to stay out of it. . . . But then, if you'll look close enough, you'll find an occasional grain of truth in these remarks which Mark and I make and which you consider merely smart. But you utter things not quite clever enough to be untrue, and while we are marveling at your profundity, you lose courage and flatly contradict yourself the next moment. Why, only that tactless and well meaning God of yours alone knows. Why any one should worry enough about the temporary meaning or construction of words to contradict himself consciously or to feel annoyed when he has done it unconsciously, is beyond me."

"Well, it is a kind of sterility—Words," Fairchild admitted.

---

5. British officers training school, comparable to West Point.
6. Mark Frost, a writer.
7. Political and literary journal; *"Dial"*: literary journal, champion of new writing, edited from 1925 to 1929 by the poet Marianne Moore.
8. Mountain climber in the Alps.

"You begin to substitute words for things and deeds, like the withered cuckold husband that took the Decameron[9] to bed with him every night, and pretty soon the thing or the deed becomes just a kind of shadow of a certain sound you make by shaping your mouth a certain way. But you have a confusion, too. I don't claim that words have life in themselves. But words brought into a happy conjunction produce something that lives, just as soil and climate and an acorn in proper conjunction will produce a tree. Words are like acorns, you know. Every one of 'em won't make a tree, but if you just have enough of 'em, you're bound to get a tree sooner or later."

"If you just talk long enough, you're bound to say the right thing some day. Is that what you mean?" the Semitic man asked.

"Let me show you what I mean." Fairchild reached again for the book.

"For heaven's sake," the other exclaimed, "let us have this one drink in peace. We'll admit your contention, if that's what you want. Isn't that what you say, Major?"

"No, really," Major Ayers protested, "I enjoyed the book. Though I rather lost the habit of reading at Sa—"

"I like the book myself," Mark Frost said. "My only criticism is that it got published."

"You can't avoid that," Fairchild told him. "It's inevitable; it happens to every one who will take the risk of writing down a thousand coherent consecutive words."

"And sooner than that," the Semitic man added, "if you've murdered your husband or won a golf championship."

"Yes," Fairchild agreed. "Cold print. Your stuff looks so different in cold print. It lends a kind of impersonal authority even to stupidity."

"That's backward," the other said. "Stupidity lends a kind of impersonal authority even to cold print."

Fairchild stared at him. "Say, what did you just tell me about contradicting myself?"

"I can afford to," the other answered. "I never authenticate mine." He drained his glass. "But as for art and artists, I prefer artists: I don't even object to paying my pro rata to feed them, so long as I am not compelled to listen to them."

"It seems to me," Fairchild rejoined, "that you spend a lot of time listening to them, for a man who professes to dislike it and who don't have to."

"That's because I'd have to listen to somebody—artist or shoe clerk. And the artist is more entertaining, because he knows less about what he is trying to do. . . . And besides, I talk a little, myself. I wonder what became of Gordon?"

1927

9. Collection of lusty tales by the Italian Giovanni Boccaccio (1313–75).

Old Man[1]

Once (it was in Mississippi, in May, in the flood year 1927) there were two convicts. One of them was about twenty-five, tall, lean, flat-stomached, with a sunburned face and Indian-black hair and pale, china-colored outraged eyes—an outrage directed not at the men who had foiled his crime, not even at the lawyers and judges who had sent him here, but at the writers,[2] the uncorporeal names attached to the stories, the paper novels—the Diamond Dicks and Jesse Jameses[3] and such—whom he believed had led him into his present predicament through their own ignorance and gullibility regarding the medium in which they dealt and took money for, in accepting information on which they placed the stamp of verisimilitude and authenticity (this so much the more criminal since there was no sworn notarised statement attached and hence so much the quicker would the information be accepted by one who expected the same unspoken good faith, demanding, asking, expecting no certification, which he extended along with the dime or fifteen cents to pay for it) and retailed for money and which on actual application proved to be impractical and (to the convict) criminally false; there would be times when he would halt his mule and plow in midfurrow (there is no walled penitentiary in Mississippi; it is a cotton plantation which the convicts work under the rifles and shotguns of guards and trusties) and muse with a kind of enraged impotence, fumbling among the rubbish left him by his one and only experience with courts and law, fumbling until the meaningless and verbose shibboleth took form at last (himself seeking justice at the same blind fount where he had met justice and been hurled back and down): Using the mails to defraud: who felt that he had been defrauded by the third-class mail system not of crass and stupid money which he did not particularly want anyway, but of liberty and honor and pride.

He was in for fifteen years (he had arrived shortly after his nineteenth birthday) for attempted train robbery. He had laid his plans

---

[1]. Afro-American nickname for the Mississippi River. This story, dramatizing the heroism of a nameless convict who rescues a pregnant woman during a Mississippi flood and assists at the birth of her child, takes the form of a frontier "tall tale." Faulkner drew attention to the combination of tragedy and comedy in *Old Man* when he declared later that the tale is about people's "aspirations and their struggles and the bizarre, the comic, and the tragic conditions they get themselves into simply coping with themselves and one another and environment" (*Faulkner in the University*, p. 177). It was originally published as part of the novel *The Wild Palms* (1939), where the chapters of *Old Man* alternated with chapters recounting a different story: the tragic love affair of an artist named Charlotte and a doctor named Harry Wilbourne who devote their lives to intense personal passion. Convinced that a child would interfere, Charlotte persuades Harry to perform an abortion and dies because he is not sufficiently skillful; Harry is tried for murder, convicted, and imprisoned in the Mississippi prison farm at Parchman, which is the setting of *Old Man*. Faulkner intended that *Old Man* serve as "counterpoint," as in music, to the other story.

[2]. Cf. Isaiah 10.1: "Woe unto them that decree unrighteous decrees, And to the writers that write perverseness."

[3]. I.e., stories of famous desperadoes, like the train robber Jesse James (1847–82).

in advance, he had followed his printed (and false) authority to the letter; he had saved the paperbacks for two years, reading and rereading them, memorising them, comparing and weighing story and method against story and method, taking the good from each and discarding the dross as his workable plan emerged, keeping his mind open to make the subtle last-minute changes, without haste and without impatience, as the newer pamphlets appeared on their appointed days as a conscientious dressmaker makes the subtle alterations in a court presentation costume as the newer bulletins appear. And then when the day came, he did not even have a chance to go through the coaches and collect the watches and the rings, the brooches and the hidden money-belts, because he had been captured as soon as he entered the express car where the safe and the gold would be. He had shot no one because the pistol which they took away from him was not that kind of a pistol although it was loaded; later he admitted to the District Attorney that he had got it, as well as the dark lantern in which a candle burned and the black handkerchief to wear over the face, by peddling among his pinehill neighbors subscriptions to the *Detectives' Gazette*. So now from time to time (he had ample leisure for it) he mused with that raging impotence, because there was something else he could not tell them at the trial, did not know how to tell them. It was not the money he had wanted. It was not riches, not the crass loot; that would have been merely a bangle to wear upon the breast of his pride like the Olympic runner's amateur medal—a symbol, a badge to show that he too was the best at his chosen gambit in the living and fluid world of his time. So that at times as he trod the richly shearing black earth behind his plow or with a hoe thinned the sprouting cotton and corn or lay on his sullen back in his bunk after supper, he cursed in a harsh steady unrepetitive stream, not at the living men who had put him where he was but at what he did not even know were pennames, did not even know were not actual men but merely the designations of shades who had written about shades.

The second convict was short and plump. Almost hairless, he was quite white. He looked like something exposed to light by turning over rotting logs or planks and he too carried (though not in his eyes like the first convict) a sense of burning and impotent outrage. So it did not show on him and hence none knew it was there. But then nobody knew very much about him, including the people who had sent him here. His outrage was directed at no printed word but at the paradoxical fact that he had been forced to come here of his own free choice and will. He had been forced to choose between the Mississippi State penal farm and the Federal Penitentiary at Atlanta, and the fact that he, who resembled a hairless and pallid slug, had chosen the out-of-doors and the sunlight was merely another manifestation of the close-guarded and solitary enigma of his character, as something recognisable roils momentarily into view from beneath stagnant and opaque water, then sinks again. None of his fellow prisoners knew what his crime had been, save that he was in for a hundred and ninety-nine years—this incredible and impossible period of punishment or restraint itself carrying a vicious and fabulous quality which indicated that his reason for being here was such that the very men, the paladins[4] and pillars of justice and equity who had sent him here had during that moment become blind apostles not of mere justice but of all human decency, blind instruments not of equity but of all human outrage and vengeance, acting in a savage personal concert, judge, lawyer and jury, which certainly abrogated justice and possibly even law. Possibly only the Federal and State's Attorneys knew what the crime actually was. There had been a woman in it and a stolen automobile transported across a state line, a filling station robbed and the attendant shot to death. There had been a second man in the car at the time and anyone could have looked once at the convict (as the two attorneys did) and known he would not even have had the synthetic courage of alcohol to pull trigger on anyone. But he and the woman and the stolen car had been captured while the second man, doubtless the actual murderer, had escaped, so that, brought to bay at last in the State's Attorney's office, harried, dishevelled and snarling, the two grimly implacable and viciously gleeful attorneys in his front and the now raging woman held by two policemen in the anteroom in his rear, he was given his choice. He could be tried in Federal Court under the Mann Act[5] and for the automobile, that is, by electing to pass through the anteroom where the woman raged he could take his chances on the lesser crime in Federal Court, or by accepting a sentence for manslaughter in the State Court he would be permitted to quit the room by a back entrance, without having to pass the woman. He had chosen; he stood at the bar and heard a judge (who looked down at him as if the District Attorney actually had turned over a rotten plank with his toe and exposed him) sentence him to a hundred and ninety-nine years at the State Farm. Thus (he had ample leisure too; they had tried to teach him to plow and had failed, they had put him in the blacksmith shop and the foreman trusty[6] himself had asked to have him removed: so that now, in a long apron like a woman, he cooked and swept and dusted in the deputy wardens' barracks) he too mused at times with that sense of impotence and outrage though it did not show on him as on the first convict since he leaned on no halted broom to do it and so none knew it was there.

It was this second convict who, toward the end of April, began to read aloud to the others from the daily newspapers when, chained

---

4. Palace officers, knights.
5. U.S. law forbidding the transportation of women across state lines for immoral

purposes.
6. Prisoner trusted with responsibility for supervising other prisoners.

ankle to ankle and herded by armed guards, they had come up from the fields and had eaten supper and were gathered in the bunkhouse. It was the Memphis newspaper which the deputy wardens had read at breakfast; the convict read aloud from it to his companions who could have had but little active interest in the outside world, some of whom could not have read it for themselves at all and did not even know where the Ohio and Missouri river basins were, some of whom had never even seen the Mississippi River although for past periods ranging from a few days to ten and twenty and thirty years (and for future periods ranging from a few months to life) they had plowed and planted and eaten and slept beneath the shadow of the levee[7] itself, knowing only that there was water beyond it from hearsay and because now and then they heard the whistles of steamboats from beyond it and during the last week or so had seen the stacks and pilot houses moving along the sky sixty feet above their heads.

But they listened, and soon even those who like the taller convict had probably never before seen more water than a horse pond would hold knew what thirty feet on a river gauge at Cairo or Memphis meant and could (and did) talk glibly of sandboils.[8] Perhaps what actually moved them was the accounts of the conscripted levee gangs, mixed blacks and whites working in double shifts against the steadily rising water; stories of men, even though they were Negroes, being forced like themselves to do work for which they received no other pay than coarse food and a place in a mudfloored tent to sleep on—stories, pictures, which emerged from the shorter convict's reading voice: the mudsplashed white men with the inevitable shotguns, the antlike lines of Negroes carrying sandbags, slipping and crawling up the steep face of the revetment to hurl their futile ammunition into the face of a flood and return for more. Or perhaps it was more than this. Perhaps they watched the approach of the disaster with that same amazed and incredulous hope of the slaves—the lions and bears and elephants, the grooms and bathmen and pastrycooks—who watched the mounting flames of Rome from Ahenobarbus'[9] gardens. But listen they did and presently it was May and the wardens' newspaper began to talk in headlines two inches tall—those black staccato slashes of ink which, it would almost seem, even the illiterate should be able to read: *Crest Passes Memphis at Midnight 4000 Homeless in White River Basin Governor Calls out National Guard Martial Law Declared in Following Counties Red Cross Train with Secretary Hoover[1] Leaves Washington Tonight*; then, three evenings later (It had been raining all day—not the vivid brief thunderous downpours of April and

---

7. Earth embankment, built to contain the swollen river so as to prevent flooding of adjacent land.
8. Bubbling springs, bursting out at the base of levees, owing to the pressure of flood water on the other side.

9. Aristocratic Roman family whose scion, the Emperor Nero (A.D. 54–68), watched Rome burn.
1. Herbert C. Hoover (1874–1964), in 1927 Secretary of Commerce; later President of the United States (1929–33).

May, but the slow steady gray rain of November and December
before a cold north wind. The men had not gone to the fields at all
during the day, and the very secondhand optimism of the almost
twenty-four-hour-old news seemed to contain its own refutation.):
*Crest Now Below Memphis 22,000 Refugees Safe at Vicksburg
Army Engineers Say Levees Will Hold.*

"I reckon that means it will bust tonight," one convict said.

"Well, maybe this rain will hold on until the water gets here," a
second said. They all agreed to this because what they meant, the
living unspoken thought among them, was that if the weather
cleared, even though the levees broke and the flood moved in upon
the Farm itself, they would have to return to the fields and work,
which they would have had to do. There was nothing paradoxical in
this, although they could not have expressed the reason for it which
they instinctively perceived: that the land they farmed and the substance they produced from it belonged neither to them who worked
it nor to those who forced them at guns' point to do so, that as far
as either—convicts or guards—were concerned, it could have been
pebbles they put into the ground and papier-mâché cotton- and
corn-sprouts which they thinned. So it was that, what between the
sudden wild hoping and the idle day and the evening's headlines,
they were sleeping restlessly beneath the sound of the rain on the
tin roof when at midnight the sudden glare of the electric bulbs
and the guards' voices waked them and they heard the throbbing of
the waiting trucks.

"Turn out of there!" the deputy shouted. He was fully dressed—
rubber boots, slicker and shotgun. "The levee went out at Mound's
Landing an hour ago. Get up out of it!"

When the belated and streaming dawn broke, the two convicts,
along with twenty others, were in a truck. A trusty drove, two
armed guards sat in the cab with him. Inside the high, stall-like topless body the convicts stood, packed like matches in an upright box
or like the pencil-shaped ranks of cordite[2] in a shell, shackled by
the ankles to a single chain which wove among the motionless feet
and swaying legs and a clutter of picks and shovels among which
they stood, and was riveted by both ends to the steel body of the
truck.

Then and without warning they saw the flood about which the
plump convict had been reading and they listening for two weeks or
more. The road ran south. It was built on a raised levee, known
locally as a dump, about eight feet above the flat surrounding land,
bordered on both sides by the barrow pits from which the earth of
the levee had been excavated. These barrow pits had held water all
winter from the fall rains, not to speak of the rain of yesterday, but
now they saw that the pit on either side of the road had vanished

2. Explosive powder, shaped into stringlike strands, used in ammunition.

and instead there lay a flat still sheet of brown water which extended into the fields beyond the pits, ravelled out into long motionless shreds in the bottom of the plow furrows and gleaming faintly in the gray light like the bars of a prone and enormous grating. And then (the truck was moving at good speed) as they watched quietly (they had not been talking much anyway but now they were all silent and quite grave, shifting and craning as one to look soberly off to the west side of the road) the crests of the furrows vanished too and they now looked at a single perfectly flat and motionless steel-colored sheet in which the telephone poles and the straight hedgerows which marked section lines seemed to be fixed and rigid as though set in concrete.

It was perfectly motionless, perfectly flat. It looked, not innocent, but bland. It looked almost demure. It looked as if you could walk on it. It looked so still that they did not realise it possessed motion until they came to the first bridge. There was a ditch under the bridge, a small stream, but ditch and stream were both invisible now, indicated only by the rows of cypress and bramble which marked its course. Here they both saw and heard movement—the slow profound eastward and upstream ("It's running backward," one convict said quietly.) set of the still rigid surface, from beneath which came a deep faint subaquean rumble which (though none in the truck could have made the comparison) sounded like a subway train passing far beneath the street and which implied a terrific and secret speed. It was as if the water itself were in three strata, separate and distinct, the bland and unhurried surface bearing a frothy scum and a miniature flotsam of twigs and screening as though by vicious calculation the rush and fury of the food itself, and beneath this in turn the original stream, trickle, murmuring along in the opposite direction, following undisturbed and unaware its appointed course and serving its Lilliputian[3] end, like a thread of ants between the rails on which an express train passes, they (the ants) as unaware of the power and fury as if it were a cyclone crossing Saturn.

Now there was water on both sides of the road and now, as if once they had become aware of movement in the water the water seemed to have given over deception and concealment, they seemed to be able to watch it rising up the flanks of the dump; trees which a few miles back had stood on tall trunks above the water now seemed to burst from the surface at the level of the lower branches like decorative shrubs on barbered lawns. The truck passed a Negro cabin. The water was up to the window ledges. A woman clutching two children squatted on the ridgepole, a man and a half-grown youth, standing waist-deep, were hoisting a squealing pig onto the slanting roof of a barn, on the ridgepole of which sat a row of

3. I.e., very small. Lilliput, in Jonathan Swift's satire, *Gulliver's Travels* (1726), was an island inhabited by miniature people.

chickens and a turkey. Near the barn was a haystack on which a cow stood tied by a rope to the center pole and bawling steadily; a yelling Negro boy on a saddleless mule which he flogged steadily, his legs clutching the mule's barrel and his body leaned to the drag of a rope attached to a second mule, approached the haystack, splashing and floundering. The woman on the housetop began to shriek at the passing truck, her voice carrying faint and melodious across the brown water, becoming fainter and fainter as the truck passed and went on, ceasing at last, whether because of distance or because she had stopped screaming those in the truck did not know.

Then the road vanished. There was no perceptible slant to it yet it had slipped abruptly beneath the brown surface with no ripple, no ridgy demarcation, like a flat thin blade slipped obliquely into flesh by a delicate hand, annealed into the water without disturbance, as if it had existed so for years, had been built that way. The truck stopped. The trusty descended from the cab and came back and dragged two shovels from among their feet, the blades clashing against the serpentining of the chain about their ankles. "What is it?" one said. "What are you fixing to do?" The trusty didn't answer. He returned to the cab, from which one of the guards had descended, without his shotgun. He and the trusty, both in hip boots and each carrying a shovel, advanced into the water, gingerly, probing and feeling ahead with the shovel handles. The same convict spoke again. He was a middle-aged man with a wild thatch of iron-gray hair and a slightly mad face. "What the hell are they doing?" he said. Again nobody answered him. The truck moved, on into the water, behind the guard and the trusty, beginning to push ahead of itself a thick slow viscid ridge of chocolate water. Then the gray-haired convict began to scream. "God damn it, unlock the chain!" He began to struggle, thrashing violently about him, striking at the men nearest him until he reached the cab, the roof of which he now hammered on with his fists, screaming. "God damn it, unlock us! Unlock us! Son of a bitch!" he screamed, addressing no one. "They're going to drown us! Unlock the chain!" But for all the answer he got the men within radius of his voice might have been dead. The truck crawled on, the guard and the trusty feeling out the road ahead with the reversed shovels, the second guard at the wheel, the twenty-two convicts packed like sardines into the truck bed and padlocked by the ankles to the body of the truck itself. They crossed another bridge—two delicate and paradoxical iron railings slanting out of the water, travelling parallel to it for a distance, then slanting down into it again with an outrageous quality almost significant yet apparently meaningless like something in a dream not quite nightmare. The truck crawled on.

Along toward noon they came to a town, their destination. The streets were paved; now the wheels of the truck made a sound like tearing silk. Moving faster now, the guard and the trusty in the cab again, the truck even had a slight bone in its teeth, its bow-wave spreading beyond the submerged sidewalks and across the adjacent lawns, lapping against the stoops and porches of houses where people stood among piles of furniture. They passed through the business district; a man in hip boots emerged knee-deep in water from a store, dragging a flat-bottomed skiff containing a steel safe.

At last they reached the railroad. It crossed the street at right angles, cutting the town in two. It was on a dump, a levee, also, eight or ten feet above the town itself; the street ran blankly into it and turned at right angles beside a cotton compress[4] and a loading platform on stilts at the level of a freight-car door. On this platform was a khaki army tent and a uniformed National Guard sentry with a rifle and bandolier.[5]

The truck turned and crawled out of the water and up the ramp which cotton wagons used and where trucks and private cars filled with household goods came and unloaded onto the platform. They were unlocked from the chain in the truck and shackled ankle to ankle in pairs they mounted the platform and into an apparently inextricable jumble of beds and trunks, gas and electric stoves, radios and tables and chairs and framed pictures which a chain of Negroes under the eye of an unshaven white man in muddy corduroy and hip boots carried piece by piece into the compress, at the door of which another guardsman stood with his rifle, they (the convicts) not stopping here but herded on by the two guards with their shotguns, into the dim and cavernous building where among the piled heterogeneous furniture the ends of cotton bales and the mirrors on dressers and sideboards gleamed with an identical mute and unreflecting concentration of pallid light.

They passed on through, onto the loading platform where the army tent and the first sentry were. They waited here. Nobody told them for what nor why. While the two guards talked with the sentry before the tent the convicts sat in a line along the edge of the platform like buzzards on a fence, their shackled feet dangling above the brown motionless flood out of which the railroad embankment rose, pristine and intact, in a kind of paradoxical denial and repudiation of change and portent, not talking, just looking quietly across the track to where the other half of the amputated town seemed to float, house shrub and tree, ordered and pageant-like and without motion, upon the limitless liquid plain beneath the thick gray sky.

After a while the other four trucks from the Farm arrived. They came up, bunched closely, radiator to tail light, with their four separate sounds of tearing silk and vanished beyond the compress. Pres-

---

4. Apparatus for compressing cotton bales.
5. Cartridge belt worn over one shoulder and diagonally across the chest under the other arm.

ently the ones on the platform heard the feet, the mute clashing of the shackles, the first truckload emerged from the compress, the second, the third; there were more than a hundred of them now in their bed-ticking overalls and jumpers and fifteen or twenty guards with rifles and shotguns. The first lot rose and they mingled, paired, twinned by their clanking and clashing umbilicals; then it began to rain, a slow steady gray drizzle like November instead of May. Yet not one of them made any move toward the open door of the compress. They did not even look toward it, with longing or hope or without it. If they thought at all, they doubtless knew that the available space in it would be needed for furniture, even if it were not already filled. Or perhaps they knew that, even if there were room in it, it would not be for them, not that the guards would wish them to get wet but that the guards would not think about getting them out of the rain. So they just stopped talking and with their jumper collars turned up and shackled in braces like dogs at a field trial they stood, immobile, patient, almost ruminant, their backs turned to the rain as sheep and cattle do.

After another while they became aware that the number of soldiers had increased to a dozen or more, warm and dry beneath rubberised ponchos, there was an officer with a pistol at his belt, then and without making any move toward it, they began to smell food and, turning to look, saw an army field kitchen set up just inside the compress door. But they made no move, they waited until they were herded into line, they inched forward, their heads lowered and patient in the rain, and received each a bowl of stew, a mug of coffee, two slices of bread. They ate this in the rain. They did not sit down because the platform was wet, they squatted on their heels as country men do, hunching forward, trying to shield the bowls and mugs into which nevertheless the rain splashed steadily as into miniature ponds and soaked, invisible and soundless, into the bread.

After they had stood on the platform for three hours, a train came for them. Those nearest the edge saw it, watched it—a passenger coach apparently running under its own power and trailing a cloud of smoke from no visible stack, a cloud which did not rise but instead shifted slowly and heavily aside and lay upon the surface of the aqueous earth with a quality at once weightless and completely spent. It came up and stopped, a single old-fashioned open-ended wooden car coupled to the nose of a pushing switch engine considerably smaller. They were herded into it, crowding forward to the other end where there was a small cast-iron stove. There was no fire in it, nevertheless they crowded about it—the cold and voiceless lump of iron stained with fading tobacco and hovered about by the ghosts of a thousand Sunday excursions to Memphis or Moorhead and return—the peanuts, the bananas, the soiled garments of infants—huddling, shoving for places near it. "Come on, come on," one of the guards shouted. "Sit down, now." At last three of the guards, laying aside their guns, came among them and broke up the huddle, driving them back and into seats.

There were not enough seats for all. The others stood in the aisle, they stood braced, they heard the air hiss out of the released brakes, the engine whistled four blasts, the car came into motion with a snapping jerk; the platform, the compress fled violently as the train seemed to transpose from immobility to full speed with that same quality of unreality with which it had appeared, running backward now though with the engine in front where before it had moved forward but with the engine behind.

When the railroad in its turn ran beneath the surface of the water, the convicts did not even know it. They felt the train stop, they heard the engine blow a long blast which wailed away un-echoed across the waste, wild and forlorn, and they were not even curious; they sat or stood behind the rain-streaming windows as the train crawled on again, feeling its way as the truck had while the brown water swirled between the trucks and among the spokes of the driving wheels and lapped in cloudy steam against the dragging fire-filled belly of the engine; again it blew four short harsh blasts filled with the wild triumph and defiance yet also with repudiation and even farewell, as if the articulated steel itself knew it did not dare stop and would not be able to return. Two hours later in the twilight they saw through the streaming windows a burning planta-tion house. Juxtaposed to nowhere and neighbored by nothing it stood, a clear steady pyre-like flame rigidly fleeing its own reflection, burning in the dusk above the watery desolation with a quality para-doxical, outrageous and bizarre.

Some time after dark the train stopped. The convicts did not know where they were. They did not ask. They would no more have thought of asking where they were than they would have asked why and what for. They couldn't even see, since the car was unlighted and the windows fogged on the outside by rain and on the inside by the engendered heat of the packed bodies. All they could see was a milky and sourceless flick and glare of flashlights. They could hear shouts and commands, then the guards inside the car began to shout; they were herded to their feet and toward the exit, the ankle chains clashing and clanking. They descended into a fierce hissing of steam, through ragged wisps of it blowing past the car. Laid-to alongside the train and resembling a train itself was a thick blunt motor launch to which was attached a string of skiffs and flat boots. There were more soldiers; the flashlights played on the rifle barrels and bandolier buckles and flicked and glinted on the ankle chains of the convicts as they stepped gingerly down into knee-deep water and entered the boats; now car and engine both vanished com-pletely in steam as the crew began dumping the fire from the firebox.

After another hour they began to see lights ahead—a faint wavering row of red pin-pricks extending along the horizon and apparently hanging low in the sky. But it took almost another hour to reach them while the convicts squatted in the skiffs, huddled into the soaked garments (they no longer felt the rain any more at all as separate drops) and watched the lights draw nearer and nearer until at last the crest of the levee defined itself; now they could discern a row of army tents stretching along it and people squatting about the fires, the wavering reflections from which, stretching across the water, revealed an involved mass of other skiffs tied against the flank of the levee which now stood high and dark overheard. Flashlights glared and winked along the base, among the tethered skiffs; the launch, silent now, drifted in.

When they reached the top of the levee they could see the long line of khaki tents, interspersed with fires about which people—men, women and children, Negro and white—crouched or stood among shapeless bales of clothing, their heads turning, their eyeballs glinting in the firelight as they looked quietly at the striped garments and the chains; further down the levee, huddled together too though untethered, was a drove of mules and two or three cows. Then the taller convict became conscious of another sound. He did not begin to hear it all at once, he suddenly became aware that he had been hearing it all the time, a sound so much beyond all his experience and his powers of assimilation that up to this point he had been as oblivious of it as an ant or a flea might be of the sound of the avalanche on which it rides; he had been travelling upon water since early afternoon and for seven years now he had run his plow and harrow and planter within the very shadow of the levee on which he now stood, but this profound deep whisper which came from the further side of it he did not at once recognise. He stopped. The line of convicts behind jolted into him like a line of freight cars stopping, with an iron clashing like cars. "Get on!" a guard shouted.

"What's that?" the convict said. A Negro man squatting before the nearest fire answered him:

"Dat's him. Dat's de Ole Man."

"The old man?" the convict said.

"Get on! Get on up there!" the guard shouted. They went on; they passed another huddle of mules, the eyeballs rolling too, the long morose faces turning into and out of the firelight; they passed them and reached a section of empty tents, the light pup tents of a military campaign, made to hold two men. The guards herded the convicts into them, three brace of shackled men to each tent.

They crawled in on all fours, like dogs into cramped kennels, and settled down. Presently the tent became warm from their bodies. Then they became quiet and then all of them could hear it, they lay listening to the bass whisper deep, strong and powerful. "The old man?" the train-robber convict said.

"Yah," another said. "He dont have to brag."[6]

At dawn the guards waked them by kicking the soles of the pro-jecting feet. Opposite the muddy landing and the huddle of skiffs an army field kitchen was set up, already they could smell the coffee. But the taller convict at least, even though he had had but one meal yesterday and that at noon in the rain, did not move at once toward the food. Instead and for the first time he looked at the River within whose shadow he had spent the last seven years of his life but had never seen before; he stood in quiet and amazed surmise and looked at the rigid steel-colored surface not broken into waves but merely slightly undulant. It stretched from the levee on which he stood, further than he could see—a slowly and heavily roiling chocolate-frothy expanse broken only by a thin line a mile away as fragile in appearance as a single hair, which after a moment he recognised. *It's another levee,* he thought quietly. *That's what we look like from there. That's what I am standing on looks like from there.* He was prodded from the rear; a guard's voice carried forward: "Go on! Go on! You'll have plenty of time to look at that!"

They received the same stew and coffee and bread as the day before; they squatted again with their bowls and mugs as yesterday, though it was not raining yet. During the night an intact wooden barn had floated up. It now lay jammed by the current against the levee while a crowd of Negroes swarmed over it, ripping off the shingles and planks and carrying them up the bank; eating steadily and without haste, the taller convict watched the barn dissolve rap-idly down to the very water-line exactly as a dead fly vanished beneath the moiling industry of a swarm of ants.

They finished eating. Then it began to rain again, as upon a signal, while they stood or squatted in their harsh garments which had not dried out during the night but had merely become slightly warmer than the air. Presently they were haled to their feet and told off into two groups, one of which was armed from a stack of mud-clogged picks and shovels nearby, and marched away up the levee. A little later the motor launch with its train of skiffs came up across what was, fifteen feet beneath its keel, probably a cotton field, the skiffs loaded to the gunwales with Negroes and a scatter-ing of white people nursing bundles on their laps. When the engine

6. On the awesome force of the Missis-sippi, Faulkner commented: "[The val-ley is] rich because the river for hundreds of years has deposited the rich silt on top of the ground, and so the river dominates not only the economy of that country but it dominates the spirit-ual life. * * * the river is Master, and any time the Old Man wants to he can break the levee and can ruin the cotton crop. * * * the planter is at armistice with him, and the superstitious planter believes that he has got to make liba-tions, make sacrifices to him * * * like the ancients with the dragon, the Mino-taur, the symbols of destructiveness which they had to placate, sacrifice" (*Faulkner in the University,* p. 178).

shut off the faint plinking of a guitar came across the water. The skiffs warped in and unloaded; the convicts watched the men and women and children struggle up the muddy slope, carrying heavy towsacks and bundles wrapped in quilts. The sound of the guitar had not ceased and now the convicts saw him—a young, black, lean-hipped man, the guitar slung by a piece of cotton plowline about his neck. He mounted the levee, still picking it. He carried nothing else, no food, no change of clothes, not even a coat.

The taller convict was so busy watching this that he did not hear the guard until the guard stood directly beside him shouting his name. "Wake up!" the guard shouted. "Can you fellows paddle a boat?"

"Paddle a boat where?" the taller convict said.

"In the water," the guard said. "Where in hell do you think?"

"I aint going to paddle no boat nowhere out yonder," the tall convict said, jerking his head toward the invisible river beyond the levee behind him.

"No, it's on this side," the guard said. He stooped swiftly and unlocked the chain which joined the tall convict and the plump hairless one. "It's just down the road a piece." He rose. The two convicts followed him down to the boats. "Follow them telephone poles until you come to a filling station. You can tell it, the roof is still above water. It's on a bayou and you can tell the bayou because the tops of the trees are sticking up. Follow the bayou until you come to a cypress snag with a woman in it. Pick her up and then cut straight back west until you come to a cotton house with a fellow sitting on the ridgepole—" He turned, looking at the two convicts, who stood perfectly still, looking first at the skiff and then at the water with intense sobriety. "Well? What are you waiting for?"

"I cant row a boat," the plump convict said.

"Then it's high time you learned," the guard said. "Get in."

The tall convict shoved the other forward. "Get in," he said. "That water aint going to hurt you. Aint nobody going to make you take a bath."

As, the plump one in the bow and the other in the stern, they shoved away from the levee, they saw other pairs being unshackled and manning the other skiffs. "I wonder how many more of them fellows are seeing this much water for the first time in their lives too," the tall convict said. The other did not answer. He knelt in the bottom of the skiff, pecking gingerly at the water now and then with his paddle. The very shape of his thick soft back seemed to wear that expression of wary and tense concern.

Some time after midnight a rescue boat filled to the guard rail with homeless men and women and children docked at Vicksburg. It was a steamer, shallow of draft; all day long it had poked up

and down cypress- and gum-choked bayous and across cotton fields
(where at times instead of swimming it waded) gathering its sorry
cargo from the tops of houses and barns and even out of trees, and
now it warped into that mushroom city of the forlorn and despairing where kerosene flares smoked in the drizzle and hurriedly strung
electrics glared upon the bayonets of martial policemen and the
Red Cross brassards of doctors and nurses and canteen-workers. The
bluff overhead was almost solid with tents, yet still there were more
people than shelter for them; they sat or lay, single and by whole
families, under what shelter they could find or sometimes under the
rain itself, in the little death of profound exhaustion while the doctors and the nurses and the soldiers stepped over and around and
among them.

Among the first to disembark was one of the penitentiary deputy
wardens, followed closely by the plump convict and another white
man—a small man with a gaunt unshaven wan face still wearing an
expression of incredulous outrage. The deputy warden seemed to
know exactly where he wished to go. Followed closely by his two
companions he threaded his way swiftly among the piled furniture
and the sleeping bodies and stood presently in a fiercely lighted and
hastily established temporary office, almost a military post of command in fact, where the Warden of the Penitentiary sat with two
army officers wearing majors' leaves. The deputy warden spoke without preamble. "We lost a man," he said. He called the tall convict's
name.

"Lost him?" the Warden said.

"Yah. Drowned." Without turning his head he spoke to the
plump convict. "Tell him," he said.

"He was the one that said he could row a boat," the plump convict said. "I never. I told him myself—" he indicated the deputy
warden with a jerk of his head "—I couldn't. So when we got to
the bayou—"

"What's this?" the Warden said.

"The launch brought word in," the deputy warden said.
"Woman in a cypress snag on the bayou, then this fellow—" he
indicated the third man; the Warden and the two officers looked at
the third man "—on a cotton house. Never had room in the launch
to pick them up. Go on."

"So we come to where the bayou was," the plump convict continued in a voice perfectly flat, without any inflection whatever. "Then
the boat got away from him. I dont know what happened. I was
just sitting there because he was so positive he could row a boat. I
never saw any current. Just all of a sudden the boat whirled clean
around and begun to run fast backward like it was hitched to a
train and it whirled around again and I happened to look up and
there was a limb right over my head and I grabbed it just in time
and that boat was snatched out from under me like you'd snatch off

a sock and I saw it one time more upside down and that fellow that said he knew all about rowing holding to it with one hand and still holding the paddle in the other—" He ceased. There was no dying fall to his voice, it just ceased and the convict stood looking quietly at a half-full quart of whiskey sitting on the table.

"How do you know he's drowned?" the Warden said to the deputy. "How do you know he didn't just see his chance to escape, and took it?"

"Escape where?" the other said. "The whole Delta's flooded. There's fifteen foot of water for fifty miles, clean back to the hills. And that boat was upside down."

"That fellow's drowned," the plump convict said. "You dont need to worry about him. He's got his pardon; it wont cramp nobody's hand signing it, neither."

"And nobody else saw him?" the Warden said. "What about the woman in the tree?"

"I dont know," the deputy said. "I aint found her yet. I reckon some other boat picked her up. But this is the fellow on the cotton house."

Again the Warden and the two officers looked at the third man, at the gaunt, unshaven wild face in which an old terror, an old blending of fear and impotence and rage still lingered. "He never came for you?" the Warden said. "You never saw him?"

"Never nobody came for me," the refugee said. He began to tremble though at first he spoke quietly enough. "I set there on that sonabitching cotton house, expecting hit to go any minute. I saw that launch and them boats come up and they never had no room for me. Full of bastard niggers and one of them setting there playing a guitar but there wasn't no room for me. A guitar!" he cried; now he began to scream, trembling, slavering, his face twitching and jerking. "Room for a bastard nigger guitar but not for me—"

"Steady now," the Warden said. "Steady now."

"Give him a drink," one of the officers said. The Warden poured the drink. The deputy handed it to the refugee, who took the glass in both jerking hands and tried to raise it to his mouth. They watched him for perhaps twenty seconds, then the deputy took the glass from him and held it to his lips while he gulped, though even then a thin trickle ran from each corner of his mouth, into the stubble on his chin.

"So we picked him and—" the deputy called the plump convict's name now "—both up just before dark and come on in. But that other fellow is gone."

"Yes," the Warden said. "Well. Here I haven't lost a prisoner in ten years, and now, like this—I'm sending you back to the Farm tomorrow. Have his family notified, and his discharge papers filled out at once."

"All right," the deputy said. "And listen, chief. He wasn't a bad fellow and maybe he never had no business in that boat. Only he did say he could paddle one. Listen. Suppose I write on his discharge, Drowned while trying to save lives in the great flood of nineteen twenty-seven, and send it down for the Governor to sign it. It will be something nice for his folks to have, to hang on the wall when neighbors come in or something. Maybe they will even give his folks a cash bonus because after all they sent him to the Farm to raise cotton, not to fool around in a boat in a flood."

"All right," the Warden said. "I'll see about it. The main thing is to get his name off the books as dead before some politician tries to collect his food allowance."

"All right," the deputy said. He turned and herded his companions out. In the drizzling darkness again he said to the plump convict: "Well, your partner beat you. He's free. He's done served his time out but you've got a right far piece to go yet."

"Yah," the plump convict said. "Free. He can have it."

As the short convict had testified, the tall one, when he returned to the surface, still retained what the short one called the paddle. He clung to it, not instinctively against the time when he would be back inside the boat and would need it, because for a time he did not believe he would ever regain the skiff or anything else that would support him, but because he did not have time to think about turning it loose. Things had moved too fast for him. He had not been warned, he had felt the first snatching tug of the current, he had seen the skiff begin to spin and his companion vanish violently upward like in a translation out of Isaiah,[7] then he himself was in the water, struggling against the drag of the paddle which he did not know he still held each time he fought back to the surface and grasped at the spinning skiff which at one instant was ten feet away and the next poised above his head as though about to brain him, until at last he grasped the stern, the drag of his body becoming a rudder to the skiff, the two of them, man and boat and with the paddle perpendicular above them like a jackstaff,[8] vanishing from the view of the short convict (who had vanished from that of the tall one with the same celerity though in a vertical direction) like a tableau snatched offstage intact with violent and incredible speed.

He was now in the channel of a slough, a bayou, in which until today no current had run probably since the old subterranean outrage which had created the country. There was plenty of current in it now though; from his trough behind the stern he seemed to see

7. Cf. Isaiah 8.7–8: "* * * and now therefore, behold, the Lord bringeth up upon them the waters of the River * * * and he shall come up over all his channels, and go over all his banks; * * * and he shall overthrow and pass through; he shall reach even to the neck; and the stretching out of his wings shall fill the breadth of thy land, O Immanuel."

8. Flag staff at the bow of a ship.

the trees and sky rushing past with vertiginous speed, looking down at him between the gouts of cold yellow in lugubrious and mournful amazement. But they were fixed and secure in something; he thought of that, he remembered in an instant of despairing rage the firm earth fixed and founded strong and cemented fast and stable forever by the generations of laborious sweat, somewhere beneath him, beyond the reach of his feet, when, and again without warning, the stern of the skiff struck him a stunning blow across the bridge of his nose. The instinct which had caused him to cling to it now caused him to fling the paddle into the boat in order to grasp the gunwale with both hands just as the skiff pivoted and spun away again. With both hands free he now dragged himself over the stern and lay prone on his face, streaming with blood and water and panting, not with exhaustion but with that furious rage which is terror's aftermath.

But he had to get up at once because he believed he had come much faster (and so farther) than he had. So he rose, out of the watery scarlet puddle in which he had lain, streaming, the soaked denim heavy as iron on his limbs, the black hair plastered to his skull, the blood-infused water streaking his jumper, and dragged his forearm gingerly and hurriedly across his lower face and glanced at it then grasped the paddle and began to try to swing the skiff back upstream. It did not even occur to him that he did not know where his companion was, in which tree among all which he had passed or might pass. He did not even speculate on that for the reason that he knew so incontestably that the other was upstream from him, and after his recent experience the mere connotation of the term upstream carried a sense of such violence and force and speed that the conception of it as other than a straight line was something which the intelligence, reason, simply refused to harbor, like the notion of a rifle bullet the width of a cotton field.

The bow began to swing back upstream. It turned readily, it outpaced the aghast and outraged instant in which he realised it was swinging far too easily, it had swung on over the arc and lay broadside to the current and began again that vicious spinning while he sat, his teeth bared in his bloody streaming face while his spent arms flailed the impotent paddle at the water, that innocent-appearing medium which at one time had held him in iron-like and shifting convolutions like an anaconda yet which now seemed to offer no more resistance to the thrust of his urge and need than so much air, like air; the boat which had threatened him and at last actually struck him in the face with the shocking violence of a mule's hoof now seemed to poise weightless upon it like a thistle bloom, spinning like a wind vane while he flailed at the water and thought of, envisioned, his companion safe, inactive and at ease in the tree with nothing to do but wait, musing with impotent and terrified fury upon that arbitrariness of human affairs which had abrogated to the one the secure tree and to the other the hysterical and unmanageable boat for the very reason that it knew that he alone of the two of them would make any attempt to return and rescue his companion.

The skiff had paid off and now ran with the current again. It seemed again to spring from immobility into incredible speed, and he thought he must already be miles away from where his companion had quitted him, though actually he had merely described a big circle since getting back into the skiff, and the object (a clump of cypress trees choked by floating logs and debris) which the skiff was now about to strike was the same one it had careened into before when the stern had struck him. He didn't know this because he had not yet ever looked higher than the bow of the boat. He didn't look higher now, he just saw that he was going to strike; he seemed to feel run through the very insentient fabric of the skiff a current of eager gleeful vicious incorrigible wilfulness; and he who had never ceased to flail at the bland treacherous water with what he had believed to be the limit of his strength now from somewhere, some ultimate absolute reserve, produced a final measure of endurance, will to endure which adumbrated mere muscle and nerves, continuing to flail the paddle right up to the instant of striking, completing one last reach thrust and recover out of pure desperate reflex, as a man slipping on ice reaches for his hat and moneypocket, as the skiff struck and hurled him once more flat on his face in the bottom of it.

This time he did not get up at once. He lay flat on his face, slightly spread-eagled and in an attitude almost peaceful, a kind of abject meditation. He would have to get up sometime, he knew that, just as all life consists of having to get up sooner or later and then having to lie down again sooner or later after a while. And he was not exactly exhausted and he was not particularly without hope and he did not especially dread getting up. It merely seemed to him that he had accidentally been caught in a situation in which time and environment, not himself, was mesmerised; he was being toyed with by a current of water going nowhere, beneath a day which would wane toward no evening; when it was done with him it would spew him back into the comparatively safe world he had been snatched violently out of and in the meantime it did not much matter just what he did or did not do. So he lay on his face, now not only feeling but hearing the strong quiet rustling of the current on the underside of the planks, for a while longer. Then he raised his head and this time touched his palm gingerly to his face and looked at the blood again, then he sat up onto his heels and leaning over the gunwale he pinched his nostrils between thumb and finger and expelled a gout of blood and was in the act of wiping his fingers on his thigh when a voice slightly above his line of sight said quietly, "It's taken you a while," and he who up to this moment had had neither reason nor time to raise his eyes higher than the bows looked up and saw, sitting in a tree and looking at him, a woman. She was not ten feet away. She sat on the lowest limb of one of the trees holding the jam he had grounded on, in a calico wrapper and an army private's tunic and a sunbonnet, a woman whom he did not even bother to examine since that first startled glance had been ample to reveal to him all the generations of her life and background, who could have been his sister if he had a sister, his wife if he had not entered the penitentiary at an age scarcely out of adolescence and some years younger than that at which even his prolific and monogamous kind married—a woman who sat clutching the trunk of the tree, her stockingless feet in a pair of man's unlaced brogans less than a yard from the water, who was very probably somebody's sister and quite certainly (or certainly should have been) somebody's wife, though this too he had entered the penitentiary too young to have had more than mere theoretical female experience to discover yet. "I thought for a minute you wasn't aiming to come back."

"Come back?"

"After the first time. After you run into this brush pile the first time and got into the boat and went on." He looked about, touching his face tenderly again; it could very well be the same place where the boat had hit him in the face.

"Yah," he said. "I'm here now though."

"Could you maybe get the boat a little closer? I taken a right sharp strain getting up here; maybe I better . . ." He was not listening; he had just discovered that the paddle was gone; this time when the skiff hurled him forward he had flung the paddle not into it but beyond it. "It's right there in them brush tops," the woman said. "You can get it. Here. Catch a holt of this." It was a grapevine. It had grown up into the tree and the flood had torn the roots loose. She had taken a turn with it about her upper body; she now loosed it and swung it out until he could grasp it. Holding to the end of the vine he warped the skiff around the end of the jam, picking up the paddle, and warped the skiff on beneath the limb and held it and now he watched her move, gather herself heavily and carefully to descend—that heaviness which was not painful but just excruciatingly careful, that profound and almost lethargic awkwardness which added nothing to the sum of that first aghast amazement which had served already for the catafalque of invincible dream since even in durance he had continued (and even with the old avidity, even though they had caused his downfall) to consume the impossible pulp-printed fables carefully censored and as carefully smuggled into the penitentiary; and who to say what Helen, what living Garbo,[9] he had not dreamed of rescuing from what craggy

9. Helen of Troy (whose beauty occasioned the Trojan War) and Greta   Garbo (b. 1905), film star.

pinnacle or dragoned keep when he and his companion embarked in the skiff. He watched her, he made no further effort to help her beyond holding the skiff savagely steady while she lowered herself from the limb—the entire body, the deformed swell of belly bulging the calico, suspended by its arms, thinking, *And this is what I get. This, out of all the female meat that walks, is what I have to be caught in a runaway boat with.*

"Where's that cottonhouse?" he said.

"Cottonhouse?"

"With that fellow on it. The other one."

"I dont know. It's a right smart of cottonhouses around here. With folks on them too, I reckon." She was examining him. "You're bloody as a hog," she said. "You look like a convict."

"Yah," he said, snarled. "I feel like I done already been hung. Well, I got to pick up my pardner and then find that cottonhouse." He cast off. That is, he released his hold on the vine. That was all he had to do, for even while the bow of the skiff hung high on the log jam and even while he held it by the vine in the comparatively dead water behind the jam, he felt steadily and constantly the whisper, the strong purring power of the water just one inch beyond the frail planks on which he squatted and which, as soon as he released the vine, took charge of the skiff not with one powerful clutch but in a series of touches light, tentative, and catlike; he realised now that he had entertained a sort of foundationless hope that the added weight might make the skiff more controllable. During the first moment or two he had a wild (and still foundationless) belief that it had; he had got the head upstream and managed to hold it so by terrific exertion continued even after he discovered that they were travelling straight enough but stern-first and continued somehow even after the bow began to wear away and swing; the old irresistible movement which he knew well by now, too well to fight against it, so that he let the bow swing on downstream with the hope of utilising the skiff's own momentum to bring it through the full circle and so upstream again, the skiff travelling broadside then bow-first then broadside again, diagonally across the channel, toward the other wall of submerged trees; it began to flee beneath him with terrific speed, they were in an eddy but did not know it; he had no time to draw conclusions or even wonder; he crouched, his teeth bared in his blood-caked and swollen face, his lungs bursting, flailing at the water while the trees stooped hugely down at him. The skiff struck, spun, struck again; the woman half lay in the bow, clutching the gunwales, as if she were trying to crouch behind her own pregnancy; he banged now not at the water but at the living sap-blooded wood with the paddle, his desire now not to go anywhere, reach any destination, but just to keep the skiff from beating itself to fragments against the tree trunks. Then something exploded, this time against the back of his head, and stooping trees and dizzy water, the woman's face and all, fled together and vanished in bright soundless flash and glare.

An hour later the skiff came slowly up an old logging road and so out of the bottom, the forest, and into (or onto) a cottonfield—a gray and limitless desolation now free of turmoil, broken only by a thin line of telephone poles like a wading millipede. The woman was now paddling, steadily and deliberately, with that curious lethargic care, while the convict squatted, his head between his knees, trying to stanch the fresh and apparently inexhaustible flow of blood from his nose with handfuls of water. The woman ceased paddling, the skiff drifted on, slowing, while she looked about. "We're done out," she said.

The convict raised his head and also looked about. "Out where?"

"I thought maybe you might know."

"I dont even know where I used to be. Even if I knowed which way was north, I wouldn't know if that was where I wanted to go." He cupped another handful of water to his face and lowered his hand and regarded the resulting crimson marbling on his palm, not with dejection, not with concern, but with a kind of sardonic and vicious bemusement. The woman watched the back of his head.

"We got to get somewhere."

"Dont I know it? A fellow on a cottonhouse. Another in a tree. And now that thing in your lap."

"It wasn't due yet. Maybe it was having to climb that tree quick yesterday, and having to set in it all night. I'm doing the best I can. But we better get somewhere soon."

"Yah," the convict said. "I thought I wanted to get somewhere too and I ain't had no luck at it. You pick out a place to get to now and we'll try yours. Gimme that oar." The woman passed him the paddle. The boat was a double-ender; he had only to turn around.

"Which way you fixing to go?" the woman said.

"Never you mind that. You just keep on holding on." He began to paddle, on across the cottonfield. It began to rain again, though not hard at first. "Yah," he said. "Ask the boat. I been in it since breakfast and I aint never knowed, where I aimed to go or where I was going either."

That was about one oclock. Toward the end of the afternoon the skiff (they were in a channel of some sort again, they had been in it for some time; they had got into it before they knew it and too late to get out again, granted there had been any reason to get out, as, to the convict anyway, there was certainly none and the fact that their speed had increased again was reason enough to stay in it) shot out upon a broad expanse of debris-filled water which the convict recognised as a river and, from its size, the Yazoo River though it was little enough he had seen of this country which he had not quitted for so much as one single day in the last seven years of his life. What he did not know was that it was now running backward.

So as soon as the drift of the skiff indicated the set of the current, he began to paddle in that direction which he believed to be downstream, where he knew there were towns—Yazoo City, and as a last resort, Vicksburg, if his luck was that bad, if not, smaller towns whose names he did not know but where there would be people, houses, something, anything he might reach and surrender his charge to and turn his back on her forever, on all pregnant and female life forever and return to that monastic existence of shotguns and shackles where he would be secure from it. Now, with the imminence of habitations, release from her, he did not even hate her. When he looked upon the swelling and unmanageable body before him it seemed to him that it was not the woman at all but rather a separate demanding threatening inert yet living mass of which both he and she were equally victims; thinking, as he had been for the last three or four hours, of that minute's—nay, second's—aberration of eye or hand which would suffice to precipitate her into the water to be dragged down to death by that senseless millstone which in its turn would not even have to feel agony, he no longer felt any glow of revenge toward her as its custodian, he felt sorry for her as he would for the living timber in a barn which had to be burned to rid itself of vermin.

He paddled on, helping the current, steadily and strongly, with a calculated husbandry of effort, toward what he believed was downstream, towns, people, something to stand upon, while from time to time the woman raised herself to bail the accumulated rain from the skiff. It was raining steadily now though still not hard, still without passion, the sky, the day itself dissolving without grief; the skiff moved in a nimbus, an aura of gray gauze which merged almost without demarcation with the roiling spittle-frothed debris-choked water. Now the day, the light, definitely began to end and the convict permitted himself an extra notch or two of effort because it suddenly seemed to him that the speed of the skiff had lessened. This was actually the case though the convict did not know it. He merely took it as a phenomenon of the increasing obfuscation, or at most as a result of the long day's continuous effort with no food, complicated by the ebbing and fluxing phases of anxiety and impotent rage at his absolutely gratuitous predicament. So he stepped up his stroke a beat or so, not from alarm but on the contrary, since he too had received that lift from the mere presence of a known stream, a river known by its ineradicable name to generations of men who had been drawn to live beside it as man always has been drawn to dwell beside water, even before he had a name for water and fire, drawn to the living water, the course of his destiny and his actual physical appearance rigidly coerced and postulated by it. So he was not alarmed. He paddled on, upstream without knowing it, unaware that all the water which for forty hours now had been pouring through the levee break to the north was somewhere ahead of him, on its way back to the River.

It was full dark now. That is, night had completely come, the gray dissolving sky had vanished, yet as though in perverse ratio surface visibility had sharpened, as though the light which the rain of the afternoon had washed out of the air had gathered upon the water as the rain itself had done, so that the yellow flood spread on before him now with a quality almost phosphorescent, right up to the instant where vision ceased. The darkness in fact had its advantages; he could now stop seeing the rain. He and his garments had been wet for more than twenty-four hours now so he had long since stopped feeling it, and now that he could no longer see it either it had in a certain sense ceased for him. Also, he now had to make no effort even not to see the swell of his passenger's belly. So he was paddling on, strongly and steadily, not alarmed and not concerned but just exasperated because he had not yet begun to see any reflection on the clouds which would indicate the city or cities which he believed he was approaching but which were actually now miles behind him, when he heard a sound. He did not know what it was because he had never heard it before and he would never be expected to hear such again since it is not given to every man to hear such at all and to none to hear it more than once in his life. And he was not alarmed now either because there was not time, for although the visibility ahead, for all its clarity, did not extend very far, yet in the next instant to the hearing he was also seeing something such as he had never seen before. This was that the sharp line where the phosphorescent water met the darkness was now about ten feet higher than it had been an instant before and that it was curled forward upon itself like a sheet of dough being rolled out for a pudding. It reared, stooping; the crest of it swirled like the mane of a galloping horse and, phosphorescent too, fretted and flickered like fire. And while the woman huddled in the bows, aware or not aware the convict did not know which, he (the convict), his swollen and blood-streaked face gaped in an expression of aghast and incredulous amazement, continued to paddle directly into it. Again he simply had not had time to order his rhythm-hypnotised muscles to cease. He continued to paddle though the skiff had ceased to move forward at all but seemed to be hanging in space while the paddle still reached thrust recovered and reached again; now instead of space the skiff became abruptly surrounded by a welter of fleeing debris—planks, small buildings, the bodies of drowned yet antic animals, entire trees leaping and diving like porpoises above which the skiff seemed to hover in weightless and airy indecision like a bird above a fleeing countryside, undecided where to light or whether to light at all, while the convict squatted in it still going through the motions of paddling, waiting for an opportunity to scream. He never found it. For an instant the skiff seemed to stand erect on its

stern and then shoot scrabbling and scrambling up the curling wall
of water like a cat, and soared on above the licking crest itself and
hung cradled into the high actual air in the limbs of a tree, from
which bower of new-leafed boughs and branches the convict, like a
bird in its nest and still waiting his chance to scream and still going
through the motions of paddling though he no longer even had the
paddle now, looked down upon a world turned to furious motion
and in incredible retrograde.

Some time about midnight, accompanied by a rolling cannonade
of thunder and lightning like a battery going into action, as though
some forty hours' constipation of the elements, the firmament itself,
were discharging in clapping and glaring salute to the ultimate
acquiescence to desperate and furious motion, and still leading its
charging welter of dead cows and mules and outhouses and cabins
and hen-coops, the skiff passed Vicksburg. The convict didn't know
it. He wasn't looking high enough above the water; he still squatted, clutching the gunwales and glaring at the yellow turmoil about
him out of which entire trees, the sharp gables of houses, the long
mournful heads of mules which he fended off with a splintered
length of plank snatched from he knew not where in passing (and
which seemed to glare reproachfully back at him with sightless eyes,
in limber-lipped and incredulous amazement) rolled up and then
down again, the skiff now travelling forward now sideways now
sternward, sometimes in the water, sometimes riding for yards upon
the roofs of houses and trees and even upon the backs of the mules
as though even in death they were not to escape that burden-
bearing doom with which their eunuch race was cursed. But he
didn't see Vicksburg; the skiff, travelling at express speed, was in a
seething gut between soaring and dizzy banks with a glare of light
above them but he did not see it; he saw the flotsam ahead of him
divide violently and begin to climb upon itself, mounting, and he
was sucked through the resulting gap too fast to recognise it as the
trestling of a railroad bridge; for a horrible moment the skiff seemed
to hang in static indecision before the looming flank of a steamboat
as though undecided whether to climb over it or dive under it,
then a hard icy wind filled with the smell and taste and sense of
wet and boundless desolation blew upon him; the skiff made one
long bounding lunge as the convict's native state, in a final paroxysm, regurgitated him onto the wild bosom of the Father of
Waters.

This is how he told about it seven weeks later, sitting in new
bed-ticking garments, shaved and with his hair cut again, on his
bunk in the barracks:

During the next three or four hours after the thunder and lightning had spent itself the skiff ran in pitch streaming darkness upon

a roiling expanse which, even if he could have seen, apparently had no boundaries. Wild and invisible, it tossed and heaved about and beneath the boat, ridged with dirty phosphorescent foam and filled with a debris of destruction—objects nameless and enormous and invisible which struck and slashed at the skiff and whirled on. He did not know he was now upon the River. At that time he would have refused to believe it, even if he had known. Yesterday he had known he was in a channel by the regularity of the spacing between the bordering trees. Now, since even by daylight he could have seen no boundaries, the last place under the sun (or the streaming sky rather) he would have suspected himself to be would have been a river; if he had pondered at all about his present whereabouts, about the geography beneath him, he would merely have taken himself to be travelling at dizzy and inexplicable speed above the largest cotton field in the world; if he who yesterday had known he was in a river, had accepted that fact in good faith and earnest, then had seen that river turn without warning and rush back upon him with furious and deadly intent like a frenzied stallion in a lane—if he had suspected for one second that the wild and limitless expanse on which he now found himself was a river, consciousness would simply have refused; he would have fainted.

When daylight—a gray and ragged dawn filled with driving scud between icy rain-squalls—came and he could see again, he knew he was in no cottonfield. He knew that the wild water on which the skiff tossed and fled flowed above no soil tamely trod by man, behind the straining and surging buttocks of a mule. That was when it occurred to him that its present condition was no phenomenon of a decade, but that the intervening years during which it consented to bear upon its placid and sleepy bosom the frail mechanicals of man's clumsy contriving was the phenomenon and this the norm and the river was now doing what it liked to do, had waited patiently the ten years in order to do, as a mule will work for you ten years for the privilege of kicking you once. And he also learned something else about fear too, something he had even failed to discover on that other occasion when he was really afraid—that three or four seconds of that night in his youth while he looked down the twice-flashing pistol barrel of the terrified mail clerk before the clerk could be persuaded that his (the convict's) pistol would not shoot: that if you just held on long enough a time would come in fear after which it would no longer be agony at all but merely a kind of horrible outrageous itching, as after you have been burned bad.

He did not have to paddle now, he just steered (who had been without food for twenty-four hours now and without any sleep to speak of for fifty) while the skiff sped on across that boiling desolation where he had long since begun to not dare believe he could possibly be where he could not doubt he was, trying with his fragment of splintered plank merely to keep the skiff intact and afloat among the houses and trees and dead animals (the entire towns, stores, residences, parks and farmyards, which leaped and played about him like fish), not trying to reach any destination, just trying to keep the skiff afloat until he did. He wanted so little. He wanted nothing for himself. He just wanted to get rid of the woman, the belly, and he was trying to do that in the right way, not for himself, but for her. He could have put her back into another tree at any time—

"Or you could have jumped out of the boat and let her and it drown," the plump convict said. "Then they could have given you the ten years for escaping and then hung you for the murder and charged the boat to your folks."

"Yah," the tall convict said.—but he had not done that. He wanted to do it the right way, find somebody, anybody he could surrender her to, something solid he could set her down on and then jump back into the river, if that would please anyone. That was all he wanted—just to come to something, anything. That didn't seem like a great deal to ask. And he couldn't do it. He told how the skiff fled on—

"Didn't you pass nobody?" the plump convict said. "No steamboat, nothing?"

"I dont know," the tall one said.—while he tried merely to keep it afloat, until the darkness thinned and lifted and revealed—

"Darkness?" the plump convict said. "I thought you said it was already daylight."

"Yah," the tall one said. He was rolling a cigarette, pouring the tobacco carefully from a new sack, into the creased paper. "This was another one. They had several while I was gone."—the skiff to be moving still rapidly up a winding corridor bordered by drowned trees which the convict recognised again to be a river running again in the direction that, until two days ago, had been upstream. He was not exactly warned through instinct that this one, like that of two days ago, was in reverse. He would not say that he now believed himself to be in the same river, though he would not have been surprised to find that he did believe this, existing now, as he did and had and apparently was to continue for an unnamed period, in a state in which he was toy and pawn on a vicious and inflammable geography. He merely realised that he was in a river again, with all the subsequent inferences of a comprehensible, even if not familiar, portion of the earth's surface. Now he believed that all he had to do would be to paddle far enough and he would come to something horizontal and above water even if not dry and perhaps even populated; and, if fast enough, in time, and that his only other crying urgency was to refrain from looking at the woman who, as vision, the incontrovertible and apparently inescapable presence of his passenger, returned with dawn, had ceased to be a human being and (you could add twenty-four more hours to the first twenty-four and the first fifty now, even counting the hen. It was dead, drowned, caught by one wing under a shingle on a roof which had rolled momentarily up beside the skiff yesterday and he had eaten some of it raw though the woman would not) had become instead one single inert monstrous sentient womb which, he now believed, if he could only turn his gaze away and keep it away, would disappear, and if he could only keep his gaze from pausing again at the spot it had occupied, would not return. That's what he was doing this time when he discovered the wave was coming.

He didn't know how he discovered it was coming back. He heard no sound, it was nothing felt nor seen. He did not even believe that finding the skiff to be now in slack water—that is, that the motion of the current which, whether right or wrong, had at least been horizontal, had now stopped that and assumed a vertical direction—was sufficient to warn him. Perhaps it was just an invincible and almost fanatic faith in the inventiveness and innate viciousness of that medium on which his destiny was now cast, apparently forever; a sudden conviction far beyond either horror or surprise that now was none too soon for it to prepare to do whatever it was it intended doing. So he whirled the skiff, spun it on its heel like a running horse, whereupon, reversed, he could not even distinguish the very channel he had come up. He did not know whether he simply could not see it or if it had vanished some time ago and he not aware at the time; whether the river had become lost in a drowned world or if the world had become drowned in one limitless river. So now he could not tell if he were running directly before the wave or quartering across its line of charge; all he could do was keep that sense of swiftly accumulating ferocity behind him and paddle as fast as his spent and now numb muscles could be driven, and try not to look at the woman, to wrench his gaze from her and keep it away until he reached something flat and above water. So, gaunt, hollow-eyed, striving and wrenching almost physically at his eyes as if they were two of those suction-tipped rubber arrows shot from the toy gun of a child, his spent muscles obeying not will now but that attenuation beyond mere exhaustion which, mesmeric, can continue easier than cease, he once more drove the skiff full tilt into something it could not pass and, once more hurled violently forward onto his hands and knees, crouching, he glared with his wild swollen face up at the man with the shotgun and said in a harsh, croaking voice: "Vicksburg? Where's Vicksburg?"

Even when he tried to tell it, even after the seven weeks and he safe, secure, riveted warranted and doubly guaranteed by the ten years they had added to his sentence for attempted escape, something of the old hysteric incredulous outrage came back into his face, his voice, his speech. He never did even get on the other boat. He told how he clung to a strake[1] (it was a dirty unpainted shanty

---

1. Plank on the bottom or side of a ship.

boat with a drunken rake of tin stove pipe, it had been moving
when he struck it and apparently it had not even changed course
even though the three people on it must have been watching him
all the while—a second man, barefoot and with matted hair and
beard also at the steering sweep, and then—he did not know how
long—a woman leaning in the door, in a filthy assortment of men's
garments, watching him too with the same cold speculation) being
dragged violently along, trying to state and explain his simple (and
to him at least) reasonable desire and need; telling it, trying to tell
it, he could feel again the old unforgettable affronting like an ague
fit as he watched the abortive tobacco rain steadily and faintly from
between his shaking hands and then the paper itself part with a
thin dry snapping report:

"Burn my clothes?" the convict cried. "Burn them?"

"How in hell do you expect to escape in them billboards?" the
man with the shotgun said. He (the convict) tried to tell it, tried
to explain as he had tried to explain not to the three people on the
boat alone but to the entire circumambience—desolate water and
forlorn trees and sky—not for justification because he needed none
and knew that his hearers, the other convicts, required none from
him, but rather as, on the point of exhaustion, he might have
picked dreamily and incredulously at a suffocation. He told the man
with the gun how he and his partner had been given the boat and
told to pick up a man and a woman, how he had lost his partner
and failed to find the man, and now all in the world he wanted was
something flat to leave the woman on until he could find an officer,
a sheriff. He thought of home, the place where he had lived almost
since childhood, his friends of years whose ways he knew and who
knew his ways, the familiar fields where he did work he had
learned to do well and to like, the mules with characters he knew
and respected as he knew and respected the characters of certain
men; he thought of the barracks at night, with screens against the
bugs in summer and good stoves in winter and someone to supply
the fuel and the food too; the Sunday ball games and the picture
shows—things which, with the exception of the ball games, he had
never known before. But most of all, his own character (Two years
ago they had offered to make a trusty of him. He would no longer
need to plow or feed stock, he would only follow those who did with
a loaded gun, but he declined. "I reckon I'll stick to plowing," he
said, absolutely without humor. "I done already tried to use a gun
one time too many."), his good name, his responsibility not only
toward those who were responsible toward him but to himself, his
own honor in the doing of what was asked of him, his pride in
being able to do it, no matter what it was. He thought of this and
listened to the man with the gun talking about escape and it
seemed to him that, hanging there, being dragged violently along
(It was here he said that he first noticed the goats' beards of moss

in the trees, though it could have been there for several days so far as he knew. It just happened that he first noticed it here.), he would simply burst.

"Cant you get it into your head that the last thing I want to do is run away?" he cried. "You can set there with that gun and watch me; I give you fair lief. All I want is to put this woman—"

"And I told you she could come aboard," the man with the gun said in his level voice. "But there aint no room on no boat of mine for nobody hunting a sheriff in no kind of clothes, let alone a penitentiary suit."

"When he steps aboard, knock him in the head with the gun barrel," the man at the sweep said. "He's drunk."

"He aint coming aboard," the man with the gun said. "He's crazy."

Then the woman spoke. She didn't move, leaning in the door, in a pair of faded and patched and filthy overalls like the two men: "Give them some grub and tell them to get out of here." She moved, she crossed the deck and looked down at the convict's companion with her cold sullen face. "How much more time have you got?"

"It wasn't due till next month," the woman in the boat said. "But I—" The woman in overalls turned to the man with the gun.

"Give them some grub," she said. But the man with the gun was still looking down at the woman in the boat.

"Come on," he said to the convict. "Put her aboard, and beat it."

"And what'll happen to you," the woman in overalls said, "when you try to turn her over to an officer? When you lay alongside a sheriff and the sheriff asks you who you are?" Still the man with the gun didn't even look at her. He hardly even shifted the gun across his arm as he struck the woman across the face with the back of his other hand, hard. "You son of a bitch," she said. Still the man with the gun did not even look at her.

"Well?" he said to the convict.

"Dont you see I cant?" the convict cried. "Cant you see that?"

Now, he said, he gave up. He was doomed. That is, he knew now that he had been doomed from the very start never to get rid of her, just as the ones who sent him out with the skiff knew that he never would actually give up; when he recognised one of the objects which the woman in overalls was hurling into the skiff to be a can of condensed milk, he believed it to be a presage, gratuitous and irrevocable as a death-notice over the telegraph, that he was not even to find a flat stationary surface in time for the child to be born on it. So he told how he held the skiff alongside the shanty-boat while the first tentative toying of the second wave made up beneath him, while the woman in overalls passed back and forth between house and rail, flinging the food—the hunk of salt meat, the ragged and filthy quilt, the scorched lumps of cold bread which she poured into the skiff from a heaped dishpan like so much garbage—while he clung to the strake against the mounting pull of the current, the new wave which for the moment he had forgotten because he was still trying to state the incredible simplicity of his desire and need until the man with the gun (the only one of the three who wore shoes) began to stamp at his hands, he snatching his hands away one at a time to avoid the heavy shoes, then grasping the rail again until the man with the gun kicked at his face, he flinging himself sideways to avoid the shoe and so breaking his hold on the rail, his weight canting the skiff off at a tangent on the increasing current so that it began to leave the shanty boat behind and he paddling again now, violently, as a man hurries toward the precipice for which he knows at last he is doomed, looking back at the other boat, the three faces sullen derisive and grim and rapidly diminishing across the widening water and at last, apoplectic, suffocating with the intolerable fact not that he had been refused but that he had been refused so little, had wanted so little, asked for so little, yet there had been demanded of him in return the one price out of all breath which (they must have known) if he could have paid it, he would not have been where he was, asking what he asked, raising the paddle and shaking it and screaming curses back at them even after the shotgun flashed and the charge went scuttering past along the water to one side.

So he hung there, he said, shaking the paddle and howling, when suddenly he remembered that other wave, the second wall of water full of houses and dead mules building up behind him back in the swamp. So he quit yelling then and went back to paddling. He was not trying to outrun it. He just knew from experience that when it overtook him, he would have to travel in the same direction it was moving in anyway, whether he wanted to or not, and when it did overtake him, he would begin to move too fast to stop, no matter what places he might come to where he could leave the woman, land her in time. Time: that was his itch now, so his only chance was to stay ahead of it as long as he could and hope to reach something before it struck. So he went on, driving the skiff with muscles which had been too tired so long they had quit feeling it, as when a man has had bad luck for so long that he ceases to believe it is even bad, let alone luck. Even when he ate—the scorched lumps the size of baseballs and the weight and durability of cannel coal even after having lain in the skiff's bilge where the shanty boat woman had thrown them—the iron-like lead-heavy objects which no man would have called bread outside of the crusted and scorched pan in which they had cooked—it was with one hand, begrudging even that from the paddle.

He tried to tell that too—that day while the skiff fled on among the bearded trees while every now and then small quiet tentative ex-

ploratory feelers would come up from the wave behind and toy for a
moment at the skiff, light and curious, then go on with a faint hissing sighing, almost a chuckling, sound, the skiff going on, driving
on with nothing to see but trees and water and solitude: until after a
while it no longer seemed to him that he was trying to put space
and distance behind him or shorten space and distance ahead but
that both he and the wave were now hanging suspended simultaneous and unprogressing in pure time, upon a dreamy desolation in
which he paddled on not from any hope even to reach anything at
all but merely to keep intact what little of distance the length of the
skiff provided between himself and the inert and inescapable mass
of female meat before him; then night and the skiff rushing on, fast
since any speed over anything unknown and invisible is too fast,
with nothing before him and behind him the outrageous idea of a
volume of moving water toppling forward, its crest frothed and
shredded like fangs, and then dawn again (another of those dreamlike alterations day to dark then back to day again with that quality
truncated, anachronic and unreal as the waxing and waning of
lights in a theatre scene) and the skiff emerging now with the
woman no longer supine beneath the shrunken soaked private's coat
but sitting bolt upright, gripping the gunwales with both hands, her
eyes closed and her lower lip caught between her teeth and he driving the splintered board furiously now, glaring at her out of his wild
swollen sleepless face and crying, croaking, "Hold on! For God's
sake hold on!"

"I'm trying to," she said. "But hurry! Hurry!" He told it, the unbelievable: hurry, hasten: the man falling from a cliff being told to
catch onto something and save himself; the very telling of it emerging shadowy and burlesque, ludicrous, comic and mad, from the
ague of unbearable forgetting with a quality more dreamily furious
than any fable behind proscenium lights:

He was in a basin now—"A basin?" the plump convict said.
"That's what you wash in."

"All right," the tall one said, harshly, above his hands. "I did."
With a supreme effort he stilled them long enough to release the
two bits of cigarette paper and watched them waft in light fluttering indecision to the floor between his feet, holding his hands motionless even for a moment longer—a basin, a broad peaceful yellow
sea which had an abruptly and curiously ordered air, giving him,
even at that moment, the impression that it was accustomed to
water even if not total submersion; he even remembered the name
of it, told to him two or three weeks later by someone: Atchafalaya—

"Louisiana?" the plump convict said. "You mean you were clean
out of Mississippi? Hell fire." He stared at the tall one. "Shucks,"
he said. "That aint but just across from Vicksburg."

"They never named any Vicksburg across from where I was," the tall one said. "It was Baton Rouge they named." And now he began to talk about a town, a little neat white portrait town nestling among enormous very green trees, appearing suddenly in the telling as it probably appeared in actuality, abrupt and airy and miragelike and incredibly serene before him behind a scattering of boats moored to a line of freight cars standing flush to the doors in water. And now he tried to tell that too: how he stood waist-deep in water for a moment looking back and down at the skiff in which the woman half lay, her eyes still closed, her knuckles white on the gunwales and a tiny thread of blood creeping down her chin from her chewed lip, and he looking down at her in a kind of furious desperation.

"How far will I have to walk?" she said.

"I dont know, I tell you!" he cried. "But it's land somewhere yonder! It's land, houses."

"If I try to move, it wont even be born inside a boat," she said. "You'll have to get closer."

"Yes," he cried, wild, desperate, incredulous. "Wait. I'll go and surrender, then they will have—" He didn't finish, wait to finish; he told that too: himself splashing, stumbling, trying to run, sobbing and gasping; now he saw it—another loading platform standing above the yellow flood, the khaki figures on it as before, identical, the same; he said how the intervening days since that first innocent morning telescoped, vanished as if they had never been, the two contiguous succeeding instants (succeeding? simultaneous) and he transported across no intervening space but merely turned in his own footsteps, plunging, splashing, his arms raised, croaking harshly. He heard the startled shout, "There's one of them!", the command, the clash of equipment, the alarmed cry: "There he goes! There he goes!"

"Yes!" he cried, running, plunging. "Here I am! Here! Here!" running on, into the first scattered volley, stopping among the bullets, waving his arms, shrieking, "I want to surrender! I want to surrender!" watching not in terror but in amazed and absolutely unbearable outrage as a squatting clump of the khaki figures parted and he saw the machine gun, the blunt thick muzzle slant and drop and probe toward him and he still screaming in his hoarse crow's voice, "I want to surrender! Cant you hear me?" continuing to scream even as he whirled and plunged splashing, ducking, went completely under and heard the bullets going thuck-thuck-thuck on the water above him and he scrabbling still on the bottom, still trying to scream even before he regained his feet and still all submerged save his plunging unmistakable buttocks, the outraged screaming bubbling from his mouth and about his face since he merely wanted to surrender. Then he was comparatively screened, out of range, though not for long. That is (he didn't tell how or where) there was a moment in which he paused, breathed for a sec-

ond before running again, the course back to the skiff open for the
time being though he could still hear the shouts behind him and
now and then a shot, and he panting, sobbing, a long savage tear in
the flesh of one hand, got when and how he did not know, and he
wasting precious breath, speaking to no one now any more than the
scream of the dying rabbit is addressed to any mortal ear but rather
an indictment of all breath and its folly and suffering, its infinite
capacity for folly and pain, which seems to be its only immortality:
"All in the world I want is just to surrender."

He returned to the skiff and got in and took up his splintered
plank. And now when he told this, despite the fury of element
which climaxed it, it (the telling) became quite simple; he now
even creased another cigarette paper between fingers which did not
tremble at all and filled the paper from the tobacco sack without
spilling a flake, as though he had passed from the machine-gun's
barrage into a bourne beyond any more amazement: so that the
subsequent part of his narrative seemed to reach his listeners as
though from beyond a sheet of slightly milky though still transparent glass, as something not heard but seen[2]—a series of shadows,
edgeless yet distinct, and smoothly flowing, logical and unfrantic
and making no sound: They were in the skiff, in the center of the
broad placid trough which had no boundaries and down which the
tiny forlorn skiff flew to the irresistible coercion of a current going
once more he knew not where, the neat small liveoak-bowered
towns unattainable and miragelike and apparently attached to
nothing upon the airy and unchanging horizon. He did not believe
them, they did not matter, he was doomed; they were less than the
figments of smoke or of delirium, and he driving his unceasing paddle without destination or even hope now, looking now and then at
the woman sitting with her knees drawn up and locked and her entire body one terrific clench while the threads of bloody saliva crept
from her teeth-clenched lower lip. He was going nowhere and
fleeing from nothing, he merely continued to paddle because he had
paddled so long now that he believed if he stopped his muscles
would scream in agony. So when it happened he was not surprised.
He heard the sound which he knew well (he had heard it but once
before, true enough, but no man needed hear it but once) and he
had been expecting it; he looked back, still driving the paddle, and
saw it, curled, crested with its strawlike flotsam of trees and debris and
dead beasts, and he glared over his shoulder at it for a full minute
out of that attenuation far beyond the point of outragement where
even suffering, the capability of being further affronted, had ceased,
from which he now contemplated with savage and invulnerable curiosity the further extent to which his now anesthetised nerves

---

2. Cf. Isaiah 32.1–4: "Behold, a king
shall reign in righteousness. * * * And
the eyes of them that see shall not be
dim, and the ears of them that hear
shall hearken. The heart also of the rash
shall understand knowledge, and the
tongue of the stammerers shall be ready
to speak plainly."

could bear, what next could be invented for them to bear, until the wave actually began to rear above his head into its thunderous climax. Then only did he turn his head. His stroke did not falter, it neither slowed nor increased; still paddling with that spent hypnotic steadiness, he saw the swimming deer. He did not know what it was nor that he had altered the skiff's course to follow it, he just watched the swimming head before him as the wave boiled down and the skiff rose bodily in the old familiar fashion on a welter of tossing trees and houses and bridges and fences, he still paddling even while the paddle found no purchase save air and still paddled even as he and the deer shot forward side by side at arm's length, he watching the deer now, watching the deer begin to rise out of the water bodily until it was actually running along upon the surface, rising still, soaring clear of the water altogether, vanishing upward in a dying crescendo of splashings and snapping branches, its damp scut flashing upward, the entire animal vanishing upward as smoke vanishes. And now the skiff struck and canted and he was out of it too, standing knee-deep, springing out and falling to his knees, scrambling up, glaring after the vanished deer. "Land!" he croaked. "Land! Hold on! Just hold on!" He caught the woman beneath the arms, dragging her out of the boat, plunging and panting after the vanished deer. Now earth actually appeared—an acclivity smooth and swift and steep, bizarre, solid and unbelievable; an Indian mound, and he plunging at the muddy slope, slipping back, the woman struggling in his muddy hands.

"Let me down!" she cried. "Let me down!" But he held her, panting, sobbing, and rushed again at the muddy slope; he had almost reached the flat crest with his now violently unmanageable burden when a stick under his foot gathered itself with thick convulsive speed. *It was a snake*, he thought as his feet fled beneath him and with the indubitable last of his strength he half pushed and half flung the woman up the bank as he shot feet first and face down back into that medium upon which he had lived for more days and nights than he could remember and from which he himself had never completely emerged, as if his own failed and spent flesh were attempting to carry out his furious unflagging will for severance at any price, even that of drowning, from the burden with which, unwitting and without choice, he had been doomed. Later it seemed to him that he had carried back beneath the surface with him the sound of the infant's first mewling cry.

When the woman asked him if he had a knife, standing there in the streaming bed-ticking garments which had got him shot at, the second time by a machine gun, on the two occasions when he had seen any human life after leaving the levee four days ago, the convict felt exactly as he had in the fleeing skiff when the woman suggested that they had better hurry. He felt the same outrageous affronting of a condition purely moral, the same raging impotence to find any answer to it; so that, standing above her, spent suffocating and inarticulate, it was a full minute before he comprehended that she was now crying, "The can! The can in the boat!" He did not anticipate what she could want with it; he did not even wonder nor stop to ask. He turned running; this time he thought, *It's another moccasin* as the thick body truncated in that awkward reflex which had nothing of alarm in it but only alertness, he not even shifting his stride though he knew his running foot would fall within a yard of the flat head. The bow of the skiff was well up the slope now where the wave had set it and there was another snake just crawling over the stern into it and as he stooped for the bailing can he saw something else swimming toward the mound, he didn't know what —a head, a face at the apex of a vee of ripples. He snatched up the can; by pure juxtaposition of it and water he scooped it full, already turning. He saw the deer again, or another one. That is, he saw a deer—a side glance, the light smoke-colored phantom in a cypress vista then gone, vanished, he not pausing to look after it, galloping back to the woman and kneeling with the can to her lips until she told him better.

It had contained a pint of beans or tomatoes, something, hermetically sealed and opened by four blows of an axe heel, the metal flap turned back, the jagged edges razor-sharp. She told him how, and he used this in lieu of a knife, he removed one of his shoelaces, and cut it in two with the sharp tin. Then she wanted warm water—"If I just had a little hot water," she said in a weak serene voice without particular hope; only when he thought of matches it was again a good deal like when she had asked him if he had a knife, until she fumbled in the pocket of the shrunken tunic (it had a darker double vee on one cuff and a darker blotch on the shoulder where service stripes and a divisional emblem had been ripped off but this meant nothing to him) and produced a match-box contrived by telescoping two shotgun shells. So he drew her back a little from the water and went to hunt wood dry enough to burn, thinking this time, *It's just another snake*, only, he said, he should have thought *ten thousand other snakes*: and now he knew it was not the same deer because he saw three at one time, does or bucks he did not know which since they were all anterless in May and besides he had never seen one of any kind anywhere before except on a Christmas card; and then the rabbit, drowned, dead anyway, already torn open, the bird, the hawk, standing upon it—the erected crest, the hard vicious patrician nose, the intolerant omnivorous yellow eye—and he kicking at it, kicking it lurching and broadwinged into the actual air.

When he returned with the wood and the dead rabbit, the baby, wrapped in the tunic, lay wedged between two cypress-knees and the woman was not in sight, though while the convict knelt in the mud, blowing and nursing his meagre flame, she came slowly and weakly from the direction of the water. Then, the water heated at last and there produced from some where he was never to know, she herself perhaps never to know until the need comes, no woman perhaps ever to know, only no woman will even wonder, that square of something somewhere between sackcloth and silk—squatting, his own wet garments steaming in the fire's heat, he watched her bathe the child with a savage curiosity and interest that became amazed unbelief, so that at last he stood above them both, looking down at the tiny terra-cotta-colored creature resembling nothing, and thought, *And this is all. This is what severed me violently from all I ever knew and did not wish to leave and cast me upon a medium I was born to fear, to fetch up at last in a place I never saw before and where I do not even know where I am.*

Then he returned to the water and refilled the bailing can. It was drawing toward sunset now (or what would have been sunset save for the high prevailing overcast) of this day whose beginning he could not even remember; when he returned to where the fire burned in the interlaced gloom of the cypresses, even after this short absence, evening had definitely come, as though darkness too had taken refuge upon that quarter-acre mound, that earthen Ark out of Genesis, that him wet cypress-choked life-teeming constricted desolation in what direction and how far from what and where he had no more idea than of the day of the month, and had now with the setting of the sun crept forth again to spread upon the waters. He stewed the rabbit in sections while the fire burned redder and redder in the darkness where the shy wild eyes of small animals— once the tall mild almost plate-sized stare of one of the deer— glowed and vanished and glowed again, the broth hot and rank after the four days; he seemed to hear the roar of his own saliva as he watched the woman sip the first canful. Then he drank too; they ate the other fragments which had been charring and scorching on willow twigs; it was full night now. "You and him better sleep in the boat," the convict said. "We want to get an early start tomorrow." He shoved the bow of the skiff off the land so it would lie level, he lengthened the painter with a piece of grapevine and returned to the fire and tied the grapevine about his wrist and lay down. It was mud he lay upon, but it was solid underneath, it was earth, it did not move; if you fell upon it you broke your bones against its incontrovertible passivity sometimes but it did not accept you substanceless and enveloping and suffocating, down and down and down; it was hard at times to drive a plow through, it sent you spent, weary, and cursing its light-long insatiable demands back to your bunk at sunset at times but it did not snatch you violently out of all familar knowing and sweep you thrall and impotent for days against any returning. *I dont know where I am and I dont reckon I know the way back to where I want to go,* he thought. *But at least the boat has stopped long enough to give me a chance to turn it around.*

He waked at dawn, the light faint, the sky jonquil-colored; the day would be fine. The fire had burned out; on the opposite side of the cold ashes lay three snakes motionless and parallel as underscoring, and in the swiftly making light others seemed to materialise: earth which an instant before had been mere earth broke up into motionless coils and loops, branches which a moment before had been mere branches now become immobile ophidian[3] festoons even as the convict stood thinking about food, about something hot before they started. But he decided against this, against wasting this much time, since there still remained in the skiff quite a few of the rocklike objects which the shanty woman had flung into it; besides (thinking this), no matter how fast nor successfully he hunted, he would never be able to lay up enough food to get them back to where they wanted to go. So he returned to the skiff, paying himself back to it by his vine-spliced painter, back to the water on which a low mist thick as cotton batting (though apparently not very tall, deep) lay, into which the stern of the skiff was already beginning to disappear although it lay with its prow almost touching the mound. The woman waked, stirred. "We fixing to start now?" she said.

"Yah," the convict said. "You aint aiming to have another one this morning, are you?" He got in and shoved the skiff clear of the land, which immediately began to dissolve into the mist. "Hand me the oar," he said over his shoulder, not turning yet.

"The oar?"

He turned his head. "The oar. You're laying on it." But she was not, and for an instant during which the mound, the island continued to fade slowly into the mist which seemed to enclose the skiff in weightless and impalpable wool like a precious or fragile bauble or jewel, the convict squatted not in dismay but in that frantic and astonished outrage of a man who, having just escaped a falling safe, is struck by the following two-ounce paper weight which was sitting on it: this the more unbearable because he knew that never in his life had he less time to give way to it. He did not hesitate. Grasping the grapevine end he sprang into the water, vanishing in the violent action of climbing, and reappeared still climbing and (who had never learned to swim) plunged and threshed on toward the almost-vanished mound, moving through the water then upon it as the deer had done yesterday and scrabbled up the muddy slope and lay gasping and panting, still clutching the grapevine end.

Now the first thing he did was to choose what he believed to be the most suitable tree (for an instant in which he knew he was insane he thought of trying to saw it down with the flange of the bailing can) and build a fire against the butt of it. Then he went to seek food. He spent the next six days seeking it while the tree

3. Pertaining to snakes.

burned through and fell and burned through again at the proper
length and he nursing little constant cunning flames along the
flanks of the log to make it paddle-shaped, nursing them at night too
while the woman and baby (it was eating, nursing now, he turning
his back or even returning into the woods each time she prepared to
open the faded tunic) slept in the skiff. He learned to watch for
stooping hawks and so found more rabbits and twice possums; they
ate some drowned fish which gave them both a rash and then a violent flux and one snake which the woman thought was turtle and
which did them no harm, and one night it rained and he got up and
dragged brush, shaking the snakes (he no longer thought, *It aint
nothing but another moccasin*, he just stepped aside for them as
they, when there was time, telescoped sullenly aside for him) out of
it with the old former feeling of personal invulnerability and built a
shelter and the rain stopped at once and did not recommence and
the woman went back to the skiff.

Then one night—the slow tedious charring log was almost a paddle now—one night and he was in bed, in his bed in the bunkhouse
and it was cold, he was trying to pull the covers up only his mule[4]
wouldn't let him, prodding and bumping heavily at him, trying to
get into the narrow bed with him and now the bed was cold too
and wet and he was trying to get out of it only the mule would not
let him, holding him by his belt in its teeth, jerking and bumping
him back into the cold wet bed and, leaning, gave him a long swipe
across the face with its cold limber musculated tongue and he
waked to no fire, no coal even beneath where the almost-finished
paddle had been charring and something else prolonged and coldly
limber passed swiftly across his body where he lay in four inches of
water while the nose of the skiff alternately tugged at the grapevine
tied about his waist and bumped and shoved him back into the
water again. Then something else came up and began to nudge at
his ankle (the log, the oar, it was) even as he groped frantically for
the skiff, hearing the swift rustling going to and fro inside the hull
as the woman began to thrash about and scream. "Rats!" she cried.
"It's full of rats!"

"Lay still!" he cried. "It's just snakes. Cant you hold still long
enough for me to find the boat?" Then he found it, he got into it
with the unfinished paddle; again the thick muscular body convulsed under his foot; it did not strike; he would not have cared,
glaring astern where he could see a little—the faint outer luminosity
of the open water. He poled toward it, thrusting aside the snake-
looped branches, the bottom of the skiff resounding faintly to thick
solid plops, the woman shrieking steadily. Then the skiff was clear
of the trees, the mound, and now he could feel the bodies whipping
about his ankles and hear the rasp of them as they went over the

4. A mule, the offspring of a horse and
an ass, is usually sterile. The dream per-
tains to the sex life of convicts.

gunwale. He drew the log in and scooped it forward along the bottom of the boat and up and out; against the pallid water he could see three more of them in lashing convolutions before they vanished. "Shut up!" he cried. "Hush! I wish I was a snake so I could get out too!"

When once more the pale and heatless wafer disc of the early sun stared down at the skiff (whether they were moving or not the convict did not know) in its nimbus of fine cotton batting, the convict was hearing again that sound which he had heard twice before and would never forget—that sound of deliberate and irresistible and monstrously disturbed water. But this time he could not tell from what direction it came. It seemed to be everywhere, waxing and fading; it was like a phantom behind the mist, at one instant miles away, the next on the point of overwhelming the skiff within the next second; suddenly, in the instant he would believe (his whole weary body would spring and scream) that he was about to drive the skiff point-blank into it and with the unfinished paddle of the color and texture of sooty bricks, like something gnawed out of an old chimney by beavers and weighing twenty-five pounds, he would whirl the skiff frantically and find the sound dead ahead of him again. Then something bellowed tremendously above his head, he heard human voices, a bell jangled and the sound ceased and the mist vanished as when you draw your hand across a frosted pane, and the skiff now lay upon a sunny glitter of brown water flank to flank with, and about thirty yards away from, a steamboat. The decks were crowded and packed with men women and children sitting or standing beside and among a homely conglomeration of hurried furniture, who looked mournfully and silently down into the skiff while the convict and the man with a megaphone in the pilot house talked to each other in alternate puny shouts and roars above the chuffing of the reversed engines:

"What in hell are you trying to do? Commit suicide?"

"Which is the way to Vicksburg?"

"Vicksburg? Vicksburg? Lay alongside and come aboard."

"Will you take the boat too?"

"Boat? Boat?" Now the megaphone cursed, the roaring waves of blasphemy and biological supposition empty cavernous and bodiless in turn, as if the water, the air, the mist had spoken it, roaring the words then taking them back to itself and no harm done, no scar, no insult left anywhere. "If I took aboard every floating sardine can you sonabitchin mushrats want me to I wouldn't even have room forrard for a leadsman.[5] Come aboard! Do you expect me to hang here on stern engines till hell freezes?"

"I aint coming without the boat," the convict said. Now another voice spoke, so calm and mild and sensible that for a moment it

5. Crewman aboard ship who ascertains the depth of the water by lowering a piece of lead on a rope.

sounded more foreign and out of place then even the megaphone's bellowing and bodiless profanity:

"Where is it you are trying to go?"

"I aint trying," the convict said. "I'm going. Parchman." The man who had spoken last turned and appeared to converse with a third man in the pilot house. Then he looked down at the skiff again.

"Carnarvon?"

"What?" the convict said. "Parchman?"

"All right. We're going that way. We'll put you off where you can get home. Come aboard."

"The boat too?"

"Yes, yes. Come along. We're burning coal just to talk to you." So the convict came alongside then and watched them help the woman and baby over the rail and he came aboard himself, though he still held to the end of the vine-spliced painter until the skiff was hoisted onto the boiler deck. "My God," the man, the gentle one, said, "is that what you have been using for a paddle?"

"Yah," the convict said. "I lost the plank."

"The plank," the mild man, (the convict told how he seemed to whisper it), "the plank. Well. Come along and get something to eat. Your boat is all right now."

"I reckon I'll wait here," the convict said. Because now, he told them, he began to notice for the first time that the other people, the other refugees who crowded the deck, who had gathered in a quiet circle about the upturned skiff on which he and the woman sat, the grapevine painter wrapped several times about his wrist and clutched in his hand, staring at him and the woman with queer hot mournful intensity, were not white people—

"You mean niggers?" the plump convict said.

"No. Not Americans."

"Not Americans? You was clean out of *America* even?"

"I dont know," the tall one said. "They called it Atchafalaya."— Because after a while he said, "What?" to the man and the man did it again, gobble-gobble—

"Gobble-gobble?" the plump convict said.

"That's the way they talked," the tall one said. "Gobble-gobble, whang, caw-caw-to-to."—And he sat there and watched them gobbling at one another and then looking at him again, then they fell back and the mild man (he wore a Red Cross brassard) entered, followed by a waiter with a tray of food. The mild man carried two glasses of whiskey.

"Drink this," the mild man said. "This will warm you." The woman took hers and drank it but the convict told how he looked at his and thought, *I aint tasted whiskey in seven years.* He had not tasted it but once before that; it was at the still itself back in a pine hollow; he was seventeen, he had gone there with four companions, two of whom were grown men, one of twenty-two or -three, the other about forty; he remembered it. That is, he remembered perhaps a third of that evening—a fierce turmoil in the hell-colored firelight, the shock and shock of blows about his head (and likewise of his own fists on other hard bone), then the waking to a splitting and blinding sun in a place, a cowshed, he had never seen before and which later turned out to be twenty miles from his home. He said he thought of this and he looked about at the faces watching him and he said,

"I reckon not."

"Come, come," the mild man said. "Drink it."

"I dont want it."

"Nonsense," the mild man said. "I'm a doctor. Here. Then you can eat." So he took the glass and even then he hesitated but again the mild man said, "Come along, down with it; you're still holding us up," in that voice still calm and sensible but a little sharp too—the voice of a man who could keep calm and affable because he wasn't used to being crossed—and he drank the whiskey and even in the second between the sweet full fire in his belly and when it began to happen he was trying to say, "I tried to tell you! I tried to!" But it was too late now in the pallid sun-glare of the tenth day of terror and hopelessness and despair and impotence and rage and outrage and it was himself and the mule, his mule (they had let him name it—John Henry) which no man save he had plowed for five years now and whose ways and habits he knew and respected and who knew his ways and habits so well that each of them could anticipate the other's very movements and intentions; it was himself and the mule, the little gobbling faces flying before them, the familiar hard skull-bones shocking against his fists, his voice shouting, "Come on, John Henry! Plow them down! Gobble them down, boy!" even as the bright hot red wave turned back, meeting it joyously, happily, lifted, poised, then hurling through space, triumphant and yelling, then again the old shocking blow at the back of his head: he lay on the deck, flat on his back and pinned arm and leg and cold sober again, his nostrils gushing again, the mild man stooping over him with behind the thin rimless glasses the coldest eyes the convict had ever seen—eyes which the convict said were not looking at him but at the gushing blood with nothing in the world in them but complete impersonal interest.

"Good man," the mild man said. "Plenty of life in the old carcass yet, eh? Plenty of good red blood too. Anyone ever suggest to you that you were hemophilic?"[6] ("What?" the plump convict said. "Hemophilic? You know what that means?" The tall convict had his cigarette going now, his body jackknifed backward into the coffinlike space between the upper and lower bunks, lean, clean,

<hr />

6. Subject to a disease that causes uncontrollable bleeding. The convicts mistakenly think the term means bisexuality or sexual ambiguity.

motionless, the blue smoke wreathing across his lean dark aquiline shaven face. "That's a calf that's a bull and a cow at the same time."

"No, it aint," a third convict said. "It's a calf or a colt that aint neither one."

"Hell fire," the plump one said. "He's got to be one or the other to keep from drounding." He had never ceased to look at the tall one in the bunk; now he spoke to him again: "You let him call you that?") The tall one had done so. He did not answer the doctor (this was where he stopped thinking of him as the mild man) at all. He could not move either, though he felt fine, he felt better than he had in ten days. So they helped him to his feet and steadied him over and lowered him onto the upturned skiff beside the woman, where he sat bent forward, elbows on knees in the immemorial attitude, watching his own bright crimson staining the mudtrodden deck, until the doctor's clean clipped hand appeared under his nose with a phial.

"Smell," the doctor said. "Deep." The convict inhaled, the sharp ammoniac sensation burned up his nostrils and into his throat. "Again," the doctor said. The convict inhaled obediently. This time he choked and spat a gout of blood, his nose now had no more feeling than a toenail, other than it felt about the size of a ten-inch shovel, and as cold.

"I ask you to excuse me," he said. "I never meant—"

"Why?" the doctor said. "You put up as pretty a scrap against forty or fifty men as I ever saw. You lasted a good two seconds. Now you can eat something. Or do you think that will send you haywire again?"

They both ate, sitting on the skiff, the gobbling faces no longer watching them now, the convict gnawing slowly and painfully at the thick sandwich, hunched, his face laid sideways to the food and parallel to the earth as a dog chews; the steamboat went on. At noon there were bowls of hot soup and bread and more coffee; they ate this too, sitting side by side on the skiff, the grapevine still wrapped about the convict's wrist. The baby waked and nursed and slept again and they talked quietly:

"Was it Parchman he said he was going to take us?"

"That's where I told him I wanted to go."

"It never sounded exactly like Parchman to me. It sounded like he said something else." The convict had thought that too. He had been thinking about that fairly soberly ever since they boarded the steamboat and soberly indeed ever since he had remarked the nature of the other passengers, those men and women definitely a little shorter than he and with skin a little different in pigmentation from any sunburn, even though the eyes were sometimes blue or gray, who talked to one another in a tongue he had never heard before and who apparently did not understand his own, people the like of whom he had never seen about Parchman nor anywhere else and who he did not believe were going there or beyond there either. But after his hillbilly country fashion and kind he would not ask, because to his raising asking information was asking a favor and you did not ask favors of strangers; if they offered them perhaps you accepted and you expressed gratitude almost tediously recapitulant, but you did not ask. So he would watch and wait, as he had done before, and do or try to do to the best of his ability what the best of his judgment dictated.

So he waited, and in midafternoon the steamboat chuffed and thrust through a willow-choked gorge and emerged from it, and now the convict knew it was the River. He could believe it now—the tremendous reach, yellow and sleepy in the afternoon—("Because it's too big," he told them soberly. "Aint no flood in the world big enough to make it do more than stand a little higher so it can look back and see just where the flea is, just exactly where to scratch. It's the little ones, the little piddling creeks that run backward one day and forward the next and come busting down on a man full of dead mules and hen houses.")—and the steamboat moving up this now (*like a ant crossing a plate*, the convict thought, sitting beside the woman on the upturned skiff, the baby nursing again, apparently looking too out across the water where, a mile away on either hand, the twin lines of levee resembled parallel unbroken floating thread) and then it was nearing sunset and he began to hear, to notice, the voices of the doctor and of the man who had first bawled at him through the megaphone now bawling again from the pilot house overhead:

"Stop? Stop? Am I running a street car?"

"Stop for the novelty then," the doctor's pleasant voice said. "I dont know how many trips back and forth you have made in yonder nor how many of what you call mushrats you have fetched out. But this is the first time you ever had two people—no, three—who not only knew the name of some place they wished to go to but were actually trying to go there." So the convict waited while the sun slanted more and more and the steamboat-ant crawled steadily on across its vacant and gigantic plate turning more and more to copper. But he did not ask, he just waited. *Maybe it was Carrollton he said*, he thought. *It begun with a C.* But he did not believe that either. He did not know where he was, but he did know that this was not anywhere near the Carrollton he remembered from that day seven years ago when, shackled wrist to wrist with the deputy sheriff, he had passed through it on the train—the slow spaced repeated shattering banging of trucks where two railroads crossed, a random scattering of white houses tranquil among trees on green hills lush with summer, a pointing spire, the finger of the hand of God. But there was no river there. *And you aint never close to this river without knowing it*, he thought. *I dont care who you are nor where you have been all your life.* Then the head of the steamboat began to swing across the stream, its shadow swinging too, travelling long before it across the water, toward the vacant ridge of willow-massed earth empty of all life. There was nothing there at all, the convict could not even see either earth or water beyond it; it was as though the steamboat were about to crash slowly through the thin low frail willow barrier and embark into space, or lacking this, slow and back and fill and disembark him into space, granted it was about to disembark him, granted this was that place which was not near Parchman and was not Carrollton either, even though it did begin with C. Then he turned his head and saw the doctor stooping over the woman, pushing the baby's eyelid up with his forefinger, peering at it.

"Who else was there when he came?" the doctor said.

"Nobody," the convict said.

"Did it all yourselves, eh?"

"Yes," the convict said. Now the doctor stood up and looked at the convict.

"This is Carnarvon," he said.

"Carnarvon?" the convict said. "That aint—" Then he stopped, ceased. And now he told about that—the intent eyes as dispassionate as ice behind the rimless glasses, the clipped quick-tempered face that was not accustomed to being crossed or lied to either. ("Yes," the plump convict said. "That's what I was aiming to ask. Them clothes. Anybody would know them. How if this doctor was as smart as you claim he was—"

"I had slept in them for ten nights, mostly in the mud," the tall one said. "I had been rowing since midnight with that sapling oar I had tried to burn out that I never had time to scrape the soot off. But it's being scared and worried and then scared and then worried again in clothes for days and days and days that changes the way they look. I dont mean just your pants." He did not laugh. "Your face too. That doctor knowed."

"All right," the plump one said. "Go on.")

"I know it," the doctor said. "I discovered that while you were lying on the deck yonder sobering up again. Now dont lie to me. I dont like lying. This boat is going to New Orleans."

"No," the convict said immediately, quietly, with absolute finality. He could hear them again—the thuck-thuck-thuck on the water where an instant before he had been. But he was not thinking of the bullets. He had forgotten them, forgiven them. He was thinking of himself crouching, sobbing, panting before running again—the voice, the indictment, the cry of final and irrevocable repudiation of the old primal faithless Manipulator of all the lust and folly and injustice: *All in the world I wanted was just to surrender;* thinking of it, remembering it but without heat now, without passion now and briefer than an epitaph: *No. I tried that once. They shot at me.*

"So you dont want to go to New Orleans. And you didn't exactly plan to go to Carnarvon. But you will take Carnarvon in preference to New Orleans." The convict said nothing. The doctor looked at him, the magnified pupils like the heads of two bridge nails. "What were you in for? Hit him harder than you thought, eh?"

"No. I tried to rob a train."

"Say that again." The convict said it again. "Well? Go on. You dont say that in the year 1927 and just stop, man." So the convict told it, dispassionately too—about the magazines, the pistol which would not shoot, the mask and the dark lantern in which no draft had been arranged to keep the candle burning so that it died almost with the match but even then left the metal too hot to carry, won with subscriptions. *Only it aint my eyes or my mouth either he's watching,* he thought. *It's like he is watching the way my hair grows on my head.* "I see," the doctor said. "But something went wrong. But you've had plenty of time to think about it since. To decide what was wrong, what you failed to do."

"Yes," the convict said. "I've thought about it a right smart since."

"So next time you are not going to make that mistake."

"I dont know," the convict said. "There aint going to be a next time."

"Why? If you know what you did wrong, they wont catch you next time."

The convict looked at the doctor steadily. They looked at each other steadily; the two sets of eyes were not so different after all. "I reckon I see what you mean," the convict said presently. "I was eighteen then. I'm twenty-five now."

"Oh," the doctor said. Now (the convict tried to tell it) the doctor did not move, he just simply quit looking at the convict. He produced a pack of cheap cigarettes from his coat. "Smoke?" he said.

"I wouldn't care for none," the convict said.

"Quite," the doctor said in that affable clipped voice. He put the cigarettes away. "There has been conferred upon my race (the Medical race) also the power to bind and to loose, if not by Jehovah perhaps, certainly by the American Medical Association—on which incidentally, in this day of Our Lord, I would put my money, at any odds, at any amount, at any time. I dont know just how far out of bounds I am on this specific occasion but I think we'll put it to the touch." He cupped his hands to his mouth, toward the pilot house overhead. "Captain!" he shouted. "We'll put these three passengers ashore here." He turned to the convict again. "Yes," he said, "I think I shall let your native state lick its own vomit. Here." Again his hand emerged from his pocket, this time with a bill in it.

"No," the convict said.

"Come, come; I dont like to be disputed either."

"No," the convict said. "I aint got any way to pay it back."

"Did I ask you to pay it back?"

"No," the convict said. "I never asked to borrow it either."

So once more he stood on dry land, who had already been toyed with twice by that risible and concentrated power of water, once more than should have fallen to the lot of any one man, any one lifetime, yet for whom there was reserved still another unbelievable recapitulation, he and the woman standing on the empty levee, the sleeping child wrapped in the faded tunic and the grapevine painter still wrapped about the convict's wrist, watching the steamboat back away and turn and once more crawl onward up the platter-like reach of vacant water burnished more and more to copper, its trailing smoke roiling in slow copper-edged gouts, thinning out along the water, fading, stinking away across the vast serene desolation, the boat growing smaller and smaller until it did not seem to crawl at all but to hang stationary in the airy substanceless sunset, dissolving into nothing like a pellet of floating mud.

Then he turned and for the first time looked about him, behind him, recoiling, not through fear but through pure reflex and not physically but the soul, the spirit, that profound sober alert attentiveness of the hillman who will not ask anything of strangers, not even information, thinking quietly, No. *This aint Carrollton neither.* Because he now looked down the almost perpendicular landward slope of the levee through sixty feet of absolute space, upon a surface, a terrain flat as a waffle and of the color of a waffle or perhaps of the summer coat of a claybank horse and possessing that same piled density of a rug or peltry, spreading away without undulation yet with that curious appearance of imponderable solidity like fluid, broken here and there by thick humps of arsenical green which nevertheless still seemed to possess no height and by writhen veins of the color of ink which he began to suspect to be actual water but with judgment reserved, with judgment still reserved even when presently he was walking in it. That's what he said, told: So they went on. He didn't tell how he got the skiff singlehanded up the revetment and across the crown and down the opposite sixty-foot drop, he just said he went on, in a swirling cloud of mosquitoes like hot cinders, thrusting and plunging through the saw-edged grass which grew taller than his head and which whipped back at his arms and face like limber knives, dragging by the vine-spliced painter the skiff in which the woman sat, slogging and stumbling knee-deep in something less of earth than water, along one of those black winding channels less of water than earth: and then (he was in the skiff too now, paddling with the charred log, what footing there had been having given away beneath him without warning thirty minutes ago, leaving only the air-filled bubble of his jumper-back ballooning lightly on the twilit water until he rose to the surface and scrambled into the skiff) the house, the cabin a little larger than a horse-box, of cypress boards and an iron roof, rising on ten-foot stilts slender as spiders' legs, like a shabby and death-stricken (and probably poisonous) wading creature which had got that far into that flat waste and died with nothing nowhere in reach or sight to lie down upon, a pirogue[7] tied to the foot of a crude lad-der, a man standing in the open door holding a lantern (it was that dark now) above his head, gobbling down at them.

He told it—of the next eight or nine or ten days, he did not re-member which, while the four of them—himself and the woman and baby and the little wiry man with rotting teeth and soft wild bright eyes like a rat or a chipmunk, whose language neither of them could understand—lived in the room and a half. He did not tell it that way, just as he apparently did not consider it worth the breath to tell how he had got the hundred-and-sixty-pound skiff single-handed up and across and down the sixty-foot levee. He just said, "After a while we come to a house and we stayed there eight or nine days then they blew up the levee with dynamite so we had to leave." That was all. But he remembered it, but quietly now, with the cigar now, the good one the Warden had given him (though not lighted yet) in his peaceful and steadfast hand, re-membering that first morning when he waked on the thin pallet be-side his host (the woman and baby had the one bed) with the fierce sun already latticed through the warped rough planking of the wall, and stood on the rickety porch looking out upon that flat fe-cund waste neither earth nor water, where even the senses doubted which was which, which rich and massy air and which mazy and impalpable vegetation, and thought quietly, *He must do something here to eat and live. But I dont know what. And until I can go on again, until I can find where I am and how to pass that town with-out them seeing me I will have to help him do it so we can eat and live too, and I dont know what.* And he had a change of clothing too, almost at once on that first morning, not telling any more than he had about the skiff and the levee how he had begged borrowed or bought from the man whom he had not laid eyes on twelve hours ago and with whom on the day he saw him for the last time he still could exchange no word, the pair of dungaree pants which even the Cajan[8] had discarded as no longer wearable, filthy, button-less, the legs slashed and frayed into fringe like that on an 1890 hammock, in which he stood naked from the waist up and holding out to her the mud-caked and soot-stained jumper and overall when the woman waked on that first morning in the crude bunk nailed into one corner and filled with dried grass, saying, "Wash them. Good. I want all them stains out. All of them."

"But the jumper," she said. "Aint he got ere old shirt too? That

7. Dug-out canoe.
8. In Louisiana, a person descended

from the French Canadians of Nova Scotia. Usually spelled "Cajun."

sun and them mosquitoes—" But he did not even answer, and she
said no more either, though when he and the Cajan returned at
dark the garments were clean, stained a little still with the old mud
and soot, but clean, resembling again what they were supposed to
resemble as (his arms and back already a fiery red which would be
blisters by tomorrow) he spread the garments out and examined
them and then rolled them up carefully in a six-months-old New
Orleans paper and thrust the bundle behind a rafter, where it remained while day followed day and the blisters on his back broke
and suppurated and he would sit with his face expressionless as a
wooden mask beneath the sweat while the Cajan doped his back
with something on a filthy rag from a filthy saucer, she still saying
nothing since she too doubtless knew what his reason was, not from
that rapport of the wedded conferred upon her by the two weeks
during which they had jointly suffered all the crises emotional social
economic and even moral which do not always occur even in the ordinary fifty married years (the old married: you have seen them, the
electroplate reproductions, the thousand identical coupled faces
with only a collarless stud or a fichu out of Louisa Alcott[9] to de-
note the sex, looking in pairs like the winning braces of dogs after a
field trial, out from among the packed columns of disaster and
alarm and baseless assurance and hope and incredible insensitivity
and insulation from tomorrow propped by a thousand morning
sugar bowls or coffee urns; or singly, rocking on porches or sitting in
the sun beneath the tobacco-stained porticoes of a thousand county
courthouses, as though with the death of the other having inherited
a sort of rejuvenescence, immortality; relict, they take a new lease
on breath and seem to live forever, as though that flesh which the
old ceremony or ritual had morally purified and made legally one
had actually become so with long tedious habit and he or she who
entered the ground first took all of it with him or her, leaving only
the old permanent enduring bone, free and trameless)—not because of this but because she too had stemmed at some point from
the same dim hill-bred Abraham.

So the bundle remained behind the rafter and day followed day
while he and his partner (he was in partnership now with his host,
hunting alligators on shares, on the halvers he called it—"Halvers?"
the plump convict said. "How could you make a business agreement
with a man you claim you couldn't even talk to?"

"I never had to talk to him," the tall one said. "Money aint got
but one language.") departed at dawn each day, at first together in
the pirogue but later singly, the one in the pirogue and the other in
the skiff, the one with the battered and pitted rifle, the other
with the knife and a piece of knotted rope and a lightwood club the

9. Three-cornered cape or neckerchief worn by 19th-century women such as those in the fiction of Louisa May Alcott (1832–88).

size and weight and shape of a Thuringian mace,[1] stalking their pleistocene nightmares up and down the secret inky channels which writhed the flat brass-colored land. He remembered that too: that first morning when turning in the sunrise from the rickety platform he saw the hide nailed drying to the wall and stopped dead, looking at it quietly, thinking quietly and soberly, *So that's it. That's what he does in order to eat and live,* knowing it was a hide, a skin, but from what animal, by association, ratiocination or even memory of any picture out of his dead youth, he did not know but knowing that it was the reason, the explanation, for the little lost spider-legged house (which had already begun to die, to rot from the legs upward almost before the roof was nailed on) set in that teeming and myriad desolation, enclosed and lost within the furious embrace of flowing mare earth and stallion sun, divining through pure rapport of kind for kind, hillbilly and bayou rat, the two one and identical because of the same grudged dispensation and niggard fate of hard and unceasing travail not to gain future security, a balance in the bank or even in a buried soda can for slothful and easy old age, but just permission to endure and endure to buy air to feel and sun to drink for each's little while, thinking (the convict), *Well, anyway I am going to find out what it is sooner than I expected to,* and did so, re-entered the house where the woman was just waking in the one sorry built-in straw-filled bunk which the Cajan had surrendered to her, and ate the breakfast (the rice, a semi-liquid mess violent with pepper and mostly fish considerably high, the chicory-thickened coffee) and, shirtless, followed the little scuttling bobbing bright-eyed rotten-toothed man down the crude ladder and into the pirogue. He had never seen a pirogue either and he believed that it would not remain upright—not that it was light and precariously balanced with its open side upward but that there was inherent in the wood, the very log, some dynamic and unsleeping natural law, almost will, which its present position outraged and violated—yet accepting this too as he had the fact that that hide had belonged to something larger than any calf or hog and that anything which looked like that on the outside would be more than likely to have teeth and claws too, accepting this, squatting in the pirogue, clutching both gunwales, rigidly immobile as though he had an egg filled with nitroglycerin in his mouth and scarcely breathing, thinking, *If that's it, then I can do it too and even if he cant tell me how I reckon I can watch him and find out.* And he did this too, he remembered it, quietly even yet, thinking, *I thought that was how to do it and I reckon I would still think that even if I had it to do again now for the first time*—the brazen day already fierce upon his naked back, the crooked channel like a voluted thread of ink, the

---

1. Spiked clublike weapon and ceremonial symbol of authority, belonging to the inhabitants of Thuringia in central Germany. "Pleistocene": geologic period in the Cenozoic era.

pirogue moving steadily to the paddle which both entered and left
the water without a sound; then the sudden cessation of the paddle
behind him and the fierce hissing gobble of the Cajan at his back
and he squatting bate-breathed and with that intense immobility of
complete sobriety of a blind man listening while the frail wooden
shell stole on at the dying apex of its own parted water. Afterward
he remembered the rifle too—the rust-pitted single-shot weapon with
a clumsily wired stock and a muzzle you could have driven a whiskey
cork into, which the Cajan had brought into the boat—but not
now; now he just squatted, crouched, immobile, breathing with infinitesimal care, his sober unceasing gaze going here and there constantly as he thought, *What? What? I not only dont know what I
am looking for, I dont even know where to look for it.* Then he felt
the motion of the pirogue as the Cajan moved and then the tense
gobbling hissing actually, hot rapid and repressed, against his neck
and ear, and glancing downward saw projecting between his own
arm and body from behind, the Cajan's hand holding the knife,
and glaring up again saw the flat thick spit of mud which as he
looked at it divided and became a thick mud-colored log which in
turn seemed, still immobile, to leap suddenly against his retinae in
three—no, four—dimensions: volume, solidity, shape, and another:
not fear but pure and intense speculation and he looking at the
scaled motionless shape, thinking not, *It looks dangerous* but *It
looks big,* thinking, *Well, maybe a mule standing in a lot looks big
to a man that never walked up to one with a halter before,* thinking,
Only if he could just tell me what to do it would save time, the
pirogue drawing nearer now, creeping now, with no ripple now even
and it seemed to him that he could even hear his companion's held
breath and he taking the knife from the other's hand now and not
even thinking this since it was too fast, a flash; it was not a surrender, not a resignation, it was too calm, it was a part of him, he had
drunk it with his mother's milk and lived with it all his life: *After
all a man cant only do what he has to do, with what he has to do it
with, with what he has learned, to the best of his judgment. And I
reckon a hog is still a hog, no matter what it looks like. So here
goes,* sitting still for an instant longer until the bow of the pirogue
grounded lighter than the falling of a leaf and stepped out of it and
paused just for one instant while the words *It does look big* stood
for just a second, unemphatic and trivial, somewhere where some
fragment of his attention could see them and vanished, and stooped
straddling, the knife driving even as he grapsed the near foreleg,
this all in the same instant when the lashing tail struck him a terrific blow upon the back. But the knife was home, he knew that
even on his back in the mud, the weight of the thrashing beast
longwise upon him, its ridged back clutched to his stomach, his arm
about its throat, the hissing head clamped against his jaw, the furious tail lashing and flailing, the knife in his other hand probing

for the life and finding it, the hot fierce gush: and now sitting beside the profound up-bellied carcass, his head again between his knees in the old attitude while his own blood freshened the other which drenched him, thinking, *It's my durn nose again.*

So he sat there, his head, his streaming face, bowed between his knees in an attitude not of dejection but profoundly bemused, contemplative, while the shrill voice of the Cajan seemed to buzz at him from an enormous distance; after a time he even looked up at the antic wiry figure bouncing hysterically about him, the face wild and grimacing, the voice gobbling and high; while the convict, holding his face carefully slanted so the blood would run free, looked at him with the cold intentness of a curator or custodian paused before one of his own glass cases, the Cajan threw up the rifle, cried "Boom-boom-boom!" flung it down and in pantomime re-enacted the recent scene then whirled his hands again, crying "Magnifique! Magnifique, Cent d'argent! Mille d'argent! Tout l'argent sous le ciel de Dieu!"[2] But the convict was already looking down again, cupping the coffee-colored water to his face, watching the constant bright carmine marble it, thinking, *It's a little late to be telling me that now,* and not even thinking this long because presently they were in the pirogue again, the convict squatting again with that unbreathing rigidity as though he were trying by holding his breath to decrease his very weight, the bloody skin in the bows before him and he looking at it, thinking, *And I cant even ask him how much my half will be.*

But this not for long either, because as he was to tell the plump convict later, money has but one language. He remembered that too (they were at home now, the skin spread on the platform, where for the woman's benefit now the Cajan once more went through the pantomime—the gun which was not used, the hand-to-hand battle; for the second time the invisible alligator was slain amid cries, the victor rose and found this time that not even the woman was watching him. She was looking at the once more swollen and inflamed face of the convict. "You mean it kicked you right in the face?" she said.

"Nah," the convict said harshly, savagely. "It never had to. I done seem to got to where if that boy was to shoot me in the tail with a bean blower my nose would bleed.")—remembered that too but he did not try to tell it. Perhaps he could not have—how two people who could not even talk to one another made an agreement which both not only understood but which each knew the other would hold true and protect (perhaps for this reason) better than any written and witnessed contract. They even discussed and agreed somehow that they should hunt separately, each in his own vessel, to double the chances of finding prey. But this was easy: the con-

2. "Magnificent! Magnificent, a hundred   silver under God's heaven!"
in silver! A thousand in silver! All the

vict could almost understand the words in which the Cajan said, "You do not need me and the rifle; we will only hinder you, be in your way." And more than this, they even agreed about the second rifle: that there was someone, it did not matter who—friend, neighbor, perhaps one in business in that line—from whom they could rent a second rifle; in their two patois, the one bastard English, the other bastard French—the one volatile, with his wild bright eyes and his voluble mouth full of stumps of teeth, the other sober, almost grim, swollen-faced and with his naked back blistered and scoriated like so much beef—they discussed this, squatting on either side of the pegged-out hide like two members of a corporation facing each other across a mahogany board table, and decided against it, the convict deciding: "I reckon not," he said. "I reckon if I had knowed enough to wait to start out with a gun, I still would. But since I done already started out without one, I dont reckon I'll change." Because it was a question of the money in terms of time, days. (Strange to say, that was the one thing which the Cajan could not tell him: how much the half would be. But the convict knew it was half.) He had so little of them. He would have to move on soon, thinking (the convict), *All this durn foolishness will stop soon and I can get on back,* and then suddenly he found that he was thinking, *Will have to get on back,* and he became quite still and looked about at the rich strange desert which surrounded him, in which he was temporarily lost in peace and hope and into which the last seven years had sunk like so many trivial pebbles into a pool, leaving no ripple, and he thought quietly, with a kind of bemused amazement, *Yes. I reckon I had done forgot how good making money was. Being let to make it.*

So he used no gun, his the knotted rope and the Thuringian mace, and each morning he and the Cajan took their separate ways in the two boats to comb and creep the secret channels about the lost land from (or out of) which now and then still other pint-sized dark men appeared gobbling, abruptly and as though by magic from nowhere, in other hollowed logs, to follow quietly and watch him at his single combats—men named Tine and Toto and Theule, who were not much larger than and looked a good deal like the muskrats which the Cajan (the host did this too, supplied the kitchen too, he expressed this too like the rifle business, in his own tongue, the convict comprehending this too as though it had been English: "Do not concern yourself about food, O Hercules. Catch alligators; I will supply the pot.") took now and then from traps as you take a shoat pig at need from a pen, and varied the eternal rice and fish (the convict did tell this: how at night, in the cabin, the door and one sashless window battened against mosquitoes—a form, a ritual, as empty as crossing the fingers or knocking on wood—sitting beside the bug-swirled lantern on the plank table in a temperature close to blood heat he would look down at the swimming segment of meat on his sweating plate and think, *It must be Theule. He was the fat one.*)—day following day, unemphatic and identical, each like the one before and the one which would follow while his theoretical half of a sum to be reckoned in pennies, dollars, or tens of dollars he did not know, mounted—the mornings when he set forth to find waiting for him like the *matador* his *aficionados* the small clump of constant and deferential pirogues, the hard noons when ringed half about by little motionless shells he fought his solitary combats, the evenings, the return, the pirogues departing one by one into inlets and passages which during the first few days he could not even distinguish, then the platform in the twilight where before the static woman and the usually nursing infant and the one or two bloody hides of the day's take the Cajan would perform his ritualistic victorious pantomime before the two growing rows of knife-marks in one of the boards of the wall; then the nights when, the woman and child in the single bunk and the Cajan already snoring on the pallet and the reeking lantern set close, he (the convict) would sit on his naked heels, sweating steadily, his face worn and calm, immersed and indomitable, his bowed back raw and savage as beef beneath the suppurant old blisters and the fierce welts of tails, and scrape and chip at the charred sapling which was almost a paddle now, pausing now and then to raise his head while the cloud of mosquitoes about it whined and whirled, to stare at the wall before him until after a while the crude boards themselves must have dissolved away and let his blank unseeing gaze go on and on unhampered, through the rich oblivious darkness, beyond it even perhaps, even perhaps beyond the seven wasted years during which, so he had just realised, he had been permitted to toil but not to work. Then he would retire himself, he would take a last look at the rolled bundle behind the rafter and blow out the lantern and lie down as he was beside his snoring partner, to lie sweating (on his stomach, he could not bear the touch of anything to his back) in the whining ovenlike darkness filled with the forlorn bellowing of alligators, thinking not, *They never gave me time to learn* but *I had forgot how good it is to work.*

Then on the tenth day it happened. It happened for the third time. At first he refused to believe it, not that he felt that now he had served out and discharged his apprenticeship to mischance, had with the birth of the child reached and crossed the crest of his Golgotha[3] and would now be, possibly not permitted so much as ignored, to descend the opposite slope free-wheeling. That was not his feeling at all. What he declined to accept was the fact that a power, a force such as that which had been consistent enough to concentrate upon him with deadly undeviation for weeks, should with all the wealth of cosmic violence and disaster to draw from, have been so barren of invention and imagination, so lacking in

3. Place outside Jerusalem where Christ was crucified.

pride of artistry and craftmanship, as to repeat itself twice. Once he had accepted, twice he even forgave, but three times he simply declined to believe, particularly when he was at last persuaded to realise that this third time was to be instigated not by the blind potency of volume and motion but by human direction and hands: that now the cosmic joker, foiled twice, had stooped in its vindictive concentration to the employing of dynamite.

He did not tell that. Doubtless he did not know himself how it happened, what was happening. But he doubtless remembered it (but quietly above the thick rich-colored pristine cigar in his clean steady hand), what he knew, divined of it. It would be evening, the ninth evening, he and the woman on either side of their host's empty place at the evening meal, he hearing the voices from without but not ceasing to eat, still chewing steadily, because it would be the same as though he were seeing them anyway—the two or three or four pirogues floating on the dark water beneath the platform on which the host stood, the voices gobbling and jabbering, incomprehensible and filled not with alarm and not exactly with rage or ever perhaps absolute surprise but rather just cacophony like those of disturbed marsh fowl, he (the convict) not ceasing to chew but just looking up quietly and maybe without a great deal of interrogation or surprise too as the Cajan burst in and stood before them, wild-faced, glaring, his blackened teeth gaped against the inky orifice of his distended mouth, watching (the convict) while the Cajan went through his violent pantomime of violent evacuation, ejection, scooping something invisible into his arms and hurling it out and downward and in the instant of completing the gesture changing from instigator to victim of that which he had set into pantomimic motion, clasping his head and, bowed over and not otherwise moving, seeming to be swept on and away before it, crying "Boom! Boom! Boom!", the convict watching him, his jaw not chewing now, though for just that moment, thinking, *What? What is it he is trying to tell me?* thinking (this a flash too, since he could not have expressed this, and hence did not even know that he have ever thought it) that though his life had been cast here, circumscribed by this environment, accepted by this environment and accepting it in turn (and he had done well here—this quietly, soberly indeed, if he had been able to phrase it, think it instead of merely knowing it—better than he had ever done, who had not even known until now how good work, making money, could be), yet it was not his life, he still and would ever be no more than the water bug upon the surface of the pond, the plumbless and lurking depths of which he would never know, his only actual contact with it being the instants when on lonely and glaring mudspits under the pitiless sun and amphitheatred by his motionless and riveted semicircle of watching pirogues, he accepted the gambit which he had not elected, entered the lashing radius of the armed tail and beat at the thrashing and hissing head with his lightwood club, or this failing, embraced without hesitation the armored body itself with the frail web of flesh and bone in which he walked and lived and sought the raging life with an eight-inch knife-blade.

So he and the woman merely watched the Cajan as he acted out the whole charade of eviction—the little wiry man gesticulant and wild, his hysterical shadow leaping and falling upon the rough wall as he went through the pantomime of abandoning the cabin, gathering in pantomime his meagre belongings from the walls and corners—objects which no other man would want and only some power or force like blind water or earthquake or fire would ever dispossess him of, the woman watching too, her mouth slightly open upon a mass of chewed food, on her face an expression of placid astonishment, saying, "What? What's he saying?"

"I dont know," the convict said. "But I reckon if it's something we ought to know we will find it out when it's ready for us to." Because he was not alarmed, though by now he had read the other's meaning plainly enough. *He's fixing to leave,* he thought. *He's telling me to leave too*—this later, after they had quitted the table and the Cajan and the woman had gone to bed and the Cajan had risen from the pallet and approached the convict and once more went through the pantomime of abandoning the cabin, this time as one repeats a speech which may have been misunderstood, tediously, carefully repetitional as to a child, seeming to hold the convict with one hand while he gestured, talked, with the other, gesturing as though in single syllables, the convict (squatting, the knife open and the almost-finished paddle across his lap) watching, nodding his head, even speaking in English: "Yah; sure. You bet. I got you."—trimming again at the paddle but no faster, with no more haste than on any other night, serene in his belief that when the time came for him to know whatever it was, that would take care of itself, having already and without even knowing it, even before the possibility, the question, ever arose, declined, refused to accept even the thought of moving also, thinking about the hides, thinking, *If there was just some way he could tell me where to carry my share to get the money* but thinking this only for an instant between two delicate strokes of the blade because almost at once he thought, *I reckon as long as I can catch them I wont have no big trouble finding whoever it is that will buy them.*

So the next morning he helped the Cajan load his few belongings —the pitted rifle, a small bundle of clothing (again they traded, who could not even converse with one another, this time the few cooking vessels, a few rusty traps by definite allocation, and something embracing and abstractional which included the stove, the crude bunk, the house or its occupancy—something—in exchange for one alligator hide)—into the pirogue, then, squatting and as two children divide sticks they divided the hides, separating them into two piles, one-for-me-and-one-for-you, two-for-me-and-two-for-you, and the Cajan loaded his share and shoved away from the platform and paused again, though this time he only put the paddle down, gathered something invisibly into his two hands and flung it violently upward, crying "Boom? Boom?" on a rising inflection, nodding violently to the half-naked and savagely scoriated man on the platform who stared with a sort of grim equability back at him and said, "Sure. Boom. Boom." Then the Cajan went on. He did not look back. They watched him, already paddling rapidly, or the woman did; the convict had already turned.

"Maybe he was trying to tell us to leave too," she said.

"Yah," the convict said. "I thought of that last night. Hand me the paddle." She fetched it to him—the sapling, the one he had been trimming at nightly, not quite finished yet though one more evening would do it (he had been using a spare one of the Cajan's. The other had offered to let him keep it, to include it perhaps with the stove and the bunk and the cabin's freehold, but the convict had declined. Perhaps he had computed it by volume against so much alligator hide, this weighed against one more evening with the tedious and careful blade.)—and he departed too with his knotted rope and mace, in the opposite direction, as though not only not content with refusing to quit the place he had been warned against, he must establish and affirm the irrevocable finality of his refusal by penetrating even further and deeper into it. And then and without warning the high fierce drowsing of his solitude gathered itself and struck at him.

He could not have told this if he had tried—this not yet mid-morning and he going on, alone for the first time, no pirogue emerging anywhere to fall in behind him, but he had not expected this anyway, he knew that the others would have departed too; it was not this, it was his very solitude, his desolation which was now his alone and in full since he had elected to remain; the sudden cessation of the paddle, the skiff shooting on for a moment yet while he thought, *What? What?* Then, *No. No. No,* as the silence and solitude and emptiness roared down upon him in a jeering bellow: and now reversed, the skiff spun violently on its heel, he the betrayed driving furiously back toward the platform where he knew it was already too late, that citadel where the very crux and dear breath of his life—the being allowed to work and earn money, that right and privilege which he believed he had earned to himself unaided, asking no favor of anyone or anything save the right to be let alone to pit his will and strength against the sauric[4] protagonist of a land, a region, which he had not asked to be projected into—was being threatened, driving the homemade paddle in grim fury, coming in sight of the platform at last and seeing the motor launch lying alongside it with no surprise at all but actually with a kind of pleas-

4. Prehistoric, pertaining to the era of the dinosaurs.

ure as though at a visible justification of his outrage and fear, the privilege of saying *I told you so* to his own affronting, driving on toward it in a dreamlike state in which there seemed to be no progress at all, in which, unimpeded and suffocating, he strove dreamily with a weightless oar, with muscles without strength or resiliency, at a medium without resistance, seeming to watch the skiff creep infinitesimally across the sunny water and up to the platform while a man in the launch (there were five of them in all) gobbled at him in that same tongue he had been hearing constantly now for ten days and still knew no word of, just as a second man, followed by the woman carrying the baby and dressed again for departure in the faded tunic and the sunbonnet, emerged from the house, carrying (the man carried several other things but the convict saw nothing else) the paper-wrapped bundle which the convict had put behind the rafter ten days ago and no other hand had touched since, he (the convict) on the platform too now, holding the skiff's painter in one hand and the bludgeon-like paddle in the other, contriving to speak to the woman at last in a voice dreamy and suffocating and incredibly calm: "Take it away from him and carry it back into the house."

"So you can talk English, can you?" the man in the launch said. "Why didn't you come out like they told you to last night?"

"Out?" the convict said. Again he even looked, glared, at the man in the launch, contriving even again to control his voice: "I aint got time to take trips. I'm busy," already turning to the woman again, his mouth already open to repeat as the dreamy buzzing voice of the man came to him and he turning once more, in a terrific and absolutely unbearable exasperation, crying, "Flood? What flood? Hell a mile, it's done passed me twice months ago! It's gone! What flood?" and then (he did not think this in actual words either but he knew it, suffered that flashing insight into his own character or destiny: how there was a peculiar quality of repetitiveness about his present fate, how not only the almost seminal crises recurred with a certain monotony, but the very physical circumstances followed a stupidly unimaginative pattern) the man in the launch said, "Take him" and he was on his feet for a few minutes yet, lashing and striking in panting fury, then once more on his back on hard unyielding planks while the four men swarmed over him in a fierce wave of hard bones and panting curses and at last the thin dry vicious snapping of handcuffs.

"Damn it, are you mad?" the man in the launch said. "Cant you understand they are going to dynamite that levee at noon today?[5] —Come on," he said to the others. "Get him aboard. Let's get out of here."

"I want my hides and boat," the convict said.

5. Levees are sometimes dynamited to flood one area so as to protect a more seriously threatened region downstream.

"Damn your hides," the man in the launch said. "If they dont get that levee blowed pretty soon you can hunt plenty more of them on the capitol steps at Baton Rouge. And this is all the boat you will need and you can say your prayers about it."

"I aint going without my boat," the convict said. He said it calmly and with complete finality, so calm, so final that for almost a minute nobody answered him, they just stood looking quietly down at him as he lay, half-naked, blistered and scarred, helpless and manacled hand and foot, on his back, delivering his ultimatum in a voice peaceful and quiet as that in which you talk to your bedfellow before going to sleep. Then the man in the launch moved; he spat quietly over the side and said in a voice as calm and quiet as the convict's:

"All right. Bring his boat." They helped the woman, carrying the baby and the paper-wrapped parcel, into the launch. Then they helped the convict to his feet and into the launch too, the shackles on his wrists and ankles clashing. "I'd unlock you if you'd promise to behave yourself," the man said. The convict did not answer this at all.

"I want to hold the rope," he said.

"The rope?"

"Yes," the convict said. "The rope." So they lowered him into the stern and gave him the end of the painter after it had passed the towing cleat, and they went on. The convict did not look back. But then, he did not look forward either, he lay half sprawled, his shackled legs before him, the end if the skiff's painter in one shackled hand. The launch made two other stops; when the hazy wafer of the intolerable sun began to stand once more directly overhead there were fifteen people in the launch; and then the convict, sprawled and motionless, saw the flat brazen land begin to rise and become a greenish-black mass of swamp, bearded and convoluted, this in turn stopping short off and there spread before him an expanse of water embraced by a blue dissolution of shoreline and glittering thinly under the noon, larger than he had ever seen before, the sound of the launch's engine ceasing, the hull sliding on behind its fading bow-wave. "What are you doing?" the leader said.

"It's noon," the helmsman said. "I thought we might hear the dynamite." So they all listened, the launch lost of all forward motion, rocking slightly, the glitter-broken small waves slapping and whispering at the hull, but no sound, no tremble even, came anywhere under the fierce hazy sky; the long moment gathered itself and turned on and noon was past. "All right," the leader said. "Let's go." The engine started again, the hull began to gather speed. The leader came aft and stooped over the convict, key in hand. "I guess you'll have to behave now, whether you want to or not," he said, unlocking the manacles. "Wont you?"

"Yes," the convict said. They went on; after a time the shore vanished completely and a little sea got up. The convict was free now but he lay as before, the end of the skiff's painter in his hand, bent now with three or four turns about his wrist; he turned his head now and then to look back at the towing skiff as it slewed and bounced in the launch's wake; now and then he even looked out over the lake, the eyes alone moving, the face grave and expressionless, thinking, *This is a greater immensity of water, of waste and desolation, than I have ever seen before;* perhaps not; thinking three or four hours later, the shoreline raised again and broken into a clutter of sailing sloops and power cruisers, *These are more boats than I believed existed, a maritime race of which I also had no cognizance* or perhaps not thinking it but just watching as the launch opened the shore gut of the ship canal, the low smoke of the city beyond it, then a wharf, the launch slowing in; a quiet crowd of people watching with that same forlorn passivity he had seen before and whose race he did recognise even though he had not seen Vicksburg when he passed it—the brand, the unmistakable hallmark of the violently homeless, he more so than any, who would have permitted no man to call him one of them.

"All right," the leader said to him. "Here you are."

"The boat," the convict said.

"You've got it. What do you want me to do—give you a receipt for it?"

"No," the convict said. "I just want the boat."

"Take it. Only you ought to have a bookstrap or something to carry it in." ("Carry it in?" the plump convict said. "Carry it where? Where would you have to carry it?")

He (the tall one) told that: how he and the woman disembarked and how one of the men helped him haul the skiff up out of the water and how he stood there with the end of the painter wrapped around his wrist and the man bustled up, saying, "All right. Next load! Next load!" and how he told this man too about the boat and the man cried, "Boat? Boat?" and how he (the convict) went with them when they carried the skiff over and racked, berthed, it with the others and how he lined himself up by a Coca-Cola sign and the arch of a draw bridge so he could find the skiff again quick when he returned, and how he and the woman (he carrying the paper-wrapped parcel) were herded into a truck and after a while the truck began to run in traffic, between close houses, then there was a big building, an armory—

"Armory?" the plump one said. "You mean a jail."

"No. It was a kind of warehouse, with people with bundles laying on the floor." And how he thought maybe his partner might be there and how he even looked about for the Cajan while waiting for a chance to get back to the door again, where the soldier was and how he got back to the door at last, the woman behind him and his chest actually against the dropped rifle.

"Gwan, gwan," the soldier said. "Get back. They'll give you some clothes in a minute. You cant walk around the streets that way. And something to eat too. Maybe your kinfolks will come for you by that time." And he told that too: how the woman said, "Maybe if you told him you had some kinfolks here he would let us out." And how he did not; he could not have expressed this either, it too deep, too ingrained; he had never yet had to think it into words through all the long generations of himself—his hillman's sober and jealous respect not for truth but for the power, the strength, of lying—not to be niggared with lying but rather to use it with respect and even care, delicate quick and strong, like a fine and fatal blade. And how they fetched him clothes—a blue jumper and overalls, and then food too (a brisk starched young woman saying, "But the baby must be bathed, cleaned. It will die if you dont," and the woman saying, "Yessum. He might holler some, he aint never been bathed before. But he's a good baby.") and now it was night, the unshaded bulbs harsh and savage and forlorn above the snorers and he rising, gripping the woman awake, and then the window. He told that: how there were doors in plenty, leading he did not know where, but he had a hard time finding a window they could use but he found one at last, he carrying the parcel and the baby too while he climbed through first—"You ought to tore up a sheet and slid down it," the plump convict said. But he needed no sheet, there were cobbles under his feet now, in the rich darkness. The city was there too but he had not seen it yet and would not— the low constant glare; Bienville had stood there too, it had been the figment of an emasculate also calling himself Napoleon but no more, Andrew Jackson had found it one step from Pennsylvania Avenue.[6] But the convict found it considerably further than one step back to the ship canal and the skiff, the Coca-Cola sign dim now, the draw bridge arching spidery against the jonquil sky at dawn: nor did he tell, any more than about the sixty-foot levee, how he got the skiff back into the water. The lake was behind him now; there was but one direction he could go. When he saw the River again he knew it at once. He should have; it was now ineradicably a part of his past, his life; it would be a part of what he would bequeath, if that were in store for him. But four weeks later it would look different from what it did now, and did: he (the Old Man) had recovered from his debauch, back in banks again, the

6. The narrator compares the convict to three famous heroes associated with New Orleans. Sieur de Bienville (Jean Baptiste Lemoyne, 1680–1768) founded New Orleans in 1718 and was twice Governor of colonial Louisiana. Napoleon Bonaparte (1769–1821), Emperor of France 1804–15, dreamed (his "figment") of ruling a French empire in America until military affairs forced him to sell the Louisiana territory to the United States in 1803. When forced into exile in 1815 he hoped to come to the United States, but was imprisoned on St. Helena Island. General Andrew Jackson (1767–1845) defeated the British at the Battle of Orleans in 1815; his ensuing fame led to his election to the U.S. presidency in 1828 and residence in the White House on Pennsylvania Avenue in Washington, D.C.

Old Man, rippling placidly toward the sea, brown and rich as chocolate between levees whose inner faces were wrinkled as though in a
frozen and aghast amazement, crowned with the rich green of summer in the willows; beyond them, sixty feet below, slick mules
squatted against the broad pull of middle-busters in the richened
soil which would not need to be planted, which would need only to
be shown a cotton seed to sprout and make; there would be the
symmetric miles of strong stalks by July, purple bloom in August, in
September the black fields snowed over, spilled, the middles
dragged smooth by the long sacks, the long black limber hands
plucking, the hot air filled with the whine of gins,[7] the September
air then but now June air heavy with locust and (the towns) the
smell of new paint and the sour smell of the paste which holds wall
paper—the towns, the villages, the little lost wood landings on stilts
on the inner face of the levee, the lower storeys bright and rank
under the new paint and paper and even the marks on spile and
post and tree of May's raging water-height fading beneath each
bright silver gust of summer's loud and inconstant rain; there was a
store at the levee's lip, a few saddled and rope-bridled mules in the
sleepy dust, a few dogs, a handful of Negroes sitting on the steps beneath the chewing tobacco and malaria medicine signs, and three
white men, one of them a deputy sheriff canvassing for votes to
beat his superior (who had given him his job) in the August primary, all pausing to watch the skiff emerge from the glitter-glare of
the afternoon water and approach and land, a woman carrying a
child stepping out, then a man, a tall man who, approaching,
proved to be dressed in a faded but recently washed and quite clean
suit of penitentiary clothing, stopping in the dust where the mules
dozed and watching with pale cold humorless eyes while the deputy
sheriff was still making toward his armpit that gesture which everyone present realised was to have produced a pistol in one flashing
motion for a considerable time while still nothing came of it. It was
apparently enough for the newcomer, however.

"You a officer?" he said.

"You damn right I am," the deputy said. "Just let me get this
damn gun—"

"All right," the other said. "Yonder's your boat, and here's the
woman. But I never did find that bastard on the cottonhouse."

One of the Governor's young men arrived at the Penitentiary the
next morning. That is, he was fairly young (he would not see thirty
again though without doubt he did not want to, there being that
about him which indicated a character which never had and never
would want anything it did not, or was not about to, possess), a Phi
Beta Kappa out of an Eastern university, a colonel on the Gover-

---

7. Machines for separating cotton from its seeds.

nor's staff who did not buy it with a campaign contribution, who
had stood in his negligent Eastern-cut clothes and his arched nose
and lazy contemptuous eyes on the galleries of any number of little
lost backwoods stores and told his stories and received the guffaws
of his overalled and spitting hearers and with the same look in his
eyes fondled infants named in memory of the last administration
and in honor (or hope) of the next, and (it was said of him and
doubtless not true) by lazy accident the behinds of some who were
not infants any longer though still not old enough to vote. He was
in the Warden's office with a briefcase, and presently the deputy
warden of the levee was there too. He would have been sent for
presently though not yet, but he came anyhow, without knocking,
with his hat on, calling the Governor's young man loudly by a nickname and striking him with a flat hand on the back and lifted one
thigh to the Warden's desk, almost between the Warden and the
caller, the emissary. Or the vizier with the command, the knotted
cord, as began to appear immediately.

"Well," the Governor's young man said, "you've played the
devil, haven't you?" The Warden had a cigar. He had offered the
caller one. It had been refused, though presently, while the Warden
looked at the back of his neck with hard immobility even a little
grim, the deputy leaned and reached back and opened the desk
drawer and took one.

"Seems straight enough to me," the Warden said. "He got swept
away against his will. He came back as soon as he could and surrendered."

"He even brought that damn boat back," the deputy said. "If
he'd a throwed the boat away he could a walked back in three days.
But no sir. He's got to bring the boat back. 'Here's your boat and
here's the woman but I never found no bastard on no
cottonhouse.'" He slapped his knee, guffawing. "Them convicts.
A mule's got twice as much sense."

"A mule's got twice as much sense as anything except a rat," the
emissary said in his pleasant voice. "But that's not the trouble."

"What is the trouble?" the Warden said.

"This man is dead."

"Hell fire, he aint dead," the deputy said. "He's up yonder in
that bunkhouse right now, lying his head off probly. I'll take you
up there and you can see him." The Warden was looking at the
deputy.

"Look," he said. "Bledsoe was trying to tell me something about
that Kate mule's leg. You better go up to the stable and—"

"I done tended to it," the deputy said. He didn't even look at
the Warden. He was watching, talking to, the emissary. "No sir.
He aint—"

"But he has received an official discharge as being dead. Not a
pardon nor a parole either: a discharge. He's either dead, or free. In

either case he doesn't belong here." Now both the Warden and the deputy looked at the emissary, the deputy's mouth open a little, the cigar poised in his hand to have its tip bitten off. The emissary spoke pleasantly, extremely distinctly: "On a report of death forwarded to the Governor by the Warden of the Penitentiary." The deputy closed his mouth, though otherwise he didn't move. "On the official evidence of the officer delegated at the time to the charge and returning of the body of the prisoner to the Penitentiary." Now the deputy put the cigar into his mouth and got slowly off the desk, the cigar rolling across his lip as he spoke:

"So that's it. I'm to be it, am I?" He laughed shortly, a stage laugh, two notes. "When I done been right three times running through three separate administrations? That's on a book somewhere too. Somebody in Jackson can find that too. And if they cant, I can show—"

"Three administrations?" the emissary said. "Well, well. That's pretty good."

"You damn right it's good," the deputy said. "The woods are full of folks that didn't." The Warden was again watching the back of the deputy's neck.

"Look," he said. "Why dont you step up to my house and get that bottle of whiskey out of the sideboard and bring it down here?"

"All right," the deputy said. "But I think we better settle this first. I'll tell you what we'll do—"

"We can settle it quicker with a drink or two," the Warden said. "You better step on up to your place and get a coat so the bottle—"

"That'll take too long," the deputy said. "I wont need no coat." He moved to the door, where he stopped and turned. "I'll tell you what to do. Just call twelve men in here and tell him it's a jury—he never seen but one before and he wont know no better—and try him over for robbing that train. Hamp can be the judge."

"You cant try a man twice for the same crime," the emissary said. "He might know that even if he doesn't know a jury when he sees one."

"Look," the Warden said.

"All right. Just call it a new train robbery. Tell him it happened yesterday, tell him he robbed another train while he was gone and just forgot it. He couldn't help himself. Besides, he wont care. He'd just as lief be here as out. He wouldn't have nowhere to go if he was out. None of them do. Turn one loose and be damned if he aint right back here by Christmas like it was a reunion or something, for doing the very same thing they caught him at before." He guffawed again. "Them convicts."

"Look," the Warden said. "While you're there, why dont you open the bottle and see if the liquor's any good. Take a drink or two. Give yourself time to feel it. If it's not good, no use in bringing it."

"O.K.," the deputy said. He went out this time.

"Couldn't you lock the door?" the emissary said. The Warden squirmed faintly. That is, he shifted his position in his chair.

"After all, he's right," he said. "He's guessed right three times now. And he's kin to all the folks in Pittman County except the niggers."

"Maybe we can work fast then." The emissary opened the briefcase and took out a sheaf of papers. "So there you are," he said.

"There what are?"

"He escaped."

"But he came back voluntarily and surrendered."

"But he escaped."

"All right," the Warden said. "He escaped. Then what?" Now the emissary said look. That is, he said,

"Listen. I'm on per diem. That's taxpayers, votes. And if there's any possible chance for it to occur to anyone to hold an investigation about this, there'll be ten senators and twenty-five representatives here on a special train maybe. On per diem. And it will be mighty hard to keep some of them from going back to Jackson by way of Memphis or New Orleans—on per diem."

"All right," the Warden said. "What does he say to do?"

"This. The man left here in charge of one specific officer. But he was delivered back here by a different one."

"But he surren—" This time the Warden stopped of his own accord. He looked, stared almost, at the emissary. "All right. Go on."

"In specific charge of an appointed and delegated officer, who returned here and reported that the body of the prisoner was no longer in his possession; that, in fact, he did not know where the prisoner was. That's correct, isn't it?" The Warden said nothing. "Isn't that correct?" the emissary said, pleasantly, insistently.

"But you cant do that to him. I tell you he's kin to half the—"

"That's taken care of. The Chief has made a place for him on the highway patrol."

"Hell," the Warden said. "He cant ride a motorcycle. I dont even let him try to drive a truck."

"He wont have to. Surely an amazed and grateful state can supply the man who guessed right three times in succession in Mississippi general elections with a car to ride in and somebody to run it if necessary. He wont even have to stay in it all the time. Just so he's near enough so when an inspector sees the car and stops and blows the horn of it he can hear it and come out."

"I still dont like it," the Warden said.

"Neither do I. Your man could have saved all of this if he had just gone on and drowned himself, as he seems to have led everybody to believe he had. But he didn't. And the Chief says do. Can you think of anything better?" The Warden sighed.

"No," he said.

"All right." The emissary opened the papers and uncapped a pen and began to write. "Attempted escape from the Penitentiary, ten years' additional sentence," he said. "Deputy Warden Buckworth transferred to highway patrol. Call it for meritorious service even if you want to. It wont matter now. Done?"

"Done," the Warden said.

"Then suppose you send for him. Get it over with." So the Warden sent for the tall convict and he arrived presently, saturnine and grave, in his new bed-ticking, his jowls blue and close under the sunburn, his hair recently cut and neatly parted and smelling faintly of the prison barber's (the barber was in for life, for murdering his wife, still a barber) pomade. The Warden called him by name.

"You had bad luck, didn't you?" The convict said nothing. "They are going to have to add ten years to your time."

"All right," the convict said.

"It's hard luck. I'm sorry."

"All right," the convict said. "If that's the rule." So they gave him the ten years more and the Warden gave him the cigar and now he sat, jackknifed backward into the space between the upper and lower bunks, the unlighted cigar in his hand while the plump convict and four others listened to him. Or questioned him, that is, since it was all done, finished, now and he was safe again, so maybe it wasn't even worth talking about any more.

"All right," the plump one said. "So you come back into the River. Then what?"

"Nothing. I rowed."

"Wasn't it pretty hard rowing coming back?"

"The water was still high. It was running pretty hard still. I never made much speed for the first week or two. After that it got better." Then, suddenly and quietly, something—the inarticulateness, the innate and inherited reluctance for speech, dissolved and he found himself, listened to himself, telling it quietly, the words coming not fast but easily to the tongue as he required them: how he paddled on (he found out by trying it that he could make better speed, if you could call it speed, next the bank—this after he had been carried suddenly and violently out to midstream before he could prevent it and found himself, the skiff, travelling back toward the region from which he had just escaped and he spent the better part of the morning getting back inshore and up to the canal again from which he had emerged at dawn) until night came and they tied up to the bank and ate some of the food he had secreted in his jumper before leaving the armory in New Orleans and the woman and the infant slept in the boat as usual and when daylight came they went

on and tied up again that night too and the next day the food gave
out and he came to a landing, a town, he didn't notice the name of
it, and he got a job. It was a cane[8] farm—

"Cane?" one of the other convicts said. "What does anybody
want to raise cane for? You cut cane. You have to fight it where I
come from. You burn it just to get shut of it."

"It was sorghum,"[9] the tall convict said.

"Sorghum?" another said. "A whole farm just raising sorghum?
Sorghum? What did they do with it?" The tall one didn't know.
He didn't ask, he just came up the levee and there was a truck wait-
ing full of niggers and a white man said, "You there. Can you run a
shovel plow?" and the convict said, "Yes," and the man said,
"Jump in then," and the convict said, "Only I've got a—"

"Yes," the plump one said. "That's what I been aiming to ask.
What did—" The tall convict's face was grave, his voice was calm,
just a little short:

"They had tents for the folks to live in. They were behind." The
plump one blinked at him.

"Did they think she was your wife?"

"I dont know. I reckon so." The plump one blinked at him.

"Wasn't she your wife? Just from time to time kind of, you
might say?" The tall one didn't answer this at all. After a moment
he raised the cigar and appeared to examine a loosening of the
wrapper because after another moment he licked the cigar carefully
near the end. "All right," the plump one said. "Then what?" So he
worked there four days. He didn't like it. Maybe that was why: that
he too could not quite put credence in that much of what he believed to be sorghum. So when they told him it was Saturday and
paid him and the white man told him about somebody who was
going to Baton Rouge the next day in a motor boat, he went to see
the man and took the six dollars he had earned and bought food
with it and tied the skiff behind the motor boat and went to Baton
Rouge. It didn't take long and even after they left the motor boat
at Baton Rouge and he was paddling again it seemed to the convict
that the River was lower and the current not so fast, so hard, so
they made fair speed, tying up to the bank at night among the willows, the woman and baby sleeping in the skiff as of old. Then the
food gave out again. This time it was a wood landing, the wood
stacked and waiting, a wagon and team being unladen of another
load. The men with the wagon told him about the sawmill and
helped him drag the skiff up the levee; they wanted to leave it there
but he would not so they loaded it onto the wagon too and he and
the woman got on the wagon too and they went to the sawmill.

8. Hollow-stemmed tall grass.
9. Cane crop raised chiefly for animal feed.

They gave them one room in a house to live in here. They paid two dollars a day and furnish. The work was hard. He liked it. He stayed there eight days.

"If you liked it so well, why did you quit?" the plump one said. The tall convict examined the cigar again, holding it up where the light fell upon the rich chocolate-colored flank.

"I got in trouble," he said.

"What trouble?"

"Woman. It was a fellow's wife."

"You mean you had been toting one piece up and down the country day and night for over a month, and now the first time you have a chance to stop and catch your breath almost you got to get in trouble over another one?" The tall convict had thought of that. He remembered it: how there were times, seconds, at first when if it had not been for the baby he might have, might have tried. But they were just seconds because in the next instant his whole being would seem to flee the very idea in a kind of savage and horrified revulsion; he would find himself looking from a distance at this millstone which the force and power of blind and risible Motion had fastened upon him, thinking, saying aloud actually, with harsh and savage outrage even though it had been two years since he had had a woman and that a nameless and not young Negress, a casual, a straggler whom he had caught more or less by chance on one of the fifth-Sunday visiting days, the man—husband or sweetheart—whom she had come to see having been shot by a trusty a week or so previous and she had not heard about it: "She aint even no good to me for that."

"But you got this one, didn't you?" the plump convict said.

"Yah," the tall one said. The plump one blinked at him.

"Was it good?"

"It's all good," one of the others said. "Well? Go on. How many more did you have on the way back? Sometimes when a fellow starts getting it it looks like he just cant miss even if—" That was all, the convict told them. They left the sawmill fast, he had no time to buy food until they reached the next landing. There he spent the whole sixteen dollars he had earned and they went on. The River was lower now, there was no doubt of it, and sixteen dollars' worth looked like a lot of food and he thought maybe it would do, would be enough. But maybe there was more current in the River still than it looked like. But this time it was Mississippi, it was cotton; the plow handles felt right to his palms again, the strain and squat of the slick buttocks against the middle-buster's blade was what he knew, even though they paid but a dollar a day here. But that did it. He told it: they told him it was Saturday again and paid him and he told about it—night, a smoked lantern in a disc of worn and barren earth as smooth as silver, a circle of crouching figures, the importunate murmurs and ejaculations, the meagre piles of

worn bills beneath the crouching knees, the dotted cubes clicking
and scuttering in the dust; that did it. "How much did you win?"
the second convict said.

"Enough," the tall one said.

"But how much?"

"Enough," the tall one said. It was enough exactly; he gave it all
to the man who owned the second motor boat (he would not need
food now), he and the woman in the launch now and the skiff towing behind, the woman with the baby and the paper-wrapped parcel
beneath his peaceful hand, on his lap; almost at once he recognised,
not Vicksburg because he had never seen Vicksburg, but the trestle
beneath which on his roaring wave of trees and houses and dead animals he had shot, accompanied by thunder and lightning, a month
and three weeks ago; he looked at it once without heat, even without interest as the launch went on. But now he began to watch the
bank, the levee. He didn't know how he would know but he knew
he would, and then it was early afternoon and sure enough the moment came and he said to the launch owner: "I reckon this will
do."

"Here?" the launch owner said. "This dont look like anywhere to
me."

"I reckon this is it," the convict said. So the launch put inshore,
the engine ceased, it drifted up and lay against the levee and the
owner cast the skiff loose.

"You better let me take you on until we come to something," he
said. "That was what I promised."

"I reckon this will do," the convict said. So they got out and he
stood with the grapevine painter in his hand while the launch
purred again and drew away, already curving; he did not watch it.
He laid the bundle down and made the painter fast to a willow root
and picked up the bundle and turned. He said no word, he
mounted the levee, passing the mark, the tide-line of the old raging,
dry now and lined, traversed by shallow and empty cracks like foolish and deprecatory senile grins, and entered a willow clump and removed the overalls and shirt they had given him in New Orleans
and dropped them without even looking to see where they fell and
opened the parcel and took out the other, the known, the desired,
faded a little, stained and worn, but clean, recognisable, and put
them on and returned to the skiff and took up the paddle. The
woman was already in it.

The plump convict stood blinking at him. "So you come back,"
he said. "Well, well." Now they all watched the tall convict as he
bit the end from the cigar neatly and with complete deliberation
and spat it out and licked the bite smooth and damp and took a
match from his pocket and examined the match for a moment as
though to be sure it was a good one, worthy of the cigar perhaps,
and raked it up his thigh with the same deliberation—a motion al-

most too slow to set fire to it, it would seem—and held it until the flame burned clear and free of sulphur, then put it to the cigar. The plump one watched him, blinking rapidly and steadily. "And they give you ten years more for running. That's bad. A fellow can get used to what they give him at first, to start off with, I dont care how much it is, even a hundred and ninety-nine years. But ten more years. Ten years more, on top of that. When you never expected it. Ten more years to have to do without no society, no female companionship—" He blinked steadily at the tall convict. But he (the tall convict) had thought of that too. He had had a sweetheart. That is, he had gone to church singings and picnics with her —a girl a year or so younger than he, short-legged, with ripe breasts and a heavy mouth and dull eyes like ripe muscadines,[1] who owned a baking-powder can almost full of earrings and brooches and rings bought (or presented at suggestion) from ten-cent stores. Presently he had divulged his plan to her, and there were times later when, musing, the thought occurred to him that possibly if it had not been for her he would not actually have attempted it—this a mere feeling, unworded, since he could not have phrased this either: that who to know what Capone's[2] uncandled bridehood she might not have dreamed to be her destiny and fate, what fast car filled with authentic colored glass and machine guns, running traffic lights. But that was all past and done when the notion first occurred to him, and in the third month of his incarceration she came to see him. She wore earrings and a bracelet or so which he had never seen before and it never became quite clear how she had got that far from home, and she cried violently for the first three minutes though presently (and without his ever knowing either exactly how they had got separated or how she had made the acquaintance) he saw her in animated conversation with one of the guards. But she kissed him before she left that evening and said she would return the first chance she got, clinging to him, sweating a little, smelling of scent and soft young female flesh, slightly pneumatic. But she didn't come back though he continued to write to her, and seven months later he got an answer. It was a postcard, a colored lithograph of a Birmingham hotel, a childish X inked heavily across one window, the heavy writing on the reverse slanted and primer-like too: *This is where were honnymonning at. Your friend (Mrs) Vernon Waldrip*

The plump convict stood blinking at the tall one, rapidly and steadily. "Yes, sir," he said. "It's them ten more years that hurt. Ten more years to do without a woman, no woman a tall a fellow wants—" He blinked steadily and rapidly, watching the tall one. The other did not move, jackknifed backward between the two bunks, grave and clean, the cigar burning smoothly and richly in his

---

1. A variety of grapes.
2. Al Capone (1899–1947), notorious American gangster.

clean steady hand, the smoke wreathing upward across his face saturnine, humorless, and calm. "Ten more years—"

"Women, —t," the tall convict said.

1939

Pantaloon in Black[1]

I

He stood in the worn, faded clean overalls which Mannie herself had washed only a week ago, and heard the first clod strike the pine box. Soon he had one of the shovels himself, which in his hands (he was better than six feet and weighed better than two hundred pounds) resembled the toy shovel a child plays with at the shore, its half cubic foot of flung dirt no more than the light gout of sand the child's shovel would have flung. Another member of his sawmill gang touched his arm and said, "Lemme have hit, Rider." He didn't even falter. He released one hand in midstroke and flung it backward, striking the other across the chest, jolting him back a step, and restored the hand to the moving shovel, flinging the dirt with that effortless fury so that the mound seemed to be rising of its own volition, not built up from above but thrusting visibly upward out of the earth itself, until at last the grave, save for its rawness, resembled any other marked off without order about the barren plot by shards of pottery and broken bottles and old brick and other objects insignificant to sight but actually of a profound meaning and fatal to touch, which no white man could have read. Then he straightened up and with one hand flung the shovel quivering upright in the mound like a javelin and turned and began to walk away, walking on even when an old woman came out of the meagre clump of his kin and friends and a few old people who had known him and his dead wife both since they were born, and grasped his forearm. She was his aunt. She had raised him. He could not remember his parents at all.

"Whar you gwine?" she said.

"Ah'm goan home," he said.

"You dont wants ter go back dar by yoself," she said. "You needs to eat. You come on home and eat."

"Ah'm goan home," he repeated, walking out from under her hand, his forearm like iron, as if the weight on it were no more than that of a fly, the other members of the mill gang whose head he was giving way quietly to let him pass. But before he reached the fence one of them overtook him; he did not need to be told it was his aunt's messenger.

1. The Pantaloon was a stock character in Italian comedy, usually the butt of cruel jokes. The story appeared in *Go Down, Moses* (1942), a unified fiction comprised of related stories originally published separately. The story is one of many in that volume that reveal the black people's profound capacity for experience and explore the violence and the tragedy that result from the estrangement of blacks from whites.

"Wait, Rider," the other said. "We gots a jug in de bushes—"
Then the other said what he had not intended to say, what he
had never conceived of himself saying in circumstances like these,
even though everybody knew it—the dead who either will not or
cannot quit the earth yet although the flesh they once lived in has
been returned to it, let the preachers tell and reiterate and affirm
how they left it not only without regret but with joy, mounting toward glory: "You dont wants ter go back dar. She be wawkin yit."

He didn't pause, glancing down at the other, his eyes red at the
inner corners in his high, slightly backtilted head. "Lemme lone,
Acey," he said. "Doan mess wid me now," and went on, stepping
over the three-strand wire fence without even breaking his stride,
and crossed the road and entered the woods. It was middle dusk
when he emerged from them and crossed the last field, stepping
over that fence too in one stride, into the lane. It was empty at this
hour of Sunday evening—no family in wagon, no rider, no walkers
churchward to speak to him and carefully refrain from looking after
him when he had passed—the pale, powder-light, powder-dry dust
of August from which the long week's marks of hoof and wheel had
been blotted by the strolling and unhurried Sunday shoes, with
somewhere beneath them, vanished but not gone, fixed and held in
the annealing dust, the narrow, splay-toed prints of his wife's bare
feet where on Saturday afternoon she would talk to the commissary to buy their next week's supplies while he took his bath; himself, his own prints, setting the period now as he strode on, moving
almost as fast as a smaller man could have trotted, his body breasting the air her body had vacated, his eyes touching the objects—
post and tree and field and house and hill—her eyes had lost.

The house was the last one in the lane, not his but rented from
Carothers Edmonds, the local white landowner. But the rent was
paid promptly in advance, and even in just six months he had re-
floored the porch and rebuilt and roofed the kitchen, doing the work
himself on Saturday afternoon and Sunday with his wife helping
him, and bought the stove. Because he made good money: sawmill-
ing ever since he began to get his growth at fifteen and sixteen and
now, at twenty-four, head of the timber gang itself because the gang
he headed moved a third again as much timber between sunup and
sundown as any other moved, handling himself at times out of the
vanity of his own strength logs which ordinarily two men would
have handled with canthooks; never without work even in the old
days when he had not actually needed the money, when a lot of
what he wanted, needed perhaps, didn't cost money—the women
bright and dark and for all purposes nameless he didn't need to buy
and it didn't matter to him what he wore and there was always food
for him at any hour of day or night in the house of his aunt who
didn't even want to take the two dollars he gave her each Saturday
—so there had been only the Saturday and Sunday dice and whis-

key that had to be paid for until that day six months ago when he saw Mannie, whom he had known all his life, for the first time and said to himself: "Ah'm thu wid all dat," and they married and he rented the cabin from Carothers Edmonds and built a fire on the hearth[2] on their wedding night as the tale told how Uncle Lucas Beauchamp, Edmonds' oldest tenant, had done on his forty-five years ago and which had burned ever since; and he would rise and dress and eat his breakfast by lamplight to walk the four miles to the mill by sunup, and exactly one hour after sundown he would enter the house again, five days a week, until Saturday. Then the first hour would not have passed noon when he would mount the steps and knock, not on post or doorframe but on the underside of the gallery roof itself, and enter and ring the bright cascade of silver dollars onto the scrubbed table in the kitchen where his dinner simmered on the stove and the galvanised tub of hot water and the baking powder can of soft soap and the towel made of scalded flour sacks sewn together and his clean overalls and shirt waited, and Mannie would gather up the money and walk the half-mile to the commissary and buy their next week's supplies and bank the rest of the money in Edmonds' safe and return and they would eat once again without haste or hurry after five days—the sidemeat, the greens, the cornbread, the buttermilk from the well-house, the cake which she baked every Saturday now that she had a stove to bake in.

But when he put his hand on the gate it seemed to him suddenly that there was nothing beyond it. The house had never been his anyway, but now even the new planks and sills and shingles, the hearth and stove and bed, were all a part of the memory of somebody else, so that he stopped in the half-open gate and said aloud, as though he had gone to sleep in one place and then waked suddenly to find himself in another: "Whut's Ah doin hyar?" before he went on. Then he saw the dog. He had forgotten it. He remembered neither seeing nor hearing it since it began to howl just before dawn yesterday—a big dog, a hound with a strain of mastiff from somewhere (he had told Mannie a month after they married: "Ah needs a big dawg. You's de onliest least thing whut ever kep up wid me one day, leff alone fo weeks.") coming out from beneath the gallery and approaching, not running but seeming rather to drift across the dusk until it stood lightly against his leg, its head raised until the tips of his fingers just touched it, facing the house and making no sound; whereupon, as if the animal controlled it, had lain guardian before it during his absence and only this instant relinquished, the shell of planks and shingles facing him solidified, filled, and for the moment he believed that he could not possibly enter it. "But Ah needs to eat," he said. "Us bofe needs to eat," he said, moving on though the dog did not follow until he turned and

2. Symbol of the home, a recurring motif in *Go Down, Moses*.

cursed it. "Come on hyar!" he said. "What you skeered of? She lacked you too, same as me," and they mounted the steps and crossed the porch and entered the house—the dusk-filled single room where all those six months were now crammed and crowded into one instant of time until there was no space left for air to breathe, crammed and crowded about the hearth where the fire which was to have lasted to the end of them, before which in the days before he was able to buy the stove he would enter after his four-mile walk from the mill and find her, the shape of her narrow back and haunches squatting, one narrow spread hand shielding her face from the blaze over which the other hand held the skillet, had already fallen to a dry, light soilure of dead ashes when the sun rose yesterday—and himself standing there while the last of light died about the strong and indomitable beating of his heart and the deep steady arch and collapse of his chest which walking fast over the rough going of woods and fields had not increased and standing still in the quiet and fading room had not slowed down.

Then the dog left him. The light pressure went off his flank; he heard the click and hiss of its claws on the wooden floor as it surged away and he thought at first that it was fleeing. But it stopped just outside the front door, where he could see it now, and the upfling of its head as the howl began, and then he saw her too. She was standing in the kitchen door, looking at him. He didn't move. He didn't breathe nor speak until he knew his voice would be all right, his face fixed too not to alarm her. "Mannie," he said. "Hit's awright. Ah aint afraid." Then he took a step toward her, slow, not even raising his hand yet, and stopped. Then he took another step. But this time as soon as he moved she began to fade. He stopped at once, not breathing again, motionless, willing his eyes to see that she had stopped too. But she had not stopped. She was fading, going. "Wait," he said, talking as sweet as he had ever heard his voice speak to a woman: "Den lemme go wid you, honey." But she was going. She was going fast now, he could actually feel between them the insuperable barrier of that very strength which could handle alone a log which would have taken any two other men to handle, of the blood and bones and flesh too strong, invincible for life, having learned at least once with his own eyes how tough, even in sudden and violent death, not a young man's bones and flesh perhaps but the will of that bone and flesh to remain alive, actually was.

Then she was gone. He walked through the door where she had been standing, and went to the stove. He did not light the lamp. He needed no light. He had set the stove up himself and built the shelves for the dishes, from among which he took two plates by feel and from the pot sitting cold on the cold stove he ladled onto the plates the food which his aunt had brought yesterday and of which he had eaten yesterday though now he did not remember when he

had eaten it nor what it was, and carried the plates to the scrubbed
bare table beneath the single small fading window and drew two
chairs up and sat down, waiting again until he knew his voice would
be what he wanted it to be. "Come on hyar, now," he said roughly.
"Come on hyar and eat yo supper. Ah aint gonter have no—" and
ceased, looking down at his plate, breathing the strong, deep pants,
his chest arching and collapsing until he stopped it presently and
held himself motionless for perhaps a half minute, and raised a
spoonful of the cold and glutinous peas to his mouth. The con-
gealed and lifeless mass seemed to bounce on contact with his lips.
Not even warmed from mouth-heat, peas and spoon spattered and
rang upon the plate; his chair crashed backward and he was standing, feeling the muscles of his jaw beginning to drag his mouth
open, tugging upward the top half of his head. But he stopped that
too before it became sound, holding himself again while he rapidly
scraped the food from his plate onto the other and took it up and
left the kitchen, crossed the other room and the gallery and set the
plate on the bottom step and went on toward the gate.

The dog was not there, but it overtook him within the first half
mile. There was a moon then, their two shadows flitting broken and
intermittent among the trees or slanted long and intact across the
slope of pasture or old abandoned fields upon the hills, the man moving almost as fast as a horse could have moved over that ground, altering his course each time a lighted window came in sight, the dog trotting at heel while their shadows shortened to the moon's curve until
at last they trod them and the last far lamp had vanished and the
shadows began to lengthen on the other hand, keeping to heel even
when a rabbit burst from almost beneath the man's foot, then lying
in the gray of dawn beside the man's prone body, beside the labored heave and collapse of the chest, the loud harsh snoring which
sounded not like groans of pain but like someone engaged without
arms in prolonged single combat.

When he reached the mill there was nobody there but the fireman—an older man just turning from the woodpile, watching quietly as he crossed the clearing, striding as if he were going to walk
not only through the boiler shed but through (or over) the boiler
too, the overalls which had been clean yesterday now draggled and
soiled and drenched to the knees with dew, the cloth cap flung onto
the side of his head, hanging peak downward over his ear as he always wore it, the whites of his eyes rimmed with red and with
something urgent and strained about them. "Whar yo bucket?" he
said. But before the fireman could answer he had stepped past him
and lifted the polished lard pail down from a nail in a post. "Ah
just wants a biscuit," he said.

"Eat hit all," the fireman said. "Ah'll eat outen de yuthers' buckets at dinner. Den you gawn home and go to bed. You dont looks
good."

"Ah aint come hyar to look," he said, sitting on the ground, his back against the post, the open pail between his knees, cramming the food into his mouth with his hands, wolfing it—peas again, also gelid and cold, a fragment of yesterday's Sunday fried chicken, a few rough chunks of this morning's fried sidemeat, a biscuit the size of a child's cap—indiscriminate, tasteless. The rest of the crew was gathering now, with voices and sounds of movement outside the boiler shed; presently the white foreman rode into the clearing on a horse. He did not look up, setting the empty pail aside, rising, looking at no one, and went to the branch and lay on his stomach and lowered his face to the water, drawing the water into himself with the same deep, strong, troubled inhalations that he had snored with, or as when he had stood in the empty house at dusk yesterday, trying to get air.

Then the trucks were rolling. The air pulsed with the rapid beating of the exhaust and the whine and clang of the saw, the trucks rolling one by one up to the skidway, he mounting the trucks in turn, to stand balanced on the load he freed, knocking the chocks out and casting loose the shackle chains and with his cant-hook squaring the sticks of cypress and gum and oak one by one to the incline and holding them until the next two men of his gang were ready to receive and guide them, until the discharge of each truck became one long rumbling roar punctuated by grunting shouts and, as the morning grew and the sweat came, chanted phrases of song tossed back and forth. He did not sing with them. He rarely ever did, and this morning might have been no different from any other —himself man-height again above the heads which carefully refrained from looking at him, stripped to the waist now, the shirt removed and the overalls knotted about his hips by the suspender straps, his upper body bare except for the handkerchief about his neck and the cap clapped and clinging somehow over his right ear, the mounting sun sweat-glinted steel-blue on the midnight-colored bunch and slip of muscles until the whistle blew for noon and he said to the two men at the head of the skidway: "Look out. Git out de way," and rode the log down the incline, balanced erect upon it in short rapid backward-running steps above the headlong thunder.

His aunt's husband was waiting for him—an old man, as tall as he was, but lean, almost frail, carrying a tin pail in one hand and a covered plate in the other; they too sat in the shade beside the branch a short distance from where the others were opening their dinner pails. The bucket contained a fruit jar of buttermilk packed in a clean damp towsack. The covered dish was a peach pie, still warm. "She baked hit fer you dis mawin," the uncle said. "She say fer you to come home." He didn't answer, bent forward a little, his elbows on his knees, holding the pie in both hands, wolfing at it, the syrupy filling smearing and trickling down his chin, blinking rapidly as he chewed, the whites of his eyes covered a little more by the creeping red. "Ah went to yo house last night, but you want dar. She sont me. She wants you to come on home. She kept de lamp burnin all last night fer you."

"Ah'm awright," he said.

"You aint awright. De Lawd guv, and He tuck away. Put yo faith and trust in Him. And she kin help you."

"Whut faith and trust?" he said. "Whut Mannie ever done ter Him? Whut He wanter come messin wid me and ——"

"Hush!" the old man said. "Hush!"

Then the trucks were rolling again. Then he could stop needing to invent to himself reasons for his breathing, until after a while he began to believe he had forgot about breathing since now he could not hear it himself above the steady thunder of the rolling logs; whereupon as soon as he found himself believing he had forgotten it, he knew that he had not, so that instead of tipping the final log onto the skidway he stood up and cast his cant-hook away as if it were a burnt match and in the dying reverberation of the last log's rumbling descent he vaulted down between the two slanted tracks of the skid, facing the log which still lay on the truck. He had done it before—taken a log from the truck onto his hands, balanced, and turned with it and tossed it onto the skidway, but never with a stick of this size, so that in a complete cessation of all sound save the pulse of the exhaust and the light free-runnig whine of the disengaged saw since every eye there, even that of the white foreman, was upon him, he nudged the log to the edge of the truckframe and squatted and set his palms against the underside of it. For a time there was no movement at all. It was as if the unrational and inanimate wood had invested, mesmerised the man with some of its own primal inertia. Then a voice said quietly: "He got hit. Hit's off de truck," and they saw the crack and gap of air, watching the infinitesimal straightening of the braced legs until the knees locked, the movement mounting infinitesimally through the belly's insuck, the arch of the chest, the neck cords, lifting the lip from the white clench of teeth in passing, drawing the whole head backward and only the bloodshot fixity of the eyes impervious to it, moving on up the arms and the straightening elbows until the balanced log was higher than his head. "Only he aint gonter turn wid dat un," the same voice said. "And when he try to put hit back on de truck, hit gonter kill him." But none of them moved. Then—there was no gathering of supreme effort—the log seemed to leap suddenly backward over his head of its own volition, spinning, crashing and thundering down the incline; he turned and stepped over the slanting track in one stride and walked through them as they gave way and went on across the clearing toward the woods even though the foreman called after him: "Rider!" and again: "You, Rider!"

At sundown he and the dog were in the river swamp four miles away—another clearing, itself not much larger than a room, a hut, a hovel partly of planks and partly of canvas, an unshaven white man standing in the door beside which a shotgun leaned, watching him as he approached, his hand extended with four silver dollars on the palm. "Ah wants a jug," he said.

"A jug?" the white man said. "You mean a pint. This is Monday. Aint you all running this week?"

"Ah laid off," he said. "Whar's my jug?" waiting, looking at nothing apparently, blinking his bloodshot eyes rapidly in his high, slightly back-tilted head, then turning, the jug hanging from his crooked middle finger against his leg, at which moment the white man looked suddenly and sharply at his eyes as though seeing them for the first time—the eyes which had been strained and urgent this morning and which now seemed to be without vision too and in which no white showed at all—and said,

"Here. Gimme that jug. You dont need no gallon. I'm going to give you that pint, give it to you. Then you get out of here and stay out. Dont come back until—" Then the white man reached and grasped the jug, whereupon the other swung it behind him, sweeping his other arm up and out so that it struck the white man across the chest.

"Look out, white folks," he said. "Hit's mine. Ah done paid you."

The white man cursed him. "No you aint. Here's your money. Put that jug down, nigger."

"Hit's mine," he said, his voice quiet, gentle even, his face quiet save for the rapid blinking of the red eyes. "Ah done paid for hit," turning on, turning his back on the man and the gun both, and recrossed the clearing to where the dog waited beside the path to come to heel again. They moved rapidly on between the close walls of impenetrable cane-stalks which gave a sort of blondness to the twilight and possessed something of that oppression, that lack of room to breathe in, which the walls of his house had had. But this time, instead of fleeing it, he stopped and raised the jug and drew the cob stopper from the fierce duskreek of uncured alcohol and drank, gulping the liquid solid and cold as ice water, without either taste or heat until he lowered the jug and the air got in. "Hah," he said. "Dat's right. Try me. Try me, big boy. Ah gots something hyar now dat kin whup you."

And, once free of the bottom's unbreathing blackness, there was the moon again, his long shadow and that of the lifted jug slanting away as he drank and then held the jug poised, gulping the silver air into his throat until he could breathe again, speaking to the jug: "Come on now. You always claim you's a better man den me. Come on now. Prove it." He drank again, swallowing the chill liquid tamed of taste or heat either while the swallowing lasted, feeling it flow solid and cold with fire, past then enveloping the strong steady panting of his lungs until they too ran suddenly free as his moving body ran in the silver solid wall of air he breasted. And he was all right, his striding shadow and the trotting one of the dog travelling swift as those of two clouds along the hill; the long cast of his motionless shadow and that of the lifted jug slanting across the slope as he watched the frail figure of his aunt's husband toiling up the hill.

"Dey tole me at de mill you was gone," the old man said. "Ah knowed whar to look. Come home, son. Dat ar cant help you."

"Hit done awready hope me," he said. "Ah'm awready home. Ah'm snakebit now and pizen cant hawm me."

"Den stop and see her. Leff her look at you. Dat's all she axes: just leff her look at you—" But he was already moving. "Wait!" the old man cried. "Wait!"

"You cant keep up," he said, speaking into the silver air, breasting aside the silver solid air which began to flow past him almost as fast as it would have flowed past a moving horse. The faint frail voice was already lost in the night's infinitude, his shadow and that of the dog scudding the free miles, the deep strong panting of his chest running free as air now because he was all right.

Then, drinking, he discovered suddenly that no more of the liquid was entering his mouth. Swallowing, it was no longer passing down his throat, his throat and mouth filled now with a solid and unmoving column which without reflex or revulsion sprang, columnar and intact and still retaining the mold of his gullet, outward glinting in the moonlight, splintering, vanishing into the myriad murmur of the dewed grass. He drank again. Again his throat merely filled solidly until two icy rills ran from his mouth-corners; again the intact column sprang silvering, glinting, shivering, while he panted the chill of air into his throat, the jug poised before his mouth while he spoke to it: "Awright. Ah'm ghy try you again. Soon as you makes up yo mind to stay whar I puts you, Ah'll leff you alone." He drank, filling his gullet for the third time and lowered the jug one instant ahead of the bright intact repetition, panting, indrawing the cool of air until he could breathe. He stoppered the cob carefully back into the jug and stood, panting, blinking, the long cast of his solitary shadow slanting away across the hill and beyond, across the mazy infinitude of all the night-bound earth. "Awright," he said. "Ah just misread de sign wrong. Hit's done done me all de help Ah needs. Ah'm awright now. Ah doan needs no mo of hit."

He could see the lamp in the window as he crossed the pasture, passing the black-and-silver yawn of the sandy ditch where he had played as a boy with empty snuff-tins and rusted harness-buckles and fragments of trace-chains and now and then an actual wheel, passing the garden patch where he had hoed in the spring days while his aunt stood sentry over him from the kitchen window, crossing the grassless yard in whose dust he had sprawled and crept before he learned to walk. He entered the house, the room, the light itself, and stopped in the door, his head backtilted a little as if he could not see, the jug hanging from his crooked finger, against his leg. "Unc Alec say you wanter see me," he said.

"Not just to see you," his aunt said. "To come home, whar we kin help you."

"Ah'm awright," he said. "Ah doan needs no help."

"No," she said. She rose from the chair and came and grasped his arm as she had grasped it yesterday at the grave. Again, as on yesterday, the forearm was like iron under her hand. "No! When Alec come back and tole me how you had wawked off de mill and de sun not half down, Ah knowed why and whar. And dat cant help you."

"Hit done awready hope me. Ah'm awright now."

"Dont lie to me," she said. "You aint never lied to me. Dont lie to me now."

Then he said it. It was his own voice, without either grief or amazement, speaking quietly out of the tremendous panting of his chest which in a moment now would begin to strain at the walls of this room too. But he would be gone in a moment.

"Nome," he said, "Hit aint done me no good."

"And hit cant! Cant nothing help you but Him! Ax Him! Tole Him about hit! He wants to hyar you and help you!"

"Efn He God, Ah dont needs to tole Him. Efn He God, He awready know hit. Awright. Hyar Ah is. Leff Him come down hyar and do me some good."

"On yo knees!" she cried. "On yo knees and ax Him!" But it was not his knees on the floor, it was his feet. And for a space he could hear her feet too on the planks of the hall behind him and her voice crying after him from the door: "Spoot! Spoot!"—crying after him across the moon-dappled yard the name he had gone by in his childhood and adolescence, before the men he worked with and the bright dark nameless women he had taken in course and forgotten until he saw Mannie that day and said, "Ah'm thu wid all dat," began to call him Rider.

It was just after midnight when he reached the mill. The dog was gone now. This time he could not remember when nor where. At first he seemed to remember hurling the empty jug at it. But later the jug was still in his hand and it was not empty, although each time he drank now the two icy runnels streamed from his mouth-corners, sopping his shirt and overalls until he walked constantly in the fierce chill of the liquid tamed now of flavor and heat and odor too even when the swallowing ceased. "Sides that," he said, "Ah wouldn't thow nothin at him. Ah mout kick him efn he needed hit and was close enough. But Ah wouldn't ruin no dog chunkin hit."

The jug was still in his hand when he entered the clearing and paused among the mute soaring of the moon-blond lumber-stacks. He stood in the middle now of the unimpeded shadow which he was treading again as he had trod it last night, swaying a little, blinking about at the stacked lumber, the skidway, the piled logs waiting for tomorrow, the boiler-shed all quiet and blanched in the moon. And then it was all right. He was moving again. But he was not moving, he was drinking, the liquid cold and swift and tasteless and requiring no swallowing, so that he could not tell if it were going down inside or outside. But it was all right. And now he was moving, the jug gone now and he didn't know the when or where of that either. He crossed the clearing and entered the boiler shed and went on through it, crossing the junctureless backloop of time's trepan, to the door of the tool-room, the faint glow of the lantern beyond the plank-joints, the surge and fall of living shadow, the mutter of voices, the mute click and scutter of the dice, his hand loud on the barred door, his voice loud too: "Open hit. Hit's me. Ah'm snakebit and bound to die."

Then he was through the door and inside the tool-room. They were the same faces—three members of his timber gang, three or four others of the mill crew, the white night-watchman with the heavy pistol in his hip pocket and the small heap of coins and worn bills on the floor before him, one who was called Rider and was Rider standing above the squatting circle, swaying a little, blinking, the dead muscles of his face shaped into smiling while the white man stared up at him. "Make room, gamblers," he said. "Make room. Ah'm snakebit and de pizen cant hawm me."

"You're drunk," the white man said. "Get out of here. One of you niggers open the door and get him out of here."

"Dass awright, boss-man," he said, his voice equable, his face still fixed in the faint rigid smiling beneath the blinking of the red eyes; "Ah aint drunk. Ah just cant wawk straight fer dis yar money weighin me down."

Now he was kneeling too, the other six dollars of his last week's pay on the floor before him, blinking, still smiling at the face of the white man opposite, then, still smiling, he watched the dice pass from hand to hand around the circle as the white man covered the bets, watching the soiled and palm-worn money in front of the white man gradually and steadily increase, watching the white man cast and win two doubled bets in succession then lose on for twenty-five cents, the dice coming to him at last, the cupped snug clicking of them in his fist. He spun a coin into the center.

"Shoots a dollar," he said, and cast, and watched the white man pick up the dice and flip them back to him. "Ah lets hit lay," he said. "Ah'm snakebit. Ah kin pass wid anything," and cast, and this time one of the negroes flipped the dice back. "Ah lets hit lay," he said, and cast, and moved as the white man moved, catching the white man's wrist before his hand reached the dice, the two of them squatting, facing each other above the dice and the money, his left hand grasping the white man's wrist, his face still fixed in the rigid and deadened smiling, his voice equable, almost deferen-

tial: "Ah kin pass even wid missouts. But dese hyar yuther boys—"
until the white man's hand sprang open and the second pair of dice
clattered onto the floor beside the first two and the white man
wrenched free and sprang up and back and reached the hand backward toward the pocket where the pistol was.

The razor hung between his shoulder-blades from a loop of cotton string round his neck inside his shirt. The same motion of the
hand which brought the razor forward over his shoulder flipped the
blade open and freed it from the cord, the blade opening on until
the back edge of it lay across the knuckles of his fist, his thumb
pressing the handle into his closing fingers, so that in the second before the half-drawn pistol exploded he actually struck at the white
man's throat not with the blade but with a sweeping blow of his
fist, following through in the same motion so that not even the first
jet of blood touched his hand or arm.

2

After it was over—it didn't take long; they found the prisoner on
the following day, hanging from the bell-rope in a negro school-
house about two miles from the sawmill, and the coroner had pronounced his verdict of death at the hands of a person or persons unknown and surrendered the body to its next of kin all within five
minutes—the sheriff's deputy who had been officially in charge of
the business was telling his wife about it. They were in the kitchen.
His wife was cooking supper. The deputy had been out of bed and
in motion ever since the jail delivery shortly before midnight of yesterday and had covered considerable ground since, and he was spent
now from lack of sleep and hurried food at hurried and curious
hours and, sitting in a chair beside the stove, a little hysterical too.

"Them damn niggers," he said. "I swear to godfrey, it's a wonder
we have as little trouble with them as we do. Because why? Because
they aint human. They look like a man and they walk on their
hind legs like a man, and they can talk and you can understand
them and you think they are understanding you, at least now and
then. But when it comes to the normal human feelings and sentiments of human beings, they might just as well be a damn herd of
wild buffaloes. Now you take this one today——"

"I wish you would," his wife said harshly. She was a stout
woman, handsome once, graying now and with a neck definitely too
short, who looked not harried at all but composed in fact, only
choleric. Also, she had attended a club rook-party that afternoon
and had won the first, the fifty-cent, prize until another member
had insisted on a recount of the scores and the ultimate throwing
out of one entire game. "Take him out of my kitchen, anyway. You
sheriffs! Sitting around that courthouse all day long, talking. It's no
wonder two or three men can walk in and take prisoners out from
under your very noses. They would take your chairs and desks and

window sills too if you ever got your feet and backsides off of them that long."

"It's more of them Birdsongs than just two or three," the deputy said. "There's forty-two active votes in that connection. Me and Maydew taken the poll-list and counted them one day. But listen —" The wife turned from the stove, carrying a dish. The deputy snatched his feet rapidly out of the way as she passed him, passed almost over him, and went into the dining room. The deputy raised his voice a little to carry the increased distance: "His wife dies on him. All right. But does he grieve? He's the biggest and busiest man at the funeral. Grabs a shovel before they even got the box into the grave they tell me, and starts throwing dirt onto her faster than a slip scraper could have done it. But that's all right—" His wife came back. He moved his feet again and altered his voice again to the altered range: "—maybe that's how he felt about her. There aint any law against a man rushing his wife into the ground, provided he never had nothing to do with rushing her to the cemetery too. But here the next day he's the first man back at work except the fireman, getting back to the mill before the fireman had his fire going, let alone steam up; five minutes earlier and he could even have helped the fireman wake Birdsong up so Birdsong could go home and go back to bed again, or he could even have cut Birdsong's throat then and saved everybody trouble.

"So he comes to work, the first man on the job, when McAndrews and everybody else expected him to take the day off since even a nigger couldn't want no better excuse for a holiday than he had just buried his wife, when a white man would have took the day off out of pure respect no matter how he felt about his wife, when even a little child would have had sense enough to take a day off when he would still get paid for it too. But not him. The first man there, jumping from one log truck to another before the starting whistle quit blowing even, snatching up ten-foot cypress logs by himself and throwing them around like matches. And then, when everybody had finally decided that that's the way to take him, the way he wants to be took, he walks off the job in the middle of the afternoon without by-your-leave or much obliged or goodbye to McAndrews or nobody else, gets himself a whole gallon of bust-skull white-mule whisky, comes straight back to the mill and to the same crap game where Birdsong has been running crooked dice on them mill niggers for fifteen years, goes straight to the same game where he has been peacefully losing a probably steady average ninety-nine percent of his pay ever since he got big enough to read the spots on them miss-out dice, and cuts Birdsong's throat clean to the neckbone five minutes later." The wife passed him again and went to the dining room. Again he drew his feet back and raised his voice:

"So me and Maydew go out there. Not that we expected to

do any good, as he had probably passed Jackson, Tennessee, about daylight; and besides, the simplest way to find him would be just to stay close behind them Birdsong boys. Of course there wouldn't be nothing hardly worth bringing back to town after they did find him, but it would close the case. So it's just by the merest chance that we go by his house; I dont even remember why we went now, but we did; and there he is. Sitting behind the barred front door with a open razor on one knee and a loaded shotgun on the other? No. He was asleep. A big pot of field peas et clean empty on the stove, and him laying in the back yard asleep in the broad sun with just his head under the edge of the porch in the shade and a dog that looked like a cross between a bear and a Polled Angus steer yelling fire and murder from the back door. And we wake him and he sets up and says, 'Awright, white folks. Ah done it. Jest dont lock me up,' and Maydew says, 'Mr Birdsong's kinfolks aint going to lock you up neither. You'll have plenty of fresh air when they get hold of you,' and he says, 'Ah done it. Jest dont lock me up'— advising, instructing the sheriff not to lock him up; he done it all right and it's too bad but it aint convenient for him to be cut off from the fresh air at the moment. So we loaded him into the car, when here come the old woman—his ma or aunt or something— panting up the road at a dog-trot, wanting to come with us too, and Maydew trying to explain to her what would maybe happen to her too if them Birdsong kin catches us before we can get him locked up, only she is coming anyway, and like Maydew says, her being in the car too might be a good thing if the Birdsongs did happen to run into us, because after all interference with the law cant be condoned even if the Birdsong connection did carry that beat for Maydew last summer.

"So we brought her along too and got him to town and into the jail all right and turned him over to Ketcham and Ketcham taken him on up stairs and the old woman coming too, right on up to the cell, telling Ketcham, 'Ah tried to raise him right. He was a good boy. He aint never been in no trouble till now. He will suffer for what he done. But dont let the white folks get him,' until Ketcham says, 'You and him ought to thought of that before he started barbering white men without using no lather first.' So he locked them both up in the cell because he felt like Maydew did, that her being in there with him might be a good influence on the Birdsong boys if anything started if he should happen to be running for sheriff or something when Maydew's term was up. So Ketcham come on back down stairs and pretty soon the chain gang come in and went on up to the bull pen and he thought things had settled down for a while when all of a sudden he begun to hear the yelling, not howling: yelling, though there wasn't no words in it, and he grabbed his pistol and run back up stairs to the bull pen where the chain gang was and Ketcham could see into the cell where the old woman was kind

of squinched down in one corner and where that nigger had done
tore that iron cot clean out of the floor it was bolted to and was
standing in the middle of the cell, holding the cot over his head
like it was a baby's cradle, yelling, and says to the old woman, 'Ah
aint goan hurt you,' and throws the cot against the wall and comes
and grabs holt of that steel barred door and rips it out of the wall,
bricks hinges and all, and walks out of the cell toting the door over
his head like it was a guaze window-screen, hollering, 'It's awright.
It's awright. Ah aint trying to git away.'

"Of course Ketcham could have shot him right there, but like he
said, if it wasn't going to be the law, then them Birdsong boys
ought to have the first lick at him. So Ketcham dont shoot. Instead,
he jumps in behind where them chain gang niggers was kind of
backed off from that steel door, hollering, 'Grab him! Throw him
down!' except the niggers hung back at first too until Ketcham gets
in where he can kick the ones he can reach, batting at the others
with the flat of the pistol until they rush him. And Ketcham says
that for a full minute that nigger would grab them as they come in
and fling them clean across the room like they was rag dolls, saying,
'Ah aint tryin to git out. Ah aint trying to git out,' until at last they
pulled him down—a big mass of nigger heads and arms and legs
boiling around on the floor and even then Ketcham says every now
and then a nigger would come flying out and go sailing through the
air across the room, spraddled out like a flying squirrel and with his
eyes sticking out like car headlights, until at last they had him
down and Ketcham went in and begun peeling away niggers until
he could see him laying there under the pile of them, laughing,
with tears big as glass marbles running across his face and down
past his ears and making a kind of popping sound on the floor
like somebody dropping bird eggs, laughing and laughing and saying, 'Hit look lack Ah just cant quit thinking. Look lack Ah just
cant quit.' And what do you think of that?"

"I think if you eat any supper in this house you'll do it in the
next five minutes," his wife said from the dining room. "I'm going
to clear this table then and I'm going to the picture show."

1942

Address to the Graduating Class, Pine Manor Junior College[1]

What's wrong with this world is, it's not finished yet. It is not
completed to that point where man can put his final signature to
the job and say, "It is finished. We made it, and it works."

Because only man can complete it. Not God, but man. It is
man's high destiny and proof of his immortality too, that his is the
choice between ending the world, effacing it from the long annal of

1. This address was delivered on June 8,   daughter.
1953, at the graduation of Faulkner's

time and space, and completing it. This is not only his right, but his privilege too. Like the phoenix it rises from the ashes of its own failure with each generation, until it is your turn now in your flash and flick of time and space which we call today, in this and in all the stations in time and space today and yesterday and tomorrow, where a handful of aged people like me, who should know but no longer can, are facing young people like you who can do, if they only knew where and how, to perform this duty, accept this privilege, bear this right.

In the beginning, God created the earth. He created it completely furnished for man. Then He created man completely equipped to cope with the earth, by means of free will and the capacity for decision and the ability to learn by making mistakes and learning from them because he had a memory with which to remember and so learn from his errors, and so in time make his own peaceful destiny of the earth. It was not an experiment. God didn't merely believe in man, He knew man. He knew that man was competent for a soul because he was capable of saving that soul and, with it, himself. He knew that man was capable of starting from scratch and coping with the earth and with himself both; capable of teaching himself to be civilized, to live with his fellow man in amity, without anguish to himself or causing anguish and grief to others, and of appreciating the value of security and peace and freedom, since our dreams at night, the very slow evolution of our bodies themselves, remind us constantly of the time when we did not have them. He did not mean freedom from fear, because man does not have the right to be free of fear. We are not so weak and timorous as to need to be free of fear; we need only use our capacity to not be afraid of it and so relegate fear to its proper perspective. He meant security and peace in which to not be afraid, freedom in which to decree and then establish security and peace. And He demanded of man only that we work to deserve and gain these things —liberty, freedom of the body and spirit both, security for the weak and helpless, and peace for all—because these were the most valuable things He could set within our capacity and reach.

During all this time, the angels (with one exception;[2] God had probably had trouble with this one before) merely looked on and watched—the serene and blameless seraphim,[3] that white and shining congeries who, with the exception of that one whose arrogance and pride God had already had to curb, were content merely to bask for eternity in the reflected glory of the miracle of man, content merely to watch, uninvolved and not even caring, while man ran his worthless and unregretted course toward and at last into that twilight where he would be no more. Because they were white, immaculate, negative, without past, without thought or grief or re-

2. I.e., Satan.
3. Angels, purifying ministers of Jehovah.

grets or hopes, except that one—the splendid dark incorrigible one, who possessed the arrogance and pride to demand with, and the temerity to object with, and the ambition to substitute with—not only to decline to accept a condition just because it was a fact, but to want to substitute another conditon in its place.

But this one's opinion of man was even worse than that of the negative and shining ones. This one not only believed that man was incapable of anything but baseness, this one believed that baseness had been inculcated in man to be used for base personal aggrandizement by them of a higher and more ruthless baseness. So God used the dark spirit too. He did not merely cast it shrieking out of the universe, as He could have done. Instead, He used it. He already presaw the long roster of the ambition's ruthless avatars[4]— Genghis and Caesar and William and Hitler and Barca and Stalin and Bonaparte and Huey Long. But He used more—not only the ambition and the ruthlessness and the arrogance to show man what to revolt against, but also the temerity to revolt and the will to change what one does not like. Because He presaw the long roster of the other avatars of that rebellious and uncompromising pride also, the long roster of names longer and more enduring than those of the tyrants and oppressors. They are the long annal of the men and women who have anguished over man's condition and who have held up to us not only the mirror of our follies and greeds and lusts and fears, but have reminded us constantly of the tremendous shape of our godhead too—the godhead and immortality which we cannot repudiate even if we dared, since we cannot rid ourselves of it but only it can rid itself of us—the philosophers and artists, the articulate and grieving who have reminded us always of our capacity for honor and courage and compassion and pity and sacrifice.

But they can only remind us that we are capable of revolt and change. They do not need, we do not need anyone to tell us what we must revolt against and efface from the earth if we are to live in peace and security on it, because we already know that. They can only remind us that man can revolt and change by telling, showing, reminding us how, not lead us, since to be led, we must surrender our free will and our capacity and right to make decisions out of our own personal soul. If we are to be led into peace and security by some individual gauleiter[5] or gang of them, like a drove of sheep through a gate in a fence, it will merely be from one enclosure to another, through another fence with another closable gate in it, and all history has shown us that this will be the gauleiter's enclosure

---

4. Incarnations, examples. The men of power are, respectively: Genghis Khan (1167–1227), the Emperor of Mongolia; Caesar Augustus (63 B.C.–A.D. 14), Roman Emperor; William the Conqueror (1027–87), French conqueror of England and King of England; Adolf Hitler (1889–1945), German dictator; Hamilcar Barca (c. 285–228 B.C.), Carthaginian General, father of Hannibal; Joseph Stalin (1879–1953), Russian dictator; and Napoleon Bonaparte (1769–1821), French Emperor; Huey P. Long (1893–1935), Louisiana Governor.

5. German Nazi district leader.

and fence and his hand which closes and locks the gate, and *that* kind of peace and security will be exactly the sort of peace and security which a flock of sheep deserve.

So He used that split part of the dark proud one's character to remind us of our heritage of free will and decision; He used the poets and philosophers to remind us, out of our own recorded anguish, of our capacity for courage and endurance. But it is we ourselves who must employ them. This time it is you, here, in this room and in all the others like it about the world at this time and occasion in your lives. It is us, we, not as groups or classes but as individuals, simple men and women individually free and capable of freedom and decision, who must decide, affirm simply and firmly and forever never to be led like sheep into peace and security, but ourselves, us, simple men and women simply and mutually confederated for a time, a purpose, an end, for the simple reason that reason and heart have both shown us that we want the same thing and must have it and intend to have it.

To do it ourselves, as individuals, not because we have to merely in order to survive, but because we wish to, will to out of our heritage of free will and decision, the possession of which has given us the right to say how we shall live, and the long proof of our recorded immortality to remind us that we have the courage to elect that right and that course.

The answer is very simple. I don't mean easy, but simple. It is so simple in fact that one's first reaction is something like this: "If that's all it takes, what you will get for it can't be very valuable, very enduring." There is an anecdote about Tolstoy,[6] I think it was, who said in the middle of a discussion on this subject: "All right, I'll start being good tomorrow—if you will too." Which was wit, and had, as wit often does, truth in it—a profound truth in fact to all of them who are incapable of belief in man. But not to them who can and do believe in man. To them, it is only wit, the despairing repudiation of man by a man exhausted into despair by his own anguish over man's condition. These do not say, *The answer is simple, but how difficult*, instead these say, *The answer is not easy, but very simple*. We do not need, the end does not even require, that we dedicate ourselves from this moment on to be Joans of Arc[7] with trumpets and banners and battle-dust toward an end which we will not even see since it will merely be a setting for the monument of martyrdom. It can be done within, concomitant with, the normal life which everyone wants and everyone should have. In fact, that normal life which everyone wants and deserves and can have—provided of course we work for it, are willing to make a reasonable amount of sacrifice commensurate with how much it is

6. Leo Tolstoy (1828–1910), Russian novelist.
7. Jeanne d'Arc (1412–31), French mystic and military heroine who led French troops against the English. Burned as a heretic, she was canonized in the 20th century as a saint.

worth and how much we want and deserve it—can be dedicated to this end and be much more efficacious than all the loud voices and the cries and the banners and trumpets and dust.

Because it begins at home. We all know what "home" means. Home is not necessarily a place fixed in geography. It can be moved, provided the old proven values which made it home and lacking which it cannot be home, are taken along too. It does not necessarily mean or demand physical ease, least of all, never in fact, physical security for the spirit, for love and fidelity to have peace and security in which to love and be faithful, for the devotion and sacrifice. Home means not just today, but tomorrow and tomorrow, and then again tomorrow and tomorrow. It means someone to offer the love and fidelity and respect to who is worthy of it, someone to be compatible with, whose dreams and hopes are your dreams and hopes, who wants and will work and sacrifice also that the thing which the two of you have together shall last forever; someone whom you not only love but like too, which is more, since it must outlast what when we are young we mean by love because without the liking and the respect, the love itself will not last.

Home is not merely four walls—a house, a yard on a particular street, with a number on the gate. It can be a rented room or an apartment—any four walls which house a marriage or a career or both the marriage and career at once. But it must be all the rooms or apartments; all the houses on that street and all the streets in that association of streets until they become a whole, an integer, of people who have the same aspirations and hopes and problems and duties. Perhaps that collection, association, integer, is set in the little spot of geography which produced us in the image of, to be the inheritors of, its problems and dreams. But this is not necessary either; it can be anywhere, so long as we accept it as home; we can even move it, providing and demanding only that we are willing to accept the new problems and duties and aspirations with which we have replaced the old ones which we left behind us, will accept the hopes and aspirations of the people already there, who had established that place as an integer worthy of being served, and are willing to accept our hopes and aspirations in return for their duties and problems. Because the duties and problems were already ours; we merely changed their designations; we cannot shed obligations by moving, because if it is home we want, we do not want to escape them. They are in fact still the same ones, performed and solved for the same reason and result: the same peace and security in which love and devotion can be love and devotion without fear of violence and outrage and change.

If we accept this to mean "home," we do not need to look further than home to find where to start to work, to begin to change, to begin to rid ourselves of the fears and pressures which are making simple existence more and more uncertain and without dignity or

peace or security, and which, to those who are incapable of believing in man, will in the end rid man of his problems by ridding him
of himself. Let us do what is within our power. It will not be easy,
of course: just simple. Let us think first of, work first toward, saving
the integer, association, collection which we call home. In fact, we
must break ourselves of thinking in the terms foisted on us by the
split-offs of that old dark spirit's ambition and ruthlessness: the
empty clanging terms of "nation" and "fatherland" or "race" or
"color" or "creed." We need look no further than home; we need
only work for what we want and deserve here. Home—the house or
even the rented room so long as it includes all the houses and
rented rooms in which hope and aspire the same hopes and aspirations—the street, then all the streets where dwell that voluntary association of people, simple men and women mutually confederated
by identical hopes and aspirations and problems and duties and
needs, to that point where they can say, "These simple things—security and freedom and peace—are not only possible, not only can
and must be, but they shall be." Home: not where *I* live or *it* lives,
but where *we* live: a thousand then tens of thousands of little integers scattered and fixed firmer and more impregnable and more solid
than rocks or citadels about the earth, so that the ruthless and ambitious split-offs of the ancient dark spirit shall look at the one and
say, "There is nothing for us here," then look further, at the rest of
them fixed and founded like fortresses about the whole inhabited
earth, and say, "There is nothing for us any more anywhere. Man
—simple unfrightened invincible men and women—has beaten us."
Then man can put that final signature to his job and say, "We finished it, and it works."

1953

Contemporary
American Prose
1945 –

W HEN IN 1942 a young critic named Alfred Kazin published his first
book, *On Native Grounds*, a survey of American writing from late
nineteenth-century realism up through the literature of the 1930s,
he judged "the greatest single fact about our modern American writing" to
be "our writers' absorption in every last detail of their American world together with their deep and subtle alienation from it." Three years later, on
August 6, 1945, the explosion of an atomic bomb over Hiroshima in Japan
brought about a hasty conclusion to World War II and also introduced into
human life a new reality so unimaginable as to make terms like "crisis" and
"alienation" seem understatements, scarcely adequate to the nature of the
postwar era. What was one to feel, what were American writers to feel
about such an event, and what difference would it make to the kind of work
they were hoping to do?

More than three decades later we can look back upon a number of
cataclysmic upheavals which followed the ones at Hiroshima and Nagasaki.
A short list might include the cold war between America and Russia which,
though never breaking into open violence, reached dangerous proportions in
the 1950s; the attendant fears of nuclear annihilation culminating in the
Cuban missile crisis of 1962; the civil rights movement of the 1960s
with its stark message that there were races in this country who lived
neither on equal nor on amicable terms; the assassination of John F. Kennedy in November of 1963, and the assassinations five years later of his
brother Robert and of Martin Luther King, chief spokesman for civil rights
and the leader of black Americans; the extended, seemingly endless war of
attrition and folly in Vietnam; violence in the urban ghettos; the killing of
four students by the National Guard at Kent State University in 1970,
bringing violence in the universities to a head; the resignation in 1974,
under intense pressure, of President Richard Nixon.

But literature is not life, even though certain episodes from our recent
history wear the aspects of both tragedy and farce; and no list of crucial
public events should be seized upon as responsible for the literature which
is contemporaneous with or which succeeded them. Even though a novel-
fantasy like Robert Coover's *The Public Burning* (1977) could not have

been written without the public events which the novelist uses as his imaginative materials—in this case the execution of the Rosenbergs in 1953 for treason, and the career of Richard Nixon—the directness of relation between literature and contemporary events depends on the books or writers one selects. In the best of postwar American novels and stories the relation has seldom been that direct. To name just three examples from serious writers in the 1950s: the work of Saul Bellow, Flannery O'Connor, and Ralph Ellison surely manifested, in Kazin's terms, "absorption in every last detail of their American world" as well as their "deep and subtle alienation from it." Yet no public event can account for why *The Adventures of Augie March* or *A Good Man Is Hard to Find* or *Invisible Man* should have occurred when they did, or indeed should have occurred at all.

Certain novels did, however, get written as a direct result of World War II, most notably Norman Mailer's *The Naked and the Dead* (1948) and James Jones's *From Here to Eternity* (1951). Mailer had been planning his novel ever since the war began; with hindsight, we can see that he got it out of his system—writing a best seller in the process—then went on to produce many different though not unrelated books. Jones, on the other hand, never found another subject; the final volume of his trilogy about the war was not published until after his death in 1978. World War II novels were long, usually swollen chronicles that looked backward to the naturalism of 1930s writers and were unambitious in their form and style. Perhaps the war novelists were intimidated by Hemingway's *A Farewell to Arms* and persuaded that there was nothing new or profound to say about their subject. Perhaps the novels sank under their conventional story lines, or perhaps it was just too soon to expect highly imaginative writing about the event. At any rate the most compellingly original treatments of that war are to be found in Joseph Heller's *Catch-22* (1961) and Thomas Pynchon's *Gravity's Rainbow* (1973), both written many years after it had ended.

SOUTHERN WRITERS

Taking the years 1945–60 as a unit, we can identify two main groupings of literary energies and principles in the postwar period. The "southern" writers are much less to be thought of as a group than as a number of individually talented novelists and short-story writers, notable for its predominance of women and generally touched by the large shadow of William Faulkner. (Faulkner remained busily at work completing the Snopes trilogy he had begun with *The Hamlet* in 1940, while visiting universities and producing other work until his death in 1962.) The older writers of this group, Katherine Anne Porter and Eudora Welty, remained active—the former occupied with the writing of a lengthy novel *Ship of Fools* (1962), the latter providing a host of distinguished short fiction and novels of which *The Golden Apples* (1947) is perhaps the finest. The younger and, at the time, highly acclaimed writers were Carson McCullers—whose first novel *The Heart Is a Lonely Hunter* (1940) was a critical success and whose short novel *The Member of the Wedding* (1946) is her best work—and Truman Capote, whose *Other Voices, Other Rooms* was published to much fanfare in 1948 when he was twenty-four (Carson McCullers was twenty-three when her first novel appeared).

The absorption of these younger writers in the grotesque, their fascination with extreme and perverse incongruities of character and scene, and their cultivation of verbal effects can be understood as a commitment to "art"—

to a use of the creative imagination and language unchecked by any presumed realities of life as it was lived in America in 1948 or 1960. On the other hand, such features of their writing may be defended as the only true and adequate response the artist can make to that bizarre life. Or so Flannery O'Connor, the most talented and humorous of younger southern writers, implied when she remarked wryly, "Of course I have found that any fiction that comes out of the South is going to be called grotesque by the Northern reader—unless it is grotesque, in which case it's going to be called realistic." In any case these artists (to whom one should add the gifted short-story writer Peter Taylor and the novelist Walker Percy) absorbed—often brilliantly created—American speech, manners, habits of eating or praying or loving, while holding back from any topical engagement with the public and social happenings around them.

NEW YORK WRITERS

With proper consciousness of the umbrellalike nature of the label, we can distinguish another main group of writers and the critics who wrote about and publicized them, as "New York." Here the milieu is urban-Jewish, the concerns recognizably more public and political—although less overtly so in the novelists than in the essayist-intellectuals who criticized them. The major periodical for these writers was *Partisan Review* (for a time *Commentary* shared some of the same interests and personnel), a magazine published monthly, bimonthly, or quarterly throughout the 1940s and 1950s and still extant. *Partisan* was remarkable for the way it managed, despite its inception in highly political circumstances and controversies in the 1930s, to maintain an extremely wide range of interests in poetry, fiction, drama, fine arts; and in Continental literature, politics, and sociological thought. Its favorite fiction writers during the postwar years were Bellow (parts of *The Adventures of Augie March* and all of *Seize the Day* appeared there), Bernard Malamud, Mailer (occasionally), and Delmore Schwartz. But *Partisan* also looked beyond urban-Jewish writing, publishing stories by Flannery O'Connor and James Baldwin and the prologue to Ellison's *Invisible Man*. Among the distinguished critics who contributed steadily to the magazine over these years on a variety of literary and political subjects, one should mention Lionel Trilling—whose *The Liberal Imagination* (1948) was perhaps the most widely read and influential of "New York" critical works—as well as Philip Rahv, Irving Howe, Elizabeth Hardwick, and Diana Trilling. Mary McCarthy reviewed plays and published some of her fiction there, and Hannah Arendt's political writing and Clement Greenberg's art criticism were regular features of the journal.

By 1960 regional and ethnic senses of identity became diluted as the various parts of America began more and more to resemble each other. This cultural dilution can be observed at work in some of the "assimilated" Jews depicted in Philip Roth's *Goodbye, Columbus* (1959) or in the southerners who inhabit Walker Percy's novels generally. To be a southern novelist in 1960 was no more exotic than to be a Jewish novelist. At about that time *Partisan Review* began to lose its distinctiveness, especially after 1963, when during a New York City newspaper strike a new magazine was formed, *The New York Review of Books*. This organ, while making use of many of the *Partisan* writers, appeared biweekly rather than quarterly and was able to give essayists and reviewers as much room as they desired. Its striking success has continued to the present day.

The subheading is taken from *Memories of West Street and Lepke*, a poem Robert Lowell published in 1958 during the years of Eisenhower's presidency (1953–61) when

> . . . even the man
> scavenging filth in the back alley trash cans,
> has two children, a beach wagon, a helpmate,
> and is a "young Republican."

They were years when attention to serious public matters probably meant attention to the cold war, and what was to be done about the real or mythical communists whom Senator Joseph McCarthy was crusading against, or whether a ban on nuclear testing could be accomplished before the United States and the Soviet Union contrived to blow up the world. At home, although there was a famously named "recession" (a Republican word brought into play so as not to recall the great economic depression of 1929 and beyond), the majority of Americans were employed, paid better than they had ever been paid, and exposed to an ever-increasing number of household "labor-saving devices" and automotive finery like the beach wagon of Lowell's poem. Citizens were generally encouraged to think well of their country, while poor people largely remained, in a phrase coined by the socialist critic Michael Harrington, "Our Invisible Poor." And although there was a flurry of confrontations over the Supreme Court's decision in 1954 that public schools could not be maintained on a segregated, "separate but equal" basis, the dramatic beginning to the civil rights struggles which were to mark the 1960s took place largely in the South and was mainly unremarked by novelists preoccupied with other matters.

For all the abuse the 1950s have received as a success-oriented, socially and ecologically irresponsible, fearfully smug decade, they look in retrospect (though they were surely not felt as such at the time) to have been a good time for serious American writers; and not the less so for the individual writer's assurance that he could not possibly be appreciated nor understood by a philistine and materialistic nation run by businessmen, generals, and golfers. So the "deep and subtle alienation" Kazin spoke of was also seen as a necessary, sometimes even an attractive, condition, which furnished a rich vein for fictional exploration. Bellow expressed the mood most masterfully in his short novel *Seize the Day* (1956) through his portrayal of a disastrous day in the life of Tommy Wilhelm, a young man surrounded by prophets, optimists, yea-sayers to family, commerce, and life, who himself cannot operate, cannot make it in, eventually cannot breathe in, this world. Or there is the hero of Ellison's *Invisible Man* (1952), who tells us in the novel's prologue that he lives underground in New York City, the city of light, serviced by a company he calls "Monopolated Light and Power" and who chooses for his hero the jazz cornetist Louis Armstrong, who has "made poetry out of being invisible." In *The Man Who Studied Yoga* (1952), Mailer inspects his unheroic hero Sam Svoboda in order to observe the sadnesses and anxieties lying not far below the surface of middle-class "ordinary" American married couples. Each of these three works lives through its detailed absorption in the urban scene from which its hero is alienated, whether as observed in Harlem, in Brooklyn, or on Manhattan's upper West Side.

OTHER CRITICISMS OF AMERICA

The most stunning fictional success of the 1950s was J. D. Salinger's *The Catcher in the Rye*, a book with a young hero who is out of step with the educational, commercial, and sexual customs of adult society and able to see through and expose its falsities and "phoniness." For a time in the late 1950s and early '60s, one could assume that all college students had read this book, as attested by their "identification" with Holden Caulfield, who summed up and rendered both poignant and funny their own presumed predicaments, enabling them to feel better about being unhappy, even to cherish the illusion that it was virtuous to be so. By 1975 this slippery and astonishing book, though never on the best-seller lists for any one year, had sold nearly six million copies.

Readers of Salinger in the 1950s were probably also reading sociological studies like David Riesman's *The Lonely Crowd* (1950), which classified American behavior as mainly "other-directed," a condition where the accepted standards and criteria for behavior came from outside the self rather than from within. Or they were learning about the "gray-flannel suit" ethos by reading Vance Packard's popular reporting or Sloan Wilson's forgotten best seller, *The Man in the Gray Flannel Suit* (1955). At a more polemical and radical level, a smaller, predominantly university audience read the social criticism of C. Wright Mills in *White Collar* (1951) and *The Power Elite* (1956). There was also much general interest in the popularized psychological, religious, or philosophical movements that surfaced after World War II. The meaning of Existentialism, as imported from France and abstracted from the novels of Albert Camus and Jean-Paul Sartre or from Mailer's novels and essays, was solemnly discussed by those in search of a post-Christian, philosophically respectable attitude toward life. There was much interest in the psychological theories of Erich Fromm or Erik Erikson or, at a lower level, in the "self-help" best sellers like Norman Vincent Peale's *The Power of Positive Thinking* (1952), which sold five million copies. One could even decide that all of Western thinking was at fault and so turn to the East and learn about Zen Buddhism through books by Alan Watts or D. T. Suzuki. The stories of Salinger increasingly featured young people unable to talk to their parents or accept "the American way of life," who became prey to extreme versions of experience, sometimes mystical and sometimes suicidal.

As the 1950s drew to a close, these criticisms of American institutional and social styles over the decade grew more extreme and more specific in the hands of radical critics. Mailer's pamphlet *The White Negro* (1957) defined the American world as essentially "square," stultifying, sickly, infected with pieties and timidities, obedient to authoritarian voices. As a cure for this sickness he proposed a "new breed of adventurer" named "the hipster" who would live according to what Mailer termed the black man's code of "ever-threatening danger" and who would dramatically confront and reject the "square" world. At a no less passionate level, though less violent in its emphasis, was Paul Goodman's *Growing Up Absurd* (1959), the most forceful of many books he wrote in opposition to the technological America he saw around him. Goodman pushed for a return to decentralized, Jeffersonian principles of social organization, to smaller cars, and to meaningful work; his plea especially focused on the "kids" (as he engagingly called them) who needed jobs more worthwhile than making tailfins for America's enormous late-Fifties automobiles if they were to respect either their country or themselves.

But the most publicized literary expression of disaffection with "official" American life was made by the "Beat" writers, of whom Jack Kerouac was the prose laureate. Advertised as "The Beat Generation" and known also, more accurately, as the San Francisco school, the group included most notably the poets Allen Ginsberg and Gregory Corso. Its influence radiated from the City Lights Bookstore run by Lawrence Ferlinghetti, who was himself a poet. Beat poets sometimes read their works to a jazz accompaniment; among their objects of veneration were Whitman, Buddha and Eastern religions generally, and (in Kerouac's case at least) large quantities of Western beer. Their experiments with drugs anticipated the more drastic and often disastrous use of them in the 1960s. The Beats were in favor of "spontaneity" and against constricting forms, poetic or political; indeed, Kerouac proved it was possible to let oneself go and write a novel (*The Subterraneans*, 1958) in three nights. Briefly, the Beat writers constituted a challenge to the many carefully worked-over lyrics or ingeniously worked-out novels which had been characteristic products of the 1950s. They were also good at clowning, and the comic touches that dot their work are probably the parts which will prove most enduring.

LETTING GO IN THE 1960S

The first years of the Sixties decade seemed truly a time when new possibilities and opportunities presented themselves on both public and private levels. The election of John F. Kennedy to the presidency brought to Washington a glamorous and humorous leader who was thought to be committed both to social justice and to culture—perhaps even bringing in the "new Augustan age of poetry and power" Robert Frost wrote about in his inaugural poem. The agreement with Russia to cease nuclear testing in the atmosphere; the increasing concern for changes in the relationship between whites and blacks; the loosening up of sexual codes and of official censorship, coincident with the marketing of an effective new oral contraceptive—these and other events seemed in the minds of some to promise a more life-affirming, less restrictive era than the preceding one. With particular regard to the matter of censorship, it may be noted that for many years Americans who wished to read Henry Miller's novels had to smuggle in from Paris their copies of *Tropic of Cancer* or *Tropic of Capricorn*, while in the mid-1950s Vladimir Nabokov's *Lolita* had to be obtained in a similar way. When in 1956, however, *Lolita* was first published in this country, there was no legal prosecution; and in 1959 the successful publication by Grove Press of D. H. Lawrence's *Lady Chatterley's Lover* cleared the way for novels of more explicit sexual reference. When Mailer published *The Naked and the Dead* in 1948, a well-known four-letter word had to be spelled "fug," evidently to spare the delicate sensibilities of its readers. By 1959, when he published his comic tour de force *The Time of Her Time*, about a sexual warrior's candidly explicit adventures with women in his Greenwich Village loft, hardly anyone raised an eyebrow.

The novelists also seemed, as in the title of Philip Roth's first novel in 1962, to be "letting go" by indulging to the fullest their verbal, storytelling propensities. Between 1961 and 1963 four novels were published (three of them first efforts) by writers whose interest was in the active, exuberant exploration of fantasies, of extremities of experience, and of comic modes which would later on come to be known as "black humor." These books, like many which followed them later in the decade, turned their back on ordinary experience, on the mundane continuities of existence in small town or big city which American writers had so devotedly investigated over the first fifty-odd years of the century. John Barth's *The Sot-Weed Factor* (1961), Joseph Heller's *Catch-22* (1961), Ken Kesey's *One Flew over the Cuckoo's Nest* (1962), and most bizarrely Thomas Pynchon's *V* (1963) all attested to the fact that no verbal resource, no gimmick or extravagance of style need be rejected in the pursuit of putting on a brilliantly entertaining performance. These novels (Kesey's perhaps excluded) were highly self-conscious, parodied other literary styles, and built those parodies into their individually odd designs, at the same time as they were ironic and playful about their own fictional assumptions.

The 1960s were also to see a corresponding "liberation" from official standards of correctness in the realm of the journalistic essay, or—as everyone who wrote in that mode called it—a "piece." Norman Podhoretz noted that everyone he knew was engaged in writing lively essays instead of laboring over novels and poems, and there were many collections of such pieces on subjects ranging from the Beat Generation phenomenon to the trial of Adolf Eichmann. Mailer's *Advertisements for Myself* (1959), the father of the mode, had shown how unconventional and various a book of essays—which also included stories, newspaper columns, interviews—might be, and he produced two more such books in the first half of the new decade. In the hands of Tom Wolfe, style became something to cultivate and exaggerate; the subject of his "New Journalism" might be the doings of a racing-car star or a New York disco celebrity, but it didn't matter since it was merely there for the style to perform upon. A young critic, Susan Sontag, entitled a group of her essays *Against Interpretation* (1966) and made the case for more playful, aesthetically oriented responses to both life and art. That the title essay was originally published in *Partisan Review*, a serious "high culture" periodical, suggested that the winds were changing; as did the fact that literary critics like Richard Poirier or Benjamin DeMott were to be observed writing full-dress "pieces" on listening to the Beatles or on the morals of *Playboy* magazine.

SATIRIC PERFORMANCES

The relation of such expansive and experimental writing to the major public disaster of this time—the assassination of John Kennedy in November 1963—we are not in a position to determine; nor can we determine the effect on literary modes of such events as the following: the increasingly desperate adventure in Vietnam; the riots in the black ghettos of our decaying cities; the turmoil in the universities consequent on the war; the murder of Robert Kennedy and Martin Luther King; the omnipresence of drugs, hard and soft; the rise of pornography as a feature of the sexual "revolution"; the decline of "the family" and the exacerbations in the relations between men and women pointed up at the decade's end by the women's movement and documented in the divorce statistics. Taken together or singly, these severe dislocations proved to be unavailable for writers to deal with in the representational and realistic modes of portrayal handed down to them by novelists such as Howells, Dreiser, or Dos Passos.

Although satire has been a traditional way of dealing with disasters or upheavals, what sort of "satire" could possibly be adequate to matter which seemed beyond the reach of even a gifted writer's words? The middle and late 1960s saw the term "black humor" employed as a tent to cover any literary creation which played fast and loose with ordinary values and standards, frequently employing elements of cruelty and shock to make us see the awful, the ugly, the "sick" in a new way, for what it was. The great humorist in this line—he was a moralist as well—may turn out to have been not a novelist at all but a stand-up comedian, Lenny Bruce, whose violent and obscene rehearsals of clichés in language and in American life gave novelists something to live up to. His was an art of solo performance, dependent (as Frost once said all poetic performance must be) on the prowess and feats of association Bruce's verbal and auditory powers were capable of.

Similar displays by the writer as satiric performer may be viewed in the works of major novelists and prose entertainers from the later 1960s and early '70s: in Mailer's speech to Lyndon Johnson (in 1965) urging him, with as much obscenity and crude familiarity as the lecturer could display, to get us out of Vietnam immediately; in the eloquent pleadings and threatening lashing of James Baldwin's attempts to make whites see and accept blacks; in the daffy brilliance of Pynchon's language throughout *The Crying of Lot 49* (1966); or in the forceful charm with which Roth as comedian came up with one amusing routine after another in *Portnoy's Complaint* (1969). The major performer of them all was undoubtedly Vladimir Nabokov, who in a series of startling novels projected his comic fantasies in a style by turns antic, icy, and weird. When at the end of the decade two of our best, but more conservative, novelists tried to render critically, in vivid detail but in a more traditional narrative, their reservations about American life in the late 1960s, they offended some readers by acting as if such a rendering by an individual imagination could still be made. Bellow's *Mr. Sammler's Planet* (1970) and John Updike's *Rabbit Redux* (1971) remain interestingly combative and tendentious views of the "liberations" of a just-ended decade.

SUMMARY: OLD AND NEW WRITERS IN THE 1970S

In retrospect the major American novelists of the past thirty years, if one agrees to list only five, are arguably Bellow, Mailer, Nabokov, Updike, and Pynchon; opposites in most things except verbal brilliance but likely candidates for positions near the top of any list. But lists are dangerous as well as provocative, and it is more important to note that the dreary cry lamenting the novel's decline is now seldom heard; rather one is impressed by the number of good novels and stories that have been written since the end of the Vietnam war. The women's movement, which became a powerful cultural fact at the end of the 1960s, undoubtedly played an important part in creating a situation where more women than ever in American history are writing fiction, memoir, cultural and social criticism in many distinctive styles and from many points of view. No single female imagination has clearly made its mark as a major one of the stature of older writers like Porter, Welty, O'Connor, or Mary McCarthy; although such a claim could plausibly be made for the work of Susan Sontag, less plausibly for Joyce Carol Oates. But it may be inadvisable to divide up writers according to sex; we can at least observe that new subjects, new materials, for fiction and memoir have been opened up, while new arguments about whether there is or should be a "feminist" criticism of literature have contributed to an enlivening of the literary situation generally.

Much of the vitality in prose writing during the years since the war is found in "nonfiction," as can be seen in this volume by examples from figures so disparate as Edmund Wilson, Malcolm X, Mailer, Updike, Baldwin, and Sontag. Concurrently, many of the best novels from the last thirty or so years are less severe or difficult, more relaxed about their own status as "art," less certain that their only task is to aspire to the condition of a masterpiece—as the great novels by modernist writers like Joyce and Faulkner surely aspired. It is a fact that Pynchon's massive *Gravity's Rainbow*, a very difficult book indeed, has had much impact on college and university readers and teachers; to what extent, however, it will become a book one rereads with pleasure, rather than plows through once as a curiosity, is very much an open question. But generally the jokier, loudly "far-out" or "trip" novels of the late 1960s have given way to more substantial blends of fantasy and realism, as in John Gardner's *The Sunlight Dialogues* (1972) and *October Light* (1976), E. M. Doctorow's *Ragtime* (1975), and Coover's *The Public Burning* (1977). In Gardner's feel for regional speech and behavior, in Robert Stone's ability (in *Dog Soldiers*, 1975) to express post-Vietnam attitudes through dialogue both funny and scarifying, in Paul Theroux's striking comic talents, we see how some of our best new novelists are both original and traditional in their conceptions. These writers and many others must be saluted by a list commemorating older writers, unjustly neglected ones, and ones just beginning to be noticed: William Styron, James Gould Cozzens, J. F. Powers, John Cheever, Evan Connell, Jr., Thomas Savage, Tillie Olsen, Grace Paley, Frederick Buechner, Maureen Howard, Richard Yates, Alison Lurie, Diane Johnson, James Alan McPherson, Cynthia Seton, Henry Bromell, Toni Morrison, Theodore Weesner, Ann Beattie. America is a large country.

EDMUND WILSON
1895–1972

Edmund Wilson's consistently interesting and varied writings touch on virtually every aspect of life and letters over the five decades from the end of World War I to his death in 1972. He addressed himself to nothing less than the major developments in literature, politics, and society of our century, while also performing as a novelist, a playwright, and, most impressively, as an indefatigable reviewer. Wilson's inexhaustible energy and curiosity, his subjective questioning of whether or not something is "true" for him commands our admiration, as well as does his possession of perhaps the most lucid, unpretentiously elegant prose style to be found anywhere in modern American letters. Nowhere are these qualities more evident than in his autobiographical writing, as witnessed by the selections here.

He was born in Red Bank, New Jersey. His father, to whom he devotes most of a retrospective essay, *The Author at Sixty* (*A Piece of My Mind,* 1956), was at one time attorney general of the state and investigated various rackets flourishing in Atlantic City. Wilson went to the Hill School, then to Princeton, where he was a good friend of F. Scott Fitzgerald, who designated Wilson his "intellectual conscience." After serving in World War I he turned to journalism in New York City and was associated with *Vanity Fair* and the *New Republic,* and later for many years with the *New Yorker.* He married a number of times, once to Mary McCarthy, whom he encouraged to write fiction. He traveled widely, among other places to the Soviet Union in 1935, to postwar Europe (celebrated and deplored in *Europe without Baedeker,* 1947) and to more remote cultures. He successfully avoided affiliations with the academy, although while writing his book on Civil War literature (*Patriotic Gore*) he taught a seminar at Harvard. Increasingly he divided his time between Wellfleet, on Cape Cod, and "the old stone house" in Talcottville, N.Y. He came to be acknowledged both here and abroad as America's most distinguished man of letters.

The fame was justified, and rests on the basis of dozens of books. Wilson's literary journalism from the 1920s and 1930s can be found in *The Shores of Light* (1952), his largest and most impressive of such collections. (*Classics and Commercials,* 1950, and *The Bit between My Teeth,* 1965, are later examples.) His sociological reports of a strike in Lawrence, Massachusetts, or of Detroit and Henry Ford, or of a day of violence in Brooklyn are notable for their strong disaffection with American capitalism and are collected along with many others in *The American Jitters* (1932) reprinted in *The American Earthquake* (1958). His novel, *I Thought of Daisy*—a valuable period piece—was published in 1929; but it was two years later, with *Axel's Castle,* that Wilson emerged as a literary critic of importance. This study in the imaginative literature of 1870–1930, with its central chapters on Yeats, Eliot, Joyce, and Proust, is probably still the best introduction to these writers and this period. The excellence of its particular insights is matched by the sweep and daring of its overall thesis: the identification of the major literature of a just-completed "period" with the tradition of symbolism.

Wilson's finest book may be *To the Finland Station*, his "study in the writing and acting of history" which is particularly memorable for its extended and subtle portraits of the great figures from the socialist-communist tradition. Along with *Patriotic Gore*, it contains his most deeply meditated and engaged thoughts about history and politics. But that same year, 1940, in a lecture at Princeton titled "The Historical Interpretation of Literature" (in *The Triple Thinkers*) Wilson argued that, for all his sympathetic commitment to historical and biographical criticism, to "factors" of explanation like Marxist or Freudian ones, the critic's task must still be to evaluate: "to estimate * * * the relative degree of success attained by the products of the various periods and the various personalities. We must be able to tell good from bad, the first-rate from the second-rate." If this insistence on evaluation set him apart from the dominant academic critical practice in 1941, it does so no less today. Much of Wilson's interest as a writer derives from the balance—or tension—he creates between the complementary but quite possibly divergent critical paths of historical understanding and personal evaluation.

One can see in *The Old Stone House* and in *Upstate* (1972), the masterpiece of Wilson's last years, how personal and public he can be in his consideration of things. Here is the individual, wandering about an old house in upstate New York, noticing this and remembering that, but being forced to locate himself—for sanity's sake—in larger historical and cultural situations, ultimately in no less a one than the inexorable passing of time. He both is and is not circumscribed by the house in which he lives, the life he is living out. We read Edmund Wilson most essentially for the way he invites us to extend our limits, while reminding us how firmly planted we must be; for the way he invites us to look at books and writers, countries or times we have never heard of, or never gotten around to considering, or even felt ignorantly superior to. He is the original man who wanted to find things out for himself, and found them over a lifetime of hard and productive labor.

The Old Stone House[1]

As I go north for the first time in years, in the slow, the constantly stopping, milk train—which carries passengers only in the back part of the hind car and has an old stove to heat it in winter—I look out through the dirt-yellowed double pane and remember how once, as a child, I used to feel thwarted in summer till I had got the windows open and there was nothing between me and the widening pastures, the great boulders, the black and white cattle, the rivers, stony and thin, the lone elms like feather-dusters, the high air which sharpens all outlines, makes all colors so breathtakingly vivid, in the clear light of late afternoon.

The little stations again: Barnevald, Stittville, Steuben—a tribute to the Prussian general who helped drill our troops for the Revolution. The woman behind me in the train talks to the conductor with a German accent. They came over here for land and freedom.

---

1. First published in *Scribner's Magazine*, December, 1933, and collected in *Travels* in *Two Democracies* (1936). Reprinted from *The American Earthquake* (1958).

Boonville: that pale boxlike building, smooth gray, with three floors of slots that look in on darkness and a roof like a flat overlapping lid—cold dark clear air, fresh water. Like nothing else but upstate New York. Rivers that run quick among stones, or, deeper, stained dark with dead leaves. I used to love to follow them—should still. A fresh breath of water off the Black River, where the blue closed gentians grow. Those forests, those boulder-strewn pastures, those fabulous distant falls!

There was never any train to Talcottville. Our house was the center of the town. It is strange to get back to this now: it seems not quite like anything else that I have ever known. But is this merely the apparent uniqueness of places associated with childhood?

The settlers of this part of New York were a first westward migration from New England. At the end of the eighteenth century, they drove ox-teams from Connecticut and Massachusetts over into the wild northern country below Lake Ontario and the St. Lawrence River, and they established here an extension of New England.

Yet an extension that was already something new. I happened last week to be in Ipswich, Mass., the town from which one branch of my family came; and, for all the New England pride of white houses and green blinds, I was oppressed by the ancient crampedness. Even the House of the Seven Gables,[2] which stimulated the imagination of Hawthorne, though it is grim perhaps, is not romantic. It, too, has the tightness and the self-sufficiency of that little provincial merchant society, which at its best produced an intense little culture, quite English in its concreteness and practicality—as the block letters of the signs along the docks make Boston look like Liverpool.[3] But life must have hit its head on those close and low-ceilinged coops. That narrowness, that meagerness, that stinginess, still grips New England today: the drab summer cottages along the shore seem almost as slit-windowed and pinched as the gray twin-houses of a mill town like Lawrence or Fall River. I can feel the relief myself of coming away from Boston to these first uplands of the Adirondacks, where, discarding the New England religion but still speaking the language of New England, the settlers found limitless space. They were a part of the new America, now forever for a century on the move; and they were to move on themselves before they would be able to build here anything comparable to the New England civilization. The country, magnificent and vast, has never really been humanized as New England has: the landscape still overwhelms the people. But this house, one of the few of its kind among later wooden houses and towns, was an attempt to found a civilization. It blends in a peculiar fashion the amenities of the

---

2. House in Salem, Mass., which provides the setting and title for Hawthorne's "Romance."

3. Major port and industrial city in northwest England. Like Liverpool, Boston was once a great port.

eastern seaboard with the rudeness and toughness of the new frontier.

It was built at the end of the eighteenth century: the first event recorded in connection with it is a memorial service for General Washington. It took four or five years in the building. The stone had to be quarried and brought out of the river. The walls are a foot and a half thick, and the plaster was applied to the stone without any intervening lattice. The beams were secured by enormous nails, made by hand and some of them eighteen inches long. Solid and simple as a fortress, the place has also the charm of something which has been made to order. There is a front porch with white wooden columns which support a white wooden balcony that runs along the second floor. The roof comes down close over the balcony, and the balcony and the porch are draped with vines. Large ferns grow along the porch, and there are stone hitching-posts and curious stone ornaments, cut out of the quarry like the house: on one side, a round-bottomed bowl in which red geraniums bloom, and on the other, an unnamable object, crudely sculptured and vaguely pagoda-like. The front door is especially handsome: the door itself is dark green and equipped with a brass knocker, and the woodwork which frames it is white; it is crowned with a wide fanlight and flanked by two narrow panes of glass, in which a white filigree of ironwork makes a webbing like ice over winter ponds. On one of the broad sides of the building, where the mortar has come off the stone, there is a dappling of dark gray under pale gray like the dappling of light in shallow water, and the feathers of the elms make dapplings of sun among their shadows of large lace on the grass.

The lawn is ungraded and uneven like the pastures, and it merges eventually with the fields. Behind, there are great clotted masses of myrtle-beds, lilac-bushes, clumps of pink phlox and other things I cannot identify; pink and white hollyhocks, some of them leaning, fine blue and purple dye of larkspur; a considerable vegetable garden, with long rows of ripe gooseberries and currants, a patch of yellow pumpkin flowers, and bushes of raspberries, both white and red—among which are sprinkled like confetti the little flimsy California poppies, pink, orange, white and red. In an old dark red barn behind, where the hayloft is almost collapsing, I find spinning-wheels, a carder, candle-molds, a patent bootjack,[4] obsolete implements of carpentry, little clusters of baskets for berry-picking and a gigantic pair of scales such as is nowadays only seen in the hands of allegorical figures.

The house was built by the Talcotts, after whom the town was named. They owned the large farm in front of the house, which

---

4. "Bootjack": device for loosening one's boots; "carder": an instrument used to disentangle and align fibers of wool or cotton in preparation for spinning.

stretches down to the river and beyond. They also had a profitable grist mill, but—I learn from the county history—were thought to have "adopted a policy adverse to the building up of a village at the point where natural advantages greatly favored," since they "refused to sell village lots to mechanics, and retained the water power on Sugar River, although parties offered to invest liberally in manufactures." In time, there were only two Talcotts left, an old maid and her widowed sister. My great-grandfather, Thomas Baker, who lived across the street and had been left by the death of his wife with a son and eight daughters, paid court to Miss Talcott and married her. She was kind to the children, and they remembered her with affection. My great-grandfather acquired in this way the house, the farm and the quarry.

All but two of my great-grandfather's daughters, of whom my grandmother was one—"six of them beauties," I understand—got married and went away. Only one of them was left in the house at the time when I first remember Talcottville: my great-aunt Rosalind, a more or less professional invalid and a figure of romantic melancholy, whose fiancé had been lost at sea. When I knew her, she was very old. It was impressive and rather frightening to call on her—you did it only by special arrangement, since she had to prepare herself to be seen. She would be beautifully dressed in a lace cap, a lavender dress and a white crocheted shawl, but she had become so bloodless and shrunken as dreadfully to resemble a mummy and reminded one uncomfortably of Miss Haversham in Dickens's *Great Expectations*. She had a certain high and formal coquetry and was the only person I ever knew who really talked like the characters in old novels. When she had been able to get about, she had habitually treated the townspeople with a condescension almost baronial. According to the family legend, the great-grandmother of great-grandmother Baker had been a daughter of one of the Earls of Essex, who had eloped with a gardener to America.

Another of my Baker great-aunts, who was one of my favorite relatives, had married and lived in the town and had suffered tragic disappointments. Only her strong intellectual interests and a mind capable of philosophic pessimism had maintained her through the wreck of her domestic life. She used to tell me how, a young married woman, she had taught herself French by the dictionary and grammar, sitting up at night alone by the stove through one of their cold and dark winters. She had read a great deal of French, subscribed to French magazines, without ever having learned to pronounce it. She had rejected revealed religion and did not believe in immortality; and when she felt that she had been relieved of the last of her family obligations—though her hair was now turning gray—she came on to New York City and lived there alone for years, occupying herself with the theater, reading, visits to her nephews and nieces—with whom she was extremely popular—and all the spectacle and news of the larger world which she had always loved so much but from which she had spent most of her life removed.

When she died, only the youngest of the family was left, the sole brother, my great-uncle Tom. His mother must have been worn out with childbearing—she died after the birth of this ninth child—and he had not turned out so well as the others. He had been born with no roof to his mouth and was obliged to wear a false gold palate, and it was difficult to understand him. He was not really simple-minded—he had held a small political job under Cleveland,[5] and he usually beat me at checkers—but he was childlike and ill-equipped to deal with life in any very effective way. He sold the farm to a German and the quarry to the town. Then he died, and the house was empty, except when my mother and father would come here to open it up for two or three months in the summer.

I have not been back here in years, and I have never before examined the place carefully. It has become for me something like a remembered dream—unearthly with the powerful impressions of childhood. Even now that I am here again, I find I have to shake off the dream. I keep walking from room to room, inside and outside, upstairs and down, with uneasy sensations of complacency that are always falling through to depression.

These rooms are very well proportioned; the white mantel-pieces are elegant and chaste, and the carving on each one is different. The larger of the two living rooms now seems a little bare because the various members of the family have claimed and taken away so many things; and there are some disagreeable curtains and carpets, for which the wife of my great-uncle Tom is to blame. But here are all the things, I take note, that are nowadays sold in antique stores: red Bohemian-glass decanters; a rusty silver snuff-box; a mirror with the American eagle painted at the top of the glass. Little mahogany tables with slim legs; a set of curly-maple furniture, deep seasoned yellow like satin; a yellow comb-backed rocker, with a design of green conch-shells that look like snails. A small bust of Dante with the nose chipped, left behind as defective by one of my cousins when its companion piece, Beethoven, was taken away; a little mahogany melodeon[6] on which my Aunt "Lin" once played. Large engravings of the family of Washington and of the "Reformers Presenting Their Famous Protest before the Diet of Spires"; a later engraving of Dickens. Old tongs and poker, impossibly heavy. A brown mahogany desk inlaid with yellow birdwood, which contains a pair of steel-rimmed spectacles and a thing for shaking sand on wet ink. Daguerreotypes in fancy cases: they seem to last much better than photographs—my grandmother looks fresh and

5. Grover Cleveland (1837–1908), 22nd and 24th President of the United States.

6. Musical instrument—a small reed organ.

cunning—I remember that I used to hear that the first time my grandfather saw her, she was riding on a load of hay—he came back up here to marry her as soon as he had got out of medical school. An old wooden flute—originally brought over from New England, I remember my great-uncle's telling me, at the time when they traveled by ox-team—he used to get a lonely piping out of it—I try it but cannot make a sound. Two big oval paintings, in tarnished gilt frames, of landscapes romantic and mountainous: they came from the Utica house of my great-grandfather Baker's brother—he married a rich wife and invented excelsior—made out of the northern lumber—and was presented with a solid-silver table service by the grateful city of Utica.

Wallpaper molded by the damp from the stone; uninviting old black haircloth furniture. A bowl of those enormous up-country sweet peas, incredibly fragrant and bright—they used to awe and trouble me—why?

In the dining room, a mahogany china closet, which originally— in the days when letters were few and great-grandfather Baker was postmaster—was the whole of the village post office. My grand-mother's pewter tea-service, with its design of oak-leaves and acorns, which I remember from her house in New Jersey. Black iron cranes, pipkins[7] and kettles for cooking in the fireplace; a kind of flat iron pitchfork for lifting the bread in and out, when they baked at the back of the hearth. On the sideboard, a glass decanter with a gilt black-letter label: "J. Rum." If there were only some rum in the decanter!—if the life of the house were not now all past!— the kitchens that trail out behind are almost too old-smelling, too long deserted, to make them agreeable to visit—in spite of the delightful brown crocks with long-tailed blue birds painted on them, a different kind of bird on each crock.

In the ample hall with its staircase, two large colored pictures of trout, one rising to bait, one leaping. Upstairs, a wooden pestle and mortar; a perforated tin box for hot coals to keep the feet warm in church or on sleigh-rides; a stuffed heron; a horrible bust of my cousin Dorothy Read in her girlhood, which her mother had done of her in Germany. The hair-ribbon and the ruffles are faithfully reproduced in marble, and the eyes have engraved pupils. It stands on a high pedestal, and it used to be possible, by pressing a button, to make it turn around. My Cousin Grace, Dorothy's mother, used to show it off and invite comparison with the original, especially calling attention to the nose; but what her mother had never known was that Dorothy had injured her nose in some rather disgraceful row with her sister. One day when the family were making an excursion, Dorothy pleaded indisposition and bribed a man with a truck to take the bust away and drop it into a pond. But Uncle Tom

---

7. "Pipkins": small earthenware pots; "cranes": iron arm used to suspend pots over a fireplace.

got this out of the man, dredged the statue up and replaced it on its pedestal. An ugly chair with a round rag back; an ugly bed with the head of Columbus sticking out above the pillows like a figurehead. Charming old bedquilts, with patterns of rhomboids in softened browns, greens and pinks, or of blue polka-dotted hearts that ray out on stiff phallic stalks. A footstool covered in white, which, however, when you step on a tab at the side, opens up into a cuspidor[8]—some relic, no doubt, of the times when the house was used for local meetings. (There used to be a musical chair, also brought back from Germany, but it seems to have disappeared.) A jar of hardly odorous dried rose-leaves, and a jar of little pebbles and shells that keep their bright colors in alcohol.

The original old panes up here have wavy lines in the glass. There are cobweb-filthy books, which I try to examine: many religious works, the annals of the state legislature, a book called *The Young Wife, or Duties of Women in the Marriage Relation*, published in Boston in 1838 and containing a warning against tea and coffee, which "loosen the tongue, fire the eye, produce mirth and wit, excite the animal passions, and lead to remarks about ourselves and others, that we should not have made in other circumstances, and which it were better for us and the world, never to have made." But there is also, I noticed downstairs, Grant Allen's *The Woman Who Did* from 1893.[9]

I come upon the *History of Lewis County* and read it with a certain pride. I am glad to say to myself that it is a creditable piece of work—admirably full in its information on geology, flora and fauna, on history and local politics; diversified with anecdotes and biographies never overflattering and often pungent; and written in a sound English style. Could anyone in the county today, I wonder, command such a sound English style? I note with gratification that the bone of a prehistoric cuttlefish, discovered in one of the limestone caves, is the largest of its kind on record, and that a flock of wild swans was seen here in 1821. In the eighties, there were still wolves and panthers. There are still bears and deer today.

I also look into the proceedings of the New York State Assembly. My great-grandfather Thomas Baker was primarily a politician and at that time a member of the Assembly. I have heard that he was a Jacksonian Democrat, and that he made a furious scene when my grandmother came back from New Jersey and announced that she had become a Republican: it "spoiled her whole visit." There is a photograph of great-grandfather Baker in an oval gilt frame, with his hair sticking out in three spikes and a wide and declamatory mouth. I look through the Assembly record to see what sort of role he played. It is the forties; the Democrats are still angry over the

---

8. Bowl used as receptacle for tobacco juice or spit.
9. Grant Allen (1848–99): Canadian-

English novelist who gave expression in this work to ideas and values of sexual freedom.

Bank of United States.[1] But when I look up Thomas Baker in the index, it turns out that he figures solely as either not being present or as requesting leave of absence. They tell me he used to go West to buy cattle.

That sealed-up space on the second floor which my father had knocked out—who did they tell me was hidden in it? I have just learned from one of the new road-signs which explain historical associations that there are caves somewhere here in which slaves were hidden. Could this have been a part of the underground route for smuggling Negroes over the border into Canada? Is the attic, the "kitchen chamber," which is always so suffocating in summer, still full of those carpetbags and crinolines and bonnets and beaver-hats that we used to get out of the old cowhide trunks and use to dress up for charades?

It was the custom for the married Baker daughters to bring their children back in the summer; and their children in time brought their children. In those days, how I loved coming up here! It was a reunion with cousins from Boston and New York, Ohio and Wisconsin, as well as with the Talcottville and Utica ones: we fished and swam in the rivers, had all sorts of excursions and games. Later on, I got to dislike it: the older generation died, the younger did not much come. I wanted to be elsewhere, too. The very fullness with life of the past, the memory of those many families of cousins and uncles and aunts, made the emptiness of the present more oppressive. Isn't it still?—didn't my gloom come from that, the night of my first arrival? Wasn't it the dread of that that kept me away? I am aware, as I walk through the rooms, of the amplitude and completeness of the place—the home of a big old-fashioned family that had to be a city in itself. And not merely did it house a clan: the whole life of the community passed through it. And now for five sixths of the year it is nothing but an unheated shell, a storehouse of unused antiques, with no intimate relation to the county.

The community itself today is somewhat smaller than the community of those days, and its condition has very much changed. It must seem to the summer traveler merely one of the clusters of houses that he shoots through along the state highway; and there may presently be little left save our house confronting, across the road, the hot-dog stand and the gasoline station.[2]

For years I have had a recurrent dream. I take a road that runs toward the west. It is summer; I pass by a strange summer forest, in

1. Jacksonian Democrats were proponents of the populist, egalitarian platform and policies of Andrew Jackson, seventh President of the U.S. Jackson abolished the Bank by letting its charter expire without renewal in 1836.
2. "This description may seem inconsistent with my account of our Talcott-ville location in another book, *A Piece of My Mind*, but the main highway was later shifted, put through along another road, and my mother had succeeded, in the meantime, in getting rid of the hot-dog stand by buying back the lot across the street" [Wilson's note].

which there are mysterious beings, though I know that, on the whole, they are shy and benign. If I am fortunate and find the way, I arrive at a wonderful river, which runs among boulders, with rapids, between alders and high spread trees, through a country-side fresh, green and wide. We go in swimming; it is miles away from anywhere. We plunge in the smooth flowing pools. We make our way to the middle of the stream and climb up on the pale round gray stones and sit naked in the sun and the air, while the river glides away below us. And I know that it is the place for which I have always longed, the place of wildness and freedom, to find which is the height of what one may hope for—the place of unal-loyed delight.

As I walk about Talcottville now, I discover that the being-haunted forest is a big grove which even in daytime used to be lonely and dark and where great white Canadian violets used to grow out of the deep black leaf-mold. Today it is no longer dark, because half the trees have been cut down. The river of my dream, I see, is simply an idealized version of the farther and less frequented and more adventurous bank of Sugar River, which had to be reached by wading. Both river and forest are west of the road that runs through the village, which accounts for my always taking that direction in my dream. I remember how Sugar River—out of the stone of which our house is built—used, in my boyhood, so to fascinate me that I had an enlargement made of one of the photo-graphs I had taken of it—a view of "the Big Falls"—and kept it in my room all winter. Today the nearer bank has been largely blasted away to get stone for the new state highway, and what we used to call "the Little Falls" is gone.

I visit the house of my favorite great-aunt, and my gloom returns and overwhelms me. The huge root of an elm has split the thick slabs of the pavement so that you have to walk over a hump; and one of the big square stone fence-posts is toppling. Her flowers, with no one to tend them, go on raggedly blooming in their seasons. There has been nobody in her house since she died. It is all too appropriate to her pessimism—that dead end she always foresaw. As I walk around the house, I remember how, once on the back porch there, she sang me old English ballads, including that grue-some one, "Oh, where have you been, Randall, my son?"—about the man who had gone to Pretty Peggy's house and been given snakes to eat:

> "What had you for supper, Randall, my son?"
> "Fresh fish fried in butter. Oh, make my bed soon!
> For I'm sick at my heart and I fain would lie down!"

She was old then—round-shouldered and dumpy—after the years when she had looked so handsome, straight-backed and with the fashionable aigrette[3] in her hair. And the song she sang seemed to have been drawn out of such barbarous reaches of the past, out of something so surprisingly different from the college-women's hotels in New York in which I had always known her as living: that England to which, far though she had come from it, she was yet so much nearer than I—that queer troubling world of legend which I knew from Percy's *Reliques*[4] but with which she had maintained a real contact through centuries of women's voices—for she sang it without a smile, completely possessed by its spirit—that it made my flesh creep, disconcerted me.

My great-aunt is dead, and all her generation are dead—and the new generations of the family have long ago left Talcottville behind and have turned into something quite different. They were already headed for the cities by the middle of the last century, as can be seen by the rapid dispersal of great-grandfather Baker's daughters. Yet there were still, in my childhood, a few who stayed on in this country as farmers. They were very impressive people, the survivors of a sovereign race who had owned their own pastures and fields and governed their own community. Today the descendants of these are performing mainly minor functions in a machine which they do not control. They have most of them become thoroughly urbanized, and they are farther from great-grandfather Baker than my grandmother, his daughter, was when she came back from New Jersey a Republican. One of her children, a retired importer in New York, was complaining to me the other day that the outrageous demands of the farmers were making business recovery impossible, and protesting that if the advocates of the income tax had their way, the best people would no longer be able to live up to their social positions. A cousin, who bears the name of one of his Ipswich ancestors, a mining engineer on the Coast and a classmate and admirer of Hoover, invested and has lost heavily in Mexican real estate and the industrial speculations of the boom. Another, with another of the old local names, is now at the head of an organization whose frankly avowed purpose is to rescue the New York manufacturers from taxation and social legislation. He has seen his native city of Utica decline as a textile center through the removal of its mills to the South, where taxes are lighter and labor is cheaper; and he is honestly convinced that his efforts are directed toward civic betterment.

Thus the family has come imperceptibly to identify its interests with those of what my great-grandfather Baker would have called the "money power." They work for it and acquiesce in it—they are

---

3. Ornamental arrangement, spray, of jewels worn on hat or in one's hair.
4. *Reliques of Ancient English Poetry,* a compilation of early English ballads, songs, and poems first published 1765 by Bishop Thomas Percy (1729–1811), antiquarian.

no longer the sovereign race of the first settlers of Lewis County, and in the cities they have achieved no sovereignty. They are much too scrupulous and decent, and their tastes are too comparatively simple for them ever to have rolled up great fortunes during the years of expansion and plunder.[5] They have still the frank accent and the friendly eye of the older American world, and they seem rather taken aback by the turn that things have been taking.

And what about me? As I come back in the train, I find that—other causes contributing—my depression of Talcottville deepens. I did not find the river and the forest of my dream—I did not find the magic of the past. I have been too close to the past: there in that house, in that remote little town which has never known industrial progress since the Talcotts first obstructed the development of the water power of Sugar River, you can see exactly how rural Americans were living a century and a half ago. And who would go back to it? Not I. Let people who have never known country life complain that the farmer has been spoiled by his radio and his Ford. Along with the memory of exaltation at the immensity and freedom of that countryside, I have memories of horror at its loneliness: houses burning down at night, sometimes with people in them, where there was no fire department to save them, and husbands or wives left alone by death—the dark nights and the prisoning winters. I do not grudge the sacrifice of the Sugar River falls for the building of the new state highway, and I do not resent the hot-dog stand. I am at first a little shocked at the sight of a transformer on the road between Talcottville and Boonville, but when I get to the Talcottville house, I am obliged to be thankful for it—no more oil-lamps in the evenings! And I would not go back to that old life if I could: that civilization of northern New York—why should I idealize it?—was too lonely, too poor, too provincial.

I look out across the Hudson and see Newburgh: with the neat-windowed cubes of its dwellings and docks, distinct as if cut by a burin,[6] built so densely up the slope of the bank and pierced by an occasional steeple, undwarfed by tall modern buildings and with only the little old-fashioned ferry to connect it with the opposite bank, it might still be an eighteenth-century city. My father's mother came from there. She was the granddaughter of a carpet-importer from Rotterdam. From him came the thick Spanish coins which the children of my father's family were supposed to cut their teeth on. The business, which had been a considerable one, declined as the sea trade of the Hudson became concentrated in New York. My father and mother went once—a good many years ago—to visit the old store by the docks, and were amazed to find a solitary old

---

5. The period following the Civil War witnessed large-scale settlement of the western U.S. and the establishment of vast private fortunes.
6. Steel tool used for engraving.

clerk still scratching up orders and sales on a slate that hung behind the counter.

And the slate and the Spanish coins, though they symbolize a kind of life somewhat different from that evoked by Talcottville, associate themselves in my mind with such things as the old post office turned china closet. And as I happen to be reading Herndon's *Life of Lincoln*,[7] that, too, goes to flood out the vision with its extension still further west, still further from the civilized seaboard, of the life of the early frontier. Through Herndon's extraordinary memoir, one of the few really great American books of its kind, which America has never accepted, preferring to it the sentimentalities of Sandburg and the ladies who write Christmas stories—the past confronts me even more plainly than through the bootjacks and daguerreotypes of Talcottville, and makes me even more uneasy. Here you are back again amid the crudeness and the poverty of the American frontier, and here is a man of genius coming out of it and perfecting himself. The story is not merely moving, it becomes almost agonizing. The ungainly boorish boy from the settler's clearing, with nobody and nothing behind him, hoping that his grandfather had been a planter as my great-aunt Rosalind hoped that she was a descendant of the Earls of Essex, the morbid young man looking passionately toward the refinement and the training of the East but unable to bring himself to marry the women who represented it for him—rejoining across days in country stores, nights in godforsaken hotels, rejoining by heroic self-discipline the creative intelligence of the race, to find himself the conscious focus of its terrible unconscious parturition—his miseries burden his grandeur. At least they do for me at this moment.

> *Old Abe Lincoln came out of the wilderness,*
> *Out of the wilderness, out of the wilderness—*[8]

The echo of the song in my mind inspires me with a kind of awe—I can hardly bear the thought of Lincoln.

Great-grandfather Baker's politics and the Talcottville general store, in which people sat around and talked before the new chain store took its place—Lincoln's school was not so very much different. And I would not go back to that.

Yet as I walk up the steps of my house in New York, I am forced to recognize, with a sinking, that I have never been able to leave it. This old wooden booth I have taken between First and Second Avenues—what is it but the same old provincial America? And as I open the door with its loose knob and breathe in the musty smell of

---

7. William Herndon (1818–91), law partner of Abraham Lincoln whose biography of him was published in 1889. Carl Sandburg's six-volume biography was published in 1926–39.

8. A popular song in the presidential campaign of 1860.

the stair-carpet, it seems to me that I have not merely stuck in the world where my fathers lived but have actually, in some ways, lost ground in it. This gray paintless clapboarded front, these lumpy and rubbed yellow walls—they were probably once respectable, but they must always have been commonplace. They have never had even the dignity of the house in Lewis County. But I have rented them because, in my youth, I had been used to living in houses and have grown to loathe city apartments.

So here, it seems, is where I must live: in an old cramped and sour frame-house—having failed even worse than my relatives at getting out of the American big-business era the luxuries and the prestige that I unquestionably should very much have enjoyed. Here is where I end by living—among the worst instead of the best of this city that took the trade away from Newburgh—the sordid and unhealthy children of my sordid and unhealthy neighbors, who howl outside my windows night and day. It is this, in the last analysis—there is no doubt about it now!—which has been rankling and causing my gloom: to have left that early world behind yet never to have really succeeded in what was till yesterday the new.

1933, 1936, 1958

From Upstate

From *Epilogue, 1970*

What I have written above[9] shows the gradual but steady expiration of the world of New York State as I knew it in my childhood and the modifications that its life has undergone. It is true that Lowville and Boonville have changed less—unless perhaps Charlottesville, Virginia—than any other part of this country that I knew when I was a child. But, as has been seen, it has reflected all the changes that, to a greater degree, have been taking place in the life of the country as a whole. I do not mean to deplore all these changes. Anyone who still takes seriously the American democratic ideal of opportunity for everybody to prosper according to his best abilities and to enjoy such advantages as he can understand ought not to complain of the many cars, the "mobile homes," of the movies and television sets, of the grills for outdoor cooking. None of these things seems to me attractive, but I probably have no right to be contemptuous about them or to blame them entirely on the people who manufacture and advertise them. If people want them, why should they not have them? Don't young people live better in trailers than they did in old-fashioned frame houses, which were often so ill-built and dreary. I remember that in Red Bank, New Jersey, a typical bourgeois suburb, the general possession of motor cars and of comfortable modern houses immensely cheered and brightened that suburban life. We were only four miles from the

---

9. In these closing pages from *Upstate* (1972) Wilson looks back on the book   he has written as well as the vanishing state as he knew it.

ocean, but nobody could get there to swim unless the family had a carriage or, later, an automobile, which at that time was expensive and required a driver. Few people habitually rode bicycles. But presently a trolley was installed, which ran between Red Bank and Seabright. And now everybody owns a car, and in summer one can go to the beach every day. Our old house in Red Bank stood not far from a kind of suburban slum, unsightly and supposed to be something of a den of immorality. My mother's new house that she bought after my father's death, more convenient and much lighter than our gloomy old place, stood in a new street called Buena Vista, and all along it were a class of people that in the past could never have lived so well. On the opposite side of the street from us was the family of a bank clerk, whose wife was pretty and well dressed and whose equally attractive daughter was a great friend of my daughter's. It is true that, when I walked along this street, the radio could be heard from every house and all were playing the same program, so that, no matter how far one walked, the continuity was never interrupted. The implications of this uniformity did not at that time escape me; but I generally approved of what was going on. This, for the people of the United States, was an improvement in their condition. Today in upstate Lewis County there is a whole community of trailers among the trees of a little woodland behind and across the road from the great mansion and mowed grounds of Constable Hall. Constable Hall is now a museum, and the big houses of the well-to-do professional men and dairy owners and merchants have now either been turned into funeral homes or are inhabited by several families. To what other uses could these places be put? And the people who ride in cars, though they are frequently killed or injured in accidents, have no longer such constricted lives. The old way of living up here threw them back on their own capacity for instructing and amusing themselves: reading, playing the piano, sentimental songs, charades, as well as making pies, jams and breadstuffs and quilting and embroidery and the other household arts. But they often, even in the bigger towns, did not see very much of the world. Our old trips in carriages to Carthage and Rome[1] now seem so slow as almost to be comic. I am able to go to Rome now as often as I like to have dinner and see a movie. I have described the quality of the dinners—though Rome has still, dating from 1908, an excellent Italian restaurant; but at worst they are better than the savorless meat and the vegetables in what we called "birds' bathtubs" of the local hotels where we used to have to eat in the course of our longer journeys. And even the worst of the movies are better than the rare melodramas that occasionally made us laugh in Boonville.

Of course there used to be a much greater difference between the

---

1. Like those of many upstate New York towns, these names have a classical reference.

"educated" and the "uneducated." Lowville Academy was once a great local center of schooling to which students came from miles around. The "Ivy League" colleges were places of training for what were called "the learned professions": law, medicine, the pulpit, certain kinds of science and the academic career. Today every young American enjoys the inalienable right to enroll at a state university and, as soon as he pleases, drop out. Negro and white children both may go all the way through primary school without ever learning to read. An "education guidance" man I know, who can certainly not in his work or his life be accused of being undemocratic, has told me that he has come to the conclusion that it is useless to try to educate a good many of the children beyond a necessary minimum. The problem of preventing the abler and more brilliant students from being retarded by the incapacity of the duller ones has sometimes been dealt with in the colleges by having special courses and classes for the former. I do not know enough about the present system to offer predictions or suggestions. I suppose that such vocational schools as the one I have described above must represent a new attempt to deal with the partially educable. It is a kind of successor to and substitute for the old apprentice system. There are in any case now relatively few examples of young people ambitious of meeting, outside the fields of technology, the higher standards of competence and culture.

My reaction to all the things that I disapprove and dislike is that of a member of a once privileged class which is being eliminated all over the world and has very little means any longer of asserting its superior "values." In this, the situation in the United States is not now very different from that in many other parts of the world—including the Soviet Union, except that in the latter the old educated and travelled and comfortable groups were less numerous and more quickly and completely suppressed. But our groups of well-to-do landowners and merchants and able professional men who made the American Revolution have now largely been reduced to the Nixons and Agnews of the present administration,[2] who are hardly superior to the mediocrities that preside over the Soviet Union. It was thought by Veblen[3] and others, that the technocrats would take over as a ruling class, and this to some extent has taken place. I cannot foresee the future, but can only go on with my old occupations.

* * *

But this passing of such splendors as New York State could pretend to has made me feel not only the transience of all forms of life in America, but at my age the constant flow and perishable character, rather than the constant renewal and hope, of everything

2. Richard M. Nixon (b. 1913), 37th President of the U.S. Spiro T. Agnew (b. 1918), his first Vice-President. Both eventually were forced to resign.

3. Thorstein Veblen (1857–1929), American social scientist and author of *Theory of the Leisure Class* (1899).

on the earth. Greece and Rome and classical France[4] left behind them much more durable monuments than our old mansions gone to ruin and our broken-off fragments of old canals; but the aeons of time required for the mammalian plantigrades of the human race to achieve what we can now see to be a very moderate and partial degree of civilization has been coming to discourage and bore me. I look at the creatures on the street and think, well, we have begun to walk upright and our toes, now more or less impractical, are shrinking like the toes of elephants' feet. We have now arrived at a skill of uttering and writing sounds that can convey rather special meanings. But our problems of future development are still absolutely appalling. I do not have any chance, and feel that I should not have the patience, to wait through the countless millennia that would get us past our ages of blind quarreling and of our blindness in sexual selection that makes so much trouble for the children we breed. How much longer must it be before the inhabitants of Russia, ignorant and easily led, spread over such enormous spaces and with so little hunger for information that at the time of the last war there were people to be found in Siberia who not only did not know that there was a war or even that there had been a revolution—how long will it be before such people can organize a modern democracy and cease to attempt to exterminate their original and creative countrymen? I speak of a modern democracy, but how long will it be, for that matter, before the United States can organize a livable society which is free from the even more modern tyranny of bureaucracy? Democracy is actually one of those vague words which are supposed to command approval without giving us a chance to take stock of what our "democracy" consists of. Can I even be sure that, in the language I use, I am formulating these issues correctly? Will these terms not seem very crude to a remotely distant future?—that future I cannot wait for. And where do we get the standards by which we judge our earthly conditions and which are bound to be subject to continual change? When I think of these struggles and transformations to come, I am almost ready to call it a day, at this time of my waning powers, for my own more or less well-meaning efforts. After all, are not my literary activities, like new roads and vocational schools, clumsy gestures in the interest of ends that can only be reached—and what then?—in the course of innumerable centuries that are now entirely unimaginable? As one grows weaker, one becomes more helpless, more lazy, and also more indifferent. Will the Soviet Union last? a Soviet citizen has just demanded. Will General Electric and General Motors—are they "Capitalism," "Democracy"?—last longer than Hyde Hall,[5] which, even in Republican America, was supposed to be still representing Feudalism? We have spent no one knows how many million years,

---

4. French culture in the 17th century was an age of classicism in the arts.

5. Hyde-Clarke Hall, 19th-century mansion in upstate New York.

as have the black widow spider, the hammerhead shark, the deadly amanita and the leaf-nosed bat, building up or assembling or creating—we do not even know how to put it—what we call our bodies and brains, our consciousness. Only now are we beginning a little to understand how these organs and members work. The process of finding out more is going to be very tedious. At least, that is how I feel toward the end of a fairly long life that has left me with the feeling—illusion?—that I have seen or sampled many kinds of experience, that I know what this planet is, what its climates in different places and at different seasons are, what its flora and fauna are, what both its more primitive men and more mechanized men are like—so that, not expecting any real novelty, I have no longer any curiosity beyond such as the satisfaction of which will keep me mildly amused while my faculties are gradually decaying. My young vision of New York State now hardly exists, though I do not think, as I did last year, that I shall sell my old place here. In spite of the encroachments of the highways and the element of impoverished ambitionless inhabitants, I have still, I think, just enough money to keep the old place going, and I am still as comfortable here as I can hope to be anywhere. That the old life is passing away, that all around me are anarchy and what seems to me stupidity, does not move me much any more. I have learned to read the papers calmly and not to hate the fools I read about. As long as my health holds out, I shall have to go on living, and I am glad to have had some share in some of the better aspects of the life of this planet and of northern New York.

1972

VLADIMIR NABOKOV
1899–1977

In Vladimir Nabokov's brilliant memoir *Speak, Memory*, he describes the composition of chess problems as "a beautiful, complex, and sterile art" related to the game itself "only insofar as, say the properties of a sphere are made use of both by a juggler in weaving a new act and by a tennis player in winning a tournament." Nabokov's art of fiction is related to the behavior of ordinary novels no less ambiguously. The best of his many books teaches us how fictional composition may be beautiful, complex, yet avoid sterility because of its fascinated attachment to human life as traced in the actions of an exiled, perverse, and doomed man—inevitably an artist.

Although he did not emigrate to the United States until 1940 (and did not begin writing novels in English until 1938), Nabokov has given us over the past fifty years a rich and ample body of work: novels, memoir, stories, poems, a book on the Russian novelist Gogol, and a translation of the Russian poet Pushkin's *Eugene Onegin*. Like the heroes of his fiction, he has lived in many places. Born in Czarist Russia (St. Petersburg) he moved with his family after the Revolution to London and Berlin, was educated at Trinity College, Cambridge, and lived in Berlin until the Nazis assumed power. After a time in Paris he came to the States, teaching and lecturing during the 1940s and '50s at Wellesley and Cornell. In 1960 he returned to Europe, establishing residence at the Palace Hotel in Montreux, Switzerland, where he eventually died. He rejected numerous invitations to return to America for lectures or residence at a university, preferring instead to pursue, in less academic circumstances, his lifetime avocation as a lepidopterist: "My pleasures are the most intense known to man: writing and butterfly hunting," as he once put it.

In one of his many interviews Nabokov announced that he "was a perfectly normal trilingual child in a family with a large library," a remark which perfectly expresses the imperious charm and sardonically eloquent tenor of his style. Over the past two decades he was partly occupied with turning into English the novels written in Russian during the 1920s and '30s, of which the two most interesting are probably *The Defence*, a poignant account of a doomed chess genius, and *Laughter in the Dark*, a painfully comic fable. Of the novels originally written in English, *Pnin* stands today as most immediately appealing, and is an excellent way to begin reading Nabokov. Its first chapter, printed here, is typical of the way his creator manages to view Timofey Pnin, an extraordinarily passionate and incompetent exile who finds himself teaching in an American college, with fondness and irony. In *Pnin* and in the much more complicated *Pale Fire* five years later, Nabokov gives us marvelously incisive scenes from academic life, as well as the look and feel of lawn, houses, streets in American small towns. Mary McCarthy insisted that *Pale Fire* is "one of the very great works of art of this century"; it is surely one of the most ingenious ones. Cast in the form of a poem, supposedly written by a dead poet named John Shade, then explicated and commented upon by the narrator, Charles Kinbote, until its meanings overwhelm the explicator, the book still manages to remain anchored to a realistic and vibrant sense of place, while giving Nabokov's superb gifts as a parodist their freest reign.

But it is to *Lolita* that appreciation of Nabokov's art most strongly directs itself. Originally published by the Olympia Press in Paris (1955), and until 1958 surreptitiously smuggled into this country as a "dirty book" (Olympia had a large list of pornography), the novel made Nabokov's reputation, indeed his notoriety. Narrated by the most famous of his doomed and duped lovers, Humbert Humbert as he usually calls himself, the book crackles with sustained inventive life, vigorous wordplay, declamation, confession, mock-confession, soliloquy, nonce poems, gibberish, outrageous puns. It is also immensely and entertainingly readable. But its most remarkable achievement is to make us "pity the monsters" (in Robert Lowell's phrase from a poem) by taking to our hearts its repulsive hero— as he himself assures us he is—with eventual sympathy and even love. We can do this only because Nabokov provides Humbert with a language dazzlingly alive to the possibilities of life and to its inevitable fadings, changings, dyings.

Lolita is Nabokov's most eloquent tribute to the power of art, but that power is charmingly saluted in some lines from John Shade's poem in *Pale Fire*, where we hear, clearly, the voice of his author:

I feel I understand
Existence, or at least a minute part
Of my existence, only through my art,
In terms of combinational delight;
And if my private universe scans right,
So does the verse of galaxies divine
Which I suspect is an iambic line.

Even when, as with the very long novel *Ada* (1969) or with his last fictional efforts, the result seems labored, it is still the "combinational delight" of words brilliantly employed that greets the reader on every page and provides both our first and our deepest pleasure in reading Nabokov.

From Pnin[1]

1

The elderly passenger sitting on the north-window side of that inexorably moving railway coach, next to an empty seat and facing two empty ones, was none other than Professor Timofey Pnin. Ideally bald, sun-tanned, and clean-shaven, he began rather impressively with that great brown dome of his, tortoise-shell glasses (masking an infantile absence of eyebrows), apish upper lip, thick neck, and strong-man torso in a tightish tweed coat, but ended, somewhat disappointingly, in a pair of spindly legs (now flanneled and crossed) and frail-looking, almost feminine feet.

His sloppy socks were of scarlet wool with lilac lozenges; his conservative black oxfords had cost him about as much as all the rest of his clothing (flamboyant goon tie[2] included). Prior to the nineteen-forties, during the staid European era of his life, he had always worn long underwear, its terminals tucked into the tops of neat silk socks, which were clocked,[3] soberly colored, and held up on his cotton-clad calves by garters. In those days, to reveal a glimpse of that white underwear by pulling up a trouser leg too high would have seemed to Pnin as indecent as showing himself to ladies minus collar and tie; for even when decayed Mme. Roux, the concierge of the squalid apartment house in the Sixteenth Arrondissement of Paris—where Pnin, after escaping from Leninized Russia and completing his college education in Prague, had spent fifteen years—happened to come up for the rent while he was without his *faux col*,[4] prim Pnin would cover his front stud with a chaste hand. All this underwent a change in the heady atmosphere of the New World. Nowadays, at fifty-two, he was crazy about sunbathing, wore sport shirts and slacks, and when crossing his legs would carefully, deliberately, brazenly display a tremendous stretch

---

1. The first chapter of Nabokov's *Pnin* (1957), first published in *The New Yorker*, November 28, 1953.
2. Large loud necktie in a loutish 1940s style.

3. Ornamented with patterns on the side.
4. Detachable collar. "Stud": ornamental fastener for dress shirt used in place of buttons.

of bare shin. Thus he might have appeared to a fellow passenger; but except for a soldier asleep at one end and two women absorbed in a baby at the other, Pnin had the coach to himself.

Now a secret must be imparted. Professor Pnin was on the wrong train. He was unaware of it, and so was the conductor, already threading his way through the train to Pnin's coach. As a matter of fact, Pnin at the moment felt very well satisfied with himself. When inviting him to deliver a Friday-evening lecture at Cremona—some two hundred versts[5] west of Waindell, Pnin's academic perch since 1945—the vice-president of the Cremona Women's Club, a Miss Judith Clyde, had advised our friend that the most convenient train left Waindell at 1:52 P.M., reaching Cremona at 4:17; but Pnin— who, like so many Russians, was inordinately fond of everything in the line of timetables, maps, catalogues, collected them, helped himself freely to them with the bracing pleasure of getting something for nothing, and took especial pride in puzzling out schedules for himself—had discovered, after some study, an inconspicuous reference mark against a still more convenient train (Lv. Waindell 2:19 P.M., Ar. Cremona 4:32 P.M.); the mark indicated that Fridays, and Fridays only, the two-nineteen stopped at Cremona on its way to a distant and much larger city, graced likewise with a mellow Italian name. Unfortunately for Pnin, his timetable was five years old and in part obsolete.

He taught Russian at Waindell College, a somewhat provincial institution characterized by an artificial lake in the middle of a landscaped campus, by ivied galleries connecting the various halls, by murals displaying recognizable members of the faculty in the act of passing on the torch of knowledge from Aristotle, Shakespeare, and Pasteur to a lot of monstrously built farm boys and farm girls, and by a huge, active, buoyantly thriving German Department which its Head, Dr. Hagen, smugly called (pronouncing every syllable very distinctly) "a university within a university."

In the Fall Semester of that particular year (1950), the enrollment in the Russian Language courses consisted of one student, plump and earnest Betty Bliss, in the Transitional Group, one, a mere name (Ivan Dub, who never materialized) in the Advanced, and three in the flourishing Elementary: Josephine Malkin, whose grandparents had been born in Minsk; Charles McBeth, whose prodigious memory had already disposed of ten languages and was prepared to entomb ten more; and languid Eileen Lane, whom somebody had told that by the time one had mastered the Russian alphabet one could practically read "Anna Karamazov" in the original. As a teacher, Pnin was far from being able to compete with those stupendous Russian ladies, scattered all over academic America, who, without having had any formal training at all, manage somehow, by dint of intuition, loquacity, and a kind of maternal

5. An Old Russian unit of measurement, the verst was .66 miles.

bounce, to infuse a magic knowledge of their difficult and beautiful tongue into a group of innocent-eyed students in an atmosphere of Mother Volga songs, red caviar, and tea; nor did Pnin, as a teacher, ever presume to approach the lofty halls of modern scientific linguistics, that ascetic fraternity of phonemes,[6] that temple wherein earnest young people are taught not the language itself, but the method of teaching others to teach that method; which method, like a waterfall splashing from rock to rock, ceases to be a medium of rational navigation but perhaps in some fabulous future may become instrumental in evolving esoteric dialects—Basic Basque and so forth—spoken only by certain elaborate machines. No doubt Pnin's approach to his work was amateurish and lighthearted, depending as it did on exercises in a grammar brought out by the Head of a Slavic Department in a far greater college than Waindell—a venerable fraud whose Russian was a joke but who would generously lend his dignified name to the products of anonymous drudgery. Pnin, despite his many shortcomings, had about him a disarming, old-fashioned charm which Dr. Hagen, his staunch protector, insisted before morose trustees was a delicate imported article worth paying for in domestic cash. Whereas the degree in sociology and political economy that Pnin had obtained with some pomp at the University of Prague around 1925 had become by midcentury a doctorate in desuetude, he was not altogether miscast as a teacher of Russian. He was beloved not for any essential ability but for those unforgettable digressions of his, when he would remove his glasses to beam at the past while massaging the lenses of the present. Nostalgic excursions in broken English. Autobiographical tidbits. How Pnin came to the *Soedinyonnïe Shtatï* (the United States). "Examination on ship before landing. Very well! 'Nothing to declare?' 'Nothing.' Very well! Then political questions. He asks: 'Are you anarchist?' I answer"—time out on the part of the narrator for a spell of cozy mute mirth—" 'First what do we understand under "Anarchism"? Anarchism practical, metaphysical, theoretical, mystical, abstractical, individual, social? When I was young,' I say, 'all this had for me signification.' So we had a very interesting discussion, in consequence of which I passed two whole weeks on Ellis Island"—abdomen beginning to heave; heaving; narrator convulsed.

But there were still better sessions in the way of humor. With an air of coy secrecy, benevolent Pnin, preparing the children for the marvelous treat he had once had himself, and already revealing, in an uncontrollable smile, an incomplete but formidable set of tawny teeth, would open a dilapidated Russian book at the elegant leatherette marker he had carefully placed there; he would open the book, whereupon as often as not a look of the utmost dismay would alter

6. Smallest unit of speech in the set of sounds that distinguish one utterance from another in a language.

his plastic features; agape, feverishly, he would flip right and left through the volume, and minutes might pass before he found the right page—or satisfied himself that he had marked it correctly after all. Usually the passage of his choice would come from some old and naïve comedy of merchant-class habitus rigged up by Ostrovski almost a century ago, or from an equally ancient but even more dated piece of trivial Leskovian jollity dependent on verbal contortions.[7] He delivered these stale goods with the rotund gusto of the classical Alexandrinka (a theater in Petersburg), rather than with the crisp simplicity of the Moscow Artists; but since to appreciate whatever fun those passages still retained one had to have not only a sound knowledge of the vernacular but also a good deal of literary insight, and since his poor little class had neither, the performer would be alone in enjoying the associative subtleties of his text. The heaving we have already noted in another connection would become here a veritable earthquake. Directing his memory, with all the lights on and all the masks of the mind a-miming, toward the days of his fervid and receptive youth (in a brilliant cosmos that seemed all the fresher for having been abolished by one blow of history), Pnin would get drunk on his private wines as he produced sample after sample of what his listeners politely surmised was Russian humor. Presently the fun would become too much for him; pear-shaped tears would trickle down his tanned cheeks. Not only his shocking teeth but also an astonishing amount of pink upper-gum tissue would suddenly pop out, as if a jack-in-the-box had been sprung, and his hand would fly to his mouth, while his big shoulders shook and rolled. And although the speech he smothered behind his dancing hand was now doubly unintelligible to the class, his complete surrender to his own merriment would prove irresistible. By the time he was helpless with it he would have his students in stitches, with abrupt barks of clockwork hilarity coming from Charles and a dazzling flow of unsuspected lovely laughter transfiguring Josephine, who was not pretty, while Eileen, who was, dissolved in a jelly of unbecoming giggles.

All of which does not alter the fact that Pnin was on the wrong train.

How should we diagnose his sad case? Pnin, it should be particularly stressed, was anything but the type of that good-natured German platitude of last century, *der zerstreute Professor.*[8] On the contrary, he was perhaps too wary, too persistently on the lookout for diabolical pitfalls, too painfully on the alert lest his erratic surroundings (unpredictable America) inveigle him into some bit of preposterous oversight. It was the world that was absent-minded and it was Pnin whose business it was to set it straight. His life was

---

7. Alexander Ostrovski (1823–86), Russian playwright. Nikolai Leskov (1831–95), Russian novelist and short-story writer.

8. The absent-minded professor.

a constant war with insensate objects that fell apart, or attacked him, or refused to function, or viciously got themselves lost as soon as they entered the sphere of his existence. He was inept with his hands to a rare degree; but because he could manufacture in a twinkle a one-note mouth organ out of a pea pod, make a flat pebble skip ten times on the surface of a pond, shadowgraph with his knuckles a rabbit (complete with blinking eye), and perform a number of other tame tricks that Russians have up their sleeves, he believed himself endowed with considerable manual and mechanical skill. On gadgets he doted with a kind of dazed, superstitious delight. Electric devices enchanted him. Plastics swept him off his feet. He had a deep admiration for the zipper. But the devoutly plugged-in clock would make nonsense of his mornings after a storm in the middle of the night had paralyzed the local power station. The frame of his spectacles would snap in mid-bridge, leaving him with two identical pieces, which he would vaguely attempt to unite, in the hope, perhaps, of some organic marvel of restoration coming to the rescue. The zipper a gentleman depends on most would come loose in his puzzled hand at some nightmare moment of haste and despair.

And he still did not know that he was on the wrong train.

A special danger area in Pnin's case was the English language. Except for such not very helpful odds and ends as "the rest is silence," "nevermore," "weekend," "who's who," and a few ordinary words like "eat," "street," "fountain pen," "gangster," "Charleston," "marginal utility," he had had no English at all at the time he left France for the States. Stubbornly he sat down to the task of learning the language of Fenimore Cooper, Edgar Poe, Edison, and thirty-one Presidents. In 1941, at the end of one year of study, he was proficient enough to use glibly terms like "wishful thinking" and "okey-dokey." By 1942 he was able to interrupt his narration with the phrase, "To make a long story short." By the time Truman entered his second term, Pnin could handle practically any topic; but otherwise progress seemed to have stopped despite all his efforts, and by 1950 his English was still full of flaws. That autumn he supplemented his Russian courses by delivering a weekly lecture in a so-called symposium ("Wingless Europe: A Survey of Contemporary Continental Culture") directed by Dr. Hagen. All our friend's lectures, including sundry ones he gave out of town, were edited by one of the younger members of the German Department. The procedure was somewhat complicated. Professor Pnin laboriously translated his own Russian verbal flow, teeming with idiomatic proverbs, into patchy English. This was revised by young Miller. Then Dr. Hagen's secretary, a Miss Eisenbohr, typed it out. Then Pnin deleted the passages he could not understand. Then he read it to his weekly audience. He was utterly helpless without the prepared text, nor could he use the ancient system of dissimulating his infirmity by moving his eyes up and down—snapping up an eyeful of words, reeling them off to his audience, and drawing out the end of the sentence while diving for the next. Pnin's worried eye would be bound to lose its bearings. Therefore he preferred reading his lectures, his gaze glued to his text, in a slow, monotonous baritone that seemed to climb one of those interminable flights of stairs used by people who dread elevators.

The conductor, a gray-headed fatherly person with steel spectacles placed rather low on his simple, functional nose and a bit of soiled adhesive tape on his thumb, had now only three coaches to deal with before reaching the last one, where Pnin rode.

Pnin in the meantime had yielded to the satisfaction of a special Pninian craving. He was in a Pninian quandary. Among other articles indispensable for a Pninian overnight stay in a strange town, such as shoe trees, apples, dictionaries, and so on, his Gladstone bag contained a relatively new black suit he planned to wear that night for the lecture ("Are the Russian People Communist?") before the Cremona ladies. It also contained next Monday's symposium lecture ("Don Quixote and Faust"), which he intended to study the next day, on his way back to Waindell, and a paper by the graduate student, Betty Bliss ("Dostoevski and Gestalt Psychology"), that he had to read for Dr. Hagen, who was her main director of cerebration. The quandary was as follows: If he kept the Cremona manuscript—a sheaf of typewriter-size pages, carefully folded down the center—on his person, in the security of his body warmth, the chances were, theoretically, that he would forget to transfer it from the coat he was wearing to the one he would wear. On the other hand, if he placed the lecture in the pocket of the suit in the bag *now*, he would, he knew, be tortured by the possibility of his luggage being stolen. On the third hand (these mental states sprout additional forelimbs all the time), he carried in the inside pocket of his present coat a precious wallet with two ten-dollar bills, the newspaper clipping of a letter he had written, with my help, to the New York Times in 1945 anent the Yalta conference,[9] and his certificate of naturalization; and it was physically possible to pull out the wallet, if needed, in such a way as fatally to dislodge the folded lecture. During the twenty minutes he had been on the train, our friend had already opened his bag twice to play with his various papers. When the conductor reached the car, diligent Pnin was perusing with difficulty Betty's last effort, which began, "When we consider the mental climate wherein we all live, we cannot but notice——"

The conductor entered; did not awake the soldier; promised the women he would let them know when they would be about to

<hr/>

9. Roosevelt, Churchill, and Stalin met in February, 1945, at Yalta in the Crimea to plan how Europe would be admin- istered by the Allies after Germany was defeated in World War II.

arrive; and presently was shaking his head over Pnin's ticket. The Cremona stop had been abolished two years before.

"Important lecture!" cried Pnin. "What to do? It is a cata-stroph!"

Gravely, comfortably, the gray-headed conductor sank into the opposite seat and consulted in silence a tattered book full of dog-eared insertions. In a few minutes, namely at 3:08, Pnin would have to get off at Whitchurch; this would enable him to catch the four-o'clock bus that would deposit him, around six, at Cremona.

"I was thinking I gained twelve minutes, and now I have lost nearly two whole hours," said Pnin bitterly. Upon which, clearing his throat and ignoring the consolation offered by the kind gray-head ("You'll make it."), he took off his reading glasses, collected his stone-heavy bag, and repaired to the vestibule of the car so as to wait there for the confused greenery skimming by to be cancelled and replaced by the definite station he had in mind.

2

Whitchurch materialized as scheduled. A hot, torpid expanse of cement and sun lay beyond the geometrical solids of various clean-cut shadows. The local weather was unbelievably summery for October. Alert, Pnin entered a waiting room of sorts, with a need-less stove in the middle, and looked around. In a solitary recess, one could make out the upper part of a perspiring young man who was filling out forms on the broad wooden counter before him.

"Information, please," said Pnin. "Where stops four-o'clock bus to Cremona?"

"Right across the street," briskly answered the employee without looking up.

"And where possible to leave baggage?"

"That bag? I'll take care of it."

And with the national informality that always nonplused Pnin, the young man shoved the bag into a corner of his nook.

"Quittance?" queried Pnin, Englishing the Russian for "receipt" (*kvitantsiya*).

"What's that?"

"Number?" tried Pnin.

"You don't need a number," said the fellow, and resumed his writing.

Pnin left the station, satisfied himself about the bus stop, and entered a coffee shop. He consumed a ham sandwich, ordered an-other, and consumed that too. At exactly five minutes to four, having paid for the food but not for an excellent toothpick which he carefully selected from a neat little cup in the shape of a pine cone near the cash register, Pnin walked back to the station for his bag.

A different man was now in charge. The first had been called home to drive his wife in all haste to the maternity hospital. He would be back in a few minutes.

"But I must obtain my valise!" cried Pnin.

The substitute was sorry but could not do a thing.

"It is there!" cried Pnin, leaning over and pointing.

This was unfortunate. He was still in the act of pointing when he realized that he was claiming the wrong bag. His index finger wavered. That hesitation was fatal.

"My bus to Cremona!" cried Pnin.

"There is another at eight," said the man.

What was our poor friend to do? Horrible situation! He glanced streetward. The bus had just come. The engagement meant an extra fifty dollars. His hand flew to his right side. *It* was there, *slava Bogu* (thank God)! Very well! He would not wear his black suit—*vot i vsyo* (that's all). He would retrieve it on his way back. He had lost, dumped, shed many more valuable things in his day. Energetically, almost lightheartedly, Pnin boarded the bus.

He had endured this new stage of his journey only for a few city blocks when an awful suspicion crossed his mind. Ever since he had been separated from his bag, the tip of his left forefinger had been alternating with the proximal edge of his right elbow in checking a precious presence in his inside coat pocket. All of a sudden he brutally yanked it out. It was Betty's paper.

Emitting what he thought were international exclamations of anxiety and entreaty, Pnin lurched out of his seat. Reeling, he reached the exit. With one hand the driver grimly milked out a handful of coins from his little machine, refunded him the price of the ticket, and stopped the bus. Poor Pnin landed in the middle of a strange town.

He was less strong than his powerfully puffed-out chest might imply, and the wave of hopeless fatigue that suddenly submerged his topheavy body, detaching him, as it were, from reality, was a sensation not utterly unknown to him. He found himself in a damp, green, purplish park, of the formal and funereal type, with the stress laid on somber rhododendrons, glossy laurels, sprayed shade trees and closely clipped lawns; and hardly had he turned into an alley of chestnut and oak, which the bus driver had curtly told him led back to the railway station, then that eerie feeling, that tingle of unreality overpowered him completely. Was it something he had eaten? That pickle with the ham? Was it a mysterious disease that none of his doctors had yet detected? My friend wondered, and I wonder, too.

I do not know if it has ever been noted before that one of the main characteristics of life is discreteness. Unless a film of flesh envelops us, we die. Man exists only insofar as he is separated from his surroundings. The cranium is a space-traveler's helmet. Stay inside or you perish. Death is divestment, death is communion. It may be wonderful to mix with the landscape, but to do so is the end of the tender ego. The sensation poor Pnin experienced was something very like that divestment, that communion. He felt porous and pregnable. He was sweating. He was terrified. A stone bench among the laurels saved him from collapsing on the sidewalk. Was his seizure a heart attack? I doubt it. For the nonce I am his physician, and let me repeat, I doubt it. My patient was one of those singular and unfortunate people who regard their heart ("a hollow, muscular organ," according to the gruesome definition in *Webster's New Collegiate Dictionary*, which Pnin's orphaned bag contained) with a queasy dread, a nervous repulsion, a sick hate, as if it were some strong slimy untouchable monster that one had to be parasitized with, alas. Occasionally, when puzzled by his tumbling and tottering pulse, doctors examined him more thoroughly, the cardiograph outlined fabulous mountain ranges and indicated a dozen fatal diseases that excluded one another. He was afraid of touching his own wrist. He never attempted to sleep on his left side, even in those dismal hours of the night when the insomniac longs for a third side after trying the two he has.

And now, in the park of Whitchurch, Pnin felt what he had felt already on August 10, 1942, and February 15 (his birthday), 1937, and May 18, 1929, and July 4, 1920—that the repulsive automaton he lodged had developed a consciousness of its own and not only was grossly alive but was causing him pain and panic. He pressed his poor bald head against the stone back of the bench and recalled all the past occasions of similar discomfort and despair. Could it be pneumonia this time? He had been chilled to the bone a couple of days before in one of those hearty American drafts that a host treats his guests to after the second round of drinks on a windy night. And suddenly Pnin (was he dying?) found himself sliding back into his own childhood. This sensation had the sharpness of retrospective detail that is said to be the dramatic privilege of drowning individuals, especially in the former Russian Navy—a phenomenon of suffocation that a veteran psychoanalyst, whose name escapes me, has explained as being the subconsciously evoked shock of one's baptism which causes an explosion of intervening recollections between the first immersion and the last. It all happened in a flash but there is no way of rendering it in less than so many consecutive words.

Pnin came from a respectable, fairly well-to-do, St. Petersburg family. His father, Dr. Pavel Pnin, an eye specialist of considerable repute, had once had the honor of treating Leo Tolstoy for a case of conjunctivitis. Timofey's mother, a frail, nervous little person with a waspy waist and bobbed hair, was the daughter of the once famous revolutionary Umov (rhymes with "zoom off") and of a German lady from Riga. Through his half swoon, he saw his mother's approaching eyes. It was a Sunday in midwinter. He was eleven. He had been preparing lessons for his Monday classes at the First Gymnasium[1] when a strange chill pervaded his body. His mother

1. European public school.

took his temperature, looked at her child with a kind of stupefaction, and immediately called her husband's best friend, the pediatrician Belochkin. He was a small, beetle-browed man, with a short beard and cropped hair. Easing the skirts of his frock coat, he sat down on the edge of Timofey's bed. A race was run between the doctor's fat golden watch and Timofey's pulse (an easy winner). Then Timofey's torso was bared, and to it Belochkin pressed the icy nudity of his ear and the sandpapery side of his head. Like the flat sole of some monopode, the ear ambulated all over Timofey's back and chest, gluing itself to this or that patch of skin and stomping on to the next. No sooner had the doctor left than Timofey's mother and a robust servant girl with safety pins between her teeth encased the distressed little patient in a strait-jacket-like compress. It consisted of a layer of soaked linen, a thicker layer of absorbent cotton, and another of tight flannel, with a sticky diabolical oilcloth—the hue of urine and fever—coming between the clammy pang of the linen next to his skin and the excruciating squeak of the cotton around which the outer layer of flannel was wound. A poor cocooned pupa, Timosha (Tim) lay under a mass of additional blankets; they were of no avail against the branching chill that crept up his ribs from both sides of his frozen spine. He could not close his eyes because his eyelids stung so. Vision was but oval pain with oblique stabs of light; familiar shapes became the breeding places of evil delusions. Near his bed was a four-section screen of polished wood, with pyrographic designs representing a bridle path felted with fallen leaves, a lily pond, an old man hunched up on a bench, and a squirrel holding a reddish object in its front paws. Timosha, a methodical child, had often wondered what that object could be (a nut? a pine cone?), and now that he had nothing else to do, he set himself to solve this dreary riddle, but the fever that hummed in his head drowned every effort in pain and panic. Still more oppressive was his tussle with the wallpaper. He had always been able to see that in the vertical plane a combination made up of three different clusters of purple flowers and seven different oak leaves was repeated a number of times with soothing exactitude; but now he was bothered by the undismissable fact that he could not find what system of inclusion and circumscription governed the horizontal recurrence of the pattern; that such a recurrence existed was proved by his being able to pick out here and there, all along the wall from bed to wardrobe and from stove to door, the reappearance of this or that element of the series, but when he tried traveling right or left from any chosen set of three inflorescences and seven leaves, he forthwith lost himself in a meaningless tangle of rhododendron and oak. It stood to reason that if the evil designer—the destroyer of minds, the friend of fever—had concealed the key of the pattern with such monstrous care, that key must be as precious as life itself and, when found, would regain for Timofey Pnin his everyday health, his everyday world; and this lucid—alas, too lucid—thought forced him to persevere in the struggle.

A sense of being late for some appointment as odiously exact as school, dinner, or bedtime added the discomfort of awkward haste to the difficulties of a quest that was grading into delirium. The foliage and the flowers, with none of the intricacies of their warp disturbed, appeared to detach themselves in one undulating body from their pale-blue background which, in its turn, lost its papery flatness and dilated in depth till the spectator's heart almost burst in response to the expansion. He could still make out through the autonomous garlands certain parts of the nursery more tenacious of life than the rest, such as the lacquered screen, the gleam of a tumbler, the brass knobs of his bedstead, but these interfered even less with the oak leaves and rich blossoms than would the reflection of an inside object in a windowpane with the outside scenery perceived through the same glass. And although the witness and victim of these phantasms was tucked up in bed, he was, in accordance with the twofold nature of his surroundings, simultaneously seated on a bench in a green and purple park. During one melting moment, he had the sensation of holding at last the key he had sought; but, coming from very far, a rustling wind, its soft volume increasing as it ruffled the rhododendrons—now blossomless, blind—confused whatever rational pattern Timofey Pnin's surroundings had once had. He was alive and that was sufficient. The back of the bench against which he still sprawled felt as real as his clothes, or his wallet, or the date of the Great Moscow Fire—1812.

A gray squirrel sitting on comfortable haunches on the ground before him was sampling a peach stone. The wind paused, and presently stirred the foliage again.

The seizure had left him a little frightened and shaky, but he argued that had it been a real heart attack, he would have surely felt a good deal more unsettled and concerned, and this roundabout piece of reasoning completely dispelled his fear. It was now four-twenty. He blew his nose and trudged to the station.

The initial employee was back. "Here's your bag," he said cheerfully. "Sorry you missed the Cremona bus."

"At least"—and what dignified irony our unfortunate friend tried to inject into that "at least"—"I hope everything is good with your wife?"

"She'll be all right. Have to wait till tomorrow, I guess."

"And now," said Pnin, "where is located the public telephone?"

The man pointed with his pencil as far out and sideways as he could without leaving his lair. Pnin, bag in hand, started to go, but he was called back. The pencil was now directed streetward.

"Say, see those two guys loading that truck? They're going to Cremona right now. Just tell them Bob Horn sent you. They'll take you."

3

Some people—and I am one of them—hate happy ends. We feel cheated. Harm is the norm. Doom should not jam. The avalanche stopping in its tracks a few feet above the cowering village behaves not only unnaturally but unethically. Had I been reading about this mild old man, instead of writing about him, I would have preferred him to discover, upon his arrival to Cremona, that his lecture was not this Friday but the next. Actually, however, he not only arrived safely but was in time for dinner—a fruit cocktail, to begin with, mint jelly with the anonymous meat course, chocolate syrup with the vanilla ice cream. And soon afterwards, surfeited with sweets, wearing his black suit, and juggling three papers, all of which he had stuffed into his coat so as to have the one he wanted among the rest (thus thwarting mischance by mathematical necessity), he sat on a chair near the lectern, while, at the lectern, Judith Clyde, an ageless blonde in aqua rayon, with large, flat cheeks stained a beautiful candy pink and two bright eyes basking in blue lunacy behind a rimless pince-nez, presented the speaker:

"Tonight," she said, "the speaker of the evening——This, by the way, is our third Friday night; last time, as you all remember, we all enjoyed hearing what Professor Moore had to say about agriculture in China. Tonight we have here, I am proud to say, the Russian-born, and citizen of this country, Professor—now comes a difficult one, I am afraid—Professor Pun-neen. I hope I have it right. He hardly needs any introduction, of course, and we are all happy to have him. We have a long evening before us, a long and rewarding evening, and I am sure you would all like to have time to ask him questions afterwards. Incidentally, I am told his father was Dostoevski's family doctor, and he has traveled quite a bit on both sides of the Iron Curtain. Therefore I will not take up your precious time any longer and will only add a few words about our next Friday lecture in this program. I am sure you will all be delighted to know that there is a grand surprise in store for all of us. Our next lecturer is the distinguished poet and prose writer, Miss Linda Lacefield. We all know she has written poetry, prose, and some short stories. Miss Lacefield was born in New York. Her ancestors on both sides fought on both sides in the Revolutionary War. She wrote her first poem before graduation. Many of her poems—three of them, at least—have been published in *Response, A Hundred Love Lyrics by American Women.* In 1922 she received the cash prize offered by——"

But Pnin was not listening. A faint ripple stemming from his recent seizure was holding his fascinated attention. It lasted only a few heartbeats, with an additional systole here and there—last, harmless echoes—and was resolved in demure reality as his distinguished hostess invited him to the lectern; but while it lasted, how limpid the vision was! In the middle of the front row of seats he saw one of his Baltic aunts, wearing the pearls and the lace and the blond wig she had worn at all the performances given by the great ham actor Khodotov, whom she had adored from afar before drifting into insanity. Next to her, shyly smiling, sleek dark head inclined, gentle brown gaze shining up at Pnin from under velvet eyebrows, sat a dead sweetheart of his, fanning herself with a program. Murdered, forgotten, unrevenged, incorrupt, immortal, many old friends were scattered throughout the dim hall among more recent people, such as Miss Clyde, who had modestly regained a front seat. Vanya Bednyashkin, shot by the Reds in 1919 in Odessa because his father had been a Liberal, was gaily signaling to his former schoolmate from the back of the hall. And in an inconspicuous situation Dr. Pavel Pnin and his anxious wife, both a little blurred but on the whole wonderfully recovered from their obscure dissolution, looked at their son with the same life-consuming passion and pride that they had looked at him with that night in 1912 when, at a school festival, commemorating Napoleon's defeat, he had recited (a bespectacled lad all alone on the stage) a poem by Pushkin.

The brief vision was gone. Old Miss Herring, retired Professor of History, author of *Russia Awakes* (1922), was bending across one or two intermediate members of the audience to compliment Miss Clyde on her speech, while from behind that lady another twinkling old party was thrusting into her field of vision a pair of withered, soundlessly clapping hands.

1953, 1957

A Discovery[1]

I found it in a legendary land
all rocks and lavender and tufted grass,
where it was settled on some sodden sand
hard by the torrent of a mountain pass.

The features it combines mark it as new   5
to science: shape and shade—the special tinge,
akin to moonlight, tempering its blue,
the dingy underside, the checquered fringe.

My needles have teased out its sculptured sex;
corroded tissues could no longer hide   10
that priceless mote now dimpling the convex
and limpid teardrop on a lighted slide.

Smoothly a screw is turned; out of the mist
two ambered hooks symmetrically slope,
or scales like battledores of amethyst   15
cross the charmed circle of the microscope.

1. Dated May 15, 1943, this poem was first published in *The New Yorker*, later in *Poems* (1957).

I found it and I named it, being versed
in taxonomic Latin; thus became
godfather to an insect and its first
describer—and I want no other fame.   20

Wide open on its pin (though fast asleep),
and safe from creeping relatives and rust,
in the secluded stronghold where we keep
type specimens it will transcend its dust.

Dark pictures, thrones, the stones like pilgrims kiss,   25
poems that take a thousand years to die
but ape the immortality of this
red label on a little butterfly.

1943, 1957

WRIGHT MORRIS

1910–

Wright Morris was born in Central City, Nebraska, and later said that since "the first ten years of my life were spent in the whistle-stops along the Platte Valley to the West," his books bore "the stamp of an object made on the plains." It is undeniably true that, whether they are set in a tiny hamlet in Nebraska, a suburb of Philadelphia (as in the selection printed here) or a beach in California, the spirit of place is central to them, and the impingement of landscape on man a major fact of Morris's imagination.

Two of his early books, published when he was in his thirties, are illustrated narratives for which he provided the photographs. They display the people, buildings, and furniture of small-town rural America, static and motionless in their solidity and their otherness. Morris's particular faith is expressed in a quotation from Henry James's *The American Scene* which he used as epigraph to *The Home Place* (1948), one of these books with photographs. James insisted that "objects and places, coherently grouped" had "a mystic meaning proper to themselves to give out: to give out, that is, to the participant at once so interested and so detached as to be moved to a report of the matter." Morris was so interested and so detached, and he combines these qualities through an ironic humor which plays over people and places, as well as over the words and phrases through which they express themselves—or are expressed.

Morris is particularly sensitive to, indeed even obsessed by, the cliché as a dead repository for something that was once, somehow, alive and breathing. The narrator of *The World in the Attic* (1949) is filled with rich nostalgia for the Nebraska places of his youth, but as he listens to the repeated phrases the inhabitants use about themselves and their surroundings, he also feels nausea. His boyhood friend, Bud Hibbard, is characterized as a visionary: "a boy, standing on this rise, or dreaming in this hollow, could close his eyes and hear music, music coming over water. * * * That the dream that might be lived, the girls that might be loved, were down there in the hollow, where the lights were blinking, just as they were across the wide green lawn of West Egg. The Great Gatsby, don't forget was born and raised out here." But Gatsby's dream is also a delusion, and though Bud Hibbard now thinks he is married to "the finest creature on God's green earth," the narrator looks at it rather differently. Yet Morris's irony manages to stay generous enough to contain sympathy and even fondness for his victimized dreamers.

His most ambitious novels, written in the 1950s, explore the legacies of heroism and nostalgia, the dreams and delusions left us by a previous generation of American writers, particularly Fitzgerald (in *The Huge Season*, 1954) and Hemingway (in *The Field of Vision*, 1956). But his work can be compared most interestingly with that of his short-lived contemporary James Agee, whose collaborations with the photographer Walker Evans in *Let Us Now Praise Famous Men* (1941) and whose deep interest in the details of provincial American life found even fuller expression in Morris's own fiction. In the story printed here, *The Ram in the Thicket*, as well as in perhaps Morris's best books—*The Works of Love* (1952) and *The Deep Sleep* (1953)—the monotony and the beauty of small-town or suburban life are examined by a restless and dedicated storyteller. Except for his teaching, mainly at San Francisco State College, Wright Morris has been devotedly and continuously a novelist, some would say a novelist's novelist. Yet despite many novels and stories, lively books of literary and social criticism, and volumes of photographs with accompanying text, his hospitable and immensely resourceful voice has not yet been appreciated as much as it deserves to be.

The Ram in the Thicket[1]

In this dream Mr. Ormsby stood in the yard—at the edge of the yard where the weeds began—and stared at a figure that appeared to be on a rise. This figure had the head of a bird with a crown of bright, exotic plumage—visible, somehow, in spite of the helmet he wore. Wisps of it appeared at the side, or shot through the top of it like a pillow leaking long sharp spears of yellow straw. Beneath the helmet was the face of a bird, a long face indescribably solemn, with eyes so pale they were like openings on the sky. The figure was clothed in a uniform, a fatigue suit that was dry at the top but wet and dripping about the waist and knees. Slung over the left arm, very casually, was a gun. The right arm was extended and above it hovered a procession of birds, an endless coming and going of all the birds he had ever seen. The figure did not speak—nor did the pale eyes turn to look at him—although it was for this, this alone, that Mr. Ormsby was there. The only sounds he heard were those his lips made for the birds, a wooing call of irresistible charm. As he

1. Published in *Harper's Bazaar* in 1948, this story, rewritten, forms the beginning of Morris's novel *Man and Boy* (1951). Its title is from Genesis 22.13: as a test of Abraham's faith, God commanded him to sacrifice his son, Isaac. In the act of offering, God saw that Abraham was obedient, and ordered that Isaac be spared. In his place God provided Abraham, for his offering, a ram tangled in a nearby thicket.

stared Mr. Ormsby realized that he was pinned to something, a specimen pinned to a wall that had quietly moved up behind. His hands were fastened over his head and from the weight he felt in his wrists he knew he must be suspended there. He knew he had been brought there to be judged, sentenced, or whatever—and this would happen when the figure looked at him. He waited, but the sky-blue eyes seemed only to focus on the birds, and his lips continued to speak to them wooingly. They came and went, thousands of them, and there were so many, and all so friendly, that Mr. Ormsby, also, extended his hand. He did this although he knew that up to that moment his hands were tied—but strange to relate, in that gesture, he seemed to be free. Without effort he broke the bonds and his hand was free. No birds came—but in his palm he felt the dull drip of the alarm clock and he held it tenderly, like a living thing, until it ran down.

In the morning light the photograph at the foot of his bed was a little startling—for the boy stood alone on a rise, and he held, very casually, a gun. The face beneath the helmet had no features, but Mr. Ormsby would have known it just by the—well, just by the stance. He would have known it just by the way the boy held the gun. He held the gun like some women held their arms when their hands were idle, like parts of their body that for the moment were not much use. Without the gun it was as if some part of the boy had been amputated; the way he stood, even the way he walked was not quite right. But with the gun—what seemed out, fell into place.

He had given the boy a gun because he had never had a gun himself and not because he wanted him to kill anything. The boy didn't want to kill anything either—he couldn't very well with his first gun because of the awful racket the bee-bees made in the barrel. He had given him a thousand-shot gun—but the rattle the bee-bees made in the barrel made it impossible for the boy to get close to anything. And *that* was what had made a hunter out of him. He had to stalk everything in order to get close enough to hit it, and after you stalk it you naturally want to hit something. When he got a gun that would really shoot, and only made a racket after he shot it, it was only natural that he shot it better than anyone else. He said shoot, because the boy never seemed to realize that when he shot and hit something the something was dead. He simply didn't realize this side of things at all. But when he brought a rabbit home and fried it—by himself, for Mother wouldn't let *him* touch it—he never kidded them about the meat they ate themselves. He never really knew whether the boy did that out of kindness for Mother, or simply because he never thought about such things. He never seemed to feel like talking much about anything. He would sit and listen to Mother—he had never once been disrespectful—nor had he ever once heeded anything she said. He would listen, respectfully, and that was all. It was a known fact that Mother knew more about birds and bird migration than anyone in the state of Pennsylvania—except the boy. It was clear to him that the boy knew more, but for years it had been Mother's business and it meant more to her—the business did—than to the boy. But it was only natural that a woman who founded the League for Wild Life Conservation would be upset by a boy who lived with a gun. It was only natural—he was upset himself by the *idea* of it—but the boy and his gun somehow never bothered him. He had never seen a boy and a dog, or a boy and anything, any closer—and if the truth were known both the boy's dogs knew it, nearly died of it. Not that he wasn't friendly, or as nice to them as any boy, but they knew they simply didn't rate in a class with his gun. Without that gun the boy himself really looked funny, didn't know how to stand, and nearly fell over if you talked to him. It was only natural that he enlisted, and there was nothing he ever heard that surprised him less than their making a hero out of him. Nothing more natural than that they should name something after him. If the boy had had his choice it would have been a gun rather than a boat, a thousand-shot non-rattle bee-bee gun named Ormsby. But it would kill Mother if she knew—maybe it would kill nearly anybody—what he thought was the most natural thing of all. Let God strike him dead if he had known anything righter, anything more natural, than that the boy should be killed. That was something he could not explain, and would certainly never mention to Mother unless he slipped up some night and talked in his sleep.

He turned slowly on the bed, careful to keep the springs quiet, and as he lowered his feet he scooped his socks from the floor. As a precaution Mother had slept the first few months of their marriage in her corset—as a precaution and as an aid to self-control. In the fall they had ordered twin beds. Carrying his shoes—today, of all days, would be a trial for Mother—he tiptoed to the closet and picked up his shirt and pants. There was simply no reason, as he had explained to her twenty years ago, why she should get up when he could just as well get a bite for himself. He had made that suggestion when the boy was just a baby and she needed her strength. Even as it was she didn't come out of it any too well. The truth was, Mother was so thorough about everything she did that her breakfasts usually took an hour or more. When he did it himself he was out of the kitchen in ten, twelve minutes and without leaving any pile of dishes around. By himself he could quick-rinse them in a little hot water, but with Mother there was the dish pan and all of the suds. Mother had the idea that a meal simply wasn't a meal without setting the table and using half the dishes in the place. It was easier to do it himself, and except for Sunday, when they had brunch, he was out of the house an hour before she got up. He had a bite of lunch at the store and at four o'clock he did the day's shopping since he was right downtown anyway. There was a time he called her up and inquired as to what she thought she wanted, but since he did all the buying he knew that better himself. As secretary for the League of Women Voters she had enough on her mind in times like these without cluttering it up with food. Now that he left the store an hour early he usually got home in the midst of her nap or while she was taking her bath. As he had nothing else to do he prepared the vegetables, and dressed the meat, as Mother had never shown much of a flair for meat. There had been a year—when the boy was small and before he had taken up that gun—when she had made several marvelous lemon meringue pies. But feeling as she did about the gun—and she told them both how she felt about it—she didn't see why she should slave in the kitchen for people like that. She always spoke to them as *they*—or as *you* plural—from the time he had given the boy the gun. Whether this was because they were both men, both culprits, or both something else, they were never entirely separate things again. When she called *they* would both answer, and though the boy had been gone two years he still felt him *there*, right beside him, when Mother said *you*.

For some reason he could not understand—although the rest of the house was as neat as a pin, too neat—the room they *lived* in was always a mess. Mother refused to let the cleaning woman set her foot in it. Whenever she left the house she locked the door. Long, long ago he had said something, and she had said something, and she had said she had wanted one room in the house where she could relax and just let her hair down. That had sounded so wonderfully human, so unusual for Mother, that he had been completely taken with it. As a matter of fact he still didn't know what to say. It was the only room in the house—except for the screened-in porch in the summer—where he could take off his shoes and open his shirt on his underwear. If the room was *clean*, it would be clean like all of the others, and that would leave him nothing but the basement and the porch. The way the boy took to the out-of-doors—he stopped looking for his cuff links, began to look for pins—was partially because he couldn't find a place in the house to sit down. They had just redecorated the house—the boy at that time was just a little shaver—and Mother had spread newspapers over everything. There hadn't been a chair in the place—except the straight-backed ones at the table—that hadn't been, that *wasn't* covered with a piece of newspaper. Anyone who had ever scrunched around on a paper knew what that was like. It was at that time that he had got the idea of having his pipe in the basement, reading in the bedroom, and the boy had taken to the out-of-doors. Because he had always wanted a gun himself, and because the boy was alone, with no kids around to play with, he had brought him home that damn gun. A thousand-shot gun by the name of Daisy—funny that he should remember the name—and five thousand bee-bees in a drawstring canvas bag. That gun had been a mistake—he began to shave himself in tepid, lukewarm water rather than let it run hot, which would bang the pipes and wake Mother up. That gun had been a mistake—when the telegram came that the boy had been killed Mother hadn't said a word, but she made it clear whose fault it was. There was never any doubt, *any* doubt, as to just whose fault it was.

He stopped thinking while he shaved, attentive to the mole at the edge of his mustache, and leaned to the mirror to avoid dropping suds on the rug. There had been a time when he had wondered about an oriental throw rug in the bathroom, but over twenty years he had become accustomed to it. As a matter of fact he sort of missed it whenever they had guests with children and Mother remembered to take it up. Without the rug he always felt just a little uneasy, a little naked, in the bathroom, and this made him whistle or turn on the water and let it run. If it hadn't been for that he might not have noticed as soon as he did that Mother did the same thing whenever anybody was in the house. She turned on the water and let it run until she was through with the toilet, then she would flush it before she turned the water off. If you happen to have old-fashioned plumbing, and have lived with a person for twenty years, you can't help noticing little things like that. He had got to be a little like that himself: since the boy had gone he used the one in the basement or waited until he got down to the store. As a matter of fact it was more convenient, didn't wake Mother up, and he could have his pipe while he was sitting there.

With his pants on, but carrying his shirt—for he might get it soiled preparing breakfast—he left the bathroom and tiptoed down the stairs.

Although the boy had gone, was gone, that is, Mother still liked to preserve her slip covers and the kitchen linoleum. It was a good piece, well worth preserving, but unless there were guests in the house he never saw it—he nearly forgot that it was there. The truth was he had to look at it once a week, every time he put down the papers—but right now he couldn't tell you what color that linoleum was! He couldn't do it, and wondering what in the world color it was he bent over and peeked at it—blue. Blue and white, Mother's favorite colors of course.

Suddenly he felt the stirring in his bowels. Usually this occurred while he was rinsing the dishes after his second cup of coffee or after the first long draw on his pipe. He was not supposed to smoke in the morning, but it was more important to be regular that way than irregular with his pipe. Mother had been the first to realize this—not in so many words—but she would rather he did anything than not be able to do *that*.

He measured out a pint and a half of water, put it over a medium fire, and added just a pinch of salt. Then he walked to the top of the basement stairs, turned on the light, and at the bottom turned it off. He dipped his head to pass beneath a sagging line of wash, the sleeves dripping, and with his hands out, for the corner was dark, he entered the cell.

The basement toilet had been put in to accommodate the help, who had to use something, and Mother would not have them on her oriental rug. Until the day he dropped some money out of his pants and had to strike a match to look for it, he had never noticed what kind of a stool it was. Mother had picked it up secondhand—she had never told him where—because she couldn't see buying something new for a place always in the dark. It was very old, with a chain pull, and operated on a principle that invariably produced quite a splash. But in spite of that, he preferred it to the one at the store and very much more than the one upstairs. This was rather hard to explain since the seat was pretty cold in the winter and the water sometimes nearly froze. But it was private like no other room in the house. Considering that the house was as good as empty, that was a strange thing to say, but it was the only way to say how he felt. If he went off for a walk like the boy, Mother would miss him, somebody would see him, and he wouldn't feel right about it anyhow. All he wanted was a dark quiet place and the feeling that for five minutes, just five minutes, nobody would be looking for him. Who would ever believe five minutes like that were so hard to come by? The closest he had ever been to the boy—after he had given him the gun—was the morning he had found him here on the stool. It was then that the boy had said, *et tu, Brutus,*[2] and they had both laughed so hard they had had to hold their sides. The boy had put his head in a basket of wash so Mother wouldn't hear. Like everything the boy said there were two or three ways to take it, and in the dark Mr. Ormsby could not see his face. When he stopped laughing the boy said, *Well, Pop, I suppose one flush ought to do,* but Mr. Ormsby had not been able to say anything. To be called Pop made him so weak that he had to sit right down on the stool, just like he was, and support his head in his hands. Just as he had never had a name for the boy, the boy had never had a name for him—none, that is, that Mother would permit him to use. Of all the names Mother couldn't stand, Pop was the worst, and he agreed with her, it was vulgar, common, and used by strangers to intimidate old men. He agreed with her, completely—until he heard the word in the boy's mouth. It was only natural that the boy would use it if he ever had the chance—but he never dreamed that any word, especially *that* word, could mean what it did. It made him weak, he had to sit down and pretend he was going about his business, and what a blessing it was that the place was dark. Nothing more was said, ever, but it remained their most important conversation—so important they were afraid to try and improve on it. Days later he remembered the rest of the boy's sentence, and how shocking it was

2. And thou, Brutus—uttered by Caesar to Brutus after Brutus has stabbed him (Shakespeare's *Julius Caesar,* 3.1.77).

but without any *sense* of shock. A blow so sharp that he had no sense of pain, only a knowing, as he had under gas, that he had been worked on. For two, maybe three minutes, there in the dark they had been what Mother called them, they were *they*—and they were there in the basement because they were so much alike. When the telegram came, and when he knew what he would find, he had brought it there, had struck a match, and read what it said. The match filled the cell with light and he saw—he couldn't help seeing —piles of tin goods in the space beneath the stairs. Several dozen cans of tuna fish and salmon, and since *he* was the one that had the points,[3] bought the groceries, there was only one place Mother could have got such things. It had been a greater shock than the telegram—that was the honest-to-God's truth and anyone who knew Mother as well as he did would have felt the same. It was unthinkable, but there it was—and there were more on top of the water closet, where he peered while precariously balanced on the stool. Cans of pineapple, crabmeat, and tins of Argentine beef. He had been stunned, the match had burned down and actually scorched his fingers, and he nearly killed himself when he forgot and stepped off the seat. Only later in the morning—after he had sent the flowers to ease the blow for Mother—did he realize how such a thing *must* have occurred. Mother knew so many influential people, and before the war they gave her so much, that they had very likely given her all of this stuff as well. Rather than turn it down and needlessly alienate people, influential people, Mother had done the next best thing. While the war was on she refused to serve it, or profiteer in any way—and at the same time not alienate people foolishly. It had been an odd thing, certainly, that he should discover all of that by the same match that he read the telegram. Naturally, he never breathed a word of it to Mother, as something like that, even though she was not superstitious, would really upset her. It was one of those things that he and the boy would keep to themselves.

It would be like Mother to think of putting it in here, the very last place that the cleaning woman would look for it. The new cleaning woman would neither go upstairs nor down, and did whatever she did somewhere else. Mr. Ormsby lit a match to see if everything was all right—hastily blew it out when he saw that the can pile had increased. He stood up—then hurried up the stairs without buttoning his pants as he could hear the water boiling. He added half a cup, then measured three heaping tablespoons of coffee into the bottom of the double boiler, buttoned his pants. Looking at his watch he saw that it was seven-thirty-five. As it would be a hard

3. During World War II Americans were issued rationing stamps and coupons ("points") with which to buy groceries and gasoline. If one lacked the necessary points, it was sometimes possible to obtain goods, for a price, on the "black market."

day—sponsoring a boat was a man-size job—he would give Mother another ten minutes or so. He took two bowls from the cupboard, sat them on blue pottery saucers, and with the grapefruit knife in his hand walked to the icebox.

As he put his head in the icebox door—in order to see he had to—Mr. Ormsby stopped breathing and closed his eyes. What had been dying for some time was now dead. He leaned back, inhaled, leaned in again. The floor of the icebox was covered with a fine assortment of jars full of leftovers Mother simply could not throw away. Some of the jars were covered with little oilskin hoods, some with saucers, and some with paper snapped on with a rubber band. It was impossible to tell, from the outside, which one it was. Seating himself on the floor he removed them one at a time, starting at the front and working toward the back. As he had done this many times before, he got well into the problem, near the middle, before troubling to sniff anything. A jar which might have been carrots—it was hard to tell without probing—was now a furry marvel of green mold. It smelled only mildly, however, and Mr. Ormsby remembered that this was penicillin, the life-giver. A spoonful of cabbage —it had been three months since they had had cabbage—had a powerful stench but was still not the one he had in mind. There were two more jars of mold, the one screwed tight he left alone as it had a frosted look and the top of the lid bulged. The culprit, however, was not that at all, but in an open saucer on the next shelf—part of an egg—Mr. Ormsby had beaten the white himself. He placed the saucer on the sink and returned all but two of the jars to the icebox; the cabbage and the explosive looking one. If it smelled he took it out, otherwise Mother had to see for herself as she refused to take *their* word for these things. When he was just a little shaver the boy had walked into the living room full of Mother's guests and showed them something in a jar. Mother had been horrified—but she naturally thought it a frog or something and not a bottle out of her own icebox. When one of the ladies asked the boy where in the world he had found it, he naturally said, *In the icebox.* Mother had never forgiven him. After that she forbade him to look in the box without permission, and the boy had not so much as peeked in it since. He would eat only what he found on the table, or ready to eat in the kitchen—or what he found at the end of those walks he took everywhere.

With the jar of cabbage and furry mold Mr. Ormsby made a trip to the garage, picked up the garden spade, walked around behind. At one time he had emptied the jars and merely buried the contents, but recently, since the war that is, he had buried it all. Part of it was a question of time—he had more work to do at the store—but the bigger part of it was to put an end to the jars. Not that it worked out that way—all Mother had to do was open a new one—but it gave him a real satisfaction to bury them. Now that the boy and his dogs were gone there was simply no one around the house to eat up all the food Mother saved.

There were worms in the fork of earth he had turned and he stood looking at them—*they* both had loved worms—when he remembered the water boiling on the stove. He dropped everything and ran, ran right into Emil Ludlow, the milkman, before he noticed him. Still on the run he went up the steps and through the screen door into the kitchen—he was clear to the stove before he remembered the door would slam. He started back, but too late, and in the silence that followed the *bang* he stood with his eyes tightly closed, his fists clenched. Usually he remained in this condition until a sign from Mother—a thump on the floor or her voice at the top of the stairs. None came, however, only the sound of the milk bottles that Emil Ludlow was leaving on the porch. Mr. Ormsby gave him time to get away, waited until he heard the horse walking, then he went out and brought the milk in. At the icebox he remembered the water—why it was he had come running in the first place—and he left the door open and hurried to the stove. It was down to half a cup but not, thank heavens, dry. He added a full pint, then returned and put the milk in the icebox; took out the butter, four eggs, and a Flori-gold grapefruit. Before he cut the grapefruit he looked at his watch and seeing that it was ten minutes to eight, an hour before train time, he opened the stairway door.

"Ohhh Mother!" he called, and then he returned to the grapefruit.

Ad astra per aspera,[4] she said, and rose from the bed. In the darkness she felt about for her corset then let herself go completely for the thirty-five seconds it required to get it on. This done, she pulled the cord to the light that hung in the attic, and as it snapped on, in a firm voice she said, *Fiat lux.*[5] Light having been made, Mother opened her eyes.

As the bulb hung in the attic, thirty feet away and out of sight, the closet remained in an afterglow, a twilight zone. It was not light, strictly speaking, but it was all Mother wanted to see. Seated on the attic stairs she trimmed her toenails with a pearl handled knife that Mr. Ormsby had been missing for several years. The blade was not so good any longer and using it too freely had resulted in ingrown nails on both of her big toes. But Mother preferred it to scissors which were proven, along with bathtubs, to be one of the most dangerous things in the home. *Even more than the battlefield, the most dangerous place in the world. Dry feet and hands before turning on lights, dry between toes.*

Without stooping she slipped into her sabots and left the closet, the light burning, and with her eyes dimmed, but not closed, went down the hall. Locking the bathroom door she stepped to the basin and turned on the cold water, then she removed several feet of paper from the toilet paper roll. This took time, as in order to keep the roller from squeaking, it had to be removed from its socket in the wall, then returned. One piece she put in the pocket of her kimono, the other she folded into a wad and used as a blotter to dab up spots on the floor. Turning up the water she sat down on the stool—then she got up to get a pencil and pad from the table near the window. On the first sheet she wrote—

Ars longa, vita brevis[6]
Wildflower club, Sun. 4 pm.

She tore this off and filed it, tip showing, right at the front of her corset. On the next page—

ROGER—
Ivory Snow
Sani-Flush on Thurs.

As she placed this on top of the toilet paper roll she heard him call "First for breakfast." She waited until he closed the stairway door, then she stood up and turned on the shower. As it rained into the tub and splashed behind her in the basin, she lowered the lid, flushed the toilet. Until the water closet had filled, stopped gurgling, she stood at the window watching a squirrel cross the yard from tree to tree. Then she turned the shower off and noisily dragged the shower curtain, on its metal rings, back to the wall. She dampened her shower cap in the basin and hung it on the towel rack to dry, dropping the towel that was there down the laundry chute. This done, she returned to the basin and held her hands under the running water, now cold, until she was awake. With her index finger she massaged her gums—*there is no pyorrhea among the Indians*— and then, with the tips of her fingers, she dampened her eyes.

She drew the blind, and in the half light the room seemed to be full of lukewarm water, greenish in color. With a piece of Kleenex, she dried her eyes, then turned it to gently blow her nose, first the left side, then with a little more blow on the right. There was nothing to speak of, nothing, so she folded the tissue, slipped it into her pocket. Raising the blind, she faced the morning with her eyes softly closed, letting the light come in as prescribed—gradually. Eyes wide, she then stared for a full minute at the yard full of grackles, covered with grackles, before she *discovered* them. Running to the door, her head in the hall, her arm in the bathroom wildly pointing, she tried to whisper, loud-whisper to him, but her voice cracked.

"Roger," she called, a little hoarsely. "The window—run!"

She heard him turn from the stove and skid on the newspapers, bump into the sink, curse, then get up and on again.

6. Art is long, life is short.

"Blackbirds?" he whispered.

"Grackles!" she said, for the thousandth time she said *Grackles*.

"They're pretty!" he said.

"Family—" she said, ignoring him, "family *icteridae* American."

"Well—" he said.

"Roger!" she said, "something's burning."

She heard him leave the window and on his way back to the stove, on the same turn, skid on the papers again. She left him there and went down the hall to the bedroom, closed the door, and passed between the mirrors once more to the closet. From five dresses—*any woman with more than five dresses, at this time, should have the vote taken away from her*—she selected the navy blue sheer with pink lace yoke and kerchief, short bolero. At the back of the closet —but in order to see she had to return to the bathroom, look for the flashlight in the drawer full of rags and old tins of shoe polish— were three shelves, each supporting ten to twelve pairs of shoes, and a large selection of slippers were piled on the floor. On the second shelf were the navy blue pumps—*we all have one weakness, but between men and shoes you can give me shoes*—navy blue pumps with a cuban heel and a small bow. She hung the dress from the neck of the floor lamp, placed the shoes on the bed. From beneath the bed she pulled a hat box—the hat was new. Navy straw with shasta daisies, pink geraniums and a navy blue veil with pink and white fuzzy dots. She held it out where it could be seen in the mirror, front and side, without seeing herself—*it's not every day that one sponsors a boat*. Not every day, and she turned to the calendar on her night table, a bird calendar featuring the natural-color male goldfinch for the month of June. Under the date of June 23rd she printed the words, *family icteridae—yardful*, and beneath it—

Met Captain Sudcliffe and gave him U.S.S. *Ormsby*

When he heard Mother's feet on the stairs Mr. Ormsby cracked her soft-boiled eggs and spooned them carefully into her heated cup. He had spilled his own on the floor when he had run to look at the black—or whatever color they were—birds. As they were very, very soft he had merely wiped them up. As he buttered the toast—the four burned slices were on the back porch airing—Mother entered the kitchen and said, "Roger—*more* toast?"

"I was watching blackbirds," he said.

"Grack-les," she said. "Any bird is a *black*bird if the males are largely or entirely black."

Talk about male and female birds really bothered Mr. Ormsby. Although she was a girl of the old school Mother never hesitated, *anywhere*, to speak right out about male and female birds. A cow was a cow, a bull was a bull, but to Mr. Ormsby a bird was a bird.

"Among the birdfolk," said Mother, "the menfolk, so to speak, wear the feathers. The female has more serious work to do."

"How does that fit the blackbirds?" said Mr. Ormsby.

"Every rule," said Mother, "has an exception."

There was no denying the fact that the older Mother got the more distinguished she appeared. As for himself, what he saw in the mirror looked very much like the Roger Ormsby that had married Violet Ames twenty years ago. As the top of his head got hard the bottom tended to get a little soft, but otherwise there wasn't much change. But it was hard to believe that Mother was the pretty little pop-eyed girl—he had thought it was her corset that popped them— whose nipples had been like buttons on her dress. Any other girl would have looked like a you-know—but there wasn't a man in Media county, or anywhere else, who ever mentioned it. A man could think what he would think, but he was the only man who really knew what Mother was like. And how little she was like *that*.

"Three-seven-four east one-one-six," said Mother.

That was the way her mind worked, all over the place in one cup of coffee—birds one moment, Mrs. Dinardo the next.

He got up from the table and went after Mrs. Dinardo's letter— Mother seldom had time to read them unless he read them to her. Returning, he divided the rest of the coffee between them, un- equally: three quarters for Mother, a swallow of grounds for him- self. He waited a moment, wiping his glasses, while Mother looked through the window at another black bird. "Cowbird," she said, "*Molothrus ater*."

"Dear Mrs. Ormsby," Mr. Ormsby began. Then he stopped to scan the page, as Mrs. Dinardo had a strange style and was not much given to writing letters. "Dear Mrs. Ormsby," he repeated, "I received your letter and I Sure was glad to know that you are both well and I know you often think of me I often think of you too—" He paused to get his breath—Mrs. Dinardo's style was not much for pauses—and to look at Mother. But Mother was still with the cowbird. "Well, Mrs. Ormsby," he continued, "I haven't a thing in a room that I know of the people that will be away from the room will be only a week next month. But come to See me I may have Something if you don't get Something." Mrs. Dinardo, for some reason, always capitalized the letter S which along with everything else didn't make it easier to read. "We are both well and he is Still in the Navy Yard. My I do wish the war was over it is So long. We are So tired of it do come and See us when you give them your boat. Wouldn't a Street be better than a boat? If you are going to name Something why not a Street? Here in my hand is news of a boat Sunk what is wrong with Orsmby on a Street? Well 116 is about the Same we have the river and its nice. If you don't find

Something See me I may have Something. Best love, Mrs. Myrtle Dinardo."

It was quite a letter to get from a woman that Mother had known, known Mother, that is, for nearly eighteen years. Brought in to nurse the boy—he could never understand why a woman like Mother, with her figure—but anyhow, Mrs. Dinardo was brought in. Something in her milk, Dr. Paige said, when it was as plain as the nose on your face it was nothing in the milk, but something in the boy. He just refused, plain refused, to nurse with Mother. The way the little rascal would look at her, but not a sound out of him but gurgling when Mrs. Dinardo would scoop him up and go upstairs to their room—the only woman—other woman, that is, that Mother ever let step inside of it. She had answered an ad that Mother had run, on Dr. Paige's suggestion, and they had been like *that* from the first time he saw them.

"I'll telephone," said Mother.

On the slightest provocation Mother would call Mrs. Dinardo by long distance—she had to come down four flights of stairs to answer—and tell her she was going to broadcast over the radio or something. Although Mrs. Dinardo hardly knew one kind of bird from another, Mother sent her printed copies of every single one of her bird-lore lectures. She also sent her hand-pressed flowers from the garden.

"I'll telephone," repeated Mother.

"My own opinion—" began Mr. Ormsby, but stopped when Mother picked up her eggcup, made a pile of her plates, and started toward the sink. "I'll take care of that," he said. "Now you run along and telephone." But Mother walked right by him and took her stand at the sink. With one hand—with the other she held her kimono close about her—she let the water run into the large dish pan. Mr. Ormsby had hoped to avoid this; now he would have to first rinse, then dry, every piece of silver and every dish they had used. As Mother could only use one hand it would be even slower than usual.

"We don't want to miss our local," he said. "You better run along and let me do it."

"Cold water," she said, "for the eggs." He had long ago learned not to argue with Mother about the fine points of washing pots, pans, or dishes with bits of egg. He stood at the sink with the towel while she went about trying to make suds with a piece of stale soap in a little wire cage. As Mother refused to use a fresh piece of soap, nothing remotely like suds ever appeared. For this purpose, he kept a box of Gold Dust Twins concealed beneath the sink, and when Mother turned her back he slipped some in.

"There now," Mother said, and placed the rest of the dishes in the water, rinsed her fingers under the tap, paused to sniff at them.

"My own opinion—" Mr. Ormsby began, but stopped when Mother raised her finger, the index finger with the scar from the wart she once had. They stood quiet, and Mr. Ormsby listened to the water drip in the sink—the night before he had come down in his bare feet to shut it off. All of the taps dripped now and there was just nothing to do about it but put a rag or something beneath it to break the ping.

"Thrush!" said Mother. "Next to the nightingale the most popular of European songbirds."

"Very pretty," he said, although he simply couldn't hear a thing. Mother walked to the window, folding the collar of her kimono over her bosom and drawing the tails into a hammock beneath her behind. Mr. Ormsby modestly turned away. He quick-dipped one hand into the Gold Dust—drawing it out he slipped it into the dish pan and worked up a suds.

As he finished wiping the dishes she came in with a bouquet for Mrs. Dinardo and arranged it, for the moment, in a tall glass.

"According to her letter," Mrs. Ormsby said, "she isn't too sure of having something—"

"Roger!" she said. "You're dripping."

Mr. Ormsby put his hands over the sink and said, "If we're going to be met right at the station I don't see where you're going to see Mrs. Dinardo. You're going to be met at the staion and then you're going to sponsor the boat. My own opinion is that after the boat we come on home."

"I know that street of hers," said Mother. "There isn't a wild-flower on it!"

On the wall above the icebox was a pad of paper and a blue pencil hanging by a string. As Mother started to write the point broke off, fell behind the icebox.

"Mother," he said, "you ever see my knife?"

"Milkman," said Mother. "If we're staying overnight we won't need milk in the morning."

In jovial tones Mr. Ormsby said, "I'll bet we're right back here before dark." That was all, that was *all* that he said. He had merely meant to call her attention to the fact that Mrs. Dinardo said—all but said—that she didn't have a room for them. But when Mother turned he saw that her mustache was showing, a sure sign that she was mad.

"Well—now," Mother said, and lifting the skirt of her kimono, swished around the cabinet and then he heard her on the stairs. From the landing at the top of the stairs she said, "In that case I'm sure there's no need for *my* going. I'm sure the Navy would just as soon have you. After all," she said, "it's *your* name on the boat!"

"Now, Mother," he said, just as she closed the door, *not* slammed it, just closed it as quiet and nice as you'd please. Although he had

been through this a thousand times it seemed he was never ready for
it, never knew when it would happen, never felt anything but nearly
sick. He went into the front room and sat down on the chair near
the piano—then got up to arrange the doily at the back of his head.
Ordinarily he could leave the house and after three or four days it
would blow over, but in all his life—their life—there had been
nothing like this. The Government of the United States—he got up
again and called, "OHHhhh Mother!"

No answer.

He could hear her moving around upstairs, but as she often went
back to bed after a spat, just moving around didn't mean much of
anything. He came back into the front room and sat down on the
milk stool near the fireplace. It was the only seat in the room not
protected with newspapers. The only thing the boy ever sat on when
he had to sit on something. Somehow, thinking about that made
him stand up. He could sit in the lawn swing, in the front yard, if
Mother hadn't told everybody in town why it was that he, Roger
Ormsby, would have to take the day off—not to sit in the lawn
swing, not by a long shot. Everybody knew—Captain Sudcliffe's
nice letter had appeared on the first page of the *Graphic*, under a
picture of Mother leading a bird-lore hike in the Poconos. This
picture bore the title LOCAL WOMAN HEADS DAWN BUSTERS, and
marked Mother's appearance on the national bird-lore scene. But it
was not one of her best pictures—it dated from way back in the
twenties and those hipless dresses and round bucket hats were not
Mother's type. Until they saw that picture, and the letter beneath it,
some people had forgotten that Virgil was missing, and most of
them seemed to think it was a good idea to swap him for a boat.
The U.S.S. *Ormsby* was a permanent sort of thing. Although he was
born and raised in the town hardly anybody knew very much about
Virgil, but they all were pretty familiar with his boat. "How's that
boat of yours coming along?" they would say, but in more than
twenty years nobody had ever asked him about *his boy*. Whose boy?
Well, that was just the point. Everyone agreed Ormsby was a fine
name for a boat.

It would be impossible to explain to Mother, maybe to anybody
for that matter, what this U.S.S. *Ormsby* business meant to him.
"The" boy and "The" *Ormsby*—it was a pretty strange thing that
they both had the definite article, and gave him the feeling he was
facing a monument.

"Oh Rog-gerrr!" Mother called.

"Coming," he said, and made for the stairs.

From the bedroom Mother said, "However I might feel personally, I do have my *own* name to think of. I am not one of these
people who can do as they please—Roger, are you listening?"

"Yes, Mother," he said.

"—with their life."

As he went around the corner he found a note pinned to the door.

> Bathroom window up
> Cellar door down
> Is it blue or brown for Navy?

He stopped on the landing and looked up the stairs.
"Did you say something?" she said.
"No, Mother—" he said, then he added, "It's blue. For the Navy, Mother, it's blue."

1948

MARY McCARTHY

1912–

In her *Paris Review* interview of 1962, Mary McCarthy, when asked about her identity, cautiously replied, "I suppose I consider myself a novelist." The "supposing" may have been her way of recognizing that, as with James Baldwin or Norman Mailer, she is as respected for her social, political, and cultural criticism as for her published fiction. She is at her best when most directly engaging us in her own life, in her responses to things around her. The autobiographical *Memories of a Catholic Girlhood*, her travel books on Venice and Florence, her accounts of the war in Vietnam and the Watergate scandal—these are obvious examples of such engagements. But her novels and stories are also persistently autobiographical. With the exception of the remarkable and usually overlooked short novel *The Oasis* (1949), we perceive things in a McCarthy fiction through the eyes of an intelligent woman to whom various things are happening at a specifiable point and space in time: New York in 1938; Cape Cod twenty or so years afterward.

Mary McCarthy has led an extraordinarily adventurous and interesting life, and it informs and shapes her books, rather than merely spilling over into them. *Memories of a Catholic Girlhood* tells the strange and complicated story of how, after being born in Seattle, she came east in 1918 with her parents and three siblings to live in Minneapolis near her father's parents (they were Catholic, whereas her maternal grandfather was a Protestant) only to encounter the influenza epidemic, which killed both father and mother. Subsequent events, culminating with her eventual entry into Vassar College, are the subject of this memoir, which, as she keeps reminding us, is suffused with fiction, the imagination having things its own way.

After graduating from Vassar, the institution which later provides the real hero of McCarthy's celebrated novel and best seller *The Group* (1963), she married, lived in New York, and embarked on a journalistic career, at one point serving as drama critic for *Partisan Review*. Her political interests —radical and critical, though never systematically defined by a creed—date from that period, as does her second marriage, to Edmund Wilson, by whom she had a child and who suggested she might be successful at writing fiction. By mutual consent the marriage ended in 1945, but with publication of *The Company She Keeps* (1942), a series of stories about a young woman, the most famous of which is called *The Man in the Brooks Brothers Shirt*, she was launched on a fictional career of lively and sometimes inspired reports on the political, sexual, and social affairs of American white middle-class, college-educated women and men.

In an appreciation of her written in 1961, the critic Elizabeth Hardwick compared her to Margaret Fuller in possessing "a subversive soul sustained by exceptional energy." Hardwick pointed out that it is not easy for a woman to make a career out of candor and dissent, that "a great measure of personal attractiveness and a high degree of romantic singularity" are necessary. This singular attractiveness Mary McCarthy has to a remarkable degree, and it beams out from her fiction, characterized throughout by a rich specification of detail that makes her evocations of paintings, food, clothes, or natural fact so substantial. Most critics agree in admiring a prose that has been called, for want perhaps of a better term, "classical" in its superbly controlled modulations of irony, contempt, cool tolerance, or heated disdain. Without Mailer's apocalyptic all-or-nothing fervor (he pugnaciously reviewed *The Group* and predictably found it wanting), McCarthy has managed rather to see things steadily and over a larger social range than most of her contemporaries.

From Memories of a Catholic Girlhood
From *To the Reader*[1]

* * *

I was born in Seattle in 1912, the first of four children. My parents had met at a summer resort in Oregon, while my mother was a coed at the University of Washington and my father, a graduate of the University of Minnesota, was in the Washington Law School. His father, J. H. McCarthy, had made a fortune in the grain-elevator business in Duluth and Minneapolis; before that, the family had been farmers in North Dakota and, before that, in Illinois. Originally, some generations back, the McCarthys had settled in Nova Scotia; the story is that they had emigrated for religious reasons and not because of the potato famine. In any case, according to legend, they became "wreckers," a common species of land pirate, off the Nova Scotia coast, tying lanterns at night to their sheep on the rocky cliffs to simulate a beaconing port and lure ships to their destruction, for the sake of plunder, or, as it is sometimes told, for the sake of the salvage contract. Plunder would be more romantic, and I hope that was it. By the time I knew them, the McCarthys had become respectable. Nevertheless, there was a wild strain in the family. The men were extraordinarily good-looking, dark and black-browed as pirates, with very fair skin and queer lit-up gray-green eyes, fringed by the "McCarthy eyelashes," long, black, and thick. There was an oddity in the hair pigmentation: my grandfather McCarthy was white by the time he was twenty, and my father was gray at the same age. The women were

---

1. From the first chapter of *Memories of a Catholic Girlhood* (1957).

pious and plain. My grandmother, Elizabeth Sheridan, looked like a bulldog. Her family, too, had originally settled in Canada, whence they had come down to Chicago.

All her sons, as if to be ornery, married pretty wives, and all married Protestants. (Her daughter, my aunt Esther, married a widower named Florence McCarthy who, freakishly, was not a Catholic either.) My mother, Therese Preston, always called "Tess" or "Tessie," was a beautiful, popular girl with an attractive, husky singing voice, the daughter of a prominent Seattle lawyer who had a big house overlooking Lake Washington. His family came originally from Vermont, of old New England stock. Harold Preston had run for United States senator and been defeated, as I always heard it, by "the interests." As state senator, he framed the first Workmen's Compensation Act passed in the United States, an act that served as a model for the workmen's compensation laws later enacted throughout the Union. He was supposed to have had a keen legal brain and was much consulted by other lawyers on points of law. He was president of the state and the city Bar Associations. He did not aspire to a judgeship; the salaries, even on the highest level, were too low, he used to say, to attract the most competent men. In professional and business circles in Seattle, his name was a byword for honesty.

The marriage between my mother and my father was opposed by both sides of the family, partly on religious grounds and partly because of my father's health. He had a bad heart, the result, I was told as a child, of playing football, and the doctors had warned him that he might die at any moment. The marriage took place, despite the opposition. It was a small wedding, with chiefly family present, in the house over the lake. My father survived seven years (during which my mother had four children and several miscarriages), but he was never very well. Nor did he make any money. Though he had a law office in the Hoge Building and a shadowy partner, he spent most of his time at home, often in bed, entertaining us children.

It sounds like a gloomy situation, yet in fact it was very gay. My mother's parents were in a state of constant apprehension that she was going to be left a young widow with a handful of children to take care of, but my mother and father seemed to be completely carefree. They were very much in love, everyone agrees, and money never worried my father. He had an allowance of eight or nine hundred dollars a month from his father, and my mother had a hundred from hers. In spite of this, they were always in debt, which was my father's fault. He was a recklessly extravagant man, who lay in bed planning treats and surprises. The reader will hear later of my little diamond rings and my ermine muff and neckpiece. I remember, too, beauty pins, picnics in the back yard, Easter egg hunts, a succession of birthday cakes and ice-cream molds, a glorious May basket my father hung on my doorknob, a hyacinth plant, parties with grab bags and fish ponds, the little electric stove on which my mother made us chocolate and cambric tea in the afternoons. My mother had a strain of extravagance in her family, too. But it was my father who insisted on turning everything into a treat. I remember his showing me how to eat a peach by building a little white mountain of sugar and then dipping the peach into it. And I remember his coming home one night with his arms full of red roses for my mother, and my mother's crying out, "Oh, Roy!" reproachfully because there was no food for dinner. Or did someone tell me this story? If we went without dinner while we were waiting for the monthly allowance, it cannot have happened often; our trouble, on the contrary, was upset stomachs due to "fancy" food, or so I am told—I have no recollection of this myself or of all the enemas and purges we are supposed to have taken. I do remember that we could not keep maids or nurses; those that stayed longest were a raw, red, homely Irishwoman with warts on her hands, the faithful Gertrude, whom I disliked because she was not pretty, and a Japanese manservant who was an artist with the pastry bag.

My father, I used to maintain, was so tall that he could not get through a door without bending his head. This was an exaggeration. He was a tall man, but not remarkably so, as I can see from pictures; like all the McCarthy men, he had a torso that was heavy-boned and a little too long for his legs. He wore his gray hair in a pompadour and carried a stick when he walked. He read to me a great deal, chiefly Eugene Field[2] and fairy tales, and I remember we heard a nightingale together, on the boulevard, near the Sacred Heart convent. But there are no nightingales in North America.

My father was a romancer, and most of my memories of him are colored, I fear, by an untruthfulness that I must have caught from him, like one of the colds that ran round the family. While my grandfather Preston was preternaturally honest, there was mendacity, somewhere, in the McCarthy blood. Many of my most cherished ideas about my father have turned out to be false. There was the legend of his football prowess. For years I believed, and repeated, that he had been captain of the Minnesota football team, but actually it was only a high-school team in Minneapolis. I suppose I must have got this impression from the boasts of my grandmother McCarthy. For years I believed that he was a Deke at college, but I think it was really Delta Upsilon. His gold watch, saved for my brother Kevin, turned out to be plated—a great disappointment. He was at the head of his class in law school, so I always heard, but I do not think this was true. As for the legend that he was a brilliant man, with marked literary gifts, alas, I once saw his diary. It was a record of heights and weights, temperatures

2. American journalist and popular, sentimental poet of childhood (1850–95).

and enemas, interspersed with slightly sententious "thoughts," like a schoolboy's; he writes out for himself, laboriously, the definitions of an atheist and an agnostic.

All the same, there was a romantic aura surrounding him, a certain mythic power that made people want to invent stories about him. My grandmother Preston, for instance, who was no special partisan of his, told me that on our fatal journey from Seattle to Minneapolis, my father drew a revolver on the train conductor, who was threatening to put our sick family off somewhere in North Dakota. I wrote this, and the reader will find it, in the memoir titled "Yonder Peasant, Who Is He?" But my Uncle Harry, who was on the train, tells me that this never happened. My father, he says, was far too sick to draw a gun on anybody, and who would have told my grandmother, except my Uncle Harry himself, since he and his wife were the only adult survivors of our party? Or did my grandmother hear it from some other passenger, on his way east during the great flu epidemic?

My last clear personal recollection of my father is one of sitting beside him on that train trip and looking out the window at the Rocky Mountains. All the rest of the party, as my memory sees it, are lying sick in bed in their compartments or drawing rooms, and I am feeling proud of the fact that my father and I, alone and still well, are riding upright in the Pullman car. As we look up at the mountains, my father tells me that big boulders sometimes fall off them, hitting the train and killing people. Listening, I start to shake and my teeth to chatter with what I think is terror but what turns out to be the flu. How vivid all this is in my mind! Yet my uncle Harry says that it was he, not my father, who was sitting with me. Far from being the last, my father was the first to fall ill. Nor does Uncle Harry recall talking about boulders.

It is the case of the gold watch, all over again. Yet how could I have mistaken my uncle for my father?

"My mother is a Child of Mary," I used to tell other children, in the same bragging spirit that I spoke of my father's height. My mother, not long after her marriage, was converted to Catholicism and though I did not know what a Child of Mary was (actually a member of a sodality of the Ladies of the Sacred Heart),[3] I knew it was something wonderful from the way my mother spoke of it. She was proud and happy to be a convert, and her attitude made us feel that it was a special treat to be a Catholic, the crowning treat and privilege. Our religion was a present to us from God. Everything in our home life conspired to fix in our minds the idea that we were very precious little persons, precious to our parents and to God, too, Who was listening to us with loving attention every night when we said our prayers. "It gave me a basic complaisancy," a psycho-

---

3. Association or group of Catholic laity.

analyst once told me (I think he meant "complacency"), but I do not recall feeling smug, exactly. It was, rather, a sense of wondering, grateful privilege. Later, we heard a great deal about having been spoiled by our parents, yet we lacked that discontent that is the real mark of the spoiled child; to us, our existence was perfect, just the way it was.

My parents' death was brought about by a decision on the part of the McCarthy family. They concluded—and who can blame them? —that the continual drain of money, and my father's monthly appeals for more, had to stop. It was decided that our family should be moved to Minneapolis, where my grandfather and grandmother could keep an eye on what was happening and try to curb my father's expenditures.

At this point, I must mention a thing that was told me, only a few years ago, by my uncle Harry, my father's younger brother. My father, he confided, was a periodical drunkard who had been a family problem from the time of his late teens. Before his marriage, while he was still in Minnesota, a series of trained nurses had been hired to watch over him and keep him off the bottle. But, like all drunkards, he was extremely cunning and persuasive. He eluded his nurses or took them with him (he had a weakness for women, too) on a series of wild bouts that would end, days or weeks later, in some strange Middle Western city where he was hiding. A trail of bad checks would lead the family to recapture him. Or a telegram for money would eventually reveal his whereabouts, though if any money was sent him, he was likely to bolt away again. The nurses having proved ineffective, Uncle Harry was summoned home from Yale to look after him, but my father evaded him also. In the end, the family could no longer handle him, and he was sent out West as a bad job. That was how he came to meet my mother.

I have no idea whether this story is true or not. Nor will I ever know. To me, it seems improbable, for I am as certain as one can be that my father did not drink when I was a little girl. Children are sensitive to such things; their sense of smell, first of all, seems sharper than other people's, and they do not like the smell of alcohol. They are also quick to notice when anything is wrong in a household. I do recall my father's trying to make some homemade wine (this must have been just before Prohibition was enacted) out of some grayish-purple bricks that had been sold him as essence of grape. The experiment was a failure, and he and my mother and their friends did a good deal of laughing about "Roy's wine." But if my father had been a dangerous drinker, my mother would not have laughed. Moreover, if he *was* a drinker, my mother's family seem not to have known it. I asked my mother's brother whether Uncle Harry's story could possibly be true. His answer was that it was news to him. It is just possible, of course, that my father reformed after his marriage, which would explain why my mother's family did not know of his habits, though as Uncle Harry pointed out, rather belligerently: "You would think they could have looked up their future son-in-law's history." Periodical drunkards, however, almost never reform, and if they do, they cannot touch wine. It remains a mystery, an eerie and troubling one. Could my father have been drinking when he came home with those red roses, for my mother, in his arms? It is a drunkard's appeasing gesture, certainly, lordly and off-balance. Was that why my mother said, "Oh, Roy!"?

If my father *was* a sort of remittance man,[4] sent out West by his family, it would justify the McCarthy's, which was, of course, Uncle Harry's motive in telling me. He felt I had defamed his mother, and he wanted me to understand that, from where *she* sat, my father's imprudent marriage was the last straw. Indeed, from the McCarthy point of view, as given by Uncle Harry, my father's marriage was just another drunkard's dodge for extracting money from his father, all other means having failed. My mother, "your lovely mother," as Uncle Harry always calls her, was the innocent lure on the hook. Perhaps so. But I refuse to believe it. Uncle Harry's derelict brother, Roy, is not the same person as my father. I simply do not recognize him.

Uncle Harry was an old man, and rather far gone in his cups himself, when he made these charges, which does not affect the point, however—in fact, might go to substantiate it. An uncanny resemblance to my father had come out in him with age, a resemblance that had not existed when he was young: his white hair stood up in a pompadour, and he had the same gray-green, electric eyes and the same animal magnetism. As a young man, Uncle Harry was the white hope of the family, the boy who went east to school, to Andover and Yale, and made a million dollars before he was thirty. It was in this capacity, of budding millionaire and family impresario, that he entrained for Seattle, in 1918, together with his pretty, social wife, my aunt Zula, to superintend our move to Minneapolis. They put up at the New Washington Hotel, the best hotel in those days, and, as my grandmother Preston told it, they brought the flu with them.[5]

We were staying at the hotel, too, since our house had been vacated—a very unwise thing, for the first rule in an epidemic is to avoid public places. Indeed, the whole idea of traveling with a sick man and four small children at the height of an epidemic seems madness, but I see why the risk was taken from an old Seattle newspaper clipping, preserved by my great-grandfather Preston: "The party left for the East at this particular time in order to see another brother, Lewis McCarthy [Louis], who is in the aviation service and had a furlough home." This was the last, no doubt, of

4. Person living away from home on money supplied ("remitted") by family.

5. Millions of people died from the influenza epidemic of 1918–19.

my father's headstrong whims. I remember the grave atmosphere in our hotel suite the night before we took the train. Aunt Zula and the baby were both sick, by this time, as I recall it, and all the adults looked worried and uncertain. Nevertheless, we went ahead, boarding the train on a Wednesday, October 30. A week later, my mother died in Minneapolis; my father survived her by a day. She was twenty-nine; he was thirty-nine (a nice difference in age, my grandmother always said).

I sometimes wonder what I would have been like now if Uncle Harry and Aunt Zula had not come on, if the journey had never been undertaken. My father, of course, might have died anyway, and my mother would have brought us up. If they had both lived, we would have been a united Catholic family, rather middle class and wholesome. I would probably be a Child of Mary. I can see myself married to an Irish lawyer and playing golf and bridge, making occasional retreats and subscribing to a Catholic Book Club. I suspect I would be rather stout. And my brother Kevin— would he be an actor today?[6] The fact is, Kevin and I are the only members of the present generation of our family who have done anything out of the ordinary, and our relations at least profess to envy us, while I do not envy them. Was it a good thing, then, that our parents were "taken away," as if by some higher design? Some of my relations philosophize to this effect, in a somewhat Panglossian style.[7] I do not know myself.

Possibly artistic talent was already dormant in our heredity and would have come out in any case. What I recall best about myself as a child under six is a passionate love of beauty, which was almost a kind of violence. I used to get cross with my mother when she screwed her hair up on top of her head in the mornings; I could not bear that she should not be beautiful all the time. My only criterion for judging candidates who presented themselves to be our nurse-maids was good looks; I remember importuning my mother, when I was about five, to hire one called Harriet—I liked her name, too— and how the world, for the first time, seemed to me cruel and inexplicable, when Harriet, who had been engaged, never materialized. She must have had a bad character, my mother said, but I could not accept the idea that anyone beautiful could be bad. Or rather, "bad" seemed to me irrelevant when put beside beauty, just as the faithful Gertrude's red warts and her ugly name made me deaf to anything alleged to me about her kindness. One of the great shocks connected with the loss of my parents was an aesthetic one; even if my guardians had been nice, I should probably not have liked them because they were so unpleasing to look at and their grammar and accents were so lacking in correctness. I had been

6. Kevin McCarthy, American actor and brother of the author.
7. Dr. Pangloss, in Voltaire's *Candide* (1759), was given to sententious philosophizing.

rudely set down in a place where beauty was not a value at all. "Handsome is as handsome does," my grandmother McCarthy's chauffeur, Frank, observed darkly, when my uncle Louis married an auburn-haired charmer from New Orleans. I hated him for saying it; it was one of those *cunning* remarks that throw cold water on life.

The people I was forced to live with in Minneapolis had a positive gift for turning everything sour and ugly. Even our flowers were hideous: we had golden glow and sickly nasturtiums in our yard. I remember one Good Friday planting sweet peas for myself next to the house, and I believe they actually blossomed—a personal triumph. I had not been an especially pretty child (my own looks were one of my few early disappointments), but, between them, my guardians and my grandmother McCarthy turned me into such a scarecrow that I could not look at myself in the mirror without despair. It was not only the braces and the glasses but a general leanness and sallowness and lankness.

Looking back, I see that it was religion that saved me. Our ugly church and parochial school provided me with my only aesthetic outlet, in the words of the Mass and the litanies and the old Latin hymns, in the Easter lilies around the altar, rosaries, ornamented prayer books, votive lamps, holy cards stamped in gold and decorated with flower wreaths and a saint's picture. This side of Catholicism, much of it cheapened and debased by mass production, was for me, nevertheless, the equivalent of Gothic cathedrals and illuminated manuscripts and mystery plays. I threw myself into it with ardor, this sensuous life, and when I was not dreaming that I was going to grow up to marry the pretender to the throne of France and win back his crown with him, I was dreaming of being a Carmelite nun, cloistered and penitential; I was also much attracted by an order for fallen women called the Magdalens.[8] A desire to excel governed all my thoughts, and this was quickened, if possible, by the parochial-school methods of education, which were based on the competitive principle. Everything was a contest; our schoolroom was divided into teams, with captains, for spelling bees and other feats of learning, and on the playground we organized ourselves in the same fashion. To win, to skip a grade, to get ahead—the nuns' methods were well adapted to the place and time, for most of the little Catholics of our neighborhood were children of poor immigrants, bent on bettering themselves and also on surpassing the Protestants, whose children went to Whittier, the public school. There was no idea of equality in the parochial school, and such an idea would have been abhorrent to me, if it had existed; equality, a sort of brutal cutting down to size, was what I was treated to at home. Equality was a species of unfairness which the good sisters of

8. Order of reformed and penitent prostitutes named after St. Mary Magdalen, reputed to have been a harlot.

St. Joseph would not have tolerated.

I stood at the head of my class and I was also the best runner and the best performer on the turning poles in the schoolyard; I was the best actress and elocutionist and the second most devout, being surpassed in this by a blond boy with a face like a saint, who sat in front of me and whom I loved; his name, which sounds rather like a Polish saint's name, was John Klosick. No doubt, the standards of the school were not very high, and they gave me a false idea of myself; I have never excelled at athletics elsewhere. Nor have I ever been devout again. When I left the competitive atmosphere of the parochial school, my religion withered on the stalk.

But in St. Stephen's School, I was not devout just to show off; I felt my religion very intensely and longed to serve God better than anyone else. This, I thought, was what He asked of me. I lived in fear of making a poor confession or of not getting my tongue flat enough to receive the Host reverently. One of the great moral crises of my life occurred on the morning of my first Communion. I took a drink of water. Unthinkingly, of course, for had it not been drilled into me that the Host must be received fasting, on the penalty of mortal sin? It was only a sip, but that made no difference, I knew. A sip was as bad as a gallon; I *could not* take Communion. And yet I had to. My Communion dress and veil and prayer book were laid out for me, and I was supposed to lead the girls' procession; John Klosick, in a white suit, would be leading the boys'. It seemed to me that I would be failing the school and my class, if, after all the rehearsals, I had to confess what I had done and drop out. The sisters would be angry; my guardians would be angry, having paid for the dress and veil. I thought of the procession without me in it, and I could not bear it. To make my first Communion later, in ordinary clothes, would not be the same. On the other hand, if I took my first Communion in a state of mortal sin, God would never forgive me; it would be a fatal beginning. I went through a ferocious struggle with my conscience, and all the while, I think, I knew the devil was going to prevail: I was going to take Communion, and only God and I would know the real facts. So it came about: I received my first Communion in a state of outward holiness and inward horror, believing I was damned, for I could not imagine that I could make a true repentance—the time to repent was now, before committing the sacrilege; afterward, I could not be really sorry for I would have achieved what I had wanted.

I suppose I must have confessed this at my next confession, scarcely daring to breathe it, and the priest must have treated it lightly: my sins, as I slowly discovered, weighed heavier on me than they did on my confessors. Actually, it is quite common for children making their first Communion to have just such a mishap as mine: they are so excited on that long-awaited morning that they hardly know what they are doing, or possibly the very taboo on food and water and the importance of the occasion drive them into an unconscious resistance. I heard a story almost identical with mine from Ignazio Silone.[9] Yet the despair I felt that summer morning (I think it was Corpus Christi Day)[1] was in a certain sense fully justified: I knew myself, how I was and would be forever; such dry self-knowledge is terrible. Every subsequent moral crisis of my life, moreover, has had precisely the pattern of this struggle over the first Communion; I have battled, usually without avail, against a temptation to do something which only I knew was bad, being swept on by a need to preserve outward appearances and to live up to other people's expectations of me. The heroine of one of my novels, who finds herself pregnant, possibly as the result of an infidelity, and is tempted to have the baby and say nothing to her husband, is in the same fix, morally, as I was at eight years old, with that drink of water inside me that only I knew was there. When I supposed I was damned, I was right—damned, that is, to a repetition or endless re-enactment of that conflict between excited scruples and inertia of will.

I am often asked whether I retain anything of my Catholic heritage. This is hard to answer, partly because my Catholic heritage consists of two distinct strains. There was the Catholicism I learned from my mother and from the simple parish priests and nuns in Minneapolis, which was, on the whole, a religion of beauty and goodness, however imperfectly realized. Then there was the Catholicism practiced in my grandmother McCarthy's parlor and in the home that was made for us down the street—a sour, baleful doctrine in which old hates and rancors had been stewing for generations, with ignorance proudly stirring the pot. The difference can be illustrated by an incident that took place when I stopped off in Minneapolis, on my way to Vassar as a freshman, in 1929. In honor of the occasion, my grandmother McCarthy invited the parish priest to her house; she wanted him to back up her opinion that Vassar was "a den of iniquity." The old priest, Father Cullen, declined to comply with her wishes and, ignoring his pewholder's angry interjections, spoke to me instead of the rare intellectual opportunities Vassar had in store for me.

Possibly Father Cullen was merely more tactful than his parishioner, but I cannot forget my gratitude to him. It was not only that he took my grandmother down a peg. He showed largeness of spirit—a quality rare among Catholics, at least in my experience, though *false* magnanimity is a common stock in trade with them. I have sometimes thought that Catholicism is a religion not suited to the laity, or not suited, at any rate, to the American laity, in whom

9. Italian novelist (1900–78).
1. Roman Catholic festival celebrating the Eucharist.

it seems to bring out some of the worst traits in human nature and to lend them a sort of sanctification. In the course of publishing these memoirs in magazines, I have received a great many letters from the laity and also from priests and nuns. The letters from the laity—chiefly women—are all alike; they might almost have been penned by the same person; I have filed them under the head of "Correspondence, Scurrilous." They are frequently full of misspellings, though the writers claim to be educated; and they are all, without exception, menacing. "False," "misrepresentation," "lying," "bigotry," "hate," "poison," "filth," "trash," "cheap," "distortion" —this is the common vocabulary of them all. They threaten to cancel their subscriptions to the magazine that published the memoir; they speak of a "great many other people that you ought to know feel as I do," i.e., they attempt to constitute themselves a pressure group. Some *demand* an answer. One lady writes: "I am under the impression that the Law forbids this sort of thing."

In contrast, the priests and nuns who have written me, apropos the same memoirs, strike a note that sounds almost heretical. They are touched, many of them say, by my "sincerity"; some of the nuns are praying for me, they write, and the priests are saying masses. One young Jesuit tells me that he has thought of me when he visited Forest Ridge Convent in Seattle and looked over the rows of girls: "I see that the startling brilliance of a slim orphan girl was fairly matched with fiery resolve and impetuous headlong drive. Nor was it easy for her those days. I suppose I should be thinking that technically you are an apostate, in bad standing, outside the gate. . . ." An older priest writes me that I am saved whether I know it or not: "I do not suggest to you where you will find your spiritual home—but that you will find it—of that I am certain—the Spirit will lead you to it. Indeed for me you have already found it, although you still must seek it." A Maryknoll nun invites me to visit her mission. None of these correspondents feels obliged to try to convert me; they seem to leave that to God to worry about. Some of them have passed through a period of doubt themselves and write me about that, to show their understanding and sympathy. Each of the letters has its own individuality. The only point of uniformity is that they all begin: "Dear Mary."

I am grateful to these priests and nuns, grateful to them for existing. They must be a minority, though they would probably deny it, even among the clergy. The idea that religion is supposed to teach you to be good, an idea that children have, seems to linger on, like a sweet treble, in their letters. Very few people appear to believe this any more, it is utterly out of style among fashionable neo-Protestants, and the average Catholic perceives no connection between religion and morality, unless it is a question of someone *else's* morality, that is, of the supposed pernicious influences of books, films, ideas, on someone else's conduct.

From what I have seen, I am driven to the conclusion that religion is only good for good people, and I do not mean this as a paradox, but simply as an observable fact. Only good people can afford to be religious. For the others, it is too great a temptation—a temptation to the deadly sins of pride and anger, chiefly, but one might also add sloth. My grandmother McCarthy, I am sure, would have been a better woman if she had been an atheist or an agnostic. The Catholic religion, I believe, is the most dangerous of all, morally (I do not know about the Moslem), because, with its claim to be the only true religion, it fosters that sense of privilege I spoke of earlier—the notion that not everyone is lucky enough to be a Catholic.

I am not sorry to have *been* a Catholic, first of all for practical reasons. It gave me a certain knowledge of the Latin language and of the saints and their stories which not everyone is lucky enough to have. Latin, when I came to study it, was easy for me and attractive, too, like an old friend; as for the saints, it is extremely useful to know them and the manner of their martyrdom when you are looking at Italian painting, to know, for instance, that a tooth is the emblem of Saint Apollonia, patron of dentistry, and that Saint Agnes is shown with a lamb, always, and Saint Catherine of Alexandria with a wheel. To read Dante and Chaucer or the English Metaphysicals or even T. S. Eliot, a Catholic education is more than a help. Having to learn a little theology as an adult in order to understand a poem of Donne or Crashaw[2] is like being taught the Bible as Great Literature in a college humanities course; it does not stick to the ribs. Yet most students in America have no other recourse than to take these vitamin injections to make good the cultural deficiency.

If you are born and brought up a Catholic, you have absorbed a good deal of world history and the history of ideas before you are twelve, and it is like learning a language early; the effect is indelible. Nobody else in America, no other group, is in this fortunate position. Granted that Catholic history is biased, it is not dry or dead; its virtue for the student, indeed, is that it has been made to come alive by the violent partisanship which inflames it. This partisanship, moreover, acts as a magnet to attract stray pieces of information not ordinarily taught in American schools. While children in public schools were studying American history, we in the convent in the eighth grade were studying English history down to the time of Lord Palmerston,[3] the reason for this was, of course, that English history, up to Henry VIII, was Catholic history, and, after that, with one or two interludes, it became anti-Catholic history. Naturally, we were taught to sympathize with Bloody Mary (never

---

2. John Donne (1573–1631), English poet and Anglican cleric. Richard Crashaw (c. 1613–49), English poet and Roman Catholic convert.

3. English Prime Minister (1784–1865) who lent support to Catholic emancipation.

called that in the convent), Mary Queen of Scots, Philip of Spain, the martyr Jesuits, Charles I (married to a Catholic princess), James II (married first to a Protestant and then to Mary of Modena), the Old Pretender, Bonnie Prince Charlie; interest petered out with Peel and Catholic Emancipation.[4] To me, it does not matter that this history was one-sided (this can always be remedied later); the important thing is to have learned the battles and the sovereigns, their consorts, mistresses, and prime ministers, to know the past of a foreign country in such detail that it becomes one's own. Had I stayed in the convent, we would have gone on to French history, and today I would know the list of French kings and their wives and ministers, because French history, up to the Revolution, was Catholic history, and Charlemagne, Joan of Arc, and Napoleon were all prominent Catholics.

Nor is it only a matter of knowing more, at an earlier age, so that it becomes a part of oneself; it is also a matter of feeling. To care for the quarrels of the past, to identify oneself passionately with a cause that became, politically speaking, a losing cause with the birth of the modern world, is to experience a kind of straining against reality, a rebellious nonconformity that, again, is rare in America, where children are instructed in the virtues of the system they live under, as though history had achieved a happy ending in American civics.

So much for the practical side. But it might be pointed out that to an American educator, my Catholic training would appear to have no utility whatever. What is the good, he would say, of hearing the drone of a dead language every day or of knowing that Saint Ursula, a Breton princess, was martyred at Cologne, together with ten thousand virgins? I have shown that such things proved to have a certain usefulness in later life—a usefulness that was not, however, intended at the time, for we did not study the lives of the saints in order to look at Italian painting or recite our catechism in order to read John Donne. Such an idea would be atrocious blasphemy. We learned those things for the glory of God, and the rest, so to speak, was added to us. Nor would it have made us study any harder if we had been assured that what we were learning was going to come in handy in later life, any more than children study arithmetic harder if they are promised it will help them later on in business. Nothing is more boring to a child than the principle of utility. The final usefulness of my Catholic training was to teach me, together with much that proved to be practical, a conception of something prior to and beyond utility ("Consider the lilies of the field; they toil not, neither do they spin"),[5] an idea of sheer wastefulness that is always shocking to non-Catholics, who cannot bear, for example, the contrast between the rich churches and the poor people of southern

---

4. Catholic Relief Acts of 1778 and 1791 granted limited but fundamental religious and educational freedom to Catholics.
5. Luke 12.27.

Europe. Those churches, agreed, are a folly; so is the life of a dirty anchorite or of a cloistered, non-teaching nun—unprofitable for society and bad for the person concerned. But I prefer to think of them that way than to imagine them as an investment, shares bought in future salvation. I never really liked the doctrine of Indulgences—the notion that you could say five Hail Marys and knock off a year in Purgatory.[6] This seemed to me to belong to my grandmother McCarthy's kind of Catholicism. What I liked in the Church, and what I recall with gratitude, was the sense of mystery and wonder, ashes put on one's forehead on Ash Wednesday, the blessing of the throat with candles on St. Blaise's Day,[7] the purple palls put on the statues after Passion Sunday, which meant they were hiding their faces in mourning because Christ was going to be crucified, the ringing of the bell at the Sanctus, the burst of lilies at Easter—all this ritual, seeming slightly strange and having no purpose (except the throat-blessing), beyond commemoration of a Person Who had died a long time ago. In these exalted moments of altruism the soul was fired with reverence.

Hence, as a lapsed Catholic, I do not trouble myself about the possibility that God may exist after all. If He exists (which seems to me more than doubtful), I am in for a bad time in the next world, but I am not going to bargain to believe in God in order to save my soul. Pascal's wager[8]—the bet he took with himself that God existed, even though this could not be proved by reasoning—strikes me as too prudential. What had Pascal to lose by behaving as if God existed? Absolutely nothing, for there was no counter-Principle to damn him in case God didn't. For myself, I prefer not to play it so safe, and I shall never send for a priest or recite an Act of Contrition in my last moments. I do not mind if I lose my soul for all eternity. If the kind of God exists Who would damn me for not working out a deal with Him, then that is unfortunate. I should not care to spend eternity in the company of such a person.

1957

6. The doctrine of Indulgences promised remission of sins, achieved through acts of contrition directed by an ecclesiastical authority. Purgatory, in Roman Catholic theology, is the place after death where souls are purged of their sins before they enter into Heaven.
7. Blaise saved a child, miraculously, from choking to death on a fishbone; his

intercession is sought for by sick people, especially those with throat problems. St. Blaise's Day is February 3.
8. Blaise Pascal (1623–62), French mathematician and mystic. The "wager" is made in terms that, since nothing can be lost and much can be won, it is prudent to bet on God's existence.

RALPH ELLISON

1914–

"If the Negro, or any other writer, is going to do what's expected of him, he's lost the battle before he takes the field." This remark of Ralph Ellison's, taken from his *Paris Review* interview of 1953, serves in more than one sense as an appropriate motto for his own career. He has not done what his critics, literary or political ones, suggested that he ought to be doing, but has insisted on being a writer rather than a spokesman for a cause or a representative figure. His importance to American letters is partly due to this independence. It is also true, however, that he has done the unexpected in not following his fine first novel with the others that were predicted; and *Invisible Man*, after a quarter of a century still stands as the sole indicator of Ellison's artistic significance.

He was born in Oklahoma, grew up in Oklahoma City, won a state scholarship and attended Tuskegee Institute where he was a music major, his instrument the trumpet. His musical life was wide enough to embrace both "serious music" and the world of Southwest-Kansas City jazz just reaching its heyday when Ellison was a young man. He became friends with Jimmy Rushing, the blues singer, and was acquainted with other members of what would be the great Count Basie band of the 1930s; this "deep, rowdy stream of jazz" figured for him as an image of the power and control that constituted art. Although he was a serious student of music and composition, his literary inclinations eventually dominated his musical ones; but testimony to his abiding knowledge and love of music may be found in some of the essays from *Shadow and Act* (1964) a collection of his prose.

When Ellison left Tuskegee he went north to make his way in New York City. There, in 1936, he met Richard Wright, who encouraged him as a writer, and Ellison began to publish reviews and short stories. *Invisible Man*, begun in 1945, was published seven years later and won the National Book Award. Ellison subsequently received a number of awards and lectureships, taught at the Salzburg Seminar, at Bard College, and at the University of Chicago, and in 1970 was named Albert Schweitzer Professor of the Humanities at New York University. Yet he has admitted to being troubled by the terms in which *Invisible Man's* success—and perhaps his own career as well—have been defined. In the *Paris Review* interview he deprecatingly referred to his novel as largely a failure, wished that rather than a "statement" about the American Negro it could be read "simply as a novel," and hoped that in twenty years it would be so read, casually adding, "if it's around that long."

That twenty-year period is now well passed and *Invisible Man* is very much around, though the attempt to view it "simply as a novel" is a complex activity. Near the beginning of the book the young hero dreams that the following message is engraved on a document presented to him at his high school graduation: "To Whom It May Concern: Keep This Nigger-Boy Running." Ellison keeps him running throughout the novel, from his term at the Southern College to his flight North into the dizzying sequence of adventures and the various brands of political and racial rhetoric he undergoes in Harlem. The novel presents a gallery of extraordinary charac-ters and circumstances, expressed through different narrative styles, against which the ordinary hero defines—or fails to define—himself. And we are to remember that the whole book is conceived and understood to be narrated from a "hole" into which the Invisible Man has retired and where he thinks about the great black jazz trumpet player, Louis Armstrong: "Perhaps I like Louis Armstrong because he's made poetry out of being invisible."

In the late 1960s some black intellectuals and writers found Ellison's work irrelevant to their more activist designs. And earlier in the decade the white critic Irving Howe published an essay praising Richard Wright for writing "protest" works like *Native Son* while (Howe claimed) Ellison and James Baldwin were evading their tragic responsibilities as black victims by being too sanguine about the possibilities of human freedom. Ellison's answer to Howe's charge is printed in an important essay called *The World and the Jug* (in *Shadow and Act*) and in essence runs like this: "I am a human being, not just the black successor to Richard Wright, and there are ways of celebrating my experience more complex than terms like 'protest' can suggest." In Ellison's own words, "To deny in the interest of revolutionary posture that * * * such possibilities of human richness exist for others" is to impoverish both life and art.

Ellison has surely felt the sting and seriousness of these charges by black and white critics; but one of the things he shares with his invisible-man protagonist is that, as with Armstrong or any good jazz improviser, he never quite stays on the beat, especially when the beat is laid down by somebody else. Although thus far only sections have been published from the long-awaited successor to *Invisible Man*, the depth and humanness of this writer's imagination make it important that readers not stop waiting.

From Invisible Man[1]

Prologue

I am an invisible man. No, I am not a spook like those who haunted Edgar Allan Poe; not am I one of your Hollywood-movie ectoplasms. I am a man of substance, of flesh and bone, fiber and liquids—and I might even be said to possess a mind. I am invisible, understand, simply because people refuse to see me. Like the bodiless heads you see sometimes in circus sideshows, it is as though I have been surrounded by mirrors of hard, distorting glass. When they approach me they see only my surroundings, themselves, or figments of their imagination—indeed, everything and anything except me.

Nor is my invisibility exactly a matter of a bio-chemical accident to my epidermis. That invisibility to which I refer occurs because of a peculiar disposition of the eyes of those with whom I come in contact. A matter of the construction of their *inner* eyes, those eyes with which they look through their physical eyes upon reality. I am not complaining, nor am I protesting either. It is sometimes advantageous to be unseen, although it is most often rather wearing on the nerves. Then too, you're constantly being bumped against by those of poor vision. Or again, you often doubt if you really exist. You wonder whether you aren't simply a phantom in other people's minds. Say, a figure in a nightmare which the sleeper tries with all his strength to destroy. It's when you feel like this that, out of

---

1. This selection from *Invisible Man* (1952) consists of the novel's Prologue and Chapter 1. Ras the Destroyer, Rine- hart, and Brother Jack, mentioned in the Prologue, are characters who will appear later.

resentment, you begin to bump people back. And, let me confess, you feel that way most of the time. You ache with the need to convince yourself that you do exist in the real world, that you're a part of all the sound and anguish, and you strike out with your fists, you curse and you swear to make them recognize you. And, alas, it's seldom successful.

One night I accidentally bumped into a man, and perhaps because of the near darkness he saw me and called me an insulting name. I sprang at him, seized his coat lapels and demanded that he apologize. He was a tall blond man, and as my face came close to his he looked insolently out of his blue eyes and cursed me, his breath hot in my face as he struggled. I pulled his chin down sharp upon the crown of my head, butting him as I had seen the West Indians do, and I felt his flesh tear and the blood gush out, and I yelled, "Apologize! Apologize!" But he continued to curse and struggle, and I butted him again and again until he went down heavily, on his knees, profusely bleeding. I kicked him repeatedly, in a frenzy because he still uttered insults though his lips were frothy with blood. Oh yes, I kicked him! And in my outrage I got out my knife and prepared to slit his throat, right there beneath the lamplight in the deserted street, holding him in the collar with one hand, and opening the knife with my teeth—when it occurred to me that the man had not *seen* me, actually; that he, as far as he knew, was in the midst of a walking nightmare! And I stopped the blade, slicing the air as I pushed him away, letting him fall back to the street. I stared at him hard as the lights of a car stabbed through the darkness. He lay there, moaning on the asphalt; a man almost killed by a phantom. It unnerved me. I was both disgusted and ashamed. I was like a drunken man myself, wavering about on weakened legs. Then I was amused: Something in this man's thick head had sprung out and beaten him within an inch of his life. I began to laugh at this crazy discovery. Would he have awakened at the point of death? Would Death himself have freed him for wakeful living? But I didn't linger. I ran away into the dark, laughing so hard I feared I might rupture myself. The next day I saw his picture in the *Daily News*, beneath a caption stating that he had been "mugged." Poor fool, poor blind fool, I thought with sincere compassion, mugged by an invisible man!

Most of the time (although I do not choose as I once did to deny the violence of my days by ignoring it) I am not so overtly violent. I remember that I am invisible and walk softly so as not to awaken the sleeping ones. Sometimes it is best not to awaken them; there are few things in the world as dangerous as sleepwalkers. I learned in time though that it is possible to carry on a fight against them without their realizing it. For instance, I have been carrying on a fight with Monopolated Light & Power for some time now. I use their service and pay them nothing at all, and they don't know it.

Oh, they suspect that power is being drained off, but they don't know where. All they know is that according to the master meter back there in their power station a hell of a lot of free current is disappearing somewhere into the jungle of Harlem. The joke, of course, is that I don't live in Harlem but in a border area. Several years ago (before I discovered the advantages of being invisible) I went through the routine process of buying service and paying their outrageous rates. But no more. I gave up all that, along with my apartment, and my old way of life: That way based upon the fallacious assumption that I, like other men, was visible. Now, aware of my invisibility, I live rent-free in a building rented strictly to whites, in a section of the basement that was shut off and forgotten during the nineteenth century, which I discovered when I was trying to escape in the night from Ras the Destroyer. But that's getting too far ahead of the story, almost to the end, although the end is in the beginning and lies far ahead.

The point now is that I found a home—or a hole in the ground, as you will. Now don't jump to the conclusion that because I call my home a "hole" it is damp and cold like a grave; there are cold holes and warm holes. Mine is a warm hole. And remember, a bear retires to his hole for the winter and lives until spring; then he comes strolling out like the Easter chick breaking from its shell. I say all this to assure you that it is incorrect to assume that, because I'm invisible and live in a hole, I am dead. I am neither dead nor in a state of suspended animation. Call me Jack-the-Bear, for I am in a state of hibernation.[2]

My hole is warm and full of light. Yes, *full* of light. I doubt if there is a brighter spot in all New York than this hole of mine, and I do not exclude Broadway. Or the Empire State Building on a photographer's dream night. But that is taking advantage of you. Those two spots are among the darkest of our whole civilization— pardon me, our whole *culture* (an important distinction, I've heard) —which might sound like a hoax, or a contradiction, but that (by contradiction, I mean) is how the world moves: Not like an arrow, but a boomerang. (Beware of those who speak of the *spiral* of history; they are preparing a boomerang. Keep a steel helmet handy.) I know; I have been boomeranged across my head so much that I now can see the darkness of lightness. And I love light. Perhaps you'll think it strange that an invisible man should need light, desire light, love light. But maybe it is exactly because I *am* invisible. Light confirms my reality, gives birth to my form. A beautiful girl once told me of a recurring nightmare in which she lay in the center of a large dark room and felt her face expand until it filled the whole room, becoming a formless mass while her eyes ran in bilious jelly up the chimney. And so it is with me. Without

2. "Jack-the-bear" is also the title of a jazz recording by Duke Ellington and his orchestra (1940).

light I am not only invisible, but formless as well; and to be unaware of one's form is to live a death. I myself, after existing some
twenty years, did not become alive until I discovered my invisibility.

That is why I fight my battle with Monopolated Light & Power.
The deeper reason, I mean: It allows me to feel my vital aliveness. I
also fight them for taking so much of my money before I learned to
protect myself. In my hole in the basement there are exactly 1,369
lights. I've wired the entire ceiling, every inch of it. And not with
fluorescent bulbs, but with the older, more-expensive-to-operate
kind, the filament type. An act of sabotage, you know. I've already
begun to wire the wall. A junk man I know, a man of vision, has
supplied me with wire and sockets. Nothing, storm or flood, must
get in the way of our need for light and ever more and brighter
light. The truth is the light and light is the truth. When I finish all
four walls, then I'll start on the floor. Just how that will go, I don't
know. Yet when you have lived invisible as long as I have you
develop a certain ingenuity. I'll solve the problem. And maybe I'll
invent a gadget to place my coffee pot on the fire while I lie in bed,
and even invent a gadget to warm my bed—like the fellow I saw in
one of the picture magazines who made himself a gadget to warm
his shoes! Though invisible, I am in the great American tradition of
tinkers. That makes me kin to Ford, Edison and Franklin. Call me,
since I have a theory and a concept, a "thinker-tinker." Yes, I'll
warm my shoes; they need it, they're usually full of holes. I'll do
that and more.

Now I have one radio-phonograph; I plan to have five. There is a
certain acoustical deadness in my hole, and when I have music I
want to *feel* its vibration, not only with my ear but with my whole
body. I'd like to hear five recordings of Louis Armstrong playing
and singing "What Did I Do to Be So Black and Blue"—all at the
same time. Sometimes now I listen to Louis while I have my favorite dessert of vanilla ice cream and sloe gin. I pour the red liquid
over the white mound, watching it glisten and the vapor rising as
Louis bends that military instrument into a beam of lyrical sound.
Perhaps I like Louis Armstrong because he's made poetry out of
being invisible. I think it must be because he's unaware that he *is*
invisible. And my own grasp of invisibility aids me to understand
his music. Once when I asked for a cigarette, some jokers gave me a
reefer, which I lighted when I got home and sat listening to my
phonograph. It was a strange evening. Invisibility, let me explain,
gives one a slightly different sense of time, you're never quite on the
beat. Sometimes you're ahead and sometimes behind. Instead of the
swift and imperceptible flowing of time, you are aware of its nodes,
those points where time stands still or from which it leaps ahead.
And you slip into the breaks and look around. That's what you hear
vaguely in Louis' music.

Once I saw a prizefighter boxing a yokel. The fighter was swift and amazingly scientific. His body was one violent flow of rapid rhythmic action. He hit the yokel a hundred times when the yokel held up his arms in stunned surprise. But suddenly the yokel, rolling about in the gale of boxing gloves, struck one blow and knocked science, speed and footwork as cold as a well-digger's posterior. The smart money hit the canvas. The long shot got the nod. The yokel had simply stepped inside of his opponent's sense of time. So under the spell of the reefer I discovered a new analytical way of listening to music. The unheard sounds came through, and each melodic line existed of itself, stood out clearly from all the rest, said its piece, and waited patiently for the other voices to speak. That night I found myself hearing not only in time, but in space as well. I not only entered the music but descended, like Dante, into its depths. *And beneath the swiftness of the hot tempo there was a slower tempo and a cave and I entered it and looked around and heard an old woman singing a spiritual as full of Weltschmerz as flamenco, and beneath that lay a still lower level on which I saw a beautiful girl the color of ivory pleading in a voice like my mother's as she stood before a group of slaveowners who bid for her naked body, and below that I found a lower level and a more rapid tempo and I heard someone shout:*

"Brothers and sisters, my text this morning is the 'Blackness of Blackness.' "

And a congregation of voices answered: "That blackness is most black, brother, most black . . ."

"In the beginning . . ."

"At the very start," they cried.

". . . there was blackness . . ."

"Preach it . . ."

". . . and the sun . . ."

"The sun, Lawd . . ."

". . . was bloody red . . ."

"Red . . ."

"Now black is . . ." the preacher shouted.

"Bloody . . ."

"I said black is . . ."

"Preach it, brother . . ."

". . . an' black ain't . . ."

"Red, Lawd, red: He said it's red!"

"Amen, brother . . ."

"Black will git you . . ."

"Yes, it will . . ."

". . . an' black won't . . ."

"Naw, it won't!"

"It do . . ."

"It do, Lawd . . ."

". . . an' it don't."

"*Halleluiah . . .*"

". . . *It'll put you, glory, glory, Oh my Lawd, in the* WHALE'S BELLY."

"*Preach it, dear brother . . .*"

". . . *an' make you tempt . . .*"

"*Good God a-mighty!*"

"*Old Aunt Nelly!*"

"*Black will make you . . .*"

"*Black . . .*"

". . . *or black will un-make you.*"

"*Ain't it the truth, Lawd?*"

And at that point a voice of trombone timbre screamed at me, "*Git out of here, you fool! Is you ready to commit treason?*"

And I tore myself away, hearing the old singer of spirituals moaning, "*Go curse your God, boy, and die.*"

I stopped and questioned her, asked her what was wrong.

"*I dearly loved my master, son,*" she said.

"*You should have hated him,*" I said.

"*He gave me several sons,*" she said, "*and because I loved my sons I learned to love their father though I hated him too.*"

"*I too have become acquainted with ambivalence,*" I said. "*That's why I'm here.*"

"*What's that?*"

"*Nothing, a word that doesn't explain it. Why do you moan?*"

"*I moan this way 'cause he's dead,*" she said.

"*Then tell me, who is that laughing upstairs?*"

"*Them's my sons. They glad.*"

"*Yes, I can understand that too,*" I said.

"*I laughs too, but I moans too. He promised to set us free but he never could bring hisself to do it. Still I loved him . . .*"

"*Loved him? You mean . . . ?*"

"*Oh yes, but I loved something else even more.*"

"*What more?*"

"*Freedom.*"

"*Freedom,*" I said. "*Maybe freedom lies in hating.*"

"*Naw, son, it's in loving. I loved him and give him the poison and he withered away like a frost-bit apple. Them boys woulda tore him to pieces with they homemade knives.*"

"*A mistake was made somewhere,*" I said, "*I'm confused.*" And I wished to say other things, but the laughter upstairs became too loud and moan-like for me and I tried to break out of it, but I couldn't. Just as I was leaving I felt an urgent desire to ask her what freedom was and went back. She sat with her head in her hands, moaning softly; her leather-brown face was filled with sadness.

"*Old woman, what is this freedom you love so well?*" I asked around a corner of my mind.

She looked surprised, then thoughtful, then baffled. "*I done for-*

*got, son. It's all mixed up. First I think it's one thing, then I think
it's another. It gits my head to spinning. I guess now it ain't nothing
but knowing how to say what I got up in my head. But it's a hard
job, son. Too much is done happen to me in too short a time. Hit's
like I have a fever. Ever' time I starts to walk my head gits to
swirling and I falls down. Or if it ain't that, it's the boys; they gits to
laughing and wants to kill up the white folks. They's bitter, that's
what they is . . ."*

"But what about freedom?"

"Leave me 'lone, boy; my head aches!"

I left her, feeling dizzy myself. I didn't get far.

*Suddenly one of the sons, a big fellow six feet tall, appeared out
of nowhere and struck me with his fist.*

"What's the matter, man?" *I cried.*

"You made Ma cry!"

"But how?" *I said, dodging a blow.*

"Askin' her them questions, that's how. Git outa here and stay,
and next time you got questions like that, ask yourself!"

*He held me in a grip like cold stone, his fingers fastening upon
my windpipe until I thought I would suffocate before he finally
allowed me to go. I stumbled about dazed, the music beating hysterically in my ears. It was dark. My head cleared and I wandered
down a dark narrow passage, thinking I heard his footsteps hurrying
behind me. I was sore, and into my being had come a profound
craving for tranquillity, for peace and quiet, a state I felt I could
never achieve. For one thing, the trumpet was blaring and the
rhythm was too hectic. A tom-tom beating like heart-thuds began
drowning out the trumpet, filling my ears. I longed for water and I
heard it rushing through the cold mains my fingers touched as I felt
my way, but I couldn't stop to search because of the footsteps
behind me.*

"Hey, Ras," *I called.* "Is it you, Destroyer? Rinehart?"

*No answer, only the rhythmic footsteps behind me. Once I tried
crossing the road, but a speeding machine struck me, scraping the
skin from my leg as it roared past.*

Then somehow I came out of it, ascending hastily from this
underworld of sound to hear Louis Armstrong innocently asking,

> What did I do
> To be so black
> And blue?

At first I was afraid; this familiar music had demanded action,
the kind of which I was incapable, and yet had I lingered there
beneath the surface I might have attempted to act. Nevertheless, I
know now that few really listen to this music. I sat on the chair's
edge in a soaking sweat, as though each of my 1,369 bulbs had
everyone become a klieg light[3] in an individual setting for a third

3. Arc light used in taking motion pictures.

degree with Ras and Rinehart in charge. It was exhausting—as
though I had held my breath continuously for an hour under the
terrifying serenity that comes from days of intense hunger. And yet,
it was a strangely satisfying experience for an invisible man to hear
the silence of sound. I had discovered unrecognized compulsions of
my being—even though I could not answer "yes" to their promptings. I haven't smoked a reefer since, however; not because they're
illegal, but because to *see* around corners is enough (that is not
unusual when you are invisible). But to hear around them is too
much; it inhibits action. And despite Brother Jack and all that sad,
lost period of the Brotherhood, I believe in nothing if not in action.

Please, a definition: A hibernation is a covert preparation for a
more overt action.

Besides, the drug destroys one's sense of time completely. If that
happened, I might forget to dodge some bright morning and some
cluck would run me down with an orange and yellow street car, or a
bilious bus! Or I might forget to leave my hole when the moment
for action presents itself.

Meanwhile I enjoy my life with the compliments of Monopolated
Light & Power. Since you never recognize me even when in closest
contact with me, and since, no doubt, you'll hardly believe that I
exist, it won't matter if you know that I tapped a power line leading
into the building and ran it into my hole in the ground. Before that
I lived in the darkness into which I was chased, but now I see. I've
illuminated the blackness of my invisibility—and vice versa. And so
I play the invisible music of my isolation. The last statement doesn't
seem just right, does it? But it is; you hear this music simply
because music is heard and seldom seen, except by musicians.
Could this compulsion to put invisibility down in black and white
be thus an urge to make music of invisibility? But I am an orator, a
rabble rouser—Am? I *was*, and perhaps shall be again. Who knows?
All sickness is not unto death, neither is invisibility.

I can hear you say, "What a horrible, irresponsible bastard!" And
you're right. I leap to agree with you. I am one of the most irresponsible beings that ever lived. Irresponsibility is part of my invisibility; any way you face it, it is a denial. But to whom can I be
responsible, and why should I be, when you refuse to see me? And
wait until I reveal how truly irresponsible I am. Responsibility rests
upon recognition, and recognition is a form of agreement. Take the
man whom I almost killed: Who was responsible for that near
murder—I? I don't think so, and I refuse it. I won't buy it. You
can't give it to me. *He* bumped *me, he* insulted *me.* Shouldn't he,
for his own personal safety, have recognized my hysteria, my "danger potential"? He, let us say, was lost in a dream world. But didn't
he control that dream world—which, alas, is only too real!—and
didn't *he* rule me out of it? And if he had yelled for a policeman,
wouldn't *I* have been taken for the offending one? Yes, yes, yes! Let

me agree with you, I was the irresponsible one; for I should have used my knife to protect the higher interests of society. Some day that kind of foolishness will cause us tragic trouble. All dreamers and sleepwalkers must pay the price, and even the invisible victim is responsible for the fate of all. But I shirked that responsibility; I became too snarled in the incompatible notions that buzzed within my brain. I was a coward . . .

But what did *I* do to be so blue? Bear with me.

Chapter I
[BATTLE ROYAL]

It goes a long way back, some twenty years. All my life I had been looking for something, and everywhere I turned someone tried to tell me what it was. I accepted their answers too, though they were often in contradiction and even self-contradictory. I was naïve. I was looking for myself and asking everyone except myself questions which I, and only I, could answer. It took me a long time and much painful boomeranging of my expectations to achieve a realization everyone else appears to have been born with: That I am nobody but myself. But first I had to discover that I am an invisible man!

And yet I am no freak of nature, nor of history. I was in the cards, other things having been equal (or unequal) eighty-five years ago. I am not ashamed of my grandparents for having been slaves. I am only ashamed of myself for having at one time been ashamed. About eighty-five years ago they were told that they were free, united with others of our country in everything pertaining to the common good, and, in everything social, separate like the fingers of the hand. And they believed it. They exulted in it. They stayed in their place, worked hard, and brought up my father to do the same. But my grandfather is the one. He was an odd old guy, my grandfather, and I am told I take after him. It was he who caused the trouble. On his deathbed he called my father to him and said, "Son, after I'm gone I want you to keep up the good fight. I never told you, but our life is a war and I have been a traitor all my born days, a spy in the enemy's country ever since I give up my gun back in the Reconstruction. Live with your head in the lion's mouth. I want you to overcome 'em with yeses, undermine 'em with grins, agree 'em to death and destruction, let 'em swoller you till they vomit or bust wide open." They thought the old man had gone out of his mind. He had been the meekest of men. The younger children were rushed from the room, the shades drawn and the flame of the lamp turned so low that it sputtered on the wick like the old man's breathing. "Learn it to the younguns," he whispered fiercely; then he died.

But my folks were more alarmed over his last words than over his dying. It was as though he had not died at all, his words caused so much anxiety. I was warned emphatically to forget what he had said and, indeed, this is the first time it has been mentioned outside the family circle. It had a tremendous effect upon me, however. I could never be sure of what he meant. Grandfather had been a quiet old man who never made any trouble, yet on his deathbed he had called himself a traitor and a spy, and he had spoken of his meekness as a dangerous activity. It became a constant puzzle which lay unanswered in the back of my mind. And whenever things went well for me I remembered my grandfather and felt guilty and uncomfortable. It was as though I was carrying out his advice in spite of myself. And to make it worse, everyone loved me for it. I was praised by the most lily-white men of the town. I was considered an example of desirable conduct—just as my grandfather had been. And what puzzled me was that the old man had defined it as *treachery.* When I was praised for my conduct I felt a guilt that in some way I was doing something that was really against the wishes of the white folks, that if they had understood they would have desired me to act just the opposite, that I should have been sulky and mean, and that that really would have been what they wanted, even though they were fooled and thought they wanted me to act as I did. It made me afraid that some day they would look upon me as a traitor and I would be lost. Still I was more afraid to act any other way because they didn't like that at all. The old man's words were like a curse. On my graduation day I delivered an oration in which I showed that humility was the secret, indeed, the very essence of progress. (Not that I believed this—how could I, remembering my grandfather?—I only believed that it worked.) It was a great success. Everyone praised me and I was invited to give the speech at a gathering of the town's leading white citizens. It was a triumph for our whole community.

It was in the main ballroom of the leading hotel. When I got there I discovered that it was on the occasion of a smoker, and I was told that since I was to be there anyway I might as well take part in the battle royal to be fought by some of my schoolmates as part of the entertainment. The battle royal came first.

All of the town's big shots were there in their tuxedoes, wolfing down the buffet foods, drinking beer and whiskey and smoking black cigars. It was a large room with a high ceiling. Chairs were arranged in neat rows around three sides of a portable boxing ring. The fourth side was clear, revealing a gleaming space of polished floor. I had some misgivings over the battle royal, by the way. Not from a distaste for fighting, but because I didn't care too much for the other fellows who were to take part. They were tough guys who seemed to have no grandfather's curse worrying their minds. No one could mistake their toughness. And besides, I suspected that fighting a battle royal might detract from the dignity of my speech. In those pre-invisible days I visualized myself as a potential Booker T. Washington. But the other fellows didn't care too much for me either, and there were nine of them. I felt superior to them in my way, and I didn't like the manner in which we were all crowded together into the servants' elevator. Nor did they like my being there. In fact, as the warmly lighted floors flashed past the elevator we had words over the fact that I, by taking part in the fight, had knocked one of their friends out of a night's work.

We were led out of the elevator through a rococo hall into an anteroom and told to get into our fighting togs. Each of us was issued a pair of boxing gloves and ushered out into the big mirrored hall, which we entered looking cautiously about us and whispering, lest we might accidentally be heard above the noise of the room. It was foggy with cigar smoke. And already the whiskey was taking effect. I was shocked to see some of the most important men of the town quite tipsy. They were all there—bankers, lawyers, judges, doctors, fire chiefs, teachers, merchants. Even one of the more fashionable pastors. Something we could not see was going on up front. A clarinet was vibrating sensuously and the men were standing up and moving eagerly forward. We were a small tight group, clustered together, our bare uppers touching and shining with anticipatory sweat; while up front the big shots were becoming increasingly excited over something we still could not see. Suddenly I heard the school superintendent, who had told me to come, yell, "Bring up the shines, gentlemen! Bring up the little shines!"

We were rushed up to the front of the ballroom, where it smelled even more strongly of tobacco and whiskey. Then we were pushed into place. I almost wet my pants. A sea of faces, some hostile, some amused, ringed around us, and in the center, facing us, stood a magnificent blonde—stark naked. There was dead silence. I felt a blast of cold air chill me. I tried to back away, but they were behind me and around me. Some of the boys stood with lowered heads, trembling. I felt a wave of irrational guilt and fear. My teeth chattered, my skin turned to goose flesh, my knees knocked. Yet I was strongly attracted and looked in spite of myself. Had the price of looking been blindness, I would have looked. The hair was yellow like that of a circus kewpie doll, the face heavily powdered and rouged, as though to form an abstract mask, the eyes hollow and smeared a cool blue, the color of a baboon's butt. I felt a desire to spit upon her as my eyes brushed slowly over her body. Her breasts were firm and round as the domes of East Indian temples, and I stood so close as to see the fine skin texture and beads of pearly perspiration glistening like dew around the pink and erected buds of her nipples. I wanted at one and the same time to run from the room, to sink through the floor, or go to her and cover her from my eyes and the eyes of the others with my body; to feel the soft thighs, to caress her and destroy her, to love her and murder her, to hide from her, and yet to stroke where below the small American flag tattooed upon her belly her thighs formed a capital V. I had a notion that of all in the room she saw only me with her impersonal eyes.

And then she began to dance, a slow sensuous movement; the smoke of a hundred cigars clinging to her like the thinnest of veils. She seemed like a fair bird-girl girdled in veils calling to me from the angry surface of some gray and threatening sea. I was transported. Then I became aware of the clarinet playing and the big shots yelling at us. Some threatened us if we looked and others if we did not. On my right I saw one boy faint. And now a man grabbed a silver pitcher from a table and stepped close as he dashed ice water upon him and stood him up and forced two of us to support him as his head hung and moans issued from his thick bluish lips. Another boy began to plead to go home. He was the largest of the group, wearing dark red fighting trunks much too small to conceal the erection which projected from him as though in answer to the insinuating low-registered moaning of the clarinet. He tried to hide himself with his boxing gloves.

And all the while the blonde continued dancing, smiling faintly at the big shots who watched her with fascination, and faintly smiling at our fear. I noticed a certain merchant who followed her hungrily, his lips loose and drooling. He was a large man who wore diamond studs in a shirtfront which swelled with the ample paunch underneath, and each time the blonde swayed her undulating hips he ran his hand through the thin hair of his bald head and, with his arms upheld, his posture clumsy like that of an intoxicated panda, wound his belly in a slow and obscene grind. This creature was completely hypnotized. The music had quickened. As the dancer flung herself about with a detached expression on her face, the men began reaching out to touch her. I could see their beefy fingers sink into the soft flesh. Some of the others tried to stop them and she began to move around the floor in graceful circles, as they gave chase, slipping and sliding over the polished floor. It was mad. Chairs went crashing, drinks were spilt, as they ran laughing and howling after her. They caught her just as she reached a door, raised her from the floor, and tossed her as college boys are tossed at a hazing, and above her red, fixed-smiling lips I saw the terror and disgust in her eyes, almost like my own terror and that which I saw in some of the other boys. As I watched, they tossed her twice and her soft breasts seemed to flatten against the air and her legs flung wildly as she spun. Some of the more sober ones helped her to escape. And I started off the floor, heading for the anteroom with the rest of the boys.

Some were still crying and in hysteria. But as we tried to leave we were stopped and ordered to get into the ring. There was nothing to do but what we were told. All ten of us climbed under the ropes and allowed ourselves to be blindfolded with broad bands of white cloth. One of the men seemed to feel a bit sympathetic and tried to cheer us up as we stood with our backs against the ropes. Some of us tried to grin. "See that boy over there?" one of the men said. "I want you to run across at the bell and give it to him right in the belly. If you don't get him, I'm going to get you. I don't like his looks." Each of us was told the same. The blindfolds were put on. Yet even then I had been going over my speech. In my mind each word was as bright as flame. I felt the cloth pressed into place, and frowned so that it would be loosened when I relaxed.

But now I felt a sudden fit of blind terror. I was unused to darkness. It was as though I had suddenly found myself in a dark room filled with poisonous cottonmouths. I could hear the bleary voices yelling insistently for the battle royal to begin.

"Get going in there!"

"Let me at that big nigger!"

I strained to pick up the school superintendent's voice, as though to squeeze some security out of that slightly more familiar sound.

"Let me at those black sonsabitches!" someone yelled.

"No, Jackson, no!" another voice yelled. "Here, somebody, help me hold Jack."

"I want to get at that ginger-colored nigger. Tear him limb from limb," the first voice yelled.

I stood against the ropes trembling. For in those days I was what they called ginger-colored, and he sounded as though he might crunch me between his teeth like a crisp ginger cookie.

Quite a struggle was going on. Chairs were being kicked about and I could hear voices grunting as with a terrific effort. I wanted to see, to see more desperately than ever before. But the blindfold was tight as a thick skin-puckering scab and when I raised my gloved hands to push the layers of white aside a voice yelled, "Oh, no you don't, black bastard! Leave that alone!"

"Ring the bell before Jackson kills him a coon!" someone boomed in the sudden silence. And I heard the bell clang and the sound of the feet scuffling forward.

A glove smacked against my head. I pivoted, striking out stiffly as someone went past, and felt the jar ripple along the length of my arm to my shoulder. Then it seemed as though all nine of the boys had turned upon me at once. Blows pounded me from all sides while I struck out as best I could. So many blows landed upon me that I wondered if I were not the only blindfolded fighter in the ring, or if the man called Jackson hadn't succeeded in getting me after all.

Blindfolded, I could no longer control my motions. I had no dignity. I stumbled about like a baby or a drunken man. The smoke had become thicker and with each new blow it seemed to sear and further restrict my lungs. My saliva became like hot bitter glue. A glove connected with my head, filling my mouth with warm blood. It was everywhere. I could not tell if the moisture I felt upon my body was sweat or blood. A blow landed hard against the nape of my neck. I felt myself going over, my head hitting the floor. Streaks of blue light filled the black world behind the blindfold. I lay prone, pretending that I was knocked out, but felt myself seized by hands and yanked to my feet. "Get going, black boy! Mix it up!" My arms were like lead, my head smarting from blows. I managed to feel my way to the ropes and held on, trying to catch my breath. A glove landed in my mid-section and I went over again, feeling as though the smoke had become a knife jabbed into my guts. Pushed this way and that by the legs milling around me, I finally pulled erect and discovered that I could see the black, sweat-washed forms weaving in the smoky-blue atmosphere like drunken dancers weaving to the rapid drum-like thuds of blows.

Everyone fought hysterically. It was complete anarchy. Everybody fought everybody else. No group fought together for long. Two, three, four, fought one, then turned to fight each other, were themselves attacked. Blows landed below the belt and in the kidney, with the gloves open as well as closed, and with my eye partly opened now there was not so much terror. I moved carefully, avoiding blows, although not too many to attract attention, fighting from group to group. The boys groped about like blind, cautious crabs crouching to protect their mid-sections, their heads pulled in short against their shoulders, their arms stretched nervously before them, with their fists testing the smoke-filled air like the knobbed feelers of hypersensitive snails. In one corner I glimpsed a boy violently punching the air and heard him scream in pain as he smashed his hand against a ring post. For a second I saw him bent over holding his hand, then going down as a blow caught his unprotected head. I played one group against the other, slipping in and throwing a punch then stepping out of range while pushing the others into the melee to take the blows blindly aimed at me. The smoke was agonizing and there were no rounds, no bells at three minute intervals to relieve our exhaustion. The room spun round me, a swirl of lights, smoke, sweating bodies surrounded by tense white faces. I bled from both nose and mouth, the blood spattering upon my chest.

The men kept yelling, "Slug him, black boy! Knock his guts out!"

"Uppercut him! Kill him! Kill that big boy!"

Taking a fake fall, I saw a boy going down heavily beside me as though we were felled by a single blow, saw a sneaker-clad foot shoot into his groin as the two who had knocked him down stumbled upon him. I rolled out of range, feeling a twinge of nausea.

The harder we fought the more threatening the men became. And yet, I had begun to worry about my speech again. How would it go? Would they recognize my ability? What would they give me?

I was fighting automatically when suddenly I noticed that one after another of the boys was leaving the ring. I was surprised, filled

with panic, as though I had been left alone with an unknown
danger. Then I understood. The boys had arranged it among themselves. It was the custom for the two men left in the ring to slug it
out for the winner's prize. I discovered this too late. When the bell
sounded two men in tuxedoes leaped into the ring and removed the
blindfold. I found myself facing Tatlock, the biggest of the gang. I
felt sick at my stomach. Hardly had the bell stopped ringing in my
ears than it clanged again and I saw him moving swiftly toward me.
Thinking of nothing else to do I hit him smash on the nose. He kept
coming, bringing the rank sharp violence of stale sweat. His face
was a black blank of a face, only his eyes alive—with hate of me
and aglow with a feverish terror from what had happened to us all.
I became anxious. I wanted to deliver my speech and he came at me
as though he meant to beat it out of me. I smashed him again and
again, taking his blows as they came. Then on a sudden impulse I
struck him lightly and as we clinched, I whispered, "Fake like I
knocked you out, you can have the prize."

"I'll break your behind," he whispered horasely.

"For *them?*"

"For *me,* sonofabitch!"

They were yelling for us to break it up and Tatlock spun me half
around with a blow, and as a joggled camera sweeps in a reeling
scene, I saw the howling red faces crouching tense beneath the
cloud of blue-gray smoke. For a moment the world wavered, unraveled, flowed, then my head cleared and Tatlock bounced before
me. That fluttering shadow before my eyes was his jabbing left
hand. Then falling forward, my head against his damp shoulder, I
whispered,

"I'll make it five dollars more."

"Go to hell!"

But his relaxed a trifle beneath my pressure and I breathed,
"Seven?"

"Give it to your ma," he said, ripping me beneath the heart.

And while I still held him I butted him and moved away. I felt
myself bombarded with punches. I fought back with hopeless desperation. I wanted to deliver my speech more than anything else in
the world, because I felt that only these men could judge truly my
ability, and now this stupid clown was ruining my chances. I began
fighting carefully now, moving in to punch him and out again with
my greater speed. A lucky blow to his chin and I had him going
too—until I heard a loud voice yell, "I got my money on the big
boy."

Hearing this, I almost dropped my guard. I was confused: Should
I try to win against the voice out there? Would not this go against
my speech, and was not this a moment for humility, for nonresis-
tance? A blow to my head as I danced about sent my right eye
popping like a jack-in-the-box and settled my dilemma. The room

went red as I fell. It was a dream fall, my body languid and fastidious as to where to land, until the floor became impatient and smashed up to meet me. A moment later I came to. An hypnotic voice said FIVE emphatically. And I lay there, hazily watching a dark red spot of my own blood shaping itself into a butterfly, glistening and soaking into the soiled gray world of the canvas.

When the voice drawled TEN I was lifted up and dragged to a chair. I sat dazed. My eye pained and swelled with each throb of my pounding heart and I wondered if now I would be allowed to speak. I was wringing wet, my mouth still bleeding. We were grouped along the wall now. The other boys ignored me as they congratulated Tatlock and speculated as to how much they would be paid. One boy whimpered over his smashed hand. Looking up front, I saw attendants in white jackets rolling the portable ring away and placing a small square rug in the vacant space surrounded by chairs. Perhaps, I thought, I will stand on the rug to deliver my speech.

Then the M.C. called to us, "Come on up here boys and get your money."

We ran forward to where the men laughed and talked in their chairs, waiting. Everyone seemed friendly now.

"There it is on the rug," the man said. I saw the rug covered with coins of all dimensions and a few crumpled bills. But what excited me, scattered here and there, were the gold pieces.

"Boys, it's all yours," the man said. "You get all you grab."

"That's right, Sambo," a blond man said, winking at me confidentially.

I trembled with excitement, forgetting my pain. I would get the gold and the bills, I thought. I would use both hands. I would throw my body against the boys nearest me to block them from the gold.

"Get down around the rug now," the man commanded, "and don't anyone touch it until I give the signal."

"This ought to be good," I heard.

As told, we got around the square rug on our knees. Slowly the man raised his freckled hand as we followed it upward with our eyes.

I heard, "These niggers look like they're about to pray!"

Then, "Ready," the man said. "Go!"

I lunged for a yellow coin lying on the blue design of the carpet, touching it and sending a surprised shriek to join those rising around me. I tried frantically to remove my hand but could not let go. A hot, violent force tore through my body, shaking me like a wet rat. The rug was electrified. The hair bristled up on my head as I shook myself free. My muscles jumped, my nerves jangled, writhed. But I saw that this was not stopping the other boys. Laughing in fear and embarrassment, some were holding back and scooping up the coins knocked off by the painful contortions of the others. The men roared above us as we struggled.

"Pick it up, goddamnit, pick it up!" someone called like a bass-voiced parrot. "Go on, get it!"

I crawled rapidly around the floor, picking up the coins, trying to avoid the coppers and to get greenbacks and the gold. Ignoring the shock by laughing, as I brushed the coins off quickly, I discovered that I could contain the electricity—a contradiction, but it works. Then the men began to push us onto the rug. Laughing embarrassedly, we struggled out of their hands and kept after the coins. We were all wet and slippery and hard to hold. Suddenly I saw a boy lifted into the air, glistening with sweat like a circus seal, and dropped, his wet back landing flush upon the charged rug, heard him yell and saw him literally dance upon his back, his elbows beating a frenzied tattoo upon the floor, his muscles twitching like the flesh of a horse stung by many flies. When he finally rolled off, his face was gray and no one stopped him when he ran from the floor amid booming laughter.

"Get the money," the M.C. called. "That's good hard American cash!"

And we snatched and grabbed, snatched and grabbed. I was careful not to come too close to the rug now, and when I felt the hot whiskey breath descend upon me like a cloud of foul air I reached out and grabbed the leg of a chair. It was occupied and I held on desperately.

"Leggo, nigger! Leggo!"

The huge face wavered down to mine as he tried to push me free. But my body was slippery and he was too drunk. It was Mr. Colcord, who owned a chain of movie houses and "entertainment palaces." Each time he grabbed me I slipped out of his hands. It became a real struggle. I feared the rug more than I did the drunk, so I held on, surprising myself for a moment by trying to topple *him* upon the rug. It was such an enormous idea that I found myself actually carrying it out. I tried not to be obvious, yet when I grabbed his leg, trying to tumble him out of the chair, he raised up roaring with laughter, and, looking at me with soberness dead in the eye, kicked me viciously in the chest. The chair leg flew out of my hand and I felt myself going and rolled. It was as though I had rolled through a bed of hot coals. It seemed a whole century would pass before I would roll free, a century in which I was seared through the deepest levels of my body to the fearful breath within me and the breath seared and heated to the point of explosion. It'll all be over in a flash, I thought as I rolled clear. It'll all be over in a flash.

But not yet, the men on the other side were waiting, red faces swollen as though from apoplexy as they bent forward in their chairs. Seeing their fingers coming toward me I rolled away as a fumbled football rolls off the receiver's fingertips, back into the coals. That time I luckily sent the rug sliding out of place and heard the coins ringing against the floor and the boys scuffling to pick them up and the M.C. calling, "All right, boys, that's all. Go get dressed and get your money."

I was limp as a dish rag. My back felt as though it had been beaten with wires.

When we had dressed the M.C. came in and gave us each five dollars, except Tatlock, who got ten for being last in the ring. Then he told us to leave. I was not to get a chance to deliver my speech, I thought. I was going out into the dim alley in despair when I was stopped and told to go back. I returned to the ballroom, where the men were pushing back their chairs and gathering in groups to talk.

The M.C. knocked on a table for quiet. "Gentlemen," he said, "we almost forgot an important part of the program. A most serious part, gentlemen. This boy was brought here to deliver a speech which he made at his graduation yesterday . . ."

"Bravo!"

"I'm told that he is the smartest boy we've got out there in Greenwood. I'm told that he knows more big words than a pocket-sized dictionary."

Much applause and laughter.

"So now, gentlemen, I want you to give him your attention."

There was still laughter as I faced them, my mouth dry, my eye throbbing. I began slowly, but evidently my throat was tense, because they began shouting, "Louder! Louder!"

"We of the younger generation extol the wisdom of that great leader and educator," I shouted, "who first spoke these flaming words of wisdom: 'A ship lost at sea for many days suddenly sighted a friendly vessel. From the mast of the unfortunate vessel was seen a signal: "Water, water; we die of thirst!" The answer from the friendly vessel came back: "Cast down your bucket where you are." The captain of the distressed vessel, at last heeding the injunction, cast down his bucket, and it came up full of fresh sparkling water from the mouth of the Amazon River.' And like him I say, and in his words, 'To those of my race who depend upon bettering their condition in a foreign land, or who underestimate the importance of cultivating friendly relations with the Southern white man, who is his next-door neighbor, I would say: "Cast down your bucket where you are"—cast it down in making friends in every manly way of the people of all races by whom we are surrounded . . .' "

I spoke automatically and with such fervor that I did not realize that the men were still talking and laughing until my dry mouth, filling up with blood from the cut, almost strangled me. I coughed, wanting to stop and go to one of the tall brass, sand-filled spittoons to relieve myself, but a few of the men, especially the superinten- dent, were listening and I was afraid. So I gulped it down, blood, saliva and all, and continued. (What powers of endurance I had during those days! What enthusiasm! What a belief in the rightness of things!) I spoke even louder in spite of the pain. But still they talked and still they laughed, as though deaf with cotton in dirty ears. So I spoke with greater emotional emphasis. I closed my ears and swallowed blood until I was nauseated. The speech seemed a hundred times as long as before, but I could not leave out a single word. All had to be said, each memorized nuance considered, ren- dered. Nor was that all. Whenever I uttered a word of three or more syllables a group of voices would yell for me to repeat it. I used the phrase "social responsibility" and they yelled:

"What's that word you say, boy?"

"Social responsibility," I said.

"What?"

"Social . . ."

"Louder."

". . . responsibility."

"More!"

"Respon—"

"Repeat!"

"—sibility."

The room filled with the uproar of laughter until, no doubt, distracted by having to gulp down my blood, I made a mistake and yelled a phrase I had often seen denounced in newspaper editorials, heard debated in private.

"Social . . ."

"What?" they yelled.

". . . equality—"

The laughter hung smokelike in the sudden stillness. I opened my eyes, puzzled. Sounds of displeasure filled the room. The M.C. rushed forward. They shouted hostile phrases at me. But I did not understand.

A small dry mustached man in the front row blared out, "Say that slowly, son!"

"What, sir?"

"What you just said!"

"Social responsibility, sir," I said.

"You weren't being smart, were you, boy?" he said, not unkindly.

"No, sir!"

"You sure that about 'equality' was a mistake?"

"Oh, yes, sir," I said. "I was swallowing blood."

"Well, you had better speak more slowly so we can understand. We mean to do right by you, but you've got to know your place at all times. All right, now, go on with your speech."

I was afraid. I wanted to leave but I wanted also to speak and I was afraid they'd snatch me down.

"Thank you, sir," I said, beginning where I had left off, and having them ignore me as before.

Yet when I finished there was a thunderous applause. I was surprised to see the superintendent come forth with a package wrapped in white tissue paper, and, gesturing for quiet, address the men.

"Gentlemen, you see that I did not overpraise this boy. He makes a good speech and some day he'll lead his people in the proper paths. And I don't have to tell you that that is important in these days and times. This is a good, smart boy, and so to encourage him in the right direction, in the name of the Board of Education I wish to present him a prize in the form of this . . ."

He paused, removing the tissue paper and revealing a gleaming calfskin brief case.

". . . in the form of this first-class article from Shad Whitmore's shop."

"Boy," he said, addressing me, "take this prize and keep it well. Consider it a badge of office. Prize it. Keep developing as you are and some day it will be filled with important papers that will help shape the destiny of your people."

I was so moved that I could hardly express my thanks. A rope of bloody saliva forming a shape like an undiscovered continent drooled upon the leather and I wiped it quickly away. I felt an importance that I had never dreamed.

"Open it and see what's inside," I was told.

My fingers a-tremble, I complied, smelling the fresh leather and finding an official-looking document inside. It was a scholarship to the state college for Negroes. My eyes filled with tears and I ran awkwardly off the floor.

I was overjoyed; I did not even mind when I discovered that the gold pieces I had scrambled for were brass pocket tokens advertising a certain make of automobile.

When I reached home everyone was excited. Next day the neighbors came to congratulate me. I even felt safe from grandfather, whose deathbed curse usually spoiled my triumphs. I stood beneath his photograph with my brief case in hand and smiled triumphantly into his stolid black peasant's face. It was a face that fascinated me. The eyes seemed to follow everywhere I went.

That night I dreamed I was at a circus with him and that he refused to laugh at the clowns no matter what they did. Then later he told me to open my brief case and read what was inside and I did, finding an official envelope stamped with the state seal; and inside the envelope I found another and another, endlessly, and I thought I would fall of weariness. "Them's years," he said. "Now

open that one." And I did and in it I found an engraved document
containing a short message in letters of gold. "Read it," my grandfather said. "Out loud!"

"To Whom It May Concern," I intoned. "Keep This Nigger-Boy
Running."

I awoke with the old man's laughter ringing in my ears.

(It was a dream I was to remember and dream again for many
years after. But at that time I had no insight into its meaning. First
I had to attend college.)

1952

SAUL BELLOW

1915–

When Saul Bellow was awarded the Nobel Prize, his citation read: "For
the human understanding and subtle analysis of contemporary culture that
are combined in his work." Except for the poet Robert Lowell, no American writer of the post-Second World War period has a better claim to these
virtues than Bellow, who has devoted himself almost exclusively and passionately to the novel and its attempt to imagine life in the United States,
particularly in the great cities of Chicago and New York.

He was born in Lachine, Quebec, grew up in the Jewish ghetto of
Montreal, and moved to Chicago when he was nine. He attended the University of Chicago, then transferred to Northwestern, where he took a
degree in anthropology and sociology, the effects of which study are everywhere evident in the novels he was to write. He taught English for a time,
served in the Merchant Marine during World War II, then after the war
spent some fifteen years away from Chicago, teaching at N.Y.U. and
Princeton, and living in Paris. In 1962 he returned to Chicago and since
then has been a lecturer at the University of Chicago. He has married four
times.

Bellow's first novel, *Dangling Man*, was not published until he was
nearly thirty and is a short series of elegantly morose meditations, told
through the journal of a young man waiting to be inducted into the army
and with the "freedom" of having nothing to do but wait. Eventually he
is drafted: "Long live regimentation," he sardonically exults. His second
novel, *The Victim* (1947), continues the investigation of ways people
strive to be relieved of self-determination. This book concerns a week in
the life of Asa Leventhal, alone in New York City while his wife visits a
relative, and suddenly confronted by a figure from the past (Kirby Allbee,
a Gentile) who succeeds in implicating Leventhal with the past and its
present manifestations. *The Victim* is Bellow's most somberly naturalistic
depiction of a man brought up against forces larger than himself; yet
from the opening sentence ("On some nights New York is as hot as
Bangkok") a poetic dimension makes itself felt and helps create the sense
of mystery and disturbance felt by both the main character and the reader.

Dangling Man and *The Victim* are highly wrought, mainly humorless
books; in two long novels published in the 1950s Bellow opened up into

new ranges of aspiration and situational zaniness which brought him respectful admiration from many critics. *The Adventures of Augie March* (1953) and *Henderson the Rain King* (1959) are each narrated by an "I" who, like his predecessor Huck Finn, is good at lighting out for the territory ahead of whoever means to tie him down. The hero's adventures, whether occurring in Chicago, Mexico, or Africa, are exuberantly delivered in an always stimulating and sometimes overactive prose. *Augie* is filled with sights and sounds, colors and surfaces; its tone is self-involved, affectionate, and affirmative in its ring; *Henderson*, Bellow's most extravagant narrative, has the even more fabulous air of a quest-romance in which the hero returns home from Africa at peace with the world he had been warring against.

The ironic motto for Bellow's novels of the 1950s may well be "Seize the Day," as in the title of perhaps his finest piece of fiction. This short novel is both painful and exhilarating because it so fully exposes its hero (Tommy Wilhelm, an aging out-of-work ex-actor) to the insults of other people who don't understand him, to a city (New York's Upper West Side) impervious to his needs, and to a narrative prose which mixes ridicule and affection so thoroughly as to make them scarcely distinguishable. *Seize the Day* combines, within Tommy's monologues, a wildness and pathos of bitter comedy which was a powerful new element in Bellow's work.

In *Where Do We Go from Here*, an essay published in 1965, Bellow pointed out that nineteenth-century American literature—Emerson, Thoreau, Whitman, Melville—was highly didactic in its efforts to "instruct a young and raw nation." Bellow sees himself in this instructive tradition, and in the international company of "didactic" novelists like Dostoyevsky, D. H. Lawrence, and Joseph Conrad; he believes also that "the imagination is looking for new ways to express virtue * * * we have barely begun to comprehend what a human being is." These concerns animate the novels Bellow has written over the past fifteen years. In *Herzog* (1964) the hero is another down-and-outer, a professor-intellectual, a student of Romanticism and of the glorification of Self which Herzog believes both modern life and modernist literature have been working to undercut. At the same time he is a comic and pathetic victim of marital disorder; like all of Bellow's heroes, Herzog has a terrible time with women, yet cannot live without them. In *Mr. Sammler's Planet* (1970), written out of the disorders of the late 1960s, the atmosphere is grimmer. Sammler, an aging Jew living (again) on New York's West Side, analyzes and judges but cannot understand the young or blacks, or the mass of people gathered at Broadway and 96th Street. He sees about him everywhere "poverty of soul" but admits that he too has "a touch of the same disease—the disease of the single self explaining what was what and who was who."

These novels and the recent *Humboldt's Gift* (1975) have been accused of parading too single-mindedly attitudes to which their author is sympathetic. But what Bellow finds moving in Theodore Dreiser's work, "his balkiness and sullenness, and then his allegiance to life," is found also in his own: complaint and weariness, fault-finding, accusation of self and others—these gestures directed at "life" also make up the stuff of life and the "allegiance" out of which Bellow's heroes are made. We read him for this range of interest, for flexibility and diversity of style and idiom, and for the eloquences of nostalgia, invective, and lamentation which make up his intensely imagined world.

Seize the Day[1]

I

When it came to concealing his troubles, Tommy Wilhelm was not less capable than the next fellow. So at least he thought, and there was a certain amount of evidence to back him up. He had once been an actor—no, not quite, an extra—and he knew what acting should be. Also, he was smoking a cigar, and when a man is smoking a cigar, wearing a hat, he has an advantage; it is harder to find out how he feels. He came from the twenty-third floor down to the lobby on the mezzanine to collect his mail before breakfast, and he believed—he hoped—that he looked passably well: doing all right. It was a matter of sheer hope, because there was not much that he could add to his present effort. On the fourteenth floor he looked for his father to enter the elevator; they often met at this hour, on the way to breakfast. If he worried about his appearance it was mainly for his old father's sake. But there was no stop on the fourteenth, and the elevator sank and sank. Then the smooth door opened and the great dark red uneven carpet that covered the lobby billowed toward Wilhelm's feet. In the foreground the lobby was dark, sleepy. French drapes like sails kept out the sun, but three high, narrow windows were open, and in the blue air Wilhelm saw a pigeon about to light on the great chain that supported the marquee of the movie house directly underneath the lobby. For one moment he heard the wings beating strongly.

Most of the guests at the Hotel Gloriana were past the age of retirement. Along Broadway in the Seventies, Eighties, and Nineties, a great part of New York's vast population of old men and women lives. Unless the weather is too cold or wet they fill the benches about the tiny railed parks and along the subway gratings from Verdi Square to Columbia University, they crowd the shops and cafeterias, the dime stores, the tea-rooms, the bakeries, the beauty parlors, the reading rooms and club rooms. Among these old people at the Gloriana, Wilhelm felt out of place. He was comparatively young, in his middle forties, large and blond, with big shoulders; his back was heavy and strong, if already a little stooped or thickened. After breakfast the old guests sat down on the green leather armchairs and sofas in the lobby and began to gossip and look into the papers; they had nothing to do but wait out the day. But Wilhelm was used to an active life and liked to go out energetically in the morning. And for several months, because he had no

---

1. The novel's title has its source in the Roman poet Horace's *carpe diem, quam minimum credula postero* (*Odes*, I.xi.7): "seize the day, put no trust in the morrow," a pervasive theme of lyric poets.

position, he had kept up his morale by rising early; he was shaved and in the lobby by eight o'clock. He bought the paper and some cigars and drank a Coca-Cola or two before he went in to breakfast with his father. After breakfast—out, out, out to attend to business. The getting out had in itself become the chief business. But he had realized that he could not keep this up much longer, and today he was afraid. He was aware that his routine was about to break up and he sensed that a huge trouble long presaged but till now formless was due. Before evening, he'd know.

Nevertheless he followed his daily course and crossed the lobby.

Rubin, the man at the newsstand, had poor eyes. They may not have been actually weak but they were poor in expression, with lacy lids that furled down at the corners. He dressed well. It didn't seem necessary—he was behind the counter most of the time—but he dressed very well. He had on a rich brown suit; the cuffs embarrassed the hairs on his small hands. He wore a Countess Mara painted necktie.[2] As Wilhelm approached, Rubin did not see him; he was looking out dreamily at the Hotel Ansonia, which was visible from his corner, several blocks away. The Ansonia, the neighborhood's great landmark, was built by Stanford White.[3] It looks like a baroque palace from Prague or Munich enlarged a hundred times, with towers, domes, huge swells and bubbles of metal gone green from exposure, iron fretwork and festoons. Black television antennae are densely planted on its round summits. Under the changes of weather it may look like marble or like sea water, black as slate in the fog, white as tufa in sunlight. This morning it looked like the image of itself reflected in deep water, white and cumulous above, with cavernous distortions underneath. Together, the two men gazed at it.

Then Rubin said, "Your dad is in to breakfast already, the old gentleman."

"Oh, yes? Ahead of me today?"

"That's a real knocked-out shirt you got on," said Rubin. "Where's it from, Saks?"

"No, it's a Jack Fagman—Chicago."

Even when his spirits were low, Wilhelm could still wrinkle his forehead in a pleasing way. Some of the slow, silent movements of his face were very attractive. He went back a step, as if to stand away from himself and get a better look at his shirt. His glance was comic, a comment upon his untidiness. He liked to wear good clothes, but once he had put it on each article appeared to go its own way. Wilhelm, laughing, panted a little; his teeth were small; his cheeks when he laughed and puffed grew round, and he looked

2. Stylish, costly, hand-painted silk necktie.
3. Distinguished American architect (1853–1906) who designed many buildings in New York City, though not the Ansonia Hotel (Broadway at 73rd St.), which is commonly misattributed to him but was actually built by W. E. D. Stokes, with Paul DuBoy the architect.

much younger than his years. In the old days when he was a college freshman and wore a raccoon coat and a beanie on his large blond head his father used to say that, big as he was, he could charm a bird out of a tree. Wilhelm had great charm still.

"I like this dove-gray color," he said in his sociable, good-natured way. "It isn't washable. You have to send it to the cleaner. It never smells as good as washed. But it's a nice shirt. It cost sixteen, eighteen bucks."

This shirt had not been bought by Wilhelm; it was a present from his boss—his former boss, with whom he had had a falling out. But there was no reason why he should tell Rubin the history of it. Although perhaps Rubin knew—Rubin was the kind of man who knew, and knew and knew. Wilhelm also knew many things about Rubin, for that matter, about Rubin's wife and Rubin's business, Rubin's health. None of these could be mentioned, and the great weight of the unspoken left them little to talk about.

"Well, y'lookin' pretty sharp today," Rubin said.

And Wilhelm said gladly, "Am I? Do you really think so?" He could not believe it. He saw his reflection in the glass cupboard full of cigar boxes, among the grand seals and paper damask and the gold-embossed portraits of famous men, García, Edward the Seventh, Cyrus the Great. You had to allow for the darkness and deformations of the glass, but he thought he didn't look too good. A wide wrinkle like a comprehensive bracket sign was written upon his forehead, the point between his brows, and there were patches of brown on his dark blond skin. He began to be half amused at the shadow of his own marveling, troubled, desirous eyes, and his nostrils and his lips. Fair-haired hippopotamus!—that was how he looked to himself. He saw a big round face, a wide, flourishing red mouth, stump teeth. And the hat, too; and the cigar, too. I should have done hard labor all my life, he reflected. Hard honest labor that tires you out and makes you sleep. I'd have worked off my energy and felt better. Instead, I had to distinguish myself—yet.

He had put forth plenty of effort, but that was not the same as working hard, was it? And if as a young man he had got off to a bad start it was due to this very same face. Early in the nineteen-thirties, because of his striking looks, he had been very briefly considered star material, and he had gone to Hollywood. There for seven years, stubbornly, he had tried to become a screen artist. Long before that time his ambition or delusion had ended, but through pride and perhaps also through laziness he had remained in California. At last he turned to other things, but those seven years of persistence and defeat had unfitted him somehow for trades and businesses, and then it was too late to go into one of the professions. He had been slow to mature, and he had lost ground, and so he hadn't been able to get rid of his energy and he was convinced that this energy itself had done him the greatest harm.

"I didn't see you at the gin game[4] last night," said Rubin.

"I had to miss it. How did it go?"

For the last few weeks Wilhelm had played gin almost nightly, but yesterday he had felt that he couldn't afford to lose any more. He had never won. Not once. And while the losses were small they weren't gains, were they? They were losses. He was tired of losing, and tired also of the company, and so he had gone by himself to the movies.

"Oh," said Rubin, "it went okay. Carl made a chump of himself yelling at the guys. This time Doctor Tamkin didn't let him get away with it. He told him the psychological reason why."

"What was the reason?"

Rubin said, "I can't quote him. Who could? You know the way Tamkin talks. Don't ask me. Do you want the *Trib*?[5] Aren't you going to look at the closing quotations?"

"It won't help much to look. I know what they were yesterday at three," said Wilhelm. "But I suppose I better had get the paper." It seemed necessary for him to lift one shoulder in order to put his hand into his jacket pocket. There, among little packets of pills and crushed cigarette butts and strings of cellophane, the red tapes of packages which he sometimes used as dental floss, he recalled that he had dropped some pennies.

"That doesn't sound so good," said Rubin. He meant to be conversationally playful, but his voice had no tone and his eyes, slack and lid-blinded, turned elsewhere. He didn't want to hear. It was all the same to him. Maybe he already knew, being the sort of man who knew and knew.

No, it wasn't good. Wilhelm held three orders of lard in the commodities market. He and Dr. Tamkin had bought this lard together four days ago at 12.96, and the price at once began to fall and was still falling. In the mail this morning there was sure to be a call for additional margin payment. One came every day.

The psychologist, Dr. Tamkin, had got him into this. Tamkin lived at the Gloriana and attended the card game. He had explained to Wilhelm that you could speculate in commodities at one of the uptown branches of a good Wall Street house without making the full deposit of margin legally required. It was up to the branch manager. If he knew you—and all the branch managers knew Tamkin—he would allow you to make short-term purchases. You needed only to open a small account.

"The whole secret of this type of speculation," Tamkin had told him, "is in the alertness. You have to act fast—buy it and sell it; sell it and buy in again. But quick! Get to the window and have them wire Chicago at just the right second. Strike and strike again! Then get out the same day. In no time at all you turn over

4. Gin rummy, a card game.
5. The New York *Herald Tribune*, a once famous daily newspaper.

fifteen, twenty thousand dollars' worth of soy beans, coffee, corn, hides, wheat, cotton." Obviously the doctor understood the market well. Otherwise he could not make it sound so simple. "People lose because they are greedy and can't get out when it starts to go up. They gamble, but I do it scientifically. This is not guesswork. You must take a few points and get out. Why, ye gods!" said Dr. Tamkin with his bulging eyes, his bald head, and his drooping lip. "Have you stopped to think how much dough people are making in the market?"

Wilhelm with a quick shift from gloomy attention to the panting laugh which entirely changed his face had said, "Ho, have I ever! What do you think? Who doesn't know it's way beyond nineteen-twenty-eight—twenty-nine and still on the rise?[6] Who hasn't read the Fulbright investigation? There's money everywhere. Everyone is shoveling it in. Money is—is—"

"And can you rest—can you sit still while this is going on?" said Dr. Tamkin. "I confess to you I can't. I think about people, just because they have a few bucks to invest, making fortunes. They have no sense, they have no talent, they just have the extra dough and it makes them more dough. I get so worked up and tormented and restless, so restless! I haven't even been able to practice my profession. With all this money around you don't want to be a fool while everyone else is making. I know guys who make five, ten thousand a week just by fooling around. I know a guy at the Hotel Pierre. There's nothing to him, but he has a whole case of Mumm's champagne at lunch. I know another guy on Central Park South— But what's the use of talking. They make millions. They have smart lawyers who get them out of taxes by a thousand schemes."

"Whereas I got taken," said Wilhelm. "My wife refused to sign a joint return. One fairly good year and I got into the thirty-two-per-cent bracket and was stripped bare. What of all my bad years?"

"It's a businessmen's government," said Dr. Tamkin. "You can be sure that these men making five thousand a week—"

"I don't need that sort of money," Wilhelm had said. "But oh! if I could only work out a little steady income from this. Not much. I don't ask much. But how badly I need—! I'd be so grateful if you'd show me how to work it."

"Sure I will. *I* do it regularly. I'll bring you my receipts if you like. And do you want to know something? I approve of your attitude very much. You want to avoid catching the money fever. This type of activity is filled with hostile feeling and lust. You should see what it does to some of these fellows. They go on the market with murder in their hearts."

"What's that I once heard a guy say?" Wilhelm remarked. "A man is only as good as what he loves."

---

6. Just before it crashed in 1929, the stock market rose to great heights.

"That's it—just it," Tamkin said. "You don't have to go about it their way. There's also a calm and rational, a psychological approach."

Wilhelm's father, old Dr. Adler, lived in an entirely different world from his son, but he had warned him once against Dr. Tamkin. Rather casually—he was a very bland old man—he said, "Wilky, perhaps you listen too much to this Tamkin. He's interesting to talk to. I don't doubt it. I think he's pretty common but he's a persuasive man. However, I don't know how reliable he may be."

It made Wilhelm profoundly bitter that his father should speak to him with such detachment about his welfare. Dr. Adler liked to appear affable. Affable! His own son, his one and only son, could not speak his mind or ease his heart to him. I wouldn't turn to Tamkin, he thought, if I could turn to him. At least Tamkin sympathizes with me and tries to give me a hand, whereas Dad doesn't want to be disturbed.

Old Dr. Adler had retired from practice; he had a considerable fortune and could easily have helped his son. Recently Wilhelm had told him, "Father—it so happens that I'm in a bad way now. I hate to have to say it. You realize that I'd rather have good news to bring you. But it's true. And since it's true, Dad— What else am I supposed to say? It's true."

Another father might have appreciated how difficult this confession was—so much bad luck, weariness, weakness, and failure. Wilhelm had tried to copy the old man's tone and made himself sound gentlemanly, low-voiced, tasteful. He didn't allow his voice to tremble; he made no stupid gesture. But the doctor had no answer. He only nodded. You might have told him that Seattle was near Puget Sound, or that the Giants and Dodgers were playing a night game, so little was he moved from his expression of healthy, handsome, good-humored old age. He behaved toward his son as he had formerly done toward his patients, and it was a great grief to Wilhelm; it was almost too much to bear. Couldn't he see—couldn't he feel? Had he lost his family sense?

Greatly hurt, Wilhelm struggled however to be fair. Old people are bound to change, he said. They have hard things to think about. They must prepare for where they are going. They can't live by the old schedule any longer and all their perspectives change, and other people become alike, kin and acquaintances. Dad is no longer the same person, Wilhelm reflected. He was thirty-two when I was born, and now he's going on eighty. Furthermore, it's time I stopped feeling like a kid toward him, a small son.

The handsome old doctor stood well above the other old people in the hotel. He was idolized by everyone. This was what people said: "That's old Professor Adler, who used to teach internal medicine. He was a diagnostician, one of the best in New York, and had a tremendous practice. Isn't he a wonderful-looking old guy? It's a pleasure to see such a fine old scientist, clean and immaculate. He stands straight and understands every single thing you say. He still has all his buttons. You can discuss any subject with him." The clerks, the elevator operators, the telephone girls and waitresses and chambermaids, the management flattered and pampered him. That was what he wanted. He had always been a vain man. To see how his father loved himself sometimes made Wilhelm madly indignant.

He folded over the *Tribune* with its heavy, black, crashing sensational print and read without recognizing any of the words, for his mind was still on his father's vanity. The doctor had created his own praise. People were primed and did not know it. And what did he need praise for? In a hotel where everyone was busy and contacts were so brief and had such small weight, how could it satisfy him? He could be in people's thoughts here and there for a moment; in and then out. He could never matter much to them. Wilhelm let out a long, hard breath and raised the brows of his round and somewhat circular eyes. He stared beyond the thick borders of the paper.

. . . love that well which thou must leave ere long.[7]

Involuntary memory brought him this line. At first he thought it referred to his father, but then he understood that it was for himself, rather. *He* should love that well. "This thou perceivest, which makes *thy* love more strong." Under Dr. Tamkin's influence Wilhelm had recently begun to remember the poems he used to read. Dr. Tamkin knew, or said he knew, the great English poets and once in a while he mentioned a poem of his own. It was a long time since anyone had spoken to Wilhelm about this sort of thing. He didn't like to think about his college days, but if there was one course that now made sense it was Literature I. The textbook was Lieder and Lovett's *British Poetry and Prose*, a black heavy book with thin pages. Did I read that? he asked himself. Yes, he had read it and there was one accomplishment at least he could recall with pleasure. He had read "Yet once more, O ye laurels." How pure this was to say! It was beautiful.

Sunk though he be beneath the wat'ry floor . . .[8]

Such things had always swayed him, and now the power of such words was far, far greater.

Wilhelm respected the truth, but he could lie and one of the things he lied often about was his education. He said he was an alumnus of Penn State; in fact he had left school before his sophomore year was finished. His sister Catherine had a B. S. degree. Wilhelm's late mother was a graduate of Bryn Mawr. He was the only member of the family who had no education. This was another sore point. His father was ashamed of him.

---

7. The last line of Shakespeare's Sonnet 73.
8. Wilhelm recalls the first and the 167th lines of *Lycidas* by John Milton (1608–1674).

But he had heard the old man bragging to another old man, saying, "My son is a sales executive. He didn't have the patience to finish school. But he does all right for himself. His income is up in the five figures somewhere."

"What—thirty, forty thousand?" said his stooped old friend.

"Well, he needs at least that much for his style of life. Yes, he needs that."

Despite his troubles, Wilhelm almost laughed. Why, that boasting old hypocrite. He knew the sales executive was no more. For many weeks there had been no executive, no sales, no income. But how we love looking fine in the eyes of the world—how beautiful are the old when they are doing a snow job! It's Dad, thought Wilhelm, who is the salesman. He's selling me. *He* should have gone on the road.

But what of the truth? Ah, the truth was that there were problems, and of these problems his father wanted no part. His father was ashamed of him. The truth, Wilhelm thought, was very awkward. He pressed his lips together, and his tongue went soft; it pained him far at the back, in the cords and throat, and a knot of ill formed in his chest. Dad never was a pal to me when I was young, he reflected. He was at the office or the hospital, or lecturing. He expected me to look out for myself and never gave me much thought. Now he looks down on me. And maybe in some respects he's right.

No wonder Wilhelm delayed the moment when he would have to go into the dining room. He had moved to the end of Rubin's counter. He had opened the *Tribune*; the fresh pages drooped from his hands; the cigar was smoked out and the hat did not defend him. He was wrong to suppose that he was more capable than the next fellow when it came to concealing his troubles. They were clearly written out upon his face. He wasn't even aware of it.

There was the matter of the different names, which, in the hotel, came up frequently. "Are you Doctor Adler's son?" "Yes, but my name is Tommy Wilhelm." And the doctor would say, "My son and I use different monickers. I uphold tradition. He's for the new." The Tommy was Wilhelm's own invention. He adopted it when he went to Hollywood, and dropped the Adler. Hollywood was his own idea, too. He used to pretend that it had all been the doing of a certain talent scout named Maurice Venice. But the scout had never made him a definite offer of a studio connection. He had approached him, but the results of the screen tests had not been good. After the test Wilhelm took the initiative and pressed Maurice Venice until he got him to say, "Well, I suppose you might make it out there." On the strength of this Wilhelm had left college and had gone to California.

Someone had said, and Wilhelm agreed with the saying, that in Los Angeles all the loose objects in the country were collected, as if America had been tilted and everything that wasn't tightly screwed down had slid into Southern California. He himself had been one of these loose objects. Sometimes he told people, "I was too mature for college. I was a big boy, you see. Well, I thought, when do you start to become a man?" After he had driven a painted flivver and had worn a yellow slicker with slogans on it, and played illegal poker, and gone out on Coke dates, he had *had* college. He wanted to try something new and quarreled with his parents about his career. And then a letter came from Maurice Venice.

The story of the scout was long and intricate and there were several versions of it. The truth about it was never told. Wilhelm had lied first boastfully and then out of charity to himself. But his memory was good, he could still separate what he had invented from the actual happenings, and this morning he found it necessary as he stood by Rubin's showcase with his *Tribune* to recall the crazy course of the true events.

I didn't seem even to realize that there was a depression. How could I have been such a jerk as not to prepare for anything and just go on luck and inspiration? With round gray eyes expanded and his large shapely lips closed in severity toward himself he forced open all that had been hidden. Dad I couldn't affect one way or another. Mama was the one who tried to stop me, and we carried on and yelled and pleaded. The more I lied the louder I raised my voice, and charged—like a hippopotamus. Poor Mother! How I disappointed her. Rubin heard Wilhelm give a broken sigh as he stood with the forgotten *Tribune* crushed under his arm.

When Wilhelm was aware that Rubin watched him, loitering and idle, apparently not knowing what to do with himself this morning, he turned to the Coca-Cola machine. He swallowed hard at the Coke bottle and coughed over it, but he ignored his coughing, for he was still thinking, his eyes upcast and his lips closed behind his hand. By a peculiar twist of habit he wore his coat collar turned up always, as though there were a wind. It never lay flat. But on his broad back, stooped with its own weight, its strength warped almost into deformity, the collar of his sports coat appeared anyway to be no wider than a ribbon.

He was listening to the sound of his own voice as he explained, twenty-five years ago in the living room on West End Avenue, "But Mother, if I don't pan out as an actor I can still go back to school."

But she was afraid he was going to destroy himself. She said, "Wilky, Dad could make it easy for you if you wanted to go into medicine." To remember this stifled him.

"I can't bear hospitals. Besides, I might make a mistake and hurt someone or even kill a patient. I couldn't stand that. Besides, I haven't got that sort of brains."

Then his mother had made the mistake of mentioning her nephew, Artie, Wilhelm's cousin, who was an honor student at

Columbia in math and languages. That dark little gloomy Artie with his disgusting narrow face, and his moles and self-sniffing ways and his unclean table manners, the boring habit he had of conjugating verbs when you went for a walk with him. "Roumanian is an easy language. You just add a *tl* to everything." He was now a professor, this same Artie with whom Wilhelm had played near the soldiers' and sailors' monument on Riverside Drive. Not that to be a professor was in itself so great. How could anyone bear to know so many languages? And Artie also had to remain Artie, which was a bad deal. But perhaps success had changed him. Now that he had a place in the world perhaps he was better. Did Artie love his languages, and live for them, or was he also, in his heart, cynical? So many people nowadays were. No one seemed satisfied, and Wilhelm was especially horrified by the cynicism of successful people. Cynicism was bread and meat to everyone. And irony, too. Maybe it couldn't be helped. It was probably even necessary. Wilhelm, however, feared it intensely. Whenever at the end of the day he was unusually fatigued he attributed it to cynicism. Too much of the world's business done. Too much falsity. He had various words to express the effect this had on him. Chicken! Unclean! Congestion! he exclaimed in his heart. Rat race! Phony! Murder! Play the Game! Buggers!

At first the letter from the talent scout was nothing but a flattering sort of joke. Wilhelm's picture in the college paper when he was running for class treasurer was seen by Maurice Venice, who wrote to him about a screen test. Wilhelm at once took the train to New York. He found the scout to be huge and oxlike, so stout that his arms seemed caught from beneath in a grip of flesh and fat; it looked as though it must be positively painful. He had little hair. Yet he enjoyed a healthy complexion. His breath was noisy and his voice rather difficult and husky because of the fat in his throat. He had on a double-breasted suit of the type then known as the pillbox; it was chalk-striped, pink on blue; the trousers hugged his ankles.

They met and shook hands and sat down. Together these two big men dwarfed the tiny Broadway office and made the furnishings look like toys. Wilhelm had the color of a Golden Grimes apple when he was well, and then his thick blond hair had been vigorous and his wide shoulders unwarped; he was leaner in the jaws, his eyes fresher and wider; his legs were then still awkward but he was impressively handsome. And he was about to make his first great mistake. Like, he sometimes thought, I was going to pick up a weapon and strike myself a blow with it.

Looming over the desk in the small office darkened by overbuilt midtown—sheer walls, gray spaces, dry lagoons of tar and pebbles —Maurice Venice proceeded to establish his credentials. He said, "My letter was on the regular stationery, but maybe you want to check on me?"

"Who, *me*?" said Wilhelm. "Why?"

"There's guys who think I'm in a racket and make a charge for the test. I don't ask a cent. I'm no agent. There ain't no commission."

"I never even thought of it," said Wilhelm. Was there perhaps something fishy about this Maurice Venice? He protested too much.

In his husky, fat-weakened voice he finally challenged Wilhelm, "If you're not sure, you can call the distributor and find out who I am, Maurice Venice."

Wilhelm wondered at him. "Why shouldn't I be sure? Of course I am."

"Because I can see the way you size me up, and because this is a dinky office. Like you don't believe me. Go ahead. Call. I won't care if you're cautious. I mean it. There's quite a few people who doubt me at first. They can't really believe that fame and fortune are going to hit 'em."

"But I tell you I do believe you," Wilhelm had said, and bent inward to accommodate the pressure of his warm, panting laugh. It was purely nervous. His neck was ruddy and neatly shaved about the ears—he was fresh from the barbershop; his face anxiously glowed with his desire to make a pleasing impression. It was all wasted on Venice, who was just as concerned about the impression *he* was making.

"If you're surprised, I'll just show you what I mean," Venice had said. "It was about fifteen months ago right in this identical same office when I saw a beautiful thing in the paper. It wasn't even a photo but a drawing, a brassière ad, but I knew right away that this was star material. I called up the paper to ask who the girl was, they gave me the name of the advertising agency; I phoned the agency and they gave me the name of the artist; I got hold of the artist and he gave me the number of the model agency. Finally, finally I got her number and phoned her and said, 'This is Maurice Venice, scout for Kaskaskia Films.' So right away she says, 'Yah, so's your old lady.' Well, when I saw I wasn't getting nowhere with her I said to her, 'Well, miss. I don't blame you. You're a very beautiful thing and must have a dozen admirers after you all the time, boy friends who like to call and pull your leg and give a tease. But as I happen to be a very busy fellow and don't have the time to horse around or argue, I tell you what to do. Here's my number, and here's the number of the Kaskaskia Distributors, Inc. Ask them who am I, Maurice Venice. The scout.' She did it. A little while later she phoned me back, all apologies and excuses, but I didn't want to embarrass her and get off on the wrong foot with an artist. I know better than to do that. So I told her it was a natural precaution, never mind. I wanted to run a screen test right away. Because I seldom am wrong about talent. If I see it, it's there. Get that, please. And do you know who that little girl is today?"

"No," Wilhelm said eagerly. "Who is she?"

Venice said impressively, " 'Nita Christenberry."

Wilhelm sat utterly blank. This was failure. He didn't know the name, and Venice was waiting for his response and would be angry.

And in fact Venice had been offended. He said, "What's the matter with you! Don't you read a magazine? She's a starlet."

"I'm sorry," Wilhelm answered. "I'm at school and don't have time to keep up. If I don't know her, it doesn't mean a thing. She made a big hit, I'll bet."

"You can say that again. Here's a photo of her." He handed Wilhelm some pictures. She was a bathing beauty—short, the usual breasts, hips, and smooth thighs. Yes, quite good, as Wilhelm recalled. She stood on high heels and wore a Spanish comb and mantilla. In her hand was a fan.

He had said, "She looks awfully peppy."

"Isn't she a divine girl? And what personality! Not just another broad in the show business, believe me." He had a surprise for Wilhelm. "I have found happiness with her," he said.

"You have?" said Wilhelm, slow to understand.

"Yes, boy, we're engaged."

Wilhelm saw another photograph, taken on the beach. Venice was dressed in a terry-cloth beach outfit, and he and the girl, cheek to cheek, were looking into the camera. Below, in white ink, was written "Love at Malibu Colony."

"I'm sure you'll be very happy. I wish you—".

"I *know*," said Venice firmly, "I'm going to be happy. When I saw that drawing, the breath of fate breathed on me. I felt it over my entire body."

"Say, it strikes a bell suddenly," Wilhelm had said. "Aren't you related to Martial Venice the producer?"

Venice was either a nephew of the producer or the son of a first cousin. Decidedly he had not made good. It was easy enough for Wilhelm to see this now. The office was so poor, and Venice bragged so nervously and identified himself so scrupulously—the poor guy. He was the obscure failure of an aggressive and powerful clan. As such he had the greatest sympathy from Wilhelm.

Venice had said, "Now I suppose you want to know where you come in. I seen your school paper, by accident. You take quite a remarkable picture."

"It can't be so much," said Wilhelm, more panting than laughing.

"You don't want to tell me my business," Venice said. "Leave it to me. I studied up on this."

"I never imagined—Well, what kind of roles do you think I'd fit?"

"All this time that we've been talking, I've been watching. Don't think I haven't. You remind me of someone. Let's see who it can be—one of the great old-timers. Is it Milton Sills? No, that's not the one. Conway Tearle, Jack Mulhall? George Bancroft? No, his face was ruggeder. One thing I can tell you, though, a George Raft type you're not—those tough, smooth, black little characters."

"No, I wouldn't seem to be."

"No, you're not that flyweight type, with the fists, from a night-club, and the glamorous sideburns, doing the tango or the bolero. Not Edward G. Robinson, either—I'm thinking aloud. Or the Cagney fly-in-your-face role, a cabbie, with that mouth and those punches."

"I realize that."

"Not suave like William Powell, or a lyric juvenile like Buddy Rogers. I suppose you don't play the sax? No. But—"

"But what?"

"I have you placed as the type that loses the girl to the George Raft type or the William Powell type.[9] You are steady, faithful, you get stood up. The older women would know better. The mothers are on your side. With what they been through, if it was up to them, they'd take you in a minute. You're very sympathetic, even the young girls feel that. You'd make a good provider. But they go more for the other types. It's as clear as anything."

This was not how Wilhelm saw himself. And as he surveyed the old ground he recognized now that he had been not only confused but hurt. Why, he thought, he cast me even then for a loser.

Wilhelm had said, with half a mind to be defiant, "Is that your opinion?"

It never occurred to Venice that a man might object to stardom in such a role. "Here is your chance," he said. "Now you're just in college. What are you studying?" He snapped his fingers. "Stuff." Wilhelm himself felt this way about it. "You may plug along fifty years before you get anywheres. This way, in one jump, the world knows who you are. You become a name like Roosevelt, Swanson.[1] From east to west, out to China, into South America. This is no bunk. You become a lover to the whole world. The world wants it, needs it. One fellow smiles, a billion people also smile. One fellow cries, the other billion sob with him. Listen, bud—" Venice had pulled himself together to make an effort. On his imagination there was some great weight which he could not discharge. He wanted Wilhelm, too, to feel it. He twisted his large, clean, well-meaning, rather foolish features as though he were their unwilling captive, and said in his choked, fat-obstructed voice, "Listen, everywhere there are people trying hard, miserable, in trouble, downcast, tired, trying and trying. They need a break, right? A break through, a help, luck or sympathy."

"That certainly is the truth," said Wilhelm. He had seized the

---

9. George Raft (b. 1903) and William Powell (b. 1892) were American film actors.

1. Franklin Delano Roosevelt (1882–1945), 32nd President. Gloria Swanson (b. 1899), celebrated film actress.

feeling and he waited for Venice to go on. But Venice had no more
to say; he had concluded. He gave Wilhelm several pages of blue
hectographed script, stapled together, and told him to prepare for
the screen test. "Study your lines in front of a mirror," he said. "Let
yourself go. The part should take ahold of you. Don't be afraid to
make faces and be emotional. Shoot the works. Because when you
start to act you're no more an ordinary person, and those things
don't apply to you. You don't behave the same way as the average."

And so Wilhelm had never returned to Penn State. His roommate
sent his things to New York for him, and the school authorities had
to write to Dr. Adler to find out what had happened.

Still, for three months Wilhelm delayed his trip to California. He
wanted to start out with the blessings of his family, but they were
never given. He quarreled with his parents and his sister. And then,
when he was best aware of the risks and knew a hundred reasons
against going and had made himself sick with fear, he left home.
This was typical of Wilhelm. After much thought and hesitation
and debate he invariably took the course he had rejected innumerable times. Ten such decisions made up the history of his life. He
had decided that it would be a bad mistake to go to Hollywood, and
then he went. He had made up his mind not to marry his wife,
but ran off and got married. He had resolved not to invest money
with Tamkin, and then had given him a check.

But Wilhelm had been eager for life to start. College was merely
another delay. Venice had approached him and said that the world
had named Wilhelm to shine before it. He was to be freed from the
anxious and narrow life of the average. Moreover, Venice had
claimed that he never made a mistake. His instinct for talent was
infallible, he said.

But when Venice saw the results of the screen test he did a quick
about-face. In those days Wilhelm had had a speech difficulty. It
was not a true stammer, it was a thickness of speech which the
sound track exaggerated. The film showed that he had many peculiarities, otherwise unnoticeable. When he shrugged, his hands
drew up within his sleeves. The vault of his chest was huge, but he
really didn't look strong under the lights. Though he called himself
a hippopotamus, he more nearly resembled a bear. His walk was
bearlike, quick and rather soft, toes turned inward, as though his
shoes were an impediment. About one thing Venice had been right.
Wilhelm was photogenic, and his wavy blond hair (now graying)
came out well, but after the test Venice refused to encourage him.
He tried to get rid of him. He couldn't afford to take a chance on
him, he had made too many mistakes already and lived in fear of
his powerful relatives.

Wilhelm had told his parents, "Venice says I owe it to myself to
go." How ashamed he was now of this lie! He had begged Venice

not to give him up. He had said, "Can't you help me out? It would kill me to go back to school now."

Then when he reached the Coast he learned that a recommendation from Maurice Venice was the kiss of death. Venice needed help and charity more than he, Wilhelm, ever had. A few years later when Wilhelm was down on his luck and working as an orderly in a Los Angeles hospital, he saw Venice's picture in the papers. He was under indictment for pandering. Closely following the trial, Wilhelm found out that Venice had indeed been employed by Kaskaskia Films but that he had evidently made use of the connection to organize a ring of call girls. Then what did he want with me? Wilhelm had cried to himself. He was unwilling to believe anything very bad about Venice. Perhaps he was foolish and unlucky, a fall guy, a dupe, a sucker. You didn't give a man fifteen years in prison, for that. Wilhelm often thought that he might write him a letter to say how sorry he was. He remembered the breath of fate and Venice's certainty that he would be happy. 'Nita Christenberry was sentenced to three years. Wilhelm recognized her although she had changed her name.

By that time Wilhelm too had taken his new name. In California he became Tommy Wilhelm. Dr. Adler would not accept the change. Today he still called his son Wilky, as he had done for more than forty years. Well, now, Wilhelm was thinking, the paper crowded in disarray under his arm, there's really very little that a man can change at will. He can't change his lungs, or nerves, or constitution or temperament. They're not under his control. When he's young and strong and impulsive and dissatisfied with the way things are he wants to rearrange them to assert his freedom. He can't overthrow the government or be differently born; he only has a little scope and maybe a foreboding, too, that essentially you can't change. Nevertheless, he makes a gesture and becomes Tommy Wilhelm. Wilhelm had always had a great longing to be Tommy. He had never, however, succeeded in feeling like Tommy, and in his soul had always remained Wilky. When he was drunk he reproached himself horribly as Wilky. "You fool, you clunk, you Wilky!" he called himself. He thought that it was a good thing perhaps that he had not become a success as Tommy since that would not have been a genuine success. Wilhelm would have feared that not he but Tommy had brought it off, cheating Wilky of his birthright. Yes, it had been a stupid thing to do, but it was his imperfect judgment at the age of twenty which should be blamed. He had cast off his father's name, and with it his father's opinion of him. It was, he knew it was, his bid for liberty, Adler being in his mind the title of the species, Tommy the freedom of the person. But Wilky was his inescapable self.

In middle age you no longer thought such thoughts about free choice. Then it came over you that from one grandfather you had inherited such and such a head of hair which looked like honey when it whitens or sugars in the jar; from another, broad thick shoulders; an oddity of speech from one uncle, and small teeth from amother, and the gray eyes with darkness diffused even into the whites, and a wide-lipped mouth like a statue from Peru. Wandering races have such looks, the bones of one tribe, the skin of another. From his mother he had gotten sensitive feelings, a soft heart, a brooding nature, a tendency to be confused under pressure.

The changed name was a mistake, and he would admit it as freely as you liked. But this mistake couldn't be undone now, so why must his father continully remind him how he had sinned? It was too late. He would have to go back to the pathetic day when the sin was committed. And where was that day? Past and dead. Whose humiliating memories were these? His and not his father's. What had he to think back on that he could call good? Very, very little. You had to forgive. First, to forgive yourself, and then general forgiveness. Didn't he suffer from his mistakes far more than his father could?

"Oh, God," Wilhelm prayed. "Let me out of my trouble. Let me out of my thoughts, and let me do something better with myself. For all the time I have wasted I am very sorry. Let me out of this clutch and into a different life. For I am all balled up. Have mercy."

II

The mail.

The clerk who gave it to him did not care what sort of appearance he made this morning. He only glanced at him from under his brows, upward, as the letters changed hands. Why should the hotel people waste courtesies on him? They had his number. The clerk knew that he was handing him, along with the letters, a bill for his rent. Wilhelm assumed a look that removed him from all such things. But it was bad. To pay the bill he would have to withdraw money from his brokerage account, and the account was being watched because of the drop in lard. According to the *Tribune*'s figures lard was still twenty points below last year's level. There were government price supports. Wilhelm didn't know how these worked but he understood that the farmer was protected and that the SEC kept an eye on the market and therefore he believed that lard would rise again and he wasn't greatly worried as yet. But in the meantime his father might have offered to pick up his hotel tab. Why didn't he? What a selfish old man he was! He saw his son's hardships; he could so easily help him. How little it would mean to him, and how much to Wilhelm! Where was the old man's heart? Maybe, thought Wilhelm, I was sentimental in the past and exaggerated his kindliness—warm family life. It may never have been there.

Not long ago his father had said to him in his usual affable, pleasant way, "Well, Wilky, here we are under the same roof again, after all these years."

Wilhelm was glad for an instant. At last they would talk over old times. But he was also on guard against insinuations. Wasn't his father saying, "Why are you here in a hotel with me and not at home in Brooklyn with your wife and two boys? You're neither a widower nor a bachelor. You have brought me all your confusions. What do you expect me to do with them?"

So Wilhelm studied the remark for a bit, then said, "The roof is twenty-six stories up. But how many years has it been?"

"That's what I was asking you."

"Gosh, Dad, I'm not sure. Wasn't it the year Mother died? What year was that?"

He asked this question with an innocent frown on his Golden Grimes, dark blond face. *What year was it!* As though he didn't know the year, the month, the day, the very hour of his mother's death.

"Wasn't it nineteen-thirty-one?" said Dr. Adler.

"Oh, was it?" said Wilhelm. And in hiding the sadness and the overwhelming irony of the question he gave a nervous shiver and wagged his head and felt the ends of his collar rapidly.

"Do you know?" his father said. "You must realize, an old fellow's memory becomes unreliable. It was in winter, that I'm sure of. Nineteen-thirty-two?"

Yes, it was age. Don't make an issue of it, Wilhelm advised himself. If you were to ask the old doctor in what year he had interned, he'd tell you correctly. All the same, don't make an issue. Don't quarrel with your own father. Have pity on an old man's failings.

"I believe the year was closer to nineteen-thirty-four, Dad," he said.

But Dr. Adler was thinking, Why the devil can't he stand still when we're talking? He's either hoisting his pants up and down by the pockets or jittering with his feet. A regular mountain of tics, he's getting to be. Wilhelm had a habit of moving his feet back and forth as though, hurrying into a house, he had to clean his shoes first on the doormat.

Then Wilhelm had said, "Yes, that was the beginning of the end, wasn't it, Father?"

Wilhelm often astonished Dr. Adler. Beginning of the end? What could he mean—what was he fishing for? Whose end? The end of family life? The old man was puzzled but he would not give Wilhelm an opening to introduce his complaints. He had learned that it was better not to take up Wilhelm's strange challenges. So he merely agreed pleasantly, for he was a master of social behavior, and said, "It was an awful misfortune for us all."

He thought, What business has he to complain to *me* of his mother's death?

Face to face they had stood, each declaring himself silently after his own way. It was: it was not, the beginning of the end—*some* end.

Unaware of anything odd in his doing it, for he did it all the time, Wilhelm had pinched out the coal of his cigarette and dropped the butt in his pocket, where there were many more. And as he gazed at his father the little finger of his right hand began to twitch and tremble; of that he was unconscious, too.

And yet Wilhelm believed that when he put his mind to it he could have perfect and even distinguished manners, outdoing his father. Despite the slight thickness in his speech—it amounted almost to a stammer when he started the same phrase over several times in his effort to eliminate the thick sound—he could be fluent. Otherwise he would never have made a good salesman. He claimed also that he was a good listener. When he listened he made a tight mouth and rolled his eyes thoughtfully. He would soon tire and begin to utter short, loud, impatient breaths, and he would say, "Oh yes . . . yes . . . yes. I couldn't agree more." When he was forced to differ he would declare, "Well, I'm not sure. I don't really see it that way. I'm of two minds about it." He would never willingly hurt any man's feelings.

But in conversation with his father he was apt to lose control of himself. After any talk with Dr. Adler, Wilhelm generally felt dissatisfied, and his dissatisfaction reached its greatest intensity when they discussed family matters. Ostensibly he had been trying to help the old man to remember a date, but in reality he meant to tell him, "You were set free when Ma died. You wanted to forget her. You'd like to get rid of Catherine, too. Me, too. You're not kidding anyone"—Wilhelm striving to put this across, and the old man not having it. In the end he was left struggling, while his father seemed unmoved.

And then once more Wilhelm had said to himself, "But man! you're not a kid. Even then you weren't a kid!" He looked down over the front of his big, indecently big, spoiled body. He was beginning to lose his shape, his gut was fat, and he looked like a hippopotamus. His younger son called him "a hummuspotamus"; that was little Paul. And here he was still struggling with his old dad, filled with ancient grievances. Instead of saying, "Good-by, youth! Oh, good-by those marvelous, foolish wasted days. What a big clunk I was—I *am*."

Wilhelm was still paying heavily for his mistakes. His wife Margaret would not give him a divorce, and he had to support her and the two children. She would regularly agree to divorce him, and then think things over again and set new and more difficult conditions. No court would have awarded her the amounts he paid. One of today's letters as he had expected, was from her. For the first time he had sent her a postdated check, and she protested. She also enclosed bills for the boys' educational insurance policies, due next week. Wilhelm's mother-in-law had taken out these policies in Beverly Hills, and since her death two years ago he had to pay the premiums. Why couldn't she have minded her own business! They were his kids, and he took care of them and always would. He had planned to set up a trust fund. But that was on his former expectations. Now he had to rethink the future, because of the money problem. Meanwhile, here were the bills to be paid. When he saw the two sums punched out so neatly on the cards he cursed the company and its IBM equipment. His heart and his head were congested with anger. Everyone was supposed to have money. It was nothing to the company. It published pictures of funerals in the magazines and frightened the suckers, and then punched out little holes, and the customers would lie awake to think out ways to raise the dough. They'd be ashamed not to have it. They couldn't let a great company down, either, and they got the scratch. In the old days a man was put in prison for debt, but there were subtler things now. They made it a shame not to have money and set everybody to work.

Well, and what else had Margaret sent him? He tore the envelope open with his thumb, swearing that he would send any other bills back to her. There was, luckily, nothing more. He put the hole-punched cards in his pocket. Didn't Margaret know that he was nearly at the end of his rope? Of course. Her instinct told her that this was her opportunity, and she was giving him the works.

He went into the dining room, which was under Austro-Hungarian management at the Hotel Gloriana. It was run like a European establishment. The pastries were excellent, especially the strudel. He often had apple strudel and coffee in the afternoon.

As soon as he entered he saw his father's small head in the sunny bay at the farther end, and heard his precise voice. It was with an odd sort of perilous expression that Wilhelm crossed the dining room.

Dr. Adler liked to sit in a corner that looked across Broadway down to the Hudson and New Jersey. On the other side of the street was a supermodern cafeteria with gold and purple mosaic columns. On the second floor a private-eye school, a dental laboratory, a reducing parlor, a veteran's club, and a Hebrew school shared the space. The old man was sprinkling sugar on his strawberries. Small hoops of brilliance were cast by the water glasses on the white tablecloth, despite a faint murkiness in the sunshine. It was early summer, and the long window was turned inward; a moth was on the pane; the putty was broken and the white enamel on the frames was streaming with wrinkles.

"Ha, Wilky," said the old man to his tardy son."You haven't met our neighbor Mr. Perls, have you? From the fifteenth floor."

"How d'do," Wilhelm said. He did not welcome this stranger; he began at once to find fault with him. Mr. Perls carried a heavy cane with a crutch tip. Dyed hair, a skinny foreheard—these were not reasons for bias. Nor was it Mr. Perls's fault that Dr. Adler was using him, not wishing to have breakfast with his son alone. But a gruffer voice within Wilhelm spoke, asking, "Who is this damn frazzle-faced herring with his dyed hair and his fish teeth and this drippy mustache? Another one of Dad's German friends. Where does he collect all these guys? What is the stuff on his teeth? I never saw such pointed crowns. Are they stainless steel, or a kind of silver? How can a human face get into this condition. Ugh!" Staring with his widely spaced gray eyes, Wilhelm sat, his broad back stooped under the sports jacket. He clasped his hands on the table with an implication of suppliance. Then he began to relent a little toward Mr. Perls, beginning at the teeth. Each of those crowns represented a tooth ground to the quick, and estimating a man's grief with his teeth as two per cent of the total, and adding to that his flight from Germany and the probable origin of his wincing wrinkles, not to be confused with the wrinkles of his smile, it came to a sizable load.

"Mr. Perls was a hosiery wholesaler," said Dr. Adler.

"Is this the son you told me was in the selling line?" said Mr. Perls.

Dr. Adler replied, "I have only this one son. One daughter. She was a medical technician before she got married—anesthetist. At one time she had an important position in Mount Sinai."

He couldn't mention his children without boasting. In Wilhelm's opinion, there was little to boast of. Catherine, like Wilhelm, was big and fair-haired. She had married a court reporter who had a pretty hard time of it. She had taken a professional name, too— Philippa. At forty she was still ambitious to become a painter. Wilhelm didn't venture to criticize her work. It didn't do much to him, he said, but then he was no critic. Anyway, he and his sister were generally on the outs and he didn't often see her paintings. She worked very hard, but there were fifty thousand people in New York with paints and brushes, each practically a law unto himself. It was the Tower of Babel in paint. *He* didn't want to go far into this. Things were chaotic all over.

Dr. Adler thought that Wilhelm looked particularly untidy this morning—unrested, too, his eyes red-rimmed from excessive smoking. He was breathing through his mouth and he was evidently much distracted and rolled his red-shot eyes barbarously. As usual, his coat collar as turned up as though he had had to go out in the rain. When he went to business he pulled himself together a little; otherwise he let himself go and looked like hell.

"What's the matter, Wilky, didn't you sleep last night?"

"Not very much."

"You take too many pills of every kind—first stimulants and then depressants, anodynes followed by analeptics, until the poor organism doesn't know what's happened. Then the luminal won't put people to sleep, and the Pervitin or Benzedrine won't wake them. God knows! These things get to be as serious as poisons, and yet everyone puts all their faith in them."

"No, Dad, it's not the pills. It's that I'm not used to New York any more. For a native, that's very peculiar, isn't it? It was never so nosiy at night as now, and every little thing is a strain. Like the alternate parking. You have to run out at eight to move your car. And where can you put it? If you forget for a minute they tow you away. Then some fool puts advertising leaflets under your windshield wiper and you have heart failure a block away because you think you've got a ticket. When you do get stung with a ticket, you can't argue. You haven't got a chance in court and the city wants the revenue."

"But in your line you have to have a car, eh?" said Mr. Perls.

"Lord knows why any lunatic would want one in the city who didn't need it for his livelihood."

Wilhelm's old Pontiac was parked in the street. Formerly, when on an expense account, he had always put it up in a garage. Now he was afraid to move the car from Riverside Drive lest he lose his space, and he used it only on Saturdays when the Dodgers were playing in Ebbets Field and he took his boys to the game. Last Saturday, when the Dodgers were out of town, he had gone out to visit his mother's grave.

Dr. Adler had refused to go along. He couldn't bear his son's driving. Forgetfully, Wilhelm traveled for miles in second gear; he was seldom in the right lane and he neither gave signals nor watched for lights. The upholstery of his Pontiac was filthy with grease and ashes. One cigarette burned in the ashtray, another in his hand, a third on the floor with maps and other waste paper and Coca-Cola bottles. He dreamed at the wheel or argued and gestured, and therefore the old doctor would not ride with him.

Then Wilhelm had come back from the cemetery angry because the stone bench between his mother's and his grandmother's grave had been overturned and broken by vandals. "Those damn teen-age hoodlums get worse and worse," he said. "Why, they must have used a sledge-hammer to break the seat smack in half like that. If I could catch one of them!" He wanted the doctor to pay for a new seat, but his father was cool to the idea. He said he was going to have himself cremated.

Mr. Perls said, "I don't blame you if you get no sleep up where you are." His voice was tuned somewhat sharp, as thought he were slightly deaf. "Don't you have Parigi the singing teacher there? God, they have some queer elements in this hotel. On which floor is that Estonian woman with all her cats and dogs? They should have made her leave long ago."

"They've moved her down to twelve," said Dr. Adler.

Wilhelm ordered a large Coca-Cola with his breakfast. Working in secret at the small envelopes in his pocket, he found two pills by touch. Much fingering had worn and weakened the paper. Under cover of a napkin he swallowed a Phenaphen sedative and a Unicap, but the doctor was sharp-eyed and said, "Wilky, what are you taking now?"

"Just my vitamin pills." He put his cigar butt in an ashtray on the table behind him, for his father did not like the odor. Then he drank his Coca-Cola.

"That's what you drink for breakfast, and not orange juice?" said Mr. Perls. He seemed to sense that he would not lose Dr. Adler's favor by taking an ironic tone with his son.

"The caffeine stimulates brain activity," said the old doctor. "It does all kinds of things to the respiratory center."

"It's just a habit of the road, that's all," Wilhelm said. "If you drive around long enough it turns your brains, your stomach, and everything else."

His father explained, "Wilky used to be with the Rojax Corporation. He was their northeastern sales representative for a good many years but recently ended the connection."

"Yes," said Wilhelm, "I was with them from the end of the war." He sipped the Coca-Cola and chewed the ice, glancing at one and the other with his attitude of large, shaky, patient dignity. The waitress set two boiled eggs before him.

"What kind of line does this Rojax company manufacture?" said Mr. Perls.

"Kiddies' furniture. Little chairs, rockers, tables, Jungle-Gyms, slides, swings, seesaws."

Wilhelm let his father do the explaining. Large and stiff-backed, he tried to sit patiently, but his feet were abnormally restless. All right! His father had to impress Mr. Perls? He would go along once more, and play his part. Fine! He would play along and help his father maintain his style. Style was the main consideration. That was just fine!

"I was with the Rojax Corporation for almost ten years," he said. "We parted ways because they wanted me to share my territory. They took a son-in-law into the business—a new fellow. It was his idea."

To himself, Wilhelm said, Now God alone can tell why I have to lay my whole life bare to this blasted herring here. I'm sure nobody else does it. Other people keep their business to themselves. Not me.

He continued, "But the rationalization was that it was too big a territory for one man. I had a monopoly. That wasn't so. The real reason was that they had gotten to the place where they would have to make me an officer of the corporation. Vice presidency. I was in line for it, but instead this son-in-law got in, and——"

Dr. Adler thought Wilhelm was discussing his grievances much too openly and said, "My son's income was up in the five figures."

As soon as money was mentioned, Mr. Perls's voice grew eagerly sharper. "Yes? What, the thirty-two-per-cent bracket? Higher even, I guess?" He asked for a hint, and he named the figures not idly but with a sort of hugging relish. Uch! How they love money, thought Wilhelm. They adore money! Holy money! Beautiful money! It was getting so that people were feeble-minded about everything except money. While if you didn't have it you were a dummy, a dummy! You had to excuse yourself from the face of the earth. Chicken! that's what it was. The world's business. If only he could find a way out of it.

Such thinking brought on the usual congestion. It would grow into a fit of passion if he allowed it to continue. Therefore he stopped talking and began to eat.

Before he struck the egg with his spoon he dried the moisture with his napkin. Then he battered it (in his father's opinion) more than was necessary. A faint grime was left by his fingers on the white of the egg after he had picked away the shell. Dr. Adler saw it with silent repugnance. What a Wilky he had given to the world! Why, he didn't even wash his hands in the morning. He used an electric razor so that he didn't have to touch water. The doctor couldn't bear Wilky's dirty habits. Only once—and never again, he swore—had he visited his room. Wilhelm, in pajamas and stockings had sat on his bed, drinking gin from a coffee mug and rooting for the Dodgers on television. "That's two and two on you, Duke. Come on—hit it, now." He came down on the mattress—bam! The bed looked kicked to pieces. Then he drank the gin as though it were tea, and urged his team on with his fist. The smell of dirty clothes was outrageous. By the bedside lay a quart bottle and foolish magazines and mystery stories for the hours of insomnia. Wilhelm lived in worse filth than a savage. When the Doctor spoke to him about this he answered, "Well, I have no wife to look after my things." And who—*who!*—had done the leaving? Not Margaret. The Doctor was certain that she wanted him back.

Wilhelm drank his coffee with a trembling hand. In his full face his abused bloodshot gray eyes, moved back and forth. Jerkily he set his cup back and put half the length of a cigarette into his mouth; he seemed to hold it with his teeth, as though it were a cigar.

"I can't let them get away with it," he said. "It's also a question of morale."

His father corrected him. "Don't you mean a moral question, Wilky?"

"I mean that, too. I have to do something to protect myself. I was promised executive standing." Correction before a stranger mortified him, and his dark blond face changed color, more pale, and then more dark. He went on talking to Perls but his eyes spied on his father. "I was the one who opened the territory for them. I could go back for one of their competitors and take away their customers. *My* customers. Morale enters into it because they've tried to take away my confidence."

"Would you offer a different line to the same people?" Mr. Perls wondered.

"Why not? I know what's wrong with the Rojax product."

"Nonsense," said his father. "Just nonsense and kid's talk, Wilky. You're only looking for trouble and embarrassment that way. What would you gain by such a silly feud? You have to think about making a living and meeting your obligations."

Hot and bitter, Wilhelm said with pride, while his feet moved angrily under the table, "I don't have to be told about my obligations. I've been meeting them for years. In more than twenty years I've never had a penny of help from anybody. I preferred to dig a ditch on the WPA[2] but never asked anyone to meet my obligations for me."

"Wilky has had all kinds of experiences," said Dr. Adler.

The old doctor's face had a wholesome reddish and almost translucent color, like a ripe apricot. The wrinkles beside his ears were deep because the skin conformed so tightly to his bones. With all his might, he was a healthy and fine small old man. He wore a white vest of a light check pattern. His hearing-aid doodad was in the pocket. An unusual shirt of red and black stripes covered his chest. He bought his clothes in a college shop farther uptown. Wilhelm thought he had no business to get himself up like a jockey, out of respect for his profession.

"Well," said Mr. Perls. "I can understand how you feel. You want to fight it out. By a certain time of life, to have to start all over again can't be a pleasure, though a good man can always do it. But anyway you want to keep on with a business you know already, and not have to meet a whole lot of new contacts."

Wilhelm again thought, Why does it have to be me and my life that's discussed, and not him and his life? He would never allow it. But I am an idiot. I have no reserve. To me it can be done. I talk. I must ask for it. Everybody wants to have intimate conversations, but the smart fellows don't give out, only the fools. The smart

---

2. Works Progress Administration, established in 1935 to provide jobs for the needy.

fellows talk intimately about the fools, and examine them all over and give them advice. Why do I allow it? The hint about his age had hurt him. No, you can't admit it's as good as ever, he conceded. Things do give out.

"In the meanwhile," Dr. Adler said, "Wilky is taking it easy and considering various propositions. Isn't that so?"

"More or less," said Wilhelm. He suffered his father to increase Mr. Perls's respect for him. The WPA ditch had brought the family into contempt. He was a little tired. The spirit, the peculiar burden of his existence lay upon him like an accretion, a load, a hump. In any moment of quiet, when sheer fatigue prevented him from struggling, he was apt to feel this mysterious weight, this growth or collection of nameless things which it was the business of his life to carry about. That must be what a man was for. This large, odd, excited, fleshy, blond, abrupt personality named Wilhelm, or Tommy, was here, present, in the present—Dr. Tamkin had been putting into his mind many suggestions about the present moment, the here and now—this Wilky, or Tommy Wilhelm, forty-four years old, father of two sons, at present living in the Hotel Gloriana, was assigned to be the carrier of a load which was his own self, his characteristic self. There was no figure or estimate for the value of this load. But it is probably exaggerated by the subject, T. W. Who is a visionary sort of animal. Who has to believe that he can know why he exists. Though he has never seriously tried to find out why.

Mr. Perls said, "If he wants time to think things over and have a rest, why doesn't he run down to Florida for a while? Off season it's cheap and quiet. Fairyland. The mangoes are just coming in. I got two acres down there. You'd think you were in India."

Mr. Perls utterly astonished Wilhelm when he spoke of fairyland with a foreign accent. Mangoes—India? What did he mean, India?

"Once upon a time," said Wilhelm, "I did some public-relations work for a big hotel down in Cuba. If I could get them a notice in Leonard Lyons[3] or one of the other columns it might be good for another holiday there, gratis. I haven't had a vacation for a long time, and I could stand a rest after going so hard. You know that's true, Father." He meant that his father knew how deep the crisis was becoming; how badly he was strapped for money; and that he could not rest but would be crushed if he stumbled; and that his obligations would destroy him. He couldn't falter. He thought, The money! When I had it, I flowed money. They bled it away from me. I hemorrhaged money. But now it's almost all gone, and where am I supposed to turn for more?

He said, "As a matter of fact, Father, I am tired as hell."

But Mr. Perls began to smile and said, "I understand from Doc-

3. New York gossip columnist.

tor Tamkin that you're going into some kind of investment with him, partners."

"You know, he's a very ingenious fellow," said Dr. Adler. "I really enjoy hearing him go on. I wonder if he really is a medical doctor."

"Isn't he?" said Perls. "Everybody thinks he is. He talks about his patients. Doesn't he write prescriptions?"

"I don't really know what he does," said Dr. Adler. "He's a cunning man."

"He's a psychologist, I understand," said Wilhelm.

"I don't know what sort of psychologist or psychiatrist he may be," said his father. "He's a little vague. It's growing into a major industry, and a very expensive one. Fellows have to hold down very big jobs in order to pay those fees. Anyway, this Tamkin is clever. He never said he practiced here, but I believe he was a doctor in California. They don't seem to have much legislation out there to cover these things, and I hear a thousand dollars will get you a degree from a Los Angeles correspondence school. He gives the impression of knowing something about chemistry, and things like hypnotism. I wouldn't trust him, though."

"And why wouldn't you?" Wilhelm demanded.

"Because he's probably a liar. Do you believe he invented all the things he claims?"

Mr. Perls was grinning.

"He was written up in *Fortune*," said Wilhelm. "Yes, in *Fortune* magazine. He showed me the article. I've seen his clippings."

"That doesn't make him legitimate," said Dr. Adler. "It might have been another Tamkin. Make no mistake, he's an operator. Perhaps even crazy."

"Crazy, you say?"

Mr. Perls put in, "He could be both sane and crazy. In these days nobody can tell for sure which is which."

"An electrical device for truck drivers to wear in their caps," said Dr. Adler, describing one of Tamkin's proposed inventions. "To wake them with a shock when they begin to be drowsy at the wheel. It's triggered by the change in blood-pressure when they start to doze."

"It doesn't sound like such an impossible thing to me," said Wilhelm.

Mr. Perls said, "To me he described an underwater suit so a man could walk on the bed of the Hudson in case of an atomic attack. He said he could walk to Albany in it."

"Ha, ha, ha, ha, ha!" cried Dr. Adler in his old man's voice. "Tamkin's Folly. You could go on a camping trip under Niagara Falls."

"This is just his kind of fantasy," said Wilhelm. "It doesn't mean a thing. Inventors are supposed to be like that. I get funny ideas myself. Everybody wants to make something. Any American does."

But his father ignored this and said to Perls, "What other inventions did he describe?"

While the frazzle-faced Mr. Perls and his father in the unseemly, monkey-striped shirt were laughing, Wilhelm could not restrain himself and joined in with his own panting laugh. But he was in despair. They were laughing at the man to whom he had given a power of attorney over his last seven hundred dollars to speculate for him in the commodities market. They had bought all that lard. It had to rise today. By ten o'clock, or half-past ten, trading would be active, and he would see.

III

Between white tablecloths and glassware and glancing silverware, through overfull light, the long figure of Mr. Perls went away into the darkness of the lobby. He thrust with his cane, and dragged a large built-up shoe which Wilhelm had not included in his estimate of troubles. Dr. Adler wanted to talk about him. "There's a poor man," he said, "with a bone condition which is gradually breaking him up."

"One of those progressive diseases?" said Wilhelm.

"Very bad. I've learned," the doctor told him, "to keep my sympathy for the real ailments. This Perls is more to be pitied than any man I know."

Wilhelm understood he was being put on notice and did not express his opinion. He ate and ate. He did not hurry but kept putting food on his plate until he had gone through the muffins and his father's strawberries, and then some pieces of bacon that were left; he had several cups of coffee, and when he was finished he sat gigantically in a state of arrest and didn't seem to know what he should do next.

For a while father and son were uncommonly still. Wilhelm's preparations to please Dr. Adler had failed completely, for the old man kept thinking, You'd never guess he had a clean upbringing, and, What a dirty devil this son of mine is. Why can't he try to sweeten his appearance a little? Why does he want to drag himself like this? And he makes himself look so idealistic.

Wilhelm sat, mountainous. He was not really so slovenly as his father found him to be. In some aspects he even had a certain delicacy. His mouth, though broad, had a fine outline, and his brow and his gradually incurved nose, dignity, and in his blond hair there was white but there were also shades of gold and chestnut. When he was with the Rojax Corporation Wilhelm had kept a small apartment in Roxbury, two rooms in a large house with a small porch and garden, and on mornings of leisure, in late spring weather like this, he used to sit expanded in a wicker chair with the sunlight pouring through the weave, and sunlight through the slug-eaten holes of the young hollyhocks and as deeply as the grass allowed into small flowers. This peace (he forgot that that time and had its troubles, too), this peace was gone. It must not have belonged to him, really, for to be here in New York with his old father was more genuinely like his life. He was well aware that he didn't stand a chance of getting sympathy from his father, who said he kept his for real ailments. Moreover, he advised himself repeatedly not to discuss his vexatious problems with him, for his father, with some justice, wanted to be left in peace. Wilhelm also knew that when he began to talk about these things he made himself feel worse, he became congested with them and worked himself into a clutch. Therefore he warned himself, Lay off, pal! It'll only be an aggravation. From a deeper source, however, came other promptings. If he didn't keep his troubles before him he risked losing them altogether, and he knew by experience that this was worse. And furthermore, he could not succeed in excusing his father on the ground of old age. No. No, he could not. I am his son, he thought. He is my father. He is as much father as I am son—old or not. Affirming this, though in complete silence, he sat, and, sitting, he kept his father at the table with him.

"Wilky," said the old man, "have you gone down to the baths here yet?"

"No, Dad, not yet."

"Well, you know the Gloriana has one of the finest pools in New York. Eighty feet, blue tile. It's a beauty."

Wilhelm had seen it. On the way to the gin game you passed the stairway to the pool. He did not care for the odor of the wall-locked and chlorinated water.

"You ought to investigate the Russian and Turkish baths, and the sunlamps and massage. I don't hold with sunlamps. But the massage does a world of good, and there's nothing better than hydrotherapy when you come right down to it. Simple water has a calming effect and would do you more good than all the barbiturates and alcohol in the world."

Wilhelm reflected that this advice was as far as his father's help and sympathy would extend.

"I thought," he said, "that the water cure was for lunatics."

The doctor received this as one of his son's jokes and said with a smile, "Well, it won't turn a sane man into a lunatic. It does a great deal for me. I couldn't live without my massages and steam."

"You're probably right. I ought to try it one of these days. Yesterday, late in the afternoon, my head was about to bust and I just had to have a little air, so I walked around the reservoir, and I sat down for a while in a playground. It rests me to watch the kids play potsy and skiprope."

The doctor said with approval, "Well, now, that's more like the idea."

"It's the end of the lilacs," said Wilhelm. "When they burn it's the beginning of summer. At least, in the city. Around the time of year when the candy stores take down the windows and start to sell sodas on the sidewalk. But even though I was raised here, Dad, I can't take city life any more, and I miss the country. There's too much push here for me. It works me up too much. I take things too hard. I wonder why you never retired to a quieter place."

The doctor opened his small hand on the table in a gesture so old and so typical that Wilhelm felt it like an actual touch upon the foundations of his life. "I am a city boy myself, you must remember," Dr. Adler explained. "But if you find the city so hard on you, you ought to get out."

"I'll do that," said Wilhelm, "as soon as I can make the right connection. Meanwhile—"

His father interrupted, "Meanwhile I suggest you cut down on drugs."

"You exaggerate that, Dad. I don't really— I give myself a little boost against—" He almost pronounced the word "misery" but he kept his resolution not to complain.

The doctor, however, fell into the error of pushing his advice too hard. It was all he had to give his son and he gave it once more. "Water and exercise," he said.

He wants a young, smart, successful son, thought Wilhelm, and he said, "Oh, Father, it's nice of you to give me this medical advice, but steam isn't going to cure what ails me."

The doctor measurably drew back, warned by the sudden weak strain of Wilhelm's voice and all that the droop of his face, the swell of his belly against the restraint of his belt intimated.

"Some new business?" he asked unwillingly.

Wilhelm made a great preliminary summary which involved the whole of his body. He drew and held a long breath, and his color changed and his eyes swam. "New?" he said.

"You make too much of your problems," said the doctor. "They ought not to be turned into a career. Concentrate on real troubles— fatal sickness, accidents." The old man's whole manner said, Wilky, don't start this on me. I have a right to be spared.

Wilhelm himself prayed for restraint; he knew this weakness of his and fought it. He knew, also, his father's character. And he began mildly, "As far as the fatal part of it goes, everyone on this side of the grave is the same distance from death. No, I guess my trouble is not exactly new. I've got to pay premiums on two policies for the boys. Margaret sent them to me. She unloads everything on me. Her mother left her an income. She won't even file a joint tax return. I get stuck. Etcetera. But you've heard the whole story before."

"I certainly have," said the old man. "And I've told you to stop giving her so much money."

Wilhelm worked his lips in silence before he could speak. The congestion was growing. "Oh, but my kids, Father. My kids. I love them. I don't want them to lack anything."

The doctor said with a half-deaf benevolence, "Well, naturally. And she, I'll bet, is the beneficiary of that policy."

"Let her be. I'd sooner die myself before I collected a cent of such money."

"Ah yes." The old man sighed. He did not like the mention of death. "Did I tell you that your sister Catherine—Philippa—is after me again."

"What for?"

"She wants to rent a gallery for an exhibition."

Stiffly fair-minded, Wilhelm said, "Well, of course that's up to you, Father."

The round-headed old man with his fine, feather-white, ferny hair said, "No, Wilky. There's not a thing on those canvases. I don't believe it; it's a case of the emperor's clothes. I may be old enough for my second childhood, but at least the first is well behind me. I was glad enough to buy crayons for her when she was four. But now she's a woman of forty and too old to be encouraged in her delusions. She's no painter."

"I wouldn't go so far as to call her a born artist," said Wilhelm, "but you can't blame her for trying something worth while."

"Let her husband pamper her."

Wilhelm had done his best to be just to his sister, and he had sincerely meant to spare his father, but the old man's tight, benevolent deafness had its usual effect on him. He said, "When it comes to women and money, I'm completely in the dark. What makes Margaret act like this?"

"She's showing you that you can't make it without her," said the doctor. "She aims to bring you back by financial force."

"But if she ruins me, Dad, how can she expect me to come back? No, I have a sense of honor. What you don't see is that she's trying to put an end to me."

His father stared. To him this was absurd. And Wilhelm thought, Once a guy starts to slip, he figures he might as well be a clunk. A real big clunk. He even takes pride in it. But there's nothing to be proud of—hey, boy? Nothing. I don't blame Dad for his attitude. And it's no cause for pride.

"I don't understand that. But if you feel like this why don't you settle with her once and for all?"

"What do you mean, Dad?" said Wilhelm, surprised. "I thought I told you. Do you think I'm not willing to settle? Four years ago when we broke up I gave her everything—goods, furniture, savings. I tried to show good will, but I didn't get anywhere. Why when I wanted Scissors, the dog, because the animal and I were so attached to each other—it was bad enough to leave the kids—she absolutely refused me. Not that she cared a damn about the animal. I don't think you've seen him. He's an Australian sheep dog. They usually have one blank or whitish eye which gives a misleading look, but they're the gentlest dogs and have unusual delicacy about eating or talking. Let me at least have the companionship of this animal. Never." Wilhelm was greatly moved. He wiped his face at all corners with his napkin. Dr. Adler felt that his son was indulging himself too much in his emotions.

"Whenever she can hit me, she hits, and she seems to live for that alone. And she demands more and more, and still more. Two years ago she wanted to go back to college and get another degree. It increased my burden but I thought it would be wiser in the end if she got a better job through it. But still she takes as much from me as before. Next thing she'll want to be a Doctor of Philosophy. She says the women in her family live long, and I'll have to pay and pay for the rest of my life."

The doctor said impatiently, "Well, these are details, not principles. Just details which you can leave out. The dog! You're mixing up all kinds of irrelevant things. Go to a good lawyer."

"But I've already told you, Dad. I got a lawyer, and she got one, too, and both of them talk and send me bills, and I eat my heart out. Oh, Dad, Dad, what a hole I'm in!" said Wilhelm in utter misery. "The lawyers—see?—draw up an agreement, and she says okay on Monday and wants more money on Tuesday. And it begins again."

"I always thought she was a strange kind of woman," said Dr. Adler. He felt that by disliking Margaret from the first and disapproving of the marriage he had done all that he could be expected to do.

"Strange, Father? I'll show you what she's like." Wilhelm took hold of his broad throat with brown-stained fingers and bitten nails and began to choke himself.

"What are you doing?" cried the old man.

"I'm showing you what she does to me."

"Stop that—stop it!" the old man said and tapped the table commandingly.

"Well, Dad, she hates me. I feel that she's strangling me. I can't catch my breath. She just has fixed herself on me to kill me. She can do it at long distance. One of these days I'll be struck down by suffocation or apoplexy because of her. I just can't catch my breath."

"Take your hands off your throat, you foolish man," said his father. "Stop this bunk. Don't expect me to believe in all kinds of voodoo."

"If that's what you want to call it, all right." His face flamed and paled and swelled and his breath was laborious.

"But I'm telling you that from the time I met her I've been a slave. The Emancipation Proclamation was only for colored people. A husband like me is a slave, with an iron collar. The churches go up to Albany and supervise the law. They won't have divorces. The court says, 'You want to be free. Then you have to work twice as hard—twice, at least! Work! you bum.' So then guys kill each other for the buck, and they may be free of a wife who hates them but they are sold to the company. The company knows a guy has got to have his salary, and takes full advantage of him. Don't talk to me about being free. A rich man may be free on an income of a million net. A poor man may be free because nobody cares what he does. But a fellow in my position has to sweat it out until he drops dead."

His father replied to this, "Wilky, it's entirely your own fault. You don't have to allow it."

Stopped in his eloquence, Wilhelm could not speak for a while. Dumb and incompetent, he struggled for breath and frowned with effort into his father's face.

"I don't understand your problems," said the old man. "I never had any like them."

By now Wilhelm had lost his head and he waved his hands and said over and over, "Oh, Dad, don't give me that stuff, don't give me that. Please don't give me that sort of thing."

"It's true," said his father. "I come from a different world. Your mother and I led an entirely different life."

"Oh, how can you compare Mother," Wilhelm said. "Mother was a help to you. Did she harm you ever?"

"There's no need to carry on like an opera, Wilky," said the doctor. "This is only your side of things."

"What? It's the truth," said Wilhelm.

The old man could not be persuaded and shook his round head and drew his vest down over the gilded shirt, and leaned back with a completeness of style that made this look, to anyone out of hearing, like an ordinary conversation between a middle-aged man and his respected father. Wilhelm towered and swayed, big and sloven, with his gray eyes red-shot and his honey-colored hair twisted in flaming shapes upward. Injustice made him angry, made him beg. But he wanted an understanding with his father, and he tried to capitulate to him. He said, "You can't compare Mother and Margaret, and neither can you and I be compared, because you, Dad, were a success. And a success—is a success. I never made a success."

The doctor's old face lost all of its composure and became hard and angry. His small breast rose sharply under the red and black shirt and he said, "Yes. Because of hard work. I was not self-indulgent, not lazy. My old man sold dry goods in Williamsburg. We were nothing, do you understand? I knew I couldn't afford to waste my chances."

"I wouldn't admit for one minute that I was lazy," said Wilhelm.

"If anything, I tried too hard. I admit I made many mistakes. Like I thought I shouldn't do things you had done already. Study chemistry. You had done it already. It was in the family."

His father continued, "I didn't run around with fifty women, either. I was not a Hollywood star. I didn't have time to go to Cuba for a vacation. I stayed at home and took care of my children."

Oh, thought Wilhelm, eyes turning upward. Why did I come here in the first place, to live near him? New York is like a gas. The colors are running. My head feels so tight, I don't know what I'm doing. He thinks I want to take away his money or that I envy him. He doesn't see what I want.

"Dad," Wilhelm said aloud, "you're being very unfair. It's true the movies was a false step. But I love my boys. I didn't abandon them. I left Margaret because I had to."

"Why did you have to?"

"Well—" said Wilhelm, struggling to condense his many reasons into a few plain words. "I had to—I had to."

With sudden and surprising bluntness his father said, "Did you have bed-trouble with her? Then you should have stuck it out. Sooner or later everyone has it. Normal people stay with it. It passes. But you wouldn't, so now you pay for your stupid romantic notions. Have I made my view clear?"

It was very clear. Wilhelm seemed to hear it repeated from various sides and inclined his head different ways, and listened and thought. Finally he said, "I guess that's the medical standpoint. You may be right. I just couldn't live with Margaret. I wanted to stick it out, but I was getting very sick. She was one way and I was another. She wouldn't be like me, so I tried to be like her, and I couldn't do it."

"Are you sure she didn't tell *you* to go?" the doctor said.

"I wish she had. I'd be in a better position now. No, it was me. I didn't want to leave, but I couldn't stay. Somebody had to take the initiative. I did. Now I'm the fall guy too."

Pushing aside in advance all the objections that his son would make, the doctor said, "Why did you lose your job with Rojax?"

"I didn't, I've told you."

"You're lying. You wouldn't have ended the connection. You need the money too badly. But you must have got into trouble." The small old man spoke concisely and with great strength. "Since you have to talk and can't let it alone, tell the truth. Was there a scandal—a woman?"

Wilhelm fiercely defended himself. "No, Dad, there wasn't any woman. I told you how it was."

"Maybe it was a man, then," the old man said wickedly.

Shocked, Wilhelm stared at him with burning pallor and dry lips. His skin looked a little yellow. "I don't think you know what you're talking about," he answered after a moment. "You shouldn't let your imagination run so free. Since you've been living here on Broadway you must think you understand life, up to date. You ought to know your own son a little better. Let's drop that, now."

"All right, Wilky, I'll withdraw it. But something must have happened in Roxbury nevertheless. You'll never go back. You're just talking wildly about representing a rival company. You won't. You've done something to spoil your reputation, I think. But you've got girl friends who are expecting you back, isn't that so?"

"I take a lady out now and then while on the road," said Wilhelm. "I'm not a monk."

"No one special? Are you sure you haven't gotten into complications?"

He had tried to unburden himself and instead, Wilhelm thought, he had to undergo an inquisition to prove himself worthy of a sympathetic word. Because his father believed that he did all kinds of gross things.

"There is a woman in Roxbury that I went with. We fell in love and wanted to marry, but she got tired of waiting for my divorce. Margaret figured that. On top of which the girl was a Catholic and I had to go with her to the priest and make an explanation."

Neither did this last confession touch Dr. Adler's sympathies or sway his calm old head or affect the color of his complexion.

"No, no, no, no; all wrong," he said.

Again Wilhelm cautioned himself. Remember his age. He is no longer the same person. He can't bear trouble. I'm so choked up and congested anyway I can't see straight. Will I ever get out of the woods, and recover my balance? You're never the same afterward. Trouble rusts out the system.

"You really *want* a divorce?" said the old man.

"For the price I pay I should be getting something."

"In that case," Dr. Adler said, "it seems to me no normal person would stand for such treatment from a woman."

"Ah, Father, Father!" said Wilhelm. "It's always the same thing with you. Look how you lead me on. You always start out to help me with my problems, and be sympathetic and so forth. It gets my hopes up and I begin to be grateful. But before we're through I'm a hundred times more depressed than before. Why is that? You have no sympathy. You want to shift all the blame on to me. Maybe you're wise to do it." Wilhelm was beginning to lose himself. "All you seem to think about is your death. Well, I'm sorry. But I'm going to die too. And I'm your son. It isn't my fault in the first place. There ought to be a right way to do this, and be fair to each other. But what I want to know is, why do you start up with me if you're not going to help me? What do you want to know about my problems for, Father? So you can lay the whole responsibility on me—so that you won't have to help me? D'you want me to comfort you for having such a son?" Wilhelm had a great knot of wrong tied tight within his chest, and tears approached his eyes but he didn't let them out. He looked shabby enough as it was. His voice was thick and hazy, and he was stammering and could not bring his awful feelings forth.

"You have some purpose of your own," said the doctor, "in acting so unreasonable. What do you want from me? What do you expect?"

"What do I expect?" said Wilhelm. He felt as though he were unable to recover something. Like a ball in the surf, washed beyond reach, his self-control was going out. "I expect *help!*" The words escaped him in a loud, wild, frantic cry and startled the old man, and two or three breakfasters within hearing glanced their way. Wilhelm's hair, the color of whitened honey, rose dense and tall with the expansion of his face, and he said, "When I suffer—you aren't even sorry. That's because you have no affection for me, and you don't want any part of me."

"Why must I like the way you behave? No, I don't like it," said Dr. Adler.

"All right. You want me to change myself. But suppose I could do it—what would I become? What could I? Let's suppose that all my life I have had the wrong ideas about myself and wasn't what I thought I was. And wasn't even careful to take a few precautions, as most people do—like a woodchuck has a few exits to his tunnel. But what shall I do now? More than half my life is over. More than half. And now you tell me I'm not even normal."

The old man too had lost his calm. "You cry about being helped," he said. "When you thought you had to go into the service I sent a check to Margaret every month. As a family man you could have had an exemption. But no! The war couldn't be fought without you and you had to get yourself drafted and be an office-boy in the Pacific theater. Any clerk could have done what you did. You could find nothing better to become than a GI."

Wilhelm was going to reply, and half raised his bearish figure from the chair, his fingers spread and whitened by their grip on the table, but the old man would not let him begin. He said, "I see other elderly people here with children who aren't much good, and they keep backing them and holding them up at a great sacrifice. But I'm not going to make that mistake. It doesn't enter your mind that when I die—a year, two years from now—you'll still be here. I do think of it."

He had intended to say that he had a right to be left in peace. Instead he gave Wilhelm the impression that he meant it was not fair for the better man of the two, and the more useful, the more admired, to leave the world first. Pehaps he meant that, too—a little; but he would not under other circumstances have come out with it so flatly.

"Father," said Wilhelm with an unusual openness of appeal.

"Don't you think I know how you feel? I have pity. I want you to live on and on. If you outlive me, that's perfectly okay by me." As his father did not answer this avowal and turned away his glance, Wilhelm suddenly burst out, "No, but you hate me. And if I had money you wouldn't. By God, you have to admit it. The money makes the difference. Then we would be a fine father and son, if I was a credit to you—so you could boast and brag about me all over the hotel. But I'm not the right type of son. I'm too old, I'm too old and too unlucky."

His father said, "I can't give you any money. There would be no end to it if I started. You and your sister would take every last buck from me. I'm still alive, not dead. I am still here. Life isn't over yet. I am as much alive as you or anyone. And I want nobody on my back. Get off! And I give you the same advice, Wilky. Carry nobody on your back."

"Just keep the money," said Wilhelm miserably. "Keep it and enjoy it yourself. That's the ticket!"

IV

Ass! Idiot! Wild boar! Dumb mule! Slave! Lousy, wallowing hippopotamus! Wilhelm called himself as his bending legs carried him from the dining room. His pride! His inflamed feelings! His begging and feebleness! And trading insults with his old father—and spreading confusion over everything. Oh, how poor, contemptible, and ridiculous he was! When he remembered how he had said, with great reproof, "You ought to know your own son"—why, how corny and abominable it was.

He could not get out of the sharply brilliant dining room fast enough. He was horribly worked up; his neck and shoulders, his entire chest ached as though they had been tightly tied with ropes. He smelled the salt odor of tears in his nose.

But at the same time, since there were depths in Wilhelm not unsuspected by himself, he received a suggestion from some remote element in his thoughts that the business of life, the real business—to carry his peculiar burden, to feel shame and impotence, to taste these quelled tears—the only important business, the highest business was being done. Maybe the making of mistakes expressed the very purpose of his life and the essence of his being here. Maybe he was supposed to make them and suffer from them on this earth. And though he had raised himself above Mr. Perls and his father because they adored money, still they were called to act energetically and this was better than to yell and cry, pray and beg, poke and blunder and go by fits and starts and fall upon the thorns of life. And finally sink beneath that watery floor—would that be tough luck, or would it be good riddance?

But he raged once more against his father. Other people with money, while they're still alive, want to see it do some good.

Granted, he shouldn't support me. But have I ever asked him to do that? Have I ever asked for dough at all, either for Margaret or for the kids or for myself? It isn't the money, but only the assistance; not even assistance, but just the feeling. But he may be trying to teach me that a grown man should be cured of such feeling. Feeling got me in dutch[4] at Rojax. I had the *feeling* that I belonged to the firm, and my *feelings* were hurt when they put Gerber in over me. Dad thinks I'm too simple. But I'm not so simple as he thinks. What about his feelings? He doesn't forget death for one single second, and that's what makes him like this. And not only is death on his mind but through money he forces me to think about it, too. It gives him power over me. He forces me that way, he himself, and then he's sore. If he was poor, I could care for him and show it. The way I *could* care, too, if I only had a chance. He'd see how much love and respect I had in me. It would make him a different man, too. He'd put his hands on me and give me his blessing."

Someone in a gray straw hat with a wide cocoa-colored band spoke to Wilhelm in the lobby. The light was dusky, splotched with red underfoot; green, the leather furniture; yellow, the indirect lighting.

"Hey, Tommy. Say, there."

"Excuse me," said Wilhelm, trying to reach a house phone. But this was Dr. Tamkin, whom he was just about to call.

"You have a very obsessional look on your face," said Dr. Tamkin.

Wilhelm thought, Here he is, Here he is. If I could only figure this guy out.

"Oh," he said to Tamkin. "Have I got such a look? Well, whatever it is, you name it and I'm sure to have it."

The sight of Dr. Tamkin brought his quarrel with his father to a close. He found himself flowing into another channel.

"What are we doing?" he said. "What's going to happen to lard today?"

"Don't worry yourself about that. All we have to do is hold on to it and it's sure to go up. But what's made you so hot under the collar, Wilhelm?"

"Oh, one of those family situations." This was the moment to take a new look at Tamkin, and he viewed him closely but gained nothing by the new effort. It was conceivable that Tamkin was everything that he claimed to be, and all the gossip false. But was he a scientific man, or not? If he was not, this might be a cause for the district attorney's office to investigate. Was he a liar? That was a delicate question. Even a liar might be trustworthy in some ways. Could he trust Tamkin—could he? He feverishly, fruitlessly sought an answer.

But the time for this question was past, and he had to trust him

4. In trouble.

now. After a long struggle to come to a decision, he had given him the money. Practical judgment was in abeyance. He had worn himself out, and the decision was no decision. How had this happened? But how had his Hollywood career begun? It was not because of Maurice Venice, who turned out to be a pimp. It was because Wilhelm himself was ripe for the mistake. His marriage, too, had been like that. Through such decisions somehow his life had taken form. And so, from the moment when he tasted the peculiar flavor of fatality in Dr. Tamkin, he could no longer keep back the money.

Five days ago Tamkin had said, "Meet me tomorrow, and we'll go to the market." Wilhelm, therefore, had had to go. At eleven o'clock they had walked to the brokerage office. On the way, Tamkin broke the news to Wilhelm that though this was an equal partnership he couldn't put up his half of the money just yet; it was tied up for a week or so in one of his patents. Today he would be two hundred dollars short; next week, he'd make it up. But neither of them needed an income from the market, of course. This was only a sporting proposition anyhow, Tamkin said. Wilhelm had to answer, "Of course." It was too late to withdraw. What else could he do? Then came the formal part of the transaction, and it was frightening. The very shade of green of Tamkin's check looked wrong; it was a false, disheartening color. His handwriting was peculiar, even monstrous; the e's were like i's, the t's and l's the same, and the h's like wasps' bellies. He wrote like a fourth-grader. Scientists, nowever, dealt mostly in symbols; they printed. This was Wilhelm's explanation.

Dr. Tamkin had given him his check for three hundred dollars. Wilhelm, in a blinded and convulsed aberration, pressed and pressed to try to kill the trembling of his hand as he wrote out his check for a thousand. He set his lips tight, crouched with his huge back over the table, and wrote with crumbling, terrified fingers, knowing that if Tamkin's check bounced his own would not be honored either. His sole cleverness was to set the date ahead by one day to give the green check time to clear.

Next he had signed a power of attorney, allowing Tamkin to speculate with his money, and this was an even more frightening document. Tamkin had never said a word about it, but here they were and it had to be done.

After delivering his signatures, the only precaution Wilhelm took was to come back to the manager of the brokerage office and ask him privately, "Uh, about Doctor Tamkin. We were in here a few minutes ago, remember?"

That day had been a weeping, smoky one and Wilhelm had gotten away from Tamkin on the pretext of having to run to the post office. Tamkin had gone to lunch alone, and here was Wilhelm, back again, breathless, his hat dripping, needlessly asking the manager if he remembered.

"Yes, sir, I know," the manager had said He was a cold, mild, lean German who dressed correctly and around his neck wore a pair of opera glasses with which he read the board. He was an extremely correct person except that he never shaved in the morning, not caring, probably, how he looked to the fumblers and the old people and the operators and the gamblers and the idlers of Broadway uptown. The market closed at three. Maybe, Wilhelm guessed, he had a thick beard and took a lady out to dinner later and wanted to look fresh-shaven.

"Just a question," said Wilhelm. "A few minutes ago I signed a power of attorney so Doctor Tamkin could invest for me. You gave me the blanks."

"Yes, sir, I remember."

"Now this is what I want to know," Wilhelm had said. "I'm no lawyer and I only gave the paper a glance. Does this give Doctor Tamkin power of attorney over any other assets of mine—money, or property?"

The rain had dribbled from Wilhelm's deformed, transparent raincoat; the buttons of his shirt, which always seemed tiny, were partly broken, in pearly quarters of the moon, and some of the dark, thick golden hairs that grew on his belly stood out. It was the manager's business to conceal his opinion of him; he was shrewd, gray, correct (although unshaven) and had little to say except on matters that came to his desk. He must have recognized in Wilhelm a man who reflected long and then made the decision he had rejected twenty separate times. Silvery, cool, level, long-profiled, experienced, indifferent, observant, with unshaven refinement, he scarcely looked at Wilhelm, who trembled with fearful awkwardness. The manager's face, low-colored, long-nostriled, acted as a unit of perception; his eyes merely did their reduced share. Here was a man, like Rubin, who knew and knew and knew. He, a foreigner, knew; Wilhelm, in the city of his birth, was ignorant.

The manager had said, "No, sir, it does not give him."

"Only over the funds I deposited with you?"

"Yes, that is right, sir."

"Thank you, that's what I wanted to find out," Wilhelm had said, grateful.

The answer comforted him. However, the question had no value. None at all. For Wilhelm had no other assets. He had given Tamkin his last money. There wasn't enough of it to cover his obligations anyway, and Wilhelm had reckoned that he might as well go bankrupt now as next month. "Either broke or rich," was how he had figured, and that formula had encouraged him to make the gamble. Well, not rich; he did not expect that, but perhaps Tamkin might really show him how to earn what he needed in the market. By now, however, he had forgotten his own reckoning and was aware only that he stood to lose his seven hundred dollars to the last cent.

Dr. Tamkin took the attitude that they were a pair of gentlemen experimenting with lard and grain futures. The money, a few hundred dollars, meant nothing much to either of them. He said to Wilhelm, "Watch. You'll get a big kick out of this and wonder why more people don't go into it. You think the Wall Street guys are so smart—geniuses? That's because most of us are psychologically afraid to think about the details. Tell me this. When you're on the road, and you don't understand what goes on under the hood of your car, you'll worry what'll happen if something goes wrong with the engine. Am I wrong?" No, he was right. "Well," said Dr. Tamkin with an expression of quiet triumph about his mouth, almost the suggestion of a jeer. "It's the same psychological principle, Wilhelm. They are rich because you don't understand what goes on. But it's no mystery, and by putting in a little money and applying certain principles of observation, you begin to grasp it. It can't be studied in the abstract. You have to take a specimen risk so that you feel the process, the money-flow, the whole complex. To know how it feels to be a seaweed you have to get in the water. In a very short time we'll take out a hundred-per-cent profit." Thus Wilhelm had had to pretend at the outset that his interest in the market was theoretical.

"Well," said Tamkin when he met him now in the lobby, "what's the problem, what is this family situation? Tell me." He put himself forward as the keen mental scientist. Whenever this happened Wilhelm didn't know what to reply. No matter what he said or did it seemed that Dr. Tamkin saw through him.

"I had some words with my dad."

Dr. Tamkin found nothing extraordinary in this. "It's the eternal same story," he said. "The elemental conflict of parent and child. It won't end, ever. Even with a find old gentleman like your dad."

"I don't suppose it will. I've never been able to get anywhere with him. He objects to my feelings. He things they're sordid. I upset him and he gets mad at me. But maybe all old men are alike."

"Sons, too. Take it from one of them," said Dr. Tamkin. "All the same, you should be proud of such a fine old patriarch of a father. It should give you hope. The longer he lives, the longer your life-expectancy becomes."

Wilhelm answered, brooding, "I guess so. But I think I inherit more from my mother's side, and she died in her fifties."

"A problem arose between a young fellow I'm treating and his dad—I just had a consultation," said Dr. Tamkin as he removed his dark gray hat.

"So early in the morning?" said Wilhelm with suspicion.

"Over the telephone, of course."

What a creature Tamkin was when he took off his hat! The indirect light showed the many complexities of his bald skull, his gull's nose, his rather handsome eyebrows, his vain mustache, his deceiver's brown eyes. His figure was stocky, rigid, short in the neck, so that the large ball of the occiput touched his collar. His bones were peculiarly formed, as though twisted twice where the ordinary human bone was turned only once, and his shoulders rose in two pagoda-like points. At midbody he was thick. He stood pigeon-toed, a sign perhaps that he was devious or had much to hide. The skin of his hands was aging, and his nails were moonless, concave, clawlike, and they appeared loose. His eyes were as brown as beaver fur and full of strange lines. The two large brown naked balls looked thoughtful—but were they? And honest—but was Dr. Tamkin honest? There was a hypnotic power in his eyes, but this was not always of the same strength, nor was Wilhelm convinced that it was completely natural. He felt that Tamkin tried to make his eyes deliberately conspicuous, with studied art, and that he brought forth his hypnotic effect by an exertion. Occasionally it failed or drooped, and when this happened the sense of his face passed downward to his heavy (possibly foolish?) red underlip.

Wilhelm wanted to talk about the lard holdings, but Dr. Tamkin said, "This father-and-son case of mine would be instructive to you. It's a different psychological type completely than your dad. This man's father thinks that he isn't his son."

"Why not?"

"Because he has found out something about the mother carrying on with a friend of the family for twenty-five years."

"Well, what do you know!" said Wilhelm. His silent thought was, Pure bull. Nothing but bull!

"You must note how interesting the woman is, too. She has two husbands. Whose are the kids? The fellow detected her and she gave a signed confession that two of the four children were not the father's."

"It's amazing," said Wilhelm, but he said it in a rather distant way. He was always hearing such stories from Dr. Tamkin. If you were to believe Tamkin, most of the world was like this. Everybody in the hotel had a mental disorder, a secret history, a concealed disease. The wife of Rubin at the newsstand was supposed to be kept by Carl, the yelling, loud-mouthed gin-rummy player. The wife of Frank in the barbershop had disappeared with a GI while he was waiting for her to disembark at the French Lines pier. Everyone was like the faces on a playing card, upside down either way. Every public figure had a character-neurosis. Maddest of all were the businessmen, the heartless, flaunting, boisterous business class who ruled this country with their hard manners and their bold lies and their absurd words that nobody could believe. They were crazier than anyone. They spread the plague. Wilhelm, thinking of the Rojax Corporation, was inclined to agree that many businessmen were insane. And he supposed that Tamkin, for all his peculiarities, spoke a kind of truth and did some people a sort of good. It confirmed Wilhelm's suspicions to hear that there was a plague, and he said, "I couldn't agree with you more. They trade on anything, they steal everything, they're cynical right to the bones."

"You have to realize," said Tamkin, speaking of his patient, or his client, "that the mother's confession isn't good. It's a confession of duress. I try to tell the young fellow he shouldn't worry about a phony confession. But what does it help him if I am rational with him?"

"No?" said Wilhelm, intensely nervous. "I think we ought to go over to the market. It'll be opening pretty soon."

"Oh, come on," said Tamkin. "It isn't even nine o'clock, and there isn't much trading the first hour anyway. Things don't get hot in Chicago until half-past ten, and they're an hour behind us, don't forget. Anyway, I say lard will go up, and it will. Take my word. I've made a study of the guilt-aggression cycle which is behind it. I ought to know *something* about that. Straighten your collar."

"But meantime," said Wilhelm, "we have taken a licking this week. Are you sure your insight is at its best? Maybe when it isn't we should lay off and wait."

"Don"t you realize," Dr. Tamkin told him, "you can't march in a straight line to the victory? You fluctuate toward it. From Euclid to Newton[5] there was straight lines. The modern age analyzes the wavers. On my own accounts, I took a licking in hides and coffee. But I have confidence. I'm sure I'll outguess them." He gave Wilhelm a narrow smile, friendly, calming, shrewd, and wizard-like, patronizing, secret, potent. He saw his fears and smiled at them. "It's something," he remarked, "to see how the competition-factor will manifest itself in different individuals."

"So? Let's go over."

"But I haven't had my breakfast yet."

"I've had mine."

"Come, have a cup of coffee."

"I wouldn't want to meet my dad." Looking through the glass doors, Wilhelm saw that his father had left by the other exit. Wilhelm thought. He didn't want to run into me, either. He said to Dr. Tamkin, "Okay, I'll sit with you, but let's hurry it up because I'd like to get to the market while there's still a place to sit. Everybody and his uncle gets in ahead of you."

"I want to tell you about this boy and his dad. It's highly absorbing. The father was a nudist. Everybody went naked in the house. Maybe the women found men *with* clothes attractive. Her husband didn't believe in cutting his hair, either. He practiced dentistry. In his office he wore riding pants and a pair of boots, and he wore a green eyeshade."

"Oh, come off it," said Wilhelm.

"This is a true case history."

---

5. Euclid (fl. 300 B.C.), Greek geometer, author of *The Elements*. Sir Isaac New-ton (1642–1727), English natural philosopher and mathematician.

Without warning, Wilhelm began to laugh. He himself had had no premonition of his change of humor. His face became warm and pleasant, and he forgot his father, his anxieties; he panted bearlike, happily, through his teeth. "This sounds like a horse-dentist. He wouldn't have to put on pants to treat a horse. Now what else are you going to tell me? Did the wife play the mandolin? Does the boy join the cavalry? Oh, Tamkin, you really are a killer-diller."

"Oh, you think I'm trying to amuse you," said Tamkin. "That's because you aren't familiar with my outlook. I deal in fact. Facts always are sensational. I'll say that a second time. Facts *always!* are sensational."

Wilhelm was reluctant to part with his good mood. The doctor had little sense of humor. He was looking at him earnestly.

"I'd bet you any amount of money," said Tamkin, "that the facts about you are sensational."

"Oh—ha, ha! You want them? You can sell them to a true confession magazine."

"People forget how sensational the things are that they do. They don't see it on themselves. It blends into the background of their daily life."

Wilhelm smiled. "Are you sure this boy tells you the truth?"

"Yes, because I've known the whole family for years."

"And you do psychological work with your own friends? I didn't know that was allowed."

"Well, I'm a radical in the profession. I have to do good wherever I can."

Wilhelm's face became ponderous again and pale. His whitened gold hair lay heavy on his head, and he clasped uneasy fingers on the table. Sensational, but oddly enough, dull, too. Now how do you figure that out? It blends with the background. Funny but unfunny. True but false. Casual but laborious, Tamkin was. Wilhelm was most suspicious of him when he took his driest tone.

"With me," said Dr. Tamkin, "I am at my most efficient when I don't need the fee. When I only love. Without a financial reward. I remove myself from the social influence. Especially money. The spiritual compensation is what I look for. Bringing people into the here-and-now. The real universe. That's the present moment. The past is no good to us. The future is full of anxiety. Only the present is real—the here-and-now. Seize the day."

"Well," said Wilhelm, his earnestness returning. "I know you are a very unusual man. I like what you say about here-and-now. Are all the people who come to see you personal friends and patients too? Like that tall handsome girl, the one who always wears those beautiful broomstick skirts and belts?"

"She was an epileptic, and a most bad and serious pathology, too. I'm curing her successfully. She hasn't had a seizure in six months, and she used to have one every week."

"And that young cameraman, the one who showed us those movies from the jungles of Brazil, isn't he related to her?"

"Her brother. He's under my care, too. He has some terrible tendencies, which are to be expected when you have an epileptic sibling. I came into their lives when they needed help desperately, and took hold of them. A certain man forty years older than she had her in his control and used to give her fits by suggestion whenever she tried to leave him. If you only knew one per cent of what goes on in the city of New York! You see, I understand what it is when the lonely person begins to feel like an animal. When the night comes and he feels like howling from his window like a wolf. I'm taking complete care of that young fellow and his sister. I have to steady him down or he'll go from Brazil to Australia the next day. The way I keep him in the here-and-now is by teaching him Greek."

This was a complete surprise! "What, do you know Greek?"

"A friend of mine taught me when I was in Cairo. I studied Aristotle with him to keep from being idle."

Wilhelm tried to take in these new claims and examine them. Howling from the window like a wolf when night comes sounded genuine to him. That was something really to think about. But the Greek! He realized that Tamkin was watching to see how he took it. More elements were continually being added. A few days ago Tamkin had hinted that he had once been in the underworld, one of the Detroit Purple Gang. He was once head of a mental clinic in Toledo. He had worked with a Polish inventor on an unsinkable ship. He was a technical consultant in the field of television. In the life of a man of genius, all of these things might happen. But had they happened to Tamkin? Was he a genius? He often said that he had attended some of the Egyptian royal family as a psychiatrist. "But everybody is alike, common or aristocrat," he told Wilhelm. "The aristocrat knows less about life."

An Egyptian princess whom he had treated in California, for horrible disorders he had described to Wilhelm, retained him to come back to the old country with her, and there he had had many of her friends and relatives under his care. They turned over a villa on the Nile to him. "For ethical reasons, I can't tell you many of the details about them," he said—but Wilhelm had already heard all these details, and strange and shocking they were, if true. *If true*— he could not be free from doubt. For instance, the general who had to wear ladies' silk stockings and stand otherwise naked before the mirror—and all the rest. Listening to the doctor when he was so strangely factual, Wilhelm had to translate his words into his own language, and he could not translate fast enough or find terms to fit what he heard.

"Those Egyptian big shots invested in the market, too, for the heck of it. What did they need extra money for? By association, I almost became a millionaire myself, and if I had played it smart there's no telling what might have happened. I could have been the ambassador." The American? The Egyptian ambassador? "A friend of mine tipped me off on the cotton. I made a heavy purchase of it. I didn't have that kind of money, but everybody there knew me. It never entered their minds that a person of their social circle didn't have dough. The sale was made on the phone. Then, while the cotton shipment was at sea, the price tripled. When the stuff suddenly became so valuable all hell broke loose on the world cotton market, they looked to see who was the owner of this big shipment. Me! They investigated my credit and found out I was a mere doctor, and they canceled. This was illegal. I sued them. But as I didn't have the money to fight them I sold the suit to a Wall Street lawyer for twenty thousand dollars. He fought it and was winning. They settled with him out of court for more than a million. But on the way back from Cairo, flying, there was a crash. All on board died. I have this guilt on my conscience, of being the murderer of that lawyer. Although he was a crook."

Wilhelm thought, I must be a real jerk to sit and listen to such impossible stories. I guess I am a sucker for people who talk about the deeper things of life, even the way he does.

"We scientific men speak of irrational guilt, Wilhelm," said Dr. Tamkin, as if Wilhelm were a pupil in his class. "But in such a situation, because of the money, I wished him harm. I realize it. This isn't the time to describe all the details, but the money made me guilty. Money and Murder both begin with M. Machinery. Mischief."

Wilhelm, his mind thinking for him at random, said, "What about Mercy? Milk-of-human-kindness?"

"One fact should be clear to you by now. Money-making is aggression. That's the whole thing. The functionalistic explanation is the only one. People come to the market to kill. They say, 'I'm going to make a killing.' It's not accidental. Only they haven't got the genuine courage to kill, and they erect a symbol of it. The money. They make a killing by a fantasy. Now, counting and number is always a sadistic activity. Like hitting. In the Bible, the Jews wouldn't allow you to count them. They knew it was sadistic."

"I don't understand what you mean," said Wilhelm. A strange uneasiness tore at him. The day was growing too warm and his head felt dim. "What makes them want to kill?"

"By and by, you'll get the drift," Dr. Tamkin assured him. His amazing eyes had some of the rich dryness of a brown fur. Innumerable crystalline hairs of spicules of light glittered in their bold surfaces. "You can't understand without first spending years on the study of the ultimates of human and animal behavior, the deep chemical, organismic, and spiritual secrets of life. I am a psychological poet."

"If you're this kind of poet," said Wilhelm, whose fingers in his pocket were feeling in the little envelopes for the Phenaphen capsules, "what are you doing on the market?"

"That's a good question. Maybe I am better at speculation because I don't care. Basically, I don't wish hard enough for money, and therefore I come with a cool head to it."

Wilhelm thought, Oh, sure! That's an answer, is it? I bet that if I took a strong attitude he'd back down on everything. He'd grovel in front of me. The way he looks at me on the sly, to see if I'm being taken in! He swallowed his Phenaphen pill with a long gulp of water. The rims of his eyes grew red as it went down. And then he felt calmer.

"Let me see if I can give you an answer that will satisfy you," said Dr. Tamkin. His flapjacks were set before him. He spread the butter on them, poured on brown maple syrup, quartered them, and began to eat with hard, active, muscular jaws which sometimes gave a creak at the hinges. He pressed the handle of his knife against his chest and said, "In here, the human bosom—mine, yours, everybody's—there isn't just one soul. There's a lot of souls. But there are two main ones, the real soul and a pretender soul. Now! Every man realizes that he has to love something or somebody. He feels that he must go outward. 'If thou canst not love, what art thou?' Are you with me?"

"Yes, Doc, I think so," said Wilhelm listening—a little skeptically but nonetheless hard.

" 'What art thou?' Nothing. That's the answer. Nothing. In the heart of hearts—Nothing! So of course you can't stand that and want to be Something, and you try. But instead of being this Something, the man puts it over on everybody instead. You can't be that strict to yourself. You love a *little*. Like you have a dog" (*Scissors!*) "or give some money to a charity drive. Now that isn't love, is it? What is it? Egotism, pure and simple. It's a way to love the pretender soul. Vanity. Only vanity, is what it is. And social control. The interest of the pretender soul is the same as the interest of the social life, the society mechanism. This is the main tragedy of human life. Oh, it is terrible! Terrible! You are not free. Your own betrayer is inside of you and sells you out. You have to obey him like a slave. He makes you work like a horse. And for what? For who?"

"Yes, for what?" The doctor's words caught Wilhelm's heart. "I couldn't agree more," he said. "When do we get free?"

"The purpose is to keep the whole thing going. The true soul is the one that pays the price. It suffers and gets sick, and it realizes that the pretender can't be loved. Because the pretender is a lie. The true soul loves the truth. And when the true soul feels like this, it wants to kill the pretender. The love has turned into hate. Then you become dangerous. A killer. You have to kill the deceiver."

"Does this happen to everybody?"

The doctor answered simply, "Yes, to everybody. Of course, for simplification purposes, I have spoken of the soul; it isn't a scientific term, but it helps you to understand it. Whenever the slayer slays, he wants to slay the soul in him which has gypped and deceived him. Who is his enemy? Him. And his lover? Also. Therefore, all suicide is murder, and all murder is suicide. It's the one and identical phenomenon. Biologically, the pretender soul takes away the energy of the true soul and makes it feeble, like a parasite. It happens unconsciously, unawaringly, in the depths of the organism. Ever take up parasitology?"

"No, it's my dad who's the doctor."

"You should read a book about it."

Wilhelm said, "But this means that the world is full of murderers. So it's not the world. It's a kind of hell."

"Sure," the doctor said. "At least a kind of purgatory. You walk on the bodies. They are all around. I can hear them cry *de profundis*[6] and wring their hands. I hear them, poor human beasts. I can't help bearing. And my eyes are open to it. I have to cry, too. This is the human tragedy-comedy."

Wilhelm tried to capture his vision. And again the doctor looked untrustworthy to him, and he doubted him. "Well," he said, "there are also kind, ordinary, helpful people. They're—out in the country. All over. What kind of morbid stuff do you read, anyway?" The doctor's room was full of books.

"I read the best of literature, science and philosophy," Dr. Tamkin said. Wilhelm had observed that in his room even the TV aerial was set upon a pile of volumes. "Korzybski, Aristotle, Freud, W. H. Sheldon, and all the great poets.[7] You answer me like a layman. You haven't applied your mind strictly to this."

"Very interesting," said Wilhelm. He was aware that he hadn't applied his mind strictly to anything. "You don't have to think I'm a dummy, though. I have ideas, too." A glance at the clock told him that the market would soon open. They could spare a few minutes yet. There were still more things he wanted to hear from Tamkin. He realized that Tamkin spoke faultily, but then scientific men were not always strictly literate. It was the description of the two souls that had awed him. In Tommy he saw the pretender. And even Wilky might not be himself. Might the name of his true soul be the one by which his old grandfather had called him—Velvel? The name of a soul, however, must be only that—soul. What did it look like? Does my soul like like me? Is there a soul that looks like Dad? Like Tamkin? Where does the true soul get its strength? Why does it have to love truth? Wilhelm was tormented, but tried to be oblivious

6. "Out of the depths"; first words of Psalm 130.
7. Count Alfred Korzybski (1879–1950), a proselytizing semanticist of dubious standing. "Sheldon": probably William Herbert Sheldon, a psychologist (b. 1898). Along with Aristotle and Freud they suggest the miscellaneous jumble of Tamkin's reading.

to his torment. Secretly, he prayed the doctor would give him some useful advice and transform his life. "Yes, I understand you," he said. "It isn't lost on me."

"I never said you weren't intelligent, but only you just haven't made a study of it all. As a matter of fact you're a profound personality with very profound creative capacities but also disturbances. I've been concerned with you, and for some time I've been treating you."

"Without my knowing it? I haven't felt you doing anything. What do you mean? I don't think I like being treated without my knowledge. I'm of two minds. What's the matter, don't you think I'm normal?" And he really was divided in mind. That the doctor cared about him pleased him. This was what he craved, that someone should care about him, wish him well. Kindness, mercy, he wanted. But—and here he retracted his heavy shoulders in his peculiar way, drawing his hands up into his sleeves; his feet moved uneasily under the table—but he was worried, too, and even somewhat indignant. For what right had Tamkin to meddle without being asked? What kind of privileged life did this man lead? He took other people's money and speculated with it. Everybody came under his care. No one could have secrets from him.

The doctor looked at him with his deadly brown, heavy, impenetrable eyes, his naked shining head, his red hanging underlip, and said, "You have lots of guilt in you."

Wilhelm helplessly admitted, as he felt the heat rise to his wide face, "Yes, I think so too. But personally," he added, "I don't feel like a murderer. I always try to lay off. It's the others who get me. You know—make me feel oppressed. And if you don't mind, and it's all the same to you, I would rather know it when you start to treat me. And now, Tamkin, for Christ's sake, they're putting out the lunch menus already. Will you sign the check, and let's go!"

Tamkin did as he asked, and they rose. They were passing the bookkeeper's desk when he took out a substantial bundle of onionskin papers and said, "These are receipts of the transactions. Duplicates. You'd better keep them as the account is in your name and you'll need them for income taxes. And here is a copy of a poem I wrote yesterday."

"I have to leave something at the desk for my father," Wilhelm said, and he put his hotel bill in an envelope with a note. *Dear Dad, Please carry me this month, Yours W.* He watched the clerk with his sullen pug's profile and his stiffnecked look push the envelope into his father's box.

"May I ask you really why you and your dad had words?" said Dr. Tamkin, who had hung back, waiting.

"It was about my future," said Wilhelm. He hurried down the stairs with swift steps, like a tower in motion, his hands in his trousers pockets. He was ashamed to discuss the matter. "He says there's a reason why I can't go back to my old territory, and there is. I told everybody I was going to be an officer of the corporation. And I was supposed to. It was promised. But then they welshed because of the son-in-law. I bragged and made myself look big."

"If you was humble enough, you could go back. But it doesn't make much difference. We'll make you a good living on the market."

They came into the sunshine of upper Broadway, not clear but throbbing through the dust and fumes, a false air of gas visible at eye-level as it spurted from the bursting buses. From old habit, Wilhelm turned up the collar of his jacket.

"Just a technical question," Wilhelm said. "What happens if your losses are bigger than your deposit?"

"Don't worry. They have ultra-modern electronic bookkeeping machinery, and it won't let you get in debt. It puts you out automatically. But I want you to read this poem. You haven't read it yet."

Light as a locust, a helicopter bringing mail from Newark Airport to La Guardia sprang over the city in a long leap.

The paper Wilhelm unfolded had ruled borders in red ink. He read:

MECHANISM VS FUNCTIONALISM
ISM VS HISM

If thee thyself couldst only see
Thy greatness that is and yet to be,
Thou would feel joy-beauty-what ecstasy.
They are at thy feet, earth-moon-sea, the trinity.

Why-forth then dost thou tarry
And partake thee only of the crust
And skim the earth's surface narry
When all creations art thy just?

Seek ye then that which art not there
In thine own glory let thyself rest.
Witness. Thy power is not bare.
Thou art King. Thou art at thy best.

Look then right before thee.
Open thine eyes and see.
At the foot of Mt. Serenity
Is thy cradle to eternity.

Utterly confused, Wilhelm said to himself explosively, What kind of mishmash, claptrap is this! What does he want from me? Damn him to hell, he might as well hit me on the head, and lay me out, kill me. What does he give me this for? What's the purpose? Is it a

deliberate test? Does he want to mix me up? He's already got me
mixed up completely. I was never good at riddles. Kiss those seven
hundred bucks good-by, and call it one more mistake in a long line
of mistakes—Oh, Mama, what a line! He stood near the shining
window of a fancy fruit store, holding Tamkin's paper, rather
dazed, as though a charge of photographer's flash powder had gone
up in his eyes.

But he's waiting for my reaction. I have to say something to him
about his poem. It really is no joke. What will I tell him? Who is
this King? The poem is written *to* someone. But who? I can't even
bring myself to talk. I feel too choked and strangled. With all the
books he reads, how come the guy is so illiterate? And why do
people just naturally assume that you'll know what they're talking
about? No. I don't know, and nobody knows. The planets don't, the
stars don't, infinite space doesn't. It doesn't square with Planck's
Constant[8] or anything else. So what's the good of it? Where's the
need of it? What does he mean here by Mount Serenity? Could it be
a figure of speech for Mount Everest? As he says people are all
committing suicide, maybe those guys who climbed Everest were
only trying to kill themselves, and if we want peace we should stay
at the foot of the mountain. In the here-and-now. But it's also here-
and-now on the slope, and on the top, where they climbed to seize
the day. Surface narry is something he can't mean, I don't believe.
I'm about to start foaming at the mouth. "Thy cradle . . ." *Who* is
resting in his cradle—in his glory? My thoughts are at an end. I feel
the wall. No more. So ——k it all! The money and everything.
Take it away! When I have the money they eat me alive, like those
piranha fish in the movie about the Brazilian jungle. It was hideous
when they ate up that Brahma bull in the river. He turned pale, just
like clay, and in five minutes nothing was left except the skeleton
still in one piece, floating away. When I haven't got it any more, at
least they'll let me alone.

"Well, what do you think of this?" said Dr. Tamkin. He gave a
special sort of wise smile, as though Wilhelm must now see what
kind of man he was dealing with.

"Nice. Very nice. Have you been writing long?"

"I've been developing this line of thought for years and years.
You follow it all the way?"

"I'm trying to figure out who this Thou is."

"Thou? Thou is you."

"Me! Why? this applies to *me?*"

"Why shouldn't it apply to you. You were in my mind when I
composed it. Of course, the hero of the poem is sick humanity. If it
would open its eyes it would be great."

"Yes, but how do I get into this?"

---

8. Max Planck (1858–1947), physicist
who postulated that energy can exist
only as quanta in multiples of an elementary quantity.

"The main idea of the poem is *construct* or *destruct*. There is no ground in between. Mechanism is *destruct*. Money of course is *destruct*. When the last grave is dug, the gravedigger will have to be paid. If you could have confidence in nature you would not have to fear. It would keep you up. Creative is nature. Rapid. Lavish. Inspirational. It shapes leaves. It rolls the waters of the earth. Man is the chief of this. All creations are his just inheritance. You don't know what you've got within you. A person either creates or he destroys. There is no neutrality . . ."

"I realized you were no beginner," said Wilhelm with propriety. "I have only one criticism to make. I think 'why-forth' is wrong. You should write 'Wherefore then dost thou . . .' " And he reflected, So? I took a gamble. It'll have to be a miracle, though, to save me. My money will be gone, then it won't be able to destruct me. He can't just take and lose it, though. He's in it, too. I think he's in a bad way himself. He must be. I'm sure because, come to think of it, he sweated blood when he signed that check. But what have I let myself in for? The waters of the earth are going to roll over me.

V

Patiently, in the window of the fruit store, a man with a scoop spread crushed ice betwee his rows of vegetables. There were also Persian melons, lilacs, tulips with radiant black at the middle. The many street noises came back after a little while from the caves of the sky. Crossing the tide of Broadway traffic, Wilhelm was saying to himself, The reason Tamkin lectures me is that somebody has lectured him, and the reason for the poem is that he wants to give me good advice. Everybody seems to know something. Even fellows like Tamkin. Many people know what to do, but how many can do it?

He believed that he must, that he could and would recover the good things, the happy things, the easy tranquil things of life. He had made mistakes, but he could overlook these. He had been a fool, but that could be forgiven. The time wasted—must be relinquished. What else could one do about it? Things were too complex, but they might be reduced to simplicity again. Recovery was possible. First he had to get out of the city. No, first he had to pull out his money. . . .

From the carnival of the street—pushcarts, accordion and fiddle, shoeshine, begging, the dust going round like a woman on stilts—they entered the narrow crowded theater of the brokerage office. From front to back it was filled with the Broadway crowd. But how was lard doing this morning? From the rear of the hall Wilhelm tried to read the tiny figures. The German manager was looking through his binoculars. Tamkin placed himself on Wilhelm's left and covered his conspicious bald head. "The guy'll ask me about the margin," he muttered. They passed, however, unobserved. "Look, the lard has held its place," he said.

Tamkin's eyes must be very sharp to read the figures over so many heads and at this distance—another respect in which he was unusual.

The room was always crowded. Everyone talked. Only at the front could you hear the flutter of the wheels within the board. Teletyped news items crossed the illuminated screen above.

"Lard. Now what about rye?" said Tamkin, rising on his toes. Here he was a different man, active and impatient. He parted people who stood in his way. His face turned resolute, and on either side of his mouth odd bulges formed under his mustache. Already he was pointing out to Wilhelm the appearance of a new pattern on the board. "There's something up today," he said.

"Then why'd you take so long with breakfast?" said Wilhelm.

There were no reserved seat in the room, only customary ones. Tamkin always sat in the second row, on the commodities side of the aisle. Some of his acquaintances kept their hats on the chairs for him.

"Thanks. Thanks," said Tamkin, and he told Wilhelm, "I fixed it up yesterday."

"That was a smart thought," said Wilhelm. They sat down.

With folded hands, by the wall, sat an old Chinese businessman in a seersucker coat. Smooth and fat, he wore a white Vandyke. One day Wilhelm had seen him on Riverside Drive pushing two little girls along in a baby carriage—his grandchildren. Then there were two women in their fifties, supposed to be sisters, shrewd and able money-makers, according to Tamkin. They had never a word to say to Wilhelm. But they would chat with Tamkin. Tamkin talked to everyone.

Wilhelm sat between Mr. Rowland, who was elderly, and Mr. Rappaport, who was very old. Yesterday Rowland had told him that in the year 1908, when he was a junior at Harvard, his mother had given him twenty shares of steel for his birthday, and then he had started to read the financial news and had never practiced law but instead followed the market for the rest of his life. Now he speculated only in soy beans, of which he had made a specialty. By his conservative method, said Tamkin, he cleared two hundred a week. Small potatoes, but then he was a bachelor, retired, and didn't need money.

"Without dependents," said Tamkin. "He doesn't have the promlems that you and I do."

Did Tamkin have dependents? He had everything that it was possible for a man to have—science, Greek, chemistry, poetry, and now dependents too. That beautiful girl with epilepsy, perhaps. He often said that she was a pure, marvelous, spiritual child who had no knowledge of the world. He protected her, and, if he was not lying, adored her. And if you encouraged Tamkin by believing him, or even if you refrained from questioning him, his hints became more daring. Sometimes he said that he paid for her music lessons. Sometimes he seemed to have footed the bill for the brother's camera expedition to Brazil. And he spoke of paying for the support of the orphaned child of a dead sweetheart. These hints, made dully as asides, grew by repetition into sensational claims.

"For myself, I don't need much," said Tamkin. "But a man can't live for himself and I need the money for certain important things. What do you figure you have to have, to get by?"

"Not less than fifteen grand, after taxes. That's for my wife and the two boys."

"Isn't there anybody else?" said Tamkin with a shrewdness almost cruel. But his look grew more sympathetic as Wilhelm stumbled, not willing to recall another grief.

"Well—there was. But it wasn't a money matter."

"I should hope!" said Tamkin. "If love is love, it's free. Fifteen grand, though, isn't too much for a man of your intelligence to ask out of life. Fools, hard-hearted criminals, and murderers have millions to squander. They burn up the world—oil, coal, wood, metal, and soil, and suck even the air and the sky. They consume, and they give back no benefit. A man like you, humble for life, who wants to feel and live, has trouble—not wanting," said Tamkin in his parenthetical fashion, "to exchange an ounce of soul for a pound of social power—he'll never make it without help in a world like this. But don't you worry." Wilhelm grasped at this assurance. "Just you never mind. We'll go easily beyond your figure."

Dr. Tamkin gave Wilhelm comfort. He often said that he had made as much as a thousand a week in commodities. Wilhelm had examined the receipts, but until this moment it had never occurred to him that there must be debit slips too; he had been shown only the credits.

"But fifteen grand is not an ambitious figure," Tamkin was telling him. "For that you don't have to wear yourself out on the road, dealing with narrow-minded people. A lot of them don't like Jews, either, I suppose?"

"I can't afford to notice. I'm lucky when I have my occupation. Tamkin, do you mean you can save our money?"

"Oh, did I forget to mention what I did before closing yesterday? You see, I closed out one of the lard contracts and bought a hedge of December rye. The rye is up three points already and takes some of the sting out. But lard will go up, too."

"Where? God, yes, you're right," said Wilhelm, eager, and got to his feet to look. New hope freshened his heart. "Why didn't you tell me before?"

And Tamkin, smiling like a benevolent magician, said, "You must learn to have trust. The slump in lard can't last. And just take a look at eggs. Didn't I predict they couldn't go any lower? They're rising and rising. If we had taken eggs we'd be far ahead."

"Then why didn't we take them?"

"We were just about to. I had a buying order in at .24, but the tide turned at .26¼ and we barely missed. Never mind. Lard will go back to last year's levels."

Maybe. But when? Wilhelm could not allow his hopes to grow too strong. However, for a little while he could breathe more easily. Late-morning trading was getting active. The shining numbers whirred on the board, which sounded like a huge cage of artificial birds. Lard fluctuated between two points, but rye slowly climbed.

He closed his strained, greatly earnest eyes briefly and nodded his Buddha's head, too large to suffer such uncertainties. For several moments of peace he was removed to his small yard in Roxbury.

He breathed in the sugar of the pure morning.

He heard the long phrases of the birds.

No enemy wanted his life.

Wilhelm thought, I will get out of here. I don't belong in New York any more. And he sighed like a sleeper.

Tamkin said, "Excuse me," and left his seat. He could not sit still in the room but passed back and forth between the stocks and commodities sections. He knew dozens of people and was continually engaging in discussions. Was he giving advice, gathering information, or giving it, or practicing—whatever mysterious profession he practiced? Hypnotism? Perhaps he could put people in a trance while he talked to them. What a rare, peculiar bird he was, with those pointed shoulders, that bare head, his loose nails, almost claws, and those brown, soft, deadly, heavy eyes.

He spoke of things that mattered, and as very few people did this he could take you by surprise, excite you, move you. Maybe he wished to do good, maybe give himself a lift to a higher level, maybe believe his own prophecies, maybe touch his own heart. Who could tell? He had picked up a lot of strange ideas; Wilhelm could only suspect, he could not say with certainty, that Tamkin hadn't made them his own.

Now Tamkin and he were equal partners, but Tamkin had put up only three hundred dollars. Suppose he did this not only once but five times; then an investment of fifteen hundred dollars gave him five thousand to speculate with. If he had power of attorney in every case, he could shift the money from one account to another. No, the German probably kept an eye on him. Nevertheless it was possible. Calculations like this made Wilhelm feel ill. Obviously Tamkin was a plunger. But how did he get by? H must be in his fifties. How did he support himself? Five years in Egypt; Hollywood before that; Michigan; Ohio; Chicago. A man of fifty has supported himself for at least thirty years. You could be sure that Tamkin had never worked in a factory or in an office. How did he make it? His taste in clothes was horrible, but he didn't buy cheap things. He wore corduroy or velvet shirts from Clyde's, painted neckties, striped socks. There was a slightly acid or pasty smell about his person; for a doctor, he didn't bathe much. Also, Dr. Tamkin had a good room at the Gloriana and had had it for about a year. But so was Wilhelm himself a guest, with an unpaid bill at present in his father's box. Did the beautiful girl with the skirts and belts pay him? Was he defrauding his so-called patients? So many questions impossible to answer could not be asked about an honest man. Nor perhaps about a sane man. Was Tamkin a lunatic, then? That sick Mr. Perls at breakfast had said that there was no easy way to tell the sane from the mad, and he was right about that in any big city and especially in New York—the end of the world, with its complexity and machinery, bricks and tubes, wires and stones, holes and heights. And was everybody crazy here? What sort of people did you see? Every other man spoke a language entirely his own, which he had figured out by private thinking; he had his own ideas and peculiar ways. If you wanted to talk about a glass of water, you had to start back with God creating the heavens and earth; the apple; Abraham; Moses and Jesus; Rome; the Middle Ages; gunpowder; the Revolution; back to Newton; up to Einstein; then war and Lenin and Hitler. After reviewing this and getting it all straight again you could proceed to talk about a glass of water. "I'm fainting, please get me a little water." You were lucky even then to make yourself understood. And this happened over and over and over with everyone you met. You had to translate and translate, explain and explain, back and forth, and it was the punishment of hell itself not to understand or be understood, not to know the crazy from the sane, the wise from the fools, the young from the old or the sick from the well. The fathers were no fathers and the sons no sons. You had to talk with yourself in the daytime and reason with yourself at night. Who else was there to talk to in a city like New York?

A queer look came over Wilhelm's face with its eyes turned up and his silent mouth with its high upper lip. He went several degrees further—when you are like this, dreaming that everybody is outcast, you realize that this must be one of the small matters. There is a larger body, and from this you cannot be separated. The glass of water fades out. You do not go from simple *a* and simple *b* to the great *x* and *y*, nor does it matter whether you agree about the glass but, far beneath such details, what Tamkin would call the real soul says plain and understandable things to everyone. There sons and fathers are themselves, and a glass of water is only an ornament; it makes a hoop of brightness on the cloth; it is an angel's mouth. There truth for everybody may be found, and confusion is only— only temporary, thought Wilhelm.

The idea of this larger body had been planted in him a few days ago beneath Times Square, when he had gone downtown to pick up tickets for the baseball game on Saturday (a doubleheader at the Polo Grounds). He was going through an underground corridor, a place he had always hated and hated more than ever now. On the walls between the advertisements were words in chalk: "Sin No More," and "Do Not Eat the Pig," he had particularly noticed. And in the dark tunnel, in the haste, heat, and darkness which disfigure and make freaks and fragments of nose and eyes and teeth, all of a sudden, unsought, a general love for all these imperfect and lurid-looking people burst out in Wilhelm's breast. He loved them. One and all, he passionately loved them. They were his brothers and his sisters. He was imperfect and disfigured himself, but what difference did that make if he was united with them by this blaze of love? And as he walked he began to say, "Oh my brothers—my brothers and my sisters," blessing them all as well as himself.

So what did it matter how many languages there were, or how hard it was to describe a glass of water? Or matter that a few minutes later he didn't feel anything like a brother toward the man who sold him the tickets?

On that very same afternoon he didn't hold so high an opinion of this same onrush of loving kindness. What did it come to? As they had the capacity and must use it once in a while, people were bound to have such involuntary feelings. It was only another one of those subway things. Like having a hard-on at random. But today, his day of reckoning, he consulted his memory again and thought, I must go back to that. That's the right clue and may do me the most good. Something very big. Truth, like.

The old fellow on the right, Mr. Rappaport, was nearly blind and kept asking Wilhelm, "What's the new figure on November wheat? Give me July soy beans too." When you told him he didn't say thank you. He said, "Okay," instead, or, "Check," and turned away until he needed you again. He was very old, older even than Dr. Adler, and if you believed Tamkin he had once been the Rockefeller of the chicken business and had retired with a large fortune.

Wilhelm had a queer feeling about the chicken industry, that it was sinister. On the road, he frequently passed chicken farms. Those big, rambling, wooden buildings out in the neglected fields; they were like prisons. The lights burned all night in them to cheat the poor hens into laying. Then the slaughter. Pile all the coops of the slaughtered on end, and in one week they'd go higher than Mount Everest or Mount Serenity. The blood filling the Gulf of Mexico. The chicken shit, acid, burning the earth.

How old—old this Mr. Rappaport was! Purple stains were buried in the flesh of his nose, and the cartilage of his ear was twisted like a cabbage heart. Beyond remedy by glasses, his eyes were smoky and faded.

"Read me that soy-bean figure now, boy," he said, and Wilhelm did. He thought perhaps the old man might give him a tip, or some useful advice or information about Tamkin. But no. He only wrote memoranda on a pad, and put the pad in his pocket. He let no one see what he had written. And Wilhelm thought this was the way a man who had grown rich by the murder of millions of animals, little chickens, would act. If there was a life to come he might have to answer for the killing of all those chickens. What if they all were waiting? But if there was a life to come, everybody would have to answer. But if there was a life to come, the chickens themselves would be all right.

Well! What stupid ideas he was having this morning. Phooey!

Finally old Rappaport did address a few remarks to Wilhelm. He asked him whether he had reserved his seat in the synagogue for Yom Kippur.

"No," said Wilhelm.

"Well, you better hurry up if you expect to say *Yiskor*[9] for your parents. I never miss."

And Wilhelm thought, Yes, I suppose I should say a prayer for Mother once in a while. His mother had belonged to the Reform congregation. His father had no religion. At the cemetery Wilhelm had paid a man to say a prayer for her. He was among the tombs and he wanted to be tipped for the *El molai rachamin*. "Thou God of Mercy," Wilhelm thought that meant. *B'gan Aden*—"in Paradise." Singing, they drew it out. *B'gan Ay-den*. The broken bench beside the grave made him wish to do something. Wilhelm often prayed in his own manner. He did not go to the synagogue but he would occasionally perform certain devotions, according to his feelings. Now he reflected, In Dad's eyes I am the wrong kind of Jew. He doesn't like the way I act. Only he is the right kind of Jew. Whatever you are, it always turns out to be the wrong kind.

Mr. Rappaport grumbled and whiffed at his long cigar, and the board, like a swarm of electrical bees, whirred.

"Since you were in the chicken business, I thought you'd speculate in eggs, Mr. Rappaport." Wilhelm, with his warm, panting laugh, sought to charm the old man.

"Oh. Yeah. Loyalty, hey?" said old Rappaport. "I should stick to them. I spent a lot of time amongst chickens. I got to be an expert chicken-sexer. When the chick hatches you have to tell the boys from the girls. It's not easy. You need long, long experience. What do you think, it's a joke? A whole industry depends on it. Yes, now and then I buy a contract eggs. What have you got today?"

Wilhelm said anxiously, "Lard. Rye."

"Buy? Sell?"

"Bought."

"Uh," said the old man. Wilhelm could not determine what he meant by this. But of course you couldn't expect him to make

9. Jewish memorial service for the dead.

himself any clearer. It was not in the code to give information to anyone. Sick with desire, Wilhelm waited for Mr. Rappaport to make an exception in his case. Just this once! Because it was critical. Silently, by a sort of telepathic concentration, he begged the old man to speak the single word that would save him, give him the merest sign. "Oh, please—please help," he nearly said. If Rappaport would close one eye, or lay his head to one side, or raise his finger and point to a column in the paper or to a figure on his pad. A hint! A hint!

A long perfect ash formed on the end of the cigar, the white ghost of the leaf with all its veins and its fainter pungency. It was ignored, in its beauty, by the old man. For it was beautiful. Wilhelm he ignored as well.

Then Tamkin said to him, "Wilhelm, look at the jump our rye just took."

December rye climbed three points as they tensely watched; the tumblers raced and the machine's lights buzzed.

"A point and a half more, and we can cover the lard losses," said Tamkin. He showed him his calculations on the margin of the *Times.*

"I think you should put in the selling order now. Let's get out with a small loss."

"Get out now? Nothing doing."

"Why not? Why should we wait?"

"Because," said Tamkin with a smiling, almost openly scoffing look, "You've got to keep your nerve when the market starts to go places. Now's when you can make something."

"I'd get out while the getting's good."

"No, you shouldn't lose your head like this. It's obvious to me what the mechanism is, back in the Chicago market. There's a short supply of December rye. Look, it's just gone up another quarter. We should ride it."

"I'm losing my taste for the gamble," said Wilhelm. "You can't feel safe when it goes up so fast. It's liable to come down just as quick."

Dryly, as though he were dealing with a child, Tamkin told him in a tone of tiring patience, "Now listen, Tommy. I have it diagnosed right. If you wish I should sell I can give the sell order. But this is the difference between healthiness and pathology. One is objective, doesn't change his mind every minute, enjoys the risk element. But that's not the neurotic character. The neurotic character—"

"Damn it, Tamkin!" said Wilhelm roughly. "Cut that out. I don't like it. Leave my character out of consideration. Don't pull any more of that stuff on me. I tell you I don't like it."

Tamkin therefore went no further; he backed down. "I meant," he said, softer, "that as a salesman you are basically an artist type.

The seller is in the visionary sphere of the business function. And then you're an actor, too."

"No matter what type I am—" An angry and yet weak sweetness rose into Wilhelm's throat. He coughed as though he had the flu. It was twenty years since he had appeared on the screen as an extra. He blew the bagpipes in a film called *Annie Laurie*. Annie had come to warn the young Laird; he would not believe her and called the bagpipers to drown her out. He made fun of her while she wrung her hands. Wilhelm, in a kilt, barelegged, blew and blew and blew and not a sound came out. Of course all the music was recorded. He fell sick with the flu after that and still suffered sometimes from chest weakness.

"Something stuck in your throat?" said Tamkin. "I think maybe you are too disturbed to think clearly. You should try some of my 'here-and-now' mental exercises. It stops you from thinking so much about the future and the past and cuts down confusion."

"Yes, yes, yes, yes," said Wilhelm, his eyes fixed on December rye.

"Nature only knows one thing, and that's the present. Present, present, eternal present, like a big, huge, giant wave—colossal, bright and beautiful, full of life and death, climbing into the sky, standing in the seas. You must go along with the actual, the Here-and-Now, the glory—"

. . . chest weakness, Wilhelm's recollection went on. Margaret nursed him. They had had two rooms of furniture, which was later seized. She sat on the bed and read to him. He made her read for days, and she read stories, poetry, everything in the house. He felt dizzy, stifled when he tried to smoke. They had him wear a flannel vest.

> Come then, Sorrow!
> Sweetest Sorrow!
> Like an own babe I nurse thee on my breast![1]

Why did he remember that? Why?

"You have to pick out something that's in the actual, immediate present moment," said Tamkin. "And say to yourself here-and-now, here-and-now, here-and-now. 'Where am I?' 'Here.' 'When is it?' 'Now.' Take an object or a person. Anybody. 'Here and now I see a person.' 'Here and now I see a man.' 'Here and now I see a man sitting on a chair.' Take me for instance. Don't let your mind wander. 'Here and now I see a man in a brown suit. Here and now I see a corduroy shirt.' You have to narrow it down, one item at a time, and not let your imagination shoot ahead. Be in the present. Grasp the hour, the moment, the instant."

Is he trying to hypnotize or con me? Wilhelm wondered. To take

1. Keats's *Endymion* 4.279–81.

my mind off selling? But even if I'm back at seven hundred bucks, then where am I?

As if in prayer, his lids coming down with raised veins, frayed out, on his significant eyes, Tamkin said, " Here and now I see a button. Here and now I see the thread that sews the button. Here and now I see the green thread.' " Inch by inch he contemplated himself in order to show Wilhelm how calm it would make him. But Wilhelm was hearing Margaret's voice as she read, somewhat unwillingly,

> Come then, Sorrow!
>
> .   .   .   .
>
> I thought to leave thee,
> And deceive thee,
> But now of all the world I love thee best.

Then Mr. Rappaport's old hand pressed his thigh, and he said, "What's my wheat? Those damn guys are blocking the way. I can't see."

VI

Rye was still ahead when they went out to lunch, and lard was holding its own.

They ate in the cafeteria with the gilded front. There was the same art inside as outside. The food looked sumptuous. Whole fishes were framed like pictures with carrots, and the salads were like terraced landscapes or like Mexican pyramids; slices of lemon and onion and radishes were like sun and moon and stars; the cream pies were about a foot thick and the cakes swollen as if sleepers had baked them in their dreams.

"What'll you have?" said Tamkin.

"Not much. I ate a big breakfast. I'll find a table. Bring me some yogurt and crackers and a cup of tea. I don't want to spend much time over lunch."

Tamkin said, "You've got to eat."

Finding an empty place at this hour was not easy. The old people idled and gossiped over their coffee. The elderly ladies were rouged and mascaraed and hennaed and used blue hair rinse and eye shadow and wore costume jewelry, and many of them were proud and stared at you with expressions that did not belong to their age. Were there no longer any respectable old ladies who knitted and cooked and looked after their grandchildren? Wilhelm's grandmother had dressed him in a sailor suit and danced him on her knee, blew on the porridge for him and said, "Admiral, you must eat." But what was the use of remembering this so late in the day?

He managed to find a table, and Dr. Tamkin came along with a tray piled with plates and cups. He had Yankee pot roast, purple cabbage, potatoes, a big slice of watermelon, and two cups of coffee. Wilhelm could not even swallow his yogurt. His chest pained him still.

At once Tamkin involved him in a lengthy discussion. Did he do it to stall Wilhelm and prevent him from selling out the rye—or to recover the ground lost when he had made Wilhelm angry by hints about the neurotic character? Or did he have no purpose except to talk?

"I think you worry a lot too much about what your wife and your father will say. Do they matter so much?"

Wilhelm replied, "A person can become tired of looking himself over and trying to fix himself up. You can spend the entire second half of your life recovering from the mistakes of the first half."

"I believe your dad told me he had some money to leave you."

"He probably does have something."

"A lot?"

"Who can tell," said Wilhelm guardedly.

"You ought to think over what you'll do with it."

"I may be too feeble to do anything by the time I get it. If I get anything."

"A thing like this you ought to plan out carefully. Invest it properly." He began to unfold schemes whereby you bought bonds, and used the bonds as security to buy something else and thereby earned twelve per cent safely on your money. Wilhelm failed to follow the details. Tamkin said, "If he made you a gift now, you wouldn't have to pay the inheritance taxes."

Bitterly, Wilhelm told him, "My father's death blots out all other considerations from his mind. He forces me to think about it, too. Then he hates me because he succeeds. When I get desperate—of course I think about money. But I don't want anything to happen to him. I certainly don't want him to die." Tamkin's brown eyes glittered shrewdly at him. "You don't believe it. Maybe it's not psychological. But on my word of honor. A joke is a joke, but I don't want to joke about stuff like this. When he dies, I'll be robbed, like. I'll have no more father."

"You love your old man?"

Wilhelm grasped at this. "Of course, of course I love him. My father. My mother—" As he said this there was a great pull at the very center of his soul. When a fish strikes the line you feel the live force in your hand. A mysterious being beneath the water, driven by hunger, has taken the hook and rushes away and fights, writhing. Wilhelm never identified what struck within him. It did not reveal itself. It got away.

And Tamkin, the confuser of the imagination, began to tell, or to fabricate, the strange history of *his* father. "He was a great singer," he said. "He left us five kids because he fell in love with an opera soprano. I never held it against him, but admired the way he followed the life-principle. I wanted to do the same. Because of unhappiness, at a certain age, the brain starts to die back." (True, true! thought Wilhelm) "Twenty years later I was doing experiments in Eastman Kodak, Rochester, and I found the old fellow. He had five more children." (False, false!) "He wept; he was ashamed. I had nothing against him. I naturally felt strange."

"My dad is something of a stranger to me, too," said Wilhelm, and he began to muse. Where is the familiar person he used to be? Or I used to be? Catherine—she won't even talk to me any more, my own sister. It may not be so much my trouble that Papa turns his back on as my confusion. It's too much. The ruins of life, and on top of that confusion—chaos and old night. Is it an easier farewell for Dad if we don't part friends? He should maybe do it angrily—"Blast you with my curse!" And why, Wilhelm further asked, should he or anybody else pity me; or why should I be pitied sooner than another fellow? It is my childish mind that thinks people are ready to give it just because you need it.

Then Wilhelm began to think about his own two sons and to wonder how he appeared to them, and what they would think of him. Right now he had an advantage through baseball. When he went to fetch them, to go to Ebbets Field, though, he was not himself. He put on a front but he felt as if he had swallowed a fistful of sand. The strange, familiar house, horribly awkward; the dog, Scissors, rolled over on his back and barked and whined. Wilhelm acted as if there were nothing irregular, but a weary heaviness came over him. On the way to Flatbush he would think up anecdotes about old Pigtown and Charlie Ebbets for the boys and reminiscences of the old stars, but it was very heavy going. They did not know how much he cared for them. No. It hurt him greatly and he blamed Margaret for turning them against him. She wanted to ruin him, while she wore the mask of kindness. Up in Roxbury he had to go and explain to the priest, who was not sympathetic. They don't care about individuals, their rules come first. Olive said she would marry him outside the Church when he was divorced. But Margaret would not let go. Olive's father was a pretty decent old guy, an osteopath, and he understood what it was all about. Finally he said, "See here, I have to advise Olive. She is asking me. I am mostly a freethinker myself, but the girl has to live in this town." And by now Wilhelm and Olive had had a great many troubles and she was beginning to dread his days in Roxbury, she said. He trembled at offending this small, pretty, dark girl whom he adored. When she would get up late on Sunday morning she would wake him almost in tears at being late for Mass. He would try to help her hitch her garters and smooth out her slip and dress and even put on her hat with shaky hands; then he would rush her to church and drive in second gear in his forgetful way, trying to apologize and to calm her. She got out a block from church to avoid gossip. Even so she loved him, and she would have married him if he had obtained the divorce. But Margaret must have sensed this. Margaret would tell him he did not really want a divorce; he was afraid of it. He cried, "Take everything I've got, Margaret. Let me go to Reno. Don't you want to marry again?" No. She went out with other men, but took his money. She lived in order to punish him.

Dr. Tamkin told Wilhelm, "Your dad is jealous of you."

Wilhelm smiled. "Of *me*? That's rich."

"Sure. People are always jealous of a man who leaves his wife."

"Oh," said Wilhelm scornfully. "When it comes to wives he wouldn't have to envy me."

"Yes, and your wife envies you, too. She thinks, He's free and goes with young women. Is she getting old?"

"Not exactly old," said Wilhelm, whom the mention of his wife made sad. Twenty years ago, in a neat blue wool suit, in a soft hat made of the same cloth—he could plainly see her. He stooped his yellow head and looked under the hat at her clear, simple face, her living eyes moving, her straight small nose, her jaw beautifully, painfully clear in its form. It was a cool day, but he smelled the odor of pines in the sun, in the granite canyon. Just south of Santa Barbara, this was.

"She's forty-some years old," he said.

"I was married to a lush," said Tamkin. "A painful alcoholic. I couldn't take her out to dinner because she'd say she was going to the ladies' toilet and disappear into the bar. I'd ask the bartenders they shouldn't serve her. But I loved her deeply. She was the most spiritual woman of my entire experience."

"Where is she now?"

"Drowned," said Tamkin. "At Provincetown, Cape Cod. It must have been a suicide. She was that way—suicidal. I tried everything in my power to cure her. Because," said Tamkin, "my real calling is to be a healer. I get wounded. I suffer from it. I would like to escape from the sicknesses of others, but I can't. I am only on loan to myself, so to speak. I belong to humanity."

Liar! Wilhelm inwardly called him. Nasty lies. He invented a woman and killed her off and then called himself a healer, and made himself so earnest he looked like a bad-natured sheep. He's a puffed-up little bogus and humbug with smelly feet. A doctor! A doctor would wash himself. He believes he's making a terrific impression, and he practically invites you to take off your hat when he talks about himself; and he thinks he has an imagination, but he hasn't, neither is he smart.

Then what am I doing with him here, and why did I give him the seven hundred dollars? thought Wilhelm.

Oh, this was a day of reckoning. It was a day, he thought, on which, willing or not, he would take a good close look at the truth. He breathed hard and his misshapen hat came low upon his congested dark blond face. A rude look. Tamkin was a charlatan, and furthermore he was desperate. And furthermore, Wilhelm had always known this about him. But he appeared to have worked it out at the back of his mind that Tamkin for thirty or forty years had gotten through many a tight place, that he would get through this crisis too and bring him, Wilhelm, to safety also. And Wilhelm realized that he was on Tamkin's back. It made him feel that he had virtually left the ground and was riding upon the other man. He was in the air. It was for Tamkin to take the steps.

The doctor, if he was a doctor, did not look anxious. But then his face did not have much variety. Talking always about spontaneous emotion and open receptors and free impulses, he was about as expressive as a pincushion. When his hypnotic spell failed, his big underlip made him look weak-minded. Fear stared from his eyes, sometimes, so humble as to make you sorry for him. Once or twice Wilhelm had seen that look. Like a dog, he thought. Perhaps he didn't look it now, but he was very nervous. Wilhelm knew, but he could not afford to recognize this too openly. The doctor needed a little room, a little time. He should not be pressed now. So Tamkin went on, telling his tales.

Wilhelm said to himself, I am on his back—his back. I gambled seven hundred bucks, so I must take this ride. I have to go along with him. It's too late. I can't get off.

"You know," Tamkin said, "that blind old man Rappaport—he's pretty close to totally blind—is one of the most interesting personalities around here. If you could only get him to tell his true story. It's fascinating. This is what he told me. You often hear about bigamists with a secret life. But this old man never hid anything from anybody. He's a regular patriarch. Now, I'll tell you what he did. He had two whole families, separate and apart, one in Williamsburg and the other in the Bronx. The two wives knew about each other. The wife in the Bronx was younger; she's close to seventy now. When he got sore at one wife he went to live with the other one. Meanwhile he ran his chicken business in New Jersey. By one wife he had four kids, and by the other six. They're all grown, but they never have met their half-brothers and sisters and don't want to. The whole bunch of them are listed in the telephone book."

"I can't believe it," said Wilhelm.

"He told me this himself. And do you know what else? While he had his eyesight he used to read a lot, but the only books he would read were by Theodore Roosevelt. He had a set in each of the places where he lived, and he brought his kids up on those books."

"Please," said Wilhelm, "don't feed me any more of this stuff, will you? Kindly do not—"

"In telling you this," said Tamkin with one of his hypnotic subtleties, "I do have a motive. I want you to see how some people free themselves from morbid guilt feelings and follow their instincts. Innately, the female knows how to cripple by sickening a man with guilt. It is a very special *de*struct, and she sends her curse to make a fellow impotent. As if she says, 'Unless I allow it, you will never more be a man.' But men like my old dad or Mr. Rappaport answer, 'Woman, what art thou to me?' You can't do that yet. You're a halfway case. You want to follow your instinct, but you're too worried still. For instance, about your kids—"

"Now look here," said Wilhelm, stamping his feet. "One thing! Don't bring up my boys. Just lay off."

"I was only going to say that they are better off than with conflicts in the home."

"I'm deprived of my children." Wilhelm bit his lip. It was too late to turn away. The anguish struck him. "I pay and pay. I never see them. They grow up without me. She makes them like herself. She'll bring them up to be my enemies. Please let's not talk about this."

But Tamkin said, "Why do you let her make you suffer so? It defeats the original object in leaving her. Don't play her game. Now, Wilhelm, I'm trying to do you some good. I want to tell you, don't marry suffering. Some people do. They get married to it, and sleep and eat together, just as husband and wife. If they go with joy they think it's adultery."

When Wilhelm heard this he had, in spite of himself, to admit that there was a great deal in Tamkin's words. Yes, thought Wilhelm, suffering is the only kind of life they are sure they can have, and if they quit suffering they're afraid they'll have nothing. He knows it. This time the faker knows what he's talking about.

Looking at Tamkin he believed he saw all this confessed from his usually barren face. Yes, yes, he too. One hundred falsehoods, but at last one truth. Howling like a wolf from the city window. No one can bear it any more. Everyone is so full of it that at last everybody must proclaim it. It! It!

Then suddenly Wilhelm rose and said, "That's enough of this. Tamkin, let's go back to the market."

"I haven't finished my melon."

"Never mind that. You've had enough to eat. I want to go back."

Dr. Tamkin slid the two checks across the table. "Who paid yesterday? It's your turn, I think."

It was not until they were leaving the cafeteria that Wilhelm remembered definitely that he had paid yesterday too. But it wasn't worth arguing about.

Tamkin kept repeating as they walked down the street that there were many who were dedicated to suffering. But he told Wilhelm, "I'm optimistic in your case, and I have seen a world of maladjustment. There's hope for you. You don't really want to destroy yourself. You're trying hard to keep your feelings open, Wilhelm. I can see it. Seven per cent of this country is committing suicide by alcohol. Another three, maybe, narcotics. Another sixty just fading away into dust by boredom. Twenty more who have sold their souls to the Devil. Then there's a small percentage of those who want to live. That's the only significant thing in the whole world of today. Those are the only two classes of people there are. Some want to live, but the great majority don't." This fantastic Tamkin began to surpass himself. "They don't. Or else, why these wars? I'll tell you more," he said. "The love of the dying amounts to one thing; they want you to die with them. It's because they love you. Make no mistake."

True, true! thought Wilhelm, profoundly moved by these revelations. How does he know these things? How can he be such a jerk, and even perhaps an operator, a swindler, and understand so well what gives? I believe what he says. It simplifies much—everything. People are dropping like flies. I am trying to stay alive and work too hard at it. That's what's turning my brains. This working hard defeats its own end. At what point should I start over? Let me go back a ways and try once more.

Only a few hundred yards separated the cafeteria from the broker's, and within that short space Wilhelm turned again, in measurable degrees, from these wide considerations to the problems of the moment. The closer he approached to the market, the more Wilhelm had to think about money.

They passed the newsreel theater where the ragged shoeshine kids called after them. The same old bearded man with his bandaged beggar face and his tiny ragged feet and the old press clipping on his fiddle case to prove he had once been a concert violinist, pointed his bow at Wilhelm, saying, "You!" Wilhelm went by with worried eyes, bent on crossing Seventy-second Street. In full tumult the great afternoon current raced for Columbus Circle, where the mouth of midtown stood open and the skyscrapers gave back the yellow fire of the sun.

As they approached the polished stone front of the new office building, Dr. Tamkin said, "Well, isn't that old Rappaport by the door? I think he should carry a white cane, but he will never admit there's a single thing the matter with his eyes."

Mr. Rappaport did not stand well; his knees were sunk, while his pelvis only half filled his trousers. His suspenders held them, gaping.

He stopped Wilhelm with an extended hand, having somehow recognized him. In his deep voice he commanded him, "Take me to the cigar store."

"You want me—? Tamkin!" Wilhelm whispered, "You take him."

Tamkin shook his head. "He wants you. Don't refuse the old gentleman." Significantly he said in a lower voice. "This minute is another instance of the 'here-and-now.' You have to live in this very minute, and you don't want to. A man asks you for help. Don't think of the market. It won't run away. Show your respect to the old boy. Go ahead. That may be more valuable."

"Take me," said the old chicken merchant again.

Greatly annoyed, Wilhelm wrinkled his face at Tamkin. He took the old man's big but light elbow at the bone. "Well, let's step on it," he said. "Or wait—I want to have a look at the board first to see how we're doing."

But Tamkin had already started Mr. Rappaport forward. He was walking, and he scolded Wilhelm, saying, "Don't leave me standing in the middle of the sidewalk. I'm afraid to get knocked over."

"Let's get a move on. Come." Wilhelm urged him as Tamkin went into the broker's.

The traffic seemed to come down Broadway out of the sky, where the hot spokes of the sun rolled from the south. Hot, stony odors rose from the subway grating in the street.

"These teen-age hoodlums worry me. I'm ascared of these Puerto Rican kids, and these young characters who take dope," said Mr. Rappaport. "They go around all hopped up."

"Hoodlums?" said Wilhelm. "I went to the cemetery and my mother's stone bench was split. I could have broken somebody's neck for that. Which store do you go to?"

"Across Broadway. That La Magnita sign next door to the Automat."

"What's the matter with this store here on this side?"

"They don't carry my brand, that's what's the matter."

Wilhelm cursed, but checked the words.

"What are you talking?"

"Those damn taxis," said Wilhelm. "They want to run everybody down."

They entered the cool, odorous shop. Mr. Rappaport put away his large cigars with great care in various pockets while Wilhelm muttered, "Come on, you old creeper. What a poky old character! The whole world waits on him." Rappaport did not offer Wilhelm a cigar, but, holding one up, he asked, "What do you say at the size of these, huh? They're Churchill-type cigars."

He barely crawls along, thought Wilhelm. His pants are dropping off because he hasn't got enough flesh for them to stick to. He's almost blind, and covered with spots, but this old man still makes money in the market. Is loaded with dough, probably. And I bet he doesn't give his children any. Some of them must be in their fifties. This is what keeps middle-aged men as children. He's master over the dough. Think—just think! Who controls everything? Old men of this type. Without needs. They don't need therefore they have. I need, therefore I don't have. That would be too easy.

"I'm older even than Churchill," said Rappaport.

Now he wanted to talk! But if you asked him a question in the market, he couldn't be bothered to answer.

"I bet you are," said Wilhelm. "Come, let's get going."

"I was a fighter, too, like Churchill," said the old man. "When we licked Spain I went into the Navy. Yes, I was a gob that time.[2] What did I have to lose? Nothing. After the battle of San Juan Hill, Teddy Roosevelt kicked me off the beach."

"Come, watch the curb," said Wilhelm.

"I was curious and wanted to see what went on. I didn't have no business there, but I took a boat and rowed myself to the beach. Two of our guys was dead, layin' under the American flag to keep the flies off. So I says to the guy on duty, there, who was the sentry, 'Let's have a look at these guys. I want to see what went on here,' and he says, 'Naw,' but I talked him into it. So he took off the flag and there were these two tall guys, both gentlemen, lying in their boots. They was very tall. The two of them had long mustaches. They were high-society boys. I think one of them was called Fish, from up the Hudson, a big-shot family. When I looked up, there was Teddy Roosevelt, with his hat off, and he was looking at these fellows, the only ones who got killed there. Then he says to me, "What's the Navy want here? Have you got orders?' 'No, sir,' I says to him. 'Well, get the hell off the beach, then.' "

Old Rappaport was very proud of this memory. "Everything he said had such snap, such class. Man! I love that Teddy Roosevelt," he said, "I love him!"

Ah, what people are! He is almost not with us, and his life is nearly gone, but T. R. once yelled at him, so he loves him. I guess it is love, too. Wilhelm smiled. So maybe the rest of Tamkin's story was true, about the ten children and the wives and the telephone directory.

He said, "Come on, come on, Mr. Rappaport," and hurried the old man back by the large hollow elbow; he gripped it through the thin cotton cloth. Re-entering the brokerage office where under the lights the tumblers were speeding with the clack of drumsticks upon wooden blocks, more than ever resembling a Chinese theater, Wilhelm strained his eyes to see the board.

The lard figures were unfamiliar. That amount couldn't be lard! They must have put the figures in the wrong slot. He traced the line back to the margin. It was down to .19, and had dropped twenty points since noon. And what about the contract of rye? It had sunk back to its earlier position, and they had lost their chance to sell.

Old Mr. Rappaport said to Wilhelm, "Read me my wheat figure."

"Oh, leave me alone for a minute," he said, and positively hid his face from the old man behind one hand. He looked for Tamkin, Tamkin's bald head, or Tamkin with his gray straw and the cocoa-colored band. He couldn't see him. Where was he? The seats next to

---

2. The U.S. defeated Spain in the Spanish-American War in 1898. A "gob" is a sailor. Winston Churchill (1874–1965) was Britain's Prime Minister during World War II.

Rowland were taken by strangers. He thrust himself over the one on the aisle, Mr. Rappaport's former place, and pushed at the back of the chair until the new occupant, a red-headed man with a thin, determined face, leaned forward to get out of his way but would not surrender the seat. "Where's Tamkin?" Wilhelm asked Rowland.

"Gee, I don't know. Is anything wrong?"

"You must have seen him. He came in a while back."

"No, but I didn't."

Wilhelm fumbled out a pencil from the top pocket of his coat and began to make calculations. His very fingers were numb, and in his agitation he was afraid he made mistakes with the decimal points and went over the subtraction and multiplication like a schoolboy at an exam. His heart, accustomed to many sorts of crisis, was now in a new panic. And, as he had dreaded, he was wiped out. It was unnecessary to ask the German manager. He could see for himself that the electronic bookkeeping device must have closed him out. The manager probably had known that Tamkin wasn't to be trusted, and on that first day he might have warned him. But you couldn't expect him to interfere.

"You get hit?" said Mr. Rowland.

And Wilhelm, quite coolly, said, "Oh, it could have been worse, I guess." He put the piece of paper into his pocket with its cigarette butts and packets of pills. The lie helped him out—although, for a moment, he was afraid he would cry. But he hardened himself. The hardening effort made a violent, vertical pain go through his chest, like that caused by a pocket of air under the collar bones. To the old chicken millionaire, who by this time had become acquainted with the drop in rye and lard, he also denied that anything serious had happened. "It's just one of those temporary slumps. Nothing to be scared about," he said, and remained in possession of himself. His need to cry, like someone in a crowd, pushed and jostled and abused him from behind, and Wilhelm did not dare turn. He said to himself, I will not cry in front of these people. I'll be damned if I'll break down in front of them like a kid, even though I never expect to see them again. No! No! And yet his unshed tears rose and rose and he looked like a man about to drown. But when they talked to him, he answered very distinctly. He tried to speak proudly.

". . . going away?" he heard Rowland ask.

"What?"

"I thought you might be going away too. Tamkin said he was going to Maine this summer for his vacation."

"Oh, going away?"

Wilhelm broke off and went to look for Tamkin in the men's toilet. Across the corridor was the room where the machinery of the board was housed. It hummed and whirred like mechanical birds, and the tubes glittered in the dark. A couple of businessmen with cigarettes in their fingers were having a conversation in the lavatory.

At the top of the closet door sat a gray straw hat with a cocoa-colored band. "Tamkin," said Wilhelm. He tried to identify the feet below the door. "Are you in there, Doctor Tamkin?" he said with stifled anger. "Answer me. It's Wilhelm."

The hat was taken down, the latch lifted, and a stranger came out who looked at him with annoyance.

"You waiting?" said one of the businessmen. He was warning Wilhelm that he was out of turn.

"Me? Not me," said Wilhelm. "I'm looking for a fellow."

Bitterly angry, he said to himself that Tamkin would pay him the two hundred dollars at least, his share of the original deposit. "And before he takes the train to Maine, too. Before he spends a penny on vacation—that liar! We went into this as equal partners."

VII

I was the man beneath; Tamkin was on my back, and I thought I was on his. He made me carry him, too, besides Margaret. Like this they ride on me with hoofs and claws. Tear me to pieces, stamp on me and break my bones.

Once more the hoary old fiddler pointed his bow at Wilhelm as he hurried by. Wilhelm rejected his begging and denied the omen. He dodged heavily through traffic and with his quick, small steps ran up the lower stairway of the Gloriana Hotel with its dark-tinted mirrors, kind to people's defects. From the lobby he phoned Tamkin's room, and when no one answered he took the elevator up. A rouged woman in her fifties with a mink stole led three tiny dogs on a leash, high-strung creatures with prominent black eyes, like dwarf deer, and legs like twigs. This was the eccentric Estonian lady who had been moved with her pets to the twelfth floor.

She identified Wilhelm. "You are Doctor Adler's son," she said. Formally, he nodded.

"I am a dear friend of your father."

He stood in the corner and would not meet her glance, and she thought he was snubbing her and made a mental note to speak of it to the doctor.

The linen-wagon stood at Tamkin's door, and the chambermaid's key with its big brass tongue was in the lock.

"Has Doctor Tamkin been here?" he asked her.

"No, I haven't seen him."

Wilhelm came in, however, to look around. He examined the photos on the desk, trying to connect the faces with the strange people in Tamkin's stories. Big, heavy volumes were stacked under the double-pronged TV aerial. *Science and Sanity*,[3] he read, and there were several books of poetry. The *Wall Street Journal* hung in separate sheets from the bed-table under the weight of the silver water jug. A bathrobe with lightning streaks of red and white was

3. A work by Korzybski.

laid across the foot of the bed with a pair of expensive batik pajamas. It was a box of a room, but from the windows you saw the river as far uptown as the bridge, as far downtown as Hoboken. What lay between was deep, azure, dirty, complex, crystal, rusty, with the red bones of new apartments rising on the bluffs of New Jersey, and huge liners in their berths, the tugs with matted beards of cordage. Even the brackish tidal river smell rose this high, like the smell of mop water. From every side he heard pianos, and the voices of men and women singing scales and opera, all mixed, and the sounds of pigeons on the ledges.

Again Wilhelm took the phone. "Can you locate Doctor Tamkin in the lobby for me?" he asked. And when the operator reported that she could not, Wilhelm gave the number of his father's room, but Dr. Adler was not in either. "Well, please give me the masseur. I say the massage room. Don't you understand me? The men's health club. Yes, Max Schilper's—how am I supposed to know the name of it?"

There a strange voice said, "Toktor Adler?" It was the old Czech prizefighter with the deformed nose and ears who was attendant down there and gave out soap, sheets, and sandals. He went away. A hollow endless silence followed. Wilhelm flickered the receiver with his nails, whistled into it, but could not summon either the attendant or the operator.

The maid saw him examining the bottles of pills on Tamkin's table and seemed suspicious of him. He was running low on Phenaphen pills and was looking for something else. But he swallowed one of his own tablets and went out and rang again for the elevator. He went down to the health club. Through the steamy windows, when he emerged, he saw the reflection of the swimming pool swirling green at the bottom of the lowest stairway. He went through the locker-room curtains. Two men wrapped in towels were playing Ping-pong. They were awkward and the ball bounded high. The Negro in the toilet was shining shoes. He did not know Dr. Adler by name, and Wilhelm descended to the message room. On the tables naked men were lying. It was not a brightly lighted place, and it was very hot, and under the white faint moons of the ceiling shone pale skins. Calendar pictures of pretty girls dressed in tiny fringes were pinned on the wall. On the first table, eyes deeply shut in heavy silent luxury lay a man with a full square beard and short legs, stocky and black-haired. He might have been an orthodox Russian. Wrapped in a sheet, waiting, the man beside him was newly shaved and red from the steambath. He had a big happy face and was dreaming. And after him was an athlete, strikingly muscled, powerful and young, with a strong white curve to his genital and a half-angry smile on his mouth. Dr. Adler was on the fourth table, and Wilhelm stood over his father's pale, slight body. His ribs were narrow and small, his belly round, white and high. It had its own being, like something separate. His thighs were weak, the muscles of his arms had fallen, his throat was creased.

The masseur in his undershirt bent and whispered in his ear, "It's your son," and Dr. Adler opened his eyes into Wilhelm's face. At once he saw the trouble in it, and by an instantaneous reflex he removed himself from the danger of contagion, and he said serenely, "Well, have you taken my advice, Wilky?"

"Oh, Dad," said Wilhelm.

"To take a swim and get a massage?"

"Did you get my note?" said Wilhelm.

"Yes, but I'm afraid you'll have to ask somebody else, because I can't. I had no idea you were so low on funds. How did you let it happen? Didn't you lay anything aside?"

"Oh, please, Dad," said Wilhelm, almost bringing his hands together in a clasp.

"I'm sorry," said the doctor. "I really am. But I have set up a rule. I've thought about it, I believe it is a good rule, and I don't want to change it. You haven't acted wisely. What's the matter?"

"Everything. Just everything. What isn't? I did have a little, but I haven't been very smart."

"You took some gamble? You lost it? Was it Tamkin? I told you, Wilky, not to build on that Tamkin. Did you? I suspect—"

"Yes, Dad, I'm afraid I trusted him."

Dr. Adler surrendered his arm to the masseur, who was using wintergreen oil.

"Trusted! And got taken?"

"I'm afraid I kind of—" Wilhelm glanced at the masseur but he was absorbed in his work. He probably did not listen to conversations. "I did. I might as well say it. I should have listened to you."

"Well, I won't remind you how often I warned you. It must be very painful."

"Yes, Father, it is."

"I don't know how many times you have to be burned in order to learn something. The same mistakes, over and over."

"I couldn't agree with you more," said Wilhelm with a face of despair. "You're so right, Father. It's the same mistakes, and I get burned again and again. I can't seem to—I'm stupid, Dad, I just can't breathe. My chest is all up—I feel choked. I just simply can't catch my breath."

He stared at his father's nakedness. Presently he became aware that Dr. Adler was making an effort to keep his temper. He was on the verge of an explosion. Wilhelm hung his face and said, "Nobody likes bad luck, eh Dad?"

"So! It's bad luck, now. A minute ago it was stupidity."

"It is stupidity—it's some of both. It's true that I can't learn. But I—"

"I don't want to listen to the details," said his father. "And I want you to understand that I'm too old to take on new burdens. I'm just too old to do it. And people who will just wait for help—must *wait* for help. They have got to stop waiting."

"It isn't all a question of money—there are other things a father can give to a son." He lifted up his gray eyes and his nostrils grew wide with a look of suffering appeal that stirred his father even more deeply against him.

He warningly said to him, "Look out, Wilky, you're tiring my patience very much."

"I try not to. But one word from you, just a word, would go a long way. I've never asked you for very much. But you are not a kind man, Father. You don't give the little bit I beg you for."

He recognized that his father was now furiously angry. Dr. Adler started to say something, and then raised himself and gathered the sheet over him as he did so. His mouth opened, wide, dark, twisted, and he said to Wilhelm, "You want to make yourself into my cross. But I am not going to pick up a cross. I'll see you dead, Wilky, by Christ, before I let you do that to me."

"Father, listen! Listen!"

"Go away from me now. It's torture for me to look at you, you slob!" cried Dr. Adler.

Wilhelm's blood rose up madly, in anger equal to his father's, but then it sank down and left him helplessly captive to misery. He said stiffly, and with a strange sort of formality, "Okay, Dad. That'll be enough. That's about all we should say." And he stalked out heavily by the door adjacent to the swimming pool and the steam room, and labored up two long flights from the basement. Once more he took the elevator to the lobby on the mezzanine.

He inquired at the desk for Dr. Tamkin.

The clerk said, "No, I haven't seen him. But I think there's something in the box for you."

"Me? Give it here," said Wilhelm and opened a telephone message from his wife. It read, "Please phone Mrs. Wilhelm on return. Urgent."

Whenever he received an urgent message from his wife he was always thrown into a great fear for the children. He ran to the phone booth, spilled out the change from his pockets and onto the little curved steel shelf under the telephone, and dialed the Digby number.

"Yes?" said his wife. Scissors barked in the parlor.

"Margaret?"

"Yes, hello." They never exchanged any other greeting. She instantly knew his voice.

"The boys all right?"

"They're out on their bicycles. Why shouldn't they be all right?

Scissors, quiet!"

"Your message scared me," he said. "I wish you wouldn't make 'urgent' so common."

"I had something to tell you."

Her familiar unbending voice awakened in him a kind of hungry longing, not for Margaret but for the peace he had once known.

"You sent me a postdated check," she said. "I can't allow that. It's already five days past the first. You dated your check for the twelfth."

"Well, I have no money. I haven't got it. You can't send me to prison for that. I'll be lucky if I can raise it by the twelfth."

She answered, "You better get it, Tommy."

"Yes? What for?" he said. "Tell me. For the sake of what? To tell lies about me to everyone? You—"

She cut him off. "You know what for. I've got the boys to bring up."

Wilhelm in the narrow booth broke into a heavy sweat. He dropped his head and shrugged while with his fingers he arranged nickels, dimes, and quarters in rows. "I'm doing my best," he said. "I've had some bad luck. As a matter of fact, it's been so bad that I don't know where I am. I couldn't tell you what day of the week this is. I can't think straight. I'd better not even try. This has been one of those days, Margaret. May I never live to go through another like it. I mean that with all my heart. So I'm not going to try to do any thinking today. Tomorrow I'm going to see some guys. One is a sales manager. The other is in television. But not to act," he hastily added. "On the business end."

"That's just some more of your talk, Tommy," she said. "You ought to patch things up with Rojax Corporation. They'd take you back. You've got to stop thinking like a youngster."

"What do you mean?"

"Well," she said, measured and unbending, remorselessly unbending, "you still think like a youngster. But you can't do that any more. Every other day you want to make a new start. But in eighteen years you'll be eligible for retirement. Nobody wants to hire a new man of your age."

"I know. But listen, you don't have to sound so hard. I can't get on my knees to them. And really you don't have to sound so hard. I haven't done you so much harm."

"Tommy, I have to chase you and ask you for money that you owe us, and I hate it."

She hated also to be told that her voice was hard.

"I'm making an effort to control myself," she told him.

He could picture her, her graying bangs cut with strict fixity above her pretty, decisive face. She prided herself on being fair-minded. We could not bear, he thought, to know what we do. Even though blood is spilled. Even though the breath of life is taken from someone's nostrils. This is the way of the weak; quiet and fair. And then smash! They smash!

"Rojax take me back? I'd have to crawl back. They don't need me. After so many years I should have got stock in the firm. How can I support the three of you, and live myself, on half the territory? And why should I even try when you won't lift a finger to help? I sent you back to school, didn't I? At that time you said—"

His voice was rising. She did not like that and intercepted him. "You misunderstood me," she said.

"You must realize you're killing me. You can't be as blind as all that. Thou shalt not kill! Don't you remember that?"

She said, "You're just raving now. When you calm down it'll be different. I have great confidence in your earning ability."

"Margaret, you don't grasp the situation. You'll have to get a job."

"Absolutely not. I'm not going to have two young children running loose."

"They're not babies," Wilhelm said. "Tommy is fourteen. Paulie is going to be ten."

"Look," Margaret said in her deliberate manner. "We can't continue this conversation if you're going to yell so, Tommy. They're at a dangerous age. There are teen-aged gangs—the parents working, or the families broken up."

Once again she was reminding him that it was he who had left her. She had the bringing up of the children as her burden, while he must expect to pay the price of his freedom.

Freedom! he thought with consuming bitterness. Ashes in his mouth, not freedom. Give me my children. For they are mine too.

Can you be the woman I lived with? he started to say. Have you forgotten that we slept so long together? Must you now deal with me like this, and have no mercy?

He would be better off with Margaret again than he was today. This was what she wanted to make him feel, and she drove it home. "Are you in misery?" she was saying. "But you have deserved it." And he could not return to her any more than he could beg Rojax to take him back. If it cost him his life, he could not. Margaret had ruined him with Olive. She hit him and hit him, beat him, battered him, wanted to beat the very life out of him.

"Margaret, I want you please to reconsider about work. You have that degree now. Why did I pay your tuition?"

"Because it seemed practical. But it isn't. Growing boys need parental authority and a home."

He begged her, "Margaret, go easy on me. You ought to. I'm at the end of my rope and feel that I'm suffocating. You don't want to be responsible for a person's destruction. You've got to let up. I feel I'm about to burst." His face had expanded. He struck a blow upon the tin and wood and nails of the wall of the booth. "You've got to let me breathe. If I should keel over, what then? And it's something I can never understand about you. How you can treat someone like this whom you lived with so long. Who gave you the best of himself. Who tried. Who loved you." Merely to pronounce the word "love" made him tremble.

"Ah," she said with a sharp breath. "Now we're coming to it. How did you imagine it was going to be—big shot? Everything made smooth for you? I thought you were leading up to this."

She had not, perhaps, intended to reply as harshly as she did, but she brooded a great deal and now she could not forbear to punish him and make him feel pains like those she had to undergo.

He struck the wall again, this time with his knuckles, and he had scarcely enough air in his lungs to speak in a whisper, because his heart pushed upward with a frightful pressure. He got up and stamped his feet in the narrow enclosure.

"Haven't I always done my best?" he yelled, though his voice sounded weak and thin to his own ears. "Everything comes from me and nothing back again to me. There's no law that'll punish this, but you are committing a crime against me. Before God—and that's no joke. I mean that. Before God! Sooner or later the boys will know it."

In a firm tone, levelly, Margaret said to him, "I won't stand to be howled at. When you can speak normally and have something sensible to say I'll listen. But not to this." She hung up.

Wilhelm tried to tear the apparatus from the wall. He ground his teeth and seized the black box with insane digging fingers and made a stifled cry and pulled. Then he saw an elderly lady staring through the glass door, utterly appalled by him, and he ran from the booth, leaving a large amount of change on the shelf. He hurried down the stairs and into the street.

On Broadway it was still bright afternoon and the gassy air was almost motionless under the leaden spokes of sunlight, and sawdust footprints lay about the doorways of butcher shops and fruit stores. And the great, great crowd, the inexhaustible current of millions of every race and kind pouring out, pressing round, of every age, of every genius, possessors of every human secret, antique and future, in every face the refinement of one particular motive or essence—I *labor, I spend, I strive, I design, I love, I cling, I uphold, I give way, I envy, I long, I scorn, I die, I hide, I want.* Faster, much faster than any man could make the tally. The sidewalks were wider than any causeway; the street itself was immense, and it quaked and gleamed and it seemed to Wilhelm to throb at the last limit of endurance. And although the sunlight appeared like a broad tissue, its actual weight made him feel like a drunkard.

"I'll get a divorce if it's the last thing I do," he swore. "As for Dad—As for Dad—I'll have to sell the car for junk and pay the hotel. I'll have to go on my knees to Olive and say, 'Stand by me a while. Don't let her win. Olive!' " And he thought, I'll try to start again with Olive. In fact, I must. Olive loves me. Olive—

Beside a row of limousines near the curb he thought he saw Dr. Tamkin. Of course he had been mistaken before about the hat with the cocoa-colored band and didn't want to make the same mistake twice. But wasn't that Tamkin who was speaking so earnestly, with pointed shoulders, to someone under the canopy of the funeral parlor? For this was a huge funeral. He looked for the singular face under the dark gray, fashionable hatbrim. There were two open cars filled with flowers, and a policeman tried to keep a path open to pedestrians. Right at the canopy-pole, now wasn't that that damned Tamkin talking away with a solemn face, gesticulating with an open hand?

"Tamkin!" shouted Wilhelm, going forward. But he was pushed to the side by a policeman clutching his nightstick at both ends, like a rolling pin. Wilhelm was even farther from Tamkin now, and swore under his breath at the cop who continued to press him back, back, belly and ribs, saying, "Keep it moving there, please," his face red with impatient sweat, his brows like red fur. Wilhelm said to him haughtily, "You shouldn't push people like this."

The policeman, however, was not really to blame. He had been ordered to keep a way clear. Wilhelm was moved forward by the pressure of the crowd.

He cried, "Tamkin!"

But Tamkin was gone. Or rather, it was he himself who was carried from the street into the chapel. The pressure ended inside, where it was dark and cool. The flow of fan-driven air dried his face, which he wiped hard with his handkerchief to stop the slight salt itch. He gave a sigh when he heard the organ notes that stirred and breathed from the pipes and he saw people in the pews. Men in formal clothes and black homburgs strode softly back and forth on the cork floor, up and down the center aisle. The white of the stained glass was like mother-of-pearl, the blue of the Star of David like velvet ribbon.

Well, thought Wilhelm, if that was Tamkin outside I might as well wait for him here where it's cool. Funny, he never mentioned he had a funeral to go to today. But that's just like the guy.

But within a few minutes he had forgotten Tamkin. He stood along the wall with others and looked toward the coffin and the slow line that was moving past it, gazing at the face of the dead. Presently he too was in this line, and slowly, slowly, foot by foot, the beating of his heart anxious, thick, frightening, but somehow also rich, he neared the coffin and paused for his turn, and gazed down. He caught his breath when he looked at the corpse, and his face swelled, his eyes shone hugely with instant tears.

The dead man was gray-haired. He had two large waves of gray hair at the front. But he was not old. His face was long, and he had a bony nose, slightly, delicately twisted. His brows were raised as though he had sunk into the final thought. Now at last he was with it, after the end of all distractions, and when his flesh was no longer flesh. And by this meditative look Wilhelm was so struck that he could not go away. In spite of the tinge of horror, and then the splash of heartsickness that he felt, he could not go. He stepped out of line and remained beside the coffin; his eyes filled silently and through his still tears he studied the man as the line of visitors moved with veiled looks past the satin coffin toward the standing bank of lilies, lilacs, roses. With great stifling sorrow, almost admiration, Wilhelm nodded and nodded. On the surface, the dead man with his formal shirt and his tie and silk lapels and his powdered skin looked so proper; only a little beneath so—black, Wilhelm thought, so fallen in the eyes.

Standing a little apart, Wilhelm began to cry. He cried at first softly and from sentiment, but soon from deeper feeling. He sobbed loudly and his face grew distorted and hot, and the tears stung his skin. A man—another human creature, was what first went through his thoughts, but other and different things were torn from him. What'll I do? I'm stripped and kicked out. . . . Oh, Father, what do I ask of you? What'll I do about the kids—Tommy, Paul? My children. And Olive? My dear! Why, why, why—you must protect me against that devil who wants my life. If you want it, then kill me. Take, take it, take it from me."

Soon he was past words, past reason, coherence. He could not stop. The source of all tears had suddenly sprung open within him, black, deep, and hot, and they were pouring out and convulsed his body, bending his stubborn head, bowing his shoulders, twisting his face, crippling the very hands with which he held the handkerchief. His efforts to collect himself were useless. The great knot of ill and grief in his throat swelled upward and he gave in utterly and held his face and wept. He cried with all his heart.

He, alone of all the people in the chapel, was sobbing. No one knew who he was.

One woman said, "Is that perhaps the cousin from New Orleans they were expecting?"

"It must be somebody real close to carry on so."

"Oh my, oh my! To be mourned like that," said one man and looked at Wilhelm's heavy shaken shoulders, his clutched face and whitened fair hair, with wide, glinting, jealous eyes.

"The man's brother, maybe?"

"Oh, I doubt that very much," said another bystander. "They're not alike at all. Night and Day."

The flowers and lights fused ecstatically in Wilhelm's blind, wet eyes; the heavy sea-like music came up to his ears. It poured into him where he had hidden himself in the center of a crowd by the great and happy oblivion of tears. He heard it and sank deeper than sorrow, through torn sobs and cries toward the consummation of his heart's ultimate need.

1956

JACK KEROUAC
1922–1969

"It made me think that everything was about to arrive—the moment when you know all and everything is decided forever." At this moment in Jack Kerouac's novel *On the Road* the narrator and his idol, Dean Moriarty, are high on marijuana and sitting in Birdland—a New York City jazz club of the 1950s—listening to the blind pianist George Shearing. " 'There he is! That's him! Old God! Old God Shearing! Yes! Yes! Yes!' " announces Dean, while the narrator is correspondingly ecstatic. Kerouac's major quality and limitation as a writer is his yearning for affirmative moments like this one in which "everything" arrives.

He was born in Lowell, Massachusetts, of Catholic French-Canadian parents. Memories of Lowell permeate his books, and in later years he moved back to live out his life there with his third wife and invalid mother. As a youth Kerouac played football in high school, then won a scholarship to Columbia University where an injury, combined with other, quite different interests soon caused him to quit the team. Alternating stretches at Columbia with stretches in the navy, his life in the early 1940s is notable mainly for the friendships he made with other aspiring and rebellious young writers, most importantly the poet Allen Ginsberg (also a student at Columbia) and the novelist William Burroughs. With these friends and others Kerouac carried out experiments with drugs and attempted to cultivate unordinary states of consciousness in which life could be transcended through visionary experiences. Such "unordinary" experience might also be gained by going "on the road"; and Kerouac's travels to California and Mexico provide the main substance for much of his fiction, particularly in *On the Road* and *Visions of Cody* (1972). These books are his liveliest versions of "road" life; they celebrate, under various fictional names, the Neal Cassady who was a friend and lover to Kerouac and Ginsberg and whose own violent death occurred just a year before Kerouac's. Other novels, such as *Dr. Sax* (1959) and *Maggie Cassidy* (1959), view with some nostalgia the landscape and people of Kerouac's idealized childhood in Lowell.

His first novel (*The Town and the City*) was published in 1950, but it was not until 1957, with *On the Road*, that be become a celebrity. Much of his fame was due to the publicity generated by what the magazines latched on to as a phenomenon called "The Beat Generation." This generation was presumably composed of young people who were disgusted with or just bored by the "conformist" mentality of the 1950s; with American society's insistence on school, career, marriage—with middle-class orientations in general. Kerouac, as quoted by John Clellon Holmes, described it thus: "It's a sort of furtiveness * * * and a weariness with all the forms, all the conventions of the world. * * * So I guess you might say we're a *beat* generation."

The "Beat" writers were very much a West Coast group with a literary center located in Lawrence Ferlinghetti's City Lights bookstore. Ginsberg, Gregory Corso, Peter Orlovsky, Kerouac, and Ferlinghetti himself gave numerous readings from their works to appreciative audiences at various coffeehouses and poetry centers. Along with Ginsberg's *Howl*, Kerouac's *On the Road* was the most widely read of these works; and although Kerouac's vision of America is much less apocalyptic and critical than Ginsberg's, they both encouraged new kinds of styles in life which were to flower in the 1960s. Kerouac, who liked to drink beer and listen to jazz, had little in common with the counterculture of the sixties; his politics were nonexistent. He never again came close to equaling the success of *On the Road*, and through excesses of various sorts, chiefly alcoholic, he died at age forty-seven, a prophet without much honor even in his own city of Lowell.

As a great affirmer Kerouac has been compared to Whitman and to Thomas Wolfe; but Whitman lived intensely within the language, as Wolfe tried to, and both believed their works had form and shape. Kerouac never succeeded in telling a sustained, interesting story. His books—scarcely novels—proceed by fits and starts, making no attempt to distinguish literature from life, so that real people mingle with fictional ones, and tenses shift from past to present for no apparent reason. He came to believe in a theory of "spontaneous prose," the writing of which he compared at one point to evacuating the bowels. His prose is best at short-range effects: remembered names of things or lists of food from a lunch counter; descriptions of the route by which he travels from one town to another.

Aside from his legendary status as a self-destructive wild man and life-affirmer, Kerouac will be remembered with affection as a comic writer who was able at times to produce charming and funny disparities between the romantic aspiration for "everything" and the realistic ways in which experience actually provides a good deal less than everything. At the beginning of *On the Road*, for example, he sets out to hitch across the country but fails to get a ride, gets rainsoaked instead and eventually takes a bus back to New York City, resolved to start again the next day. "It was my dream that screwed up," the narrator reflects. Kerouac's career and early death suggest a similar pattern. His influences on other writers has not been large; but his undisciplined, passionately enthusiastic version of a dreamed American life remains in the mind.

From On the Road[1]

2

In the month of July 1947, having saved about fifty dollars from old veteran benefits, I was ready to go to the West Coast. My friend Remi Boncoeur had written me a letter from San Francisco, saying

---

1. Chapters 2, 4, and 14 from Part I of *On the Road* deal with the narrator's fiasco of a departure for the West, with a typical moment along the way, and with his return home.

I should come and ship out with him on an around-the-world liner. He swore he could get me into the engine room. I wrote back and said I'd be satisfied with any old freighter so long as I could take a few long Pacific trips and come back with enough money to support myself in my aunt's house while I finished my book. He said he had a shack in Mill City and I would have all the time in the world to write there while we went through the rigmarole of getting the ship. He was living with a girl called Lee Ann; he said she was a marvelous cook and everything would jump. Remi was an old prep-school friend, a Frenchman brought up in Paris and a really mad guy—I didn't know how mad at this time. So he expected me to arrive in ten days. My aunt was all in accord with my trip to the West; she said it would do me good, I'd been working so hard all winter and staying in too much; she even didn't complain when I told her I'd have to hitchhike some. All she wanted was for me to come back in one piece. So, leaving my big half-manuscript sitting on top of my desk, and folding back my comfortable home sheets for the last time one morning, I left with my canvas bag in which a few fundamental things were packed and took off for the Pacific Ocean with the fifty dollars in my pocket.

I'd been poring over maps of the United States in Paterson[2] for months, even reading books about the pioneers and savoring names like Platte and Cimarron and so on, and on the road-map was one long red line called Route 6 that led from the tip of Cape Cod clear to Ely, Nevada, and there dipped down to Los Angeles. I'll just stay on 6 all the way to Ely, I said to myself and confidently started. To get to 6 I had to go up to Bear Mountain. Filled with dreams of what I'd do in Chicago, in Denver, and then finally in San Fran, I took the Seventh Avenue subway to the end of the line at 242nd Street, and there took a trolley into Yonkers; in downtown Yonkers I transferred to an outgoing trolley and went to the city limits on the east bank of the Hudson River. If you drop a rose in the Hudson River at its mysterious source in the Adirondacks, think of all the places it journeys by as it goes to sea forever—think of that wonderful Hudson Valley. I started hitching up the thing. Five scattered rides took me to the desired Bear Mountain Bridge, where Route 6 arched in from New England. It began to rain in torrents when I was let off there. It was mountainous. Route 6 came over the river, wound around a traffic circle, and disappeared into the wilderness. Not only was there no traffic but the rain came down in buckets and I had no shelter. I had to run under some pines to take cover; this did no good; I began crying and swearing and socking myself on the head for being such a damn fool. I was forty miles north of New York; all the way up I'd been worried about the fact that on this, my big opening day, I was only moving north instead

2. Paterson, N.J., birthplace of Kerouac's friend Allen Ginsberg, and the subject of William Carlos Williams's long poem, *Paterson* (1948, 1958).

of the so-longed-for west. Now I was stuck on my northernmost hangup. I ran a quarter-mile to an abandoned cute English-style filling station and stood under the dripping eaves. High up over my head the great hairy Bear Mountain sent down thunderclaps that put the fear of God in me. All I could see were smoky trees and dismal wilderness rising to the skies. "What the hell am I doing up here?" I cursed, I cried for Chicago. "Even now they're all having a big time, they're doing this, I'm not there, when will I get there!"— and so on. Finally a car stopped at the empty filling station; the man and the two women in it wanted to study a map. I stepped right up and gestured in the rain; they consulted; I looked like a maniac, of course, with my hair all wet, my shoes sopping. My shoes, damn fool that I am, were Mexican huaraches, plantlike sieves not fit for the rainy night of America and the raw road night. But the people let me in and rode me *back* to Newburgh, which I accepted as a better alternative than being trapped in the Bear Mountain wilderness all night. "Besides," said the man, "there's no traffic passes through 6. If you want to go to Chicago you'd do better going across the Holland Tunnel in New York and head for Pittsburgh," and I knew he was right. It was my dream that screwed up, the stupid hearthside idea that it would be wonderful to follow one great red line across America instead of trying various roads and routes.

In Newburgh it had stopped raining. I walked down to the river, and I had to ride back to New York in a bus with a delegation of schoolteachers coming back from a weekend in the mountains— chatter-chatter blah-blah, and me swearing for all the time and the money I'd wasted, and telling myself, I wanted to go west and here I've been all day and into the night going up and down, north and south, like something that can't get started. And I swore I'd be in Chicago tomorrow, and made sure of that, taking a bus to Chicago, spending most of my money, and didn't give a damn, just as long as I'd be in Chicago tomorrow.

4

The greatest ride in my life was about to come up, a truck, with a flatboard at the back, with about six or seven boys sprawled out on it, and the drivers, two young blond farmers from Minnesota, were picking up every single soul they found on that road—the most smiling, cheerful couple of handsome bumpkins you could ever wish to see, both wearing cotton shirts and overalls, nothing else; both thick-wristed and earnest, with broad howareyou smiles for anybody and anything that came across their path. I ran up, said "Is there room?" They said, "Sure, hop on, 'sroom for everybody."

I wasn't on the flatboard before the truck roared off; I lurched, a rider grabbed me, and I sat down. Somebody passed a bottle of rotgut, the bottom of it. I took a big swig in the wild, lyrical, drizzling air of Nebraska. "Whooee, here we go!" yelled a kid in a baseball cap, and they gunned up the truck to seventy and passed everybody on the road. "We been riding this sonofabitch since Des Moines. These guys never stop. Every now and then you have to yell for pisscall, otherwise you have to piss off the air, and hang on, brother, hang on."

I looked at the company. There were two young farmer boys from North Dakota in red baseball caps, which is the standard North Dakota farmer-boy hat, and they were headed for the harvests; their old men had given them leave to hit the road for a summer. There were two young city boys from Columbus, Ohio, high-school football players, chewing gum, winking, singing in the breeze, and they said they were hitchhiking around the United States for the summer. "We're going to LA!" they yelled.

"What are you going to do there?"

"Hell, we don't know. Who cares?"

Then there was a tall slim fellow who had a sneaky look. "Where you from?" I asked. I was lying next to him on the platform; you couldn't sit without bouncing off, it had no rails. And he turned slowly to me, opened his mouth, and said, "Mon-ta-na."

Finally there were Mississippi Gene and his charge. Mississippi Gene was a little dark guy who rode freight trains around the country, a thirty-year-old hobo but with a youthful look so you couldn't tell exactly what age he was. And he sat on the boards crosslegged, looking out over the fields without saying anything for hundreds of miles, and finally at one point he turned to me and said, "Where *you* headed?"

I said Denver.

"I got a sister there but I ain't seed her for several couple years." His language was melodious and slow. He was patient. His charge was a sixteen-year-old tall blond kid, also in hobo rags; that is to say, they wore old clothes that had been turned black by the soot of railroads and the dirt of boxcars and sleeping on the ground. The blond kid was also quiet and he seemed to be running away from something, and it figured to be the law the way he looked straight ahead and wet his lips in worried thought. Montana Slim spoke to them occasionally with a sardonic and insinuating smile. They paid no attention to him. Slim was all insinuation. I was afraid of his long goofy grin that he opened up straight in your face and held there half-moronically.

"You got any money?" he said to me.

"Hell no, maybe enough for a pint of whisky till I get to Denver. What about you?"

"I know where I can get some."

"Where?"

"Anywhere. You can always folly a man down an alley, can't you?"

"Yeah, I guess you can."

"I ain't beyond doing it when I really need some dough. Headed up to Montana to see my father. I'll have to get off this rig at Cheyenne and move up some other way. These crazy boys are going to Los Angeles."

"Straight?"

"All the way—if you want to go to LA you got a ride."

I mulled this over; the thought of zooming all night across Nebraska, Wyoming, and the Utah desert in the morning, and then most likely the Nevada desert in the afternoon, and actually arriving in Los Angeles within a foreseeable space of time almost made me change my plans. But I had to go to Denver. I'd have to get off at Cheyenne too, and hitch south ninety miles to Denver.

I was glad when the two Minnesota farmboys who owned the truck decided to stop in North Platte and eat; I wanted to have a look at them. They came out of the cab and smiled at all of us. "Pisscall!" said one. "Time to eat!" said the other. But they were the only ones in the party who had money to buy food. We all shambled after them to a restaurant run by a bunch of women, and sat around over hamburgers and coffee while they wrapped away enormous meals just as if they were back in their mother's kitchen. They were brothers; they were transporting farm machinery from Los Angeles to Minnesota and making good money at it. So on their trip to the Coast empty they picked up everybody on the road. They'd done this about five times now; they were having a hell of a time. They liked everything. They never stopped smiling. I tried to talk to them—a kind of dumb attempt on my part to befriend the captains of our ship—and the only responses I got were two sunny smiles and large white corn-fed teeth.

Everybody had joined them in the restaurant except the two hobo kids, Gene and his boy. When we all got back they were still sitting in the truck, forlorn and disconsolate. Now the darkness was falling. The drivers had a smoke; I jumped at the chance to go buy a bottle of whisky to keep warm in the rushing cold air of night. They smiled when I told them. "Go ahead, hurry up."

"You can have a couple shots!" I reassured them.

"Oh no, we never drink, go ahead."

Montana Slim and the two high-school boys wandered the streets of North Platte with me till I found a whisky store. They chipped in some, and Slim some, and I bought a fifth. Tall, sullen men watched us go by from false-front buildings; the main street was lined with square box-houses. There were immense vistas of the plains beyond every sad street. I felt something different in the air in North Platte, I didn't know what it was. In five minutes I did. We got back on the truck and roared off. It got dark quickly. We all had a shot, and suddenly I looked, and the verdant farmfields of the Platte began to disappear and in their stead, so far you couldn't see to the end, appeared long flat wastelands of sand and sagebrush. I was astounded.

"What in the hell is this?" I cried out to Slim.

"This is the beginning of the rangelands, boy. Hand me another drink."

"Whoopee!" yelled the high-school boys. "Columbus, so long! What would Sparkie and the boys say if they was here. Yow!"

The drivers had switched up front; the fresh brother was gunning the truck to the limit. The road changed too: humpy in the middle, with soft shoulders and a ditch on both sides about four feet deep, so that the truck bounced and teetered from one side of the road to the other—miraculously only when there were no cars coming the opposite way—and I thought we'd all take a somersault. But they were tremendous drivers. How that truck disposed of the Nebraska nub—the nub that sticks out over Colorado! And soon I realized I was actually at last over Colorado, though not officially in it, but looking southwest toward Denver itself a few hundred miles away. I yelled for joy. We passed the bottle. The great blazing stars came out, the far-receding sand hills got dim. I felt like an arrow that could shoot out all the way.

And suddenly Mississippi Gene turned to me from his cross-legged, patient reverie, and opened his mouth, and leaned close, and said, "These plains put me in the mind of Texas."

"Are you from Texas?"

"No sir, I'm from Green-vell Muzz-sippy." And that was the way he said it.

"Where's that kid from?"

"He got into some kind of trouble back in Mississippi, so I offered to help him out. Boy's never been out on his own. I take care of him best as I can, he's only a child." Although Gene was white there was something of the wise and tired old Negro in him, and something very much like Elmer Hassel, the New York dope addict, in him, but a railroad Hassel, a traveling epic Hassel, crossing and recrossing the country every year, south in the winter and north in the summer, and only because he had no place he could stay in without getting tired of it and because there was nowhere to go but everywhere, keep rolling under the stars, generally the Western stars.

"I been to Og-den a couple times. If you want to ride on to Ogden I got some friends there we could hole up with."

"I'm going to Denver from Cheyenne."

"Hell, go right straight thru, you don't get a ride like this every day."

This too was a tempting offer. "What was in Ogden?" "What's Ogden?" I said.

"It's the place where most of the boys pass thru and always meet there; you're liable to see anybody there."

In my earlier days I'd been to sea with a tall rawboned fellow from Louisiana called Big Slim Hazard, William Holmes Hazard, who was hobo by choice. As a little boy he'd seen a hobo come up to ask his mother for a piece of pie, and she had given it to him, and when the hobo went off down the road the little boy had said, "Ma, what is that fellow?" "Why, that's a ho-bo." "Ma, I want to be a ho-bo someday." "Shet your mouth, that's not for the like of the Hazards." But he never forgot that day, and when he grew up, after a short spell playing football at LSU, he did become a hobo. Big Slim and I spent many nights telling stories and spitting tobacco juice in paper containers. There was something so indubitably reminiscent of Big Slim Hazard in Mississippi Gene's demeanor that I said, "Do you happen to have met a fellow called Big Slim Hazard somewhere?"

And he said, "You mean the tall fellow with the big laugh?"

"Well, that sounds like him. He came from Ruston, Louisiana."

"That's right. Louisiana Slim he's sometimes called. Yessir, I shore have met Big Slim."

"And he used to work in the East Texas oil fields?"

"East Texas is right. And now he's punching cows."

And that was exactly right; and still I couldn't believe Gene could have really known Slim, whom I'd been looking for, more or less, for years. "And he used to work in tugboats in New York?"

"Well now, I don't know about that."

"I guess you only knew·him in the West."

"I reckon. I ain't never been to New York."

"Well, damn me, I'm amazed you know him. This is a big country. Yet I knew you must have known him."

"Yessir, I know Big Slim pretty well. Always generous with his money when he's got some. Mean, tough fellow, too; I seen him flatten a policeman in the yards at Cheyenne, one punch." That sounded like Big Slim; he was always practicing that one punch in the air; he looked like Jack Dempsey,[3] but a young Jack Dempsey who drank.

"Damn!" I yelled into the wind, and I had another shot, and by now I was feeling pretty good. Every shot was wiped away by the rushing wind of the open truck, wiped away of its bad effects, and the good effect sank in my stomach. "Cheyenne, here I come!" I sang. "Denver, look out for your boy."

Montana Slim turned to me, pointed at my shoes, and commented, "You reckon if you put them things in the ground something'll grow up?"—without cracking a smile, of course, and the other boys heard him and laughed. And they were the silliest shoes in America; I brought them along specifically because I didn't want my feet to sweat in the hot road, and except for the rain in Bear

---

3. American heavyweight boxing champion 1919–26.

Mountain they proved to be the best possible shoes for my journey. So I laughed with them. And the shoes were pretty ragged by now, the bits of colored leather sticking up like pieces of fresh pineapple and my toes showing through. Well, we had another shot and laughed. As in a dream we boomed through small crossroads towns smack out of the darkness, and passed long lines of lounging harvest hands and cowboys in the night. They watched us pass in one motion of the head, and we saw them slap their thighs from the continuing dark the other side of town—we were a funny-looking crew.

A lot of men were in this country at that time of the year; it was harvest time. The Dakota boys were fidgeting. "I think we'll get off at the next pisscall; seems like there's a lot of work around here."

"All you got to do is move north when it's over here," counseled Montana Slim, "and jes follow the harvest till you get to Canada." The boys nodded vaguely; they didn't take much stock in his advice.

Meanwhile the blond young fugitive sat the same way; every now and then Gene leaned out of his Buddhistic trance over the rushing dark plains and said something tenderly in the boy's ear. The boy nodded. Gene was taking care of him, of his moods and his fears. I wondered where the hell they would go and what they would do. They had no cigarettes. I squandered my pack on them, I loved them so. They were grateful and gracious. They never asked, I kept offering. Montana Slim had his own but never passed the pack. We zoomed through another crossroads town, passed another line of tall lanky men in jeans clustered in the dim light like moths on the desert, and returned to the tremendous darkness, and the stars overhead were pure and bright because of the increasingly thin air as we mounted the high hill of the western plateau, about a foot a mile, so they say, and no trees obstructing any low-leveled stars anywhere. And once I saw a moody whitefaced cow in the sage by the road as we flitted by. It was like riding a railroad train, just as steady and just as straight.

By and by we came to a town, slowed down, and Montana Slim said, "Ah, pisscall," but the Minnesotans didn't stop and went right on through. "Damn, I gotta go," said Slim.

"Go over the side," said somebody.

"Well, I *will*," he said, and slowly, as we all watched, he inched to the back of the platform on his haunch, holding on as best he could, till his legs dangled over. Somebody knocked on the window of the cab to bring this to the attention of the brothers. Their great smiles broke as they turned. And just as Slim was ready to proceed, precarious as it was already, they began zigzagging the truck at seventy miles an hour. He fell back a moment; we saw a whale's spout in the air; he struggled back to a sitting position. They swung the truck. Wham, over he went on his side, watering all over himself. In the roar we could hear him faintly cursing, like the whine of a man far across the hills. "Damn . . . damn . . ." He never knew we were doing this deliberately; he just struggled, as grim as Job. When he was finished, as such, he was wringing wet, and now he had to edge and shimmy his way back, and with a most woebegone look, and everybody laughing, except the sad blond boy, and the Minnesotans roaring in the cab. I handed him the bottle to make up for it.

"What the hail," he said, "was they doing that on purpose?"

"They sure were."

"Well, damn me, I didn't know that. I know I tried it back in Nebraska and didn't have half so much trouble."

We came suddenly into the town of Ogallala, and here the fellows in the cab called out, "*Pisscall!*" and with great good delight. Slim stood sullenly by the truck, ruing a lost opportunity. The two Dakota boys said good-by to everybody and figured they'd start harvesting here. We watched them disappear in the night toward the shacks at the end of town where lights were burning, where a watcher of the night in jeans said the employment men would be. I had to buy more cigarettes. Gene and the blond boy followed me to stretch their legs. I walked into the least likely place in the world, a kind of lonely Plains soda fountain for the local teenage girls and boys. They were dancing, a few of them, to the music on the jukebox. There was a lull when we came in. Gene and Blondey just stood there, looking at nobody; all they wanted was cigarettes. There were some pretty girls, too. And one of them made eyes at Blondey and he never saw it, and if he had he wouldn't have cared, he was so sad and gone.

I bought a pack each for them; they thanked me. The truck was ready to go. It was getting on midnight now, and cold. Gene, who'd been around the country more times than he could count on his fingers and toes, said the best thing to do now was for all of us to bundle up under the big tarpaulin or we'd freeze. In this manner, and with the rest of the bottle, we kept warm as the air grew icecold and pinged our ears. The stars seemed to get brighter the more we climbed the High Plains. We were in Wyoming now. Flat on my back, I stared straight up at the magnificent firmament, glorying in the time I was making, in how far I had come from sad Bear Mountain after all, and tingling with kicks at the thought of what lay ahead of me in Denver—whatever, whatever it would be. And Mississippi Gene began to sing a song. He sang it in a melodious, quiet voice, with a river accent, and it was simple, just "I got a purty little girl, she's sweet six-teen, she's the purti-est thing you ever seen," repeating it with other lines thrown in, all concerning how far he'd been and how he wished he could go back to her but he done lost her.

I said, "Gene, that's the prettiest song."

"It's the sweetest I know," he said with a smile.

"I hope you get where you're going, and be happy when you do."

"I always make out and move along one way or the other."

Montana Slim was asleep. He woke up and said to me, "Hey, Blackie, how about you and me investigatin' Cheyenne together tonight before you go to Denver?"

"Sure thing." I was drunk enough to go for anything.

As the truck reached the outskirts of Cheyenne, we saw the high red lights of the local radio station, and suddenly we were bucking through a great crowd of people that poured along both sidewalks. "Hell's bells, it's Wild West Week," said Slim. Big crowds of businessmen, fat businessmen in boots and ten-gallon hats, with their hefty wives in cowgirl attire, bustled and whoopeed on the wooden sidewalks of old Cheyenne; farther down were the long stringy boulevard lights of new downtown Cheyenne, but the celebration was focusing on Oldtown. Blank guns went off. The saloons were crowded to the sidewalk. I was amazed, and at the same time I felt it was ridiculous: in my first shot at the West I was seeing to what absurd devices it had fallen to keep its proud tradition. We had to jump off the truck and say good-by; the Minnesotans weren't interested in hanging around. It was sad to see them go, and I realized that I would never see any of them again, but that's the way it was. "You'll freeze your ass tonight," I warned. "Then you'll burn 'em in the desert tomorrow afternoon."

"That's all right with me long's as we get out of this cold night," said Gene. And the truck left, threading its way through the crowds, and nobody paying attention to the strangeness of the kids inside the tarpaulin, staring at the town like babes from a coverlet. I watched it disappear into the night.

14

At dawn my bus was zooming across the Arizona desert—Indio, Blythe, Salome[4] (where she danced); the great dry stretches leading to Mexican mountains in the south. Then we swung north to the Arizona mountains, Flagstaff, clifftowns. I had a book with me I stole from a Hollywood stall, "*Le Grand Meaulnes*" by Alain-Fournier,[5] but I preferred reading the American landscape as we went along. Every bump, rise, and stretch in it mystified my longing. In inky night we crossed New Mexico; at gray dawn it was Dalhart, Texas; in the bleak Sunday afternoon we rode through one Oklahoma flat-town after another; at nightfall it was Kansas. The bus roared on. I was going home in October. Everybody goes home in October.

4. As a reward for dancing at the request of King Herod, Salome asked for and was presented with John the Baptist's severed head (Mark 6.21–28).
5. French novelist (1886–1914). Alain-Fournier's poetic novel (in English, *The Wanderer*) has been regarded as a classic expression of youthful longings by French adolescents and their teachers.

We arrived in St. Louis at noon. I took a walk down by the Mississippi River and watched the logs that came floating from Montana in the north—grand Odyssean[6] logs of our continental dream. Old steamboats with their scrollwork more scrolled and withered by weathers sat in the mud inhabited by rats. Great clouds of afternoon overtopped the Mississippi Valley. The bus roared through Indiana cornfields that night; the moon illuminated the ghostly gathered husks; it was almost Halloween. I made the acquaintance of a girl and we necked all the way to Indianapolis. She was nearsighted. When we got off to eat I had to lead her by the hand to the lunch counter. She bought my meals; my sandwiches were all gone. In exchange I told her long stories. She was coming from Washington State, where she had spent the summer picking apples. Her home was on an upstate New York farm. She invited me to come there. We made a date to meet at a New York hotel anyway. She got off at Columbus, Ohio, and I slept all the way to Pittsburgh. I was wearier than I'd been for years and years. I had three hundred and sixty-five miles yet to hitchhike to New York, and a dime in my pocket. I walked five miles to get out of Pittsburgh, and two rides, an apple truck and a big trailer truck, took me to Harrisburg in the soft Indian-summer rainy night. I cut right along. I wanted to get home.

It was the night of the Ghost of the Susquehanna. The Ghost was a shriveled little old man with a paper satchel who claimed he was headed for "Canady." He walked very fast, commanding me to follow, and said there was a bridge up ahead we could cross. He was about sixty years old; he talked incessantly of the meals he had, how much butter they gave him for pancakes, how many extra slices of bread, how the old men had called him from a porch of a charity home in Maryland and invited him to stay for a weekend, how he took a nice warm bath before he left; how he found a brand-new hat by the side of the road in Virginia and that was it on his head; how he hit every Red Cross in town and showed them his World War I credentials; how the Harrisburg Red Cross was not worthy of the name; how he managed in this hard world. But as far as I could see he was just a semi-respectable walking hobo of some kind who covered the entire Eastern Wilderness on foot, hitting Red Cross offices and sometimes bumming on Main Street corners for a dime. We were bums together. We walked seven miles along the mournful Susquehanna. It is a terrifying river. It has bushy cliffs on both sides that lean like hairy ghosts over the unknown waters. Inky night covers all. Sometimes from the railyards across the river rises a great red locomotive flare that illuminates the horrid cliffs. The little man said he had a fine belt in his satchel and we stopped for him to fish it out. "I got me a fine belt here somewheres—got it in

---

6. Odysseus was a legendary Greek voyager and hero of Homer's *Odyssey*.

Frederick, Maryland. Damn, now did I leave that thing on the counter at Fredericksburg?"

"You mean Frederick."

"No, no Fredericksburg, *Virginia!*" He was always talking about Frederick, Maryland, and Fredericksburg, Virginia. He walked right in the road in the teeth of advancing traffic and almost got hit several times. I plodded along in the ditch. Any minute I expected the poor little madman to go flying in the night, dead. We never found that bridge. I left him at a railroad underpass and, because I was so sweaty from the hike, I changed shirts and put on two sweaters; a roadhouse illuminated my sad endeavors. A whole family came walking down the dark road and wondered what I was doing. Strangest thing of all, a tenorman was blowing very fine blues in this Pennsylvania hick house; I listened and moaned. It began to rain hard. A man gave me a ride back to Harrisburg and told me I was on the wrong road. I suddenly saw the little hobo standing under a sad streetlamp with his thumb stuck out—poor forlorn man, poor lost sometimeboy, now broken ghost of the penniless wilds. I told my driver the story and he stopped to tell the old man.

"Look here, fella, you're on your way west, not east."

"Heh?" said the little ghost. "Can't tell me I don't know my way around here. Been walking this country for years. I'm headed for Canady."

"But this ain't the road to Canada, this is the road to Pittsburgh and Chicago." The little man got disgusted with us and walked off. The last I saw of him was his bobbing little white bag dissolving in the darkness of the mournful Alleghenies.

I thought all the wilderness of America was in the West till the Ghost of the Susquehanna showed me different. No, there is a wilderness in the East; it's the same wilderness Ben Franklin plodded in the oxcart days when he was postmaster, the same as it was when George Washington was a wildbuck Indian-fighter, when Daniel Boone told stories by Pennsylvania lamps and promised to find the Gap, when Bradford built his road and men whooped her up in log cabins.[7] There were not great Arizona spaces for the little man, just the bushy wilderness of eastern Pennsylvania, Maryland, and Virginia, the backroads, the black-tar roads that curve among the mournful rivers like Susquehanna, Monongahela, old Potomac and Monocacy.

That night in Harrisburg I had to sleep in the railroad station on a bench; at dawn the station master threw me out. Isn't it true that you start your life a sweet child believing in everything under your

7. Daniel Boone (1734?–1820), famous explorer and settler of Kentucky. Cumberland Gap, a pass through the Appalachian Mts. into Kentucky and the West. "Braddock's Road" was the name given to the wagon trail which provided the original cleared route of travel through the Gap; Kerouac substitutes Bradford for Braddock.

father's roof? Then comes the day of the Laodiceans, when you know you are wretched and miserable and poor and blind and naked,[8] and with the visage of a gruesome grieving ghost you go shuddering through nightmare life. I stumbled haggardly out of the station; I had no more control. All I could see of the morning was a whiteness like the whiteness of the tomb. I was starving to death. All I had left in the form of calories were the last of the cough drops I'd bought in Shelton, Nebraska, months ago; these I sucked for their sugar. I didn't know how to panhandle. I stumbled out of town with barely enough strength to reach the city limits. I knew I'd be arrested if I spent another night in Harrisburg. Cursed city! The ride I proceeded to get was with a skinny, haggard man who believed in controlled starvation for the sake of health. When I told him I was starving to death as we rolled east he said. "Fine, fine, there's nothing better for you. I myself haven't eaten for three days. I'm going to live to be a hundred and fifty years old." He was a bag of bones, a floppy doll, a broken stick, a maniac. I might have gotten a ride with an affluent fat man who'd say, "Let's stop at this restaurant and have some pork chops and beans." No, I had to get a ride that morning with a maniac who believed in controlled starvation for the sake of health. After a hundred miles he grew lenient and took out bread-and-butter sandwiches from the back of the car. They were hidden among his salesman samples. He was selling plumbing fixtures around Pennsylvania. I devoured the bread and butter. Suddenly I began to laugh. I was all alone in the car, waiting for him as he made business calls in Allentown, and I laughed and laughed. Gad. I was sick and tired of life. But the madman drove me home to New York.

Suddenly I found myself on Times Square. I had traveled eight thousand miles around the American continent and I was back on Times Square; and right in the middle of a rush hour, too, seeing with my innocent road-eyes the absolute madness and fantastic hoorair of New York with its millions and millions hustling forever for a buck among themselves, the mad dream—grabbing, taking, giving, sighing, dying, just so they could be buried in those awful cemetery cities beyond Long Island City. The high towers of the land—the other end of the land, the place where Paper America is born. I stood in a subway doorway, trying to get enough nerve to pick up a beautiful long butt, and every time I stooped great crowds rushed by and obliterated it from my sight, and finally it was crushed. I had no money to go home in the bus. Paterson is quite a few miles from Times Square. Can you picture me walking those last miles through the Lincoln Tunnel or over the Washington Bridge and into New Jersey? It was dusk. Where was Hassel? I dug the square for Hassel; he wasn't there, he was in Riker's Island,[9] be-

---

8. Cf. Revelation 3.14–18.　　　9. Island in New York harbor with a jail.

hind bars. Where Dean?[1] Where everybody? Where life? I had my
home to go to, my place to lay my head down and figure the losses
and figure the gain that I knew was in there somewhere too. I had to
panhandle two bits for the bus. I finally hit a Greek minister who
was standing around the corner. He gave me a quarter with a
nervous lookaway. I rushed immediately to the bus.

When I got home I ate everything in the icebox. My aunt got up
and looked at me. "Poor little Salvatore," she said in Italian.
"You're thin, you're thin. Where have you been all this time?" I had
on two shirts and two sweaters; my canvas bag had torn cottonfield
pants and the tattered remnants of my huarache shoes in it. My
aunt and I decided to buy a new electric refrigerator with the
money I had sent her from California; it was to be the first one in
the family. She went to bed, and late at night I couldn't sleep and
just smoked in bed. My half-finished manuscript was on the desk. It
was October, home, and work again. The first cold winds rattled the
windowpane, and I had made it just in time. Dean had come to my
house, slept several nights there, waiting for me; spent afternoons
talking to my aunt as she worked on a great rag rug woven of all
the clothes in my family for years, which was now finished and
spread on my bedroom floor, as complex and as rich as the passage
of time itself; and then he had left, two days before I arrived,
crossing my path probably somewhere in Pennsylvania or Ohio, to
go to San Francisco. He had his own life there; Camille had just
gotten an apartment. It had never occurred to me to look her up
while I was in Mill City. Now it was too late and I had also missed
Dean.

                                                                1957

1. Dean Moriarty, the narrator's much admired friend, modeled on Kerouac's friend
Neal Cassady.

NORMAN MAILER

1923–

"The sour truth is that I am imprisoned with a perception which will
settle for nothing less than making a revolution in the consciousness of
our time. Whether rightly or wrongly, it is then obvious that I should go
so far as to think it is my present and future work which will have the
deepest influence of any work being done by an American novelist in these
years." Taken from the introductory "advertisement" in Norman Mailer's
first collection of his occasional journalism, reviews, and stories, these two
sentences lay out the terms in which the writer insists his work be considered and judged. As Richard Poirier has put it, Mailer "has exhibited a
literary ambition that can best be called imperialistic. He has wanted to
translate his life into a literary career and then to translate that literary

career into history." To a remarkable degree this writer has succeeded in realizing his aim.

He was born in New Jersey, grew up in Brooklyn, went to Harvard College, where by the end of his first semester (and just before turning seventeen) he "formed the desire to be a major writer." Mailer took a number of writing courses at Harvard (as well as ones in engineering), won various literary prizes, then upon graduation entered the army with the intention of writing a "great war novel" about either the European or the Pacific conflict, whichever was to be his personal fate. He served in the Pacific and came home to write, over the course of fifteen months, *The Naked and the Dead*. If not obviously a "great war novel," it is a good one, strong when it evokes place and action, lively as a drama of debate, of ideas in conflict. It was also a best-seller and got Mailer off to a success which would take some work to live up to.

His uncertain and turbulent career in the ten years after the war is described in *Advertisements for Myself* (1959): marriages and divorces, disillusionment with leftist politics (Mailer supported former Vice-President Henry Wallace's ill-fated campaign for the presidency in 1948), experiments with drugs and with new fictional styles. The novels from these years, *Barbary Shore* (1951) and *The Deer Park* (1955), were largely treated as fallings-off from his first book. But in *Barbary Shore* Mailer ambitiously attempted and at least partially succeeded in weaving an eerie Cold War fantasy about sex, power, and totalitarianism, all played out within a Brooklyn rooming house. And *The Deer Park* moved across country to Hollywood, continuing to explore relationships among sex, politics, and money, as well as demonstrating Mailer's stylistic debt to F. Scott Fitzgerald.

After *The Deer Park* appeared in 1955, Mailer began to write a column for the *Village Voice*, a Greenwich Village weekly he had helped found. Concurrently he became fascinated with a phenomenon he called "Hip" and with its embodiment in the Hipster, a heroic, cool, but potentially violent figure whose essential being contradicted everything Mailer saw as the dull pieties of social adjustment fashionable in the years of Eisenhower's presidency. "The shits are killing us," was Mailer's war cry, as he set out to confound the "square" mentality by finding suitable antagonists for it, such as the "Existential hero" he saw in John F. Kennedy, or the comic warrior Sergius O'Shaugnessy who appears in Mailer's fiction; or (most luridly and pompously) in the notion of himself as an investigator of "psychic mysteries" like rape, suicide, and orgasm. The fullest development of these theories is found in his essay *The White Negro* (1959); while his culminating fictional portrayal of the hero-as-hipster is Stephen Rojack, the narrator of *An American Dream* (1964) who murders his wife in the novel's second chapter. Adverse critics of the book saw Rojack as no more than a crude projection of his author's destructive fantasies. But Mailer is larger than his character, and the novel an ingenious attempt to create a more human and healthier consciousness.

As his work became increasingly subversive of traditional distinctions among "fiction," "essay," "poetry," or "sociology," Mailer's style grew bolder in metaphor, more daring in its improvisations. His powerful originality as a literary critic can be observed in *The Dynamic of American Letters* (printed here) where he analyzes the American novel in this century. And as the country plunged ever deeper into the Vietnam tragedy, his imagination was stung to the composition of a brilliantly obscene improvisation (officially a novel) *Why Are We in Vietnam?* (1967), then to perhaps his finest book, *The Armies of the Night* (1968). Here, for once, the power of the man and of the moment came together in an extended piece of writing that is at once history, fiction, and prophecy. Springing from Mailer's involvement in the 1967 march on the Pentagon in protest of the war, it plays off private, even ignoble concerns against the public significances borne by the event. The "Mailer" who moves through these pages is a less-than-heroic figure, often available for comic and satiric treatment by the author, though not exclusively so; and in that quality *Armies* resembles no book in American letters so much as *The Education of Henry Adams*. Thick with often humorously observed particularity, its tone is eventually graver and more serious than anything he had written before or has written since.

Since 1967 he has been at work on a gigantic novel to end all American novels. Meanwhile he has run for mayor of New York City, and made a number of films—of which perhaps the most interesting is *Maidstone*, to whose published text he wrote a long introduction. He has also, along with a book on spaceflight (*A Fire on the Moon*, 1970), written a polemic against Kate Millett and certain aspects of the women's movement (*The Prisoner of Sex*, 1971), a biography of Marilyn Monroe, and an account of the Foreman-Ali heavyweight struggle in Zaire. Throughout these books, as well as in his personal appearances on late-night talk shows, his comic sense has shown to good advantage the ability in uncertain or unpleasant situations to interpolate, mimic, turn a phrase against the world or himself, sometimes against both at the same time. Whether Mailer's literary production has as yet or will ever live up to the immense promise he made for himself—to make "a revolution in the consciousness of our time"—there is fertility and variety in his performances as an entertainer, diagnostician, and prophet committed to nothing less than what Emerson called the "conversion of the world."

The Man Who Studied Yoga[1]

I

I would introduce myself if it were not useless. The name I had last night will not be the same as the name I have tonight. For the moment, then, let me say that I am thinking of Sam Slovoda. Obligatorily, I study him, Sam Slovoda who is neither ordinary nor extraordinary, who is not young nor yet old, not tall nor short. He is sleeping, and it is fit to describe him now, for like most humans he prefers sleeping to not sleeping. He is a mild pleasant-looking man who has just turned forty. If the crown of his head reveals a little bald spot, he has nourished in compensation the vanity of a

---

1. This short novel, as Mailer calls it, was written in 1952 and published in *Advertisements for Myself* (1959). Originally it was conceived as the prologue to a mammoth eight-part novel (never completed) that would revolve around "the adventures of a mythical hero, Sergius O'Shaugnessy." *The Deer Park* (1955) was to have been its first part.

mustache. He has generally when he is awake an agreeable manner, at least with strangers; he appears friendly, tolerant, and genial. The fact is that like most of us, he is full of envy, full of spite, a gossip, a man who is pleased to find others are as unhappy as he, and yet—this is the worst to be said—he is a decent man. He is better than most. He would prefer to see a more equitable world, he scorns prejudice and privilege, he tries to hurt no one, he wishes to be liked. I will go even further. He has one serious virtue—he is not fond of himself, he wishes he were better. He would like to free himself of envy, of the annoying necessity to talk about his friends, he would like to love people more: specifically, he would like to love his wife more, and to love his two daughters without the tormenting if nonetheless irremediable vexation that they closet his life in the dusty web of domestic responsibilities and drudging for money.

How often he tells himself with contempt that he has the cruelty of a kind weak man.

May I state that I do not dislike Sam Slovoda; it is just that I am disappointed in him. He has tried too many things and never with a whole heart. He has wanted to be a serious novelist and now merely indulges the ambition; he wished to be of consequence in the world, and has ended, temporarily perhaps, as an overworked writer of continuity for comic magazines; when he was young he tried to be a bohemian and instead acquired a wife and family. Of his appetite for a variety of new experience I may say that it is matched only by his fear of new people and novel situations.

I will give an instance. Yesterday, Sam was walking along the street and a bum approached him for money. Sam did not see the man until too late; lost in some inconsequential thought, he looked up only in time to see a huge wretch of a fellow with a red twisted face and an outstretched hand. Sam is like so many; each time a derelict asks for a dime, he feels a coward if he pays the money, and is ashamed of himself if he doesn't. This once, Sam happened to think, I will not be bullied, and hurried past. But the bum was not to be lost so easily. "Have a heart, Jack," he called after in a whisky voice, "I need a drink bad." Sam stopped, Sam began to laugh. "Just so it isn't for coffee, here's a quarter," he said, and he laughed, and the bum laughed. "You're a man's man," the bum said. Sam went away pleased with himself, thinking about such things as the community which existed between all people. It was cheap of Sam. He should know better. He should know he was merely relieved the situation had turned out so well. Although he thinks he is sorry for bums, Sam really hates them. Who knows what violence they can offer?

At this time, there is a powerful interest in Sam's life, but many would ridicule it. He is in the process of being psychoanalyzed. Myself, I do not jeer. It has created the most unusual situation between Sam and me. I could go into details but they are perhaps premature. It would be better to watch Sam awaken.

His wife, Eleanor, has been up for an hour, and she has shut the window and neglected to turn off the radiator. The room is stifling. Sam groans in a stupor which is neither sleep nor refreshment, opens one eye, yawns, groans again, and lies twisted, strangled and trussed in pajamas which are too large for him. How painful it is for him to rise. Last night there was a party, and this morning, Sunday morning, he is awakening with a hangover. Invariably, he is depressed in the morning, and it is no different today. He finds himself in the flat and familiar dispirit of nearly all days.

It is snowing outside. Sam finally lurches to the window, and opens it for air. With the oxygen of a winter morning clearing his brain, he looks down six stories into the giant quadrangle of the Queens housing development in which he lives, staring morosely at the inch of slush which covers the monotonous artificial park that separates his apartment building from an identical structure not two hundred feet away. The walks are black where the snow has melted, and in the children's playground, all but deserted, one swing oscillates back and forth, pushed by an irritable little boy who plays by himself among the empty benches, swaddled in galoshes, muffler, and overcoat. The snow falls sluggishly, a wet snow which probably will turn to rain. The little boy in the playground gives one last disgusted shove to the swing and trudges away gloomily, his overshoes leaving a small animal track behind him. Back of Sam, in the four-room apartment he knows like a blind man, there is only the sound of Eleanor making breakfast.

Well, thinks Sam, depression in the morning is a stage of his analysis, Dr. Sergius has said.

This is the way Sam often phrases his thoughts. It is not altogether his fault. Most of the people he knows think that way and talk that way, and Sam is not the strongest of men. His language is doomed to the fashion of the moment. I have heard him remark mildly, almost apologetically, about his daughters: "My relation with them still suffers because I haven't worked through all my feminine identifications." The saddest thing is that the sentence has meaning to Sam even if it will not have meaning to you. A great many ruminations, discoveries, and memories contribute their connotation to Sam. It has the significance of a cherished line of poetry to him.

Although Eleanor is not being analyzed, she talks in a similar way. I have heard her remark in company, "Oh, you know Sam, he not only thinks I'm his mother, he blames me for being born." Like most women, Eleanor can be depended upon to employ the idiom of her husband.

What amuses me is that Sam is critical of the way others speak. At the party last night he was talking to a Hollywood writer, a young man with a great deal of energy and enthusiasm. The young man spoke something like this: "You see, boychick, I can spike any script with yaks, but the thing I can't do is heartbreak. My wife says she's gonna give me heartbreak. The trouble is I've had a real solid-type life. I mean I've had my ups and downs like all of humanity, but there's never been a shriek in my life. I don't know how to write shrieks."

On the trip home, Sam had said to Eleanor, "It was disgraceful. A writer should have some respect for language."

Eleanor answered with a burlesque of Sam's indignation. "Listen, I'm a real artist-type. Culture is for comic-strip writers."

Generally, I find Eleanor attractive. In the ten years they have been married she has grown plump, and her dark hair which once was long is now cropped in a mannish cut of the prevailing mode. But, this is quibbling. She still possesses her best quality, a healthy exuberance which glows in her dark eyes and beams in her smile. She has beautiful teeth. She seems aware of her body and pleased with it. Sam tells himself he would do well to realize how much he needs her. Since he has been in analysis he has come to discover that he remains with Eleanor for more essential reasons than mere responsibility. Even if there were no children, he would probably cleave to her.

Unhappily, it is more complicated than that. She is always—to use their phrase—competing with him. At those times when I do not like Eleanor, I am irritated by her lack of honesty. She is too sharp-tongued, and she does not often give Sam what he needs most, a steady flow of uncritical encouragement to counteract the harshness with which he views himself. Like so many who are articulate on the subject, Eleanor will tell you that she resents being a woman. As Sam is disappointed in life, so is Eleanor. She feels Sam has cheated her from a proper development of her potentialities and talent, even as Sam feels cheated. I call her dishonest because she is not so ready as Sam to put the blame on herself.

Sam, of course, can say all this himself. It is just that he experiences it in a somewhat different way. Like most men who have been married for ten years, Eleanor is not quite real to him. Last night at the party, there were perhaps half a dozen people whom he met for the first time, and he talked animatedly with them, sensing their reactions, feeling their responses, aware of the life in them, as they were aware of the life in him. Eleanor, however, exists in his nerves. She is a rather vague embodiment, he thinks of her as "she" most of the time, someone to conceal things from. Invariably, he feels uneasy with her. It is too bad. No matter how inevitable, I am always sorry when love melts into that pomade of affection, resentment, boredom and occasional compassion which is the best we may expect of a man and woman who have lived together a long time. So often, it is worse, so often no more than hatred.

They are eating breakfast now, and Eleanor is chatting about the party. She is pretending to be jealous about a young girl in a strapless evening gown, and indeed, she does not have to pretend altogether. Sam, with liquor inside him, had been leaning over the girl; obviously he had coveted her. Yet, this morning, when Eleanor begins to talk about her, Sam tries to be puzzled.

"Which girl was it now?" he asks a second time.

"Oh, you know, the hysteric," Eleanor says, "the one who was parading her bazooms in your face." Eleanor has ways of impressing certain notions upon Sam. "She's Charlie's new girl."

"I didn't know that," Sam mutters. "He didn't seem to be near her all evening."

Eleanor spreads marmalade over her toast and takes a bite with evident enjoyment. "Apparently, they're all involved. Charles was funny about it. He said he's come to the conclusion that the great affairs of history are between hysterical women and detached men."

"Charles hates women," Sam says smugly. "If you notice, almost everything he says about them is a discharge of aggression." Sam has the best of reasons for not liking Charles. It takes more than ordinary character for a middle-aged husband to approve of a friend who moves easily from woman to woman.

"At least Charles discharges his aggression," Eleanor remarks.

"He's almost a classic example of the Don Juan complex. You notice how masochistic his women are?"

"I know a man or two who's just as masochistic."

Sam sips his coffee. "What made you say the girl was an hysteric?"

Eleanor shrugs. "She's an actress. And I could see she was a tease."

"You can't jump to conclusions," Sam lectures. "I had the impression she was a compulsive. Don't forget you've got to distinguish between the outer defenses, and the more deeply rooted conflicts."

I must confess that this conversation bores me. As a sample it is representative of the way Sam and Eleanor talk to each other. In Sam's defense I can say nothing; he has always been too partial to jargon.

I am often struck by how eager we are to reveal all sorts of supposedly ugly secrets about ourselves. We can explain the hatred we feel for our parents, we are rather pleased with the perversions to which we are prone. We seem determinedly proud to be superior to ourselves. No motive is too terrible for our inspection. Let someone hint, however, that we have bad table manners and we fly into a rage. Sam will agree to anything you may say about him, provided it is sufficiently serious—he will be the first to agree he has fantasies of murdering his wife. But tell him that he is afraid of waiters, or imply to Eleanor that she is a nag, and they will be quite annoyed.

Sam has noticed this himself. There are times when he can hear the jargon in his voice, and it offends him. Yet, he seems powerless to change his habits.

An example: He is sitting in an armchair now, brooding upon his breakfast, while Eleanor does the dishes. The two daughters are not home; they have gone to visit their grandmother for the weekend. Sam had encouraged the visit. He had looked forward to the liberty Eleanor and himself would enjoy. For the past few weeks the children had seemed to make the most impossible demands upon his attention. Yet now they are gone and he misses them, he even misses their noise. Sam, however, cannot accept the notion that many people are dissatisfied with the present, and either dream of the past or anticipate the future. Sam must call this "ambivalence over possessions." Once he even felt obliged to ask his analyst, Dr. Sergius, if ambivalence over possessions did not characterize him almost perfectly, and Sergius whom I always picture with the flat precision of a coin's head—bald skull and horn-rimmed glasses— answered in his German accent, "But, my dear Mr. Slovoda, as I have told you, it would make me happiest if you did not include in your reading, these psychoanalytical text-works."

At such rebukes, Sam can only wince. It is so right, he tells himself, he is exactly the sort of ambitious fool who uses big words when small ones would do.

2

While Sam sits in the armchair, gray winter light is entering the windows, snow falls outside. He sits alone in a modern seat, staring at the gray, green, and beige décor of their living room. Eleanor was a painter before they were married, and she has arranged this room. It is very pleasant, but like many husbands, Sam resents it, resents the reproductions of modern painters upon the wall, the slender coffee table, a free-form poised like a spider on wire legs, its feet set onto a straw rug. In the corner, most odious of all, is the playmate of his children, a hippopotamus of a television-radio-and-phonograph cabinet with the blind monstrous snout of the video tube.

Eleanor has set the Sunday paper near his hand. Soon, Sam intends to go to work. For a year, he has been giving a day once or twice a month to a bit of thought and a little writing on a novel he hopes to begin sometime. Last night, he told himself he would work today. But he has little enthusiasm now. He is tired, he is too depressed. Writing for the comic strips seems to exhaust his imagination.

Sam reads the paper as if he were peeling an enormous banana. Flap after flap of newsprint is stripped away and cast upon the straw rug until only the Magazine Section is left. Sam glances through it with restless irritability. A biography of a political figure runs its flatulent prose into the giant crossword puzzle at the back. An account of a picturesque corner of the city becomes lost in statistics and exhortations on juvenile delinquency, finally to emerge with photographs about the new style of living which desert architecture provides. Sam looks at a wall of windows in rotogravure with a yucca tree framing the pool.

There is an article about a workingman. His wife and his family are described, his apartment, his salary and his budget. Sam reads a description of what the worker has every evening for dinner, and how he spends each night of the week. The essay makes its point; the typical American workingman must watch his pennies, but he is nonetheless secure and serene. He would not exchange his life for another.

Sam is indignant. A year ago he had written a similar article in an attempt to earn some extra money. Subtly, or so he thought, he had suggested that the average working man was raddled with insecurity. Naturally, the article had been rejected.

Sam throws the Magazine Section away. Moments of such anger torment him frequently. Despite himself, Sam is enraged at editorial dishonesty, at the smooth strifeless world which such articles present. How angry he is—how angry and how helpless. "It is the actions of men and not their sentiments which make history," he thinks to himself, and smiles wryly. In his living room he would go out to tilt the windmills of a vast, powerful, and hypocritical society; in his week of work he labors in an editorial cubicle to create spaceships, violent death, women with golden tresses and wanton breasts, men who act with their fists and speak with patriotic slogans.

I know what Sam feels. As he sits in the armchair, the Sunday papers are strewn around him, carrying their war news, their murders, their parleys, their entertainments, mummery of a real world which no one can grasp. It is terribly frustrating. One does not know where to begin.

Today, Sam considers himself half a fool for having been a radical. There is no longer much consolation in the thought that the majority of men who succeed in a corrupt and acquisitive society are themselves obligatorily corrupt, and one's failure is therefore the price of one's idealism. Sam cannot recapture the pleasurable bitterness which resides in the notion that one has suffered for one's principles. Sergius is too hard on him for that.

They have done a lot of work on the subject. Sergius feels that Sam's concern with world affairs has always been spurious. For example, they have uncovered in analysis that Sam wrote his article about the worker in such a way as to make certain it would be refused. Sam, after all, hates editors; to have such a piece accepted would mean he is no better than they, that he is a mediocrity. So long as he fails he is not obliged to measure himself. Sam, therefore, is being unrealistic. He rejects the world with his intellect, and this enables him not to face the more direct realities of his present life.

Sam will argue with Sergius but it is very difficult. He will say,

"Perhaps you sneer at radicals because it is more comfortable to ignore such ideas. Once you became interested it might introduce certain unpleasant changes in your life."

"Why," says Sergius, "do you feel it so necessary to assume that I am a bourgeois interested only in my comfort?"

"How can I discuss these things," says Sam, "if you insist that my opinions are the expression of neurotic needs, and your opinions are merely dispassionate medical advice?"

"You are so anxious to defeat me in an argument," Sergius will reply. "Would you admit it is painful to relinquish the sense of importance which intellectual discussion provides you?"

I believe Sergius has his effect. Sam often has thoughts these days which would have been repellent to him years ago. For instance, at the moment, Sam is thinking it might be better to live the life of a worker, a simple life, to be completely absorbed with such necessities as food and money. Then one could believe that to be happy it was necessary only to have more money, more goods, less worries. It would be nice, Sam thinks wistfully, to believe that the source of one's unhappiness comes not from oneself, but from the fault of the boss, or the world, or bad luck.

Sam has these casual daydreams frequently. He likes to think about other lives he might have led, and he envies the most astonishing variety of occupations. It is easy enough to see why he should wish for the life of an executive with the power and sense of command it may offer, but virtually from the same impulse Sam will wish himself a bohemian living in an unheated loft, his life a catch-as-catch-can from day to day. Once, after reading an article, Sam even wished himself a priest. For about ten minutes it seemed beautiful to him to surrender his life to God. Such fancies are common, I know. It is just that I, far better than Sam, know how serious he really is, how fanciful, how elaborate, his imagination can be.

The phone is ringing. Sam can hear Eleanor shouting at him to answer. He picks up the receiver with a start. It is Marvin Rossman who is an old friend, and Marvin has an unusual request. They talk for several minutes, and Sam squirms a little in his seat. As he is about to hang up, he laughs. "Why, no, Marvin, it gives me a sense of adventure," he says.

Eleanor has come into the room toward the end of this conversation. "What is it all about?" she asks.

Sam is obviously a bit agitated. Whenever he attempts to be most casual, Eleanor can well suspect him. "It seems," he says slowly, "that Marvin has acquired a pornographic movie."

"From whom?" Eleanor asks.

"He said something about an old boy friend of Louise's."

Eleanor laughs. "I can't imagine Louise having an old boy friend with a dirty movie."

"Well, people are full of surprises," Sam says mildly.

"Look, here," says Eleanor suddenly. "Why did he call us?"

"It was about our projector."

"They want to use it?" Eleanor asks.

"That's right." Sam hesitates. "I invited them over."

"Did it ever occur to you I might want to spend my Sunday some other way?" Eleanor asks crossly.

"We're not doing anything," Sam mumbles. Like most men, he feels obliged to act quite nonchalantly about pornography. "I'll tell you, I am sort of curious about the film. I've never seen one, you know."

"Try anything once, is that it?"

"Something of the sort." Sam is trying to conceal his excitement. The truth is that in common with most of us, he is fascinated by pornography. It is a minor preoccupation, but more from lack of opportunity than anything else. Once or twice, Sam has bought the sets of nude photographs which are sold in marginal bookstores, and with guilty excitement has hidden them in the apartment.

"Oh, this is silly," Eleanor says. "You were going to work today."

"I'm just not in the mood."

"I'll have to feed them," Eleanor complains. "Do we have enough liquor?"

"We can get beer." Sam pauses. "Alan Sperber and his wife are coming too."

"Sam you're a child."

"Look, Eleanor," says Sam, controlling his voice, "if it's too much trouble, I can take the projector over there."

"I ought to make you do that."

"Am I such an idiot that I must consult you before I invite friends to the house?"

Eleanor has the intuition that Sam, if he allowed himself, could well drown in pornography. She is quite annoyed at him, but she would never dream of allowing Sam to take the projector over to Marvin Rossman's where he could view the movie without her—that seems indefinably dangerous. Besides she would like to see it, too. The mother in Eleanor is certain it cannot hurt her.

"All right, Sam," she says, "but you are a child."

More exactly, an adolescent, Sam decides. Ever since Marvin phoned, Sam has felt the nervous glee of an adolescent locking himself in the bathroom. Anal fixation, Sam thinks automatically.

While Eleanor goes down to buy beer and cold cuts in a delicatessen, Sam gets out the projector and begins to clean it. He is far from methodical in this. He knows the machine is all right, he has shown movies of Eleanor and his daughters only a few weeks ago, but from the moment Eleanor left the apartment, Sam has been consumed by an anxiety that the projection bulb is burned out. Once he has examined it, he begins to fret about the motor. He wonders if it needs oiling, he blunders through a drawer of household tools looking for an oilcan. It is ridiculous. Sam knows that what he is trying to keep out of his mind are the reactions Sergius will have. Sergius will want to "work through" all of Sam's reasons for seeing the movie. Well, Sam tells himself, he knows in advance what will be discovered: detachment, not wanting to accept Eleanor as a sexual partner, evasion of responsibility, etc. etc. The devil with Sergius. Sam has never seen a dirty movie, and he certainly wants to.

He feels obliged to laugh at himself. He could not be more nervous, he knows, if he were about to make love to a woman he had never touched before. It is really disgraceful.

When Eleanor comes back, Sam hovers about her. He is uncomfortable with her silence. "I suppose they'll be here soon," Sam says.

"Probably."

Sam does not know if he is angry at Eleanor or apprehensive that she is angry at him. Much to his surprise he catches her by the waist and hears himself saying, "You know, maybe tonight when they're gone . . . I mean, we do have the apartment to ourselves." Eleanor moves neither toward him nor away from him. "Darling, it's not because of the movie," Sam goes on, "I swear. Don't you think maybe we could . . ."

"Maybe," says Eleanor.

3

The company has arrived, and it may be well to say a word or two about them. Marvin Rossman who has brought the film is a dentist, although it might be more accurate to describe him as a frustrated doctor. Rossman is full of statistics and items of odd information about the malpractice of physicans, and he will tell these things in his habitually gloomy voice, a voice so slow, so sad, that it almost conceals the humor of his remarks. Or, perhaps, that is what creates his humor. In his spare time, he is a sculptor, and if Eleanor may be trusted, he is not without talent. I often picture him working in the studio loft he has rented, his tall bony frame the image of dejection. He will pat a piece of clay to the armature, he will rub it sadly with this thumb, he will shrug, he does not believe that anything of merit could come from him. When he talked to Sam over the phone, he was pessimistic about the film they were to see. "It can't be any good," he said in his melancholy voice. "I know it'll be a disappointment." Like Sam, he has a mustache, but Rossman's will droop at the corners.

Alan Sperber who has come with Rossman is the subject of some curiosity for the Slovodas. He is not precisely womanish; in fact, he is a large plump man, but his voice is too soft, his manners too precise. He is genial, yet he is finicky; waspish, yet bland; he is fond of telling long rather affected stories, he is always prepared with a new one, but to general conversation he contributes little. As a lawyer, he seems miscast. One cannot imagine him inspiring a client to confidence. He is the sort of heavy florid man who seems boyish at forty, and the bow ties and gray flannel suits he wears do not make him appear more mature.

Roslyn Sperber, his wife, used to be a schoolteacher, and she is a quiet nervous woman who talks a great deal when she is drunk. She is normally quite pleasant, and has only one habit which is annoying to any degree. It is a little flaw, but social life is not unlike marriage in that habit determines far more than vice or virtue. This mannerism which has become so offensive to the friends of the Sperbers is Roslyn's social pretension. Perhaps I should say intellectual prentension. She entertains people as if she were conducting a salon, and in her birdlike voice is forever forcing her guests to accept still another intellectual canapé. "You must hear Sam's view of the world market," she will say, or "Has Louise told you her statistics on divorce?" It is quite pathetic for she is so eager to please. I have seen her eyes fill with tears at a sharp word from Alan.

Marvin Rossman's wife, Louise, is a touch grim and definite in her opinions. She is a social welfare worker, and will declare herself with force whenever conversation impinges on those matters where she is expert. She is quite opposed to psychoanalysis, and will say without quarter, "It's all very well for people in the upper-middle area"—she is referring to the upper middle class—"but, it takes more than a couch to solve the problems of . . ." and she will list narcotics, juvenile delinquency, psychosis, relief distribution, slum housing, and other descriptions of our period. She recites these categories with an odd anticipation. One would guess she was ordering a meal.

Sam if fond of Marvin but he cannot abide Louise. "You'd think she discovered poverty," he will complain to Eleanor.

The Slovodas do feel superior to the Rossmans and the Sperbers. If pressed, they could not offer the most convincing explanation why. I suppose what it comes down to is that Sam and Eleanor do not think of themselves as really belonging to a class, and they feel that the Sperbers and Rossmans are petit-bourgeois. I find it hard to explain their attitude. Their company feels as much discomfort and will apologize as often as the Slovodas for the money they have, and the money they hope to earn. They are all of them equally concerned with progressive education and the methods of raising children to be well adjusted—indeed, they are discussing that now—they consider themselves relatively free of sexual taboo, or put more properly, Sam and Eleanor are no less possessive than the others. The Slovodas' culture is not more profound; I should be hard put to say that Sam is more widely read, more seriously informed, than Marvin or Alan, or for that matter, Louise. Probably, it comes to this: Sam, in his heart, thinks himself a rebel, and there are few rebels who do not claim an original mind. Eleanor has been a bohemian and considers herself more sophisticated than her friends who merely went to college and got married. Louise Rossman could express it most soundly. "Artists, writers, and people of the creative layer have in their occupational ideology the belief that they are classless."

One thing I might remark about the company. They are all being the most unconscionable hypocrites. They have rushed across half the city of New York to see a pornographic film, and they are not at all interested in each other at the moment. The women are giggling like tickled children at remarks which cannot possibly be so funny. Yet, they are all determined to talk for a respectable period of time. No less, it must be serious talk. Roslyn has said once, "I feel so funny at the thought of seeing such a movie," and the others have passed her statement by.

At the moment, Sam is talking about value. I might note that Sam loves conversation and thrives when he can expound an idea.

"What are our values today?" he asks. "It's really fantastic when you stop to think of it. Take any bright talented kid who's getting out of college now."

"My kid brother, for example," Marvin interposes morosely. He passes his bony hand over his sad mustache, and somehow the remark has become amusing, much as if Marvin had said, "Oh, yes, you have reminded me of the trials, the worries, and the cares which my fabulous younger brother heaps upon me."

"All right, take him," Sam says. "What does he want to be?"

"He doesn't want to be anything," says Marvin.

"That's my point," Sam says excitedly. "Rather than work at certain occupations, the best of these kids would rather do nothing at all."

"Alan has a cousin," Roslyn says, "who swears he'll wash dishes before he become a businessman."

"I wish that were true," Eleanor interrupts. "It seems to me everybody is conforming more and more these days."

They argue about this. Sam and Eleanor claim the country is suffering from hysteria; Alan Sperber disagrees and says it's merely a reflection of the headlines; Louise says no adequate criteria exist to measure hysteria; Marvin says he doesn't know anything at all.

"More solid liberal gains are being made in this period," says Alan, "than you would believe. Consider the Negro—"

"Is the Negro any less maladjusted?" Eleanor shouts with passion.

Sam maneuvers the conversation back to his thesis. "The values of the young today, and by the young, I mean the cream of the kids, the ones with ideas, are a reaction of indifference to the culture crisis. It really is despair. All they know is what they don't want to do."

"That is easier," Alan says genially.

"It's not altogether unhealthy," Sam says. "It's a corrective for smugness and the false value of the past, but it has created new false value." He thinks it worth emphasizing. "False value seems always to beget further false value."

"Define your terms," says Louise, the scientist.

"No, look," Sam says, "there's no revolt, there's no acceptance. Kids today don't want to get married, and—"

Eleanor interrupts. "Why should a girl rush to get married? She loses all chance for developing herself."

Sam shrugs. They are all talking at once. "Kids don't want to get married," he repeats, "and they don't want not to get married. They merely drift."

"It's a problem we'll all have to face with our own kids in ten years," Alan says, "although I think you make too much of it, Sam."

"My daughter," Marvin states. "She's embarrassed I'm a dentist. Even more embarrassed than I am." They laugh.

Sam tells a story about his youngest, Carol Ann. It seems he had a fight with her, and she went to her room. Sam followed, he called through the door.

"No answer," Sam says. "I called her again, 'Carol Ann.' I was a little worried you understand, because she seemed so upset, so I said to her, 'Carol-Ann, you know I love you.' What do you think she answered?"

"What?" asks Roslyn.

"She said, 'Daddie, why are you so anxious?' "

They all laugh again. There are murmurs about what a clever thing it was to say. In the silence which follows, Roslyn leans forward and says quickly in her high voice, "You must get Alan to tell you his wonderful story about the man who studied yogi."

"Yoga," Alan corrects. "It's too long to tell."

The company prevails on him.

"Well," says Alan, in his genial courtroom voice, "it concerns a friend of mine named Cassius O'Shaugnessy."

"You don't mean Jerry O'Shaugnessy, do you?" asks Sam.

Alan does not know Jerry O'Shaugnessy. "No, no, this is Cassius O'Shaugnessy," he says. "He's really quite an extraordinary fellow." Alan sits plumply in his chair, fingering his bow tie. They are all used to his stories, which are told in a formal style and exhibit the attempt to recapture a certain note of urbanity, wit, and élan[2] which Alan has probably copied from someone else. Sam and

2. Spirit.

Eleanor respect his ability to tell these stories, but they resent the fact that he talks *at* them.

"You'd think we were a jury of his inferiors," Eleanor has said. "I hate being talked down to." What she resents is Alan's quiet implication that his antecedents, his social position, in total his life outside the room is superior to the life within. Eleanor now takes the promise from Alan's story by remarking, "Yes, and let's see the movie when Alan has finished."

"Sssh," Roslyn says.

"Cassius was at college a good while before me," says Alan, "but I knew him while I was an undergraduate. He would drop in and visit from time to time. An absolutely extraordinary fellow. The most amazing career. You see, he's done about everything."

"I love the way Alan tells it," Roslyn pipes nervously.

"Cassius was in France with Dos Passos and Cummings, he was even arrested with e.e. After the war, he was one of the founders of the Dadaist school, and for a while I understand he was Fitzgerald's guide to the gold of the Côte D'Azur. He knew everybody, he did everything. Do you realize that before the twenties had ended, Cassius had managed his father's business and then entered a monastery? It is said he influenced T. S. Eliot."[3]

"Today, we'd call Cassius a psychopath," Marvin observes.

"Cassius called himself a great dilettante," Alan answers, "although perhaps the nineteenth-century Russian conception of the great sinner would be more appropriate. What do you say if I tell you this was only the beginning of his career?"

"What's the point?" Louise asks.

"Not yet," says Alan, holding up a hand. His manner seems to say that if his audience cannot appreciate the story, he does not feel obliged to continue. "Cassius studied Marx in the monastery. He broke his vows, quit the church, and became a Communist. All though the thirties he was a figure in the Party, going to Moscow, involved in all the Party struggles. He left only during the Moscow trials."[4]

Alan's manner while he relates such stories is somewhat effeminate. He talks with little caresses of his hand, he mentions names and places with a lingering ease as if to suggest that his audience and he are aware, above all, of nuance. The story as Alan tells it is drawn overlong. Suffice it that the man about whom he is talking, Cassius O'Shaughnessy, becomes a Trotskyist, becomes an anarchists, is a pacifist during the second World War, and suffers it from a prison cell.

"I may say," Alan goes on, "that I worked for his defense, and was successful in getting him acquitted. Imagine my dolor when I

---

3. This improbable combination of literary feats suggests the legendary or mythical status of Cassius's reputation.
4. Trials of the followers of Leon Trotsky, 1879–1940 (an exiled Soviet dissi-

dent eventually assassinated), for alleged acts of treason against the Soviet government. Most of the defendants were executed.

learned that he had turned his back on his anarchist friends and was living with gangsters."

"This is weird," Eleanor says.

"Weird, it is," Alan agrees. "Cassius got into some scrape, and disappeared. What could you do with him? I learned only recently that he had gone to India and was studying yoga. In fact, I learned it from Cassius himself. I asked him of his experiences at Brahna-puth-thar, and he told me the following story."

Now Alan's voice alters, he assumes the part of Cassius and speaks in a tone weary of experience, wise and sad in its knowledge. " 'I was sitting on my haunches contemplating my navel,' Cassius said to me, 'when of a sudden I discovered my navel under a different aspect. It seemed to me that if I were to give a counter-clockwise twist, my navel would unscrew.' "

Alan looks up, he surveys his audiences which is now rapt and uneasy, not certain as yet whether a joke is to come. Alan's thumb and forefinger pluck at the middle of his ample belly, his feet are crossed upon the carpet in symbolic suggestion of Cassius upon his haunches.

" 'Taking a deep breath, I turned, and the abysses of Vishtarni loomed beneath. My navel had begun to unscrew. I knew I was about to accept the reward of three years of contemplation. So,' said Cassius, 'I turned again, and my navel unscrewed a little more. I turned and I turned,' " Alan's fingers now revolving upon his belly, " 'and after a period I knew that with one more turn my navel would unscrew itself forever. At the edge of revelation, I took one sweet breath, and turned my navel free.' "

Alan looks up at his audience.

" 'Damn,' said Cassius, 'if my ass didn't fall off.' "

4

The story has left the audience in an exaspereated mood. It has been a most untypical story for Alan to tell, a little out of place, not offensive exactly, but irritating and inconsequential. Sam is the only one to laugh with more than bewildered courtesy, and his mirth seems excessive to everyone but Alan, and of course, Roslyn, who feels as if she has been the producer. I suppose what it reduces to, is a lack of taste. Perhaps that is why Alan is not the lawyer one would expect. He does not have that appreciation—as necessary in his trade as for an actor—of what is desired at any moment, of that which will encourage as opposed to that which does not encourage a stimulating but smooth progression of logic and sentiment. Only a fool would tell so long a story when everyone is awaiting the movie.

Now, they are preparing. The men shift armchairs to correspond with the couch, the projector is set up, the screen is unfolded. Sam attempts to talk while he is threading the film, but no one listens. They seem to realize suddenly that a frightful demand has been placed upon them. One does not study pornography in a living room with a beer glass in one's hand, and friends at the elbow. It is the most unsatisfactory of compromises; one can draw neither the benefits of solitary contemplation nor of social exchange. There is, at bottom, the same exasperated fright which one experiences in turning the slower tap and receiving cold water when the flesh has been prepared for heat. Perhaps that is why they are laughing so much now that the movie is begun.

A title, *The Evil Act*, twitches on the screen, shot with scars, holes, and the dustlines of age. A man and woman are sitting on a couch, they are having coffee. They chat. What they say is conveyed by printed words upon an ornately flowered card, interjected between glimpses of their casual gestures, a cup to the mouth, a smile, a cigarette being lit. The man's name, it seems, is Frankie Idell; he is talking to his wife, Magnolia. Frankie is dark, he is sinister, he confides in Magnolia, his dark counterpart, with a grimace of his brows, black from make-up pencil.

This is what the titles read:

FRANKIE: She will be here soon.
MAGNOLIA: This time the little vixen will not escape.
FRANKIE: No, my dear, this time we are prepared.
(He looks at his watch.)
FRANKIE: Listen, she knocks!

There is a shot of a tall blond woman knocking on the door. She is probably over thirty, but by her short dress and ribboned hat it is suggested that she is a girl of fifteen.

FRANKIE: Come in, Eleanor.

As may be expected, the audience laughs hysterically at this. It is so wonderful a coincidence. "How I remember Frankie," says Eleanor Slovoda, and Roslyn Sperber is the only one not amused. In the midst of the others' laughter, she says in a worried tone, obviously a drift upon her own concerns, "Do you think we'll have to stop the film in the middle to let the bulb cool off?" The others hoot, they giggle, they are weak from the combination of their own remark and the action of the plot.

Frankie and Magnolia have sat down on either side of the heroine, Eleanor. A moment passes. Suddenly stiffly, they attack. Magnolia from her side kisses Eleanor, and Frankie commits an indecent caress.

ELEANOR; How dare you? Stop!
MAGNOLIA: Scream, my little one. It will do you no good. The walls are soundproofed.
FRANKIE: We've fixed a way to make you come across.

ELEANOR: This is hideous. I am hitherto undefiled. Do not touch me!

The captions fade away. A new title takes their place. It says, *But There Is No Escape From The Determined Pair.* On the fade-in, we discover Eleanor in the most distressing situation. Her hands are tied to loops running from the ceiling, and she can only writhe in helpless perturbation before the deliberate and progressive advances of Frankie and Magnolia. Slowly they humiliate her, with relish they probe her.

The audience laughs no longer. A hush has come upon them. Eyes unblinking they devour the images upon Sam Slovoda's screen.

Eleanor is without clothing. As the last piece is pulled away, Frankie and Magnolia circle about her in a grotesque of pantomime, a leering of lips, limbs in a distortion of desire. Eleanor faints. Adroitly, Magnolia cuts her bonds. We see Frankie carrying her inert body.

Now, Eleanor is trussed to a bed, and the husband and wife are tormenting her with feathers. Bodies curl upon the bed in postures so complicated, in combinations so advanced, that the audience leans forward, Sperbers, Rossmans, and Slovodas, as if tempted to embrace the moving images. The hands trace abstract circles upon the screen, passes and recoveries upon a white background so illumined the hollows and swells, limb to belly and mouth to undescribables, tip of a nipple, orb of a navel, swim in giant magnification, flow and slide in a lurching yawing fall, blotting out the camera eye.

A little murmur, all unconscious, passes from their lips. The audience sways, each now finally lost in himself, communing hungrily with shadows, violated or violating, fantasy triumphant.

At picture's end, Eleanor the virgin whore is released from the bed. She kisses Frankie, she kisses Magnolia. "You dears," she says, "let's do it again." The projector lamp burns empty light, the machine keeps turning, the tag of film goes *slap-tap, slap-tap, slap-tap, slap-tap, slap-tap, slap-tap.*

"Sam, turn it off," says Eleanor.

But when the room lights are on, they cannot look at one another. "Can we see it again?" someone mutters. So, again, Eleanor knocks on the door, is tied, defiled, ravished, and made rapturous. They watch it soberly now, the room hot with the heat of their bodies, the darkness a balm for orgiastic vision. To the Deer Park, Sam is thinking, to the Deer Park of Louis XV[5] were brought the most beautiful maidens of France, and there they stayed, dressed in fabulous silks, perfumed and wigged, the mole drawn upon their cheek, ladies of pleasure awaiting the pleasure of the king. So Louis

5. Louis XV (1710–74) kept a "deer park" as one of his royal residences.

had stripped an empire, bankrupt a treasury, prepared a deluge, while in his garden on summer evenings the maidens performed their pageants, eighteenth-century tableau of the evil act, beauteous instruments of one man's desire, lewd translation of a king's power. That century men sought wealth so they might use its fruits; this epoch men lusted for power in order to amass more power, a compounding of power into pyramids of abstraction whose yield are cannon and wire enclosure, pillars of statistics to the men who are the kings of this century and do no more in power's leisure time than go to church, claim to love their wives, and eat vegetables.

Is it possible, Sam wonders, that each of them here, two Rossmans, two Sperbers, two Slovodas, will cast off their clothes when the movie is done and perform the orgy which tickles at the heart of their desire? They will not, he knows, they will make jokes when the projector is put away, they will gorge the plate of delicatessen Eleanor provides, and swallow more beer, he among them. He will be the first to make jokes.

Sam is right. The movie has made him extraordinarily alive to the limits of them all. While they sit with red faces, eyes bugged, glutting sandwiches of ham, salami, and tongue, he begins the teasing.

"Roslyn," he calls out, "is the bulb cooled off yet?"

She cannot answer him. She chokes on beer, her face glazes, she is helpless with self-protecting laughter.

"Why are you so anxious, Daddie?" Eleanor says quickly.

They begin to discuss the film. As intelligent people they must dominate it. Someone wonders about the actors in the piece, and discussion begins afresh. "I fail to see," says Louise, "why they should be hard to classify. Pornography is a job to the criminal and prostitute element."

"No, you won't find an ordinary prostitute doing this," Sam insists. "It requires a particular kind of personality."

"They have to be exhibitionists," says Eleanor.

"It's all economic," Louise maintains.

"I wonder what those girls felt?" Roslyn asks. "I feel sorry for them."

"I'd like to be the cameraman," says Alan.

"I'd like to be Frankie," says Marvin sadly.

There is a limit to how long such a conversation may continue. The jokes lapse into silence. They are all busy eating. When they begin to talk again, it is of other things. Each dollop of food sops the agitation which the movie has spilled. They gossip about the party the night before, they discuss which single men were interested in which women, who got drunk, who got sick, who said the wrong thing, who went home with someone else's date. When this is exhausted, one of them mentions a play the others have not seen.

Soon they are talking about books, a concert, a one-man show by an artist who is a friend. Dependably, conversation will voyage its orbit. While the men talk of politics, the women are discussing fashions, progressive schools, and recipes they have attempted. Sam is uncomfortable with the division; he knows Eleanor will resent it, he knows she will complain later of the insularity of men and the basic contempt they feel for women's intelligence.

"But you collaborated," Sam will argue. "No one forced you to be with the women."

"Was I to leave them alone?" Eleanor will answer.

"Well, why do the women always have to go off by themselves?"

"Because the men aren't interested in what we have to say."

Sam sighs. He has been talking with interest, but really he is bored. These are nice pleasant people, he thinks, but they are ordinary people, exactly the sort he has spent so many years with, making little jokes, little gossip, living little everyday events, a close circle where everyone mothers the other by his presence. The womb of middle-class life, Sam decides heavily. He is in a bad mood indeed. Everything is laden with dissatisfaction.

Alan has joined the women. He delights in preparing odd dishes when friends visit the Sperbers, and he is describing to Eleanor how he makes blueberry pancakes. Marvin draws closer to Sam.

"I wanted to tell you," he says, "Alan's story reminded me. I saw Jerry O'Shaugnessy the other day."

"Where was he?"

Marvin is hesitant. "It was a shock, Sam. He's on the Bowery. I guess he's become a wino."

"He's always drank a lot," says Sam.

"Yeah." Marvin cracks his bony knuckles. "What a stinking time this is, Sam."

"It's probably like the years after 1905 in Russia,"[6] Sam says.

"No revolutionary party will come out of this."

"No," Sam says, "nothing will come."

He is thinking of Jerry O'Shaugnessy. What did he look like? what did he say? Sam asks Marvin, and clucks his tongue at the dispiriting answer. It is a shock to him. He draws closer to Marvin, he feels a bond. They have, after all, been through some years together. In the thirties they have been in the Communist Party, they have quit together, they are both weary of politics today, still radicals out of habit, but without enthusiasm and without a cause. "Jerry was a hero to me," Sam says.

"To all of us," says Marvin.

The fabulous Jerry O'Shaugnessy, thinks Sam. In the old days, in the Party, they had made a legend of him. All of them with their

6. A reference to the violent and abortive insurrection in 1905 among Russian workers and peasants against the Czar's repressions.

middle-class origins and their desire to know a worker-hero.

I may say that I was never as fond of Jerry O'Shaugnessy as was Sam. I thought him a showman and too pleased with himself. Sam, however, with his timidity, his desire to travel, to have adventure and know many women, was obliged to adore O'Shaugnessy. At least he was enraptured with his career.

Poor Jerry who ends as a bum. He has been everything else. He has been a trapper in Alaska, a chauffeur for gangsters, an officer in the Foreign Legion, a labor organizer. His nose was broken, there were scars on his chin. When he would talk about his years at sea or his experiences in Spain, the stenographers and garment workers, the radio writers and unemployed actors would listen to his speeches as if he were the prophet of new romance, and their blood would be charged with the magic of revolutionary vision. A man with tremendous charm. In those days it had been easy to confuse his love for himself with his love for all underprivileged workingmen.

"I thought he was still in the Party," Sam says.

"No," says Marvin, "I remember they kicked him out a couple of years ago. He was supposed to have piddled some funds, that's what they say."

"I wish he'd taken the treasury," Sam remarks bitterly. "The Party used him for years."

Marvin shrugs. "They used each other." His mustache droops. "Let me tell you about Sonderson. You know he's still in the Party. The most progressive dentist in New York." They laugh.

While Marvin tells the story, Sam is thinking of other things. Since he has quit Party work, he has studied a great deal. He can tell you about prison camps and the secret police, political murders, the Moscow trials, the exploitation of Soviet labor, the privileges of the bureaucracy; it is all painful to him. He is straddled between the loss of a country he has never seen, and his repudiation of the country in which he lives. "Doesn't the Party seem a horror now?" he bursts out.

Marvin nods. They are trying to comprehend the distance between Party members they have known, people by turn pathetic, likable, or annoying—people not unlike themselves—and in contrast the immensity of historic logic which deploys along statistics of the dead.

"It's all schizoid," Sam says. "Modern life is schizoid."

Marvin agrees. They have agreed on this many times, bored with the petulance of their small voices, yet needing the comfort of such complaints. Marvin asks Sam if he has given up his novel, and Sam says, "Temporarily." He cannot find a form, he explains. He does not want to write a realistic novel, because reality is no longer realistic. "I don't know what it is," says Sam. "To tell you the truth, I think I'm kidding myself. I'll never finish this book. I just like to entertain the idea I'll do something good some day." They sit there in friendly depression. Conversation has cooled. Alan and the women are no longer talking.

"Marvin," asks Louise, "what time is it?"

They are ready to go. Sam must say directly what he had hoped to approach by suggestion. "I was wondering," he whispers to Rossman, "would you mind if I held onto the film for a day or two?"

Marvin looks at him. "Oh, why of course, Sam," he says in his morose voice. "I know how it is." He pats Sam on the shoulder as if, symbolically, to convey the exchange of ownership. They are fellow conspirators.

"If you ever want to borrow the projector," Sam suggests.

"Nah," says Marvin, "I don't know that it would make much difference."

5

It has been, when all is said, a most annoying day. As Sam and Eleanor tidy the apartment, emptying ash trays and washing the few dishes, they are fond neither of themselves nor each other. "What a waste today has been," Eleanor remarks, and Sam can only agree. He has done no writing, he has not been outdoors, and still it is late in the evening, and he has talked too much, eaten too much, is nervous from the movie they have seen. He knows that he will watch it again with Eleanor before they go to sleep; she has given her assent to that. But as is so often the case with Sam these days, he cannot await their embrace with any sure anticipation. Eleanor may be in the mood or Eleanor may not; there is no way he can control the issue. It is depressing; Sam knows that he circles about Eleanor at such times with the guilty maneuvers of a sad hound. Resent her as he must, be furious with himself as he will, there is not very much he can do about it. Often, after they have made love, they will lie beside each other in silence, each offended, each certain the other is to blame. At such times, memory tickles them with a cruel feather. Not always has it been like this. When they were first married, and indeed for the six months they lived together before marriage, everything was quite different. Their affair was very exciting to them; each told the other with some hyperbole but no real mistruth that no one in the past had ever been comparable as lover.

I suppose I am a romantic. I always feel that this is the best time in people's lives. There is, after all, so little we accomplish, and that short period when we are beloved and triumph as lovers is sweet with power. Rarely are we concerned then with our lack of importance; we are too important. In Sam's case, disillusion means even more. Like so many young men, he entertained the secret conceit that he was an extraordinary lover. One cannot really believe this without supporting at the same time the equally secret conviction that one is fundamentally inept. It is—no matter what Sergius would say—a more dramatic and therefore more attractive view of oneself than the sober notion which Sam now accepts with grudging wisdom, that the man as lover is dependent upon the bounty of the woman. As I say, he accepts the notion, it is one of the lineaments of maturity, but there is a part of him which, no matter how harried by analysis, cannot relinquish the antagonism he feels that Eleanor has respected his private talent so poorly, and has not allowed him to confer its benefits upon more women. I mock Sam, but he would mock himself on this. It hardly matters; mockery cannot accomplish everything, and Sam seethes with that most private and tender pain: even worse than being unattractive to the world is to be unattractive to one's mate; or, what is the same and describes Sam's case more accurately, never to know in advance when he shall be undesirable to Eleanor.

I make perhaps too much of the subject, but that is only because it is so important to Sam. Relations between Eleanor and him are not really that bad—I know other couples who have much less or nothing at all. But comparisons are poor comfort to Sam; his standards are so high. So are Eleanor's. I am convinced the most unfortunate people are those who would make an art of love. It sours other effort. Of all artists, they are certainly the most wretched.

Shall I furnish a model? Sam and Eleanor are on the couch and the projector, adjusted to its slowest speed, is retracing the elaborate pantomime of the three principals. If one could allow these shadows a life . . . but indeed such life has been given them. Sam and Eleanor are no more than an itch, a smart, a threshold of satisfaction; the important share of themselves has steeped itself in Frankie-, Magnolia-, and Eleanor-of-the-film. Indeed the variations are beyond telling. It is the most outrageous orgy performed by five ghosts.

Self-critical Sam! He makes love in front of a movie, and one cannot say that it is unsatisfactory any more than one can say it is pleasant. It is dirty, downright porno dirty, it is a lewd slop-brush slapped through the middle of domestic exasperations and breakfast eggs. It is so dirty that only half of Sam—he is quite divisible into fractions—can be exercised at all. The part that is his brain worries along like a cuckolded burgher. He is taking the pulse of his anxiety. Will he last long enough to satisfy Eleanor? Will the children come back tonight? He cannot help it. In the midst of the circus, he is suddenly convinced the children will walk through the door. "Why are you so anxious, Daddie?"

So it goes. Sam the lover is conscious of exertion. One moment he is Frankie Idell, destroyer of virgins—take that! you whore!—the next, body moving, hands caressing, he is no more than some lines from a psychoanalytical text. He is thinking about the sensitivity of his scrotum. He has read that this is a portent of femininity in a male. How strong is his latent homosexuality worries Sam, thrusting stiffly, warm sweat running cold. Does he identify with Eleanor-of-the film.

Technically, the climax is satisfactory. They lie together in the dark, the film ended, the projector humming its lonely revolutions in the quiet room. Sam gets up to turn it off; he comes back and kisses Eleanor upon the mouth. Apparently, she has enjoyed herself more than he; she is tender and fondles the tip of his nose.

"You know, Sam," she says from her space beside him, "I think I saw this picture before."

"When?"

"Oh, you know when. That time."

Sam thinks dully that women are always most loving when they can reminisce about infidelity.

"That time!" he repeats.

"I think so."

Racing forward from memory like the approaching star which begins as a point on the mind and swells to explode the eyeball with its odious image, Sam remembers, and is weak in the dark. It is ten years, eleven perhaps, before they were married, yet after they were lovers. Eleanor has told him, but she has always been vague about details. There had been two men it seemed, and another girl, and all had been drunk. They had seen movie after movie. With reluctant fascination, Sam can conceive the rest. How it had pained him, how excited him. It is years now since he has remembered, but he remembers. In the darkness he wonders at the unreasonableness of jealous pain. That night was impossible to imagine any longer— therefore it is more real; Eleanor his plump wife who presses a pigeon's shape against her housecoat, forgotten heroine of black orgies. It had been meaningless, Eleanor claimed; it was Sam she loved, and the other had been no more than a fancy of which she wished to rid herself. Would it be the same today, thinks Sam, or had Eleanor been loved by Frankie, by Frankie of the other movies, by Frankie of the two men she never saw again on that night so long ago?

The pleasure I get from this pain, Sam thinks furiously.

It is not altogether perverse. If Eleanor causes him pain, it means after all that she is alive for him. I have often observed that the reality of a person depends upon his ability to hurt us; Eleanor as the vague accusing embodiment of the wife is different, altogether different, from Eleanor who lies warmly in Sam's bed, an attractive Eleanor who may wound his flesh. Thus, brother to the pleasure of pain, is the sweeter pleasure which follows pain. Sam, tired, lies in Eleanor's arms, and they talk with the cozy trade words of old professionals, agreeing that they will not make love again before a movie, that it was exciting but also not without detachment, that all in all it has been good but not quite right, that she had loved this action he had done, and was uncertain about another. It is their old familiar critique, a sign that they are intimate and well disposed. They do not talk about the act when it has failed to fire; then they go silently to sleep. But now, Eleanor's enjoyment having mollified Sam's sense of no enjoyment, they talk with the apologetics and encomiums of familiar mates. Eleanor falls asleep, and Sam falls almost asleep, curling next to her warm body, his hand over her round belly with the satisfaction of a sculptor. He is drowsy, and he thinks drowsily that these few moments of creature-pleasure, this brief compassion he can feel for the body that trusts itself to sleep beside him, his comfort in its warmth, is perhaps all the meaning he may ask for his life. That out of disappointment, frustration, and the passage of dreary years come these few moments when he is close to her, and their years together possess a connotation more rewarding than the sum of all which has gone into them.

But then he thinks of the novel he wants to write, and he is wide-awake again. Like the sleeping pill which fails to work and leaves one warped in an exaggeration of the ills which sought the drug, Sam passes through the promise of sex-emptied sleep, and is left with nervous loins, swollen jealousy of an act ten years dead, and sweating irritable resentment of the woman's body which hinders his limbs. He has wasted the day, he tells himself, he has wasted the day as he has wasted so many days of his life, and tomorrow in the office he will be no more than his ten fingers typing plot and words for Bramba the Venusian and Lee-Lee Deeds, Hollywood Star, while that huge work with which he has cheated himself, holding it before him as a covenant of his worth, that enormous novel which would lift him at a bound from the impasse in which he stifles, whose dozens of characters would develop a vision of life in bountiful complexity, lies foundered, rotting on a beach of purposeless effort. Notes here, pages there, it sprawls through a formless wreck of incidental ideas and half-episodes, utterly without shape. He has not even a hero for it.

One could not have a hero today, Sam thinks, a man of action and contemplation, capable of sin, large enough for good, a man immense. There is only a modern hero damned by no more than the ugliness of wishes whose satisfaction he will never know. One needs a man who could walk the stage, someone who—no matter who, not himself. Someone, Sam thinks, who reasonably could not exist.

The novelist, thinks Sam, perspiring beneath blankets, must live in paranoia and seek to be one with the world; he must be terrified of experience and hungry for it; he must think himself nothing and believe he is superior to all. The feminine in his nature cries for proof he is a man; he dreams of power and is without capacity to gain it; he loves himself above all and therefore despises all that he is.

He is that, thinks Sam, he is part of the perfect prescription, and yet he is not a novelist. He lacks energy and belief. It is left for him to write an article some day about the temperament of the ideal novelist.

In the darkness, memories rise, yeast-swells of apprehension. Out of bohemian days so long ago, comes the friend of Eleanor, a girl who had been sick and was committed to an institution. They visited her, Sam and Eleanor, they took the suburban train and sat on the lawn of the asylum grounds while patients circled about intoning a private litany, or shuddering in boob-blundering fright from an insect that crossed their skin. The friend had been silent. She had smiled, she had answered their questions with the fewest words, and had returned again to her study of sunlight and blue sky. As they were about to leave, the girl had taken Sam aside. "They violate me," she said in a whisper. "Every night when the doors are locked, they come to my room and they make the movie. I am the heroine and am subjected to all variety of sexual viciousness. Tell them to leave me alone so I may enter the convent." And while she talked, in a horror of her body, one arm scrubbed the other. Poor tortured friend. They had seen her again, and she babbled, her face had coarsened into an idiot leer.

Sam sweats. There is so little he knows, and so much to know. Youth of the depression with its economic terms, what can he know of madness or religion? They are both so alien to him. He is the mongrel, Sam thinks, brought up without religion from a mother half Protestant and half Catholic, and a father half Catholic and half Jew. He is the quarter-Jew, and yet he is a Jew, or so he feels himself, knowing nothing of Gospel, tabernacle, or Mass, the Jew through accident, through state of mind. What . . . whatever did he know of penance? self-sacrifice? mortification of the flesh? the love of his fellow man? Am I concerned with my relation to God? ponders Sam, and smiles sourly in the darkness. No, that has never concerned him, he thinks, not for better nor for worse. "They are making the movie," says the girl into the ear of memory, "and so I cannot enter the convent."

How hideous was the mental hospital. A concentration camp, decides Sam. Perhaps it would be the world some day, or was that only his projection of feelings of hopelessness? "Do not try to solve the problems of the world," he hears from Sergius, and pounds a lumpy pillow.

However could he organize his novel? What form to give it? It is so complex. Too loose, thinks Sam, too scattered. Will he ever fall asleep? Wearily, limbs tense, his stomach too keen, he plays again the game of putting himself to sleep. "I do not feel my toes," Sam says to himself, "my toes are dead, my calves are asleep, my calves are sleeping . . ."

In the middle from wakefulness to slumber, in the torpor which floats beneath blankets, I give an idea to Sam. "Destroy time, and chaos may be ordered," I say to him.

"Destroy time, and chaos may be ordered," he repeats after me, and in desperation to seek his coma, mutters back, "I do not feel my nose, my nose is numb, my eyes are heavy, my eyes are heavy."

So Sam enters the universe of sleep, a man who seeks to live in such a way as to avoid pain, and succeeds merely in avoiding pleasure. What a dreary compromise is life!

1952, 1959

[The Dynamic of American Letters]¹

Reader, a telegram: SHIFT MCNAMARA LAMBS FROM WARS OF JELLIED FIRE TO LIONS IN BURNING BUSH.

Everything in this book is attached to everything else. Trust me for a time. Indulge me:

Assume I am a lecturer in the fields of Fellowship surrounding Literature (American) and am trying to draw some grand design in twenty minutes on a talk devoted to "The Dynamic of American Letters." Knowing attention is iron for the blood of a Fellow, I will not be so foolish as to perish without a look at the topical and the interesting. No, I will use "The Dynamic of American Letters" as preparation for a lightning discussion of Herzog and Terry Southern, with a coda on the art of the absurd.² Let me then have my first sentence as lecturer: "There has been a war at the center of American letters for a long time." That is not so poor. The look of absolute comprehension on the face of the audience encourages the lecturer to go on.

The war began as a class war; an upper-middle class looked for a development of its taste, a definition of its manners, a refinement of itself to prepare a shift to the aristocratic; that was its private demand upon culture. That demand is still being made by a magazine called *The New Yorker*. This upper-class development of literature was invaded a long time ago, however, back at the cusp of the century, by a counter-literature whose roots were found in poverty, industrial society, and the emergence of new class. It was a literature which grappled with a peculiarly American phenomenon—a tendency of American society to alter more rapidly than the ability of its artists to record that change. Now, of course, one might go back two thousand years into China to find a society which did not alter more rapidly than its culture, but the American phenomenon

1. As Mailer tells us later on, this was originally a talk delivered in December, 1964, to a large assembly of professors of literature and American Studies. It was later incorporated in *Cannibals and Christians* (1966), a collection of essays and occasional pieces. In Mailer's mythology, "Christians" are the inhabitants of small-town America; "Cannibals" are the immigrant exploiters of America. His discussion of what has happened to the American novel is set against the mounting horror of the Vietnam war.

2. Saul Bellow's *Herzog* was published in 1964; Terry Southern's *The Magic Christian* in 1959. The former is a long, tragicomic exploration of a mid-20th-century American Jewish intellectual; the latter is a short satiric fantasy, grotesque and outrageous in its humor.

had to do with the very rate of acceleration. The order of magnitude in this rate had shifted. It was as if everything changed ten times as fast in America, and this made for extraordinary difficulty in creating a literature. The sound, sensible, morally stout delineation of society which one found in Tolstoy and Balzac and Zola, in Thackeray and in Trollope, had become impossible.[3] The American novelist of manners had to content himself with manners—he could not put a convincing servant into his work, and certainly not a workingman, because they were moving themselves in one generation out from the pantry into the morning dress of the lady in the parlor and up from the foundry to the master of the factory. The novelist of manners could not go near these matters—they promised to take over all of his book. So the job was left to Howells, Stephen Crane, to Dreiser, and in lesser degree to such writers as Norris, Jack London, Upton Sinclair—let us say it was left to Dreiser.[4] A fundamental irony of American letters had now presented itself. For in opposition to Dreiser was the imperfectly developed countertradition of the genteel. The class which wielded the power which ran America, and the class which most admired that class, banded instinctively together to approve a genteel literature which had little to do with power or the secrets of power. They encouraged a literature about courtship and marriage and love and play and devotion and piety and style, a literature which had to do finally with the *excellence* of belonging to their own genteel tradition. Thus it was a literature which borrowed the forms of its conduct from European models. The people who were most American by birth, and who had the most to do with managing America, gave themselves a literature which had the least to say about the real phenomena of American life, most particularly the accelerated rate, the awful rate, of growth and anomaly through all of society. That sort of literature and that kind of attempt to explain America was left to the sons of immigrants who, if they were vigorous enough, and fortunate enough to be educated, now had the opportunity to see that America was a phenomenon never before described, indeed never before visible in the record of history. There was something going on in American life which was either grand or horrible or both, but it was going on—at a dizzy rate—and the future glory or doom of the world was not necessarily divorced from it. Dreiser labored like a titan to capture the phenomenon; he became a titan; Thomas Wolfe, his only peer as giant (as the novelist-as-giant), labored also like a titan, but for half as long and died in terror of the gargantuan proportions of the task. Yet each failed in one part of the job. They

3. Leo Tolstoy (1828–1910), Russian novelist. Honoré de Balzac (1799–1850), and Emile Zola (1840–1902), French novelists. W. M. Thackeray (1811–1863) and Anthony Trollope (1815–82), British novelists.

4. Mailer names several late 19th-century American novelists, of whom the most important for his argument is Theodore Dreiser (1871–1945), author of *An American Tragedy* (1925) and other books.

were able to describe society—Wolfe like the greatest five-year-old who ever lived,[5] an invaluable achievement, and Dreiser like some heroic tragic entrepreneur who has reasoned out through his own fatigue and travail very much how everything works in the iron mills of life, but is damned because he cannot pass on the knowledge to his children. Dreiser and Wolfe were up from the people, and Dreiser particularly came closer to understanding the social machine than any American writer who ever lived, but he paid an unendurable price—he was forced to alienate himself from manner in order to learn the vast amount he learned. Manner insists one learn at a modest rate, that one learn each step with grace before going on to the next. Dreiser was in a huge hurry, he had to learn everything—that was the way he must have felt his mission, so there is nothing of manner in his work; which is to say, nothing of tactics.

If the upper-class quite naturally likes a literature which is good for them, a literature at the surface perhaps trivial, but underneath amusing, elucidative, *fortifying*, it is because this kind of literature elaborates and clarifies the details of their life, and thus adjusts their sense of power, their upper-class sense of power, which is invariably lubricated by a sense of detail. So too does that other class of readers in American literature, that huge, loose, all but unassociated congregation of readers—immigrant, proletarian, entrepreneur—wish in turn for a literature which is equally good for them. That is where Dreiser had to fail. He was only half-good for such readers. He taught them strategy as Americans had never gotten it before in a novel. If they were adventurers, he was almost as useful to them as Stendhal[6] was exceptionally useful to a century of French intellectuals who had come to Paris from the provinces. But not quite. Dreiser, finally, is not quite as useful, and the difference is crucial. Because a young adventurer reads a great novel in the unvoiced hope it is a grindstone which sharpens his axe sufficiently to smash down doors now locked to him. Dreiser merely located the doors and gave warnings about the secret padlocks and the traps. But he had no grindstone, no manner, no eye for the deadly important manners of the rich, he was obliged to call a rich girl "charming"; he could not make her charming when she spoke, as Fitzgerald could, and so he did not really prepare the army of his readers for what was ahead. His task was doubly difficult—it was required of him to give every upstart fresh strategy and tactics. No less than the secret sociology of society is what is needed by the upstart and that

5. "This Argument was delivered, originally, as a talk to The American Studies Association and the M.L.A. This remark brought laughter from the audience. Since I did not wish to insult the memory of Wolfe, it would have been happier and perhaps more accurate to have said: like the greatest fifteen-year-old alive" [Mailer's note]. Thomas Wolfe (1900–38), American novelist, author of *Look Homeward, Angel* (1929).

6. Pseudonym of Marie Henri Beyle (1783–1842), French novelist whose *The Red and the Black* (1831) is about just such an adventurer.

strategy Dreiser gave him. But tactics—the manners of the drawing room, the deaths and lifes of the drawing room, the cocktail party, the glorious tactics of the individual kill—that was all beyond him. Dreiser went blind climbing the mountains of society, so he could not help anyone to see what was directly before him—only what had happened and what was likely to come next.

That was the initial shape of the war, Naturalism versus the Genteel Tradition it has been called, and one might pose Henry James against Dreiser, but James is sufficiently great a writer to violate the generalizations one must make about the novel of manners which must always—precisely because it deals with manners— eschew the overambitious, plus extremes of plot—which James of course did not. So let us say the war was between Dreiser and Edith Wharton, Dreiser all strategy, no tactics; and Wharton all tactics. Marvelous tactics they were—a jewel of a writer and stingy as a parson—she needed no strategy. The upper-class writer had all strategy provided him by the logic of his class. Maybe that is why the war never came to decision, or even to conclusion. No upper-class writer went down into the pits to bring back the manner alive of the change going on *down there*, certainly not Edith Wharton, not James Branch Cabell, of course not, nor Hergesheimer nor even Cather or Glasgow, not Elinor Wylie, no, nor Carl Van Vechten, and no diamond in the rough was ever reshaped by the cutters of Newport. The gap in American letters continued. Upper-class writers like John Dos Passos[7] made brave efforts to go down and get the stuff and never quite got it, mainly in Dos Passos's case because they lacked strategy for the depths—manners may be sufficient to delineate the rich but one needs a vision of society to comprehend the poor, and Dos Passos had only revulsion at injustice, which is ultimately a manner. Some upper-class writers like Fitzgerald turned delicately upon the suppositions of their class, lost all borrowed strategy and were rudderless, were forced therefore to become superb in tactics, but for this reason perhaps a kind of hysteria lived at the center of their work; lower-class writers like Farrell and Steinbeck[8] described whole seas of the uncharted ocean but their characters did not push from one milieu into another, and so the results were more taxonomic than apocalyptic.

Since then the war has shifted. No writer succeeded in doing the single great work which would clarify a nation's vision of itself as Tolstoy had done perhaps with *War and Peace* or *Anna Karenina*, and Stendhal with *The Red and the Black*, no one novel came along which was grand and daring and comprehensive and detailed, able

---

7. John Dos Passos (1896–1960), American novelist, author of the trilogy *U.S.A.* Mailer has been naming various American "upper-class" novelists and poets who were incapable of writing adequately about the working class.

8. James T. Farrell (b. 1904), American novelist, author of *Studs Lonigan* (1932). John Steinbeck (1902–68), American novelist, author of *The Grapes of Wrath* (1939).

to give sustenance to the adventurer and merriment to the rich, leave compassion in the icechambers of the upper class and energy as alms for the poor. (Not unless it was *Tropic of Cancer*.)[9] Dreiser came as close as any, and never got close at all, for he could not capture the moment, and no country in history has lived perhaps so much for the moment as America. After his heroic failure, American literature was isolated—it was necessary to give courses in American literature to Americans, either because they would not otherwise read it, or because reading it, they could not understand it. It was not quite vital to them. It did not save their lives, make them more ambitious, more moral, more tormented, more audacious, more ready for love, more ready for war, for charity and for invention. No, it tended to puzzle them. The realistic literature had never caught up with the rate of change in American life, indeed it had fallen further and further behind, and the novel gave up any desire to be a creation equal to the phenomenon of the country itself; it settled for being a metaphor. Which is to say that each separate author made a separate peace. He would no longer try to capture America, he would merely try to give life to some microcosm in American life, some metaphor—in the sense that a drop of water is a metaphor of the seas, or a hair of the beast is for some a metaphor of the beast—and in that metaphor he might—if he were very lucky—have it all, rich and poor, strategy and tactics, insight and manner, detail, authority, the works. He would have it all for a particular few. It was just that he was no longer writing about the beast but, as in the case of Hemingway (if we are to take the best of this), about the paw of the beast, or in Faulkner about the dreams of the beast. What a paw and what dreams! Perhaps they are the two greatest writers America ever had, but they had given up on trying to do it all. Their vision was partial, determinedly so, they saw that as the first condition for trying to be great— that one must not try to save. Not souls, and not the nation. The desire for majesty was the bitch which licked at the literary loins of Hemingway and Faulkner: the country could be damned. Let it take care of itself.

And of course the country did. Just that. It grew by itself. Like a weed and a monster and a beauty and a pig. And the task of explaining America was taken over by Luce magazines.[1] Those few aristocratic novelistic sensibilities which had never seen the task of defining the country as one for them—it was finally most unamusing as a task—grew smaller and smaller and more and more superb. Edith Wharton reappeared as Truman Capote,[2] even more of a jewel, even stingier. Of writers up from the bottom there were

9. Novel (1931) by American writer Henry Miller, adept at portraying working-class and unemployed poor in Paris.
1. Magazines like *Time* and *Life*, published by the Henry Luce Corporation.

2. Truman Capote (b. 1924), American writer, author of *Other Voices, Other Rooms*, a rather "precious" novel, and *In Cold Blood* (1965).

numbers: Dreiser's nephews were as far apart as Saul Bellow and James Jones.[3] But the difference between the two kinds of writers had shifted. It had begun to shift somewhere after the Second World War, and the shift had gone a distance. One could not speak at all now of aristocratic writers and novelists whose work was itself the protagonist to carry the writer and his readers through the locks of society; no, the work had long since retreated, the great ambition was gone, and then it was worse, even the metaphor was gone, the paw of the beast and the dreams of the beast, no, literature was down to the earnest novel and the perfect novel, to moral seriousness and Camp. Herzog and Candy had become the protagonists.[4]

Frank Cowperwood[5] once amassed an empire. Herzog, his bastard great-nephew, diddled in the ruins of an intellectual warehouse. Where once the realistic novel cut a swath across the face of society, now its reality was concentrated into moral seriousness. Where the original heroes of naturalism had been active, bold, self-centered, close to tragic, and up to their nostrils in their exertions to advance their own life and force the webs of society, so the hero of moral earnestness, the hero Herzog and the hero Levin in Malamud's *A New Life,* are men who represent the contrary—passive, timid, other-directed, pathetic, up to the nostrils in anguish: the world is stronger than they are; suicide calls.

Malamud's hero is more active than Herzog, he is also more likable, but these positive qualities keep the case from being so pure. There is a mystery about the reception of *Herzog.* For beneath its richness of texture and its wealth of detail, the fact remains: never has a novel been so successful when its hero was so dim. Not one of the critics who adored the book would ever have permitted Herzog to remain an hour in his house. For Herzog was defeated, Herzog was an unoriginal man, Herzog was a fool—not an attractive God-anointed fool like Gimpel the Fool,[6] his direct progenitor, but a sodden fool, over-educated and inept, unable to fight, able to love only when love presented itself as a gift. Herzog was intellectual but not bright, his ideas not original, his style as it appeared in his letters unendurable—it had exactly the leaden-footed sense of phrase which men laden with anxiety and near to going mad put into their communications. Herzog was hopeless. We learned nothing about society from him, not even anything about his life. And he is the only figure in the book. His wives, his mistress, his family, his children, his friends, even the man who cuckolds him are seen on the periphery of a dimming vision. Like all men near to being mad, his attention is within, but the inner attention is without

---

3. James Jones (1921–77), American novelist, author of *From Here to Eternity* (1951), usually not admired (as is Bellow) for his style.
4. Hero and heroine respectively of Bellow's *Herzog* and Southern's *Candy* (1964). The latter novel pretends to follow, sympathetically, the bizarre sexual adventures of its heroine, Candy Christian, in a manner far removed from "moral seriousness."
5. Hero of Dreiser's *The Financier* (1927).
6. Hero of a story by Isaac Bashevis Singer: *Gimpel the Fool* (1950).

genius. Herzog is dull, he is unendurably dull—he is like all those bright pedagogical types who have a cavity at the center of their brain.

Yet the novel succeeds. There is its mystery. One reads it with compassion. With rare compassion. Bored by Herzog, still there is a secret burning of the heart. One's heart turns over and produces a sorrow. Hardly any books are left to do that.

Of course, Herzog is alive on sufferance. He is a beggar, an extraordinary beggar who fixes you with his eye, his breath, his clothing, his dank near-corrupt presence; he haunts. Something goes on in Herzog's eye. It says: I am debased, I am failed, I am near to rotten, and yet something just as good and loving resides in me as the tenderest part of your childhood. If the prophet Elijah[7] sent me, it is not to make you feel guilt but to weep. Suddenly, Herzog inspires sorrow—touch of alchemy to the book—Herzog is at the center of the modern dilemma. If we do not feel compassion for him, a forceful compassion which sends blood to warm the limbs and the heart, then we are going to be forced to shoot him. Because if Herzog does not arouse your compassion there is no other choice —he is too intolerable a luxury to keep alive in his mediocrity unless he arouses your love. The literary world chose to love him. We were not ready to shoot Herzog. It all seemed too final if we did. Because then there would be nothing left but Camp, and Camp is the art of the cannibal, Camp is the art which evolved out of the bankruptcy of the novel of-manners. It is the partial thesis of these twenty minutes that the pure novel of manners had watered down from *The House of Mirth* to the maudlin middle reaches of *The Rector of Justin*; had in fact gone all the way down the pike from *The Ambassadors* to *By Love Possessed*.[8] So, one does not speak of the novel of manners any longer—one is obliged to look at the documentary, *In Cold Blood*—or one is obliged to look at satire. The aristocratic impulse turned upon itself produced one classic— Terry Southern's *The Magic Christian*. Never had distaste for the habits of a mass mob reached such precision, never did wit falter in its natural assumption that the idiocies of the mass were attached breath and kiss to the hypocrisies, the weltering grandeurs, and the low stupidities of the rich, the American rich. The aristocratic impulse to define society by evocations of manner now survived only in the grace of any cannibal sufficiently aristocratic to sup upon his own family. *The Magic Christian* was a classic of Camp.

Note then: The two impulses in American letters had failed, the realistic impulse never delivered the novel which would ignite a nation's consciousness of itself, and the aristocratic impulse clawed at the remaining fabric of a wealthy society it despised and no

---

7. Old Testament prophet, herald of the Messiah and the Day of Judgment (1 and 2 Kings).
8. *The House of Mirth* (1905), by Edith Wharton; *The Rector of Justin* (1964), by Louis Auchincloss; *The Ambassadors* (1903), by Henry James; *By Love Possessed* (1957), by James Gould Cozzens.

longer wished to sustain. Like a Tinguely machine[9] which destroys itself, Camp amused by the very act of its destruction. Since it was also sentimental, the artifacts were necrophiliac.

Literature then had failed. The work was done by the movies, by television. The consciousness of the masses and the culture of the land trudged through endless mud.

The American consciousness in the absence of a great tradition in the novel ended by being developed by the bootlicking pieties of small-town newspaper editors and small-town educators, by the worst of organized religion, a formless force filled with the terrors of all the Christians left to fill the spaces left by the initial bravery of the frontiersman, and these latterday Christians were simply not as brave. That was one component of the mud. The other was the sons of the immigrants. Many of them hated America, hated it for what it offered and did not provide, what it revealed of opportunity and what it excluded from real opportunity. The sons of these immigrants and the sons' sons took over the cities and began to run them, high up in the air and right down into the ground, they plucked and they plundered and there was not an American city which did not grow more hideous in the last fifty years. Then they spread out—they put suburbs like blight on the land—and piped mass communications into every home. They were cannibals selling Christianity to Christians, and because they despised the message and mocked at it in their own heart, they succeeded in selling something else, a virus perhaps, an electronic nihilism went through the mass media of America and entered the Christians and they were like to being cannibals, they were a tense and livid people, swallowing their own hate with the tranquilizers and the sex in the commercials, whereas all the early cannibals at the knobs of the mass-media made the mistake of passing on their bleak disease and were left now too gentle, too liberal, too programmatic, filled with plans for social welfare, and they looked and talked in Show Biz styles which possessed no style and were generally as unhealthy as Christians who lived in cellars and caves.

Yes, the cannibal sons of the immigrants had become Christians, and the formless form they had evolved for their mass-media, the hypocritical empty and tasteless taste of the television arts they beamed across the land encountered the formless form and the all but tasteless taste of the small-town tit-eating cannibal mind at its worst, and the collision produced schizophrenia in the land. Half of America went insane with head colds and medicaments and asthmas and allergies, hospitals and famous surgeons with knives to cut into the plague, welfares and plans and committees and cooperations and boredom, boredom plague deep upon the land; and the other part of America went ape, and the motorcycles began to roar like

9. Jean Tinguely (b. 1925) created a work of sculpture with moving parts which eventually destroyed itself.

lions across the land and all the beasts of all the buried history of America turned in their circuit and prepared to slink toward the market place, there to burn the mother's hair and bite the baby to the heart. One thought of America and one thought of aspirin, kitchen-commercials, and blood. One thought of Vietnam. And the important art in America became the art of the absurd.

1964, 1966

From The Armies of the Night[1]
Part I
5. TOWARD A THEATER OF IDEAS

The guests were beginning to leave the party for the Ambassador, which was two blocks away. Mailer did not know this yet, but the audience there had been waiting almost an hour. They were being entertained by an electronic folk rock guitar group, so presumably the young were more or less happy, and the middle-aged dim. Mailer was feeling the high sense of clarity which accompanies the light show of the aurora borealis when it is projected upon the inner universe of the chest, the lungs, and the heart. He was happy. On leaving, he had appropriated a coffee mug and filled it with bourbon. The fresh air illumined the bourbon, gave it a cerebrative edge; words entered his brain with the agreeable authority of fresh minted coins. Like all good professionals, he was stimulated by the chance to try a new if related line of work. Just as professional football players love sex because it is so close to football, so he was fond of speaking in public because it was thus near to writing. An extravagant analogy? Consider that a good half of writing consists of being sufficiently sensitive to the moment to reach for the next promise which is usually hidden in some word or phrase just a shift to the side of one's conscious intent. (Consciousness, that blunt tool, bucks in the general direction of the truth; instinct plucks the feather. Cheers!) Where public speaking is an exercise from prepared texts to demonstrate how successfully a low order of consciousness can beat upon the back of a collective flesh, public speaking being, therefore, a sullen expression of human possibility metaphorically equal to a bugger on his victim, speaking-in-public (as Mailer liked to describe any speech which was more or less improvised, impromptu, or dangerously written) was an activity like writing; one had to trick or seize or submit to the grace of each moment, which, except for those unexpected and sometimes well-

---

1. The following selection consists of Chapters 5 and 6 (Part I) and Chapters 2 and 3 (Part II) from *The Armies of the Night* (1968). The occasion is the anti-Vietnam war march to the Pentagon in October, 1967. Mailer, despite some reservations, has agreed to participate in this march, and also in a premarch evening rally at a Washington theater. In the first two chapters, which describe that evening, the principal actors are Mailer; the poet Robert Lowell; Dwight Macdonald, a leading American critic and journalist of politics and literature; Paul Goodman, poet and cultural critic, author of *Growing Up Absurd* (1959); and Ed de Grazia, one of the organizers of the march.

deserved moments when consciousness and grace came together (and one felt on the consequence, heroic) were usually occasions of some mystery. The pleasure of speaking in public was the sensitivity it offered: with every phrase one was better or worse, close or less close to the existential promise of truth, *it feels true,* which hovers on good occasions like a presence between speaker and audience. Sometimes one was better, and worse, at the same moment; so strategic choices on the continuation of the attack would soon have to be decided, a moment to know the blood of the gambler in oneself.

Intimations of this approaching experience, obviously one of Mailer's preferred pleasures in life, at least when he did it well, were now connected to the professional sense of intrigue at the new task: tonight he would be both speaker and master of ceremonies. The two would conflict, but interestingly. Already he was looking in his mind for kind even celebrative remarks about Paul Goodman which would not violate every reservation he had about Goodman's dank glory. But he had it. It would be possible with no violation of truth to begin by saying that the first speaker looked very much like Nelson Algren,[2] because in fact the first speaker was Paul Goodman, and both Nelson Algren and Paul Goodman looked like old cons. Ladies and Gentlemen, without further ado let me introduce one of young America's favorite old cons, Paul Goodman! (It would not be necessary to add that where Nelson Algren looked like the sort of skinny old con who was in on every make in the joint, and would sign away Grandma's farm to stay in the game, Goodman looked like the sort of old con who had first gotten into trouble in the YMCA, and hadn't spoken to anyone since.)

All this while, Mailer had in clutch *Why Are We in Vietnam?*[3] He had neglected to bring his own copy to Washington and so had borrowed the book from his hostess on the promise he would inscribe it. (Later he was actually to lose it—working apparently on the principle that if you cannot make a hostess happy, the next best charity is to be so evil that the hostess may dine out on tales of your misconduct.) But the copy of the book is now noted because Mailer, holding it in one hand and the mug of whisky in the other, was obliged to notice on entering the Ambassador Theater that he had an overwhelming urge to micturate. The impulse to pass urine, being for some reason more difficult to restrain when both hands are occupied, there was no thought in the Master of Ceremonies' mind about the alternatives—he would have to find The Room before he went on stage.

That was not so immediately simple as one would have thought. The twenty guests from the party, looking a fair piece subdued under the fluorescent lights, had therefore the not unhaggard look

2. Chicago-based contemporary American novelist, author of *The Man with the Golden Arm* (1949) and other works.

3. Mailer's most recent novel (1967).

of people who have arrived an hour late at the theater. No matter that the theater was by every evidence sleazy (for neighborhood movie houses built on the dream of the owner that some day Garbo or Harlow or Lombard would give a look in, aged immediately they were not used for movies anymore) no matter, the guests had the uneasiness of very late arrivals. Apologetic, they were therefore in haste for the speakers to begin.

Mailer did not know this. He was off already in search of The Room, which, it developed was up on the balcony floor. Imbued with the importance of his first gig as Master of Ceremonies, he felt such incandescence of purpose that he could not quite conceive it necessary to notify de Grazia he would be gone for a minute. Incandescence is the *satori*[4] of the Romantic spirit which spirit would insist—this is the essence of the Romantic—on accelerating time. The greater the power of any subjective state, the more total is a Romantic's assumption that everyone understands exactly what he is about to do, therefore waste not a moment by stopping to tell them.

Flush with his incandescence, happy in all the anticipations of liberty which this Götterdämmerung[5] of a urination was soon to provide, Mailer did not know, but he had already and unwitting to himself metamorphosed into the Beast. Wait and see!

He was met on the stairs by a young man from *Time* magazine, a stringer presumably, for the young man lacked that I-am-damned look in the eye and rep tie of those whose work for *Time* has become a life addiction. The young man had a somewhat ill-dressed look, a map showed on his skin of an old adolescent acne, and he gave off the unhappy furtive presence of a fraternity member on probation for the wrong thing, some grievous mis-deposit of vomit, some hanky panky with frat-house tickets.

But the Beast was in a great good mood. He was soon to speak; that was food for all. So the Beast greeted the *Time* man with the geniality of a surrogate Hemingway unbending for the Luce-ites (Loo-sights was the pun)[6] made some genial cryptic remark or two about finding Herr John, said cheerfully in answer to why he was in Washington that he had come to protest the war in Vietnam, and taking a sip of bourbon from the mug he kept to keep all fires idling right, stepped off into the darkness of the top balcony floor, went through a door into a pitch-black men's room, and was alone with his need. No chance to find the light switch for he had no matches, he did not smoke. It was therefore a matter of locating what's what with the probing of his toes. He found something finally which seemed appropriate, and pleased with the precision of these generally unused senses in his feet, took aim between them at a point twelve inches ahead, and heard in the darkness the sound of his water striking the floor. Some damn mistake had been made, an assault from the side doubtless instead of the front, the bowl was relocated now, and Master of Ceremonies breathed deep of the great reveries of this utterly non-Sisyphian[7] release—at last!!—and thoroughly enjoyed the next forty-five seconds, being left on the aftermath not a note depressed by the condition of the premises. No, he was off on the Romantic's great military dream, which is: seize defeat, convert it to triumph. Of course, pissing on the floor was bad; very bad; the attendant would probably gossip to the police, (if the *Time* man did not sniff it out first) and The Uniformed in turn would report it to The Press who were sure to write about the scandalous condition in which this meeting had left the toilets. And all of this contretemps merely because the management, bitter with their lost dream of Garbo and Harlow and Lombard, were now so pocked and stingy they doused the lights. (Out of such stuff is a novelist's brain.)

Well, he could convert this deficiency to an asset. From gap to gain is very American. He would confess straight out to all aloud that he was the one who wet the floor in the men's room, he alone! While the audience was recovering from the existential anxiety of encountering an orator who confessed to such a crime, he would be able—their attention now riveted—to bring them up to a contemplation of deeper problems, of, indeed, the deepest problems, the most chilling alternatives, and would from there seek to bring them back to a restorative view of man. Man might be a fool who peed in the wrong pot, man was also a scrupulous servant of the self-damaging admission; man was therefore a philosopher who possessed the magic stone; he could turn loss to philosophical gain, and so illumine the deeps, find the poles, and eventually learn to cultivate his most special fool's garden: *satori*, incandescence, and the hard gemlike flame[8] of bourbon burning in the furnaces of metabolism.

Thus composed, illumined by these first stages of Emersonian transcendence, Mailer left the men's room, descended the stairs, entered the back of the orchestra, all opening remarks held close file in his mind like troops ranked in order before the parade, and then suddenly, most suddenly saw, with a cancerous swoop of albatross wings, that de Grazia was on the stage, was acting as M.C., was— no calling it back—launched into the conclusion of a gentle stammering stumbling—small orator, de Grazia!—introduction of Paul Goodman. All lost! The magnificent opening remarks about the forces gathered here to assemble on Saturday before the Pentagon, this historic occasion, let us hold it in our mind and focus on a

---

7. Sisyphus was condemned to push a huge boulder up a hill with, unlike Mailer, no prospect of relief.
8. The English critic Walter Pater (1839– 94) advocated in *Studies in the History of the Renaissance* that one should cultivate such an intense response to art.

puddle of passed water on the floor above and see if we assembled here can as leftists and proud dissenters contain within our minds the grandeur of the two—all lost!—no chance to do more than pick up later—later! after de Grazia and Goodman had finished dead-assing the crowd. Traitor de Grazia! Sicilian de Grazia!

As Mailer picked his way between people sitting on the stone floor (orchestra seats had been removed—the movie house was a dance hall now with a stage) he made a considerable stir in the orchestra. Mailer had been entering theaters for years, mounting stages—now that he had put on weight, it would probably have been fair to say that he came to the rostrum like a poor man's version of Orson Welles,[9] some minor note of the same contemplative presence. A titter and rise of expectation followed him. He could not resist its appeal. As he passed de Grazia, he scowled, threw a look from Lower Shakespearian "Et tu Bruté," and proceeded to slap the back of his hand against de Grazia's solar plexus. It was not a heavy blow, but then de Grazia was not a heavy man; he wilted some hint of an inch. And the audience pinched off a howl, squeaked on their squeal. It was not certain to them what had taken place.

Picture the scene two minutes later from the orchestra floor. Paul Goodman, now up at the microphone with no podium or rostrum, is reading the following lines:

> . . . these days my contempt for the misrulers of my country is icy and my indignation raucous.

It is impossible to tell what he is reading. Off at the wing of the stage where the others are collected—stout Macdonald, noble Lowell, beleaguered de Grazia, and Mailer, Prince of Bourbon, the acoustics are atrocious. One cannot hear a word the speaker is saying. Nor are there enough seats. If de Grazia and Macdonald are sitting in folding chairs, Mailer is squatting on his haunches, or kneeling on one knee like a player about to go back into the ball game. Lowell has the expression on his face of a dues payer who is just about keeping up with the interest on some enormous debt. As he sits on the floor with his long arms clasped mournfully about his long Yankee legs, "I am here," says his expression, "but I do not have to pretend I like what I see." The hollows in his cheeks give a hint of the hanging judge. Lowell is of a good weight, not too heavy, not too light, but the hollows speak of the great Puritan gloom in which the country was founded—man was simply not good enough for God.

At this moment, it is hard not to agree with Lowell. The cavern of the theater seems to resonate behind the glare of the footlights, but this is no resonance of a fine bass voice—it is rather electronics

9. Actor and film director (b. 1915) of large bulk.

on the march. The public address system hisses, then rings in a random chorus of electronic music, sounds of cerebral mastication from some horror machine of Outer Space (where all that electricity doubtless comes from, child!) then a hum like the squeak in the hinges of the gates of Hell—we are in the penumbra of psychedelic netherworlds, ghost-odysseys from the dead brain cells of adolescent trysts with LSD, some ultrapurple spotlight from the balcony (not ultraviolet—ultrapurple, deepest purple one could conceive) there out in the dark like some neon eye of the night, the media is the message,[1] and the message is purple, speaks of the monarchies of Heaven, madnesses of God, and clam-vaults of people on a stone floor. Mailer's senses are now tuned to absolute pitch or sheer error—he marks a ballot for absolute pitch—he is certain there is a profound pall in the audience. Yes, they sit there, stricken, inert, in terror of what Saturday will bring, and so are unable to rise to a word the speaker is offering them. It will take dynamite to bring life. The shroud of burned-out psychedelic dreams is in this audience, Cancer Gulch with open maw—and Mailer thinks of the vigor and the light (from marijuana?) in the eyes of those American soldiers in Vietnam who have been picked by the newsreel cameras to say their piece, and the happy healthy never unintelligent faces of all those professional football players he studies so assiduously on television come Sunday (he has neglected to put his bets in this week) and wonders how they would poll out on sentiment for the war.

HAWKS 95   DOVES 6

NFL Footballers Approve Vietnam War

Doubtless. All the healthy Marines, state troopers, professional athletes, movie stars, rednecks, sensuous life-loving Mafia, cops, mill workers, city officials, nice healthy-looking easy-grafting politicians full of the light (from marijuana?) in their eye of a life they enjoy—yes, they would be for the war in Vietnam. Arrayed against them as hard-core troops: an elite! the Freud-ridden embers of Marxism, good old American anxiety strata—the urban middle-class with their proliferated monumental adenoidal resentments, their secret slavish love for the oncoming hegemony of the computer and the suburb, yes, they and their children, by the sheer ironies, the sheer ineptitude, the *kinks* of history, were now being compressed into more and more militant stands, their resistance to the war some hopeless melange, somehow firmed, of Pacifism and closet Communism. And their children—on a freak-out from the suburbs to a love-in on the Pentagon wall.

It was the children in whom Mailer had some hope, a gloomy

---

1. Herbert Marshall McLuhan (b. 1911), a Canadian critic and communications theorist, coined this slogan in *Understanding Media* (1964) to say that each medium of communication (TV, print, etc.) determines its appropriate mode of response, whatever the "subject" of its address.

hope. These mad middle-class children with their lobotomies from sin, their nihilistic embezzlement of all middle-class moral funds, their innocence, their lust for apocalypse, their unbelievable indifference to waste: twenty generations of buried hopes perhaps engraved in their chromosomes, and now conceivably burning like faggots in the secret inquisitional fires of LSD. It was a devil's drug—designed by the Devil to consume the love of the best, and leave them liver-wasted, weeds of the big city. If there had been a player piano, Mailer might have put in a quarter to hear "In the Heart of the City Which Has No Heart."

Yes, these were the troops: middle-class cancer-pushers and drug-gutted flower children. And Paul Goodman to lead them. Was he now reading this?

> Once American faces were beautiful to me but now they look cruel and as if they had narrow thoughts.

Not much poetry, but well put prose. And yet there was always Goodman's damnable tolerance for all the varieties of sex. Did he know nothing of evil or entropy? Sex was the superhighway to your own soul's entropy if it was used without a constant sharpening of the taste. And orgies? What did Goodman know of orgies, real ones, not lib-lab college orgies to carry out the higher program of the Great Society, but real ones with murder in the air, and witches on the shoulder. The collected Tory[2] in Mailer came roaring to the surface like a cocked hat in a royal coach.

"When Goodman finishes, I'm going to take over as M.C.," he whispered to de Grazia. (The revery we have just attended took no more in fact than a second. Mailer's melancholy assessment of the forces now mounting in America took place between two consecutive lines of Goodman's poem—not because Mailer cerebrated that instantly, but because he had had the revery many a time before— he had to do no more than sense the audience, whisper Cancer Gulch to himself and the revery went by with a mental ch-ch-ch Click! reviewed again.) In truth, Mailer was now in a state. He had been prepared to open the evening with apocalyptic salvos to announce the real gravity of the situation, and the intensely peculiar American aspect of it—which is that the urban and suburban middle class were to be offered on Saturday an opportunity for glory— what other nation could boast of such option for its middle class? Instead—lost. The benignity and good humor of his planned opening remarks now subjugated to the electronic hawking and squabbling and *hum* of the P.A., the maniacal necessity to *wait* was on this hiatus transformed into a violent concentration of purpose, all intentions reversed. He glared at de Grazia. "How could you do

2. Member of the Conservative party in England, generally in support of established authority.

this?" he whispered to his ear.

De Grazia looked somewhat confused at the intensity. Meetings to de Grazia were obviously just meetings, assemblages of people who coughed up for large admissions or kicked in for the pitch; at best, some meetings were less boring than others. De Grazia was much too wise and guilty-spirited to brood on apocalypse. "I couldn't find you," he whispered back.

"You didn't trust me long enough to wait one minute?"

"We were over an hour late," de Grazia whispered again. "We had to begin."

Mailer was all for having the conversation right then on stage: to hell with reciprocal rights and polite incline of the ear to the speaker. The Beast was ready to grapple with the world. "Did you think I wouldn't show up?" he asked de Grazia.

"Well, I was wondering."

In what sort of mumbo-jumbo of promise and betrayal did de Grazia live? How could de Grazia ever suppose he would not show up? He had spent his life showing up at the most boring and onerous places. He gave a blast of his eyes to de Grazia. But Macdonald gave a look at Mailer, as if to say, "You're creating disturbance."

Now Goodman was done.

Mailer walked to the stage. He did not have any idea any longer of what he would say, his mind was empty, but in a fine calm, taking for these five instants a total rest. While there was no danger of Mailer ever becoming a demagogue since if the first idea he offered could appeal to a mob, the second in compensation would be sure to enrage them, he might nonetheless have made a fair country orator, for he loved to speak, he loved in fact to holler, and liked to hear a crowd holler back. (Of how many New York intellectuals may that be said?)

"I'm here as your original M.C., temporarily displaced owing to a contretemps"—which was pronounced purposefully as contretempse —"in the men's room," he said into the microphone for opening, but the gentle high-strung beast of a device pushed into a panic by the electric presence of a real Beast, let loose a squeal which shook the welds in the old foundation of the Ambassador. Mailer immediately decided he had had enough of public address systems, electronic fields of phase, impedance, and spooks in the circuitry. A hex on collaborating with Cancer Gulch. He pushed the microphone away, squared off before the audience. "Can you hear me?" he bellowed.

"Yes."

"Can you hear me in the balcony?"

"Yes."

"Then let's do away with electronics," he called out.

Cries of laughter came back. A very small pattern of applause. (Not too many on his side for electrocuting the public address system, or so his orator's ear recorded the vote.)

"Now I missed the beginning of this occasion, or I would have been here to introduce Paul Goodman, for which we're all sorry, right?"

Confused titters. Small reaction.

"What are you, dead-heads?" he bellowed at the audience. "Or are you all"—here he put on his false Irish accent—"in the nature of becoming dead ahsses?" Small laughs. A whistle or two. "No," he said, replying to the whistles, "I invoke these dead asses as part of the gravity of the occasion. The middle class plus one hippie surrealistic symbolic absolutely insane March on the Pentagon, bless us all," beginning of a big applause which offended Mailer for it came on "bless" and that was too cheap a way to win votes, "bless us all—shit!" he shouted, "I'm trying to say the middle class plus shit, I mean plus revolution, is equal to one big collective dead ass." Some yells of approval, but much shocked curious rather stricken silence. He had broken the shank of his oratorical charge. Now he would have to sweep the audience together again. (Perhaps he felt like a surgeon delivering a difficult breech—nothing to do but plunge to the elbows again.)

"To resume our exposition," a good warm titter, then a ripple of laughter, not unsympathetic to his ear; the humor had been unwitting, but what was the life of an orator without some bonus? "To resume this orderly marshalling of concepts"—a conscious attempt at humor which worked less well; he was beginning to recognize for the first time that bellowing without a mike demanded a more forthright style—"I shall now *engage* in confession." More Irish accent. (He blessed Brendan Behan[3] for what he had learned from him.) "A public speaker may offer you two opportunities. Instruction or confession." Laughter now. "Well, you're all college heads, so my instruction would be as pearls before—I dare not say it." Laughs. Boos. A voice from the balcony: "Come on, Norman, say something!"

"Is there a black man in the house?" asked Mailer. He strode up and down the stage pretending to peer at the audience. But in fact they were illumined just well enough to emphasize one sad discovery—if black faces there were they were certainly not in plenty. "Well ah'll just have to be the *impromptu* Black Power for tonight. Woo-eeeeee! Woo-eeeeee! HMmmmmmmm." He grunted with some partial success, showing hints of Cassius Clay.[4] "Get your white butts moving."

"The confession. The confession!" screamed some adolescents from up front.

---

3. Large, loud Irish playwright and performer (1925–1964).

4. Muhammad Ali (b. 1942), boxer and world heavyweight champion.

He came to a stop, shifted his voice. Now he spoke in a relaxed tone. "The confession, yeah!" Well, at least the audience was awake. He felt as if he had driven away some sepulchral phantoms of a variety which inhabited the profound middle-class schist. Now to charge the center of vested spookery.

"Say," he called out into the semidarkness with the ultrapurple light coming off the psychedelic lamp on the rail of the balcony, and the spotlights blaring against his eyes, "say," all happiness again, "I think of Saturday, and that March and do you know, fellow carriers of the holy unendurable grail, for the first time in my life I don't know whether I have the piss or the shit scared out of me most." It was an interesting concept, thought Mailer, for there was a difference between the two kinds of fear—pursue the thought, he would, in quieter times—"we are up, face this, all of you, against an existential situation—we do not know how it is going to turn out, and what is even more inspiring of dread is that the government doesn't know either."

Beginning of a real hand, a couple of rebel yells. "We're going to try to stick it up the government's ass," he shouted, "right into the sphincter of the Pentagon." Wild yells and chills of silence from different reaches of the crowd. Yeah, he was cooking now. "Will reporters please get every word accurately," he called out dryly to warm the chill.

But humor may have been too late. *The New Yorker* did not have strictures against the use of sh*t for nothing; nor did Dwight Macdonald love *The New Yorker* for nothing, he also had stricture against sh*t's metaphorical associations. Mailer looked to his right to see Macdonald approaching, a book in his hands, arms at his side, a sorrowing look of concern in his face. "Norman," said Macdonald quietly, "I can't possibly follow you after all this. Please introduce me, and get it over with."

Mailer was near to stricken. On the one hand interrupted on a flight; on the other, he had fulfilled no duty whatsoever as M.C. He threw a look at Macdonald which said: give me this. I'll owe you one.

But de Grazia was there as well. "Norman, let me be M.C. now," he said.

They were being monstrous unfair, thought Mailer. They didn't understand what he had been doing, how good he had been, what he would do next. Fatal to walk off now—the verdict would claim he was unbalanced. Still, he could not hold the stage by force. That was unthinkably worse.

For the virtuous, however, deliverance (like buttercups) pops up everywhere. Mailer now took the microphone and turned to the audience. He was careful to speak in a relaxed voice. "We are having a disagreement about the value of the proceedings. Some think de Grazia should resume his post as Master of Ceremonies. I would like to keep the position. It is an existential moment. We do not know how it will turn out. So let us vote on it." Happy laughter from the audience at these comic effects. Actually Mailer did not believe it was an existential situation any longer. He reckoned the vote would be well in his favor. "Will those," he asked, "who are in favor of Mr. de Grazia succeeding me as Master of Ceremonies please say aye."

A good sound number said aye.

Now for the ovation. "Will those opposed to this, please say no." The no's to Mailer's lack of pleasure were no greater in volume. "It seems the ayes and no's are about equal," said Mailer. (He was thinking to himself that he had posed the issue all wrong—the ayes should have been reserved for those who would keep him in office.) "Under the circumstances," he announced, "I will keep the chair." Laughter at this easy cheek. He stepped into the middle of such laughter. "You have all just learned an invaluable political lesson." He waved the microphone at the audience. "In the absence of a definitive vote, the man who holds the power, keeps it."

"Hey, de Grazia," someone yelled from the audience, "why do you let him have it?"

Mailer extended the microphone to de Grazia who smiled sweetly into it. "Because if I don't," he said in a gentle voice, "he'll beat the shit out of me." The dread word had been used again.

"Please, Norman," said Macdonald retreating.

So Mailer gave his introduction to Macdonald. It was less than he would have attempted if the flight had not been grounded, but it was certainly respectable. Under the military circumstances, it was a decent cleanup operation. For about a minute he proceeded to introduce Macdonald as a man with whom one might seldom agree, but could never disrespect because he always told the truth as he saw the truth, a man therefore of the most incorruptible integrity. "Pray heaven, I am right," said Mailer to himself, and walked past Macdonald who was on his way to the mike. Both men nodded coolly to each other.

In the wing, visible to the audience, Paul Goodman sat on a chair clearly avoiding any contaminatory encounter with The Existentialist. De Grazia gave his "It's tough all over" smile. Lowell sat in a mournful hunch on the floor, his eyes peering over his glasses to scrutinize the metaphysical substance of his boot, now hide? now machine? now, where the joining and to what? foot to boot, boot to earth—cease all speculations as to what was in Lowell's head. "The one mind a novelist cannot enter is the mind of a novelist superior to himself," said once to Mailer by Jean Malaquais.[5] So, by corollary, the one mind a minor poet may not enter . . .

Lowell looked most unhappy. Mailer, minor poet, had often ob-

___
5. French novelist whose *Reflections on Hip* Mailer admired.

served that Lowell had the most disconcerting mixture of strength and weakness in his presence, a blending so dramatic in its visible sign of conflict that one had to assume he would be sensationally attractive to women. He had something untouchable, all insane in its force; one felt immediately there were any number of causes for which the man would be ready to die, and for some he would fight, with an axe in his hand and a Cromwellian[6] light in his eye. It was even possible that physically he was very strong—one couldn't tell at all—he might be fragile, he might have the sort of farm mechanic's strength which could manhandle the rear axle and differential off a car and into the back of a pickup. But physical strength or no, his nerves were all too apparently delicate. Obviously spoiled by everyone for years, he seemed nonetheless to need the spoiling. These nerves—the nerves of a consummate poet—were not tuned to any battering. The squalls of the mike, now riding up a storm on the erratic piping breath of Macdonald's voice, seemed to tear along Lowell's back like a gale. He detested tumult—obviously. And therefore saw everything which was hopeless in a rife situation: the dank middle-class depths of the audience, the strident squalor of the mike, the absurdity of talent gathered to raise money—for what, dear God? who could finally know what this March might convey, or worse, purvey, and worst of all—to be associated now with Mailer's butcher boy attack. Lowell's eyes looked up from the shoe, and passed one withering glance by the novelist, saying much, saying, "Every single bad thing I have ever heard about you is not exaggerated."

Mailer, looking back, thought bitter words he would not say: "You, Lowell, beloved poet of many, what do you know of the dirt and the dark deliveries of the necessary? What do you know of dignity hard-achieved, and dignity lost through innocence, and dignity lost by sacrifice for a cause one cannot name. What do you know about getting fat against your will, and turning into a clown of an arriviste baron when you would rather be an eagle or a count, or rarest of all, some natural aristocrat from these damned democratic states. No, the only subject we share, you and I, is that species of perception which shows that if we are not very loyal to our unendurable and most exigent inner light, then some day we may burn. How dare you condemn me! You know the diseases which inhabit the audience in this accursed psychedelic house. How dare you scorn the explosive I employ?"

And Lowell with a look of the greatest sorrow as if all this *mess* were finally too shapeless for the hard Protestant smith of his own brain, which would indeed burst if it could not forge his experience into the iron edge of the very best words and the most unsinkable relation of words, now threw up his eyes like an epileptic as if

6. Oliver Cromwell (1599–1658) led the Puritan revolt against Charles I.

turned out of orbit by a turn of the vision—and fell backward, his head striking the floor with no last instant hesitation to cushion the blow, but like a baby, downright sudden, savagely to himself, as if from the height of a foot he had taken a pumpkin and dropped it splat on the floor. "There, much-regarded, much-protected brain, you have finally taken a blow," Lowell might have said to himself, for he proceeded to lie there, resting quietly, while Macdonald went on reading from "The White Man's Burden," Lowell seeming as content as if he had just tested the back of his cranium against a policeman's club. What a royal head they had all to lose!

6. A TRANSFER OF POWER

That evening went on. It was in fact far from climax. Lowell, resting in the wing on the floor of the stage, Lowell recuperating from the crack he had given his head, was a dreamy figure of peace in the corner of the proscenium, a reclining shepherd contemplating his flute, although a Washington newspaper was to condemn him on Saturday in company with Mailer for "slobbish behavior" at this unseemly lounging.

Now Macdonald finished. What with the delays, the unmanageable public address system, and the choppy waters of the audience at his commencement, for Mailer had obviously done him no good, Macdonald had been somewhat less impressive than ever. A few people had shown audible boredom with him. (Old-line Communists perhaps. Dwight was by now one of the oldest anti-Communists in America.)

> Take up the White Man's burden—
> Ye dare not stoop to less—
> Nor call too loud on Freedom
> To cloak your weariness;
> By all ye cry or whisper,
> By all ye leave or do,
> The silent, sullen peoples
> Shall weigh your Gods and you.[7]

read Macdonald from Kipling's poem, and the wit was in the selection, never the presentation.

He was done. He walked back to the wings with an air of no great satisfaction in himself, at most the sense of an obligation accomplished. Lowell's turn had arrived. Mailer stood up to introduce him.

The novelist gave a fulsome welcome to the poet. He did not speak of his poetry (with which he was not conspicuously familiar) nor of his prose which he thought excellent—Mailer told instead of

---

7. Penultimate stanza of Rudyard Kipling's poem *The White Man's Burden* (1899), usually considered an imperialist utterance.

why he had respect for Lowell as a man. A couple of years ago, the poet had refused an invitation from President Johnson to attend a garden party for artists and intellectuals, and it had attracted much attention at the time for it was one of the first dramatic acts of protest against the war in Vietnam, and Lowell was the only invited artist of first rank who had refused. Saul Bellow, for example, had attended the garden party. Lowell's refusal could not have been easy, the novelist suggested, because artists were attracted to formal afternoons of such elevated kind since that kind of experience was often stimulating to new perception and new work. So, an honorific occasion in full panoply was not easy for the mature artist to eschew. Capital! Lowell had therefore bypassed the most direct sort of literary capital. Ergo, Mailer respected him—he could not be certain he would have done the same himself, although, of course, he assured the audience he would not probably have ever had the opportunity to refuse. (Hints of merriment in the crowd at the thought of Mailer on the White House lawn.)

If the presentation had been formal up to here, it had also been somewhat graceless. On the consequence, our audience's amusement tipped the slumbering Beast. Mailer now cranked up a vaudeville clown for finale to Lowell's introduction. "Ladies and gentlemen, if novelists come from the middle class, poets tend to derive from the bottom and the top. We all know good poets at the bot'—ladies and gentlemen, here is a poet from the top, Mr. Robert Lowell." A large vigorous hand of applause, genuine enthusiasm for Lowell, some standing ovation.

But Mailer was depressed. He had betrayed himself again. The end of the introduction belonged in a burlesque house—he worked his own worst veins, like a man on the edge of bankruptcy trying to collect hopeless debts. He was fatally vulgar! Lowell passing him on the stage had recovered sufficiently to cast him a nullifying look. At this moment, they were obviously far from friends.

Lowell's shoulders had a slump, his modest stomach was pushed forward a hint, his chin was dropped to his chest as he stood at the microphone, pondering for a moment. One did not achieve the languid grandeurs of that slouch in one generation—the grandsons of the first sons had best go through the best troughs in the best eating clubs at Harvard before anyone in the family could try for such elegant note. It was now apparent to Mailer that Lowell would move by instinct, ability, and certainly by choice, in the direction most opposite from himself.

"Well," said Lowell softly to the audience, his voice dry and gentle as any New England executioner might ever hope to be, "this has been a zany evening." Laughter came back, perhaps a little too much. It was as if Lowell wished to reprove Mailer, not humiliate him. So he shifted, and talked a bit uneasily for perhaps a minute about very little. Perhaps it was too little. Some of the audience, encouraged by earlier examples, now whistled. "We can't hear you," they shouted, "speak louder."

Lowell was annoyed. "I'll bellow," he said, "but it won't do any good." His firmness, his distaste for the occasion, communicated some subtle but impressive sense of his superiority. Audiences are moved by many cues but the most satisfactory to them is probably the voice of their abdomen. There are speakers who give a sense of security to the abdomen, and they always elicit the warmest kind of applause. Mailer was not this sort of speaker; Lowell was. The hand of applause which followed this remark was fortifying. Lowell now proceeded to read some poetry.

He was not a splendid reader, merely decent to his own lines, and he read from that slouch, that personification of ivy climbing a column, he was even diffident, he looked a trifle helpless under the lights. Still, he made no effort to win the audience, seduce them, dominate them, bully them, amuse them, no, they were there for him, to please *him*, a sounding board for the plucked string of his poetic line, and so he endeared himself to them. They adored him— for his talent, his modesty, his superiority, his melancholy, his petulance, his weakness, his painful, almost stammering shyness, his noble strength—*there* was the string behind other strings.

> O to break loose, like the chinook
> salmon jumping and falling back,
> nosing up to the impossible
> stone and bone-crushing waterfall—
> raw-jawed, weak-fleshed there, stopped by ten
> steps of the roaring ladder, and then
> to clear the top on the last try,
> alive enough to spawn and die.[8]

Mailer discovered he was jealous. Not of the talent. Lowell's talent was very large, but then Mailer was a bulldog about the value of his own talent. No, Mailer was jealous because he had worked for this audience, and Lowell without effort seemed to have stolen them: Mailer did not know if he was contemptuous of Lowell for playing *grand maître*,[9] or admiring of his ability to do it. Mailer knew his own version of *grand maître* did not compare. Of course no one would be there there to accept his version either. Then pain of bad reviews was not in the sting, but in the subsequent pressure which, like water on a joint, collected over the decade. People who had not read your books in fifteen years were certain they were missing nothing of merit. A buried sorrow, not very attractive, (for bile was in it and the bitterness of unrequited literary injustice)

8. First stanza of Lowell's *Waking Early Sunday Morning* (from *Near the Ocean*, 1967). After the next paragraph the final stanza is quoted.
9. Grand master.

released itself from some ducts of the heart, and Mailer felt hot anger at how Lowell was loved and he was not, a pure and surprising recognition of how much emotion, how much simple and child-like bitter sorrowing emotion had been concealed from himself for years under the manhole cover of his contempt for bad reviews.

> Pity the planet, all joy gone
> from this sweet volcanic cone;
> peace to our children when they fall
> in small war on the heels of small
> war—until the end of time
> to police the earth, a ghost
> orbiting forever lost
> in our monotonous sublime.

They gave Lowell a good standing ovation, much heartiness in it, much obvious pleasure that they were there on a night in Washington when Robert Lowell had read from his work—it was as nice as that—and then Lowell walked back to the wings, and Mailer walked forward. Lowell did not seem particularly triumphant. He looked still modest, still depressed, as if he had been applauded too much for too little and so the reservoir of guilt was still untapped.

Nonetheless, to Mailer it was now *mano a mano.*[1] Once, on a vastly larger scale of applause, perhaps people had reacted to Manolete[2] not unlike the way they reacted to Lowell, so stirred by the deeps of sorrow in the man, that the smallest move produced the largest emotion. If there was any value to the comparison then Mailer was kin to the young Dominguin, taking raucous chances, spitting in the eye of the bull, an excess of variety in his passes. But probably there was no parallel at all. He may have felt like a matador in the flush of full competition, going out to do his work after the other torero has had a triumph, but for fact he was probably less close in essence now to the bullfighter than the bull. We must not forget the Beast. He had been sipping the last of the bourbon out of the mug. He had been delayed, piqued, twisted from his purpose and without anything to eat in close to ten hours. He was on the hunt. For what, he hardly knew. It is possible the hunt existed long before the victim was ever conceived.

"Now, you may wonder who I am," he said to the audience, or bellowed to them, for again he was not using the mike, "and you may wonder why I'm talking in a Southern accent which is phony" —the Southern accent as it sounded to him in his throat, was actually not too bad at this moment—"and the reason is that I want to make a presentation to you." He did not have a notion of what he would say next, but it never occurred to him something would

---

1. Hand to hand.
2. Manolete and his younger countryman Dominguin were famous matadors.

not come. His impatience, his sorrow, his jealousy were gone, he just wanted to live on the edge of that rhetorical sword he would soon try to run through the heart of the audience. "We are gathered here"—shades of Lincoln in hippieland—"to make a move on Saturday to invest the Pentagon and halt and slow down its workings, and this will be at once a symbolic act and a real act"—he was roaring—"for real heads may possibly get hurt, and soldiers will be there to hold us back, and some of us may be arrested"—how, wondered the wise voice at the rear of this roaring voice, could one ever leave Washington now without going to jail?—"some blood conceivably will be shed. If I were the man in the government responsible for controlling this March, I would not know what to do." Sonorously—"I would not wish to arrest too many or hurt anyone for fear the repercussions in the world would be too large for my bureaucrat's heart to bear—it's so full of shit." Roars and chills from the audience again. He was off into obscenity. It gave a heartiness like the blood of beef tea to his associations. There was no villainy in obscenity for him, just—paradoxically, characteristically—his love for America: he had first come to love America when he served in the U.S. Army, not the America of course of the flag, the patriotic unendurable fix of the television programs and the newspapers, no, long before he was ever aware of the institutional oleo of the most suffocating American ideas he had come to love what editorial writers were fond of calling the democratic principle with its faith in the common man. He found that principle and that man in the Army, but what none of the editorial writers ever mentioned was that that noble common man was obscene as an old goat, and his obscenity was what saved him. The sanity of said common democratic man was in his humor, his humor was in his obscenity. And his philosophy as well—a reductive philosophy which looked to restore the hard edge of proportion to the overblown values overhanging each small military existence—viz: being forced to salute an overconscientious officer with your back stiffened into an exaggerated posture. "That Lieutenant is chickenshit," would be the platoon verdict, and a blow had somehow been struck for democracy and the sanity of good temper. Mailer once heard a private end an argument about the merits of a general by saying, "his spit don't smell like ice cream either," only the private was not speaking of spit. Mailer thought enough of the line to put it into *The Naked and the Dead*, along with a good many other such lines the characters in his mind and his memory of the Army had begun to offer him. The common discovery of America was probably that Americans were the first people on earth to live for their humor; nothing was so important to Americans as humor. In Brooklyn, he had taken this for granted, at Harvard he had thought it was a by-product of being at Harvard, but in the Army he discovered that the humor was probably in the veins and the roots of the local history of every state and county in America—the truth of the way it really felt over the years passed on a river of obscenity from small-town storyteller to storyteller there down below the bankers and the books and the educators and the legislators—so Mailer never felt more like an American than when he was naturally obscene—all the gifts of the American language came out in the happy play of obscenity upon concept, which enabled one to go back to concept again. What was magnificent about the word shit is that it enabled you to use the word noble: a skinny Southern cracker with a beatific smile on his face saying in the dawn in a Filipino rice paddy, "Man, I just managed to take me a noble shit." Yeah, that was Mailer's America. If he was going to love something in the country, he would love that. So after years of keeping obscene language off to one corner of his work, as if to prove after *The Naked and the Dead* that he had many an arrow in his literary quiver, he had come back to obscenity again in the last year—he had kicked goodbye in his novel *Why Are We in Vietnam?* to the old literary corset of good taste, letting his sense of language play on obscenity as freely as it wished, so discovering that everything he knew about the American language (with its incommensurable resources) went flying in and out of the line of his prose with the happiest beating of wings—it was the first time his style seemed at once very American to him and very literary in the best way, at least as he saw the best way. But the reception of the book had been disappointing. Not because many of the reviews were bad (he had learned, despite all sudden discoveries of sorrow, to live with that as one lived with smog) no, what was disappointing was the crankiness across the country. Where fusty conservative old critics had once defended the obscenity in *The Naked and the Dead*, they, or their sons, now condemned it in the new book, and that *was* disappointing. The country was not growing up so much as getting a premature case of arthritis.

At any rate, he had come to the point where he liked to use a little obscenity in his public speaking. Once people got over the shock, they were sometimes able to discover that the humor it provided was not less powerful than the damage of the pain. Of course he did not do it often and he tried not to do it unless he was in good voice—Mailer was under no illusion that public speaking was equal to candid conversation; an obscenity uttered in a voice too weak for its freight was obscene, since obscenity probably resides in the quick conversion of excitement to nausea—which is why Lyndon Johnson's speeches are called obscene by some. The excitement of listening to the American President alters abruptly into the nausea of wandering down the blind alleys of his voice.

This has been a considerable defense of the point, but then the point was at the center of his argument and it could be put thus: the American corporation executive, who was after all the foremost representative of Man in the world today, was perfectly capable of burning unseen women and children in the Vietnamese jungles, yet felt a large displeasure and fairly final disapproval at the generous use of obscenity in literature and in public.

The apology may now be well taken, but what in fact did Mailer say on the stage of the Ambassador before the evening was out? Well, not so very much, just about enough to be the stuff of which footnotes are made, for he did his best to imitate a most high and executive voice.

"I had an experience as I came to the theater to speak to all of you, which is that before appearing on this stage I went upstairs to the men's room as a prelude to beginning this oratory so beneficial to all"—laughs and catcalls—"and it was dark, so—ahem—I missed the bowl—all men will know what I mean. Forgiveness might reign. But tomorrow, they will blame that puddle of water on Communists which is the way we do things here in Amurrica, anyone of you pinko poos want to object, lemme tell ya, the reason nobody was in the men's room, and it so dark, is that if there been a light they'd had to put a CIA man in there and the hippies would grope him silly, see here, you know who I am, why it just came to me, ah'm so phony, I'm as full of shit as Lyndon Johnson. Why, man, I'm nothing but his little old alter ego. That's what you got right here working for you, Lyndon Johnson's little old *dwarf* alter ego. How you like him? How you like him?" (Shades of Cassius Clay again.)

And in the privacy of his brain, quiet in the glare of all that sound and spotlight, Mailer thought quietly, "My God, that is probably exactly what you are at this moment, Lyndon Johnson with all his sores, sorrows, and vanity, squeezed down to five foot eight," and Mailer felt for the instant possessed, as if he had seized some of the President's secret soul, or the President seized some of his—the bourbon was as luminous as moonshine to the spores of insanity in the flesh of his brain, a smoke of menace swished in the air, and something felt real, almost as if he had caught Lyndon Johnson by the toe and now indeed, bugger the rhyme, should never let him go.

"Publicity hound," shouted someone from the upper balcony.

"Fuck you," cried Mailer back with absolute delight, all the force of the Texas presidency in his being. Or was it Lucifer's fire? But let us use asterisks for these obscenities to emphasize how happily he used the words, they went off like fireworks in his orator's heart, and asterisks look like rocket-bursts and the orbs from Roman candles * * *. F*ck you he said to the heckler but with such gusto the vowel was doubled. F*-*ck you! was more like it. So, doubtless, had the President disposed of all opposition in private session. Well, Mailer was here to bring the presidency to the public.

"This yere dwarf alter ego has been telling you about his imbroglio with the p*ssarooney up on the top floor, and will all the reporters please note that I did not talk about defecation commonly known as sheeee-it!"—full imitation of LBJ was attempted there—"but to the contrary, speak of you-rye-nation! I p*ssed on the floor. Hoo-ee! Hoo-ee! How's that for Black Power full of white p*ss? You just know all those reporters are going to say it was sh*t tomorrow. F*ck them. F*ck all of them. Reporters, will you stand up and be counted?"

A wail of delight from the students in the audience. What would the reporters do? Would they stand?

One lone figure arose.

"Where are *you* from?" asked Mailer.

"Washington *Free Press*." A roar of delight from the crowd. It was obviously some student or hippie paper.

"Ah want *The Washington Post*," said Mailer in his best Texas tones, "and the *Star*. Ah know there's a *Time* magazine man here for one, and twenty more like him no doubt." But no one stood. So Mailer went into a diatribe. "Yeah, people," he said, "watch the reporting which follows. Yeah, these reporters will kiss Lyndon Johnson's *ss and Dean Rusk's *ss and Man Mountain Mc-Namara's *ss,[3] they will rush to kiss it, but will they stand up in public? No! Because they are the silent assassins of the Republic. They alone have done more to destroy this nation than any force in it." They will certainly destroy me in the morning, he was thinking. But it was for this moment worth it, as if two very different rivers, one external, one subjective, had come together; the frustrated bile, piss, pus, and poison he had felt at the progressive contamination of all American life in the abscess of Vietnam, all of that, all heaped in lighted coals of brimstone on the press' collective ear, represented one river, and the other was the frustrated actor in Mailer—ever since seeing *All the King's Men* years ago he had wanted to come on in public as a Southern demagogue.

The speech went on, and a few fine things possibly were said next to a few equally obscene words, and then Mailer thought in passing of reading a passage from *Why Are We in Vietnam?* but the passage was full of plays of repetition on the most famous four-letter word of them all, and Mailer thought that was conceivably redundant now and so he ended modestly with a final, "See you on Saturday!"

The applause was fair. Not weak, but empty of large demonstration. No standing ovation for certain. He felt cool, and in a quiet, pleasant, slightly depressed mood. Since there was not much conversation between Macdonald, Lowell, and himself, he turned after a moment, left the stage, and walked along the floor where the

3. Dean Rusk (b. 1909), Secretary of State during the Kennedy and Johnson administrations, 1961–69. Robert Mc-Namara (b. 1916), Secretary of Defense during the Kennedy and Johnson administrations, 1961–68. The two cabinet officials held most responsible for perpetuating the war in Vietnam.

audience had sat. A few people gathered about him, thanked him, shook his hand. He was quiet and reserved now, with genial slightly muted attempts to be cordial. He had noticed this shift in mood before, even after readings or lectures which had been less eventful. There was a mutual embarrassment between speaker and audience once the speaker had left the stage and walked through the crowd. It was due no doubt to the intimacy—that most special intimacy— which can live between a speaker and the people he has addressed, yes they had been so intimate then, that the encounter now, after- ward, was like the eye-to-the-side maneuvers of client and whore once the act is over and dressing is done.

Mailer went on from there to a party of more liberal academics, and drank a good bit more and joked with Macdonald about the superiority of the introduction he had given to Lowell over the introduction Dwight had received.

"Next time don't interrupt me," he teased Macdonald, "and I'll give you a better introduction."

"Goodness, I couldn't hear a word you said," said Macdonald, "you just sounded awful. Do you know, Norman, the acoustics were terrible on the wing. I don't think any of us heard anything anyone else said."

Some time in the early morning, or not so early, Mailer got to bed at the Hay-Adams and fell asleep to dream no doubt of fancy parties in Georgetown when the Federal period in architecture was young. Of course if this were a novel, Mailer would spend the rest of the night with a lady. But it is history, and so the Novelist is for once blissfully removed from any description of the hump-your- backs of sex. Rather he can leave such matters to the happy or unhappy imagination of the reader.

Part II
2. THE MARSHAL AND THE NAZI[4]

They put him in the rear seat of a Volkswagen camper and he welcomed the opportunity to relax. Soon they would drive him, he guessed, to some nearby place where he would be arraigned, fined, and released. He kept searching the distance for sight of Lowell and Macdonald whom he assumed would be following any minute. The thought that they might not have been picked up was depressing, for he could only guess at the depths of Lowell's dejection if he had botched his arrest, and now, with each twenty seconds, he became more gloomily certain that Lowell and Macdonald had been turned back, had failed to get arrested, and blamed himself now for the rush with which he had set out—he should have warned them the arrest might not be automatic, that one might have to steal it—he

---

4. In this section and in the next, *Grandma with Orange Hair*, Mailer has been arrested for transgressing a police line near the Pentagon and finds himself in a Volkswagen camper on his way to be arraigned.

felt somehow incompetent at not having properly prepared them.

Now a new man entered the Volkswagen. Mailer took him at first for a Marshal or an official, since he was wearing a dark suit and a white motorcycle helmet, and had a clean-cut stubborn face with short features. But he was carrying something which looked like a rolled-up movie screen over five feet long, and he smiled in the friendliest fashion, sat down next to Mailer, and took off his helmet. Mailer thought he was about to be interrogated and he looked forward to that with this friendly man, no less! (of course the prisoner often looks forward to his interrogation) but then another man carrying a clipboard came up to them, and leaning through the wide double door of the camper, asked questions of them both. When Mailer gave his name, the man with the clipboard acted as if he had never heard of him, or at least pretended never to have heard of him, the second possibility seeming possible since word traveled quickly from reporters.

"How do you spell it?"

"M.A.I.L.E.R."

"Why were you arrested, Mr. Miller?"

"For transgressing a police line as a protest against the war in Vietnam."

The Clipboard then asked a question of the man sitting next to him. "And why were *you* arrested?"

"As an act of solidarity with oppressed forces fighting for liberty against this country in Southeast Asia."

The Clipboard nodded drily, as if to say, "Yeah, we're all crazy here." Then he asked, pointing to the object which looked like a rolled-up movie screen. "You want that with you?"

"Yessir," said the man next to Mailer. "I'd like to take it along."

The Clipboard gave a short nod, and walked off. Mailer would never see him again. If the History has therefore spent a pointless exchange with him, it is to emphasize that the first few minutes of an arrest such as this are without particular precedent, and so Mailer, like a visitor from Mars, or an adolescent entering polite society, had no idea of what might be important next and what might not. This condition of innocence was not, however, particularly disagreeable since it forced him to watch everything with the attention, let us say, of a man like William Buckley[5] spending his first hour in a Harlem bar—no, come! things are far safer for Mailer at the Pentagon.

He chatted with his fellow prisoner, Teague, Walter Teague was the name, who had been in the vanguard of the charge Mailer had seen from the parking lot. But before any confused impressions were to be sorted, they were interrupted by the insertion of the next prisoner put into the Volkswagen, a young man with straight blond

5. William F. Buckley, Jr. (b. 1925), conservative political columnist.

hair and a Nazi armband on his sleeve. He was installed in the rear, with a table between, but Mailer was not happy, for his eyes and the Nazi's bounced off each other like two heads colliding—the novelist discovered he was now in a hurry for them to get this stage of the booking completed. He was also privately indignant at the U.S. Army (like a private citizen, let us say, who writes a letter to his small-town newspaper) at the incredible stupidity of putting a Nazi in the same Volkswagen camper with Pentagon demonstrators— there were two or three other cars available, at least!—next came the suspicion that this was not an accident, but a provocation in the making. If the Nazi started trouble, and there was a fight, the newspaper accounts would doubtless state that Norman Mailer had gotten into an altercation five minutes after his arrest. (Of course, they would not say with whom.) This is all doubtless most paranoid of Mailer, but then he had had nearly twenty years of misreporting about himself, and the seed of paranoia is the arrival of the conviction that the truth about oneself is never told. (Mailer might have done better to pity the American populace—receiving misinformation in systematic form tends to create mass schizophrenia: poor America—Eddie and Debbie are True Love.)[6]

Now they were moved out of the camper and over to an Army truck. There was Teague, and the novelist, and another arrestee—a tall Hungarian who quickly told Mailer how much he liked his books and in much the same breath that he was a Freedom Fighter —there was also a new U. S. Marshal, and the Nazi. The prisoners climbed one by one over the high tailgate, Mailer finding it a touch awkward for he did not wish to dirty his dark blue pinstripe suit, and then they stood in the rear of the truck, a still familiar 2½ ton 6-by of a sort which the novelist hadn't been in for twenty-one years, not since his Army discharge.

Standing in the truck, a few feet apart from each other, all prisoners regarding one another, the Nazi fixed on Mailer. Their eyes locked like magnets coming into line, and for perhaps twenty seconds they stared at each other. Mailer looked into a pair of yellow eyes so compressed with hate that back of his own eyes he could feel the echo of such hatred ringing. The Nazi was taller than Mailer, well-knit, and with neatly formed features and a shock of blond hair, would have been handsome but for the ferocity of his yellow eyes which were sunk deep in their sockets. Those eyes made him look like an eagle.

Yet Mailer had first advantage in this eye-staring contest. Because he had been prepared for it. He had been getting into such confrontations for years, and rarely lost them, even though he sometimes thought they were costing him eyesight. Still, some developed instinct had made him ready an instant before the Nazi. Every bit

6. Reference to the highly publicized marriage in the 1950s between singer Eddie Fisher and actress Debbie Reynolds which later ended in divorce.

of intensity he possessed—with the tremors of the March and the Marshal's arm still pent in him—glared forth into the other's eyes: he was nonetheless aghast at what he saw. The American Nazis were all fanatics, yes, poor mad tormented fanatics, their psyches twisted like burning leaves in the fire of their hatreds, yes, indeed! but this man's conviction stood in his eyes as if his soul had been focused to a single point of light. Mailer could feel violence behind violence rocking through his head. If the two of them were ever alone in an alley, one of them might kill the other in a fight—it was not unlike holding an electric wire in the hand. And the worst of it was that he was not even feeling violent himself—whatever violence he possessed had gone to his eyes—by that route had he projected himself on the Nazi.

After the first five seconds of the shock had passed, he realized he might be able to win—the Nazi must have taken too many easy contests, and had been too complacent in the first moment, yes it was like wrestlers throwing themselves on each other: one knuckle of one finger a little better able to be worked on a grip could make the difference—now he could feel the hint of force ebbing in the other's eyes, and could wonder at his own necessity to win. He did not hate the Nazi nearly so much as he was curious about him, yet the thought of losing had been intolerable as if he had been *obliged* not to lose, as if the duty of his life at this particular moment must have been to look into that Nazi's eye, and say with his own, "You claim you have a philosophical system which comprehends all—you know nothing! My eyes encompass yours. My philosophy contains yours. You have met the wrong man!" And the Nazi looked away, and was hystérical with fury on the instant.

"You Jew bastard," he shouted. "Dirty Jew with kinky hair."

They didn't speak that way. It was too corny. Yet he could only answer, "You filthy Kraut."

"Dirty Jew."

"Kraut pig."

A part of his mind could actually be amused at this choice—he didn't even hate Germans any more. Indeed Germans fascinated him now. Why they liked his books more than Americans did. Yet here he could think of nothing better to return than "Kraut pig."

"I'm not a Kraut," said the Nazi, "I'm a Norwegian." And then as if the pride of his birth had tricked him into communication with an infidel, thus into sacrilege, the Nazi added quickly, "Jew bastard red," then cocked his fists. "Come here, you coward," he said to Mailer, "I'll kill you."

"Throw the first punch, baby," said Mailer, "you'll get it all."

They were both absolutely right. They had a perfect sense of the other. Mailer was certainly not brave enough to advance on the Nazi—it would be like springing an avalanche on himself. But he also knew that if the Nazi jumped him, one blond youth was very

likely to get massacred. In retrospect, it would appear not uncomic
—two philosophical monomaniacs with the same flaw—they could
not help it, they were counterpunchers.

"Jew coward! Red bastard!"

"Go fuck yourself, Nazi baby."

But now a tall U. S. Marshal who had the body and insane look
of a very good rangy defensive end in professional football—that
same hard high-muscled build, same coiled spring of wrath, same
livid conviction that everything opposing the team must be wrecked,
sod, turf, grass, uniforms, helmets, bodies, yes even bite the football
if it will help—now leaped into the truck and jumped between them.
"Shut up," he said, "or I'll wreck both of you." He had a long
craggy face somewhere in the physiognomical land between Steve
McQueen and Robert Mitchum, but he would never have made
Hollywood, for his skin was pocked with the big boiling craters of a
red lunar acne, and his eyes in Cinemascope[7] would have blazed an
audience off their seat for such gray-green flame could only have
issued from a blowtorch. Under his white Marshal's helmet, he was
one impressive piece of gathered wrath.

Speaking to the Marshal at this point would have been dangerous.
The Marshal's emotions had obviously been marinating for a week
in the very special bile waters American Patriotism reserves for its
need. His feelings were now caustic as a whip—too gentle the
simile!—he was in agonies of frustration because the honor of his
profession kept him from battering every prisoner's head to a
Communist pulp. Mailer looked him over covertly to see what he
could try if the Marshal went to work on him. All reports: negative.
He would not stand a chance with this Marshal—there seemed no
place to hit him where he'd be vulnerable; stone larynx, leather
testicles, ice cubes for eyes. And he had his Marshal's club in his
hand as well. Brother! Bring back the Nazi!

Whether the Marshal had been once in the Marine Corps, or in
Vietnam, or if half his family were now in Vietnam, or if he just
hated the sheer Jew York presumption of that slovenly, drug-ridden
weak contaminating America-hating army of termites outside this
fortress' walls, he was certainly any upstanding demonstrator's
nightmare. Because he was full of American rectitude and was
fearless, and savage, savage as the exhaust left in the wake of a
motorcycle club, gasoline and cheap perfume were one end of his
spectrum, yeah, this Marshal loved action, but he was also in that
no man's land between the old frontier and the new ranch home—
as they, yes *they*—the enemies of the Marshal—tried to pass bills to
limit the purchase of hunting rifles, so did *they* try to kill America,
inch by inch, all the forces of evil, disorder, mess and chaos in the
world, and *cowardice*! and city ways, and slick shit, and despolia-

---

7. By using special-lens cameras and extrawide curved screen, Cinemascope achieved
massive and realistic effects.

tion of national resources, all the subtle invisible creeping paralyses
of Communism which were changing America from a land where
blood was red to a land where water was foul—yes in this Marshal's
mind—no lesser explanation could suffice for the Knight of God
light in the flame of his eye—the evil was without, America was
threatened by a foreign disease, and the Marshal was threatened to
the core of his sanity by any one of the first fifty of Mailer's ideas
which would insist that the evil was within, that the best in America
was being destroyed by what in itself seemed next best, yes American heroism corrupted by American know-how—no wonder murder
stood out in his face as he looked at the novelist—for the Marshal
to lose his sanity was no passing psychiatric affair: think rather of a
rifleman on a tower in Texas and a score of his dead on the street.[8]

But now the Nazi began to play out the deepest of ceremonies.
The truck standing still, another Marshal at the other end of the van
(the one indeed who had arrested Mailer) and Teague and the
Hungarian to different sides, everyone had their eyes on the Norwegian. He now glared again at Mailer, but then whipped away his
eyes before a second contest could begin, and said, "All right, Jew,
come over here if you want a fight."

The Marshal took the Nazi and threw him against the side-wall
of the truck. As he bounced off, the Marshal gave him a rap below
the collarbone with the butt of his club. "I told you to shut up.
Now, just shut up." His rage was intense. The Nazi looked back at
him sullenly, leaned on the butt of the club almost defiantly as if the
Marshal didn't know what foolish danger he was in to treat the Nazi
so, the Nazi had a proud curved hint of a smile, as if he were
recording the features of this Marshal forever in the history of his
mind, the Nazi's eyes seemed to say to the Marshal, "You are really
on my side although you do not admit it—you would like to beat
me now because in the future you know you will yet kiss my
boots!" And the Marshal traveling a high edge of temper began to
slam the Nazi against the wall of the truck with moderate force, but
rhythmically, as if he would pacify them both by this act, bang, and
bang, step by step, the imaginary dialogue of the Marshal to the
Nazi now sounding in Mailer's ear somewhat like this, "Listen,
Nazi, you're nothing but a rat fart who makes my job harder, and
gives the scum around me room to breathe, cause they look at you
and feel righteous. You just keep me diverted from the real danger."

And the Nazi looked back with a full sullen pouting defiance as if
from deep in himself he was all unconsciously saying to the Marshal, "You know I am beautiful, and you are frightened of me. I
have a cause, and I am ready to die for it, and you are just ready to
die for a uniform. Join me where the real war is. Already the

8. University of Texas student C. J.
Whitman, firing from the observation
tower on the Austin campus, killed 12
people and wounded 33 others in 1966.

strongest and wildest men in America wear our symbol on their motorcycle helmets."

And the Marshal, glaring back at the Nazi, butt of his club transfixing him against the wall of the van, gave a contemptuous look, as if to drop him with the final unspoken word. "Next to strong wild men, you're nothing but a bitch."

Then the truck began to move, and the Marshal calmer now, stood silently between Mailer and the Nazi; and the Nazi also quiet now, stood in place looking neither at the Marshal nor Mailer. Some small storm of hysteria seemed to have worked itself out of the van.

3. GRANDMA WITH ORANGE HAIR

There was not much to see through the canvas arch of the vehicle. A view of a service road they passed along, a little bumping, a bit of swaying—in two minutes they arrived at the next stop. It was the southwest wall of the Pentagon, so much was obvious, for the sun shone brightly here.

Probably they were at the rear of a large mess hall or cafeteria, since a loading platform extended for a considerable distance to either side of where the truck had come in. There were MPs and Marshals on the platform, maybe twenty or thirty, as many again in the back-up area where they had come in. At a long desk at the base of the loading platform, the prisoners were being booked. Each had a Marshal beside him. It was quiet and orderly. The Nazi was standing next to Mailer, but now neither looked at the other. It was indeed all over. The Nazi looked quietly spent, almost gentle—as if the outbursts had been his duty, but duty done, he was just a man again—no need to fight.

They took Mailer's name, having trouble with the spelling again. He was now certain it was not trivial harassment but simple unfamiliarity. The clerk, a stout Marshal with the sort of face that belonged to a cigar, worked carefully at his sheets. The questions were routine—name, address, why arrested—but he entered them with a slow-moving pen which spoke of bureaucratic sacraments taken up, and records set down in perpetuity.

When this was over, Mailer was led by the Marshal who had first arrested him, over to the open door of a sort of school bus painted olive-drab. There was, however, a delay in boarding it, and the Marshal said, "I'm sorry, Mr. Mailer, we have to wait here for a minute to get your number."

"I don't mind."

They were being particularly polite with each other. Mailer had a clear opportunity to look again at this Marshal's face; the *vibrations* of the arrest now utterly discharged, he had an agreeable face indeed, quiet, honest, not unintelligent, not unhumorous. And he talked with the pleasant clipped integrity of a West Virginia accent.

Mailer was going to ask him if he came from West Virginia, then out of some random modesty about putting too intensive a question and being wrong, he said instead, "May I ask your name?" It was as one might have expected, a name like Tompkins or Hudkins. "May I ask which state you're from, Marshal?"

"It's West Virginia, Mr. Mailer."

"My wife and I had a young lady work for us once who came from West Virginia. Your accent is similar to hers."

"Is that a fact?"

"Yes, I was wondering if you might be related. There's a suggestion of family resemblance." He mentioned the name. No relation.

Now the necessary paper was delivered to the Marshal. He signed it, and Mailer could board the bus. He had been given the number 10. He was the tenth man arrested at the Pentagon.

"Well, goodbye, Mr. Mailer. Nice talking to you."

"Yes."

Perhaps they were troubled partisans. Or did each wish to show the other that the enemy possessed good manners?

No, thought Mailer, it was ritual. At the moment of the arrest, cop and criminal knew each other better than mates, or at least knew some special *piece* of each other better than mates, yes an arrest was carnal. Not sexual, carnal—of the meat, strangers took purchase of each other's meat. Then came the reciprocal tendency to be pleasant. Beneath all those structures advertised as majestic in law and order there was this small carnal secret which the partners of a bust could share. It was tasty to chat afterward, all sly pleasures present that the secret was concealed. Mailer thought of a paragraph he had written once about police—it had probably acted upon him as much as anything else to first imagine his movie.[9] Now his mind remembered the approximate sense of the paragraph, which actually (indulging Mailer's desire to be quoted) went exactly like this:

> . . . they contain explosive contradictions within themselves. Supposed to be law-enforcers, they tend to conceive of themselves as the law. They are more responsible than the average man, they are more infantile. They are attached umbilically to the concept of honesty, they are profoundly corrupt. They possess more physical courage than the average man, they are unconscionable bullies; they serve the truth, they are psychopathic liars . . . their work is authoritarian, they are cynical; and finally if something in their heart is deeply idealistic, they are also bloated with greed. There is no human creation so contradictory, so finally enigmatic, as the character of the average cop . . .

Yes, and without an arrest, he would never have known that this very nice Marshal from West Virginia with his good American face

9. Probably *Beyond the Law* (1967).

and pleasant manners and agreeable accent, had also a full quiver of sadism and a clammy sweat of possession as he put the arm on you. But indeed, what knowledge had the Marshal of him?

Inside the bus, at the rear of the aisle, was a locked cage and three or four protesters were enclosed there; jailed within their jailing. They greeted him with jeers, cat-calls, hellos, requests for cigarettes, water—after the first impact, it was not ill-spirited. "Hey, look," said one of the kids behind the bars, "they got older people in with us too."

"What time does this bus leave for Plainfield?" Mailer asked. The laughter came back. It was going to be all right. He could hear them whispering.

"You Norman Mailer?" asked one.

"Yes."

"Hey, great. Listen, man, we got to talk."

"I hope we don't have too much time." More laughter. He was beginning to feel good for the first time since his arrest. "What did you gentlemen do to be given such honor?" asked Mailer with a wave at their cage.

"We're the ones who were resisting arrest."

"Did you resist it much?"

"Are you kidding?" said one dark-haired gloomy thin young pirate with a large Armenian mustache and a bloodied handkerchief on his head, "if we put our hands in front of our face to keep from being beaten to death, they said we were resisting." Hoots and jeers at the fell accuracy of this.

"Well, did you all just sit there and take it?"

"I got in a couple of good shots at my Marshal," said one of the kids. It was hard to tell if he was lying. Something about their incarceration in the cage made it difficult to separate them, or perhaps it was that they seemed part of a team, of a musical group—the Monsters, or the Freaks, or the Caged Kissers—they had not known each other an hour ago, but the cage did the work of making them an ensemble.

The rest of the bus was slowly filling. Mailer had first taken a seat next to a young minister wearing his collar, and they chatted not unhappily for a few minutes, and then both crossed the aisle to sit on the side of the bus which looked out on the loading platform and the table where they had been booked. From these seats, Mailer had a view of the Marshals and MPs outside, of new arrests arriving in trucks, and of the prisoners coming into the bus, one by one, every couple of minutes. After a while, he realized the bus would not move until it was filled, and this, short of massive new arrests, would take at least an hour.

It was not disagreeable waiting. Each new prisoner was obliged to make an entrance like an actor coming on stage for his first appearance: since prisoners in transit are an enforced audience, new entrance automatically becomes theater. Some new men sauntered on the bus, some bowed to the faces in the aisle, some grinned, some scowled and sat down immediately; one or two principled pacifists practicing total noncooperation were dragged off the 2½-ton trucks, bumped along the ground, tugged over to the bus, and thrown in by the Marshals. Bleeding a little, looking dazed, the three or four young men who arrived by this route were applauded with something not unlike the enthusiasm a good turn gets in a music hall. Handsome young boys got on the bus, and slovenly oafs, hippies, and walking wounded. One boy had a pant leg soaked in blood. A fat sad fellow with a huge black beard now boarded; a trim and skinny kid who looked like he played minor league short-stop took a seat, a Japanese boy, androgynous in appearance, told a few prisoners around him that none of the Marshals had been able to decide if he was a boy or a girl, so they had not known—for he would not tell them—whether a Marshal or a Matron should search him. This was quickly taken up with pleasure and repeated down the bus.

Outside, a truck would arrive every five or ten minutes and some boys and girls would dismount and go to the base of the loading platform to be booked, the boys to enter the bus, the girls to go off to another bus. Still no sign of Lowell or Macdonald. Mailer kept hoping they would appear in the next haul of prisoners. After a while he began to study the Marshals.

Their faces were considerably worse than he had expected. He had had the fortune to be arrested by a man who was incontestably one of the pleasanter Marshals on duty at the Pentagon, he had next met what must be the toughest Marshal in the place—the two had given him a false spectrum. The gang of Marshals now studied outside the bus were enough to firm up any fading loyalty to his own cause: they had the kind of faces which belong to the bad guys in a Western. Some were fat, some were too thin, but nearly all seemed to have those subtle anomalies of the body which come often to men from small towns who have inherited strong features, but end up, by their own measure, in failure. Some would have powerful chests, but abrupt paunches, the skinny ones would have a knob in the shoulder, or a hitch in their gait, their foreheads would have odd cleaving wrinkles, so that one man might look as if an ax had struck him between the eyes, another paid tithe to ten parallel deep lines rising in ridges above his eye brows. The faces of all too many had a low cunning mixed with a stroke of rectitude: if the mouth was slack, the nose was straight and severe; should the lips be tight, the nostrils showed an outsize greed. Many of them looked to be ex-First Sergeants, for they liked to stand with the heels of their hands on the top of their hips, or they had that way of walking, belly forward, which a man will promote when he is in comfortable circumstances with himself and packing a revolver in a belt holster. The toes turn out; the belly struts. They were older men than he might have expected, some in their late thirties, more in their forties, a few looked to be over fifty, but then that may have been why they were here to receive prisoners rather than out on the line—in any case they emitted a collective spirit which, to his mind, spoke of little which was good, for their eyes were blank and dull, that familiar small-town cast of eye which speaks of apathy rising to fanaticism only to subside in apathy again. (Mailer had wondered more than once at that curious demand of small-town life which leaves something good and bright in the eyes of some, is so deadening for others—it was his impression that people in small towns had eyes which were generally livelier or emptier than the more concentrated look of city vision.) These Marshals had the dead eye and sour cigar, that sly shuffle of propriety and rut which so often comes out in a small-town sheriff as patriotism and the sweet stink of a crooked dollar. Small-town sheriffs sidled over to a crooked dollar like a High Episcopalian hooked on a closet queen. If one could find the irredeemable madness of America (for we are a nation where weeds will breed in the gilding tank)[1] it was in those late afternoon race track faces coming into the neon lights of the parimutuel windows, or those early morning hollows in the eye of the soul in places like Vegas where the fevers of America go livid in the hum of the night, and Grandmother, the church-goer, orange hair burning bright now crooned over the One-Arm Bandit, pocketbook open, driving those half-dollars home, home to the slot.

"Madame, we are burning children in Vietnam."

"Boy, you must go get yourself lost. Grandma's about ready for a kiss from the jackpot."

The burned child is brought into the gaming hall on her hospital bed.

"Madame, regard our act in Vietnam."

"I hit! I hit! Hot deedy, I hit. Why, you poor burned child—you just brought me luck. Here, honey, here's a lucky half-dollar in reward. And listen sugar, tell the nurse to change your sheets. Those sheets sure do stink. I hope you ain't got gangrene. Hee hee, hee hee. I get a supreme pleasure mixing with gooks in Vegas."

One did not have to look for who would work in the concentration camps and the liquidation centers—the garrison would be filled with applicants from the pages of a hundred American novels, from *Day of the Locust* and *Naked Lunch* and *The Magic Christian*,[2] one could enlist half the Marshals outside this bus, simple, honest, hard-working government law-enforcement agents, yeah! There was something at loose now in American life, the poet's beast slinking to

1. Metaphorically, a place where deceptive veneer is applied to give something a showy or pleasing appearance.
2. *The Day of the Locust* (1939), by Nathanael West; *Naked Lunch* (1959), by William S. Burroughs; *The Magic Christian* (1959) by Terry Southern. Novels filled with freaks, grotesques, and unsavory types generally.

the marketplace. The country had always been wild. It had always been harsh and hard, it had always had a fever—when life in one American town grew insupportable, one could travel, the fever to travel was in the American blood, so said all, but now the fever had left the blood, it was in the cells, the cells traveled, and the cells were as insane as Grandma with orange hair. The small towns were disappearing in the bypasses and the supermarkets and the shopping centers, the small town in America was losing its sense of the knuckle, the herb, and the root, the walking sticks were no longer cut from trees, nor were they cured, the schools did not have crazy old teachers now but teaching aids, and in the libraries, *National Geographic* gave way to *TV Guide*. Enough of the old walled town had once remained in the American small town for gnomes and dwarfs and knaves and churls (yes, and owls and elves and crickets) to live in the constellated cities of the spiders below the eaves in the old leaning barn which—for all one knew—had been a secret ear to the fevers of the small town, message center for the inhuman dreams which passed through the town at night in sleep and came to tell their insane tale of the old barbarian lust to slaughter villages and drink their blood, yes who knew which ghosts, and which crickets, with which spider would commune—which prayers and whose witch's curses would travel those subterranean trails of the natural kingdom about the town, who knows which fevers were forged in such communion and returned on the blood to the seed, it was an era when the message came by the wind and not by the wire (for the town gossip began to go mad when the telephone tuned its buds to the tip of her tongue) the American small town grew out of itself, and grew out of itself again and again, harmony between communication and the wind, between lives and ghosts, insanity, the solemn reaches of nature where insanity could learn melancholy (and madness some measure of modesty) had all been lost now, lost to the American small town. It had grown out of itself again and again, its cells traveled, worked for government, found security through wars in foreign lands, and the nightmares which passed on the winds in the old small towns now traveled on the nozzle tip of the flame thrower, no dreams now of barbarian lusts, slaughtered villages, battles of blood, no, nor any need for them—technology had driven insanity out of the wind and out of the attic, and out of all the lost primitive places: one had to find it now wherever fever, force, and machines could come together, in Vegas, at the race track, in pro football, race riots for the Negro, suburban orgies— none of it was enough—one had to find it in Vietnam; that was where the small town had gone to get its kicks.

That was on the faces of the Marshals. It was a great deal to read on the limited evidence before him, but he had known these faces before—they were not so different from the cramped, mean, stern, brave, florid, bestial, brutish, narrow, calculating, incurious, hardy, wily, leathery, simple, good, stingy, small-town faces he had once been familiar with in his outfit overseas, all those Texans from all those small towns, it was if he could tell—as at a college reunion—the difference these more than twenty years had made. If it were legitimate to read the change in American character by the change in the faces of one's classmates, then he could look at these Marshals like men he had known in the Army, but now revisited, and something had gone out of them, something had come in. If there was a common unattractive element to the Southern small-town face, it was in that painful pinch between their stinginess and their greed. No excess of love seemed ever to come off a poor white Southerner, no fats, no riches, no sweets, just the avidity for such wealth. But there had been sadness attached to this in the old days, a sorrow; in the pinch of their cheeks was the kind of abnegation and loneliness which spoke of what was tender and what was lost forever. So they had dignity. Now the hollows in their faces spoke of men who were rabid and toothless, the tenderness had turned corrosive, the abnegation had been replaced by hate, dull hate, cloud banks of hate, the hatred of failures who had not lost their greed. So he was reminded of a probability he had encountered before: that, nuclear bombs all at hand, the true war party of America was in all the small towns, even as the peace parties had to collect in the cities and the suburbs. Nuclear warfare was dividing the nation. The day of power for the small-town mind was approaching—who else would be left when atomic war was done would reason the small-town mind, and in measure to the depth of their personal failure, would love Vietnam, for Vietnam was the secret hope of a bigger war, and that bigger war might yet clear the air of races, faces, in fact—technologies—all that alienation they could not try to comprehend.

It was not a happy meditation. Among the soldiers he had known, there was the chance to talk. He did not see many faces here who would ever talk. Cheers. They were dragging a girl out of one of the trucks now. Pale-skinned, with light brown hair, no lipstick, dungarees, she had that unhappy color which came from too many trips to marijuana garden. Nonetheless, she waved to her boyfriend while being dragged along the ground. He was eventually dragged into their bus.

Mailer began to chat with the young clergyman. His name was John Boyle, and he was Presbyterian Chaplain at Yale. The number of his arrest was nine. They joked about this—he had beaten Mailer to the Bench. Actually he had seen the Protagonist get arrested, had followed to see if he were being treated properly (a sign of Mailer's age, a proper sign of status!) was turned back with assurances, wandered behind Pentagon lines, and in the course of protesting the arrest of a demonstrator, was apprehended himself (although the Marshal had wanted to release him when he saw his collar).

"Well," said Mailer, "at least we have low numbers."

"Do you think that will mean much?"

"We should be the first to get out."

From where he sat in the bus, he could see square vertical columns back of the loading platform, columns reminiscent of Egyptian architecture: Mailer now had a rumination about the nature of Egyptian architecture and its relation to the Pentagon, those ultra-excremental forms of ancient Egyptian architecture, those petrified excrements of the tomb and the underground chambers here at the Pentagon, but he was not an Egyptologist, no sir, and the connection eluded him. He must pursue it later. Something there. But the rumination running down, we may quickly leave his thoughts.

1968

JAMES BALDWIN

1924–

James Baldwin was born in Harlem, the first of nine children. From his novel *Go Tell It on the Mountain* (1951) and his story *The Rockpile*, we learn how extremely painful was the relationship between the father and his eldest son. David Baldwin, son of a slave, was a lay preacher rigidly committed to a vengeful God who would eventually judge white people as they deserved; in the meantime much of the vengeance was taken out on James. His father's "unlimited capacity for introspection and rancor," as the son later put it, must have had a profound effect on the sermonizing style Baldwin was to develop. Just as important was his conversion and resulting service as a preacher in his father's church, as we can see from both the rhythm and message of his prose—which is very much a *spoken* prose.

Baldwin did well in school and having received a hardship deferment from military service (his father was dying) began to attach himself to Greenwich Village, where he concentrated on the business of becoming a writer. In 1944 he met Richard Wright, at that time "the greatest black writer in the world for me," in whose early books Baldwin "found expressed, for the first time in my life, the sorrow, the rage, and the murderous bitterness which was eating up my life and the lives of those about me." Wright helped him win a Eugene Saxton Fellowship, and in 1948, when Baldwin went to live in Paris, he was following Wright's footsteps (Wright had become an expatriate to the same city two years earlier). It is perhaps for this reason that in his early essays written for *Partisan Review* and published in 1955 as *Notes of a Native Son* (with the title's explicit reference to Wright's novel) Baldwin dissociated himself from the image of American life found in Wright's "protest work" and, as Ralph Ellison was also doing, went about protesting in his own way.

As far as his novels are concerned, Baldwin's way involved a preoccupation with the intertwining of sexual with racial concerns, particularly in America. His interest in what it means to be black and homosexual in relation to white society is most fully and interestingly expressed in his long and somewhat ragged third novel, *Another Country* (1962). (He had previously written *Go Tell It on the Mountain*, and a second novel, *Giovanni's Room* [1956] about a white expatriate in Paris and his male lover.) *Another Country* contains scenes full of lively detail and intelligent reflection, though it lacks—as do all his novels—a compelling design that draws the book together. Thus far Baldwin has made little fictional use of the talents for irony and sly teasing he is master of in his essays; nor, unlike Ellison or Mailer, has he shown much interest in stylistic experimentation.

Baldwin's imagination is intensely social and reveals itself most passionately and variously in his collections of essays, of which *Notes of a Native Son* is probably the best, and in what many would judge his finest piece of writing, *Letter from a Region of My Mind* (in *The Fire Next Time*, 1963). This essay, the first half of which is printed here, was first published in the *New Yorker* and probably had a greater effect on white liberals than on the blacks who read it. In its firm rejection of separatism between the races as preached by the Black Muslims and their leader, Elijah Muhammad, it spoke out for love as the difficult and necessary way out of slavery and race hatred. Today, with all that has happened since its appearance, it is still a fresh and moving utterance, directed as the best of Baldwin's essays are by a beautifully controlled speaking voice, alternately impressing upon us its accents of polite directness, sardonic irony, or barely controlled fury.

Like Mailer, Baldwin risks advertising himself too strenuously, and sometimes falls into stridency and sentimentality. Like Ellison he has experienced many pressures to be something more than just a novelist; but he has produced a respectable series of novels, stories, and a play, even if no single fiction of his is comparable in breadth and daring to *Invisible Man*. There is surely no black writer better able to imagine white experience, to speak in various tones of different kinds and behaviors of people or places other than his own. In its sensitivity to shades of discrimination and moral shape, and in its commitment—despite everything—to America, his voice is comparable in importance to that of any person of letters writing today.

From The Fire Next Time[1]

[Part I]

I underwent, during the summer that I became fourteen, a prolonged religious crisis. I use the word "religious" in the common, and arbitrary, sense, meaning that I then discovered God, His saints and angels, and His blazing Hell. And since I had been born in a Christian nation, I accepted this Deity as the only one. I supposed Him to exist only within the walls of a church—in fact, of *our* church—and I also supposed that God and safety were synonymous. The word "safety" brings us to the real meaning of the word

1. *Letter from a Region of My Mind*, of which the first half is printed here, was originally published in the *New Yorker* in 1962, then combined with a shorter essay to make up *The Fire Next Time* (1963). In the second half of the *Letter* Baldwin describes in detail his impressions of the Black Muslims and their leader, Elijah Muhammad. The book's epigraph—"God gave Noah the rainbow sign,/No more water, the fire next time!" —alludes to what Baldwin terms at the book's conclusion "the fulfilment of that prophecy, recreated from the Bible in song by a slave," which we will suffer if we do not "end the racial nightmare, and achieve our country."

"religious" as we use it. Therefore, to state it in another, more accurate way, I became, during my fourteenth year, for the first time in my life, afraid—afraid of the evil within me and afraid of the evil without. What I saw around me that summer in Harlem was what I had always seen; nothing had changed. But now, without any warning, the whores and pimps and racketeers on the Avenue[2] had become a personal menace. It had not before occurred to me that I could become one of them, but now I realized that we had been produced by the same circumstances. Many of my comrades were clearly headed for the Avenue, and my father said that I was headed that way, too. My friends began to drink and smoke, and embarked—at first avid, then groaning—on their sexual careers. Girls, only slightly older than I was, who sang in the choir or taught Sunday school, the children of holy parents, underwent, before my eyes, their incredible metamorphosis, of which the most bewildering aspect was not their budding breasts or their rounding behinds but something deeper and more subtle, in their eyes, their heat, their odor, and the inflection of their voices. Like the strangers on the Avenue, they became, in the twinkling of an eye, unutterably different and fantastically *present*. Owing to the way I had been raised, the abrupt discomfort that all this aroused in me and the fact that I had no idea what my voice or my mind or my body was likely to do next caused me to consider myself one of the most depraved people on earth. Matters were not helped by the fact that these holy girls seemed rather to enjoy my terrified lapses, our grim, guilty, tormented experiments, which were at once as chill and joyless as the Russian steppes and hotter, by far, than all the fires of Hell.

Yet there was something deeper than these changes, and less definable, that frightened me. It was real in both the boys and the girls, but it was, somehow, more vivid in the boys. In the case of the girls, one watched them turning into matrons before they had become women. They began to manifest a curious and really rather terrifying single-mindedness. It is hard to say exactly how this was conveyed: something implacable in the set of the lips, something farseeing (seeing what?) in the eyes, some new and crushing determination in the walk, something peremptory in the voice. They did not tease us, the boys, any more; they reprimanded us sharply, saying, "You better be thinking about your soul!" For the girls also saw the evidence on the Avenue, knew what the price would be, for them, of one misstep, knew that they had to be protected and that we were the only protection there was. They understood that they must act as God's decoys, saving the souls of the boys for Jesus and binding the bodies of the boys in marriage. For this was the beginning of our burning time, and "It is better," said St. Paul—who elsewhere, with a most unusual and stunning exactness, described

2. Lenox Avenue, the main street running through Harlem.

2116 ★ James Baldwin

himself as a "wretched man"—"to marry than to burn."[3] And I began to feel in the boys a curious, wary, bewildered despair, as though they were now settling in for the long, hard winter of life. I did not know then what it was that I was reacting to; I put it to myself that they were letting themselves go. In the same way that the girls were destined to gain as much weight as their mothers, the boys, it was clear, would rise no higher than their fathers. School began to reveal itself, therefore, as a child's game that one could not win, and boys dropped out of school and went to work. My father wanted me to do the same. I refused, even though I no longer had any illusions about what an education could do for me; I had already encountered too many college-graduate handymen. My friends were now "downtown," busy, as they put it, "fighting the man." They began to care less about the way they looked, the way they dressed, the things they did; presently, one found them in twos and threes and fours, in a hallway, sharing a jug of wine or a bottle of whiskey, talking, cursing, fighting, sometimes weeping: lost, and unable to say what it was that oppressed them, except that they knew it was "the man"—the white man. And there seemed to be no way whatever to remove this cloud that stood between them and the sun, between them and love and life and power, between them and whatever it was that they wanted. One did not have to be very bright to realize how little one could do to change one's situation; one did not have to be abnormally sensitive to be worn down to a cutting edge by the incessant and gratuitious humiliation and danger one encountered every working day, all day long. The humiliation did not apply merely to working days, or workers; I was thirteen and was crossing Fifth Avenue on my way to the Forty-second Street library, and the cop in the middle of the street muttered as I passed him, "Why don't you niggers stay uptown where you belong?" When I was ten, and didn't look, certainly, any older, two policemen amused themselves with me by frisking me, making comic (and terrifying) speculations concerning my ancestry and probable sexual prowess, and for good measure, leaving me flat on my back in one of Harlem's empty lots. Just before and then during the Second World War, many of my friends fled into the service, all to be changed there, and rarely for the better, many to be ruined, and many to die. Others fled to other states and cities—that is, to other ghettos. Some went on wine or whiskey or the needle, and are still on it. And others, like me, fled into the church.

For the wages of sin were visible everywhere, in every wine-stained and urine-splashed hallway, in every clanging ambulance bell, in every scar on the faces of the pimps and their whores, in every helpless, newborn baby being brought into this danger, in every knife and pistol fight on the Avenue, and in every disastrous bulletin: a cousin, mother of six, suddenly gone mad, the children

3. 1 Corinthians 7.8–9.

parcelled out here and there; an indestructible aunt rewarded for years of hard labor by a slow, agonizing death in a terrible small room; someone's bright son blown into eternity by his own hand; another turned robber and carried off to jail. It was a summer of dreadful speculations and discoveries, of which these were not the worst. Crime became real, for example—for the first time—not as *a* possibility but as *the* possibility. One would never defeat one's circumstances by working and saving one's pennies; one would never, by working, acquire that many pennies, and, besides, the social treatment accorded even the most successful Negroes proved that one needed, in order to be free, something more than a bank account. One needed a handle, a lever, a means of inspiring fear. It was absolutely clear that the police would whip you and take you in as long as they could get away with it, and that everyone else— housewives, taxi-drivers, elevator boys, dishwashers, bartenders, lawyers, judges, doctors, and grocers—would never, by the operation of any generous human feeling, cease to use you as an outlet for his frustrations and hostilities. Neither civilized reason nor Christian love would cause any of those people to treat you as they presumably wanted to be treated; only the fear of your power to retaliate would cause them to do that, or to seem to do it, which was (and is) good enough. There appears to be a vast amount of confusion on this point, but I do not know many Negroes who are eager to be "accepted" by white people, still less to be loved by them; they, the blacks, simply don't wish to be beaten over the head by the whites every instant of our brief passage on this planet. White people in this country will have quite enough to do in learning how to accept and love themselves and each other, and when they have achieved this—which will not be tomorrow and may very well be never—the Negro problem will no longer exist, for it will no longer be needed.

People more advantageously placed than we in Harlem were, and are, will no doubt find the psychology and the view of human nature sketched above dismal and shocking in the extreme. But the Negro's experience of the white world cannot possibly create in him any respect for the standards by which the white world claims to live. His own condition is overwhelming proof that white people do not live by these standards. Negro servants have been smuggling odds and ends out of white homes for generations, and white people have been delighted to have them do it, because it has assuaged a dim guilt and testified to the intrinsic superiority of white people. Even the most doltish and servile Negro could scarcely fail to be impressed by the disparity between his situation and that of the people for whom he worked; Negroes who were neither doltish nor servile did not feel that they were doing anything wrong when they robbed white people. In spite of the Puritan-Yankee equation of virtue with well-being, Negroes had excellent reasons for doubting that money was made or kept by any very striking adherence to the Christian virtues; it certainly did not work that way for black Christians. In any case, white people, who had robbed black people of their liberty and who profited by this theft every hour that they lived, had no moral ground on which to stand. They had the judges, the juries, the shotguns, the law—in a word, power. But it was a criminal power, to be feared but not respected, and to be outwitted in any way whatever. And those virtues preached but not practiced by the white world were merely another means of holding Negroes in subjection.

It turned out, then, that summer, that the moral barriers that I had supposed to exist between me and the dangers of a criminal career were so tenuous as to be nearly nonexistent. I certainly could not discover any principled reason for not becoming a criminal, and it is not my poor, God-fearing parents who are to be indicted for the lack but this society. I was icily determined—more determined, really, than I then knew—never to make my peace with the ghetto but to die and go to Hell before I would let any white man spit on me, before I would accept my "place" in this republic. I did not intend to allow the white people of this country to tell me who I was, and limit me that way, and polish me off that way. And yet, of course, at the same time, I *was* being spat on and defined and described and limited, and could have been polished off with no effort whatever. Every Negro boy—in my situation during those years, at least—who reaches this point realizes, at once, profoundly, because he wants to live, that he stands in great peril and must find, with speed, a "thing," a gimmick, to lift him out, to start him on his way. *And it does not matter what the gimmick is.* It was this last realization that terrified me and—since it revealed that the door opened on so many dangers—helped to hurl me into the church. And, by an unforeseeable paradox, it was my career in the church that turned out, precisely, to be my gimmick.

For when I tried to assess my capabilities, I realized that I had almost none. In order to achieve the life I wanted, I had been dealt, it seemed to me, the worst possible hand. I could not become a prizefighter—many of us tried but very few succeeded. I could not sing. I could not dance. I had been well conditioned by the world in which I grew up, so I did not yet dare take the idea of becoming a writer seriously. The only other possibility seemed to involve my becoming one of the sordid people on the Avenue, who were not really as sordid as I then imagined but who frightened me terribly, both because I did not want to live that life and because of what they made me feel. Everything inflamed me, and that was bad enough, but I myself had also become a source of fire and temptation. I had been far too well raised, alas, to suppose that any of the extremely explicit overtures made to me that summer, sometimes by boys and girls but also, more alarmingly, by older men and women, had anything to do with my attractiveness. On the contrary, since the Harlem idea of seduction is, to put it mildly, blunt, whatever these people saw in me merely confirmed my sense of my depravity.

It is certainly sad that the awakening of one's senses should lead to such a merciless judgment of oneself—to say nothing of the time and anguish one spends in the effort to arrive at any other—but it is also inevitable that a literal attempt to mortify the flesh should be made among black people like those with whom I grew up. Negroes in this country—and Negroes do not, strictly or legally speaking, exist in any other—are taught really to despise themselves from the moment their eyes open on the world. This world is white and they are black. White people hold the power, which means that they are superior to blacks (intrinsically, that is: God decreed it so), and the world has innumerable ways of making this difference known and felt and feared. Long before the Negro child perceives this difference, and even longer before he understands it, he has begun to react to it, he has begun to be controlled by it. Every effort made by the child's elders to prepare him for a fate from which they cannot protect him causes him secretly, in terror, to begin to await, without knowing that he is doing so, his mysterious and inexorable punishment. He must be "good" not only in order to please his parents and not only to avoid being punished by them; behind their authority stands another, nameless and impersonal, infinitely harder to please, and bottomlessly cruel. And this filters into the child's consciousness through his parents' tone of voice as he is being exhorted, punished, or loved; in the sudden, uncontrollable note of fear heard in his mother's or his father's voice when he has strayed beyond some particular boundary. He does not know what the boundary is, and he can get no explanation of it, which is frightening enough, but the fear he hears in the voices of his elders is more frightening still. The fear that I heard in my father's voice, for example, when he realized that I really *believed* I could do anything a white boy could do, and had every intention of proving it, was not at all like the fear I heard when one of us was ill or had fallen down the stairs or strayed too far from the house. It was another fear, a fear that the child, in challenging the white world's assumptions, was putting himself in the path of destruction. A child cannot, thank Heaven, know how vast and how merciless is the nature of power, with what unbelievable cruelty people treat each other. He reacts to the fear in his parents' voices because his parents hold up the world for him and he has no protection without them. I defended myself, as I imagined, against the fear my father made me feel by remembering that he was very old-fashioned. Also, I prided myself on the fact that I already knew how to outwit him. To defend oneself against a fear is simply to insure that one will, one day, be conquered by it; fears must be faced. As for one's wits, it is just not true that one can live by them—not, that is, if one wishes really to live. That summer, in any case, all the fears with which I had grown up, and which were now a part of me and controlled my vision of the world, rose up like a wall between the world and me, and drove me into the church.

As I look back, everything I did seems curiously deliberate, though it certainly did not seem deliberate then. For example, I did not join the church of which my father was a member and in which he preached. My best friend in school, who attended a different church, had already "surrendered his life to the Lord," and he was very anxious about my soul's salvation. (I wasn't, but any human attention was better than none.) One Saturday afternoon, he took me to his church. There were no services that day, and the church was empty, except for some women cleaning and some other women praying. My friend took me into the back room to meet his pastor—a woman. There she sat, in her robes, smiling, an extremely proud and handsome woman, with Africa, Europe, and the America of the American Indian blended in her face. She was perhaps forty-five or fifty at this time, and in our world she was a very celebrated woman. My friend was about to introduce me when she looked at me and smiled and said, "Whose little boy are you?" Now this, unbelievably, was precisely the phrase used by pimps and racketeers on the Avenue when they suggested, both humorously and intensely, that I "hang out" with them. Perhaps part of the terror they had caused me to feel came from the fact that I unquestionably wanted to be *somebody's* little boy. I was so frightened, and at the mercy of so many conundrums, that inevitably, that summer, *someone* would have taken me over; one doesn't, in Harlem, long remain standing on any auction block. It was my good luck—perhaps—that I found myself in the church racket instead of some other, and surrendered to a spiritual seduction long before I came to any carnal knowledge. For when the pastor asked me, with that marvellous smile, "Whose little boy are you?" my heart replied at once, "Why, yours."

The summer wore on, and things got worse. I became more guilty and more frightened, and kept all this bottled up inside me, and naturally, inescapably, one night, when this woman had finished preaching, everything came roaring, screaming, crying out, and I fell to the ground before the altar. It was the strangest sensation I have ever had in my life—up to that time, or since. I had not known that it was going to happen, or that it could happen. One moment I was on my feet, singing and clapping and, at the same time, working out in my head the plot of a play I was working on then; the next moment, with no transition, no sensation of falling, I was on my back, with the lights beating down into my face and all the vertical saints above me. I did not know what I was doing down so low, or how I had got there. And the anguish that filled me cannot be described. It moved in me like one of those floods that devastate counties, tearing everything down, tearing children from their parents and lovers from each other, and making everything an unrecognizable waste. All I really remember is the pain, the unspeakable pain; it was as though I were yelling up to Heaven and Heaven would not hear me. And if Heaven would not hear me, if love could not descend from Heaven—to wash me, to make me clean—then utter disaster was my portion. Yes, it does indeed mean something—something unspeakable—to be born, in a white country, an Anglo-Teutonic, antisexual country, black. You very soon, without knowing it, give up all hope of communion. Black people, mainly, look down or look up but do not look at each other, not at you, and white people, mainly, look away. And the universe is simply a sounding drum; there is no way, no way whatever, so it seemed then and has sometimes seemed since, to get through a life, to love your wife and children, or your friends, or your mother and father, or to be loved. The universe, which is not merely the stars and the moon and the planets, flowers, grass, and trees, but *other people*, has evolved no terms for your existence, has made no room for you, and if love will not swing wide the gates, no other power will or can. And if one despairs—as who has not?—of human love, God's love alone is left. But God—and I felt this even then, so long ago, on that tremendous floor, unwillingly—is white. And if His love was so great, and if He loved all His children, why were we, the blacks, cast down so far? Why? In spite of all I said thereafter, I found no answer on the floor—not *that* answer, anyway—and I was on the floor all night. Over me, to bring me "through," the saints sang and rejoiced and prayed. And in the morning, when they raised me, they told me that I was "saved."

Well, indeed I was, in a way, for I was utterly drained and exhausted, and released, for the first time, from all my guilty torment. I was aware then only of my relief. For many years, I could not ask myself why human relief had to be achieved in a fashion at once so pagan and so desperate—in a fashion at once so unspeakably old and so unutterably new. And by the time I was able to ask myself this question, I was also able to see that the principles governing the rites and customs of the churches in which I grew up did not differ from the principles governing the rites and customs of other churches, white. The principles were Blindness, Loneliness, and Terror, the first principle necessarily and actively cultivated in order to deny the two others. I would love to believe that the principles were Faith, Hope, and Charity, but this is clearly not so for most Christians, or for what we call the Christian world.

I was saved. But at the same time, out of a deep, adolescent cunning I do not pretend to understand, I realized immediately that I could not remain in the church merely as another worshipper. I would have to give myself something to do, in order not to be too bored and find myself among all the wretched unsaved of the Avenue. And I don't doubt that I also intended to best my father on his own ground. Anyway, very shortly after I joined the church, I became a preacher—a Young Minister—and I remained in the pulpit for more than three years. My youth quickly made me a much bigger drawing card than my father. I pushed this advantage ruthlessly, for it was the most effective means I had found of breaking his hold over me. That was the most frightening time of my life, and quite the most dishonest, and the resulting hysteria lent great passion to my sermons—for a while. I relished the attention and the relative immunity from punishment that my new status gave me, and I relished, above all, the sudden right to privacy. It had to be recognized, after all, that I was still a schoolboy, with my schoolwork to do, and I was also expected to prepare at least one sermon a week. During what we may call my heyday, I preached much more often than that. This meant that there were hours and even whole days when I could not be interrupted—not even by my father. I had immobilized him. It took rather more time for me to realize that I had also immobilized myself, and had escaped from nothing whatever.

The church was very exciting. It took a long time for me to disengage myself from this excitement, and on the blindest, most visceral level, I never really have, and never will. There is no music like that music, no drama like the drama of the saints rejoicing, the sinners moaning, the tambourines racing, and all those voices coming together and crying holy unto the Lord. There is still, for me, no pathos quite like the pathos of those multicolored, worn, somehow triumphant and transfigured faces, speaking from the depths of a visible, tangible, continuing despair of the goodness of the Lord. I have never seen anything to equal the fire and excitement that sometimes, without warning, fill a church, causing the church, as Leadbelly[4] and so many others have testified, to "rock." Nothing that has happened to me since equals the power and the glory that I sometimes felt when, in the middle of a sermon, I knew that I was somehow, by some miracle, really carrying, as they said, "the Word"—when the church and I were one. Their pain and their joy were mine, and mine were theirs—they surrendered their pain and joy to me, I surendered mine to them—and their cries of "Amen!" and "Hallelujah!" and "Yes, Lord!" and "Praise His name!" and "Preach it, brother!" sustained and whipped on my solos until we all became equal, wringing wet, singing and dancing, in anguish and rejoicing, at the foot of the altar. It was, for a long time, in spite of—or, not inconceivably, because of—the shabbiness of my motives, my only sustenance, my meat and drink. I rushed home from school, to the church, to the altar, to be alone there, to commune with Jesus, my dearest Friend, who would never fail me, who knew

4. Huddie Ledbetter (1888–1949) or Leadbelly: folk and blues singer who had enormous influence on other singers.

all the secrets of my heart. Perhaps He did, but I didn't, and the bargain we struck, actually, down there at the foot of the cross, was that He would never let me find out.

He failed His bargain. He was a much better Man than I took Him for. It happened, as things do, imperceptibly, in many ways at once. I date it—the slow crumbling of my faith, the pulverization of my fortress—from the time, about a year after I had begun to preach, when I began to read again. I justified this desire by the fact that I was still in school, and I began, fatally, with Dostoevski. By this time, I was in a high school that was predominantly Jewish. This meant that I was surrounded by people who were, by definition, beyond any hope of salvation, who laughed at the tracts and leaflets I brought to school, and who pointed out that the Gospels had been written long after the death of Christ. This might not have been so distressing if it had not forced me to read the tracts and leaflets myself, for they were indeed, unless one believed their message already, impossible to believe. I remember feeling dimly that there was a kind of blackmail in it. People, I felt, ought to love the Lord *because* they loved Him, and not because they were afraid of going to Hell. I was forced, reluctantly, to realize that the Bible itself had been written by men, and translated by men out of languages I could not read, and I was already, without quite admitting it to myself, terribly involved with the effort of putting words on paper. Of course, I had the rebuttal ready: These men had all been operating under divine inspiration. *Had* they? *All* of them? And I also knew by now, alas, far more about divine inspiration than I dared admit, for I knew how I worked myself up into my own visions, and how frequently—indeed, incessantly—the visions God granted to me differed from the visions He granted to my father. I did not understand the dreams I had at night, but I knew that they were not holy. For that matter, I knew that my waking hours were far from holy. I spent most of my time in a state of repentance for things I had vividly desired to do but had not done. The fact that I was dealing with Jews brought the whole question of color, which I had been desperately avoiding, into the terrified center of my mind. I realized that the Bible had been written by white men. I knew that, according to many Christians, I was a descendant of Ham,[5] who had been cursed, and that I was therefore predestined to be a slave. This had nothing to do with anything I was, or contained, or could become; my fate had been sealed forever, from the beginning of time. And it seemed, indeed, when one looked out over Christendom, that this was what Christendom effectively believed. It was certainly the way it behaved. I remembered the Italian priests and bishops blessing Italian boys who were on their way to Ethiopia.

5. One of the sons of Noah, Ham was cursed with slavery for seeing his drunken father's nakedness (Genesis 9. 18–27). He was also regarded as the progenitor of the African peoples.

Again, the Jewish boys in high school were troubling because I could find no point of connection between them and the Jewish pawnbrokers and landlords and grocery-store owners in Harlem. I knew that these people were Jews—God knows I was told it often enough—but I thought of them only as white. Jews, as such, until I got to high school, were all incarcerated in the Old Testament, and their names were Abraham, Moses, Daniel, Ezekiel, and Job, and Shadrach, Meshach, and Abednego. It was bewildering to find them so many miles and centuries out of Egypt, and so far from the fiery furnace.[6] My best friend in high school was a Jew. He came to our house once, and afterward my father asked, as he asked about everyone, "Is he a Christian?"—by which he meant "Is he saved?" I really do not know whether my answer came out of innocence or venom, but I said coldly, "No. He's Jewish." My father slammed me across the face with his great palm, and in that moment everything flooded back—all the hatred and all the fear, and the depth of a merciless resolve to kill my father rather than allow my father to kill me—and I knew that all those sermons and tears and all that repentance and rejoicing had changed nothing. I wondered if I was expected to be glad that a friend of mine, or anyone, was to be tormented forever in Hell, and I also thought, suddenly, of the Jews in another Christian nation, Germany. They were not so far from the fiery furnace after all, and my best friend might have been one of them. I told my father, "He's a better Christian than you are," and walked out of the house. The battle between us was in the open, but that was all right; it was almost a relief. A more deadly struggle had begun.

Being in the pulpit was like being in the theatre; I was behind the scenes and knew how the illusion was worked. I knew the other ministers and knew the quality of their lives. And I don't mean to suggest by this the "Elmer Gantry"[7] sort of hypocrisy concerning sensuality; it was a deeper, deadlier, and more subtle hypocrisy than that, and a little honest sensuality, or a lot, would have been like water in an extremely bitter desert. I knew how to work on a congregation until the last dime was surrendered—it was not very hard to do—and I knew where the money for "the Lord's work" went. I knew, though I did not wish to know it, that I had no respect for the people with whom I worked. I could not have said it then, but I also knew that if I continued I would soon have no respect for myself. And the fact that I was "the young Brother Baldwin" increased my value with those same pimps and racketeers who had helped to stampede me into the church in the first place. They still saw the little boy they intended to take over. They were

---

6. Shadrach, Meshach, and Abednego appear in the Old Testament (Book of Daniel 3.19–24), where they are cast into the fiery furnace for refusing to worship the divinities of Babylon and disobeying King Nebuchadnezzar.

7. Hero of Sinclair Lewis's novel of that title whose preaching is at odds with his lechery.

waiting for me to come to my senses and realize that I was in a very lucrative business. They knew that I did not yet realize this, and also that I had not yet begun to suspect where my own needs, *coming up* (they were very patient), could drive me. They themselves did know the score, and they knew that the odds were in their favor. And, really, I knew it, too. I was even lonelier and more vulnerable than I had been before. And the blood of the Lamb had not cleansed me in any way whatever. I was just as black as I had been the day that I was born. Therefore, when I faced a congregation, it began to take all the strength I had not to stammer, not to curse, not to tell them to throw away their Bibles and get off their knees and go home and organize, for example, a rent strike. When I watched all the children, their copper, brown, and beige faces staring up at me as I taught Sunday school, I felt that I was committing a crime in talking about the gentle Jesus, in telling them to reconcile themselves to their misery on earth in order to gain the crown of eternal life. Were only Negroes to gain this crown? Was Heaven, then, to be merely another ghetto? Perhaps I might have been able to reconcile myself even to this if I had been able to believe that there was any loving-kindness to be found in the haven I represented. But I had been in the pulpit too long and I had seen too many monstrous things. I don't refer merely to the glaring fact that the minister eventually acquires houses and Cadillacs while the faithful continue to scrub floors and drop their dimes and quarters and dollars into the plate. I really mean that there was no love in the church. It was a mask for hatred and self-hatred and despair. The transfiguring power of the Holy Ghost ended when the service ended, and salvation stopped at the church door. When we were told to love everybody, I had thought that that meant *everybody*. But no. It applied only to those who believed as we did, and it did not apply to white people at all. I was told by a minister, for example, that I should never, on any public conveyance, under any circumstances, rise and give my seat to a white woman. White men never rose for Negro women. Well, that was true enough, in the main—I saw his point. But what was the point, the purpose, of *my* salvation if it did not permit me to behave with love toward others, no matter how they behaved toward me? What others did was their responsibility, for which they would answer when the judgment trumpet sounded. But what *I* did was *my* responsibility, and I would have to answer, too—unless, of course, there was also in Heaven a special dispensation for the benighted black, who was not to be judged in the same way as other human beings, or angels. It probably occurred to me around this time that the vision people hold of the world to come is but a reflection, with predictable wishful distortions, of the world in which they live. And this did not apply only to Negroes, who were no more "simple" or "spontaneous" or "Christian" than anybody else—who were merely more oppressed.

In the same way that we, for white people, were the descendants of Ham, and were cursed forever, white people were, for us, the descendants of Cain. And the passion with which we loved the Lord was a measure of how deeply we feared and distrusted and, in the end, hated almost all strangers, always, and avoided and despised ourselves.

But I cannot leave it at that; there is more to it than that. In spite of everything, there was in the life I fled a zest and a joy and a capacity for facing and surviving disaster that are very moving and very rare. Perhaps we were, all of us—pimps, whores, racketeers, church members, and children—bound together by the nature of our oppression, the specific and peculiar complex of risks we had to run; if so, within these limits we sometimes achieved with each other a freedom that was close to love. I remember, anyway, church suppers and outings, and, later, after I left the church, rent and waistline parties[8] where rage and sorrow sat in the darkness and did not stir, and we ate and drank and talked and laughed and danced and forgot all about "the man." We had the liquor, the chicken, the music, and each other, and had no need to pretend to be what we were not. This is the freedom that one hears in some gospel songs, for example, and in jazz. In all jazz, and especially in the blues, there is something tart and ironic, authoritative and double-edged. White Americans seem to feel that happy songs are *happy* and sad songs are *sad*, and that, God help us, is exactly the way most white Americans sing them—sounding, in both cases, so helplessly, defenselessly fatuous that one dare not speculate on the temperature of the deep freeze from which issue their brave and sexless little voices. Only people who have been "down the line," as the song puts it, know what this music is about. I think it was Big Bill Broonzy[9] who used to sing "I Feel So Good," a really joyful song about a man who is on his way to the railroad station to meet his girl. She's coming home. It is the singer's incredibly moving exuberance that makes one realize how leaden the time must have been while she was gone. There is no guarantee that she will stay this time, either, as the singer clearly knows, and, in fact, she has not yet actually arrived. Tonight, or tomorrow, or within the next five minutes, he may very well be singing "Lonesome in My Bedroom," or insisting, "Ain't we, ain't we, going to make it all right? Well, if we don't today, we will tomorrow night." White Americans do not understand the depths out of which such an ironic tenacity comes, but they suspect that the force is sensual, and they are terrified of sensuality and do not any longer understand it. The word "sensual" is not intended to bring to mind quivering dusky maidens or priapic black studs. I am referring to something much simpler and much less fanciful. To be sensual, I think, is to respect and rejoice in the

---

8. Gatherings held in houses or apartments in order to raise money to pay the rent.

9. Blues singer and guitarist (1893–1958).

force of life, of life itself, and to be *present* in all that one does, from the effort of loving to the breaking of bread. It will be a great day for America, incidentally, when we begin to eat bread again, instead of the blasphemous and tasteless foam rubber that we have substituted for it. And I am not being frivolous now, either. Something very sinister happens to the people of a country when they begin to distrust their own reactions as deeply as they do here, and become as joyless as they have become. It is this individual uncertainty on the part of white American men and women, this inability to renew themselves at the fountain of their own lives, that makes the discussion, let alone elucidation, of any conundrum—that is, any reality—so supremely difficult. The person who distrusts himself has no touchstone for reality—for this touchstone can be only oneself. Such a person interposes between himself and reality nothing less than a labyrinth of attitudes. And these attitudes, furthermore, though the person is usually unaware of it (is unaware of so much!), are historical and public attitudes. They do not relate to the present any more than they relate to the person. Therefore, whatever white people do not know about Negroes reveals, precisely and inexorably, what they do not know about themselves.

White Christians have also forgotten several elementary historical details. They have forgotten that the religion that is now identified with their virtue and their power—"God is on our side," says Dr. Verwoerd[1]—came out of a rocky piece of ground in what is now known as the Middle East before color was invented, and that in order for the Christian church to be established, Christ had to be put to death, by Rome, and that the real architect of the Christian church was not the disreputable, sun-baked Hebrew who gave it his name but the mercilessly fanatical and self-righteous St. Paul. The energy that was buried with the rise of the Christian nations must come back into the world; nothing can prevent it. Many of us, I think, both long to see this happen and are terrified of it, for though this transformation contains the hope of liberation, it also imposes a necessity for great change. But in order to deal with the untapped and dormant force of the previously subjugated, in order to survive as a human, moving, moral weight in the world, America and all the Western nations will be forced to reexamine themselves and release themselves from many things that are now taken to be sacred, and to discard nearly all the assumptions that have been used to justify their lives and their anguish and their crimes so long.

"The white man's Heaven," sings a Black Muslim minister, "is the black man's Hell." One may object—possibly—that this puts the matter somewhat too simply, but the song is true, and it has been true for as long as white men have ruled the world. The Africans

---

1. Dr. Henrik Verwoerd was a dedicated proponent of *apartheid* (separation of the races) and Prime Minister of South Africa in the late 1950s.

put it another way: When the white man came to Africa, the white man had the Bible and the African had the land, but now it is the white man who is being, reluctantly and bloodily, separated from the land, and the African who is still attempting to digest or to vomit up the Bible. The struggle, therefore, that now begins in the world is extremely complex, involving the historical role of Christianity in the realm of power—that is, politics—and in the realm of morals. In the realm of power, Christianity has operated with an unmitigated arrogance and cruelty—necessarily, since a religion ordinarily imposes on those who have discovered the true faith the spiritual duty of liberating the infidels. This particular true faith, moreover, is more deeply concerned about the soul than it is about the body, to which fact the flesh (and the corpses) of countless infidels bears witness. It goes without saying, then, that whoever questions the authority of the true faith also contests the right of the nations that hold this faith to rule over him—contests, in short, their title to his land. The spreading of the Gospel, regardless of the motives or the integrity or the heroism of some of the missionaries, was an absolutely indispensable justification for the planting of the flag. Priests and nuns and schoolteachers helped to protect and sanctify the power that was so ruthlessly being used by people who were indeed seeking a city, but not one in the heavens, and one to be made, very definitely, by captive hands. The Christian church itself—again, as distinguished from some of its ministers—sanctified and rejoiced in the conquests of the flag, and encouraged, if it did not formulate, the belief that conquest, with the resulting relative well-being of the Western populations, was proof of the favor of God. God had come a long way from the desert—but then so had Allah, though in a very different direction. God, going north, and rising on the wings of power, had become white, and Allah, out of power, and on the dark side of Heaven, had become—for all practical purposes, anyway—black. Thus, in the realm of morals the role of Christianity has been, at best, ambivalent. Even leaving out of account the remarkable arrogance that assumed that the ways and morals of others were inferior to those of Christians, and that they therefore had every right, and could use any means, to change them, the collision between cultures—and the schizophrenia in the mind of Christendom—had rendered the domain of morals as chartless as the sea once was, and as treacherous as the sea still is. It is not too much to say that whoever wishes to become a truly moral human being (and let us not ask whether or not this is possible; I think we must *believe* that it is possible) must first divorce himself from all the prohibitions, crimes, and hypocrisies of the Christian church. If the concept of God has any validity or any use, it can only be to make us larger, freer, and more loving. If God cannot do this, then it is time we got rid of Him.

1962, 1963

MALCOLM X
1925–1965

He was born Malcolm Little, in Omaha, Nebraska, seventh child of a Baptist preacher who admired Marcus Garvey and his doctrines of black separatism and who (Malcolm came to believe) was murdered by white men, his death made to look like suicide. Malcolm grew up in Lansing, Michigan, where he was an extraordinarily bright and successful student. At age fifteen he moved to Boston to live with his half-sister; a few years later he was launched on a career of hustling and drug-peddling which resulted in his incarceration for twenty years in various prisons. While in prison he began to read voraciously and was converted to the Islamic religion as expounded by the Black Muslim leader, Elijah Muhammad. Upon his release from prison he became Malcolm X, the "X" standing for—in Elijah Muhammad's doctrine—the unknown African name which was truly his and would be recovered some day. He was a powerful lecturer, traveler, and spokesman for the new faith, but eventually broke with his leader, and in his last months became less convinced by Muhammad's doctrine of the necessary separation of the races and the essential evil of all whites. His life ended when he was gunned down by assassins while preparing to speak in Harlem's Audubon Ballroom. At his funeral the actor Ossie Davis spoke of "that brave, black, ironic gallantry, which was his style and hallmark, that shocking *zing* of fire-and-be-damned-to-you, so absolutely absent in every other Negro man I know."

In the years since its publication after his death, the *Autobiography* has lost none of its power to shock and awe us. The shock comes at the ranges of brutality and meanness revealed in a society where white men are in control; the awe is at the strength of one man, by his own admission sunken to depths of brutality and meanness, who suddenly discovers himself, is rescued and transformed into an individual spirit of rare quality. But the only way we have of approaching Malcolm's achievement as it expresses itself in words is (aside from a collection of speeches) the *Autobiography*; and since this is both an "as-told-to" narrative published with the assistance of Alex Haley, and the narrative of a conversion, readers may feel they must operate under different assumptions from those they bring to a novel or memoir by a professional writer. How can the convert, the saved man, portray his earlier unconverted self without constantly simplifying and distorting it, or his present self without glorifying it? And how much distortion or alteration of the "truth" about Malcolm's life should we attribute to his amanuensis?

The as-told-to nature of the *Autobiography* can best be handled by ignoring it, since the voice which speaks in Malcolm's book is entirely identifiable and consistent: "I looked like Li'l Abner. Mason, Michigan, was written all over me. My kinky, reddish hair was cut hick style, and I didn't even use grease in it." This plain style can accommodate both the ironic gallantry spoken of by Ossie Davis and the "shocking *zing* of fire-and-be-damned-to-you" as well, so that the reader feels it is not "literature" but just a man speaking to us. Yet it is feat of literary art to create this impression.

No one who attempts to put his past into words in order to make it live for someone else can be simply and wholly contemptuous of that unreconstructed life. Malcolm's art is in the unfailing liveliness with which his memory plays over his now discredited life of shoeshine boy, pimp, railway porter, thief, rebellious convict. His imagination warms to the memories of the great dance bands which appeared regularly at Roseland ballroom in Boston, playing for whites one night, blacks the next. The shame and disgust at submitting to the required "conk" that would deny one's heritage by changing the quality of one's hair is embarrassingly real to the converted Muslim looking back; but the painful memory of the ingredients carefully assembled to pour into that hair—eggs, potatoes, vaseline and Red Devil lye—take on an interest all out of proportion to the moral of the story.

As the book proceeds through Malcolm's prison conversion, his tone, style, and experience naturally become indistinguishable from the present day rememberer—the author; and the book, as it concludes in 1965, becomes a direct sermon to America. But there is an important moment in the chapter "Saved" when Malcolm tells how he began in prison to read, study, even copy out pages from the dictionary which he then read aloud to himself. His own struggle with and eventual respect for the use of words suggests that along with whatever tribute we pay to him as a hero and a myth, we owe as well our serious attention to the words of his book.

From The Autobiography of Malcolm X
Chapter Three. "Homeboy"[1]

I looked like Li'l Abner.[2] Mason, Michigan, was written all over me. My kinky, reddish hair was cut hick style, and I didn't even use grease in it. My green suit's coat sleeves stopped above my wrists, the pants legs showed three inches of socks. Just a shade lighter green than the suit was my narrow-collared, three-quarter length Lansing department store topcoat. My appearance was too much for even Ella. But she told me later she had seen countrified members of the Little family come up from Georgia in even worse shape than I was.

Ella had fixed up a nice little upstairs room for me. And she was truly a Georgia Negro woman when she got into the kitchen with her pots and pans. She was the kind of cook who would heap up your plate with such as ham hock, greens, black-eyed peas, fried fish, cabbage, sweet potatoes, grits and gravy, and cornbread. And the more you put away, the better she felt. I worked out at Ella's kitchen table like there was no tomorrow.

Ella still seemed to be as big, black, outspoken and impressive a woman as she had been in Mason and Lansing. Only about two weeks before I arrived, she had split up with her second husband— the soldier, Frank, whom I had met there the previous summer; but she was taking it right in stride. I could see, though I didn't say, how any average man would find it almost impossible to live for

---

1. In this third chapter from Malcolm X's *Autobiography* he has come to live in Roxbury, Massachusetts, with his half-sister Ella. Wilfred, Hilda, Philbert, and Reginald are his brothers and sisters back home in Lansing, Michigan.
2. "Hillbilly" hero of a comic strip by Al Capp.

very long with a woman whose every instinct was to run everything
and everybody she had anything to do with—including me. About
my second day there in Roxbury, Ella told me that she didn't want
me to start hunting for a job right away, like most newcomer
Negroes did. She said that she had told all those she'd brought
North to take their time, to walk around, to travel the buses and the
subway, and get the feel of Boston, before they tied themselves
down working somewhere, because they would never again have the
time to really see and get to know anything about the city they were
living in. Ella said she'd help me find a job when it was time for me
to go to work.

So I went gawking around the neighborhood—the Waumbeck
and Humboldt Avenue Hill section of Roxbury, which is something
like Harlem's Sugar Hill, where I'd later live. I saw those Roxbury
Negroes acting and living differently from any black people I'd ever
dreamed of in my life. This was the snooty-black neighborhood;
they called themselves the "Four Hundred," and looked down their
noses at the Negroes of the black ghetto, or so-called "town" section
where Mary, my other half-sister, lived.

What I thought I was seeing there in Roxbury were high-class,
educated, important Negroes, living well, working in big jobs and
positions. Their quiet homes sat back in their mowed yards. These
Negroes walked along the sidewalks looking haughty and dignified,
on their way to work, to shop, to visit, to church. I know now, of
course, that what I was really seeing was only a big-city version of
those "successful" Negro bootblacks and janitors back in Lansing.
The only difference was that the ones in Boston had been brainwashed even more thoroughly. They prided themselves on being
incomparably more "cultured," "cultivated," "dignified," and better
off than their black brethren down in the ghetto, which was no
further away than you could throw a rock. Under the pitiful mis-
apprehension that it would make them "better," these Hill Negroes
were breaking their backs trying to imitate white people.

Any black family that had been around Boston long enough to
own the home they lived in was considered among the Hill elite. It
didn't make any difference that they had to rent out rooms to make
ends meet. Then the native-born New Englanders among them
looked down upon recently migrated Southern home-owners who
lived next door, like Ella. And a big percentage of the Hill dwellers
were in Ella's category—Southern strivers and scramblers, and West
Indian Negroes, whom both the New Englanders and the Southerners called "Black Jews." Usually it was the Southerners and the
West Indians who not only managed to own the places where they
lived, but also at least one other house which they rented as income
property. The snooty New Englanders usually owned less than they.

In those days on the Hill, any who could claim "professional"
status—teachers, preachers, practical nurses—also considered them-

selves superior. Foreign diplomats could have modeled their conduct on the way the Negro postmen, Pullman porters, and dining car waiters of Roxbury acted, striding around as if they were wearing top hats and cutaways.

I'd guess that eight out of ten of the Hill Negroes of Roxbury, despite the impressive-sounding job titles they affected, actually worked as menials and servants. "He's in banking," or "He's in securities." It sounded as though they were discussing a Rockefeller or a Mellon—and not some gray-headed, dignity-posturing bank janitor, or bond-house messenger. "I'm with an old family" was the euphemism used to dignify the professions of white folks' cooks and maids who talked so affectedly among their own kind in Roxbury that you couldn't even understand them. I don't know how many forty- and fifty-year-old errand boys went down the Hill dressed like ambassadors in black suits and white collars, to downtown jobs "in government," "in finance," or "in law." It has never ceased to amaze me how so many Negroes, then and now, could stand the indignity of that kind of self-delusion.

Soon I ranged out of Roxbury and began to explore Boston proper. Historic buildings everywhere I turned, and plaques and markers and statues for famous events and men. One statue in the Boston Commons astonished me: a Negro named Crispus Attucks, who had been the first man to fall in the Boston Massacre.[3] I had never known anything like that.

I roamed everywhere. In one direction, I walked as far as Boston University. Another day, I took my first subway ride. When most of the people got off, I followed. It was Cambridge, and I circled all around in the Harvard University campus. Somewhere, I had already heard of Harvard—though I didn't know much more about it. Nobody that day could have told me I would give an address before the Harvard Law School Forum some twenty years later.

I also did a lot of exploring downtown. Why a city would have *two* big railroad stations—North Station and South Station—I couldn't understand. At both of the stations, I stood around and watched people arrive and leave. And I did the same thing at the bus station where Ella had met me. My wanderings even led me down along the piers and docks where I read plaques telling about the old sailing ships that used to put into port there.

In a letter to Wilfred, Hilda, Philbert, and Reginald back in Lansing, I told them about all this, and about the winding, narrow, cobblestoned streets, and the houses that jammed up against each other. Downtown Boston, I wrote them, had the biggest stores I'd

---

3. Crispus Attucks was killed in the Boston Massacre (1770), a violent engagement between British soldiers and revolutionary colonists that preceded the War of Independence.

ever seen, and white people's restaurants and hotels. I made up my mind that I was going to see every movie that came to the fine, air-conditioned theaters.

On Massachusetts Avenue, next door to one of them, the Loew's State Theater, was the huge, exciting Roseland State Ballroom. Big posters out in front advertised the nationally famous bands, white and Negro, that had played there. "COMING NEXT WEEK," when I went by that first time, was Glenn Miller. I remember thinking how nearly the whole evening's music at Mason High School dances had been Glenn Miller's records. What wouldn't that crowd have given, I wondered, to be standing where Glenn Miller's band was actually going to play? I didn't know how familiar with Roseland I was going to become.

Ella began to grow concerned, because even when I had finally had enough sight-seeing, I didn't stick around very much on the Hill. She kept dropping hints that I ought to mingle with the "nice young people my age" who were to be seen in the Townsend Drug-store two blocks from her house, and a couple of other places. But even before I came to Boston, I had always felt and acted toward anyone my age as if they were in the "kid" class, like my younger brother Reginald. They had always looked up to me as if I were considerably older. On weekends back in Lansing where I'd go to get away from the white people in Mason, I'd hung around in the Negro part of town with Wilfred's and Philbert's set. Though all of them were several years older than me, I was bigger, and I actually looked older than most of them.

I didn't want to disappoint or upset Ella, but despite her advice, I began going down into the town ghetto section. That world of grocery stores, walk-up flats, cheap restaurants, poolrooms, bars, storefront churches, and pawnshops seemed to hold a natural lure for me.

Not only was this part of Roxbury much more exciting, but I felt more relaxed among Negroes who were being their natural selves and not putting on airs. Even though I did live on the Hill, my instincts were never—and still aren't—to feel myself any better than any other Negro.

I spent my first month in town with my mouth hanging open. The sharp-dressed young "cats" who hung on the corners and in the poolrooms, bars and restaurants, and who obviously didn't work anywhere, completely entranced me. I couldn't get over marveling at how their hair was straight and shiny like white men's hair; Ella told me this was called a "conk." I had never tasted a sip of liquor, never even smoked a cigarette, and here I saw little black children, ten and twelve years old, shooting craps, playing cards, fighting, getting grown-ups to put a penny or a nickel on their number for them, things like that. And these children threw around swear words I'd never heard before, even, and slang expressions that were just as new to me, such as "stud" and "cat" and "chick" and "cool" and "hip." Every night as I lay in bed I turned these new words over in my mind. It was shocking to me that in town, especially after dark, you'd occasionally see a white girl and a Negro man strolling arm in arm along the sidewalk, and mixed couples drinking in the neon-lighted bars—not slipping off to some dark corner, as in Lansing. I wrote Wilfred and Philbert about that, too.

I wanted to find a job myself, to surprise Ella. One afternoon, something told me to go inside a poolroom whose window I was looking through. I had looked through that window many times. I wasn't yearning to play pool; in fact, I had never held a cue stick. But I was drawn by the sight of the cool-looking "cats" standing around inside, bending over the big, green, felt-topped tables, making bets and shooting the bright-colored balls into the holes. As I stared through the window this particular afternoon, something made me decide to venture inside and talk to a dark, stubby, conk-headed fellow who racked up balls for the pool-players, whom I'd heard called "Shorty." One day he had come outside and seen me standing there and said "Hi, Red," so that made me figure he was friendly.

As inconspicuously as I could, I slipped inside the door and around the side of the poolroom, avoiding people, and on to the back, where Shorty was filling an aluminum can with the powder that pool players dust on their hands. He looked up at me. Later on, Shorty would enjoy teasing me about how with that first glance he knew my whole story. "Man, that cat still *smelled* country!" he'd say, laughing. "Cat's legs was so long and his pants so short his knees showed—an' his head looked like a briar patch!"

But that afternoon Shorty didn't let it show in his face how "country" I appeared when I told him I'd appreciate it if he'd tell me how could somebody go about getting a job like his.

"If you mean racking up balls," said Shorty, "I don't know of no pool joints around here needing anybody. You mean you just want any slave you can find?" A "slave" meant work, a job.

He asked what kind of work I had done. I told him that I'd washed restaurant dishes in Mason, Michigan. He nearly dropped the powder can. "My homeboy! Man, gimme some skin! I'm from Lansing!"

I never told Shorty—and he never suspected—that he was about ten years older than I. He took us to be about the same age. At first I would have been embarrassed to tell him, later I just never bothered. Shorty had dropped out of first-year high school in Lansing, lived a while with an uncle and aunt in Detroit, and had spent the last six years living with his cousin in Roxbury. But when I mentioned the names of Lansing people and places, he remembered many, and pretty soon we sounded as if we had been raised in the same block. I could sense Shorty's genuine gladness, and I don't have to say how lucky I felt to find a friend as hip as he obviously was.

"Man, this is a swinging town if you dig it," Shorty said. "You're my homeboy—I'm going to school you to the happenings." I stood there and grinned like a fool. "You got to go anywhere now? Well, stick around until I get off."

One thing I liked immediately about Shorty was his frankness. When I told him where I lived, he said what I already knew—that nobody in town could stand the Hill Negroes. But he thought a sister who gave me a "pad," not charging me rent, not even running me out to find "some slave," couldn't be all bad. Shorty's slave in the poolroom, he said, was just to keep ends together while he learned his horn. A couple of years before, he'd hit the numbers and bought a saxophone. "Got it right in there in the closet now, for my lesson tonight." Shorty was taking lessons "with some other studs," and he intended one day to organize his own small band. "There's a lot of bread to be made gigging right around here in Roxbury," Shorty explained to me. "I don't dig joining some big band, one-nighting all over just to say I played with Count or Duke or somebody."[4] I thought that was smart. I wished I had studied a horn; but I never had been exposed to one.

All afternoon, between trips up front to rack balls, Shorty talked to me out of the corner of his mouth: which hustlers—standing around, or playing at this or that table—sold "reefers," or had just come out of prison, or were "second-story men."[5] Shorty told me that he played at least a dollar a day on the numbers. He said as soon as he hit a number, he would use the winnings to organize his band.

I was ashamed to have to admit that I had never played the numbers. "Well, you ain't never had nothing to play with," he said, excusing me, "but you start when you get a slave, and if you hit, you got a stake for something."

He pointed out some gamblers and some pimps. Some of them had white whores, he whispered. "I ain't going to lie—I dig them two-dollar white chicks," Shorty said. "There's a lot of that action around here, nights: you'll see it." I said I already had seen some. "You ever had one?" he asked.

My embarrassment at my inexperience showed. "Hell, man," he said, "don't be ashamed. I had a few before I left Lansing—them Polack chicks that used to come over the bridge. Here, they're mostly Italians and Irish. But it don't matter what kind, they're something else! Ain't no different nowhere—there's nothing they love better than a black stud."

Through the afternoon, Shorty introduced me to players and

4. Count Basie (b. 1909) and Duke Ellington (1899–1974), great black American bandleaders.
5. I.e., burglars.

loungers. "My homeboy," he'd say, "he's looking for a slave if you hear anything." They all said they'd look out.

At seven o'clock, when the night ball-racker came on, Shorty told me he had to hurry to his saxophone lesson. But before he left, he held out to me the six or seven dollars he had collected that day in nickel and dime tips. "You got enough bread, homeboy?"

I was okay, I told him—I had two dollars. But Shorty made me take three more. "Little fattening for your pocket," he said. Before we went out, he opened his saxophone case and showed me the horn. It was gleaming brass against the green velvet, an alto sax. He said, "Keep cool, homeboy, and come back tomorrow. Some of the cats will turn you up a slave."

When I got home, Ella said there had been a telephone call from somebody named Shorty. He had left a message that over at the Roseland State Ballroom, the shoeshine boy was quitting that night, and Shorty had told him to hold the job for me.

"Malcolm, you haven't had any experience shining shoes," Ella said. Her expression and tone of voice told me she wasn't happy about my taking that job. I didn't particularly care, because I was already speechless thinking about being somewhere close to the greatest bands in the world. I didn't even wait to eat any dinner.

The ballroom was all lighted when I got there. A man at the front door was letting in members of Benny Goodman's band. I told him I wanted to see the shoeshine boy, Freddie.

"You're going to be the new one?" he asked. I said I thought I was, and he laughed, "Well, maybe you'll hit the numbers and get a Cadillac, too." He told me that I'd find Freddie upstairs in the men's room on the second floor.

But downstairs before I went up, I stepped over and snatched a glimpse inside the ballroom. I just couldn't believe the size of that waxed floor! At the far end, under the soft, rose-colored lights, was the bandstand with the Benny Goodman musicians moving around, laughing and talking, arranging their horns and stands.

A wiry, brown-skinned, conked fellow upstairs in the men's room greeted me. "You Shorty's homeboy?" I said I was, and he said he was Freddie. "Good old boy," he said. "He called me, he just heard I hit the big number, and he figured right I'd be quitting." I told Freddie what the man at the front door had said about a Cadillac. He laughed and said, "Burns them white cats up when you get yourself something. Yeah, I told them I was going to get me one— just to bug them."

Freddie then said for me to pay close attention, that he was going to be busy and for me to watch but not get in the way, and he'd try to get me ready to take over at the next dance, a couple of nights later.

As Freddie busied himself setting up the shoeshine stand, he told

me, "Get here early . . . your shoeshine rags and brushes by this
footstand . . . your polish bottles, paste wax, suede brushes over
here . . . everything in place, you get rushed, you never need to
waste motion. . . ."

While you shined shoes, I learned, you also kept watch on customers inside, leaving the urinals. You darted over and offered a
small white hand towel. "A lot of cats who ain't planning to wash
their hands, sometimes you can run up with a towel and shame
them. Your towels are really your best hustle in here. Cost you a
penny apiece to launder—you always get at least a nickel tip."

The shoeshine customers, and any from the inside rest room who
took a towel, you whiskbroomed a couple of licks. "A nickel or a
dime tip, just give 'em that," Freddie said. "But for two bits, Uncle
Tom a little—white cats especially like that. I've had them to come
back two, three times a dance."

From down below, the sound of the music had begun floating up.
I guess I stood transfixed. "You never seen a big dance?" asked
Freddie. "Run on awhile, and watch."

There were a few couples already dancing under the rose-colored
lights. But even more exciting to me was the crowd thronging in.
The most glamorous-looking white women I'd ever seen—young
ones, old ones, white cats buying tickets at the window, sticking big
wads of green bills back into their pockets, checking the women's
coats, and taking their arms and squiring them inside.

Freddie had some early customers when I got back upstairs.
Between the shoeshine stand and thrusting towels to me just as they
approached the wash basin, Freddie seemed to be doing four things
at once. "Here, you can take over the whiskbroom," he said, "just
two or three licks—but let 'em feel it."

When things slowed a little, he said, "You ain't seen nothing
tonight. You wait until you see a spooks' dance! Man, our own
people carry *on!*" Whenever he had a moment, he kept schooling
me. "Shoelaces, this drawer here. You just starting out, I'm going to
make these to you as a present. Buy them for a nickel a pair, tell
cats they need laces if they do, and charge two bits."

Every Benny Goodman record I'd ever heard in my life, it
seemed, was filtering faintly into where we were. During another
customer lull, Freddie let me slip back outside again to listen. Peggy
Lee was at the mike singing. Beautiful! She had just joined the band
and she was from North Dakota and had been singing with a group
in Chicago when Mrs. Benny Goodman discovered her, we had
heard some customers say. She finished the song and the crowd
burst into applause. She was a big hit.

"It knocked me out, too, when I first broke in here," Freddie
said, grinning, when I went back in there. "But, look, you ever
shined any shoes?" He laughed when I said I hadn't, excepting my

own. "Well, let's get to work. I never had neither." Freddie got on
the stand and went to work on his own shoes. Brush, liquid polish,
brush, paste wax, shine rag, lacquer sole dressing . . . step by step,
Freddie showed me what to do.

"But you got to get a whole lot faster. You can't waste time!"
Freddie showed me how fast on my own shoes. Then, because
business was tapering off, he had time to give me a demonstration
of how to make the shine rag pop like a firecracker. "Dig the
action?" he asked. He did it in slow motion. I got down and tried it
on his shoes. I had the principle of it. "Just got to do it faster,"
Freddie said. "It's a jive noise, that's all. Cats tip better, they figure
you're knocking yourself out!"

By the end of the dance, Freddie had let me shine the shoes of
three or four stray drunks he talked into having shines, and I had
practiced picking up my speed on Freddie's shoes until they looked
like mirrors. After we had helped the janitors to clean up the ballroom after the dance, throwing out all the paper and cigarette butts
and empty liquor bottles, Freddie was nice enough to drive me all
the way home to Ella's on the Hill in the second-hand maroon
Buick he said he was going to trade in on his Cadillac. He talked to
me all the way. "I guess it's all right if I tell you, pick up a couple
of dozen packs of rubbers, two-bits apiece. You notice some of
those cats that came up to me around the end of the dance? Well,
when some have new chicks going right, they'll come asking you for
rubbers. Charge a dollar, generally you'll get an extra tip."

He looked across at me. "Some hustles you're too new for. Cats
will ask you for liquor, some will want reefers. But you don't need
to have nothing except rubbers—until you can dig who's a cop.

"You can make ten, twelve dollars a dance for yourself if you
work everything right," Freddie said, before I got out of the car in
front of Ella's. "The main thing you got to remember is that everything in the world is a hustle. So long, Red."

The next time I ran into Freddie I was downtown one night a few
weeks later. He was parked in his pearl gray Cadillac, sharp as a
tack, "cooling it."

"Man, you sure schooled me!" I said, and he laughed; he knew
what I meant. It hadn't taken me long on the job to find out that
Freddie had done less shoeshining and towel-hustling than selling
liquor and reefers, and putting white "Johns" in touch with Negro
whores. I also learned that white girls always flocked to the Negro
dances—some of them whores whose pimps brought them to mix
business and pleasure, others who came with their black boy
friends, and some who came in alone, for a little freelance lusting
among a plentiful availability of enthusiastic Negro men.

At the white dances, of course, nothing black was allowed, and
that's where the black whores' pimps soon showed a new shoeshine

boy what he could pick up on the side by slipping a phone number or address to the white Johns who came around the end of the dance looking for "black chicks."

Most of Roseland's dances were for whites only, and they had white bands only. But the only white band ever to play there at a Negro dance to my recollection, was Charlie Barnet's. The fact is that very few white bands could have satisfied the Negro dancers. But I know that Charlie Barnet's "Cherokee" and his "Redskin Rhumba" drove those Negroes wild. They'd jampack that ballroom, the black girls in way-out silk and satin dresses and shoes, their hair done in all kinds of styles, the men sharp in their zoot suits and crazy conks, and everybody grinning and greased and gassed.

Some of the bandsmen would come up to the men's room at about eight o'clock and get shoeshines before they went to work. Duke Ellington, Count Basie, Lionel Hampton, Cootie Williams, Jimmie Lunceford were just a few of those who sat in my chair. I would really make my shine rag sound like someone had set off Chinese firecrackers. Duke's great alto saxman, Johnny Hodges—he was Shorty's idol—still owes me for a shoeshine I gave him. He was in the chair one night, having a friendly argument with the drummer, Sonny Greer, who was standing there, when I tapped the bottom of his shoes to signal that I was finished. Hodges stepped down, reaching his hand in his pocket to pay me, but then snatched his hand out to gesture, and just forgot me, and walked away. I wouldn't have dared to bother the man who could do what he did with "Daydream" by asking him for fifteen cents.

I remember that I struck up a little shoeshine-stand conversation with Count Basie's great blues singer, Jimmie Rushing. (He's the one famous for "Sent for You Yesterday, Here You Come Today" and things like that.) Rushing's feet, I remember, were big and funny-shaped—not long like most big feet, but they were round and roly-poly like Rushing. Anyhow, he even introduced me to some of the other Basie cats, like Lester Young, Harry Edison, Buddy Tate, Don Byas, Dickie Wells, and Buck Clayton. They'd walk in the rest room later, by themselves. "Hi, Red." They'd be up there in my chair, and my shine rag was popping to the beat of all of their records, spinning in my head. Musicians never have had, anywhere, a greater shoeshine-boy fan than I was. I would write to Wilfred and Hilda and Philbert and Reginald back in Lansing, trying to describe it.

I never got any decent tips until the middle of the Negro dances, which is when the dancers started feeling good and getting generous. After the white dances, when I helped to clean out the ballroom, we would throw out perhaps a dozen empty liquor bottles.

But after the Negro dances, we would have to throw out cartons full of empty fifth bottles—not rotgut, either, but the best brands, and especially Scotch.

During lulls up there in the men's room, sometimes I'd get in five minutes of watching the dancing. The white people danced as though somebody had trained them—left, one, two; right, three, four—the same steps and patterns over and over, as though somebody had wound them up. But those Negroes—nobody in the world could have choreographed the way they did whatever they felt—just grabbing partners, even the white chicks who came to the Negro dances. And my black brethren today may hate me for saying it, but a lot of black girls nearly got run over by some of those Negro males scrambling to get at those white women; you would have thought God had lowered some of his angels. Times have sure changed; if it happened today, those same black girls would go after those Negro men—and the white women, too.

Anyway, some couples were so abandoned—flinging high and wide, improvising steps and movements—that you couldn't believe it. I could feel the beat in my bones, even though I had never danced.

"*Showtime!*" people would start hollering about the last hour of the dance. Then a couple of dozen really wild couples would stay on the floor, the girls changing to low white sneakers. The band now would really be blasting, and all the other dancers would form a clapping, shouting circle to watch that wild competition as it began, covering only a quarter or so of the ballroom floor. The band, the spectators and the dancers, would be making the Roseland Ballroom feel like a big rocking ship. The spotlight would be turning, pink, yellow, green, and blue, picking up the couples lindy-hopping as if they had gone mad. "*Wail, man, wail!*" people would be shouting at the band; and it *would* be wailing, until first one and then another couple just ran out of strength and stumbled off toward the crowd, exhausted and soaked with sweat. Sometimes I would be down there standing inside the door jumping up and down in my gray jacket with the whiskbroom in the pocket, and the manager would have to come and shout at me that I had customers upstairs.

The first liquor I drank, my first cigarettes, even my first reefers, I can't specifically remember. But I know they were all mixed together with my first shooting craps, playing cards, and betting my dollar a day on the numbers, as I started hanging out at night with Shorty and his friends. Shorty's jokes about how country I had been made us all laugh. I still was country, I know now, but it all felt so great because I was accepted. All of us would be in somebody's place, usually one of the girls', and we'd be turning on, the reefers making everybody's head light, or the whisky aglow in our middles. Everybody understood that my head had to stay kinky a while longer, to grow long enough for Shorty to conk it for me. One of these nights, I remarked that I had saved about half enough to get a zoot.[6]

"*Save?*" Shorty couldn't believe it. "Homeboy, you never heard of credit?" He told me he'd call a neighborhood clothing store the first thing in the morning, and that I should be there early.

A salesman, a young Jew, met me when I came in. "You're Shorty's friend?" I said I was; it amazed me—all of Shorty's contacts. The salesman wrote my name on a form, and the Roseland as where I worked, and Ella's address as where I lived. Shorty's name was put down as recommending me. The salesman said, "Shorty's one of our best customers."

I was measured, and the young salesman picked off a rack a zoot suit that was just wild: sky-blue pants thirty inches in the knee and angle-narrowed down to twelve inches at the bottom, and a long coat that pinched my waist and flared out below my knees.

As a gift, the salesman said, the store would give me a narrow leather belt with my initial "L" on it. Then he said I ought to also buy a hat, and I did—blue, with a feather in the four-inch brim. Then the store gave me another present: a long, thick-linked, gold-plated chain that swung down lower than my coat hem. I was sold forever on credit.

When I modeled the zoot for Ella, she took a long look and said, "Well, I guess it had to happen." I took three of those twenty-five-cent sepia-toned, while-you-wait pictures of myself, posed the way "hipsters" wearing their zoots would "cool it"—hat dangled, knees drawn close together, feet wide apart, both index fingers jabbed toward the floor. The long coat and swinging chain and the Punjab pants were much more dramatic if you stood that way. One picture, I autographed and airmailed to my brothers and sisters in Lansing, to let them see how well I was doing. I gave another one to Ella, and the third to Shorty, who was really moved: I could tell by the way he said, "Thanks, homeboy." It was part of our "hip" code not to show that kind of affection.

Shorty soon decided that my hair was finally long enough to be conked. He had promised to school me in how to beat the barber-shops' three- and four-dollar price by making up congolene, and then conking ourselves.

I took the little list of ingredients he had printed out for me, and went to a grocery store, where I got a can of Red Devil lye, two eggs, and two medium-sized white potatoes. Then at a drugstore near the poolroom, I asked for a large jar of vaseline, a large bar of soap, a large-toothed comb and a fine-toothed comb, one of those rubber hoses with a metal spray-head, a rubber apron and a pair of gloves.

6. A "zoot suit" was an outlandishly styled three-piece suit of the times.

"Going to lay on that first conk?" the drugstore man asked me. I proudly told him, grinning, "Right!"

Shorty paid six dollars a week for a room in his cousin's shabby apartment. His cousin wasn't at home. "It's like the pad's mine, he spends so much time with his woman," Shorty said. "Now, you watch me—"

He peeled the potatoes and thin-sliced them into a quart-sized Mason fruit jar, then started stirring them with a wooden spoon as he gradually poured in a little over half the can of lye. "Never use a metal spoon; the lye will turn it black," he told me.

A jelly-like, starchy-looking glop resulted from the lye and potatoes, and Shorty broke in the two eggs, stirring real fast—his own conk and dark face bent down close. The congolene turned pale-yellowish. "Feel the jar," Shorty said. I cupped my hand against the outside, and snatched it away. "Damn right, it's hot, that's the lye," he said. "So you know it's going to burn when I comb it in—it burns *bad*. But the longer you can stand it, the straighter the hair."

He made me sit down, and he tied the string of the new rubber apron tightly around my neck, and combed up my bush of hair. Then, from the big vaseline jar, he took a handful and massaged it hard all through my hair and into the scalp. He also thickly vaselined my neck, ears and forehead. "When I get to washing out your head, be sure to tell me anywhere you feel any little stinging," Shorty warned me, washing his hands, then pulling on the rubber gloves, and tying on his own rubber apron. "You always got to remember that any congolene left in burns a sore into your head."

The congolene just felt warm when Shorty started combing it in. But then my head caught fire.

I gritted my teeth and tried to pull the sides of the kitchen table together. The comb felt as if it was raking my skin off.

My eyes watered, my nose was running. I couldn't stand it any longer; I bolted to the washbasin. I was cursing Shorty with every name I could think of when he got the spray going and started soap-lathering my head.

He lathered and spray-rinsed, lathered and spray-rinsed, maybe ten or twelve times, each time gradually closing the hot-water faucet, until the rinse was cold, and that helped some.

"You feel any stinging spots?"

"No," I managed to say. My knees were trembling.

"Sit back down, then. I think we got it all out okay."

The flame came back as Shorty, with a thick towel, started drying my head, rubbing hard. "*Easy, man, easy!*" I kept shouting.

"The first time's always worst. You get used to it better before long. You took it real good, homeboy. You got a good conk."

When Shorty let me stand up and see in the mirror, my hair hung down in limp, damp strings. My scalp still flamed, but not as badly;

I could bear it. He draped the towel around my shoulders, over my rubber apron, and began again vaselining my hair.

I could feel him combing, straight back, first the big comb, then the fine-tooth one.

Then, he was using a razor, very delicately, on the back of my neck. Then, finally, shaping the sideburns.

My first view in the mirror blotted out the hurting. I'd seen some pretty conks, but when it's the first time, on your *own* head, the transformation, after the lifetime of kinks, is staggering.

The mirror reflected Shorty behind me. We both were grinning and sweating. And on top of my head was this thick, smooth sheen of shining red hair—real red—as straight as any white man's.

How ridiculous I was! Stupid enough to stand there simply lost in admiration of my hair now looking "white," reflected in the mirror in Shorty's room. I vowed that I'd never again be without a conk, and I never was for many years.

This was my first really big step toward self-degradation: when I endured all of that pain, literally burning my flesh to have it look like a white man's hair. I had joined that multitude of Negro men and women in America who are brainwashed into believing that the black people are "inferior"—and white people "superior"—that they will even violate and mutilate their God-created bodies to try to look "pretty" by white standards.

Look around today, in every small town and big city, from two-bit catfish and soda-pop joints into the "integrated" lobby of the Waldorf-Astoria, and you'll see conks on black men. And you'll see black women wearing these green and pink and purple and red and platinum-blonde wigs. They're all more ridiculous than a slapstick comedy. It makes you wonder if the Negro has completely lost his sense of identity, lost touch with himself.

You'll see the conk worn by many, many so-called "upper class" Negroes, and, as much as I hate to say it about them, on all too many Negro entertainers. One of the reasons that I've especially admired some of them, like Lionel Hampton and Sidney Poitier, among others, is that they have kept their natural hair and fought to the top. I admire any Negro man who has never had himself conked, or who has had the sense to get rid of it—as I finally did.

I don't know which kind of self-defacing conk is the greater shame—the one you'll see on the heads of the black so-called "middle class" and "upper class," who ought to know better, or the one you'll see on the heads of the poorest, most downtrodden, ignorant black men. I mean the legal-minimum-wage ghetto-dwelling kind of Negro, as I was when I got my first one. It's generally among these poor fools that you'll see a black kerchief over the man's head, like Aunt Jemima; he's trying to make his conk last longer, between trips to the barbershop. Only for special occasions is this kerchief-protected conk exposed—to show off how "sharp" and "hip" its owner is. The ironic thing is that I have never heard any woman, white or black, express any admiration for a conk. Of course, any white woman with a black man isn't thinking about his hair. But I don't see how on earth a black woman with any race pride could walk down the street with any black man wearing a conk—the emblem of his shame that he is black.

To my own shame, when I say all of this I'm talking first of all about myself—because you can't show me any Negro who ever conked more faithfully than I did. I'm speaking from personal experience when I say of any black man who conks today, or any white-wigged black woman, that if they gave the brains in their heads just half as much attention as they do their hair, they would be a thousand times better off.

1965

FLANNERY O'CONNOR
1925–1964

Flannery O'Connor, one of this century's finest writers of short stories, was born in Savannah, lived with her mother in Milledgeville, Georgia, for much of her life, and died before her fortieth birthday—victim like her father of disseminated lupus, a rare and incurable blood disease. She was stricken with the disease in 1950 while at work on her first novel, but injections of a cortisone derivative managed to arrest it, though the cortisone weakened her bones to the extent that from 1955 on she got around on aluminum crutches. She was able to write, travel, and lecture until 1964 when the lupus reactivated itself and killed her. A Roman Catholic throughout her life, she is quoted as having remarked, apropos a trip to Lourdes, "I had the best-looking crutches in Europe." This remark suggests the kind of hair-raising jokes which centrally inform her writing, as well as a refusal to indulge in self-pity over her fate.

She published two novels, *Wise Blood* (1952) and *The Violent Bear It Away* (1960), both weighty with symbolic and religious concerns, and ingeniously contrived in the black-humored manner of Nathanael West, her American predecessor in this mode. But her really memorable creations of characters and actions take place in the stories, which are extremely funny, sometimes unbearably so, and finally we may wonder just what it is we are laughing at. Upon consideration the jokes are seen to be dreadful ones, as with Manley Pointer's treatment of Joy Hopewell's artificial leg in *Good Country People* or Mr. Head's trials and tribulations in *The Artificial Nigger*.

Another American "regionalist," the poet Robert Frost, whose own work contains its share of "dreadful jokes," once confessed to being more interested in people's speech than in the people themselves. A typical Flannery O'Connor story consists at its most vital level in people talking, clucking their endless reiterations of clichés about life, death, and the universe. These clichés are captured with beautiful accuracy by an artist who had spent her life listening to them, lovingly and maliciously keeping track until she could put them to use. Early in her life she hoped to be a cartoonist, and there is cartoonlike mastery in her vivid renderings of character through speech and other gesture. Critics have called her a maker of grotesques, a label which like other ones—Regionalist, Southern Lady, or Roman Catholic Novelist—might have annoyed if it didn't obviously amuse her too. She once remarked tartly that "anything that comes out of the South is going to be called grotesque by the Northern reader, unless it is grotesque, in which case it is going to be called realistic."

Of course this capacity for mockery, along with a facility in portraying perverse behavior, may work against other demands we make of the fiction writer; and it is true that Flannery O'Connor seldom suggests that her characters have inner lives that are imaginable, let alone worth respect. Instead the emphasis is on the sharp eye and the ability to tell a tale and keep it moving inevitably toward completion. These completions are usually violent, occurring when the character—in many cases a woman—must confront an experience which she cannot handle by the old trustworthy language and habit-hardened responses. O'Connor's art lies partly in making it impossible for us merely to scorn the banalities of expression and behavior by which these people get through their lives. However dark the comedy, it keeps in touch with the things of this world, even when some force from another world threatens to annihilate the embattled protagonist. And although the stories are filled with religious allusions and parodies, they do not try to inculcate a doctrine. One of her best ones is titled *Revelation*, but a reader often finishes a story with no simple, unambiguous sense of what has been revealed. Instead we must trust the internal fun and richness of each tale to reveal what it has to reveal. We can agree also, in sadness, with the critic Irving Howe's conclusion to his review of her posthumous collection of stories that it is intolerable for such a writer to have died at the age of thirty-nine.

Good Country People[1]

Besides the neutral expression that she wore when she was alone, Mrs. Freeman had two others, forward and reverse, that she used for all her human dealings. Her forward expression was steady and driving like the advance of a heavy truck. Her eyes never swerved to left or right but turned as the story turned as if they followed a yellow line down the center of it. She seldom used the other expression because it was not often necessary for her to retract a statement, but when she did, her face came to a complete stop, there was an almost imperceptible movement of her black eyes, during which they seemed to be receding, and then the observer would see that Mrs. Freeman, though she might stand there as real as several grain sacks thrown on top of each other, was no longer there in spirit. As for getting anything across to her when this was the case, Mrs. Hopewell had given it up. She might talk her head off. Mrs. Freeman could never be brought to admit herself wrong on any point.

1. From *A Good Man Is Hard to Find* (1955).

She would stand there and if she could be brought to say anything, it was something like, "Well, I wouldn't of said it was and I wouldn't of said it wasn't," or letting her gaze range over the top kitchen shelf where there was an assortment of dusty bottles, she might remark, "I see you ain't ate many of them figs you put up last summer."

They carried on their important business in the kitchen at breakfast. Every morning Mrs. Hopewell got up at seven o'clock and lit her gas heater and Joy's. Joy was her daughter, a large blonde girl who had an artificial leg. Mrs. Hopewell thought of her as a child though she was thirty-two years old and highly educated. Joy would get up while her mother was eating and lumber into the bathroom and slam the door, and before long, Mrs. Freeman would arrive at the back door. Joy would hear her mother call, "Come on in," and then they would talk for a while in low voices that were indistinguishable in the bathroom. By the time Joy came in, they had usually finished the weather report and were on one or the other of Mrs. Freeman's daughters, Glynese or Carramae, Joy called them Glycerin and Caramel. Glynese, a redhead, was eighteen and had many admirers; Carramae, a blonde, was only fifteen but already married and pregnant. She could not keep anything on her stomach. Every morning Mrs. Freeman told Mrs. Hopewell how many times she had vomited since the last report.

Mrs. Hopewell liked to tell people that Glynese and Carramae were two of the finest girls she knew and that Mrs. Freeman was a *lady* and that she was never ashamed to take her anywhere or introduce her to anybody they might meet. Then she would tell how she had happened to hire the Freemans in the first place and how they were a godsend to her and how she had had them four years. The reason for her keeping them so long was that they were not trash. They were good country people. She had telephoned the man whose name they had given as a reference and he had told her that Mr. Freeman was a good farmer but that his wife was the nosiest woman ever to walk the earth. "She's got to be into everything," the man said. "If she don't get there before the dust settles, you can bet she's dead, that's all. She'll want to know all your business. I can stand him real good," he had said, "but me nor my wife neither could have stood that woman one more minute on this place." That had put Mrs. Hopewell off for a few days.

She had hired them in the end because there were no other applicants but she had made up her mind beforehand exactly how she would handle the woman. Since she was the type who had to be into everything, then, Mrs. Hopewell had decided, she would not only let her be into everything, she would *see to it* that she was into everything—she would give her the responsibility of everything, she would put her in charge. Mrs. Hopewell had no bad qualities of her own but she was able to use other people's in such a constructive way that she never felt the lack. She had hired the Freemans and she had kept them four years.

Nothing is perfect. This was one of Mrs. Hopewell's favorite sayings. Another was: that is life! And still another, the most important, was: well, other people have their opinions too. She would make these statements, usually at the table, in a tone of gentle insistence as if no one held them but her, and the large hulking Joy, whose constant outrage had obliterated every expression from her face, would stare just a little to the side of her, her eyes icy blue, with the look of someone who has achieved blindness by an act of will and means to keep it.

When Mrs. Hopewell said to Mrs. Freeman that life was like that, Mrs. Freeman would say, "I always said so myself." Nothing had been arrived at by anyone that had not first been arrived at by her. She was quicker than Mr. Freeman. When Mrs. Hopewell said to her after they had been on the place a while, "You know, you're the wheel behind the wheel," and winked, Mrs. Freeman had said, "I know it. I've always been quick. It's some that are quicker than others."

"Everybody is different," Mrs. Hopewell said.

"Yes, most people is," Mrs. Freeman said.

"It takes all kinds to make the world."

"I always said it did myself."

The girl was used to this kind of dialogue for breakfast and more of it for dinner; sometimes they had it for supper too. When they had no guest they ate in the kitchen because that was easier. Mrs. Freeman always managed to arrive at some point during the meal and to watch them finish it. She would stand in the doorway if it were summer but in the winter she would stand with one elbow on top of the refrigerator and look down on them, or she would stand by the gas heater, lifting the back of her skirt slightly. Occasionally she would stand against the wall and roll her head from side to side. At no time was she in any hurry to leave. All this was very trying on Mrs. Hopewell but she was a woman of great patience. She realized that nothing is perfect and that in the Freemans she had good country people and that if, in this day and age, you get good country people, you had better hang onto them.

She had had plenty of experience with trash. Before the Freemans she had averaged one tenant family a year. The wives of these farmers were not the kind you would want to be around you for very long. Mrs. Hopewell, who had divorced her husband long ago, needed someone to walk over the fields with her; and when Joy had to be impressed for these services, her remarks were usually so ugly and her face so glum that Mrs. Hopewell would say, "If you can't come pleasantly, I don't want you at all," to which the girl, standing square and rigid-shouldered with her neck thrust slightly forward, would reply, "If you want me, here I am—LIKE I AM."

Mrs. Hopewell excused this attitude because of the leg (which had been shot off in a hunting accident when Joy was ten). It was hard for Mrs. Hopewell to realize that her child was thirty-two now and that for more than twenty years she had had only one leg. She thought of her still as a child because it tore her heart to think instead of the poor stout girl in her thirties who had never danced a step or had any *normal* good times. Her name was really Joy but as soon as she was twenty-one and away from home, she had had it legally changed. Mrs. Hopewell was certain that she had thought and thought until she had hit upon the ugliest name in any language. Then she had gone and had the beautiful name, Joy, changed without telling her mother until after she had done it. Her legal name was Hulga.

When Mrs. Hopewell thought the name, Hulga, she thought of the broad blank hull of a battleship. She would not use it. She continued to call her Joy to which the girl responded but in a purely mechanical way.

Hulga had learned to tolerate Mrs. Freeman who saved her from taking walks with her mother. Even Glynese and Carramae were useful when they occupied attention that might otherwise have been directed at her. At first she had thought she could not stand Mrs. Freeman for she had found that it was not possible to be rude to her. Mrs. Freeman would take on strange resentments and for days together she would be sullen but the source of her displeasure was always obscure; a direct attack, a positive leer, blatant ugliness to her face—these never touched her. And without warning one day, she began calling her Hulga.

She did not call her that in front of Mrs. Hopewell who would have been incensed but when she and the girl happened to be out of the house together, she would say something and add the name Hulga to the end of it, and the big spectacled Joy-Hulga would scowl and redden as if her privacy had been intruded upon. She considered the name her personal affair. She had arrived at it first purely on the basis of its ugly sound and then the full genius of its fitness had struck her. She had a vision of the name working like the ugly sweating Vulcan who stayed in the furnace and to whom, presumably, the goddess had to come when called.[2] She saw it as the name of her highest creative act. One of her major triumphs was that her mother had not been able to turn her dust into Joy, but the greater one was that she had been able to turn it herself into Hulga. However, Mrs. Freeman's relish for using the name only irritated her. It was as if Mrs. Freeman's beady steel-pointed eyes had penetrated far enough behind her face to reach some secret fact. Something about her seemed to fascinate Mrs. Freeman and then one day Hulga realized that it was the artificial leg. Mrs. Freeman had a

2. Vulcan was the Greek god of fire whom Venus, goddess of love, "presumably" obeyed as her consort.

special fondness for the details of secret infections, hidden deformities, assaults upon children. Of diseases, she preferred the lingering or incurable. Hulga had heard Mrs. Hopewell give her the details of the hunting accident, how the leg had been literally blasted off, how she had never lost consciousness. Mrs. Freeman could listen to it any time as if it had happened an hour ago.

When Hulga stumped into the kitchen in the morning (she could walk without making the awful noise but she made it—Mrs. Hopewell was certain—because it was ugly-sounding), she glanced at them and did not speak. Mrs. Hopewell would be in her red kimono with her hair tied around her head in rags. She would be sitting at the table, finishing her breakfast and Mrs. Freeman would be hanging by her elbow outward from the refrigerator, looking down at the table. Hulga always put her eggs on the stove to boil and then stood over them with her arms folded, and Mrs. Hopewell would look at her—a kind of indirect gaze divided between her and Mrs. Freeman —and would think that if she would only keep herself up a little, she wouldn't be so bad looking. There was nothing wrong with her face that a pleasant expression wouldn't help. Mrs Hopewell said that people who looked on the bright side of things would be beautiful even if they were not.

Whenever she looked at Joy this way, she could not help but feel that it would have been better if the child had not taken the Ph.D. It had certainly not brought her out any and now that she had it, there was no more excuse for her to go to school again. Mrs. Hopewell thought it was nice for girls to go to school to have a good time but Joy had "gone through." Anyhow, she would not have been strong enough to go again. The doctors had told Mrs. Hopewell that with the best of care, Joy might see forty-five. She had a weak heart. Joy had made it plain that if it had not been for this condition, she would be far from these red hills and good country people. She would be in a university lecturing to people who knew what she was talking about. And Mrs. Hopewell could very well picture her there, looking like a scarecrow and lecturing to more of the same. Here she went about all day in a six-year-old skirt and a yellow sweat shirt with a faded cowboy on a horse embossed on it. She thought this was funny; Mrs. Hopewell thought it was idiotic and showed simply that she was still a child. She was brilliant but she didn't have a grain of sense. It seemed to Mrs. Hopewell that every year she grew less like other people and more like herself—bloated, rude, and squint-eyed. And she said such strange things! To her own mother she had said—without warning, without excuse, standing up in the middle of a meal with her face purple and her mouth half full—"Woman! do you ever look inside? Do you ever look inside and see what you are *not?* God!" she had cried sinking down again and staring at her plate, "Malebranche[3]

3. Nicolas Malebranche, French philosopher (1638–1715).

was right: we are not our own light. We are not our own light!" Mrs. Hopewell had no idea to this day what brought that on. She had only made the remark, hoping Joy would take it in, that a smile never hurt anyone.

The girl had taken the Ph.D. in philosophy and this left Mrs. Hopewell at a complete loss. You could say, "My daughter is a nurse," or "My daughter is a schoolteacher," or even, "My daughter is a chemical engineer." You could not say, "My daughter is a philosopher." That was something that had ended with the Greeks and Romans. All day Joy sat on her neck in a deep chair, reading. Sometimes she went for walks but she didn't like dogs or cats or birds or flowers or nature or nice young men. She looked at nice young men as if she could smell their stupidity.

One day Mrs. Hopewell had picked up one of the books the girl had just put down and opening it at random, she read, "Science, on the other hand, has to assert its soberness and seriousness afresh and declare that it is concerned solely with what-is. Nothing—how can it be for science anything but a horror and a phantasm? If science is right, then one thing stands firm: science wishes to know nothing of nothing. Such is after all the strictly scientific approach to Nothing. We know it by wishing to know nothing of Nothing." These words had been underlined with a blue pencil and they worked on Mrs. Hopewell like some evil incantation in gibberish. She shut the book quickly and went out of the room as if she were having a chill.

This morning when the girl came in, Mrs. Freeman was on Carramae. "She thrown up four times after supper," she said, "and was up twict in the night after three o'clock. Yesterday she didn't do nothing but ramble in the bureau drawer. All she did. Stand up there and see what she could run up on."

"She's got to eat," Mrs. Hopewell muttered, sipping her coffee, while she watched Joy's back at the stove. She was wondering what the child had said to the Bible salesman. She could not imagine what kind of a conversation she could possibly have had with him.

He was a tall gaunt hatless youth who had called yesterday to sell them a Bible. He had appeared at the door, carrying a large black suitcase that weighted him so heavily on one side that he had to brace himself against the door facing. He seemed on the point of collapse but he said in a cheerful voice. "Good morning, Mrs. Cedars!" and set the suitcase down on the mat. He was not a bad-looking young man though he had on a bright blue suit and yellow socks that were not pulled up far enough. He had prominent face bones and a streak of sticky-looking brown hair falling across his forehead.

"I'm Mrs. Hopewell," she said.

"Oh!" he said, pretending to look puzzled but with his eyes sparkling, "I saw it said 'The Cedars' on the mailbox so I thought you was Mrs. Cedars!" and he burst out in a pleasant laugh. He picked up the satchel and under cover of a pant, he fell forward into her hall. It was rather as if the suitcase had moved first, jerking him after it. "Mrs. Hopewell!" he said and grabbed her hand. "I hope you are well!" and he laughed again and then all at once his face sobered completely. He paused and gave her a straight earnest look and said, "Lady, I've come to speak of serious things."

"Well, come in," she muttered, none too pleased because her dinner was almost ready. He came into the parlor and sat down on the edge of a straight chair and put the suitcase between his feet and glanced around the room as if he were sizing her up by it. Her silver gleamed on the two sideboards; she decided he had never been in a room as elegant as this.

"Mrs. Hopewell," he began, using her name in a way that sounded almost intimate, "I know you believe in Christian service."

"Well yes," she murmured.

"I know," he said and paused, looking very wise with his head cocked on one side, "that you're a good woman. Friends have told me."

Mrs. Hopewell never liked to be taken for a fool. "What are you selling?" she asked.

"Bibles," the young man said and his eye raced around the room before he added, "I see you have no family Bible in your parlor, I see that is the one lack you got!"

Mrs. Hopewell could not say, "My daughter is an atheist and won't let me keep the Bible in the parlor." She said, stiffening slightly, "I keep my Bible by my bedside." This was not the truth. It was in the attic somewhere.

"Lady," he said, "the word of God ought to be in the parlor."

"Well, I think that's a matter of taste," she began. "I think . . ."

"Lady," he said, "for a Christian, the word of God ought to be in every room in the house besides in his heart. I know you're a Christian because I can see it in every line of your face."

She stood up and said, "Well, young man, I don't want to buy a Bible and I smell my dinner burning."

He didn't get up. He began to twist his hands and looking down at them, he said softly, "Well lady, I'll tell you the truth—not many people want to buy one nowadays and besides, I know I'm real simple. I don't know how to say a thing but to say it. I'm just a country boy." He glanced up into her unfriendly face. "People like you don't like to fool with country people like me!"

"Why!" she cried, "good country people are the salt of the earth! Besides, we all have different ways of doing, it takes all kinds to make the world go 'round. That's life!"

"You said a mouthful," he said.

"Why, I think there aren't enough good country people in the world!" she said, stirred. "I think that's what's wrong with it!"

His face had brightened. "I didn't inraduce myself," he said. "I'm Manley Pointer from out in the country around Willohobie, not even from a place, just from near a place."

"You wait a minute," she said. "I have to see about my dinner." She went out to the kitchen and found Joy standing near the door where she had been listening.

"Get rid of the salt of the earth," she said, "and let's eat."

Mrs. Hopewell gave her a pained look and turned the heat down under the vegetables. "I can't be rude to anybody," she murmured and went back into the parlor.

He had opened the suitcase and was sitting with a Bible on each knee.

"You might as well put those up," she told him. "I don't want one."

"I appreciate your honesty," he said. "You don't see any more real honest people unless you go way out in the country."

"I know," she said, "real genuine folks!" Through the crack in the door she heard a groan.

"I guess a lot of boys come telling you they're working their way through college," he said, "but I'm not going to tell you that. Somehow," he said, "I don't want to go to college. I want to devote my life to Chrustian service. See," he said, lowering his voice, "I got this heart condition. I may not live long. When you know it's something wrong with you and you may not live long, well then, lady . . ." He paused, with his mouth open, and stared at her.

He and Joy had the same condition! She knew that her eyes were filling with tears but she collected herself quickly and murmured, "Won't you stay for dinner? We'd love to have you!" and was sorry the instant she heard herself say it.

"Yes mam," he said in an abashed voice, "I would sher love to do that!"

Joy had given him one look on being introduced to him and then throughout the meal had not glanced at him again. He had addressed several remarks to her, which she had pretended not to hear. Mrs. Hopewell could not understand deliberate rudeness, although she lived with it, and she felt she had always to overflow with hospitality to make up for Joy's lack of courtesy. She urged him to talk about himself and he did. He said he was the seventh child of twelve and that his father had been crushed under a tree when he himself was eight year old. He had been crushed very badly, in fact, almost cut in two and was practically not recognizable. His mother had got along the best she could by hard working and she had always seen that her children went to Sunday School and that they read the Bible every evening. He was now nineteen year old and he had been selling Bibles for four months. In that time he had sold seventy-seven Bibles and had the promise of two more sales. He wanted to become a missionary because he thought that was the way you could do most for people. "He who losest his life shall find it," he said simply and he was so sincere, so genuine and earnest that Mrs. Hopewell would not for the world have smiled. He prevented his peas from sliding onto the table by blocking them with a piece of bread which he later cleaned his plate with. She could see Joy observing sidewise how he handled his knife and fork and she saw too that every few minutes, the boy would dart a keen appraising glance at the girl as if he were trying to attract her attention.

After dinner Joy cleared the dishes off the table and disappeared and Mrs. Hopewell was left to talk with him. He told her again about his childhood and his father's accident and about various things that had happened to him. Every five minutes or so she would stifle a yawn. He sat for two hours until finally she told him she must go because she had an appointment in town. He packed his Bibles and thanked her and prepared to leave, but in the doorway he stopped and wrung her hand and said that not on any of his trips had he met a lady as nice as her and he asked if he could come again. She had said she would always be happy to see him.

Joy had been standing in the road, apparently looking at something in the distance, when he came down the steps toward her, bent to the side with his heavy valise. He stopped where she was standing and confronted her directly. Mrs. Hopewell could not hear what he said but she trembled to think what Joy would say to him. She could see that after a minute Joy said something and that then the boy began to speak again, making an excited gesture with his free hand. After a minute Joy said something else at which the boy began to speak once more. Then to her amazement, Mrs. Hopewell saw the two of them walk off together, toward the gate. Joy had walked all the way to the gate with him and Mrs. Hopewell could not imagine what they had said to each other, and she had not yet dared to ask.

Mrs. Freeman was insisting upon her attention. She had moved from the refrigerator to the heater so that Mrs. Hopewell had to turn and face her in order to seem to be listening. "Glynese gone out with Harvey Hill again last night," she said. "She had this sty."

"Hill," Mrs. Hopewell said absently, "is that the one who works in the garage?"

"Nome, he's the one that goes to chiropracter school," Mrs. Freeman said. "She had this sty. Been had it two days. So she says when he brought her in the other night he says, 'Lemme get rid of that sty for you,' and she says, 'How?' and he says, 'You just lay yourself down acrost the seat of that car and I'll show you.' So she done it and he popped her neck. Kept on a-popping it several times until she made him quit. This morning," Mrs. Freeman said, "she ain't got no sty. She ain't got no traces of a sty."

"I never heard of that before," Mrs. Hopewell said.

"He ast her to marry him before the Ordinary,"[4] Mrs. Freeman went on, "and she told him she wasn't going to be married in no *office.*"

"Well, Glynese is a fine girl," Mrs. Hopewell said. "Glynese and Carramae are both fine girls."

"Carramae said when her and Lyman was married Lyman said it sure felt sacred to him. She said he said he wouldn't take five hundred dollars for being married by a preacher."

"How much would he take?" the girl asked from the stove.

"He said he wouldn't take five hundred dollars," Mrs. Freeman repeated.

"Well we all have work to do," Mrs. Hopewell said.

"Lyman said it just felt more sacred to him," Mrs. Freeman said. "The doctor wants Carramae to eat prunes. Says instead of medicine. Says them cramps is coming from pressure. You know where I think it is?"

"She'll be better in a few weeks," Mrs. Hopewell said.

"In the tube," Mrs. Freeman said. "Else she wouldn't be as sick as she is."

Hulga had cracked her two eggs into a saucer and was bringing them to the table along with a cup of coffee that she had filled too full. She sat down carefully and began to eat, meaning to keep Mrs. Freeman there by questions if for any reason she showed an inclination to leave. She could perceive her mother's eye on her. The first round-about question would be about the Bible salesman and she did not wish to bring it on. "How did he pop her neck?" she asked.

Mrs. Freeman went into a description of how he had popped her neck. She said he owned a '55 Mercury but that Glynese said she would rather marry a man with only a '36 Plymouth who would be married by a preacher. The girl asked what if he had a '32 Plymouth and Mrs. Freeman said what Glynese had said was a '36 Plymouth.

Mrs. Hopewell said there were not many girls with Glynese's common sense. She said what she admired in those girls was their common sense. She said that reminded her that they had had a nice visitor yesterday, a young man selling Bibles. "Lord," she said, "he bored me to death but he was so sincere and genuine I couldn't be rude to him. He was just good country people, you know," she said, "—just the salt of the earth."

"I seen him walk up," Mrs. Freeman said, "and then later—I seen him walk off," and Hulga could feel the slight shift in her voice, the slight insinuation, that he had not walked off alone, had he? Her face remained expressionless but the color rose into her

---

4. Justice of the Peace who performs the marriage ceremony in his chambers rather than in public.

neck and she seemed to swallow it down with the next spoonful of egg. Mrs. Freeman was looking at her as if they had a secret together.

"Well, it takes all kinds of people to make the world go 'round," Mrs. Hopewell said. "It's very good we aren't all alike."

"Some people are more alike than others," Mrs. Freeman said.

Hulga got up and stumped, with about twice the noise that was necessary, into her room and locked the door. She was to meet the Bible salesman at ten o'clock at the gate. She had thought about it half the night. She had started thinking of it as a great joke and then she had begun to see profound implications in it. She had lain in bed imagining dialogues for them that were insane on the surface but that reached below to depths that no Bible salesman would be aware of. Their conversation yesterday had been of this kind.

He had stopped in front of her and had simply stood there. His face was bony and sweaty and bright, with a little pointed nose in the center of it, and his look was different from what it had been at the dinner table. He was gazing at her with open curiosity, with fascination, like a child watching a new fantastic animal at the zoo, and he was breathing as if he had run a great distance to reach her. His gaze seemed somehow familiar but she could not think where she had been regarded with it before. For almost a minute he didn't say anything. Then on what seemed an insuck of breath, he whispered, "You ever ate a chicken that was two days old?"

The girl looked at him stonily. He might have just put this question up for consideration at the meeting of a philosophical association. "Yes," she presently replied as if she had considered it from all angles.

"It must have been mighty small!" he said triumphantly and shook all over with little nervous giggles, getting very red in the face, and subsiding finally into his gaze of complete admiration, while the girl's expression remained exactly the same.

"How old are you?" he asked softly.

She waited some time before she answered. Then in a flat voice she said, "Seventeen."

His smiles came in succession like waves breaking on the surface of a little lake. "I see you got a wooden leg," he said. "I think you're brave. I think you're real sweet."

The girl stood blank and solid and silent.

"Walk to the gate with me," he said. "You're a brave sweet little thing and I liked you the minute I seen you walk in the door."

Hulga began to move forward.

"What's your name?" he asked, smiling down on the top of her head.

"Hulga," she said.

"Hulga," he murmured, "Hulga. Hulga. I never heard of anybody name Hulga before. You're shy, aren't you, Hulga?" he asked.

She nodded, watching his large red hand on the handle of the giant valise.

"I like girls that wear glasses," he said. "I think a lot. I'm not like these people that a serious thought don't ever enter their heads. It's because I may die."

"I may die too," she said suddenly and looked up at him. His eyes were very small and brown, glittering feverishly.

"Listen," he said, "don't you think some people was meant to meet on account of what all they got in common and all? Like they both think serious thoughts and all?" He shifted the valise to his other hand so that the hand nearest her was free. He caught hold of her elbow and shook it a little. "I don't work on Saturday," he said. "I like to walk in the woods and see what Mother Nature is wearing. O'er the hills and far away. Pic-nics and things. Couldn't we go on a pic-nic tomorrow? Say yes, Hulga," he said and gave her a dying look as if he felt his insides about to drop out of him. He had even seemed to sway slightly toward her.

During the night she had imagined that she seduced him. She imagined that the two of them walked on the place until they came to the storage barn beyond the two back fields and there, she imagined, that things came to such a pass that she very easily seduced him and that then, of course, she had to reckon with his remorse. True genius can get an idea across even to an inferior mind. She imagined that she took his remorse in hand and changed it into a deeper understanding of life. She took all his shame away and turned it into something useful.

She set off for the gate at exactly ten o'clock, escaping without drawing Mrs. Hopewell's attention. She didn't take anything to eat, forgetting that food is usually taken on a picnic. She wore a pair of slacks and a dirty white shirt, and as an afterthought, she had put some Vapex on the collar of it since she did not own any perfume. When she reached the gate no one was there.

She looked up and down the empty highway and had the furious feeling that she had been tricked, that he had only meant to make her walk to the gate after the idea of him. Then suddenly he stood up, very tall, from behind a bush on the opposite embankment. Smiling, he lifted his hat which was new and wide-brimmed. He had not worn it yesterday and she wondered if he had bought it for the occasion. It was toast-colored with a red and white band around it and was slightly too large for him. He stepped from behind the bush still carrying the black valise. He had on the same suit and the same yellow socks sucked down in his shoes from walking. He crossed the highway and said, "I knew you'd come!"

The girl wondered acidly how he had known this. She pointed to the valise and asked, "Why did you bring your Bibles?"

He took her elbow, smiling down on her as if he could not stop. "You can never tell when you'll need the word of God, Hulga," he said. She had a moment in which she doubted that this was actually happening and then they began to climb the embankment. They went down into the pasture toward the woods. The boy walked lightly by her side, bouncing on his toes. The valise did not seem to be heavy today; he even swung it. They crossed half the pasture without saying anything and then, putting his hand easily on the small of her back, he asked softly, "Where does your wooden leg join on?"

She turned an ugly red and glared at him and for an instant the boy looked abashed. "I didn't mean you no harm," he said. "I only meant you're so brave and all. I guess God takes care of you."

"No," she said, looking forward and walking fast, "I don't even believe in God."

At this he stopped and whistled. "No!" he exclaimed as if he were too astonished to say anything else.

She walked on and in a second he was bouncing at her side, fanning with his hat. "That's very unusual for a girl," he remarked, watching her out of the corner of his eye. When they reached the edge of the wood, he put his hand on her back again and drew her against him without a word and kissed her heavily.

The kiss, which had more pressure than feeling behind it, produced that extra surge of adrenalin in the girl that enables one to carry a packed trunk out of a burning house, but in her, the power went at once to the brain. Even before he released her, her mind, clear and detached and ironic anyway, was regarding him from a great distance, with amusement but with pity. She had never been kissed before and she was pleased to discover that it was an unexceptional experience and all a matter of the mind's control. Some people might enjoy drain water if they were told it was vodka. When the boy, looking expectant but uncertain, pushed her gently away, she turned and talked on, saying nothing as if such business, for her, were common enough.

He came along panting at her side, trying to help her when he saw a root that she might trip over. He caught and held back the long swaying blades of thorn vine until she had passed beyond them. She led the way and he came breathing heavily behind her. Then they came out on a sunlit hillside, sloping softly into another one a little smaller. Beyond, they could see the rusted top of the old barn where the extra hay was stored.

The hill was sprinkled with small pink weeds. "Then you ain't saved?" he asked suddenly, stopping.

The girl smiled. It was the first time she had smiled at him at all. "In my economy," she said, "I'm saved and you are damned but I told you I didn't believe in God."

Nothing seemed to destroy the boy's look of admiration. He gazed at her now as if the fantastic animal at the zoo had put its paw through the bars and given him a loving poke. She thought he looked as if he wanted to kiss her again and she walked on before he had the chance.

"Ain't there somewheres we can sit down sometime?" he murmured, his voice softening toward the end of the sentence.

"In that barn," she said.

They made for it rapidly as if it might slide away like a train. It was a large two-story barn, cool and dark inside. The boy pointed up the ladder that led into the loft and said, "It's too bad we can't go up there."

"Why can't we?" she asked.

"Yer leg," he said reverently.

The girl gave him a contemptuous look and putting both hands on the ladder, she climbed it while he stood below, apparently awestruck. She pulled herself expertly through the opening and then looked down at him and said, "Well, come on if you're coming," and he began to climb the ladder, awkwardly bringing the suitcase with him.

"We won't need the Bible," she observed.

"You never can tell," he said, panting. After he had got into the loft, he was a few seconds catching his breath. She had sat down in a pile of straw. A wide sheath of sunlight, filled with dust particles, slanted over her. She lay back against a bale, her face turned away, looking out the front opening of the barn where hay was thrown from a wagon into the loft. The two pink-speckled hillsides lay back against a dark ridge of woods. The sky was cloudless and cold blue. The boy dropped down by her side and put one arm under her and the other over her and began methodically kissing her face, making little noises like a fish. He did not remove his hat but it was pushed far enough back not to interfere. When her glasses got in his way, he took them off of her and slipped them into his pocket.

The girl at first did not return any of the kisses but presently she began to and after she had put several on his cheek, she reached his lips and remained there, kissing him again and again as if she were trying to draw all the breath out of him. His breath was clear and sweet like a child's and the kisses were sticky like a child's. He mumbled about loving her and about knowing when he first seen her that he loved her, but the mumbling was like the sleepy fretting of a child being put to sleep by his mother. Her mind, throughout this, never stopped or lost itself for a second to her feelings. "You ain't said you loved me none," he whispered finally, pulling back from her. "You got to say that."

She looked away from him off into the hollow sky and then down at a black ridge and then down farther into what appeared to be two green swelling lakes. She didn't realize he had taken her glasses but this landscape could not seem exceptional to her for she seldom paid any close attention to her surroundings.

"You got to say it," he repeated. "You got to say you love me."

She was always careful how she committed herself. "In a sense," she began, "if you use the word loosely, you might say that. But it's not a word I use. I don't have illusions. I'm one of those people who see *through* to nothing."

The boy was frowning. "You got to say it. I said it and you got to say it," he said.

The girl looked at him almost tenderly. "You poor baby," she murmured. "It's just as well you don't understand," and she pulled him by the neck, face-down, against her. "We are all damned," she said, "but some of us have taken off our blindfolds and see that there's nothing to see. It's a kind of salvation."

The boy's astonished eyes looked blankly through the ends of her hair. "Okay," he almost whined, "but do you love me or don'tcher?"

"Yes," she said and added, "in a sense. But I must tell you something. There mustn't be anything dishonest between us." She lifted his head and looked him in the eye. "I am thirty years old," she said. "I have a number of degrees."

The boy's look was irritated but dogged. "I don't care," he said. "I don't care a thing about what all you done. I just want to know if you love me or don'tcher?" and he caught her to him and wildly planted her face with kisses until she said, "Yes, yes."

"Okay then," he said, letting her go. "Prove it."

She smiled, looking dreamily out on the shifty landscape. She had seduced him without even making up her mind to try. "How?" she asked, feeling that he should be delayed a little.

He leaned over and put his lips to her ear. "Show me where your wooden leg joins on," he whispered.

The girl uttered a sharp little cry and her face instantly drained of color. The obscenity of the suggestion was not what shocked her. As a child she had sometimes been subject to feelings of shame but education had removed the last traces of that as a good surgeon scrapes for cancer; she would no more have felt it over what he was asking than she would have believed in his Bible. But she was as sensitive about the artificial leg as a peacock about his tail. No one ever touched it but her. She took care of it as someone else would his soul, in private and almost with her own eyes turned away. "No," she said.

"I known it," he muttered, sitting up. "You're just playing me for a sucker."

"Oh no no!" she cried. "It joins on at the knee. Only at the knee. Why do you want to see it?"

The boy gave her a long penetrating look. "Because," he said, "it's what makes you different. You ain't like anybody else."

She sat staring at him. There was nothing about her face or her round freezing-blue eyes to indicate that this had moved her; but she felt as if her heart had stopped and left her mind to pump her blood. She decided that for the first time in her life she was face to face with real innocence. This boy, with an instinct that came from beyond wisdom, had touched the truth about her. When after a minute, she said in a hoarse high voice, "All right," it was like surrendering to him completely. It was like losing her own life and finding it again, miraculously, in his.

Very gently he began to roll the slack leg up. The artificial limb, in a white sock and brown flat shoe, was bound in a heavy material like canvas and ended in an ugly jointure where it was attached to the stump. The boy's face and his voice were entirely reverent as he uncovered it and said, "Now show me how to take it off and on."

She took it off for him and put it back on again and then he took it off himself, handling it as tenderly as if it were a real one. "See!" he said with a delighted child's face. "Now I can do it myself!"

"Put it back on," she said. She was thinking that she would run away with him and that every night he would take the leg off and every morning put it back on again. "Put it back on," she said.

"Not yet," he murmured, setting it on its foot out of her reach. "Leave it off for a while. You got me instead."

She gave a little cry of alarm but he pushed her down and began to kiss her again. Without the leg she felt entirely dependent on him. Her brain seemed to have stopped thinking altogether and to be about some other function that it was not very good at. Different expressions raced back and forth over her face. Every now and then the boy, his eyes like two steel spikes, would glance behind him where the leg stood. Finally she pushed him off and said, "Put it back on me now."

"Wait," he said. He leaned the other way and pulled the valise toward him and opened it. It had a pale blue spotted lining and there were only two Bibles in it. He took one of these out and opened the cover of it. It was hollow and contained a pocket flask of whiskey, a pack of cards, and a small blue box with printing on it. He laid these out in front of her one at a time in an evenly-spaced row, like one presenting offerings at the shrine of a goddess. He put the blue box in her hand. THIS PRODUCT TO BE USED ONLY FOR THE PREVENTION OF DISEASE, she read, and dropped it. The boy was unscrewing the top of the flask. He stopped and pointed, with a smile, to the deck of cards. It was not an ordinary deck but one with an obscene picture on the back of each card. "Take a swig," he said, offering her the bottle first. He held it in front of her, but like one mesmerized, she did not move.

Her voice when she spoke had an almost pleading sound. "Aren't you," she murmured, "aren't you just good country people?"

The boy cocked his head. He looked as if he were just beginning to understand that she might be trying to insult him. "Yeah," he said, curling his lip slightly, "but it ain't held me back none. I'm as good as you any day in the week."

"Give me my leg," she said.

He pushed it farther away with his foot. "Come on now, let's begin to have us a good time," he said coaxingly. "We ain't got to know one another good yet."

"Give me my leg!" she screamed and tried to lunge for it but he pushed her down easily.

"What's the matter with you all of a sudden?" he asked, frowning as he screwed the top on the flask and put it quickly back inside the Bible. "You just a while ago said you didn't believe in nothing. I thought you was some girl!"

Her face was almost purple. "You're a Christian!" she hissed. "You're a fine Christian! You're just like them all—say one thing and do another. You're a perfect Christian, you're . . ."

The boy's mouth was set angrily. "I hope you don't think," he said in a lofty indignant tone, "that I believe in that crap! I may sell Bibles but I know which end is up and I wasn't born yesterday and I know where I'm going!"

"Give me my leg!" she screeched. He jumped up so quickly that she barely saw him sweep the cards and the blue box into the Bible and throw the Bible into the valise. She saw him grab the leg and then she saw it for an instant slanted forlornly across the inside of the suitcase with a Bible at either side of its opposite ends. He slammed the lid shut and snatched up the valise and swung it down the hole and then stepped through himself.

When all of him had passed but his head, he turned and regarded her with a look that no longer had any admiration in it. "I've gotten a lot of interesting things," he said. "One time I got a woman's glass eye this way. And you needn't to think you'll catch me because Pointer ain't really my name. I use a different name at every house I call at and don't stay nowhere long. And I'll tell you another thing, Hulga," he said, using the name as if he didn't think much of it, "you ain't so smart. I been believing in nothing ever since I was born!" and then the toast-colored hat disappeared down the hole and the girl was left, sitting on the straw in the dusty sunlight. When she turned her churning face toward the opening, she saw his blue figure struggling successfully over the green speckled lake.

Mrs. Hopewell and Mrs. Freeman, who were in the back pasture, digging up onions, saw him emerge a little later from the woods and head across the meadow toward the highway. "Why, that looks like that nice dull young man that tried to sell me a Bible yesterday," Mrs. Hopewell said, squinting. "He must have been selling them to the Negroes back in there. He was so simple," she said, "but I guess the world would be better off if we were all that simple."

Mrs. Freeman's gaze drove forward and just touched him before he disappeared under the hill. Then she returned her attention to the evil-smelling onion shoot she was lifting from the ground. "Some can't be that simple," she said. "I know I never could."

1955

JOHN BARTH

1930–

During a prolonged student strike at the State University of New York in Buffalo, John Barth, teaching there at the time, when asked his opinion of the strike answered that it was important but boring. To judge from his fiction, this response also characterizes Barth's attitude toward everyday human affairs. Although gifted with strong representational powers, as demonstrated in his first two novels, he is uninterested in providing carefully rendered imitations of life but does care passionately about the activity of storytelling, of narrative itself—to the extent that a reviewer of one of his most elaborate pieces of fiction (*Chimera*, 1972) called him a "narrative chauvinist pig."

He was born in Cambridge, Maryland, and after a brief time spent at the Juilliard School of Music, entered Johns Hopkins University in Baltimore, from which he graduated and where he currently teaches writing. In the first three and the last three months of 1955, Barth accomplished the noteworthy feat of writing his first two novels, books preoccupied with "ultimate" philosophical and moral questions a gifted young man might have asked at Johns Hopkins. The hero of *The Floating Opera* (1956) is such a young man named Todd Andrews who plans to kill himself on the day of which the novel treats, and who describes the title thus: "It's a floating opera, friend, chock-full of curiosities, melodrama, spectacle, instruction and entertainment, but it floats willy-nilly on the tide of my vagrant prose." No better description has been made of Barth's work as a whole.

The Floating Opera was nominated for the National Book Award and remains compelling for its playful, colloquial speech, and for Barth's ability to spin marvelously funny yarns fringed with metaphysical speculation. It is also notable for its intimate feeling for the Maryland coastal region, at moments reminding us of Melville's similarly genial treatment of New England in *Moby-Dick*, our literature's grandest floating opera. Barth's second novel, *The End of the Road* (1958) was to be his last "realistic" one, though it is also filled with narrative games. In the manic monologues and dialectical skirmishes with others, engaged in by its hero Jacob Horner, Barth practices an inventive and amusing questioning of moral and philosophical values. This extremely funny book turns suddenly grim at its conclusion, when Horner is left with nothing but words (he is an evasive teacher of grammar) to deal with the horror of an event beyond them and for which he is in part responsible.

After the rapid composition of these books, Barth ceased to be interested in writing even as minimally tied to conventionally realistic fiction as they were. In the immensely long and sometimes labored books which followed—*The Sot-Weed Factor* (1960) and *Giles Goat-Boy* (1966)—he constructed gigantic parody-histories filled with gags, sexual bawdy, and lore of all sorts in order to dislocate and entertain the reader. Barth is saying in these books, among other things, that fiction is stranger than "fiction," that the reader must understand he is not reading about Life— events which really take place in a world out there—but is instead reading words. So *Giles* is as much "about" itself as a book can be: its comically pedantic and self-footnoting procedure and its strategy of pretending that the Universe is really the University are only two of the devices by which Barth attempts to dazzle and ensnare us.

The selection printed here is taken from a volume (*Lost in the Funhouse*, 1968) subtitled *Fiction for Print, Tape, Live Voice,* and at one point a voice addresses us as follows: "The reader! You, dogged, uninsultable, print-oriented bastard, it's you I'm addressing, who else, from inside this monstrous fiction." *Life-Story* is one of Barth's most extreme attempts to confuse the realms of art and life, imagination and reality. How much further he can go along the disruptively playful line taken by this story, or by the recent retelling and complicating of classical legends in *Chimera,* is anybody's guess. But Barth has never yet lacked the resourcefulness to create something beyond what we had hitherto imagined as possible or proper narrative behavior, and he will probably do it again.

Life-Story[1]

I

Without discarding what he'd already written he began his story afresh in a somewhat different manner. Whereas his earlier version had opened in a straight-forward documentary fashion and then degenerated or at least modulated intentionally into irrealism and dissonance he decided this time to tell his tale from start to finish in a conservative, "realistic," unself-conscious way. He being by vocation an author of novels and stories it was perhaps inevitable that one afternoon the possibility would occur to the writer of these lines that his own life might be a fiction, in which he was the leading or an accessory character. He happened at the time[2] to be in his study attempting to draft the opening pages of a new short story; its general idea had preoccupied him for some months along with other general ideas, but certain elements of the conceit, without which he could scarcely proceed, remained unclear. More specifically: narrative plots may be imagined as consisting of a "ground-situation" (Scheherazade desires not to die) focused and dramatized by a "vehicle-situation" (Scheherazade beguiles the King with endless stories), the several incidents of which have their final value in terms of their bearing upon the "ground-situation." In our author's case it was the "vehicle" that had vouchsafed itself, first as a germinal proposition in his commonplace book—D comes to suspect that the world is a novel, himself a fictional personage—subsequently as an articulated conceit explored over several pages of the workbook in which he elaborated more systematically his casual inspirations: since D is writing a fictional account of this conviction he has indisputably a fictional existence in his account, replicating what he suspects to be his own situation. Moreover E, hero of D's account,

1. From *Lost in the Funhouse: Fiction for Print, Tape, Live Voice* (1968). 2. "9:00 A.M., Monday, June 20, 1966" [Barth's note].

is said to be writing a similar account, and so the replication is in both ontological directions, et cetera. But the "ground-situation"— some state of affairs on D's part which would give dramatic resonance to his attempts to prove himself factual, assuming he made such attempts obstinately withheld itself from his imagination. As is commonly the case the question reduced to one of stakes: what were to be the consequences of D's—and finally E's—disproving or verifying his suspicion, and why should a reader be interested?

What a dreary way to begin a story he said to himself upon reviewing his long introduction. Not only is there no "ground-situation," but the prose style is heavy and somewhat old-fashioned, like an English translation of Thomas Mann,[3] and the so-called "vehicle" itself is at least questionable: self-conscious, vertiginously arch, fashionably solipsistic, unoriginal—in fact a convention of twentieth-century literature. Another story about a writer writing a story! Another regressus in infinitum! Who doesn't prefer art that at least overtly imitates something other than its own processes? That doesn't continually proclaim "Don't forget I'm an artifice!"? That takes for granted its mimetic nature instead of asserting it in order (not so slyly after all) to deny it, or vice-versa? Though his critics sympathetic and otherwise described his own work as avant-garde, in his heart of hearts he disliked literature of an experimental, self-despising, or overtly metaphysical character, like Samuel Beckett's, Marian Cutler's, Jorge Borges's.[4] The logical fantasies of Lewis Carroll pleased him less than straight-forward tales of adventure, subtly sentimental romances, even densely circumstantial realisms like Tolstoy's. His favorite contemporary authors were John Updike, Georges Simenon, Nicole Riboud.[5] He had no use for the theater of absurdity, for "black humor," for allegory in any form, for apocalyptic preachments meretriciously tricked out in dramatic garb.

Neither had his wife and adolescent daughters, who for that matter preferred life to literature and read fiction when at all for entertainment. Their kind of story (his too, finally) would begin if not once upon a time at least with arresting circumstance, bold character, trenchant action. C flung away the whining manuscript and pushed impatiently through the french doors leading to the terrace from his oak-wainscoted study. Pausing at the stone balustrade to light his briar he remarked through a lavender cascade of wisteria that lithe-limbed Gloria, Gloria of timorous eye and militant breast, had once again chosen his boat-wharf as her basking-place.

<hr>

3. German novelist (1875–1955), author of *The Magic Mountain* and others.
4. Samuel Beckett (b. 1906), Irish writer, dramatist, poet. Marian Cutler, one of Barth's invented authors. Jorge Luis Borges (b. 1899), Argentinian short-story writer.
5. Georges Simenon (b. 1903), Belgian-Swiss writer of detective novels. Nicole Riboud, another of Barth's invented authors.

By Jove he exclaimed to himself. It's particularly disquieting to suspect not only that one is a fictional character but that the fiction one's in—the fiction one is—is quite the sort one least prefers. His wife entered the study with coffee and an apple-pastry, set them at his elbow on his work table, returned to the living room. Ed' pelut' kondo nedode; nyoing nyang.[6] One manifestation of schizophrenia as everyone knows is the movement from reality toward fantasy, a progress which not infrequently takes the form of distorted and fragmented representation, abstract formalism, an increasing pre-occupation, even obsession, with pattern and design for their own sakes—especially patterns of a baroque, enormously detailed char-acter—to the (virtual) exclusion of representative "content." There are other manifestations. Ironically, in the case of graphic and plastic artists for example the work produced in the advanced stages of their affliction may be more powerful and interesting than the realistic productions of their earlier "sanity." Whether the artists themselves are gratified by this possibility is not reported.

B called upon a literary acquaintance, B———, summering with Mrs. B and children on the Eastern Shore of Maryland. "You say you lack a ground-situation. Has it occurred to you that that cir-cumstance may be your ground-situation? What occurs to me is that if it is it isn't. And conversely. The case being thus, what's really wanting after all is a well-articulated vehicle, a foreground or up-stage situation to dramatize the narrator's or author's grundlage. His what. To write merely C comes to suspect that the world is a novel, himself a fictional personage is but to introduce the vehicle; the next step must be to initiate its uphill motion by establishing and com-plicating some conflict. I would advise in addition the eschewal of overt and self-conscious discussion of the narrative process. I would advise in addition the eschewal of overt and self-conscious discus-sion of the narrative process. The via negativa and its positive counterpart are it is to be remembered poles after all of the same cell. Returning to his study.

If I'm going to be a fictional character G declared to himself I want to be in a rousing good yarn as they say, not some piece of avant-garde preciousness. I want passion and bravura action in my plot, heroes I can admire, heroines I can love, memorable speeches, colorful accessory characters, poetical language. It doesn't matter to me how naively linear the anecdote is; never mind modernity! How reactionary J appears to be. How will such nonsense sound thirty-six years from now?[7] As if. If he can only get K through his story I reflected grimly; if he can only retain his self-possession to the end of this sentence; not go mad; not destroy himself and/or others. Then what I wondered grimly. Another sentence fast, another story. Scheherazade my only love! All those nights you kept your secret

6. Nonsense words.
7. "10:00 A.M., Monday, June 20, 1966" [Barth's note].

from the King my rival, that after your defloration he was unnecessary, you'd have killed yourself in any case when your invention failed.

Why could he not begin his story afresh X wondered, for example with the words why could he not begin his story afresh et cetera? Y's wife came into the study as he was about to throw out the baby with the bathwater. "Not for an instant to throw out the baby while every instant discarding the bathwater is perhaps a chief task of civilized people at this hour of the world.[8] I used to tell B_____ that without success. What makes you so sure it's not a film he's in or a theater-piece?

Because U responded while he certainly felt rather often that he was merely acting his own role or roles he had no idea who the actor was, whereas even the most Stanislavsky-methodist would presumably if questioned closely recollect his offstage identity even onstage in mid-act. Moreover a great part of T's "drama," most of his life in fact, was non-visual, consisting entirely in introspection, which the visual dramatic media couldn't manage easily. He had for example mentioned to no one his growing conviction that he was a fictional character, and since he was not given to audible soliloquizing a "spectator" would take him for a cheerful, conventional fellow, little suspecting that et cetera. It was of course imaginable that much goes on in the mind of King Oedipus in addition to his spoken sentiments; any number of interior dramas might be being played out in the actors' or characters' minds, dramas of which the audience is as unaware as are V's wife and friends of his growing conviction that he's a fictional character. But everything suggested that the medium of his life was prose fiction—moreover a fiction narrated from either the first-person or the third-person-omniscient point of view.

Why is it L wondered with mild disgust that both K and M for example choose to write such stuff when life is so sweet and painful and full of such a variety of people, places, situations, and activities other than self-conscious and after all rather blank introspection? Why is it N wondered et cetera that both M and O et cetera when the world is in such parlous explosive case? Why et cetera et cetera et cetera when the word, which was in the beginning, is now evidently nearing the end of its road? Am I being strung out in this ad libitum fashion I wondered merely to keep my author from the pistol? What sort of story is it whose drama lies always in the next frame out? If Sinbad sinks it's Scheherazade who drowns; whose neck one wonders is on her line?

2

Discarding what he'd already written as he could wish to discard the mumbling pages of his life he began his story afresh, resolved

8. "11:00 A.M., Monday, June 20, 1966" [Barth's note].

this time to eschew overt and self-conscious discussion of his narrative process and to recount instead in the straight-forwardest manner possible the several complications of his character's conviction that he was a character in a work of fiction, arranging them into dramatically ascending stages if he could for his readers' sake and leading them (the stages) to an exciting climax and dénouement if he could.

He rather suspected that the medium and genre in which he worked—the only ones for which he felt any vocation—were moribund if not already dead. The idea pleased him. One of the successfullest men he knew was a blacksmith of the old school who et cetera. He meditated upon the grandest sailing-vessel ever built, the *France II*, constructed in Bordeaux in 1911 not only when but because the age of sail had passed. Other phenomena that consoled and inspired him were the great flying-boat *Hercules*, the zeppelin *Hindenburg*, the *Tsar Pushka* cannon, the then-record Dow-Jones industrial average of 381.17 attained on September 3, 1929.

He rather suspected that the society in which he persisted—the only one with which he felt any degree of identification—was moribund if not et cetera. He knew beyond any doubt that the body which he inhabited—the only one et cetera—was et cetera. The idea et cetera. He had for thirty-six years lacking a few hours been one of our dustmote's three billion tenants give or take five hundred million, and happening to be as well a white male citizen of the United States of America he had thirty-six years plus a few hours more to cope with one way or another unless the actuarial tables were mistaken, not bloody likely, or his term was unexpectedly reduced.

Had he written for his readers' sake? The phrase implied a thitherto-unappreciated metaphysical dimension. Suspense. If his life was a fictional narrative it consisted of three terms—teller, tale, told—each dependent on the other two but not in the same ways. His author could as well tell some other character's tale or some other tale of the same character as the one being told as he himself could in his own character as author; his "reader" could as easily read some other story, would be well advised to; but his own "life" depended absolutely on a particular author's original persistence, thereafter upon some reader's. From this consideration any number of things followed, some less tiresome than others. No use appealing to his author, of whom he'd come to dislike even to think. The idea of his playing with his characters' and his own self-consciousness! He himself tended in that direction and despised the tendency. The idea of his or her smiling smugly to himself as the "words" flowed from his "pen" in which his the protagonist's unhappy inner life was exposed! Ah he had mistaken the nature of his narrative; he had thought it very long, longer than Proust's, longer than any German's, longer than *The Thousand Nights and a Night* in ten quarto volumes. Moreover he'd thought it the most prolix and pedestrian *tranche-de-vie* realism, unredeemed by even the limited virtues of colorful squalor, solid specification, an engaging variety of scenes and characters—in a word a bore, of the sort he himself not only would not write but would not read either. Now he understood that his author might as probably resemble himself and the protagonist of his own story-in-progress. Like himself, like his character afore-mentioned, his author not impossibly deplored the obsolescence of humanism, the passing of *savoir-vivre*, et cetera; admired the out-moded values of fidelity, courage, tact, restraint, amiability, self-discipline, et cetera; preferred fictions in which were to be found stirring actions, characters to love as well as ditto to despise, speeches and deeds to affect us strongly, et cetera. He too might wish to make some final effort to put by his fictional character and achieve factuality or at least to figure in if not be hero of a more attractive fiction, but be caught like the writer of these lines in some more or less desperate tour de force. For him to attempt to come to an understanding with such an author were as futile as for one of his own creations to et cetera.

But the reader! Even if his author were his only reader as was he himself of his work-in-progress as of the sentence-in-progress and his protagonist of his, et cetera, his character as reader was not the same as his character as author, a fact which might be turned to account. What suspense.

As he prepared to explore this possibility one of his mistresses whereof he had none entered his brown study unannounced. "The passion of love," she announced, "which I regard as no less essential to a satisfying life than those values itemized above and which I infer from my presence here that you too esteem highly, does not in fact play in your life a role of sufficient importance to sustain my presence here. It plays in fact little role at all outside your imagina-tive and/or ary life. I tell you this not in a criticizing spirit, for I judge you to be as capable of the sentiment aforementioned as any other imagin[ative], deep-feeling man in good physical health more or less precisely in the middle of the road of our life. What hampers, even cripples you in this regard is your final preference, which I refrain from analyzing, for the sedater, more responsible pleasures of monogamous fidelity and the serener affections of domesticity, notwithstanding the fact that your enjoyment of these is correspond-ingly inhibited though not altogether spoiled by an essentially romantical, unstable, irresponsible, death-wishing fancy. V. S. Pritchett,[9] English critic and author, will put the matter succinctly in a soon-to-be-written essay on Flaubert, whose work he'll say depicts the course of ardent longings and violent desires that rise from the horrible, the sensual, and the sadistic. They turn into the virginal and mystical, only to become numb by satiety. At this point

9. English literary critic and autobiographer (b. 1900).

pathological boredom leads to a final desire for death and nothingness—the Romantic syndrome. If, not to be unfair, we qualify
somewhat the terms horrible and sadistic and understand satiety to
include a large measure of vicariousness, this description undeniably
applies to one aspect of yourself and your work; and while your
ditto has other, even contrary aspects, the net fact is that you have
elected familial responsibilities and rewards—indeed, straight-laced
middle-classness in general—over the higher expenses of spirit and
wastes of shame attendant upon a less regular, more glamorous
style of life. So to elect is surely admirable for the layman, even
essential if the social fabric, without which there can be no culture,
is to be preserved. For the artist, however, and in particular the
writer, whose traditional material has been the passions of men and
women, the choice is fatal. You having made it I bid you goodnight
probably forever."

Even as she left he reached for the sleeping pills cached conveniently in his writing desk and was restrained from their administration only by his being in the process of completing a sentence,
which he cravenly strung out at some sacrifice of rhetorical effect
upon realizing that he was et cetera. Moreover he added hastily he
had not described the intruder for his readers' vicarious satiety: a
lovely woman she was, whom he did not after all describe for his
readers' et cetera inasmuch as her appearance and character were
inconstant. Her interruption of his work inspired a few sentences
about the extent to which his fiction inevitably made public his
private life, though the trespasses in this particular were as nothing
beside those of most of his profession. That is to say, while he did
not draw his characters and situations directly from life nor permit
his author-protagonist to do so, any moderately attentive reader of
his oeuvre, his what, could infer for example that its author feared
for example schizophrenia, impotence creative and sexual, suicide—
in short living and dying. His fictions were preoccupied with these
fears among their other, more serious preoccupations. Hot dog. As
of the sentence-in-progress he was not in fact unmanageably
schizophrenic, impotent in either respect, or dead by his own hand,
but there was always the next sentence to worry about. But there
was always the next sentence to worry about. In sum he concluded
hastily such limited self-exposure did not constitute a misdemeanor,
representing or mis as it did so small an aspect of his total self,
negligible a portion of his total life—even which totalities were they
made public would be found remarkable only for their being so
unremarkable. Well shall he continue.

Bearing in mind that he had not developed what he'd mentioned
earlier about turning to advantage his situation vis-à-vis his "reader"
(in fact he deliberately now postponed his return to that subject,
sensing that it might well constitute the climax of his story) he
elaborated one or two ancillary questions, perfectly aware that he

was trying, even exhausting, whatever patience might remain to whatever readers might remain to whoever elaborated yet another ancillary question. Was the novel of his life for example a *roman à clef*.[1]? Of that genre he was as contemptuous as of the others aforementioned; but while in the introductory adverbial clause it seemed obvious to him that he didn't "stand for" anyone else, any more than he was an actor playing the role of himself, by the time he reached the main clause he had to admit that the question was unanswerable, since the "real" man to whom he'd correspond in a *roman à clef* would not be also in the *roman à clef* and the characters in such works were not themselves aware of their irritating correspondences.

Similarly unanswerable were such questions as when "his" story (so he regarded it for convenience and consolement though for all he knew he might be not the central character; it might be his wife's story, one of his daughters's, his imaginary mistress's, the man-who-once-cleaned-his-chimney's) began. Not impossibly at his birth or even generations earlier: a *Bildungsroman*, an *Erziehungsroman*, a *roman fleuve*.[2]! More likely at the moment he became convinced of his fictional nature: that's where he'd have begun it, as he'd begun the piece currently under his pen. If so it followed that the years of his childhood and younger manhood weren't "real," he'd suspected as much, in the first-order sense, but a mere "background" consisting of a few well-placed expository insinuations, perhaps misleading, or inferences, perhaps unwarranted, from strategic hints in his present reflections. God so to speak spare his readers from heavy-footed forced expositions of the sort that begin in the countryside near ———— in May of the year ———— it occurred to the novelist ————— that his own life might be a ————, in which he was the leading or an accessory character. He happened at the time to be in the oak-wainscoted study of the old family summer residence; through a lavender cascade of hysteria he observed that his wife had once again chosen to be the subject of this clause, itself the direct object of his observation. A lovely woman she was, whom he did not describe in keeping with his policy against drawing characters from life as who should draw a condemnee to the gallows. Begging his pardon. Flinging his tiresome tale away he pushed impatiently through the french windows leading from his study to a sheer drop from the then-record high into a nearly fatal depression.

He clung onto his narrative depressed by the disproportion of its ratiocination to its dramatization, reflection to action. One had heard *Hamlet* criticized as a collection of soliloquies for which the implausible plot was a mere excuse; witnessed Italian operas whose dramatic portions were no more than interstitial relief and arbitrary

1. Novel about "real" persons and "actual" events.
2. "*Bildungsroman*": novel about education and development of its hero.

"*Erziehungsroman*": novel with a thesis.
"*Roman fleuve*": extended chronicle novel about related people.

continuity between the arias. If it was true that he didn't take his "real" life seriously enough even when it had him by the throat, the fact didn't lead him to consider whether the fact was a cause or a consequence of his tale's tedium or both.

Concluding these reflections he concluded these reflections: that there was at this advancèd page still apparently no ground-situation suggested that his story was dramatically meaningless. If one regarded the absence of a ground-situation, more accurately the protagonist's anguish at that absence and his vain endeavors to supply the defect, as itself a sort of ground-situation, did his life-story thereby take on a kind of meaning? A "dramatic" sort he supposed, though of so sophistical a character as more likely to annoy than to engage.

3

The reader! You, dogged, uninsultable, print-oriented bastard, it's you I'm addressing, who else, from inside this monstrous fiction. You've read me this far, then? Even this far? For what discreditable motive? How is it you don't go to a movie, watch TV, stare at a wall, play tennis with a friend, make amorous advances to the person who comes to your mind when I speak of amorous advances? Can nothing surfeit, saturate you, turn you off? Where's your shame?

Having let go this barrage of rhetorical or at least unanswered questions and observing himself nevertheless in midst of yet another sentence he concluded and caused the "hero" of his story to conclude that one or more of three things must be true: 1) his author was his sole and indefatigable reader; 2) he was in a sense his own author, telling his story to himself, in which case in which case; and/or 3) his reader was not only tireless and shameless but sadistic, masochistic if he was himself.

For why do you suppose—you! you!—he's gone on so, so relentlessly refusing to entertain you as he might have at a less desperate than this hour of the world[3] with felicitous language, exciting situation, unforgettable character and image? Why has he as it were ruthlessly set about not to win you over but to turn you away? Because your own author bless and damn you his life is in your hands! He writes and reads himself; don't you think he knows who gives his creatures their lives and deaths? Do they exist except as he or others read their words? Age except we turn their pages? And can he die until you have no more of him? Time was obviously when his author could have turned the trick; his pen had once to left-to-right it through these words as does your kindless eye and might have ceased at any one. This. This. And did not as you see but went on like an Oriental torturemaster to the end.

But you needn't! He exclaimed to you. In vain. Had he petitioned

3. "11:00 P.M., Monday, June 20, 1966" [Barth's note].

you instead to read slowly in the happy parts, what happy parts, swiftly in the painful no doubt you'd have done the contrary or cut him off entirely. But as he longs to die and can't without your help you force him on, force him on. Will you deny you've read this sentence? This? To get away with murder doesn't appeal to you, is that it? As if your hands weren't inky with other dyings! As if he'd know you'd killed him! Come on. He dares you.

In vain. You haven't: the burden of his knowledge. That he continues means that he continues, a fortiori you too. Suicide's impossible: he can't kill himself without your help. Those petitions aforementioned, even his silly plea for death—don't you think he understands their sophistry, having authored their like for the wretches he's authored? Read him fast or slow, intermittently, continuously, repeatedly, backward, not at all, he won't know it; he only guesses someone's reading or composing his sentences, such as this one, because he's reading or composing sentences such as this one; the net effect is that there's a net effect, of continuity and an apparently consistent flow of time, though his pages do seem to pass more swiftly as they near his end.

To what conclusion will he come? He'd been about to append to his own tale inasmuch as the old analogy between Author and God, novel and world, can no longer be employed unless deliberately as a false analogy, certain things follow: 1) fiction must acknowledge its fictiousness and metaphoric invalidity or 2) choose to ignore the question or deny its relevance or 3) establish some other, acceptable relation between itself, its author, its reader. Just as he finished doing so however his real wife and imaginary mistresses entered his study; "It's a little past midnight" she announced with a smile; "do you know what that means?"

Though she'd come into his story unannounced at a critical moment he did not describe her, for even as he recollected that he'd seen his first light just thirty-six years before the night incumbent he saw his last: that he could not after all be a character in a work of fiction inasmuch as such a fiction would be of an entirely different character from what he thought of as fiction. Fiction consisted of such monuments of the imagination as Cutler's *Morganfield*, Riboud's *Tales Within Tales*, his own creations; fact of such as for example read those fictions. More, he could demonstrate by syllogism that the story of his life was a work of fact: though assaults upon the boundary between life and art, reality and dream, were undeniably a staple of his own and his century's literature as they'd been of Shakespeare's and Cervantes's, yet it was a fact that in the corpus of fiction as far as he knew no fictional character had become convinced as had he that he was a character in a work of fiction. This being the case and he having in fact become thus convinced it followed that his conviction was false. "Happy birthday," said his wife et cetera, kissing him et cetera to obstruct his view of the end of the sentence he was nearing the end of, playfully refusing to be nay-said so that in fact he did at last as did his fictional character end his ending story endless by interruption, cap his pen.

1968

JOHN UPDIKE

1932–

"To transcribe middleness with all its grits, bumps and anonymities, in its fullness of satisfaction and mystery: is it possible * * * or worth doing?" John Updike's novels and stories give a positive answer to the question he asks in his memoir, *The Dogwood Tree: A Boyhood;* for he is arguably the most significant transcriber, or creator rather, of "middleness" in American writing since William Dean Howells. Falling in love in high school, meeting a college roommate, going to the eye-doctor or dentist, eating supper on Sunday night, visiting your mother with your wife and son— these activities are made to yield up their possibilities to a writer as responsively curious in imagination and delicately precise in his literary expression as Updike has shown himself to be.

Born in Reading, Pennsylvania, an only child, he grew up in the small town of Shillington. He was gifted at drawing and caricaturing, and after graduating summa cum laude from Harvard in 1954 he spent a year studying art in England, then returned to America and went to work for the *New Yorker*, where his first stories appeared and to which he is still a regular contributor. When later in the 1950s he left the magazine, he also left New York City and with his wife and children settled in Ipswich, Massachusetts. There he pursued "his solitary trade as methodically as the dentist practiced his" (*The Dogwood Tree*), resisting the temptations of university teaching as successfully as the blandishments of media talk-shows. Like Howells, his ample production has been achieved through dedicated, steady work; his books are the fruit of patience, leisure, and craft.

Since 1958 when his first novel, *The Poorhouse Fair*, appeared, Updike has published not only many novels and stories but also four books of poems, a play, and much occasional journalism. He is most admired by some readers as the author of the "Olinger" stories, about life in an imaginary Pennsylvania town which takes on its colors from the real Shillington of his youth. The heroes of these stories are adolescents straining to break out of their fast-perishing environments, as they grow up and as their small town turns into something else. Updike treats them with a blend of affection and ironic humor that is wonderfully assured in its touch, while his sense of place, of growing up in the Depression and the years of World War II, is always vividly present. Like Howells (whose fine memoir of his youthful days in Ohio, *A Boy's Town*, is an ancestor of Updike's *The Dogwood Tree*) he shows how one's spirit takes on its coloration from the material circumstances—houses, clothes, landscape, food, parents—one is bounded by.

This sense of place, which is also a sense of life, is found in the stories and in the novels too, although Updike has found it harder to invent convincing forms in which to tell longer tales. His most ambitious novel is probably *The Centaur* (1964), memorable for its portrayal of three days of confusion and error in the life of an American high-school teacher seen through his son's eyes; but the book is also burdened with an elaborate set of mythical trappings that seem less than inevitable. *Couples* (1968), a novel which gained him a good deal of notoriety as a chronicler of sexual relationships, marital and adulterous, is jammed with much interesting early-1960s lore about suburban life but seems uncertain whether it is an exercise in realism or a creative fantasy, as does his recent *Marry Me* (1976).

It is in the two "Rabbit" novels that Updike found his most congenial and engaging subject for longer fiction. In each book he has managed to render the sense of an era—the 1950s in *Rabbit, Run*; the late sixties in *Rabbit Redux*—through the eyes of a hero who both is and is not like his creator. Harry "Rabbit" Angstrom, ex-high school basketball star, a prey to nostalgia and in love with his own past, perpetually lives in a present he can't abide. *Rabbit, Run* shows him trying to escape from his town, his job, his wife and child, by a series of disastrously sentimental and humanly irresponsible actions; yet Updike makes us feel Rabbit's yearnings even as we judge the painful consequences of yielding to them. Ten years later, the fading basketball star has become a fortyish, dispirited printer with a way-ward wife and a country (America in summer, 1970) which is both land-ing on the moon and falling to pieces. *Rabbit Redux* is masterly in pre-senting a Pennsylvania small town rotting away from its past certainties; it also attempts to deal with the Vietnam war and the black revolution. With respect to these large public events there is sometimes an identity, sometimes a divergence, at other times a confusion between Rabbit's con-sciousness and the larger one of his author, resulting in a book one must argue with as well as about. Still, his best work is in his stories: *Of the Farm* is a distinguished short novel, and *Separating* (printed here) an ex-ample of his careful, poised sense of how things work, a sense which can also be observed at work in the poem *Dog's Death*.

Near the end of his memoir he summarized his boyish dream of becoming an artist:

> He saw art—between drawing and writing he ignorantly made no distinction—as a method of riding a thin pencil line out of Shillington, out of time altogether, into an infinity of unseen and even unborn hearts. He pictured this infinity as radiant. How innocent!

Most writers would name that innocence only to deplore it. Updike main-tains instead that, as with the Christian faith he still professes, succeeding years have given him no better assumptions with which to replace it. In any case his fine sense of fact has protected him from fashionable extrava-gances in black humor and experimental narratives, while enabling him to be both a satirist and a celebrator of our social and domestic conditions.

The Dogwood Tree[1]

A BOYHOOD

When I was born, my parents and my mother's parents planted a dogwood tree in the side yard of the large white house in which we

1. From *Assorted Prose* (1965).

lived throughout my boyhood. This tree, I learned quite early, was exactly my age, was, in a sense, me. But I never observed it closely, am not now sure what color its petals were; its presence was no more distinct than that of my shadow. The tree was my shadow, and had it died, had it ceased to occupy, each year with increasing volume and brilliance, its place in the side yard, I would have felt that a blessing like the blessing of light had been withdrawn from my life.

Though I cannot ask you to see it more clearly than I myself saw it, yet mentioning it seems to open the possibility of my boyhood home coming again to life. With a sweet damp rush the grass of our yard seems to breathe again on me. It is just cut. My mother is pushing the mower, to which a canvas catch is attached. My grandmother is raking up the loose grass in thick heaps, small green haystacks impregnated with dew, and my grandfather stands off to one side, smoking a cigar, elegantly holding the elbow of his right arm in the palm of his left hand while the blue smoke twists from under his mustache and dissolves in the heavy evening air—that misted, too-rich Pennsylvania air. My father is off, doing some duty in the town; he is a conscientious man, a schoolteacher and deacon, and also, somehow, a man of the streets.

In remembering the dogwood tree I remember the faintly speckled asbestos shingles of the chicken house at the bottom of our yard, fronting on the alley. We had a barn as well, which we rented as a garage, having no car of our own, and between the chicken house and the barn there was a narrow space where my grandfather, with his sly country ways, would urinate. I, a child, did also, passing through this narrow, hidden-feeling passage to the school grounds beyond our property; the fibrous tan-gray of the shingles would leap up dark, silky and almost black, when wetted.

The ground in this little passsage seems a mysterious trough of pebbles of all colors and bits of paper and broken glass. A few weeds managed to grow in the perpetual shadow. All the ground at the lower end of the yard had an ungrateful quality; we had an ash heap on which we used to burn, in an extravagant ceremony that the war's thrift ended, the preceding day's newspaper. The earth for yards around the ashpile was colored gray. Chickens clucked in their wire pen. My grandmother tended them, and when the time came, beheaded them with an archaic efficiency that I don't recall ever witnessing, though I often studied the heavy log whose butt was ornamented with fine white neck-feathers pasted to the wood with blood.

A cat crosses our lawn, treading hastily on the damp grass, crouching low with distaste. Tommy is the cat's name; he lives in our chicken house but is not a pet. He is perfectly black; a rarity, he has no white dab on his chest. The birds scold out of the walnut tree and the apple and cherry trees. We have a large grape arbor, and a stone birdbath, and a brick walk, and a privet hedge the height of a child and many bushes behind which my playmates hide. There is a pansy bed that in winter we cover with straw. The air is green, and heavy, and flavored with the smell of turned earth; in our garden grows, among other vegetables, a bland, turniplike cabbage called kohlrabi, which I have never seen, or eaten, since the days when, for a snack, I would tear one from its row with my hands.

History

My boyhood was spent in a world made tranquil by two invisible catastrophes: the Depression and World War II. Between 1932, when I was born, and 1945, when we moved away, the town of Shillington changed, as far as I could see, very little. The vacant lot beside our home on Philadelphia Avenue remained vacant. The houses along the street were neither altered nor replaced. The high-school grounds, season after season, continued to make a placid plain visible from our rear windows. The softball field, with its triptych backstop, was nearest us. A little beyond, on the left, were the school and its boilerhouse, built in the late 1920s of the same ochre brick. In the middle distance a cinder track circumscribed the football field. At a greater distance there were the tennis courts and the poor farm fields and the tall double rows of trees marking the Poorhouse Lane. The horizon was the blue cloud, scarred by a gravel pit's orange slash, of Mount Penn, which overlooked the city of Reading.

A little gravel alley, too small to be marked with a street sign but known in the neighborhood as Shilling Alley, wound hazardously around our property and on down, past an untidy sequence of back buildings (chicken houses, barns out of plumb, a gunshop, a small lumber mill, a shack where a blind man lived, and the enchanted grotto of a garage whose cement floors had been waxed to the lustre of ebony by oil drippings and in whose greasy-black depths a silver drinking fountain spurted the coldest water in the world, silver water so cold it made your front teeth throb) on down to Lancaster Avenue, the main street, where the trolley cars ran. All through those years, the trolley cars ran. All through those years Pappy Shilling, the surviving son of the landowner after whom the town was named, walked up and down Philadelphia Avenue with his thin black cane and his snow-white bangs; a vibrating chain of perfect-Sunday-school-attendance pins dangled from his lapel. Each autumn the horse-chestnut trees dropped their useless, treasurable nuts; each spring the dogwood tree put forth a slightly larger spread of blossoms; always the leaning walnut tree in our back yard fretted with the same tracery of branches the view we had.

Within our house, too, there was little change. My grandparents did not die, though they seemed very old. My father continued to teach at the high school; he had secured the job shortly after I was born. No one else was born. I was an only child. A great many only children were born in 1932; I make no apologies. I do not remember ever feeling the space for a competitor within the house. The five of us already there locked into a star that would have shattered like crystal at the admission of a sixth. We had no pets. We fed Tommy on the porch, but he was too wild to set foot in the kitchen, and only my grandmother, in a way wild herself, could touch him. Tommy came to us increasingly battered and once did not come at all. As if he had never existed: that was death. And then there was a squirrel, Tilly, that we fed peanuts to; she became very tame, and under the grape arbor would take them from our hands. The excitement of those tiny brown teeth shivering against my fingertips: that was life. But she, too, came from the outside, and returned to her tree, and did not dare intrude in our house.

The arrangement inside, which seemed to me so absolute, had been achieved, beyond the peripheries of my vision, drastically and accidentally. It may, at first, have been meant to be temporary. My father and grandfather were casualties of the early thirties. My father lost his job as a cable splicer with the telephone company; he and my mother had been living—for how long I have never understood—in boarding-houses and hotels throughout western Pennsylvania, in towns whose names (Hazleton, Altoona) even now make their faces light up with youth, a glow flowing out of the darkness preceding my birth. They lived through this darkness, and the details of the adventure that my mother recalls—her lonely closeted days, the games of solitaire, the novels by Turgenev, the prostitutes downstairs, the men sleeping and starving in the parks of Pittsburgh —seem to waken in her an unjust and unreasonable happiness that used to rouse jealousy in my childish heart. I remember waiting with her by a window for my father to return from weeks on the road. It is in the Shillington living room. My hands are on the radiator ridges, I can see my father striding through the hedge toward the grape arbor, I feel my mother's excitement beside me mingle with mine. But she says this cannot be; he had lost his job before I was born.

My grandfather came from farming people in the south of the county. He prospered, and prematurely retired; the large suburban house he bought to house his good fortune became his fortune's shell, the one fragment of it left him. The two men pooled their diminished resources of strength and property and, with their women, came to live together. I do not believe they expected this arrangement to last long. For all of them—for all four of my adult guardians—Shillington was a snag, a halt in a journey that had begun elsewhere. Only I belonged to the town. The accidents that had planted me here made uneasy echoes in the house, but, like Tilly and Tommy, their source was beyond my vision.

Geography

As in time, so it was in space. The town was fringed with things that appeared awesome and ominous and fantastic to a boy. At the end of our street there was the County Home—an immense yellow poorhouse, set among the wide orchards and lawns, surrounded by a sandstone wall that was low enough on one side for a child to climb easily, but that on the other side offered a drop of twenty or thirty feet, enough to kill you if you fell. Why this should have been, why the poorhouse grounds should have been so deeply recessed on the Philadelphia Avenue side, puzzles me now. What machinery, then, could have executed such a massive job of grading I don't know. But at the time it seemed perfectly natural, a dreadful pit of space congruent with the pit of time into which the old people (who could be seen circling silently in the shade of the trees whose very tops were below my feet) had been plunged by some mystery that would never touch me. That I too would come to their condition was as unbelievable as that I would really fall and break my neck. Even so, I never acquired the daring that some boys had in racing along the top of the wall. In fact—let it be said now—I was not a very daring boy.

The poorhouse impinged on us in many ways. For one thing, my father, whose favorite nightmare was poverty, often said that he liked living so close to a poorhouse; if worse came to worse, he could walk there. For another, the stench of the poorhouse pigs, when the wind was from the east, drifted well down Philadelphia Avenue. Indeed, early in my life the poorhouse livestock were still herded down the street on their way to the slaughterhouse on the other side of town. Twice, in my childhood, the poorhouse barn burnt, and I remember my father (he loved crowds) rushing out of the house in the middle of one night, and my begging to go and my mother keeping me with her, and the luckier, less sheltered children the next day telling me horrific tales of cooked cows and screaming horses. All I saw were the charred ruins, still smoldering, settling here and there with an unexpected crackle, like the underbrush the morning after an ice storm.

Most whiffs of tragedy came, strangely, from the east end of the street. I remember two, both of them associated with the early morning and with the same house a few doors away in the neighborhood. When I was a baby, a man was run over and crushed by a milk wagon—a horse-drawn milk wagon. It had happened within sight of our windows, and I grew to know the exact path of asphalt, but could never picture it. I believed all horse-drawn milk wagons were as light as the toy one I had; by the time I understood about this accident they had vanished from the streets. No matter how many times I visited the patch of asphalt, I could not understand how it had happened. And then, the family that succeeded the widow in her house—or it may have been in the other side; it was a brick semi-detached, set back and beclouded by several tall fir or cedar trees—contained a young man who, while being a counsellor at a summer camp, had had one of his boys dive into shallow water and, neck broken, die in his arms. The young counsellor at dawn one day many months later put a bullet through his head. I seem to remember hearing the shot; certainly I remember hearing my parents bumping around in their bedroom, trying to locate what had wakened them.

Beyond the poorhouse, where Philadelphia Avenue became a country lane, and crossed a little brook where water cress grew, there was a path on the right that led to the poorhouse dam. It was a sizable lake, where people fished and swam. Its mud bottom bristled with broken bottles and jagged cans. A little up from one of its shores, the yellow walls and rotten floor of the old pesthouse survived. Beyond the lake was a woods that extended along the south of the town. Here my parents often took me on walks. Every Sunday afternoon that was fair, we would set out. Sun, birds, and treetops rotated above us as we made our way. There were many routes. Farther down the road, toward Grille, another road led off, and went past a gravel cliff and sad little composition-shingled farmhouses whose invisible inhabitants I imagined as gravel-colored skeletons. By way of a lane we could leave this road and walk down toward the dam. Or we could walk up by the dam until we struck this road, and walk on until we came to a road that took us back into the town by way of the cemetery. I disliked these walks. I would lag farther and farther behind, until my father would retrace his steps and mount me on his shoulders. Upon this giddy, swaying perch—I hesitated to grip his ears and hair as tightly as I needed to—I felt as frightened as exultant, and soon confusedly struggled to be put down. In the woods I would hurl myself against dead branches for the pleasure of feeling them shatter and of disturbing whatever peace and solace my parents were managing to gather. If, at moments, I felt what they wanted me to feel—the sweet moist breath of mulching leaves, the delicate scratch of some bird in the living silence, the benevolent intricacy of moss and rocks and roots and ferns all interlocked on some bank torn by an old logging trail—I did not tell them. I was a small-town child. Cracked pavements and packed dirt were my ground.

This broad crescent of woods is threaded with our walks and suffused with images of love. For it was here, on the beds of needles under the canopies of low pine boughs, that our girls—and this is later, not boyhood at all, but the two have become entangled—were rumored to give themselves. Indeed, I was told that one of the girls in our class, when we were in the ninth grade, had boasted that she liked nothing so much as skinny-dipping in the dam and then making love under the pines. As for myself, this was beyond me, and may be myth, but I do remember, when I was seventeen, taking a girl on one of those walks from my childhood so (then) long ago. We had moved from town, but only ten miles, and my father and I drove in to the high school every day. We walked, the girl and I, down the path where I had smashed so many branches, and sat down on a damp broad log—it was early spring, chilly, a timid froth of leaves overhead—and I dared lightly embrace her from behind and cup my hands over her breasts, small and shallow within the stiffness of her coat, and she closed her eyes and tipped her head back, and an adequate apology seemed delivered for the irritable innocence of these almost forgotten hikes with my parents.

The road that came down into Shillington by way of the cemetery led past the Dives estate, another ominous place. It was guarded by a wall topped with spiky stones. The wall must have been a half-mile long. It was so high my father had to hold me up so I could look in. There were so many buildings and greenhouses I couldn't identify the house. All the buildings were locked and boarded up; there was never anybody there. But in the summer the lawns were mowed; it seemed by ghosts. There were tennis courts, and even— can it be?—a few golf flags. In any case there was a great deal of cut lawn, and gray driveway, and ordered bushes; I got the impression of wealth as a vast brooding absence, like God Himself. The road here was especially overshadowed by trees, so a humid, stale, cloistered smell flavored my glimpses over the wall.

The cemetery was on the side of a hill, bare to the sun, which quickly faded the little American flags and killed the potted geraniums. It was a holiday place; on Memorial Day the parade, in which the boys participated mounted on bicycles whose wheels were threaded with tricolor crêpe paper, ended here, in a picnic of speeches and bugle music and leapfrog over the tombstones. From here you had a perfect view of the town, spread out in the valley between this hill and Slate Hill, the chimneys smoking like just-snuffed cigarettes, the cars twinkling down on Lancaster Avenue, the trolleys moving with the dreamlike slow motion distance imposes.

A little to one side of the cemetery, just below the last trees of the love-making woods, was a small gravel pit where, during the war, we played at being guerrillas. Our leader was a sickly and shy boy whose mother made him wear rubbers whenever there was dew on the grass. His parents bought him a helmet and khaki jacket and even leggings, and he brought great enthusiasm to the imitation of war. G.I.'s and Japs, shouting "Geronimo!" and "Banzai!," we leaped and scrambled over boulders and cliffs in one of whose clefts I always imagined, for some reason, I was going to discover a great deal of money, in a tan cloth bag tied with a leather thong. Though I visualized the bag very clearly, I never found it.

Between this pit and the great quarry on the far edge of town, I lose track of Shillington's boundaries. I believe it was just fields, in which a few things were still farmed. The great quarry was immense, and had a cave, and an unused construction covered with fine gray dust and filled with mysterious gears, levers, scoops, and stairs. The quarry was a mile from my home; I seldom went there. It wears in memory a gritty film. The tougher section of town was nearby. Older boys with .22s used the quarry as a rifle range, and occasionally wounded each other, or smaller children. To scale its sides was even more dangerous than walking along the top of the poorhouse wall. The legends of love that scattered condums along its grassy edges seemed to be of a coarser love than that which perfumed the woods. Its cave was short, and stumpy, yet long enough to let you envision a collapse blocking the mouth of light and sealing you in; the walls were of a greasy golden clay that seemed likely to collapse. The one pure, lovely thing about the quarry, beside its grand size, was the frozen water that appeared on its floor in the winter, and where you could skate sheltered from the wind, and without the fear of drowning that haunted the other skating place, the deep dam. Though the area of ice was smaller, the skaters seemed more skillful down at the quarry: girls in red tights and bouncy short skirts that gave their fannies the effect of a pompon turned and swirled and braked backward to a stop on their points, sparkling ice chips sprinkling in twin fans of spray.

Near the quarry was the Shillington Friday Market, where the sight of so many naked vegetables depressed me, and the Wyomissing Creek, a muddy little thing to skip pebbles in, and the hilly terrain where, in those unbuilding years, a few new houses were built. The best section of town, called Lynoak, was farther on, more toward Reading, around the base of Slate Hill, where I sometimes sledded. It was a long walk back through the streets, under the cold street lights, the sled runners rattling on the frozen ruts, my calves aching with the snow that always filtered through my galoshes. This hill in summer was another place my parents hiked to. The homes of the well-off (including an amazingly modern house, of white brick, with a flat roof, and blue trim, like something assembled from the two dimensions of a Hollywood movie) could be seen climbing its sides, but there was still plenty of room for, during the war, Victory gardens,[2] and above that, steep wilderness. The top was a bare, windy, primeval place. Looking north, you saw the roofs of Shillington merge with the roofs of other suburbs in a torn carpet that went right into the bristling center of Reading, under the blue silhouette of Mount Penn. As Shillington on the south faced the country, northward it faced the city.

---

2. Vegetable plots planted and used by civilians during World War II.

Reading: a very powerful and fragrant and obscure city—who has ever heard of it? Wallace Stevens was born there, and John Philip Sousa died there.[3] For a generation it had a Socialist mayor. Its railroad is on the Monopoly Board. It is rumored to be endeared to gangsters, for its citizens make the most tolerant juries in the East. Unexpectedly, a pagoda overlooks it from the top of Mount Penn. This is the meagre list of its singularities as I know them. Larger than Harrisburg and Wilkes-Barre and Lancaster, it is less well known. Yet to me Reading is the master of cities, the one at the center that all others echo. How rich it smelled! Kresge's swimming in milk chocolate and violet-scented toilet water, Grant's barricaded with coconut cookies, the vast velveted movie theatres dusted with popcorn and a cold whiff of leather, the bakeshops exhaling hearty brown drafts of molasses and damp dough and crisp grease and hot sugar, the beauty parlors with their gingerly stink of singeing, the bookstores glistening with fresh paper and bubbles of hardened glue, the shoe-repair nooks blackened by Kiwi Wax and aromatic shavings, the public lavatory with its emphatic veil of soap, the hushed, brick-red side streets spiced with grit and the moist seeds of maples and ginkgos, the goblin stench of the trolley car that made each return to Shillington a race with nausea—Reading's smells were most of what my boyhood knew of the Great World that was suspended, at a small but sufficient distance, beyond my world.

For the city and the woods and the ominous places were peripheral; their glamour and menace did not intrude into the sunny area where I lived, where the seasons arrived like issues of a magazine and I moved upward from grade to grade and birthday to birthday on a notched stick that itself was held perfectly steady. There was the movie house, and the playground, and the schools, and the grocery stores, and our yard, and my friends, and the horse-chestnut trees. My geography went like this: in the center of the world lay our neighborhood of Shillington. Around it there was greater Shillington, and around that, Berks County. Around Berks County there was the State of Pennsylvania, the best, the least eccentric, state in the Union. Around Pennsylvania, there was the United States, with a greater weight of people on the right and a greater weight of land on the left. For clear geometrical reasons, not all children could be born, like me, at the center of the nation. But that some children chose to be born in other countries and even continents seemed sad and fantastic. There was only one possible nation: mine. Above this vast, rectangular, slightly (the schoolteachers insisted) curved field of the blessed, there was the sky, and the flag, and, mixed up with both, Roosevelt.

3. Wallace Stevens (1879–1955), American poet. John Philip Sousa (1854–1932), American bandmaster, composer of band marches.

Democrats

We were Democrats. My grandfather lived for ninety years, and always voted, and always voted straight Democrat. A marvellous chain of votes, as marvellous as the chain of Sunday-school-attendance pins that vibrated from Pappy Shilling's lapel. The political tradition that shaped his so incorruptible prejudice I am not historian enough to understand; it had something to do with Lincoln's determination to drive all the cattle out of this section of Pennsylvania if Lee won the Battle of Gettysburg.

My parents are closer to me. The events that shaped their views are in my bones. At the time when I was conceived and born, they felt in themselves a whole nation stunned, frightened, despairing. With Roosevelt, hope returned. This simple impression of salvation is my political inheritance. That this impression is not universally shared amazes me. It is as if there existed a class of people who deny that the sun is bright. To me as a child Republicans seemed blind dragons; their prototype was my barber—an artist, a charmer, the only man, my mother insists, who ever cut my hair properly. Nimble and bald, he used to execute little tap-dance figures on the linoleum floor of his shop, and with engaging loyalty he always had the games of Philadelphia's two eighth-place teams tuned in on the radio. But on one subject he was rabid; the last time he cut my hair he positively asserted that our President had died of syphilis. I cannot to this day hear a Republican put forth his philosophy without hearing the snip of scissors above my ears and feeling the little ends of hair crawling across my hot face, reddened by shame and the choking pressure of the paper collar.

Now

Roosevelt was for me the cap on a steadfast world, its emblem and crown. He was always there. Now he is a weakening memory, a semi-legend; it has begun to seem fabulous—like an episode in a medieval chronicle—that the greatest nation in the world was led through the world's greatest war by a man who could not walk. Now, my barber has retired, my hair is a wretched thatch grizzled with gray, and, of the two Philadelphia ball clubs, one has left Philadelphia and one is not always in last place. Now the brick home of my boyhood is owned by a doctor, who has added an annex to the front, to contain his offices. The house was too narrow for its lot and its height; it had a pinched look from the front that used to annoy my mother. But that thin white front with its eyes of green window sash and its mouth of striped awning had been a face to me; it has vanished. My dogwood tree still stands in the side yard, taller than ever, but the walnut tree out back has been cut down. My grandparents are dead. Pappy Shilling is dead. Shilling

Alley has been straightened, and hardtopped, and rechristened Brobst Street. The trolley cars no longer run. The vacant lots across the town have been filled with new houses and stores. New homes have been built far out Philadelphia Avenue and all over the poorhouse property. The poorhouse has been demolished. The poorhouse dam and its aphrodisiac groves have been trimmed into a town park and a chlorinated pool where all females must sheathe their hair in prophylactic bathing caps. If I could go again into 117 Philadelphia Avenue and look out the rear windows, I would see, beyond the football field and the cinder track, a new, two-million-dollar high school, and beyond it, where still stands one row of the double line of trees that marked the Poorhouse Lane, a gaudy depth of postwar housing and a Food Fair like a hideous ark breasting an ocean of parked cars. Here, where wheat grew, loudspeakers unremittingly vomit commercials. It has taken me the shocks of many returnings, more and more widely spaced now, to learn, what seems simple enough, that change is the order of things. The immutability, the steadfastness, of the site of my boyhood was an exceptional effect, purchased for me at unimaginable cost by the paralyzing calamity of the Depression and the heroic external effort of the Second World War.

Environment

The difference between a childhood and a boyhood must be this: our childhood is what we alone have had; our boyhood is what any boy in our environment would have had. My environment was a straight street about three city blocks long, with a slight slope that was most noticeable when you were on a bicycle. Though many of its residents commuted to Reading factories and offices, the neighborhood retained a rural flavor. Corn grew in the strip of land between the alley and the school grounds. We ourselves had a large vegetable garden, which we tended not as a hobby but in earnest, to get food to eat. We sold asparagus and eggs to our neighbors. Our peddling things humiliated me, but then I was a new generation. The bulk of the people in the neighborhood were not long off the farm. One old lady down the street, with an immense throat goiter, still wore a bonnet. The most aristocratic people in the block were the full-fashioned knitters; Reading's textile industry prospered in the Depression. I felt neither prosperous nor poor. We kept the food money in a little recipe box on top of the icebox, and there were nearly always a few bills and coins in it. My father's job paid him poorly but me well; it gave me a sense of, not prestige, but *place*. As a schoolteacher's son, I was assigned a role; people knew me. When I walked down the street to school, the houses called, "Chonny." I had a place to be.

Schools

The elementary school was a big brick cube set in a square of black surfacing chalked and painted with the diagrams and runes of children's games. Wire fences guarded the neighboring homes from the playground. Whoever, at soccer, kicked the ball over the fence into Snitzy's yard had to bring it back. It was very terrible to have to go into Snitzy's yard, but there was only one ball for each grade. Snitzy was a large dark old German who might give you the ball or lock you up in his garage, depending upon his mood. He did not move like other men; suddenly the air near your head condensed, and his heavy hands were on you.

On the way to school, walking down Lancaster Avenue, we passed Henry's, a variety store where we bought punch-out licorice belts and tablets with Edward G. Robinson and Hedy Lamarr smiling on the cover. In October, Halloween masks appeared, hung on wire clotheslines. Hanging limp, these faces of Chinamen and pirates and witches were distorted, and, thickly clustered and rustling against each other, they seemed more frightening masking empty air than they did mounted on the heads of my friends—which was frightening enough. It is strange how fear resists the attacks of reason, how you can know with absolute certainty that it is only Mark Wenrich or Jimmy Trexler whose eyes are moving so weirdly in those almond-shaped holes, and yet still be frightened. I abhorred that effect of double eyes a mask gives; it was as bad as seeing a person's mouth move upside down.

I was a Crow. That is my chief memory of what went on inside the elementary school. In music class the singers were divided into three groups: Nightingales, Robins, and Crows. From year to year the names changed. Sometimes the Crows were Parrots. When visitors from the high school, or elsewhere "outside," came to hear us sing, the Crows were taken out of the room and sent upstairs to watch with the fifth grade an educational film about salmon fishing in the Columbia River. Usually there were only two of us, me and a girl from Philadelphia Avenue whose voice was in truth very husky. I never understood why I was a Crow, though it gave me a certain derisive distinction. As I heard it, I sang rather well.

The other Crow was the first girl I kissed. I just did it, one day, walking back from school along the gutter where the water from the ice plant ran down, because somebody dared me to. And I continued to do it every day, when we reached that spot on the pavement, until a neighbor told my mother, and she, with a solemn weight that seemed unrelated to the airy act, forbade it.

I walked to school mostly with girls. It happened that the mothers of Philadelphia Avenue and, a block up, of Second Street had borne female babies in 1932. These babies now teased me, the lone boy in their pack, by singing the new song, "Oh, Johnny, oh Johnny, how you can love!" and stealing my precious rubber-lined bookbag. The queen of these girls later became the May Queen of our senior class. She had freckles and thick pigtails and green eyes and her mother made her wear high-top shoes long after the rest of us had switched to low ones. She had so much vitality that on the way back from school her nose would start bleeding for no reason. We would be walking along over the wings of the maple seeds and suddenly she would tip her head back and rest it on a wall while someone ran and soaked a handkerchief in the ice-plant water and applied it to her streaming, narrow, crimson-shining nostrils. She was a Nightingale. I loved her deeply, and ineffectually.

My love for that girl carries through all those elementary-school cloakrooms; they always smelled of wet raincoats and rubbers. That tangy, thinly resonant, lonely smell: can love have a better envelope? Everything I did in grammar school was meant to catch her attention. I had a daydream wherein the stars of the music class were asked to pick partners and she, a Nightingale, picked me, a Crow. The teacher was shocked; the class buzzed. To their amazement I sang superbly; my voice, thought to be so ugly, in duet with hers was beautiful. Still singing, we led some sort of parade.

In the world of reality, my triumph was getting her to slap me once, in the third grade. She was always slapping boys in those years; I could not quite figure out what they did. Pull her pigtails, untie her shoes, snatch at her dress, tease her (they called her "Pug")—this much I could see. But somehow there seemed to be under these offensive acts a current running the opposite way; for it was precisely the boys who behaved worst to her that she talked to solemnly at recess, and walked with after school, and whose names she wrote on the sides of her books. Without seeing this current, but deducing its presence, I tried to jump in; I entered a tussle she was having with a boy in homeroom before the bell. I pulled the bow at the back of her dress, and was slapped so hard that children at the other end of the hall heard the crack. I was overjoyed; the stain and pain on my face seemed a badge of initiation. But it was not. The distance between us remained as it was. I did not really want to tease her, I wanted to rescue her, and to be rescued by her. I lacked—and perhaps here the only child suffers a certain deprivation—that kink in the instincts on which childish courtship turns. He lacks a certain easy roughness with other children.

All the years I was at the elementary school the high school loomed large in my mind. Its students—tall, hairy, smoke-breathing —paced the streets seemingly equal with adults. I could see part of its immensity from our rear windows. It was there that my father performed his mysteries every day, striding off from breakfast, down through the grape arbor, his coat pocket bristling with defective pens. He now and then took me over there; the incorruptible smell of varnish and red sweeping wax, the size of the desks, the height of the drinking fountains, the fantastic dimensions of the combination gymnasium-auditorium made me feel that these were halls in which a race of giants had ages ago labored through lives of colossal bliss. At the end of each summer, usually on Labor Day Monday, he and I went into his classroom, Room 201, and unpacked the books and arranged the tablets and the pencils on the desks of his homeroom pupils. Sharpening forty pencils was a chore, sharing it with him a solemn pleasure. To this day I look up at my father through the cedar smell of pencil shavings. To see his key open the front portals of oak, to share alone with him for an hour the pirate hoard of uncracked books and golden pencils, to switch off the lights and leave the room and walk down the darkly lustrous perspective of the corridor and perhaps halt for a few words by an open door that revealed another teacher, like a sorcerer in his sanctum, inscribing forms beside a huge polished globe of the Earth—such territories of wonder boyhood alone can acquire.

The Playground

The periphery I have traced; the center of my boyhood held a calm collection of kind places that are almost impossible to describe, because they are so fundamental to me, they enclosed so many of my hours, that they have the neutral color of my own soul, which I have always imagined as a pale oblong just under my ribs. In the town where I now live, and where I am writing this, seagulls weep overhead on a rainy day. No seagulls found their way inland to Shillington; there were sparrows, and starlings, and cowbirds, and robins, and occasionally a buzzard floating high overhead on immobile wings like a kite on a string too high to be seen.

The playground: up from the hardball diamond, on a plateau bounded on three sides by cornfields, a pavilion contained some tables and a shed for equipment. I spent my summer weekdays there from the age when I was so small that the dust stirred by the feet of roof-ball players got into my eyes. Roof ball was the favorite game. It was played with a red rubber ball smaller than a basketball. The object was to hit it back up on the roof of the pavilion, the whole line of children in succession. Those who failed dropped out. When there was just one person left, a new game began with the cry "Noo-oo *gay*-ame," and we lined up in the order in which we had gone out, so that the lines began with the strongest and tallest and ended with the weakest and youngest. But there was never any doubt that everybody could play; it was perfect democracy. Often the line contained as many as thirty pairs of legs, arranged chronologically. By the time we moved away, I had become a regular front-runner; I knew how to flick the ball to give it spin, how to leap up and send the ball skimming the length of the roof edge, how to plump it with my knuckles when there was a high bounce. Somehow the game never palled. The sight of the ball bouncing along the tarpaper of the foreshortened roof was always important. Many days I was at the playground from nine o'clock, when they ran up the American flag, until four, when they called the equipment in, and played nothing else.

If you hit the ball too hard, and it went over the peak of the roof, you were out, and you had to retrieve the ball, going down a steep bank into a field where the poorhouse men had stopped planting corn because it all got mashed down. If the person ahead of you hit the ball into the air without touching the roof, or missed it entirely, you had the option of "saving," by hitting the ball onto the roof before it struck the ground; this created complex opportunities for strategy and gallantry. I would always try to save the Nightingale, for instance, and there was a girl who came from Louisiana with a French name whom everybody wanted to save. At twelve, she seemed already mature, and I can remember standing with a pack of other boys under the swings looking up at the undersides of her long tense dark-skinned legs as she kicked into the air to give herself more height, the tendons on the underside of her smooth knees jumping, her sneakered feet pointing like a ballerina's shoes.

The walls of the pavilion shed were scribbled all over with dirty drawings and words and detailed slanders on the prettier girls. After hours, when the supervisors were gone, if you were tall enough you could grab hold of a cross beam and get on top of the shed, where there was an intimate wedge of space under the slanting roof; here no adult ever bothered to scrub away the pencillings, and the wood fairly breathed of the forbidden. The very silence of the pavilion, after the day-long click of checkers and *pokabok* of ping-pong, was like a love-choked hush.

Reality seemed more intense at the playground. There was a dust, a daring. It was a children's world; nowhere else did we gather in such numbers with so few adults over us. The playground occupied a platform of earth; we were exposed, it seems now, to the sun and sky. Looking up, one might see a buzzard or witness a portent.

The Enormous Cloud

Strange, that I remember it. One day, playing roof ball—and I could be six, nine, or twelve when it happened—my head was tipped back and there was an enormous cloud. Someone, maybe I, even called, "Look at the cloud!" It was a bright day; out of nowhere had materialized a cloud, roughly circular in shape, as big as a continent, leaden-blue in the mass, radiant silver along the edges. Its size seemed overwhelming; it was more than a portent, it was the fulfillment of one. I had never seen, and never saw again, such a big cloud.

For of course what is strange is that clouds have no size. Moving in an immaterial medium at an indeterminate distance, they offer no hold for measurement, and we do not even judge them relative to each other. Even, as on a rainy day, when the sky is filled from horizon to horizon, we do not think, "What an enormous cloud." It is as if the soul is a camera shutter customarily set at "ordinary"; but now and then, through some inadvertence, it is tripped wide open and the film is flooded with an enigmatic image.

Another time the sky spoke at the playground, telling me that treachery can come from above. It was our Field Day. One of the events was a race in which we put our shoes in a heap, lined up at a distance, ran to the heap, found our shoes, put them on, and raced back. The winner got a ticket to the Shillington movie theatre. I was the first to find my shoes, and was tying my laces when, out of the ring of adults and older children who had collected to watch, a voice urged, "Hurry! Don't tie the laces." I didn't, and ran back, and was disqualified. My world reeled at the treachery of that unseen high voice: I loved the movies.

The Movie House

It was two blocks from my home; I began to go alone from the age of six. My mother, so strict about my kissing girls, was strangely indulgent about this. The theatre ran three shows a week, for two days each, and was closed on Sundays. Many weeks I went three times. I remember a summer evening in our yard. Supper is over, the walnut tree throws a heavy shadow. The fireflies are not out yet. My father is off, my mother and her parents are turning the earth in our garden. Some burning sticks and paper on our ash heap fill the damp air with low smoke; I express a wish to go to the movies, expecting to be told No. Instead, my mother tells me to go into the house and clean up; I come into the yard again in clean shorts, the shadows slightly heavier, the dew a little wetter; I am given eleven cents and run down Philadelphia Avenue in my ironed shorts and fresh shirt, down past the running ice-plant water, the dime and the penny in my hand. I always ran to the movies. If it was not a movie with Adolphe Menjou, it was a horror picture. People turning into cats—fingers going stubby into paws and hair being blurred in with double exposure—and Egyptian tombs and English houses where doors creak and wind disturbs the curtains and dogs refuse to go into certain rooms because they sense something supersensory. I used to crouch down into the seat and hold my coat in front of my face when I sensed a frightening scene coming, peeking through the buttonhole to find out when it was over. Through the buttonhole Frankenstein's monster glowered; lightning flash; sweat poured over the bolts that held his face together. On the way home, I ran again, in terror now. Darkness had come, the first show was from seven to nine, by nine even the longest summer day was ending. Each porch along the street seemed to be a tomb crammed with shadows, each shrub seemed to shelter a grasping arm. I ran with a frantic high step, trying to keep my ankles away from the reaching hand. The last and worst terror was our own porch; low brick walls on either side concealed possible cat people. Leaping high, I launched myself at the door and, if no one was in the front of the house, fled through suffocating halls past gaping doorways to the kitchen, where there was always someone working, and a light bulb burning. The icebox. The rickety worn table, oilcloth-covered, where we ate. The windows painted solid black by the interior brightness. But even then I kept my legs away from the furry space beneath the table.

These were Hollywood's comfortable years. The theatre, a shallowly sloped hall too narrow to have a central aisle, was usually crowded. I liked it most on Monday nights, when it was emptiest. It seemed most mine then. I had a favorite seat—rear row, extreme left—and my favorite moment was the instant when the orange side lights, Babylonian in design, were still lit, and the curtain was closed but there was obviously somebody up in the projection room, for the camera had started to whir. In the next instant, I knew, a broad dusty beam of light would fill the air above me, and the titles of the travelogue would appear on the curtains, their projected steadiness undulating as with an unhurried, composed screech the curtains were drawn back, revealing the screen alive with images that then would pass through a few focal adjustments. In that delicate, promissory whir was my favorite moment.

On Saturday afternoons the owner gave us all Hershey bars as we came out of the matinee. On Christmas morning he showed a free hour of cartoons and the superintendent of the Lutheran Sunday school led us in singing carols, gesticulating in front of the high blank screen, no bigger than the shadow of the moth that sometimes landed on the lens. His booming voice would echo curiously on the bare walls, usually so dark and muffling but that on this one morning, containing a loud sea of Christmas children, had a bare, clean, morning quality that echoed. After this special show we all went down to the Town Hall, where the plumpest borough employee, disguised as Santa Claus, gave us each a green box of chocolates. Shillington was small enough to support such traditions.

Three Boys

A, B, and C, I'll say, in case they care. A lived next door; he *loomed* next door, rather. He seemed immense—a great wallowing fatso stuffed with possessions; he was the son of a full-fashioned knitter. He seemed to have a beer-belly; after several generations beer-bellies may become congenital. Also his face had no features. It was just a blank ball on his shoulders. He used to call me "Ostrich," after Disney's Ollie Ostrich. My neck was not very long; the name seemed horribly unfair; it was its injustice that made me cry. But nothing I could say, or scream, would make him stop. And I still, now and then—in reading, say, a book review by one of the

apple-cheeked savants of the quarterlies or one of the pious grem-
lins who manufacture puns for *Time*—get the old sensations: my
ears close up, my eyes go warm, my chest feels thin as an eggshell,
my voice churns silently in my stomach. From A I received my first
impression of the smug, chinkless, irresistible *power* of stupidity; it
is the most powerful force on earth. It says "Ostrich" often enough,
and the universe crumbles.

A was more than a boy, he was a force-field that could manifest
itself in many forms, that could take the wiry, disconsolate shape of
wide-mouthed, tiny-eared boys who would now and then beat me
up on the way back from school. I did not greatly mind being
beaten up, though I resisted it. For one thing, it firmly involved me,
at least during the beating, with the circumambient humanity that
so often seemed evasive. Also, the boys who applied the beating
were misfits, periodic flunkers, who wore corduroy knickers with
threadbare knees and men's shirts with the top button buttoned—
this last an infallible sign of deep poverty. So that I felt there was
some justice, some condonable revenge, being applied with their
fists to this little teacher's son. And then there was the delicious
alarm of my mother and grandmother when I returned home
bloody, bruised, and torn. My father took the attitude that it was
making a boy of me, an attitude I dimly shared. He and I both were
afraid of me becoming a sissy—he perhaps more afraid than I.

When I was eleven or so I met B. It was summer and I was down
at the playground. He was pushing a little tank with moving rubber
treads up and down the hills in the sandbox. It was a fine little toy,
mottled with camouflage green; patriotic manufacturers produced
throughout the war millions of such authentic miniatures which we
maneuvered with authentic, if miniature, militance. Attracted by the
toy, I spoke to him; though taller and a little older than I, he had
my dull straight brown hair and a look of being also alone. We
became fast friends. He lived just up the street—toward the poorhouse, the east part of the street, from which the little winds of
tragedy blew. He had just moved from the Midwest, and his mother
was a widow. Beside wage war, we did many things together. We
played marbles for days at a time, until one of us had won the
other's entire coffee-canful. With jigsaws we cut out of plywood
animals copied from comic books. We made movies by tearing the
pages from Big Little Books[4] and coloring the drawings and pasting
them in a strip, and winding them on toilet-paper spools, and making a cardboard carton a theatre. We rigged up telephones, and
racing wagons, and cities of the future, using orange crates and
cigar boxes and peanut-butter jars and such potent debris. We loved
Smokey Stover[5] and were always saying "Foo." We had an intense
spell of Monopoly. He called me "Uppy"—the only person who

4. Small, squat children's books, usually
featuring comic-strip heroes. Popular before and during World War II.
5. Comic-strip character.

ever did. I remember once, knowing he was coming down that afternoon to my house to play Monopoly, in order to show my joy I set up the board elaborately, with the Chance and Community Chest cards fanned painstakingly, like spiral staircases. He came into the room, groaned, "Uppy, what are you doing?" and impatiently scrabbled the cards together in a sensible pile. The older we got, the more the year between us told, and the more my friendship embarrassed him. We fought. Once, to my horror, I heard myself taunting him with the fact that he had no father. The unmentionable, the unforgivable. I suppose we patched things up, children do, but the fabric had been torn. He had a long, pale, serious face, with buck-teeth, and is probably an electronics engineer somewhere now, doing secret government work.

So through B I first experienced the pattern of friendship. There are three stages. First, acquaintance: we are new to each other, making each other laugh in surprise, and demand nothing beyond politeness. The death of the one would startle the other, no more. It is a pleasant stage, a stable stage; on austere rations of exposure it can live a lifetime, and the two parties to it always feel a slight gratification upon meeting, will feel vaguely confirmed in their human state. Then comes intimacy: now we laugh before two words of the joke are out of the other's mouth, because we know what we will say. Our two beings seem marvellously joined, from our toes to our heads, along tingling points of agreement; everything we venture is right, everything we put forth lodges in a corresponding socket in the frame of the other. The death of one would grieve the other. To be together is to enjoy a mounting excitement, a constant echo and amplification. It is an ecstatic and unstable stage, bound of its own agitation to tip into the third: revulsion. One or the other makes a misjudgment; presumes; puts forth that which does not meet agreement. Sometimes there is an explosion; more often the moment is swallowed in silence, and months pass before its nature dawns. Instead of dissolving, it grows. The mind, the throat, are clogged; forgiveness, forgetfulness, that have arrived so often, fail. Now everything jars and is distasteful. The betrayal, perhaps a tiny fraction in itself, has inverted the tingling column of agreement, made all pluses minuses. Everything about the other is hateful, despicable; yet he cannot be dismissed. We have confided in him too many minutes, too many words; he has those minutes and words as hostages, and his confidences are embedded in us where they cannot be scraped away, and even rivers of time cannot erode them completely, for there are indelible stains. Now—though the friends may continue to meet, and smile, as if they had never trespassed beyond acquaintance—the death of the one would please the other.

An unhappy pattern to which C is an exception. He was my friend before kindergarten, he is my friend still. I go to his home now, and he and his wife serve me and my wife with alcoholic drinks and slices of excellent cheese on crisp crackers, just as twenty years ago he served me with treats from his mother's refrigerator. He was a born host, and I a born guest. Also he was intelligent. If my childhood's brain, when I look back at it, seems a primitive mammal, a lemur or shrew, his brain was an angel whose visitation was widely hailed as wonderful. When in school he stood to recite, his cool rectangular forehead glowed. He tucked his right hand into his left armpit and with his left hand mechanically tapped a pencil against his thigh. His answers were always correct. He beat me at spelling bees and, in another sort of competition, when we both collected Big Little Books, he outbid me for my supreme find (in the attic of a third boy), the first Mickey Mouse. I can still see that book, I wanted it so badly, its paper tan with age and its drawings done in Disney's primitive style, when Mickey's black chest is naked like a child's and his eyes are two nicked oblongs. Losing it was perhaps a lucky blow; it helped wean me away from hope of ever having possessions.

C was fearless. He deliberately set fields on fire. He engaged in rock-throwing duels with tough boys. One afternoon he persisted in playing quoits with me although—as the hospital discovered that night—his appendix was nearly bursting. He was enterprising. He peddled magazine subscriptions door-to-door; he mowed neighbors' lawns; he struck financial bargains with his father. He collected stamps so well his collection blossomed into a stamp company that filled his room with steel cabinets and mimeograph machinery. He collected money—every time I went over to his house he would get out a little tin box and count the money in it for me: $27.50 one week, $29.95 the next, $30.90 the next—all changed into new bills nicely folded together. It was a strange ritual, whose meaning for me was: since he was doing it, I didn't have to. His money made me richer. We read Ellery Queen[6] and played chess and invented board games and discussed infinity together. In later adolescence, he collected records. He liked the Goodman quintets but loved Fats Waller.[7] Sitting there in that room so familiar to me, where the machinery of the Shilco Stamp Company still crowded the walls and for that matter the tin box of money might still be stashed, while my thin friend grunted softly along with that dead dark angel on "You're Not the Only Oyster in the Stew," I felt, in the best sense, patronized: the perfect guest of the perfect host. What made it perfect was that we had both spent our entire lives in Shillington.

Concerning the Three Great Secret Things: (1) Sex

In crucial matters, the town was evasive. Sex was an unlikely, though persistent, rumor. My father slapped my mother's bottom and made a throaty noise and I thought it was a petty form of

6. Fictional crime investigator-hero of many novels and a weekly radio program.
7. Benny Goodman (b. 1909), swing clarinetist and orchestra leader. Thomas ("Fats") Waller (1904–1943), jazz pianist, singer, composer whose *You're Not the Only Oyster in the Stew* is one of his best recordings.

sadism. The major sexual experience of my boyhood was a section of a newsreel showing some women wrestling in a pit of mud. The mud covered their bathing suits so they seemed naked. Thick, interlocking, faceless bodies, they strove and fell. The sight was so disturbingly resonant that afterward, in any movie, two women pulling each other's hair or slapping each other—there was a good deal of this in movies of the early forties; Ida Lupino was usually one of the women—gave me a tense, watery, drawn-out feeling below the belt. Thenceforth my imaginings about girls moved through mud. In one recurrent scene I staged in my bed, the girl and I, dressed in our underpants and wrapped around with ropes, had been plunged from an immense cliff into a secret pond of mud, by a villain who resembled Peg-Leg Pete.[8] I usually got my hands free and rescued her; sometimes she rescued me; in any case there hovered over our spattered, elastic-clad bodies the idea that these were the last minutes of our lives, and all our shames and reservations were put behind us. It turned out that she had loved me all along. We climbed out, into the light. The ropes had hurt our wrists; yet the sweet kernel of the fantasy lay somehow in the sensations of being tightly bound, before we rescued each other.

(2) Religion

Pragmatically, I have become a Congregationalist, but in the translucent and tactful church of my adoption my eyes sting, my throat goes grave, when we sing—what we rarely sang in the Lutheran church of my childhood—Luther's mighty hymn:

> For still our ancient foe
> Doth seek to work us woe;
> His craft and power are great,
> And arm'd with cruel hate,
> On earth is not his equal.[9]

This immense dirge of praise for the Devil and the world, thunderous, slow, opaquely proud, nourishes a seed in me I never knew was planted. How did the patently vapid and drearily businesslike teachings to which I was lightly exposed succeed in branding me with a Cross? And a brand so specifically Lutheran, so distinctly Nordic; an obdurate insistence that at the core of the core there is a right-angled clash to which, of all verbal combinations we can invent, the Apostles' Creed[1] offers the most adequate correspondence and response.

Of my family, only my father attended the church regularly,

---

8. Villainous tormentor of Mickey Mouse in comic strips.

9. *"Ein Feste Burg"* ("A mighty fortress is our God") is a famous hymn composed by Martin Luther (1483–1546),

German leader of the Protestant Reformation.

1. Christian statement of belief ascribed to the Twelve Apostles ("I believe in God the Father Almighty * * *").

returning every Sunday with the Sunday Reading *Eagle* and the complaint that the minister prayed too long. My own relations with the church were unsuccessful. In Sunday school, I rarely received the perfect attendance pin, though my attendance seemed to me and my parents as perfect as anybody's. Instead, I was given a pencil stamped KINDT'S FUNERAL HOME. Once, knowing that a lot of racy social activity was going on under its aegis, I tried to join the Luther League; but I had the misfortune to arrive on the night of their Halloween party, and was refused admittance because I was not wearing a costume. And, the worst rebuff, I was once struck by a car on the way to Sunday school. I had the collection nickel in my hand, and held on to it even as I was being dragged fifteen feet on the car's bumper. For this heroic churchmanship I received no palpable credit; the Lutheran Church seemed positively to dislike me.

Yet the crustiness, the inhospitality of the container enhanced the oddly lucid thing contained. I do not recall my first doubts; I doubted perhaps abnormally little. And when they came, they never roosted on the branches of the tree, but attacked the roots; if the first article of the Creed stands, the rest follows as water flows downhill. That God, at a remote place and time, took upon Himself the form of a Syrian carpenter and walked the earth willfully healing and abusing and affirming and grieving, appeared to me quite in the character of the Author of the grass. The mystery that more puzzled me as a child was the incarnation of my ego—that omnivorous and somehow preëxistent "I"—in a speck so specifically situated amid the billions of history. Why was I I? The arbitrariness of it astounded me; in comparison, nothing was too marvellous.

Shillington bred a receptivity to the supernatural unrelated to orthodox religion. This is the land of the hex signs, and in the neighboring town of Grille a "witch doctor" hung out a shingle like a qualified M.D. I was struck recently, on reading Frazer's contemptuous list of superstitions in *The Golden Bough*,[2] by how many of them seemed good sense. My grandmother was always muttering little things; she came from a country world of spilled salt and cracked mirrors and new moons and omens. She convinced me, by contagion, that our house was haunted. I punished her by making her stand guard outside the bathroom when I was in it. If I found she had fallen asleep in the shadowy hallway crawling with ghosts, I would leap up on her back and pummel her with a fury that troubles me now.

Imagine my old neighborhood as an African village; under the pointed roofs tom-toms beat, premonitions prowl, and in the darkness naked superstition in all her plausibility blooms:

---

2. *The Golden Bough*, by Sir James Frazer (1854–1941), a Scottish anthro- pologist who traced the primitive origin of myths.

The Night-blooming Cereus

It was during the war; early in the war, 1942. *Collier's* had printed a cover showing Hirohito, splendidly costumed and fanged, standing malevolently in front of a bedraggled, bewildered Hitler and an even more decrepit and craven Mussolini. Our troops in the Pacific reeled from island to island; the Japanese seemed a race of demons capable of anything. The night-blooming cereus was the property of a family who lived down the street in a stucco house that on the inside was narrow and dark in the way that houses in the middle of the country sometimes are. The parlor was crowded with obscure furniture decked out with antimacassars and porcelain doodads. At Christmas a splendiferous tree appeared in that parlor, hung with pounds of tinsel and strung popcorn and paper chains and pretzels and balls and intricate, figurative ornaments that must have been rescued from the previous century.

The blooming of the cereus was to be an event in the neighborhood; for days we had been waiting. This night—a clear warm night, in August or September—word came, somehow. My mother and grandmother and I rushed down Philadelphia Avenue in the dark. It was late; I should have been in bed. I remembered the night I was refused permission to go to the poorhouse fire. The plant stood at the side of the house, in a narrow space between the stucco wall and the hedge. A knot of neighborhood women had already gathered; heavy shoulders and hair buns were silhouetted in an indeterminate light. On its twisted, unreal stem the flower had opened its unnaturally brilliant petals. But no one was looking at it. For overhead, in the north of a black sky strewn with stars like thrown salt, the wandering fingers of an aurora borealis gestured, now lengthening and brightening so that shades of blue and green could be distinguished, now ebbing until it seemed there was nothing there at all. It was a rare sight this far south. The women muttered, sighed, and, as if involuntarily, out of the friction of their bodies, moaned. Standing among their legs and skirts, I was slapped by a sudden cold wave of fear. "Is it the end of the world?" one of the women asked. There was no answer. And then a plane went over, its red lights blinking, its motors no louder than the drone of a wasp. Japanese. The Japanese were going to bomb Shillington, the center of the nation. I waited for the bomb, and without words prayed, expecting a miracle, for the appearance of angels and Japanese in the sky was restrained by the same impossibility, an impossibility that the swollen waxy brilliant white of the flower by my knees had sucked from the night.

The plane of course passed; it was one of ours; my prayer was answered with the usual appearance of absence. We went home, and the world reconstituted its veneer of reason, but the moans of the women had rubbed something in me permanently bare.

(3) Art

Leafing through a scrapbook my mother long ago made of my childhood drawings, I was greeted by one I had titled "Mr. Sun talking to Old Man Winter in his Office." Old Man Winter, a cloud with stick legs, and his host, a radiant ball with similar legs, sit at ease, both smiling, on two chairs that are the only furniture of the solar office. That the source of all light should have, somewhere, an office, suited my conception of an artist, who was someone who lived in a small town like Shillington, and who, equipped with pencils and paper, practiced his solitary trade as methodically as the dentist practiced his. And indeed, that is how it is at present with me.

Goethe[3]—probably among others—says to be wary of our youthful wishes, for in maturity we are apt to get them. I go back, now, to Pennsylvania, and on one of the walls of the house in which my parents now live there hangs a photograph of myself as a boy. I am smiling, and staring with clear eyes at something in the corner of the room. I stand before that photograph, and am disappointed to receive no flicker, not the shadow of a flicker, of approval, of gratitude. The boy continues to smile at the corner of the room, beyond me. That boy is not a ghost to me, he is real to me; it is I who am a ghost to him. I, in my present state, was one of the ghosts that haunted his childhood. Like some phantom conjured by this child from a glue bottle, I have executed his commands; acquired pencils, paper, and an office. Now I wait apprehensively for his next command, or at least a nod of appreciation, and he smiles through me, as if I am already transparent with failure.

He saw art—between drawing and writing he ignorantly made no distinction—as a method of riding a thin pencil line out of Shillington, out of time altogether, into an infinity of unseen and even unborn hearts. He pictured this infinity as radiant. How innocent! But his assumption here, like his assumptions on religion and politics, is one for which I have found no certain substitute. He loved blank paper and obedience to this love led me to a difficult artistic attempt. I reasoned thus: just as the paper is the basis for the marks upon it, might not events be contingent upon a never-expressed (because featureless) ground? Is the true marvel of Sunday skaters the pattern of their pirouettes or the fact that they are silently upheld? Blankness is not emptiness; we may skate upon an intense radiance we do not see because we see nothing else. And in fact there is a color, a quiet but tireless goodness that things at rest, like a brick wall or a small stone, seem to affirm. A wordless reassurance these things are pressing to give. An hallucination? To transcribe middleness with all its grits, bumps, and anonymities, in its fullness of satisfaction and mystery: is it possible or, in view of the suffering

3. Johann Wolfgang von Goethe (1749–1832), German poet and dramatist.

that violently colors the periphery and that at all moments threatens to move into the center, worth doing? Possibly not; but the horse-chestnut trees, the telephone poles, the porches, the green hedges recede to a calm point that in my subjective geography is still the center of the world.

End of Boyhood

I was walking down this Philadelphia Avenue one April and was just stepping over the shallow little rain gutter in the pavement that could throw you if you were on roller skates—though it had been years since I had been on roller skates—when from the semide-tached house across the street a boy broke and ran. He was the youngest of six sons. All of his brothers were in the armed services, and five blue stars hung in his home's front window.[4] He was several years older than I, and used to annoy my grandparents by walking through our yard, down past the grape arbor, on his way to high school. Long-legged, he was now running diagonally across the high-crowned street. I was the only other person out in the air. "Chonny!" he called. I was flattered to have him, so tall and grown, speak to me. "Did you hear?"

"No. What?"

"On the radio. The President is dead."[5]

That summer the war ended, and that fall, suddenly mobile, we moved away from the big white house. We moved on Halloween night. As the movers were fitting the last pieces of furniture, furniture that had not moved since I was born, into their truck, little figures dressed as ghosts and cats flitted in and out of the shadows of the street. A few rang our bell, and when my mother opened the door they were frightened by the empty rooms they saw behind her, and went away without begging. When the last things had been packed, and the kitchen light turned off, and the doors locked, the three of us—my grandparents were already at the new house—got into the old Buick my father had bought—in Shillington we had never had a car, for we could walk everywhere—and drove up the street, east, toward the poorhouse and beyond. Somewhat self-consciously and cruelly dramatizing my grief, for I was thirteen and beginning to be cunning, I twisted and watched our house recede through the rear window. Moonlight momentarily caught in an upper pane; then the reflection passed, and the brightest thing was the white brick wall itself. Against the broad blank part where I used to bat a tennis ball for hours at a time, the silhouette of the dogwood tree stood confused with the shapes of the other bushes in

4. During World War II some American families displayed "service flags" in their windows, each star denoting a son in one of the branches of the armed forces. When a serviceman was killed, a gold star was substituted for the blue.

5. Franklin Delano Roosevelt (1882–1945) served as President for 12 years (1933–45). His death, after reelection to a fourth term, came as a grievous shock to many Americans, as though a long period of stability had ended.

our side yard, but taller. I turned away before it would have disappeared from sight; and so it is that my shadow has always remained in one place.

Separating[1]

The day was fair. Brilliant. All that June the weather had mocked the Maples' internal misery with solid sunlight—golden shafts and cascades of green in which their conversations had wormed unseeing, their sad murmuring selves the only stain in Nature. Usually by this time of the year they had acquired tans; but when they met their elder daughter's plane on her return from a year in England they were almost as pale as she, though Judith was too dazzled by the sunny opulent jumble of her native land to notice. They did not spoil her homecoming by telling her immediately. Wait a few days, let her recover from jet lag, had been one of their formulations, in that string of gray dialogues—over coffee, over cocktails, over Cointreau—that had shaped the strategy of their dissolution, while the earth performed its annual stunt of renewal unnoticed beyond their closed windows. Richard had thought to leave at Easter; Joan had insisted they wait until the four children were at last assembled, with all exams passed and ceremonies attended, and the bauble of summer to console them. So he had drudged away, in love, in dread, repairing screens, getting the mowers sharpened, rolling and patching their new tennis court.

The court, clay, had come through its first winter pitted and windswept bare of redcoat. Years ago the Maples had observed how often, among their friends, divorce followed a dramatic home improvement, as if the marriage were making one last twitchy effort to live; their own worst crisis had come amid the plaster dust and exposed plumbing of a kitchen renovation. Yet, a summer ago, as canary-yellow bulldozers gaily churned a grassy, daisy-dotted knoll into a muddy plateau, and a crew of pigtailed young men raked and tamped clay into a plane, this transformation did not strike them as ominous, but festive in its impudence; their marriage could rend the earth for fun. The next spring, waking each day at dawn to a sliding sensation as if the bed were being tipped, Richard found the barren tennis court, its net and tapes still rolled in the barn, an environment congruous with his mood of purposeful desolation, and the crumbling of handfuls of clay into cracks and holes (dogs had frolicked on the court in a thaw; rivulets had evolved trenches) an activity suitably elemental and interminable. In his sealed heart he hoped the day would never come.

Now it was here. A Friday. Judith was reacclimated; all four children were assembled, before jobs and camps and visits again scattered them. Joan thought they should be told one by one. Richard was for making an announcement at the table. She said, "I

1. From the *New Yorker*, June 23, 1975.

think just making an announcement is a cop-out. They'll start quarrelling and playing to each other instead of focussing. They're each individuals, you know, not just some corporate obstacle to your freedom."

"O.K., O.K. I agree." Joan's plan was exact. That evening, they were giving Judith a belated welcome-home dinner, of lobster and champagne. Then, the party over, they, the two of them, who nineteen years before would push her in a baby carriage along Tenth Street to Washington Square,[2] were to walk her out of the house, to the bridge across the salt creek, and tell her, swearing her to secrecy. Then Richard Jr., who was going directly from work to a rock concert in Boston, would be told, either late when he returned on the train or early Saturday morning before he went off to his job; he was seventeen and employed as one of a golf-course maintenance crew. Then the two younger children, John and Margaret, could, as the morning wore on, be informed.

"Mopped up, as it were," Richard said.

"Do you have any better plan? That leaves you the rest of Saturday to answer any questions, pack, and make your wonderful departure."

"No," he said, meaning he had no better plan, and agreed to hers, though it had an edge of false order, a plea for control in the semblance of its achievement, like Joan's long chore lists and financial accountings and, in the days when he first knew her, her too copious lecture notes. Her plan turned one hurdle for him into four—four knife-sharp walls, each with a sheer blind drop on the other side.

All spring he had been morbidly conscious of insides and outsides, of barriers and partitions. He and Joan stood as a thin barrier between the children and the truth. Each moment was a partition, with the past on one side and the future on the other, a future containing this unthinkable *now*. Beyond four knifelike walls a new life for him waited vaguely. His skull cupped a secret, a white face, a face both frightened and soothing, both strange and known, that he wanted to shield from tears, which he felt all about him, solid as the sunlight. So haunted, he had become obsessed with battening down the house against his absence, replacing screens and sash cords, hinges and latches—a Houdini[3] making things snug before his escape.

The lock. He had still to replace a lock on one of the doors of the screened porch. The task, like most such, proved more difficult than he had imagined. The old lock, aluminum frozen by corrosion, had been deliberately rendered obsolete by manufacturers. Three hardware stores had nothing that even approximately matched the mortised hole its removal (surprisingly easy) left. Another hole had to be gouged, with bits too small and saws too big, and the old hole fitted with a block of wood—the chisels dull, the saw rusty, his fingers thick with lack of sleep. The sun poured down, beyond the porch, on a world of neglect. The bushes already needed pruning, the windward side of the house was shedding flakes of paint, rain would get in when he was gone, insects, rot, death. His family, all those he would lose, filtered through the edges of his awareness as he struggled with screw holes, splinters, opaque instructions, minutiae of metal.

Judith sat on the porch, a princess returned from exile. She regaled them with stories of fuel shortages, of bomb scares in the Underground, of Pakistani workmen loudly lusting after her as she walked past on her way to dance school. Joan came and went, in and out of the house, calmer than she should have been, praising his struggles with the lock as if this were one more and not the last of their chain of shared chores. The younger of his sons, John, now at fifteen suddenly, unwittingly handsome, for a few minutes held the rickety screen door while his father clumsily hammered and chiselled, each blow a kind of sob in Richard's ears. His younger daughter, having been at a slumber party, slept on the porch hammock through all the noise—heavy and pink, trusting and forsaken. Time, like the sunlight, continued relentlessly; the sunlight slowly slanted. Today was one of the longest days. The lock clicked, worked. He was through. He had a drink; he drank it on the porch, listening to his daughter. "It was so sweet," she was saying, "during the worst of it, how all the butcher's and bakery shops kept open by candlelight. They're all so plucky and cute. From the papers, things sounded so much worse here—people shooting people in gas lines, and everybody freezing."

Richard asked her, "Do you still want to live in England forever?" *Forever:* the concept, now a reality upon him, pressed and scratched at the back of his throat.

"No," Judith confessed, turning her oval face to him, its eyes still childishly far apart, but the lips set as over something succulent and satisfactory. "I was anxious to come home. I'm an American." She was a woman. They had raised her; he and Joan had endured together to raise her, alone of the four. The others had still some raising left in them. Yet it was the thought of telling Judith—the image of her, their first baby, walking between them arm in arm to the bridge—that broke him. The partition between himself and the tears broke. Richard sat down to the celebratory meal with the back of his throat aching; the champagne, the lobster seemed phases of sunshine; he saw them and tasted them through tears. He blinked, swallowed, croakily joked about hay fever. The tears would not stop leaking through; they came not through a hole that could be plugged but through a permeable spot in a membrane, steadily, purely, endlessly, fruitfully. They became, his tears, a shield for himself against these others—their faces, the fact of their assembly, a last time as innocents, at a table where he sat the last time as head. Tears dropped from his nose as he broke the lobster's back; salt flavored his champagne as he sipped it; the raw clench at the back of his throat was delicious. He could not help himself.

His children tried to ignore his tears. Judith, on his right, lit a cigarette, gazed upward in the direction of her too energetic, too sophisticated exhalation; on her other side, John earnestly bent his face to the extraction of the last morsels—legs, tail segments—from the scarlet corpse. Joan, at the opposite end of the table, glanced at him surprised, her reproach displaced by a quick grimace, of forgiveness, or of salute to his superior gift of strategy. Between them, Margaret, no longer called Bean, thirteen and large for her age, gazed from the other side of his pane of tears as if into a shop-window at something she coveted—at her father, a crystalline heap of splinters and memories. It was not she, however, but John who, in the kitchen, as they cleared the plates and carapaces away, asked Joan the question: "*Why is Daddy crying?*"

Richard heard the question but not the murmured answer. Then he heard Bean cry, "Oh, no-oh!"—the faintly dramatized exclamation of one who had long expected it.

John returned to the table carrying a bowl of salad. He nodded tersely at his father and his lips shaped the conspiratorial words "She told."

"Told what?" Richard asked aloud, insanely.

The boy sat down as if to rebuke his father's distraction with the example of his own good manners and said quietly, "The separation."

Joan and Margaret returned; the child, in Richard's twisted vision, seemed diminished in size, and relieved, relieved to have had the boogeyman at last proved real. He called out to her—the distances at the table had grown immense—"You knew, you always knew," but the clenching at the back of his throat prevented him from making sense of it. From afar he heard Joan talking, levelly, sensibly, reciting what they had prepared: it was a separation for the summer, an experiment. She and Daddy both agreed it would be good for them; they needed space and time to think; they liked each other but did not make each other happy enough, somehow.

Judith, imitating her mother's factual tone, but in her youth off-key, too cool, said, "I think it's silly. You should either live together or get divorced."

Richard's crying, like a wave that has crested and crashed, had become tumultuous; but it was overtopped by another tumult, for John, who had been so reserved, now grew larger and larger at the table. Perhaps his younger sister's being credited with knowing set him off. "Why didn't you *tell* us?" he asked, in a large round voice quite unlike his own. "You should have *told* us you weren't getting along."

Richard was startled into attempting to force words through his tears. "We *do* get along, that's the trouble, so it doesn't show even to us—" "That we do not love each other" was the rest of the sentence; he couldn't finish it.

Joan finished for him, in her style. "And we've always, *especially*, loved our children."

John was not mollified. "What do you care about *us?*" he boomed. "We're just little things you *had.*" His sisters' laughing forced a laugh from him, which he turned hard and parodistic: "Ha ha *ha.*" Richard and Joan realized simultaneously that the child was drunk, on Judith's homecoming champagne. Feeling bound to keep the center of the stage, John took a cigarette from Judith's pack, poked it into his mouth, let it hang from his lower lip, and squinted like a gangster.

"You're not little things we had," Richard called to him. "You're the whole point. But you're grown. Or almost."

The boy was lighting matches. Instead of holding them to his cigarette (for they had never seen him smoke; being "good" had been his way of setting himself apart), he held them to his mother's face, closer and closer, for her to blow out. Then he lit the whole folder—a hiss and then a torch, held against his mother's face. Prismed by his tears, the flame filled Richard's vision; he didn't know how it was extinguished. He heard Margaret say, "Oh stop showing off," and saw John, in response, break the cigarette in two and put the halves entirely into his mouth and chew, sticking out his tongue to display the shreds to his sister.

Joan talked to him, reasoning—a fountain of reason, unintelligible. "Talked about it for years . . . our children must help us . . . Daddy and I both want . . ." As the boy listened, he carefully wadded a paper napkin into the leaves of his salad, fashioned a ball of paper and lettuce, and popped it into his mouth, looking around the table for the expected laughter. None came. Judith said, "Be mature," and dismissed a plume of smoke.

Richard got up from this stifling table and led the boy outside. Though the house was in twilight, the outdoors still brimmed with light, the long waste light of high summer. Both laughing, he supervised John's spitting out the lettuce and paper and tobacco into the pachysandra.[4] He took him by the hand—a square gritty hand, but for its softness a man's. Yet, it hold on. They ran together up into the field, past the tennis court. The raw banking left by the bulldozers was dotted with daisies. Past the court and a flat stretch where they used to play family baseball stood a soft green rise glorious in the sun, each weed and species of grass distinct as illumination on parchment. "I'm sorry, so sorry," Richard cried.

4. Green, leafy plant, frequently used as ground cover.

"You were the only one who ever tried to help me with all the goddam jobs around this place."

Sobbing, safe within his tears and the champagne, John explained, "It's not just the separation, it's the whole crummy year, I *hate* that school, you can't make any friends, the history teacher's a scud."[5]

They sat on the crest of the rise, shaking and warm from their tears but easier in their voices, and Richard tried to focus on the child's sad year—the weekdays long with homework, the weekends spent in his room with model airplanes, while his parents murmured down below, nursing their separation. How selfish, how blind, Richard thought; his eyes felt scoured. He told his son, "We'll think about getting you transferred. Life's too short to be miserable."

They had said what they could, but did not want the moment to heal, and talked on, about the school, about the tennis court, whether it would ever again be as good as it had been that first summer. They walked to inspect it and pressed a few more tapes more firmly down. A little stiltedly, perhaps trying to make too much of the moment, to prolong it, Richard led the boy to the spot in the field where the view was best, of the metallic blue river, the emerald marsh, the scattered islands velvet with shadow in the low light, the white bits of beach far away. "See," he said. "It goes on being beautiful. It'll be here tomorrow."

"I know," John answered, impatiently. The moment had closed.

Back in the house, the others had opened some white wine, the champagne being drunk, and still sat at the table, the three females, gossiping. Where Joan sat had become the head. She turned, showing him a tearless face, and asked, "All right?"

"We're fine," he said, resenting it, though relieved, that the party went on without him.

In bed she explained, "I couldn't cry I guess because I cried so much all spring. It really wasn't fair. It's your idea, and you made it look as though I was kicking you out."

"I'm sorry," he said. "I couldn't stop. I wanted to but couldn't."

"You *didn't* want to. You loved it. You were having your way, making a general announcement."

"I love having it over," he admitted. "God, those kids were great. So brave and funny." John, returned to the house, had settled to a model airplane in his room, and kept shouting down to them, "I'm O.K. No sweat." "And the way," Richard went on, cozy in his relief, "they never questioned the reasons we gave. No thought of a third person. Not even Judith."

"That *was* touching," Joan said.

He gave her a hug. "You were great too. Thank you." Guiltily, he realized he did not feel separated.

5. Disagreeable, objectionable person.

"You still have Dickie to do," she told him. These words set before him a black mountain in the darkness; its cold breath, its near weight affected his chest. Of the four children Dickie was most nearly his conscience. Joan did not need to add, "That's one piece of your dirty work I won't do for you."

"I know. I'll do it. You go to sleep."

Within minutes, her breathing slowed, became oblivious and deep. It was quarter to midnight. Dickie's train from the concert would come in at one-fourteen. Richard set the alarm for one. He had slept atrociously for weeks. But whenever he closed his lids some glimpse of the last hours scorched them—Judith exhaling toward the ceiling in a kind of aversion, Bean's mute staring, the sunstruck growth of the field where he and John had rested. The mountain before him moved closer, moved within him; he was huge, momentous. The ache at the back of his throat felt stale. His wife slept as if slain beside him. When, exasperated by his hot lids, his crowded heart, he rose from bed and dressed, she awoke enough to turn over. He told her then, "If I could undo it all, I would."

"Where would you begin?" she asked. There was no place. Giving him courage, she was always giving him courage. He put on shoes without socks in the dark. The children were breathing in their rooms, the downstairs was hollow. In their confusion they had left lights burning. He turned off all but one, the kitchen overhead. The car started. He had hoped it wouldn't. He met only moonlight on the road; it seemed a diaphanous companion, flickering in the leaves along the roadside, haunting his rearview mirror like a pursuer, melting under his headlights. The center of town, not quite deserted, was eerie at this hour. A young cop in uniform kept company with a gang of T-shirted kids on the steps of the bank. Across from the railroad station, several bars kept open. Customers, mostly young, passed in and out of the warm night, savoring summer's novelty. Voices shouted from cars as they passed; an immense conversation seemed in progress. Richard parked and in his weariness put his head on the passenger seat, out of the commotion and wheeling lights. It was as when, in the movies, an assassin grimly carries his mission through the jostle of a carnival—except the movies cannot show the precipitous, palpable slope you cling to within. You cannot climb back down; you can only fall. The synthetic fabric of the car seat, warmed by his cheek, confided to him an ancient, distant scent of vanilla.

A train whistle caused him to lift his head. It was on time; he had hoped it would be late. The slender drawgates descended. The bell of approach tingled happily. The great metal body, horizontally fluted, rocked to a stop, and sleepy teen-agers disembarked, his son among them. Dickie did not show surprise that his father was meeting him at this terrible hour. He sauntered to the car with two friends, both taller than he. He said "Hi" to his father and took the

passenger's seat with an exhausted promptness that expressed gratitude. The friends got into the back, and Richard was grateful; a few
more minutes' postponement would be won by driving them home.

He asked, "How was the concert?"

"Groovy," one boy said from the back seat.

"It bit," the other said.

"It was O.K.," Dickie said, moderate by nature, so reasonable
that in his childhood the unreason of the world had given him
headaches, stomach aches, nausea. When the second friend had
been dropped off at his dark house, the boy blurted, "Dad, my eyes
are killing me with hay fever! I'm out there cutting that mothering
grass all day!"

"Do we still have those drops?"

"They didn't do any good last summer."

"They might this." Richard swung a U-turn on the empty street.
The drive home took a few minutes. The mountain was here, in his
throat. "Richard," he said, and felt the boy, slumped and rubbing
his eyes, go tense at his tone, "I didn't come to meet you just to
make your life easier. I came because your mother and I have some
news for you, and you're a hard man to get ahold of these days. It's
sad news."

"That's O.K." The reassurance came out soft, but quick, as if
released from the tip of a spring.

Richard had feared that his tears would return and choke him,
but the boy's manliness set an example, and his voice issued forth
steady and dry. "It's sad news, but it needn't be tragic news, at least
for you. It should have no practical effect on your life, though it's
bound to have an emotional effect. You'll work at your job, and go
back to school in September. Your mother and I are really proud of
what you're making of your life; we don't want that to change at
all."

"Yeah," the boy said lightly, on the intake of his breath, holding
himself up. They turned the corner; the church they went to loomed
like a gutted fort. The home of the woman Richard hoped to marry
stood across the green. Her bedroom light burned.

"Your mother and I," he said, "have decided to separate. For the
summer. Nothing legal, no divorce yet. We want to see how it feels.
For some years now, we haven't been doing enough for each other,
making each other as happy as we should be. Have you sensed
that?"

"No," the boy said. It was an honest, unemotional answer: true
or false in a quiz.

Glad for the factual basis, Richard pursued, even garrulously, the
details. His apartment across town, his utter accessibility, the split
vacation arrangements, the advantages to the children, the added
mobility and variety of the summer. Dickie listened, absorbing. "Do
the others know?"

Richard described how they had been told.

"How did they take it?"

"The girls pretty calmly. John flipped out; he shouted and ate a cigarette and made a salad out of his napkin and told us how much he hated school."

His brother chuckled. "He did?"

"Yeah. The school issue was more upsetting for him than Mom and me. He seemed to feel better for having exploded."

"He did?" The repetition was the first sign that he was stunned.

"Yes. Dickie, I want to tell you something. This last hour, waiting for your train to get in, has been about the worst of my life. I hate this. *Hate* it. My father would have died before doing it to me." He felt immensely lighter, saying this. He had dumped the mountain on the boy. They were home. Moving swiftly as a shadow, Dickie was out of the car, through the bright kitchen. Richard called after him, "Want a glass of milk or anything?"

"No thanks."

"Want us to call the course tomorrow and say you're too sick to work?"

"No, that's all right." The answer was faint, delivered at the door to his room; Richard listened for the slam of a tantrum. The door closed normally. The sound was sickening.

Joan had sunk into that first deep trough of sleep and was slow to awake. Richard had to repeat, "I told him."

"What did he say?"

"Nothing much. Could you go say good night to him? Please."

She left their room, without putting on a bathrobe. He sluggishly changed back into his pajamas and walked down the hall. Dickie was already in bed, Joan was sitting beside him, and the boy's bedside clock radio was murmuring music. When she stood, an inexplicable light—the moon?—outlined her body through the nightie. Richard sat on the warm place she had indented on the child's narrow mattress. He asked him, "Do you want the radio on like that?"

"It always is."

"Doesn't it keep you awake? It would me."

"No."

"Are you sleepy?"

"Yeah."

"Good. Sure you want to get up and go to work? You've had a big night."

"I want to."

Away at school this winter he had learned for the first time that you can go short of sleep and live. As an infant he had slept with an immobile, sweating intensity that had alarmed his babysitters. As the children aged, he became the first to go to bed, earlier for a time than his younger brother and sister. Even now, he would go slack in the middle of a television show, his sprawled legs hairy and brown. "O.K. Good boy, Dickie, listen. I love you so much, I never knew how much until now. No matter how this works out, I'll always be with you. Really."

Richard bent to kiss an averted face but his son, sinewy, turned and with wet cheeks embraced him and gave him a kiss, on the lips, passionate as a woman's. In his father's ear he moaned one word, the crucial, intelligent word: "*Why?*"

Why. It was a whistle of wind in a crack, a knife thrust, a window thrown open on emptiness. The white face was gone, the darkness was featureless. Richard had forgotten why.

1975

Dog's Death[1]

She must have been kicked unseen or brushed by a car.
Too young to know much, she was beginning to learn
To use the newspapers spread on the kitchen floor
And to win, wetting there, the words, "Good dog! Good dog!"

We thought her shy malaise was a shot reaction.   5
The autopsy disclosed a rupture in her liver.
As we teased her with play, blood was filling her skin
And her heart was learning to lie down forever.

Monday morning, as the children were noisily fed
And sent to school, she crawled beneath the youngest's bed.   10
We found her twisted and limp but still alive.
In the car to the vet's, on my lap, she tried

To bite my hand and died. I stroked her warm fur
And my wife called in a voice imperious with tears.
Though surrounded by love that would have upheld her,   15
Nevertheless she sank and, stiffening, disappeared.

Back home, we found that in the night her frame,
Drawing near to dissolution, had endured the shame
Of diarrhoea and had dragged across the floor
To a newspaper carelessly left there. *Good dog.*   20

1969

1. From *Midpoint* (1969).

PHILIP ROTH

1933–

From the moment Philip Roth's collection of stories *Goodbye, Columbus* won the Houghton-Mifflin Literary Fellowship for 1959, his career has received the ambiguous reward of much anxious concern, directed at it by critics and centered on whether he would develop the promise displayed in this first book. Ten years later, with *Portnoy's Complaint*, Roth became overnight the famous author of a "dirty" best-seller, yet his success only made his critics more uneasy. Was this gifted portrayer of Jewish middle-class life really more interested in scoring points off caricatures than in creating and exploring characters? Did his very facility with words inhibit the exercise of deeper sympathies and more humanly generous purposes?

Roth grew up in Newark, New Jersey, attended the branch of Rutgers University there, graduated from Bucknell University, took an M.A. in English literature at the University of Chicago, then served in the army. Over the years he has taught at a number of universities while receiving many awards and fellowships. Like John Barth, another "university" writer, Roth is an ironic humorist, although the impulse behind his early stories is darker and less playful. *Goodbye, Columbus* is about Jews on the verge of being or already having been assimilated into the larger American culture, and the stories confidently take the measure of their embattled heroes, as in *The Conversion of the Jews* or *Epstein* or the long title story. *Defender of the Faith* (printed here), arguably the best piece in the collection, is distinguished for the way Roth explores rather than exploits the conflict between personal feelings and religious loyalties as they are felt by Nathan Marx, a U.S. army sergeant in a Missouri training company near the end of World War II. Throughout *Goodbye, Columbus* the narrator's voice is centrally important: in some stories it is indistinguishable from that of a campus wiseguy; in others it reaches out to a calmer and graver sense of disparities between promises and performance.

Roth's first two novels, *Letting Go* (1962) and *When She Was Good* (1967), markedly extended the territory charted in *Goodbye, Columbus* and showed him eager and equipped to write about people other than Jews. *Letting Go* is conventional in technique and in its subjects—love, marriage, university life—but Roth's easy mastery of the look and feel of places and things is everywhere evident. F. Scott Fitzgerald is the American writer whose presence in these early novels is most strongly felt; in particular, the section from *Letting Go* told in the first person by a graduate student in English betrays its indebtedness to Fitzgerald's Nick Carraway, the narrator of *The Great Gatsby*. This Fitzgeraldian atmosphere, with its nostalgic presentation of adolescence and early romantic visions, is even more evident in *When She Was Good*, which is strong in its rendering of middle-American living rooms and kitchens, the flushed atmosphere of late-night 1950s sex in parked cars, or the lyrics of popular songs—bits of remembered trivia which Roth, like his predecessor, has a genius for bringing to life.

The less than overwhelming reception of his second novel probably helped Roth move away from relatively sober realism; certainly *Portnoy's Complaint* (1969) is a louder and more virtuoso performance than the earlier books. Alexander Portnoy's recollections of early childhood miseries are really a pretext for Roth to perform a succession of clever numbers in the inventive mode of a stand-up comic. Memories of growing up in New Jersey, listening to radio programs, playing softball, ogling girls at the ice-skating rink, or (most sensationally) masturbating in outlandish ways add up to an entertaining narrative which is sometimes crude but more often delicate and precise.

More recently Roth has moved toward fantasy and further showmanly operations: *Our Gang* (1970) attempted to do for Richard Nixon and his associates what actual events were to do one better; *The Breast* (1971) is a rather unamusing fable about a man's metamorphosis into that object; *The Great American Novel* (1973) sank under its weight of baseball lore dressed up in tall tales. But in *My Life As a Man* (1974) and *The Professor of Desire* (1977) Roth returned to matters which have traditionally preoccupied the social novelist and which inform his own best work: marriage, divorce, the family, being a Jew, and being psychoanalyzed—the pressures of civilization and the resultant individual discontents. And the more generous purposes and human sympathies necessary to deal seriously with such matters are in evidence as they have not always been.

Defender of the Faith[1]

In May of 1945, only a few weeks after the fighting had ended in Europe, I was rotated back to the States, where I spent the remainder of the war with a training company at Camp Crowder, Missouri. We had been racing across Germany so swiftly during the late winter and spring that when I boarded the plane that drizzly morning in Berlin, I couldn't believe our destination lay to the west. My mind might inform me otherwise, but there was an inertia of the spirit that told me we were flying to a new front where we would disembark and continue our push eastward—eastward until we'd circled the globe, marching through villages along whose twisting, cobbled streets crowds of the enemy would watch us take possession of what up till then they'd considered their own. I had changed enough in two years not to mind the trembling of the old people, the crying of the very young, the uncertain fear in the eyes of the once-arrogant. After two years I had been fortunate enough to develop an infantryman's heart which, like his feet, at first aches and swells, but finally grows horny enough for him to travel the weirdest paths without feeling a thing.

Captain Paul Barrett was to be my C. O. at Camp Crowder. The day I reported for duty he came out of his office to shake my hand. He was short, gruff, and fiery, and indoors or out he wore his polished helmet liner[2] down on his little eyes. In Europe he had received a battlefield commission and a serious chest wound, and had been returned to the States only a few months before. He spoke easily to me, but was, I thought, unnecessarily abusive towards the troops. At the evening formation, he introduced me.

"Gentlemen," he called. "Sergeant Thurston, as you know, is no longer with this Company. Your new First Sergeant is Sergeant Nathan Marx here. He is a veteran of the European theater and consequently will take no shit."

I sat up late in the orderly room that evening, trying halfheartedly to solve the riddle of duty rosters, personnel forms, and morn-

---

1. From *Goodbye, Columbus* (1959).
2. Plastic liner worn under a helmet to prevent chafing or bruising.

ing reports. The CQ[3] slept with his mouth open on a mattress on the floor. A trainee stood reading the next day's duty roster, which was posted on the bulletin board directly inside the screen door. It was a warm evening and I could hear the men's radios playing dance music over in the barracks.

The trainee, who I knew had been staring at me whenever I looked groggily into the forms, finally took a step in my direction.

"Hey, Sarge—we having a G.I. party tomorrow night?" A G.I. party is a barracks-cleaning.

"You usually have them on Friday nights?"

"Yes," and then he added mysteriously, "that's the whole thing."

"Then you'll have a G.I. party."

He turned away and I heard him mumbling. His shoulders were moving and I wondered if he was crying,

"What's your name, soldier?" I asked.

He turned, not crying at all. Instead his green-speckled eyes, long and narrow, flashed like fish in the sun. He walked over to me and sat on the edge of my desk.

He reached out a hand. "Sheldon," he said.

"Stand on your own two feet, Sheldon."

Climbing off the desk, he said, "Sheldon Grossbart." He smiled wider at the intimacy into which he'd led me.

"You against cleaning the barracks Friday night, Grossbart? Maybe we shouldn't have G.I. parties—maybe we should get a maid." My tone startled me: I felt like a Charlie McCarthy, with every top sergeant I had ever known as my Edgar Bergen.[4]

"No, Sergeant." He grew serious, but with a seriousness that seemed only to be the stifling of a smile. "It's just G.I. parties on Friday night, of all nights . . ."

He slipped up to the corner of the desk again—not quite sitting, but not quite standing either. He looked at me with those speckled eyes flashing and then made a gesture with his hand. It was very slight, no more than a rotation back and forth of the wrist, and yet it managed to exclude from our affairs everything else in the orderly room, to make the two of us the center of the world. It seemed, in fact, to exclude everything about the two of us except our hearts. "Sergeant Thurston was one thing," he whispered, an eye flashing to the sleeping CQ, "but we thought with you here, things might be a little different."

"We?"

"The Jewish personnel."

"Why?" I said, harshly.

He hesitated a moment, and then, uncontrollably, his hand went up to his mouth. "I mean . . ." he said.

3. Noncommissioned officer in charge of quarters at night or on weekends.
4. Bergen, a ventriloquist, and Charlie

McCarthy, his dummy, were a popular radio comedy team.

"What's on your mind?" Whether I was still angry at the "Sheldon" business or something else, I hadn't a chance to tell—but clearly I was angry.

". . . we thought you . . . Marx, you know, like Karl Marx. The Marx brothers. Those guys are all . . . M-A-R-X, isn't that how you spell it, Sergeant?"

"M-A-R-X."

"Fishbein said—" He stopped. "What I mean to say, Sergeant—" His face and neck were red, and his mouth moved but no words came out. In a moment, he raised himself to attention, gazing down at me. It was as though he had suddenly decided he could expect no more sympathy from me than from Thurston, the reason being that I was of Thurston's faith and not his. The young man had managed to confuse himself as to what my faith really was, but I felt no desire to straighten him out. Very simply, I didn't like him.

When I did nothing but return his gaze, he spoke, in an altered tone. "You see, Sergeant," he explained to me, "Friday nights, Jews are supposed to go to services."

"Did Sergeant Thurston tell you you couldn't go to them when there was a G.I. party?"

"No."

"Did he say you had to stay and scrub the floors?"

"No, Sergeant."

"Did the Captain say you had to stay and scrub the floors?"

"That isn't it, Sergeant. It's the other guys in the barracks." He leaned toward me. "They think we're goofing off. But we're not. That's when Jews go to services, Friday night. We have to."

"Then go."

"But the other guys make accusations. They have no right."

"That's not the Army's problem, Grossbart. It's a personal problem you'll have to work out yourself."

"But it's un*fair*."

I got up to leave. "There's nothing I can do about it," I said.

Grossbart stiffened in front of me. "But this is a matter of *religion*, sir."

"Sergeant."

"I mean 'Sergeant,' " he said, almost snarling.

"Look, go see the chaplain. The I.G.[5] You want to see Captain Barrett, I'll arrange an appointment."

"No, no. I don't want to make trouble, Sergeant. That's the first thing they throw up to you. I just want my rights!"

"Damn it, Grossbart, stop whining. You have your rights. You can stay and scrub floors or you can go to *shul*—"[6]

The smile swam in again. Spittle gleamed at the corners of his mouth. "You mean church, Sergeant."

"I mean *shul*, Grossbart!" I walked past him and outside. Near me I heard the scrunching of a guard's boots on gravel. In the lighted windows of the barracks the young men in T-shirts and fatigue pants were sitting on their bunks, polishing their rifles. Suddenly there was a light rustling behind me. I turned and saw Grossbart's dark frame fleeing back to the barracks, racing to tell his Jewish friends that they were right—that like Karl and Harpo, I was one of them.

The next morning, while chatting with the Captain, I recounted the incident of the previous evening, as if to unburden myself of it. Somehow in the telling it seemed to the Captain that I was not so much explaining Grossbart's position as defending it.

"Marx, I'd fight side by side with a nigger if the fellow proved to me he was a man. I pride myself," the Captain said looking out the window, "that I've got an open mind. Consequently, Sergeant, nobody gets special treatment here, for the good *or* the bad. All a man's got to do is prove himself. A man fires well on the range, I give him a weekend pass. He scores high in PT, he gets a weekend pass. He *earns* it." He turned from the window and pointed a finger at me. "You're a Jewish fellow, am I right, Marx?"

"Yes, sir."

"And I admire you. I admire you because of the ribbons on your chest, not because you had a hem stitched on your dick before you were old enough to even know you had one. I judge a man by what he shows me on the field of battle, Sergeant. It's what he's got *here*," he said, and then, though I expected he would point to his heart, he jerked a thumb towards the buttons straining to hold his blouse across his belly. "Guts," he said.

"Okay, sir, I only wanted to pass on to you how the men felt."

"Mr. Marx, you're going to be old before your time if you worry about how the men feel. Leave that stuff to the Chaplain—pussy, the clap, church picnics with the little girls from Joplin, that's all his business, not yours. Let's us train these fellas to shoot straight. If the Jewish personnel feels the other men are accusing them of goldbricking . . . well, I just don't know. Seems awful funny how suddenly the Lord is calling so loud in Private Grossman's ear he's just got to run to church."

"Synagogue," I said.

"Synagogue is right, Sergeant. I'll write that down for handy reference. Thank you for stopping by."

That evening, a few minutes before the company gathered outside the orderly room for the chow formation, I called the CQ, Corporal Robert LaHill, in to see me. LaHill was a dark burly fellow whose hair curled out of his clothes wherever it could. He carried a glaze in his eyes that made one think of caves and dinosaurs. "LaHill," I said, "when you take the formation, remind the men that they're free to attend church services *whenever* they are held, provided they report to the orderly room before they leave the area."

LaHill didn't flicker; he scratched his wrist, but gave no indication that he'd heard or understood.

"LaHill," I said, *"church.* You remember? Church, priest, Mass, confession . . ."

He curled one lip into a ghastly smile; I took it for a signal that for a second he had flickered back up into the human race.

"Jewish personnel who want to attend services this evening are to fall out in front of the orderly room at 1900." And then I added, "By order of Captain Barrett."

A little while later, as a twilight softer than any I had seen that year dropped over Camp Crowder, I heard LaHill's thick, inflectionless voice outside my window: "Give me your ears, troopers. Toppie says for me to tell you that at 1900 hours all Jewish personnel is to fall out in front here if they wants to attend the Jewish Mass."

At seven o'clock, I looked out of the orderly-room window and saw three soldiers in starched khakis standing alone on the dusty quadrangle. They looked at their watches and fidgeted while they whispered back and forth. It was getting darker, and alone on the deserted field they looked tiny. When I walked to the door I heard the noises of the G.I. party coming from the surrounding barracks —bunks being pushed to the wall, faucets pounding water into buckets, brooms whisking at the wooden floors. In the windows big puffs of cloth moved round and round, cleaning the dirt away for Saturday's inspection. I walked outside and the moment my foot hit the ground I thought I heard Grossbart, who was now in the center, call to the other two, "Ten-*hut!*" Or maybe when they all three jumped to attention, I imagined I heard the command.

At my approach, Grossbart stepped forward. "Thank you, sir," he said.

"Sergeant, Grossbart," I reminded him. "You call officers 'Sir.' I'm not an officer. You've been in the Army three weeks—you know that."

He turned his palms out at his sides to indicate that, in truth, he and I lived beyond convention. "Thank you, anyway," he said.

"Yes," the tall boy behind him said. "Thanks a lot."

And the third whispered, "Thank you," but his mouth barely fluttered so that he did not alter by more than a lip's movement, the posture of attention.

"For what?" I said.

Grossbart snorted, happily. "For the announcement before. The Corporal's announcement. It helped. It made it . . ."

"Fancier." It was the tall boy finishing Grossbart's sentence.

Grossbart smiled. "He means formal, sir. Public," he said to me.

"Now it won't seem as though we're just taking off, goldbricking, because the work has begun."

"It was by order of Captain Barrett," I said.

"Ahh, but you pull a little weight . . ." Grossbart said. "So we thank you." Then he turned to his companions. "Sergeant Marx, I want you to meet Larry Fishbein."

The tall boy stepped forward and extended his hand. I shook it. "You from New York?" he asked.

"Yes."

"Me too." He had a cadaverous face that collapsed inward from his cheekbone to his jaw, and when he smiled—as he did at the news of our communal attachment—revealed a mouthful of bad teeth. He blinked his eyes a good deal, as though he were fighting back tears. "What borough?" he asked.

I turned to Grossbart. "It's five after seven. What time are services?"

"*Shul*," he smiled, "is in ten minutes. I want you to meet Mickey Halpern. This is Nathan Marx, our Sergeant."

The third boy hopped forward. "Private Michael Halpern." He saluted.

"Salute officers, Halpern." The boy dropped his hand, and in his nervousness checked to see if his shirt pockets were buttoned on the way down.

"Shall I march them over, sir?" Grossbart asked, "or are you coming along?"

From behind Grossbart, Fishbein piped up. "Afterwards they're having refreshments. A Ladies' Auxiliary from St. Louis, the rabbi told us last week."

"The chaplain," whispered Halpern.

"You're welcome to come along," Grossbart said.

To avoid his plea, I looked away, and saw, in the windows of the barracks, a cloud of faces staring out at the four of us.

"Look, hurry out of here, Grossbart."

"Okay, then," he said. He turned to the others. "Double time, *march!*" and they started off, but ten feet away Grossbart spun about, and running backwards he called to me, "Good *shabus,*[7] sir." And then the three were swallowed into the Missouri dusk.

Even after they'd disappeared over the parade grounds, whose green was now a deep twilight blue, I could hear Grossbart singing the double-time cadence, and as it grew dimmer and dimmer it suddenly touched some deep memory—as did the slant of light— and I was remembering the shrill sounds of a Bronx playground, where years ago, beside the Grand Concourse,[8] I had played on long spring evenings such as this. Those thin fading sounds . . . It was a pleasant memory for a young man so far from peace and home, and it brought so very many recollections with it that I began

7. Sabbath.   8. Bronx, New York, expressway.

to grow exceedingly tender about myself. In fact, I indulged myself
to a reverie so strong that I felt within as though a hand had opened
and was reaching down inside. It had to reach so very far to touch
me. It had to reach past those days in the forests of Belgium and the
dying I'd refused to weep over; past the nights in those German
farmhouses whose books we'd burned to warm us, and which I
couldn't bother to mourn; past those endless stretches when I'd shut
off all softness I might feel for my fellows, and managed even to
deny myself the posture of a conqueror—the swagger that I, as a
Jew, might well have worn as my boots whacked against the rubble
of Münster, Braunschweig, and finally Berlin.

But now one night noise, one rumor of home and time past, and
memory plunged down through all I had anesthetized and came to
what I suddenly remembered to be myself. So it was not altogether
curious that in search of more of me I found myself following
Grossbart's tracks to Chapel No. 3 where the Jewish services were
being held.

I took a seat in the last row, which was empty. Two rows in front
sat Grossbart, Fishbein, and Halpern, each holding a little white
dixie cup. Fishbein was pouring the contents of his cup into Grossbart's, and Grossbart looked mirthful as the liquid drew a purple arc
between his hand and Fishbein's. In the glary yellow light, I saw the
chaplain on the pulpit chanting the first line of the responsive reading. Grossbart's prayerbook remained closed on his lap; he swished
the cup around. Only Halpern responded in prayer. The fingers of
his right hand were spread wide across the cover of the book, and
his cap was pulled down low onto his brow so that it was round like
a *yarmulke*[9] rather than long and pointed. From time to time,
Grossbart wet his lips at the cup's edge; Fishbein, his long yellow
face, a dying light bulb, looked from here to there, leaning forward
at the neck to catch sight of the faces down the row, in front—then
behind. He saw me and his eyelids beat a tattoo. His elbow slid into
Grossbart's side, his neck inclined towards his friend, and then,
when the congregation responded, Grossbart's voice was among
them. Fishbein looked into his book now too; his lips, however,
didn't move.

Finally it was time to drink the wine. The chaplain smiled down
at them as Grossbart swigged in one long gulp, Halpern sipped,
meditating, and Fishbein faked devotion with an empty cup.

At last the chaplain spoke: "As I look down amongst the congregation—" he grinned at the word, "this night, I see many new
faces, and I want to welcome you to Friday night services here at
Camp Crowder. I am Major Leo Ben Ezra, your chaplain . . ."
Though an American, the chaplain spoke English very deliberately,
syllabically almost, as though to communicate, above all, to the lip-
readers in the audience. "I have only a few words to say before we

9. Skullcap.

adjourn to the refreshment room where the kind ladies of the Temple Sinai, St. Louis, Missouri, have a nice setting for you."

Applause and whistling broke out. After a momentary grin, the chaplain raised his palms to the congregation, his eyes flicking upward a moment, as if to remind the troops where they were and Who Else might be in attendance. In the sudden silence that followed, I thought I heard Grossbart's cackle—"Let the goyim[1] clean the floors!" Were those the words? I wasn't sure, but Fishbein, grinning, nudged Halpern. Halpern looked dumbly at him, then went back to his prayerbook, which had been occupying him all through the rabbi's talk. One hand tugged at the black kinky hair that stuck out under his cap. His lips moved.

The rabbi continued. "It is about the food that I want to speak to you for a moment. I know, I know, I know," he intoned, wearily, "how in the mouths of most of you the *trafe*[2] food tastes like ashes. I know how you gag, some of you, and how your parents suffer to think of their children eating foods unclean and offensive to the palate. What can I tell you? I can only say close your eyes and swallow as best you can. Eat what you must to live and throw away the rest. I wish I could help more. For those of you who find this impossible, may I ask that you try and try, but then come to see me in private where, if your revulsion is such, we will have to seek aid from those higher up."

A round of chatter rose and subsided; then everyone sang "Ain Kelohanoh", after all those years I discovered I still knew the words.

Suddenly, the service over, Grossbart was upon me. "Higher up? He means the General?"

"Hey, Shelly," Fishbein interrupted, "he means God." He smacked his face and looked at Halpern. "How high can you go!"

"Shhh!" Grossbart said. "What do you think, Sergeant?"

"I don't know. You better ask the chaplain."

"I'm going to. I'm making an appointment to see him in private. So is Mickey."

Halpern shook his head. "No, no, Sheldon . . ."

"You have rights, Mickey. They can't push us around."

"It's okay. It bothers my mother, not me . . ."

Grossbart looked at me. "Yesterday he threw up. From the hash. It was all ham and God knows what else."

"I have a cold—that was why," Halpern said. He pushed his *yamalkah* back into a cap.

"What about you, Fishbein?" I asked. "You kosher too?"

He flushed, which made the yellow more gray than pink. "A little. But I'll let it ride. I have a very strong stomach. And I don't eat a lot anyway . . ." I continued to look at him, and he held up his wrist to re-enforce what he'd just said. His watch was tightened to

---

1. Gentiles.   2. Unkosher—unfit to eat.

the last hole and he pointed that out to me. "So I don't mind."

"But services are important to you?" I asked him.

He looked at Grossbart. "Sure, sir."

"Sergeant."

"Not so much at home," said Grossbart, coming between us, "but away from home it gives one a sense of his Jewishness."

"We have to stick together," Fishbein said.

I started to walk towards the door; Halpern stepped back to make way for me.

"That's what happened in Germany," Grossbart was saying, loud enough for me to hear. "They didn't stick together. They let themselves get pushed around."

I turned. "Look, Grossbart, this is the Army, not summer camp."

He smiled. "So?" Halpern tried to sneak off, but Grossbart held his arm. "So?" he said again.

"Grossbart," I asked, "how old are you?"

"Nineteen."

"And you?" I said to Fishbein.

"The same. The same month even."

"And what about him?" I pointed to Halpern, who'd finally made it safely to the door.

"Eighteen," Grossbart whispered. "But he's like he can't tie his shoes or brush his teeth himself. I feel sorry for him."

"I feel sorry for all of us, Grossbart, but just act like a man. Just don't overdo it."

"Overdo what, sir?"

"The sir business. Don't overdo that," I said, and I left him standing there. I passed by Halpern but he did not look up. Then I was outside, black surrounded me—but behind I heard Grossbart call, "Hey, Mickey, *liebschen*,[3] come on back. Refreshments!"

Liebschen! My grandmother's word for me!

One morning, a week later, while I was working at my desk, Captain Barrett shouted for me to come into his office. When I entered, he had his helmet liner squashed down so that I couldn't even see his eyes. He was on the phone, and when he spoke to me, he cupped one hand over the mouthpiece.

"Who the fuck is Grossbart?"

"Third platoon, Captain," I said. "A trainee."

"What's all this stink about food? His mother called a goddam congressman about the food . . ." He uncovered the mouthpiece and slid his helmet up so I could see the curl of his bottom eyelash. "Yes, sir," he said into the phone. "Yes, sir. I'm still here, sir. I'm asking Marx here right now . . ."

He covered the mouthpiece again and looked back to me. "Light-foot Harry's on the phone," he said, between his teeth. "This congressman calls General Lyman who calls Colonel Sousa who calls

3. Darling.

the Major who calls me. They're just dying to stick this thing on me. What's a matter," he shook the phone at me, "I don't feed the troops? What the hell is this?"

"Sir, Grossbart is strange . . ." Barrett greeted that with a mockingly indulgent smile. I altered my approach. "Captain, he's a very orthodox Jew and so he's only allowed to eat certain foods."

"He throws up, the congressman said. Every time he eats something his mother says he throws up!"

"He's accustomed to observing the dietary laws, Captain."

"So why's his old lady have to call the White House!"

"Jewish parents, sir, they're apt to be more protective than you expect. I mean Jews have a very close family life. A boy goes away from home, sometimes the mother is liable to get very upset. Probably the boy *mentioned* something in a letter and his mother misinterpreted."

"I'd like to punch him one right in the mouth. There's a goddam war on and he wants a silver platter!"

"I don't think the boy's to blame, sir. I'm sure we can straighten it out by just asking him. Jewish parents worry—"

"*All* parents worry, for Christ sake. But they don't get on their high horse and start pulling strings—"

I interrupted, my voice higher, tighter than before. "The home life, Captain, is so very important . . . but you're right, it may sometimes get out of hand. It's a very wonderful thing, Captain, but because it's so close, this kind of thing—"

He didn't listen any longer to my attempt to present both myself and Lightfoot Harry with an explanation for the letter. He turned back to the phone. "Sir?" he said. "Sir, Marx here tells me Jews have a tendency to be pushy. He says he thinks he can settle it right here in the Company . . . Yes, sir . . . I *will* call back, sir, soon as I can . . ." He hung up. "Where are the men, Sergeant?"

"On the range."

With a whack on the top, he crushed his helmet over his eyes, and charged out of his chair. "We're going for a ride."

The Captain drove and I sat beside him. It was a hot spring day and under my newly starched fatigues it felt as though my armpits were melting down onto my sides and chest. The roads were dry and by the time we reached the firing range, my teeth felt gritty with dust though my mouth had been shut the whole trip. The Captain slammed the brakes on and told me to get the hell out and find Grossbart.

I found him on his belly, firing wildly at the 500 feet target. Waiting their turns behind him were Halpern and Fishbein. Fishbein, wearing a pair of rimless G.I. glasses I hadn't seen on him before, gave the appearance of an old peddler who would gladly have sold you the rifle and cartridges that were slung all over him. I stood back by the ammo boxes, waiting for Grossbart to finish spraying the distant targets. Fishbein straggled back to stand near me.

"Hello, Sergeant Marx."

"How are you?" I mumbled.

"Fine, thank you. Sheldon's really a good shot."

"I didn't notice."

"I'm not so good, but I think I'm getting the hang of it now . . . Sergeant, I don't mean to, you know, ask what I shouldn't . . ." The boy stopped. He was trying to speak intimately but the noise of the shooting necessitated that he shout at me.

"What is it?" I asked. Down the range I saw Captain Barrett standing up in the jeep, scanning the line for me and Grossbart.

"My parents keep asking and asking where we're going. Everybody says the Pacific. I don't care, but my parents . . . If I could relieve their minds I think I could concentrate more on my shooting."

"I don't know where, Fishbein. Try to concentrate anyway."

"Sheldon says you might be able to find out—"

"I don't know a thing, Fishbein. You just take it easy, and don't let Sheldon—"

"*I'm* taking it easy, Sergeant. It's at home—"

Grossbart had just finished on the line and was dusting his fatigues with one hand. I left Fishbein's sentence in the middle.

"Grossbart, the Captain wants to see you."

He came toward us. His eyes blazed and twinkled. "Hi!"

"Don't point that goddam rifle!"

"I wouldn't shoot you, Sarge." He gave me a smile wide as a pumpkin as he turned the barrel aside.

"Damn you, Grossbart—this is no joke! Follow me."

I walked ahead of him and had the awful suspicion that behind me Grossbart was *marching*, his rifle on his shoulder, as though he were a one-man detachment.

At the jeep he gave the Captain a rifle salute. "Private Sheldon Grossbart, sir."

"At ease, Grossman." The captain slid over to the empty front seat, and crooking a finger, invited Grossbart closer.

"Bart, sir. Sheldon Gross*bart*. It's a common error." Grossbart nodded to me—*I understand*, he indicated. I looked away, just as the mess truck pulled up to the range, disgorging a half dozen K.P.'s with rolled-up sleeves. The mess sergeant screamed at them while they set up the chow line equipment.

"Grossbart, your mama wrote some congressman that we don't feed you right. Do you know that?" the Captain said.

"It was my father, sir. He wrote to Representative Franconi that my religion forbids me to eat certain foods."

"What religion is that, Grossbart?"

"Jewish."

"Jewish, *sir*," I said to Grossbart.

"Excuse me, sir. 'Jewish, sir.'"

"What have you been living on?" the Captain asked. "You've been in the Army a month already. You don't look to me like you're falling to pieces."

"I eat because I have to, sir. But Sergeant Marx will testify to the fact that I don't eat one mouthful more than I need to in order to survive."

"Marx," Barrett asked, "is that so?"

"I've never seen Grossbart eat, sir," I said.

"But you heard the rabbi," Grossbart said. "He told us what to do, and I listened."

The Captain looked at me. "Well, Marx?"

"I still don't know what he eats and doesn't eat, sir."

Grossbart raised his rifle, as though to offer it to me. "But, Sergeant—"

"Look, Grossbart, just answer the Captain's questions!" I said sharply.

Barrett smiled at me and I resented it. "All right, Grossbart," he said, "What is it you want? The little piece of paper? You want out?"

"No, sir. Only to be allowed to live as a Jew. And for the others, too."

"What others?"

"Fishbein, sir, and Halpern."

"They don't like the way we serve either?"

"Halpern throws up, sir. I've seen it."

"I thought *you* threw up."

"Just once, sir. I didn't know the sausage was sausage."

"We'll give menus, Grossbart. We'll show training films about the food, so you can identify when we're trying to poison you."

Grossbart did not answer. Out before me, the men had been organized into two long chow lines. At the tail end of one I spotted Fishbein—or rather, his glasses spotted me. They winked sunlight back at me like a friend. Halpern stood next to him, patting inside his collar with a khaki handkerchief. They moved with the line as it began to edge up towards the food. The mess sergeant was still screaming at the K.P.'s, who stood ready to ladle out the food, bewildered. For a moment I was actually terrorized by the thought that somehow the mess sergeant was going to get involved in Grossbart's problem.

"Come over here, Marx," the Captain said to me. "Marx, you're a Jewish fella, am I right?"

I played straight man. "Yes, sir."

"How long you been in the Army? Tell this boy."

"Three years and two months."

"A year in combat, Grossbart. Twelve goddam months in combat all through Europe. I admire this man," the Captain said, snapping a wrist against my chest. But do you hear him peeping about the food? Do you? I want an answer, Grossbart. Yes or no."

"No, sir."

"And why not? He's a Jewish fella."

"Some things are more important to some Jews than other things to other Jews."

Barrett blew up. "Look, Grossbart, Marx here is a good man, a goddam *hero*. When you were sitting on your sweet ass in high school, Sergeant Marx was killing Germans. Who does more for the Jews, you by throwing up over a lousy piece of sausage, a piece of firstcut meat—or Marx by killing those Nazi bastards? If I was a Jew, Grossbart, I'd kiss this man's feet. He's a goddam hero, you know that? And *he* eats what we give him. Why do you have to cause trouble is what I want to know! What is it you're buckin' for, a discharge?"

"No, sir."

"I'm talking to a *wall*! Sergeant, get him out of my way." Barrett pounced over to the driver's seat. "I'm going to see the chaplain!" The engine roared, the jeep spun around, and then, raising a whirl of dust, the Captain was headed back to camp.

For a moment, Grossbart and I stood side by side, watching the jeep. Then he looked at me and said, "I don't want to start trouble. That's the first thing they toss up to us."

When he spoke I saw that his teeth were white and straight, and the sight of them suddenly made me understand that Grossbart actually did have parents: that once upon a time someone had taken little Sheldon to the dentist. He was someone's son. Despite all the talk about his parents, it was hard to believe in Grossbart as a child, an heir—as related by blood to anyone, mother, father, or, above all, to me. This realization led me to another.

"What does your father do, Grossbart?" I asked, as we started to walk back towards the chow line.

"He's a tailor."

"An American?"

"Now, yes. A son in the Army," he said, jokingly.

"And your mother?" I asked.

He winked. "A *ballabusta*[4]—she practically sleeps with a dust-cloth in her hand."

"She's also an immigrant?"

"All she talks is Yiddish, still."

"And your father too?"

"A little English. 'Clean,' 'Press,' 'Take the pants in . . .' That's

4. Good housekeeper.

the extent of it. But they're good to me . . ."

"Then, Grossbart—" I reached out and stopped him. He turned towards me and when our eyes met his seemed to jump back, shiver in their sockets. He looked afraid. "Grossbart, then you were the one who wrote that letter, weren't you?"

It took only a second or two for his eyes to flash happy again. "Yes." He walked on, and I kept pace. "It's what my father *would* have written if he had known how. It was his name, though. *He* signed it. He even mailed it. I sent it home. For the New York postmark."

I was astonished, and he saw it. With complete seriousness, he thrust his right arm in front of me. "Blood is blood, Sergeant," he said, pinching the blue vein in his wrist.

"What the hell *are* you trying to do, Grossbart? I've seen you eat. Do you know that? I told the Captain I don't know what you eat, but I've seen you eat like a hound at chow."

"We work hard, Sergeant. We're in training. For a furnace to work, you've got to feed it coal."

"If you wrote the letter, Grossbart, then why did you say you threw up all the time?"

"I was really talking about Mickey there. But he would never write, Sergeant, though I pleaded with him. He'll waste away to nothing if I don't help. Sergeant, I used my name, my father's name, but it's Mickey and Fishbein too I'm watching out for."

"You're a regular Messiah, aren't you?"

We were at the chow line now.

"That's a good one, Sergeant." He smiled. "But who knows? Who can tell? Maybe you're the Messiah . . . a little bit. What Mickey says is the Messiah is a collective idea. He went to Yeshivah, Mickey, for a while. He says *together* we're the Messiah.[5] Me a little bit, you a little bit . . . You should hear that kid talk, Sergeant, when he gets going."

"Me a little bit, you a little bit. You'd like to believe that, wouldn't you, Grossbart? That makes everything so clean for you."

"It doesn't seem too bad a thing to believe, Sergeant. It only means we should all give a little, is all . . ."

I walked off to eat my rations with the other noncoms.

Two days later a letter addressed to Captain Barrett passed over my desk. It had come through the chain of command—from the office of Congressman Franconi, where it had been received, to General Lyman, to Colonel Sousa, to Major Lamont, to Captain Barrett. I read it over twice while the Captain was as the officers' mess. It was dated May 14th, the day Barrett had spoken with Grossbart on the rifle range.

---

5. "Messiah": the deliverer who will rule over the people of Israel at the end of time. "Yeshivah": Jewish institution of learning.

Dear Congressman:

First let me thank you for your interest in behalf of my son, Private Sheldon Grossbart. Fortunately, I was able to speak with Sheldon on the phone the other night, and I think I've been able to solve our problem. He is, as I mentioned in my last letter, a very religious boy, and it was only with the greatest difficulty that I could persuade him that the religious thing to do—what God Himself would want Sheldon to do—would be to suffer the pangs of religious remorse for the good of his country and all mankind. It took some doing, Congressman, but finally he saw the light. In fact, what he said (and I wrote down the words on a scratch pad so as never to forget), what he said was, "I guess you're right, Dad. So many millions of my fellow Jews gave up their lives to the enemy, the least I can do is live for a while minus a bit of my heritage so as to help end this struggle and regain for all the children of God dignity and humanity." That, Congressman, would make any father proud.

By the way, Sheldon wanted me to know—and to pass on to you—the name of a soldier who helped him reach this decision: SERGEANT NATHAN MARX. Sergeant Marx is a combat veteran who is Sheldon's First Sergeant. This man has helped Sheldon over some of the first hurdles he's had to face in the Army, and is in part responsible for Sheldon's changing his mind about the dietary laws. I know Sheldon would appreciate any recognition Marx could receive.

Thank you and good luck. I look forward to seeing your name on the next election ballot.

> Respectfully,
> Samuel E. Grossbart

Attached to the Grossbart communiqué was a communiqué addressed to General Marshall Lyman, the post commander, and signed by Representative Charles E. Franconi of the House of Representatives. The communiqué informed General Lyman that Sergeant Nathan Marx was a credit to the U.S. Army and the Jewish people.

What was Grossbart's motive in recanting? Did he feel he'd gone too far? Was the letter a strategic retreat—a crafty attempt to strengthen what he considered our alliance? Or had he actually changed his mind, via an imaginary dialogue between Grossbart *père* and *fils*? I was puzzled, but only for a few days—that is, only until I realized that whatever his reasons, he had actually decided to disappear from my life: he was going to allow himself to become just another trainee. I saw him at inspection but he never winked; at chow formations but he never flashed me a sign; on Sundays, with the other trainees, he would sit around watching the noncoms' softball team, for whom I pitched, but not once did he speak an unnecessary or unusual word to me. Fishbein and Halpern retreated from sight too, at Grossbart's command I was sure. Apparently he'd seen that wisdom lay in turning back before he plunged us over into the ugliness of privilege undeserved. Our separation allowed me to forgive him our past encounters, and, finally, to admire him for his good sense.

Meanwhile, free of Grossbart, I grew used to my job and my administrative tasks. I stepped on a scale one day and discovered I had truly become a noncombatant: I had gained seven pounds. I found patience to get past the first three pages of a book. I thought about the future more and more, and wrote letters to girls I'd known before the war—I even got a few answers. I sent away to Columbia for a Law School catalogue. I continued to follow the war in the Pacific, but it was not my war and I read of bombings and battles like a civilian. I thought I could see the end in sight and sometimes at night I dreamed that I was walking on the streets of Manhattan—Broadway, Third Avenue, and 116th Street, where I had lived those three years I'd attended Columbia College. I curled myself around these dreams and I began to be happy.

And then one Saturday when everyone was away and I was alone in the orderly room reading a month-old copy of *The Sporting News*, Grossbart reappeared.

"You a baseball fan, Sergeant?"

I looked up. "How are you?"

"Fine," Grossbart said. "They're making a soldier out of me."

"How are Fishbein and Halpern?"

"Coming along," he said. "We've got no training this afternoon. They're at the movies."

"How come you're not with them?"

"I wanted to come over and say hello."

He smiled—a shy, regular-guy smile, as though he and I well knew that our friendship drew its sustenance from unexpected visits, remembered birthdays, and borrowed lawnmowers. At first it of-fended me, and then the feeling was swallowed by the general uneasiness I felt at the thought that everyone on the post was locked away in a dark movie theater and I was here alone with Grossbart. I folded my paper.

"Sergeant," he said, "I'd like to ask a favor. It is a favor and I'm making no bones about it."

He stopped, allowing me to refuse him a hearing—which, of course, forced me into a courtesy I did not intend. "Go ahead."

"Well, actually it's two favors."

I said nothing.

"The first one's about these rumors. Everybody says we're going to the Pacific."

"As I told your friend Fishbein, I don't know. You'll just have to wait to find out. Like everybody else."

"You think there's a chance of any of us going East?"

"Germany," I said, "maybe."

"I meant New York."

"I don't think so, Grossbart. Offhand."

"Thanks for the information, Sergeant," he said.

"It's not information, Grossbart. Just what I surmise."

"It certainly would be good to be near home. My parents . . . you know." He took a step towards the door and then turned back. "Oh the other thing. May I ask the other?"

"What is it?"

"The other thing is—I've got relatives in St. Louis and they say they'll give me a whole Passover dinner if I can get down there. God, Sergeant, that'd mean an awful lot to me."

I stood up. "No passes during basic, Grossbart."

"But we're off from now till Monday morning, Sergeant. I could leave the post and no one would even know."

"I'd know. You'd know."

"But that's all. Just the two of us. Last night I called my aunt and you should have heard her. 'Come, come,' she said. 'I got gefilte fish, *chrain*[6] the works!' Just a day, Sergeant, I'd take the blame if anything happened."

"The captain isn't here to sign a pass."

"You could sign."

"Look, Grossbart—"

"Sergeant, for two months practically I've been eating *trafe* till I want to die."

"I thought you'd made up your mind to live with it. To be minus a little bit of heritage."

He pointed a finger at me. "You!" he said. "That wasn't for you to read!"

"I read it. So what."

"That letter was addressed to a congressman."

"Grossbart, don't feed me any crap. You *wanted* me to read it."

"Why are you persecuting me, Sergeant?"

"Are you kidding!"

"I've run into this before," he said, "but never from my own!"

"Get out of here, Grossbart! Get the hell out of my sight!"

He did not move. "Ashamed, that's what you are. So you take it out on the rest of us. They say Hitler himself was half a Jew. Seeing this, I wouldn't doubt it!"

"What are you trying to do with me, Grossbart? What are you after? You want me to give you special privileges, to change the

6. Horseradish.

food, to find out about your orders, to give you weekend passes."

"You even talk like a goy!" Grossbart shook his fist. "Is this a weekend pass I'm asking for? Is a Seder[7] sacred or not?"

Seder! It suddenly occurred to me that Passover had been celebrated weeks before. I confronted Grossbart with the fact.

"That's right," he said. "Who says no? A month ago, and *I* was in the field eating hash! And now all I ask is a simple favor—a Jewish boy I thought would understand. My aunt's willing to go out of her way—to make a Seder a month later—" He turned to go, mumbling.

"Come back here!" I called. He stopped and looked at me. "Grossbart, why can't you be like the rest? Why do you have to stick out like a sore thumb? Why do you beg for special treatment?"

"Because I'm a Jew, Sergeant. I *am* different. Better, maybe not. But different."

"This is a war, Grossbart. For the time being *be* the same."

"I refuse."

"What?"

"I refuse. I can't stop being me, that's all there is to it." Tears came to his eyes. "It's a hard thing to be a Jew. But now I see what Mickey says—it's a harder thing to stay one." He raised a hand sadly toward me. "Look at you."

"Stop crying!"

"Stop this, stop that, stop the other thing! You stop, Sergeant. Stop closing your heart to your own!" And wiping his face with his sleeve, he ran out the door. "The least we can do for one another . . . the least . . ."

An hour later I saw Grossbart headed across the field. He wore a pair of starched khakis and carried only a little leather ditty bag. I went to the door and from the outside felt the heat of the day. It was quiet—not a soul in sight except over by the mess hall four K.P.'s sitting round a pan, sloped forward from the waists, gabbing and peeling potatoes in the sun.

"Grossbart!" I called.

He looked toward me and continued walking.

"Grossbart, get over here!"

He turned and stepped into his long shadow. Finally he stood before me.

"Where are you going?" I said.

"St. Louis. I don't care."

"You'll get caught without a pass."

"So I'll get caught without a pass."

"You'll go to the stockade."

"I'm in the stockade." He made an about-face and headed off.

I let him go only a step: "Come back here," I said, and he

7. Ceremonial dinner on the first evening of Passover.

followed me into the office, where I typed out a pass and signed the Captain's name and my own initials after it.

He took the pass from me and then, a moment later, he reached out and grabbed my hand. "Sergeant, you don't know how much this means to me."

"Okay. Don't get in any trouble."

"I wish I could show you how much this means to me."

"Don't do me any favors. Don't write any more congressmen for citations."

Amazingly, he smiled. "You're right. I won't. But let me do something."

"Bring me a piece of that gefilte fish. Just get out of here."

"I will! With a slice of carrot and a little horseradish. I won't forget."

"All right. Just show your pass at the gate. And don't tell *any-body*."

"I won't. It's a month late, but a good Yom Tov to you."

"Good Yom Tov,[8] Grossbart," I said.

"You're a good Jew, Sergeant. You like to think you have a hard heart, but underneath you're a fine decent man. I mean that."

Those last three words touched me more than any words from Grossbart's mouth had the right to. "All right, Grossbart. Now call me 'sir' and get the hell out of here."

He ran out the door and was gone. I felt very pleased with myself—it was a great relief to stop fighting Grossbart. And it had cost me nothing. Barrett would never find out, and if he did, I could manage to invent some excuse. For a while I sat at my desk, comfortable in my decision. Then the screen door flew back and Grossbart burst in again. "Sergeant!" he said. Behind him I saw Fishbein and Halpern, both in starched khakis, both carrying ditty bags exactly like Grossbart's.

"Sergeant, I caught Mickey and Larry coming out of the movies. I almost missed them."

"Grossbart, did I say tell no one?"

"But my aunt said I could bring friends. That I should, in fact."

"I'm the Sergeant, Grossbart—not your aunt!"

Grossbart looked at me in disbelief; he pulled Halpern up by his sleeve. "Mickey, tell the Sergeant what this would mean to you."

"Grossbart, for God's sake, spare us—"

"Tell him what you told me, Mickey. How much it would mean."

Halpern looked at me and, shrugging his shoulders, made his admission. "A lot."

Fishbein stepped forward without prompting. "This would mean a great deal to me and my parents, Sergeant Marx."

"No!" I shouted.

8. Praise the day.

Grossbart was shaking his head. "Sergeant, I could see you denying me, but how you can deny Mickey, a Yeshivah boy, that's beyond me."

"I'm not denying Mickey anything. You just pushed a little too hard, Grossbart. *You* denied him."

"I'll give him my pass, then," Grossbart said. "I'll give him my aunt's address and a little note. At least let him go."

In a second he had crammed the pass into Halpern's pants' pocket. Halpern looked at me, Fishbein too. Grossbart was at the door, pushing it open. "Mickey, bring me a piece of gefilte fish at least." And then he was outside again.

The three of us looked at one another and then I said, "Halpern, hand that pass over."

He took it from his pocket and gave it to me. Fishbein had now moved to the doorway, where he lingered. He stood there with his mouth slightly open and then pointed to himself. "And me?" he asked.

His utter ridiculousness exhausted me. I slumped down in my seat and I felt pulses knocking at the back of my eyes. "Fishbein," I said, "you understand I'm not trying to deny you anything, don't you? If it was my Army I'd serve gefilte fish in the mess hall. I'd sell kugel[9] in the PX, honest to God."

Halpern smiled.

"You understand, don't you, Halpern?"

"Yes, Sergeant."

"And you, Fishbein? I don't want enemies. I'm just like you—I want to serve my time and go home. I miss the same things you miss."

"Then, Sergeant," Fishbein interrupted, "Why don't you come too?"

"Where?"

"To St. Louis. To Shelley's aunt. We'll have a regular Seder. Play hide-the-matzah." He gave a broad, black-toothed smile.

I saw Grossbart in the doorway again, on the other side of the screen.

"Pssst!" He waved a piece of paper. "Mickey, here's the address. Tell her I couldn't get away."

Halpern did not move. He looked at me and I saw the shrug moving up his arms into his shoulders again. I took the cover off my typewriter and made out passes for him and Fishbein. "Go," I said, "the three of you."

I thought Halpern was going to kiss my hand.

That afternoon, in a bar in Joplin, I drank beer and listened with half an ear to the Cardinal game. I tried to look squarely at what I'd become involved in, and began to wonder if perhaps the struggle

---

9. Baked pudding of noodles or potatoes.

with Grossbart wasn't much my fault as his. What was I that I had to *muster* generous feelings? Who was I to have been feeling so grudging, so tight-hearted? After all, I wasn't being asked to move the world. Had I a right, then, or a reason, to clamp down on Grossbart, when that meant clamping down on Halpern, too? And Fishbein, that ugly agreeable soul, wouldn't he suffer in the bargain also? Out of the many recollections that had tumbled over me these past few days, I heard from some childhood moment my grand-mother's voice: "What are you making a *tsimas*?"[1] It was what she would ask my mother when, say, I had cut myself with a knife and her daughter was busy bawling me out. I would need a hug and a kiss and my mother would moralize! But my grandmother knew—mercy overrides justice. I should have known it, too. Who was Nathan Marx to be such a pennypincher with kindness? Surely, I thought, the Messiah himself—if he should ever come—won't niggle over nickels and dimes. God willing, he'll hug and kiss.

The next day, while we were playing softball over on the Parade Grounds, I decided to ask Bob Wright, who was noncom in charge over at Classification and Assignment, where he thought our train-ees would be sent when their cycle ended in two weeks. I asked casually, between innings, and he said, "They're pushing them all into the Pacific. Shulman cut the orders on your boys the other day."

The news shocked me, as though I were father to Halpern, Fish-bein, and Grossbart.

That night I was just sliding into sleep when someone tapped on the door. "What is it?"

"Sheldon."

He opened the door and came in. For a moment I felt his pres-ence without being able to see him. "How was it?" I asked, as though to the darkness.

He popped into sight before me. "Great, Sergeant." I felt my springs sag; Grossbart was sitting on the edge of the bed. I sat up.

"How about you?" he asked. "Have a nice weekend?"

"Yes."

He took a deep paternal breath. "The others went to sleep . . ." We sat silently for a while, as a homey feeling invaded my ugly little cubicle: the door was locked, the cat out, the children safely in bed.

"Sergeant, can I tell you something? Personal?"

I did not answer and he seemed to know why. "Not about me. About Mickey. Sergeant, I never felt for anybody like I feel for him. Last night I heard Mickey in the bed next to me. He was crying so, it could have broken your heart. Real sobs."

"I'm sorry to hear that."

---

1. Side dish made of mixed cooked vegetables and fruit; i.e., *tsimas* = fuss.

"I had to talk to him to stop him. He held my hand, Sergeant—he wouldn't let it go. He was almost hysterical. He kept saying if he only knew where we were going. Even if he knew it *was* the Pacific, that would be better than nothing. Just to know."

Long ago, someone had taught Grossbart the sad law that only lies can get the truth. Not that I couldn't believe in Halpern's crying—his eyes *always* seemed red-rimmed. But, fact or not, it became a lie when Grossbart uttered it. He was entirely strategic. But then—it came with the force of indictment—so was I! There are strategies of aggression, but there are strategies of retreat, as well. And so, recognizing that I myself, had been without craft and guile, I told him what I knew. "It is the Pacific."

He let out a small gasp, which was not a lie. "I'll tell him. I wish it was otherwise."

"So do I."

He jumped on my words. "You mean you think you could do something? A change maybe?"

"No, I couldn't do a thing."

"Don't you know anybody over at C & A?"

"Grossbart, there's nothing I can do. If your orders are for the Pacific then it's the Pacific."

"But Mickey."

"Mickey, you, me—everybody, Grossbart. There's nothing to be done. Maybe the war'll end before you go. Pray for a miracle."

"But—"

"Good night, Grossbart." I settled back, and was relieved to feel the springs upbend again as Grossbart rose to leave. I could see him clearly now; his jaw had dropped and he looked like a dazed prizefighter. I noticed for the first time a little paper bag in his hand.

"Grossbart"—I smiled—"my gift?"

"Oh, yes, Sergeant. Here, from all of us." He handed me the bag. "It's egg roll."

"Egg roll?" I accepted the bag and felt a damp grease spot on the bottom. I opened it, sure that Grossbart was joking.

"We thought you'd probably like it. You know, Chinese egg roll. We thought you'd probably have a taste for—"

"Your aunt served egg roll?"

"She wasn't home."

"Grossbart, she invited you. You told me she invited you and your friends."

"I know. I just reread the letter. *Next* week."

I got out of bed and walked to the window. It was black as far off as I could see. "Grossbart," I said. But I was not calling him.

"What?"

"What are you, Grossbart? Honest to God, what are you?"

I think it was the first time I'd asked him a question for which he didn't have an immediate answer.

"How can you do this to people?" I asked.

"Sergeant, the day away did us all a world of good. Fishbein, you should see him, he *loves* Chinese food."

"But the Seder," I said.

"We took second best, Sergeant."

Rage came charging at me. I didn't sidestep—I grabbed it, pulled it in, hugged it to my chest.

"Grossbart, you're a liar! You're a schemer and a crook! You've got no respect for anything! Nothing at all! Not for me, for the truth, not even for poor Halpern! You use us all—"

"Sergeant, Sergeant, I feel for Mickey, honest to God, I do. I *love* Mickey. I try—"

"You try! You feel!" I lurched towards him and grabbed his shirt front. I shook him furiously. "Grossbart, get out. Get out and stay the hell away from me! Because if I see you, I'll make your life miserable. *You understand that?*"

"Yes."

I let him free, and when he walked from the room I wanted to spit on the floor where he had stood. I couldn't stop the fury from rising in my heart. It engulfed me, owned me, till it seemed I could only rid myself of it with tears or an act of violence. I snatched from the bed the bag Grossbart had given me and with all my strength threw it out the window. And the next morning, as the men policed the area around the barracks, I heard a great cry go up from one of the trainees who'd been anticipating only this morning handful of cigarette butts and candy wrappers. "Egg roll!" he shouted. "Holy Christ, Chinese goddam egg roll!"

A week later when I read the orders that had come down from C & A I couldn't believe my eyes. Every single trainee was to be shipped to Camp Stoneham, California, and from there to the Pacific. Every trainee but one: Private Sheldon Grossbart was to be sent to Fort Monmouth, New Jersey. I read the mimeographed sheet several times. Dee, Farrell, Fishbein, Fuselli, Fylypowycz, Glinicki, Gromke, Gucwa, Halpern, Hardy, Helebrandt . . . right down to Anton Zygadlo, all were to be headed West before the month was out. All except Grossbart. He had pulled a string and I wasn't it.

I lifted the phone and called C & A.

The voice on the other end said smartly, "Corporal Shulman, sir."

"Let me speak to Sergeant Wright."

"Who is this calling, sir?"

"Sergeant Marx."

And to my surprise, the voice said, "*Oh.*" Then: "Just a minute, Sergeant."

Shulman's *oh* stayed with me while I waited for Wright to come to the phone. Why *oh*? Who was Shulman? And then, so simply, I knew I'd discovered the string Grossbart had pulled. In fact, I could hear Grossbart the day he'd discovered Shulman, in the PX, or the bowling alley, or maybe even at services. "Glad to meet you. Where you from? Bronx? Me too. Do you know so-and-so? And so-and-so? Me too! You work at C & A? Really? Hey, how's chances of getting East? Could you do something? Change something? Swindle, cheat, lie? We gotta help each other, you know . . . if the Jews in Germany . . ."

At the other end Bob Wright answered. "How are you, Nate? How's the pitching arm?"

"Good. Bob, I wonder if you could do me a favor." I heard clearly my own words and they so reminded me of Grossbart that I dropped more easily than I could have imagined into what I had planned. "This may sound crazy, Bob, but I got a kid here on orders to Monmouth who wants them changed. He had a brother killed in Europe and he's hot to go to the Pacific. Says he'd feel like a coward if he wound up stateside. I don't know, Bob, can anything be done? Put somebody else in the Monmouth slot?"

"Who?" he asked cagily.

"Anybody. First guy on the alphabet. I don't care. The kid just asked if something could be done."

"What's his name?"

"Grossbart, Sheldon."

Wright didn't answer.

"Yeah," I said, "he's a Jewish kid, so he thought I could help him out. You know."

"I guess I can do something," he finally said. "The Major hasn't been around here for weeks—TDY[2] to the golf course. I'll try, Nate that's all I can say."

"I'd appreciate it, Bob. See you Sunday," and I hung up, perspiring.

And the following day the corrected orders appeared: Fishbein, Fuselli, Fylypowycz, Glinicki, Grossbart, Gucwa, Halpern, Hardy . . . Lucky Private Harley Alton was to go to Fort Monmouth, New Jersey, where for some reason or other, they wanted an enlisted man with infantry training.

After chow that night I stopped back at the orderly room to straighten out the guard duty roster. Grossbart was waiting for me. He spoke first.

"You son of a bitch!"

I sat down at my desk and while he glared down at me I began to make the necessary alterations in the duty roster.

"What do you have against me?" he cried. "Against my family? Would it kill you for me to be near my father, God knows how many months he has left to him."

2. Temporary Duty, an Army orders term used ironically here.

"Why?"

"His heart," Grossbart said. "He hasn't had enough troubles in a lifetime, you've got to add to them. I curse the day I ever met you, Marx! Shulman told me what happened over there. There's no limit to your anti-Semitism, is there! The damage you've done here isn't enough. You have to make a special phone call! You really want me dead!"

I made the last few notations in the duty roster and got up to leave. "Good night, Grossbart."

"You owe me an explanation!" He stood in my path.

"Sheldon, you're the one who owes explanations."

He scowled. "To *you*?"

"To me, I think so, yes. Mostly to Fishbein and Halpern."

"That's right, twist things around. I owe nobody nothing, I've done all I could do for them. Now I think I've got the right to watch out for myself."

"For each other we have to learn to watch out, Sheldon. You told me yourself."

"You call this watching out for me, what you did?"

"No. For all of us."

I pushed him aside and started for the door. I heard his furious breathing behind me, and it sounded like steam rushing from the engine of his terrible strength.

"You'll be all right," I said from the door. And, I thought, so would Fishbein and Halpern be all right, even in the Pacific, if only Grossbart could continue to see in the obsequiousness of the one, the soft spirituality of the other, some profit for himself.

I stood outside the orderly room, and I heard Grossbart weeping behind me. Over in the barracks, in the lighted windows, I could see the boys in their T-shirts sitting on their bunks talking about their orders, as they'd been doing for the past two days. With a kind of quiet nervousness, they polished shoes, shined belt buckles, squared away underwear, trying as best they could to accept their fate. Behind me, Grossbart swallowed hard, accepting his. And then, resisting with all my will an impulse to turn and seek pardon for my vindictiveness, I accepted my own.

1959

SUSAN SONTAG

1933–

Susan Sontag's career as a writer reveals a restless, highly modernized sensibility trying out a number of different though related modes of understanding twentieth-century reality. After graduating from the University of

Chicago, she first studied religion and philosophy at Harvard and at Union Theological Seminary. Then in the early 1960s she began to write (and publish in the *Partisan Review*) speculative and polemical essays about art which she collected in 1966 as *Against Interpretation*, the title of the most provocative of these essays. Here and elsewhere, Sontag announced herself and encouraged others to be "against interpretation"—against the attempt to criticize art by turning it into a critical paraphrase which then became the subject of concern rather than the work it presumably set out to illuminate. Another essay, *Notes on Camp*, argued in defense of the kinds of pleasure we take in less-than-good art, often in creations so outrageous or inept that they turn out to be interesting in new and different ways.

A further volume of essays, *Styles of Radical Will* (1969) continued to show her interest in an art—now strongly slanted toward the film—which overturned conventional "realistic" expectations and delivered instead a radically new object, untranslatable into well-worn interpretive categories. By this time she had also published two novels, *The Benefactor* (1964) and *Death Kit* (1967), which were indebted to French models in their anti-realistic, dreamlike, and abstract atmosphere. Intelligent and inventive (particularly at moments in *Death Kit*), the novels were nonetheless a good deal less powerful than the essays; and *Trip to Hanoi* (included in *Styles of Radical Will*), an account of Sontag's visit to North Vietnam in 1967, showed how vivid and lively her rendering of people and place could be when she set aside complicated fictional strategies and wrote merely out of the sense of having something to describe, something to say.

Trip to Hanoi was also a "trip" in the 1960s drug-culture sense of the word; for at the end of the essay Sontag comes back to the United States with a sense of new possibilities for "revolution," the opening up of new feelings, the extension of consciousness as a reprieve from society-induced inhibitions. As if to capitalize on this sense, she devoted herself whole-heartedly to film, writing and directing *Duet for Cannibals* in 1970 and *Brother Karl* the following year. Then little was heard from her, as she became ill with cancer. She recovered, however, and in 1977–78 published three new books: *On Photography*; *I, Etc.*, a collection of stories; and *Illness as Metaphor*, a book about various uses of the "disease" metaphor.

On Photography received sharp criticism from professional photographers who resented Sontag's attempt to speak authoritatively about their discipline, and from critics who faulted her penchant for large cultural generalizations. Actually, her purpose is to puncture some of the more vapid and sentimental notions about why photography is "good"—that it somehow aids understanding and tolerance by "explaining" the nature of human reality. In the selection printed here Sontag shows, through a careful review of Diane Arbus's photographs, how such an account will simply not do. *On Photography* is interesting for the way it shows that a principled animus toward a subject can be productive of incisive, revealing commentary about it. As always in Sontag's writings, her wide reading and crisply stated prose style are evident, as are her polemical verve and lack of interest in careful qualifications or cautious reservations. Her powers are very much tied up with her ability to provoke discussion and argument, once again opening up new possibilities for "revolutionary" thinking.

On Photography
America, Seen through Photographs, Darkly[1]

As Walt Whitman gazed down the democratic vistas of culture, he tried to see beyond the difference between beauty and ugliness, importance and triviality. It seemed to him servile or snobbish to make any discriminations of value, except the most generous ones. Great claims were made for candor by our boldest, most delirious prophet of cultural revolution. Nobody would fret about beauty and ugliness, he implied, who was accepting a sufficiently large embrace of the real, of the inclusiveness and vitality of actual American experience. All facts, even mean ones, are incandescent in Whitman's America—that ideal space, made real by history, where "as they emit themselves facts are showered with light."[2]

The Great American Cultural Revolution heralded in the preface to the first edition of *Leaves of Grass* (1855) didn't break out, which has disappointed many but surprised none. One great poet alone cannot change the moral weather; even when the poet has millions of Red Guards[3] at his disposal, it is still not easy. Like every seer of cultural revolution, Whitman thought he discerned art already being overtaken, and demystified, by reality. "The United States themselves are essentially the greatest poem." But when no cultural revolution occurred, and the greatest of poems seemed less great in days of Empire than it had under the Republic, only other artists took seriously Whitman's program of populist transcendence, of the democratic transvaluation of beauty and ugliness, importance and triviality. Far from having been themselves demystified by reality, the American arts—notably photography—now aspired to do the demystifying.

In photography's early decades, photographs were expected to be idealized images. This is still the aim of most amateur photographers, for whom a beautiful photograph is a photograph of something beautiful, like a woman, a sunset. In 1915 Edward Steichen[4] photographed a milk bottle on a tenement fire escape, an early example of a quite different idea of the beautiful photograph. And since the 1920s, ambitious professionals, those whose work gets into museums, have steadily drifted away from lyrical subjects, conscientiously exploring plain, tawdry, or even vapid material. In recent decades, photography has succeeded in somewhat revising, for everybody, the definitions of what is beautiful and ugly—along the lines that Whitman had proposed. If (in Whitman's words) "each

---

1. The second chapter of Sontag's *On Photography* (1977). Its title refers to St. Paul's description (1 Corinthians 13.12) of how we see as human beings ("through a glass, darkly").
2. From the preface to the first edition of Whitman's *Leaves of Grass* (1855) as are the quotations in the following para-graphs.
3. A cadre of militants in the People's Republic of China organized "spontaneously" to combat kinds of cultural deviation.
4. A pioneer American photographer (1879–1973) whose earlier works are characterized by soft focus.

precise object or condition or combination or process exhibits a beauty," it becomes superficial to single out some things as beautiful and others as not. If "all that a person does or thinks is of consequence," it becomes arbitrary to treat some moments in life as important and most as trivial.

To photograph is to confer importance. There is probably no subject that cannot be beautified; moreover, there is no way to suppress the tendency inherent in all photographs to accord value to their subjects. But the meaning of value itself can be altered—as it has been in the contemporary culture of the photographic image which is a parody of Whitman's evangel. In the mansions of predemocratic culture, someone who gets photographed is a celebrity. In the open fields of American experience, as catalogued with passion by Whitman and as sized up with a shrug by Warhol,[5] everybody is a celebrity. No moment is more important than any other moment; no person is more interesting than any other person.

The epigraph for a book of Walker Evans's[6] photographs published by the Museum of Modern Art is a passage from Whitman that sounds the theme of American photography's most prestigious quest:

> I do not doubt but the majesty & beauty of the world are latent in any iota of the world . . . I do not doubt there is far more in trivialities, insects, vulgar persons, slaves, dwarfs, weeds, rejected refuse, than I have supposed. . . .

Whitman thought he was not abolishing beauty but generalizing it. So, for generations, did the most gifted American photographers, in their polemical pursuit of the trivial and the vulgar. But among American photographers who have matured since World War II, the Whitmanesque mandate to record in its entirety the extravagant candors of actual American experience has gone sour. In photographing dwarfs, you don't get majesty & beauty. You get dwarfs.

Starting from the images reproduced and consecrated in the sumptuous magazine *Camera Work* that Alfred Stieglitz[7] published from 1903 to 1917 and exhibited in the gallery he ran in New York from 1905 to 1917 at 291 Fifth Avenue (first called the Little Gallery of the Photo-Secession, later simply "291")—magazine and gallery constituting the most ambitious forum of Whitmanesque judgments—American photography has moved from affirmation to erosion to, finally, a parody of Whitman's program. In this history the most edifying figure is Walker Evans. He was the last great photographer to work seriously and assuredly in a mood deriving

---

5. Andy Warhol (b. 1928), graphic artist and film-maker, a major figure in the American Pop Art movement of the 1960s. Totally passive and accepting in his attitude toward experience.
6. American photographer (b. 1903) whose pictures catch ordinary people in characteristic and revealing attitudes.
7. American photographer (1864–1946) of international reputation who pioneered the use of the hand camera; self-constituted leader of the first generation of "art" photographers.

from Whitman's euphoric humanism, summing up what had gone on before (for instance, Lewis Hine's[8] stunning photographs of immigrants and workers), anticipating much of the cooler, ruder, bleaker photography that has been done since—as in the prescient series of "secret" photographs of anonymous New York subway riders that Evans took with a concealed camera between 1939 and 1941. But Evans broke with the heroic mode in which the Whitmanesque vision had been propagandized by Stieglitz and his disciples, who had condescended to Hine. Evans found Stieglitz's work arty.

Like Whitman, Stieglitz saw no contradiction between making art an instrument of identification with the community and aggrandizing the artist as a heroic, romantic, self-expressing ego. In his florid, brilliant book of essays, *Port of New York* (1924), Paul Rosenfeld[9] hailed Stieglitz as one "of the great affirmers of life. There is no matter in all the world so homely, trite, and humble that through it this man of the black box and chemical bath cannot express himself entire." Photographing, and thereby redeeming the homely, trite, and humble is also an ingenious means of individual expression. "The photographer," Rosenfeld writes of Stieglitz, "has cast the artist's net wider into the material world than any man before him or alongside him." Photography is a kind of overstatement, a heroic copulation with the material world. Like Hine, Evans sought a more impersonal kind of affirmation, a noble reticence, a lucid understatement. Neither in the impersonal architectural still lifes of American façades and inventories of rooms that he loved to make, nor in the exacting portraits of Southern sharecroppers he took in the late 1930s (published in the book done with James Agee,[1] *Let Us Now Praise Famous Men*), was Evans trying to express himself.

Even without the heroic inflection, Evans's project still descends from Whitman's: the leveling of discriminations between the beautiful and the ugly, the important and the trivial. Each thing or person photographed becomes—a photograph; and becomes, therefore, morally equivalent to any other of his photographs. Evans's camera brought out the same formal beauty in the exteriors of Victorian houses in Boston in the early 1930s as in the store buildings on main streets in Alabama towns in 1936. But this was a leveling up, not down. Evans wanted his photographs to be "literate, authoritative, transcendent." The moral universe of the 1930s being no longer ours, these adjectives are barely credible today. Nobody demands that photography be literate. Nobody can imagine how it could be authoritative. Nobody understands how anything, least of all a photograph, could be transcendent.

8. American sociologist (1874–1940) who photographed children working in factories, immigrants, and New York City slums.

9. Music and cultural critic (1890–1946).
1. American poet, novelist, and critic (1909–55).

Whitman preached empathy, concord in discord, oneness in diversity. Psychic intercourse with everything, everybody—plus sensual union (when he could get it)—is the giddy trip that is
proposed explicitly, over and over and over, in the prefaces and the
poems. This longing to proposition the whole world also dictated his
poetry's form and tone. Whitman's poems are a psychic technology
for chanting the reader into a new state of being (a microcosm of
the "new order" envisaged for the polity); they are functional, like
mantras—ways of transmitting charges of energy. The repetition,
the bombastic cadence, the run-on lines, and the pushy diction are a
rush of secular afflatus, meant to get readers psychically airborne, to
boost them up to that height where they can identify with the past
and with the community of American desire. But this message of
identification with other Americans is foreign to our temperament
now.

The last sigh of the Whitmanesque erotic embrace of the nation,
but universalized and stripped of all demands, was heard in the
"Family of Man" exhibit organized in 1955 by Edward Steichen,
Stieglitz's contemporary and co-founder of Photo-Secession. Five
hundred and three photographs by two hundred and seventy-three
photographers from sixty-eight countries were supposed to converge
—to prove that humanity is "one" and that human beings, for all
their flaws and villainies, are attractive creatures. The people in the
photographs were of all races, ages, classes, physical types. Many of
them had exceptionally beautiful bodies; some had beautiful faces.
As Whitman urged the readers of his poems to identify with him
and with America, Steichen set up the show to make it possible for
each viewer to identify with a great many of the people depicted
and, potentially, with the subject of every photograph: citizens of
World Photography all.

It was not until seventeen years later that photography again
attracted such crowds at the Museum of Modern Art: for the retrospective given Diane Arbus's work in 1972.[2] In the Arbus show, a
hundred and twelve photographs all taken by one person and all
similar—that is, everyone in them looks (in some sense) the same
—imposed a feeling exactly contrary to the reassuring warmth of
Steichen's material. Instead of people whose appearance pleases,
representative folk doing their human thing, the Arbus show lined
up assorted monsters and borderline cases—most of them ugly;
wearing grotesque or unflattering clothing; in dismal or barren
surroundings—who have paused to pose and, often, to gaze frankly,
confidentially at the viewer. Arbus's work does not invite viewers to
identify with the pariahs and miserable-looking people she photographed. Humanity is not "one."

2. American photographer (1923–71).

The Arbus photographs convey the anti-humanist message which people of good will in the 1970s are eager to be troubled by, just as they wished, in the 1950s, to be consoled and distracted by a sentimental humanism. There is not as much difference between these messages as one might suppose. The Steichen show was an up and the Arbus show was a down, but either experience serves equally well to rule out a historical understanding of reality.

Steichen's choice of photographs assumes a human condition or a human nature shared by everybody. By purporting to show that individuals are born, work, laugh, and die everywhere in the same way, "The Family of Man" denies the determining weight of history —of genuine and historically embedded differences, injustices, and conflicts. Arbus's photographs undercut politics just as decisively, by suggesting a world in which everybody is an alien, hopelessly isolated, immobilized in mechanical, crippled identities and relationships. The pious uplift of Steichen's photograph anthology and the cool dejection of the Arbus retrospective both render history and politics irrelevant. One does so by universalizing the human condition, into joy; the other by atomizing it, into horror.

The most striking aspect of Arbus's work is that she seems to have enrolled in one of art photography's most vigorous enterprises —concentrating on victims, on the unfortunate—but without the compassionate purpose that such a project is expected to serve. Her work shows people who are pathetic, pitiable, as well as repulsive, but it does not arouse any compassionate feelings. For what would be more correctly described as their dissociated point of view, the photographs have been praised for their candor and for an unsentimental empathy with their subjects. What is actually their aggressiveness toward the public has been treated as a moral accomplishment: that the photographs don't allow the viewer to be distant from the subject. More plausibly, Arbus's photographs—with their acceptance of the appalling—suggest a naïveté which is both coy and sinister, for it is based on distance, on privilege, on a feeling that what the viewer is asked to look at is really *other*. Buñuel,[3] when asked once why he made movies, said that it was "to show that this is not the best of all possible worlds." Arbus took photographs to show something simpler—that there is another world.

The other world is to be found, as usual, inside this one. Avowedly interested only in photographing people who "looked strange," Arbus found plenty of material close to home. New York, with its drag balls and welfare hotels, was rich with freaks. There was also a carnival in Maryland, where Arbus found a human pincushion, a hermaphrodite with a dog, a tattooed man, and an albino sword-swallower; nudist camps in New Jersey and in Pennsylvania; Disneyland and a Hollywood set, for their dead or fake landscapes without people; and the unidentified mental hospital

3. Luis Buñuel (b. 1900), Spanish film director.

where she took some of her last, and most disturbing, photographs. And there was always daily life, with its endless supply of oddities —if one has the eye to see them. The camera has the power to catch so-called normal people in such a way as to make them look abnormal. The photographer chooses oddity, chases it, frames it, develops it, titles it.

"You see someone on the street," Arbus wrote, "and essentially what you notice about them is the flaw." The insistent sameness of Arbus's work, however far she ranges from her prototypical subjects, shows that her sensibility, armed with a camera, could insinuate anguish, kinkiness, mental illness with any subject. Two photographs are of crying babies; the babies look disturbed, crazy. Resembling or having something in common with someone else is a recurrent source of the ominous, according to the characteristic norms of Arbus's dissociated way of seeing. It may be two girls (not sisters) wearing identical raincoats whom Arbus photographed together in Central Park; or the twins and triplets who appear in several pictures. Many photographs point with oppressive wonder to the fact that two people form a couple; and every couple is an odd couple: straight or gay, black or white, in an old-age home or in a junior high. People looked eccentric because they didn't wear clothes, like nudists; or because they did, like the waitress in the nudist camp who's wearing an apron. Anybody Arbus photographed was a freak—a boy waiting to march in a pro-war parade, wearing his straw boater and his "Bomb Hanoi" button; the King and Queen of a Senior Citizens Dance; a thirtyish suburban couple sprawled in their lawn chairs; a widow sitting alone in her cluttered bedroom. In "A Jewish giant at home with his parents in the Bronx, NY, 1970," the parents look like midgets, as wrong-sized as the enormous son hunched over them under their low living-room ceiling.

The authority of Arbus's photographs derives from the contrast between their lacerating subject matter and their calm, matter-of-fact attentiveness. This quality of attention—the attention paid by the photographer, the attention paid by the subject to the act of being photographed—creates the moral theater of Arbus's straight-on, contemplative portraits. Far from spying on freaks and pariahs, catching them unawares, the photographer has gotten to know them, reassured them—so that they posed for her as calmly and stiffly as any Victorian notable sat for a studio portrait by Julia Margaret Cameron.[4] A large part of the mystery of Arbus's photographs lies in what they suggest about how her subjects felt after consenting to be photographed. Do they see themselves, the viewer wonders, like *that*? Do they know how grotesque they are? It seems as if they don't.

The subject of Arbus's photographs is, to borrow the stately Hegelian label, "the unhappy consciousness." But most characters

4. English portrait photographer (1815–79).

in Arbus's Grand Guignol[5] appear not to know that they are ugly.
Arbus photographs people in various degrees of unconscious or
unaware relation to their pain, their ugliness. This necessarily limits
what kinds of horrors she might have been drawn to photograph: it
excludes sufferers who presumably know they are suffering, like
victims of accidents, wars, famines, and political persecutions.
Arbus would never have taken pictures of accidents, events that
break into a life; she specialized in slow-motion private smashups,
most of which had been going on since the subject's birth.

Though most viewers are ready to imagine that these people, the
citizens of the sexual underworld as well as the genetic freaks, are
unhappy, few of the pictures actually show emotional distress. The
photographs of deviates and real freaks do not accent their pain but,
rather, their detachment and autonomy. The female impersonators
in their dressing rooms, the Mexican dwarf in his Manhattan hotel
room, the Russian midgets in a living room on 100th Street, and
their kin are mostly shown as cheerful, self-accepting, matter-of-
fact. Pain is more legible in the portraits of the normals: the quarreling elderly couple on a park bench, the New Orleans lady bartender at home with a souvenir dog, the boy in Central Park
clenching his toy hand grenade.

Brassaï[6] denounced photographers who try to trap their subjects
off-guard, in the erroneous belief that something special will be
revealed about them.[7] In the world colonized by Arbus, subjects are
always revealing themselves. There is no decisive moment. Arbus's
view that self-revelation is a continuous, evenly distributed process
is another way of maintaining the Whitmanesque imperative: treat
all moments as of equal consequence. Like Brassaï, Arbus wanted
her subjects to be as fully conscious as possible, aware of the act in
which they were participating. Instead of trying to coax her subjects
into a natural or typical position, they are encouraged to be
awkward—that is, to pose. (Thereby, the revelation of self gets
identified with what is strange, odd, askew.) Standing or sitting
stiffly makes them seem like images of themselves.

Most Arbus pictures have the subjects looking straight into the
camera. This often makes them look even odder, almost deranged.
Compare the 1912 photograph by Lartigue[8] of a woman in a
plumed hat and veil ("Racecourse at Nice") with Arbus's "Woman
with a Veil on Fifth Avenue, NYC, 1968." Apart from the char-

5. Series of short, sensational stage-
pieces, bloody and monstrous in their
intent.
6. Gyula Brassaï (b. 1899), French photographer of Parisian city life.
7. "Not an error, really. There is something on people's faces when they don't
know they are being observed that never
appears when they do. If we did not
know how Walker Evans took his subway photographs (riding the New York
subways for hundreds of hours, standing,

with the lens of his camera peering between two buttons of his topcoat), it
would be obvious from the pictures
themselves that the seated passengers, although photographed close and frontally,
didn't know they were being photographed; their expressions are private
ones, not those they would offer to the
camera" [Sontag's note].
8. Jacques Henri Lartigue (1896–   ),
French photographer, particularly of
racecourses.

acteristic ugliness of Arbus's subject (Lartigue's subject is, just as characteristically, beautiful), what makes the woman in Arbus's photograph strange is the bold unselfconsciousness of her pose. If the Lartigue woman looked back, she might appear almost as strange.

In the normal rhetoric of the photographic portrait, facing the camera signifies solemnity, frankness, the disclosure of the subject's essence. That is why frontality seems right for ceremonial pictures (like weddings, graduations) but less apt for photographs used on billboards to advertise political candidates. (For politicians the three-quarter gaze is more common: a gaze that soars rather than confronts, suggesting instead of the relation to the viewer, to the present, the more ennobling abstract relation to the future.) What makes Arbus's use of the frontal pose so arresting is that her subjects are often people one would not expect to surrender themselves so amiably and ingenuously to the camera. Thus, in Arbus's photographs, frontality also implies in the most vivid way the subject's cooperation. To get these people to pose, the photographer has had to gain their confidence, has had to become "friends" with them.

Perhaps the scariest scene in Tod Browning's[9] film *Freaks* (1932) is the wedding banquet, when pinheads, bearded women, Siamese twins, and living torsos dance and sing their acceptance of the wicked normal-sized Cleopatra, who has just married the gullible midget hero. "One of us! One of us! One of us!" they chant as a loving cup is passed around the table from mouth to mouth to be finally presented to the nauseated bride by an exuberant dwarf. Arbus had a perhaps oversimple view of the charm and hypocrisy and discomfort of fraternizing with freaks. Following the elation of discovery, there was the thrill of having won their confidence, of not being afraid of them, of having mastered one's aversion. Photographing freaks "had a terrific excitement for me," Arbus explained. "I just used to adore them."

Diane Arbus's photographs were already famous to people who follow photography when she killed herself in 1971; but, as with Sylvia Plath, the attention her work has attracted since her death is of another order—a kind of apotheosis. The fact of her suicide seems to guarantee that her work is sincere, not voyeuristic, that it is compassionate, not cold. Her suicide also seems to make the photographs more devastating, as if it proved the photographs to have been dangerous to her.

She herself suggested the possibility. "Everything is so superb and breathtaking. I am creeping forward on my belly like they do in war movies." While photography is normally an omnipotent viewing from a distance, there is one situation in which people do get killed for taking pictures: when they photograph people killing each other.

9. American film director (1882–1962) of *Dracula* (1931) and *Freaks* (1932).

Only war photography combines voyeurism and danger. Combat photographers can't avoid participating in the lethal activity they record; they even wear military uniforms, though without rank badges. To discover (through photographing) that life is "really a melodrama," to understand the camera as a weapon of aggression, implies there will be casualties. "I'm sure there are limits," she wrote. "God knows, when the troops start advancing on you, you do approach that stricken feeling where you perfectly well can get killed." Arbus's words in retrospect describe a kind of combat death: having trespassed certain limits, she fell in a psychic ambush, a casualty of her own candor and curiosity.

In the old romance of the artist, any person who has the temerity to spend a season in hell[1] risks not getting out alive or coming back psychically damaged. The heroic avant-gardism of French literature in the late nineteenth and early twentieth centuries furnishes a memorable pantheon of artists who fail to survive their trips to hell. Still, there is a large difference between the activity of a photographer, which is always willed, and the activity of a writer, which may not be. One has the right to, may feel compelled to, give voice to one's own pain—which is, in any case, one's own property. One volunteers to seek out the pain of others.

Thus, what is finally most troubling in Arbus's photographs is not their subject at all but the cumulative impression of the photographer's consciousness: the sense that what is presented is precisely a private vision, something voluntary. Arbus was not a poet delving into her entrails to relate her own pain but a photographer venturing out into the world to *collect* images that are painful. And for pain sought rather than just felt, there may be a less than obvious explanation. According to Reich,[2] the masochist's taste for pain does not spring from a love of pain but from the hope of procuring, by means of pain, a strong sensation; those handicapped by emotional or sensory analgesia only prefer pain to not feeling anything at all. But there is another explanation of why people seek pain, diametrically opposed to Reich's, that also seems pertinent: that they seek it not to feel more but to feel less.

Insofar as looking at Arbus's photographs is, undeniably, an ordeal, they are typical of the kind of art popular among sophisticated urban people right now: art that is a self-willed test of hardness. Her photographs offer an occasion to demonstrate that life's horror can be faced without squeamishness. The photographer once had to say to herself, Okay, I can accept that; the viewer is invited to make the same declaration.

Arbus's work is a good instance of a leading tendency of high art in capitalist countries: to suppress, or at least reduce, moral and

---

1. The French poet Arthur Rimbaud (1854–99) wrote *Une Saison en enfer* (*A Season in Hell*) in 1873.

2. Wilhelm Reich (1897–1957), psychologist and sexual theorist.

sensory queasiness. Much of modern art is devoted to lowering the threshold of what is terrible. By getting us used to what, formerly, we could not bear to see or hear, because it was too shocking, painful, or embarrassing, art changes morals—that body of psychic custom and public sanctions that draws a vague boundary between what is emotionally and spontaneously intolerable and what is not. The gradual suppression of queasiness does bring us closer to a rather formal truth—that of the arbitrariness of the taboos constructed by art and morals. But our ability to stomach this rising grotesqueness in images (moving and still) and in print has a stiff price. In the long run, it works out not as a liberation of but as a subtraction from the self: a pseudo-familiarity with the horrible reinforces alienation, making one less able to react in real life. What happens to people's feelings on first exposure to today's neighborhood pornographic film or to tonight's televised atrocity is not so different from what happens when they first look at Arbus's photographs.

The photographs make a compassionate response feel irrelevant. The point is not to be upset, to be able to confront the horrible with equanimity. But this look that is not (mainly) compassionate is a special, modern ethical construction: not hardhearted, certainly not cynical, but simply (or falsely) naïve. To the painful nightmarish reality out there, Arbus applied such adjectives as "terrific," "interesting," "incredible," "fantastic," "sensational"—the childlike wonder of the pop mentality. The camera—according to her deliberately naïve image of the photographer's quest—is a device that captures it all, that seduces subjects into disclosing their secrets, that broadens experience. To photograph people, according to Arbus, is necessarily "cruel," "mean." The important thing is not to blink.

"Photography was a license to go wherever I wanted and to do what I wanted to do," Arbus wrote.[3] The camera is a kind of passport that annihilates moral boundaries and social inhibitions, freeing the photographer from any responsibility toward the people photographed. The whole point of photographing people is that you are not intervening in their lives, only visiting them. The photographer is supertourist, an extension of the anthropologist, visiting natives and bringing back news of their exotic doings and strange gear. The photographer is always trying to colonize new experiences or find new ways to look at familiar subjects—to fight against boredom. For boredom is just the reverse side of fascination: both depend on being outside rather than inside a situation, and one leads to the other. "The Chinese have a theory that you pass through boredom into fascination," Arbus noted. Photographing an appalling underworld (and a desolate, plastic overworld), she had no intention of entering into the horror experienced by the

3. These quotations are from Arbus's foreword to her 1972 retrospective.

denizens of those worlds. They are to remain exotic, hence "terrific." Her view is always from the outside.

"I'm very little drawn to photographing people that are known or even subjects that are known," Arbus wrote. "They fascinate me when I've barely heard of them." However drawn she was to the maimed and the ugly, it would never have occurred to Arbus to photograph Thalidomide babies[4] or napalm victims—public horrors, deformities with sentimental or ethical associations. Arbus was not interested in ethical journalism. She chose subjects that she could believe were found, just lying about, without any values attached to them. They are necessarily ahistorical subjects, private rather than public pathology, secret lives rather than open ones.

For Arbus, the camera photographs the unknown. But unknown to whom? Unknown to someone who is protected, who has been schooled in moralistic and in prudent responses. Like Nathanael West,[5] another artist fascinated by the deformed and mutilated, Arbus came from a verbally skilled, compulsively health-minded, indignation-prone, well-to-do Jewish family, for whom minority sexual tastes lived way below the threshold of awareness and risk-taking was despised as another goyish craziness. "One of the things I felt I suffered from as a kid," Arbus wrote, "was that I never felt adversity. I was confined in a sense of unreality. . . . And the sense of being immune was, ludicrous as it seems, a painful one." Feeling much the same discontent, West in 1927 took a job as a night clerk in a seedy Manhattan hotel. Arbus's way of procuring experience, and thereby acquiring a sense of reality, was the camera. By experience was meant, if not material adversity, at least psychological adversity—the shock of immersion in experiences that cannot be beautified, the encounter with what is taboo, perverse, evil.

Arbus's interest in freaks expresses a desire to violate her own innocence, to undermine her sense of being privileged, to vent her frustration at being safe. Apart from West, the 1930s yield few examples of this kind of distress. More typically, it is the sensibility of someone educated and middle-class who came of age between 1945 and 1955—a sensibility that was to flourish precisely in the 1960s.

The decade of Arbus's serious work coincides with, and is very much of, the sixties, the decade in which freaks went public, and became a safe, approved subject of art. What in the 1930s was treated with anguish—as in *Miss Lonelyhearts* and *The Day of the Locust*—would in the 1960s be treated in a perfectly deadpan way, or with positive relish (in the films of Fellini, Arrabal, Jodorowsky,

---

4. Thalidomide, an antinausea drug given to pregnant women in the early 1960s, caused grotesque birth defects in their offspring.

5. American novelist (1902–40), author of *Miss Lonelyhearts* (1933) and *Day of the Locust* (1939).

in underground comics, in rock spectacles).[6] At the beginning of the sixties, the thriving Freak Show at Coney Island was outlawed; the pressure is on to raze the Times Square turf of drag queens and hustlers and cover it with skyscrapers. As the inhabitants of deviant underworlds are evicted from their restricted territories—banned as unseemly, a public nuisance, obscene, or just unprofitable—they increasingly come to infiltrate consciousness as the subject matter of art, acquiring a certain diffuse legitimacy and metaphoric proximity which creates all the more distance.

Who could have better appreciated the truth of freaks than someone like Arbus, who was by profession a fashion photographer—a fabricator of the cosmetic lie that masks the intractable inequalities of birth and class and physical appearance. But unlike Warhol, who spent many years as a commercial artist, Arbus did not make her serious work out of promoting and kidding the aesthetic of glamour to which she had been apprenticed, but turned her back on it entirely. Arbus's work is reactive—reactive against gentility, against what is approved. It was her way of saying fuck *Vogue*, fuck fashion, fuck what's pretty. This challenge takes two not wholly compatible forms. One is a revolt against the Jews' hyper-developed moral sensibility. The other revolt, itself hotly moralistic, turns against the success world. The moralist's subversion advances life as a failure as the antidote to life as a success. The aesthete's subversion, which the sixties was to make peculiarly its own, advances life as a horror show as the antidote to life as a bore.

Most of Arbus's work lies within the Warhol aesthetic, that is, defines itself in relation to the twin poles of boringness and freakishness; but it doesn't have the Warhol style. Arbus had neither Warhol's narcissism and genius for publicity nor the self-protective blandness with which he insulates himself from the freaky nor his sentimentality. It is unlikely that Warhol, who comes from a working-class family, ever felt any of the ambivalence toward success which afflicted the children of the Jewish upper middle classes in the 1960s. To someone raised as a Catholic, like Warhol (and virtually everyone in his gang), a fascination with evil comes much more genuinely than it does to someone from a Jewish background. Compared with Warhol, Arbus seems strikingly vulnerable, innocent—and certainly more pessimistic. Her Dantesque vision of the city (and the suburbs) has no reserves of irony. Although much of Arbus's material is the same as that depicted in, say, Warhol's *Chelsea Girls* (1966), her photographs never play with horror, milking it for laughs; they offer no opening to mockery, and no possibility of finding freaks endearing, as do the films of Warhol and Paul Morrissey.[7] For Arbus, both freaks and Middle America

6. Federico Fellini (b. 1921), Italian film director whose works often feature grotesque people. Fernando Arrabal (b. 1932), Spanish playwright with Surrealist affiliations.

7. A protégé of Warhol's, and director of *Flesh* (1968).

were equally exotic: a boy marching in a pro-war parade and a Levittown housewife were as alien as a dwarf or a transvestite; lower-middle-class suburbia was as remote as Times Square, lunatic asylums, and gay bars. Arbus's work expressed her turn against what was public (as she experienced it), conventional, safe, reassuring—and boring—in favor of what was private, hidden, ugly, dangerous, and fascinating. These contrasts, now, seem almost quaint. What is safe no longer monopolizes public imagery. The freakish is no longer a private zone, difficult of access. People who are bizarre, in sexual disgrace, emotionally vacant are seen daily on the newsstands, on TV, in the subways. Hobbesian man[8] roams the streets, quite visible, with glitter in his hair.

Sophisticated in the familiar modernist way—choosing awkwardness, naïveté, sincerity over the slickness and artificiality of high art and high commerce—Arbus said that the photographer she felt closest to was Weegee,[9] whose brutal pictures of crime and accident victims were a staple of the tabloids in the 1940s. Weegee's photographs are indeed upsetting, his sensibility is urban, but the similarity between his work and Arbus's ends there. However eager she was to disavow standard elements of photographic sophistication such as composition, Arbus was not unsophisticated. And there is nothing journalistic about her motives for taking pictures. What may seem journalistic, even sensational, in Arbus's photographs places them, rather, in the main tradition of Surrealist art—their taste for the grotesque, their professed innocence with respect to their subjects, their claim that all subjects are merely *objets trouvés*.[1]

"I would never choose a subject for what it meant to me when I think of it," Arbus wrote, a dogged exponent of the Surrealist bluff. Presumably, viewers are not supposed to judge the people she photographs. Of course, we do. And the very range of Arbus's subjects itself constitutes a judgment. Brassaï, who photographed people like those who interested Arbus—see his "La Môme Bijou" of 1932— also did tender cityscapes, portraits of famous artists. Lewis Hine's "Mental Institution, New Jersey, 1924" could be a late Arbus photograph (except that the pair of Mongoloid children posing on the lawn are photographed in profile rather than frontally); the Chicago street portraits Walker Evans took in 1946 are Arbus material, as are a number of photographs by Robert Frank.[2] The difference is in the range of other subjects, other emotions that

---

8. Thomas Hobbes (1588–1679) wrote *Leviathan* (1651) in which the life of man in a state of nature was characterized as brutish and untamed.
9. Arthur Felling ("Weegee") (1900–68), sensationalistic American news photographer.
1. Found objects. The insistence that

there are no "artistic" subjects, that anything will do if one makes something of it.
2. Swiss photographer (b. 1924) whose pictures of everyday American life can be found in *The Americans* (1959), with text by Jack Kerouac.

Hine, Brassaï, Evans, and Frank photographed. Arbus is an *auteur*[3] in the most limiting sense, as special a case in the history of photography as is Giorgio Morandi,[4] who spent a half century doing still lifes of bottles, in the history of modern European painting. She does not, like most ambitious photographers, play the field of subject matter—even a little. On the contrary, all her subjects are equivalent. And making equivalences between freaks, mad people, suburban couples, and nudists is a very powerful judgment, one in complicity with a recognizable political mood shared by many educated, left-liberal Americans. The subjects of Arbus's photographs are all members of the same family, inhabitants of a single village. Only, as it happens, the idiot village is America. Instead of showing identity between things which are different (Whitman's democratic vista), everybody is shown to look the same.

Succeeding the more buoyant hopes for America has come a bitter, sad embrace of experience. There is a particular melancholy in the American photographic project. But the melancholy was already latent in the heyday of Whitmanesque affirmation, as represented by Stieglitz and his Photo-Secession circle. Stieglitz, pledged to redeem the world with his camera, was still shocked by modern material civilization. He photographed New York in the 1910s in an almost quixotic spirit—camera/lance against skyscraper/windmill. Paul Rosenfeld described Stieglitz's efforts as a "perpetual affirmation." The Whitmanesque appetites have turned pious: the photographer now patronizes reality. One needs a camera to show patterns in that "dull and marvelous opacity called the United States."

Obviously, a mission as rotten with doubt about America—even at its most optimistic—was bound to get deflated fairly soon, as post–World War I America committed itself more boldly to big business and consumerism. Photographers with less ego and magnetism than Stieglitz gradually gave up the struggle. They might continue to practice the atomistic visual stenography inspired by Whitman. But, without Whitman's delirious powers of synthesis, what they documented was discontinuity, detritus, loneliness, greed, sterility. Stieglitz, using photography to challenge the materialist civilization, was, in Rosenfeld's words, "the man who believed that a spiritual America existed somewhere, that America was not the grave of the Occident." The implicit intent of Frank and Arbus, and of many of their contemporaries and juniors, is to show that America *is* the grave of the Occident.

Since photography cut loose from the Whitmanesque affirmation —since it has ceased to understand how photographs could aim at being literate, authoritative, transcendent—the best of American photography (and much else in American culture) has given itself over to the consolations of Surrealism, and America has been dis-

---

3. Creator, artist. The term is used by some film critics to describe the total control of the director over his film.
4. Italian painter (1890–1964).

covered as the quintessential Surrealist country. It is obviously too easy to say that America is just a freak show, a wasteland—the cut-rate pessimism typical of the reduction of the real to the surreal. But the American partiality to myths of redemption and damnation remains one of the most energizing, most seductive aspects of our national culture. What we have left of Whitman's discredited dream of cultural revolution are paper ghosts and a sharp-eyed witty program of despair.

1977

Contemporary American Poetry 1945–

M ORE THAN a decade after the end of World War II, two important and transforming shocks were administered to American poetry: Allen Ginsberg's *Howl* (1956) and Robert Lowell's *Life Studies* (1959). Ginsberg, in a single stroke and with the energy of a reborn Whitman, made poetry one of the rallying points for underground protest and prophetic denunciation of the prosperous, complacent, gray-spirited Eisenhower years. Lowell, a more "difficult," less popular poet, brought a new autobiographical intensity into American poetry by exposing the neuroses and bouts with insanity suffered by an inbred New Englander. The connection between such volumes and the times in which they were written is direct and apparent. The poems anticipated and explored strains in American social relationships which were to issue in the open conflicts of the 1960s and 1970s: public unrest about the uses of government and industrial power; the institutions of marriage and the family; the rights and powers of racial minorities, of women, and of homosexuals; the use of drugs; and the causes and consequences of mental disorders.

But social pressures cannot fully explain why American poets such as Lowell and Ginsberg felt ready to claim new authority and new areas of experience in their writing. However radical the changes in the style and content of American poetry of the 1950s and 1960s, its assurance was rooted in subtle, far-reaching developments of the decade before. American poetry had flourished in the late 1940s because of a new light in which American poets perceived themselves and because of the confidence they drew from the achievements of their predecessors in the first half of the century. Some paradoxes about what was "American," of course, remained. A prominent critic, referring to T. S. Eliot and Ezra Pound, could still assert: "During the past generation we have seen our two chief poets make their escape from America, the one to become an English subject and the other a partisan of Mussolini and, ultimately, a prisoner of our government." Arguably the best "American" poem of the 1940s proved to be Eliot's *Four Quartets* (1943), which had been written in England.

Nevertheless the accomplishments of other members of the generation of Pound and Eliot—poets who had remained in America and whose early reputations these two expatriates had overshadowed—were becoming solidly recognized and evaluated. Robert Frost, whose first *Collected Poems* (1930) received the Pulitzer Prize, was already well known. But William Carlos Williams and Wallace Stevens became influential for younger poets only through the major works they published after the war. The first two books of Williams's *Paterson* appeared in 1946 and 1948; Stevens published *Transport to Summer* in 1947, *The Auroras of Autumn* in 1950, and his *Collected Poems* in 1954. Younger poets who were to prove themselves the strongest of their generation began publishing notable books just after 1945: Elizabeth Bishop's first volume, *North & South* (1946); Robert Lowell's *Lord Weary's Castle* (1946); Richard Wilbur's *The Beautiful Changes* (1947); John Berryman's *The Dispossessed* (1948); and the important second volume by Theodore Roethke, *The Lost Son* (1948). After the death of the great Irish poet W. B. Yeats in 1939 and the immigration to the United States of his most notable English successor, W. H. Auden, it became clear that the center of poetic activity in the English language had shifted from Britain to America.

If there was a new confidence expressed by American poetry after World War II, there was also a new visibility for American poets. Earlier poets had been relatively isolated from the American public: Pound and Eliot lived in Europe; Wallace Stevens was a businessman in Hartford; William Carlos Williams was a small-town doctor in New Jersey. Poetry readings had been relatively rare performances by the few famous poets of the familiar poems the audience already knew but wanted to hear from the illustrious presence himself. After the war, writers' conferences and workshops, recordings, published and broadcast interviews became more common. A network of poets traveling to give readings and of poets-in-residence at universities began to form. In the 1960s and 1970s, readings became less formal, more numerous and accessible, held not only in auditoriums but in coffee houses, bars, and lofts. The purpose of these more casual readings was often to introduce new poets or, perhaps, new poems by an already recognized writer. The poet coming of age after the war was, as one of them, Richard Wilbur, put it, more a "poet-citizen" than an alienated artist. He often made his living by putting together a combination of teaching positions, readings, and foundation grants.

A poet's education in the 1950s probably differed from that of poets in an earlier generation. Writing poetry in the postwar years became firmly linked to the English literature curriculum in ways that it had not been in the past. Many of the young poets were taught to read verse and sometimes to write it by influential literary critics who were often poets themselves: John Crowe Ransom, Yvor Winters, Robert Penn Warren, R. P. Blackmur, Allen Tate. There was, for better or worse, the college major in English literature, as there had not been in so narrow and disciplined a sense for the poetic giants of a generation earlier. Eliot, for example, had done graduate work in philosophy, Pound in Romance philology, Williams had gone to medical school; and each had forged his own literary criticism. A younger poet, on the other hand, *studied* Eliot's essays, or learned critical approaches to literature in English courses such as the ones Allen Ginsberg took from Mark Van Doren and Lionel Trilling at Columbia or James Merrill from Reuben Brower at Amherst. A popular critical text, *Understanding Poetry* (1938) by Cleanth Brooks and Robert Penn Warren, taught students to be close readers of English metaphysical poems of the seventeenth century, such as those by John Donne and Andrew Marvell. As the poet W. D. Snodgrass testifies, "In school we had been taught to write a very difficult and very intellectual poem. We tried to achieve the obscure and dense texture of the French symbolists (very intuitive and often deranged poets), but by using methods similar to those of the very intellectual and conscious poets of the English Renaissance, especially the Metaphysical poets."

A young writer, thus trained to read intricate traditional lyrics, did not expect to encounter much, if any, contemporary verse in the classroom. The student had to seek out modern poems in the literary quarterlies or come upon them through the chance recommendations of informed friends and teachers. And whether a beginning poet fell, in this private, accidental way, under the influence of Eliot's ironic elegies or Stevens's high rhapsodies or William Carlos Williams's homemade documentaries, he was prepared to think of a poem as something "other" than the poet himself, objective, free from the quirks of the personal.

In the 1950s, while there was no dominant prescription for a poem, the short lyric meditation was held in high regard. Avoiding the first person, poets would find an object, a landscape, or an observed encounter which epitomized and clarified their feelings. A poem was the product of retrospection, a gesture of composure following the initial shock or stimulus which provided the occasion for writing. Often composed in intricate stanzas and skillfully rhymed, such a poem deployed its mastery of verse form as one sign of the civilized mind's power to explore, tame, and distill raw experience. Richard Wilbur's verse was especially valued for its speculative neatness, a poise which was often associated with the awareness of the historical values of European culture. It was a time of renewed travel in Europe; there were Fulbright fellowships for American students to study abroad, prizes for writers who wanted to travel and write in Europe. Wilbur and others wrote poems about European art and artifacts and landscapes as a way of testing American experience against the alternative ways of life, for example, American Puritanism or notions of virtue, viewed against such complicated pleasures as those embodied in the seventeenth-century sculpted fountain described in Wilbur's *A Baroque Wall-Fountain in the Villa Sciarra*. Unlike the pessimistic Eliot of *The Waste Land*, such poets found the treasures of the past—its art and literature—nourishing in poems whose chief pleasure was that of evaluation and balancing, of weighing such alternatives as spirituality and worldliness.

That was one side of the picture. The other side, equally important, was the way many of these same young poets reacted to (*to*, rather than *against*) their training. Richard Howard, in a happy phrase, calls this postwar generation of poets "the children of Midas." He is thinking of the last phases of the classical myth, when King Midas, having discovered that everything he touches ("his food, his women, his words") inconveniently turns to gold, prays to lose the gift of the golden touch. "What seems to me especially proper to these poets," Howard says, "* * * is the last development, the longing to *lose* the gift of order, despoiling the self of all that had been, merely, *propriety*." In the 1950s and 1960s there were some very extreme examples of poets transforming themselves: Allen Ginsberg, who began by writing formal quatrains, became the free and rambunctious poet of *Howl*; Sylvia Plath, who began as a well-mannered imitator of

Eliot and Dylan Thomas, turned into the intense suicidal protagonist of *Ariel* (1966). It is a special mark of this period that a poet as bookish, as literary, as academic as John Berryman, who started out writing like Auden and Yeats, should also have written the wildest and most disquieting lyrics of his time, *The Dream Songs* (1964, 1968).

The new confidential and technical sophistication of American poetry in the 1940s fostered the more exploratory styles of the 1950s and 1960s. Some changes were more noticeable and notorious than others. For one thing, poetry seemed to be extending its subject matter to more explicit and extreme areas of autobiography: insanity, sex, divorce, alcoholism. The convenient but not very precise label "confessional" came to be attached to certain books: Robert Lowell's *Life Studies*, which explored the disorders of several generations of his New England family; Anne Sexton's *To Bedlam and Part Way Back* (1960) and *All My Pretty Ones* (1962), which dealt openly with abortion, the sex life of women, the poet's own life in mental hospitals; W. D. Snodgrass's *Heart's Needle* (1969), whose central lyric sequence chronicled the stages of divorce from the point of view of a husband separated from his wife and child; John Berryman's *Dream Songs*, which exposed his alcoholism and struggle with insanity. Allen Ginsberg's *Howl* celebrated his homosexuality. Sylvia Plath's *Ariel* explored the frantic energies of a woman on the edge of suicide.

Some of the poetry of this period was avowedly political, tending in the 1950s to general protest and in the 1960s to more specifically focused critiques. The Beats of the 1950s—with *Howl* as their manifesto—had no one particular object of protest. Their work envisioned freer life styles and explored underground alternatives to life in a standardized or mechanized society. The pun on the word "Beat" linked them on the one side to a downtrodden drifting underground community—drugs, homosexuality, political radicalism—and, on the other, to a new "beatitude," made available by Eastern religious cults that many members of this generation espoused. Gary Snyder, who in the 1950s was with the Beats in San Francisco, is one example of how their protests were extended and focused in the next decades. In his books of the Sixties and Seventies such as *Earth House Hold* and *Turtle Island* he dramatizes a very specific alternative to American suburban and urban sprawl: he describes and advocates a life of almost Thoreauvian simplicity in a commune in the Sierras.

Many poets in the 1960s identified themselves with specific reform and protest movements. Denise Levertov, Adrienne Rich, and Robert Lowell, among others, directed poems against American participation in the Vietnam war and our government's support of the corrupt South Vietnam regime. Robert Lowell publicly refused President Johnson's invitation to a White House dinner and was a participant in the 1967 march against the Pentagon which Norman Mailer describes in *Armies of the Night*. Robert Bly and others used the occasion of receiving poetry prizes to make anti-war statements. The important freedom movements of the 1960s—advocating black power, women's liberation, and gay rights—had spokesmen among committed poets. Black poets such as Gwendolyn Brooks and LeRoi Jones (later Imamu Baraka) who had already had considerable success with white audiences, turned to address exclusively black constituencies. Small presses, notably the Broadside Press, were founded for the publication of black poets, and others devoted themselves to feminist writing.

Some poetry of the late 1960s had the insistence, urgency, and singlemind-edness of political tracts. But the more enduring effect of political protest on poetry was to make a broader, more insistent range of voices available to verse; poems dramatized individual predicaments, stressing the under-lying angers and desires that also issue in political action. Black poets experimented in bringing out the distinctive speech rhythms of Black English; they stressed the oral values of verse—its openness to song, to angry chant, and to the cadenced complaint of the "blues." Among feminists, Adrienne Rich, in books such as *Diving into the Wreck* and *The Dream of a Common Language,* stressed the power of poetic language to explore the fan-tasies, buried rage, and special awareness of women.

In an indirect but vital sense the heightened energies of almost all po-etry in the 1960s and 1970s had political implications. With the increasing standardization of speech, a documented decline in reading skills in the schools, the dominance of nationwide television, poems provided a special resource for individual expression, a resistance to the leveling force of official language, and access to profoundly individual areas of consciousness. In that context poets are superficially apolitical as James Wright, W. S. Mer-win, James Merrill, and John Ashberry were by their very cultivation of private vision making distinctly political choices.

In response to the pressures, inner and outer, of the Fifties and Sixties, new kinds of poems took their place alongside the favored "objective" poems of the late Forties. As some poets aimed more at exposing than at composing the self, they demanded more open forms to suggest vagaries, twists, and confusions of mind or else its potential directness and sponta-neity. Their poems depended on less rhyme, sparer use of regular stanzas and metrics, even new ways of spacing a poem on the page. Critics talked of organic form, using free verse which took its length of line or its visual form on the page from the poet's provisional or intense feelings at the moment of composition. The most insistent formulations of this attitude are to be found in the manifestoes of the so-called Black Mountain School, a group of poets gathered at Black Mountain College in North Carolina and very much influenced by its rector, Charles Olson. Olson's famous pro-nouncements on "Projective Verse" were first published in 1950. Ordinary lineation, straight left-hand margins, regular meters and verse forms were to be discarded in favor of a free placement of lines and phrases over the page. The unit of poetic expression was to be not a predetermined metrical foot but the poet's "breath"; breaks in the line corresponded to the mental and physical energy enlisted to get the words on the page. Olson's purpose was to put the poem in touch—as in certain forms of meditation or yoga—with an individual poet's natural rhythms, often buried by acquired verbal skills. The poet was not to revise his poems to any great extent; he might make considerable mental preparation or store up intense feeling before writing, but the poem itself was to represent feeling at the moment of composition. Another corollary of Olson's theories, not part of the Black Mountain credo but growing logically from it, was the notion that a poem was in some way provisional. In contrast to the notion of the 1940s that a poem was a completed and permanent object, some poets saw their work as transitory, incomplete, an instrument of passage. Allen Ginsberg and Adrienne Rich carefully date each of their poems as if to suggest that the feelings involved are peculiarly subject to revision by later experience.

A parallel development—only very loosely related to the San Francisco Beat explosion and Black Mountain manifestoes—took place among a group of poets involved with and inspired by the work of nonrepresentational or Abstract Expressionist painters in New York. The so-called New York School included John Ashbery, Kenneth Koch, James Schuyler, and the figure whose friendship and enthusiasm held them all together, Frank O'Hara. It was O'Hara with his breezy diary poems, almost throwaways, who most typified their belief in the poem as a chronicle of its occasion and of the act of composing it. As O'Hara said in his offhand parody of sober poetic credos, *Personism: A Manifesto* (1959); "The poem is at last between two persons instead of two pages. * * * In all modesty, I confess that it may be the death of literature as we know it."

American poetry emerged from the 1960s enriched, its technical and thematic range enormously expanded. The only single common denominator among these various directions of change was the desire to make poetry less distant—in both sound and subject matter—from its potential readers. The poems of the 1970s were not to be, indeed could not be, as technically innovative as those of the previous decade. The political impulse behind much radical poetry had waned; the main exception was women's poetry, which, especially in response to the work of Adrienne Rich, continued to explore areas special to feminism.

The 1960s had changed the face of American poetry, and it seemed the task of poets in the 1970s not so much to innovate as to consolidate and perhaps reinterpret the achievement of the previous three decades. What characterized the world of American poetry was its pluralism and the power of its best poets to absorb a variety of influences. Traditional verse and metrical forms had not been left behind, but they took their place among a number of poetic resources rather than as obligatory models of poetic decorum. The single perfect and self-contained lyric ceased to define the boundary of poetic ambitions, and the high ambitions of Pound in his *Cantos* or William Carlos Williams in *Paterson* (reaching back to Whitman and *Leaves of Grass*) stood out in bold relief as extensions of poetic possibility. Robert Lowell in *Notebook* showed one of the ways the poetic virtues of the three decades since the war might be combined: it consisted of a series of unrhymed sonnets, which served as a journal. "If I saw something one day, I wrote it that day, or the next, or the next. Things I felt or saw or read were drift to the whirlpool, the squeeze of the sonnet and the loose ravel of blank verse." Berryman's *Dream Songs*, however strict their stanzaic form and their use of rhyme, was a sequence with enormous flexibility of voice and richly varied exposures of the self. Sequences of poems provided one way of countering neat closure and of suggesting both the fluidity of external life and the complexity of consciousness. Long poems provided another alternative. In a bold stroke James Merrill's series of three book-length "Divine Comedies" was a sign that poetic ambitions were taking a new direction. Many American poets did not want to think of their poems as the shards or fragments of modern literature. They perhaps remembered that Wallace Stevens, whose first published volume was *Harmonium*, wanted to call his collected poems *The Whole of Harmonium*. For some writers the poem was once again to fulfill the Romantic poet Wordsworth's ambition to record "the growth of a poet's mind" in a modern epic of consciousness. As poetry moved away from the single lyrics of the immediate postwar period, ambitions once again focused on allowing shorter poetic efforts to grow into larger construction; the strength of longer poems or related series of poems lay not in their paraphrasable message or their power to project an "objective correlative" for a small poetic truth but in their extended power to present particularized models of the mind's continuing struggle for insight.

THEODORE ROETHKE
1908–1963

Theodore Roethke was born in Saginaw, Michigan, where both his German grandfather and his father kept greenhouses for a living. "I was born under a glass heel and have always lived there," he was to remark. He was haunted not only by the ordered, protected world of the paternal greenhouse and its cultivated flowers, but also by the desolate landscape of that part of Michigan. "The marsh, the mire, the Void, is always there, immediate and terrifying. It is a splendid place for schooling the spirit. It is America."

Roethke's poetry often re-enacted this "schooling" of the spirit by revisiting the landscapes of his childhood: the nature poems which make up the largest part of his early work try to bridge the distance between a child's consciousness and the adult mysteries presided over by his father. Roethke arranged and rearranged these poems to give the sense of a spiritual autobiography, especially in preparing the volumes *The Lost Son* (1948), *Praise to the End!* (1951), and *The Waking* (1953). The greenhouse world emerged as a "reality harsher than reality," the cultivator's activity pulsating and threatening. Its overseers, like "Frau Bauman, Frau Schmidt, and Frau Schwartze," emerge as gods, fates, and witches all in one. It was by focusing on the minute processes of botanical growth—the rooting, the budding—that the poet found a way of participating in the mysteries of this once alien world, "alive in a slippery grave."

Another of Roethke's ways of regenerating himself was to explore prerational speech, like children's riddles, to recapture a nonlogical state of being. One of the sections of *The Lost Son* is called "The Gibber," a pun referring both to meaningless utterance and to the technical name for the pouch at the base of the calyx of a flower. The pun identifies a principle of growth with prehuman and childish speech. *The Lost Son* suggests that recapturing a childlike merger with nature might revive the spirit of an adult life: "A lively understandable spirit / Once entertained you. / It will come again. / Be still. / Wait."

If the nature poems of Roethke's first four books explore the anxieties with him since childhood, his later love poems show him in periods of release and momentary pleasure.

> And I dance round and round,
> A fond and foolish man,
> And see and suffer myself
> In another being at last.

The love poems, many of them included in *Words for the Wind* (1958) and *The Far Field* (1964), are among the most appealing in recent American verse. They stand in sharp relief to the suffering Roethke experienced in other areas of his personal life—several mental breakdowns and periods of alcoholism—which led to a premature death. *The Far Field*, a posthumous volume, includes fierce, strongly rhymed lyrics in which Roethke tried "bare, even terrible statement." In these last great poems he moves beyond nature and physical sensation, pressing the senses toward the threshold of spiritual insight:

> I teach my eyes to hear, my ears to see
> How body from spirit slowly does unwind
> Until we are pure spirit at the end.

Even the nature poems of this last volume, gathered as "The North American Sequence" (from which *The Far Field* is taken) are "journeys to the interior." They use extended landscape to find natural analogies for the human passage toward death, hoping "in their rhythms to catch the very movement of the mind itself."

Roethke is remembered as one of the great teachers of poetry, especially by those young poets and critics who studied with him at the University of Washington from 1948 until the time of his death in 1963. James Wright, David Wagoner, and Richard Hugo, among others, attended his classes. He was noted for his mastery of sound and metrics. Though his own poetry was intensely personal, his starting advice to students always de-emphasized undisciplined self-expression. "Write like someone else," was his instruction to beginners. His own apprenticeship to Blake and to Yeats had shown him how their lyric voices allowed him to discover related but unsuspected voices within himself.

Roethke was much honored later in his career: a Pulitzer Prize for *The Waking* (1953); a National Book Award and Bollingen Prize for the collected poems, *Words for the Wind* (1958), and a posthumous National Book Award for *The Far Field* (1964).

Cuttings

> Sticks-in-a-drowse droop over sugary loam,
> Their intricate stem-fur dries;
> But still the delicate slips keep coaxing up water;
> The small cells bulge;
>
> One nub of growth   5
> Nudges a sand-crumb loose,
> Pokes through a musty sheath
> Its pale tendrilous horn.

1948

Cuttings

(*later*)

> This urge, wrestle, resurrection of dry sticks,
> Cut stems struggling to put down feet,
> What saint strained so much,
> Rose on such lopped limbs to a new life?
>
> I can hear, underground, that sucking and sobbing,   5
> In my veins, in my bones I feel it,—
> The small waters seeping upward,

The tight grains parting at last.
When sprouts break out,
Slippery as a fish   10
I quail, lean to beginnings, sheath-wet.

                                                      1948

Weed Puller

Under the concrete benches,
Hacking at black hairy roots,—
Those lewd monkey-tails hanging from drainholes,—
Digging into the soft rubble underneath,
Webs and weeds,   5
Grubs and snails and sharp sticks,
Or yanking tough fern-shapes,
Coiled green and thick, like dripping smilax,[1]
Tugging all day at perverse life:
The indignity of it!—   10
With everything blooming above me,
Lilies, pale-pink cyclamen, roses,
Whole fields lovely and inviolate,—
Me down in that fetor[2] of weeds,
Crawling on all fours,   15
Alive, in a slippery grave.

                                                      1948

Frau Bauman, Frau Schmidt,
and Frau Schwartze[1]

Gone the three ancient ladies
Who creaked on the greenhouse ladders,
Reaching up white strings
To wind, to wind
The sweet-pea tendrils, the smilax,   5
Nasturtiums, the climbing
Roses, to straighten
Carnations, red
Chrysanthemums; the stiff
Stems, jointed like corn,   10
They tied and tucked,—
These nurses of nobody else.
Quicker than birds, they dipped
Up and sifted the dirt;
They sprinkled and shook;   15
They stood astride pipes,
Their skirts billowing out wide into tents,
Their hands twinkling with wet;
Like witches they flew along rows
Keeping creation at ease;   20
With a tendril for needle
They sewed up the air with a stem;

---

1. A type of fern.
2. Stench.

1. Women who worked in the greenhouse
owned by Roethke's father.

They teased out the seed that the cold kept asleep,—
All the coils, loops, and whorls.
They trellised the sun; they plotted for more than themselves. 25
I remember how they picked me up, a spindly kid,
Pinching and poking my thin ribs
Till I lay in their laps, laughing,
Weak as a whiffet;[2]
Now, when I'm alone and cold in my bed, 30
They still hover over me,
These ancient leathery crones,
With their bandannas stiffened with sweat,
And their thorn-bitten wrists,
And their snuff-laden breath blowing lightly over me in my first
    sleep. 35

1948

My Papa's Waltz

The whiskey on your breath
Could make a small boy dizzy;
But I hung on like death:
Such waltzing was not easy.

We romped until the pans 5
Slid from the kitchen shelf;
My mother's countenance
Could not unfrown itself.

The hand that held my wrist
Was battered on one knuckle; 10
At every step you missed
My right ear scraped a buckle.

You beat time on my head
With a palm caked hard by dirt,
Then waltzed me off to bed 15
Still clinging to your shirt.

1948

The Lost Son

1. The Flight

At Woodlawn[1] I heard the dead cry:
I was lulled by the slamming of iron,
A slow drip over stones,
Toads brooding wells.
All the leaves stuck out their tongues; 5
I shook the softening chalk of my bones,
Saying,
Snail, snail, glister me forward,
Bird, soft-sigh me home,

2. A small, young or unimportant person (probably from *whippet*, a small   dog).
1. A cemetery.

Worm, be with me. 10
This is my hard time.

Fished in an old wound,
The soft pond of repose;
Nothing nibbled my line,
Not even the minnows came. 15

Sat in an empty house
Watching shadows crawl,
Scratching.
There was one fly.

Voice, come out of the silence. 20
Say something.
Appear in the form of a spider
Or a moth beating the curtain.

Tell me:
Which is the way I take; 25
Out of what door do I go,
Where and to whom?

Dark hollows said, lee to the wind,
The moon said, back of an eel,
The salt said, look by the sea, 30
Your tears are not enough praise,
You will find no comfort here,
In the kingdom of bang and blab.

Running lightly over spongy ground,
Past the pasture of flat stones, 35
The three elms,
The sheep strewn on a field,
Over a rickety bridge
Toward the quick-water, wrinkling and rippling.

Hunting along the river, 40
Down among the rubbish, the bug-riddled foliage,
By the muddy pond-edge, by the bog-holes,
By the shrunken lake, hunting, in the heat of summer.

The shape of a rat?
It's bigger than that. 45
It's less than a leg
And more than a nose,
Just under the water
It usually goes.

Is it soft like a mouse? 50
Can it wrinkle its nose?

Could it come in the house
On the tips of its toes?

Take the skin of a cat
And the back of an eel,—   55
Then roll them in grease,—
That's the way it would feel.

It's sleek as an otter
With wide webby toes
Just under the water   60
It usually goes.

2. The Pit

Where do the roots go?
        Look down under the leaves.
Who put the moss there?
        These stones have been here too long.   65
Who stunned the dirt into noise?
        Ask the mole, he knows.
I feel the slime of a wet nest.
        Beware Mother Mildew.
Nibble again, fish nerves.   70

3. The Gibber

At the wood's mouth,
By the cave's door,
I listened to something
I had heard before.

Dogs of the groin   75
Barked and howled,
The sun was against me,
The moon would not have me.

The weeds whined,
The snakes cried,   80
The cows and briars
Said to me: Die.

What a small song. What slow clouds. What dark water.
Hath the rain a father? All the caves are ice. Only the snow's here.
I'm cold. I'm cold all over. Rub me in father and mother.   85
Fear was my father, Father Fear.
His look drained the stones.

        What gliding shape
        Beckoning through halls,
        Stood poised on the stair,   90
        Fell dreamily down?

From the mouths of jugs
Perched on many shelves,
I saw substance flowing
That cold morning.   95

Like a slither of eels
That watery cheek
As my own tongue kissed
My lips awake.

Is this the storm's heart? The ground is unstilling itself.   100
My veins are running nowhere. Do the bones cast out their fire?
Is the seed leaving the old bed? These buds are live as birds.
Where, where are the tears of the world?
Let the kisses resound, flat like a butcher's palm;
Let the gestures freeze; our doom is already decided.   105
All the windows are burning! What's left of my life?
I want the old rage, the lash of primordial milk!
Goodbye, goodbye, old stones, the time-order is going,
I have married my hands to perpetual agitation,
I run, I run to the whistle of money.   110

Money money money
Water water water

How cool the grass is.
Has the bird left?
The stalk still sways.   115
Has the worm a shadow?
What do the clouds say?

These sweeps of light undo me.
Look, look, the ditch is running white!
I've more veins than a tree!   120
Kiss me, ashes, I'm falling through a dark swirl.

4. The Return

The way to the boiler was dark,
Dark all the way,
Over slippery cinders
Through the long greenhouse.   125

The roses kept breathing in the dark.
They had many mouths to breathe with.
My knees made little winds underneath
Where the weeds slept.

There was always a single light   130
Swinging by the fire-pit,
Where the fireman pulled out roses,
The big roses, the big bloody clinkers.[2]

2. Large cinders; the residue left in burning coal.

Once I stayed all night.
The light in the morning came slowly over the white   135
Snow.
There were many kinds of cool
Air.
Then came steam.

Pipe-knock.   140

Scurry of warm over small plants.
Ordnung! ordnung![3]
Papa is coming!

A fine haze moved off the leaves;
Frost melted on far panes;   145
The rose, the chrysanthemum turned toward the light.
Even the hushed forms, the bent yellowy weeds
Moved in a slow up-sway.

5. *"It was beginning winter"*

It was beginning winter,
An in-between time,   150
The landscape still partly brown:
The bones of weeds kept swinging in the wind,
Above the blue snow.

It was beginning winter,
The light moved slowly over the frozen field,   155
Over the dry seed-crowns,
The beautiful surviving bones
Swinging in the wind.

Light traveled over the wide field;
Stayed.   160
The weeds stopped swinging.
The mind moved, not alone,
Through the clear air, in the silence.

Was it light?
Was it light within?   165
Was it light within light?
Stillness becoming alive,
Yet still?

A lively understandable spirit
Once entertained you.   170
It will come again.
Be still.
Wait.

                                                             1948

3. A call to order.

The Waking[1]

I wake to sleep, and take my waking slow.
I feel my fate in what I cannot fear.
I learn by going where I have to go.

We think by feeling. What is there to know?
I hear my being dance from ear to ear.
I wake to sleep, and take my waking slow.

Of those so close beside me, which are you?
God bless the Ground! I shall walk softly there,
And learn by going where I have to go.

Light takes the Tree; but who can tell us how?
The lowly worm climbs up a winding stair;
I wake to sleep, and take my waking slow.

Great Nature has another thing to do
To you and me; so take the lively air,
And, lovely, learn by going where to go.

This shaking keeps me steady. I should know.
What falls away is always. And is near.
I wake to sleep, and take my waking slow.
I learn by going where I have to go.

1953

I Knew a Woman

I knew a woman, lovely in her bones,
When small birds sighed, she would sigh back at them;
Ah, when she moved, she moved more ways than one:
The shapes a bright container can contain!
Of her choice virtues only gods should speak,
Or English poets who grew up on Greek
(I'd have them sing in chorus, cheek to cheek).

How well her wishes went! She stroked my chin,
She taught me Turn, and Counter-turn, and Stand;[1]
She taught me Touch, that undulant white skin;
I nibbled meekly from her proffered hand;
She was the sickle; I, poor I, the rake,
Coming behind her for her pretty sake
(But what prodigious mowing we did make).

Love likes a gander, and adores a goose:
Her full lips pursed, the errant note to seize;
She played it quick, she played it light and loose;
My eyes, they dazzled at her flowing knees;

---

1. The poem's form is that of a villanelle. 1. Parts of a Pindaric ode.

Her several parts could keep a pure repose,
Or one hip quiver with a mobile nose   20
(She moved in circles, and those circles moved).

Let seed be grass, and grass turn into hay:
I'm martyr to a motion not my own;
What's freedom for? To know eternity.
I swear she cast a shadow white as stone.   25
But who would count eternity in days?
These old bones live to learn her wanton ways:
(I measure time by how a body sways).

                                                   1958

The Far Field[1]

1

I dream of journeys repeatedly:
Of flying like a bat deep into a narrowing tunnel,
Of driving alone, without luggage, out a long peninsula,
The road lined with snow-laden second growth,
A fine dry snow ticking the windshield,   5
Alternate snow and sleet, no on-coming traffic,
And no lights behind, in the blurred side-mirror,
The road changing from glazed tarface to a rubble of stone,
Ending at last in a hopeless sand-rut,
Where the car stalls,   10
Churning in a snowdrift
Until the headlights darken.

2

At the field's end, in the corner missed by the mower,
Where the turf drops off into a grass-hidden culvert,
Haunt of the cat-bird, nesting-place of the field-mouse,   15
Not too far away from the ever-changing flower-dump,
Among the tin cans, tires, rusted pipes, broken machinery,—
One learned of the eternal;
And in the shrunken face of a dead rat, eaten by rain and
       groundbeetles
(I found it lying among the rubble of an old coal bin)   20
And the tom-cat, caught near the pheasant-run,
Its entrails strewn over the half-grown flowers,
Blasted to death by the night watchman.

I suffered for birds, for young rabbits caught in the mower,
My grief was not excessive.   25
For to come upon warblers in early May
Was to forget time and death:
How they filled the oriole's elm, a twittering restless cloud,
       all one morning,

1. The penultimate of six poems in Roethke's "North American Sequence" from *The Far Field.*

And I watched and watched till my eyes blurred from the
    bird shapes,—
Cape May, Blackburnian, Cerulean,[2]—   30
Moving, elusive as fish, fearless,
Hanging, bunched like young fruit, bending the end branches,
Still for a moment,
Then pitching away in half-flight,
Lighter than finches,   35
While the wrens bickered and sang in the half-green hedgerows,
And the flicker drummed from his dead tree in the chicken-yard.

—Or to lie naked in sand,
In the silted shallows of a slow river,
Fingering a shell,   40
Thinking:
Once I was something like this, mindless,
Or perhaps with another mind, less peculiar;
Or to sink down to the hips in a mossy quagmire;
Or, with skinny knees, to sit astride a wet log,   45
Believing:
I'll return again,
As a snake or a raucous bird,
Or, with luck, as a lion.

I learned not to fear infinity,   50
The far field, the windy cliffs of forever,
The dying of time in the white light of tomorrow,
The wheel turning away from itself,
The sprawl of the wave,
The on-coming water.   55

3

The river turns on itself,
The tree retreats into its own shadow.
I feel a weightless change, a moving forward
As of water quickening before a narrowing channel
When banks converge, and the wide river whitens;   60
Or when two rivers combine, the blue glacial torrent
And the yellowish-green from the mountainy upland,—
At first a swift rippling between rocks,
Then a long running over flat stones
Before descending to the alluvial plain,[3]   65
To the clay banks, and the wild grapes hanging from the elmtrees.
The slightly trembling water
Dropping a fine yellow silt where the sun stays;
And the crabs bask near the edge,
The weedy edge, alive with small snakes and bloodsuckers,—   70

I have come to a still, but not a deep center,
A point outside the glittering current;

2. Names of warblers.
3. Soil deposited by flowing water, as in river deltas.

My eyes stare at the bottom of a river,
At the irregular stones, iridescent sandgrains,
My mind moves in more than one place,   75
In a country half-land, half-water.

I am renewed by death, thought of my death,
The dry scent of a dying garden in September,
The wind fanning the ash of a low fire.
What I love is near at hand,   80
Always, in earth and air.

                                  4

The lost self changes,
Turning toward the sea,
A sea-shape turning around,—
An old man with his feet before the fire,   85
In robes of green, in garments of adieu.

A man faced with his own immensity
Wakes all the waves, all their loose wandering fire.
The murmur of the absolute, the why
Of being born falls on his naked ears.   90
His spirit moves like monumental wind
That gentles on a sunny blue plateau.
He is the end of things, the final man.

All finite things reveal infinitude:
The mountain with its singular bright shade   95
Like the blue shine on freshly frozen snow,
The after-light upon ice-burdened pines;
Odor of basswood on a mountain-slope,
A scent beloved of bees;
Silence of water above a sunken tree: 100
The pure serene of memory in one man,—
A ripple widening from a single stone
Winding around the waters of the world.

                                                          1964

Her Longing

          Before this longing,
          I lived serene as a fish,
          At one with the plants in the pond,
          The mare's tail, the floating frogbit,
          Among my eight-legged friends,   5
          Open like a pool, a lesser parsnip,
          Like a leech, looping myself along,
          A bug-eyed edible one,
          A mouth like a stickleback,—
          A thing quiescent!   10

          But now—
          The wild stream, the sea itself cannot contain me:

I dive with the black hag, the cormorant,[1]
Or walk the pebbly shore with the humpbacked heron,
Shaking out my catch in the morning sunlight,   15
Or rise with the gar-eagle, the great-winged condor.[2]
Floating over the mountains,
Pitting my breast against the rushing air,
A phoenix, sure of my body,
Perpetually rising out of myself,   20
My wings hovering over the shorebirds,
Or beating against the black clouds of the storm,
Protecting the sea-cliffs.

                                                    1964

Her Time

When all
My waterfall
Fancies sway away
From me, in the sea's silence;
In the time   5
When the tide moves
Neither forward nor back,
And the small waves
Begin rising whitely,
And the quick winds   10
Flick over the close whitecaps,
And two scoters fly low,
Their four wings beating together,
And my salt-laden hair
Flies away from my face   15
Before the almost invisible
Spray, and the small shapes
Of light on the far
Cliff disappear in a last
Glint of the sun, before   20
The long surf of the storm booms
Down on the near shore,
When everything—birds, men, dogs—
Runs to cover:
I'm one to follow,   25
To follow.

                                                    1964

Wish for a Young Wife

My lizard, my lively writher,
May your limbs never wither,
May the eyes in your face
Survive the green ice
Of envy's mean gaze;   5

---

1. A large, black, voracious seabird.   2. Mountain birds of prey.

May you live out your life
Without hate, without grief,
And your hair ever blaze,
In the sun, in the sun,
When I am undone,   10
When I am no one.

                                                   1964

In a Dark Time

In a dark time, the eye begins to see,
I meet my shadow in the deepening shade;
I hear my echo in the echoing wood—
A lord of nature weeping to a tree.
I live between the heron and the wren,   5
Beasts of the hill and serpents of the den.

What's madness but nobility of soul
At odds with circumstance? The day's on fire!
I know the purity of pure despair,
My shadow pinned against a sweating wall.   10
That place among the rocks—is it a cave,
Or winding path? The edge is what I have.

A steady storm of correspondences!
A night flowing with birds, a ragged moon,
And in broad day the midnight come again!   15
A man goes far to find out what he is—
Death of the self in a long, tearless night,
All natural shapes blazing unnatural light.

Dark, dark my light, and darker my desire.
My soul, like some heat-maddened summer fly,   20
Keeps buzzing at the sill. Which I is *I*?
A fallen man, I climb out of my fear.
The mind enters itself, and God the mind,
And one is One, free in the tearing[1] wind.

                                                   1964

Infirmity

In purest song one plays the constant fool
As changes shimmer in the inner eye.
I stare and stare into a deepening pool
And tell myself my image cannot die.
I love myself: that's my one constancy.   5
Oh, to be something else, yet still to be!

Sweet Christ, rejoice in my infirmity;
There's little left I care to call my own.

---

1. With a pun, referring to "tearless" in line 17 (according to Roethke's note).

Today they drained the fluid from a knee
And pumped a shoulder full of cortisone;   10
Thus I conform to my divinity
By dying inward, like an aging tree.

The instant ages on the living eye;
Light on its rounds, a pure extreme of light
Breaks on me as my meager flesh breaks down—   15
The soul delights in that extremity.
Blessed the meek; they shall inherit wrath;[1]
I'm son and father of my only death.

A mind too active is no mind at all;
The deep eye sees the shimmer on the stone;   20
The eternal seeks, and finds, the temporal,
The change from dark to light of the slow moon,
Dead to myself, and all I hold most dear,
I move beyond the reach of wind and fire.

Deep in the greens of summer sing the lives   25
I've come to love. A vireo whets its bill.
The great day balances upon the leaves;
My ears still hear the bird when all is still;
My soul is still my soul, and still the Son,
And knowing this, I am not yet undone.   30

Things without hands take hands: there is no choice,—
Eternity's not easily come by.
When opposites come suddenly in place,
I teach my eyes to hear, my ears to see
How body from spirit slowly does unwind   35
Until we are pure spirit at the end.

                                                    1964

1. This is a paraphrase of Jesus' words in   the meek, for they shall inherit the earth"
the Sermon on the Mount, "Blessed are   (Matthew 5.4).

CHARLES OLSON

1910–1970

Charles Olson was not only a poet but the energizing critical force in a group of poets whose work was beginning to be known in the 1950s: Denise Levertov, Robert Creeley, and Robert Duncan among them. More than any other contemporary poet, Olson assumed for his admirers the status of guru, a combination of teacher, cultural theorist, literary critic, and anthropologist. His enthusiastic followers gathered from tapes and transcripts a record of his lectures and fugitive remarks which is equal in bulk to his collected poetry. Olson's influence grew out of his years at Black Mountain, an experimental college in North Carolina where he had served as an instructor and then as head or rector, succeeding the artist Josef Albers. In its flourishing years under the direction of Olson, the college included among its teachers and students key figures of the avant-garde: John Cage in music, Merce Cunningham in dance, Franz Kline and Robert Rauschenberg in painting.

Olson had made his mark, just before going to Black Mountain, with a critical study of Herman Melville and *Moby-Dick, Call Me Ishmael* (1947). The book, in one sense, declared Olson's personal independence of the formal academic system in which he had been closely involved up to that point. He had been, as he put it, "uneducated" at Wesleyan, Yale, and Harvard, had taught at Clark University in Worcester, Mass., and had taken an advanced degree in American Civilization at Harvard. *Call Me Ishmael*, unlike most literary studies coming out of universities at that time, was fiercely personal and unorthodox—almost a prose poem or collage, which, in prophetic tones, proclaimed new bearings in American literature. Olson credited Melville with discovering the symbolic importance of the Pacific; *Moby-Dick* gave access to the "unwarped primal world" which, according to the poet, was the true center of the American experience.

Olson claimed that "the substances of history now useful lie outside, under, right here, anywhere but in the direct continuum of society as we have had it." Therefore, his own work, as he makes clear in *The Kingfishers*, sharply cultivates the primitive sources of energy almost buried by civilized responses and instruments. "If I have any taste," he says, echoing the French poet Rimbaud, "it is only because I have interested myself / in what was slain in the sun. * * * I hunt among stones."

As a sometime archaeologist, Olson literally "hunted among stones." He spent some time studying earlier North American cultures and worked among the Mayan ruins in the Yucatán, trying to recover the living elements of an archaic way of life, the surviving elements of its language and the relation of its speech to the natural environment of that part of Mexico. Olson was concerned with how one broke through the crust of civilization and inherited perceptions to the instinctive and intimate connections between man and nature which Western cultures had buried or concealed.

In his lifetime poetic project, the Maximus poems, Olson sought to do for his own life what the anthropologist does for a lost civilization; he aimed at recapturing or reinstating lost links to the unconscious sources of his being. Ezra Pound's *Cantos*, with their mosaic of disjoined and recurrent images, provided a formal model; but, in Olson's eyes, Pound was too devoted to reviving the values of European culture. The Maximus poems were designed to capture the mythical spirit of place—the fishing town of Gloucester, Massachusetts, where Olson grew up in a neighborhood called Dogtown. Maximus is an enlarged version of its author. The facts of Olson's own life in Gloucester (including perhaps even a joking allusion in the name Maximus to the fact that Olson was six-feet-eight) are used as a point of departure for an ambitious effort to project the entire historical, geological, and social presence of the town. Through the heightened awareness of Maximus, Olson tries to find the hidden energies which shape consciousness, "the primal features of those founders who lie buried in us." These features include the backgrounds and racial inheritance of his own Swedish father and Irish-American mother. They also include the communal dependence upon and subjection to the sea around the town. So, for example, when Gloucester celebrates the blessing of the fleet, or when tourists come to see a famous "bad statue of the Gloucester fisherman" in the town square (*Maximus, to Gloucester, Sunday, July* 19), Olson under-cuts such ceremonies by evoking the violence of the fisherman's life, the reality of death and danger at sea.

What was most radical about Olson's work was the way he attempted to recapture the direct energies of experience. He outlined a poetic tech-nique for accomplishing this aim in an influential manifesto called *Projective Verse* (1950). In Olson's proposed "open form," ordinary lineation, straight left-hand margin, regular meters and verse forms are to be dis-carded in favor of a free placement of lines and phrases over the page. This "composition by field" would allow, through typographical adjust-ments, for something like a musical score in which the length of pauses, the degree of emphasis, even changes of speed could be indicated. The unit of poetic expression was not a predetermined metrical foot, but the length of breath of the particular poet. The arrangement of words on the page would convey rhythms of thinking, breathing, and gesturing. Olson hoped to get closer to the individuality of a poet by making the poem a graph of the process through which it was produced. "A poem is energy transferred from where the poet got it * * * by way of the poem itself to, all the way over to, the reader." The poet expresses himself "as a creature of nature" and so regains his undistorted relation to "those other creations of nature which we may, with no derogation, call objects."

Like certain techniques of meditation and yoga, Olson's theory seems an effort to bring mental activity (here writing) in touch with its in-stinctive physical origins. Poetry was to be in no sense a summary or a description, but a notation of the self at a particular moment. Whether Olson realized this idea in his own writing or not, he influenced poets far beyond his immediate circle at Black Mountain. The theory justified a new stress on poetry of the present tense and on poetry which attempted to reproduce the fragmentation of mental activity. Though Olson extended many of Ezra Pound's notions of poetic immediacy, he transferred the authority for perceiving mythic truth from the mind dependent on Euro-pean culture to the mind striving to get in touch with the instinctive roots of its own behavior.

The Kingfishers

1

What does not change / is the will to change

He woke, fully clothed, in his bed. He
remembered only one thing, the birds, how
when he came in, he had gone around the rooms
and got them back in their cage, the green one first,   5
she with the bad leg, and then the blue,
the one they had hoped was a male

Otherwise? Yes, Fernand, who had talked
              lispingly of Albers[1] & Angkor Vat.[2]

---

1. Josef Albers (b. 1888), artist and teacher, first at the Bauhaus in Germany, then at Black Mountain College in North Carolina.

2. Or Wat, ruined temple complex built in the 12th century in the ancient Cam-bodian city of Angkor.

He had left the party without a word.   10
                              How he got up, got into his coat,
I do not know. When I saw him, he was
                        at the door, but it did not matter,
he was already sliding along the wall of the night, losing himself
in some crack of the ruins. That it should have   15
                        been he who said, "The kingfishers!

who cares
for their feathers
now?"

His last words had been, "The pool is slime." Suddenly everyone,   20
ceasing their talk, sat in a row around him, watched
they did not so much hear, or pay attention, they
wondered, looked at each other, smirked, but listened,
he repeated and repeated, could not go beyond his thought
"The pool   the kingfishers' feathers were wealth   why   25
did the export stop?"

It was then he left

                                   2
I thought of the E on the stone, and of what Mao[3] said
la lumiere"
                        but the kingfisher   30
de l'aurore"
                        but the kingfisher flew west
est devant nous![4]
                        he got the color of his breast
                        from the heat of the setting sun!   35

The features are, the feebleness of the feet
                              (syndactylism[5] of the 3rd & 4th digit)
the bill, serrated, sometimes a pronounced beak, the wings
where the color is, short and round, the tail
inconspicuous.   40

But not these things were the factors. Not the birds.
The legends are
legends. Dead, hung up indoors, the kingfisher
will not indicate a favoring wind,
or avert the thunderbolt. Nor, by its nesting,   45
still the waters, with the new year, for seven days.
It is true, it does nest with the opening
                              year, but not on the waters.
It nests at the end of a tunnel bored by itself in a bank. There,

3. Mao Tse-tung (1893–1976), revolutionary leader and political philosopher of
The People's Republic of China.
4. *"La lumière de l'aurore est devant*

nous": "The dawn's light is before us."
5. The condition of having two or more
digits joined partially or totally.

six or eight white and translucent eggs are laid, on fishbones   50
not on bare clay, on bones thrown up in pellets by the birds.

On these rejectamenta[6]
(as they accumulate they form a cup-shaped
structure) the young are born.
And, as they are fed and grow, this   55
nest of excrement and decayed fish becomes
a dripping, fetid mass
Mao concluded:
nous devons
nous lever   60
et agir![7]

3
When the attentions change / the jungle
leaps in
even the stones are split
they rive   65

Or,
enter
that other conqueror we more naturally recognize
he so resembles ourselves

But the E   70
cut so rudely on that oldest stone
sounded otherwise,
was differently heard

as, in another time, were treasures used:

(and, later, much later, a fine ear thought   75
a scarlet coat)

"of green feathers   feet, beaks and eyes
of gold

"animals likewise,
resembling snails   80

"a large wheel, gold,
with figures of unknown four-foots,
and worked with tufts of leaves, weight
3800 ounces

"last, two birds, of thread and featherwork, the quills   85
gold, the feet
gold, the two birds perched on two reeds

---

6. Rejects; rubbish.   7. "We must get up and act!"

gold, the reeds arising from two embroidered mounds,
one yellow, the other
white.   90

       "And from each reed hung
       seven feathered tassels.

In this instance, the priests
(in dark cotton robes, and dirty,
their dishevelled hair matted with blood, and flowing wildly   95
over their shoulders)
rush in among the people, calling on them
to protect their gods

And all now is war
where so lately there was peace,   100
and the sweet brotherhood, the use
of tilled fields.

                    4

Not one death but many,
not accumulation but change, the feed-back proves,   105
                   the feed-back is
the law

     Into the same river no man steps twice
     When fire dies air dies
     No one remains, nor is, one

Around an appearance, one common model, we grow up   110
many. Else how is it,
if we remain the same,
we take pleasure now
in what we did not take pleasure before? love
contrary objects? admire and / or find fault? use   115
other words, feel other passions, have
nor figure, appearance, disposition, tissue
the same?

     To be in different states without a change
     is not a possibility   120

We can be precise. The factors are
in the animal and / or the machine the factors are
communication and / or control, both involve
the message. And what is the message? The message is
a discrete or continuous sequence of measurable   125
                  events distributed in time

is the birth of air, is
the birth of water, is
a state between
the origin and   130

the end, between
birth and the beginning of
another fetid nest

is change, presents
no more than itself   135

And the too strong grasping of it,
when it is pressed together and condensed,
loses it

This very thing you are

II

They buried their dead in a sitting posture   140
serpent   cane   razor   ray of the sun

And she sprinkled water on the head of the child, crying
"Cioa-coatl! Cioa-coatl!"
with her face to the west

Where the bones are found, in each personal heap   145
with what each enjoyed, there is always
the Mongolian louse

The light is in the east. Yes. And we must rise, act. Yet
in the west, despite the apparent darkness (the whiteness
which covers all), if you look, if you can bear, if you can,   150
                                        long enough

        as long as it was necessary for him, my guide
        to look into the yellow of that longest-lasting rose

so you must, and, in that whiteness, into that face,
        with what candor, look   155

and, considering the dryness of the place
        the long absence of an adequate race

            (of the two who first came, each a conquistador,
                        one healed, the other
            tore the eastern idols down, toppled   160
            the temple walls, which, says the excuser
            were black from human gore)

hear
hear, where the dry blood talks
        where the old appetite walks   165

                        la piu saporita et migliore
                        che si possa truovar al mondo[8]

8. "The most flavorful and best that can be found in the world."

where it hides, look
in the eye how it runs
in the flesh / chalk   170

> but under these petals
> in the emptiness
> regard the light, contemplate
> the flower

whence it arose   175

> with what violence benevolence is bought
> what cost in gesture justice brings
> what wrongs domestic rights involve
> what stalks
> this silence   180

what pudor pejorocracy affronts
how awe, night-rest and neighborhood can rot
what breeds where dirtiness is law
what crawls
below   185

III

> I am no Greek, hath not th'advantage.
> And of course, no Roman:
> he can take no risk that matters,
> the risk of beauty least of all.

> But I have my kin, if for no other reason than   190
> (as he said, next of kin) I commit myself, and,
> given my freedom, I'd be a cad
> if I didn't. Which is most true.

> It works out this way, despite the disadvantage.
> I offer, in explanation, a quote: 195
> si j'ai du goût, ce n'est guères
> que pour la terre et les pierres[9]

> Despite the discrepancy (an ocean   courage   age)
> this is also true: if I have any taste
> it is only because I have interested myself   200
> in what was slain in the sun

> I pose you your question:

shall you uncover honey / where maggots are?

> I hunt among stones

1960

9. "If I care for anything, it is for little besides earth and stones," from Arthur Rimbaud's *A Season in Hell* (1873).

The Distances

So the distances are Galatea[1]
             and one does fall in love and desires

mastery

      old Zeus[2]—young Augustus[3]

Love knows no distance, no place   5
            is that far away or heat changes
into signals, and control

      old Zeus—young Augustus

          Death is a loving matter, then, a horror
             we cannot bide, and avoid   10
by greedy life

      we think all living things are precious
      —Pygmalions

          a German inventor in Key West
who had a Cuban girl, and kept her, after her death   15
in his bed
         after her family retrieved her
he stole the body again from the vault

Torso on torso in either direction,
    young Augustus   20
         out via nothing where messages
are
  or in, down La Cluny's steps to the old man sitting[4]
a god throned on torsoes,

      old Zeus   25

Sons go there hopefully as though there was a secret, the object to
undo distance?
          They huddle there, at the bottom
of the shaft, against one young bum
         or two loving cheeks,   30

     Augustus?

You can teach the young nothing
           all of them go away, Aphrodite

---

1. In Greek mythology, Pygmalion fell in love with an ivory statue he had carved. Answering his prayers, Aphrodite, the goddess of love, brought the statue to life; the sculptor married his creation.
2. In Greek mythology, ruler of the gods.
3. Augustus Caesar, nephew of Julius Caesar and first Roman Emperor (63 B.C.– A.D. 14).
4. Probably refers to a statue of the Roman Emperor Julian (331/332–363) in the Musée de Cluny in Paris.

tricks it out,
        old Zeus—young Augustus   35

You have love, and no object
                  or you have all pressed to your nose
which is too close,

       old Zeus hiding in your chin your young
       Galatea   40

the girl who makes you weep, and you keep the corpse live by all
your arts

       whose cheek do you stroke when you
                        stroke the stone face
      of young Augustus, made for bed in   45
                   a military camp, o Caesar?

O love who places all where each is, as they are, for every moment,
yield
      to this man
                        that the impossible distance   50
be healed,
      that young Augustus
      and old Zeus
be enclosed

      "I wake you,   55
stone. Love this man."

                                    1960

Maximus, to Gloucester,[1] Sunday, July 19

and they stopped before that bad sculpture of a fisherman

—"as if one were to talk to a man's house,
knowing not what gods or heroes are"—

not knowing what a fisherman is
instead of going straight to the Bridge   5
and doing no more than—saying no more than—
in the Charybdises[2] of the
Cut waters the flowers tear off

---

1. A fishing town in Massachusetts, where Olson spent his boyhood; on July 19 each year townspeople conduct a service at the foot of a memorial statue to fishermen lost at sea, casting wreaths of flowers into the Cut (the inner harbor).

2. In *The Odyssey*, the Greek hero Odysseus, returning from the Trojan War, had to navigate between the twin perils of the sea monster Scylla and the whirlpool Charybdis.

the wreaths

the flowers   10
turn
the character of the sea   The sea jumps
the fate of the flower   The drowned men are undrowned
in the eddies
                    of the eyes   15
                    of the flowers
                    opening
                    the sea's eyes

The disaster
is undone   20
What was received as alien
—the flower
on the water, that a man drowns
that he dies in water as he dies on earth, the impossible
        that this gross fact can return to us   25
            in this upset
on a summer day
of a particular tide

that the sensation is true,
that the transformations of fire are, first of all, sea—   30
        "as gold for wares wares for gold"

        Let them be told who stopped first
        by a bronze idol

        A fisherman is not a successful man
        he is not a famous man he is not a man   35
        of power, these are the damned by God

                        II

whose surface bubbles
with these gimlets
which screw-in like

potholes, caustic   40
caked earth of painted
pools, Yellowstone

Park[3] of holes
is death the diseased
presence on us, the spilling lesion   45

---

3. Largest and best-known American national park, located in northwestern Wyoming, noted for its mud volcanoes,
Mammoth Hot Springs, and 10,000 gey-
sers (which erupt regularly, from holes
in the ground, spewing boiling water into
the air).

of the brilliance
it is to be alive: to walk onto it,
as Jim Bridger the first into it,[4]

it is more true a scabious
field than it is a pretty   50
meadow

> When a man's coffin is the sea
> the whole of creation shall come to his funeral,

> it turns out; the globe
> is below, all lapis   55

> and its blue surface golded
> by what happened

> this afternoon: there are eyes
> in this water

the flowers   60
from the shore,

awakened
the sea

> Men are so sure they know very many things,
> they don't even know night and day are one   65

> A fisherman works without reference to
> that difference. It is possible he also

> by lying there when he does lie, jowl
> to the sea, has another advantage: it is said,

"You rectify what can be rectified," and when a man's heart   70
cannot see this, the door of his divine intelligence is shut

> let you who paraded to the Cut today
> to hold memorial services to all fishermen
> who have been lost at sea in a year
> when for the first time not one life was lost   75

>> radar sonar radio telephone good engines
>> bed-check seaplanes goodness over and under us

no difference
when men come back

1960

4. Fur trader and later government In- been the first white man to visit the Great
dian scout (1804–81), believed to have Salt Lake in Utah (1824).

ELIZABETH BISHOP

1911–

Elizabeth Bishop has often been praised for her "famous eye," her direct and unflinching descriptive powers, as if her accuracy were an end in itself. Yet, however detailed her immersion in a particular scene, her poems often end by reminding us, as Wallace Stevens did, that "we live in a place / that is not our own and much more, not ourselves, / and hard it is in spite of blazoned days." Practicing shifts of physical scale, opening long perspectives of time which dwarf the merely human, Bishop does more than merely observe; she emphasizes the dignified frailty of a human observer and the pervasive mysteries which surround her. Examining her own case, she traces the observer's instinct to early childhood. *In the Waiting Room*, a poem written in the early 1970s, probes the sources and motives behind her interest in detail. Using an incident from 1918 when she was seven—a little girl waits for her aunt in the dentist's ante-room—Bishop shows how in the course of the episode she became aware, as if wounded, of the utter strangeness and engulfing power of the world. The spectator in that poem hangs on to details as a kind of life-jacket; she observes because she has to. In a related autobiographical story, *In the Village*, she tells of a little girl haunted by the screams of her mother, just back from a sanitarium. Like *In the Waiting Room*, the story is told through the child's eyes. It links childhood losses to a maturing need to recapture the physicality of the world and to reclaim vanished primal pleasures, "the elements speaking: earth, air, fire, water."

Elizabeth Bishop was born in 1911 in Worcester, Massachusetts. Her father died when she was eight months old. When she was five, her mother was taken to a sanitarium and Bishop never saw her again. Thereafter she lived with relatives in New England and in Nova Scotia. She graduated from Vassar College in 1934, where while a student she had been introduced to Marianne Moore. Moore's meticulous taste for fact was to influence Bishop's poetry, but more immediately Moore's independent life as a poet made that life seem an alternative to Bishop's vaguer intentions to attend medical school. Bishop lived in New York City and in Key West, Florida; a traveling fellowship took her to Brazil, which so appealed to her that she stayed there for over sixteen years.

Exile and travel were at the heart of Bishop's poems from the very start. The title of her very first book, *North & South* (1946), looks forward to the tropical worlds she was to choose so long as home—Florida and, later, Brazil—and backward to her childhood and the northern seas of Nova Scotia. Her poems are set among these landscapes where she can stress the sweep and violence of encircling and eroding geological powers or, in the case of Brazil, a bewildering botanical plenty. *Questions of Travel* (1965), her third volume, constitutes a sequence of poems initiating her, with her botanist-geologist-anthropologist's curiosity, into the life of Brazil and the mysteries of what questions a traveler-exile should ask. In this series with its increasing penetration of a new country, a process is at work similar to one Bishop identifies in the great English zoologist and naturalist Charles Darwin, of whom Bishop once said: "One admires the beautiful solid case being built up out of his endless, heroic observations, almost unconscious or automatic—and then comes a sudden relaxation, a forgetful phrase, and one feels the strangeness of his undertaking, sees the lonely young man, his eyes fixed on facts and minute details, sinking or sliding giddily off into the unknown."

In 1969 Bishop's *Complete Poems* appeared, an ironic title in light of the fact that she has continued to write and publish new poetry. *Geography III* (1976) contains some of her very best work, poems which, from the settled perspective of her return to America, look back at and evaluate the appetite for exploration apparent in her earlier verse. Having left Brazil, Bishop has lived in Boston since 1970 and taught at Harvard University until 1977. She received the Pulitzer Prize for the combined volume *North & South and A Cold Spring* (1955); the National Book Award for *The Complete Poems*; and in 1976 was the first woman and the first American to receive the Books Abroad Neutsadt International Literary Prize.

The Man-Moth[1]

       Here, above,
cracks in the buildings are filled with battered moonlight.
The whole shadow of Man is only as big as his hat.
It lies at his feet like a circle for a doll to stand on,
and he makes an inverted pin, the point magnetized to the moon. 5
He does not see the moon; he observes only her vast properties,
feeling the queer light on his hands, neither warm nor cold,
of a temperature impossible to record in thermometers.

      But when the Man-Moth
pays his rare, although occasional, visits to the surface,   10
the moon looks rather different to him. He emerges
from an opening under the edge of one of the sidewalks
and nervously begins to scale the faces of the buildings.
He thinks the moon is a small hole at the top of the sky,
proving the sky quite useless for protection.   15
He trembles, but must investigate as high as he can climb.

      Up the façades,
his shadow dragging like a photographer's cloth behind him,
he climbs fearfully, thinking that this time he will manage
to push his small head through that round clean opening   20
and be forced through, as from a tube, in black scrolls on the light.
(Man, standing below him, has no such illusions.)
But what the Man-Moth fears most he must do, although
he fails, of course, and falls back scared but quite unhurt.

      Then he returns   25
to the pale subways of cement he calls his home. He flits,

1. Newspaper misprint for "mammoth" [Bishop's note].

he flutters, and cannot get aboard the silent trains
·fast enough to suit him. The doors close swiftly.
The Man-Moth always seats himself facing the wrong way
and the train starts at once at its full, terrible speed,   30
without a shift in gears or a gradation of any sort.
He cannot tell the rate at which he travels backwards.

      Each night he must
be carried through artificial tunnels and dream recurrent dreams.
Just as the ties recur beneath his train, these underlie   35
his rushing brain. He does not dare look out the window,
for the third rail,[2] the unbroken draught of poison,
runs there beside him. He regards it as a disease
he has inherited the susceptibility to. He has to keep
his hands in his pockets, as others must wear mufflers.   40

      If you catch him,
hold up a flashlight to his eye. It's all dark pupil,
an entire night itself, whose haired horizon tightens
as he stares back, and closes up the eye. Then from the lids
one tear, his only possession, like the bee's sting, slips.   45
Slyly he palms it, and if you're not paying attention
he'll swallow it. However, if you watch, he'll hand it over,
cool as from underground springs and pure enough to drink.

                                        1946

Seascape

This celestial seascape, with white herons got up as angels,
flying as high as they want and as far as they want sidewise
in tiers and tiers of immaculate reflections;
the whole region, from the highest heron
down to the weightless mangrove island   5
with bright green leaves edged neatly with bird-droppings
like illumination in silver,
and down to the suggestively Gothic arches of the mangrove[1] roots
and the beautiful pea-green back-pasture
where occasionally a fish jumps, like a wild-flower   10
in an ornamental spray of spray;
this cartoon by Raphael for a tapestry for a Pope:[2]
it does look like heaven.
But a skeletal lighthouse standing there
in black and white clerical dress,   15
who lives on his nerves, thinks he knows better.
He thinks that hell rages below his iron feet,
that that is why the shallow water is so warm,
and he knows that heaven is not like this.

2. Allusion to the exposed electrified source of power on modern subways.

1. Trees whose interlacing roots are visible above ground in semi-tropical and tropical areas such as the Florida Everglades.

2. Raphael (1483–1520) was a painter of the Italian Renaissance whose sometime patron was Pope Julius II. Raphael prepared several initial sketches, called "cartoons," for the figures on landscapes in tapestries for the Vatican.

Heaven is not like flying or swimming,   20
but has something to do with blackness and a strong glare
and when it gets dark he will remember something
strongly worded to say on the subject.

                                                    1946

The Fish

I caught a tremendous fish
and held him beside the boat
half out of water, with my hook
fast in a corner of his mouth.
He didn't fight.   5
He hadn't fought at all.
He hung a grunting weight,
battered and venerable
and homely. Here and there
his brown skin hung in strips   10
like ancient wallpaper,
and its pattern of darker brown
was like wallpaper:
shapes like full-blown roses
stained and lost through age.   15
He was speckled with barnacles,
fine rosettes of lime,
and infested
with tiny white sea-lice,
and underneath two or three   20
rags of green weed hung down.
While his gills were breathing in
the terrible oxygen
—the frightening gills,
fresh and crisp with blood,   25
that can cut so badly—
I thought of the coarse white flesh
packed in like feathers,
the big bones and the little bones,
the dramatic reds and blacks   30
of his shiny entrails,
and the pink swim-bladder
like a big peony.
I looked into his eyes
which were far larger than mine   35
but shallower, and yellowed,
the irises backed and packed
with tarnished tinfoil
seen through the lenses
of old scratched isinglass.[1]   40
They shifted a little, but not
to return my stare.

1. A whitish, semitransparent substance, originally obtained from the swim-blad- ders of some fresh-water fishes and occasionally used for windows.

—It was more like the tipping
of an object toward the light.
I admired his sullen face,   45
the mechanism of his jaw,
and then I saw
that from his lower lip
—if you could call it a lip—
grim, wet, and weaponlike,   50
hung five old pieces of fish-line,
or four and a wire leader
with the swivel still attached,
with all their five big hooks
grown firmly in his mouth.   55
A green line, frayed at the end
where he broke it, two heavier lines,
and a fine black thread
still crimped from the strain and snap
when it broke and he got away.   60
Like medals with their ribbons
frayed and wavering,
a five-haired beard of wisdom
trailing from his aching jaw.
I stared and stared   65
and victory filled up
the little rented boat,
from the pool of bilge
where oil had spread a rainbow
around the rusted engine   70
to the bailer rusted orange,
the sun-cracked thwarts,
the oarlocks on their strings,
the gunnels—until everything
was rainbow, rainbow, rainbow!   75
And I let the fish go.

1946

Over 2000 Illustrations and a Complete Concordance[1]

Thus should have been our travels:
serious, engravable.
The Seven Wonders of the World are tired
and a touch familiar, but the other scenes,
innumerable, though equally sad and still,   5
are foreign. Often the squatting Arab,
or group of Arabs, plotting, probably,
against our Christian Empire,
while one apart, with outstretched arm and hand

---

1. Part of the title of an old edition of the Bible described in the opening lines of the poem. (It is illustrated with a series of sepia engravings of the Holy Land.) A concordance is a guide to occurrences of words and proper names and places in a book.

points to the Tomb, the Pit, the Sepulcher.[2]   10
The branches of the date-palms look like files.
The cobbled courtyard, where the Well is dry,
is like a diagram, the brickwork conduits
are vast and obvious, the human figure
far gone in history or theology,   15
gone with its camel or its faithful horse.
Always the silence, the gesture, the specks of birds
suspended on invisible threads above the Site,
or the smoke rising solemnly, pulled by threads.
Granted a page alone or a page made up   20
of several scenes arranged in cattycornered rectangles
or circles set on stippled gray,
granted a grim lunette,[3]
caught in the toils of an initial letter,
when dwelt upon, they all resolve themselves.   25
The eye drops, weighted, through the lines
the burin[4] made, the lines that move apart
like ripples above sand,
dispersing storms, God's spreading fingerprint,
and painfully, finally, that ignite   30
in watery prismatic white-and-blue.

Entering the Narrows at St. Johns[5]
the touching bleat of goats reached to the ship.
We glimpsed them, reddish, leaping up the cliffs
among the fog-soaked weeds and butter-and-eggs.   35
And at St. Peter's[6] the wind blew and the sun shone madly.
Rapidly, purposefully, the Collegians marched in lines,
crisscrossing the great square with black, like ants.
In Mexico the dead man lay
in a blue arcade; the dead volcanoes   40
glistened like Easter lilies.
The jukebox went on playing "Ay, Jalisco!"
And at Volubilis[7] there were beautiful poppies
splitting the mosaics; the fat old guide made eyes.
In Dingle[8] harbor a golden length of evening   45
the rotting hulks held up their dripping plush.
The Englishwoman poured tea, informing us
that the Duchess was going to have a baby.
And in the brothels of Marrakesh[9]
the little pockmarked prostitutes   50
balanced their tea-trays on their heads
and did their belly-dances; flung themselves
naked and giggling against our knees,
asking for cigarettes. It was somewhere near there

---

2. The burial place of Christ, depicted
(along with other places associated with
the life of Jesus, such as the Well and
the Site) among the "2000 illustrations"
of the title.
3. The oval, often a segment of an enlarged initial letter, framing an illustration.

4. Engraver's tool.
5. In Newfoundland.
6. The papal basilica in Rome; the Collegians are members of constituent orders of the Church.
7. A ruined city in Morocco.
8. A town in southwest Ireland.
9. City in Morocco.

I saw what frightened me most of all: 55
A holy grave, not looking particularly holy,
one of a group under a keyhole-arched stone baldaquin[1]
open to every wind from the pink desert.
An open, gritty, marble trough, carved solid
with exhortation, yellowed   60
as scattered cattle-teeth;
half-filled with dust, not even the dust
of the poor prophet paynim[2] who once lay there.
In a smart burnoose Khadour looked on amused.

Everything only connected by "and" and "and."   65
Open the book. (The gilt rubs off the edges
of the pages and pollinates the fingertips.)
Open the heavy book. Why couldn't we have seen
this old Nativity[3] while we were at it?
—the dark ajar, the rocks breaking with light,   70
an undisturbed, unbreathing flame,
colorless, sparkless, freely fed on straw,
and, lulled within, a family with pets,
—and looked and looked our infant[4] sight away.

                                                                         1955

At the Fishhouses

Although it is a cold evening,
down by one of the fishhouses
an old man sits netting,
his net, in the gloaming almost invisible
a dark purple-brown,   5
and his shuttle worn and polished.
The air smells so strong of codfish
it makes one's nose run and one's eyes water.
The five fishhouses have steeply peaked roofs
and narrow, cleated gangplanks slant up   10
to storerooms in the gables
for the wheelbarrows to be pushed up and down on.
All is silver: the heavy surface of the sea,
swelling slowly as if considering spilling over,
is opaque, but the silver of the benches,   15
the lobster pots, and masts, scattered
among the wild jagged rocks,
is of an apparent translucence
like the small old buildings with an emerald moss
growing on their shoreward walls.   20
The big fish tubs are completely lined
with layers of beautiful herring scales
and the wheelbarrows are similarly plastered
with creamy iridescent coats of mail,

---

1. Architectural canopy.
2. Archaic literary word for pagan, especially Moslem.
3. A scene of the adoration of the infant
Christ.
4. The Latin root of "infant" (*infans*) means "speechless."

with small iridescent flies crawling on them.   25
Up on the little slope behind the houses,
set in the sparse bright sprinkle of grass,
is an ancient wooden capstan,[1]
cracked, with two long bleached handles
and some melancholy stains, like dried blood,   30
where the ironwork has rusted.
The old man accepts a Lucky Strike.[2]
He was a friend of my grandfather.
We talk of the decline in the population
and of codfish and herring   35
while he waits for a herring boat to come in.
There are sequins on his vest and on his thumb.
He has scraped the scales, the principal beauty,
from unnumbered fish with that black old knife,
the blade of which is almost worn away.   40

Down at the water's edge, at the place
where they haul up the boats, up the long ramp
descending into the water, thin silver
tree trunks are laid horizontally
across the gray stones, down and down   45
at intervals of four or five feet.

Cold dark deep and absolutely clear,
element bearable to no mortal,
to fish and to seals . . . One seal particularly
I have seen here evening after evening.   50
He was curious about me. He was interested in music;
like me a believer in total immersion,[3]
so I used to sing him Baptist hymns.
I also sang "A Mighty Fortress Is Our God."
He stood up in the water and regarded me   55
steadily, moving his head a little.
Then he would disappear, then suddenly emerge
almost in the same spot, with a sort of shrug
as if it were against his better judgment.
Cold dark deep and absolutely clear,   60
the clear gray icy water . . . Back, behind us,
the dignified tall firs begin.
Bluish, associating with their shadows,
a million Christmas trees stand
waiting for Christmas. The water seems suspended   65
above the rounded gray and blue-gray stones.
I have seen it over and over, the same sea, the same,
slightly, indifferently swinging above the stones,
icily free above the stones,
above the stones and then the world.   70
If you should dip your hand in,

---

1. Cylindrical drum around which rope is   2. Brand of cigarettes.
wound, used for hauling.   3. Form of baptism used by Baptists.

your wrist would ache immediately,
your bones would begin to ache and your hand would burn
as if the water were a transmutation of fire
that feeds on stones and burns with a dark gray flame.   75
If you tasted it, it would first taste bitter,
then briny, then surely burn your tongue.
It is like what we imagine knowledge to be:
dark, salt, clear, moving, utterly free,
drawn from the cold hard mouth   80
of the world, derived from the rocky breasts
forever, flowing and drawn, and since
our knowledge is historical, flowing, and flown.

                                                          1955

Questions of Travel

There are too many waterfalls here; the crowded streams
hurry too rapidly down to the sea,
and the pressure of so many clouds on the mountaintops
makes them spill over the sides in soft slow-motion,
turning to waterfalls under our very eyes.   5
—For if those streaks, those mile-long, shiny, tearstains,
aren't waterfalls yet,
in a quick age or so, as ages go here,
they probably will be.
But if the streams and clouds keep travelling, travelling,   10
the mountains look like the hulls of capsized ships,
slime-hung and barnacled.

Think of the long trip home.
Should we have stayed at home and thought of here?
Where should we be today?   15
Is it right to be watching strangers in a play
in this strangest of theatres?
What childishness is it that while there's a breath of life
in our bodies, we are determined to rush
to see the sun the other way around?   20
The tiniest green hummingbird in the world?
To stare at some inexplicable old stonework,
inexplicable and impenetrable,
at any view,
instantly seen and always, always delightful?   25
Oh, must we dream our dreams
and have them, too?
And have we room
for one more folded sunset, still quite warm?

But surely it would have been a pity   30
not to have seen the trees along this road,
really exaggerated in their beauty,
not to have seen them gesturing
like noble pantomimists, robed in pink.

—Not to have had to stop for gas and heard   35
the sad, two-noted, wooden tune
of disparate wooden clogs
carelessly clacking over
a grease-stained filling-station floor.
(In another country the clogs would all be tested.   40
Each pair there would have identical pitch.)
—A pity not to have heard
the other, less primitive music of the fat brown bird
who sings above the broken gasoline pump
in a bamboo church of Jesuit baroque: 45
three towers, five silver crosses.
—Yes, a pity not to have pondered,
blurr'dly and inconclusively,
on what connection can exist for centuries
between the crudest wooden footwear   50
and, careful and finicky,
the whittled fantasies of wooden cages.
—Never to have studied history in
the weak calligraphy of songbirds' cages.
—And never to have had to listen to rain   55
so much like politicians' speeches:
two hours of unrelenting oratory
and then a sudden golden silence
in which the traveller takes a notebook, writes:

"Is it lack of imagination that makes us come   60
to imagined places, not just stay at home?
Or could Pascal[1] have been not entirely right
about just sitting quietly in one's room?

Continent, city, country, society:
the choice is never wide and never free.   65
And here, or there . . . No. Should we have stayed at home,
wherever that may be?"

1965

The Armadillo

FOR ROBERT LOWELL

This is the time of year
when almost every night
the frail, illegal fire balloons appear.
Climbing the mountain height,

rising toward a saint   5
still honored in these parts,
the paper chambers flush and fill with light
that comes and goes, like hearts.

---

1. French mathematician and philosopher (1623–62), who said, "* * * man's misfortunes spring from the single cause that they are unable to stay quietly in one room" (*Pensées*, translated by J. M. Cohen).

Once up against the sky it's hard
to tell them from the stars—   10
planets, that is—the tinted ones:
Venus going down, or Mars,

or the pale green one. With a wind,
they flare and falter, wobble and toss;
but if it's still they steer between   15
the kite sticks of the Southern Cross,

receding, dwindling, solemnly
and steadily forsaking us,
or, in the downdraft from a peak,
suddenly turning dangerous.   20

Last night another big one fell.
It splattered like an egg of fire
against the cliff behind the house.
The flame ran down. We saw the pair

of owls who nest there flying up   25
and up, their whirling black-and-white
stained bright pink underneath, until
they shrieked up out of sight.

The ancient owls' nest must have burned.
Hastily, all alone,   30
a glistening armadillo left the scene,
rose-flecked, head down, tail down,

and then a baby rabbit jumped out,
short-eared, to our surprise.
So soft!—a handful of intangible ash   35
with fixed, ignited eyes.

Too pretty, dreamlike mimicry!
O falling fire and piercing cry
and panic, and a weak mailed fist[1]
clenched ignorant against the sky!   40

1965

In the Waiting Room

In Worcester, Massachusetts,
I went with Aunt Consuelo
to keep her dentist's appointment
and sat and waited for her
in the dentist's waiting room.   5

---

1. The armadillo, curled tight. It is protected against everything but fire.

It was winter. It got dark
early. The waiting room
was full of grown-up people,
arctics and overcoats,
lamps and magazines.   10
My aunt was inside
what seemed like a long time
and while I waited I read
the *National Geographic*
(I could read) and carefully   15
studied the photographs:
the inside of a volcano,
black, and full of ashes;
then it was spilling over
in rivulets of fire.   20
Osa and Martin Johnson[1]
dressed in riding breeches,
laced boots, and pith helmets.
A dead man slung on a pole
—"Long Pig,"[2] the caption said.   25
Babies with pointed heads
wound round and round with string;
black, naked women with necks
wound round and round with wire
like the necks of light bulbs.   30
Their breasts were horrifying.
I read it right straight through.
I was too shy to stop.
And then I looked at the cover:
the yellow margins, the date.   35

Suddenly, from inside,
came an *oh!* of pain
—Aunt Consuelo's voice—
not very loud or long.
I wasn't at all surprised;   40
even then I knew she was
a foolish, timid woman.
I might have been embarrassed,
but wasn't. What took me
completely by surprise   45
was that it was *me:*
my voice, in my mouth.
Without thinking at all
I was my foolish aunt,
I—we—were falling, falling,   50
our eyes glued to the cover
of the *National Geographic,*
February, 1918.

1. Famous explorers and travel writers.
2. Polynesian cannibals' name for the human carcass.

I said to myself: three days
and you'll be seven years old.   55
I was saying it to stop
the sensation of falling off
the round, turning world
into cold, blue-black space.
But I felt: you are an *I*,   60
you are an *Elizabeth*,
you are one of *them*.
Why should you be one, too?
I scarcely dared to look
to see what it was I was.   65
I gave a sidelong glance
—I couldn't look any higher—
at shadowy gray knees,
trousers and skirts and boots
and different pairs of hands   70
lying under the lamps.
I knew that nothing stranger
had ever happened, that nothing
stranger could ever happen.
Why should I be my aunt,   75
or me, or anyone?
What similarities—
boots, hands, the family voice
I felt in my throat, or even
the *National Geographic*   80
and those awful hanging breasts—
held us all together
or made us all just one?
How—I didn't know any
word for it—how "unlikely" . . .   85
How had I come to be here,
like them, and overhear
a cry of pain that could have
got loud and worse but hadn't?

The waiting room was bright   90
and too hot. It was sliding
beneath a big black wave,
another, and another.

Then I was back in it.
The War[3] was on. Outside,   95
in Worcester, Massachusetts,
were night and slush and cold,
and it was still the fifth
of February, 1918.

---

3. World War I.

One Art

The art of losing isn't hard to master;
so many things seem filled with the intent
to be lost that their loss is no disaster.

Lose something every day. Accept the fluster
of lost door keys, the hour badly spent.   5
The art of losing isn't hard to master.

Then practice losing farther, losing faster:
places, and names, and where it was you meant
to travel. None of these will bring disaster.

I lost my mother's watch. And look! my last, or   10
next-to-last, of three loved houses went.
The art of losing isn't hard to master.

I lost two cities, lovely ones. And, vaster,
some realms I owned, two rivers, a continent.
I miss them, but it wasn't a disaster.   15

—Even losing you (the joking voice, a gesture
I love) I shan't have lied. It's evident
the art of losing's not too hard to master
though it may look like (*Write* it!) like disaster.

1976

RANDALL JARRELL
1914–1965

"The gods who had taken away the poet's audience had given him students," said Randall Jarrell. He was describing the state of American poetry after World War II, and from any other poet it would have been an entirely bitter statement. In fact, among the American poets and critics emerging after 1945, Jarrell enjoyed being *the* teacher, both in and out of the classroom. The novelist Peter Taylor recalls that when he came to Vanderbilt University as a freshman in the mid-1930s, Jarrell, then a graduate student, had already turned the literary students into disciples; he held court even on the sidelines of touch football games, where Taylor heard him deliver brilliant analyses of Chekhov short stories. Later in life, he was to give unrelenting attention, as poet and friend, to works-in-progress by his contemporaries—such writers as Robert Lowell, Delmore Schwartz, and John Berryman.

Jarrell was born in Nashville, Tennessee, but spent much of his childhood in Long Beach, California. When his parents divorced, the child, then eleven, remained for a year with his grandparents in Hollywood, then returned to live with his mother in Nashville. He majored in psychology at Vanderbilt and stayed on there to do graduate work in English. In 1937 he left Nashville to teach at Kenyon College (Gambier, Ohio) on the invitation of his old Vanderbilt professor, John Crowe Ransom, the New Critic and Fugitive poet. From that time on, Jarrell almost always had some connection with a university: after Kenyon, the University of Texas, Sarah Lawrence College, and from 1947 until his death, the Women's College of the University of North Carolina at Greensboro. But, as his novel *Pictures from an Institution* (1954) with its mixed satiric and tender views of academic life suggests, he was never satisfied with a cloistered education. His literary criticism and teaching were aimed at recapturing and re-educating an audience either lost to poetry or upon whom poetry was lost. As poetry editor of *The Nation* (1946), and then in a series of essays and reviews collected as *Poetry and the Age* (1953), he introduced readers to the work of their contemporaries—Elizabeth Bishop, Robert Lowell, John Berryman, the William Carlos Williams of *Paterson*—and influentially reassessed the reputations of Whitman and Robert Frost.

Jarrell was not only the ablest critic of verse but also one of the best poets to emerge after World War II. While others—Richard Wilbur and Robert Lowell among them—were writing highly structured poems with complicated imagery, Jarrell was writing with a rare colloquial plainness. Many of his poems are dramatic monologues whose speakers express disappointment with the "dailiness of life." These figures of loneliness and aging are to be found especially in the collection *The Woman at the Washington Zoo* (1960), the heroine of whose title poem sees her frustrations mirrored in the caged animals around her. Jarrell often adopts the points of view of women and children or of the soldiers in his extraordinary war poems, the strongest to come out of the 1941–45 conflict. He had been trained as an Army Air Force pilot, and after that as a control tower operator, hence his sense of the war's special casualties—what one critic calls "the soldier-technician * * * the clumsy mechanical animals and their child-guardians," so often portrayed in Jarrell's volumes *Little Friend, Little Friend* (1945) and *Losses* (1948). In *The Death of the Ball Turret Gunner,* nothing seems to have happened to the soldier-protagonist between conception and the moment he is shot down, which is presented as if it were an abortion.

Against the blasted or unrealized possibilities of adult life Jarrell often poised the rich mysteries of childhood. Many of the poems, like *Cinderella,* reinterpret fairy tales. Jarrell himself translated Grimms' fairy tales and wrote several children's books, among them *The Bat-Poet.* The title poem of his last book, *The Lost World* (1965), looks back to his Los Angeles playtime, the movie sets and plaster dinosaurs and pterodactyls against whose eternal gay presence he measures his own aging: "I hold in my own hands in happiness, / Nothing: the nothing for which there's no reward."

Jarrell suffered a nervous breakdown in February, 1965, but returned to teaching that fall. In October he was struck down by a car and died. His *Complete Poems* were published posthumously (1969) as was a translation of Goethe's *Faust,* Part I, in preparation at his death.

90 North[1]

> At home, in my flannel gown, like a bear to its floe,
> I clambered to bed; up the globe's impossible sides

1. The latitude of the North Pole.

I sailed all night—till at last, with my black beard,
My furs and my dogs, I stood at the northern pole.

There in the childish night my companions lay frozen,   5
The stiff furs knocked at my starveling throat,
And I gave my great sigh: the flakes came huddling,
Were they really my end? In the darkness I turned to my rest.

—Here, the flag snaps in the glare and silence
Of the unbroken ice. I stand here,   10
The dogs bark, my beard is black, and I stare
At the North Pole . . .
                         And now what? Why, go back.

Turn as I please, my step is to the south.
The world—my world spins on this final point
Of cold and wretchedness: all lines, all winds   15
End in this whirlpool I at last discover.

And it is meaningless. In the child's bed
After the night's voyage, in that warm world
Where people work and suffer for the end
That crowns the pain—in that Cloud-Cuckoo-Land[2]   20

I reached my North and it had meaning.
Here at the actual pole of my existence,
Where all that I have done is meaningless,
Where I die or live by accident alone—

Where, living or dying, I am still alone;   25
Here where North, the night, the berg of death
Crowd me out of the ignorant darkness,
I see at last that all the knowledge

I wrung from the darkness—that the darkness flung me—
Is worthless as ignorance: nothing comes from nothing,   30
The darkness from the darkness. Pain comes from the darkness
And we call it wisdom. It is pain.

                                                            1942

The Death of the Ball Turret Gunner[1]

From my mother's sleep I fell into the State,
And I hunched in its belly till my wet fur froze.
Six miles from earth, loosed from its dream of life,

---

2. A fantasy world; in Aristophanes'
comedy *The Birds* (414 B.C.), an imaginary city the cuckoos build in the sky.
1. "A ball turret was a plexiglass sphere
set into the belly of a B-17 or B-24
[bomber], and inhabited by two .50 caliber machine-guns and one man, a short,
small man. When this gunner tracked
with his machine-guns a fighter attacking
his bomber from below, he revolved with
the turret; hunched upside-down in his
little sphere, he looked like the foetus in
the womb. The fighters which attacked
him were armed with cannon firing explosive shells. The hose was a steam
hose" [Jarrell's note].

I woke to black flak[2] and the nightmare fighters.
When I died they washed me out of the turret with a hose.   5

                                                                    1945

Second Air Force

Far off, above the plain the summer dries,
The great loops of the hangars sway like hills.
Buses and weariness and loss, the nodding soldiers
Are wire, the bare frame building, and a pass
To what was hers; her head hides his square patch   5
And she thinks heavily: My son is grown.
She sees a world: sand roads, tar-paper barracks,
The bubbling asphalt of the runways, sage,
The dunes rising to the interminable ranges,
The dim flights moving over clouds like clouds.   10
The armorers in their patched faded green,
Sweat-stiffened, banded with brass cartridges,
Walk to the line; their Fortresses,[1] all tail,
Stand wrong and flimsy on their skinny legs,
And the crews climb to them clumsily as bears.   15
The head withdraws into its hatch (a boy's),
The engines rise to their blind laboring roar,
And the green, made beasts run home to air.
Now in each aspect death is pure.
(At twilight they wink over men like stars   20
And hour by hour, through the night, some see
The great lights floating in—from Mars, from Mars.)
How emptily the watchers see them gone.

They go, there is silence; the woman and her son
Stand in the forest of the shadows, and the light   25
Washes them like water. In the long-sunken city
Of evening, the sunlight stills like sleep
The faint wonder of the drowned; in the evening,
In the last dreaming light, so fresh, so old,
The soldiers pass like beasts, unquestioning,   30
And the watcher for an instant understands
What there is then no need to understand;
But she wakes from her knowledge, and her stare,
A shadow now, moves emptily among
The shadows learning in their shadowy fields   35
The empty missions.
                    Remembering,
She hears the bomber calling, *Little Friend!*[2]
To the fighter hanging in the hostile sky,

---

2. Antiaircraft fire.
1. Flying Fortresses, a type of bomber in World War II.
2. "In 'Second Air Force' the woman visiting her son remembers what she has read on the front page of her newspaper the week before, a conversation between a bomber, in flames over Germany, and one of the fighters protecting it: 'Then I heard the bomber call me in: "Little Friend, Little Friend, I got two engines on fire. Can you see me, Little Friend?" I said, "I'm crossing right over you. Let's go home" ' " [Jarrell's note].

And sees the ragged flame eat, rib by rib,
Along the metal of the wing into her heart: 40
The lives stream out, blossom, and float steadily
To the flames of the earth, the flames
That burn like stars above the lands of men.

She saves from the twilight that takes everything
A squadron shipping, in its last parade—   45
Its dogs run by it, barking at the band—
A gunner walking to his barracks, half-asleep,
Starting at something, stumbling (above, invisible,
The crews in the steady winter of the sky
Tremble in their wired fur); and feels for them   50
The love of life for life. The hopeful cells
Heavy with someone else's death, cold carriers
Of someone else's victory, grope past their lives
Into her own bewilderment: The years meant *this?*

But for them the bombers answer everything.   55
                                                              1945

A Girl in a Library[1]

An object among dreams, you sit here with your shoes off
And curl your legs up under you; your eyes
Close for a moment, your face moves toward sleep . . .
You are very human.
                    But my mind, gone out in tenderness,
Shrinks from its object with a thoughtful sigh.   5
This is a waist the spirit breaks its arm on.
The gods themselves, against you, struggle in vain.[2]
This broad low strong-boned brow; these heavy eyes;
These calves, grown muscular with certainties;
This nose, three medium-sized pink strawberries   10
—But I exaggerate. In a little you will leave:
I'll hear, half squeal, half shriek, your laugh of greeting—
Then, *decrescendo*,[3] bars of that strange speech
In which each sound sets out to seek each other,
Murders its own father, marries its own mother,[4]   15
And ends as one grand transcendental vowel.

(Yet for all I know, the Egyptian Helen spoke so.)
As I look, the world contracts around you:

1. "*A Girl in a Library* is a poem about
the New World and the Old: about a
girl, a student of Home Economics and
Physical Education, who has fallen asleep
in the library of a Southern college; about
a woman who looks out of one book,
Pushkin's *Eugen Onegin*, at the girl
asleep among so many; and about the *I*
of the poem, a man somewhere between
the two" [Jarrell's note].

2. From *The Maid of Orleans*, a play by
Friedrich Schiller (1759–1805): "With
stupidity the Gods themselves struggle in
vain."
3. Musical term for diminishing volume.
4. Describing the chaotic effect of the
girl's speech pattern; an allusion to Oedipus, who, in Greek legend, murdered his
father and married his mother.

I see Brünnhilde had brown braids and glasses
She used for studying; Salome straight brown bangs,[5]   20
A calf's brown eyes, and sturdy light-brown limbs
Dusted with cinnamon, an apple-dumpling's . . .
Many a beast has gnawn a leg off and got free,
Many a dolphin curved up from Necessity—
The trap has closed about you, and you sleep.   25
If someone questioned you, *What doest thou here?*
You'd knit your brows like an orangoutang
(But not so sadly; not so thoughtfully)
And answer with a pure heart, guilelessly:
I'm studying. . . .
            If only you were not!   30
Assignments,
        recipes,
            the *Official Rulebook*
Of Basketball—ah, let them go; you needn't mind.
The soul has no assignments, neither cooks
Nor referees: it wastes its time.
                It wastes its time.
Here in this enclave there are centuries   35
For you to waste: the short and narrow stream
Of Life meanders into a thousand valleys
Of all that was, or might have been, or is to be.
The books, just leafed through, whisper endlessly . . .
Yet it is hard. One sees in your blurred eyes   40
The "uneasy half-soul" Kipling saw in dogs'.[6]
One sees it, in the glass, in one's own eyes.
In rooms alone, in galleries, in libraries,
In tears, in searchings of the heart, in staggering joys
We memorize once more our old creation,   45
Humanity: with what yawns the unwilling
Flesh puts on its spirit,[7] O my sister!

So many dreams! And not one troubles
Your sleep of life? no self stares shadowily
From these worn hexahedrons, beckoning   50
With false smiles, tears? . . .
              Meanwhile Tatyana[8]
Larina (gray eyes nickel with the moonlight
That falls through the willows onto Lensky's tomb;
Now young and shy, now old and cold and sure)
Asks, smiling: "But what is she dreaming of, fat thing?"   55

---

5. Helen, Brünnhilde, and Salome are legendary, passionate heroines, also central figures in operas by Richard Strauss (1864–1949) (*The Egyptian Helen* and *Salome*) and Richard Wagner (1813–83) (*The Ring of the Nibelungen*).
6. The English poet Rudyard Kipling (1865–1936), in his poem *Supplication of the Black Aberdeen*: "This dim, distressed half-soul that hurts me so."
7. A paraphrase of Jesus' words: "The spirit is willing but the flesh is weak."
8. In the Russian novel *Eugen Onegin* (1830), by Alexander Pushkin (1799–1837), Lensky is killed in a duel by Onegin. Lensky was hopelessly in love with Tatyana, who had nourished an unrequited love for Onegin when she was very young. Later, however, she marries someone else and rejects Onegin.

I answer: She's not fat. She isn't dreaming.
She purrs or laps or runs, all in her sleep;
Believes, awake, that she is beautiful;
She never dreams.
    Those sunrise-colored clouds
Around man's head—that inconceivable enchantment 60
From which, at sunset, we come back to life
To find our graves dug, families dead, selves dying:
Of all this, Tanya,[9] she is innocent.
For nineteen years she's faced reality:
They look alike already.
      They say, man wouldn't be 65
The best thing in this world—and isn't he?—
If he were not too good for it. But she
—She's good enough for it.
      And yet sometimes
Her sturdy form, in its pink strapless formal,
Is as if bathed in moonlight—modulated 70
Into a form of joy, a Lydian mode;[1]
This Wooden Mean's[2] a kind, furred animal
That speaks, in the Wild of things, delighting riddles
To the soul that listens, trusting . . .
      Poor senseless Life:
When, in the last light sleep of dawn, the messenger 75
Comes with his message, you will not awake.
He'll give his feathery whistle, shake you hard,
You'll look with wide eyes at the dewy yard
And dream, with calm slow factuality:
"Today's Commencement. My bachelor's degree 80
In Home Ec., my doctorate of philosophy
In Phys. Ed.
   [Tanya, they won't even *scan*]
Are waiting for me. . . ."
      Oh, Tatyana,
The Angel comes: better to squawk like a chicken
Than to say with truth, "But I'm a *good* girl,"
And Meet his Challenge with a last firm strange 85
Uncomprehending smile; and—then, then!—see
The blind date that has stood you up: your life.
(For all this, if it isn't, perhaps, life,
Has yet, at least, a language of its own
Different from the books'; worse than the books'.) 90
And yet, the ways we miss our lives are life.
Yet . . . yet . . . .
    to have one's life add up to *yet!*

You sigh a shuddering sigh. Tatyana murmurs,
 "Don't cry, little peasant"; leaves us with a swift

---

9. Diminutive of Tatyana.
1. A musical scale associated with religious tranquility.
2. As contrasted to the Golden Mean, the perfect medium.

"Good-bye, good-bye . . . Ah, don't think ill of me . . ."   95
Your eyes open: you sit here thoughtlessly.

I love you—and yet—and yet—I love you.

Don't cry, little peasant. Sit and dream.
One comes, a finger's width beneath your skin,
To the braided maidens singing as they spin;   100
There sound the shepherd's pipe, the watchman's rattle
Across the short dark distance of the years.
I am a thought of yours: and yet, you do not think . . .
The firelight of a long, blind, dreaming story
Lingers upon your lips; and I have seen   105
Firm, fixed forever in your closing eyes,
The Corn King beckoning to his Spring Queen.[3]

1951

Cinderella

Her imaginary playmate was a grown-up
In sea-coal[1] satin. The flame-blue glances,
The wings gauzy as the membrane that the ashes
Draw over an old ember—as the mother
In a jug of cider—were a comfort to her.   5
They sat by the fire and told each other stories.

"What men want. . . ." said the godmother softly—
How she went on it is hard for a man to say.
Their eyes, on their Father, were monumental marble.
Then they smiled like two old women, bussed[2] each other,   10
Said, "Gossip, gossip"; and, lapped in each other's looks,
Mirror for mirror, drank a cup of tea.

Of cambric tea.[3] But there is a reality
Under the good silk of the good sisters'
Good ball gowns. *She* knew. . . . Hard-breasted, naked-eyed,   15
She pushed her silk feet into glass, and rose within
A gown of imaginary gauze. The shy prince drank
A toast to her in champagne from her slipper

And breathed, "Bewitching!" Breathed, "I am bewitched!"
—She said to her godmother, "Men!"   20
And, later, looking down to see her flesh
Look back up from under lace, the ashy gauze
And pulsing marble of a bridal veil,
She wished it all a widow's coal-black weeds.[4]

3. "The Corn King and the Spring Queen went by many names; in the beginning they were the man and woman who, after ruling for a time, were torn to pieces and scattered over the fields in order that the grain might grow" [Jarrell's note]. The braided maidens, shepherd, and watchman mentioned earlier in this stanza are background figures in Wagner operas, through whom meaning is conveyed without their being aware of its implications.
1. Black.
2. Kissed.
3. A drink made of hot water, milk, and sugar.
4. Mourning garb.

A sullen wife and a reluctant mother,   25
She sat all day in silence by the fire.
Better, later, to stare past her sons' sons,
Her daughters' daughters, and tell stories to the fire.
But best, dead, damned, to rock forever
Beside Hell's fireside—to see within the flames   30

The Heaven to whose gold-gauzed door there comes
A little dark old woman, the God's Mother,
And cries, "Come in, come in! My son's out now,
Out now, will be back soon, may be back never,
Who knows, eh? *We* know what they are—men, men!   35
But come, come in till then! Come in till then!"

                                             1960

Next Day

Moving from Cheer to Joy, from Joy to All,
I take a box
And add it to my wild rice, my Cornish game hens.
The slacked or shorted, basketed, identical
Food-gathering flocks
Are selves I overlook. Wisdom, said William James,[1]   5

Is learning what to overlook. And I am wise
If that is wisdom.
Yet somehow, as I buy All from these shelves
And the boy takes it to my station wagon,   10
What I've become
Troubles me even if I shut my eyes.

When I was young and miserable and pretty
And poor, I'd wish
What all girls wish: to have a husband,   15
A house and children. Now that I'm old, my wish
Is womanish:
That the boy putting groceries in my car

See me. It bewilders me he doesn't see me.
For so many years   20
I was good enough to eat: the world looked at me
And its mouth watered. How often they have undressed me,
The eyes of strangers!
And, holding their flesh within my flesh, their vile

Imaginings within my imagining,   25
I too have taken
The chance of life. Now the boy pats my dog
And we start home. Now I am good.

---

1. From *Principles of Psychology*, by the American philosopher William James (1842–1910).

The last mistaken,
Ecstatic, accidental bliss, the blind   30

Happiness that, bursting, leaves upon the palm
Some soap and water—
It was so long ago, back in some Gay
Twenties, Nineties, I don't know . . . Today I miss
My lovely daughter   35
Away at school, my sons away at school,

My husband away at work—I wish for them.
The dog, the maid,
And I go through the sure unvarying days
At home in them. As I look at my life,   40
I am afraid
Only that it will change, as I am changing:

I am afraid, this morning, of my face.
It looks at me
From the rear-view mirror, with the eyes I hate,   45
The smile I hate. Its plain, lined look
Of gray discovery
Repeats to me: "You're old." That's all, I'm old.

And yet I'm afraid, as I was at the funeral
I went to yesterday.   50
My friend's cold made-up face, granite among its flowers,
Her undressed, operated-on, dressed body
Were my face and body.
As I think of her I hear her telling me

How young I seem; I *am* exceptional;   55
I think of all I have.
But really no one is exceptional,
No one has anything, I'm anybody,
I stand beside my grave
Confused with my life, that is commonplace and solitary.   60
                                                                      1965

Well Water

What a girl called "the dailiness of life"
(Adding an errand to your errand. Saying,
"Since you're up . . ." Making you a means to
A means to a means to) is well water.
Pumped from an old well at the bottom of the world.   5
The pump you pump the water from is rusty
And hard to move and absurd, a squirrel-wheel
A sick squirrel turns slowly, through the sunny
Inexorable hours. And yet sometimes
The wheel turns of its own weight, the rusty   10
Pump pumps over your sweating face the clear

Water, cold, so cold! you cup your hands
And gulp from them the dailiness of life.

1965

The Player Piano[1]

I ate pancakes one night in a Pancake House
Run by a lady my age. She was gay.
When I told her that I came from Pasadena
She laughed and said, "I lived in Pasadena
When Fatty Arbuckle[2] drove the El Molino bus."   5

I felt that I had met someone from home.
No, not Pasadena, Fatty Arbuckle.
Who's that? Oh, something that we had in common
Like—like—the false armistice.[3] Piano rolls.
She told me her house was the first Pancake House   10

East of the Mississippi, and I showed her
A picture of my grandson. Going home—
Home to the hotel—I began to hum,
"Smile a while, I bid you sad adieu,
When the clouds roll back I'll come to you."[4]   15

Let's brush our hair before we go to bed,
I say to the old friend who lives in my mirror.
I remember how I'd brush my mother's hair
Before she bobbed[5] it. How long has it been
Since I hit my funnybone? had a scab on my knee?   20

Here are Mother and Father in a photograph,
Father's holding me. . . . They both look so *young*.
I'm so much older than they are. Look at them,
Two babies with their baby. I don't blame you,
You weren't old enough to know any better;   25

If I could I'd go back, sit down by you both,
And sign our true armistice: you weren't to blame.
I shut my eyes and there's our living room.
The piano's playing something by Chopin,
And Mother and Father and their little girl   30

Listen. Look, the keys go down by themselves!
I go over, hold my hands out, play I play—
If only, somehow, I had learned to live!
The three of us sit watching, as my waltz
Plays itself out a half-inch from my fingers.   35

1969

---

1. A piano which, when fitted with perforated rolls, plays automatically.
2. A corpulent actor of the silent film
era, whose career was destroyed when
he was involved in a sex-murder scandal.
3. Truce.
4. Lines from a popular song of the 1920s.
5. Popular short hairstyle of the period.

JOHN BERRYMAN

1914–1972

From a generation whose ideal poem was short, self-contained, and ironic, John Berryman emerged as the author of two extended and passionate works: *Homage to Mistress Bradstreet* and the lyric sequence called *The Dream Songs*. It was as if Berryman needed more space than the single lyric provided—a larger theater to play out an unrelenting psychic drama. He had written shorter poems—songs and sonnets—but it was his discovery of large-scale dramatic situations and strange new voices that astonished his contemporaries.

Berryman seemed fated to intense suffering and self-preoccupation. His father, a banker, shot himself outside his son's window when the boy was twelve. The suicide haunted Berryman to the end of his own life, which also came by suicide. He turns to the subject obsessively in *The Dream Songs*.

> I spit upon this dreadful banker's grave
> who shot his heart out in a Florida dawn
> O ho alas alas
> When will indifference come, I moan and rave

Berryman, who was born John Smith, took a new name from his step-father, also a banker. His childhood was a series of displacements: ten years near McAlester, Oklahoma, then Tampa, Florida, and, after his father's suicide, Gloucester, Massachusetts, and New York City. His mother's second marriage ended in divorce, but his stepfather sent him to private school in Connecticut. Berryman graduated from Columbia College in 1936 and won a fellowship to Clare College, Cambridge, England.

He was later to say of himself, "I masquerade as a writer. Actually I am a scholar." However misleading this may be about his poetry, it reminds us that all his life Berryman drew nourishment from teaching—at Wayne State, at Harvard (1940–43), then off and on at Princeton, and, from 1955 until his death, at the University of Minnesota. He chose to teach, not creative writing, but literature and the "history of civilization," and claimed that such teaching forced him into areas in which he wouldn't otherwise have done detailed work. A mixture of bookishness and wildness characterizes all his writing: five years of research lay behind the intensities of *Homage to Mistress Bradstreet*, while an important constituent of "huffy Henry's" personality in *The Dream Songs* is his professorial awkwardness and exhibitionism.

Berryman seemed drawn to borrowing identities in his poetry. In his first important volume, *The Dispossessed* (1948), he had experimented with various dramatic voices in short *Nervous Songs: The Song of the Demented Priest, A Professor's Song, The Song of the Tortured Girl, The Song of the Man Forsaken and Obsessed*. The "dispossession" of the book's title had two opposite and urgent meanings for him: "the miserable, *put out of one's own*, and the relieved, saved, undevilled, de-spelled." Taking on such roles was for Berryman both a revelation of his cast-out, fatherless state, and an exorcism of it. It was perhaps in that spirit that he entered into an imaginative dialogue with what he felt as the kindred nature of the Puritan poet Anne Bradstreet. "Both of our worlds unhanded us." What started out to be a poem of fifty lines emerged as the fifty-seven stanzas of *Homage to Mistress Bradstreet* (1956), a work so absorbing that after completing it Berryman claimed to be "a ruin for two years." It was not Bradstreet's poetry which engaged him. Quite the contrary: he was fascinated by the contrast between her "bald abstract rime" and her life of passionate suffering. The poem explores the kinship between Bradstreet and Berryman as figures of turbulence and rebellion.

Berryman took literary encouragement from another American poet of the past, Stephen Crane, about whom he wrote a book-length critical study in 1950. Crane's poems, he said, have "the character of a 'dream,' something seen naively in a new relation. * * * His poetry has the inimitable sincerity of a frightened savage anxious to learn what his dream means." Berryman's attraction to a poetry which accommodated the nightmare antics of the dream world became apparent in his own long work, *The Dream Songs.* It was modeled, he claimed, on "the greatest American poem," Whitman's *Song of Myself,* a less tortured long poem but one in which the speaker assumes, as Berryman's protagonist does, a number of roles and a fluid, ever-changing persona. *77 Dream Songs* was published in 1964. Additional poems, to a total of 385, appeared in *His Toy, His Dream, His Rest* (1968). (Some uncollected "Dream Songs" were published posthumously in *Henry's Fate,* 1977, and drafts of others remain in manuscript.) There are obvious links between Berryman and other so-called confessional writers such as Robert Lowell, Sylvia Plath, and Anne Sexton. But the special autobiographical flavor of *The Dream Songs* is that of a psychic vaudeville; as in dreams, the poet represents himself through a fluid series of *alter egos,* whose voices often flow into one another in single poems. Despite the suffering which these poems enact, Berryman seemed to find a secret strength through the staginess, variety, resourcefulness, and renewals of these almost 400 poems.

The Dream Songs brought Berryman a success which was not entirely beneficial. The collection *Love and Fame* (1970) shows him beguiled by his own celebrity and wrestling with some of its temptations. In an unfinished, posthumously published novel, *Recovery,* he portrays himself as increasingly prey to alcoholism. Berryman had been married twice before and his hospitalization for drinking and for periods of insanity had put a strain on his third marriage. He came to distrust his poetry as a form of exhibitionism and was clearly, in his use of the discipline of prose and in the prayers which crowd his last two volumes of poetry (*Delusions, Etc.* appeared posthumously) in search of some new and humbling style. Having been raised a strict Catholic and fallen away from the church, he tried to return to it in his last years, speaking of his need for a "God of rescue." On January 7, 1972, Berryman committed suicide by leaping from a Minneapolis bridge onto the frozen Mississippi River.

Homage to Mistress Bradstreet

Anne Bradstreet ("Born 1612 Anne Dudley, married at 16 Simon Bradstreet, a Cambridge man, steward to the Countess of Warwick and protege of her father Thomas Dudley secretary to the Earl of Lincoln. Crossed in the *Arbella,* 1630, under Governor

Winthrop" [Berryman's note]) came to the Massachusetts Bay Colony
when she was eighteen years old. She was one of the first poets on American
soil. Of this poem, Berryman says, "An American historian somewhere observes that all colonial settlements are intensely conservative, *except* in the
initial break-off point (whether religious, political, legal, or whatever). Trying to do justice to both parts of this obvious truth—which I came upon
only after the poem was finished—I concentrated upon the second and the
poem laid itself out in a series of rebellions. I had her rebel first against the
new environment and above all against her barrenness (which in fact
lasted for years), then against her marriage (which in fact seems to have
been brilliantly happy), and finally against her continuing life of illness,
loss, and age. These are the three large sections of the poem; they are preceded and followed by an exordium and coda, of four stanzas each, spoken
by the 'I' of the twentieth-century poet, which modulates into her voice,
who speaks most of the poem. Such is the plan. Each rebellion, of course,
is succeeded by submission, although even in the moment of the poem's
supreme triumph—the presentment, too long to quote now, of the birth of
her first child—rebellion survives" [Quoted in *Poets on Poetry*, ed. by
Howard Nemerov, New York: Basic Books, 1966].

Berryman wrote two stanzas of the poem and found himself stalled for
five years, during which he gathered material. "I had this incredible mass
of stuff and a very good idea of the shape of the poem, with the exception
of one crucial point, which was this * * * it did not occur to me to have a
dialogue between them * * * to insert me, in my own person, John Berryman, *I*, into the poem" [Quoted in *Paris Review* #53, Winter 1972 edition, in an interview].

Homage to Mistress Bradstreet was first published in *Partisan Review* in
1953 but did not appear as a book until 1956.

In his exordium (stanzas 1–4), the poet makes an intense identification
between himself and Bradstreet, both of them alienated by hardship or
circumstance from those around them: "We are on each other's hands /
who care. Both of our worlds unhanded us." The identification is so complete that in the subsequent stanzas he hears her voice recounting the
tribulations of life in a new country, her yearnings for the England she
left behind, her lonely dedication to her poetry, and the personal suffering
in her early barrenness and miscarriages. Stanza 17 continues in Bradstreet's voice.

From Homage to Mistress Bradstreet

* * *

17

The winters close, Springs open, no child stirs
under my withering heart, O seasoned heart   130
God grudged his aid.
All things else soil like a shirt.
Simon is much away. My executive[1] stales.
The town came through for the cartway by the pales,[2]
but my patience is short,   135
I revolt from, I am like, these savage foresters

---

1. Power to act.   2. Stockade fence.

18

whose passionless dicker in the shade, whose glance
impassive & scant, belie their murderous cries
when quarry seems to show.
Again I must have been wrong, twice.[3]   140
Unwell in a new way. Can that begin?
God brandishes. O love, O I love. Kin,
gather. My world is strange
and merciful, ingrown months, blessing a swelling trance.[4]

19

So squeezed, wince you I scream? I love you & hate   145
off with you. Ages! *Useless.* Below my waist
he has me in Hell's vise.
Stalling. He let go. Come back: brace
me somewhere. No. No. Yes! everything down
hardens I press with horrible joy down   150
my back cracks like a wrist
shame I am voiding oh behind it is too late

20

hide me forever I work thrust I must free
now I all muscles & bones concentrate
what is living from dying?   155
Simon I must leave you so untidy
Monster you are killing me Be sure
I'll have you later Women do endure
I can *can* no longer
and it passes the wretched trap whelming and I am me   160

21

drencht & powerful, I did it with my body!
One proud tug greens Heaven. Marvellous,
unforbidding Majesty.
Swell, imperious bells. I fly.
Mountainous, woman not breaks and will bend: 165
sways God nearby: anguish comes to an end.
Blossomed Sarah,[5] and I
blossom. Is that thing alive? I hear a famisht howl.

22

Beloved household, I am Simon's wife,
and the mother of Samuel—whom greedy yet I miss   170
out of his kicking place.
More in some ways I feel at a loss,
freer. Cantabanks & mummers,[6] nears
longing for you. Our chopping[7] scores my ears,
our costume bores my eyes.   175
St. George[8] to the good sword, rise! chop-logic's rife

---

3. One of several allusions to her failure
to become pregnant.
4. "Her first child was not born until
about 1633" [Berryman's note].
5. Wife of Abraham, barren until old
age, when she gave birth to Isaac (Genesis 17.18).
6. Ballad-singers and mimes.
7. "*Chopping*: disputing, snapping, hag-
gling; axing" [Berryman's note].
8. Patron saint of England, the slayer of
dragons.

23

& fever & Satan & Satan's ancient fere.[9]
Pioneering is not feeling well,
not Indians, beasts.
Not all their riddling can forestall   180
one leaving. Sam, your uncle has had to
go from us to live with God. 'Then Aunt went too?'
Dear, she does wait still.
Stricken: 'Oh. Then he takes us one by one.' My dear.

24

Forswearing it otherwise, they starch their minds.   185
Folkmoots,[1] & blether, blether. John Cotton rakes[2]
to the synod of Cambridge.[3]
Down from my body my legs flow,
out from it arms wave, on it my head shakes.
Now Mistress Hutchinson rings forth a call—   190
should she? many creep out at a broken wall—
affirming the Holy Ghost
dwells in one justified. Factioning passion blinds

25

all to all her good, all—can she be exiled?
Bitter sister, victim! I miss you.   195
—I miss you, Anne,[4]
day or night weak as a child,
tender & empty, doomed, quick to no tryst.
—I hear you. Be kind, you who leaguer[5]
my image in the mist.   200
—Be kind you, to one unchained eager far & wild

26

and if, O my love, my heart is breaking, please
neglect my cries and I will spare you. Deep
in Time's grave, Love's, you lie still.
Lie still.—Now? That happy shape   205
my forehead had under my most long, rare,
ravendark, hidden, soft bodiless hair
you award me still.
You must not love me, but I do not bid your cease.

27

Veiled my eyes, attending. How can it be I?   210
Moist, with parted lips, I listen, wicked.
I shake in the morning & retch.

---

9. "*Fere*: his friend Death" [Berryman's note].
1. A town assembly for debate. "Blether": nonsense.
2. "Rakes: inclines, as a mast; bows" [Berryman's note].
3. In the first synod (a body for religious debate), Cotton agreed to the condemnation and banishment of his follower Anne Hutchinson. Her heresies included a de-emphasis of perfect moral conduct as evidence of the justification for Christian salvation.
4. "One might say: He [the poet] is en-abled to speak, at last, in the fortune of an echo of her—and when she is loneliest (her former spiritual adviser [John Cotton] having deserted Anne Hutchinson, and this her [Bradstreet's] closest friend banished), as if she had summoned him; and only thus, perhaps, is she enabled to hear him. This second section of the poem is a dialogue, his voice however ceasing well before it ends at [line] 307, and hers continuing for the whole third part until the coda ([stanzas] 54–57)" [Berryman's note].
5. Beleaguer, besiege.

Brood I do on myself naked.
A fading world I dust, with fingers new.
—I have earned the right to be alone with you.   215
—What right can that be?
Convulsing, if you love, enough, like a sweet lie.

28

Not that, I know, you can. This cratered skin,
like the crabs & shells of my Palissy[6] ewer, touch!
Oh, you do, you do?   220
Falls on me what I like a witch,
for lawless holds, annihilations of law
which Time and he and man abhor, foresaw:
sharper than what my Friend[7]
brought me for my revolt when I moved smooth & thin,   225

29

faintings black, rigour, chilling, brown
parching, back, brain burning, the grey pocks
itch, a manic stench
of pustules snapping, pain floods the palm,
sleepless, or a red shaft with a dreadful start   230
rides at the chapel, like a slipping heart.
My soul strains in one qualm
ah but *this* is not to save me but to throw me down.

30

And out of this I lull. It lessens. Kiss me.
That once. As sings out up in sparkling dark   235
a trail of a star & dies,
while the breath flutters, sounding, mark,
so shorn ought such caresses to us be
who, deserving nothing, flush and flee
the darkness of that light,   240
a lurching frozen from a warm dream. Talk to me.

31[8]

—It is Spring's New England. Pussy willows wedge
up in the wet. Milky crestings, fringed
yellow, in heaven, eyed
by the melting hand-in-hand or mere   245
desirers single, heavy-footed, rapt,
make surge poor human hearts. Venus is trapt—
the hefty pike shifts, sheer[9]—
in Orion blazing. Warblings, odours, nudge to an edge—

32

—Ravishing, ha, what crouches outside ought,   250
flamboyant, ill, angelic. Often, now,
I am afraid of you.

6. Bernard Palissy (1510–90), French
Protestant ceramicist, noted for special
glazes and highly ornamented pieces.
7. Alludes to the punishments of God visited on those who rebel against Him (cf.
Isaiah 1.5).
8. Berryman (in *Poets on Poetry*) called
this speech of the poet to Bradstreet "an

only half-subdued aria-stanza."
9. Lines 246–47 are opposed images of
the bottom of the sea against the summit of the sky (Venus). "Sheer" in the
sense of "invisible" [quoted from comments by Berryman in the Italian translation of *Mistress Bradstreet* by Sergio
Perosa].

I am a sobersides; I know.
I *want* to take you for my lover.—Do.
—I hear a madness. Harmless I to you   255
am not, not I?—No.
—I cannot but be. Sing a concord of our thought.

                                33
—Wan dolls in indigo on gold:[1] refrain
my western lust. I am drowning in this past.
I lose sight of you   260
who mistress me from air. Unbraced
in delirium of the grand depths,[2] giving away
haunters what kept me, I breathe solid spray.
—I am losing you!
Straiten me on.[3]—I suffered living like a stain: 265

                                34
I trundle the bodies, on the iron bars,
over that fire backward & forth; they burn;
bits fall. I wonder if
I killed them. Women serve my turn.
—Dreams! You are good.—No.—Dense with hardihood   270
the wicked are dislodged, and lodged the good.
In green space we are safe.
God awaits us (but I am yielding) who Hell wars.

                                35
—I cannot feel myself God waits. He flies
nearer a kindly world; or he is flown.   275
One Saturday's rescue[4]
won't show. Man is entirely alone
may be. I am a man of griefs & fits
trying to be my friend. And the brown smock splits,
down the pale flesh a gash   280
broadens and Time holds up your heart against my eyes.

                                36
—Hard and divided heaven! creases me. Shame
is failing. My breath is scented, and I throw
hostile glances towards God.
Crumpling plunge of a pestle, bray:[5]   285

---

1. "Cf., on Byzantine icons [here, the impassive Madonnas painted against gold backgrounds in Medieval altarpieces of the Eastern Church], Frederick Rolfe ('Baron Corvo'): 'Who ever dreams of praying (with expectation of response) for the prayer of a Tintoretto or a Titian, or a Bellini, or a Botticelli? But who can refrain from crying "O Mother!" to these unruffleable wan dolls in indigo on gold?' (quoted from *The Desire and Pursuit of the Whole* by Graham Greene in *The Last Childhood*)" [Berryman's note].
2. " 'Délires des grandes profondeurs', described by [Jacques] Cousteau and others; a euphoria, sometimes fatal in which the hallucinated diver offers passing fish his line, helmet, anything" [Berryman's note; he translates the French phrase in line 262].
3. I.e., tighten your embrace.
4. "As of cliffhangers, movie serials wherein each week's episode ends with a train bearing down on the strapped heroine or with the hero dangling over an abyss into which Indians above him peer with satisfaction before they hatchet the rope; *rescue*: forcible recovery (by the owner) of goods distrained" [Berryman's note].
5. Punning (according to Berryman's notes) on (1) the pulverizing action of a mortar and pestle, (2) the strident noise of a donkey.

sin cross & opposite, wherein I survive
nightmares of Eden. Reaches foul & live
he for me, this soul
to crunch, a minute tangle of eternal flame.

37

I fear Hell's hammer-wind. But fear does wane.   290
Death's blossoms grain my hair; I cannot live.
A black joy clashes
joy, in twilight. The Devil said
'I will deal toward her softly, and her enchanting cries[6]
will fool the horns of Adam.' Father of lies,   295
a male great pestle smashes
small women swarming towards the mortar's rim in vain.

38

I see the cruel spread Wings black with saints!
Silky my breasts not his, mine, mine to withhold
or tender, tender.
I am sifting, nervous, and bold.   300
The light is changing. Surrender this loveliness
you cannot make me do. *But* I will. Yes.
What horror, down stormy air,
warps towards me? My threatening promise faints   305

39[7]

torture me, Father, lest not I be thine!
Tribunal terrible & pure, my God,
mercy for him and me.
Faces half-fanged, Christ drives abroad,
and though the crop hopes, Jane[8] is so slipshod   310
I cry. Evil dissolves, & love, like foam;
that love. Prattle of children powers me home,
my heart claps like the swan's
under a frenzy of *who* love me & who shine.[9]

* * *

1953, 1956

A Professor's Song

(. . rabid or dog-dull.) Let me tell you how
The Eighteenth Century couplet ended. Now
Tell me. Troll[1] me the sources of that Song—
Assigned last week—by Blake.[2] Come, come along,
Gentlemen. (Fidget and huddle, do. Squint soon.)   5
I want to end these fellows all by noon.

---

6. Referring to Satan's temptation of
Eve, who was to eat the apple from the
Tree of Knowledge and then convince
Adam to do so (cf. Genesis 3).
7. "The stanza is unsettled, like [stanza]
24, by a middle line, signaling a broad
transition" [Berryman's note].
8. A servant.
9. The final stanzas present Bradstreet's
intensified vision of death and damnation
and include the death of her father, blas-
pheming. But in the last four stanzas the
poem modulates back into the poet's
voice and his vow to keep Bradstreet
alive in his loving memory and in his
writing. "Hover, utter, still, a sourcing
whom my lost candle like the firefly
loves."
1. Chant merrily.
2. William Blake (1757–1827), English
Romantic poet, author of *Songs of Innocence and Experience.*

'That deep romantic[3] chasm'—an early use;
The word is from the French, by our abuse
Fished out a bit. (Red all your eyes. O when?)
'A poet is a man speaking to men':[4]   10
But I am then a poet, am I not?—
Ha ha. The radiator, please. Well, what?

Alive now—no—Blake would have written prose,
But movement following movement crisply flows,
So much the better, better the much so,   15
As burbleth Mozart.[5] Twelve. The class can go.
Until I meet you, then, in Upper Hell
Convulsed, foaming immortal blood: farewell.

                                                              1958

From DREAM SONGS[1]

I

Huffy Henry hid   the day,
unappeasable Henry sulked.
I see his point,—a trying to put things over.
It was the thought that they thought
they could *do* it made Henry wicked & away.   5
But he should have come out and talked.

All the world like a woolen lover
once did seem on Henry's side.
Then came a departure.
Thereafter nothing fell out as it might or ought.   10
I don't see how Henry, pried
open for all the world to see, survived.

What he has now to say is a long
wonder the world can bear & be.
Once in a sycamore I was glad   15

---

3. The Professor is lecturing about the adaptation of European conventions by the English Romantics, such as William Blake, William Wordsworth, and Samuel Taylor Coleridge (1772–1834). In this phrase, quoted from his poem *Kubla Khan* (1816), Coleridge uses the word "romantic" to mean "mysterious" or "savage"; the French word *romantique* meant more strictly "pertaining to Medieval romances and tales."
4. From William Wordsworth's (1770–1850) preface to the second edition of *Lyrical Ballads* (1800).
5. Wolfgang Amadeus Mozart (1756–91), the great Austrian composer of the Classical movement which, in music, preceded the Romantic movement. In the preceding line, Berryman is imitating the symmetry of classical form.
1. These poems were written over a pe-

riod of 13 years. (77 *Dream Songs* was published in 1964, and the remaining poems appeared in *His Toy, His Dream, His Rest* in 1968. Some uncollected Dream Songs were included in the volume *Henry's Fate*, which appeared five years after Berryman committed suicide in 1972.) Berryman placed an introductory note at the head of *His Toy, His Dream, His Rest*: "The poem then, whatever its wide cast of characters, is essentially about an imaginary character (not the poet, not me) named Henry, a white American in early middle age sometimes in blackface, who has suffered an irreversible loss and talks about himself sometimes in the first person, sometimes in the third, sometimes even in the second; he has a friend, never named, who addresses him as Mr. Bones and variants thereof. Requiescant in pace."

all at the top, and I sang.
Hard on the land wears the strong sea
and empty grows every bed.

14

Life, friends, is boring. We must not say so.
After all, the sky flashes, the great sea yearns,
we ourselves flash and yearn,
and moreover my mother told me as a boy
(repeatedly) 'Ever to confess you're bored   5
means you have no

Inner Resources.' I conclude now I have no
inner resources, because I am heavy bored.
Peoples bore me,
literature bores me, especially great literature,   10
Henry bores me, with his plights & gripes
as bad as achilles,[1]

who loves people and valiant art, which bores me.
And the tranquil hills, & gin, look like a drag
and somehow a dog   15
has taken itself & its tail considerably away
into mountains or sea or sky, leaving
behind: me, wag.

29

There sat down, once, a thing on Henry's heart
so heavy, if he had a hundred years
& more, & weeping, sleepless, in all them time
Henry could not make good.
Starts again always in Henry's ears   5
the little cough somewhere, an odour, a chime.

And there is another thing he has in mind
like a grave Sienese face[1] a thousand years
would fail to blur the still profiled reproach of. Ghastly,
with open eyes, he attends, blind.   10
All the bells say: too late. This is not for tears;
thinking.

But never did Henry, as he thought he did,
end anyone and hacks her body up
and hide the pieces, where they may be found.   15
He knows: he went over everyone, & nobody's missing.

---

1. Greek hero of Homer's *The Iliad*, who, angry at slights against his honor, sulked in his tent and refused to fight against the Trojans.

1. Alluding to the somber, austere mosaic-like religious portraits by the Italian painters who worked in Siena during the 13th and 14th centuries.

Often he reckons, in the dawn, them up.
Nobody is ever missing.

40

I'm scared a lonely. Never see my son,
easy be not to see anyone,
combers[1] out to sea
know they're goin somewhere but not me.
Got a little poison, got a little gun,   5
I'm scared a lonely.

I'm scared a only one thing, which is me,
from othering I don't take nothin, see,
for any hound dog's sake.
But this is where I livin, where I rake   10
my leaves and cop my promise,[2] this' where we
cry oursel's awake.

Wishin was dyin but I gotta make
it all this way to that bed on these feet
where peoples said to meet.   15
Maybe but even if I see my son
forever never, get back on the take,
free, black & forty-one.[3]

45

He stared at ruin. Ruin stared straight back.
He thought they was old friends. He felt on the stair
where her papa found them bare
they became familiar. When the papers were lost
rich with pals' secrets, he thought he had the knack   5
of ruin. Their paths crossed

and once they crossed in jail; they crossed in bed;
and over an unsigned letter their eyes met,
and in an Asian city
directionless & lurchy at two & three,   10
or trembling to a telephone's fresh threat,
and when some wired his head

to reach a wrong opinion, 'Epileptic'.
But he noted now that: they were not old friends.
He did not know this one.   15
This one was a stranger, come to make amends
for all the imposters, and to make it stick.
Henry nodded, un-.

---

1. Waves which roll over and break with
a foamy crest.
2. Slang for "pile up potential."

3. Playing on "free, white, and 21," colloquial for legally independent.

76. Henry's Confession

Nothin very bad happen to me lately.
How you explain that? —I explain that, Mr Bones,
terms o' your bafflin odd sobriety,
Sober as man can get, no girls, no telephones,
what could happen bad to Mr Bones?   5
—*If* life is a handkerchief sandwich,

in a modesty of death I join my father
who dared so long agone leave me.
A bullet on a concrete stoop
close by a smothering southern sea   10
spreadeagled on an island, by my knee.
—You is from hunger, Mr Bones,

I offers you this handkerchief, now set
your left foot by my right foot,
shoulder to shoulder, all that jazz,   15
arm in arm, by the beautiful sea,[1]
hum a little, Mr Bones.
—I saw nobody coming, so I went instead.

143

—That's enough of that, Mr Bones. *Some* lady you make.
Honour the burnt cork,[2] be a vaudeville man,
I'll sing you now a song
the like of which may bring your heart to break:
he's gone! and we don't know where. When he began   5
taking the pistol out & along,

you was just a little; but gross fears
accompanied us along the beaches, pal.
My mother was scared almost to death.
He was going to swim out, with me, forevers,   10
and a swimmer strong he was in the phosphorescent   Gulf,
but he decided on lead.

That mad drive wiped out my childhood. I put him down
while all the same on forty years I love him
stashed in Oklahoma   15
besides his brother Will. Bite the nerve of the town
for anyone so desperate. I repeat: I love him
until *I* fall into coma.

---

1. Phrase from a popular song.   2. Used by actors to blacken the face.

384

The marker slants, flowerless, day's almost done,
I stand above my father's grave with rage,
often, often before
I've made this awful pilgrimage to one
who cannot visit me, who tore his page   5
out: I come back for more,

I spit upon this dreadful banker's grave
who shot his heart out in a Florida dawn
O ho alas alas
When will indifference come, I moan & rave   10
I'd like to scrabble till I got right down
away down under the grass

and ax the casket open ha to see
just how he's taking it, which he sought so hard
we'll tear apart   15
the mouldering grave clothes ha & then Henry
will heft the ax once more, his final card,
and fell it on the start.

385

My daughter's heavier. Light leaves are flying.
Everywhere in enormous numbers turkeys will be dying
and other birds, all their wings.
They never greatly flew. Did they wish to?
I should know. Off away somewhere once I knew   5
such things.

Or good Ralph Hodgson[1] back then did, or does.
The man is dead whom Eliot[2] praised. My praise
follows and flows too late.
Fall is grievy, brisk. Tears behind the eyes   10
almost fall. Fall comes to us as a prize
to rouse us toward our fate.

My house is made of wood and it's made well,
unlike us. My house is older than Henry;
that's fairly old.   15
If there were a middle   ground between things and the soul
or if the sky resembled more the sea,
I wouldn't have to scold

                          my heavy daughter.
                          1968

1. Ralph Hodgson (1871–1962), an English poet who wrote balladlike lyrics. Berryman may be alluding to Hodgson's *Hymn to Moloch*, in which the poet protests the slaughter of birds for commercial uses.
2. T. S. Eliot (1888–1965), American poet and critic.

ROBERT LOWELL

1917–1977

In 1964 a literary critic called Robert Lowell "our truest historian." Lowell had earned that emblematic position not simply because his poetry was often concerned with historical and political issues but because the poet himself was a figure of historical interest. Descendant of a long line of New Englanders, he bore powerful witness to their traditions, memories, eccentricities, and neuroses. He was born into a secure world, but his poetry records instability and change: personal rebellion, mental illness, and political stress. Writing under those pressures, he helped give American poetry a new autobiographical cast, a new urgency and directness of speech, and a new openness to public subjects.

Lowell came from patrician families closely associated with Boston. His grandfather, another R. T. S. Lowell, was a well-known Episcopal minister and head of the fashionable St. Mark's School which the poet was later to attend. His great-granduncle, James Russell Lowell, had been a poet and ambassador to England. Another relation, A. Lawrence, was president of Harvard just before the young poet came there as a freshman. Perhaps the only light note in the family was struck by the poet Amy Lowell, "big and a scandal, as if Mae West were a cousin." Robert Lowell's father was a naval officer who, after his retirement, did badly in business. Much of the poet's life was a reaction against his background of Bostonian eminence and public service. At first he turned angrily against it, but later in life he tried to draw upon its strength without being crippled by it.

Lowell's first act of separation was to leave the East after two years at Harvard (1935–37) in order to study at Kenyon College with John Crowe Ransom, the poet and critic. The move brought him in closer touch with the New Criticism and its predilections for "formal difficult poems," the wit and irony of English metaphysical writers such as John Donne. He also, through Ransom and the poet Allen Tate, came into contact with (though never formally joined) the Fugitive movement, whose members were southern agrarians opposed to what they regarded as the corrupting values of northern industrialism.

Even more decisive was his conversion in 1940 to Roman Catholicism and his resistance to American policies in World War II. Although he did try to enlist in the navy, he refused to be drafted into the army. He opposed the saturation bombing of Hamburg and the Allied policy of unconditional surrender and was as a result sentenced to a year's confinement in New York's West Street jail and admonished by the presiding judge for "marring" his family traditions. In his first book, *Lord Weary's Castle* (1946), Lowell's Catholicism and antagonism to Protestant mercantile Boston were most sharply expressed. Catholicism, he was later to say, gave him not so much a subject as "some kind of form, and I could begin a poem and build it to a climax." It provided a set of ritual symbols and a distanced platform from which to attack "our sublunary secular sprawl," the commercial-minded Boston of *Children of Light*. The climaxes to which Lowell refers are the apocalyptic conclusions of these early poems—

devastating sentences such as: "The Lord survives the rainbow of His will"; "The blue kingfisher dives on you in fire."

Alongside those poems drawing upon Old Testament anger, there was another strain in *Lord Weary's Castle*. In poems such as *After the Surprising Conversions* and *Jonathan Edwards and the Spider*, he explored from within the nervous intensity which underlay Puritan revivalism. Similarly in later dramatic narratives with modern settings such as *The Mills of the Kavanaghs* and *Falling Asleep over the Aeneid* he exposed his morbid fascination with and psychological interest in ruined New England families.

In *Life Studies* (1959) his subjects became explicitly autobiographical. In 1957 he had been giving poetry readings on the West Coast. Allen Ginsberg and the other Beats had just made their strongest impact in San Francisco, and Lowell felt that by contrast to their candid, breezy writing, his own style seemed "distant, symbol-ridden, and willfully difficult. * * * I felt my old poems hid what they were really about, and many times offered a stiff, humorless and even impenetrable surface." His own new style was to be more controlled and severe than "Beat" writing, but he was stimulated by Ginsberg's self-revelations to write more openly than he had about his parents and grandparents, about the mental breakdowns he suffered in the 1950s, and about the difficulties of marriage. (Lowell had divorced his first wife, the novelist Jean Stafford, and had married the critic Elizabeth Hardwick in 1949.)

Life Studies opens with a poem, *Beyond the Alps*, which recalls Lowell's departure from the Catholic Church (1950). The book touches on his prison experience during World War II. But by and large it records his ambivalence toward the New England where he resettled after the war, on Boston's "hardly passionate Marlborough Street." He no longer denounces the city of his fathers as if he were a privileged outsider. In complicated psychological portraits of his childhood, his relation to his parents and his wives, he assumes a portion of the weakness and vulnerability for himself.

In 1960 Lowell left Boston to live in New York City. *For the Union Dead* (1964), the book that followed, continued the autobiographical vein of *Life Studies*. Lowell called it a book about "witheredness * * * lemony, soured and dry, the drouth I had touched with my own hands." These poems seem more carefully controlled than his earlier "life studies." Poems like *Neo-Classical Urn* and *For the Union Dead* consist much less in the miscellaneous memories of dreams and jagged experience; instead they present data as a skilled psychoanalyst might organize it, finding key images from the past which explain the present. The book includes a number of political or public poems, such as *July in Washington*, which uses Lowell's scarred personal past and his sense of the nourishing traditions of the Republic as a way of criticizing the bland or evasive politics of the Eisenhower years.

Lowell's *History* (1973) is again a new departure. He had begun these Poems like *Neo-Classical Urn* and *For the Union Dead* consist much less in editions of *Notebooks*. These unrhymed fourteen-line poems were reactions to his reading, his personal life, and the Vietnam war, of which he was an outspoken critic. "Things I felt or saw, or read were drift in the whirlpool." The poems were more committed to the present than to the recollections which had been the subjects of *Life Studies* and *For the Union Dead*:

"always the instant, something changing to the lost. A flash of haiku to lighten the distant." In 1973, in a characteristic act of self-assessment, Lowell rearranged and revised these poems which had begun as a diary. Those dealing with public subjects, present and past, were published, along with some new poems, as *History*. The more personal poems, recording the breakup of his second marriage and separation from his wife and daughter, were published under the title *For Lizzie and Harriet*. At the same time a new collection of sonnets, *The Dolphin*, records his remarriage to Lady Caroline Blackwood. He divided his time between her home in England and periods of teaching writing and literature at Harvard—a familiar pattern for him in which the old tensions between New England and "elsewhere" were being constantly explored and renewed. His last book, *Day by Day* (1977), records those stresses as well as new marital difficulties. It also contains some of his most powerful poems about his childhood.

Lowell had been active in the theater with a version of *Prometheus Bound* and a translation of Racine's *Phaedra*, as well as adaptations of Melville and Hawthorne stories gathered as *The Old Glory*. He translated from modern European poetry and the classics, often freely as "imitations" which brought important poetic voices into English currency. His *Selected Poems* (his own choices) appeared in 1976. When he died suddenly at the age of sixty, he was the dominant and most honored poet of his generation—not only for his ten volumes of verse but for his broad activity as a man of letters. He stood out as one who kept alive—sometimes at great psychological cost—the notion of the poet's public responsibility. He was with the group of writers who led Vietnam war protesters against the Pentagon in 1967, where Norman Mailer, a fellow protester, observed that "Lowell gave off at times the unwilling haunted saintliness of a man who was repaying the moral debts of ten generations of ancestors."

Colloquy in Black Rock[1]

Here the jack-hammer[2] jabs into the ocean;
My heart, you race and stagger and demand
More blood-gangs for your nigger-brass percussions,
Till I, the stunned machine of your devotion,
Clanging upon this cymbal of a hand,   5
Am rattled screw and footloose. All discussions

End in the mud-flat detritus of death.
My heart, beat faster, faster. In Black Mud[3]
Hungarian workmen give their blood
For the martyre Stephen,[4] who was stoned to death.   10

Black Mud, a name to conjure with: O mud
For watermelons gutted to the crust,

1. A section of Bridgeport, Connecticut, where Lowell went to live in 1944 after serving his term as a conscientious objector. It has a large Hungarian population.
2. Rock drill operated by compressed air.
3. The speaker's name for mud flats near Black Rock.
4. A reference (1) to the wartime blood donations of the workmen, (2) to the patron saint of Hungary, King Stephen I (977–1038) and probably (3) to St. Stephen Promartyr, the first Christian to sacrifice himself for Christ.

Mud for the mole-tide[5] harbor, mud for mouse,
Mud for the armored Diesel fishing tubs that thud
A year and a day[6] to wind and tide; the dust   15
Is on this skipping heart that shakes my house,

House of our Savior who was hanged till death.
My heart, beat faster, faster. In Black Mud
Stephen the martyre was broken down to blood:
Our ransom is the rubble of his death.   20

Christ walks on the black water. In Black Mud
Darts the kingfisher.[7] On Corpus Christi,[8] heart,
Over the drum-beat of St. Stephen's choir
I hear him, *Stupor Mundi*,[9] and the mud
Flies from his hunching wings and beak—my heart,   25
The blue kingfisher dives on you in fire.

1946

The Quaker Graveyard in Nantucket

[FOR WARREN WINSLOW,[1] DEAD AT SEA]

Let man have dominion over the fishes of the sea and the fowls of the
air and the beasts of the whole earth, and every creeping creature that
moveth upon the earth.[2]

I

A brackish reach of shoal off Madaket—[3]
The sea was still breaking violently and night
Had steamed into our North Atlantic Fleet,
When the drowned sailor clutched the drag-net. Light
Flashed from his matted head and marble feet,   5
He grappled at the net
With the coiled, hurdling muscles of his thighs:
The corpse was bloodless, a botch of reds and whites,
Its open, staring eyes
Were lustreless dead-lights[4]   10
Or cabin-windows on a stranded hulk
Heavy with sand. We weight the body, close
Its eyes and heave it seaward whence it came[5]
Where the heel-headed dogfish barks its nose
On Ahab's[6] void and forehead; and the name   15

5. Special currents produced by a mole (breakwater).
6. Perhaps the "year and a day" of Lowell's prison sentence.
7. A short-tailed bird that dives for fish; associated in the poem's last line with Christ, the "fisher of men."
8. Body of Christ; a feast day of the Christian year celebrating the Eucharist, the transformation of the Host into the body of Christ.
9. Marvel of the world.
1. A cousin of Lowell's who died in the sinking of a naval vessel during World War II.

2. From Genesis 1.26, the account of the Creation of Man.
3. On Nantucket Island.
4. Shutters over portholes to keep out water in a storm. The images in lines 4–11 come from "The Shipwreck," the opening chapter of *Cape Cod* by Henry David Thoreau (1817–62).
5. The sea is imagined as the primitive source of life as well as the agent of Winslow's destruction.
6. The single-minded pursuer of the white whale Moby-Dick, in the novel by Herman Melville (1819–91).

Is blocked in yellow chalk.
Sailors, who pitch this portent at the sea
Where dreadnaughts shall confess
Its hell-bent deity,
When you are powerless   20
To sand-bag this Atlantic bulwark, faced
By the earth-shaker, green, unwearied, chaste
In his steel scales: ask for no Orphean lute
To pluck life back.[7] The guns of the steeled fleet
Recoil and then repeat   25
The hoarse salute.

II

Whenever winds are moving and their breath
Heaves at the roped-in bulwarks of this pier,
The terns and sea-gulls tremble at your death
In these home waters. Sailor, can you hear   30
The Pequod's[8] sea wings, beating landward, fall
Headlong and break on our Atlantic wall
Off 'Sconset, where the yawing S-boats[9] splash
The bellbuoy, with ballooning spinnakers,
As the entangled, screeching mainsheet clears   35
The blocks: off Madaket, where lubbers lash
The heavy surf and throw their long lead squids
For blue-fish? Sea-gulls blink their heavy lids
Seaward. The winds' wings beat upon the stones,
Cousin, and scream for you and the claws rush   40
At the sea's throat and wring it in the slush
Of this old Quaker graveyard where the bones
Cry out in the long night for the hurt beast
Bobbing by Ahab's whaleboats in the East.

III

All you recovered from Poseidon[1] died   45
With you, my cousin, and the harrowed brine
Is fruitless on the blue beard of the god,
Stretching beyond us to the castles in Spain,
Nantucket's westward haven. To Cape Cod
Guns, cradled on the tide,   50
Blast the eelgrass about a waterclock
Of bilge and backwash, roil the salt and sand
Lashing earth's scaffold, rock
Our warships in the hand
Of the great God, where time's contrition blues   55
Whatever it was these Quaker[2] sailors lost
In the mad scramble of their lives. They died
When time was open-eyed,
Wooden and childish; only bones abide

---

7. In Greek mythology, Orpheus through
his music tried to win the freedom of his
bride Eurydice from the Underworld.
8. Ahab's ship, destroyed by Moby-Dick.
9. A type of large racing sailboat;
"yawing": steering wildly in heavy seas;
"lubber": sailor's term for an awkward
seaman.
1. In Greek mythology, god of the sea.
2. The whaling population of Nantucket
included many Quakers.

There, in the nowhere, where their boats were tossed   60
Sky-high, where mariners had fabled news
Of IS,[3] the whited monster. What it cost
Them is their secret. In the sperm-whale's slick
I see the Quakers drown and hear their cry:
"If God himself had not been on our side,   65
If God himself had not been on our side,
When the Atlantic rose against us, why,
Then it had swallowed us up quick."

IV

This is the end of the whaleroad[4] and the whale
Who spewed Nantucket bones on the thrashed swell   70
And stirred the troubled waters to whirlpools
To send the Pequod packing off to hell:
This is the end of them, three-quarters fools,
Snatching at straws to sail
Seaward and seaward on the turntail whale,   75
Spouting out blood and water as it rolls,
Sick as a dog to these Atlantic shoals:
Clamavimus,[5] O depths. Let the sea-gulls wail

For water, for the deep where the high tide
Mutters to its hurt self, mutters and ebbs.   80
Waves wallow in their wash, go out and out,
Leave only the death-rattle of the crabs,
The beach increasing, its enormous snout
Sucking the ocean's side.
This is the end of running on the waves;   85
We are poured out like water. Who will dance
The mast-lashed master of Leviathans[6]
Up from this field of Quakers in their unstoned graves?

V

When the whale's viscera go and the roll
Of its corruption overruns this world   90
Beyond tree-swept Nantucket and Woods Hole[7]
And Martha's Vineyard, Sailor, will your sword
Whistle and fall and sink into the fat?
In the great ash-pit of Jehoshaphat[8]
The bones cry for the blood of the white whale,   95
The fat flukes arch and whack about its ears,
The death-lance churns into the sanctuary, tears

---

3. The white whale is here imagined as a force like the God of Exodus 3.14, who, when asked his name by Moses, replies, "I AM THAT I AM." Also an abbreviation of Jesus Salvator. The whale is imagined as the sacrificial victim of the materialist Quakers.
4. An Anglo-Saxon epithet for the sea.
5. Latin: "We have called." Adapting the opening of Psalm 130: "Out of the depths have I cried unto thee, O Lord."
6. An Old Testament sea monster, here identified with Ahab's pursuit of the white whale. "Who will dance" alludes to the absence of a poet like Orpheus to rescue drowned figures (see note 7, above).
7. On the coast of Massachusetts near the island of Martha's Vineyard.
8. "The day of judgment. The world, according to some prophets, will end in fire" [Lowell's note]. In Joel 3, the Last Judgment takes place in the valley of Jehoshaphat.

The gun-blue swingle,[9] heaving like a flail,
And hacks the coiling life out: it works and drags
And rips the sperm-whale's midriff into rags,   100
Gobbets of blubber spill to wind and weather,
Sailor, and gulls go round the stoven timbers
Where the morning stars sing out together
And thunder shakes the white surf and dismembers
The red flag hammered in the mast-head.[1] Hide,   105
Our steel, Jonas Messias, in Thy side.[2]

VI. OUR LADY OF WALSINGHAM[3]

There once the penitents took off their shoes
And then walked barefoot the remaining mile;
And the small trees, a stream and hedgerows file
Slowly along the munching English lane,   110
Like cows to the old shrine, until you lose
Track of your dragging pain.
The stream flows down under the druid[4] tree,
Shiloah's[5] whirlpools gurgle and make glad
The castle of God. Sailor, you were glad   115
And whistled Sion by that stream. But see:

Our Lady, too small for her canopy,
Sits near the altar. There's no comeliness
At all or charm in that expressionless
Face with its heavy eyelids. As before,   120
This face, for centuries a memory,
Non est species, neque decor,[6]
Expressionless, expresses God: it goes
Past castled Sion. She knows what God knows,
Not Calvary's Cross nor crib at Bethlehem   125
Now, and the world shall come to Walsingham.

VII

The empty winds are creaking and the oak
Splatters and splatters on the cenotaph,
The boughs are trembling and a gaff
Bobs on the untimely stroke   130
Of the greased wash exploding on a shoal-bell
In the old mouth of the Atlantic. It's well;
Atlantic, you are fouled with the blue sailors,
Sea-monsters, upward angel, downward fish:
Unmarried and corroding, spare of flesh   135

---

9. Knifelike wooden instrument for beating flax.
1. At the end of *Moby-Dick*, the arm of the Indian Tashtego appears from the waves and nails Ahab's flag to the sinking mast.
2. The Old Testament figure of Jonah, who had been swallowed by a whale, is here merged with the New Testament Christ (Messiah). He is imagined inside the whale pierced by a harpoon as Christ was pierced by the spear of the Roman centurion. Both symbolize salvation: Jonah emerged alive from the whale and Jesus was resurrected from the dead.
3. Lowell took these details from E. I. Watkin's *Catholic Art and Culture*, which includes a description of the medieval shrine of the Virgin at Walsingham.
4. One of the pre-Christian religions in England.
5. The stream which flows past God's Temple on Mount Sion (Isaiah 8.6). In Isaiah 51.2, the redeemed come "singing into Zion."
6. "There is no ostentation or elegance."

Mart once of supercilious, wing'd clippers,
Atlantic, where your bell-trap guts its spoil
You could cut the brackish winds with a knife
Here in Nantucket, and cast up the time
When the Lord God formed man from the sea's slime ¹⁴⁰
And breathed into his face the breath of life,
And blue-lung'd combers lumbered to the kill.
The Lord survives the rainbow⁷ of His will.

1946

Children of Light¹

Our fathers wrung their bread from stocks and stones
And fenced their gardens with the Redman's bones;
Embarking from the Nether Land of Holland,
Pilgrims unhouseled² by Geneva's night,
They planted here the Serpent's seeds³ of light;   5
And here the pivoting searchlights probe to shock
The riotous glass houses⁴ built on rock,
And candles gutter by an empty altar,
And light is where the landless blood of Cain⁵
Is burning, burning the unburied grain.   10

1946

Mr. Edwards and the Spider¹

I saw the spiders marching through the air,
Swimming from tree to tree that mildewed day
    In latter August when the hay
    Came creaking to the barn. But where
        The wind is westerly,   5
Where gnarled November makes the spiders fly
Into the apparitions of the sky,
    They purpose nothing but their ease and die
Urgently beating east to sunrise and the sea;

    What are we in the hands of the great God?²   10
It was in vain you set up thorn and briar
    In battle array against the fire
    And treason crackling in your blood;

---

7. Alluding to God's covenant with Noah after the Flood. The rainbow symbolized the fact that mankind would never again be destroyed by flood (Genesis 9.11).

1. In Luke 16, the children of this world are distinguished from the children of light, the Lord's chosen.

2. I.e., not having received Holy Communion. John Calvin's theology was strongly established in Geneva. He denied that in Holy Communion the Eucharistic bread and wine actually became the body and blood of Christ.

3. Alluding to the channeling of Protestant energies into business. The serpent, associated with Satan the tempter or Eve, seems to pervert the "seeds," the elect or "children of light."

4. Modern houses by the shore.

5. Likening the modern descendants of the Puritans to the race of Cain, presumably because, in dispossessing the Indians, they had committed a crime like Cain's against his brother.

1. Jonathan Edwards, Puritan preacher and theologian (1703–58). Lowell quotes his writings throughout. The details of the first stanza come from his youthful essay *Of Insects* ("The Habits of Spiders").

2. This stanza draws upon Edwards's sermon "Sinners in the Hands of an Angry God," whose point of departure is Ezekiel 22.14: "Can thine heart endure or can thine hands be strong in the days that I shall deal with thee" (cf. line 18).

For the wild thorns grow tame
And will do nothing to oppose the flame;   15
Your lacerations tell the losing game
You play against a sickness past your cure.
How will the hands be strong? How will the heart endure?

A very little thing, a little worm,
Or hourglass-blazoned spider,³ it is said,   20
    Can kill a tiger. Will the dead
    Hold up his mirror and affirm
        To the four winds the smell
And flash of his authority? It's well
If God who holds you to the pit of hell,   25
Much as one holds a spider, will destroy,
Baffle and dissipate your soul. As a small boy

On Windsor Marsh,⁴ I saw the spider die
When thrown into the bowels of fierce fire:
    There's no long struggle, no desire   30
    To get up on its feet and fly—
        It stretches out its feet
And dies. This is the sinner's last retreat;
Yes, and no strength exerted on the heat
Then sinews the abolished will, when sick   35
And full of burning, it will whistle on a brick.

But who can plumb the sinking of that soul?
Josiah Hawley,⁵ picture yourself cast
    Into a brick-kiln where the blast
    Fans your quick vitals to a coal—   40
        If measured by a glass,
How long would it seem burning! Let there pass
A minute, ten, ten trillion; but the blaze
Is infinite, eternal: this is death,
To die and know it. This is the Black Widow, death.   45
                                                    1946

After the Surprising Conversions¹

September twenty-second, Sir: today
I answer. In the latter part of May,

---

3. The poisonous black widow spider has, on the underside of its abdomen, a red marking which resembles an hourglass.
4. East Windsor, Connecticut, Edwards's childhood home.
5. Edwards's uncle, Joseph Hawley, whose suicide is described in *After the Surprising Conversions.*
1. This poem draws upon letters and ac-

counts by the Puritan preacher and theologian Jonathan Edwards (1703–58). Edwards describes the effects of an amazing religious revival, the "surprising conversions" of 1734–35. On June 1, 1735, his uncle, Joseph Hawley, slit his own throat; the suicide channeled and countered the effects of the revival in ways that Lowell describes.

Hard on our Lord's Ascension,[2] it began
To be more sensible.[3] A gentleman
Of more than common understanding, strict
In morals, pious in behavior, kicked
Against our goad. A man of some renown,
An useful, honored person in the town,
He came of melancholy parents; prone
To secret spells, for years they kept alone—
His uncle, I believe, was killed of it:
Good people, but of too much or little wit.
I preached one Sabbath on a text from Kings;
He showed concernment for his soul. Some things
In his experience were hopeful. He
Would sit and watch the wind knocking a tree
And praise this countryside our Lord has made.
Once when a poor man's heifer died, he laid
A shilling on the doorsill; though a thirst
For loving shook him like a snake, he durst
Not entertain much hope of his estate
In heaven. Once we saw him sitting late
Behind his attic window by a light
That guttered on his Bible; through that night
He meditated terror, and he seemed
Beyond advice or reason, for he dreamed
That he was called to trumpet Judgment Day
To Concord. In the latter part of May
He cut his throat. And though the coroner
Judged him delirious, soon a noisome stir
Palsied our village. At Jehovah's nod
Satan seemed more let loose amongst us: God
Abandoned us to Satan, and he pressed
Us hard, until we thought we could not rest
Till we had done with life. Content was gone.
All the good work was quashed. We were undone.
The breath of God had carried out a planned
And sensible withdrawal from this land;
The multitude, once unconcerned with doubt,
Once neither callous, curious nor devout,
Jumped at broad noon, as though some peddler groaned
At it in its familiar twang: "My friend,
Cut your own throat. Cut your own throat. Now! Now!"
September twenty-second, Sir, the bough
Cracks with the unpicked apples, and at dawn
The small-mouth bass breaks water, gorged with spawn.

        1946

5

10

15

20

25

30

35

40

45

---

2. Christ's ascension into Heaven, celebrated 40 days after Easter.
3. I.e., apparent to the senses. In a letter of May 30, 1735, Edwards wrote, "It
began to be very sensible that the spirit
of God was gradually withdrawing from
us."

For George Santayana[1]
1863–1952

In the heydays of 'forty-five,
bus-loads of souvenir-deranged
G.I.'s and officer-professors of philosophy
came crashing through your cell,
puzzled to find you still alive,   5
free-thinking Catholic infidel,[2]
stray spirit, who'd found
the Church too good to be believed.
Later I used to dawdle
past Circus and Mithraic Temple[3]   10
to *Santo Stefano* grown paper-thin
like you from waiting. . . .
There at the monastery hospital,
you wished those geese-girl sisters[4] wouldn't bother
their heads and yours by praying for your soul: 15
"There is no God and Mary is His Mother."

Lying outside the consecrated ground
forever now, you smile
like Ser Brunetto running for the green
cloth at Verona[5]—not like one   20
who loses, but like one who'd won . . .
as if your long pursuit of Socrates'
demon, man-slaying Alcibiades,[6]
the demon of philosophy, at last had changed
those fleeting virgins into friendly laurel trees   25
at *Santo Stefano Rotondo*, when you died
near ninety,
still unbelieving, unconfessed and unreceived,
true to your boyish shyness of the Bride.[7]
Old trooper, I see your child's red crayon pass,   30
bleeding deletions on the galleys[8] you hold
under your throbbing magnifying glass,
that worn arena, where the whirling sand

1. Philosopher, poet, and novelist who taught at Harvard from 1889 to 1912. He spent his last years abroad and died in a monastery in Rome where, among his visitors, were American soldiers from the victorious Allied armies.
2. Santayana, born Catholic, became an atheist.
3. Ruins of a Roman arena, the Circus Maximus, and of temples in the Roman forum devoted to the worship of the God of Light (a rival to early Christian worship). "Santo Stefano": Roman church near the monastery hospital where Santayana died.
4. The wimple (headdress) worn by the nuns looks like a bird in flight.
5. In *Inferno* XV, Dante (1265–1321), bidding farewell to his teacher, Brunetto Latini, compares him to a runner in a footrace in Verona, in which the prize for the winner is a green cloth.
6. Athenian general (450–404 B.C.), beloved by his teacher Socrates (470?–399 B.C.). Lowell is probably alluding to the challenge of mortal beauty and sensuality to philosophers (Santayana's first book was *The Sense of Beauty*, 1896). The "fleeting virgins" allude to myths of nymphs such as that of Daphne, turned into laurel trees. Apollo, the god of poetry, pursued Daphne for her beauty; instead the laurel came as a reward for his poetry.
7. The Catholic Church, the "Bride of Christ."
8. Printer's proofs.

and broken-hearted lions lick your hand
refined by bile as yellow as a lump of gold.   35

                                                                          1959

Memories of West Street and Lepke[1]

Only teaching on Tuesdays, book-worming
in pajamas fresh from the washer each morning,
I hog a whole house on Boston's
"hardly passionate Marlborough Street,"[2]
where even the man   5
scavenging filth in the back alley trash cans,
has two children, a beach wagon, a helpmate,
and is a "young Republican."
I have a nine months' daughter,
young enough to be my granddaughter.   10
Like the sun she rises in her flame-flamingo infants' wear.

These are the tranquillized *Fifties*,
and I am forty. Ought I to regret my seedtime?
I was a fire-breathing Catholic C.O.,[3]
and made my manic statement,   15
telling off the state and president, and then
sat waiting sentence in the bull pen
beside a Negro boy with curlicues
of marijuana in his hair.

                                                                           20
Given a year,
I walked on the roof ot the West Street Jail, a short
enclosure like my school soccer court,
and saw the Hudson River once a day
through sooty clothesline entanglements
and bleaching khaki tenements.   25
Strolling, I yammered metaphysics with Abramowitz,
a jaundice-yellow ("it's really tan")
and fly-weight pacifist,
so vegetarian,
he wore rope shoes and preferred fallen fruit.   30
He tried to convert Bioff and Brown,
the Hollywood pimps, to his diet.
Hairy, muscular, suburban,
wearing chocolate double-breasted suits,
they blew their tops and beat him black and blue.   35

I was so out of things, I'd never heard
of the Jehovah's Witnesses.[4]

1. In 1943 Lowell was sentenced to a year in New York's West Street jail for his refusal to serve in the armed forces. Among the prisoners was Lepke Buchalter, head of Murder Incorporated, an organized crime syndicate, who had been convicted of murder.

2. William James's phrase for a street in the elegant Back Bay section of Boston, where Lowell lived in the 1950s.
3. Conscientious objector (to war).
4. A Christian revivalist sect strongly opposed to war and denying the power of the state in matters of conscience.

"Are you a C.O.?" I asked a fellow jailbird.
"No," he answered, "I'm a J.W."
He taught me the "hospital tuck,"[5]   40
and pointed out the T-shirted back
of *Murder Incorporated's* Czar Lepke,
there piling towels on a rack,
or dawdling off to his little segregated cell full
of things forbidden the common man: 45
a portable radio, a dresser, two toy American
flags tied together with a ribbon of Easter palm.
Flabby, bald, lobotomized,
he drifted in a sheepish calm,
where no agonizing reappraisal   50
jarred his concentration on the electric chair—
hanging like an oasis in his air
of lost connections. . . .

                                                                        1959

Man and Wife

Tamed by *Miltown*,[1] we lie on Mother's bed;
the rising sun in war paint dyes us red;
in broad daylight her gilded bed-posts shine,
abandoned, almost Dionysian.[2]
At last the trees are green on Marlborough Street,[3]   5
blossoms on our magnolia ignite
the morning with their murderous five days' white.
All night I've held your hand,
as if you had
a fourth time faced the kingdom of the mad—   10
its hackneyed speech, its homicidal eye—
and dragged me home alive. . . . Oh my *Petite*,
clearest of all God's creatures, still all air and nerve:
you were in your twenties, and I,
once hand on glass   15
and heart in mouth,
outdrank the Rahvs[4] in the heat
of Greenwich Village, fainting at your feet—
too boiled and shy
and poker-faced to make a pass,   20
while the shrill verve
of your invective scorched the traditional South.

Now twelve years later, you turn your back.
Sleepless, you hold

---

5. The authorized, efficient way of making beds in a hospital.
1. Brand name of a barbiturate tranquilizer.
2. Orgiastic, as in the Greek celebration honoring Dionysus, the god of wine.
3. In Boston's once elegant Back Bay section.
4. Philip Rahv (1908–74), a literary critic and one of the founders of *Partisan Review*, and a friend from the period when Lowell was courting his second wife, Elizabeth Hardwick.

your pillow to your hollows like a child;   25
your old-fashioned tirade—
loving, rapid, merciless—
breaks like the Atlantic Ocean on my head.

1959

"To Speak of Woe That Is in Marriage"[1]

*"It is the future generation that presses into being by means of these
exuberant feelings and supersensible soap bubbles of ours."*
—SCHOPENHAUER[2]

"The hot night makes us keep our bedroom windows open.
Our magnolia blossoms. Life begins to happen.
My hopped up husband drops his home disputes,
and hits the streets to cruise for prostitutes,
free-lancing out along the razor's edge.   5
This screwball might kill his wife, then take the pledge.
Oh the monotonous meanness of his lust. . . .
It's the injustice . . . he is so unjust—
whiskey-blind, swaggering home at five.
My only thought is how to keep alive.   10
What makes him tick? Each night now I tie
ten dollars and his car key to my thigh. . . .
Gored by the climacteric[3] of his want,
he stalls above me like an elephant."

1959

Skunk Hour

[FOR ELIZABETH BISHOP][1]

Nautilus Island's[2] hermit
heiress still lives through winter in her Spartan cottage;
her sheep still graze above the sea.
Her son's a bishop. Her farmer
is first selectman in our village;   5
she's in her dotage.

Thirsting for
the hierarchic privacy
of Queen Victoria's century,
she buys up all   10
the eyesores facing her shore,
and lets them fall.

The season's ill—
we've lost our summer millionaire,

---

1. "The Wife of Bath's Prologue," line
3, from *The Canterbury Tales* by English poet Geoffrey Chaucer (1340?–1400).
2. Arthur Schopenhauer (1788–1860),
German philosopher noted for his pessimism and misogyny.

3. Any critical period.
1. Lowell's poem is a response to Elizabeth Bishop's *The Armadillo*.
2. The poem is set in Castine, Maine,
where Lowell had a summer house.

who seemed to leap from an L. L. Bean   15
catalogue.[3] His nine-knot yawl
was auctioned off to lobstermen.
A red fox stain covers Blue Hill.

And now our fairy
decorator brightens his shop for fall;   20
his fishnet's filled with orange cork,
orange, his cobbler's bench and awl;
there is no money in his work,
he'd rather marry.

One dark night,   25
my Tudor Ford climbed the hill's skull;
I watched for love-cars. Lights turned down,
they lay together, hull to hull,
where the graveyard shelves on the town. . . .
My mind's not right.   30

A car radio bleats,
"Love, O careless Love. . . ." I hear
my ill-spirit sob in each blood cell,
as if my hand were at its throat. . . .
I myself am hell;[4]   35
nobody's here—

only skunks, that search
in the moonlight for a bite to eat.
They march on their soles up Main Street:
white stripes, moonstruck eyes' red fire   40
under the chalk-dry and spar spire
of the Trinitarian Church.

I stand on top
of our back steps and breathe the rich air—
a mother skunk with her column of kittens swills the garbage pail.   45
She jabs her wedge-head in a cup
of sour cream, drops her ostrich tail,
and will not scare.

1959

Eye and Tooth

My whole eye was sunset red,
the old cut cornea throbbed,
I saw things darkly,
as through an unwashed goldfish globe.

3. A mail-order house in Maine, which deals primarily with sporting and camping goods.

4. "Which way I fly is Hell, myself am Hell" (Satan in Milton's *Paradise Lost*, IV.75).

I lay all day on my bed.
I chain-smoked through the night,
learning to flinch
at the flash of the matchlight.

Outside, the summer rain,
a simmer of rot and renewal,
fell in pinpricks.
Even new life is fuel.

My eyes throb.
Nothing can dislodge
the house with my first tooth
noosed in a knot to the doorknob.

Nothing can dislodge
the triangular blotch
of rot on the red roof,
a cedar hedge, or the shade of a hedge.

No ease from the eye
of the sharp-shinned hawk in the birdbook there,
with reddish-brown buffalo hair
on its shanks, one ascetic talon

clasping the abstract imperial sky.
It says:
an eye for an eye,
a tooth for a tooth.[1]

No ease for the boy at the keyhole,
his telescope,
when the women's white bodies flashed
in the bathroom. Young, my eyes began to fail.

Nothing! No oil
for the eye, nothing to pour
on those waters or flames.
I am tired. Everyone's tired of my turmoil.

1964

The Neo-Classical Urn

I rub my head and find a turtle shell
stuck on a pole,
each hair electrical
with charges, and the juice alive
with ferment. Bubbles drive
the motor, always purposeful . . .

---

1. Exodus 21.24.

Poor head!
How its skinny shell once hummed,
as I sprinted down the colonnade
of bleaching pines, cylindrical   10
clipped trunks without a twig between them. Rest!
I could not rest. At full run on the curve,
I left the cast stone statue of a nymph,
her soaring armpits and her one bare breast,
gray from the rain and graying in the shade,   15
as on, on, in sun, the pathway now a dyke,
I swerved between two water bogs,
two seines[1] of moss, and stooped to snatch
the painted turtles on dead logs.
In that season of joy,   20
my turtle catch
was thirty-three,
dropped splashing in our garden urn,
like money in the bank,
the plop and splash   25
of turtle on turtle,
fed raw gobs of hash . . .

Oh neo-classical white urn, Oh nymph,
Oh lute![2] The boy was pitiless who strummed
their elegy,   30
for as the month wore on,
the turtles rose,
and popped up dead on the stale scummed
surface—limp wrinkled heads and legs withdrawn
in pain. What pain? A turtle's nothing. No   35
grace, no cerebration, less free will
than the mosquito I must kill—
nothings! Turtles! I rub my skull,
that turtle shell,
and breathe their dying smell,   40
still watch their crippled last survivors pass,
and hobble humpbacked through the grizzled grass.

1964

July in Washington

The stiff spokes of this wheel[1]
touch the sore spots of the earth.

On the Potomac, swan-white
power launches keep breasting the sulphurous wave.

---

1. A type of fishnet.
2. **The** ornamental garden urn of his
childhood is addressed in tones reminiscent of the English Romantic poet
John Keats's (1795–1821) *Ode on a*

Grecian Urn.
1. I.e., Washington, D.C., which is laid
out in a formal plan of concentric circles. Some of the intersecting circles
contain equestrian statues (line 7).

Otters slide and dive and slick back their hair,   5
raccoons clean their meat in the creek.

On the circles, green statues ride like South American
liberators above the breeding vegetation—

prongs and spearheads of some equatorial
backland that will inherit the globe.   10

The elect, the elected . . . they come here bright as dimes,
and die disheveled and soft.

We cannot name their names, or number their dates—
circle on circle, like rings on a tree—

but we wish the river had another shore,   15
some farther range of delectable mountains,[2]

distant hills powdered blue as a girl's eyelid.
It seems the least little shove would land us there,

that only the slightest repugnance of our bodies
we no longer control could drag us back.   20

                                                                    1964

Night Sweat

Work-table, litter, books and standing lamp,
plain things, my stalled equipment, the old broom—
but I am living in a tidied room,
for ten nights now I've felt the creeping damp
float over my pajamas' wilted white . . .   5
Sweet salt embalms me and my head is wet,
everything streams and tells me this is right;
my life's fever is soaking in night sweat—
one life, one writing! But the downward glide
and bias of existing wrings us dry—   10
always inside me is the child who died,
always inside me is his will to die—
one universe, one body . . . in this urn
the animal night sweats of the spirit burn.
Behind me! You! Again I feel the light   15
lighten my leaded eyelids, while the gray
skulled horses whinny for the soot of night.
I dabble in the dapple of the day,
a heap of wet clothes, seamy, shivering,
I see my flesh and bedding washed with light,   20

2. In *Inferno*, Canto I, Dante is separated by his sins from the Delectable
Mountain, representing Virtue. Perhaps
this is also an allusion to the passage
from Hell to the mountain of Purgatory.

my child exploding into dynamite,
my wife . . . your lightness alters everything,
and tears the black web from the spider's sack,
as your heart hops and flutters like a hare.
Poor turtle, tortoise, if I cannot clear   25
the surface of these troubled waters here,
absolve me, help me, Dear Heart, as you bear
this world's dead weight and cycle on your back.

                                                                 1964

For the Union Dead[1]

"Relinquunt Omnia Servare Rem Publicam."[2]

The old South Boston Aquarium stands
in a Sahara of snow now. Its broken windows are boarded.
The bronze weathervane cod has lost half its scales.
The airy tanks are dry.

Once my nose crawled like a snail on the glass;   5
my hand tingled
to burst the bubbles
drifting from the noses of the cowed, compliant fish.

My hand draws back. I often sigh still
for the dark downward and vegetating kingdom   10
of the fish and reptile. One morning last March,
I pressed against the new barbed and galvanized

fence on the Boston Common. Behind their cage,
yellow dinosaur steamshovels were grunting
as they cropped up tons of mush and grass   15
to gouge their underworld garage.

Parking spaces luxuriate like civic
sandpiles in the heart of Boston.
A girdle of orange, Puritan-pumpkin colored girders
braces the tingling Statehouse,   20

shaking over the excavations, as it faces Colonel Shaw
and his bell-cheeked Negro infantry
on St. Gaudens' shaking Civil War relief,
propped by a plank splint against the garage's earthquake.

1. First published under the title *Colonel Shaw and the Massachusetts' 54th* in a paperback edition of *Life Studies* (1960). With a change of title, it became the title poem of *For the Union Dead* (1964).
2. Robert Gould Shaw (1837–63) led the first all-Negro regiment in the North during the Civil War. He was killed in the attack against Fort Wagner, South Carolina. A bronze relief by the sculptor Augustus Saint-Gaudens (1848–97), dedicated in 1897, standing opposite the Massachusetts State House on Boston Common, commemorates the deaths. A Latin inscription on the monument reads *"Omnia Reliquit Servare Rem Publicam"* —"He leaves all behind to serve the Republic." Lowell's epigraph alters the inscription slightly, changing the third person singular ("he") to the third person plural: *"They* give up everything to serve the Republic."

Two months after marching through Boston,   25
half the regiment was dead;
at the dedication,
William James[3] could almost hear the bronze Negroes breathe.

Their monument sticks like a fishbone
in the city's throat.   30
Its Colonel is as lean
as a compass-needle.

He has an angry wrenlike vigilance,
a greyhound's gentle tautness;
he seems to wince at pleasure,   35
and suffocate for privacy.

He is out of bounds now. He rejoices in man's lovely,
peculiar power to choose life and die—
when he leads his black soldiers to death,
he cannot bend his back.   40

On a thousand small town New England greens,
the old white churches hold their air
of sparse, sincere rebellion; frayed flags
quilt the graveyards of the Grand Army of the Republic.

The stone statues of the abstract Union Soldier   45
grow slimmer and younger each year—
wasp-waisted, they doze over muskets
and muse through their sideburns . . .

Shaw's father wanted no monument
except the ditch,   50
where his son's body was thrown[4]
and lost with his "niggers."

The ditch is nearer.
There are no statues for the last war[5] here;
on Boylston Street,[6] a commercial photograph   55
shows Hiroshima boiling

over a Mosler Safe, the "Rock of Ages"
that survived the blast. Space is nearer.
When I crouch to my television set,
the drained faces of Negro school-children rise like balloons.[7]   60

Colonel Shaw
is riding on his bubble,

3. Philosopher and psychologist (1842–
1910) who taught at Harvard.
4. By the Confederate soldiers at Fort
Wagner.
5. World War II.

6. In Boston, where the poem is set.
7. Probably news photographs connected
with contemporary civil rights demonstrations to secure desegregation of schools
in the South.

he waits
for the blessed break.

The Aquarium is gone. Everywhere,   65
giant finned cars nose forward like fish;
a savage servility
slides by on grease.

1960, 1964

Ezra Pound[1]

Horizontal on a deckchair in the ward
of the criminal mad. . . . A man without shoestrings clawing
the Social Credit[2] broadside from your table, you saying,
". . . here with a black suit and black briefcase; in the brief,
an abomination, Possum's *hommage* to Milton."[3]   5
Then sprung; Rapallo,[4] and the decade gone;
and three years later, Eliot dead, you saying,
"Who's left alive to understand my jokes?
My old Brother in the arts . . . besides, he was a smash of a poet."
You showed me your blotched, bent hands, saying, "Worms.   10
When I talked that nonsense about Jews on the Rome
wireless,[5] Olga knew it was shit, and still loved me."
And I, "Who else has been in Purgatory?"
You, "I began with a swelled head and end with swelled feet."

1969, 1973

Robert Frost[1]

Robert Frost at midnight,[2] the audience gone
to vapor, the great act laid on the shelf in mothballs,
his voice is musical and raw—he writes in the flyleaf:
For Robert from Robert, his friend in the art.
"Sometimes I feel too full of myself," I say.   5
And he, misunderstanding, "When I am low,
I stray away. My son[3] wasn't your kind. The night
we told him Merrill Moore[4] would come to treat him,
he said, 'I'll kill him first.' One of my daughters thought things,
thought every male she met was out to make her;   10
the way she dressed, she couldn't make a whorehouse."
And I, "Sometimes I'm so happy I can't stand myself."

1. Pound was held as criminally insane
in St. Elizabeth's Hospital, Washington,
D.C., from 1945 to 1958.
2. A crackpot scheme for economic reform which Pound vehemently supported.
3. "Possum" was an affectionate name
for Pound's friend and fellow poet, T. S.
Eliot (1888–1965), who had written *Old
Possum's Book of Practical Cats*. Eliot
had been critical of Milton's influence on
poetry, but in the essay mentioned reverses his opinion.
4. After Pound's release ("sprung") from
St. Elizabeth's, he returned to Italy,
where one of his homes was Rapallo.
5. During World War II Pound's broadcasts over Italian radio ("wireless," line
12) in favor of the Fascist dictator
Mussolini included anti-Semitic remarks.
Olga Rudge was Pound's mistress and
companion until his death in 1972.
1. American poet (1874–1963).
2. Alludes to the poem *Frost at Midnight*
by Samuel Taylor Coleridge (1772–1834),
in which the English poet celebrates a
peaceful moment with his infant son.
3. Frost's son committed suicide.
4. Poet and psychiatrist (b. 1903).

And he, "When I am too full of joy, I think
how little good my health did anyone near me."

1969, 1973

Ulysses[1]

Shakespeare stand-ins,[2] same string hair, gay, dirty . . .
there's a new poetry in the air, it's youth's
patent, lust coolly led on by innocence—
late-flowering Garden, far from Eden fallen,
and still fair! None chooses as his model   5
Ulysses landhugging from port to port for girls . . .
his marriage a cover for the underworld,
dark harbor of suctions and the second chance.
He won Nausicaa twenty years too late. . . .
Scarred husband and wife sit naked, one Greek smile,   10
thinking *we were bound to fall in love*
if only we stayed married long enough—
because our ships are burned and all friends lost
How we wish we were friends with half our friends!

1969, 1973

Reading Myself

Like thousands, I took just pride and more than just,
struck matches that brought my blood to a boil;
I memorized the tricks to set the river on fire—
somehow never wrote something to go back to.
Can I suppose I am finished with wax flowers   5
and have earned my grass on the minor slopes of Parnassus.[3] . . .
No honeycomb is built without a bee
adding circle to circle, cell to cell,
the wax and honey of a mausoleum—
this round dome proves its maker is alive;   10
the corpse of the insect lives embalmed in honey,
prays that its perishable work live long
enough for the sweet-tooth bear to desecrate—
this open book . . . my open coffin.

1969, 1973

In the Ward

[FOR ISRAEL CITKOVITZ][1]

Ten years older in an hour—

I see your face smile,
your mouth is stepped on without bruising.

---

1. The protagonist of *The Odyssey*, by the Greek poet Homer (8th century B.C.); the epic poem recounts the adventures of its hero on his return to Ithaca and his wife, Penelope, 20 years after the fall of Troy. Lowell imagines Ulysses as a Don Juan in search of sexual adventures (as with the nymph Nausicaa, line 9) before he returns to his patient wife.
2. The so-called "flower children" of the 1960s, whose characteristic long hair and colorful outfits remind Lowell of minor actors in Shakespearean plays.
3. In mythology, the mountain home of Pegasus, the winged horse of poetry, and traditionally symbol of the summits of poetic achievement.
1. American composer (1909–74) and friend of the poet; Lowell is visiting him in a hospital ward.

You are very frightened by the ward,
your companions are chosen for age;   5
you are the youngest
and sham-flirt with your nurse—
your chief thought is scheming
the elaborate surprise of your escape.

Being old in good times is worse   10
than being young in the worst.

Five days
on this grill, this mattress
over nothing—
the wisdom of this sickness   15
is piously physical,
ripping up memory
to find your future—
old beauties, old masters
hoping to lose their minds before they lose
        their friends.   20

Your days are dark,
your nights imaginary—
the child says,
heaven is a big house
with lots of water and flowers—   25
you go in in a trunk.

Your feet are wired above your head.
If you could hear the glaring lightbulb
sing
your old modernist classics—   30
they are for a lost audience.

Last year
in buoyant unrest,
you gathered two or three young friends
in the *champagne room*   35
of your coldwater flat,
to explore the precision
and daimonic lawlessness
of Arnold Schönberg[2] born
when music was still imperfect science—   40
Music,
its ever retreating borderlines of being,
as treacherous, perhaps, to systems,
to fecundity,
as to silence.   45

_____
2. Austrian composer (1874–1951), one of the pioneers of modern 12-tone music.

Die Sprache ist unverstanden
doch nicht unverständlich?[3]

If you keep cutting your losses,
you have no loss to cut.

Nothing you see now   50
can mean anything;
your will is fixed on the lightbulb,
its blinding impassivity
withholding disquiet,
the art of the possible   55
that art abhors.

It's an illusion death or technique
can wring the truth from us like water.

What helpless paperishness,
if vocation   60
is only shouting what we will.

Somewhere your spirit
led the highest life;
all places matched
with that place   65
come to nothing.

1977

Epilogue[1]

Those blessèd structures, plot and rhyme—
why are they no help to me now
I want to make
something imagined, not recalled?
I hear the noise of my own voice: 5
The painter's vision is not a lens,
it trembles to caress the light.
But sometimes everything I write
with the threadbare art of my eye
seems a snapshot,   10
lurid, rapid, garish, grouped,
heightened from life,
yet paralyzed by fact.
All's misalliance.
Yet why not say what happened?   15
Pray for the grace of accuracy

---

3. A quotation from Schönberg: "The language is not understandable yet not unintelligible."

1. The poem is printed as the last piece (excluding a few translations) in Lowell's last book, *Day by Day* (1977).

Vermeer[2] gave to the sun's illumination
stealing like the tide across a map
to his girl solid with yearning.
We are poor passing facts, 20
warned by that to give
each figure in the photograph
his living name.

1977

2. Jan Vermeer (1632–75), Dutch painter noted for his subtle handling of the effects of light.

GWENDOLYN BROOKS

1917–

The career of Gwendolyn Brooks links two very different generations of black poets. For the greater part of her writing life, she followed the example of the older writers of the "Harlem Renaissance," Langston Hughes and Countee Cullen among them, who honored the ideal of an integrated society. However much her poetry drew on the street language of blacks, and on rhythms of jazz and the blues, Brooks had strong links as well to the more formal diction of English poetry. Before 1967 most of the support for her poetry and readings came from white audiences. Since 1967, Brooks has worked with and backed militant black writers who intend their work for a primarily Afro-American audience.

Brooks was born in Topeka, Kansas; she grew up in Chicago and is closely identified with the energies and problems of its black community. She went to Chicago's Englewood High School and graduated from Wilson Junior College. Brooks remembers writing poetry from the time she was seven and keeping poetry notebooks from the time she was eleven. She got her education in the moderns—Pound and Eliot—under the guidance of a rich Chicago socialite, Inez Cunningham Stark, who was a reader for *Poetry* magazine and taught a poetry class at the Southside Community Art Center. Her first book, *A Street in Bronzeville* (1945), took its title from the name journalists gave to the Chicago Negro ghetto. Her poems portrayed the waste and loss which are the inevitable result of what Langston Hughes called the blacks' "dream deferred." Or as Brooks put it:

> But could a dream send up through onion fumes
> Its white and violet, fight with fried potatoes
> And yesterday's garbage ripening in the hall,
> Flutter, or sing an aria down these rooms
>
> Even if we were willing to let it in,
> Had time to warm it, keep it very clean,
> Anticipate a message, let it begin?

With her second book of poems, *Annie Allen* (1949), Brooks became the first black to receive the Pulitzer Prize for poetry.

In *Annie Allen* and in her Bronzeville poems (*Bronzeville Boys and Girls*, 1956, continued the work begun in *A Street in Bronzeville*), Brooks concentrated not so much on protest or anger as on portraits of what Langston Hughes called "the ordinary aspects of black life." In character sketches she stressed the vitality and the often subversive morality of ghetto figures; good girls who wanted to be bad, the boredom of the children of hard-working pious mothers, the laments of suffering women abandoned by their men. She has a keen satirical eye for such details as (in *The Lovers of the Poor*) the encounter between blacks and whites during a visit of the Ladies' Betterment League to ghetto flats. Brooks's diction was a combination of the florid Biblical speech of black Protestant preachers, street talk, and the main speech patterns of English and American verse. She writes vigorous, strongly accented and strongly rhymed lines with a great deal of alliteration. She also cultivates traditional lyric forms; for example, she is one of the few modern poets to write extensively in the sonnet form.

A great change in Brooks's life came with the Second Black Writers' Conference at Fisk University in 1967, in whose charged activist atmosphere she encountered many of the new young black poets. After this, Brooks became interested in writing poetry exclusively for black audiences. She drew closer to militant political groups as a result of conducting poetry workshops for some members of the Blackstone Rangers, a teenage gang in Chicago. In autobiographical writings such as her prose *Report from Part One*, Brooks became more self-conscious about the special problems of black women and her own potential role as a leader of black feminists. She left her New York publisher in order to have her work printed by black publishers, especially the Broadside Press. Brooks's poetry, too, has changed, in both its focus and its technique. Her subjects, as in *Boy Breaking Glass*, tend to be more explicitly political, and to deal with the question of revolutionary violence. In style, too, she has left behind the narratives and character sketches of her earlier writing. The poems set jagged phrases of anger, defiance, and bafflement beside one another and seem to be sets of elliptical images put together by a radical and restless mind.

Kitchenette Building[1]

We are things of dry hours and the involuntary plan,
Grayed in, and gray. "Dream" makes a giddy sound, not strong
Like "rent," "feeding a wife," "satisfying a man."

But could a dream send up through onion fumes
Its white and violet, fight with fried potatoes   5
And yesterday's garbage ripening in the hall,
Flutter, or sing an aria down these rooms

Even if we were willing to let it in,
Had time to warm it, keep it very clean,
Anticipate a message, let it begin?   10

---

1. The first of 11 poems in the sequence *A Street in Bronzeville*.

We wonder. But not well! not for a minute!
Since Number Five is out of the bathroom now,
We think of lukewarm water, hope to get in it.

1945

A Song in the Front Yard

I've stayed in the front yard all my life.
I want a peek at the back
Where it's rough and untended and hungry weed grows.
A girl gets sick of a rose.

I want to go in the back yard now   5
And maybe down the alley,
To where the charity children play.
I want a good time today.

They do some wonderful things.
They have some wonderful fun.   10
My mother sneers, but I say it's fine
How they don't have to go in at quarter to nine.
My mother, she tells me that Johnnie Mae
Will grow up to be a bad woman.
That George'll be taken to Jail soon or late   15
(On account of last winter he sold our back gate.)

But I say it's fine. Honest, I do.
And I'd like to be a bad woman, too,
And wear the brave stockings of night-black lace
And strut down the streets with paint on my face.   20

1945

The Vacant Lot

Mrs. Coley's three-flat brick
Isn't here any more.
All done with seeing her fat little form
Burst out of the basement door;
And with seeing her African son-in-law   5
(Rightful heir to the throne)
With his great white strong cold squares of teeth
And his little eyes of stone;
And with seeing the squat fat daughter
Letting in the men   10
When majesty has gone for the day—
And letting them out again.

1945

Maxie Allen

Maxie Allen always taught her
Stipendiary little daughter
To thank her Lord and lucky star
For eye that let her see so far,

For throat enabling her to eat   5
Her Quaker Oats and Cream-of-Wheat,
For tongue to tantrum for the penny,
For car to hear the haven't-any,
For arm to toss, for leg to chance,
For heart to hanker for romance.   10

Sweet Annie tried to teach her mother
There was somewhat of something other.
And whether it was veils and God
And whistling ghosts to go unshod
Across the broad and bitter sod,   15
Or fleet love stopping at her foot
And giving her its never-root
To put into her pocket-book,
Or just a deep and human look,
She did not know; but tried to tell.   20

Her mother thought at her full well,
In inner voice not like a bell
(Which though not social has a ring
Akin to wrought bedevilling)
But like an oceanic thing: 25
What do you guess I am?
You've lots of jacks and strawberry jam.
And you don't have to go to bed, I remark,
With two dill pickles in the dark,
Nor prop what hardly calls you honey   30
And gives you only a little money.

                                                     1949

The Lovers of the Poor

arrive. The Ladies from the Ladies' Betterment
    League
Arrive in the afternoon, the late light slanting
In diluted gold bars across the boulevard brag
Of proud, seamed faces with mercy and murder hinting   5
Here, there, interrupting, all deep and debonair,
The pink paint on the innocence of fear;
Walk in a gingerly manner up the hall.
Cutting with knives served by their softest care,
Served by their love, so barbarously fair.   10
Whose mothers taught: You'd better not be cruel!
You had better not throw stones upon the wrens!
Herein they kiss and coddle and assault
Anew and dearly in the innocence
With which they baffle nature. Who are full,   15
Sleek, tender-clad, fit, fiftyish, a-glow, all
Sweetly abortive, hinting at fat fruit,
Judge it high time that fiftyish fingers felt

Beneath the lovelier planes of enterprise.
To resurrect. To moisten with milky chill.   20
To be a random hitching-post or plush.
To be, for wet eyes, random and handy hem.
                    Their guild is giving money to the poor.
The worthy poor. The very very worthy
And beautiful poor. Perhaps just not too swarthy?   25
Perhaps just not too dirty nor too dim
Nor—passionate. In truth, what they could wish
Is—something less than derelict or dull.
Not staunch enough to stab, though, gaze for gaze!
God shield them sharply from the beggar-bold!   30
The noxious needy ones whose battle's bald
Nonetheless for being voiceless, hits one down.
                    But it's all so bad! and entirely too much for
                            them.
The stench; the urine, cabbage, and dead beans,
Dead porridges of assorted dusty grains,   35
The old smoke, *heavy* diapers, and, they're told,
Something called chitterlings. The darkness. Drawn
Darkness, or dirty light. The soil that stirs.
The soil that looks the soil of centuries.
And for that matter the general oldness. Old   40
Wood. Old marble. Old tile. Old old old.
Not homekind Oldness! Not Lake Forest, Glencoe.[1]
Nothing is sturdy, nothing is majestic,
There is no quiet drama, no rubbed glaze, no
Unkillable infirmity of such   45
A tasteful turn as lately they have left,
Glencoe, Lake Forest, and to which their cars
Must presently restore them. When they're done
With dullards and distortions of this fistic
Patience of the poor and put-upon.   50
                    They've never seen such a make-do-ness as
Newspaper rugs before! In this, this "flat,"
Their hostess is gathering up the oozed, the rich
Rugs of the morning (tattered! the bespattered. . . .)
Readies to spread clean rugs for afternoon.   55
Here is a scene for you. The Ladies look,
In horror, behind a substantial citizeness
Whose trains clank out across her swollen heart.
Who, arms akimbo, almost fills a door.
All tumbling children, quilts dragged to the floor   60
And tortured thereover, potato peelings, soft-
Eyed kitten, hunched-up, haggard, to-be-hurt.
                    Their League is allotting largesse to the Lost.
But to put their clean, their pretty money, to put
Their money collected from delicate rose-fingers   65

---

1. Prosperous suburbs north of Chicago.

Tipped with their hundred flawless rose-nails seems . . .
         They own Spode, Lowestoft, candelabra,
Mantels, and hostess gowns, and sunburst clocks,
Turtle soup, Chippendale, red satin "hangings,"
Aubussons and Hattie Carnegie.[2] They Winter   70
In Palm Beach; cross the Water in June; attend,
When suitable, the nice Art Institute;
Buy the right books in the best bindings; saunter
On Michigan, Easter mornings, in sun or wind.
Oh Squalor! This sick four-story hulk, this fibre   75
With fissures everywhere! Why, what are bringings
Of loathe-love largesse? What shall peril hungers
So old old, what shall flatter the desolate?
Tin can, blocked fire escape and chitterling
And swaggering seeking youth and the puzzled wreckage   80
Of the middle passage, and urine and stale shames
And, again, the porridges of the underslung
And children children children. Heavens! That
Was a rat, surely, off there, in the shadows? Long
And long-tailed? Gray? The Ladies from the Ladies'   85
Betterment League agree it will be better
To achieve the outer air that rights and steadies,
To hie to a house that does not holler, to ring
Bells elsetime, better presently to cater
To no more Possibilities, to get   90
Away. Perhaps the money can be posted.
Perhaps they two may choose another Slum!
Some serious sooty half-unhappy home!—
Where loathe-love likelier may be invested.
         Keeping their scented bodies in the center   95
Of the hall as they walk down the hysterical hall,
They allow their lovely skirts to graze no wall,
Are off at what they manage of a canter,
And, resuming all the clues of what they were,
Try to avoid inhaling the laden air.   100
                1960

Naomi

Too foraging to blue-print or deploy!—
To lift her brother;
Or tell dull mother
That is not it among the dishes and brooms,
It is damper   5
Than what you will wipe out of sills and down from
      the mouldings of rooms
And dump from the dirty-clothes hamper;

2. "Spode, Lowestoft": English china; "Chippendale": 18th-century English furniture; "Aubussons": 18th-century French rugs; "Hattie Carnegie": fashionable American designer of the 1950s.

Or say "Do not bother
To hug your cheese and furniture"
To her small father;   10

Or to register at all the hope of her hunt or say what
It was not.

(It was, by diligent caring,
To find out what life was for.

For certainly what it was not for was forbearing.)   15

                                                        1968

Boy Breaking Glass

TO MARC CRAWFORD, FROM WHOM THE COMMISSION

Whose broken window is a cry of art
(success, that winks aware
as elegance, as a treasonable faith)
is raw: is sonic: is old-eyed première.
Our beautiful flaw and terrible ornament.   5
Our barbarous and metal little man.

"I shall create! If not a note, a hole.
If not an overture, a desecration."

Full of pepper and light
and Salt and night and cargoes.   10

"Don't go down the plank
if you see there's no extension.
Each to his grief, each to
his loneliness and fidgety revenge.
Nobody knew where I was and now I am no longer there." 15

The only sanity is a cup of tea.
The music is in minors.

Each one other
is having different weather.

"It was you, it was you who threw away my name!   20
And this is everything I have for me."

Who has not Congress, lobster, love, luau,
the Regency Room, the Statue of Liberty,
runs. A sloppy amalgamation.
A mistake.   25
A cliff.
A hymn, a snare, and an exceeding sun.

                                                        1968

ROBERT DUNCAN

1919–

Like Ezra Pound and Charles Olson, two writers he admires, Robert Duncan is an educated iconoclast. He has a strong bias against established universities, the "academy," and an equally strong urge, in his extensive critical writings, to be a learned teacher himself.

Duncan was born in Oakland, California, and studied at the University of California, Berkeley, in 1936–38. He left after his sophomore year to pursue a homosexual love affair in the East. In his own thinking there was a strong connection between his homosexuality and his poetic stance: "Perhaps the sexual irregularity underlay and led to the poetic; neither as homosexual nor as poet could one take over readily the accepted paradigms of the Protestant ethic."

Poetry would provide the grounds for his release. "Working in words I am an escapist. But I want every part of the actual world involved in my escape." More concretely, Duncan found support and encouragement in the work of a new generation of poets, strongly influenced by Charles Olson and including figures such as Denise Levertov and Robert Creeley. Olson's *Maximus* poems encouraged him to think in long-range inclusive terms, so that all the poems of a lifetime might be considered as building one swelling "poem" such as Whitman's *Leaves of Grass*. The very titles of Duncan's principal books suggest a continuing and overarching effort, one imagined as accommodating a cresting natural process: *The Opening of the Field* (1960); *Roots and Branches* (1964); *Bending the Bow* (1968).

This last title refers us to Duncan's notions of poetic composition: "our instant knowing of fitness as we work in the poem, where the descriptive or analytic mind would falter. Here the true is beautiful as an arrow flies from its bow with exact aim." His emphasis is on allowing moments of excitement and ecstasy to dictate the shape and rhythm of the poem. He compares finding the right cadence or meter to a dancer losing awareness of himself and entering into the rhythmic impulse of the dance. So, for example, wanting to write about the death of a favorite cat, he says he did not find the proper shape for his feelings until one day on the beach he stared at the rhythm of the incoming breakers. The resulting poem, *A Storm of White*, includes the inexorable "moving whiteness":

> White white white   like
>   a boundary in death advancing
> That is our life

Duncan stresses the power of poetry to capture ritual meanings or feelings behind particular moments. For example, *Two Presentations* tries to recapture feelings about the death of the mother who had adopted him after his real mother had died in childbirth. The poem characteristically tries to get back to mythic sources, "the Mother in back of my mothers." Though it was triggered by a dream, the poem also shows how ritual responses are released in the materials of everyday life—in this case an overheard conversation in a bus and a coincidence involving his name and the name of the bus line. By the end accidents of identity and name drop away as the poem presses to a larger mythical connection: "But, of that other Great Mother / or metre, of the matter * * *" Duncan reminds himself that all poetic utterance for him is a kind of exhalation of and letter to the Mother from whom he had been separated. He learns thus to connect her with the Great Mother of primitive mysteries. Very often, in this fashion, Duncan will superimpose contemporary events on ritual programs drawn from Egyptian, Oriental, and Greek mythology, as if to stress the hidden and enduring profile of a particular moment. But behind the theory is the simpler intention he set out as early as *The Years as Catches* (1942–43):

> Catch from the years the line of joy,
> impatient & repeated day,
> my heart, break, Eye
> break open and set free
> His world, my ecstasy.

Duncan lives in San Francisco and continues his political radicalism. He was morally and politically opposed to war long before the Vietnam protests of the 1960s. Though he served briefly in the army during World War II, he bitterly disapproved of what he called Roosevelt's "Permanent War Economy." "I saw the State and the War as diseases, eternal enemies of man's universal humanity and of the individual volition." He has edited experimental magazines and has also taught at various colleges, including San Francisco State, the University of California at Berkeley, and the University of British Columbia.

King Haydn of Miami Beach

1

In the rustling shelter of Japanese peach
with the blacks and the plum-colored lady apes
dances King Haydn of Miami Beach
the now, the now, of never perhaps,
bows to Death, bows to Death,   5
plans next week wonderfully pretend
a temporary pleasurable boat-trip & ride
round the capes, round the capes,
and back again.

2

King Haydn abandons the dance of his do.   10
With joy he resumes
the half-waltz and rumba of never
come true. But
Mr Responsible Person
booms in the head of Mr Do Why.   15
Love-waltz and rumba come

stop.
King Haydn abandons
the never come true.
Hops.   20
To the tune of Mr. Do Why
vacations and oceans grow tired and die.

Fixt with a joyless partner motion
King Haydn and Mr
Dandruff Why   25
do the why do do why do.

3. Paradise Club

This is the Heaven-House Everyday Do
that Mr Responsible Person God
built in a day.

This is Mr Responsible Who   30
looks out for the welfare of me and you,
of Eve, of you, of Adam, of me.
This is the Absolute Person we fear.
This is His hot round biggish sun.
This is the middle of next year.   35
This is the bird on its wounded wing
that fell out of Heaven and started to sing,
that fell into soul, into single
extraordinary badly and poor.

This is the Other Place, the Miami Beach lure,   40
beyond the Absolute Door of Why
where each fallen birdie is six feet high.

This is the eye of Mr Responsible,
the Comprehensible,
sees each birdling that falles from grace   45
lose wits, lose form, lose time and face.
This is Mr Responsible Person.
This is His ordinary only Heaven.
King Haydn in the Other Place
dances away his chance for grace.   50

4. Psychoanalysis

Death is a sin, Death is a sin,
leaves a taste after of oil and tin.
In the fiery hell of Miami beach
the sun can glare like a red hot peach
but the night comes in   55
and the life goes out.
The boys and the girls play Turn About.
King Haydn and Mr Why begin

to deal the cards and play at Death.
The game is long and the chance is brief.   60
Among the cards and the chattering dead
the blacks and the plum-colord lady apes
change and then again change shapes.

Death is a sin, Death is a sin.
The sorry old sun can glower and pout   65
but Death comes in
and the life goes out
and leaves a taste after of oil and tin.

5

How many miles to Love and back,
Hobbyhorse Wise? askt Mr Why.   70

You can never get there.
To where? to there?

Hobbyhorse Poor, said Mr Why:
to Lack from Lack to Lack and back.

New York City, 1943   1947

Often I Am Permitted to Return to a Meadow

as if it were a scene made-up by the mind,
that is not mine, but is a made place,

that is mine, it is so near to the heart,
an eternal pasture folded in all thought
so that there is a hall therein   5

that is a made place, created by light
wherefrom the shadows that are forms fall.

Wherefrom fall all architectures I am
I say are likenesses of the First Beloved
whose flowers are flames lit to the Lady.   10

She it is Queen Under The Hill
whose hosts are a disturbance of words within words
that is a field folded.

It is only a dream of the grass blowing
east against the source of the sun   15
in an hour before the sun's going down

whose secret we see in a children's game
of ring a round of roses told.

Often I am permitted to return to a meadow
as if it were a given property of the mind   20
that certain bounds hold against chaos,

that is a place of first permission,
everlasting omen of what is.

1960

Poetry, a Natural Thing

    Neither our vices nor our virtues
further the poem. "They came up
    and died
just like they do every year
    on the rocks."   5

    The poem
feeds upon thought, feeling, impulse,
    to breed   itself,
a spiritual urgency at the dark ladders leaping.

This beauty is an inner persistence   10
    toward the source
striving against (within) down-rushet of the river,
    a call we heard and answer
in the lateness of the world
    primordial bellowings   15
from which the youngest world might spring,

salmon not in the well where the
    hazelnut falls
but at the falls battling, inarticulate,
    blindly making it.   20

This is one picture apt for the mind.

A second: a moose painted by Stubbs,[1]
where last year's extravagant antlers
    lie on the ground.
The forlorn moosey-faced poem wears   25
    new antler-buds,
    the same,

"a little heavy, a little contrived,"

his only beauty to be
    all moose.   30

1960

---

1. George Stubbs (1724–1806), English painter of animals.

Two Presentations

1

[After my mother's death in December 1960, there were two returns of her presence in February and March of 1961. The first came in a dream.]

"We send you word of the Mother."
Was it my mother? our mother?
In the dream it was a blessing or a key
she brought, a message.
Was it H.D.'s[1] frail script?   5

It was she, I thought, but the sign
was of another. It was a help
(for my mind is in great trouble)
to receive the letter.

But I was cold, lying in the narrow bed,   10
naked. When did I lie there so?
        The first light of morning
came in over me, a cold thin wave
where nerves shrank back from the bruise.

Who gave me the note? Only I   15
accuse myself of lying here in the cold,
shaking in the drafts of light,
hugging to the scant cover.

For I have lost heart,
my mind is divided.   20

[AFTERTHOUGHTS, November 1961. Working on the H.D. Book,[2] I had begun to fear her death as a forfeit or foundation of the work.

My first mother in whom I took my first nature, the formal imperative of my physical body and signature, died when I was born. I was motherless then, "in the cold," for six months before my second mother found and adopted me. But the "When did I lie there so?" seems to refer to some cold back of this period of loss, as, in turn, "the Mother" is back of my mothers.

When I was born, what gave birth to me fell back dead or died in the labor towards my success. Was she alive or dead when I drew my first "breath" and utterd, threw out, my first cry? In taking heart, another heart was lost. What blessing, what key then?]

---

1. Hilda Doolittle (1886–1961), American poet who, along with Ezra Pound, helped formulate the doctrine of Imagism.

2. A compressed history of Imagism, published by Duncan in periodicals (1966–69), and which he dedicated to H.D.

2

[*In the change from my birth name, Edward Howard Duncan, to
my name by adoption, Robert Edward Symmes, the hidden or lost
name is Howard.*

*The second presentation came while I was riding the Union-
Howard busline from the Marina to North Beach. I had begun a
poem addresst to my mother, when the hysterical talk of a school-
girl broke in, dictating fragments of a message that seemd meant
for me and at the same time to direct the poem.*]

> You are gone and I send
> as I used to
>   with the salutation *Dear Mother*
>   the beginning of a letter   25
>   as if it could reach you.
>
> Yet *Dear Mother* could catch at my heart to say
>   —and did when I was a child, as you
> are now a child among shades—
>   as if the words betrayd
> a painful nearness and separation.   30
>
> "It's this poem I wrote and I calld it *My Soul!*"
> Was she talking to me? Her voice carries
> above the din of high-school girls chattering,
> crowding the bus with shrill bird voices.
>
> "It's this poem I wrote, see!"   35
>
> She waits, and when I look up from where I am writing . . .
> Did she see me writing here? How did I hear
>   her voice if not directed in the crowd to me?
> Laughing, the fat little Hindu girl
> turns her eyes from my glance, triumphant.   40
>
> "I write so many, see, all the time.
> And this one I lost. That's why I say
> I lost *My Soul.*"
>
> Does she say anything that comes into her head
> to hold my attention?   45
> "Well, you didnt go over and pull me out,"
> she shouts to some girl I can't see.
>
> "I had such a cramp in my leg
> and I almost drownd.
> I thought I was all alone."   50
>
> Like *that* then. Her voice, too,
> came thru to me,

swimming in the flood of voices as if alone,
catching my attention
—a sheaf of poems hysterical girls   55
might carry about, carry-on about,
their souls or names . . .
loves? "You'll never love anyone," you said, Mother,
so long ago.

        Caught in the swirl of waters,   60
bobbing heads of the young girls, pubescent,
    descending from the bus,
pass on or out, into the street beyond
      —one dark Hindu face among them passes
      out of my ken.   65

Are you out there alone then like that?
Or did your own mother come, close in,
to meet you. As your sister, looking forward or back
from her eighty years, said,
"Mother will be there when I die,   70
waiting for me." Her throat
catching at the evocation.

    But, of that other Great Mother
or metre, of the matter . . .

My letter always went alone   75
    to where
I never knew you reading.

                                   1964

Bending the Bow

We've our business to attend Day's duties,
bend back the bow in dreams as we may
til the end rimes in the taut string
with the sending. Reveries are rivers and flow
where the cold light gleams reflecting the window upon the
    surface of the table,   5
the presst-glass creamer, the pewter sugar bowl, the litter
    of coffee cups and saucers,
carnations painted growing upon whose surface. The whole
composition of surfaces leads into the other
        current disturbing
what I would take hold of. I'd been   10
in the course of a letter—I am still
in the course of a letter—to a friend,
who comes close in to my thoughts so that
the day is hers. My hand writing here
there shakes in the currents of . . . of air?   15
of an inner anticipation of . . . ? reaching to touch
ghostly exhilarations in the thought of her.

At the extremity of this
design
"there is a connexion working in both directions, as in   20
the bow and the lyre"—
only in that swift fulfillment of the wish
that sleep
can illustrate my hand
sweeps the string.   25

You stand behind the where-I-am.
The deep tones and shadows I will call a woman.
The quick high notes . . . You are a girl there too,
    having something of sister and of wife,
        inconsolate,   30
    and I would play Orpheus[1] for you again,
        recall the arrow or song
        to the trembling daylight
        from which it sprang.

1968

Where It Appears

I'd cut the warp
to weave that web

    in the air

   and here

let image perish in image,   5

leave writer and reader

   up in the air

     to draw
        momentous

           inconclusions,   10

ropes of the first water
    returnd by a rhetoric

   the rain swells.

Statistically insignificant as a locus of creation
   I have in this   my own   15

      intense

     area of self creation,

1. In Greek mythology, Orpheus descended into Hades to retrieve his wife Eurydice from the dead with the aid of his music.

the Sun itself
insignificant among suns.

The magi[1] of the probable   20
bring forth a mirror,   an

iridescence,   an ocean

which I hold in the palm of my hand   ·

as if I could cast a shadow   ·

to surround   ·   25

what is boundless   ·

as if I could handle   ·   this pearl   ·   that touches

upon every imagination of what

I am   ·

wrong about the web,   the   30

reflection,   the lure of the world

I love.

1968

1. Wise men or sorcerers; especially the magi who came to witness the birth of the
Christ Child in Bethlehem.

RICHARD WILBUR

1921–

Richard Wilbur was born in New York City, the son of a painter, and
grew up in the country in New Jersey. He was educated at Amherst College,
where Robert Frost was a frequent guest and teacher. Whether through the
direct influence of the older poet or not, Wilbur is recognized, along with
Frost, as probably the most accomplished prosodist in recent American poetry. Of the effects of those years, Wilbur says: "Most American poets of
my generation were taught to admire the English metaphysical poets of the
seventeenth century and such contemporary masters of irony as John Crowe
Ransom. We were led by our teachers and by the critics whom we read to
feel that the most adequate and convincing poetry is that which accommodates mixed feelings, clashing ideas, and incongruous images." Wilbur was
to remain true to this preference for the ironic meditative lyric, the single
perfect poem, rather than longer narratives or dramatic sequences.

After graduation and service in the infantry in Italy and France (1943–

45), Wilbur returned to study for an M.A. at Harvard, with a firm notion of what he expected to get out of poetry. "My first poems were written in answer to the inner and outer disorders of the second World War and they helped me * * * to take ahold of raw events and convert them, provisionally, into experience." He reasserted the balance of mind against instinct and violence: "The praiseful, graceful soldier / Shouldn't be fired by his gun." The poised lyrics in *The Beautiful Changes* (1947) and *Ceremony* (1950) also reclaimed a sense of Europe obscured by the war: the value of pleasure, defined as an interplay of intelligence with sensuous enjoyment. Whether looking at a real French landscape, as in *Grasse: The Olive Trees*, or a French landscape painting, as in *Ceremony*, the point was to show the witty shaping power of the mind in nature. Hence the importance of "emblem" poems: poems which develop the symbolic significance of a natural object (the "unearthly" pallor of olive trees which "teach the South it is not paradise") or of works of art that incorporate nature (*A Baroque Wall-Fountain in the Villa Sciarra*).

Wilbur prefers strict stanzaic forms and meters; "limitation makes for power: the strength of the genie comes of his being confined in a bottle." In individual lines and the structure of an entire poem, his emphasis is on a civilized balancing of perceptions. *A World without Objects Is a Sensible Emptiness* begins with the "tall camels of the spirit," but qualifies our views of lonely spiritual impulses. The poem summons us back to find visionary truth grasped through sensual experience. "All shining things need to be shaped and borne." Wilbur favors "a spirituality which is not abstracted, not dissociated and world-renouncing. A good part of my work could, I suppose, be understood as a public quarrel with the aesthetics of Edgar Allan Poe"—presumably with Poe's notion that poetry provided *indefinite* sensations and aspired to the abstract condition of music.

Wilbur was among the first of the younger postwar poets to adopt a style of living and working different from the masters of an earlier generation—from Eliot, ironic priestlike modernist who lived as a publisher-poet in England, or William Carlos Williams, a doctor in Paterson, or Wallace Stevens, a remote insurance executive in Hartford. Wilbur was a teacher-poet and gave frequent readings. Instead of thinking of himself as an alienated artist, he came to characterize himself as a "poet-citizen," part of what he judged a widening community of poets addressing themselves to an audience increasingly responsive to poetry. Wilbur's taste for civilized wit and his metrical skill made him an ideal translator of the seventeenth-century satirical comedies of Molière, *Tartuffe* (1963) and *The Misanthrope* (1955). They are frequently played, as is the musical version of Voltaire's *Candide* for which Wilbur was one of the collaborating lyricists. Wilbur, who teaches at Smith, received the Pulitzer Prize for his volume *Things of This World* (1956) and has since published *Advice to a Prophet* (1961) and *Walking to Sleep* (1969).

Grasse:[1] The Olive Trees

FOR MARCELLE AND FERDINAND SPRINGER

Here luxury's the common lot. The light
Lies on the rain-pocked rocks like yellow wool

---

1. A city in southern France.

And around the rocks the soil is rusty bright
From too much wealth of water, so that the grass
Mashes under the foot, and all is full   5
Of heat and juice and a heavy jammed excess.

Whatever moves moves with the slow complete
Gestures of statuary. Flower smells
Are set in the golden day, and shelled in heat,
Pine and columnar cypress stand. The palm   10
Sinks its combs in the sky. This whole South swells
To a soft rigor, a rich and crowded calm.

Only the olive contradicts. My eye,
Traveling slopes of rust and green, arrests
And rests from plenitude where olives lie   15
Like clouds of doubt against the earth's array.
Their faint disheveled foliage divests
The sunlight of its color and its sway.

Not that the olive spurns the sun; its leaves
Scatter and point to every part of the sky,   20
Like famished fingers waving. Brilliance weaves
And sombers down among them, and among
The anxious sliver branches, down to the dry
And twisted trunk, by rooted hunger wrung.

Even when seen from near, the olive shows   25
A hue of far away. Perhaps for this
The dove brought olive back, a tree which grows
Unearthly pale, which ever dims and dries,
And whose great thirst, exceeding all excess,
Teaches the South it is not paradise.   30

1950

The Death of a Toad

A toad the power mower caught,
Chewed and clipped of a leg, with a hobbling hop has got
   To the garden verge, and sanctuaried him
   Under the cineraria leaves, in the shade
      Of the ashen heartshaped leaves, in a dim,   5
         Low, and a final glade.

The rare original heartsblood goes,
Spends on the earthen hide, in the folds and wizenings, flows
   In the gutters of the banked and staring eyes. He lies
   As still as if he would return to stone,   10
      And soundlessly attending, dies
         Toward some deep monotone,

Toward misted and ebullient seas
And cooling shores, toward lost Amphibia's emperies.[1]
  Day dwindles, drowning, and at length is gone   15
In the wide and antique eyes, which still appear
    To watch, across the castrate lawn,
      The haggard daylight steer.

                       1950

Ceremony

A striped blouse in a clearing by Bazille[2]
Is, you may say, a patroness of boughs
Too queenly kind[3] toward nature to be kin.
But ceremony never did conceal,
  Save to the silly[4] eye, which all allows,   5
How much we are the woods we wander in.

Let her be some Sabrina[5] fresh from stream,
Lucent as shallows slowed by wading sun,
Bedded on fern, the flowers' cynosure:[6]
Then nymph and wood must nod and strive to dream 10
That she is airy earth, the trees, undone,
Must ape her languor natural and pure.

Ho-hum. I am for wit and wakefulness,
And love this feigning lady by Bazille.
What's lightly hid is deepest understood,   15
And when with social smile and formal dress
She teaches leaves to curtsey and quadrille,[7]
I think there are most tigers in the wood.

                       1950

"A World without Objects
Is a Sensible Emptiness"[1]

    The tall camels of the spirit
  Steer for their deserts, passing the last groves loud
With the sawmill shrill of the locust, to the whole honey
      of the arid
    Sun. They are slow, proud,

1. Archaic for *empires*. Amphibia is imagined to be the spiritual ruler of the toad's universe.
2. Jean Frédéric Bazille (1841–71), French painter noted for painting figures in forest landscapes; he was associated with the Impressionists.
3. An original meaning of "Nature" was "kind."
4. Innocent, homely.
5. A nymph, the presiding deity of the river Severn in Milton's masque *Comus* (1634).
6. Center of attraction; also from the constellation Ursa Minor, whose center is the Pole Star.
7. A square dance, of French origin, performed by four couples.
1. From *Second Century*, Meditation 65, by Thomas Traherne (c. 1638–74): "Life without objects is sensible emptiness, and that is a greater misery than death or nothing." "Sensible" is used to mean "palpable to the senses."

And move with a stilted stride   5
To the land of sheer horizon, hunting Traherne's
Sensible emptiness, there where the brain's lantern-slide
  Revels in vast returns.

O connoisseurs of thirst,
  Beasts of my soul who long to learn to drink   10
Of pure mirage, those prosperous islands are accurst
  That shimmer on the brink

Of absence; auras, lustres,
  And all shinings need to be shaped and borne.
Think of those painted saints, capped by the early masters   15
  With bright, jauntily-worn

Aureate plates, or even
  Merry-go-round rings. Turn, O turn
From the fine sleights of the sand, from the long empty oven
  Where flames in flamings burn   20

Back to the trees arrayed
  In bursts of glare, to the halo-dialing run
Of the country creeks, and the hills' bracken tiaras made
  Gold in the sunken sun,

Wisely watch for the sight   25
  Of the supernova[2] burgeoning over the barn,
Lampshine blurred in the steam of beasts, the spirit's right
  Oasis, light incarnate.

                                                  1950

Year's End

Now winter downs the dying of the year,
  And night is all a settlement of snow;
From the soft street the rooms of houses show
  A gathered light, a shapen atmosphere,
Like frozen-over lakes whose ice is thin   5
And still allows some stirring down within.

I've known the wind by water banks to shake
  The late leaves down, which frozen where they fell
And held in ice as dancers in a spell
  Fluttered all winter long into a lake;   10
Graved on the dark in gestures of descent,
They seemed their own most perfect monument.

There was perfection in the death of ferns
  Which laid their fragile cheeks against the stone

---

2. A scientific term for an exploding star, here associated with the Star of Bethlehem.

A million years. Great mammoths overthrown   15
Composedly have made their long sojourns,
Like palaces of patience, in the gray
And changeless lands of ice. And at Pompeii[3]

The little dog lay curled and did not rise
But slept the deeper as the ashes rose   20
And found the people incomplete, and froze
The random hands, the loose unready eyes
Of men expecting yet another sun
To do the shapely thing they had not done.

These sudden ends of time must give us pause.   25
We fray into the future, rarely wrought
Save in the tapestries of afterthought.
More time, more time. Barrages of applause
Come muffled from a buried radio.
The New-year bells are wrangling with the snow.   30

1950

A Black November Turkey

TO A.M. AND A.M.

Nine white chickens come
With haunchy walk and heads
Jabbing among the chips, the chaff, the stones
And the cornhusk-shreds,

And bit by bit infringe   5
A pond of dusty light,
Spectral in shadow until they bobbingly one
By one ignite.

Neither pale nor bright,
The turkey-cock parades   10
Through radiant squalors, darkly auspicious as
The ace of spades,

Himself his own cortège[1]
And puffed with the pomp of death,
Rehearsing over and over with strangled râle[2]   15
His latest breath.

The vast black body floats
Above the crossing knees
As a cloud over thrashed branches, a calm ship
Over choppy seas,   20

---

3. Roman city buried by and partly preserved in lava after the eruption of Mount Vesuvius (A.D. 79).

1. Funeral procession.
2. An abnormal breathing sound, associated with ill health.

Shuddering its fan and feathers
In fine soft clashes
With the cold sound that the wind makes, fondling
    Paper-ashes.

The pale-blue bony head   25
Set on its shepherd's-crook
Like a saint's death-mask, turns a vague, superb
    And timeless look

Upon these clocking hens
And the cocks that one by one,   30
Dawn after mortal dawn, with vulgar joy
    Acclaim the sun.

                        1956

A Baroque Wall-Fountain in the Villa Sciarra[1]

FOR DORE AND ADJA

Under the bronze crown
Too big for the head of the stone cherub whose feet
    A serpent has begun to eat,
Sweet water brims a cockle[2] and braids down

    Past spattered mosses, breaks   5
On the tipped edge of a second shell, and fills
    The massive third below. It spills
In threads then from the scalloped rim, and makes

    A scrim or summery tent
For a faun-ménage[3] and their familiar goose.   10
    Happy in all that ragged, loose
Collapse of water, its effortless descent

    And flatteries of spray,
The stocky god upholds the shell with ease,
    Watching, about his shaggy knees,   15
The goatish innocence of his babes at play;

    His fauness all the while
Leans forward, slightly, into a clambering mesh
    Of water-lights, her sparkling flesh
In a saecular[4] ecstasy, her blinded smile   20

    Bent on the sand floor
Of the trefoil[5] pool, where ripple-shadows come

1. A park in Rome, rich in 17th-century statues and fountains.
2. Sculptured shell.
3. A faun is a rural god, usually represented with a goat's tail and legs, and thought of as lusty. "Faun-ménage" is here taken to mean household.
4. Lasting for ages (with pun on secular, "worldly").
5. Triple-leaved.

And go in swift reticulum.[6]
More addling to the eye than wine, and more

    Interminable to thought   25
Than pleasure's calculus. Yet since this all
    Is pleasure, flash, and waterfall,
Must it not be too simple? Are we not

    More intricately expressed
In the plain fountains that Maderna[7] set   30
    Before St. Peter's—the main jet
Struggling aloft until it seems at rest

    In the act of rising, until
The very wish of water is reversed,
    That heaviness borne up to burst   35
In a clear, high, cavorting head, to fill

    With blaze, and then in gauze
Delays, in a gnatlike shimmering, in a fine
    Illumined version of itself, decline,
And patter on the stones its own applause?   40

    If that is what men are
Or should be, if those water-saints display
    The pattern of our areté,[8]
What of these showered fauns in their bizarre,

    Spangled, and plunging house?   45
They are at rest in fulness of desire
    For what is given, they do not tire
Of the smart of the sun, the pleasant water-douse

    And riddled pool below,
Reproving our disgust and our ennui   50
    With humble insatiety.
Francis,[9] perhaps, who lay in sister snow

    Before the wealthy gate
Freezing and praising, might have seen in this
    No trifle, but a shade of bliss—   55
That land of tolerable flowers, that state

    As near and far as grass
Where eyes become the sunlight, and the hand

6. In a netlike structure.
7. Carlo Maderna (1556–1629), one of the architects of St. Peter's Basilica in Rome, and the designer of one of its two fountains.
8. "A Greek word meaning roughly 'virtue' " [Wilbur's note].
9. St. Francis (b. 1182) lived a life of poverty and regarded all natural creatures as his brothers and sisters.

Is worthy of water: the dreamt land
Toward which all hungers leap, all pleasures pass.   60

1956

In the Field

This field-grass brushed our legs
Last night, when out we stumbled looking up,
    Wading as through the cloudy dregs
        Of a wide, sparkling cup,

Our thrown-back heads aswim   5
In the grand, kept appointments of the air,
    Save where a pine at the sky's rim
        Took something from the Bear.[1]

Black in her glinting chains,
Andromeda[2] feared nothing from the seas,   10
    Preserved as by no hero's pains,
        Or hushed Euripides',

And there the dolphin glowed,
Still flailing through a diamond froth of stars,
    Flawless as when Arion[3] rode   15
        One of its avatars.

But none of that was true.
What shapes that Greece or Babylon discerned
    Had time not slowly drawn askew
        Or like cat's cradles[4] turned?   20

And did we not recall
That Egypt's north was in the Dragon's tail?[5]
    As if a form of type[6] should fall
        And dash itself like hail,

The heavens jumped away,   25
Bursting the cincture of the zodiac[7]
    Shot flares with nothing left to say
        To us, not coming back

Unless they should at last,
Like hard-flung dice that ramble out the throw,   30

---

1. The constellation Ursa Major.
2. In mythology, a princess rescued from a sea monster by Perseus. According to Wilbur, "Some think that Euripides' lost play *Andromeda* told of the transformation of Andromeda * * * into the constellation bearing [that] name."
3. In mythology, Arion, a Greek poet and musician cast out to sea, rode to safety on a dolphin's back. The dolphin is also a northern constellation; "ava-

tars": incarnations.
4. Children's game in which string is transferred from one player's hands to another's in a seemingly endless series of symmetrical patterns.
5. In the Ptolemaic system of astronomy, north was reckoned with reference to a star in the constellation (the dragon).
6. Printers' type, set into a frame.
7. I.e., the "belt" of the celestial sphere.

Be gathered for another cast.
  Whether that might be so

  We could not say, but trued[8]
Our talk awhile to words of the real sky,
  Chatting of class or magnitude,   35
    Star-clusters, nebulae,

  And how Antares,[9] huge
As Mars' big roundhouse swing, and more, was fled
  As in some rimless centrifuge
    Into a blink of red.   40

  It was the nip of fear
That told us when imagination caught
  The feel of what we said, came near
    The schoolbook thoughts we thought,

  And faked a scan of space   45
Blown black and hollow by our spent grenade,
  All worlds dashed out without a trace,
    The very light unmade.

  Then, in the late-night chill,
We turned and picked our way through outcrop stone 50
  By the faint starlight, up the hill
    To where our bed-lamp shone.

  Today, in the same field,
The sun takes all, and what could lie beyond?
  Those holes in heaven have been sealed 55
    Like rain-drills in a pond,

  And we, beheld in gold,
See nothing starry but these galaxies
  Of flowers, dense and manifold,
    Which lift about our knees—   60

  White daisy-drifts where you
Sink down to pick an armload as we pass,
  Sighting the heal-all's[1] minor blue
    In chasms of the grass,

  And strews of hawkweed where,   65
Amongst the reds or yellows as they burn,
  A few dead polls[2] commit to air
    The seeds of their return.

8. Adjusted accurately.
9. A giant red star, so named because of
its resemblance to Mars (Ares in Greek).

1. A wild flower.
2. Heads of flowers.

We could no doubt mistake
These flowers for some answer to that fright   70
We felt for all creation's sake
In our dark talk last night,

Taking to heart what came
Of the heart's wish for life, which, staking here
In the least field an endless claim,   75
Beats on from sphere to sphere

And pounds beyond the sun,
Where nothing less peremptory can go,
And is ourselves, and is the one
Unbounded thing we know.   80

1969

JAMES DICKEY

1923–

James Dickey was born in Atlanta, Georgia, and grew up in one of its suburbs. Six-feet-three, he had been a high-school football star and "a wild
motorcycle rider." After a year at Clemson College, S. C. (1942), he enlisted in the Air Force. As a young man he had admired the Romantic poet
Byron largely for what he symbolized: bold, masculine swagger and a love
of martial and sexual adventure. During off hours from combat missions in
the South Pacific, Dickey became acquainted with modern poetry in an
anthology by Louis Untermeyer, one of the first influential collections. But
it was not until after the war, at Vanderbilt College and through the encouragement of one of his professors, Monroe Spears, that Dickey seriously
began to write poetry himself.

His first poem was published in *Sewanee Review* while he was still a
senior in college; his first book of verse, *Into the Stone*, appeared in 1960.
Since that time Dickey has consistently regarded poetry as the center of
his career, although he has at different periods been an advertising man for
Coca-Cola in New York and Atlanta, a college teacher, a training officer for
pilots during the Korean War, a best-selling novelist (*Deliverance*, 1970),
and a film writer (adapting *Deliverance* for Hollywood).

Over the years the look of Dickey's poems on the page has changed, and
the poetry has become more and more interested in the courting of danger
and violence. But the essential focus of the poems remains the same:
Dickey is concerned with the instincts, the unconscious, and the primitive.
He explores "the forfeited animal grace of human beings * * * and the
hunter's sense of understanding with the hunted animal." Many of his
earlier poems (in *Drowning with Others*, 1962, and *Helmets*, 1964) deal
with special physical skills and the strengths remembered from his wartime
experiences. Other poems adopt what he terms "country surrealism."
Human spectators fall into states of fantasy or hallucination, visionary mo-

ments when they feel themselves taking on the energy of animals. The poet in *A Dog Sleeping on My Feet* seems to share the dog's dreams of the chase so completely that he can imagine the end of his own poem in these terms:

> * * * my hand, which speaks in a daze
> The hypnotized language of beasts,
> Shall falter, and fail
>
> Back into the human tongue

In *The Heaven of Animals* the speaker imagines a world where the beasts fulfill themselves as hunter or hunted, but without blood or pain, in a kind of deadly joy in which "They fall, they are torn, / They rise, they walk again."

In Dickey's earlier poems the speaker was primarily an observer, describing as if from outside these states of animal and instinctual grace. The poet tended to write in short lines—three accents or beats per line. With *Buckdancer's Choice* (1965) Dickey became interested in longer "split lines," which he has used ever since. The line of verse is splintered into phrases, each group of words separated from the next by spaces designed to take the place of punctuation. The purpose is to approximate the way the mind "associates in bursts of words, in jumps." Instead of speaking through a distanced observer, the poem is placed within the mind of someone who is caught in a moment of crisis or excitement.

Dickey seems to be interested, increasingly, in violence and power as subjects. As the apocalyptic title of his 1970 volume might suggest—*The Eye Beaters, Blood, Victory, Madness, Buckhead and Mercy*—many of his new poems are designed to administer shocks to the reader's system. His novel *Deliverance* recounts the regression to an animal-like state by a group of ostensibly civilized men when they fall into danger on a canoe trip. In a more humorous vein, his poems *Cherrylog Road* and *Power and Light* look at the force of machines and electricity as a clue to the charged energies underlying our everyday lives.

Dickey enjoys cutting a flamboyant public figure with a reputation for hard drinking and fast motorcycles. He also enjoys being a publicist for the life of the poet, as if he were indeed a latter-day Byron. This involves him in paradoxical activity, a cross between serious literary criticism and advertisements for himself. He has published a series of *Self-Interviews* as well as a penetrating collection of reviews of other poets, *Babel to Byzantium* (1968). In 1967–69 he held the chair of poetry at the Library of Congress.

A Dog Sleeping on My Feet

Being his resting place,
I do not even tense
The muscles of a leg
Or I would seem to be changing.
Instead, I turn the page
Of the notebook, carefully not

5

Remembering what I have written,
For now, with my feet beneath him
Dying like embers,
The poem is beginning to move   10
Up through my pine-prickling legs
Out of the night wood,

Taking hold of the pen by my fingers.
Before me the fox floats lightly,
On fire with his holy scent.   15
All, all are running.
Marvelous is the pursuit,
Like a dazzle of nails through the ankles,

Like a twisting shout through the trees
Sent after the flying fox   20
Through the holes of logs, over streams
Stock-still with the pressure of moonlight.
My killed legs,
My legs of a dead thing, follow,

Quick as pins, through the forest,   25
And all rushes on into dark
And ends on the brightness of paper.
When my hand, which speaks in a daze
The hypnotized language of beasts,
Shall falter, and fail   30

Back into the human tongue,
And the dog gets up and goes out
To wander the dawning yard,
I shall crawl to my human bed
And lie there smiling at sunrise,   35
With the scent of the fox

Burning my brain like an incense,
Floating out of the night wood,
Coming home to my wife and my sons
From the dream of an animal,   40
Assembling the self I must wake to,
Sleeping to grow back my legs.

                                                       1962

The Heaven of Animals

Here they are. The soft eyes open.
If they have lived in a wood
It is a wood.
If they have lived on plains
It is grass rolling   5
Under their feet forever.

Having no souls, they have come,
Anyway, beyond their knowing.
Their instincts wholly bloom
And they rise.   10
The soft eyes open.

To match them, the landscape flowers,
Outdoing, desperately
Outdoing what is required:
The richest wood,   15
The deepest field.

For some of these,
It could not be the place
It is, without blood.
These hunt, as they have done,   20
But with claws and teeth grown perfect,

More deadly than they can believe.
They stalk more silently,
And crouch on the limbs of trees,
And their descent   25
Upon the bright backs of their prey

May take years
In a sovereign floating of joy.
And those that are hunted
Know this as their life,   30
Their reward: to walk

Under such trees in full knowledge
Of what is in glory above them,
And to feel no fear,
But acceptance, compliance.   35
Fulfilling themselves without pain

At the cycle's center,
They tremble, they walk
Under the tree,
They fall, they are torn,   40
They rise, they walk again.

1962

Cherrylog Road

Off Highway 106
At Cherrylog Road I entered
The '34 Ford without wheels,
Smothered in kudzu,[1]

---

1. A vine introduced to the United States from Japan, which often grows over whole fields.

With a seat pulled out to run   5
Corn whiskey down from the hills,

And then from the other side
Crept into an Essex
With a rumble seat of red leather
And then out again, aboard   10
A blue Chevrolet, releasing
The rust from its other color,

Reared up on three building blocks.
None had the same body heat;
I changed with them inward, toward   15
The weedy heart of the junkyard,
For I knew that Doris Holbrook
Would escape from her father at noon

And would come from the farm
To seek parts owned by the sun   20
Among the abandoned chassis,
Sitting in each in turn
As I did, leaning forward
As in a wild stock-car race

In the parking lot of the dead.   25
Time after time, I climbed in
And out the other side, like
An envoy or movie star
Met at the station by crickets.
A radiator cap raised its head,   30

Become a real toad or a kingsnake
As I neared the hub of the yard,
Passing through many states,
Many lives, to reach
Some grandmother's long Pierce-Arrow[2]   35
Sending platters of blindness forth

From its nickel hubcaps
And spilling its tender upholstery
On sleepy roaches,
The glass panel in between   40
Lady and colored driver
Not all the way broken out,

The back-seat phone
Still on its hook.
I got in as though to exclaim,   45
"Let us go to the orphan asylum,

---

2. Vintage luxury car.

John; I have some old toys
For children who say their prayers."

I popped with sweat as I thought
I heard Doris Holbrook scrape   50
Like a mouse in the southern-state sun
That was eating the paint in blisters
From a hundred car tops and hoods.
She was tapping like code,

Loosening the screws,   55
Carrying off headlights,
Sparkplugs, bumpers,
Cracked mirrors and gear-knobs,
Getting ready, already,
To go back with something to show   60

Other than her lips' new trembling
I would hold to me soon, soon,
Where I sat in the ripped back seat
Talking over the interphone,
Praying for Doris Holbrook   65
To come from her father's farm

And to get back there
With no trace of me on her face
To be seen by her red-haired father
Who would change, in the squalling barn,   70
Her back's pale skin with a strop,
Then lay for me

In a bootlegger's roasting car
With a string-triggered 12-gauge shotgun
To blast the breath from the air.   75
Not cut by the jagged windshields,
Through the acres of wrecks she came
With a wrench in her hand,

Through dust where the blacksnake dies
Of boredom, and the beetle knows   80
The compost has no more life.
Someone outside would have seen
The oldest car's door inexplicably
Close from within:

I held her and held her and held her,   85
convoyed at terrific speed
By the stalled, dreaming traffic around us,
So the blacksnake, stiff
With inaction, curved back
Into life, and hunted the mouse   90

With deadly overexcitement,
The beetles reclaimed their field
As we clung, glued together,
With the hooks of the seat springs
Working through to catch us red-handed   95
Amidst the gray breathless batting

That burst from the seat at our backs.
We left by separate doors
Into the changed, other bodies
Of cars, she down Cherrylog Road   100
And I to my motorcycle
Parked like the soul of the junkyard

Restored, a bicycle fleshed
With power, and tore off
Up Highway 106, continually   105
Drunk on the wind in my mouth,
Wringing the handlebar for speed,
Wild to be wreckage forever.

                                                          1964

Power and Light

... only connect . . .1
—E. M. FORSTER

I may even be
A man, I tell my wife: all day I climb myself

Bowlegged up those damned poles   rooster-heeled in all
Kinds of weather   and what is there when I get
Home? Yes, woman trailing ground-oil   5
Like a snail, home is where I climb down,
And this is the house I pass through on my way

To power and light.
Going into the basement is slow, but the built-on smell of home
Beneath home gets better with age   the ground fermenting   10
And spilling through the barrel-cracks of plaster   the dark
Lying on the floor, ready for use   as I crack
The seal on the bottle   like I tell you it takes
A man to pour whiskey in the dark and CLOSE THE DOOR
    between

The children and me.   15
The heads of nails drift deeper through their boards
And disappear. Years in the family dark have made me good
At this   nothing else is so good   pure fires of the Self
Rise crooning in lively blackness   and the silence around them,

1. From *Howards End*, by E. M. Forster, the English novelist (1879–1970),
who is offering an axiom for achieving
satisfying personal and social relations.

Like the silence inside a mouth, squirms with colors,   20
The marvellous worms of the eye float out into the real

World   sunspots
Dancing as though existence were
One huge closed eye   and I feel the wires running
Like the life-force along the limed rafters   and all connections   25
With poles   with the tarred naked belly-buckled black
Trees I hook to my heels   with the shrill phone calls leaping
Long distance   long distances through my hands   all connections

Even the one
With my wife, turn good   turn better than good   turn good   30
Not quite, but in the deep sway of underground   among the roots
That bend like branches   all things connect   and stream
Toward light and speech   tingle   rock like a powerline in wind,
Like a man working, drunk on pine-moves   the sun in the socket
Of his shoulder   and on his neck dancing like dice-dots,   35

And I laugh
Like my own fate watching over me night and day   at home
Underground   or flung up on towers walking
Over mountains   my charged hair standing on end   crossing
The sickled, slaughtered alleys of timber   40
Where the lines loop and crackle on their gallows.
Far under the grass of my grave, I drink like a man

The night before
Resurrection Day. My watch glows with the time to rise
And shine. Never think I don't know my profession   45
Will lift me: why, all over hell the lights burn in your eyes,
People are calling each other   weeping with a hundred thousand
Volts   making deals   pleading   laughing like fate,
Far off, invulnerable   or with the right word pierced

To the heart   50
By wires I held, shooting off their ghostly mouths,
In my gloves. The house spins   I strap crampons to my shoes
To climb the basement stairs, sinking my heels in the tree-
life of the boards. Thorns! Thorns! I am bursting
Into the kitchen, into the sad way-station   55
Of my home, holding a double handful of wires

Spitting like sparklers
On the Fourth of July. Woman, I know the secret of sitting
In light   of eating a limp piece of bread   under
The red-veined eyeball of a bulb. It is all in how you are   60
Grounded. To bread I can see, I say, as it disappears and agrees
With me   the dark is drunk   and I am a man
Who turns on. I am a man.

                                                                    1967

DENISE LEVERTOV

1923–

Although she was born in England and published her first book of poems there (*The Double Image*, 1946), Denise Levertov really belongs to the history of contemporary American poetry. She married an American, the writer Mitchell Goodman, she has lived here since 1948, and she has increasingly interested herself in American radical politics. More important, even before she published her first book in the United States (*Here and Now*, 1957) she underwent a formative apprenticeship in American verse.

Behind her was a rich European heritage. One of Levertov's ancestors was the Welsh tailor and mystic Angel Jones; her father was descended from the Russian rabbi Schneour Zaimon, a follower of the Hasidic movement which believes in the radiance of everyday experience. She honors these two mystics in *Illustrious Ancestors* and hopes to emulate their lessons in her poems. Levertov tries to coax the element of mystery out of ordinary occurrences, cityscapes and landscapes, the intricacies of human relationships, sexual rapport and sexual difficulties.

The most decisive influence on her work was William Carlos Williams, about whom she wrote: "he made available to us the whole range of the language, he showed us the rhythms of speech as *poetry*—the rhythms and idioms not only of what we say aloud but of what we say in our thoughts." She gives Williams credit for making an American poet out of "a British Romantic with almost Victorian background." Levertov also admires and shares some of the concerns of the "Black Mountain poets," Charles Olson, Robert Duncan, and Robert Creeley, with whom critics sometimes group her. Like them she sees poetry as a way of rediscovering mythic dimensions in daily life.

Central to her poem *Clouds*, for example, is a terrifying moment when the lover beside her feels cold to the touch. But she is "brought to speech," as the experience is crystallized for her by real and imagined visions of the sky. Staring at the gray heavens, she begins to see the radiant colors which mix to a single dull shade, and with that illumination she turns back to think about the "colors of truth" behind the "death's chill" of her relationship. It is this kind of penetration of common experiences that she refers to in *The Room*: "I don't want to escape, only to see / the enactment of rites."

Levertov tries to find an "organic form," a rhythm which grows from a poet's "inner voice." Each poem is to have "a rhythmic norm peculiar to [itself]. * * * I heard Henry Cowell [an American composer] tell that the drone in Indian music is known as the horizon note. Al Kresch, the painter, sent me a quotation from Emerson: 'The health of the eye demands a horizon.' This sense of the beat or pulse underlying the whole I think of as the horizon note of the poem."

During the late 1960s Levertov's husband, Mitchell Goodman, actively opposed the Vietnam war and was prosecuted for his protest activities. Levertov herself participated in antiwar demonstrations and devoted many of her poems in *The Sorrow Dance* (1968) and *Relearning the Alphabet*

(1970) to political protest. She has come increasingly to feel that a vital poetry must be politically engaged. Much of her literary criticism, as well as a report of her trip to North Vietnam, has been collected in *The Poet in the World* (1973).

The Room

With a mirror
I could see the sky.

With two mirrors or three
justly placed, I could see
the sun bowing to the evening chimneys.   5

Moonrise—the moon itself might appear
in a fourth mirror placed high
and close to the open window.

       With enough mirrors within
and even without the room, a cantilever   10
supporting them, mountains
and oceans might be manifest.

I understand perfectly
that I could encounter my own eyes
too often—I take account   15
of the danger—.
       If the mirrors
are large enough, and arranged
with bravura, I can look
beyond my own glance.   20

With one mirror
how many stars could I see?

I don't want to escape, only to see
the enactment of rites.

                 1959

Terror

Face-down; odor
of dusty carpet. The grip
of anguished stillness.

Then your naked voice, your
head knocking the wall, sideways,   5
the beating of trapped thoughts against iron.

If I remember, how is it
my face shows

barely a line? Am I
a monster, to sing   10
in the wind on this sunny hill

and not taste the dust always,
and not hear
that rending, that retching?
How did morning come, and the days   15
that followed, and quiet nights?

                                                                    1959

At the Edge

How much I should like to begin
a poem with And—presupposing
the hardest said—
the moss cleared off the stone,
the letters plain.   5
How the round moon
would shine into all the corners
of such a poem and show
the words! Moths and dazzled
awakened birds   10
would freeze in its light!
The lines would be
an outbreak of bells
and I swinging on the rope!

Yet, not desiring apocrypha[1]   15
but true revelation,
what use to pretend the stone discovered,
anything visible?
That poem indeed
may not be carved there, may lie   20
—the quick of mystery—
in animal eyes gazing
from the thicket,
a creature of unknown size,
fierce, terrified, having teeth or   25
no defense, but whom
no And may approach suddenly.

                                                                    1959

A Map of the Western Part of the County of Essex in England

Something forgotten for twenty years: though my fathers
and mothers came from Cordova and Vitepsk and Caernarvon,[2]
and though I am a citizen of the United States and less a
stranger here than anywhere else, perhaps,

---

1. The Apocrypha consist of Biblical books of doubtful authority, as distinguished from the books of the Bible considered to be "true revelations."
2. Towns in Spain, Russia, and Wales, respectively.

I am Essex-born: 5
Cranbrook Wash[3] called me into its dark tunnel,
the little streams of Valentines heard my resolves,
Roding held my head above water when I thought it was
drowning me; in Hainault only a haze of thin trees
stood between the red doubledecker buses and the boar-hunt, 10
the spirit of merciful Philippa[4] glimmered there.
Pergo Park knew me, and Clavering, and Havering-atte-Bower,
Stanford Rivers lost me in osier[5] beds, Stapleford Abbots
sent me safe home on the dark road after Simeon[6]-quiet even-
song,
Wanstead drew me over and over into its basic poetry, 15
in its serpentine lake I saw bass-viols among the golden dead
leaves,
through its trees the ghost of a great house. In
Ilford High Road I saw the multitudes passing pale under the
light of flaring sundown, seven kings
in somber starry robes gathered at Seven Kings 20
the place of law
where my birth and marriage are recorded
and the death of my father. Woodford Wells
where an old house was called The Naked Beauty (a white
statue forlorn in its garden) 25
saw the meeting and parting of two sisters,
(forgotten? and further away
the hill before Thaxted? where peace befell us? not once
but many times?).
All the Ivans dreaming of their villages 30
all the Marias dreaming of their walled cities,
picking up fragments of New World slowly,
not knowing how to put them together nor how to join
image with image, now I know how it was with you, an old
map
made long before I was born shows ancient 35
rights of way where I walked when I was ten burning with desire
for the world's great splendors, a child who traced voyages
indelibly all over the atlas, who now in a far country
remembers the first river, the first
field, bricks and lumber dumped in it ready for building, 40
that new smell, and remembers
the walls of the garden, the first light.

1961

---

3. In the county of Essex, England, as are all the other towns subsequently mentioned in the poem.
4. Philippa of Hainault (c. 1314–69), queen consort of English King Edward III (1327–77), known for her gentleness and compassion and credited with helping to maintain peace during Edward's long reign. In 1347 she interceded with her husband and saved the lives of six city burghers of Calais whom he had threatened to execute.
5. A species of willow, often used for basket-weaving.
6. St. Simeon is usually depicted receiving the infant Jesus into the Temple. The reference is to Simeon's awe when he realized that he held the Messiah in his hands.

Clouds

The clouds as I see them, rising
urgently, roseate in the
mounting of somber power

surging in evening haste over
roofs and hermetic   5
grim walls—

             Last night
As if death had lit a pale light
in your flesh, you flesh
was cold to my touch, or not cold   10
but cool, cooling, as if the last traces
of warmth were still fading in you.
My thigh burned in cold fear where
yours touched it.

But I forced to mind my vision of a sky   15
close and enclosed, unlike the space in which
      these clouds move—
a sky of gray mist it appeared—
and how looking intently at it we saw
its gray was not gray but a milky white
in which radiant traces of opal greens,   20
fiery blues, gleamed, faded, gleamed again,
and how only then, seeing the color in the gray,
a field sprang into sight, extending
between where we stood and the horizon,

a field of freshest deep spiring grass   25
starred with dandelions,
green and gold
gold and green alternating in closewoven
chords, madrigal field.

Is death's chill that visited our bed   30
other than what it seemed, is it
a gray to be watched keenly?

Wiping my glasses and leaning westward,
clearing my mind of the day's mist and leaning
into myself to see   35
the colors of truth

I watch the clouds as I see them
in pomp advancing, pursuing
the fallen sun.

                        1961

Illustrious Ancestors[1]

The Rav
of Northern White Russia declined,
in his youth, to learn the
language of birds, because
the extraneous did not interest him; nevertheless   5
when he grew old it was found
he understood them anyway, having
listened well, and as it is said, 'prayed
        with the bench and the floor.' He used
what was at hand—as did   10
Angel Jones of Mold,[2] whose meditations
were sewn into coats and britches.
        Well, I would like to make,
thinking some line still taut between me and them,
poems direct as what the birds said,   15
hard as a floor, sound as a bench,
mysterious as the silence when the tailor
would pause with his needle in the air.

        1961

The Unknown

FOR MURIEL RUKEYSER[3]

The kettle changes its note,
the steam sublimed.

Supererogatory[4] divinations one is
lured on by!
        The routine   5
is decent. As if the white page
were a clean tablecloth,
as if the vacuumed floor were
a primed canvas, as if
new earrings made from old shells   10
of tasty abalone were nose rings for the two most beautiful
girls of a meticulous island, whose bodies are oiled as one oils
a table of teak . . . Hypocrisies
of seemly hope, performed to make a place
for miracles to occur; and if the day   15
is no day for miracles, then the preparations
are an order one may rest in.

        But one doesn't want
rest, one wants miracles. Each time that note
changes (which is whenever you let it)—the kettle   20

1. Rabbi (or Rav) Schneour Zaimon and Angel Jones were mystics who were also the "illustrious ancestors," respectively, of Levertov's father and mother.
2. A town in Wales.
3. Fellow poet (b. 1913) and friend of Levertov.
4. Superfluous, not required.

(already boiling) passing into enlightenment without
a moment's pause, out of fury into
quiet praise—desire
wakes again. *Begin over.*
        It is to hunt a white deer   25
        in snowy woods. Beaten
        you fall asleep in the afternoon
on a sofa.
        And wake to witness,
softly backing away from you, mollified,   30
all that the room had insisted on—
        eager furniture, differentiated planes . . .
Twilight has come, the windows
are big and solemn, brimful of the afterglow;
and sleep has swept through the mind, loosening   35
brown leaves from their twigs to drift
        out of sight
beyond the horizon's black rooftops.
A winter's dirt
makes Indian silk squares of the windowpanes,   40
semi transparent, a designed
middle distance.
        The awakening is
to transformation,
word after word.   45

        1966

The Willows of Massachusetts

Animal willows of November
in pelt of gold enduring when all else
has let go all ornament
and stands naked in the cold.
Cold shine of sun on swamp water   5
cold caress of slant beam on bough,
gray light on brown bark.
Willows—last to relinguish a leaf,
curious, patient, lion-headed, tense
with energy, watching   10
the serene cold through a curtain
of tarnished strands.

        1966

From Olga Poems
(OLGA LEVERTOFF, 1914–1964)[1]

i
By the gas-fire, kneeling
to undress,

---

1. The poet's sister.

scorching luxuriously, raking
her nails over olive sides, the red
waistband ring—   5

(And the little sister
beady-eyed in the bed—
or drowsy, was I? My head
a camera—)

Sixteen. Her breasts   10
round, round, and
dark-nippled—

who now these two months long
is bones and tatters of flesh in earth.

ii
The high pitch of   15
nagging insistence, lines
creased into raised brows—

Ridden, ridden—
the skin around the nails
nibbled sore—   20

You wanted
to shout the world to its senses,
did you?—to browbeat

the poor into joy's
socialist republic—   25
What rage

and human shame swept you
when you were nine and saw
the Ley Street houses,

grasping their meaning as *slum*.   30
Where I, reaching that age,
teased you, admiring

architectural probity, circa
eighteen-fifty, and noted
pride in the whitened doorsteps.   35

Black one, black one,
there was a white
candle in your heart.

iii

i

Everything flows
                she muttered into my childhood,   40
pacing the trampled grass where human puppets
rehearsed fates that summer,
stung into alien semblances by the lash of her will—

everything flows—
I looked up from my Littlest Bear's cane armchair   45
and knew the words came from a book
and felt them alien to me

but linked to words we loved
                        from the hymnbook—*Time
like an ever-rolling stream / bears all its sons away*—   50

ii

Now as if smoke or sweetness were blown my way
I inhale a sense of her livingness in that instant,
feeling, dreaming, hoping, knowing boredom and zest like anyone
                                                        else—
a young girl in the garden, the same alchemical[2] square
I grew in, we thought sometimes   55
too small for our grand destinies—
                        But dread
was in her, a bloodbeat, it was against the rolling dark
oncoming river she raised bulwarks, setting herself
to sift cinders after early Mass all of one winter,   60

labelling her desk's normal disorder, basing
her verses on Keble's[3] *Christian Year*, picking
those endless arguments, pressing on

to manipulate lives to disaster . . . To change,
to change the course of the river! What rage for order   65
disordered her pilgrimage—so that for years at a time

she would hide among strangers, waiting
to rearrange all mysteries in a new light.

iii

Black one, incubus—
                she appeared   70
riding anguish as Tartars[4] ride mares

over the stubble of bad years.

In one of the years
        when I didn't know if she were dead or alive

---

2. Turning base metal into gold.
3. John Keble (1792–1866), English divine and poet.

4. Central Asian barbarians led by Genghis Khan in the 13th century.

I saw her in dream   75
haggard and rouged
      lit by the flare
from an eel- or cockle-stand on a slum street—

was it a dream? I had lost

all sense, almost, of   80
     who she was, what—inside of her skin,
under her black hair
         dyed blonde—

it might feel like to be, in the wax and wane of the moon,
in the life I feel as unfolding, not flowing, the pilgrim years—   85
            * * *
vi
Your eyes were the brown gold of pebbles under water.
I never crossed the bridge over the Roding, dividing
the open field of the present from the mysteries,
the wraiths and shifts of time-sense Wanstead Park held suspended,
without remembering your eyes. Even when we were estranged   90
and my own eyes smarted in pain and anger at the thought of you.
And by other streams in other countries; anywhere where the light
reaches down through shallows to gold gravel. Olga's
brown eyes. One rainy summer, down in the New Forest,
when we could hardly breathe for ennui[5] and the low sky,   95
you turned savagely to the piano and sightread
straight through all the Beethoven sonatas, day after day—
weeks, it seemed to me. I would turn the pages some of the time,
go out to ride my bike, return—you were enduring in the
falls and rapids of the music, the arpeggios[6] rang out, the rectory   100
trembled, our parents seemed effaced.
I think of your eyes in that photo, six years before I was born,
the fear in them. What did you do with your fear,
later? Through the years of humiliation,
of paranoia and blackmail and near-starvation, losing   105
the love of those you loved, one after another,
parents, lovers, children, idolized friends, what kept
compassion's candle alight in you, that lit you
clear into another chapter (but the same book) a clearing
in the selva oscura,[7]   110
a house whose door
swings open, a hand beckons
in welcome'?
      I cross
so many brooks in the world, there is so much light   115

---

5. Boredom.
6. Component notes of a musical chord played successively.
7. Literally "dark wood," translating Dante's phrase from the opening of his *Inferno,* in which he depicts the sinner lost in the midst of life. "The quoted lines in the sixth section are an adaptation of some lines in 'Selva Oscura' by the late Louis MacNeice, a poem much beloved by my sister" [Levertov's note].

dancing on so many stones, so many questions my eyes
smart to ask of your eyes, gold brown eyes,
the lashes short but the lids
arched as if carved out of olivewood, eyes with some vision
of festive goodness in back of their hard, or veiled, or shining,   120
unknowable gaze . . .
May–August, 1964   1966

ROBERT CREELEY

1926–

Robert Creeley's poems are easily recognizable on the page; most of them
are brief and use short lines. Yet their brevity belies their intensity: a poem
is, for him, "a kind of absolute seizure." His notions of the origin of a
poem seem crystallized in a sentence he is fond of quoting from William
Carlos Williams: "In our family we stammer until, half mad, we come to
speech." Williams's work taught Creeley that the poet thinks not *before*,
but *with* his poem.

In 1954 the poet Charles Olson invited Creeley to teach at Black Mountain College, a seedbed of advanced activity in painting, literature, and
music. For two years Creeley edited *The Black Mountain Review*. He was
later to edit some of Olson's writings (after Olson's death), and he responded powerfully to Olson's theory of "projective verse." As Creeley
understood it, the line of poetry was to take its measure from no externally
imposed system, but rather from the "breath, from the breathing of the
man who writes." Himself an articulate critic of art, Creeley helped to
connect Olson's literary theory with some of the discoveries of Abstract
Expressionist (nonrepresentational) painting. From the "action painting"
of Jackson Pollock, Creeley drew the notion that art—poetry as well as
painting—need not be "about" anything other than the gestures expressing
the artist's bodily and emotional energies *at one moment* of grappling
with his materials.

Creeley, along with his fellow poets Olson and Robert Duncan, thought
of verse not as dealing with consciously chosen subjects but as something
"given," forced upon the writer by a resonant experience. (*The Rain*, for
example, begins with insomnia on a rainy night and only comes to rest
when the writer has learned through his poem to connect those insistent
physical disturbances with their psychological sources, a demand for love.)
Creeley came to believe that a poem should not be much revised, if at all;
it was "composed" in the time required to write it out, although, of course,
a semiconscious preparatory period leads up to composition.

The weight and seriousness of Creeley's literary theory shouldn't blind
readers to the fact that his poems keep to personal relationships, "the terms
of marriage, relations of men and women, senses of isolation, senses of place
in the intimate measure." He avoids the larger mythical dimensions which
Olson and Duncan try to find in everyday life. "Embarrassed for a larger
vision," he accordingly gives his books titles of modest dimensions: *For
Love* (1962); *Words* (1967); *Pieces* (1969); *A Day Book* (1972).

Creeley was born in Arlington, Massachusetts. His father, a doctor, died when the poet was very young, and Creeley remembers how, for the child growing up without a father, the doctor's black bag came to stand for all those professions "which could travel * * * with all you needed in your hands." In becoming a poet, he chose such a profession for himself, and has led an unusually itinerant life. His education included two periods at Harvard, with an interim serving in the American Field Service in Burma and India. With his first wife, he lived in New Hampshire, in France, and in Mallorca, where he started the Divers Press. He has also lived in Taos, San Francisco, and Guatemala. He now teaches at the State University of New York in Buffalo.

Air: "Cat Bird Singing"

Cat bird singing
makes music like sounds coming

at night. The trees, goddamn them,
are huge eyes. They

watch, certainly, what   5
else should they do? My love

is a person of rare refinement,
and when she speaks,

there is another air,
melody—what Campion[1] spoke of   10

with his
follow thy fair sunne unhappie shadow . . .

Catbird, catbird.
O lady hear me. I have no

other   15
voice left.

                                      1959

Somewhere

The galloping collection of boards
are the house which I afforded
one evening to walk into
just as the night came down.

Dark inside, the candle   5
lit of its own free will, the attic

---

1. Thomas Campion (1567–1620), English poet and composer, who wrote the lyric *Follow thy fair sunne unhappie shadow.*

groaned then, the stairs
led me up into the air.

From outside, it must have seemed
a wonder that it was   10
the inside *he* as *me* saw
in the dark there.

1959

The Rain

All night the sound had
come back again,
and again falls
this quiet, persistent rain.

What am I to myself   5
that must be remembered,
insisted upon
so often? Is it

that never the ease,
even the hardness,   10
of rain falling
will have for me

something other than this,
something not so insistent—
am I to be locked in this   15
final uneasiness.

Love, if you love me,
lie next to me.
Be for me, like rain,
the getting out   20

of the tiredness, the fatuousness, the semi-
lust of intentional indifference.
Be wet
with a decent happiness.

1962

The Rhythm

It is all a rhythm,
from the shutting
door, to the window
opening,

the seasons, the sun's   5
light, the moon,

the oceans, the
growing of things,

the mind in men
personal, recurring   10
in them again,
thinking the end

is not the end, the
time returning,
themselves dead, but   15
someone else coming,

If in death I am dead,
then in life also
dying, dying . . .
And the women cry and die.   20

The little children
grow only to old men.
The grass dries,
the force goes.

But is met by another   25
returning, oh not mine,
not mine, and
in turn dies.

The rhythm which projects
from itself continuity   30
bending all to its force
from window to door,
from ceiling to floor,
light at the opening,
dark at the closing.   35

1967

Song

The grit
of things,
a measure
resistant—

times walk-   5
ing, talk-
ing, telling
lies and

all the other
places, no   10

one ever
quite the same.

1967

One Way

Of the two, one
faces one. In
the air there is

no tremor, no
odor. There is   5
a house around them,

of wood, of walls.
The mark is silence.
Everything hangs.

As he raises   10
his hand to
not strike her, as

again his hand
is raised, she has
gone, into another   15

room. In the room
left by her, he
cannot see himself

as in a mirror, as
a feeling of reflection.   20
He thinks he thinks,

of something else.
All the locked time,
all the letting go

down into it, as a   25
locked room, come to.
This time not changed,

but the way of feeling
secured by walls and books,
a picture hanging down,   30

a center shifted, dust
on all he puts his hand on,
disorder, papers and letters

and accumulations of clothing,
and bedclothes, and under his   35
feet the rug bunches.

1967

A Place

The wetness of that street, the light,
the way the clouds were heavy is
not description. But in the memory I fear

the distortion. I do not feel
what it was I was feeling. I am im-   5
patient to begin again, open

whatever door it was, find the weather
is out there, grey, the rain then and
now falling from the sky to the wet ground.

1967

The World

I wanted so ably
to reassure you, I wanted
the man you took to be me,

to comfort you, and got
up, and went to the window   5
pushed back, as you asked me to,

the curtain, to see
the outline of the trees
in the night outside.

The light, love,   10
the light we felt then,
greyly, was it, that

came in, on us, not
merely my hands or yours,
or a wetness so comfortable,   15

but in the dark then
as you slept, the grey
figure came so close

and leaned over,
between us, as you   20
slept, restless, and

my own face had to
see it, and be seen by it,
the man it was, your

grey lost tired bewildered   25
brother, unused, untaken—
hated by love, and dead,

but not dead, for an
instant, saw me, myself
the intruder, as he was not.   30

I tried to say, it is
all right, she is
happy, you are no longer

needed. I said,
he is dead, and he   35
went as you shifted

and woke, at first afraid,
then knew by my own knowing
what had happened—

and the light then   40
of the sun coming
for another morning
in the world.

1967

ALLEN GINSBERG
1926–

"Hold back the edges of your gowns, Ladies, we are going through hell."
William Carlos Williams's introduction to Allen Ginsberg's *Howl* (1956)
was probably the most auspicious public welcome from one poet to another
since Emerson had hailed the unknown Whitman in a letter that Whitman
prefaced to the second edition of *Leaves of Grass* one hundred years before.
Howl combined apocalyptic criticism of the dull, prosperous Eisenhower
years with exuberant celebration of an emerging counterculture. It was the
best known and most widely circulated book of poems of its time, and with
its appearance Ginsberg became part of the history of publicity as well as
the history of poetry. *Howl* and Jack Kerouac's novel *On the Road* were
the pocket Bibles of the generation whose name Kerouac had coined—
"Beat," with its punning overtones of "beaten down" and "beatified."

Allen Ginsberg was born in 1926, son of Louis Ginsberg, a schoolteacher
in New Jersey, himself a poet, and of Naomi Ginsberg, a Russian émigrée,
whose madness and eventual death her son memorialized in *Kaddish*

(1959). His official education took place at Columbia University, but for him as for Jack Kerouac the presence of William Burroughs in New York was equally influential. Burroughs (b. 1914), later the author of *Naked Lunch*, one of the most inventive experiments in American prose, was at that time a drug addict about to embark on an expatriate life in Mexico and Tangier. He helped Ginsberg discover modern writers: Kafka, Yeats, Céline, Rimbaud. Ginsberg responded to Burroughs's liberated kind of life, to his comic-apocalyptic view of American society, and to his bold literary use of autobiography, as when writing about his own experience with addicts and addiction in *Junkie*, whose chapters Ginsberg was reading in manuscript form in 1950.

Ginsberg's New York career has passed into mythology. In 1945, his sophomore year, he was expelled from Columbia: he had sketched some obscene drawings and phrases in the dust of his dormitory window to draw the attention of a neglectful cleaning woman to the grimy state of his room. Then, living periodically with Burroughs and Kerouac, he shipped out for short trips as a messman on merchant tankers and worked in addition as a welder, a night-porter, and a dishwasher.

One summer, in a Harlem apartment, Ginsberg underwent what he was always to represent as the central conversion experience of his life. He had an "auditory vision" of the English poet William Blake reciting his poems: first *Ah! Sunflower*, and then a few minutes later the same oracular voice intoning *The Sick Rose*. It was "like hearing the doom of the whole universe, and at the same time the inevitable beauty of that doom." Ginsberg was convinced of the presence of "this big god over all * * * and that the whole purpose of being born was to wake up to Him."

Ginsberg eventually finished Columbia in 1948 with high grades but under a legal cloud. Herbert Huncke, a colorful but irresponsible addict friend, had been using Ginsberg's apartment as a storage depot for the goods he stole to support his "habit." To avoid prosecution as an accomplice, Ginsberg had to plead insanity and spent eight months in Columbia Psychiatric Institute.

After more odd jobs—a ribbon factory in New Jersey, a local AFL newspaper—and a considerable success as a market researcher in San Francisco, Ginsberg left the "straight," nine-to-five world for good. He was drawn to San Francisco, he said, by its "long honorable * * * tradition of Bohemian—Buddhist—Wobbly [the I.W.W., an early radical labor movement]—mystical—anarchist social involvement." In the years after 1954 he met San Francisco poets such as Robert Duncan, Kenneth Rexroth, Gary Snyder (who was studying Chinese and Japanese at Berkeley) and Lawrence Ferlinghetti, whose City Lights Bookshop became the publisher of *Howl*. The night Ginsberg read the new poem aloud at the Six Gallery has been called "the birth trauma of the Beat Generation"; it focused and released an angry call for attention to the spirited "misfits" and downtrodden talents of American life.

Howl's spontaneity of surface conceals but grows out of Ginsberg's care and self-consciousness about rhythm and meter. Under the influence of William Carlos Williams, who had befriended him in Paterson after he left the mental hospital, Ginsberg had started carrying around a notebook to record the rhythms of voices around him. Kerouac's *On the Road* gave him further examples of "frank talk," and in addition of an "oceanic" prose "sometimes as sublime as epic line." Under Kerouac's influence Ginsberg began the long tumbling lines which were to become his trademark. He carefully explained that all of *Howl and Other Poems* was an experiment in what could be done with the long line, the longer unit of breath which seemed natural for him. "My feeling is for a big long clanky statement," one which accommodates "not the way you would *say* it, a thought, but the way you would think it—i.e., we think rapidly, in visual images as well as words, and if each successive thought were transcribed in its confusion * * * you get a slightly different prosody than if you were talking slowly."

The long line is something Ginsberg learned as well from Biblical rhetoric, from the 18th-century English poet Christopher Smart, and, above all, from Whitman and Blake. His first book pays tribute to both these latter poets. A *Supermarket in California*, with its movement from exclamations to sad questioning, is Ginsberg's melancholy reminder of what has become, after a century, of Whitman's vision of American plenty. In *Sunflower Sutra* he celebrates the battered nobility beneath our industrial "skin of grime." Ginsberg at his best gives a sense of both doom and beauty, whether in the denunciatory impatient prophecies of *Howl* or in the catalogue of suffering in *Kaddish*. His disconnected phrases can accumulate as narrative shrieks or, at other moments, can build as a litany of praise.

By the end of the 1960s Ginsberg was widely known and widely traveled. For him it was a decade in which he conducted publicly his own pursuit of inner peace during a long stay with Buddhist instructors in India and at home served as a kind of guru himself for many young people disoriented by the Vietnam war. Ginsberg read his poetry and held "office hours" in universities all over America, a presence at everything from "be-ins"—mass outdoor festivals of chanting, costumes, and music—to antiwar protests. He was a gentle and persuasive presence at hearings for many kinds of reform: revision of severe drug laws and laws against homosexuality. Ginsberg himself had lived for years with the poet Peter Orlovsky and wrote frankly about their relationship. His poems record his drug experiences as well, and *The Change*, written in Japan in 1963, marks his decision to keep away from what he considered the nonhuman domination of drugs and to lay new stress on "living in and inhabiting the human form."

In *The Fall of America* (1972) Ginsberg turned to "epic," a poem including history and registering the ups and downs of his travels across the United States. These "transit" poems sometimes seem like tape-recorded random lists of sights, sounds, and names, but at their best they give a sense of how far America has fallen, by measuring the provisional and changing world of nuclear America against the traces of nature still visible in our landscape and place names. Ginsberg now lives on a farm near Woodstock, New York, and has added ecology to the causes for which he is a patient and attractive spokesman.

From Howl[1]

FOR CARL SOLOMON

I

I saw the best minds of my generation destroyed by madness, starving hysterical naked,

---

1. With Jack Kerouac's *On the Road* (1957), *Howl* is a central document of the Beat Movement of the 1950s, drawing on incidents in the lives of Ginsberg,

dragging themselves through the negro streets at dawn looking for an
   angry fix,
angelheaded hipsters[2] burning for the ancient heavenly connection[3]
   to the starry dynamo in the machinery of night,
who poverty and tatters and hollow-eyed and high sat up smoking in
   the supernatural darkness of cold-water flats floating across the
   tops of cities contemplating jazz,
who bared their brains to Heaven under the El[4] and saw Mohammedan angels staggering on tenement roofs illuminated,   5
who passed through universities with radiant cool eyes hallucinating
   Arkansas and Blake-light[5] tragedy among the scholars of war,
who were expelled from the academies for crazy & publishing
   obscene odes on the windows of the skull,[6]
who cowered in unshaven rooms in underwear, burning their money
   in wastebaskets and listening to the Terror through the wall,
who got busted in their pubic beards returning through Laredo with
   a belt of marijuana for New York,
who ate fire in paint hotels or drank turpentine in Paradise Alley,[7]
   death, or purgatoried their torsos night after night   10
with dreams, with drugs, with waking nightmares, alcohol and cock
   and endless balls,
incomparable blind streets of shuddering cloud and lightning in the
   mind leaping toward poles of Canada & Paterson,[8] illuminating
   all the motionless world of Time between,
Peyote solidities of halls, backyard green tree cemetery dawns, wine
   drunkenness over the rooftops, storefront boroughs of teahead
   joyride neon blinking traffic light, sun and moon and tree
   vibrations in the roaring winter dusks of Brooklyn, ashcan rant-
   ings and kind king light of mind,
who chained themselves to subways for the endless ride from Battery
   to holy Bronx[9] on benzedrine until the noise of wheels and
   children brought them down shuddering mouth-wracked and
   battered bleak of brain all drained of brilliance in the drear
   light of Zoo,
who sank all night in submarine light of Bickford's[1] floated out and

---

Kerouac, and their friends. Ginsberg met
Carl Solomon (b. 1928) while both were
patients in Columbia Psychiatric Institute
in 1949, and called him "an intuitive
Bronx Dadaist and prose-poet." Many
details in *Howl* come from the "apocryphal history" which Solomon told Ginsberg in 1949. In *More Mishaps* (1968),
Solomon admits that these adventures
were "compounded partly of truth, but
for the most [of] raving self-justification,
crypto-bohemian boasting * * * effeminate prancing and esoteric aphorisms."
2. The Beats who went "on the road" in
the 1950s; "hip": slang for "aware."
3. Person who supplies dope.
4. Elevated railway in New York City.
5. Referring to Ginsberg's apocalyptic
vision of the English poet William Blake
(1757–1827).

6. In 1945, Ginsberg was expelled from
Columbia for drawing obscene pictures
and phrases in the grime of his dormitory windows, in an effort to attract the
cleaning woman's attention to the filth in
the room. In 1948; in danger of prosecution as an accessory to burglary, Ginsberg volunteered to undergo psychiatric
treatment.
7. A tenement courtyard in New York's
East Village; setting of Kerouac's *The
Subterraneans* (1958).
8. Ginsberg's hometown, also the town
celebrated by William Carlos Williams
in his long poem *Paterson.*
9. Opposite ends of a New York subway
line; the Bronx Zoo was the northern
terminus.
1. All-night cafeteria where Ginsberg
worked during his college years.

sat through the stale beer afternoon in desolate Fugazzi's,[2]
listening to the crack of doom on the hydrogen jukebox,   15
who talked continuously seventy hours from park to pad to bar to
    Bellevue[3] to museum to the Brooklyn Bridge,
a lost battalion of platonic conversationalists jumping down the
    stoops off fire escapes off windowsills off Empire State out of
    the moon,
yacketayakking screaming vomiting whispering facts and memories
    and anecdotes and eyeball kicks and shocks of hospitals and
    jails and wars,
whole intellects disgorged in total recall for seven days and nights
    with brilliant eyes, meat for the Synagogue cast on the pave-
    ment,
who vanished into nowhere Zen New Jersey leaving a trail of am-
    biguous picture postcards of Atlantic City Hall,   20
suffering Eastern sweats and Tangerian bone-grindings and migraines
    of China[4] under junk-withdrawal in Newark's bleak furnished
    room,
who wandered around and around at midnight in the railroad yard
    wondering where to go, and went, leaving no broken hearts,
who lit cigarettes in boxcars boxcars boxcars racketing through snow
    toward lonesome farms in grandfather night,
who studied Plotinus Poe St. John of the Cross[5] telepathy and bop
    kaballa[6] because the cosmos instinctively vibrated at their feet
    in Kansas,
who loned it through the streets of Idaho seeking visionary indian
    angels who were visionary indian angels,   25
who thought they were only mad when Baltimore gleamed in super-
    natural ecstasy,
who jumped in limousines with the Chinaman of Oklahoma on the
    impulse of winter midnight streetlight smalltown rain,
who lounged hungry and lonesome through Houston seeking jazz
    or sex or soup, and followed the brilliant Spaniard to converse
    about America and Eternity, a hopeless task, and so took ship
    to Africa,
who disappeared into the volcanoes of Mexico leaving behind noth-
    ing but the shadow of dungarees and the lava and ash of
    poetry scattered in fireplace Chicago,
who reappeared on the West Coast investigating the F.B.I. in beards
    and shorts with big pacifist eyes sexy in their dark skin passing
    out incomprehensible leaflets,   30
who burned cigarette holes in their arms protesting the narcotic
    tobacco haze of Capitalism,
who distributed Supercommunist pamphlets in Union Square[7]

---

2. Bar near Greenwich Village frequented
by the Beats.
3. New York public hospital to which
mental patients are generally committed.
4. African and Asian sources of drugs.
5. Spanish visionary and poet (1542–91),
author of *The Dark Night of the Soul*;
Edgar Allan Poe (1809–49), American
poet and author of supernatural tales;

Plotinus (205–70), visionary philosopher.
Ginsberg was interested in these figures
because of their mysticism.
6. Bop was the jazz style of the 1940s;
the kaballa is a mystical tradition of interpretation of Hebrew scripture.
7. A gathering spot for radical speakers
in New York in the 1930's.

weeping and undressing while the sirens of Los Alamos[8] wailed them down, and wailed down Wall,[9] and the Staten Island ferry also wailed,

who broke down crying in white gymnasiums naked and trembling before the machinery of other skeletons,

who bit detectives in the neck and shrieked with delight in police-cars for committing no crime but their own wild cooking pederasty and intoxication,

who howled on their knees in the subway and were dragged off the roof waving genitals and manuscripts,   35

who let themselves be fucked in the ass by saintly motorcyclists, and screamed with joy,

who blew and were blown by those human seraphim, the sailors, caresses of Atlantic and Caribbean love,

who balled in the morning in the evenings in rosegardens and the grass of public parks and cemeteries scattering their semen freely to whomever come who may,

who hiccupped endlessly trying to giggle but wound up with a sob behind a partition in a Turkish Bath when the blonde & naked angel came to pierce them with a sword,

who lost their loveboys to the three old shrews of fate the one eyed shrew of the heterosexual dollar the one eyed shrew that winks out of the womb and the one eyed shrew that does nothing but sit on her ass and snip the intellectual golden threads of the craftsman's loom,   40

who copulated ecstatic and insatiate with a bottle of beer a sweetheart a package of cigarettes a candle and fell off the bed, and continued along the floor and down the hall and ended fainting on the wall with a vision of ultimate cunt and come eluding the last gyzym of consciousness,

who sweetened the snatches of a million girls trembling in the sunset, and were red eyed in the morning but prepared to sweeten the snatch of the sunrise, flashing buttocks under barns and naked in the lake,

who went out whoring through Colorado in myriad stolen nightcars, N.C.,[1] secret hero of these poems, cocksman and Adonis of Denver—joy to the memory of his innumerable lays of girls in empty lots & diner backyards, moviehouses' rickety rows, on mountaintops in caves or with gaunt waitresses in familiar roadside lonely petticoat upliftings & especially secret gasstation solipsisms[2] of johns, & hometown alleys too,

who faded out in vast sordid movies, were shifted in dreams, woke on a sudden Manhattan, and picked themselves up out of basements hungover with heartless Tokay and horrors of Third Avenue iron dreams & stumbled to unemployment offices,

who walked all night with their shoes full of blood on the snowbank

---

8. In New Mexico, a center for the development of the atomic bomb.
9. Wall Street, but also alludes to the Wailing Wall, a place of public lamentation in Jerusalem.
1. Neal Cassady, "hip" companion of Jack Kerouac and the original Dean Moriarty, one of the leading figures in *On the Road*.
2. A solipsism is the philosophical notion that all truth is subjective.

docks waiting for a door in the East River to open to a room full of steamheat and opium, 45

who created great suicidal dramas on the apartment cliff-banks of the Hudson[3] under the wartime blue floodlight of the moon & their heads shall be crowned with laurel in oblivion,

who ate the lamb stew of the imagination or digested the crab at the muddy bottom of the rivers of Bowery,[4]

who wept at the romance of the streets with their pushcarts full of onions and bad music,

who sat in boxes breathing in the darkness under the bridge, and rose up to build harpsichords in their lofts,

who coughed on the sixth floor of Harlem crowned with flame under the tubercular sky surrounded by orange crates of theology, 50

who scribbled all night rocking and rolling over lofty incantations which in the yellow morning were stanzas of gibberish,

who cooked rotten animals lung heart feet tail borsht & tortillas dreaming of the pure vegetable kingdom,

who plunged themselves under meat trucks looking for an egg,

who threw their watches off the roof to cast their ballot for Eternity outside of Time, & alarm clocks fell on their heads every day for the next decade,

who cut their wrists three times successively unsuccessfully, gave up and were forced to open antique stores where they thought they were growing old and cried, 55

who were burned alive in their innocent flannel suits on Madison Avenue[5] amid blasts of leaden verse & the tanked-up clatter of the iron regiments of fashion & the nitroglycerine shrieks of the fairies of advertising & the mustard gas of sinister intelligent editors, or were run down by the drunken taxicabs of Absolute Reality,

who jumped off the Brooklyn Bridge this actually happened and walked away unknown and forgotten into the ghostly daze of Chinatown soup alleyways & firetrucks, not even one free beer,

who sang out of their windows in despair, fell out of the subway window, jumped in the filthy Passaic,[6] leaped on negroes, cried all over the street, danced on broken wineglasses barefoot smashed phonograph records of nostalgic European 1930's German jazz finished the whiskey and threw up groaning into the bloody toilet, moans in their ears and the blast of colossal steamwhistles,

who barreled down the highways of the past journeying to each other's hotrod-Golgotha[7] jail-solitude watch or Birmingham jazz incarnation,

who drove crosscountry seventytwo hours to find out if I had a vision or you had a vision or he had a vision to find out Eternity, 60

3. The steep apartment-lined embankments of the Hudson River along Riverside Drive in New York City.
4. Southern extension of Third Avenue in New York City; traditional haunt of derelicts and alcoholics.
5. Center of New York advertising agencies, and of the stereotype "Man in the Gray Flannel Suit."
6. River flowing past Paterson, New Jersey.
7. Site of Christ's crucifixion.

who journeyed to Denver, who died in Denver, who came back to
Denver & waited in vain, who watched over Denver & brooded
& loned in Denver and finally went away to find out the
Time, & now Denver is lonesome for her heroes,

who fell on their knees in hopeless cathedrals praying for each
other's salvation and light and breasts, until the soul illumi-
ated its hair for a second,

who crashed through their minds in jail waiting for impossible criminals with golden heads and the charm of reality in their
hearts who sang sweet blues to Alcatraz,

who retired to Mexico to cultivate a habit, or Rocky Mount to
tender Buddha or Tangiers[8] to boys or Southern Pacific to the
black locomotive or Harvard to Narcissus to Woodlawn[9] to the
daisychain or grave,

who demanded sanity trials accusing the radio of hypnotism &
were left with their insanity & their hands & a hung jury,   65

who threw potato salad at CCNY lecturers[1] on Dadaism[2] and
subsequently presented themselves on the granite steps of the
madhouse with shaven heads and harlequin speech of suicide,
demanding instantaneous lobotomy,

and who were given instead the concrete void of insulin metrasol
electricity hydrotherapy psychotherapy occupational therapy
pingpong & amnesia,

who in humorless protest overturned only one symbolic pingpong
table, resting briefly in catatonia,

returning years later truly bald except for a wig of blood, and tears
and fingers, to the visible madman doom of the wards of the
madtowns of the East,

Pilgrim State's Rockland's and Greystone's[3] foetid halls, bickering
with the echoes of the soul, rocking and rolling in the midnight solitude-bench dolmen-realms of love, dream of life a
nightmare, bodies turned to stone as heavy as the moon,   70

with mother finally ******, and the last fantastic book flung out of
the tenement window, and the last door closed at 4 AM and
the last telephone slammed at the wall in reply and the last
furnished room emptied down to the last piece of mental
furniture, a yellow paper rose twisted on a wire hanger in the
closet, and even that imaginary, nothing but a hopeful little
bit of hallucination—

ah, Carl,[4] while you are not safe I am not safe, and now you're
really in the total animal soup of time—

---

8. William Burroughs (b. 1914), homosexual author, drug addict, and Ginsberg's fellow Beat, lived in Mexico and
Tangier, Morocco; Kerouac lived for a
while in Rocky Mount, North Carolina;
Neal Cassady worked for the Southern
Pacific Railroad.
9. A cemetery in the Bronx; Narcissus,
in Greek mythology, fell in love with his
own reflection in a pool.
1. This and the following incidents probably derived from the "apocryphal history of my adventures" related by Solo-

mon to Ginsberg.
2. Artistic cult of absurdity (c. 1916–
20); "CCNY": City College of New
York.
3. Three mental hospitals near New
York. Solomon was institutionalized at
Pilgrim State and Rockland; Ginsberg's
mother, Naomi, was permanently institutionalized at Greystone after years of
suffering hallucinations and paranoid attacks. She died there in 1956, the year
after *Howl* was written.
4. Solomon.

and who therefore ran through the icy streets obsessed with a sudden
flash of the alchemy of the use of the ellipse the catalog the
meter & the vibrating plane,
who dreamt and made incarnate gaps in Time & Space through
images juxtaposed, and trapped the archangel of the soul between 2 visual images and joined the elemental verbs and set
the noun and dash of consciousness together jumping with
sensation of Pater Omnipotens Aeterna Deus[5]
to recreate the syntax and measure of poor human prose and stand
before you speechless and intelligent and shaking with shame,
rejected yet confessing out the soul to conform to the rhythm
of thought in his naked and endless head,   75
the madman bum and angel beat in Time, unknown, yet putting
down here what might be left to say in time come after death,
and rose reincarnate in the ghostly clothes of jazz in the goldhorn
shadow of the band and blew the suffering of America's
naked mind for love into an eli eli lamma lamma sabacthani[6]
saxophone cry that shivered the cities down to the last radio
with the absolute heart of the poem of life butchered out of their
own bodies good to eat a thousand years.

                                                         1956

A Supermarket in California

What thoughts I have of you tonight, Walt Whitman,[1] for I
walked down the sidestreets under the trees with a headache self-
conscious looking at the full moon.

In my hungry fatigue, and shopping for images, I went into the
neon fruit supermarket, dreaming of your enumerations!

What peaches and what penumbras![2] Whole families shopping at
night! Aisles full of husbands! Wives in the avocados, babies in the
tomatoes!—and you, Garcia Lorca,[3] what were you doing down by
the watermelons?

I saw you, Walt Whitman, childless, lonely old grubber, poking
among the meats in the refrigerator and eyeing the grocery boys.

I heard you asking questions of each: Who killed the pork
chops? What price bananas? Are you my Angel?   5

I wandered in and out of the brilliant stacks of cans following
you, and followed in my imagination by the store detective.

We strode down the open corridors together in our solitary

5. "All Powerful Father, Eternal God."
An allusion to a phrase used by the
French painter Paul Cézanne (1839–
1906), in a letter describing the effects of
nature (1904). Ginsberg, in an interview, compared his own method of
sharply juxtaposed images to Cézanne's
foreshortening of perspective in landscape
painting.
6. Christ's last words on the Cross: "My
God, my God, why have you forsaken

me?"
1. American poet (1819–92), author of
Leaves of Grass, against whose homosexuality and vision of American plenty
Ginsberg measures himself.
2. Partial shadows.
3. Spanish poet and dramatist (1899–
1936), author of *A Poet in New York*,
whose work is characterized by surrealist and homoerotic inspiration.

fancy tasting artichokes, possessing every frozen delicacy, and never
passing the cashier.

Where are we going, Walt Whitman? The doors close in an
hour. Which way does your beard point tonight?
    (I touch your book and dream of our odyssey in the supermarket
and feel absurd.)
    Will we walk all night through solitary streets? The trees add
shade to shade, lights out in the houses, we'll both be lonely.   10

Will we stroll dreaming of the lost America of love past blue
automobiles in driveways, home to our silent cottage?
    Ah, dear father, graybeard, lonely old courage-teacher, what
America did you have when Charon quit poling his ferry and you
got out on a smoking bank and stood watching the boat disappear on
the black waters of Lethe?[4]
Berkeley 1955   1956

Sunflower Sutra[1]

I walked on the banks of the tincan banana dock and sat down
    under the huge shade of a Southern Pacific locomotive to look
    at the sunset over the box house hills and cry.
Jack Kerouac[2] sat beside me on a busted rusty iron pole, companion,
    we thought the same thoughts of the soul, bleak and blue
    and sad-eyed, surrounded by the gnarled steel roots of trees of
    machinery.
The oily water on the river mirrored the red sky, sun sank on top of
    final Frisco peaks, no fish in that stream, no hermit in those
    mounts, just ourselves rheumy-eyed and hungover like old
    bums on the riverbank, tired and wily.
Look at the Sunflower, he said, there was a dead gray shadow
    against the sky, big as a man, sitting dry on top of a pile of
    ancient sawdust—
—I rushed up enchanted—it was my first sunflower, memories of
    Blake[3]—my visions—Harlem   5
and Hells of the Eastern rivers, bridges clanking Joes Greasy Sand-
    wiches, dead baby carriages, black treadless tires forgotten and
    unretreaded, the poem of the riverbank, condoms & pots, steel
    knives, nothing stainless, only the dank muck and the razor
    sharp artifacts passing into the past—
and the gray Sunflower poised against the sunset, crackly bleak and
    dusty with the smut and smog and smoke of olden locomotives
    in its eye—

---

4. Forgetfulness. In Greek mythology,
one of the rivers of Hades; Charon was
the boatman who ferried the dead to
Hell.
1. Sanskrit for "thread"; the word refers to Brahmin or Buddhist religious
texts of ritual instruction.

2. Fellow Beat (1922–69), author of *On
the Road* (1957).
3. In Harlem in 1948, Ginsberg had had
a hallucinatory revelation in which he
heard the English poet William Blake
(1757–1827) reciting his poem *Ah! Sunflower*.

corolla[4] of bleary spikes pushed down and broken like a battered
crown, seeds fallen out of its face, soon-to-be-toothless mouth
of sunny air, sunrays obliterated on its hairy head like a dried
wire spiderweb,

leaves stuck out like arms out of the stem, gestures from the sawdust
root, broke pieces of plaster fallen out of the black twigs, a
dead fly in its ear,

Unholy battered old thing you were, my sunflower O my soul, I
loved you then!   10

The grime was no man's grime but death and human locomotives,

all that dress of dust, that veil of darkened railroad skin, that smog
of cheek, that eyelid of black mis'ry, that sooty hand or
phallus or protuberance of artificial worse-than-dirt—industrial
—modern—all that civilization spotting your crazy golden
crown—

and those blear thoughts of death and dusty loveless eyes and ends
and withered roots below, in the home-pile of sand and sawdust, rubber dollar bills, skin of machinery, the guts and
innards of the weeping coughing car, the empty lonely tincans
with their rusty tongues alack, what more could I name, the
smoked ashes of some cock cigar, the cunts of wheelbarrows and
the milky breasts of cars, wornout asses out of chairs &
sphincters of dynamos—all these

entangled in your mummied roots—and you there standing before
me in the sunset, all your glory in your form!

A perfect beauty of a sunflower! a perfect excellent lovely sunflower existence! a sweet natural eye to the new hip moon, woke
up alive and excited grasping in the sunset shadow sunrise
golden monthly breeze!   15

How many flies buzzed round you innocent of your grime, while
you cursed the heavens of the railroad and your flower soul?

Poor dead flower? when did you forget you were a flower? when did
you look at your skin and decide you were an impotent dirty
old locomotive? the ghost of a locomotive? the specter and
shade of a once powerful mad American locomotive?

You were never no locomotive, Sunflower, you were a sunflower!

And you Locomotive, you are a locomotive, forget me not!

So I grabbed up the skeleton thick sunflower and stuck it at my
side like a scepter,   20

and deliver my sermon to my soul, and Jack's soul too, and anyone
who'll listen,

—We're not our skin of grime, we're not our dread bleak dusty
imageless locomotive, we're all beautiful golden sunflowers
inside, we're blessed by our own seed & golden hairy naked
accomplishment-bodies growing into mad black formal sunflowers in the sunset, spied on by our eyes under the shadow
of the mad locomotive riverbank sunset Frisco hilly tincan
evening sitdown vision.

Berkeley 1955   1956

---

4. Petals forming the inner envelope of a flower.

Kaddish[1]

FOR NAOMI GINSBERG 1894–1956

I

Strange now to think of you, gone without corsets & eyes, while I
    walk on the sunny pavement of Greenwich Village.
downtown Manhattan, clear winter noon, and I've been up all
    night, talking, talking, reading the Kaddish aloud, listening to
    Ray Charles[2] blues shout blind on the phonograph
the rhythm the rhythm—and your memory in my head three years
    after—And read Adonais'[3] last triumphant stanzas aloud—
    wept, realizing how we suffer—
And how Death is that remedy all singers dream of, sing, remem-
    ber, prophesy as in the Hebrew Anthem, or the Buddhist
    Book of Answers—and my own imagination of a withered leaf
    at dawn—
Dreaming back thru life, Your time—and mine accelerating toward
    Apocalypse,   5
the final moment—the flower burning in the Day—and what comes
    after,
looking back on the mind itself that saw an American city
a flash away, and the great dream of Me or China, or you and a
    phantom Russia, or a crumpled bed that never existed—
like a poem in the dark—escaped back to Oblivion—
No more to say, and nothing to weep for but the Beings in the
    Dream, trapped in its disappearance,   10
sighing, screaming with it, buying and selling pieces of phantom,
    worshipping each other,
worshipping the God included in it all—longing or inevitability?—
    while it lasts, a Vision—anything more?
It leaps about me, as I go out and walk the street, look back over
    my shoulder, Seventh Avenue, the battlements of window
    office buildings shouldering each other high, under a cloud,
    tall as the sky an instant—and the sky above—an old blue
    place.
or down the Avenue to the South, to—as I walk toward the Lower
    East Side—where you walked 50 years ago, little girl[4]—from
    Russia, eating the first poisonous tomatoes of America—
    frightened on the dock—
then struggling in the crowds of Orchard Street toward what?—
    toward Newark—   15

1. In Judaism, a prayer, usually recited by mourners, as part of the daily religious service. The term comes from the Hebrew word for "holy." Naomi Ginsberg had suffered hallucinations since the time her son was young. She was separated from her husband, the poet Louis Ginsberg, was hospitalized several times, and finally died in Greystone Hospital, to which she had been committed in the late 1940s.
2. A blind blues singer (b. 1932).

3. An elegy written by the English Romantic poet Percy Bysshe Shelley (1792–1822) for his recently dead friend, the poet John Keats (1795–1821).
4. Before moving to Newark, an industrial town in northern New Jersey, Naomi lived on the Lower East Side of Manhattan (Orchard Street was its business center), as did many Jewish immigrants from Eastern Europe in the early 1900s.

toward candy store, first home-made sodas of the century, hand-
    churned ice cream in backroom on musty brownfloor boards—
Toward education marriage nervous breakdown, operation, teaching
    school, and learning to be mad, in a dream—what is this life?
Toward the Key in the window—and the great Key lays its head
    of light on top of Manhattan, and over the floor, and lays down
    on the sidewalk—in a single vast beam, moving, as I walk
    down First[5] toward the Yiddish Theater—and the place of
    poverty
you knew, and I know, but without caring now—Strange to have
    moved thru Paterson, and the West, and Europe and here
    again,[6]
with the cries of Spaniards now in the doorstoops doors and dark
    boys on the street, fire escapes old as you   20
—Tho you're not old now, that's left here with me—
Myself, anyhow, maybe as old as the universe—and I guess that
    dies with us—enough to cancel all that comes—What came is gone
    forever every time—
That's good! That leaves it open for no regret—no fear radiators,
    lacklove, torture even toothache in the end—
Though while it comes it is a lion that eats the soul—and the lamb,
    the soul, in us, alas offering itself in sacrifice to change's
    fierce hunger—hair and teeth—and the roar of bonepain, skull
    bare, break rib, rot-skin, braintricked Implacability.
Ai! ai! we do worse! We are in a fix! And you're out, Death let you
    out, Death had the Mercy, you're done with your century,
    done with God, done with the path thru it—Done with your-
    self at last—Pure—Back to the Babe dark before your Father,
    before us all—before the world—   25
There, rest. No more suffering for you. I know where you've
    gone, it's good.
No more flowers in the summer fields of New York, no joy now,
    no more fear of Louis,
and no more of his sweetness and glasses, his high school decades,
    debts, loves, frightened telephone calls, conception beds, rela-
    tives, hands—
No more of sister Elanor,—she gone before you—we kept it secret
    —you killed her—or she killed herself to bear with you—an
    arthritic heart—But Death's killed you both—No matter—
Nor your memory of your mother, 1915 tears in silent movies
    weeks and weeks—forgetting, agrieve watching Marie Dressler
    address humanity, Chaplin dance in youth,[7]   30
or Boris Godinov, Chaliapin's at the Met,[8] halling his voice of a

---

5. First Avenue. There were a number of
theaters on the Lower East Side which
performed in Yiddish (a combination of
Hebrew and Low German), the vernacular language of the Eastern European
Jewish immigrants.
6. The poet grew up in Paterson, New
Jersey. He became popular as a poet
with *Howl*, which he first read in San
Francisco; his fame as a poet led to a
European tour.

7. Charles Spencer Chaplin (1889–1977)
and Marie Dressler (1869–1934), silent-
film stars.
8. Feodor Chaliapin (1873–1938), Russian bass who sang at the Metropolitan
Opera in New York, famous for his role
in the Russian opera *Boris Godunov* by
Modest Mussorgsky (1839–81). "halling": "voicing through the hall" [Gins-
berg's note, letter of June 16, 1978].

weeping Czar—by standing room with Elanor & Max[9]—watching also the Capitalists take seats in Orchestra, white furs, diamonds,

with the YPSL's[1] hitch-hiking thru Pennsylvania, in black baggy gym skirts pants, photograph of 4 girls holding each other round the waste,[2] and laughing eye, too coy, virginal solitude of 1920

all girls grown old, or dead, now, and that long hair in the grave—lucky to have husbands later—

You made it—I came too—Eugene my brother before (still grieving now and will gream[3] on to his last stiff hand, as he goes thru his cancer—or kill—later perhaps—soon he will think—)

And it's the last moment I remember, which I see them all, thru myself, now—tho not you   35

I didn't foresee what you felt—what more hideous gape of bad mouth came first—to you—and were you prepared?

To go where? In that Dark—that—in that God? a radiance? A Lord in the Void? Like an eye in the black cloud in a dream? Adonoi[4] at last, with you?

Beyond my remembrance! Incapable to guess! Not merely the yellow skull in the grave, or a box of worm dust, and a stained ribbon—Deathshead with Halo? can you believe it?

Is it only the sun that shines once for the mind, only the flash of existence, than none ever was?

Nothing beyond what we have—what you had—that so pitiful—yet Triumph,   40

to have been here, and changed, like a tree, broken, or flower—fed to the ground—but mad, with its petals, colored, thinking Great Universe, shaken, cut in the head, leaf stript, hid in an egg crate hospital, cloth wrapped, sore—freaked in the moon brain, Naughtless.

No flower like that flower, which knew itself in the garden, and fought the knife—lost

Cut down by an idiot Snowman's icy—even in the Spring—strange ghost thought—some Death—Sharp icicle in his hand—crowned with old roses—a dog for his eyes—cock of a sweatshop—heart of electric irons.

All the accumulations of life, that wear us out—clocks, bodies, consciousness, shoe, breasts—begotten sons—your Communism—'Paranoia' into hospitals.

You once kicked Elanor in the leg, she died of heart failure later. You of stroke. Asleep? within a year, the two of you, sisters in death. Is Elanor happy?   45

Max grieves alive in an office on Lower Broadway, lone large mustache over midnight Accountings, not sure. His life passes—as he sees—and what does he doubt now? Still dream of making money, or that might have made money, hired nurse, had children, found even your Immortality, Naomi?

---

9. Husband of Naomi's sister, Elanor.
1. Young People's Socialist League.
2. A pun on *waste* and *waist* (death and age) [Ginsberg's note].

.3. "Grieve + dream = gream" [Ginsberg's note].
4. Hebrew designation for God (means "Lord").

I'll see him soon. Now I've got to cut through—to talk to you—
as I didn't when you had a mouth.
Forever. And we're bound for that, Forever—like Emily Dickinson's horses[5]—headed to the End.
They know the way—These Steeds—run faster than we think—it's
our own life they cross—and take with them.

Magnificènt, mourned no more, marred of heart, mind behind,
married dreamed, mortal changed—Ass and face done with murder.   50
In the world, given, flower maddened, made no Utopia, shut
under pine, almed in Earth, balmed in Lone, Jehovah, accept.
Nameless, One Faced, Forever beyond me, beginningless, endless, Father in death. Tho I am not there for this Prophecy, I am
unmarried, I'm hymnless, I'm Heavenless, headless in blisshood I
would still adore
Thee, Heaven, after Death, only One blessed in Nothingness, not
light or darkness, Dayless Eternity—
Take this, this Psalm, from me, burst from my hand in a day,
some of my Time, now given to Nothing—to praise Thee—But
Death
This is the end, the redemption from Wilderness, way for the
Wonderer, House sought for All, black handkerchief washed clean
by weeping—page beyond Psalm—Last change of mine and Naomi
—to God's perfect Darkness—Death, stay thy phantoms!   55

II

Over and over—refrain—of the Hospitals—still haven't written
your history—leave it abstract—a few images
run thru the mind—like the saxophone chorus of houses and
years—remembrance of electrical shocks,[6]
By long nites as a child in Paterson apartment, watching over
your nervousness—you were fat—your next move—
By that afternoon I stayed home from school to take care of
you—once and for all—when I vowed forever that once man disagreed with my opinion of the cosmos, I was lost—
By my later burden—vow to illuminate mankind—this is release
of particulars—(mad as you)—(sanity a trick of agreement)—   5
But you stared out the window on the Broadway Church corner, and spied a mystical assassin from Newark,
So phoned the Doctor—'OK go way for a rest'—so I put on my
coat and walked you downstreet—On the way a grammarschool
boy screamed, unaccountably—'Where you goin Lady to Death'?
I shuddered—
and you covered your nose with motheaten fur collar, gas mask
against poison sneaked into downtown atmosphere, sprayed by
Grandma—

5. American poet (1830–86), whose
poem *Because I could not stop for
Death* speaks of the carriage of Death
whose "Horses' Heads/Were toward
Eternity." (*The Poems of Emily Dickinson*, ed. Thomas Johnson, Poem 712.)
6. I.e., electric shock treatments for paranoia undergone by Naomi.

And was the driver of the cheesebox Public Service bus a member of the gang? You shuddered at his face, I could hardly get you on—to New York, very Times Square, to grab another Greyhound—

where we hung around 2 hours fighting invisible bugs and jewish sickness—breeze poisoned by Roosevelt—   10

out to get you—and me tagging along, hoping it would end in a quiet room in a victorian house by a lake.

Ride 3 hours thru tunnels past all American industry, Bayonne preparing for World War II, tanks, gas fields, soda factories, diners, locomotive roundhouse fortress—into piney woods New Jersey Indians—calm towns—long roads thru sandy tree fields—

Bridges by deerless creeks, old wampum loading the streambed— down there a tomahawk or Pocahantas[7] bone—and a million old ladies voting for Roosevelt in brown small houses, roads off the Madness highway—

perhaps a hawk in a tree, or a hermit looking for an owl-filled branch—

All the time arguing—afraid of strangers in the forward double seat, snoring regardless—what busride they snore on now?   15

'Allen, you don't understand—it's—ever since those 3 big sticks up my back—they did something to me in Hospital, they poisoned me, they want to see me dead—3 big sticks, 3 big sticks—

'The Bitch! Old Grandma! Last week I saw her, dressed in pants like an old man, with a sack on her back, climbing up the brick side of the apartment

'On the fire escape, with poison germs, to throw on me—at night—maybe Louis is helping her—he's under her power—

'I'm your mother, take me to Lakewood' (near where Graf Zeppelin had crashed before, all Hitler in Explosion)[8] 'where I can hide.'

We got there—Dr. Whatzis rest home—she hid behind a closet —demanded a blood transfusion.   20

We were kicked out—tramping with Valise to unknown shady lawn houses—dusk, pine trees after dark—long dead street filled with crickets and poison ivy—

I shut her up by now—big house REST HOME ROOMS— gave the landlady her money for the week—carried up the iron valise—sat on bed waiting to escape—

Neat room in attic with friendly bedcover—lace curtains— spinning wheel rug—Stained wallpaper old as Naomi. We were home.

I left on the next bus to New York—lay my head back in the last seat, depressed—the worst yet to come?—abandoning her, rode in torpor—I was only 12.

Would she hide in her room and come out cheerful for breakfast? Or lock her door and stare thru the window for side-

---

7. Indian princess who saved the life of Captain John Smith, one of the early English settlers of Virginia.
8. Probably a loose reference to the explosion of the passenger airship zeppelin

Hindenburg at Lakeville, New Jersey, in 1936. Many of Naomi's paranoid fantasies centered on Hitler and were rooted in his persecution of the Jews.

street spies? Listen at keyholes for Hitlerian invisible gas? Dream
in a chair—or mock me, by—in front of a mirror, alone?   25
    12 riding the bus at nite thru New Jersey, have left Naomi to
Parcae[9] in Lakewood's haunted house—left to my own fate bus—
sunk in a seat—all violins broken—my heart sore in my ribs—
mind was empty—Would she were safe in her coffin—
    Or back at Normal School in Newark, studying up on America in
a black skirt—winter on the street without lunch—a penny a
pickle—home at night to take care of Elanor in the bedroom—
    First nervous breakdown was 1919—she stayed home from
school and lay in a dark room for three weeks—something bad—
never said what—every noise hurt—dreams of the creaks of Wall
Street—
    Before the grey Depression[1]—went upstate New York—recov-
ered—Lou took photo of her sitting crossleg on the grass—her long
hair wound with flowers—smiling—playing lullabies on mandoline
—poison ivy smoke in left-wing summer camps and me in infancy
saw trees—
    or back teaching school, laughing with idiots, the backward
classes—her Russian speciality—morons with dreamy lips, great
eyes, thin feet & sicky fingers, swaybacked, rachitic[2]—   30
    great heads pendulous over Alice in Wonderland, a blackboard
full of C A T.
    Naomi reading patiently, story out of a Communist fairy book—
Tale of the Sudden Sweetness of The Dictator—Forgiveness of
Warlocks—Armies Kissing—
    Deathsheads Around the Green Table—The King & the Workers
—Paterson Press printed them up in the 30's till she went mad,
or they folded, both.
    O Paterson! I got home late that nite. Louis was worried. How
could I be so—didn't I think? I shouldn't have left her. Mad in
Lakewood. Call the Doctor. Phone the home in the pines. Too
late.
    Went to bed exhausted, wanting to leave the world (probably
that year newly in love with R——my high school mind hero, jewish boy who came a doctor later—then silent neat kid—   35
    I later laying down life for him, moved to Manhattan—followed
him to college—Prayed on ferry to help mankind if admitted—
vowed, the day I journeyed to Entrance Exam—
    by being honest revolutionary labor lawyer—would train for that
—inspired by Sacco Vanzetti, Norman Thomas, Debs, Altgeld,
Sandburg, Poe—Little Blue Books.[3] I wanted to be President, or
Senator.

---

9. Latin: the (three) Fates, who control human destiny.
1. The economic depression of the 1930s.
2. With rickets, a spinal deformity.
3. Socialist pamphlets; Ginsberg has
listed his literary and political heroes:
Nicola Sacco (1891–1927) and Bartolo-
meo Vanzetti (1887–1927), immigrant
anarchists involved in a controversial
murder trial, whose conviction and execution were considered to be politically

motivated as a punishment for their leftist activities; Norman Thomas (1884–
1968), head of the U.S. Socialist party;
Eugene V. Debs (1855–1926), labor
leader and Socialist candidate for President; John Altgeld (1847–1902), Governor of Illinois, known for his progressive
views; Carl Sandburg (1878–1967) and
Edgar Allan Poe (1809–49), American
poets.

ignorant woe—later dreams of kneeling by R's shocked knees declaring my love of 1941—What sweetness he'd have shown me, tho, that I'd wished him & despaired—first love—a crush—

Later a mortal avalanche, whole mountains of homosexuality, Matterhorns of cock, Grand Canyons of asshole—weight on my melancholy head—

meanwhile I walked on Broadway imagining Infinity like a rubber ball without space beyond—what's outside?—coming home to Graham Avenue still melancholy passing the lone green hedges across the street, dreaming after the movies—)   40

The telephone rang at 2AM—Emergency—she'd gone mad—Naomi hiding under the bed screaming bugs of Mussolini[2]—Help! Louis! Buba! Fascists! Death!—the landlady frightened—old fag attendant screaming back at her—

Terror, that woke the neighbors—old ladies on the second floor recovering from menopause—all those rags between thighs, clean sheets, sorry over lost babies—husbands ashen—children sneering at Yale, or putting oil in hair at CCNY—or trembling in Montclair State Teachers College like Eugene—

Her big leg crouched to her breast, hand outstretched Keep Away, wool dress on her thighs, fur coat dragged under the bed—she barricaded herself under bedspring with suitcases.

Louis in pyjamas listening to phone, frightened—do now?—Who could know?—my fault, delivering her to solitude?—sitting in the dark room on the sofa, trembling, to figure out—

He took the morning train to Lakewood, Naomi still under bed—thought he brought poison Cops—Naomi screaming—Louis what happened to your heart then? Have you been killed by Naomi's ecstasy?   45

Dragged her out, around the corner, a cab, forced her in with valise, but the driver left them off at drugstore. Bus stop, two hours' wait.

I lay in bed nervous in the 4-room apartment, the big bed in living room, next to Louis' desk—shaking—he came home that nite, late, told me what happened.

Naomi at the prescription counter defending herself from the enemy—racks of children's books, douche bags, aspirins, pots, blood—'Don't come near me—murderers! Keep away! Promise not to kill me!'

Louis in horror at the soda fountain—with Lakewood girlscouts—coke addicts—nurses—busmen hung on schedule—Police from country precinct, dumbed—and a priest dreaming of pigs on an ancient cliff?

Smelling the air—Louis pointing to emptiness?—Customers vomiting their cokes—or staring—Louis humiliated—Naomi triumphant—The Announcement of the Plot. Bus arrives, the drivers won't have them on trip to New York.   50

Phonecalls to Dr. Whatzis, 'She needs a rest,' The mental hospital—State Greystone Doctors—'Bring her here, Mr. Ginsberg.'

Naomi, Naomi—sweating, bulge-eyed, fat, the dress unbuttoned

---

4. "Mussolini": Fascist dictator of Italy, 1922–43; "Buba": Naomi's mother.

at one side—hair over brow, her stocking hanging evilly on her legs
—screaming for a blood transfusion—one righteous hand
upraised—a shoe in it—barefoot in the Pharmacy—
The enemies approach—what poisons? Tape recorders? FBI?
Zhdanov hiding behind the counter? Trotsky mixing rat bacteria in
the back of the store?[5] Uncle Sam in Newark, plotting deathly
perfumes in the Negro district? Uncle Ephraim, drunk with murder
in the politician's bar, scheming of Hague? Aunt Rose passing water
thru the needles of the Spanish Civil War?
till the hired $35 ambulance came from Red Bank——Grabbed
her arms—strapped her on the stretcher—moaning, poisoned by
imaginaries, vomiting chemicals thru Jersey, begging mercy from
Essex County to Morristown—
And back to Greystone where she lay three years—that was the
last breakthrough, delivered her to Madhouse again——   55
On what wards—I walked there later, oft—old catatonic ladies,
grey as cloud or ash or walls—sit crooning over floorspace—Chairs
—and the wrinkled hags acreep, accusing—begging my 13-year-old
mercy—
'Take me home'—I went alone sometimes looking for the lost
Naomi, taking Shock—and I'd say, 'No, you're crazy Mama,—
Trust the Drs.'—

And Eugene, my brother, her elder son, away studying Law in a
furnished room in Newark—
came Paterson-ward next day—and he sat on the broken-down
couch in the living room—'We had to send her back to Greystone'—
—his face perplexed, so young, then eyes with tears—then crept
weeping all over his face—'What for?' wail vibrating in his cheek-
bones, eyes closed up, high voice—Eugene's face of pain.   60
Him faraway, escaped to an Elevator in the Newark Library, his
bottle daily milk on windowsill of $5 week furn room downtown
at trolley tracks—
He worked 8 hrs. a day for $20/wk—thru Law School years—
stayed by himself innocent near negro whorehouses.
Unlaid, poor virgin—writing poems about Ideals and politics
letters to the editor Pat Eve News—(we both wrote, denouncing
Senator Borah and Isolationists[6]—and felt mysterious toward
Paterson City Hall—
I sneaked inside it once—local Moloch[7] tower with phallus spire
& cap o' ornament, strange gothic Poetry that stood on Market
Street—replica Lyons' Hotel de Ville[8]—

5. A. A. Zhdanov (1896–1948), Soviet
political leader and General; Leon Trotsky (1879–1940), a leader of the Russian
(Bolshevist) Revolution in 1917 who subsequently fled to America and was murdered in Mexico.
6. William Edgar Borah (1865–1940),
U.S. Senator from Idaho, a leader of
the isolationist group opposed to U.S.
intervention in the defense of Western

Europe in the period preceding World
War II.
7. In the Bible, a god of the Phoenicians
to whom children were sacrificed. Ginsberg often uses him as a symbol of the
capitalist god mercilessly consuming its
children.
8. Town hall of Lyons, France (like Paterson, a silk manufacturing center).

wings, balcony & scrollwork portals, gateway to the giant city clock, secret map room full of Hawthorne—dark Debs in the Board of Tax—Rembrandt smoking in the gloom[9]—   65

Silent polished desks in the great committee room—Aldermen? Bd of Finance? Mosca the hairdresser aplot—Crapp the gangster issuing orders from the john—The madmen struggling over Zone, Fire, Cops & Backroom Metaphysics—we're all dead—outside by the bus-stop Eugene stared thru childhood—

where the Evangelist preached madly for 3 decades, hard-haired, cracked & true to his mean Bible—chalked Prepare to Meet Thy God on civic pave—

or God is Love on the railroad overpass concrete—he raved like I would rave, the lone Evangelist—Death on City Hall—)

But Gene, young,—been Montclair Teachers College 4 years— taught half year & quit to go ahead in life—afraid of Discipline Problems—dark sex Italian students, raw girls getting laid, no English, sonnets disregarded—and he did not know much—just that he lost—

so broke his life in two and paid for Law—read huge blue books and rode the ancient elevator 13 miles away in Newark & studied up hard for the future   70

just found the Scream of Naomi on his failure doorstep, for the final time, Naomi gone, us lonely—home—him sitting there—

Then have some chicken soup, Eugene. The Man of Evangel wails in front of City Hall. And this year Lou has poetic loves of suburb middle-age—in secret—music from his 1937 book[1]—Sincere —he longs for beauty—

No love since Naomi screamed—since 1923?—now lost in Grey-stone[2] ward—new shock for her—Electricity, following the 40 Insulin.

And Metrasol had made her fat.

So that a few years later she came home again—we'd much advanced and planned—I waited for that day—my Mother again to cook &—play the piano—sing at mandoline—Lung Stew, & Stenka Razin,[3] & the communist line on the war with Finland—and Louis in debt—suspected to be poisoned money—mysterious capitalisms   75

—& walked down the long front hall & looked at the furniture. She never remembered it all. Some amnesia. Examined the doilies —and the dining room set was sold—

the Mahogany table—20 years love—gone to the junk man—we still had the piano—and the book of Poe—and the Mandolin, tho needed some string, dusty—

---

9. Ginsberg's youthful fantasies about the mysterious interiors of the Paterson City Hall include Eugene Debs, Nathaniel Hawthorne (1804–64), and the Dutch painter Rembrandt (1606–69).
1. In 1937 Louis Ginsberg published a book of poems, *The Everlasting Minute*.
2. A mental hospital. Insulin and metrasol are drugs used, sometimes along with electric shock, in shock treatment for psychoses.
3. A Russian folk hero, about whom many stories were told. "Lung stew": since an animal's innards were considered unfit to eat according to Jewish dietary rules, this was a very inexpensive dish.

She went to the backroom to lay down in bed and ruminate, or
nap, hide—I went in with her, not leave her by herself—lay in bed
next to her—shades pulled, dusky, late afternoon—Louis in front
room at desk, waiting—perhaps boiling chicken for supper—
    'Don't be afraid of me because I'm just coming back home
from the mental hospital—I'm your mother—'
    Poor love, lost—a fear—I lay there—Said, 'I love you Naomi,'—
stiff, next to her arm. I would have cried, was this the comfortless
lone union?—Nervous, and she got up soon.   80
    Was she ever satisfied? And—by herself sat on the new couch by
the front windows, uneasy—cheek leaning on her hand—narrowing
eye—at what fate that day—
    Picking her tooth with her nail, lips formed an O, suspicion—
thought's old worn vagina—absent sideglance of eye—some evil
debt written in the wall, unpaid—& the aged breasts of Newark
come near—
    May have heard radio gossip thru the wires in her head, con-
trolled by 3 big sticks left in her back by gangsters in amnesia, thru
the hospital—caused pain between her shoulders—
    Into her head—Roosevelt should know her case, she told me—
Afraid to kill her, now, that the government knew their names—
traced back to Hitler—wanted to leave Louis' house forever.
    One night, sudden attack—her noise in the bathroom—like croak-
ing up her soul—convulsions and red vomit coming out of her
mouth—diarrhea water exploding from her behind—on all fours
in front of the toilet—urine running between her legs—left retching
on the tile floor smeared with her black feces—unfainted—   85
    At forty, varicosed, nude, fat, doomed, hiding outside the apart-
ment door near the elevator calling Police, yelling for her girl-friend
Rose to help—
    Once locked herself in with razor or iodine—could hear her
cough in tears at sink—Lou broke through glass green-painted door,
we pulled her out to the bedroom.
    Then quiet for months that winter—walks, alone, nearby on
Broadway, read Daily Worker[4]—Broke her arm, fell on icy street—
    Began to scheme escape from cosmic financial murder plots—
later she ran away to the Bronx to her sister Elanor. And there's
another saga of late Naomi in New York.

    Or thru Elanor or the Workman's Circle, where she worked,
addressing envelopes, she made out—went shopping for Campbell's tomato soup—saved money Louis mailed her—   90
    Later she found a boyfriend, and he was a doctor—Dr. Isaac
worked for National Maritime Union—now Italian bald and pudgy
old doll—who was himself an orphan—but they kicked him out—
Old cruelties—
    Sloppier, sat around on bed or chair, in corset dreaming to her-
self—'I'm hot—I'm getting fat—I used to have such a beautiful

4. Newspaper of the American Communist party.

figure before I went to the hospital—You should have seen me in Woodbine—' This in a furnished room around the NMU hall, 1943.

Looking at naked baby pictures in the magazine—baby powder advertisements, strained lamb carrots—'I will think nothing but beautiful thoughts.'

Revolving her head round and round on her neck at window light in summertime, in hypnotize, in doven[5]-dream recall—

'I touch his cheek, I touch his cheek, he touches my lips with his hand, I think beautiful thoughts, the baby has a beautiful hand.'—   95

Or a No-shake of her body, disgust—some thought of Buchenwald[6]—some insulin passes thru her head—a grimace nerve shudder at Involuntary (as shudder when I piss)—bad chemical in her cortex—'No don't think of that. He's a rat.'

Naomi, 'And when we die we become an onion, a cabbage, a carrot, or a squash, a vegetable.' I come downtown from Columbia and agree. She reads the Bible, thinks beautiful thoughts all day.

'Yesterday I saw God. What did he look like? Well, in the afternoon I climbed up a ladder—he has a cheap cabin in the country, like Monroe, NY the chicken farms in the wood. He was a lonely old man with a white beard.

'I cooked supper for him. I made him a nice supper—lentil soup, vegetables, bread & butter—miltz—he sat down at the table and ate, he was sad.

'I told him, Look at all those fightings and killings down there, What's the matter? Why don't you put a stop to it?   100

'I try, he said—That's all he could do, he looked tired. He's a bachelor so long, and he likes lentil soup.'

Serving me meanwhile, a plate of cold fish—chopped raw cabbage dript with tapwater—smelly tomatoes—week-old health food—grated beets & carrots with leaky juice, warm—more and more disconsolate food—I can't eat it for nausea sometimes—the Charity of her hands stinking with Manhattan, madness, desire to please me, cold undercooked fish—pale red near the bones. Her smells—and oft naked in the room, so that I stare ahead, or turn a book ignoring her.

One time I thought she was trying to make me come lay her—flirting to herself at sink—lay back on huge bed that filled most of the room, dress up round her hips, big slash of hair, scars of operations, pancreas, belly wounds, abortions, appendix, stitching of incisions pulling down in the fat like hideous thick zippers—ragged long lips between her legs—What, even, smell of asshole? I was cold—later revolted a little, not much—seemed perhaps a good idea to try—know the Monster of the Beginning Womb—Perhaps—that way. Would she care? She needs a lover.

5. Intoned, as in private prayer.
6. Nazi concentration camp in central Germany.

Yisborach, v'yistabach, v'yispoar, v'yisroman, v'yisnaseh, v'yishador, v'yishalleh v'yishallol, sh'meh d'kudsho, b'rich hu.[7]

And Louis reestablishing himself in Paterson grimy apartment in negro district—living in dark rooms—but found himself a girl he later married, falling in love again—tho sere & shy—hurt with 20 years Naomi's mad idealism.   105

Once I came home, after longtime in N.Y., he's lonely—sitting in the bedroom, he at desk chair turned round to face me—weeps, tears in red eyes under his glasses—

That we'd left him—Gene gone strangely into army—she out on her own in NY, almost childish in her furnished room. So Louis walked downtown to postoffice to get mail, taught in highschool— stayed at poetry desk, forlorn—ate grief at Bickford's[8] all these years—are gone.

Eugene got out of the Army, came home changed and lone— cut off his nose in jewish operation—for years stopped girls on Broadway for cups of coffee to get laid—Went to NYU,[9] serious there, to finish Law.—

And Gene lived with her, ate naked fishcakes, cheap, while she got crazier—He got thin, or felt helpless, Naomi striking 1920 poses at the moon, half-naked in the next bed.

bit his nails and studied—was the weird nurse-son—Next year he moved to a room near Columbia—though she wanted to live with her children—   110

'Listen to your mother's plea, I beg you'—Louis still sending her checks—I was in bughouse that year 8 months—my own visions unmentioned in this here Lament—

But then went half mad—Hitler in her room, she saw his mustache in the sink—afraid of Dr. Isaac now, suspecting that he was in on the Newark plot—went up to Bronx to live near Elanor's Rheumatic Heart—

And Uncle Max never got up before noon, tho Naomi at 6 AM was listening to the radio for spies—or searching the windowsill,

for in the empty lot downstairs, an old man creeps with his bag stuffing packages of garbage in his hanging black overcoat.

Max's sister Edie works—17 years bookeeper at Gimbels— lived downstairs in apartment house, divorced—so Edie took in Naomi on Rochambeau Ave—   115

Woodlawn Cemetery across the street, vast dale of graves where Poe once—Last stop on Bronx subway—lots of communists in that area.

Who enrolled for painting classes at night in Bronx Adult High School—walked alone under Van Cortlandt Elevated line to class—paints Naomiisms—

Humans sitting on the grass in some Camp No-Worry summers yore—saints with droopy faces and long-ill-fitting pants, from hospital—

7. A section of the Kaddish: "Praised and glorified be the name of the Holy One though He be above all the praises which we can utter."

8. A chain of coffee shops in New York City.
9. New York University.

Brides in front of Lower East Side with short grooms—lost El
trains running over the Babylonian apartment rooftops in the
Bronx—

Sad paintings—but she expressed herself. Her mandolin gone,
all strings broke in her head, she tried. Toward Beauty? or some old
life Message? 120

But started kicking Elanor, and Elanor had heart trouble—came
upstairs and asked her about Spydom for hours,—Elanor frazzled.
Max away at office, accounting for cigar stores till at night.

'I am a great woman—am truly a beautiful soul—and because of
that they (Hitler, Grandma, Hearst, the Capitalists, Franco, Daily
News, the 20's, Mussolini, the living dead) want to shut me up—
Buba's the head of a spider network—'

Kicking the girls, Edie & Elanor—Woke Edie at midnite to
tell her she was a spy and Elanor a rat. Edie worked all day and
couldn't take it—She was organizing the union.—And Elanor began
dying, upstairs in bed.

The relatives call me up, she's getting worse—I was the only
one left—Went on the subway with Eugene to see her, ate stale
fish—

'My sister whispers in the radio—Louis must be in the apartment—his mother tells him what to say—LIARS!—I cooked for
my two children—I played the mandolin—' 125

Last night the nightingale woke me / Last night when all was
still/ it sang in the golden moonlight/ from on the wintry hill.
She did.

I pushed her against the door and shouted 'DON'T KICK
ELANOR!'—she stared at me—Contempt—die—disbelief her sons
are so naive, so dumb—'Elanor is the worst spy! She's taking
orders!'

'—No wires in the room!'—I'm yelling at her—last ditch,
Eugene listening on the bed—what can he do to escape that
fatal Mama—'You've been away from Louis years already—Grandma's too old to walk—'

We're all alive at once then—even me & Gene & Naomi in one
mythological Cousinesque room—screaming at each other in the
Forever—I in Columbia jacket, she half undressed.

I banging against her head which saw Radios, Sticks, Hitlers—
the gamut of Hallucinations—for real—her own universe—no
road that goes elsewhere—to my own—No America, not even a
world— 130

That you go as all men, as Van Gogh,[1] as mad Hannah, all the
same—to the last doom—Thunder, Spirits, Lightning!

I've seen your grave! O strange Naomi! My own—cracked grave!
Shema Y'Israel[2]—I am Svul Avrum—you—in death?

Your last night in the darkness of the Bronx—I phone-called—
thru hospital to secret police.

---

1. Vincent Van Gogh (1853–90), Dutch
painter who died insane.

2. In the Hebrew service, "Hear, O
Israel."

That came, when you and I were alone, shrieking at Elanor in my ear—who breathed hard in her own bed, got thin—

Nor will forget, the doorknock, at your fright of spies,—Law advancing, on my honor—Eternity entering the room—you running to the bathroom undressed, hiding in protest from the last heroic fate—   135

staring at my eyes, betrayed—the final cops of madness rescuing me—from your foot against the broken heart of Elanor,

your voice at Edie weary of Gimbels coming home to broken radio—and Louis needing a poor divorce, he wants to get married soon—Eugene dreaming, hiding at 125 St., suing negros for money on crud furniture, defending black girls—

Protests from the bathroom—Said you were sane—dressing in a cotton robe, your shoes, then new, your purse and newspaper clippings—no—your honesty—

as you vainly made your lips more real with lipstick, looking in the mirror to see if the Insanity was Me or a carful of police.

or Grandma spying at 78—Your vision—Her climbing over the walls of the cemetery with political kidnapper's bag—or what you saw on the walls of the Bronx, in pink nightgown at midnight, staring out the window on the empty lot—   140

Ah Rochambeau Ave—Playground of Phantoms—last apartment in the Bronx for spies—last home for Elanor or Naomi, here these communist sisters lost their revolution—

'All right—put on your coat Mrs.—let's go—We have the wagon downstairs—you want to come with her to the station?'

The ride then—held Naomi's hand, and held her head to my breast, I'm taller—kissed her and said I did it for the best—Elanor sick—and Max with heart condition—Needs—

To me—'Why did you do this?'—'Yes Mrs., your son will have to leave you in an hour'—The Ambulance

came in a few hours—drove off at 4 AM to some Bellevue[3] in the night downtown—gone to the hospital forever. I saw her led away—she waved, tears in her eyes.   145

Two years, after a trip to Mexico—bleak in the flat plain near Brentwood, scrub brush and grass around the unused RR train track to the crazyhouse—

new brick 20 story central building—lost on the vast lawns of madtown on Long Island—huge cities of the moon.

Asylum spreads out giant wings above the path to a minute black hole—the door—entrance thru crotch—

I went in—smelt funny—the halls again—up elevator—to a glass door on a Woman's Ward—to Naomi—Two nurses buxom white— They led her out, Naomi stared—and I gaspt—She'd had a stroke—

Too thin, shrunk on her bones—age come to Naomi—now broken into white hair—loose dress on her skeleton—face sunk, old! withered—cheek of crone—   150

3. New York municipal hospital, often used for emergency mental cases.

One hand stiff—heaviness of forties & menopause reduced by one heart stroke, lame now—wrinkles—a scar on her head, the lobotomy—ruin, the hand dipping downwards to death—

O Russian faced, woman on the grass, your long black hair is crowned with flowers, the mandolin is on your knees—
Communist beauty, sit here married in the summer among daisies, promised happiness at hand—
holy mother, now you smile on your love, your world is born anew, children run naked in the field spotted with dandelions,
they eat in the plum tree grove at the end of the meadow and find a cabin where a white-haired negro teaches the mystery of his rainbarrel—   155
blessed daughter come to America, I long to hear your voice again, remembering your mother's music, in the Song of the Natural Front—
O glorious muse that bore me from the womb, gave suck first mystic life & taught me talk and music, from whose pained head I first took Vision—
Tortured and beaten in the skull—What mad hallucinations of the damned that drive me out of my own skull to seek Eternity till I find Peace for Thee, O Poetry—and for all humankind call on the Origin
Death which is the mother of the universe!—Now wear your nakedness forever, white flowers in your hair, your marriage sealed behind the sky—no revolution might destroy that maidenhood—
O beautiful Garbo[4] of my Karma—all photographs from 1920 in Camp Nicht-Gedeiget here unchanged—with all the teachers from Newark—Nor Elanor be gone, nor Max await his specter—nor Louis retire from this High School—   160

Back! You! Naomi! Skull on you! Gaunt immortality and revolution come—small broken woman—the ashen indoor eyes of hospitals, ward greyness on skin—
'Are you a spy?' I sat at the sour table, eyes filling with tears—'Who are you? Did Louis send you?—The wires—'
in her hair, as she beat on her head—'I'm not a bad girl—don't murder me!—I hear the ceiling—I raised two children—'
Two years since I'd been there—I started to cry—She stared—nurse broke up the meeting a moment—I went into the bathroom to hide, against the toilet white walls
'The Horror' I weeping—to see her again—'The Horror'—as if she were dead thru funeral rot in—'The Horror!'   165
I came back she yelled more—they led her away—'You're not Allen—' I watched her face—but she passed by me, not looking—
Opened the door to the ward,—she went thru without a glance back, quiet suddenly—I stared out—she looked old—the verge of the grave—'All the Horror!'

---

4. Greta Garbo (b. 1905), glamorous film star with a reputation for mystery who went into seclusion at the height of her career; "Karma": destiny.

Another year, I left NY—on West Coast in Berkeley cottage dreamed of her soul—that, thru life, in what form it stood in that body, ashen or manic, gone beyond joy—

near its death—with eyes—was my own love in its form, the Naomi, my mother on earth still—sent her long letter—& wrote hymns to the mad—Work of the merciful Lord of Poetry.

that causes the broken grass to be green, or the rock to break in grass—or the Sun to be constant to earth—Sun of all sunflowers and days on bright iron bridges—what shines on old hospitals—as on my yard—   170

Returning from San Francisco one night, Orlovsky in my room— Whalen in his peaceful chair⁵—a telegram from Gene, Naomi dead—

Outside I bent my head to the ground under the bushes near the garage—knew she was better—

at last—not left to look on Earth alone—2 years of solitude— no one, at age nearing 60—old woman of skulls—once long-tressed Naomi of Bible—

or Ruth who wept in America—Rebecca aged in Newark— David remembering his Harp, now lawyer at Yale

or Svul Avrum—Israel Abraham—myself—to sing in the wilderness toward God—O Elohim!⁶—so to the end—2 days after her death I got her letter—   175

Strange Prophecies anew! She wrote—'The key is in the window, the key is in the sunlight at the window—I have the key—Get married Allen don't take drugs—the key is in the bars, in the sunlight in the window.

Love,
your mother'

which is Naomi—

HYMMNN

In the world which He has created according to his will Blessed
    Praised
Magnified Lauded Exalted the Name of the Holy One Blessed
    is He!
In the house in Newark Blessed is He! In the madhouse Blessed
    is He! In the house of Death Blessed is He!
Blessed be He in homosexuality! Blessed be He in Paranoia!
    Blessed be He in the city! Blessed be He in the Book!
Blessed be He who dwells in the shadow! Blessed be He!
    Blessed be He!   5
Blessed be you Naomi in tears! Blessed be you Naomi in fears!
    Blessed Blessed Blessed in sickness!
Blessed be you Naomi in Hospitals! Blessed be you Naomi in
    solitude! Blest be your triumph! Blest be your bars! Blest be
    your last years' loneliness!
Blest be your failure! Blest be your stroke! Blest be the close of

---

5. Peter Orlovsky (b. 1933), fellow poet   (b. 1923), West Coast poet.
and Ginsberg's lover; Philip Whalen   6. God, in the Old Testament.

your eye!   Blest be the gaunt of your cheek!   Blest be your
    withered thighs!
Blessed be Thee Naomi in Death!   Blessed be Death!   Blessed
    be Death!
Blessed be He Who leads all sorrow to Heaven!   Blessed be He
    in the end!   10
Blessed be He who builds Heaven in Darkness!   Blessed Blessed
    Blessed be He!   Blessed be He!   Blessed be Death on us All!

III

Only to have not forgotten the beginning in which she drank
    cheap sodas in the morgues of Newark,
only to have seen her weeping on grey tables in long wards of her
    universe
only to have known the weird ideas of Hitler at the door, the
    wires in her head, the three big sticks
rammed down her back, the voices in the ceiling shrieking out her
    ugly early lays for 30 years,
only to have seen the time-jumps, memory lapse, the crash of wars,
    the roar and silence of a vast electric shock,   5
only to have seen her painting crude pictures of Elevateds[7] running
    over the rooftops of the Bronx
her brothers dead in Riverside or Russia, her lone in Long Island
    writing a last letter—and her image in the sunlight at the
    window
'The key is in the sunlight at the window in the bars the key
    is in the sunlight,'
only to have come to that dark night on iron bed by stroke when
    the sun gone down on Long Island
and the vast Atlantic roars outside the great call of Being to its
    own   10
to come back out of the Nightmare—divided creation—with her
    head lain on a pillow of the hospital to die
—in one last glimpse—all Earth one everlasting Light in the fa-
    miliar blackout—no tears for this vision—
But that the key should be left behind—at the window—the key
    in the sunlight—to the living—that can take
that slice of light in hand—and turn the door—and look back
    see
Creation glistening backwards to the same grave, size of universe,
size of the tick of the hospital's clock on the archway over the
    white door—   15

IV

O mother
what have I left out
O mother
what have I forgotten

7. Railway elevated above New York City streets.

O mother   5
farewell
with a long black shoe
farewell
with Communist Party and a broken stocking
farewell   10
with six dark hairs on the wen of your breast
farewell
with your old dress and a long black beard around the vagina
farewell
with your sagging belly   15
with your fear of Hitler
with your mouth of bad short stories
with your fingers of rotten mandolines
with your arms of fat Paterson porches
with your belly of strikes and smokestacks   20
with your chin of Trotsky and the Spanish War
with your voice singing for the decaying overbroken workers
with your nose of bad lay with your nose of the smell of the pickles
    of Newark
with your eyes
with your eyes of Russia   25
with your eyes of no money
with your eyes of false China
with your eyes of Aunt Elanor
with your eyes of starving India
with your eyes pissing in the park   30
with your eyes of America taking a fall
with your eyes of your failure at the piano
with your eyes of your relatives in California
with your eyes of Ma Rainey[8] dying in an ambulance
with your eyes of Czechoslovakia attacked by robots   35
with your eyes going to painting class at night in the Bronx
with your eyes of the killer Grandma you see on the horizon from
    the Fire-Escape
with your eyes running naked out of the apartment screaming into
    the hall
with your eyes being led away by policemen to an ambulance
with your eyes strapped down on the operating table   40
with your eyes with the pancreas removed
with your eyes of appendix operation
with your eyes of abortion
with your eyes of ovaries removed
with your eyes of shock   45
with your eyes of lobotomy
with your eyes of divorce
with your eyes of stroke
with your eyes alone

8. Negro blues singer (1866–1939).

with your eyes   50
with your eyes
with your Death full of Flowers

V

Caw caw caw crows shriek in the white sun over grave stones in
    Long Island
Lord Lord Lord Naomi underneath this grass my halflife and my
    own as hers
caw caw my eye be buried in the same Ground where I stand in
    Angel
Lord Lord great Eye that stares on All and moves in a black
    cloud
caw caw strange cry of Beings flung up into sky over the waving
    trees   5
Lord Lord O Grinder of giant Beyonds my voice in a boundless
    field in Sheol[9]
Caw caw the call of Time rent out of foot and wing an instant in
    the universe
Lord Lord an echo in the sky the wind through ragged leaves the
    roar of memory
caw caw all years my birth a dream caw caw New York the bus
    the broken shoe the vast highschool caw caw all Visions of the
    Lord
Lord Lord Lord caw caw caw Lord Lord Lord caw caw caw
    Lord   10
NY 1959   1961

To Aunt Rose

Aunt Rose—now—might I see you
with your thin face and buck tooth smile and pain
     of rheumatism—and a long black heavy shoe
      for your bony left leg
limping down the long hall in Newark on the running carpet 5
     past the black grand piano
      in the day room
        where the parties were
    and I sang Spanish loyalist[1] songs
     in a high squeaky voice   10
      (hysterical) the committee listening
    while you limped around the room
      collected the money—
Aunt Honey, Uncle Sam, a stranger with a cloth arm
    in his pocket   15

---

9. Name for the underworld in early
Hebrew writings.
1. During the Spanish Civil War (1936–
39), many left-wing Americans—among
them Ginsberg's relatives in Newark—
sympathized with the Spanish loyalists
who were resisting Francisco Franco's
(1892–1975) efforts to become dictator
of Spain.

and huge young bald head
  of Abraham Lincoln Brigade[2]

—your long sad face
  your tears of sexual frustration
   (what smothered sobs and bony hips   20
    under the pillows of Osborne Terrace)
—the time I stood on the toilet seat naked
  and you powdered my thighs with Calomine
   against the poison ivy—my tender
    and shamed first black curled hairs   25
what were you thinking in secret heart then
   knowing me a man already—
and I an ignorant girl of family silence on the thin pedestal
  of my legs in the bathroom—Museum of Newark.
       Aunt Rose   30
Hitler is dead, Hitler is in Eternity; Hitler is with
  Tamburlane and Emily Brontë[3]

Though I see you walking still, a ghost on Osborne Terrace
  down the long dark hall to the front door
   limping a little with a pinched smile   35
   in what must have been a silken
    flower dress
welcoming my father, the Poet, on his visit to Newark
   —see you arriving in the living room
    dancing on your crippled leg   40
   and clapping hands his book
    had been accepted by Liveright[4]

Hitler is dead and Liveright's gone out of business
The Attic of the Past and *Everlasting Minute* are out of print
   Uncle Harry sold his last silk stocking   45
   Claire quit interpretive dancing school
    Buba sits a wrinkled monument in Old
     Ladies Home blinking at new babies

last time I saw you was the hospital
   pale skull protruding under ashen skin   50
    blue veined unconscious girl
     in an oxygen tent
   the war in Spain has ended long ago
     Aunt Rose

Paris 1958   1961

---

2. American volunteers who fought against the Fascists in the Spanish Civil War.
3. English poet and novelist (1818–48), author of *Wuthering Heights*; Tamburlane was the Mideastern "scourge" and conqueror (hero of Christopher Marlowe's *Tamburlane*, 1588).

4. Leading American publisher of the 1920s and 1930s (now a subsidiary of W. W. Norton & Company), published *The Everlasting Minute* (1937), poems by Allen Ginsberg's father Louis (b. 1895), whose first book was *The Attic of the Past* (Boston, 1920).

On Burroughs' Work[1]

The method must be purest meat
and no symbolic dressing,
actual visions & actual prisons
as seen then and now.

Prisons and visions presented   5
with rare descriptions
corresponding exactly to those
of Alcatraz and Rose.[2]

A naked lunch is natural to us,
we eat reality sandwiches.   10
But allegories are so much lettuce.
Don't hide the madness.

San Jose 1954   1963

Continuation of a Long Poem of These States:[1]
S.F. Southward[2]

Stage-lit streets
    Downtown Frisco whizzing past, buildings
  ranked by Freeway balconies
      Bright Johnny Walker neon
         sign Christmastrees   5
And Christmas and its eves
    in the midst of the same deep wood
      as every sad Christmas before, surrounded
        by forests of stars—
Metal columns, smoke pouring cloudward,   10
    yellow-lamp horizon
      warplants move, tiny
    planes lie in Avionic fields[3]
Meanwhile Working Girls sort mail into the red slot
  Rivers of newsprint to soldiers' *Vietnam*   15
    Infantry Journal, Kanackee
      Social Register, Wichita Star
And Postoffice Christmas the same brown place
    mailhandlers' black fingers
    dusty mailbags filled   20
      1948 N.Y. Eighth Avenue was

1. William Burroughs (b. 1914), a senior member of the Beat Generation, homosexual, former heroin addict, and author of the novels *Junkie* (1953, 1964) and *Naked Lunch* (1959).
2. Referring to the "prisons and visions" of lines 3 and 5. Alcatraz was the island prison in San Francisco Bay; one of Ginsberg's hallucinatory visions of the English poet William Blake (1757–1827) had been of the poet reciting *The Sick Rose*.
1. Part of a series of what Ginsberg called "transit poems" in *The Fall of America* (1972).
2. I.e., driving southward from San Francisco.
3. Outside the warplants of the previous line.

> or when Peter[4] drove the mailtruck 1955
>> from Rincon Annex—
> Bright lights' windshield flash,
>> adrenalin shiver in shoulders   25
>>> Around the curve
>> crawling a long truck
>>> 3 bright green signals on forehead
> Jewelled Bayshore passing the Coast Range
>
>> one architect's house light on hill crest   30
> . . . . negro voices rejoice over radio
>> Moonlight sticks of tea[5]
> Moss Landing Power Plant
>> shooting its cannon smoke
>>> across the highway, Red tailight   35
>>>> speeding the white line and a mile away
>> Orion's[6] muzzle
>>> raised up
>>>> to the center of Heaven.

December 18, 1965   1972

4. Peter Orlovsky (b. 1933), Ginsberg's   5. Marijuana cigarettes.
long-time lover and fellow poet.   6. The constellation.

A. R. AMMONS
1926–

A. R. Ammons writes that he "was born big and jaundiced (and ugly) on February 18, 1926, in a farmhouse 4 miles southwest of Whiteville, N.C., and 2 miles northwest of New Hope Elementary School and New Hope Baptist Church." It is characteristic of Ammons to be laconic, self-deprecating, unfailingly local, and unfailingly exact. He belongs to the "home-made" strain of American writers rather than the Europeanized or cosmopolitan breed. His poems are filled with the landscapes in which he has lived: North Carolina, the South Jersey coast, and the surroundings of Ithaca, New York, where he now lives and teaches in the English department of Cornell University.

Ammons's career did not start out with a traditional literary education. At Wake Forest College in North Carolina he studied mostly scientific subjects, especially biology and chemistry, and that scientific training has strongly colored his poems. Only later (1951–52) did he study English literature for three semesters at the University of California in Berkeley. He had worked briefly as a high school principal in North Carolina. When he returned from Berkeley he spent twelve years as an executive for a firm which made biological glass in southern New Jersey.

In 1955, his thirtieth year, Ammons published his first book of poems, *Ommateum*. The title refers to the compound structure of an insect's eye and foreshadows a twofold impulse in Ammons's work. On one hand he is involved in the minute observation of natural phenomena; on the other hand he is frustrated by the physical limitations analogous to those of the insects' vision. We see the world, as insects do, in small portions and in impulses which take in but do not totally resolve the many images we receive. "Overall is beyond me," says Ammons in *Corsons Inlet*, a important poem in which the shifting details of shoreline and dunes represent a severe challenge to the poet-observer. There are no straight lines. The contours differ every day, every hour, and they teach the poet the endless adjustments he must make to nature's fluidity.

"A poem is a walk," Ammons has said, and in even the most casual of such encounters he looks closely at things: vegetation, small animals, the minute shifts of wind and weather and light. Yet over and over he seems drawn to Emerson's visionary aspirations for poetry. "Poetry," Emerson remarked, "was all written before time was, and whenever we are so finely organized that we can penetrate into that region where the air is music, we hear those primal warnings and attempt to write them down." Much of Ammons's poetry is given over to testing such transcendental promise for a glimpse of supernatural order and calm.

A typical Ammons poem may move, like *Gravelly Run*, from visionary promptings to sober rebukes from a nature more complicated than the poet dare imagine. At the outset Ammons relaxes and gives himself over: "I don't know somehow it seems sufficient / to see and hear whatever coming and going is, / losing the self to the victory / of stones and trees." By the end of the poem he is in a more embattled position: "so I look and reflect, but the air's glass / jail seals each thing in its entity." The word *reflect*, offered as a gesture of understanding, is drained of its meditative meaning before our eyes. Human gesture becomes nothing but a reflection, a mirror. The poem turns everything brutally physical, a world of unconnected particles; the poet's visionary effort becomes merely that of the "surrendered self among unwelcoming forms."

Ammons began his career writing short lyrics, almost journal entries in an unending career of observation. But the laconic notations—of a landslide, a shift in the shoreline from one day to the next—often bore abstract titles—*Clarity, Saliences*—as if to suggest his appetite for more extended meanings. Ammons has been driven to many kinds of poetic experiments in his effort to make his verse fully responsive to the engaging but evasive particularity of natural process. "Stop on any word and language gives way: / the blades of reason, unlightened by motion, sink in," he remarks in his *Essay on Poetics*. Preparing *Tape for the Turn of the Year* (1965) he typed a book-length day-to-day verse diary along an adding machine tape. The poem ended when the tape did. This was his first and most flamboyant attempt to turn his verse into something beyond mere gatherings. Since then he has discovered that the long poem is the form best adapted to his continuing, indeed endless, dialogue between the specific and the general. As punctuation, the poems tend to use the colon instead of the period so as to keep the poem from grinding to a complete halt or stopping the flow in which the mind feverishly suggests analogies among its minutely perceived experiences. Ammons published several notable examples (*Hibernaculum, Extremes and Moderations*) in his *Collected Poems 1951–1971*. But his intention has been most fully realized in *Sphere: the Form of a Motion*, a single poem, book-length, with no full stops, 155 sections of four tercets each, whose very title suggests its ambition to be what Wallace Stevens would call "the poem of the act of the mind." *Sphere* is committed, as Ammons himself is, to the provisional, the self-revising, its only unity the mind's power to make analogies between the world's constant "diversifications."

So I Said I Am Ezra

So I said I am Ezra
and the wind whipped my throat
gaming for the sounds of my voice
    I listened to the wind
go over my head and up into the night   5
Turning to the sea I said
        I am Ezra
but there were no echoes from the waves
The words were swallowed up
    in the voice of the surf   10
or leaping over the swells
lost themselves oceanward
    Over the bleached and broken fields
I moved my feet and turning from the wind
    that ripped sheets of sand   15
    from the beach and threw them
    like seamists across the dunes
swayed as if the wind were taking me away
and said
        I am Ezra   20
As a word too much repeated
falls out of being
so I Ezra went out into the night
like a drift of sand
and splashed among the windy oats   25
that clutch the dunes
of unremembered seas

        1955

Bridge

A tea garden shows you how:

        you sit in rhododendron shade
at table
on a pavilion-like lawn

        the sun midafternoon through the blooms   5
and you

watch lovers and single people
go over the steep moonbridge at the pond's narrows

where flies nip circles

  in the glass   10
and vanish in the widening sight except for an uncertain

   gauze memory of wings

and as you sip from the small thick cup
   held bird-warm
   in the hands   15

   you watch
the people
rising on the bridge

descend into the pond,

   where bridge and mirrorbridge merge   20

   at the bank
returning their images to themselves:
   a grove
of pepper trees (sgraffito)[1]
   screens them into isolations of love or loneliness: 25

it is enough from this to think in the green tea scent
and turn to farther things:

when the spirit comes to the bridge of consciousness
and climbs higher and higher
   toward the peak no one reaches live   30
but where ascension
   and descension meet
completing the idea of a bridge

think where the body is,
   that going too deep   35

it may lose touch,
   wander a ghost in hell
   sing irretrievably in gloom,
and think

how the spirit silvery with vision may   40
break loose in high wind

   and go off weightless

body never to rise or spirit fall again to unity,
to lovers strolling through pepper-tree shade:

---

1. A method of decoration by scratches through a superficial layer or glazing to a ground of a different color.

paradise was when
Dante[2]
regathered from height and depth
    came out onto the soft, green, level earth   45

into the natural light, come, sweat, bloodblessings,
    and thinning sheaf of days.   50

1963

Gravelly Run

I don't know somehow it seems sufficient
to see and hear whatever coming and going is,
losing the self to the victory
    of stones and trees,
of bending sandpit lakes, crescent   5
round groves of dwarf pine:

for it is not so much to know the self
as to know it as it is known
    by galaxy and cedar cone,
as if birth had never found it   10
and death could never end it:

the swamp's slow water comes
down Gravelly Run fanning the long
    stone-held algal[1]
hair and narrowing roils[2] between   15
the shoulders of the highway bridge:

holly grows on the banks in the woods there,
and the cedars' gothic-clustered
    spires could make
    green religion in winter bones: 20

so I look and reflect, but the air's glass
jail seals each thing in its entity:

no use to make any philosophies here:
    I see no
god in the holly, hear no song from   25
    the snowbroken weeds: Hegel[3] is not the winter
yellow in the pines: the sunlight has never
heard of trees: surrendered self among
    unwelcoming forms: stranger,
hoist your burdens, get on down the road.   30

1965

2. Dante Alighieri (1265–1321), author
of *The Divine Comedy*, emerging from
his journey through Hell, Purgatory, and
Paradise.
1. From algae: aquatic weeds such as
kelp.
2. Grows agitated.
3. Georg Wilhelm Friedrich Hegel (1770–
1831), German philosopher who believed
in a unifying spirit immanent in Nature.

Corsons Inlet

I went for a walk over the dunes again this morning
to the sea,
then turned right along
    the surf
                rounded a naked headland   5
                and returned

    along the inlet shore:

it was muggy sunny, the wind from the sea steady and high,
crisp in the running sand,
    some breakthroughs of sun   10
    but after a bit

continuous overcast:

the walk liberating, I was released from forms,
from the perpendiculars,
    straight lines, blocks, boxes, binds   15
of thought
into the hues, shadings, rises, flowing bends and blends
    of sight:

                I allow myself eddies of meaning:
yield to a direction of significance   20
running
like a stream through the geography of my work:
    you can find
in my sayings
                swerves of action   25
            like the inlet's cutting edge:
    there are dunes of motion,
organizations of grass, white sandy paths of remembrance
in the overall wandering of mirroring mind:
but Overall is beyond me: is the sum of these events   30
I cannot draw, the ledger I cannot keep, the accounting
beyond the account:

in nature there are few sharp lines: there are areas of
primrose
    more or less dispersed;   35
disorderly orders of bayberry; between the rows
of dunes,
irregular swamps of reeds,
though not reeds alone, but grass, bayberry, yarrow, all . . .
predominantly reeds: 40

I have reached no conclusions, have erected no boundaries,
shutting out and shutting in, separating inside

from outside: I have
drawn no lines:
as   45

manifold events of sand
change the dune's shape that will not be the same shape
tomorrow,

so I am willing to go along, to accept
the becoming   50
thought, to stake off no beginnings or ends, establish
        no walls:

by transitions the land falls from grassy dunes to creek
to undercreek: but there are no lines, though
        change in that transition is clear   55
        as any sharpness: but "sharpness" spread out,
allowed to occur over a wider range
than mental lines can keep:

the moon was full last night: today, low tide was low:
black shoals of mussels exposed to the risk   60
of air
and, earlier, of sun,
waved in and out with the waterline, waterline inexact,
caught always in the event of change:
        a young mottled gull stood free on the shoals   65
        and ate
to vomiting: another gull, squawking possession, cracked a crab,
picked out the entrails, swallowed the soft-shelled legs, a ruddy
turnstone[1] running in to snatch leftover bits:

risk is full: every living thing in   70
siege: the demand is life, to keep life: the small
white blacklegged egret, how beautiful, quietly stalks and spears
            the shallows, darts to shore
                to stab—what? I couldn't
        see against the black mudflats—a frightened   75
        fiddler crab?

            the news to my left over the dunes and
reeds and bayberry clumps was
        fall: thousands of tree swallows
        gathering for flight: 80
        an order held
        in constant change: a congregation
rich with entropy: nevertheless, separable, noticeable
        as one event,

1. A plover-like migratory bird.

not chaos: preparations for   85
flight from winter,
cheet, cheet, cheet, cheet, wings rifling the green clumps,
beaks
at the bayberries
   a perception full of wind, flight, curve,   90
   sound:
   the possibility of rule as the sum of rulelessness:
the "field" of action
with moving, incalculable center:

in the smaller view, order tight with shape: 95
blue tiny flowers on a leafless weed: carapace of crab:
snail shell:
      pulsations of order
      in the bellies of minnows: orders swallowed,
broken down, transferred through membranes   100
to strengthen larger orders: but in the large view, no
lines or changeless shapes: the working in and out, together
     and against, of millions of events: this,
         so that I make
         no form of   105
         formlessness:

orders as summaries, as outcomes of actions override
or in some way result, not predictably (seeing me gain
the top of a dune,
the swallows   110
could take flight—some other fields of bayberry
     could enter fall
     berryless) and there is serenity:

     no arranged terror: no forcing of image, plan,
or thought: 115
no propaganda, no humbling of reality to precept:

terror pervades but is not arranged, all possibilities
of escape open: no route shut, except in
   the sudden loss of all routes:

     I see narrow orders, limited tightness, but will   120
not run to that easy victory:
     still around the looser, wider forces work:
     I will try
    to fasten into order enlarging grasps of disorder, widening
scope, but enjoying the freedom that   125
Scope eludes my grasp, that there is no finality of vision,
that I have perceived nothing completely,
     that tomorrow a new walk is a new walk.

                   1965

Saliences[1]

Consistencies rise
and ride
the mind down
hard routes
    walled   5
with no outlet and so
to open a variable geography,
    proliferate
possibility, here
is this dune fest   10
    releasing
mind feeding out,
gathering clusters,
fields of order in disorder,
where choice   15
can make beginnings,
    turns,
    reversals,
where straight line
and air-hard thought   20
can meet
unarranged disorder,
    dissolve
before the one event that
creates present time   25
in the multi-variable
    scope:
a variable of wind
among the dunes,
making variables   30
of position and direction and sound
of every reed leaf
and bloom,
running streams of sand,
winding, rising, at a depression   35
falling out into deltas,
weathering shells with blast,
striking hiss into clumps of grass,
against bayberry leaves,
    lifting   40
the spider from footing to footing
hard across the dry even crust
toward the surf:
wind, a variable, soft wind, hard
steady wind, wind   45
shaped and kept in the
bent of trees,

---

1. Outcroppings, projections.

the prevailing dipping seaward
of reeds,
the kept and erased sandcrab trails: 50
wind, the variable to the gull's flight,
how and where he drops the clam
and the way he heads in, running to loft:
wind, from the sea, high surf
and cool weather;   55
from the land, a lessened breakage
and the land's heat:
wind alone as a variable,
as a factor in millions of events,
leaves no two moments   60
on the dunes the same:
        keep
free to these events,
bend to these
changing weathers: 65
multiple as sand, events of sense
alter old dunes
of mind,
release new channels of flow,
free materials   70
to new forms:
wind alone as a variable
takes this neck of dunes
out of calculation's reach:
come out of the hard   75
routes and ruts,
pour over the walls
of previous assessments: turn to
the open,
the unexpected, to new saliences of feature.   80

The reassurance is
that through change
continuities sinuously work,
cause and effect
        without alarm,   85
gradual shadings out or in,
motions that full
        with time
do not surprise, no
abrupt leap or burst: possibility,   90
with meaningful development
of circumstance:

when I went back to the dunes today,
        saliences,
congruent to memory,   95
spread firmingly across my sight:

the narrow white path
rose and dropped over
grassy rises toward the sea:
sheets of reeds,   100
tasseling now near fall,
filled the hollows
with shapes of ponds or lakes:
bayberry, darker, made wandering
chains of clumps, sometimes pouring   105
into heads, like stopped water:
        much seemed
constant, to be looked
forward to, expected:
from the top of a dune rise,   110
look of ocean salience: in
        the hollow,
where a runlet
        makes in
at full tide and fills a bowl,   115
extravagance of pink periwinkle
along the grassy edge,
and a blue, bunchy weed, deep blue,
deep into the mind the dark blue
        constant: 120
minnows left high in the tide-deserted pocket,
        fiddler crabs
bringing up gray pellets of drying sand,
disappearing from air's faster events
at any close approach: 125
certain things and habits
        recognizable as
having lasted through the night:
though what change in
a day's doing!   130
desertions of swallows
        that yesterday
ravaged air, bush, reed, attention
in gatherings wide as this neck of dunes:
now, not a sound   135
or shadow, no trace of memory, no remnant
explanation:
summations of permanence!
where not a single single thing endures,
the overall reassures,   140
deaths and flights,
shifts and sudden assaults claiming
limited orders,
the separate particles:
earth brings to grief   145
much in an hour that sang, leaped, swirled,
yet keeps a round

    quiet turning,
beyond loss or gain,
beyond concern for the separate reach.   150

           1966

Laser[1]

An image comes
and the mind's light, confused
as that on surf
or ocean shelves,
gathers up,   5
parallelizes, focuses
and in a rigid beam illuminates the image:

the head seeks in itself
fragments of left-over light
to cast a new   10
direction,
any direction,
to strike and fix
a random, contradicting image:

but any found image falls   15
back to darkness or
the lesser beams splinter and
go out:
the mind tries to
dream of diversity, of mountain   20
rapids shattered with sound and light,

of wind fracturing brush or
bursting out of order against a mountain
range: but the focused beam

folds all energy in,   25
the image glares filling all space:
the head falls and
hangs and cannot wake itself.

           1970

The City Limits

When you consider the radiance, that it does not withhold
itself but pours its abundance without selection into every
nook and cranny not overhung or hidden; when you consider

that birds' bones make no awful noise against the light but
lie low in the light as in a high testimony; when you consider   5
the radiance, that it will look into the guiltiest

---

1. Electromagnetic device employing the natural oscillations of atoms to generate a rigidly focused light.

swervings of the weaving heart and bear itself upon them,
not flinching into disguise or darkening; when you consider
the abundance of such resource as illuminates the glow-blue

bodies and gold-skeined wings of flies swarming the dumped   10
guts of a natural slaughter or the coil of shit and in no
way winces from its storms of generosity; when you consider

that air or vacuum, snow or shale, squid or wolf, rose or lichen,
each is accepted into as much light as it will take, then
the heart moves roomier, the man stands and looks about, the   15

leaf does not increase itself above the grass, and the dark
work of the deepest cells is of a tune with May bushes
and fear lit by the breadth of such calmly turns to praise.

1971

Triphammer Bridge

I wonder what to mean by *sanctuary*, if a real or
apprehended place, as of a bell rung in a gold
surround, or as of silver roads along the beaches

of clouds seas don't break or black mountains
overspill; jail: ice here's shapelier than anything,   5
on the eaves massive, jawed along gorge ledges, solid

in the plastic blue boat fall left water in: if I
think the bitterest thing I can think of that seems like
reality, slickened back, hard, shocked by rip-high wind:

sanctuary, sanctuary, I say it over and over and the   10
word's sound is the one place to dwell: that's it, just
the sound, and the imagination of the sound—a place.

1972

JAMES MERRILL

1926–

When James Merrill's *First Poems* were published in 1950, he was immediately recognized as one of the most gifted and polished poets of his generation. But it was not until *Water Street* (1962), his third volume of poems, that Merrill began to enlist his brilliant technique and sophisticated tone in developing a poetic autobiography. The book takes its title from the street where he lives in the seaside village of Stonington, Connecticut. The opening poem, *An Urban Convalescence*, explores his decision to leave New York, which he sees as a distracting city that destroys its past. He portrays his move as a rededication to his personal past, and an attempt through poetry "to make some kind of house / Out of the life lived, out of the love spent."

The metaphor of "home" is an emotional center to which Merrill's writing often returns, as in *Lost in Translation,* where the narrator recalls a childhood summer in a home mysteriously without parents. *The Broken Home* similarly recalls elements of Merrill's own experience as the son of parents who divorced when he was young. He had been born to the second marriage of Charles E. Merrill, financier and founder of the best known brokerage firm in America. In the short narrative poems of *Water Street* and the book that followed he returns again and again to inner dramas connected to key figures of his childhood and to key childhood scenes. *The Broken Home* and *Lost in Translation* were to show how memory and the act of writing have the power to reshape boyhood pain and conflict so as to achieve "the unstiflement of the entire story." Such an attitude distinguishes Merrill from his contemporaries (Robert Lowell, Anne Sexton, Sylvia Plath), whose autobiographical impulse expresses itself primarily in the present tense and the use of poems as an urgent journal true to the moment.

As an undergraduate at Amherst College, Merrill had written an honors thesis on the French novelist Marcel Proust (1871–1922). His poetry was clearly affected by Proust's notion that the literary exercise of memory slowly discloses the patterns of childhood experience that we are destined to relive. Proust showed in his novel how such power over chaotic material of the past is often triggered involuntarily by an object or an episode in the present whose associations reach back into formative childhood encounters. The questions he asked were asked by Freud as well: What animates certain scenes—and not others—for us? It is to answer such questions that some of Merrill's poems are told from the viewpoint of an observant child. In other poems the poet is explicitly present, at his desk, trying to incorporate into his adult understanding of the contours of his life the pain and freshness of childhood memories. The poems are narrative (one of his early books was called *Short Stories*) as often as lyric, in the hope that dramatic *action* will reveal the meanings with which certain objects have become charged. As Merrill sees it, "You hardly ever need to *state* your feelings. The point is to feel and keep the eyes open. Then what you feel is expressed, is mimed back at you by the scene. A room, a landscape. I'd go a step further. We don't *know* what we feel until we see it distanced by this kind of translation."

Merrill has traveled extensively and has presented landscapes from his travels not as external descriptions but rather as ways of exploring alternative or buried states of his own mind, the "translations" of which he speaks above. Poems such as *Days of 1964* and *After the Fire* reflect his experience of Greece, his home for a portion of each year. They respectively anticipate and comment on *The Fire Screen* (1969), a sequence of poems describing the rising and falling curve of a love affair partly in terms of an initiation into Greece with its power to strip away urban sophistication. The books that followed served as initiations into other psychic territories. Problems of family relationships and erotic entanglements previously seen on an intimate scale were in *Braving the Elements* (1972) acted out against a wider backdrop: the long landscapes, primitive geological perspectives, and erosions of the American Far West. Here human experience, examined in his earlier work in close-up, is seen as part of a longer process of evolution comprehensible in terms of enduring nonhuman patterns.

In *Divine Comedies* (which received the Pulitzer Prize in 1977) Merrill began his most ambitious work: two thirds of it is devoted to *The Book of Ephraim*, a long narrative, the first of a trilogy of book-length poems. It is not only a recapitulation of his career but also an attempt to locate individual psychic energies as part of a larger series of nourishing influences: friends living and dead, literary predecessors, scientific theories of the growth of the universe and the mind, the life of other periods and even other universes—all conducted through a set of encounters with the "other world" in seances at the Ouija board. It is a witty and original and assured attempt to take the intimate material of the short lyric which has characterized his earlier work and cast it onto an epic scale.

An Urban Convalescence

Out for a walk, after a week in bed,
I find them tearing up part of my block
And, chilled through, dazed and lonely, join the dozen
In meek attitudes, watching a huge crane
Fumble luxuriously in the filth of years.   5
Her jaws dribble rubble. An old man
Laughs and curses in her brain,
Bringing to mind the close of *The White Goddess*.[1]

As usual in New York, everything is torn down
Before you have had time to care for it.   10
Head bowed, at the shrine of noise, let me try to recall
What building stood here. Was there a building at all?
I have lived on this same street for a decade.

Wait. Yes. Vaguely a presence rises
Some five floors high, of shabby stone   15
—Or am I confusing it with another one
In another part of town, or of the world?—
And over its lintel into focus vaguely
Misted with blood (my eyes are shut)
A single garland sways, stone fruit, stone leaves,   20
Which years of grit had etched until it thrust
Roots down, even into the poor soil of my seeing.
When did the garland become part of me?
I ask myself, amused almost,
Then shiver once from head to toe,   25

Transfixed by a particular cheap engraving of garlands
Bought for a few francs long ago,

1. The book (1948) in which English poet Robert Graves sets forth the impassioned theory that authentic poetry is inspired by a primitive goddess who is both creative and destructive. The crane is her sacred bird, which through a pun the poet here associates with the mechanical crane. Its operator seems like a crazed parody poet, committed only to demolition.

All calligraphic tendril[2] and cross-hatched rondure,
Ten years ago, and crumpled up to stanch
Boughs dripping, whose white gestures filled a cab,　　　30
And thought of neither then nor since.
Also, to clasp them, the small, red-nailed hand
Of no one I can place. Wait. No. Her name, her features
Lie toppled underneath that year's fashions.
The words she must have spoken, setting her face　　　35
To fluttering like a veil, I cannot hear now,
Let alone understand.

So that I am already on the stair,
As it were, of where I lived,
When the whole structure shudders at my tread　　　40
And soundlessly collapses, filling
The air with motes of stone.
Onto the still erect building next door
Are pressed levels and hues—
Pocked rose, streaked greens, brown whites.　　　45
Who drained the pousse-café?[3]
Wires and pipes, snapped off at the roots, quiver.

Well, that is what life does. I stare
A moment longer, so. And presently
The massive volume of the world　　　50
Closes again.

Upon that book I swear
To abide by what it teaches:
Gospels of ugliness and waste,
Of towering voids, of soiled gusts,　　　55
Of a shrieking to be faced
Full into, eyes astream with cold—

With cold?
All right then. With self-knowledge.

Indoors at last, the pages of *Time* are apt　　　60
To open, and the illustrated mayor of New York,
Given a glimpse of how and where I work,
To note yet one more house that can be scrapped.

Unwillingly I picture
My walls weathering in the general view.　　　65
It is not even as though the new
Buildings did very much for architecture.

Suppose they did. The sickness of our time requires
That these as well be blasted in their prime.

2. Delicately engraved and shaded vines
and curving boughs.　　　3. An after-dinner drink made up of layers of different colored cordials.

You would think the simple fact of having lasted   70
Threatened our cities like mysterious fires.

There are certain phrases which to use in a poem
Is like rubbing silver with quicksilver. Bright
But facile, the glamour deadens overnight.
For instance, how 'the sickness of our time'   75

Enhances, then debases, what I feel.
At my desk I swallow in a glass of water
No longer cordial, scarcely wet, a pill
They had told me not to take until much later.

With the result that back into my imagination   80
The city glides, like cities seen from the air,
Mere smoke and sparkle to the passenger
Having in mind another destination

Which now is not that honey-slow descent
Of the Champs-Elysées,[4] her hand in his,   85
But the dull need to make some kind of house
Out of the life lived, out of the love spent.

                                                                1962

The Broken Home

Crossing the street,
I saw the parents and the child
At their window, gleaming like fruit
With evening's mild gold leaf.

In a room on the floor below,   5
Sunless, cooler—a brimming
Saucer of wax, marbly and dim—
I have lit what's left of my life.

I have thrown out yesterday's milk
And opened a book of maxims.   10
The flame quickens. The word stirs.

Tell me, tongue of fire,
That you and I are as real
At least as the people upstairs.

My father, who had flown in World War I,   15
Might have continued to invest his life
In cloud banks well above Wall Street and wife.
But the race was run below, and the point was to win.

Too late now, I make out in his blue gaze
(Through the smoked glass of being thirty-six)   20

---

4. A stylish boulevard in Paris.

The soul eclipsed by twin black pupils, sex
And business; time was money in those days.

Each thirteenth year he married. When he died
There were already several chilled wives
In sable orbit—rings, cars, permanent waves.   25
We'd felt him warming up for a green bride.

He could afford it. He was "in his prime"
At three score ten. But money was not time.

                                ●

When my parents were younger this was a popular act:
A veiled woman would leap from an electric, wine-dark car   30
To the steps of no matter what—the Senate or the Ritz Bar—
And bodily, at newsreel speed, attack

No matter whom—Al Smith[1] or José Maria Sert[2]
Or Clemenceau[3]—veins standing out on her throat
As she yelled *War mongerer! Pig! Give us the vote!*,   35
And would have to be hauled away in her hobble skirt.

What had the man done? Oh, made history.
Her business (he had implied) was giving birth,
Tending the house, mending the socks.

Always that same old story—   40
Father Time and Mother Earth,[4]
A marriage on the rocks.

                                ●

One afternoon, red, satyr-thighed
Michael, the Irish setter, head
Passionately lowered, led   45
The child I was to a shut door. Inside,

Blinds beat sun from the bed.
The green-gold room throbbed like a bruise.
Under a sheet, clad in taboos
Lay whom we sought, her hair undone, outspread,   50

And of a blackness found, if ever now, in old
Engravings where the acid bit.
I must have needed to touch it
Or the whiteness—was she dead?
Her eyes flew open, startled strange and cold.   55
The dog slumped to the floor. She reached for me. I fled.

                                ●

1. Alfred E. Smith (1873–1944), a Governor of New York and in 1928 candidate for the presidency.
2. Spanish painter (1876–1945) who decorated the lobby of the Waldorf Astoria hotel in New York (1930).
3. Georges Clemenceau (1841–1929), Premier of France during World War I, visited the U.S. in 1922.
4. In one sense a reference to Cronus (Greek for Time) and Rhea, Mother of the Gods, the parents of Zeus, who dethroned his father.

Tonight they have stepped out onto the gravel.
The party is over. It's the fall
Of 1931. They love each other still.

She: Charlie, I can't stand the pace.   60
He: Come on, honey—why, you'll bury us all!

A lead soldier guards my windowsill:
Khaki rifle, uniform, and face.
Something in me grows heavy, silvery, pliable.

How intensely people used to feel!   65
Like metal poured at the close of a proletarian novel,[5]
Refined and glowing from the crucible,
I see those two hearts, I'm afraid,
Still. Cool here in the graveyard of good and evil,
They are even so to be honored and obeyed.   70

⋅

... Obeyed, at least, inversely. Thus
I rarely buy a newspaper, or vote.
To do so, I have learned, is to invite
The tread of a stone guest[6] within my house.

Shooting this rusted bolt, though, against him,   75
I trust I am no less time's child than some
Who on the heath impersonate Poor Tom[7]
Or on the barricades risk life and limb.

Nor do I try to keep a garden, only
An avocado in a glass of water—   80
Roots pallid, gemmed with air. And later,

When the small gilt leaves have grown
Fleshy and green, I let them die, yes, yes,
And start another. I am earth's no less.

⋅

A child, a red dog roam the corridors,   85
Still, of the broken home. No sound. The brilliant
Rag runners halt before wide-open doors.
My old room! Its wallpaper—cream, medallioned
With pink and brown—brings back the first nightmares,
Long summer colds, and Emma, sepia-faced,   90
Perspiring over broth carried upstairs
Aswim with golden fats I could not taste.

The real house became a boarding-school.
Under the ballroom ceiling's allegory

5. I.e., a novel dealing with labor, here with making iron and steel.
6. The commendatore in Mozart's *Don Giovanni* (1787) returns as a statue to get his revenge.
7. Edgar, in Shakespeare's *King Lear*, disowned by his father, wanders the heath as a madman.

Someone at last may actually be allowed   95
To learn something; or, from my window, cool
With the unstiflement of the entire story,
Watch a red setter stretch and sink in cloud.

                                                                    1966

Days of 1964[1]

Houses, an embassy, the hospital,
Our neighborhood sun-cured if trembling still
In pools of the night's rain . . .
Across the street that led to the center of town
A steep hill kept one company part way   5
Or could be climbed in twenty minutes
For some literally breathtaking views,
Framed by umbrella pines, of city and sea.
Underfoot, cyclamen, autumn crocus grew
Spangled as with fine sweat among the relics   10
Of good times had by all. If not Olympus,[2]
An out-of-earshot, year-round hillside revel.

I brought home flowers from my climbs.
Kyria[3] Kleo who cleans for us
Put them in water, sighing *Virgin, Virgin*.   15
Her legs hurt. She wore brown, was fat, past fifty,
And looked like a Palmyra[4] matron
Copied in lard and horsehair. How she loved
You, me, loved us all, the bird, the cat!
I think now she *was* love. She sighed and glistened   20
All day with it, or pain, or both.
(We did not notably communicate.)
She lived nearby with her pious mother
And wastrel son. She called me her real son.

I paid her generously, I dare say.   25
Love makes one generous. Look at us. We'd known
Each other so briefly that instead of sleeping
We lay whole nights, open, in the lamplight,
And gazed, or traded stories.

One hour comes back—you gasping in my arms   30
With love, or laughter, or both,
I having just remembered and told you
What I'd looked up to see on my way downtown at noon:
Poor old Kleo, her aching legs,

1. This poem takes place in Athens. The Alexandrian poet Cavafy (1863–1933) wrote a number of Greek love poems having the form of this title (*Days of* . . . .)
2. In Greek mythology, the mountain home of the gods.
3. A form of address ("Mrs.").
4. A style of sculpture relatively crude and with sharply defined lines, which flourished in the ancient Syrian city of Palmyra (later part of the Roman Empire and today famous for its ruins).

Trudging into the pines. I called,   35
Called three times before she turned.
Above a tight, skyblue sweater, her face
Was painted. Yes. Her face was painted
Clown-white, white of the moon by daylight,
Lidded with pearl, mouth a poinsettia leaf,   40
Eat me, pay me—the erotic mask
Worn the world over by illusion
To weddings of itself and simple need.
Startled mute, we had stared—was love illusion?—
And gone our ways. Next, I was crossing a square   45
In which a moveable outdoor market's
Vegetables, chickens, pottery kept materializing
Through a dream-press of hagglers each at heart
Leery lest he be taken, plucked,
The bird, the flower of that November mildness,   50
Self lost up soft clay paths, or found, foothold,
Where the bud throbs awake
The better to be nipped, self on its knees in mud—
Here I stopped cold, for both our sakes;

And calmer on my way home bought us fruit.   55

Forgive me if you read this. (And may Kyria Kleo,
Should someone ever put it into Greek
And read it aloud to her, forgive me, too.)
I had gone so long without loving,
I hardly knew what I was thinking.   60
Where I hid my face, your touch, quick, merciful,
Blindfolded me. A god breathed from my lips.
If that was illusion, I wanted it to last long;
To dwell, for its daily pittance, with us there,
Cleaning and watering, sighing with love or pain.   65
I hoped it would climb when it needed to the heights
Even of degradation, as I for one
Seemed, those days, to be always climbing
Into a world of wild
Flowers, feasting, tears—or was I falling, legs   70
Buckling, heights, depths,
Into a pool of each night's rain?
But you were everywhere beside me, masked,
As who was not, in laughter, pain, and love.

                                                                       1966

After the Fire

Everything changes; nothing does. I am back,
The doorbell rings, my heart leaps out of habit,
But it is only Kleo[1]—how thin, how old!—
Trying to smile, lips chill as the fallen dusk.

---

1. The same Greek housekeeper who appears in *Days of 1964*.

She has brought a cake "for tomorrow" 5
As if tomorrows were still memorable.
We sit down in the freshly-painted hall
Once used for little dinners. (The smoke cleared
On no real damage, yet I'd wanted changes,
Balcony glassed in, electric range, 10
And wrote to have them made after the fire.)
Now Kleo's eyes begin to stream in earnest—
Tears of joy? Ah, troubles too, I fear.
Her old mother has gone off the deep end.

From their basement window the yiayia,[2] nearly ninety, 15
Hurls invective at the passing scene,
Tea bags as well, the water bill, an egg
For emphasis. A strange car stops outside?
She cackles *Here's the client! Paint your face,*
Putana![3] to her daughter moistening 20
With tears the shirt she irons. Or locks her out
On her return from watering, with tears,
My terrace garden. (I will see tomorrow
The white oleander burst from its pot in the rains.)
Nor is darling Panayioti, Kleo's son, 25
Immune. Our entire neighbourhood now knows
As if they hadn't years before
that he is a *Degenerate!* a *Thieving*
Faggot! just as Kleo is a *Whore!*

I press Kleo's cold hand and wonder 30
What could the poor yiayia have done
to deserve this terrible gift of hindsight,
These visions that possess her of a past
When Kleo really was a buxom armful
And "Noti" cruised the Naval Hospital, 35
slim then, with teased hair. Now he must be forty,
Age at which degeneration takes
Too much of one's time and strength and money.
My eyes brim with past evenings in this hall,
Gravy-spattered cloth, candles minutely 40
Guttering in the love-blinded gaze.
The walls' original oldfashioned colors,
Cendre de rose,[4] warm flaking ivory—
Colors last seen as by that lover's ghost
Stumbling downstairs wound in a sheet of flame— 45
Are hidden now forever but not lost
Beneath this quiet sensible light gray.

Kleo goes on. The yiayia's *warm*,
What can it mean? She who sat blanketed
In mid-July now burns all day, 50

2. A Greek grandmother.   4. Dusty pink.
3. Whore.

Eats only sugar, having ascertained
Poison in whatever Kleo cooks.
Kill me, there'll be an autopsy,
Putana, matricide, I've seen to that!
I mention my own mother's mother's illness,   55
Querulous temper, lucid shame.
Kleo says weeping that it's not the same,
There's nothing wrong, according to the doctor,
Just that she's old and merciless. And warm.

Next day I visit them. Red-eyed Kleo   60
Lets me in. Beyond her, bedclothes disarrayed,
The little leaden oven-rosy witch
Fastens her unrecognizing glare
Onto the lightest line that I can spin.
"It's me, yiayia! Together let us plumb   65
Depths long dry"—getting no further, though,
Than Panayioti's anaconda arms:

"Ah Monsieur Tzim, bon zour et bon retour!
Excuse mon déshabillé. Toute la nuit
Z'ai décoré l'église pour la fête   70
Et fait l'amour, le prêtre et moi,
Dans une alcove derrière la Sainte Imaze.
Tiens, z'ai un cadeau pour toi,
Zoli foulard qui me va pas du tout.
Mais prends-le donc, c'est pas volé—   75
Ze ne suis plus voleur, seulement volaze!"[5]

Huge, powerful, bland, he rolls his eyes and r's.
Glints of copper wreathe his porcelain brow
Like the old-time fuses here, that blow so readily.
I seem to know that crimson robe,   80
And on his big fat feet—my slippers, ruined.
Still, not to complicate affairs,
Remembering also the gift of thumb-sized garnet
Bruises he clasped round Aleko's throat,
I beam with gratitude. Meanwhile   85
Other translated objects one by one
Peep from hiding: teapot, towel, transistor.
Upon the sideboard an old me
Scissored from its glossy tavern scene—
I know that bare arm too, flung round my shoulder—   90
Buckles against a ruby glass ashtray.
(It strikes me now, as happily it did not
The insurance company, that P caused the fire.
Kleo's key borrowed for a rendezvous,

---

5. **Badly spoken French:** "Ah, Mr. Jim, hello and welcome back. Excuse my sloppy appearance. All night I decorated the church for the holiday and made love, the priest and I, in a nook behind the Holy Image. Look, I have a gift for you, a pretty scarf that isn't at all right for me. Please take it. It's not stolen. I'm not a thief, only fickle."

A cigarette left burning . . . Never mind.)   95
Life like the bandit Somethingopoulos
Gives to others what it takes from us.
Some of those embers can't be handled yet.

I mean to ask whose feast it is today
But the room brightens, the yiayia shrieks my name—   100
It's Tzimi! He's returned!
—And with that she returns to human form,
The snuffed-out candle-ends grow tall and shine,
Dead flames encircle us, which cannot harm,
The table's spread, she croons, and I   105
Am kneeling pressed to her old burning frame.

                                                           1972

Lost in Translation

FOR RICHARD HOWARD[1]

Diese Tage, die leer dir scheinen
und wertlos für das All,
haben Wurzeln zwischen den Steinen
und trinken dort überall.[2]

A card table in the library stands ready
To receive the puzzle which keeps never coming.
Daylight shines in or lamplight down
Upon the tense oasis of green felt.
Full of unfulfillment, life goes on,   5
Mirage arisen from time's trickling sands
Or fallen piecemeal into place:
German lesson, picnic, see-saw, walk
With the collie who "did everything but talk"—
Sour windfalls of the orchard back of us.   10
A summer without parents is the puzzle,
Or should be. But the boy, day after day,
Writes in his Line-a-Day No *puzzle*.

He's in love, at least. His French Mademoiselle,[3]
In real life a widow since Verdun,   15
Is stout, plain, carrot-haired, devout.
She prays for him, as does a curé in Alsace,
Sews costumes for his marionettes,
Helps him to keep behind the scene
Whose sidelit goosegirl, speaking with his voice,   20
Plays Guinevere as well as Gunmoll Jean.
Or else at bedtime in his tight embrace
Tells him her own French hopes, her German fears,

1. American poet and translator from the French (b. 1929).
2. Part of a translation by the Austrian poet Rainer Maria Rilke (1875–1926) of *Palme* by the French poet Paul Valéry (1871–1945). See lines 32, 33. "These days which seem empty and entirely fruitless to you have roots between the stones and drink from everywhere."
3. A French-speaking governess; "Verdun": site of a battle in World War I; "curé": a French priest.

Her—but what more is there to tell?
Having known grief and hardship, Mademoiselle   25
Knows little more. Her languages. Her place.
Noon coffee. Mail. The watch that also waited
Pinned to her heart, poor gold, throws up its hands—
No puzzle! Steaming bitterness
Her sugars draw pops back into his mouth, translated: 30
"Patience, chéri. Geduld, mein Schatz."[4]
(Thus, reading Valéry the other evening
And seeming to recall a Rilke version of "Palme,"
That sunlit paradigm whereby the tree
Taps a sweet wellspring of authority,   35
The hour came back. Patience dans l'azur.
Geduld im . . . Himmelblau? Mademoiselle.)

Out of the blue, as promised, of a New York
Puzzle-rental shop the puzzle comes—
A superior one, containing a thousand hand-sawn,   40
Sandal-scented pieces. Many take
Shapes known already—the craftsman's repertoire
Nice in its limitation—from other puzzles:
Witch on broomstick, ostrich, hourglass,
Even (surely not just in retrospect)   45
An inchling, innocently branching palm.
These can be put aside, made stories of
While Mademoiselle spreads out the rest face-up,
Herself excited as a child; or questioned
Like incoherent faces in a crowd,   50
Each with its scrap of highly colored
Evidence the Law must piece together.
Sky-blue ostrich? Likely story.
Mauve of the witch's cloak white, severed fingers
Pluck? Detain her. The plot thickens   55
As all at once two pieces interlock.

Mademoiselle does borders—(Not so fast.
A London dusk, December last.
Chatter silenced in the library
This grown man reenters, wearing grey.   60
A medium. All except him have seen
Panel slid back, recess explored,
An object at once unique and common
Displayed, planted in a plain tole
Casket the subject now considers   65
Through shut eyes, saying in effect:
"Even as voices reach me vaguely
A dry saw-shriek drowns them out,
Some loud machinery—a lumber mill?

---

4. French and German phrases for "Have
patience, my dear." The recalled phrases
remind him of a line in Valéry's *Palme*
and Rilke's translation; "Patience in the
blue": a way of characterizing the slow
nurture of the palm tree.

Far uphill in the fir forest   70
Trees tower, tense with shock,
Groaning and cracking as they crash groundward.
But hidden here is a freak fragment
Of a pattern complex in appearance only.
What it seems to show is superficial   75
Next to that long-term lamination
Of hazard and craft, the karma that has
Made it matter in the first place.
Plywood. Piece of a puzzle." Applause
Acknowledged by an opening of lids   80
Upon the thing itself. A sudden dread—
But to go back. All this lay years ahead.)

Mademoiselle does borders. Straight-edge pieces
Align themselves with earth or sky
In twos and threes, naive cosmogonists   85
Whose views clash. Nomad inlanders meanwhile
Begin to cluster where the totem
Of a certain vibrant egg-yolk yellow
Or pelt of what emerging animal
Acts on the straggler like a trumpet call   90
To form a more sophisticated unit.
By suppertime two ragged wooden clouds
Have formed. In one, a Sheik with beard
And flashing sword hilt (he is all but finished)
Steps forward on a tiger skin. A piece   95
Snaps shut, and fangs gnash out at us!
In the second cloud—they gaze from cloud to cloud
With marked if undecipherable feeling—
Most of a dark-eyed woman veiled in mauve
Is being helped down from her camel (kneeling)   100
By a small backward-looking slave or page-boy
(Her son, thinks Mademoiselle mistakenly)
Whose feet have not been found. But lucky finds
In the last minutes before bed
Anchor both factions to the scene's limits   105
And, by so doing, orient
Them eye to eye across the green abyss.
The yellow promises, oh bliss,
To be in time a sumptuous tent.

Puzzle begun I write in the day's space,   110
Then, while she bathes, peek at Mademoiselle's
Page to the curé: ". . . cette innocente mère,
Ce pauvre enfant, que deviendront-ils?"[5]
Her azure script is curlicued like pieces
Of the puzzle she will be telling him about.   115
(Fearful incuriosity of childhood!

---

5. "This innocent mother, this poor child, what will become of them?"

"Tu as l'accent allemand,"[6] said Dominique.
Indeed. Mademoiselle was only French by marriage.
Child of an English mother, a remote
Descendant of the great explorer Speke,   120
And Prussian father. No one knew. I heard it
Long afterwards from her nephew, a UN
Interpreter. His matter-of-fact account
Touched old strings. My poor Mademoiselle,
With 1939 about to shake   125
This world where "each was the enemy, each the friend"
To its foundations, kept, though signed in blood,
Her peace a shameful secret to the end.)
"Schlaf wohl, chéri." Her kiss. Her thumb
Crossing my brow against the dreams to come.   130

This World that shifts like sand, its unforeseen
Consolidations and elate routine,
Whose Potentate had lacked a retinue?
Lo! it assembles on the shrinking Green.

Gunmetal-skinned or pale, all plumes and scars,   135
Of Vassalage the noblest avatars—
The very coffee-bearer in his vair
Vest is a swart Highness, next to ours.

Kef[7] easing Boredom, and iced syrups, thirst,
In guessed-at glooms old wives who know the worst   140
Outsweat that virile fiction of the New:
"Insh'Allah, he will tire—" "—or kill her first!"

(Hardly a proper subject for the Home,
Work of—dear Richard, I shall let *you* comb
Archives and learned journals for his name—   145
A minor lion attending on Gérôme.)[8]

While, thick as Thebes[9] whose presently complete
Gates close behind them, Houri and Afreet[1]
Both claim the Page. He wonders whom to serve,
And what his duties are, and where his feet,   150

And if we'll find, as some before us did,
That piece of Distance deep in which lies hid
Your tiny apex sugary with sun,
Eternal Triangle, Great Pyramid!

Then Sky alone is left, a hundred blue   155
Fragments in revolution, with no clue

6. "You have a German accent."
7. A narcotic made from Indian hemp.
8. French painter (1824–1904), noted for his historical paintings, often of Near Eastern scenes.
9. The ancient capital of Upper Egypt.
1. Near Eastern mythological figures: "Houri": a virgin awarded to those who attain paradise; "Afreet": an evil genie.

To where a Niche will open. Quite a task,
Putting together Heaven, yet we do.

It's done. Here under the table all along
Were those missing feet. It's done.   160

The dog's tail thumping. Mademoiselle sketching
Costumes for a coming harem drama
To star the goosegirl. All too soon the swift
Dismantling. Lifted by two corners,
The puzzle hung together—and did not.   165
Irresistibly a populace
Unstitched of its attachments, rattled down.
Power went to pieces as the witch
Slithered easily from Virtue's gown.
The blue held out for time, but crumbled, too.   170
The city had long fallen, and the tent,
A separating sauce mousseline,
Been swept away. Remained the green
On which the grown-ups gambled. A green dusk.
First lightning bugs. Last glow of west   175
Green in the false eyes of (coincidence)
Our mangy tiger safe on his bared hearth.

Before the puzzle was boxed and readdressed
To the puzzle shop in the mid-Sixties,
Something tells me that one piece contrived   180
To stay in the boy's pocket. How do I know?
I know because so many later puzzles
had missing pieces—Maggie Teyte's[2] high notes
Gone at the war's end, end of the vogue for collies,
A house torn down; and hadn't Mademoiselle   185
Kept back her pitiful bit of truth as well?
I've spent the last days, furthermore,
Ransacking Athens for that translation of "Palme."
Neither the Goethehaus nor the National Library
Seems able to unearth it. Yet I can't   190
Just be imagining. I've seen it. Know
How much of the sun-ripe original
Felicity Rilke made himself forego
(Who loved French words—verger, mûr, parfumer)[3]
In order to render its underlying sense.   195
Know already in that tongue of his
What Pains, what monolithic Truths
Shadow stanza to stanza's symmetrical
Rhyme-rutted pavement. Know that ground plan left
Sublime and barren, where the warm Romance   200
Stone by stone faded, cooled; the fluted nouns
Made taller, lonelier than life

2. English soprano (1888–1976), famous   songs.
for her singing of French opera and   3. "Orchard, ripe, to scent."

By leaf-carved capitals in the afterglow.
The owlet umlaut[4] peeps and hoots
Above the open vowel. And after rain   205
A deep reverberation fills with stars.

Lost, is it, buried? One more missing piece?

But nothing's lost. Or else: all is translation
And every bit of us is lost in it
(Or found—I wander through the ruin of S[5]   210
Now and then, wondering at the peacefulness)
And in that loss a self-effacing tree,
Color of context, imperceptibly
Rustling with its angel, turns the waste
To shade and fiber, milk and memory.   215

                                                                   1976

4. A German accent mark (¨).   5. Initial of former lover.

FRANK O'HARA
1926–1966

After Frank O'Hara's death, when the critic Donald Allen gathered O'Hara's *Collected Poems*, he was surprised to discover that there were more than 500, many not published before. Some had to be retrieved from letters or from scraps of paper in boxes and trunks. O'Hara's poems were often spontaneous acts, revised minimally or not at all, then scattered generously, half forgotten. His work was published, not by large commercial presses but by art galleries such as Tibor de Nagy and by small presses. These influential but fugitive paperbacks—*A City Winter* (1952), *Meditations in an Emergency* (1956), *Lunch Poems* (1964), and *Second Avenue* (1960)—included love poems, "letter" poems, "post-cards," and odes, each bearing the mark of its occasion: a birthday, a thank you, memories of a lunch hour, or simply *Having a Coke with You*. They are filled, like diaries, with the names of Manhattan streets, writers, artists, restaurants, cafés, and films. O'Hara practiced what he once called, in mockery of sober poetic manifestoes, "personism." The term came to him one day at the office when he was writing a poem for someone he loved. "While I was writing it I was realizing that if I wanted to I could use the telephone instead of writing the poem, and so Personism was born. * * * It puts the poem squarely between the poet and the person, Lucky Pierre style, and the poem is correspondingly gratified. The poem is at last between two persons instead of two pages."

O'Hara came to live in New York in 1951. He was born in Baltimore and grew up in Worcester, Massachusetts. He was in the navy for two years (with service in the South Pacific and Japan), then at Harvard, where he majored in music and English. In New York he became involved in the art world, working at different times as an editor and critic for *Art News* and a curator for the Museum of Modern Art. But this was more than a way of making a living; it was also making a life. These were the years in which Abstract Expressionism—nonrepresentational painting—flourished, and New York replaced Paris as the art capital of the world. O'Hara met and wrote about painters such as Willem de Kooning, Franz Kline, and Jackson Pollock, then producing their most brilliant work. After 1955, as a special assistant in the International Program of the Museum of Modern Art, O'Hara helped organize important traveling exhibitions which introduced and impressed the new American painting upon the art world abroad.

As friends, many of these painters and sculptors were the occasion for and recipients of O'Hara's poems. Even more important, their way of working served as a model for his own style of writing. As the poet John Ashbery puts it, "The poem [is] the chronicle of the creative act that produces it." At the simplest level this means including the random jumps, distractions, and loose associations involved in writing about a particular moment, and sometimes recording the pauses in the writing of the poem. ("And now that I have finished dinner I can continue.") In O'Hara's work the casual is often, unexpectedly, the launching point for the visionary. The offhand chronicle of a lunch-hour walk can suddenly crystallize around a thunderclap memory of three friends, artists who died young: "First / Bunny died, then John Latouche, / then Jackson Pollock. But is the / earth as full as life was full, of them?"

Frank O'Hara was indisputably, for his generation, *the* poet of New York. The very title of one of his poems, *To the Mountains in New York,* suggests that the city was for him what pastoral or rural worlds were for other writers, a source of refreshment and fantasy.

> I love this hairy city.
> It's wrinkled like a detective story
> and noisy and getting fat and smudged
> lids hood the sharp hard black eyes.

Behind the exultation of O'Hara's cityscapes, a reader can often sense the melancholy which is made explicit in poems such as A *Step Away from Them.* Part of the city's allure was that it answered O'Hara's driving need to reach out for friends, events, animation. His eagerness is balanced on "the wilderness wish / of wanting to be everything to everybody everywhere." There is also in O'Hara's poetry an understanding of how urban life and the world of machines can devour the spirit; he was fascinated with, and wrote several poems about, the young actor James Dean, whose addiction to racing culminated in a fatal automobile accident.

O'Hara's example encouraged other poets—John Ashbery, Kenneth Koch, and James Schuyler. Loosely known as the New York School of Poets, they occasionally collaborated on poems, plays, and happenings. O'Hara's bravado was a rallying point for these writers outside the more traditional and historically conscious modernism of Pound and Eliot. As John Ashbery remembers, "He was more influenced by contemporary music and art than by what had been going on in American poetry." His poems were like "inspired rambling," open to all levels and areas of experience, expressed in a colloquial tone which could easily shade into Surrealistic dream. "I'm too blue, / An elephant takes up his trumpet, / money flutters from the windows of cries."

A few days after his fortieth birthday in 1966, O'Hara was struck down at night by a beach-buggy on Fire Island, New York. He died a few hours later. With his death, the nourishing interaction of painting and writing in New York, as well as their fertilizing effect on dance and theater, seemed over. Without his central communicating figure, the fields tended to seal themselves off once more.

To the Harbormaster

I wanted to be sure to reach you;
though my ship was on the way it got caught
in some moorings. I am always tying up
and then deciding to depart. In storms and
at sunset, with the metallic coils of the tide   5
around my fathomless arms, I am unable
to understand the forms of my vanity
or I am hard alee with my Polish rudder[1]
in my hand and the sun sinking. To
you I offer my hull and the tattered cordage   10
of my will. The terrible channels where
the wind drives me against the brown lips
of the reeds are not all behind me. Yet
I trust the sanity of my vessel; and
if it sinks, it may well be in answer   15
to the reasoning of the eternal voices,
the waves which have kept me from reaching you.

1954?   1957

Sleeping on the Wing

Perhaps it is to avoid some great sadness,
as in a Restoration tragedy[1] the hero cries "Sleep!
O for a long sound sleep and so forget it!"
that one flies, soaring above the shoreless city,
veering upward from the pavement as a pigeon   5
does when a car honks or a door slams, the door
of dreams, life perpetuated in parti-colored loves
and beautiful lies all in different languages.

Fear drops away too, like the cement, and you
are over the Atlantic. Where is Spain? where is   10
who? The Civil War was fought to free the slaves,
was it? A sudden down-draught reminds you of gravity
and your position in respect to human love. But

1. Probably a submerged comic reference to "The Polish Rider" by Rembrandt. O'Hara said this poem was about his friend, the contemporary painter Larry Rivers, who expressed a continuing fascination with Rembrandt's painting of a knight on horseback. "Hard alee": a movement toward the lee or sheltered side of a sailboat; i.e., away from the wind.
1. An especially melodramatic or rhetorical brand of tragedy from the period of English history after the restoration of Charles II to the throne (1660).

here is where the gods are, speculating, bemused.
Once you are helpless, you are free, can you believe   15
that? Never to waken to the sad struggle of a face?
to travel always over some impersonal vastness,
to be out of, forever, neither in nor for!
The eyes roll asleep as if turned by the wind
and the lids flutter open slightly like a wing.   20
The world is an iceberg, so much is invisible!
and was and is, and yet the form, it may be sleeping
too. Those features etched in the ice of someone
loved who died, you are a sculptor dreaming of space
and speed, your hand alone could have done this.   25
Curiosity, the passionate hand of desire. Dead,
or sleeping? Is there speed enough? And, swooping,
you relinquish all that you have made your own,
the kingdom of your self sailing, for you must awake
and breathe your warmth in this beloved image   30
whether it's dead or merely disappearing,
as space is disappearing and your singularity.

1955   1957

In Memory of My Feelings

TO GRACE HARTIGAN[1]

1

My quietness has a man in it, he is transparent
and he carries me quietly, like a gondola, through the streets.
He has several likenesses, like stars and years, like numerals.
My quietness has a number of naked selves,
so many pistols I have borrowed to protect myselves   5
from creatures who too readily recognize my weapons
and have murder in their heart!
                  though in winter
they are warm as roses, in the desert
taste of chilled anisette.   10
              At times, withdrawn,
I rise into the cool skies
and gaze on at the imponderable world with the simple identification
of my colleagues, the mountains. Manfred[2] climbs to my nape,
speaks, but I do not hear him,   15
                I'm too blue.
An elephant takes up his trumpet,
money flutters from the windows of cries, silk stretching its mirror
across shoulder blades. A gun is "fired."
                    One of me rushes   20
to window #13 and one of me raises his whip and one of me
flutters up from the center of the track amidst the pink flamingoes,
and underneath their hooves as they round the last turn my lips
are scarred and brown, brushed by tails, masked in dirt's lust,

1. American Abstract Expressionist painter (b. 1922) and friend of the poet.
2. Tortured Romantic hero of Lord By-

ron's poetic drama of the same name.
Manfred, an exile, is pictured solitary
high in the mountains.

definition, open mouths gasping for the cries of the bettors for the
lungs of earth.   25
        So many of my transparencies could not resist the race!
Terror in earth, dried mushrooms, pink feathers, tickets,
a flaking moon drifting across the muddied teeth,
the imperceptible moan of covered breathing,   30
                love of the serpent!
I am underneath its leaves as the hunter crackles and pants
and bursts, as the barrage balloon drifts behind a cloud
and animal death whips out its flashlight,
                whistling   35
and slipping the glove off the trigger hand. The serpent's eyes
redden at sight of those thorny fingernails, he is so smooth!
          My transparent selves
flail about like vipers in a pail, writhing and hissing
without panic, with a certain justice of response   40
and presently the aquiline serpent comes to resemble the Medusa.[3]

2

The dead hunting
and the alive, ahunted.
       My father, my uncle,
my grand-uncle and the several aunts. My   45
grand-aunt dying for me, like a talisman, in the war,
before I had even gone to Borneo
her blood vessels rushed to the surface
and burst like rockets over the wrinkled
invasion of the Australians, her eyes aslant   50
like the invaded, but blue like mine.
An atmosphere of supreme lucidity,
          humanism,
the mere existence of emphasis,
         a rusted barge   55
painted orange against the sea
full of Marines reciting the Arabian ideas
which are a proof in themselves of seasickness
which is a proof in itself of being hunted.
A hit? *ergo* swim   60
      My 10   my 19,
my 9,   and the several years. My
12 years since they all died, philosophically speaking.
And now the coolness of a mind
like a shuttered suite in the Grand Hotel   65
where mail arrives for my incognito,[4]
         whose façade
has been slipping into the Grand Canal[5] for centuries;
rockets splay over a *sposalizio*,[6]

---

3. In Greek mythology, a female figure
with serpents growing out of her head,
whose glance turned men to stone.
4. Assumed identity.

5. Main waterway lined with crumbling
palaces in Venice.
6. Wedding.

fleeing into night   70
from their Chinese memories, and it is a celebration,
the trying desperately to count them as they die.
But who will stay to be these numbers
when all the lights are dead?

3

The most arid stretch is often richest,   75
the hand lifting towards a fig tree from hunger
                                        digging
and there is water, clear, supple, or there
deep in the sand where death sleeps, a murmurous bubbling
proclaims the blackness that will ease and burn.   80
You preferred the Arabs? but they didn't stay to count
their inventions, racing into sands, converting themselves into
so many,
             embracing, at Ramadan,[7] the tenderest effigies of
themselves with penises shorn by the hundreds, like a camel   85
ravishing a goat.
                       And the mountainous-minded Greeks could speak
of time as a river[8] and step across it into Persia, leaving the pain
at home to be converted into statuary. I adore the Roman copies.[9]
And the stench of the camel's spit I swallow,   90
and the stench of the whole goat. For we have advanced, France,
together into a new land, like the Greeks, where one feels nostalgic
for mere ideas, where truth lies on its deathbed like an uncle
and one of me has a sentimental longing for number,
as has another for the ball gowns of the Directoire and yet   95
another for "Destiny, Paris, destiny!"
                                    or "Only a king may kill a king."[1]

How many selves are there in a war hero asleep in names? under
a blanket of platoon and fleet, orderly. For every seaman
with one eye closed in fear and twitching arm at a sigh for Lord
          Nelson,[2]   100
he is all dead; and now a meek subaltern[3] writhes in his bedclothes
with the fury of a thousand, violating an insane mistress
who has only herself to offer his multitudes.
                                    Rising,
he wraps himself in the burnoose[4] of memories against the heat
          of life   105
and over the sands he goes to take an algebraic position *in re*[5]
a sun of fear shining not too bravely. He will ask himselves to
vote on fear before he feels a tremor,
                              as runners arrive from the mountains

7. Ninth month of the Mohammedan year, consisting of 30 days during which strict fasting is observed in daylight hours.
8. According to the Greek philosopher Heracleitus (c. 540–c. 480 B.C.).
9. I.e., of the original Greek statues.
1. Style popular during the French Di-
rectory (the revolutionary executive body, 1796); slogans having to do with controversies of the Napoleonic period.
2. Viscount Horatio Nelson (1758–1805), famous British naval hero.
3. Of subaltern rank.
4. Flowing Arab desert garment.
5. In reference to.

bearing snow, proof that the mind's obsolescence is still capable   110
of intimacy. His mistress will follow him across the desert
like a goat, towards a mirage which is something familiar about
one of his innumerable wrists,

                      and lying in an oasis one day,
playing catch with coconuts, they suddenly smell oil.   115

4

Beneath these lives
the ardent lover of history hides,

                   tongue out
leaving a globe of spit on a taut spear of grass
and leaves off rattling his tail a moment   120
to admire this flag.

             I'm looking for my Shanghai Lil.[6]
Five years ago, enamored of fire-escapes, I went to Chicago,
an eventful trip: the fountains! the Art Institute, the Y
for both sexes, absent Christianity.   125

             At 7, before Jane
was up, the copper lake stirred alainst the sides
of a Norwegian freighter; on the deck a few dirty men,
tired of night, watched themselves in the water
as years before the German prisoners on the *Prinz Eugen*   130
dappled the Pacific with their sores, painted purple
by a Naval doctor.

             Beards growing, and the constant anxiety
over looks. I'll shave before she wakes up. Sam Goldwyn
spent $2,000,000 on Anna Sten, but Grushenka left America.[7]   135
One of me is standing in the waves, an ocean bather,
or I am naked with a plate of devils at my hip.

             Grace
to be born and live as variously as possible. The conception
of the masque barely suggests the sordid identifications.   140
I am a Hittite[8] in love with a horse. I don't know what blood's
in me I feel like an African prince I am a girl walking downstairs
in a red pleated dress with heels I am a champion taking a fall
I am a jockey with a sprained ass-hole I am the light mist

                  in which a face appears   145
and it is another face of blonde I am a baboon eating a banana
I am a dictator looking at his wife I am a doctor eating a child
and the child's mother smiling I am a Chinaman climbing a
      mountain
I am a child smelling his father's underwear I am an Indian
sleeping on a scalp   150
           and my pony is stamping in the birches,

---

6. Femme fatale role played by Marlene Dietrich in the film *Shanghai Express* (1932).
7. In 1933, the powerful film producer Samuel Goldwyn (1882–1974) imported actress Anna Sten (b. 1908) to the United States in the hope of creating a new international star. (Sten was already celebrated in her native Russia, where, in 1931, she had starred as Grushenka in the film version of *The Brothers Karamazov*.) Goldwyn's plan failed.
8. Member of an ancient nomadic tribe of Asia Minor and Syria (1600–1200 B.C.).

and I've just caught sight of the *Niña,* the *Pinta* and the *Santa*
Maria.[9]
What land is this, so free?
I watch
the sea at the back of my eyes, near the spot where I think   [155]
in solitude as pine trees groan and support the enormous winds,
they are humming *L'Oiseau de feu!*[1]
They look like gods, these whitemen,
and they are bringing me the horse I fell in love with on the frieze.[2]
5
And now it is the serpent's turn.   [160]
I am not quite you, but almost, the opposite of visionary.
You are coiled around the central figure,
the heart
that bubbles with red ghosts, since to move is to love
and the scrutiny of all things is syllogistic,   [165]
the startled eyes of the dikdik,[3] the bush full of white flags
fleeing a hunter,
which is our democracy
but the prey
is always fragile and like something, as a seashell can be   [170]
a great Courbet,[4] if it wishes. To bend the ear of the outer world.

When you turn your head
can you feel your heels, undulating? that's what it is
to be a serpent. I haven't told you of the most beautiful things
in my lives, and watching the ripple of their loss disappear   [175]
along the shore, underneath ferns,
face downward in the ferns
my body, the naked host to my many selves, shot
by a guerrilla warrior or dumped from a car into ferns
which are themselves *journalières.*[5]   [180]
The hero, trying to unhitch his parachute,
stumbles over me. It is our last embrace.
And yet
I have forgotten my loves, and chiefly that one, the cancerous
statue which my body could no longer contain,   [185]
against my will
against my love
become art,
I could not change it into history
and so remember it,   [190]
and I have lost what is always and everywhere
present, the scene of my selves, the occasion of these ruses,
which I myself and singly must now kill
and save the serpent in their midst.

1956   1960

9. Columbus's three ships.
1. *The Firebird,* a ballet by Igor Stravinsky, premiered in 1910.
2. A band of sculptured decoration.

3. A small African antelope.
4. I.e., like a painting by the French Realist painter (1819–77).
5. Daylaborers.

A Step Away from Them

It's my lunch hour, so I go
for a walk among the hum-colored
cabs. First, down the sidewalk
where laborers feed their dirty
glistening torsos sandwiches   5
and Coca-Cola, with yellow helmets
on. They protect them from falling
bricks, I guess. Then onto the
avenue where skirts are flipping
above heels and blow up over   10
grates. The sun is hot, but the
cabs stir up the air. I look
at bargains in wristwatches. There
are cats playing in sawdust.
                            On   15
to Times Square, where the sign[1]
blows smoke over my head, and higher
the waterfall pours lightly. A
Negro stands in a doorway with a
toothpick, languorously agitating.   20
A blonde chorus girl clicks: he
smiles and rubs his chin. Everything
suddenly honks: it is 12:40 of
a Thursday.
                    Neon in daylight is a   25
great pleasure, as Edwin Denby[2] would
write, as are light bulbs in daylight.
I stop for a cheeseburger at JULIET'S
CORNER. Giulietta Masina, wife of
Federico Fellini, *è bell' attrice*.[3]   30
And chocolate malted. A lady in
foxes on such a day puts her poodle
in a cab.
              There are several Puerto
Ricans on the avenue today, which   35
makes it beautiful and warm. First
Bunny died, then John Latouche,
then Jackson Pollock.[4] But is the
earth as full as life was full, of them?
And one has eaten and one walks,   40
past the magazines with nudes
and the posters for BULLFIGHT and
the Manhattan Storage Warehouse,

1. Famous steam-puffing billboard advertising cigarettes.
2. Fellow poet (b. 1923) and influential
ballet critic.
3. "A beautiful actress." Masina starred
in many of director Fellini's best-known
films, such as *La Strada* (1954) and
Nights of Cabiria (1956).
4. V. R. Lang (1924–56), poet and director of The Poets' Theater in Cambridge, Massachusetts, where she produced
several of O'Hara's plays; Latouche
(1917–56), lyricist for several New York
musicals, such as *The Golden Apple*;
Pollock (1912–1956), Abstract Expressionist painter, considered the originator
of "action" painting. All three were gifted
friends of the poet who met tragic deaths.

which they'll soon tear down. I
used to think they had the Armory[5]   45
Show there.
                A glass of papaya juice
and back to work. My heart is in my
pocket, it is Poems by Pierre Reverdy.[6]

1956   1964

The Day Lady[1] Died

It is 12:20 in New York a Friday
three days after Bastille day,[2] yes
it is 1959 and I go get a shoeshine
because I will get off the 4:19 in Easthampton[3]
at 7:15 and then go straight to dinner   5
and I don't know the people who will feed me

I walk up the muggy street beginning to sun
and have a hamburger and a malted and buy
an ugly NEW WORLD WRITING to see what the poets
in Ghana are doing these days   10
                        I go on to the bank
and Miss Stillwagon (first name Linda I once heard)
doesn't even look up my balance for once in her life
and in the GOLDEN GRIFFIN[4] I get a little Verlaine
for Patsy with drawings by Bonnard although I do   15
think of Hesiod, trans. Richmond Lattimore or
Brendan Behan's new play or *Le Balcon* or *Les Nègres*
of Genet, but I don't, I stick with Verlaine
after practically going to sleep with quandariness

and for Mike I just stroll into the PARK LANE   20
Liquor Store and ask for a bottle of Strega and
then I go back where I came from to 6th Avenue
and the tobacconist in the Ziegfeld Theatre and
casually ask for a carton of Gauloises and a carton
of Picayunes, and a NEW YORK POST with her face on it 25

and I am sweating a lot by now and thinking of
leaning on the john door in the 5 SPOT
while she whispered a song along the keyboard
to Mal Waldron[5] and everyone and I stopped breathing

1959   1960

5. Site of the influential and controversial first American showing of European Post-Impressionist painters in 1913.
6. French poet (1899–1960), whose work strongly influenced O'Hara's writing.
1. Billie Holiday (1915–59), also known as Lady Day, the immortal black singer of jazz and the blues.
2. July 14, the French national holiday.
3. Town in eastern Long Island, popular summer resort among New York artists.
4. A bookstore close to the Museum of Modern Art. The attractions for O'Hara's intellectual hostess (the artist Patsy Southgate) of the books listed might be that the ones by Behan and Genêt were new plays recently done in New York. The edition of poems by French poet Paul Verlaine (1844–96) was illustrated by the equally famous French artist Pierre Bonnard (1867–1947). The Hesiod was a new translation by poet Richmond Lattimore.
5. Billie Holiday's accompanist (b. 1925).

Ave Maria[1]

Mothers of America
          let your kids go to the movies!
get them out of the house so they won't know what you're up to
it's true that fresh air is good for the body
                but what about the soul   5
that grows in darkness, embossed by silvery images
and when you grow old as grow old you must
                   they won't hate you
they won't criticize you they won't know
               they'll be in some glamorous country   10
they first saw on a Saturday afternoon or playing hookey

they may even be grateful to you
               for their first sexual experience
which only cost you a quarter
             and didn't upset the peaceful home 15
they will know where candy bars come from
              and gratuitous bags of popcorn
as gratuitous as leaving the movie before it's over
with a pleasant stranger whose apartment is in the Heaven on Earth
    Bldg
near the Williamsburg Bridge[2]   20
             oh mothers you will have made the little tykes
so happy because if nobody does pick them up in the movies
they won't know the difference
             and if somebody does it'll be sheer gravy
and they'll have been truly entertained either way   25
instead of hanging around the yard
          or up in their room
                 hating you
prematurely since you won't have done anything horribly mean yet
except keeping them from the darker joys   30
             it's unforgivable the latter
so don't blame me if you won't take this advice
             and the family breaks up
and your children grow old and blind in front of a TV set
               seeing 35
movies you wouldn't let them see when they were young
1960
                       1964

1. Ironic reference to the Catholic prayer addressed to the Virgin Mary, Mother of God.

2. Bridge connecting lower Manhattan with the Williamsburg section of Brooklyn.

JOHN ASHBERY
1927–

John Ashbery has described his writing this way: "I think that any one of my poems might be considered to be a snapshot of whatever is going on in my mind at the time—first of all the desire to write a poem, after that wondering if I've left the oven on or thinking about where I must be in the next hour." Ashbery has developed a style hospitable to quicksilver changes in tone and attention, to the awkward comedy of the unrelated thoughts and things at any given moment pressing in on what we say or do. So, for example, *Grand Galop* (1965) begins:

> All things seem mention of themselves
> And the names which stem from them branch out to
> > other referents.
> Hugely, spring exits again. The weigela does its
> > dusty thing
> In fire-hammered air. And garbage cans are heaved against
> The railing as the tulips yawn and crack open and fall apart.

The poem goes on to give some lunch menus which include "sloppy joe on bun." The proximity of "fire-hammered air" and "sloppy joe on bun" suggest a tension central to Ashbery's work: intuitions of vision and poetic ecstasy side by side with the commonplace. Ashbery's work implies that the two kinds of experience are inseparable in the mind.

Ashbery's poetry was not always so open to contradictory notions and impulses. His early books rejected the mere surfaces of realism and the momentary in order to get at "remoter areas of consciousness." The protagonist of *Illustration* (from his first book, *Some Trees*) is a cheerful nun about to leave behind the irrelevancies of the world by leaping from a skyscraper. Her act implies that "Much that is beautiful must be discarded / So that we may resemble a taller / impression of ourselves." To reach the "remoter areas of consciousness," Ashbery tried various technical experiments. He used highly patterned forms such as the sestina in *Some Trees* and *The Tennis Court Oath* (1962) not with any show of mechanical brilliance, but to explore: "I once told somebody that writing a sestina was rather like riding downhill on a bicycle and having the pedals push your feet. I wanted my feet to be pushed into places they wouldn't normally have taken. * * *"

Ashbery was born in Rochester, N.Y., in 1927. He attended Deerfield Academy and Harvard, graduating in 1949. He received an M.A. in English from Columbia in 1951. As a Fulbright scholar in French literature, Ashbery lived in Montpellier and Paris (1955–57) and wrote about the French avant-garde novelist Raymond Roussel. Again in France (1958–65), he was art critic for the European edition of the New York *Herald Tribune* and reported the European shows and exhibitions for *Art News and Arts International*. He returned to New York in 1965 to be executive editor of *Art News*, a position he held until 1972. He is currently a professor of English in the creative writing program at Brooklyn College.

Ashbery's interest in art played a formative role in his poetry. He is often associated with Frank O'Hara, James Schuyler, and Kenneth Koch as part of the "New York School" of poets. The name refers to their common interest in the New York school of abstract painters of the 1940s and 1950s, whose energies and techniques they wished to adapt in poetry. These painters avoided realism in order to stress the work of art as a representation of the creative act which produced it—as in the "action paintings" of Jackson

Pollock. Ashbery's long poem *Self-Portrait in a Convex Mirror* gives as much attention to the rapidly changing feelings of the poet in the act of writing his poem as it does to the Renaissance painting which inspired him. The poem moves back and forth between the distracted energies which feed a work of art and the completed composition, which the artist feels as both a triumph and as a falsification of complex feelings. Ashbery shares with O'Hara a sense of the colloquial brilliance of daily life in New York and sets this in tension with the concentration and stasis of art.

The book *Self-Portrait in a Convex Mirror* (1975) won the three major poetry prizes of its year; a tribute to the fact that it had perfected the play of contrasting voices—visionary and colloquial—which had long characterized Ashbery's work. He has since published *Houseboat Days* (1977).

Illustration

I

A novice[1] was sitting on a cornice
High over the city. Angels

Combined their prayers with those
Of the police, begging her to come off it.

One lady promised to be her friend.   5
"I do not want a friend," she said.

A mother offered her some nylons
Stripped from her very legs. Others brought

Little offerings of fruit and candy,
The blind man all his flowers. If any   10

Could be called successful, these were,
For that the scene should be a ceremony

Was what she wanted. "I desire
Monuments," she said. "I want to move

Figuratively, as waves caress   15
The thoughtless shore. You people I know

Will offer me every good thing
I do not want. But please remember

I died accepting them." With that, the wind
Unpinned her bulky robes, and naked   20

As a roc's[2] egg, she drifted softly downward
Out of the angels' tenderness and the minds of men.

---

1. Student in the first stage of instruction to be a nun.
2. Legendary bird of prey.

II

Much that is beautiful must be discarded
So that we may resemble a taller

Impression of ourselves. Moths climb in the flame,   25
Alas, that wish only to be the flame:

They do not lessen our stature.
We twinkle under the weight

Of indiscretions. But how could we tell
That of the truth we know, she was   30

The somber vestment? For that night, rockets sighed
Elegantly over the city, and there was feasting:

There is so much in that moment!
So many attitudes toward that flame,

We might have soared from earth, watching her glide   35
Aloft, in her peplum³ of bright leaves.

But she, of course, was only an effigy
Of indifference, a miracle

Not meant for us, as the leaves are not
Winter's because it is the end.   40

1956

Some Trees

These are amazing: each
Joining a neighbor, as though speech
Were a still performance.
Arranging by chance

To meet as far this morning   5
From the world as agreeing
With it, you and I
Are suddenly what the trees try

To tell us we are:
That their merely being there   10
Means something; that soon
We may touch, love, explain.

And glad not to have invented
Such comeliness, we are surrounded:
A silence already filled with noises,   15
A canvas on which emerges

3. In ancient Greece, a drapery about the upper part of the body.

A chorus of smiles, a winter morning.
Placed in a puzzling light, and moving,
Our days put on such reticence
These accents seem their own defense.   20

1956

Soonest Mended

Barely tolerated, living on the margin
In our technological society, we were always having to be rescued
On the brink of destruction, like heroines in *Orlando Furioso*[1]
Before it was time to start all over again.
There would be thunder in the bushes, a rustling of coils,   5
And Angelica, in the Ingres painting,[2] was considering
The colorful but small monster near her toe, as though wondering
    whether forgetting
The whole thing might not, in the end, be the only solution.
And then there always came a time when
Happy Hooligan[3] in his rusted green automobile   10
Came plowing down the course, just to make sure everything was
    O.K.
Only by that time we were in another chapter and confused
About how to receive this latest piece of information.
Was it information? Weren't we rather acting this out
For someone else's benefit, thoughts in a mind   15
With room enough to spare for our little problems (so they began
    to seem),
Our daily quandary about food and the rent and bills to be paid?
To reduce all this to a small variant,
To step free at last, minuscule on the gigantic plateau—
This was our ambition: to be small and clear and free.   20
Alas, the summer's energy wanes quickly,
A moment and it is gone. And no longer
May we make the necessary arrangements, simple as they are.
Our star was brighter perhaps when it had water in it.
Now there is no question even of that, but only   25
Of holding on to the hard earth so as not to get thrown off,
With an occasional dream, a vision: a robin flies across
The upper corner of the window, you brush your hair away
And cannot quite see, or a wound will flash
Against the sweet faces of the others, something like: 30
This is what you wanted to hear, so why
Did you think of listening to something else? We are all talkers
It is true, but underneath the talk lies
The moving and not wanting to be moved, the loose
Meaning, untidy and simple like a threshing floor.[4]   35

1. Fantastic epic poem by Ludovico Ariosto (1474–1533), whose romantic heroine Angelica is constantly being rescued from imminent perils such as monsters and ogres.
2. *Roger Delivering Angelica* (1819), a painting based on a scene from Ariosto, by the French artist Jean Auguste Dominique Ingres (1780–1867).
3. The good-natured, simple title character of a popular comic strip of the 1920s and 1930s.
4. Used at harvest time to separate the wheat from the chaff, which is to be discarded.

These then were some hazards of the course,
Yet though we knew the course *was* hazards and nothing else
It was still a shock when, almost a quarter of a century later,
The clarity of the rules dawned on you for the first time.
They were the players, and we who had struggled at the game   40
Were merely spectators, though subject to its vicissitudes
And moving with it out of the tearful stadium, borne on shoulders, at last.
Night after night this message returns, repeated
In the flickering bulbs of the sky, raised past us, taken away from us,
Yet ours over and over until the end that is past truth,   45
The being of our sentences, in the climate that fostered them,
Not ours to own, like a book, but to be with, and sometimes
To be without, alone and desperate.
But the fantasy makes it ours, a kind of fence-sitting
Raised to the level of an esthetic ideal. These were moments, years,   50
Solid with reality, faces, namable events, kisses, heroic acts,
But like the friendly beginning of a geometrical progression
Not too reassuring, as though meaning could be cast aside some day
When it had been outgrown. Better, you said, to stay cowering
Like this in the early lessons, since the promise of learning   55
Is a delusion, and I agreed, adding that
Tomorrow would alter the sense of what had already been learned,
That the learning process is extended in this way, so that from this standpoint
None of us ever graduates from college,
For time is an emulsion,[5] and probably thinking not to grow up   60
Is the brightest kind of maturity for us, right now at any rate.
And you see, both of us were right, though nothing
Has somehow come to nothing; the avatars[6]
Of our conforming to the rules and living
Around the home have made—well, in a sense, "good citizens" of us,   65
Brushing the teeth and all that, and learning to accept
The charity of the hard moments as they are doled out,
For this is action, this not being sure, this careless
Preparing, sowing the seeds crooked in the furrow,
Making ready to forget, and always coming back   70
To the mooring of starting out, that day so long ago.

                                                                    1970

Definition of Blue

The rise of capitalism parallels the advance of romanticism
And the individual is dominant until the close of the nineteenth century.
In our own time, mass practices have sought to submerge the personality

---

5. A chemical solution in which the particles of one liquid are suspended in another.
6. Incarnations.

By ignoring it, which has caused it instead to branch out in all di-
    rections
Far from the permanent tug that used to be its notion of "home."   5
These different impetuses are received from everywhere
And are as instantly snapped back, hitting through the cold atmo-
    sphere
In one steady, intense line.

There is no remedy for this "packaging" which has supplanted the
    old sensations.
Formerly there would have been architectural screens at the point
    where the action became most difficult   10
As a path trails off into shrubbery—confusing, forgotten, yet contin-
    uing to exist.
But today there is no point in looking to imaginative new methods
Since all of them are in constant use. The most that can be said for
    them further
Is that erosion produces a kind of dust or exaggerated pumice[1]
Which fills space and transforms it, becoming a medium   15
In which it is possible to recognize oneself.

Each new diversion adds its accurate touch to the ensemble, and so
A portrait, smooth as glass, is built up out of multiple corrections
And it has no relation to the space or time in which it was lived.
Only its existence is a part of all being, and is therefore, I suppose,
    to be prized   20
Beyond chasms of night that fight us
By being hidden and present.

And yet it results in a downward motion, or rather a floating one
In which the blue surroundings drift slowly up and past you
To realize themselves some day, while, you, in this nether world that
    could not be better,
Waken each morning to the exact value of what you did and said,
    which remains.

                                                          1970

Summer

There is that sound like the wind
Forgetting in the branches that means something
Nobody can translate. And there is the sobering "later on,"
When you consider what a thing meant, and put it down.

For the time being the shadow is ample   5
And hardly seen, divided among the twigs of a tree,
The trees of a forest, just as life is divided up
Between you and me, and among all the others out there.

---

1. The cooled, spongy residue of volcanic lava used as an abrasive to polish surfaces.

And the thinning-out phase follows
the period of reflection. And suddenly, to be dying 10
Is not a little or mean or cheap thing,
Only wearying, the heat unbearable,

And also the little mindless constructions put upon
Our fantasies of what we did: summer, the ball of pine needles,
The loose fates serving our acts, with token smiles, 15
Carrying out their instructions too accurately—

Too late to cancel them now—and winter, the twitter
Of cold stars at the pane, that describes with broad gestures
This state of being that is not so big after all.
Summer involves going down as a steep flight of steps 20

To a narrow ledge over the water. Is this it, then,
This iron comfort, these reasonable taboos,
Or did you mean it when you stopped? And the face
Resembles yours, the one reflected in the water.

1970

Self-Portrait in a Convex Mirror[1]

As Parmigianino did it, the right hand
Bigger than the head, thrust at the viewer
And swerving easily away, as though to protect
What it advertises. A few leaded panes, old beams,
Fur, pleated muslin, a coral ring run together 5
In a movement supporting the face, which swims
Toward and away like the hand
Except that it is in repose. It is what is
Sequestered. Vasari[2] says, "Francesco one day set himself
To take his own portrait, looking at himself for that purpose 10
In a convex mirror, such as is used by barbers . . .
He accordingly caused a ball of wood to be made
By a turner, and having divided it in half and
Brought it to the size of the mirror, he set himself
With great art to copy all that he saw in the glass," 15
Chiefly his reflection, of which the portrait
Is the reflection once removed.
The glass chose to reflect only what he saw
Which was enough for his purpose: his image
Glazed, embalmed, projected at a 180-degree angle. 20
The time of day or the density of the light
Adhering to the face keeps it
Lively and intact in a recurring wave

1. This self-portrait by the Italian Mannerist Parmigianino (Girolamo Francesco Mazzola, 1503–40) on a convex piece of poplar wood hangs in the Kunsthistorisches Museum in Vienna.
2. Giorgio Vasari (1511–74), Italian architect, painter, and art historian, whose *Lives of the Most Eminent Italian Painters, Sculptors, and Architects* is the principal source of information about those artists.

Of arrival. The soul establishes itself.
But how far can it swim out through the eyes   25
And still return safely to its nest? The surface
Of the mirror being convex, the distance increases
Significantly; that is, enough to make the point
That the soul is a captive, treated humanely, kept
In suspension, unable to advance much farther   30
Than your look as it intercepts the picture.
Pope Clement and his court were "stupefied"
By it,[3] according to Vasari, and promised a commission
That never materialized. The soul has to stay where it is,
Even though restless, hearing raindrops at the pane,   35
The sighing of autumn leaves thrashed by the wind,
Longing to be free, outside, but it must stay
Posing in this place. It must move
As little as possible. This is what the portrait says.
But there is in that gaze a combination   40
Of tenderness, amusement and regret, so powerful
In its restraint that one cannot look for long.
The secret is too plain. The pity of it smarts,
Makes hot tears spurt: that the soul is not a soul,
Has no secret, is small, and it fits   45
Its hollow perfectly: its room, our moment of attention.
That is the tune but there are no words.
The words are only speculation
(From the Latin *speculum*, mirror):
They seek and cannot find the meaning of the music.   50
We see only postures of the dream,
Riders of the motion that swings the face
Into view under evening skies, with no
False disarray as proof of authenticity.
But it is life englobed.   55
One would like to stick one's hand
Out of the globe, but its dimension,
What carries it, will not allow it.
No doubt it is this, not the reflex
To hide something, which makes the hand loom large   60
As it retreats slightly. There is no way
To build it flat like a section of wall:
It must join the segment of a circle,
Roving back to the body of which it seems
So unlikely a part, to fence in and shore up the face   65
On which the effort of this condition reads
Like a pinpoint of a smile, a spark
Or star one is not sure of having seen
As darkness resumes. A perverse light whose
Imperative of subtlety dooms in advance its   70
Conceit to light up: unimportant but meant.

---

3. When Parmigianino moved from his
native Parma to Rome in 1524, he presented the self-portrait to Pope Clement
VII as a credential for papal patronage.

Francesco, your hand is big enough
To wreck the sphere, and too big,
One would think, to weave delicate meshes
That only argue its further detention.   75
(Big, but not coarse, merely on another scale,
Like a dozing whale on the sea bottom
In relation to the tiny, self-important ship
On the surface.) But your eyes proclaim
That everything is surface. The surface is what's there   80
And nothing can exist except what's there.
There are no recesses in the room, only alcoves,
And the window doesn't matter much, or that
Sliver of window or mirror on the right, even
As a gauge of the weather, which in French is   85
Le temps, the word for time, and which
Follows a course wherein changes are merely
Features of the whole. The whole is stable within
Instability, a globe like ours, resting
On a pedestal of vacuum, a ping-pong ball   90
Secure on its jet of water.
And just as there are no words for the surface, that is,
No words to say what it really is, that it is not
Superficial but a visible core, then there is
No way out of the problem of pathos vs. experience.   95
You will stay on, restive, serene in
Your gesture which is neither embrace nor warning
But which holds something of both in pure
Affirmation that doesn't affirm anything.

The balloon pops, the attention   100
Turns dully away. Clouds
In the puddle stir up into sawtoothed fragments.
I think of the friends
Who came to see me, of what yesterday
Was like. A peculiar slant   105
Of memory that intrudes on the dreaming model
In the silence of the studio as he considers
Lifting the pencil to the self-portrait.
How many people came and stayed a certain time,
Uttered light or dark speech that became part of you   110
Like light behind windblown fog and sand,
Filtered and influenced by it, until no part
Remains that is surely you. Those voices in the dusk
Have told you all and still the tale goes on
In the form of memories deposited in irregular   115
Clumps of crystals. Whose curved hand controls,
Francesco, the turning seasons and the thoughts
That peel off and fly away at breathless speeds
Like the last stubborn leaves ripped
From wet branches? I see in this only the chaos   120
Of your round mirror which organizes everything

Around the polestar[4] of your eyes which are empty,
Know nothing, dream but reveal nothing.
I feel the carousel starting slowly
And going faster and faster: desk, papers, books,   125
Photographs of friends, the window and the trees
Merging in one neutral band that surrounds
Me on all sides, everywhere I look.
And I cannot explain the action of leveling,
Why it should all boil down to one   130
Uniform substance, a magma[5] of interiors.
My guide in these matters is your self,
Firm, oblique, accepting everything with the same
Wraith of a smile, and as time speeds up so that it is soon
Much later, I can know only the straight way out,   135
The distance between us. Long ago
The strewn evidence meant something,
The small accidents and pleasures
Of the day as it moved gracelessly on,
A housewife doing chores. Impossible now   140
To restore those properties in the silver blur that is
The record of what you accomplished by sitting down
"With great art to copy all that you saw in the glass"
So as to perfect and rule out the extraneous
Forever. In the circle of your intentions certain spars[6]   145
Remain that perpetuate the enchantment of self with self:
Eyebeams, muslin, coral. It doesn't matter
Because these are things as they are today
Before one's shadow ever grew
Out of the field into thoughts of tomorrow.   150

Tomorrow is easy, but today is uncharted,
Desolate, reluctant as any landscape
To yield what are laws of perspective
After all only to the painter's deep
Mistrust, a weak instrument though   155
Necessary. Of course some things
Are possible, it knows, but it doesn't know
Which ones. Some day we will try
To do as many things as are possible
And perhaps we shall succeed at a handful   160
Of them, but this will not have anything
To do with what is promised today, our
Landscape sweeping out from us to disappear
On the horizon. Today enough of a cover burnishes
To keep the supposition of promises together   165
In one piece of surface, letting one ramble
Back home from them so that these
Even stronger possibilities can remain

---

4. The North Star, hence the magnetic
center.
5. Soft mixture of organic or mineral

materials.
6. Pieces of lustrous mineral; also, round
timbers used to extend a sail.

Whole without being tested. Actually
The skin of the bubble-chamber's as tough as   170
Reptile eggs; everything gets "programmed" there
In due course: more keeps getting included
Without adding to the sum, and just as one
Gets accustomed to a noise that
Kept one awake but now no longer does,   175
So the room contains this flow like an hourglass
Without varying in climate or quality
(Except perhaps to brighten bleakly and almost
Invisibly, in a focus sharpening toward death—more
Of this later). What should be the vacuum of a dream   180
Becomes continually replete as the source of dreams
Is being tapped so that this one dream
May wax, flourish like a cabbage rose,
Defying sumptuary laws,[7] leaving us
To awake and try to begin living in what   185
Has now become a slum. Sydney Freedberg in his
Parmigianino[8] says of it: "Realism in this portrait
No longer produces an objective truth, but a *bizarria*. . . .
However its distortion does not create
A feeling of disharmony. . . . The forms retain   190
A strong measure of ideal beauty," because
Fed by our dreams, so inconsequential until one day
We notice the hole they left. Now their importance
If not their meaning is plain. They were to nourish
A dream which includes them all, as they are   195
Finally reversed in the accumulating mirror.
They seemed strange because we couldn't actually see them.
And we realize this only at a point where they lapse
Like a wave breaking on a rock, giving up
Its shape in a gesture which expresses that shape.   200
The forms retain a strong measure of ideal beauty
As they forage in secret on our idea of distortion.
Why be unhappy with this arrangement, since
Dreams prolong us as they are absorbed?
Something like living occurs, a movement   205
Out of the dream into its codification.

As I start to forget it
It presents its stereotype again
But it is an unfamiliar stereotype, the face
Riding at anchor, issued from hazards, soon   210
To accost others, "rather angel than man" (Vasari).
Perhaps an angel looks like everything
We have forgotten, I mean forgotten
Things that don't seem familiar when
We meet them again, lost beyond telllng,   215

---

7. Laws regulating private behavior, in   *His Works in Painting* (Cambridge,
this case mode of dress.   Mass.: 1950); *"bizarria"*: distortion.
8. Sydney J. Freedberg, *Parmigianino:*

Which were ours once. This would be the point
Of invading the privacy of this man who
"Dabbled in alchemy, but whose wish
Here was not to examine the subtleties of art
In a detached, scientific spirit: he wished through them   220
To impart the sense of novelty and amazament to the spectator"
(Freedberg). Later portraits such as the Uffizi
"Gentleman," the Borghese "Young Prelate" and
The Naples "Antea" issue from Mannerist
Tensions,[9] but here, as Freedberg points out,   225
The surprise, the tension are in the concept
Rather than its realization.
The consonance of the High Renaissance[1]
Is present, though distorted by the mirror.
What is novel is the extreme care in rendering   230
The velleities[2] of the rounded reflecting surface
(It is the first mirror portrait),
So that you could be fooled for a moment
Before you realize the reflection
Isn't yours. You feel then like one of those   235
Hoffmann[3] characters who have been deprived
Of a reflection, except that the whole of me
Is seen to be supplanted by the strict
Otherness of the painter in his
Other room. We have surprised him   240
At work, but no, he has surprised us
As he works. The picture is almost finished,
The surprise almost over, as when one looks out,
Startled by a snowfall which even now is
Ending in specks and sparkles of snow.   245
It happened while you were inside, asleep,
And there is no reason why you should have
Been awake for it, except that the day
Is ending and it will be hard for you
To get to sleep tonight, at least until late.   250

The shadow of the city injects its own
Urgency: Rome where Francesco
Was at work during the Sack:[4] his inventions
Amazed the soldiers who burst in on him;
They decided to spare his life, but he left soon after;   255
Vienna where the painting is today, where
I saw it with Pierre in the summer of 1959; New York

9. Mannerism was a style of painting in 16th-century Italy in which proportions or the laws of perspective were distorted to produce effects of tension or disturbance. "Uffizi," "Borghese": galleries in Florence and Rome, respectively.
1. In Italian painting and architecture, the period in the late 15th and early 16th centuries in which the harmonious proportions ("consonance") of Classical art were recaptured and honored.
2. Loosely, caprices.
3. E. T. A. Hoffman (1776–1822), German author, whose tales often had to do with the supernatural.
4. In 1527, the Hapsburg Emperor Charles V sacked Rome in an assertion of power against Pope Clement VII.

Where I am now, which is a logarithm[5]
Of other cities. Our landscape
Is alive with filiations, shuttlings;   260
Business is carried on by look, gesture,
Hearsay. It is another life to the city,
The backing of the looking glass of the
Unidentified but precisely sketched studio. It wants
To siphon off the life of the studio, deflate   265
Its mapped space to enactments, island it.
That operation has been temporarily stalled
But something new is on the way, a new preciosity
In the wind. Can you stand it,
Francesco? Are you strong enough for it?   270
This wind brings what it knows not, is
Self-propelled, blind, has no notion
Of itself. It is inertia that once
Acknowledged saps all activity, secret or public:
Whispers of the word that can't be understood   275
But can be felt, a chill, a blight
Moving outward along the capes and peninsulas
Of your nervures and so to the archipelagoes
And to the bathed, aired secrecy of the open sea.
This is its negative side. Its positive side is   280
Making you notice life and the stresses
That only seemed to go away, but now,
As this new mode questions, are seen to be
Hastening out of style. If they are to become classics
They must decide which side they are on.   285
Their reticence has undermined
The urban scenery, made its ambiguities
Look willful and tired, the games of an old man.
What we need now is this unlikely
Challenger pounding on the gates of an amazed   290
Castle. Your argument, Francesco,
Had begun to grow stale as no answer
Or answers were forthcoming. If it dissolves now
Into dust, that only means its time had come
Some time ago, but look now, and listen: 295
It may be that another life is stocked there
In recesses no one knew of; that it,
Not we, are the change; that we are in fact it
If we could get back to it, relive some of the way
It looked, turn our faces to the globe as it sets   300
And still be coming out all right:
Nerves normal, breath normal. Since it is a metaphor
Made to include us, we are a part of it and
Can live in it as in fact we have done,
Only leaving our minds bare for questioning   305
We now see will not take place at random

5. Mathematical term defining the relationship between two other terms.

But in an orderly way that means to menace
Nobody—the normal way things are done,
Like the concentric growing up of days
Around a life: correctly, if you think about it.   310

A breeze like the turning of a page
Brings back your face: the moment
Takes such a big bite out of the haze
Of pleasant intuition it comes after.
The locking into place is "death itself,"   315
As Berg said of a phrase in Mahler's Ninth;[6]
Or, to quote Imogen in *Cymbeline*, "There cannot
Be a pinch in death more sharp than this,"[7] for,
Though only exercise or tactic, it carries
The momentum of a conviction that had been building.   320
Mere forgetfulness cannot remove it
Nor wishing bring it back, as long as it remains
The white precipitate[8] of its dream
In the climate of sighs flung across our world,
A cloth over a birdcage. But it is certain that   325
What is beautiful seems so only in relation to a specific
Life, experienced or not, channeled into some form
Steeped in the nostalgia of a collective past.
The light sinks today with an enthusiasm
I have known elsewhere, and known why   330
It seemed meaningful, that others felt this way
Years ago. I go on consulting
This mirror that is no longer mine
For as much brisk vacancy as is to be
My portion this time. And the vase is always full   335
Because there is only just so much room
And it accommodates everything. The sample
One sees is not to be taken as
Merely that, but as everything as it
May be imagined outside time—not as a gesture   340
But as all, in the refined, assimilable state.
But what is this universe the porch of
As it veers in and out, back and forth,
Refusing to surround us and still the only
Thing we can see? Love once   345
Tipped the scales but now is shadowed, invisible,
Though mysteriously present, around somewhere.
But we know it cannot be sandwiched
Between two adjacent moments, that its windings
Lead nowhere except to further tributaries   350
And that these empty themselves into a vague
Sense of something that can never be known

---

6. Alban Berg (1885–1935), Viennese
composer of 12-tone music, speaking
of the Ninth Symphony of his Austrian
predecessor, the composer Gustav Mahler (1860–1911).
7. Shakespeare, *Cymbeline* 1.2.61–62.
8. In chemistry, a solid deposit separated
from a solution.

Even though it seems likely that each of us
Knows what it is and is capable of
Communicating it to the other. But the look   355
Some wear as a sign makes one want to
Push forward ignoring the apparent
Naïveté of the attempt, not caring
That no one is listening, since the light
Has been lit once and for all in their eyes   360
And is present, unimpaired, a permanent anomaly,
Awake and silent. On the surface of it
There seems no special reason why that light
Should be focused by love, or why
The city falling with its beautiful suburbs   365
Into space always less clear, less defined,
Should read as the support of its progress,
The easel upon which the drama unfolded
To its own satisfaction and to the end
Of our dreaming, as we had never imagined   370
It would end, in worn daylight with the painted
Promise showing through as a gage, a bond.
This nondescript, never-to-be defined daytime is
The secret of where it takes place
And we can no longer return to the various   375
Conflicting statements gathered, lapses of memory
Of the principal witnesses. All we know
Is that we are a little early, that
Today has that special, lapidary[9]
Todayness that the sunlight reproduces   380
Faithfully in casting twig-shadows on blithe
Sidewalks. No previous day would have been like this.
I used to think they were all alike,
That the present always looked the same to everybody
But this confusion drains away as one   385
Is always cresting into one's present.
Yet the "poetic," straw-colored space
Of the long corridor that leads back to the painting,
Its darkening opposite—is this
Some figment of "art," not to be imagined   390
As real, let alone special? Hasn't it too its lair
In the present we are always escaping from
And falling back into, as the waterwheel of days
Pursues its uneventful, even serene course?
I think it is trying to say it is today   395
And we must get out of it even as the public
Is pushing through the museum now so as to
Be out by closing time. You can't live there.
The gray glaze of the past attacks all know-how:
Secrets of wash and finish that took a lifetime   400
To learn and are reduced to the status of

---

9. Pertaining to an inscription in stone, hence condensed or concentrated.

Black-and-white illustrations in a book where colorplates
Are rare. That is, all time
Reduces to no special time. No one
Alludes to the change; to do so might   405
Involve calling attention to oneself
Which would augment the dread of not getting out
Before having seen the whole collection
(Except for the sculptures in the basement:
They are where they belong).   410
Our time gets to be veiled, compromised
By the portrait's will to endure. It hints at
Our own, which we were hoping to keep hidden.
We don't need paintings or
Doggerel written by mature poets when   415
The explosion is so precise, so fine.
Is there any point even in acknowledging
The existence of all that? Does it
Exist? Certainly the leisure to
Indulge stately pastimes doesn't,   420
Any more. Today has no margins, the event arrives
Flush with its edges, is of the same substance,
Indistinguishable. "Play" is something else;
It exists, in a society specifically
Organized as a demonstration of itself.   425
There is no other way, and those assholes
Who would confuse everything with their mirror games
Which seem to multiply stakes and possibilities, or
At least confuse issues by means of an investing
Aura that would corrode the architecture   430
Of the whole in a haze of suppressed mockery,
Are beside the point. They are out of the game,
Which doesn't exist until they are out of it.
It seems like a very hostile universe
But as the principle of each individual thing is   435
Hostile to, exists at the expense of all the others
As philosophers have often pointed out, at least
This thing, the mute, undivided present,
Has the justification of logic, which
In this instance isn't a bad thing   440
Or wouldn't be, if the way of telling
Didn't somehow intrude, twisting the end result
Into a caricature of itself. This always
Happens, as in the game where
A whispered phrase passed around the room   445
Ends up as something completely different.
It is the principle that makes works of art so unlike
What the artist intended. Often he finds
He has omitted the thing he started out to say
In the first place. Seduced by flowers,   450
Explicit pleasures, he blames himself (though
Secretly satisfied with the result), imagining

He had a say in the matter and exercised
An option of which he was hardly conscious,
Unaware that necessity circumvents such resolutions.   455
So as to create something new
For itself, that there is no other way,
That the history of creation proceeds according to
Stringent laws, and that things
Do get done in this way, but never the things   460
We set out to accomplish and wanted so desperately
To see come into being. Parmigianino
Must have realized this as he worked at his
Life-obstructing task. One is forced to read
The perfectly plausible accomplishment of a purpose   465
Into the smooth, perhaps even bland (but so
Enigmatic) finish. Is there anything
To be serious about beyond this otherness
That gets included in the most ordinary
Forms of daily activity, changing everything   470
Slightly and profoundly, and tearing the matter
Of creation, any creation, not just artistic creation
Out of our hands, to install it on some monstrous, near
Peak, too close to ignore, too far
For one to intervene? This otherness, this   475
"Not-being us" is all there is to look at
In the mirror, though no one can say
How it came to be this way. A ship
Flying unknown colors has entered the harbor.
You are allowing extraneous matters   480
To break up your day, cloud the focus
Of the crystal ball. Its scene drifts away
Like vapor scattered on the wind. The fertile
Thought-associations that until now came
So easily, appear no more, or rarely. Their   485
Colorings are less intense, washed out
By autumn rains and winds, spoiled, muddied,
Given back to you because they are worthless.
Yet we are such creatures of habit that their
Implications are still around *en permanence*, confusing   490
Issues. To be serious only about sex
Is perhaps one way, but the sands are hissing
As they approach the beginning of the big slide
Into what happened. This past
Is now here: the painter's   495
Reflected face, in which we linger, receiving
Dreams and inspirations on an unassigned
Frequency, but the hues have turned metallic,
The curves and edges are not so rich. Each person
Has one big theory to explain the universe   500
But it doesn't tell the whole story
And in the end it is what is outside him
That matters, to him and especially to us

Who have been given no help whatever
In decoding our own man-size quotient and must rely   505
On second-hand knowledge. Yet I know
That no one else's taste is going to be
Any help, and might as well be ignored.
Once it seemed so perfect—gloss on the fine
Freckled skin, lips moistened as though about to part   510
Releasing speech, and the familiar look
Of clothes and furniture that one forgets.
This could have been our paradise: exotic
Refuge within an exhausted world, but that wasn't
In the cards, because it couldn't have been   515
The point. Aping naturalness may be the first step
Toward achieving an inner calm
But it is the first step only, and often
Remains a frozen gesture of welcome etched
On the air materializing behind it,   520
A convention. And we have really
No time for these, except to use them
For kindling. The sooner they are burnt up
The better for the roles we have to play.
Therefore I beseech you, withdraw that hand,   525
Offer it no longer as shield or greeting,
The shield of a greeting, Francesco:
There is room for one bullet in the chamber:
Our looking through the wrong end
Of the telescope as you fall back at a speed   530
Faster than that of light to flatten ultimately
Among the features of the room, an invitation
Never mailed, the "it was all a dream"
Syndrome, though the "all" tells tersely
Enough how it wasn't. Its existence   535
Was real, though troubled, and the ache
Of this waking dream can never drown out
The diagram still sketched on the wind,
Chosen, meant for me and materialized
In the disguising radiance of my room.   540
We have seen the city; it is the gibbous[1]
Mirrored eye of an insect. All things happen
On its balcony and are resumed within,
But the action is the cold, syrupy flow
Of a pageant. One feels too confined,   545
Sifting the April sunlight for clues,
In the mere stillness of the ease of its
Parameter.[2] The hand holds no chalk
And each part of the whole falls off
And cannot know it knew, except   550

1. Irregularly rounded or convex (for example, the form of the moon between half moon and full moon).
2. A constant whose values characterize the variables in a system.

Here and there, in cold pockets
Of remembrance, whispers out of time.

1975

Wet Casements

> *When Eduard Raban, coming along the passage,*
> *walked into the open doorway, he saw that it*
> *was raining. It was not raining much.*
> —KAFKA,[1] *Wedding Preparations in the Country*

The conception is interesting: to see, as though reflected
In streaming windowpanes, the look of others through
Their own eyes. A digest of their correct impressions of
Their self-analytical attitudes overlaid by your
Ghostly transparent face. You in falbalas[2]　　　　　　　5
Of some distant but not too distant era, the cosmetics,
The shoes perfectly pointed, drifting (how long you
Have been drifting; how long I have too for that matter)
Like a bottle-imp[3] toward a surface which can never be approached,
Never pierced through into the timeless energy of a present　　10
Which would have its own opinions on these matters,
Are an epistemological[4] snapshot of the processes
That first mentioned your name at some crowded cocktail
Party long ago, and someone (not the person addressed)
Overheard it and carried that name around in his wallet　　15
For years as the wallet crumbled and bills slid in
And out of it. I want that information very much today,

Can't have it, and this makes me angry.
I shall use my anger to build a bridge like that
Of Avignon, on which people may dance for the feeling　　20
Of dancing on a bridge.[5] I shall at last see my complete face
Reflected not in the water but in the worn stone floor of my bridge.

I shall keep to myself.
I shall not repeat others' comments about me.

1977

1. Franz Kafka (1883–1924), Czech writer known for his surreal and bleak vision of life.
2. Furbelows, ruffles.
3. A figure suspended in liquid. When pressure is exerted above, the figure sinks to the bottom and is then sent back to the top by counterpressure.
4. Having to do with the nature and limits of knowledge.
5. A reference to the French folksong: *"Sur le pont d'Avignon, l'on y danse.* * * * (On the bridge of Avignon, one dances there)."

W. S. MERWIN

1927–

As a child W. S. Merwin wrote hymns for his father, a Presbyterian minister in Union, New Jersey, and Scranton, Pennsylvania. Apart from that he had almost no acquaintance with poetry until, on a scholarship, he entered Princeton University. There he read verse steadily and began to write with the encouragement of the poet John Berryman and the critic R. P. Blackmur. Then Merwin's extensive study of foreign languages and literatures enabled him to find work as a tutor abroad. He remained, like Ezra Pound, apart from American literary institutions and became a translator of European literature, especially medieval romance and modern symbolist poetry.

Merwin's continuing activity as a translator has been a resource and stimulus for his own poetry. In translating two great medieval epics, the French *Song of Roland* (1963) and the Spanish *The Poem of the Cid* (1959), his object was to bring into English a diction "rough, spare, sinewy, rapid" which would transmit the directness and energy of the world of chivalric imagination. His first book, *A Masque for Janus* (1952), includes ballads, songs, and carols—often based on medieval verse forms— whose slightly antique diction gives an air of simple mystery to poems about love, inner heroism, and death. So, for example, from *The Rime of the Palmers*:

> And these palmers that on
> A field of summer went
> Are perfect and lie down
> Thus, lest the land repent.

A Masque for Janus was chosen by W. H. Auden as the best book submitted in its year for the Yale Series of Younger Poets. Merwin went on to publish *The Dancing Bears* (1954) and *Green with Beasts* (1956). In later books he was to draw his subjects from a more clearly contemporary context. Many of the poems in *The Drunk in the Furnace* (1960) and *The Moving Target* (1963) are about members of his family and memories of his boyhood in Scranton. A further change came with *The Lice* (1967) and the volumes which followed it. His poems became briefer and more prophetic, less tied to details of biography, history, or social occasion. As always, Merwin is trying to reach below the surface of urban American experience, but this time without the benefit of narrative or pre-established metrical forms. He will speak through humble figures, as in *Peasant: His Prayer to the Powers of This World*. Or he will use the most commonplace occurrences as a point of departure for meditation: *Evening*, or *Daybreak*. Such poems quickly become parables, spoken in a voice less concerned with descriptive detail than with archetypal elements: the ways in which each evening prefigures death, each dawn the passing of time.

Of these short poems Merwin says: "What is needed for any particular nebulous unwritten hope that may become a poem is not a manipulable, more or less predictable recurring pattern, but an unduplicatable resonance, something that would be like an echo except that it is repeating no sound." Hence his unpunctuated lines of varying lengths, which seem a series of related oracular phrases, each corresponding to a breath. The poems frequently use the metaphor of a threshold or door, locating the reader at a moment between life and death, or between life and a visionary afterlife. The poet is stationed at that imagined spot where he appreciates the world ("surprised at the earth"), but also understands that any given day may be one in which he might write *For the Anniversary of My Death*.

In 1973 Merwin prepared a series of adaptations of Asian proverbs, *Asian Figures*, which reflect his interest in compact meditative forms, such as Oriental rituals and prayers. This mode seems now to be his settled choice and characterizes the poems of *The Carrier of Ladders* (1970), *Writings to an Unfinished Accompaniment* (1973), and *The Compass Flower* (1977).

The Drunk in the Furnace

For a good decade
The furnace stood in the naked gully, fireless
And vacant as any hat. Then when it was
No more to them than a hulking black fossil
To erode unnoticed with the rest of the junk-hill   5
By the poisonous creek, and rapidly to be added
    To their ignorance.

    They were afterwards astonished
To confirm, one morning, a twist of smoke like a pale
Resurrection, staggering out of its chewed hole,   10
And to remark then other tokens that someone,
Cosily bolted behind the eye-holed iron
Door of the drafty burner, had there established
    His bad castle.

    Where he gets his spirits   15
It's a mystery. But the stuff keeps him musical:
Hammer-and-anvilling with poker and bottle
To his jugged bellowings, till the last groaning clang
As he collapses onto the rioting
Springs of a litter of car-seats ranged on the grates,   20
    To sleep like an iron pig.

    In their tar-paper church
On a text about stoke-holes that are sated never
Their Reverend lingers. They nod and hate trespassers.
When the furnace wakes, though, all afternoon   25
Their witless offspring flock like piped[1] rats to its siren
Crescendo, and agape on the crumbling ridge
    Stand in a row and learn.

                            1960

To My Brother Hanson

B. Jan. 28, 1926   D. Jan. 28, 1926

My elder,
Born into death like a message into a bottle,
The tide
Keeps coming in empty on the only shore.

---

1. Allusion to the Pied Piper of Hamelin, whose piping lured the rats from the town; when he was not paid, he lured away the children as well.

Maybe it has lovers but it has few friends.   5
It is never still but it keeps its counsel, and

If I address you whose curious stars
Climbed to the tops of their houses and froze,
It is in hope of no
Answer, but as so often, merely   10
For want of another, for
I have seen catastrophe taking root in the mirror,
And why waste my words there?

Yes, now the roads themselves are shattered
As though they had fallen from a height, and the sky   15
Is cracked like varnish. Hard to believe,
Our family tree
Seems to be making its mark everywhere.
I carry my head high
On a pike that shall be nameless.   20

Even so, we had to give up honor entirely,
But I do what I can. I am patient
With the woes of the cupboards, and God knows—
I keep the good word close to hand like a ticket.
I feed the wounded lights in their cages.   25
I wake up at night on the penultimate stroke, and with
My eyes still shut I remember to turn the thorn
In the breast of the bird of darkness.
I listen to the painful song
Dropping away into sleep.   30

Blood
Is supposed to be thicker. You were supposed to be there
When the habits closed in pushing
Their smiles in front of them, when I was filled
With something else, like a thermometer,   35
When the moment of departure, standing
On one leg, like a sleeping stork, by the doorway,
Put down the other foot and opened its eye.
I
Got away this time for a while. I've come
Again to the whetted edge of myself where I   40
Can hear the hollow waves breaking like
Bottles in the dark. What about it? Listen, I've

Had enough of this. Is there nobody
Else in the family
To take care of the tree, to nurse the mirror,   45
To fix up a bite for hope when the old thing
Comes to the door,
To say to the pans of the balance
Rise up and walk?

1963

Daybreak

Again this procession of the speechless
Bringing me their words
The future woke me with its silence
I join the procession
An open doorway 5
Speaks for me
Again

1963

Evening

I am strange here and often I am still trying
To finish something as the light is going
Occasionally as just now I think I see
Off to one side something passing at that time
Along the herded walls under the walnut trees 5
And I look up but it is only
Evening again the old hat without a head
How long will it be till he speaks when he passes

1967

For the Anniversary of My Death

Every year without knowing it I have passed the day
When the last fires will wave to me
And the silence will set out
Tireless traveller
Like the beam of a lightless star 5

Then I will no longer
Find myself in life as in a strange garment
Surprised at the earth
And the love of one woman
And then shamelessness of men 10
As today writing after three days of rain
Hearing the wren sing and the falling cease
And bowing not knowing to what

1967

The Judgment of Paris[1]

FOR ANTHONY HECHT

Long afterwards
the intelligent could deduce what had been offered

and not recognized
and they suggest that bitterness should be confined
to the fact that the gods chose for their arbiter 5

1. In Greek legend, Paris was asked to give a golden apple to the fairest of three goddesses who, to obtain the apple, each offered him a reward. In the poem the goddesses speak in this order: Athena offers him wisdom and power; Hera offers martial glory; and Aphrodite offers the most beautiful woman in the world. In the poem, as in the legend, Paris's reward for choosing Aphrodite is Helen, wife of Menelaus (in the legend their elopement to Troy occasioned the Trojan War and downfall of that city).

a mind and character so ordinary
albeit a prince

and brought up as a shepherd[2]
a calling he must have liked
for he had returned to it   10

when they stood before him
the three
naked feminine deathless
and he realized that he was clothed
in nothing but mortality   15
the strap of his quiver of arrows crossing
between his nipples
making it seem stranger

and he knew he must choose
and on that day   20

the one with the gray eyes spoke first
and whatever she said he kept
thinking he remembered
but remembered it woven with confusion and fear
the two faces that he called father   25
the first sight of the palace
where the brothers were strangers
and the dogs watched him and refused to know him
she made everything clear she was dazzling she
offered it to him   30
to have for his own but what he saw
was the scorn above her eyes
and her words of which he understood few
all said to him *Take wisdom*
take power   35
you will forget anyway

the one with the dark eyes spoke
and everything she said
he imagined he had once wished for
but in confusion and cowardice   40
the crown
of his father the crowns the crowns bowing to him
his name everywhere like grass
only he and the sea
triumphant   45
she made everything sound possible she was
dazzling she offered it to him
to hold high but what he saw
was the cruelty around her mouth

2. Paris had been abandoned on Mount
Ida by his parents, Priam and Hecuba,
rulers of Troy, because it had been foretold that he would bring the downfall of
the city. He was rescued and brought up
as a shepherd.

and her words of which he understood more   50
all said to him *Take pride*
take glory
you will suffer anyway

the third one the color of whose eyes
later he could not remember   55
spoke last and slowly and
of desire and it was his
though up until then he had been
happy with his river nymph[3]
here was his mind   60
filled utterly with one girl gathering
yellow flowers
and no one like her
the words
made everything seem present   65
almost present
present
they said to him *Take*
her
you will lose her anyway   70

it was only when he reached out to the voice
as though he could take the speaker
herself
that his hand filled with
something to give   75
but to give to only one of the three
an apple as it is told
discord itself in a single fruit its skin
already carved
To the fairest   80

then a mason working above the gates of Troy
in the sunlight thought he felt the stone
shiver

in the quiver on Paris's back the head
of the arrow for Achilles' heel[4]   85
smiled in its sleep

and Helen stepped from the palace to gather
as she would do every day in that season
from the grove the yellow ray[5] flowers tall
as herself   90

whose roots are said to dispel pain

                                                            1970

---

3. Oenone, the nymph Paris deserted to
claim Helen.
4. The hero of the Greek army, who was
killed when Paris shot him in the heel—

the only vulnerable point in his otherwise
indestructible body.
5. Probably rue, often used for medicinal
purposes.

The Piper

It is twenty years
since I first looked for words
for me now
whose wisdom or something would stay me
I chose to   5
trouble myself about the onset
of this
it was remote it was grievous
it is true I was still a child

I was older then   10
than I hope ever to be again
that summer sweating in the attic
in the foreign country
high above the piper but hearing him
once   15
and never moving from my book
and the narrow
house full of pregnant women
floor above floor
waiting   20
in that city
where the sun was the one bell

It has taken me till now
to be able to say
even this   25
it has taken me this long
to know what I cannot say
where it begins
like the names of the hungry

Beginning   30
I am here
please
be ready to teach me
I am almost ready to learn

1970

JAMES WRIGHT

1927–

James Wright was born in Martin's Ferry, Ohio, and the unmemorialized
towns and townspeople of this part of the Midwest appear frequently in
his poetry. He portrayed these lonely, fated figures in a manner which
owed a lot to the isolated New Englanders of Robert Frost and Edwin

Arlington Robinson and the country solitaries of the English poet and novelist Thomas Hardy. In *At Thomas Hardy's Birthplace, 1953,* Wright meditates the "secret" which the earlier poet "learned from the ground." He must have admired the patient suffering of the doomed rural characters in Hardy's writings, and he spoke of their closeness to "the ache and sorrow of darkened earth."

Wright identified a special power for vision in troubled figures and outcasts; they came to embody an unearthly energy which defied the tumbledown surroundings of the ramshackle towns in which his dramas took place. A lesbian, discovered and taunted by her neighbors (*Sappho*), concludes her monologue by imagining herself freed of pain and the flesh: "Until my soul flares outward like a blue / Blossom of gas fire dancing in mid-air: / Free of the body's work of twisted iron."

When not searching out these visionary resources, Wright's early poems are often deeply elegiac; consolation comes in a survivor's power to identify with nature's bleaker laws. For example, Wright's advice *To a Troubled Friend* has its harsh dimensions: "you must feel the summer's rage of fire, / Beyond this frigid season's empty storms, / Banished to bloom, and bear the bird's desire."

Wright's first books of poems, *The Green Wall* and *Saint Judas,* similar in tone and subject, were published in 1957 and 1959 respectively. *The Green Wall* had been chosen by W. H. Auden as the best book submitted in its year to the Yale Series of Younger Poets. But there was a considerable change in Wright's manner by the time his next books appeared: *The Branch Will Not Break* (1963) and *Shall We Gather at the River?* (1968). The poems were more colloquial in diction, used open forms rather than regular stanzas, and appeared to be more random in their organization. Contributing to this change was Wright's deliberate effort to find nourishment and new voices through translating foreign poets. He worked with Spanish poems (by Neruda, Guillen, and Vallejo, among others) and translated from the Austrian Georg Trakl. He learned from them how to organize poems through the abrupt placement of surreal images in apparently familiar natural settings:

> The unwashed shadows
> Of blast furnaces from Moundsville, West Virginia,
> Are sneaking across the pits of strip mines
> To steal grapes
> In heaven.

In Wright's later work, the poems are less elegiac. Though still deeply conscious of mortality, these poems also allow for sudden bursts of exaltation, as if prompted by the threat of death. *Having Lost My Sons, I Confront the Wreckage of the Moon: Christmas,* 1960 uses a surreal image in both the title and body of the poem to suggest the shattered confusion of a survivor, bereft, yet aware of an admixture of vitality and joy: "This cold winter / Moon spills the inhuman fire / Of jewels / Into my hands."

Wright has taught at several universities, most recently at Hunter College in the City University of New York. He has always thought of himself as a teacher of literature and resists teaching creative writing courses and workshops. During his undergraduate career at Kenyon College, he studied with the literary critic and poet John Crowe Ransom. Wright has a Ph.D. from the University of Washington, where he knew Theodore Roethke, to whose nature poetry his own bears a strong likeness. As a Fulbright scholar he studied at the University of Vienna. In 1972 his *Collected Poems* won the Pulitzer Prize. In 1973 he published a further volume of poems, *Two Citizens*.

Devotions

I longed to kill you once, when I was young,
Because you laughed at me before my friends.
    And now the baffled prose
Of a belated vengeance numbs my tongue.
    Come back, before the last wind bends   5
Your body to the void beyond repose.

Standing alone before your grave, I read
The name, the season, every decent praise
    A chisel might devise—
Deliberate scrawls to guard us from the dead.   10
    And yet I lift my strength, to raise
Out of the mossy wallow your pig's eyes.

The summons fell, but I could not come home
To gloat above the hackling and the rasp
    Caught in your corded throat;   15
And, many towns away, I heard your doom
    Tolling the hate beyond my grasp,
Thieving the poisons of my angry thought.

After so many years to lose the vision
Of your last anguish! Furious at the cheat,   20
    After your burial
I traveled here, to lay my weak derision
    Fresh as a garland at your feet.
All day I have gathered curses, but they fail.

I cannot even call to mind so clearly,   25
As once I could, your confident thin voice
    Banishing me to nothing.
Your hand crumbles, your sniffing nostrils barely
    Evoke the muscles of my loathing;
And I too die, who came here to rejoice.   30

Lost mocker of my childhood, how the moss
Softens your hair, how deeply nibbling fangs
    Sink in the careless ground.
Seasons of healing grasses weave across
    Your caving lips, and dull my strange   35
Terror of failures. Shaken, I have found

Nothing to mark you off in earth but stone.
Walking here lonely and strange now, I must find
    A grave to prod my wrath
Back to its just devotions. Miserable bone,   40
    Devouring jaw-hinge, glare gone blind,
Come back, be damned of me, your aftermath.

             1959

The Jewel

There is this cave
In the air behind my body
That nobody is going to touch:
A cloister, a silence
Closing around a blossom of fire.   5
When I stand upright in the wind,
My bones turn to dark emeralds.

             1963

Having Lost My Sons, I Confront the Wreckage of the Moon: Christmas, 1960

After dark
Near the South Dakota border,
The moon is out hunting, everywhere,
Delivering fire,
And walking down hallways   5
Of a diamond.

Behind a tree,
It lights on the ruins
Of a white city:
Frost, frost.   10

Where are they gone,
Who lived there?

Bundled away under wings
And dark faces.

I am sick   15
Of it, and I go on,
Living, alone, alone,
Past the charred silos, past the hidden graves
Of Chippewas[1] and Norwegians.

This cold winter   20
Moon spills the inhuman fire
Of jewels
Into my hands.

---

1. An Indian tribe.

Dead riches, dead hands, the moon
Darkens,   25
And I am lost in the beautiful white ruins
Of America.

1963

A Blessing

Just off the highway to Rochester, Minnesota,
Twilight bounds softly forth on the grass.
And the eyes of those two Indian ponies
Darken with kindness.
They have come gladly out of the willows   5
To welcome my friend and me.
We step over the barbed wire into the pasture
Where they have been grazing all day, alone.
They ripple tensely, they can hardly contain their happiness
That we have come.   10
They bow shyly as wet swans. They love each other.
There is no loneliness like theirs.
At home once more,
They begin munching the young tufts of spring in the darkness.
I would like to hold the slenderer one in my arms,   15
For she has walked over to me
And nuzzled my left hand.
She is black and white,
Her mane falls wild on her forehead,
And the light breeze moves me to caress her long ear   20
That is delicate as the skin over a girl's wrist.
Suddenly I realize
That if I stepped out of my body I would break
Into blossom.

1963

Old Age Compensation

There are no roads but the frost,
And the pumpkins look haggard.
The ants have gone down to the grave, crying
God spare them one green blade.
Failing the grass, they have abandoned the grass.   5
All creatures who have died today of old age
Have gone more than ten miles already.
All day I have slogged behind
And dreamed of them praying for one candle,
Only one.   10
Fair enough. Only, from where I stand,
I can see one last night nurse shining in one last window
In the Home for Senior Citizens.
The white uniform flickers, the town is gone.
What do I do now? I have one candle,   15
But what's the use?
If only they can catch up with twilight,

They'll be safe enough.
Their boats are moored there, among the cattails
And the night-herons' nests.   20
All they have to do now
Is to get one of those lazy birds awake long enough
To guide them across the river.
Herons fly low, too.
All it will take is one old man trawling one oar.   25
Anybody can follow a blue wing,
They don't need my candle.
But I do.

                                                                  1968

Late November in a Field

Today I am walking alone in a bare place,
And winter is here.
Two squirrels near a fence post
Are helping each other drag a branch
Toward a hiding place; it must be somewhere   5
Behind those ash trees.
They are still alive, they ought to save acorns
Against the cold.
Frail paws rifle the troughs between cornstalks
    when the moon
Is looking away.   10
The earth is hard now,
The soles of my shoes need repairs.
I have nothing to ask a blessing for,
Except these words.
I wish they were   15
Grass.

                                                                  1968

To the Poets in New York

You strolled in the open, leisurely and alone,
Daydreaming of a beautiful human body
That had undressed quietly and slipped into the river
And become the river:
The proud body of an animal that would transform   5
The snaggled gears and the pulleys
Into a plant that grows under water.
You went searching gently for the father of your own agony,
The camellia of your death,
The voice that would call out to you clearly and name the fires   10
Of your hidden equator.

Solitary,
Patient for the last voices of the dusk to die down, and the dusk
To die down, listener waiting for courteous rivers

To rise and be known,   15
You kept a dark counsel.
It is not seemly a man should rend open by day
The huge roots of his blood trees.
A man ought to hide sometimes on the banks
Of the sky,   20
And some human beings
Have need of lingering back in the fastidious half-light
Even at dawn.

                                                                    1968

To the Muse

It is all right. All they do
Is go in by dividing
One rib from another. I wouldn't
Lie to you. It hurts
Like nothing I know. All they do   5
Is burn their way in with a wire.
It forks in and out a little like the tongue
Of that frightened garter snake we caught
At Cloverfield, you and me, Jenny
So long ago.   10

I would lie to you
If I could.
But the only way I can get you to come up
Out of the suckhole, the south face
Of the Powhatan pit,[1] is to tell you   15
What you know:

You come up after dark, you poise alone
With me on the shore.
I lead you back to this world.

Three lady doctors in Wheeling open   20
Their offices at night.
I don't have to call them, they are always there.
But they only have to put the knife once
Under your breast.
Then they hang their contraption.   25
And you bear it.

It's awkward a while. Still, it lets you
Walk about on tiptoe if you don't
Jiggle the needle.
It might stab your heart, you see.   30
The blade hangs in your lung and the tube
Keeps it draining.

---

1. A coal mine, probably in West Virginia.

That way they only have to stab you
Once. Oh Jenny,
I wish to God I had made this world, this scurvy   35
And disastrous place. I
Didn't, I can't bear it
Either, I don't blame you, sleeping down there
Face down in the unbelievable silk of spring,
Muse of black sand,   40
Alone.

I don't blame you, I know
The place where you lie.
I admit everything. But look at me.
How can I live without you?   45
Come up to me, love,
Out of the river, or I will
Come down to you.

                                                     1968

Northern Pike

All right. Try this,
Then. Every body
I know and care for,
And every body
Else is going   5
To die in a loneliness
I can't imagine and a pain
I don't know. We had
To go on living. We
Untangled the net, we slit   10
The body of this fish
Open from the hinge of the tail
To a place beneath the chin
I wish I could sing of.
I would just as soon we let   15
The living go on living.
An old poet whom we believe in
Said the same thing, and so
We paused among the dark cattails and prayed
For the muskrats,   20
For the ripples below their tails,
For the little movements that we knew the crawdads[1]
    were making under water,
For the right-hand wrist of my cousin who is a policeman.
We prayed for the game warden's blindness.
We prayed for the road home.   25
We ate the fish.
There must be something very beautiful in my body,
I am so happy.

                                                     1971

1. Crayfish.

You and I Saw Hawks Exchanging the Prey

They did the deed of darkness
In their own mid-light.

He plucked a gray field mouse
Suddenly in the wind.

The small dead fly alive   5
Helplessly in his beak,

His cold pride, helpless.
All she receives is life.

They are terrified. They touch.
Life is too much.   10

She flies away sorrowing.
Sorrowing, she goes alone.

Then her small falcon, gone,
Will not rise here again.

Smaller than she, he goes   15
Claw beneath claw beneath
Needles and leaning boughs,

While she, the lovelier
Of these brief differing two,
Floats away sorrowing,   20

Tall as my love for you,

And almost lonelier.

Delighted in the delighting,
I love you in mid-air,
I love myself the ground.   25

The great wings sing nothing
Lightly. Lightly fall.

1973

ANNE SEXTON
1928–1975

Anne Sexton's first book of poems, *To Bedlam and Part Way Back* (1960),
was published at a time when the label "confessional" came to be attached

to poems more frankly autobiographical than had been usual in American verse. For Sexton the term "confessional" is particularly apt. Though she had abandoned the Roman Catholicism into which she was born, her poems enact something analogous to preparing for and receiving religious absolution. She dedicates a poem to a friend who "urges me to make an appointment for the Sacrament of Confession,"

> My friend, my friend, I was born
> doing reference work in sin, and born
> confessing it. This is what poems are;
> with mercy
> for the greedy,
> they are the tongue's wrangle,
> the world's pottage, the rat's star.

Sexton's own confessions were to be made in terms more startling than the traditional Catholic images of her childhood. The purpose of her poems was not to analyze or explain behavior but to make it palpable in all its ferocity of feeling. Poetry "should be a shock to the senses. It should also hurt." This is apparent both in the themes she chooses and the particular ways in which she chooses to exhibit her subjects. Sexton writes about sex, illegitimacy, guilt, madness, suicide. Her first book portrays her own mental breakdown, her time in a mental hospital, her efforts at reconciliation with her young daughter and husband when she returns. Her second book, *All My Pretty Ones* (1962) takes its title from *Macbeth* and refers to the death of both her parents within three months of one another. Later books act out a continuing debate about suicide: *Live or Die* (1967), *The Death Notebooks* (1974), and *The Awful Rowing toward God* (1975—posthumous), titles that prefigure the time when she took her own life (1975).

Sexton spoke of images as "the heart of poetry. Images come from the unconscious. Imagination and the unconscious are one and the same." In the mental hospital she sees herself as "the laughing bee on a stalk / of death"; after an operation, as a little girl sent out to play "my stomach laced up like a football / for the game." The poems are very often addressed to other people or entities with whom she is trying to reconnect herself: her parents, her husband, a lover, her child, even her own public self or her body. Powerful images substantiate the strangeness of her own feelings, and attempt to redefine experiences so as to gain understanding, absolution, or revenge. These poems poised between, as her titles suggest, life and death, or "bedlam and part way back" are efforts at establishing a middle ground of self-assertion, substituting surreal images for the reductive versions of life visible to the exterior eye.

Anne Sexton was born in 1928 in Newton, Massachusetts, and attended Garland Junior College. She came to poetry fairly late—when she was twenty-eight, after seeing the critic I. A. Richards lecturing about the sonnet on television. In the late 1950s she attended poetry workshops in the Boston area, including Robert Lowell's poetry seminars at Boston University. One of her fellow students was Sylvia Plath, whose suicide she commemorated in a poem and whose fate she later followed. Sexton claimed that she was less influenced by Lowell's *Life Studies* than by W. D. Snodgrass's autobiographical *Heart's Needle* (1959), but certainly Lowell's support and the association with Plath left their mark upon her and made it possible for her to publish. Though her career was relatively brief, she received several major literary prizes, including the Pulitzer Prize for *Live or Die* and an American Academy of Arts and Letters traveling fellowship. Her suicide came after a series of mental breakdowns.

You, Doctor Martin[1]

You, Doctor Martin, walk
 from breakfast to madness. Late August,
I speed through the antiseptic tunnel
  where the moving dead still talk
of pushing their bones against the thrust   5
of cure. And I am queen of this summer hotel
  or the laughing bee on a stalk

  of death. We stand in broken
lines and wait while they unlock
the door and count us at the frozen gates   10
  of dinner. The shibboleth[2] is spoken
and we move to gravy in our smock
of smiles. We chew in rows, our plates
  scratch and whine like chalk

  in school. There are no knives   15
for cutting your throat. I make
moccasins all morning. At first my hands
  kept empty, unraveled for the lives
they used to work. Now I learn to take
them back, each angry finger that demands   20
  I mend what another will break

  tomorrow. Of course, I love you;
you lean above the plastic sky,
god of our block, prince of all the foxes.
  The breaking crowns are new   25
that Jack wore.[3] Your third eye[4]
moves among us and lights the separate boxes
  where we sleep or cry.

  What large children we are
here. All over I grow most tall   30
in the best ward. Your business is people,
  you call at the madhouse, an oracular
eye in our nest. Out in the hall

1. Sexton's doctor in a mental hospital, the setting of the poem.
2. Password (as contrasted to saying grace before meals).
3. As in the nursery rhyme *Jack and Jill*, where "Jack fell down and broke his crown."
4. In Buddhism, the doorway of the soul, located between and above the two eyes, between the prefrontal lobes of the brain.

the intercom pages you. You twist in the pull
    of the foxy children who fall   35

       like floods of life in frost.
    And we are magic talking to itself,
noisy and alone. I am queen of all my sins
    forgotten. Am I still lost?
    Once I was beautiful. Now I am myself,   40
counting this row and that row of moccasins
    waiting on the silent shelf.

                                           1960

All My Pretty Ones[1]

Father, this year's jinx rides us apart
where you followed our mother to her cold slumber;
a second shock boiling its stone to your heart,
leaving me here to shuffle and disencumber
you from the residence you could not afford: 5
a gold key, your half of a woolen mill,
twenty suits from Dunne's, an English Ford,
the love and legal verbiage of another will,
boxes of pictures of people I do not know.
I touch their cardboard faces. They must go.   10

But the eyes, as thick as wood in this album,
hold me. I stop here, where a small boy
waits in a ruffled dress for someone to come . . .
for this soldier who holds his bugle like a toy
or for this velvet lady who cannot smile.   15
Is this your father's father, this commodore
in a mailman suit? My father, time meanwhile
has made it unimportant who you are looking for.
I'll never know what these faces are all about.
I lock them into their book and throw them out.   20

This is the yellow scrapbook that you began
the year I was born; as crackling now and wrinkly
as tobacco leaves: clippings where Hoover outran
the Democrats, wiggling his dry finger at me
and Prohibition;[2] news where the *Hindenburg* went   25
down[3] and recent years where you went flush

1. From the epigraph to the volume of
which this is the title poem. In Shakespeare's *Macbeth* 4.3.216 ff. Macduff reacts to the news that Macbeth has had
his wife and children slaughtered: "All
my pretty ones? / Did you say all? O
hell-kite! All? / What! all my pretty
chickens and their dam / At one fell
swoop? * * * / I cannot but remember
such things were, / That were most precious to me."
Macduff later kills Macbeth. Sexton's
poem is an elegy for her father, who died
in June, 1959, four months after the death
of his wife.
2. Herbert Hoover (1874–1964) won the
presidential election in 1928; "Prohibition": the period (1920–33) when the
sale of alcoholic beverages was outlawed.
3. The *Hindenburg* was a German passenger zeppelin, which exploded and
crashed in flames at Lakeville, New Jersey, in 1936.

on war. This year, solvent but sick, you meant
to marry that pretty widow in a one-month rush.
But before you had that second chance, I cried
on your fat shoulder. Three days later you died.   30

These are the snapshots of marriage, stopped in places.
Side by side at the rail toward Nassau[4] now;
here, with the winner's cup at the speedboat races,
here, in tails at the Cotillion[5], you take a bow,
here, by our kennel of dogs with their pink eyes,   35
running like show-bred pigs in their chain-link pen;
here, at the horseshow where my sister wins a prize;
and here, standing like a duke among groups of men.
Now I fold you down, my drunkard, my navigator,
my first lost keeper, to love or look at later.   40

I hold a five-year diary that my mother kept
for three years, telling all she does not say
of your alcoholic tendency. You overslept,
she writes. My God, father, each Christmas Day
with your blood, will I drink down your glass   45
of wine? The diary of your hurly-burly years
goes to my shelf to wait for my age to pass.
Only in this hoarded span will love persevere.
Whether you are pretty or not, I outlive you,
bend down my strange face to yours and forgive you.   50

                                                      1962

Letter Written on a Ferry While
Crossing Long Island Sound[1]

I am surprised to see
that the ocean is still going on.
Now I am going back
and I have ripped my hand
from your hand as I said I would   5
and I have made it this far
as I said I would
and I am on the top deck now
holding my wallet, my cigarettes
and my car keys   10
at 2 o'clock on a Tuesday
in August of 1960.

Dearest,
although everything has happened,
nothing has happened.   15

---

4. In the Bahamas.
5. Usually a ball at which debutantes (age 18) are presented to society.

1. From Orient Point, Long Island, to New London, Connecticut.

The sea is very old.
The sea is the face of Mary,[2]
without miracles or rage
or unusual hope,
grown rough and wrinkled   20
with incurable age.

Still,
I have eyes.
These are my eyes:
the orange letters that spell   25
ORIENT on the life preserver
that hangs by my knees;
the cement lifeboat that wears
its dirty canvas coat;
the faded sign that sits on its shelf   30
saying KEEP OFF.
Oh, all right, I say,
I'll save myself.

Over my right shoulder
I see four nuns   35
who sit like a bridge club,
their faces poked out
from under their habits,
as good as good babies who
have sunk into their carriages.   40
Without discrimination
the wind pulls the skirts
of their arms.
Almost undressed,
I see what remains: 45
that holy wrist,
that ankle,
that chain.

Oh God,
although I am very sad,   50
could you please
let these four nuns
loosen from their leather boots
and their wooden chairs
to rise out   55
over this greasy deck,
out over this iron rail,
nodding their pink heads to one side,
flying four abreast
in the old-fashioned side stroke;   60
each mouth open and round,

2. The Virgin Mary, mother of Christ.

breathing together
as fish do,
singing without sound.

Dearest,   65
see how my dark girls sally forth,
over the passing lighthouse of Plum Gut,
its shell as rusty
as a camp dish,
as fragile as a pagoda   70
on a stone;
out over the little lighthouse
that warns me of drowning winds
that rub over its blind bottom
and its blue cover;   75
winds that will take the toes
and the ears of the rider
or the lover.

There go my dark girls,
their dresses puff   80
in the leeward air.
Oh, they are lighter than flying dogs
or the breath of dolphins;
each mouth opens gratefully,
wider than a milk cup.   85
My dark girls sing for this.
They are going up.

See them rise
on black wings, drinking
the sky, without smiles   90
or hands
or shoes.
They call back to us
from the gauzy edge of paradise,
good news, good news.   95

1962

Flee on Your Donkey

*Ma faim, Anne, Anne,
Fuis sur ton âne . . .*
—RIMBAUD[1]

Because there was no other place
to flee to,
I came back to the scene of the disordered senses,
came back last night at midnight,

---

1. "My hunger, Anne, Anne, / Flee on your donkey * * *" From a poem (*Feasts of Hunger*) by Arthur Rimbaud (1854–91), French Symbolist poet, author of *A Season in Hell* and *Illuminations.*

arriving in the thick June night   5
without luggage or defenses,
giving up my car keys and my cash,
keeping only a pack of Salem cigarettes
the way a child holds on to a toy.
I signed myself in where a stranger   10
puts the inked-in X's—
for this is a mental hospital,
not a child's game.

Today an interne knocks my knees,
testing for reflexes.   15
Once I would have winked and begged for dope.
Today I am terribly patient.
Today crows play black-jack
on the stethoscope.

Everyone has left me   20
except my muse,
that good nurse.
She stays in my hand,
a mild white mouse.

The curtains, lazy and delicate,   25
billow and flutter and drop
like the Victorian skirts
of my two maiden aunts
who kept an antique shop.

Hornets have been sent.   30
They cluster like floral arrangements on the screen.
Hornets, dragging their thin stingers,
hover outside, all knowing,
hissing: *the hornet knows.*
I heard it as a child   35
but what was it that he meant?
The hornet knows!
What happened to Jack and Doc and Reggy?
Who remembers what lurks in the heart of man?
What did The Green Hornet mean, *he knows?*   40
Or have I got it wrong?
Is it The Shadow who had seen
me from my bedside radio?

Now it's *Dinn, Dinn, Dinn!*
while the ladies in the next room argue   45
and pick their teeth.
Upstairs a girl curls like a snail;
in another room someone tries to eat a shoe;
meanwhile an adolescent pads up and down
the hall in his white tennis socks.   50

A new doctor makes rounds
advertising tranquilizers, insulin, or shock
to the uninitiated.

Six years of such small preoccupations!
Six years of shuttling in and out of this place!   55
O my hunger! My hunger!
I could have gone around the world twice
or had new children—all boys.
It was a long trip with little days in it
and no new places.   60

In here,
it's the same old crowd,
the same ruined scene.
The alcoholic arrives with his golf clubs.
The suicide arrives with extra pills sewn   65
into the lining of her dress.
The permanent guests have done nothing new.
Their faces are still small
like babies with jaundice.

Meanwhile,   70
they carried out my mother,
wrapped like somebody's doll, in sheets,
bandaged her jaw and stuffed up her holes.
My father, too. He went out on the rotten blood
he used up on other women in the Middle West.   75
He went out, a cured old alcoholic
on crooked feet and useless hands.
He went out calling for his father
who died all by himself long ago—
that fat banker who got locked up,   80
his genes suspended like dollars,
wrapped up in his secret,
tied up securely in a straitjacket.

But you, my doctor, my enthusiast,
were better than Christ;   85
you promised me another world
to tell me who
I was.

I spent most of my time,
a stranger,   90
damned and in trance—that little hut,
that naked blue-veined place,
my eyes shut on the confusing office,
eyes circling into my childhood,
eyes newly cut.   95
Years of hints

strung out—a serialized case history—
thirty-three years of the same dull incest
that sustained us both.
You, my bachelor analyst, 100
who sat on Marlborough Street,[2]
sharing your office with your mother
and giving up cigarettes each New Year,
were the new God,
the manager of the Gideon Bible. 105

I was your third-grader
with a blue star on my forehead.
In trance I could be any age,
voice, gesture—all turned backward
like a drugstore clock. 110
Awake, I memorized dreams.
Dreams came into the ring
like third string fighters,
each one a bad bet
who might win 115
because there was no other.

I stared at them,
concentrating on the abyss
the way one looks down into a rock quarry,
uncountable miles down, 120
my hands swinging down like hooks
to pull dreams up out of their cage.
O my hunger! My hunger!

Once,
outside your office, 125
I collapsed in the old-fashioned swoon
between the illegally parked cars.
I threw myself down,
pretending dead for eight hours.
I thought I had died 130
into a snowstorm.
Above my head
chains cracked along like teeth
digging their way through the snowy street.
I lay there 135
like an overcoat
that someone had thrown away.
You carried me back in,
awkwardly, tenderly,
with the help of the red-haired secretary 140
who was built like a lifeguard.
My shoes,

2. In Boston.

I remember,
were lost in the snowbank
as if I planned never to walk again.   145

That was the winter
that my mother died,
half mad on morphine,
blown up, at last,
like a pregnant pig.   150
I was her dreamy evil eye.
In fact,
I carried a knife in my pocketbook—
my husband's good L. L. Bean³ hunting knife.
I wasn't sure if I should slash a tire   155
or scrape the guts out of some dream.

You taught me
to believe in dreams;
thus I was the dredger.
I held them like an old woman with arthritic fingers,   160
carefully straining the water out—
sweet dark playthings,
and above all, mysterious
until they grew mournful and weak.
O my hunger! My hunger!   165
I was the one
who opened the warm eyelid
like a surgeon
and brought forth young girls
to grunt like fish.   170

I told you,
I said—
but I was lying—
that the knife was for my mother . . .
and then I delivered her.   175

The curtains flutter out
and slump against the bars.
They are my two thin ladies
named Blanche and Rose.
The grounds outside   180
are pruned like an estate at Newport.
Far off, in the field,
something yellow grows.

Was it last month or last year
that the ambulance ran like a hearse   185
with its siren blowing on suicide—
Dinn, dinn, dinn!—

3. Sporting-goods dealer in Maine.

a noon whistle that kept insisting on life
all the way through the traffic lights?

I have come back   190
but disorder is not what it was.
I have lost the trick of it!
The innocence of it!
That fellow-patient in his stovepipe hat
with his fiery joke, his manic smile—   195
even he seems blurred, small and pale.
I have come back,
recommitted,
fastened to the wall like a bathroom plunger,
held like a prisoner   200
who was so poor
he fell in love with jail.

I stand at this old window
complaining of the soup,
examining the grounds,   205
allowing myself the wasted life.
Soon I will raise my face for a white flag,
and when God enters the fort,
I won't spit or gag on his finger.
I will eat it like a white flower.   210
Is this the old trick, the wasting away,
the skull that waits for its dose
of electric power?

This is madness
but a kind of hunger.   215
What good are my questions
in this hierarchy of death
where the earth and the stones go
Dinn! Dinn! Dinn!
It is hardly a feast.   220
It is my stomach that makes me suffer.

Turn, my hungers!
For once make a deliberate decision.
There are brains that rot here
like black bananas.   225
Hearts have grown as flat as dinner plates.
Anne, Anne,
flee on your donkey,
flee this sad hotel,
ride out on some hairy beast,   230
gallop backward pressing
your buttocks to his withers,
sit to his clumsy gait somehow.
Ride out

any old way you please!   235
In this place everyone talks to his own mouth.
That's what it means to be crazy.
Those I loved best died of it—
the fool's disease.

June 1962   1966

Sylvia's Death

FOR SYLVIA PLATH[1]

O Sylvia, Sylvia,
with a dead box of stones and spoons,

with two children, two meteors
wandering loose in the tiny playroom,

with your mouth into the sheet,   5
into the roofbeam, into the dumb prayer,

(Sylvia, Sylvia,
where did you go
after you wrote me
from Devonshire   10
about raising potatoes
and keeping bees?)

what did you stand by,
just how did you lie down into?

Thief!—   15
how did you crawl into,

crawl down alone
into the death I wanted so badly and for so long,

the death we said we both outgrew,
the one we wore on our skinny breasts,   20

the one we talked of so often each time
we downed three extra dry martinis in Boston,

the death that talked of analysts and cures,
the death that talked like brides with plots,

the death we drank to,   25
the motives and then the quiet deed?

(In Boston
the dying

---

1. American poet (1932–63), friend of
Sexton's, and a suicide. Plath was living
in Devonshire, England, with her husband, the poet Ted Hughes, at the time
of her death.

ride in cabs,
yes death again,   30
that ride home
with *our* boy.)

O Sylvia, I remember the sleepy drummer
who beat on our eyes with an old story,

how we wanted to let him come   35
like a sadist or a New York fairy

to do his job,
a necessity, a window in a wall or a crib,

and since that time he waited
under our heart, our cupboard,   40

and I see now that we store him up
year after year, old suicides

and I know at the news of your death,
a terrible taste for it, like salt.

(And me,   45
me too.
And now, Sylvia,
you again
with death again,
that ride home   50
with *our* boy.)

And I say only
with my arms stretched out into that stone place,

what is your death
but an old belonging,   55

a mole that fell out
of one of your poems?

(O friend,
while the moon's bad,
and the king's gone,   60
and the queen's at her wit's end
the bar fly ought to sing!)

O tiny mother,
you too!
O funny duchess!   65
O blonde thing!
February 17, 1963   1966

Cinderella

You always read about it:
the plumber with twelve children
who wins the Irish Sweepstakes.
From toilets to riches.
That story.   5

Or the nursemaid,
some luscious sweet from Denmark
who captures the oldest son's heart.
From diapers to Dior.[1]
That story.   10

Or a milkman who serves the wealthy,
eggs, cream, butter, yogurt, milk,
the white truck like an ambulance
who goes into real estate
and makes a pile.   15
From homogenized to martinis at lunch.

Or the charwoman
who is on the bus when it cracks up
and collects enough from the insurance.
From mops to Bonwit Teller.[2]   20
That story.

Once
the wife of a rich man was on her deathbed
and she said to her daughter Cinderella:
Be devout. Be good. Then I will smile   25
down from heaven in the seam of a cloud.
The man took another wife who had
two daughters, pretty enough
but with hearts like blackjacks.
Cinderella was their maid.   30
She slept on the sooty hearth each night
and walked around looking like Al Jolson[3]
Her father brought presents home from town,
jewels and gowns for the other women
but the twig of a tree for Cinderella.   35
She planted that twig on her mother's grave
and it grew to a tree where a white dove sat.
Whenever she wished for anything the dove
would drop it like an egg upon the ground.
The bird is important, my dears, so heed him.   40

Next came the ball, as you all know.
It was a marriage market.

---

1. **Christian Dior,** French designer of
elegant clothes.
2. **A fashionable** department store.

3. American singer (1886–1950), famous
for his appearance in blackface in the
first talking film, *The Jazz Singer* (1927).

The prince was looking for a wife.
All but Cinderella were preparing
and gussying up for the big event.   45
Cinderella begged to go too.
Her stepmother threw a dish of lentils
into the cinders and said: Pick them
up in an hour and you shall go.
The white dove brought all his friends;   50
all the warm wings of the fatherland came,
and picked up the lentils in a jiffy.
No, Cinderella, said the stepmother,
you have no clothes and cannot dance.
That's the way with stepmothers.   55

Cinderella went to the tree at the grave
and cried forth like a gospel singer:
Mama! Mama! My turtledove,
send me to the prince's ball!
The bird dropped down a golden dress   60
and delicate little gold slippers.
Rather a large package for a simple bird.
So she went. Which is no surprise.
Her stepmother and sisters didn't
recognize her without her cinder face   65
and the prince took her hand on the spot
and danced with no other the whole day.

As nightfall came she thought she'd better
get home. The prince walked her home
and she disappeared into the pigeon house   70
and although the prince took an axe and broke
it open she was gone. Back to her cinders.
These events repeated themselves for three days.
However on the third day the prince
covered the palace steps with cobbler's wax   75
and Cinderella's gold shoe stuck upon it.

Now he would find whom the shoe fit
and find his strange dancing girl for keeps
He went to their house and the two sisters
were delighted because they had lovely feet.   80
The eldest went into a room to try the slipper on
but her big toe got in the way so she simply
sliced it off and put on the slipper.
The prince rode away with her until the white dove
told him to look at the blood pouring forth.   85
That is the way with amputations.
They don't just heal up like a wish.
The other sister cut off her heel
but the blood told as blood will.
The prince was getting tired.   90
He began to feel like a shoe salesman.

But he gave it one last try.
This time Cinderella fit into the shoe
like a love letter into its envelope.

At the wedding ceremony   95
the two sisters came to curry favor
and the white dove pecked their eyes out.
Two hollow spots were left
like soup spoons.

Cinderella and the prince   100
lived, they say, happily ever after,
like two dolls in a museum case
never bother by diapers or dust,
never arguing over the timing of an egg,
never telling the same story twice,   105
never getting a middle-aged spread,
their darling smiles pasted on for eternity.
Regular Bobbsey Twins.[4]
That story.

                                                             1971

4. Title characters of a popular series of children's books, known for their innocuous adventures.

ADRIENNE RICH

1929–

Adrienne Rich began her career with a prize particularly important for poets of her generation. She was chosen, as were James Wright, John Ashbery, and W. S. Merwin in other years, to have her first book of poems published in the Yale Series of Younger Poets. W. H. Auden, judge for the series in the 1950s, said of Rich's volume, *A Change of World* (1951), that her poems "were neatly and modestly dressed * * * respect their elders but are not cowed by them, and do not tell fibs." Rich, looking back at that period from the vantage of 1972, gives a more complicated sense of it. In an influential essay on women writers, *When We Dead Awaken*, she remembers this period during and just after her years at Radcliffe College as one in which the chief models for young women who wanted to write poetry were the admired male poets of the time: Robert Frost, Dylan Thomas, W. H. Auden, Wallace Stevens, W. B. Yeats. From their work she learned her craft. Even in looking at the poetry of older women writers she found herself "looking * * * for the same things I found in the poetry of men, because I wanted women poets to be the equals of men, and to be equal was still confused with sounding the same." She felt then—and was to feel even more sharply in the years following her marriage (in 1953 to the economist Alfred Conrad)—"the split * * * between the girl * * * who defined herself in writing poems, and the girl who was to define herself by her relationships with men."

Rich has worked, first tentatively and then more securely, to describe and explore this conflict. Twenty years and five volumes after *A Change of World* she published a collection called *The Will to Change*. Those titles accurately reflect the important turn in Rich's work: from acceptance of change as the way of the world to a resolute relocation of power and decision within the self. Speaking twenty years later of *Storm Warnings* from *A Change of World*, Rich remarked, "I'm amazed at the number of images of glass breaking—as if you're the one on the inside and the glass is being broken from without. You're somehow menaced. Now I guess I think of it in reverse. I think of the whole necessity of smashing panes if you're going to save yourself from a burning building."

In her twenties, Rich gave birth to three children within four years; "a radicalizing experience" she said and the chief transforming event in both her personal and writing life. Trying to be the ideal faculty wife and hostess, undergoing difficult pregnancies, and taking care of three small sons, she had little time or energy for writing. In 1955 her second book, *The Diamond Cutters*, appeared; but eight years were to pass before she published another. It was during this time that Rich experienced most severely that gap between what she calls the "energy of creation" and the "energy of relation. * * * In those early years I always felt the conflict as a failure of love in myself." The identification of the writer's imagination with feelings of guilt and cold egotism is voiced in the poem *Orion*, in which a young housewife leaves the demands of home, husband, and children behind and twins herself in fantasy with a male persona, her childhood hero, the giant constellation Orion.

With her third and fourth books, *Snapshots of a Daughter-in-Law* (1963) and *Necessities of Life* (1966), Rich began explicitly to treat problems which have engaged her ever since. The title poem of *Snapshots* exposes the gap between literary versions of women's experience and the day-to-day truths of their lives. Fragments of familiar poems praising and glamorizing women are juxtaposed with scenes from ordinary home life— in a way which adapts the technique of Eliot's *The Waste Land* to more overtly social protest.

When Rich and her husband moved to New York City in 1966 they became increasingly involved in radical politics, especially in the opposition to the Vietnam war. These new concerns are reflected in the poems of *Leaflets* (1969) and *The Will to Change* (1971). But along with new subject matter came equally important changes in style. Rich's poems throughout the 1960s moved away from formal verse patterns to more jagged utterance. Sentence fragments, lines of varying length, irregular spacing to mark off phrases—all these devices emphasized a voice of greater urgency. Ever since *Snapshots of a Daughter-in-Law* Rich had been dating each poem, as if to mark them as provisional, true to the moment but instruments of passage, like entries in a journal where feelings are subject to continual revision. Rich experimented with forms which would give greater prominence to the images in her poetry. Hence, in *The Will to Change*, she refers to and tries to find verbal equivalents for the devices of films, such as quick cuts, close-ups. (One of the poems is called *Shooting Script*.) In speeded-up and more concentrated attention to images, she saw a more intense way to expose the contradictions of consciousness, the simultaneity of opposing emotions.

Rich sees a strong relation between poetry and feminism. Poetry becomes a means for discovering the inner world of women, just as the telescope was for exploring the heavens. As she says in *Planetarium,*

> I am an instrument in the shape
> of a woman trying to translate pulsations
> into images   for the relief of the body
> and the reconstruction of the mind.

The kind of communication Rich most values is envisioned in *Face to Face.* The speaker, a nineteenth-century American pioneer woman, waits in stillness on the frontier for a reunion with her absent husband. Her winter's isolation has allowed her privacy and a concentration to find "plain words." The two will meet

> each with his God-given secret,
> spelled out through months of snow and silence,
> burning under the bleached scalp; behind dry lips
> a loaded gun.

The last line, quoted from Emily Dickinson, suggests how such meetings with loved ones are both dreaded and desired, how they are potentially explosive but also reach out for understanding, "a poetry of dialogue and of the furious effort to break through to dialogue," as one critic remarks. Rich's poems aim at self-definition, at establishing boundaries of the self, but they also fight off the notion that insights remain solitary and unshared. Many of her poems proceed in a tone of intimate argument, as if understanding, political as well as personal, is only manifest in the terms with which we explain ourselves to lovers, friends, and our closest selves. Others give full and powerful expression to the stored-up angers and resentments in women's experience.

In the 1970s Rich's increasing commitment to feminism and to the study of the writings of women resulted in a book of prose, *Of Woman Born: Motherhood as Experience and Institution* (1976). Partly autobiographical and partly historical and anthropological, the book weighs the actual feelings involved in bearing and rearing children against the myths and expectations fostered by our medical, social, and political institutions. Like Rich's poetry, *Of Woman Born* refuses to separate the immediacy of private feelings from political commentary and decision; it suggests that all change originates in changes of individual consciousness.

Storm Warnings

The glass[1] has been falling all the afternoon,
And knowing better than the instrument
What winds are walking overhead, what zone
Of gray unrest is moving across the land,
I leave the book upon a pillowed chair   5

1. Barometer.

And walk from window to closed window, watching
Boughs strain against the sky

And think again, as often when the air
Moves inward toward a silent core of waiting,
How with a single purpose time has traveled   10
By secret currents of the undiscerned
Into this polar realm. Weather abroad
And weather in the heart alike come on
Regardless of prediction.

Between foreseeing and averting change   15
Lies all the mastery of elements
Which clocks and weatherglasses cannot alter.
Time in the hand is not control of time,
Nor shattered fragments of an instrument
A proof against the wind; the wind will rise,   20
We can only close the shutters.

I draw the curtains as the sky goes black
And set a match to candles sheathed in glass
Against the keyhole draught, the insistent whine
Of weather through the unsealed aperture.   25
This is our sole defense against the season;
These are the things that we have learned to do
Who live in troubled regions.

                                                      1951

The Roofwalker

FOR DENISE LEVERTOV

Over the half-finished houses
night comes. The builders
stand on the roof. It is
quiet after the hammers,
the pulleys hang slack.   5
Giants, the roofwalkers,
on a listing deck, the wave
of darkness about to break
on their heads. The sky
is a torn sail where figures   10
pass magnified, shadows
on a burning deck.

I feel like them up there:
exposed, larger than life,
and due to break my neck.   15

Was it worth while to lay—
with infinite exertion—
a roof I can't live under?

—All those blueprints,
closings of gaps,   20
measurings, calculations?
A life I didn't choose
chose me: even
my tools are the wrong ones
for what I have to do.   25
I'm naked, ignorant,
a naked man fleeing
across the roofs
who could with a shade of difference
be sitting in the lamplight   30
against the cream wallpaper
reading—not with indifference—
about a naked man
fleeing across the roofs.

1961   1962

Face to Face

Never to be lonely like that—
the Early American figure on the beach
in black coat and knee-breeches
scanning the didactic storm in privacy,

never to hear the prairie wolves   5
in their lunar hilarity
circling one's little all, one's claim
to be Law and Prophets

for all that lawlessness,
never to whet the appetite   10
weeks early, for a face, a hand
longed-for and dreaded—

How people used to meet!
starved, intense, the old
Christmas gifts saved up till spring,   15
and the old plain words,

and each with his God-given secret,
spelled out through months of snow and silence,
burning under the bleached scalp; behind dry lips
a loaded gun.[1]   20

1965   1966

Orion[1]

Far back when I went zig-zagging
through tamarack pastures

---

1. Allusion to Emily Dickinson's poem,   popularly known as the Hunter, which
My Life had stood—a Loaded Gun—.   appears as a giant with a belt and sword.
1. A constellation of the winter sky,

you were my genius, you
my cast-iron Viking, my helmed
lion-heart king[2] in prison.   5
Years later now you're young

my fierce half-brother, staring
down from that simplified west
your breast open, your belt dragged down
by an oldfashioned thing, a sword   10
the last bravado you won't give over
though it weighs you down as you stride

and the stars in it are dim
and maybe have stopped burning.
But you burn, and I know it;   15
as I throw back my head to take you in
an old transfusion happens again:
divine astronomy is nothing to it.

Indoors I bruise and blunder,
break faith, leave ill enough   20
alone, a dead child born in the dark.
Night cracks up over the chimney,
pieces of time, frozen geodes[3]
come showering down in the grate.

A man reaches behind my eyes   25
and finds them empty
a woman's head turns away
from my head in the mirror
children are dying my death
and eating crumbs of my life.   30

Pity is not your forte.
Calmly you ache up there
pinned aloft in your crow's nest,[4]
my speechless pirate!
You take it all for granted   35
and when I look you back

it's with a starlike eye
shooting its cold and egotistical[5] spear
where it can do least damage.
Breathe deep! No hurt, no pardon   40

2. Allusion to King Richard the Lion-
Heart of England (1157–99), imprisoned
in Austria on his return from the Crusades.
3. Small, spheroid stones, with a cavity
usually lined with crystals.
4. Lookout post on the mast of old ships.
5. "One of two phrases suggested by
Gottfried Benn's essay, *Artists and Old*

Age in *Primal Vision*, edited by E. B.
Ashton, New Directions" [Rich's note].
Benn's advice to the modern artist is:
"Don't lose sight of the cold and egotistical element in your mission. * * *
With your back to the wall, care-worn
and weary, in the gray light of the void,
read Job and Jeremiah and keep going"
(pp. 206–7).

out here in the cold with you
you with your back to the wall.

1965   1969

Charleston in the Eighteen-Sixties

DERIVED FROM THE DIARIES OF MARY BOYKIN CHESNUT

He seized me by the waist and kissed my throat . . .
Your eyes, dear, are they grey or blue,
eyes of an angel?
The carts have passed already with their heaped
night-soil, we breathe again . . .   5
Is this what war is? Nitrate . . .
But smell the pear,
the jasmine, the violets.
Why does this landscape always sadden you?
Now the freshet is up on every side,   10
the river comes to our doors,
limbs of primeval trees dip in the swamp.

So we fool on into the black
cloud ahead of us.
Everything human glitters fever-bright—   15
the thrill of waking up
out of a stagnant life?
There seems a spell upon
your lovers,—all dead of wounds
or blown to pieces . . . Nitrate!   20
I'm writing, blind with tears of rage.
In vain. Years, death, depopulation, fears,
bondage—these shall all be borne.
No imagination to forestall woe.

1966   1969

Planetarium

THINKING OF CAROLINE HERSCHEL (1750–1848)
ASTRONOMER, SISTER OF WILLIAM,[1] AND OTHERS.

A woman in the shape of a monster
a monster in the shape of a woman
the skies are full of them

a woman   'in the snow
among the Clocks and instruments   5
or measuring the ground with poles'

in her 98 years to discover
8 comets

---

1. William Herschel (1738–1822), discoverer of the planet Uranus.

she whom the moon ruled
like us
levitating into the night sky
riding the polished lenses

Galaxies of women, there
doing penance for impetuousness
ribs chilled
in those spaces   of the mind

An eye,

     'virile, precise and absolutely certain'
     from the mad webs of Uranusborg[2]

         encountering the NOVA[3]

every impulse of light exploding
from the core
as life flies out of us

     Tycho whispering at last
     'Let me not seem to have lived in vain'

What we see, we see
and seeing is changing

the light that shrivels a mountain
and leaves a man alive

Heartbeat of the pulsar[4]
heart sweating through my body

The radio impulse
pouring in from Taurus[5]

     I am bombarded yet   I stand

I have been standing all my life in the
direct path of a battery of signals
the most accurately transmitted most
untranslatable language in the universe
I am a galactic[6] cloud so deep   so involuted that a light wave could take 15
years to travel through me   And has
taken   I am an instrument in the shape

2. Uranienborg, an observatory built by
Danish astronomer Tycho Brahe (1546–
1601).
3. A new star discovered by Brahe in
1573 in the constellation Cassiopeia.

4. Interstellar short period radio signal.
5. The constellation in the northern
hemisphere.
6. Pertaining to the Milky Way.

of a woman trying to translate pulsations
into images   for the relief of the body
and the reconstruction of the mind.   45
1968
                                                                      1971

The Burning of Paper Instead of Children

> *I was in danger of*
> *verbalizing my moral*
> *impulses out of existence.*
>
> —*Daniel Berrigan,*[1] *on trial in Baltimore*

1. My neighbor, a scientist and art-collector, telephones me in a
state of violent emotion. He tells me that my son and his, aged
eleven and twelve, have on the last day of school burned a mathematics textbook in the backyard. He has forbidden my son to come
to his house for a week, and has forbidden his own son to leave the
house during that time. "The burning of a book," he says, "arouses
terrible sensations in me, memories of Hitler; there are few things
that upset me so much as the idea of burning a book."

Back there: the library, walled
with green Britannicas[2]   10
Looking again

in Dürer's *Complete Works*
for MELANCOLIA,[3] the baffled woman

the crocodiles in Herodotus[4]
the Book of the Dead[5]   15
the *Trial of Jeanne d'Arc*,[6] so blue
I think, It is her color

and they take the book away
because I dream of her too often

love and fear in a house   20
knowledge of the oppressor
I know it hurts to burn

2. To imagine a time of silence
or few words
a time of chemistry and music   25

the hollows above your buttocks
traced by my hand
or, *hair is like flesh*, you said

1. Jesuit priest, opponent of the Vietnam war, tried and convicted for burning draft records at a Selective Service
office in Catonsville, Maryland.
2. British encyclopedia.
3. Melancholy personified as a woman
in an engraving by German painter

Albrecht Dürer (1471–1528).
4. Greek historian, fifth century B.C.
5. Ancient Egyptian mystical work.
6. Transcript of the trial of Joan of Arc
(1411–31), French peasant girl considered the savior of France, burned at the
stake for witchcraft and later canonized.

an age of long silence

relief   30

from this tongue   this slab of limestone
or reinforced concrete
fanatics and traders
dumped on this coast wildgreen clayred   35
that breathed once
in signals of smoke
sweep of the wind

knowledge of the oppressor
this is the oppressor's language

yet I need it to talk to you   40

3. *People suffer highly in poverty and it takes dignity and intelli-*
gence to overcome this suffering. Some of the suffering are: a child
did not had dinner last night: a child steal because he did not have
money to buy it: to hear a mother say she do not have money to buy
food for her children and to see a child without cloth it will make
tears in your eyes.[7]

(the fracture of order
the repair of speech
to overcome this suffering)

4. We lie under the sheet   50
after making love, speaking
of loneliness
relieved in a book
relived in a book
so on that page   55
the clot and fissure
of it appears
words of a man
in pain
a naked word   60
entering the clot
a hand grasping
through bars:

deliverance

What happens between us   65
has happened for centuries
we know it from literature

---

7. This paragraph is quoted from an
essay by one of Rich's black students in
the open admissions program at the City
College of New York.

still it happens

sexual jealousy
outflung hand   70
beating bed

dryness of mouth
after panting

there are books that describe all this
and they are useless   75

You walk into the woods behind a house
there in that country
you find a temple
built eighteen hundred years ago
you enter without knowing   80
what it is you enter

so it is with us

no one knows what may happen
though the books tell everything

burn the texts   said Artaud[8]   85

5. I am composing on the typewriter late at night, thinking of
today. How well we all spoke. A language is a map of our failures.
Frederick Douglass[9] wrote an English purer than Milton's. People
suffer highly in poverty. There are methods but we do not use them.
Joan, who could not read, spoke some peasant form of French.
Some of the suffering are: it is hard to tell the truth; this is America;
I cannot touch you now. In America we have only the present tense.
I am in danger. You are in danger. The burning of a book arouses
no sensation in me. I know it hurts to burn. There are flames of
napalm in Catonsville, Maryland. I know it hurts to burn. The
typewriter is overheated, my mouth is burning, I cannot touch you
and this is the oppressor's language.
1968
                                                                          1971

A Valediction Forbidding Mourning[1]

My swirling wants. Your frozen lips.
The grammar turned and attacked me.

8. Antonin Artaud (1896–1948), French
Surrealist poet who appeared in Carl
Dreyer's film *The Passion of Joan of
Arc*. Considered the founder of the Theater of the Absurd, Artaud called for
the destruction of traditional texts in
order to heighten the modern theater's
focus on contemporary problems.
9. Former slave (1817–98) who escaped
to the North during the Civil War and
became a leading abolitionist. John
Milton (1608–74), English poet, author
of *Paradise Lost*.
1. Title of a famous poem by John
Donne (1572–1631), in which the English poet forbids his wife to lament his
departure on a trip to the Continent.

Themes, written under duress.
Emptiness of the notations.

They gave me a drug that slowed the healing of wounds.   5

I want you to see this before I leave:
the experience of repetition as death
the failure of criticism to locate the pain
the poster in the bus that said:
my bleeding is under control.   10

A red plant in a cemetery of plastic wreaths.

A last attempt: the language is a dialect called metaphor.
These images go unglossed: hair, glacier, flashlight.
When I think of a landscape I am thinking of a time.
When I talk of taking a trip I mean forever.   15
I could say: those mountains have a meaning
but further than that I could not say.

To do something very common, in my own way.

1970   1971

The Mirror in Which Two Are Seen as One

1

She is the one you call sister.
Her simplest act has glamor,
as when she scales a fish the knife
flashes in her long fingers
no motion wasted or when   5
rapidly talking of love
she steel-wool burnishes
the battered kettle

Love apples cramp you sideways
with sudden emptiness   10
the cereals glutting you, the grains
ripe clusters picked by hand
Love: the refrigerator
with open door
the ripe steaks bleeding   15
their hearts out in plastic film
the whipped butter, the apricots
the sour leftovers

A crate is waiting in the orchard
for you to fill it   20
your hands are raw with scraping
the sharp bark, the thorns
of this succulent tree

Pick, pick, pick
this harvest is a failure   25
the juice runs down your cheekbones
like sweat or tears

2

She is the one you call sister
you blaze like lightning about the room
flicker around her like fire   30
dazzle yourself in her wide eyes
listing her unfelt needs
thrusting the tenets of your life
into her hands

She moves through a world of India print   35
her body dappled
with softness, the paisley swells at her hip
walking the street in her cotton shift
buying fresh figs because you love them
photographing the ghetto because you took her there   40

Why are you crying dry up your tears
we are sisters
words fail you in the stare of her hunger
you hand her another book
scored by your pencil   45
you hand her a record
of two flutes in India reciting

3

Late summer night the insects
fry in the yellowed lightglobe
your skin burns gold in its light   50
In this mirror, who are you? Dreams of the nunnery
with its discipline, the nursery
with its nurse, the hospital
where all the powerful ones are masked
the graveyard where you sit on the graves   55
of women who died in childbirth
and women who died at birth
Dreams of your sister's birth
your mother dying in childbirth over and over
not knowing how to stop   60
bearing you over and over

your mother dead and you unborn
your two hands grasping your head
drawing it down against the blade of life
your nerves the nerves of a midwife   65
learning her trade

1971   1973

Diving into the Wreck

First having read the book of myths,
and loaded the camera,
and checked the edge of the knife-blade,
I put on
the body-armor of black rubber   5
the absurd flippers
the grave and awkward mask.
I am having to do this
not like Cousteau[1] with his
assiduous team   10
aboard the sun-flooded schooner
but here alone.

There is a ladder.
The ladder is always there
hanging innocently   15
close to the side of the schooner.
We know what it is for,
we who have used it.
Otherwise
it's a piece of maritime floss   20
some sundry equipment.

I go down.
Rung after rung and still
the oxygen immerses me
the blue light   25
the clear atoms
of our human air.
I go down.
My flippers cripple me,
I crawl like an insect down the ladder   30
and there is no one
to tell me when the ocean
will begin.

First the air is blue and then
it is bluer and then green and then   35
black I am blacking out and yet
my mask is powerful
it pumps my blood with power
the sea is another story
the sea is not a question of power   40
I have to learn alone
to turn my body without force
in the deep element.

1. Jacques-Yves Cousteau (b. 1910), a French underwater explorer and author.

And now: it is easy to forget
what I came for   45
among so many who have always
lived here
swaying their crenellated fans
between the reefs
and besides   50
you breathe differently down here.

I came to explore the wreck.
The words are purposes.
The words are maps.
I came to see the damage that was done   55
and the treasures that prevail.
I stroke the beam of my lamp
slowly along the flank
of something more permanent
than fish or weed   60

the thing I came for:
the wreck and not the story of the wreck
the thing itself and not the myth
the drowned face[2] always staring
toward the sun   65
the evidence of damage
worn by salt and sway into this threadbare beauty
the ribs of the disaster
curving their assertion
among the tentative haunters.   70

This is the place.
And I am here, the mermaid whose dark hair
streams black, the merman in his armored body
We circle silently
about the wreck   75
we dive into the hold.
I am she: I am he

whose drowned face sleeps with open eyes
whose breasts still bear the stress
whose silver, copper, vermeil[3] cargo lies   80
obscurely inside barrels
half-wedged and left to rot
we are the half-destroyed instruments
that once held to a course
the water-eaten log   85
the fouled compass

We are, I am, you are
by cowardice or courage

2. Referring to the ornamental female   many old sailing ships.
figurehead which formed the prow of   3. Gilded silver or bronze.

the one who find our way
back to this scene   90
carrying a knife, a camera
a book of myths
in which
our names do not appear.

1972   1973

For the Dead

I dreamed I called you on the telephone
to say: *Be kinder to yourself*
but you were sick and would not answer

The waste of my love goes on this way
trying to save you from yourself   5

I have always wondered about the leftover
energy, water rushing down a hill
long after the rains have stopped

or the fire you want to go to bed from
but cannot leave, burning-down but not burnt-down   10
the red coals more extreme, more curious
in their flashing and dying
than you wish they were
sitting there long after midnight

1972   1973

Blood-Sister

FOR CYNTHIA

Shoring up the ocean. A railroad track
ran close to the coast for miles
through the potato-fields, bringing us
to summer. Weeds blur the ties,
sludge clots the beaches.   5

During the war, the shells we found—
salmon-and-silver coins
sand dollars dripping sand
like dust. We were dressed
in navy dotted-swiss dresses in the train   10
not to show the soot. Like dolls
we sat with our dolls in the station.

When did we begin to dress ourselves?

Now I'm wearing jeans spider-webbed
with creases, a black sweater bought years ago   15
worn almost daily since

the ocean has undergone a tracheotomy
and lost its resonance
you wear a jersey the color of
Navaho turquoise and sand   20
you are holding a naked baby girl
she laughs into your eyes
we sit at your table drinking coffee
light flashes off unwashed sheetglass
you are more beautiful than you have ever been   25

we talk of destruction and creation
ice fits itself around each twig of the lilac
like a fist of law and order
your imagination burns like a bulb in the frozen soil
the fierce shoots knock   30
at the roof of waiting

when summer comes the ocean may be closed for good
we will turn
to the desert
where survival   35
takes naked and fiery forms

1973   1975

Toward the Solstice

The thirtieth of November.
Snow is starting to fall.
A peculiar silence is spreading
over the fields, the maple grove.
It is the thirtieth of May,   5
rain pours on ancient bushes, runs
down the youngest blade of grass.
I am trying to hold in one steady glance
all the parts of my life.
A spring torrent races   10
on this old slanting roof,
the slanted field below
thickens with winter's first whiteness.
Thistles dried to sticks in last year's wind
stand nakedly in the green,   15
stand sullenly in the slowly whitening,
field.

      My brain glows
more violently, more avidly
the quieter, the thicker
the quilt of crystals settles,   20
the louder, more relentlessly
the torrent beats itself out
on the old boards and shingles.
It is the thirtieth of May,   25

the thirtieth of November,
a beginning or an end,
we are moving into the solstice
and there is so much here
I still do not understand.   30
If I could make sense of how
my life is still tangled
with dead weeds, thistles,
enormous burdocks, burdens
slowly shifting under   35
this first fall of snow,
beaten by this early, racking rain
calling all new life to declare itself strong
or die,
   if I could know   40
in what language to address
the spirits that claim a place
beneath these low and simple ceilings,
tenants that neither speak nor stir
yet dwell in mute insistence   45
till I can feel utterly ghosted in this house.

If history is a spider-thread
spun over and over though brushed away
it seems I might some twilight
or dawn in the hushed country light   50
discern its greyness stretching
from molding or doorframe, out
into the empty dooryard
and following it climb
the path into the pinewoods,   55
tracing from tree to tree
in the failing light, in the slowly
lucidifying day
its constant, purposive trail,
till I reach whatever cellar hole   60
filling with snowflakes or lichen,
whatever fallen shack
or unremembered clearing
I am meant to have found
and there, under the first or last   65
star, trusting to instinct
the words would come to mind
I have failed or forgotten to say
year after year, winter
after summer, the right rune[1]   70
to ease the hold of the past
upon the rest of my life
and ease my hold on the past.

---

1. I.e., spell, incantation.

If some rite of separation
is still unaccomplished   75
between myself and the long-gone
tenants of this house,
between myself and my childhood,
and the childhood of my children,
it is I who have neglected   80
to perform the needed acts,
set water in corners, light and eucalyptus
in front of mirrors,
or merely pause and listen
to my own pulse vibrating   85
lightly as falling snow,
relentlessly as the rainstorm,
and hear what it has been saying.
It seems I am still waiting
for them to make some clear demand   90
some articulate sound or gesture,
for release to come from anywhere
but from inside myself.

A decade of cutting away
dead flesh, cauterizing   95
old scars ripped open over and over
and still it is not enough.
A decade of performing
the loving humdrum acts
of attention to this house   100
transplanting lilac suckers,
washing panes, scrubbing
wood-smoke from splitting paint,
sweeping stairs, brushing the thread
of the spider aside,   105
and so much yet undone,
a woman's work, the solstice nearing,
and my hand still suspended
as if above a letter
I long and dread to close.   110

1977   1978

GARY SNYDER

1930–

Gary Snyder, who has called himself "a hobo and a worker," was loosely
associated with Allen Ginsberg, Jack Kerouac, and others in forming what
came to be called the Beat movement of the 1950s (in *The Dharma Bums*,
Kerouac models a central character after Snyder). But what marked Snyder
off from the others of his generation who went "on the road" was the rigor

with which he pursued alternatives to city life and Western systems of value. He combined his wanderings with periods of studying linguistics, mythology, and Oriental languages.

Snyder grew up on a farm in Washington and studied anthropology at Reed College in Oregon. Living in the Pacific Northwest, he developed a serious interest in the folklore and mythology of the American Indians. He did graduate work in linguistics at Indiana University and classical Chinese at the University of California in Berkeley. In 1956–57 and again in the mid-1960s, Snyder took formal instruction in Buddhism under Zen masters in Japan.

Like Thoreau at Walden Pond, Snyder writes artful journals of a life in nature—"an ecological survival technique," he prefers to call it. "The rhythms of my poems follow the rhythms of the physical work I'm doing and life I'm leading at any given time." His experience as a logger and forest ranger in the Pacific Northwest are reflected in the *Myths and Texts* he was writing from 1952 to 1956 and in poems such as *Piute Creek* and *Milton by Firelight*. *The Back Country* includes poems from the Far West and from his years at a monastery in Japan. Snyder's service on a tanker in the South Pacific is treated in some of the prose journals of *Earth House Hold* (1969). *Turtle Island* (1974) grows out of his life as a hunter and gatherer of food, a member—along with his wife and children—of a commune in the foothills of the Sierras.

Though the material of his poems is what the naturalist, hunter, and logger would observe, the experiences Snyder tries to capture are those of ritual feelings and natural power. He describes poetry as "the skilled use of the voice and language to embody rare and powerful states of mind that are in immediate origin personal to the singer, but at deep levels common to all who listen." A quenching of a forest fire in the American West—one of his "Texts"—will lead in the accompanying "Myth" to parallels with the burning of Troy and allusions to Buddhist ritual silence and incense. He more characteristically refers to poetry as a "riprap." This is a forester's term, the title of his first book (1959). A riprap, he explains, is "a cobble of stone laid on steep slick rock to make a trail for horses in the mountains." The combination of know-how and ascent appeals to him, and symbolizes his belief that awakened spiritual insight is inseparable from a strong documentary impulse; "Poetry a riprap on the slick rock of metaphysics." It is a statement Thoreau would have understood and a use of poetry he would have endorsed.

Piute Creek[1]

One granite ridge
A tree, would be enough
Or even a rock, a small creek,
A bark shred in a pool.
Hill beyond hill, folded and twisted   5
Tough trees crammed
In thin stone fractures
A huge moon on it all, is too much.

1. In the Sierra Mountains of the American West.

The mind wanders. A million
Summers, night air still and the rocks   10
Warm. Sky over endless mountains.
All the junk that goes with being human
Drops away, hard rock wavers
Even the heavy present seems to fail
This bubble of a heart.   15
Words and books
Like a small creek off a high ledge
Gone in the dry air.

A clear, attentive mind
Has no meaning but that   20
Which sees is truly seen.
No one loves rock, yet we are here.
Night chills. A flick
In the moonlight
Slips into Juniper shadow: 25
Back there unseen
Cold proud eyes
Of Cougar or Coyote
Watch me rise and go.

                                           1959

Milton[1] by Firelight

PIUTE CREEK, AUGUST 1955

"O hell, what do mine eyes
            with grief behold?"[2]
Working with an old
Singlejack miner, who can sense
The vein and cleavage   5
In the very guts of rock, can
Blast granite, build
Switchbacks[3] that last for years
Under the beat of snow, thaw, mule-hooves.
What use, Milton, a silly story   10
Of our lost general[4] parents,
            eaters of fruit?

The Indian, the chainsaw boy,
And a string of six mules
Came riding down to camp   15
Hungry for tomatoes and green apples.
Sleeping in saddle-blankets
Under a bright night-sky
Han River slantwise by morning.

1. John Milton (1608–74), major English poet and author of *Paradise Lost*,
which retells the Biblical story of the
Fall of Man.
2. Satan's words when he first sees
Adam and Eve in the Garden of Eden
(*Paradise Lost*, IV.358).
3. Roads ascending a steep incline in a
zigzag pattern.
4. I.e., of our race.

Jays squall 20
Coffee boils

In ten thousand years the Sierras
Will be dry and dead, home of the scorpion.
Ice-scratched slabs and bent trees.
No paradise, no fall, 25
Only the weathering land
The wheeling sky,
Man, with his Satan
Scouring the chaos of the mind.
Oh Hell! 30

Fire down
Too dark to read, miles from a road
The bell-mare clangs in the meadow
That packed dirt for a fill-in
Scrambling through loose rocks 35
On an old trail
All of a summer's day.[5]

1959

Riprap[1]

Lay down these words
Before your mind like rocks.
          placed solid, by hands
In choice of place, set
Before the body of the mind 5
          in space and time:
Solidity of bark, leaf, or wall
          riprap of things:
Cobble of milky way,
          straying planets, 10
These poems, people,
          lost ponies with
Dragging saddles—
          and rocky sure-foot trails.
The worlds like an endless 15
          four-dimensional
Game of Go.[2]
          ants and pebbles
In the thin loam, each rock a word
          a creek-washed stone 20
Granite: ingrained
          with torment of fire and weight

---

5. Alludes to an epic simile describing Satan's fall: "From morn / to noon he fell, from noon to dewy eve, / A summer's day" (*Paradise Lost*, I.742–44).
1. "A cobble of stone laid on steep slick rock to make a trail for horses in the mountains" [Snyder's note].
2. An ancient Japanese game played with black and white stones, placed one after the other on a checkered board.

Crystal and sediment linked hot
  all change, in thoughts,
As well as things.   25

          1959

From Myths and Texts: Burning, Section 17

THE TEXT

Sourdough mountain called a fire in:
Up Thunder Creek, high on a ridge.
Hiked eighteen hours, finally found
A snag and a hundred feet around on fire:
All afternoon and into night   5
Digging the fire line
Falling the burning snag
It fanned sparks down like shooting stars
Over the dry woods, starting spot-fires
Flaring in wind up Skagit valley   10
From the Sound.
Toward morning it rained.
We slept in mud and ashes,
Woke at dawn, the fire was out,
The sky was clear, we saw   15
The last glimmer of the morning star.

THE MYTH

Fire up Thunder Creek and the mountain—troy's burning!
The cloud mutters
The mountains are your mind.
The woods bristle there,
Dogs barking and children shrieking   5
Rise from below.

Rain falls for centuries
Soaking the loose rocks in space
Sweet rain, the fire's out
The black snag glistens in the rain   10
& the last wisp of smoke floats up
Into the absolute cold
Into the spiral whorls of fire
The storms of the Milky Way
"Buddha incense in an empty world"   15
Black pit cold and light-year
Flame tongue of the dragon
Licks the sun

The sun is but a morning star[1]

          1960

---

1. The last words of *Walden* by the American Transcendentalist author Henry David
Thoreau (1817–62).

Fire in the Hole

Squatting a day in the sun,
    one hand turning the steeldrill,
one, swinging the four pound singlejack hammer
        down.
three inches an hour   5
granite bullhump boulder
        square in the trail.
above, the cliffs,
        of Piute Mountain waver.
sweat trickles down my back.   10

why does this day keep coming into mind.
a job in the rock hills
    aching arms
        the muletracks
            arching blinding sky, 15
    noon sleep under
        snake-scale juniper limbs.
that the mind
    entered the tip of steel.
the arm fell   20
    like breath.
the valley, reeling,
        on the pivot of that drill—
twelve inches deep we packed the charge
    dynamite on mules   25
        like frankincense.
Fire in the hole !
Fire in the hole !
Fire in the hole !

jammed the plunger down.   30
thru dust
        and sprinkling stone
strolld back to see:
hands and arms and shoulders
free.   35
      1968

Vapor Trails

Twin streaks twice higher than cumulus,
Precise plane icetracks in the vertical blue
Cloud-flaked light-shot shadow-arcing
Field of all future war, edging off to space.

Young expert U.S. pilots waiting   5
The day of criss-cross rockets
And white blossoming smoke of bomb,

The air world torn and staggered for these
Specks of brushy land and ant-hill towns—

I stumble on the cobble rockpath,   10
Passing through temples,
Watching for two-leaf pine
　　—spotting that design.

in Daitoku-ji[1]   1968

The Old Dutch Woman

The old dutch woman would spend half a day
Pacing the backyard where I lived
　　　　　in a fixed-up shed,
What did she see.
Wet leaves, the rotten tilted-over   5
　　　　over-heavy heads
Of domesticated flowers.
　　　　　I knew Indian Paintbrush
Thought nature meant mountains,
Snowfields, glaciers and cliffs,   10
White granite waves underfoot.

Heian ladies[1]
Trained to the world of the garden,
　　　　　poetry,
　　lovers slippt in with at night—   15

My Grandmother standing wordless
　　fifteen minutes
Between rows of loganberries,
　　clippers poised in her hand.

New leaves on the climbing rose   20
Planted last fall.
　　—tiny bugs eating the green—

Like once watching
　　　　mountaingoats:
Far over a valley   25
Half into the
　　　　shade of the headwall,
　　Pick their way over the snow.

1968

I Went into the Maverick Bar

I went into the Maverick Bar
In Farmington, New Mexico.

---

1. In Japan (where Snyder studied Buddhism).

1. Japanese court ladies of the 12th century.

And drank double shots of bourbon
            backed with beer.
My long hair was tucked up under a cap   5
I'd left the earring in the car.

Two cowboys did horseplay
            by the pool tables,
A waitress asked us
            where are you from?   10
a country-and-western band began to play
"We don't smoke Marijuana in Muskokie"
And with the next song,
            a couple began to dance.

They held each other like in High School dances   15
            in the fifties;
I recalled when I worked in the woods
            and the bars of Madras, Oregon.
That short-haired joy and roughness—
            America—your stupidity.   20
I could almost love you again.

We left—onto the freeway shoulders—
            under the tough old stars—
In the shadow of bluffs
            I came back to myself,   25
To the real work, to
            "What is to be done."[1]

                    1974

1. Title of a revolutionary pamphlet by Lenin (1902).

SYLVIA PLATH
1932–1963

Sylvia Plath is best known for those poems she wrote feverishly, two or three a day, in the last months of her life. Most of them were collected in a volume called *Ariel*, published in 1965, two years after her suicide in London. The book had an eloquent preface by Robert Lowell, who commented on the astonishing transformation which had overtaken Plath's work in a relatively brief period before her death. Lowell had known the young women in 1958 when she and another poet, Anne Sexton, made regular visits to his poetry seminar at Boston University. He remembered her "air of maddening docility * * * I sensed her abashment and distinction, and never guessed her later appalling and triumphant fulfillment."

    Lowell's impression was characteristic of most of the witnesses of Plath's life. Even when she retold her story in the autobiographical novel *The Bell Jar* (1963), there seemed to be a terrible gap between the tone and behavior of a gifted, modest suburban girl of the 1950s and the hidden turmoil which burst out in a nervous breakdown and a first suicide attempt when she was nineteen. Like Plath, the heroine of *The Bell Jar* won the chance to spend one summer in New York as a guest editor of a young women's magazine (in real life *Mademoiselle*). *The Bell Jar* details the trivial stereotyping of women's roles in both the business and social worlds. Then, with little psychological preparation for the reader, Esther Greenwood, the heroine, attempts suicide and has to be hospitalized (as was Plath herself between her junior and senior years in college). What is astonishing about *The Bell Jar* is that although it was written just before the *Ariel* poems, it betrays very little of the strong feeling, the ferocity, that Plath was able to discover and express through her last poetry.

As the poem *Daddy* suggests, Plath's final outburst had a great deal to do with the breakup of her marriage to the English poet Ted Hughes and its connection to buried feelings about her childhood and her parents' marriage. Otto Plath died in 1940, when his daughter was eight years old. A Prussian, Sylvia's father was twenty-one years older than her mother and had been his wife's German professor. He was a biologist, author of a treatise on bumblebees, and, in his household, an autocrat. His death from diabetes might have been prevented if he had consented to see a doctor when signs of physical deterioration set in. Instead, diagnosing his own condition as cancer, he virtually turned their home into a hospital, demanded constant family attendance, and for several years kept his wife and children under the strain of living with what he insisted was an incurable disease.

After his death the strain became financial. Sylvia's mother, left penniless with two small children, worked hard as a teacher and reinforced her daughter's ambitions to be literary, successful, and well rounded. On scholarship Sylvia went to Smith College, from which she graduated *summa cum laude*. On a Fulbright grant she studied in England at Cambridge University, where she met and married Ted Hughes. For the first years the marriage seemed to fulfill a romantic dream—a handsome English husband, two poets beginning careers together, encouraging one another's work. (Plath's first book, *The Colossus*, appeared in 1960.) They were known in literary circles in London and spent time in New England when Plath returned for a year to teach at Smith.

In 1960, back in England, their daughter Frieda was born and, in 1962, a son Nicholas. Hughes began seeing another woman; Plath spent two harsh winters in their country house in Devon and finally asked Hughes for a legal separation. It was under the stress of repeating her mother's experience, left alone with two small children, that Plath's deep anger against and attachment to her father surfaced in poetry. In *Daddy* he is identified with her husband and made partially responsible for her blasted marriage.

From Robert Lowell and Anne Sexton, Plath adopted the license to write about "private and taboo subjects," such as their experiences of breakdowns and mental hospitals. In her case the poems touch deep suspicions of family life, voiced resentments of her young children as well as of her husband. But the *Ariel* poems, unlike Lowell's melancholy, often speak through figures of grotesque gaiety. In *Lady Lazarus* Plath was able to refer to her suicide attempts through the mask of a "sort of walking miracle." "Out of the ash / I rise with my red hair / And I eat men like air."

The other side of Plath's disappointment with failed human relationships was to imagine herself and others absorbed by nature. Human contacts become small and unreal while natural processes go on, palpable,
unruffled by human pain. Like death, this was another way to escape living
with a flawed self. Through writing Plath faced that problem very clearly:
"I cannot sympathize with those cries from the heart that are informed
by nothing except a needle or a knife. * * * I believe that one should be
able to control and manipulate experiences, even the most terrifying * * *
with an informed and intelligent mind. * * * Certaintly it [experience]
shouldn't be a kind of shut-box and mirror-looking, narcissistic experience."
Her lucid stanzas, clear diction, and resolute dramatic speakers embodied
those beliefs. Before she died, Plath had managed through poetry to discover, express, and control the hidden violence of her inner experience.
Whether she would have been able to sustain those truths in her day-to-
day living is an unanswerable question. She took her life on February 11,
1963.

Black Rook in Rainy Weather

On the stiff twig up there
Hunches a wet black rook
Arranging and rearranging its feathers in the rain.
I do not expect miracle
Or an accident   5

To set the sight on fire
In my eye, nor seek
Any more in the desultory weather some design,
But let spotted leaves fall as they fall,
Without ceremony, or portent   10

Although, I admit, I desire,
Occasionally, some backtalk
From the mute sky, I can't honestly complain:
A certain minor light may still
Leap incandescent   15

Out of kitchen table or chair
As if a celestial burning took
Possession of the most obtuse objects now and then—
Thus hallowing an interval
Otherwise inconsequent   20

By bestowing largesse, honor,
One might say love. At any rate, I now walk
Wary (for it could happen
Even in this dull, ruinous landscape); skeptical,
Yet politic; ignorant   25

Of whatever angel may choose to flare
Suddenly at my elbow. I only know that a rook

Ordering its black feathers can so shine
As to seize my senses, haul
My eyelids up, and grant   30

A brief respite from fear
Of total neutrality. With luck,
Trekking stubborn through this season
Of fatigue, I shall
Patch together a content   35

Of sorts. Miracles occur,
if you care to call those spasmodic
Tricks of radiance miracles. The wait's begun again,
The long wait for the angel,
For that rare, random descent.[1]   40

1960

Morning Song

Love set you going like a fat gold watch.
The midwife slapped your footsoles, and your bald cry
Took its place among the elements.

Our voices echo, magnifying your arrival. New statue.
In a drafty museum, your nakedness   5
Shadows our safety. We stand round blankly as walls.

I'm no more your mother
Than the cloud that distils a mirror to reflect its own slow
Effacement at the wind's hand.

All night your moth-breath   10
Flickers among the flat pink roses. I wake to listen:
A far sea moves in my ear.

One cry, and I stumble from bed, cow-heavy and floral
In my Victorian nightgown.
Your mouth opens clean as a cat's. The window square   15

Whitens and swallows its dull stars. And now you try
Your handful of notes;
The clear vowels rise like balloons.

1961   1966

The Applicant

First, are you our sort of a person?
Do you wear
A glass eye, false teeth or a crutch,
A brace or a hook,
Rubber breasts or a rubber crotch,   5

---

1. At Pentecost, the Holy Ghost descended in the form of fiery tongues upon
Christ's disciples (Acts 2.1–5).

Stitches to show something's missing? No, no? Then
How can we give you a thing?
Stop crying.
Open your hand.
Empty? Empty. Here is a hand   10

To fill it and willing
To bring teacups and roll away headaches
And do whatever you tell it.
Will you marry it?
It is guaranteed   15

To thumb shut your eyes at the end
And dissolve of sorrow.
We make new stock from the salt.
I notice you are stark naked.
How about this suit——   20

Black and stiff, but not a bad fit.
Will you marry it?
It is waterproof, shatterproof, proof
Against fire and bombs through the roof.
Believe me, they'll bury you in it.   25

Now your head, excuse me, is empty.
I have the ticket for that.
Come here, sweetie, out of the closet.
Well, what do you think of *that?*
Naked as paper to start   30

But in twenty-five years she'll be silver,
In fifty, gold.[2]
A living doll, everywhere you look.
It can sew, it can cook,
It can talk, talk, talk.   35

It works, there is nothing wrong with it.
You have a hole, it's a poultice.
You have an eye, it's an image.
My boy, it's your last resort.
Will you marry it, marry it, marry it.   40

1966

Lady Lazarus[1]

I have done it again.
One year in every ten
I manage it——

---

2. Silver and gold are the commemorative metals for the 25th and 50th wedding anniversaries.

1. Lazarus was raised from the dead by
Jesus (John 11.1–45).

A sort of walking miracle, my skin
Bright as a Nazi lampshade,[2]   5
My right foot

A paperweight,
My face a featureless, fine
Jew linen.

Peel off the napkin   10
O my enemy.
Do I terrify?——

The nose, the eye pits, the full set of teeth?
The sour breath
Will vanish in a day.   15

Soon, soon the flesh
The grave cave ate will be
At home on me

And I a smiling woman.
I am only thirty.   20
And like the cat I have nine times to die.

This is Number Three.
What a trash
To annihilate each decade.

What a million filaments.   25
The peanut-crunching crowd
Shoves in to see

Them unwrap me hand and foot——
The big strip tease.
Gentleman, ladies,   30

These are my hands,
My knees.
I may be skin and bone,

Nevertheless, I am the same, identical woman.
The first time it happened I was ten.   35
It was an accident.

The second time I meant
To last it out and not come back at all.
I rocked shut

2. In the Nazi death camps, the skins of victims were sometimes used to make
lampshades.

As a seashell.   40
They had to call and call
And pick the worms off me like sticky pearls.

Dying
Is an art, like everything else.
I do it exceptionally well.   45

I do it so it feels like hell.
I do it so it feels real.
I guess you could say I've a call.

It's easy enough to do it in a cell.
It's easy enough to do it and stay put.   50
It's the theatrical

Comeback in broad day
To the same place, the same face, the same brute
Amused shout:

"A miracle!"   55
That knocks me out.
There is a charge

For the eyeing of my scars, there is a charge
For the hearing of my heart——
It really goes.   60

And there is a charge, a very large charge,
For a word or a touch
Or a bit of blood

Or a piece of my hair or my clothes.
So, so, Herr[3] Doktor.   65
So, Herr Enemy.

I am your opus,
I am your valuable,
The pure gold baby

That melts to a shriek.   70
I turn and burn.
Do not think I underestimate your great concern.

Ash, ash—
You poke and stir.
Flesh, bone, there is nothing there——   75

3. Mr.

A cake of soap,
A wedding ring,
A gold filling.

Herr God, Herr Lucifer,
Beware
Beware.   80

Out of the ash[4]
I rise with my red hair
And I eat men like air.

1962   1966

Ariel[1]

Stasis in darkness.
Then the substanceless blue
Pour of tor[2] and distances.

God's lioness,
How one we grow,   5
Pivot of heels and knees!—The furrow

Splits and passes, sister to
The brown arc
Of the neck I cannot catch,

Nigger-eye   10
Berries cast dark
Hooks——

Black sweet blood mouthfuls,
Shadows.
Something else   15

Hauls me through air——
Thighs, hair;
Flakes from my heels.

White
Godiva,[3] I unpeel——   20
Dead hands, dead stringencies.

And now I
Foam to wheat, a glitter of seas.
The child's cry

---

4. An allusion to the phoenix, a mythical bird (the only one of its kind) said to live in the Arabian desert; after 500–600 years, the bird dies by fire and is reborn out of its own ashes.
1. The spirit of fire and air in Shakespeare's *The Tempest*. Ariel was also the name of the horse Plath rode weekly in 1961–62, when she lived in Devon, England.
2. A rocky peak.
3. Lady Godiva rode naked on horseback through the streets of Coventry (1040) to win a remission of feudal obligations and taxes.

Melts in the wall.   25
And I
Am the arrow,

The dew that flies
Suicidal, at one with the drive
Into the red   30

Eye, the cauldron of morning.

1962   1966

Daddy

You do not do, you do not do
Any more, black shoe
In which I have lived like a foot
For thirty years, poor and white,
Barely daring to breathe or Achoo.   5

Daddy, I have had to kill you.
You died before I had time——
Marble-heavy, a bag full of God,
Ghastly statue with one grey toe[1]
Big as a Frisco seal   10

And a head in the freakish Atlantic
Where it pours bean green over blue
In the waters off beautiful Nauset.[2]
I used to pray to recover you.
Ach, du.[3]   15

In the German tongue, in the Polish town[4]
Scraped flat by the roller
Of wars, wars, wars.
But the name of the town is common.
My Polack friend   20

Says there are a dozen or two.
So I never could tell where you
Put your foot, your root,
I never could talk to you.
The tongue stuck in my jaw.   25

It stuck in a barb wire snare.
Ich, ich, ich, ich,[5]
I could hardly speak.
I thought every German was you.
And the language obscene   30

---

1. Plath's father's toe turned black from diabetes.
2. Beach north of Boston.
3. Ah, you: the first of a series of references to her father's German origins.
4. Grabow, the birthplace of Otto Plath, the poet's father.
5. I.

An engine, an engine
Chuffing me off like a Jew.
A Jew to Dachau, Auschwitz, Belsen.[6]
I began to talk like a Jew.
I think I may well be a Jew.   35

The snows of the Tyrol,[7] the clear beer of Vienna
Are not very pure or true.
With my gypsy ancestress and my weird luck
And my Taroc[8] pack and my Taroc pack
I may be a bit of a Jew.   40

I have always been scared of *you*,
With your Luftwaffe,[9] your gobbledygoo.
And your neat moustache
And your Aryan eye, bright blue.
Panzer-man, panzer-man,[1] O You——   45

Not God but a swastika
So black no sky could squeak through.
Every woman adores a Fascist,
The boot in the face, the brute
Brute heart of a brute like you.   50

You stand at the blackboard, daddy,
In the picture I have of you,
A cleft in your chin instead of your foot
But no less a devil for that, no not
Any less the black man who   55

Bit my pretty red heart in two.
I was ten when they buried you.
At twenty I tried to die
And get back, back, back to you.
I thought even the bones would do.   60

But they pulled me out of the sack,
And they stuck me together with glue.[2]
And then I knew what to do.
I made a model of you,
A man in black with a Meinkampf[3] look   65

---

6. German concentration camps, where millions of Jews were murdered during World War II.
7. Austrian Alpine region.
8. Variant of Tarot, ancient fortune-telling cards.
9. The German air force.
1. Hitler, who had a neat moustache, preached the superiority of the Aryan race—persons with blond hair and blue eyes, as opposed to those with darker, Semitic characteristics. "Panzer" means "armor" in German.
2. An allusion to Plath's first suicide attempt.
3. A reference to Hitler's political autobiography, *Mein Kampf* (*My Struggle*), written and published before his rise to power, in which the future dictator outlined his plans for world conquest.

And a love of the rack and the screw.
And I said I do, I do.
So daddy, I'm finally through.
The black telephone's off at the root,
The voices just can't worm through. 70

If I've killed one man, I've killed two——
The vampire who said he was you
And drank my blood for a year,
Seven years, if you want to know.
Daddy, you can lie back now. 75

There's a stake in your fat black heart
And the villagers never liked you.
They are dancing and stamping on you.
They always *knew* it was you.
Daddy, daddy, you bastard, I'm through. 80

1962 1966

Edge[1]

The woman is perfected.
Her dead

Body wears the smile of accomplishment,
The illusion of a Greek necessity

Flows in the scrolls of her toga, 5
Her bare

Feet seem to be saying:
We have come so far, it is over.

Each dead child coiled, a white serpent,
One at each little 10

Pitcher of milk, now empty.
She has folded

Them back into her body as petals
Of a rose close when the garden

Stiffens and odours bleed 15
From the sweet, deep throats of the night flower.

1. According to the poet's husband, Ted Hughes ("Notes on the Chronological Order of Sylvia Plath's Poems," *Tri-Quarterly*, Fall, 1966), this poem was written a week before the poet's suicide. Plath seems to be contemplating a design on the "edge" of a piece of classical pottery (real or imagined); the design apparently depicts the death of a woman and her children. The last line possibly refers to the way the moon is represented in the scene.

The moon has nothing to be sad about,
Staring from her hood of bone.

She is used to this sort of thing.
Her blacks crackle and drag.   20

1963   1966

Words

Axes
After whose stroke the wood rings,
And the echoes!
Echoes travelling
Off from the centre like horses.   5

The sap
Wells like tears, like the
Water striving
To re-establish its mirror
Over the rock   10

That drops and turns,
A white skull,
Eaten by weedy greens.
Years later I
Encounter them on the road——   15

Words dry and riderless,
The indefatigable hoof-taps.
While
From the bottom of the pool, fixed stars
Govern a life.   20

1963   1966

Blackberrying

Nobody in the lane, and nothing, nothing but blackberries,
Blackberries on either side, though on the right mainly,
A blackberry alley, going down in hooks, and a sea
Somewhere at the end of it, heaving. Blackberries
Big as the ball of my thumb, and dumb as eyes   5
Ebon in the hedges, fat
With blue-red juices. These they squander on my fingers.
I had not asked for such a blood sisterhood; they must love me.
They accommodate themselves to my milkbottle, flattening their
    sides.

Overhead go the choughs[1] in black, cacophonous flocks—   10
Bits of burnt paper wheeling in a blown sky.

1. Small, chattering birds of the crow family.

Theirs is the only voice, protesting, protesting.
I do not think the sea will appear at all.
The high, green meadows are glowing, as if lit from within.
I come to one bush of berries so ripe it is a bush of flies,   15
Hanging their bluegreen bellies and their wing panes in a Chinese
    screen.
The honey-feast of the berries has stunned them; they believe in
    heaven.
One more hook, and the berries and bushes end.

The only thing to come now is the sea.
From between two hills a sudden wind funnels at me,   20
Slapping its phantom laundry in my face.
These hills are too green and sweet to have tasted salt.
I follow the sheep path between them. A last hook brings me
To the hills' northern face, and the face is orange rock
That looks out on nothing, nothing but a great space   25
Of white and pewter lights, and a din like silversmiths
Beating and beating at an intractable metal.

                                   1971

IMAMU AMIRI BARAKA (LeRoi Jones)

1934–

The poet who in 1966 returned to the slums of Newark, New Jersey, as a
black activist named Imamu Baraka had been born in that city thirty-two
years before as LeRoi Jones. Baraka came to say that "the Black Artists's
role in America is to aid in the destruction of America as he knows it."
But he arrived at that attitude after almost fifteen years of attempting to
make a go of the idea of an integrated society, or at least of a multiracial
literary world.

    Jones was a precocious child who graduated from high school two
years early. He attended Howard University, spent two and a half years
as an aerial-climatographer in the Air Force, then studied at Columbia,
taking an M.A. in German literature. He associated himself with Beat
poets such as Allen Ginsberg and with poets of the New York School such
as Frank O'Hara. "For me, Lorca, Williams, Pound, and Charles Olson
have had the greatest influence," Jones said in 1959. At that time his
desire was to find a poetic style that would fully and freely express "whatever I think I am." In more particular terms, this meant new metrics and
ways of notation on the page so that the poet could stress the way he
sounds, his individual cadence. It was natural that he should turn for
tonal models on the one side to the "projective verse" of Olson, and on
the other to the rhythms he knew from black music like the blues.

    Jones's early poems tried to describe or convey a personal anguish for
which the poet projected no political solution. "I am inside someone— /
who hates me, I look / out from his eyes." He returns over and over to
the predicament of a divided self, part of whose pain stems from being a

black intellectual in a white world. For the most part, the speakers in these poems as in *I Substitute for the Dead Lecturer*, are paralyzed by their guilt and fears:

> And I am frightened
> that the flame of my sickness
> will burn off my face. And leave
> the bones, my stewed black skull,
> an empty cage of failure.

Jones's first two volumes of poetry were *Preface to a Twenty Volume Suicide Note* (1961) and *The Dead Lecturer* (1964). Later in his career, he was to look back at those earlier poems as symptomatic not of personal disorders but of a sick society. "You notice the preoccupation with death, with suicide. * * * Always my own, caught up in the deathurge of the twisted society. The work a cloud of abstraction and disjointedness, that was just whiteness. * * * There is a spirituality always trying to get through, to triumph, to walk across those dead bodies like stuntin for disciples, walking the water of dead bodies europeans call their minds."

Looking back at his university and army experience, Jones was to say: "The Howard thing let me understand the Negro sickness. They teach you how to pretend to be white. But the Air Force made me understand the white sickness."

Feeling these pressures, Jones became increasingly outspoken and separate from the white literary circles of which he was an important part. In 1958 with his first wife, who was white, he had started *Yugen* magazine and then the Totem Press, printing work by poets such as Charles Olson, Robert Duncan, Gary Snyder, and Frank O'Hara. But in a series of influential plays in the mid-1960s, Jones turned to explore the violent bases of relationships between blacks and whites. In *Dutchman* (1964), an encounter involving a young black and a white woman in a subway ends in the gratuitous murder of the black.

In his book reviews, Jones became strongly critical of what he called "The Myth of a Negro Literature." He claimed that most Negro literature was mediocre because "most of the Negroes who've found themselves in a position to become writers were middle-class Negroes who thought of literature as a way of proving they were not 'inferior' (and quite a few who wanted to prove they were)."

The answer was to move out of the range of white literary institutions. He first went to Harlem and began the Black Arts Repertory Theater. Then the focus of his activities became avowedly social and political. In 1966 he set up Spirit House in Newark. Jones was involved in the Newark riots in the summer of 1967 and, after appealing a stiff sentence, acquitted of carrying a concealed weapon. His book of poems *Black Magic* (1969) marked a real point of departure in his writings. The titles of its three sections tell a great deal about its concerns: Sabotage, Target Study, and Black Art. "We want a black poem. And a / Black World. / Let all the world be a Black Poem" he says at the conclusion of "Black Art," "And Let All Black People Speak This Poem / Silently / or LOUD." The capital letters suggest how strongly the poems have moved toward chant, oral presentation, and political rallying. Taking a Muslim name, Imamu Amiri Baraka,

Jones helped found in 1968 the Black Community Development and Defense Organization, an enclave in Newark which has remained strongly
separatist and politically and economically radical.

An Agony. As Now.

I am inside someone—
who hates me. I look
out from his eyes. Smell
what fouled tunes come in
to his breath. Love his   5
wretched women.

Slits in the metal, for sun. Where
my eyes sit turning, at the cool air
the glance of light, or hard flesh
rubbed against me, a woman, a man,   10
without shadow, or voice, or meaning.

This is the enclosure (flesh,
where innocence is a weapon. An
abstraction. Touch. (Not mine.
Or yours, if you are the soul I had   15
and abandoned when I was blind and had
my enemies carry me as a dead man
(if he is beautiful, or pitied.

It can be pain. (As now, as all his
flesh hurts me.) It can be that. Or   20
pain. As when she ran from me into
that forest.
            Or pain, the mind
silver spiraled whirled against the
sun, higher than even old men thought   25
God would be. Or pain. And the other. The
yes. (Inside his books, his fingers. They
are withered yellow flowers and were never
beautiful.) The yes. You will, lost soul, say
'beauty.' Beauty, practiced, as the tree. The   30
slow river. A white sun in its wet sentences.
Or, the cold men in their gale. Ecstasy. Flesh
or soul. The yes. (Their robes blown. Their bowls
empty. They chant at my heels, not at yours.) Flesh
or soul, as corrupt. Where the answer moves too quickly. 35
Where the God is a self, after all.)

Cold air blown through narrow blind eyes. Flesh,
white hot metal. Glows as the day with its sun.
It is a human love, I live inside. A bony skeleton
you recognize as words or simple feeling.   40

But it has no feeling. As the metal, is hot, it is not,
given to love.

It burns the thing
inside it. And that thing
screams.   45

1964

I Substitute for the Dead Lecturer

*What is most precious, because it is lost. What is lost, because it is most
precious.*

They have turned, and say that I am dying. That
I have thrown
my life
away. They
have left me alone, where   5
there is no one, nothing
save who I am. Not a note
nor a word.

       Cold air batters
the poor (and their minds   10
turn open
like sores). What kindness
What wealth
can I offer? Except
what is, for me,   15
ugliest. What is
for me, shadows, shrieking
phantoms. Except
they have need
of life. Flesh   20
at least,
       should be theirs.

The Lord has saved me
to do this. The Lord
has made me strong. I   25
am as I must have
myself. Against all
thought, all music, all
my soft loves.

       For all these wan roads   30
I am pushed to follow, are
my own conceit. A simple muttering
elegance, slipped in my head
pressed on my soul, is my heart's

worth. And I am frightened   35
that the flame of my sickness
will burn off my face. And leave
the bones, my stewed black skull,
an empty cage of failure.

                                                              1964

Political Poem

(FOR BASIL)

Luxury, then, is a way of
being ignorant, comfortably
An approach to the open market
of least information. Where theories
can thrive, under heavy tarpaulins   5
without being cracked by ideas.

(I have not seen the earth for years
and think now possibly "dirt" is
negative, positive, but clearly
social. I cannot plant a seed, cannot   10
recognize the root with clearer dent
than indifference. Though I eat
and shit as a natural man. (Getting up
from the desk to secure a turkey sandwich
and answer the phone: the poem undone   15
undone by my station, by my station,
and the bad words of Newark.[1]) Raised up
to the breech, we seek to fill for this
crumbling century. The darkness of love,
in whose sweating memory all error is forced.   20

Undone by the logic of any specific death. (Old gentlemen
who still follow fires, tho are quieter
and less punctual. It is a polite truth
we are left with. Who are you? What are you
saying? Something to be dealt with, as easily.   25
The noxious game of reason, saying, "No, No,
you cannot feel," like my dead lecturer
lamenting thru gipsies his fast suicide.

                                                              1964

After the Ball

The magic dance

of the second ave ladies,
                    in the artificial glare
                    of the world, silver-green curls sparkle

---

1. The poet's birthplace.

and the ladies' arms jingle 5
with new Fall pesos, sewn on grim bracelets
the poet's mother-in-law thinks are swell.

So much for America, let it sweep in grand style
up the avenues of its failure. Let it promenade smartly
beneath the marquees of its despair. 10
Bells swing lazily in New Mexico
ghost towns. Where the wind celebrates
afternoon, and leftover haunts stir a little
out of vague instinct,
hanging their messy sheets 15
in slow motion against the intrepid dust
or the silence
which they cannot scare.

1969

Three Modes of History and Culture

Chalk mark sex of the nation, on walls we drummers
know
as cathedrals. Cathedra,[1] in a churning meat milk.

Women glide through looking for telephones. Maps
weep 5
and are mothers and their daughters listening to

music teachers. From heavy beginnings. Plantations,
learning
America, as speech, and a common emptiness. Songs knocking

inside old women's faces. Knocking through cardboard trunks. 10
Trains
leaning north, catching hellfire in windows, passing through

the first ignoble cities of missouri, to illinois, and the panting
Chicago.
And then all ways, we go where flesh is cheap. Where factories 15

sit open, burning the chiefs. Make your way! Up through fog and
history
Make your way, and swing the general, that it come flash open

and spill the innards of that sweet thing we heard, and gave theory
to. 20
Breech, bridge, and reach, to where all talk is energy. And there's

enough, for anything singular. All our lean prophets and rhythms.
Entire
we arrive and set up shacks, hole cards,[2] Western hearts at the edge

1. Literally, chairs of authority, here referring to graffiti as official pronouncements.
2. Probably punched computer cards.

of saying. Thriving to balance the meanness of particular skies. 25
Race
of madmen and giants.

Brick songs. Shoe songs. Chants of open weariness.
Knife wiggle early evenings of the wet mouth. Tongue
dance midnight, any season shakes our house. Don't 30
tear my clothes! To doubt the balance of misery
ripping meat hug shuffle fuck. The Party of Insane
Hope. I've come from there too. Where the dead told lies
about clever social justice. Burning coffins voted
and staggered through cold white streets listening 35
to Willkie or Wallace or Dewey[3] through the dead face
of Lincoln. Come from there, and belched it out.

I think about a time when I will be relaxed.
When flames and non-specific passion wear themselves
away. And my eyes and hands and mind can turn 40
and soften, and my songs will be softer
and lightly weight the air.

1969

Major Bowes' Diary[1]

Flesh chase night, weather booming and dark
hosts of fear pushing the windows even in
plastics land. Meat spells stir the funk
false messages seal the eery light and hook it
to the mind, or a mind, if the identity of pain 5
must be personal. No one understands masks
and invention, except masqueraders and inventors.
The circle of seeing is that limited, and the thing seen
will look like anything. (With the morning's rise
snow will substitute for music, and the cold pavement 10
for the scrape of thought. Hands lips moving. Legs
and the bottoms of coats; whipped around in the
midnight wind.

Stars at six, just the two, one dim, the other bright
up near the crescent moon (a lighted mouth static 15
as consciousness or the soft skin of love. A head
will be filled with someone else's voice. The tips
of the fingers will smell, like that someone.

1969

3. Wendell Willkie (1892–1944), Henry
Wallace (1888–1965), and Thomas Dewey
(1902–71), presidential candidates defeated in the elections of the 1940s. Politicians appear to be capitalizing on the
image of strong leadership offered by

Abraham Lincoln.
1. "Major" Bowes (1874–1946) was the
master of ceremonies of a radio "Amateur Hour" popular in the 1930s and
1940s.

Cant

The walls are made of rain. The city's walls
of scattered paper, and autographed photos
of Hobbes.[1]
> (Last remnant of idealness, open
> ness. Political theorists in brown suede   5
> beautiful shoes. Lurch from left to right
> along the corridors of predicted Grace.
> Having lost . . . the flags droop, and cling
> to their wet poles. Booker Washington
> and Gunga Din, dry lipped, in hell   10
> adding their myth to the fortifiers' bulk.[2])
Knowing the season
as a change of heart.
Black to gold. Thread of reason
whipped against the walls. New winds,   15
of a complex weather. The naked seek clothes,
the holy, a faster God, to keep the known
in line.
> Mystery
> > loves company. The popes and witches   20
caught in paint and metal. "This is a picture
of a beer can. We are no longer
concerned
with light."[3]
> Make do,   25
> with what we have.

> Tools, like arks.[4]
> At the mercy of Aristotle,[5]
> or any missionary/ confusing what we are
for what we could become.   30

1969

Will They Cry When You're Gone, You Bet

> You leave dead friends in
> a desert. But they've deserted
> you, and them-
> selves, and are leaving
> themselves,   5
> in the foot paths

1. Thomas Hobbes (1588–1679), English political philosopher, author of *Leviathan*, here used as a symbol of the manipulative power of political theorists. 2. Booker T. Washington (1856–1905), black leader and author of *Up from Slavery*, preached accommodation as a means of achieving reforms for blacks; Gunga Din, the hero of a poem by Rudyard Kipling (1865–1936), was a native water-carrier who sacrificed himself for his white masters. Baraka's point is that they both contributed to the myth of white supremacy. 3. An apology for Pop Art, a form of photographically realistic painting which flourished in the early 1960s. 4. I.e., Noah's Ark, which saved a remnant of mankind from the Great Flood (Genesis 6.9 ff.). 5. Greek philosopher (384–322 B.C.), here used as a symbol of an arbitrary realism that precludes the possibility of positive change.

of madmen and saints
enough sense to get away
from the dryness and uselessness
of such relaxation, dying in the dry   10
light, sand packed in their mouths
eyes burning, white women serenade them
in mystic deviousness, which is another
way of saying they're seeing things, which
are not really there, except for them,   15
never to find an oasis, even bitter water
which we get used to, is better than
white drifting fairies, muses, singing
to us, in calm tones, about how it is better to die
etcetera, than go off from them, how it is better to   20
lie in the cruel sun with your eyes turning to dunes
than leave them alone in that white heat,

                                                    1969

Selected Bibliographies

The best general handbook for research in the literature contained in this volume of *The Norton Anthology of American Literature* is Clarence Gohdes's *Bibliographical Guide to the Study of the Literature of the U.S.A.*, 4th ed. (1976). Lists of significant works are given under such general headings as "American studies or American civilization," "American history: general tools," "American history: some special studies," "Selected histories of ideas in the U.S.," "Philosophy and psychology in the U.S.," "Transcendentalism in the U.S.," "Religion in the U.S.," "Arts other than literature," "Chief general bibliographies of American literature," "Chief general histories and selected critical discussions of American literature," "Studies of 20th-century literature," "Selected studies of re-gional literature," and "Literature on or by racial and other minorities." Other useful, critically annotated guides are Lewis Leary's *American Literature: A Study and Research Guide* (1976) and Robert C. Schweik and Die-ter Riesner's *Reference Sources in English and American Literature: An Annotated Bibliography* (1977). Two valuable encyclopedic reference volumes are James D. Hart's *Oxford Companion to American Literature*, 4th ed. (1965) and Max J. Herzberg's *The Reader's Encyclopedia of American Literature* (1962).

The most ambitious comprehensive history is *Literary History of the United States*, ed. Robert E. Spiller *et al.* (1948, 1974). The discursive bibliographical supplements to this volume may also be recommended.

AMERICAN LITERATURE 1865–1914

The titles of the following highly selective list of general historical and critical studies suggest their coverage within this period: Daniel Aaron, *The Unwritten War: American Writers and the Civil War* (1973); Louis Au-chincloss, *Pioneers and Caretakers: A Study of Nine American Woman Novelists* (1965); Warner Berthoff, *The Ferment of Realism: American Literature, 1884–1919* (1965); Richard Bridgman, *The Colloquial Style in America* (1966); Edwin H. Cady, *The Light of Common Day* (1971); Richard Chase, *The American Novel and Its Tradition* (1957); Henry Steele Commager, *The American Mind: An Interpretation of American Thought and Character since the 1880's* (1950); Marcus Cunliffe, *The Literature of the United States* (1961); Robert Falk, *The Victorian Mode in American Fiction, 1865–1885* (1965); Leslie A. Fiedler, *Love and Death in the American Novel* (1960); Seymour L. Gross and John Edward Hardy, eds., *Images of the Negro in American Literature* (1966); Daniel Hoffman, *Form and Fable in American Fiction* (1961); Leon Howard, *Literature and the American Tradition* (1960); Howard Mumford Jones, *The Age of Energy: Varieties of American Experience, 1865–1915* (1971); Alfred Kazin, *On Native Grounds: An Interpretation of Modern American Prose Literature* (1942); Jay Martin, *Harvests of Change: American Literature, 1865–1914* (1967); Leo Marx, *The Machine in the Garden: Technology and the Pastoral Ideal in America* (1964); Ruth Miller, *Backgrounds to Black American Literature* (1971); Vernon L. Parrington, *Main Currents in American Thought: An Interpretation of American Literature from the Beginnings to 1920*, 3 vols. (1927–1930); Roy Harvey Pearce, *The Continuity of American Poetry* (1961); Donald Pizer, *Realism and Naturalism in Nineteenth-Century American Literature* (1966); Richard Poirier, *A World Elsewhere: The Place of Style in American Literature* (1966); Constance Rourke, *American Humor: A Study of the National Character* (1931); Henry Nash Smith, *Virgin Land: The American West as Symbol and Myth* (1950) and *Democracy and the Novel: Popular Resistance to Classic American Writers* (1978); Tony Tanner, *The Reign of Wonder* (1965); Hyatt H. Waggoner, *American Poets from the Puritans to the Present* (1968); Charles C. Walcutt, *American Literary Naturalism: A Divided Stream* (1956); Edmund Wilson, *Patriotic Gore: Studies in the Literature of the American Civil War* (1962); Larzer Ziff, *The American 1890's* (1966).

Eight American Authors: A Review of Research and Criticism, rev. ed., ed. James Woodress (1971), contains discursive chapters that had appeared, up to 1969, on two authors in this period—Clemens and James; *Fifteen American Authors before 1900: Bibliographic*

Essays on Research and Criticism, ed. Robert A. Rees and Earl N. Harbert (1971), contains chapters on Adams, Stephen Crane, Howells, and Norris.

Henry Adams

No uniform, authoritatively edited collection of Henry Adams's writings exists. Ernest Samuels's annotated edition of *The Education* sets a high standard for those who would undertake such a project in the future. In 1920, 1930, and 1938, Worthington C. Ford edited three volumes of Adams's excellent letters. The standard biography is a trilogy by Ernest Samuels: *The Young Henry Adams* (1948); *Henry Adams, the Middle Years* (1958); and *Henry Adams, the Major Phase* (1964). A sound one-volume life is Elizabeth Stevenson's *Henry Adams, a Biography* (1956).

George Hochfield's *Henry Adams: An Introduction and Interpretation* (1962) delivers well what its title promises. Different aspects of Adams are dealt with in Max I. Baym's *The French Education of Henry Adams* (1951); John J. Conder's *A Formula of His Own: Henry Adams's Literary Experiment* (1970); William H. Jordy's *Henry Adams: Scientific Historian* (1952); J. C. Levenson's *The Mind and Art of Henry Adams* (1957), a difficult and distinguished work; Ernest Scheyer's *The Circle of Henry Adams: Art and Artists* (1970); and Vern Wagner's *The Suspension of Henry Adams: A Study of Manner and Matter* (1969), which effectively treats Adams's humor.

Ambrose Bierce

The best edition of Bierce's writings, *Collected Works of Ambrose Bierce* (1909–1912), was edited by Walter Neale. The largest collection of Bierce's letters is available in Bertha C. Pope's edition of *The Letters of Ambrose Bierce* (1921).

Vincent Starrett's pioneer appreciative biography *Ambrose Bierce* (1920) should be supplemented by Walter Neale's *Life of Ambrose Bierce;* by Carey McWilliams's *Ambrose Bierce: A Biography* (1929); by the standard critical biography, Paul Fatout's *Ambrose Bierce, the Devil's Lexicographer* (1951); and by Mary Elizabeth Grenander's *Ambrose Bierce* (1971).

Charles W. Chesnutt

There is no uniform edition of Chesnutt's writings. Sylvia L. Render edited (with an excellent introduction) *The Short Fiction of Charles W. Chesnutt* (1974). The first full-length biography was written by his daughter: Helen M. Chesnutt, *Charles Waddel Chesnutt: Pioneer of the Color Line* (1952). Heermance J. Noel's *Charles W. Chesnutt: America's First Great Black Novelist* (1974) is a useful critical biography. The best guide to the mostly shorter appraisals of Chesnutt's fiction is Curtis W. Ellison and Eugene W. Metcalf, Jr.'s thorough, annotated *Charles W. Chesnutt: A Reference Guide* (1977).

Kate Chopin

The Complete Works of Kate Chopin (1969) was edited in two volumes by Per Seyersted, who also wrote the excellent *Kate Chopin: A Critical Biography* (1969), the most important full-length study of this rediscovered author. An early critical biography is Daniel Rankin's *Kate Chopin and Her Creole Stories* (1932).

Samuel Clemens

The present standard edition of *The Writings of Mark Twain* (1922–1925), 37 vols., ed. Albert Bigelow Paine, is being superseded by the ongoing editions of *The Mark Twain Papers* (1969–), under the supervision of Frederick Anderson, and *The Works of Mark Twain* (1972–), under the supervision of John Gerber. Two volumes of letters have appeared so far in the *Papers*, and other Twain letters are available in several scattered volumes, the most interesting of which is *The Correspondence of Samuel L. Clemens and William Dean Howells, 1872–1910*, ed. Henry Nash Smith and William M. Gibson (1960).

Albert Bigelow Paine's *Mark Twain, a Biography* (1912) is vivid, unreliable, and still indispensable. Justin Kaplan's *Mr. Clemens and Mark Twain, a Biography* (1966) is a lively, popular account. Van Wyck Brooks's polemical and controversial *The Ordeal of Mark Twain* (1920) should be read together with Bernard De Voto's corrective *Mark Twain's America* (1932). De Lancey Ferguson's *Mark Twain: Man and Legend* (1943) is still the best full-length critical biography.

The criticism of Mark Twain is enormous in quantity, variety, and quality. Two excellent general studies are Henry Nash Smith's *Mark Twain: The Development of a Writer* (1962) and William M. Gibson's *The Art of Mark Twain*. James Cox's perceptive *Mark Twain: The Fate of Humor* (1966) and Gladys Bellamy's *Mark Twain as a Literary Artist* (1950), Edgar M. Branch's *The Literary Apprenticeship of Mark Twain* (1950) and Albert E. Stone's *The Innocent Eye: Childhood in Mark Twain's Imagination* (1961) are all distinguished contributions to Twain scholarship. More specialized studies of distinction include Henry Seidel Canby's *Turn West, Turn East* (1951), which concentrates on Twain and Henry James; Louis J. Budd's *Mark Twain: Social Philosopher* (1962); Bernard De Voto's *Mark Twain at Work* (1942); Paul Fatout's *Mark Twain on the Lecture Circuit* (1960); Sydney J. Krause's *Mark Twain as Critic* (1967); Paul Baetzhold's *Mark Twain and John Bull* (1970); and Walter Blair's *Mark Twain and Huckleberry Finn* (1960).

Stephen Crane

Fredson Bowers is the textual editor of *The Works of Stephen Crane* (1969–1976), a complete edition which has come in for some criticism despite its endorsement by the Center for Editions of American Authors. *Stephen Crane: Letters* (1960) was edited by R. W. Stallman and Lillian Gilkes. Joseph Katz edited both *The Portable Stephen Crane* (1969) and *The Poems of Stephen Crane: A Critical Edition* (1966).

Thomas Beer's early biography *Stephen Crane: A Study in American Letters* (1923) is still important, though it lacks documentation. The poet John Berryman prepared a stimulating and more factually reliable biography in 1950, and R. W. Stallman's massive, polemical *Stephen Crane: A Critical Biography* (1968) incorporates the substantial new material discovered in the interim.

Edwin H. Cady's *Stephen Crane* (1962) is an excellent critical introduction to Crane's life and work. Eric Solomon's *Stephen Crane: From Parody to Realism* (1966), Donald B. Gibson's *The Fiction of Stephen Crane*

(1968), Daniel G. Hoffman's *The Poetry of Stephen Crane* (1957), Marston La France's *A Reading of Stephen Crane* (1971), and Frank Bergon's *Stephen Crane's Artistry* are among the best of the surprisingly few significant book-length studies.

Theodore Dreiser

Most of Dreiser's novels and short stories are in print, but his poetry, plays, and other writings generally are not, and a well-edited uniform edition of Dreiser's writings is badly needed. Robert H. Elias has edited three volumes of *Letters of Theodore Dreiser* (1959).

The most complete biography is W. A. Swanberg's lively *Dreiser* (1965), but Robert H. Elias's *Theodore Dreiser: Apostle of Nature* (1949) is still valuable. Marguerite Tjader's *Theodore Dreiser: A New Dimension* (1965) sheds light on his later life especially. Ellen Moers's *Two Dreisers* (1969) examines the biographical circumstances surrounding (and the compositional histories of) *Sister Carrie* and *An American Tragedy*.

Good introductions to Dreiser's life and work may be found in Philip L. Gerber's *Theodore Dreiser* (1964) and John J. McAleer's *Theodore Dreiser: An Introduction and Interpretation*. F. O. Matthiessen's *Theodore Dreiser* (1951) is still illuminating, but more recent critical studies by Charles Shapiro, *Theodore Dreiser: Our Bitter Patriot* (1962), Richard Lehan, *Theodore Dreiser: His World and His Novels* (1969), R. N. Mookerjee, *Theodore Dreiser: His Thought and Social Criticism* (1974), and Donald Pizer, *The Novels of Theodore Dreiser* (1976), have advanced our appreciation and understanding considerably.

A bibliographical study may be found in Jackson R. Bryer's *Fifteen Modern American Authors* (1969), later reissued as *Sixteen Modern American Authors* (1973).

W. E. B. DuBois

There is no collected edition of DuBois's prolific output. Four interesting collections of DuBois's writings are available: Philip S. Foner's *W. E. B. DuBois Speaks: Speeches and Addresses* (1970); Meyer Weinberg's *W. E. B. DuBois: A Reader* (1970); Andrew G. Paschol, *A W. E. B. DuBois Reader* (1971); and Herbert Lee Moon's *The Emerging Thought of W. E. B. DuBois: Essays and Editorials from the "Crisis"* (1972). Herbert Aptheker has edited three volumes of *The Correspondence of W. E. B. DuBois* (1973–1978).

Significant background to DuBois's place in American intellectual thought may be found in August Meier's *Negro Thought in America, 1880–1915* (1963) and John Hope Franklin's *From Slavery to Freedom: A History of American Negroes* (1967). In the past decade several biographies of DuBois have appeared: Leslie A. Lacey's *Cheer the Lonesome Traveller: The Life of W. E. B. DuBois* (1970); Shirley Graham's *His Day Is Marching On: A Memoir of W. E. B. DuBois* (1971); and Arnold Rampersad's excellent critical study, *The Art and Imagination of W. E. B. DuBois* (1976). Two specialized studies of value are Francis Broderick's *W. E. B. DuBois, Negro Leader in a Time of Crisis* (1959) and Elliot M. Rudwick's *W. E. B. DuBois: A Study in Minority Group Leadership* (1961).

Mary E. Wilkins Freeman

The only collection of Freeman's work, *The Best Stories of Mary E. Wilkins* (1927), was edited by Henry W. Lanier. Perry D. Westbrook's full-length study, *Mary Wilkins Freeman* (1967), is a good introduction to Freeman's life and work.

Emma Goldman

A number of Goldman's works are out of print, but Alix Kates Shulman has edited *Red Emma Speaks: Selected Writings and Speeches* (1972). *Anarchism and Other Essays* (1910), an important early collection, *The Social Significance of Modern Drama* (1914), *My Disillusionment in Russia* (1923), and *My Further Disillusionment in Russia* (1924) are Goldman's chief early works. Her vivid autobiography, *Living My Life*, was first published in two volumes in 1931 and in one volume in 1934. Richard and Anna Maria Drinnon edited *Nowhere at Home: Letters from Exile of Emma Goldman and Alexander Berkman* (1975). Two useful biographies are Richard Drinnon's *Rebel in Paradise* (1961) and Alix Kates Shulman's *To the Barricades: The Anarchist Life of Emma Goldman* (1971).

Hamlin Garland

Donald Pizer is preparing *The Works of Hamlin Garland* in 44 volumes. Pizer has already edited *Hamlin Garland's Diaries* (1968).

The most comprehensive biography of Garland is in French: Robert Mane's *Hamlin Garland: l'homme et l'oeuvre* (1968). Jean Holloway's full-scale critical biography *Hamlin Garland* (1960) may be supplemented by Donald Pizer's *Hamlin Garland's Early Work and Career* (1960). Extensive treatment of Garland by Ahnebrink, Walcutt, Parrington, Pizer, and Martin also appears in those authors' more general studies of the period and of realism and naturalism.

Joel Chandler Harris

The Complete Tales of Uncle Remus (1955) is the most complete one-volume edition. Julia Collier Harris edited *Joel Chandler Harris, Editor and Essayist: Miscellaneous Literary, Political, and Social Writings* (1931). Three important biographies, the last of which is critical and interpretive, are Robert L. Wiggins's *The Life of Joel Chandler Harris from Obscurity in Boyhood to Fame in Early Manhood* (1918), Julia Collier Harris's *The Life and Letters of Joel Chandler Harris* (1918), and Paul M. Cousins's *Joel Chandler Harris: A Biography* (1968). S. Brooks's *Joel Chandler Harris, Folklorist* (1950) is a specialized study.

Bret Harte

The most complete collection is *The Works of Bret Harte* (1914) in 25 volumes. Harte's poetry may be found in *The Complete Poetical Works of Bret Harte* (1899). Geoffrey Bret Harte edited *The Letters of Bret Harte* (1926).

The standard life is George R. Stewart, Jr.'s *Bret Harte: Argonaut and Exile* (1931). Among the most important studies are Franklin Walker's in his *San Francisco's Literary Frontier* (1939) and Margaret Duckett's *Mark Twain and Bret Harte* (1964).

W. D. Howells

A Selected Edition of W. D. Howells (1968–) will provide the first authoritatively edited collection (in 30 or more volumes) of this major figure's enormous literary production. In the meantime, individual reprints must be sought out and may be supplemented by such collections of his letters as the two volumes edited by Henry Nash Smith and William M. Gibson, *The Correspondence of Samuel L. Clemens and William Dean Howells, 1872–1910* (1960) and his daughter Mildred Howells's edition in two volumes of *Life in Letters of William Dean Howells* (1928) and by Walter J. Meserve's *The Complete Plays of W. D. Howells* (1960).

The standard critical biography is Edwin H. Cady's two-volume work, *The Road to Realism: The Early Years, 1837–1885* (1956) and *The Realist at War: The Mature Years, 1885–1920* (1958). Van Wyck Brooks's *Howells: His Life and Work* (1959) reveals Howells in relation to his contemporaries. A more recent biography is Kenneth S. Lynn's *William Dean Howells: An American Life* (1971).

In the last three decades critical studies of Howells have appeared regularly. The introduction to Clara M. and Rudolph Kirk's *William Dean Howells: Representative Selections*** (1950) contains much useful information. An excellent brief introduction is William M. Gibson's *William Dean Howells* (1967). Everett Carter's *Howells and the Age of Realism* (1954) was one of the first to argue Howells's centrality to his age and its chief literary development. Other general studies of interest are George N. Bennett's *William Dean Howells: The Development of a Novelist* (1959); George C. Carrington's *The Immense Complex Drama* (1966); William McMurray's *The Literary Realism of William Dean Howells* (1967); and Robert L. Hough's *The Quiet Rebel: William Dean Howells as a Social Commentator* (1959). Kermit Vanderbilt's fresh and illuminating *The Achievement of William Dean Howells: A Reinterpretation* (1968) concentrates on five of Howells's novels. Three important, more specialized studies are James Woodress's *Howells and Italy* (1952); Olov W. Fryckstedt's *In Quest of America: A Study of Howells' Early Development as a Novelist* (1958); and James L. Dean's *Howells' Travels toward Art* (1970).

Henry James

The Novels and Tales of Henry James (The New York Edition) in 26 volumes, originally published 1907–1917, was reissued 1962–1965. Other collections of James's diverse writings are available in Leon Edel's edition of *The Complete Plays of Henry James* (1949); R. P. Blackmur's *The Art of the Novel* (1935); Morris Shapiro's edition of *Selected Literary Criticism* (1963); Morton D. Zabel's edition of James's travel writings, *The Art of Travel* (1958); F. O. Matthiessen and Kenneth B. Murdoch's *The Notebooks of Henry James* (1947); F. W. Dupee's edition of the three volumes of *Henry James: Autobiography* (1956); and in various collections of essays and letters edited by Leon Edel.

Edel is also author of the definitive, "Freudian" biography of James in five volumes, published between 1953 and 1972. F. O. Matthiessen's *The James Family* (1947) reveals Henry's relationships to this extraordinary American family, which included his brother William, the celebrated psychologist and philosopher.

F. W. Dupee's *Henry James* (1951) and Bruce McElderry's *Henry James* (1965) are among the best of the introductory books that survey the life and career. Since the 1940s, critical studies of James have abounded. Among the best of these, in chronological order, are J. W. Beach's pioneering *The Method of Henry James* (1918); Morris Roberts's *Henry James's Criticism* (1929); F. O. Matthiessen's *Henry James, the Major Phase* (1944); Quentin Anderson's *The American Henry James* (1957); Richard Poirier's *The Comic Sense of Henry James* (1960); Oscar Cargill's thorough *The Novels of Henry James* (1961); Dorothea Krook's *The Ordeal of Consciousness in Henry James* (1962); Laurence B. Holland's *The Expense of Vision* (1964); J. A. Ward's *Search for Form: Studies in the Structure of James's Fiction* (1967); Sallie Sears's *The Negative Imagination: Form and Perspective in the Novels of Henry James* (1968); James Kraft's *The Early Tales of Henry James* (1969); and Viola Hopkins Winner's *Henry James and the Visual Arts* (1970).

Sarah Orne Jewett

There is no collected edition of Jewett's writings. Jewett's *Stories and Tales* were published in seven volumes in 1910, but a more readily available collection, *The Best Stories of Sarah Orne Jewett* (1925), was edited in two volumes with a foreword by Willa Cather. Richard Cary edited *The Uncollected Short Stories of Sarah Orne Jewett* (1971). Cary also edited *Sarah Orne Jewett Letters*, rev. and enlarged ed. (1967).

The standard critical biography is F. O. Matthiessen's *Sarah Orne Jewett* (1929). A more complete critical survey of her life and work is Richard Cary's *Sarah Orne Jewett* (1962). Margaret Thorp's brief *Sarah Orne Jewett* (1966) is a good introductory study.

Jack London

No standard edition in English of London's voluminous writings is available; the rare (and incomplete) Sonoma edition (1928) printed 28 titles in 21 volumes; the British Fitzroy *Works* reprinted 20 titles in the 1960s. The best collection of London's letters is King Hendricks and Irvin Shepard's *Letters from Jack London* (1965).

The most substantial early biography of London was written by his daughter Joan: *Jack London and His Times: An Unconventional Biography* (1939). Earl Labor's *Jack London* (1974) effectively combines biography and criticism and is the best introduction to London.

Specialized studies of special merit are Philip S. Foner's *Jack London, American Rebel* (1947); Franklin Walker's *Jack London and the Klondike* (1966); and James I. McClintock's *White Logic: Jack London's Short Stories* (1975). Joan R. Sherman's *Jack London: A Reference Guide* (1977) is an especially useful review of the secondary literature.

Frank Norris

There are two important editions of Frank Norris: *The Complete Edition of Frank Norris* (1928) and Donald Pizer's *The Literary Criticism of Frank Norris* (1964). Franklin Walker edited *The Letters of Frank Norris* (1956).

The only biography is Franklin Walker's *Frank Norris: A Biography* (1932), fortunately a reliable one. A lively introduction is Warren French's *Frank Norris* (1962). Other important critical studies include Ernest Marchand's *Frank Norris: A Study* (1942); Lars Ahnebrink's *The Beginnings of Naturalism in American Fiction* (1950); Donald Pizer's fresh and acute *The Novels of Frank Norris* (1966); and William B. Dillingham's *Frank Norris: Instinct and Art* (1969).

Booker T. Washington

Louis R. Harlan is editing *The Booker T. Washington Papers* (1972–). August Meier's *Negro Thought in America, 1880–1915* (1963) and John Hope Franklin's *From Slavery to Freedom: A History of American Negroes* (1967) are two useful background books. E. L. Thornborough's biographical study *Booker T. Washington* (1969) should be supplemented by the fine critical biography by Louis R. Harlan, *Booker T. Washington: The Making of a Black Leader, 1865–1901* (1972). Specialized studies of interest are Basil Matthews's *Booker T. Washington: Educator and Interracial Interpreter* (1948) and G. R. Spencer's *Booker T. Washington and the Negro's Place in American Life* (1955).

Edith Wharton

There is no uniform edition of Wharton's writings. Louis Auchincloss edited *The Edith Wharton Reader* (1965), and R. W. B. Lewis edited in two volumes *The Collected Short Stories of Edith Wharton* (1968).

R. W. B. Lewis, using the extensive Wharton Papers at Yale, prepared the definitive *Edith Wharton: A Biography* (1975). Millicent Bell's *Edith Wharton and Henry James: The Story of Their Friendship* (1965) is still useful.

Two excellent introductory studies are Louis Auchincloss's brief *Edith Wharton* (1961) and Margaret B. McDowell's *Edith Wharton* (1976). Book-length studies of importance include Blake Nevins's *Edith Wharton: A Study of Her Fiction* (1953); Marilyn J. Lyde's *Edith Wharton: Convention and Morality in the Work of a Novelist* (1959); Geoffrey Walton's *Edith Wharton: A Critical Interpretation* (1971); and Cynthia Griffin Wolff's *A Feast of Words: The Triumph of Edith Wharton* (1977).

AMERICAN LITERATURE BETWEEN THE WARS 1914–1945

The best treatments of American literature during the period are Frederick J. Hoffman, *The Twenties: American Writing in the Post-war Decade* (1955); and two books by Hugh Kenner: *The Pound Era* (1971) and *A Homemade World: The American Modernist Writers* (1975). Graham Hough, in *Image and Experience: Studies in a Literary Revolution* (1960), explores modernism in the context of British literature. Two brief surveys are Louise Brogan's *Achievement in American Poetry, 1900–1950* (1951) and Alan S. Downer's *Fifty Years of American Drama, 1900–1950* (1951). Extensive treatments of separate areas are in Alfred Kazin, *On Native Grounds: An Interpretation of Modern American Prose Literature* (1942); Maxwell Geismar, *Writers in Crisis: The American Novel between Two Wars* (1942) and *The Last of the Provincials: The American Novel between Two Wars* (1948); Roy Harvey Pearce, *The Continuity of American Poetry* (1961); *Literary History of the United States*, ed. Robert E. Spiller *et al.*, vol. III (1948); and Walter Sutton, *Modern American Criticism* (1963).

Interpretations of special aspects of American writing against the backgrounds of their traditions are Daniel Aaron's *Writers on the Left* (1961); Richard Bridgman's *The Colloquial Style in America* (1966); Nathan L. Huggins's *Harlem Renaissance* (1971); and Wright Morris's *The Territory Ahead* (1958).

The critic Malcolm Cowley, in *After the Genteel Tradition: American Writers, 1910–1930* (1937), gathered essays by important writers and critics commenting on contemporary literary issues, and wrote *Exile's Return: A Narrative of Ideas* (1934; rev. ed., 1951), an analysis of the 1920s from the standpoint of a participant. Edmund Wilson, in *The Shock of Recognition* (1943), presents writings by American writers about each other. His collections of his own essays and book reviews provide a lively survey of the period: *Classics and Commercials: A Literary Chronicle of the Thirties* (1951) and *The Shores of Light: A Literary Chronicle of the Twenties and Thirties*

(1952). In *Earthly Delights, Unearthly Adornments: American Writers as Image-Makers* (1978), Wright Morris comments on his contemporaries and predecessors from the standpoint of a novelist writing after World War II.

Full bibliographical material on several authors in this period may be found in *Fifteen Modern American Authors: A Survey of Research and Criticism*, ed. Jackson R. Bryer (1969): Anderson, Cather, Hart Crane, Eliot, Faulkner, Fitzgerald, Frost, Hemingway, Pound, Robinson, Steinbeck, and Stevens; a revised and updated edition was issued in 1973 as *Sixteen Modern American Authors* (Williams being added). See also *Bibliography*, ed. Richard M. Ludwig, Supplement to *Literary History of the United States* (1963), and *American Literary Scholarship: An Annual*, ed. James Woodress (1965–).

Sherwood Anderson

There is no collected edition of Anderson's writing. In addition to works mentioned in the author's introduction, Anderson published *The Modern Writer* (1925); *Sherwood Anderson's Notebook* (1925); *Alice and the Lost Novel* (1929); *Nearer the Grass Roots* (1929); *The American Country Fair* (1930); and *Home Town* (1940). *The Letters of Sherwood Anderson* (1953) were edited by Howard Mumford Jones and Walter Rideout. Eugene P. Seehy and Kenneth A. Lohf compiled *Sherwood Anderson: A Bibliography* (1960). For commentary see David D. Anderson, *Sherwood Anderson: An Introduction and Interpretation* (1967); *Homage to Sherwood Anderson*, ed. Paul P. Appel (1970); Rex Burbank, *Sherwood Anderson* (1964); Irving Howe, *Sherwood Anderson* (1951); James Schevill, *Sherwood Anderson* (1951); Brom Weber, *Sherwood Anderson* (1964); and *The Achievement of Sherwood Anderson: Essays in Criticism*, ed. R. L. White (1966).

Willa Cather

Cather's volume of verse, *April Twilights* (1903; rev. ed., 1923), and her collection of essays, *Not under Forty* (1936), supplement the standard edition of her fiction, *The Novels and Stories of Willa Cather* (1937–1941). Other sources include *The Old Beaty and Others*, posthumously collected short stories (1948); *Willa Cather on Writing* (1949); *Writings from Willa Cather's Campus Years*, ed. James Shively (1950); *Collected Short Fiction, 1892–1912*, ed. Virginia Faulkner (1965); and *The Kingdom of Art: Willa Cather's First Principles and Critical Statements*, ed. Bernice Slote (1967). A bibliography by Bernice Slote is in *Fifteen Modern American Authors*, ed. Jackson R. Bryer (1969). Astute brief studies of Cather are David Daiches's *Willa Cather* (1951) and Dorothy Van Ghent's *Willa Cather* (1964). Personal memoirs include Edith Lewis's *Willa Cather Living* (1953) and Elizabeth Sergeant's *Willa Cather: A Memoir* (1953). E. K. Brown's *Willa Cather* (1953) and James Woodress's *Willa Cather* (1970) are full-length critical biographies. Commentaries on Cather are gathered in *Willa Cather and Her Critics*, ed. James Schroeter (1967).

Hart Crane

'Brom Weber edited *The Complete Poems and Selected Letters and Prose of Hart Crane* (1966), the best current text. Crane's *Collected Poems*, edited by his friend Waldo Frank, appeared in 1933. Other sources of primary and bibliographical material are *The Letters of Hart Crane*, ed. Brom Weber (1965); *The Letters of Hart Crane and His Family*, ed. Thomas S. W. Lewis (1974); *Hart Crane: An Annotated Critical Bibliography*, ed. Joseph Schwartz (1970); and *Hart Crane: A Descriptive Bibliography*, ed. Joseph Schwartz and Robert C. Schweik (1972). Gary Lane compiled *A Concordance to the Poems of Hart Crane* (1972).

Philip Horton's moving biography, *Hart Crane: The Life of an American Poet* (1937; reprint, 1957), was followed by Brom Weber's *Hart Crane: A Biographical and Critical Study* (1948) and John Unterecker's detailed *Voyager: A Life of Hart Crane* (1969). Susan Jenkins Brown, *Robber Rocks: Letters and Memories of Hart Crane, 1923–1932* (1969), provides an unusual portrait of Crane from the perspective of three close friends.

Three critics, themselves poets, contributed important early essays on Crane: Richard P. Blackmur in *The Double Agent* (1935); Allen Tate in *Reactionary Essays on Poetry and Ideas* (1936); and Yvor Winters in *In Defense of Reason* (1947). For more recent studies, see L. S. Dembo's *Hart Crane's Sanscrit Charge: A Study of "The Bridge"* (1960); Richard W. B. Lewis's *The Poetry of Hart Crane* (1967); and Helge N. Nilsen's *Hart Crane's "The Bridge": A Study in Sources and Interpretations* (1976). Brief introductions are Vincent Quinn's *Hart Crane* (1963); Samuel Hazo's *Hart Crane: An Introduction and Interpretation* (1963); Monroe K. Spears's *Hart Crane* (1965); and Herbert A. Leibowitz's *Hart Crane: An Introduction to the Poetry* (1968). R. W. Butterfield's *The Broken Arc: A Study of Hart Crane* (1969) and M. D. Uroff's *Hart Crane: The Patterns of His Poetry* (1974) analyze the often-neglected Key West poems. Hunce Voelcker's *The Hart Crane Voyages* (1967) is an impressionistic re-creation of Crane's process of composing *Voyages*.

Countee Cullen

For extended studies of Cullen see Stephen H. Bronz, *Roots of Negro Racial Consciousness—the 1920's: Three Harlem Renaissance Authors* (1954); Helen J. Dinger, *A Study of Countee Cullen* (1953); Margaret Perry, *A Bio-Bibliography of Countee P. Cullen* (1969); and Blanche E. Ferguson, *Countee Cullen and the Negro Renaissance* (1966).

E. E. Cummings

Complete Poems, 1913–1962 appeared in a two-volume edition in 1968 and in a single volume in 1972. George J. Firmage edited *Three Plays and a Ballet* (1967). Cummings's prose fiction includes *The Enormous Room* (1922) and *EIMI* (1933). *E. E. Cummings: A Miscellany Revised*, ed. George J. Firmage (1965), contains previously uncollected short prose pieces. *Six Nonlectures* (1953) consists of the talks that Cummings delivered at Harvard in the same year. *Selected Letters of E. E. Cummings* (1969) was edited by F. W. Dupee and George Stade. George J. Firmage edited *E. E. Cummings: A Bibliography* (1960).

Several of Cummings's earlier individual works have been re-edited by George J. Firmage in the Cummings Typescript Editions. These include *Tulips & Chimneys* (1976), *No Thanks* (1978), *The Enormous Room*, including illustrations by Cummings (1978), *ViVa* (1979), and *XAIPE* (1979).

The Magic Maker, a biography by Cummings's friend Charles Norman, was published in 1958 and reissued after the poet's death. A new biography is *Dreams in the Mirror*, by Richard S. Kennedy (1979). Norman Friedman's *E. E. Cummings: The Art of His Poetry* (1960) focuses on Cummings's language and the techniques of his poetry. Friedman's second book, *E. E. Cummings: The Growth of a Writer* (1964), discusses Cummings's texts in roughly chronological order. Barry A. Marks's *E. E. Cummings* (1964) analyzes individual poems and considers the relation between Cummings's graphic art and the principles of his poetry. Robert E. Wegner's *The Poetry and Prose of E. E. Cummings* (1965) and Bethany K. Dumas's *E. E. Cummings: A Remembrance of Miracles* (1974) provide introductions to Cummings's work.

E. E. Cummings and the Critics, ed. S. V. Baum (1962), traces critical response to Cummings over the course of his career. *Harvard Wake*, Vol. I (1946), is devoted to Cummings and contains commentaries by prominent literary figures. Norman Friedman edited *E. E. Cummings: A Collection of Critical Essays* (1972).

Hilda Doolittle (H. D.)

Collected Poems of H. D. was published in 1925. Subsequent volumes of poetry include *Red Rose for Bronze* (1931); the trilogy of war poems *The Walls Do Not Fall* (1944), *Tribute to the Angels* (1945), and *The Flowering of the Rod* (1946); and the dramatic monologue *Helen in Egypt* (1961). H. D.'s other book-length verse dramas are *Hippolytus Temporizes* (1927) and the translation of Euripides' *Ion* (1937). *Palimpsest* (1926), *Hadylus* (1928), and *Bid Me to Live* (1961) comprise her major prose fiction. *By Avon River* (1949) celebrates Shakespeare in prose and verse.

Tribute to Freud (1956) is her account of her psychoanalysis by Freud.

Thomas Burnett Swann's *The Classical World of H. D.* (1962) and Vincent Quinn's *Hilda Doolittle* (1967) are the only full-length studies of H. D. H. D. figures prominently in *The Heart to Artemis: A Writer's Memoirs* (1962), the autobiography of her closest friend and traveling companion, Bryher (Winifred Ellerman). A chapter entitled "The Perfect Imagist" in Glenn Hughes's *Imagism and the Imagists* (1931) considers H. D.'s early poetry. In "H. D. and the Age of Myth," *The Sewanee Review*, Vol. LVI (1948), Harold H. Watts discusses the war poems and H. D.'s use of history. The autumn, 1969, issue of *Contemporary Literature* is devoted exclusively to H. D. and contains an interview with her literary executor Norman Holmes Pearson, articles by various critics, and a selection of her poetry, prose, and letters. In the same issue, Jackson R. Bryer and Pamela Roblyer present the best bibliography of material by and about H. D.

John Dos Passos

In addition to works mentioned in the author's introduction, Dos Passos's works include the novels *Streets of Night* (1923) and *Chosen Country* (1951) and the collections of political and historical commentary *In All Countries* (1934), *Journeys between Two Wars* (1938), *The Living Thoughts of Tom Paine* (1940), *The Ground We Stand On* (1941), *The Theme Is Freedom* (1956), and *Occasions and Protests* (1964). Jack Potter's *A Bibliography of John Dos Passos* appeared in 1950, and *Dos Passos: A Collection of Critical Essays*, ed. Andrew Hook, in 1974. Full-length studies include George-Albert Astre, *Thèmes et structures dans l'oeuvre de John Dos Passos* (1956); John D. Brantley, *The Fiction of John Dos Passos* (1968); John H. Wrenn, *John Dos Passos* (1961); and Melvile Landsberg, *Dos Passos' Path to U.S.A.* (1970).

T. S. Eliot

Eliot's poetic works have been collected in *Collected Poems, 1909–1962* (1963) and *The Complete Poems and Plays of T. S. Eliot* which includes *Poems Written in Early Youth* (1969). The indispensable manuscript to *The Waste Land* is in *The Waste Land: A Facsimile and Transcript of the Original Drafts Including the Annotations of Ezra Pound*, ed. Valerie Eliot (1971). Collections of Eliot's criticism include *Selected Essays*, 3rd ed. (1951), and *Selected Prose of T. S. Eliot*, ed. Frank Kermode (1975). Other important critical writings include *The Use of Poetry and the Use of Criticism* (1933); *Poetry and Drama* (1951); *The Three Voices of Poetry* (1953); *On Poetry and Poets* (1957); and *To Criticize the Critic and Other Writings* (1965). Three volumes of social commentary are *After Strange Gods* (1934); *The Idea of a Christian Society* (1939); and *Notes toward the Definition of Culture* (1948). Eliot's Ph.D. dissertation was published as *Knowledge and Experience in the Philosophy of F. H. Bradley* in 1964.

There are biographical materials in *T. S. Eliot: A Symposium*, ed. Richard Marsh and Thurairajah Tambimuttu (1948); Herbart Howarth's *Notes on Some Figures behind T. S. Eliot* (1964); *T. S. Eliot: The Man and His Work*, ed. Allen Tate (1967); and *Affectionately, T. S. Eliot*, ed. William Turner Levy and

Victor Scherle (1968). Full-length studies include Russell Kirk's *Eliot and His Age* (1971); Robert Sencourt's *T. S. Eliot: A Memoir* (1971); Lyndall Gordon's *Eliot's Early Years* (1977); and James E. Miller's *T. S. Eliot's Personal Waste Land: Exorcism of the Demons* (1977), a psychosexual study.

Of the countless critical studies of Eliot, the best are F. O. Matthiessen's *The Achievement of T. S. Eliot*, rev. ed. (1947); Helen Gardner's *The Art of T. S. Eliot* (1950); Hugh Kenner's *The Invisible Poet* (1959); Northrup Frye's *T. S. Eliot* (1963); Bernard Bergonzi's *T. S. Eliot* (1972); and Stephen Spender's *T. S. Eliot* (1976). Useful introductions include Elizabeth Drew's *T. S. Eliot: The Design of His Poetry* (1949); George Williamson's *A Reader's Guide to T. S. Eliot* (1953); and Grover Smith's *T. S. Eliot's Poetry and Plays* (1956). Special studies include Carol Smith's *T. S. Eliot's Dramatic Theory and Practice* (1963); David E. Jones's *The Plays of T. S. Eliot* (1960); John Margolies's *T. S. Eliot's Intellectual Development, 1922–1939* (1972); and Helen Gardner's *The Composition of Four Quartets* (1978). A recent study is Derek Traversi's *T. S. Eliot: The Longer Poems* (1976). For collections of critical essays about Eliot, see *T. S. Eliot: A Study of His Writings by Various Hands*, ed. B. Rajan (1947); *T. S. Eliot, a Selected Critique*, ed. Leonard Unger (1948); Hugh Kenner's *T. S. Eliot: A Collection of Critical Essays* (1962); *Twentieth Century Interpretations of The Waste Land*, ed. Jay Martin (1968); and *T. S. Eliot: A Collection of Criticism*, ed. Linda W. Wagner (1974).

Donald C. Gallup compiled the standard bibliography, *T. S. Eliot: A Bibliography*, rev. ed. (1969).

William Faulkner

There is no collected edition of Faulkner's works. In addition to volumes mentioned in the author's introduction are *Early Prose and Poetry*, ed. Carvel Collins (1962); *Dr. Martino and Other Stories* (1934); *Pylon* (1935); *The Unvanquished* (1938); *Intruder in the Dust* (1948); *Knight's Gambit* (1949); *Collected Stories of William Faulkner* (1950); *Requiem for a Nun* (1951); *Notes on a Horsethief* (1951); *Big Woods* (1955); and *Essays, Speeches, and Public Letters*, ed. James B. Meriwether (1965). Transcripts of discussion sessions and interviews with Faulkner include *Faulkner at Nagano*, ed. Robert A. Jelliffe (1956); *Faulkner in the University*, ed. Frederick L. Gwynn and Joseph L. Blotner (1959); *Faulkner at West Point*, ed. Joseph L. Fant and Robert Ashley (1964); and *The Lion in the Garden*, ed. James B. Meriwether and Michael Millgate (1968). Letters are collected in *The Faulkner–Cowley File*, ed. Malcolm Cowley (1961), and *Selected Letters of William Faulkner*, ed. Joseph L. Blotner (1977).

The full-length *Faulkner: A Biography*, 2 vols. (1974), by Joseph L. Blotner, may be supplemented by biographical material and memoirs in John Cullen and Floyd C. Watkins's *Old Times in the Faulkner Country* (1961); John Faulkner's *My Brother Bill* (1963); *William Faulkner of Oxford*, ed. James B. Webb and A. Wigfall Green (1965); and Murry C. Falkner's *The Falkners of Mississippi* (1967).

Full-length critical studies include Michael Millgate's *The Achievement of William Faulk-*

ner (1963); Cleanth Brooks's *The Yok-napatawpha Country* (1963), and *Toward Yok-napatawpha and Beyond* (1978); Olga Vickery's *The Novels of William Faulkner* (1959; rev. ed., 1964); and Richard P. Adams's *Faulkner: Myth and Motion* (1968). Others are Irving Howe's *William Faulkner* (1952; rev. ed., 1962); Hyatt H. Waggoner's *William Faulkner* (1959); Walter Slatoff's *Quest for Failure* (1960); Frederick J. Hoffman's *William Faulkner* (1961); Lawrance Thompson's *William Faulkner, an Introduction and Interpretation* (1963; rev. ed., 1967); and Edward L. Volpe's *A Reader's Guide to William Faulkner* (1964). More specialized studies include Warren Beck's *Man in Motion: Faulkner's Trilogy* (1961); John Longley, Jr.'s *The Tragic Mask: A Study of Faulkner's Heroes* (1963); John Hunt's *William Faulkner: Art in Theological Tension* (1965); Peter Swiggert's *The Art of Faulkner's Novels* (1962); Charles H. Nilon's *Faulkner and the Negro* (1965); Melvin Backman's *Faulkner: The Major Years* (1966); Walter Brylowski's *Faulkner's Olympian Laugh* (1968); H. Richardson's *William Faulkner, the Journey to Self-Discovery* (1969); and John T. Irwin's *Doubling and Incest, Repetition and Revenge: A Speculative Reading of Faulkner* (1975).

Collections of critical essays include *William Faulkner: Two Decades of Criticism*, ed. Frederick J. Hoffman and Olga Vickery (1951); Hoffman and Vickery's *William Faulkner: Three Decades of Criticism* (1960); Linda Wagner's *William Faulkner: Four Decades of Criticism* (1973); *Faulkner: A Collection of Critical Essays*, ed. Robert Penn Warren (1966); and *William Faulkner: A Collection of Criticism*, ed. Dean M. Schmitter (1973). Useful reference books include Robert W. Kirk and Marvin Klots's *Faulkner's People: A Complete Guide and Index* (1963); Harry Runyan's *A Faulkner Glossary* (1964); Dorothy Tuck's *Apollo Handbook of Faulkner* (1964); I. L. Sleeth's *William Faulkner: A Bibliography of Criticism* (1962); and the authoritative bibliography by James B. Meriwether, *The Literary Career of William Faulkner: A Bibliographic Study* (1961).

F. Scott Fitzgerald

Fitzgerald's novels are *This Side of Paradise* (1920); *The Beautiful and Damned* (1922); *The Great Gatsby* (1925); *Tender Is the Night* (1934; rev. ed. 1939; reprint, 1953); and the unfinished *The Last Tycoon* (1941). His collections of stories are *Flappers and Philosophers* (1921); *Tales of the Jazz Age* (1922); *All the Sad Young Men* (1926); and *Taps at Reveille* (1935). A satirical play, *The Vegetable, or From President to Postman*, was published in 1923. Among the valuable collections of Fitzgerald's writings are *The Apprentice Fiction of F. Scott Fitzgerald*, ed. John Kuehl (1965); *F. Scott Fitzgerald in His Own Time: A Miscellany*, ed. Jackson R. Bryer and Matthew J. Bruccoli (1971); and *Afternoon of an Author*, ed. Arthur Mizener (1957). *The Crack-Up*, ed. Edmund Wilson (1945), collects essays, notebook entries, and letters from the 1930s which provide an indispensable firsthand impression of Fitzgerald's early success and subsequent emotional, economic, and marital collapse.

The Letters of F. Scott Fitzgerald (1963) was edited by Andrew Turnbull. Other volumes of letters are *Dear Scott/Dear Max: The Fitzgerald–Perkins Correspondence*, ed. John Kuehl and Jackson R. Bryer (1971); and *As Ever, Scott Fitz*—(letters between Fitzgerald and his literary agent, Harold Ober), ed. Matthew J. Bruccoli and Jennifer McCabe Atkinson (1972); Fitzgerald's biographers are Arthur Mizener, *The Far Side of Paradise* (1951; rev. ed., 1965), and Andrew Turnbull, *Scott Fitzgerald* (1962). Other sources of biographical information include Sheila Graham's reminiscences (*Beloved Infidel* [1958] and *College of One* [1967]) of her affair with Fitzgerald; Nancy Milford's *Zelda* (1970); and Aaron Latham's *Crazy Sundays: F. Scott Fitzgerald in Hollywood* (1971).

Critical introductions to Fitzgerald's work include Kenneth Eble's *F. Scott Fitzgerald* (1963); Sergio Perosa's *The Art of F. Scott Fitzgerald* (1965); Henry Dan Piper's *F. Scott Fitzgerald: A Critical Portrait* (1965) and Richard D. Lehan's *F. Scott Fitzgerald and the Craft of Fiction* (1966). *The Fictional Technique of F. Scott Fitzgerald* (1957) by James E. Miller offers close readings of the first three novels. Robert Sklar's *F. Scott Fitzgerald: The Last Laocoön* (1967) sees the effort to master the genteel tradition as an impetus for complex artistry, while Milton R. Stern's *The Golden Moment: The Novels of F. Scott Fitzgerald* (1970) focuses on autobiography and personality in the fiction. Other useful works include William Goldhurst's *F. Scott Fitzgerald and His Contemporaries* (1963), which studies the relations between Fitzgerald and four influential contemporaries—Wilson, Mencken, Lardner, and Hemingway; Matthew J. Bruccoli's *The Composition of Tender Is the Night* (1963); and John F. Callahan's *The Illusions of a Nation: Myth and History in the Novels of F. Scott Fitzgerald* (1972). *F. Scott Fitzgerald: The Man and His Work*, ed. Alfred Kazin (1951), and *F. Scott Fitzgerald*, ed. Arthur Mizener (1963), are collections of critical essays. Jackson R. Bryer has edited *The Critical Reputation of F. Scott Fitzgerald: A Bibliographical Study* (1967).

Robert Frost

The Poetry of Robert Frost (1969) incorporated *Complete Poems* (1949) and Frost's last volume, *In the Clearing* (1962). Eleven early essays on farming, edited by Edward C. Lathem and Lawrance Thompson, appear in *Robert Frost: Farm Poultryman* (1963). Important collections of letters appear in *Selected Letters of Robert Frost*, ed. Lawrance Thompson (1964); *The Letters of Robert Frost to Louis Untermeyer* (1963); and Margaret Anderson, *Robert Frost and John Bartlett: The Record of a Friendship* (1963). His critical essays have been collected in *Selected Prose*, ed. Hyde Cox and Edward C. Lathem (1966). Collections of conversations and interviews with Frost include Edward C. Lathem's *Interviews with Robert Frost* (1966); Reginald L. Cook's *The Dimensions of Robert Frost* (1964); Daniel Smythe's *Robert Frost Speaks* (1954); and Louis Mertin's *Robert Frost: Life and Talks—Walking* (1965).

Lawrance Thompson finished two volumes of the authorized biography before his death: *Robert Frost: The Early Years, 1874–1915* (1966) and *Robert Frost: The Years of Triumph, 1915–1938* (1970). The early *Robert Frost: A Bibliography*, ed. W. B. Shubrick

Clymer and Charles Green (1937), must be supplemented by Una Parameswaran, "Robert Frost: A Bibliography of Articles and Books, 1958–1964," *Bulletin of Bibliography* (January/Spring, May/August, 1967), and by W. B. S. Clymer, *Robert Frost: A Bibliography* (1972).

A brief critical introduction to Frost's poetry is Lawrance Thompson's *Robert Frost* (1964). The best full-length critical studies are Reuben Brower's *The Poetry of Robert Frost: Constellations of Intention* (1963) and John F. Lynen's *The Pastoral Art of Robert Frost* (1964). Other useful studies are Reginald L. Cook's *The Dimensions of Robert Frost* (1958); Radcliffe Squires's *The Major Themes of Robert Frost* (1963); Philip L. Gerber's *Robert Frost* (1966); George W. Nitchie's adversely critical *Human Values in the Poetry of Robert Frost* (1960); and John R. Doyle, Jr.'s *The Poetry of Robert Frost: An Analysis* (1962). Collections of critical essays include *Robert Frost: An Introduction,* ed. Robert A. Greenberg and James G. Hepburn (1961); *Robert Frost: A Collection of Critical Essays,* ed. James M. Cox (1962); and *Recognition of Robert Frost,* ed. Richard Thornton (1970).

Ernest Hemingway

There is no collected edition of Hemingway's writings. In addition to works mentioned in the author's introduction, his fiction includes *Today Is Friday* (1926) and *God Rest You Merry Gentlemen* (1933). His tribute to Spain, *The Spanish Earth,* and his play *The Fifth Column* appeared in 1938, the latter in a collection *The Fifth Column and the First Forty-nine Stories.* His journalism has been collected in *The Wild Years,* ed. Gene Z. Hanrahan (1962), and *By-Line: Ernest Hemingway, Selected Articles and Dispatches of Four Decades,* ed. William White (1967). Audre Hanneman's *Ernest Hemingway: A Comprehensive Bibliography* (1967) is exceptionally thorough.

The authorized biography is Carlos Baker's *Ernest Hemingway: A Life Story* (1969). Of numerous memoirs by relatives and acquaintances, the best are Leicester Hemingway's *My Brother, Ernest Hemingway* (1962); Marcelline Hemingway Sanford's *At the Hemingways: A Family Portrait* (1962); and Gregory H. Hemingway's *Papa* (1976).

Philip Young, *Ernest Hemingway* (1959), Earl Rovit, *Ernest Hemingway* (1963), and Sheridan Baker, *Ernest Hemingway* (1967) are introductory critical studies. Full-length critical works include Carlos Baker's *Ernest Hemingway: The Writer As Artist* (1952; rev. ed., 1956) and Philip Young's *Ernest Hemingway* (1952; rev. ed., 1966). For collections of critical essays on Hemingway, see *Ernest Hemingway: The Man and His Work,* ed. John K. M. McCaffery (1950); *Hemingway and His Critics,* ed. Carlos Baker (1961); *Hemingway: A Collection of Critical Essays,* ed. Robert P. Weeks (1962); and *The Literary Reputation of Hemingway in Europe,* ed. Roger Asselineau (1965). Specialized studies include Charles A. Fenton's *The Apprenticeship of Ernest Hemingway: The Early Years* (1954); Robert W. Lewis's *Hemingway on Love* (1965); Robert O. Stephen's *Hemingway's Nonfiction: The Public Voice* (1968); and Emily A. Watts's *Ernest Hemingway and the Arts* (1971).

Langston Hughes

The Selected Poems of Langston Hughes (1959 and 1965) draws on his earlier volumes, the most important of which were *The Weary Blues* (1926); *Fine Clothes to the Jew* (1927); *The Dream Keeper and Other Poems* (1932); *Scottsboro Limited: Four Poems and a Play in Verse* (1932); and *Montage of a Dream Deferred* (1951). More recent is *The Panther and the Lash: Poems of Our Times* (1967). Faith Berry has edited *Good Morning Revolution: Uncollected Social Protest Writings by Langston Hughes* (1973). Hughes's autobiographical volumes include *The Big Sea* (1940) and *I Wonder as I Wander* (1956).

Biographies of Hughes include Milton Meltzer's *Langston Hughes: A Biography* (1968); C. Rollins's *Black Troubador* (1970); and James S. Haskins's *Always Movin' On: The Life of Langston Hughes* (1976). James A. Emmanuel's *Langston Hughes* (1967) is an excellent introduction to Hughes's writing. Full-length critical studies are Onwuchekwa Jemie's *Langston Hughes: An Introduction to the Poetry* (1976) and Richard K. Barksdale's *Langston Hughes: The Poet and His Critics* (1977). Therman B. O'Daniel has edited *Langston Hughes, Black Genius: A Critical Evaluation* (1972). Useful reference works include Donald C. Dickinson's *A Bio-Bibliography of Langston Hughes, 1902–1967* (1967) and the compilation by Peter Mandelik and Stanley Schatt, *A Concordance to the Poetry of Langston Hughes* (1975).

Archibald MacLeish

An early collection of MacLeish's poetry, *Poems, 1924–1933* (1933), was superseded by *Collected Poems, 1917–1952* (1952; rev. ed., 1963). *The Human Season: Selected Poems, 1926–1972* (1972) drew on the later volumes *Songs for Eve* (1954) and *The Wild Old Wicked Man and Other Poems* (1967) as well as on earlier verse. The most complete collection is *New and Collected Poems, 1917–1976* (1976). His plays include two war-time radio dramas, *The Fall of the City* (1937) and *Air Raid* (1938), and a successful Broadway dramatization of the book of Job, *J. B.* (1958). For his literary essays and manifestoes, see *The Irresponsibles: A Declaration* (1940); *Poetry and Opinion: The Pisan Cantos of Ezra Pound, a Dialogue on the Role of Poetry* (1950); *Poetry and Experience* (1960); *The Dialogues of Archibald MacLeish and Mark Van Doren* (1964); and the following collections: *A Time to Speak: The Selected Prose of Archibald MacLeish* (1941); *A Time to Act: Selected Addresses* (1943); and *The American Story: Ten Broadcasts* (1944).

Two studies of his writing are Signi Falk's *Archibald MacLeish* (1965) and Grover Smith's *Archibald MacLeish* (1971). Bibliographical aids include the Library of Congress's *Bibliography* (1972) and Edward Mullaly's *Archibald MacLeish: A Checklist* (1973).

Edna St. Vincent Millay

Millay's *Collected Sonnets* (1941) and *Collected Lyrics* (1943) were followed by *Collected Poems: Edna St. Vincent Millay,* ed. Norma Millay (1956). Her prose sketches, *Distressing Dialogues,* published under the pseudonym Nancy Boyd, appeared in 1924. Her three verse plays (*Aria da Capa* [1920]; *The Lamp and the Bell* [1921]; *Two Slatterns and a King* [1921]) were collected in *Three Plays* (1926).

Karl Yost compiled *A Bibliography of the Works of Edna St. Vincent Millay* in 1937; Allan Ross Macdougall edited *Letters of Edna St. Vincent Millay* in 1952. The most recent biographical study is in Joan Dash's *A Life of One's Own: Three Gifted Women and the Men They Married* (1973). Fuller treatments are Jean Gould's *The Poet and Her Book* (1969) and Miriam Gurko's *Restless Spirit* (1957). Useful brief introductions are Norman A. Brittin's *Edna St. Vincent Millay* (1967) and James Gray's *Edna St. Vincent Millay* (1967). Elizabeth Atkins's *Edna St. Vincent Millay and Her Times* (1936) is an earlier critical study.

Marianne Moore

No collection of Moore's verse is authoritative because each excluded some earlier poems while subjecting others to extensive revisions and changes in format. Her separate volumes include *Poems* (1921); *Observations* (1924); *The Pangolin and Other Verse* (1936); *What Are Years?* (1941); *Nevertheless* (1944); *Like a Bulwark* (1956); *O to Be a Dragon* (1959); and *Tell Me, Tell Me* (1966). Collections include *Selected Poems* (1935); *Collected Poems* (1951); and *The Complete Poems of Marianne Moore* (1967), which included selections from her translation of *The Fables of La Fontaine* (1954). She also translated Adalbert Stifter's *Rock Crystal: A Christmas Tale* (1945). A collection of her critical essays, *Predilections*, appeared in 1955.

Four important and perceptive essays on Moore are by poet-critics: T. S. Eliot's introduction to Moore's *Selected Poems;* Richard P. Blackmur's "The Method of Marianne Moore," in *The Double Agent* (1935); Kenneth Burke's "Motives and Motifs in the Poetry of Marianne Moore," reprinted in *A Grammar of Motives* (1945); and Randall Jarrell's "Thoughts about Marianne Moore," reprinted in *Poetry and the Age* (1953). Hugh Kenner's incisive essay "Disliking It" is in *A Homemade World: The American Modernist Writers* (1975). Book-length studies include Bernard F. Engel's *Marianne Moore* (1963); Jean Garrigue's *Marianne Moore* (1965); George W. Nitchie's *Marianne Moore: An Introduction to the Poetry* (1969); Pamela W. Hadas's *Marianne Moore, Poet of Affection* (1977); and Donald Hall's *Marianne Moore: The Cage and the Animal* (1970). The most recent is Laurence Stapleton's *Marianne Moore: The Poet's Advance* (1978). M. J. Tambimuttu edited *Festschrift for Marianne Moore's Seventy-fifth Birthday—by Various Hands* in 1964, and Charles Tomlinson edited *Marianne Moore: A Collection of Critical Essays* in 1969. Eugene P. Sheehy and Kenneth A. Lohf compiled *The Achievement of Marianne Moore: A Bibliography, 1907–1957* in 1958, and Craig S. Abbott compiled *Marianne Moore: A Descriptive Bibliography* in 1977. Gary Lane's *A Concordance to the Poems of Marianne Moore* appeared in 1972.

Katherine Anne Porter

There is no standard collection of Porter's works, nor a biography. In addition to the works mentioned in the author's introduction, she published an expanded edition of *Flowering Judas* in 1935, edited a translation from the Spanish by her second husband, Eugene Pressly, of J. F. Lizardi's *The Itching Parrot* (1942), and published *The Collected Essays and Occasional Writings* (1970) and essays and reviews in *The Never Ending Wrong* (1977).

The bibliographies are Edward Schwartz's *Katherine Anne Porter, a Critical Bibliography: Bulletin of the New York Public Library* (1957), and *A Bibliography of the Works of Katherine Anne Porter*, ed. Louise Waldrip and Shirley Ann Bauer (1969). Two important essays on Porter are in Glenway Wescott's *Images of Truth* (1962) and Robert P. Warren's *Selected Essays* (1958). *Katherine Anne Porter: A Critical Symposium* was edited by Lodwicj Hartley and George Gore (1969). An interview with Porter by George Plimpton appeared in the *Paris Review Interviews* (1963). For surveys of her career and writings, see Ray West's *Katherine Anne Porter* (1963); George Hendrick's *Katherine Anne Porter* (1965); M.M. Liberman's *Katherine Anne Porter's Fiction* (1971); Harry J. Mooney's *The Fiction and Criticism of Katherine Anne Porter* (1962); William L. Nance's *Katherine Anne Porter and the Art of Rejection* (1964); W. S. Emmons's *Katherine Anne Porter: The Regional Stories* (1967); and Paul R. Baumgarter's *Katherine Anne Porter* (1969).

Ezra Pound

Pound's early poetry, from *A Lume Spento* (1908) through *Ripostes* (1912), has been collected in the authoritative *Collected Early Poems of Ezra Pound*, ed. Michael King (1976). The same volumes, along with later volumes *Hugh Selwyn Mauberley* and *Homage to Sextus Propertius*, are collected in *Personae: The Collected Poems*, rev. ed., with appendices (1949). Earlier editions of *The Cantos* have been superseded by *The Cantos*, I through CXX with the exception of LXXII and LXXIII, which have never been published (1976). The most important of Pound's critical writings are *The Spirit of Romance*, rev. ed. (1952); *Gaudier-Brzeska: A Memoir* (1916); *Instigations* (1920); *Make It New* (1934); *Guide to Kulchur* (1938); and *Patria Mia* (1950). His criticism has been collected in *Literary Essays of Ezra Pound*, ed. T. S. Eliot (1954), and *Selected Prose, 1909–1965*, ed. William Cookson (1973). *Ezra Pound Speaking: Radio Speeches of World War II*, ed. Leonard W. Doob (1978), is a collection of wartime radio addresses. D. D. Paige edited *The Letters of Ezra Pound, 1907–1941* (1950). A revised edition of *Selected Poems of Ezra Pound* (1949) and *Ezra Pound: Selected Cantos* appeared in 1957 and 1967 respectively.

There is biographical material in Pound's autobiographical pamphlet *Indiscretions* (1923); Noel Stock's *Ezra Pound's Pennsylvania* (1976); Michael Reck's *Ezra Pound: A Close-Up* (1967); Harry M. Meachman's *The Caged Panther: Ezra Pound at St. Elizabeth's* (1968); *The Trial of Ezra Pound* (1966) by Pound's lawyer, Julien Cornell; and the memoir by Pound's daughter, Mary de Rachewiltz, *Discretions* (1972). Full-length biographies are Charles Norman's *Ezra Pound* (1960); Noel Stock's *The Life of Ezra Pound* (1970); and C. David Haymann's *Ezra Pound, the Last Rower: A Political Profile* (1976).

The best critical volumes on Pound are Hugh Kenner's *The Pound Era* (1972); Donald Davie's brief *Pound* (1975); and the latter's *Ezra Pound: Poet as Sculptor* (1964). M. L. Rosenthal's *A Primer of Ezra Pound* (1960) is a good introduction, and Christine Brooke-Rose's *A ZBC of Ezra Pound* (1971) is a perceptive study. Collections of essays on Pound include *Ezra Pound: A Collection of Critical Essays*, ed. Walter Sutton (1963); *New Approaches to Ezra Pound*, ed. Eva Hesse (1969); and *Ezra Pound: The Critical Heritage*, ed. Eric Homberger (1972). On Pound's early verse see N. Christophe de Nagy's *The Poetry of Ezra Pound: The Pre-Imagist Stage*, rev. ed. (1968); Thomas H. Jackson's *The Early Poetry of Ezra Pound* (1968); Hugh Witemeyer's *The Poetry of Ezra Pound: Forms and Renewal, 1908–1920* (1969); and K. K. Ruthven's *A Guide to Ezra Pound's Personae* (1969). Studies of particular works include John Espey's *Ezra Pound's Mauberley: A Study in Composition* (1955); J. P. Sullivan's *Ezra Pound and Sextus Propertius: A Study in Creative Translation* (1964); L. S. Dembo's *The Confucian Odes of Ezra Pound* (1963); the indispensable *Annotated Index to the Cantos of Ezra Pound* (through Canto LXXXIV), ed. John H. Edwards and William W. Vasse (1957); and the following books on *The Cantos: Motive and Method in the Cantos of Ezra Pound*, ed. Lewis Leary (1954); Clark Emery's *Ideas into Action* (1958); George Dekker's *The Cantos of Ezra Pound* (1963); Noel Stock's *Reading the Cantos* (1967); Walter Baumann's *The Rose in the Steel Dust: An Examination of the Cantos of Ezra Pound* (1967); Daniel D. Pearlman's *The Barb of Time: The Unity of Pound's Cantos* (1969); Eugene P. Nasser's *The Cantos of Ezra Pound* (1975); and Ronald Bush's *The Genesis of Pound's Cantos* (1976).

Donald C. Gallup's *A Bibliography of Ezra Pound* appeared in 1963, and Gary Lane issued *A Concordance to Personae: The Shorter Poems of Ezra Pound* in 1974.

John Crowe Ransom

There is no collected edition of Ransom's writings. A selection from his first two volumes, *Poems about God* (1919) and *Chills and Fever* (1924), appeared as *Grace after Meat* in 1924. *Selected Poems* (1945) excluded many of his previously published poems. *Selected Poems* (1963), a more generous selection, included many revisions of his earlier works. His critical volumes are *God without Thunder: An Unorthodox Defense of Orthodoxy* (1931); *The World's Body* (1938); and *Beating the Bushes: Selected Essays, 1941–1970* (1972).

Writings about Ransom include *John Crowe Ransom: Critical Essays and a Bibliography*, ed. Thomas D. Young (1968); John L. Stewart's *John Crowe Ransom* (1962); Thornton H. Parsons's *John Crowe Ransom* (1969); Robert Buffington's *The Equilibrist: A Study of John Crowe Ransom's Poems, 1916–1963* (1976); Karl F. Knight's *The Poetry of John Crowe Ransom: A Study of Diction, Metaphor, and Symbol* (1971); Miller Williams's *The Poetry of John Crowe Ransom* (1972); and Thomas D. Young's *Gentleman in a Dustcoat: A Biography of John Crowe Ransom* (1976).

Edwin Arlington Robinson

Collected Poems of Edwin Arlington Robinson (1921) was enlarged periodically through 1937. In addition to a considerable body of shorter verse, Robinson wrote a number of long narrative poems. *Merlin* (1917), *Lancelot* (1920), and *Tristram* (1927) evoke an Arthurian world embroiled in "modern" moral and political crises. Robinson's other explorations of human character in modern life include *Roman Bartholomew* (1923); *The Man Who Died Twice* (1924); *Cavender's House* (1929); *The Glory of the Nightingales* (1930); *Matthias at the Door* (1931); *Talifer* (1933); *Amaranth* (1934); and *King Jasper* (1935). Ridgely Torrence compiled *Selected Letters* (1940). Denham Sutcliffe edited *Untriangulated Stars: Letters of Edwin Arlington Robinson to Harry de Forest Smith, 1890–1905* (1947). Richard Cary edited *Edwin Arlington Robinson's Letters to Edith Brower* (1968). *A Bibliography of Edwin Arlington Robinson*, ed. Charles Bescher Hogan, appeared in 1936. William White compiled *Edwin Arlington Robinson: A Supplementary Bibliography* (1971).

Two biographies, both entitled *Edwin Arlington Robinson*, are by Hermann Hagedorn (1938) and Emery Neff (1948). Three early critical studies, all entitled *Edwin Arlington Robinson*, were written by Mark Van Doren (1927), Charles Cestre (1930), and Yvor Winters (1946). Ellsworth Barnard's *Edwin Arlington Robinson: A Critical Study* (1952) is the best introduction to Robinson's work. Others include Chard Powers Smith's *Where the Light Falls: A Portrait of Edwin Arlington Robinson* (1965); Wallace L. Anderson's *Edwin Arlington Robinson: A Critical Introduction* (1967); Hoyt C. Franchere's *Edwin Arlington Robinson* (1968); and Louis O. Coxe's *Edwin Arlington Robinson: The Life of Poetry* (1969). Edwin S. Fussell examines the cultural and intellectual influences on Robinson in *Edwin Arlington Robinson: The Literary Background of a Traditional Poet* (1954). W. R. Robinson's *Edwin Arlington Robinson: A Poetry of the Act* (1967) focuses on the poet's aesthetics and on his methods of constructing and exploring philosophical themes and motifs. Ellsworth Barnard edited *Edwin Arlington Robinson: Centenary Essays* (1969). Other collections are *Appreciation of Edwin Arlington Robinson: Twenty-eight Interpretive Essays*, ed. Richard Cary (1969), and *Edwin Arlington Robinson: A Collection of Critical Essays*, ed. Francis Murphy (1970).

Carl Sandburg

The Complete Poems of Carl Sandburg (1950) was revised and expanded in 1969. In addition to seven full-length volumes of poetry, Sandburg wrote a Pulitzer Prize–winning study of Abraham Lincoln (*Abraham Lincoln: The Prairie Years*, 2 vols. [1926], and *Abraham Lincoln: The War Years*, 4 vols. [1939]), two collections of journalism and social commentary, a novel, and several books for children. *The Letters of Carl Sandburg* (1968) was edited by Herbert Mitgang. Mark Van Doren published *Carl Sandburg: With a Bibliography of Sandburg Materials in the Collections of the Library of Congress* (1969).

Always the Young Strangers (1952) is Sandburg's autobiography. Other sources of biographical information are Karl Detzer's *Carl Sandburg: A Study in Personality and Background* (1941); Harry Golden's *Carl Sandburg* (1961); and North Callahan's *Carl Sandburg: Lincoln of Our Literature* (1970). Critical studies include Richard Crowder's *Carl Sandburg* (1964); Hazell Durnell's *The America of Carl Sandburg* (1965); and Gay Wilson Allen's *Carl Sandburg* (1972). Sandburg's work has occasioned numerous reviews, journal articles, and anthology pieces.

Gertrude Stein

There is no complete edition of Gertrude Stein's profuse and eclectic writings. *The Yale Edition of the Unpublished Writings of Gertrude Stein*, ed. Carl Van Vechten (1951–1958), contains eight volumes of poetry, prose fiction, portraits, essays, and miscellany. Among the works published during Stein's lifetime are *Tender Buttons* (1914), cycles of prose poems on objects, food, and rooms; and the children's book *The World Is Round* (1926). Her prose fiction includes *Three Lives* (1909); *The Making of Americans* (1925); *Lucy Church Amiably* (1930); *Ida: A Novel* (1941); and *Brewsie and Willie* (1946). *Geography and Plays* (1922), *Operas and Plays* (1932), and *Last Operas and Plays*, ed. Carl Van Vechten (1949), contain dramatic pieces. Biographical material and portraits of Stein's contemporaries may be found in *The Autobiography of Alice B. Toklas* (1933); *Portraits and Prayers* (1934); *Everybody's Autobiography* (1937); and *Wars I Have Seen* (1945). Other works, including meditations, essays, sketches, and sociolinguistic treatises, are *Useful Knowledge* (1928); *How to Write* (1931); *Lectures in America* (1935); *Narration: Four Lectures by Gertrude Stein* (1935); *What Are Masterpieces* (1940); and *Four in America* (1947). Donald C. Gallup has edited *Fernhurst, Q.E.D. and Other Early Writings by Gertrude Stein* (1971), and also a collection of letters to Gertrude Stein, *The Flowers of Friendship* (1953). Julian Sawyer's *Gertrude Stein: A Bibliography* (1940) was published before the end of Stein's career.

Biographical studies of Gertrude Stein are Elizabeth Sprigge's *Gertrude Stein: Her Life and Work* (1957); John Malcolm Brinnin's *The Third Rose: Gertrude Stein and Her World* (1959); Howard Greenfield's *Gertrude Stein: A Biography* (1973); and J. Michael Hoffman's *The Development of Abstractionism in the Writings of Gertrude Stein* (1965). W. G. Rogers's *When This You See Remember Me: Gertrude Stein in Person* (1948) and Alice B. Toklas's *What Is Remembered* (1963) are reminiscences of Stein by friends. Critical studies include Donald Sutherland's *Gertrude Stein: A Biography of Her Work* (1951); Allegra Stewart's *Gertrude Stein and the Present* (1967); Norman Weinstein's *Gertrude Stein and the Literature of the Modern Consciousness* (1970); and Robert B. Haas's *A Primer for the Gradual Understanding of Gertrude Stein* (1971). A number of recent essays on Stein's work are collected in a special issue of *Widening Circle*, Vol. I, No. 4 (1973). The most recent biographical and critical studies are Richard Bridgman's *Gertrude Stein in Pieces* (1970); Janet Hobhouse's *Everybody Who Was Anybody* (1975); and James R. Mellow's *Charmed Circle: Gertrude Stein and Company* (1974).

John Steinbeck

There is no collected edition of Steinbeck's writings. In addition to titles mentioned in the text, his works of fiction are the collection of stories, *The Long Valley* (1938), and two novels, *The Short Reign of Pippin IV* (1957) and *The Winter of Our Discontent* (1961). His nonfiction includes *A Russian Journal*, with Robert Capa (1947); *Once There Was a War* (1958); and *America and Americans* (1966). His short novels (minus *Burning Bright*) are collected in *The Short Novels of John Steinbeck* (1953). Critical studies of Steinbeck include Harry T. Moore's *The Novels of John Steinbeck: A First Critical Study* (1939); Peter Lisca's *The Wide World of John Steinbeck* (1958); Warren French's *John Steinbeck* (1961); and Joseph Fontenrose's *John Steinbeck: An Introduction and Interpretation* (1963). A thorough but inaccurate bibliography is Tetsumaro Hayaski, *John Steinbeck: A Concise Bibliography (1930–1965)* (1967).

Wallace Stevens

The Collected Poems of Wallace Stevens was published in 1954. *Opus Posthumous*, ed. Samuel French Morse (1957), includes previously uncollected poems, plays, and essays primarily found among Stevens's numerous contributions to magazines and anthologies. Holly Stevens arranges a large selection of her father's poems in their probable order of composition and makes various textual corrections in editing *The Palm at the End of the Mind* (1971). *The Necessary Angel: Essays on Reality and the Imagination* (1951) is Stevens's prose statement on poetry. Other sources of primary and bibliographical material are *Letters of Wallace Stevens*, ed. Holly Stevens (1966); *Concordance to the Poetry of Wallace Stevens*, ed. Thomas Walsh (1963); and *Wallace Stevens: A Descriptive Bibliography*, compiled by J. M. Edelstein (1973).

Samuel French Morse's *Wallace Stevens: Poetry as Life* (1970) is a critical biography. Two early studies, William Van O'Connor's *The Shaping Spirit* (1950) and Robert Pack's *Wallace Stevens* (1958), provide introductions to Stevens's work. Robert Buttel's *Wallace Stevens: The Making of Harmonium* (1967) and Walton A. Litz's *Introspective Voyager: The Poetic Development of Wallace Stevens* (1972) trace the maturation of Stevens's thought and style through his early and middle years. Frank Doggett's *Stevens' Poetry of Thought* (1966), Michel Benamou's *Wallace Stevens and the Symbolist Imagination* (1972), and Harold Bloom's *Wallace Stevens: The Poems of Our Climate* (1977) consider some intellectual influences on Stevens. John J. Enck's *Wallace Stevens: Images and Judgments* (1964), Joseph N. Riddle's *The Clairvoyant Eye: The Poetry and Poetics of Wallace Stevens* (1965), Ronald Sukenick's *Wallace Stevens: Musing the Obscure* (1967), and Merle E. Brown's *Wallace Stevens: The Poem as Act* (1971) offer readings of many individual poems. Other useful full-length studies include Daniel Fuchs's *The Comic Spirit of Wallace Stevens* (1963); Eugene Paul Nassar's *Wallace Stevens: An Anatomy of Figuration* (1965); James Baird's *The Dome and the Rock: Structure in the Poetry of Wallace Stevens* (1968); and Helen H. Vendler's *On Extended Wings: Wallace Stevens' Longer Poems* (1969).

Allen Tate

Poems (1960), collecting the poetry of eight previous volumes, was followed by *The Swimmers and Other Selected Poems* in 1970. The two most inclusive volumes of Tate's essays are *Collected Essays* (1959) and *Essays of Four Decades* (1968). Tate wrote two biographies: *Stonewall Jackson: The Good Soldier* (1928) and *Jefferson Davis: His Rise and Fall* (1929). *The Fathers* (1938) is his only novel. Among the books he co-authored or edited are *I'll Take My Stand: The South and the Agrarian Tradition* (1930); *Who Owns America: A New Declaration of Independence* (1936); and *The Vigil of Venus* (1943), which he translated from the Latin.

Biographical information may be found in Radcliffe Squires's *Allen Tate: A Literary Biography* (1971). Tate is a central figure in two studies of the literary magazine *The Fugitive*: John M. Bradbury's *The Fugitives: A Critical Account* (1958) and Louise Cowan's *The Fugitive Group: A Literary History* (1959). Critical studies of Tate's work are R. K. Meiners's *The Last Alternatives: A Study of the Works of Allen Tate* (1963); George Hemphill's *Allen Tate* (1964); Ferman Bishop's *Allen Tate* (1967); and M. E. Bradford's *Rumors of Mortality: An Introduction to Allen Tate* (1969). Important essays on Tate's work and life are contained in *Allen Tate and His Work*, ed. Radcliffe Squires (1972). This volume also offers a full bibliography of writings by and about Tate.

Jean Toomer

Toomer's published works include *Cane* (1923, 1975); *Essentials* (1931); *Portage Potential* (1932); and an address, "The Flavor of Man" (1949). On Toomer, see Arna Bontemps's "Jean Toomer and the Harlem Writers of the 1920's," in *Anger and Beyond: The Negro Writer in the United States*, ed. Herbert Hill (1966); Edward Margolies's *Native Sons* (1968); Hugh M. Gloster's *Negro Voices in American Fiction* (1948); and Robert A. Bone's *The Negro Novel in America*, rev. ed. (1965).

Eudora Welty

There is no collected edition of Eudora Welty's fiction. In addition to the volumes mentioned in the author's introduction, she has written *Delta Wedding* (1946) and *The Golden Apples* (1949) and one book for children, *The Shoe Bird* (1964).

The best introduction to her writing is Joseph A. Bryant, Jr.'s *Eudora Welty* (1968). Ruth M. Vande Kieft's *Eudora Welty* (1962) and Alfred Appel's *A Season of Dreams: The Fiction of Eudora Welty* (1965) are more thorough but less up to date. Valuable essays are Katherine Anne Porter's introduction to *Selected Stories of Eudora Welty* (1954); Robert Penn Warren's "Love and Separateness in Eudora Welty," in *Selected Essays* (1958); Louis D. Rubin's "The Golden Apples of the Sun," in *Writers of the Modern South* (1963); and Burnice Glenn's "Fantasy in the Fiction of Eudora Welty," in *A Southern Vanguard*, ed. Allen Tate (1947). Seymour L. Gross compiled "Eudora Welty: A Bibliography of Criticism and Comment," *Secretary's News Sheet*, Bibliographical Society, University of Virginia, No. 45 (April, 1960).

Nathanael West

West's novels have been collected in *The Complete Works of Nathanael West*, ed. Alan Ross (1957). William White has compiled two bibliographies: "Nathanael West: A Bibliography," *Studies in Bibliography*, Vol. 11 (1958), pp. 207–224; and "Nathanael West: Further Bibliographical Notes," *Serif*, Vol. 2 (1965), pp. 28–31. The best study of West's work is Randall Reid's *The Fiction of Nathanael West: No Redeemer, No Promised Land* (1971). Other full-length studies are James F. Light's *Nathanael West: An Interpretive Study* (1961); Stanley E. Hyman's *Nathanael West* (1962); and Victor Comerchero's *Nathanael West: The Ironic Prophet* (1964). Jay Martin has written a biography, *Nathanael West: The Art of His Life* (1970), and has edited *Nathanael West: A Collection of Critical Essays* (1971).

William Carlos Williams

Williams's poems have been collected in three volumes: *Collected Earlier Poems of William Carlos Williams* (1951); *Collected Later Poems of William Carlos Williams* (1950); and *Pictures from Brueghel* (1962). The five books of Williams's long poem *Paterson*, published individually between 1946 and 1958, were issued in one volume in 1963. Williams's short stories are collected in *Make Light of It* (1950) and again, with several additions, in *The Farmers' Daughters* (1961). His novels are *A Voyage to Pagany* (1928); *White Mule* (1937); *In the Money* (1940); and *The Build Up* (1946). His dramatic pieces were published together in *Many Loves and Other Plays* (1961). His most important essays are contained in *In the American Grain* (1925; reissued, 1940); *Selected Essays of William Carlos Williams* (1954); and *Imaginations*, ed. Webster Schott (1970). Williams's prose also includes *The Autobiography of William Carlos Williams* (1951); a book of recollections dictated to Edith Heal, *I Wanted to Write a Poem* (1958); and *Yes, Mrs. Williams* (1959), a portrait of the poet's mother. J. C. Thirlwall edited *The Selected Letters of William Carlos Williams* (1957); Ron Loewinsohn edited *William Carlos Williams: The Embodiment of Knowledge* (1974); and Emily Mitchell Wallace compiled *A Bibliography of William Carlos Williams* (1968).

James E. Breslin's *William Carlos Williams: An American Artist* (1970) is the best overview of Williams's work. Other general introductions are Linda Wagner's *The Poems of William Carlos Williams* (1964); Alan Ostrom's *The Poetic World of William Carlos Williams* (1966); Thomas Whitaker's *William Carlos Williams* (1968); and James Guimond's *The Art of William Carlos Williams: A Discovery and Possession of America* (1968). Bram Dijkstra's *The Hieroglyphics of a New Speech: Cubism, Stieglitz, and the Early Poetry of William Carlos Williams* (1969) and Mike Weaver's *William Carlos Williams: The American Background* (1971) focus on the social, intellectual, and aesthetic influences on Williams and on the milieu in which he wrote. Joseph N. Riddel's *The Inverted Bell: Modernism and the Counter-Poetics of William Carlos Williams* (1974) considers the problematic of language for Williams the theorist and experimenter. Reed Whittemore's *William Carlos*

Williams: Poet from Jersey (1975) is a critical biography.

Linda Wagner, *The Prose of William Carlos Williams* (1970), and Robert Coles, *William Carlos Williams: The Knack of Survival in America* (1975), discuss Williams's prose. Other full-length studies are W. S. Peterson's *An Approach to Paterson* (1967); Joel Conarroe's *William Carlos Williams' Paterson: Language and Landscape* (1970); Benjamin Sankey's *A Companion to William Carlos Williams's Paterson* (1971); Sherman Paul's *The Music of Survival: A Biography of a Poem by William Carlos Williams* (1968); and Jerome Mazzaro's *William Carlos Williams: The Later Poems* (1973). J. Hillis Miller's *Poets of Reality* (1966) and Hugh Kenner's *A Homemade World: The American Modernist Writers* (1975) contain valuable chapters on Williams. Paul Mariani, *William Carlos Williams: The Poet and His Critics* (1975), considers Williams's critical reception.

Richard Wright

No standard edition of Wright's works exists. His fiction includes *Uncle Tom's Children* (1938); *Native Son* (1940); *The Outsider* (1953); *Savage Holiday* (1954); *The Long Dream* (1958); *Eight Men* (1961); and *Lawd Today* (written in 1936; published in 1963). His full-length works of nonfiction are *Twelve Million Black Voices* (1941); *Black Boy* (1945); *Black Power* (1954); *The Color Curtain* (1956); *Pagan Spain* (1957); and *White Man, Listen!* (1957). Among his important essays are "The Ethics of Living Jim Crow," in *American Stuff: A WPA Writers' Anthology* (1937), reprinted in the Harper Perennial paperback edition of *Uncle Tom's Children* (1965); "Blueprint for Negro Literature," in *New Challenge* (1937), reprinted in *Armistad 2*, ed. John A. Williams and Charles F. Harris (1971); *How Bigger Was Born*, a pamphlet (1940), reprinted in the Harper Perennial paperback edition of *Native Son* (1966); and the chapter "Black Boy," Wright's account of his membership in the Communist party, in Richard Crossman's *The God That Failed* (1949). Full-length critical and biographical studies are Dan McCall's *The Example of Richard Wright* (1969); Edward Margolies's *The Art of Richard Wright* (1969); Michele Febre's *The Unfinished Quest of Richard Wright*, trans. Isabel Benson (1973); Con-

stance Webb's *Richard Wright: A Biography* (1968). Important essays on Wright include Irving Howe's "Black Boys and Native Sons," *Dissent* (1963), reprinted in *A World More Attractive* (1963); Ralph Ellison's reply to Howe in "The World and the Jug," *New Leader* (1963), reprinted in *Shadow and Act* (1964); James Baldwin's "Everybody's Protest Novel" and "Many Thousands Gone," *Partisan Review* (1949 and 1951), reprinted in *Notes of a Native Son* (1955), and "Alas, Poor Richard," in *Nobody Knows My Name* (1961); and Eldridge Cleaver's "Notes on a Native Son," in *Soul on Ice* (1968). *American Hunger* (1977) is an autobiographical fragment, originally intended to be part of *Black Boy*, which covers Wright's experience in the Communist party.

Elinor Wylie

Elinor Wylie's brief publishing career spanned just eight years, from her first volume, *Nets to Catch the Wind* (1921), to the collection completed at the time of her death, *Angels and Earthly Creatures* (1929). In between she published two books of poetry—*Black Armor* (1923) and *Trivial Breath* (1928)—as well as four novels—*Jenifer Lorn* (1924); *The Venetian Glass Nephew* (1925); *The Orphan Angel* (1926); and *Mr. Hodge and Mr. Hazard* (1928). In 1912 her mother had privately printed in London *Incidental Numbers*, containing her youthful verse. *The Collected Poems of Elinor Wylie*, ed. William Rose Benét, appeared in 1932, and her *Collected Prose* came out the following year. *Last Poems* (1943) brought together previously uncollected poetry as well as some juvenilia from *Incidental Numbers* and transcriptions from manuscripts, with an appreciation by the English novelist Edith Olivier.

There is no full-length biography. Personal memoirs and appreciations include Carl Van Doren's *Three Worlds* (1936); William Rose Benét's *The Prose and Poetry of Elinor Wylie* (1934); Edmund Wilson's reviews and eulogy in *Shores of Light* (1952); Mary Colum's *Life and the Dream* (1947); Elizabeth S. Sergeant's *Fire under the Andes: A Group of North American Portraits* (1927); and Nancy Hoyt's portrait of her sister, *Elinor Wylie: Portrait of an Unknown Lady* (1935). A comprehensive critical study is Thomas Gray's *Elinor Wylie* (1969).

CONTEMPORARY AMERICAN PROSE 1945–

There are no indispensable surveys or histories of the period, and the most useful discussions of books and writers are found in collections of essays by several critics. Warner Berthoff's *Fictions and Events* (1971) has an excellent study of Edmund Wilson as well as an essay on books by Mailer and Malcolm X. *A Literature without Qualities: American Writing since 1945* (1979), also by Warner Berthoff, is a brilliantly succinct consideration of, among other things, postwar novelists. Richard Poirier's *The Performing Self* (1971) has material on Barth, Pynchon, and others of recent reputation. In *Bright Book of Life* (1973), Alfred Kazin discusses American novelists and storytellers from Hemingway to Mailer. Tony Tanner's *City of Words: American Fiction 1935–1970* (1971) provides a full treatment of many figures from this period, while Frank MacConnell's *Four Postwar*

American Novelists (1977) contains analyses of the literary careers of Bellow, Mailer, Barth, and Pynchon. Irving Howe's essay on Ralph Ellison and on "The New York Intellectuals" may be found in his *Decline of the New* (1971). Leslie Fiedler's *Collected Essays* (1971) and Norman Podhoretz's *Doings and Undoings* (1964) include essays on and reviews of most of the writers anthologized here. Arthur Mizener's *The Sense of Life in the Modern Novel* (1964) is useful on Salinger and Updike. Roger Sale's *On Not Being Good Enough* (1979) has lively writing about many recent novelists, some of them not very well known. *Black Fiction* (1974), by Roger Rosenblatt, is thoughtful and incisive. Morris Dickstein's *Gates of Eden: American Culture in the Sixties* (1977) is a wide-ranging, personal view of the period. Finally, the 26 issues of *The New American Review*, edited by

Theodore Solotaroff, is an excellent place to encounter much interesting fiction and other prose published between 1968 and 1978.

James Baldwin

Baldwin has written five novels: *Go Tell It on the Mountain* (1953); *Giovanni's Room* (1956); *Another Country* (1962); *Tell Me How Long the Train's Been Gone* (1968); and *If Beale Street Could Talk* (1974). A collection of short stories, *Going to Meet the Man*, was published in 1965.

In addition to *The Fire Next Time* (1963), Baldwin has published two collections of essays: *Notes of a Native Son* (1955) and *Nobody Knows My Name* (1961). *No Name in the Street* (1972) is a later and grimmer look at the racial situation. *The Devil Finds Work* (1976) is a book about the movies.

The Furious Passage of James Baldwin by Fern Eckman (1966) contains biographical information. Louis H. Pratt's *James Baldwin* (1978) is a more recent study. Kenneth Kinnamon has edited the Prentice-Hall collection of critical essays on Baldwin (1974). *Squaring Off: Mailer vs. Baldwin* by W. J. Weatherby (1976) is a lively account of their relationship.

John Barth

Barth is the author of four novels, the first three of which were altered when republished: *The Floating Opera* (1956, 1967); *The End of the Road* (1958, 1967); *The Sot-Weed Factor* (1960, 1967); *Giles Goat-Boy; or, The Revised New Syllabus* (1966). *Lost in the Funhouse: Fiction for Print, Tape, Live Voice* (1968) is a collection of stories. *Chimera* (1972) consists of three novellas.

John Barth, by Gerhard Joseph (1970) is a biographical and critical pamphlet in the University of Minnesota series. *John Barth: An Introduction* by David Morell (1976) is an intelligent survey of Barth's work, containing much lively information and manuscript material plus an excellent bibliography. The first two chapters of Richard Poirier's *The Performing Self* (1971) are also relevant.

Saul Bellow

Among Bellow's works are the following novels: *Dangling Man* (1944); *The Victim* (1947); *The Adventures of Augie March* (1953); *Henderson the Rain King* (1959); *Herzog* (1964); *Mr. Sammler's Planet* (1970); *Humboldt's Gift* (1975). His play, *The Last Analysis*, produced in New York in 1964, was published in 1965. *To Jerusalem and Back* (1976) is an account of a visit to Israel. Also of interest is a lecture, "Some Notes on Recent American Fiction," *Encounter* (November, 1963).

A useful collection of critical essays on Bellow's work which also includes his essay "Where Do We Go from Here: The Future of Fiction" is *Saul Bellow and the Critics*, ed. Irving Malin (1967). Books about him include *Saul Bellow* by Robert Dutton (1971), which takes him up through *Mr. Sammler's Planet* and provides a selective bibliography of further studies. *Saul Bellow: A Comprehensive Bibliography* has been compiled by B. A. Sokoloff and Mark E. Posner (1973).

Ralph Ellison

Ellison's two books are *Invisible Man* (1952) and *Shadow and Act* (1964). There are also a number of uncollected short stories and excerpts from a novel in progress. (See Bernard Benoit and Michel Fabre, "A Bibliography of Ralph Ellison's Published Writings," in *Studies in Black Literature* [1971].)

The Prentice-Hall collection of critical essays (1974), edited by John Hersey, has a number of useful items, including interviews with Ellison by Hersey and James McPherson and a further selected bibliography. *Studies in Invisible Man*, ed. Ronald Gottesman (1971), is a shorter collection. Irving Howe's essay contrasting Ellison with Richard Wright appears in *A World More Attractive* (1963).

Jack Kerouac

Among Kerouac's novels are *The Town and the City* (1950; reissued, 1973); *The Subterraneans* (1958); *The Dharma Bums* (1958); *Doctor Sax* (1959); *Desolation Angels* (1965); *Visions of Cody* (1972). There are also poems, *Mexico City Blues* (1959), and a screenplay, *Pull My Daisy* (1959).

Kerouac: A Biography by Ann Charters (1973) is a sympathetic and knowledgeable treatment of his life. Ann Charters has also provided *A Bibliography of Works by Jack Kerouac* (1967). John Clellon Holmes's *Nothing More to Declare* (1967) is a splendid memoir in which Kerouac figures. *The Beat Generation* (1971) by Bruce Cook is a sympathetic consideration of the West Coast milieu in which Kerouac and his fellow writers for a time flourished. *Naked Angels* (1976) by John Lytell is a useful study of the Beats with emphasis on Kerouac, Ginsberg, and William Burroughs. *Jack's Book: An Oral Biography* by Barry Gifford and Lawrence Lee (1978) is of interest.

Mary McCarthy

Mary McCarthy has published two collections of stories: *The Company She Keeps* (1942) and *Cast a Cold Eye* (1950). *The Oasis* (1948) is a short novel. Her four novels are *The Groves of Académe* (1952); *A Charmed Life* (1955); *The Group* (1963); and *Birds of America* (1971). Her autobiographical *Memories of a Catholic Girlhood* appeared in 1957.

On the Contrary (1961) and *The Writing on the Wall* (1970) are collections of essays on literary and cultural topics. Travel books are *Venice Observed* (1956) and *The Stones of Florence* (1959). Her essays on Vietnam and the Watergate hearings are found in *The Seventeenth Degree* (1974). *Sights and Spectacles* (1956) has been republished and enlarged as *Mary McCarthy's Theater Chronicles 1937–1962* (1963).

Critical and biographical writing about her includes *The Company She Kept* (1967) by Doris Grumbach; *Mary McCarthy* by Irwin Stock (1968); and essays by Elizabeth Hardwick in *A View of My Own* (1963). *Mary McCarthy: A Bibliography* by Sherli Goldman was published in 1968.

Norman Mailer

Mailer's novels are *The Naked and the Dead* (1948); *Barbary Shore* (1951); *The Deer Park* (1955); *An American Dream* (1965); and *Why Are We in Vietnam?* (1967). Among collections of essays and miscellaneous materials are *Advertisements for Myself* (1959); *The Presidential Papers* (1963); and *Cannibals and Christ-*

ians (1966). *The Armies of the Night: History as a Novel, the Novel as History*, was published in 1968. His writings about political conventions are collected in *Some Honorable Men* (1975). Some further titles are *Of a Fire on the Moon* (1971); *The Prisoner of Sex* (1972); and *Marilyn* (1973). His most ambitious film is *Maidstone* (1968), for which he later wrote a preface (in *Existential Essays* [1972]).

The best study is Richard Poirier's *Norman Mailer* in the Modern Masters series (1973). Also good is *Down Mailer's Way* (1974) by Robert Solotaroff. *Squaring Off* (1976) by W. J. Weatherby has some interesting personal glimpses.

Malcolm X

Malcolm X Speaks (1965) is a collection of speeches. The best discussion of the *Autobiography* as an imaginative work is by Warner Berthoff in his essay "Witness and Testament: Two Contemporary Classics," in *Fictions and Events* (1971).

Wright Morris

Among Wright Morris's many novels are *My Uncle Dudley* (1942); *The World in the Attic* (1949); *Man and Boy* (1951); *The Works of Love* (1952); *The Deep Sleep* (1953); *The Huge Season* (1954); *The Field of Vision* (1956); *Ceremony in Lone Tree* (1960); *One Day* (1965); *In Orbit* (1967); and *Fire Sermon* (1971). Books of photographs with accompanying texts include *The Home Place* (1948) and *God's Country and My People* (1968).

Morris's literary and social criticism is found in *The Territory Ahead* (1958); *A Bill of Rites, a Bill of Wrongs, a Bill of Goods* (1967); *About Fiction* (1975); and *Earthly Delights, Unearthly Adornments* (1978).

There is a book on Morris by David Madden (1964) and a pamphlet in the University of Minnesota series by Leon Howard (1968). Granville Hicks's preface to *Wright Morris, a Reader* (an anthology of his works) is a good appreciation. A recent full-length study is G. B. Crump's *The Novels of Wright Morris: A Critical Interpretation* (1978).

Vladimir Nabokov

Among Nabokov's many novels are *The Defense* (1930; translated into English, 1964); *Laughter in the Dark* (1933; translated into English, 1961); *The Real Life of Sebastian Knight* (1941); *Lolita* (1955, 1958); *Pnin* (1957); *Pale Fire* (1962); *Ada* (1969); *Look at the Harlequins!* (1974). He published a number of volumes of short stories, of which the most recent was *Tyrants Destroyed and Other Stories* (1975). Among his other works are *Poems* (1959); *Speak Memory: An Autobiography Revisited* (1966, originally published 1951); and *Strong Opinions*, essays and interviews (1973). He wrote a critical book, *Nikolai Gogol* (1944), and edited and translated Pushkin's *Eugene Onegin* (1964).

Andrew Field has compiled *Nabokov: A Bibliography* (1974) and has written a partial biography, *Nabokov: His Life in Part* (1977). Critical studies include Page Stegner's *The Art of Vladimir Nabokov: Escape into Aesthetics* (1966); Andrew Field's *Nabokov: His Life in Art* (1967); *Nabokov: The Man and His Work*, ed. L. S. Dembo (1967); and *For Vladimir Nabokov on His Seventieth Birthday*, ed.

Charles Newman and Alfred Appel, Jr. (1970). Julian Moynahan's *Vladimir Nabokov* (1971) is a short introduction. *The Viking Portable Nabokov*, ed. Page Stegner (1968, 1971) is a good selection from the work. Martin Green's *Yeats's Blessings on Von Hügel* (1967) has a fine essay on *Lolita*.

Flannery O'Connor

Flannery O'Connor's novels are *Wise Blood* (1952) and *The Violent Bear It Away* (1960). Two collections of stories, *A Good Man Is Hard to Find* (1955) and *Everything That Rises Must Converge* (1965), are included— plus some earlier previously uncollected stories—in *Complete Stories* (1971). Her letters are collected in *The Habit of Being: The Letters of Flannery O'Connor* (1979).

A collection of her essays and other occasional prose is *Mystery and Manners*, ed. Sally and Robert Fitzgerald (1969). There are a number of books about her fiction, the most interesting of which is probably *The Added Dimension: The Art and Mind of Flannery O'Connor*, ed. M. J. Freedman and L. A. Lawson (1966). Robert Fitzgerald's memoir, prefaced to *Everything That Rises Must Converge*, is an excellent portrait. Stanley Edgar Hyman's pamphlet in the University of Minnesota series (1966) is a good short introduction.

Philip Roth

Roth's fiction consists of *Goodbye, Columbus* (1959), a novella and five short stories, and the following novels: *Letting Go* (1962); *When She Was Good* (1967); *Portnoy's Complaint* (1969); *Our Gang* (1971); *The Breast* (1972); *The Great American Novel* (1973); *My Life As a Man* (1974); and *The Professor of Desire* (1977). *Reading Myself and Others* (1975) is a collection of essays and interviews.

Interesting essays about Roth are Theodore Solotaroff's "The Journey of Philip Roth," in *The Red Hot Vacuum* (1970), and Irving Howe's adversely critical "Philip Roth Reconsidered," in *The Critical Point* (1973). John N. McDaniel's *The Fiction of Philip Roth* (1974) is a longer treatment.

Susan Sontag

Susan Sontag has published two novels, *The Benefactor* (1964) and *Death Kit* (1967), plus a collection of stories, *I, etcetera* (1978). Her essays about art, culture, and politics are found in *Against Interpretation* (1966) and *Styles of Radical Will* (1969). She has written the screenplays for and directed the films *Duet for Cannibals* (1970) and *Brother Karl* (1971). *On Photography* was published in 1977, *Illness As Metaphor* in 1978.

John Updike

Updike's novels are *The Poorhouse Fair* (1958); *Rabbit, Run* (1961); *The Centaur* (1963); *Of the Farm* (1965); *Couples* (1968); *Rabbit Redux* (1971); *A Month of Sundays* (1975); *Marry Me* (1976); and *Coup* (1978). Collections of short fiction are *The Same Door* (1959); *Pigeon Feathers* (1962); *The Music School* (1966); *Bech: A Book* (1970); and *Museums and Women* (1973). *Midpoint* (1969) and *Tossing and Turning* (1977) are collections of poems. His occasional articles, interviews, and reviews are found in *Assorted Prose* (1965) and *Picked-Up Pieces* (1975).

Charles Thomas Samuels's pamphlet in the University of Minnesota series (1969) is usefully critical. Alfred Kazin's discussion of Updike in *Bright Book of Life* (1973) is also of interest.

Edmund Wilson

Among Wilson's numerous books are *To the Finland Station* (1940) and *Patriotic Gore* (1962), works of political and social criticism. *Axel's Castle* (1931) is his major essay in literary criticism, while *The Wound and the Bow* (1941) and *The Triple Thinkers* (1938; rev. and expanded, 1948) are collections of literary and cultural essays. *The Shores of Light* (1952), *Classics and Commercials* (1950), and *The Bit*

between My Teeth (1965) reprint Wilson's literary reviews and essays from the 1920s to 1960. His fiction includes a novel, *I Thought of Daisy* (1929), and a collection of stories, *Memoirs of Hecate County* (1946). Travel and miscellaneous books include *Europe without Baedeker* (1947); *A Piece of My Mind* (1956); and *Upstate* (1972).

Letters on Literature and Politics, ed. Elena Wilson (1977), is a large selection from Wilson's letters over his career.

Warner Berthoff's *Edmund Wilson* (1968) and Leonard Kriegel's *Edmund Wilson* (1972) are excellent critical studies. See also *Edmund Wilson, a Bibliography*, comp. Richard David Ramsey (1971).

CONTEMPORARY AMERICAN POETRY 1945–

Randall Jarrell's *Poetry and the Age* (1953) is still the most engaging general introduction for the student of contemporary American poetry. Valuable studies of the period and of particular poets are to be found in Harold Bloom's *The Ringers in the Tower* (1971) and *Figures of Capable Imagination* (1976); *The Survival of Poetry*, ed. Martin Dodsworth (1970); Richard Howard's *Alone with America* (1969); David Kalstone's *Five Temperaments* (1977); Howard Nemerov's *Figures of Thought* (1978); and Robert Pinsky's *The Situation of Poetry* (1976). Useful interview material is to be found in Anthony Ostroff's *The Contemporary Poet as Artist and Critic: Eight Symposia* (1964); *Preferences*, ed. Richard Howard and Thomas Victor (1974); and the various volumes of *Writers at Work: The Paris Review Interviews*.

A. R. Ammons

Ammons's *Collected Poems: 1951–1971* (1972) were followed by several shorter volumes: *Sphere: The Form of a Motion* (1974); *Diversifications* (1975); and *The Snow Poems* (1977). There are useful critical essays on his work in Richard Howard, *Alone with America* (1969) and in Harold Bloom, *The Ringers in the Tower* (1971). An interview with Ammons appeared in a special issue of *Diacritics*, Vol. III, No. 5 (Winter, 1973), devoted to studies of his work.

John Ashbery

John Ashbery's volumes of poetry include *Some Trees* (1956); *The Tennis Court Oath* (1962); *Rivers and Mountains* (1966); *The Double Dream of Spring* (1970); *Three Poems* (1972); *Self-Portrait in a Convex Mirror* (1975); and *Houseboat Days* (1977). With James Schuyler he is co-author of the comic novel *A Nest of Ninnies* (1969). Among useful critical essays are the chapters on Ashbery in Richard Howard's *Alone with America* (1969) and David Kalstone's *Five Temperaments* (1977), and a study by Harold Bloom in *Contemporary Poetry in America: Essays and Introductions*, ed. Robert Boyers (1973). David K. Kermani's *John Ashbery: A Comprehensive Bibliography* (1975) is indispensable and amusing.

Imamu Amiri Baraka (LeRoi Jones)

Baraka's volumes of poetry include *Preface to a Twenty Volume Suicide Note* (1961); *The Dead Lecturer* (1965); *Black Art* (1966); *Black Magic: Poetry 1961–1967* (1969). He is

the author of several important plays including *Dutchman* and *Slave* (1964), *The Baptism* and *The Toilet* (1967) and *Four Black Revolutionary Plays* (1969). His prose writings include *Home: Social Essays* (1966) and *Raise Race Rays Raze* (1972).

John Berryman

Homage to Mistress Bradstreet (1956) and a selection of Berryman's *Short Poems* (1948) were issued together in paperback format in 1968. His other volumes of poetry include *77 Dream Songs* (1964); *Berryman's Sonnets* (1967); *His Toy, His Dream, His Rest* (1968); *Love and Fame* (1970; rev. ed., 1972); *Delusions, Etc.* (1972); and a posthumous volume, *Henry's Fate* (1977). Berryman's critical biography, *Stephen Crane*, appeared in 1950, and a collection of his short fiction and literary essays was issued under the title *The Freedom of the Poet* (1976). Berryman's unfinished novel about his alcoholism, *Recovery*, appeared in 1973. A valuable critical introduction to Berryman's poetry is to be found in Martin Dodsworth's essay on him in *The Survival of Poetry*, ed. Martin Dodsworth (1970). Joel Conarroe's *John Berryman* (1977) is a book-length biographical and critical study.

Elizabeth Bishop

The Complete Poems of Elizabeth Bishop were published in 1969. Since then she has written another book of poems, *Geography III* (1976). The moving and important short story "In the Village" was included in her *Questions of Travel* (1965), and another story, "In Prison," has been reprinted in *The Poet's Story*, ed. Howard Moss (1973). Bishop has translated from the Portuguese *The Diary of Helena Morley* (1957, 1977), an enchanting memoir of provincial life in Brazil. Anne Stevenson's biographical and critical study *Elizabeth Bishop* appeared in 1966. Useful critical essays on Bishop's poetry appear in the issue of *World Literature Today* (1976) devoted to her and in David Kalstone's *Five Temperaments* (1977).

Gwendolyn Brooks

Gwendolyn Brooks's volumes of poetry include *A Street in Bronzeville* (1945); *Annie Allen* (1949); *Bronzeville Boys and Girls* (1956); *Selected Poems* (1963); *In the Mecca* (1968); *Riot* (1969); *Family Pictures* (1970); *The World of GB* (1971); *Aloneness* (1972). She is the author of a prose autobiography, the first installment of which is *Report from Part One* (1972).

Robert Creeley

Robert Creeley's *Selected Poems* were published in 1976 and include verse from *For Love* (1962), *Words* (1967), and *Pieces* (1969). Creeley's early and uncollected poems are available in *The Charm* (1969). His collected notes and essays were published in *A Quick Graph* (1970). His fiction includes *The Gold Diggers* (1954), a collection of short stories, and *The Island* (1963), a novel.

James Dickey

The most convenient single volume of Dickey's poetry is *Poems 1957–1967*, which includes selections from *Into the Stone* (1957), *Drowning with Others* (1962), *Helmets* (1964), *Two Poems of the Air* (1964), and *Buckdancer's Choice* (1965). Later volumes of poetry include *The Eye-Beaters, Blood, Victory, Madness, Buckhead and Mercy* (1970) and *The Zodiac* (1976). Dickey's literary criticism includes *The Suspect in Poetry* (1964), *Babel to Byzantium* (1968), and *The Self as Agent* (1970). His novel *Deliverance* was published in 1970. Two autobiographical collections, *Self-Interviews* and *Sorties: Journals and New Essays*, appeared in 1970 and 1971 respectively.

Robert Duncan

Duncan's poems have not yet been collected in a single volume, but there are a number of useful selected volumes chosen from his many fugitive pamphlet publications. The volumes of selections include *The Years as Catches, First Poems 1939–41* (1966); *Selected Poems 1942–1950* (1959); *The First Decade: Selected Poems*, Vol. 1 (1968); and *Derivations: Selected Poems, 1950–1956* (1968). Other important books of his poetry are *The Opening of the Field* (1960); *Roots and Branches* (1964); and *Bending the Bow* (1968).

Allen Ginsberg

Ginsberg's poems have, with the exception of *Empty Mirror* (early poems collected in 1961), been issued in the now unmistakable City Lights paperbacks. They include *Howl* (1956); *Kaddish and Other Poems, 1958–1960* (1961); *Reality Sandwiches* (1963); *Planet News, 1961–1967* (1968); *The Fall of America, Poems of These States, 1965–1971* (1973); and *Mind Breaths, Poems 1972–1977* (1977). Ginsberg has published a great number of pages from his journals, dealing with his travels, such as the *Indian Journals* (1970). *Allen Verbatim* (1974) includes transcripts of some of his "lectures on poetry." In 1977 he published *Letters Early Fifties Early Sixties* (1977). Among the many interviews, the Paris Review dialogue conducted by Tom Clarkin, *Writers at Work: Third Series* (1967), is extremely valuable. Jane Kramer's *Allen Ginsberg in America* (1969) is a brilliant documentary piece on Ginsberg in the 1960s.

Randall Jarrell

Randall Jarrell's *Complete Poems* were published in 1969. His novel satirizing American academic life, *Pictures from an Institution*, appeared in 1954. Jarrell's critical essays have been collected in *Poetry and the Age* (1953), *A Sad Heart at the Supermarket* (1962), and *The Third Book of Criticism* (1969). Some of the most valuable commentary on Jarrell's life and work are to be found in a memorial volume of essays edited by Robert Lowell, Peter Taylor, and Robert Penn Warren, *Randall Jarrell, 1914–1965* (published in 1967). Suzanne Ferguson's *The Poetry of Randall Jarrell* is a useful book-length study.

Denise Levertov

Levertov's books of poems include *The Double Image* (1946); *Here and Now* (1957); *Overland to the Islands* (1958); *With Eyes at the Back of Our Heads* (1960); *The Jacob's Ladder* (1962); *O Taste and See* (1964); *The Sorrow Dance* (1967); *Relearning the Alphabet* (1970); *To Stay Alive* (1971); *Footprints* (1972); and *The Freedom of the Dust* (1973). *The Poet in the World* (1973) includes essays on her own work, her reviews of other poets, and some theoretical essays on poetry.

Robert Lowell

In 1976, the year before his death, Lowell prepared his *Selected Poems*, which drew upon all his volumes of poetry except *Day by Day* which appeared in 1977. The interested reader will still have to look back to individual volumes since Lowell frequently revised his poems and could only print a small proportion of his work in *Selected Poems*. His earlier books of verse include *Lord Weary's Castle* (1946); *The Mills of the Kavenaughs* (1951); *Life Studies* (1959); *Imitations* (1961); *For the Union Dead* (1964); *Near the Ocean* (1967); *Notebook* (1969; rev. and expanded, 1970); *The Dolphin* (1973); *For Lizzie and Harriet* (1973); and *History* (1973). For the stage Lowell prepared adaptations of Racine's *Phaedra* (1961) and Aeschylus's *Prometheus Bound* (1969) as well as versions of Hawthorne and Melville stories grouped under the title *The Old Glory* (1965). Among the many useful critical works on Lowell are Philip Cooper's *The Autobiographical Myth of Robert Lowell* (1970); Jerome Mazzaro's *The Poetic Themes of Robert Lowell* (1965); Hugh B. Staples's *Robert Lowell, the First Twenty Years* (1962); Stephen Yenser's *Circle to Circle* (1975); and Steven Axelrod's *Robert Lowell: Life and Art* (1978). *Robert Lowell: A Collection of Critical Essays*, ed. Thomas Parkinson (1968) includes an important interview with the poet. A partial bibliography of Lowell's work can be found in Jerome Mazzaro, *The Achievement of Robert Lowell, 1939–1959* (1960).

James Merrill

Merrill has published the following volumes of poetry: *First Poems* (1951); *The Country of a Thousand Years of Peace* (1959; rev. ed., 1970); *Water Street* (1962); *Nights and Days* (1966); *The Fire Screen* (1969); *Braving the Elements* (1972); *Divine Comedies* (1976); and *Mirabell: Books of Number* (1978). He has also written two novels: *The Seraglio* (1957) and *The (Diblos) Notebook* (1965). Among useful critical essays are the chapters on Merrill in Richard Howard's *Alone with America* (1969) and in David Kalstone's *Five Temperaments* (1977) as well as "James Merrill's Oedipal Fire," an article by Richard Saez in *Parnassus: Poetry in Review* (Fall–Winter, 1974), pp. 159–184.

W. S. Merwin

The First Four Books of Poems (1975) is a convenient reissue of all the verse Merwin published from 1952 through 1960. His other volumes of poetry include *The Moving Target* (1963); *The Lice* (1967); *The Carrier of Ladders* (1970); *Writings to an Unfinished Accompaniment* (1973); and *The Compass Flower* (1977). His prose includes two volumes of sketches or parables: *The Miner's Pale Children* (1970) and *Houses and Travellers* (1977). He has done translations of poetry from many languages, including *The Song of Roland* (1963) and *The Poem of the Cid* (1959). A useful introduction to his work can be found in Richard Howard's *Alone with America* (1969).

Frank O'Hara

The Collected Poems of Frank O'Hara was published in 1971. It has since been supplemented by two volumes: *Early Poems* (1977) and *Poems Retrieved* (1977). O'Hara's critical articles and other prose can be found in *Art Chronicles 1954–1966* (1975) and *Standing Still and Walking in New York* (1975). A volume of anecdotes and reminiscences, *Homage to Frank O'Hara*, ed. Bill Berkson and Joe LeSueur, appeared in 1978. An informative critical study is Marjorie Perloff's *Frank O'Hara: Poet among Painters* (1977).

Charles Olson

The best single introduction to Charles Olson is Robert Creeley's *Selected Writings of Charles Olson* (1967). *The Distances*, a collection of poems, appeared in 1960. Olson's *Maximus Poems* appeared in sections from 1953 through 1968. Among his prose works are *Call Me Ishmael* (1947), a study of Melville; *Mayan Letters* (1953); and *Letters for Origin* (1970).

Sylvia Plath

Plath's books of poetry include *The Colossus and Other Poems* (1962); *Ariel* (1966); *Crossing the Water* (1971); and *Winter Trees* (1972). Her novel *The Bell Jar* was first published in England in 1963. Plath's mother Aurelia Schober Plath selected and edited the useful *Letters Home: Correspondence 1950–63* (1975). A number of informative essays appeared in *The Art of Sylvia Plath*, ed. Charles Newman (1970). Among the book-length studies, *Chapters in a Mythology* by Judith Kroll (1976) is especially helpful.

Adrienne Rich

A convenient starting point is Rich's *Poems Selected and New, 1950–1974*, which draws poems from the poet's earlier books: *A Change of World* (1951); *The Diamond Cutters* (1955); *Snapshots of a Daughter-in-Law* (1963); *Necessities of Life* (1966); *Leaflets* (1969); *The Will to Change* (1971); and *Diving into the Wreck* (1973). Since then, Rich has published a further book of poems, *The Dream of a Common Language* (1978). There are valuable critical essays and an interview in *Adrienne Rich's Poetry*, ed. Barbara Charlesworth Gelpi and Albert Gelpi (1975). Rich is also the author of an important study, *Of Woman Born: Motherhood as Experience and Institution* (1976). She has collected her essays, lectures, and speeches in *On Lies, Secrets, and Silence: Selected Prose 1966–1979* (1979).

Theodore Roethke

The Collected Poems of Theodore Roethke was published in 1966. Useful comments on poetic tradition and his own poetic practice are to be found in several collections of Roethke's prose: *On the Poet and His Craft: Selected Prose of Theodore Roethke*, ed. Ralph J. Mills, Jr. (1965); *Straw for the Fire: From the Notebooks of Theodore Roethke, 1948–63*, ed. David Wagoner (1972); and *The Selected Letters of Theodore Roethke*, ed. Ralph J. Mills, Jr. (1970). Among the useful studies of Roethke's work are *Theodore Roethke: An Introduction to the Poetry* by Karl Malkoff (1966); Rosemary Sullivan's *Theodore Roethke: The Garden Master* (1975); and *Theodore Roethke: Essays on the Poetry*, ed. Arnold Stein (1965). Allan Seager's *The Glass House* (1968) contains useful biographical material.

Anne Sexton

Sexton's books of poems include *To Bedlam and Part Way Back* (1960); *All My Pretty Ones* (1962); *Live or Die* (1966); *Love Poems* (1969); *Transformations* (1971); *The Book of Folly* (1973); *The Death Notebooks* (1974); and *The Awful Rowing toward God* (1975). *A Self-Portrait in Letters* (1977) gives useful biographical material. Important interviews and critical essays are to be found in J. D. McClatchy's *Anne Sexton: The Artist and Her Critics* (1978).

Gary Snyder

Snyder's poems have been published by several different presses, often with duplication of poems. *Riprap*, originally published in 1959, is most easily obtained in *Riprap, and Cold Mountain Poems* (1965). *Myths and Texts* first appeared in 1960. Other volumes include *The Back Country* (1968); *Regarding Wave* (1970); *Six Sections from Mountains and Rivers without End plus One* (1970); and *Turtle Island* (1974). Snyder's book of prose dealing with ecology, *Earth House Hold*, was published in 1969.

Richard Wilbur

The most convenient single volume is *The Poems of Richard Wilbur* (1963), which draws from *The Beautiful Changes* (1947), *Ceremony and Other Poems* (1950), *Things of This World* (1956), and *Advice to a Prophet* (1961). Since then, he has published *Walking to Sleep* (1969) and *The Mind-Reader* (1976). His translations from Molière include *The Misanthrope* (1955) and *Tartuffe* (1963). A selection of prose is available in *Responses: Prose Pieces, 1948–1976* (1976).

James Wright

James Wright's *Collected Poems* (1971) included poems from his earlier volumes *The Green Wall* (1956), *Saint Judas* (1959), *The Branch Will Not Break* (1963), and *Shall We Gather at the River* (1968). Since then he has published *Two Citizens* (1973) and *To a Blossoming Pear Tree* (1977). Wright has translated from German and Spanish in versions of *The Rider on the White Horse: Selected Short Fiction of Theodor Storm* (1964), *Twenty Poems of Georg Trakl* (1963), *Twenty Poems of Cesar Vallejo* (1964), *Twenty Poems of Pablo Neruda* (with Robert Bly, 1968), and Herman Hesse's *Poems* (1970). A helpful introduction to Wright's work can be found in Richard Howard's *Alone with America* (1969).

Index